SOCIAL SECURITY LEGISLATION 2005

VOLUME II: INCOME SUPPORT, JOBSEEKER'S ALLOWANCE, STATE PENSION CREDIT AND THE SOCIAL FUND

AUSTRALIA
Law Book Co.
Sydney

CANADA and USA
Carswell
Toronto

HONG KONG
Sweet & Maxwell Asia

NEW ZEALAND
Brookers
Auckland

SINGAPORE and MALAYSIA
Sweet & Maxwell Asia
Singapore and Kuala Lumpur

SOCIAL SECURITY LEGISLATION 2005

General Editor
David Bonner, LL.B, LL.M

VOLUME II:
INCOME SUPPORT, JOBSEEKER'S ALLOWANCE, STATE PENSION CREDIT AND THE SOCIAL FUND

Consultant
John Mesher, B.A., B.C.L., LL.M
Barrister, Professor Associate of Law,
University of Sheffield, Social Security and Child Support Commissioner

Commentary By

Penny Wood, LL.B., M.Sc.
Solicitor, District Chairman,
Appeal Tribunals

Richard Poynter, B.C.L., M.A.(Oxon.)
Solicitor, District Chairman, Appeal Tribunals
Deputy Social Security Commissioner

Nick Wikeley, M.A. (Cantab)
Barrister, Professor of Law, University of Southampton
Deputy Social Security Commissioner, Deputy District Chairman, Appeal Tribunals

David Bonner, LL.B., LL.M.
Senior Lecturer in Law, University of Leicester,
Formerly Member, Social Security Appeal Tribunals

Consultant Editor
Child Poverty Action Group

LONDON
SWEET & MAXWELL
2005

Published in 2005 by
Sweet & Maxwell Limited of
100 Avenue Road, Swiss Cottage,
London NW3 3PF
www.sweetandmaxwell.co.uk
Typeset by Servis Filmsetting Ltd, Manchester

Printed and bound in Great Britain by MPG Books, Bodmin, Cornwall

No natural forests were destroyed to make this product;
only farmed timber was used and replanted.

A CIP catalogue record for this book is
available from the British Library

ISBN 0 421 920 505

CHILD POVERTY ACTION GROUP

The Child Poverty Action Group (CPAG) is a charity, founded in 1965, which campaigns for the relief of poverty in the United Kingdom. It has a particular reputation in the field of welfare benefits law derived from its legal work, publications, training and parliamentary and policy work, and is widely recognised as the leading organisation for taking test cases on social security law.

CPAG is therefore ideally placed to act as Consultant Editor to this 4-volume work—**Social Security Legislation 2005**. CPAG is not responsible for the detail of what is contained in each volume, and the authors' views are not necessarily those of CPAG. The Consultant Editor's role is to act in an advisory capacity on the overall structure, focus and direction of the work.

For more information about CPAG, its rights and policy publications or training courses, its address is 94 White Lion Street, London, N1 9PF (telephone: 020 7837 7979—website: *www.cpag.org.uk*).

FOREWORD

I am once again grateful to all those involved in the compilation and publication of these volumes of Social Security Legislation. They are an indispensable guide to all those who work in this field, including those who sit on tribunals. This new edition builds on the excellence of its predecessors so as to provide an exhaustive and up to date exegesis of this most complex area of law. They provide us with an indispensable source of information and guidance to inform the decisions we make. I welcome its publication most warmly.

His Honour Judge Michael Harris
President of Appeal Tribunals

PREFACE

Income Support, Jobseeker's Allowance, State Pension Credit and the Social Fund is Volume II of the four volume series: *Social Security Legislation 2005*. The companion volumes are: Bonner, Hooker and White, *Volume I: Non-Means Tested Benefits*; Rowland and White, *Volume III: Administration, Adjudication and the European Dimension* and Wikeley and Williams, *Volume IV: Tax Credits and Employer-Paid Social Security Benefits*.

Each of the volumes in the series provides a legislative text, clearly showing the form and date of amendments, and commentary up to date to April 14, 2005. The commentary in this volume includes caselaw developments up to the end of June 2005.

No doubt related to the long anticipated general election on May, 5, 2005, this year has been characterised more by Government prouncements of its vision for the future (*e.g.* the Prime Minister's speech on October 12, 2004 on reforming the welfare state) and statements announcing large-scale reform, *e.g.* of incapacity benefit and pensions, than by the implementation of any major legislative developments. However, that is not to say that there have not been any significant changes to the regulations governing means-tested benefits this year. Two in particular should be mentioned. The first was the amendment on May 1, 2004 of the habitual residence test aimed at ensuring that a person will not be treated as habitually resident unless he or she has a right to reside in the UK. The lack of any definition within the regulations of what is meant by "right to reside" in this context, the limited transitional protection provisions, and recent ECJ caselaw which indicates that the principle of non-discrimination on the basis of nationality can increasingly be relied upon to prevent Member States denying access to benefits even to non-nationals who are economically inactive, means that this new requirement is likely to be a fertile ground of future Commissioner and court decisions. However, in the meantime it will be left to tribunals to grapple with the problems created by the new test. The other important development, which has not attracted a great deal of attention, but which will be of considerable assistance to certain claimants, was the expansion of the definition of "existing housing costs" with effect from November 28, 2004.

In addition, the phased transfer of financial support for children to child tax credit for those claimants who are still receiving amounts for children in their income support/income-based JSA which was planned to start in October 2004 has suffered the same fate that seems to beset other staged changes, *e.g.* the conversion of "old" child support cases to the "new" scheme, although it must be said that the delay in this case is not of the same scale. The transfer will now not commence until 2006 and will not be completed until December 31, 2006. As discussed in the note to regulation 17 of the Income Support Regulations, the transfer procedure may well be problematical, as indeed were the transitional provisions for those income support and income-based JSA claimants who claimed child tax credit in

2003/2004. See *CIS/1064/2004* in which the Commissioner conducts a detailed analysis of these convoluted provisions.

In terms of caselaw, the decisions of the Court of Appeal in *Hockenjos* and of the Commissioner in *CIS/3280/2003*, *CIS/1124/2004* and *CIS/1840/2004* (under appeal to the Court of Appeal *sub nom. Secretary of State for Work and Pensions v Bhakta*) are perhaps the most significant this year. In *Hockenjos* the Court of Appeal ruled that the linking of child additions in income-based JSA to child benefit indirectly discriminated against a substantial minority carer (such as Mr Hockenjos) in breach of EC Directive 79/7. The important development in *Bhakta* was the Commissioner's approach to the "date of decision" rule in s.12(8)(b) of the Social Security Act 1998. The Commissioner held that a tribunal has power to make an advance award from the date on which habitual residence is likely to be established and is not bound to dismiss the appeal if the claimant has not become habitually resident by the date of the Secretary of State's decision. However, also of note are the recent decisions of the Court of Appeal in *Secretary of State for Work and Pensions v W* (on the meaning of "abandoned" in para.8(3)(b) of Sch.3 to the Income Support Regulations), in *Ahmed v Secretary of State for Work and Pensions* (on sponsorship undertakings) and in *Secretary of State for Work and Pensions v Arathoon* (on the calculation of the "add back" for the purpose of housing costs).

Besides these highlighted developments, there have also been the usual crop of more minor legislative changes and the continuing flow of Commissioners' decisions, and to a lesser extent, court judgments.

As always, revising and updating the legislative text and commentary, has required considerable flexibility on the part of the publisher and a great deal of help from a number of sources, including CPAG as advisory editor to the series, for which we express our sincere appreciation. Thanks are also due to Miranda Bayliss, Peter Banks and Jill Walker. But particular mention must be made here of the debt owed by all of us to John Mesher, who began the provision of annotated legislation for tribunals, has given wise advice on the development of this series, and who happily remains on call as consultant in respect of this Volume.

To maximise space for explanatory commentary we have provided lists of definitions only where the commentary to the provision is substantial, or where reference to definitions is essential for its proper understanding. Users of this book should always check whether particular words or phrases they are called on to apply have a particular meaning ascribed to them in the legislation. Generally, the first or second regulation in each set of regulations contains definitions of key terms (check the 'Arrangement of Regulations' at the beginning of each set for an indication of the subject matter covered by each regulation). There are also definition or 'interpretation' sections in each of the Acts (check 'Sections Reproduced' at the beginning of each Act for an indication of the subject matter covered by each section or Schedule).

Users of the original three volumes in this series, and their predecessors, have over the years provided valuable comments which have invariably been helpful to us in ensuring that the selection of legislative material for inclusion and the commentary upon it reflect the sort of difficulties encountered in practice. In so doing, readers have thus helped shape the content of each of the volumes in the current series. We hope that readers will continue that tradition. Please write to the General Editor of the series, David Bonner,

Faculty of Law, The University, Leicester LE1 7RH, who will pass on any comments received to the appropriate commentator.

Our gratitude also goes to the President of Appeal Tribunals, Judge Harris, and his staff for continuing the tradition of help and encouragement.

June 30, 2005

Penny Wood
Richard Poynter
Nick Wikeley
David Bonner

CONTENTS

Contents

Contents

PART III
JOBSEEKER'S ALLOWANCE

PART IV
STATE PENSION CREDIT

PART V
THE SOCIAL FUND

USING THIS BOOK, USING LEGAL AUTHORITY AND FINDING OTHER SOURCES OF INFORMATION

Introduction

This book is not designed as an introduction to, or general textbook on, the law relating to social security. Inevitably some familiarity with the social security system has been assumed. This note is designed to assist readers who are not lawyers—and also those lawyers who are not familiar with this particular field of law—by identifying the sources of social security law and showing how to find them. Volume IV also deals with income tax law, and its version of this section contains additional comments about that.

Primary sources of social security law

Social security law is based on legislation, consisting of *Acts of Parliament*, which are primary legislation and are also known as statutes, and *statutory instruments*, which are secondary or delegated legislation made by ministers acting under powers conferred by primary legislation and are also known as regulations (or, occasionally, orders). Another source of the law lies in *judicial decisions*, made, in this context, principally by Social Security Commissioners who hear appeals from appeal tribunals although some decisions of the courts are also relevant. Such judicial decisions provide authoritative interpretation of the legislation. The precise mixture of the three sources differs from benefit to benefit.

The scope of this book and the status of the commentary

This book contains an up-to-date text of the principal statutes and statutory instruments relevant to the work of appeal tribunals and Commissioners. It also contains a commentary on that legislation, referring to relevant decisions of Commissioners and the courts. The commentary aims to help readers understand the legislation and its implications. The focus in decision-making, however, must remain on the actual words of the legislation as applied by the Commissioners and courts, because the commentary merely reflects the opinion of the commentator on what the law is.

Finding a particular section in a statute

Statutes consist of numbered sections (sometimes grouped in Parts, which may in turn be divided into Chapters) and they often have schedules at the end.

Suppose you wanted to find section 137 of the Social Security Contributions and Benefits Act 1992. Sometimes the word "section" is abbreviated to "s."; so you could refer to the Social Security Contributions and Benefits Act 1992, s.137.

To find this provision, you can use the contents pages to find where provisions of the Social Security Contributions and Benefits Act 1992 are printed. You can also use the running heads at the top of each page; the header on the left-hand page gives the name of the Act while the header on the right-hand page gives the year and chapter number (abbreviated "c.") as well as the section dealt with on that page. The chapter number simply indicates the order in the Parliamentary year of the statute; the Social Security Contributions and Benefits Act 1992 is chapter 4, meaning that it was the fourth statute to be passed by Parliament in 1992.

After the text of the section comes a note of the AMENDMENTS made to the provision, reference to relevant DEFINITIONS, and the commentary, which appears under the heading GENERAL NOTE. Where the section is re-enacted in consolidating legislation, that is, legislation drawing together all the amendments over time in a new statute, the DERIVATION, or source, of the provision is also given so that you can see where the provision originally appeared. This can be helpful in considering any decisions of Commissioners or the courts on the earlier form of the provision.

Finding a particular regulation

Statutory instruments consist of numbered regulations (or articles where the statutory instrument is in the form of an order rather than being a set of regulations) and, like statutes, they sometimes have schedules at the end.

Suppose you wanted to find regulation 42 of the Income Support (General) Regulations 1987. Sometimes the word "regulation" is abbreviated to "reg."; so you could refer to the Income Support (General) Regulations 1987, reg.42.

To find this provision, use the contents pages to find the Income Support (General) Regulations 1987. Then move forward within the regulations until you find the one you want. Again the running headers at the top of each page will assist you. The header on the right-hand page gives the statutory instrument number, that is the year of publication and the number, as in SI 1987/1967, indicating that these regulations were the 1967th statutory instrument made by Ministers and approved by Parliament in 1987.

As with statutes, after the text of the regulation comes a note of the AMENDMENTS made to the provision, reference to relevant DEFINITIONS, and the commentary which appears under the heading GENERAL NOTE Where the regulation is re-enacted in consolidating regulations, that is, legislation drawing together all the amendments made over time in a new set of regulations, the DERIVATION or source, of the provision is also given so that you can see where the provision originally appeared. This can be helpful in considering any decisions of Commissioners or the courts on the earlier form of the provision.

Commissioners' decisions

Both reported and unreported decisions of Commissioners are important sources of guidance on the interpretation and application of legislation relating to social security benefits and their administration. Where relevant, these are binding on both decision-makers and on tribunals. The binding nature of Commissioners' decisions is discussed below. A single Commissioner hears most appeals, though the Chief Commissioner does occasionally direct that three Commissioners sitting together should hear cases of special importance. This is then known as a Tribunal of Commissioners.

Reported decisions

About 40 to 50 decisions a year are selected to be "reported". Selection used to be a decision of the Chief Commissioner acting alone. Later he made his selection on advice from a committee of Commissioners, but, since 2002, selection of decisions to report has been the task of an Editorial committee chaired by the Chief Commissioner. Decisions are selected for reporting only if they are of general importance and command the assent of at least a majority of Commissioners. They are published in biennial bound volumes by The Stationery Office and in looseleaf form (contact Margaret Drummond, Print Solutions, Room B0202, Benton Park Road, Newcastle-upon- Tyne NE98 1YX (tel. 0191 225 5422)) and on the world wide web (*www.dwp.gov.uk/advisers/docs/commdecs/index.asp*) by the Department for Work and Pensions (replacing the DSS). They can also be accessed via the Commissioners' website (*www.osscsc.gov.uk*). These decisions are available in all tribunal venues and can be consulted in local social security offices, and some main libraries.

Reported decisions are renumbered with the initial letter "R" for "reported". *R(IB) 1/00* was the first decision on incapacity benefit to be reported in 2000. A decision of a Tribunal of Commissioners is often identified by adding a letter "T" in brackets after the reference, as in *R(IB) 2/99(T)*. Scottish decisions are not specifically identified as such.

Unreported decisions

Reported decisions are selected from a greater body of decisions in the cases dealt with by the Commissioners. Those not reported are known as unreported decisions but still have precedential value. Each Commissioner's decision is given a file number in the Commissioners' Office, which is a unique identification number. From 1997 cases have been registered consecutively by number within a calendar year, without a separate range of numbers for each benefit. Prior to 1995, there was a separate range of numbers for each benefit. So Commissioner's decision *CU/23/1992* is the 23rd case on unemployment benefit registered in 1992. The letters "CU" indicate that the decision is that of a Commissioner (C) and that the benefit in question is unemployment benefit (U). Between 1995 and 1997, there had been a change of approach, reflecting computerisation. The system of numbering consecutively within benefits in a particular year ceased. The lettering system remained the same, but the number after the letters, as in *CU/7328/1995*, indicated that this was the 7328th case on any benefit registered since the beginning of 1995.

Scottish decisions have an "S" after the "C" (*e.g. CSI/26/98*) and, until the Welsh office of the Commissioners was closed, Welsh decisions could be identified as having a "W" after the "C". The "W" will be added again in 2005.

Until the end of 2001, some 100 decisions a year were "starred" because it was considered that they raised points of significance or interest and deserved wider circulation. They did not, however, acquire any enhanced precedential status from being starred. The practice of starring was discontinued from the start of 2002. Instead decisions that Commissioners believe should have wider currency are available on the Commissioners' new website (*www.osscsc.gov.uk*). Some decisions are selected as of particular interest and highlighted for a time in the Most Recent Decisions part of the Decisions section of that website. As with "starring", however, a decision does not gain enhanced precedential status through "highlighting".

Other sources of/on Commissioners' decisions

There are a number of other sources of valuable information or commentary on Commissioners' decisions, whether reported or unreported: publications such as the *Journal of Social Security Law*, the *Journal of Social Welfare and Family Law*, *Legal Action*, *The Law Society's Gazette*, the *Disability Rights Bulletin* and CPAG's *Welfare Rights Bulletin*. A range of reported and unreported decisions and many valuable updates and comments were also available on the website maintained by Commissioner Howell (*www.hywels.clara.co.uk/commrs/decns.htm*). This website is remaining in existence for the time being (although it has not been updated since April 28, 2002), despite the advent of the Commissioners' new website referred to above. To quote Commissioner Howell, this is "in the hope that the improved arrangements on the official website . . . will prove permanent".

What does it mean to say that a case is binding?

Reference to decisions being binding means that where a similar point is raised in a later case before an adjudicating authority bound by the decision, that adjudicating authority must accept the interpretation of the law contained in the decision. So a Commissioner's decision explaining what a term in a particular regulation means, lays down the definition of that term in much the same way as if the term had been defined in the regulations themselves. The decision may also help in deciding what the same term means when it is used in a different set of regulations, provided that the term appears to have been used in a similar text.

Appeals to the Commissioners are now available only on points of law, but before April 1987 appeals were available on points of fact as well as law. Care should be taken in reading older decisions to appreciate that some were concerned with fact rather than law, though the reported decisions invariably contain points of general application. Relevant decisions of the Commissioners and the courts are explained in the commentary to the statutory provisions in this volume, together with guidance on their significance for decision-making in the tribunals. Users of the book should remember that it is the decision itself which is binding and not the explanation of it in the commentary; that is merely the opinion of the commentator.

Using Commissioners' decisions: the hierarchy of authority

Although the Chief Commissioner has directed that, so far as possible, reference should be made to reported decisions only, the legal position is that all decisions of Commissioners are binding on decision-makers and tribunals. Where there is a conflict, a decision of a Tribunal of Commissioners should be preferred to a decision of a single Commissioner and a reported decision should generally be preferred to an unreported decision (*R(I)*

12/75(T)), unless the unreported decision was the later decision and the Commissioner expressly decided not to follow the earlier reported decision (see the Northern Ireland decision, *(R 1/00(FC))*. Decisions of Commissioners are not binding on other Commissioners. However, a single Commissioner will always follow a decision of a Tribunal of Commissioners and will generally follow a decision of another single Commissioner *(R(I) 12/75(T))*. A Tribunal of Commissioners will generally follow a decision of another such Tribunal but is not bound to do so *(R(U) 4/88(T))*.

There are separate Commissioners in Northern Ireland considering legislation that is often indistinguishable from the legislation in Great Britain. Decisions of Northern Ireland Commissioners are not binding in Great Britain *(R(SB) 1/90(T))* but are persuasive. Such decisions are included in the decisions published on the website of the Great Britain Commissioners but the selection of decisions to be reported is made by the Chief Commissioner in Northern Ireland. Looseleaf publication by The Stationery Office and on the world wide web by the Department for Social Development *(www.dsdni.gov.uk)* is separate from the publication of Great Britain decisions. So was the publication of bound volumes by The Stationery Office until 1999. From 2000, reported Northern Ireland decisions are included in the same bound volumes as reported decisions of Commissioners in Great Britain. References to decisions of Northern Ireland Commissioners can always be distinguished from references to decisions of Commissioners in Great Britain because the former are numbered differently with the letters identifying the type of benefit always being in brackets after the numbers, as in *C12/98(IS)*, which has been reported as *R1/00(IS)*. Unreported decisions of the Northern Ireland Commissioners can be found on the Department for Social Development website at *www.dsdni.gov.uk*.

Using Commissioners' decisions at Tribunals and before the Commissioners

Decision-makers and claimants are entitled to assume that tribunals and Commissioners have immediate access to reported decisions of Commissioners and they need not provide copies, although it may sometimes be helpful to do so. However, where either a decision-maker or a claimant intends to rely on an unreported decision, it will be necessary to provide a copy of the decision to the tribunal or Commissioner. A copy of the decision should also be provided to the other party before the hearing because otherwise it may be necessary for there to be an adjournment to enable that party to take advice on the significance of the decision.

Decisions of the Courts

Decisions of the superior courts in Great Britain and Northern Ireland on questions of legal principle are almost invariably followed by decision-makers, tribunals and Commissioners, even when they are not strictly binding because the relevant court was in a different part of the United Kingdom or exercised a parallel—but not superior—jurisdiction (see the note to section 14 of the Social Security Act 1998 in Part I of *Vol. III: Adminstration, Adjudication and the European Dimension*.

Decisions of the courts on social security matters are generally included among the reports of Commissioners' decisions. So, for example, *R(I)1/00*

contains Commissioner's decisions *CSI 12/98*, the decision of the Court of
Session upholding the Commissioner's decision and the decision of the
House of Lords in *Chief Adjudication Officer v Faulds*, reversing the decision
of the Court of Session. Some of them can also be found in the various series
of law reports familiar to lawyers (in particular, in the *Law Reports*, the
Weekly Law Reports, the *All England Law Reports*, the *Industrial Cases Reports*
and the *Family Law Reports*. Decisions of the House of Lords since mid-
November 1996 are available on the world wide web (*http://www.parlia-
ment.uk/judicial_work/judicial_work5.cfm*). Very recent ones are available
there only hours after delivery of their Lordships' opinions. Some Court of
Appeal decisions can be obtained on the Court Service website
(*http://www.courtservice.gov.uk/judgments/judg_home.htm*). Sweet and
Maxwell's online subscription service *Westlaw* is another valuable source
(*www.westlaw.co.uk/*), as is Smith Bernal's *Casetrack* (*www.casetrack.com*)
and LexisNexis' *Lexis* (*www.lexis.com/*).

European Community Law

The European Community is part of the European Union. European
Community Law affecting social security is covered in the third volume in
this series: Rowland and White, *Social Security Legislation 2004: Vol.III.
Administration, Adjudication and the European Dimension.*

The European Union has two courts: the Court of Justice of the
European Communities, and the Court of First Instance. Decision-
makers, tribunals and Commissioners are under a duty by reason of
Article 10 (ex.5) of the EC Treaty to apply decisions of the Luxembourg
courts, where relevant to cases before them, in preference to other authorities binding on them.

Decisions of the Court of Justice of the European Communities come in
two parts: the Opinion of the Advocate General and the decision of the
Court. It is the decision of the Court which is binding. The Court is assisted
by hearing the Opinion of the Advocate General before itself coming to a
conclusion on the issue before it. The Court does not always follow its
Advocate General. Where it does, the Opinion of the Advocate General
often elaborates the arguments in greater detail than the single collegiate
judgment of the Court. No dissenting judgments appear in reports from the
Court of Justice.

Decisions of the Luxembourg courts are available on the world wide web
at *www.curia.eu.int/*.

The European Convention on Human Rights, the Strasbourg Court and the Human Rights Act 1998

The Court of Human Rights in Strasbourg is quite separate from the
Luxembourg courts and serves a different purpose: interpreting and applying the European Convention on Human Rights, which is incorporated into
United Kingdom law by the Human Rights Act 1998. From October 2,
2000, public authorities, including courts, Commissioners, tribunals and
decision-makers (the Secretary of State) must act in accordance with the
incorporated provisions of the Convention, unless statute prevents this.
They must take into account the Strasbourg case law. They are required to
interpret legislation, so far as is possible to do so, to give effect to the incorporated Convention rights. Any court or tribunal may declare secondary

legislation incompatible with those rights and, in certain circumstances, invalidate it. Only the higher courts can declare a provision of primary legislation to be incompatible with those rights, but no court or tribunal can invalidate primary legislation.

The work of the Court and the impact of the Human Rights Act 1998 on social security are discussed in the third volume in this series: *Administration, Adjudication and the European Dimension.*

Judgments of the Court of Human Rights are made by majority, and separate concurring or dissenting judgments are included with the decision of the majority where the Court is not unanimous.

Decisions of the Court of Human Rights are available on the world wide web at *www.echr.coe.int/.*

Official guidance on Social Security Law

The law has been translated into a more civil servant friendly format. Prior to the decision-making and appeals changes made by the Social Security Act 1998, guidance on benefits and their administration was set out in the thirteen volume *Adjudication Officers Guide (AOG)* published by The Stationery Office. This has now been replaced by a fourteen volume *Decision Makers Guide (DMG).* This is available on the world wide web at *http://www.dwp.gov.uk/publications/dwp/dmg/index.asp.*

The coverage of the DMG is as follows:

Volume 1   Decision Making and Appeals

Volume 2   International Subjects

Volume 3   Subjects Common to all Benefits

Volume 4   Jobseeker's Allowance and Income Support

Volume 5   Jobseeker's Allowance and Income Support

Volume 6   Jobseeker's Allowance and Income Support

Volume 7   Jobseeker's Allowance and Income Support

Volume 8   No longer issued

Volume 9   No longer issued

Volume 10 Benefits for Incapacity, Disability and Maternity

Volume 11 Industrial Injuries Benefits

Volume 12 Widow's Benefit and Retirement Pension

Volume 13 State Pension Credit

Volume 14 State Pension Credit

It should be noted that the DMG is not binding on tribunals and Commissioners; it is internal guidance for the use of decision-makers within the Department.

Child Benefit and Guardian's Allowance are now administered by the HM Revenue and Customs, as are tax credits. A range of useful material can be found on its website at *www.hmrc.gov.uk/practitioners/index.shtml.*

Unofficial guidance on Social Security Law

There are a large number of guides. CPAG's *Welfare Benefits Handbook*, published annually each spring, is unrivalled as a practical and comprehensive introduction from the claimant's viewpoint.

CHANGE OF NAME FROM DEPARTMENT OF SOCIAL SECURITY TO DEPARTMENT FOR WORK AND PENSIONS

The Secretaries of State for Education and Skills and for Work and Pensions Order 2002 (SI 2002/1397) makes provision for the change of name from the Department of Social Security to Department for Work and Pensions. Article 9(5) provides:

"(5) Subject to article 12 [which makes specific amendments], any enactment or instrument passed or made before the coming into force of this Order shall have effect, so far as may be necessary for the purposes of or in consequence of the entrusting to the Secretary of State for Work and Pensions of the social security functions, as if any reference to the Secretary of State for Social Security, to the Department of Social Security or to an officer of the Secretary of State for Social Security (including any reference which is to be construed as such as reference) were a reference to the Secretary of State for Work and Pensions, to the Department for Work and Pensions or, as the case may be, to an officer of the Secretary of State for Work and Pensions."

TABLE OF CASES

TABLE OF STATUTES

TABLE OF STATUTORY INSTRUMENTS

TABLE OF SOCIAL SECURITY COMMISSIONERS' DECISIONS

TABLE OF ABBREVIATIONS USED IN THIS SERIES

AA	Attendance Allowance
ADHD	Attention Deficit Hyperactivity Disorder
Adjudication Regulations	Social Security (Adjudication) Regulations 1986
All E.R.	All England Law Reports (Butterworths)
AO	Adjudication Officer
AOG	HMSO, *Adjudication Officers Guide*
Attendance Allowance Regulations	Social Security (Attendance Allowance) Regulations 1991
BAMS	Benefits Agency Medical Service
Blue Books	HMSO, *The Law Relating to Social Security*, Vols. 1–11
CAO	Chief Adjudication Officer
CBA 1975	Child Benefit Act 1975
CCA 2001	Capital Allowance Act 2001
CP	Carer Premium
CPAG	Child Poverty Action Group
CPR	Civil Procedure Rules
CRU	Compensation Recovery Unit
CSA 1995	Child Support Act 1995
CS(NI)O 1995	Child Support (Northern Ireland) Order 1995
CSO	Child Support Officer
CSPSSA	Child Support, Pensions and Social Security Act 2000
CTC	Child Tax Credit
Claims and Payments Regulations 1979	Social Security (Claims and Payments) Regulations 1979
Claims and Payments Regulations 1987	Social Security (Claims and Payments) Regulations 1987
C.M.L.R.	Common Market Law Reports
Commissioners Procedure Regulations	Social Security Commissioners (Procedure) Regulations 1999
Computation of Earnings Regulations 1978	Social Security Benefit (Computation of Earnings) Regulations 1978
Computation of Earnings Regulations 1996	Social Security Benefit (Computation of Earnings) Regulations 1996
Council Tax Benefit Regulations	Council Tax Benefit (General) Regulations 1992 (SI 1992/1814)
DAT	Disability Appeals Tribunal
DCP	Disabled Child Premium

Table of Abbreviations used in this Series

Decisions and Appeals Regulations 1999	Social Security and Child Support (Decision and Appeals) Regulations 1999
Dependency Regulations	Social Security Benefit (Dependency) Regulations 1977
DLA	Disability Living Allowance
DLADWAA 1991	Disability Living Allowance and Disability Allowance (Consequential Provisions) Regulations 1991
DM	Decision Maker
DMA	Decision-making and Appeals
DMG	HMSO, *Decision-Makers Guide*
DMP	Delegated Medical Practitioner
Disability Working Allowance Regulations	Disability Working Allowance (General) Regulations 1991
DPTC	Disabled Persons Tax Credit
DSS	Department of Social Security
DWA	Disability Working Allowance
E.C.R.	European Court Reports
ECHR	European Court of Human Rights
EEA	European Economic Area
E.H.R.R.	European Human Rights Reports
EMA	Education Maintenance Allowance
EMO	Examining Medical Officer
EMP	Examining Medical Practitioner
ERA	Evoked Response Audiometry
ERA 1996	Employers Rights Act 1996
ER(NI)O 1996	Employers Rights (Northern Ireland) Order 1996
Eur.L.Rev.	European Law Review
FA	Finance Act
Family Credit Regulations	Family Credit (General) Regulations 1987
FIS	Family Income Supplement
G.P.	General Practitioner
GRP	Graduated Retirement Pension
GA Regulations	Social Security (Guardian's Allowance) Regulations 1975
General Benefit Regulations	Social Security (General Benefit) Regulations 1982
HASSASSA	Health and Social Services and Social Security Adjudication Act 1983
HNCIP	(Housewives) Non-Contributory Invalidity Pension
Hospital In-Patients Regulations	Social Security (Hospital In-Patients) Regulations 1975
Housing Benefit Regulations	Housing Benefit (General) Regulations 1987 (SI 1987/1971)
HPP	Higher Pensioner Premium

Table of Abbreviations used in this Series

HRA 1998	Human Rights Act 1998
Income Support Regulations	Income Support (General) Regulations 1987
IB Regulations	Social Security (Incapacity Benefit) Regulations 1994
IBS	Irritable Bowel Syndrome
ICA	Invalid Care Allowance
ICTA	Income and Corporation Taxes Act
IIAC	Industrial Injuries Advisory Council
I.L.J.	Industrial Law Journal
IRRA	Inland Revenue Act 1890
ITEPA 2003	Income Tax (Earnings and Pensions) Act 2003
ITS	Independent Tribunal Service
IWA	Social Security (Incapacity for Work) Act 1994
IW (General) Regulations	Social Security (Incapacity for Work) (General) Regulations 1995
IW (Transitional) Regulations	Social Security (Incapacity for Work) (Transitional) Regulations 1995
Invalid Care Allowance Regulations	Social Security (Invalid Care Allowance) Regulations 1976
JSA	Jobseeker's Allowance
JSA 1995	Jobseekers Act 1995
JS(NI)O 1995	Jobseekers (Northern Ireland) Act 1995
JSA Regulations	Jobseeker's Allowance Regulations 1996
JSA (Transitional) Regulations	Jobseeker's Allowance (Transitional) Regulations 1996
J.S.W.L.	Journal of Social Welfare Law
J.S.W.F.L.	Journal of Social Welfare and Family Law
J.S.S.L.	Journal of Social Security Law
LEL	Lower Earnings Limit
MA	Maternity Allowance
MAT	Medical Appeal Tribunal
Maternity Benefit Regulations	Social Security (Maternity Benefit) Regulations 1975
Medical Evidence Regulations	Social Security (Medical Evidence) Regulations 1976
NCIP	Non-Contributory Invalidity Pension
NI	National Insurance
OPA 1973	Overseas Pensions Act 1973
OPB	One Parent Benefit
OPSSAT	Office of the President of the Social Security Appeals Tribunal
Ogus, Barendt and Wikeley	A. Ogus, E. Barendt and N. Wikeley, *The Law of Social Security* (4th ed., Butterworths, 1995)
Overlapping Benefits Regulations	Social Security (Overlapping Benefits) Regulations 1979

Overpayments Regulations	Social Security (Payments on account, Overpayments and Recovery) Regulations
PAYE	Pay as You Earn
P.D.	Practice Direction
PD	Prescribed Disease
PIE	Period of Interruption of Employment
PIW	Period of Incapacity for Work
Persons Abroad Regulations	Social Security Benefit (Persons Abroad) Regulations 1975
Persons Residing Together Regulations	Social Security Benefit (Persons Residing Together) Regulations 1977
Prescribed Diseases Regulations	Social Security (Industrial Injuries) (Prescribed Diseases) Regulations 1985
PTA	Pure Tone Audiometry
Recoupment Regulations	Social Security (Recoupment) Regulations 1990
REA	Reduced Earnings Allowance
RMO	Regional Medical Officer
RSI	Repetitive Strain Injury
SAP	Statutory Adoption Pay
SDA	Severe Disablement Allowance
SDP	Severe Disability Premium
Severe Disablement Allowance Regulations	Social Security (Severe Disablement Allowance) Regulations 1984
SMP	Statutory Maternity Pay
SPCA 2002	State Pension Credit Act 2002
SPCA(NI) 2002	State Pension Credit Act (Northern Ireland) 2002
SPP	Statutory Paternity Pay
SSA 1975	Social Security Act 1975
SSA 1980	Social Security Act 1980
SSA 1981	Social Security Act 1981
SSA 1985	Social Security Act 1985
SSA 1986	Social Security Act 1986
SSA 1988	Social Security Act 1988
SSA 1989	Social Security Act 1989
SSA 1998	Social Security Act 1998
SS (No.2) A 1980	Social Security (No.2) Act 1980
SSAA 1992	Social Security Administration Act 1992*
SSAC	Social Security Advisory Committee
SSAT	Social Security Appeal Tribunal
SSCBA 1992	Social Security Contributions and Benefits Act 1992*
SSCB(NI) 1992	Social Security Contributions and Benefits (Northern Ireland) Act 1992

Table of Abbreviations used in this Series

SSHBA	Social Security and Housing Benefits Act 1982
SS (MP) A 1977	Social Security (Miscellaneous Provisions) Act 1977
SSP	Statutory Sick Pay
SSPA 1975	Social Security Pensions Act 1975
SSCBA 1992	Social Security Contributions and Benefits Act 1992*
SSAA 1992	Social Security Administration Act 1992*
SS(CP)A 1992	Social Security (Consequential Provisions) Act 1992
STC	Simon's Tax Cases
TC	Tax Cases
TCA 1999	Tax Credits Act 1999
TCA 2002	Tax Credits Act 2002
TCGA 1992	Taxation of Chargeable Gains Act 1992
TCTM	Tax Credits Technical Manual
TMA 1970	Taxes Management Act 1970
USI Regulations	Social Security (Unemployment, Sickness and Invalidity Benefit) Regulations 1983
VERA 1992	Vehicle Excise and Registration Act 1992
WFTC	Working Family Tax Credit
White Paper	Jobseeker's Allowance, Cm.2687 (October 1994)
Widow's Benefit and Retirement Pension Regulations	Social Security (Widow's Benefit and Retirement Pensions) Regulations 1979
Wikeley, Annotations	N. Wikeley, "Annotations to Jobseekers Act 1995 (c.18)" in *Current Law Statutes Annotated* (1995)
Wikeley, Ogus and Barendt	Wikeley, Ogus and Barendt *The Law of Social Security* (5th ed., Butterworths, 2002)
W.L.R.	Weekly Law Reports
Workmen's Compensation Acts	Workmen's Compensation Acts 1925 to 1945
WRPA 1999	Welfare Reform and Pensions Act 1999
WRP(NI)O 1999	Welfare Reform and Pensions (Northern Ireland) Order 1999
WTC	Working Tax Credit

*Where the context makes it seem more appropriate these could also be referred to as Contributions and Benefits Act 1992, Administration Act 1992

CHANGE OF NAME FROM DEPARTMENT OF SOCIAL SECURITY TO DEPARTMENT FOR WORK AND PENSIONS

The Secretaries of State for Education and Skills and for Work and Pensions Order 2002 (SI 2002/1397) makes provision for the change of name from the Department of Social Security to Department for Work and Pensions. Article 9(5) provides:

"(5) Subject to article 12 [which makes specific amendments], any enactment or instrument passed or made before the coming into force of this Order shall have effect, so far as may be necessary for the purposes of or in consequence of the entrusting to the Secretary of State for Work and Pensions of the social security functions, as if any reference to the Secretary of State for Social Security, to the Department of Social Security or to an officer of the Secretary of State for Social Security (including any reference which is to be construed as such a reference) were a reference to the Secretary of State for Work and Pensions, to the Department for Work and Pensions or, as the case may be, to an officer of the Secretary of State for Work and Pensions."

PART I

BENEFITS ACTS

Social Security Contributions and Benefits Act 1992

(1992 C.4)

SECTIONS REPRODUCED

PART VII

INCOME-RELATED BENEFITS

General

Income support

Family credit

Disability working allowance

General

PART VIII

THE SOCIAL FUND

PART XIII

GENERAL

Interpretation

Subordinate legislation

Short title, commencement and extent

PART VII

INCOME-RELATED BENEFITS

General

Income-related benefits

1.10   **123.**—(1) Prescribed schemes shall provide for the following benefits (in this Act referred to as "income-related benefits")—

(a) income support;
(b) [⁴. . .];
(c) [⁴. . .];
(d) housing benefit; and
[¹(e) council tax benefit.]

(2) The Secretary of State shall make copies of schemes prescribed under subsection (1)(a), (b) or (c) above available for public inspection at local offices of [³ the Department of Work and Pensions] at all reasonable hours without payment.

[Subss. (3) to (6) omitted as applying only to housing benefit and council tax benefit.]

AMENDMENTS

1.11   1. Local Government Finance Act 1992, Sch.9, para.1(1) (April 1, 1993).
2. Tax Credits Act 1999, Sch.1, paras 1 and 2(f) (October 5, 1999).
3. Secretaries of State for Education and Skills and for Work and Pensions Order 2002 (SI 2002/1397), art.12 and Sch., para.9 (June 27, 2002).
4. Tax Credits Act 2002, s.60 and Sch.3 (April 8, 2003).

DERIVATION
Social Security Act 1986, s.20(1) and (2).

1.12

Income support

Income support

124.—(1) A person in Great Britain is entitled to income support if—   1.13
[¹(a) he is of or over the age of 16;]
[⁴(aa) he has not attained the qualifying age for state pension credit;]
  (b) he has no income or his income does not exceed the applicable amount;
  (c) he is not engaged in remunerative work and, if he is a member of a married or unmarried couple, the other member is not so engaged; [¹. . .]
[¹(d) except in such circumstances as may be prescribed, he is not receiving relevant education;
  (e) he falls within a prescribed category of person; [⁵ . . .]
  (f) he is not entitled to a jobseeker's allowance and, if he is a member of a married or unmarried couple, the other member of the couple is not [³, and the couple are not,] entitled to an income-based jobseeker's allowance.] [⁴ and
  (g) if he is a member of a married or unmarried couple, the other member of the couple is not entitled to state pension credit.]
  (2) [². . .].
  (3) [². . .].
  (4) Subject to subsection (5) below, where a person is entitled to income support, then—
  (a) if he has no income, the amount shall be the applicable amount; and
  (b) if he has income, the amount shall be the difference between his income and the applicable amount.
  (5) Where a person is entitled to income support for a period to which this subsection applies, the amount payable for that period shall be calculated in such manner as may be prescribed.
  (6) Subsection (5) above applies—
  (a) to a period of less than a week which is the whole period for which income support is payable; and
  (b) to any other period of less than a week for which it is payable.

AMENDMENTS

1. Jobseekers Act 1995, Sch.2, para.30 (October 7, 1996).
2. Jobseekers Act 1995, Sch.3 (October 7, 1996).
3. Welfare Reform and Pensions Act 1999, Sch.8, para.28 (March 19, 2001).
4. State Pension Credit Act 2002, s.14 and Sch.2 paras 1 and 2 (October 6, 2003).
5. State Pension Credit Act 2002, s.21 and Sch.3 (October 6, 2003).

DERIVATION

Subs. (1): Social Security Act 1986, s.20(3).   1.14
Subs. (2): 1986 Act, s.20(4N).

5

Subs. (3): 1986 Act, s.20(4).
Subss. (4) to (6): 1986 Act, s.21(1) to (1B).

DEFINITIONS

"Great Britain"—see s.172(a).
"income-based jobseeker's allowance"—see s.137(1) and Jobseekers Act, s.35(1).
"married couple"—see s.137(1).
"prescribed"—*ibid.*
"qualifying age for state pension credit"—*ibid.*
"unmarried couple"—*ibid.*

GENERAL NOTE

Subs. (1)

1.15   Here the general conditions of entitlement to income support are set out. Note the amendments made on October 7, 1996 as a consequence of the introduction of jobseeker's allowance ("JSA") (see below). All of the conditions must be satisfied for there to be entitlement to income support (*CIS 166/1994*). There is also a capital test under s.134(1).

If there is entitlement under this subsection, the amount of income support is laid down in subss.(4) to (6).

There is no contributions test or requirement of citizenship (but see section 115 of the Immigration and Asylum Act 1999 on "persons subject to immigration control"). However, although a person qualifies if he is in Great Britain, an habitual residence condition was introduced on August 1, 1994. See the definition of "person from abroad" in reg.21(3) of the Income Support (General) Regulations, and the notes to that definition. Regulation 4 of the Income Support Regulations allows an award to continue for a short period of temporary absence from Great Britain, but otherwise income support cannot be paid to a person outside Great Britain. See *R(IS) 4/99* and *R(IS) 9/98*, which hold that income support is not a social security benefit within Art.4(1) of EC Regulation 1408/71. Although income support has been listed by the UK government as included in the new category of "special non-contributory benefits" to which Regulation 1408/71 applies from June 1, 1992 (see Art.4(2a) and Annex IIa), such benefits cannot be "exported" (*i.e.* paid where the claimant is in another Member State) (Art.10a). Article 10a provides for the granting of such benefits "exclusively in the territory of the Member State in which [the person] reside[s], in accordance with the legislation of that State". ("Resides" means "habitually resides": Art.1(h).) It was argued in *Perry v Chief Adjudication Officer, The Times*, October 20, 1998, also reported as part of *R(IS) 4/99*, that Art.10a conferred a positive right to income support on the claimant because of his habitual residence in the UK, and that he remained entitled to income support by virtue of that right, even during periods of temporary absence. But the Court of Appeal rejected this argument. The language of Art.10a made it clear that special non-contributory benefits were to be granted in accordance with the domestic law of the Member State. Presence in Great Britain was a requirement of the UK's legislation (subject to the exceptions in reg.4 of the Income Support Regulations) and this was not incompatible with Art.10a. The Court of Appeal also agreed with the Commissioner that the claimant could not rely on Art.2(4) of EC Regulation 1247/92 (the Regulation which introduced the June 1992 amendment) to export an entitlement to income support in respect of periods before June 1, 1992.

Para. (a)

1.16   From October 7, 1996 the minimum age for income support is again 16 (as it was until September 1988 before most 16- and 17-year-olds were excluded). But to be entitled a person must fall within a prescribed category (para.(e)). See reg.4ZA of and Sch.1B to the Income Support Regulations for these categories. Note that a person aged 16 to 18 in relevant education is still only entitled to income support in certain circumstances (para.(d) and reg.13 of the Income Support Regulations).

The reduction in the lower age limit is a consequence of the replacement from October 7, 1996 of income support by income-based JSA for people who are required to be available for work as a condition of receiving benefit. To be entitled to income-based JSA a person must in general be at least 18 (Jobseekers Act, s.3(1)(f)(i)), although there are exceptions, which are similar, but not identical, to those that used to operate for income support (see the 1996 edition of Mesher and Wood, *Income Support, the Social Fund and Family Credit: the Legislation* for reg.13A of and Sch.1A to the Income Support Regulations and the further escape under s.25; these provisions were revoked on October 7, 1996). Entitlement to JSA excludes entitlement to income support (para.(f)).

Para.(aa)

State Pension Credit was introduced on October 6, 2003. Paragraph (aa) rules out any possibility that a claimant could be entitled to both state pension credit and income support by providing that no person who has reached "the qualifying age for state pension credit" can be entitled to income support. "The qualifying age for state pension credit" is defined by s.137(1) below. The effect of that definition is that the qualifying age is 60 for both men and women until April 2010 after which it will increase by stages to 65 in line with the increase in pensionable age for a woman. It remains possible for the partner of a person over 60 to claim income support in some circumstances—see para.(g) below.

Para.(b)

The person's income (which includes the income of the claimant's family) must be less than the applicable amount (effectively the figure set for the family's requirements under s.135). However, note that as a consequence of the removal of amounts for children from income support (with effect from April 6, 2004, except in "transitional cases"—see the note to reg. 17 of the Income Support Regulations), only a partner's income will count as that of the claimant and the applicable amount will no longer include any personal allowances for children, the family premium, the disabled child premium or an enhanced disability premium for a child. 1.17

CIS 166/1994 confirms that the conditions in subs.(1) are cumulative. The fact that the claimant was not working in his business and so para.(c) did not apply, did not mean that income from that business could not potentially disentitle him under para.(b). See the notes to reg.30 of the Income Support Regulations.

Para.(c)

The introduction of the condition in para.(c) marked an important change from the supplementary benefit rules. If either the claimant or his partner is in remunerative work (defined in regs 5 and 6 of the Income Support Regulations) there is no entitlement to income support. For supplementary benefit, this condition was only applied to the claimant. The transitional protection announced on April 28, 1988 (see p.198 of the 1998 edition of *Mesher and Wood*) has remained on an extra-statutory basis. 1.18

Note that from October 7, 1996 the limit for remunerative work in the case of a partner is 24 hours or more a week (Income Support Regulations, reg.5(1A)). It remains 16 or more for the claimant.

Para.(d)

See regs 12 and 13 of the Income Support Regulations. 1.19

Para.(e)

From October 7, 1996 only certain categories of people are entitled to income support. See reg.4ZA of and Sch.1A to the Income Support Regulations for these categories. They are similar to those groups who formerly were exempt from the 1.20

requirement to be available for work for the purposes of income support (see Sch.1 to the Income Support Regulations which was revoked on October 7, 1996), but there are some differences.

Para. (f)

1.21   Entitlement to JSA excludes entitlement to income support (any "top-up" to a person's contribution-based JSA will be by way of income-based JSA, not income support); if the claimant is a member of a couple, he will also not qualify for income support if his partner is entitled to income-based JSA or if he and his partner are entitled together to "joint-claim" JSA. But although entitlement to income support and JSA is mutually exclusive, some people may be eligible for either, *i.e.* those who fall into a prescribed category for income support but who also satisfy the labour market conditions for JSA. See the notes to reg.4ZA of the Income Support Regulations for discussion of the position of such claimants and of the fact that the raising of the limit for remunerative work for partners to 24 hours a week from October 7, 1996 may create a "better-off" problem for some claimants.

Para. (g)

By virtue of para.(aa) above, a claimant who is aged over 60 years cannot be entitled to income support. Claimants who are aged 59 or less themselves, but who have partners above that age, may claim income support as long as their partners are not actually entitled to state pension credit. Since, under s. 1 SSAA 1992, there can be no entitlement to state pension credit without making a claim, the effect is that a couple with one member aged over 60 and the other aged under 60 (and who are not already in receipt of state pension credit) can choose to claim either income support, JSA or state pension credit. It will normally be advantageous to claim state pension credit.

Subs. (4)

1.22   This provision sets out the basic means test calculation for income support. Providing that the conditions of entitlement imposed by subs.(1) and the capital test under s.134(1) are satisfied, the claimant's income is set against his applicable amount, calculated according to regs 17 to 22 of the Income Support (General) Regulations. The difference is the amount of benefit. The claimant's income includes that of the other members of his family, except in prescribed cases (s. 136(1)). Note that as a consequence of the removal of amounts for children from income support (with effect from April 6, 2004, except in "transitional cases"—see further the note to reg.17 of the Income Support Regulations), only a partner's income will count as that of the claimant.

Subss. (5) and (6)

1.23   These provisions allow regulations to deal with entitlement for part-weeks. See regs 73 to 77 of the Income Support (General) Regulations.

Severe hardship cases

1.24   **125.** [¹. . .]

AMENDMENT

1. Jobseekers Act 1995, Sch.3 (October 7, 1996).

Trade disputes

1.25   **126.**—(1) This section applies to a person, other than a child or a person of a prescribed description—
         (a) who [² is prevented from being entitled to a jobseeker's allowance by section 14 of the Jobseekers Act 1995 (trade disputes)]; or

(b) who would be so [² prevented] if otherwise entitled to that benefit, except during any period shown by the person to be a period of incapacity for work [¹ . . .] or to be within the maternity period.

(2) In subsection (1) above "the maternity period" means the period commencing at the beginning of the 6th week before the expected week of confinement and ending at the end of the 7th week after the week in which confinement takes place.

(3) For the purposes of calculating income support—

(a) so long as this section applies to a person who is not a member of a family, the applicable amount shall be disregarded;

(b) so long as it applies to a person who is a member of a family but is not a member of a married or unmarried couple, the portion of the applicable amount which is included in respect of him shall be disregarded;

(c) so long as it applies to one of the members of a married or unmarried couple—

(i) if the applicable amount consists only of an amount in respect of them, it shall be reduced to one half; and

(ii) if it includes other amounts, the portion of it which is included in respect of them shall be reduced to one-half and any further portion of it which is included in respect of the member of the couple to whom this section applies shall be disregarded;

(d) so long as it applies to both members of a married or unmarried couple—

(i) if neither of them is responsible for a child or person of a prescribed description who is a member of the same household, the applicable amount shall be disregarded; and

(ii) in any other case, the portion of the applicable amount which is included in respect of them and any further portion of it which is included in respect of either of them shall be disregarded.

(4) Where a reduction under subsection (3)(c) above would not produce a sum which is a multiple of 5p, the reduction shall be to the nearest lower sum which is such a multiple.

(5) Where this section applies to a person for any period, then, except so far as regulations provide otherwise—

(a) in calculating the entitlement to income support of that person or a member of his family the following shall be treated as his income and shall not be disregarded—

(i) any payment which he or a member of his family receives or is entitled to obtain by reason of the person to whom this section applies being without employment for that period; and

(ii) without prejudice to the generality of sub-paragraph (i) above, any amount which becomes or would on an application duly made, become available to him in that period by way of repayment of income tax deducted from his [³ taxable earnings (as defined by section 10 of the Income Tax (Earnings and Pensions) Act 2003 under PAYE regulations]; and

(b) any payment by way of income support for that period or any part of it which apart from this paragraph would be made to him, or to a person whose applicable amount is aggregated with his—

(i) shall not be made if the weekly rate of payment is equal to or less than the relevant sum; or

(ii) if it is more than the relevant sum, shall be at a weekly rate equal to the difference.

(6) In respect of any period less than a week, subsection (5) above shall have effect subject to such modifications as may be prescribed.

(7) Subject to subsection (8) below, the "relevant sum" for the purposes of subsection (5) above shall be [⁴£30.50].

(8) If an order under section 150 of the Administration Act (annual up-rating) has the effect of increasing payments of income support, from the time when the order comes into force there shall be substituted, in subsection (5)(b) above, for the references to the sum for the time being mentioned in it references to a sum arrived at by—

(a) increasing that sum by the percentage by which the personal allowance under paragraph 1(1) of Part I of Schedule 2 to the Income Support (General) Regulations 1987 for a single person aged not less than 25 has been increased by the order; and

(b) if the sum so increased is not a multiple of 50p, disregarding the remainder if it is 25p and, if it is not, rounding it up or down to the nearest 50p,

and the order shall state the substituted sum.

AMENDMENTS

1.26   1. Social Security (Incapacity for Work) Act 1994, Sch.1, para.31 (April 13, 1995).

2. Jobseekers Act 1995, Sch.2, para.31 (October 7, 1996).

3. Income Tax (Earnings and Pensions) Act 2003, Sch.6, Pt 2, para.179 (April 6, 2003).

4. Social Security Benefits Up-rating Order 2005 (SI 2005/522), art.18 (April 11, 2005).

DERIVATION

Social Security Act 1986, s.23.

DEFINITIONS

1.27   "child"—see s.137(1).
"family"—*ibid.*
"married couple"—*ibid.*
"prescribed"—*ibid.*
"the Administration Act"—see s.174.
"unmarried couple"—see s.137(1).

GENERAL NOTE

The trade dispute rule, long an important part of the supplementary benefit scheme, was considerably simplified in the income support rules, although most of the stringency remains.

Subs. (1)

1.28   The rule applies to anyone other than a child or young person (Income Support (General) Regulations, reg.14) who is disentitled to JSA, or would be disentitled, under s.14 of the Jobseekers Act. Thus the income support rule depends directly on the JSA rule. Note that if the decision-maker considers that he does not have enough information to decide this question, it will be assumed that the person is involved in the trade dispute (Decisions and Appeals Regulations 1999, reg.13(2)).

The rule does not apply when the person involved is incapable of work. There is no trade dispute disqualification for incapacity benefit. The rule also does not apply in the maternity period, defined in subs.(2).

If the rule applies there are consequences for the way in which applicable amounts are calculated. This is dealt with in subs.(3). There are also consequences for the way in which income is calculated. This is dealt with in subs.(5) and in a number of regulations. The most immediate effect is that the person is treated as in remunerative work for the seven days following the first day of the stoppage of work or the day on which the claimant withdrew his labour (Income Support Regulations, reg.5(4)). The result is that neither the person nor his partner can be entitled to income support at all for those days (s.124(1)(c)).

Subs. (3)

This provision sets out the effect on the applicable amount if the claimant is not excluded by the conditions of entitlement.   **1.29**

(a) A single claimant with no child or young person in the household is to have no applicable amount, and so cannot be entitled to any benefit. There is the possibility of a crisis loan under the social fund but only for expenses that result from a disaster or for items for cooking or heating (including fireguards) (Social Fund Direction, 17(a) and (g)).

(b) For a single claimant with a child or young person in the household, the "portion of the applicable amount included in respect of" the claimant is disregarded. It is clear that the personal allowance for the claimant is taken out, and so is any premium payable on account of the claimant's disability or age or because she is a carer. Arguably the family premium and the lone parent element of the family premium (if payable) are not included "in respect of" the claimant and so remain, but the *Decision Makers Guide* only accepts this in the case of the basic family premium (see para.32639).

(c) For a couple where the trade dispute rule applies to only one of them, if they have no premiums on top of their personal allowance, that allowance is reduced by a half. This is a different rule from supplementary benefit, which would have left the other partner with the appropriate personal allowance for a single claimant. If there are any premiums, then the rule in para.(b) applies. Thus any premium payable solely for the person involved in the dispute (*e.g.* a carer premium) is taken out, but according to para.32642 of the *Decision Makers Guide* such a premium will be included in full if it is for the person not involved in the dispute. Any premium paid for the couple (*e.g.* a pensioner premium) is reduced by half. But para.32642 accepts that the family premium is payable in full. It is easier to argue for the retention of the family premium here, since that would be paid to the remaining partner if the partner involved in the trade dispute disappeared.

(d) For a couple where the trade dispute rule applies to both of them, the applicable amount is nil if there is no child or young person in the house- hold. If there is a child or young person, then the family premium and any premium paid for that person's disability is allowed on top of the personal allowance for that person.

Note that housing costs are payable, provided that at least one member of the family (*e.g.* a child or young person) is not involved in the dispute. The housing costs are treated as the responsibility of the member or members not involved in the dispute (Income Support Regulations, Sch.3, para.2(2)).

Further note that the above explanation of the provisions in subs.(3) needs to be modified to take into account the removal of amounts for children and young persons from income support with effect from April 6, 2004, except for "transitional cases". Transitional cases in this context are claimants who immediately before

11

April 6, 2004 are in receipt of income support and have a child or young person who is a member of their family but who have not been awarded (and whose partners have not been awarded) child tax credit for a period which begins before April 6, 2004 (see further the note to reg.17 of the Income Support Regulations). Such claimants will continue to receive personal allowances, the family premium and premiums for their children as part of their income support until they apply for or are transferred onto child tax credit (this phased transfer was intended to start in October 2004 but has been delayed and will not be completed until December 31, 2006). Where the new rules apply the income support applicable amount will no longer include personal allowances for any child or young person, the family premium, the disabled child premium or an enhanced disability premium for a child.

Subs. (5)

1.30   If the trade dispute rule applies, the normal rules about income are modified. Under para.(a) any payment that a member of the family receives, or is entitled to obtain by reason of the person involved in the trade dispute being without employment, must be taken into account. In *R(SB) 29/85* a loan from a local authority Social Work Department (the Scottish equivalent of a Social Services Department) to meet arrears of hire purchase repayments was held to be capable of being such a payment. The claimant had not been in arrears before the dispute and the loan was to be repaid on his return to work. But on the facts it was a payment of capital, not income. Now reg.41(3) of the Income Support (General) Regulations secures that, in trade dispute cases, payments under s.17 or 24 of the Children Act 1989 or s.12, 24 or 26 of the Social Work (Scotland) Act 1968 (now the Children (Scotland) Act 1995) (payments to families to prevent children being taken into care, etc.) are treated as income, not capital. Nor does the disregard of such income in para.28 of Sch.9 to the Income Support (General) Regulations apply in trade dispute cases. Other categories of income normally disregarded but counted here are income in kind (para.21) and charitable or voluntary payments (para.15). Holiday pay paid more than four weeks after the termination of employment (normally capital) is earnings (reg.35(1)(d)).

The other main category under para.(a) is income tax refunds paid or due. The effect of reg.48(2) is that in trade dispute cases refunds do not count as capital. The assumption is then that they count as income, but this does not seem to be provided for expressly.

Under para.(b) there is the final automatic deduction of the "relevant sum." This is the sum specified in subs.(6). as increased in future years under subs.(7). The sum was increased to £30.50 in April 2005. The relevant sum is often called "assumed strike pay," but is deducted regardless of whether the person involved is entitled to strike pay, a member of a union, or even on strike.

The "compensation" for this rule is that any payment from a trade union up to the amount of £30.50 is disregarded (Sch.9, para.34).

The cumulative result of these income rules, plus the reductions in applicable amounts, is that even married strikers will often receive very little benefit indeed (if any). Their only resort is the social fund for crisis loans in disasters or for items for cooking or heating (including fireguards) (Social Fund Direction, 17(a) and (g)).

Effect of return to work

1.31   **127.** If a person returns to work with the same employer after a period during which section 126 above applies to him, and whether or not his return is before the end of any stoppage of work in relation to which he is or would be [¹ prevented from being entitled to a jobseeker's allowance]—

(a) that section shall cease to apply to him at the commencement of the day on which he returns to work; and

(b) until the end of the period of 15 days beginning with that day section 124(1) above shall have effect in relation to him as if the following paragraph were substituted for paragraph (c)—"(c) in the case of a member of a married or unmarried couple, the other member is not engaged in remunerative work; and"; and

(c) any sum paid by way of income support for that period of 15 days to him or, where he is a member of a married or unmarried couple, to the other member of that couple, shall be recoverable in the pre-scribed manner from the person to whom it was paid or from any pre-scribed person or, where the person to whom it was paid is a member of a married or unmarried couple, from the other member of the couple.

AMENDMENT

1. Jobseekers Act 1995, Sch.2, para.32 (October 7, 1996).

DERIVATION

Social Security Act 1986, s.23A.   1.32

DEFINITIONS

"married couple"—see s.137(1).
"prescribed"—*ibid.*
"unmarried couple"—*ibid.*

GENERAL NOTE

This section allows income support to be paid for the first 15 days following a   1.33
return to work from a trade dispute. Normally the work would exclude entitlement to benefit under s.124(1)(c) regardless of whether any wages were payable or not. The rules about the relevant sum and income tax refunds under s.126 do not apply, but the other adjustments to the income rules do apply. Applicable amounts are cal-culated in the ordinary way. Note that any advance of earnings or loan made by the employer counts as earnings (Income Support (General) Regulations, reg.48(5) and (6)). In addition, any payment of benefit under this section is recoverable under subs.(c) and Part VIII of the Payments Regulations.

Family Credit

Family credit

128. [¹ . . .]   1.34

AMENDMENT

1. Tax Credits Act 2002, s.60 and Sch.6 (April 8, 2003).   1.35

Disability working allowance

Disability working allowance

129. [¹ . . .]   1.36

AMENDMENT

1. Tax Credits Act 2002, s.60 and Sch.6 (April 8, 2003).   1.37

GENERAL NOTE

1.38   Sections 128 and 129 originally dealt with family credit and disability working allowance respectively. As a result of amendments made by the Tax Credits Act 1999, these sections then provided the legislative basis for working families' tax credit (WFTC) and disabled person's tax credit (DPTC) with effect from October 5, 1999. However, the Tax Credits Act 2002 replaced WFTC and DPTC with a new tax credits regime comprising working tax credit (WTC) and child tax credit (CTC). Consequently, ss.128 and 129 were repealed with effect from April 8, 2003 by s.60 of and Sch.6 to the Tax Credits Act 2002 (see further Tax Credits Act 2002 (Commencement No.4, Transitional Provisions and Savings) Order 2003, art. 2(4)(e) and Sch.2).

The text of and commentary on ss.128 and 129 have accordingly been omitted from this volume for 2003 and subsequent years. For the full annotated text of these provisions, see paras 1.34–1.62 of the 2002 edition of this volume; see also Part IV of that volume for the Family Credit (General) Regulations 1987 (SI 1987/1973) and the Disability Working Allowance (General) Regulations 1991 (SI 1991/2887). The 2002 commentary on ss.128 and 129 and on those (and other relevant) regulations should be read together with the Updating Material at paras 6.1–6.35 in the 2003 edition. That section included the updating material on WFTC and DPTC in the 2002/2003 Supplement as well as subsequent developments.

For detailed commentary on WTC and CTC, see the new Vol. IV in this series, *Tax Credits and Employer-paid Social Security Benefits.*

General

Exclusions from benefit

1.39   **134.**—(1) No person shall be entitled to an income-related benefit if his capital or a prescribed part of it exceeds the prescribed amount.

(2) Except in prescribed circumstances the entitlement of one member of a family to any one income-related benefit excludes entitlement to that benefit for any other member for the same period.

(3) [¹ . . .]

(4) Where the amount of any income-related benefit would be less than a prescribed amount, it shall not be payable except in prescribed circumstances.

AMENDMENT

1. Local Government Finance Act 1992, Sch.9, para.7 (April 1, 1993).

DERIVATION

1.40   Subs.(1): Social Security Act 1986, s.22(6).
Subs.(2): 1986 Act, s.20(9).
Subs.(4): 1986 Act, s.21(7).

DEFINITIONS

"family"—see s.137(1).
"prescribed"—*ibid.*

GENERAL NOTE

Subs. (1)

1.41   The capital limit for income support was raised to £8,000 from £6,000 in April 1990 (Income Support Regulations, reg.45). From April 8, 1996 the capital limit for income support was further raised to £16,000 for claimants living permanently in residential care or nursing homes, residential accommodation or Polish resettlement homes (Income Support Regulations, regs 45(b) and 53(1B)). In addition, on April 9, 2001, the income support limit was increased to £12,000 in the case of a claimant who, or whose partner, is aged 60 or over (Income Support Regulations, regs 45(aa) and 53(IZA)). As a consequence of the start of the state pension credit scheme on October 6, 2003 this now only applies if the claimant's partner is aged 60 or over; if the claimant has reached the qualifying age for state pension credit (defined in s.137(1)—the effect of that definition is that the qualifying age is 60 for both men and women until April 2010 after which it will increase by stages to 65 in line with the increase in pensionable age for a woman) he will not be entitled to income support (s.124(1)(aa)). The limit for housing benefit and council tax benefit (the other two remaining income-related benefits within the meaning of s.123 after the abolition of working families' tax credit and disabled person's tax credit on April 8, 2003) is £16,000. There is no capital limit for working tax credit and child tax credit (which started on April 6, 2003) and state pension credit (introduced on October 6, 2003).

Since the capital rule operates as an exclusion to benefit it is arguable that the burden of proof that a claimant's capital exceeds the limit is on the Secretary of State. The Tribunal of Commissioners in *CIS 417/1992*, reported as part of *R(IS) 26/95*, treat satisfaction of the capital rule as part of what the claimant has to prove in showing entitlement to income support. However, the contrary argument was not put to the Tribunal. But once it has been shown that the claimant possesses an item of capital, it is for him to prove that one of the disregards in Sch.10 applies (*CIS 240/1992*). Similarly, if it has been established that the claimant is the legal owner of a property, the burden is on him to show that the beneficial ownership does not follow the legal ownership (*CIS 30/1993*).

Subs. (4)
See reg.26(4) of the Claims and Payments Regulations in Vol. III of this series.   1.42

The applicable amount

135.—(1) The applicable amount, in relation to any income-related   1.43
benefit, shall be such amount or the aggregate of such amounts as may be prescribed in relation to that benefit.

(2) The power to prescribe applicable amounts conferred by subsection (1) above includes power to prescribe nil as an applicable amount.

[[1](3) In prescribing, for the purposes of income support, amounts under subsection (1) above in respect of accommodation in any area for qualifying persons in cases where prescribed conditions are fulfilled, the Secretary of State shall take into account information provided by local authorities or other prescribed bodies or persons with respect to the amounts which they have agreed to pay for the provision of accommodation in relevant premises in that area.

(4) In subsection (3) above—
"accommodation" includes any board or care;
"local authority"—
  (a) in relation to areas in England and Wales, has the same meaning as it has in Part III of the National Assistance Act 1948; and
  (b) in relation to areas in Scotland, has the meaning given by section 1(2) of the Social Work (Scotland) Act 1968;
"qualifying person" means any person who falls within—
  (a) subsection (1) of section 26A of the National Assistance Act 1948

(which is inserted by the National Health Service and Community Care Act 1990 and relates to persons ordinarily resident in residential care or nursing homes immediately before the commencement of that section); or

(b) subsection (1) of section 86A of the Social Work (Scotland) Act 1968 (the corresponding provision for Scotland), or who would fall within either of those subsections apart from any regulations under subsection (3) of the section in question;

"relevant premises"—

(a) in relation to areas in England and Wales, has the meaning given by section 26A(2) of the National Assistance Act 1948; and

(b) in relation to areas in Scotland, has the meaning given section 86A(2) of the Social Work (Scotland) Act 1968.]

(5) [³ . . .] The applicable amount for a severely disabled person shall include an amount in respect of his being a severely disabled person.

(6) Regulations may specify circumstances in which persons are to be treated as being or as not being severely disabled.

AMENDMENTS

1.44   1. To be omitted until s.9 of the Social Security Act 1990 is brought into force: Social Security (Consequential Provisions) Act 1992, s.6 and Sch.4, Pt I.

2. Local Government Finance Act 1992, Sch.9, para.8 (April 1, 1993).

3. Tax Credits Act 2002, s.60 and Sch.3 (April 8, 2003).

DERIVATION

1.45   Social Security Act 1986, s.22(1) to (4).

DEFINITION

"prescribed"—see s.137(1).

GENERAL NOTE

Subs. (1)

1.46   See regs 17 to 22A of and Sch.2 to the Income Support (General) Regulations.

CIS 683/1993 confirms that a claimant's applicable amount can only consist of elements specified in the relevant regulations. It cannot be increased by the amount of maintenance (or insurance premiums) the claimant is required to pay.

Subs. (2)

See reg.21 of and Sch.7 to the Income Support Regulations.

Subss. (3) and (4)

1.47   The predecessors of these subsections were inserted into s.22 of the 1986 Act by s.9 of the Social Security Act 1990 and are closely bound up with the Government's community care reforms. Those reforms under the National Health Service and Community Care Act 1990 were intended to come into force in April 1991, but after the passage of the Social Security Act 1990, it was announced that they would not come into effect until April 1993. These amendments have not yet come into force (see Social Security (Consequential Provisions) Act 1992, Sch.4, paras 1 and 4).

Subss. (5) and (6)

1.48   See para.13 of Sch.2 to the Income Support (General) Regulations. A provision requiring the payment of a community care addition to income support to very severely disabled people was put into the 1986 Act when it was going through the

House of Lords. Although the Government did not wish to have this requirement in the legislation it did not seek to remove its spirit when the Bill returned to the House of Commons. But it put in its own amendments, which have now become subss.(5) and (6).

In *R(IS) 22/93* the Commissioner held that s.22(4) of the 1986 Act (the predecessor of subs.(6)) did not authorise the making of regulations prescribing conditions to be satisfied before a person counts as severely disabled other than conditions relating to the extent of that person's disablement. Otherwise, the mandatory provision of s.22(3) (the predecessor of subs.(5)) would be undermined. He therefore went on to hold that heads (ii) and (iii) of para.13(2)(a) of Sch.2, on the severe disability premium, were not validly part of the General Regulations. This was because they referred to the presence of a non-dependant in the claimant's household and to the receipt of invalid care allowance by another person, and not to the claimant's disability.

On appeal, the majority of the Court of Appeal took the opposite view, that s.22(4) gave the Secretary of State power to specify financial and domestic conditions as part of the circumstances in which a person was or was not to be treated as severely disabled (*Chief Adjudication Officer v Foster* [1992] Q.B. 31, [1991] 3 All E.R. 846). Therefore the provisions were valid. Lord Donaldson M.R. dissented trenchantly, saying that if s.22(4) allowed regulations to specify conditions not relating to the severity of disability this would "emasculate the imperative contained in subs.(3) and indeed . . . render it otiose."

The House of Lords ([1993] A.C. 754, [1993] 1 All E.R. 705) also held the provisions to be valid. Lord Bridge agreed that subs.(3) (now subs.(5)) required the applicable amount for a severely disabled person to include some amount in respect of being such a person. But subs.(4) (now subs.(6)) was a deeming provision that allowed the Secretary of State to define who was to be treated as severely disabled. He could do this by reference to circumstances that either related to the degree of disability or affected the extent of need for income support arising from the disability. If the only power intended to be given by subs.(4) was a power to define the degree of disability that qualified as severe, the language used was totally inappropriate for that purpose (especially compared with the precise code for determining the degree of disability which qualified someone for severe disablement allowance).

Lord Bridge would have reached this conclusion without looking at the Parliamentary history of the subsections in Hansard, but following *Pepper v Hart* [1993] A.C. 593, [1992] 3 W.L.R. 1032 this could be consulted. The statements of Ministers in both Houses of Parliament on the government amendments made clear that it was intended to use the regulation-making power to prescribe that the severe disability premium should only be applicable where the person was receiving the higher rate of attendance allowance, was living in a household with no other adult able to care for him and had noone eligible for invalid care allowance in respect of him. Therefore, the ambiguity in the regulation-making power was to be resolved so as to authorise that use of the power.

The House of Lords' decision settled the scope of subss.(5) and (6). See the notes to para.13 of Sch.2 to the Income Support (General) Regulations for the conditions for the severe disability premium. On the powers of the Social Security Commissioners, tribunals and decision-makers to determine the validity or otherwise of regulations, see Vol. III of this series.

Income and capital

136.—(1) Where a person claiming an income-related benefit is a member of a family, the income and capital of any member of that family shall, except in prescribed circumstances, be treated as the income and capital of that person.

(2) Regulations may provide that capital not exceeding the amount

1.49

prescribed under section 134(1) above but exceeding a prescribed lower amount shall be treated, to a prescribed extent, as if it were income of a prescribed amount.

(3) Income and capital shall be calculated or estimated in such manner as may be prescribed.

(4) A person's income in respect of a week shall be calculated in accordance with prescribed rules; and the rules may provide for the calculation to be made by reference to an average over a period (which need not include the week concerned).

(5) Circumstances may be prescribed in which—

(a)   a person is treated as possessing capital or income which he does not possess;

(b)   capital or income which a person does possess is to be disregarded;

(c)   income is to be treated as capital;

(d)   capital is to be treated as income.

DERIVATION

1.50   Subs.(1): Social Security Act 1986, s.22(5).
Subss.(2) to (5): 1986 Act, s.22(7) to (9).

DEFINITIONS

"family"—see s.137(1).
"prescribed"—*ibid.*

GENERAL NOTE

Subs. (1)

1.51   This provides that the general rule for income support is that all of the family's (as defined in s.137(1)) income and capital should be aggregated together and treated as the claimant's. The modifications to this rule for children and young persons were in regs.44 and 47 of the Income Support Regulations (see the 2003 edition of this volume for those regulations and the notes to those regulations). However, as a consequence of the removal of amounts for children and young persons from income support (with effect from April 6, 2004, except in "transitional cases"— see the note to reg.17 of the Income Support Regulations), a child's income and capital will be totally ignored and only a partner's income and capital will count as that of the claimant (see the amended form of reg.23(1) of the Income Support Regulations).

Subs. (2)

1.52   Reg.53 of the Income Support Regulations provides for an income to be assumed to be produced from capital between £3,000 and £8,000. For those income support claimants for whom the capital limit was raised to £16,000 on April 8, 1996 (see regs 45(b) and 53(1B) of the Income Support Regulations), the tariff income rule only applies to capital over £10,000. Similarly, from April 9, 2001 it has only applied to capital over £6,000 for a claimant who, or whose partner, is aged 60 or over, following the increase in the capital limit to £12,000 for those claimants (see Income Support Regulations, regs 45(aa) and 53(IZA)). Note that from October 6, 2003 when the state pension credit scheme commenced this will only apply if the claimant's partner is 60 or over since a claimant who has reached the qualifying age for state pension credit (defined in s.137(1) – the effect of that definition is that the qualifying age is 60 for both men and women until April 2010 after which it will increase by stages to 65 in line with the increase in pensionable age for a woman) is not entitled to income support (s.124(1)(aa)).

Subss.(3) to (5)
Large parts of the regulations deal with the matters covered by these subsections.   **1.53**

Interpretation of Part VII and supplementary provisions

137.—(1) In this Part of this Act, unless the context otherwise requires—   **1.54**
[¹"billing authority" has the same meaning as in Part I of the Local Government Finance Act 1992;]
"child" means a person under the age of 16;
[¹. . .]
"dwelling" means any residential accommodation, whether or not consisting of the whole or part of a building and whether or not comprising separate and self-contained premises;
"family" means—
  (a) a married or unmarried couple;
  (b) a married or unmarried couple and a member of the same household for whom one of them is or both are responsible and who is a child or a person of a prescribed description;
  (c) except in prescribed circumstances, a person who is not a member of a married or unmarried couple and a member of the same household for whom that person is responsible and who is a child or a person of a prescribed description;
[²"income-based jobseeker's allowance" has the same meaning as in the Jobseekers Act 1995;]
"industrial injuries scheme" means a scheme made under Schedule 8 to this Act or section 159 of the 1975 Act or under the Old Cases Act;
[¹"levying authority" has the same meaning as in Part II of the Local Government Finance Act 1992;]
"married couple" means a man and woman who are married to each other and are members of the same household;
[³"pensionable age" has the meaning given by the rules in paragraph 1 of Schedule 4 to the Pensions Act 1995 (c. 26);]
"prescribed" means specified in or determined in accordance with regulations;
[³"state pension credit" means state pension credit under the State Pension Credit Act 2002;
"the qualifying age for state pension credit" is (in accordance with section 1(2)(b) and (6) of the State Pension Credit Act 2002)—
  (a) in the case of a woman, pensionable age; or
  (b) in the case of a man, the age which is pensionable age in the case of a woman born on the same day as the man;]
"unmarried couple" means a man and woman who are not married to each other but are living together as husband and wife otherwise than in prescribed circumstances;
"war pension scheme" means a scheme under which war pensions (as defined in section 25 of the Social Security Act 1989) are provided;
"week", in relation to [¹council tax benefit], means a period of seven days beginning with a Monday.
(2) Regulations may make provision for the purposes of this Part of this Act—
  (a) as to circumstances in which a person is to be treated as being or not being in Great Britain;

(b) continuing a person's entitlement to benefit during periods of temporary absence from Great Britain;

(c) as to what is or is not to be treated as remunerative work or as employment;

[²(d) as to circumstances in which a person is or is not to be treated as engaged or normally engaged in remunerative work;]

(e) as to what is or is not to be treated as relevant education;

(f) as to circumstances in which a person is or is not to be treated as receiving relevant education;

(g) specifying the descriptions of pension increases under war pension schemes or industrial injuries schemes that are analogous to the benefits mentioned in section 129(2)(b)(i) to (iii) above;

(h) as to circumstances in which a person is or is not to be treated as occupying a dwelling as his home;

(i) for treating any person who is liable to make payments in respect of a dwelling as if he were not so liable;

(j) for treating any person who is not liable to make payments in respect of a dwelling as if he were so liable;

(k) for treating as included in a dwelling any land used for the purposes of the dwelling;

(l) as to circumstances in which persons are to be treated as being or not being members of the same household;

(m) as to circumstances in which one person is to be treated as responsible or not responsible for another.

AMENDMENTS

1. Local Government Finance Act 1992, Sch.9, para.9 (April 1, 1993).
2. Jobseekers Act 1995, Sch.2, para.35 (October 7, 1996).
3. State Pension Credit Act 2002, s.14 and Sch.2 paras 1 and 4 (October 6, 2003).

DERIVATION

1.55

Subs.(1): Social Security Act, ss.20(11) and 84(1).
Subs.(2): 1986 Act, s.20(12).

DEFINITIONS

"the 1975 Act"—see s.174.
"the Old Cases Act"—*ibid.*

GENERAL NOTE

Subs. (1)

1.56

These definitions are important throughout the income support scheme.

"*child*". Note the restricted definition that gives rise to the need to define "young persons" in regulations, to cater for the over-15s.

"*dwelling*". See the notes to the definition of "dwelling occupied as the home" in reg.2(1) of the Income Support (General) Regulations.

"*family*". The definition effectively covers couples with or without children and single claimants with children. It may be that some contexts in the regulations require that single claimants without children are also included where a "family" is referred to.

Under para.(a), see the later definitions of married couple and unmarried couple.

Para.(b) covers couples and any child or young person (see reg.14 of the Income Support Regulations) in the household for whom one of the couple is responsible. On the general test of membership of the household and children, see *England v Secretary of State for Social Services* [1982] 3 F.L.R. 222, *R(FIS) 4/83* and *R(SB) 14/87*. See also the notes under "married couple" and "unmarried couple". There are deeming rules in reg.16 of the Income Support Regulations.

Para.(c) covers a single claimant who is responsible for a child in the same household.   1.57

"*income-based jobseeker's allowance*". See ss.35(1) and 1(4) of the Jobseekers Act.

"*married couple*". The crucial question here is whether the couple are members of the same household. In *Santos v Santos* [1972] 2 All E.R. 246 at 255 it was said that "household" refers to "people held together by a particular kind of tie". No doubt the approach taken in *R(SB) 13/82*, *R(SB) 4/83* and *CSB 463/1986* would apply here, subject to the deeming regulations mentioned above. The basic point of these and other decisions is that a house can contain a number of households. According to *R(SB) 4/83*, the concept of a household is a matter of commonsense and common experience. If a person in practice has exclusive occupation of separate accommodation from another person they do not live in the same household. In *CSB 463/1986* two claimants physically shared one room in a house as well as other facilities, but otherwise lived separately. They were in separate households. Thus a husband and wife can maintain separate households under the same roof. If the couple have decided to live apart in the same house, there can be separate households even if the husband is still maintaining the wife (*CIS 72/1994*). In *CIS 671/1992* the claimant and his wife shared a room in a home for the mentally ill. Both suffered from senile dementia and they did not understand that they were husband and wife. It is held that there must be some communality, something that can be identified as a domestic establishment. Mere presence in the same room did not turn them into a household. It is a question of fact in each case. In *CIS 81/1993* the same Commissioner similarly concludes that a husband and wife (who were not mentally incapacitated) were not members of the same household where they lived in separate rooms in a nursing home, were billed separately and had only limited contact with each other.

In *CIS 671/1992* the Commissioner also considers whether the claimant and his   1.58
wife could be said to be members of some other household (the home as a whole). He refers to the decision of the House of Lords in *Simmons v Pizzey* [1979] A.C. 37 (occupants of a woman's refuge not a single household), and concludes that all the residents of the home were not one household.

These decisions are followed in *R(IS) 1/99*, which also concerned a married couple who shared a double room in a residential home (for which they were billed separately). The room was furnished with their own furniture and they had a kettle and a toaster to make breakfast, although they ate their main meals in the communal dining room. They spent much of their time together and were able to wash and dress themselves, apart from needing assistance to get out of the bath. They had entered the home because it was becoming difficult to cope on their own and so they needed someone else to undertake the organisation of their domestic and personal activities. The Commissioner agrees with *CIS 671/1992* that for there to be a "household" there had to be a domestic establishment. This meant two or more people living together as a unit and enjoying a reasonable level of independence and self-sufficiency. If the degree of independence and self-sufficiency fell below a certain level, there was no longer a domestic establishment and therefore no longer a household. The point at which this occurred was a matter for the common sense of the tribunal. The tribunal had correctly concluded in this case that the claimants were not members of the same household.

Although a person cannot simultaneously have two households he can spend, for example, six months of the year in one household and six in another (*CIS 11304/1995*).

A person under 16 cannot be a member of a married or unmarried couple (*CFC*   1.59
7/1992).

"*the qualifying age for state pension credit*". See note to s.124(1)(aa) above.

"unmarried couple". The meaning and effect of this definition raises one of the most contentious issues in the whole of the law of social security—the cohabitation rule. The term "cohabitation" is now replaced by "living together as husband and wife," which is thought to be more neutral. The "rule" arises from the facts that the applicable amount for a couple is less than that for two single claimants and that a claimant is excluded from entitlement to income support if her partner is in remunerative work. The principle of aggregation between husband and wife is itself controversial, but while it remains, so it is argued, a couple living together as husband and wife must be treated in the same way. This is despite the fact that the legal position of such a couple in many other respects is different from that of a married couple.

While the law remains as it is, it is crucial to identify when a couple are living together as husband and wife. The first point to note is that the income support scheme recognises other ways of living together and has specific rules for determining the entitlement of claimants who live in someone else's household or have someone else living in their household. Webster J. put this very well in *Robson v Secretary of State for Social Services* [1982] 3 F.L.R. 232 at 236, when he said that "the legislation provides for three different situations: two persons who are living together being husband and wife is the first; two persons living together as husband and wife is the second; and two persons living together not as husband and wife is the third. It seems to me that where the facts show that there are two persons living together not being husband and wife, then both the second and third situations must be considered." Thus to show that a couple are living together is only the first step, not the final one, as so often happens in practice (see also, *e.g. Crake v SBC, Butterworth v SBC* [1982] 1 All E.R. 498 at 502, SB 38).

1.60   There have been a number of Commissioner's decisions on a similar rule in widow's benefit (the test is held to be the same in *R(SB) 17/81* and *R(G) 3/81* and the same principles will apply for the income-related benefits), but the position reached is fairly vague. Early attempts to obtain a judicial definition of "cohabitation" were unsuccessful ("for my part it is so well-known that nothing I could say about it could possibly assist in its interpretation hereafter", Lord Widgery C. J. in *R. v S. W. London A. T. Ex p. Barnett*, SB 4). The examination of three main matters is required in deciding if a woman is cohabiting with a man as his wife: "(1) their relationship in relation to sex: (2) their relationship in relation to money: (3) their general relationship. Although all three are as a rule relevant, no single one of them is necessarily conclusive" (*R(G) 3/71*). In *CIS 87/1993*, however, the Commissioner expresses the view that it is the parties' general relationship that is most important (see below).

In response to criticisms about the operation of the cohabitation rule the Supplementary Benefits Commission produced published guidelines. The last formulation in summary form was in the 1984 edition of the *Supplementary Benefits Handbook*. A previous form of these guidelines had been approved as "an admirable signpost; the approach cannot be faulted" (Woolf J. in *Crake v SBC, Butterworth v SBC*, above) and were found to correspond to the *R(G) 3/71* test in *R(SB) 17/81*. The Handbook said (para.2.13) that the main criteria are:

"1. *Members of the same household*
    The couple must be living in the same household and neither partner will usually have any other home where they normally live. This implies that the couple live together, apart from absences necessary for employment, visits to relatives, etc.
2. *Stability*
    Living together as husband and wife clearly implies more than an occasional or very brief association. When a couple first live together, it may be clear from the start that the relationship is similar to that of husband and wife (for example, if the woman has taken the man's name and borne his child), but in cases where at the outset the nature of the relationship is less clear it may be right not to regard the couple as living together as husband and wife until it is apparent that a stable relationship has been formed.

3. *Financial support*

In most husband and wife relationships one would expect to find financial support of one party by the other, or sharing of household expenses, but the absence of any such arrangement does not of itself prove that a couple are not living together.

4. *Sexual relationship*

Similarly, a sexual relationship is a normal part of a marriage and therefore of living together as husband and wife. But its absence at any particular time does not necessarily prove that a couple are not living as husband and wife.

5. *Children*

When a couple are caring for a child of their union, there is a strong presumption that they are living together as husband and wife.

6. *Public acknowledgment*

Whether the couple have represented themselves to other people as husband and wife is relevant. However, many couples living together do not wish to pretend that they are actually married. The fact that they retain their identity publicly as unmarried people does not mean that they cannot be regarded as living together as husband and wife."

The Handbook was wrong to claim that these guidelines had been approved by courts and a Commissioner, for there had been changes in form. The most important, in the paragraph on "sexual relationship", are devastatingly set out by the Commissioner in *R(SB) 35/85*. It was the 1979 version that was approved in *Crake* and *Butterworth* and in *R(SB) 17/81* and that referred to a sexual relationship as an important as well as a normal part of marriage and also noted that the presence of a sexual relationship did not necessarily prove that a couple were living as husband and wife. The 1982 edition added a new sentence "However, if a couple have never had such a relationship it is most unlikely that they should be regarded as living together as husband and wife." The 1983 edition "watered down" that sentence to suggesting that "it may be wrong" to regard the couple as living together as husband and wife in such circumstances. In the 1984 edition this final sentence disappeared altogether, along with the suggestion that the presence of a sexual relationship does not necessarily prove that a couple are living as husband and wife. In the meantime, the law has remained exactly the same. However, it is correct to stress that there is no single way by which the issue can be decided in every case. For the criteria tend not to help in making the basic distinction between couples living together as husband and wife and those living together in other ways. As *CIS 87/1993* emphasises, it is important to consider *why* the couple are living together. **1.61**

The issues are now dealt with in Pt 11 of the DMG, where the issues are discussed quite fully and with reference to a range of decisions. It is notable that in para.11045 a sexual relationship is now described as an important part of marriage, and the presence of a sexual relationship is said not to be conclusive in itself of living together as husband and wife.

Household

Being members of the same household is obviously necessary. The approach to the meaning of "household" in the definition of "householder" for supplementary benefit purposes (see the notes on "married couple") may be relevant. In *R(SB) 30/83* the Commissioner holds that the issue is not decided on a week-by-week basis. So where the woman was absent during University terms living in a rented bedsitter, the couple were living together throughout. This principle was implicitly applied in *R(SB) 8/85*. The claimant lived with a Mr G, whose employment brought him to the area and was said to go back to his wife at weekends. The Commissioner holds that a person can only be a member of one couple, and so of one household, at a time. This appears to leave open, to be determined according to the circumstances, whether Mr G was **1.62** living with the claimant for five days a week and with his wife for two days, or with only one of them. *CIS 11304/1995* explicitly states that there can be two households in these circumstances. Mr K lived with his wife in Zimbabwe for six months of the year and with the claimant in England for the other half of the year. Although Mr K could not simultaneously have two households, he could spend six months of the year in one household and six in another. If a person maintains and from time to time lives in the same house as his lawful spouse there is an initial presumption that they form a married couple.

In *R(SB) 19/85* the claimant had been living together with (another) Mr G as his wife in Manchester. She did not move with him to London because there was no place available in a London hospital for her to have dialysis on a kidney machine. Although *R(SB) 30/83* holds that the relationship can continue despite temporary absences, the Commissioner holds that the situation here was different. Effectively, the claimant and Mr G had ceased to live together in the same accommodation. At the time, reg.2(2) of the Supplementary Benefit (Aggregation) Regulations, deeming a couple still to be members of the same household through temporary absences, only applied to married couples, not as later also to unmarried couples. Now see reg.16(1) of the Income Support Regulations.

Stability

1.63   Stability of a relationship is only of great weight if the relationship is one like husband and wife. There is no reason why a stable landlady-lodger relationship or flat-sharing relationship should not last for many years (see, for example, *CP 8001/1995*). However, it is sometimes suggested that an element of permanency in a relationship may differentiate it from, say, an employer-housekeeper relationship (*e.g. Campbell v Secretary of State for Social Services* [1983] 4 F.L.R. 138, where the "housekeeper" had sold her furniture and intended to apply for a joint local authority tenancy with the man). This forward-looking approach does make sense. But, as *CP 8001/1995* points out, even if an arrangement has become an established and settled one after some years, it does not follow that it has been on the same footing since the couple first started living together.

Financial support

1.64   The approach to financial support seems to make almost any arrangement point the same way, except a very clearly fixed commercial rate. If the man pays a lot, he is supporting the woman. If he pays very little, this shows that the relationship is more than a commercial one. This makes it very difficult for parties who are friends, or where the man pays what he can afford, where the proper conclusion may merely be that the two people share a household.

Sexual relationship

1.65   There has been an attempt to decrease reliance on the existence of a sexual relationship, partly in response to criticism of "sex snoopers" and methods of investigation. Officers are now instructed not to initiate questions about sexual relationships and not to seek to inspect sleeping arrangements, but to note statements and evidence presented by the claimant. However, if a rule is to distinguish people living together as husband and wife from people living together in some other way it seems impossible not to give great significance to the nature of the sexual relationship. By playing down its importance, either as being present or absent, the Handbook inevitably shifted the test closer to one which simply tested whether the couple were living together in one household. The Commissioner in *CIS 87/1993* considers that where there has never been a sexual relationship, strong alternative grounds are needed to reach the conclusion that the relationship is akin to that of husband and wife. In his view, the instruction to DSS officers not to ask about the physical aspects of the relationship is inappropriate in an inquisitorial system, and if the information is not volunteered, such questions may have to be asked. But care will need to be taken to prevent any such investigation becoming over-intrusive.

In *CSB 150/1985* the Commissioner held that an unmarried couple who refrained on principle from any sexual relationship could not be described as living together as husband and wife. The claimant and his fiancee lived in the same house, but were Mormons. That religion forbids sexual relationships before marriage.

Children and public acknowledgment

The shared care of children, especially children of the couple, and public acknowl-   **1.66**
edgment are obviously important factors. In *R(G) 1/79*, the adoption of the same name on the electoral register was decisive. Other elements might be whether the couple visit relatives or friends, or go on holiday, together.

What these points come to is that the so-called "objective facts" of a relationship may be capable of being interpreted either way. This, then, leaves the authorities in a difficulty, although it is clear that the burden of proof (where relevant: see *CIS 317/1994* below) is on the DSS, at least when the rule operates as a disqualification. In two decisions the Divisional Court has stressed the importance of looking at the intention of the parties in explaining the "objective facts". In *Butterworth v SBC*, above, the claimant was disabled following a serious accident, and invited the man, whom she had known for five years, to move into her house, since she was then on her own. The man had his own bedroom, with a lock on the door. He did the cooking and household tasks, and they lived as one household. Woolf J. says:

> "If the only reason that [the man] went to that house temporarily was to look after Mrs. Butterworth in her state of illness and, albeit, while doing so, acted in the same way as an attentive husband would behave towards his wife who suffered an illness, this does not amount to living together as husband and wife because it was not the intention of the parties that there should be such a relationship. Looked at without knowing the reason for the man going to live there, it would appear that they were living together as husband and wife, but when the reason was known that would explain those circumstances."

In *Robson*'s case (above), the parties were both seriously disabled, needing wheelchairs and invalid cars. They had been friends for a long time before they were widowed. They moved together into a two-bedroom maisonette at their social worker's suggestion. They lived as one household. As so often the SBAT assumed that this was conclusive, and this was an error of law. In order to provide guidance to tribunals, Webster J. says that often it is only possible to decide into which category a relationship falls by considering the objective facts,

> "because usually the intention of the parties is either unascertainable, or, if ascertainable, is not to be regarded as reliable. But if it is established to the satisfaction of the tribunal that the two persons concerned did not intend to live together as husband and wife and still do not intend to do so, in my judgment it would be a very strong case indeed sufficient to justify a decision that they are, or ought to be treated as if they are, husband and wife."

Although subsequent Divisional Court decisions (*e.g. Kaur v Secretary of State for*   **1.67**
Social Services [1982] 3 F.L.R. 237) have not referred to intention as a factor, it has not been rejected either. However, in *R(SB) 17/81* the Commissioner says that Webster J.'s words are of no real assistance to tribunals. For, he says, it is "the conduct of the person concerned to which regard has to be paid", *i.e.* "what he or she does or says at the relevant time." If *R(SB) 17/81* is taken as deciding that only the "objective facts" as identified by the Handbook criteria are relevant, and that the intention of the parties is not relevant, it need not be followed as being inconsistent with persuasive decisions of the Divisional Court. If *R(SB) 17/81* is taken as a reminder of the difficulties of establishing intention it is in line with those decisions, although evidence of intention should not be as limited as suggested. On the facts of *R(SB) 17/81* the couple shared a sexual relationship and one household, but

said that there was nothing permanent about the relationship. The Commissioner points out that the fact that they did not intend to marry did not mean that they did not intend to live together as though they were married.

It is the second view of *R(SB) 17/81* that seems to have been applied in recent Commissioners' decisions, although AOs (now decision-makers) commonly rely on the first view in submissions to tribunals. *CSSB 145/1983* is a decision on facts reminiscent of *Robson*'s case. Two disabled people living in a sheltered housing scheme moved into one flat to share living expenses and provide mutual support. At the beginning the Housing Association running the flats did not have the funds to divide the one bedroom. There was no sexual relationship. The SSAT had decided that the situation was no different from that of a married couple where one partner had a serious disability. The Commissioner holds this to be a wrong approach. A sharing of expenses and mutual support can arise between people of the same sex, or between brother and sister, and does not in itself amount to living together as husband and wife.

1.68   In *R(SB) 35/85* the claimant was a widow in her seventies. She had taken over the tenancy of her bungalow in 1976, on the death of her brother, with whom she had lived for some years. In 1974, Mr W, who needed care and help, had moved into the household. By August 1984, he was a widower. The claimant did the cooking and there was a sharing of household expenses. The Commissioner holds that the SSAT, in finding the claimant and Mr W to be living together as husband and wife, had failed to see that the existence of a common household was only one ingredient in the decision. He adopts as helpful guidance the approach of Woolf J. in *Butterworth's* case that it is impossible to categorise all the kinds of explanation of why two people were sharing a household, which would mean that the two were not living together as husband and wife.

In *CIS 87/1993* the claimant maintained that the only relationship between him and Mrs B, with whom he was living, was that of patient and carer. The Commissioner decides that the SSAT had failed to consider their general relationship and *why* they were living together. He expresses reservations about the "criteria" relied upon by AOs in cohabitation cases. He points out that Woolf J. in *Crake* and *Butterworth* considered it wrong to refer to them as "criteria" and preferred the description "admirable signposts". There was nothing in *R(SB) 17/81* to suggest that only these admirable signposts had to be considered. In the Commissioner's view, the admirable signposts failed to emphasise the significance of the parties' "general relationship". It was arguable that it was the parties' general relationship that was of paramount importance and that their sexual and their financial relationship were only relevant for the light they threw upon the general relationship.

The importance of looking at the totality of the parties' relationship and of not simply using the criteria as items on a checklist to be ticked off one by one is emphasised in *CP 8001/1995*. The claimant was a widow who had taken in a lodger. He paid her rent and a contribution towards expenses, but they did not pool resources, even though she had a right to draw cheques on his bank account. As time passed, they became friends, watched TV and ate together and went on holiday together with a group of friends. There was no sexual relationship, but on occasion they went halves on a twin-bedded room when staying in a hotel. The Commissioner decides that even though there were elements in the arrangement that matched those found in a normal marriage, it was equally akin to that of a brother and sister living in the same household, and that the totality of the evidence did not add up to a husband and wife relationship.

Burden of proof

1.69   In *CIS 317/1994* the Commissioner decides that the question of onus of proof did not arise where the question of whether the claimant was living together as husband and wife with her alleged partner fell to be determined on an *initial* claim for income support. What had to be considered was all the relevant facts.

He pointed to the duty on the claimant to provide such information as may be required to decide the claim (see reg.7(1) of the Claims and Payments Regulations). The Commissioner also considered that although living together as husband and wife operated as a disqualification for widow's benefit it did not do so for income support. But, with respect, this distinction seems more apparent than real. Even though cohabitation is not an automatic bar in all cases, if the claimant's alleged partner is in remunerative work, or has income or capital that disentitles them to income support, or has himself already claimed income support, the effect of a living together decision will be to disqualify the claimant from income support. Thus it is suggested that the burden of proof (on the decision-maker) may come into play in marginal cases (if the claimant otherwise satisfies the conditions of entitlement to income support), even on initial claims. If benefit is stopped on a review on the grounds of alleged cohabitation, the burden of proof will be on the DM. However, as pointed out above, it is often not so much the facts that may be at issue as the interpretation of those facts. Here the intention of the parties and the reason why they are living together may be the deciding factors (and see *CIS 87/1993* above).

PART VIII

THE SOCIAL FUND

Payments out of the social fund

138.—(1) There may be made out of the social fund, in accordance with this Part of this Act—   1.70
  (a) Payments of prescribed amounts, whether in respect of prescribed items or otherwise, to meet, in prescribed circumstances, maternity expenses and funeral expenses; and
  (b) . . . *[Omitted as relating solely to the discretionary social fund.]*
  (2) Payments may also be made out of that fund, in accordance with this Part of this Act, of a prescribed amount or a number of prescribed amounts to prescribed descriptions of persons, in prescribed circumstances, to meet expenses for heating, which appear to the Secretary of State to have been or to be likely to be incurred in cold weather.
  (3) . . . *[Omitted as relating solely to the discretionary social fund.]*
  (4) In this section "prescribed" means specified in or determined in accordance with regulations.
  (5) . . . *[Omitted as relating solely to the discretionary social fund.]*

DERIVATIONS

Subss.(1) and (2): Social Security Act 1986, s.32(2) and (2A).   1.71
Subs.(3): 1986 Act, s.33(1A).
Subs.(4): 1986 Act, s.84(1).

GENERAL NOTE

This book cannot contain any real discussion of the general social fund scheme.   1.72
It is concerned with claims that can lead to an appeal to a tribunal. Only the payments for maternity and funeral expenses under subs.(1)(a) and for cold weather and winter fuel under subs.(2) are dealt with by decision-makers and tribunals.

Subs. (1) (a)

1.73   Subsection (1)(a) is re-enacted by s.70(1)(a) of the 1998 Act with effect from April 5, 1999. This part of the social fund scheme was originally brought into operation in April 1987 to enable payments to be made for maternity and funeral expenses. These are made under the ordinary system of adjudication and under regulations required to be made by subs.(1)(a). They are not subject to any budget. See the Social Fund Maternity and Funeral Expenses (General) Regulations 1987. The death grant and the maternity grant, formerly payable under the Social Security Act 1975, were abolished (1986 Act, ss.38 and 41) and the provisions for maternity and funeral expenses under the supplementary benefit regulations were removed in April 1987 (General Regulations, regs 13 to 15).

Subsection (1)(a) does little more than provide the framework for the detailed entitlement set out in the General Regulations. See s.78(4) of the Administration Act on the recovery of funeral payments from the estate of the deceased.

New restrictions on payments for funeral expenses were introduced on June 5, 1995 and there was further clarification and tightening-up of the rules on April 7, 1997 (see regs 7 and 7A of the General Regulations and the notes to those regulations). Note also the changes introduced on November 17, 1997.

The argument that maternity (or funeral) expenses that do not qualify under subs.(1)(a) can be met from the discretionary social fund under subs.(1)(b) was rejected in *R. v Social Fund Inspector Ex p. Harper*, High Court, February 7, 1997. Harrison J. held that subss.(1)(a) and (b) provided mutually exclusive methods of meeting particular needs and that maternity and funeral expenses were only intended to be met to the extent laid down in the General Regulations.

Subs. (2)

1.74   Although the predecessor of this subsection was in force from April 1988, the regulations it required were not in place until November 7, 1988 (Social Fund Cold Weather Payments (General) Regulations 1988). The form of the scheme, as embodied in the 1988 Regulations, has been amended several times. The current form does not require a separate claim to be made for a severe weather payment. As for maternity and funeral expenses, the decisions are made by decision-makers, with appeals to a tribunal, and are not subject to any budget.

See also the notes to the Social Fund Winter Fuel Payment Regulations 2000.

PART XIII

GENERAL

Interpretation

Application of Act in relation to territorial waters

1.75   **172.** In this Act—

(a) any reference to Great Britain includes a reference to the territorial waters of the United Kingdom adjacent to Great Britain;

(b) any reference to the United Kingdom includes a reference to the territorial waters of the United Kingdom.

DERIVATION

Social Security Act 1986, s.84(4).   1.76

Age

173. For the purposes of this Act a person—   1.77
(a) is over or under a particular age if he has or, as the case may be, has not attained that age; and
(b) is between two particular ages if he has attained the first but not the second;

and in Scotland (as in England and Wales) the time at which a person attains a particular age expressed in years is the commencement of the relevant anniversary of the date of his birth.

DERIVATION

Social Security Act 1975, Sch.20.   1.78

References to Acts

174. In this Act—   1.79
"the 1975 Act" means the Social Security Act 1975;
"the 1986 Act" means the Social Security Act 1986;
"the Administration Act" means the Social Security Administration Act 1992;
"the Consequential Provisions Act" means the Social Security (Consequential Provisions) Act 1992;
"the Northern Ireland Contributions and Benefits Act" means the Social Security Contributions and Benefits (Northern Ireland) Act 1992;
"the Old Cases Act" means the Industrial Injuries and Diseases (Old Cases) Act 1975; and
"the Pensions Act" means the Social Security Pensions Act 1975.

Subordinate legislation

Regulations, orders and schemes

175.—(1) Subject to [²subsection (1A) below], regulations and orders   1.80
under this Act shall be made by the Secretary of State.
[²(1A) Subsection (1) above has effect subject to—
(a) any provision of Part I or VI of this Act providing for regulations or an order to be made by the Treasury or by the Commissioners of Inland Revenue, and
(b) section 145(5) above.]
(2) Powers under this Act to make regulations, orders or schemes shall be exercisable by statutory instrument.
(3) Except in the case of an order under section 145(3) above and in so far as this Act otherwise provides, any power under this Act to make regulations or an order may be exercised—

(a) either in relation to all cases to which the power extends, or in relation to those cases subject to specified exceptions, or in relation to any specified cases or classes of case;

(b) so as to make, as respects the cases in relation to which it is exercised—

   (i) the full provision to which the power extends or any less provision (whether by way of exception or otherwise),

   (ii) the same provision for all cases in relation to which the power is exercised, or different provision for different cases or different classes of case or different provision as respects the same case or class of case for different purposes of this Act;

   (iii) any such provision either unconditionally or subject to any specified condition;

and where such a power is expressed to be exercisable for alternative purposes it may be exercised in relation to the same case for any or all of those purposes; and powers to make regulations or an order for the purposes of any one provision of this Act are without prejudice to powers to make regulations or an order for the purposes of any other provision.

(4) Without prejudice to any specific provision in this Act, any power conferred by this Act to make regulations or an order (other than the power conferred in section 145(3) above) includes power to make thereby such incidental, supplementary, consequential or transitional provision as appears to the [² person making the regulations or order] to be expedient for the purposes of the regulations or order.

(5) Without prejudice to any specific provisions in this Act, a power conferred by any provision of this Act except—

(a) sections 30, 47(6), [¹25B(2)(a)] and 145(3) above and paragraph 3(9) of Schedule 7 to this Act;

(b) section 122(1) above in relation to the definition of "payments by way of occupational or personal pension"; and

(c) Part XI,

to make regulations or an order includes power to provide for a person to exercise a discretion in dealing with any matter.

(6) *[Omitted as relating only to housing benefit and community charge benefit.]*

(7) Any power of the Secretary of State under any provision of this Act, except the provisions mentioned in subsection (5)(a) and (b) above and Part IX, to make any regulations or order, where the power is not expressed to be exercisable with the consent of the Treasury, shall if the Treasury so direct be exercisable only in conjunction with them.

(8) and (9) *[Omitted as relating only to ss.116 to 120.]*

(10) Any reference in this section or section 176 below to an order or regulations under this Act includes a reference to an order or regulations made under any provision of an enactment passed after this Act and directed to be construed as one with this Act; but this subsection applies only so far as a contrary intention is not expressed in the enactment so passed, and without prejudice to the generality of any such direction.

AMENDMENTS

1.81
   1. Social Security (Incapacity for Work) Act 1994, Sch.1, para.36 (April 13, 1995).
   2. Social Security Contributions (Transfer of Functions, etc.) Act 1999, s.2 and Sch.3, para.29 (April 1, 1999).

DERIVATION

Social Security Act 1986, ss.83(1) and 84(1).   1.82

Parliamentary control

176.—(1) and (2) [*Omitted as not applying to income-related benefits.*]   1.83
(3) A statutory instrument—
(a) which contains (whether alone or with other provisions) any order, regulations or scheme made under this Act by the Secretary of State, [¹the Treasury or the Commissioners of Inland Revenue,] other than an order under section 145(3) above; and
(b) which is not subject to any requirement that a draft of the instrument shall be laid before and approved by a resolution of each House of Parliament,
shall be subject to annulment in pursuance of a resolution of either House of Parliament.

AMENDMENT

1. Social Security Contributions (Transfer of Functions, etc.) Act 1999, s.2 and   1.84
Sch.3, para.30 (April, 1999).

DERIVATION

Social Security Act 1986, s.83(4).   1.85

[Short title, commencement and extent]

Short title, commencement and extent

177.—(1) This Act may be cited as the as the Social Security Contri-   1.86
butions and Benefits Act 1992.
(2) This Act is to be read, where appropriate, with the Administration Act and the Consequential Provisions Act.
(3) The enactments consolidated by this Act are repealed, in consequence of the consolidation, by the Consequential Provisions Act.
(4) Except as provided in Schedule 4 to the Consequential Provisions Act, this Act shall come into force on 1st July 1992.
(5) The following provisions extend to Northern Ireland—
section 16 and Schedule 2;
section 116(2); and
this section.
(6) Except as provided by this section, this Act does not extend to Northern Ireland.

DEFINITIONS

"the Administration Act"—see s.174.
"the Consequential Provisions Act"—*ibid.*

31

Jobseekers Act 1995

(1995 c. 18)

SECTIONS REPRODUCED

PART I

THE JOBSEEKER'S ALLOWANCE

Denial of jobseeker's allowance

Miscellaneous

PART II

BACK TO WORK SCHEMES

PART III

MISCELLANEOUS AND SUPPLEMENTAL

SCHEDULE

An Act to provide for a jobseeker's allowance and to make other provision   **1.91**
to promote the employment of the unemployed and the assistance of
persons without a settled way of life. [June 28, 1995]

GENERAL NOTE

Jobseeker's Allowance: A Brief Overview
   On October 7, 1996 ("commencement"), jobseeker's allowance ("JSA")   **1.92**
replaced two separate benefits, unemployment benefit ("UB") and income

support ("IS"), as the benefit for those unemployed persons whom the state requires to remain in the labour market as a condition of receiving state support. UB disappeared entirely. IS remains as means-tested assistance for those whose personal circumstances are such that they are not required to seek work as a condition of receiving state support: principally pensioners, the sick and disabled, single parents. (For a full list see Income Support (General) Regulations 1987, reg.4ZA, Sch.1B.)

JSA was introduced by the Jobseekers Act 1995 ("the Act"), which remains a freestanding source rather than (on the model of incapacity benefit) effecting its ends by inserting new sections in the SSCBA 1992. The Act, however, is very much a skeleton, with the bulk of the key detail found in two sets of regulations: in the voluminous Jobseeker's Allowance Regulations 1996 (SI 1996/207) (172 regulations and eight Schedules) ("the JSA Regs") and in the fortunately less extensive but somewhat complex Jobseeker's Allowance (Transitional Provisions) Regulations 1995 ("the JSA (Transitional) Regs"). Both sets have been quite heavily amended.

The Government's aim in introducing JSA was to depart from the previous confusing regime under which the unemployed could be eligible for either or both of two different benefits (UB and IS), based on different principles (one a contributory benefit as of right, the other based on test of means), each with its own set of rules (albeit that there was a degree of commonalty), one administered by the Employment Service ("ES"), the other by the Benefits Agency ("BA"). JSA is a single benefit, embodying both a contributory and a means-tested component, with unified rules on such key aspects as labour market tests, the treatment of earnings and days of benefit payment, and claimants dealing (so far as possible) with a single office. On the implications of JSA as a single benefit see further *Hockenjos v Secretary of State for Social Security*, Court of Appeal, May 2, 2001, approving *CJSA 1920/1999*. It was designed also to emphasise the responsibilities of the unemployed to take every advantage of the opportunities open to them to return to the world of work (*Jobseeker's Allowance*, Cm. 2687 (October 1994), Foreword by Peter Lilley and Michael Portillo, at p.2 ("White Paper")). The new benefit structure and administration are supposed to be simpler and clearer, affording better value for the taxpayer, and a better service to claimants. JSA is to help people return to work by strengthening incentives to work; by creating a framework of support within which the ES can give more effective advice and help; by increasing understanding among the unemployed about their obligations and encouraging effective action to meet them, in part by providing effective and timely sanctions for those who do not take the required steps; and by supporting the effectiveness for the unemployed of active labour market policies (White Paper, para.2.9). JSA, like incapacity benefit, was expected to help target available money on those who need it most and effect significant financial savings (White Paper, para.3.3). JSA can better respond to changing circumstances than its predecessors since the Act has enabled the Government to pilot rule changes locally before implementing successful ones nationally, but only ones made with a view to ascertaining their effectiveness in terms of encouraging and helping claimants to find or retain work (White Paper, para.3.3; s.2.9). See, *e.g.* the Jobseeker's Allowance (Pilot Scheme) Regulations 1996 (SI 1996/1307) applying to JSA the Income Support (Pilot Scheme) Regulations 1996 (SI 1996/1252) with respect to Project Work, an employment programme.

1.93   This introductory overview examines the main elements of the conditions of entitlement to JSA for those wholly new claimants claiming for the very first time on or after commencement (*i.e.* those without any links to previous benefits regimes), concentrating on conditions common to both components of JSA, and highlighting major areas of difference between JSA and the UB and/or IS regime of benefits for unemployed people.

JSA is a weekly benefit, payable on a weekly basis, with only limited provision for part-weeks. It thus emulates IS rather than UB, a daily benefit. But, following the

UB pattern, claimants must generally serve three waiting days in any jobseeking period before entitlement begins (those intermittently unemployed being aided here by a 12-week "linking" rule and the provision for "linked periods" such as ones of incapacity or entitlement to maternity allowance or periods of training that do not "break" a jobseeking period) (s.21, Sch.1, para.4; JSA Regs, regs 46–49).

There are two types of JSA: contribution-based JSA (CBJSA) and income-based JSA (IBJSA). Both have common "core" conditions of entitlement, but also some peculiar to each type. The former focus only on the claimant, as do the conditions specific to CBJSA. IBJSA has a wider focus; it deploys the IS concept of aggregation of resources (those of members of his family being, generally, treated as those of the claimant) and applies some of its specific conditions of entitlement to members of the claimant's family.

To deal first with *the common "core" conditions*: a person in Great Britain, and under pensionable age, who is out of work (not working 16 or more hours per week) but capable of it, is not receiving relevant education, and satisfies the labour market conditions (available for employment; actively seeking employment; entry into a jobseeker's agreement), will be eligible for JSA. *Such a person will be entitled to CBJSA*, for a maximum of six months in an unbroken period of unemployment (longer in calendar terms with intermittent but "linked" unemployment)—a marked and controversial reduction from the one-year entitlement to UB—provided that he satisfies the contribution conditions (the insurance-based element, which will—save in unusual circumstances—exclude those under 18), that he does not earn more than the prescribed amount each week and that he is not entitled to income support (ss.1, 2). **1.94**

The rules on determining the amount of CBJSA payable to a claimant entitled to CBJSA are markedly different from UB. CBJSA is a basic benefit with no increases for dependants. More surprisingly for an insurance-based benefit, nominally paid as of right and commonly seen (albeit mistakenly) as "earned" by the payment of contributions into the insurance scheme, the amount will vary as between claimants who have satisfied the same contribution conditions to be eligible for it. The amount is determined by first ascertaining the age-related amount applicable to the claimant (the lowest rate for those under 18, a middle rate for those aged 18–24, and the highest rate for those aged 25 or over), and then making prescribed deductions in respect of *his* earnings and pension payments (no concept of aggregation of family resources is here applicable) (s.4(1), (2); JSA Regs, regs 79–81). The concept of abatement of benefit (even to nil) in respect of pension payments is familiar to students of UB, but with CBJSA applies regardless of age, unlike UB where it affected only those aged 55 or over (SSCBA 1992, s.30 (now repealed)). Taken with s.2(1)(c) (earnings in excess of the prescribed amount precluding entitlement), these elements of age-relating and abatement on account of earnings as well as pension payments confirm the awkward hybrid nature of CBJSA: neither a fully-fledged contributory benefit receivable as of right and regardless of means, nor a fully-fledged income-related benefit. Although abatement of CBJSA because of earnings represents a further extension of means-testing into the contributory sphere, CBJSA cannot properly be described as an income-related benefit in the same sense as IS or IBJSA. These rules on CBJSA look to a much narrower range of "means": capital is totally ignored while, with respect to income only earnings are regarded for s.2(1)(c) purposes, although pension payments are in addition taken into account in terms of abatement or reduction of CBJSA. Furthermore, the rules look only to the claimant's resources and not, like income-related benefits, to those of his family (partner, child, young person).

A claimant satisfying the common "core" conditions will be eligible for IBJSA if neither he nor any member of his family is entitled to income support and no one else in his family is entitled to IBJSA (ss.1, 3(1)(b)-(d)). Generally speaking, he must be 18 or over, but certain 16 and 17-year-olds can be entitled in cases of hardship, if the Secretary of State so directs, or in a variety of prescribed circumstances (*e.g.* as a **1.95** couple with a child, or as someone laid off from, or kept on short time in his employment, or as a person leaving care) (ss.3(1)(f), 16; JSA Regs, Pt IV (Young Persons)). His partner, if any, must not be engaged in remunerative work (s.3(1)(e)). Capital over a prescribed limit precludes entitlement to IBJSA altogether (s.13; JSA Regs, reg.107 (usually £8,000 but £16,000 for those living permanently in certain residential care homes, nursing homes and residential accommodation providing board and personal care by reason, for example, of disability, and £12,000 where claimant or partner is 60 or over) (see further reg.116(1ZA), (1B)). But, as with other income-related benefits, his income (including tariff income from capital) must not exceed the applicable amount (here made up, on the IS model and following rules borrowed from that benefit, of appropriate personal allowances, premiums and eligible housing costs, with modifications in respect of persons in residential care and nursing homes and of special cases (*e.g.* persons from abroad)) (s.3(1)(a)).

In relation to income based JSA, the means test is broadly the same as that for income support and many of the other rules mirror those that apply to income support. Where there are differences, these are noted at the appropriate places in the commentary. One important change that was made to the income support rules alongside the introduction of JSA is that from October 7, 1996, in the case of a claimant's partner, remunerative work is defined as 24 (not 16) hours a week. This also applies to income-based JSA.

1.96   An unemployed claimant may thus merely get CBJSA, having, for example, capital resources that preclude entitlement to IBJSA (although he may later move on to IBJSA when those resources fall below the capital limit), or having an income exceeding his IBJSA applicable amount. Or, because of an inadequate contribution record denying access to CBJSA, he may simply be entitled to IBJSA. Alternatively, a claimant may be entitled to both components at the same time. In that situation, the amount of JSA payable is the income-based element unless that is lower than the contribution-based element, in which case the latter is the amount payable. Whatever the amount payable, however, the entitlement to CBJSA erodes the claimant's maximum six months' entitlement to that component of JSA (ss.4(6)–(11), 5(1)).

An otherwise existing entitlement to JSA will be defeated where the claimant's unemployment is due to a stoppage of work due to a trade dispute, in which he has a direct interest, at his place of work, or because he has withdrawn his labour in furtherance of any trade dispute (s.14). The period affected, not being one of entitlement, will not count towards his six months' entitlement to CBJSA, thus reaffirming the benefit system's supposed neutrality in trade disputes.

1.97   Even where entitlement to JSA exists, the allowance is not payable for varying periods in a number of situations in which the person's unemployment might be said to be voluntary both in terms of how it came about and his behaviour whilst unemployed (s.19; JSA Regs, regs 69–75). Where in such situations there is an underlying entitlement to CBJSA, however, such periods of preclusion from payment eat into the maximum period of entitlement to CBJSA (s.5(1); JSA Regs, reg.47(4))—a position in marked contrast to UB where periods of disqualification for voluntary unemployment merely delayed the start of, or interrupted, the one year's maximum entitlement.

Unsurprisingly, non-entitlement to JSA generally means no allowance can be paid. In a number of situations there is no entitlement to JSA because of failure to meet one or more of the labour market conditions (availability; actively seeking work; entry into a jobseeker's agreement). Nonetheless, a reduced rate of IBJSA is payable in cases of hardship (s.21, Sch.1, para.8; JSA Regs, regs 140–146). Under the UB/IS regime, those subject to sanctions for voluntary unemployment would (a) be suspended from benefit while the matter was determined, but (b) could receive a reduced rate of IS until that point and also during the period of imposition of the sanction. The JSA regime is different. JSA remains payable pending determination of whether a sanction should be imposed but, once imposed there is no automatic entitlement to a reduced rate of benefit; a reduced rate of IBJSA is only payable in cases of hardship (ss.19, 20(4)–(6); JSA Regs, regs 140–146).

The basic rules are modified significantly in their application to share fishermen and members of the forces (s.21, Sch.1, para.17; JSA Regs, Pt XII).

The standard JSA picture has been one of a claimant claiming in his own right a contribution-based jobseeker's allowance and of a claimant claiming income-based jobseeker's allowance for himself, and any spouse and/or children, with consequent aggregation of needs and resources. From March 19, 2001, a new dimension was added: the requirement that a "joint-claim couple" make a joint claim for jobseeker's allowance (what in reality is a joint-claim income-based jobseeker's allowance) (s.1(2B)–(2D)). This aspect of the scheme goes beyond the familiar notion of aggregation of needs and resources (although "joint-claim jobseeker's allowance" embodies that too (see ss.3A, 4)) since that traditional model embodies the notion of one partner in a couple being dependent on the other, the latter being the claimant having to fulfil the conditions of entitlement. The "joint-claim couple" aspect goes further than this in that each partner is party to the claim and each must satisfy the conditions of entitlement in s.1(2)(a)–(c) and (e) to (i). In other words, each partner of a joint-claim couple must (i) be available for employment; (ii) have entered into a jobseeker's agreement; (iii) be actively seeking employment; (iv) not be engaged in remunerative work; (v) be capable of work; (vi) not be receiving relevant education; (vii) be under pensionable age; and (viii) be in Great Britain. **1.98**

The "joint-claim" scheme has, legislatively speaking, required the adaptation of rules designed for a single claimant to deal instead with two people. Of particular note are the provisions for entitlement notwithstanding that one member of the couple does not meet the "labour market conditions" (see JSA Regulations, reg.3D) and the provision enabling one member of the couple to receive a reduced rate jobseeker's allowance where the other is caught by a fixed or discretionary period sanction in s.20A. This makes analogous provision for the application to members of a joint claim couple of the sanctions applicable to claimants under s.19, *e.g.* for non compliance with a jobseeker's direction [fixed period sanction] or for loss of employment through misconduct or for having voluntarily left employment without just cause [discretionary period sanctions].

A "joint-claim couple" is defined in s.1(4) as a married or unmarried couple, of a prescribed description, who are not members of any family that includes someone for whom one of the members of the couple is entitled to child benefit. JSA Regulations, reg.3A gives the prescribed description: initially where one of the members of the couple was born after March 19, 1976, but being 18 or over (reg.3A(1)). From October 28, 2002, subject to reg.3E(2)(l), it covers such a person born after October 28, 1957. Such a couple, however, will not be of a prescribed description if there is a child but no one is as yet entitled to child benefit, because there has been no claim or one has only just been made; if the couple has care of a child or young person as fosterers or with a view to adoption; or if a child or young person is living with the couple when he is away from home while at school (reg.3A(1)). **1.99**

In short, the central idea of the "joint-claim scheme" is that certain childless couples—young childless couples at least one of whom is (in the initial scheme under 25, later extended to under 45)—will have to make joint claims for income-based jobseeker's allowance. The change is aimed at preventing benefits dependency at a young age by ensuring that both partners are directly involved in the labour market, so that, for example, each will have to be available for and actively seeking work. Rather than one being the dependant of the other, both members of the couple will be claimants having equal rights and responsibilities.

Note also the power in s.29 to pilot new regulations and the back to work bonus scheme introduced by s.26. See the notes to those sections.

PART I

THE JOBSEEKER'S ALLOWANCE

Entitlement

The jobseeker's allowance

1.100   **1.**—(1) An allowance, to be known as a jobseeker's allowance, shall be payable in accordance with the provisions of this Act.

(2) Subject to the provisions of this Act, a claimant is entitled to a jobseeker's allowance if he—

(a) is available for employment;

(b) has entered into a jobseeker's agreement, which remains in force;

(c) is actively seeking employment;

[¹(d) satisfies the conditions set out in section 2;]

(e) is not engaged in remunerative work;

(f) is capable of work;

(g) is not receiving relevant education;

(h) is under pensionable age; and

(i) is in Great Britain.

[¹(2A) Subject to the provisions of this Act, a claimant who is not a member of a joint-claim couple is entitled to a jobseeker's allowance if he satisfies—

(a) the conditions set out in paragraphs (a) to (c) and (e) to (i) of subsection (2); and

(b) the conditions set out in section 3.

(2B) Subject to the provisions of this Act, a joint-claim couple are entitled to a jobseeker's allowance if—

(a) a claim for the allowance is made jointly by the couple;

(b) each member of the couple satisfies the conditions set out in paragraphs (a) to (c) and (e) to (i) of subsection (2); and

(c) the conditions set out in section 3A are satisfied in relation to the couple.

(2C) Regulations may prescribe circumstances in which subsection (2A) is to apply to a claimant who is a member of a joint-claim couple.

(2D) Regulations may, in respect of cases where a person would (but for the regulations) be a member of two or more joint-claim couples, make provision for only one of those couples to be a joint-claim couple; and the provision which may be so made includes provision for the couple which is to be the joint-claim couple to be nominated—

(a) by the persons who are the members of the couples, or

(b) in default of one of the couples being so nominated, by the Secretary of State.]

(3) A jobseeker's allowance is payable in respect of a week.

(4) In this Act—

"a contribution-based jobseeker's allowance" means a jobseeker's allowance entitlement to which is based on the claimant's satisfying conditions, which include those set out in section 2; [². . .]

"an income-based jobseeker's allowance" means a jobseeker's allowance entitlement to which is based on the claimant's satisfying conditions, which include those set out in section 3 [¹ or a joint-claim jobseeker's allowance;

"a joint-claim couple" means a married or unmarried couple who—

(a) are not members of any family whose members include a person in respect of whom a member of the couple is entitled to child benefit, and

(b) are of a prescribed description;

"a joint-claim jobseeker's allowance" means a jobseeker's allowance entitlement to which arises by virtue of subsection (2B).]

AMENDMENTS

1. Welfare Reform and Pensions Act 1999, Sch.7, para.2 (March 19, 2001).   1.101
2. Welfare Reform and Pensions Act 1999, Sch.13, Pt V (April 2, 2000).

DEFINITIONS

"a joint-claim couple": see subs.(4).
"a joint-claim jobseeker's allowance": see subs.(4).
"actively seeking employment": see s.7(1).
"available for employment": see s.6(1).
"capable of work": see s.35(2), Sch.1, para.2, and SSCBA 1992, Pt XIIA.
"claimant": see s.35(1).
"contribution-based jobseeker's allowance": see subs.(4).
"employment" (except in section 7): see s.35(1), JSA Regs, regs 3, 4.
"employment" (in section 7): see s.7(8).
"entitled" see s.35(1) and SSAA 1992, ss.1, 68.
"Great Britain": see s.35(1).
"income-based jobseeker's allowance": see subs.(4).
"jobseeker's agreement": see ss. 9(1), 35(1).
"pensionable age": see s.35(1), JSA Regs, reg. 3 and SSCBA 1992, s.122(1).
"relevant education": see s.35(2), Sch.1, para.14, and JSA Regs, reg.54.
"remunerative work": see s.35(2), Sch.1, para.1, and JSA Regs, reg.51.
"week": see s.35(1).
"work": *ibid.*

GENERAL NOTE

This section provides the legislative basis for payment of the new jobseeker's   1.102
allowance, a weekly benefit (subs.(3)) and a single benefit (see *Hockenjos v Secretary of State for Social Security*, Court of Appeal, May 2, 2001, approving *CJSA 1920/1999*) taking two forms (subs.(4)): (1) a "contribution-based jobseeker's allowance" (in essence the replacement for the insurance based unemployment benefit); and (2) an "income-based jobseeker's allowance" (in essence the income-related benefit that takes over the role that income support previously played for unemployed people of insufficient means). Subsection (2) sets out the conditions of entitlement to the components of the new benefit. Note that there are several common conditions (paras (a)–(c) and (e)–(i)), that must be fulfilled, as well as the separate conditions for each component (para.(d), subs.(2A) or (2B), as the case maybe): those set out in s.2 for a "contribution-based jobseeker's allowance" and those found in s.3 for an "income based jobseeker's allowance" for a claimant who is not a member of a joint-claim couple and those found in s.3A for an income-based jobseeker's allowance for a joint-claim couple. On joint-claim couple, see "Overview of JSA", above, and the notes to subs.(4), below.

Subs.(2)

This sets out the basic conditions of entitlement to the new benefit, in either of its   1.103
forms. It is merely a "framework", amplified by other sections of and Schedules to

the Act (subs.(2) begins, "Subject to the provisions of this Act") and in the detail of the Jobseeker's Allowance Regulations 1996 (the JSA Regs). Many of the central conditions will be familiar to those who previously dealt with unemployment benefit and/or income support for the unemployed. But conditions previously only applicable to the income support aspect of benefits for the unemployed and not to unemployment benefit are now applied also to the replacement for unemployment benefit: the "contribution-based jobseeker's allowance". In addition, and reflecting the new ethos of a benefit for "jobseeker's" rather than the "unemployed", a central condition for both components of the new allowance is that the claimant has entered into a jobseeker's agreement, which remains in force (para.(b)).

The conditions of entitlement, the sources in which they are "fleshed out", and some of the principles they reflect and the problem areas they deal with are considered in the remainder of this annotation (unless stated otherwise, each condition must be satisfied by *both* members of a "joint-claim couple", on which see further "Overview of JSA", above, and the notes to subs.(4), below):

(1) *"is available for employment"* (para.(a)): see further s.6 and the JSA Regs, Pt II, Chs I and II (regs 4–17). This "labour market" condition is one aspect of the central underlying principle, common to regimes of benefit for unemployed people, that the claimant's unemployment must be involuntary.

(2) *"has entered into a jobseeker's agreement which remains in force"* (para.(b)): see further ss.9–10 and the JSA Regs, Pt II, Chs I and V, regs 31–45. Note, in particular, that a claimant is to be treated as having satisfied this condition in any of the circumstances set out in JSA Regs, reg.34. This is a further aspect of the underlying principle, common in regimes of benefit for the unemployed, that the claimant's unemployment must be involuntary: he is a jobseeker, looking to return to work, and must agree a programme of activity, the better to enable him to do so. The jobseeker's agreement is an integral part of identifying what steps back to work are appropriate for the claimant and to enable regular and effective monitoring of his activities to that end, reviewing and altering the terms of the agreement as necessary over a period (see White Paper, para.4.16, and ss.10, 11). Note, in particular, that "employment officers" (usually Employment Service personnel: see s.9(13)) cannot enter into an agreement the terms of which are such that the claimant acting in accordance with them would fail to satisfy either of the key requirements to be available for and actively seeking work, thus placing such officers at the heart of policing these central requirements of the system (s.9(5)). Whether this will give rise to a higher profile on "actively seeking work" and more appeals to tribunals than hitherto remains to be seen.

(3) *"is actively seeking employment"* (para.(b)): see further s.7 and the JSA Regs, Pt II, Chs I and III (regs 4, 18–22). This second "labour market" condition is a further aspect of the central underlying principle, common to regimes of benefit for unemployed people, that the claimant's unemployment must be involuntary. In any week a person is actively seeking work if during that week he takes such steps as he can reasonably be expected to take in order to have *the best prospects of securing employment*, thereby stressing the requirements of taking positive action to secure work.

(4) *satisfies either (a) the conditions set out in s.2 or (b) (i) (as a non-joint-claim claimant) those in s.3 or (ii) (as joint-claim couple) those in s.3A.*

1.104   *The conditions set out in s.2 (contribution-based jobseeker's allowance) (para.(1)(d))*: The concept of "joint-claim couple" is not of relevance here. Each claimant for contribution-based jobseeker's allowance is treated as a separate individual. The conditions enumerated in s.2 deal with the further conditions of entitlement particular to the "contribution-based jobseeker's allowance", and JSA Regs, reg.56, provides some amplification. Regulations 47 and 48 are also relevant, and it is necessary to cross-refer to some of the provisions of the SSCBA 1992 dealing with contribution conditions. In essence the contribution conditions (the claimant's insurance) record are much the same as those under unemployment benefit from 1988 onwards, but there is greater protection of the position of carers who left the labour market to care for an invalid and now wish to return to the world of employment. But s.2 also establishes the mutual exclusivity of income support and contribution-based JSA and in addition embodies a preclusive earnings rule.

The conditions set out in s.3 (income-based jobseeker's allowance for a claimant who is not   **1.105**
a member of a joint-claim couple) (subs.(2A)): those set out in s.3 are particular to income-based jobseeker's allowance for a claimant who is not a member of a joint-claim couple. On "joint-claim couple" see "Overview of JSA", above, and notes to subs.(4), below. Amplification is found in the JSA Regs, Pts VI–XI, regs 76–155. The rules on means test are essentially the same as for income support.

The conditions set out in s.3A ((income-based jobseeker's allowance for a joint-claim   **1.106**
couple) (subss.(2B)–(2D)): Broadly speaking, these adapt the means-test and other provisions in s.3 to become conditions to be met by both members of the joint-claim couple. On "joint-claim couple", see "Overview of JSA", above, and the notes to subs.(4), below.

(5) *"is not engaged in remunerative work"*, (para.(e)): see further s.21 and Sch.1, para.1, which together enabled the making of the amplificatory regulations, the JSA Regs, regs 51–53. It may seem obvious that those who have a job cannot be said to be unemployed. But previous regimes have always catered for partial unemployment, and it is inevitably a matter of controversy at what point a line is to be drawn saying a claimant is working to such an extent that he cannot properly be said to be unemployed and need state support. The remunerative work rules draw that line; once the threshold is reached the JSA system will no longer regard a working claimant as "unemployed". The remunerative work rules as applicable to contribution-based JSA set the threshold at 16 hours per week: "remunerative work" means in the case of the claimant (the only person relevant for contribution-based JSA), work in which he is engaged or, where his hours of work fluctuate, is engaged on average, for not less than 16 hours per week; and work here means work for which payment is made or which is done in expectation of payment (JSA Regs, reg.51(1)(a)). Provision is made in JSA Regs, reg.51(2), (3) for determining the number of hours for which a person is engaged in work, essentially along the same line as provisions applicable to the issue in income support prior to its replacement as a benefit for unemployed people (Income Support (General) Regulations 1987, reg.5).

JSA Regs, reg.52 deals with those who are to be treated as engaged in remunerative work, notwithstanding that they may not at the time at issue be doing any work at all and, indeed, may be wholly without employment. In this way, the remunerative work condition becomes a vehicle for excluding the following claimants from both types of JSA:

(a) those who are without good cause absent from what constitutes remunerative work under reg.51 (those on maternity leave or absent from work through illness are protected);

(b) those absent from what constitutes remunerative work under reg.51 by reason of a recognised, customary or other holiday (those on maternity leave or absent from work through illness are protected);

(c) for varying periods in which those payments are taken into account, those who were, or were treated as being, in remunerative work whose employment has terminated but who received a "compensation payment" in respect of its termination or who have been paid holiday pay in respect of it.

Regulation 53 protects a range of claimants who *are* working by treating them as   **1.107**
not engaged in remunerative work: charity or voluntary workers paid only expenses; those engaged on a scheme for which a training allowance is paid; certain persons living in or temporarily absent from residential accommodation, a nursing home or

a residential care home; (as regards the performance of their duties) part-time firemen, auxiliary coastguards, lifeboatmen, members of a fire brigade, members of a prescribed territorial or reserve force; councillors as regards the performance of their duties; those engaged in boarding and fostering children; those mentally or physically disabled whose earning capacity or hours of work are in consequence reduced below 75 per cent of the normal threshold.

As noted above, for contribution-based JSA, only the claimant is relevant. Note in contrast that a claimant who is a member of a married or unmarried couple (but not a joint-claim couple) will be excluded from income-based JSA, despite his not being engaged (or treated as engaged) in remunerative work, if his partner is so engaged (or treated as so engaged), but the hours' threshold in respect of the partner is 24 rather than 16 (s.3(1)(e), JSA Regs, reg.51(1)(b)). As regards a joint-claim couple, both must satisfy the remunerative work condition. Failure of one to do so would, in principle, be expected to result in disentitlement of both. But see JSA Regulations, reg.3E, enabling the other member of a joint-claim couple to claim as a "standard" ss.1(2A) and 3 claimant in certain circumstances where the other member fails to meet one or more of the conditions of entitlement in s.1(2)(a)–(c) and (e)–(i). One such circumstance is where the "failing" member is engaged, or has agreed to be engaged, in remunerative work for more than 16 but less than 24 hours per week (JSA Regulations, reg.3E(2)(g)).

(6) *"is capable of work"* (para.(f)): this represents, as in the past, a demarcation line between benefits for those able to work but unable to find employment (previously unemployment/now jobseeker's benefits) and benefits for those incapable of work (incapacity benefits). However, complications inevitably did occur when claimants had to transfer from one type of benefit to the other, particularly in respect of periods of short-term incapacity. Hence the demarcation is no longer as strict as in the past; s.21 and Sch.1, para.2 enabled the making of JSA Regs, reg.55, which allows someone to remain in receipt of JSA whilst incapable of work for up to two weeks. No more than two such periods are permitted in any jobseeking period of less than 12 months. Where a jobseeking period lasts longer than 12 months, in effect one is entitled to no more than two such "short-term incapacity periods" in any 12 months.

1.108

(7) *"is not receiving relevant education"* (para.(g)): see further s.21 and Sch.1, para.14 and the regulation they enabled, JSA Regs, reg.54, which defines it to cover only full-time education, not being a course of advanced education, which is undertaken by a child or young person. Someone treated as a child for child benefit purposes or who is receiving full-time education as far as the child benefit system is concerned (see SSCBA 1992, s.142) is treated as receiving full-time education for the purposes of jobseeker's allowance (JSA Regs, reg.54(2)). Because this exclusion covers persons under 19, the effect of the contribution conditions (the claimant's insurance record) is to make this in practice a hurdle much more relevant to income-based than contribution-based JSA. Those on a full-time course of advanced education, it should be noted, will be excluded from JSA because they are treated as not available for employment (see s.6, JSA Regs, regs 1(3), 15(a)).

(8) *"is under pensionable age"* (para.(h)): "pensionable age" is defined as in the SSCBA 1992, s.122(1) (see s.35(1) and JSA Regs, reg.3). This inability of those over pensionable age to obtain JSA represents a significant change from the unemployment benefit regime, where those who had deferred retirement or had elected to "de-retire" in order to enhance their eventual retirement pension could receive unemployment benefit while seeking work. The change, however, is thought to affect a very small number of people each year (*per* Mr R. Evans, Parliamentary Under Secretary of State, *House of Commons Standing Committee Debates on the Jobseeker's Bill*, col. 133).

(9) *"is in Great Britain"* (para. (i)): see further s.21 and Sch.1, para.11, which enabled JSA Regs, reg.50 to treat temporary absence for certain specified purposes (*e.g.* to attend an employment interview) as presence in Great Britain and the amendment effected by JSA Regs, reg.165 to reg.11 of the Persons Abroad

Regulations 1975 to enable entitlement notwithstanding absence in the circumstances covered by reg.11. Note that for contribution-based JSA there is no requirement of "residence", whether ordinary or habitual; the condition is one of presence. But rules on habitual residence apply to restrict or deny the access of some people to income-based JSA. Note further that this condition of presence in Great Britain cannot prevail against the entitlements afforded under EC law: see, *e.g.* EC Regulation 1408/71, below.

Subs. (2A)

This deals with what is termed in this commentary the "standard" claimant for income-based jobseeker's allowance: that is, the claimant who is not a member of a joint-claim couple (on "joint-claim couple" see "Overview of JSA", above, and notes to subs.(4), below). In other words, broadly speaking, he is a single person, a member of a couple with children, or a member of a childless couple neither of whom was born after March 19, 1976 (*i.e.* neither is under 25) or, since October 2002, neither of whom was born after October 28, 1957 (*i.e.* neither is under 45). This claimant must meet the common conditions of entitlement in s.1(2)(a)–(c) and (e)–(i), plus those in s.3.

    1.109

Subs. (2B)

This deals with the entitlement of a joint-claim couple (see notes to subs.(4)) to income-based jobseeker's allowance. The couple must make a claim for the allowance jointly. Each member of the couple must meet the common conditions of entitlement in s.1(2)(a)–(c) and (e)–(i), plus those in s.3A. An allowance, entitlement to which is obtained pursuant to this subsection, is called a "joint-claim jobseeker's allowance" (subs.(4)).

    1.110

Subs. (2C)

This rule-making power enables regulations to stipulate circumstances in which a member of a joint-claim couple (see further notes to subs.(4)) is instead to be treated as a "standard" claimant under subs.(2A). JSA Regs, reg.3E is the product of the exercise of this power. It enables one member of a joint-claim couple to claim as a "standard" ss.1(2A) and 3 claimant in certain circumstances where the other member (described here as the "failing" member) does not satisfy one or more of the conditions of entitlement in s.1(2)(a)–(c) and (e)–(i). One such circumstance is where the "failing" member is engaged, or has agreed to be engaged, in remunerative work for more than 16 but less than 24 hours per week (JSA Regs, reg.3E(2)(g)). Others include where the "failing" member is pregnant and claiming maternity allowance or statutory maternity pay (reg.3E(2)(h)); or in receipt of statutory sick pay (reg.3E(2)(k)); or who is over pensionable age (reg.3E(2)(f)). See further the notes on that regulation.

    1.111

Subs. (2D)

This power enables regulations to be made where someone would otherwise be a member of two joint-claim couples. JSA Regs, reg.3(2) is the product of the exercise of this power. Where someone would otherwise be a member of more than one joint-claim couple, he will be regarded as a member of the couple he nominates or (in default) that the Secretary of State nominates. That nominated couple operates to the exclusion of any other couple of which he may be a member.

    1.112

Subs. (3)

This stipulates that jobseeker's allowance is one paid in respect of a week, whereas unemployment benefit was, of course, a daily benefit. Note, however, that s.21 and Sch.1, para.5 enable the making of regulations to permit payment of JSA for a period of less than a week. The circumstances in which this may be done are contained in JSA Regs, Pt XI, regs 150–155.

    1.113

Subs.(4)

1.114
This specifies that there are two types of jobseeker's allowance: (1) a "contribution-based jobseeker's allowance", entitlement to which depends on fulfilling the common conditions in subs.(2) plus the specific ones in section two; and (2) an "income-based jobseeker's allowance", entitlement to which is dependent on meeting the particular conditions set out in section three (standard claimant) or s.3A (joint-claim couple) as well as the common conditions in subs.(2).

Just as with the old regime of benefits for unemployed people, where a person might, depending on the circumstances, be entitled to only one or to both of unemployment benefit and income support, so with the jobseeker's allowance: section four contains complicated provisions on amounts of each type of allowance and the situation, common in practice, where the allowance received by an unemployed person looking for work is an amalgam of both types.

The subsection also defines "joint-claim couple" as a married or unmarried couple, *of a prescribed description,* who are not members of any family that includes someone for whom one of the members of the couple is entitled to child benefit. JSA Regs, reg.3A, as amended from October 28, 2002 gives the prescribed description: where one of the members of the couple was born after October 28, 1957, but being 18 or over. Subject to reg.3E(1), below, it thus now covers a member aged between 18 and 45. Initially coverage was for those aged between 18 and 25. Such a couple, however, will not be of a prescribed description if:

(a) under JSA Regs, reg.77(3), one of its members is treated as responsible for a child or young person (where no one is as yet entitled to child benefit, for example, because a claim has only just been made);

(b) the couple has care of a child or young person in one or more of the circumstances mentioned in JSA Regs, reg.78(4) (where they are fosterers or the child has been placed with them for adoption);

(c) a child or young person is living with the couple in the circumstances mentioned in JSA Regs, reg.78(8) (a child living with the couple when he is away from home while at school).

"Joint-claim jobseeker's allowance" is also defined in this subsection. It means an allowance entitlement to which arises through subs.(2B), above.

The contribution-based conditions

1.115
2.—(1) The conditions referred to in [² section 1(2)(d)] are that the claimant—

(a) has actually paid Class 1 contributions in respect of one ("the base year") of the last two complete years before the beginning of the relevant benefit year and satisfies the additional conditions set out in subsection (2);

(b) has, in respect of the last two complete years before the beginning of the relevant benefit year, either paid Class 1 contributions or been credited with earnings and satisfies the additional condition set out in subsection (3);

(c) does not have earnings in excess of the prescribed amount; and

(d) is not entitled to income support.

(2) The additional conditions mentioned in subsection (1)(a) are that—

(a) the contributions have been paid before the week for which the jobseeker's allowance is claimed;

(b) the earnings factor derived from earnings upon which primary Class 1 contributions have been paid, or treated as paid, is not less than the base year's lower earnings limit multiplied by 25.

(3) The additional condition mentioned in subsection (1)(b) is that the earnings factor derived from earnings upon which primary Class 1 contributions have been paid or treated as paid or from earnings credited is not less, in each of the two complete years, than the lower earnings limit for the year multiplied by 50.

[[1](3A) Where primary Class 1 contributions have been paid or treated as paid on any part of a person's earnings, subsections (2)(b) and (3) above shall have effect as if such contributions had been paid or treated as paid on so much of the earnings as did not exceed the upper earnings limit.]

(4) For the purposes of this section—

(a) "benefit year" means a period which is a benefit year for the purposes of Part II of the Benefits Act or such other period as may be prescribed for the purposes of this section;

(b) "the relevant benefit year" is the benefit year which includes—

    (i) the beginning of the jobseeking period, which includes the week for which a jobseeker's allowance is claimed, or

    (ii) (if earlier) the beginning of any linked period; and

(c) other expressions which are used in this section and the Benefits Act have the same meaning in this section as they have in that Act.

AMENDMENTS

1. Social Security Act 1998, Sch.7, para.133 (April 6, 1999). **1.116**
2. Welfare Reform and Pensions Act 1999, Sch.7, para.3 (March 19, 2001).

DEFINITIONS

"base year": see subs.(1)(a).
"Benefits Act": see s.35(1).
"benefit year": see subs.(4)(a) and s.35(1); SSCBA 1992, s.21(6).
"claimant": see s.35(1).
"earnings": see s.35(3), Sch.1, para.6; SSCBA 1992, s.3.
"earnings factor": subs.(4)(c) and SSCBA 1992, ss.22, 23.
"jobseeking period": see s.35(1) and JSA Regs, reg.47.
"linked period": see s.35(2) and Sch.1, para.3; JSA Regs, reg.48(2).
"lower earnings limit": see subs.(4)(c) and SSCBA 1992, s.5(1)(a).
"prescribed": see s.35(1).
"primary Class 1 contributions": see subs.(4)(c) and SSCBA 1992, ss.6, 8.
"relevant benefit year": see subs.(4)(b).
"upper earnings limit": see SSCBA 1992, ss.122(1) and 5(1).
"week": see s.35(1).
"year": see subs.(4)(c), s.35(1) and SSCBA 1992, s.122(1).

GENERAL NOTE

Section 1 stipulates that to be entitled to a contribution-based jobseeker's **1.117** allowance, a person must fulfil not only the common conditions set out in s.1(2)(a)–(c) and (e)–(i), but also those particular to that contribution-based component of JSA set out in this section (see s.1(2)(d)).

The particular conditions are threefold. First, and unsurprisingly in an insurance- or contribution-based benefit, the claimant must satisfy conditions relating to his past contribution record in terms of a specified mixture of paid and credited Class 1 social security contributions (those paid by employed earners) (subs.(1)(a), (b)). Secondly, his earnings with respect to the week of claim must not exceed a prescribed amount (subs.(1)(c)). Thirdly, the claimant must not be entitled to income support (subs.(1)(d)).

Each of these conditions will be examined in turn.

Subss. (1) (a) and (b), (2)–(4); particular condition one: the contribution conditions

1.118   These set out, or provide the necessary interpretative arrangements for, the insurance-or contribution-based conditions of entitlement particular to contribution-based JSA. In essence, they reproduce those that have been applicable to unemployment benefit since 1988, when those contribution conditions were tightened (with at least one unintended effect, now remedied in the JSA system) to require a more recent and extensive contact with the world of employment (see SSCBA 1992, s.25(1), (2)(a), Sch.3, Pt I, para.1 as in force immediately prior to commencement).

As with all contributory benefits, whether someone satisfies the contribution conditions for the benefit is a decision for the Secretary of State and now appealable to a tribunal as a decision on a claim for or award of benefit not otherwise rendered non-appealable (SSA 1998, s.12 and Sch.2; Decisions and Appeals Regs, reg.27 and Sch.2). From April 1, 1999, this has to some extent been affected by the entry into force of the Social Security (Transfer of Functions, etc.) Act 1999, below, which transfers certain functions from the Secretary of State to the Board of Inland Revenue. Certain matters as to categorisation of earners, which class of contributions a person is liable or entitled to pay, and whether they been paid in respect of any period become decisions for officers of the Board of Inland Revenue, thus impacting to some degree on the Secretary of State's decision as to whether the conditions specific to benefit entitlement are met. It would seem that for now such decisions on contribution conditions for benefit purposes remain ones for the Secretary of State. But s.8(1)(m) of that Act enables such an officer to decide such issues relating to contributions as may be prescribed by regulations. So the decision-maker could change. In any event, it would, given that appeals on this aspect will be rare, be inappropriate to go into too much detail in this work. But a brief outline may be of assistance in understanding the nature of contribution-based JSA and in considering the matter of when someone, having exhausted his title to such an allowance in accordance with the provisions of s.5(1) (after 26 weeks in a case of continuous unemployment), can become entitled to a further contribution-based jobseeker's allowance in accordance with the provisions of s.5(2). Some knowledge is also useful to identify the groups excluded by these contribution conditions from access to contribution-based JSA.

1.119   *Applying the contribution conditions*: the first step in applying the contribution conditions is to identify the relevant benefit year: the one including the beginning of the jobseeking period or any linked period (as will be seen below, the concept of linked period is crucial in helping qualify for contribution-based JSA those persons who left the labour market in order to care for an invalid, many of whom who had inadvertently been ruled out of unemployment benefit by the tightening of the contribution conditions in 1988). A benefit year runs generally from the first Sunday in January in one calendar year until the first Saturday in January in the next calendar year. So, if someone's first ever claim for any benefit was for JSA in October 2002, the relevant benefit year is 2002–2003. The second step in applying the conditions is to ascertain the two contribution/tax years (April 6 in one calendar year to April 5 in the next) in which the requisite level of contributions must be met: the last two *complete* tax/contribution years *before the start of the relevant benefit year*. So if the benefit year is 2002–2003 (Jan.–Jan.), the tax/contribution years are 1999–2000 and 2000–2001 (April–April), since tax/contribution year 2001–2002 was not complete at the start of the relevant benefit year. The final steps are to determine whether in one of those tax/contribution years (the "base year") the requisite level of *paid* contributions has been met (the first contribution condition) (subss.(1)(a), (2)(b)) and, if so, whether the requisite level of paid and/or credited contributions has also been met in respect of each of the two tax years (the second contribution condition) (subss.(1)(b), (3)). Paid (or treated as paid) means paid (or treated as paid) on so much of the earnings in the relevant years as did not exceed the upper earnings limit for contributions payment purposes (subs.(3A)). See further commentary to SSCBA 1992, Sch.3 in *Social Security Legislation 2005: Vol. I: Non Means Tested Benefits*.

The effect of the contribution conditions (potentially problematic groups): although one   **1.120**
must always be careful to avoid an over-simplistic approach in such a complex area, one can readily identify a number of groups either denied entitlement by the contribution conditions or who will have significant difficulties satisfying them:

(a) *The self-employed*—it is too simplistic to say that no self-employed person can have title to a contribution-based JSA; it depends on when he is/was self-employed. Since the contribution conditions can only be satisfied by Class 1 contributions (those paid by employed earners or credited during periods of unemployment or incapacity), the effect is to exclude from contribution-based JSA those who were self-employed throughout either of the relevant tax/contribution years.

(b) *Those who have never been employed*—the requirement in the first contribution condition for payment of contributions effectively excludes those who, whether through unemployment, incapacity or disability, have been unable to build a contribution record in terms of paid contributions.

(c) *Those unemployed or incapable of work during the relevant tax/contribution years but in work since the end of the second year*—if insufficient contributions have been paid in either of the years to satisfy condition one, these groups will be excluded, despite a prior full record in terms of paid contributions, unless the period of unemployment or incapacity forms a linked period with the current jobseeking period (see JSA Regs, reg. 48): a gap of more than 12 weeks precludes linking.

(d) *Persons under 18*—the conditions of entitlement to contribution-based JSA contain no explicit lower age limit, unlike income-based JSA, which specifically excludes most persons under 18 (see s.3(1)(f)). The contribution conditions do, however, tend to preclude entitlement to contribution-based JSA for those under 18 save in highly unusual circumstances; even a claim at the very beginning of a benefit year requires looking back to a tax year beginning almost three years earlier, so that for the bulk of the period focused on, the person will have been under 16, generating neither paid nor credited Class 1 contributions.

(e) *The low-paid*—those whose earnings fall below the lower earnings limit for the whole or the main part of a tax year will not satisfy the contribution conditions since there is no liability or ability to pay Class 1 contributions where earnings fall below that limit, and, because the person is in work, no Class 1 credits are generated.

(f) *Those married women or widows paying reduced rate contributions*—these do not generate any earnings factor (and so do not count) for UB/JSA purposes (SSCBA 1992, s.22(4)).

Contribution-based JSA: an improved position for carers: From 1988, the first contri-   **1.121**
bution condition for unemployment benefit required looking back to one of two recent tax years, rather than, as was the case prior to 1988, to any tax/contribution year. This impacted adversely on those (usually women) who, possibly with a full contribution record, left the secure world of employment to care for an invalid. Whilst receipt of invalid care allowance (ICA) produced credited Class 1 contributions to help fulfil the second contribution condition, if the person sought to return to the job market and claimed unemployment benefit pending finding work, say, some five years later, s/he would be precluded from entitlement since in neither of

the relevant tax/contribution years had s/he paid any contributions; from 1988 a complete record of paid contributions in earlier tax years did not count. This was an unintended effect of the 1988 changes (see Mr R. Evans, Parliamentary Under Secretary of State, *House of Commons Standing Committee B Debates on the Jobseeker's Bill*, cols 161–162 (1994–95)), and is not carried over into contribution-based JSA because the concept of "linked period" (see subs.(4)(b)(ii), s.21 and Sch.1, para.3, and JSA Regs, reg.48) includes, for purposes of helping someone to satisfy the contribution conditions, periods of receipt of ICA (see JSA Regs, reg.48(2), (3)), so that in our example the "relevant benefit year" becomes that in which the period of entitlement to ICA began (see subs.(4)(b)), and the relevant tax/contribution years, being determined by reference to that benefit year, are years in which the person had a full contribution record of paid contributions.

Subs. (1) (c): particular condition two: the earnings condition

1.122   In the White Paper, government presented contribution-based JSA as a benefit receivable for a period, irrespective of means, by those unemployed people who had paid contributions whilst in employment (para.4.21). Despite that, but in line with other statements in the White Paper (*ibid.*), this second particular condition specifies that a claimant for a contribution-based JSA "must not have earnings in excess of the prescribed amount".

The prescribed amount is not the same for everyone, but is determined for a particular claimant in accordance with the formula set out in JSA Regs, reg.56: a level equal to the claimant's personal age-related rate of contribution-based JSA (determined in accordance with s.4(1)(a) and JSA Regs, reg.79) plus the appropriate disregards from his earnings, minus one penny. Only the claimant's earnings are taken into account. On what constitutes "earnings" and their calculation, see s.35(3), which requires the term to be construed in accordance with SSCBA 1992, s.3 (earnings includes any remuneration or profit derived from an employment) and in accordance with Sch.1, para.6, which enables the making of regulations to treat as earnings specified employment protection payments and payments analogous to them. Furthermore, given that s.35(3) was one of the powers under which the JSA Regs were made, it appears to direct one for detail to JSA Regs, regs 98 (earnings of employed earners) and 100 (earnings of self-employed earners) and related regulations in JSA Regs, Pt VIII including appropriate disregards under Sch.6.

The idea is to preclude from entitlement to contribution-based JSA someone whose earnings, after taking account of any earnings disregards under the JSA scheme, would exceed his contributory entitlement. It is important to note that the earnings condition precludes entitlement, rather than allowing underlying entitlement but precluding payment. This preclusion of entitlement means that weeks covered by it do not eat into a claimant's maximum 182 days of entitlement to contribution-based JSA (see s.5).

1.123   In *CJSA/3928 & 3931/2003*, Commissioner Howell applied this earnings condition, using the Computation of Earnings Regulations so as to spread forward the payment received at the end of a month in respect of a range of past work (the claimant's hours were irregular), thus ruling out the particular weeks of claim because the earnings thus assessed were in each week above the prescribed amount.

1.124   One way of looking at this earnings condition (and to some extent reconciling the rule with conceptions of this as a benefit paid irrespective of means) might be to regard it as a statement that those earning in excess of the prescribed amount cannot in reality be said to be unemployed (*cf.* the "weekly earnings in excess of the lower earnings limit" rule and justification for it in USI Regs, reg.7(1)(o), (5A), pp.722–23 and 740 of Bonner, Hooker and White, *Non-Means Tested Benefits: The Legislation* (1996)) but are, in effect, deemed to be "employed". Thus the earnings rule plays a parallel role to that of the "remunerative work" condition which, as regards contribution-based JSA, rules out claimants working 16 or more hours per week. Both rules deal with the area of partial unemployment (the claimant actually works for some of the week). That on remunerative work denies title to those working more than the specified hours, whilst the earnings rule denies entitlement to those whose part-week employment, albeit falling within the 15hours permitted, is quite well-paid. Both rules thus deal with an area of difficulty once covered by the complexities and uncertainties of the "full extent normal rule" (see USI Regs, regs 7(1)(e), (2), pp.719, 722 and 730–35 of the 1996 edition of *Non Means Tested Benefits: The Legislation.*

But this role of dealing with partial unemployment is not the only one played by the preclusive "earnings limit", albeit that it may be the most obvious. The JSA Regs on earnings and their calculation define "earnings" widely. For example, reg. 98 states that employed earners' earnings include any "compensation payment" ("any payment made in respect of the termination of the employment other than" certain specified payments, for example, a statutory redundancy payment), certain Employment Protection (Consolidation) Act payments (guarantee payments, remuneration while suspended from work on medical or maternity grounds and remedies for unfair dismissal and compensation) as well as compensation for unfair dismissal or redundancy on grounds of involvement in trade union activities and protective awards under the Trade Union and Labour Relations (Consolidation) Act 1992. Related regulations prescribe the period for which such payments can be taken into account, and for calculating a weekly equivalent (see JSA Regs, regs 94, 97). So that, clearly, another purpose of this preclusive earnings condition could be, as was the case with unemployment benefit, to deny entitlement where some other system has compensated the person for the loss of his job (*cf.* the "terminal/compensation payments" rule in USI Regs, reg.7(1)(d), (5), (6), [pp.719, 723–24, 724–30 of the 1996 edition of *Non Means Tested Benefit: The Legislation*] and the rules on certain employment protection payments in USI Regs, reg.7(1)(k) [pp.721–22, 737–38 of the 1996 edition of this work]), thus ruling out of JSA for a period persons who are actually without work but are actively seeking and available for it, and in effect treating them as if they were still employed. But the remunerative work condition (s.1(2)(e) and JSA Regs, reg.52(3)) deals with the matter of "compensation payments" on termination of remunerative work, leaving this rule a possible role to play only with respect to payments on termination of part-time employment and with respect to the matter of the employment protection payments referred to above.

Another way of looking at this condition, however, especially when one reads it alongside the rules contained in s.4(1) on reduction or abatement of contribution-based JSA because of earnings and pension payments, is to see this earnings condition as a further intrusion of elements of "means-testing" into contributory benefits, something increasing stealthily since 1980 (see Wikeley, annotations to s.2). That said, however, it is equally clear that, despite such elements of "means-testing", contribution-based JSA (like its predecessor unemployment benefit) cannot properly be regarded as an "income-related" or fully-fledged "means-tested benefit" in the same way as income support, working tax credit or income-based JSA. These rules on contribution-based JSA look to a much narrower range of "means": capital is totally ignored, while, with respect to income only earnings are regarded for subs.(1)(c) purposes, although pension payments are in addition taken account of under s.4(1) (abatement or reduction of contribution-based JSA). Furthermore, the rules look only to the claimant's resources and not, like income-related benefits, to those of his partner or dependants. In short, contribution-based JSA is an uneasy hybrid benefit. It remains to be seen whether the degree of means-testing will be increased in the future: the White Paper appeared to envisage abatement or reduction of contribution-based JSA by other benefits (see para.4.21), but this has not been carried forward into the Act or the Regulations (indeed JSA Regs, reg.98(2)(a) specifically precludes from ranking as earnings of an employed earner "any remuneration paid by or on behalf of an employer to the claimant in respect of a period throughout which the claimant is on maternity leave or is absent from work because s/he is ill").

1.125

Subs. (1)(d): particular condition three: the claimant must not be entitled to income support

1.126   Read with s.3(1)(b) and SSCBA 1992, s.124(1)(f) (inserted by Sch.2, para.30 of the JSA), this establishes that JSA and income support are mutually exclusive benefits: one cannot have both at the same time. JSA is the benefit for those who are expected to seek work as a condition of receiving state benefit; income support is the residual income-related benefit for those who are not: principally pensioners, lone parents, men aged 60–64, sick and disabled people and those with significant caring responsibilities (for a full list see the Income Support (General) Regulations 1987, reg.4ZA and Sch.1B [prescribed categories of person] inserted by the Income Support (General) (Jobseeker's Allowance Consequential Amendments) Regulations 1996). So, under the income support scheme as amended by this Act and by regulations, requirements that (save in prescribed cases) claimants be available for and actively seeking work have gone, the minimum age of entitlement drops to 16, and persons able to claim entitlement (those in a prescribed category of person [see SSCBA 1992, s.124(1)(e)] are listed exhaustively in the new reg.4ZA of and Sch.1B to the Income Support (General) Regulations 1987. See the notes to reg.4ZA for discussion of the position of claimants who may be able to claim either JSA or income support and of the fact that the 24-hour limit for remunerative work for partners under JSA (the same limit applies to income support from October 7, 1996) may lead to a "better-off" problem for some claimants.

The income-based conditions

1.127   **3.**—(1) The conditions referred to in [¹ section 1(2A)(b)] are that the claimant—

  (a) has an income which does not exceed the applicable amount (determined in accordance with regulations under section 4) or has no income;

  (b) is not entitled to income support [² or state pension credit];

  (c) is not a member of a family one of whose members is entitled to income support;

  (d) is not a member of a family one of whose members is entitled to an income-based jobseeker's allowance;

  [² (dd) is not a member of a married or unmarried couple the other member of which is entitled to state pension credit;]

  (e) is not a member of a married or unmarried couple the other member of which is engaged in remunerative work; and

  (f) is a person—

   (i) who has reached the age of 18; or

   (ii) in respect of whom a direction under section 16 is in force; or

   (iii) who has, in prescribed circumstances to be taken into account for a prescribed period, reached the age of 16 but not the age of 18.

  (2) Regulations may provide for one or both of the following conditions to be included in the income-based conditions, in the case of a person to whom subsection (1)(f)(ii) or (iii) applies—

  (a) a condition that the claimant must register for employment;

  (b) a condition that the claimant must register for training.

  (3) In subsection (1)(f)(iii) "period" includes—

  (a) a period of a determinate length;

  (b) a period defined by reference to the happening of a future event; and

  (c) a period of a determinate length but subject to earlier determination upon the happening of a future event.

(4) Regulations under subsection (2) may, in particular, make provision by reference to persons designated by the Secretary of State for the purpose of the regulations.

AMENDMENTS

1. Welfare Reform and Pensions Act 1999, s.59 and Sch.7, para.4(1) (March 19, 2001).

1.128

2. State Pension Credit Act 2002, s.14 and Sch.2, para.37 (October 6, 2003).

DEFINITIONS

"claimant"—see s.35(1).
"employment"—*ibid.*, JSA Regs, reg.4.
"family"—see s.35(1).
"income-based conditions"—*ibid.*
"income-based jobseeker's allowance"—see s.1(4).
"married couple"—see s.35(1).
"prescribed"—*ibid.*
"training"—*ibid.*
"unmarried couple"—*ibid.*

GENERAL NOTE

Subs. (1)

1.129

This contains the further conditions for entitlement to income-based JSA for a claimant who is not a member of a "joint-claim couple" in addition to those in s.1 and the capital rule under s.13(1). See s.3A for the further conditions of entitlement for a joint-claim couple. For who constitutes a "joint-claim couple", see s.1(4) and reg.3A(1) of the JSA Regulations.

Under para.(a), the person's income (which includes the income of his family: s.13(2) and reg.88(1) of the JSA Regulations) must be less than the applicable amount (effectively the figure set for the family's requirements under s.4(5)). Note that as a consequence of the removal of amounts for children from income-based JSA (with effect from April 6, 2004, except in "transitional cases"—see the note to reg.17 of the Income Support Regulations and the note to reg.83 of the JSA Regulations), only a partner's income will count as that of the claimant and the applicable amount will no longer include any personal allowances for children, the family premium, the disabled child premium or the enhanced disability premium for a child. The person must in general be at least 18 (para.(f)(i)), except if he comes within certain categories (para.(f)(iii)), or the Secretary of State has directed that he will otherwise suffer severe hardship (para.(f)(ii) and s.16). (See regs 57–68 of the JSA Regulations for those 16- and 17-year-olds who are entitled to income-based JSA and the conditions of their eligibility.) If the person is a member of a couple, his partner must not be engaged in remunerative work (in the case of a partner remunerative work is work of 24 hours or more a week: reg.51(1)(b) of the JSA Regulations) (para.(e)). Paras (b) and (c) confirm that income-based JSA is not payable if the claimant, or any member of his family, is entitled to income support. See the corresponding amendment to s.124(1) of the Contributions and Benefits Act as regards the conditions of entitlement to income support. In addition, para.(d) excludes entitlement if another member of the family is entitled to income-based JSA. Following the introduction of state pension credit on October 6, 2003, entitlement to income-based JSA is also excluded if the claimant is entitled to state pension credit (para.(b)) or if he is a member of a couple and his partner is entitled to state pension credit (para.(dd)).

Subs. (2)

See reg.62 of the JSA Regulations.

[¹ The conditions for claims by joint-claim couples

1.130

3A.—(1) The conditions referred to in section 1(2B)(c) are—

(a) that the income of the joint-claim couple does not exceed the applicable amount (determined in accordance with regulations under section 4) or the couple have no income;

(b) that no member of a family of which the couple are members is entitled to income support;

(c) that no member of any such family (other than the couple) is entitled to an income-based jobseeker's allowance;

[² (cc) that neither member of the couple is entitled to state pension credit;]

(d) that at least one member of the couple has reached the age of 18; and

(e) that if only one member of the couple has reached the age of 18, the other member of the couple is a person—

(i) in respect of whom a direction under section 16 is in force; or

(ii) who has, in prescribed circumstances to be taken into account for a prescribed period, reached the age of 16.

(2) Subsections (2) and (4) of section 3 shall apply in relation to a member of the couple to whom subsection (1)(e)(i) or (ii) above applies as they apply in relation to a claimant to whom subsection (1)(f)(ii) or (iii) of that section applies.

(3) In subsection (1)(e)(ii) above "period" shall be construed in accordance with section 3(3).]

AMENDMENTS

1.131

1. Welfare Reform and Pensions Act 1999, s.59 and Sch.7, para.4(2) (March 19, 2001).

2. State Pension Credit Act 2002, s.14 and Sch.2, para.38 (October 6, 2003).

DEFINITIONS

"claimant"—see s.35(1).

"family"—*ibid.*

"income-based jobseeker's allowance"—see s.1(4).

"joint-claim couple"—*ibid.*

"prescribed"—see s.35(1).

GENERAL NOTE

Subs. (1)

1.132

In addition to the requirements in s.1 and the capital rule under s.13(1), this sets out the further conditions for entitlement to income-based JSA in the case of a joint-claim couple (defined in s.1(4) and see reg.3A(1) of the JSA Regulations). For a claimant for income-based JSA who is not a member of a joint-claim couple, see. s.3.

The conditions in subs.(1) more or less mirror those in s.3(1), with the necessary adjustments in the wording due to the fact that this section is only concerned with claims by a couple who both have to meet the conditions (except in certain circumstances—see reg.3E of the JSA Regulations). The amendment made on October 6, 2003 as a consequence of the introduction of state pension credit excludes entitlement to income-based JSA in the case of a joint-claim couple if either member of the couple is entitled to state pension credit (para.(cc)).

[¹ Joint-claim couples: the nominated member

3B.—(1) Where a joint-claim couple make a claim for a joint-claim job-seeker's allowance, they may nominate one of them as the member of the couple to whom the allowance is to be payable.

(2) In default of one of them being so nominated, the allowance shall be payable to whichever of them is nominated by the Secretary of State.

(3) Subsections (1) and (2) have effect subject to section 4A(4) and (7).

(4) In this Act references to the nominated member of a joint-claim couple are, except where section 20A(7) applies, to the member of the couple nominated under subsection (1) or (2) above; and where section 20A(7) applies, references to the nominated member of such a couple are to the member of the couple to whom section 20A(7) provides for the allowance to be payable.

(5) Nothing in this section or section 20A(7) affects the operation of any statutory provision by virtue of which any amount of the allowance is required or authorised to be paid to someone other than the nominated member of the couple.]

1.133

AMENDMENT

1. Welfare Reform and Pensions Act 1999, s.59 and Sch.7, para.4(2) (March 19, 2001).

1.134

DEFINITIONS

"joint-claim couple"—see s.1(4).
"joint-claim jobseeker's allowance"—*ibid.*

Amount payable by way of jobseeker's allowance

4.—(1) In the case of a contribution-based jobseeker's allowance, the amount payable in respect of a claimant ("his personal rate") shall be calculated by—

(a) determining the age-related amount applicable to him; and

(b) making prescribed deductions in respect of earnings and pension payments.

(2) The age-related amount applicable to a claimant, for the purposes of subsection (1)(a), shall be determined in accordance with regulations.

(3) In the case of an income-based jobseeker's allowance [² (other than a joint-claim jobseeker's allowance)], the amount payable shall be—

(a) if a claimant has no income, the applicable amount;

(b) if a claimant has an income, the amount by which the applicable amount exceeds his income.

[² (3A) In the case of a joint-claim jobseeker's allowance, the amount payable in respect of a joint-claim couple shall be—

(a) if the couple have no income, the applicable amount;

(b) if the couple have an income, the amount by which the applicable amount exceeds the couple's income.]

(4) Except in prescribed circumstances, a jobseeker's allowance shall not be payable where the amount otherwise payable would be less than a prescribed minimum.

(5) The applicable amount shall be such amount or the aggregate of such amounts as may be determined in accordance with regulations.

1.135

(6) Where a claimant [¹is entitled to both a contribution-based job-seeker's allowance and an income-based jobseeker's allowance] but has no income, the amount payable [¹ by way of a jobseeker's allowance] shall be—

    (a) the applicable amount, if that is greater than his personal rate; and

    (b) his personal rate, if it is not.

(7) Where the amount payable to a claimant to whom subsection (6) applies is the applicable amount, the amount payable to him by way of a job-seeker's allowance shall be taken to consist of two elements—

    (a) one being an amount equal to his personal rate; and

    (b) the other being an amount equal to the excess of the applicable amount over his personal rate.

(8) Where a claimant [¹ is entitled to both a contribution-based job-seeker's allowance and an income-based jobseeker's allowance] and has an income, the amount payable [¹ by way of a jobseeker's allowance] shall be—

    (a) the amount by which the applicable amount exceeds his income, if the amount of that excess is greater than his personal rate; and

    (b) his personal rate, if it is not.

(9) Where the amount payable to a claimant to whom subsection (8) applies is the amount by which the applicable amount exceeds his income, the amount payable to him by way of a jobseeker's allowance shall be taken to consist of two elements—

    (a) one being an amount equal to his personal rate; and

    (b) the other being an amount equal to the amount by which the difference between the applicable amount and his income exceeds his personal rate.

(10) The element of a jobseeker's allowance mentioned in subsection (7)(a) and that mentioned in subsection (9)(a) shall be treated, for the purpose of identifying the source of the allowance, as attributable to the claimant's entitlement to a contribution-based jobseeker's allowance.

(11) The element of a jobseeker's allowance mentioned in subsection (7)(b) and that mentioned in subsection (9)(b) shall be treated, for the purpose of identifying the source of the allowance, as attributable to the claimant's entitlement to an income-based jobseeker's allowance.

[² (11A) In subsections (6) to (11) "claimant" does not include—

    (a) a joint-claim couple, or

    (b) a member of such a couple (other than a person to whom regulations under section 1(2C) apply);

but section 4A, which contains corresponding provisions relating to joint-claim couples, applies instead.]

(12) Regulations under subsection (5) may provide that, in prescribed cases, an applicable amount is to be nil.

AMENDMENTS

1.136

1. Welfare Reform and Pensions Act 1999, s.70 and Sch.8, para.29 (November 11, 1999).

2. Welfare Reform and Pensions Act 1999, Sch.7, para.5 (March 19, 2001).

DEFINITIONS

    "claimant"—see s.35(1).

    "contribution-based conditions"—*ibid.*

    "contribution-based jobseeker's allowance"—see s.1(4).

    "earnings"—see s.35(3).

"income-based conditions"—see s.35(1).
"income-based jobseeker's allowance"—see s.1(4).
"joint-claim couple"—see s.1(4).
"pension payments"—see s.35(1).
"prescribed"—*ibid.*

GENERAL NOTE

This section is concerned with the amount of a jobseeker's allowance. The various   1.137
rules it contains arise out of the fact that JSA is a single benefit with two different
elements: contribution-based JSA and income-based JSA. Thus, for example, when
both components are payable it is necessary to identify each element for accounting
purposes, contribution-based JSA being payable out of the National Insurance Fund
and income-based JSA out of general taxation (see subss.(7), (9), (10) and (11)),
and because of the 182-day limit on entitlement for contribution-based JSA (see
s.5(1)). Subs.(1) provides the basic framework for the calculation of the amount
payable by way of contribution-based JSA (the "personal rate") and subs.(3) does
the same for income-based JSA (by setting the person's income, if any, against his
applicable amount). If the claimant satisfies the conditions of entitlement for both
contribution-based and income-based JSA and his personal rate is either greater
than his applicable amount if he has no income, or is greater than his applicable
amount minus his income, the amount of JSA payable will be the personal rate
(subss.(6)(b) and (8)(b)). This reflects the fact that contribution-based JSA,
although subject to increased (when compared with unemployment benefit) reduction in respect of the *claimant's* own earnings and pension payments, still falls considerably short of being a totally means-tested benefit.

Subss.(1) and (2)

If the claimant is entitled to contribution-based JSA, the amount payable ("his   1.138
personal rate") is calculated by deducting from the age-related amount appropriate
to him (see reg.79 of the JSA Regulations) any earnings that he has (see reg.80) and
pension payments under reg.81.

The end result may be that such deductions result in no amount being payable,
despite an underlying entitlement. In other words, the concept of abatement of
benefit, confined in unemployment benefit cases to pension payments in respect of
claimants 55 or over, has been carried over into JSA, irrespective of the age of the
claimant, and extended to also cover earnings. Further, it would appear that even
where the personal rate is nil because of such abatement, nevertheless, because there
remains an underlying entitlement, that period still counts towards the maximum
period of entitlement to contribution-based JSA (182 days in any period for which
the person's entitlement is established by reference (under s.2(1)(b)) to the same two
years—see s.5(1)). This contrasts with the position under s.2(1)(c) where the weekly
earnings (on their own) exceed the prescribed amount; in that situation there is no
entitlement (the person in effect is treated as if employed) and the periods covered
do not eat into the 182 days' maximum entitlement (26 weeks, assuming continuous unemployment).

Subs.(3)

This provision sets out the basic means test calculation for income-based JSA
(other than a joint-claim jobseeker's allowance). Provided that the conditions of
entitlement imposed by ss. 1 and 3 and the capital test under s.13(1) are satisfied,
the claimant's income is set against his applicable amount, calculated according to
regs 82 to 87 of the JSA Regulations. The difference is the amount of benefit. The
claimant's income includes that of the other members of his family (s.13(2)),
although note the modifications to this rule for children and young persons which
were in regs. 106 and 109 of the JSA Regulations (see the 2003 edition of this
volume for those regulations and the notes to those regulations). However, as

a consequence of the removal of amounts for children and young persons from income-based JSA (with effect from April 6, 2004, except in "transitional cases"—see further the note to reg. 17 of the Income Support Regulations and the note to reg.83 of the JSA Regulations), a child's income and capital will be totally ignored and only a partner's income and capital will count as that of the claimant (see the amended form of reg. 88(1) of the JSA Regulations).

Subs. (3A)

1.139   This sets out the basic means test calculation for a joint-claim jobseeker's allowance. Provided that the conditions of entitlement imposed by ss.1 and 3A-B and the capital test under s.13(1) are satisfied, the joint-claim couple's income is set against its applicable amount, calculated according to regs 86A-D of the JSA Regulations. The difference is the amount of benefit, so that, if the couple have no income the amount payable is its applicable amount.

Subs. (4)

See reg.87A of the JSA Regulations.

Subs. (5)

See regs 82 to 87 of and Schs 1 to 5 to the JSA Regulations. These adopt the income support model, although there are some changes to the premiums to reflect the fact that people over pensionable age have never been entitled to JSA.

Subs. (11A)

This provides that subss.(6)–(11) do not apply to a joint-claim couple. Instead, similar provision is made for such a couple in s.4A, below.

Subs. (12)

See reg.85 of and Sch.5 to the JSA Regulations.

[¹ Amount payable in respect of joint-claim couple

1.140   **4A.**—(1) This section applies where—

(a) a joint-claim couple are entitled to a joint-claim jobseeker's allowance; and

(b) one or each of the members of the couple is in addition entitled to a contribution-based jobseeker's allowance;

and in such a case the provisions of this section have effect in relation to the couple in place of section 4(3A).

(2) If a joint-claim couple falling within subsection (1) have no income, the amount payable in respect of the couple by way of a jobseeker's allowance shall be—

(a) the applicable amount, if that is greater than the couple's personal rate; and

(b) the couple's personal rate, if it is not.

(3) Where the amount payable in accordance with subsection (2) is the applicable amount, the amount payable in respect of the couple by way of a jobseeker's allowance shall be taken to consist of two elements—

(a) one being an amount equal to the couple's personal rate; and

(b) the other being an amount equal to the excess of the applicable amount over the couple's personal rate.

(4) Where the amount payable in accordance with subsection (2) is the couple's personal rate, then—

    (a) if each member of the couple is entitled to a contribution-based job-seeker's allowance, an amount equal to the member's own personal rate shall be payable in respect of the member by way of such an allowance;

    (b) if only one of them is so entitled, an amount equal to that member's personal rate shall be payable in respect of the member by way of such an allowance;

and in either case nothing shall be payable in respect of the couple by way of a joint claim jobseeker's allowance.

(5) If a joint-claim couple falling within subsection (1) have an income, the amount payable in respect of the couple by way of a jobseeker's allowance shall be—

    (a) the amount by which the applicable amount exceeds the couple's income, if the amount of that excess is greater than the couple's personal rate; and

    (b) the couple's personal rate, if it is not.

(6) Where the amount payable in accordance with subsection (5) is the amount by which the applicable amount exceeds the couple's income, the amount payable in respect of the couple by way of a jobseeker's allowance shall be taken to consist of two elements—

    (a) one being an amount equal to the couple's personal rate; and

    (b) the other being an amount equal to the amount by which the difference between the applicable amount and the couple's income exceeds the couple's personal rate.

(7) Where the amount payable in accordance with subsection (5) is the couple's personal rate, subsection (4) shall apply as it applies in a case where the amount payable in accordance with subsection (2) is that rate.

(8) The element of a jobseeker's allowance mentioned in subsection (3)(a) and that mentioned in subsection (6)(a) shall be treated, for the purpose of identifying the source of the allowance, as attributable—

    (a) in a case where only one member of the joint-claim couple is entitled to a contribution-based jobseeker's allowance, to that member's entitlement to such an allowance; and

    (b) in a case where each member of the couple is entitled to a contribution-based jobseeker's allowance, rateably according to their individual entitlements to such an allowance.

(9) The element of a jobseeker's allowance mentioned in subsection (3)(b) and that mentioned in subsection (6)(b) shall be treated, for the purpose of identifying the source of the allowance, as attributable to the couple's entitlement to a joint-claim jobseeker's allowance.

(10) In this section, "the couple's personal rate", in relation to a joint-claim couple, means—

    (a) where only one member of the couple is entitled to a contribution-based jobseeker's allowance, that member's personal rate;

    (b) where each member of the couple is entitled to such an allowance, the aggregate of their personal rates.]

Amendment

1. Welfare Reform and Pensions Act 1999, s.59 and Sch.7, para.6 (March 19, 2001).

           1.141

"contribution-based jobseeker's allowance"—see s.1(4).
"joint-claim couple"—*ibid.*
"joint-claim jobseeker's allowance"—*ibid.*

GENERAL NOTE

1.142   This section is concerned with the amount of JSA in the case of a joint-claim couple where either or both members of the couple are entitled to contribution-based JSA. If there is no entitlement to contribution-based JSA, see s.4(3A). Its provisions have a similar effect to those in s.4(6)–(11). See the notes to s.4 as to why there is a need for these rules. Note the definition of "the couple's personal rate" in subs.(10). The "personal rate" is the amount payable by way of contribution-based JSA (see. s.4(1)).

Duration of a contribution-based jobseeker's allowance

1.143   **5.**—(1) The period for which a person is entitled to a contribution-based jobseeker's allowance shall not exceed, in aggregate, 182 days in any period for which his entitlement is established by reference (under section 2(1)(b)) to the same two years.

(2) The fact that a person's entitlement to a contribution-based jobseeker's allowance ("his previous entitlement") has ceased as a result of subsection (1), does not prevent his being entitled to a further contribution-based jobseeker's allowance if—

(a) he satisfies the contribution-based conditions; and
(b) the two years by reference to which he satisfies those conditions includes at least one year which is later than the second of the two years by reference to which his previous entitlement was established.

(3) Regulations may provide that a person who would be entitled to a contribution-based jobseeker's allowance but for the operation of prescribed provisions of, or made under, this Act shall be treated as if entitled to the allowance for the purposes of this section.

DEFINITIONS

1.144   "contribution-based conditions": see ss.2 and 35(1).
"contribution-based jobseeker's allowance": see ss.1(4) and 35(1).
"his previous entitlement": see subs.(2).
"prescribed": see s.35(1).
"regulations": *ibid.*
"year": *ibid.*

GENERAL NOTE

1.145   This section deals only with entitlement to a contribution-based jobseeker's allowance. It has no direct relevance to the income-based component of JSA, but will have consequences where there was entitlement to both elements of JSA and the amount payable was, in effect, that from the income-based component of JSA (see further annotations to s.4(6)–(11)).

Entitlement to contribution-based jobseeker's allowance (a benefit obtainable as of right rather than income-related) is time-limited, as was its predecessor, unemployment benefit. Title to the latter expired when someone had been entitled to it for 312 days in a single period of interruption of employment (after 12 months in a case of continuous unemployment, although the calendar period would be longer where the single period of unemployment was composed of several spells, separated in time, but "linked" for benefit purposes). But that person could requalify for consideration for another "year" of entitlement (actual entitlement depending on satisfaction of the standard conditions of entitlement) once he had worked for a specified number of hours per week for a specified number of weeks in a specified time period.

This section similarly provides for a time-based expiry of entitlement to contribution-based JSA and for an ability to qualify for further, in turn time-limited, spells of entitlement to it. The rules in their specifics, however, afford a marked contrast with the unemployment benefit regime. The time limit on entitlement is in effect halved to 26 weeks (six months) in a case of continuous unemployment (longer in calendar terms in cases of intermittent unemployment—see annotation to subs. (1)), and the rules on requalification for a further spell of entitlement are linked, not to hours of work done, but in essence to less readily understandable matters of the claimant's contribution record in particular years, albeit in a manner that in effect will tend to require a return to employment in order to requalify (see annotation to subs.(2)).

Tribunals will need more knowledge of contributions than before (if only to understand the Secretary of State's decision communicated to them), since both the "exhaustion rule" (subs.(1)) and the "requalification rule" (subs.(2)) refer to the contribution-based conditions in s.2, the central ones for requalification purposes being those dealing with the claimant's contribution record. See further the annotations to that section.

Subs.(1): the exhaustion rule

This stipulates that the period for which a person can be entitled to a contribution-based jobseeker's allowance cannot exceed in total 182 days *in any period for which his entitlement is established by reference (under s.2(1)(b): the second contribution condition) to the same two tax/contribution years.*

1.146

In the simplest case of continuous unemployment, this effectively means that after serving the three "waiting days" (s.21, Sch.1, para.4; JSA Regs, reg.46) the exhaustion point is reached after 26 weeks (six months) since JSA generally operates on a full week basis. This is, perhaps, the most striking change from the unemployment benefit regime.

But more complicated cases can arise. Some people suffer intermittent unemployment, with spells of unemployment being interspersed with a variety of other spells: periods of incapacity for work, spells of employment, periods of training, periods caring for an invalid, periods of pregnancy. How is one to ascertain whether the days in an initial spell of unemployment are to be aggregated with ones in a later spell for purposes of this exhaustion rule? The answer lies in the rubric: *182 days in any period for which his entitlement is established by reference (under s.2(1)(b): the second contribution condition) to the same two tax/contribution years.* Translating and applying this requires some understanding of the concepts, "jobseeking period" (see further JSA Regs, reg.47) "linking" (see further JSA Regs, reg.48(1)) and "linked period" (see further JSA Regs, reg.48(2), (3)). It also requires some understanding of the contribution-record conditions in s.2 ("his entitlement is established by reference . . . to the same two years").

Basically a "jobseeking period" is one in which the claimant satisfies or is treated as satisfying the conditions of entitlement common to both types of JSA, set out in s.1(2)(a)–(c) and (e)–(i) (see JSA Regs, reg.47). Notions of "linking" may be familiar from the unemployment benefit regime and from incapacity benefit. But the "linking rule" for JSA is somewhat different as to specifics. It requires two or more ostensibly distinct jobseeking periods to be treated as one period where they are separated by a period comprising only (a) any period of not more than 12 weeks, (b) a linked period, (c) any period of not more than 12 weeks falling between any two linked periods or between a jobseeking period and a linked period or (d) a period of summons for jury service requiring attendance at court (see JSA Regs, reg.48(1)). A "linked period" embraces periods of incapacity for work, of entitlement to a maternity allowance, of engagement in training for which a training allowance is payable and (for more limited purposes) of entitlement to invalid care allowance (see JSA Regs, reg.48(2)). Note, however, that the rubric does not refer to "jobseeking period" or to "linked period" but deliberately to "*any period* for which his entitlement is established by reference (under s.2(1)(b)) to the same two [tax/contribution] years" (emphasis supplied by annotator). So that days of entitlement to contribution-based jobseeker's allowance in wholly separate jobseeking periods can still be aggregated for purposes of the exhaustion rule provided that entitlement to contribution-based jobseeker's allowance in each is determined by reference to the same two tax/contribution years. Which brings us to the essentials of the contribution-record conditions (see further the annotations to s.2).

Under s.2, the two tax/contribution years (April to April) relevant for a claim are the last two *complete* tax/contribution years before the *start* of the benefit year (generally first Sunday in January in one calendar year to the first Saturday in January in the next), which includes the beginning of the *jobseeking period* in respect of which JSA is being claimed or, if earlier, the beginning of any *linked period* (see s.2(1), (4)).

All this is much less readily understandable in terms of application to real life than the unemployment benefit regime. Some illustrative and non-exhaustive examples may help show how all this works.

Example I:

1.147   Let us assume a claim for JSA as a first ever claim for any benefit in November 2003. The benefit year is 2003/2004, and the tax years are 2000/2001 and 2001/2002. In a continuous spell of unemployment the claimant is entitled to contribution-based JSA for 82 days. He then works for 10 weeks and again becomes unemployed, and claims JSA. This second spell of unemployment lasts 200 days. This second spell of unemployment "links" with the first to become one; the tax/contribution years remain, as before, determined by the start of the benefit year, which included the beginning of the period (the first spell); and the tax/contribution years are the same. So the exhaustion point for entitlement to contribution-based JSA is reached once the claimant has been entitled to contribution-based JSA for 100 days in this second spell.

Example II:

1.148   The claim for JSA at the beginning of February 2003 is that person's first ever claim for any benefit. The relevant benefit year is 2003/2004, the relevant tax/contribution are 2000/2001 and 2001/2002. In this first jobseeking period, he is entitled to contribution-based JSA for 100 days. He then becomes incapable of work for 84 days. Thereafter he is still without work and claims JSA. That second spell of unemployment lasts indefinitely. For two weeks (14 days of the period of incapacity) he will remain entitled to contribution-based JSA unless he elects to claim or has claimed incapacity benefit, severe disablement allowance or income support (JSA Regs, reg.55). Assuming he does remain so entitled (14 days), the two apparently separate jobseeking periods "link" to form one, being separated only by a "linked period", title in the second spell of no work still depends on the same two tax/contribution years (being determined by the start of the single jobseeking period formed by the linking rule) and he will reach the exhaustion point for contribution-based JSA after 68 days.

Example III:

1.149   The first ever claim for any benefit is for JSA at the beginning of February 2003. The relevant benefit year is 2003/2004 and the relevant tax years are 2000/2001 and 2001/2002. In that first jobseeking period he is entitled to contribution-based JSA for 70 days. He then is in full-time employment for 14 weeks at the end of which he is again unemployed, and claims JSA. This spell of unemployment lasts indefinitely. Here the two jobseeking periods do not link to form one, being separated by more than 12 weeks and by a period (employment), which is not a "linked period". But the relevant benefit year is still 2003/2004 and the relevant tax years are thus still 2000/2001 and 2001/2002, the same as for the first jobseeking period. The determinative rubric reads "*any period* for which his entitlement is established by reference (under s.2(1)(b)) to the same two [tax/contribution] years" (emphasis supplied by annotator), so that the days of entitlement to contribution-based jobseeker's allowance in each of our jobseeking periods must be aggregated. So that his title to contribution-based JSA will be exhausted after 112 days of entitlement in the second jobseeking period, entitlement starting after service of three waiting days (see s.21, Sch.1, para.4 and JSA Regs, reg.46).

Interpreting and applying the rubric "any period for which a person is entitled to a contribution-based jobseeker's allowance" requires making and maintaining the important distinction between "entitled" and "payable". While an allowance cannot be payable without entitlement, a person can be entitled to an allowance but, nevertheless, it may not be payable to him. So, if his weekly earnings exceed the prescribed amount, there is no entitlement (s.2(1)(c)). If, in contrast, a combination of his earnings and pension payments merely reduce the amount otherwise payable to nil under the abatement provisions of s.4, there is entitlement, but no payable amount. Similarly, a claimant caught by the trade dispute provision is not entitled to an allowance, whereas in contrast the approach is that no allowance is payable to a person who loses his job through misconduct, despite his satisfying the conditions of entitlement to JSA. How does this relate to the exhaustion rule under subs.(1)? Obviously, days of entitlement to JSA count towards the period, days of non-entitlement cannot. So a period in which a person's earnings exceed the prescribed amount does not erode the maximum period of entitlement, but a period in which an amount otherwise payable to an entitled claimant is reduced to nil does count towards and eat into that 182-day maximum. The period in which the claimant is caught by the trade dispute provision does not affect the 182-day maximum, but one in which, despite entitlement to contribution-based JSA, an allowance is not payable because he is caught by s.19 (*e.g.* for leaving a job through misconduct), does erode the 182-day period (something confirmed, unnecessarily, by JSA Regs, reg.47(4)).

Note finally that regulations under subs.(3) can treat someone, for the purposes of the exhaustion and requalification rules, as entitled to a contribution-based jobseeker's allowance, where specified provisions of the Act (that is, specified in regulations—"prescribed") or under the Act (*i.e.* contained in Regulations) have removed what would otherwise have been an actual underlying entitlement. See further the annotation to subs.(3), below.

Subs.(2): the requalification rule

Requalification here does not mean that the person will be entitled to benefit or   1.150
that it will in fact be payable even if there is an entitlement. Actual entitlement will depend on fulfilling the conditions of entitlement, common to both components of JSA, which are set out in s.1, while the amount payable depends as normal on the principles in s.4. Requalification essentially means getting back on track for reconsideration of possible entitlement to a contribution-based JSA.

In order to requalify for consideration, the claimant must satisfy the conditions specific to contribution-based jobseeker's allowance that are set out in s.2: he must not be entitled to income support (one cannot have IS and JSA at the same time); his weekly earnings must not exceed a prescribed amount; and he must satisfy the contribution-record conditions (subs.(2)(a)). Further, however, the two tax/contribution years by reference to which the contribution-record conditions are satisfied must include at least one tax/contribution year which is later than the second tax/contribution year by reference to which "his previous entitlement" to contribution-based jobseeker's allowance (now exhausted applying subs.(1)) was established. So if, as in Examples II and III (annotation to subs.(1), above), the previous entitlement in benefit year 2003/2004 rested on the 2000/2001 and the 2001/2002 tax/contribution years, requalification for a further period of entitlement to contribution-based jobseeker's allowance could come in a time-period based on tax/contribution years 2001/2002 and 2002/2003. That could come about in benefit year 2004/2005, but only if the jobseeking period in question did not "link" with the one in 2003/2004. So someone who remains continuously unemployed after exhausting his title, or whose spells of intermittent unemployment are not separated by periods that break the link, cannot requalify. But if, in contrast, the claimant breaks the link back to the previous period (for example by working for 16 or more hours per week for a continuous period of at least 13 weeks) in a way that moves his new claim into benefit year 2004/2005 then if he is thereafter without work, or working less than 16 hours per week, he can requalify, provided that (i) the contribution record in tax/contribution years 2001/2002 and 2002/2003 reaches the requisite level, (ii) his weekly earnings do not exceed the prescribed amount, and (iii) he is not entitled to income support (one cannot have IS and JSA at the same time). The link would also be broken by not claiming JSA for a continuous 13-week period, since a period of no claim cannot be a jobseeking period (JSA Regs, reg.47(3)(a)), but that apparent ability to move a new claim into a benefit year more favourable for requalification purposes is not one open to those without work who need an income from the state in terms of income-related JSA. Periods in excess of 12 weeks of non-entitlement because of being caught by the trade dispute provision (s.14, JSA Regs, reg. 47(3)(d)) or where entitlement ceased because of a failure to comply with, for example, attendance conditions (see JSA Regs, regs 25, 47(3)(c)) also have the effect of breaking the link, but, given their effect on income replacement, will tend to do fortuitously rather than as a matter of deliberate choice to assist requalification.

Subs. (3)

1.151 The jobseeker's allowance regime draws a crucial distinction between entitlement to an allowance, on the one hand, and an allowance being payable on the other (see further the annotations to subs.(1), above). While an allowance cannot be payable without entitlement, a person can be entitled to an allowance but nevertheless it may not be payable to him. So, if his weekly earnings exceed the prescribed amount, there is no entitlement (s.2(1)(c)). If in contrast, a combination of his earnings and pension payments merely reduce the amount otherwise payable to nil under the abatement provisions of s.4, there is entitlement, but no payable amount. Similarly, a claimant caught by the trade dispute provision is not entitled to an allowance, whereas in contrast the approach is that no allowance is payable to a person who loses his job through misconduct, despite his satisfying the conditions of entitlement to JSA. Under subs.(1), obviously, days of entitlement to JSA count towards the period, days of non-entitlement cannot. So a period in which a person's earnings exceed the prescribed amount does not erode the maximum period of entitlement, but a period in which an amount otherwise payable to an entitled claimant is reduced to nil does count towards and eat into that 182-day maximum. The period in which the claimant is caught by the trade dispute provision does not affect the 182-day maximum, but one in which, despite entitlement, an allowance is not payable because he is caught by s.19 (*e.g.* for leaving a job through misconduct) does erode the 182-day period.

1.152 All this seems obvious but is a necessary precursor to understanding the role of this subsection and of the regulation made under it.

This subsection enables the making of regulations to treat someone, for the purposes of the exhaustion and requalification rules, as entitled to a contribution-based jobseeker's allowance, where specified provisions of the Act (that is, specified in regulations—"prescribed") or under the Act (*i.e.* contained in regulations) have removed what would otherwise have been an actual underlying entitlement. In other words, although in the situation covered there may be no entitlement such as to enable the award of any or the full amount of benefit, nevertheless the period covered in the regulations will eat into the maximum 182 days' entitlement.

The regulation made under subs.(3) is JSA Regs, reg.47(4). Sub-paras (a) and (b) of reg.47(4) provide that a day in a jobseeking period (see reg.47(1)–(3)) in respect of which the person satisfies the contribution-record conditions (in s.2(1)(a), (b)) counts for the purposes of the exhaustion rule in this section as a day of entitlement to a contribution-based jobseeker's allowance even though no JSA is payable by virtue of s.19. However, a day of entitlement in respect of which payment is precluded under s.19 already ranks for the purposes of the exhaustion rule in subs.(1) by virtue of the "entitlement/payability" distinction discussed in the annotations to that subsection. Thus reg.47(4) was unnecessary to secure that aim. But whether this is taken from this subsection and reg.47(4)(a) and (b) or simply from the consequences of the distinction s.19 draws between entitlement, on the one hand, and the allowance not being payable on the other (examined above), one thing is abundantly clear: the days for which someone is ruled out of receiving benefit under s.19 (*e.g.* because of losing employment through misconduct) now count in determining when title to contribution-based jobseeker's allowance is exhausted, whereas under the unemployment benefit regime, such days of disqualification did not so count (not being days of unemployment) (see ss.26, 28; USI Regs, reg.7(1)(b)(i) in Bonner, Hooker and White *Non-Means Tested Benefits: The Legislation* (1996)). So that if someone with an underlying entitlement to contribution-based jobseeker's allowance is denied payment for the maximum period of preclusion (26 weeks), that preclusion not only prevents payment, but extinguishes entitlement to such an allowance based on the tax/contribution years relevant to that claim and, to gain another period of entitlement, the claimant will have to satisfy the requalification rule (subs.(2)). So reaching the right and proper decision on what under the unemployment benefit regime would have been called "disqualification" and determining the appropriate period of preclusion is even more important than before (see further the annotations to s.19).

Regulation 47(4)(a) and (c) read with para.(2) of that regulation achieve another purpose: that stated in the joint Employment Department/Department of Social Security memorandum to the House of Lords Select Committee on the Scrutiny of Delegated Powers (HL 50, 1994–1995, Annex I). That memorandum suggested that the subsection **1.153**

"enables regulations to provide for certain classes of person to be treated as entitled to a contribution-based jobseeker's allowance. *It will be used to ensure that claimants who are receiving payments of an income-based jobseeker's allowance under the provisions of paragraphs 8 and 9 of Schedule 1 have their contributory entitlement of 182 days eroded, in cases where a contributory entitlement would have existed.*" (para.31, emphasis added by annotator.)

JSA Regs, reg.47(4)(a) and (c), read together, mean that any period in which someone who satisfies the contribution-record conditions (see s.2(1)(a), (b)) is denied benefit because they are not available for or actively seeking work or because no jobseeker's agreement is in force, but nonetheless is awarded a reduced payment because of severe hardship (see JSA Regs, Pt IX), counts towards the 182-day maximum entitlement period to contribution-based jobseeker's allowance.

Jobseeking

Availability for employment

6.—(1) For the purposes of this Act, a person is available for employment **1.154** if he is willing and able to take up immediately any employed earner's employment.

(2) Subsection (1) is subject to such provisions as may be made by regulations; and those regulations may, in particular, provide that a person—

    (a) may restrict his availability for employment in any week in such ways as may be prescribed; or

(b) may restrict his availability for employment in any week in such circumstances as may be prescribed (for example, on grounds of conscience, religious conviction or physical or mental condition or because he is caring for another person) and in such ways as may be prescribed.

(3) The following are examples of restrictions for which provision may be made by the regulations—

(a) restrictions on the nature of the employment for which a person is available;

(b) restrictions on the periods for which he is available;

(c) restrictions on the terms or conditions of employment for which he is available;

(d) restrictions on the locality or localities within which he is available.

(4) Regulations may prescribe circumstances in which, for the purposes of this Act, a person is or is not to be treated as available for employment.

(5) Regulations under subsection (4) may, in particular, provide for a person who is available for employment—

(a) only in his usual occupation,

(b) only at a level of remuneration not lower than that which he is accustomed to receive, or

(c) only in his usual occupation and at a level of remuneration not lower than that which he is accustomed to receive,

to be treated, for a permitted period, as available for employment.

(6) Where it has been determined [1 . . .] that a person is to be treated, for the purposes of this Act, as available for employment in any week, the question whether he is available for employment in that week may be subsequently determined [1under section 9 or 10 of the Social Security Act 1998].

(7) In this section "permitted period", in relation to any person, means such period as may be determined in accordance with the regulations made under subsection (4).

(8) Regulations under subsection (4) may prescribe, in relation to permitted periods—

(a) the day on which any such period is to be regarded as having begun in any case;

(b) the shortest and longest periods which may be determined in any case;

(c) factors which [2the Secretary of State] may take into account in determining the period in any case.

(9) For the purposes of this section "employed earner's employment" has the same meaning as in the Benefits Act.

AMENDMENTS

1.155 1. Social Security Act 1998, Sch.7, para.134(1) (October 18, 1999).

2. Social Security Act 1998, Sch.7, para.134(2) (October 18, 1999).

DEFINITIONS

"Benefits Act": see s.35(1).

"claimant": see *ibid.*

"employed earner's employment": see subs.(9) and SSCBA 1992, s.2.

"employment": see s.35(1).
"the first determination": see subs.(6).
"permitted period": see subs.(7).
"prescribed": see s.35(1).
"regulations": see *ibid.*
"week": see *ibid.*

General Note

This section and ss.7 to 10 expand on the "labour market conditions" for   **1.156**
entitlement to JSA in s.1(2)(a) to (c). However, much of the key detail remains in
the regulations made under these sections (see Part II of the JSA Regulations). Note
that regulations made under ss.6 and 7 are subject to the affirmative procedure
(s.37(1)(c)).

The benefits regimes for unemployed people have always embodied an underlying principle that the unemployment must be involuntary, one aspect of which is that
the claimant without work must want to and seek to return to the world of employment. One element giving effect to that principle has been the requirement that the
claimant, as a condition of receiving benefit, must be "available for employment"
(examined here). The other is that the claimant must actively be seeking employment (examined in the annotations to s.7). The availability requirement formed an
integral part both of unemployment benefit and of income support. But, while the
central concept of availability was the same for each benefit, the detailed rules and
approaches were not.

This section, amplifying the basic statement of availability as a condition of entitlement to JSA (whether contribution- or income-based) set out in s.1(2)(a), gives a
basic definition of the "available for employment" requirement (subs.(1), (9)). But
that relatively straightforward approach, encapsulating the essence of case law (decisions of courts and commissioners on the availability concept in its manifestations in
earlier regimes of benefits for the unemployed) is itself made "subject to such provisions as may be made by regulations" made under the other provisions of this section,
which consist of rule-making powers (subs.(2)–(5)), definitions (subs.(7), (9)), and
one dealing with the scope of revision or supersession of a decision that a person is
to be treated as available (subs.(6)). The regulations made under this section are the
JSA Regs, Pt II, Chs I and II, regs 4, 5–17, which are detailed and rendered complex
by "legislation by reference" and the manner in which they often qualify each other.

Subs.(1)

This sets out what might be called the general principle of availability; in effect a   **1.157**
statutory endorsement of the basic case law propositions that to be available a
claimant must be prepared to accept at once any offer of suitable employment
brought to his notice (*R(U)1/53*) and must be able to accept such an offer (*Shaukat
Ali v CAO, App. to R(U)1/85*). The general principle stated in the subsection requires
a claimant:

(i)   to be *willing* to take up *any employed earner's employment*;

(ii)   to be *able* to take it up;

(iii)   to be willing and able to do so *immediately.*

Each of these elements requires some further comment, undertaken below. It
must be recalled, however, that this general statement, important as it is in emphasising requirements to be flexible to meet the needs of the labour market, is qualified by the regulations. The essence of those qualifications are noted in the
annotation to this section, with the detail being reserved for the annotations to the
particular regulations.

Non-availability precludes entitlement to JSA (see s.1(2)(a)). But it is not crystal
clear from that provision or from subs.(1) whether the matter is to be looked at on a
weekly or, like unemployment benefit, a daily basis. Granted s.1(3) further stipulates

that JSA "is payable in respect of a week", but the scheme also provides for part-week entitlement (s.21, Sch.1, para.5, JSA Regs, regs 150–155). But the question arises whether a claimant unavailable on one or two days in a particular week loses entitlement for that whole week or just for the days of non-availability, retaining title to a proportionately reduced rate of benefit for the remaining days of the week on which he is available. The Departmental view is apparently that one must read this subsection with s.1. Taking the absolute availability rule ("a person is available for employment if he is willing and able to take up immediately any employed earner's employment") in this subsection with the weekly basis of JSA ("a jobseeker's allowance is payable in respect of a week": s.1(3)), the requirement is that one be available throughout the week in the absolute terms set by this subsection, unless specifically relieved from that requirement by means of the concessions set out in the JSA Regs dealing with availability: so that, a single unprotected day of non-availability precludes entitlement for that benefit week. The matter is further explored in the annotations to JSA Regs, reg.7(3).

1.158   *"any employed earner's employment"*: As was the case with the previous regime of benefits for unemployed people *(R(U)14/51)*, availability for self-employment does not suffice; the section requires availability for employed earner's employment, on the definition of which see subsection (9) and SSCBA 1992, ss.2, 122(1). Note in contrast that in some circumstances a claimant can confine his jobsearch to self-employment and still be actively seeking employment under s.7 and JSA Regs, reg.20. But he must always still be available for *employment* as opposed to *self-employment*.

The rubric refers to *"any"* employed earner's employment. The apparent width of this indicates graphically the need for claimants to be flexible in a changing labour market. But subs.(2) and resultant regulations enable the imposition of a range of restrictions on availability, both for the generality of claimants throughout their claim (JSA Regs, regs 7, 8), for the generality of claimants during a "permitted period" of up to 13 weeks (JSA Regs, reg.16), for those laid off or kept on short-time (JSA Regs, reg.17) and for particular groups of claimants (JSA Regs, reg.13), examined in more depth in the annotations to the particular regulations themselves.

Under the previous regime of benefits for the unemployed, being available for part-time work only did not of itself necessarily preclude availability *(CU109/48(KL);CU22/91,* paras 9, 10). That is *not* the position under JSA. Subject to regulations enabling restriction of hours to less, in order to be regarded as available for employment, a person must be willing and able (see below) to take up employment for a minimum of 40 hours per week (JSA Regs, reg.6(1)) but also be willing and able to take up employment of less than 40 hours per week (JSA Regs, reg.6(2)). In other words, being available merely for part-time employment (less than 40 hours per week) does not suffice, but to be available one must not only be available for full-time employment (40 hours or more per week) but be willing and able to accept part-time employment (less than 40 hours per week), if offered. Generally, no claimant is able to restrict his availability to less than the 40 hours minimum (JSA Regs, reg.7(1)), but there are exceptions for those with caring responsibilities *(ibid.,* reg.13(4), (5)), for those on short-time *(ibid.,* reg.17(2)) and for anyone whose physical or mental condition makes reasonable such a restriction *(ibid.,* reg.13(3)). Furthermore, JSA Regs, reg.7 allows a claimant to agree a pattern of availability ("the times at which he is available to take up employment") for 40 hours or more across a week, even though this may effect some reduction in his prospects of securing employment, provided that the pattern of availability is such as to afford him reasonable prospects of securing employment and that those prospects are not reduced considerably by the restriction embodied in the pattern of availability.

1.159   *"willing . . . to take up"*: What a claimant is willing and not willing to do can, of course, most obviously be judged from his professions of willingness on claim forms, in interviews with the Employment Service, and in his jobseeker's agreement. But it can also be inferred from his conduct (see *R(U)4/53*).

"able to take up": Problem areas under previous regimes of benefits for unemployed people afford likely instances where this requirement will prove problematic. Because of the different wording of the primary legislation, and the detail of new specific regulations, however, it cannot readily be assumed that the case law solutions propounded under the old regime will necessarily carry over into the new. But, bearing that very much in mind, obvious instances of inability to take up employment are where immigration law precludes the claimant working (*Shaukat Ali v CAO*, Appendix to *R(U)1/85*), or the claimant is about to go abroad (*R(U)2/90(T)*—dealing with the position of wives of servicemen about to join their husbands for a posting abroad), or he is contractually bound to another employer (*R(U)11/51*), for example, to be on call each working day. As regards this last category, note, however, the specific rules treating "a person who is laid-off " and "a person who is kept on short time" (both terms specifically defined in JSA Regs, reg.4) as available in certain circumstances (*ibid.*, reg.17). Another instance of possible inability would be going away on holiday. The position as respects unemployment benefit, of course, was that a claimant could still be regarded as available if, having made prior arrangements with the Employment Service, he could be readily contacted, would be willing and able to cut short the holiday to accept employment and could show that there was nothing to prevent him accepting such suitable employment as might be notified (*R(U)1/55*). But there is now in the legislation itself (as opposed to one merely in case law, as was the position under the unemployment benefit regime) an explicit statutory requirement of being able to take up *immediately* any employment, with only a few exceptions enshrined in legislation (JSA Regs, reg.5). So it would appear that a harsher approach may have to be taken than in the past. See further *CJSA/1279/98*.

1.160

"immediately": Just as case law on unemployment benefit generally required a claimant to be able to accept *at once* a suitable position, so the JSA statutory formulation of availability generally requires willingness and ability to take up *immediately* any employed earner's employment. A person is able to take up employment immediately even if he first has to obtain clearance in respect of any job, where that clearance is more or less a formality and normally a telephone call would suffice (*CSU 182/1997*, which concerned a former Inland Revenue employee who had taken early retirement and so was subject to the "Rules on the acceptance of outside appointments by Crown Servants").

1.161

But, just as the requirement under unemployment benefit was modified by regulations (see USI Regs, reg.12), so exceptions are provided in JSA Regs, reg.5, made under the width of the enabling power in subs.(2), below. Regulation 5 provides exceptions, giving varying periods of grace within which one must be willing and able to take up employment, for a range of groups: (a) for persons with caring responsibilities; (b) for those engaged in voluntary work; (c) for others providing a service with or without remuneration; (d) for certain persons employed for less than 16 hours per week and under a specific statutory obligation to provide notice. It also prevents the "immediately" requirement being used to negate the protective effect of reg.7, 13 or 17, allowing certain claimants periods of non-availability (in effect agreeing a "pattern of availability") by providing that the "immediately" condition cannot be used to require a claimant to be available at a time of permitted non-availability pursuant to his pattern of availability, so long as he is willing and able to take up employment immediately that permitted spell ends. See further the annotations to JSA Regs, reg.5.

Subss. (2), (3)
Subsection (2) enables the basic availability rule in subs.(1) to be modified by regulations, particularly (but not exclusively) by enabling a person to restrict his availability in prescribed ways and by enabling someone to restrict his availability both in prescribed circumstances (*e.g.* on grounds of his physical or mental condition) and

1.162

in prescribed ways. Subsection (3) sets out examples of restrictions which can be provided for in regulations: on the nature of employment; on periods of availability; on terms and conditions of employment; and on the locality or localities of availability. But clearly neither subsection so limits the modifications that can be made.

Leaving aside the "deemed available" and "deemed not available" regulations examined under subs.(4), the regulations made (a) provide for exceptions to the "immediately" available requirements (JSA Regs, reg.5), and (b) set out permitted restrictions (JSA Regs, regs 6–13, 17). The former have been noted in the annotation to subs.(1). The latter set a standard minimum hours (40) per week requirement, and enable a claimant to place a range of restrictions on his availability in a week without endangering his entitlement through failure to surmount the availability hurdle (see in particular regs 7, 8, 13, 17). Some groups of claimants are allowed more restrictions than others. See further the annotations to the specific regulations, but note here a central requirement (not applicable to those who impose only restrictions reasonable in light of physical or mental condition) that the claimant establish that he has reasonable prospects of securing employment despite (generally all) the restrictions he has imposed.

Subss. (4), (5), (7), (8)

1.163
Subsection (4) enables the making of regulations treating someone either as available or, as the case may be, not available for JSA purposes, whatever might be the result of applying to him the standard test of actual availability. See further JSA Regs, regs 14 (treated as available) and 15 (treated as not available, *i.e.* excluded from JSA). Subsection (5) provides that regulations under subs.(4) can in particular enable a claimant to restrict availability to his usual occupation for a "permitted period", defined in subs.(7) as "in relation to any person, such period as may be determined in accordance with regulations", which regulations, pursuant to subs.(8), can prescribe the day on which the period begins, its minimum and maximum lengths and the factors that a decision-maker may take into account in determining the period in any particular case. JSA Regs, reg.16 is the product. There is a specific "deeming" regulation dealing with those laid-off or kept on short time (reg.17). Another "deeming" regulation deals with full-time students following a "qualifying course" (an employment related course of further or higher education, or a standard above that, lasting no more than 12 months) (reg.17A).

Note further that, unlike the position with unemployment benefit, where full benefit remained in payment pending resolution of the issue (see USI Regs, reg.12A), if there remains an unresolved issue as to the claimant's availability for work there will be no entitlement to benefit under JSA, although the person excluded may be eligible for a hardship payment (on which see further JSA Regs, regs 140–146).

Subs. (6)

1.164
This provides that where it had been decided that a person is to be treated as available for employment in any benefit week, a subsequent revision or supersession of that decision can embrace also the question whether, in that week, the person was actually available for employment.

Subs. (9)

1.165
This stipulates that "employed earner's employment" has the same meaning for purposes of this section as it does in SSCBA 1992, s.2. See Bonner, Hooker and White, *Social Security Legislation 2005: Vol. I: Non Means Tested Benefits.*

Actively seeking employment

1.166
7.—(1) For the purposes of this Act, a person is actively seeking employment in any week if he takes in that week such steps as he can reasonably be

expected to have to take in order to have the best prospects of securing employment,

(2) Regulations may make provision—

(a) with respect to steps which it is reasonable, for the purposes of sub-section (1), for a person to be expected to have to take in any week;

(b) as to circumstances (for example, his skills, qualifications, abilities and physical or mental limitations) which, in particular, are to be taken into account in determining whether, in relation to any steps taken by a person, the requirements of subsection (1) are satisfied in any week.

(3) Regulations may make provision for acts of a person which would otherwise be relevant for purposes of this section to be disregarded in such circumstances (including circumstances constituted by, or connected with, his behaviour or appearance) as may be prescribed.

(4) Regulations may prescribe circumstances in which, for the purposes of this Act, a person is to be treated as actively seeking employment.

(5) Regulations under subsection (4) may, in particular, provide for a person who is actively seeking employment—

(a) only in his usual occupation,

(b) only at a level of remuneration not lower than that which he is accus-tomed to receive, or

(c) only in his usual occupation and at a level of remuneration not lower than that which he is accustomed to receive,

to be treated, for the permitted period determined in his case for the pur-poses of section 6(5), as actively seeking employment during that period.

(6) Regulations may provide for this section, and any regulations made under it, to have effect in relation to a person who has reached the age of 16 but not the age of 18 as if "employment" included "training".

(7) Where it has been determined [¹. . .] that a person is to be treated, for the purposes of this Act, as actively seeking employment in any week, the question whether he is actively seeking employment in that week may sub-sequently be determined [¹under section 9 or 10 of the Social Security Act 1998].

(8) For the purposes of this section—

"employment" means employed earner's employment or, in prescribed cir-cumstances

(a) self-employed earner's employment; or

(b) employed earner's employment and self-employed earner's employ-ment;

and "employed earners employment" and "self-employed earner's employ-ment" have the same meaning as in the Benefits Act.

AMENDMENT

1. Social Security Act 1998, Sch.7, para.135 (October 18, 1999).   **1.167**

DEFINITIONS

"Benefits Act": see s.35(1).
"employer earner's employment": see subs.(8) and SSCBA 1992, ss.2(1), 122(1).
"employment": see subs.(8).
"the first determination": see subs.(7).
"prescribed": see s.35(1).
"regulations": *ibid.*

"self-employed earner's employment": see subs.(8) and SSCBA 1992, ss.2(1), 122(1).

"training": see s.35(1); JSA Regs, reg.65(6).

"week": see s.35(1); JSA Regs, reg.4.

GENERAL NOTE

1.168   The actively seeking work test as a "labour market" condition of entitlement to JSA, like availability for work (the other "labour market" condition) set out in s.6, is a concrete manifestation of the underlying principle governing benefit regimes for unemployed people; that the unemployment must be involuntary. Dropped from the regime in the 1930s, it was reintroduced amidst considerable controversy in 1989. Contrary to expectations, it did not generate a flood of appeals to SSATs. Whether it attains a higher profile as a crucial element of JSA remains to be seen.

Where the matter of whether the claimant is actively seeking work remains unresolved, there is no entitlement to JSA and none will be payable until the Secretary of State has decided the matter in the claimant's favour. However, pending resolution of the question a claimant may be eligible for reduced rate hardship payments: see further s.21, Sch.1, para.8 and JSA Regs, regs 140–146. In that regard, the position under JSA is not significantly different from that under the unemployment benefit and/or income support regime for unemployed people.

Subs. (1)

1.169   As regards unemployment benefit, the test for actively seeking work was contained in subordinate legislation: to be actively seeking work in any week, a person had to take such steps, reasonable in his case, as to offer him *the best prospects of receiving offers of employment* (USI Regs, reg.12B(1)). For JSA, this subsection contains a similarly formulated test: in any week a person is actively seeking work if during that week he takes such steps as he can reasonably be expected to take in order to have *the best prospects of securing employment,* perhaps thereby stressing more strongly the requirement of taking positive action to secure work. Note that here "employment" is not confined to "employed earner's employment" but can in some circumstances embrace self-employment (subs.(8)): see further JSA Regs, regs 18(3)(i), 19(1)(r), 20(2), (3)).

It is for the claimant to establish that he is actively seeking work. As Northern Ireland Commissioner Brown stated in *C1/00–01(JSA)* and *C2/00–01 (JSA),* "it is . . . in the claimant's interest to keep a record and to have as far as possible further corroborative proof of the steps he has taken to seek employment" (para.29). Note, however, that the claimant's oral or written statement that he did this or that constitutes 'evidence', so that in that case the tribunal erred insofar as it appeared to have rejected the claimant's statement merely because it was uncorroborated: "a claimant does not have to produce corroborative evidence though obviously his case will be strengthened if he can do so" (para.30). She continued:

> "the tribunal was of course entitled to reject any evidence if it did not find it reliable. What it was not entitled to do however was to conclude that the claimant's evidence was not evidence. The claimant's evidence could have been accepted by the Tribunal and could, at its height, have, if accepted, established that he was actively seeking work. Instead, however, the Tribunal appeared to ignore this evidence and appeared to have the view that corroborative evidence must always be produced" (para.34).

The terms of a jobseeker's agreement may mean it is reasonable to take no active steps in a particular period: see *CJSA/2162/2001,* noted in the commentary to s.9, below.

Subs. (2)

1.170   This enabling power authorises regulations to be made with respect to the steps it is reasonable for someone to be expected to have to take in order to be regarded as actively seeking work and as to the circumstances that in particular are to be taken into account in determining whether the steps actually taken by a person are such as to satisfy the actively seeking work test. See further JSA Regs, reg.18, which builds on USI Regs, reg.12B.

Subs. (3)

This remarkable and controversial provision has no direct parallel in the prede-   1.171
cessor provisions on actively seeking work that governed unemployment benefit and income support for unemployed people. It enables regulations to be made prescribing circumstances in which acts of a person that would otherwise be relevant in applying the actively seeking work test are to be disregarded. Those circumstances include ones constituted by, or connected with, the person's behaviour or appearance, but the range of circumstances is not restricted to those categories. The aim was to "enable a person's jobseeking activity to be disregarded if he behaves or presents himself in such a way as deliberately to reduce or extinguish his chance of receiving offers of employment" (DSS, *Notes on Clauses* [with respect to the Jobseeker's Bill]). JSA Regs, reg.18(4) is the material provision. It provides that an otherwise relevant act of a person is to be disregarded in a number of circumstances unless the circumstances were due to reasons beyond his control: (i) where in taking the act he acted in a violent or abusive manner; (ii) where the act comprised the completion of an application for employment and he spoiled the application; (iii) where, by his behaviour or appearance he otherwise undermined his prospects of securing the employment in question.

The regulation, particularly in head (iii), thus involves a more explicit "policing" of behaviour, appearance and, possibly, form-filling competence by Employment Service personnel, decision-makers and tribunals. The concept of "spoiled the application" in head (ii) is by no means crystal clear. The saving for circumstances beyond one's control will presumably protect the dyslexic and the illiterate, but what about the semi-literate? Electoral law, of course, has the concept of the "spoilt ballot paper", which covers the situation in which the voter has inadvertently dealt with his ballot paper in such a manner that it cannot conveniently be used as a ballot paper, but whether that in any way provides a valid analogy for "spoiled" in this regulation remains to be seen. Given the aim of the provision, it might have been better to have worded it "deliberately spoiled". A further sanction for some such behaviour lies in the preclusion of payment of benefit under s.19(6)(c) in respect of the person having, without good cause, neglected to avail himself of a reasonable opportunity of employment; the equivalent provision in the unemployment benefit regime enabled disqualification of a claimant who had attended an interview for a job as a parcel porter in a "dirty and unshaven state" (*R(U)28/55*). Care will have to be taken to avoid applying the provision in a manner discriminatory on grounds of sex or race (*e.g.* to penalise men with long hair or Rastafarians with dreadlocks).

Subss. (4), (5)

Subsection (4) enables the making of regulations treating a person as actively   1.172
seeking work. Subsection (5) amplifies this by providing that such regulations can, for the "permitted period" for availability purposes (see s.6(5) and JSA Regs, reg.16), enable a person to be treated as actively seeking employment where he is actually doing so only in his usual occupation, or only at a level of remuneration not lower than that which he is accustomed to receive, or only in that occupation and at such a level of remuneration. See JSA Regs, regs 19–21A.

Subs. (6)

This enables regulations to be made so that in respect of payment of incomebased   1.173
JSA to 16-and 17-year-olds "employment" for actively seeking work purposes extends to training. See further JSA Regs, reg.65.

Subs. (7)

1.174   This deals with the situation where in accordance with the Act it has been decided that a person is to be treated as actively seeking employment in any week. It enables a subsequent revision or supersession of that decision to embrace also the question whether in that week the person was actually actively seeking employment.

Subs. (8)

1.175   This makes clear that employment, for actively seeking work purposes, covers both employed earner's and self-employed earner's employment. For definitions of these terms, see SSCBA 1992, ss.2(1), 122(1). See Bonner, Hooker and White, *Social Security Legislation 2005:Vol. I: Non Means Tested Benefits.*

Attendance, information and evidence

1.176   **8.**—(1) Regulations may make provision for requiring a claimant [²(other than a joint-claim couple claiming a joint-claim jobseeker's allowance)]—

(a) to attend at such place and at such time as [¹an employment officer] may specify; and

(b) to provide information and such evidence as may be prescribed as to his circumstances, his availability for employment and the extent to which he is actively seeking employment.

[²(1A) Regulations may make provision—

(a) for requiring each member of a joint-claim couple claiming a joint-claim jobseeker's allowance to attend at such place and such time as the Secretary of State may specify;

(b) for requiring a member of such a couple to provide information and such evidence as may be prescribed as to his circumstances, his availability for employment and the extent to which he is actively seeking employment;

(c) for requiring such a couple to jointly provide information and such evidence as may be prescribed as to the circumstances of each or either member of the couple, the availability for employment of each or either member of the couple and the extent to which each or either member of the couple is actively seeking employment;

(d) where any requirement to provide information or evidence is imposed on such a couple by virtue of paragraph (c), for the joint obligation of the couple to be capable of being discharged by the provision of the information or evidence by one member of the couple.]

(2) Regulations under subsection (1) [²or (1A)] may, in particular—

(a) prescribe circumstances in which entitlement to a jobseeker's allowance is to cease in the case of a claimant who, [² or (as the case may be) a joint-claim couple claiming a joint-claim jobseeker's allowance a member of which,] fails to comply with any regulations made under that subsection;

(b) provide for entitlement to cease at such time (after he [²or, as the case may be, a member of the joint-claim couple] last attended in compliance with requirements of the kind mentioned in subsection (1)(a) [²or (1A)(a)]) as may be determined in accordance with any such regulations;

[²(c) provide for entitlement not to cease if the claimant or (as the case may be) either member of the joint-claim couple shows, within a prescribed period of the failure to comply on the part of the claimant or (as the case may be) a member of the couple, that the claimant or (as the case may be) the defaulting member of the couple had good cause for that failure; and]

(d) prescribe—

    (i) matters which are, or are not, to be taken into account in determining whether a person has, or does not have, good cause for failing to comply with any such regulations; and

    (ii) circumstances in which a person is, or is not, to be regarded as having, or not having, good cause for failing to comply with any such regulations.

[[1](3) In subsection (1) "employment officer" means an officer of the Secretary of State or such other person as may be designated for the purposes of that subsection by an order made by the Secretary of State.]

AMENDMENTS

1. Welfare Reform and Pensions Act 1999, s.70 and Sch.8, para.29 (November 11, 1999).

    2. Welfare Reform and Pensions Act 1999, Sch.7, para.7 (March 19, 2001).

      1.177

DEFINITIONS

"a joint-claim couple": see s.1(4).
"a joint-claim jobseeker's allowance": see s.1(4).
"claimant": see s.35(1).
"employment": see s.35(1); JSA Regs, reg.4.
"prescribed": see s.35(1).
"regulations": *ibid.*

GENERAL NOTE

This section provides a range of rule-making powers with respect to requiring a claimant (and the members of a joint-claim couple) (hereinafter "claimant" or "he") to attend at the place and time specified by the Secretary of State and to provide information and evidence on his circumstances, his availability for employment and the extent to which he is actively seeking employment (subs.(1)). In short, to provide through attendance, etc., the wherewithal whereby his claim can continue to be monitored and assessed. In particular the regulations can provide sanctions against non-conforming claimants, through denial of entitlement, subject to a saving for showing, within a specified time-period, good cause for the non-compliance (subs.(2)). In common with other parts of the scheme (compare s.19), the regulations can prescribe circumstances in which a person does or does not have good cause for any act or omission, and can set out the circumstances that are or are not to be taken into account in determining the good cause issue (subs.(2)).

    1.178

The relevant regulations are the JSA Regs, Pt II, Ch. IV (regs 23–30). Only an outline can be given here. For detail see those regs and commentary thereto.

A claimant must attend at such place and at such time as is specified by the Secretary of State (in practice a civil servant) in a notification given or sent to him (reg.23). The notification may be given in writing, by telephone or by electronic means (e-mail). This will set a normal "signing" day for the purposes of keeping up his claim, and is important for applying the definition of "benefit week" (see reg.1(3)): generally the period of seven days ending with the day corresponding to his normal (usually fortnightly) "signing" day. Regulation 24 generally requires the claimant to provide such information, evidence, certificates and documents as the Secretary of State requests for the purposes of his claim (paras (1)–(5)). He must, if required by the Secretary of State to do so, provide a signed declaration about his availability, his actively seeking work, and with respect to changes of circumstances (*e.g.* there have been none), in each case covering the period since he claimed or since he last signed a declaration (para.(6)). Changes of circumstances (including ones known to be likely to occur) must be reported promptly to the Secretary of State (para.(7)).

The matter of sanctions for non-compliance is dealt with by regs 25–30. Non-attendance and attending at the wrong time on the signing day are both penalised, subject to a saving for good cause. So is failing to provide a signed declaration on the specified day, again subject to a saving for good cause.

1.179 If the claimant fails to attend on the specified day, entitlement will cease on the earlier of the day he should have attended or the day after the last day in respect of which he has provided information or evidence showing that he continues to be entitled to JSA, but not earlier than the day he last attended (his last actual "signing" day) (regs 25(1)(a), 26). Given the rewording of the regulation, effective March 25, 1999, it now appears clear that in this situation there is no need for a formal written warning of the consequences, followed by a repetition of the default, before entitlement can cease (see *CJSA/4775/1997* on the previous wording). If he fails to attend at the specified time (but does attend on the day), and is duly warned in writing that repeating such conduct next time may result in entitlement being withdrawn, and on the next occasion again fails to attend at the specified time, entitlement will cease on the earlier of the days he should have attended or the day after the last day in respect of which he has provided information or evidence showing that he continues to be entitled to JSA, but not earlier than the day he last attended (his last actual "signing" day) (regs 25(1)(b), 26). In both of the above situations, the decision that entitlement is to cease must be made by an adjudication officer (now "decision-maker") (*CJSA/4775/1997*). However, in neither situation is entitlement to cease if the claimant shows, before the end of the fifth working day after that of non-compliance, that he had "good cause" for the failure (reg.27(1)). "Working day" is any day on which the appropriate office (Department of Education and Employment office or any other specified place of attendance with respect to him) is not closed (reg.27(2), (4)). He will be regarded as having "good cause" (i) if, being a carer or a voluntary worker, he was required to attend at a time less than 48 hours from his receipt of the notification; (ii) if, being someone providing a service with or without remuneration, he was required to attend at a time less than 24 hours from his receipt of the notification [thus aligning these rules with the "immediacy" exceptions in the context of availability for employment (regs 30(a), (b), 5(1), (2))]; or (iii) if the day of failure to attend was one of "deemed availability" or "deemed actively seeking employment" pursuant to certain specified provisions of the deeming regulations (reg.30(c), (d)). Otherwise, matters to be taken into account in determining "good cause" in these contexts include (*i.e.* the list is not exhaustive): (i) whether the claimant misunderstood the requirement on him due to misleading information given him by an employment officer or due to any learning, language or literacy difficulties of the claimant; (ii) any difficulty with the claimant's normal mode of transport and whether there was any reasonable available alternative; (iii) the established customs and practices of any religion to which the claimant belongs; (iv) whether the claimant was attending an interview for employment [or, in some cases, self-employment: see reg.28(2)]; and (v) whether he was attending, or accompanying someone for whom he has caring responsibilities, to a medical or dental appointment, and whether it would have been unreasonable in the circumstances to rearrange the appointment (reg.28(1)).

1.180 Where a claimant who was required to provide a signed declaration (as to availability, etc.: see above) fails to provide it on the due day, then entitlement ceases on the earlier of that due day or the day after the last day in respect of which he has provided information or evidence showing that he continues to be entitled to JSA, but not earlier than the day he last attended (his last actual "signing" day) (regs 25(1)(c), 26). The decision that entitlement is to cease must be made by an adjudication officer (decision-maker) (*CJSA/4775/1997*). However, entitlement is not to cease if the claimant shows, before the end of the fifth working day after that of non-compliance, that he had "good cause" for the failure (reg.27(1)). "Working day" is any day on which the "appropriate office" (Department of Education and Employment office or any other specified place of attendance with respect to him) is not closed (regs 27(2), 4). In this context, no regulation specifies what constitutes "good cause"; reg.29 merely stipulates that the matters to be taken into account in determining whether the claimant had it in respect of his failure to supply a signed declaration on the due date include (*i.e.* the list is not exhaustive); (i) whether there were adverse postal conditions; (ii) whether the claimant misunderstood the requirement on him due to any of his learning, language or literacy difficulties or due to any misleading information given to him by an employment officer (reg.29).

The jobseeker's agreement

9.—(1) An agreement which is entered into by a claimant and an employment officer and which complies with the prescribed requirements in force at the time when the agreement is made is referred to in this Act as "a jobseeker's agreement".

(2) A jobseeker's agreement shall have effect only for the purposes of section 1.

(3) A jobseeker's agreement shall be in writing and be signed by both parties.

(4) A copy of the agreement shall be given to the claimant.

(5) An employment officer shall not enter into a jobseeker's agreement with a claimant unless, in the officer's opinion, the conditions mentioned in section 1(2)(a) and (c) would be satisfied with respect to the claimant if he were to comply with, or be treated as complying with, the proposed agreement.

(6) The employment officer may, and if asked to do so by the claimant shall forthwith, refer a proposed jobseeker's agreement to [¹the Secretary of State] for him to determine—

(a) whether, if the claimant concerned were to comply with the proposed agreement, he would satisfy—
  (i) the condition mentioned in section 1(2)(a); or
  (ii) the condition mentioned in section 1(2)(c); and

(b) whether it is reasonable to expect the claimant to have to comply with the proposed agreement.

(7) [¹On a reference under subsection (6) the Secretary of State]—

(a) shall, so far as practicable, dispose of it in accordance with this section before the end of the period of 14 days from the date of the reference;

(b) may give such directions, with respect to the terms on which the employment officer is to enter into a jobseeker's agreement with the claimant, as [¹the Secretary of State] considers appropriate;

(c) may direct that, if conditions as he considers appropriate are satisfied, the proposed jobseeker's agreement is to be treated (if entered into) as having effect on such date, before it would other- wise have effect, as may be specified in the direction.

(8) Regulations may provide—

(a) for such matters as may be prescribed to be taken into account by [¹the Secretary of State] in giving a direction under subsection (7)(c); and

(b) for such persons as may be prescribed to be notified of—
  (i) any determination of an adjudication officer under this section;
  (ii) any direction giver by an adjudication officer under this section.

(9) [¹ . . .].

1.181

(10) Regulations may provide that, in prescribed circumstances, a claimant is to be treated as having satisfied the condition mentioned in section 1(2)(b).

(11) Regulations may provide that, in prescribed circumstances, a jobseeker's agreement is to be treated as having effect on a date, to be determined in accordance with the regulations, before it would otherwise have effect.

(12) Except in such circumstances as may be prescribed, a jobseeker's agreement entered into by a claimant shall cease to have effect on the coming to an end of an award of a jobseeker's allowance made to him [²or to a joint-claim couple of which he is a member.].

(13) In this section and section 10 "employment officer" means an officer of the Secretary of State or such other person as may be designated for the purposes of this section by an order made by the Secretary of State.

AMENDMENTS

1.182   1. Social Security Act 1998, Sch.7, para.136 (October 18, 1999).
2. Welfare Reform and Pensions Act 1999, Sch.7, para.8 (March 19, 2001).

DEFINITIONS

"a joint-claim couple": see s.1(4).
"a joint-claim jobseeker's allowance": see s.1(4).
"claimant": see s.35(1).
"employment officer": see subs.(13).
"jobseeker's agreement": see subs.(1).
"prescribed": see s.35(1).
"regulations": *ibid.*

GENERAL NOTE

1.183   This section, containing and enabling the making of further important provisions on the jobseeker's agreement, needs to be read in the light of the amplification and clarification provided by JSA Regs, regs 31–36, made under it; and of s.10 supplemented by regs 37–40, which provide for the variation of a jobseeker's agreement. This note attempts to blend the provisions of this section and the JSA Regs with statements in the White Paper and/or in parliament on the administrative process, to give a coherent account of how the arrangements with respect to jobseeker's agreements will operate. On some points of finer detail, however, readers will have to scrutinise closely the exact terms of the JSA Regs referred to.

Perhaps the most obvious and striking difference between unemployment benefit and JSA is the central requirement that, in order to be entitled to JSA, the claimant must have entered into a jobseeker's agreement that remains in force (s.1(2)(b)). Note, however, that a person may be treated as having done so in any of the circumstances set out in JSA Regs, reg.34. Might an example be where the office had a backlog of claims because a town's major employer (a factory) had closed down (see JSA Regs, reg.34(d))?

That a person must enter (or be treated as having entered) into such an agreement is the way in which previously voluntary arrangements (the Back to Work plan) are translated into legal requirements for the purposes of JSA. A jobseeker's agreement has effect only for the purposes of entitlement to JSA ("the purposes of section 1") (subs.(2)) and hence does not give rise to any contractual or other private law obligations or relationship.

1.184   Subsection (1) defines "a jobseeker's agreement" as one entered into by a claimant and an "employment officer", complying with the "prescribed requirements" as in force at the time it is made. The jobseeker's agreement must be in writing and signed by both parties to it (the claimant and the employment officer) (subs.(3)). The claimant signs a declaration that he understands and agrees to the conditions set out in the agreement (White Paper, para.4.19), but the declaration is not specified in regulations as one of the "prescribed requirements". The "prescribed requirements" are listed in JSA Regs, reg.31. The agreement must contain: (i) the claimant's name; (ii) unless he is available for any hours at any times, the total number of hours for which he is available for employment and any pattern of availability ("the times at which he is available to take up employment": see reg.7); (iii) any restrictions on availability as permitted by the scheme; (iv) a description of the type of employment he is seeking; (v) the action he will take to seek employment and to improve his prospects of finding employment; (vi) the start and finish of the "permitted period" in which he is allowed to restrict his availability and jobsearch to his usual occupation and/or his usual rate of remuneration; (vii) a statement of his rights to have a proposed agreement referred to the Secretary State (decision-maker), to have a decision-maker's decision and/or directions reviewed by another decision-maker, and of his right of appeal to a tribunal in respect of the decision and/or direction given on that review; and (viii) the date of the agreement. A copy of the agreement must be given to him (subs.(4)).

The jobseeker's agreement is an integral part of identifying what steps back to work are appropriate for the claimant and to enable regular and effective monitoring of his activities to that end, reviewing and altering the terms of the agreement as necessary over a period (see White Paper, para.4.16, and ss.10, 11). Note, in particular, that "employment officers" (usually Employment Service personnel: see subs.(13)) cannot enter into an agreement the terms of which are such that the claimant acting in accordance with them would fail to satisfy either of the key requirements to be available for and actively seeking work, thus placing such officers at the heart of policing these central requirements of the system (subs.(5)). Whether this will give rise to a higher profile on "actively seeking work" and more appeals to tribunals than hitherto remains to be seen.

Given that failing to enter into the agreement results in no JSA, tribunals may discover that claimants find it difficult to see this as a genuine agreement, freely entered into rather than imposed. That the agreement will contain useful information on the facilities provided by the Employment Service and the standards of service the claimant is entitled to receive under the Jobseeker's Charter (see White Paper, para.4.17) is hardly a consolation: this valuable information would presumably have been provided even if, as with unemployment benefit, the JSA scheme lacked the requisite of a jobseeker's agreement as a condition of entitlement to benefit. Whether the jobseeker's agreement proves to be a standard *pro forma* document or one which accurately reflects the particular claimant's circumstances remains to be seen.

The basic rule on when the agreement comes into effect would appear to be the day it is signed, but that is a deduction from the effect of other rules rather than finding expression in a particular provision. In some cases, no doubt, the claimant and the employment officer will reach ready agreement on the terms of the jobseeker's agreement, which will be signed on the day of claim, and take effect then. Where it is not signed until a date later than the day of claim, JSA Regs, reg.35, made pursuant to subs.(11), provides that the agreement is to be automatically backdated to the day of claim, unless the agreement (in reality a proposed agreement) is referred to the Secretary of State (decision-maker) in accordance with subs.(6).

The most common situation in which a proposed jobseeker's agreement will be referred to a decision-maker is likely to be where there is a dispute between the parties over the availability and/or actively seeking work aspects of it or over whether it is reasonable to expect the claimant to have to comply with it. In such a situation, the employment officer *must* refer the proposed agreement to a decision-maker if the claimant asks him to do so (subs.(6)). In addition, the employment officer always has power to refer such matters to the decision-maker (subs.(6)), and doubtless will

1.185

do so particularly where he is unsure about the availability and/or actively seeking work aspects.

1.186   In *CJSA/2162/2001*, Commissioner Williams held that:

> "a valid jobseeker's agreement continues in force until it is varied or brought to an end in accordance with the 1995 Act and the Jobseeker's Allowance Regulations. It cannot unilaterally be ignored by the Secretary of State. While in force it is relevant not only to section 1 but also to other parts of the Act including section 7. Section 7 incorporates a test of reasonableness in considering whether someone is actively seeking work for the purposes of section 1. Section 7(1) allows for the possibility that someone can meet the section 1(2)(c) test without taking any step to seek work if that is reasonable. Regulation 18 of the Regulations does not, when read as a whole, preclude that possibility in considering whether the test in section 7(1) is satisfied. The terms of the jobseeker's agreement are relevant to the consideration of the reasonableness of the steps taken by the claimant. I do not decide if the agreement is determinative of that issue (para.40)."

So in an unusual case (the claimant should really have been directed to income support as a person in ill health), where the agreement in force in effect did not require her to take any steps actively to seek work, she was entitled to benefit because of the agreement in force and the fact that she was both available for and actively seeking work. It was in fact reasonable for her to take no active steps as none had been asked for. But in fact she had taken some, had participated in the reviews and had actively found part-time work. The Secretary of State should have taken steps to revise the agreement using s.10, but had not.

1.187   If a proposed agreement is referred to a decision-maker, he must, so far as is practicable, dispose of it (determine it) within 14 days of the reference (subs.(7)(a)). In determining it, he may also give such directions with respect to the terms on which the employment officer is to enter into a jobseeker's agreement with the claimant as the decision-maker considers appropriate (subs.(7)(b)). If the decision-maker considers it appropriate, he can give directions that the proposed agreement (if entered into) is to be back-dated (subs.(7)(c)). In considering whether back-dating is appropriate, JSA Regs, reg.32 (made under subs.(8)(a)) stipulates that he must take into account all relevant matters, including those specifically listed in the regulation (*i.e.* that list is not exhaustive). The matters so listed are: (i) whether the claimant was reasonable in refusing to accept the proposed agreement; (ii) whether the terms of the agreement which the claimant has indicated, to the decision-maker or the employment officer, that he is prepared to accept, are reasonable; (iii) the fact that the claimant has signified to the decision-maker or the employment officer that he is prepared to accept the proposed agreement; (iv) the date on which, taking account of all the circumstances, the decision-maker considers the claimant was prepared to enter into an agreement the decision-maker considers reasonable; (v) the fact that the date on which the claimant first had an opportunity to sign a jobseeker's agreement was later than the date of claim. Notification of the decision-maker's determination and any directions given by him will doubtless be given to the employment officer as a matter of the arrangements within the JSA administrative structure, and must be given to the claimant under JSA Regs, reg.33. Any determination of the Secretary of State (decision-maker) under this section is binding (subs.(9)) but not final, because of the possibility of revision and appeal under the DMA arrangements.

Generally, a jobseeker's agreement ceases to have effect when the claimant's award of JSA comes to an end (subs. (12)). JSA Regs, reg.36 prescribes the circumstances in which a jobseeker's agreement shall not so cease to have effect (for example where a further claim for JSA is made within 14 days of the previous award coming to an end: see reg.36(a)).

Variation of jobseeker's agreement

10.—(1) A jobseeker's agreement may be varied, in the prescribed manner, by agreement between the claimant and any employment officer.

(2) Any agreement to vary a jobseeker's agreement shall be in writing and be signed by both parties.

(3) A copy of the agreement, as varied, shall be given to the claimant.

(4) An employment officer shall not agree to a variation of a jobseeker's agreement, unless, in the officer's opinion, the conditions mentioned in section 1(2)(a) and (c) would continue to be satisfied with respect to the claimant if he were to comply with, or be treated as complying with, the agreement as proposed to be varied.

(5) The employment officer may, and if asked to do so by the claimant shall forthwith, refer a proposed variation of a jobseeker's agreement to [¹ the Secretary of State] for him to determine—

- (a) whether, if the claimant concerned were to comply with the agreement as proposed to be varied, he would satisfy—
    - (i) the condition mentioned in section 1(2)(a), or
    - (ii) the condition mentioned in section 1(2)(c); and
- (b) whether it is reasonable to expect the claimant to have to comply with the agreement as proposed to be varied.

(6) [¹On a reference under subsection (5) the Secretary of State]—

- (a) shall, so far as practicable, dispose of it in accordance with this section before the end of the period of 14 days from the date of the reference;
- (b) shall give such directions as he considers appropriate as to—
    - (i) whether the jobseeker's agreement should be varied, and
    - (ii) if so, the terms on which the claimant and the employment officer are to enter into an agreement to vary it;
- (c) may bring the jobseeker's agreement to an end where the claimant fails, within a prescribed period, to comply with a direction given under paragraph (b)(ii);
- (d) may direct that, if—
    - (i) the jobseeker's agreement is varied, and
    - (ii) such conditions as he considers appropriate are satisfied,

the agreement as varied is to be treated as having effect on such date, before it would otherwise have effect, as may be specified in the direction.

(7) Regulations may provide—

- (a) for such matters as may be prescribed to be taken into account by [¹the Secretary of State] in giving a direction under section (6)(b) or (d); and
- (b) for such persons as may be prescribed to be notified of—
    - (i) any determination of [¹the Secretary of State] under this section;
    - (ii) any direction given by [¹the Secretary of State] under this section.

(8) [¹ . . .].

<small>AMENDMENT</small>

1. Social Security Act 1998, Sch.7, para.137 (October 18, 1999).

<small>DEFINITIONS</small>

"claimant": see s.35(1).
"employment officer": see s.9(13).

1.188

1.189

"jobseeker's agreement": see ss.35(1), 9(1).
"prescribed": see s.35(1).
"regulations": see s.35(1).

GENERAL NOTE

1.190   This section enables a jobseeker's agreement to be varied, with the aim of ensuring that it reflects the claimant's changing circumstances and the labour market. The section also provides for the mode and manner of decision-making and is amplified by JSA Regs, regs 37–40.

A jobseeker's agreement can, on the proposal of either the employment officer or the claimant, be varied with the consent of both parties (subs.(1); JSA Regs, reg.37). An agreement to vary must, like the varied agreement itself, be in writing and signed by both parties (subs.(2); JSA Regs, reg. 37). The claimant must get a copy of the varied agreement (subs.(3)). An employment officer cannot agree a variation unless satisfied that under its terms the claimant would continue to be available for and actively seeking employment (subs.(4)), once more emphasising the central role for Employment Service personnel in monitoring those crucial "labour market" conditions of entitlement.

Some cases will be the subject of decisions and directions of decision-makers. The most common situation in which a proposed variation of a jobseeker's agreement will be referred to a decision-maker is likely to be where there is a dispute between the parties over the availability and/or the actively seeking work aspects of it, or over whether it is reasonable to expect the claimant to have to comply with it. In such a situation, the employment officer *must* refer the proposed variation of the agreement to a decision-maker if the claimant asks him to do so (subs.(5)). In addition, the employment officer always has power to refer such matters to the decision-maker (subs.(5), and doubtless will do so particularly where he is unsure about the availability and/or the actively seeking work aspects.

A decision-maker is, so far as is practicable, to determine the reference within 14 days. He must give such directions as he considers appropriate as to whether the agreement should be varied and if so the terms on which the parties are to agree a varied agreement. Should the claimant fail to do so within 21 days of the direction, the decision-maker can bring the jobseeker's agreement to an end, thus disentitling the claimant to JSA since s.1(2)(b) requires a jobseeker's agreement to be in force (subs.(6)(a)–(c)). The decision-maker can also backdate the varied agreement (subs.(6)(d)). In giving directions under subs.(6)(b) or (d) the decision-maker must take into account the preference of the claimant if he considers that both the claimant's proposals and those of the employment officer meet the requirements of subs.(5) (the "labour market" conditions and the "reasonableness" requirement) (JSA Regs, reg.38).

Notification of the decision-maker's determination and any directions given by him will doubtless be given to the employment officer as a matter of the arrangements within the JSA administrative structure, and must be given to the claimant under JSA Regs, reg.40, made pursuant to subs.(7)(b).

A decision-maker can bring a jobseeker's agreement to an end (thus denying benefit) where, within 21 days, a claimant has not agreed the terms of a varied agreement as indicated by the decision maker. In *CJSA/4435/1998*, Commissioner Levenson was of the view that an appeal against the decision-maker's direction on the terms of the agreement necessarily involved also an appeal against his decision to terminate the agreement (para.8). In the particular case, dealing only with the type of work for which the claimant should be available, he noted that the relevant standard was that of "reasonable prospects of employment", notwithstanding imposed restrictions, pursuant to JSA Regs, regs 8, 10. The tribunal applied a different test of "good prospects" when rejecting his appeal, and so erred in law in imposing on the claimant a higher degree of proof than that stipulated in the regulations.

Jobseeker's agreement: reviews and appeals

11.—[¹ . . .].   1.191

REPEAL

1. Social Security Act 1998, Sch.7, para.138 (October 18, 1999).   1.192

Income and capital

Income and capital: general

12.—(1) In relation to a claim for a jobseeker's allowance, the income and   1.193
capital of a person shall be calculated or estimated in such manner as may
be prescribed.

(2) A person's income in respect of a week shall be calculated in accordance with prescribed rules.

(3) The rules may provide for the calculation to be made by reference to
an average over a period (which need not include the week concerned).

(4) Circumstances may be prescribed in which—
  (a) a person is treated as possessing capital or income which he does not
       possess;
  (b) capital or income which a person does possess is to be disregarded;
  (c) income is to be treated as capital;
  (d) capital is to be treated as income.

DEFINITIONS

  "prescribed"—see s.35(1).
  "week"—*ibid.*

GENERAL NOTE

  This section is very similar to subss.(3) to (5) of s.136 of the Contributions and   1.194
Benefits Act and contains extensive powers to prescribe how a claimant's capital and
income is to be calculated for the purposes of JSA. See Part VIII of and Schs 6, 6A,
7 and 8 to the JSA Regulations.

  See also s.13.

Income and capital: income-based jobseeker's allowance

13.—(1) No person shall be entitled to an income-based jobseeker's   1.195
allowance if his capital, or a prescribed part of it, exceeds the prescribed
amount.

(2) Where a person claiming an income-based jobseeker's allowance is a
member of a family, the income and capital of any member of that family
shall, except in prescribed circumstances, be treated as the income and
capital of the claimant.

[¹ (2A) Subsections (1) and (2) do not apply as regards a joint-claim jobseeker's allowance; but a joint-claim couple shall not be entitled to a joint-
claim jobseeker's allowance if the couple's capital, or a prescribed part of it,
exceeds the prescribed amount.

(2B) Where a joint-claim couple claim a joint-claim jobseeker's
allowance—
  (a) the couple's income and capital includes the separate income and
       capital of each of them; and

(b) the income and capital of any other person who is a member of any family of which the couple are members shall, except in prescribed circumstances, be treated as income and capital of the couple.]

(3) Regulations may provide that capital not exceeding the amount prescribed under subsection (1) [¹or (2A)], but exceeding a prescribed lower amount, shall be treated, to a prescribed extent, as if it were income of a prescribed amount.

AMENDMENT

1.196   1. Welfare Reform and Pensions Act 1999, s.59 and Sch.7, para.9 (March 19, 2001).

DEFINITIONS

"claimant"—see s.35(1).
"family"—*ibid.*
"income-based jobseeker's allowance"—see s.1(4).
"joint-claim couple"—*ibid.*
"joint-claim jobseeker's allowance"—*ibid.*
"prescribed"—see s.35(1).
"regulations"—*ibid.*

GENERAL NOTE

1.197   The provisions in this section are similar to those in ss.134(1) and 136(1) and (2) of the Contributions and Benefits Act 1992. Note the amendments made on March 19, 2001 relating to the introduction of joint claims for JSA for certain childless couples (see the notes at the beginning of this Act and to s.1(4)).

Subs. (1)
The rules are similar (although since October 6, 2003 not quite identical) to income support. The capital limit for income-based JSA is £8,000, except where the claimant or any partner is aged 60 or over when it is £12,000, or where the claimant lives permanently in a residential care or nursing home, residential accommodation or a Polish resettlement home when it is £16,000 (JSA Regulations, regs 107 and 116(1ZA) and (1B)).
See the note to s.134(1) of the Contributions and Benefits Act 1992.

Subs. (2)
This provides that the general rule for income-based JSA (as for income support) is that all of the family's (as defined in s.35(1)) income and capital is aggregated together and treated as the claimant's. The modifications to this rule for children and young persons were in regs. 106 and 109 of the Jobseeker's Allowance Regulations (see the 2003 edition of this volume for those regulations and the notes to those regulations). However, as a consequence of the removal of amounts for children and young persons from income-based JSA (with effect from April 6, 2004, except in "transitional cases"—see the note to reg. 17 of the Income Support Regulations and the note to reg.83 of the JSA Regulations), a child's income and capital will be totally ignored and only a partner's income and capital will count as that of the claimant (see the amended form of reg. 88(1) of the JSA Regulations).

Subss. (2A) and (2B)
Subss.(1) and (2) do not apply to joint-claim JSA but the effects of subss.(2A) and (2B) is to apply similar rules to those in subss.(1) and (2) to joint-claim JSA. On subs.(2B), see reg.88ZA of the JSA Regulations.

Subs. (3)
This enables a similar "tariff income" rule to the one that operates for income support to be applied to income-based (including joint-claim) JSA. Reg.116 of the

JSA Regulations provides for an income to be assumed to be produced from capital between £3,000 and £8,000 (£6,000 and £12,000 if the claimant or any partner is aged 60 or over or £10,000 and £16,000 in the case of claimants living permanently in residential care or nursing homes, etc.).

Trade disputes

Trade disputes

14.—(1) Where— 1.198
- (a) there is a stoppage of work which causes a person not to be employed on any day, and
- (b) the stoppage is due to a trade dispute at his place of work, that person is not entitled to a jobseeker's allowance for the week which includes that day unless he proves that he is not directly interested in the dispute.

(2) A person who withdraws his labour on any day in furtherance of a trade dispute, but to whom subsection (1) does not apply, is not entitled to a jobseeker's allowance for the week which includes that day.

(3) If a person who is prevented by subsection (1) from being entitled to a jobseeker's allowance proves that during the stoppage—
- (a) he became bona fide employed elsewhere;
- (b) his employment was terminated by reason of redundancy within the meaning of [¹section 139 of the Employment Rights Act 1996,] or
- (c) he bona fide resumed employment with his employer but subsequently left for a reason other than the trade dispute,

subsection (1) shall be taken to have ceased to apply to him on the occurrence of the event referred to in paragraph (a) or (b) or (as the case may be) the first event referred to in paragraph (c).

(4) In this section "place of work", in relation to any person, means the premises or place at which he was employed.

(5) Where separate branches of work which are commonly carried on as separate businesses in separate premises or at separate places are in any case carried on in separate departments on the same premises or at the same place, each of those departments shall, for the purposes of subsection (4), be deemed to be separate premises or (as the case may be) a separate place.

AMENDMENT

1. Employment Rights Act 1996, Sch.1, para.67(2)(a) (August 22, 1996). 1.199

DEFINITIONS

"employment": see s.35(1); JSA Regs, regs 3, 4.
"entitled": see s.35(1).
"place of work": see subs.(4).
"trade dispute": see s.35(1).
"week": *ibid.*

GENERAL NOTE

This section denies entitlement to JSA to certain persons affected by or involved in 1.200
trade disputes in two situations. First, where a stoppage of work due to a trade dispute

at the claimant's place of work causes him not to be employed on any day, he will not be entitled to JSA for the week which includes that day, unless either he can establish that he is not directly interested in the dispute or he can invoke one of the escape routes provided by subs.(3) (subs.(1)). The second situation where entitlement is denied throughout a week is where in furtherance of a trade dispute the claimant withdraws his labour on any day in that week, but not in such a way as to be caught by subs.(1) (the first situation of denial of entitlement) (subs.(2)).

In many respects the section replicates the trade dispute disqualification from unemployment benefit in SSCBA 1992, s.27 and, as noted below, case law interpreting that and its precursor provisions will still be relevant in interpreting this JSA provision. There has been some change of terminology without apparent change of meaning (*e.g.* "place of work" rather than "place of employment"). That one day affected bars title for the whole week rather than just for the day, as would have been the case with unemployment benefit, is unsurprising; it reflects the change from a daily benefit (UB) to a weekly benefit (JSA). Like the trade dispute disqualification from unemployment benefit, this provision denies entitlement. Hence weeks ruled out do not constitute a jobseeking period (JSA Regs, reg.48(3)(e)), but nor do they erode the 182-day maximum period of entitlement to contribution-based JSA founded on a contribution record in a single set of two tax/contribution years (see further notes to ss.2 and 5). This is in marked contrast to the double penalty suffered by the person who, for example, loses his job through misconduct, precluded from payment of JSA by s.19, who not only is denied payment but has the 182-day period eroded by the period of preclusion imposed under that section (see further notes to ss.5 and 19). This differential can to some degree be rationalised on the basis that the role of s.19 is to preclude payment to those who are in some way responsible for their own unemployment, whereas, as shown below, the trade dispute preclusion can catch the innocent, and in part the trade dispute preclusion in denying benefit to those affected is said to manifest state neutrality in the dispute, the merits of which should not concern the benefit system.

Subs.(1)

1.201   To bring the trade dispute preclusion in subs.(1) into operation, the Secretary of State (decision-maker) must prove on the balance of probabilities that:

(1) there was a *trade dispute*;

(2) at the claimant's *place of work*;

(3) which resulted in a *stoppage of work*;

(4) and that stoppage caused the claimant not to be employed on a day.

This adapts for this section the approach to the unemployment benefit trade dispute disqualification set out in *R(U)17/52(T)*.

Each of these conditions contains terms (highlighted above) whose interpretation is vital to the correct application of the section's denial of entitlement to JSA.

Trade dispute

1.202   Determining the existence of a trade dispute seems logically the first task of the adjudicating authorities, because in the absence of a trade dispute the other conditions cannot apply. The basic definition, which is very broad, is now to be found in s.35(1), rather than in the section itself, as was the case in unemployment benefit, but the definitions are identical. The definition clearly includes strikes, whether official or unofficial (*R(U)5/59*), lockouts (*R(U)17/52*) and demarcation disputes (*R(U)14/64*). There is no requirement that the claimant be a party to the trade dispute: *R(U)3/69* and see below. It has been held that there can be a trade dispute between an employer and employees of another employer who picket the employer's premises and persuade his employees to strike: *R(U)1/74*. There is a requirement in the definition of trade dispute in s.35(1) that the dispute concern employment or non-employment of persons or conditions or terms of employment. Disputes outside these parameters are not trade disputes for the purpose of this section. It is now clearly established that a dispute about safety procedures is within the definition: *R(U)3/71, R(U)5/77* and *R. v National Insurance Commissioner Ex p. Thompson* (1977), reported as an Appendix to *R(U)5/77*. In *R(U)5/87* Commissioner Rice held that the words "any dispute . . . which is connected with the employment . . . of any person" are wide enough to include any dispute connected with the manner in which the employment is carried out, and in that case covered the dispute over the employees' "go slow". In most cases establishing the existence of a trade dispute is unlikely to be problematic. But note that in *R(U)21/59*, para.6, the Commissioner indicated that a dispute between an employer and an employee must have reached "a certain stage of contention before it may properly be termed a [trade] dispute". In the case before the Commissioner he was clearly satisfied that evidence that the workforce had met to consider their response to their employer's rejection of their claims concerning their terms of employment amounted to a trade dispute and suggested that one may well have existed some time before the meeting took place.

It should be noted that in determining the existence of a trade dispute it is no part of the adjudicating authorities' task to make any assessment of the merits of the dispute: *Ex p. Thompson* (cited above) and *R(SSP)1/86*. It may be necessary to make findings of fact about when the trade dispute started and ended, but it should be remembered that the more important dates relate to when the stoppage of work started and ended. This is discussed below. There is a clear distinction to be drawn between a trade dispute and a stoppage of work under the section.

Place of work

The trade dispute must be at the claimant's place of work as defined in subs.(4). Read with subs.(5) this allows some separation of departments within a range of employment operated by a single employer. It will usually be a straightforward task to identify the premises or place at which the claimant is employed. Obviously each case must be determined on its own facts. How broadly or narrowly the place will be defined will vary according to the circumstances of each case. In *R(U)4/58* the place of employment of an employee loading ships was held to be the whole of the docks.

1.203

Where the decision-maker shows on the balance of probabilities a place of work, it will be for the claimant to prove on the balance of probabilities that there are separate branches of work and that the trade dispute is not at his place of work so construed: *R(U)1/70*, para.14. The escape route is complex because the claimant, who may not be best placed to do so, must adduce evidence to show that

(a) there are separate branches of work at his place of work; a claimant is unlikely to succeed unless he can show that the branch is engaged in work that is not part of an integrated process of production: *R(U)4/62*, para.7;

(b) the separate branches of work are commonly carried on as separate businesses in separate premises or at separate places; this necessarily involves adducing evidence as to patterns in other similar businesses: *R(U)4/62* and *R(U)1/70*, para.17; and

(c) at his place of employment the branches of work are in fact carried out in separate departments at the same premises or place.

In cases involving such arguments, clear findings of fact are obviously vital. *CU66/1986(T)* affords an illustration. There the claimant successfully appealed her trade dispute disqualification to a tribunal of commissioners. She was a colliery canteen worker at Frickley Colliery, laid off during the miner's strike in 1984–1985. The commissioners held that there was carried on in the canteen a separate branch of work, and one which is commonly carried on as a separate business in separate premises or at a separate place. But was the canteen a separate department? The evidence of the NUM Branch Secretary at the colliery was that the canteen was inside

1.204

the colliery gates and had been attached to or added to the pit-head baths that had been built in 1937. It was managed by the manageress who was appointed by and answerable to the NCB Catering Manager at Doncaster. While applications for jobs at the canteen would be made to the colliery's personnel manager, the area canteen manager would be responsible for making the appointment. As regards disciplinary matters with respect to canteen workers, again, the area manager would be involved but the colliery manager would also have to be informed. Profits and losses in the canteen did not appear to feature in figures about the profitability of the colliery. The commissioners, in the light of this evidence, decided that the work carried on in the canteen was a separate branch of work carried on in a separate department on the same premises or at the same place as the colliery. Accordingly, since the trade dispute that caused the stoppage of work was not at the claimant's place of employment she would not be disqualified from benefit. The commissioners also referred to an umpire's decision (Case 2185/29, *Umpires Decisions,* Vol. VIII, p.88) under the equivalent provision in s.8(1) of the Unemployment Insurance Act 1920. There, a blacksmith employed in the blacksmiths' department at a colliery, which department did both wagon repairing and general colliery work, was able to rely on the escape route, notwithstanding that only some work in that department was carried on as a separate department from coal-mining.

Stoppage of work

1.205   Generally defining a stoppage of work is relatively easy. But defining when it begins may be more problematic and a useful approach may be to adopt the reverse of the principles laid down in the decisions on the ending of stoppages of work discussed below. The starting point will always be to consider the definition given by the tribunal of commissioners in *R(U)17/52(T)*:

> ". . . a stoppage of work must be in the nature of a strike or lockout, that is to say it must be a move in a contest between an employer and his employees, the object of which is that employment shall be resumed on certain conditions."

In *R(U)7/58* it was held that a stoppage of work occurred when 38 production workers out of a total of 90 withdrew their labour. In *R(U)1/87* Commissioner Skinner said that "stoppage of work" means "a situation in which operations are being stopped or hindered otherwise than to a negligible extent" (paragraph 7). There the closure of the furriers' fleshing shop on May 2, 1984, causing a 60 per cent loss of production, resulted in a stoppage from that date. In *R(U)1/65*, following a long line of commissioners' decisions, it was held that where there was a trade dispute and subsequently the employer indicates that he will never re-employ the strikers, the stoppage of work continues to be due to the trade dispute despite the high improbability that the strikers will be re-employed and despite their acceptance of that position. In effect the disqualification can only end when they become bona fide employed elsewhere or when the stoppage ends. In *R(U)25/57*, the commissioner adopted the approach taken by the umpire in 1926 as establishing the principles to be applied in determining when the end of a stoppage of work occurred:

> ". . . a stoppage of work may come to an end without any settlement of the dispute, by the workers returning to work in a body, or by driblets, or by their places being taken by other men. In such cases the stoppage of work comes to an end when the employers have got all the workers they require, that is, when work is no longer being stopped or hindered by the refusal of workers to work on the employer's terms or the refusal of employers to employ the workers on the workers' terms . . . When work is again proceeding normally and is not being held up, either by the men holding back or by circumstances directly resulting from the stoppage of work, the stoppage of work is at an end." (para.6.)

This approach was cited with approval in *R(U)1/65*. It is consistent with this approach that, where a dispute had ended but work was needed to industrial plant to carry out repairs necessitated by the stoppage, a lay-off while those repairs were carried out was a part of the stoppage due to the trade dispute: *R. v National Insurance Commissioner Ex p. Dawber* (published as an Appendix to *R(U)9/80*).

The stoppage causes the claimant not to be employed on a day

If the stoppage causes him not to be employed on any day, the claimant loses enti-   1.206
tlement to JSA for the week including that day (unless he can invoke one of the escape routes), a change reflecting the weekly character of JSA as opposed to the daily benefit structure of unemployment benefit.

It has already been noted that the claimant need not be a party to the trade dispute to be caught by the disqualification. A claimant is caught if the stoppage is the effective cause of his not working. So, if enough people stay away from work for a stoppage to occur, all those losing days of employment, whether by their own choice or by force of circumstances, such as picketing or being laid off by the employer, are to be regarded as having lost their employment by reason of the stoppage.

Escape routes

There are four escape routes for avoiding the preclusive effect of subs.(1): the   1.207
proviso in the subsection itself and the three exceptions set out in subs.(3).

(1) *The proviso*: The claimant can avoid the disqualification by proving that he has no direct interest in the trade dispute. In determining what constitutes a direct interest in the trade dispute, it is necessary to look no further than the decision of the House of Lords in *Presho v Insurance Officer* [1984] 1 All E.R. 97 (published as Appendix 2 to *R(U)1/84*), followed by the Court of Appeal in *Cartlidge v Chief Adjudication Officer* [1986] 2 All E.R. 1. In *Presho* Lord Brandon said that the words should be given their natural and ordinary meaning, and continued:

". . . where different groups of workers, belonging to different unions, are employed by the same employers at the same place of work and there is a trade dispute between the common employers and one of the unions to which one of the groups of workers belong, those in the other groups of workers belonging to other unions are directly, and not merely indirectly, interested in that trade dispute provided that two conditions are fulfilled. The first condition is that, whatever may be the outcome of the trade dispute, it will be applied by the common employers not only to the group of workers belonging to the one union participating in the dispute, but also to the other groups of workers belonging to the other unions concerned. The second condition is that the application of the outcome of the dispute 'across the board' . . . should come about automatically as a result of one or other of three things: first, a collective agreement which is legally binding; or, second, a collective agreement which is not legally binding; or, third, established industrial custom and practice at the place of work concerned. [These issues involve] a question of fact of a kind which insurance officers, local tribunals and the commissioner, are by reason of their wide knowledge and experience of matters pertaining to industrial relations, exceptionally well qualified to answer." (At 101–102.)

In *Cartlidge*, the commissioner had found that the miner's dispute concerned both   1.208
pay and pit closures, and so Mr Cartlidge was directly interested in the trade dispute. It follows that it will be extremely difficult for claimants to take advantage of this escape route. However, the fact that the claimant was at one time directly interested in the trade dispute (and thus then unable to invoke the proviso) does not preclude him from successfully invoking it later during the stoppage should he cease to have a direct interest. The proviso is not invocable once and once only during a stoppage (*R(U)1/87*, para.9, relying on *R(U)5/86(T)*, paras 15–28, where a tribunal of commissioners disapproved statements to the contrary in *R(U)4/79(T)* because a line of commissioners' authority running contrary to that relied on in *R(U)4/79(T)* had not

been cited or considered in *R(U)4/79(T)*). A claimant, initially directly interested in the trade dispute (and therefore rightly denied benefit), can cease to be so interested and thus claim the benefit of the proviso to conclude the period of denial, where his dismissal by his employer genuinely indicates the employer's intention to sever all relations with him and is not just a tactical manoeuvre in the dispute. In *R(U)1/87* the hindsight available to the commissioner showed that the claimant's dismissal on the first day of the stoppage was part of plans to trim the size of the workforce and thus a genuine severance of all relations with the claimant rather than a tactical move in the dispute. Accordingly, the claimant was not subject to disqualification after that first day. Of course, were that case being decided now, with respect to JSA, the whole week in which that day occurred would be ruled out by subs.(1).

(2) Bona fide employment elsewhere (subs.(3)(a)): If someone caught by the subs.(1) preclusion proves that during the stoppage he became bona fide employed elsewhere, subs.(1) is to be taken to cease to apply to him from the point at which he became so employed elsewhere.

The burden of proof is on the claimant to establish the *bona fide* nature of the employment. Bona fide means that the employment must not merely be a device to avoid the disqualification; both the employment and the reason for taking it must be genuine *(R(U)6/74)*. There is no objection to the taking of temporary employment so long as it is genuine. It will usually be necessary to show that the relationship with the former employer with whom there was a trade dispute has been permanently severed. So a former boiler-maker who obtained intermittent work in his usual occupation in a different port, but returned to his former employer on the ending of the dispute was held not to have established that he was bona fide employed elsewhere *(R(U)39/56)*.

1.209   *(3) Employment terminated by reason of redundancy (subs.(3)(b))*: If someone caught by the subs.(1) preclusion proves that during the stoppage his employment was terminated by reason of redundancy within the meaning of s.139(1) of the Employment Rights Act 1996, subs.(1) is to be taken to have ceased to apply to him from the point of such termination. As to "by reason of redundancy within the meaning of section 139(1)", termination will be by reason of redundancy if it is attributable wholly or mainly to (a) the fact that the employer has ceased, or intends to cease, to carry on that business in the place where the employee [the JSA claimant] was employed, or (b) the fact that the requirements of that business for employees to carry out work of a particular kind, or for employees to carry out work of a particular kind in the place where [the claimant] was employed, have ceased or diminished or are expected to cease or diminish.

The precursor of this provision was inserted into the unemployment benefit trade dispute disqualification scheme, to remove the injustice perceived to exist in the *Cartlidge* case. Mr Cartlidge had volunteered for redundancy prior to the start of the miners' dispute in 1984. Between receiving his notice of redundancy and its taking effect, a stoppage due to a trade dispute at his place of work caused him to not to be employed on some days. He had tried to work and had done so for much of the period but had lost some days work because of the picketing of his pit. The Court of Appeal reluctantly held that the trade dispute disqualification extended beyond the termination of his employment because the stoppage of work was still continuing (the relevant provision then disqualified "for any day during the stoppage"). The effect of this provision is that subs.(1) can have no preclusive effect beyond the point of termination of employment by reason of redundancy. It is perhaps worth noting that the current formulation of subs.(1) would have worked to benefit someone in Mr Cartlidge's position prior to the termination in that if, despite a stoppage of work, he managed to work throughout the week (not losing a day of employment) he would not be precluded from JSA for that week, even though loss of a day's employment due to the stoppage in the preceding and subsequent weeks had precluded title to JSA for those weeks.

(4) Bona fide resumption of employment and subsequent leaving for another reason (subs.(3)(c)): If someone caught by the subs.(1) preclusion proves that during the stoppage he bona fide resumed employment with his employer, subs.(1) is to be taken to have ceased to apply to him from the point at which he bona fide resumed his employment.

This is an escape route for the claimant who has withdrawn his labour, subsequently returned to work, but then left it for a reason unconnected with the trade dispute. The reason will usually be something other than leaving his job to take another: subs.(3)(a) would there afford an easier escape route. Bona fide is to be interpreted as in subs.(3)(a). But otherwise it is not easy to see how this provision will work in practice. Does resumption mean that the employment was terminated and re-employment offered, or merely that the claimant returned to work during the trade dispute, or both? There appears to be no case law on the precursor of this provision, so many points await interpretation.

Subs.(2)

This subsection makes it clear that anyone not falling within subs.(1) who withdraws their labour on any day in furtherance of a trade dispute is not entitled to JSA for the week which includes that day. It fills a gap in the test in subs.(1)(a) because it does not require any stoppage of work to have occurred; nor does it require the trade dispute to be at the claimant's place of employment. As long as the withdrawal of labour is in furtherance of a trade dispute, the preclusion operates. It could require the authorities to draw a distinction between a "withdrawal of labour" and a "lock-out" (Ogus, Barendt and Wikeley, p.141), risking an opinion on the merits of the dispute.

1.210

Effect on other claimants

15.—(1) Except in prescribed circumstances, subsection (2) applies in relation to a claimant for an income-based jobseeker's allowance where a member of his family ("A") is, or would be, prevented by section 14 from being entitled to a jobseeker's allowance.

1.211

(2) For the purposes of calculating the claimant's entitlement to an income based jobseeker's allowance—

(a) any portion of the applicable amount which is included in respect of A shall be disregarded for the period for which this subsection applies to the claimant;

(b) where the claimant and A are a married or unmarried couple, any portion of the applicable amount which is included in respect of them shall be reduced to one half for the period for which this subsection applies to the claimant;

(c) except so far as regulations provide otherwise, there shall be treated as the claimant's income—

(i) any amount which becomes, or would on an application duly made become, available to A in relation to that period by way of repayment of income tax deducted from A's [¹ taxable earnings (as defined by section 10 of the Income Tax (Earnings and Pensions) Act 2003 under PAYE regulations]; and

(ii) any other payment which the claimant or any member of his family receives or is entitled to obtain because A is without employment for that period; and

(d) any payment by way of a jobseeker's allowance for that period or any part of it which apart from this paragraph would be made to the claimant—

(i) shall not be made, if the weekly rate of payment ("the rate") would be equal to or less than the prescribed sum; and

(ii) shall be at a weekly rate equal to the difference between the rate and the prescribed sum, if the rate would be more than the prescribed sum.

(3) Where a reduction under subsection (2)(b) would not produce a sum which is a multiple of 5p, the reduction shall be to the nearest lower sum which is such a multiple.

(4) Where A returns to work with the same employer after a period during which subsection (2) applied to the claimant (whether or not his return is before the end of any stoppage of work in relation to which he is, or would be, prevented from being entitled to a jobseeker's allowance), subsection (2) shall cease to apply to the claimant at the commencement of the day on which A returns to work.

(5) In relation to any period of less than a week, subsection (2) shall have effect subject to such modifications as may be prescribed.

(6) Subsections (7) to (9) apply where an order made under section 150 of the Administration Act (annual up-rating of benefits) has the effect of increasing the sum prescribed in regulations made under section 4(5) as the personal allowance for a single person aged not less than 25("the personal allowance").

(7) For the sum prescribed in regulations made under subsection (2)(d) there shall be substituted, from the time when the order comes into force, a sum arrived at by increasing the prescribed sum by the percentage by which the personal allowance has been increased by the order.

(8) If the sum arrived at under subsection (7), is not a multiple of 50p—

(a) any remainder of 25p or less shall be disregarded;

(b) any remainder of more than 25p shall be rounded up to the nearest 50p.

(9) The order shall state the sum substituted for the sum prescribed in regulations made under subsection (2)(d).

(10) Nothing in subsection (7) prevents the making of further regulations under subsection (2)(d) varying the prescribed sum.

AMENDMENT

1. Income Tax (Earnings and Pensions) Act 2003, Sch.6, Pt 2, para.229 (April 6, 2003).

DEFINITIONS

1.212
"applicable amount"—see s.35(1).
"the Administration Act"—*ibid.*
"claimant"—*ibid.*
"employment"—*ibid.*, JSA Regs., regs 3 and 4.
"family"—see s.35(1).
"income-based jobseeker's allowance"—*ibid.*, s.1(4).
"married couple"—see s.35(1).
"prescribed"—*ibid.*
"unmarried couple"—*ibid.*

GENERAL NOTE

Subs. (1)

1.213
This provision applies where the partner of an income-based JSA claimant is involved in a trade dispute. Although subs.(1) refers to a member of the claimant's

family, the effect of reg.171(b)(i) of the JSA Regulations is that subs.(2) can only apply to the claimant's partner. Note that benefit will not be affected if the claimant's partner is incapable of work or within the "maternity period" (six weeks before and seven weeks after confinement) (reg.171(b)(ii) of the JSA Regulations). If the *claimant* is involved in a trade dispute see s.14.

Note also reg.52(2) of the JSA Regulations, which treats a partner as in remunerative work for the seven days following the first day of the stoppage of work or the first day on which the partner withdrew his labour if the claimant was not entitled to income-based JSA when the partner became involved in the dispute. The result is to disentitle the claimant for those days (s.3(1)(e)). The partner is not treated as in remunerative work outside this period (reg.53(g)).

Subs.(2)

This follows the rules for income support in s.126(3)(c) and (5) of the Contributions and Benefits Act 1992. See the notes to s.126. The basic principle is that where the claimant's partner is involved in a trade dispute, no benefit is payable in respect of him (paras (a) and (b)). The "prescribed sum" for the purposes of para.(d) is £30.50 from April 11, 2005 (reg.172 of the JSA Regulations).

Subs.(4)

Subs.(2) ceases to apply from the day the claimant's partner returns to work.

[¹Trade disputes: joint-claim couples

15A.—(1) Sections 14 and 15 shall, in relation to a joint-claim couple 1.214
claiming a joint-claim jobseeker's allowance, apply in accordance with this section.

(2) Where each member of the couple is prevented by section 14 from being entitled to a jobseeker's allowance, the couple are not entitled to a joint-claim jobseeker's allowance.

(3) But where only one member of the couple is prevented by that section from being entitled to a jobseeker's allowance, the couple are not for that reason alone prevented from being entitled to a joint-claim jobseeker's allowance.

(4) Section 15(1) does not have effect in relation to the couple but, except in prescribed circumstances, section 15(2) applies for the purposes of calculating the couple's entitlement to a joint-claim jobseeker's allowance where—

(a) a member of the couple, or

(b) any other person who is a member of any family of which the couple are members,

is, or would be, prevented by section 14 from being entitled to a jobseeker's allowance.

(5) Where section 15(2) applies in relation to the couple by virtue of subsection (4) above, that provision and section 15(4) apply with the following modifications—

(a) references to the claimant are to be taken as references to the couple;

(b) references to "A" are to the person mentioned in subsection (4)(a) or (b) above;

(c) section 15(2)(b) has effect as if for "where the claimant and A are a married or unmarried couple," there were substituted "where A is a member of the couple,"; and

(d) section 15(2)(c)(ii) has effect as if for "of his family" there were substituted "of any family of which the couple are members".]

AMENDMENT

1.215   1. Welfare Reform and Pensions Act 1999, s.59 and Sch.7, para.10 (March 19, 2001).

DEFINITIONS

"claimant"—see s.35(1).
"family"—*ibid.*
"joint-claim couple"—see s.1(4).
"joint-claim jobseeker's allowance"—*ibid.*

GENERAL NOTE

1.216   This applies the rules in ss.14 and 15 (subject to minor modifications, see subss.(4) and (5)) to joint-claim couples (*i.e.* certain childless couples, see the notes at the beginning of this Act and to s.1(4)).

Persons Under 18

Severe hardship

1.217   **16.**—(1) If it appears to the Secretary of State—
(a) that a person—
   (i) has reached the age of 16 but not the age of 18;
   (ii) is not entitled to a jobseeker's allowance or to income support; and
   (iii) is registered for training but is not being provided with any training; and
(b) that severe hardship will result to him unless a jobseeker's allowance is paid to him,
the Secretary of State may direct that this section is to apply to him.
   (2) A direction may be given so as to have effect for a specified period.
   (3) The Secretary of State may revoke a direction if—
(a) it appears to him that there has been a change of circumstances as a result of which failure to receive a jobseeker's allowance need no longer result in severe hardship to the person concerned;
[¹(b) it appears to him that the person concerned has, without good cause—
   (i) neglected to avail himself of a reasonable opportunity of a place on a training scheme; or
   (ii) after a place on such a scheme has been notified to him by an employment officer as vacant or about to become vacant, refused or failed to apply for it or to accept it when offered to him; or]
(c) he is satisfied that it was given in ignorance of some material fact or was based on a mistake as to some material fact and considers that, but for that ignorance or mistake, he would not have given the direction.
[¹(4) In this section—
"employment officer" means an officer of the Secretary of State or such other person as may be designated for the purposes of this section by an order made by the Secretary of State;

"period" includes—
   (a) a period of a determinate length;
   (b) a period defined by reference to the happening of a future event; and
   (c) a period of a determinate length but subject to earlier determination upon the happening of a future event;
"training scheme" has such meaning as may be prescribed.]

AMENDMENT

1. Social Security Act 1998, s.86(1) and Sch.7 para.139 (October 18, 1999).   **1.218**

DEFINITION

"training"—see s.35(1), JSA Regs, reg.57(1).

GENERAL NOTE

Subs. (1) and (2)
   This provision is similar to the former s.125 of the Contributions and Benefits Act   **1.219**
(revoked on October 7, 1996), which dealt with income support severe hardship directions.
   Subs.(1) requires that the person under 18 is not entitled to income support or JSA, so the person must fall outside the categories covered in regs 59 to 61 of the JSA Regulations and not be eligible for income support under reg.4ZA of and Sch.1B to the Income Support Regulations. (He must also not be entitled to contribution-based JSA, but this is very unlikely in the case of a person under 18.) The other main conditions are that the person is registered for, but not receiving, training and that severe hardship will (not may) result if JSA is not paid. The question of whether these conditions are satisfied is for the Secretary of State, and even if they are, there is a discretion whether or not to allow benefit. There is no right of appeal to an appeal tribunal from the Secretary of State's decision.
   To claim JSA on the grounds of severe hardship, the person should first register for work and training with the Careers Service where he will be given an ES9 referral form to take to the JobCentre (but see reg.62 of the JSA Regulations for the exceptions to this rule). Staff are instructed that all 16- and 17-year-old claimants should be allowed to make an application for JSA and should not be turned away by the JobCentre. An initial check will be made to see if the young person is eligible for JSA as of right (see regs 59 to 61 of the JSA Regulations). If not, and the application on the grounds of severe hardship fails at this stage, it will automatically be referred to the Severe Hardship Claims Unit for consideration. The Employment Service has produced detailed guidance on JSA for 16 and 17 year-olds (*Employment Service Guidance, JSA for 16 and 17 year olds*). Chapter 7, which deals with the severe hardship interview, states that the young person should be informed of the need to contact parents, whether or not the young person is living with them, or a third party, in order to verify the information he or she has given. The young person's consent to do this is required, but refusal of permission without good reason may mean that there will not be enough evidence on which to make a direction (although all such potential "nil" decisions still have to go to the Severe Hardship Claims Unit). At the same time no "undue pressure" is to be placed on the young person to give permission. This could be difficult to implement in practice. However, the guidance also states (more flexibly) that evidence from a responsible third party (*e.g.* a relative, social worker or voluntary worker), either in person, by telephone or in writing, may mean that contact with the young person's parents is not necessary.
   A direction may be made for a definite period (subs.(2)) (usually eight weeks, but this can be varied according to the circumstances). It can be renewed and it may be

revoked if any of the conditions in subs.(3) apply. If a direction is made the decision-maker must consider all the other conditions of entitlement.

Note that the three-day waiting period for JSA does not apply if a s.16 direction has been made (reg.46(1) of the JSA Regulations).

Subs. (3)

1.220   Once a direction is made under this section the claimant satisfies s.3(1)(f) (iii). If the claimant ceases to satisfy the other conditions of entitlement, entitlement will cease. The Secretary of State has a general discretion to revoke a direction whenever there is a change of circumstances, which means that severe hardship no longer need follow from non-payment of JSA (para.(a)). This emphasises the strictness of the test under subs.(1). If severe hardship will not definitely follow from the non-payment of JSA, subs.(1) cannot operate. It appears that the revocation of the direction may be retrospective from the date of the change of circumstances, and, if there was a failure to disclose facts constituting the change, the overpayment is recoverable under s.71A of the Administration Act. A direction may also be revoked if it was originally given in ignorance of or under a mistake as to a material fact that would have altered the decision on the inevitability of severe hardship (para.(c)). If there was misrepresentation of or failure to disclose that material fact, recovery under s.71A may arise.

In addition, para.(b) allows for revocation of a direction where the person has failed to pursue or refused a training opportunity without good cause ("good cause" for these purposes is not defined, so the existing case law on its meaning will be relevant).

Note that in such a case the sanctions provided for in s.19(5) do not apply (s.20(2)). The young person's "offence" will be dealt with by revocation of the direction, if this is considered appropriate, or by reduction of his JSA under reg.63(1)(b), if this applies. If a direction is revoked the young person can apply for another severe hardship direction to be made but it seems that it will be subject to a 40 per cent reduction (20 per cent if the young person is pregnant or seriously ill) of the appropriate personal allowance under para.1 of Sch.1 to the JSA Regulations for the first two weeks (s.17(3)(a) and reg.63(1)(a)). See the notes to s.17 and reg.63.

Note that the sanctions in s.19(5) also do not apply if a young person who is the subject of a severe hardship direction commits the lesser "misdemeanour" of failing to complete a training course without good cause (s.20(2)). Instead his JSA will be reduced in accordance with s.17 and reg.63 of the JSA Regulations, if applicable. But note that the sanctions in s.19(6) do apply.

Reduced payments

1.221   **17.**—(1) Regulations may provide for the amount of an income-based jobseeker's allowance [³ payable in respect of] any young person to whom this section applies to be reduced—

(a) in such circumstances;

(b) by such a percentage; and

(c) for such a period.

as may be prescribed.

[²(1A) Regulations may provide for the amount of a joint-claim jobseeker's allowance payable in respect of any joint-claim couple where a member of the couple is a young person to whom this section applies to be reduced—

(a) in such circumstances;

(b) by such a percentage; and

(c) for such a period,

as may be prescribed.]

(2) This section applies to any young person in respect of whom—

(a) a direction is in force under section 16; and

(b) [¹ any] of the conditions mentioned in subsection (3) is satisfied.

(3) The conditions are that—

(a) the young person was previously entitled to an income-based job-seeker's allowance and that entitlement ceased by virtue of the revocation of a direction under section 16;

[¹(b) he has given up a place on a training scheme, or failed to attend such a scheme on which he has been given a place, and no certificate has been issued to him under subsection (4);

(c) he has lost his place on such a scheme through misconduct.

(4) Where a young person who has given up a place on a training scheme, or failed to attend such a scheme on which he has been given a place—

(a) claims that there was good cause for his doing so; and

(b) applies to the Secretary of State for a certificate under this subsection, the Secretary of State shall, if he is satisfied that there was good cause, issue a certificate to that effect and give a copy of it to the young person.

(5) In this section—

"training scheme" has such meaning as may be prescribed;

"young person" means a person who has reached the age of 16 but not the age of 18.]

AMENDMENTS

1. Social Security Act 1998, s.86(1) and Sch.7, para.140 (October 18, 1999).   **1.222**

2. Welfare Reform and Pensions Act 1999, s.70 and Sch.8, para.29 (November 11, 1999).

3. Welfare Reform and Pensions Act 1999, Sch.7, para.11 (March 19, 2001).

GENERAL NOTE

Under this section regulations can provide for JSA that is being paid because a   **1.223**
severe hardship is in force to be paid at a reduced rate. See reg.63 of the JSA Regulations that has been made under this section. Note that although subs.(3)(a) refers to revocation of a s.16 direction generally, it is only where a direction has been revoked under s.16(3)(b) that a reduction will be applied under reg.63 (see reg.63(1)(a)).

Note the escape-route in para.(4) whereby the Secretary of State can decide that the young person had good cause for failing to complete the training and issue a certificate to that effect. A decision as to whether or not to issue a certificate of good cause under para.(4) is one against which there is no right of appeal (para.1(b) of Sch.2 to the Social Security Act 1998). There is no definition of "good cause" so presumably the extensive caselaw on good cause will apply. See reg.7(24) of the Decisions and Appeals Regulations in relation to supersessions where a sanction has been imposed under reg.63 of the JSA Regulations but the Secretary of State then issues a good cause certificate under s.17(4).

Note also that if a young person who is the subject of a severe hardship direction fails to pursue or refuses a training opportunity without good cause (so that the direction is liable to be revoked under s.16(3)(b)), or fails to complete a training course without good cause, or loses his place through misconduct, the sanctions provided for in s.19(5) do not apply (s.20(2)). The young person's "offence" will be dealt with under s.16, or this section and reg.63 of the JSA Regulations, as appropriate. See the notes to reg.63.

1.224 **Recovery of overpayments**

18. *[Omitted. See s.71A of the Social Security Administration Act 1992 in Vol. III.]*

Denial of jobseeker's allowance

1.225 **Circumstances in which a jobseeker's allowance is not payable**

19.—(1) Even though the conditions for entitlement to a jobseeker's allowance are satisfied with respect to a person, the allowance shall not be payable in any of the circumstances mentioned in subsection (5) or (6).

[⁴(1A) Subject to section 20A(9), this section does not apply as regards a joint-claim jobseeker's allowance (but sections 20A and 20B make, in relation to such an allowance, provision corresponding to that made by this section and section 20).]

(2) If the circumstances are any of those mentioned in subsection (5), the period for which the allowance is not to be payable shall be such period (of at least one week but not more than 26 weeks) as may be prescribed.

(3) If the circumstances are any of those mentioned in subsection (6), the period for which the allowance is not to be payable shall be such period (of at least one week but not more than 26 weeks) as may be determined by [²the Secretary of State].

(4) Regulations may prescribe—

(a) circumstances which [³ the Secretary of State] is to take into account, and

(b) circumstances which he is not to take into account,

in determining a period under subsection (3).

(5) The circumstances referred to in subsections (1) and (2) are that the claimant—

(a) has, without good cause, refused or failed to carry out any jobseeker's direction which was reasonable, having regard to his circumstances;

(b) has, without good cause—

(i) neglected to avail himself of a reasonable opportunity of a place on a training scheme or employment programme;

(ii) after a place on such a scheme or programme has been notified to him by an employment officer as vacant or about to become vacant, refused or failed to apply for it or to accept it when offered to him;

(iii) given up a place on such a scheme or programme; or

(iv) failed to attend such a scheme or programme on which he has been given a place; or

(c) has lost his place on such a scheme or programme through misconduct.

(6) The circumstances referred to in subsections (1) and (3) are that the claimant—

(a) has lost his employment as an employed earner through misconduct;

(b) has voluntarily left such employment without just cause;

(c) has, without good cause, after a situation in any employment has been notified to him by an employment officer as vacant or about to become vacant, refused or failed to apply for it or to accept it when offered to him; or

(d) has, without good cause, neglected to avail himself of a reasonable opportunity of employment.

(7) In such circumstances as may be prescribed, including in particular where he has been dismissed by his employer by reason of redundancy within the meaning of [¹ section 139(1) of the Employment Rights Act 1996] after volunteering or agreeing to be so dismissed, a person who might otherwise be regarded as having left his employment voluntarily is to be treated as not having left voluntarily.

(8) Regulations may—

(a) prescribe matters which are, or are not, to be taken into account in determining whether a person—
  (i) has, or does not have, good cause for any act or omission; or
  (ii) has, or does not have, just cause for any act or omission; or

(b) prescribe circumstances in which a person—
  (i) is, or is not, to be regarded as having, or not having, good cause for any act or omission; or
  (ii) is, or is not, to be regarded as having, or not having, just cause for any act or omission.

(9) Subject to any regulations under subsection (8), in determining whether a person has, or does not have, good cause or (as the case may be) just cause for any act or omission, any matter relating to the level of remuneration in the employment in question shall be disregarded.

(10) In this section—

(a) "employment officer" means an officer of the Secretary of State or such other person as may be designated for the purposes of this section by an order made by the Secretary of State;

(b) "jobseeker's direction" means a direction in writing given by an employment officer with a view to achieving one or both of the following—
  (i) assisting the claimant to find employment;
  (ii) improving the claimant to find employment; and

(c) "training scheme" and "employment programme" have such meaning as may be prescribed.

AMENDMENTS

1. Employment Rights Act 1996, Sch.1, para.67(2) (August 22, 1996).   1.226
2. Social Security Act 1998, Sch.7, para.141(1) (October 18, 1999).
3. Social Security Act 1998, Sch.7, para.141(2) (October 18, 1999).
4. Welfare Reform and Pensions Act 1999, Sch.7, para.12 (March 19, 2001).

DEFINITIONS

"a joint-claim jobseeker's allowance": see s.1(4).
"claimant": see s.35(1).
"employed earner": see s.35(1); JSA Regs, reg.3; SSCBA 1992, s.2(1)(a).
"employment": see s.35(1).
"employment officer": subs.(10).
"employment programme": see subs.(10), JSA Regs, reg.75(1)(a).
"jobseeker's direction": see subs.(10), JSA Regs, reg.75(1)(b).
"prescribed": see s.35(1).
"regulations": *ibid.*

"training scheme": see subs.(10).
"week" (except subs.(2)): see s.35(1), JSA Regs, reg.75(2).
"week" (in subs.(2)): see s.35(1), JSA Regs, reg.75(3).

GENERAL NOTE

Aims and structure of the section

1.227   This section underpins the requirement, common to JSA and the previous benefit regimes for the unemployed, that the claimant's unemployment be involuntary. Like disqualification under the now repealed SSCBA 1992, s.28 (with which section it has some affinities), this section provides sanctions by precluding, for varying periods, payment of JSA to which the claimant is otherwise be entitled (subs.(1)), where the claimant falls within the circumstances covered in either subs.(5) or (6). It thereby penalises those whose unemployment is voluntary both in terms of how the unemployment came about and in terms of behaviour whilst unemployed.

Subsection (5) provides grounds for precluding payment, which are concerned with the claimant's failure to comply with a jobseeker's direction issued by an employment officer or with avoidable loss or refusal of a training scheme or employment programme opportunity.

Subsection (6), essentially echoing the "heads" of disqualification from unemployment benefit in SSCBA 1992, s.28(1)(a)–(c), provides grounds for precluding payment of JSA, which are concerned with the avoidable loss or refusal of employment.

The section and the approach it embodies, however, differ in a number of significant respects from disqualification under SSCBA 1992, s.28. Under the latter, days of disqualification were not days of unemployment (not days of entitlement) and so did not count towards the 312-day maximum period of entitlement. The position under JSA is very different. As noted in the annotations to s.5 above, days on which, despite entitlement, an allowance is not payable because the claimant is caught by s.19 (*e.g.* for leaving a job through misconduct) *do* erode the 182-day maximum period of entitlement to contribution-based JSA, so that, if someone with an underlying entitlement to contribution-based jobseeker's allowance is denied payment for the maximum period of preclusion (26 weeks), that preclusion not only prevents payment, but extinguishes entitlement to such an allowance based on the tax/contribution years relevant to that claim, and, to gain another period of entitlement, the claimant will have to satisfy the requalification rule set out in s.5(2). So reaching the right and proper decision on what under the unemployment benefit regime would have been called "disqualification", and determining in subs.(6) situations the appropriate period of preclusion, is even more important than before. Another significant point of difference is that the degree of discretion available to the Secretary of State and Appeals Tribunals under this section is reduced in comparison with the unemployment regime in a number of ways:

(a)   the appropriate period of preclusion in subs.(5) situations has been fixed by regulations (subs.(2), JSA Regs, reg.69) and set at either two, four or 26 weeks;

(b)   the Secretary of State has exercised his power under subs.(4) to prescribe factors to be taken into account under subs.(3) in fixing the appropriate period of preclusion for those caught by subs.(6) (see JSA Regs, reg.70);

(c)   the Secretary of State now has power not only to define what is and what is not "good cause" for the purposes of escaping from the preclusive effects of some of the "heads" in subs.(5) and (6) (see JSA Regs, regs 72, 73), something familiar from the unemployment benefit regime, but also to define what constitutes and does not constitute "just cause" for the purposes of escaping the "voluntarily leaving employment" preclusion in subs.(6)(b) (although as yet he has not done so); and

(d) he has power to prescribe situations in which someone who might otherwise be regarded as having left employment voluntarily is to be treated as not having done so, particularly in "voluntary redundancy" contexts (subs.(7) and JSA Regs, reg.71).

Finally, in approaching s.19, it should be noted that s.20 provides a range of relief **1.228** from the effects of this section. Thus, s.20 should carefully be scrutinised before imposing any period of preclusion under s.19 or regulations made under it. The reliefs afforded through s.20 confer protection against being penalised for refusing to act as a strike-breaker (s.20(1)); protect those leaving "employment on trial" (s.20(3), (7), (8)); with respect to subs.(5) situations, protect those 16-and 17-year-olds subject to severe hardship directions regulations, leaving their position to be regulated by ss. 16 and 17 rather than subs.(5) of this section; and enable receipt of hardship payments of income-based JSA (s.20(4)–(6)). Unlike the voluntary unemployment context in income support, there is now no question of automatic entitlement to a "reduced rate" income-based JSA in cases where a s.19 preclusion operates, although on establishing hardship a person so precluded can obtain a reduced rate hardship payment of income-based JSA payable at once for some (*e.g.* a pregnant single claimant, some carers) but for others only after the first 14 days of the s.19 preclusion (see s.20(4), (5), JSA Regs, regs 140–146). See further the annotations to s.20.

Subs.(1)

This provides that, despite entitlement to it, JSA is not payable where the claimant **1.229** is caught by any of the preclusive "heads" of subs.(5) or (6). The implications of the distinction between entitlement and payability have been examined above and in the annotations to s.5 (the exhaustion and requalification rules in respect of contribution-based JSA).

Subs.(1A)

This provides that the preclusive effect of this section applies only to "standard" **1.230** claims for JSA (see notes to Jobseekers Act 1995, s.1). It does not cover "joint-claim couples". Instead analogous provision is made in ss.20A and 20B replicating for the members of such a couple the preclusive effects of this section and the saving effect of s.20. This is, however, "subject to section 20A(9)", the effect of which is to apply subss.(7) to (10) of s.19 (a variety of rule-making powers and definitions—see notes to those subss., below) to joint-claim couples for the purposes of s.20A. This necessitates reading subss. (10)(b) (the definition of jobseeker's direction) as if the reference there to the claimant were instead a reference to the member of the joint-claim couple caught by s.20A(2)(a) (*i.e.* where he has, without good cause, refused or failed to carry out any jobseeker's direction that was reasonable, having regard to his circumstances).

Subs.(2)

This provides that where the claimant is caught by one of the "heads" of preclu- **1.231** sion in subs.(5) (jobseeker's direction, training scheme or employment programme), the period for which JSA is not payable is to be set by regulations at not less than one week but not more than 26 weeks. A distinction is drawn between defaults in respect of New Deal options (see further JSA Regs, regs 1(3) and 75) and those in respect of jobseeker's directions or other employment programmes or training schemes. As regards defaults in respect of the New Deal options, the penalty for a first offence is set at two weeks. A further "New Deal" offence within 12 months attracts four weeks, while for a third offence within 12 months of the second, the sanction increases to 26 weeks. So long as no more than 12 months elapse between "offences" that much enhanced penalty would thereafter apply to the fourth and any subsequent New Deal "offence". As regards, sanctions in respect of a jobseeker's direction or other employment programmes or training schemes, the regulation sets the period at four weeks in the case of a claimant falling foul of s.19(5) within 12 months of last having done so (even where the other default was in respect of a New Deal option), otherwise at two weeks. Both in subs.(2) and reg.69, "week" means "benefit week" (s.35(1), JSA Regs, reg.75(3)). "Benefit week" is defined in a complex fashion in JSA Regs, reg.1(3): in its basic form, it is the period of seven days ending with the day of the week specified in the claimant's attendance notice (colloquially, the day corresponding to his "signing on" day).

The prescribed period of preclusion begins on the first day of the week following the date of the determination that a jobseeker's allowance is not payable under subs.(5) (JSA Regs, reg.69(2)(b); Decisions and Appeals Regulations 1999, reg.7(8)(a)). However, where benefit is paid otherwise than fortnightly in arrears, the sanction begins on the day after the end of the last benefit week in respect of which JSA was paid (JSA Regs, reg.69(2)(a); Decisions and Appeals Regulations 1999, reg.7(8)(b)).

There is, of course, also the question: when does the period finish? The short answer is whenever the period of preclusion expires. But this raises the matter of supervening or interrupting events. It is submitted that, as with the old regime, any period of preclusion, once begun, continues for an unbroken period until its duly calculated end (the same rule as in unemployment benefit: see *R(U)24/56*). So where a claimant takes other employment or training, loses it and claims again during the period of preclusion, he will still be caught by the remaining days of the period even though the loss of this other employment or training would not itself warrant preclusion under subs.(6) (*cf. R(U)13/64*). Note, however, the effect of JSA Regs, reg.69(3) and (4), which makes income-based JSA payable, notwithstanding this section, where a 26-week preclusion is in force in respect of a New Deal option and during that period the Secretary of State gives the claimant written notice that he need no longer participate in those options.

Unlike subs.(3), subs.(2) makes no reference to the decision-maker, probably because of the period of preclusion and its starting date being prescribed. But this has not produced a two-tier system of decision-making (see Wikeley, *Annotations*); while jobseeker's directions are, of course, issued by employment officers and those officers will doubtless also be concerned with the claimant's access to training schemes and employment programmes, SSA 1998, s.8 has the effect that any question whether a jobseeker's allowance is not payable to a person by virtue of this section is one for the Secretary of State (decision-maker), thus opening up the usual channels of appeal.

Subss.(3), (4)

1.232   These set the period of preclusion in subs.(6) cases. Where a scheme provides for periods of preclusion from benefit, two main questions arise: (a) what is the length of the period; (b) when does it begin and end? Discussion is divided accordingly.

1.233   *(a) Fixing the length of the period*: If a claimant is caught by one of the payment precluding "heads" of subs.(6), the period of preclusion is at the discretion of the decision-maker (and thus tribunals), with the subsection setting a minimum of one week (as opposed to one day for unemployment benefit) and a maximum of 26 weeks (the same ceiling as for unemployment benefit and income support for unemployed people). "Week" here means any period of seven consecutive days (s.35(1), JSA Regs, reg.75(2)). Since JSA, unlike unemployment benefit, is a weekly benefit (s.1(3)), the specification of a one-week minimum is unsurprising, representing (generally) the smallest unit for benefit purposes. It might, therefore, be convenient if the periods of preclusion imposed were expressed in terms of weeks. But there is no requirement that the period of preclusion imposable must be so expressed; the Jobseekers Act and the JSA Regs make provision for part-weeks, and it is expressly recognised in JSA Regs, reg.152(1)(c) that a part-week may occur because of a period of non-payability under this section; and, indeed, the circumstances to be taken into account when fixing the appropriate period may point to a preclusion involving part-weeks.

Under the previous regimes of benefits for unemployed people, setting the period was a matter for the discretion of the statutory authorities guided statutorily only by the maximum limit imposable and otherwise by case law (almost entirely decisions of the Commissioners). As for JSA, subs.(4) enables the making of regulations specifying circumstances to be taken, or not to be taken, into account by the decision-maker (and hence the tribunal) in determining the preclusive period under subs.(3). JSA Regs, reg.70 provides that the decision-maker (and hence a tribunal) must take into account all the circumstances of the case. It further specifies the following particular circumstances to be taken into account, some of which reflect previous Commissioners' decisions on unemployment benefit (added in square brackets by the annotator):

(1) Where the employment would have lasted less than 26 weeks, the length of time that it was likely to have lasted must be taken into account [*R(U)5/54* held that where the employment was due to end after another three weeks anyway, it was right to limit the period of disqualification to three weeks].

(2) In a case of preclusion for loss of employment through misconduct, where the employer has indicated an intention to re-engage the claimant, the date when he is to be re-engaged is to be taken into account. [In *R(U)10/71* where misconduct had only resulted in suspension from work for four weeks (nonetheless a loss of employment) the disqualification period was limited to that of the suspension, thus adequately protecting the National Insurance Fund against an unjustified claim.]

(3) Where the claimant left voluntarily an employment of 16 hours per week or less, the rate of pay and hours of employment which he left must be taken into account.

(4) There must be taken into account in a voluntary leaving or neglect to avail case ("heads" (b) and (d) of subs. (6)), any mitigating circumstances of physical or mental stress connected with his employment.

Otherwise, the regulation rules nothing out or in. *Its core is that the decision-maker [and hence the tribunal] must take account of all the circumstances of the case.* That was also the central message of Commissioners' decisions on fixing the period of disqualification in unemployment benefit cases. These decisions stressed that the discretion was to be exercised judicially and sensibly, taking due account of all the circumstances, including those relevant to the anterior question of whether disqualification was required at all and the justice and merits of each case (*R(U)8/74(T)*), bearing in mind the purpose of disqualification; the protection of the National Insurance Fund against avoidable claims (*R(U)27/52*). In *CJSA/3875/2002*, Commissioner Turnbull, while accepting that a principal rationale of sanctions is the protection of the national insurance fund as stated in *R(U)8/74*, considered that the degree of blame attaching to the claimant's conduct can also be taken into account in fixing the period of sanction, thus enabling valid distinctions to be drawn between one case and another, between failure to apply for a vacancy through mistake or forgetfulness, on the one hand, and deliberate failure on the other (paras 19–21). Tribunals must indicate in their decisions that they have considered the matter of the appropriate period of preclusion (*R(U)3/79*). A tribunal's failure to indicate conscious exercise of discretion and to state the facts taken into account in exercising it is an error of law (*R(U)4/87*; *CSJSA/261/1987*). "Since the tribunal has to consider the whole matter afresh, it is clear that the length of the "disqualification" should be considered by the tribunal even although it is not raised by the appellant" (*CSJSA/261/1987*, para. 21). The tribunal must stay within the bounds of reasonableness. In *CJSA/2931/2003*, Commissioner Howell upheld

1.234

a tribunal decision disqualifying the claimant for 18 weeks as fully justified on the facts. It had thought suspect the claimant's credibility in claiming that he had telephoned and been told that the vacancy was filled whereas in fact it had remained open. The sanction imposed was well within those bounds in a case where a long-term claimant is found to have made no real effort to follow up a vacancy notified to him.

In the unemployment benefit cases, the focus in disqualification cases, both in terms of the issue of disqualification itself and the matter of the appropriate period, was on the time the claimant did the act relied on to ground disqualification (*e.g.* the course of conduct said to constitute misconduct, leaving employment voluntarily, refusing a suitable job). Not in isolation, of course; that act must often be set in the context of events leading up to it (*e.g.* the claimant having been warned about such conduct, the employment relationship in voluntary cases) and sometimes in the context of subsequent events which might, at the very least, throw light on the claimant's intentions or motives at the time of doing the act relied on to ground disqualification (see Deputy Commissioner Mesher's examples in *CU/89/1991*, paras 9, 10). There is nothing in the JSA regime to dictate a different approach; indeed, the particularised factors in JSA Regs, reg.70 look forward as well as back. It is further submitted that the factors found relevant and irrelevant by Commissioners in the context of unemployment benefit disqualifications should also be given due weight in fixing the appropriate period of preclusion in subs.(6) situations, bearing in mind the rationale of preclusion: to protect the National Insurance Fund against avoidable claims; to strengthen the sanction against voluntary unemployment; and to remind claimants that they are "jobseekers":

Relevant factors:

1.235   —in misconduct cases, the seriousness of the misconduct (*CU/90/1988*), how closely it is connected with work (*R(U)1/71*) and any mitigating circumstances (*R(U)13/53*);

—how close the claimant came to avoiding "disqualification" by establishing "just cause" (*R(U)20/64(T)*) or "good cause";

—the reasons for leaving employment (*R(U)8/74(T)*);

—in voluntary leaving cases, attempts to find other work before leaving (*R(U)8/74(T)*); *R(U)20/64(T)*; *R(U)4/70*) or to withdraw notice (*R(U) 27/59*) or that the claimant's departure served some public need or interest (*R(U)4/87*)

—that voluntarily leaving a job involves some cost to be borne by the claimant rather than the National Insurance Fund (*R(U)4/87*).

Irrelevant factors:

1.236   —a conflict of evidence (*R(U)2/72*) (see notes to subs.(6), [C] Conflicting Evidence, etc.);

—the claimant has already been punished through criminal sanctions (*R(U)27/52*) or, arguably by analogy, loss of employment (but see *CU/72/1993*).

The shorter, prescribed periods of disqualification under subs.(5) are not directly relevant since they refer to particular situations. Although the 2 or 4 week periods provided for in relation to that subsection are indicative of the response to the types of conduct set out there and thus give some indication of the view taken of situations which might be seen as slightly analogous to a failure to apply for a job vacancy, the duty of the decision-maker and the appeal tribunal as regards subs.(6) cases is to weigh this "misconduct" up in the scale of one to 26 weeks (*CSJSA/261/1998*, para.23).

(b) Commencement and termination of the period: If, on a claim for JSA, a s.19 question arises, the Secretary of State can determine the question there and then. But if, as must quite often be the case, he is unable for the time being to determine the question, he has the further option of determining the claim ("determination one") on the assumption that s.19 does not restrict payment of benefit, so that if the conditions of entitlement to JSA are met, JSA will be payable until the Secretary of State is able to determine the s.19 question in what is a supersession of "determination one" (SSA 1998 s.100, Decisions and Appeals Regulations 1999, regs 6(2)(f) and 7(8)). If the Secretary of State takes this option, then any period of preclusion under s.19 starts on the day the determination on supersession takes effect. That determination takes effect, in the usual class of case, from the day immediately following the end of the benefit week in which the determination on supersession was made (see Decisions and Appeals Regulations 1999, reg.7(8)(a)–see reg.7(8)(b) for the less common type of case). Otherwise, the JSA regime is statutorily silent on the point of commencement of the period of preclusion in subs.(6). The intention in immediate determination or reference to SSAT situations, appears to be to fall back on to the case law "rules" that regulated the matter in the unemployment benefit context (see further Bonner, Hooker and White, *Non Means Tested Benefits: The Legislation* (1996), p.146). The first such "rule" is that, usually, the period should begin from the day following the loss of employment, where subs.(6)(a) or (b) applies [misconduct or voluntary leaving], or the refusal, failure, neglect to avail etc, where subs.(6)(c) or (d) is involved (*R(U)11/59*; *CU19/48*; *CU155/50*). The second rule is that where someone has received JSA because the authorities were unaware of or failed to appreciate the circumstances, the period of preclusion should begin on the first day of the benefit week following the decision to preclude ("disqualify") (*CU155/50*; *R(U)35/53*). The third such "rule" in unemployment benefit was that, if the claimant had been held not entitled to benefit for a period following the termination of the employment, because he had received compensation (*e.g.* money in lieu of notice) on termination of that employment, the disqualification period (*e.g.* for misconduct) began at the end of the "ineligible period" (now the end of the period for which the claimant is treated as in remunerative work under JSA Regs, reg.52(3)). The final "rule" was that where someone as it were "serves his time" by not claiming benefit, knowing that he would be disqualified if he did, he was not required to serve the period again by disqualifying from the point of claim. Rather the period of disqualification began on the date he would have been disqualified had he claimed immediately after, for example, the loss of employment (*CU19/48*, para.6). This final rule is more problematical with respect to contribution-based JSA in so far as it would remove one part of the double penalty, intended by having days of preclusion erode the maximum period of 182 days' entitlement to contribution-based JSA in respect of a contribution record based on the same two tax/contribution years (see further notes to ss.2 and 5). On the other hand, of course, in such a situation the claimant has already suffered a period of no state benefits.

Of course, it remains to be seen what the actual approach of decision-maker will be. Perhaps it would have been simpler just to have the period of preclusion start on the first day of the benefit week after the decision to preclude because of a subs.(6) circumstance, just as it does in subs.(5) circumstances or those contemplated by Decisions and Appeals Regulations 1999, reg.7(8) with respect to supersession.

There is of course, the question: when does the period finish? The short answer is whenever the period of preclusion expires. But this raises the matter of supervening or interrupting events. It is submitted that, as with the old regime, any period of preclusion, once begun, continues for an unbroken period until its duly calculated end (the same rule as in unemployment benefit: see *R(U)24/56*). So where a claimant takes other employment, loses it and claims again during the period of preclusion, he will still be caught by the remaining days of the period even though the loss of this other employment would not itself warrant preclusion under subs.(6) (*cf. R(U) 13/64*).

Subs. (5)

1.238   Paragraph (a) operates with respect to a "jobseeker's direction", paras (b) and (c) with respect to "training schemes" and "employment programmes". Discussion is divided accordingly.

1.239   *(a) Preclusions in respect of a jobseeker's direction*: Payment of JSA must be precluded for the prescribed period (see subss.(1), (2)) where, without good cause, the claimant has refused or failed to carry out any jobseeker's direction, which direction was reasonable having regard to his circumstances. The provision has some affinities with the more convoluted disqualification in SSCBA 1992, s.28(1)(d) which had rather fallen into disuse. The White Paper suggests a higher profile for the new power; it contemplated that the widened power to issue directions would "enable advisers ['employment officers'] to direct jobseeker's to improve their employability through, for example, attending a course to improve jobseeking skills or motivation, or taking steps to present themselves acceptably to employers. This [jobseeker's direction] will be an important means of ensuring that jobseeker's are taking the right steps to get back to work" (para.4.18). Attendance at previously voluntary courses might thus be rendered compulsory (Wikeley, *Annotations*, 18–37).

A "jobseeker's direction" is a written direction given by an "employment officer" which is aimed at assisting the claimant to find employment and/or improving his prospects of being employed (subs.(10)(b)). An "employment officer" is an officer of the Secretary of State (a civil servant in the Department of Work and Pensions) or such other person designated as such for these purposes by order made by the Secretary of State (subs.(10)(a)).

There will inevitably be some overlap between the requirement that the direction be "reasonable, having regard to the claimant's circumstances" and the "good cause" exemption, so that "excusing" factors might be argued as constituting "good cause" for the refusal/failure or as rendering the direction "unreasonable". Although it is, strictly speaking, legally possible to do so, it will in practice be hard to argue successfully that a factor legislatively precluded from constituting "good cause" under provisions examined below, nonetheless renders the direction "unreasonable".

On "good cause", subs.(8) enables regulations to prescribe what is and what is not good cause for the purposes of this preclusive head, and also to prescribe matters to be taken into account in determining whether the claimant had good cause. The relevant regulation for purposes of this head of preclusion is JSA Regs.72. Subject to those Regulations, however, subs.(9) stipulates that one must disregard any matter relating to the remuneration level in the employment in question (in the context of a jobseeker's direction this, if it applies here at all, must mean the type of employment the direction aims to help him find).

1.240   *(b) Preclusions in respect of training schemes or employment programmes*: There are a number of "heads" dictating preclusion for the prescribed period (see subss.(1), (2)). They cover inappropriate behaviour by persons who have a place on a training scheme or employment programme and also those who, in a variety of ways, decline to go on one.

The term "employment programme" is defined in JSA Regs, reg.75(1)(a), and is often amended to reflect new initiatives, such as Gateway to Work or employment zone programmes. A "training scheme" is defined in JSA Regs, reg.75(1)(b) and amendments to it reflect changes in the names of the bodies responsible for arranging and delivering training.

Subsection (5)(b) covers (i) a claimant's neglect to avail himself of a reasonable opportunity of a place on a training scheme or employment programme; or (ii) after an employment officer has notified him of a vacant place on such a scheme or programme, his failure to apply for such a place or to accept it when offered to him; or (iii) his giving up his place; or (iv) his failure to attend having been given a place. In all such cases, there is a saving for "good cause".

As regards "good cause" in subs.(5) (6) (b), JSA Regs, reg.73, made pursuant to subs.(8), merely lists a number of circumstances which, if and to the extent that the act or omission is attributable to them, will constitute good cause for an act or omission relevant to para.(b). The regulation does not rule out any particular circumstance from ranking as good cause; it lists the circumstances which do so rank "without prejudice to any other circumstances in which a person may be regarded as having good cause for any act or omission" for para.(b) purposes. Nor does it list factors relevant to deciding the good cause question, again leaving that matter at large and at the discretion of the Secretary of State and/or Appeals tribunal. **1.241**

Furthermore, where the act or omission relates to an employment programme, certain full-time students (see JSA Regs, reg.17A(2)) undertaking a qualifying course will have good cause for the act or omission where they were, or would have been, required to attend the programme at a time which would have precluded attendance at the qualifying course (JSA Regs, reg.75(2B)(a)). Essentially a "qualifying course" is an employment-related course of further or higher education, or a standard above that, lasting no more than 12 months (see JSA Regs, reg.17A(7), (8)). As regards sub-paras (i) and (ii) of s.19(5)(b) (respectively giving up a place on, or failing to attend, a training scheme, in this case, the qualifying course), such persons will have good cause where the giving up or failing to attend the qualifying course came within the first four weeks of the period of study, or was due to lack of ability, or to the course being unsuitable for the person in vocationally relevant respects (JSA Regs, reg.75(2B)(b), (4)).

Subsection (5)(c) covers the claimant who through his misconduct has lost his place on a training scheme or employment programme. There is, naturally, no saving for "good cause". "Misconduct" is not defined in the legislation, but in principle it ought to bear, with appropriate adaptation for context, the same meaning as under the unemployment benefit scheme disqualification for losing employment through misconduct, carried over into JSA by subs.(6)(a) (an approach endorsed in *CJSA/3790/2001*). The conduct must, in short, be blameworthy, reprehensible and wrong, having regard to appropriate standards in the relevant set of relationships in the training scheme or the employment programme. See further the annotations to subs.(6)(a), below (section [B]).

Subs.(6)

[A] INTRODUCTION

If the facts of the case meet the criteria in one of the heads in the subsection, some period of preclusion of payment must be imposed—subs.(1) reads "shall not be payable". The discretion vested in the statutory authorities (Secretary of State, Appeal tribunal, Commissioner) goes to what should be the period of preclusion once one of the heads dictating preclusion is made out in the case at hand: minimum one week, maximum 26 weeks (see further notes to subs.(3)). **1.242**

These heads replicate those of the "voluntary unemployment" disqualification under the unemployment benefit regime (see SSCBA 1992, s.28(1)(a)–(c)), and the approach taken in this note is that interpretations adopted by courts and commissioners there are authoritative also for JSA, unless some specific statutory provision with respect to JSA dictates otherwise or some marked difference between the nature of the benefits suggests that a particular principle is inappropriate to carry over into the JSA scheme. In *CJSA/3304/1999*, Commissioner Levenson considered the case of someone who had left employment A for unspecified reasons, then found employment with employer B, from which he was dismissed, and only then claimed jobseeker's allowance. The tribunal allowed the claimant's appeal against preclusion of payment founded on his having voluntarily left employment A without just cause.

Commissioner Levenson upheld the tribunal. In his opinion, a preclusion of payment can only be made under s.19(3) and (6) where a claim for benefit has been made and only "in respect of the employment immediately preceding the claim" (para.16). Insofar as *R(U)13/64* might be thought to say otherwise, Commissioner Levenson, drawing support from Commissioner Goodman in para.9 in *CU/64/1994*, declined to follow it. Citing Bonner, Hooker and White, *Non Means Tested Benefits:The Legislation* (1999) (the precursor of this part of Vol. II), he noted that preclusion of payment in jobseeker's allowance was significantly different from disqualification under the unemployment benefit regime with which *R(U)13/64* dealt: firstly the period of preclusion ate into and eroded the maximum period of entitlement to contribution-based JSA; and secondly, a claimant who was caught could only look to hardship payments rather than, as before, have an entitlement to reduced rate social assistance (income support). Accordingly, decisions on the unemployment regime of disqualification are not necessarily binding in what otherwise is the analogous context of s.19 preclusion (para.16).

In the same case the facts could meet the criteria in more than one of the heads (see, *e.g. R(U)2/54*). The Secretary of State can rely for the first time at the Appeals tribunal on a different head to that initially relied on or to that set out in the appeal papers. Indeed, the tribunal can reject a case on the head relied on by the Secretary of State but impose preclusion on another head (*R(U)2/71*), although very special precautions are necessary. The chairman should ensure that any change in contention or shift of ground to be considered by the tribunal is clearly explained to the claimant and that the written records show that this has been done (*R(U)2/71*, para.7; *CU/77/1993*).

This annotation examines first each of the grounds which dictate preclusion of payment (section [B]) and concludes with a note on some problems of evidence, resolving matters according to the onus of proof and recording such decisions (section [C]).

[B] GROUNDS OF PRECLUSION

1.243   *(1) "Lost his employment . . . through misconduct" (subs.(6)(a))*: "Lost his employment": this concept is not confined to dismissal, but will also embrace persons claiming benefit while suspended from work for misconduct (*R(U)10/71*) and the person who accepts the chance to resign rather than be dismissed as a result of his misconduct (*R(U)2/76*, where the claimant used a company car without permission to give driving lessons and was found at home in the bath when he should have been out selling). In *CU/056/1989*, Commissioner Heggs, dealing with a situation in which the claimant had been allowed to resign rather than be dismissed, noted:

> "In Decision *R(U)17/64* it was held that 'loss of employment' is a more comprehensive phrase than 'leaving voluntarily' because loss of employment may result either from voluntarily leaving or from dismissal. In considering whether employment has been lost through misconduct, therefore, it is not always necessary to determine categorically whether the claimant left voluntarily or was dismissed. In the present case the tribunal, in my view, correctly concluded that the claimant lost his employment through misconduct" (para.7).

The claimant had been allowed to resign rather than be dismissed after he had been caught eating company products (pies) at his workplace in violation of a general prohibition on eating company products in the production area. He had previously violated this rule and been warned about his conduct. He had also received a final written warning that future misconduct would result in his summary dismissal. Unfortunately, the SSAT decision was erroneous in law because (a) the decision contained no explanation of why the claimant's admitted conduct constituted misconduct and (b) it failed to record the reasons for imposing the maximum period of disqualification (see *R(U)4/87*, noted in the annotation to subs. (3)).

"As an employed earner": see s.35(1); JSA Regs, reg.3; SSCBA 1992, s.2(1)(a). The disqualification does not cover misconduct in self-employment.

"Through misconduct": the loss of employment must be brought about because of the claimant's misconduct. The change from "his misconduct" in SSCBA 1992, s.28(1)(a) to merely "misconduct" in subs.(6)(a) of this section, cannot, it is submitted, be read so as to justify penalising a claimant who lost his job through someone else's misconduct. Any such reading would be absurd and unjust and contrary to the aim of penalising "voluntary unemployment".

Authorities directly in point because they deal with the situation where there were several reasons for the loss of employment state that misconduct need not be the sole cause of the loss of employment so long as it is a contributory cause, a necessary element in bringing about the loss *(R(U)1/57; R(U)14/57; CU/34/92)*. Suggestions that it must be the main cause in order to ground disqualification read too much into *R(U)20/59*, where the Commissioner's statement that misconduct (trouble with the police) was there the main cause seems to be no more than a finding of fact in that particular case in which the multiple cause point was not really an issue. A Northern Ireland authority *(R8/60(UB))* requiring that misconduct be the decisive cause cannot stand against British authorities directly in point, being of persuasive authority only.

The meaning and scope of misconduct. "Misconduct" is not statutorily defined. **1.244** Commissioners' decisions on unemployment benefit offer such definition as there is. The term has to be interpreted in a common-sense manner and applied with due regard to the circumstances of each case *(R(U)24/56; R(U)8/57, para.6)*. It is narrower than unsatisfactory conduct *(124/51(UB))*. Misconduct is "conduct which is causally but not necessarily directly connected with the employment, and having regard to the relationship of employer and employee and the rights and duties of both, can fairly be described as blameworthy, reprehensible and wrong". *(R(U)2/77,* para.15). The Commissioner in *R(U)2/77* (para.6) saw nothing wrong with a tribunal's description of it as an indictment of the claimant's character as an employee. A useful test, particularly where the conduct in question occurred away from work, would be: was the claimant's blameworthy, reprehensible or wrong conduct such as would cause a reasonable employer to dispense with his services on the ground that, having regard to this conduct he was not a fit person to hold that appointment *(R(U)7/57,* para.6).

The act or omission alleged to constitute misconduct need not have been deliberate or intentional, although such might often be the case. Misconduct can consist in carelessness or negligence, but there it is necessary to discriminate between that type and degree of carelessness which may have to be put up with in human affairs, and the more deliberate or serious type of carelessness which justifies withholding benefit because the claimant has lost his employment through his own avoidable fault. In *R(U)8/57* the claimant, a manager of a branch pharmacy, was dismissed for "negligence in the discharge of responsible duties" when a number of cash shortages were discovered over a period of weeks. Serious carelessness could legitimately be inferred and his disqualification was upheld, notwithstanding his acquittal on a charge of embezzlement arising out of the same situation. It is quite clear that a claimant who acts on a genuine misunderstanding cannot properly be said to be guilty of misconduct; the behaviour cannot there be described as "blameworthy, reprehensible and wrong" *(CU/122/92,* para.6, citing *R(U)14/56)*.

This head of disqualification is sometimes referred to as "industrial misconduct", a term denoting that the misconduct must be causally connected with the employment whose loss is under consideration, rather than requiring its connection with a particular type of employment. Misconduct which occurred before the claimant took up the employment, the loss of which is under consideration but which caused its loss, cannot disqualify him: see *R(U)26/56*, where an accountant was dismissed when his employers learned of a conviction for fraud which occurred before he commenced employment with them. In *R(U)26/56, both* the conduct and its consequences (the criminal conviction) occurred before the employment was taken up. *R(U)1/58*, however, also applies the non-preclusion principle where the conduct occurred before the taking-up of the employment, but the consequences came after its commencement. There a civil engineer and buyer was awaiting trial for certain acts committed before he entered the employment. By agreement with his employer he ceased work pending the result of the trial. On conviction he simply did not return to the employment. Nor, however, was he pressed to do so. The Commissioner held that "acts or omissions occurring before the commencement of the employment do not constitute 'misconduct'" (para.4), citing *R(U)26/56*, so the only matter remaining was the issue of voluntary leaving without just cause. The leaving was not voluntary: "he merely anticipated a decision by his employers to dispense with his services; he was not altogether a free agent when deciding or agreeing not to attend further at his place of business" (paras 5, 6). So, to refer to a case of interest notified to the authors, an SSAT was correct in holding that a van driver, dismissed after conviction of a drink-driving offence and disqualification from driving, could not be disqualified from benefit because the conduct constituting the offence had taken place before he took up the employment in question, even though the conviction came after he had done so.

1.245   Subject to that, the causal connection with the employment need not be direct (*R(U)2/77*, para.15). The conduct need not have taken place at work or in working hours, though cases where it did would be common. In *R(U)1/71* the Commissioner upheld the disqualification of a local authority parks' gardener dismissed for an act of gross indecency with another man, away from work and out of working hours. The Commissioner said,

> "If a person loses his employment by reason of misconduct which has a sufficient connection with the employment it may not matter that it was committed outside the employment. Common examples are those of the man employed as a motor vehicle driver who loses his licence as a result of his driving outside his employment and is disqualified from driving: there is an obvious link between the misconduct and the work. [See, *e.g. R(U)7/57* and *R(U)24/64*.] Similarly a person who commits offences of dishonesty outside his work may be disqualified, since most employers regard a thief as unsuitable to have about their premises. [See, *e.g. R(U)10/53*.]" (Case references added by annotator.)

Sexual offences outside the employment were said to present considerable difficulty but can rank as misconduct in *special circumstances* where they can be said to have something to do with the employment:

> "*The commercial traveller case [CU38/51]* is a good instance. The employers may well have thought that there was a real danger that when visiting houses trying to sell ribbons, probably to women who might often be alone in the house, the claimant might attempt some sort of liberties."

The Commissioner further opined that:

> "there are some employments where the employer has a legitimate interest in the conduct of employees even outside the employment. One example may be that of a person who holds a special position, *e.g.* a schoolteacher. Another may be that of a government department who rightly feel that their employees should maintain a high standard of conduct at all times."

In *R(U)1/71* itself, even though there was no evidence of direct contact with the public in the claimant's job, the Commissioner, in a case he thought close to the line, was not prepared to overturn the tribunal's view that the claimant had lost his employment through misconduct.

1.246   *Examples of misconduct.* Apart from those already noted, instances have been: persistent absenteeism without permission (*R(U)22/52, R(U)8/61*); unauthorised absence through ill health and/or domestic circumstances when coupled with failure to notify the employer (*R(U)23/58*; *R(U)11/59*); repeated unauthorised absence to seek work more suited to the claimant's state of health in circumstances in which the claimant gave the employer no reasons for his absences and he had received previous warning about his conduct (*R(U)8/61*); overstaying a holiday without permission (*R(U)2/74*; *R(U)11/59*). Theft from fellow workers at a works' social function has been held to be misconduct (*R(U)10/53*). So has offensive behaviour to fellow employees, consisting of obscene language and an element of what would now be termed sexual harassment (suggestive remarks to and, in their presence, about, female colleagues) (*R(U)12/56*). By analogy, one would today expect racial abuse and discrimination to be capable of constituting misconduct. Recklessly or knowingly making false allegations about superiors or colleagues can be misconduct, and where a false criminal charge is so laid it would plainly be misconduct (*R(U)24/55*, para.13), but it was not enough to prove misconduct to show that the employee's charge of assault by his supervisor had been dismissed in the magistrates' court (*ibid.*). Refusal to obey a reasonable instruction *in line with the claimant's contract of employment* (*e.g.* a refusal to work overtime) has been held to be misconduct (*R(U)38/58*), even where obeying the instruction would conflict with trade union policies (*R(U)41/53*). However, disobedience of such an order due to a genuine misunderstanding has been held not to constitute misconduct (*R(U)14/56*), and not every breach of every trivial rule would suffice (*R(U)24/56*). And, of course, the claimant can legitimately refuse to obey instructions not contractually stipulated for without its constituting misconduct (*R(U)9/59*; *R9/60(UB)*). Where an employee was dismissed for refusing to join a trade union as part of a closed-shop arrangement negotiated after his employment commenced, he did not lose his job through misconduct (*R(U)2/77*).

Establishing misconduct, matters of proof and the duties of the statutory authorities **1.247**
(decision-makers, appeal tribunals and commissioners). The Secretary of State (decision-maker) bears the onus of proof of establishing misconduct, and it must be clearly proved by the best available evidence. As a general rule, of course, hearsay evidence can be accepted by the statutory authorities, but particularly where a claimant is charged with misconduct and he disputes the facts which are alleged to constitute it, "it is desirable that the most direct evidence of those facts should be adduced, so that the allegations may be properly tested" (*R(U)2/60*, para.7). Given that the statutory authorities apparently have no powers to force employers to supply information or to compel the attendance of witnesses, it may be difficult to get to the truth of the matter. In some cases the statutory authorities may be able to have regard to what has happened in other legal or disciplinary proceedings arising out of the same situation now said to show misconduct. Where such proceedings are pending one option in difficult cases where the available evidence about the relevant conduct conflicts would be to postpone a decision on the "disqualification" issue until the outcome of such proceedings as are pending is known. There is no obligation to await their outcome (*R(U)10/54*), and one must always keep in view the relationship between those proceedings and the tasks of the statutory authorities. Another option would be to try to resolve the matter by weighing and comparing the evidence available (*e.g.* does the tribunal believe the direct evidence given by the claimant it has seen and questioned and how does that compare with the indirect and/or hearsay evidence in any written material from the employer or others which is relied on by the decision-maker) and ultimately, where doubts persist, allow the matter to be settled by application of the rules on onus of proof (see further, below section [C] of this annotation). It would presumably be open to the decision-maker to revise the tribunal's decision if new material facts came to light in the course of those other proceedings. The other legal proceedings could be criminal proceedings, court proceedings for breach of contract, or complaints of unfair dismissal heard in industrial tribunals. Disciplinary proceedings may take place before a much wider variety of bodies. An important issue is what is the relationship to the decision-making task of the statutory authorities, of decisions given by these bodies on a matter relevant to the claimant's case?

1.248   While in varying degrees decisions given by such bodies certainly can constitute relevant evidence for the statutory authorities, they are not, legally speaking, conclusive of the outcome before the statutory authorities, who are duty bound to make up their own minds as to what constitutes misconduct grounding disqualification from benefit, irrespective of the conclusions reached by employers, the courts or disciplinary bodies (*R(U)10/54*, para.6: *R(U)2/74*, para.15). The other proceedings do not deal with the exact issue dealt with by the statutory authorities. For example, a motoring conviction as a private motorist which did not attract a ban from driving would not necessarily constitute misconduct warranting the disqualification of a lorry-driver who had been sacked by his employer as a result. It would depend on the nature of the conduct constituting the offence: the claimant might be able to show that notwithstanding the conviction his conduct was not "blameworthy" (*R(U)22/64*, para.6). It must be remembered too that the standard of proof of guilt in criminal cases is proof beyond reasonable doubt, a higher standard than that applicable here—proof on the balance of probabilities. So an acquittal on a criminal charge arising out of the conduct now said to constitute misconduct does not necessarily preclude a finding of misconduct. Thus in *R(U)8/57*, where the manager of the branch pharmacy was acquitted of embezzlement in relation to the cash shortages, he nonetheless lost his employment through misconduct since his inadequate supervision of staff amounted to serious carelessness. Similarly, there are important differences between proceedings before appeals tribunals and the Commissioner on the one hand, and unfair dismissal proceedings in the industrial tribunal on the other. In unfair dismissal, while the employee's conduct is relevant, the main issue before the industrial tribunal concerns the employer's behaviour in consequence. Before the statutory authorities, in contrast, the emphasis is more on the employee's conduct, although that of the employer is also relevant. The issue of loss of employment through misconduct raises issues of what is fair between claimant and the other contributors to the insurance fund and not what is fair as between employer and employee. Commissioners have stressed that social security tribunals when dealing with misconduct cases should not express their decisions in such terms as fair or unfair dismissal or proper or improper dismissal. The onus of proof in industrial tribunal proceedings may not be the same on issues relevant to the statutory authorities' task as they are in proceedings before those authorities. Equally, while the issue before the statutory authorities is one of substance, the industrial tribunal can find a dismissal unfair on procedural grounds. Hence, while the decision of the industrial tribunal is conclusive of the matters it had to decide, it does not conclude anything in proceedings before the statutory authorities, and its findings of fact are not binding on them, even where some of the facts before the industrial tribunals are identical with facts relevant to the proceedings before those authorities:

> "There will, therefore, be cases where a claimant succeeds before an industrial tribunal on the unfair dismissal question, but the relevant adjudicating authority has decided that disqualification must be imposed by reason of misconduct, and *vice versa*" (*per* Commissioner Rice in *CU/90/1988*, para.4).

1.249   The findings of fact in the industrial tribunal are, however, cogent evidence on which those authorities can act (*CU/17/1993*), since it may well be that with both employer and employee present and examined the industrial tribunal, a judicial authority presided over by a lawyer, reaching its deliberate findings of fact after due inquiry, is better placed than the statutory authorities to fully investigate the facts of the matter. But the statutory authorities are not bound to decide the facts in the same way as the industrial tribunal (*R(U)2/74*, paras 14 and 15 and see generally on the relationship between the two sets of proceedings: *R(U)4/78* and *R(U)3/79*). For similar reasons on ability to obtain and to probe evidence, decisions of the criminal courts on matters relevant to the case before the statutory authorities are entitled to great respect. Thus where it is clear that a criminal court has decided the identical issue which the claimant needs to reopen before the judicial authorities (social security tribunal or Commissioner) if he is to succeed in his appeal, the decision of that court is likely *in practice* to be dispositive of the issue before those authorities. This is almost certainly so if one follows the view of the Commissioner in *R(U)24/55* that in such a situation, save in exceptional cases, the statutory authorities must treat a conviction by a criminal court as conclusive proof that the act or omission which constitutes the offence was done or made. It is also likely to be so if one prefers to *R(U)24/55* the more recent view of a Commissioner in a sickness benefit case dealing with a similar issue (*R(S)2/80*). It has always been for the person relying on it to prove the fact of a conviction, and it is preferably done through official certification (*R(U)24/64*). In *R(S)2/80* it was said that the initial onus was on the adjudication officer [now Secretary of State/decision-maker] to show that the conviction directly related to points at issue in the appeal, and if that were done the onus passed to the claimant to show on the balance of probabilities that he was nevertheless entitled to the benefit; that is, by analogy in this context, that he did not lose his job through misconduct (*e.g.* by showing that the true facts were not as found by the court or, if they were, that they do not constitute misconduct).

Where the decisions of disciplinary bodies (which may well examine a wide range of witnesses) are concerned, it appears that although never binding on the statutory authorities, they are entitled to an increasing degree of respect the more their proceedings approximate to proceedings in a court of law. Thus a finding by a chief constable after police disciplinary proceedings was cogent evidence that the claimant had committed particular acts (*R(U)10/63*), but a decision by a hospital management committee, the precise reasons for which were not disclosed to the Commissioner, was not so regarded (*R(U)7/61*). Whether one is concerned with decisions of the courts, of industrial tribunals or disciplinary proceedings it is submitted that crucial questions for the statutory authorities will be: what was the decision; by what sort of body, how, by what process, and on what sort(s) of evidence was the decision made; and how closely does the matter involved in that decision relate to that before those authorities?

(2) "Has voluntarily left such employment without just cause" (subs. (6) (b)): Note at the **1.250** outset that s.20(3) and JSA Regs, reg.74 made under it protect from disqualification under this head or under that in subs.(6)(d) certain persons who leave employed earner's employment voluntarily and without just cause at any time within the "trial period" (that is, between the beginning of the fifth week and the end of the twelfth week of the employment in question, with some provision to ignore certain weeks). The approach to such cases must be first to consider, in the light of the case law principles elaborated below, whether the claimant voluntarily left without just cause and, if he did so, then to consider whether s.20(3) and JSA Regs, reg.74 protect him from preclusion of payment of JSA. In *CJSA/3304/1999*, Commissioner Levenson considered the case of someone who had left employment A for unspecified reasons, then found employment with employer B, from which he was dismissed, and only then claimed jobseeker's allowance. The tribunal allowed the claimant's appeal against preclusion of payment founded on his having voluntarily left employment A without just cause. Commissioner Levenson upheld the tribunal. A preclusion of payment can only be made under s.19(3) and (6) where a claim for benefit has been made and only "in respect of the employment immediately preceding the claim" (para.16). Insofar as *R(U)13/64* might be thought to say otherwise, Commissioner Levenson, drawing support from Commissioner Goodman in para.9 in *CU/64/1994*, declined to follow it, for reasons noted in the introduction to the commentary on subs.(6), above.

"Such employment". The restriction ("such" referring back to para.(a)) to employed earners' employment means that leaving self-employment cannot ground disqualification under this head.

(a) Onus of proof. Those who assert that the claimant left his employment volun- **1.251** tarily must prove it. Once done the onus passes to the claimant to prove that he had

just cause for so leaving. In both cases the onus is discharged on the balance of probabilities (*R(U)20/64(T)*). See further, below, section [C] of this annotation.

1.252   *(b) "Has voluntarily left"*. The commonest case of voluntarily leaving will be when the claimant of his own accord handed in his notice or otherwise terminated his contract of employment. Indeed, in many cases there will be no dispute about this aspect of the case; the real issue will be that of just cause. But voluntarily leaving also embraces other means by which employment was lost. So the actors who threatened to leave unless certain demands were met and were then treated by their employers as having given notice left voluntarily (*R(U)33/51*). It is still voluntarily leaving where the employment ends because the employer refuses to accept the claimant's withdrawal of notice (*R(U)27/59*). It can also embrace in limited instances cases where the loss of employment took the form of a dismissal brought about by conduct of the claimant which would inevitably lead to termination of the employment (*R(U)16/52; R(U)2/54, R(U)9/59, R(U)7/74*), but such situations must be looked at with caution and restraint (*R(U)2/77*). Thus, in *R(U)6/52* the claimant's appointment was conditional on her completing a satisfactory medical. She refused to undergo X-ray examination and was given notice. The commissioner stated as a general rule of unemployment insurance law that if a person deliberately and knowingly acts in a way that makes it necessary for his employer to dismiss him, he may be regarded as having left his employment voluntarily. But another commissioner has since made clear in *R(U)7/74* that "this would normally require a finding that the employee had acted, or was threatening to act, in a manner involving a deliberate repudiation of his contract of employment". So in that case an employee whose written terms of employment made no reference to a requirement to work overtime, did not leave voluntarily when he was dismissed for refusing to work overtime (*cf. R(U)9/59*). Similarly, dismissal of an existing employee for refusal to join a trade union when a closed shop agreement was negotiated was not voluntary leaving (*R(U)2/77*). Nor was dismissal for refusing for good reason to pay a trade union subscription (*R(U)4/51*). Leaving was not voluntary where the claimant who departed had no effective choice but to quit, *e.g.* because dismissal appeared inevitable (*R(U)1/58: cf. R(U)2/76* noted further, below, section [C] of the annotation). In *R(U)1/96*, Commissioner Goodman considered the case of a female nursery assistant who gave her employer four weeks' notice, was prepared to work out those weeks, but whose employer, after an unsuccessful attempt to persuade her to stay on, told her to leave after two days. The commissioner considered and applied *CU/155/50* and *R(U)2/54* so as to reject the argument that the claimant had not left voluntarily but had been dismissed (and could therefore only be disqualified if misconduct could be proved). He regarded *British Midland Airways v Lewis* [1978] I.C.R. 782 (a decision of the Employment Appeal Tribunal in the context of dismissal under labour legislation) as not laying down "any categorical proposition of law" but as merely being a decision on the facts of that case, and continued:

> "In my view the ruling in *CU/155/50* and *R(U)2/54* that there is a voluntary leaving applies equally, whether it is a case of an employer not allowing an employee to work out his or her notice or whether it is a case of actual notice to leave given first by the employee, followed by a notice of termination given during the currency of the employee's notice by the employer. In the latter case, once the employee has given in his notice to leave it is a unilateral termination of the employment contract and cannot be withdrawn without the consent of the employer (*Riordan v War Office* [1959] 1 W.L.R. 1046). It follows that in the present case, when the claimant gave her four weeks notice in on Wednesday December 9, 1992 she had herself terminated the employment and thereby left it voluntarily. Even if what the employer did on Friday December 11, 1992 can be construed as giving in a counter-notice requiring her to leave on that day and not to work out her four weeks notice, that does not, in my view, alter the fact that the effective termination of the employment was a voluntary leaving by the claimant" (para.12).

Taking early retirement can constitute voluntarily leaving (*R(U)26/51, R(U)20/64,* **1.253**
R(U)4/70, R(U)1/81). Even where a schoolteacher retired three years early in
response to the generalised encouragement to take early retirement offered to teachers in his position by his local education authority, which further certified that his
retirement was in the interests of the efficient discharge of the education authority's
functions, it was still voluntarily leaving (*Crewe v Social Security Commissioner* [1982]
2 All E.R. 745, CA, published as an Appendix to *R(U)3/81).* However, in *R(U)1/83*
the commissioner distinguished *Crewe* and held that a civil servant who acceded to
his employer's specific request that *he* retire early should not be regarded as having
left his employment voluntarily. Since these cases were decided, subs.(7) has been
added to the section, enabling regulations to be made treating someone who might
otherwise be regarded as having left his employment voluntarily as not having left
voluntarily. Whether this in effect exempts from preclusion under this head a
claimant on the *Crewe* side of the line depends on whether in the circumstances of
his particular case, including the nature and terms of his early retirement scheme,
he can bring himself within the terms of the protection for voluntary redundancy set
out in JSA Regs, reg.71, a matter explored below in the annotations to subs.(7) and
to reg.71. For early retirement cases not saved by that regulation and subsection, the
fine distinction between the *Crewe* type of case and those of the type considered in
R(U)1/83 may still be important. In *CSU/22/94,* Commissioner Mitchell applied
R(U)1/83 in favour of a claimant (a principal teacher) who had been pressured by
his employers to accept an early retirement package, in a context in which his only
alternative was to accept a lower status position (albeit one without loss of income)
(being placed on a long-term supply teacher basis). That alternative was one which
"a teacher of the claimant's experience and standing could not reasonably be
expected to accept" (para.5). The decision thus stresses the need for tribunals carefully to consider whether the claimant can be said to have left voluntarily before
moving on to the "without just cause" aspect.

In *CU/70/94,* Commissioner Rice makes it clear that one cannot base a finding of
voluntary leaving without just cause on the notion that the claimant who left, not
considering herself up to the job for medical reasons, ought to have found out more
about, or to have known more about, the demands of the job before she accepted it.

(c) "Without just cause". There is no definition of "just cause" in the Act. Nor, **1.254**
despite the power given by subs.(8), is there any in the regulations (compare "good
cause"). Subsection (9) stipulates that, subject to any regulations made under
subs.(8), any matter relating to the level of remuneration in the employment in question in the case, must be disregarded in determining whether the claimant does or
does not have "just cause". Otherwise, court and commissioners' decisions on
unemployment benefit offer such interpretation as there is, and courts and commissioners have avoided laying down hard and fast rules on it for all circumstances.

"Just cause" involves balancing the interests of the claimant with those of the community of fellow contributors to the National Insurance Fund. It is not a matter of
what is in the best interests of the claimant, or of what is just as between employee
and employer, or of what is in the public interest generally. To establish that he did
not leave without just cause (that phraseology giving the proper emphasis) the
claimant must show that in leaving he acted reasonably in circumstances that make
it just that the burden of his unemployment should be cast on the National Insurance
Fund (*Crewe v Social Security Commissioner* [1982] 2 All E.R. 745, *per* Slade L.J. at
752; *per* Donaldson L.J. at 750–751, explaining *R(U)20/64(T),* para.8; *per* Lord
Denning M.R. at 749). Was what he did right and reasonable in the context of the
risk of unemployment? Was his voluntary leaving such as to create an unreasonable
risk of unemployment, bearing in mind that there may be circumstances that leave
a person no reasonable alternative but to leave his employment (*per* Donaldson L.J.
at 750)? Establishing just cause may well be a heavier burden than showing "good
cause" (*per* Slade L.J. at 751). In *R(U)4/87,* Commissioner Monroe stated that "the
analogy with insurance seems now the paramount criterion of just cause" (para.8).
His examination of decisions on the matter led him "to think that in general it is only

where circumstances are such that a person has virtually no alternative to leaving voluntarily that he will be found to have had just cause for doing so, rather as a person who throws his baggage overboard to make room in the lifeboat can claim on his baggage insurance" (para.9).

Whether the claimant succeeds in discharging the burden of showing just cause depends essentially on all the circumstances of his case, including the reasons for leaving and such matters as whether he had another job to go to, whether before he left he had made reasonable inquiries about other work or its prospects, or whether there were in his case good prospects of finding other work. Such elements should not be considered in water-tight compartments (*R(U)20/64(T)*), para.9). His previous claims record is not directly relevant (*ibid.*, para.18). In R(U)/4/87 Commissioner Monroe, following para.10 of R(U)*3/81* (approved in *Crewe*), ruled as remote from and irrelevant to the just cause issue long-term considerations prayed in aid by the claimant who had "urged that his leaving had in the long run actually benefited the national insurance fund, in that he had made available a vacancy for someone who would otherwise have continued unemployed, and that he was now earning more so that he was paying higher contributions" (para.10). Such factors had nothing to do with the issue of being forced to leave (*ibid.*). In CU/048/90, Commissioner Sanders considered the appeal of a claimant who had, as a result of his employer's attitude, become dissatisfied with his employment and had sought alternative employment by circulating his curriculum vitae to 30 companies. During interviews with Barclays Bank he was given the impression that his application for a particular post would be successful, and he resigned from his employment. In the event he was not offered the other post. Commissioner Sanders considered the correct approach to "just cause" to be that set out in R(U)4/87 (para.9). He thought that the "circumstances have to be very demanding before a claimant can establish just cause for leaving" (para.3). It seemed to the commissioner "that in the circumstances of the case the claimant had reason to leave because he thought he was not progressing in his career" but took the view "that the circumstances were not so pressing as to justify his leaving, from an unemployment benefit point of view, before he had secured the job with Barclays Bank even though he had been led to believe that his application for that job would be successful" (*ibid.*). He agreed with the SSAT that the claimant did not have just cause for leaving voluntarily and had to be disqualified, but found their decision erroneous in law in failing to explain why they had imposed a period of 13 weeks.

1.255   In some cases, probably rare in practice, an actual promise of immediate suitable new employment (which then falls through after the employment was left or the start of which is delayed) may afford just cause in the absence of other justificatory circumstances (*R(U)20/64(T)*, para.17; *Crewe, per* Donaldson L.J. at 750). There is no rule of law saying that just cause cannot be established where the claimant leaves without another job to go to. Indeed, in *R(U)20/64(T)* a tribunal of commissioners suggested that there could be circumstances in the claimant's personal or domestic life which become so pressing that they justify him leaving employment "without regard to the question of other employment" (para.12) and they cited as illustrations *R(U)14/52, R(U)19/52* and *R(U)31/59*, all noted below. Equally, it was clearly established that some feature of the claimant's existing employment may justify him in leaving it immediately without any regard to the question of other employment (para.11) and here the commissioners quoted as instances *CU248/49, R(U)15/53, R(U)38/53* and *R(U)18/57*, considered below. But there must be some urgency in the matter and, as regards the latter class of case, the circumstances must be so pressing that it cannot be reasonable to expect the claimant to take such steps as are open to him to resolve before leaving the grievance connected with work through the proper channels of existing grievance procedures. *CU106/1987* makes it clear that a tribunal cannot merely rely on the Secretary of State's (decision-maker's) suggestion that there would be such a grievance procedure in the circumstances of the claimant's employment. It was wrong in law to take account of a suggested grievance procedure to reject the claimant's appeal without having proper findings of fact as to the existence of such a grievance procedure. One would equally have thought that a tribunal should also consider whether any procedure found to exist could cover the claimant's complaint and whether it was reasonable in the circumstances to expect the claimant to have resort to it. A simple desire to change jobs is not usually enough to warrant putting the burden of one's unemployment on the Fund. Nor does moving house without more constitute just cause; it depends on the reasons for the move *(R(U)20/64(T)*, para.15). Rather than approaching the just cause issue from the angle of considering it necessary for the claimant to be assured of suitable alternative employment, unless there were circumstances justifying him in leaving without it (the approach in *R(U)14/52*), the commissioners in *R(U)20/64(T)* preferred a different perspective. They preferred to look (1) to whether the reasons for leaving themselves amounted to just cause (*i.e.* leaving aside the matter of alternative employment or its prospects), and (2) where the reasons did not of themselves establish just cause to then consider whether the

"promises or prospects of other employment may be effective as an *additional* factor which may help the claimant establish just cause. For example, where a man *almost* establishes just cause [in relation to, *e.g.* pressing personal or domestic circum-stances] the fact that he has a promise or prospects of other employment may serve to tip the scale in his favour, or alternatively may provide grounds for reducing the period of disqualification. In considering these matters of course the strength of his chances of employment and the gap, if any, likely to occur between the two employ-ments must be taken into account" (para.17).

The Commissioners stated: 1.256

"that it is impossible to lay down any period of time representing a gap between employments, or any degree of probability of fresh employment which will give an automatic answer to the question whether the claimant has shown just cause for leaving."

They drew

"a distinction between on the one hand, having suitable employment to go to, as where there is an actual promise of employment, and having only prospects of employment on the other. It may be reasonable to expect a claimant who has only prospects to take some steps before leaving, such as communicating with the employment exchange to see whether his prospects cannot be made more certain."

It is probably true to say that the claimant's chances of establishing just cause are stronger where there are promises or good prospects of employment, or where the reasons for leaving are in themselves quite strong and he can show efforts made to ascertain job prospects before leaving the old employment.

A number of cases concerning, on the one hand, grievances about existing employment and, on the other, personal or domestic circumstances, can usefully be quoted as *instances* in which just cause was established, and it may be useful to note in contrast a number of examples in each category where it was not. But the import-ance of looking to the precise circumstances of each and every case cannot be too strongly stressed. Note that whether a given set of facts constitutes "just cause" for leaving is a question of mixed fact and law, making it one that commissioners can deal with under their jurisdiction to correct errors of law by tribunals (*CU/53/1991*).

(i) Grievances about work. In *R(U)/15/53* a piece-worker who lost his job when he   1.257
refused to accept a substantial reduction in earnings thrust on him by his employer had just cause for leaving. In *R(U)38/53* the claimant left after subjection to pres-sure to join a trade union and was able to establish just cause; it would have been intolerable if he had to remain. In *R(U)18/57* an apprentice ordered to do work clearly outside the scope of his apprenticeship had only the options of doing as he was told or leaving immediately. In choosing the latter he had just cause. But mere

failure to get on with colleagues (*R(U)17/54*) or strained relations with one's employer (*R(U)8/74*) has been held not enough. Not feeling oneself capable of the work, where one's employer was satisfied, is unlikely to be enough without clear medical evidence of that fact (*R(U)13/52*), but leaving employment during a probationary period because the claimant considered himself unsuited to the work and that it was unfair to his employer to continue training him was more generously treated in *R(U)3/73*. Indeed, in *CU43/87* Commissioner Davenport said that "a person who is experimenting in trying a new line of work should not lightly be penalised if that experiment fails". Persons should be encouraged to try new types of employment where work in their usual field is not available:

"It must be recognised that in such circumstances a person may find that he cannot stay in his employment and it may be that he is reasonable in leaving that employment, whereas a person who had more experience in the field in question would not be held to have acted reasonably if he gave up the employment. Not everyone finds that new and unfamiliar employment is such that she or he can reasonably stay in it" (para.7).

CU/90/91 further illustrates that persons who leave employment as unsuitable after a trial period can have just cause for doing so and be protected from preclusion of payment without having to rely on the time-limited "trial period" concept found in s.20(3) and JSA Regs, reg.74. Commissioner Hallett stated:

"It is clear from the evidence, which I accept, that the claimant took the job with Fords (which would have been permanent) on trial, conditionally on his being able to obtain accommodation in the area. It is well-settled in social security unemployment law that claimants should be encouraged to take jobs on trial and that if, after trial, the job proves unsuitable, they do have just cause for leaving. It is in the interests of the national insurance fund, and of public policy, to encourage persons to obtain employment and not penalise them if, after fair trial, the job proves unsuitable" (para.10).

The claimant had just cause for leaving.

1.258   *(ii) Personal or domestic circumstances.* In *R(U)14/52* the claimant had just cause for leaving his job in order to be with his elderly and sick wife who lived alone. It was not possible for her to move to live with him so as to be near enough to his work. He also thought his chances of employment would be good in his wife's area, but there was little evidence in the case of searching inquiries about those prospects. In *R(U)19/52* the claimant who left her job to move with her service-man husband to a new posting, likely to be more than short-term, had just cause. Had the posting been short-term, however, she would have had to make inquiries about job prospects in the new area before leaving. See further *R(U)4/87* and *CU110/1987*. In *CU110/1987* the claimant's serviceman husband received telephone notice of posting to Germany on February 14, 1986. He went there on March 1, 1986. On February 14, 1986, the claimant gave the one week's notice required under her contract of employment and ceased work on February 21, claiming benefit the next day. She had to be available to vacate the married quarters in Aldershot from March 1. However, she did not join her husband in Germany until March 25, since repairs were needed to the married quarters there. Commissioner Monroe held that in these circumstances she had just cause for leaving when she did [February 21] rather than later, that, rather than whether she should have left at all, being the real issue in the case, since in the commissioner's view it could hardly be said that she did not have just cause to leave (whenever she could) to join her husband in Germany. She was not to be disqualified from benefit. Actual entitlement to benefit, however, would turn on the unresolved matter of her availability for work. On this issue of availability in that context, see *R(U)2/90(T)*. In *R(U)31/59* the reason for leaving was the move to a new home, too far from the job, because the existing home (two small attic rooms) was wholly unsuitable for his family. By contrast, in *R(U)6/53* the 21-year-old girl who left her job to move with her rather strict parents to a new area did not have just cause; it was reasonable to expect her to live alone, at least until she could find work in the new area.

Leaving for a financial advantage (*e.g.* to draw a marriage gratuity only payable on resignation (*R(U)14/55*), or to take early retirement, even where this was encouraged by the employer and might be said to be in the public interest in terms of opening the way for younger teachers and promoting the efficiency of the education service, has been held not to rank as just cause (*Crewe v Social Security Commissioner* [1982] 2 All E.R. 745; *R(U)26/51*; *R(U)23/59*; *R(U)20/64(T)*; *R(U)4/70*; *R(U)1/81*; *CU/170/1992* (which is not to be reported), which noted that *CU/95/1989* was either very different or decided against the weight of established authority). Subsection (7) and JSA Regs, reg.71, below, may provide assistance for some such claimants by treating them as not having left voluntarily thus obviating the just cause issue.

(3) "After a situation . . . offered to him" (subs. (6)(c)): This head of preclusion covers **1.259** the claimant who has been notified by an "employment officer" that a situation in employment is vacant or about to become so. It penalises him where, without good cause, (i) he has refused to apply for that situation, or (ii) he has failed to apply for it, or (iii) he has refused to accept it when offered to him.

"Refusal" clearly covers outright rejection of an offer or of the opportunity to apply for the post. Accepting an offer but then telling lies which caused the employer to withdraw it was treated as refusal in a Northern Ireland decision (*R6/50(UB)*).

On the meaning of "accept a situation in any employment", see *CSU 7/1995*. The claimant was offered the job of a lampshade maker at a wage of £79 per week, having been informed of the vacancy by the Employment Service. But she changed her mind and did not start the job because the wage was too low to meet her commitments. The tribunal decided that since she did accept the offer of employment, s.28(1)(b) of the Contributions and Benefits Act (whose terms were substantially similar to subs.(6)(c)) did not operate to disqualify her from receiving unemployment benefit. However, the Commissioner held that although, normally, acceptance of an offer of a situation would be tantamount to accepting the situation it could not have been intended that it would be possible to defeat the operation of s.28(1)(b) by an acceptance in theory but a repudiation in practice. The claimant had not "accepted the situation" within the meaning of s.28(1)(b).

See also *CJSA 4179/1997* in which the claimant was offered a "trial" as a part-time car washer. The tribunal dealt with the case under subs.(6)(c) but the Commissioner expressed doubt as to whether the "trial" was an offer of a "situation in any employment". The tribunal should have investigated what the trial involved. If subs.(6)(c) did not apply, subs.(6)(d) should then have been considered.

The claimant must have been notified of the actual or impending vacancy by an "employment officer": an officer of the Secretary of State (a civil servant in the Department of Work and Pensions) or such other person designated as such for these purposes by order made by the Secretary of State (subs.(10)(a)). Some aspects of decisions on the equivalent provision in the unemployment benefit context are still relevant (although that referred to "properly notified" that was merely a way of limiting the bodies or persons who could notify for the purposes of that provision since "properly notified" merely meant "notified by" a range of specified persons or bodies) on what constitutes notification. There need not be much detail, provided that the broad nature of the situation is made clear (*R(U)32/52*). It will then be up to the claimant to ascertain such further particulars as he requires (*ibid.*). A verbal notification suffices (*CU40/1987*).

A failure properly to complete an application form can amount to a failure to apply (*CJSA 2692/1999*). However, where the applicant disputed the necessity of including a photograph on the employer's application form, contending that it would be accepted without one, the employment officer, without clear information to the contrary from the employer, should have tested the matter by forwarding the form without photograph to see if that indeed was the case. He had not done so and, in *CJSA*

/2082/2002 and *CJSA/5415/2002*, Commissioner Rowland allowed the appeal against the sanction imposed.

1.260   In *CJSA/4665/01*, Commissioner Howell held that the "failed to apply" head could not catch someone who had filled in application forms which the employment service then refused to pass on because of criticisms of the employment service and government training initiatives, on the faith of which he had left his last job and felt badly let down. The service refused to pass them on because of these criticisms they saw as directed against themselves. Since the forms were otherwise properly completed, and there was no evidence of any intention to spoil his chances or that any employers had been or would be put off by the comments from considering him for employment, it had not been shown that he had "failed to apply" for the posts in question. The Commissioner noted that the claimant might be wise to take the advice of the employment service and remove the comments so as to maximise his chances of employment. He noted also that there will be other cases:

> "where the way a claimant completes or spoils a job application will be unsatis-factory and unfit to be put in front of any employer so as to prevent it counting as a genuine application at all, so that he or she will have 'failed to apply': it is all a question of fact (para.5)."

In *CJSA/2931/2003*, Commissioner Howell upheld a tribunal decision disqualify-ing the claimant for 18 weeks as fully justified on the facts. It had thought suspect the claimant's credibility in claiming that he had telephoned and been told that the vacancy was filled whereas in fact it had remained open. The sanction imposed was well within the bounds of reasonableness in a case where a long-term claimant is found to have made no real effort to follow up a vacancy notified to him.

There is now no requirement that the employment be "suitable", but there is, across all the sub-heads of the paragraph, a saving for "good cause". In the past, however, questions of the suitability of the employment and of good cause for the refusal or failure to apply, or refusal or failure to accept, tended to intertwine and the case authorities tended not to distinguish between them (see *e.g. R(U)26/52*) to the extent that it almost appeared that the sole basis for "good cause", at least as reflected in reported decisions, was the non-suitability of the employment in the claimant's cir-cumstances. A general merging of the suitability and good cause heads was evident in the case authorities. The heads focused on such matters as the location of the employment (*R(U)41/51, R(U)34/58*), the claimant's personal and family circum-stances (*R(U)13/52, R(U)20/60, R(U)2/77, R2/63(UB)*) and on the terms of the employment. That intertwining of the issues may mean that some issues sometimes characterised as "suitability" issues in the past may still be raised, despite the dele-tion of "suitable" from the statutory text, as "good cause" issues. But here one must proceed with extreme care and caution, since "good cause" is no longer a matter regu-lated solely by principle in case law but has been restricted and regulated by subss.(8) and (9) and JSA Regs, reg.72 made pursuant to them. Generally speaking, but subject to the specifics in reg.72 (and any other regulations which may be made in that behalf), subs.(9) provides that no regard is to be paid to the level of remuneration in the employment in question in determining "good cause". Regulation 72 does several things: (i) it specifies certain circumstances in which a person is to be regarded as having "good cause"; (ii) subject to that, it precludes certain reasons ranking as "good cause"; and (iii) sets out a non-exhaustive list of factors to be taken into account in determining the "good cause" issue. It is submitted that other factors, including ones suggested by earlier case law, whether on suitability or good cause, will still be rele-vant so long as they are not ruled out of account for the good cause issue by the preclusive clauses of subs.(8) and (9) and JSA Regs, reg.72. See further the notes to subs.(8) and (9), below; and see JSA Regs, reg.72.

1.261   *(4) "He has neglected ... employment" (subs. (6) (d))*: Note at the outset that s.20(3) and JSA Regs, reg.74 made under it protect from disqualification under this head or under that in subs.(6)(b) certain persons who leave employed earner's employment voluntarily and without just cause at any time within the "trial period" (that is, between the beginning of the fifth week and the end of the twelfth week of the employment in question, with some provision to ignore certain weeks). In short, in cases covered by s.20(3) and JSA Regs, reg.74, characterising (as one could) the voluntary leaving as a "neglect to avail" will be pointless; those provisions will prevent preclusion.

This head of disqualification overlaps somewhat with subs.(6)(c). Preclusion is to be imposed where the claimant has neglected to avail himself of a reasonable opportunity of employment. There is now a saving for good cause, on which see also the notes to subs.(6)(c), above, subss.(8) and (9), below, and JSA Regs, reg.72 (noted more fully, and covering this head in the same way as subs.(6)(c), in the annotations to that regulation relating to this paragraph of this subsection). The effect of JSA Regs, reg.72(8), (9) is that a claimant will have good cause under subs.(5)(d) for neglecting to avail himself of an opportunity of employment unless the situation is a "qualifying former employment" of his. See further the notes to JSA Regs, reg.72. And even where the situation is such a former employment, there are other provisions on good cause in reg.72, applicable to subs.(5), para.(d), which come into play in deciding whether there was good cause for neglecting to avail himself of such a former employment (see reg.72, paras (2)–(7)). The submission made in the note to subs.(6)(c) on the relevance of suitability/good cause case law also applies here, so that decisions like *R(U)2/77* which protected the person, who could have had his old job back if he would, contrary to his convictions, join a trade union, would still be relevant. An excusing factor mentioned in *R(U)5/71*, namely, a conscientious objection to a job, connected with religion or morals, is reflected as a factor to be taken into account in determining good cause in JSA Regs, reg.72(2)(c).

This head of disqualification seems designed to cater for the person who literally complies with subs.(6)(c) in that he applies for the post, and does not explicitly refuse it, but who behaves in such a way that he would never get it, for example, by turning up at an interview in a dirty or unkempt condition, unwashed and unshaved (*R(U)28/55*). Neglect to avail will also cover an explicit refusal to take a job or to fulfill a key condition for getting it (*e.g.* the requirement in Scotland that teachers be registered: *R(U)5/71*).

[C] CONFLICTING EVIDENCE: RESOLVING MATTERS IN ACCORDANCE WITH THE ONUS OF PROOF, AND RECORDING SUCH DECISIONS

In *CU/109/1988* Commissioner Rice considered an alleged case of voluntary leaving in which the SSAT had been faced with conflicting written, but no oral, evidence from employer and claimant. The employer had alleged that the claimant had left his job of his own accord, giving no reason other than his desire to leave their service. The claimant's letter of appeal merely referred to unspecified pressures resulting in his leaving on a basis "which cannot be described as voluntary". Further inquiries by means of form UB86B merely elicited as the reason for leaving, "sudden and serious disagreement with superior over policy issues", but no further details. The SSAT upheld the disqualification, deciding that the AO had discharged his onus of proving voluntary leaving by means of the employers' statement which was not countered by any *specific* evidence from the claimant in rebuttal. Moreover, since he had given no details of what had happened, the claimant had failed to establish just cause for voluntarily leaving. Commissioner Rice held that the SSAT were not entitled to reach that conclusion. The Commissioner considered that:

1.262

> "there was not enough evidence to justify the tribunal's conclusion that the adjudication officer had established his case. The adjudication officer could not himself give evidence (see *R(SB)10/86*, para.5) and contradictory statements, as between the employers and the claimant, without the backup of any oral evidence and cross-examination, were not sufficient to establish the case, on the balance of probability, in favour of the adjudication officer's submission."

The Commissioner found in the claimant's statements an indication that his departure was not voluntary but enforced, that the proper characterisation of his departure might be as a form of dismissal (the Commissioner used the term, "constructively dismissed") rather than voluntary leaving. This was possibly a generous interpretation; others might rather have regarded the same statements as relevant to the "just cause" issue, as indicating departure in consequence of an irresoluble grievance about work, as in the cases cited under "grievances about work" (see above, annotation to subs.(6)(b) on "without just cause"). Perhaps the Commissioner had in mind here, although he did not refer to them, instances of enforced departure such as *R(U)1/58* and *R(U)2/76* where the claimants who departed had no effective choice but to quit, *e.g.* because dismissal appeared inevitable. Such situations can then raise the issue of whether disqualification was nonetheless appropriate because of loss of employment through misconduct, as was held to be the case in *R(U)2/76*. There the claimant used a company car without permission to give driving lessons and was found at home in the bath when he should have been out selling. He accepted the chance to resign rather than be dismissed as a result of his misconduct. Commissioner Watson stated in that case:

> "It is not uncommon for a person to be given an opportunity to resign instead of being discharged in circumstances which employers consider constitute misconduct. Faced with the prospect of dismissal for his misconduct, the claimant has stated that he chose to resign 'as it enhanced better opportunity for future re-employment.' The reason for the termination of an employment has to be considered and the claimant's leaving his employment was not of a voluntary nature since he was faced with the prospect of disciplinary action and possible, or even probable, dismissal. It is not necessary that the claimant was certain to have been dismissed as the local tribunal appear to have thought. *The form by which an employment is terminated is not necessarily decisive as to whether leaving an employment was voluntary or was the result of misconduct.* The claimant stated in his letter, dated July 9, 1975, that he considered that he would have been discharged anyway." (para.4; emphasis added by commentator)

1.263   In *CU/109/1988*, Commissioner Rice set aside the decision and remitted it for reconsideration and determination by a differently constituted tribunal, expressing the hope that the claimant and/or a representative of the employers might appear to supply new evidence.

This Commissioner's decision is useful in telling tribunals what is insufficient to make out a case for voluntary leaving, but does not otherwise give assistance in how to proceed in this difficult but not uncommon situation, where one cannot choose between the conflicting statements since each is internally consistent in that insufficient detail is provided to show up internal contradictions which might raise doubts about it. In such a case, perhaps the fairest approach when the appeal first comes on, would be to adjourn, expressing the wish that the parties appear to help the tribunal. That wish would be made known to the claimant when the written decision to adjourn is communicated to him, and could be made known to the employer through the Secretary of State (decision-maker). Since there are no powers of compulsion, that approach will not necessarily bear fruit in many cases, so that when the appeal is next heard, the tribunal will have to decide on the basis of the conflicting evidence. In such a case as *CU/109/88*, it is submitted that, since there is no way the tribunal can be satisfied as to the accuracy of either contention, the correct decision is that the adjudication officer has not discharged his onus of establishing voluntary leaving, and the claimant's appeal against disqualification must be allowed. This appears the inevitable consequence of the allocation of onus of proof in a context in which the decision-maker and the tribunal lack power to compel the attendance of witnesses. The problem is not unique to the voluntary leaving issue; where one is satisfied that the departure was voluntary and the issue of "just cause" arises, an irreconcilable conflict of evidence would result in a decision that the claimant had failed to establish "just cause", to discharge the onus lying on him on that matter. The problem can also arise in cases of disqualification for misconduct, although adjournments there might bear more fruit where other proceedings (*e.g.* for unfair dismissal) are pending, since the evidence accepted there would be cogent evidence on which the tribunal could proceed further. But where no such proceedings take place, a decision on the basis of the onus of proof would go in favour of the claimant, since the decision-maker bears the onus of establishing misconduct, and it must be clearly proved by the best available evidence, and it is desirable that in disputed cases this be done by direct evidence (*R(U)2/60*, para.7). In *CU/16/1991*, Commissioner Hoolahan set aside as erroneous in law an SSAT decision that the claimant be disqualified for loss of employment through misconduct but for a period less than that imposed by the AO. The reduction was effected because of certain doubts about the evidence that the claimant had falsified his timesheet. In the Commissioner's judgement,

> "it was incumbent upon the appeal tribunal to make a finding of fact as to whether or not the time sheet had been falsified. It was not sufficient to state in their reasons that the question 'could not be resolved on the evidence avail able to the tribunal.' If they required further evidence it was open to them to adjourn for that purpose. (Although I appreciate that there had already been one adjournment to enable the employer's evidence to be adduced 'relating to the disciplinary hearing, the evidence taken and the evidence found proved warranting instant dismissal.') If no further evidence was to be available, it was incumbent upon the appeal tribunal to reach a decision on the evidence that was available. The onus was on the adjudication officer to prove the case on the balance of probabilities. The case does not have to be proved beyond a reasonable doubt, although, of course, a serious allegation such as falsifying a time sheet does require cogent evidence for its proof. If, at the end of the day, the appeal tribunal is not satisfied that the allegation has been proved, then it is open to them so to find." (para.7.)

Where appeals are decided on this basis, how should the decision be recorded on the tribunal record? It is submitted that such evidence as there is should be noted, that the tribunal record should state that no findings of fact have been made (the tribunal has not been able to ascertain what happened), that the decision should be recorded in full, while the reason for the decision should state that the party bearing the onus of proof on the relevant issue has failed to discharge it.

Subs.(7)

This enables the making of regulations setting out circumstances in which a person who might otherwise be regarded, under the normal rules discussed above, as having left employment voluntarily, is to be treated as *not* having left voluntarily.

1.264

In making particular reference to the situation in which a person has been "dismissed by his employer by reason of redundancy within the meaning of section 139(1) of the Employment Rights Act 1996 after volunteering or agreeing to be so dismissed", the section reveals as its immediate ancestor s.28(4) of the SSCBA 1992, which was meant to remove the threat of disqualification from unemployment benefit which would, given the interpretation of just cause in *Crewe v Social Security Commissioner* ([1982] 2 All E.R. 745: see notes to subs.(6)(b), above), apply to persons who volunteered for or agreed to redundancy and thereby lost their employment. That threat might discourage what might be thought to be the economically and socially desirable policy of shedding labour as painlessly as possible. Unfortunately, the language chosen worked against the full achievement of that intent, and commissioners were divided in their decisions on whether the section was confined to dismissals in the technical sense used in the then applicable statute (the Employment Protection (Consolidation) Act 1978) (excluding terminations by mutual consent) or extended to a broader concept, embracing such terminations, covering the situation "where the employer has made clear that some employees of the claimant's category must either immediately or in the near future leave the employment by reason of the redundancy" so that mutual agreements on when the claimant left, even if the claimant volunteered to be one of those made redundant, were protected by the provision (*R(U)3/91*). The case law had probably reached the stage where Commissioner Goodman's decision in *R(U)3/91* had disposed of that particular problem. But even the wider approach could not help those who, laid off from work, apply for and receive a redundancy payment under s.88 of the 1978 Act (now ss.149–152 of the Employment Rights Act 1996), unless there were evidence of an actual or constructive dismissal by the employer either at the time of lay off or subsequently (*CU/71/94*, para.18). In *CU/71/94*, there had been no dismissal either in the narrower or the broader sense, but Commissioner Goodman held that on the facts the particular claimant had just cause for leaving his employment and was not to be disqualified.

One aim of subs.(7) is thus the same as its precursor. But it is by no means confined to that context, enabling regulations to treat a person as not having left voluntarily "in such circumstances as may be prescribed". To date, however, rule-making has been confined to the circumstance of "voluntary redundancy". The regulation made, JSA Regs, reg.71 is fortunately better worded to achieve its ends than the provision which caused the Commissioners so much difficulty, and protects a broader range of voluntary redundancy situations than previously. See the notes to that regulation.

Subs.(8)

1.265   A number of the heads of preclusion in subss.(5) and (6), above, contain savings for "good cause". This subsection enables the Secretary of State to make regulations setting out what is and what is not "good cause" and to stipulate factors to be taken into account in determining the "good cause" issue. The regulations made, JSA Regs, regs 72 and 73, have been referred to in the notes to subss.(5) and (6) and are annotated at their location in this volume. Where this subsection goes further than its predecessor (SSCBA 1992, s.28(5)) is in giving the Secretary of State power to do the same in respect of "just cause", a saving for which is found in the preclusion in subs.(6)(b) (voluntarily leaving employment without "just cause"). To date, no such regulations have been made. So the matter of "just cause" has to be interpreted in the light of previous case law on unemployment benefit and in the light of the limitation set by subs.(9).

Subs.(9)

1.266   This stipulates that, subject to any regulations made under subs.(8), any matter relating to the level of remuneration in the employment in question in the case, must be disregarded in determining whether the claimant does or does not have "good cause" or "just cause". In also covering "just cause" the provision goes wider than its predecessor, SSCBA 1992, s.28(5).

Note also that since April 1, 1999 there has been a national minimum wage for most workers (broadly £4.85 per hour for those aged 22 or over; £4.10 per hour for those aged 18 to 21; and, for the first time from October 1, 2004, workers aged below 18 who have ceased to be of compulsory school age qualify for the national minimum wage at an hourly rate of £3.00). It is suggested that as a consequence of the national minimum wage legislation subs.(9) should not prevent a claimant from being able to show, *e.g.* just cause for leaving voluntarily, if his employer refuses to pay him at his appropriate minimum rate, or, *e.g.* good cause for refusing employment, if the proposed rate of pay is not at least at the minimum wage level that applies to him. This is on the basis that the rule in subs.(9) should not be applied in a way that runs contrary to the National Minimum Wage Act 1998.

Exemptions from section 19

1.267   **20.**—(1) Nothing in section 19, or in regulations under that section, shall be taken to prevent payment of a jobseeker's allowance merely because the claimant refuses to seek or accept employment in a situation which is vacant in consequence of a stoppage of work due to a trade dispute.

(2) Section 19 does not apply, in the circumstances mentioned in subsection (5) of that section, if—

(a) a direction is in force under section 16 with respect to the claimant; and

(b) he has acted in such a way as to risk—

(i) having that direction revoked under subsection (3)(b) of section 16; or

(ii) having the amount of his jobseeker's allowance reduced by virtue of section 17, because [¹the condition mentioned in section 17(3)(b) or (c) is satisfied].

(3) Regulations shall make provisions for the purpose of enabling any person of a prescribed description to accept any employed earner's employment without falling within section 19(6)(b) or (d) should he leave that employment voluntarily and without just cause at any time during a trial period.

(4) In such circumstances as may be prescribed, an income-based jobseeker's allowance shall be [²payable in respect of] a claimant even though section 19 prevents payment of a jobseeker's allowance to him.

(5) A jobseeker's allowance shall be payable by virtue of subsection (4) only if the claimant has complied with such requirements as to the provision of information as may be prescribed for the purposes of this subsection.

(6) Regulations under subsection (4) may, in particular, provide for a jobseeker's allowance payable by virtue of that subsection to be—

(a) payable at a prescribed rate;

(b) payable for a prescribed period (which may differ from the period fixed under section 19(2) or (3)).

(7) In subsection (3), "trial period" has such meaning as may be prescribed.

(8) Regulations may make provision for determining, for the purposes of this section, the day on which a person's employment is to be regarded as commencing.

AMENDMENTS

1. Social Security Act 1998, Sch.7, para.142 (October 18, 1999). **1.268**
2. Welfare Reform and Pensions Act 1999, s.70 and Sch.8, para.29 (November 11, 1999).

DEFINITIONS

"claimant": see s.35(1).
"employment": see s.35(1), JSA Regs, reg.4.
"income-based jobseeker's allowance": see ss.1(4) and 35(1).
"jobseeker's agreement": see ss.9(1) and 35(1).
"regulations": see s.35(1).
"trade dispute": *ibid.*
"trial period": see subs.(7), JSA Regs, reg.74(4).

GENERAL NOTE

Like its precursor, SSCBA 1992, s.29, this section affords a number of exemp- **1.269**
tions from the preclusive effect of s.19, but goes further than its predecessor by enabling the making of regulations providing for hardship payments of a reduced rate

of income-based JSA for those precluded from full JSA by s.19. See further JSA Regs, regs 140–146.

Subs. (1)

1.270
This provides that nothing in s.19 or regulations made under it can prevent payment of JSA merely because the claimant refuses to seek or accept employment vacant in consequence of a stoppage of work due to a trade dispute. On the definition of "trade dispute", see s.35(1) and the notes to s.14(1). On "stoppage of work", see the notes to s.14(1).

This maintains the traditional "neutral" approach to trade disputes taken in social security law. A claimant is not required to be a strike-breaker and so will not be sanctioned for refusing work that is vacant because of a trade dispute.

Subs. (2)

1.271
If a young person who is the subject of a severe hardship direction fails to pursue or refuses a training opportunity without good cause or fails to complete a training course without good cause, or loses his place through misconduct, s.19(5) does not apply. The young person's "offence" will be dealt with by revocation of the direction under s.16(3) or reduction in his JSA under s.17 as appropriate. See reg.63 of the JSA Regulations.

Subss. (3), (7) and (8)

1.272
This has parallels with SSCBA 1992, s.29(2), (3), but unlike that section relegates the "meat" to regulations. Like s.29(2), (3), this provision and JSA Regs, reg.74 made under it protect certain persons who leave employment voluntarily without just cause at any time during a trial period from preclusion from JSA under the voluntarily leaving employment without just cause head of s.19(6)(b) or under s.19(6)(d) (neglect to avail oneself of a reasonable opportunity of employment).

Subss. (4), (5) and (6)

1.273
In the past a claimant suspended or disqualified from unemployment benefit under s.28(1) of the Contributions and Benefits Act, or who would have been so disqualified if otherwise entitled, could (if eligible) receive reduced payments of income support (see reg.22 of the Income Support Regulations (now revoked) in the 1996 edition of *Mesher and Wood, Income-related Benefits: The Legislation*; see also reg.21A (also now revoked) which provided for claimants' income support to be reduced in the case of failure to attend certain compulsory courses). Under the new scheme, however, there is no automatic entitlement to reduced income-based JSA where a sanction is imposed under s.19. Benefit will only be paid if a claimant can show that he, or a member of his household, will suffer hardship as a result of the sanction. If a "hardship payment" is made, it will be subject to a 40 per cent or 20 per cent reduction of the appropriate personal allowance for a single claimant and will not be payable for the first two weeks, except to certain claimants (*i.e.* those who come within one of the "vulnerable" groups listed in reg.140(1)). In the case of a "New Deal" sanction (see the notes to JSA Regs, reg.69) hardship payments will not be available at all (even if the sanction is for four weeks), except to claimants in one of the vulnerable groups (see regs 140(4A) and 140A(1)). For a claimant who is not in one of the vulnerable groups there is the possibility of a crisis loan from the Social Fund during the period of a New Deal sanction, but only for expenses arising out of a disaster or for items for cooking or heating (including fireguards) (Social Fund Direction 17(d) and (g)). In the case of a non-New Deal sanction a claimant who is not getting hardship payments will only have access to a crisis loan for expenses resulting from a disaster or for items for cooking or heating for 14 days starting on the first day of the benefit week following the end of the sanction (Social Fund Direction 17(c) and (g)). (Note Direction 18(2) for crisis loans for a partner's living expenses in such a case). Because JSA is paid fortnightly in arrears, if, for example, such a sanction is for two weeks, this will mirror the period when the effect

of the sanction is actually felt. This restricted access to crisis loans does not apply to claimants in one of the vulnerable groups who have been awarded hardship payments (Direction 17(f)).

Note that where a s.19 sanction is imposed, the effect is that JSA is not *payable* (see s.19(1)). *Entitlement* to JSA continues during the period of the sanction. It thus eats into the 182-day maximum period of entitlement for contribution-based JSA: see s.5. On the other hand, full housing benefit and council tax benefit will continue to be payable (see reg.2(3A) of the Housing Benefit Regulations 1987 and the Council Tax Benefit Regulations 1992 respectively), for claimants who would otherwise be getting income-based JSA. Claimants awarded hardship payments will also be entitled to full housing/council tax benefit because hardship payments count as payments of income-based JSA.

See regs 140–146 of the JSA Regulations for the rules governing hardship payments and the notes to those regulations. Under subs.(5) see reg.144.

[¹Denial or reduction of joint-claim jobseeker's allowance

20A.—(1) Where this section applies to a member of a joint-claim couple, that member of the couple shall be subject to sanctions for the purposes of this section.   1.274

(2) This section applies to a member of a joint-claim couple if that member of the couple—

(a) has, without good cause, refused or failed to carry out any jobseeker's direction which was reasonable, having regard to his circumstances;

(b) has, without good cause—

  (i) neglected to avail himself of a reasonable opportunity of a place on a training scheme or employment programme;

  (ii) after a place on such a scheme or programme has been notified to him by an employment officer as vacant or about to become vacant, refused or failed to apply for it or to accept it when offered to him;

  (iii) given up a place on such a scheme or programme; or

  (iv) failed to attend such a scheme or programme on which he has been given a place;

(c) has lost his place on such a scheme or programme through misconduct;

(d) has lost his employment as an employed earner through misconduct;

(e) has voluntarily left such employment without just cause;

(f) has, without good cause, after a situation in any employment has been notified to him by an employment officer as vacant or about to become vacant, refused or failed to apply for it or to accept it when offered to him; or

(g) has, without good cause, neglected to avail himself of a reasonable opportunity of employment.

(3) Where this section applies to a member of a joint-claim couple by virtue of any of paragraphs (a) to (c) of subsection (2), the period for which he is to be subject to sanctions shall be such period (of at least one week but not more than 26 weeks) as may be prescribed.

(4) Where this section applies to a member of a joint-claim couple by virtue of any of paragraphs (d) to (g) of subsection (2), the period for which he is to be subject to sanctions shall be such period (of at least one week but not more than 26 weeks) as may be determined by the Secretary of State.

(5) Even though the conditions for entitlement to a joint-claim jobseeker's allowance are satisfied in relation to a joint-claim couple—

    (a) the allowances shall not be payable for any period during which both members of the couple are subject to sanctions; and

    (b) the amount of the allowance payable in respect of the couple for any period during which only one member of the couple is subject to sanctions shall be reduced to an amount calculated by the prescribed method ("the reduced amount").

(6) The method prescribed for calculating the reduced amount may, in particular, involve—

    (a) deducting amounts from, or making percentage reductions of, the amount which would be the amount of the allowance if neither member of the couple were subject to sanctions;

    (b) disregarding portions of the applicable amount;

    (c) treating amounts as being income or capital of the couple.

(7) During any period for which the amount of a joint-claim jobseeker's allowance payable in respect of a joint-claim couple is the reduced amount, the allowance shall be payable to the member of the couple who is not subject to sanctions.

(8) Regulations may prescribe—

    (a) circumstances which the Secretary of State is to take into account, and

    (b) circumstances which he is not to take into account,

in determining a period under subsection (4).

(9) Subsections (7) to (10) of section 19 apply for the purposes of this section as for those of that section but as if references in subsection (10)(b) of that section to the claimant were to the member of the joint-claim couple to whom subsection (2)(a) above applies.]

AMENDMENT

1.275   1. Welfare Reform and Pensions Act 1999, Sch.7, para.13 (March 19, 2001).

GENERAL NOTE

1.276   This section, together with s.20B below, makes "provision corresponding to that made by . . . section [19] and section 20" in relation to a joint-claim jobseeker's allowance (see s.19(1A) above). So, subs.(2) of this section corresponds to subss.(5) and (6) of s.19 and subss.(3), (4) and (8) correspond to subss.(2), (3) and (4) respectively. By subs.(9), subss.(7)–(10) of s.19 apply (with necessary modification) to this section. Reference should be made to the notes to the appropriate provision of s.19.

If any of the circumstances listed in subs.(2) applies to a member of a joint claim couple, s/he is "subject to sanctions" under subs.(1). The consequences of this are stated in subss.(5) and (6). Subject to the hardship provisions in s.20B and Part IXA of the JSA Regulations:

•   if both members of a joint-claim couple are subject to sanctions, then no JSA is payable; and

•   if only one member of the couple is subject to sanctions, JSA is payable at a reduced rate calculated in accordance with reg.74B of the JSA Regulations and, under subs.(7), is paid to the member who is not so subject.

1.277   [¹ **20B.**—(1) Section 20A shall not be taken to apply to a member of a joint-claim couple merely because he has refused to seek or accept employment in a situation which is vacant in consequence of a stoppage of work due to a trade dispute.

(2) Section 20A does not apply to a member of a joint-claim couple by virtue of any of paragraphs (a) to (c) of subsection (2) of that section if—

    (a) a direction is in force under section 16 with respect to that member of the couple; and

    (b) he has acted in such a way as to risk—

        (i) having that direction revoked under subsection (3)(b) of section 16; or

        (ii) having the amount of the couple's entitlement to a joint-claim jobseeker's allowance reduced by virtue of section 17 because the condition in section 17(3)(b) or (c) is established.

(3) Regulations shall make provision for the purpose enabling any person of a prescribed description to accept any employed earner's employment without section 20A applying to him by virtue of paragraph (e) or (g) of subsection (2) of that section should he leave that employment voluntarily and without just cause at any time during a trial period.

(4) In such circumstances as may be prescribed, a joint-claim jobseeker's allowance shall be payable in respect of a joint-claim couple even though section 20A(5)(a) prevents payment of such a jobseeker's allowance to the couple.

(5) A jobseeker's allowance shall be payable by virtue of subsection (4) only if the couple have complied with such requirements as to the provision of information as may be prescribed for the purposes of this subsection.

(6) Regulations under subsection (4) may, in particular, provide for a jobseeker's allowance payable by virtue of that subsection to be—

    (a) payable at a prescribed rate;

    (b) payable for a prescribed period (which may differ from the period during which both members of the couple are subject to sanctions for the purposes of section 20A).

(7) In subsection (3), "trial period" has such meaning as may be prescribed.

(8) Regulations may make provision for determining, for the purposes of this section, the day on which a person's employment is to be regarded as commencing.]

AMENDMENT

1. Welfare Reform and Pensions Act 1999, Sch.7, para.11 (March 19, 2001).   **1.278**

GENERAL NOTE

This section establishes exemptions from the rules in s.20A for claimants who are members of a joint claim couple which are substantially similar to the exemptions from s.19 which are established for other claimants by s.20. See the commentary to s.20 for further details.

Miscellaneous

Supplementary provisions

21. Further provisions in relation to a jobseeker's allowance are set out in Schedule 1.   **1.279**

Members of the forces

1.280   **22.**—(1) Regulations may modify any provision of this Act, in such manner as Secretary of State thinks proper, in its application to persons who are or have been members of Her Majesty's forces.

(2) The regulations may, in particular, provide for section 19(6)(b) not to apply in relation to a person who is discharged from Her Majesty's forces at his own request.

(3) For the purposes of this section, Her Majesty's forces shall be taken to consist of such establishments and organisations in which persons serve under the control of the Defence Council as may be prescribed.

Recovery of sums in respect of maintenance

1.281   **23.**—(1) Regulations may make provision for the court to have power to make a recovery order against any person where an award of income-based jobseeker's allowance has been made to that person's spouse.

(2) In this section "recovery order" means an order requiring the person against whom it is made to make payments to the Secretary of State or to such other person or persons as the court may determine.

(3) Regulations under this section may make provision for the transfer by the Secretary of State of the right to receive payments under, and to exercise rights in relation to, a recovery order.

(4) Regulations made under this section may, in particular, include provision—

(a) as to the matters to which the court is, or is not, to have regard in determining any application under the regulations; and

(b) as to the enforcement of recovery orders.

(5) In this section, "the court" means—

(a) in relation to England and Wales, a magistrates' court; and

(b) in relation to Scotland, the sheriff.

DEFINITIONS

1.282   "income-based jobseeker's allowance"—see s.1(4).
"regulations"—see s.35(1).

GENERAL NOTE

This section is concerned with the enforcement of a person's liability to maintain his spouse where an award of JSA has been made to that spouse (compare ss.106 and 107 of the Administration Act in relation to income support). It is not known how often these powers to recover spousal maintenance are in fact used since the child support maintenance system introduced by the Child Support Act 1991 has been in operation.

PART II

BACK TO WORK SCHEMES

The back to work bonus

1.283   **26.**—(1) Regulations may make provision for the payment, in prescribed circumstances, of sums to or in respect of persons who are or have been entitled to a Jobseeker's allowance or to income support.

(2) A sum payable under the regulations shall be known as "a back to work bonus".

(3) [¹Subject to section 677 of the Income Tax (Earnings and Pensions) Act 2003 (which provides for a back to work bonus not to be taxable)], a back to work bonus shall be treated for all purposes as payable by way of a jobseeker's allowance or (as the case may be) income support.

(4) The regulations may, in particular, provide for—

(a) a back to work bonus to be payable only on the occurrence of a prescribed event;

(b) a bonus not to be payable unless a claim is made before the end of the prescribed period;

(c) the amount of a bonus (subject to any maximum prescribed by virtue of paragraph (g)) to be determined in accordance with the regulations;

(d) enabling amounts to be calculated by reference to periods of entitlement to a jobseeker's allowance and periods of entitlement to income support;

(e) treating a bonus as payable wholly by way of income support or wholly by way of a jobseeker's allowance, in a case where amounts have been calculated in accordance with provision made by virtue of paragraph (d);

(f) keeping persons who may be entitled to a bonus informed of the amounts calculated in accordance with any provision of the regulations made by virtue of paragraph (c);

(g) the amount of a bonus not to exceed a prescribed maximum;

(h) a bonus not to be payable if the amount of the bonus which would otherwise be payable is less than the prescribed minimum;

(i) prescribed periods to be disregarded for prescribed purposes;

(j) a bonus which has been paid to a person to be treated, in prescribed circumstances and for prescribed purposes, as income or capital of his or of any other member of his family;

(k) treating the whole or a prescribed part of an amount which has accrued towards a person's bonus—

(i) as not having accrued towards his bonus; but

(ii) as having accrued towards the bonus of another person;

(l) the whole or a prescribed part of a back to work bonus to be payable, in such circumstances as may be prescribed, to such person, other than the person who is or had been entitled to a jobseeker's allowance or to income support, as may be determined in accordance with the regulations.

AMENDMENT

1. Income Tax (Earnings and Pensions) Act 2003, Sch.6, Pt 2, para.230 (April 6, 2003).

DEFINITIONS

"prescribed"—see s.35(1).   1.284
"regulations"—*ibid.*

GENERAL NOTE

The detailed rules relating to the back to work bonus scheme that was introduced on October 7, 1996 were contained in the Social Security (Back to Work Bonus) (No. 2) Regulations 1996 (SI 1996/2570) (see the 2004 edition of this volume for those Regulations). The scheme was abolished on October 25, 2004 and the 1996 Regulations were revoked with effect from that date by reg.8 of the Social Security (Back to Work Bonus and Lone Parent Run-on) (Amendment and Revocation) Regulations 2003 (SI 2003/1589), subject to a transitional provision in reg. 10. The effect of reg.10 is to continue the 1996 Regulations in force (subject to certain modifications) in order to enable claimants to claim the bonus during a further period. For reg.10 of the 2003 Regulations and the note to that regulation, see p. 723.

The Government's justification for the abolition of the back to work bonus was that evaluation of the scheme had shown that it did not act as an incentive for claimants to take up full-time work and that its complex rules and eligibility criteria had contributed to low levels of awareness of the existence of the scheme. It has been replaced by, among other measures, an expansion of the Job Grant scheme (paid under arrangements made under s. 2(2) of the Employment and Training Act 1973). From October 2004 the new Job Grant (a one-off payment of £100 or £250) has been payable to people who start full-time work after they have been getting certain benefits for at least six months and who satisfy the other qualifying conditions.

Pilot schemes

1.285   **29.**—(1) Any regulations to which this subsection applies may be made so as to have effect for a specified period not exceeding 12 months.

(2) Any regulations which, by virtue of subsection (1), are to have effect for a limited period are referred to in this section as "a pilot scheme".

(3) A pilot scheme may provide that its provisions are to apply only in relation to—

    (a) one or more specified areas or localities;

    (b) one or more specified classes of person;

    (c) persons selected—

        (i) by reference to prescribed criteria; or

        (ii) on a sampling basis.

(4) A pilot scheme may make consequential or transitional provision with respect to the cessation of the scheme on the expiry of the specified period.

(5) A pilot scheme ("the previous scheme") may be replaced by a further pilot scheme making the same, or similar, provision (apart from the specified period) to that made by the previous scheme.

(6) Subject to subsection (8), subsection (1) applies to—

    (a) regulations made under this Act, other than—

        (i) regulations made under section 4(2) or (5) which have the effect of reducing any age-related amount or applicable amount; or

        (ii) regulations made under section 27;

    (b) regulations made under the Administration Act, so far as they relate to a jobseeker's allowance;

    (c) regulations made under Part VII of the Benefits Act (income-related benefits), other than any mentioned in subsection (7); and

    (d) regulations made under the Administration Act, so far as they relate to income-related benefits payable under Part VII of the Benefits Act.

(7) The regulations referred to in subsection (6)(c) are—

    (a) and (b) [² . . .]

    (c) regulations under section 130(4) of that Act which have the effect of reducing the appropriate maximum housing benefit;

(d) regulations under section 131(10)(a) of that Act which have the effect of reducing the appropriate maximum council tax benefit; and

(e) regulations reducing any of the sums prescribed under section 135(1) of that Act.

(8) Subsection (1) applies only if the regulations are made with a view to ascertaining whether their provisions will, or will be likely to, encourage persons to obtain or remain in work or will, or will be likely to, facilitate the obtaining by persons of work or their remaining in work.

AMENDMENTS

1. Tax Credits Act 1999, Sch.1, paras 1 and 6(h) (October 5, 1999)   **1.286**
2. Tax Credits Act 2002, s.60 and Sch.3 (April 8, 2003).

DEFINITIONS

"the Administration Act"—see s.35(1).
"the Benefits Act"—*ibid.*
"regulations"—*ibid.*

GENERAL NOTE

This important provision contains a new power to "pilot" changes in regulations   **1.287**
across particular geographical areas and/or specified categories of claimants for a
period of up to 12 months (this period can be extended: see subs.(5)). The power can
only be exercised in relation to the types of regulations listed in subs.(6) and with a
view to assessing whether the proposed changes are likely to encourage or help people
to find or remain in work (subs.(8)). Regulations made under this section are subject
to the affirmative resolution procedure (s.37(1)(c)). The early indications were that
this power would be used on a fairly regular basis and this has continued to be the case.

PART III

MISCELLANEOUS AND SUPPLEMENTAL

Termination of awards

31.—(1) Regulations may make provision allowing, in prescribed circum-   **1.288**
stances, an award of income support to be brought to an end by [¹ the
Secretary of State] where the person to whom it was made, or where he is a
member of a married or unmarried couple his partner [² or the couple], will
be entitled to a jobseeker's allowance if the award is brought to an end.

(2) Regulations may make provision allowing, in prescribed circumstances, an award of a jobseeker's allowance to be brought to an end by[¹ the
Secretary of State] where the person to whom it was made, or where he is a
member of a married or unmarried couple his partner, [² or where the award
was made to a couple a member of the couple,] will be entitled to income
support if the award is brought to an end.

(3) In this section "partner" means the other member of the couple concerned.

AMENDMENTS

1. Social Security Act 1998, s.86(1) and Sch.7, para.143 (October 18, 1999).   **1.289**

2. Welfare Reform and Pensions Act 1999, s.59 and Sch.7, para.14 (March 19, 2001).

<small>DEFINITIONS</small>

"married couple"—*ibid.*
"unmarried couple"—*ibid.*

Interpretation

1.290

35.—(1) In this Act—
[².. .]
"the Administration Act" means the Social Security Administration Act 1992;
"applicable amount" means the applicable amount determined in accordance with regulations under section 4;
"benefit year" has the meaning given by section 2(4);
"the Benefits Act" means the Social Security Contributions and Benefits Act 1992;
"child" means a person under the age 16;
"claimant" means a person who claims a jobseeker's allowance; [³except that in relation to a joint-claim couple claiming a joint-claim jobseeker's allowance it means the couple, or each member of the couple, as the context requires;]
"continental shelf operations" has the same meaning as in section 120 of the Benefits Act;
"contribution-based conditions" means the conditions set out in section 2;
"contribution-based jobseeker's allowance" has the meaning given in section 1(4);
"employed earner" has the meaning prescribed for the purposes of this Act;
"employment", except in section 7, has the meaning prescribed for the purposes of this Act;
"entitled", in relation to a jobseeker's allowance, is to be construed in accordance with—
   (a) the provisions of this Act relating to entitlement; and
   (b) [²section 1 of the Administration Act and section 27 of the Social Security Act 1998]
"family" means—
   (a) a married or unmarried couple;
   (b) a married or unmarried couple and a member of the same household for whom one of them is, or both are, responsible and who is a child or a person of a prescribed description;
   (c) except in prescribed circumstances, a person who is not a member of a married or unmarried couple and a member of the same household for whom that person is responsible and who is a child or a person of a prescribed description;
"Great Britain" includes the territorial waters of the United Kingdom adjacent to Great Britain;
"income-based conditions" means the conditions set out in section 3;
"income-based jobseeker's allowance" has the meaning given in section 1(4);
"jobseeker's agreement" has the meaning given by section 9(1);

"jobseeking period" has the meaning prescribed for the purposes of this Act;

[³"joint-claim couple" and "joint-claim jobseeker's allowance" have the meanings given by section 1(4);]

"married couple" means a man and woman who are married to each other and are members of the same household;

[³"the nominated member", in relation to a joint-claim couple, shall be construed in accordance with section 3B(4);]

"occupational pension scheme" has the same meaning as it has in the Pension Schemes Act 1993 by virtue of section 1 of that Act;

"pensionable age" has the meaning prescribed for the purposes of this Act;

"pension payments" means—

    (a) periodical payments made in relation to a person, under a personal pension scheme or, in connection with the coming to an end of an employment of his, under an occupational pension scheme or a public service pension scheme; and

    (b) such other payments as may be prescribed;

"personal pension scheme" means—

    (a) a personal pension scheme as defined by section 1 of the Pension Schemes Act 1993;

    (b) a contract or trust scheme approved under Chapter III of Part XIV of the Income and Corporation Taxes Act 1988; and

    (c) a personal pension scheme approved under Chapter IV of that Part of that Act;

"prescribed" [¹, except in section 27 (and in section 36 so far as relating to regulations under section 27),] means specified in or determined in accordance with regulations;

"public service pension scheme" has the same meaning as it has in the Pension Schemes Act 1993 by virtue of section 1 of that Act;

"regulations" [¹, except in section 27 (and in section 36 so far as relating to regulations under section 27),] means regulations made by the Secretary of State;

"tax year" means the 12 months beginning with 6th April in any year;

"trade dispute" means any dispute between employers and employees, or between employees and employees, which is connected with the employment or non-employment or the terms of employment or the conditions of employment of any persons, whether employees in the employment of the employer with whom the dispute arises, or not;

"training" has the meaning prescribed for the purposes of this Act and, in relation to prescribed provisions of this Act, if regulations so provide, includes assistance to find training or employment, or to improve a person's prospects of being employed, of such a kind as may be prescribed;

"unmarried couple" means a man and woman who are not married to each other but are living together as husband and wife otherwise than in prescribed circumstances;

"week" means a period of 7 days beginning with a Sunday or such other period of 7 days as may be prescribed;

"work" has the meaning prescribed for the purposes of this Act;

"year", except in the expression "benefit year", means a tax year.

(2) The expressions "capable of work", "linked period", "relevant education" and "remunerative work" are to be read with paragraphs 2, 3, 14 and 1 of Schedule 1.

(3) Subject to any regulations made for the purposes of this subsection, "earnings" is to be construed for the purposes of this Act in accordance with section 3 of the Benefits Act and paragraph 6 of Schedule 1 to this Act.

AMENDMENTS

1.291   1. Social Security Contributions (Transfer of Functions, etc.) Act 1999, s.2 and Sch.3, para.62 (April 1, 1999).

2. Social Security Act 1998, Sch.7, para.144 (October 18, 1999).

3. Welfare Reform and Pensions Act 1999, s.59 and Sch.7, para.15 (March 19, 2001).

GENERAL NOTE

1.292   This section defines certain terms used in the legislation, but leaves some to be construed in accordance with specified paragraphs of Sch.1 and others to be defined through regulations, some of which definitions relate to the whole of the JSA Regulations (see regs 1(3) and 3) and some of which only apply to specified Parts.

"*child*". The restriction to a person under 16 gives rise to the need to define "young person" in the JSA Regulations to cater for the over-15s (see JSA Regs, regs 57(1) and 76(1)).

"*employed earner*". See reg.3 of the JSA Regulations.

"*employment*". This is defined for purposes of "actively seeking employment" in s.7(8) to cover both employed and self-employed earner's employment as those terms are used in SSCBA 1992, but otherwise "employment" has the meaning prescribed in regulations: see JSA Regs, regs 3, 4.

"*family*". The definition is the same as in s.137(1) of the Contributions and Benefits Act 1992. See the notes to that definition. For "person of a prescribed description" see reg.76(1) of the JSA Regulations.

"*married couple*". The definition is the same as in s.137(1) of the Contributions and Benefits Act 1992. See the notes to that definition.

"*occupational pension scheme*". An "occupational pension scheme" is:

> "any scheme or arrangement which is comprised in one or more instruments or agreements and which has, or is capable of having, effect in relation to one or more description or categories of employment so as to provide benefits, in the form of pensions or otherwise, payable on termination of service, or on death or retirement, to or in respect of earners with qualifying service in an employment of any such description or category" (Pension Schemes Act 1993, s.1).

"*pensionable age*". See reg.3 of the JSA Regulations.

"*personal pension scheme*". A "personal pension scheme" embraces a contract or trust scheme approved under Ch. III of Part XIV of the Income and Corporation Taxes Act 1988; a personal pension scheme approved under Ch. IV of that Part of that Act; and a personal pension scheme as defined in s.1 of the Pension Schemes Act 1993 ("any scheme or arrangement which is comprised in one or more instruments or agreements and which has, or is capable of having, effect so as to provide benefits, in the form of pensions or otherwise, payable on death or retirement to or in respect of employed earners who have made arrangements with the trustees or managers of the scheme for them to become members of it").

"*public service pension scheme*". A "public service pension scheme" is:

"an occupational pension scheme [as defined above] established by or under an enactment or the Royal prerogative or a Royal charter, being a scheme (a) all the particulars of which are set out in, or in a legislative instrument made under, an enactment, Royal warrant or charter, or (b) which cannot come into force, or be amended, without the scheme or amendment being approved by a Minister of the Crown or government department."

The term includes:

"any occupational pension scheme established, with the concurrence of the Treasury, by or with the approval of any Minister of the Crown and any occupational pension scheme prescribed by regulations made by the Secretary of State and the Treasury jointly as being a scheme which ought in their opinion to be treated as a public service pension scheme for the purposes of this Act" (Pension Schemes Act 1993, s.1).

"training". See reg.57(1) of the JSA Regulations.
"unmarried couple". The definition is the same as in s.137(1) of the Contributions and Benefits Act 1992. See the notes to that definition.

Regulations and orders

36.—(1) Any power under this Act to make regulations or orders, other than an order under section [² 8(3),] 9(13) or 19(10)(a), shall be exercisable by statutory instrument.   1.293

(2) Any such power may be exercised—

(a) either in relation to all cases to which it extends, or in relation to those cases subject to specified exceptions, or in relation to any specified cases or classes of case;

(b) so as to make, as respects the cases in relation to which it is exercised—

   (i) the full provision to which the power extends or any less provision (whether by way of exception or otherwise),

   (ii) the same provision for all cases in relation to which it is exercised, or different provision for different cases or different classes of case or different provision as respects the same case or class of case for different purposes of this Act,

   (iii) any such provision either unconditionally or subject to any specified condition.

(3) Where any such power is expressed to be exercisable for alternative purposes it may be exercised in relation to the same case for any or all of those purposes.

(4) Any such power includes power—

(a) to make such incidental, supplemental, consequential or transitional provision as appears to the Secretary of State [¹, or (in the case of regulations made by the Treasury) to the Treasury,] to be expedient; and

(b) to provide for a person to exercise a discretion in dealing with any matter.

(5) Any power to make regulations or an order for the purposes of any provision of this Act is without prejudice to any power to make regulations or an order for the purposes of any other provision.

AMENDMENTS

1. Social Security Contributions (Transfer of Functions, etc.) Act 1999, s.2 and Sch.3, para.63 (April 1, 1999).   1.294

2. Welfare Reform and Pensions Act 1999, s.70 and Sch.8, para.29 (November 11, 1999).

"regulations"—see s.35(1).

GENERAL NOTE

See s.37 for the regulations which require approval by affirmative resolution.

Parliamentary control

1.295   **37.**—(1) Subsection (2) applies in relation to the following regulations (whether made alone or with other regulations)—

(a) regulations made under, or by virtue of, any provision of this Act other than—
   (i) section 6, 7, 26, 29 or 40;
   (ii) paragraph (b) of the definition of "pension payments" in section 35(1), or
   (iii) paragraph 17 of Schedule 1, before the date on which jobseeker's allowances first become payable;

(b) the first regulations to be made under section 26;

(c) regulations made under section 6, 7, 29, paragraph (b) of the definition of "pension payments" in section 35(1) or paragraph 17 of Schedule 1.

(2) No regulations to which this subsection applies shall be made unless a draft of the statutory instrument containing the regulations has been laid before Parliament and approved by a resolution of each House.

(3) Any other statutory instrument made under this Act, other than one made under section 41(2), shall be subject to annulment in pursuance of a resolution of either House of Parliament.

DEFINITIONS

1.296   "pension payments"—see s.35(1).
"regulations"—*ibid.*

GENERAL NOTE

Note in particular that regulations governing availability for, and actively seeking, employment and pilot schemes have to be approved by affirmative resolution (subs.(1)(c)).

General financial arrangements

1.297   **38.**—*[Omitted as not relevant.]*

Provision for Northern Ireland

1.298   **39.**—*[Omitted as not relevant.]*

Transitional provisions

1.299   **40.**—(1) The Secretary of State may by regulations make such transitional provision, consequential provision or savings as he considers necessary or expedient for the purposes of or in connection with—

(a) the coming into force of any provision of this Act; or

(b) the operation of any enactment repealed or amended by any such provision during any period when the repeal or amendment is not wholly in force;

(2) Regulations under this section may in particular make provision—

(a) for the termination or cancellation of awards of unemployment benefit or income support;

(b) for a person whose award of unemployment benefit or income support has been terminated or cancelled under regulations made by virtue of paragraph (a) to be treated as having been awarded a job-seeker's allowance (a "transitional allowance")—

   (i) of such a kind,

   (ii) for such period,

   (iii) of such an amount, and

   (iv) subject to such conditions,

as may be determined in accordance with the regulations;

(c) for a person's continuing entitlement to a transitional allowance to be determined by reference to such provision as may be made by the regulations;

(d) for the termination of an award of a transitional allowance;

(e) for the review of an award of a transitional allowance;

(f) for a contribution-based jobseeker's allowance not to be payable for a prescribed period where a person is disqualified for receiving unemployment benefit;

(g) that days which were days of unemployment for the purposes of entitlement to unemployment benefit, and such other days as may be prescribed, are to be treated as having been days during which a person was, or would have been, entitled to a jobseeker's allowance;

(h) that days which were days of entitlement to unemployment benefit, and such other days as may be prescribed, are to be treated as having been days of entitlement to a contribution-based job-seeker's allowance;

(i) that the rate of a contribution-based transitional allowance is to be calculated by reference to the rate of unemployment benefit paid or payable.

DEFINITIONS

"contribution-based jobseeker's allowance"—see s.1(4).   **1.300**
"prescribed"—see s.35(1).
"regulations"—*ibid.*

GENERAL NOTE

See the Jobseeker's Allowance (Transitional Provisions) Regulations 1996 (SI 1996/2657) which are consolidating regulations that replaced the Jobseeker's Allowance (Transitional Provisions) Regulations 1995 (SI 1995/3276), as amended, from November 4, 1996. The text and commentary can be found in the 2000 edition of this volume.

Short title, commencement, extent etc.

41.—(1) This Act may be cited as the Jobseekers Act 1995.   **1.301**
(2) Section 39 and this section (apart from subsections (4) and (5)) come

into force on the passing of this Act, but otherwise the provisions of this Act come into force on such day as the Secretary of State may by order appoint.

(3) Different days may be appointed for different purposes.

(4) Schedule 2 makes consequential amendments.

(5) The repeals set out in Schedule 3 shall have effect.

(6) Apart from this section, section 39 and paragraphs 11 to 16, 28, 67 and 68 of Schedule 2, this Act does not extend to Northern Ireland.

GENERAL NOTE

Subss. (4) and (5)

1.302   The amendments and repeals effected by, respectively, Schs 2 and 3 have been taken into account in the appropriate places in this book.

SCHEDULE 1

SUPPLEMENTARY PROVISIONS

Remunerative work

1.303   **1.**—(1) For the purposes of this Act, "remunerative work" has such meaning as may be prescribed.

(2) Regulations may prescribe circumstances in which, for the purposes of this Act—

(a) a person who is not engaged in remunerative work is to be treated as engaged in remunerative work; or

(b) a person who is engaged in remunerative work is to be treated as not engaged in remunerative work.

Capacity for work

1.304   **2.**—(1) The question whether a person is capable or incapable of work shall be determined, for the purposes of this Act, in accordance with the provisions of Part XIIA of the Benefits Act.

(2) References in Part XIIA of the Benefits Act to the purposes of that Act shall be construed, where those provisions have effect for the purposes of this Act by virtue of sub-paragraph (1), as references to the purposes of this Act.

(3) Section 171B of the Benefits Act (incapacity for work: the own occupation test) shall have effect, as applied by sub-paragraph (1) for the purposes of this Act, as if for the references in subsection (3) and (4)(a) to any purpose of the Benefits Act there were substituted references to any purpose of this Act.

Linking periods

1.305   **3.** Regulations may provide—

(a) for jobseeking periods which are separated by not more than a prescribed number of weeks to be treated, for purposes of this Act, as one jobseeking period;

(b) for prescribed periods ("linked periods") to be linked, for purposes of this Act, to any jobseeking period.

Waiting days

1.306   **4.** Except in prescribed circumstances, a person is not entitled to a jobseeker's allowance in respect of a prescribed number of days at the beginning of a jobseeking period.

5. Regulations may make provision in relation to—

(a) entitlement to a jobseeker's allowance, or

(b) the amount payable by way of such an allowance, in respect of any period of less than a week.

Employment protection sums

1.307   **6.**—(1) In relation to any contribution-based jobseeker's allowance, regulations may make provision—

(a) for any employment protection sum to be treated as earnings payable by such person, to such person and for such period as may be determined in accordance with the regulations; and

(b) for any such period, so far as it is not a period of employment, to be treated as a period of employment.

(2) In this paragraph "employment protection sum" means—

(a) any sum, or a prescribed part of any sum—

    (i) payable, in respect of arrears of pay, under an order for reinstatement or re-engagement made under[¹the Employment Rights Act 1996];

    (ii) payable, by way of pay, under an order made under that Act for the continuation of a contract of employment;

    (iii) payable, by way of remuneration, under a protective award made under section 189 of the Trade Union and Labour Relations (Consolidation) Act 1992; and

(b) any prescribed sum which the regulations provide is to be treated as related to any sum within paragraph (a).

Pension payments

1.308

7. Regulations may make provision, for the purposes of any provision of, or made under, this Act—

(a) for such sums by way of pension payments to be disregarded for prescribed purposes;

(b) as to the week in which any pension payments are to be treated as having begun;

(c) for treating, in a case where—

    (i) a lump sum is paid to a person in connection with a former employment of his or arrangements are made for a lump sum to be so paid; or

    (ii) benefits of any description are made available to a person in connection with a former employment of his or arrangements are made for them to be made so available; or

    (iii) pension payments to a person are assigned, reduced or postponed or are made otherwise than weekly,

such payments as being made to that person by way of weekly pension payments as are specified in or determined under the regulations;

(d) for the method of determining whether pension payments are made to a person for any week and their amount.

Exemptions

1.309

8. Regulations may prescribe circumstances in which a person may be entitled to an income-based jobseeker's allowance without—

(a) being available for employment;

(b) having entered into a jobseeker's agreement; or

(c) actively seeking employment.

[³ **8A.**—(1) Regulations may prescribe circumstances in which a joint-claim couple may be entitled to a joint-claim jobseeker's allowance without each member of the couple satisfying all the conditions referred to in section 1(2B)(b).

(2) Regulations may prescribe circumstances in which, and a period for which, a transitional case couple may be entitled to a joint-claim jobseeker's allowance without having jointly made a claim for it.

(3) In sub-paragraph (2)—

(a) "a transitional case couple" means a joint-claim couple a member of which is entitled to an income-based jobseeker's allowance on the coming into force of Schedule 7 to the Welfare Reform and Pensions Act 1999; and

(b) "period" shall be construed in accordance with section 3(3).]

9. Regulations may provide—

(a) for an income-based jobseeker's allowance to which a person is entitled by virtue of regulations under paragraph 8 [³ or 8A] to be payable at a prescribed rate;

(b) for it to be payable for a prescribed period.

[³ *Continuity of claims and awards: persons ceasing to be a joint-claim couple*

1.310

9A.—(1) Regulations may make provision about the entitlement to a jobseeker's allowance of persons ("ex-members") who cease to be members of a joint-claim couple.

(2) Regulations under this paragraph may, in particular, provide—

(a) for treating each or either of the ex-members as having made any claim made by the couple or, alternatively, for any such claim to lapse;

(b) for any award made in respect of the couple to be replaced by an award (a "replacement award") in respect of each or either of the ex-members of the couple or, alternatively, for any such award to lapse.

Continuity of claims and awards: persons again becoming a joint-claim couple

9B.—(1) Regulations may make provision about the entitlement to a jobseeker's allowance of persons ("ex-members") who, having ceased to be members of a joint-claim couple, again become the members of a joint-claim couple.

(2) Regulations under this paragraph may, in particular, provide—

(a) for any claim made by the ex-members when they were previously a joint-claim couple to be revived or otherwise given effect as a claim made by the couple;

(b) for any award made in respect of the ex-members when they were previously a joint-claim couple to be restored;

(c) for any such award, or any replacement award (within the meaning of paragraph 9A) made in respect of either of them, to be replaced by an award (a "new award") in respect of the couple.

Continuity of claims and awards: couple becoming a joint-claim couple

9C.—(1) Regulations may make provision about the entitlement to a jobseeker's allowance of persons who become members of a joint-claim couple as a result of the married or unmarried couple of which they are members becoming a joint-claim couple.

(2) Regulations under this paragraph may, in particular, provide—

(a) for any claim made by either member of the couple before the couple became a joint-claim couple to be given effect as a claim made by the couple;

(b) for any award, or any replacement award (within the meaning of paragraph 9A), made in respect of either member of the couple before the couple became a joint-claim couple to be replaced by an award (a "new award") in respect of the couple.

Paragraphs 9A to 9C: supplementary

9D.—(1) Regulations may provide, in relation to any replacement award (within the meaning of paragraph 9A) or new award (within the meaning of paragraph 9B or 9C)—

(a) for the award to be of an amount determined in a prescribed manner;

(b) for entitlement to the award to be subject to compliance with prescribed requirements as to the provision of information and evidence.

(2) In paragraphs 9A to 9C and this paragraph—

"award" means an award of a jobseeker's allowance;

"claim" means a claim for a jobseeker's allowance.]

Claims yet to be determined and suspended payments

[³ **10.**—(1) In such circumstances as may be prescribed—

(a) a claimant for a jobseeker's allowance other than a joint-claim jobseeker's allowance;

(b) a joint-claim couple claiming a joint-claim jobseeker's allowance; or

(c) a member of such a couple,

may be treated as being entitled to an income-based jobseeker's allowance before his or (as the case may be) the couple's claim for the allowance has been determined.]

(2) In such circumstances as may be prescribed, an income-based jobseeker's allowance shall be payable [³ to—

(a) a claimant for a jobseeker's allowance other than a joint-claim jobseeker's allowance;

(b) a joint-claim couple claiming a joint-claim jobseeker's allowance; or

(c) a member of such a couple,

even though payment to him or (as the case may be) the couple] of a jobseeker's allowance has been suspended by virtue of regulations under [²section 5(1)(n) or (nn)] of the Administration Act.

(3) A jobseeker's allowance shall be payable by virtue of sub-paragraph (1) or (2) only if the claimant [³ or (as the case may be) the couple or the member of the couple] has complied with such requirements as to the provision of information as may be prescribed for the purposes of this paragraph.

(4) Regulations may make provision for a jobseeker's allowance payable by virtue of sub-paragraph (1) or (2) to be—

(a) payable at a prescribed rate;

(b) payable for a prescribed period;

(c) treated as being a contribution-based jobseeker's allowance for the purposes of section 5 of this Act.

(5) Regulations may make provision—

(a) for the recovery, by prescribed means and in prescribed circumstances, of the whole or part of any amount paid by virtue of sub-paragraph (1) or (2);

(b) for the whole or part of any amount paid by virtue of sub-paragraph (1) to be treated, if an award is made on the claim referred to there, as having been paid on account of the jobseeker's allowance awarded;

(c) for the whole or part of any amount paid by virtue of sub-paragraph (2) to be treated, if the suspension referred to there is lifted, as having been paid on account of the suspended allowance.

Presence in and absence from Great Britain

11.—(1) Regulations may provide that in prescribed circumstances a claimant who is not in Great Britain may nevertheless be entitled to a contribution-based jobseeker's allowance.

(2) Regulations may make provision for the purposes of this Act as to the circumstances in which a person is to be treated as being or not being in Great Britain.

1.315

Households

12. Regulations may make provision for the purposes of this Act as to the circumstances in which persons are to be treated as being or not being members of the same household.

1.316

Responsibility for another person

13. Regulations may make provision for the purposes of this Act as to the circumstances in which one person is to be treated as responsible or not responsible for another.

1.317

Relevant education

14. Regulations may make provision for the purposes of this Act—

(a) as to what is or is not to be treated as relevant education; and

(b) as to the circumstances in which a person is or is not to be treated as receiving relevant education.

1.318

Calculation of periods

15. Regulations may make provision for calculating periods for any purpose of this Act.

1.319

Employment on ships etc.

16.—(1) Regulations may modify any provision of this Act in its application to any person who is, has been, or is to be—

(a) employed on board any ship, vessel, hovercraft or aircraft,

(b) outside Great Britain at any prescribed time or in any prescribed circumstances, or

(c) in prescribed employment in connection with continental shelf operations,

so far as that provision relates to a contribution-based jobseeker's allowance.

(2) The regulations may in particular provide—

(a) for any such provision to apply even though it would not otherwise apply;

(b) for any such provision not to apply even though it would otherwise apply;

(c) for the taking of evidence, in a country or territory outside Great Britain, by a British consular official or other prescribed person;

(d) for enabling payment of the whole, or any part of a contribution-based jobseeker's allowance to be paid to such of the claimant's dependants as may be prescribed.

1.320

Additional conditions

17. Regulations may require additional conditions to be satisfied with respect to the payment of a jobseeker's allowance to any person who is, has been, or is to be, in employment which falls within a prescribed description.

1.321

Benefits Act purposes

18. Regulations may provide for—

(a) a jobseeker's allowance;

1.322

(b)   a contribution-based jobseeker's allowance; or

(c)   an income-based jobseeker's allowance,

to be treated, for prescribed purposes of the Benefits Act, as a benefit, or a benefit of a prescribed description.

AMENDMENTS

1. Employment Rights Act 1996, Sch.1, para.67(3) (August 22, 1996).
2. Social Security Act 1998, Sch.7, para.146 (October 18, 1999).
3. Welfare Reform and Pensions Act 1999, Sch.7, para.16 (March 19, 2001).

DEFINITIONS

"a joint-claim couple": see s.1(4).
"a joint-claim jobseeker's allowance: see s.1(4).
"a transitional case couple": see para.8A(3).
"the Benefits Act": see s.35(1).
"contribution-based jobseeker's allowance": see s.35(1), 1(4).
"employment": see s.35(1).
"employment protection sum": see para.6(2).
"ex-members": see paras 9A(1), 9B(1).
"Great Britain": see s.35(1).
"income-based jobseeker's allowance": see ss.35(1), 1(4).
"jobseeker's agreement": see ss.35(1), 9(1).
"jobseeking period": see s.35(1), JSA Regs, reg.47.
"pension payments": see s.35(1).
"prescribed": see s.35(1).
"regulations": see s.35(1).
"week": see s.35(1).

GENERAL NOTE

Para. 1

1.323   Where a claimant is engaged in remunerative work, there can be no entitlement to JSA (s.1(2)(e)). If only his partner is so engaged, he can still be eligible for contribution-based JSA but not for income-based JSA (s.3(1)(e)). This provision enables regulations to define "remunerative work" (in fact setting a threshold of 16 hours for the claimant and 24 hours for his partner). Those regulations can also define situations in which, despite not being so engaged, a person is to be treated as if engaged in remunerative work and conversely, to prescribe situations in which someone who would on the usual rules be regarded as being in remunerative work is to be treated as if he were not. See further JSA Regs, regs 51–53.

Para. 2

1.324   To be entitled to JSA, a claimant must be capable of work (s.1(2)(f)). This provision ensures that the assessment of capacity/incapacity for work for JSA purposes is to be determined, as appropriate, by either the "own occupation" or the "personal capability assessment" (formerly the "all work test" of incapacity for work) found in Pt XIIA of the SSCBA 1992.

Para. 3

1.325   This makes provision which benefits those whose unemployment is intermittent, interspersed with, say, periods of employment, of incapacity for work, of training for work or periods when pregnant, by providing, somewhat after the fashion of unemployment benefit and its notion of "period of interruption of employment" ("PIE"), for the concepts of "linking" and "linked periods" whereby apparently separate jobseeking periods are fused into one and certain periods ("linked periods") do not "break" a jobseeking period.

"Linking", and through it the creation of a single jobseeking period, is important for two reasons: (1) the "waiting days" (see para.4, below) only have to be served once in a jobseeking period; (2) in determining "the relevant benefit year" for purposes of identifying which tax/contribution years have to be looked at in order to ascertain if the claimant satisfies the contribution-record conditions of entitlement to contribution-based JSA (see further annotation to s.2, above).

A "jobseeking period" is basically any period throughout which the claimant satisfies (or is treated as satisfying) the conditions of entitlement to JSA set out in s.1(2)(a)–(c) and (e)–(i): available for employment; a current jobseeker's agreement; actively seeking employment; not in remunerative work; not receiving relevant education; under pensionable age; and in Great Britain (s.35(1); JSA Regs, reg.47(1)). Where a hardship payment under Pt IX of those Regulations is paid to a claimant who does not satisfy a labour market condition (any of the conditions in s.1(2)(a)–(c): availability; actively seeking; jobseeker's agreement), he is to be treated as satisfying them for purposes of applying the above definition of jobseeking period (JSA Regs, reg.47(2)). He is also treated as satisfying the conditions in s.1(2)(a)–(c) and (e)–(i) when entitled to JSA under reg.13(3) of the JSA (Transitional) Regulations (JSA Regs, reg.47(2A)). Certain periods cannot constitute, or be part of, a jobseeking period: (i) any period in which no claim for JSA has been made or treated as made; (ii) any period before the day on which a claim is made or before the earliest date in which good cause for a late claim is shown; (iii) a period caught by the 12-month limit on backdating entitlement under s.1(2) of the SSAA 1992; (iv) a period of disentitlement under JSA Regs, regs 25, 26; (v) any week of disentitlement because the claimant is caught by the trade dispute rule in s.14 (JSA Regs, reg.47(3)). Note also JSA Regs, reg.47A on periods of interruption of employment prior to October 7, 1996.

"Linked periods" comprise (i) any period throughout which the claimant is, or is treated as, incapable of work under Part XIIA of the SSCBA 1992; (ii) any period throughout which she was entitled to a maternity allowance under s.35 of that Act; (iii) any period throughout which the claimant was engaged in training for which a training allowance is payable; (iv) (but only for contributions-conditions purposes) any period throughout which the claimant was entitled to an invalid care allowance (now "carer's allowance") under s.70 of the SSCBA 1992; (v) a period of attending court in response to a jury summons, which period includes October 6, 1996 and was immediately preceded by a period of entitlement to unemployment benefit; (vi) certain periods of participation in the Employment Option, the Voluntary Sector Option or the Environment Task Force Option of the New Deal and various Intensive Activity Period Programmes; (vii) certain periods of participation in an employment zone programme (JSA Regs, reg.48(2), (3)).

Two or more jobseeking periods "link" and are treated as one jobseeking period where they are separated by a period comprising only (i) one of 12 weeks; (ii) a linked period; (iii) a period of not more than 12 weeks falling between any two linked periods or between a jobseeking period and a linked period; (iv) any period in respect of which the claimant is summoned for jury service and is required to attend court (JSA Regs, reg.48(1)).

Para.4

Unemployment benefit was a daily benefit payable in respect of a six-day week. JSA is a weekly benefit. Nonetheless, through this provision, as amplified by JSA Regs, reg.46(2), it deploys the concept of "waiting days", familiar from unemployment benefit but never part of income support, whereby, despite meeting the other conditions of entitlement to JSA, there is no entitlement to it for a number of days (currently three, but alterable by regulations) at the start of a jobseeking period. On "jobseeking period" and the effect of "linking", see notes to para.3, above. Note further that the "waiting days" rule does not apply where the claimant's entitlement to JSA begins within 12 weeks of the ending of his entitlement to income support, incapacity benefit or invalid care allowance, nor where the claim for income-based

1.326

JSA has to be determined by reference to s.3(1)(f)(ii), (*i.e.* the person is 16 or 17, registered for training but is not being provided with any, severe hardship will result to him if JSA is not paid, and the Secretary of State directs that s.16 is to apply to him) (JSA Regs, reg.46(1)).

Para.5

1.327   Although JSA is a weekly rather than a daily benefit, provision is made through regulations made under this paragraph for entitlement to JSA and the amount payable in respect of a period less than a week. See JSA Regs, regs 150–155 (regs 150(2), (3) and 152 are the ones relevant to contribution-based JSA).

Para.6

1.328   This enables regulations to treat as earnings with respect to contribution-based JSA for prescribed periods, certain employment protection sums under the Employment Rights Act 1996 and the Trade Union and Labour Relations (Consolidation) Act 1992 (or treated by regulations as related to those specific sums). It also enables regulations to treat those periods as ones of employment. See JSA Regs, reg.98(1)(f), (ff), (g) and related regulations on calculating net earnings (reg.99), determining the date on which they are treated for JSA purposes as paid (reg.96), the period over which they are taken into account (reg.94), and a weekly amount (reg.97).

Para.7

1.329   This enables regulations to deal with the listed aspects of taking into account pension payments. As regards contribution-based JSA, the scheme incorporates the concept of abatement of benefit (even to nil) in respect of pension payments, familiar from unemployment benefit, but extends it to all claimants (not just those 55 or over) and raises the weekly amount at which they are to be taken into account to £50 per week. See further notes to s.4(1) and JSA Regs, reg.81.

Paras 8, 8A, and 9

1.330   These enable regulations allowing access to reduced rates of income-based JSA for "persons in hardship", both in respect of standard cases and those of joint-claim couples, without having to meet the "labour market" conditions (availability; actively seeking; jobseeker's agreement). See further, JSA Regs, regs 140–146 (standard cases) and regs 146A–146H (joint-claim couples). In addition, para.8A enables regulations for a "transitional case couple" to be entitled to a joint-claim jobseeker's allowance for a period without having made a claim for it. A "transitional case couple" is a "joint-claim couple where one member was entitled to income-based JSA when the joint claim changes came into effect (March 19, 2001). JSA Regs, reg.3F is the product of the exercise of this rule-making power.

Paras 9A–9D

1.331   These rule-making powers deal with matters of continuity where a couple cease to be a joint-claim couple (*e.g.* because of the birth of a child)(a "replacement award") (para.9A), where a couple again become a joint-claim couple (*e.g.* because of the death of a child) (para.9B) and where two people newly become one (*e.g.* because a child has become 16 and left education)(para.9C) (in both cases a "new award"). See further JSA Regs, regs 3B (ceasing to be a joint-claim couple), 3C (a couple again or newly becoming a joint-claim couple).

Para.10

1.332   This enables regulations allowing access to reduced rate payments of income-based JSA for a "person in hardship" before the claim or the joint-claim for JSA has been determined and where payment of JSA has been suspended by virtue of regulations under s.5(1)(n) or (nn) of the SSAA 1992. See further JSA Regs, regs 140–146 (standard cases) and 146A–146H (joint-claim couples).

Para. 11

Generally, to be entitled to JSA, a claimant must be in Great Britain (s.1(2)(i)). **1.333** Sub-paragraph (1) enables regulations to be made prescribing circumstances in which someone not in Great Britain can nevertheless be entitled to contribution-based JSA. See JSA Regs, regs 165and 166. The former effected amendments to reg.11 of the Persons Abroad Regulations (see below). The latter amended the Social Security (Mariners' Benefits) Regulations 1975, which are not reproduced in this book.

Sub-paragraph (2) enables the making of regulations treating a person as being, or as not being, in Great Britain. See JSA Regs, reg.50 which in the circumstances there set out treat someone temporarily absent from Great Britain as if he were present in Great Britain, thus enabling him to remain eligible for JSA while temporarily absent.

Para. 12

This enables regulations to set out when persons are or are not to be regarded for **1.334** JSA purposes as members of the same household. See reg.78 of the JSA Regulations.

Para. 13

This enables regulations setting out when someone is to be treated as responsible **1.335** for a child or young person. See reg.77 of the JSA Regulations.

Para. 14

A person cannot be entitled to JSA if receiving relevant education (s.1(2)(g)). This **1.336** paragraph enables regulations to provide for what does and does not constitute relevant education and for when someone is, or is not, to be treated as receiving it. See further JSA Regs, reg.54, which defines it to cover only full-time education, not being a course of advanced education, which is undertaken by a child or young person. Someone treated as a child for child benefit purposes or who is receiving full-time education as far as the child benefit system is concerned (see SSCBA 1992, s.142), is treated as receiving full-time education for purposes of jobseeker's allowance (JSA Regs, reg.54(2)). Because this exclusion covers persons under 19, the effect of the contribution conditions (the claimant's insurance record) is to make this in practice a hurdle much more relevant to income-based than contribution-based JSA. Those on a full-time course of advanced education, it should be noted will be excluded from JSA because treated as not available for employment (see s.6, JSA Regs, regs 1(3), 15(a)).

Para. 16

This enables regulations to modify any provision of this Act, so far as it relates to **1.337** contribution-based JSA, in its application to those employed on ships, vessels, hovercraft or aircraft, to those outside Great Britain, or to those in prescribed employment in connection with continental shelf operations. See further JSA Regs, Pt XII (not reproduced in this work), dealing with share fishermen and persons outside Great Britain, including mariners.

Para. 17

This enables regulations to require additional conditions to be satisfied with **1.338** respect to payment of JSA to those in, or who have been in, or who are to be in, employment of a prescribed description. See further JSA Regs, Pt XII (not reproduced in this work), dealing with share fishermen and persons outside Great Britain, including mariners.

State Pension Credit Act 2002

(2002, c.16)

ARRANGEMENT OF SECTIONS

SCHEDULES

Schedules 1–3 [*omitted.*]   1.346

INTRODUCTION AND GENERAL NOTE

The prime purpose of this Act, embodied in ss.1–17, is to set the framework for   1.347
the new state pension credit that has been available to people aged 60 and over as
from October 6, 2003. It also makes, in s.18, an unconnected minor amendment to
the Pensions Schemes Act 1993. This corrects an oversight in the Welfare Reform
and Pensions Act 1999 as regards widowers' entitlements to benefits on bereavement, in order to avoid an element of double recovery in some cases. This latter provision is not included here as it falls outside the remit of this Volume.

State Pension Credit

The bulk of this Act is concerned with a new social security benefit, the state   1.348
pension credit, which is the latest phase in the government's pensions reforms. The
issue of poverty amongst pensioners has been high on the political agenda in recent
years. The Labour government elected in 1997 set out its initial proposals in *A New
Contract for Welfare: Partnership in Pensions* (Cm. 4179, 1998). This led to the introduction of stakeholder pensions under Part I of the Welfare Reform and Pensions
Act 1999, with effect from April 2001, as a new option for private pension provision for those on moderate incomes. The previous State Earnings Related Pension
Scheme ("SERPS") was replaced as from April 2002 by the new State Second
Pension under the Child Support, Pensions and Social Security Act 2000.

So far as the poorest pensioners were concerned, the government resisted
demands from its own backbenchers and supporters to restore the link between the
state retirement pension and increases in average earnings. Instead, the value of
income support for pensioners was dramatically increased and that benefit relabelled
as the minimum income guarantee (or "MIG") for that client group. (This was
purely a marketing change and involved no drafting amendments to the primary or
secondary legislation other than the inclusion of the new higher rates for pensioners.) This had the effect of increasing the gap between the (higher) MIG entitlement
and the (lower) basic state retirement pension respectively for a single pensioner.
The disparity increased from £5.75 in April 1998 (when the basic pension represented 92 per cent of the MIG rate) to £22.65 by April 2002 (by which time the
basic pension had fallen to 77 per cent of the MIG level). This exacerbated the long-
standing problem that pensioners with small amounts of private incomes on top of
their state retirement pension saw no benefit from such thrift as any such income is
deducted pound-for-pound under income support rules.

The proposal for a pension credit was first canvassed in a DSS consultation paper
in November 2000 (DSS, *The Pension Credit: a consultation paper*, Cm. 4900), which
was followed by the publication of a further paper entitled *The Pension Credit: the government's proposals* (DWP, 2001). The pension credit both continues the existing
income support arrangements (or MIG) for pensioners in a modified form and provides some reward for those with small private incomes. Thus the state pension
credit comprises two quite distinct elements. The first is the "guarantee credit",
which is intended to provide a minimum level of income to those aged 60 or over.
This replaces the MIG, the marketing name for income support for pensioners. The
second is the "savings credit", which is designed to provide an additional form of
income for pensioners from the age of 65 who have low or modest private incomes
(*e.g.* an occupational pension and/or income from savings) in addition to the basic
state retirement pension.

Section 1 specifies the common conditions for access to the pension credit,   1.349
whilst ss.2 and 3 respectively stipulate the extra conditions which must be satisfied
in order to qualify for either or both of the guarantee credit and the savings credit.

This legislative framework will be familiar to those readers acquainted with the structure of the Jobseekers Act 1995 (c.18), which likewise sets out the common conditions in s.1 and the additional criteria for the income-based and contribution-based elements respectively in ss.2 and 3. The common conditions for state pension credit in s.1 are that the claimant is in Great Britain and has reached the qualifying age (set at the pensionable age for women, and so for the time being at 60). In addition, s.4 includes a number of exclusions from entitlement to the pension credit and s.5 confirms that a claimant's resources must be aggregated with those of their partner.

The calculation of the guarantee credit entitlement under s.2 essentially works in the same way as the income support scheme. Moreover, by virtue of transitional provisions made under s.13(2), existing income support pensioner claimants may be treated as having made a claim for the pension credit (State Pension Credit (Consequential, Transitional and Miscellaneous Provisions) Regulations 2002 (SI 2002/3019, reg.36). There are, however, two important differences in the substantive rules of entitlement to the guarantee credit when contrasted with those that apply to income support. Income support is not available to those who work for 16 hours or more a week and is subject to an upper capital limit. Neither rule applies to the new pension credit.

The savings credit under s.3, comprising the second potential element in the state pension credit, is an entirely novel form of benefit. It works in completely the opposite way to the traditional means-test which applies for the purposes of income support. Previously a pensioner who had a small private income over and above the state retirement pension saw their MIG or income support reduced pound-for-pound by any such income. In contrast, the savings credit provides a small weekly supplement to reward those with modest savings or private incomes. Section 3 sets out the two extra criteria for the award of the savings credit (in addition to the common rules contained in s.1 for the pension credit as a whole). The first of these is that the claimant (or their partner) is at least 65. The second is effectively a complicated mathematical formula which is translated into text form. This can only really be understood by following the example provided in the annotation to s.3. Its effect is to provide a small savings credit of up to £16.44 at 2005/06 rates for a single pensioner for those with incomes which are just above the MIG level.

The other important difference from the current arrangements concerns the duration of awards of any pension credit (of either type) and the effects of change in circumstances. Income support is a weekly benefit and any changes in circumstances (*e.g.* in the amount of an occupational pension) must be reported to the DWP. Where the pension credit is awarded, the Secretary of State must specify an "assessed income period" (s.6), which will typically be for five years (s.9). The statutory assumption under s.7(4) is that the claimant's income will then remain constant throughout this period, subject to any deemed increases of a foreseeable and regular nature, such as the arrangements for indexation of any occupational or other private pension (*e.g.* in line with the Retail Price Index); see also s.10. The remarkable effect of these provisions is that where the claimant receives a windfall increase during the period of the award, any such increases are disregarded (s.7(5)) and accordingly do not give rise to any obligation to report such a change to the Department. In the event that the pensioner's income falls, a fresh assessment can be applied for (s.8).

1.350 The remaining provisions of the Act which relate to the state pension credit are of a supplementary nature. Section 11 introduces Sch.1, which applies the social security claims, decisions and appeals procedures to the state pension credit. Section 12 makes special provision for the few polygamous marriages that may fall within the ambit of the new scheme whilst s.13 enables the Secretary of State to make regulations governing transitional arrangements. Section 14 introduces Sch.2, which makes minor and consequential amendments. Sections 15–17 provide definitions of a number of key terms, such as "income" (s.15) and "retirement pension income" (s.16), as well as other general expressions (s.17), but also grant the Secretary of State extensive regulation-making powers to provide further definitions of certain terms. The relevant regulations, also in this Volume (see paras **4.1** *et seq.*), are the State Pension Credit Regulations 2002 (SI 2002/1792), as amended.

The final point to note about the state pension credit is a matter of nomenclature. Throughout the 2002 Act the new benefit is referred to as the *state* pension credit. This formula is required because s.29 of the Welfare Reform and Pensions Act 1999 makes provision for the creation of "pension credits" as a mechanism for effecting pension sharing on divorce. This Act, therefore, could not describe the new benefit simply as the pension credit. However, the new benefit is known as the *state* pension credit purely for the purposes of statutory drafting. The Department's publicity material describes the new benefit as the Pension Credit *simpliciter.* For the reasons explained in the General Note to s.3, the "savings credit", one of the constituent elements in the pension credit, is itself something of a misnomer, as it is not merely a credit on savings. It should also be made clear that the state pension credit has nothing whatsoever to do with the working tax credit and the child tax credit which were introduced in April 2003 by the Tax Credits Act 2002 (see Vol. IV in this series). Those *tax* credits are administered by the Inland Revenue; the state pension credit remains firmly in the province of the DWP and its new Pension Service, the Department's operational arm which now has responsibility for all pensions matters.

The DWP has published its estimates as to the likely long-term costs of the pension credit (DWP, *The Pension Credit: long-term projections,* 2002). In addition, the House of Commons Work and Pensions Committee has published a detailed report on the prospects for the pension credit (*Second Report,* Session 2001–02, HC 638–I and 638–II). Whilst welcoming the extra expenditure involved in the pension credit and the recognition which the new scheme accords to saving, the report raises a number of questions about the government's strategy. These include concerns about the administration and delivery of the pension credit by the Pension Service and the extent of take-up amongst pensioners. (The government's working assumption is that take-up of the pension credit will be 67 per cent in its first year of operation.) The government's response to the report has been published as the Select Committee's *Second Special Report* (Session 2001–02, HC 1006). See further Report by the Comptroller and Auditor General, *Tackling Pensioner Poverty: Encouraging take-up of entitlements* (HC 37, Session 2002–03) and Select Committee on Public Accounts, *Twelfth Report* (HC 565, Session 2002–03); see also N. Wikeley "State Pension Credit: completing the pensions jigsaw?" (2004) 11 *Journal of Social Security Law* 12. For the Select Committee's report on the implementation of the pension credit scheme, see Pension Credit (Third Report, Session 2004–05, HC 43–I and HC 43–II).

Other provisions

As mentioned in the introduction, s.18 relates to an amendment to the Pensions Schemes Act 1993. Section 19 contains the general regulation-making power and also specifies which regulations are to be subject to the affirmative procedure. Section 20 concerns the relevant financial provisions, s.21 (and Sch.3) make a number of minor repeals while s.22 deals with the short title, commencement and extent (which is Great Britain only: s.22(6); parallel provision is made for Northern Ireland).   **1.351**

Commencement

The Act received the Royal Assent on June 25, 2002. Sections 19, 20 and 22 came into effect on that date (s.22(2)). Other provisions come into effect as the Secretary of State may order (s.22(3)).   **1.352**

The State Pension Credit Act 2002 (Commencement No.1) Order 2002 (SI 2002/1691 (C.51)) provided that July 2, 2002 was the day appointed for the coming into force of the regulation making powers under ss.1 to 7, 9 and 11–17 (except for certain provisions in s.14). The relevant regulations are the State Pension Credit Regulations 2002 (SI 2002/1792, as amended), which came into force on October 6, 2003.

Section 18, which is not covered in this Volume for the reasons explained above, came into force on September 3, 2002 (State Pension Credit Act 2002 (Commencement No.2) Order 2002 (SI 2002/2248 (C.72)).

Further regulation making powers came into force on January 27, 2003 (State Pension Credit Act 2002 (Commencement No.3) Order 2002 (SI 2003/83 (C.4)).

Provisions relating to claims and decisions, and some repeals, came into force on April 7, 2003 (State Pension Credit Act 2002 (Commencement No.4) Order 2002 (SI 2003/966 (C.52)).

The final Commencement Order was the State Pension Credit Act 2002 (Commencement No.5) and Appointed Day Order 2003 (SI 2003/1766 (C.75)). This brought into force on October 6, 2003 all those provisions of the Act which were not already in force and appointed that day as the "appointed day" for the purposes of s.13 of the Act (transitional provisions).

State pension credit: entitlement and amount

Entitlement

1.353   **1.**—(1) A social security benefit to be known as state pension credit shall be payable in accordance with the following provisions of this Act.

(2) A claimant is entitled to state pension credit if—
(a) he is in Great Britain;
(b) he has attained the qualifying age; and
(c) he satisfies—
  (i) the condition in section 2(1) (guarantee credit); or
  (ii) the conditions in section 3(1) and (2) (savings credit).

(3) A claimant who is entitled to state pension credit is entitled—
(a) to a guarantee credit, calculated in accordance with section 2, if he satisfies the condition in subsection (1) of that section, or
(b) to a savings credit, calculated in accordance with section 3, if he satisfies the conditions in subsections (1) and (2) of that section,
(or to both, if he satisfies both the condition mentioned in paragraph (a) and the conditions mentioned in paragraph (b)).

(4) Subsections (2) and (3) are subject to the following provisions of this Act.

(5) Regulations may make provision for the purposes of this Act—
(a) as to circumstances in which a person is to be treated as being or not being in Great Britain; or
(b) continuing a person's entitlement to state pension credit during periods of temporary absence from Great Britain.

(6) In this Act "the qualifying age" means—
(a) in the case of a woman, pensionable age; or
(b) in the case of a man, the age which is pensionable age in the case of a woman born on the same day as the man.

Definitions

"claimant"—see s.17(1).
"entitled"—*ibid.*
"guarantee credit"—*ibid.*

"pensionable age"—*ibid.*
"the qualifying age"—see subs.(6).
"regulations"—see s.17(1).
"savings credit"—*ibid.*

GENERAL NOTE

This section sets out the entitlement criteria for the state pension credit. The 1.354
conditions laid down by this section are the common entitlement rules. These are
that the claimant is in Great Britain (subs.(2)(a); see further subs.(5)) and has
reached the qualifying age (subs.(2)(b), as defined by subs.(6)). In addition, a
claimant must satisfy either or both of the additional rules relating to eligibility for
the guarantee credit (s.2) and the savings credit (s.3) (see subs.(2)(c)). The guarantee credit replaces the MIG (or, in other words, income support) for the pensioner population. The calculation of the guarantee credit itself works in the same
way as the MIG and is designed to bring a pensioner's income up to a minimum
threshold, which for 2005/06 is £109.45 for a single claimant and £167.05 for a
couple. The savings credit, which may be payable additionally to or independently
of the guarantee credit, seeks to provide a reward for those pensioner claimants who
have a modest private income over and above the basic state retirement pension. A
claimant's entitlement thus comprises either or both such components, depending
on which conditions are met (subs.(3)). These requirements are obviously subject
to the remaining provisions of the Act (subs.(4)).

Subs.(5)

This power enables regulations to make further provision in respect to the resi- 1.355
dence requirement. The government have used power in the same way as for income
support (see State Pension Credit Regulations 2002 (SI 2002/1792), regs 2 and 3).
Thus pension credit claimants are required to be habitually resident but may retain
their entitlement for four weeks (or exceptionally eight weeks) during a period of
temporary absence abroad.

Subs.(6)

This definition of "qualifying age" must be read together with the definition of 1.356
"pensionable age" in s.17(1). Its effect is that the qualifying age for both men and
women is the pensionable age for women. This is currently 60, but between 2010 and
2020 will rise gradually until it reaches 65, in line with men (Pensions Act 1995, s.126
and Sch.4). The basic requirement under subs.(2)(a) is that a pension credit claimant
must have reached this qualifying age; this is also sufficient for entitlement to the
guarantee credit under s.2. However, a claimant must actually be 65 (or their partner
must be) in order to claim the savings credit (s.3(1)). The government's justification
for this distinction is that "the age of 65 is the first point at which we judge that the
savings credit can be fairly and equally paid to ensure that we are not open to legal
challenge in respect of gender equality" (Ms M. Eagle MP, Parliamentary Under-
Secretary for Work and Pensions, Standing Committee A, col.104). Thus retired
single women aged between 60 and 64 may claim the guarantee credit but not the
savings credit, even though they may have a small private income. Women of this age
who are members of a married or unmarried couple may claim the savings credit if
their partner is aged 65 or over, and so may see some benefit from private savings.

Guarantee credit

2.—(1) The condition mentioned in section 1(2)(c)(i) is that the 1.357
claimant—

(a) has no income; or
(b) has income which does not exceed the appropriate minimum
    guarantee.

151

(2) Where the claimant is entitled to a guarantee credit, then—

(a) if he has no income, the guarantee credit shall be the appropriate minimum guarantee; and

(b) if he has income, the guarantee credit shall be the difference between the appropriate minimum guarantee and his income.

(3) The appropriate minimum guarantee shall be the total of—

(a) the standard minimum guarantee; and

(b) such prescribed additional amounts as may be applicable.

(4) The standard minimum guarantee shall be a prescribed amount.

(5) The standard minimum guarantee shall be—

(a) a uniform single amount in the case of every claimant who is a member of a married or unmarried couple; and

(b) a lower uniform single amount in the case of every claimant who is not a member of such a couple.

(6) Regulations may provide that, in prescribed cases, subsection (3) shall have effect with the substitution for the reference in paragraph (a) to the standard minimum guarantee of a reference to a prescribed amount.

(7) Where the claimant is severely disabled, there shall be included among the additional amounts prescribed under subsection (3)(b) an amount in respect of that circumstance.

(8) Where—

(a) the claimant is entitled to an allowance under section 70 of the Contributions and Benefits Act, or

(b) if the claimant is a member of a married or unmarried couple, the other member of the couple is entitled to such an allowance,

there shall be included among the additional amounts prescribed under subsection (3)(b) an amount in respect of that circumstance.

(9) Except for the amount of the standard minimum guarantee, the powers conferred by this section to prescribe amounts include power to prescribe nil as an amount.

DEFINITIONS

1.358

"appropriate minimum guarantee"—see subs.(3) and s.17(1).

"claimant"—see s.17(1).

"Contributions and Benefits Act"—*ibid.*

"entitled"—*ibid.*

"guarantee credit"—*ibid.*

"income"—*ibid.*

"married couple"—*ibid.*

"prescribed"—*ibid.*

"regulations"—*ibid.*

"standard minimum guarantee"—see subss. (4), (5) and s.17(1).

"unmarried couple"—see s.17(1).

GENERAL NOTE

1.359

This section sets out the extra condition (further to the common conditions in s.1) which a pension credit claimant must satisfy in order to be entitled to the guarantee credit (which replaces the MIG, or income support, for pensioners). The extra condition is that the claimant either has no income or has an income which does not exceed the "appropriate minimum guarantee" (subs.(1)). "Income" is defined in accordance with ss.15 and 16 (and see State Pension Credit Regulations 2002 (SI 2002/1792, Part III)); but note also that the claimant's income is to be aggregated with that of any partner (s.5). The "appropriate minimum guarantee" is equivalent to the applicable amount in the income support scheme. It therefore comprises the "standard minimum guarantee" and other prescribed amounts (subs.(3)). The former is a standard prescribed amount (subss.(4) and (5)) which in 2005/06 is £109.45 for a single person and £167.05 for a couple (State Pension Credit Regulations 2002 (SI 2002/1792), reg.6(1)). The other prescribed amounts mirror the premiums in the income support scheme. Specific provision is made for two particular types of extra prescribed amounts under subs.(3)(b), namely for those who are severely disabled (subs.(7); this is based on SSCBA 1992, s.135(5)) and for those who are entitled to a carer's allowance (formerly invalid care allowance) under SSCBA 1992, s.70 (subs.(8)). The extra amounts under subs.(3)(b) also include other elements, *e.g.* prescribed sums for owner-occupiers as regards their housing costs (see generally State Pension Credit Regulations 2002 (SI 2002/1792), Schs. I and II).

The Secretary of State also has the power to substitute a prescribed amount for the uniform standard minimum guarantee (subs.(6)). This only has effect for the purpose of calculating the appropriate minimum guarantee for that person under subs.(3)(a), which is then based on the prescribed amount plus any other prescribed additional amounts. It does not, therefore, affect the standard minimum guarantee for other purposes in the Act, most notably the assessment of the maximum savings credit under s.3(7). This power has been inserted to enable a different rate to be applied where the claimant (or their partner) remains in hospital for more than 52 weeks. The previous regime provided for "hospital downrating" to apply after six weeks in hospital, but the government initially increased this period to 13 weeks and then subsequently to 52 weeks by the Social Security (Hospital In-Patients and Miscellaneous Amendments) Regulations 2003 (SI 2003/1195); see now State Pension Credit Regulations 2002 (SI 2002/1792), Sch.III, para.2.

The Secretary of State also has the power, taking subss. (6) and (9) together, to prescribe nil as the amount of the standard minimum guarantee in subs.(3)(a). The wording of subs.(9) is not entirely clear, but its import (when read with subs.(6)) appears to be that nil can be prescribed as the amount of the standard minimum guarantee under subs.(3)(a) but not as the rate of the normal standard minimum guarantee under subss. (4) and (5). This enables a nil amount to be specified for prisoners and members of religious orders who are fully maintained by their orders (both being groups who are currently excluded from income support; see now State Pension Credit Regulations 2002 (SI 2002/1792), reg.6(2) and (3)).

Three important differences with the rules governing entitlement to income support should be noted. First, there is no provision in the Act for a "16-hour rule" in the state pension credit scheme. Thus, unlike those of working age who claim income support or jobseeker's allowance, pensioners are not disentitled if they work 16 hours or more a week. Secondly, there is no upper capital limit for the pension credit (see further s.15); moreover the deemed rate of return by virtue of the tariff income rule is halved (State Pension Credit Regulations 2002 (SI 2002/1792), reg.15(6)). Finally, the traditional weekly means-test for income support has not been replicated in the arrangements for the pension credit; instead the typical award will be made for an "assessed income period" of five years (see further s.7).

Savings credit

3.—(1) The first of the conditions mentioned in section 1(2)(c)(ii) is that the claimant—   **1.360**

    (a) has attained the age of 65; or

    (b) is a member of a married or unmarried couple, the other member of which has attained that age.

(2) The second of the conditions mentioned in section 1(2)(c)(ii) is that—

    (a) the claimant's qualifying income exceeds the savings credit threshold; and

(b) the claimant's income is such that, for the purposes of subsection (3), amount A exceeds amount B.

(3) Where the claimant is entitled to a savings credit, the amount of the savings credit shall be the amount by which amount A exceeds amount B.

(4) For the purposes of subsection (3)—

"amount A" is the smaller of—

(a) the maximum savings credit; and

(b) a prescribed percentage of the amount by which the claimant's qualifying income exceeds the savings credit threshold; and

"amount B" is—

(a) a prescribed percentage of the amount (if any) by which the claimant's income exceeds the appropriate minimum guarantee; or

(b) if there is no such excess, nil.

(5) Where, by virtue of regulations under section 2(6), the claimant's appropriate minimum guarantee does not include the standard minimum guarantee, regulations may provide that the definition of "amount B" in subsection (4) shall have effect with the substitution for the reference in paragraph (a) to the appropriate minimum guarantee of a reference to a prescribed higher amount.

(6) Regulations may make provision as to income which is, and income which is not, to be treated as qualifying income for the purposes of this section.

(7) For the purposes of this section—

"the savings credit threshold" is such amount as may be prescribed;

"the maximum savings credit" is a prescribed percentage of the difference between—

(a) the standard minimum guarantee; and

(b) the savings credit threshold.

(8) Regulations may prescribe descriptions of persons in whose case the maximum savings credit shall be taken to be nil.

DEFINITIONS

1.361   "appropriate minimum guarantee"—see ss.2(3) and 17(1).
"claimant"—see s.17(1).
"entitled"—*ibid.*
"income"—*ibid.*
"married couple"—*ibid.*
"maximum savings credit"—see subs.(7).
"prescribed"—see s.17(1).
"regulations"—*ibid.*
"savings credit"—*ibid.*
"savings credit threshold"—see subs.(7).
"standard minimum guarantee"—ss.2(4), (5) and 17(1)
"unmarried couple"—s.17(1)

GENERAL NOTE

1.362   This section sets out the extra conditions (further to the common conditions in s.1) which a pension credit claimant must satisfy in order to be entitled to the savings credit. A claimant may be entitled to the savings credit even if he or she is not entitled to the guarantee credit (s.1(3)). In order to qualify for a savings credit there are two additional requirements that must be satisfied. The first is that the claimant (or their partner) is at least 65 (subs.(1)). This is in contrast to the conditions for the guarantee credit, for which the qualifying age is the basic age of 60 specified in the common criteria for the pension credit (s.1(2)(a) and (6)). The second additional condition is more complex. The claimant's "qualifying income" (including that of their partner: see further ss.5, 15 and 16 and State Pension Credit Regulations 2002 (SI 2002/1792), reg.9) must exceed the "savings credit threshold" and must be such that "amount A exceeds Amount B" (subs.(2)), the difference being the amount of savings credit entitlement (subs.(3)). The complexity is the inevitable consequence of the draftsman's attempt to reduce an arithmetical calculation into comprehensible prose. The good news is that this formula does not require the same skills in advanced algebra as did the original child support scheme.

The term "savings credit" is itself something of a misnomer, as will be seen from the examples discussed below. The savings credit is not a credit that is payable simply because a pensioner has savings, *e.g.* in a bank account. Rather, it is a supplement that is payable to pensioners who have small amounts of private income, whether in the form of an occupational or other private pension or indeed by way of income which is generated from savings.

Subs. (1)

See further the annotation to s.1(6).   **1.363**

Subss. (2)–(4)

The additional condition in subs.(2) can be understood better if it is broken down   **1.364**
into its four constituent terms: qualifying income, the savings credit threshold and amounts A and B respectively, although the component parts of these terms also require further definition.

Qualifying income

The expression "qualifying income" is further defined by regulations (subs.(6):   **1.365**
see State Pension Credit Regulations 2002 (SI 2002/1792), regs 15–18). The claimant's qualifying income includes those elements of their income which arise from contributions to the National Insurance scheme (*e.g.* the basic state retirement pension and any additional pension such as SERPS) and from their own private provision (*e.g.* an occupational pension or income from capital). After considerable debate, the government announced that income from work is to be treated in the same way as income from an occupational pension or savings. The term "income" is further defined by ss.15 and 16, and such income must be aggregated with that of any partner (s.5).

Savings credit threshold

The "savings credit threshold" is "such amount as may be prescribed" (subs.(7)).   **1.366**
This threshold for 2005/06 is £82.05 for a single person and £131.20 for a couple (State Pension Credit Regulations 2002 (SI 2002/1792), reg.7(2)), *i.e.* the basic state retirement pension for a single person and a couple respectively. This means that pensioners whose qualifying income is less than this level, even though they have, *e.g.* a small occupational pension or income from savings, are unable to claim the savings credit. This is likely to be the case with those women who are not entitled to a full retirement pension because of gaps in their contributions records. Thus these women pensioners may claim the guarantee credit to bring their income up to the appropriate minimum guarantee under s.2, but see no extra benefit for their thrift as their combined income from other sources does not exceed the basic retirement pension.

Amount A

"Amount A" is the *smaller* of the "maximum savings credit" and "a prescribed   **1.367**
percentage of the amount by which the claimant's qualifying income exceeds the savings credit threshold" (subs.(4)). The "maximum savings credit" is a prescribed percentage (60 per cent: State Pension Credit Regulations 2002 (SI 2002/1792),

reg.7(1)(a)) of the difference between the standard minimum guarantee and the savings credit threshold (subs.(7)). By this stage (if not before) the reader of these annotations might appreciate a simple algebraic notation. An example may therefore assist.

For 2005/06 the maximum savings credit is 60 per cent of the difference between the standard minimum guarantee (£109.45 for a single person, £167.05 for a couple) and the savings credit threshold (£82.05 for a single person and £131.20 for a couple). The difference for a single person is thus £27.40, of which 60 per cent is £16.44. For a couple the difference is £35.85, of which 60 per cent is £21.51. The maximum savings credit is accordingly £16.44 for single claimants and £21.51 for couples.

This figure must then be compared with a second figure representing "a pre-scribed percentage of the amount by which the claimant's qualifying income exceeds the savings credit threshold". In this context the prescribed percentage is also 60 per cent (State Pension Credit Regulations 2002 (SI 2002/1792), reg.7(1)(b)). The savings credit threshold is aligned with the basic state retirement pension and so, as we have seen, for 2005/06 is £82.05 for a single person and £131.20 for a couple. The "qualifying income" is to be calculated in accordance with ss.15 and 16 and with regulations under subs.(6) (see also above). If a single claimant's qualifying weekly income is £92.05, comprising the basic state retirement pension and a small occupational pension, then this second figure is £6 (being 60 per cent of the differ-ence between £92.05 and £82.05). As £6 is less than £16.44 in this scenario, Amount A is the former, *i.e.* £6.

Amount B

1.368   Amount B is "a prescribed percentage of the amount (if any) by which the claimant's income exceeds the appropriate minimum guarantee" or, if there is no such excess, nil (subs.(4)). The prescribed percentage in this calculation is 40 per cent in this instance, not 60 per cent (State Pension Credit Regulations 2002 (SI 2002/1792), reg.7(1)(c)). It is also important to note that in this calculation the ref-erence is to the claimant's income, not their *qualifying* income (which may be a lower figure). The appropriate minimum guarantee is defined by s.2(3), and represents the current minimum income guarantee for pensioners. Let us assume that in the scen-ario under discussion the claimant's appropriate minimum guarantee consists of the standard minimum guarantee (*i.e.* there are no extra sums equivalent to further premiums) and is £109.45 in 2005/06. In this example the claimant's income (£92.05) is clearly less than the appropriate minimum guarantee (£109.45) and so amount B must be nil.

In the hypothetical case set out above, amount A is £6 and amount B is nil. We have already established that the claimant's qualifying income (£92.05) exceeds the savings credit threshold (£82.05) and so subs.(2)(a) is met. As amount A exceeds amount B, the requirement in subs.(2)(b) is also satisfied. Assuming that the claimant (or partner) is over 65, this means that both conditions for the award of the savings credit are fulfilled. The amount of the savings credit in such a case is the amount by which amount A exceeds amount B, namely £6 (subs.(3)).

If, however, a single pensioner's total income and qualifying income in 2005/06 is £109.45, *e.g.* comprising the state retirement pension and an occupational pension, then amount A is £16.44. This figure is both the maximum savings credit, *i.e.* a figure which is both 60 per cent of the difference between the standard minimum guarantee and the savings credit threshold and 60 per cent of the amount by which this individual's qualifying income exceeds the savings credit threshold. In such a scenario the claimant's income is the same as the appropriate minimum guarantee and so amount B is nil. The excess of amount A over amount B is therefore £16.44 and this sum is payable by way of a savings credit under subs.(3). The pensioner's income is thus £125.89 (retirement pension and occupational pension together with £16.44 savings credit), whereas under the previous arrangements there would have been no entitlement to income support, leaving such a pensioner in the same pos-ition as a pensioner claimant whose sole income was the state retirement pension.

Once a pensioner's income starts to exceed the appropriate minimum guarantee, then the way in which amounts A and B are defined is such that the claimant's entitlement to the savings credit is gradually withdrawn as their income increases. A further simple example will suffice. Assume that a single pensioner's total weekly income is £119.45, comprising the state retirement pension and an occupational pension. On these facts amount A is the smaller of the maximum savings credit (£16.44) and 60 per cent of the amount by which the claimant's income (£119.45) exceeds the savings credit threshold (£82.05). The latter figure is £22.44 (60 per cent of the difference, being £37.40). As this obviously is more than £16.44, amount A will be £16.44. Amount B is 40 per cent of the amount by which the claimant's income (and again, for the purposes of exposition, we assume that income and qualifying income are identical) exceeds the appropriate minimum guarantee (*i.e.* £109.45). The difference between those two figures in this example is £10, of which 40 per cent is £4. Both the conditions set out in subs.(2) are therefore satisfied, and so the claimant's savings credit is the amount by which amount A (£16.44) exceeds amount B (£4), namely £12.44. The claimant, on this scenario, thus has a final income of £131.89: £119.45 by way of retirement pension and occupational pension topped up by £12.44 savings credit). Thus the value of the savings credit will gradually diminish as the claim-ant's combined income from other sources rises. At 2005/06 rates this means that no savings credit is payable for a single pensioner with a total income of £151 a week or more or for a couple whose joint income is £221 a week or more. The Explanatory Notes to the Act (at Annex B) and the Department's publicity material includes ready reckoner tables which illustrate the outcomes for these types of calculations.

Subs.(5)

Section 2(6) enables the Secretary of State to provide for a different rate for the guarantee credit to be applied in place of the standard minimum guarantee where the claimant (or their partner) remains in hospital for more than 52 weeks. If this same principle were to be carried over into the calculation of the savings credit, the effect would be that amount B would be much higher and might well exceed amount A, which would extinguish any entitlement to the savings credit by virtue of subs.(3). This provision allows regulations to be made to provide for a higher figure to be stipulated in place of the reference to the appropriate minimum guarantee in the definition of amount B. This will reduce amount B and accordingly increase the likelihood that amount A will exceed amount B and so result in the savings credit being payable (State Pension Credit Regulations 2002 (SI 2002/1792), Sch.III, para.2). 1.369

Subs.(8)

This power enables a nil amount to be specified as the maximum savings credit for prisoners and members of religious orders who are fully maintained by their orders. This mirrors the power under s.2(9) and reflects the fact that both groups who are currently excluded from income support (see State Pension Credit Regulations 2002 (SI 2002/1792), reg.7(3)). 1.370

Exclusions

4.—(1) A claimant is not entitled to state pension credit if he is a member of a married or unmarried couple the other member of which is entitled to state pension credit. 1.371

(2) In section 115(1) of the Immigration and Asylum Act 1999 (c.33) (exclusion of certain persons from benefits) in the words preceding paragraph (a), after "Jobseekers Act 1995" insert "or to state pension credit under the State Pension Credit Act 2002".

(3) Where the amount payable by way of state pension credit would (apart from this subsection) be less than a prescribed amount, it shall not be payable except in prescribed circumstances.

DEFINITIONS

"claimant"—see s.17(1).
"entitled"—*ibid.*
"married couple"—*ibid.*
"prescribed"—*ibid.*
"unmarried couple"—*ibid.*

GENERAL NOTE

1.372   Only one member of a married or unmarried couple is entitled to the pension credit, so preventing double provision from public funds (subs.(1), modelled on SSCBA 1992, s.134(2)). The general exclusion of persons who are "subject to immigration control" from access to the benefits system is extended to the pension credit scheme (subs.(2); for the limited exceptions to the rule in s.115 of the Immigration and Asylum Act 1999, see the Social Security (Immigration and Asylum) Consequential Amendments Regulations 2000 (SI 2000/636)).

Provision is also made to set a minimum threshold for payment of the pension credit. Entitlement of less than 10 pence a week is not payable, unless it can be combined with another benefit (subs.(3)), modelled on SSCBA 1992, s.134(4); see State Pension Credit Regulations 2002 (SI 2002/1792), reg.13).

Aggregation

Income and capital of claimant, spouse, etc.

1.373   **5.**—Where the claimant is a member of a married or unmarried couple, the income and capital of the other member of the couple shall, except in prescribed circumstances, be treated for the purposes of this Act as income and capital of the claimant.

DEFINITIONS

"capital"—see s.17(1).
"claimant"—*ibid.*
"income"—*ibid.*
"prescribed"—*ibid.*
"married couple"—*ibid.*
"unmarried couple"—*ibid.*

GENERAL NOTE

1.374   This section provides for the aggregation of the income and capital resources of the claimant and his or her partner, whether married or otherwise (but note that the definition of both married and unmarried couples in s.17(1) assumes a heterosexual relationship). This is in line with standard means-tested benefit principles. Indeed, this provision is closely modelled on SSCBA 1992, s.136(1). The definitions of both married and unmarried couples assumes that the partners are living in the same household. For special cases where persons are treated as either being or not being members of the same household, see State Pension Credit Regulations 2002 (SI 2002/1792), reg.5).

Retirement provision

Duty to specify assessed income period

6.—(1) In any case falling within subsection (3) or (4), the Secretary of State shall, on the making of the relevant decision, specify a period as the assessed income period, unless prevented by subsection (2).

(2) The Secretary of State is prevented from specifying a period as the assessed income period under subsection (1)—

(a) if the relevant decision takes effect at a time when an assessed income period is in force in the case of the claimant by virtue of a previous application of this section; or

(b) in such other circumstances as may be prescribed.

(3) The first case is where—

(a) the Secretary of State determines the amount of a claimant's income for the purposes of a decision relating to state pension credit;

(b) the decision is a decision under section 8(1), 9 or 10 of the Social Security Act 1998 (c.14) (decisions on claims etc, and decisions revising or superseding decisions);

(c) the decision takes effect on or after—

(i) the day on which the claimant attains the age of 65; or

(ii) if earlier, in a case where the claimant is a member of a married or unmarried couple, the day on which the other member of the couple attains that age; and

(d) the decision is not to the effect that the claimant is not entitled to state pension credit.

(4) The second case is where—

(a) the amount of the claimant's income is determined on, or for the purposes of, an appeal against a decision that the claimant is not entitled to state pension credit;

(b) on the appeal, it is decided that the claimant is entitled to state pension credit; and

(c) the decision takes effect as mentioned in subsection (3)(c).

(5) In this section "the relevant decision" means—

(a) so far as relating to the first case, the decision mentioned in subsection (3)(a);

(b) so far as relating to the second case, the decision on appeal mentioned in subsection (4)(b).

(6) This section is subject to section 9.

(7) This section and sections 7 to 10 shall be construed as one.

1.375

Definitions

"assessed income period"—see s.17(1).

"claimant"—*ibid.*

"entitled"—*ibid.*

"income"—*ibid.*

"married couple"—*ibid.*

"prescribed"—*ibid.*

"the relevant decision"—see subs.(5).

"unmarried couple"—see s.17(1).

1.376

1.377 When making a decision that a person is entitled to the pension credit, the Secretary of State is also required to specify an "assessed income period" in relation to the claimant (subs.(1)). Such a decision may be made in the first instance by the Secretary of State (subs.(3)) or following an appeal (subs.(4)). The Secretary of State is prevented from so doing where an assessed income period is currently in force (subs.(2)(a)). For circumstances prescribed under subs.(2)(b), see State Pension Credit Regulations 2002 (SI 2002/1792), reg.10(1). The significance of the "assessed income period" is that it is used as the basis for a long-term award of the pension credit (see s.7). It should also be noted that this section is subject to s.9 (see subs.(6)), which specifies that the "assessed income period" is normally five years, and that ss.7 to 10 "shall be construed as one" (subs.(7)).

Fixing of claimant's retirement provision for assessed income period

1.378 **7.**—(1) This section applies where, pursuant to section 6(1), the Secretary of State on the making of the relevant decision specifies a period as the assessed income period.

(2) This section has effect for the purpose of determining, as at any time in the assessed income period—

(a) the claimant's entitlement to state pension credit; or

(b) the amount of state pension credit to which the claimant is entitled.

(3) Where the claimant's income, as determined for the purposes of the relevant decision, includes an amount (the "assessed amount") in respect of an element of the claimant's retirement provision, the amount of that element as at any time in the assessed income period shall be taken to be the assessed amount as for the time being varied in accordance with regulations under subsection (4).

(4) The assessed amount shall be deemed, except in prescribed circumstances—

(a) to increase, or

(b) in the case of income from capital, to increase or decrease,

on such date or dates and by such amounts as may be prescribed.

(5) Where it is determined for the purposes of the relevant decision that the claimant's income does not include any, or any further, elements of retirement provision, the claimant's income throughout the assessed income period shall be taken not to include those elements.

(6) For the purposes of this Act "retirement provision" means income of any of the following descriptions—

(a) retirement pension income, other than benefit under the Contributions and Benefits Act;

(b) income from annuity contracts (other than retirement pension income);

(c) income from capital;

and an "element" of a person's retirement provision is income of any of those descriptions from a particular source.

(7) For the purposes of this section, regulations may make provision—

(a) for treating income of any particular description as income of another description; or

(b) for treating income from different sources as income from the same source.

(8) Nothing in subsections (3) to (5) prevents the revision under section 9 of the Social Security Act 1998 (c.14) of the relevant decision or of any earlier or later decision under section 10 of that Act.

(9) This section is subject to section 8.

DEFINITIONS

"assessed amount"—see subs.(3).　　　　　　　　　　　　　　　　　　1.379
"assessed income period"—see s.17(1).
"capital"—*ibid.*
"claimant"—*ibid.*
"Contributions and Benefits Act"—*ibid.*
"element"—see subs.(6) and s.17(1).
"entitled"—see s.17(1).
"income"—*ibid.*
"regulations"—*ibid.*
"relevant decision"—see s.6(5).
"retirement pension income"—see ss.16 and 17(1).
"retirement provision"—see s.7(6) and s.17(1).

GENERAL NOTE

This provision is the key to understanding how the new pension credit scheme　　1.380
fundamentally differs from other means-tested benefits in terms of the usual requirement to report changes in income during the period of an award. Once the Secretary
of State has specified the "assessed income period" under s.6 (which is typically five
years: s.9(1)), this has the effect of fixing the "assessed amount" derived from the
claimant's "retirement provision" (effectively their income: see subs.(6)) for the
duration of that period (subs.(3)). This assessed amount is subject to deemed
increases or decreases (reflecting, *e.g.* the terms of a claimant's pension arrangements, such as a cost-of-living increase) (subs.(4); for further detail on this, see State
Pension Credit Regulations 2002 (SI 2002/1792), reg.10(2)–(7)). Any further elements of retirement provision which are acquired at some later date within the
assessed income period are then disregarded (subs.(5)). Such changes accordingly
need not be reported during the lifetime of the award. Even if the changes deemed
under subs.(4) work in favour of the claimant (*i.e.* their actual increase is more than
the deemed increase), the effect of subs.(3) is that there is no overpayment and no
need to report the change.

The implications of this radical change were spelt out by Mr Ian McCartney MP,
the Minster for Pensions:

> "Let us be clear about this: if a pensioner wins the lottery in the second week of
> his or her assessed income period, the increase in capital, be it £10 or £1 million,
> will not be reflected in the pension credit entitlement until the end of the assessed
> income period—in four years and 50 weeks' time . . . We can live with ignoring
> a few individuals' good fortune for the sake of simplification for the overwhelm-
> ing majority of pensioners" (Standing Committee A, cols 166 and 184).

But if the claimant actually loses out, in that the deemed increase is more than their
actual increase, a new decision can be sought (s.8(1)). The normal powers to effect
a revision of an initial decision under s.9 of the SSA 1998 remain in place (subs.(8)).

Fresh determinations increasing claimant's entitlement

8.—(1) Subsections (3) to (5) of section 7 do not prevent the making of　　1.381
fresh determinations as to the elements, or any of the elements, or the
amount of any of the elements, of the claimant's retirement provision as at
any time during the assessed income period, if—

    (a) the fresh determinations are for the purpose of making a decision under section 10 of the Social Security Act 1998 (c.14) ("the new decision");

    (b) the new decision increases the amount of state pension credit to which the claimant is entitled; and

    (c) the increase is in whole or in part the result of the fresh determinations (taken as a whole).

(2) The conditions in paragraphs (b) and (c) of subsection (1) shall be taken to be satisfied if—

    (a) the new decision reduces the amount of state pension credit to which the claimant is entitled; but

    (b) the reduction is less than it would have been apart from the fresh determinations (taken as a whole).

(3) Where a fresh determination is made by virtue of subsection (1), then, as respects the part of the assessed income period that begins with the day on which the new decision takes effect, subsections (3) to (5) of section 7 shall have effect in accordance with the fresh determination, instead of the determination which it replaces, but as if—

    (a) the fresh determination were (and the determination which it replaces were not) a determination for the purposes of the relevant decision;

    (b) any assessed amount resulting from the fresh determination were not subject to variation under subsection (4) of that section at any time before the day on which the new decision takes effect; and

    (c) the claimant's income, as determined for the purposes of the relevant decision, were constituted accordingly.

DEFINITIONS

1.382
    "assessed income period"—see ss.9(1) and 17(1).
    "claimant"—see s.17(1).
    "element"—*ibid.*
    "entitled"—*ibid.*
    "income"—*ibid.*
    "retirement provision"—see ss.7(6) and 17(1).

GENERAL NOTE

The presumption under s.7 is that the assessment of the claimant's "retirement provision" will remain unchanged during the typical five-year award of pension credit, subject to the usual uprating. However, a fresh determination can be made by way of a supersession decision within the assessed income period to increase the claimant's entitlement. This will not affect the assessed income period (subs.(1)). The assessed income period can also continue where the effect of the supersession decision is to reduce entitlement to the pension credit, but the reduction is less than it would otherwise have been because of the recalculation of some other element of the claimant's income (subs.(2)). Where a supersession decision is made, the remaining elements of the retirement provision are treated as unchanged for the rest of the assessed income period (subs.(3)). See also State Pension Credit Regulations 2002 (SI 2002/1792), reg.11.

Duration of assessed income period

1.383
    9.—(1) An assessed income period shall (subject to subsections (2) to (4)) be the period of five years beginning with the day on which the relevant decision takes effect.

(2) If the Secretary of State considers that the particulars of the claimant's retirement provision as determined for the purposes of the relevant decision are not likely, after taking account of any assumed variations under subsection (3), to be typical of the claimant's retirement provision throughout the period of 12 months beginning with the day on which that decision takes effect—

(a) he need not specify a period under section 6(1); and

(b) if he does so, he may specify a period shorter than five years (but beginning as mentioned in subsection (1)).

(3) It shall be assumed for the purposes of subsection (2) that the same variations fall to be made in relation to the amount of an element of the claimant's retirement provision as determined for the purposes of the relevant decision as would fall to be made under section 7(4) if an assessed income period were to be specified in accordance with subsection (1).

(4) An assessed income period shall, except in prescribed circumstances, end at any time at which—

(a) the claimant becomes a member of a married or unmarried couple;

(b) the claimant ceases to be a member of a married or unmarried couple;

(c) the claimant attains the age of 65; or

(d) in a case where the claimant is a member of a married or unmarried couple, the other member of the couple attains the age of 65.

(5) Regulations may prescribe further times at which, or circumstances in which, an assessed income period shall end.

DEFINITIONS

"assessed income period"—see subs.(1) and s.17(1).   1.384
"claimant"—see s.17(1).
"element"—*ibid.*
"married couple"—*ibid.*
"prescribed"—*ibid.*
"regulations"—see s.17(1).
"relevant decision"—see s.6(5).
"retirement provision"—see ss.7(6) and 17(1).
"unmarried couple"—see s.17(1).

GENERAL NOTE

The normal rule is that the "assessed income period" for the purposes of an award of the pension credit is five years (subs.(1)). Throughout this period the claimant's "retirement provision" (see s.7), *i.e.* their standard income during retirement, is treated as remaining the same, subject only to uprating in line with inflation. This is in contrast to the requirement that claimants of other means-tested benefits report any changes in income which affect their benefit entitlement. However, if the Secretary of State takes the view that the claimant's retirement provision as assessed is not likely to be typical of their actual income over the next 12 months, a period shorter than five years may be specified (subs.(2)). Foreseeable increases in income on retirement (*e.g.* in line with inflation) are not treated as making the assessment atypical (subs.(3)). Whatever its initial duration, an assessed income period terminates if the claimant becomes a member of a couple, separates from their partner or reaches 65 (or any partner does so) (subs.(4)). Further circumstances which will result in the termination of an assessed income period, as prescribed under subs.(5), are specified in the State Pension Credit Regulations 2002 (SI 2002/1792), reg.12.

Effect of variations under section 7(4)

1.385

10.—(1) This section applies where—

(a) an assessed income period is in force; and

(b) there is an alteration in an element of the claimant's retirement provision which affects the computation of the amount of state pension credit to which the claimant is entitled.

(2) Where, as a result of the alteration, the amount of state pension credit to which the claimant is entitled is increased or reduced, then, as from the commencing date, the amount of state pension credit payable in the case of the claimant shall be the increased or reduced amount, without any further decision of the Secretary of State (and the award of state pension credit shall have effect accordingly).

(3) Where, notwithstanding the alteration, the claimant continues on and after the commencing date to be entitled to the same amount of state pension credit as before, the award shall continue in force accordingly.

(4) In this section—

"alteration" means a variation in the amount of an element of the claimant's retirement provision in accordance with regulations under section 7(4);

"commencing date", in relation to an alteration, means the date on which the alteration comes into force.

DEFINITIONS

1.386

"alteration"—see subs.(4).

"assessed income period"—see s.17(1).

"claimant"—*ibid.*

"commencing date"—see subs.(4).

"element"—see s.17(1).

"entitled"—*ibid.*

"regulations"—*ibid.*

"retirement provision"—*ibid.*

GENERAL NOTE

Section 7(4) provides for the assessed amount of a claimant's retirement provision to be increased or decreased during the assessed income period. This provision deals with the consequences of such a change (subs. (1)). Subs.(2) allows the amount of the pension credit payable to be increased or decreased accordingly without the need for a further decision by the Secretary of State. If the level of the award remains the same, the award continues in force unaffected (subs.(3)). See also State Pension Credit Regulations 2002 (SI 2002/1792), reg.11.

Miscellaneous and supplementary

Administration

1.387

11.—Schedule 1 shall have effect and in that Schedule—

Part 1 makes amendments to Part 1 of the Administration Act (claims for, and payments and general administration of, benefit);

Part 2 makes amendments to Part 1 of the Social Security Act 1998 (c.14) (decisions and appeals); and

Part 3 makes miscellaneous and supplementary provision.

DEFINITION

"the Administration Act"—see s.17(1).

GENERAL NOTE

This section introduces Sch.1 to the Act. This makes amendments to the SSAA 1992 and the SSA 1998 which are designed to apply the normal social security rules for claims, decisions and appeals to the state pension credit scheme.

Polygamous marriages

12.—(1) This section applies to any case where—   **1.388**
  (a) a person ("the person in question") is a husband or wife by virtue of a marriage entered into under a law which permits polygamy;
  (b) either party to the marriage has for the time being any spouse additional to the other party; and
  (c) the person in question, the other party to the marriage and the additional spouse are members of the same household.
  (2) Regulations under this section may make provision—
  (a) as to the entitlement of the person in question to state pension credit;
  (b) as to any guarantee credit or savings credit to which that person is entitled;
  (c) for prescribing a different amount as the standard minimum guarantee in the case of the person in question;
  (d) in a case where the person in question is the claimant, for treating the income and capital of the other party and of the additional spouse as income and capital of the person in question.
  (3) Any such regulations may provide—
  (a) that prescribed provisions shall apply instead of prescribed provisions of this Act; or
  (b) that prescribed provisions of this Act shall not apply or shall apply subject to prescribed modifications or adaptations.
  (4) Except in relation to the amount of the standard minimum guarantee, any power to prescribe amounts by virtue of this section includes power to prescribe nil as an amount.

DEFINITIONS

  "capital"—see s.17(1).   **1.389**
  "claimant"—*ibid.*
  "entitled"—*ibid.*
  "guarantee credit"—*ibid.*
  "income"—*ibid.*
  "prescribed"—*ibid.*
  "regulations"—*ibid.*
  "savings credit"—*ibid.*
  "standard minimum guarantee"—*ibid.*

GENERAL NOTE

This section makes special provision for claimants who are parties to polygamous marriages. See also State Pension Credit Regulations 2002 (SI 2002/ 1792), reg.8 and Sch.III, para.1.

Transitional provisions

1.390   **13.**—(1) The Secretary of State may by regulations make such transitional provision, consequential provision or savings as he considers necessary or expedient for the purposes of, or in connection with—

(a) the coming into force of any of the state pension credit provisions of this Act; or

(b) the operation of any enactment repealed or amended by any of those provisions during any period when the repeal or amendment is not wholly in force.

(2) The provision that may be made by regulations under this section includes in particular—

(a) provision for a person who attains or has attained the qualifying age on or before the appointed day and who immediately before that day is entitled to income support—

(i) to be treated as having been awarded on, and with effect as from, that day state pension credit of an amount specified in or determined in accordance with the regulations; or

(ii) to be treated as having made a claim for state pension credit; and

(b) provision for an assessed income period under section 6 of such length as may be specified in or determined in accordance with the regulations (which may be longer than the maximum period provided for by section 9(1)) to have effect in the case of a person who attains or has attained the qualifying age on or before the appointed day.

(3) In this section—

"the appointed day" means such day as the Secretary of State may by order appoint;

"the state pension credit provisions of this Act" means this Act other than section 18.

DEFINITIONS

1.391   "the appointed day"—see subs.(3).
"the qualifying age"—see s.1(6).
"regulations"—see s.17(1).
"the state pension credit provisions of this Act"—see subs.(3).

GENERAL NOTE

This section enables regulations to be made governing the transitional arrangements for the introduction of the pension credit. The new scheme came into force on October 6, 2003 (the "appointed day": see State Pension Credit Act 2002 (Commencement No.5) and Appointed Day Order 2003 (SI 2003/1766 (C.75)) and all claims made before October 2004 should be backdated to October 2003 (see State Pension Credit (Consequential, Transitional and Miscellaneous Provisions) Regulations 2002 (SI 2002/3019, reg.38(4)). Those regulations permit existing income support pensioner claimants to be treated as having claimed or having been awarded pension credit to ensure continuity (subs.(2)(a)). They also allow awards to be based on a longer period than the standard assessed income period of five years, so allowing awards to be staggered (subs.(2)(b); the limit is seven years: see State Pension Credit (Consequential, Transitional and Miscellaneous Provisions) Regulations 2002 (SI 2002/3019, reg.37). This will avoid the significant operational problems that would otherwise inevitably arise in 2008 if a large number of claims came up for renewal at the same time.

The 12 month automatic backdating rule, which originally applied just in the first year of the scheme, has now been made a permanent feature for pension credit claims: Social Security (Claims and Payments) Regulations 1987 (SI 1987/1968), reg.19 and Sch.4, as amended by Social Security (Claims and Payments) Amendment (No. 2) Regulations 2004 (SI 2004/1821), reg.2.

Minor and consequential amendments

14.—Schedule 2 (which makes minor and consequential amendments relating to state pension credit) shall have effect.   1.392

GENERAL NOTE

This section introduces Sch.2 to the Act, which makes a series of minor and consequential amendments to the SSCBA 1992, the SSAA 1992 and other statutes. These include amendments to SSCBA 1992, s.124 to exclude those who have reached the qualifying age for the pension credit from entitlement to income support (Sch.2, para.2) and to Jobseekers Act 1995, s.3 to ensure that those entitled to the pension credit are excluded from jobseeker's allowance (Sch.2, paras 36–38).

Interpretation of state pension credit provisions

Income and capital

15.—(1) In this Act "income" means income of any of the following descriptions—   1.393
  (a) earnings;
  (b) working tax credit;
  (c) retirement pension income;
  (d) income from annuity contracts (other than retirement pension income);
  (e) prescribed social security benefits (other than retirement pension income and state pension credit);
  (f) foreign social security benefits of any prescribed description;
  (g) a war disablement pension or war widow's or widower's pension;
  (h) a foreign war disablement pension or foreign war widow's or widower's pension;
  (i) income from capital;
  (j) income of any prescribed description.
  (2) Regulations may provide that a person's capital shall be deemed to yield him income at a prescribed rate.
  (3) Income and capital shall be calculated or estimated in such manner as may be prescribed.
  (4) A person's income in respect of any period shall be calculated in accordance with prescribed rules.
  (5) The rules may provide for the calculation to be made by reference to an average over a period (which need not consist of or include the whole or any part of the period concerned).
  (6) Circumstances may be prescribed in which—
  (a) a person is treated as possessing capital or income which he does not possess;
  (b) capital or income which a person does possess is to be disregarded;
  (c) income is to be treated as capital; or
  (d) capital is to be treated as income.
  (7) Subsections (2) to (6) have effect for the purposes of this Act.

1.394

"capital"—see s.17(1).
"earnings"—*ibid.*
"foreign social security benefits"—*ibid.*
"foreign war disablement pension"—*ibid.*
"foreign war widow's or widower's pension"—*ibid.*
"income"—see subs.(1).
"prescribed"—see s.17(1).
"regulations"—*ibid.*
"retirement pension income"—see s.16(1).
"social security benefits"—see s.17(1).
"war disablement pension"—*ibid.*
"war widow's or widower's pension"—*ibid.*
"working tax credit"—*ibid.*

GENERAL NOTE

1.395
The term "income" is given a very broad definition in subs.(1) for the purposes of the pension credit scheme. In particular, the Secretary of State has the power under subs.(1)(e) to specify which social security benefits count as income (see State Pension Credit Regulations 2002 (SI 2002/1792), reg.15(1), (3) and (4); and for foreign social security benefits see *ibid.*, reg.15(2)). The Secretary of State may also extend the definition of income to include "income of any prescribed description" (subs.(1)(j)). This latter power has been used to include less commonly found forms of income that some pensioners have (*e.g.* maintenance payments); see State Pension Credit Regulations 2002 (SI 2002/1792, reg.15(5)).

There is, however, no upper capital limit for the purposes of entitlement to the pension credit. Instead, capital is deemed, by regulations made under subs.(2), to have an assumed rate of return for the purposes of assessing entitlement to both forms of the pension credit. This rate is set at £1 for every £500 (or part thereof) in excess of the relevant lower threshold (£6,000 in most cases but £10,000 for those in residential care or nursing homes: see State Pension Credit Regulations 2002 (SI 2002/1792), reg.15(6)–(8)). Any capital below these thresholds is disregarded, as is the case with income support. The net result is that pensioners are treated markedly more favourably than those persons of working age in receipt of means-tested benefits, who are subject both to the capital rule and to a harsher tariff income rule on capital below that threshold.

Note that for the purposes of claiming housing benefit (or council tax benefit), pension credit claimants receiving the guarantee credit have the whole of their capital and income disregarded (see the Housing Benefit Regulations, reg.22, as substituted by the Housing Benefit and Council Tax Benefit (State Pension Credit) Regulations 2003 (SI 2003/325), reg.8). For claimants receiving solely the savings credit, the local authority is required to use the DWP's calculations for claimants' capital and income (see reg.23 of the Housing Benefit Regulations, as substituted). For these reasons it is important that a tribunal reaching a decision on the amount of capital or income in a pension credit case should specify the amount of such capital or income in the Decision Notice.

The extensive powers contained in subss.(3)–(6) replicate those which apply to means-tested benefits by virtue of SSCBA 1992, s.136(3)–(5).

Retirement pension income

1.396
16.—(1) In this Act "retirement pension income" means any of the following—

    (a) a Category A or Category B retirement pension payable under sections 43 to 55 of—

(i) the Contributions and Benefits Act; or

(ii) the Social Security Contributions and Benefits (Northern Ireland) Act 1992 (c.7);

(b) a shared additional pension payable under section 55A of either of those Acts (utilisation of State scheme pension credits on divorce);

(c) graduated retirement benefit payable under section 62 of either of those Acts;

(d) a Category C or Category D retirement pension payable under section 78 of either of those Acts;

(e) age addition payable under section 79 of either of those Acts;

(f) income from an occupational pension scheme or a personal pension scheme;

(g) income from an overseas arrangement;

(h) income from a retirement annuity contract;

(i) income from annuities or insurance policies purchased or transferred for the purpose of giving effect to rights under a personal pension scheme or an overseas arrangement;

(j) income from annuities purchased or entered into for the purpose of discharging liability under—

(i) section 29(1)(b) of the Welfare Reform and Pensions Act 1999 (c.30) (pension credits on divorce); or

(ii) Article 26(1)(b) of the Welfare Reform and Pensions (Northern Ireland) Order 1999 (SI 1999/3147 (NI 11)) (corresponding provision for Northern Ireland).

(2) The Secretary of State may by regulations amend subsection (1); and any such regulations may—

(a) add to or vary the descriptions of income for the time being listed in that subsection; or

(b) remove any such description from that subsection.

(3) In this section—

"overseas arrangement" has the meaning given by section 181(1) of the Pension Schemes Act 1993 (c.48);

"retirement annuity contract" means a contract or scheme approved under Chapter 3 of Part 14 of the Income and Corporation Taxes Act 1988 (c.1).

DEFINITIONS

"the Contribution and Benefits Act"—see s.17(1).

"occupational pension scheme"—*ibid.*

"overseas arrangement"—see subs.(3).

"personal pension scheme"—*ibid.*

"regulations"—see s.17(1).

"retirement annuity contract"—see subs.(3).

1.397

GENERAL NOTE

This section provides a comprehensive definition of the term "retirement pension income" for the purposes of this Act (subs.(1)). The extensive list includes both social security benefits paid to pensioners as well as various forms of private income received by pensioners. The Secretary of State may by regulations add to, vary or remove any of the descriptions so listed (subs.(2); see further State Pension Credit Regulations 2002 (SI 2002/1792), reg.16). This power provides the necessary flexibility to accommodate other social security benefits or private financial products for pensioners that may become available in the future. But it also includes the power to remove matters listed in subs.(1).

Other interpretation provisions

1.398   **17.**—(1) In this Act—

"the Administration Act" means the Social Security Administration Act 1992 (c.5);

"assessed income period" shall be construed in accordance with sections 6 and 9;

"appropriate minimum guarantee" shall be construed in accordance with section 2(3);

"capital" shall be construed in accordance with section 15;

"claimant" means a claimant for state pension credit;

"the Contributions and Benefits Act" means the Social Security Contributions and Benefits Act 1992 (c.4);

"earnings" has the same meaning as in Parts 1 to 5 of the Contributions and Benefits Act (see sections 3(1) and 112, and the definition of "employment" in section 122, of that Act);

"element", in relation to the claimant's retirement provision, shall be construed in accordance with section 7(6);

"entitled", in relation to state pension credit, shall be construed in accordance with—

    (a) this Act,

    (b) section 1 of the Administration Act (entitlement to be dependent on making of claim, etc.), and

    (c) section 27 of the Social Security Act 1998 (c.14) (restrictions on entitlement to benefit in certain cases of error),

(and, in relation to any other benefit within the meaning of section 1 of the Administration Act or section 27 of the Social Security Act 1998, in accordance with that section or (as the case may be) both of those sections in addition to any other conditions relating to that benefit);

"foreign social security benefit" means any benefit, allowance or other payment which is paid under the law of a country outside the United Kingdom and is in the nature of social security;

"foreign war disablement pension" means any retired pay, pension, allowance or similar payment granted by the government of a country outside the United Kingdom—

    (a) in respect of disablement arising from forces' service or war injury; or

    (b) corresponding in nature to any retired pay or pension to which [¹section 641 of the Income Tax (Earnings and Pensions) Act 2003] applies;

"foreign war widow's or widower's pension" means any pension, allowance or similar payment granted to a widow or widower by the government of a country outside the United Kingdom—

    (a) in respect of a death due to forces' service or war injury; or

    (b) corresponding in nature to a pension or allowance for a widow or widower under any scheme mentioned in [¹section 641(1)(e) or (f) of the Income Tax (Earnings and Pensions) Act 2003];

"guarantee credit" shall be construed in accordance with sections 1 and 2;

"income" shall be construed in accordance with section 15;

"married couple" means a man and a woman who are married to each other and are members of the same household;

"occupational pension scheme" has the meaning given by section 1 of the Pension Schemes Act 1993 (c.48);

"pensionable age" has the meaning given by the rules in paragraph 1 of Schedule 4 to the Pensions Act 1995 (c.26) (equalisation of pensionable ages for men and women);

"personal pension scheme" means a personal pension scheme—
  (a) as defined in section 1 of the Pension Schemes Act 1993; or
  (b) as defined in section 1 of the Pension Schemes (Northern Ireland) Act 1993 (c.49);

"prescribed" means specified in, or determined in accordance with regulations;

"the qualifying age" has the meaning given by section 1(6);

"regulations" means regulations made by the Secretary of State;

"retirement pension income" shall be construed in accordance with section 16;

"retirement provision" shall be construed in accordance with section 7(6);

"savings credit" shall be construed in accordance with sections 1 and 3;

"social security benefits" means benefits payable under the enactments relating to social security in any part of the United Kingdom;

"standard minimum guarantee" shall be construed in accordance with section 2(3) to (5) and (9);

"unmarried couple" means a man and a woman who are not married to each other but are living together as husband and wife otherwise than in prescribed circumstances;

"war disablement pension" means—
  (a) any retired pay, pension or allowance granted in respect of disablement under powers conferred by or under—
    (i) the Air Force (Constitution) Act 1917 (c.51);
    (ii) the Personal Injuries (Emergency Provisions) Act 1939 (c.82);
    (iii) the Pensions (Navy, Army, Air Force and Mercantile Marine) Act 1939 (c.83);
    (iv) the Polish Resettlement Act 1947 (c.19); or
    (v) Part 7 or section 151 of the Reserve Forces Act 1980 (c.9); or
  (b) without prejudice to paragraph (a), any retired pay or pension to which [¹ any of paragraphs (a) to (f) of section 641(1) of the Income Tax (Earnings and Pensions) Act 2003] applies;

"war widow's or widower's pension" means—
  (a) any widow's or widower's pension or allowance granted in respect of a death due to service or war injury and payable by virtue of any enactment mentioned in paragraph (a) of the definition of "war disablement pension"; or
  (b) a pension or allowance for a widow or widower granted under any scheme mentioned in [¹section 641(1)(e) or (f) of the Income Tax (Earnings and Pensions) Act 2003];

"working tax credit" means a working tax credit under the Tax Credits Act 2002 to which a person is entitled whether alone or jointly with another.

(2) Regulations may make provision for the purposes of this Act—

(a) as to circumstances in which persons are to be treated as being or not being members of the same household;

(b) as to circumstances in which persons are to be treated as being or not being severely disabled.

(3) The following provisions of the Contributions and Benefits Act, namely—

(a) section 172 (references to Great Britain or United Kingdom to include reference to adjacent territorial waters, etc.), and

(b) section 173 (meaning of attaining an age, etc.), shall apply for the purposes of this Act as they apply for the purposes of that Act.

AMENDMENT

1.399   1. Income Tax (Earnings and Pensions) Act 2003, Sch.6, para.263 (October 6, 2003).

GENERAL NOTE

This is the general definition section for the Act. For definitions of "income" and "retirement pension income", see ss.15 and 16 respectively.

18. *[Omitted.]*

Regulations and orders

1.400   **19.**—(1) Subject to the following provisions of this section, subsections (1), (2) to (5) and (10) of section 175 of the Contributions and Benefits Act (regulations and orders etc) shall apply in relation to any power conferred on the Secretary of State by any provision of this Act to make regulations or an order as they apply in relation to any power conferred on him by that Act to make regulations or an order, but as if for references to that Act (other than references to specific provisions of it) there were substituted references to this Act.

(2) A statutory instrument containing (whether alone or with other provisions) the first regulations under—

(a) section 2(3)(b), (4) or (6),

(b) section 3(4), (5), (6), (7) or (8),

(c) section 4(3),

(d) section 12, or

(e) section 15(1)(e), (f) or (j), (2), (3), (4) or (6),

shall not be made unless a draft of the instrument has been laid before, and approved by a resolution of, each House of Parliament.

(3) A statutory instrument—

(a) which contains regulations under this Act (whether alone or with other provisions), and

(b) which is not subject to any requirement that a draft of the instrument be laid before, and approved by a resolution of, each House of Parliament,

shall be subject to annulment in pursuance of a resolution of either House of Parliament.

"the Contribution and Benefits Act"—see s.17(1).   1.401
"regulations"—*ibid.*

GENERAL NOTE

This section applies the usual regulation-making powers for social security benefits under SSCBA 1992, s.175 to the pension credit scheme (subs.(1)). The first
regulations made under the various powers listed in subs.(2) were subject to the
affirmative procedure (see further State Pension Credit Regulations 2002 (SI
2002/1792) and Third Standing Committee on Delegated Legislation, Session
2001–02, July 8, 2002). The inclusion of regulations made under the provisions
specified in s.15 (subs.(2)(e)) follows a recommendation in the *Ninth Report* of the
Select Committee on Delegated Powers and Regulatory Reform. Other regulations
remain subject to the usual negative resolution procedure (subs.(3)).

Financial provisions

20.—(1) There shall be paid out of money provided by Parliament—   1.402
(a) any sums payable by way of state pension credit;
(b) any expenditure incurred by the Secretary of State or other govern-
    ment department under or by virtue of this Act; and
(c) any increase attributable to this Act in the sums payable out of money
    so provided under any other Act.

(2) There shall be paid into the Consolidated Fund any increase attributable to this Act in the sums which under any other Act are payable into
that Fund.

Enactments repealed

21.—The enactments specified in Schedule 3 to this Act are repealed to   1.403
the extent there specified.

GENERAL NOTE

Schedule 3 to the Act made a small number of minor repeals to existing social
security legislation which appeared to be unconnected with the introduction of the
pension credit. The repeals mostly involved the removal of the word "and" or "or"
in particular statutory provisions. The one exception is a minor but substantive
repeal to the conditions of entitlement for the Christmas bonus. This is the removal
of the requirement that a claimant whose only qualifying benefit is income support
should have reached pensionable age not later than the end of the relevant week
(SSCBA 1992, s.148(4)). This repeal is genuinely consequential upon the introduction of the pension credit. See also further the amendments made to SSCBA
1992, ss.148–150 by Sch.2, paras 5–7.

Short title, commencement and extent

22.—(1) This Act may be cited as the State Pension Credit Act 2002.   1.404
(2) This section and sections 19 and 20 come into force on the passing of
this Act.
(3) Except as provided by subsection (2), this Act shall come into force
on such day as the Secretary of State may by order appoint; and different
days may be so appointed for different purposes.

(4) Any order under this section may make such transitional provision as appears to the Secretary of State to be necessary or expedient in connection with the provisions brought into force by the order.

(5) Any amendment or repeal made by this Act has the same extent as the enactment to which it relates (unless otherwise provided).

(6) Subject to that, this Act extends to England and Wales and Scotland only.

GENERAL NOTE

For the reasons explained in the Introduction and General Note, although this Act is to be known as the State Pension Credit Act 2002 (subs.(1)), the credit itself is described in official literature as the pension credit. This section (along with ss.19 and 20) came into force on Royal Assent (June 25, 2002) (subs.(2)).

SCHEDULES

1.405   **Sch.1. to Sch.3.** *[Omitted.]*

Asylum and Immigration Act 1996

(1996 c. 49)

SECTION REPRODUCED

1.406   11. Saving for social security regulation.

SCHEDULE REPRODUCED

Schedule 1, Pt I.

GENERAL NOTE

1.407   Section 11 of this Act was introduced in response to the Court of Appeal's decision in *R. v Secretary of State for Social Security Ex p. Joint Council for the Welfare of Immigrants and another* [1996] 4 All E.R. 385. This had challenged the validity of the Social Security (Persons from Abroad) Miscellaneous Amendments Regulations 1996 (SI 1996/30) in so far as they drastically curtail the benefit entitlement of asylum seekers. The Court of Appeal (by a majority) held that the regulations were indeed *ultra vires* as (*per* Simon Brown L.J.) they were so "uncompromisingly draconian in effect . . . Parliament cannot have intended a significant number of genuine asylum seekers to be impaled on the horns of so intolerable a dilemma: the need either to abandon their claims to refugee status or alternatively to maintain them as best they can but in a state of utter destitution".

Section 11(1) specifically authorises the making of regulations to exclude asylum seekers from benefits, while s.11(4) and para.2 of Sch.1 reinstate the invalid parts of the 1996 Regulations with effect from July 24, 1996. Note also para.6 of Sch.1 which concerns asylum seekers who are excluded from benefit by the reinstatement effected by para.2.

For discussion of these provisions see the notes to reg.70 of the Income Support Regulations and see reg.12(1) of the Social Security (Persons from Abroad) Miscellaneous Amendments Regulations 1996 (p.689).

On s.11(2) see reg.21ZB (and formerly reg.21ZA) of the Income Support Regulations.

Saving for social security regulations

11.—(1) Notwithstanding any enactment or rule of law, regulations may exclude any person who has made a claim for asylum from entitlement to any of the following benefits, namely—

(a) income support, housing benefit and council tax benefit under the Social Security Contributions and Benefits Act 1992;

(b) [*Omitted as applying only to Northern Ireland*]; and

(c) jobseeker's allowance under the Jobseekers Act 1995or [*omitted as applying only to Northern Ireland*].

(2) Regulations may provide that, where such a person who is so excluded is subsequently recorded by the Secretary of State as a refugee within the meaning of the Convention—

(a) that person may, within a prescribed period, claim the whole or any prescribed proportion of any income support, housing benefit or council tax benefit to which he would have been entitled had he been recorded as a refugee immediately after he made the claim for asylum; and

[*Subss. (2) (b) and (3) are omitted as not relevant to the benefits covered by this book*].

(4) Schedule 1 to this Act—

(a) Part I of which modifies the Social Security (Persons from Abroad) Miscellaneous Amendments Regulations 1996; and

(b) [*Omitted as applying only to Northern Ireland*] shall have effect.

(5) The Jobseeker's Allowance (Amendment) Regulations 1996 shall have effect as if they had been made on the day on which this Act is passed.

(6) In this section—

"claim for asylum" and "the Convention" have the same meanings as in the 1993 Act;

"prescribed" means prescribed by regulations;

"regulations"—

(a) in relation to income support, housing benefit or council tax benefit under the Social Security Contributions and Benefits Act 1992, means regulations under that Act or the Social Security Administration Act 1992;

(b) [*omitted as applying only to Northern Ireland*];

(c) in relation to jobseeker's allowance under the Jobseekers Act 1995, means regulations under that Act or the Social Security Administration Act 1992;

(d) [*omitted as applying only to Northern Ireland*].

1.408

DEFINITIONS

"claim for asylum"—see the Asylum and Immigration Appeals Act 1993.
"the Convention"—*ibid.*

1.409

SCHEDULE 1

MODIFICATIONS OF SOCIAL SECURITY REGULATIONS

PART I

SOCIAL SECURITY (PERSONS FROM AROAD)MISCELLANEOUS
AMENDMENTS REGULATIONS 1996

Preliminary

1.410   **1.** In this Part of this Schedule—
(a) "the 1996 Regulations" means the Social Security (Persons from Abroad) Miscellaneous Amendments Regulations 1996; and
(b) expressions which are used in the 1996 Regulations have the same meanings as in those Regulations.

Income Support

1.411   **2.** In regulation 8 of the 1996 Regulations (amendment of the Income Support Regulations)—
(a) paragraph (2) so far as relating to the sub-paragraph added to regulation 21(3) of the Income Support Regulations as sub-paragraph (j); and
(b) paragraph (3)(c) and (d),
shall have effect as if the 1996 Regulations had been made, and had come into force, on the day on which this Act is passed.

[Paras 3 and 4 are omitted as not relevant to the benefits covered by this book].

General

1.412   **5.** Regulation 12(1) of the 1996 Regulations (saving) shall have effect as if after the words "shall continue to have effect" there were inserted the words "(both as regards him and as regards persons who are members of his family at the coming into force of these Regulations)".

6.—(1) Subject to sub-paragraph (2) below, any person who is excluded from entitlement to income support, housing benefit or council tax benefit by any of the provisions which are modified by the preceding provisions of this Part of this Schedule—
(a) shall not be entitled to the benefit for any period beginning on or after the day on which this Act is passed; and
(b) shall not be entitled to the benefit for any period beginning on or after 5th February 1996 except on a claim made before the day on which this Act is passed, or an application made before that day for the review of a decision.

(2) Nothing in this paragraph shall apply in any case where a person is entitled to the benefit in question either—
(a) by virtue of regulation 12(1) of the 1996 Regulations (saving); or
(b) by virtue of regulations making such provision as is mentioned in section 11(2) of this Act.

Immigration and Asylum Act 1999

(1999 C. 33)

Exclusion from benefits

115.—(1) No person is entitled to income-based jobseeker's allowance   1.414
under the Jobseekers Act 1995 or to—
   (a) attendance allowance,
   (b) severe disablement allowance,
   (c) [¹carer's allowance],
   (d) disability living allowance,
   (e) income support,
   (f) [²...]
   (g) [²...]
   (h) a social fund payment,
   (i) child benefit,
   (j) housing benefit, or
   (k) council tax benefit,
under the Social Security Contributions and Benefits Act 1992 while he is
a person to whom this section applies.
   (2) No person in Northern Ireland is entitled to—
   (a) income-based jobseeker's allowance under the Jobseekers (Northern
       Ireland) Order 1995, or
   (b) any of the benefits mentioned in paragraphs (a) to (j) of subsection (1),
under the Social Security Contributions and Benefits (Northern Ireland)
Act 1992 while he is a person to whom this section applies.
   (3) This section applies to a person subject to immigration control unless
he falls within such category or description, or satisfies such conditions, as
may be prescribed.
   (4) Regulations under subsection (3) may provide for a person to be
treated for prescribed purposes only as not being a person to whom this
section applies.
   (5) In relation to the benefits mentioned in subsection (1)(f) or (g), "prescribed" means prescribed by regulations made by the Treasury.
   (6) In relation to the matters mentioned in subsection (2) (except so far
as it relates to the benefits mentioned in subsection (1)(f) or (g)), "prescribed" means prescribed by regulations made by the Department.

(7) Section 175(3) to (5) of the Social Security Contributions and Benefits Act 1992 (supplemental powers in relation to regulations) applies to regulations made by the Secretary of State or the Treasury under subsection (3) as it applies to regulations made under that Act.

(8) Sections 133(2), 171(2) and 172(4) of the Social Security Contributions and Benefits (Northern Ireland) Act 1992 apply to regulations made by the Department under subsection (3) as they apply to regulations made by the Department under that Act.

(9) "A person subject to immigration control" means a person who is not a national of an EEA State and who—

(a) requires leave to enter or remain in the United Kingdom but does not have it;

(b) has leave to enter or remain in the United Kingdom which is subject to a condition that he does not have recourse to public funds;

(c) has leave to enter or remain in the United Kingdom given as a result of a maintenance undertaking; or

(d) has leave to enter or remain in the United Kingdom only as a result of paragraph 17 of Schedule 4.

(10) "Maintenance undertaking", in relation to any person, means a written undertaking given by another person in pursuance of the immigration rules to be responsible for that person's maintenance and accommodation.

AMENDMENTS

1. Regulatory Reform (Carer's Allowance) Order 2002 (SI 2002/1457), art.2(1) and Sch., para. 3(c) (April 1, 2003).
2. Tax Credits Act 2002, s.60 and Sch.6 (April 8, 2003).

GENERAL NOTE

1.415   See the Social Security (Immigration and Asylum) Consequential Amendments Regulations 2000 and the notes to reg.21(3) of the Income Support (General) Regulations 1987.

Paragraph 17 of Sch.4 to the Act (referred to in s.115(9)(d)) provides for the automatic continuation of leave to enter or remain pending an appeal:

(i) against a decision to vary (or a refusal to vary) limited leave to enter or remain in the UK (under s.61); or

(ii) by an asylum seeker against a decision to vary (or a refusal to vary) limited leave to enter or remain in the UK (under s.69(2) of the Act).

Back-dating of benefits where person recorded as refugee

1.416   **123.**—(1) This section applies if—

(a) a person is recorded by the Secretary of State as a refugee within the meaning of the Refugee Convention; and

(b) before the refugee was so recorded, he or his dependant was a person to whom section 115 applied.

(2) Regulations may provide that a person mentioned in subsection (1)(b) may, within a prescribed period, claim the whole, or any prescribed proportion, of any benefit to which he would have been entitled had the refugee been so recorded when he made his claim for asylum.

(3)–(6) *[Omitted as relating only to housing benefit and council tax benefit].*

(7) The regulations may make provision in relation to a person who has received support under this Part or who is a dependant of such a person—

(a) for the determination, or for criteria for the calculation, of the value of that support; and

(b) for the sum which he would be entitled to claim under the regulations to be reduced by the whole, or any prescribed proportion, of that valuation.

(8) The reductions permitted by subsection (7) must not exceed the amount of the valuation.

(9) "Regulations" means—

(a) in relation to jobseeker's allowance under the Jobseekers Act 1995, regulations made by the Secretary of State under that Act or the Social Security Administration Act 1992;

(b) in relation to jobseeker's allowance under the Jobseekers (Northern Ireland) Order 1995, regulations made by the Department under that Order or the Social Security Administration (Northern Ireland) Act 1992;

(c) in relation to a benefit under the Social Security Contributions and Benefits Act 1992 [¹ or state pension credit], regulations made by the Secretary of State under that Act [¹, the Social Security Administration Act 1992 (c. 5) or the State Pension Credit Act 2002];

(d) in relation to a benefit under the Social Security Contributions and Benefits (Northern Ireland) Act 1992, regulations made by the Department under that Act or the Social Security Administration (Northern Ireland) Act 1992.

AMENDMENT

1. State Pension Credit Act 2002, s.14 and Sch.2 para.42 (October 6, 2003).

GENERAL NOTE

See reg.21ZB of the Income Support Regulations.   1.417

Children (Leaving Care) Act 2000

(2000 c. 35)

SECTIONS REPRODUCED

GENERAL NOTE

The Children (Leaving Care) Act 2000, which came into effect on October 1, 2001, places new duties on local authorities in connection with the provision of support and assistance to those who are leaving local authority care (ie whom the local authority is ceasing to "look after"). The Act replaces the arrangements previously contained in s.24 of the Children Act 1989. Its provisions are amplified in the Children (Leaving Care) (England) Regulations 2001 (SI 2001/ 2874) and the   1.419

Children (Leaving Care) (Wales) Regulations 2001 (SI 2001/ 2189), both of which also came into force on October 1, 2001. The Act does not apply to Scotland, with the exception of s.6. It was originally intended that equivalent legislation would be introduced in Scotland in 2002. However a decision was taken to delay the implementation of the changes in Scotland and the relevant provisions (see the Support and Assistance of Young People Leaving Care (Scotland) Regulations 2003 (SSI 2003/608)) only came into force on April 1, 2004.

The effect of s.6 of the Act is to exclude an "eligible child" (defined in the new para.19B of Sch.2 to the Children Act 1989, inserted by s.1) or a "relevant child" (defined in the new s.23A of the 1989 Act, inserted by s.2) from entitlement to income-based JSA, income support and housing benefit. Section 6(3) allows regulations to provide for exceptions to this rule: see the Children (Leaving Care) Social Security Benefits Regulations 2001 (SI 2001/3074) (p.744). In addition regulations under s.6(4) can extend the exclusion from these benefits to children who have been looked after by a local authority in Scotland. Such regulations have now been made and came into force on April 1, 2004 (see the Children (Leaving Care) Social Security Benefits (Scotland) Regulations 2004 (SI 2004/747) (p. 747).

For a discussion of s.6 and of the relevant definitions, see the note to reg.2 of the Children (Leaving Care) Social Security Benefits Regulations 2001 (p.745). See also the note to reg. 2 of the Children (Leaving Care) Social Security Benefits (Scotland) Regulations 2004 (p. 784).

Further duties of local authorities towards children whom they are looking after

1.420   **1.** In Part II of Schedule 2 to the Children Act 1989 ("the 1989 Act"), which contains provision as to children being looked after by local authorities, after paragraph 19 insert—

> "*Preparation for ceasing to be looked after*
> **19A.** *[Omitted.]*
> **19B.**—(1) A local authority shall have the following additional functions in relation to an eligible child whom they are looking after.
> (2) In sub-paragraph (1) "eligible child" means, subject to subparagraph (3), a child, who—
>
> > (a) is aged sixteen or seventeen; and
> > (b) has been looked after by a local authority for a prescribed period, or periods amounting in all to a prescribed period, which began after he reached a prescribed age and ended after he reached the age of sixteen.
>
> (3) The Secretary of State may prescribe—
>
> > (a) additional categories of eligible children; and
> > (b) categories of children who are not to be eligible children despite falling within sub-paragraph (2).
>
> (4)–(8) *[Omitted.]*
> **19C.** *[Omitted.]*."

Additional functions of local authorities in respect of certain children

1.421   **2.**—(1) The 1989 Act is amended as follows.

(2) *[Omitted.]*

(3) In the heading before section 24, at the end insert "and young persons".

(4) After that heading insert the following new sections—

"**The responsible authority and relevant children.**

23A.—(1) The responsible local authority shall have the functions set out in section 23B in respect of a relevant child.

(2) In subsection (1) "relevant child" means (subject to subsection (3)) a child who—

    (a) is not being looked after by any local authority;

    (b) was, before last ceasing to be looked after, an eligible child for the purposes of paragraph 19B of Schedule 2; and

    (c) is aged sixteen or seventeen.

(3) The Secretary of State may prescribe –

    (a) additional categories of relevant children; and

    (b) categories of children who are not to be relevant children despite falling within subsection (2).

(4)–(5) *[Omitted.]*

23B. *[Omitted.]*

23C. *[Omitted.]*"

Exclusion from benefits

6.—(1) No person is entitled to income-based jobseeker's allowance under the Jobseekers Act 1995, or to income support or housing benefit under the Social Security Contributions and Benefits Act 1992, while he is a person to whom this section applies.

    1.422

(2) Subject to subsection (3), this section applies to—

    (a) an eligible child for the purposes of paragraph 19B of Schedule 2 to the Children Act 1989;

    (b) a relevant child for the purposes of section 23A of that Act; and

    (c) any person of a description prescribed in regulations under subsection (4).

(3) The Secretary of State may by regulations provide that this section does not apply to a person who falls within subsection (2)(a) or (b) but who also falls within such category or description, or satisfies such conditions, as may be prescribed in the regulations.

(4) The Secretary of State may make regulations prescribing descriptions of persons who do not fall within subsection (2)(a) or (b) but who—

    (a) have been looked after by a local authority in Scotland (within the meaning of section 17(6) of the Children (Scotland) Act 1995); and

    (b) otherwise correspond (whether or not exactly) to eligible or relevant children.

(5) The Secretary of State may in regulations make such transitional, consequential and saving provision as he considers necessary or expedient in connection with the coming into force of this section.

(6) Section 175(3) to (5) of the Social Security Contributions and Benefits Act 1992 (supplemental power in relation to regulations) applies to regulations made under this section as it applies to regulations made under that Act.

(7) Powers to make regulations under this section include power to make different provision for different areas.

(8) Powers to make regulations under this section are exercisable by statutory instrument.

(9) No statutory instrument containing regulations under subsection (4) is to be made unless a draft of the instrument has been laid before Parliament and approved by a resolution of each House of Parliament.

(10) A statutory instrument containing regulations under subsection (3) or (5) shall be subject to annulment in pursuance of a resolution of either House of Parliament.

Age-Related Payments Act 2004

(2004 c. 10)

SECTIONS REPRODUCED

Payments for 2004

GENERAL NOTE

1.426   The Age-Related Payments Act 2004 came into force on July 8, 2004 and provides for a one-off payment—to be made during the Winter of 2004—to "qualifying individuals" (see s.1) who were aged 70 or over on September 26, 2004 and were ordinarily resident in Great Britain for at least one day in the preceding week ("the qualifying week"). It also includes a general power for the Secretary of State to make "regulations providing for the making of payments by him to persons who have attained the age of 60 years". The provisions relating to the 2004 payment are included because it is possible that they have given rise to disputes which remain unresolved during 2005. It is understood that the general power will be used to make the payment of £200 to pensioners (supposedly as a form of council tax rebate) that was announced in the March 2005 budget.

The rules for the 2004 payment are similar, but not identical, to those for winter fuel payments from the social fund (see Part V below). The payment is, in the most usual cases, £100 for each household that contains a qualifying individual, but the rate of payment, and the identity of the payee, can vary according to the rules set out in ss. 2 and 3. There is no entitlement if the qualifying individual has been a hospital in-patient for 52 continuous weeks ending with the qualifying week or was in custody or subject to immigration control throughout that week (s.4). As with winter fuel payments, the Secretary of State may make an age-related payment without a receiving a claim.

However, anyone who is entitled but who has not received the payment by December 31, 2004 must make a claim for it by March 31, 2005 or lose entitlement (s.5). The normal rules for revision, supersession and appeal to an appeal tribunal apply.

The general power to make payments to (s.7) is not limited by any specification of the purposes for which the payment is to be made, is to be contrasted with the more limited power to make payments "to meet expenses for heating, which appear likely to the Secretary of State to have been or likely to be incurred in cold weather" in s.138(2) of SSCBA 1992 which is used to make cold weather payments and winter fuel payments.

Payments for 2004

"Qualifying individual" and "relevant week"

1—(1) In this Act "qualifying individual" means an individual who—   **1.427**
(a) is ordinarily resident in Great Britain on at least one day in the relevant week, and
(b) attains the age of 70 years on or before the last day of the relevant week.
(2) In this Act "the relevant week" means the week beginning with Monday 20th September 2004 and ending with Sunday 26th September 2004.

Entitlement: basic cases

2—(1) A qualifying individual shall be entitled to a payment of £100 if at any time in the relevant week—
(a) he is single, and
(b) either—
    (i) he is not living with another qualifying individual, or
    (ii) he is in receipt of state pension credit.
(2) A qualifying individual shall be entitled to a payment of £50 if at any time in the relevant week—
(a) he is single,
(b) he is not in receipt of state pension credit, and
(c) he is living with another qualifying individual.
(3) A qualifying individual shall be entitled to a payment of £100 if at any time in the relevant week he is part of a couple and—
(a) the other member of the couple is not a qualifying individual, or
(b) either member of the couple is in receipt of—
    (i) state pension credit,
    (ii) an income-based jobseeker's allowance, or
    (iii) income support.
(4) A qualifying individual shall be entitled to a payment of £50 if at any time in the relevant week he is part of a couple and—
(a) the other member of the couple is a qualifying individual, and
(b) neither member of the couple is in receipt of state pension credit.
(5) This section is subject to section 3.

Entitlement: special cases

3—(1) Where—   **1.428**
(a) two or more couples live together, and

(b) two or more individuals, each of whom is part of one of the couples, would (but for this subsection) be entitled to a payment under section 2(3)(a) (and not under section 2(3)(b)),

then each of those individuals shall instead be entitled to a payment of £50.

(2) Where each member of a couple would (but for this subsection) be entitled to a payment under section 2(3)(b)—

(a) the member who is to receive a payment in 2004 under the Social Fund Winter Fuel Payment Regulations 2000 (SI 2000/729) shall be entitled to the payment under section 2(3)(b), and

(b) the other member shall not be entitled to a payment under section 2(3)(b).

(3) Where—

(a) only one member of a couple is a qualifying individual,

(b) he would (but for this subsection) be entitled to a payment under section 2(3),

(c) the other member of the couple is to receive a payment in 2004 under the Social Fund Winter Fuel Payment Regulations 2000, and

(d) the qualifying individual is not to receive a payment in 2004 under those regulations,

then—

(i) that other member of the couple shall be entitled to a payment of £100, and

(ii) the qualifying individual shall not be entitled to a payment under section 2(3).

(4) Subsection (5) applies to a qualifying individual if—

(a) on the last day of the relevant week he is living in a care home, and

(b) throughout the period of 13 weeks ending with the relevant week his ordinary place of residence was a care home.

(5) Where this subsection applies to a qualifying individual—

(a) if he is not in receipt of state pension credit at any time in the relevant week, he shall be entitled to a payment of £50 (and he shall not be entitled to a payment under section 2), and

(b) if at any time in the relevant week he is in receipt of state pension credit, he shall not be entitled to a payment under section 2 or this section.

(6) Where a person to whom subsection (5) applies is part of a couple, in the application of section 2(3) and (4) to the other member of the couple the person to whom subsection (5) applies shall be treated as a non—qualifying individual.

Disqualifications

1.429   4—(1) A qualifying individual who would (but for this section) be entitled to a payment under section 2 or 3 shall not be entitled to the payment if—

(a) he is in receipt of free in-patient treatment throughout the period of 52 weeks ending with the relevant week,

(b) he is in custody throughout the relevant week, or

(c) he is subject to immigration control throughout the relevant week.

(2) For the purposes of subsection (1)—

(a) the reference to receipt of free in-patient treatment shall be construed in accordance with regulation 2(2) and (2A) of the Social Security (Hospital In-patients) Regulations 1975 (SI 1975/555),

(b) a person is in custody if he is detained in custody under a sentence imposed by a court, and

(c) the reference to being subject to immigration control shall be construed in accordance with section 115(9) of the Immigration and Asylum Act 1999 (c. 33).

(3) Where a person to whom this section applies is part of a couple, in the application of section 2(3) and (4) to the other member of the couple the person to whom this section applies shall be treated as a non-qualifying individual.

Procedure

5—(1) Where before 31st December 2004 the Secretary of State thinks that a person is entitled to a payment under section 2 or 3, the Secretary of State shall make the payment before that date (without a claim being required).

1.430

(2) A person who is entitled to a payment under section 2 or 3 and who does not receive it before 31st December 2004, may claim the payment.

(3) A claim under subsection (2) must—

(a) be in writing to the Secretary of State,

(b) be received by the Secretary of State before 31st March 2005, and

(c) specify—

(i) the claimant's name, address, date of birth and national insurance number (if he has one), and

(ii) the date on which the claim is sent to the Secretary of State, and

(d) include a declaration that the claimant was ordinarily resident in Great Britain on at least one day in the relevant week.

(4) If the Secretary of State thinks that a person making a claim under subsection (2) is entitled to a payment under section 2 or 3, the Secretary of State shall make the payment.

(5) The provisions of Chapter II of Part I of the Social Security Act 1998 (c. 14) (revision, appeal, &c.) shall apply to a decision of the Secretary of State about a person's entitlement to a payment under section 2 or 3 (whether or not following a claim) as they apply to a decision of the Secretary of State under section 8 of that Act.

Payment to be disregarded for tax and social security

6. No account shall be taken of entitlement to a payment under section 2 or 3 in considering a person's—

1.431

(a) liability to tax,

(b) entitlement to benefit under an enactment relating to social security (irrespective of the name or nature of the benefit), or

(c) entitlement to a tax credit.

Future payments

Power to provide for payments

7—(1) The Secretary of State may make regulations providing for the making of payments by him to persons who have attained the age of 60 years.

1.432

(2) Regulations under subsection (1) may provide for payments to be made—

(a) to persons in a specified class (which may be defined by reference to age or otherwise);

(b) in specified circumstances.

(3) Regulations under subsection (1) may, in particular—

(a) provide for payments to be made only once, at specified times or over a specified period,

(b) provide for exceptions,

(c) apply (with or without modifications) an enactment relating to social security (including, in particular, an enactment relating to claims, payments, evidence, revision of decisions, appeals or recovery of payment in error), and

(d) make different provision for different cases or circumstances.

(4) Regulations under this section—

(a) shall be made by statutory instrument, and

(b) may not be made unless a draft has been laid before and approved by resolution of each House of Parliament.

(5) [Omitted]

General

Interpretation

8—(1) In this Act—

1.433 "care home"—

(a) in relation to England and Wales, has the same meaning as that given by section 3 of the Care Standards Act 2000 (c. 14), and

(b) in relation to Scotland, means accommodation provided by a care home service within the meaning of section 2(3) of the Regulation of Care (Scotland) Act 2001 (asp 8)—

"couple" means a man and a woman who share a household and who are, or who live as, husband and wife,

"income—based jobseeker's allowance" has the meaning given by section 1(1) and (4) of the Jobseekers Act 1995 (c. 18),

"income support" means income support under section 124 of the Social Security Contributions and Benefits Act 1992 (c. 4),

"qualifying individual" has the meaning given by section 1,

"the relevant week" has the meaning given by section 1,

"single", in relation to an individual, means not part of a couple, and

"state pension credit" has the meaning given by section 1(1) of the State Pension Credit Act 2002 (c. 16).

(2) The provisions of this Act shall apply, with any necessary modifications, to the parties to a polygamous marriage as if they together formed one couple.

Money

1.434 9. Expenditure of the Secretary of State under or by virtue of this Act shall be paid out of money provided by Parliament.

Extent

1.435 10—This Act shall extend only to—

(a) England and Wales, and

(b) Scotland.

Citation

11. This Act may be cited as the Age-Related Payments Act 2004.

1.436

Child Support Act 1991

(1991 c. 48)

SECTIONS REPRODUCED

6.	Applications by those claiming or receiving benefit.	1.437
43.	Recovery of child support maintenance by deduction from benefit.	
46.	Reduced benefit decisions.	

SCHEDULES REPRODUCED

Sch.1, paras 4 and 8

GENERAL NOTE

This book does not deal directly with the system of child support maintenance. For a full treatment, see Jacobs and Douglas, *Child Support: the Legislation.*

1.438

Since its inception the child support legislation has provided for certain income-related benefits to be reduced where a parent on benefit fails to cooperate in the process of assessing maintenance from an absent parent (now referred to as a non-resident parent). However, from October 5, 1999 this has only applied to income support and income-based JSA. Moreover, since the introduction of the new tax credits regime on April 6, 2003, and in particular child tax credit (CTC), some parents may be better off claiming CTC rather than income support or income-based JSA, as any maintenance that they do receive is ignored in full for the purposes of CTC (and working tax credit). For full details of the new tax credits scheme see Vol. IV in this series, *Tax Credits and Employer-paid Social Security Benefits.* It is only income support claimants and income-based JSA claimants who are *required* to use the Child Support Agency to obtain maintenance for their children. For details of the current provisions relating to reduced benefit decisions (replacing the former reduced benefit directions), see ss.6 and 46 below and the notes to those provisions, together with Part IV of the Child Support (Maintenance Calculation Procedure) Regulations).

In addition, where an absent parent was on income support or income-based JSA, a deduction could be made from his income support or income-based JSA as a contribution towards child support maintenance. This deduction will still apply in cases which have not yet been "converted" to the new child support scheme introduced by the Child Support, Pensions and Social Security Act 2000 (see below). (This deduction can also be made from an absent parent's contribution-based JSA if he would be entitled to income-based JSA at the same rate but for the fact that he is getting contribution-based JSA; in addition, deductions for arrears of child support maintenance can be made from contribution-based JSA in certain circumstances (see further the note to s.43)). However, for those cases to which the new child support rules apply, a deduction of £5 in respect of the flat-rate of child support maintenance can be made from a greatly expanded list of benefits (see further the note to s.43).

Those parts of the child support legislation relevant to the reduction and the deduction are included in this book.

Furthermore, from April 1997 s.10 of the Child Support Act 1995 has provided for income support and income-based JSA claimants receiving child maintenance to build up a "child maintenance bonus". See the Social Security (Child Maintenance Bonus) Regulations 1996 (SI 1996/3195). However, as part of the changes to the child support scheme under the 2000 Act, the child maintenance bonus is being abolished and replaced by a child maintenance "premium" (in effect a disregard) (see further the note to s.10 of the 1995 Act below). These provisions are also covered in this book.

1.439   On March 3, 2003 the long-delayed changes to the child support scheme introduced by the Child Support, Pensions and Social Security Act 2000 finally came into force (see the Child Support, Pensions and Social Security Act 2000 (Commencement No.12) Order 2003 (SI 2003/192), as amended by the Child Support, Pensions and Social Security Act 2000 (Commencement No.13) Order 2003 (SI 2003/346)). The new rules only apply to all new (and non-linking) child support applications (a new application is one with an effective date on or after March 3, 2003); most existing cases will be "converted" at a future date (still not announced and likely to be delayed for a number of years), although some may transfer earlier. Thus, for example, if after March 3, 2003, a person with a existing child support assessment makes a new application for a different child with a different non-resident parent the new scheme will be applied to both applications. For full details of the new scheme and when it applies, see Jacobs and Douglas, *Child Support: the Legislation.*

Since the child support changes are coming into force in stages depending on the type of case, this means that the old rules will continue to apply for some claimants. However, for reasons of space, only the new provisions relating to reduced benefit decisions and deductions for child support maintenance are included in this edition. Readers are referred to the 2002 edition of this volume for the former provisions relating to reduced benefit directions and deductions as a contribution towards child maintenance. However, for ease of reference both the provisions relating to the child maintenance bonus and the child maintenance premium are included. The notes to the relevant sections of the Child Support Act 1991 and 1995 reproduced below contain details of the relevant commencement provisions.

[¹ Applications by those claiming or receiving benefit

1.440   **6.**—(1) This section applies where income support, an income-based jobseeker's allowance or any other benefit of a prescribed kind is claimed by or in respect of, or paid to or in respect of, the parent of a qualifying child who is also a person with care of the child.

(2) In this section, that person is referred to as "the parent".

(3) The Secretary of State may—

(a) treat the parent as having applied for a maintenance calculation with respect to the qualifying child and all other children of the non-resident parent in relation to whom the parent is also a person with care; and

(b) take action under this Act to recover from the non-resident parent, on the parent's behalf, the child support maintenance so determined.

(4) Before doing what is mentioned in subsection (3), the Secretary of State must notify the parent in writing of the effect of subsections (3) and (5) and section 46.

(5) The Secretary of State may not act under subsection (3) if the parent asks him not to (a request which need not be in writing).

(6) Subsection (1) has effect regardless of whether any of the benefits mentioned there is payable with respect to any qualifying child.

(7) Unless she has made a request under subsection (5), the parent shall, so far as she reasonably can, comply with such regulations as may be made by the Secretary of State with a view to the Secretary of State's being provided with the information which is required to enable—

(a) the non-resident parent to be identified or traced;

(b) the amount of child support maintenance payable by him to be calculated; and

(c) that amount to be recovered from him.

(8) The obligation to provide information which is imposed by subsection (7)—

(a) does not apply in such circumstances as may be prescribed; and

(b) may, in such circumstances as may be prescribed, be waived by the Secretary of State.

(9) If the parent ceases to fall within subsection (1), she may ask the Secretary of State to cease acting under this section, but until then he may continue to do so.

(10) The Secretary of State must comply with any request under subsection (9) (but subject to any regulations made under subsection (11)).

(11) The Secretary of State may by regulations make such incidental or transitional provision as he thinks appropriate with respect to cases in which he is asked under subsection (9) to cease to act under this section.

(12) The fact that a maintenance calculation is in force with respect to a person with care does not prevent the making of a new maintenance calculation with respect to her as a result of the Secretary of State's acting under subsection (3).]

AMENDMENT

1. Child Support, Pensions and Social Security Act 2000, s.3 (March 3, 2003).   **1.441**

DEFINITIONS

"child": see Child Support Act 1991, s.55.
"child support maintenance": see Child Support Act 1991, s.54.
"non-resident parent": *ibid.*
"person with care": *ibid.*
"qualifying child": *ibid.*

GENERAL NOTE

The long-delayed changes to the child support scheme introduced by the Child   **1.442**
Support, Pensions and Social Security Act 2000 finally came into force on March 3, 2003. The changes are being implemented in stages depending on the type of case (see the note at the beginning of the Child Support Act 1991 above). They include the substitution of this section and of s.46. The new form of this section and of s.46 contain some significant differences from the previous provisions.

Article 4 of the Child Support, Pensions and Social Security Act 2000 (Commencement No.12) Order 2003 (SI 2003/192) provides that the new form of this section and of s.46 apply in cases where (i) on or after March 3, 2003 income support or income-based JSA is claimed by or for, or paid to or for, the parent with care of a qualifying child and there is no maintenance assessment or maintenance calculation in force in respect of that parent and has been no maintenance assessment in force during the previous eight weeks in respect of the child; (ii) on or after March 3, 2003 a parent with care withdraws her authorisation under the previous form of s.6(1) and a maintenance assessment has been made with an effective date before March 3, 2003; (iii) immediately before March 3, 2003 the previous form of s.6(1) applied and a maintenance assessment has not been made because the Secretary of State was considering whether the parent with care should be required to give authorisation, or had accepted that she should not be so required because of the risk of harm or undue distress, or was in the process of serving notice or considering reasons before imposing a reduced benefits direction, or had imposed a reduced benefits direction.

See also reg.31(3)–(8) of the Child Support (Maintenance Calculation Procedure) Regulations 2000 for the transitional provisions relating to reduced benefit decisions.

For the previous form of s.6 see the 2002 edition of this volume.

Under the new form of s.6, a parent with care of a qualifying child who has claimed, or is being paid ("paid" means "actually paid", not "lawfully paid": *Secretary of State for Social Security v Harmon, Carter and Cocks* [1999] 1 W.L.R. 163, also reported as *R(CS) 4/99*; on June 9, 2005 the Northern Ireland Court of Appeal reached the same conclusion (*Department for Social Development v MacGeagh* [2005] NICA 28)) income support or income-based JSA (or for whom these benefits are claimed or paid) is *deemed* to have applied for child support maintenance (subss.(1) and (3)). It is no longer necessary for the parent with care to authorise the Secretary of State to take action to recover child support maintenance, as was the case under the old form of s.6. Note that the Secretary of State is only empowered to act under subs.(3); he is not obliged to do so (although in practice he is likely to). The Secretary of State will not be in breach of his obligation to consider the welfare of any child under s.2 of the Child Support Act 1991 if he does not first seek the views of the non-resident parent before acting under this section (*R(CS) 1/98*; see also *R. v Secretary of State for Social Security Ex p. Lloyd* [1995] 1 F.L.R. 856).

Under the new provisions the parent with care can "opt out" (*i.e.* request the Secretary of State not to act), which need not be done in writing (subs.(5)). However, this is likely to trigger an inquiry in her reasons (see s.46(2)). The Secretary of State has to serve a notice giving the parent with care four weeks to provide her reasons for opting out. If the Secretary of State does not consider that there are reasonable grounds for believing that there would be a risk of harm or undue distress to the parent with care or any children living with her if he acted under s.6, this may result in her becoming subject to a reduced benefit decision (see s.46(3)–(5)). Note s.46(6) which allows the Secretary of State to make periodic inquiries into her reasons for opting out.

1.443 Unless she has opted out, the parent with care is obliged to provide the necessary information (subs.(7)), although this does not apply/can be waived in prescribed circumstances (subs.(8)). Part II of the Child Support (Information, Evidence and Disclosure) Regulations 1992 (SI 1992/1812), as amended, prescribes the information required. Failure to provide the information required under subs.(7) may also result in the parent with care becoming subject to a reduced benefit decision (see s.46).

Note that subs.(7)(a) refers to providing information to enable the non-resident parent to be traced or *identified* (the old form of s.6 (see subs.(9)(a)) had only required information to enable him to be traced). This reverses the result in *CCS 15221/1996*. The parent with care in *CCS 15221/1996* had given particulars of the absent parent but when he did not accept paternity she refused to give further details of their relationship or to undergo DNA testing or to consent to it for her child. The Commissioner held that the obligation to provide information to allow the absent parent to be traced did not require the parent with care to submit herself or her child to scientific tests. "Tracing" related to the whereabouts of an alleged parent and not to the determination of parentage. The new wording in subs.(7)(a), however, is intended to encompass such tests (and any other means of identification).

Note also that under the new s.46 an additional ground on which a reduced benefit decision can be made is the refusal by a parent with care to submit to a DNA test.

If the parent stops getting income support or income-based JSA, or she is no longer the parent of a qualifying child, or the parent with care of the child, the Secretary must cease acting if she requests this (subss.(9) and (10); see *CCS 4725/1995*).

There is a right of appeal to a tribunal against a reduced benefit decision (s.20(1)(c) of the Child Support Act 1991, see Jacobs and Douglas, *Child Support: the Legislation*). However, it is not possible to appeal to a tribunal against a decision to reduce a person's benefit in accordance with a reduced benefit decision (see para.8 of Sch.2 to the Social Security Act 1998 in Vol. III of this series).

Special Cases

[¹ Recovery of child support maintenance by deduction from benefit

43.—(1) This section applies where—

(a) a non-resident parent is liable to pay a flat rate of child support main-   1.444
    tenance (or would be so liable but for a variation having been agreed
    to), and that rate applies (or would have applied) because he falls
    within paragraph 4(1)(b) or (c) or 4(2) of Schedule 1; and

(b) such conditions as may be prescribed for the purposes of this section
    are satisfied.

(2) The power of the Secretary of State to make regulations under section 5 of the Social Security Administration Act 1992 by virtue of subsection (1)(p) (deductions from benefits) may be exercised in relation to cases to which this section applies with a view to securing that payments in respect of child support maintenance are made or that arrears of child support maintenance are recovered.

(3) For the purposes of this section, the benefits to which section 5 of the 1992 Act applies are to be taken as including war disablement pensions and war widows' pensions (within the meaning of section 150 of the Social Security Contributions and Benefits Act 1992 (interpretation)).]

AMENDMENT

1. Child Support, Pensions and Social Security Act 2000, s.21 (March 3, 2003).   1.445

DEFINITIONS

"child support maintenance": see Child Support Act 1991, s.54.
"non-resident parent": *ibid.*

GENERAL NOTE

The long-delayed changes to the child support scheme introduced by the Child   1.446
Support, Pensions and Social Security Act 2000 finally came into force on March 3, 2003. The changes are being implemented in stages depending on the type of case (see the note at the beginning of the Child Support Act 1991 above). They include the substitution of this section and of Pt I of Sch.1 to the 1991 Act. The new form contains some significant differences from the previous provisions.

The new form of s.43 and para.4 of Pt I of Sch.1 to the 1991 Act apply in those cases to which the new child support scheme applies (see art.3 of and the Schedule to the Child Support, Pensions and Social Security Act 2000 (Commencement No.12) Order 2003 (SI 2003/192) – broadly these are applications for child support maintenance with an effective date on or after March 3, 2003 and certain cases where there is an existing assessment).

Under the new scheme, unless the nil rate is applicable, a £5 flat rate of child support maintenance applies for non-resident parents in receipt of certain prescribed benefits (although a different amount may apply under the transitional arrangements when a case converts to the new system). (For when the nil rate is applicable see para.5 of Sch.1 to the 1991 Act and reg.5 of the Child Support (Maintenance Calculations and Special Cases) Regulations 2000 (SI 2001/155) in Jacobs and Douglas, *Child Support: the Legislation*).

This section, Sch.1, paras 4 and 8 and reg.4 of the Child Support (Maintenance Calculations and Special Cases) Regulations 2000, together with Sch.9B to the Claims and Payments Regulations 1987 (see Vol. III of this series), provide for the deduction of the £5 flat rate from the non-resident parent's benefit and its payment to the parent with care. The deduction will be made if either the non-resident parent or his partner is getting income support, income-based JSA or state pension credit. It is halved if the non-resident parent's partner is also a non-resident parent with a child support maintenance calculation in force. The flat-rate deduction will also be made if the non-resident parent is in receipt of any of the following: contribution-based JSA, incapacity benefit, severe disablement allowance, retirement pension, carer's allowance, maternity allowance, industrial injuries benefit, bereavement allowance, widowed mother's allowance, widowed parent's allowance, widow's pension, war disablement pension, war widow's or widower's pension, a social security benefit paid by a country other than the UK, or a training allowance (other than Work-Based Learning for Young People). In addition, except where income support, income-based JSA or state pension credit is payable to the non-resident parent or his partner, a deduction of £1 for arrears of child support maintenance can be made from any of those benefits or allowances. A deduction can only be made from one benefit in any one week (para.2(2) of Sch.9B to the Claims and Payment Regulations). No deduction will be made if this would result in less than 10p of the benefit remaining payable (para.2(3) of Sch.9B). Note also that if the non-resident parent is regarded as having "shared care" (*i.e.* for at least 52 nights in a year), the amount of child support maintenance payable will be nil and no deduction will be made (see para.8(2) of Sch.1 to the 1991 Act). For a discussion of the priority to be given to the flat-rate deduction in relation to other deductions, see the note to reg.35 of the Claims and Payments Regulations in Vol. III of this series.

1.447   There is a right of appeal to a tribunal against a decision to make deductions from benefit in respect of child support maintenance, although there may be little scope for argument if the legislation has been correctly applied.

For the previous form of s.43, Sch.1, para.5(4) and regs 13 and 28 and Schs.4 and 5 of the Child Support (Maintenance Assessments and Special Cases) Regulations 1992, under which (together with para. 7A of Sch. 9 to the Claims and Payments Regulations 1987 (see Vol. III of this series)) a deduction of £5.70 can be made from the income support, income-based JSA or state pension credit of an absent parent (or contribution-based JSA if the absent parent would be entitled to income-based JSA at the same rate but for the fact that he is getting contribution-based JSA: see para.1(1), definition of "specified benefit", and para.1(2) of Sch.9 to the Claims and Payments Regulations 1987 in Vol. III of this series) as a contribution towards the maintenance of his children, see the 2002 edition of this volume. These provisions still apply for existing cases that have not been converted to the new child support scheme (see the note at the beginning of the Child Support Act 1991, above). Note also that in existing cases deductions for arrears of child support maintenance can be made from contribution-based JSA (even where there would be no entitlement to income-based JSA) in certain circumstances (see para.7B of Sch.9 to the Claims and Payments Regulations). If the full £5.70 cannot be deducted because other deductions are being made which have a higher priority, £2.85 can be deducted (see paras 7A(4), 8(1) and 9 of Sch.9 to the Claims and Payments Regulations). Contributions towards child maintenance have the lowest priority of the deductions covered by Sch.9.

In *CCS/16904/1996* the Commissioner conducted a detailed analysis of the legislation on deductions in place of child support maintenance. He referred to the fact that s.43(2) allowed regulations to be made for deducting payments in place of child support maintenance from various benefits and reg.28(2) of the Child Support (Maintenance Assessments and Special Cases) Regulations 1992 (SI 1992/1815) (see the 2002 edition of this volume for this regulation) defined the amount of the payments (now see para.4 of Sch.1, together with reg.4(3) of the Child Support (Maintenance Calculations and Special Cases) Regulations) but there was nothing that in so many words imposed an obligation on an absent parent to make such payments. He concluded that the legal basis for liability to make payments in place of child support maintenance was provided by the general duty to maintain a child under s.1 of the 1991 Act. This required the payment of such "maintenance" (not just child support maintenance) as determined in accordance with the provisions of the Act. Thus if it was decided that s.43 applied, this gave rise to a liability on the absent parent to make payment and a corresponding entitlement of the parent with care to receive the amounts deducted by the Secretary of State. The decision was appealed to the Court of Appeal under the name of *Dollar v Child Support Officer*, reported as *R(CS) 7/99*, but there was no specific challenge to the Commissioner's conclusion on this issue. The Court of Appeal proceeded on the basis that there was a liability to make the payments identified in s.43(2). The Commissioner states in *CCS/3488/2004* that he therefore sees no reason to depart from what he said in *CCS/16904/1996*.

Note also *R(Plumb) v Secretary of State for Work and Pensions* [2002] EWHC 1125 (Admin), March 22, 2002, unreported (Admin. Ct). The claimant contended that the £5.10 deduction (as it then was) from his JSA made as a contribution towards the maintenance of his child affected the quality and extent of his contact with his daughter and thus was in breach of Art.8 of the European Convention on Human Rights (right to family life). The Court accepted that such a deduction was capable of amounting to an interference with an Art.8 right but on the facts of this case this was far from being established. Furthermore, any interference with the claimant's right under Art.8(1) was justified under Art.8(2).

[¹ Reduced benefit decisions

46.—(1) This section applies where any person ("the parent")—

    1.448

(a) has made a request under section 6(5);

(b) fails to comply with any regulation made under section 6(7); or

(c) having been treated as having applied for a maintenance calculation under section 6, refuses to take a scientific test (within the meaning of section 27A).

(2) The Secretary of State may serve written notice on the parent requiring her, before the end of a specified period—

(a) in a subsection (1)(a) case, to give him her reasons for making the request;

(b) in a subsection (1)(b) case, to give him her reasons for failing to do so; or

(c) in a subsection (1)(c) case, to give him her reasons for her refusal.

(3) When the specified period has expired, the Secretary of State shall consider whether, having regard to any reasons given by the parent, there are reasonable grounds for believing that—

(a) in a subsection (1)(a) case, if the Secretary of State were to do what is mentioned in section 6(3);

(b) in a subsection (1)(b) case, if she were to be required to comply; or

(c) in a subsection (1)(c) case, if she took the scientific test,

there would be a risk of her, or of any children living with her, suffering harm or undue distress as a result of his taking such action, or her complying or taking the test.

(4) If the Secretary of State considers that there are such reasonable grounds, he shall—

(a) take no further action under this section in relation to the request, the failure or the refusal in question; and

(b) notify the parent, in writing, accordingly.

(5) If the Secretary of State considers that there are no such reasonable grounds, he may, except in prescribed circumstances, make a reduced benefit decision with respect to the parent.

(6) In a subsection (1)(a) case, the Secretary of State may from time to time serve written notice on the parent requiring her, before the end of a specified period—

(a) to state whether her request under section 6(5) still stands; and

(b) if so, to give him her reasons for maintaining her request,

and subsections (3) to (5) have effect in relation to such a notice and any response to it as they have effect in relation to a notice under subsection (2)(a) and any response to it.

(7) Where the Secretary of State makes a reduced benefit decision he must send a copy of it to the parent.

(8) A reduced benefit decision is to take effect on such date as may be specified in the decision.

(9) Reasons given in response to a notice under subsection (2) or (6) need not be given in writing unless the Secretary of State directs in any case that they must.

(10) In this section—

(a) "comply" means to comply with the requirement or with the regulation in question; and "complied" and "complying" are to be construed accordingly;

(b) "reduced benefit decision" means a decision that the amount payable by way of any relevant benefit to, or in respect of, the parent concerned be reduced by such amount, and for such period, as may be prescribed;

(c) "relevant benefit" means income support or an income-based job-seeker's allowance or any other benefit of a kind prescribed for the purposes of section 6; and

(d) "specified", in relation to a notice served under this section, means specified in the notice; and the period to be specified is to be determined in accordance with regulations made by the Secretary of State.]

AMENDMENT

1.449   1. Child Support, Pensions and Social Security Act 2000, s.19 (March 3, 2003).

DEFINITION

"maintenance calculation"—see Child Support Act 1991, s.54.

GENERAL NOTE

1.450   The long-delayed changes to the child support scheme introduced by the Child Support, Pensions and Social Security Act 2000 finally came into force on March 3, 2003. The changes are being implemented in stages according to the type of case (see the note at the beginning of the Child Support Act 1991 above). They include the substitution of this section and of s.6. The new forms of s.6 and this section contain some significant differences from the previous provisions. See the note to s.6 above for the cases to which the new forms of s.6 and this section apply from March 3, 2003. Note also the transitional provisions relating to reduced benefit decisions in reg.31(3)–(8) of the Child Support (Maintenance Calculation Procedure) Regulations 2000.

For the previous form of s.46 see the 2002 edition of this volume.

The new form of this section applies where the parent with care has (i) requested the Secretary of State not to act under s.6, (ii) failed to comply with her obligation to provide information under s.6(7), or (iii) refused to take a DNA test (subs.(1)). The written notice under subs.(2) to give reasons must give four weeks to do so (Child Support (Maintenance Calculation Procedure) Regulations 2000, reg.9).

When the four weeks has expired, the Secretary of State must consider whether there are reasonable grounds for believing that there would be a risk of harm or undue distress to the parent with care or any children living with her if (i) he did take action under s.6, (ii) she was required to provide the information, or (iii) she took the test (subs.(3)). (On risk of harm or undue distress see *CCS 1037/1995, CCS 6096/1995, CCS 7003/1995, CCS 12609/1996, CCS 588/1998* and *CCS 7559/1999*). If not, he may give a reduced benefit decision (subs.(5)). However, he cannot do so if the parent's (or any partner's) income support or income-based JSA includes a disability, higher pensioner or disabled child premium or the parent (or any partner) has an award of child tax credit that includes the element for a child/young person with a disability (Child Support (Maintenance Calculation Procedure) Regulations 2000, reg.10).

CCS 1037/1995 confirmed that the discretion in subs.(5) means that there are two stages to these considerations. Even if in the Secretary of State's view there is no risk of harm or undue distress, he then has to go on to decide whether or not to issue a reduced benefit decision. In exercising that discretion, he must, in accordance with s.2 of the 1991 Act, "have regard to the welfare of any child likely to be affected by his decision". Thus he should look to see if there is some exceptional or special factor that suggests that the welfare of a child would be adversely affected by a reduced benefit decision. The Commissioner gives as examples of such special factors the age or state of health of the child or parent. These are now covered, to some extent at least, by reg.10, but it may be that there are other relevant factors, depending on the circumstances of the particular case.

1.451

Note subs.(6) under which a parent with care who has requested the Secretary of State not to act under s.6 can be required to restate her reasons from time to time; the Secretary of State will then reconsider them in accordance with subss.(3)–(5).

The reduced benefit decision, once made, requires the amount of income support or income-based JSA payable to or in respect of the parent to be reduced. See Part IV of the Child Support (Maintenance Calculation Procedure) Regulations for the amount of the reduction, its length and the provisions for its suspension or termination. At April 2005 benefit rates the reduction is £22.48 per week (this will be adjusted, if necessary, so as not reduce the amount of income support or income-based JSA below 10p); it lasts for three years.

There is a right of appeal to a tribunal against a reduced benefit decision (s.20(1)(c) of the Child Support Act 1991, see Jacobs and Douglas, *Child Support: the Legislation*). However, it is not possible to appeal to a tribunal against a decision to reduce a person's benefit in accordance with a reduced benefit decision (see para.8 of Sch.2 to the Social Security Act 1998 in Vol. III of this series).

SCHEDULE 1   **Section 11**

Maintenance Assessments

[¹ Part I

Calculation of Weekly Amount of Child Support Maintenance

Flat rate

4.—(1) Except in a case falling within sub-paragraph (2), a flat rate of £5 is payable if the nil rate does not apply and—

1.452

(a) the non-resident parent's net weekly income is £100 or less; or

(b) he receives any benefit, pension or allowance prescribed for the purposes of this para-graph of this sub-paragraph; or

(c) he or his partner (if any) receives any benefit prescribed for the purposes of this para-graph of this sub-paragraph.

(2) A flat rate of a prescribed amount is payable if the nil rate does not apply and—

(a) the non-resident parent has a partner who is also a non-resident parent;

(b) the partner is a person with respect to whom a maintenance calculation is in force; and

(c) the non-resident parent or his partner receives any benefit prescribed under sub-para-graph (1)(c).

(3) The benefits, pensions and allowances which may be prescribed for the purposes of sub-paragraph (1)(b) include ones paid to the non-resident parent under the law of a place outside the United Kingdom.

[Paras 5 to 7 not reproduced.]

Shared care – flat rate

1.453   **8.**—(1) This paragraph applies only if—

(a) the rate of child support maintenance payable is a flat rate; and

(b) that rate applies because the non-resident parent falls within paragraph 4(1)(b) or (c) or 4(2).

(2) If the care of a qualifying child is shared as mentioned in paragraph 7(2) for at least 52 nights during a prescribed 12-month period, the amount of child support maintenance payable by the non-resident parent to the person with care of that child is nil.]

[The rest of the Schedule has not been reproduced.]

AMENDMENT

1.454   1. Child Support, Pensions and Social Security Act 2000, s.1(3) and Sch.1 (March 3, 2003).

Child Support Act 1995

(1995 c. 34)

SECTION REPRODUCED

1.455   10.   The child maintenance bonus

The child maintenance bonus

1.456   **10.**—(1) The Secretary of State may by regulations make provision for the payment, in prescribed circumstances, of sums to persons—

(a) who are or have been in receipt of child maintenance; and

(b) to or in respect of whom income support or a jobseeker's allowance is or has been paid.

(2) A sum payable under the regulations shall be known as "a child main-tenance bonus".

(3) A child maintenance bonus shall be treated for all purposes as payable by way of income support or (as the case may be) a jobseeker's allowance.

[[1] (4) Subsection (3) is subject to section 677 of the Income Tax (Earnings and Pensions) Act 2003 (which provides for a back to work bonus not to be taxable).]

(5) The regulations may, in particular, provide for—

(a) a child maintenance bonus to be payable only on the occurrence of a prescribed event;

(b) a bonus not to be payable unless a claim is made before the end of the prescribed period;

(c) the amount of a bonus (subject to any maximum prescribed by virtue of paragraph (f)) to be determined in accordance with the regulations;

(d) enabling amounts to be calculated by reference to periods of entitlement to income support and periods of entitlement to a jobseeker's allowance;

(e) treating a bonus as payable wholly by way of a jobseeker's allowance or wholly by way of income support, in a case where amounts have been calculated in accordance with provision made by virtue of paragraph (d);

(f) the amount of a bonus not to exceed a prescribed maximum;

(g) a bonus not to be payable if the amount of the bonus which would otherwise be payable is less than the prescribed minimum;

(h) prescribed periods to be disregarded for prescribed purposes;

(i) a bonus which has been paid to a person to be treated, in prescribed circumstances and for prescribed purposes, as income or capital of hers or of any other member of her family;

(j) treating the whole or a prescribed part of an amount which has accrued towards a person's bonus—

    (i) as not having accrued towards her bonus; but

    (ii) as having accrued towards the bonus of another person.

(6) The Secretary of State may by regulations provide—

(a) for the whole or a prescribed part of a child maintenance bonus to be paid in such circumstances as may be prescribed to such person, other than the person who is or had been in receipt of child maintenance, as may be determined in accordance with the regulations;

(b) for any payments of a prescribed kind which have been collected by the Secretary of State, and retained by him, to be treated for the purposes of this section as having been received by the appropriate person as payments of child maintenance.

(7) In this section—

"appropriate person" has such meaning as may be prescribed;

"child" means a person under the age of 16;

"child maintenance" has such meaning as may be prescribed;

"family" means—

(a) a married or unmarried couple;

(b) a married or unmarried couple and a member of the same household for whom one of them is, or both are, responsible and who is a child or a person of a prescribed description;

(c) except in prescribed circumstances, a person who is not a member of a married or unmarried couple and a member of the same household for whom that person is responsible and who is a child or a person of a prescribed description;

"married couple" means a man and woman who are married to each other and are members of the same household; and

"unmarried couple" means a man and woman who are not married to each other but are living together as husband and wife otherwise than in prescribed circumstances.

(8) For the purposes of this section, the Secretary of State may by regulations make provision as to the circumstances in which—

(a) persons are to be treated as being or not being members of the same household;

(b) one person is to be treated as responsible or not responsible for another.

AMENDMENT

1. Income Tax (Earnings and Pensions) Act 2003, Sch.6, Pt 2, para.231 (April 6, 2003).

GENERAL NOTE

1.457   See the Social Security (Child Maintenance Bonus) Regulations 1996.

As part of the child support reforms introduced by the Child Support, Pensions and Social Security Act 2000, the child maintenance bonus is being abolished. It is replaced by a child maintenance "premium" (in effect a disregard) of £10 per week for income support and income-based JSA claimants.

The long-delayed start to the commencement of the new child support scheme finally began on March 3, 2003. The changes are being implemented in stages depending on the type of case (see the note at the beginning of the Child Support Act 1991 above).

Under the new scheme s.10 is repealed by s.23 of the 2000 Act. Article 6 of the Child Support, Pensions and Social Security Act 2000 (Commencement No.12) Order 2003 (SI 2003/192), as substituted by art.2 of the Child Support, Pensions and Social Security Act 2000 (Commencement No.13) Order 2003 (SI 2003/346), brings s.23 into force in relation to those cases to which the new rules for child support apply (see arts 3 and 4 of the Commencement No.12 Order referred to in the notes to s.6 and s.43 above for those cases). It also brings s.23 into force in relation to cases where child maintenance which is not child support maintenance is first paid under an agreement or court order on or after March 3, 2003. This has the effect of abolishing the child maintenance bonus for income support or income-based JSA claims on the day on or after March 3, 2003 that such child maintenance is first paid.

1.458   For those cases in respect of which s.23 has come into force, it will no longer be possible for the person to accrue a child maintenance bonus. See reg.4 of the Social Security (Child Maintenance Premium and Miscellaneous Amendments) Regulations 2000 (SI 2000/3176), as substituted by reg.2 of the Social Security (Child Maintenance Premium and Miscellaneous Amendments) Amendment Regulations 2003 (SI 2003/231) (p.739) and the note at the beginning of the Child Maintenance Bonus Regulations for the transitional provisions relating to bonuses that have accrued before s.23 comes into force for a particular case.

Income support and income-based JSA claimants for whom the child maintenance bonus has been abolished will be eligible for the child maintenance premium from the date of the abolition. See para.73 of Sch.9 to the Income Support Regulations, and the note to that paragraph, and para.70 of Sch.7 to the JSA Regulations.

Since it will be possible for income support and income-based JSA claimants receiving child maintenance to continue to accrue a child maintenance bonus until their case is converted to the new child support regime, this section and the Social Security (Child Maintenance Bonus) Regulations 1996 are being retained in this edition.

PART II

INCOME SUPPORT

Income Support (General) Regulations 1987

(SI 1987/1967)

Made by the Secretary of State under ss.20(1), (3)(d), (4), (9), (11) and (12), *22(1), (2), (4) and (5) to (9), 23(1), (3) and (5), 51(1)(n) and 84(1) of the* *Social Security Act 1986 and ss.114, 166(1) to (3A) of the Social Security Act* *1975.*

2.1

ARRANGEMENT OF REGULATIONS

PART I

GENERAL

2.2

PART II

CONDITIONS OF ENTITLEMENT

2.3

PART III

MEMBERSHIP OF A FAMILY

2.4

PART IV

APPLICABLE AMOUNTS

PART V

INCOME AND CAPITAL

CHAPTER I

GENERAL

CHAPTER II

INCOME

CHAPTER III

EMPLOYED EARNERS

CHAPTER IV

SELF-EMPLOYED EARNERS

CHAPTER IVA

PARTICIPANTS IN THE SELF-EMPLOYMENT ROUTE

CHAPTER V

OTHER INCOME

CHAPTER VI

CAPITAL

Chapter VII

Liable Relatives

Chapter VIIA

Child Support

Chapter VIII

Students

PART VI

APPLICABLE AMOUNTS AND ASSESSMENT OF INCOME AND CAPITAL
IN URGENT CASES

PART VII

CALCULATION OF INCOME SUPPORT FOR PART-WEEKS

SCHEDULES

PART I

GENERAL

Citation and commencement

   1. These Regulations may be cited as the Income Support (General)   **2.19**
Regulations 1987 and shall come into force on 11th April 1988.

Interpretation

2.20   **2.**—(1) In these Regulations, unless the context otherwise requires
"the Act" means the Social Security Act 1986;
[⁴⁸ "adoption leave" means a period of absence from work on ordinary or
additional adoption leave by virtue of section 75A or 75B of the
Employment Rights Act 1996;]
[⁵⁷ "the Armed Forces and Reserve Forces Compensation Scheme"
means the scheme established under section 1(2) of the Armed Forces
(Pensions and Compensation) Act 2004;]
"attendance allowance" means:—

    (a) an attendance allowance under section 35 of the Social Security
Act [SSCBA, s.64];

    (b) an increase of disablement pension under section 61 or 63 of that
Act [SSCBA, s.104 or 105];

    (c) a payment under regulations made in exercise of the power con-
ferred by section 159(3)(b) of that Act;

    (d) an increase of an allowance which is payable in respect of constant
attendance under section 5 of the Industrial Injuries and Diseases
(Old Cases) Act 1975;

    (e) a payment by virtue of articles 14, 15, 16, 43 or 44 of the Personal
Injuries (Civilians) Scheme 1983 or any analogous payment; or

    (f) any payment based on need for attendance which is paid as part of
a war disablement pension;

[²⁶"the benefit Acts" means the Contributions and Benefits Act and the
Jobseekers Act 1955;]
"benefit week" has the meaning prescribed in paragraph 4 of Schedule 7 to
the Social Security (Claims and Payments) Regulations 1987 [⁴and for
the purposes of calculating any payment of income and of regulation
74(2)(a) "benefit week" shall also mean the period of 7 days ending on
the day before the first day of the first benefit week following the date of
claim or the last day on which income support is paid if it is in payment
for less than a week;]
[⁶"board and lodging accommodation" means—

    (a) accommodation provided to a person or, if he is a member of a
family, to him or any other member of his family, for a charge
which is inclusive of the provision of that accommodation and at
least some cooked or prepared meals which both are cooked or prepared (by a person other than the person to whom the accommodation is provided or a member of his family) and are consumed in
that accommodation or associated premises; or

    (b) accommodation provided to a person in a hotel, guest house,
lodging house or some similar establishment,

except accommodation provided by a close relative of his or of any
other member of his family, or other than on a commercial basis;]
[⁴⁹ "child tax credit" means a child tax credit under section 8 of the Tax
Credits Act 2002;]
[³¹"the Children Order" means the Children (Northern Ireland) Order
1995;]
"claimant" means a person claiming income support;
"close relative" means a parent, parent-in-law, son, son-in-law, daughter,
daughter-in-law, step-parent, step-son, step-daughter, brother, sister,

or the spouse of any of the preceding persons or, if that person is one of an unmarried couple, the other member of that couple;

[[19]"community charge benefit" means community charge benefits under Part VII of the Contributions and Benefits Act as originally enacted;]

"concessionary payment" means a payment made under arrangements made by the Secretary of State with the consent of the Treasury which is charged either to the National Insurance Fund or to a Departmental Expenditure Vote to which payments of benefit under the Act, the Social Security Act or the Child Benefit Act 1975 are charged;

[[19]the "Contributions and Benefits Act" means the Social Security Contributions and Benefits Act 1992;]

"co-ownership scheme" means a scheme under which a dwelling is let by a housing association and the tenant, or his personal representative, will, under the terms of the tenancy agreement or of the agreement under which he became a member of the association, be entitled, on his ceasing to be a member and subject to any condition stated in either agreement, to a sum calculated by reference directly or indirectly to the value of the dwelling;

"couple" means a married or an unmarried couple;

[[38] "course of study" means any course of study, whether or not it is a sandwich course (within the meaning prescribed in regulation 61(1)) and whether or not a grant is made for attending or undertaking it;]

"Crown tenant" means a person who occupies a dwelling under a tenancy or licence where the interest of the landlord belongs to Her Majesty in right of the Crown or to a government department or is held in trust for Her Majesty for the purposes of a government department, except (in the case of an interest belonging to Her Majesty in right of the Crown) where the interest is under the management of the Crown Estate Commissioners;

[[22]"date of claim" means the date on which the claimant makes, or is treated as making, a claim for income support for the purposes of regulation 6 of the Social Security (Claims and Payments) Regulations 1987;]

[[15]"disability living allowance" means a disability living allowance under section 37ZA of the Social Security Act [SSCBA, s.71];

[[49] . . .]

"dwelling occupied as the home" means the dwelling together with any garage, garden and outbuildings, normally occupied by the claimant as his home including any premises not so occupied which it is impracticable or unreasonable to sell separately, in particular, in Scotland, any croft land on which the dwelling is situated;

"earnings" has the meaning prescribed in regulation 35 or, as the case may be, 37;

[[28] [[58] . . .]]

[[28] [[58] . . .]]

"employed earner" shall be construed in accordance with section 2(1)(a) of the Social Security Act [SSCBA, s.2(1)a];

[[4]"employment" except for the purposes of section 20(3)(d) of the Act [SSCBA, s.124(1)(d)], includes any trade, business, profession, office or vocation;]

[[37]"employment zone" means an area within Great Britain designated for the purposes of section 60 of the Welfare Reform and Pensions Act 1999 and an "employment zone programme" means a programme established for such an area or areas designed to assist claimants for a jobseeker's allowance to obtain sustainable employment;

"employment zone contractor" means a person who is undertaking the provision of facilities in respect of an employment zone programme on behalf of the Secretary of State for Education and Employment;]

[52[54 . . .]]

[39"full-time student" has the meaning prescribed in regulation 61(1);]

[57 "a guaranteed income payment" means a payment made under article 14(1)(b) or article 21(1)(a) of the Armed Forces and Reserve Forces (Compensation Scheme) Order 2005;]

"housing association" has the meaning assigned to it by section 1(1) of the Housing Associations Act 1985;

[30"housing benefit expenditure" means expenditure in respect of which housing benefit is payable as specified in regulation 10(1) of the Housing Benefit (General) Regulations 1987 but does not include any such expenditure in respect of which an amount is applicable under regulation 17(1)(e) or 18(1)(f) (housing costs);]

[35"Immigration and Asylum Act" means the Immigration and Asylum Act 1999;]

[35 . . .]

[43"the Intensive Activity Period for 50 plus" means the programme known by that name and provided in pursuance of arrangements made by or on behalf of the Secretary of State under section 2 of the Employment and Training Act 1973, being a programme lasting for up to 52 weeks for any one individual aged 50 years or over on the day that he or she first joined any such programme, and consisting for that individual of any one or more of the following elements, namely assistance in pursuing self-employed earner's employment, education and training, work experience, assistance with job search, motivation and skills training;]

"invalid carriage or other vehicle" means a vehicle propelled by petrol engine or by electric power supplied for use on the road and to be controlled by the occupant;

[38"last day of the course" has the meaning prescribed in regulation 61(1);]

"liable relative" has the meaning prescribed in regulation 54;

"lone parent" means a person who has no partner and who is responsible for, and a member of the same household as, a child or young person;

"long tenancy" means a tenancy granted for a term of years certain exceeding twenty one years, whether or not the tenancy is, or may become, terminable before the end of that term by notice given by or to the tenant or by re-entry, forfeiture (or, in Scotland, irritancy) or otherwise and includes a lease for a term fixed by law under a grant with a covenant or obligation for perpetual renewal unless it is a lease by subdemise from one which is not a long tenancy;

[6"lower rate" where it relates to rates of tax has the same meaning as in the Income and Corporation Taxes Act 1988 by virtue of section 832(1) of that Act;]

[22"maternity leave" means a period during which a woman is absent from work because she is pregnant or has given birth to a child, and at the end of which she has a right to return to work either under the terms of her contract of employment or under Part III of the Employment Protection (Consolidation) Act 1978;]

"mobility allowance" means an allowance under section 37A of the Social Security Act;

"mobility supplement" means any supplement under article 26A of the Naval, Military and Air Forces etc (Disablement and Death) Service Pensions Order 1983 including such a supplement by virtue of any other scheme or order or under Article 25A of the Personal Injuries (Civilians) Scheme 1983;

"net earnings" means such earnings as are calculated in accordance with regulation 36

"net profit" means such profit as is calculated in accordance with regulation 38;

[[41]"the New Deal options" means the employment programmes specified in regulation 75(1)(a)(ii) of the Jobseeker's Allowance Regulations 1996 and the training scheme specified in regulation 75(1)(b)(ii) of those Regulations;]

"non-dependant" has the meaning prescribed in regulation 3;

"non-dependant deduction" means a deduction that is to be made under regulation 17(*e*) and paragraph 11 of Schedule 3;

[[44] "nursing home" means—
  (a) premises which are a nursing home or mental nursing home within the meaning of the Registered Homes Act 1984 and which are either registered under Part II of that Act or exempt from registration under section 37 thereof (power to exempt Christian Science Homes); or
  (b) any premises used or intended to be used for the reception of such persons or the provision of such nursing or services as is mentioned in any paragraph of subsection (1) of section 21 or section 22(1) of the Registered Homes Act 1984 (meaning of nursing home or mental nursing home) or, in Scotland, as are mentioned in section 10(2) of the Nursing Homes Registration (Scotland) Act 1938 (interpretation) and which are maintained or controlled by a body instituted by special Act of Parliament or incorporated by Royal Charter;
  (c) in Scotland—
      (i) premises which are a nursing home within the meaning of section 10 of the Nursing Homes Registration (Scotland) Act 1938 which are either registered under that Act or exempt from registration under section 6 or 7 thereof (general power to exempt homes and power to exempt Christian Science Homes);
      (ii) premises which are a private hospital within the meaning of section 12 of the Mental Health (Scotland) Act 1984 (private hospitals), and which are registered under that Act;]

"occupational pension" means any pension or other periodical payment under an occupational pension scheme but does not include any discretionary payment out of a fund established for relieving hardship in particular cases;

"partner" means where a claimant—
  (a) is a member of a married or an unmarried couple, the other member of that couple;
  (b) is married polygamously to two or more members of his household, any such member;

[⁴⁸ "paternity leave" means a period of absence from work on leave by virtue of section 80A or 80B of the Employment Rights Act 1996;] "payment" includes a part of a payment;

[²³"pay period" means the period in respect of which a claimant is, or expects to be, normally paid by his employer, being a week, a fortnight, four weeks, a month or other shorter or longer period as the case may be;]

[²⁵"pension fund holder" means with respect to a personal pension scheme or retirement annuity contract, the trustees, managers or scheme administrators, as the case may be, of the scheme or contract concerned;]

[³⁸ "period of study" means the period beginning with the date on which a person starts attending or undertaking a course of study and ending with the last day of the course or such earlier date (if any) such as he finally abandons it or is dismissed from it;]

[²²"personal pension scheme" has the same meaning as in [²⁵section 1 of the Pension Schemes Act 1993] and, in the case of a self-employed earner, includes a scheme approved by the Inland Revenue under Chapter IV of Part XIV of the Income and Corporation Taxes Act 1988;]

"policy of life insurance" means any instrument by which the payment of money is assured on death (except death by accident only) or the happening of any contingency dependent on human life, or any instrument evidencing a contract which is subject to payment of premiums for a term dependent on human life;

[⁵"polygamous marriage" means any marriage during the subsistence of which a party to it is married to more than one person and the ceremony of marriage took place under the law of a country which permits polygamy;]

[⁴⁴. . .]

¹⁶"qualifying person" means a person in respect of whom payment has been made from the Fund [²¹[⁵⁶ the Eileen Trust or the Skipton Fund]]

[²⁶. . .]

"relative" means close relative, grand-parent, grand-child, uncle, aunt, nephew or niece;

"relevant enactment" has the meaning prescribed in regulation 16(8)(a);

"remunerative work" has the meaning prescribed in regulation 5;

[⁴"residential accommodation" except in [⁸ [⁴⁴. . .] Schedule 3B] has the meaning prescribed in regulation 21(3);]

[¹⁸[⁵⁰ . . .]]

[⁴⁴ "residential care home" means an establishment—

    (a) which is required to be registered under Part I of the Registered Homes Act 1984 and is so registered, or is deemed to be registered under section 2(3) of the Registered Homes (Amendment) Act 1991 (which refers to the registration of small homes where the application for registration has not been determined); or

    (b) run by the Abbeyfield Society including all bodies corporate or incorporate which are affiliated to that Society; or

    (c) which provides residential accommodation with both board and personal care and is managed or provided by a body incorporated by Royal Charter or constituted by Act of Parliament other than a local social services authority; or

(d) in Scotland, which is a home registered under section 61 of the Social Work (Scotland) Act 1968 or is an establishment provided by a housing association registered with Scottish Homes established by the Housing (Scotland) Act 1988 which provides care equivalent to that given in residential accommodation provided under Part IV of the Social Work (Scotland) Act 1968; or

(e) which is exempt from registration under Part I of the Registered Homes Act 1984 pursuant to section 1(4)(a) of that Act (exemption from registration in respect of certain homes) because one or more of the residents are treated as relatives pursuant to section 19(4) of that Act;

and in paragraph (c) of this definition, "personal care" means personal care for persons in need of personal care by reason of old age, disablement, past or present dependence on alcohol or drugs or past or present mental disorder;]

[25"retirement annuity contract" means a contract or trust scheme approved under Chapter III of Part XIV of the Income and Corporation Taxes Act 1988;]

"self-employed earner" shall be construed in accordance with section 2(1)(b) of the Social Security Act [SSCBA, s.2(1)(b)];

[40 "self-employment route" means—

[55 "self-employment route" means assistance in pursuing self-employed earner's employment whilst participating in—

(a) an employment zone programme; or

(b) a programme provided or other arrangements made pursuant to section 2 of the Employment and Training Act 1973 (functions of the Secretary of State) or section 2 of the Enterprise and New Towns (Scotland) Act 1990 (functions in relation to training for employment etc.)]

"single claimant" means a claimant who neither has a partner nor is a lone parent;

"Social Security Act" means the Social Security Act 1975;

[34"sports award" means an award made by one of the Sports Councils named in section 23(2) of the National Lottery *etc.* Act 1993 out of sums allocated to it for distribution under that section;]

[38 . . .]

[37"subsistence allowance" means an allowance which an employment zone contractor has agreed to pay to a person who is participating in an employment zone programme;]

"supplementary benefit" means a supplementary pension or allowance under section 1 or 4 of the Supplementary Benefits Act 1976;

"terminal date" in respect of a claimant means the terminal date in his case for the purpose of regulation 7 of the Child Benefit (General) Regulations 1976;

[21"the Eileen Trust" means the charitable trust of that name established on 29th March 1993 out of funds provided by the Secretary of State for the benefit of persons eligible for payment in accordance with its provisions;]

[16"the Fund" means moneys made available from time to time by the Secretary of State for the benefit of persons eligible for payment in accordance with the provisions of a scheme established by him on 24th April 1992 or, in Scotland, on 10th April 1992;]

[20"the Independent Living (Extension) Fund" means the Trust of that name established by a deed dated 25th February 1993 and made between the Secretary of State for Social Security of the one part and Robin Glover Wendt and John Fletcher Shepherd of the other part;]

[2"the Independent Living Fund" means the charitable trust established out of funds provided by the Secretary of State for the purpose of providing financial assistance to those persons incapacitated by or otherwise suffering from very severe disablement who are in need of such assistance to enable them to live independently;]

[20"the Independent Living (1993) Fund" means the Trust of that name established by a deed dated 25th February 1993 and made between the Secretary of State for Social Security of the one part and Robin Glover Wendt and John Shepherd of the other part;]

[20"the Independent Living Funds" means the Independent Living Fund, the Independent Living (Extension) Fund and the Independent Living (1993) Fund;]

[9"the Macfarlane (Special Payments) Trust" means the trust of that name, established on 29th January 1990 partly out of funds provided by the Secretary of State, for the benefit of certain persons suffering from haemophilia;]

[13"the Macfarlane (Special Payments) (No.2) Trust" means the trust of that name, established on 3rd May 1991 partly out of funds provided by the Secretary of State, for the benefit of certain persons suffering from haemophilia and other beneficiaries;]

[1"the Macfarlane Trust" means the charitable trust, established partly out of funds provided by the Secretary of State to the Haemophilia Society, for the relief of poverty or distress among those suffering from haemophilia;]

[56 "the Skipton Fund" means the ex-gratia payment scheme administered by the Skipton Fund Limited, incorporated on 25th March 2004, for the benefit of certain persons suffering from hepatitis C and other persons eligible for payment in accordance with the scheme's provisions;]

"training allowance" means an allowance (whether by way of periodical grants or otherwise) payable—.

(a) out of public funds by a Government department or by or on behalf of the [12 Secretary of State for Employment] [11, Scottish Enterprise or Highlands and Islands Enterprise] [42, the Learning and Skills Council for England or the National Assembly for Wales];

(b) to a person for his maintenance or in respect of a member of his family; and

(c) for the period, or part of the period, during which he is following a course of training or instruction provided by, or in pursuance of arrangements made with, that department or approved by that department in relation to him or so provided or approved by or on behalf of [12the Secretary of State for Employment] [11, Scottish Enterprise or Highlands and Islands Enterprise], [42 or the National Assembly for Wales]

but it does not include an allowance paid by any Government department to or in respect of a person by reason of the fact that he is following a course of full-time education [7, other than under arrangements made under section 2 of the Employment and Training Act 1973,] or is training as a teacher;

[[24]"voluntary organisation" means a body, other than a public or local authority, the activities of which are carried on otherwise than for profit;]

[[45] "war widower's pension" means any widower's pension or allowance granted in respect of a death due to service or war injury and payable by virtue of the Air Force (Constitution) Act 1917, the Personal Injuries (Emergency Provisions) Act 1939, the Pensions (Navy, Army, Air Force and Mercantile Marine) Act 1939, the Polish Resettlement Act 1947 or Part VII or section 151 of the Reserve Forces Act 1980 or a pension or allowance for a widower granted under any scheme mentioned in section 315(2)(e) of the Income and Corporation Taxes Act 1988;]

[[19]"water charges" means—
  (a) as respects England and Wales, any water and sewerage charges under Chapter 1 of Part V of the Water Act 1991;
  (b) as respects Scotland, any water and sewerage charges under Schedule 11 to the Local Government Finance Act 1992;
  in so far as such charges are in respect of the dwelling which a person occupies as his home.]

[[32]"welfare to work beneficiary" means a person—
  (a) to whom regulation 13A(1) of the Social Security (Incapacity for Work) (General) Regulations 1995 applies; and
  (b) who again becomes incapable of work for the purposes of Part XIIA of the Contributions and Benefits Act 1992;]

[[49] "working tax credit" means a working tax credit under section 10 of the Tax Credits Act 2002;]

[[49] . . .]

[[23]"year of assessment" has the meaning prescribed in section 832(1) of the Income and Corporation Taxes Act 1988;]

"young person" has the meaning prescribed in regulation 14,

[[3]"youth training scheme [[12] or youth training]" means—
  (a) arrangements made under section 2 of the Employment and Training Act 1973 (functions of the Secretary of State); or
  (b) arrangements made by the Secretary of State for persons enlisted in Her Majesty's forces for any special term of service specified in regulations made under section 2 of the Armed Forces Act 1966 (power of Defence Council to make regulations as to engagement of persons in regular forces),
  for purposes which include the training of persons who, at the beginning of their training, are under the age of 18.]

[[44] (1A) For the purposes of these Regulations, where a person's principal place of residence is a residential care home or a nursing home and he is temporarily absent from that home, he shall be regarded as continuing to reside in that home—
(a) where he is absent because he is a patient, for the first [[51] 52] weeks of any such period of absence and for this purpose—
    (i) "patient" has the meaning it has in Schedule 7 by virtue of regulation 21(3); and
    (ii) periods of absence separated by not more than 28 days shall be treated as a single period of absence equal in duration to all those periods; and

(b) for the first three weeks of any other period of absence.]

(2) In these Regulations, unless the context otherwise requires, a reference—

(a) to a numbered Part is to the Part of these Regulations bearing that number;

(b) to a numbered regulation or Schedule is to the regulation in or Schedule to these Regulations bearing that number;

(c) in a regulation or Schedule to a numbered paragraph is to the paragraph in that regulation or Schedule bearing that number;

(d) in a paragraph to a lettered or numbered sub-paragraph is to the sub-paragraph in that paragraph bearing that letter or number.

(3) Unless the context requires otherwise, any reference to the claimant's family or, as the case may be, to being a member of his family, shall be construed for the purposes of these Regulations as if it included in relation to a polygamous marriage a reference to any partner and any child or young person who is treated as the responsibility of the claimant or his partner, where that child or young person is a member of the claimant's household.

[29(4) [58 . . .]]

AMENDMENTS

2.21   1. Income Support (General) Amendment Regulations 1988 (SI 1988/663), reg.2 (April 11, 1988).

2. Family Credit and Income Support (General) Amendment Regulations 1988 (SI 1988/999), reg.4 (June 9, 1988).

3. Income Support (General) Amendment No.3 Regulations 1988 (SI 1988/1228), reg.2 (August 29, 1988).

4. Income Support (General) Amendment No.4 Regulations 1988 (SI 1988/1445), reg.2 (September 12, 1988).

5. Income Support (General) Amendment No.5 Regulations 1988 (SI 1988/2022), reg.2(b) (December 12, 1988).

6. Income Support (General) Amendment No.5 Regulations 1988 (SI 1988/2022), reg.2(a) (April 10, 1989).

7. Income Support (General) Amendment No.2 Regulations 1989 (SI 1989/1323), reg.2 (August 21, 1989).

8. Income Support (General) Amendment Regulations 1989 (SI 1989/534), Sch.I para.1 (October 9, 1989).

9. Income-related Benefits Schemes Amendment Regulations 1990 (SI 1990/127), reg.3 (January 31, 1990).

11. Enterprise (Scotland) Consequential Amendments Order 1991 (SI 1991/387), art.9 (April 1, 1991).

12. Income Support (General) Amendment Regulations 1991 (SI 1991/236), reg.2 (April 8, 1991).

13. Income-related Benefits Schemes and Social Security (Recoupment) Amendment Regulations 1991 (SI 1991/1175), reg.5 (May 11, 1991).

15. Disability Living Allowance and Disability Working Allowance (Consequential Provisions) Regulations 1991 (SI 1991/2742), reg.11(2) (April 6, 1992).

16. Income-related Benefits Schemes and Social Security (Recoupment) Amendment Regulations 1992 (SI 1992/1101), reg.6(2) (May 7, 1992).

17. Income-related Benefits Schemes (Miscellaneous Amendments) (No.3) Regulations 1992 (SI 1992/2155), reg.12 (October 5, 1992).

19. Income-related Benefits Schemes (Miscellaneous Amendments) Regulations 1993 (SI 1993/315), reg.3 (April 12, 1993).

20. Social Security Benefits (Miscellaneous Amendments) (No. 2) Regulations 1993 (SI 1993/963), reg.2 (April 22, 1993).

214

21. Income-related Benefits Schemes and Social Security (Recoupment) Amendment Regulations 1993 (SI 1993/1249), reg.4 (May 14, 1993).

22. Income-related Benefits Schemes (Miscellaneous Amendments) (No. 4) Regulations 1993 (SI 1993/2119), reg.2 (October 4, 1993).

23. Income-related Benefits Schemes (Miscellaneous Amendments) (No. 5) Regulations 1994 (SI 1994/2139), reg.22 (October 3, 1994).

24. Income-related Benefits Schemes (Miscellaneous Amendments) Regulations 1995 (SI 1995/516), reg.17 (April 10, 1995).

25. Income-related Benefits Schemes and Social Security (Claims and Payments) (Miscellaneous Amendments) Regulations 1995 (SI 1995/2303), reg.6(2) (October 2, 1995).

26. Income Support (General) (Jobseeker's Allowance Consequential Amendments) Regulations 1996 (SI 1996/206), reg.2 (October 7, 1996).

28. Income-related Benefits Schemes and Social Fund (Miscellaneous Amendments) Regulations 1996 (SI 1996/1944), reg.13 and Sch., para.1 (October 7, 1996).

29. Income-related Benefits Schemes and Social Fund (Miscellaneous Amendments) Regulations 1996 (SI 1996/1944), reg.13 and Sch., para.2 (October 7, 1996).

30. Income-related Benefits and Jobseeker's Allowance (Miscellaneous Amendments) Regulations 1997 (SI 1997/65), reg.4(1) (April 7, 1997).

31. Social Security (Miscellaneous Amendments) Regulations 1998 (SI 1998/563), reg.5(1) and (2)(e) (April 6, 1998).

32. Social Security (Welfare to Work) Regulations 1998 (SI 1998/2231), reg.13(2) (October 5, 1998).

33. Social Security and Child Support (Tax Credits) Consequential Amendments Regulations 1999 (SI 1999/2566), reg.2(3) and Sch.2, Part III (October 5, 1999).

34. Social Security Amendment (Sports Awards) Regulations 1999 (SI 1999/2165), reg.2(1) and 2(e) (August 23, 1999).

35. Social Security (Immigration and Asylum) Consequential Amendments Regulations 2000 (SI 2000/636), reg.3(2) (April 3, 2000).

37. Social Security Amendment (Employment Zones) Regulations 2000 (SI 2000/724), reg.2 (April 3, 2000).

38. Social Security Amendment (Students) Regulations 2000 (SI 2000/1981), reg.5(1) and (2) (July 31, 2000).

39. Social Security Amendment (Students) Regulations 2000 (SI 2000/1981), reg.5(1) and (2)(b) (July 31, 2000). The new definition was moved to its present—and alphabetically correct—place in the regulation by the Social Security (Students and Income-related Benefits) (No. 2) Regulations 2000 (SI 2000/ 2422), reg.4 (October 9, 2000).

40. Social Security Amendment (Employment Zones) (No. 2) Regulations 2000 (SI 2000/2910), reg.2(1) and (2) (November 27, 2000).

41. Social Security (Miscellaneous Amendments) Regulations 2001 (SI 2001/488), reg.2 (April 9, 2001).

42. Social Security (Miscellaneous Amendments) (No. 2) Regulations 2001 (SI 2001/652), reg.2 (March 26, 2001).

43. Social Security Amendment (New Deal) Regulations 2001 (SI 2001/ 1029), reg.15(2) and (3)(c) (April 9, 2001).

44. Social Security Amendment (Residential Care and Nursing Homes) Regulations 2001 (SI 2001/3767), reg.2 and Sch. Pt I para.1 (April 8, 2002).

45. Social Security (Miscellaneous Amendments) Regulations 2002 (SI 2002/841), reg.2 (April 8, 2002).

46. Income Support (General) and Jobseeker's Allowance Amendment Regulations 2002 (SI 2002/1411), reg.2 (June 17, 2002).

47. Social Security Amendment (Employment Programme) Regulations 2002 (SI 2002/2314), reg.3(2) (October 14, 2002).

48. Social Security (Paternity and Adoption) Amendment Regulations 2002 (SI 2002/2689), reg.2 (December 8, 2002).

49. Income-related Benefits and Jobseeker's Allowance (Working Tax Credit and Child Tax Credit) (Amendment) Regulations 2002 (SI 2002/2402), reg.2 and Sch.1, para.1 (April 6, 2003).

50. Social Security (Removal of Residential Allowance and Miscellaneous Amendments) Regulations 2003 (SI 2003/1121), reg.2 and Sch.1 (October 6, 2003).

51. Social Security (Hospital In-Patients and Miscellaneous Amendments) Regulations 2003 (SI 2003/1195), reg.3(2) (May 21, 2003).

52. Social Security (Miscellaneous Amendments) (No.2) Regulations 2003 (SI 2003/2279), reg.2(2) (October 1, 2003).

53. Social Security (Miscellaneous Amendments) Regulations 2004) (SI 2004/565), reg.2(2) (April 1, 2004).

54. Social Security (Miscellaneous Amendments) Regulations 2004 (SI 2004/565), reg.2(2) (April 1, 2004).

55. Social Security (Income-Related Benefits Self-Employment Route Amendment) Regulations 2004 (SI 2004/963), reg.2 (May 4, 2004).

56. Social Security (Miscellaneous Amendments) (No. 2) Regulations 2004 (SI 2004/1141), reg.2 (May 12, 2004).

57. Social Security (Miscellaneous Amendments) Regulations 2005 (SI 2005/574), reg.2 (April 4, 2005).

58. Social Security (Miscellaneous Amendments) Regulations 2005 (SI 2005/574), reg.3 (April 4, 2005).

DEFINITIONS

2.22
"dwelling"—see 1986 Act, s.84(1) (SSCBA, s.137(1)).
"family"—see 1986 Act, s.20(11) (SSCBA, s.137(1)).
"married couple"—*ibid.*
"occupational pension scheme"—see 1986 Act, s.84(1) (PSA, s.1).
"unmarried couple"—see 1986 Act, s.20(11) (SSCBA, s.137(1)).

GENERAL NOTE

2.23
The significance of most of these definitions is mentioned in the notes to the regulations in which they occur. A few points are noted here.

"Armed Forces and Reserve Forces Compensation Scheme": This scheme replaces the War Pensions Scheme ("WPS") for those who suffer injuries, ill health or death due to service in the Armed Forces on or after April 6, 2005. However, the WPS continues to operate for existing beneficiaries and for claims where the cause of the injury, illness or death is due to service before April 6, 2005. The new scheme will make three types of payment: tariff based lump sums, regular "guaranteed income payments" and bereavement grants. See the definition of "guaranteed income payment" below which covers payments made to the injured person under art.14(1)(b) of the Armed Forces and Reserve Forces (Compensation Scheme) Order 2005 (SI 2005/439) and payments to "a surviving spouse, civil partner or his surviving adult dependant" under art.21(1)(a) of the Order (note that by art.65 of the Order the reference to civil partner is omitted until s.1 of the Civil Partnership Act 2004 comes into force). A "surviving adult dependant" means someone with whom the deceased was "cohabiting as partners in a substantial and exclusive relationship" (see art.22 of and Sch.1 to the Order). The £10 disregard that applies to war disablement, war widows and war widowers' pensions paid under the WPS scheme will apply to guarantee income payments (see the new para.16(cc) of Sch.9). No special provision is made in respect of the lump sum payments but since they are made in respect of personal injury presumably they will be treated in the same way as other personal injury payments (note the disregards in para.15 of sch.9 and para.12 of Sch.10).

"*Board and lodging accommodation*": Now that since April 1989 there are no special calculations of benefit for claimants in board and lodging accommodation (as opposed to residential care or nursing homes), the definition is of less significance than in the past. Either the accommodation must be in some establishment like a hotel or lodging house or the charge must include the provision of some cooked or prepared meals in the accommodation or associated premises. The requirement in para.(a) that a charge is made for the accommodation has logically to be considered before the exclusion of non-commercial arrangements. In *CSB 1163/1988* the claimant moved with her two children into a house owned by the Jesus Fellowship Church (Baptist), where 17 other people also lived. Meals were provided. The terms of her occupation were that she should put all her income into a "common purse." A basic charge to cover food, accommodation and running costs was set, but any excess of the claimant's income was regarded as a donation to the Church. The Commissioner holds that the claimant was not a boarder because she did not pay a "charge." She was one of a joint community of persons, all sharing their income and outgoings. See also *R. v Sheffield Housing Benefits Review Board Ex p. Smith, Rugby Borough Council Housing Benefits Review Board Ex p. Harrison and Daventry District Council Housing Benefits Review Board Ex p. Bodden*, below. Some family arrangements may be of this kind. Similarly, if a person makes a contribution of whatever he can afford week by week to the household expenses, this is probably not a charge. On the other hand, a fixed, but low, amount may require the non-commercial basis exception to be examined. Recent cases on the meaning of "board" in the Rent Acts (*e.g. Otter v Norman* [1988] 2 All E.R. 897, HL) indicate that merely providing the ingredients will not amount to preparing a meal. This was specifically decided in the supplementary benefit context in *CSB 950/1987*. The argument that getting a packet of cornflakes out of a cupboard constituted preparation was rejected.

If this primary definition is met there is an exclusion either if the accommodation is provided by a close relative (see definition below) of the claimant or any member of his family (see s.137(1)) or if it is provided on other than a commercial basis. Provision by a limited company, of which a close relative of the resident is a director or a shareholder, is not provision by a close relative (*R(SB) 9/89*). In this case the company was formed well before the resident went into the home. It might be different if the company was a mere facade or had been formed for a fraudulent or improper purpose. In *R(IS) 2/91* the claimant became a resident in a nursing home of which his daughter was the sole proprietor. He was actually cared for by the staff employed by his daughter. Nonetheless, his accommodation and meals were "provided" by his daughter. "Provided" means "made available."

2.24

What is a commercial basis is unclear, although the *Decision Makers Guide* suggests that the phrase should be interpreted broadly, not simply that a profit has to be made (Ch. 24, App. 5, paras 49–50). If the charge and the arrangements are as one would expect in a commercial relationship it can clearly be argued that the basis is commercial. The *DMG* considers that if the intention is to cover the cost of food plus a reasonable amount for accommodation, the arrangement should also be regarded as commercial. This approach is confirmed by *CSB 1163/1988* (above), where the tribunal had decided that "commercial basis" contained an element of profit. The Commissioner holds that this was an error of law and that the phrase means a basis that is intended to be more or less self-financing and not provided as part of a quasi "family" setting. On the facts, the lack of the intention to make a profit by the Church did not prevent the basis being commercial, but the "community" nature of the arrangement did. It was probable that if the claimant paid no income in for at least a short time, she would not have been asked to leave. In *R. v Sheffield Housing Benefits Review Board Ex p. Smith, Rugby Borough Council Housing Benefits Review Board Ex p. Harrison and Daventry District Council Housing Benefits Review Board, Ex p. Bodden, The Times*, December 28, 1994, (housing benefit cases which also concerned the Jesus Fellowship Church) Blackburne J. reaches a similar conclusion. In deciding whether an arrangement was on a commercial basis, it was necessary to look at the arrangement as a whole. It was not correct only to consider the amount payable for the accommodation and to ignore the other terms of the agreement. See also *Campbell & Ors v (1) South Northamptonshire District Council (2) Secretary of State for the Department of Work and Pensions* [2004] EWCA Civ 409, reported as *R(H) 8/04* (the appeal from *CH/5125, CH/5126, CH/5129 and CH/5130/02*) which again concerned the Jesus Fellowship. As far as family arrangements are concerned, all the circumstances must be considered. If money has been spent adapting accommodation to a disabled person's needs, this may be relevant. It is not the case, as is often argued by decision-makers, that if a person enters into an arrangement with a friend or a non-close relative it is automatically non-commercial. In *CIS 1951/1991* (confirmed in *R(IS) 17/94* and in *R(IS) 11/98*) whether a family arrangement was on a commercial basis is held to be entirely a question of fact for the tribunal, which has to consider whether it is similar to that which might have been arranged with a paying lodger (see the notes to reg.3).

2.25   *"close relative"*: The words "brother" and "sister" include half-brothers and half-sisters (*R(SB) 22/87*). The same decision confirms that if a child is adopted it becomes the child of its adoptive parents and ceases to have any legal relationship with its natural parents or brothers or sisters. It is legal relationships which are referred to in the definition of "close relative."

"couple": "Married couple" and "unmarried couple" are defined in s.137(1) of the Contributions and Benefits Act.

"date of claim": See the notes to reg.6 of the Social Security (Claims and Payments) Regulations in Vol III of this series.

"dwelling occupied as the home": "Home" is no longer defined, but the present definition contains many similarities to that of "home" in the old Supplementary Benefit (Requirements) Regulations and (Resources) Regulations. Instead of referring to accommodation, it refers to a dwelling, but since the definition of "dwelling" in s.137(1) of the Contributions and Benefits Act refers to residential accommodation, there is probably not much difference. The s.137(1) definition does specify that a dwelling can be the whole or part of a building and need not comprise separate and self-contained premises. The dwelling must be normally occupied as the home by the claimant. There is no reference here to the claimant's family, but presumably if the claimant has a family within s.137(1) of the Contributions and Benefits Act, the family's home will normally be his home, although see *CIS 81/1991* below.

2.26   The question whether the reference to "the dwelling" means that only one dwelling at a time can meet the definition or whether in certain circumstances two physically separate buildings may constitute one dwelling has been the subject of several decisions. *R(SB) 30/83* decided that two completely separate units could not constitute one home. However, *R(SB) 10/89* held that two units about 600 yards apart, neither of which on their own could accommodate the assessment unit were one home. The Commissioner relied on some Rent Act cases on when something is let as a separate dwelling (in particular, *Langford Property Co Ltd v Goldrich* [1949] 1 K.B. 511). She took account of the fact that the mode of life of the assessment unit was such that one house was an "extension" or "annexe" of the other, that the two houses were within walking distance of each other, and that neither had been purchased as an investment. In *CIS 299/1992* it was held that a bungalow and an adjoining caravan constituted one dwelling. But in *CIS 81/1991*, where the claimant lived in one house and members of his family slept in another, the second house did not come within the definition in reg.2(1). This was because it was not occupied by the *claimant* as his home. The Commissioner distinguished *R(SB) 10/89* on the grounds that it was decided in relation to what in his view was the significantly different definition of "home" in the Supplementary Benefit Regulations, which referred to ". . . the accommodation . . . normally occupied by the assessment unit . . .". He also held that the reference in the definition of dwelling in s.137(1) to "separate and self-contained premises" did not mean that a dwelling could be spread over separate buildings. This decision may be correct where only members of the claimant's family live in the other property (and now see para.52 of *Secretary of State for Work and Pensions v Miah* [2003] EWCA Civ 1111; [2003] 4 All ER 702 (below) in which Mance LJ expresses the view that in those circumstances a claimant would probably not be able to claim that both houses were normally occupied by him). However, it was suggested in previous editions that where a claimant occupies two physically separate properties, both could still constitute the dwelling normally occupied by the claimant as his home depending on the circumstances. This has now been confirmed by the Court of Appeal in *Secretary of State for Work and Pensions v Miah*, upholding the decision of the Commissioner in *CJSA 4620/2000*. The Commissioner had disagreed with *CIS 81/1991* and concluded that a "dwelling occupied as the home" could comprise more than one building. However, he emphasised that for the definition (and therefore the disregard in para.1 of Sch.8 to the JSA Regulations, the equivalent of para.1 of Sch.10) to apply the claimant had to personally occupy the dwelling as his home. The Commissioner directed the new tribunal to have particular regard to para.13 of *R(SB) 10/89* (see above) and to consider whether the situation was in effect that of a single home on a split site. But he pointed out that occasional use of the second house by the claimant would not suffice, since the second house also had to be "normally" occupied by the claimant as his home. The Court of Appeal upheld the Commissioner's approach. It took the view that the use of the phrase "dwelling occupied as the home" indicated that the focus should be the functions served by the concept of a dwelling rather than its constituent elements and that function was a place serving as a home for the claimant. Commonsense, justice and fairness also supported this approach. If the claimant had been living in one property which was large enough to accommodate him and his family then it would have been disregarded. It could not be fair that he should suffer when the purpose of having two properties was exactly the same. The Court also pointed to the difficulties, if the disregard only applied to one property, of determining which of the properties was to be disregarded in a case where the claimant was occupying both as his home (which, as the Court pointed out, was not the situation in *CIS 81/1991*).

Para.3(6) of Sch.3 allows payments to be made for two homes in limited circumstances. It also appears that accommodation cannot be normally occupied until some person has actually moved in (*R(SB) 27/84, R(SB) 7/86*), given the special rule created in para.3(7) for periods before anyone moves in. But this raises the question as to what is meant by "moved in" (and see *CH/2957/2004*, to be reported as *R(H) 9/05*, below). In an unstarred decision, *CIS 4/1990*, the Commissioner doubts the existence of a rule that occupation requires residence. The same point was made in the supplementary benefit context in *CSB 524/1985* (not quoted by the Commissioner) and *CSSB 34/1987*. While it is right that the word used in the legislation is "occupy" and not "reside," it must also be noted that the definition requires not simply occupation, but occupation as the home. This point was the basis of *R(SB) 7/86* also not mentioned in *CIS 4/1990*. However, it is suggested that the issue of what is sufficient to amount to occupation will be one of fact depending on the particular circumstances of the case. Thus, for example in *CH 2521/2002*, a case on the meaning of "dwelling normally occupied as his home" in reg.5(1) of the Housing Benefit Regulations, the Commissioner decided that the claimant did not so occupy a flat when he only slept there a few nights a week while he was decorating it and had not moved in any clothing or possessions (other than a cooker which he did not use and a camp bed).

However, in *CH/2957/2004*, to be reported as *R(H) 9/05*, the Deputy Commissioner reached the opposite conclusion. The claimant, who was elderly and disabled, entered into a tenancy agreement of a flat near her relatives on February 12, 2004, intending to move in on March 15, 2004 after the flat had been adapted to meet her needs. The work was carried out and her furniture was moved in on March 15, 2004. The claimant gave up her previous accommodation but did not physically go to the flat herself on March 15 because she had been admitted to hospital. Following a rehabilitation period the claimant went to live in the flat on August 9, 2004. The Deputy Commissioner holds that the claimant was normally occupying the flat as her home from March 15, 2004. She was not occupying any other home from that date and the flat had become her new permanent address. The local authority had contended that normal occupation involved physical presence in a property but since the claimant had a physical presence in the shape of her furniture it was difficult to see how she could be said not to have occupied it. As a matter of general law occupation did not require the personal presence of the tenant if the property was under her control and being used by her to store her goods and for no other purpose. The Deputy Commissioner therefore rejected the local authority's submission that it was necessary (but sufficient) for the claimant to spend one night at the property in order to normally occupy it as her home. In his view, if "normally" was intended to refer to some degree of regularity of occupation, far more than one night would be needed. But he did not consider that the word "normally" was directed to any question of length of occupation but was being used to deal with the case where there might be more than one dwelling that was the claimant's home. The local authority had also relied on various references in other parts of reg.5 of the Housing Benefit Regulations (which contains similar, although not identical, provisions to para.3 of Sch.3) to the claimant moving into the property as inferring that occupation meant physically moving in. But "moving in" was not part of the definition in reg.5(1) (the equivalent of para.3(1)). The subsequent paragraphs modified the general rule in reg.5(1) by spelling out certain circumstances in which a claimant could be treated as occupying a dwelling as her home for housing benefit purposes before she had moved in. But this did not answer the question as to what a claimant had to do in order to "move into" a property. In the Deputy Commissioner's view the claimant in this case had moved into the flat on the date that she removed her furniture from her previous home and moved it into her new flat. A more significant issue in his view was the fact that for the claimant to take advantage of the temporary absence provisions in reg.5(8B) and (8C) (the equivalent of paras 3(11) and (12)) she had to be said to intend to *return* to occupy the flat as her home after her stay in hospital. However, the Deputy Commissioner concludes that because she had occupied the flat through the acts of her agents moving her furniture in she could be said to be returning there when she left hospital. Although this strained the use of the word "return", the alternative construction would be to draw an artificial distinction between a person who spent ten minutes at the property before becoming unwell and a person who became unwell before arriving in person at the property.

2.27   The definition extends to any garden or outbuildings which are occupied as part of the home (like the toilet and coalstore in outbuildings in *R(SB) 13/84* or the "development land" in *R(SB) 27/84* which might have been part of the garden). *CIS 427/1991* holds that the line between a garden and other land occupied with a dwelling is to be drawn according to the view of the ordinary man in the street.

If a building or a garden is occupied as part of the home it does not matter that they could be sold separately. This only comes into play when some buildings or land are not so occupied. Then those premises still count as part of the home if it is impracticable or unreasonable to sell them separately. (Note *C3/99-00(FC) (T)* which draws attention to the different definition in the Northern Ireland legislation.) A potential limit to this extension is exposed by *CSB 965/ 1986*, where the claimant was a tenant of a council house and owned a half-share in a small-holding two fields away. The small-holding was clearly not occupied as part of the home. The Commissioner holds that the extension could not apply since the home could not be sold and therefore the question of separate sale could not arise. This decision seems dubious, especially since the definition refers by way of example to croft land in Scotland, where the crofter is often only a tenant. But perhaps *CSB 965/1986* can be supported on the basis that if the small-holding was the only premises actually owned by the claimant it could not be unreasonable or impracticable to sell it separately. In *CIS 427/1991* the Commissioner holds that *R(SB) 13/84* was wrong in suggesting that property outside Scotland which is comparable to croft land is to be treated on the same principles. In considering reasonableness and practicability all the circumstances must be considered, including the use to which the premises are put, any profit made from them, etc. (*R(SB) 13/84* and *R(SB) 27/84*). In *CIS 427/1991* the state of health of the claimant's wife was a factor of which account could be taken in assessing whether it was unreasonable to sell land held with the home but not occupied as the home (she was a manic depressive who needed the adjoining fields for therapeutic walking). Medical evidence as to the therapeutic benefit would obviously be highly desirable in these circumstances.

CIS 616/1992 holds that the common parts of a block of flats (*e.g.* the entrance hall or staircases) do not come within the definition. It is not impracticable or unreasonable to sell such areas separately but quite simply impossible to do so.

"employed earner": The meaning in s.2(1)(a) of the Contributions and Benefits Act   **2.28**
1992, as amended by the Income Tax (Earnings and Pensions) Act 2003, Sch.6, Pt 2, para.171 with effect from April 6, 2003, is "a person who is gainfully employed in Great Britain either under a contract of service, or in an office (including elective office) with general earnings" (for the definition of "general earnings" see s.7(3) of the 2003 Act).

On the tests for deciding whether a person is an employed earner or in self-employment, see *CJSA 4721/2001* and the other cases discussed in the notes to reg.30.

"a guarantee income payment": See the note to *"the Armed Forces and Reserve Forces Compensation Scheme"* above.

"nursing home": The definitions of "nursing home" and "residential care home" were   **2.29**
moved from reg.19 to reg.2(1) on April 8, 2002 when the former regulation was repealed. One week before that on April 1, 2002 the Registered Homes Act 1984 to which both regulations refer was repealed by s.117 of and Sch.6 to the Care Standards Act 2000 (see art.3(7)(j) of SI 2001/3852 (C.125)). Under the 1984 Act "residential care homes" and "nursing homes" were obliged to register with local authorities. The Care Standards Act replaced that scheme with a different regime under which "care homes" must register (in England) with the new National Care Standards Commission or (in Wales) with the National Assembly for Wales.

Presumably, the failure to update the wording of the definitions to refer to the Care Standards Act and to adopt its terminology, is a deliberate reflection of a different change in policy, namely that special payments of income support in order to meet accommodation charges in care and nursing homes (whether run privately, or by the voluntary sector or by local authorities) are to be phased out. The repeal of reg.19 and Sch.4 abolishes the special rules for "preserved rights" payments where the claimant had been in a home from before April 1, 1993 and from April 8, 2002, payments of residential allowances under para.2A of Sch.2 are restricted to those who were entitled to them on April 7, 2002 (see para.2A(6)). This process has now been completed by the Social Security (Removal of Residential Allowances and Miscellaneous Amendments) Regulations 2003 (SI 2003/1121) which came into force on October 6, 2003 (see the note to reg.17).

The issue of whether or not a particular institution was or was not a "nursing home" or "a residential care home" should shortly be of historical interest only. However, as it may still give rise to disputes in relation to periods before April 8, 2002, it should be noted that in England and Wales to be a "nursing home" most homes had both to be within the category of nursing home under the 1984 Act *and* actually registered under that Act. There were exceptions to this rule where the home was a Christian Science Home or was run by a body set up by a special Act of Parliament or by Royal Charter. In Scotland paras (b) and (c) of the definition achieved the same result by reference to Scottish legislation.

"occupational pension": Section 1 of the Pension Schemes Act 1993 defines an "occu-   **2.30**
pational pension scheme" as "any scheme or arrangement which is comprised in one or more instruments or agreements and which has, or is capable of having, effect in

relation to one or more descriptions or categories of employments so as to provide benefits, in the form of pensions or otherwise, payable on termination of service, or on death or retirement, to or in respect of earners with qualifying service in an employment of any such description or category".

"personal pension scheme": The meaning in s.1 of the Pension Schemes Act 1993 is "any scheme or arrangement which is comprised in one or more instruments or agreements and which has, or is capable of having, effect so as to provide benefits, in the form of pensions or otherwise, payable on death or retirement to or in respect of employed earners who have made arrangements with the trustees or managers of the scheme for them to become members of it".

"residential care home": For the repeal of the Registered Homes Act 1984 and the policy changes affecting payments of IS to those in residential care homes from April 8, 2002, see the definition of "nursing home" (above). The following commentary is taken from pp.264–265 of the 2001 edition.

Under para.(a) of the definition, the basic test is registration by the local authority. The local authority will apply the criteria of board and personal care at that stage. A small home can be deemed to be registered while waiting for registration.

2.31   Categories (b) and (c) do not require registration. Under (c) all Abbeyfield Homes are included whether or not they provide board and personal care and whether or not they meet the conditions for registration (*R(SB) 11/91*). In category (c), a decision is necessary on whether board and personal care is provided. By analogy with cases on the Rent Acts (see *Otter v Norman* [1988] 2 All E. R. 897 for a discussion), "board" requires the provision of some prepared food and drink which goes beyond the trivial. It does not require any particular standard of substantiality, but a cup of cocoa, say, would not do on its own. "Personal care" is only defined to the extent of limiting the reasons why it has to be provided. The *Decision Makers Guide* (para.24041) suggests that "personal care" means "all that the proprietors must do to preserve and promote the health, safety and well-being of the residents. [It] is broadly the same as the care which might be provided by a competent carer, which includes washing, bathing, dressing, toiletry needs, administration of medicines and when a resident falls sick, the kind of attention someone would receive from a carer under the guidance of a GP, a nurse, or any other member of the primary health care service." This is helpful but should not be seen to imply that a particular level of personal care must be provided. If something beyond the trivial which counts as personal care is provided, then personal care is provided, even though much more care would be desirable.

Category (e) was added from October 4, 1993 to include small homes not required to register because one or more residents are *treated as relatives* for the purposes of Part I of the Registered Homes Act 1984. Under s.1(4)(a), as amended by the Registered Homes (Amendment) Act 1991, and s.19(4) of the 1984 Act, homes with less than four residents are not required to register where the only residents are those who run the home, employees, their relatives or people who are treated as relatives because they have lived there for at least five years. Thus homes which are not required to register because the residents are genuine relatives are not covered by this category.

2.32   *"self-employed earner"*: The meaning in s.2(1)(b) of the Contributions and Benefits Act 1992 is "a person who is gainfully employed in Great Britain otherwise than in employed earner's employment (whether or not he is also employed in such employment)."

On the tests for deciding whether a person is an employee or self-employed see *CJSA 4721/2001* and the other cases discussed in the notes to reg.30.

"self-employment route": The new form of the definition of *"self-employment route"* is intended to encompass assistance in pursuing self-employed earner's employment

while participating in *any* programme provided or other arrangement made under s.2 of the Employment and Training Act 1973 or s.2 of the Enterprise and New Towns (Scotland) Act 1990 (it has been introduced so as to avoid the need to amend the definition each time a new scheme is created). It also covers such assistance while taking part in an employment zone programme (such programmes do not come under those provisions but s.60 of the Welfare Reform and Pensions Act 1999). A person who is receiving assistance under the self-employment route is not regarded as being in remunerative work (this was previously achieved by Orders made by the Secretary of State under s.26 of the Employment Act 1988 in relation to individual schemes under s.2 of the 1973 Act but now see the new sub-para.(dd) of reg.6(1) and the amended form of reg.53(bb) of the JSA Regulations).

The other main consequence of participating in programmes under the self-employment route is that the normal rules for the treatment of income do not apply to receipts from trading (see reg.23A); such receipts are only to be taken into account as income in accordance with regs 39A to 39D. Note the disregards in para.64 of Sch.9 and para.6(3) and (4) and para.52 of Sch.10 and of discretionary payments for those participating in an employment zone programme in para.72 of Sch.9 and para.58 of Sch.10.

See also para.13 of Sch.9 which from April 1, 2004 has provided for a single disregard of the various allowances, grants and other payments made under s.2 of the Employment and Training Act 1973 or s.2 of the Enterprise and New Towns (Scotland) Act 1990 to people participating in New Deals and other training and welfare to work schemes. For the capital disregard see para.30 of Sch.10. These disregards have replaced, among other provisions, para.62 of Sch.9 and para.50 of Sch.10 which had previously contained a disregard of top-up grants for people participating in the self-employment route; such grants will now be ignored under the blanket provisions in para.13 of Sch.9 and para.30 of Sch.10.

"the Skipton Fund": This is government-funded and has been set up to make lump sum ex-gratia payments to people (or their dependants if the person died after August 29, 2003) who have contracted hepatitis C from NHS blood, blood products or tissue. Such payments are fully disregarded (see para.22 of Sch.10; note also the disregard in para.39(2)–(7) of Sch.9 to cover income payments to close family members that derive from a Skipton Fund payment).

"training allowance": *R(IS) 10/98* holds that payments from the European Social Fund can fall within this definition. As part of his part-time course the claimant went on a two-week placement in Brussels and Strasbourg, for which funds were provided by the European Social Fund. The Commissioner decided that this meant that he was in receipt of a training allowance and so could continue to be paid income support during his absence abroad (under reg.4(2)(c)(i) and para.11 of Sch.1 in force at that time; see the 1996 edition of Mesher and Wood: *Income-Related Benefits: The Legislation*). The payment from the European Social Fund was out of "public funds" administered in the UK by the Department of Employment and so could be said to be made "by or on behalf of the Secretary of State for Employment"; the Secretary of State would also have to have been satisfied that the course, or at least the placement, came within the ambit of the European Social Fund and so could be said to have "approved" the course.

In *R(TC) 1/03* the "training allowance" paid to the claimant was funded from the local authority's budget, not by external funding. It therefore did not fall within the definition in reg.2(1) of the Family Credit Regulations (which paralleled this definition) (see the 2002 edition of this volume for the Family Credit Regulations which were revoked in April 2003).

"welfare to work beneficiary": Under reg.13A(1) of the Social Security (Incapacity for Work) (General) Regulations 1995 a person is a "welfare to work beneficiary" if (i) he has ceased to be entitled to a benefit (other than statutory sick pay) on or after

2.33

October 5, 1998 which he was getting on the grounds of incapacity for work ("benefit" for this purpose includes incapacity benefit, severe disablement allowance, income support paid on the basis of incapacity for work, or any of the income support, income-based JSA, housing benefit or council tax benefit disability premiums awarded on that ground, or national insurance credits for incapacity for work: reg.13A(4) of the Incapacity for Work Regulations); (ii) he had been incapable of work for more than 28 weeks (his "previous period of incapacity for work") when his benefit entitlement stopped (it is not necessary for the person to have been in receipt of benefit for the whole of the period); (iii) the previous period of incapacity for work ended 28 weeks or more after the end of any earlier "linking term" (see below) (reg.13A(3)(b)); (iv) he started a training course for which he receives a training allowance under s.2(1) of the Employment and Training Act 1973 or s.2(3) of the Enterprise and New Towns (Scotland) Act 1990 or work for which he is paid or expects to be paid within a week (*i.e.* any period of seven days: reg.2(1) of the Incapacity for Work Regulations) of benefit entitlement ending (exempt work under reg.17 of the Incapacity for Work Regulations does not count but otherwise "work" is not further defined); and (v) *either* notified the Secretary of State (verbally or in writing) that he had started work or training within a month (*i.e.* a calendar month: Interpretation Act 1978, Sch.1) of benefit ceasing *or* successfully appealed against a decision that he was capable of work under the "own occupation test" or the "all work test" (now the personal capability assessment) (see Vol.I of this series for the details of these tests) and the resulting period of incapacity for work was more than 28 weeks. Note that if the previous period of incapacity for work stopped because the person was found capable of work (other than a capacity decision made solely because the person started work), and any appeal was unsuccessful, the intention is that reg.13A(1) will not apply (reg.13A(3)(a)). Nor will it do so, it seems, if the person's previous period of incapacity ended because he was treated as capable of work under reg.7 or 8 of the Incapacity for Work Regulations for failing without good cause to return the all work test questionnaire or attend for a medical examination, even in that case in the event of a successful appeal.

If the person satisfies these conditions, he counts as a "welfare to work beneficiary" for 52 weeks starting on the first day after the end of his previous period of incapacity for work (the "linking term"). This is a fixed period and it is irrelevant whether the person stops work or training or if there are any further days of incapacity in that period. The effect is to provide a 52-week linking rule between periods of incapacity for work for the purpose of access to the disability and higher pensioner premiums and payment of housing costs (see the new paras 10(4) and 12(1A) inserted into Sch.2 and the new paras 7(10) and 14(10) inserted into Sch.3 with effect from October 5, 1998 and the notes to those paragraphs). In addition, if a welfare to work beneficiary becomes incapable of work and reclaims benefit within the linked term, he will be treated as incapable of work for up to 91 days if (i) during his previous period of incapacity for work he passed the all work test (now the personal capability assessment) or was exempt from the test under reg.10 of the Incapacity for Work Regulations (severe conditions) (note this will not apply if the person was treated as incapable of work under reg.27 of those Regulations (exceptional circumstances)) and (ii) he submits medical evidence of his incapacity for work. The 91 days need not be consecutive but must fall within the 52-week linking period or the first 13 weeks after the end of that period. After 91 days the person will have to satisfy the normal rules for incapacity for work.

2.34   Once the 52-week linking period expires, a person can requalify as a welfare to work beneficiary if he meets the requirements for this, including the fact that at least 28 weeks have passed since the end of the previous linking term. Note that days of incapacity within that linking term can count towards satisfying the condition of 28 weeks incapacity (under the normal eight week linking rule: see s.30(1)(c) of the Contributions and Benefits Act).

"year of assessment": The meaning in s.832(1) of the Income and Corporation Taxes Act 1988 is "with reference to any tax year, the year for which such tax was granted

by any Act granting income tax." A tax year is the 12 months beginning with April 6 in any year.

Para. (3)

Note that special provision is only made for polygamous marriages. If the claimant is not married, the ordinary living together as husband and wife rules apply (Contributions and Benefits Act, s.137(1); 1986 Act, s.20(11)).

[¹Disapplication of section 1(1A) of the Administration Act

2A. Section 1(1A) of the Administration Act (requirement to state national insurance number) shall not apply—   2.35
  (a) [³ . . .]
  (b) to a partner in respect of whom a claim for income support is made or treated as made before [² 5th October 1998].]

AMENDMENTS

1. Social Security (National Insurance Number Information: Exemption)   2.36
Regulations 1997 (SI 1997/2676), reg.10 (December 1, 1997).
2. Social Security (National Insurance Number Information: Exemption) (No.2) Regulations 1997 (SI 1997/2814), reg.2 (December 1, 1997).
3. Social Security (Working Tax Credit and Child Tax Credit) (Consequential Amendments) Regulations 2003 (SI 2003 No. 455), reg.2 and Sch.1, para.1 (April 6, 2004, except in "transitional cases" and see further the note to reg.17 of the Income Support Regulations).

DEFINITION

"partner"—see reg.2(1).

GENERAL NOTE

Subs.(1A), together with subss.(1B) and (1C), was inserted into s.1 of the   2.37
Administration Act by s.19 of the Social Security Administration (Fraud) Act 1997 and came into force on December 1, 1997. The effect of these provisions is that where s.1(1)(a) of the Administration Act (no entitlement to benefit unless a claim for it is made) applies, *i.e.* generally, there will also be no entitlement to benefit unless the claimant provides a national insurance (NI) number, together with information or evidence to show that it is his, *or* provides evidence or information to enable his NI number to be traced, *or* applies for a NI number and provides sufficient information or evidence for one to be allocated to him. A P45 or P60 form will be evidence of a person's NI number but these may not always be available; other evidence which shows the person's number should also be sufficient. This requirement for an NI number applies to both the claimant and any person for whom he is claiming, except in prescribed circumstances (subss.(1A) and (1C)). The effect of reg.2A is that where a claim for income support was made, or treated as made, before October 5, 1998 (but not on or after that date) the national insurance number requirement did not apply to any partner of the claimant. Between December 1, 1997 and April 5, 2004 any child or young person included in the claim was also exempt from the requirement under para.(a). That exemption became unnecessary—and para.(a) was therefore repealed—on April 6, 2004 when support for children and young persons was removed from income support and transferred to child tax credit. See the note to reg.17 for the circumstances in which para.(a) remains in force on a transitional basis.

Note *CIS 345/2003* which confirms that a decision refusing to allocate an NI number (or alternatively if such a refusal is a determination, not a decision, a decision denying income support on the basis of such a determination) is appealable

(*CIS 3692/2001* which decided that a tribunal only had a restricted jurisdiction as regards such a decision not followed). The Commissioner considered that the new tribunal would find the following observations from an officer on behalf of the Secretary of State helpful:

> "It is to be hoped that the Secretary of State's representatives in the claimant's local social security office will in the meantime reconsider its refusal to provide to the tribunal the evidence on which its refusal of the claimant's claim under section 1(1B) of the Social Security [Administration Act 1992 was based]. If not, the new tribunal will, in my submission, be at liberty firstly to direct the Secretary of State to produce the evidence in question and secondly, in the event of a refusal to comply with that direction, to consider whether the Secretary of State is thereby seeking to shelter from scrutiny an indefensible decision."

Definition of non-dependant

2.38   **3.**—(1) In these Regulations, "non-dependant" means any person, except someone [³ to whom paragraph (2), (2A) or (2B) applies], who normally resides with a claimant [⁴or with whom a claimant normally resides.]

[³(2) This paragraph applies to—

(a) any member of the claimant's family;

(b) a child or young person who is living with the claimant but who is not a member of his household by virtue of regulation 16 (circumstances in which a person is to be treated as being or not being a member of the household);

(c) a person who lives with the claimant in order to care for him or for the claimant's partner and who is engaged for that purpose by a charitable or [⁵voluntary organisation] which makes a charge to the claimant or the claimant's partner for the care provided by that person;

(d) the partner of a person to whom sub-paragraph (c) applies.

(2A) This paragraph applies to a person, other than a close relative of the claimant or the claimant's partner,—

(a) who is liable to make payments on a commercial basis to the claimant or the claimant's partner in respect of his occupation of the claimant's dwelling;

(b) to whom the claimant or the claimant's partner is liable to make payments on a commercial basis in respect of his occupation of that person's dwelling;

(c) who is a member of the household of a person to whom sub-paragraph (a) or (b) applies.

(2B) Subject to paragraph (2C), this paragraph applies to—

(a) a person who jointly occupies the claimant's dwelling and who is either—

    (i) a co-owner of that dwelling with the claimant or the claimant's partner (whether or not there are other co-owners); or

    (ii) jointly liable with the claimant or the claimant's partner to make payments to a landlord in respect of his occupation of that dwelling,

(b) a partner of a person whom sub-paragraph (a) applies.

(2C) Where a person is a close relative of the claimant or the claimant's partner, paragraph (2B) shall apply to him only if the claimant's, or the claimant's partner's, co-ownership, or joint liability to make payments to a landlord in respect of his occupation, of the dwelling arose either before 11th April 1988, or, if later, on or before the date upon which the claimant or the claimant's partner first occupied the dwelling in question.]

(3) [² . . .].

(4) For the purposes of this regulation a person resides with another only if they share any accommodation except a bathroom, a lavatory or a communal area [¹ but not if each person is separately liable to make payments in respect of his occupation of the dwelling to the landlord].

(5) In this regulation "communal area" means any area (other than rooms) of common access (including halls and passageways) and rooms of common use in sheltered accommodation.

AMENDMENTS

1. Income Support (General) Amendment Regulations 1989 (SI 1989/534), reg.2   **2.39**
(April 10, 1989).
2. Income Support (General) Amendment Regulations 1989 (SI 1989/534), Sch.1, para.2 (October 9, 1989).
3. Income Support (General) Amendment No. 6 Regulations 1991 (SI 1991/ 2334), reg.2 (November 11, 1991).
4. Income-related Benefits Schemes (Miscellaneous Amendments) (No. 6) Regulations 1994 (SI 1994/3061), reg.2(2) (December 2, 1994).
5. Income-related Benefits Schemes (Miscellaneous Amendments) Regulations 1995 (SI 1995/516), reg.18 (April 10, 1995).

DEFINITIONS

"child"—see 1986 Act, s.20(11) (SSCBA, s.137(1)).
"claimant"—see reg.2(1).
"dwelling"—see 1986 Act, s.84(1) (SSCBA, s.137(1)).
"family"—*ibid.*
"partner"—see reg.2(1).
"voluntary organisation"—*ibid.*
"young person"—*ibid.*, reg.14.

GENERAL NOTE

Para. (1)
The definition of "non-dependant" is important for a number of purposes, par-   **2.40**
ticularly deductions from housing costs and qualification for the severe disability premium. Its use for different purposes causes difficulties. What might be a sensible test for determining when a contribution towards accommodation costs ought to be assumed from an independent person who shares the claimant's accommodation might be less sensible in determining a severely disabled person's financial needs.

A person who normally resides with the claimant, or with whom the claimant normally resides, (*Chief Adjudication Officer and Another v Bate* [1996] 2 All E.R. 790, HL also reported as *R(IS) 12/96*), unless within the important exceptions in paras (2) to (2C), is a non-dependant.

The December 1994 amendment to para.(1) was the government's immediate (within 48 hours) response to the Court of Appeal's decision in *Bate v Chief Adjudication Officer and Secretary of State for Social Security* on November 30, 1994 (*The Times*, December 12, 1994). Ms Bate was a severely disabled person who lived in her parents' home. The Court of Appeal decided that because her parents were the "householders", in the sense that it was they who jointly occupied the home as tenants, they did not normally reside with *her*, but she normally resided with *them*. Thus they did not come within the definition of non-dependant at all. The Court recognised that this construction did not fit easily with the amendment to reg.3(2)(d) on April 10,

227

1989 (now recast in para.(2A)), but did not consider that the meaning of the initial regulation could be determined by later amendments. The April 1989 amendment simply showed that the draftsman had assumed that "residing with the claimant" had the meaning which the Court had rejected. However, the House of Lords disagreed, holding that "resides with" meant no more than that the claimant and the other person lived in the same dwelling. It was not limited to the situation where it was the *claimant's* household or dwelling.

The December 2, 1994 regulations (SI 1994/3061) were introduced without first being referred to the Social Security Advisory Committee. Section 173(1)(a) of the Administration Act permits this if the Secretary of State considers it inexpedient to refer proposed regulations by reason of urgency. The failure to refer these proposed regulations was challenged by Ms Bate (see Welfare Rights Bulletin 125). It was argued that the Court of Appeal had decided that it was Parliament's intention that people in Ms Bate's position should be entitled to a severe disability premium (and therefore it intended that financial provision should be made for this) and so the Secretary of State could not say that it was urgent that payment of the premium should stop. In addition, the Secretary of State should not be allowed to sidestep the consultation procedure, which Parliament clearly considered important, in this way. (See the comment of Hobhouse L.J. in *Chief Adjudication Officer v Palfrey and Others* (reported as part of *R(IS) 26/95*) that one reason at least for the consultation procedure is the "remarkable latitude" given to the maker of regulations in the Social Security Acts.) But leave to bring judicial review was refused both by the High Court and the Court of Appeal.

2.41   Paras (4) and (5) provide a partial definition of "resides with." In its original form, para.(4) put forward only one necessary, but not on its own sufficient, condition about sharing accommodation. But the general test of para.(1) still had to be satisfied. On "sharing of accommodation" see *CSIS 185/1995* in the note to para.(4). The post-April 1989 form of para.(4) specifically excludes from the definition a situation where co-residents are separately liable to make payments to a landlord. Such a person is already paying for accommodation costs. "Landlord" does not require there to be a tenancy; licensees can come within the exclusion (*CSIS 43/1992*).

Outside this exclusion the arrangement must still come within the general meaning of "residing with" and be the normal situation to come within the definition in para.(1). In *CSIS 100/1993* the claimant's daughter sometimes stayed in her mother's home and used that address for official correspondence. The Commissioner says that where correspondence is sent is a possible indicator that the daughter normally resided with the claimant, but equally, having regard to the other places the daughter stayed, it could be that she had no "fixed abode" (and thus did not normally reside with the claimant). This is further expanded on in *CIS 14850/1996* where the Commissioner states that for a person to be "normally resident" it was necessary for him to have lived in the house concerned, if not permanently, for a sufficient length of time for it to be regarded as his usual abode. The question of normal residence was a practical one to be determined in the light of common sense (see *CSIS 76/1991*). It would be relevant to consider why the residence started, its duration, the relationship, if any, between the people concerned, including its history; the reason why the residence had been taken up and whether it had lasted longer than its original purpose; and whether there was any alternative residence the person could take up. In that case a woman who was previously unknown to the claimant but who may have been his daughter came to live with him on the breakdown of her marriage. The matrimonial proceedings were protracted and she was also waiting for a council house. When the claimant applied for his income support to be reviewed to include a severe disability premium she had been living in his house for nine months. The Commissioner considered that since they had not previously known each other normal residence might take longer to establish and even longer if they were not in fact close relatives. If "the daughter" was waiting for alternative accommodation her residence could be quite lengthy without necessarily becoming normal. Questions such as what steps she had taken to find other accommodation, or with regard to her former matrimonial home, would also need to be investigated.

Paras (2) to (2C)

These provisions except those who would otherwise count as non-dependants **2.42** from coming within that category. The exceptions have been through a convoluted series of forms, whose meaning has been a matter of great controversy. The convolutions are traced in previous editions of Mesher and Wood, *Income-related Benefits: the Legislation,* and great care must be taken in identifying what form of the regulation is in effect at particular dates which may be relevant to outstanding claims and appeals. See *CIS 20034/1997* for a useful summary of the position in relation to each of the periods from October 9, 1989 for a severely disabled claimant living with his family. The House of Lords in *Foster v Chief Adjudication Officer* [1993] A.C. 754; [1993] 1 All E.R. 705 holds that the amendment made on October 9, 1989 (to add the conditions now substantially contained in para.(2B)(a)(i) and (ii)) was not *ultra vires* on the ground of irrationality.

Note that regs 4 to 6 of the Income Support (General) Amendment No.6 Regulations 1991 provide transitional protection for claimants who were entitled to the severe disability premium before October 21, 1991, by virtue of the pre-November 1991 form of reg.3 (see p.664).

In *R(IS) 17/94* a Tribunal of Commissioners states that SSATs, when considering, for example, a claimant's right to a severe disability premium, should deal with the position from the date of claim down to the date when the issues are finally decided (preferring the approach of *R(IS) 26/95* to that of *CIS 649/1992,* where the Commissioner held that an adjudicating authority should only consider the position as at the date from which benefit is sought). *CIS 649/1992* is also inconsistent with, for example, *R(IS) 13/93* (see the notes to reg.23(2) of the Adjudication Regulations). But in relation to appeals lodged on or after May 21, 1998, note the effect of s.22(8) of the Administration Act inserted by para.3 of Sch.6 to the Social Security Act 1998 where there is a change of circumstances after the date of the decision under appeal, and now see s.12(8)(b) of the 1998 Act. In addition, *R(IS) 17/94* dealt with an argument that once a claimant had acquired a right to a severe disability premium, its removal by subsequent amendment of reg.3(2) was prevented by s.16(1)(c) of the Interpretation Act (protection of acquired rights). Section 16 applies unless the contrary intention appears. The Commissioners hold that the words "shall come into force in relation to a particular claimant" in reg.1(1) of SI 1989/534 (the regulations at issue) indicated that the regulations were intended to apply to existing claimants. A claim made after the regulations came into force would be subject to them without the need for these words. Thus they were clearly intended to provide for existing claimants.

Para. (2)

These four categories excluded from the definition of non-dependant have been in **2.43** the regulation since 1988 and are relatively straightforward. They cover those who are not sufficiently independent of the claimant to be a non-dependant.

(a) A member of the family. This, by reference to s.137(1) of the Contributions and Benefits Act (1986 Act, s.20(11)), covers children and 16–18 year-olds treated as in full time secondary level education as well as partners, but only if members of the same household.

(b) Children who are not members of the family under the operation of the special rules in reg.16.

(c) and (d) Certain carers provided at a charge by charities or voluntary bodies, plus the carer's partner.

Para. (2A)

This is a recasting in November 1991 of the previous para.(2)(d) to (db). The dif- **2.44** ference is that a close relative (defined in reg.2(1)) of the claimant or his partner does not come within para.(2A). Thus, for instance, the parents of a severely disabled person may no longer come within para.(2A). If they are not to be non-dependants from November 1991, they must come within paras (2B) and (2C). Outside the close relative exception, the effect of para.(2A) now is that where the relationship between the claimant (or the claimant's partner) and the other person (or a member of that person's household) is a commercial one, that person is not a non-dependant. No further contribution to accommodation costs is therefore appropriate.

There must be a legal liability (as distinct from a moral or ethical obligation *(CIS 754/1991)*) to make payments for accommodation, *i.e.* rent or a board and lodging charge, on a commercial basis. The first question is whether there is a liability to pay. It has been held on the pre-November 1991 version of para.(2A) that a severely disabled claimant living with, for example, his parents can be their licensee and therefore liable to pay for his accommodation in the sense that if no payment is made the licence could terminate *(CIS 195/1991, CIS 754/ 1991)*. In deciding whether such a liability exists there would need to be findings as to the terms on which a claimant lives in his parents' home, the amount and regularity of the payments and the use made of the claimant's contributions. If the payments go towards rent or a mortgage that would be a stronger case than if they are used for the claimant's own personal needs *(CIS 754/1991)*, but they need not be applied directly to accommodation costs. If the claimant's contributions go into a general fund used for household costs (including accommodation) that will suffice *(R(IS)17/94)*. It will then be necessary to conclude on the basis of the relevant findings whether there was an intention to create legal relations. Such an intention can be inferred from a course of conduct (see Scarman L.J. in *Horrocks v Forray* [1976] 1 W.L.R. 230 at 239). *CIS 754/1991* holds that this might not be too difficult to infer where an adult member of the family is making regular payments in respect of his occupation. It may be easier to infer where the parents depend on the claimant's contributions because of their own financial circumstances. In his directions to the new SSAT in *CIS 754/1991* the Commissioner concludes:

> "In essence there should be what I might call a broad approach to satisfaction of the condition keeping in mind that the AO has throughout accepted that in [*CIS 195/1991*] it was right to conclude that the claimant [had a liability to make payments in respect of his occupation]. I should have thought that the facts in many of the cases are likely to be essentially indistinguishable from those in [*CIS/195/1991*]."

2.45   The facts in *CIS/195/1991* were that the claimant's parents took £20 per week from his benefit. The rest of the money was used for his own needs. The SSAT found that the claimant lived in his parents' house as a licensee and paid them £20 in respect of his occupation of it.

But what of the situation where there can be no contractual liability because one of the parties lacks the capacity to make a contract? In *CIS 195/1991* the claimant was held to be capable of incurring a liability to make payment, despite his mental disability. Under English law the contract was voidable because of his mental disability, not void. However, in Scottish law an "incapax" is not capable of making any personal contract. *R(IS) 17/94* holds that in Scottish cases ATs must first consider whether a claimant is so mentally incapacitated as to be incapax. But if this is the case, the doctrine of recompense may well apply to establish a liability on the incapax, so that the result is similar in practical terms to that in *CIS 195/1991* (see 1993 Supplement for fuller discussion of *R(IS) 17/94*, the reported version of *CSIS 28/1992* and *CSIS 40/1992*). The doctrine of recompense is also considered in *CSIS 641/1995*, although on the particular facts of that case (see the summary in the 1998 Supplement to Mesher and Wood, *Income-related Benefits: the Legislation*) it did not apply. In *CIS 754/1991* the Commissioner expresses the *obiter* view that where a person has no contractual capacity at all, the doctrine of restitution does not seem available to assist claimants in England in the way that recompense can in Scotland. Thus in English cases for mentally disabled claimants it will generally be necessary for there to be a finding of sufficient contractual capacity. On the facts of both *CIS*

195/1991 and *CIS 754/1991* the capacity required does not seem to be of a very high order. The claimant in *CIS 754/1991* was found to have sufficient contractual capacity despite having Downs syndrome and needing an appointee to act for her in social security matters.

Since October 1, 1990, the liability to pay has had to be on a commercial basis. **2.46** The words "commercial basis" govern the nature of the liability, not just the quality of the payments made *(R(IS) 17/94)*. For a discussion of "commercial basis" see *CSB 1163/1988* and the notes to the definition of "board and lodging accommodation" in reg.2(1). In *CIS 195/1991* (approved in *R(IS) 17/94*) the Commissioner held that the question of whether an arrangement is on a commercial basis was entirely one of fact for the SSAT. What has to be considered is whether the arrangement is the sort that might have been entered into if the parents had taken in a lodger, instead of, in *CIS 195/1991*, their physically and mentally handicapped son. This approach was also expressly approved by another Tribunal of Commissioners in *R(IS) 11/98*. The claimant, who was severely disabled, lived with her parents and paid them £25 per week. The Commissioners emphasise that *CIS 195/1991* had only considered that a commercial arrangement in a family situation was unlikely, not that it was impossible or even improbable. They also confirm that a profit element is not necessary, nor was it relevant whether the family depended financially on the payments or whether they would take any action if the claimant did not pay (although these last two factors were relevant to the question of whether there was a liability to make payments, see *CIS 754/1991*). The Commissioners rejected the AO's contention that in considering the adequacy of the claimant's payments a deduction should be made for the value of the care provided by the parents, pointing out that reg.3 referred to payments in respect of the *occupation* of the dwelling.

Although there might still be some scope for structuring an informal relationship to get within para.(2A), the requirement of a commercial basis (since October 1, 1990) and the exclusion of close relatives (from November 11, 1991) provide quite a stringent control. Note the transitional protection in regs 4 to 6 of the Income Support (General) Amendment No. 6 Regulations 1991 (see p.664) for claimants entitled to the severe disability premium before October 21, 1991.

Tribunals faced with sorting out severe disability premium entitlement, in particular for the periods October 9, 1989 to September 30, 1990 and October 1, 1990 to November 10, 1991, will need to pay particular regard to the Commissioners' decisions discussed above. There is a useful summary of the position in relation to each of the periods from October 9, 1989 in *CIS 20034/1997*.

Paras (2B) to (2C)

These provisions replace the previous para.(2)(c) on joint occupiers, and impose **2.47** a considerably stricter test. The biggest change in November 1991 was to exclude joint occupiers who are close relatives (see reg.2(1)) from the operation of para.(2B) except in restricted circumstances. This is done by para.(2C). If the close relative met the conditions of para.(2B) either before April 11, 1988, or as soon as the claimant or partner moved to the current home, then advantage can be taken of para.(2B). The aim is to exclude arrangements made within a family (in the non-income support sense) designed to take advantage of the definition of a non-dependant. The thinking is that if the arrangement was the basis on which the occupation of the home by the claimant started it is likely to be a genuine one. Existing claimants excluded by this rule may particularly benefit from the transitional protection mentioned above. *CIS 80/1994* rejects the argument that para.(2C) is invalid on the ground that it operates retrospectively. The Commissioner states that para.(2C) imposes a new condition of future eligibility (though with reference to past events). Thus it does not take away any vested right or create any new obligation in regard to events that have already passed.

In *CIS 650/1993* the claimant had been a joint tenant of her home with her husband. When he died in 1990 she became the sole tenant. Later her sister came to live with her and they became joint tenants. The Commissioner rejects the claimant's contention that the previous joint liability of the claimant and her husband meant that para.(2C) was satisfied. In the context of reg.3, para.(2C) only referred to the joint liability of the claimant and the person currently residing with her and not to any other joint liability.

In *CIS 216/1997* the claimant who was in receipt of the severe disability premium gave up the tenancy of her local authority home (with effect from January 22, 1995) and went to live with her daughter and her family. She moved to her daughter's home on January 16, 1995 and became a joint tenant with her of that home on January 23, 1995. During the week from January 16 to 22, the claimant was moving her belongings from her old home to her new, although she slept at her daughter's home from January 16. The Commissioner decides that the claimant was to be regarded as having "first occupied" her new home when she first normally resided there. It was clear from the evidence that arrangements for the joint tenancy had been made with the local authority before the claimant moved in with her daughter. The move and the creation of the joint tenancy were inextricably linked. In his view the claimant did not finally become an occupier of her new home until January 23, 1995 and so para.(2C) applied.

2.48 The rest of para.(2B) is based on the provisions in force from October 1989. First, there must be joint occupation of the claimant's home. In *CIS 180/1989* the claimant was a single woman in receipt of attendance allowance, severe disablement allowance and income support. She lived with her parents, who owned the house. The Commissioner held that "jointly occupies" is not to be given a technical meaning, but its ordinary meaning. The phrase applies where "persons who normally reside together jointly occupy the premises in the sense of equality of access and use as distinct from a situation where restrictions are imposed in relation to those matters." It did not matter, under the legislation in force at the relevant time, that the claimant did not have any proprietary interest in the house. *CIS 180/1989* (approved by the Tribunal of Commissioners in *R(IS) 17/94*) has governed the position, particularly in severe disability premium cases, for the period before October 9, 1989, when amendments to impose the extra conditions now substantially contained in para.(2B)(a)(i) and (ii) were made. Indeed, it has been usual for AOs to concede that for the period before October 9, 1989, parents or other family members are not non-dependants.

It might be objected that the approach of *CIS 180/1989* expanded the exception on joint occupation so far that it excluded everyone who would be caught by the primary definition of a non-dependant. This is not so. People can reside together, but without the equality of access and use stressed by the Commissioner. The House of Lords in the *Foster* case, where it was conceded that the claimant's parents were joint occupiers up to October 9, 1989, expressed similar doubts that the exception, if widely construed, might eat up the rule, but did not reach any authoritative conclusion. In a decision on the equivalent housing benefit provision (*Fullwood v Chesterfield Borough Council, The Times*, June 15, 1993) the Court of Appeal specifically rejected the basis of *CIS 180/1989*, holding that "jointly occupies" is a technical legal phrase, meaning "occupies by right jointly with one or more persons". Thus, joint occupation entails either a joint tenancy or joint liability to make payments under an agreement for occupation. This decision strictly only related to housing benefit, but both the Court of Appeal and the House of Lords in *Bate* (see above) accepted that the phrase should be given the same meaning for the purposes of income support. It connoted a legal relationship and not merely factual co-residence.

From October 9, 1989, it has been specifically provided that one of two extra conditions must be satisfied. One is that the claimant (or partner) is a co-owner of the home with the other person (or partner). This is unchanged since October 9, 1989. The other condition is that there is joint liability to make payments in respect of the occupation of the home to a landlord. This was changed in November 1991 from the October 9, 1989 form to specify that the payments must be to a landlord. The result is broadly to confirm the outcome of *CIS 299/1990* (discussed in the 1991 edition of Mesher and Wood, *Income-related Benefits: the Legislation*), and to remove the problem of interpretation addressed in that decision. These conditions narrowed the scope of para.(2B) considerably. Where there is separate, rather than joint, liability a person is deemed not to be residing with the claimant (para.(4)).

Para. (3)
The revocation removes the special rule for boarders and hostel-dwellers.　　2.49

Para. (4)
The original form of para.(4) merely meant that if accommodation other than bathroom, lavatory or a communal area was not shared, one person was not "residing with" another. It did not mean that the person was "residing with" the other just because such accommodation was shared. The general test of para.(1) still has to be satisfied. See *CSIS 100/1993* and *CIS 14850/1996* above. See also *Kadhim v London Borough of Brent Housing Benefit Review Board* (CA, unreported, December 20, 2000) which reaches the same view on the similar provision in reg.3(4) of the Housing Benefit Regulations. Para.(4) now also excludes from the definition of non-dependant a person who is separately liable to make payments to the landlord. See *CSIS 43/1992* above. Joint tenants and co-owners (other than close relatives of the claimant or partner) are excluded by para.(2B)(a).

CSIS 185/1995 holds that a person does not share a kitchen with another if it is not used physically by him but only by a third party to prepare food on his behalf. The Commissioner also points out that the issue is whether there is a "sharing of *accommodation*". So deciding whether the claimant shared a room simply because some of her clothes were stored there, would depend on what use, if any, the claimant made of the room, by considering what was stored there, in what, and to what extent, if any, the claimant herself went in and out of the room to deal with her property.

[1Permitted period

3A.—(1) For the purposes of regulation 17(6), [2. . .], paragraph 7(6) of　　2.50
Schedule 3A, paragraph 6(3) of Schedule 3B and paragraphs 4 and 6 of Schedule 8 (applicable amounts, mortgage interest, protected sums and earnings to be disregarded), where a claimant has ceased to be entitled to income support—
  (a) because he or his partner becomes engaged in remunerative work the permitted period, [3. . .] shall be 12 weeks; or
  (b) for any other reason, the permitted period shall be eight weeks.
  (2) [3. . .].
  (3) [3. . .].

AMENDMENTS

1. Income Support (General) Amendment No.3 Regulations 1989 (SI 1989/　　2.51
1678), reg.2 (October 9, 1989).
2. Social Security (Income Support, Claims and Payments and Adjudication) Amendment Regulations 1995 (SI 1995/2927), reg.4 (December 12, 1995).
3. Income Support (General) (Jobseeker's Allowance Consequential Amendments) Regulations 1996 (SI 1996/206), reg.3 (October 7, 1996).

GENERAL NOTE

Reg.3A provides a definition of the maximum permitted period of break in　　2.52
entitlement for the application of the various provisions set out in para.(1).
The omission of paras (2) and (3) is a consequence of the introduction of jobseeker's allowance on October 7, 1996.

PART II

CONDITIONS OF ENTITLEMENT

[¹Prescribed categories of person

2.53 **4ZA.**—(1) Subject to the following provisions of this regulation, a person to whom any paragraph of Schedule 1B applies falls within a prescribed category of person for the purposes of section 124(1)(e) of the Contributions and Benefits Act (entitlement to income support).

(2) Paragraph (1) does not apply to a [⁴ full-time student] during the period of study.

(3) A[⁴ full-time student] during the period of study falls within a prescribed category of person for the purposes of section 124(1)(e) of the Contributions and Benefits Act only if—

(a) [³ paragraph 1 of Part I of the Schedule to the Social Security (Immigration and Asylum) Consequential Amendments Regulations 2000] applies to him; or

(b) paragraph 1, 2, 10, 11, 12, or 18 of Schedule 1B applies to him; or

(c) any other paragraph of Schedule 1B applies to him and he has a partner who is also a [⁴ full-time student], and either he or his partner is treated as responsible for a child or young person, but this provision shall apply only for the period of the summer vacation appropriate to his course.]

[⁵(3A) Paragraph (1) does not apply to a person to whom section 6 of the Children (Leaving Care) Act 2000 (exclusion from benefits) applies.]

[²(4) A person who falls within a prescribed category in Schedule 1B for the purposes of this regulation for any day in a benefit week, shall fall within that category for the whole of that week.]

AMENDMENTS

2.54 1. Income Support (General) (Jobseeker's Allowance Consequential Amendments) Regulations 1996 (SI 1996/206), reg.4 (October 7, 1996).

2. Income-related Benefits and Jobseeker's Allowance (Amendment) (No. 2) Regulations 1997 (SI 1997/2197), reg.5(2) (October 6, 1997).

3. Social Security (Immigration and Asylum) Consequential Amendments Regulations 2000 (SI 2000/636), reg.3(3) (April 3, 2000).

4. Social Security Amendment (Students) Regulations 2000 (SI 2000/1981), reg.5(5) and Sch.(July 31, 2000).

5. Children (Leaving Care) Act 2000 (Commencement No. 2 and Consequential Provisions) Order 2001 (SI 2001/3070), art.3(2) and Sch.1, para.(a) (October 1, 2001).

DEFINITIONS

"child"—see SSCBA, s.137(1).
"benefit week"—see reg.2(1).
"full-time student"—see reg.61(1).
"partner"—see reg.2(1).
"period of study"—*ibid.*
"young person"—see reg.14.

GENERAL NOTE

Para. (1)

As a consequence of the introduction of JSA on October 7, 1996, the income   2.55
support scheme had to undergo a fundamental restructuring. Income support is no
longer available to people who are claiming benefit because they are unemployed.
People who have to be available for, and actively seeking, work as a condition of
receiving benefit have to claim JSA. Since October 7, 1996, in order to qualify for
income support a person has to fall within a "prescribed category" (see SSCBA
s.124(1)(e)). These categories are set out in Sch.1B. The categories in Sch.1B
broadly resemble most of those in the former Sch.1 (people not required to be available for employment) which was revoked on October 7, 1996, but there are some
differences. See the notes to Sch.1B. For the position of full-time students, see paras
(2) and (3). Note also para.(3A) (see below).

Schedule 1B provides an exhaustive list of the circumstances in which a person
will be entitled to income support. There is no category of analogous circumstances
or provision for a reduced rate of benefit on the ground of hardship for people who
do not come within these categories (compare the former reg.8(3), see the 1996
edition of *Mesher & Wood, Income-related Benefits: the Legislation*). Moreover, the provision for hardship payments under JSA is considerably restricted (see regs 140–146
of the JSA Regulations and the notes to those regulations (regs 146A–146D in the
case of joint-claim couples)). For the very limited provision for urgent cases outside
the normal scope of the income support rules see reg.70.

Note that entitlement to income support and JSA is mutually exclusive, although
some people may be eligible for either. Section 124(1)(f) of the Contributions and
Benefits Act provides that entitlement to JSA excludes entitlement to income
support (any "top-up" to a person's contribution-based JSA will be by way of
income-based JSA). Similarly, a person will not be entitled to JSA (contribution- or
income-based) if he is entitled to income support (ss.2(1)(d) and 3(1)(b) of the
Jobseekers Act). However, there is nothing to prevent a person who qualifies for
income support claiming JSA if he also fulfils the conditions of entitlement for JSA.
But in most circumstances it will be better for him to claim income support so as to
avoid the risk of being "sanctioned" for not complying with the labour market conditions. If the claimant is a member of a couple he will not be entitled to income
support if his partner is claiming *income-based* JSA (SSCBA s.124(1)(f)). If his
partner is claiming *contribution-based* JSA he will be able to claim income support if
he is eligible for this, or his partner (or, from March 19, 2001, he and his partner in
the case of certain childless couples) can claim income-based JSA. If the claimant is
incapable of work it will be better for him to claim income support in order to qualify
for the disability premium under para.12(1)(b) of Sch.2 after serving the appropriate waiting period. If the only basis for qualifying for the premium is incapacity for
work for 364 days (or 196 days if he is terminally ill), his partner will not be able to
get a JSA disability premium for him (see para.14 of Sch.1 to the JSA Regulations).
Moreover, note the "better-off" problem for some claimants as a result of the limit
for remunerative work for partners being 24 hours a week from October 7, 1996 (see
reg.5(1A), JSA Regs, reg.51(1)(b)). The consequence of this is that if the claimant's
partner is working between 16 and 24 hours a week the couple will have to consider
whether they will gain more by claiming working tax credit; see further Vol. IV of
this series.

A further substantial contraction in the number of people covered by income
support occurred on October 6, 2003 when the state pension credit scheme commenced. Claimants who have reached the qualifying age for state pension credit
(this is currently 60 but will gradually rise between 2010 and 2020 until it reaches
65: see further the note to s.1(6) of the State Pension Credit Act 2002), are no
longer entitled to income support (see s.124(aa) of the Contributions and Benefits
Act 1992). Such claimants now have to claim state pension credit. A claimant whose
partner is entitled to (ie who has claimed and been awarded) state pension credit is

also ineligible (s.124(g) of the 1992 Act). Thus a couple with one member aged over 60 and the other aged under 60 (who are not already in receipt of state pension credit) can chose to claim either income support (or JSA) or state pension credit. It will normally be advantageous to claim state pension credit. For an overview of the state pension credit scheme see the Introduction and General Note at the beginning of the State Pension Credit Act 2002.

Paras (2) and (3)

2.56   The effect of paras (2) and (3) is to exclude most full-time students (defined in reg.61(1)) from entitlement to income support from the beginning of their course to the end (see the definition of period of study in reg.2(1)). A full-time student will only be entitled during his period of study if he is a "person subject to immigration control" entitled to urgent cases payments because he is temporarily without funds (para.(3)(a)), or a lone parent, a single foster parent, a student who qualifies for the disability or severe disability premium, or who has been incapable of work for 28 weeks (two or more periods separated by not more than eight weeks count as continuous), or who is disabled and entitled under para.11 of Sch.1B, or deaf, or a refugee learning English (para.(3)(b)). Full-time student couples with a child who fall within any of the other paragraphs in Sch.1B may claim but only in the summer vacation (para.(3)(c)).

Para.(3A)

2.57   Section 6 of the Children (Leaving Care) Act 2000 (p.181) excludes certain 16 and 17 year olds who have been looked after by a local authority in England or Wales on or after October 1, 2001, or by a local authority in Scotland on or after April 1, 2004, from entitlement to income support, income-based JSA and housing benefit. Regulation 2 of the Children (Leaving Care) Social Security Benefits Regulations 2001 (SI 2001/3074) and reg.2 of the Children (Leaving Care) Social Security Benefits (Scotland) Regulations 2004 (SI 2004/747) provide for exceptions to the exclusion from income support and income-based JSA (but not housing benefit). For a discussion of s.6, the relevant definitions and the exceptions, see the notes to reg.2 of the Children (Leaving Care) Social Security Benefits Regulations 2001 (p.745) and to reg.2 of the Children (Leaving Care) Social Security Benefits (Scotland) Regulations 2004 (p.749).

Para.(4)

2.58   This confirms that if a person satisfies any of the paragraphs in Sch.1B on any day in a benefit week, he is treated as doing so for the whole of that week.

Temporary absence from Great Britain

2.59   **4.**—(1) Where a claimant is entitled to income support for a period immediately preceding a period of temporary absence from Great Britain, his entitlement to income support [² shall continue only—

   (a)   in the circumstances specified in paragraph (2), during the first 4 weeks of that period of temporary absence; and

   (b)   in the circumstances specified in paragraph (3), during the first 8 weeks of that period.]

   (2) The circumstances in which a claimant's entitlement to income support is to continue during the first four weeks of a temporary absence from Great Britain are that—

   (a)   the period of absence is unlikely to exceed 52 weeks; and

   (b)   while absent from Great Britain, the claimant continues to satisfy the other conditions of entitlement to income support; and

(c) any one of the following conditions apply—
    (i) the claimant falls within one or more of the prescribed categories of person listed in Schedule 1B other than paragraphs 7, 15, 20, 21, 24, 25, 26 or 27 of that Schedule; or
    (ii) the claimant falls within paragraph 7 of Schedule 1B (persons incapable of work) and his absence from Great Britain is for the sole purpose of receiving treatment from an appropriately qualified person for the incapacity by reason of which he satisfies the conditions of that paragraph; or]
    (iii) he is in Northern Ireland; or
    (iv) he is a member of a couple and he and his partner are both absent from Great Britain, and a premium referred to in paragraphs 9, [⁵9A,] 10, 11 or 13 of Schedule 2 (applicable amounts) is applicable in respect of his partner; [¹ or
  [³(v) on the day on which the absence began he had satisfied the provisions of [⁴ paragraph 7 of Schedule 1B] (persons incapable of work) for a continuous period of not less than—
    (aa) 196 days in the case of a claimant who is terminally ill within the meaning of section 30B(4) of the Contributions and Benefits Act, or who is entitled to the highest rate of the care component of disability living allowance; or
    (bb) 364 days in any other case,
and for this purpose any two or more separate periods separated by a break of not more than 56 days shall be treated as one continuous period.]]

[²(3) The circumstances in which a claimant's entitlement to income support is to continue during the first 8 weeks of a temporary absence from Great Britain are that—
(a) the period of absence is unlikely to exceed 52 weeks; and
(b) the claimant continues to satisfy the other conditions of entitlement to income support; and
(c) the claimant is, or the claimant and any other member of his family are, accompanying a member of the claimant's family who is a child or young person solely in connection with arrangements made for the treatment of that child or young person for a disease or bodily or mental disablement; and
(d) those arrangements relate to treatment—
    (i) outside Great Britain;
    (ii) during the period whilst the claimant is, or the claimant and any member of his family are, temporarily absent from Great Britain; and
    (iii) by, or under the supervision of, a person appropriately qualified to carry out that treatment.

[⁶(3A) A claimant's entitlement to income support shall continue during a period of temporary absence from Great Britain if—
(a) he satisfied the conditions of entitlement to income support immediately before the beginning of that period of temporary absence; and
(b) that period of temporary absence is for the purpose of the claimant receiving treatment at a hospital or other institution outside Great Britain where that treatment is being provided—
    (i) under section 3 of the National Health Service Act 1977 (services generally);

> (ii) pursuant to arrangements made under section 23 of that Act (voluntary organisations and other bodies); or
>
> (iii) pursuant to arrangements made under paragraph 13 of Schedule 2 to the National Health Service and Community Care Act 1990 (National Health Service Trusts—specific powers).]
>
> (4) In paragraphs (2) and (3) "appropriately qualified" means qualified to provide medical treatment, physiotherapy or a form of treatment which is similar to, or related to, either of those forms of treatment.]

AMENDMENTS

2.60   1. Income Support (General) Amendment Regulations 1988 (SI 1988/663), reg.3 (April 11, 1988).

2. Income Support (General) Amendment Regulations 1990 (SI 1990/547), reg.3 (April 9, 1990).

3. Disability Working Allowance and Income Support (General) Amendment Regulations 1995 (SI 1995/482), reg.5 (April 13, 1995).

4. Income Support (General) (Jobseeker's Allowance Consequential Amendments) Regulations 1996 (SI 1996/206), reg.5 (October 7, 1996).

5. Income-related Benefits Schemes and Social Fund (Miscellaneous Amendments) Regulations 1996 (SI 1996/1944), reg.6(3) (October 7, 1996).

6. Social Security (Income Support and Jobseeker's Allowance) Amendment Regulations 2004 (SI 2004/1869), reg.2 (October 4, 2004).

DEFINITIONS

"claimant"—see reg.2(1).
"couple"—*ibid.*
"disability living allowance"—*ibid.*
"partner"—*ibid.*

GENERAL NOTE

2.61   This provision takes over from reg.3 of the old Conditions of Entitlement Regulations a limited right to benefit during the claimant's absence from Great Britain (normally excluded by s.124(1) of the Contributions and Benefits Act; 1986 Act, s.20(3)); see *Perry v Chief Adjudication Officer, The Times,* October 20, 1998, also reported as *R(IS) 4/99,* in the note to s.124(1)). Great Britain means England, Scotland and Wales. If it is the claimant's partner who is temporarily absent, see Sch.7, para.11.

Para. (1)

2.62   The absence must be temporary, on the meaning of which see *Chief Adjudication Officer v Ahmed & Others, The Times,* April 6, 1994 (Court of Appeal). In *R. v Social Security Commissioner, Ex p. Akbar, The Times,* November 6, 1991, Hodgson J. had decided that temporary meant "not permanent". The Court of Appeal in *Ahmed* says that this is wrong, although the decision in *Akbar* itself was correct. However, the Court does agree with Hodgson J. that an absence can be temporary, even though the intended date for return remains uncertain. Thus *R(S) 1/85* should not be followed on this point. The Court of Appeal holds that the decision as to whether a person is temporarily absent is one of fact for the adjudicating authority concerned. Relevant factors include the claimant's intention (although this is not decisive) and the length of the absence. If a person initially has the intention of not returning or an intention to stay for some fixed period which goes beyond the temporary (*e.g.* a matter of years), the absence is not temporary from the outset. In practice, the 52-week period referred to in paras (2)(a) and (3)(a) is likely to be the most important test.

The claimant must have been entitled to income support immediately before the temporary absence. Since the reference is to entitlement, it does not seem that income support must actually have been received. But a claim must have been made for that period before entitlement can arise (Administration Act, s.1).

If the conditions set out in para.(2) are met, entitlement at the rate which would have been payable if the claimant had remained in Great Britain, can continue for the first four weeks of the temporary absence. If the conditions of para.(3) are met, entitlement can continue for the first eight weeks of absence. When calculating periods of absence from Great Britain the day of leaving and the day of return are both days on which the person is in Great Britain (see para.070642 of the *Decision Makers Guide* and *R(S) 1/66*).

If the claimant does not satisfy the conditions for continuing entitlement or the four or eight weeks are exhausted, any partner remaining in Great Britain may claim. If the absence is temporary, the couple ought on principle to remain members of the same household (although the effect of reg.16(3)(d) is obscure).

Para. (2)

Sub-paras (a) and (b) are self-explanatory. It is important that all the other conditions of entitlement must continue to be satisfied. The five conditions in sub-para.(c) are alternatives.   **2.63**

Head (i) covers claimants eligible for income support, apart from by reason of incapacity for work (but see (ii) and (v)), secondary education, trade disputes or being a person from abroad.

Some of the conditions which lead to eligibility for income support will obviously continue during absence abroad (*e.g.* pregnancy) but others may not (*e.g.* temporarily looking after children, if the children are left behind). Since the October 1993 change in the test of responsibility for a child, a lone parent who goes abroad temporarily without her children should continue to be eligible for income support under para.1 of Sch.1B. This is because reg.15(1) now makes receipt of child benefit the primary test of responsibility. Child benefit can continue to be paid while a claimant is temporarily absent from Great Britain for up to eight weeks. Only if no claim for child benefit has been made is the person with whom the child usually lives treated as responsible under reg.15(2)(a). The matter has to be tested week by week (*CIS 49/1991*). See the 1993 edition of Mesher, *Income-related Benefits: the Legislation* for the potential problems for lone parents absent abroad prior to October 4, 1993.

Head (ii) covers incapacity for work, but only subject to these conditions (as applied to incapacity benefit by reg.2(1) of the Social Security (Persons Abroad) Regulations 1975). See *R(S) 2/86* and *R(S) 1/90* for the conditions and head (v). Para.(4) defines when the person providing treatment is appropriately qualified.

Head (iii) is self explanatory.

Head (iv) refers to the pensioner and disability premiums, but only applies to couples who are both abroad. It requires the premium to be "applicable". It is clearly arguable that "applicable" means "ought to be applied", so that entitlement to the premium, even if it is not actually in payment, will do.

Head (v) allows those incapable of work for at least 52 weeks, or 28 weeks if they are terminally ill (*i.e.* expected to die from a progressive disease within six months) or entitled to the highest rate care component of disability living allowance, to use the regulation free of the conditions of head (ii). Two or more periods of incapacity count as one continuous period unless there is a break of more than eight weeks. Before April 13, 1995 the minimum period was 28 weeks for all claimants, but it has been increased for most claimants in line with the changes following the introduction of incapacity benefit. For the details of incapacity benefit see Vol. I of this series. Note reg.8(1) of the Income-related Benefits Schemes and Social Security (Claims and Payments) (Miscellaneous Amendments) Regulations 1995 (p.654), which provides that in deciding whether a claimant can satisfy head (v) on or after October 2, 1995, a period of incapacity immediately before April 13, 1995 can count towards the 52 (or 28) weeks, provided it is linked to, or part of, the current period. See also the transitional provision in reg.27(2) of the Income Support (General) (Jobseeker's Allowance Consequential Amendments) Regulations 1996 (p.675) in relation to the October 1996 changes to income support that are a consequence of the introduction of JSA.

Para. (3)

2.64   The conditions in heads (a) and (b) are the same as in para.(2)(a) and (b). Then the effect of heads (c) and (d) is that where the claimant is accompanying a child or young person in their family abroad for that child or young person to receive treatment, entitlement can continue for eight weeks. The claimant's absence must be solely for that purpose. The treatment must be for a medical condition and be carried out by an appropriately qualified person within the meaning of para.(4). There seems to be no reason why a claimant accompanying a child should be more deserving than a claimant going abroad for treatment for himself.

Para (3A)

2.65   From October 4, 2004 claimants who are temporarily absent from Great Britain in order to receive NHS treatment at a hospital (or similar institution) in another country, and who were entitled to IS immediately before their departure, continue to be so entitled during their absence.

Persons treated as engaged in remunerative work

2.66   **5.**—(1) Subject to the following provisions of this regulation, for the purposes of section 20(3)(c) of the Act [SSCBA, s.124(1)(c)] (conditions of entitlement to income support), remunerative work is work in which a person is engaged, or, where his hours of work fluctuate, he is engaged on average, for [⁶not less than 16 hours] a week being work for which payment is made or which is done in expectation of payment.

[⁹(1A) In the case of any partner of the claimant paragraph (1) shall have effect as though for the words "16 hours" there were substituted the words "24 hours".]

(2) [⁸Subject to paragraph (3B),] the number of hours for which a person is engaged in work shall be determined—

  (a) where no recognisable cycle has been established in respect of a person's work, by reference to the number of hours or, where those hours are likely to fluctuate, the average of the hours, which he is expected to work in a week;

  (b) where the number of hours for which he is engaged fluctuate, by reference to the average of hours worked over—

    (i) if there is a recognisable cycle of work, the period of one complete cycle (including, where the cycle involves periods in which the person does no work, those periods but disregarding any other absences);

    (ii) in any other case, the period of five weeks immediately before the date of claim or the date [¹¹ on which a superseding decision is made under section 10 (decisions superseding earlier decisions) of the Social Security Act 1998] or such other length of time as may, in the particular case, enable the person's average hours of work to be determined more accurately.

(3) A person shall be treated as engaged in remunerative work during any period for which he is absent from work referred to in paragraph (1) if the absence is either without good cause or by reason of a recognised, customary or other holiday.

[⁷(3A) A person shall not be treated as engaged in remunerative work on any day on which the person is on maternity leave [¹⁴, paternity leave or adoption leave] or is absent from work because he is ill.]

[⁸(3B) Where for the purpose of paragraph (2)(b)(i), a person's recognisable cycle of work at a school, other educational establishment or other place of employment is one year and includes periods of school holidays or similar vacations during which he does not work, those periods and any other periods not forming part of such holidays or vacations during which he is not required to work shall be disregarded in establishing the average hours for which he is engaged in work.]

(4) A person who makes a claim and to whom or whose partner section 23 of the Act [SSCBA, s.126] (trade disputes) applies [¹or applied] shall, for the period of seven days following the date on which the stoppage of work due to a trade dispute at his or his partner's place of work commenced or, if there is no stoppage, the date on which he or his partner first withdrew his labour in furtherance of a trade dispute, be treated as engaged in remunerative work.

(5) A person who was, or was treated as being, engaged in remunerative work and in respect of that work earnings to which [⁴regulation 35(1)(b) to (d) and (i)] (earnings of employed earners) applies are [³paid] shall be treated as engaged in remunerative work for the period for which those earnings are taken into account in accordance with Part V.

[²(6) For the purposes of this regulation, in determining the number of hours in which a person is engaged or treated as engaged in remunerative work, no account shall be taken of any hours in which the person is engaged in an employment or a scheme to which [¹². . . regulation 6(1)] (persons not treated as engaged in remunerative work) applies.]

[⁵(7) For the purposes of paragraphs (1) and (2), in determining the number of hours for which a person is engaged in work, that number shall include any time allowed to that person by his employer for a meal or for refreshment, but only where that person is, or expects to be, paid earnings in respect of that time.]

[¹³(8)–(10) . . .]

AMENDMENTS

1. Income Support (General) Amendment Regulations 1988 (SI 1988/663), reg.4 (April 11, 1988).

2. Income Support (General) Amendment No.4 Regulations 1988 (SI 1988/1445), reg.3 (September 9, 1988).

3. Income Support (General) Amendment No.5 Regulations 1988 (SI 1988/2022), reg.3 (December 12, 1988).

4. Income Support (General) Amendment No.2 Regulations 1989 (SI 1989/1323), reg.3 (October 9, 1989).

5. Income Support (General) Amendment Regulations 1990 (SI 1990/547), reg.4 (April 9, 1990).

6. Income Support (General) Amendment No.4 Regulations 1991 (SI 1991/1559), reg.3 (April 7, 1992).

7. Income-related Benefits Schemes (Miscellaneous Amendments) (No. 4) Regulations 1993 (SI 1993/2119), reg.3 (October 4, 1993).

8. Income-related Benefits Schemes (Miscellaneous Amendments) Regulations 1995 (SI 1995/516), reg.19 (April 10, 1995).

9. Income-related Benefits Schemes and Social Fund (Miscellaneous Amendments) Regulations 1996 (SI 1996/1944), reg.6(4) (October 7, 1996).

2.67

10. Social Security (Miscellaneous Amendments) (No.2) Regulations 1999 (SI 1999/2556), reg.2(2) (October 4, 1999).

11. Social Security Act 1998 (Commencement No. 12, and Consequential and Transitional Provisions) Order 1999 (SI 1999/3178), art.3(5) and Sch.5, para.1 (November 29, 1999)

12. Social Security (Miscellaneous Amendments) Regulations 2000 (SI 2000/681), reg.2(a) (April 3, 2000).

13. Social Security (Miscellaneous Amendments) Regulations 2001 (SI 2001/488), reg.3 (April 9, 2001).

14. Social Security (Paternity and Adoption) Amendment Regulations 2002 (SI 2002/2689), reg.2 (December 8, 2002).

DEFINITIONS

"the Act"—see reg.2(1).
"adoption leave"—*ibid.*
"date of claim"—*ibid.*
"maternity leave"—*ibid.*
"partner"—*ibid.*
"paternity leave"—*ibid.*

GENERAL NOTE

2.68   Under s.124(1)(c) of the SSCBA 1992, and ss 1(2)(e) and 3(1)(e) of the Jobseekers Act 1995, it is a condition of entitlement to income support and income-based JSA that neither the claimant nor her/his partner is in remunerative work. It is also a condition of entitlement to contribution-based JSA that the claimant should not be in remunerative work. Remunerative work is also relevant to the amount of any non-dependant deduction from the claimant's housing costs (see para.18 of Sch.3) and (in transitional cases, see the note to reg.17) to whether the earnings of certain children and young persons are disregarded under para.15 of Sch.8.

The rules governing remunerative work are set out, for income support purposes, in this regulation and reg.6, and, for income-based JSA purposes, in regs 51–53 of the JSA Regulations, which are in similar—though not identical—terms. Since the introduction of JSA on October 7, 1996, the principal rule has been that a claimant (and, where relevant, a non-dependant or a child or young person) is in remunerative work if s/he works for not less than 16 hours a week and the claimant's partner is in remunerative work if s/he works for not less than 24 hours a week (except in those cases where the couple is obliged to make a joint claim for JSA, in which case the 16-hour rule applies to both members because both are claimants). Where the hours of work fluctuate, an average is taken using the rules in para.(2).

2.69   In cases (other than joint-claim JSA cases) where the claimant's partner is working between 16 and 24 hours a week, it may be possible for the couple to claim both working tax credit (see Vol.IV) and income support or income-based JSA. In such cases, there is an automatic entitlement to maximum WTC but the claimant's income-based JSA will be reduced pound for pound by the WTC that is paid.

Because income support is normally paid in arrears, the disentitlement applies immediately a person starts remunerative work, regardless of whether wages have been paid or when they will be paid. This situation is specifically mentioned in the Social Fund Guide as one in which a crisis loan might be payable if no other resources are available. The details of the test are therefore important. Note the exceptions in reg.6, brought in by para.(6).

Para. (1)

2.70   First note that the test is in terms of work, not employment. Therefore, the precise categorisation of the activities carried out may not be crucial. This is illustrated in two family credit decisions (remunerative work is a qualification for family credit). In *CFC 7/1989* the claimant's husband was working in connection with

Moral Re-Armament, a Christian charity, for about 38 hours a week. He received payment by persuading individuals to covenant income to him. He was not employed by Moral Re-Armament or the covenantors, nor did he contract with them on a self-employed basis. But this did not matter, because what he did was undoubtedly work and he was paid for it. In *R(FC) 2/90* both the claimant and her husband were officers of the Salvation Army. It was accepted, following the decision of the Court of Appeal in *Rogers v Booth* [1937] 2 All E.R. 751, that the relationship of officers to the Salvation Army is spiritual, not contractual. Nevertheless, the onerous duties of officers were "work."

Remunerative

Work is remunerative if payment is made for it, or it is done in the expectation of payment. There is a significant difference from the common law test (on which see *R(FIS) 1/83*), because the mere hope of or desire for payment is not the same as expectation (although note that in *R(IS) 13/99* the Commissioner comments that he did not see any fundamental distinction between "hope of" and "expectation of" payment). Thus in *CFC 3/1989*, the claimant's husband, who regarded himself as a self-employed writer, but who had not sold any manuscripts and did not anticipate any sales in the next six months, was not in remunerative work. The Commissioner puts forward a rule of thumb, not a binding principle, that for work to be done in the expectation of payment some payment must be expected within 26 weeks of the relevant date. This was based partly on the length of a family credit award, but there clearly should be one dividing line between the income support and family credit systems. In *R(IS) 1/93* the Commissioner holds that the guiding principle on when there is an expectation of payment should be common sense and an appreciation of the realities of the situation. The claimant, another writer, had sent several works to publishers, but had had negligible success in selling anything. She was working "on spec," with only the hope of payment, not an expectation. In *Kevin Smith v Chief Adjudication Officer (R(IS) 21/95)* the claimant's partner, who was in receipt of an enterprise allowance, wished to establish herself as an agent for pop groups and spent a lot of time building up contacts in the pop music world. The Court of Appeal, having said that the question is really one of fact, distinguishes between work done to set up a business, which is not done in expectation of payment, and work carried out once the business is established, which it would be reasonable to infer was done in expectation of payment. On the facts of that case the claimant's partner was not engaged in remunerative work. On the other side of the line, see *CIS 434/1994* in which a person who had started an estate agent's business and was working without pay until the business became profitable was held to be in remunerative work. In *CIS 929/1995* the two or three hours a freelance musician spent practising each day did not count as hours of work for the purposes of reg.5(1).

In *R(IS) 22/95* the claimant's wife worked in a general shop owned by the two of them. For several months she had worked without pay and had no expectation of receiving any in the future because the business was making a loss. The Commissioner holds that the SSAT had been correct in concluding that on the facts she was not in remunerative work. This decision was upheld by the Court of Appeal in *Chief Adjudication Officer v Ellis* (reported as part of *R(IS) 22/95*). In *Ellis* the Court gives some general guidance on the questions to be considered when deciding whether a person is in remunerative work. In particular, the Court draws a distinction between a person providing a service (such as the claimant carrying on a translation agency in *Perrot v SBC* [1980] 3 All E.R. 110 where the unprofitability of her business was irrelevant) and the position of a retail shop. The Court points out that the price paid for goods sold in a shop is not payment for the work of the salesman, but the price of the goods sold. Thus simply carrying on a retail business did not necessarily mean that a person was in remunerative work (so *CSIS 39/1994* should not be followed on this point). But if the person was not expecting to make any money the question had to be asked why the shop was being kept open. In this

2.71

case the answer was clear. The claimant's wife was carrying on the business in the hope of disposing of the goodwill. She was not in remunerative work.

In *R(IS) 5/95* the claimant who was both a director and an employee of a small limited company had also worked for some months without pay, due to financial difficulties. The Commissioner states that it was necessary to consider in relation to each week whether he was working in his capacity as an employee or a director (although the functions of a director of a small private company were quite slight (*R(U) 1/93*, para.5)). If this work had been done as an employee it was only remunerative if any payment expected was in that capacity (although reg.42(6) (notional earnings) would also need to be considered). Moreover expectation of payment meant payment for current work. It may be that this is not the case for the self-employed, although the Court of Appeal in *Ellis* states that the question of whether work is done in expectation of payment is to be decided at the time the work is done, not at the end of the year or other accounting period.

If a claimant deliberately arranges to work for no remuneration (and therefore has no expectation of payment) then, unsurprisingly, that work does not qualify as remunerative work. In *CTC 626/2001* a husband went into partnership with his wife. He worked 30 hours a week in the partnership business and she worked six. However, in order to save income tax the partners agreed that 100 per cent of the profits was allocated to the wife leaving the husband with no income from the business. The Commissioner upheld the decision of the tribunal that there was no entitlement to WFTC: the wife was in remunerative work but for less than 16 hours a week and the husband, though he worked far more than 16 hours a week, was not in remunerative work at all. As *CTC 626/2001* related to a tax credit the conclusion that the husband was not in remunerative work was to his disadvantage. However, one logical consequence of the decision is the possibility that a similar arrangement could be used by a self-employed claimant who was in fact working for more than 16 hours a week to retain entitlement to IS or income-based JSA. It is suggested that such an arrangement would not in fact be effective because, following the remarks of Millet L.J. in *Ellis*, it would be appropriate in such circumstances "to treat the partnership as a single economic unit just as if it were carried on by a sole trader".

The payment must be in return for the work (*R(FIS) 1/86*), but need not derive from an employer. Thus the payments by covenantors in *CFC 7/1989* (see above) counted. So too did the payments from the Salvation Army in *R(FC) 2/90*, although they were not paid under contract and were aimed at providing for the officers' actual needs. There was a distinction from the maintenance grant paid to a student. Provision for actual needs went beyond mere maintenance. A grant is not in return for work (*R(FIS) 1/86*), so that students and trainees (*R(FIS) 1/83*) will still not be said to be in remunerative work. The argument that enterprise allowance is paid in return for work was rejected by the Court of Appeal in *Kevin Smith v Chief Adjudication Officer* (above). The Court holds that it is a payment to enable people to establish themselves in business, not for work. This conclusion was indicated both by the terms of the enterprise allowance scheme and reg.37(1). If receipt of enterprise allowance by itself meant that a person had to be treated as engaged in remunerative work, the inclusion in reg.37(1) of enterprise allowance as earnings was unnecessary since the calculation stage envisaged by reg.37 would never be reached.

A payment in kind will count in the same way as a payment in cash. In *CFC 33/1993* the provision of rent-free accommodation and the payment of gas and electricity bills meant that the claimant's work was done for payment.

Engaged in work

2.72   It is hours during which the person is engaged in work and is paid (or at least expects payment) which are crucial. The calculation is usually relatively easy for employees. Thus in *CIS 3/1989* the claimant's paid one hour lunch break did not count towards the limit. He was not "engaged in" work for that hour. The precise result is reversed from April 1990, by para.(7), but the principle might apply in other situations. *R(FC) 1/92* suggests that where the nature of the job requires a person to work beyond the contractually specified hours, the longer hours count. But it is not clear just how this translates from the old family credit provision to income support. For the self-employed the test is not of hours costed and charged to a client, but of hours of activities which are essential to the undertaking (*R(FIS) 6/85*). Thus time spent in preparation, research, doing estimates and accounts, travel for the purposes of the undertaking, keeping a shop open, etc., must all count. But activities carried on merely in the hope, rather than expectation, of payment are not remunerative. The actual hours of work must be considered. In *R(IS) 22/95*, although the shop in which the claimant's wife worked was open from 8.30am to 6.30pm Monday to Friday, she only spent three hours a day in it. The rest of the time she was in her home (which was in the same premises), ready to go into the shop if the shop bell rang. The Commissioner expresses the view (without finally deciding the point) that on the particular facts of that case (a small shop with little stock and fewer customers) the hours "on call" may not be hours of work. The decision in *R(IS) 22/95* was upheld by the Court of Appeal in *Chief Adjudication Officer v Ellis* (see above), but the Court of Appeal does not deal with this particular point. But in *R(IS) 13/99* the same Commissioner decides that the time spent by a self-employed minicab driver waiting at the cab office for potential customers (which he was not obliged to do) was work done in expectation of payment. This seems somewhat dubious, in that it was not essential to his work for him to spend that time there. However, the decision was upheld by the Court of Appeal (*Kazantzis v Chief Adjudication Officer*, reported as part of *R(IS) 13/ 99*). In *R(IS) 12/95* all the hours that a share fisherman was at sea (including those that he was not on watch or was sleeping) counted. The Commissioner referred to *Suffolk County Council v Secretary of State for the Environment and another* [1984] I.C.R. 882 in which the House of Lords had distinguished between a regular fireman required to remain in the station while on duty and a retained fireman free to do as he pleases until called upon. The claimant could not do as he pleased during his rest period. He had to stay on the trawler and could be summoned to assist if, for example, there was a storm. In the *Suffolk* case the House of Lords held that a retained fireman's waiting time could not be taken into account in calculating his contractual hours of employment. The claimant in *R(IS) 13/99* had attempted to rely on this decision but the Commissioner points out that the circumstances were not analogous. The issue under para.(1) was not whether the claimant was employed during his waiting time but whether he was "at work" during that time.

CIS 514/1990 holds that although recipients of enterprise allowance must undertake to work for at least 36 hours a week in their business, that does not mean that they must automatically be treated as doing so for benefit purposes (see *Kevin Smith v Chief Adjudication Officer* (*R(IS) 21/95*)) above on whether enterprise allowance is paid in return for work).

Paras (2) to (3A)

Where a person works a fixed number of hours, week in, week out, there is no difficulty in applying the weekly limits in para.(1) to his or her claim. But what if a person does not work the same hours each week? What, indeed, if there are some weeks in which s/he does no work at all? This is the problem addressed by paras (2) to (3A) and also, for those who work in schools or other places of education and who wish to claim income support (but not JSA) during school holidays, by para.(3B) (see the note on "Term-time only workers" below).

Although these provisions (and those that preceded them) have been the subject of a considerable number of Commissioners' decisions, consideration of paras (2) to (3A) must now begin with the decision of the Tribunal of Commissioners in *R(JSA) 5/03*, dealing with the equivalent provisions of regs 51 and 52 of the JSA Regulations. The appeals before the Tribunal of Commissioners concerned people who were employees and the principles laid down in its decision must be seen in that context. Other considerations may be relevant in cases where the claimant is "self-employed" (see below).

2.73

The Tribunal's starting point was that:

"11. Defining 'remunerative work' as being work in which someone is engaged for not less than 16 hours a week (24 hours in the case of a claimant's partner) is simple enough. But how do you arrive at the appropriate number of hours when the working hours fluctuate? And how do you deal with those periods during most people's working year, when for some reason or other they are absent from work (and, therefore, not engaged in work at all)?

12. The first step in any analysis is to recognise that periods when a person does no work fall into various categories. Consideration of regulations 51(2) and 52(1) suggests that the relevant categories are:

    (a) periods during which someone is without work because he or she is between jobs,

    (b) periods of no work (other than holidays) during which someone is without work because work is not provided by his or her employer,

    (c) periods during which someone can properly be regarded as being on holiday,

    (d) periods of absence due to sickness and maternity leave.

    (e) periods of unauthorised absence 'without good cause'.

In these appeals, we are not concerned with periods of absence due to sickness or maternity leave, but it is apparent from the terms of regulation 52(1) that a person who is otherwise in remunerative work ceases temporarily to be so engaged during such absences. We are also not concerned with periods of absence without good cause, but it is equally apparent that such absences are to be treated in the same way as holidays."

The Tribunal's approach to those issues was to look first at whether the person's employment had ended. In doing so, "regard should be had to reality" (para.25) and not just to the formal legal position:

"22. In our view, the approach taken by decision-makers should be as follows. Where a contract of employment comes to an end at the beginning of what would be a period of absence from work even if the contract continued, the person should be taken still to be in employment if is expected that he or she will resume employment after that period, either because there is some express arrangement, though not necessarily an enforceable contract, or because it is reasonable to assume that a long standing practice of re-employment will continue."

If it is determined that the person is no longer in employment then no question of remunerative work arises. If, on the other hand, the employment relationship is—as a matter of reality—still subsisting, it becomes necessary to decide whether the person is absent from work due to a holiday or for some other reason. This issue is to be decided on the basis that a person is on holiday during those periods of absence for which they are entitled to be paid—either by contract or, from October 1, 1998, under the Working Time Regulations 1998.

The Tribunal continues:

"28. Applying regulation 51(2) [i.e., of the JSA Regulations—equivalent to reg.5(2) of the IS Regulations] is relatively straightforward once it has been established that a person is still engaged in employment and his or her entitlement to holidays has been ascertained. If he works the same number of hours each week when not on holiday, that is the number of hours to be taken into account for the purpose of regulation 51(1). If the number of hours fluctuates, an average is taken. How the average is calculated when there is no cycle of work is determined under regulation 51(2)(b)(ii) [or reg.5(2)(b)(ii)] which allows some discretion as to the period over which the average is to be calculated. Regulation 51(2)(b)(i) [or reg.5(2)(b)(i)] makes more specific provision in a case where there is a recognisable cycle of work."

Specifically, when there is a recognisable cycle of work of one year the requirement in reg.51(2)(b)(i) [or 5(2)(b)(i)] to calculate the average taking into account "periods in which the person does no work . . . but disregarding other absences" means:

"dividing the total number of hours worked . . . by 52 less the number of weeks of holiday to which the particular claimant is entitled. The result determines whether the person concerned is in remunerative work or not for the whole period of the cycle *(R(IS) 8/95)* so that it is not necessary where there is a cycle to attribute the holiday entitlement to any particular weeks."

The same approach should presumably be adopted to established cycles of work of less than 52 weeks but which include periods in which the person does no work.

On that basis, unpaid "holidays" are "periods in which the person does no work" for the purposes of reg.51(2)(b)(i) [reg.5(2)(b)(i)] and paid holidays and periods of absence through sickness etc. are "other absences". In cases which pre-date the Working Time Regulations 1998—or to which those Regulations do not apply, see for example *CJSA/4764/2002*—in which the employee has no holiday entitlement, neither the fact that payment of their salary may be spread over the year in equal monthly instalments nor the fact that the rate at which they are paid has been enhanced to reflect the absence of any formal holiday entitlement alters the position that there is no holiday entitlement (although the latter circumstance is relevant to the issue of the claimant's earnings (see para.42)).

In consequence, the Tribunal of Commissioners held that the reasoning in (though not the result of) *R(IS) 15/94* was incorrect and that *R(IS) 7/96* which had followed that reasoning was wrongly decided and should no longer be followed.

Term-time only workers—para.(3B)

For JSA the position of those who only work during term-time is governed by reg.51(2)(a) and (b) of the JSA Regulations as interpreted by the decision of the Tribunal of Commissioners in *R(JSA) 5/03*. This is because, in *R(JSA) 4/03*, reg.51(2)(c) of the JSA Regulations was held by the same Tribunal to be of no legal effect because it discriminated indirectly against women and could not be objectively justified by reference to factors other than sex. It was therefore inconsistent with EC Directive 79/7/EEC (see Vol.III). However, unlike JSA, income support is not within the material scope of that Directive because it provides protection against poverty rather than against any of the risks listed in Art.3 of the Directive—see C.-63/91 and C.-64/91 *Jackson and Cresswell v Chief Adjudication Officer* [1992] E.C.R. I-4737 (also reported as an appendix to *R(IS) 10/91*). Therefore reg.5(3B) of the income support Regulations (equivalent to reg.52(2)(c)) is unaffected by the decision in *R(JSA) 4/03* and needs to be applied.

In the past the application of reg.5 to term-time-only workers has been a matter of acute controversy and readers are referred to the more detailed historical note at pp.213-219 of Vol.II of the 2000 edition. The law as it relates to income support has, however, now been settled by the decision of the House of Lords in *Chief Adjudication Officer v Stafford and Banks* [2001] UKHL 33, HL, June 28, 2001 (also reported as *R(IS) 5/01*).

The issue in *Stafford and Banks* may conveniently be illustrated using the facts of Mr Banks' appeal. He was employed as an assistant for children with special needs at a junior school. During the 38 weeks of term time each year, he worked a regular 20 hour week but during the 14 weeks of the school holidays he did not work at all and was not paid. He had a continuing contract of employment with the same employer and all parties approached the case on the basis that he had a recognisable cycle of work of one year including both term-time and school holidays. It was common ground that in these circumstances, the combined effect of para.(2)(b)(i) and (3B) (which had been introduced to reverse the effect of the decision in *R(IS) 15/94*) was to average Mr Banks' working hours across the cycle but that school holidays had to be disregarded when calculating that average. The effect was that Mr Banks' hours were averaged over term-time only and were accordingly 20 hours

2.74

a week (20 × 38 ÷ 38) rather than 14.6 hours per week (20 × 38 ÷ 52) which would have been the case if they had been averaged over the whole year including school holidays.

Up to this point, there was no dispute. What divided the parties and the House of Lords was whether or not—in addition to this averaging process—*the two paragraphs also had the effect of treating Mr Banks as being engaged in remunerative work during the 14 weeks of school holiday when he was not actually working*. In other words, was it possible for Mr Banks to say that he was not engaged in remunerative work at all during those weeks in the cycle which had not been included in the calculation of his average hours?

2.75   The majority of the House of Lords (Lord Slynn, Hope and Millet) held that it was not. The disregard in para.(3B) only applied to the calculation of the average number of hours and did not alter the length of the cycle of work. The decision as to whether or not the claimant was engaged in remunerative work was to be applied to the full period of the cycle. The decision is, perhaps, best summarised in the judgment of Lord Millet (at paras 63 and 65):

". . . To my mind the critical point is that paras (2)(b)(i) is not replaced by paragraph (3B) but merely made subject to it. Paragraph 2(b) remains in full force save only to the extent to which it is modified by paragraph (3B). The two paragraphs must be read together. They are both concerned with persons who have a regular cycle of work. Neither of them is concerned with the question when a person is to be treated as being engaged in work, but only with the determination of the average number of hours for which he is engaged in work for the purpose of determining whether the work (in which ex hypothesi he must be treated as being engaged) is remunerative work. Paragraph 2(b)(i) directs that the average number of hours is to be determined by reference to a complete cycle including periods during which he does no work, and there is nothing in paragraph (3B) which modifies this. It does not affect the duration of the cycle or exclude periods during which he does no work. In the case of the present claimant, therefore, the cycle of work remains the complete year . . . and the claimant continues to be treated (by paragraph (2)(b)(i)) as engaged in work throughout the cycle including periods when he does no work. Paragraph (3B) directs that the school holidays are to be disregarded, not for the purpose of determining when a person is to be treated as engaged in work, but merely for the purpose of establishing the average number of hours worked during the cycle."

In the circumstances, the decision of the Commissioner in *CSJSA/395/1998* must be followed in preference to the decisions in *CIS/1118/1997, CIS/3216/1997* and *CJSA/3218/1997* which had held (with Lord Cooke who dissented in *Stafford and Banks*) that para.(3B) restricted the weeks during which a claimant is treated as engaged in remunerative work to those which were included in the averaging calculation. Similarly, the persuasive dissent of Lord Scott (who would have held that neither para.(2) nor para.(3B) had the effect of treating a claimant as being engaged in remunerative work when he was not actually working) cannot be taken as representing the law.

2.76   The decision of the majority in *Stafford and Banks* considerably narrows the scope for further dispute about the benefit entitlements of term-time only workers. However, it should be noted that para.(3B) (and hence the *Stafford and Banks* ruling) only applies if it is first established that there is a "recognisable cycle of work". In three appeals decided since the decision of the House of Lords in *Stafford and Banks* (*CIS/914/1997, CJSA/2759/1998* and *CJSA/1772/2002*), Mr Commissioner Rowland held that such a cycle had not been established. The Commissioner pointed out that where a person is employed on a casual or relief basis "it may be clear that [he or she] will not work during school holidays *but it may not be clear that he or she will work during the whole of the terms* and for that reason a cycle may not be established" (emphasis added). There may come a time when a pattern of regular employment in practice will establish an annual cycle but in *CIS/914/1997* the Commissioner refused to accept that this had occurred when the claimant had only worked for part of a year before claiming benefit and in *CJSA/2759/1998* he expressed the view that establishing a cycle in practice "is likely to require the completion of two cycles".

It should also be noted that in *Stafford and Banks*, the House of Lords was dealing with a case in which it was not disputed that the employment relationship between the claimant and his employer continued to exist over the holiday period. This issue must now be approached in accordance with *R(JSA) 5/03* (above), *i.e.* by having regard to the reality of the position rather than a strict analysis of the status of the contract of employment. Even so, there may be cases in which it will not be reasonable to expect that the person will resume employment. In such cases, any recognisable cycle of work that may have been established will be broken with the effect that *Stafford and Banks* no longer applies.

Self-employment

In the case of a self-employed worker who has periods of work interspersed with periods of no work the position is less clear. Para.(1) does not state what is the appropriate period to look at when determining whether a person is engaged in remunerative work. Each case will therefore depend to some extent on its own facts. If, for example, a person carries on a business for six months of the year and does no work in connection with that business for the rest of the year, it must be arguable that the period to be looked at is the six months when his business is dormant and that during that time he is not engaged in work. This is the approach taken in the *Decision Makers Guide*, paras 20151–2. However, this is not the conclusion reached by the Commissioner in *CIS 493/1993*. The claimant ran a guest house with a six-month season and did a minimal amount of work during the closed season. The claimant had argued that there were two cycles, or periods, one in which he worked more than 16 hours every week and the second during which he was not engaged in work at all. The Commissioner states that the first question was whether there was a recognisable cycle, and the second was whether the claimant's hours fluctuated within that cycle. The basis of this approach seems to have been that para.(2) is to be used to determine the number of hours for which a person is engaged in work. But para.(2) does not provide a rule for deciding the number of hours worked per week in all cases. It applies in the circumstances described in the opening words of sub-paras (a) and (b) (*R(IS) 8/95*). It is suggested that the first question is what is the appropriate period for deciding whether a claimant is engaged in remunerative work, which will depend on the facts of each case, before going on to consider whether the particular circumstances referred to in para.(2) apply. Note that para.(3B) would not seem to apply to the self-employed. 2.77

Para.(4)

See the notes to s.126 of the Contributions and Benefits Act (1986 Act, s.23). 2.78

Para.(5)

Where income payments in lieu of notice or remuneration are paid or (within four weeks of termination) holiday pay, the person is treated as in remunerative work for the period covered. See regs 29 and 31. 2.79

Para.(7)

Paid meal or refreshment breaks count in the calculation of the hours for which a person is engaged in work. 2.80

Persons not treated as engaged in remunerative work

6. [[10]—(1)] A person shall not be treated as engaged in [[2] remunerative work in so far as—] 2.81

[³(a) [¹². . .]]
  (b) he is engaged in child minding in his home;
  (c) he is engaged by a charity or [⁷voluntary organisation [⁸—],] or is a volunteer where the only payment received by him or due to be paid to him, is a payment which is to be disregarded under regulation 40(2) and paragraph 2 of Schedule 9 (sums to be disregarded in the calculation of income other than earnings);
  (d) he is engaged on a scheme for which a training allowance is being paid; [⁴. . .]
[¹⁵(dd) he is receiving assistance under the self-employment route;]
  (e) [¹². . .]
[⁹(f) [¹². . .]]
[⁶(g) [¹². . .]]
[⁴(h) he is engaged in any one of the employments mentioned in heads (a) to (d) of sub-paragraph (1) of paragraph 7 of Schedule 8 (which relates to persons serving as firemen, in coastal rescue activities etc); [⁵. . .]
  (j) he is performing his duties as a councillor, and for this purpose "councillor" has the same meaning as in [¹²section 171F(2) of the Contributions and Benefits Act];] [⁵ or
  (k) he is engaged in caring for a person who is accommodated with him by virtue of arrangements made under any of the provisions referred to in paragraph 26 [⁷ or in accordance with paragraph 27] of Schedule 9 (sums to be disregarded in the calculation of income other than earnings) and is in receipt of any payment specified in [⁷those paragraphs].]
  (l) [*Omitted*]
[¹⁰ (m) he is engaged in an activity in respect of which—
    (i) a sports award has been made, or is to be made, to him; and
    (ii) no other payment is made or is expected to be made to him]
  [¹] [¹⁶. . .]
[¹² (4) The following persons shall not be treated as engaged in remunerative work—
  (a) a person who is mentally or physically disabled and by reason of that disability—
    (i) his earnings are reduced to 75 per cent, or less of what a person without that disability and working the same number of hours would reasonably be expected to earn in that employment or in comparable employment in the area; or
    (ii) his number of hours of work are 75 per cent, or less of what a person without that disability would reasonably be expected to undertake in that employment or in comparable employment in the area;
  (b) subject to regulation 5(4) and (5) (persons treated as engaged in remunerative work), a person to whom section 126 of the Contributions and Benefits Act (trade disputes) applies or in respect of whom section 124(1) of that Act (conditions of entitlement to income support) has effect as modified by section 127(b) of that Act (effect of return to work);
  (c) a person to whom paragraph 4 of Schedule 1B applies;
[¹⁴(d) a person who is in employment, who lives in, or is temporarily absent from, a residential care home, a nursing home or residential

accommodation and who requires personal care by reason of old age, disablement, past or present dependence on alcohol or drugs, past or present mental disorder or a terminal illness.]]

[[13]](5) A person shall not be treated as engaged in remunerative work for the period specified in paragraph (6) in so far as—

  (a) he or his partner is engaged in work which—

    (i) is remunerative work; and

    (ii) he, or his partner, is expected to be engaged in remunerative work for a period of no less than five weeks;

  (b) he or his partner had, for a continuous period of 26 weeks ending on the day before the day on which he commenced the work referred to in sub-paragraph (a), been entitled to and in receipt of income support or an income-based jobseeker's allowance;

  (c) he or his partner had, as at the day before the day on which he commenced the work referred to in sub-paragraph (a), an applicable amount which included—

    (i) an amount determined in accordance with Schedule 3 (housing costs) as applicable to him in respect of a loan which qualifies under paragraph 15 or 16 of that Schedule; or

    (ii) an amount determined in accordance with Schedule 2 to the Jobseeker's Allowance Regulations 1996 (housing costs) as applicable to him in respect of a loan which qualifies under paragraph 14 or 15 of that Schedule; and

  (d) he or his partner remain liable to make payments on such a loan.

(6) A person referred to in paragraph (5) shall not be treated as engaged in remunerative work for—

  (a) the period of four weeks commencing with the day on which he was first engaged in the work referred to in sub-paragraph (a) of that paragraph; [[16]. . .]

(7) In calculating the period of benefit entitlement referred to in paragraph [[16]. . .] (5)(b), no account shall be taken of entitlement arising by virtue of paragraph [[16]. . .] (6).

(8) In paragraph (5), a reference to the claimant or his partner being entitled to and in receipt of an income-based jobseeker's allowance or to an amount being applicable to either of them under the Jobseeker's Allowance Regulations 1996 shall include a reference to the claimant and his partner being entitled to, and in receipt of, a joint-claim jobseeker's allowance and to an amount being applicable to that couple under those Regulations.]

AMENDMENTS

1. Income Support (General) Amendment Regulations 1988 (SI 1988/663), reg.5 (April 11, 1988).   **2.82**

2. Income Support (General) Amendment No.4 Regulations 1988 (SI 1988/1445), reg.4 (September 12, 1988).

3. Income Support (General) Amendment No.4 Regulations 1991 (SI 1991/1559), reg.4 (October 7, 1991).

4. Income Support (General) Amendment Regulations 1992 (SI 1992/468), reg.2 (April 6, 1992).

5. Income-related Benefits Schemes (Miscellaneous Amendments) (No.3) Regulations 1992 (SI 1992/2155), reg.13 (October 5, 1992).

6. Social Security Benefits (Miscellaneous Amendments) Regulations 1993 (SI 1993/518), reg.5 (April 1, 1993).

7. Income-related Benefits Schemes (Miscellaneous Amendments) (No.5) Regulations 1994 (SI 1994/2139), reg.23 (October 3, 1994).

8. Income-related Benefits Schemes (Miscellaneous Amendments) Regulations 1995 (SI 1995/516), reg.20 (April 10, 1995).

9. Income Support (General) (Jobseeker's Allowance Consequential Amendments) Regulations 1996 (SI 1996/206), reg.6 (October 7, 1996).

10. Social Security Amendment (Sports Award) Regulations 1999 (SI 1999/2165), reg.6(2) (August 23, 1999)

11. Social Security (Miscellaneous Amendments) (No.2) Regulations 1999 (SI 1999/2556, reg.2(3) (October 4, 1999)

12. Social Security (Miscellaneous Amendments) Regulations 2000 (SI 2000/681), reg.2(b)(i) (April 3, 2000)

13. Social Security (Miscellaneous Amendments) Regulations 2001 (SI 2001/488), reg.4 (April 9, 2001).

14. Social Security Amendment (Residential Care and Nursing Homes) Regulations 2001 (SI 2001/3767), reg.2 and Sch., Pt I, para.2 (April 8, 2002).

15. Social Security (Income-Related Benefits Self-Employment Route Amendment) Regulations 2004 (SI 2004/963), reg.3 (May 4, 2004).

16. Social Security (Back to Work Bonus and Lone Parent Run-on) (Amendment and Revocation) Regulations 2003 (SI 2003/1589), reg.2(a) (October 25, 2004).

DEFINITIONS

"the Act"—see reg.2(1).
"remunerative work"—*ibid.*
"training allowance"—*ibid.*
"voluntary organisation"—*ibid.*

GENERAL NOTE

2.83   These categories must be deemed not to be in remunerative work for the time engaged in these activities, although the "not" could be better placed. The effect is that there is not an automatic exclusion from entitlement under s.124(1)(c) of the Contributions and Benefits Act (1986 Act, s.20(3)(c)). Any earnings from employment must still be taken into account as income. Most of the categories are self-explanatory.

Para.(1)(b) deems a person who is childminding in her own home not to be in remunerative work. However, there is no specific provision in Sch.1B to enable childminders to qualify for income support. If a claimant who is a childminder does not come within any other paragraph of Sch.1B, it may be possible to argue that para.3 applies (looking after a child whose parent is temporarily absent from home). This would be along the lines that a parent who is out at work is absent from home on a temporary basis. Para.3 does not seem to require that the person should be looking after the child all the time; as long as this is done on a regular basis this should suffice.

Under para.(1)(c), para.2 of Sch.9 refers to payments solely of expenses to volunteers or people working for charitable or voluntary bodies. A volunteer is someone who without any legal obligation performs a service for another person without expectation of payment (*R(IS)12/92*).

Under para.(1)(d), training allowances are most commonly paid to people on Work Based Learning for Young People (in Scotland "Skillseekers"), which has replaced Youth Training, Modern Apprenticeships, etc.

Under para (1)(dd) those receiving assistance under the "self-employment route" are treated as not being in remunerative work. See the annotation to the definition of "self-employment route" in reg.2(1) and the General Note to reg.39A.

In addition, reg.2(2)(a) of the New Deal (Lone Parents) (Miscellaneous Provisions) Order 2001 (SI 2001/2915), has the effect that from September 13,

2001, top-up payments made to those participating in the self-employment route of the New Deal for Lone Parents and other payments made to assist with the expenses of such participation are to be treated as a training allowance for the purpose of reg.6(1)(d).

Under para.(1)(j), the definition of "councillor" is—

"(a) in relation to England and Wales, a member of a London borough council, a county council, a district council, a parish or community council, the Common Council of the City of London or the Council of the Isles of Scilly; and

(b) in relation to Scotland, a member of a regional, islands or district council."

Under para.(1)(k) foster-parents who receive statutory payments for fostering, or people receiving payments for providing temporary care in their home, are deemed not to be in remunerative work by reason of those payments.

Para.(1)(m) provides that a person will be deemed not to be in remunerative work while engaged in activity for which the only payment he is, or will be, receiving is a "sports award" (defined in reg.2(1)). See also reg.37(2)(c) which ensures that the sports award is not treated as self-employed earnings. A sports award is disregarded as income other than earnings under para.69 of Sch.9 except to the extent that it has been made for any of the items listed in para.69(2). There is a similar disregard where the sports award counts as capital (see para.56 of Sch.10) but in this case the disregard only applies for 26 weeks from the date of receipt.

Paras (2) and (3) *Lone-parent run-on*: The "lone-parent run-on" previously estab‑ **2.84** lished by these paras was abolished on October 25, 2004. For details of the former run-on see p.262 of Vol. II of the 2004 edition.

Para.(4) *Disabled workers*: See *CIS/1657/2004* (to be reported as *R(IS) 10/05* and the note to para.8 of Sch.1B.

Paras (5) to (8) *Mortgage interest run-on*: under paras (5) to (8), some claimants who have been receiving IS or JSA housing costs are treated as not in remunerative work (and hence still entitled to IS) for the first four weeks of full-time work (*i.e.*, 16 hours for the claimant or 24 for the claimant's partner—see reg.5(1) and (1A)). Before October 25, 2004, those claimants who qualified for the "lone-parent run-on" under the former paras (2) and (3) were potentially entitled to the mortgage interest run-on for two weeks after the end of the two week lone-parent run-on period (under para.6(b)). However, with the abolition of the lone-parent run-on, para.(6)(b) was revoked, so that in all cases the mortgage interest run-on now lasts for the four week period specified in para.(6)(a). To qualify, a claimant (or her/his partner) must have been in receipt of IS or income-based JSA for a continuous period of 26 weeks (not including any earlier run-on periods—see para.(7)) ending on the day before the commencement of full-time work and must have been entitled to housing costs for mortgage interest or interest on a home improvement loan on that day. In addition, the full-time work must be expected to last for a period of at least five weeks.

During the run-on period, IS is paid at the lower of the weekly amount of housing costs which was payable immediately before the claimant or her/his partner com‑menced full-time work or the rate of IS or income-based JSA which was being paid (or would have been paid but for the receipt of a training allowance) in the benefit week before full-time work commenced (see para.19A of Sch.7).

Under para.9A of Sch.1B a person to whom para.(5) applies is in a prescribed category and therefore eligible for IS even if they were previously receiving JSA.

Meaning of employment

7.—[¹. . .]   **2.85**

AMENDMENT

1. Income Support (General) (Jobseeker's Allowance Consequential Amendments) Regulations 1996 (SI 1996/206), reg.28 and Sch.3 (October 7, 1996).

Persons not required to be available for employment

2.86   **8.**—[¹...]

AMENDMENT

1. Income Support (General) (Jobseeker's Allowance Consequential Amendments) Regulations 1996 (SI 1996/206), reg.28 and Sch.3 (October 7, 1996).

Persons treated as available for employment

2.87   **9.**—[¹...]

AMENDMENT

1. Income Support (General) (Jobseeker's Allowance Consequential Amendments) Regulations 1996 (SI 1996/206), reg.28 and Sch.3 (October 7, 1996).

Circumstances in which claimants are not to be treated as available for employment

2.88   **10.**—[¹...]

AMENDMENT

1. Income Support (General) (Jobseeker's Allowance Consequential Amendments) Regulations 1996 (SI 1996/206), reg.28 and Sch.3 (October 7, 1996).

[¹Actively seeking employment

2.89   **10A.**—[²...]

AMENDMENTS

1. Income Support (General) Amendment No.2 Regulations 1989 (SI 1989/1323), reg.6 (October 9, 1989).
2. Income Support (General) (Jobseeker's Allowance Consequential Amendments) Regulations 1996 (SI 1996/206), reg.28 and Sch.3 (October 7, 1996).

Registration for employment

2.90   **11.**—[¹...]

AMENDMENT

1. Income Support (General) (Jobseeker's Allowance Consequential Amendments) Regulations 1996 (SI 1996/206), reg.28 and Sch.3 (October 7, 1996).

[¹Relevant Education

2.91   **12.**—(1) For the purposes of these Regulations a child or young person is to be treated as receiving relevant education if, and only if—
    (a) he is not receiving advanced education; but
    (b) he is receiving full-time education for the purposes of section 2 of the Child Benefit Act 1975 [SSCBA, s.142] (meaning of child) or, as the case may be, he is treated as a child for the purposes of that section.

(2) For the purposes of this regulation "receiving advanced education" means participating in any course (whether full-time or part-time)—

(a) leading to a postgraduate degree or comparable qualification, a first degree or comparable qualification, a diploma of higher education, a higher national diploma, [²a higher national certificate] or a teaching qualification; or

[²(b) any other course which is a course of a standard above advanced GNVQ or equivalent, including a course which is of a standard above a general certificate of education (advanced level) or a Scottish national qualification (higher or advanced higher).]]

AMENDMENTS

1. Income Support (General) Amendment Regulations 1990 (SI 1990/547), reg.5 (April 9, 1990).

2. Social Security (Miscellaneous Amendments) (No. 3) Regulations 2004 (SI 2004/2308), reg.5(1) (October 4, 2004).

2.92

DEFINITIONS

"child"—see 1986 Act, s.20(11) (SSCBA, s.137(1)).
"young person"—see regs 2(1) and 14.

GENERAL NOTE

The general rule under s.124(1)(d) of the Contributions and Benefits Act is that if a claimant is receiving relevant education he is not entitled to income support. Regulation 12 provides an exhaustive test of when a person is to be treated as receiving relevant education. The 1990 formulation is a tidying-up. Note that only a child or young person can qualify and that relevant education does not include a course of advanced education. There is a reference over to the child benefit legislation and the reg.12 question is one to which the assumption in reg.13(2) of the Decisions and Appeals Regulations 1999 (see Vol.III of this series) applies. If the Secretary of State considers that he does not have all the relevant information or evidence to decide whether the person should count as in relevant education, he will proceed on the basis that the child benefit decision would be adverse to the claimant in the income support sense.

See on the child benefit test, regs 5 to 11 of the Child Benefit (General) Regulations 2003 (SI 2003/493) (which revoke and replace the Child Benefit (General) Regulations 1976) in Vol.I of this series. Contact hours of at least 12 per week are required. See *R(F) 1/93* in which the Commissioner held that supervised study (in reg.5 of the Child Benefit Regulations 1976) "would normally be understood to import the presence or close proximity of a teacher or tutor". A different approach is taken in *Flemming v Secretary of State for Work and Pensions* [2002] EWCA Civ 641, Court of Appeal, May 10, 2002 (agreeing with the Northern Ireland Court of Appeal's decision in *Bronwyn Wright-Turner v Department of Social Development* (January 11, 2002, unreported)) in relation to the similar provision in reg.5 of the Invalid Care Regulations 1976 (see Vol.I of this series) but note that this was in a different context, namely that of full-time university education. Relevant education continues through temporary interruptions, like school holidays. When a person ceases actually to receive relevant education he is treated as doing so (unless he is in remunerative work of 24 hours or more a week and in certain other circumstances) until the next terminal date after he reaches compulsory school leaving age, or after he leaves relevant education if he stays on beyond compulsory school leaving age, or until he reaches 19 if this is earlier. The terminal date is the Sunday after the first Monday in January, the first Monday after Easter Monday, or the first Monday in September. For England and Wales (but not Scotland) there is now a single school leaving date: the last Friday in June in the school year in which the child's 16th birthday falls (see the Education (School Leaving Date) Order (SI 1997/1970)). Thus in 2005 children

2.93

in England and Wales who reach 16 before September 1, 2005 can leave school on Friday, June 24, 2005; their terminal date will be Sunday, September 11, 2005 and they count as being in relevant education until that date (unless the exceptions apply). For a child who stays on beyond compulsory school leaving age the three terminal dates are still applicable. There is also the possibility of a person remaining a "child" for an extension period of 12 weeks beyond the terminal date (or 16 weeks if the terminal date is the Sunday after the first Monday in September) if he is under 18, registered for work or training, not in remunerative work of 24 hours or more a week, not in receipt of income support/income-based JSA in his own right and not on Work Based Learning for Young People. In England and Wales for a child whose school leaving date is June 24, 2005 the extension period will be September 12, 2005 to January 1, 2006.

Note that reg.13 allows certain claimants to receive income support though in relevant education.

Circumstances in which persons in relevant education may be entitled to income support

2.94   **13.**—(1) Notwithstanding that a person is to be treated as receiving relevant education under regulation 12 (relevant education) he shall, if paragraph (2) applies to him and he satisfies the other conditions of entitlement to income support, be entitled to income support.

(2) This paragraph applies to [³a person aged 16 or over but under 19 (hereinafter referred to as an eligible person)] who—

(a) is the parent of a child for whom he is treated as responsible under regulation 15 (circumstances in which a person is to be treated as responsible or not responsible for another) and who is treated as a member of his household under regulation 16 (circumstances in which a person is to be treated as being or not being a member of the household); or

(b) is severely mentally or physically handicapped and because of that he would be unlikely, even if he were available for employment, to obtain employment within the next 12 months; or

(c) has no parent nor any person acting in the place of his parents; or

[¹(d) of necessity has to live away from his [²parents and any] person acting in the place of his parents because—

   (i) he is estranged from his [²parents and that person]; or
   (ii) he is in physical or moral danger; or
   (iii) there is a serious risk to his physical or mental health;] or

[⁴(dd) has ceased to live in accommodation provided for him by a local authority under Part III of the Children Act 1989 (local authority support for children and families) and is of necessity living away from his parents and any person acting in place of his parents;]

(e) is living away from his parents and any person acting in the place of his parents in a case where his parents are or, as the case may be, that person is unable financially to support him and—

   (i) chronically sick or mentally or physically disabled; or
   (ii) detained in custody pending trial or sentence upon conviction or under a sentence imposed by a court; or
   (iii) prohibited from entering or re-entering Great Britain; or

(f) [⁶. . .]

(g) [⁶. . .]

[⁶(h) is a person to whom paragraph 18 of Schedule 1B (refugees) applies.]

(3) In this regulation—

[⁵(a) any reference to a person acting in the place of an eligible person's parents includes—

    (i) for the purposes of paragraph (2)(c), (d) and (dd), a reference to a local authority or voluntary organisation where the eligible person is being looked after by them under a relevant enactment or where the eligible person is placed by the local authority or voluntary organisation with another person, that other person whether or not a payment is made to him;

    (ii) for the purposes of paragraph (2)(e), the person with whom the person is so placed;]

  (b) "chronically sick or mentally disabled" means, in relation to a person to whom that expression refers, a person—

    (i) in respect of whom the condition specified in paragraph 12(1) of Schedule 2 (additional condition for the higher pensioner and disability premiums) is satisfied; or

    (ii) in respect of whom an amount under article 26 of the Naval, Military and Air Forces etc. (Disablement and Death) Services Pension Order 1983 (provision of expenses in respect of appropriate aids for disabled living) is payable in respect of the cost of providing a vehicle, or maintaining a vehicle to a disabled person; or

    (iii) who is substantially and permanently disabled.

AMENDMENTS

1. Family Credit and Income Support (General) Amendment Regulations 1989 (SI 1989/1034), reg.4 (July 10, 1989).
  2.95

2. Income Support (General) Amendment Regulations 1991 (SI 1991/236), reg.5 (April 8, 1991).

3. Income Support (General) Amendment No. 4 Regulations 1991 (SI 1991/1559), reg.6 August 5, 1991).

4. Income Support (General) Amendment Regulations 1992 (SI 1992/468), reg.3 (April 6, 1992).

5. Income Support (General) Amendment Regulations 1992 (SI 1992/468), Sch. para.2 April 6, 1992).

6. Income Support (General) (Jobseeker's Allowance Consequential Amendments) Regulations 1996 (SI 1996/206), reg.7 (October 7, 1996).

DEFINITIONS

"child"—see 1986 Act, s.20(11) (SSCBA, s.137(1)).
"relevant enactment"—see reg.2(1), reg.16(8)(a).

GENERAL NOTE

In the circumstances set out in para.(2) a claimant, if he satisfies the other conditions of entitlement, is entitled to income support although in relevant education. The regulation can only benefit someone aged from 16 to 18 inclusive. If a claimant satisfies any of para.(2)(a) to (e), he will be eligible for income support under para.15 of Sch.1B. If he comes within para.(2)(h), he will qualify under para.18.
  2.96

Para. (2)

Sub-para. (a): A person of at least 16 who is the parent of a child who is in the same household can claim although in relevant education.
  2.97

Sub-para. (b): Severe mental or physical handicap has no special meaning. Qualification for one of the higher levels of the care component of disability living allowance would certainly do, although the *Decision Makers Guide* requires medical evidence to be provided in support of the claim (paras 20647–20654). See *CIS 632/1994*.

Sub-para. (c): A parent presumably means a natural parent or an adoptive parent. A person acting in place of parents may include some informal relationships, for example, where a child's parents have died and the child is brought up by another member of the family, but see the decisions referred to below. If a person is claiming child benefit in respect of a pupil, this would be a strong factor. However, a sponsor under the Immigration Act 1971 is not a person acting in place of parents. A sponsor's duties are restricted to the maintenance and accommodation of the dependant without recourse to public funds and there is no responsibility for other aspects of the dependant's life (*R(IS) 9/94*).

Para. (3)(a)(i) specifically includes for this purpose local authorities and voluntary organisations who are looking after children (what used to be known as having them in care) under a relevant enactment (defined in reg.16(8)(a)), and foster parents with whom the pupil has been placed by *the* local authority or voluntary organisation. Since head (i) refers to pupils placed by "the", not "a", local authority or voluntary organisation, it would seem that head (i) only applies where the pupil is being looked after by the local authority or voluntary organisation under a relevant enactment. In *CIS 447/1994* the claimant was estranged from his parents. A local authority social worker gave him a list of approved accommodation and he went to lodge at an address on the list. The Commissioner decides that "placed" in the second limb of para. (3)(a)(i) referred to placement under the Children Act. But even if it did not, in the Commissioner's view, providing the claimant with a list of approved accommodation did not constitute "placing" him (even in a non-technical sense) with another person. This did not mean that the second limb was redundant. Its purpose was to make clear that where a claimant had been placed with a person by a local authority, it was estrangement, etc., from that person, not from the local authority, that was relevant. *CIS 11766/1996* concerned the position of a claimant who had continued to live with his ex-foster parents after his care order had ended. The Commissioner follows the approach of *CSB 325/1985* and holds that ex-foster parents cease to be acting in place of parents when their fostering contract comes to an end.

Sub-para. (d): See sub-para. (c) above for the meaning of parent and of person acting in place of a parent. The 1991 amendment to the effect that the pupil must be living away from parents *and* substitutes (and see head (i) on estrangement) was described by the DSS as technical. However, this was a change of substance. The previous form referred to living away from or estrangement from parents *or* substitutes. When the Conditions of Entitlement Regulations were in this form, *CSB 677/1983* decided that the pupil qualified if estranged from his parents even though he was not estranged from a person acting in their place. Now the pupil has to be living away from or estranged from both. See sub-para. (dd) on pupils leaving care.

2.98 *Head (i)*: Estrangement has "connotations of emotional disharmony" (*R(SB) 2/87*) and it seems that it can exist although financial support is being provided. The 1989 form of sub-para. (d) is an attempt to provide a test of "genuine estrangement." It is in some respects stricter than the previous form because in addition to showing estrangement, the person in relevant education must also show that as a result, at least partly, of that he has of necessity to live away from his parents and any substitute. It is obviously a matter of judgment when estrangement is serious enough to necessitate that the young person leaves home. There is perhaps some widening in the addition of two extra categories which may lead to a need to leave home.

CIS 11441/1995 decides that estrangement from a local authority can exist. The claimant, aged 16, was in the care of a local authority but because of her violent and aggressive behaviour in a community home it had been decided that she should live in rented accommodation by herself. She was given help to find suitable accommodation and the authority met her liability for council tax and because income support had been refused provided her with a payment equivalent to her income support entitlement. Her rent was met through housing benefit. The care order remained in place as the claimant wished it to continue for "emotional" reasons. The Commissioner decides that sub-para.(dd) did not apply because the local authority were continuing to provide the claimant with accommodation by supervising and assisting in the arrangements for her rented accommodation (see s.23(2)(f) of the Children Act 1989). But sub-para.(d) did apply. The claimant was "living away" from the local authority because she was living away from the people who represented the authority, *i.e.* the community home (the terms of reg.13 were clearly intended to reverse *R(SB) 2/87* which had held that it was not possible for a person to live away from a local authority). Further it was "necessary" for her to do this because it had been accepted that it was not possible for the claimant to live in a community home or with foster parents. Moreover she was "estranged" from the local authority because she was estranged from the community home where the local authority had placed her. The fact that she continued to have some contact with and received some assistance from the local authority did not alter the fact of the estrangement.

Head (ii): Under head (ii), the meaning of "physical or moral danger" is again a matter of judgment. It is not a term of art with an established meaning. Obvious points are that a person can be in danger from himself or from others and that a danger can exist before any harm has actually occurred (see *Kelly v Monklands District Council* 1986 S.L.T. 169 on the phrase "at risk of sexual or financial exploitation" in the Code of Guidance on Homelessness). Nor is the danger specified to be immediate, but the test will no doubt be whether the danger is sufficient to necessitate living away from parents or their substitute. The danger does not have to emanate from the pupil's parents. In *R(IS) 9/94* the claimant's parents were in a refugee camp in Ethiopia, having fled there after civil war broke out in Somalia. It is held that he had to live away from his parents in view of the situation in Somalia, as otherwise he was in physical or moral danger; in addition, there was a serious risk to his physical or mental health under head (iii).   **2.99**

Head (iii): Under head (iii) there is an echo of the "serious risk to health" test of reg.30 of the Supplementary Benefit (Single Payments) Regulations. There was there some dispute about how closely a tribunal had to define the seriousness of the risk (compare *R(SB) 5/81* and *CSB 11/81* with *R(SB) 3/82* and *R(SB) 8/82*). The nature of the risk must no doubt be identified (as the danger must be under head (ii)) and some reason given why it is serious enough to necessitate living away from parents or their substitute. See *R(IS) 9/94* in the notes to head (ii).   **2.100**

Sub-para. (dd): This provision protects the entitlement of pupils leaving local authority care who need to live away from their parents and any substitute without the necessity of proving estrangement or moral danger or one of the other conditions in sub-para.(d). See the note to sub-para.(c) for the meaning of parent and person acting in place of a parent.

Sub-para. (e): Here the pupil must be living away from both parents and persons acting in place of parents, and they must be unable to provide financial support. The reason for this inability must be one of those listed. See para.(3)(b) for the definition of chronically sick or mentally or physically disabled. See the note to sub-para.(c) for the meaning of parent and person acting in place of a parent.

Head (iii): In *R(IS) 9/94* the claimant's parents who were in a refugee camp in Ethiopia had no leave to enter the UK at the date of the claim. Under s.3 of the

Immigration Act 1971 (subject to certain exceptions) all persons who are not British citizens require leave to enter the UK. The claimant's parents were thus prohibited from entering Great Britain.

Sub-para. (h): This is a special case of refugees.

Para. (3)

2.101   The previous form of sub-para.(a) (see the Supplement to the 1991 edition of *Mesher, Income Support, The Social Fund and Family Credit: the Legislation*) remains in force in Scotland. The new form was introduced on April 6, 1992, as a consequence of the Children Act, 1989.

See the note to para.(2)(c).

[¹Persons under 18 years

2.102   **13A.**—[². . .],]

AMENDMENTS

1. Income Support (General) Amendment No.3 Regulations 1988 (SI 1988/1228), reg.4 (September 12, 1988).
2. Income Support (General) (Jobseeker's Allowance Consequential Amendments) Regulations 1996 (SI 1996/206), reg.28 and Sch.3 (October 7, 1996).

PART III

MEMBERSHIP OF THE FAMILY

Persons of a prescribed description

2.103   **14.**—(1) Subject to paragraph (2), a person of a prescribed description for the purposes of section 20(11) of the Act [SSCBA, s.137(1)] as it applies to income support (definition of the family) and section 23(1) [¹and (3)] of the Act [SSCBA, s.126(1) and (3)] is a person aged 16 or over but under 19 who is treated as a child for the purposes of section 2 of the Child Benefit Act 1975 [SSCBA, s.142] (meaning of child), and in these Regulations such a person is referred to as a "young person".

[³ (2) Paragraph (1) shall not apply to a person who is—
   (a) receiving advanced education within the meaning of regulation 12(2) (relevant education);
   (b) entitled to income support or would, but for section 134(2) (provision against dual entitlement of members of family) of the Contributions and Benefits Act, be so entitled; or
   (c) a person to whom section 6 of the Children (Leaving Care) Act 2000 (exclusion from benefits) applies.]

[⁴ (3) A person of a prescribed description for the purposes of section 137(1) of the Contributions and Benefits Act as it applies to income support (definition of family) includes a child or young person in respect of whom section 145A of that Act applies for the purposes of entitlement to child benefit but only for the period prescribed under section 145A(1) of that Act.]

AMENDMENTS

1. Income Support (General) Amendment No. 4 Regulations 1988 (SI 1988/ 1445), reg.5 (September 12, 1988).

2.104

2. Income Support (General) Amendment Regulation 1990 (SI 1990/547), reg.6 (April 9, 1990).

3. Children (Leaving Care) Act 2000 (Commencement No. 2 and Consequential Provisions) Order 2001 (SI 2001/3070), art.3(2) and Sch.1, para.(b) (October 1, 2001).

4. Income-related Benefits and Jobseeker's Allowance (Working Tax Credit and Child Tax Credit) (Amendment) Regulations 2002 (SI 2002/2402), reg.2 and Sch.1, para.2 (April 6, 2003).

DEFINITION

"the Act"—see reg.2(1).

GENERAL NOTE

For the circumstances in which a person of 16 to 18 is treated as a child for child benefit purposes, see reg.12. If such a person is receiving advanced education (para.(2)(a)); could be entitled to income support in their own right (see reg.13) (para.(2)(b)); or is a 16 or 17 year old who has been looked after by a local authority in England or Wales on or after October 1, 2001 or a local authority in Scotland on or after April 1, 2004 and is excluded from income support, income-based JSA and housing benefit (see the notes to reg.2 of the Children (Leaving Care) Social Security Benefits Regulations 2001 (SI 2001/3074) (p.745) and to reg.2 of the Children (Leaving Care) Social Security Benefits (Scotland) Regulations 2004 (SI 2004/747) (p.749)) (para.(2)(c)), that person does not come within reg.14. Under s.145A of SSCBA 1992 and reg.20 of the Child Benefit (General) Regulations 2003 (see Vol. I) a claimant who is entitled to child benefit for a child who dies continues to receive that benefit for the following eight weeks or until the end of the week which would have included the child's nineteenth birthday (whichever is the shorter period). Paragraph (3) taken together with the amendment to reg.15(1), has the effect that such a claimant will also continue to get income support in respect of the dead child for the same period.

2.105

Circumstances in which a person is to be treated as responsible or not responsible for another

15.—[¹(1) Subject to the following provisions of this regulation, a person is to be treated as responsible for a child or young person for whom he is receiving child benefit [² and this includes a child or young person to whom paragraph (3) of regulation 14 applies.].

2.106

(1A) In a case where a child ("the first child") is in receipt of child benefit in respect of another child ("the second child"), the person treated as responsible for the first child in accordance with the provisions of this regulation shall also be treated as responsible for the second child.

(2) In the case of a child or young person in respect of whom no person is receiving child benefit, the person who shall be treated as responsible for that child or young person shall be—

(a) except where sub-paragraph (b) applies, the person with whom the child or young person usually lives; or

(b) where only one claim for child benefit has been made in respect of the child or young person, the person who made that claim.]

(3) Where regulation 16(6) (circumstances in which a person is to be treated as being or not being a member of the household) applies in respect

of a child or young person, that child or young person shall be treated as the responsibility of the claimant for that part of the week for which he is under that regulation treated as being a member of the claimant's household.

(4) Except where paragraph (3) applies, for the purposes of these Regulations a child or young person shall be treated as the responsibility of only one person in any benefit week and any person other than the one treated as responsible for the child or young person under this regulation shall be treated as not so responsible.

AMENDMENTS

2.107
1. Income-related Benefits Schemes (Miscellaneous Amendments) (No.4) Regulations 1993 (SI 1993/2119), reg.5 (October 4, 1993).

2. Income-related Benefits and Jobseeker's Allowance (Working Tax Credit and Child Tax Credit) (Amendment) Regulations 2002 (SI 2002/2402), reg.2 and Sch.1, para.2 (April 6, 2003).

DEFINITIONS

"benefit week"—see reg.2(1).
"child"—see 1986 Act, s.20(11) (SSCBA, s.137(1)).
"claimant"—see reg.2(1).
"young person"—*ibid*, reg.14.

GENERAL NOTE

Para. (1)

2.108
This regulation sets out the circumstances in which a person is "responsible" for a child or young person for the purposes of income support. Before April 6, 2004 that question determined whether or not the claimant could claim an applicable amount for the child or young person under regs 17(b) or 18(c) and a family premium under regs 17(c) or 18(d) (because of the definition of "family" in s.137(1) of the Contributions and Benefits Act). Subject to exceptions in transitional cases (as to which see the note to reg.17), income support became an "adults only" benefit on April 6, 2004 with all support for the costs of bringing up children and young persons transferred to child tax credit and regs 17(b) and (c) and 18(c) and (d) were repealed. Regulation 15 has not, however, been repealed, because it continues to be of relevance to the issue of whether or not a claimant is a "lone parent" within para.1 of Sch.1B and in the transitional cases referred to above.

The definition of family in s.137(1) of the Contributions and Benefits Act (1986 Act, s.20(11)) refers to a person being responsible for a child or young person (on which see reg.14). Reg.15 makes the test of responsibility receipt of child benefit. Up to October 4, 1993, the test was "primary responsibility", and receipt of child benefit was only relevant in cases of doubt. See the notes to reg.15 in the 1993 edition and *Whelan v Chief Adjudication Officer, The Independent*, November 14, 1994. The Court of Appeal confirmed that the question of who had "primary responsibility" for a child had to be assessed on a week to week basis. On the facts, the claimant had primary responsibility for the children in the three weeks in the summer when they stayed with her.

In *C2/01–02(IS)(T)*, a Tribunal of Commissioners in Northern Ireland rejected a challenge to the *vires* of the Northern Ireland equivalent of reg.15(1). The regulation was held not to conflict either with the requirement under art.3 of the Children Order (Northern Ireland) 1995 (equivalent to s.1 of the Children Act 1989) that where a Court determines a question with respect to the upbringing of a child, that child's welfare is to be the paramount consideration or with the provisions of the Northern Ireland Act 1998 which apply the European Convention on Human Rights within the province.

Para.(1A)

If a child (B) for whom a person (A) is responsible gets child benefit for another child (C), (A) is also treated as responsible for (C).

2.109

Para.(2)

If no one is receiving child benefit for the child, then if one claim only has been made, the person who made that claim is responsible. Otherwise the person responsible is the person with whom the child usually lives. (See the notes to reg.7 of the Family Credit (General) Regulations in the 2002 edition of this volume on "living with".) Since para.(4) refers to consideration of responsibility on the basis of benefit weeks, the test of where a child usually lives should be applied week by week and not on some kind of overall assessment on a long-term basis (*CIS 49/1991*). In the vast majority of cases, however, the question of who is responsible for a child for the purposes of income support will now be determined by who is receiving child benefit. The rules for child benefit include methods of establishing priorities between claimants, and a child benefit claimant can agree that someone with lower priority should be paid it.

2.110

Paras (3) and (4)

Para.(4) provides that only one person can be treated as responsible for a child in any one benefit week. There is no provision for dividing up income support where a child spends time in different households. The only exceptions are under para.(3), which allows a person to be treated as responsible for a child for the part of the week in which he is in the household, but only where the child is being looked after by a local authority or is in custody (reg.16(6)). The result of the new test is that if someone else is in receipt of child benefit for a child in any one benefit week, an income support claimant cannot be treated as responsible for that child even if the child spends most of, or even all, his time with the claimant. This may provide for even greater administrative simplicity than the previous test of primary responsibility but at a cost of a lack of justice in certain situations.

2.111

In this connection note *R.(Chester) v Secretary of State for Social Security* [2001] EWHC Admin 1119, High Court, December 7, 2001. The claimant and her husband had separated and a contact order provided that the children should reside with her husband during the week in school term times and with the claimant over the weekends and for half of the school holidays. Both the claimant and her husband applied for child benefit. The Secretary of State awarded child benefit to the husband and the claimant applied for judicial review, relying largely on Art.8 of the ECHR (right to respect for family life). Collins J. held that the Secretary of State had erred in law because he could have made an award which reflected more closely the division of care (for example, a fairer result could have been achieved by awarding the claimant child benefit for one child for the whole period of the school holidays). Collins J. also pointed to the power in reg.34 of the Claims and Payments Regulations under which benefit can be paid to a third party on behalf of a beneficiary. However, the question as to the effect that that would have on the claimant's JSA was left open. Although Collins J. did not consider that it was necessary for the claimant to rely on Art.8 of the ECHR in order to succeed, his judgment does indicate that payment of child benefit to only one parent in shared care cases is capable of amounting to a breach of Art.8. In *Hockenjos v Secretary of State for Social Security* [2004] EWCA Civ 1749, the Court of Appeal held (on appeal from *CJSA/4890/1998*) that regs 77(1)-(3) and (5) of the JSA Regulations (equivalent to paras (1)-(2) and (4)) discriminated against men contrary to Art.4 of EC Directive 79/7 (see Vol.III) and therefore could not be applied to Mr Hockenjos and, by implication, to any man within the personal scope of that Directive—see further the note to reg.77 of the JSA Regulations. Note, however, that although that decision applies to both income-based and contribution-based JSA—see the earlier decision of the Court of Appeal in the same case (*Hockenjos v Secretary of State for Social Security* [2001] EWCA Civ 624, [2001] 2 C.M.L.R. 51, [2001] I.C.R. 966)— it does *not* apply to income support because that benefit is not within the material scope of the Directive (see C.–63/91 and C.–64/91 *Jackson and Cresswell v Chief Adjudication Officer* [1992] E.C.R. I-4737 (also reported as an appendix to *R(IS) 10/91*).

Circumstances in which a person is to be treated as being or not being a member of the household

2.112   **16.**—(1) Subject to paragraphs (2) and (5), the claimant and any partner and, where the claimant or his partner is treated as responsible under regulation 15 (circumstances in which a person is to be treated as responsible or not responsible for another) for a child or young person, that child or young person and any child of that child or young person shall be treated as members of the same household [¹notwithstanding that any of them] [⁷is temporarily living away from the other members of his family].

[⁷(2) Paragraph (1) shall not apply to a person who is living away from the other members of his family where—

    (a) that person does not intend to resume living with the other members of his family; or

    (b) his absence from the other members of his family is likely to exceed 52 weeks, unless there are exceptional circumstances (for example the person is in hospital or otherwise has no control over the length of his absence), and the absence is unlikely to be substantially more than 52 weeks.]

(3) Paragraph (1) shall not apply in respect of any member of a couple or of a polygamous marriage where—

    (a) one, both or all of them are patients detained in a hospital provided under section 4 of the National Health Service Act 1977 (special hospitals) or section 90(1) of the Mental Health (Scotland) Act 1984 (provision of hospitals for patients requiring special security); or

  [⁹(b) one, both or all of them are—

      (i) detained in custody pending trial or sentence upon conviction or under a sentence imposed by a court; or

     (ii) on temporary release in accordance with the provisions of the Prison Act 1952 or the Prisons (Scotland) Act 1989;]

    (c) [⁶. . .]

    (d) the claimant is abroad and does not satisfy the conditions of regulation 4 (temporary absence from Britain); or

    (e) one of them is permanently in residential accommodation or in a residential care or a residential nursing home.

(4) A child or young person shall not be treated as a member of the claimant's household where he is—

  [⁵(a) placed with the claimant or his partner by a local authority under section 23(2)(a) of the Children Act 1989 or by a voluntary organisation under section 59(1)(a) of that Act; or

    (b) placed with the claimant or his partner prior to adoption; or]

    (c) placed for adoption with the claimant or his partner pursuant to a decision under the Adoption Agencies Regulations 1983 or the Adoption Agencies (Scotland) Regulations 1984.

(5) Subject to paragraph (6), paragraph (1) shall not apply to a child or young person who is not living with the claimant[¹ and who]—

    (a) [⁴in a case which does not fall within sub-paragraph (aa),] has been continuously absent from Great Britain for a period of more than four weeks commencing—

(i) [⁸ subject to paragraph (5A),] where he went abroad before the date of claim for income support, with that date;

(ii) in any other case, [⁴on the day which immediately follows the day] on which he went abroad; or

[⁴(aa) where regulation 4(3) or paragraph 11A or 12A of Schedule 7 (temporary absence abroad for the treatment of a child or young person) applies, has been continuously absent from Great Britain for a period of more than eight weeks, that period of eight weeks commencing—

(i) [⁸ subject to paragraph (5A),] where he went abroad before the date of the claim for income support, on the date of that claim;

(ii) in any other case, on the day which immediately follows the day on which he went abroad; or]

(b) has been an in-patient or in [¹accommodation provided under any of the provisions referred to in [²any of sub-paragraphs (a) to (d) [³(excluding heads (i) and (ii)] of sub-paragraph (d)) of the definition of residential accommodation] in regulation 21(3)] for a continuous period of more than 12 weeks commencing—

(i) [⁸ subject to paragraph (5A),] where he became an in-patient or, as the case may be, entered that accommodation, before the date of the claim for income support, with that date; or

(ii) in any other case, with the date on which he became an in-patient or entered that accommodation,

and, in either case, has not been in regular contact with either the claimant or any member of the claimant's household; or

[⁵(c) is being looked after by a local authority under a relevant enactment; or

(d) has been placed with a person other than the claimant prior to adoption; or]

(e) has been placed for adoption pursuant to a decision under the Adoption Agencies Regulations 1983 or the Adoption Agencies (Scotland) Regulations 1984; or

(f) is detained in custody pending trial or sentence upon conviction or under a sentence imposed by a court.

[⁸(5A) Sub-paragraphs (a)(i), (aa)(i) and (b)(i) of paragraph (5) shall not apply in a case where immediately before the date of claim for income support the claimant was entitled to an income-based jobseeker's allowance.]

(6) A child or young person to whom any of the circumstances mentioned in sub-paragraphs (c) or (f) of paragraph (5) applies shall be treated as being a member of the claimant's household only for that part of any benefit week where that child or young person lives with the claimant.

(7) Where a child or young person for the purposes of attending the educational establishment at which he is receiving relevant education is living with the claimant or his partner and neither one is treated as responsible for that child or young person that child or young person shall be treated as being a member of the household of the person treated as responsible for him and shall not be treated as a member of the claimant's household.

(8) In this regulation—

[⁵(a) "relevant enactment" means the Army Act 1955, the Social Work (Scotland) Act 1968, the Matrimonial Causes Act 1973, the Adoption (Scotland) Act 1978, the Family Law Act 1986 and the Children Act 1989;]

(b) "voluntary organisation" has the meaning assigned to it in the [⁵Children Act 1989] or, in Scotland, the Social Work (Scotland) Act 1968.

2.113   1. Income Support (General) Amendment Regulations 1988 (SI 1988/663), reg.8 (April 11, 1988).

2. Income Support (General) Amendment Regulations 1989 (SI 1989/534), reg.3 (April 10, 1989).

3. Income Support (General) Amendment Regulations 1989 (SI 1989/534), Sch.1, para.3 (October 9, 1989).

4. Income Support (General) Amendment Regulations 1990 (SI 1990/547), reg.7 (April 9, 1990).

5. Income Support (General) Amendment Regulations 1992 (SI 1992/468), Sch. para.3 (April 6, 1992). *Note:* The previous form (see the 1991 edition) of sub-paras (4)(a) and (b), (5)(c) and (d) and (8)(a) and (b) remains in force in Scotland. The new form was introduced on April 6, 1992, as a consequence of the Children Act 1989.

6. Social Security Benefits (Amendments Consequential Upon the Introduction of Community Care) Regulations 1992 (SI 1992/3147), Sch.1, para.1 (April 1, 1993).

7. Income-related Benefits Schemes (Miscellaneous Amendments) (No.4) Regulations 1993 (SI 1993/2119), reg.6 (October 4, 1993).

8. Income Support (General) (Jobseeker's Allowance Consequential Amendments) Regulations 1996 (SI 1996/206), reg.8 (October 7, 1996).

9. Income-related Benefits Schemes and Social Fund (Miscellaneous Amendments) Regulations 1996 (SI 1996/1944), reg.6(5) (October 7, 1996).

DEFINITIONS

2.114   "child"—see 1986 Act, s.20(11) (SSCBA, s.137(1)).
"claimant"—see reg.2(1).
"couple"—*ibid.*
"date of claim"—*ibid.*
"dwelling occupied as the home"—*ibid.*
"nursing home"—see reg.2(1), reg.19(3).
"partner"—see reg.2(1).
"polygamous marriage"—*ibid.*
"residential accommodation"—*ibid.*, reg.21(3).
"residential care home"—*ibid.*, reg.19(3).
"young person"—*ibid.*, reg.14.

GENERAL NOTE

Para. (1)

2.115   This provision does two things. The first is to provide that a claimant and partner are deemed to be members of the same household, notwithstanding that they are temporarily apart. Before October 4, 1993, the deeming applied notwithstanding one partner's absence from the dwelling occupied as the home (see below). Since a partner is one of a married or unmarried couple and it is an essential part of the definition of both kinds of couple that the parties should be members of the same household, para.(1) cannot subvert the general meaning of household referred to in the notes to s.137(1) of the Contributions and Benefits Act (see *CIS 671/1992*). Para.(1) must only mean that because one partner is temporarily living elsewhere this does not in itself mean that membership of the same household ceases. This means that the exceptions in para.(3) perhaps do not achieve much, but probably indicate that those circumstances do terminate membership of the household.

The other thing done by para.(1) is to deem that where an adult is responsible for a child or young person under reg.15, the child or young person is to be treated as in the same household as the adult, notwithstanding that one of them is temporarily living elsewhere (again, before October 4, 1993, the test was absence from the home). After

April 6, 2004, this deeming provision is only of relevance in relation to transitional cases (see the notes to reg.15 and reg.17). There are exceptions in paras (4) and (5).

Thus the test under para.(1) is now one of absence from other members of the family, rather than from the home. *CIS 209/1989* held that the old form of para.(1) only applied if there was a dwelling which could be regarded as the home of both partners. This is no longer required, but it is still necessary for the family to have previously lived as members of the same household. (See notes to s.137(1) of the Contributions and Benefits Act under "*married couple*" on the meaning of household.) The Commissioner in *CIS 508/1992* seems to have accepted that the home need not have been in this country; how this applies to the new test of absence from other members of the family is not entirely clear. Temporarily is not defined and each case will need to be decided on its particular facts. However, adjudicating authorities still need to investigate whether either of the conditions in para.(2) applies. Note in particular *CIS 13805/1996* in the note to para.(2).

The difficulties which can arise when one member of a couple is living temporarily in a residential care home (or in any of the other types of accommodation listed in para.9 of Sch.7) while the other member continues to live at the couple's home were considered by the Commissioner in *CIS/1544/2001*. In those circumstances, para.9 provides that claimant's applicable amount is to be the higher of the applicable amount to which he would be entitled as a member of the couple or the aggregate of the applicable amounts to which he and his partner would be entitled as a single claimant or (in an appropriate case) as a lone parent. Previous DWP Guidance (now replaced—see *DMG Letter 05/02*) stated that for the purpose of carrying out this calculation, each member of the couple was to be treated as a non-dependent of the other. One consequence of this approach was that—under para.13(2)(a)(ii) of Sch.2—neither partner was entitled to the severe disability premium. The Commissioner held that there was no justification for such an approach. As long as the absence was only temporary, the claimant and his wife remained members of the same household by virtue of reg.16(1). Each therefore remained the partner of the other and could not be each other's non-dependant because of reg.3(2)(a). The notional calculation required by the second alternative in para.9 (which treated the couple as if they were single claimants and therefore did imply that they were to be treated as normally living apart) *only* applied for the purpose of calculating the applicable amount. Applying that approach, the claimant was entitled to have the severe disability premium to which his wife would have been entitled as a single claimant normally living on her own, included in her applicable amount. **2.116**

Para.(2)

Para.(1) does not apply where the person living away does not intend to resume living together with the other members of the family or is likely to be away for more than 52 weeks (or longer in exceptional circumstances, provided it is not substantially longer). When either of these conditions applies membership of the same household immediately ceases. **2.117**

In *CIS 13805/1996* the Commissioner points out that the "not" in para.(2)(a) relates to "intend" rather than "resume". This was significant because it was possible for a person to have no intention one way or the other. For example, where a couple had agreed to live apart for a couple of months, and neither had an intention to resume living with the other, but equally neither had an intention not to do so, para.(2)(a) could apply. This interpretation was further supported by the fact that once an intention not to resume living together had been formed, a separation was no longer temporary and so para.(1) ceased to apply in any event; thus para.(2)(a) would serve no function (other perhaps than to provide a partial definition of "temporary") if it was read as only operating when there was an intention not to resume living together. The facts in *CIS 13805/1996* were that the claimant's husband was in Pakistan. He had applied for permission to enter the UK but it had not yet been granted. They intended to resume living together, as long as permission was granted for the claimant's husband to join her. The Commissioner states that the question therefore was whether such intention counted for the purposes of para.(2)(a). *CIS 508/1992* and *CIS 484/1993* had held in relation to para.4(8) of the former Sch.3 (now para.3(10)) that the intention to return must not be a contingent one. In the Commissioner's view the same interpretation applied for the purposes of para.(2)(a), since there was no material distinction between that provision and para.(2)(a). Thus para.(2)(a) applied because the claimant's intention to resume living in the same household as her husband was not an unqualified one. Therefore the fact that the claimant's husband was in remunerative work did not bar her from entitlement to income support.

Para. (3)

2.118   Para.(1) does not apply in these circumstances, as between partners and poly-gamous marriages. The intention seems to be that the members of the couple or marriage cease to be partners in these circumstances, but para.(3) does not exactly say so. Under sub-para.(b) a person required to live in a bail hostel is not "detained in custody" pending trial *(R(IS) 17/93)*; see Sch.7, para.9 as to how his applicable amount is calculated if he is a member of a couple. However, once a person has been charged, he is detained in custody pending trial, even if subsequently no trial takes place *(R(IS) 1/94)*.In *Chief Adjudication Officer v Carr, The Times*, June 2, 1994, also reported as *R(IS) 20/95*, the Court of Appeal held that a person on home leave while serving a prison sentence was not "detained in custody" during the leave period. The definition of "prisoner" in reg.21(3) was amended with effect from April 10, 1995, so as to include periods of temporary release, and sub-para.(b) has now been similarly amended with effect from October 7, 1996.

Para. (4)

2.119   Children or young persons are not to be members of the household of their foster-parents or the people they are placed with for adoption. They therefore cannot be a member of the family.

Para. (5)

2.120   Para.(1) does not apply to a child or young person who is not living with the claimant when one of heads (a) to (f) applies. Again, the intention seems to be that in these circumstances the child or young person is to be treated as not a member of the household, but para.(5) does not expressly say so. It may be that the general test of membership of the household is relevant. See para.(8) for the meaning of "relevant enactment".

In *Secretary of State for Work & Pensions v Bobezes* [2005] EWCA Civ. 111, CA (Pill & Buxton L.JJ. and Lord Slynn of Hadley), February 16, 2005 (also reported as *R(IS) 6/05*), the claimant was denied an applicable amount for his sixteen year-old step-daughter who was staying temporarily with her grandparents in Portugal. He argued that if he had been British it was probable that the grandparents would have been living in Great Britain with the consequence that para.(5)(a) would not have applied and the general rule in para.(1) would have treated his daughter as continuing to be a member of his household during her temporary absence. The issue before the Commissioner (*CIS/825/2001*) had been whether the fact that income support was a special non-contributory benefit within Art.4(2)(a) of Council Regulation (EEC) 1408/71 (see Vol.III) (and therefore, under Art.10a payable "exclusively . . . in accordance with the legislation of" Great Britain), prevented Mr Bobezes from arguing that para.(5)(a) therefore discriminated against him indirectly on the grounds of his Portuguese nationality contrary to Art.7 of Council Regulation (EEC) 1612/68 (see Vol.III). The Commissioner held that it did not but, by the time the case reached the Court of Appeal, it was appreciated that nothing actually turned on this point because, even if Regulation 1408/71 applied to the exclusion of Regulation 1612/68, Art.3 of the former Regulation had substantially the same effect as Art.7 of the latter.

The issue before the Court of Appeal therefore became whether the jurisprudence of the ECJ required Mr Bobezes to produce detailed statistical evidence, which would not in practice be available, in order to establish discrimination. The Court held that it did not and that, in contrast to the position where discrimination on the ground of sex is alleged, "the Commissioners and the court are entitled to take a broad approach and to find that indirect discrimination is liable to affect a significant number of migrant workers on the ground of nationality without statistical proof being available."

In Mr Bobezes' case, the Court considered that:

> "the proper approach is to compare the children of migrant workers with British children whose families are normally resident here. It is intrinsically likely that significantly more of the former than the latter will be prejudiced by paragraph 16(5) of the Regulation."

and therefore remitted the appeal to a tribunal to decide the question of whether such discrimination could be justified by the Secretary of State.

Para. (6)

This provision provides a limited exception to para.(5), allowing a claimant to receive benefit for children or young persons being looked after by a local authority or in custody for the days on which they are in the claimant's home.   **2.121**

Para. (7)

This is a special rule where children live away from home while at school.   **2.122**

PART IV

APPLICABLE AMOUNTS

Applicable amounts

17. Subject to regulations [⁸ 18 to 22A] and 70 (applicable amounts in   **2.123** other cases and reductions in applicable amounts and urgent cases), a claimant's weekly applicable amount shall be the aggregate of such of the following amounts as may apply in his case:

(a) an amount in respect of himself or, if he is a member of a couple, an amount in respect of both of them, determined in accordance with paragraph 1(1), (2) or (3), as the case may be, of Schedule 2;

(b) [¹¹ . . .]

[⁶ (bb) [¹⁰ . . .]]

(c) [¹¹ . . .]

(d) the amount of any premiums which may be applicable to him, determined in accordance with Parts III and IV of Schedule 2 (premiums);

(e) any amounts determined in accordance with Schedule 3 (housing costs) which may be applicable to him in respect of mortgage interest payments or such other housing costs as are prescribed in that Schedule.

[¹(f) any amounts determined in accordance with [²paragraphs (2) to (7)].

[²(g) the amount of the protected sum which may be applicable to him determined in accordance with Schedule 3A [³or, as the case may be, 3B].]

(2) Where—

(a) a claimant has throughout the period beginning on 11th April 1988 and ending immediately before the coming into force of paragraphs 25 to 28 of Schedule 10 (capital to be disregarded) failed to satisfy the capital condition in section 22(6) of the Act (no entitlement to benefit if capital exceeds prescribed amount); and

(b) as a consequence he is not entitled to any transitional addition, special transitional addition or personal expenses addition under Part II of the Transitional Regulations; and

(c) had those paragraphs been in force on 11th April 1988 he would have satisfied that condition and been entitled to any such addition,

the amount applicable under this paragraph shall, subject to paragraph (3) be equal to the amount of any transitional addition, special transitional addition and personal expenses addition to which he would be entitled under Part II of the Transitional Regulations had he been entitled to any such addition in the week commencing 11th April 1988.

(3) For the purposes of paragraph (2), in determining a claimant's total benefit income in his second benefit week for the purpose of calculating the amount of any transitional addition to which he would have been entitled, no account shall be taken of any payment referred to in paragraph (1)(j) of regulation 9 of the Transitional Regulations (total benefit income) which is made in respect of that week to compensate for the loss of entitlement to income support.

(4) Subject to paragraph (6), where—

(a) the claimant or any member of his family was temporarily absent from his home in the claimant's first or second benefit week (or both), because he was—

   (i) a patient; or

  (ii) outside Great Britain for the purpose of receiving treatment for any disease or bodily or mental disablement or for the purpose of accompanying a child or young person who is outside Great Britain for the purpose of receiving such treatment; or

 (iii) in a residential care or nursing home or in accommodation provided under any of the provisions referred to in any of subparagraphs (a) to [⁹(c)] of the definition of residential accommodation in regulation 21(3) (special cases); or

 (iv) in the care of a local authority under a relevant enactment; or

  (v) staying with a person who was contributing to his maintenance; and

(b) as a result—

   (i) in the claimant's first benefit week his requirements for the purpose of calculating his entitlement to supplementary benefit were increased or reduced or he was not entitled to that benefit; or

  (ii) in the claimant's second benefit week his applicable amount was increased or reduced or he was not entitled to income support; and

(c) the period during which his requirements were, or his applicable amount was, increased or reduced, or he was not entitled to benefit, or any one or more of those circumstances existed, did not exceed eight weeks,

the amount applicable under this paragraph (4) shall be equal to the amount determined under paragraph (5).

(5) The amount for the purposes of paragraph (4) shall be an amount equal to the difference between—

(a) the amount that his total benefit income in his first benefit week would have been had he been entitled in respect of that week to

supplementary benefit calculated on the basis that he or any member of his family had not been absent from the home; and, if less,
(b) the amount of his total benefit income in the first complete week after the period of temporary absence ends; but for the purpose of calculating his total benefit income in that week—
  (i) no account shall be taken of any payment referred to in paragraph (1)(j) of regulation 9 of the Transitional Regulations which is made in respect of that week to compensate for the loss (in whole or in part) of entitlement to income support; and
  (ii) if the period of temporary absence ends after the coming into force of paragraph (4), the amount of income support to be taken into account shall, notwithstanding regulation 9(6) of the Transitional Regulations, be calculated as if that paragraph were not in force.

(6) The amount under paragraph (4) shall cease to be applicable to a claimant if he ceases to be entitled to income support for a period exceeding [⁴the permitted period determined in accordance with regulation 3A (permitted period)].

[⁴(6A) For the purposes of paragraph (6), where a claimant has ceased to be entitled to income support because he or his partner is participating in arrangements for training made under section 2 of the Employment and Training Act 1973 [⁵or section 2 of the Enterprise and New Towns (Scotland) Act 1990] or attending a course at an employment rehabilitation centre established under that section [⁵of the 1993 Act], he shall be treated as if he had been entitled to income support for the period during which he or his partner is participating in such arrangements or attending such a course.]

(7) In this Regulation—

"first benefit week" and "second benefit week" have the meanings given to those expressions in regulations 2(1) of the Transitional Regulations and shall also include the week which would have been the claimant's "first benefit week" or, as the case may be, "second benefit week" had he been entitled to supplementary benefit or, as the case may be, income support in that week;

"total benefit income" has, subject to paragraphs (3) and (5)(b), the same meaning as in regulation 9 of the Transitional Regulations;

"Transitional Regulations" means the Income Support (Transitional Regulations 1987.]

AMENDMENTS

1. Income Support (General) Amendment No.2 Regulations 1988 (SI 1988/910), reg.2 (May 30, 1988).

2. Income Support (General) Amendment No.4 Regulations 1988 (SI 1988/1445), Sch.1, para.11 (April 10, 1989).

3. Income Support (General) Amendment Regulations 1989 (SI 1989/534), Sch.1, para.17 (October 9, 1989).

4. Income Support (General) Amendment No.3 Regulations 1989 (SI 1989/1678), reg.4 (October 9, 1989).

5. Enterprise (Scotland) Consequential Amendments Order 1991 (SI 1991/387), art.2 and 9 (April 1, 1991).

6. Social Security Benefits (Amendments Consequential Upon the Introduction of Community Care) Regulations 1992 (SI 1992/3147), reg.2(1) (April 1, 1993).

7. Income-related Benefits Schemes (Miscellaneous Amendments) (No. 4) Regulations 1993 (SI 1993/2119), reg.7 (October 4, 1993).

2.124

8. Income Support (General) (Jobseeker's Allowance Consequential Amendments) Regulations 1996 (SI 1996/206), reg.9 (October 7, 1996).

9. Social Security Amendment (Residential Care and Nursing Homes) Regulations 2001 (SI 2001/3767), reg.2 and Sch., Pt I, para.3 (April 8, 2002).

10. Social Security (Removal of Residential Allowance and Miscellaneous Amendments) Regulations 2003 (SI 2003/1121), reg.2 and Sch.1, para.2 (October 6, 2003).

11. Social Security (Working Tax Credit and Child Tax Credit) (Consequential Amendments) Regulations 2003 (SI 2003 No. 455), reg.2 and Sch.1, para.2 (April 6, 2004, except in "transitional cases" and see further the note to reg.17 of the Income Support Regulations).

DEFINITIONS

2.125   "child"—see 1986 Act, s.20(11) (SSCBA, s.137(1)).
"claimant"—see reg.2(1).
"couple"—*ibid.*
"family"—see 1986 Act, s.20(11) (SSCBA, s.137(1)).
"young person"—see reg.2(1), reg.14.

GENERAL NOTE

2.126   Reg.17 sets out the categories which go towards the total applicable amount, which is then set against the claimant's income to determine entitlement.

The categories cover first a personal allowance for the claimant, as a single person or a member of a couple. The amount of the allowance is specified in Sch.2.

Although the text of reg.1(2), (3) and (4) of the Social Security (Working Tax Credit and Child Tax Credit) (Consequential Amendments) Regulations 2003 (SI 2003/455) is set out at p.685 below, it is convenient to note the effect of those provisions in the commentary to this regulation. Before April 6, 2004, a further personal allowance (specified in Sch.2) was added under para.(b) of reg.17 for each child or young person who was a member of the family (see s.137(1) of the Contributions and Benefits Act and regs.14–16). With effect from April 6, 2004, the process of transferring all financial support for children and young persons from income support to child tax credit ("CTC") began.

2.127   It was originally intended that the transfer would be completed by April 6, 2005, but that did not happen and it is now envisaged that action to transfer existing claimants will not even begin until 2006. On December 31, 2006, the income support and income-based JSA personal allowances for children and young persons, the family premium, the enhanced disability premium in respect of a child or young person and the disabled child premium will be abolished by a combination of s.1(3)(d) of the Tax Credit Act 2002, the Tax Credits Act 2002 (Commencement No. 4, Transitional and Savings) Order 2003 (SI 2003/962) and the Tax Credits Act 2002 (Commencement No. 4, Transitional Provisions and Savings) (Amendment) Order 2005 (SI 2005/1106) (see Vol. IV). Those amounts will be referred to in this note as "the child elements": (recent statutory instruments have taken to describing them as "the child premia"—see SI 2005/773 and SI 2005/776—but that description is inaccurate both because a personal allowance for a child or young person is not a "premium" and because, in any event, the plural of "premium" is "premiums", not "premia").

2.128   The transfer process appears to be in two stages. First, under reg.1(2),(3) and (4) of SI 2003/455—the provisions of which are analysed in more detail below— entitlement is to the child elements is withdrawn for all claimants other than those whom this book describes as "transitional cases" i.e. those who were in receipt of the child elements on April 6, 2004 and have not subsequently been awarded CTC and, possibly, those claimants whose families included a child or young person on April 6, 2004, who have not been awarded CTC and who make a new claim for income support or income-based JSA after that date.

The transitional cases are then to be transferred following the procedure in the Tax Credits Act (Transitional Provisions) Order 2005 (SI 2005/773) (see Vol. IV). The drafting of that Order is problematical. The operative provision is art.3, which deems a "specified person", as defined in art.4—effectively those described in this book as "transitional cases"—to make a claim for CTC on the "specified date", which is defined by art.5 as the day following the date on which the DWP notifies the Inland Revenue as the proposed final day of the last benefit week in respect of which the child elements are to be paid to the claimant. By art.6, an award on the deemed claim begins either on the "specified date" or on the date on which the Board notifies the DWP of an award of CTC. This is subject to the transitional provision in art.7 (which, bizarrely, appears to be in identical terms to that made in art.2 of the Tax Credits Act 2002 (Transitional Provisions) (No.2) Order 2005 (SI 2005/776) made on the very same day, and by the same department of state, as SI 2005/773).

2.129

The potential problem arises because the definition of "the specified date" does not contain a long-stop provision stating that if no specified date has arisen in relation to a particular case by December 31, 2006 (when the child elements are abolished), that date will be the specified date. It is clear from art.5 that it is intended that the notification from the DWP to the Board is to be given, and therefore that the deemed CTC claim will arise, on a case-by-case basis. This can be seen from the fact that the notification is to be of the:

2.130

> "the proposed final day of the last benefit week for which the child premia [sic] in respect of income support or income based jobseeker's allowance is to be paid *to the specified person*" (emphasis added).

If the italicised words did not put the matter beyond doubt, the need to specify the last day of the benefit week, which will vary from one claimant to the next, will make an individual notification necessary.

On that basis, consider the position of a claimant in respect of whom, by oversight, no such notification is given. Such a claimant cannot continue to be entitled to the child elements after December 31, 2006 because they will have been abolished for all purposes by s.1(3)(d). However, because the deemed claim for CTC is based on the notification from the DWP to the Board rather than on the actual cessation of entitlement to the child elements, a claimant for whom no notification is given will not have made a deemed claim for CTC either and, unless an actual claim is then made within the three month period allowed by reg.7 of the Tax Credits (Claims and Notifications) Regulations 2002, will lose benefit. The same problem arises if the notification is made by the DWP but the Board does not get round to processing the deemed claim until after December 31, 2006 and therefore does not give the notification to the DWP that is required by art.6(b) of SI 2005/773: the CTC claim takes effect from the date of notification by the Board if that is later than the specified date.

Particularly given the catalogue of delay and error that has attended the introduction of the tax credits to date, it seems optimistic to assume that the procedures of the DWP and the Revenue will invariably operate as is intended. The absence of a provision deeming any claimant in a transitional case who has not previously made a CTC claim (deemed or actual) to make such a claim on December 31, 2006 is a fiasco waiting to happen.

2.131

The transitional provision in art.7 of SI 2005/773/art.2 of SI 2005/776 also appears to be technically defective. Its purpose is to prevent the automatic backdating provisions in reg.7 of the Tax Credits (Claims and Notifications) Regulations 2002 from operating so as to produce a backdated entitlement to CTC that would overlap with a period of actual entitlement to the child elements of income support/income-based JSA. However, although the drafting covers the circumstances where a CTC claim is made by a claimant who was entitled to income support/income-based JSA for a child and where a CTC claim is made by a claimant whose partner was entitled to JSA for a child, where the claimant and partner were a joint-claim couple for JSA purposes, it does not appear to cover the circumstances in which a CTC claim is made by a claimant who was not herself entitled to income

2.132

support/income-based JSA but who was covered by an income support/income-based JSA claim made by a partner. The practical implications would appear to be that if such a person were well advised, he or she could obtain three months' double benefit. This would be of particular benefit to anyone who happened to be splitting up from their partner at the appropriate time and therefore was unconcerned at the possibility that the Secretary of State might seek to recover an IS/JSA overpayment from his/her former partner.

Until such time as the DWP takes steps to complete the transfer to CTC, the current position is governed by reg.1(2),(3) and (4) of SI 2003/455 and appears to be as follows:

- for claimants who do not have a child or young person who is a member of their family before April 6, 2004, para.(b) of reg.17 (and also reg.18(b) and paras 2, 14 and the relevant parts of para.13A of Sch.2) was revoked with effect from April 6, 2004 (reg.1(4) of SI 2003/455).

- for claimants who have a child or young person who is a member of their family and who are (or whose partners are) in receipt of CTC prior to April 6, 2004, para.(b) of reg.17 (and also reg.18(b) and paras 2, 14 and the relevant parts of para.13A of Sch.2) was revoked with effect from April 6, 2004 (reg.1(2) of SI 2003/455). From the first day of the first benefit week beginning on or after that date, such claimants are not entitled to the child elements;

- for claimants who have a child or young person who is a member of their family and who were not (and whose partners were not) in receipt of CTC prior to April 6, 2004, but who subsequently become (or whose partners subsequently become) entitled to CTC in respect of a period which precedes that date (*i.e.*, under reg.7 of the Tax Credits (Claims and Notifications) Regulations 2002—see Vol. IV), reg.7 of SI 2003/455 (which provides that, subject to limited disregards, CTC counts as income for income support purposes between April 7, 2003 and April 6, 2004—see p.702) applies from the first day of the first benefit week beginning on or after the commencement date of the CTC award. (This may mean that there will have been an overpayment for the period before CTC was awarded which, it would seem, would be recoverable under s.74(1) of the Administration Act.) For such claimants, para.(b) of reg.17 (and the other provisions referred to above) are revoked with effect from April 6, 2004 (reg.1(2) of SI 2003/455) with the same consequences as are set out in the previous paragraph.

- for claimants who have a child or young person who is a member of their family and who are in receipt of income support but have not been awarded (and whose partners have not been awarded) CTC as at April 6, 2004 and who do not subsequently become entitled to CTC for a period which begins before that date, para.(b) of reg.17 (and the other provisions referred to above) remain in force until CTC is awarded. They are then revoked with effect from the first day of the first benefit week beginning on or after the day on which the CTC award begins. For convenience the commentary in this Volume refers to such claimants as "transitional cases" during the period from April 6, 2004 to the date on which the old rules are revoked in their case.

- it is unclear whether claimants who have a child or young person who is a member of their family but who were not in receipt of income support before April 6, 2004 can make a new claim for income support on or after that date and be awarded the child elements on that claim. This depends on whether the words "for the purposes of his claim for income support" in reg.1(3)(a) of SI 2003/455 merely define the phrase "member of his family" (*i.e.*, by specifying that that phrase is used in the sense defined by s.137(1) of the Contributions and Benefits Act and regs 14–16) or whether they are to be taken as requiring that an actual claim for income support must be in existence before reg.1(3)(a) can apply. Under the latter interpretation, a claimant who did not have (or whose partner did not have) an extant claim for income support before

April 6, 2004 is a person to whom reg.1(4) of SI 2003/455 applies so that reg.17(b) and the other provisions referred to above were revoked with effect from the first day of the first benefit week beginning on or after that date. The consequence would be that any new claim could not include the child elements. Under the former interpretation, if a claimant's family includes a child or young person as defined by s.137(1), then reg.17(b) and the other provisions remain in force until CTC is awarded and until that time a new claim for income support should include the child elements. Under this interpretation, reg.1(4) of SI 2003/455 only applies to claimants whose families (at least before April 6, 2004) do not include a child or a young person at all. As the substantive amendments made by reg.2 of and Sch.1 to SI 2003/455 with effect from April 6, 2004 concern children or young persons, this interpretation would mean that reg.1(4) served two purposes: first, to prevent personal allowances etc. for children and young persons being included for income support claimants who were not previously responsible for a child or young person but become so on or after April 6, 2004 (*e.g.*, as the result of the birth of a baby or through adoption) and, secondly, as a tidying up measure to ensure that the rules governing personal allowances etc. for children and young persons were completely revoked in all cases. In the view of the editors the former interpretation represents the more natural meaning of the provision but it is unclear which interpretation represents the policy intention. Official guidance (DMG Memos JSA/IS 64 and JSA/IS 96) assume that the former interpretation is correct but this is contradicted by other official literature and statements. For further consideration of whether claimants would be better off asserting a claim for the child elements or claiming CTC, and for a practical assessment of the obstacles they may face if they choose the former course, see *Children and IS/I-B JSA—In or Out?* in *Welfare Rights Bulletin 186.*

Until October 5, 2003, claimants living in residential care homes or nursing homes also received a "residential allowance" under para.(bb) (for further details, see pp.486–488 of Vol. II of the 2003 Edition). With effect from October 6, 2003, para.(bb) was revoked and residential allowances abolished. All financial help with the costs of care is now provided by local authority social services departments.

The second main category covers premiums. The former family premium under paragraph (c) (payable if the claimant's family included a child or a young person) was also abolished with effect from April 6, 2004 subject to the same transitional provisions.

The other premiums are in Parts III and IV of Sch.2.

The third category covers housing costs, set out in Sch.3. Note reg.13(1) of the Decisions and Appeals Regulations 1999 (see Vol. III of this series).

The fourth category, in sub-paras.(f) and (g), covers transitional protection for a number of groups. Sub-para.(f) first deals with those assisted by paras 25 to 28 of Sch.10 on disregarded capital, which were inserted from May 30, 1988. The details are in paras (2) and (3). Sub-para.(f) secondly deals with groups who lost out on the ordinary transitional protection because of temporary absence from home around April 11, 1988. Here the details are in paras (4) to (6). Sub-para.(g) applies Schs 3A and 3B, giving transitional protection to certain claimants in board and lodging accommodation on the change in the income support system on April 10, 1989, and to hostel-dwellers and operators on the changes in October 1989. See the notes to Sch.3A and 3B.

Paras (2) and (3)

These provisions apply where a person was continuously excluded from entitlement to income support by the capital rule before the additional disregards were added with effect from May 30, 1988. If the person would have satisfied the capital rule on April 11, 1988, if those disregards had been in the regulations and would have been entitled to some transitional protection, then the amount of that protec-

2.133

tion is applicable from May 30, 1988. There is no statutory provision for filling the gap between April 11 and May 30, but extra-statutory payments were made. The effect of para.(3) is that in doing the calculations of total benefit income in the second benefit week around April 11, any extra-statutory payment is to be ignored.

Paras (4) to (6A)

2.134   Where the calculation of total benefit income in either the first or second benefit week is affected by a person's temporary absence from home (for one of the reasons set out in para.(4)(a)), then the calculation can be done as if the person was still at home. The absence must not exceed eight (or sometimes 12) weeks (para.(4)(c)) and the addition applied will cease if there is a subsequent break in entitlement of more than eight (or sometimes 12) weeks (para.(6)).

There are special rules for particular categories in regs 18 to 22A, in particular for residents in residential care and nursing homes.

Polygamous marriages

2.135   **18.**—[¹(1) Subject to paragraph (2) and [⁹regulations 21] [⁸ to 22A] and 70 (applicable amounts in other cases and reductions in applicable amounts and urgent cases), where a claimant is a member of a polygamous marriage his weekly applicable amount shall be the aggregate of such of the following amounts as may apply in his case:

(a) the highest amount applicable to him and one of his partners determined in accordance with paragraph 1(3) of Schedule 2 as if he and that partner were a couple;

(b) an amount equal to the differences between the amounts specified in [⁸sub-paragraph (3)(d)][⁴and (1)(e)] of paragraph 1 of Schedule 2 in respect of each of his other partners;

(c) [¹¹ . . .]

[⁶ (cc) ¹⁰ . . .]]

(d) [¹¹ . . .]

(e) the amount of any premiums which may be applicable to him determined in accordance with Parts III and IV of Schedule 2 (premiums);

(f) any amounts determined in accordance with Schedule 3 (housing costs) which may be applicable to him in respect of mortgage interest payments or such other housing costs as are prescribed in that Schedule.

[²(g) any amount determined in accordance with regulation 17(1)(f) (applicable amounts);]

[³(h) the amount of the protected sum which may be applicable to him determined in accordance with Schedule 3A [⁵or, as the case may be, 3B].]

[¹(2) In the case of a partner who is aged less than 18, the amount which applies in respect of that partner shall be nil unless—

(a) that partner is treated as responsible for a child, or [⁸(b) that partner is a person who—

(i) had he not been a member of a polygamous marriage would have qualified for income support under regulation 4ZA; or

(ii) satisfies the requirements of section 3(1)(f)(iii) of the Jobseekers Act 1995 (prescribed circumstances for persons aged 16 but less than 18); or

(iii) is the subject of a direction under section 16 of the Jobseekers Act 1995 (persons under 18: severe hardship).]

AMENDMENTS

1. Income Support (General) Amendment No.3 Regulations 1988 (SI 1988/   **2.136**
1228), reg.5 (September 9, 1988).
2. Income Support (General) Amendment No.4 Regulations 1988 (SI 1988/
1445), reg.6 (September 9, 1988).
3. Income Support (General) Amendment No.4 Regulations 1988 (SI 1988/
1445), Sch.1, para.12 (April 10, 1989).
4. Family Credit and Income Support (General) Amendment Regulations 1989
(SI 1989/1034), reg.5 (July 10, 1989)
5. Income Support (General) Amendment Regulations 1989 (SI 1989/534),
Sch.1, para.17 (October 9, 1989).
6. Social Security Benefits (Amendments Consequential Upon the Introduction
of Community Care) Regulations 1992 (SI 1992/3147), reg.2(1) (April 1, 1993).
7. Income-related Benefits Schemes (Miscellaneous Amendments) (No. 4)
Regulations 1993 (SI 1993/2119) reg.8 (October 4, 1993).
8. Income Support (General) (Jobseeker's Allowance Consequential
Amendments) Regulations 1996 (SI 1996/206), reg.10 (October 7, 1996).
9. Social Security Amendment (Residential Care and Nursing Homes)
Regulations 2001 (SI 2001/3767), reg.2 and Sch., Pt I, para.4 (April 8, 2002).
10. Social Security (Removal of Residential Allowance and Miscellaneous
Amendments) Regulations 2003 (SI 2003/1121), reg.2 and Sch.1, para.3
(October 6, 2003).
11. Social Security (Working Tax Credit and Child Tax Credit) (Consequential
Amendments) Regulations 2003 (SI 2003 No. 455), reg.2 and Sch.1, para.3 (April
6, 2004, except in "transitional cases" and see further the note to reg.17 of the
Income Support Regulations).

DEFINITIONS

"the Act"—see reg.2(1).
"child"—see 1986 Act, s.20(11) (SSCBA, s.137(1)).
"claimant"—see reg.2(1).
"couple"—*ibid.*
"partner"—*ibid.*
"polygamous marriage"—*ibid.*
"young person"—*ibid.*, reg.14.

GENERAL NOTE

Reg.18 contains special rules for polygamous marriages, but not for other kinds   **2.137**
of relationships. There the ordinary living together as husband and wife rule in
s.137(1) of the Contributions and Benefits Act (1986 Act, s.20(11)) applies.

Applicable amounts for persons in residential care and nursing homes

19.—[¹ . . .]   **2.138**

AMENDMENT

1. Social Security Amendment (Residential Care and Nursing Homes)
Regulations 2001 (SI 2001/3767), reg.2 and Sch., Pt I para.5 (April 8, 2002).

GENERAL NOTE

The revocation of reg.19 abolished the system of "preserved rights" for those who   **2.139**
were resident in a nursing or residential care home on March 31, 1993 (*i.e.*, immediately before the introduction of care in the community). For details of the operation of that system see pp. 255–265 of Vol II of the 2001 Edition.

Applicable amounts for persons on board and lodging accommodation and hostels

2.140   **20.**—[¹. . .]

AMENDMENT

1. Income Support (General) Amendment Regulations 1989 (SI 1989/534), Sch.1, para.4 (October 9, 1989).

GENERAL NOTE

2.141   As from October 1989, most hostel-dwellers, unless their accommodation comes within the amended definition of residential accommodation in reg.21(3), are entitled to the ordinary income support personal allowances and premiums and to housing benefit for their accommodation. See Sch.3B for transitional protection from October 1989 and April 1990.

Boarders had already been transferred to a similar system from April 1989. Their transitional protection is under Sch.3A.

Special cases

2.142   **21.**—(1) Subject to [²⁷paragraph (1B)] [²¹[²⁵regulation 21ZB] (treatment of refugees) and][¹⁹regulation 22A] (reductions in applicable amounts) in the case of a person to whom any paragraph in column (1) of Schedule 7 applies (applicable amounts in special cases), the amount included in the claimant's weekly amount in respect of him shall be the amount prescribed in the corresponding paragraph in column (2) of that Schedule [³⁰ . . .].

[⁶(1A) Except where the amount prescribed in Schedule 7 in respect of a person to whom paragraph (1) applies includes an amount applicable under regulation 17(1)(d) or 18(1)(e), a person to whom paragraph (1) applies shall be treated as not being severely disabled.]

[²⁷(IB)[²⁹. . .[²⁸ . . .]]]

(2) In Schedule 7, for the purposes of [²⁹paragraph 1, 2 or 3 (patients)], where a person has been a patient for two or more distinct periods separated by one or more intervals each not exceeding 28 days, he shall be treated as having been a patient continuously for a period equal in duration to the total of those distinct periods.

(3) [¹⁸ [³¹ Subject to paragraphs (3F) and (3G)]] in Schedule 7—

[²⁵. . .]

[²⁵"partner of a person subject to immigration control" means a person—

   (i)   who is not subject to immigration control within the meaning of section 115(9) of the Immigration and Asylum Act; or

   (ii) to whom section 115 of that Act does not apply by virtue of regulation 2 of the Social Security (Immigration and Asylum) Consequential Amendments Regulations 2000; and

   (iii) who is a member of a couple and his partner is subject to immigration control within the meaning of section 115(9) of that Act and section 115 of that Act applies to her for the purposes of exclusion from entitlement to income support;]

[¹⁴"person from abroad" [²⁵ . . .] means a claimant who is not habitually resident in the United Kingdom, [²⁰ the Channel Islands, the Isle of Man or the Republic of Ireland], but for this purpose, no claimant shall be treated as not habitually resident in the United Kingdom who is—

(a) a worker for the purposes of Council Regulation (EEC) No. 1612/68 or (EEC) No. 1251/70 or a person with a right to reside in the United Kingdom pursuant to Council Directive No. 68/360/EEC or No. 73/148/EEC; or [[31] a person who is an accession State worker requiring registration who is treated as a worker for the purpose of the definition of "qualified person" in regulation 5(1) of the Immigration (European Economic Area) Regulations 2000 pursuant to regulation 5 of the Accession (Immigration and Worker Registration) Regulations 2004].

(b) a refugee within the definition in Article 1 of the Convention relating to the Status of Refugees done at Geneva on 28th July 1951, as extended by Article 1(2) of the Protocol relating to the Status of Refugees done at New York on 31st January 1967; or

(c) a person who has been granted exceptional leave [[24] to enter the United Kingdom by an immigration officer within the meaning of the Immigration Act 1971, or] to remain in the United Kingdom by the Secretary of State [[26];or

(d) a person who is not a person subject to immigration control within the meaning of section 115(9) of the Immigration and Asylum Act and who is in the United Kingdom as a result of his deportation, expulsion or other removal by compulsion of law from another country to the United Kingdom;]

"patient" means a person (other than a prisoner) who is regarded as receiving free in-patient treatment within the meaning of the Social Security (Hospital In-Patients) Regulations 1975;

[[16]"prisoner" means a person who—

(a) is detained in custody pending trial or sentence upon conviction or under a sentence imposed by a court; or

(b) is on temporary release in accordance with the provisions of the Prison Act 1952 or the Prisons (Scotland) Act 1989,

other than a person [[23] who is detained in hospital under the provisions of the Mental Health Act 1983, or, in Scotland, under the provisions of the Mental Health (Scotland) Act 1984 or the Criminal Procedure (Scotland) Act 1995;]]

[[9]"residential accommodation" means, subject to the following provisions of this regulation, accommodation provided by a local authority in a home owned or managed by that or another local authority—

(a) under sections 21 to 24 [[16]. . .] of the National Assistance Act 1948 (provision of accommodation); or

(b) in Scotland, under section 13B or 59 of the Social Work (Scotland) Act 1968 (provision of residential and other establishments) [[15]. . .]; or

(c) under section 7 of the Mental Health (Scotland) Act 1984 (functions of local authorities),

where the accommodation is provided for a person whose stay in that accommodation has become other than temporary.]

[[7](3A) Where on or after 12th August 1991 a person is in, or only temporarily absent from, residential accommodation within the meaning of paragraph (3) and that accommodation subsequently becomes a residential care home [[27] . . .] that person shall continue to be treated as being in residential accommodation within the meaning of paragraph (3) if, and for so long as, he remains in the same accommodation [[22]. . .].]

[[10](3B) In a case where on 31st March 1993 a person was in or was temporarily absent from accommodation provided under section 26 of the National Assistance Act 1948, the definition of "residential accommodation" in paragraph (3) shall have effect in relation to that case as if for the words "provided by a local authority in a home owned or managed by that or another authority" there were substituted the words "provided in accordance with arrangements made by a local authority", and for the words in sub-paragraph (a) "under sections 21 to 24 [[16]. . .]" there were substituted the words "under section 26".

(3C) In a case where on 31st March 1993 a person was in or was temporarily absent from accommodation provided by a local authority under section 21 of the National Assistance Act 1948, the definition of "residential accommodation" in paragraph (3) shall have effect in relation to that case as if, after the words "by that or another [[12]local] authority" there were inserted the words "or provided in accordance with arrangements made by a local authority".]

[[15](3D) In Scotland, in a case where on the 31st March 1993 a person was in or was temporarily absent from accommodation provided under section 13B in a private or voluntary sector home, section 59(2)(c) of the Social Work (Scotland) Act 1968 or section 7 of the Mental Health (Scotland) Act 1984 in a voluntary or private sector home, the definition of "residential accommodation" in paragraph (3) shall have effect in that case as if—

    (a) for the words "provided by a local authority in a home owned or managed by that or another local authority" there were substituted the words "provided in accordance with arrangements made by a local authority"; and

    (b) for the words in sub-paragraph (b) "under section 13B or 59" there were substituted the words "under section 13B or 59(2)(c)";

and for the purpose of this paragraph the definition of "residential accommodation" above shall continue to have effect as though the words "other than in premises registered under section 61 of that Act (registration) and which are used for the rehabilitation of alcoholics or drug addicts." were retained at the end of sub-paragraph (b) of the definition.

(3E) In Scotland, in a case where on 31st March 1993 a person was in or was temporarily absent from accommodation the provision of which was secured by a local authority under section 13B in a home owned or managed by that or another local authority, section 59(2)(a) or (b) of the Social Work (Scotland) Act 1968, or section 7 of the Mental Health (Scotland) Act 1984 in a home owned or managed by that or another local authority, the definition of "residential accommodation" in paragraph (3) shall have effect in relation to that case as if, after the words "by that or another local authority" there were inserted the words "or provided in accordance with arrangements made by a local authority".]

[[18](3F) In paragraph (3) "person from abroad" does not include any person in Great Britain who left the territory of Montserrat after 1st November 1995 because of the effect on that territory of a volcanic eruption.]

[[31](3G) In paragraph (3), for the purposes of the definition of a person from abroad no person shall be treated as habitually resident in the United Kingdom, the Channel Islands, the Isle of Man or the Republic of Ireland if he does not have a right to reside in the United Kingdom, the Channel Islands, the Isle of Man or the Republic of Ireland.]

(4) A person who would, but for this paragraph, be in residential accommodation within the meaning of paragraph (3) shall not be treated as being in residential accommodation if he is a person—

(a) who is under the age of 18 and in the care of a local authority under Part II or III of the Social Work (Scotland) Act 1968 (promotion of social welfare of children in need of care), or

(b) [[16]. . .]

(c) for whom board is not provided.]

[[8](4A) [[9]In paragraph (4), sub-paragraph (c)] shall apply only to accommodation—

(a) where no cooked or prepared food is made available to the claimant in consequence solely of his paying the charge for the accommodation or any other charge which he is required to pay as a condition of occupying the accommodation, or both of those charges, or

(b) where such food is actually made available for his consumption on payment of a further charge or charges.]

[[10](4B) In the case of a person who on 31st March 1993 was either in or only temporarily absent from, residential accommodation within the meaning of regulation 21(3) as then in force, paragraph (4) shall apply as if sub-paragraph (c) was omitted.]

(5) A claimant to whom paragraph 19 of Schedule 7 (disability premium) applies shall be entitled to income support for the period in respect of which that paragraph applies to him notwithstanding that his partner was also entitled to income support for that same period.

AMENDMENTS

1. Income Support (General) Amendment No.4 Regulations 1988 (SI 1988/1445), Sch.1, para.1 (April 10, 1989).

2. Income Support (General) Amendment Regulations 1989 (SI 1989/534), Sch.1, para.5 (October 9, 1989).

3. Income Support (General) Amendment Regulations 1990 (SI 1990/547), reg.8 (April 9, 1990).

4. Income Support (General and Transitional) Amendment Regulations 1990 (SI 1990/2324), reg.2 (December 17, 1990).

5. Income Support (General) Amendment Regulations 1991 (SI 1991/236), reg.7 (April 8, 1991).

6. Income Support (General) Amendment (No.3) Regulations 1991 (SI 1991/1033), reg.2 (May 20, 1991).

7. Income Support (General) Amendment (No.5) Regulations 1991 (SI 1991/1656), reg.2 (August 12, 1991).

8. Income-related Benefits Schemes (Miscellaneous Amendments) (No.3) Regulations 1992 (SI 1992/2155), reg.15 (October 5, 1992).

9. Social Security Benefits (Amendments Consequential Upon the Introduction of Community Care) Regulations 1992 (SI 1992/3147), Sch.1, para.3 (April 1, 1993).

10. Social Security Benefits (Miscellaneous Amendments) Regulations 1993 (SI 1993/518), reg.5 (April 1, 1993).

11. Income-related Benefits Schemes (Miscellaneous Amendments) Regulations 1993 (SI 1993/315), reg.4 (April 12, 1993).

12. Income-related Benefits Schemes (Miscellaneous Amendments) (No.4) Regulations 1993 (SI 1993/2119), reg.10 (October 4, 1993).

13. Income-related Benefits Schemes (Miscellaneous Amendments) Regulations 1994 (SI 1994/527), reg.3 (April 11, 1994).

14. Income-related Benefits Schemes (Miscellaneous Amendments) (No.3) Regulations 1994 (SI 1994/1807), reg.4(1) (August 1, 1994).

2.143

15. Income-related Benefits Schemes (Miscellaneous Amendments) (No.5) Regulations 1994 (SI 1994/2139), reg.25 (October 3, 1994).

16. Income-related Benefits Schemes (Miscellaneous Amendments) Regulations 1995 (SI 1995/516), reg.21 (April 10, 1995).

17. Social Security (Persons from Abroad) Miscellaneous Amendments Regulations 1996 (SI 1996/30), reg.8(2) (February 5, 1996).

18. Income-related Benefits (Montserrat) Regulations 1996 (SI 1996/2006), reg.4 (August 28, 1996).

19. Income Support (General) (Jobseeker's Allowance Consequential Amendments) Regulations 1996 (SI 1996/206), reg.12 (October 7,1996).

20. Income-related Benefits Schemes and Social Fund (Miscellaneous Amendments) Regulations 1996 (SI 1996/1944), reg.6(6) (October 7, 1996).

21. Income Support and Social Security (Claims and Payments) (Miscellaneous Amendments) Regulations 1996 (SI 1996/2431), reg.2 (October 15, 1996).

22. Income Support (General) Amendment (No.3) Regulations 1996 (SI 1996/2614), reg.2 (November 8, 1996).

23. Social Security (Miscellaneous Amendments) Regulations 1998 (SI 1998/563), reg.8(1) and (2)(c)(i) (April 6, 1998).

24. Social Security (Miscellaneous Amendments) Regulations 1998 (SI 1998/563), reg.18(3) and (4)(c) (April 6, 1998).

25. Social Security (Immigration and Asylum) Consequential Amendments Regulations 2000 (SI 2000/636), reg.3(4)(a) (April 3, 2000).

26. Income-related Benefits and Jobseeker's Allowance (Amendment) Regulations 2000 (SI 2000/979), reg.2 (May 2, 2000).

27. Social Security Amendment (Residential Care and Nursing Homes) Regulations 2001 (SI 2001/3767), reg.2 and Sch., Pt I, para.6 (April 8, 2002).

28. Social Security (Removal of Residential Allowance and Miscellaneous Amendments) Regulations 2003 (SI 2003/1121), reg.2 and Sch.1 para.4 (October 6, 2003).

29. Social Security (Third Party Deductions and Miscellaneous Amendments) Regulations 2003 (S.I. 2003/2325), reg.3 (October 6, 2003).

30. Social Security (Working Tax Credit and Child Tax Credit) (Consequential Amendments) Regulations 2003 (SI 2003 No. 455), reg.2 and Sch.1, para.4 (April 6, 2004), except in "transitional cases" and see further the note to reg.17 of the Income Support Regulations.

31. Social Security (Habitual Residence) Amendment Regulations 2004 (SI 2004/1232), reg.3 (May 1, 2004).

DEFINITIONS

2.144   "child"—see 1986 Act, s.20(11) (SSCBA, s.137(1)).
"claimant"—see reg.2(1).
"local authority"—*ibid.*
"residential care home"—*ibid.*, reg.19(3).
"young person"—*ibid.*, reg.14.

GENERAL NOTE

Para.(1)

2.145   Applicable amounts in special cases are to be as prescribed in Sch.7.

Under para.6 of Sch.7 a person "without accommodation" is only entitled to a personal allowance for himself (or the allowance for a couple, if he is a member of a couple). In *R(IS) 23/98* the claimant had lived in his car for approximately two weeks. He was refused a disability premium as part of his income support. The Commissioner decides that a car could not be regarded as accommodation in the context of para.6. He approved of the following description of accommodation in para.29503 of the *Adjudication Officer's Guide*: "An effective shelter from the elements which is capable of being heated; and in which the occupants can sit, lie down, cook and eat; and which is reasonably suited for continuous occupation". While there is force in the Commissioner's reasoning in relation to a car, his (*obiter*) view that an ordinary tent or touring caravan may not constitute accommodation is more surprising (particularly in the light of the AO's concession to the contrary). It is suggested that the AO's distinction between a car as a means of transport and a tent (or caravan) as a means of shelter is correct. In this connection, note also para.17(1)(f) of Sch.3 under which payments in respect of a tent count as allowable housing costs (without any restriction as to the kind of tent).

On para.9 of Sch.7 see *CIS 1544/2001* in the notes to reg.16(1).

Para. (1A)

This provision secures that, except where the particular paragraph of Sch.7   **2.146** expressly allows the payment of a premium, a person whose entitlement falls under Sch.7 does not qualify for the severe disability premium.

Para. (2)

This provision supplies a linking rule for hospital patients (see para.(3)) who come   **2.147** out of hospital for short periods.

Para. (3)

This paragraph contains some important definitions for Sch.7, which are also   **2.148** referred to in other parts of the Regulations.

"Partner of a person subject to immigration control"

For a discussion of "person subject to immigration control" see the note to "person from abroad" below. In *CIS 1159/2004*, the claimant had been entitled to the severe disability premium under para.13(2)(a) of Sch.2. Subsequently his wife, who was a person subject to immigration control, came to live with him and he therefore became a "partner of a person subject to immigration control". The consequence was that whilst he retained his own personal allowance, he could not claim for his wife because, under para.16A of Sch.7, her personal allowance was nil. Ms Commissioner Fellner held that despite this circumstance, his wife was still the claimant's "partner" as defined by reg.2(1) with the effect that—as she herself was not entitled to the severe disability premium—para.13(2)(b) of Sch.2 disentitled the claimant to the premium. The Commissioner also rejected the claimant's argument that the SDP provisions were *ultra vires*.

"Person from abroad"

The definition of "person from abroad" has been considerably narrowed with effect   **2.149** from April 3, 2000. This is because many of the exclusions from benefit previously to be found in this paragraph are now contained in s.115 of the Immigration and Asylum Act 1999. The framework of the law is now as follows:

(1) under s.115(1) and (3) a "person subject to immigration control" is not entitled to a wide range of benefits including income support, income-based jobseeker's allowance, working families' tax credit, disabled person's tax credit and social fund payments;

(2) this general rule is subject to limited exceptions which are set out in the Social Security (Immigration and Asylum) Consequential Amendments Regulations 2000 (SI 2000/636);

(3) even if a claimant is not a "person subject to immigration control" (or if he is so subject, but is not excluded from benefit because of SI 2000/636) he may nevertheless be a "person from abroad"—and therefore not entitled to income

support or income-based jobseeker's allowance—if, broadly speaking, he is not habitually resident in the UK.

2.150 *"Person subject to immigration control"* is defined by s.115(9). Note first of all that a person who is a national of a European Economic Area ("EEA") state (*i.e.*, of the 25 EU countries—Austria, Belgium, Cyprus, the Czech Republic, Denmark, Estonia, Finland, France, Germany, Greece, Hungary, Ireland, Italy, Latvia, Lithuania, Luxembourg, Malta, the Netherlands, Poland, Portugal, Slovakia, Slovenia, Spain, Sweden and the UK—or of Iceland, Liechtenstein or Norway) can *never* be a person subject to immigration control for social security purposes. Nationals of other countries are subject to immigration control if they are within one of the following four categories:

2.151 *(a) a person who requires leave to enter or remain in the UK but does not have it*
This category (s.115(9)(a)) covers those who would have come within heads (b) to (g) of the pre-April 3, 2000 definition of "person from abroad", *i.e.*, illegal entrants, overstayers, people who are subject to a deportation order, those allowed temporary admission to the UK and, subject to *R(SB) 11/88* (below), anyone whose immigration status has yet to be determined.
The practice of the Immigration and Nationality Directorate of the Home Office ("IND") is to grant temporary admission to asylum seekers (except those who are detained) pending investigation of their claims (see *CIS 3108/97*). Section 115 therefore has the effect of excluding all asylum seekers from benefit with effect from April 3, 2000. The intention is that asylum seekers who are destitute will instead receive support from a Home Office agency, the National Asylum Support Service, under ss.95–100 of the Immigration and Asylum Act. Note however that reg.70(2A) of the IS Regulations, reg.147(2A) of the JSA Regulations, reg.12(1) of the Social Security (Persons From Abroad) Miscellaneous Amendments Regulations 1996 (SI 1996/30) and regs 2(4)(a) and (5) and 12(3) of SI 2000/636 contain important transitional protection for claimants who became asylum seekers on or before April 2, 2000.
For social security purposes, whether or not a person requires leave to enter or remain in the UK is a matter for the decision-maker (or, on appeal, for the appeal tribunal or Commissioner) to determine and any decision by the IND is not binding (*R(SB) 11/88* but see *R(SB) 2/85* and *R(SB) 25/85* as to the terms on which leave is granted).
Nationals of the Isle of Man and the Channel Islands have freedom of travel within the UK and do not require leave to enter or remain (Immigration Act 1971, s.1(3)). Certain commonwealth citizens cannot be deported (Immigration Act 1971, s.7(1)).

(b) a person who has leave to enter or remain but subject to a condition that he does not have recourse to public funds
2.152 Limited leave to enter or remain subject to there being no recourse to public funds is given under s.33(1) of the Immigration Act 1971. "Public funds" are currently defined by rule 6 of the Immigration Rules as attendance allowance, severe disablement allowance, carer's allowance, disability living allowance, income support, council tax benefit and housing benefit, a social fund payment, child benefit, income based JSA, state pension credit, child tax credit, working tax credit and certain publicly-funded housing.
Such a condition is typically applied to those seeking to join relatives who are settled in the UK, to people coming to the UK to study, to work or just for a visit.
For this category (s.115(9)(b)) and the following two (s.115(9)(c) and (d)) to apply, it is necessary that the person should actually require leave to enter or remain in the U.K. So, for example, if the IND mistakenly grants conditional leave to a person who is in fact a British citizen and does not require leave at all the mistake does not cause that person to become subject to immigration control for social security purposes (see *R(SB) 11/88*). However, where it is clear that leave is required, the decision of the IND as to the terms on which leave is granted is conclusive (see

R(SB) 2/85 and *R(SB) 25/85*). A proper statement of the terms of leave should be obtained from the Home Office (*CSSB 137/82*).

There is one exception to the exclusion from benefit in s.115(9)(b). This is established by reg.2(1) and para.1 of Part I of the Schedule to SI 2000/636, and applies to those who have previously supported themselves without recourse to public funds and find themselves temporarily without money because remittances from abroad have been disrupted. In such circumstances, income support, income-based jobseeker's allowance and social fund payments can be paid as long as there is a reasonable expectation that the supply of funds will be resumed.

(c) a person who has leave to enter or remain which was given as a result of
a maintenance undertaking

"Maintenance undertaking" is defined by s.115(10) as "a written undertaking given by another person in pursuance of the immigration rules to be responsible for [the claimant's] maintenance and accommodation".

2.153

Under Rule 35 of the Immigration Rules such undertakings may be demanded from "a sponsor of a person seeking leave to enter or variation of leave to enter or remain in the United Kingdom" but are normally only required from the sponsors of elderly or other dependent relatives. The purpose of the undertaking is to reinforce a condition that the person seeking leave to enter or remain should not have recourse to public funds by

- demonstrating that the sponsor has sufficient resources to maintain and accommodate the relative without the latter claiming public funds;

- making the sponsor legally "liable to maintain" the relative. This has the effect that, if the Secretary of State does for any reason have to pay income support to the relative (and, in most cases, the mere existence of an undertaking will mean that the relative has no such entitlement), the sponsor may, in certain circumstances, be subject to a criminal penalty and the Secretary of State may recoup the benefit paid by making a complaint in a magistrates' court (see, respectively ss. 105 and 106 SSAA 1992 in Vol. III)

The requirement in the definition that the undertaking has been given "in pursuance of the immigration rules" has the effect that only *formal* sponsorship undertakings required by the IND before leave is granted prevent access to benefit. But it does not mean that the undertaking must be given on one of the official Home Office forms (either Form RON 112 or the Form SET(F) that replaced it)—see *R. (Begum) v Social Security Commissioner* [2003] EWHC 3380 (Admin), QBD (Sir Christopher Bellamy), November 6, 2003 confirming *CIS/2474/1999*, *CIS/2816/2002* and, on this point, *CIS/47/2002*. Those forms "are expressly in the language of undertaking and emphasise the significance of such undertakings" (see Rix L.J. at para.36 of *Ahmed v Secretary of State for Work & Pensions* [2005] EWCA Civ 535, CA (May, Rix and Jacob L.JJ.), April 19, 2005 (to be reported as *R(IS) 8/05*). But if an official form is not used, consideration may need to be given to whether the document signed by the sponsor amounts to an "undertaking" at all. In *Ahmed* the Court of Appeal held (upholding the Commissioner in *CIS/426/2003* and disagreeing, on this point, with the Commissioner in *CIS/47/2002* in which the disputed document was in similar terms) that the issue is one of substance rather than form and that the legal test is whether or not the document contains a promise or agreement about what the sponsor will do in the future rather than a statement about his or her present abilities and intentions:

"47. . . . It seems to me that an undertaking has to be something in the nature of a promise or agreement and the language that "I am able and willing to maintain and accommodate" is language which has reference, essentially, to current ability and intention and does not amount to a promise for the future. The essence of an undertaking is a promise as to the future, as typically found in the language 'I will.'

48. I accept that the use of any particular language is not a condition precedent. The absence of an express reference to "I undertake", such as is found in the Home Office's forms, or to "I promise" or "I agree", will not necessarily be critical if it is still clear that the substance of what is said is a promise for the future." (*per* Rix L.J.)

So, the declaration in the *Ahmed* case that the sponsor was "able and willing to maintain and accommodate the applicant without recourse to public funds and in suitable accommodation" was not an undertaking because it only related to present facts and intentions.

In *CIS 3508/2001* it was held that leave to enter or remain was given "as a result of" a maintenance undertaking if the existence of that undertaking was a factor in the decision to grant leave. It does not have to be the only, or even a major, factor. It is sufficient that it was of some relevance. It seems that that will almost always be the case if the immigration decision maker acts within the Immigration Rules.

People who are granted leave to enter or remain as a result of a maintenance undertaking are not entitled to income support income-based JSA until they have been resident in the UK for a period of at least five years from the date of entry or the date on which the undertaking was given, whichever is later. The only exception is where the person (or all the people if there was more than one) who gave the maintenance undertaking has died before the end of the five year period. See para.3 of Part I of the Schedule to SI 2000/636.

Sponsored immigrants are not excluded from social fund payments (see para.4 of Part II of the Schedule to SI 2000/636) but in practice are unlikely to be eligible for anything other than a crisis loan or a winter fuel payment. This is because, as persons subject to immigration control, they are excluded from the qualifying benefits for maternity and funeral expenses payments, community care grants, budgeting loans and cold weather payments. Sponsored immigrants are also not excluded from entitlement to attendance allowance, severe disablement allowance, carer's allowance or disability living allowance.

Recent guidance from the Secretary of State (DMG Memo JSA/IS 101) clarifies that family members of those granted refugee status or (in certain circumstances) exceptional leave to remain, discretionary leave or humanitarian protection, who come to the UK for settlement under the "family reunion" rules, will have indefinite leave to remain in the UK without restrictions and are not sponsored immigrants even though their visas will include the indorsement "VISA FAMILY REUNION (Sponsor)". Such claimants are not persons subject to immigration control and will be entitled to income-related benefits as soon as they have become habitually resident.

(d) a person who has leave to enter or remain only because he is appealing against certain immigration decisions

2.154   Under s.61 of the Immigration and Asylum Act 1999, a person with limited leave to enter or remain in the UK has a right of appeal against a decision to vary, or to refuse to vary, his leave. The right arises if the consequence of the decision is that the person may be required to leave the UK within 28 days of being notified of it. A similar right is given to asylum seekers by s.69(2). Paragraph 17 of Sch.4 to the 1999 Act provides that while an appeal under s.61 or 69(2) is pending, the leave to which the appeal relates and any conditions subject to which it was granted continue to have effect. Section 115(9)(d) provides that those whose leave has automatically been extended by para.17 are persons subject to immigration control.

The ECSMA Agreement and the European Social Charter

2.155   Nationals of those countries which are not members of the EEA but which have ratified the European Convention on Social and Medical Assistance ("the ECSMA

Agreement") or the European Social Charter (both of which are treaties concluded under the auspices of the Council of Europe (ETS Nos 14 and 35 respectively) are subject to immigration control but are not excluded from income support, income-based jobseeker's allowance or social fund payments as long as they are "lawfully present" in the UK (see para.4 of Part I of the Schedule to SI 2000/636). This affects nationals of Turkey (ECSMA Agreement) and of Romania, Switzerland, Turkey and Ukraine (Social Charter).

The meaning of "lawfully present" was considered by the Court of Appeal in *Kaya v London Borough of Haringey and Secretary of State for Social Security*, (CA, May 1, 2001) [2001] EWCA Civ 677. The case concerned the interpretation of that phrase in the context of Mrs Kaya's entitlement to housing assistance under s.185(2) of the Housing Act 1992 and Class E of reg.3 of the Homelessness (England) Regulations 2000 but the judgments consider SI 2000 No. 636 and the Secretary of State for Social Security intervened in the case because of its potential implications for the social security system. The issue was whether a Turkish asylum seeker who had been given temporary admission to the UK under para.21 of Sch.2 to the Immigration Act 1971 pending a decision on her asylum claim was "lawfully present in the United Kingdom" as required by Class E. The Court decided unanimously that she was not. Under s.11(1) of that Act a person "who has not otherwise entered the United Kingdom shall be deemed not to do so as long as he is detained, *or temporarily admitted* or released while liable to detention, under the power conferred by Schedule 2". Following the decision of the House of Lords in *R. v Home Secretary Ex parte Bugdaycay* [1987] A.C. 514, it was held that the purpose of a grant of temporary admission was to prevent the commission of the criminal offence of entering without leave under s.24(1)(a) and that this purpose was achieved by the legal fiction of treating a person with temporary admission as being not present at all.

Any attempt to apply the Court's decision to the IS scheme necessarily encounters an unusual conceptual difficulty. Under s.124 of the Contributions and Benefits Act, no-one can be entitled to IS in the first place unless they are "[a] person in Great Britain". To treat those with temporary admission as *ipso facto* not being "in Great Britain" has the consequence that it was unnecessary for them to have been expressly excluded from income support as "persons from abroad" until April 3, 2000. It would also render otiose the former (and, in transitional cases, continuing) entitlement of certain categories of asylum seeker to urgent cases payments under reg.70. The Court's decision in *Kaya* thus appears to imply a class of claimants who are "in Great Britain" for the purposes of s.124 without also being "present" here for the purposes of the Immigration Act. Be that as it may, it has been confirmed in *CIS 2091/2001* that *Kaya* does apply in the field of social security and that it is binding on Commissioners and on tribunals.

That decision was confirmed by the Court of Appeal in *Szoma v Secretary of State for Work and Pensions* [2003] EWCA Civ 1131 (July 30, 2003) (Pill and Carnwath L.JJ. and Kay J.). The majority of the Court (Pill L.J. and Kay J.) also expressly rejected a submission that *Kaya* was wrongly decided. Mr Szoma is petitioning the House of Lords for leave to appeal.

Spouses and family members of EEA nationals

A person who is not an EEA national but who is a family member of such a national is not excluded from social fund payments (para.1 of Part II of the Schedule to SI 2000/636—but see note on sponsored immigrants (above) as to the practical restrictions on eligibility). Such people do not need to rely on this provision if they themselves are nationals of ECSMA or European Social Charter states.   **2.156**

EEA reciprocal agreements

Under Art.310 (formerly Art.238) of the Treaty establishing the European Community (as amended by the Treaty of Amsterdam), the EC "may conclude with one or more States or international organisations agreements establishing an association   **2.157** involving reciprocal rights and obligations, common action and special procedure". Paragraphs 2 and 3 of Part II to SI 2000/636 apply when such a reciprocal agreement provides for equal treatment in the field of social security of workers who are nationals of the signatory State and their families. In those circumstances, nationals of the non–EC State who are lawfully working in the UK and members of their families who are living with them are not excluded by s.115 from entitlement to social fund payments. For an example of how an association agreement affected entitlement to family credit under the pre-April 3, 2000 law see *R(FC 1/01)* which also decides that where such an Agreement does not provide for equal treatment in the field of social security but a Decision of an Association Council constituted under the Agreement and required by the Agreement to adopt social security measures does so provide, the Decision of the Association Council must be regarded as made under the Agreement so that (in terms of the current law) paras 2 and 3 of Part II of the Schedule would apply.

From time to time, tribunals can be called on to decide legal issues arising under the terms of the individual Association Agreements and the Decisions of the Association Councils established by those Agreements. Useful guidance for those who need to apply the Agreement between the EC and Turkey may be found in two decisions of Mr Commissioner Mesher, *CJSA 4705/1999* and *CIS 5707/1999*. In the latter appeal, the Commissioner holds that income support is not within the material scope of Decision 3/80 of the Association Council under that Agreement (and therefore that IS claimants may not benefit from its terms). In the former appeal, it was held that JSA *was* within the material scope of the Decision but, following the decision of the ECJ in *Sürül v Bundesanstalt für Arbeit* (C–262/96) [1999] E.C.R. I-2685, a person may only rely on the Decision if authorised to reside in the Member State concerned and lawfully resident there. In *CJSA 4705/1999*, the claimant was an overstayer and therefore not authorised to reside in the United Kingdom. He could not therefore benefit from Decision 3/80.

Habitual Residence Test

2.158   Claimants who are not subject to immigration control (or who are protected from exclusion from income support or income-based JSA by SI 2000/636) may nevertheless be refused benefit unless they are "habitually resident" in the common travel area ("CTA"—see rule 15 of the Immigration Rules) of the UK, Channel Islands, Isle of Man or Republic of Ireland. This includes UK nationals and nationals of other EEA States unless they fall within one of the exempted groups (see below). Claimants who are neither exempt nor habitually resident in the CTA are defined as "persons from abroad" and (except for those asylum seekers who are transitionally entitled to urgent case payments under reg.70(2A)) have applicable amount of nil and hence no entitlement to income support or income-based jobseeker's allowance (see para.17 of Sch.7 and para.14 of Sch.5 to the JSA Regulations). The requirement to be habitually resident only applies to the claimant, not to a partner or dependant.

The test applies to all new and repeat claims for income support on and after August 1, 1994. Existing claimants were not affected (see reg.4(2) of the Income-related Benefits Schemes (Miscellaneous Amendments) (No.3) Regulations 1994 (SI 1994/1807). In the early days of the test there were a number of challenges to its validity both on the grounds that it was *ultra vires* s.124(1) of the Contributions and Benefits Act and as being unlawful under EC law. However, these challenges were all unsuccessful (see pp. 290–291 of the 1999 edition of *Mesher and Wood, Income-related Benefits: the Legislation*) and there can be no real doubt as to the test's validity.

Since May 1, 2004, a person cannot be habitually resident for the purpose of the definition of "person from abroad" in para.(3) unless s/he also has a "right to reside" in the CTA—see para.(3F) and the notes on "Right to reside" below.

Who is exempt?

2.159   Certain groups are treated as habitually resident without reference to the circumstances of individual claimants. These are set out in sub-paragraphs (a) to (d).

Sub-para. (a)

A person who is a "worker" for the purposes of EC Regulations 1612/68 or 1251/70, **2.160** or who has a right of residence under EC Directives 68/360 or 73/148, is exempt. These Regulations and Directives apply to all EEA nationals, including UK nationals who are exercising Community rights: *R. v Immigration Appeal Tribunal and Surinder Singh Ex parte Secretary of State for the Home Department*, ECJ Case C-370/90, [1992] 3 All E.R. 798. Community rights include the right to move in order to work, or to seek work (Art. 48 of the Treaty of Rome—now, following amendment, Art. 39 EC). A UK National who has moved to another EEA country to work and then returns to the UK in order to seek work is thus exercising his right to freedom of movement, and this is so whether or not he claims income support/income-based JSA (contrary to the assertion frequently made by decision-makers); exemption from the habitual residence test will, however, depend on whether he counts as a worker (see below) or can otherwise satisfy or be treated as satisfying the habitual residence test. But note that as a result of the ECJ's decision in *Swaddling*, such a person may count as actually habitually resident immediately on his return (see below). Obviously in most cases a person who is a worker or work seeker will now have to claim income-based JSA rather than income support (unless, for example, he is incapable of work).

EC Regs 1612/68 and 1251/70

Regulation 1612/68 provides for freedom of movement for workers and their **2.161** families.

The main question is what is meant by "worker" in this context. "Worker" is not defined in Regulation 1612/68 (or in the EC Treaty). However, the word is to be interpreted broadly and as a matter of Community, not national, law (*Levin* [1982] E.C.R. 1035). A person's motives for working in another Member State are not relevant (*Bettray* [1989] E.C.R. 1621). "Worker" includes those who work part-time or whose pay is below subsistence level, provided that they are pursuing an activity that is "genuine and effective" and not on such a small scale as to be "marginal and ancillary" (*Levin*, and *Kempf* [1986] E.C.R. 1741). If the work is very limited *and* only on an irregular or occasional basis, this may indicate that it is a marginal and ancillary activity (*Raulin* [1992] E.C.R. 1–1027). But if it can be described as an economic activity (*Levin*), as opposed to, for example, a hobby, this should count as work, even if it is for only a few hours a week. In *R(IS) 12/98* an au pair who had worked for five weeks (being paid £35 for a 13 hour week, plus free board and lodging) was held to be a worker.

Thus if the person has genuinely worked, even for a very short period, they can count as a worker. There seems to be no reason why this should not include work done during a previous stay in the UK (even if on this occasion the person has not yet obtained employment) although this will depend on the length of time which has passed since the previous stay and the extent to which it can be said that the work now sought is connected to the work previously undertaken—see the discussion of *Collins* in the note to reg. 85 of the JSA Regulatons. And see further the question referred to the ECJ by the Commissioner in *Swaddling* (below), although this was not answered by the Court. It was accepted by the Advocate General in *Scrivner* [1985] E.C.R. 1027 that if a worker becomes unemployed or incapable of work, they remain a worker for the purposes of Regulation 1612/68. (The ECJ itself did not comment on the point because the national court had accepted that Mr Scrivner still had the status of worker and so no question on this issue was put to the ECJ.) Mr Scrivner had worked in Belgium but had given up his job for personal reasons and then registered as in search of work. The ECJ held that he was entitled to the Belgian "minimex" (a benefit which provided a "minimum means of subsistence"), as this was a social advantage within Article 7(2) of Regulation 1612/68 which could not be denied to migrant workers. However, the DSS took the view that an unemployed worker does not retain worker status. In *R(IS) 3/97*, the AO submitted that the ECJ's judgments in *Lair* [1988] E.C.R. 3161 and *Raulin* meant that immediately on ceasing employment a person lost the status of worker and became merely a work seeker. But this is rejected by the Commissioner. He points out that *Lair* had held that worker status was retained by a person who had voluntarily given up work in order to take up vocational training which was linked to the previous job. In *Raulin* it was decided that if the training had no link with the previous occupation, worker status was only retained in the case of a migrant worker who was involuntarily unemployed. But those cases were dealing with situations where people could be said to have taken themselves out of the labour market by undertaking full-time studies. The ECJ recognised that nevertheless those concerned could be regarded as retaining the status of worker under certain conditions. Those cases did not deal at all with the situation where a person ceased voluntarily or involuntarily to be in an employment relationship but remained in the labour market, *e.g.* by making genuine efforts to find work. In such circumstances a person did not immediately lose the status of "worker" for the purposes of Regulation 1612/68. However the claimant in *R(IS) 3/97* had never been employed in the UK, so the Commissioner did not actually have to directly decide whether sub-para.(a) applied in these circumstances.

2.162   But the question did directly arise in *R(IS) 12/98*. The claimant was a French national who after coming to the UK had worked as an au pair with a family (being paid £35 for a 13-hour week, with free board and lodging) for about five weeks before she claimed income support on July 31, 1995. It was accepted that the claimant had been a "worker" for the purposes of Regulation 1612/68 before she claimed income support. But the AO contended that if a person left employment voluntarily the status of worker was lost. The Commissioner concludes, having regard in particular to para.29 of the ECJ's judgment in *Lair*, that a person who had left employment but remained in the labour market retained the status of worker for the purposes of Regulation 1612/68. It did not in itself matter whether the previous employment was left voluntarily or involuntarily. The issue was whether the circumstances of the leaving, and in particular the person's intentions and actions at the time, indicated whether or not the person was still in the labour market. The claimant in this case had continued to seek work after her employment had ended; she thus continued to be a "worker" and so was to be treated as habitually resident under sub-para.(a). *R(IS) 12/98* is followed in *R(IS) 9/99*.

R(IS) 3/97 also deals with the position of a person seeking work who has not previously worked in the UK. The claimant was a national of the Republic of Ireland. In 1991 he went to France where he worked as an agricultural labourer. In October 1994 he came to the UK, registered as unemployed and claimed income support. The Commissioner holds that it was plain from the ECJ's judgment in *Lebon* [1987] E.C.R. 2811 that a person who was simply a work seeker, that is, who had moved from one Member State to another to seek employment, was not a worker for the purposes of Regulation 1612/68. In *Lebon* the ECJ decided that the right to equal treatment as regards social and tax advantages (which would include income support) in Art.7(2) of Regulation 1612/68 only applied to workers and not to those who moved to seek employment. The ECJ stated that people who moved in order to seek employment only enjoyed equal treatment as regards access to such employment in accordance with Article 39 EC (formerly, prior to amendment, Article 48 of the Treaty) and Articles 2 and 5 of Regulation 1612/68. Moreover, as the ECJ had ruled in *Raulin*, in deciding whether a person was a worker for the purposes of Regulation 1612/68, account could only be taken of occupational activities pursued in the host State but not activities pursued elsewhere in the Community. Thus, as the claimant had never worked in the UK, he was not a worker for the purposes of Regulation 1612/68. In *Collins* (at para.32), the Court held that the concept of "worker" is not used in Regulation 1612/68 in a uniform manner and that, although other parts of the Regulation used the term in a broader sense, in Title II of Part I (which contains Art.7, the relevant anti-discrimination provision) "this term covers only persons who have already entered the employment market". It was for the UK courts or tribunals to decide whether the phrase "worker for the purposes of Council Regulation (EEC) No. 1612/68" in head (a) of the definition of "person from abroad" was to be interpreted as meaning "worker for the purpose of *Title II of Part I of* Council Regulation (EEC) No. 1612/68". Commissioner Mesher has now decided (*CJSA/4065/1999*) that it is to be so interpreted.

Regulation 1251/70, *inter alia*, grants a right of residence after termination of employment to certain retired or incapacitated workers. For this to apply, a worker must have reached pension age when he stopped work, been employed in the host State for the last 12 months and lived there for more than three years, or ceased work due to a permanent incapacity and lived in the host State for more than two years (if the incapacity resulted from an accident at work or occupational disease entitling him to benefit there is no residence condition). If his spouse is a national there are no required periods of employment or residence (article 2). However, as the Commissioner in *R(IS) 12/98* points out, the test under sub-para.(a) is not whether the claimant has a right to remain in the UK under Regulation 1251/70. It is whether the claimant counts as a worker for the purposes of that Regulation. Article 1 of Regulation 1251/70 states that the provisions of the Regulation apply to "nationals of a Member State who have worked as employed persons in the territory of another Member State" and to their families. Thus the Commissioner in *R(IS) 12/98* thought it possible (although he did not express a firm conclusion on the point) that a national of a Member State who had worked as an employed person in the UK could be "a worker for the purposes of Regulation 1251/70". This was especially in view of Art.4(2), which treats periods of involuntary unemployment (and absences due to illness or accident) as periods of employment for the purposes of Art.2 (and see also para.34 of the ECJ's judgment in *Lair*). If this is the case, this would be a less onerous test than under Regulation 1612/68. *R(IS) 3/97* confirms that only employment in the host State in question is relevant to the assessment of whether someone is a worker for the purposes of Regulation 1251/70.

EC Directives 68/360 and 73/148

People who have a right to reside under EC Directives 68/360 or 73/148 are also treated as habitually resident. (The I(EEA) Order implements, *inter alia*, Directives 68/360 and 73/148.) Directive 68/360 covers workers and members of their families who come within Regulations 1612/68 or 1251/70. Members of the worker's family who have a right to "install" themselves with the worker are his spouse, their children who are under the age of 21 or dependent, and their ascendant relatives who are dependent (Art.10(1) of Regulation 1612/68). In addition, Art.10(2) provides that Member States shall "facilitate the admission of" other members of a worker's family who are either dependent or who were living under his roof in the previous country. It is not clear whether the latter also have a right of residence for these purposes (see Wyatt and Dashwood, *European Community Law* (3rd ed.), pp. 246 and 282).

Directive 68/360 is concerned with the issue of residence permits, but the right to reside does not derive from the permit but from Community law itself (*Royer* [1976] E.C.R. 497, *Echternach* [1989] E.C.R. 723, *Raulin, Roux* [1991] E.C.R. 1–273; and see *R(IS) 9/99* below). Thus workers who satisfy the conditions for obtaining (or retaining) a residence permit are covered, even if they have not applied for one. Residence permits are issued on the basis of confirmation from the employer of the worker's employment. They are for five years unless the employment is expected to last less than one year; where the expected period of the worker's employment is more than three months but less than a year a permit *may* be (but is not automatically: *R(IS) 9/99*) limited to this period. A worker whose employment is not expected to last more than three months has a right of residence without a residence permit for the expected duration of the employment. Seasonal workers, and frontier workers (*i.e.* those who return to another Member State at least once a week) also have a right of residence without a residence permit. A residence permit does not end if the worker becomes involuntarily unemployed or temporarily incapablé of work. It would seem to follow that it *may* be withdrawn if the person becomes *voluntarily* unemployed but clearly all the circumstances would need to be taken into account. Presumably such a decision should be taken by the Home Office. A residence permit may also be withdrawn if the person leaves the UK for more than six months (unless this is for military service).

2.163

2.164

It should be remembered, as *R(IS) 9/99* points out (and see *Royer*, etc., above), that a worker's right of residence derives directly from Art.39 (ex 48) EC and not from the Directive, which does not of itself impose any conditions on that right. As the Commissioner in *R(IS) 9/99* states, a right of residence under Directive 68/360 will thus primarily be of relevance for someone who was not a worker, for example, a member of a worker's family. Similarly *R(IS) 3/97* confirms that Directive 68/630 does not provide a right of residence for work seekers. The right of EEA Nationals to stay in other Member States for the purpose of seeking employment derives not from that Directive but from Art.48(3) of the Treaty of Rome (now, after amendment, Art.39 EC). That decision has now been conclusively confirmed by the ECJ in *Collins* (at paras 36–44 of the judgment).

2.165   Directive 73/148, which is very similar to Directive 68/360, covers the self-employed and those who are providing or receiving services, and their families. It also applies to EEA nationals who are seeking self-employment, or to provide or receive services. As in the case of Directive 68/360, the permit does not create the right to reside which derives from the Treaty itself, but only confirms it. Residence permits for the self-employed are to be granted for at least five years; for providers or recipients of services they may be limited to the duration of the service. A permit is not to be withdrawn because the person is temporarily incapable of work. Services are those that are normally paid for, and include industrial, commercial, craft and professional activities (Art.60 of the Treaty). The ECJ has held that tourism, medical treatment and education are covered (*Luisi* [1984] E.C.R. 377). The Directive does not, for example, specify the level of service, or impose any qualifying period, in order for a right of residence to be granted. Thus its application could be quite wide. However, it does not extend to a person who has taken no steps towards seeking self-employment or offering services to the public beyond arriving in a Member State with the wish to do (see *R(IS) 6/00* and *C10/95(IS)*). The scope of Directive 73/148 was also considered by the Commissioner in *CIS 4727/1999*. He decided (following *Steymann v Staatssecretaris van Justitie* [1988] E.C.R. 6519 and *Sodemare SA v Regione Lombardia* [1997] E.C.R. I-3395) that a claimant who wished to bring herself within the personal scope of the Directive on the basis of receipt of services must have moved from one Member State to another *for the purpose of* receiving those services (see Art.1(1)(b)). A person who comes to the UK for the purpose of settlement takes herself outside the scope of the Directive: it is not relevant that she may actually receive services here following her arrival.

Note that sub-para.(a) does not refer to EC Directive 75/34 under which those who have retired from self-employment because of old age or incapacity have a right to reside; the rules are similar to those that apply to retired workers under Regulation 1251/70. It is not clear why this Directive has not been included.

A8 nationals treated as workers

For "a person who is an accession State worker requiring registration who is treated as a worker for the purpose of the definition of "qualified person" in regulation 5(1) of the Immigration (European Economic Area) Regulations 2000 pursuant to regulation 5 of the Accession (Immigration and Worker Registration) Regulations 2004" see the commentary to para.(3G) ("Right to reside") below.

Sub-paras (b) and (c)

2.166   Refugees and people who have been granted exceptional leave to enter, or to remain in, the UK are treated as habitually resident (note that before April 6, 1998 sub-para.(c) only referred to those who had been granted exceptional leave to *remain* in (not to enter) the UK)

In *R(IS) 9/98* the Commissioner confirms that a person counts as a refugee entitled to the protection of the 1951 Convention from the time he fulfills the criteria contained in the definition in the Convention. It is not necessary for his status as a refugee to have been recognised by the Home Office, since such recognition does not make the person a refugee but merely declares him to be one.

Sub-para. (d)

From May 2, 2000, people who are deported, expelled or otherwise compulsorily **2.167** removed from another country to the UK are automatically treated as habitually resident in the CTA unless they fall within the categories of claimant who are subject to immigration control under s.115(9) of the Immigration and Asylum Act.

Meaning of habitual residence

"Habitual residence" is not defined in the regulation and therefore the words must **2.168** be given their natural and ordinary meaning (see *Shah v Barnet London Borough Council* [1983] 2 A.C. 309, [1983] 1 All E.R. 226, *Re J (A Minor)* [1990] 2 A.C. 562, *R(IS) 6/96* and *R(IS) 2/00*). Whether a person is habitually resident is a question of fact to be decided by reference to all the circumstances in each case (*Re J*). Habitual residence is not the same as domicile (*R(U) 8/88*). It is possible to be habitually resident in more than one country (although it is unusual); it is also possible to be habitually resident in none. A person does not have to be continually present in a country in order to be habitually resident. There is no time limit after which habitual residence is established, but the longer the length of stay the more likely the person is to be habitually resident. On the other hand, a person may be habitually resident shortly after arriving in a country depending on the circumstances. For people who are "re-establishing ties" in the UK, see *Swaddling* and *Nessa* (below). Originally the practice was that if a person stated on their income support claim form that they had not entered the UK within the last five years habitual residence would be assumed. The SSAC had recommended that the trigger point for generating inquiries into habitual residence should be reduced to two years. This has now been accepted by the Government.

The concept of habitual residence occurs in European law, in particular in EC Regulation 1408/71 dealing with social security for migrant workers, and has been considered in several Commissioners' decisions on unemployment benefit (see *R(U) 7/85, R(U) 4/86, CU 285/1985* and in particular *R(U) 8/88* which has appendices summarising these decisions together with references to the relevant European provisions and case law). However, it is important to remember that the context of this case law is that of returning workers claiming to have retained their "habitual residence" while working elsewhere, in order to qualify for unemployment benefit. It is thus mainly concerned with looking at the past. In *Di Paolo v Office National de L'Emploi* [1977] E.C.R. 315 the ECJ stated that account had to be taken of factors such as the nature of a person's occupation, the reasons for moving to another State to work and the length of residence before the person moved. The Court also held that stable employment could outweigh other factors in determining habitual residence. But as the Commissioner in *R(IS) 2/00* points out, that decision was concerned with the particular context of Article 71(1)(b)(ii) of Regulation 1408/71 (the exception to the general rule that an unemployed person should receive unemployment benefit from the State where he was last employed) and the ECJ was not suggesting that the factors mentioned were the only ones to be taken into account in determining habitual residence. In his view *Di Paolo* should not be used to illustrate the meaning of habitual residence except with great caution. Furthermore, as the SSAC's report said, the case law's emphasis on the length and stability of employment does not take account of the fact that part-time or temporary work, or short fixed-term contracts, may be the only available option for many people coming to the UK. In addition, where availability is not a condition for receiving benefit, as is now the case for income support, employment related factors may be of little assistance in determining whether a person is habitually resident. Note, however, that the ECJ in *Swaddling* apparently adopts a similar approach to the meaning of "residence" (*i.e.* habitual residence: see Art.1(h) of Regulation 1408/71) for the purpose of Art.10a, as it had laid down in *Di Paolo* (although the emphasis on stable employment is much reduced). But it seems questionable whether the approach used to determine whether habitual residence has been *retained* during an absence is necessarily appropriate when the issue is whether habitual residence has been (*re-*) *established*.

2.169   The concept of habitual residence also occurs in certain areas of UK law, *e.g.* tax, family and child support law. Here it has sometimes been equated to "ordinarily resident". See, for example *Kapur v Kapur* [1984] F.L.R. 920, a case on the meaning of habitual residence in the Domicile and Matrimonial Proceedings Act 1973, which holds that there is no real distinction between "ordinary" and "habitual" residence. Bush J. in *Kapur* refers to the House of Lords' decision in *Shah* (which concerned the interpretation of "ordinarily resident" in the Education Act 1962) where ordinary residence was held to include habitual residence. Lord Scarman states that the words "ordinarily resident" were to be given their natural and ordinary meaning which was "habitually and normally resident, apart from temporary or occasional absences of long or short duration". Habitually meant that the residence had to be adopted voluntarily and for a settled purpose (see *IRC v Lysaght* [1928] A.C. 234). In the light of the House of Lords' decision in *Shah* Bush J. declined to follow *Cruse v Chittum* [1974] 2 All E.R. 940 which had held that habitual residence was something more than ordinary residence. In *Shah* Lord Scarman points out that a settled purpose could be for a limited period; there was no need to intend to stay indefinitely. Such a purpose could include education, employment, health, family or "merely love of the place". Thus in *CA 35/1992* a woman, who had gone to Malta for health reasons, intending to return within 18 months, was held to be ordinarily resident there. The fact that a person has a restricted right to stay in the UK does not prevent him from being habitually resident (*Shah* and *Kapur*), and see *R(IS) 6/96*, where the Commissioner states that the test focuses on the fact and nature of the residence and not on the legal right of abode. Thus an asylum seeker may become habitually resident before his status as a refugee is recognised by the Home Office (*R(IS)9/98*). The residence must, however, be lawful (*Shah*). It is clear from these cases that habitual residence can be acquired quite quickly. In the domestic context, as the law currently stands, it probably cannot be acquired in a single day (*Macrae v Macrae* [1949] 2 All E.R. 34, which held that habitual residence could be gained as easily as it is lost, is of doubtful authority in the light of *Re J*, see below), but certainly where there is a settled purpose a short period may suffice, depending on the circumstances.

The SSAC expressed regret that the chosen test was not ordinary residence as this was the test for family credit and disability working allowance and one with which UK adjudicators were more familiar. They understood that the DSS's view was that habitual residence implied "a stronger, more regular physical presence in the country and association with it" than ordinary residence did. But they considered that the difference between the two was one of emphasis and they were unable to find any uniquely distinguishing factor. The concept of habitual residence also arises in the context of child support. A recent example of this can be seen in the decision of the Inner House of the Court of Session in *L.A. v Secretary of State for Work and Pensions and T.V.I.* (Lords Hamilton, Cosgrove and Bonomy), March 25, 2004. However, child support decisions must be applied with caution in the context of income support as they concern the *jurisdiction* of the Child Support Agency rather than *entitlement* to a benefit.

The test in the context of income support

2.170   The meaning of habitual residence in the context of income support has been considered in a number of Commissioners, decisions, most notably in *R(IS) 6/96*, and by the House of Lords in *Nessa v Chief Adjudication Officer*. It has also been considered by the ECJ in relation to people who are covered by Regulation 1408/71 (*Swaddling v Adjudication Officer*, Case C-90/97, ECJ, February 25, 1999, *The Times*, March 4, 1999, also reported as *R(IS) 6/99*). However, the point is made forcibly in *R(IS) 6/00* (para.18) that there is no reason to interpret the meaning of habitual residence in domestic UK law by reference to EC legislation: it is the UK domestic law meaning which must be applied except to the extent that some specific provision of EC law requires otherwise. See also para.20 of *CIS 1304/1997 & CJSA 5394/1998* where a different Commissioner agrees that the European concept does not replace the domestic concept and *Gingi v Secretary of State for Work and Pensions* [2001] EWCA Civ 1685, CA, November 14, 2001 where the Court rejected the argument that *Swaddling* had established a meaning of "habitually resident" for the purposes of British law and that, as those words could only have one meaning which could not change according to the facts of the case, that meaning must be applied in every habitual residence case. This, it was said, was "a gallant attempt to extend the protection of Community Law to a case containing no Community element, and which does not fall within the reach of the Community legal order." In view of the decision in *Nessa* that in most cases—and certainly in the case of someone coming to the UK for the first time—it is necessary to take up residence and live here for a period before habitual residence is established, it is clear that there are differences between the test as it applies to those exercising community rights and as it applies to others. However unsatisfactory this may seem, it represents the current state of the law and the DSS Guidance, referred to at p.171 of the 1999 edition of *Mesher and Wood, Income-related Benefits: the Legislation*, which seeks to assimilate the different tests by treating all those returning to the UK to re-establish ties here as being habitually resident immediately upon their return, is not consistent with what was said in *Nessa*.

R(IS) 6/96

In *R(IS) 6/96* the claimant was a British National who had been born in Burma   2.171
and lived there all her life until she came to the UK in June 1992. Her husband and children remained in Burma. She obtained employment in July 1992 but was made redundant in May 1994. She then claimed income support. In July 1994 she returned to Burma as her husband was thought to be terminally ill. She returned on August 20, 1994 and claimed income support on August 31. Her claim was refused on the grounds that she was not habitually resident in the UK. The Commissioner allowed her appeal because on the facts she had clearly become habitually resident in the UK by July 1994 and this was not affected by her temporary absence for a month. See Lord Scarman in *Shah* who refers to temporary or occasional absences of long or short duration not affecting ordinary residence and the ECJ's judgment in *Di Paolo* where the Court takes a similar view in relation to habitual residence. See also *CIS 14591/1996* below.

However, the Commissioner also gives general guidance on the principles to be adopted in applying the habitual residence test for the purposes of income support. He emphasises that the facts of each case had to be considered and that it was not possible to provide a complete definition of habitual residence or to list all the relevant factors. It was for the adjudicating authorities to be satisfied that a claimant was not habitually resident, rather than for the claimant to prove his habitual residence (although a tribunal should try to decide the issue by further investigation of the facts rather then relying on the burden of proof). To be resident a person had to be seen to be making a "genuine home for the time being" here but it need not be his only home or a permanent one. (Actual residence in two places is perfectly possible: *R(IS) 9/99*.) In deciding whether the person had become habitually resident, the most important factors were the length, continuity and general nature of the actual residence. An appreciable period of time, together with a settled intention, were necessary to establish habitual residence. What counted as an "appreciable period of time" depended on the facts of each case. It should be a period which showed "a settled and viable pattern of living here as a resident". Thus the practicality of a person's arrangements for residence had to be considered. In determining whether the plans were viable, the possibility of claiming income support had to be left out of account (although this did not mean that there must be no conceivable circumstances in which a person might need to resort to income support). The Commissioner recognised that since habitual residence could be abandoned in a day (see *Re J*), there could be a period when the claimant was not habitually resident anywhere.

The Commissioner's approach in *R(IS) 6/96* was largely based on Lord Brandon's comments in *Re J*, which was a child abduction case. Lord Brandon stated *inter alia* that whether a person was habitually resident was a question of fact to be decided by reference to all the circumstances of any particular case and that an appreciable period of time and a settled intention were necessary to establish habitual residence. Since the question the House of Lords was deciding was whether J had *ceased* to be habitually resident in Western Australia (which Lord Brandon held could happen in a single day if a person left with a settled intention not to return but to take up long-term residence elsewhere), the point that "an appreciable period of time and a settled intention" were needed to establish habitual residence was technically *obiter*. However, Lord Brandon's comments are clearly strong dicta and have been adopted in a large number of subsequent family law cases (see *R(IS) 2/00*). The Commissioner in *R(IS) 6/96* did not consider that there was any inconsistency between the approach taken in *Re J* and what was said by Lord Scarman in *Shah* and the ECJ in *Di Paolo*. All emphasised that the correct approach was a factual and practical one, taking into account all the individual's circumstances. In his view, however, where habitual residence may differ from ordinary residence was in the need for there to be an appreciable period of actual residence before a person became habitually resident.

Nessa

2.172   Mrs Nessa came to the UK in August 1994 when aged 55. She had previously lived all her life in Bangladesh. Her father-in-law in whose house she had been living had died and she had come to the UK for the emotional support of her late husband's brother and his family. Her husband had lived and worked in the UK until his death in 1975 and she had a right of abode here. She claimed income support in September 1994.

The Commissioner in *R(IS) 2/00* held that when the habitual residence test was introduced into the income support scheme the intention was to use the same legal concept as was already in use in other contexts. In his view the Child Support Commissioner in *R(CS) 5/96* was not suggesting that habitual residence had a different meaning in different statutory contexts, but merely that the significance of factors may vary in different circumstances. He therefore decided *R(IS) 6/96* had been right to hold, following *Re J*, that for a person to be habitually resident an appreciable period of residence as well as a settled intention had to be shown. However, he did not agree with all the reasoning in *R(IS) 6/96* and he added two important qualifications.

The first concerned the examples given in *R(IS) 6/96* of what might amount to an appreciable period in certain circumstances. Because of the danger of examples being read as minimum or normal periods, he did not think that any periods should be mentioned. There was no minimum period necessary to establish habitual residence (see *Cameron v Cameron* 1996 S.L.T. 306). Even Lord Brandon's statement that a person could not become habitually resident in a single day had to be read in its context, that of "a sharp-edged leaving of the country of existing habitual residence with the intention to take up long-term residence in another country". The context and all the circumstances had to be considered in each case. Thus, *e.g.* if a person lived in different countries for part of each year, he could simultaneously be habitually resident in both. Moreover, periods spent in the UK prior to the date of the latest arrival here could be relevant in assessing what was an appreciable period under the *Re J* principle. The appreciable period did not need to be continuous and periods spent in this country while the person was still habitually resident in another country could count as part of the appreciable period to be taken into account after the actual arrival, as long as they were connected with the settled intention to reside here. Thus visits for the purpose of making arrangements to live here could count, but not those that were merely holidays or to see relatives.

The second qualification was that the viability of a person's residence in the UK, either generally or with or without assistance from public funds, was only one relevant factor among others, to be given the appropriate weight according to the circumstances. In his view *R(IS) 6/96* should not be read as imposing an additional condition that only residence without resort to income support or public assistance was relevant to the *Re J* test. See also *CIS 1459/1996* and *CIS 16097/1996* which agree that the question of whether the residence is viable in the UK without recourse to public funds is only one factor, and not by itself decisive.

The Commissioner did not consider that *Shah* supported the conclusion that, for the purposes of applying the ordinary residence test, evidence of past residence on an established and settled basis was always necessary. (The students in *Shah* had already been resident for three years because in order to be eligible for local authority grants they had to show three years' ordinary residence.) But he did consider that a habit took time to establish and that residence only changed its quality at the point at which it became habitual. Thus he rejected the argument that once sufficient time had elapsed for the residence to become habitual that showed that it had been habitual from the outset. However, he did state that subsequent conduct could act as confirmation that a claimant's intentions were settled from the outset. He also points out that the ECJ did not decide in *Di Paolo* that a person's habitual residence was where he had his habitual centre of interests. The location of a person's centre of interests might be one relevant factor in determining habitual residence but the two concepts were not synonymous.   **2.173**

Mrs Nessa appealed to the Court of Appeal but her appeal was dismissed (*Nessa v Chief Adjudication Officer* [1998] 2 All E.R. 728). The Court of Appeal (by a majority) followed *Re J* and held that in order to establish habitual residence it was necessary for a claimant not only to have been in the UK voluntarily, and for settled purposes, but also to have fulfilled those conditions for an appreciable period of time. However, the appreciable period need not be particularly long. The dissenting judge (Thorpe L.J.) considered that Lord Brandon's comments in *Re J* were clearly *obiter* and that an appreciable period was not an essential ingredient of habitual residence. In his view the adjective "habitual" ensured that "the connection [to the country] is not transitory or temporary but enduring and the necessary durability can be judged prospectively in exceptional cases".

Mrs Nessa appealed again to the House of Lords which unanimously upheld the majority in the Court of Appeal. Lord Slynn of Hadley, with whom all the other judges agreed reviewed the authorities discussed above and stated:

> "With the guidance of these cases it seems to me plain that as a matter of ordinary language a person is not habitually resident in any country unless he has taken up residence and lived there for a period.. . . If Parliament had intended that a person seeking to enter the United Kingdom or such a person declaring his intention to settle here is to have income support on arrival, it could have said so. It seems to me impossible to accept the argument at one time advanced that a person who has never been here before who says on landing, 'I intend to settle in the United Kingdom' and who is fully believed is automatically a person who is habitually resident here. Nor is it enough to say I am going to live at X or with Y. He must show residence in fact for a period which shows that the residence has become "habitual" and, as I see it, will or is likely to continue to be habitual."

Lord Slynn did accept that there might be "special cases where the person concerned is not coming here for the first time, but is resuming an habitual residence previously had . . . On such facts the Adjudication Officer may or of course may not be satisifed that the previous habitual residence has been resumed. This position is quite different from that of someone coming to the United Kingdom for the first time." Although *Swaddling* was cited by Lord Slynn as one example of this type of case the exception seems to be considerably narrower than the principle of Community law established by that case, namely that the length of residence in a Member State could not be regarded as an intrinsic element of the concept of habitual residence where a claimant comes within Regulation 1408/71. Lord Slynn appears to be saying no more than that in some cases it will be possible to say on the facts that a returning resident is merely resuming a habitual residence which has   **2.174** already been established. The reference to the possibility that the AO (now decision-maker) "may not be satisfied" clearly indicates that this will not always be the case and that some returning residents will need to re-establish habitual residence by living in the CTA for a period of time.

Lord Slynn's opinion also contains interesting observations on how long the appreciable period of time should be. Whilst recognising that the period is not fixed and "may be longer where there are doubts", he also stated that "it may be short" and quoted with approval the statement of Butler Sloss L.J. in *Re F (A Minor) (Child Abduction)* [1994] F.L.R. 548 at 555 that "A month can be . . . an appreciable period of time". He also agreed with the Commissioner that there were factors which indicated that habitual residence had been established in Mrs Nessa's case "even by the date of the tribunal hearing *or as I see it, even earlier*" (emphasis added). At the date of her tribunal hearing on December 6, 1994, Mrs Nessa had been in the UK for 15 weeks. It must be stressed that the House of Lords clearly regarded this issue as one to be determined by tribunals on the facts of individual cases; however the view of the Commissioner in *CIS 15927/1996* that the establishment of habitual residence would normally require residence of at least some months must now be read in the light of Lord Slynn's comments.

2.175   As the issue of what is an "appreciable period" is one of fact and degree, and the decisions highlighted by Commissioners for wider circulation normally concern issues of law, there are few public examples of how the Commissioners approach that issue when exercising their discretion under s.14(8)(a) of SSA 1998. However, post-*Nessa* examples can be found in the decisions of Commissioner Jacobs in *CIS 1304/1997* and *CJSA 5394/1998* and of Commissioner Howell in *CIS 376/2002* all of which involved returning residents.

In Commissioner Jacobs' decision guidance was given that in a typical case tribunals should conduct a three stage enquiry into (i) the circumstances in which the claimant's earlier habitual residence was lost; (ii) the links between the claimant and the UK while abroad; and (iii) the circumstances of his return to the UK. So, for example, if the claimant's departure from the UK was temporary (albeit long-term) or conditional or if habitual residence was lost only as a result of events which occurred after the claimant's departure, those would be factors favouring a resumption of habitual residence immediately on return. On the facts of those appeals, the Commissioner held that the claimants, both British nationals who—as was accepted—had previously been habitually resident here but had lost that habitual residence during an extended period of absence abroad nevertheless resumed their previous habitual residence on the very day of their return to Britain. The relevant extracts from *CIS 1304/1997* and *CJSA 5394/1998* were recently reissued as an Appendix to *CIS 4474/2003* (see below).

By contrast the claimant in *CIS 376/2002* who was a naturalised British citizen who had worked in Britain for many years but had spent no more than 11 months here in the five years before the claims for benefit which were under consideration, was held not to have become habitually resident immediately. Commissioner Howell QC accepted the tribunal's finding that although the claimant had been habitually resident he had ceased to be so over that five year period but rejected the tribunal's doubts about whether he had a settled intention to remain here. On that basis, the Commissioner held that the claimant had not been resident for an appreciable period of time when his claim for IS was made (some three days after his arrival) but had become habitually resident by the date of the decision on that claim approximately five weeks later. In reaching his decision the Commissioner denied the possiblity that a claimant who had lost his or her habitual residence could resume it immediately without first being present for an appreciable period of time. He stated (at para.12):

"Everything therefore depends on what counts as an "appreciable period" of resumed residence in this context so that his residence in the United Kingdom can be said to have become established as habitual . . . As has been said many times in the cases where judges from the House of Lords down to more humble levels have had to struggle with the meaning of this expression, this is ultimately a question of fact and degree, depending on the individual circumstances of each case, and there are no hard and fast rules to apply. For a returning citizen of this country coming back to live here again after a period of residence overseases . . ., the period may be short: as little as a month or so. But it is not zero or minimal, since even a returning expatriate may change his plans again and there is therefore at least some space of time after actual arrival when one simply has to wait and see."

CIS 4474/2003 contains helpful guidance on the proper approach to be taken to the test and in weighing the relevant factors. In particular, Mr Commissioner Jacobs warns (at para.16) of the danger of overemphasising viability as a factor:

"16. The danger of overemphasising viability is this. A claimant needs to establish habitual residence in order to claim an income-related benefit. A claim would not be necessary if the claimant has a guaranteed source of funds sufficient for survival. The danger is that the only claimants who can establish habitual residence will be those who have sufficient access to funds not to need it. That cannot be right. Habitual residence is a test of entitlement, not a bar to entitlement. It must be applied in a way that allows for the possibility of a claimant establishing both habitual residence and an entitlement to income support."

The Commissioner also noted that the approach taken by Commissioners to the length of the appreciable period had developed since *R(IS) 6/96* and gave (at para.19) the following guidance:

"19. What is an appreciable period depends on the circumstances of the particular case. But I agree with the Secretary of State that in the general run of cases the period will lie between one and three months. *I would certainly require cogent reasons from a tribunal to support a decision that a significantly longer period was required*" (emphasis added).

In *CIS/3280/2003, CIS/1124/2004* and *CIS/1840/2004* (to be appealed to the Court of Appeal on another issue *sub nom. Secretary of State for Work and Pensions v Bhakta*—see below under "Habitual residence" and "down to the date of decision"), Commissioner Rowland indicated his broad agreement with the approach in *CIS/4474/2003*:

"I am content to accept that, where a claimant is likely to remain in the United Kingdom permanently or for a substantial period of time, the conventional period that must have elapsed between his arrival and his establishing habitual residence is between one month and three months. However, those are not rigid limits. In an exceptional case, a person with a right of abode in the United Kingdom who, although not falling within the scope of regulation 21(3)(d), has been forced to flee another country and is nonetheless able to show a settled intention to remain in the United Kingdom might be accepted as habitually resident after less than a month of residence. Perhaps less exceptionally, a person with no ties to the United Kingdom and making no effort to become established here despite a vague intention to remain might be found not to be habitually resident in the United Kingdom until considerably longer than three months had elapsed."

However, disagreement with that approach was expressed in the decision of Commissioner Williams in *CIS 1972/2003* (at para.14):

". . . I comment only that I have seen tribunals decide on shorter periods than a month and longer periods than three months without being appealed, or appealed successfully. Too much should not be read into the facts of individual decisions or, I suggest, trends in the small number of—usually difficult—cases that Commissioners come to decide on the facts. It does not help when Commissioners' decisions are used to play a forensic game (for it is no more than that) of finding the longest, or the shortest, period endorsed by a Commissioner and then claiming some general rule from it. Parliament could have set a specific time limit. It did not. Advisors cannot seek certainty where it does not exist."

In *CIS 1972/2003* the Commissioner also considered a submission that the requirement to be resident for an appreciable period of time could in some cases be in contravention of the UN Convention on the Rights of the Child. He stated (at para.18):

". . . The claim for the children is relevant to the overall assessment of Mrs H's claim. That could raise several factual issues, though none were explored here. In terms of compliance with the Convention, attention should be paid to the award of child benefit and other benefits. More broadly, the other rights of the children, and the rights and obligations of the father, may be relevant in assessing whether the move of the mother and children to the United Kingdom is permanent. For example, does it take place in accordance with all relevant child protection laws? That may be a reason for hesitation in an individual case. In any event, the settlement of the children must be part of the total story. But I do not think that references to the Convention take the matter any further than that."

Settled intention and appreciable period—the test following R(IS) 6/96 and Nessa

2.176   Thus it is clear that whether a person is habitually resident in the UK (more technically in the CTA) is a question of fact to be decided by reference to all the circumstances of the particular case (recently emphasised by the Court of Appeal in *Re M (A Minor) (Habitual Residence), The Times*, January 3, 1996). Habitual residence can continue during absences of long or short duration. It is for the tribunal to be satisfied that the claimant is not habitually resident (*R(IS) 2/00*). Some of the relevant factors will include the length of time in the UK, the reason for coming (or returning) here, the claimant's intentions, the location of his possessions and family, where he has previously worked, the length and purpose of any absence from the UK, etc. The intention to reside here does not need to be permanent or indefinite but can be for a limited period (*e.g.*, for the purposes of education as in *Shah*; see also *Cameron v Cameron* quoted in *R(IS) 2/00* where the Court of Appeal said that the settled intention necessary under *Re J* was an intention to reside here for an appreciable period). But if the claimant's intention is conditional, *e.g.* on benefit being awarded, this is not a settled intention to stay (*CIS 12703/1996*). The question to be asked is whether "in all the circumstances, including the settledness of the person's intentions as to residence, the residence has continued for a sufficient period for it to be said to be habitual" (*R(IS) 2/00*). There is no minimum appreciable period and in some circumstances it will be quite short. See, *e.g. Re F (A Minor) (Child Abduction)* (above). In *Re B (Minors) (Abduction) (No. 2)* [1993] 1 F.L.R. 993, Waite J., after referring to the assumption of habitual residence requiring an appreciable period of time and a settled intention, states that ". . . Logic would suggest that provided the purpose was settled, the period of habitation need not be long". So if the settle intention is very strong, the appreciable period may shrink. It may be that if the claimant is returning to a country where he has lived before, habitual residence can be acquired more quickly (in this connection note the DSS's view in para.11 of its original memorandum to SSAC (Cm 2609) that ". . . In some circumstances, for instance returning UK nationals, it will be possible to become habitually resident from the moment of entry"). Equally, if the claimant has come to the UK, *e.g.* because he needs to be near relatives due to failing health and has severed all ties with his previous country, it is difficult to see why such a person should not become habitually resident at a very early stage. It may be that it was these kinds of situations that the Commissioner in *Nessa* had in mind when he said that subsequent conduct could act as confirmation of a claimant's stated intentions and help to show that they were settled from the outset. But in those circumstances it does not seem to be the quality of the residence that has changed, only the evidence about it.

2.177   One other point should be made. The Commissioner's dilution in *Nessa* of the statement in *R(IS) 6/96* that for the residence to count the claimant's plans for living in the UK had to be "viable", in the sense of viable without resort to income support, is to be welcomed. Such a requirement, if that was what it was intended to be, could have the effect of preventing some people (*e.g.* those who are unable to work because of age or ill-health) from ever becoming habitually resident because they could never bridge the viability gap. It also carries with it the danger of imposing a condition that a person be self-supporting (at least for a time), when the chosen test is that of habitual residence rather than "without recourse to public funds". It seems to add a substantial gloss to the *Re J* test. The Commissioner in *Nessa* considered that viability might be relevant in assessing whether a person's intentions were truly settled. That seems less controversial, but for the reasons already stated, whether the person's need to resort to public funds should enter into the consideration, is highly questionable.

Note that a person can remain habitually resident during periods of even comparatively lengthy absence. See, for example, *CIS 14591/1996*. In June 1993 the claimant and his wife came to the UK with the intention of living here permanently. But in October 1994 they returned to India to be with their daughter-in-law until she could obtain entry clearance. This was finally granted after some 13 months. The claimant's claim for income support made on his return to the UK in November 1995 was refused on the ground that he was not habitually resident. However, the Commissioner decided that the claimant had become habitually resident before he went to India in October 1994 and had remained so throughout the period of his absence. He had retained a settled intention to live in the UK permanently and his absence was always intended to be temporary.

Swaddling

The claimant was a British national who until he was 23 had lived and worked in the UK. From 1980 to 1994 for the majority of the time he worked in France. In late 1994 he was made redundant. After failing to find further employment in France, he returned to the UK in January 1995 to live with his brother and in order to obtain work here. His claim for income support made on January 9, 1995 was refused on the ground that he was not habitually resident in the UK. The Commissioner held that the appropriate appreciable period in all the circumstances was eight weeks from the date of his return to the UK. Under the terms of purely domestic law the claimant was thus not entitled to income support for the period January 9 to March 3, 1995. The Commissioner rejected an argument put forward by the claimant that under Art.10a(2) of EC Regulation 1408/71 he could rely on his period of residence in France to satisfy the habitual residence condition. The Commissioner decided that Article 10a(2) did not assist the claimant since the habitual residence test did not make entitlement to income support subject to *completion* of a period of employment, self-employment or residence (note that in Regulation 1408/71 "residence" means "habitual residence": Art.1(h)) but went to whether habitual residence had been established initially.

But the Commissioner did refer to the ECJ the question whether the application of a habitual residence test (involving the requirement of an appreciable period of residence) to a person who had exercised his right to freedom of movement and had worked and been habitually resident in another Member State and then returned to the UK to seek work infringed Art.48 of the Treaty of Rome. It was contended on behalf of the claimant that the test had the effect of deterring a person from exercising his Community rights since he had been made worse off by its application than if he had worked throughout in the UK. For the AO it was submitted that the principle in Art.48 did not extend to conditions for acquiring entitlement to a non-contributory benefit like income support.

However the ECJ (Case C-90/97, *The Times*, March 4, 1999, also reported as *R(IS)6/99*) did not answer the question as to whether there had been an infringement of Art.48 since it considered that the case could be dealt with under Regulation 1408/71. It was accepted that Mr Swaddling was a person covered by Regulation 1408/71 (as an employed person he had been subject to both the British and French social security schemes). Art.10a(1) provides that a person to whom the Regulation

2.178

applies is to be granted certain special non-contributory benefits (which include income support) in the territory of the Member State in which he resides. "Reside" means "habitually reside": Art.1(h). The Court stated that in deciding where a person habitually resided, account had to be taken in particular of his family situation; the reasons which had led him to move; the length and continuity of his residence; the fact (where this was the case) that he was in stable employment; and his intention as it appeared from all the circumstances. However, the Court also held that the length of residence in the Member State in which payment of benefit was sought could not be regarded as an intrinsic element of the concept of residence within the meaning of Art.10a.

The result of the ECJ's judgment would thus seem to be that a person covered by Regulation 1408/71 can be habitually resident in a Member State for the purposes of Art.10a on the day of arrival if the circumstances as a whole, including the other factors referred to by the Court, lead to that conclusion. The Community meaning of "habitually resident" therefore differs from the interpretation that currently applies in a domestic context. The ECJ's interpretation also seems to be inherently discriminatory, since it will normally be easier for returning nationals to show that they are re-establishing ties with their country of origin than it will be for, *e.g.* other EEA nationals. One question that arises is to whom does the ECJ's judgment apply? Clearly it covers returning British nationals who come within the scope of Regulation 1408/71 and, as already indicated, it is difficult to see how non-British EEA nationals in a similar position could be excluded without breaching Art.7 of Regulation 1612/68.

Habitual residence and "down to the date of decision"

2.179   If a person fails the habitual residence test this does not mean to say that s/he cannot satisfy it at a subsequent date, particularly if further information is produced or there is a change in circumstances, or simply due to passage of time. However, in relation to appeals brought on or after May 21, 1998 (the date on which the SSA 1998 received Royal Assent) a tribunal may not take into account any circumstance that arose for the first time after the date of the decision—see s.12(8)(b) of the SSA 1998 and the commentary to that provision in Vol. III. (For the position before May 21, 1998, see *CIS/11481/1995* and *CIS/17208/1996*.)

Circumstances often arise in which a claimant, who was not habitually resident by the date of the Secretary of State's decision, has undoubtedly become so by the hearing of his or her appeal against that decision. Until recently, it was believed that s.12(8)(b) required the tribunal to dismiss such an appeal and suggest the claimant made a fresh claim, which—unless it could be brought within the restrictive rules for backdating—would then leave a gap in the claimant's entitlement.

However, Commissioner Rowland has now held in *CIS/3280/2003, CIS/1124/2004* and *CIS/1840/2004*, that a tribunal has power in such circumstances to make an advance award of benefit from the date on which habitual residence is likely to be established. That power arises either under reg.13 of the Social Security (Claims and Payments) Regulations 1987 (see Vol. III) (in which case the power is subject to an advance time limit of three months) or under the power in reg.6(2)(a)(ii) of the Social Security and Child Support (Decisions and Appeals) Regulations 1999 (see Vol. III) to supersede on the ground of an anticipated change in circumstances. The regulations impose a discretionary power to make an advance award, rather than a duty to do so, but that power has to be exercised judicially and it would seem from the actual outcome in those appeals that a failure to consider its exercise will be an error of law that would entitle the Commissioner to substitute his own decision—as presumably will an irrational exercise or non-exercise of the power or the failure to give adequate reasons for the tribunal's decision to exercise or not to exercise the power. For an example of a Commissioner considering, but refusing to exercise, the power see *CJSA/4065/1999*.

CIS/1840/2004 is to be appealed to the Court of Appeal on another issue *sub nom. Secretary of State for Work and Pensions v Bhakta*. Decision makers have been given guidance by the Secretary of State (DMG Letter 08/05) advising them to stay making decisions on claims and revisions—and to seek the postponement of any existing appeals—in look-alike cases.

Para. (3F): Montserrat

Those who came to Great Britain from Montserrat after November 1, 1995, fol- **2.179.1**
lowing the volcanic eruption there are deemed not to be persons from abroad and are therefore not subject to the habitual residence test.

Para. (3G): Right to reside

On May 1, 2004, the regulations were amended by the insertion of para.(3G) **2.179.2**
which introduces a new restriction into the habitual residence test. No person "shall be treated as habitually resident" in the CTA unless s/he has a "right to reside there". Conceptually, the "right to reside" test applies to all claimants but, in practical terms it will only affect nationals of the EEA states and, in particular of eight of the ten states which acceded to the EU on that date, the so-called "A8 states" (the Czech Republic, Estonia, Hungary, Latvia, Lithuania, Poland, Slovakia and Slovenia). Nationals of Cyprus and Malta, sometimes referred to as the "A2 states", which also acceded to the EU on May 1, 2004, are not affected by the test, except to the extent that it applies to all EEA nationals.

The right to reside test does not affect non-EEA nationals in practice because such people will either have a right of abode in the UK, in which case, they will obviously also have a right to reside here; or they will have some type of leave to remain here, in which case, they will have a right to reside here for the duration of that leave—and any extension of it (although they will not necessarily be entitled to income-related benefits); or they will be illegal entrants or overstayers, in which case they are already excluded from benefit as persons subject to immigration control so that the additional requirement that they have should have the right to reside before being entitled to such benefits has no practical effect.

The EU law affecting social security is covered in more detail in Vol. III. For present purposes, the starting point must be that under Art.17 (ex 8) of the EC Treaty "[e]very person holding the nationality of a Member State shall be a citizen of the Union" and that, under Art.18 (ex 8a) EC:

"1. Every citizen of the Union shall have the right to move and reside freely within the territory of the Member States, subject to the limitations and conditions laid down in this Treaty and by the measures adopted to give it effect. . . ."

It is also of potential relevance that, under Art.12 (ex 6) EC:

"Within the scope of application of this Treaty, and without prejudice to any special provisions contained therein, any discrimination on grounds of nationality shall be prohibited"

and that, under Art.39 (ex 48) EC:

"1. Freedom of movement for workers shall be secured within the Community.
2. Such freedom of movement shall entail the abolition of any discrimination based on nationality between workers of the Member States as regards employment, remuneration and other conditions of work and employment.
3. It shall entail the right, subject to limitations justified on grounds of public policy, public security or public health:
. . .
(c) to stay in a Member State for the purpose of employment in accordance with the provisions governing the employment of nationals of that State laid down by law, regulation or administrative action;
(d) to remain in the territory of a Member State after having been employed in that State, subject to conditions which shall be embodied in implementing regulations to be drawn up by the Commission."

Nationals of the three EEA states that are not EU members enjoy the same rights under the EEA Treaty.

As is hinted at by Art.39(3)(d), although it is sometimes possible for EU citizens to rely directly on rights conferred by the EC Treaty, it is normally regarded as establishing the general principles on which the EC is based, which are then given practical effect through being implemented by Directives and Regulations made by the Commission. In particular, the principle of the free movement of workers has been implemented by (among others) the various EC Directives and Regulations referred to in head (a) of the definition of "person from abroad" and discussed above. EC Regulations have direct effect in all Member States and do not require further implementation at national level. However, the relevant Directives have been implemented (and some of the Regulations reflected) in the domestic legislation of the UK by the Immigration (European Economic Area) Regulations 2000 (SI 2000/2326). It will therefore be convenient to consider first the general position of EEA nationals under those Regulations; then to discuss the special rules that apply to A8 nationals and, finally, to consider whether there may be other occasions when either an EEA national might be regarded as having a right to reside (*i.e.*, on the basis that the I (EEA) Regulations fail fully to implement the EC Directives—or to reflect the Regulations—that form part of directly applicable Community law) or, even though the EEA national does not have a right to reside, it may nevertheless amount to unlawful discrimination to deny him or her benefit on that basis.

The I(EEA) Regulations

2.179.3   Under reg.14 of the I(EEA) Regulations:

"Right of residence

14.—(1) A qualified person is entitled to reside in the United Kingdom, without the requirement for leave to remain under the 1971 Act, for as long as he remains a qualified person.

(2) A family member of a qualified person is entitled to reside in the United Kingdom, without the requirement for such leave, for as long as he remains the family member of a qualified person.

(3) A qualified person and the family member of such a person may reside and pursue economic activity in the United Kingdom notwithstanding that his application for a residence permit or residence document (as the case may be) has not been determined by the Secretary of State.

(4) However, this regulation is subject to regulation 21(3)(b)."

Regulation 21(3)(b) contains a power for the Secretary of State to remove a "qualified person" from the UK if he "has decided that his removal is justified on the grounds of public policy, public security or public health".

"The "qualified persons" who have the right to reside under reg.14(1) are specified in reg.5 as being "a person who is an EEA national and in the United Kingdom" in one of the following capacities:

Workers: A worker is defined by reg.3(1)(a) as being "a worker within the meaning of Article 39 of the EC Treaty"—see the discussion of the concept under "EC Regs 1612/68 and 12571/70" above. Regulation 5(2) spells out that, as would in any event be the case under ECJ case law, a worker does not cease to be a qualified person solely because he becomes temporarily incapable of work as a result of illness or accident or he is involuntarily unemployed "if that fact is duly recorded by the relevant employment office". The practical effect of the words in quotation marks would appear to be that an EEA national who becomes involuntarily unemployed will have to claim JSA even if s/he might otherwise fall within one of the prescribed categories of those who are entitled to claim IS.

The self-employed: For the rights of the self-employed under EC law, see the discussion of Directive 73/148 above. For the purposes of the I(EEA) Regulations, "self-employed person" is defined by reg.3(1)(b) as "a person who establishes himself in order to pursue activity as a self-employed person in accordance with

Article 43 of the EC Treaty, or who seeks to do so". Regulation 5(3) provides that such a person does not cease to be a qualified person solely because he is temporarily incapable of work as a result of illness or accident.

Providers of, and recipients of, services: These are defined by reg.3(1)(c) and (d) as respectively "a person who provides, or seeks to provide, services within the meaning of Art.50 of the EC Treaty" and "a person who receives, or seeks to receive, services within the meaning of Art.50 of the EC Treaty". See the discussion of Directive 73/148 above.

The self-sufficient: "self-sufficient person" is defined by reg.3(1)(e) as meaning a person who has sufficient resources to avoid his becoming a burden on the social assistance system of the United Kingdom and is covered by sickness insurance in respect of all risks in the United Kingdom. That definition follows the wording of Art.1 of Directive 90/364/EEC and of 90/365/EEC, both of which then specify that resources are deemed to be "sufficient where they are higher than the level of resources which the host Member State may grant social assistance to its nationals, taking into account the personal circumstances of the applicant" and, where appropriate any relevant family members. That test is repeated in slightly different words in reg.3(2) of the I(EEA) Regulations.

It may seem self-evident that a person who has been driven by circumstances to claim an income-related benefit, no longer satisfies that definition of a "self-sufficient person". However, DWP Guidance (DMG Memo Vol. 2 02/04, paras 24-26) advises decision makers—it is suggested, correctly—that this is a matter for the Home Office to decide: if a person has acquired the right to reside in the UK by residing here as a self-sufficient person—and the issue of a residence permit under Part IV of the I(EEA) Regulations will be conclusive proof of that status, although the absence of such a permit may not mean that the claimant automatically has no right to reside—then he or she satisfies the right to reside test until the IND takes steps to bring that right of residence to an end under Arts 21(3)(a) and/or 22(2)(b) of I(EEA) Regulations.

The retired: a "retired person" is defined by reg.3(1)(f) as meaning someone who has previously been employed or self-employed in the UK and who now has a pension or other social security benefit that is sufficient to prevent him becoming entitled to "social assistance"—a phrase that is not defined but which would certainly cover the income-related benefits. Again, it would seem that once a retired person has acquired a right of residence on that basis, the right subsists unless there is a decision by the IND that that right has come to an end because income-related benefits have been claimed.

Students: The students who have a right of residence are those who are "enrolled at a recognised educational establishment in the United Kingdom for the principal purpose of following a vocational training course", who make a declaration to the Secretary of State (or satisfy him in some other manner) that they have" sufficient resources to avoid . . . becoming a burden on the social assistance system of the United Kingdom" and who are "covered by sickness insurance in respect of all risks in the United Kingdom" (reg.3(1)(g)).

The formerly self-employed: Those who, in the past, have been self-employed in the United Kingdom but have now permanently ceased such activity may still have a right of residence if they fall into one of four categories set out in reg.4(1):

- they are over pensionable age on the day on which they cease to be self-employed in the UK, have been self-employed for at least 12 months prior to that date and have resided continuously in the UK for more than three years (unless they are married to a UK national, in which case the 12 months and three years requirements do not apply—reg.4(2)).

- they gave up self-employment in the UK because they had become permanently incapable of work and have resided continuously in the UK for more than two years (unless they are married to a UK national in which case the two years requirement does not apply—reg.4(2)).

- they have resided in the UK (no minimum period of residence is specified) and gave up self-employment in the UK because they had become permanently incapable of work following an accident at work or an occupational illness which entitles them to a pension payable in whole or in part by the state. As industrial injuries disablement benefit, the UK benefit for those injured at work or suffering from prescribed occupational diseases, is only payable to employed earners (*i.e.* not the self-employed), the scope for this category is limited. It could perhaps apply if a person was both employed and self-employed and had to give up self-employment as a result of permanent incapacity following an accident suffered as an employee.

- they have been "continuously resident and continuously active as a self-employed person in the United Kingdom for three years", are still self-employed in another EEA state but reside in the UK and return to their residence at least once a week.

In calculating continuous residence periods of up to three months absence from the UK in any year are not taken into account. Periods spent outside the UK on military service are also ignored—reg.4(4)(a). In calculating continuous self-employed activity, periods of inactivity caused by circumstances outside the control of the claimant or by illness or accident are counted as periods of activity— reg.4(4)(b).

Family members of dead self-employed people: As to family members generally, see below. However certain family members of certain qualifying persons who have died become qualifying persons in their own right under reg.5(4). This only applies if the original qualifying person qualified as being self-employed or formerly self-employed under the rules explained above and the family member satisfies the other conditions specified in Arts 4(4)(b) and 5.

Family members

2.179.4   Under reg.14(2) of the I(EEA) Regulations, the family members of qualifying persons also have a right of residence if they are themselves EEA nationals (see reg.9). "Family member" is defined by reg.6. In most cases, the phrase means the qualifying person's spouse, the children and grandchildren of the qualifying person (or of the spouse) who are either their dependants or are under the age of 21, and the parents and grandparents etc. of the qualifying person (or of the spouse) who are "dependant relatives". The exceptions are:

- where the qualifying person is a student, in which case only the qualifying person's spouse and the qualifying person's dependent children are "family members", and

- where a former qualifying person has ceased to reside in the UK, his or her spouse—or divorced spouse—is a "family member" provided s/he is the primary carer of their dependent child who is under 19 and attending an educational course within the scope of Article 12 of Regulation (EEC) No. 1612/68 in the United Kingdom, and descendants of his or of his spouse who are under 21 or are their dependants are "family members", provided that they were attending such an educational course in the UK when the qualified person was residing in the UK and are continuing to attend such a course.

For the position of dependants and household members of EEA nationals and UK nationals who are not themselves EEA nationals (and therefore cannot qualify as "family members") see Arts 10 and 11.

The special position of A8 nationals

2.179.5   When considering the position of A8 Nationals, it is important to begin with the premise that they are Citizens of the Union, and have the same rights under EC law as the nationals of other Member States unless some provision of EC law removes or restricts those rights either expressly or by implication. A8 nationals have different rules applied to them under the national law of the UK (and of other Member States that were members of the EU before it was enlarged on May 1, 2004) because the Treaty of Accession permitted the existing Member States to derogate from the full rights of A8 nationals for a limited period (for further details see the commentary to Art.39 EC in Vol. III). The UK government restricted the residence rights of A8 nationals as set out in Accession (Immigration and Worker Registration) Regulations 2004 (SI 2004/1219) and, at the same time, introduced the right to reside test that is under discussion in this note to prevent most A8 nationals from becoming entitled to out-of-work benefits during the first 12 months of their residence in the UK. Disputes may well arise as to whether the restrictions on the rights of A8 nationals in SI/2004/1219 exceed what is permitted under the derogations in the Treaty of Accession. Discussion of those issues would require detailed examination of the terms of the derogations concerned and is therefore beyond the scope of this book. It should, however, be noted that there are no derogations from Regulation 1408/71 and that the only derogations permitted from Regulation 1612/68 relate to Arts 1–6 and do not cover, for example, the anti-discrimination principle in Art.7.

The Accession (Immigration and Worker Registration) Regulations 2004

The text of these regulations is set out in full later in this Volume. The scheme of those regulations is to derogate from Art.39 EC, Regulation 68/360 and parts of Regulation 1612/68 by requiring (reg.7) most A8 nationals to register with the Home Office (under reg.8) in order to work lawfully in the UK. The I(EEA) Regulations are modified (by reg.5) so that such an A8 national is only a "worker" *i.e.* with the right to reside, during periods in which s/he is actually working in accordance with the registration scheme. During such periods is exempt from the habitual residence test under the amendment to head (a) of the definition of "person from abroad". By reg.6 a work-seeker from an A8 country who would be required to register if s/he were to find employment does not have a right to reside other than as a self-sufficient person. The effect is that affected A8 nationals cannot receive benefits while first looking for work in the UK. If they find a job and register with the Home Office in accordance with the rules of the registration scheme, they may receive any in-work benefits to which they might be entitled while actually working but will not be entitled to benefits if, for any reason, they cease work before they have worked continuously for 12 months (reg.2(4)). **2.179.6**

The following A8 nationals are permitted to work without registering with the Home Office and enjoy the full rights enjoyed by other EEA nationals (reg.2(2)–(6)):

- those who, on April 30, 2004, had leave to enter or remain in the UK that was not subject to an condition restricting their employment.

- those who were working legally in the UK on April 30, 2004 and who had been so working without interruption throughout the preceding 12 months.

- those who have worked legally in the UK without interruption for a period of 12 months falling partly or wholly after April 30, 2004.

- those who are also nationals of the UK, another EEA State that is not an A8 State or of Switzerland.

- those who are "posted workers" (*i.e.*, workers in the UK for employers that are not established here).

- those who are family members of (non-A8) EEA or Swiss nationals who are in the UK as workers or self-sufficient persons, retired persons or students.

The definition of "legally working" in reg.2(7) excludes asylum seekers who work—even those with Home Office permission to do so—because they do not have leave to enter or remain under the Immigration Act—see the discussion of the *Kaya* case (under "Lawfully present" above). When deciding whether a claimant has worked for 12 months without interruption, up to 30 days on which s/he was not working can be ignored as long as s/he was working at the beginning and end of the period.

Compatibility of the right to reside test with EC law.

2.179.7   It is controversial whether certain parts of the right to reside test, both as it appears to affect A8 nationals and as it affects some economically inactive nationals of all Member States, is fully in accordance with EC law. In particular, there are no express derogations from any part of Regulation 1408/71 (see Vol.III). It is true that there are derogations from Art.39 EC (under which those Regulations were made) but express derogations were apparently felt to be necessary in respect of Directive 68/360 and Regulation 1612/68. On that basis, it is arguable that if an A8 national can establish a right to benefit under the provisions of Regulation 1408/71, the fact that the 2004 Regulations appear to deny him or her the right to reside (and hence a right to benefit under domestic British law) is neither here nor there.

The position of A8 nationals who work in the UK (and register with the Home Office) but become involuntarily unemployed before they have worked for 12 months requires particular comment. Any other EEA national would be regarded in those circumstances as continuing to be a "worker" with an entitlement to benefit. The effect of the 2004 Regulations is that an A8 national in the same position is to be treated as a "work-seeker" with no such entitlement. The effect of the 2004 Regulations would therefore seem to be to discriminate directly against the A8 national on the grounds of nationality. Article 7 of Regulation 1612/68 would appear to prohibit such an outcome. And, as has already been noted, the Treaty of Accession does not permit Member States to derogate from Art.7. See also in this respect, the decision of the CA in *R(D) v Secretary of State for Work and Pensions* [2004] EWCA Civ 1468, CA (Mummery and Kay L.JJ.), October 11, 2004, which while rejecting the submissions made by a Latvian work-seeker accepted that Art.7 would apply if he became and remained, a "worker".

More generally, the case law of the ECJ increasingly suggests that the principle of non-discrimination in Art.12 (ex 6) EC can be used, even by those who are economically inactive, to prevent Member States of which they are not nationals from denying them access to social security benefits on the basis of nationality—see, for example, the discussion of *Grzelczyk v Centre public d'aide sociale d'Ottignies-Louvain-la-Veuve*, Case C.-184/999, *Baumbast and R. v Secretary of State for the Home Department*, Case C.-314/99 and *Trojani v Centre public d'aide sociale de Bruxelles*, Case C.-456-02 in Part III of Vol.III. The type of argument accepted by the ECJ in those decisions seems to be capable of application to the right to reside test in appropriate circumstances. Although it is difficult to be sure from the brief judgments of the Court, it does not appear that those decisions were cited to the Court of Appeal in the *D* case.

Transitional protection

2.179.8   Note, finally, that reg.6 of the Social Security (Habitual Residence) Amendment Regulations 2004 (reproduced later in this Volume) establishes transitional protection from the right to reside test for those who were entitled (or who subsequently prove to have been entitled) to income support, JSA, state pension credit, housing benefit or council tax benefit on April 30, 2004. The transitional protection continues until the last day on which entitlement to any of those benefits ceases.

"Patient"

2.180   Reg.2(2) of the Hospital In-Patients Regulations requires that the person is or has been maintained free of charge while undergoing treatment in a NHS hospital or a similar institution. There have been amendments in November 1987 and November

1992 so that in all cases a person is to be regarded as maintained free of charge unless the accommodation and services are provided under s.65 of the National Health Service Act 1987 (or the Scottish equivalent) or para.14 of Sch.2 to the National Health Service and Community Care Act 1990, which relate only to fee-paying patients in NHS and Trust hospitals. In *CS 249/1989* and *R(IS) 7/92* the Commissioners regretfully apply the unambiguous effect of the 1987 amendment, which means that even where considerable contributions to maintenance are made, the person is still treated as a patient, with the consequent reduction in income support specified in Sch.7. However, it was decided in *CIS 3325/2000* that reg.2(2) only applies in circumstances where the NHS is providing an element of maintenance as well as treatment or nursing care. The Commissioner said (at para.44):

". . . before regulation 2(2) can operate to deprive a person receiving treatment of entitlement to income support it must be shown that the provision under the National Health Service Act itself, or under "arrangements" made by the Secretary of State or on his behalf under that Act, extends not only to healthcare services in the form of medical treatment or additional day care, but also to the provision of *maintenance* in the institution where he is receiving that treatment or care. In other words the expression . . . "under the National Health Service Act 1977" in paragraph (a) . . . qualify not only the word "treatment" but also the word "maintained" nine words before."

There is also doubt as to whether the deeming provision of reg.2(2) operates when a claimant is in hospital for less that 24 hours a day. *CSA 249/1989* holds that it does not but the Commissioner in *CIS 192/1991* disagrees, holding that the deeming applies despite the person's absence from the hospital during each period of 24 hours. In her view *R(S) 4/84* was not authority for holding that anything less than 24 hours' actual presence in a hospital took the person outside the provisions of reg.2(2). In fact, as *CDLA 11099/1995* points out, *R(S) 4/84* is positive authority to the contrary. In *R(S) 4/84* the claimant spent every night in hospital receiving treatment but attended a college during the day. The Commissioner held that she satisfied the condition of under-going treatment as an in-patient but that she was not maintained free of charge by the hospital because she had to maintain herself during the day. It was for that reason that the claimant succeeded in *R(S) 4/84*. The effect of the 1987 amendment to the "full-out" words in reg.2(2) had been to deem the condition of being maintained free of charge to be satisfied if a person was undergoing treatment as an in-patient (except in the case of a private patient in a NHS hospital). *R(S) 4/84* had clearly accepted that the claimant's treatment overnight as an in-patient was sufficient for the purposes of reg.2(2).

In *R(IS) 8/96* the Commissioner approaches the issue in a different way. In relation to whether a person counts as a patient if he is absent from hospital during the day, however, the result is the same as in *CIS 192/1991*. In *R(IS) 8/96* the claimant had been in hospital between April and September 1993 but had had various periods of home leave and could go out during the day. The Commissioner holds, following *CIS 13/1949* (reported), *R(S) 8/51* and *R(S) 9/52*, that in deciding whether a person was an in-patient, the circumstances existing at the beginning of a day were to be treated as continuing throughout that day. Thus a day on which a person was admitted, or returned, to hospital was not a day on which a person was to be treated as an in-patient, but a day on which a person was discharged from, or left, hospital did count as such a day. The rule in *R(S) 1/66* (disqualification only for days throughout which a person was absent from Great Britain) did not apply in this context. The provision at issue in that case employed a different phrase "for any period *during* which" (which the Commissioner had decided meant "throughout"), whereas reg.2(2) merely referred to any period "for which" the person receives free inpatient treatment.

However, in *CSS 617/1997* the Commissioner considered that the approach in *R(S) 1/66* did apply for the benefit at issue in that case (severe disablement allowance (SDA)). The claimant came home from hospital on a Friday morning

2.181

and returned on the following Monday evening. The AO decided that he was only entitled to the full rate of SDA for three days (Saturday to Monday). The Commissioner points out that the claimant remained entitled to SDA while in hospital, albeit that it was paid at the reduced personal expenses rate; the question therefore was for what period that partial suspension of *payment* was lifted. One of the powers under which the Hospital In-Patients Regulations were made was s.82(6) of the SSA 1975 [s.113(2) of the SSCBA]. That power authorised regulations to suspend payment of benefit to a person *during* any period in which he was undergoing treatment as an in-patient. Applying the approach in *R(S) 1/66*, the Commissioner concluded that there was only authority to suspend payment of benefit in this case for days throughout which the claimant was an in-patient, with the consequence that he was entitled to the full rate of SDA for all four days at home. The Commissioner expressed the view, however, that the effect of the Hospital In-patient Regulations might be different where the question was one of basic entitlement to benefit. It is not clear that this attempt to reconcile the various conflicting decisions on this issue works, since, for example, entitlement to income support may well continue while a person is an in-patient, although the rate of payment will be reduced in accordance with the rules in Sch.7. The current guidance to decision-makers in relation to income support/income-based JSA is that the circumstances that exist at the start of the day should be treated as continuing throughout the day (see the *Decision Makers Guide*, paras 24372–4).

In *White v Chief Adjudication Officer, The Times*, August 2, 1993, the Health Authority had made an agreement with a nursing home under which the home agreed to reserve 18 places for people nominated by the Health Authority in return for a grant. The claimant who had been in hospital for some years was transferred to the nursing home under this arrangement. The Court of Appeal agreed with *R(IS) 7/92* that the definition of "hospital" in s.128 of the National Health Service Act 1977 applied. In s.128 "hospital" includes "any institution for the reception and treatment of persons suffering from illness", and "illness" is defined to include mental disorder and "any injury or disability requiring medical or dental treatment or nursing". The claimant was mentally ill and required appropriate nursing. The nursing home had agreed to maintain appropriate staffing, including qualified mental nurses. Medication was dispensed (although not prescribed) by the nursing home. Thus the home was a hospital within the meaning of the Hospital In-Patient Regulations. It was not maintained under the National Health Service Act 1977, but the claimant was receiving treatment there pursuant to arrangements made by the Health Authority on behalf of the Secretary of State under the 1977 Act which was enough to bring the hospital within reg.2(2)(b). The claimant was therefore not entitled to income support as his income exceeded his reduced applicable amount as a hospital in-patient. Note that reg.2(2) of the Hospital In-Patient Regulations was amended on November 16, 1992. It is not clear whether such an arrangement will still fall within the terms of reg.2(2) as amended.

2.182   See also *Botchett v Chief Adjudication Officer, The Times*, May 8, 1996 (*R(IS) 10/96*). The claimant had severe learning disabilities and was resident in a registered nursing home. The nursing home had been part of a hospital but in 1991 was transferred to a trust which was funded by the health authority. The Court of Appeal held that the claimant's disability came within the definition of mental disorder, the care and assistance she received from nursing as opposed to domestic staff was to be regarded as "medical or other treatment" within reg.2(2) and that the home was a "similar institution" to a hospital. She was therefore a "patient" for the purposes of income support.

However, in *CDLA 7980/1995* (which concerned the almost identical provision to reg.2(2) in reg.8(1) of the Social Security (Disability Living Allowance) Regulations 1991) the Commissioner points out that to bring the definition into play the medical or other treatment has to be provided "in a hospital or similar institution". In that case the claimant, who had severe learning difficulties and was an epileptic, left long-term hospital accommodation and went to live in a privately-rented house with five other tenants. Staff employed by Stockport Health Trust provided 24-hour care for the tenants but medication was prescribed by their individual GPs. The rent and other outgoings of the house were met from the tenants' benefits and the tenants were free to come and go as they wished. Having noted that paras (a) and (c) of the definition of "hospital" in s.128 of the National Health Service Act 1977 begin with the words "any institution", the Commissioner holds that used in connection with the word "hospital", those words connoted "some sort of formal body or structure which controls all aspects of the treatment or care that is provided including the premises in which that treatment or care is carried out. They mean more than just a building in which care and treatment takes place". There was no institution in that sense on the facts of this case. The treatment and care took place in a house let to the six occupants who were responsible for the rent and other outgoings. The fact that their money and affairs were managed on their behalf did not mean that they ceased to be responsible for the cost of accommodation, food, etc., ordered in their names. Leave to appeal against this decision was granted by the Commissioner but the appeal did not proceed.

"Prisoner"

A person is detained in custody pending trial once he has been charged. It does 2.183 not matter that in fact no trial takes place because the proceedings are discontinued. For the period he was in custody he was a prisoner (*R(IS) 1/94*). However, a person required to live in a bail hostel is not detained in custody pending trial (*R(IS) 17/93*); see Sch.7, para.9 as to how his applicable amount is calculated if he is a member of a couple.

Sub-para.(b) of the definition has been added to reverse the effect of *Chief Adjudication Officer v Carr, The Times*, June 2, 1994, also reported as *R(IS) 20/95*. A majority of the Court of Appeal had upheld the Commissioner's decision that a person serving a prison sentence who was released for a period of home leave was not a prisoner during that leave period. A person on temporary release will now continue to count as a prisoner and will not be eligible for income support. A person on income support with whom the prisoner stays while released on temporary licence can apply for a community care grant for his living expenses (see Social Fund Direction 4(a)(iv)).

Only people detained in custody awaiting trial or sentence have a limited entitlement to income support (see Sch.7, para.8(b)).

"Residential accommodation"

This definition applies where the person's stay is more than temporary and con- 2.184 trols the application of the so-called "Part III rate" under para.13 of Sch.7. That rate is being phased out as from April 8, 2002—see the commentary to para.(1B) above. Note that para.(4) excludes from the definition under-18s in care in Scotland (sub-para.(a)), and accommodation where board is not provided (sub-para.(c)). The effect of sub-para.(c) is that residents of some types of local authority hostels are not shifted onto ordinary income support and housing benefit with other hostel-dwellers. If board is available, residents remain entitled to the "Part III rate" under para.13 of Sch.7. See the notes to the definition of "residential care home" in reg.19 for "board". Para.(4A) in effect provides that board is available where any cooked or prepared food is provided in return for an inclusive charge. The intention is that if residents buy their own food or meals when they want them they are not restricted to the Part III rate.

Section 21(1) of the National Assistance Act 1948 obliges a local authority to provide accommodation for local residents "who by reason of age, illness, disability or other circumstances are in need of care and attention which is not otherwise available to them" (note that with effect from April, 1, 1993, s.21 only covers cases of illness and disability: see s.42 of, and Schs 9 and 10 to, the National Health Service and Community Care Act 1990). In *CA 2985/1997* the tribunal erred in law for not investigating whether the local authority had power to act under s.21(1), since this had been put directly in issue by the claimant. The claimant contended that accommodation was "otherwise available". The Commissioner refers to *R. v Sefton MBC Ex p. Help the*

Aged and Charlotte Blanchard [1997] 4 All E.R. 532 which had clearly established that accommodation was "not otherwise available" if the claimant did not have the means to pay for it. Subject to this, in his view it was a question of fact in each case. A key aspect, apart from means, would be whether the claimant or some other appropriate person was capable of organising the accommodation (see Department of Health Circular (LAC (98) 19)).

See also *CSIS 453/1995* which concerned s.59 of the Social Work (Scotland) Act 1968. The Commissioner concludes on the facts that the claimant's accommodation had not been secured by the local authority within s.59(2)(c) and that accordingly she was entitled to income support at the residential care home rate.

Note the increased upper and lower capital limits for most people living permanently in residential accommodation from April 1996 (regs 45(b) and 53(1A), see the note to reg.53; note reg.53(4)).

Para.(3A)

2.185   Local authorities have duties to provide accommodation under the statutes mentioned in the definition of residential accommodation in para.(3), either in their own homes or by meeting the costs of independent homes. Residents then make a contribution to the costs. By agreement between the Government and local authorities the minimum weekly charge has been set at 80 per cent of the basic rate of retirement pension. The resident can qualify for the ordinary rates of income support.

The Government was concerned that some local authorities had transferred their own homes to independent bodies (or were planning to do so) and required residents who did not wish to move to sign undertakings to arrange their own accommodation. If this had the effect of absolving the local authority from their duty to provide accommodation, the costs would be transferred from the local authorities to the income support budget. There was concern that the long-term welfare of existing residents was at risk if the local authority's responsibility was removed. Thus para.(3A) was introduced to provide that if residential accommodation became a residential care home after August 11, 1991, existing residents continue to be treated as if they were still in residential accommodation. There were originally two conditions to this. The first was that the person stays in the same accommodation. This condition remains. (There may be scope for manipulation here.) The second condition was that the local authority remained under a duty to provide or arrange for accommodation for the person. (This requirement has been removed with effect from November 8, 1996, see below). At the same time as reg.21 was amended the Secretary of State issued Directions under the National Assistance Act 1948 and the National Health Service Act 1977 that in these circumstances of transfer the local authority remains under a duty. *R(IS) 13/96* decides that para.(3A) did effect a material change in the law and was not (as the AO had argued) merely declaratory. In both cases the claimants were resident in "Part III" homes for the elderly, the management of which was transferred by the local authority to a voluntary organisation before August 12, 1991. The residents were given the option of staying in the same home or moving to another home still run by the local authority. Both claimants stayed in their current home. The Commissioner holds that the evidence showed that the agreement between the local authority and the voluntary organisation in both cases did not come within s.26 of the National Assistance Act 1948. Thus the claimants were entitled to income support at the residential care home rate. The general approach of *R(IS) 13/96* is followed by the Commissioner in *R(A) 3/96*, but he also points out that in deciding whether an arrangement is made under s.26 of the 1948 Act, s.26(2) is of central importance. Section 26(2) required that the arrangement provide for payments by the local authority to the voluntary organisation. This was because the essence of a s.26 arrangement was that the accommodation was provided in fulfilment of the local authority's duty under s.21(1) and so under s.26(3) the person concerned was under no liability to pay the voluntary organisation for the accommodation, but was obliged to refund the local authority for the payments made to the voluntary organisation (the obligation was subject to reduction on the grounds of the person's inability to pay). Thus if the residents were liable to make payments for their accommodation to the voluntary organisation a necessary characteristic of a s.26 arrangement was missing and the continued provision of accommodation was not pursuant to Part III of the 1948 Act. The Commissioner's decision in *R(IS) 13/96* was confirmed by the Court of Appeal in *Chief Adjudication Officer v Harris* and *Chief Adjudication Officer v Gibbon* (April 15, 1994, unreported). The Court of Appeal also upheld the decision in *R(A) 3/96* in *Chief Adjudication Officer v Steane, The Times*, December 19, 1995. The CAO appealed to the House of Lords in both cases but the appeals were dismissed (*Chief Adjudication Officer and another v Quinn (on behalf of Jane Harris, Deceased), Same v Gibbon* and *Same v Steane* [1996] 4 All E.R. 72, also reported as part of *R(A) 3/96*). The House of Lords held that none of the arrangements had been made under s.26 because there was no provision for the local authority to make payments to the voluntary organisations concerned in accordance with s.26(2).

Following the House of Lords' judgment in *Quinn (Harris), Gibbon* and *Steane*, para.(3A) has been amended with effect from November 8, 1996 (despite the fact that Lord Slynn did consider that it had effected a change in the law; the transfers in *Harris, Gibbon* and *Steane* had all taken place *before* para.(3A) was introduced in August 1991). It is now no longer a condition that for the rule in para.(3A) to apply the local authority has to remain under a duty to provide or arrange for accommodation for the person concerned.

Paras (3B) to (3E)

The intention of these paragraphs is that where a local authority accepted responsibility for accommodating a person prior to April 1, 1993, they remain responsible for them.

2.186

[¹ Treatment of refugees

[²**21ZB.**—(1) This paragraph applies to a person who has submitted a claim for asylum on or after 3rd April 2000 and who is notified that he has been recorded by the Secretary of State as a refugee within the definition in Article 1 of the Convention relating to the Status of Refugees done at Geneva on 28th July 1951 as extended by Article 1(2) of the Protocol relating to the Status of Refugees done at New York on 31st January 1967.

(2) Subject to paragraph (3), a person to whom paragraph (1) applies, who claims income support within 28 days of receiving the notification referred to in paragraph (1), shall have his claim for income support determined as if he had been recorded as a refugee on the date when he submitted his claim for asylum.

(3) The amount of support provided under section 95 or 98 of the Immigration and Asylum Act, including support provided by virtue of regulations made under Schedule 9 to that Act, by the Secretary of State in respect of essential living needs of the claimant and his [³ partner] (if any) as specified in regulations made under paragraph 3 of Schedule 8 to the Immigration and Asylum Act shall be deducted from any award of income support due to the claimant by virtue of paragraph (2).]]

2.187

AMENDMENTS

1. Income Support and Social Security (Claims and Payments) (Miscellaneous Amendments) Regulations 1996 (SI 1996/2431), reg.3 (October 15, 1996).

2. Social Security (Immigration and Asylum) Consequential Amendments Regulations 2000 (SI 2000/636), reg.3 (5) (April 3, 2000).

2.188

3. Social Security (Working Tax Credit and Child Tax Credit) (Consequential Amendments) Regulations 2003 (SI 2003/455), reg.2 and Sch.1, para.5 (April 6, 2004), except in "transitional cases" and see further the note to reg.17 of the Income Support Regulations.

GENERAL NOTE

2.189   Regulation 21ZB replaces the former reg.21ZA for people who claim asylum after April 3, 2000. Its effect is to allow asylum seekers whose refugee status is subsequently recognised by the IND to claim income support retrospectively. The claim for IS must be made within 28 days of the claimant receiving notice that he has been granted refugee status but if this time limit is met, the date of claim is taken as being the date on which the claim for asylum was recorded as having been made (see regs 6(4D) and 19(8) of the Social Security (Claims and Payments) Regulations 1987 in Vol. III of this series). The refugee therefore receives a lump sum equal to his income support entitlement throughout the period he was waiting for his asylum claim to be determined less (under para.(3)) the amount of any asylum support which he has received under s.95 or 98 of the Immigration and Asylum Act 1999. The lump sum is disregarded as income and, for a period of 52 weeks, as capital (see para.57 of Sch.9 and para.49 of Sch.10 respectively).

This provision is more favourable to refugees than the former reg.21ZA which only entitled them to make a retrospective claim for income support at the lower urgent cases rate (see the former reg.21ZA(3) and *R(IS) 9/98*).

Regulations 21ZA remains in force for those claimants who claimed asylum before April 3, 2000 and are subsequently recognised as refugees (see reg.12(1) and (2) of SI 2000/636). For the text of the regulation see p.182 of the 1999 edition of *Mesher and Wood, Income-related Benefits: the Legislation*. Is it necessary for a refugee to state expressly in his or her claim for income support that s/he wishes to be given the benefit of this provision? That question was considered by a Deputy Commissioner in *CIS 579/2004*, in the context of the former reg.21ZA (which, for these purposes, is in the same terms as the present regulation). The Deputy Commissioner held, applying *CIS 371/1993* that, whilst an express claim was clearly sufficient, it was not necessary. If—as would usually be the case—the words used by the claimant on the claim form were enough in themselves to raise the issue of backdating then that amounted to an implied claim which the Secretary of State was obliged to decide. On the facts of the appeal, the claim form had disclosed that the claimant and her husband were foreign nationals, that the husband needed permission to work, that the couple had been supported by social services while the claim for refugee status was pending but that support had ended when the claimant had been granted indefinite leave to remain and that the claimant had recently been notified of her refugee status. The Deputy Commissioner held that those facts were sufficient to establish an implied claim for the past period specified in the regulation. The Deputy Commissioner went on to hold that simply making a claim for income support (*i.e.*, without expressly or impliedly including a claim for the past period) within the 28 day time limit was not sufficient for the purposes of reg.21ZA. Given her decision that an implied claim had been made on the facts of the case, the Deputy Commissioner's comments on this issue were *obiter* and may need further consideration if a future appeal arises in which no implied claim has been made on the facts.

In *CJSA/4843/2003* another Deputy Commissioner held that a refugee who fails to make a claim for income support within the 28 day period prescribed by reg.21ZB(2) (and therefore does not qualify for backdating to the date on which s/he applied for asylum) may nevertheless qualify for up to three months' backdating if s/he satisfies reg.19(4) and (5) of the Social Security (Claims and Payments) Regulations 1987 (see Vol. III).

CIS/3438/2004 considers the position where a claimant submits a properly completed claim form for income support within 28 days of having been granted refugee status but does not submit some necessary piece of supporting evidence within that period. The Commissioner expressed doubt as to whether reg.6(1A) of the Claims and Payments Regulations (which provides that a claim for income support is normally to be treated as made only when the "evidence requirements" of reg.4(1A) are satisfied— see Vol.III) overrode the specific provision for refugees in reg.6(4D) (which provides that the claim is to be treated as made when the application for asylum was recorded as having been made). But even if it did, a tribunal was required fully to investigate the exceptions to the evidence requirements in reg.4(1B), In this case, the form required by the Secretary of State did not exist at the time of the claim and was not generated by the Home Office until many weeks later. Under reg.4(1B)(b), the claimant was not to be penalised for not having produced a non-existent piece of evidence.

[1Reductions in applicable amounts in certain cases of failure to attend courses

21A.—[² . .].]

2.190

AMENDMENTS

1. Income Support (General and Transitional) Amendment Regulations 1990 (SI 1990/2324), reg.3 (December 17, 1990).
2. Income Support (General) (Jobseeker's Allowance Consequential Amendments) Regulations 1996 (SI 1996/206), reg.28 and Sch.3 (October 7, 1996).

[Reductions in applicable amounts in certain cases of actual or notional unemployment benefit disqualification

22.—[¹. . .]

2.191

AMENDMENT

1. Income Support (General) (Jobseeker's Allowance Consequential Amendments) Regulations 1996 (SI 1996/206), reg.28 and Sch.3 (October 7, 1996).

[1Reduction in applicable amount where the claimant is appealing against a decision [²which embodies a determination] that he is not incapable of work

22A.—(1) Subject to paragraph (3), where a claimant falls within para-
graph 25 of Schedule 1B (persons appealing against a decision [²which embodies a determination] that they are not incapable of work under the [³personal capability assessment]), and none of the other paragraphs of that Schedule applies to him, his applicable amount shall be reduced by a sum equivalent to 20 per cent, of the following amount—
  (a) in the case of a person to whom regulation 17 or 18 or paragraphs 6, 9 to 12, 16, 17(c)(i) or (d)(i) of Schedule 7 applies—
    (i) where he is a single claimant aged less than 18 or a member of a couple or a polygamous marriage where all the members, in either case, are less than 18, the amount specified in paragraph 1(1)(a), (b) or (c), as the case may be, of Schedule 2 (applicable amounts);
    (ii) where he is a single claimant aged not less than 18 but less than 25 or a member of a couple or a polygamous marriage where one member is aged not less than 18 but less than 25 and the other member, or in the case of a polygamous marriage each other member, is a person under 18 who—

2.192

(aa) does not qualify for income support under regulation 4ZA, or who would not so qualify if he were to make a claim; and

(bb) does not satisfy the requirements of section 3(1)(f)(iii) of the Jobseekers Act 1995 (prescribed circumstances for persons aged 16 but less than 18); and

(cc) is not the subject of a direction under section 16 of the Jobseekers Act 1995 (persons under 18: severe hardship), the amount specified in paragraph 1(1)(d) of that Schedule;

(iii) where he is a single claimant aged not less than 25 or a member of a couple or a polygamous marriage (other than a member of a couple or a polygamous marriage to whom head (ii) of this sub-paragraph applies) at least one of whom is aged not less than 18, the amount specified in paragraph 1(1)(e) of that Schedule;

(b) [⁵. . .].

(2) A reduction under paragraph (1) shall, if it is not a multiple of 5p, be rounded to the nearest such multiple or, if it is a multiple of 2.5p but not of 5p, to the next lower multiple of 5p.

(3) Paragraph (1) shall not apply to a claimant who is appealing against a decision [²which embodies a determination] that he is not incapable of work under the [³personal capability assessment] where that [²determination] was [⁴ the first determination made in accordance with, the all work test before 3rd April 2000 or, after that date, the personal capability assessment, in relation to the claimant], and the claimant was, immediately prior to 13th April 1995, either—

(a) in receipt of invalidity pension under Part II of the Contributions and Benefits Act as then in force, or severe disablement allowance; or

(b) incapable of work in accordance with paragraph 5 of Schedule 1 as in force on 12th April 1995 and had been so for a continuous period of 28 weeks.]

AMENDMENTS

2.193   1. Income Support (General) (Jobseeker's Allowance Consequential Amendments) Regulations 1996 (SI 1996/206), reg.13 (October 7, 1996).

2. Social Security Act 1998 (Commencement No.9 and Savings and Consequential and Transitional Provisions) Order 1999 (SI 1999/2422 (C.61)), art.3(7) and Sch.6, para.1 (September 6, 1999).

3. Social Security (Incapacity for Work) Miscellaneous Amendments Regulations 1999 (SI 1999/3109), reg.6 (April 3, 2000).

4. Social Security (Incapacity) Miscellaneous Amendments Regulations 2000 (SI 2000/590), reg.5 (April 3, 2000).

5. Social Security Amendment (Residential Care and Nursing Homes) Regulations 2001 (SI 2001/3767), reg.2(1) and Part I of Sch. para.7 (April 8, 2002).

DEFINITION

"personal capability assessment"—SSCBA s.171C, Incapacity for Work Regs., reg.24.

GENERAL NOTE

2.194   Paras (1) and (2) of this regulation replace the provisions formerly in regs 8(2A) and 22 (now revoked). Para.(3) repeats the transitional protection in reg.19(5) of the Disability Working Allowance and Income Support (General) Amendment Regulations 1995 (see p.669).

The regulation applies where a claimant is appealing against a decision that he is fit for work on the basis of the "personal capability assessment" (which has replaced the "all work test" from April 3, 2000) and so is eligible for income support under para.25 of Sch.1B (and does not qualify under any of the other paragraphs in Sch.1B). See Vol. I of this series for full details of the personal capability assessment and when it applies. A claimant will be eligible for income support under para.25 until the appeal is determined (which means the final determination of the appeal, *e.g.* if it is taken to the Social Security Commissioner, confirmed in *CIS 2654/1999,* see further the notes to para.25 of Sch.1B). However, his income support will be reduced by 20 per cent of the appropriate personal allowance for a single claimant of his age (para.(1)). (If the appeal is successful the reduction will be repaid). But full income support was paid where the claimant had appealed after failing his first all work test or personal capability assessment if he had been incapable of work for 28 weeks or in receipt of invalidity benefit or severe disablement allowance immediately before April 13, 1995 (para.(3)). Note also reg.27(3) of the Income Support (General) (Jobseeker's Allowance Consequential Amendments) Regulations 1996 which provided for the reduction under para.(1) not to apply to people covered by reg.19(5) of the Disability Working Allowance and Income Support (General) Amendment Regulations 1995 as originally made (see the notes to reg.19(5) and (6) of those Regulations).

In order to receive full benefit the person will have to sign on as available for work and claim JSA while waiting for his appeal to be decided. The fact that a person has been available for employment will not prejudice the appeal about incapacity as it will be a change of circumstances that has occurred after the date of decision under appeal (s.12(8)(b) SSA 1998). See further the notes to para.25 of Sch.1B.

In *Smyth* (High Court of Northern Ireland, July 6, 2001) it was argued that the reduction under the equivalent Northern Ireland provision to para.(1) constituted "an impermissible clog" on the exercise of the right to appeal and was therefore a violation of Art.6 of the European Convention on Human Rights. However, this was rejected by Kerr J. In his view, the reduction was "a proportionate means of discouraging unmeritorious or frivolous appeals" and was not such a disincentive that it destroyed the essence of the right to appeal. He considered that a claimant's Art.6 rights were "sufficiently safeguarded by the existence of the right of appeal, the availability of income support (albeit at a reduced level) while the appeal is pending, and the backdated repayment of the full amount on a successful outcome for the appeal".

Part V

Income and capital

Chapter I

General

Calculation of income and capital of members of claimant's family and of a polygamous marriage

2.195   **23.**—(1) [³Subject to paragraph (4), the income and capital of a claimant's partner which by virtue of section 136(1) of the Contributions and Benefits Act] is to be treated as income and capital of the claimant, shall be calculated in accordance with the following provisions of this Part in like manner as for the claimant; and any reference to the "claimant" shall, except where the context otherwise requires, be construed, for the purposes of this Part, as if it were a reference to his partner [³. . .].

[³(2) Subject to the following provisions of this Part, the income paid to, or in respect of, and capital of, a child or young person who is a member of the claimant's family shall not be treated as the income or capital of the claimant.]

(3) [¹Subject to paragraph (5)] where a claimant or the partner of a claimant is married polygamously to two or more members of his household—

(a) the claimant shall be treated as possessing capital and income belonging to each such member [³. . .]; and

(b) the income and capital of that member [³. . .] shall be calculated in accordance with the following provisions of this Part in like manner as for the claimant [³. . .].

[¹(4) Where at least one member of a couple is aged less than 18 and the applicable amount of the couple falls to be determined under [²paragraphs 1(3)(b), (c), (f) or (g)] of Schedule 2 (applicable amounts), the income of the claimant's partner shall not be treated as the income of the claimant to the extent that—

(a) in the case of a couple where both members are aged less than 18, the amount specified in paragraph 1(3)(a) of that Schedule exceeds the amount specified in [²paragraph 1(3)(c)] of that Schedule; and

(b) in the case of a couple where only one member is aged less than 18, the amount specified in paragraph 1(3)(d) of that Schedule exceeds the amount which applies in that case which is specified in [²paragraph 1(3)(f) or (g)] of that Schedule.

(5) Where a member of a polygamous marriage is a partner aged less than 18 and the amount which applies in respect of him under regulation 18(2) (polygamous marriages) is nil, the claimant shall not be treated as possessing the income of that partner to the extent that an amount in respect of him would have been included in the applicable amount if he had fallen within the circumstances set out in regulation 18(2)(a) or (b).]

AMENDMENTS

1. Income Support (General) Amendment No.3 Regulations 1988 (SI 1988/   **2.196**
1228), reg.6 (September 12, 1988).
2. Income Support (General) (Jobseeker's Allowance Consequential
Amendments) Regulations 1996 (SI 1996/206), reg.14 (October 7, 1996).
3. Social Security (Working Tax Credit and Child Tax Credit) (Consequential
Amendments) Regulations 2003 (SI 2003/455), reg.2 and Sch.1, para.6 (April 6,
2004, except in "transitional cases" and see further the note to reg.17 of the Income
Support Regulations).

DEFINITIONS

"child"—see 1986 Act, s.20(11) (SSCBA, s.137(1)).
"claimant"—see reg.2(1).
"family"—see 1986 Act, s.20(11) (SSCBA, s.137(1)).
"partner"—see reg.2(1).
"polygamous marriage"—*ibid.*
"young person"—*ibid.*, reg.14.

GENERAL NOTE

Resources are to be either capital or income. There is nothing in between. The   **2.197**
distinction between capital and income is one which has given a good deal of trouble
in the past, and in many other legal contexts. There is no attempt at any general definition in the Regulations, although see regs 35, 41 and 48. The approach tends to
be that around the borderlines a decision can go either way, and it is only if a decision is completely unreasonable that it embodies an error of law (*R. v W. London
SBAT Ex p. Taylor* [1975] 2 All E. R. 790). But ultimately the question is one of law
(see *Lillystone v SBC* [1982] 3 F.L.R. 52, CA). However, note *CIS 2537/1997* in
which the Commissioner queries whether the question is one of law. He points to
Gallagher v Jones [1994] Ch. 107, CA and *Herbert Smith v Honour* [1999] S.T.C. 173
as authority for the proposition that for income tax and similar purposes the principal guide to whether something is income or capital is by reference to accounting
principles. See also *CIS 5481/1997* below.

So far as general principle goes it has been said that the "essential feature of
receipts by way of income is that they display an element of periodic recurrence.
Income cannot include ad hoc receipts." (Bridge J. in *R. v Supplementary Benefits
Commission Ex p. Singer* [1973] 1 W.L.R. 713). This links the notion of recurrence
(which may only be expected in the future) with the notion of a period to which the
income is linked. Similar notions are applied by the Commissioner in *R(SB) 29/85*
where the issue was the proper treatment of a £15 loan made to a striking miner by
a local authority Social Work Department to meet arrears on hire purchase agreements. The Commissioner holds that this was a capital payment, since it was a "one-
off" advance and there was no evidence that it was one of a series of payments.
Earlier he had referred to income payments normally bearing a readily identifiable
relationship with a period. However, periodic recurrence alone is not enough. The
nature of the obligation (if any) under which a payment is made must be looked at.
A capital payment may be made by instalments. Then in general each instalment is
a capital payment, so that reg.41 is necessary. The general rule is supported by the
Court of Appeal in *Lillystone v SBC* where the purchase price of a house was to be
paid in monthly instalments over 10 years. It was agreed that each £70 instalment,
when it was paid, was capital, not income. See also *CIS 5481/1997* which concerned
the assets of a business partnership. The Commissioner emphasised that some of the
assets would be income, not capital; the distinction was to be drawn in accordance
with accounting practice. This provided that the key principle was what the expenditure was calculated to effect from a practical and business point of view, and the
same also applied to receipts (see *CIR v Wattie* [1998] S.T.C. 1160).

2.198   A similar approach was taken by the Court of Appeal in *Morrell v Secretary of State for Work and Pensions* [2003] EWCA Civ 526, reported as *R(IS) 6/03*. Following her divorce, the claimant had been receiving regular sums of money from her mother, either paid to her to help her pay her rent and other living expenses, or paid directly to her landlord in respect of her rent. It was not in dispute that the payments were made to the claimant by way of loan, although the repayment terms were quite vague, the mother merely expecting reimbursement gradually as her daughter's problems decreased. The claimant argued that because the payments made by her mother were a loan, they were not income payments but should have been treated as capital. However, the Court rejected this argument. Referring to *Chief Adjudication Officer v Leeves*, November 6, 1998, CA, reported as *R(IS) 5/99* (see the note to reg.40), it said that the word "income" was to be given its ordinary and natural meaning. There was no general principle (in tax cases or elsewhere) that loans should be treated as capital rather than income. The regular monthly receipts from her mother clearly had the character of income. The Court agreed with *Leeves* that a sum received under a certain and immediate obligation to repay did not amount to income. However, there was no such obligation in this case and so the payments counted as income.

In *R(SB) 2/83* the Tribunal of Commissioners says "In most cases capital resources arise out of income resources. They represent savings out of past earnings. However, before they undergo the metamorphosis from income to capital all relevant debts, including, in particular, tax liabilities, are first deducted." In *R(SB) 35/83* the Commissioner holds that accumulated earnings will not become capital until all relevant liabilities are deducted. Since the "relevant liabilities" seems to mean the deductions appropriate under the benefit legislation, presumably it is only the categories mentioned in reg.36(3), if not already deducted, which can be considered, plus, it seems, expenses necessarily incurred in obtaining the earnings (*R(FC) 1/90* and *R(IS) 16/93*—see the note to reg.36(3)). *CIS 563/1991* decides that such expenses are not deductible in the case of income other than earnings (see the note to reg.40(1)). There is no provision for deducting amounts which are to be used for ordinary current expenditure (*R(IS) 3/93*).

2.199   *R(IS) 3/93* also confirms that a payment does not metamorphose into capital until the end of the period to which it is attributed as income. Thus, for example, payment of a month's salary, attributable for a forward period of a month from the date it was due to be paid, would retain its character as income until the end of that period. This principle should apply to other forms of income as it does to earnings. Thus if, for instance, arrears of a social security benefit are paid, then any amount of those arrears left after the end of the period to which the benefit is properly attributed as income comes into the category of capital. *R(SB) 4/89*, holding arrears of special hardship allowance to be income, did not deal with this point.

However, in *CIS/2467/2003* the Commissioner holds that the principle does not apply to self-employed earnings (although he confirms that it does apply to income other than earnings, such as incapacity benefit and disability living allowance which were in issue in that case, as well as earnings from employment). This was because the calculation of earnings from self-employment did not turn on when particular receipts came in but was, under reg.30(1), to be calculated as average weekly earnings (net profit, subject to deductions for income tax and social security) over a period of normally a year. Those average weekly earnings are then taken into account for income support purposes for an equivalent period into the future. There was therefore no period of attribution to be attached to any particular business receipt and the basis of the *R(IS) 3/93* principle did not exist. In the Commissioner's view it would be artificial and wrong to regard all business receipts as retaining the character of income until the expiry of the period for which earnings calculated over the whole period were taken into account. Instead the protection for self-employed earners in relation to the capital rules lay in the disregard of the value of business assets under para.6 of Sch.10. The Commissioner also held that the *R(IS) 3/93* principle did not apply to self-employed earnings covered by the special attribution rule in reg.30(2) (royalties, etc). The claimant in *CIS/2467/2003* was a self-employed author who received advances on contracting to write a book and subsequent royalties on sales. His claim for income support was refused on the ground that he had capital in excess of the prescribed limit. The Commissioner rejected his argument that money paid by way of advances was not legally owned by him because the advances were repayable if he did not fulfill the contract. In his view the advances fully belonged to the claimant as soon as they were received. The Commissioner further concluded that the claimant's business receipts had the character of capital as soon as they were paid to him and that the disregard of business assets in para.6 of Sch.10 did not apply (for further discussion of this case see the note to reg.30 and the note to para.6 of Sch.10).

On the meaning of "income" see also *R(IS) 4/01*. The Commissioner decides, applying *Chief Adjudication Officer v Leeves*, November 6, 1998, CA, reported as *R(IS) 5/99* (see the note to reg.40), that the part of the claimant's occupational pension that was being paid to his former wife under an attachment of earnings order did not count as his income for the purposes of income support. He concluded that in the absence of a statutory definition, income meant "money paid regularly to the recipient or to his order but not money which is being paid and which he cannot prevent from being paid directly to a third party instead of him". The Commissioner also held that the notional income rule in reg.42(4)(a) did not apply: see the note to reg.42(4)(a).

In addition see *CIS 5479/1999* in which an overpayment of an occupational pension was being recovered by the Italian authorities by withholding the monthly payments of the pension. The Commissioner refers to *Leeves* as confirming his own view that in the general context of the income support scheme income to be taken into account is income that is actually paid to a claimant. If a claimant who has not actually received income is to be treated as having that income, that has to be achieved by a specific provision in the legislation. In *R(IS) 4/02* the same Commissioner applies this approach to conclude, contrary to the view taken in para.9 of *CIS 212/1989* (and followed with some hesitation in *CIS 295/1994*), that payments of the claimant's husband's annuity which had vested in his trustee in bankruptcy under s.306 of the Insolvency Act 1986 were not part of his income (and thus not part of the claimant's income) for the purposes of income support. See also *R(IS) 2/03*, which agrees with *R(IS) 4/02* (on the basis of the principle in *Re Landau* [1998] Ch.223, affirmed in *Krasner v Dennison* [2001] Ch. 76) that *CIS 212/1989* should no longer be followed. Thus the payments under the claimant's self-employed pension annuity that were being applied entirely for the benefit of his creditors were not his actual income (see the note to reg.42(4) and (4ZA) for the position in relation to notional income). Note that the law has now changed on the exclusion of pension rights from a bankrupt's estate (Welfare Reform and Pensions Act 1999, s.11), but only for bankruptcy orders made on or after May 29, 2000. Regulation 42(4) and (4ZA) were also amended on November 9, 1999 to make specific provision for pensions paid to third parties (see the note to reg.42(4) and (4ZA) and in particular *R(IS) 4/01* discussed in that note). The general principle of the meaning of "income", however, will remain of significance.

A similar approach was taken in *CH/3013/2003*, to be reported as *R(H) 5/05*, in relation to bank overdrafts. The Commissioner referred to the fact that the standard terms of a bank overdraft were that it was repayable on demand, although the demand might not be made while the amount stayed within an agreed limit. Those terms brought the repayment obligation within the *Leeves* principle. The obligation was certain, as the amount overdrawn could be identified day by day, and was immediate, even though the bank choose not to enforce the immediate obligation. Thus the resources provided by the use of the claimant's overdraft facility did not amount to income. The Commissioner commented that that result was also in accord with the ordinary and natural meaning of "income". One would not naturally speak of a person having an income from incurring expenditure and running up an overdraft. (Note that the Commissioner did not refer to the Court of Appeal's decision in *R v West Dorset DC Ex p. Poupard* [1998] 28 R.V.R. 40 which had held that borrowings by way of a bank overdraft secured by capital and used for living expenses constituted income for the purposes of the housing benefit scheme as it then existed. But arguably this decision

2.200

is no longer pertinent, bearing in mind that it concerned the former housing benefit scheme, and in the light of *Leeves*.) The Commissioner left open the question of whether the same would apply to credit cards (although he did refer to *CH/3393/2003* in which it was accepted that the juggling of credit card balances, where there was no immediate liability to repay beyond the minimum monthly payment, created a regular funding facility to be taken into account as income; however in the circumstances of the case before him there was no need to decide whether or not *CH/3393/2003* was correctly decided or whether it depended on its particular facts).

Paras (1) and (2)

2.201   These provisions contain the basic rule on the aggregation of resources. With effect from April 6, 2004 (except in "transitional cases"—see the note to reg.17), only the income and capital of the claimant's partner is treated as the claimant's. Note that the definition of partner refers on to married and unmarried couples, defined in s.137(1) of the Contributions and Benefits Act (and see para.(3) for polygamous marriages). It is an essential part of the definition of both kinds of couple that the parties should be members of the same household, so that reg.16 may also be relevant. There are special rules for couples where at least one member is under 18 (paras (4) and (5)).

2.202   Under the form of reg.23 in force before April 6, 2004 (the old form continues to apply for "transitional cases"—see the note to reg.17) the income (but not the capital) of a child or young person who was a member of the clamaint's family was aggregated with the claimant's (see the 2003 edition of this volume for the old form of reg.23 and the notes to that regulation for further details of the former rules relating to treatment of a child or young person's income and capital). However, with effect from April 6, 2004 (except in "transitional cases"—see the note to reg.17) amounts for children and young persons have been removed from the income support scheme; financial assistance to help with the cost of bringing up a child or young person is now to be provided through the child tax credit system, see Vol. IV of this series. As a consequence the new form of para.(2) provides that income paid to, or in respect of, and the capital of, a child or young person does not count as that of the claimant. Note the new disregards of child benefit and child tax credit (see para.5B of Sch.9) (for income support claimants who had an award of child tax credit before April 6, 2004 see reg.7 of the Social Security (Working Tax Credit and Child Tax Credit) (Consequential Amendments) Regulations 2003 (SI 2003/455) (as amended) on p. 686 and the notes to that regulation).

References to "the claimant" in the following regulations are to be treated as references to any partner. However, see *R(IS) 3/03* discussed in the note to para.12 of Sch.10.

Para. (4)

2.203   This paragraph applies where a couple receives less than the ordinary couple's rate of personal allowance because of the ineligibility of one partner who is under 18 (this is the effect of the reference to para.1(3)(b), (c), (f) and (g) of Sch.2). The income of the ineligible partner is not treated as the claimant's except to the extent that it exceeds the difference between the reduced rate of personal allowance and the ordinary rate. The aggregation of capital is not affected.

Para. (5)

2.204   This makes similar provision for polygamous marriages.

[¹ Income of participants in the self-employment route [² . . .]

2.205   **23A.** Chapters II, III, IV, V, VII and VIIA of this Part and regulations 62 to 66A, 68 and 69 shall not apply to any income which is to be calculated in accordance with Chapter IVA of this Part (participants in the self-employment route [² . . .]).]

AMENDMENTS

1. Social Security (Miscellaneous Amendments) (No.4) Regulations 1998 (SI 1998/1174), reg.6(2) (June 1, 1998).
2. Social Security Amendment (Employment Zones) (No.2) Regulations 2000 (SI 2000/2910), reg.5(1)(a) (November 27, 2000).

DEFINITION

"self-employment route"—see reg.2(1).

GENERAL NOTE

Regulation 23A takes any gross receipts from trading while on the "self-employment route" out of the categories of earnings, self-employed earnings and income other than earnings for the purposes of any claim for income support. The rules for liable relative payments, payments of child support maintenance and student income (except reg.67) also do not apply. Any such receipts may only be taken into account in accordance with regs 39A to 39D. For the definition of the "self-employment route", see reg.2(1).   2.206

Treatment of charitable or voluntary payments

24.—[[1] . . .]   2.207

AMENDMENT

1. Income Support (General) Amendment No.5 Regulations 1988 (SI 1988/2022), reg.5 (December 12, 1988).

Liable relative payments

25. Regulations 29 to [[1]42], 46 to 52 and Chapter VIII of this Part shall not apply to any payment which is to be calculated in accordance with Chapter VII thereof (liable relatives).   2.208

AMENDMENT

1. Social Security (Working Tax Credit and Child Tax Credit) (Consequential Amendments) Regulations 2003 (SI 2003/455), reg.2 and Sch.1, para.7 (April 6, 2004, except in "transitional cases" and see further the note to reg.17 of the Income Support Regulations).

[[1]Child support

25A. Regulations 29, 31, 32, 40 and 42 and Chapter VII of this Part shall not apply to any payment which is to be calculated in accordance with chapter VIIA of this Part (child support).]   2.209

AMENDMENT

1. Social Security (Miscellaneous Provisions) Amendment Regulations 1993 (SI 1993/846), reg.2 (April 19, 1993).

GENERAL NOTE

Reg.25A takes payments of child support maintenance, paid under an assessment carried out in accordance with the Child Support Acts 1991–1995, out of the categories of income other than earnings and of liable relative payments. They may only be taken into account for income support purposes in accordance with regs 60A to 60D.   2.210

Calculation of income and capital of students

2.211   **26.** The provisions of Chapters II to VI of this Part (income and capital) shall [¹ have effect in relation to students and their partners subject to the modifications set out in Chapter VIII thereof(students)].

Amendment

1. Income Support (General) Amendment Regulations 2001 (SI 2001/721), reg.2(a) (March 29, 2001).

Definitions

"partner"—see reg.2(1).
"student"—*ibid.*, reg.61(1).

[¹Rounding of fractions

2.212   **27.** Where any calculation under this Part results in a fraction of a penny that fraction shall, if it would be to the claimant's advantage, be treated as a penny, otherwise it shall be disregarded.]

Amendment

1. Income Support (General) Amendment Regulations 1988 (SI 1988/663), reg.13 (April 11, 1988).

Chapter II

Income

Calculation of income

2.213   **28.**—(1) For the purposes of section 20(3) of the Act [SSCBA, s.124(1)] (conditions of entitlement to income support), the income of a claimant shall be calculated on a weekly basis—

(a) by determining in accordance with this Part, other than Chapter VI, the weekly amount of his income; and

(b) by adding to that amount the weekly income calculated under regulation 53 (calculation of tariff income from capital).

[¹(2) For the purposes of paragraph (1) "income" includes capital treated as income under regulations 41 (capital treated as income) and income which a claimant is treated as possessing under regulation 42 (notional income).]

Amendment

1. Income Support (General) Amendment No.4 Regulations 1991 (SI 1991/1559), reg.7 (October 7, 1991).

Definitions

"the Act"—see reg.2(1).
"claimant"—*ibid.*

Reg.28 simply confirms that all resources which would come under the descrip- **2.214**
tion of income, including resources specifically treated as earnings or income, are to
be taken into account in the income calculation.

Calculation of earnings derived from employed earner's employment and income other than earnings

29.—(1) [¹. . .] Earnings derived from employment as an employed earner **2.215**
and income which does not consist of earnings shall be taken into account
over a period determined in accordance with the following paragraphs and
at a weekly amount determined in accordance with regulation 32 (calculation of weekly amount of income).

(2) Subject to [⁴the following provisions of this regulation], the period
over which a payment is to be taken into account shall be—

(a) in a case where it is payable in respect of a period, a period equal to
the length of that period;

(b) in any other case, a period equal to such number of weeks as is equal
to the number obtained (and any fraction shall be treated as a corresponding fraction of a week) by dividing the net earnings, or in the
case of income which does not consist of earnings, the amount of that
income [³less any amount paid by way of tax on that income which is
disregarded under paragraph 1 of Schedule 9 (income other than
earnings to be disregarded)] by the amount of income support which
would be payable had the payment not been made plus an amount
equal to the total of the sums which would fall to be disregarded from
that payment under Schedule 8 [³(earnings to be disregarded) or, as
the case may be, any paragraph of Schedule 9 other than paragraph
1 of that Schedule,] as is appropriate in the claimant's case;

and that period shall begin on the date on which the payment is treated as
paid under regulation 31 (date on which income is treated as paid).

[⁴(2A) The period over which a Career Development Loan, which is paid
pursuant to section 2 of the Employment and Training Act 1973, shall be
taken into account shall be the period of education and training intended to
be supported by that loan.

(2B) Where grant income as defined in Chapter VIII of this Part
has been paid to a person who ceases to be a [⁸ full-time student] before
the end of the period in respect of which that income is payable and, as a
consequence, the whole or part of that income falls to be repaid by
that person, that income shall be taken into account over the period
beginning on the date on which that income is treated as paid under
regulation 31 and ending—

(a) on the date on which repayment is made in full; or

[⁵(aa) where the grant is paid in instalments, on the day before the next
instalment would have been paid had the claimant remained a [⁸ full-
time student]; or]

(b) on the last date of the academic term or vacation during which that
person ceased to be a [⁸ full-time student],

whichever shall first occur.]

(3) Where earnings not of the same kind are derived from the same source
and the periods in respect of which those earnings would, but for this paragraph, fall to be taken into account—

(a) overlap, wholly or partly, those earnings shall be taken into account over a period equal to the aggregate length of those periods;

(b) and that period shall begin with the earliest date on which any part of those earnings would otherwise be treated as paid under regulation 31 (date on which income is treated as paid).

[²(4) In a case to which paragraph (3) applies, earnings under regulation 35 (earnings of employed earners) shall be taken into account in the following order of priority—

(a) earnings normally derived from the employment;

(b) any payment to which paragraph (1)(b) or (c) of that regulation applies;

(c) any payment to which paragraph (1)(i) of that regulation applies;

(d) any payment to which paragraph (1)(d) of that regulation applies.]

[¹(4A) Where earnings to which regulation 35(1)(b) to (d) (earnings of employed earners) applies are paid in respect of part of a day, those earnings shall be taken into account over a period equal to a day.]

[²(4B) Where earnings to which regulation 35(1)(i)(i) applies (earnings of employed earners) are paid in respect of or on the termination of any employment which is not part-time employment, the period over which they are to be taken into account shall be—

(a) a period equal to such number of weeks as is equal to the number (less any fraction of a whole number) obtained by dividing the net earnings by the maximum weekly amount which, on the date on which the payment of earnings is made, is specified in paragraph 8(1)(c) of Schedule 14 to the Employment Protection (Consolidation) Act 1978; or

(b) a period equal to the length of the specified period,

whichever is the shorter, and that period shall begin on the date on which the payment is treated as paid under regulation 31 (date on which income is treated as paid).

(4C) Any earnings to which regulation 35(1)(i)(ii) applies which are paid in respect of or on the termination of part-time employment, shall be taken into account over a period equal to one week.

(4D) In this regulation—

(a) "part-time employment" means employment in which a person is not to be treated as engaged in remunerative work under regulation 5 or [⁶6(1)[⁷ and (4)]] (persons treated, or not treated, as engaged in remunerative work);

(b) "specified period" means a period equal to—

(i) the period of notice which is applicable to a person, or would have been applicable if it had not been waived; less

(ii) any part of that period during which the person has continued to work in the employment in question or in respect of which he has received a payment to which regulation 35(1)(c) applies,

and for the purposes of this definition "period of notice" means the period of notice of termination of employment to which a person is entitled by statute or by contract, whichever is the longer, or, if he is not entitled to such notice, the period of notice which is customary in the employment in question.]

(5) For the purposes of this regulation the claimant's earnings and income which does not consist of earnings shall be calculated in accordance with Chapters III and V respectively of this Part.

AMENDMENTS

1. Income Support (General) Amendment No.5 Regulations 1988 (SI 1988/ 2022), reg.7 (December 12, 1988).
2. Income Support (General) Amendment No.2 Regulations 1989 (SI 1989/ 1323), reg.9 (October 9, 1989).
3. Income Support (General) Amendment Regulations 1990 (SI 1990/547), reg.10 (April 9, 1990).
4. Income-related Benefits and Jobseeker's Allowance (Miscellaneous Amendments) Regulations 1997 (SI 1997/65), reg.5 (April 7, 1997).
5. Social Security (Miscellaneous Amendments) Regulations 1998 (SI 1998/ 563), reg.12 (April 6, 1998).
6. Social Security (Miscellaneous Amendments) (No.2) Regulations 1999 (SI 1999/2556), reg.2(4) (October 4, 1999).
7. Social Security (Miscellaneous Amendments) Regulations 2000 (SI 2000/ 681), reg.2(c) (April 3, 2000).
8. Social Security Amendment (Students) Regulations 2000 (SI 2000/1981), reg.5(5) and Sch. (July 31, 2000).

2.216

DEFINITIONS

"claimant"—see reg.2(1), reg.23(1).
"employed earner"—see reg.2(1).
"full-time student"—see reg.61(1).
"grant income"—*ibid.*

GENERAL NOTE

Paras (1) to (2B)

This regulation applies to the earnings of employees and income other than earnings. Thus it covers other social security benefits. Earnings from self-employment are dealt with in reg.30. It defines the period over which income is to be taken into account and the date on which that period starts. The general rule is set out in para.(2). The first part (familiar from reg.9(2)(a) of the old Resources Regulations) is that where a payment is in respect of a period it is to be taken into account for an equal period. A fortnight's unemployment benefit is to be taken into account for a fortnight *(R(SB) 17/82)*, a month's salary for a month, an annual covenant for a year *(R(SB) 25/86,* but see Chapter VIII for students). There will be problems in determining the period in respect of which a payment is made in some cases. For instance, is holiday pay in terms of days, to be attributed to each of the seven days in a week (as done in *R(SB) 11/85* and *CSB 1004/1988*), or is it in terms of weeks, so that only five days' worth is attributed to each week? The Commissioner in *CJSA/1589/2004* adopts the former approach, preferring *CJSA/3438/1998* to *CJSA/4508/1998* (the latter decision had accepted that holiday pay should be attributed on the basis of "working days"). The claimant who had been contracted to work a three day week was paid 11.115 days holiday pay on the termination of his employment. The Commissioner holds that he was by virtue of that holiday pay (which counted as earnings: see reg.98(1)(c) of the JSA Regulations) to be treated as being in remunerative work (see reg.52(3) of the JSA Regulations) for 12 days (see reg.94(5) of the JSA Regulations, the equivalent of para.(4A) where earnings are paid in respect of part of a day), namely from November 28 to December 9, 2002, and not for four weeks as the tribunal had decided. A further example could be that of a supply teacher who works for a varying number of days in each month and is paid at the end of the month. Is that payment in respect of the month or in respect of the number of days worked? Much will turn on the precise contractual situation and the terms used by the parties, as confirmed by *R(IS) 3/93*. Decisions on the former reg.7(1)(g) of the Social Security (Unemployment, Sickness and Invalidity Benefit) Regulations 1983 (like *R(U) 3/84*) may be helpful.

2.217

The question in relation to supply teachers was specifically considered in *R(IS) 10/95*. The claimant had worked as a supply teacher for five days in the month of June. She was paid for work done in a month at the end of the following month. The Commissioner accepts that the claimant's contract with the local education authority was on a daily basis (see *R(U) 2/87*). But he rejected her argument that the period for which payment was made was five days. He holds that since she was employed on a daily basis, she was in fact paid for five different periods in June. Para.(2)(a) clearly only envisaged payment in respect of a single period, since neither para.(2) nor reg.32(1) could operate satisfactorily if a single payment could be in respect of two or more periods. Thus the payment for the days worked in a particular month had to be attributed to the period of a month. *R(IS) 10/95* is followed with some reluctance in *CIS 167/1992*. The result of this approach is that the period is determined by the employer's administrative arrangements for payment, rather than the terms of the employment. But it is surely arguable that the period in respect of which the payment was payable was one day. The terms of the claimant's employment were that she was paid £42.23 per session (*i.e.* day). The Commissioner's approach equates the period in respect of which a payment is *payable* with the period for which payment is *due to be made*, which is not necessarily the same. Moreover, the Commissioner does not seem to have taken account of the fact that "payment" can include part of a payment (see reg.2(1)). Thus some of the operational difficulties referred to by the Commissioner could be overcome by dividing the claimant's monthly payment by the number of days worked in that month and attributing this on a daily basis. However, this does not deal with the point that all the payments would be due on one day. If the payments were due before the date of the claim, reg.31(1)(a) would apply to attribute them all to that day; if they were paid during a claim see reg.32(5) and reg.31(1)(b). See also para.13 of Sch.8.

2.218   Para.(2A) relates to Career Development Loans.

Para.(2B), in force from April 7, 1997, concerns the situation where a person is due to repay part or all of a student grant because he leaves or is dismissed from his course before it finishes. Note *CIS 4201/2003* which confirms that para.(2B) has no application if the claimant has already left the course by the time the grant (or instalment of the grant) is paid (see further below). If para.(2B) does apply, the grant income (defined in reg.61(1)) will be taken into account from the date it is treated as paid under reg.31 until full repayment has been made, or, where the grant is paid in instalments, the day before the next instalment would be due, or the last day of the term or vacation in which the person ceases to be a full-time student, whichever is earlier. See reg.32(6A) for calculation of the weekly amount to be taken into account and note reg.40(3B). Para.(2B) thus confirms the effect of the decision in *CIS 5185/1995*. The claimant who had been a full-time student left his course and claimed income support on January 10, 1994. The education authority did not inform him of the amount of the grant he had to repay until March 20, 1994. The Commissioner holds that the claimant was not entitled to income support because until the grant was repaid it was income that remained available to the claimant and had to be taken into account (see *R. v Bolton SBAT Ex p. Fordham* [1981] 1 All E.R. 50 and *CSB 1408/1988*) and it exceeded his applicable amount. Moreover, once the claimant had ceased to be a student, the disregards in reg.62 did not apply (but now see reg.32(6A)). The Commissioner rejects the argument that the grant income could be disregarded under the principle in *Barclays Bank v Quistclose Investments Ltd* [1970] A.C. 567. That principle did not apply because the education authority retained no beneficial interest in the grant. They merely reserved the right to demand repayment of a sum calculated in accordance with how much of the relevant term had expired when the claimant ceased to be a student.

However, in *CIS 12263/1996* the Commissioner took the view that as soon as a student had abandoned his course and an obligation to repay the balance of his grant to the education authority arose, he held the money on constructive trust for the authority. Thus in assessing the claimant's entitlement to income support the repayable balance of the grant was not to be taken into account as his income. The Commissioner in *CIS 12263/1996* considered that the *Quistclose* case was concerned with a "purpose trust" (*i.e.* where a grant or loan was impressed with a particular purpose from the beginning), whereas in this situation a constructive trust had arisen because the grant had been paid on the condition that the claimant continued to be a student. He also distinguished the Court of Appeal's decision in *Fordham* on the ground that in that case there had been uncertainty as to the obligation to repay (there was none here). Moreover, an alternative approach was that once the balance of the grant became repayable it could no longer be regarded as the claimant's income at all (see para.9(7) of *R(SB) 20/83*).

Leave to appeal against the decision in *CIS 5185/1995* was granted by the Court of Appeal but the appeal was not pursued for financial reasons. However, an appeal was brought by the AO against the decision in *CIS 12263/1996* (*Chief Adjudication Officer v Leeves*, November 6, 1998, CA, reported as *R(IS) 5/99*). It was conceded on behalf of the claimant that there was no constructive trust in these circumstances, since no proprietary right had been retained by the education authority, nor had any fiduciary obligation been created. However, the Court of Appeal held that money that the claimant was under a "certain and immediate liability" to repay did not amount to income. Thus once the claimant had received a request for immediate repayment of a specified sum from the local education authority the grant ceased to count as his income (although it fell to be treated as such until that time, even though he had abandoned his course). The Court distinguished its decision in *Fordham* as the liability to repay in that case had been uncertain. The Court's approach in *Leeves* was affirmed in *Morrell v Secretary of State for Work and Pensions* [2003] EWCA Civ 526, reported as *R(IS) 6/03* (see the note to reg.23).

Thus in relation to periods before April 7, 1997, the repayable balance of a grant will not count as a claimant's income from the date that the liability to repay has "crystallised" (*Leeves*). As regards periods after April 6, 1997, para.(2B) will apply. However, it is suggested that this is subject to the preliminary question of whether the repayable grant counts as the claimant's income at all. If it does not do so because there is a "certain and immediate" liability to repay, it is arguable that para.(2B) will not (or will cease to) apply. This is because neither para.(2B), nor reg.40(3B) or reg.32(6A), would seem to have the effect of deeming the grant to be income but simply provide for the period over which the grant is to be taken into account *if* it does count as income, and the method of calculating that income. Compare the wording of the former reg.40(3A) (in force until August 1, 2001; see Social Security Legislation 2001, Vol. II, p.337) (treatment of student loans where a claimant has ceased to be a full-time student): this required "a sum equal to the weekly amount" to be taken into account as income.

Where para.(2B) is applicable (for example, where repayment is not required immediately, or the amount of the repayment has not been calculated), note that the disregards for grant income in reg.62 will apply (reg.32(6A)); see also reg.40(3B).

Note that para.(2B) will not apply if the claimant has already ceased to be a full-time student by the time the grant (or the instalment of the grant) is paid (*CIS 4201/2003*). In *CIS 4201/2003* the question of whether the third instalment of the claimant's dependants' grant for the year 2000/1 which had been paid to her after she left her course was income for the purposes of her income support claim therefore had to be determined in accordance with *Leeves*. The Commissioner analyses the relevant provisions of the Education (Student Support) Regulations 2000 and concludes that on the facts of that case there was no obligation to repay an ascertained amount until the request for repayment had been made by the Student Loan Company (which was almost a year later). The instalment therefore fell to be taken into account as income until the middle of June 2001 (presumably under reg.40(3AA) although the Commissioner does not refer to this provision).

Any grant or covenant income or student loan left over at the end of the person's course is disregarded as income (see para.61 of Sch.9).

2.219

Note the special rules set out in paras (4B) to (4D) for calculating the period over which compensation payments (see reg.35(1)(i) and (3)) are to be taken into account.

If the payment is not in respect of a period then there is a mechanical rule in para.(2)(b) spreading it at the rate of income support which would otherwise be payable, taking account of any disregards.

Once the period is fixed, it begins on the date specified in reg.31.

Paras (3) and (4)

2.220
Para.(3) establishes an exception in the case of earnings only, to the rule about the date from which a payment is to be taken into account. It is to deal mainly with the situation on the termination of employment when a claimant may be entitled to regular earnings, week in hand payments, pay in lieu of notice or compensation for breach of contract and holiday pay. The effect is that each payment which is not disregarded (Sch.8, paras 1 to 3) is to be taken into account for the appropriate period, and the periods are to be put together consecutively. Then the aggregate period starts on the earliest date which would be fixed for any of the periods under reg.31. Note that para.(3) only applies where the earnings are of different kinds, and derive from the same source. Thus it would not apply to payments from different employers.

Para.(4) deals with the order in which payments in lieu of notice, compensation payments and holiday pay are to be taken into account in conjunction with ordinary earnings.

Para. (4A)

2.221
Earnings paid in respect of a part of a day are taken into account for a day.

Para. (4B)

2.222
This provision defines the length of the period for which a payment of compensation on the termination of full-time employment is to be taken into account. The line between full-time and part-time is drawn by para.(4D)(a) and reg.35(3)(c). What is a payment of compensation is defined in reg.35(3)(a). There are two alternative periods, whichever is the shorter being applied. The first is obtained by dividing the amount of the payment by the maximum weekly sum specified at the relevant time for the purposes of calculating statutory redundancy payments and the basic award for unfair dismissal. From April 1, 1989, the sum was £172, from April 1, 1990, it was £184, from April 1, 1991, it was £198, from April 1, 1992 (not increased in 1993 or 1994), it was £205, from September 27, 1995 (not increased in 1996 or 1997) it was £210, from April 1, 1998 it was £220 (not increased in 1999), from February 1, 2000 it was £230, from February 1, 2001 it was £240, from February 1, 2002 it was £250, from February 1, 2003 it was £260, from February 1, 2004 it was £270 and from February 1, 2005 it has been £280. This calculation will give an advantage to lower paid workers, for whom the period may be shorter than the number of weeks' wages represented by the payment. The second alternative is the "specified period", defined in para.(4D)(b) as the period of notice to which the person was legally entitled (or customarily entitled for civil servants with no contractual entitlement) less any period worked out or already covered by a payment in lieu of notice. This secures that if a person receives a payment which is larger than would be required to make up for the uncovered period of notice, he is not affected beyond the legal notice period.

Although the end of para.(4B) provides that the payment is to be treated as paid on the date fixed by reg.31, this result may well be displaced by the operation of paras (3) and (4).

Para. (4C)

2.223
Where a payment of compensation is made on the termination of part-time employment (para.(4D)(a) and reg.35(3)(c)) it is to be taken into account for one week. See also reg.32(7).

Calculation of earnings of self-employed earners

30.—(1) Except where paragraph (2) applies, where a claimant's income consists of earnings from employment as a self-employed earner the weekly amount of his earnings shall be determined by reference to his average weekly earnings from that employment—

(a) over a period of[[1]one year]; or

(b) where the claimant has recently become engaged in that employment or there has been a change which is likely to affect the normal pattern of business, over such other period [[1]. . .] as may, in any particular case, enable the weekly amount of his earnings to be determined more accurately.

(2) Where the claimant's earnings consist of royalties or sums paid periodically for or in respect of any copyright those earnings shall be taken into account over a period equal to such number of weeks as is equal to the number obtained (and any fraction shall be treated as a corresponding fraction of a week) by dividing the earnings by the amount of income support which would be payable had the payment not been made plus an amount equal to the total of the sums which would fall to be disregarded from the payment under Schedule 8 (earnings to be disregarded) as is appropriate in the claimant's case.

(3) For the purposes of this regulation the claimant's earnings shall be calculated in accordance with Chapter IV of this Part.

2.224

AMENDMENT

1. Income-related Benefits Schemes (Miscellaneous Amendments) (No.4) Regulations 1993 (SI 1993/2119), reg.11 (October 4, 1993).

2.225

DEFINITIONS

"claimant"—see reg.2(1), reg.23(1).
"self-employed earner"—see reg.2(1).

GENERAL NOTE

Reg.30 applies to earnings from self-employment. A person is a self-employed earner if he is in "gainful employment", other than employed earner's employment (SSCBA, s.2(1)(b), imported by reg.2(1)). In *CIS 166/1994* the claimant was a self-employed builder, whose work had dried up, although he had not ceased trading. The Commissioner points out that a person can be in gainful employment, even though he is not working or receiving any money from the employment (see *e.g.* *Vandyk v Minister of Pensions and National Insurance* [1955] 1 Q.B. 29). Whether the claimant was in gainful employment depended on his current and prospective activities and intentions. The Commissioner endorsed a detailed list of factors put forward by the AO for determining this. He also held that *R(FC) 2/90* which decided that the question whether a person was employed, or self-employed, for the purposes of income support or family credit, was for decision by the adjudicating authorities, not the Secretary of State, had not been affected by the 1992 consolidating legislation.

CIS 14409/1996 further confirmed that it was for the adjudicating authorities to decide whether particular earnings were self-employed earnings falling within reg.30, without being bound by the way they had been treated for contribution purposes. This was despite s.2(3) of the Contributions and Benefits Act 1992 (person treated as an employed earner in relation to a particular employment to be so treated for all contribution and benefit purposes). If the adjudicating authorities took a different view from the Secretary of State it was a matter for her what action she took in order to ensure compliance with s.2(3). The claimant in *CIS 14409/1996* was an

2.226

actor. Although his general status was that of a self-employed earner, his gross receipts for the previous year included earnings from radio and television engagements from which Class 1 national insurance contributions as a employed earner had been deducted. The SSAT decided that because the majority of his earnings were as a self-employed earner all his earnings fell to be calculated under reg.30. The Commissioner holds that this was plainly wrong (see s.2 of the 1992 Act and *Fall v Hitchen* [1973] 1 W.L.R. 286) and that what the tribunal should have addressed was the question of the nature of these particular earnings. On the facts the claimant was quite clearly carrying out his broadcasting work as a person in business on his own account (see *Market Investigations v Ministry of Social Security* [1969] 2 Q.B. 173). Thus the AO had been correct to treat the earnings from the radio and television contracts as self-employed earnings. On the tests for deciding whether a person is an employee or self-employed see further *CJSA 4721/2001*.

CJSA 1039/1999 concerned the application of regs 95 and 101(11) of the JSA Regulations (the equivalent of this regulation and reg.38(10)) in the context of a self-employed fairground stallholder working the summer season only. The Commissioner adopts the conclusion in *CIS 166/1994* (although not all its reasoning) that the period for working out a claimant's earnings under reg.95 is not the same period in law (though it may be in fact) as the period during which the claimant is engaged in remunerative work, or the period during which he was, or was not, gainfully employed as a self-employed earner. The question whether the claimant was or was not in remunerative work was to be kept separate from the question whether his earnings from self-employment were to be apportioned over a full year or some other period. See also *R(JSA) 1/03*.

Note that if the self-employment has ceased, earnings from that self-employment (other than royalty or copyright payments) are ignored (para.3 of Sch.8). Note also the disregard of business assets in para.6 of Sch.10 and see *CIS/2467/2003* below.

2.227   The earnings (calculated under regs 37 to 39) are generally to be averaged over a period of one year. It does not seem necessary that the period immediately precedes the benefit week in question. Any one year period—normally the last year for which accounts are available—will do. The alternative period under para.(1)(b) can only be chosen if there has been a change likely to affect the normal pattern of business or if the self-employment has recently started. In *CIS 166/1994* the Commissioner accepts that where such a change had produced, or was likely to produce, a substantial reduction in the claimant's earnings, it was appropriate for the period to start from the date of the change (with the likely result that no earnings fell to be taken into account). See also *CIS 14409/1996*. Note also the more general exception hidden in reg.38(10), which allows the amount of any item of income or expenditure to be calculated over a different period if that will produce a more accurate figure.

CJSA 1039/1999 applies these provisions in the context of a seasonal worker. The Commissioner points out that the general rule in reg.95(1)(a) of the JSA Regulations (the equivalent of para.(1)(a)) operates on the assumption that someone who is self-employed remains as such on a continuing basis. But that assumption did not apply to a seasonal worker. In the case of a seasonal worker, the status of being self-employed started and then stopped once or twice, at least, each year. In such cases, the engagement in self-employment would in many cases, in a broad sense, always be recent. Alternatively, any change in the seasonal patterns would activate the other proviso in reg.95(1)(b) (the equivalent of para.(1)(b)). In addition the flexibility in reg.101(11) had to be borne in mind (for income support see reg.38(10)). It was a question of fact for the new tribunal to decide whether the earnings period was the whole year or the summer season, and if the latter, when that season started and ended. If the earnings were to be spread over a year, they had to be offset against the claimant's entitlement to JSA in the off-season but this would not apply if they were averaged over the summer season only. For a case involving a seasonal worker in which the Commissioner did accept that the seasonal earnings should be spread over the whole year, see *R(JSA) 1/03*.

Para.(2) supplies a special rule for payments of royalties or for copyright, which are to be spread in the same way as income of an employee not in respect of a period (reg.29(2)(b)).

CIS/2467/2003 concerned a self-employed author who received advances on contracting to write a book and subsequent royalties on sales above the amount of the advance. However he had not been able to undertake any writing for some months due to illness, although he intended to resume this activity as soon as he had recovered. His income support claim was refused on the ground that he had capital above the prescribed limit. The Commissioner rejected his argument that money paid by way of advances was not legally owned by him because the advances were repayable if he did not fulfill the contract. In his view the advances fully belonged to the claimant as soon as they were received. The Commissioner then went on to consider whether the principle in *R(IS) 3/93* that a payment does not metamorphose into capital until the end of the period to which it is attributed as income applied to self-employed earnings. He concluded that it did not. This was because the calculation of earnings from self-employment did not turn on when particular receipts came in but was, under para.(1), to be calculated as average weekly earnings (net profit, subject to deductions for income tax and social security) over a period of normally a year. Those average weekly earnings were then taken into account for an equivalent period into the future. There was therefore no period of attribution to be attached to any particular business receipt and the basis of the *R(IS) 3/93* principle did not exist. In the Commissioner's view it would be artificial and wrong to regard all business receipts as retaining the character of income until the expiry of the period for which earnings calculated over the whole period were taken into account. Instead the protection for self-employed earners in relation to the capital rules lay in the disregard of the value of business assets under para.6 of Sch.10. The Commissioner also held that the fact that para.(2) did provide a special rule for the attribution of the kind of self-employed earnings in issue in this case did not make a difference in relation to capital. First, there was still the protection of the disregard in para.6 of Sch.10. Second, the attribution rule in para.(2) (which was very difficult to apply) was an artificial one, not linked to any assessment of the period in respect of which any particular payment was made. The rationale for the operation of the *R(IS) 3/93* principle was therefore also missing in relation to these types of self-employed earnings. The Commissioner accordingly concluded that the claimant's business receipts had the character of capital as soon as they were paid to him (although he did accept that payments of VAT which the claimant had a liability to pay over to Customs and Excise did not form part of his capital). The Commissioner finally considered whether the disregard in para.6 applied but decided that it did not (see further the note to para.6 of Sch.10).

Note that the profit simply derived from a capital asset is not earnings, which must be derived from some employment or occupation. See *R(U) 3/77*. Note also *R(FC) 2/92* and the other decisions in the note to para.6 of Sch.10 on the question of whether ownership of a tenanted house is a business.

Date on which income is treated as paid

31.—(1) Except where paragraph (2) [⁵ or (3)] applies, a payment of income to which regulation 29 (calculation of earnings derived from employed earner's employment and income other than earnings) applies shall be treated as paid—   2.228

    (a) in the case of a payment which is due to be paid before the first benefit week pursuant to the claim, on the date on which it is due to be paid;

    (b) in any other case, on the first day of the benefit week in which it is due to be paid or the first succeeding benefit week in which it is practicable to take it into account.

    (2) Income support, [⁴Jobseeker's allowance], [²maternity allowance,] [³short-term or long term incapacity benefit], or severe disablement

allowance [³. . .], shall be treated as paid on the day of the benefit week in respect of which [¹it is payable].

[⁶(3)Working tax credit or child tax credit shall be treated as paid—

(a) where the award of that tax credit begins on the first day of a benefit week, on that day, or

(b) on the first day of the benefit week that follows the date the award begins, or

(c) on the first day of the first benefit week that follows the date an award of income support begins, if later,

until the last day of the last benefit week that coincides with or immediately follows the last day for which the award of that tax credit is made.]

AMENDMENTS

2.229   1. Income Support (General) Amendment Regulations 1988 (SI 1988/663), reg.14 (April 11, 1988).

2. Income Support (General) Amendment No.4 Regulations 1988 (SI 1988/1445), reg.8 (September 12, 1988).

3. Disability Working Allowance and Income Support (General) Amendment Regulations 1995 (SI 1995/482), reg.10 (April 13, 1995).

4. Income Support (General) (Jobseeker's Allowance Consequential Amendments) Regulations 1996 (SI 1996/206), reg.15 (October 7, 1996).

5. Social Security (Miscellaneous Amendments) Regulations 2000 (SI 2000/681), reg.3(1) (April 3, 2000).

6. Social Security (Working Tax Credit and Child Tax Credit) (Consequential Amendments) (No. 3) Regulations 2003 (SI 2003/1731), reg.2(2) (August 8, 2003).

DEFINITIONS

"benefit week"—see reg.2(1).
"child tax credit"—*ibid.*
"working tax credit"—*ibid.*

GENERAL NOTE

Para. (1)
2.230   This provision applies to determine when the period of attribution of earnings from employment and income (other than the benefits specified in para.(2) and working tax credit and child tax credit (para.(3)) fixed in reg.29 begins. The crucial date is that on which the payment is due to be paid. This date may well be different from the date of actual payment. Legal obligations must be considered, *e.g.* the terms of a contract of employment *(R(SB) 33/83)*. If a claimant's contract of employment is terminated without due notice any deferred holiday pay and wages withheld under week-in-hand arrangements are due immediately. So are any agreed payments in lieu of notice *(R(SB) 23/84* and *R(SB) 11/85)*. Note the operation of regs 29(3) and (4) when different kinds of earnings are received for overlapping periods.

For an example of a case where payment was not due to be made when the claimant was laid off, see *CJSA/4261/2003*. The claimant was a "core casual" dock worker who was laid off and claimed JSA the next day. His employers said that six days' holiday pay was due to him and a decision-maker therefore treated him as in remunerative work for that period. However, evidence was provided by his union which confirmed that as a core casual worker his employment was not terminated when he was laid off. He could chose, but was not obliged, to take his holiday when he was laid off. Furthermore, if he did not take his holiday when laid off (or by agreement at other times), he could not receive payment for any accrued holiday entitlement until more than four weeks after the termination or interruption of his employment. Thus the terms of his contract clearly showed that no holiday pay was due when he was laid off and he was entitled to JSA from the day he claimed, subject to the three waiting days rule.

In *CIS 590/1993* the claimant had been dismissed from her employment in April 1991 because she was pregnant. In June 1992 she was awarded compensation by an industrial tribunal under the Sex Discrimination Act 1975 which included one month's loss of earnings. The tribunal had deducted the income support paid to the claimant for the month after her dismissal. It is held that the loss of earnings element of the award was to be taken into account as earnings under reg.35 (see the notes to reg.35). For the purpose of reg.31(1), the date on which it was due to be paid was the date when the lost earnings were due to be paid, not when the award was made. This was because the award was to be regarded as a payment in lieu of remuneration and the purpose of the sex discrimination legislation was to put the claimant in the position she would have been if the employer had not acted unlawfully. If the payment was treated as due at the date of the award this could produce unfairness. The result was that the earnings were to be attributed to a period of one month in April/May 1991 and she was to be treated as in remunerative work for that period. However, the income support that had been paid to the claimant for that period was not recoverable as there had been no failure to disclose or misrepresentation. It had in any event been recouped.

If the payment is due before the first week pursuant to the claim (on which see Sch.7 to the Claims and Payments Regulations), it is treated as paid on the date it is due. This date then starts the period under reg.29. In other cases the payment is treated as paid on the first day of the benefit week in which it is due (or the next week if the main rule is impracticable).

Para. (2)

It seems that the effect of para.(2) is that all these benefits are treated as paid on a daily basis. A proportion of the weekly rate is treated as paid for each day covered by the entitlement. This should avoid overlaps of the kind revealed in *R(SB) 15/82*. See regs 75(b) and 32(4). 2.231

Para. (3)

This provides the rules for attributing an award of working tax credit or child tax credit. At the start of an award it will be treated as paid on the first day of the benefit week after the date of the award unless the award begins on the first day of a benefit week when it is treated as paid on that day (sub-paras.(a) and (b)). If an award of working tax credit or child tax credit is already in payment when income support is claimed, it is treated as paid on the first day of the first benefit week that follows the date income support is awarded (sub-para.(c)). At the end of an award it is treated as paid "until the last day of the last benefit week that coincides with or immediately follows the last day for which the award of that tax credit is made". The Commissioner in *CIS/1064/2004* considered that this meant that it was to be treated as paid until the end of the benefit week in which the last day of the tax credit award fell (despite the apparent absurdity of asking whether a week coincides with a day). 2.232

However, as *CIS/1064/2004* points out, para.(3) does not supply a complete rule for the taking into account of income arising from awards of child tax credit and working tax credit. This is because it does not say how a weekly amount of income is to be derived from the amount of a tax credit award. The Commissioner therefore considered that reg.32, substituting for the word "payment" in that regulation the amount of the tax credit award, should be applied (either directly or by a process of analogy to flesh out para.(3)). If an award had been amended, the period of the most recent child tax credit or working tax credit award had to be considered. Where there had been an amended award, the period over which the amount of the amended award would be taken into account would be only the period after the effective date of the amendment. The weekly amount of the award, or amended award, so calculated had then to be taken into account, but only from the first day of the benefit week identified under para.(3). The weekly amount had to be attributed to all the benefit weeks in the period from the effective date of the award, or amended award, to the end of the award, regardless of the way in which payments of tax credit were actually being made. If after para.(3) had been applied a tax credit award was terminated or amended there would either no longer be any amount to be taken into account or there would have to be a fresh application of reg.32 and para.(3)(b) or (c).

Calculation of weekly amount of income

2.233   **32.**—(1) For the purposes of regulation 29 (calculation of earnings derived from employed earner's employment and income other than earnings), subject to [³paragraphs (2) to (7)][¹. . .], where the period in respect of which a payment is made—

(a) does not exceed a week, the weekly amount shall be the amount of that payment;

(b) exceeds a week, the weekly amount shall be determined—

(i) in a case where that period is a month, by multiplying the amount of the payment by 12 and dividing the product by 52;

(ii) in a case where that period is three months, by multiplying the amount of the payment by 4 and dividing the product by 52;

(iii) in a case where that period is a year by dividing the amount of the payment by 52;

(iv) in any other case by multiplying the amount of the payment by 7 and dividing the product by the number equal to the number of days in the period in respect of which it is made.

(2) Where a payment for a period not exceeding a week is treated under regulation 31(1)(a) (date on which income is treated as paid) as paid before the first benefit week and a part is to be taken into account for some days only in that week (the relevant days), the amount to be taken into account for the relevant days shall be calculated by multiplying the amount of the payment by the number equal to the number of relevant days and dividing the product by the number of days in the period in respect of which it is made.

(3) Where a payment is in respect of a period equal to or in excess of a week and a part thereof is to be taken into account for some days only in a benefit week (the relevant days), the amount to be taken into account for the relevant days shall, except where paragraph (4) applies, be calculated by multiplying the amount of the payment by the number equal to the number of relevant days and dividing the product by the number of days in the period in respect of which it is made.

(4) In the case of a payment of—

(a) [⁵. . .] [²maternity allowance], [⁴short-term or long-term incapacity benefit], or severe disablement allowance [⁴. . .], the amount to be taken into account for the relevant days shall be the amount of benefit [¹payable] in respect of those days;

(b) income support [⁵or jobseeker's allowance], the amount to be taken into account for the relevant days shall be calculated by multiplying the weekly amount of the benefit by the number of relevant days and dividing the product by seven.

(5) Except in the case of a payment which it has not been practicable to treat under regulation 31(1)(b) as paid on the first day of the benefit week in which it is due to be paid, where a payment of income from a particular source is or has been paid regularly and that payment falls to be taken into account in the same benefit week as a payment of the same kind and from the same source, the amount of that income to be taken into account in any one benefit

week shall not exceed the weekly amount determined under paragraph (1)(a) or (b), as the case may be, of the payment which under regulation 31(1)(b) (date on which income is treated as paid) is treated as paid first.

(6) Where the amount of the claimant's income fluctuates and has changed more than once, or a claimant's regular pattern of work is such that he does not work every week, the foregoing paragraphs may be modified so that the weekly amount of his income is determined by reference to his average weekly income—

(a) if there is a recognisable cycle of work, over the period of one complete cycle (including, where the cycle involves periods in which the claimant does no work, those periods but disregarding any other absences);

(b) in any other case, over a period of five weeks or such other period as may, in the particular case, enable the claimant's average weekly income to be determined more accurately.

[6(6A) Where income is taken into account under paragraph (2B) of regulation 29 over the period specified in that paragraph, the amount of that income to be taken into account in respect of any week in that period shall be an amount equal to the amount of that income which would have been taken into account under regulation 62 had the person to whom that income was paid not ceased to be a[7 full-time student].]

[3(7) Where any payment of earnings is taken into account under paragraph (4C) of regulation 29 (calculation of earnings derived from employed earner's employment and income other than earnings), over the period specified in that paragraph, the amount to be taken into account shall be equal to the amount of the payment.]

AMENDMENTS

1. Income Support (General) Amendment Regulations 1988 (SI 1988/663), reg.15 (April 11, 1988).   2.234

2. Income Support (General) Amendment Regulations 1988 (SI 1988/1445), reg.8 (September 12, 1988).

3. Income Support (General) Amendment No. 2 Regulations 1989 (SI 1989/1323), reg.10 (October 9, 1989).

4. Disability Working Allowance and Income Support (General) Amendment Regulations 1995 (SI 1995/482), reg.11 (April 13, 1995).

5. Income Support (General) (Jobseeker's Allowance Consequential Amendments) Regulations 1996 (SI 1996/206), reg.16 (October 7, 1996).

6. Income-related Benefits and Jobseeker's Allowance (Miscellaneous Amendments) Regulations 1997 (SI 1997/65), reg.6 (April 7, 1997).

7. Social Security Amendment (Students) Regulations 2000 (SI 2000/1981), reg.5(5) and Sch. (July 31, 2000).

DEFINITIONS

"benefit week"—see reg.2(1).
"claimant"—*ibid.*, reg.23(1).
"full-time student"—see reg.61(1).

GENERAL NOTE

Para. (1)

This provision gives a straightforward method of converting payments to be taken   2.235
into account for various periods to a weekly equivalent. Reg.75 deals with the calculation for part-weeks of entitlement.

Para. (2) to (4)

2.236   These provisions establish the rules where the period for which a payment is to be taken into account under regs 29 and 31 does not coincide with a benefit week and some odd days ("the relevant days") come into a benefit week.

Para. (5)

2.237   There are two different rules, according to whether two payments from the same regular source fall to the same benefit week because of the rules of attribution or because of the operation of reg.31(1)(b). The general rule is the first one, under which the maximum amount to be taken into account in the benefit week is the weekly amount of the payment due first. The *Decision Makers Guide* (para.25081) gives an example of how this could arise. A claimant has been receiving statutory sick pay from his employer every two weeks. He receives a payment for two weeks on November 15. This is attributed to the period November 15 to November 28 inclusive. The claimant is to return to work on December 2 and receives a final payment of two weeks' sick pay on November 22. The AO treats this as paid on November 22 for the period November 22 to December 5. For the income support benefit week from November 22 to November 28 the amount of sick pay to be taken into account is limited to the weekly amount of the payment made on November 15. There is an exception to this rule in that if the first payment was due to be paid before the date of claim it is to be disregarded (Sch.8, para.13 and Sch.9, para.35). Then there will no longer be an overlap. The second rule applies where under reg.31(1)(b) it has not been practicable to take a payment into account in the benefit week in which it was due to be paid. The payment then is taken into account in the first practicable benefit week. In this situation both payments can be taken into account in the same week, although each payment can have the appropriate disregard applied (Sch.8, para.10 and Sch.9, para.37). The disregards in para.13 of Sch.8 and para.35 of Sch.9 (see above) may also apply.

Para. (6)

2.238   This paragraph is oddly placed because it only allows the preceding paragraphs to be modified, not any of the other regulations on the calculation or attribution of income.

Para. (6A)

2.239   Reg.29(2B) deals with the period over which a student grant is to be taken into account in the case of a person who has left or been dismissed from his course before it finishes and so has to repay part or all of his grant. Para.(6A) provides that where reg.29(2B) applies, the weekly amount of the income to be taken into account is to be calculated in accordance with reg.62. This means that the grant income will be apportioned over the period of study (*i.e.* from the beginning of the academic year to the day before the summer vacation), except for those elements which are apportioned over 52 weeks, and the disregards in reg.62(2), (2A) and (2B) will apply. See further reg.62 and the notes to that regulation. See also reg.40(3B) which provides that the amount of the grant income to be taken into account is to be calculated on the basis that none of it has been repaid. But note *Chief Adjudication Officer v Leeves* (November 6, 1998, CA, reported as *R(IS) 5/99*) in the notes to reg.29(2B) and the argument discussed in those notes as to when reg.29(2B) applies.

    Any grant or covenant income or student loan left over at the end of the person's course is disregarded as income (see para.61 of Sch.9).

Para. (7)

2.240   Where a payment of compensation (reg.35(3)(a)) is made on the termination of part-time employment (reg.29(4D)(a) and reg.35(3)(c)) it is taken into account for a week (reg.29(4C)). This provision confirms that the whole payment is taken into account for that week.

Weekly amount of charitable or voluntary payment

33.—(1)[¹ . . .]   2.241

AMENDMENT

1. Income Support (General) Amendment No.5 Regulations 1988 (SI 1988/2022), reg.8 (December 12, 1988).

Incomplete weeks of benefit

34.[¹ . . .]   2.242

AMENDMENT

1. Income Support (General) Amendment Regulations 1988 (SI 1988/663), reg.16 (April 11. 1988).

CHAPTER III

EMPLOYED EARNERS

Earnings of employed earners

35.—(1) [²Subject to paragraphs (2) and (3),] "earnings" means in the   2.243
case of employment as an employed earner, any remuneration or profit
derived from that employment and includes—
(a) any bonus or commission;
(b) any payment in lieu of remuneration except any periodic sum paid to
     a claimant on account of the termination of his employment by
     reason of redundancy;
(c) any payment in lieu of notice [² . . .];
(d) any holiday pay except any payable more than four weeks after the
     termination or interruption of employment but this exception shall
     not apply to a claimant to whom [¹section 23 of the Act [SSCBA,
     s.126] (trade disputes) applies or in respect of whom section 20(3) of
     the Act [SSCBA, s.124(1)] (conditions of entitlement to income
     support) has effect as modified by section 23A(*b*) of the Act [SSCBA,
     s.127(b)] (effect to return to work)];
(e) any payment by way of a retainer;
(f) any payment made by the claimant's employer in respect of expenses
     not wholly, exclusively and necessarily incurred in the performance
     of the duties of the employment, including any payment made by the
     claimant's employer in respect of—
       (i) travelling expenses incurred by the claimant between his home
            and place of employment;
      (ii) expenses incurred by the claimant under arrangements made for
            the care of a member of his family owing to the claimant's
            absence from home;
(g) any award of compensation made under section 68(2) or 71(2)(a) of
     the Employment Protection (Consolidation) Act 1978 (remedies for
     unfair dismissal and compensation);

(h) any such sum as is referred to in section 18(2) of the Social Security (Miscellaneous Provisions) Act 1977 (certain sums to be earnings for social security purposes).

[²(i) where—

 (i) a payment of compensation is made in respect of employment which is not part-time employment and that payment is not less than the maximum weekly amount, the amount of the compensation less the deductible remainder, where that is applicable;

 (ii) a payment of compensation is made in respect of employment which is part-time, the amount of the compensation.]

[⁶(j) the amount of any payment by way of a non-cash voucher which has been taken into account in the computation of a person's earnings in accordance with regulation 18(22) to (25) of the Social Security (Contributions) Regulations 1979.]

[²(1A) For the purposes of paragraph (1)(i)(i) the "deductible remainder"—

(a) applies in cases where dividing the amount of compensation by the maximum weekly amount produces a whole number plus a fraction; and

(b) is equal to the difference between—

 (i) the amount of the compensation; and

 (ii) the product of the maximum weekly amount multiplied by the whole number.]

(2) "Earnings" shall not include—

(a) [⁶ Subject to paragraph (2A),] any payment in kind;

(b) any remuneration paid by or on behalf of an employer to the claimant [⁴in respect of a period throughout which the claimant is on maternity leave [⁹, paternity leave or adoption leave] or is absent from work because he is ill];

(c) any payment in respect of expenses wholly, exclusively and necessarily incurred in the performance of the duties of the employment;

(d) any occupational pension.

[⁵(e) any lump sum payment made under the Iron and Steel Re-adaptation Benefits Scheme].

[⁶(2A) Paragraph (2)(a) shall not apply in respect of any non-cash voucher referred to in paragraph (1)(j).]

[²(3) In this regulation—

(a) "compensation" means any payment made in respect of or on the termination of employment in a case where a person has not received or received only part of a payment in lieu of notice due or which would have been due to him had he not waived his right to receive it, other than—

 (i) any payment specified in paragraph (1)(a) to (h);

 (ii) any payment specified in paragraph (2)(a) to [⁵(e)];

 (iii) any redundancy payment within the meaning of section 81(1) of the Employment Protection (Consolidation) Act 1978, and

 (iv) any refund of contributions to which that person was entitled under an occupational pension scheme within the meaning of section 66(1) of the Social Security Pensions Act 1975;

 [³(v) any compensation payable by virtue of section 173 or section 178(3) or (4) of the Education Reform Act 1988;]

(b) "maximum weekly amount" means the maximum weekly amount which, on the date on which the payment of compensation is made, is specified in paragraph 8(1)(c) of Schedule 14 to the Employment Protection (Consolidation) Act 1978;

(c) "part-time employment" means employment in which a person is not to be treated as engaged in remunerative work under regulation 5 or [⁷ 6(1) [⁸ and (4)]]] (persons treated, or not treated, as engaged in remunerative work).]

AMENDMENTS

1. Income Support (General) Amendment Regulations 1988 (SI 1988/663), reg.17 (April 11, 1988).   **2.244**

2. Income Support (General) Amendment No.2 Regulations 1989 (SI 1989/1323), reg.11 (October 9, 1989).

3. Education (Inner London Education Authority) (Transitional and Supplementary Provisions) (No.2) Order 1990 (SI 1990/774), art.2 (April 1, 1990).

4. Income-related Benefits Schemes (Miscellaneous Amendments) (No.4) Regulations 1993 (SI 1993/2119), reg.12 (October 4, 1993).

5. Social Security (Miscellaneous Amendments) Regulations 1997 (SI 1997/454), reg.7 (April 7, 1997).

6. Social Security Amendment (Non-Cash Vouchers) Regulations 1999 (SI 1999/1509), reg.2(5) (July 1, 1999).

7. Social Security (Miscellaneous Amendments) (No.2) Regulations 1999 (SI 1999/2556), reg.2(4) (October 4, 1999).

8. Social Security (Miscellaneous Amendments) Regulations 2000 (SI 2000/681), reg.2(c) (April 3, 2000).

9. Social Security (Paternity and Adoption) Amendment Regulations 2002 (SI 2002/2689), reg.2(4) (December 8, 2002).

DEFINITIONS

"the Act"—see reg.2(1).
"adoption leave"—*ibid.*
"claimant"—*ibid.*, reg.23(1).
"employed earner"—see reg.2(1).
"family"—see 1986 Act, s.20(11) (SSCBA, s.137(1)).
"maternity leave"—see reg.2(1).
"occupational pension"—see reg.2(1).
"paternity leave"—*ibid.*

GENERAL NOTE

Reg.35 applies to earnings from employment as an employed earner. See the definition in reg.2(1). On the tests for deciding whether a person is an employed earner or in self-employment, see *CJSA 4721/2001* and the other cases discussed in the notes to reg.30. The category of office-holder includes holders of elective office, such as local councillors. Some payments made to councillors (*e.g.* for travelling expenses and subsistence allowances: *CIS 89/1989*) will be excluded under para.(2)(c), but attendance allowances, which are not paid to meet specific expenses, count as earnings (*R(IS) 6/92*). *CIS 77/1993* decides that basic allowances are also earnings, but applies the disregard in para.(2)(c), reg.40(4) (now reg.40(4)(a)) and Sch.9, para.3. The purpose of the basic allowance is to compensate the councillor for his time and to cover the expenses incurred in the execution of his duties. The expenses may, as in that case, absorb the total allowance. The Commissioner points out that since March 18, 1992, basic allowances had been disregarded for the purposes of the former reg.7(1)(g)(i) of the Social Security (Unemployment, Sickness and Invalidity   **2.245**

Benefit) Regulations 1983. The allowance was therefore treated differently depending on whether unemployment benefit or income support was claimed. However, its treatment under JSA is the same as for income support.

See also the notes to reg.36(3) for discussion of the application of the principle of *Parsons v Hogg* [1985] 2 All E.R. 897, CA to the meaning of "gross earnings". This allows the deduction from earnings of necessary, etc., expenses incurred by the employee.

Note in addition *R(TC) 2/03* discussed below which concerned deductions for previously overpaid salary.

Para.(1)

2.246

This paragraph first provides a general definition of earnings from employment as an employee—any remuneration or profit derived from that employment—and then deems certain payments to be earnings. Para.(2) provides a number of exceptions and Sch.8 lists items which would otherwise count as earnings which are to be disregarded. In particular under paras 1 to 3 final earnings due on the termination or interruption of employment are disregarded.

The general test covers straightforward wages or salary, but can extend to other remuneration derived from employment. According to *R(SB) 21/86*, these are wide words, which mean "having their origin in." Thus if it had been necessary to decide whether a compensatory award for unfair dismissal by an Industrial Tribunal was derived from employment, the Commissioner would have held that it did. *R(SB) 21/86* is followed in *CIS 590/1993*, which concerned the loss of earnings element in a compensation award for sex discrimination. Payments to a NCB employee in lieu of concessionary coal constituted remuneration derived from employment (*R(SB) 2/86*). Tips and gratuities would be an example of payments from third parties which are nonetheless derived from employment (see Williams, *Social Security Taxation*, paras 4.21 to 4.22 for discussion of the income tax cases).

See also *CH 2387/2002*, a case on the equivalent council tax benefit provision (reg.19(1) of the Council Tax Benefit Regulations). The company accounts showed that the claimant had drawn £6,400 for the year 1999/2000, whereas he had actually received less than half that amount, the remainder having been loaned by him to the company. The Commissioner rejects the claimant's contention that only the amount he received constituted earnings and confirms that for the purpose of council tax benefit his earnings were £6,400. But the repayment of a loan by a company to a director is not a profit derived from employment (*CCS 3671/2002*). The Commissioner in *CCS 3671/2002* refers to *Shilton v Wilmshurst (Inspector of Taxes)* [1991] 1 AC 684 in which the House of Lords stated that an emolument was not "from" employment if it was not paid as a reward for past services or as an inducement to enter into employment and provide future services. It was not enough on its own that the payment came from the employer.

Note *R(TC) 2/03* which concerned the meaning of "earnings" in reg.19(1) of the Family Credit Regulations (the working families' tax credit equivalent of this provision—see the 2002 edition of this volume for these Regulations). The claimant's partner's employer had made deductions from his current salary in order to recover an earlier overpayment. His payslips showed his "gross for tax" figure as £76 less than his usual salary. The Commissioner held that his gross earnings for the months the deduction was made was the reduced figure. The most likely analysis was that there had been a consensual variation of the contract of employment for those months, making the lower figure the remuneration or profit derived from that employment. In so doing, the Commissioner declined to follow *CCS 4378/2001* (a child support case) which had also concerned an overpayment by the employer that was being recovered by deductions from current salary. The Commissioner in *CCS 4378/2001* held that the whole of the absent parent's salary before deductions counted as "earnings". However, he suggested that the solution to the apparent unfairness of that conclusion lay in the fact that an overpayment of salary paid by mistake and to which the person was not entitled was not "earnings" at the time it was made because it was not "remuneration or profit *derived from* . . . employment". He therefore directed the new tribunal to consider whether it had jurisdiction to go back to the period of the overpayment and alter the maintenance assessment. The Commissioner in *R(TC) 2/03*, however, did not see why the overpayment was not derived from employment at least for any period before the mistake was identified and recovery required by the employer. He therefore preferred his own approach. Certainly the solution adopted in *R(TC) 2/03* has the merit of focusing on the earnings that are actually being received for the period in question and avoids the need to attempt to revisit earlier periods in a claim.

The particular categories in sub-paras (a) to (j) are deemed to be earnings, whether they would in general count as earnings or not (*R(SB) 21/86*). Only a few categories require comment.

Sub-para.(b): A payment in lieu of remuneration will in its nature be an income   **2.247** payment. Capital payments (*e.g.* for the loss of the job itself) are excluded. *R(SB) 21/86* held that a compensatory award for unfair dismissal made by an Industrial Tribunal was a payment in lieu of remuneration, to be taken into account for the number of weeks specified in the award. Such an award is now expressly included in sub-para.(g), but if it can also fall into (b) it will lead to complete disentitlement to income support under reg.5(5), regardless of the weekly amount of the award. In *CIS 590/1993* the claimant's award of compensation under the Sex Discrimination Act included amounts for injured feelings, the loss of a tax rebate and one month's loss of earnings. It was accepted that the first two items counted as capital. The Commissioner follows *R(SB) 21/86* and holds that the loss of earnings element fell to be treated as earnings under sub-para.(b). There was no reason for drawing a distinction between a compensatory award for unfair dismissal and that part of a sex discrimination award that was for loss of earnings. The fact that only the former was referred to in sub-para.(g) did not imply that the loss of earnings elements in sex (or race) discrimination awards (or indeed awards made by county courts for breach of employment contracts) were excluded from para.(1), since the categories listed in sub-paras (a) to (i) were only included as examples. See the notes to reg.31(1) as to when the earnings were treated as due to be paid.

Sub-para.(c): This sub-paragraph is now confined to payments in lieu of notice,   **2.248** whether full or partial. Presumably, it covers payments expressly in lieu of notice (see *CIS 400/1994*). "Global" payments will fall under sub-para.(i). If earnings under this sub-paragraph are received, entitlement is excluded under reg.5(5) for the period covered.

Sub-para.(d): Holiday pay which is payable (*i.e* due to be paid, not received or paid: **2.249** *R(SB) 15/82, R(SB) 33/83, R(SB) 11/85*) within four weeks of termination or interruption of employment counts as earnings. In cases of termination holiday pay will be due immediately, unless the contract of employment expressly provides otherwise. Therefore, whenever it is paid (and presumably it cannot count until it is actually paid) it will count as earnings to be taken into account for the benefit week in which it was due to be paid. Then s.74 of the Administration Act (1986 Act, s.27) might come into play. If employment is merely interrupted it is more likely that holiday pay will not be payable immediately. Earnings received under this sub-paragraph lead to disentitlement under reg.5(5).

CJSA/1589/2004 concerned the attribution of holiday pay where the claimant was to be treated as in remunerative work under reg.52(3) of the JSA Regulations (the equivalent of reg.5(5)). The claimant who had been contracted to work a three day week was paid 11.115 days holiday pay when his employment terminated. The question was whether the holiday pay was to be attributed in terms of days, that is to each of the seven days in a week, or on the basis of "working days". The Commissioner, preferring *CJSA/3438/1998* to *CJSA/4508/1998*, holds that the claimant was to be treated as being in remunerative work for 12 days (see reg.94(5) of the JSA

Regulations, the equivalent of reg.29(4A), where earnings are paid in respect of part of a day), namely from November 28 to December 9, 2002, and not for four weeks as the tribunal had decided. See also *R(SB) 11/85* on this approach to attribution of holiday pay.

Holiday pay outside this sub-paragraph is capital (reg.48(3)).

CIS 894/1994 holds that for a payment to be holiday pay there has to be entitlement to holidays under the contract of employment. The claimant worked on a North Sea oil rig. His contract of employment provided that there was no entitlement to holidays but that he would accrue 42 hours vacation pay per quarter. He could ask for this pay at any time and payment would be made at the end of the quarter. On the termination of his employment he was paid 100 days accrued vacation pay. The Commissioner decides that the vacation pay was not holiday pay in the ordinary sense of the word. It had nothing to do with the taking of holidays but was in reality compensation for the fact that there was no holiday entitlement. The consequence was that it fell to be disregarded under para.1(a)(ii) of Sch.8.

2.250   *Sub-para.(e)*: *R(IS) 9/95* decides that a guarantee payment under s.12 of the Employment Protection (Consolidation) Act 1978 is a payment by way of a retainer.

2.251   *Sub-para.(f)*: The conditions here are in line with those under which expenses are deductible from earnings for income tax purposes. Payment for all items beyond those solely necessary for *the performance of* the duties of the employment are caught. It is not enough if the expenses are incurred in order to enable the person to perform those duties (*Smith v Abbott* [1994] 1 All E.R. 673). The express mention of the expenses of travel to and from work and of looking after a family member merely spells this out. (On child care expenses see *Jackson and Cresswell v Chief Adjudication Officer* Joined Cases C-63/91 and C-64/91 [1992] E.C.R. I-4737, also reported as Appendix 2 to *R(IS) 10/91*, and *R(FC) 2/98 (Meyers)*, in the notes to reg.36(3)). The reimbursement of a local councillor's home telephone expenses in *CIS 38/1989* is an example. On the evidence, the expenses were necessarily incurred, but not wholly or exclusively, in the performance of his duties as a councillor. On other evidence, such expenses could be apportioned between personal and employment purposes (*cf. R(FC) 1/91, CFC 26/1989* and *R(FIS) 13/91* on reg.38(3)). See also *CFC 836/1995* in the notes to reg.38(11) on apportionment of expenses between earnings as an employee and from self-employment. There is helpful guidance in *R(FIS) 4/85*.

CIS 89/1989 holds that travel and subsistence allowances paid to a local councillor, which included travel from home to the place of employment, were for necessary etc. expenses, because a councillor's home is also a place of employment. *R(IS) 6/92* confirms this result, because under s.174(1) of the Local Government Act 1972 payments of travelling and subsistence allowances can only be made where the expenses have been necessarily incurred for the performance of any duty as a councillor. Therefore, such a payment must fall outside sub-para.(f) and within para.(2)(c). In *CIS 77/1993* it was accepted that a local councillor's expenses (*e.g.* the use of his home and telephone) could lead to the whole of his basic allowance being disregarded (see above). The approach taken in the *Decision Makers Guide* applies these decisions (see paras 26072–5). See also the notes to reg.36(3).

2.252   *Sub-para.(g)*: If awards of compensation can only come under this sub-paragraph and not (b) they do not lead to complete disentitlement, but the amount must be considered. The reference to the Employment Protection (Consolidation) Act 1978 needs to be updated to the currrent Act (Employment Rights Act 1996).

2.253   *Sub-para.(h)*: The sums referred to in s.18(2) of the 1977 Act are maternity pay under s.40 of the Employment Protection (Consolidation) Act 1978; arrears of pay under s.122(3)(a); arrears of pay under an order for reinstatement or re-engagement; a sum payable under an award for the continuation of a contract; and remuneration under a protective award.

Sub-para. (i): There was a significant change in 1989 in the treatment of lump sum payments made on the termination of employment, which was designed to simplify decision-making. It was along similar lines to the change in the UB rules, but introduced several differences. In *CIS 400/1994* the Commissioner drew attention to the different ways that termination payments at the end of a period of employment were treated by the income support and unemployment benefit legislation. In particular, the definition of "compensation" was not the same (*e.g.*, for unemployment benefit purposes "compensation" could include payments in lieu of notice; for income support it cannot). For the position under JSA, see reg.98(1)(b) and (3) of the JSA Regulations.

2.254

There are separate provisions depending whether it is full-time or part-time employment which is terminated. The dividing line is defined in para.(3)(c) and reg.29(4D)(a) by adopting the test of remunerative work in regs 5 and 6(1) and (4).

Full-time employment: This new category of earnings is added to the list while sub-para.(c) is restricted to payments in lieu of notice and not payments of compensation for loss of employment. For full-timers sub-para.(i) applies to a payment of "compensation" which equals or exceeds the "maximum weekly amount".

"Compensation" is defined in para.(3)(a). First, the person must not have received a payment in lieu of all the notice to which he was legally entitled. If this has happened, no other payment can be "compensation" within sub-para.(i) (confirmed in *CIS 400/1994*). Second, all the payments already counted as earnings by para.(1)(a) to (h) or excluded from that category by para.(2), refunds of pension contributions and "any redundancy payment within the meaning of s.81(1) of the Employment Protection (Consolidation) Act 1978" are excluded. On the meaning of "any redundancy payment . . .", see *CJSA 82/1998* (which concerned the same phrase in reg.98(2)(f) of the JSA Regulations). In the Commissioner's view, a payment "within the meaning of . . ." was wider than a payment "made under . . .". He concludes that the exemption under reg.98(2)(f) applied to all payments genuinely made in lieu of a redundancy payment up to the level of entitlement that would arise under the statutory duty to make a redundancy payment (now contained in s.135 of the Employment Rights Act 1996). The same should apply to the exclusion under para.(3)(a)(iii).

Other payments made in respect of or on the termination of employment count as compensation. It does not particularly matter what the employer calls the payment, providing that it is connected to the termination (*cf. R(U) 4/92* and *R(U) 5/92*), so that merely calling the payment a capital payment (*e.g.* for loss of the job as a capital asset) does not take it outside sub-para.(i). The main categories will be payments from employers which are not precisely categorised (*e.g.* the ubiquitous *"ex gratia"* payment) and payments made in settlement of claims for unfair or wrongful dismissal (providing that a payment in lieu of full notice has not already been paid). But a payment solely in relation to racial discrimination during employment is not within the definition (*CU 88/1991*).

2.255

The "maximum weekly amount" is defined in para.(3)(b) and is the amount specified at the relevant time as the maximum to be used in calculating the basic award for unfair dismissal and redundancy payments. The figure in effect from April 1, 1989, was £172, from April 1, 1990, was £184, from April 1, 1991, was £198, from April 1, 1992 (not increased in 1993 or 1994) was £205, from September 27, 1995 (not increased in 1996 or 1997) was £210, from April 1, 1998 was £220 (not increased in 1999), from February 1, 2000 was £230, from February 1, 2001 was £240, from February 1, 2002 was £250, from February 1, 2003 was £260, from February 1, 2004 was £270 and from February 1, 2005 is £280.

If a payment is "compensation" then its amount has to be divided by the maximum weekly amount. If this division produces a whole number plus a fraction the portion of the amount of the compensation representing that fraction is ignored as earnings. It is the "deductible remainder" (para.(1B)). But it appears to be capital (reg.48(11)). The payment less any deductible remainder is taken into account as income for the same number of weeks as the whole number (reg.29(4B)(a)). However, the rigid application of this rule could result in the payment being taken into account for longer than the claimant's notice period. Therefore, under reg.29(4B)(b) the payment is to be taken into account for a period equal to the person's notice entitlement (less any days of notice worked or covered by a payment in lieu of notice) if this is shorter. This is the "specified period" (reg.29(4D)(b)).

The date on which this period is to start is defined by reg.31 (reg.29(4B)). Often this will be the date of termination, but it may be later, *e.g.* where there is a settlement of an unfair dismissal claim. But see *CIS 590/1993* referred to above and in the notes to reg.31(1). If there is an identifiable loss of earnings element in the settlement, such a payment may come within para.(1)(a) to (h) (and thus fall outside the definition of "compensation") and be due to be paid on the date when the lost earnings, etc., were due to be paid. Note the effect of reg.29(3) and (4).

Where the payment is small, less in total than the "maximum weekly amount," these provisions do not apply and the payment is treated as capital (reg.48(11)).

2.256   *Part-time employment*: For part-time employment the whole payment of "compensation" is to be taken into account in one week (reg.35(1)(i)(ii) and reg.29(4C)), generally the week in which it is due to be paid (reg.31).

Sub.para. (j): The effect of this sub-paragraph, together with para.(2A), is that non-cash vouchers liable for Class 1 national insurance contributions will be treated as earnings. This does not apply to non-cash vouchers that are not taken into account for national insurance purposes. As payments in kind they will count as other income (see reg.40(4)(a)) but note the disregard in para.21 of Sch.9.

Note that reg.2(2) of the Social Security Amendment (Non-Cash Vouchers) Regulations 1999 (SI 1999/1509) provides that where a claimant has an existing award of income support (or JSA) on June 30, 1999, sub-para.(j) and para.(2A) will not operate until the date that the first decision on review of that award after June 30, 1999 takes effect.

Para. (2)

2.257   These amounts—payments in kind, sick, maternity, paternity or adoption leave pay, reimbursement of necessary expenses and occupational pensions—are not earnings, but do count as other income (reg.40(4)(a)). It is apparently intended that lump sum payments covered by sub-para.(e) should count as capital (as their nature would indicate), although reg.40(4) (now reg.40(4)(a)) has not also been amended. Note that income in kind is disregarded (Sch.9, para.21) and so are payments of necessary expenses (Sch.9, para.3). There is no provision for the disregard of ill-health payments or occupational pensions (confirmed in *CIS 6/1989*). If a person is remunerated by payments in kind, there is the possibility of notional earnings being attributed to the person under reg.42(6).

See the notes to para.(1)(f) for what are necessary, etc., expenses. In a decision on the equivalent provision in the Family Credit Regulations (reg.19(2)), the Commissioner suggested that its effect is that expenditure by the employee on necessary etc. expenses is to be deducted from the amount of his earnings (*CFC 2/1989*). This does not seem to be consistent with the pattern of reg.35, which is otherwise concerned with payments to the employee, and is rejected in *R(FC) 1/90*, *R(IS) 16/93* and *CIS 77/1993*. See the notes to reg.19(2) of the Family Credit Regulations in the 2002 edition of this volume for full discussion of the point. The payment can be by way of reimbursement to the employee for expenses initially met by him (*CIS 77/1993*). But the application of the principle of *Parsons v Hogg* to the meaning of "gross earnings" in reg.36 will, it seems, permit the deduction from earnings of necessary, etc., expenses incurred by the employee. See the notes to reg.36(3). *CJSA 2402/2003* confirms that a trade union subscription is not deductible as such an expense and that this does not infringe Art.11 ECHR (right of assembly and association).

CIS 4317/1997 has highlighted an anomaly in the legislation that results from sick or maternity pay, etc. not being treated as earnings. The claimant stopped work in September 1996 because of illness. He was paid four weeks' statutory and contractual sick pay on October 31, 1996 and his contract of employment was terminated on the same day. He claimed income support on November 1 but was treated as having income for four weeks from October 31 under regs 29(1) and (2) and 31(1). The Commissioner confirmed that this was correct. Although final earnings were disregarded under para.1 of Sch.8, there was no equivalent disregard in Sch.9 (or elsewhere) to enable final payments of sick pay to be ignored. He rejected the argument that reg.29(2) was *ultra vires*. This argument was renewed before the Court of Appeal but was dismissed (*Owen v Chief Adjudication Officer*, April 29, 1999). The claimant had contended that the power in s.136(5)(a) (person can be treated as possessing income or capital which he does not possess) did not apply where the person in fact possessed the income; it therefore did not authorise a provision treating income received by the claimant at one time as available to him at another time. In addition, reg.29(2) was outside the power in s.136(3) (income to be calculated or estimated in prescribed manner). It was contended that simply shifting income from one period to another was neither "calculation" nor "estimation". But the Court of Appeal held that reg.29(2) was within the power in s.136(5)(a). A deeming provision by its very nature had the effect of treating a fact or state of affairs as existing for a stated purpose when that fact or state of affairs did not in truth exist. Section 136(5)(a) was sufficiently widely framed to authorize a provision that spread or apportioned income to a stated period. The Court also rejected the contention that reg.29(2) was *ultra vires* on the ground of irrationality. However, the Court of Appeal (like the Commissioner and the tribunal) expressed disquiet at the anomalous result arising from the different treatment of sick pay and final earnings and voiced the hope that the operation of the regulations in these circumstances would be reconsidered.

Calculation of net earnings of employed earners

36.—(1) For the purposes of regulation 29 (calculation of earnings of employed earners) the earnings of a claimant derived from employment as an employed earner to be taken into account shall, subject to paragraph (2), be his net earnings.

2.258

(2) There shall be disregarded from a claimant's net earnings, any sum specified in paragraphs 1 to 13 [²[³ or 15A]] of Schedule 8.

(3) For the purposes of paragraph (1) net earnings shall be calculated by taking into account the gross earnings of the claimant from that employment less—

(a) any amount deducted from those earnings by way of—
   (i) income tax;
   (ii) primary Class 1 contributions under the Social Security Act; and
(b) one-half of any sum paid by the claimant [¹in respect of a pay period] by way of a contribution towards an occupational or personal pension scheme.

AMENDMENTS

1. Income-related Benefits Schemes (Miscellaneous Amendments) (No.5) Regulations 1994 (SI 1994/2139), reg.26 (October 3, 1994).

2.259

2. Social Security (Miscellaneous Amendments) (No. 2) Regulations 1999 (SI 1999/2556), reg.2(5) (October 4, 1999).

3. Social Security (Back to Work Bonus and Lone Parent Run-on) (Amendment and Revocation) Regulations 2003 (SI 2003/1589), reg.2(b) (October 25, 2004).

DEFINITIONS

"claimant"—see reg.2(1), reg.23(1).
"employed earner"—see reg.2(1).
"occupational pension scheme"—see Pension Schemes Act 1993, s.1.
"pay period"—see reg.2(1).
"personal pension scheme"—*ibid.*
"Social Security Act"—*ibid.*

GENERAL NOTE

Para. (1)

2.260   Earnings defined in reg.35 are to be converted to net earnings before being taken into account. This is to be done according to para.(3).

Para. (2)

2.261   After the conversion to net earnings has been carried out, the amounts specified in paras 1 to 13 or 15A of Sch.8 are to be disregarded. For the position relating to earnings of a child or young person see the note to para.14 of Sch.8.

Para. (3)

2.262   Only this limited list of deductions for payments made by the employee may be made from gross earnings. Nothing is to be deducted for travel costs (see *CJSA 4721/2001*), child care expenses or meals at work. This leads to a much simpler calculation than under supplementary benefit. The compensation was an increase in the basic disregard from its previous £4 to £5.

   R(FC) 1/90 holds that if the employee makes contributions to both an occupational and a personal pension scheme, half of both contributions can be deducted. See also *R(CS) 3/00* which decides that half of the contributions made under retirement annuity contracts by employed earners were to be deducted from gross earnings under para.1(3)(c) of Sch.1 to the Child Support (Maintenance Assessments and Special Cases) Regulations 1992. Such contracts came within the meaning of "personal pension scheme" for employed earners. The same definition of "personal pension scheme" is used for income support (see reg.2(1)) and the Commissioner's reasoning should apply to deductions under para.(3)(b).

   There was, however, some doubt about the meaning of "gross earnings." In *R(FC) 1/90* the Commissioner refers to the principle adopted by the Court of Appeal in *Parsons v Hogg* [1985] 2 All E.R. 897, appendix to *R(FIS) 4/85*, and by the Commissioner in *R(FIS) 4/85*, that "earnings," even associated with the word "gross," in the Family Income Supplements (General) Regulations 1980 meant not the remuneration actually received, but the receipts after payment of expenses wholly and necessarily incurred in the course of winning those receipts. He applies this principle to the equivalent provision to reg.36 in the Family Credit Regulations (reg.20) (see the 2002 edition of this volume for the Family Credit Regulations) and holds that expenses necessarily wholly and exclusively incurred by the employee in the performance of the duties of employment are to be deducted from the gross receipts to produce a figure of gross earnings. The same Commissioner applies the principle to income other than earnings in *CIS 25/1989*, but this has not been followed in *CIS 563/1991* and *R(IS) 13/01* (see the note to reg.40(1)). In *R(FC) 1/90*, the claimant's expenditure on work equipment might be deducted, but not child-care expenses (*R(FIS) 2/88*).

   The wording of reg.36 is not the same as was considered in *Parsons v Hogg*, so that there was some doubt about the application of the principle. In *R(IS) 6/92* the Commissioner held that an attendance allowance paid to a local councillor had to be taken into account as earnings, subject only to the £5 disregard, although the councillor incurred necessary, etc., expenses on such things as stationery and telephone calls. However, the Commissioner referred only to reg.35 and not to reg.36 or any of the decisions cited in the previous paragraph. In *CIS 77/1993*, which concerned a local councillor's basic allowance, the same Commissioner considered that *Parsons v Hogg* did not apply, but decided that the allowance fell within reg.35(2)(c). However, the application of *Parsons v Hogg* does produce a result where only resources actually available to the person are counted. It is also the approach taken in para.26016 of the *Decision Makers Guide*. *R(IS) 16/93* has now expressly decided that the principle of *Parsons v Hogg* applies to reg.36. This has been followed in *CIS 507/1994*.

Parsons v Hogg* has also been applied to "gross earnings" in para.1(3) of Sch.I to the Child Support (Maintenance Assessments and Special Cases) Regulations 1992 (SI 1992/1815) in *R(CS) 2/96*. Moreover, *CCS 3882/1997* has held that the principle of *Parsons v Hogg* is not restricted to expenses wholly, exclusively and necessarily incurred in the performance of the duties of the employment but can extend to subscriptions to professional bodies or learned societies which are tax-deductible under s.201 of the Income and Corporation Taxes Act 1988, provided that they have to be incurred in order to win the earnings in question. *CJSA 2402/2003* confirms that this would not apply to a trade union subscription since there was (as far as the Commissioner was aware) no specific provision of the income tax legislation under which the union subscription would be deductible in computing the amount of income for income tax purposes.   **2.263**

See also *CCS 318/1995* which decided that an armed forces "local overseas allowance" could be deducted on the ground that it covered the special expenses of working abroad, whereas a lodgings allowance for those stationed in the UK was not allowable (*CCS 5352/1995*). Rent allowances for police officers would seem not to be a deductible expense (*R(CS) 2/99, CCS 101/1994* and *R(CS) 10/98*, although *CCS 12769/1996* is to the contrary. See also *CCS 2561/1998* which "entirely agrees" with the approach taken in *R(CS) 2/99*.

In calculating the amount of necessary, etc., expenses to be deducted the principle established in *R(FC) 1/91, CFC 26/1989* and *R(IS) 13/91* should be applied. That is that if items have a dual private and work use, and that use can be apportioned on a time basis, the appropriate proportion should be deducted. See the note to reg.38(3). See also *CFC 836/1995* in the notes to reg.38(11) on apportionment of expenses between two employments.

In *R(IS) 10/91*, a challenge to the inability to deduct child-care expenses from earnings as being discriminatory and therefore contrary to E.C. Directive 79/7 was rejected. On appeal, the Court of Appeal referred the question whether supplementary benefit and/or income support fall within art.3 of the Directive to the European Court of Justice (*Cresswell v Chief Adjudication Officer, Jackson v Chief Adjudication Officer*, reported as Appendix 1 to *R(IS) 10/91*).

A similar question in relation to housing benefit had been referred by the Divisional Court in *R. v Secretary of State for Social Security Ex parte Smithson* (June 26, 1990). The Advocate General's opinion in *Smithson* (delivered on November 20, 1991) was that the provisions on higher pensioner premium were part of the statutory scheme protecting against the risks of invalidity and old age, so that they came within art.3. The ECJ (February 4, 1992) (Case 243/90) disagreed, finding that the higher pensioner premium was an inseparable part of the whole scheme of housing benefit, which was intended to compensate for the fact that the beneficiary's income was insufficient to meet housing costs and not to provide protection against one of the risks specified in art.3(1) (*e.g.* sickness, invalidity, old age). Although criteria concerning protection against old age and sickness were part of the criteria for determining the level against which the beneficiary's income was tested, that did not affect the purpose of the whole scheme.

Once that decision had been made, the ECJ's decision in *Cresswell and Jackson* (July 16, 1992) [1992] E.C.R. I–4737, [1993] 3 All E.R. 265, also reported as Appendix 2 to *R(IS) 10/91*, followed fairly inevitably. Benefits such as supplementary benefit and income support could be granted in a variety of personal situations to persons whose means are insufficient to meet their needs as defined by statute.   **2.264**

Therefore they did not come within art.3(1) of the Directive. In the particular cases the claimants' theoretical needs were set independently of any consideration of any of the risks specified in art.3(1). Nor did the fact that the conditions of entitlement to a benefit affected a single parent's ability to take up access to vocational training or part-time employment bring that benefit within EC Directive 76/207 on equal treatment for men and women as regards access to employment, vocational training and promotion, and working conditions. Benefit schemes only come within Directive 76/207 if their subject matter is access to employment, etc., or working conditions.

These decisions seem to rule out challenges to the income support scheme under either Directive, as accepted in *CIS 8/1990* and *CIS 375/1990*. (But the position is different under JSA. In *Hockenjos v Secretary of State*, [2001] EWCA Civ 624, [2001] 2.C.M.L.R. 51, [2001] I.C.R. 966 the Court of Appeal held that the Jobseekers Act 1995 had set up a unitary statutory scheme to provide against the risk of unemployment which was covered by Art.3(1)(a) of EC Directive 79/7. The result is that both contribution-based and income-based JSA are within the scope of Directive 79/7.)

However, the possibility of a challenge to the family credit scheme (now abolished) under Directive 76/207 remained. Family credit similarly did not, until October 4, 1994, permit the offsetting of any child care expenses against earnings. In *R(FC) 2/98 (Meyers)*, the claimant argued that the family credit rule before October 4, 1994, was discriminatory and in breach of Directive 76/207. The contention was that since the main purpose of family credit was to supplement the income of low-paid workers, family credit was directly concerned with access to employment and/or working conditions. The Commissioner referred the question as to whether family credit was covered by Directive 76/207 to the ECJ. On July 13, 1995 the ECJ (*Meyers v Adjudication Officer*, Case C-116/94, [1995] All E.R.(EC) 705, also reported as *R(FC) 2/98*) held that family credit was concerned with both access to employment and working conditions and so fell within the scope of Directive 76/207. The case then went back to the Commissioner for him to consider whether the family credit rules did indirectly discriminate against women and, if so, whether this was objectively justifiable. The Commissioner accepted that the absence of a child care costs disregard had a disparate impact on women but found that this discrimination was objectively justified and so the family credit rules were compatible with Directive 76/207.

In addition, there may be a possibility of challenge under art.7 of EC Regulation 1612/68 on social and tax advantages. In *O'Flynn v Chief Adjudication Officer (R(IS)4/98)* the Court of Appeal accepted that a social fund funeral payment is a social advantage within the Regulation. See the notes to reg.7(1) of the Social Fund Maternity and Funeral Expenses Regulations.

Chapter IV

Self-Employed Earners

Earnings of self-employed earners

2.265 **37.**—(1) Subject to paragraph (2), "earnings", in the case of employment as a self-employed earner, means the gross receipts of the employment and shall include any allowance paid under section 2 of the Employment and Training Act 1973 [[1]or section 2 of the Enterprise and New Towns (Scotland) Act 1990] to the claimant for the purpose of assisting him in carrying on his business.

[²(2) "Earnings" shall not include—

(a) where a claimant is involved in providing board and lodging accommodation for which a charge is payable, any payment by way of such a charge;

[³(b) any payment to which paragraph 26 or 27 of Schedule 9 refers (payments in respect of a person accommodated with the claimant under an arrangement made by a local authority or voluntary organisation and payments made to the claimant by a health authority, local authority or voluntary organisation in respect of persons temporarily in the claimant's care).]]

[⁴(c) any sports award.]

AMENDMENTS

1. Enterprise (Scotland) Consequential Amendments Order 1991 (SI 1991/ 387), art.2 (April 1, 1991).   **2.266**
2. Income-related Benefits Schemes (Miscellaneous Amendments) (No.3) Regulations 1992 (SI 1992/2155), reg.16 (October 5, 1992).
3. Income-related Benefits Schemes (Miscellaneous Amendments) (No.5) Regulations 1994 (SI 1994/2139), reg.27 (October 3, 1994).
4. Social Security Amendment (Sports Awards) Regulations 1999 (SI 1999/ 2165), reg.6(3) (August 23, 1999).

DEFINITIONS

"board and lodging accommodation"—see reg.2(1).
"claimant"—see reg.2(1), reg.23(1).
"self-employed earner"—see reg.2(1).
"sports award"—*ibid*.
"voluntary organisation"—*ibid*.

GENERAL NOTE

Para. (1)

On the tests for deciding whether a person is an employee or self-employed, see **2.267** *CJSA 4721/2001* and the other cases discussed in the notes to reg.30.

The starting point for the self-employed is the figure of gross receipts, including Business Start-up Allowance (previously enterprise allowance), to be reduced to net profits under reg.38.

In *CFC 4/1991*, the claimant's husband had recently started a construction business. He received a loan of £5,500 from a relative and made part repayment of £4,000 not long afterwards. The AO and the SSAT treated the loan as part of the "gross receipts" of the self-employment. The repayment could not be deducted from the gross receipts because of reg.22(5)(a) of the Family Credit Regulations (the equivalent of reg.38(5)(a) below). (See the 2002 edition of this volume for the Family Credit Regulations.) The result was that the net profit so calculated took the claimant above family credit level. The Commissioner found that the loan was a capital receipt, but concluded that the words of reg.21(1) of the Family Credit Regulations (the equivalent of reg.37(1)) were unambiguous and included capital receipts. On appeal under the name of *Kostanczwk*, an order of the Registrar of the Court of Appeal (dated August 21, 1992) allowed the appeal by consent and directed that capital receipts not generated by a claimant's business do not form part of the gross receipts of that employment for the purposes of reg.21 of the Family Credit Regulations. As *R(FC) 1/97* confirmed, since that direction was contained in an Order made by consent and without argument it was not binding on anyone other than the parties to the Order and the tribunal to whom the direction was made. But as the decision in *CFC 4/1991* had been set aside by the Court of Appeal, *CFC 24/1989* remained at that time the only authoritative Commissioner's decision on the point. In *CFC 24/1989* it was held that a grant of £900 from the Prince's Youth Business Trust to assist in the setting up of a business was not part of the gross receipts. The Commissioner focuses on the bizarre consequences if a capital receipt has to count as part of the gross receipts, when capital expenditure cannot be deducted from the gross receipts. The approach of *CFC 24/1989* was to be preferred as a matter of principle. In *CFC 23/1991* a legacy used to keep the claimant's business afloat was not a receipt of the business. The argument that since reg.37 is placed within the income section of the regulations, gross receipts must mean "revenue receipts" and exclude loans or receipts from the sale of capital assets, etc., did seem to be a convincing one. This has now been confirmed by *R(FC) 1/97*. In a comprehensive decision the Commissioner holds that neither a loan for business purposes nor the proceeds of sale of capital assets (in that case a car and a computer printer) form part of the gross receipts of the employment for the purposes of reg.21 of the Family Credit Regulations (the equivalent of reg.37).

Para.(2)

2.268   *CIS 55/1989* decided that the predecessor of sub-para.(a), which referred to a claimant "employed" in providing board and lodging accommodation (defined in reg.2(1)), applied whenever the claimant made a charge for providing the accommodation. It was not necessary for the claimant to provide it by way of business. The substitution of the word "involved" reinforces this conclusion. The payments received count as income under reg.40(4)(a), but subject to disregards.

But equally sub-para.(a) will apply where the claimant is engaged in a board and lodging business. In *CIS 521/2002* the claimant was one of four partners who ran a hotel providing board and lodging accommodation for the homeless. The consequence of sub-para.(a) was that rather than her share of the net partnership profits (after deducting income tax, NI contributions and half of any pension contributions) falling under reg.38(1)(b), the gross amount of the receipts from the tenants had to be taken into account under reg.40(4)(a), subject to any disregard in Sch.9. As the claimant lived in the hotel (and on the basis that she was to be regarded as living in the whole hotel as her home) para.20 of Sch.9 applied. The issue was how the claimant's income was to be calculated. The tribunal applied the disregard under para.20(b) to the total of the receipts from the boarders and then divided by four to obtain the claimant's share. The result of this calculation was that the claimant was not entitled to income support because her income exceeded her applicable amount. However, the Commissioner concluded that the disregard under para.20(b) fell to be applied *after* the claimant's gross income had been calculated. Her gross income was her partnership share, not the total of the board and lodging charges. Furthermore, as para.20 made no provision for partnerships or for taking into account only a proportion of the number of boarders, the disregard to be set against the claimant's quarter share under para.20(b) was £20 plus 50% of any excess for each of the 16 boarders. On this basis, the claimant had no income to be taken into account for the purpose of income support.

Sub-para.(b) applies to payments to foster-parents and to people for providing temporary care in their home. Those payments are disregarded as income other than earnings under paras 26 and 27 of Sch.9. Sub-para.(b) ensures that they are not treated as earnings. See also reg.6(1)(k).

On sub-para.(c), see reg.6(1)(m) and the note to that provision. See also the disregards in para.69 of Sch.9 and para.56 of Sch.10.

Calculation of net profit of self-employed earners

2.269   **38.**—(1) For the purposes of regulation 30 (calculation of earnings of self-employed earners), the earnings of a claimant to be taken into account shall be—

(a) in the case of a self-employed earner who is engaged in employment on his own account, the net profit derived from that employment;

(b) in the case of a self-employed earner whose employment is carried on in partnership or is that of a share fisherman within the meaning of the Social Security (Mariners' Benefits) Regulations 1975, his share of the net profit derived from that employment less—
   (i) an amount in respect of income tax and of social security contributions payable under the Social Security Act [SSCBA] calculated in accordance with regulation 39 (deduction of tax and contributions for self-employed earners); and
   (ii) [¹one half of any premium paid [²in the period that is relevant under regulation 30] in respect of a retirement annuity contract or a personal pension scheme].

(2) There shall be disregarded from a claimant's net profit any sum, where applicable, specified in paragraphs 1 to 13 [⁴ [⁶ . . .]] of Schedule 8.

(3) For the purposes of paragraph (1)(a) the net profit of the employment shall, except where paragraph (9) applies, be calculated by taking into account the earnings of the employment over the period determined under regulation 30 (calculation of earnings of self-employed earners) less—
(a) subject to paragraphs (5) to (7), any expenses wholly and exclusively defrayed in that period for the purposes of that employment;
(b) an amount in respect of—
   (i) income tax; and
   (ii) social security contributions payable under the Social Security Act [SSCBA],
calculated in accordance with regulation 39 (deduction of tax and contributions for self-employed earners); and
(c) [¹one half of any premium paid [²in the period that is relevant under regulation 30] in respect of a retirement annuity contract or a personal pension scheme].

(4) For the purposes of paragraph (1)(b), the net profit of the employment shall be calculated by taking into account the earnings of the employment over the period determined under regulation 30 less, subject to paragraphs (5) to (7), any expenses wholly and exclusively defrayed in that period for the purposes of that employment.

(5) Subject to paragraph (6), no deduction shall be made under paragraph (3)(a) or (4) in respect of—
(a) any capital expenditure;
(b) the depreciation of any capital asset;
(c) any sum employed or intended to be employed in the setting up or expansion of the employment;
(d) any loss incurred before the beginning of the period determined under regulation 30 (calculation of earnings of self-employed earners);
(e) the repayment of capital on any loan taken out for the purposes of the employment;
(f) any expenses incurred in providing business entertainment.

(6) A deduction shall be made under paragraph (3)(a) or (4) in respect of the repayment of capital on any loan used for—
(a) the replacement in the course of business of equipment or machinery; and
(b) the repair of an existing business asset except to the extent that any sum is payable under an insurance policy for its repair.

(7) [⁵The Secretary of State] shall refuse to make a deduction in respect of any expenses under paragraph (3)(a) or (4) where he is not satisfied that

the expense has been defrayed or, having regard to the nature of the expense and its amount, that it has been reasonably incurred.

(8) For the avoidance of doubt—

(a) a deduction shall not be made under paragraph (3)(a) or (4) in respect of any sum unless it has been expended for the purposes of the business;

(b) a deduction shall be made thereunder in respect of—

(i) the excess of any VAT paid over VAT received in the period determined under regulation 30 (calculation of earnings of self-employed earners);

(ii) any income expended in the repair of an existing asset except to the extent that any sum is payable under an insurance policy for its repair;

(iii) any payment of interest on a loan taken out for the purposes of the employment.

(9) Where a claimant is engaged in employment as a child minder the net profit of the employment shall be one-third of the earnings of that employment, less—

(a) an amount in respect of—

(i) income tax; and

(ii) social security contributions payable under the Social Security Act [SSCBA],

calculated in accordance with regulation 39 (deduction of tax and contributions for self-employed); and

(b) [¹one half of any premium paid in respect of a retirement annuity contract or personal pension scheme].

(10) Notwithstanding regulation 30 (calculation of earnings of self-employed earners) and the foregoing paragraphs, [⁵the Secretary of State] may assess any item of a claimant's income or expenditure over a period other than that determined under regulation 30 as may, in the particular case, enable the weekly amount of that item of income or expenditure to be determined more accurately.

(11) For the avoidance of doubt where a claimant is engaged in employment as a self-employed earner and he is also engaged in one or more other employments as a self-employed or employed earner any loss incurred in any one of his employments shall not be offset against his earnings in any other of his employments.

(12)[³. . .].

AMENDMENTS

2.270   1. Income-related Benefits Schemes (Miscellaneous Amendments) (No.4) Regulations 1993 (SI 1993/2119), reg.13 (October 4, 1993).

2. Income-related Benefits Schemes (Miscellaneous Amendments) (No.5) Regulations 1994 (SI 1994/2139), reg.28 (October 3, 1994).

3. Income-related Benefits Schemes and Social Security (Claims and Payments) (Miscellaneous Amendments) Regulations 1995 (SI 1995/2303), reg.6(3) (October 2, 1995).

4. Social Security (Miscellaneous Amendments) (No.2) Regulations 1999 (SI 1999/2556), reg.2(6) (October 4, 1999).

5. Social Security Act 1998 (Commencement No. 12 and Consequential and Transitional Provisions) Order 1999 (SI 1999/3178 (C.81)), art.3(5) and Sch.5, para.2 (November 29, 1999).

6. Social Security (Back to Work Bonus and Lone Parent Run-on) (Amendment and Revocation) Regulations 2003 (SI 2003/1589), reg.2(c) (October 25, 2004).

DEFINITIONS

"claimant"—see reg.2(1), reg.23(1).
"personal pension scheme"—see reg.2(1).
"retirement annuity contract"—*ibid.*
"self-employed earner"—*ibid.*
"Social Security Act"—*ibid.*

GENERAL NOTE

The structure is as follows: 2.271
(1) General rule.
(2) Disregards.
(3) Net profit of sole traders.
(4) Net profit of partners and share fishermen.
(5) Deductions are not allowed.
(6) Deductions allowed.
(7) Tests for (3), (4) and (6).
(8) Tests for (3), (4) and (6).
(9) Child minders.
(10) Period of calculation to be adjusted.
(11) Two employments.

Para. (1)
This provision sets up two categories—   2.272

(a) those in employment on their own account ("sole traders") and

(b) partners and share fishermen.

For both, the earnings to be taken into account under reg.30 are to be net profits. Under (b) the deductions for income tax, social security contributions and personal pension or retirement annuity (see reg.2(1)) premiums are put under para.(1). For (a), these appear in para.(3).

Para. (2)
See the notes to reg.36(2). The difference is that para.(2) does not refer to the dis-   2.273
regard in para.15A of Sch.8 as this is not relevant to self-employed earnings.

Para. (3)
For sole traders apart from child minders (para.(9)) the starting point in calculat-   2.274
ing net profit under para.(1) is earnings, *i.e.* gross receipts (see notes to reg.37(1) on the meaning of gross receipts). From that are deducted expenses. Any expenses wholly and exclusively defrayed may be deducted providing that they are reasonably incurred (para.(7)) and the rules of paras (5) and (6) are applied. The expenses must have been actually defrayed, so that unpaid liabilities cannot be deducted (*CIS 212/1988*).
There has been considerable doubt about whether the cost of items which have a dual use, for business and private purposes, can be apportioned. *The Adjudication Officer's Guide* originally suggested that the cost of telephone calls, units of gas or electricity consumption and petrol could be apportioned (because consumption can be identified as for business or private purposes), but not, for instance, standing charges or road fund tax or insurance for a car. In a series of appeals heard together, the Commissioner convincingly demolished this approach (*R(FC) 1/91, CFC 26/1989* and *R(IS) 13/91*). He holds that where expenses can be apportioned on a time basis, this can identify the amount wholly and exclusively defrayed on business expenses. There remain some expenses, like the cost of lunches for clients, which

are not capable of apportionment. The Commissioner also holds that the apportionment made by the Inspector of Taxes is cogent evidence of the amounts wholly and exclusively incurred for the purposes of the business, which should be accepted in the absence of evidence to the contrary. The *Adjudication Officer's Guide* was subsequently amended to reflect this decision. Now see para.26029 of the *Decision Makers Guide*. See also *CFC 836/1995* in the note to para.(11).

The standard deductions for tax and social security contributions (see reg.39) and personal pension or retirement annuity (see reg.2(1)) premiums are made.

Para. (4)

2.275   For partners and share fishermen the calculation is effectively the same apart from the standard deductions already in para.(1)(b).

Para. (5)

2.276   No deductions are allowed for these items, many of which will appear in profit and loss accounts. But see para.(6) for exceptions to (e).

Para. (6)

2.277   Deductions can be made for the repayment of capital on loans for these repairs or replacements. The interest on such a loan will be an allowable expense under the general test (and see para.(8)(b)(iii)).

Para. (7)

2.278   This provision confirms that an expense must have been actually paid out (*CIS 212/1988*), and imposes a general test of reasonableness.

Para. (8)

2.279   The test of business purpose merely confirms the general requirement under paras (3) and (4). It is useful to have the categories in (b) expressly confirmed.

Para. (9)

2.280   For child-minders the simple rule of taking profit as one third of gross receipts is used. The standard deductions are then made. Child-minders who work at home are treated as not in remunerative work (reg.6(1)(b)). See the note to reg.6(1)(b).

Para. (10)

2.281   This provision gives a very general power to average items over different periods from that set in reg.30, where the basic rule is to take the previous one year.

Para. (11)

2.282   *R(FC) 1/93* applies the principle that a loss in one employment cannot be set off against a profit or earnings in another separate employment. The claimant ran a sub-post office and a shop in the same premises. The Commissioner decides that carrying out the office of sub-postmistress was employment as an employed earner, while running the shop was employment as a self-employed earner. The loss made by the shop could not be set off against the claimant's earnings as a sub-postmistress. *CFC 836/1995* concerned similar facts. However, the Commissioner went on to consider the apportionment of expenses between the two employments. Applying by analogy *R(FC) 1/91* (apportionment of expenses between business and personal use), he held that expenses which were not solely attributable to the shop could be apportioned between the shop and the claimant's husband's employment as a sub-postmaster. The basis of the apportionment in that case was 75 per cent to the post office and 25 per cent to the shop, since the primary reason most customers visited the premises was for the post office services. Thus 75 per cent of the expenses relating to the general running of the premises and the two activities and the repayments on a loan to acquire the post office and shop could be deducted from the earnings as a sub-postmaster, as the Commissioner accepted that these had been wholly, exclusively and necessarily incurred in the performance of the duties of sub-postmaster (see *R(FC) 1/90*, applying *Parsons v Hogg*). See also *CFC 4238/1997*.

Deduction of tax and contributions for self-employed earners

39.—(1) The amount to be deducted in respect of income tax under regulation 38(1)(b)(i), (3)(b)(i) or (9)(a)(i) (calculation of net profit of self-employed earners) shall be calculated on the basis of the amount of chargeable income and as if that income were assessable to income tax at [¹the lower rate or, as the case may be, the lower rate and the basic rate of tax] less only the personal relief to which the claimant is entitled under sections 8(1) and (2) and 14(1)(a) and (2) of the Income and Corporation Taxes Act 1970 (personal relief) as is appropriate to his circumstances; but, if the period determined under regulation 30 (calculation of earnings of self-employed earners) is less than a year, [¹the earnings to which the lower rate [³. . .] of tax is to be applied and] the amount of the personal relief deductible under this paragraph shall be calculated on a pro rata basis.

(2) The amount to be deducted in respect of social security contributions under regulation 38(1)(b)(i), (3)(b)(ii) or (9)(a)(ii) shall be the total of—

[²(a)   the amount of Class 2 contributions payable under section 11(1) or, as the case may be, 11(3) of the Contributions and Benefits Act at the rate applicable at the date of claim except where the claimant's chargeable income is less than the amount specified in section 11(4) of that Act (small earnings exception) for the tax year in which the date of claim falls; but if the assessment period is less than a year, the amount specified for that tax year shall be reduced pro rata; and

(b)   the amount of Class 4 contributions (if any) which would be payable under section 15 of that Act (Class 4 contributions recoverable under the Income Tax Acts) at the percentage rate applicable at the date of claim on so much of the chargeable income as exceeds the lower limit but does not exceed the upper limit of profits and gains applicable for the tax year in which the date of claim falls; but if the assessment period is less than a year, those limits shall be reduced pro rata.]

(3) In this regulation "chargeable income" means—

(a)   except where sub-paragraph (b) applies, the earnings derived from the employment less any expenses deducted under paragraph (3)(a) or, as the case may be, (4) of regulation 38;

(b)   in the case of employment as a child minder, one-third of the earnings of that employment.

AMENDMENTS

1. Income-related Benefits Schemes (Miscellaneous Amendments) (No.3) Regulations 1992 (SI 1992/2155), reg.17 (October 5, 1992).

2. Income-related Benefits Schemes (Miscellaneous Amendments) (No.4) Regulations 1993 (SI 1993/2119), reg.14 (October 4, 1993).

3. Income-related Benefits Schemes (Miscellaneous Amendments) (No.5) Regulations 1994 (SI 1994/2139), reg.29 (October 3, 1994).

DEFINITIONS

"claimant"—see reg.2(1), reg.23(1).
"date of claim"—see reg.2(1).
"lower rate"—see reg.2(1).
"Social Security Act"—*ibid.*

2.283

2.284

Para. (1)

2.285   The deduction for income tax from the amount of earnings calculated under reg.38 is to be made by applying the lower and basic rates of tax (*i.e.* currently 10 and 22 per cent respectively) and the personal relief as a single or married person. This figure may well be higher than the actual tax payable. The references to the Income and Corporation Taxes Act 1970 need to be updated to the current Act.

Para. (2)

2.286   Deductions are made for the Class 2 and Class 4 Social Security contributions payable on the amount calculated under reg.38.

[¹ Chapter IVA

Participants in the Self-Employment Route [³ . . .]

Interpretation

2.287   **39A.** In this Chapter—
"[² . . .]
"special account" means, where a person was carrying on a commercial activity in respect of which assistance is received under the self-employment route, the account into which the gross receipts from that activity were payable during the period in respect of which such assistance was received.]

AMENDMENTS

1. Social Security (Miscellaneous Amendments) (No.4) Regulations 1998 (SI 1998/1174), reg.6(3) (June 1, 1998).
2. Social Security Amendment (Employment Zones) (No.2) Regulations 2000 (SI 2000/2910), reg.5(1)(b) (November 27, 2000).
3. Social Security Amendment (Employment Zones) (No.2) Regulations 2000 (SI 2000/2910), reg.5(1)(c) (November 27, 2000).

DEFINITION

"self-employment route"—see reg.2(1).

GENERAL NOTE

2.288   Regulations 39A to 39D are the same in substance as regs 102A to 102D of the JSA Regulations (apart from necessary differences in cross-references). They apply to the income from "test-trading" of people who have taken part in the "self-employment route" (defined in reg.2(1)). See the notes to reg.102C of the JSA Regulations.

See also reg.23A, the effect of which is that the normal rules for the treatment of income do not apply to receipts from trading while on the self-employment route; such receipts are only to be taken into account as income in accordance with regs 39A to 39D.

Note the disregards in para.64 of Sch.9 and para.6(3) and (4) and para.52 of Sch.10.

[¹ Treatment of gross receipts of participants in the self-employment route [². . .]

39B. The gross receipts of a commercial activity carried on by a person   2.289
in respect of which assistance is received under the self-employment route,
shall be taken into account in accordance with the following provisions of
this Chapter.]

AMENDMENTS

1. Social Security (Miscellaneous Amendments) (No.4) Regulations 1998 (SI
1998/1174), reg.6(3) (June 1, 1998).
2. Social Security Amendment (Employment Zones) (No.2) Regulations 2000 (SI
2000/2910), reg.5(1)(c) (November 27, 2000).

DEFINITION

"self-employment route"—see reg.2(1).

GENERAL NOTE

See the note to reg.39A.   2.290

[¹ Calculation of income of participants in the self-employment route [². . .]

39C.—(1) The income of a person who has received assistance under the   2.291
self-employment route shall be calculated by taking into account the whole
of the monies in the special account at the end of the last day upon which
such assistance was received and deducting from those monies—
   (a) an amount in respect of income tax calculated in accordance with
       regulation 39D (deduction in respect of tax for participants in the
       self-employment route [². . .]); and
   (b) any sum to which paragraph (4) refers.

(2) Income calculated pursuant to paragraph (1) shall be apportioned
equally over a period which starts on the date the income is treated as
paid under paragraph (3) and is equal in length to the period beginning
with the day upon which assistance was first received under the
self-employment route and ending on the last day upon which such assistance was received.

(3) Income calculated pursuant to paragraph (1) shall be treated as
paid—
   (a) in the case where it is due to be paid before the first benefit week
       in respect of which the participant or his partner first claims
       income support following the last day upon which assistance was
       received under the self-employment route, on the day in the week
       in which it is due to be paid which corresponds to the first day of
       the benefit week;
   (b) in any other case, on the first day of the benefit week in which it is
       due to be paid.

(4) This paragraph refers, where applicable in each benefit week in respect
of which income calculated pursuant to paragraph (1) is taken into account
pursuant to paragraphs (2) and (3), to the sums which would have been disregarded under paragraphs 4 to 6B and 9 of Schedule 8 had the income been
earnings.]

AMENDMENTS

1. Social Security (Miscellaneous Amendments) (No.4) Regulations 1998 (SI 1998/1174), reg.6(3) (June 1, 1998).
2. Social Security Amendment (Employment Zones) (No.2) Regulations 2000 (SI 2000/2910), reg.5(1)(c) (November 27, 2000).

DEFINITION

"self-employment route"—see reg.2(1).

GENERAL NOTE

See the note to reg.39A.

[¹Deduction in respect of tax for participants in the self-employment route [². . .]

2.292
39D.—(1) The amount to be deducted in respect of income tax under regulation 39C(1)(a) (calculation of income of participants in the self-employment route [². . .]) in respect of the period determined under regulation 39C(2) shall be calculated as if—

(a) the chargeable income is the only income chargeable to tax:
(b) the personal reliefs which are applicable to the person receiving assistance under the self-employment route by virtue of sections 257(1), 257A(1) and 259 of the Income and Corporation Taxes Act 1988 (personal reliefs) are allowable against that income; and
(c) the rate at which the chargeable income less the personal relief is assissable to income tax is the lower rate of tax or, as the case may be, the lower rate and the basic rate of tax.

(2) For the purpose of paragraph (1), the lower rate of tax to be applied and the amount of the personal relief deductible shall, where the period determined under regulation 39C(2) is less than a year, be calculated on a pro rata basis.

(3) In this regulation, "chargeable income" means the monies in the special account at the end of the last day upon which assistance was received under the self-employment route.]

AMENDMENTS

1. Social Security (Miscellaneous Amendments) (No.4) Regulations 1998 (SI 1998/1174), reg.6(3) (June 1, 1998).
2. Social Security Amendment (Employment Zones) (No.2) Regulations 2000 (SI 2000/2910), reg.5(1)(c) (November 27, 2000).

DEFINITION

"self-employment route"—see reg.2(1).

GENERAL NOTE

2.293
See the note to reg.39A.

Chapter V

Other Income

Calculation of income other than earnings

40.—(1) For the purposes of regulation 29 (calculation of income other   2.294
than earnings) the income of a claimant which does not consist of earnings to
be taken into account shall, subject to [⁶paragraphs (2) to (3B)], be his gross
income and any capital treated as income under [¹⁰regulation 41 (capital
treated as income)].

(2) There shall be disregarded from the calculation of a claimant's gross
income under paragraph (1), any sum, where applicable, specified in
Schedule 9.

(3) Where the payment of any benefit under the benefit Acts is subject to
any deduction by way of recovery the amount to be taken into account under
paragraph (1) shall be the gross amount payable.

[⁹ (3A) Paragraph (3AA) applies where—

(a) a relevant payment has been made to a person in an academic
year; and

(b) that person abandons, or is dismissed from, his course of study before
the payment to him of the final instalment of the relevant payment.

(3AA) The amount of a relevant payment to be taken into account for the
assessment period for the purposes of paragraph (1) in respect of a person to
whom paragraph (3A) applies, shall be calculated by applying the formula—

$$\frac{A - (B \times C)}{D}$$

where—

A = the total amount of the relevant payment which that person would
have received had he remained a student until the last day of the academic term in which he abandoned, or was dismissed from, his course,
less any deduction under regulation 66A(5);

B = the number of benefit weeks from the benefit week immediately
following that which includes the first day of that academic year to the
benefit week immediately before that which includes the day on which
the person abandoned, or was dismissed from, his course;

C = the weekly amount of the relevant payment, before the application of
the £10 disregard, which would have been taken into account as
income under regulation 66A(2) had the person not abandoned or been
dismissed from, his course and, in the case of a person who was not
entitled to income support immediately before he abandoned or was
dismissed from his course, had that person, at that time, been entitled
to income support;

D = the number of benefit weeks in the assessment period.

(3AB) In paragraphs (3A) and (3AA)—

"academic year" and "student loan" shall have the same meanings as for
the purposes of Chapter VIII of this Part;

"assessment period" means the period beginning with the benefit week
which includes the day on which the person abandoned, or was dis-

missed from, his course and ending with the benefit week which includes the last day of the last quarter for which an instalment of the relevant payment was payable to that person and for the purposes of this definition, "quarter" shall have the same meaning as for the purposes of the Education (Student Support) Regulations 2001;

"relevant payment" means either a student loan or an amount intended for the maintenance of dependants referred to in regulation 62(3B) or both.]

[⁴(3B) In the case of income to which regulation 29(2B) applies (calculation of income of former students), the amount of income to be taken into account for the purposes of paragraph (1) shall be the amount of that income calculated in accordance with regulation 32(6A) and on the basis that none of that income has been repaid.]1

(4) [⁷Subject to paragraph (5)] for the avoidance of doubt there shall be included as income to be taken into account under paragraph (1)

[⁷(a) any payment to which regulation 35(2) or 37(2) (payments not earnings) applies; or

(b) in the case of a claimant who is receiving support provided under section 95 or 98 of the Immigration and Asylum Act including support provided by virtue of regulations made under Schedule 9 to that Act, the amount of such support provided in respect of essential living needs of the claimant and his [¹⁰ partner] (if any) as is specified in regulations made under paragraph 3 of Schedule 8 to the Immigration and Asylum Act;

(5) In the case of a claimant who is the partner of a person subject to immigration control and whose partner is receiving support provided under section 95 or 98 of the Immigration and Asylum Act including support provided by virtue of regulations made under Schedule 9 to that Act, there shall not be included as income to be taken into account under paragraph (1) the amount of support provided in respect of essential living needs of the partner of the claimant and his dependants (if any) as is specified in regulations made under paragraph 3 of Schedule 8 to the Immigration and Asylum Act.]

AMENDMENTS

2.295 1. Income Support (General) Amendment No.5 Regulations 1988 (SI 1988/2022), reg.9 (December 12, 1988).

2. Social Security Benefits (Student Loans and Miscellaneous Amendments) Regulations 1990 (SI 1990/1549), reg.5(4) (September 1, 1990).

3. Income Support (General) Amendment Regulations 1991 (SI 1991/236), reg.9 (March 13, 1991).

4. Income-related Benefits and Jobseeker's Allowance (Miscellaneous Amendments) Regulations 1997 (SI 1997/65), reg.7 (April 7, 1997).

5. Income-related Benefits and Jobseeker's Allowance (Amendment) (No.2) Regulations 1997 (SI 1997/2197), reg.5(3) (October 6, 1997).

6. Social Security (Miscellaneous Amendments) Regulations 1998 (SI 1998/563), reg.13(1)(a) (April 6, 1998).

7. Social Security (Immigration and Asylum) Consequential Amendments Regulations 2000 (SI 2000/636), reg.3(6) (April 3, 2000).

8. Social Security Amendment (Students) Regulations 2000 (SI 2000/1981), reg.5(5) and Sch.(July 31, 2000).

9. Social Security Amendment (Students and Income-related Benefits) Regulations 2001 (SI 2001/2319), reg.5(1) (August 1, 2001).

10. Social Security (Working Tax Credit and Child Tax Credit) (Consequential Amendments) Regulations 2003 (SI 2003/455), reg.2 and Sch.1, para.8 (April 6,

2004, except in "transitional cases" and see further the note to reg.17 of the Income Support Regulations).

DEFINITIONS

"academic year"—see reg.61(1).
"benefit Acts"—see reg.2(1).
"benefit week"—*ibid.*
"claimant"—see reg.2(1), reg.23(1).
"full-time student"—see reg.61(1).
"Immigration and Asylum Act"—see reg.61(1).
"partner of a person subject to immigration control"—see reg.21(3).
"student"—see reg.61(1).
"student loan"—*ibid.*

GENERAL NOTE

Para. (1)

This paragraph mainly confirms that all forms of income other than earnings fall into this category, and provides that the gross amount is to be taken into account.   2.296

The first point is that the income must of course be the claimant's (or his partner's—as a consequence of the removal of amounts for children and young persons from income support (with effect from April 6, 2004, except in "transitional cases"—see the note to reg.17) the income of a child or young person who is a member of the claimant's family is no longer aggregated with the claimant's—see further the note to reg.23). A loan can constitute income (*R(SB) 20/83, R(SB) 7/88, Morrell v Secretary of State for Work and Pensions* [2003] EWCA Civ 526, reported as *R(IS) 6/03), CJSA 1134/2003,* to be reported as *R(JSA) 4/04,* (student loan paid (whether properly or otherwise) to part-time student)) but money that a claimant is under a "certain and immediate liability" to repay does not amount to income (see *Chief Adjudication Officer v Leeves* (November 6, 1998, CA, reported as *R(IS) 5/99*) in the notes to reg.29(2B)). Thus resources provided by the use of an overdraft facility do not amount to income since the standard terms of a bank overdraft are that it is repayable on demand, even though that demand may not be made while the amount stays within an agreed limit (*CH/3013/2003,* to be reported as *R(H) 5/05*— see further the note to reg 23). See also *R(IS) 4/01* which decides, applying *Leeves,* that the part of the claimant's occupational pension that was being paid to his former wife under an attachment of earnings order did not count as his income for the purposes of income support. The notional income rule in reg.42(4)(a) also did not apply: see the note to reg.42(4)(a). A similar approach was taken in *CIS 5479/1999* (where an overpayment of an occupational pension was being recovered by the Italian authorities by withholding the monthly payments of the pension) and in *R(IS) 4/02* (both decided by the same Commissioner). In *R(IS) 4/02* the Commissioner decides, contrary to the view taken in para.9 of *CIS 212/1989* (and followed with some hesitation in *CIS 295/1994*), that payments of the claimant's husband's annuity which had vested in his trustee in bankruptcy under s.306 of the Insolvency Act 1986 were not part of his income (and thus not part of the claimant's income) for the purposes of income support. In his view, in the general context of the income support scheme income to be taken into account is income that is actually paid to a claimant. Note also *R(IS) 2/03,* that concerned payments under the claimant's self-employed pension annuity that were being applied for the benefit of his creditors, which agrees with *R(IS) 4/02* (on the basis of the principle in *Re Landau* [1998] Ch. 223, affirmed in *Krasner v Dennison* [2001] Ch. 76) that *CIS 212/1989* should no longer be followed. See further the note to reg.23.

Secondly, the amount of the gross income has to be calculated. *CIS 25/1989* held that, applying the principle of *Parsons v Hogg* [1985] 2 All E.R. 897, appendix to *R(FIS) 4/85,* expenditure necessary to produce the income is to be deducted to   2.297

produce a figure of gross income. The claimant was entitled to £21.60 per month sickness benefit from the Ideal Benefit Society only while he continued to pay £60 annual payment to the Society. The monthly equivalent (£5) was to be deducted from the £21.60. However, in *CIS 563/1991* the Commissioner disagrees with *CIS 25/1989* and holds that gross income in para.(1) means without any deduction of the expenses incurred in gaining that income, except to the extent expressly allowed by Sch.9. He considers that the various provisions in Sch.9 relating to deduction of expenses incurred by the claimant would not be necessary if "gross income" meant income after deducting the expenses of obtaining it. In his view *CIS 25/1989*, in applying *Parsons v Hogg* in this context, had not paid sufficient regard to the fact that that case was concerned with earnings of employed earners and involved different statutory provisions. The phrase "gross income" was an equivocal one, as indicated by the Court of Appeal's decision in *Parsons v Hogg*, and the statutory context had to be considered. The principle of *Parsons v Hogg* had been applied to earnings in *R(FC) 1/90* and *R(IS) 16/93*, (but apparently not to attendance and basic allowances paid to councillors, which are counted as earnings, in *R(IS) 6/92* and *CIS 77/1993*). (On the application of *Parsons v Hogg* to the meaning of "gross earnings", see further the notes to reg.36(3)). The Commissioner in *CIS 563/1991* considered that the statutory context of earnings of employed earners and income other than earnings was sufficiently different not to necessitate a uniform approach to the deduction of expenses.

This question was considered again in *R(IS) 13/01*. The Commissioner opined that arguably the principle in *Parsons v Hogg* should apply to income other than earnings in the light of the fact that so few of the paragraphs in Sch.9 were concerned with expenses. However, he followed *CIS 563/1991* rather than *CIS 25/1989* on the basis of *Colchester Estates (Cardiff) v Carlton Industries Plc* [1986] Ch. 80. In that case Nourse L.J. had said that where there were two conflicting decisions of equal status and the earlier decision was fully considered in the later decision, the later decision should be followed unless the judge was convinced that the later decision was wrong because, for instance, some binding or persuasive authority had not been cited in either of the two cases. The Commissioner considered that the same approach should be applied by Commissioners and therefore followed *CIS 563/1991* which had considered *CIS 25/1989* in detail and not followed it.

Certain kinds of income are disregarded under Sch.9 (para.(2)). With the revocation of reg.24 there is now no special rule for charitable or voluntary payments. Note reg.48 on income treated as capital.

A major form of income for income support claimants will be from other social security benefits. All benefits of an income nature (presumably benefits like disablement gratuity and widow's payment continue to be treated as capital although there is now no classification in the regulations (*cf. R(SB) 4/89*)) count in full as income unless disregarded under Sch.9. Benefits disregarded include housing benefit (para.5), the mobility component of disability living allowance or mobility supplement (paras 6 and 8), attendance allowance or the care component of disability living allowance (para.9), social fund payments (para.31), council tax benefit (para.52) and from April 7, 2003, guardian's allowance (para.5A). In addition, with effect from April 6, 2004 (except in "transitional cases"—see the note to reg.17) child benefit and child tax credit are ignored (para.5B) (for income support claimants who had an award of child tax credit before April 6, 2004 see reg.7 of the Social Security (Working Tax Credit and Child Tax Credit) (Consequential Amendments) Regulations 2003 (SI 2003/455) (as amended) on p.686 and the notes to that regulation).

Benefits which count as income are income whether they are paid on time or in the form of arrears (*R(SB) 4/89*). Then reg.31 defines the date on which the income is treated as paid. The fact that there is a partial disregard of some kinds of benefit arrears as capital in para.7 of Sch.10 does not affect this conclusion. This is because the conclusion, and *R(SB) 4/89*, must be subject to the principle of *R(SB) 2/83* and *R(SB) 35/83* that at some point accumulated income turns into capital. The sensible approach would be that if any amount of income is still possessed after the end of the period to which it is properly attributed as income under regs 29 and 31, then it becomes capital, subject to the deduction of relevant liabilities under *R(SB) 2/83* and *R(SB) 35/83*. See *R(IS) 3/93*. Thus there is still something for para.7 of Sch.10 to bite on.

Para. (2)

This paragraph authorises the disregards in Sch.9. See *CIS 563/1991* discussed in the note to para.22 of Sch.9 and *CIS 82/1993* and *CIS 13059/1996* in the notes to paras 19 and 30 where more than one disregard applies. *CIS 683/1993* confirms that income can only be disregarded to the extent allowed for by Sch.9. Therefore, no deduction could be made for the maintenance payments made by the claimant, whether under a court order or otherwise, or for his insurance premiums, in calculating his income. But see *R(IS) 4/01* in the note to reg.42(4). If the maintenance payments are made under an attachment of earnings order rather than by the claimant out of his own income they will not count as his income. However, the deprivation of income rule in reg.42(1) might be applicable if the claimant has deliberately provoked an attachment of earnings order in order to secure benefit.

2.298

Para. (3)

If deductions are made from social security benefits for recovery of overpayments or social fund loans the gross amount of benefit is used in the calculation of income support. A deduction for child support maintenance is a deduction by way of recovery for the purposes of para.(3) (and reg.103(3) of the JSA Regulations) (Social Security (Claims and Payments) Regulations 1987, Sch.9B, para.8, see Vol. III in this series).

2.299

Para. (3A)–(3AB)

The new paras (3A)–(3AB) contain precise rules for calculating the amount of a student loan and/or any non-repayable amount for dependants (paid to students who started their course after September 1, 1998) to be taken into account as income where a student abandons or is dismissed from his course. Note the definitions in para.(3AB) and see the notes to reg.66A for a discussion of the current system for student support. For an example of how the provisions in paras (3A)–(3AB) work in practice see Annex D to HB/CTB Circular A31/2001. Note that the calculation can result in a nil income figure, depending on the point in the term at which the student abandoned or was dismissed from his course.

2.300

If the former student repays the loan this does not constitute a change of circumstances so as to provide grounds for supersession (see reg.6(6)(a) of the Decisions and Appeals Regulations 1999 in vol. III of this series). The intention is that the amount calculated under para.(3AA) should still be taken into account as income. However the guidance to decision-makers does state that if the Student Loan Company demands immediate repayment (*e.g.* because the loan instalment should not have been paid because the student had abandoned or been dismissed from the course), no loan income should be taken into account from the date that demand is made (see DMG Memo, Vol. 6 02/01, paras 17–18). This is on the basis that the student is under a "certain and immediate liability" to repay the loan and so it should not be treated as his income (see *Chief Adjudication Officer v Leeves*, reported as *R(IS) 5/99*, discussed in the notes to reg.29(2B)). But this would not apply if the former student voluntarily repaid the loan, as confirmed in *CJSA 549/2003*. The Commissioner considered that the particularly harsh effect of these provisions in such circumstances where no account was taken of any repayment and it was simply assumed that the loan could still be used for living expenses merited the attention of the Secretary of State (but so far the Commissioner's suggestion remains unheeded).

Note para.61 of Sch.9 under which any part of a student loan or grant left over at the end of a course is ignored.

See also para.(3B).

Para. (3B)

2.301   See the notes to regs 29(2B) and 32(6A). But note *Chief Adjudication Officer v Leeves* (November 6, 1998, CA, reported as *R(IS) 5/99*) and the argument discussed in the notes to reg.29(2B) as to when that provision applies.

Note also para.61 of Sch.9 under which any grant or covenant income or student loan left over at the end of the person's course is disregarded.

Para. (4) (a)

2.302   These amounts, which do not count as earnings, do count as other income. However, note the disregards in paras 1, 3, 4, 4A, 18, 20, 21, 26 and 27 of Sch.9. See also *CIS 521/2002* discussed in the note to reg.37(2).

Paras (4) (b) and (5)

2.303   See the notes to reg.21(3).

Capital treated as income

2.304   **41.**—[8(1) Capital which is payable by instalments which are outstanding on—

(a) the first day in respect of which income support is payable or the date of the determination of the claim, whichever is earlier; or

(b) in the case of a supersession, the date of that supersession,

shall be treated as income if the aggregate of the instalments outstanding and the amount of the claimant's capital otherwise calculated in accordance with Chapter VI of this Part exceeds £8,000 [9 or, in a case where regulation 45(aa) applies, £12,000] or, in a case where regulation 45(b) applies, £16,000.]

(2) Any payment received under an annuity shall be treated as income.

(3) [12. . .]

[2(4) In the case of a person to whom section 20(3) of the Act [SSCBA, s.124(1)] (conditions of entitlement to income support) has effect as modified by section 23A(b) of that Act [SSCBA, s.127(b)] (effect of return to work), any amount by way of repayment of income tax deducted from his emoluments in pursuance of section 203 of the Income and Corporation Taxes Act 1988, shall be treated as income.]

[4(5) Any earnings to the extent that they are not a payment of income shall be treated as income.]

[7(6) Any Career Development Loan paid pursuant to section 2 of the Employment and Training Act 1973 shall be treated as income.]

[11(7) Where an agreement or court order provides that payments shall be made to the claimant in consequence of any personal injury to the claimant and that such payments are to be made, wholly or partly, by way of periodical payments, any such periodical payments received by the claimant (but not a payment which is treated as capital by virtue of this Part), shall be treated as income.]

AMENDMENTS

2.305   1. Income Support (General) Amendment Regulations 1988 (SI 1988/663), reg.18 (April 11, 1988).

2. Income Support (General) Amendment No.4 Regulations 1988 (SI 1988/1445), reg.9 (September 12, 1988).

3. Family Credit and Income Support (General) Amendment Regulations 1989 (SI 1989/104), reg.7 (July 10, 1989).

4. Income Support (General) Amendment No.2 Regulations 1989 (SI 1989/1323), reg.13 (October 9, 1989).

5. Income-related Benefits (Miscellaneous Amendments) Regulations 1990 (SI 1990/671), reg.5 (April 9, 1990).

6. Income Support (General) Amendment Regulations 1992 (SI 1992/468), Sch. para.4 (April 6, 1992).

7. Income-related Benefits and Jobseeker's Allowance (Miscellaneous Amendments) Regulations 1997 (SI 1997/65), reg.3 (April 7, 1997).

8. Social Security Act 1998 (Commencement No.12 and Consequential and Transitional Provisions) Order 1999 (SI 1999/3178 (C.81)), art.3(5) and Sch.5, para.3 (November 29, 1999)

9. Social Security Amendment (Capital Limits and Earnings Disregards) Regulations 2000 (SI 2000/2545), reg.2(1)(a) (April 9, 2001).

10. Children (Leaving Care) Act 2000 (Commencement No.2 and Consequential Provisions) Order 2001 (SI 2001/3070), art.3(2) and Sch.1, para.(c) (October 1, 2001).

11. Social Security Amendment (Personal Injury Payments) Regulations 2002 (SI 2002/2442), reg.2 (October 28, 2002).

12. Social Security (Working Tax Credit and Child Tax Credit) (Consequential Amendments) Regulations 2003 (SI 2003/455), reg.2 and Sch.1, para.9 (April 6, 2004, except in "transitional cases" and see further the note to reg.17 of the Income Support Regulations).

DEFINITIONS

"the Act"—see reg.2(1).
"claimant"—*ibid.*

GENERAL NOTE

Para. (1)

2.306

The value of the right to receive any outstanding instalments of capital payable by instalments is disregarded (Sch.10, para.16). See the notes to reg.23 on the line between capital and income. Normally each instalment, when it is paid, would add to the claimant's capital (*Lillystone v SBC* [1982] 3 F.L.R. 52). The literal efect of para.(1) is that if the amount of the instalments outstanding plus the claimant's (including partner's: reg.23) other capital comes to more than £8,000 (£12,000 if the claimant's partner is aged 60 or over (regs 45(aa) and 53(IZA)), £16,000 in the case of claimants living permanently in residential care or nursing homes, residential accommodation or Polish resettlement homes: regs 45(b) and 53(1B)), the whole amount outstanding is to be treated as income. What para.(1) does not say is what this means. A capital sum cannot simply be treated as income. The common sense rule would be that each instalment, when paid, was treated as a payment of income (as suggested in paras 28532 and 28536 of the *Decision Makers Guide*), but this is not expressed in para.(1). For an example of where the rule in para.(1) applied see *R(IS) 7/98* in the notes to para.15 of Sch.10 and see *R(IS) 10/01* referred to in the note to para.(2).

Para. (2)

2.307–2.30

The value of the right to receive income under an annuity is disregarded as capital (Sch.10, para.11). The income under some "home income" schemes is disregarded under para.17 of Sch.9.

The general rule, however, is that payments under an annuity count as income.

In *R(IS) 10/01* part of the claimant's damages award following a road traffic accident was in the form of two structured settlement annuities. The monthly annuity payments were used for the claimant's substantial care needs. However, as these fell squarely within para.(2) they counted as income with the result that the claimant was not entitled to income support. The Commissioner also accepted that they came within para.(1). The claimant appealed but the Court of Appeal dismissed the appeal and upheld the decision of the Commissioner (*Beattie v Secretary of State for Social Security*, April 9, 2001, *The Times*, May 3, 2001, reported as part of *R(IS) 10/01*).

However, note that from October 28, 2002 the problem highlighted by *Beattie* has been ameliorated by the introduction of a disregard for payments from annuities purchased from funds derived from personal injury awards (see para.15 of Sch.9). Regular payments from such annuities will now be disregarded unless they are used for the items listed in para.15(2) of Sch.9, in which case a £20 disregard (subject to the overall £20 disregard in para.36 of Sch.9) will apply.

Para. (3)

2.309   This paragraph was omitted with effect from April 6, 2004 by reg.2 of and para.9 of Sch.1 to the Social Security (Working Tax Credit and Child Tax Credit) (Consequential Amendments) Regulations 2003 (SI 2003/455), except in "transitional cases" (*i.e.* those cases in which the claimant is still receiving amounts for his children in his income support—see further the note to reg.17). For "transitional cases" para.(3) continues in force (see the 2003 edition of this volume for this provision). With effect from May 12, 2004, reg.5 of the Social Security (Miscellaneous Amendments) (No. 2) Regulations 2004 (SI 2004/1141) substituted the words "section 12 of the Social Work (Scotland) Act 1968 or sections 29 or 30 of the Children (Scotland) Act 1995" for the words "section 12, 24 or 26 of the Social Work (Scotland) Act 1968" in para.(3). The effect of this amendment is simply to update the references to the Scottish legislation referred to in para.(3).

Para. (4)

2.310   In trade dispute cases repayments of PAYE tax, normally capital, are to be treated as income.

Para. (5)

2.311   This seems merely to confirm that sums which are defined as earnings in reg.35 which might under the general law be categorised as capital are income.

Para. (6)

2.313   This treats Career Development Loans, which are provided in order to help adults pay for vocational education or training, as income. However, the income will be disregarded under para.13 of Sch.9 (replacing the previous disregards in paras 59 and 60 of Sch.9 which were revoked on April 1, 2004), except any part of the loan that was intended to meet the cost of food, ordinary clothing or footwear, household fuel, rent for which housing benefit is payable, housing costs met by income support, council tax or water charges during the period of training or education. On "ordinary clothing or footwear" see paras 28671–2 of the *Decision Makers Guide*. In addition, any part of the loan left over at the end of the course is ignored.

For treatment of career development loans before these rules were introduced on April 7, 1997, see *CIS 507/1997*.

Para. (7)

2.314   See the note to para.(2) above. Para.(7) provides that any periodical payments paid under an agreement or court order to a claimant in consequence of personal injury to him, other than payments that are treated as capital (see reg.48(4)), count as income. However, from October 28, 2002, such payments are disregarded under para.15 of Sch.9 unless they are used for food, ordinary clothing or footwear, fuel, housing costs met by income support or housing benefit, council tax or water charges, in which case £20 is disregarded (see further the note to para.15 of Sch.9).

Notional income

2.315   **42.**—(1) A claimant shall be treated as possessing income of which he has deprived himself for the purpose of securing entitlement to income support or increasing the amount of that benefit.

(2) Except in the case of—

(a) a discretionary trust;

(b) a trust derived from a payment made in consequence of a personal injury;

[²³(c) jobseeker's allowance; or]

[²⁵(d) [⁵¹. . .]]

[⁸(e) [⁴⁸ working tax credit];

(f) [⁴⁹ child tax credit],]

[²⁰(g) a personal pension scheme or retirement annuity contract where the claimant is aged under 60,]

[²⁴(h) [⁵⁴. . .]] [²⁶ or

(i) any sum to which paragraph 44(a) or 45(a) of Schedule 10 (disregard of compensation for personal injuries which is administered by the Court) refers,] [³⁰ or

(j) rehabilitation allowance made under section 2 of the Employment and Training Act 1973],

income which would become available to the claimant upon application being made but which has not been acquired by him shall be treated as possessed by him but only from the date on which [¹it could be expected to be acquired were an application made.]

[²⁰(2A) Where a person, aged not less than 60, is a member of, or a person deriving entitlement to a pension under, a personal pension scheme, or is a party to, or a person deriving entitlement to a pension under, a retirement annuity contract, and—

(a) in the case of a personal pension scheme, he fails to purchase an annuity with the funds available in that scheme where—

(i) he defers, in whole or in part, the payment of any income which would have been payable to him by his pension fund holder;

(ii) he fails to take any necessary action to secure that the whole of any income which would be payable to him by his pension fund holder upon his applying for it, is so paid; or

(iii) income withdrawal is not available to him under that scheme; or

(b) in the case of a retirement annuity contract, he fails to purchase an annuity with the funds available under that contract,

the amount of any income foregone shall be treated as possessed by him, but only from the date on which it could be expected to be acquired were an application for it to be made.

(2B) The amount of any income foregone in a case to which either head (2A)(a)(i) or (ii) applies shall be the maximum amount of income which may be withdrawn from the fund and shall be determined by the [³⁹ Secretary of State] who shall take account of information provided by the pension fund holder in accordance with regulation 7(5) of the Social Security (Claims and Payments) Regulations 1987.

(2C) The amount of any income foregone in a case to which either head (2A)(a)(iii) or sub-paragraph (2A)(b) applies shall be the income that the [⁵⁰ person] could have received without purchasing an annuity had the funds held under the relevant personal pension scheme or retirement annuity contract been held under a personal pension scheme where income withdrawal was available and shall be determined in the manner specified in paragraph (2B).]

[²⁵(2D) [⁵¹ . . .]]

(3) Except in the case of a discretionary trust, or a trust derived from a payment made in consequence of a personal injury, any income which is due to be paid to the claimant but—

(a) has not been paid to him;

(b) is not a payment prescribed in regulation [⁴⁴8 or 9] of the Social Security (Payments on Account, Overpayment and Recovery) Regulations [⁴⁴ 1988] (duplication and prescribed payments or maintenance payments) and not made on or before the date prescribed in relation to it,

shall [¹⁰except for any amount to which paragraph (3A) [⁴¹, (3B) or (3C)] applies] be treated as possessed by the claimant.

[¹⁰(3A) This paragraph applies to an amount which is due to be paid to the claimant under an occupational pension scheme but which is not paid because the trustees or managers of the scheme have suspended or ceased payments [¹³. . .] due to an insufficiency of resources.

(3B) This paragraph applies to any amount by which a payment made to the claimant from an occupational pension scheme falls short of the payment to which he was due under the scheme where the shortfall arises because the trustees or managers of the scheme have insufficient resources available to meet in full the scheme's liabilities [¹³. . .].]

[⁴¹(3C) This paragraph applies to any earnings which are due to an employed earner on the termination of his employment by reason of redundancy but which have not been paid to him.]

[²(4) [³² Any payment of income, other than a payment of income specified in paragraph (4ZA)], made—

(a) to a third party in respect of a single claimant or [⁵¹ his partner] (but not a member of the third party's family) shall be treated—

(i) in a case where the payment is derived from a payment of any benefit under the benefit Acts,[⁵³ a payment from the Armed Forces and Reserve Forces Compensation Scheme,] a war disablement pension [²¹, war widow's pension [⁴⁷ or war widower's pension] or a pension payable to a person as a widow [⁴⁷ or widower] under the Naval, Military and Air Forces Etc. (Disablement and Death) Service Pensions Order 1983 insofar as that Order is made under the Naval and Marine Pay and Pensions Act 1865 [²²or the Pensions and Yeomanry Pay Act 1884], or is made only under section 12(1) of the Social Security (Miscellaneous Provisions) Act 1977 and any power of Her Majesty otherwise than under an enactment to make provision about pensions for or in respect of persons who have been disabled or have died in consequence of service as members of the armed forces of the Crown,] as possessed by that single claimant, if it is paid to him, [⁵¹ or by his partner, if it is paid to his partner];

[³⁶(ia) in a case where that payment is a payment of an occupational pension or is a pension or other periodical payment made under a personal pension scheme, as possessed by that single claimant or, as the case may be, by [⁵¹ the claimant's partner];]

(ii) in any other case, as possessed by that single claimant [⁵¹ or his partner] to the extent that it is used for the food, ordinary clothing or footwear, household fuel, rent [⁵⁵. . .] for which housing benefit is payable, [¹⁶or] [⁷. . .] any housing costs to the extent that they are met under regulations 17(1)(e) or 18(1)(f) (housing costs) [16. . .] [4. . .] [3. . .] [4. . .], of that single claimant or, as the case may be, [51 of his partner] [7, or is used for any [12council tax] or water charges for which that claimant or [51 partner is liable]];

[51 (b) to a single claimant or his partner in respect of a third party (but not in respect of another member of his family) shall be treated as possessed by that single claimant or, as the case may be, his partner, to the extent that it is kept or used by him or used by or on behalf of his partner;]

but, except where sub-paragraph (a)(i) applies and in the case of a person to whom section 23 of the Act [SSCBA, s.126] (trade disputes) applies, this paragraph shall not apply to any payment in kind.]

[32 (4ZA) Paragraph (4) shall not apply in respect of a payment of income made—

(a) under the Macfarlane Trust, the Macfarlane (Special Payments) Trust, the Macfarlane (Special Payments) (No. 2) Trust, the Fund, the Eileen Trust or the Independent Living Funds;

(b) pursuant to section 19(1)(a) of the Coal Industry Act 1994 (concessionary coal); or

(c) pursuant to section 2 of the Employment and Training Act 1973 in respect of a person's participation—

    (i) in an employment programme specified in regulations 75(1)(a)(ii) of the Jobseeker's Allowance Regulations 1996;

    (ii) in a training scheme specified in regulation 75(1)(b)(ii) of those Regulations; or

    [45 (iia) in the Intensive Activity Period specified in regulation 75(1)(a)(iv) of those Regulations or in the Intensive Activity Period for 50 plus; or]

    (iii) in a qualifying course within the meaning specified in regulation 17A(7) of those Regulations.]

    (iv) [*Omitted.*]

[37(d) under an occupational pension scheme or in respect of a pension or other periodical payment made under a personal pension scheme where—

    (i) a bankruptcy order has been made in respect of the person in respect of whom the payment has been made or, in Scotland, the estate of that person is subject to sequestration or a judicial factor has been appointed on that person's estate under section 41 of the Solicitors (Scotland) Act 1980;

    (ii) the payment is made to the trustee in bankruptcy or any other person acting on behalf of the creditors; and

    (iii) the person referred to in (i) and [51 his partner (if any)] does not possess, or is not treated as possessing, any other income apart from that payment.]

[16(4A) Where the claimant lives in a residential care home or a nursing home, or is temporarily absent from such a home, any payment made by a person other than the claimant or a member of his family in respect of some or all of the cost of maintaining the claimant [51 or his partner in that home shall be treated as possessed by the claimant or his partner].]

(5) Where a claimant's earnings are not ascertainable at the time of the determination of the claim or of any [40 revision or supersession the Secretary of State] shall treat the claimant as possessing such earnings as

is reasonable in the circumstances of the case having regard to the number of hours worked and the earnings paid for comparable employment in the area.

[⁴³(5A) Where the amount of a subsistence allowance paid to a claimant in a benefit week is less than the amount of income-based jobseeker's allowance that person would have received in that benefit week had it been payable to him, less 50p, he shall be treated as possessing the amount which is equal to the amount of income-based jobseeker's allowance which he would have received in that week, less 50p.]

(6) [³³Subject to paragraph (6A),] where—

(a) a claimant performs a service for another person; and

(b) that person makes no payment of earnings or pays less than that paid for a comparable employment in the area,

the [³⁹Secretary of State] shall treat the claimant as possessing such earnings (if any) as is reasonable for that employment unless the claimant satisfies him that the means of that person are insufficient for him to pay or to pay more for the service [³³. . .].

[³³(6A) Paragraph (6) shall not apply—

(a) to a claimant who is engaged by a charitable or voluntary organisation or who is a volunteer if the [³⁸Secretary of State] is satisfied in any of those cases that it is reasonable for him to provide the service free of charge;

[⁴²(b) in a case where the service is performed in connection with—

(i) the claimant's participation in an employment or training programme in accordance with regulation 19(1)(q) of the Jobseeker's Allowance Regulations 1996 ,[⁴⁶, other than where the service is performed in connection with the claimant's participation in the Intensive Activity Period specified in regulation 75(1)(a)(iv) of those Regulations or in the Intensive Activity Period for 50 plus]; or

(ii) the claimant's or the claimant's partner's participation in an employment or training programme as defined in regulation 19(3) of those Regulations for which a training allowance is not payable or, where such an allowance is payable, it is payable for the sole purpose of reimbursement of travelling or meal expenses to the person participating in that programme; or]

(c) to a claimant who is engaged in work experience whilst participating in—

(i) the New Deal for Lone Parents; or

(ii) a scheme which has been approved by the Secretary of State as supporting the objectives of the New Deal for Lone Parents [⁵². . .].

(6B) [⁵². . .]

(6C) [⁵². . .]]

(6D) [*Omitted.*]

(7) Where a claimant is treated as possessing any income under any of [³¹ paragraphs (1) to (4A)] the foregoing provisions of this Part shall apply for the purposes of calculating the amount of that income as if a payment had actually been made and as if it were actual income which he does possess.

(8) Where a claimant is treated as possessing any earnings under paragraph (5) or (6) the foregoing provisions of this Part shall apply for the

purposes of calculating the amount of those earnings as if a payment had actually been made and as if they were actual earnings which he does possess except that paragraph (3) of regulation 36 (calculation of net earnings of employed earners) shall not apply and his net earnings shall be calculated by taking into account the earnings which he is treated as possessing, less—

(a) an amount in respect of income tax equivalent to an amount calculated by applying to those earnings [¹¹the lower rate or, as the case may be, the lower rate and the basic rate of tax] in the year of assessment less only the personal relief to which the claimant is entitled under sections 8(1) and (2) and 14(1)(a) and (2) of the Income and Corporation Taxes Act 1970 (personal relief) as is appropriate to his circumstances; but, if the period over which those earnings are to be taken into account is less than a year, [¹¹the earnings to which the lower rate [¹⁸. . .] of tax is to be applied and] the amount of the personal relief deductible under this paragraph shall be calculated on a pro rata basis;

[¹⁶(b) where the weekly amount of those earnings equals or exceeds the lower earnings limit, an amount representing primary Class 1 contributions under the Contributions and Benefits Act, calculated by applying to those earnings the initial and main primary percentages in accordance with sections 8(1) (a) and (b) of that Act; and]

(c) one-half of any sum payable by the claimant [¹⁷in respect of a pay period] by way of a contribution towards an occupational or personal pension scheme.

[¹⁰(8A) In paragraphs (3A) and (3B) the expression "resources" has the same meaning as in the Social Security Pensions Act 1975 by virtue of section 66(1) of that Act.]

[²(9) In paragraph (4) the expression "ordinary clothing or footwear" means clothing or footwear for normal daily use, but does not include school uniforms, or clothing or footwear used solely for sporting activities.]

AMENDMENTS

1. Income Support (General) Amendment Regulations 1988 (SI 1988/663), reg.19 (April 11, 1988).

2. Income Support (General) Amendment (No.4) Regulations 1988 (SI 1988/1445), reg.10 (September 12, 1988).

3. Income Support (General) Amendment (No.4) Regulations 1988 (SI 1988/1445), Sch.1, para.4 (April 10, 1989).

4. Income Support (General) Amendment Regulations 1989 (SI 1989/534), Sch.1, para.7 (October 9, 1989).

5. Income-related Benefits Schemes Amendment Regulations 1990 (SI 1990/127), reg.3 (January 31, 1990).

6. Income-related Benefits Schemes and Social Security (Recoupment) Amendment Regulations 1991 (SI 1991/1175), reg.5 (May 11, 1991).

7. Income Support (General) Amendment No. 4 Regulations 1991 (SI 1991/1559), reg.8 (October 7, 1991).

8. Income Support (General) Amendment Regulations 1992 (SI 1992/468), reg.4 (April 6, 1992).

9. Income-related Benefits Schemes and Social Security (Recoupment) Amendment Regulations 1992 (SI 1992/1101), reg.6 (May 7, 1992).

10. Income Support (General) Amendment (No.2) Regulations 1992 (SI 1992/1198), reg.2 (May 22, 1992).

2.316

11. Income-related Benefits Schemes (Miscellaneous Amendments) (No. 3) Regulations 1992 (SI 1992/2155), reg.18 (October 5, 1992).

12. Income-related Benefits Schemes (Miscellaneous Amendments) Regulations 1993 (SI 1993/315), Sch. para.2 (April 1, 1993).

13. Income-related Benefits Schemes (Miscellaneous Amendments) Regulations 1993 (SI 1993/315), reg.6 (April 12, 1993).

14. Social Security Benefits (Miscellaneous Amendments) (No. 2) Regulations 1993 (SI 1993/963), reg.2(3) (April 22, 1993).

15. Income-related Benefits Schemes and Social Security (Recoupement) Amendment Regulations 1993 (SI 1993/1249), reg.4(3) (May 14, 1993).

16. Income-related Benefits Schemes (Miscellaneous Amendments) Regulations 1994 (SI 1994/527), reg.4 (April 11, 1994).

17. Income-related Benefits Schemes (Miscellaneous Amendments) (No.5) Regulations 1994 (SI 1994/2139), reg.26 (October 3, 1994).

18. Income-related Benefits Schemes (Miscellaneous Amendments) (No.5) Regulations 1994 (SI 1994/2139), reg.29 (October 3, 1994).

19. Income-related Benefits Schemes (Miscellaneous Amendments) Regulations 1995 (SI 1995/516), reg.22 (April 10, 1995).

20. Income-related Benefits Schemes and Social Security (Claims and Payments) (Miscellaneous Amendments) Regulations 1995 (SI 1995/2303), reg.6(4) (October 2, 1995).

21. Income-related Benefits Schemes Amendment (No.2) Regulations 1995 (SI 1995/2792), reg.6(2) (October 28, 1995).

22. Income-related Benefits Schemes (Widows' etc. Pensions Disregards) Amendment Regulations 1995 (SI 1995/3282), reg.2 (December 20, 1995).

23. Income Support (General) (Jobseeker's Allowance Consequential Amendments) Regulations 1996 (SI 1996/206), reg.17 (October 7, 1996).

24. Income-related Benefits Schemes and Social Fund (Miscellaneous Amendments) Regulations 1996 (SI 1996/1944), reg.13 and Sch. para.3 (October 7, 1996).

25. Child Benefit, Child Support and Social Security (Miscellaneous Amendments) Regulations 1996 (SI 1996/1803), reg.37 (April 7, 1997).

26. Income-related Benefits and Jobseeker's Allowance (Amendment) (No.2) Regulations 1997 (SI 1997/2197), reg.5(4) (October 6, 1997).

27. Income-related Benefits and Jobseeker's Allowance (Amendment) (No.2) Regulations 1997 (SI 1997/2197), reg.7(3) and (4)(e) (October 6, 1997).

28. Social Security Amendment (New Deal) Regulations 1997 (SI 1997/ 2863), reg.17(1) and (2)(e) (January 5, 1998).

29. Social Security Amendment (New Deal) Regulations 1997 (SI 1997/ 2863), reg.17(3) and (4)(e) (January 5, 1998).

30. Social Security (Miscellaneous Amendments) Regulations 1998 (SI 1998/ 563), reg.6(1) and (2)(e) (April 6, 1998).

31. Social Security (Miscellaneous Amendments) Regulations 1998 (SI 1998/ 563), reg.13(1)(b) (April 6, 1998).

32. Social Security Amendment (New Deal) (No.2) Regulations 1998 (SI 1998/2117), reg.2(2) (September 24, 1998).

33. Income Support (General) Amendment Regulations 1999 (SI 1999/ 2554), reg.2(2)(a) and (b) (October 4, 1999).

34. Social Security and Child Support (Tax Credits) Consequential Amendments Regulations 1999 (SI 1999/2566), reg.2(1) and Sch.2, Pt I (October 5, 1999).

35. Social Security and Child Support (Tax Credits) Consequential Amendments Regulations 1999 (SI 1999/2566), reg.2(2) and Sch.2, Pt II (October 5, 1999).

36. Social Security Amendment (Notional Income and Capital) Regulations 1999 (SI 1999/2640), reg.2(1) (a) (November 15, 1999).

37. Social Security Amendment (Notional Income and Capital) Regulations 1999 (SI 1999/2640), reg.2(3) (c) (November 15, 1999).

38. Income Support (General) Amendment Regulations 1999 (SI 1999/ 2554), reg.2(2) (c) (November 29, 1999).

39. Social Security Act 1998 (Commencement No. 12 and Consequential and Transitional Provisions) Order 1999 (SI 1999/3178 (C.81)), art.3(5) and Sch.5, para.4(a) (November 29, 1999).

40. Social Security Act 1998 (Commencement No. 12 and Consequential and Transitional Provisions) Order 1999 (SI 1999/3178 (C.81)), art.3(5) and Sch.5, para.4(b) (November 29, 1999).

41. Income Support (General) and Jobseeker's Allowance Amendment (No. 2) Regulations 1999 (SI 1999/3324), reg.2 (January 7, 2000).

42. Social Security (Approved Work) Regulations 2000 (SI 2000/678), reg.2(2) (April 3, 2000).

43. Social Security Amendment (Employment Zones) Regulations 2000 (SI 2000/724), reg.3(1) (April 3, 2000).

44. Social Security (Miscellaneous Amendments) (No.3) Regulations 2001 (SI 2001/859), reg.3(2) (April 9, 2001).

45. Social Security Amendment (New Deal) Regulations 2001 (SI 2001/ 1029), reg.15(4) and (5)(c) (April 9, 2001).

46. Social Security Amendment (New Deal) Regulations 2001 (SI 2001/ 1029), reg.15(6) and (7)(c) (April 9, 2001).

47. Social Security (Miscellaneous Amendments) Regulations 2002 (SI 2002/ 841), reg.2(2) (April 8, 2002).

48. Social Security (Working Tax Credit and Child Tax Credit) (Consequential Amendments) Regulations 2003 (SI 2003/455), reg.2 and Sch.1, para.10(b) (April 7, 2003).

49. Social Security (Working Tax Credit and Child Tax Credit) (Consequential Amendments) Regulations 2003 (SI 2003/455), reg.2 and Sch.1, para.10(c) (April 7, 2003).

50. State Pension Credit (Consequential, Transitional and Miscellaneous Provisions) Regulations 2002 (SI 2002/3019), reg.29(2) (October 6, 2003).

51. Social Security (Working Tax Credit and Child Tax Credit) (Consequential Amendments) Regulations 2003 (SI 2003/455), reg.2 and Sch.1, para.10 (except sub-paras. (b) and (c)) (April 6, 2004, except in "transitional cases" and see further the note to reg.17 of the Income Support Regulations).

52. Social Security (Miscellaneous Amendments) (No. 3) Regulations 2004 (SI 2004/2308), reg.5(2) (October 4, 2004).

53. Social Security (Miscellaneous Amendments) Regulations 2005 (SI 2005/574), reg.2(5) (April 4, 2005).

54. Social Security (Miscellaneous Amendments) Regulations 2005 (SI 2005/574), reg.3(3)(a) (April 4, 2005).

55. Social Security (Miscellaneous Amendments) Regulations 2005 (SI 2005/ 574), reg.3(3)(b) (April 4, 2005).

DEFINITIONS

"the Act"—see reg.2(1).   2.317
"the Armed Forces and Reserve Forces Compensation Scheme"—*ibid.*
"benefit Acts"—*ibid.*
"child tax credit"—*ibid.*
"claimant"—see reg.2(1), reg.23(1).
"earnings"—see reg.2(1).
"family"—see 1986 Act, s.20(11) (SSCBA, s.137(1)).
"Intensive Activity Period for 50 plus"—see reg.2(1).
"lower rate"—*ibid.*
"occupational pension"—*ibid.*
"occupational pension scheme"—see Pension Schemes Act 1993, s.1.
"partner"—see reg.2(1).
"pay period"—*ibid.*
"payment"—*ibid.*

"pension fund holder"—*ibid.*
"personal pension scheme"—*ibid.*
"retirement annuity contract"—*ibid.*
"single claimant"—*ibid.*
"Social Security Act"—*ibid.*
"subsistence allowance"—*ibid.*
"the Eileen Trust"—*ibid.*
"the Fund"—*ibid.*
"the Independent Living Funds"—*ibid.*
"the Macfarlane (Special Payments) Trust"—*ibid.*
"the Macfarlane (Special Payments) (No.2) Trust"—*ibid.*
"the Macfarlane Trust"—*ibid.*
"training allowance"—*ibid.*
"voluntary organisation"—*ibid.*
"war widow's pension"—*ibid.*
"war widower's pension"—*ibid.*
"water charges"—*ibid.*
"working tax credit"—*ibid.*
"year of assessment"—*ibid.*

GENERAL NOTE

2.318   The structure is as follows:

(1) Deprivation of income.

(2)–(2C) Income available on application.

(3) Income due.

(3A) and (3B) Income from occupational pension schemes not paid.

(3C) Unpaid earnings due on termination of employment by reason of redundancy.

(4)–(4A) Third parties.

(5) Earnings not ascertainable.

(5A) Subsistence allowances paid to people participating in employment zone programmes.

(6)–(6C) Underpaid services.

(7) Calculation.

(8) Deductions.

(8A) and (9) Definitions.

Para. (1)
2.319   See notes to reg.51(1). A social security benefit is "income" which a claimant may be treated as still possessing under para.(1) (*CSIS 57/1992*). But a refusal to take up an offer of employment would not be a deprivation of income (see *CCS 7967/1995* decided under the child support legislation).

Note that the corresponding regulation under JSA (reg.105(1) of the JSA Regulations) applies if a person has deprived himself of income in order to secure entitlement to or increase the amount of JSA *or income support*. That avoids the question that might otherwise have arisen on a claimant transferring from income support to JSA as to whether a deprivation which had only been for the purposes of income support could be caught by reg.105(1). But para.(1) has not been similarly amended.

Paras (2) to (2C)
2.320   See notes to reg.51(2). There are some extra excluded categories here. The fact that a number of social security benefits are excluded suggests that social security benefits

generally are caught by the rule. It is not at all clear that such benefits "would become available upon application being made" if an award has not already been made. Stages of the gathering of evidence and a decision by a decision-maker are necessary before a claimant becomes entitled to payment. The words "would become" may be broad enough to cover that process, but that could only be the case where entitlement is straightforward. See *CIS 16271/1996*. The income available to be acquired by the claimant must be for his own benefit (and not, for example, rent under a sub-lease that had to be paid straight over to the head landlord) (*CIS 15052/1996*).

Note the exclusion of working tax credit (para.(2)(e)). Its various predecessors, working families' tax credit, disabled person's tax credit, family credit and disability working allowance had similarly been exempted. Child tax credit is also excluded (para.(2)(f)). Para.(2)(d) and para.(2D) (which exempted the additional amount of child benefit for a lone parent (if any)) was revoked with effect from April 6, 2004 (except in "transitional cases"—see the note to reg.17) as part of the amendments consequential on the removal of amounts for children and young persons from income support.

2.321

Under para.(2)(g) income available on request from a personal pension scheme or under a retirement annuity contract is exempt from the notional income rules until a person reaches 60. If after he becomes 60 the person fails to purchase an annuity with the money available from, and (if this is an option) does not draw the income from, such a pension fund, he will be assumed to have an amount of income determined in accordance with paras (2B) or (2C) (para.(2A)). No notional capital will be assumed (see reg.51(2)(d)) and any actual capital is disregarded (see Sch.10, para.23A). See also the amendments to regs 7 and 32 of the Claims and Payments Regulations. Note that para.(2A) only applies to existing claimants from the date their income support is reviewed following provision of the relevant information about their pension fund, or October 1, 1998, if that is sooner; for new claims it has effect from the date of the claim (reg.1(5) of the amending regulations).

For an illustration of the operation of the provisions in paras (2A)–(2C), see *CIS 4080/2001*. In *CIS 4501/2002* para.(2A) applied even though the claimant was not drawing on her pension because it was a pension mortgage which she needed to retain in order to pay her mortgage. The argument that para.(2A) contravenes Art.14, when read with Art.1 of Protocol 1, ECHR because it interferes with a claimant's ability to leave funds in a pension scheme to accumulate was rejected in *R(IS)12/04*. The Commissioner holds that even if Art.1 of Protocol 1 (or Art.8) was engaged for the purposes of Art.14 (which had not been established), the claimant had not shown a sufficient basis of comparison of his position with that of a woman for Art.14 to be invoked.

On para.(2)(i), see the notes to paras 44 and 45 of Sch.10.

The purpose of para.(2)(j) is to enable a claimant who is on a full-time rehabilitation course and so eligible for rehabilitation allowance from the DfEE to choose whether to claim the allowance or remain on income support. Rehabilitation courses are designed to assist people who have been incapable of work for a prolonged period to return to the labour market. If a person claims the allowance he is treated as capable of work and so would cease to be entitled to income support on the ground of incapacity for work (although he could claim JSA).

Para.(3)

To start with the exclusion in sub-para.(b), the reference to the revoked 1987 Payments Regulations has finally been updated, so that it is no longer necessary to rely on the Interpretation Act 1978 to read the references in sub-para.(b) as being to the 1988 Regulations. Sub-para.(b) excludes almost all social security benefits from the operation of this paragraph (although abandoning entitlement might be a deprivation of income under para.(1)). The other exclusions are of income due, but not paid, under discretionary trusts and trusts of personal injury compensation, entitlements under occupational pension schemes covered by paras (3A) and (3B) and earnings due but not paid where employment has ended due to redundancy (para.(3C)).

2.322

Outside these exclusions if income is due, *i.e.* legally due, it is to be treated as possessed by the claimant, and as income. The value of a debt would normally be a capital asset. Note that there is no discretion. An example would be of wages legally due but not paid but note the effect of para.(3C) where earnings are due but not paid on the termination of employment by reason of redundancy. However, the income that is due to be paid must be payable to the claimant for his own benefit (and not, for example, rent under a sub-lease that has to be paid straight over to the head landlord) (*CIS 15052/1996*).

See reg.70(2)(b) (urgent cases) for the possibility of payment when notional income is attributed under para.(3).

Paras (3A) and (3B)

2.323   Where a payment due from an occupational pension scheme is either not made or is not made in full because of a deficiency in the scheme's resources (defined in para.(8A)) the amount not paid does not fall within para.(3). The original form of the provisions applied only where the scheme stopped making payments to members of the scheme. The amendment puts beyond doubt that if payments to relatives or dependants of members are stopped, para.(3) does not apply.

Para. (3C)

2.324   For the definition of earnings see reg.35. The intention is that when the earnings are paid any benefit that would not have been paid if the earnings had been paid at the right time will be recovered (see SSAA, s.74 and Overpayments Regulations, reg.7).

Paras (4) and (4ZA)

2.325   See the notes to reg.51(3) and (3A).

In *R(FC) 4/98* (which concerned the similar provision in the Family Credit Regulations (reg.26(3)); see the 2002 edition of this volume for the Family Credit Regulations) the claimant's husband, from whom she was separated, was paying the mortgage payments on her home. They were joint owners of the property. The Commissioner held that only one half of the payments should be regarded as her notional income. Although the claimant and her husband were jointly and severally liable to the lender for the repayment of the mortgage, as between themselves they were each only responsible for repaying one half.

In *CJSA 3411/1998* the claimant was on a one year residential training course. He was in receipt of an adult education bursary, part of which was paid directly to the college. The Commissioner decides that no notional income was to be attributed to the claimant under reg.105(10)(a)(ii) of the JSA Regulations (the equivalent of para.(4).(a)(ii)). Of the listed items only "food" was covered by the payment to the college (the power supplies used in the college did not constitute "household fuel"). But this was not caught by reg.105(10)(a)(ii) as the food provided by the college was a "payment in kind". These words referred to any payment to, or income of, the claimant in kind as well as any payment to the third party in kind.

R(IS) 4/01 considers the effect of head (ia) inserted into para.(4)(a) with effect from November 15, 1999. In that case virtually all of the claimant's occupational pension was paid over to his former wife under an attachment of earnings order. The Commissioner points out that before November 15, 1999 the effect of head (ii) was that payments of occupational pensions to third parties would be treated as the claimant's income only to the extent that the payments had been used for the support of the claimant. After that date head (ia) removed that limitation but it was still necessary to consider if the payments were made "in respect of" the claimant. In the Commissioner's view, the context of all three provisions in para.(4)(a) indicated that the payments caught by head (ia) were restricted to those payments which were made for the support of the claimant so as to reduce the need for him to be supported by income support. The payments in this case did nothing to support the claimant. The consequence was that the payments did not count as the claimant's income either before or after November 15, 1999. *R(IS) 2/03* agrees as to the effect of the phrase "in respect of" in the opening part of para.(4)(a). The result in that case was that payments under the claimant's self-employed pension annuity that were being applied entirely for the benefit of his creditors did not count as notional income (see further the note to reg.23 as to whether such payments count as actual income). *R(IS) 4/02* further refers to these somewhat problematic provisions, pointing out that even if heads (i) and (ii) of para.(4ZA)(d) are satisfied, head (iii) will not be if the claimant (or any member of his family, from April 6, 2004 (except in "transitional cases"—see the note to reg.17) only his partner) has, or is treated as having, any other income.

Para. (4A)

Where the claimant lives in a residential care or nursing home, any payment made by a third party towards the cost of the claimant's or any partner's residential care or nursing home fees (with effect from April 6, 2004—the old form of this paragraph which also applied to the cost of any other member of the claimant's family's residential care or nursing home fees remains in existence for "transitional cases"—see the note to reg.17) counts as the claimant's income. However, under paras 15, 15A, 30, 30A and 66 of Sch.9 certain "top-up" payments to people in residential care and nursing homes are disregarded. "Person" in para.(4A) will include a local authority (Sch.1 to the Interpretation Act 1978).

2.326

Para. (5)

This is a very general discretion. The decision-maker (or tribunal) must have regard to the number of hours worked and the going rate locally for comparable employment in deciding what is reasonable, but is not prevented from considering all relevant circumstances (*R(SB) 25/83, R(SB) 15/86, R(SB) 6/88*).

2.327

Para. (5A)

This concerns claimants who are participating in an "employment zone" (defined in reg.2(1)) programme established under s.60 of the Welfare Reform and Pensions Act 1999 and being paid a "subsistence allowance" (reg.2(1)). The aim is that the subsistence allowance will be taken into account as income at the time it is due to be paid (see reg.105(11A) of the JSA Regulations for the income-based JSA provision). Note the corresponding disregard in para.71 of Sch.9 (para.68 of Sch.7 to the JSA Regulations) where the amount of a subsistence allowance exceeds the amount of income-based JSA that the person would have received. Any arrears of a subsistence allowance paid as a lump sum are treated as capital (reg.48(12); JSA Regulations, reg.110(11)) and ignored for 52 weeks from the date of receipt (para.59 of Sch.10; JSA Regulations, para.54 of Sch.8). Any discretionary payment from an "employment zone contractor" (defined in reg.2(1)) is also disregarded, but if the payment counts as capital only for 52 weeks from the date of receipt (see para.72 of Sch.9 and para.58 of Sch.10; JSA Regulations, para.69 of Sch.7 and para.53 of Sch.8).

2.328

Paras (6) to (6C)

These paragraphs are concerned with what is commonly referred to as the "notional earnings" rule. Para.(6) was restructured in October 1999 so that it only contains the basic rule while the specific exceptions are now in para.(6A). Para.(6A)(a) and (b)(i) are simply a reordering of the exceptions that were previously set out in para.(6) itself but paras (6A)(c) and (b)(ii) (the latter was added on April 3, 2000) are new.

2.329

Para. (6)

If the two conditions in sub-paras. (a) and (b) are met there is no discretion whether or not to apply the rule, unless the claimant comes within the proviso in para.(6) itself or one of the exceptions in para.(6A). However, the application of both the rule and the exception in para.(6A)(a) involve a number of value judgments (*e.g.* in relation to

2.330

"comparable employment", what earnings (if any) are "reasonable" to treat the claimant as possessing and whether it is "reasonable" for the claimant to provide the service free of charge if he is a volunteer or working for a charitable or voluntary body). See *CIS 2916/1997* in which the claimant was spending time in her mother's shop to keep her mother company following recent bereavements. The Commissioner says that whether this amounted to a "service" was a question of fact and degree, having regard, *inter alia*, to the effort and time put in (see *Clear v Smith* [1981] 1 W.L.R. 399) but in particular to the advantage derived by the mother. If the help given was substantial, the claimant was providing a service. However, when deciding whether it was reasonable for her to provide this service free of charge, it was necessary to consider whether what the claimant was doing amounted to "work".

In *R(SB) 3/92* (on the supplementary benefit predecessor of this provision) the Commissioner held that the rule applied where a mother provided services to her disabled adult son out of love and affection. On appeal in *Sharrock v Chief Adjudication Officer* (March 26, 1991; appendix to *R(SB) 3/92*) the Court of Appeal agreed that such relationships came within the old provision, providing that the service provided was of a character for which an employer would be prepared to pay. In *CIS 93/1991* the Commissioner holds that the principle of *Sharrock* applies to reg.42(6), which thus covers services provided within informal family relationships without any contract. Under supplementary benefit there was no proviso exempting volunteers etc. at the time. Now unpaid carers can be defined as volunteers (*CIS 93/1991*), so that there is a discretion not to apply the rule (see below). In *CIS 422/1992* (which again concerned Mrs Sharrock), the Commissioner held that she was a volunteer and that it was reasonable for her to provide her services free. The evidence was that her son made a substantial contribution to the household expenses. If she were to charge for her services the whole basis of the arrangement between them would have to change, which could have a deleterious effect on their relationship. (However, the part of the son's contribution that was not in respect of *his* living and accommodation costs could not be disregarded under para.18 of Sch.9.) It is difficult to see how in most cases it can be unreasonable for carers to look after a relative without payment. This is acknowledged by paras 26200-1 of the *Decision Makers Guide* which also lists factors to be considered in cases of doubt which are broadly in line with those suggested in *CIS 93/1991* (see below).

Under sub-para.(b) the "employer" must either make no payment or pay less than is paid for comparable employment in the area. Since the amount of notional earnings is set according to what is reasonable for that comparable employment, it seems that some comparable employment must exist in all cases.

2.331   Some of the points made in *R(SB) 13/86* on the previous supplementary benefit provision also apply to para.(6). It must be necessary to identify the employer for whom the services were provided. "Person" includes a company or other corporate employer (Interpretation Act 1978). Thus in *R(IS) 5/95* where the claimant, who was an employee and director of a small company, was working unpaid because of the company's financial difficulties, it was necessary to consider whether para.(6) applied. See also *CCS 4912/1998* which holds that a similar child support rule applied where a person provided his services through a personal service company that he had set up himself and which was paying him a very low hourly rate.

Particulars of the services provided and any payments made must be ascertained. See *CIS 701/1994* on the factors to consider when assessing comparable employment (the claimant in that case was again a carer) and the amount of notional earnings.

It was suggested in earlier editions (of "*Mesher*") that although payments of earnings in kind are disregarded in the calculation of income (reg.35(2)(a) and Sch.9, para.21), payments in kind should be considered in testing whether a claimant is paid at all or is paid less than the rate for comparable employment. However, *CIS 11482/1995* decides that this is not correct. The claimant's wife worked as a shop assistant for 12 hours a week for which she was paid £5 in cash and took goods to the value of £36 from the shelves. The Commissioner, after deciding that earnings in para.(6) meant earnings as defined in regs 35 or 37 (see reg.2(1)), holds that since earnings in kind were ignored when considering whether any payment at all of earnings had been made, this must also be the case when deciding whether a person was paid less than the rate for comparable employment. Thus in considering whether the claimant's wife was paid less than the rate for comparable employment, the £36 that she received in goods was to be left out of account. But to avoid unfair double counting it was necessary to deduct any cash payments in the calculation of her notional earnings under para.(6). This was permissible because para.(6) allowed the amount of earnings which would be paid for comparable employment to be adjusted where circumstances made it reasonable. However, it would not be "reasonable" to deduct the earnings in kind because that did not involve a double counting as the actual value of the earnings in kind was disregarded.

The claimant can then escape if he proves (on the balance of probabilities) that the person to whom he has provided the services has insufficient means to pay more. This could well cause difficulties for claimants reluctant to make embarrassing enquiries. But there is an interest in preventing employers from economising at the expense of the income support budget. The Court of Appeal in *Sharrock v Chief Adjudication Officer* suggests that "means" refers simply to monetary resources and is a matter of broad judgment. No automatic test of ignoring certain benefits or regarding an income above income support level as available should be adopted. In *CIS 93/1991*, the claimant looked after his elderly and severely disabled father, but declined to give any information about the father's means. The Commissioner confirms that in such circumstances the basic rule of para.(6) must be applied, but subject to the exception for volunteers.

Paras (6A)–(6C)

Para.(6A) specifies four situations in which the rule in para.(6) will not apply. Firstly, sub-para.(a) allows volunteers or those engaged by charities or voluntary organisations not to have any notional earnings if it is reasonable for them to provide their services free of charge. Volunteer in this context means someone who without any legal obligation performs a service for another person without expectation of payment (*R(IS) 12/92*). Thus, it would seem that if any payment is made to the claimant, the proviso cannot apply. The Commissioner in *CIS 93/1991* holds that the means of the "employer" is a factor here, but other factors are relevant too. It may be more reasonable for close relatives to provide services free of charge than for others to do so. The basis on which the arrangement was made, the expectations of the family members concerned, the housing arrangements and the reason why the carer gave up any paid work might need to be considered. Anomalies like the loss of invalid care allowance (now carer's allowance) if the carer accepted payment should be considered. So should the question of what alternatives would be available if the relative ceased to provide the care. If there was no realistic alternative to the relative continuing to provide the care and the person would not agree to make any payment, that would point to it being reasonable for the claimant to provide the services free of charge (*CIS 701/1994*). In *CIS 93/1991* the tribunal went wrong in not properly considering their discretion under the exception and concentrating on the legitimate inference that the "employer" could afford to pay the going rate. In *CIS 701/1994* the Commissioner expresses the view that if a person had substantial resources that were genuinely surplus to requirements, that would be different from the situation, for example, of a person saving towards the costs of future residential care. It should be noted that the test is whether it is reasonable for the person to provide his services free of charge, rather than whether it is reasonable for payment not to be made for the service, although this is a factor (*CIS 147/1993*). If the claimant was receiving training while, or by doing, the work, this may be relevant (*R(IS) 12/92*).

In *CIS 93/1991* the Commissioner points out that the aim of the rule is clearly to prevent an employer who has the means to pay the going rate profiting at the expense of the public purse. If, therefore, a claimant volunteers to undertake painting work (as in *CIS 147/1993*), which otherwise would have remained undone, there is no

2.332

element of financial profit to the employer in the claimant doing the work. If, however, the employer would have paid the claimant if he had not said he did not wish to be paid, it may be concluded that it was not reasonable for the claimant to offer his services free of charge.

2.333   Secondly, para.(6A)(b)(i) covers the situation where a person is on an employment programme or training scheme for three or more days in any benefit week and is not paid a training allowance. This may occur, for example, if the person is on a "taster" of a New Deal option (see further the notes to reg.19(1)(q) of the JSA Regulations). Sub-para.(b)(i) ensures that a person who is on such a programme or scheme will not be treated as possessing notional earnings by virtue of providing a service for which he is not being paid. (For income support purposes this provision will usually only be relevant to the claimant's partner rather than the claimant himself). The third exception in para.(6A)(b)(ii) prevents the attribution of notional earnings where the claimant, or his partner, is taking part in an employment or training programme of any length, for which no training allowance, or one that only reimburses travelling or meal expenses, is payable. An example would be a work trial or work placement under the New Deal for 50 plus or the New Deal for Disabled People.

The fourth exclusion from the notional earnings rule applies to lone parents who are on work experience while participating in the New Deal for Lone Parents or a related pilot scheme (para.(6A)(c)). The exemption originally only lasted for up to 150 hours, or six months, work with the same employer, but the October 2004 amendments mean that this exemption now applies without limit.

Paras (7) to (8)

2.334   If notional income counts it is to be calculated as though it was actual income. Notional deductions are to be made from earnings to get a net figure.

Para.(9)

2.335   The examples given in paras 28671–2 of the *Decision Makers Guide* suggest that football boots are not for "normal daily use", and that when applying the test of "for normal daily use" the wide needs of all claimants should be considered.

Notional earnings of seasonal workers

2.336   **43.**[¹. . .].

AMENDMENT

1. Income Support (General) Amendment No. 2 Regulations 1989 (SI 1989/1323), reg.14 (October 9, 1989).

GENERAL NOTE

2.337   When the special rules for seasonal workers were removed from the unemployment benefit scheme this was consequently also done for income support.

Modifications in respect of children and young persons

2.338   **44.**[¹. . .]

AMENDMENT

2.339   1. Social Security (Working Tax Credit and Child Tax Credit) (Consequential Amendments) Regulations 2003 (SI 2003/455), reg.2 and Sch.1, para.11 (April 6, 2004, except in "transitional cases" and see further the note to reg.17 of the Income Support Regulations).

GENERAL NOTE

This regulation contained the special rules for treatment of the income of a child   **2.339.1**
or young person who was a member of the claimant's family (see the 2003 edition
of this Volume for this regulation and the notes to it). However, with effect from
April 6, 2004 (except in "transitional cases"—see the note to reg.17) amounts for
children and young persons have been removed from the income support scheme;
financial assistance to help with the cost of bringing up a child or young person is
now to be provided through the child tax credit system, see Volume IV of this series.
As a consequence, the income of a child or young person is no longer aggregated
with the claimant's (see the new form of reg.23 and the notes to that regulation) and
therefore most of the modifications made by reg.44 are no longer needed (but see
below). Regulation 44 does however remain in force for "transitional cases"—see the
note to reg.17.

For income support claimants who had an award of child tax credit before April
6, 2004 see reg.7 of the Social Security (Working Tax Credit and Child Tax Credit)
(Consequential Amendments) Regulations 2003 (SI 2003/455) (as amended) on
p.686 and the notes to that regulation.

Paragraph (2) of reg.44 was concerned with payments to residential schools for a
child's or young person's maintenance. Since there is a continuing need to make provision for such payments, a new disregard (see para.25A of Sch.9) has been introduced with effect from April 6, 2004 (except in "transitional cases"—see the note to
reg.17). This provides that payments to a boarding school for the maintenance of a
child or young person who is a member of the claimant's family made by a third party
or out of funds provided by a third party are ignored in full.

Chapter VI

Capital

Capital limit

[¹**45.** For the purposes of section 134(1) of the Contributions and   **2.340**
Benefits Act as it applies to income support (no entitlement to benefit if
capital exceeds prescribed amount)—

  (a) except where paragraph [²(aa) or] (b) applies, the prescribed amount
      is £8,000;
[²(aa) where the circumstances prescribed in regulation 53(1ZA) apply in
      the claimant's case, the prescribed amount is £12,000;]
  (b) where the circumstances prescribed in regulation 53(1B) apply in the
      claimant's case, the prescribed amount is £16,000.]

AMENDMENTS

1. Income-related Benefits Schemes (Miscellaneous Amendments) Regulations
1996 (SI 1996/462), reg.12(1) (April 8, 1996).

2. Social Security Amendment (Capital Limits and Earnings Disregards)
Regulations 2000 (SI 2000/2545), reg.2(1)(b) (April 9, 2001).

DEFINITION

"claimant"—see reg.2(1), reg.23(1).

2.341 Under s.134(1) of the Contributions and Benefits Act there is no entitlement to income support if the claimant's capital exceeds the prescribed amount. £8,000 has been prescribed since April 9, 1990 and this remains the same for most claimants. However, from April 8, 1996 the upper limit was raised to £16,000 for claimants living permanently in residential care or nursing homes, residential accommodation or Polish resettlement homes (para.(b)). In addition, the tariff income rule only applies to capital over £10,000 for these claimants. See the notes to reg.53. The capital limit was also raised to £12,000 from April 9, 2001 where the claimant or any partner is aged 60 or over. Note that as a consequence of the start of the state pension credit scheme on October 6, 2003 this now only applies if the claimant's partner is aged 60 or over; if the claimant has reached the qualifying age for state pension credit (defined in s.137(1) of the Contributions and Benefits Act—the effect of that definition is that the qualifying age is 60 for both men and women until April 2010 after which it will increase by stages to 65 in line with the increase in pensionable age for a woman) he will not be entitled to income support (s. 124(1)(aa) of the 1992 Act). If the capital limit is £12,000, the tariff income rule applies to capital over £6,000 (see reg.53(1ZA) and the notes to reg.53). The capital of a claimant's partner is aggregated with the claimant's (reg.23(1)), but not that of children or young persons (reg.23(2), replacing the rule formerly in reg.47 with effect from April 6, 2004, except for "transitional cases"—see the note to reg.17).

In *CIS 127/1993* the Commissioner raises the question of where the burden of proof lies when considering whether the capital rule is satisfied. The Tribunal of Commissioners in *CIS 417/1992* (reported as part of *R(IS) 26/95*) treat this as part of what the claimant has to prove in showing entitlement to income support. However, the argument that the capital rule operates as an exception to the conditions of basic entitlement does not appear to have been put. See sidenote to s.134 which is entitled "Exclusions from benefit". But once it has been shown that the claimant possesses an item of capital, it is for him to prove that one of the disregards in Sch.10 applies (*CIS 240/1992*). Similarly, once it has been established that the claimant is the legal owner of a property, the burden is on her to show that she does not have any or all of the beneficial interest (*CIS 30/1993*).

Calculation of capital

2.342 **46.**—(1) For the purposes of Part II of the Act [SSCBA, Part VII] as it applies to income support, the capital of a claimant to be taken into account shall, subject to paragraph (2), be the whole of his capital calculated in accordance with this Part and any income treated as capital under [¹regulation 48 (income treated as capital)].

(2) There shall be disregarded from the calculation of a claimant's capital under paragraph (1) any capital, where applicable, specified in Schedule 10.

1. Income Support (General) Amendment No. 5 Regulations 1988 (SI 1988/2022), reg.10 (December 12, 1988).

"the Act"—see reg.2(1).
"claimant"—*ibid.*, reg.23(1).

2.343 All the claimant's (and partner's) capital, both actual and notional, counts towards the £8,000 (£12,000: see reg.45(aa) or £16,000: see reg.45(b)) limit, subject to the disregards in Sch.10. In *R(IS) 15/96* the Commissioner considers that claimants should be advised by the Benefits Agency of the existence of the disregards so that they can take advantage of them (the claimant had received a criminal injuries compensation award so that the trust disregard in para.12 of Sch.10 could have been relevant).

There is a good deal of law on actual capital.

The first condition is of course that the capital resource is the claimant's or his partner's. This is not as simple as it sounds. In *CIS 634/1992* the claimant was made bankrupt on November 29, 1990. However, his trustee in bankruptcy was not appointed until April 1991. Between November 29 and December 28, 1990, when he claimed income support the claimant divested himself of most of his capital. Under the Insolvency Act 1986 (subject to certain exceptions) a bankrupt's property does not vest in his trustee in bankruptcy on the making of a bankruptcy order, but only when the trustee is appointed. The appointment does not have retrospective effect. It is held that since he had failed to give a satisfactory account of how he had disposed of his capital he was to be treated as still possessing it (*R(SB) 38/85* referred to in the notes to reg.51(1)). Thus the claimant was not entitled to income support prior to the appointment of the trustee in bankruptcy because until then he possessed actual capital over the income support limit.

See also *CIS 1189/2003* which concerned a claimant who was the sole residuary beneficiary under her mother's will. The estate had remained unadministered for several years so that her mother's property had not actually vested in the claimant. However, the property counted as the claimant's actual capital for the purposes of income support since, subject only to the formalities needed to perfect her title, she had for all practical purposes an entitlement in respect of the property that was equivalent to full beneficial ownership.

R(IS) 9/04 confirms that assets being administered on a patient's behalf either at the Court of Protection or by his or her receiver remain the patient's assets which have to be valued at their current market value (see reg.49) (following *CIS 7127/1995*). Such assets are held under a "bare trust" with the entire beneficial ownership remaining with the patient. The fact that the Court had discretionary powers of *control* over the management of the patient's property for his or her benefit did not mean that the patient's beneficial *ownership* had ceased.

Note that money that a claimant is under a "certain and immediate liability" to repay will not count as his capital (see *Chief Adjudication Officer v Leeves*, November 6, 1998, CA, reported as *R(IS) 5/99*, (affirmed in *Morrell v Secretary of State for Work and Pensions* [2003] EWCA Civ 526, reported as *R(IS) 6/03*), below).

Beneficial ownership
The mere fact that an asset or a bank or building society account is in the claimant's name alone does not mean that it belongs to the claimant. It is the "beneficial ownership" which matters. The claimant may hold the asset under a trust which means that he cannot simply treat the asset as his, but must treat it as if it belonged to the beneficiary or beneficiaries under the trust. It is they who are "beneficially entitled." A trustee may also be a beneficiary, in which case the rule in reg.52 may come into play, or may have no beneficial interest at all.

2.344

These issues often arise in the context of attributing the beneficial ownership of former matrimonial assets. One example where the first situation applied is *R(IS) 2/93*. The claimant had a building society account in her sole name, which she had had since before her marriage. Her husband deposited the bulk of the money in it, including his salary. On their separation, the AO and the SSAT treated the entire amount in the account as part of the claimant's capital. The Commissioner holds that she was not solely beneficially entitled to the money so that reg.52 had to operate. There is helpful guidance on the limited circumstances in which the "presumption of advancement" (*i.e.* that when a husband puts an asset into his wife's name he intends to make an outright gift of it) will operate in modern circumstances. And see *CIS 982/2002* (which concerns the valuation of a share in a frozen joint bank account) in the notes to reg.52. Note also *R(IS) 10/99* below. In *CIS 553/1991* where a house was in the husband's sole name it is held that its valuation should take into account the wife's statutory right of occupation under the Matrimonial Homes Act 1967. See also *R(IS) 1/97*, in the note to para.5 of Sch.10. In most cases of spouses, in whoever's name the asset is, there will be some degree of joint ownership. But if an asset is in the sole name of one, arguably the other should not be treated as having a half share under reg.52 until it has been established that s/he does own at least part of it. On this see *R(IS) 1/03* which holds that a person's right to seek a lump sum payment or property transfer order under the Matrimonial Causes Act 1973 is not a capital asset. Moreover, *CIS 984/2002* should also be noted in this context. This holds that money held by the claimant's solicitor pending quantification of the statutory charge to the Legal Services Commission under s.10(7) of the Access to Justice Act 1999 was not part of the claimant's capital. Until that quantification had been carried out, it was not possible to identify any particular amount as the claimant's capital. Another way of looking at it was to treat the statutory charge as an incumbrance for the purpose of reg.49(a)(ii) (see *CIS 368/1993*). Nor was any part of the money available to the claimant on application for the purposes of reg.51(2).

2.345   There have been several examples in other contexts of the second situation, where the claimant has no beneficial interest at all. In *R(SB) 49/83* the claimant had bought a house, but said that this was on behalf of his son, who was paying off the loan. The Commissioner held that if this could be established, the claimant would hold the house on a resulting trust for his son. It would not then be part of his capital resources. See *CSB 200/1985* (applying *Cowcher v Cowcher* [1972] 1 W.L.R. 425) for the position where another person provides part of the money. In *R(SB) 53/83* the claimant's son had paid him £2,850 to be used for a holiday in India. The claimant died without taking the holiday or declaring the existence of the money to the DHSS. The Commissioner, applying the principle of *Barclays Bank Ltd v Quistclose Investments Ltd* [1970] A.C. 567, held that there was a trust to return the money to the son if the primary purpose of the loan was not carried out. Since the Commissioner held that there had been no overpayment while the claimant was alive, this must mean that the claimant held the money on trust to use it for the specified purpose or to return it. It was not part of the claimant's resources. This is an important decision, which overtakes some of the reasoning of *R(SB) 14/81* (see below). The actual decision in *R(SB) 53/83* was reversed (by consent) by the Court of Appeal, because the Commissioner had differed from the appeal tribunal on a point of pure fact. *R(SB) 1/85* holds that this does not affect its authority on the issue of principle. In *R(SB) 1/85*, the claimant's mother-in-law had some years previously provided the money for the purchase of the lease of a holiday chalet for the use of the claimant's mentally handicapped son, Keith. The lease was in the claimant's name and its current value was probably about £5,000. The AO's initial statement of the facts was that the mother-in-law had bought the chalet in the claimant's name. The Commissioner holds that this would give rise to a presumption of a resulting trust in her favour, so that the claimant would have no beneficial interest in the chalet—nothing he could sell. The presumption could be rebutted if in fact the mother-in-law had made an outright gift to the claimant, or to Keith. In the second case the claimant again would have no beneficial interest. In the first, he would be caught, for even if he had said that he intended to use the chalet purely for Keith, he had not made the necessary written declaration of trust (Law of Property Act 1925, s.53). Another possibility was that the mother-in-law had made a gift to the claimant subject to an express (but unwritten) trust in favour of Keith, when again the claimant clearly would not be the beneficial owner. This is a very instructive decision, which will give valuable guidance in sorting out many family-type arrangements. *CIS 30/1993* also sets out helpful guidance on the points to consider when deciding whether a resulting trust has been created. The claimant had purchased her flat with the proceeds of sale of her previous home. She had bought that home as a sitting tenant with the aid of a loan, the repayments on which had been made by her children. The Commissioner states that the children's contributions indicated a resulting trust in their favour in the beneficial interest in the house in proportion to their and the claimant's contributions to the purchase price. If the claimant had, as a sitting tenant, received a discount on the price, that would be treated as a contribution. The resulting trust would transfer to the flat on the sale of the house. However, the presumption of a resulting trust created by the children's contributions could be rebutted by proof of the purchasers' true intentions, *e.g.* that an outright gift was, or different beneficial interests under the trust than those created by the presumption were, intended.

The *Quistclose* principle was re-affirmed in *R(SB) 12/86*, where £2,000 was lent to the claimant on condition that she did not touch the capital amount, but only took the interest, and repaid the £2,000 on demand. The £2,000 was not part of her capital, never having been at her disposal. The Commissioner in *CSB 975/1985* was prepared to apply the principle to a loan on mortgage from a Building Society for property renovation. But it would have to be found that the loan was made for no other purpose and was to be recoverable by the Building Society if for any reason the renovations could not be carried out. However, *CIS 5185/1995* decides that it does not apply to a student grant which the claimant became liable to repay to the education authority when he left his course early (for the treatment of student grants in these circumstances now see reg.29(2B) but note the argument discussed in the notes to reg.29(2B) as to when that provision applies). The Commissioner holds that the grant was income that remained available to him until it was repaid to the authority (see *R. v Bolton SBAT Ex parte Fordham* [1981] 1 All E.R. 50 and *CSB 1408/1988*). It could not be disregarded under the *Quistclose* principle because the education authority retained no beneficial interest in the grant. The authority merely reserved the right to demand repayment of a sum calculated according to the unexpired balance of the relevant term when the person ceased to be a student. But in *CIS 12263/1996* the Commissioner took the view that as soon as a student had abandoned his course and an obligation to repay the balance of his grant to the education authority arose, he held the money on constructive trust for the authority. The Commissioner in *CIS 12263/1996* considered that the *Quistclose* case was concerned with a "purpose trust" (*i.e.* where a grant or loan was impressed with a particular purpose from the beginning), whereas in this situation a constructive trust had arisen because the grant been paid on the condition that the claimant continued to be a student. An appeal was brought against this decision by the AO (*Chief Adjudication Officer v Leeves*, November 6, 1998, CA, reported as *R(IS) 5/99*). It was conceded on behalf of the claimant that there was no constructive trust in these circumstances, since no proprietary right had been retained by the education authority, nor had any fiduciary obligation been created. However, the Court of Appeal held that money that the claimant was under a "certain and immediate liability" to repay did not amount to income. Thus once the claimant had received a request for immediate repayment of a specified sum from the local education authority the grant ceased to count as his income (although it fell to be treated as such until that time, even though he had abandoned his course). The Court distinguished its decision in *Fordham* as the liability to repay in that case had been uncertain. The same principle will apply to capital that the claimant is under an obligation to repay. Once the liability to repay has "crystallised" (*Leeves*), it will cease to be part of the claimant's resources.

2.346

The dangers and difficulties of *Quistclose* are further pointed out in *CSB 1137/ 1985*, particularly where family transactions are concerned. If a gift or loan is made with a particular motive, the whole sum becomes part of the recipient's resources. The intention to impose a trust must appear expressly (as in *R(SB) 12/86*) or by implication from the circumstances. Perhaps it is easier to prove (*e.g.* by contemporaneous documents) such an intention in business transactions. Often such evidence will be lacking in domestic situations, but the issue is one of proof, as is shown in *R(IS) 1/90*. There, the claimant established a Building Society account in his own name which was to be used solely to finance his son's medical education. He executed no documents about the account. It was argued that there was sufficient evidence of a declaration of trust over the account, but the Commissioner holds that the claimant had not unequivocally

2.347

renounced his beneficial interest in the sum in the account. Although he had ear-marked the money for the son's education, the situation was like an uncompleted gift and there was insufficient evidence of a declaration of trust. There is a thin line between an outright gift or loan, and one subject to an implied trust. In *R(IS) 5/98* where the claimant had transferred her flat to her daughter partly on the condition that her daughter looked after her, it is held that the gift failed when this condition was not fulfilled and the daughter held the flat on trust for her mother. An appeal against this decision was dismissed by the Court of Appeal (*Ellis v Chief Adjudication Officer, The Times*, May 14, 1997, also reported as part of *R(IS) 5/98*). The claimant had argued that the condition was void for uncertainty but this was rejected by the Court.

The furthest extension so far of the *Quistclose* principle is in *CFC 21/1989*. The claimant's father paid her each month an amount to meet her mortgage obligation to a building society. The Commissioner accepts that the money was impressed with a trust that it should be used only for that purpose and did not form part of her capital. The extension is that the purpose was to meet expenditure on an item which could be covered by income support.

2.348 For the position under Scots law see *R(IS) 10/99*. The claimant agreed that he would pay his former wife (from whom he was separated) £22,250, representing a share of his pension. When he claimed income support, the claimant had £15,500 in his bank account which he said he was holding for his wife. The Commissioner decides that the £15,500 was not subject to a trust. This was because there had been no delivery of the subject of the trust, nor any satisfactory equivalent to delivery, "so as to achieve irrevocable divestiture of the truster and investiture of the trustee in the trust estate", as required by Scots law (see *Clark Taylor & Co. Ltd v Quality Site Development (Edinburgh) Ltd.* 1981 S.C. 11). There was no separate bank account and had been no clear indication to the claimant's wife that the money was held on trust for her. In addition, the Requirements of Writing (Scotland) Act 1995 required the trust to be proved in writing and the signature of the grantor. This had not been done here. The Commissioner also decided that the money could not be regarded as matrimonial property for the purposes of the Family Law (Scotland) Act 1995, since the claimant's severance package (which was being used to pay his wife) only came into existence after the parties ceased to cohabit and thus did not satisfy the definition of matrimonial property in s.10(3) and (4) of the Act. It was also clear that the claimant was not holding the sum as his wife's agent as there was no evidence of her consent to this. Finally, there was no "incumbrance" within the meaning of reg.49(a)(ii) preventing the claimant disposing of the money. The consequence was that the £15,500 counted as the claimant's capital. (*Note*: as (1999) 6 *J.S.S.L.* D41 points out, the outcome of this case is in fact unlikely to have been different if the principles of trust law in England and Wales had been applied. However, capital that a claimant is under a "certain and immediate liability" to repay will not count as his capital (see *Leeves* above).)

See also the doctrine of secret trusts, under which a person who receives property under an intestacy when the deceased refrained from making a will in reliance on that person's promise to carry out his expressed intentions, holds the property on trust to carry out those intentions (*CSB 989/1985*).

Another example of the legal owner having nothing to sell is *R(SB) 23/85*. The claimant's wife in a home-made and legally ineffective deed of gift purported to give an uninhabitable property to her son. He, as intended, carried out the works to make it habitable. The Commissioner holds that although a court will not normally "complete" such an "uncompleted gift" in favour of someone who has not given valuable consideration, one of the situations in which a transfer of the property will be ordered is where the intended recipient is induced to believe that he has or will have an interest in the property and acts on that belief to his detriment. Thus in the meantime the claimant's wife held the property merely as a "bare trustee" and could not lawfully transfer it to anyone but the son. There is discussion of what kind of action might give rise to the right to complete the gift in *R(SB) 7/87*. See also *CIS 807/1991* on proprietary estoppel.

Choses in action

There is also a remarkable range of interests in property which do have a present 2.349
market value and so are actual capital resources. These are usually things in action
(or choses in action), rights to sue for something. Debts, even where they are not
due to be paid for some time, are things in action which can be sold. A good example
is *R(SB) 31/83* where the claimant in selling a house allowed the purchaser a mortgage of £4,000, to be redeemed in six months. The debt conferred a right to sue and
had to be valued at what could be obtained on the open market. In *CJSA 204/2002*
the claimant had lent her son £8,500 for the deposit on a flat. The Commissioner
holds that the legal debt owed by the son to the claimant had to be valued in order
to decide whether the claimant had actual capital in excess of £8,000. The terms of
the loan, including the rate of any interest and whether there was any security for the
loan, as well as the terms of repayment, were clearly relevant to this valuation. Once
the value of the loan had been determined, the question of deprivation of capital then
had to be considered. To the extent that the value of the loan was less than £8,500,
to that extent the claimant had deprived herself of capital. However, on the facts the
Commissioner found that the claimant had not deprived herself of the capital for the
purpose of securing entitlement to, or increasing the amount of, jobseeker's
allowance (see further the note to reg.51(1)).

Similarly, a life interest in a trust fund is a present asset which can be sold and has
a market value (*R(SB) 2/84, R(SB) 43/84, R(SB) 15/86* and *R(SB) 13/87*). The practical effect is reversed by para.13 of Sch.10. An action for breach of fiduciary duty
against an attorney appointed under the Enduring Powers of Attorney Act 1985 who
had used the claimant's capital to repay her own debts also constitutes actual capital;
so too would a claim against the attorney for misapplication of capital on the ground
that she had made gifts outside the circumstances sanctioned by s.3(5) of the 1985
Act (this allows an attorney to make gifts (to herself or others) "provided that the
value of each such gift is not unreasonable having regard to all the circumstances and
in particular the size of the donor's estate") (*R(IS) 17/98*).

Bank or building society accounts

A more direct way of holding capital is in a bank or building society account. In 2.350
CSB 296/1985 the claimant's solicitor received £12,000 damages on behalf of the
claimant and placed the money on deposit, presumably in the solicitor's client
account. The Commissioner held that the £12,000 was an actual resource of the
claimant, on the basis that there was no difference in principle between monies being
held by a solicitor on behalf of a client and monies held by a bank or building society
on behalf of a customer. This decision was upheld by the Court of Appeal in *Thomas
v Chief Adjudication Officer* (reported as *R(SB) 17/87*). Russell L.J. says "the possession of this money by the solicitors as the agent for the claimant was, in every sense
of the term, possession by the claimant." However, note *CIS 984/2002* which holds
that money held by the claimant's solicitor pending quantification of the statutory
charge to the Legal Services Commission under s.10(7) of the Access to Justice Act
1999 was not part of the claimant's capital. Until that quantification had been
carried out, it was not possible to identify any particular amount as the claimant's
capital. Another way of looking at it was to treat the statutory charge as an incumbrance for the purpose of reg.49(a)(ii) (see *CIS 368/1993*). Nor was any part of the
money available to the claimant on application for the purposes of reg.51(2).

The approach taken in *Thomas* seems to involve valuing the amount of money
directly, not as a technical chose in action. However, the importance of the legal relationship between a bank and a customer being one of debtor and creditor was
revealed in *CSB 598/1987*. A large cheque was paid into the claimant's wife's bank
account on October 9, 1987. The amount was credited to her account on that date,
but the cheque was not cleared until October 15. The bank's paying-in slips reserved
the bank's right to "postpone payment of cheques drawn against uncleared effects
which may have been credited to the account." The effect was that the bank did not
accept the relationship of debtor and creditor on the mere paying in of a cheque.

Thus the amount did not become part of the claimant's actual resources until October 15. A person who deliberately refrains from paying in a cheque may be fixed with notional capital under reg.51.

CIS/255/2005 concerned the effect on capital of the issue of a cheque. The Commissioner holds that the claimant's capital was reduced from the date that the cheque was issued (this would not apply if the cheque was postdated). After that time she could not honestly withdraw money from her bank account so as to leave insufficient funds to meet the cheque.

In *R(IS) 15/96* the Commissioner confirms that money in a building society or bank (or solicitor's client) account is an actual resource in the form of a chose in action. It is not, as the SSAT had decided, held in trust. If the money is in an account from which it can be withdrawn at any time, its value is the credit balance (less any penalties for early withdrawal, etc.). But if the money cannot be withdrawn for a specified term the value will be less (although the notional capital rules may come into play in respect of the difference in value: *CIS 494/1990;* see also *CIS 2208/2003*).

Interests in trusts

2.351   The nature of interests in capital under trusts gives rise to several problems. It is clear that a person may have an absolute vested interest under a trust, although payment is deferred, *e.g.* until the age of 21. This was the case in *R(SB) 26/86*, where the resource was held to be the person's share of the fund. However, an interest may be contingent on reaching a particular age. This appears to have been one of the assumptions on which the Court of Appeal decided the unsatisfactory case of *Peters v Chief Adjudication Officer, R(SB) 3/89*. It was conceded that sums were held on trust to be paid over to each of three sisters on attaining the age of 18, with the power to advance up to 50 per cent. of the capital before then. In the end, the Court of Appeal accepted the valuation of half of the full value for each sister under 18. The precise finding may depend on the supplementary benefit rule on discretionary trusts, which has not been translated into the income support legislation. But some statements about the general market value of such interests are made. May L. J. says "in an appropriate market a discretionary entitlement of up to 50 per cent. now and at least 50 per cent. in, say, six months in a given case, or three to four years in another, could well be said to have a value greater than 50 per cent. of the capital value of the trust." This clearly supports the view that a contingent interest has a market value and so is actual capital. See also *CTC 4713/2002* which concerned a similar trust in favour of the claimant's son to that in *Peters* (although in this case the trustees had power to advance the whole of the fund). The Commissioner notes that in *Peters* the Court of Appeal had accepted the valuation agreed by the parties without argument. He acknowledged that each case must turn on its facts and that valuation of different interests would differ depending on such factors as the nature of the underlying investments (there was evidence in this case that due to lack of investor confidence the market value of the fund was much diminished); in addition in this case, unlike *Peters*, the whole of the fund could be advanced. However, he concluded that the Court of Appeal's approach in *Peters* lead to a valuation of the claimant's son's equitable interest as being more or less equal to the whole net value of the trust fund (less 10 per cent. for the expenses of sale).

All interests which can be sold or borrowed against will need to be considered. However, in the case of an interest under a discretionary trust, the DSS will normally only take payments of capital (or income) into account when they are actually made.

In *R(IS) 9/04* it was argued that funds held by the Court of Protection were analogous to those held by a discretionary trustee. Since neither the claimant nor her receiver could insist on the Court releasing any part of the funds it was contended that the market value of the claimant's actual interest was so small as to be negligible. However, the Commissioner followed *CIS 7127/1995* in holding that the entire beneficial interest in the funds administered by the Court remained with the claimant to whom alone they belonged. The fact the Court had discretionary powers of *control* over the management of a patient's property for his or her benefit did not mean that the patient's beneficial *ownership* had ceased. The funds therefore had to be valued at their current market value, less any appropriate allowance for sale expenses, in the normal way (see reg.49).

Realisation of assets

R(SB) 18/83 stresses that there are more ways of realising assets than sale. In par-   2.352
ticular, assets can be charged to secure a loan which can be used to meet requirements. In that case the asset was a minority shareholding in a family company. The
Commissioner says that only a person prepared to lend money without security would
do so in such circumstances. The articles of association of the company provided that
if a shareholder wanted to sell shares they were to be offered to the existing shareholders at the fair value fixed by the auditors. The Commissioner holds that the regulations do not require assets to be valued at a figure higher than anything the person
would realise on them, *i.e.* the auditor's fair value. This is in line with the purpose of
the capital cut-off that a claimant can draw on resources until they fall below the limit.

This approach to valuation can usefully deal with unrealisable assets. See the notes
to reg.49. However, it is no part of the definition of capital that it should be immediately realisable, although its market value may be affected by such factors. It thus
remains possible (especially in circumstances like those imposed by reg.52 below)
for a claimant to be fixed with a large amount of capital which is not available to him.
If this takes the claimant over the £8,000 (£12,000: see reg.45(aa) or £16,000: see
reg.45(b)) limit, a crisis loan may be appropriate while the claimant attempts to
realise the asset or raise a commercial loan (*Social Fund Guide*, para.4717–8).

Deduction of liabilities

The general rule is that the whole of a capital resource is to be taken into account.   2.353
Liabilities are not to be deducted from the value (*R(SB) 2/83*). Otherwise, it is only
if a debt is secured on the capital asset that it can be deducted, at the stage specifi-
cially required by reg.49 or 50 (*R(IS) 21/93*). See the notes to reg.49.

Disregard of capital of child or young person

47. [¹. . .]   2.354

AMENDMENT

1. Social Security (Working Tax Credit and Child Tax Credit) (Consequential   2.355
Amendments) Regulations 2003 (SI 2003/455), reg.2 and Sch.1, para.11 (April 6,
2004, except in "transitional cases" and see further the note to reg.17 of the Income
Support Regulations).

GENERAL NOTE

This regulation provided that the capital of a child or young person who was a   2.355.1
member of the claimant's family was not to be treated as the claimant's (see the 2003
edition of this Volume for this regulation and the notes to it). However, with effect
from April 6, 2004 (except in "transitional cases"—see the note to reg.17) amounts
for children and young persons have been removed from the income support scheme;
financial assistance to help with the cost of bringing up a child or young person is now
to be provided through the child tax credit system, see Volume IV of this series. As a
consequence, under the new form of reg.23 (in force from April 6, 2004, except for
"transitional cases"—see the note to reg.17) neither the income nor the capital of a
child or young person counts as the claimant's (see the new form of reg.23(2) and the
notes to that regulation). This regulation has therefore been revoked. It does however,
remain in force for "transitional cases"—see the note to reg.17.

For income support claimants who had an award of child tax credit before April
6, 2004 see reg.7 of the Social Security (Working Tax Credit and Child Tax Credit)
(Consequential Amendments) Regulations 2003 (SI 2003/455) (as amended) on
p.686 and the notes to that regulation.

Income treated as capital

2.356   **48.**—(1) Any [². . .] bounty derived from employment to which paragraph 7 of Schedule 8 applies [²and paid at intervals of at least one year] shall be treated as capital.

(2) Except in the case of an amount to which section 23(5)(a)(ii) of the Act [SSCBA, s.126(5)(a)(ii)] (refund of tax in trade dispute cases) [²or regulation 41(4) (capital treated as income)] applies, any amount by way of a refund of income tax deducted from profit or emoluments chargeable to income tax under Schedule D or E shall be treated as capital.

(3) Any holiday pay which is not earnings under regulation 35(1)(d) (earnings of employed earners) shall be treated as capital.

(4) Except any income derived from capital disregarded under paragraph 1, 2, 4, 6, [³12 or 25 to 28] of Schedule 10, any income derived from capital shall be treated as capital but only from the date it is normally due to be credited to the claimant's account.

(5) Subject to paragraph (6), in the case of employment as an employed earner, any advance of earnings or any loan made by the claimant's employer shall be treated as capital.

[¹(6) Paragraph (5) shall not apply to a person to whom section 23 of the Act [SSCBA, s.126] (trade disputes) applies or in respect of whom section 20(3) of the Act [SSCBA, s.124(1)] (conditions of entitlement to income support) has effect as modified by section 23A(b) [SSCBA, s.127(b)] (effect of return to work).]

(7) Any payment under section 30 of the Prison Act 1952 (payments for discharged prisoners) or allowance under section 17 of the Prisons (Scotland) Act 1952 (allowances to prisoners on discharge) shall be treated as capital.

[¹¹(8) [¹³. . .]

(8A) [¹³. . .].]

[³(9) Any charitable or voluntary payment which is not made or not due to be made at regular intervals, other than one to which paragraph (10) applies, shall be treated as capital.

(10) This paragraph applies to a payment—

(a) which is made to a person to whom section 23 of the Act [SSCBA, s.126] (trade disputes) applies or in respect of whom section 20(3) of the Act [SSCBA, s.124(1)] (conditions of entitlement to income support) has effect as modified by section 23A(b) of the Act [SSCBA, s.127(b)] (effect of return to work) [¹³ or to the partner] of such a person;

(b) [¹³. . .]

(c) which is made under the Macfarlane Trust[⁵, or the Macfarlane (Special Payments) Trust][⁶, the Macfarlane (Special Payments) (No. 2) Trust][⁸, the Fund][¹⁰, the Eileen Trust] or [⁹ the Independent Living Funds].]

[⁴(11) Any compensation within the meaning of regulation 35(3) (earnings of employed earners) which is made in respect of employment which is not part-time employment within the meaning of that regulation, to the extent that it is not earnings by virtue of regulation 35(1)(i)(i) shall be treated as capital.]

[¹²(12) Any arrears of subsistence allowance which are paid to a claimant as a lump sum shall be treated as capital.]

AMENDMENTS

1. Income Support (General) Amendment Regulations 1988 (SI 1988/663),   **2.357**
reg.21 (April 11, 1988).
2. Income Support (General) Amendment No.4 Regulations 1988 (SI 1988/
1445), reg.11 (September 12, 1988).
3. Income Support (General) Amendment No.5 Regulations 1988 (SI 1988/
2022), reg.11 (December 12, 1988).
4. Income Support (General) Amendment No.2 Regulations 1989 (SI 1989/
1323), reg.15 (October 9, 1989).
5. Income-related Benefits Schemes Amendment Regulations 1990 (SI 1990/
127), reg.33 (January 31, 1990).
6. Income-related Benefits Schemes and Social Security (Recoupment)
Amendment Regulations 1991 (SI 1991/1175), reg.5 (May 11, 1991).
7. Income Support (General) Amendment Regulations 1992 (SI 1992/468), Sch.
para.5 (April 6, 1992).
8. Income-related Benefits Schemes and Social Security (Recoupment)
Amendment Regulations 1992 (SI 1992/1101) reg.6 (May 7, 1992).
9. Social Security Benefits (Miscellaneous Amendments) (No.2) Regulations
1993 (SI 1993/963), reg.2(3) (April 22, 1993).
10. Income-related Benefits Schemes and Social Security (Recoupment)
Amendment Regulations 1993 (SI 1993/1249), reg.4(3) (May 14, 1993).
11. Social Security (Miscellaneous Amendments) Regulations 1998 (SI 1998/
563), reg.4(1) (April 6, 1998).
12. Social Security Amendment (Employment Zones) Regulations 2000 (SI
2000/724), reg.3(2) (April 3, 2000).
13. Social Security (Working Tax Credit and Child Tax Credit) (Consequential
Amendments) Regulations 2003 (SI 2003/455), reg.2 and Sch.1, para.12
(April 6, 2004, except in "transitional cases" and see further the note to reg.17 of
the Income Support Regulations).

DEFINITIONS

"the Act"—see reg.2(1).   **2.358**
"child"—see 1986 Act, s.20(11) (SSCBA, s.137(1)).
"the Children Order"—see reg.2(1).
"claimant"—see 1986 Act, s.20(11), (SSCBA, s.137(1)), reg.23(1).
"employed earner"—see reg.2(1).
"family"—see 1986 Act, s.20(11) (SSCBA, s.137(1)).
"subsistence allowance"—see reg.2(1).
"the Eileen Trust"—*ibid.*
"the Fund"—*ibid.*
"the Independent Living Funds"—*ibid.*
"the Macfarlane (Special Payments) Trust"—*ibid.*
"the Macfarlane (Special Payments) (No. 2) Trust"—*ibid.*
"the Macfarlane Trust"—*ibid.*

GENERAL NOTE

Most of these categories deemed to be capital are self-explanatory. They are then   **2.359**
disregarded as income (Sch.9, para.32).

Para. (4)

The general rule is that the income from capital is not to be treated as income, but   **2.360**
is added to the capital when it is credited. The excepted cases are premises and business assets plus trusts of personal injury compensation.

Note that paras 44 and 45 of Sch.10 have not been added to the list of excepted cases.
Thus payments to a claimant from funds held in court that derive from damages for

personal injury or compensation for the death of a parent will count as capital, whatever the nature of those payments. The words "income derived from capital" would seem wide enough to cover payments of income that are made to the claimant from such funds. Such payments may also fall under para.12 of Sch.10 (see *CIS 368/1994* in the note to para.12). But in such a case, following *CIS 563/1991* (see below), the disregard in para.44 or 45 should take precedence and the payments count as capital. This is confirmed in *CIS 2211/2002*, which follows *CIS 929/2000*. In *CIS 929/2000* the Commissioner agrees with *Bell v Todd and Tyneside Metropolitan Borough Council*, High Court, June 29, 2001, unreported, and *CIS 4037/1999* which had held that since the disregard for funds held (for example) in the Court of Protection was more specific, this should prevail over the more general disregard in para.12 of Sch.10. (*CIS 929/2000* also contains a useful summary of the changes in the treatment of personal injury compensation for the purposes of income support since 1988). The Commissioner in *CIS 2211/2002* refers to *Ryan v Liverpool Health Authority* [2002] Lloyd's Med Rep. 23 (which like *Bell* was concerned with the provisions for assessing a person's resources for the purpose of services under Part III of the National Assistance Act 1948 which in this respect parallel the income support provisions). Munby J in *Ryan* had suggested that the rationale for treating the general class of personal injury claimants whose funds are held in trust differently from those who are under a disability and whose funds are accordingly held in court was that in the former case they should be expected to use their trust income for their accommodation whereas the latter should have their trust income wholly disregarded. The Commissioner in *CIS 2211/2002* agreed with this explanation but not with the conclusion that the consequence was that payments from funds held in court were totally disregarded. The effect of para.22(1) of Sch.9 was that such payments were disregarded as income but they counted as capital under para.(4). The result in *CIS 2211/2000* was that the tariff income rule applied as the monthly payment authorised by the Court was £5,000 (but presumably this should only have operated until the "capital" had been used to meet the claimant's expenses). However, if the payments do not take the claimant's capital over £3,000 (£6,000 where the claimant or any partner (from October 6, 2003, where the claimant's partner) is aged 60 or over, or £10,000 for claimants permanently in residential care), they should not affect the claimant's income support.

2.361   The income must be derived from some capital asset of the claimant (*CIS 25/ 1989*). A twelve-month assured shorthold tenancy is not a capital asset and income from the subletting of rooms is not "derived from" the tenancy (*CIS 82/1993*).

The income covered by this provision is disregarded as income (Sch.9, para.22), but remember that capital over £3,000 (£6,000 where the claimant or any partner (from October 6, 2003, where the claimant's partner) is aged 60 or over, or £10,000 for claimants permanently in residential care) is deemed to produce a tariff income under reg.53.

In *CIS 563/1991* the Commissioner considers that the effect of para.(4) is to treat a payment of income as capital for the same length of time as it would have been taken into account as income. So, for example, a payment of a month's rent from a property let out to tenants counts as capital for a month from the date that the claimant is due to receive it. After that, reg.48(4) ceases to have effect. Money spent during that month cannot form part of the claimant's actual capital at the end of the month (subject to the possible effect of the notional capital rule in reg.51(1)). Although saved-up income only metamorphoses into capital after deducting all relevant debts (see the notes to reg.23), the Commissioner considers that where para.(4) has effected a statutory metamorphosis, any unspent money at the end of the period covered by para.(4) continues to count as capital; it does not change into income and then immediately back into capital. Thus any outstanding debts will only reduce the amount of the capital if they are secured on the capital itself (reg.49(a)(ii)). *CIS 563/1991* also deals with the situation where more than one disregard in Sch.10 could apply. If a property was disregarded under para.26 (taking steps to dispose of premises) the rental income from it would count as income and would only be ignored to the extent allowed for by para.22(2) of Sch.9. But if the property was let by the claimant and the para.5 disregard also applied (as was possible under the form of para.5 in force before October 2, 1995: see the 1995 edition of *Mesher and Wood, Income-related Benefits: the Legislation*) the rental income would count as capital. The Commissioner concludes that considering reg.48(4) and para.22 of Sch.9 together, the primary rule was that income derived from capital was to be treated as capital. The disregard in para.5 therefore took precedence, and the rental income counted as capital, even during periods when the property could also be disregarded under one or more of the provisions listed in para.22 and para.(4). Note that under the new form of para.5 a property let to tenants by the claimant is no longer disregarded (see the note to para.5); the rent will still generally count as capital under the normal rule in para.(4) (unless one of the exceptions applies). See also *CIS 2211/2002* above.

Paras (8) and (8A)

These paragraphs provided that arrears of payments made by local authorities in Great Britain (para.(8)) and authorities in Northern Ireland (para.(8A)) towards the maintenance of children were treated as capital, but arguably they were capital in any event. For the disregard of current payments see para.25(1)(b)–(d) of Sch.9. With effect from April 6, 2004 (except in "transitional cases"—see the note to reg.17) amounts for children and young persons have been removed from the income support scheme; financial assistance to help with the cost of bringing up a child or young person is now to be provided through the child tax credit system, see Volume IV of this series. The revocation of paras (8) and (8A) is another of the consequential changes that apply from April 6, 2004 (except in "transitional cases"—see the note to reg.17) as a result of income support becoming an "adults only" benefit. **2.362**

Paras (9) and (10)

Regs. 24 and 33 on charitable or voluntary payments were revoked from December 1988. See the notes to para.15 of Sch.9 for the meaning of "charitable" and "voluntary." The general rule in para.(9) is that such payments not made or due to be made at regular intervals are to be treated as capital. This rule does not apply to the three kinds of payments set out in para.(10). However, there is nothing to say how such payments are to be treated. Presumably they must be treated as capital or income according to general legal principles (on which see the notes to reg.23). Similarly, there is nothing expressly to say how payments which are made or due to be made regularly are to be treated, but no doubt they will usually have the character of income. **2.363**

Para. (11)

The elements of compensation on the termination of full-time employment which do not count as earnings under reg.35(1)(i) are payments of less than the "maximum weekly amount" and "deductible remainders" (see the notes to reg.35). **2.364**

Para. (12)

"Subsistence allowances" (reg.2(1)) are paid to claimants participating in an "employment zone" (defined in reg.2(1)) programme. Any arrears paid as a lump sum are treated as capital and ignored for 52 weeks from the date of receipt (para.59 of Sch.10). See further the note to reg.42(5A). **2.365**

Calculation of capital in the United Kingdom

49. Capital which a claimant possesses in the United Kingdom shall be calculated— **2.366**
  (a) except in a case to which sub-paragraph (b) applies, at its current market or surrender value, less—
      (i) where there would be expenses attributable to sale, 10 per cent.; and

(ii) the amount of any incumbrance secured on it;
(b) in the case of a National Savings Certificate—
(i) if purchased from an issue the sale of which ceased before 1st July last preceding the first day on which income support is payable or the date of the determination of the claim, whichever is the earlier, or in the case of a [¹supersession,the date of that supersession], at the price which it would have realised on that 1st July had it been purchased on the last day of that issue;
(ii) in any other case, at its purchase price.

AMENDMENT

2.367   1. Social Security Act 1998 (Commencement No.12 and Consequential and Transitional Provisions) Order 1999 (SI 1999/3178 (C.81)), art.3(5) and Sch.5, para.6 (November 29, 1999).

DEFINITION

"claimant"—see reg.2(1), reg.23(1).

GENERAL NOTE

2.368   The general rule is that the market value of the asset is to be taken. The surrender value will be taken if appropriate (although the surrender value of life insurance policies and of annuities is totally disregarded (Sch.10, paras 15 and 11)). The value at this stage does not take account of any incumbrances secured on the assets, since those come in under para.(a)(ii) (*R(IS) 21/93*). In *R(SB) 57/83* and *R(SB) 6/84* the test taken is the price that would be commanded between a willing buyer and a willing seller at a particular date. In *R(SB) 6/84* it is stressed that in the case of a house it is vital to know the nature and extent of the interest being valued. Also, since what is required is a current market value, the Commissioner holds that an estate agent's figure for a quick sale was closer to the proper approach than the District Valuer's figure for a sale within three months. All the circumstances must be taken into account in making the valuation. In *CIS 553/1991* it is held that in valuing a former matrimonial home the wife's statutory right of occupation under the Matrimonial Homes Act 1967 has to be taken into account. Similarly, if personal possessions are being valued, it is what the possessions could be sold for which counts, not simply what was paid for them (*CIS 494/1990, CIS 2208/2003*). Sometimes a detailed valuation is not necessary, such as where the value of an asset is on any basis clearly over the £8,000 (£12,000: see reg.45(aa) or £16,000: see reg.45(b)) limit (*CSIS 40/1989*).

It is accepted that the test of the willing buyer and the willing seller is the starting point for the valuation of shares (*R(SB) 57/83, R(SB) 12/89* and *R(IS) 2/90*). The latter case emphasises that in the income support context the value must be determined on the basis of a very quick sale, so that the hypothetical willing seller would be at a corresponding disadvantage. In the case of private companies there is often a provision in the articles of association that a shareholder wishing to sell must first offer the shares to other shareholders at a "fair value" fixed by the auditors (this was the case in *R(SB) 18/83* and *R(IS) 2/90*). Then the value of the shares ought not to be higher than the fair value, but for income support purposes may well be less. The possible complications are set out in *CSB 488/1982* (quoted with approval in *R(SB) 12/89* and *R(IS) 2/90*). In *R(IS) 8/92* it is suggested that the market value is what a purchaser would pay for the shares subject to the same restriction. Whether the shareholding gives a minority, equal or controlling interest is particularly significant. All the circumstances of the share structure of the company must be considered. For instance, in *R(SB) 12/89* shares could only be sold with the consent of the directors, which it was indicated would not be forthcoming. It seems to be agreed that valuation according to Inland Revenue methods is not appropriate (*R(SB) 18/83* and *R(IS) 2/90*), although it is suggested in *R(SB) 12/89* that the Inland Revenue Shares Valuation Division might be able to assist tribunals. It is not known if this is so. What is absolutely clear is that the total value of the company's shareholding cannot simply be divided in proportion to the claimant's holding (*R(SB) 18/83*). However, in the case of shares in companies quoted on the London Stock Exchange the Inland Revenue method of valuation should be used (*R(IS) 18/95*). This involves looking at all the transactions relating to the relevant share during the previous day, taking the lowest figure and adding to this a quarter of the difference between the lowest and the highest figure. The Commissioner considered that decision-makers could use the valuation quoted in newspapers (which is the mean between the best bid and best offer price at the close of business the previous day) to obtain approximate valuations. However, where a completely accurate valuation was essential, the Inland Revenue method would need to be adopted.

The proper approach to valuation can usefully deal with unrealisable assets. 2.369
Sometimes their market value will be nil (*e.g.* a potential interest under a discretionary trust: *R(SB) 25/83*); sometimes it will be very heavily discounted. However, if the asset will be realisable after a time, it may have a current value. The claimant may be able to sell an option to purchase the asset in the future (see *R(IS) 8/92*) or borrow, using the asset as security. But the valuation must reflect the fact that the asset is not immediately realisable. In *R(IS) 4/96* the claimant had on his divorce transferred his interest in the former matrimonial home to his wife in return for a charge on the property which could only be enforced if she died, remarried or cohabited for more than six months. The claimant's former wife was 46 and in good health. A discount had to be applied to the present day value of the charge to reflect the fact that it might not be realisable for as long as 40 years or more; consequently it was unlikely to be worth more than £3,000. See also *CIS 982/2002* in which the Commissioner sets out a number of detailed questions that had to be considered when valuing the claimant's share (if any) in a joint bank account that had been frozen following the claimant's separation from her husband. It should similarly be remembered that if, exceptionally, personal possessions are being taken into account (*e.g.* they have been bought to secure benefit), their value is not what was paid for them, but what could be obtained for them if sold as second-hand (*CIS 494/1990, CIS 2208/2003*). As the Tribunal of Commissioners in *R(SB) 45/83* point out, the market value (in this case of an interest in an entire trust fund) must reflect the outlay the purchaser would expect to incur in obtaining transfer of the assets and the profit he would expect as an inducement to purchase. If there might be some legal difficulty in obtaining the underlying asset (as there might have been in *R(SB) 21/83* and in *R(IS) 13/95*) where shares were held in the names of the claimant's children) this must be taken into account.

The general rule is that the whole of a capital resource is to be taken into account. Liabilities are not to be deducted from the value (*R(SB) 2/83*). Otherwise, it is only where a debt is secured on the capital asset that it is deducted under para.(a)(ii). The standard case would be a house that is mortgaged. The amount of capital outstanding would be deducted from the market value of the house. In *R(SB) 14/81* (see Sch.10, para.8) the claimant had been lent £5,000 for work on his bungalow, which was mortgaged to secure the debt. He had £3,430 left. Although he was obliged to make monthly repayments this liability could not be deducted from the £3,430, for the debt was not secured on the money. However, the principle of *R(SB) 53/83* (see the notes to reg.46) would make the money not part of the claimant's resources. In *R(SB) 18/83* the Commissioner says that personal property such as shares (or money) can be charged by a contract for valuable consideration (*e.g.* a loan) without any writing or the handing over of any title documents. But this is not the case in Scots law (*R(SB) 5/88*). In *R(IS) 18/95* the claimant's brokers had a lien on his shares for the cost of acquisition and their commission which fell to be offset against the value of the shares. *CIS 368/1993* concerned money held under a solicitor's undertaking. £40,000 of the proceeds of sale of the claimant's house was retained by his solicitors in pursuance of an undertaking to his bank given because of a previous charge on the property. The Commissioner decides that the undertaking was an incumbrance within para.(a)(ii). It was the equivalent of a pledge or lien and was secured on the proceeds of sale. Thus the £40,000 did not count as part of the claimant's resources. See also *CIS 984/2002* which concerned money held by the claimant's solicitor pending quantification of the statutory charge to the Legal Services Commission under s.10(7) of the Access to Justice Act 1999. The Commissioner holds that this was not part of the claimant's capital until the charge had been quantified as until then it was not possible to identify any particular amount as the claimant's capital. He added that another way of looking at it was to treat the statutory charge as an incumbrance for the purpose of para.(a)(ii).

2.370 In *R(IS) 5/98* the claimant transferred her flat to her daughter on the understanding that the daughter would care for her in the flat and pay off the mortgage. The daughter complied with the second condition, but evicted her mother from the flat. The Commissioner decides that the gift of the flat to the daughter had been subject to the condition that she looked after her mother. As that condition had not been fulfilled, the gift failed and the daughter held the property on trust for the claimant. In valuing the claimant's interest under para.(a), the mortgage was to be deducted because the daughter was to be treated as subrogated to the rights of the mortgagee. In addition, the costs of the litigation to recover the property from the daughter also fell to be deducted. The claimant appealed against this decision to the Court of Appeal but her appeal was dismissed (*Ellis v Chief Adjudication Officer, The Times*, May 14, 1997, also reported as part of *R(IS) 5/98*).

The first deduction to be made under para.(a) is a standard 10 per cent. if there would be any expenses attributable to sale, as there almost always will be. The second is the amount of any incumbrance secured on the asset. There is particularly full and helpful guidance on the nature of incumbrances on real property and the evidence which should be examined in *R(IS) 21/93*, and see above. In *R(IS) 10/99* the Commissioner points out that the word "incumbrance" is unknown to the law of Scotland, but goes on to interpret para.(a)(ii) as meaning that there must be something attached to the capital in question that prevents the claimant from disposing of it.

Calculation of capital outside the United Kingdom

2.371 **50.** Capital which a claimant possesses in a country outside the United Kingdom shall be calculated—

    (a) in a case in which there is no prohibition in that country against the transfer to the United Kingdom of an amount equal to its current market or surrender value in that country, at that value;

    (b) in a case where there is such a prohibition, at the price which it would realise if sold in the United Kingdom to a willing buyer,

less, where there would be expenses attributable to sale, 10 per cent. and the amount of any incumbrance secured on it.

DEFINITION

"claimant"—see reg.2(1), reg.23(1).

GENERAL NOTE

2.372 There had been problems under supplementary benefit in valuing overseas assets. Now the standard rules about the deduction of 10 per cent for sale expenses and the deduction of the amount of any incumbrance secured on the asset apply. But then there are two separate situations. Under para.(a), if there is no prohibition in the country where the asset is located against transferring to the UK an amount of money equal to the asset's value in that country, the market value there is the test.

CH 4972/2002 confirms that under para.(a) it is the local market value that is taken, not the value that could be obtained by marketing the asset in the UK. If there are merely restrictions or delays in transfer this does not seem to come within para.(a). If there is such a prohibition, under para.(b) the value is the market value in the UK.

Notional capital

51.—(1) A claimant shall be treated as possessing capital of which he has deprived himself for the purpose of securing entitlement to income support or increasing the amount of that benefit [6 except—

   (a) where that capital is derived from a payment made in consequence of any personal injury and is placed on trust for the benefit of the claimant; or

   (b) to the extent that the capital which he is treated as possessing is reduced in accordance with regulation 51A (diminishing notional capital rule)] [15or

   (c) any sum to which paragraph 44(a) or 45(a) of Schedule 10 (disregard of compensation for personal injuries which is administered by the Court) refers].

   (2) Except in the case of—

   (a) a discretionary trust;

   (b) a trust derived from a payment made in consequence of a personal injury; or

   (c) any loan which would be obtainable if secured against capital disregarded under Schedule 10, [13 or

   (d) a personal pension scheme or retirement annuity contract,] [15 or

   (e) any sum to which paragraph 44(a) or 45(a) of Schedule 10 (disregard of compensation for personal injuries which is administered by the Court) refers,]

any capital which would become available to the claimant upon application being made but which has not been acquired by him shall be treated as possessed by him but only from the date on which [1 it could be expected to be acquired were an application made.]

   [2(3) [17 Any payment of capital, other than a payment of capital specified in paragraph (3A)], made—

   (a) to a third party in respect of a single claimant or [23 his partner] (but not a member of the third party's family) shall be treated—

      (i) in a case where that payment is derived from a payment of any benefit under the benefit Acts, [25 a payment from the Armed Forces and Reserve Forces Compensation Scheme,] a war disablement pension [14, war widow's pension [22 or war widower's pension] or a pension payable to a person as a widow [22 or widower] under the Naval, Military and Air Forces Etc. (Disablement and Death) Service Pensions Order 1983 in so far as that Order is made under the Naval and Marine Pay and Pensions Act 1865 or the Pensions and Yeomanry Pay Act 1884, or is made only under section 12(1) of the Social Security (Miscellaneous Provisions) Act 1977 and any power of Her Majesty otherwise than under an enactment to make provision about pensions for or in respect of persons who have been disabled or who have died in consequence of service as members of the armed forces of the Crown,] as possessed by that single claimant, if it is paid to him, [23 or by his partner, if it is paid to his partner];

[18(ia) in a case where that payment is a payment of an occupational pension or is a pension or other periodical payment made under a personal pension scheme, as possessed by that single claimant or, as the case may be, by [23 the claimant's partner];]

(ii) in any other case, as possessed by that single claimant [23 or his partner] to the extent that it is used for the food, ordinary clothing or footwear, household fuel, rent [26. . .] for which housing benefit [21 is payable or] [8. . .] any housing costs to the extent that they are met under regulation 17(1)(e) and 18(1)(f) (housing costs) [21 . . .] of that single claimant or, as the case may be, [23 of his partner] [8, or is used for any [10council tax] or water charges for which that claimant or [23 partner is liable]];

[23 (b) to a single claimant or his partner in respect of a third party (but not in respect of another member of his family) shall be treated as possessed by that single claimant or, as the case may be, his partner, to the extent that it is kept or used by him or used by or on behalf of his partner.]].

[17(3A) Paragraph (3) shall not apply in respect of a payment of capital made—

(a) under the Macfarlane Trust, the Macfarlane (Special Payments) Trust, the Macfarlane (Special Payments) (No. 2) Trust, the Fund, the Eileen Trust [24, the Independent Living Funds or the Skipton Fund];

(b) pursuant to section 2 of the Employment and Training Act 1973 in respect of a person's participation—

(i) in an employment programme specified in regulation 75(1)(a)(ii) of the Jobseeker's Allowance Regulations 1996;

(ii) in a training scheme specified in regulation 75(1)(b)(ii) of those Regulations; or

[20(iia) in the Intensive Activity Period specified in regulation 75(1)(a)(iv) of those Regulations or in the Intensive Activity Period for 50 plus; or]

(iii) in a qualifying course within the meaning specified in regulation 17A(7) of those Regulations.]

(iv) [*Omitted.*]

[19(c) under an occupational pension scheme or in respect of a pension or other periodical payment made under a personal pension scheme where—

(i) a bankruptcy order has been made in respect of the person in respect of whom the payment has been made or, in Scotland, the estate of that person is subject to sequestration or a judicial factor has been appointed on that person's estate under section 41 of the Solicitors (Scotland) Act 1980;

(ii) the payment is made to the trustee in bankruptcy or any other person acting on behalf of the creditors; and

(iii) the person referred to in (i) and [23 his partner (if any)] does not possess, or is not treated as possessing, any other income apart from that payment.]

(4) Where a claimant stands in relation to a company in a position analogous to that of a sole owner or partner in the business of that company, he shall be treated as if he were such sole owner or partner and in such a case—

(a) the value of his holding in that company shall, notwithstanding regulation 46 (calculation of capital), be disregarded; and

(b) he shall, subject to paragraph (5), be treated as possessing an amount of capital equal to the value or, as the case may be, his share of the value of the capital of that company and the foregoing provisions of this Chapter shall apply for the purposes of calculating that amount as if it were actual capital which he does possess.

(5) For so long as the claimant undertakes activities in the course of the business of the company, the amount which he is treated as possessing under paragraph (4) shall be disregarded.

(6) Where a claimant is treated as possessing capital under any of paragraphs (1) to (4), the foregoing provisions of this Chapter shall apply for the purposes of calculating its amount as if it were actual capital which he does possess.

[[1](7) For the avoidance of doubt a claimant is to be treated as possessing capital under paragraph (1) only if the capital of which he has deprived himself is actual capital.]

[[2](8) In paragraph (3) the expression "ordinary clothing or footwear" means clothing or footwear for normal daily use, but does not include school uniforms, or clothing or footwear used solely for sporting activities]].

AMENDMENTS

1. Income Support (General) Amendment Regulations 1988 (SI 1988/663), reg.22 (April 11, 1988).

2. Income Support (General) Amendment No.4 Regulations 1988 (SI 1988/1445), reg.12 (September 12, 1988).

3. Income Support (General) Amendment No.4 Regulations (SI 1988/1445), Sch.1, para.4 (April 10, 1989).

4. Income Support (General) Amendment Regulations 1989 (SI 1989/534), Sch.1, para.7 (October 9, 1989).

5. Income-related Benefits Schemes Amendment Regulations 1990 (SI 1990/127), reg.3 (January 31, 1990).

6. Income Support (General) Amendment No. 3 Regulations 1990 (SI 1990/1776), reg.5 (October 1, 1990).

7. Income-related Benefits Schemes and Social Security (Recoupment) Amendment Regulations 1991 (SI 1991/1175), reg.5 (May 11, 1991).

8. Income Support (General) Amendment No.4 Regulations 1991 (SI 1991/1559), reg.8 (August 5, 1991).

9. Income-related Benefits Schemes and Social Security (Recoupment) Amendment Regulations 1992 (SI 1992/1101), reg.6 (May 7, 1992).

10. Income-related Benefits Schemes (Miscellaneous Amendments) Regulations 1993 (SI 993/315), Sch. para.3 (April 1, 1993).

11. Social Security Benefits (Miscellaneous Amendments) (No.2) Regulations 1993 (SI 1993/963), reg.2(3) (April 22, 1993).

12. Income-related Benefits Schemes and Social Security (Recoupment) Amendment Regulations 1993 (SI 1993/1249), reg.4(3) (May 14, 1993).

13. Income-related Benefits Schemes and Social Security (Claims and Payments) (Miscellaneous Amendments) Regulations 1995 (SI 1995/2303), reg.6(5) (October 2, 1995).

14. Income-related Benefits and Jobseeker's Allowance (Miscellaneous Amendments) Regulations 1997 (SI 1997/65), reg.9 (April 7, 1997).

15. Income-related Benefits and Jobseeker's Allowance (Amendment) (No. 2) Regulations 1997 (SI 1997/2197), reg.5(4) (October 6, 1997).

16. Social Security Amendment (New Deal) Regulations 1997 (SI 1997/2863), reg.17(5) and (6)(e) (January 5, 1998).

2.374

17. Social Security Amendment (New Deal) (No.2) Regulations 1998 (SI 1998/2117), reg.3(2) and (3)(c) (September 24, 1998).

18. Social Security Amendment (Notional Income and Capital) Regulations 1999 (SI 1999/2640), reg.2(1)(a) (November 15, 1999).

19. Social Security Amendment (Notional Income and Capital) Regulations 1999 (SI 1999/2640), reg.2(3)(c) (November 15, 1999).

20. Social Security Amendment (New Deal) Regulations 2001 (SI 2001/1029), reg.15(8) and (9)(c) (April 9, 2001).

21. Social Security Amendment (Residential Care and Nursing Homes) Regulations 2001 (SI 2001/3767), reg.2(1) and Pt I of Sch., para.8 (April 8, 2002).

22. Social Security (Miscellaneous Amendments) Regulations 2002 (SI 2002/841), reg.2(3) (April 8, 2002).

23. Social Security (Working Tax Credit and Child Tax Credit) (Consequential Amendments) Regulations 2003 (SI 2003/455), reg.2 and Sch.1, para.13 (April 6, 2004, except in "transitional cases" and see further the note to reg.17 of the Income Support Regulations).

24. Social Security (Miscellaneous Amendments) (No. 3) Regulations 2004 (SI 2004/2308), reg.3(1) and (2)(a) (October 4, 2004).

25. Social Security (Miscellaneous Amendments) Regulations 2005 (SI 2005/574), reg.2(5) (April 4, 2005).

26. Social Security (Miscellaneous Amendments) Regulations 2005 (SI 2005/574), reg.3(4) (April 4, 2005).

DEFINITIONS

2.375
"the Armed Forces and Reserve Forces Compensation Scheme"—see reg.2(1).
"the benefit Acts"—*ibid.*
"claimant"—see reg.2(1), reg.23(1).
"family"—see 1986 Act, s.20(11) (SSCBA, s.137(1)).
"Intensive Activity Period for 50 plus"—see reg.2(1).
"occupational pension"—*ibid.*
"payment"—*ibid.*
"personal pension scheme"—*ibid.*
"retirement annuity contract"—*ibid.*
"the Eileen Trust"—*ibid.*
"the Fund"—*ibid.*
"the Independent Living Funds"—see reg.2(1).
"the Macfarlane (Special Payments) Trust"—*ibid.*
"the Macfarlane (Special Payments) (No. 2) Trust"—*ibid.*
"the Macfarlane Trust"—*ibid.*
"the Skipton Fund"—*ibid.*
"water charges"—see reg.2(1).

GENERAL NOTE

Para. (1)
2.376
In order for para.(1) to apply, only two elements must be proved by the AO—that the person has deprived himself of actual capital (see para.(7)) and that his purpose was to secure entitlement to or increase the amount of income support. It is clear that the principles applied to these questions for supplementary benefit purposes are to be applied to para.(1) *(CIS 24/1988, CIS 40/1989* and *R(IS) 1/91*, although the first decision is in error in failing to note the crucial difference identified in the next sentence). There is now no discretion (the regulation says "shall," not "may"). This was thought to give rise to the problems mentioned at the end of this note. These problems led to the insertion of reg.51A, applying a diminishing capital rule. Capital subject to that rule is excluded from reg.51(1) by sub-para.(b). *R(IS) 1/91* over-turned the previous understanding of the effect of reg.51(1) and is discussed at the

end of this note and in the note to reg.51A. Sub-para.(a) excludes the operation of reg.51(1) where money derived from compensation for personal injury is placed on trust for the claimant. Sub-para.(c) does the same in respect of funds held in court on behalf of a person that derive from damages for personal injury to that person. See also the note to para.12 of Sch.10.

Note *CIS/2540/2004* which confirms that a finding by a tribunal that a claimant is to be treated as having notional capital is not binding in relation to a subsequent claim. Section 17 of the Social Security Act 1998 draws a distinction between a decision which by s.17(1) is made "final" and a finding of fact necessary to the decision which under s.17(2) is only conclusive for the purpose of further decisions to the extent that regulations so provide; no regulations providing for any such conclusive effect have been made in this context. A subsequent tribunal hearing an appeal against the refusal of income support when the claimant made a further claim was not therefore bound by the previous tribunal's finding on the issue of deprivation of capital but could consider the issue afresh.

Deprivation

Here the onus of proof is complicated by the relationship with the claimant's actual capital. Once it is shown that a person did possess, or received, an asset, the burden shifts to him to show that it has ceased to be a part of his actual capital, to be valued under reg.49 *(R(SB) 38/85)*. Therefore, para.(1) can only come into play after these two stages have been passed, with the second stage depending on the claimant. If he cannot satisfactorily account for the way in which an asset or a sum of money which he says he no longer has was disposed of, the proper conclusion is that it remains a part of his actual capital. In *CIS 634/1992* the claimant was made bankrupt on November 29, 1990. Between November 29 and December 28, 1990, when he claimed income support the claimant divested himself of most of his capital. His trustee in bankruptcy was not appointed until April 1991. Under the Insolvency Act 1986 (subject to certain exceptions) a bankrupt's property does not vest in his trustee on the making of a bankruptcy order but only when the trustee is appointed. However, s.284 of the Insolvency Act 1986 makes any disposal of property or payment by a bankrupt between the presentation of a bankruptcy petition and the vesting of his estate in his trustee void (except with the consent or later ratification of the court). The claimant could not therefore in law deprive himself of any resources from November 29, onwards and reg.51(1) could not apply. However, since he had failed to give a satisfactory account of how he had disposed of his capital, he was to be treated as still possessing it *(R(SB) 38/85)*. Thus he was not entitled to income support prior to the appointment of the trustee in bankruptcy because until then he possessed actual capital over the income support limit.

"Deprive" is an ordinary English word and is not to be given any special legal definition *(R(SB) 38/85, R(SB) 40/85)*. The result is that a person deprives himself of a resource if he ceases to possess it, regardless of the reason for doing so or the fact that he receives some other resource in return. This is the clear assumption in *R(SB) 38/85* and is expressly decided in *R(SB) 40/85*. That decision holds that the approach in the *S Manual* (para.6042—set out on p.177 of the second edition of *Mesher, Supplementary Benefit and Family Income Supplement: the Legislation* (1985)), that a person had not deprived himself of a resource if he spent money or changed it into another form which is still available to him, was wrong. The effect is to put the main emphasis on the purpose of the deprivation.

However, this raises the question of the interaction of reg.51(1) with para.10 of Sch.10. Under para.10 the value of personal possessions is disregarded except those that have been acquired with the intention of reducing capital so as to gain entitlement to income support. This interaction was discussed in *CIS 494/1990* and has now been further explored in *R(IS) 8/04*. Both cases concerned the use of capital to buy a vehicle, for the purpose of securing entitlement to income support. In *CIS 494/1990* the Commissioner points out that the value of the vehicle will be considerably less than the purchase price and treats only this "depreciation" as notional

2.377

capital under reg.51(1). He proceeded on the assumption that there was an immediate depreciation of £1,000. The Commissioner in *R(IS) 8/04* agrees that where capital is used, for a purpose caught by reg.51(1), to buy personal possessions, the value of the assets as actual capital must be taken into account in calculating the amount of notional capital under reg.51(1). It would be unfair to treat a claimant as still having all the capital used to buy the possessions and also as having the market value of the possessions. He acknowledges that the mechanism for reaching this result was not entirely clear as reg.51(1) and the exception in para.10 of Sch.10 appear to operate independently. However he was satisfied that the general principle that actual capital should be looked at before notional capital supported the approach taken in *CIS 494/1990*. But he did not agree with *CIS 494/1990* that as the value of the car further depreciated over time there was a corresponding increase in the claimant's notional capital. The amount of the capital of which the claimant had deprived himself had to be fixed at the date of the deprivation, since it was only that amount to which the prohibited purpose in reg.51(1) could be attached. Any future depreciation could only fairly be said to result from the operation of the market and not from the claimant's original purpose to gain entitlement to benefit. The Commissioner added that the same principles would apply to other factors which resulted in a difference between the amount of capital spent on an asset and the amount to be taken into account for the asset as actual capital (*e.g.* the effect of expenses that would be incurred in selling the asset). See also under *Diminishing capital*, below.

It is arguable that a person cannot deprive himself of something which he has never possessed, but it may be that a deliberate failure to acquire an asset is also a deprivation. In *CSB 598/1987* it is suggested that a deliberate failure to pay a cheque into a bank account could be a deprivation. See also *CIS 1586/1997* which states that a sale at a known undervalue and the release of a debtor from a debt were capable of a mounting to deprivation. However, a person does not deprive herself of an asset by failing to seek a lump sum payment or property transfer order under the Matrimonial Causes Act 1973, since the right to make an application under the Act is not a capital asset (*R(IS) 1/03*). Moreover, even if this had constituted deprivation, the claimant's reasons for not bringing proceedings (which included, *inter alia*, fear of her abusive husband) clearly indicated that her purpose had not been to secure entitlement to income support.

If the claimant's attorney appointed under the Enduring Powers of Attorney Act 1985 repays a loan or makes gifts of the claimant's capital this may amount to deprivation by the claimant, since the attorney is the agent of the claimant *(CIS 12403/1991)*. In that case there was a question as to whether the loan was the responsibility of the claimant or the attorney and whether the gifts were allowable under s.3(5) of the 1985 Act which permits the making of gifts "provided that the value of each such gift is not unreasonable having regard to all the circumstances and in particular the size of the donor's estate". The Commissioner states that the new tribunal would have to consider whether the payments were properly made; if not, there would be a claim against the attorney which would constitute actual capital; if they were properly made the question of deprivation would have to be considered.

Purpose

2.378   Here the AO must show that the person's purpose is one of those mentioned in para.(1). There is unlikely to be direct evidence of purpose (although there might be contemporary letters or documents), so that primary facts must be found from which an inference as to purpose can be drawn (*CSB 200/1985, R(SB) 40/85*).

The view put forward in *CSB 28/81* that the test is of the person's predominant purpose, is rejected in *R(SB) 38/85* and *R(SB) 40/85*. In *R(SB) 38/85* it was suggested that it was enough that a subsidiary purpose was to obtain supplementary benefit. In *R(SB) 40/85* the Commissioner says that this must be a "significant operative purpose." If the obtaining of benefit was a foreseeable consequence of the transaction then, in the absence of other evidence, it could be concluded that this was the person's purpose. This would exclude some cases caught by the width of the approach to deprivation, *e.g.* where a resource is converted into another form in which it is still taken into account. For then there would be no effect on eligibility for benefit. But beyond that situation there remain great difficulties. The Commissioners mention a number of relevant factors, *e.g.* whether the deprivation was a gift or in return for a service, the personal circumstances of the person (*e.g.* age, state of health, employment prospects, needs), whether a creditor was pressing for repayment of a loan. It must be an issue of fact when these other factors indicate that the reasonably foreseeable consequence of obtaining benefit was not a significant operative factor. As *CH/3169/2004* (a case on the equivalent housing benefit provision) confirms, the test is a subjective one, which depends upon the evidence about the particular claimant in question (the claimant in that case was a schizophrenic whose mental state was such that he was unlikely to fully appreciate the implications of his behaviour and had limited capacity to plan for the future). The length of time since the disposal of the capital may be relevant (*CIS 264/1989*). However, in *CJSA/1425/2004* the Commissioner states that the question whether the purpose of obtaining benefit was a significant operative purpose had to be determined by deciding whether it was reasonable for the claimant to act in the way that he did, despite the fact that the timing of the payment of the claimant's credit card debts indicated that one purpose of the payments was to obtain benefit (see below for a fuller discussion of *CJSA/1425/2004*). Where the claimant had been warned about the consequences of a transaction by the local DSS office (*i.e.* that reg.51(1) would be applied) and still went ahead, this showed that he could not have as any part of his purpose securing of entitlement, or continued entitlement, to income support (*CIS 621/1991*). In effect, the test seems to be whether the person would have carried out the transaction at the same time if there had been no effect on eligibility for benefit. The onus of proof on the Secretary of State may come into play in marginal cases.

A number of recent decisions have firmed up the principles to be applied. *CIS 124/1990* holds that it must be proved that the person actually knew of the capital limit rule, otherwise the necessary deliberate intention to obtain benefit could not have been present. It is not enough that the person ought to have known of the rule. The crunch comes, and the resolution with the approach in *R(SB) 40/85* (where it was suggested that the existence of some limit might be said to be common knowledge), in the assessment of the evidence about the person's knowledge. The Commissioner stresses that the person's whole background must be considered, including experience of the social security system and advice which is likely to have been received from the family and elsewhere. The burden of proof is on the Secretary of State, but in some circumstances a person's assertion that they did not know of the rule will not be credible. In *CIS 124/1990* itself the claimant was illiterate and spoke and understood only Gujerati. The Commissioner says that this should put her in no better or worse situation than a literate claimant whose mother tongue was English, but that the possibility of misunderstandings in interpretation should be considered. *CIS 124/1990* is followed in *R(SB) 12/91*, where the necessity of a positive finding of fact, based on sufficient evidence, that the person knew of the capital limit is stressed. Evidence that the person had been in receipt of supplementary benefit or income support for some years was not in itself enough. But information which the person has received, together with his educational standing and other factors, will be material in deciding whether actual knowledge exists or not. *CIS 30/1993* similarly holds that it is not possible to infer actual knowledge of the capital limits simply from the claimant signing a claim form which contained that information. The claimant was partially sighted and had not completed the claim form herself but merely signed it. It was necessary for the tribunal to indicate what evidence satisfied it that the claimant did know of the capital limits.

The Commissioner in *R(SB) 9/91* stresses that a positive intention to obtain benefit must be shown to be a significant operative purpose. It is not enough for the AO merely to prove that the obtaining of benefit was a natural consequence of the

2.379

transaction in question. The claimant had transferred her former home to her two daughters. Evidence was given that her sole intention was to make a gift to her daughters, as she intended to leave the property to them in her will and it was no longer of any use to her (she being permanently in need of residential nursing care). The Commissioner notes that this did not explain why the transfer was made when it was, why the proceeds of sale of the property would not have been of use to the claimant and what she thought she would live on if she gave the property away. She had been in receipt of supplementary benefit for several years. On the evidence the obtaining of benefit was a significant operative purpose. As *CJSA 1395/2002* confirms, *R(SB) 9/91* thus endorses the attribution of an intention to a claimant by implication from all the circumstances but the conclusion must be in terms of the claimant's purpose, not in terms of the natural consequences of the transaction in question. See *CH/3619/2004* (applied in *CIS/218/2005*) referred to above, which reiterates that it is necessary for a tribunal to determine the claimant's actual (*i.e.* subjective) intention.

In *CIS 242/1993*, another case where the claimant had gone into residential care, the Commissioner reaches the opposite conclusion on the facts to that in *R(SB) 9/91*. The claimant's son had cared for his mother for 15 years. When she went into a residential care home, she gave her share of the proceeds of sale of their jointly owned home to her son to be used towards the purchase of his flat. The Commissioner accepts that she had relinquished her share in gratitude to her son and not to secure income support.

In *R(IS) 13/94* the claimant's capital was in excess of the statutory limit when he purchased his council house. The deposit used up enough of his capital to bring him below the limit. It was necessary to consider whether para.(1) applied to this use of the capital since the claimant was apparently dependent on income support to meet the mortgage interest. But in *R(IS) 15/96* using a criminal injuries compensation award to pay off part of a mortgage was not caught by para.(1). The SSAT had found that the claimant's purpose had been to secure his future and to reduce the burden on the DSS for his mortgage payments. This was a matter for the judgment of the tribunal.

A further example is *CJSA 204/2002*. The claimant had agreed to provide the deposit for a flat that she and her son would buy. In the event the claimant did not move into the new flat with her son and his girlfriend because of a disagreement but she still lent her son the deposit. The claimant did correspond with her solicitor about obtaining security for the loan but no formal agreement or legal charge was entered into. The Commissioner holds that the claimant clearly had reasons for keeping her promise to lend the deposit (for example, so as not to let her son down or sour relations further) and in his view there had been no deprivation within reg.51(1). See also *R(IS) 1/03* above.

2.380   In *CIS 109/1994* and *CIS 112/1994* the claimants had used their capital to purchase an annuity and a life insurance policy respectively. In *CIS 109/1994* the claimant was both physically and mentally frail and lived in a nursing home. The tribunal found that at the material time she had no knowledge of the income support capital and deprivation of capital rules, and entered into the transaction on her son's advice, who considered that this was the best use of her capital to enable her to stay in the nursing home. The Commissioner holds that the tribunal had not erred in concluding that she had not purchased the annuity in order to obtain income support. In *CIS 112/1994* the Commissioner decides that para.(1) did apply, but that para.15 of Sch.10 applied to disregard the life policy. The Commissioner also deals with "double counting" of notional and actual capital (see below). See also *R(IS) 7/98* where capital had been used to purchase an "investment bond". The Commissioner decides that the bond fell within the definition of "policy of life insurance" in reg.2(1) and so could be disregarded under para.15 of Sch.10. But the claimant's intention at the time of the investment had to be considered to see whether para.(1) applied.

If capital is used to repay debts which are immediately payable then this cannot be said to be for the purpose of obtaining benefit (*R(SB) 12/91* and *Jones v Secretary of*

State for Work and Pensions, see below). (Note also that capital that a claimant is under a "certain and immediate liability" to repay should not in fact be treated as his capital: *Chief Adjudication Officer v Leeves,* November 6, 1998, CA, reported as *R(IS) 5/99,* affirmed in *Morrell v Secretary of State for Work and Pensions* [2003] EWCA Civ 526, reported as *R(IS) 6/03).* In *R(SB) 12/91* there were doubts whether the alleged debts, to members of the family, were legally enforceable debts and whether they were owed by the claimant personally. But the fact that a debt is not legally enforceable and/or immediately repayable does not mean that repayment of it must be for the purpose of securing income support. As *CJSA 1395/2002* points out, what the Commissioner said in para.14 of *R(SB) 12/91* was that in such circumstances "the question will arise" of whether the securing of benefit or an increased amount was a significant operative purpose. It is still necessary to consider the claimant's purpose in repaying the debt *(CIS 2627/1995, Jones v Secretary of State for Work and Pensions* [2003] EWCA Civ 964). In *Jones* the Court of Appeal emphasizes that the issue as to whether or not repayment of a debt was for the purpose of obtaining income support was a question of fact to be determined according to the circumstances in each case. Thus, even if a debt was not immediately repayable, this did not necessarily mean that its repayment was made in order to obtain income support. Conversely (and more rarely) there could be cases where repayment of an immediately repayable debt was for the purpose of securing entitlement to income support—an example might be where the debtor thought the creditor would not call in the debt for some time but still made immediate repayment. It was a question of fact in each case.

The facts in *Jones* were unusual. The claimant and her husband had sold some land and used the money to pay off a number of their many debts. One of those debts was for £17,000 which was owed to a friend, Mr S. The claimant's husband and Mr S came to an arrangement whereby the claimant purchased a BMW car for £13,500 as security for this debt. The car was to be Mr S's property but he allowed the claimant and her husband full use of it on the basis that they paid all the running costs. The issue was whether the claimant's significant operative purpose in entering into this arrangement was the retention of entitlement to income support.

The Court of Appeal held that since the tribunal had accepted that the car belonged to Mr S, the effect of the transaction had been that the debt to Mr S had been repaid. The fact that Mr S was content for the money to be used to buy him a car was irrelevant, as was the fact that Mr S was content for the claimant and her husband to use the car. On the facts Mr S had been pressing for repayment of the debt and so the claimant had not deprived herself of capital for the purpose of securing entitlement to income support. However, even if the true position was that the claimant had not repaid Mr S and the car was hers, it was subject to a charge by way of security in favour of Mr S for £17,000 and so under reg.49(a)(ii) the charge had to be deducted from the value of the car (with the result that its value was nil). It could not be said that in creating the charge on the car the claimant had deprived herself of capital for the purpose of securing entitlement to income support since clearly this was the only way the claimant could secure use of the car and if the arrangement had not been made the claimant and her husband would have had to repay the £17,000 loan.

2.381

CJSA/1425/2004 concerned payment of credit card debts. The claimant had been made redundant and claimed JSA three months later. His claim was initially processed as a claim for contribution-based JSA only but was later "reviewed" and income-based JSA was awarded from the date of the initial claim. Between the date of the initial claim and the application for "review" the claimant paid £6,000 to three credit card accounts and £3,000 to his mother. The Commissioner accepts that the timing of the payments indicated that the claimant knew that this would reduce his capital to a level that would entitle him to benefit and that this was one purpose of the payments. However it did not follow that the claimant did not intend to pay the credit card bills in order to settle his debts and avoid the interest that would otherwise be charged on them. If the claimant had mixed motives, the question whether the purpose of obtaining benefit was a significant operative purpose had to be determined by deciding whether it was reasonable for the claimant to act in the way that he did. In the Commissioner's view, the threat of having to make high-interest payments was just as capable of making it reasonable to pay a debt as the threat of enforcement of a liability to pay. He considered that any other view would be contrary to public policy as expressed in s.94 of the Consumer Credit Act 1974 which entitles a debtor under a regulated consumer credit agreement to discharge his indebtedness at any time. The plain purpose of that provision was to allow a debtor to escape further interest payments. The Commissioner commented that it "would be anomalous if the benefit system were to require people to incur additional liability for interest. I can see no reason why the benefit system should treat differently a person who has just cleared his debts to avoid them growing and a person who never had any debts". He therefore concluded that payment of the credit cards debts was reasonable and was for the purpose of avoiding further substantial liabilities for interest payments and not for the purpose of obtaining or increasing entitlement to income-based JSA. However, the Commissioner did not find it reasonable for the claimant to have repaid his mother (the appellant's own evidence to the tribunal had been that "[i]t wasn't a loan but I felt obliged to give it back when she asked") and that this had been done for the purpose of increasing entitlement to income-based JSA.

CIS 40/1989 provides an interesting example on its facts of the securing or increase of benefit not being a significant operative purpose. The claimant had been on supplementary benefit and then income support since 1978. Her father died intestate. The estate consisted almost entirely of a house in which the claimant's sister had lived with the father. The claimant and her sister were the sole beneficiaries of the estate. Legal proceedings had to be taken to enforce a sale of the house. In March 1988 the claimant received £38,000 net of costs, which her solicitor divided equally between the claimant, her son, her daughter and her grand-daughter. After repaying a number of debts and buying a secondhand car, the amount possessed by the claimant quickly fell below £6,000. The AO and the SSAT found that she should be treated as still possessing the amounts given to her children and grandchild. The Commissioner, having heard the claimant give evidence and be cross-examined, accepted that her purpose was to carry out her father's wishes, which were that the house should be used to provide for his grandchildren and great-grandchildren. She had originally intended to take nothing, but had been encouraged by her children to take a quarter share. She knew of the capital limit, but did not know of the effect her actions would have on her benefit entitlement. On these particular facts, the Commissioner found that para.(1) did not apply. See also *CJSA 1395/2002* in which the claimant considered herself under a moral obligation to give £10,000 to her mother, brother and sister after her grandmother had made the claimant the sole beneficiary under her will, allegedly to spite the rest of the family.

2.382   In many cases of alleged deprivation of capital there will have been a course of spending, often on various items, and sometimes over a considerable period of time. In *CH/3169/2004* (a case on the equivalent housing benefit provision), the Commissioner emphasises the need to go through all the various items of expenditure, taking account of any explanations put forward by the claimant, and to reach a specific determination as to (i) what amounts (if any) represent deprivation of capital in excess of a reasonable level of general expenditure in the claimant's circumstances; and as regards *those* (ii) what had been the claimant's purpose at the time and whether this included an intention to obtain benefit. The tribunal had erred in simply expressing its decision in generalised terms without attempting to analyse the movements on the claimant's account during the relevant period.

2.383   There may be a problem in the transfer from the corresponding supplementary benefit regulation (Resources Regulations, reg.4(1)). reg.51(1) only mentions income support. What if a person deprived himself of capital in December 1987, thinking only of supplementary benefit. On a claim for income support, can he be caught by reg.51(1)? In *CIS 259/1990* (which was to be reported as *R(IS) 8/91*, but was withdrawn from reporting) the Commissioner accepts that the purpose must be to secure or increase income support, but held that the claimant in March 1987 knew enough about the effect of depleting her resources on her means-tested benefit for her purpose to satisfy reg.51(1). The Commissioner found that the claimant was aware that the existing means-tested benefit was to be replaced by another means-tested benefit (although the evidential basis for this finding does not appear). There was an appeal to the Court of Appeal, but the decision was set aside by consent. In *R(IS) 14/93* the Commissioner does not accept the reliance in *CIS 259/1990* on the enactment of the Social Security Act 1986 well before the income support scheme came into operation. He holds that a provision of a statute has no legal existence until it comes into force. Therefore, when in that case the claimant in November/December 1987, divested himself of capital he could not have done it with the intention of obtaining income support, because at that time it did not exist. Nor can the words "income support" be taken to refer to means-tested benefits which previously went under the name of supplementary benefit. This approach has the merit of not making the result depend on the vagaries of the particular claimant's advance knowledge of the nature of the income support reforms in April 1988.

Note that the corresponding regulation under JSA (reg.113(1) of the JSA Regulations) applies if a person has deprived himself of capital in order to secure entitlement to or increase the amount of JSA *or income support*. That avoids the question that might otherwise have arisen on a claimant transferring from income support to JSA as to whether a deprivation which had only been for the purposes of income support could be caught by reg.113(1). But para.(1) has not been similarly amended.

Diminishing capital

There were problems from the removal of discretion in the shift to income support. Under the Supplementary Benefit (Resources) Regulations this was used in particular for two purposes. One was to avoid double counting with the rule about personal possessions, now contained in para.10 of Sch.10. The value of personal possessions is not disregarded if they were acquired with the intention of reducing capital so as to gain entitlement to benefit. With no discretion at either end a claimant could have the market value of the possessions counted as part of his actual capital and the money he spent on them counted as notional capital under this paragraph. The Commissioner in *CIS 494/1990* avoided this problem by treating only the shortfall between the market value of the personal possessions from time to time and the purchase price (the "depreciation") as the notional capital to be imputed under reg.51(1). This is followed in part in *R(IS)8/04*. The Commissioner in *R(IS)8/04* agrees that only the shortfall should be treated as notional capital but does not agree that the notional capital should be deemed to increase over time in line with the reduction in the market value of the asset. In his view the amount of the capital of which the claimant had deprived himself had to be fixed at the date of the deprivation, since it was only that amount to which the prohibited purpose in reg.51(1) could be attached. Any future depreciation could only fairly be said to result from the operation of the market and not from the claimant's original purpose to gain entitlement to benefit. It would also seem to be difficult to combine such an increase with the diminishing capital rule under reg.51A.

In *CIS 112/1994* the Commissioner had also recognised the gross unfairness to a claimant if she were to be penalised twice because of the lack of discretion in reg.51(1). In the Commissioner's view this was not the intention of the regulation. But in that case double counting did not arise. The claimant had purchased a life insurance policy with a legacy. Although she was to be treated as still possessing the notional capital by virtue of reg.51(1), the actual capital (the life policy) could be disregarded under para.15 of Sch.10.

The second problem for which the use of discretion was useful was that it was unfair to fix a claimant with an amount of notional capital for eternity. If he had still had the capital and not been entitled to benefit, he would have had to use up the capital for living expenses. Thus the figure of notional capital could be reduced by the equivalent of the weekly benefit lost by the capital counting (*R(SB) 38/85, R(SB) 40/85*). There had seemed no possibility of such a process applying to reg.51(1) until

2.384

2.385

the decision of the Tribunal of Commissioners in *R(IS) 1/91*. The Tribunal concluded that the diminishing capital rule did apply. This is because para.(6) provides that regs 45 to 50 apply to the calculation of notional capital as if it was actual capital. If a claimant has capital over the prescribed limit, reasonable expenditure on living and other sensible expenses (not necessarily limited to income support rates) will reduce the amount of capital until it falls below the limit. He will then be entitled to income support. The same situation is held to apply where it is notional capital, rather than actual, which is held initially. The decision is wrong in principle, because if actual capital is held, the actual amount, reduced by any expenditure, must be considered week by week. This is not a consequence of any of regs 45 to 50 and there is no analogy with the notional reduction of notional capital. Para.(6) is primarily concerned with the calculation of the market value of assets. Nonetheless, *R(IS) 1/91* must be followed in relation to weeks before October 1, 1990.

With effect from October 1, 1990, reg.51A provides an express diminishing notional capital rule. *R(IS) 9/92* decides that while the principles of *R(IS) 1/91* apply up to that date, they do not apply thereafter. They are superseded by the rules laid down in reg.51A. See also *CIS 3268/2002*, discussed in the notes to reg.51A, as to the date when the rule in reg.51A comes into play and as to the position before that rule operates. *R(IS)8/04* confirms that reg.51A only applies if the claimant is not entitled to income support or entitled to a reduced amount of income support because of notional capital; it does not operate if for example his actual capital exceeds the prescribed limit (see further the notes to reg.51A).

Para. (2)

2.386   It is not at all clear what sort of capital would be caught by this rule. It must be available simply on application, with no other conditions, but not amount to actual capital (*cf. R(SB) 26/86* and *R(SB) 17/87*). Examples might be money held in court which would be released on application or arrears of employer's sick pay which needed to be applied for. Note the exclusions. Although discretionary trusts are specifically excluded, a potential beneficiary would not seem to be caught by para.(2) anyway. More than an application is needed for payment to be made: the discretion has to be exercised. On sub-para.(d) see the note to reg.42(2) to (2C). On sub-para.(e) see the notes to paras 44 and 45 of Sch.10.

Paras (3) and (3A)

2.387   Note that if the conditions are met, there is no discretion whether or not to apply para.(3). In this respect, as in others, *R(SB) 6/88* would be decided differently under income support.

Para.(3)(a) applies where payments are made to a third party in respect of the claimant or any partner. (The form of this provision in force before April 6, 2004, and which remains in force for "transitional cases"—see the note to reg.17, also applied if payments were made to a third party in respect of any child or young person who was a member of the claimant's family. However, with effect from April 6, 2004 (except in "transitional cases"—see the note to reg.17) amounts for children and young persons were removed from the income support scheme (financial support for children and young persons is now to be provided through the child tax credit system, see Vol IV in this series) and income support became in effect an "adults only" benefit. Thus the new form of para.(3)(a) only applies to payments made to a third party in respect of the claimant or his partner, if any.)

If the payment is derived from a benefit or pension listed in head (i) it counts as the claimant's. From November 15, 1999 this also applies to a payment from an occupational or personal pension (head (ia)), but not if the payment is made to the trustee in bankruptcy (or other person acting on the creditors' behalf) of a person who is bankrupt (or the subject of sequestration) and he (and his partner (before April 6, 2004, and still in "transitional cases"—see the note to reg.17, his family)) has no other actual or notional income (para.(3A)(c)). See *R(IS) 4/01* in the note to reg.42(4) and (4ZA) on the effect of head (ia).

In other cases the payment counts as the claimant's in so far as it is actually used for food, ordinary clothing or footwear, fuel, housing costs met by income support or housing benefit, council tax or water charges (head (ii)). "Ordinary clothing or footwear" is defined in para.(8). Para.29867 of the *Decision Makers Guide* suggests that wellington boots are not for "normal daily use", nor are special shoes needed because of a disability (as these are not worn by people in general on a daily basis).

If the payment is used for items or costs other than those listed in head (ii), it does not form part of the claimant's capital. However, *CJSA 1458/2002* holds that the exclusion from capital in head (ii) will not apply and money used for other items or costs will count as the claimant's if the money is paid to a third party at the claimant's own direction. The facts in *CJSA 1458/2002* were that the claimant had devised a scheme whereby rent from his tenant was paid into a particular account to be used "(either directly or indirectly) in respect of any of the landlords costs relating to the premises and (either directly or indirectly) in respect of any of the landlords mortgage capital repayments". The account into which the money was paid was a PEP (which the claimant had tried to open in the name of his mortgagee but had found this to be impossible in law). The Commissioner confirms the tribunal's decision that the claimant's deliberate failure to acquire an asset was a deprivation caught by para.(1). The claimant also contended that the payments into the PEP were excluded from his capital under head (ii) because they were being used for capital repayments on his mortgage. However, the tribunal had rejected this argument on the ground that the payments were not made to a third party but into an investment vehicle that was beneficially owned by the claimant. The Commissioner agreed with that analysis but stated that he would also reach the same result by another route, namely that the money was paid to the third party at the claimant's own direction and therefore the exclusion from capital in para.(3)(a) was not applicable. However, with respect to the Commissioner, it is suggested that there is nothing in the wording of para.(3)(a) that requires such an interpretation. Furthermore, it would seem to depart from the approach previously taken to this provision (and its income counterpart in reg.42(4)(a)(ii)), since it has long been recognised that the rules about payments to third parties do allow for some "benefit planning", as a means of meeting expenditure that is not covered by income support.

The operation of para.(3)(b) is clear. In these circumstances the payment would not form part of the claimant's actual capital in view of the obligation to use it for a third party.　　2.388

Paragraph (3) does not apply to payments from the listed Trusts and Funds nor to payments made in respect of an 18–25 year-old who is on a "New Deal" option, a person in the Intensive Activity Period (IAP) of the New Deal for those aged 25 or over, or the IAP for 50 plus, or a person aged 25 or over who is undertaking a "qualifying course" (para.(3A)). On "qualifying course", see the note to reg.17A of those Regulations. Regulation 17A allows a person aged 25 or over to be treated as available for work (see reg.21A of the JSA Regulations for the parallel provision in relation to the active seeking of work) while attending a full-time employment-related course. This concession is part of the Government's scheme to assist that age group to find work. While taking part in a New Deal option, a person may be eligible to receive a grant (spread over six months) or be able to apply for payments from a Discretionary Fund operated by the Employment Service to cover exceptional costs; payments may also be made from the Discretionary Fund in respect of people on a "qualifying course". Such payments may be paid to the provider of the employment or training rather than to the person himself. They will not count as notional capital for the purposes of any claim for income support.

Paras (4) and (5)

These two paragraphs establish an artificial method of dealing with one person companies or similar. The basic legal position is that if there is a company, the shareholders' assets are the value of the shares, not the value of the company's assets (*R(SB) 57/83*). But under para.(4), if the claimant is in a position analogous to a　　2.389

sole owner or partner in the business of the company (on which, see *R(IS) 8/92*), the value of his shareholding is disregarded, and he is treated as possessing a proportionate share of the capital of the company. The value is the net worth of the company's total assets taken together (*R(IS) 13/93*). The value of one particular asset within the total is not relevant in itself. However, as long as the claimant undertakes activities in the course of the business of the company, the amount produced by para.(4) is disregarded (para.(5)). Temporary interruptions in activity (*e.g.* holidays, short-term sickness) ought not to prevent para.(5) from applying. It is accepted in *R(IS) 13/93* that any activities which are more than *de minimis* satisfy para.(4).

Para.(6)

2.390   One of the effects of para.(6) is that the disregards in Sch.10 can apply to notional capital. However, *CIS 30/1993* decides that the disregard in para.26 of Sch.10 (taking steps to dispose of premises) could not apply where the claimant had already disposed of the capital so as to trigger reg.51(1). reg.51(6) did not provide any authority for altering the provisions of Sch.10 which could only apply where their conditions were met. This is a different view from that taken in some other decisions. See the note to para.26 of Sch.10.

CIS 231/1991 confirms that it is not necessary for the disregard under Sch.10 to have been applicable before the claimant deprived himself of the capital. The claimant had transferred his former home to his parents who were both over 60. When he claimed income support his parents were living in the home. The Commissioner holds that the former home fell to be disregarded under para.4(a) of Sch.10; the disregard in para.4 applied to notional, as well as actual, capital.

Para.(7)

2.391   The capital of which a person has deprived himself must be actual capital. In *CIS 240/1992* and *CIS 30/1993* the Commissioner raises the question (without expressing a conclusion) as to whether para.(1) can apply when a claimant is deemed to possess an equal share in a capital asset under reg.52. In *CIS 240/1992* the claimant had a quarter share in a property, but the effect of reg.52 was to treat him as having a half-share. The claimant's parents (his mother owned the other three-quarters of the property) then bought his share for £5,000, out of which he repaid them loans of £3,883. The Commissioner points out that as reg.52 operated to treat the claimant as having a notional equal share in the property, his actual share should not also count, since otherwise there would be double counting. Therefore, when he sold his actual share to his parents, was there no disposal of *actual* capital at all, or no disposal to the extent that his notional share exceeded his actual share? Para. 29809 of the *Decision Makers Guide* assumes that the rule in para.(1) can only apply to the claimant's actual share of the capital, even though the effect of reg.52 is to deem him to own a larger share. But this does not entirely deal with the Commissioner's point. In fact in *CIS 240/1992*, since the property was subject to a tenancy, even if under para.(1) the claimant was treated as still possessing his actual interest, the disregard in para.5 of Sch.10 (as in force at that time) would result in him having no capital. The new tribunal would also have to consider whether para.(1) applied when the claimant repaid the loans (see *R(SB) 12/91* above).

[¹Diminishing notional capital rule

2.392   **51A.**—(1) Where a claimant is treated as possessing capital under regulation 51(1) (notional capital), the amount which he is treated as possessing—

(a) in the case of a week that is subsequent to—

(i) the relevant week in respect of which the conditions set out in paragraph (2) are satisfied, or

(ii) a week which follows that relevant week and which satisfies those conditions,

shall be reduced by an amount determined under paragraph (2);

(b) in the case of a week in respect of which paragraph (1)(a) does not apply but where—

    (i) that week is a week subsequent to the relevant week, and

    (ii) that relevant week is a week in which the condition in paragraph (3) is satisfied,

shall be reduced by the amount determined under paragraph (3).

(2) This paragraph applies to a benefit week or part week where the claimant satisfies the conditions that—

(a) he is in receipt of income support; and

(b) but for regulation 51(1), he would have received an additional amount of income support in that benefit week or, as the case may be, that part week;

and in such a case, the amount of the reduction for the purposes of paragraph (1)(a) shall be equal to that additional amount.

(3) Subject to paragraph (4), for the purposes of paragraph (1)(b) the condition is that the claimant would have been entitled to income support in the relevant week, but for regulation 51(1), and in such a case the amount of the reduction shall be equal to the aggregate of—

(a) the amount of income support to which the claimant would have been entitled in the relevant week but for regulation 51(1); and for the purposes of this sub-paragraph if the relevant week is a part-week that amount shall be determined by dividing the amount of income support to which he would have been so entitled by the number equal to the number of days in the part-week and multiplying the quotient by 7;

(b) the amount of housing benefit (if any) equal to the difference between his maximum housing benefit and the amount (if any) of housing benefit which he is awarded in respect of the benefit week, within the meaning of regulation 2(1) of the Housing Benefit (General) Regulations 1987 (interpretation), which includes the last day of the relevant week;

(c) the amount of community charge benefit (if any) equal to the difference between his maximum community charge benefit and the amount (if any) of community charge benefit which he is awarded in respect of the benefit week, within the meaning of regulation 2(1) of the Community Charge Benefits (General) Regulations 1989 (interpretation) which includes the last day of the relevant week.

[²(d) the amount of council tax benefit (if any) equal to the difference between his maximum council tax benefit and the amount (if any) of council tax benefit which he is awarded in respect of the benefit week which includes the last day of the relevant week, and for this purpose "benefit week" has the same meaning as in regulation 2(1) of the Council Tax Benefit (General) Regulations 1992 (interpretation).]

(4) The amount determined under paragraph (3) shall be redetermined under that paragraph if the claimant makes a further claim for income support and the conditions in paragraph (5) are satisfied, and in such a case—

(a) sub-paragraphs [³(a) to (d)] of paragraph (3) shall apply as if for the words "relevant week" there were substituted the words "relevant subsequent week"; and

413

(b) subject to paragraph (6), the amount as re-determined shall have effect from the first week following the relevant subsequent week in question.

(5) The conditions are that—

(a) a further claim is made 26 or more weeks after—

(i) the date on which the claimant made a claim for income support in respect of which he was first treated as possessing the capital in question under regulation 51(1); or

(ii) in a case where there has been at least one re-determination in accordance with paragraph (4), the date on which he last made a claim for income support which resulted in the weekly amount being re-determined; or

(iii) the date on which he last ceased to be in receipt of income support; whichever last occurred; and

(b) the claimant would have been entitled to income support but for regulation 51(1).

(6) The amount as re-determined pursuant to paragraph (4) shall not have effect if it is less than the amount which applied in that case immediately before the re-determination and in such a case the higher amount shall continue to have effect.

(7) For the purpose of this regulation—

(a) "part-week" means a period to which sub-section (1A) of section 21 of the Act [SSCBA, s.124(5)] (amount etc. of income support) applies;

(b) "relevant week" means the benefit week or part-week in which the capital in question of which the claimant has deprived himself within the meaning of regulation 51(1)—

(i) was first taken into account for the purpose of determining his entitlement to income support; or

(ii) was taken into account on a subsequent occasion for the purpose of determining or re-determining his entitlement to income support on that subsequent occasion and that determination or re-determination resulted in his beginning to receive, or ceasing to receive, income support;

and where more than one benefit week or part-week is identified by reference to heads (i) and (ii) of this sub-paragraph the later or latest such benefit week or, as the case may be, the later or latest such part-week;

(c) "relevant subsequent week" means the benefit week or part-week which includes the day on which the further claim or, if more than one further claim has been made, the last such claim was made.]

AMENDMENTS

2.393 1. Income Support (General) Amendment No.3 Regulations 1990 (SI 1990/1776), reg.6 (October 1, 1990).

2. Income-related Benefits Schemes (Miscellaneous Amendments) Regulations 1993 (SI 1993/315), Sch., para.4 (April 1, 1993).

3. Social Security (Miscellaneous Amendments) (No.3) Regulations 2001 (SI 2001/859), reg.6(2) (April 9, 2001).

DEFINITIONS

2.394 "benefit week"—see reg.2(1).
"claimant"—*ibid.*
"community charge benefit"—*ibid.*

GENERAL NOTE

See the note to reg.51(1) for the general background. Reg.51A provides for the   **2.395**
reduction of the amount of notional capital fixed by reg.51(1). If the amount of
notional capital remaining is not sufficient to remove entitlement to income support
altogether, it is to be treated as reducing each week by the amount by which income
support would be increased if it did not exist at all (paras (1)(a) and (2)). If the
amount does remove entitlement it is to be treated as reducing each week by the
amount of income support the person would receive if the notional capital had not
been fixed plus the proportion of rent and council tax not met by housing benefit or
council tax benefit (paras (1)(b) and (3)). There are complicated provisions for redetermination and recalculation.

Note that the reduction required by reg.51A does not start to operate until there
is a week in which the claimant either would have been in receipt of income support
(para.(3)) or would have been in receipt of an increased amount of income support
(para.(2)), *but for* reg.51(1). Thus in *R(IS) 8/04*, where the claimant had used capital
to purchase a car for the purpose of securing entitlement to income support and it
seemed likely that the value of the car (once this was established) would result in his
actual capital exceeding £8,000, reg.51A did not apply to reduce his notional
capital. This was because it could not be said that "but for" the notional capital he
would have been in receipt of income support.

The inter-relationship of this regulation, which ties the reduction in notional
capital very much to income support rates, and *R(IS) 1/91* is of considerable difficulty. The Tribunal of Commissioners' diminishing capital rule works on reasonable
expenditure not necessarily limited to income support rates. Could a claimant take
the benefit of this more generous rule, or had its implication from the regulations
been destroyed by the introduction of this express provision? *R(IS) 9/92* holds that
the second alternative is correct.

Another pertinent issue is the date from which the diminishing notional capital
rule applies. If reg.51A only operates from the date of the claim for income support,
as its terms imply and as *CIS 3268/2002* confirms, it would seem unfair for some
equivalent diminishing notional capital rule not to apply to amounts of notional
capital during any gap between the date of the intentional deprivation and the claim
for income support. This point is considered in *CIS 3268/2002*. However, the
Commissioner concludes that in many cases it is a "red herring". This is because
expenses such as living and household expenses which could be taken into account
in applying a diminishing notional capital rule will often have already been taken into
account in calculating the amount of actual capital of which a claimant deprived
himself. If such expenses have already been taken into account there is no justification for making any further deduction from the amount of the notional capital. The
Commissioner recognises that there may be a problem where a claimant has
deprived himself of the entire amount of his actual capital in one transaction and
then does not claim income support for some time. However, this did not arise on
the facts of the case before him.

Capital jointly held

52. Except where a claimant possesses capital which is disregarded under   **2.396**
regulation 51(4) (notional capital), where a claimant and one or more
persons are beneficially entitled in possession to any capital asset they shall
be treated as if each of them were entitled in possession [¹to the whole beneficial interest therein in an equal share and the foregoing provisions of this
Chapter shall apply for the purposes of calculating the amount of capital
which the claimant is treated as possessing as if it were actual capital which
the claimant does possess.]

2.397   1. Social Security Amendment (Capital) Regulations 1998 (SI 1998/2250), reg.2 (October 12, 1998).

DEFINITION

"claimant"—see reg.2(1), reg.23(1).

GENERAL NOTE

2.398   This regulation was amended on October 12, 1998 following the decision in *CIS 15936/1996, CIS 263/1997* and *CIS 3283/1997* (see the common Appendix). In that decision the Commissioner held that the October 1995 amendment to the regulation was *ultra vires* (see also *CIS 2575/1997* below). The October 1995 amendment had provided that the value of a claimant's actual or deemed share of jointly-owned capital was to be calculated by dividing the net value of the capital as a whole by the number of co-owners. The aim of that amendment had been to reverse the effect of the Court of Appeal's decision in *Chief Adjudication Officer v Palfrey and others, The Times*, February 17, 1995, also reported as part of *R(IS) 26/95* (see below). See the 1998 edition of *Mesher and Wood, Income-related Benefits: the Legislation* for the October 1995 form of reg.52. The Government decided not to appeal against the decision in *CIS 15936/1996, CIS 263/1997* and *CIS 3283/1997* but (somewhat unusually) to restore the form of the regulation that existed before October 2, 1995. A similar amendment was made to the JSA Regulations, the Family Credit Regulations and Disability Working Allowance Regulations (both now revoked), the Housing Benefit Regulations and the Council Tax Benefit Regulations.

The result, broadly, is that there is no double "deeming" under this regulation. The first "deeming" remains, *i.e.* joint owners are still deemed to have equal shares in the property (although see the Court of Appeal's decision in *Hourigan* under "*Scope of the rule*" below for the limited meaning of joint-owner in this context). But the second, that the value of the share was to be "deemed" by reference to the value of the property as a whole, does not. Thus instead of attributing what could be a totally artificial value to the deemed (or actual) share, it will, following *Palfrey*, have to be given its true market value. This, together with the Court of Appeal's decision in *Hourigan*, will have the effect of mitigating the worst effects of this rule in certain cases but it will still have arbitrary and unfair consequences for some claimants.

2.399   The basis of the Commissioner's decision in *CIS 15936/1996, CIS 263/1997* and *CIS 3283/1997* was that the October 1995 amendment was outside the powers in s.136(3) and (5)(a) of the Contributions and Benefits Act 1992. He held that the power in s.136(3) to provide for the calculation or estimation of capital did not allow assets to be valued in a way that had no relationship to their actual value. In addition, s.136(5)(a) did not authorise the amendment because the amendment was concerned with valuation, not the actual capital or income which a person did or did not possess. In *CIS 2575/1997* the Commissioner confirms that his decision in *CIS 15936/1996, CIS 263/1997* and *CIS 3283/1997* equally applies to land outside the UK and to all forms of co-ownership.

The decision in *CIS 15936/1996, CIS 263/1997* and *CIS 3283/1997* was given on May 21, 1998. The guidance to AOs on the effect of this decision expressed the view that it could not be applied for any period before May 21, 1998 because of s.69 of the Administration Act 1992 (the "anti-test case rule"). However, it is by no means certain that s.69 was applicable in cases of *ultra vires* regulations. There is indeed provision for this in s.27(5) of the Social Security Act 1998 (which has replaced s.69) but s.69 was silent on the matter. Given the nature of *ultra vires* declarations, it is certainly arguable that in the absence of an express provision, s.69 did not apply in this situation. The Commissioner in *CIS 2575/1997* refers to but does not rule on this question, although he does draw attention to *CA 73/1994* which apparently held that s.69 did bite on an *ultra vires* decision by a Commissioner.

As has been suggested to me by Nick Wikeley, there was another complication   **2.400**
arising out of the Government's decision to restore the pre-October 1995 form of
reg.52. Because JSA was not introduced until October 7, 1996, there was no pre-
October 1995 formulation to which the parallel JSA provision (reg.115 of the JSA
Regulations) could revert. Since the effect of the decision in *CIS 15936/1996,
CIS 263/1997* and *CIS 3283/1997* was to remove the last part of reg.115, it followed
that there was no sensible provision dealing with the valuation of jointly-owned
assets for the purposes of JSA at least from May 21, 1998 (and possibly from the
commencement of the JSA scheme if an *ultra vires* decision was not caught by s.69)
until the 1998 amendment came into force on October 12, 1998.

The validity of reg.52 had also been challenged before the Tribunal of
Commissioners in *R(IS) 26/95 (Palfrey)* on the ground of irrationality. But the
Commissioners held, given their ruling on valuation under reg.52, that irrationality
had not been made out and that reg.52 was validly made. The Court of Appeal in
Palfrey did not express a view as to whether reg.52 was invalid, as this argument only
became relevant if the CAO's construction of reg.52 was correct; nor did the Court
of Appeal in *Hourigan*.

Scope of the rule

Previous editions of Mesher and Wood, *Income-related Benefits: the Legislation* have   **2.401**
described this regulation as containing an extraordinary rule (a view endorsed in *CIS
408/1990*). In *CIS 807/1991* the rule is described as draconian. In the words of
Brooke L.J. in *Hourigan* (see below): "The intention of this statutory scheme is that
people should be expected to dip into their capital rather than be reliant on the state
for income support. Why should Parliament have expected people to dip into capital
which they did not in fact possess?" Shared interests in assets had caused difficult
problems of valuation under supplementary benefit. The intention of reg.52 was to
provide a solution which is simple to apply, but the conceptual difficulties posed are
formidable.

The intended effect of reg.52 is that except in the case of deemed ownership of a
company's assets under reg.51(4), if the claimant has any share of the beneficial interest (*i.e.* the right to dispose of something) in an asset he is treated as having an equal
share in the interest, regardless of the legal and equitable position. ("In possession"
means that ownership is enjoyed at present, rather than on the happening of some
event in the future.) Thus if a person has a 10 per cent interest in a house, and another
person has a 90 per cent interest, each is treated as having a 50 per cent interest.
There are many situations in which such a division might occur. The same could
apply to, say, joint bank accounts or Building Society accounts. The result could
easily be, in conjunction with the rules on disregards in Sch.10, that a claimant is
fixed with capital assets which he is not legally entitled to at all, let alone able to realise
immediately. Although crisis loans under the social fund may be available (Social
Fund Guide, para.4717–8), the guidance presently given is in terms of short-term
support while assets are realised, which does not meet the case. Normally the
claimant's "remedy" for the artificial effects of reg.52 would be to dispose of his share
in the asset, when he will receive an amount appropriate to his actual legal share. But
this will not always be possible. The deprivation rule in reg.51(1) should not apply in
these circumstances: see reg.51(7) and the note to that paragraph and para.29809 of
the *Decision Makers Guide*.

However, doubt as to the ambit of reg.52 was raised as a result of the decision in
CIS 7097/1995. The claimant's husband went to live in a nursing home on a permanent basis. In order to help finance the cost of this, £7,000 National Savings
belonging to him was cashed in and paid into their joint bank account. It was never
intended that this should thereby become part of the joint money in the account; it
had simply been paid into the account so that the nursing home fees could be paid
by direct debit. A separate tally was kept of this money which had been declared as
the husband's own money for the purposes of his application to the local authority
for help with the nursing home fees. The AO treated the claimant as entitled to half

of the balance in the joint account (including her husband's National Savings) which when added to her other capital meant that she did not qualify for income support. However, the Commissioner holds that reg.52 did not apply to her husband's National Savings. Reg.52 only operated where property was held in joint beneficial ownership because it was only then that two or more people were "beneficially entitled in possession" to a given capital asset. Reg.52 was needed because of the special nature of joint beneficial ownership and deemed a joint beneficial owner to have the equal share that he would by law have if the joint ownership was severed. But cases where property was held in undivided shares fell outside reg.52 because under such an arrangement each co-owner was beneficially and individually entitled to his own share of the actual capital. His share was a different asset from the shares belonging to the others; and in contrast to the joint right of a joint owner was an asset which was separately disposable by him. On the facts of this case, there was clear evidence that the normal presumption of joint beneficial ownership between a husband and wife operating a joint bank account did not apply. It was obviously intended that the balance of the husband's National Savings was to remain his sole property and that it had merely been paid into the joint account for convenience. The consequence was that the claimant was entitled to income support as her capital did not include any of her husband's National Savings.

2.402   The question whether reg.52 also applies to deem actual unequal shares in a capital asset to be equal shares was, as the Commissioner in *CIS 7097/1995* points out, expressly reserved by the Tribunal of Commissioners in *CIS 417/1992*, reported as part of *R(IS) 26/95*, and there was no argument on the point before the Court of Appeal. But it was considered, albeit briefly, in *CIS 240/1992*. In that case the claimant and his mother were tenants in common of a property, the claimant's share being one quarter. The Commissioner accepted that a situation where a claimant had an unequal share of the beneficial interest fell within the scope of reg.52, so that the claimant was to be treated as having a half-share in the property. See also *CIS 127/1993*. Moreover, in *CIS 15936/1996*, *CIS 263/1997* and *CIS 3283/1997* the Commissioner expressly dissents from any general statement in *CIS 7097/1995* that reg.52 was confined to joint tenancies. In his view, reg.52 applied to all kinds of co-ownership, including joint tenancies and tenancies in common. He repeats this view in *CIS 2575/1997*.

    Clearly the policy intention is that reg.52 has effect beyond the fairly limited role of deeming a person to have an equal share of a capital asset that is in joint beneficial ownership. However, the Secretary of State's contention that reg.52 does also apply to tenancies in common was unanimously rejected by the Court of Appeal in *Hourigan v Secretary of State for Work and Pensions* [2002] EWCA Civ 1890, reported as *R(IS) 4/03* (which was the appeal from *CIS 5906/1999*). The claimant had purchased her home from the local authority with the help of her son who contributed five-sixths of the purchase price. When she went into a residential care home her income support was stopped on the basis that she had capital in excess of £8,000 because she was deemed to be the beneficial owner of half the house under reg.52.

    Brooke L.J. accepted that the language of reg.52 lent itself naturally to the situation in which two or more people were jointly entitled to the equitable interest in the same capital asset since they did not each possess a separate share in the equitable interest. In that situation the effect of reg.52 was to treat the joint tenancy as severed and to deem the claimant as having an equal share (with the other joint tenants) of the whole beneficial interest. However, in relation to tenancies in common, there was no need for such a deemed severing as the beneficial interest that a tenant in common owned was a separately disposable asset. It was a misuse of language to say that the claimant and her son were beneficially entitled to the house within the meaning of reg.52 as they were not. To interpret the provision in the way contended for by the Secretary of State would require very much clearer words. The Court acknowledged that a crude deeming of equal apportionment where property is jointly-owned could produce unjust results, not only against claimants but also in some cases in their favour, as it could in the case of a tenancy in common. Its approach therefore was to restrict the manifest unfairness that could result from reg.52 to the situation where its wording clearly did apply, that is in relation to property held in joint beneficial ownership. The consequence was that it was the claimant's one sixth share that fell to be valued with the result that she did not have capital in excess of £8,000.

The Secretary of State decided not to apply for leave to appeal to the House of Lords against the decision in *Hourigan*. Thus the consequence is that it has now been authoritively established that reg.52 only applies to property held under a joint tenancy, not a tenancy in common.

Note that reg.52 only applies where the beneficial interest is jointly-owned. It does not apply merely because there is a separation between legal and beneficial interests, for instance where one person holds assets on trust for another. But if an interest in a trust fund is jointly-owned, then reg.52 may apply. This was the case in *R(IS)2/93*, where a building society account in the claimant's sole name was in fact a joint asset of herself and her (separated) husband. She had to be treated as possessing half of the amount in the account, regardless of how it might be dealt with in matrimonial proceedings. But it is arguable that in the case of assets that are the subject of matrimonial dispute, reg.52 should not apply and their value should be disregarded, until ownership is resolved. See *Welfare Rights Bulletin* 108 p.5, referring to *CIS 298/1989* (a decision given without reasons). This should apply whether or not a couple were married. However, note *CIS 982/2002* which states that there is no general rule that property which is frozen or the subject of a dispute is to be disregarded or taken as having no value. The claimant and her husband, from whom she was separated, had a savings account in their joint names. The account was subject to a "matrimonial difficulties stop", the effect of which was that the claimant had no access to the funds without her husband's consent or an order from the court. The decision sets out a number of detailed questions that had to be considered in deciding whether the funds in the account were part of the claimant's capital and, if so, how her share was to be valued.

Valuation under reg.52

2.403
The restoration of reg.52 to its original form on October 12, 1998 means that it is the deemed equal share that has to be valued, *not* the proportionate share of the overall value that has to be taken (see the Court of Appeal's decision in *Chief Adjudication Officer v Palfrey and others, The Times*, February 17, 1995, also reported as part of *R(IS) 26/95*, which had upheld the Tribunal of Commissioners' decisions in *CIS 391/1992* and *CIS 417/1992* (reported as part of *R(IS) 26/95*). The Tribunal of Commissioners gave detailed guidance as to the basis of a proper valuation of such a share (paras 53 and 54 in *CIS 391/1992*). In both *CIS 391/1992* and *CIS 417/1992* ownership was shared with relatives who were unable or unwilling to sell the property or buy the claimant's interest. The Commissioners recognised, as did the Court of Appeal, that the market value in such cases may well be nil.

See *Mesher and Wood, Income-related Benefits: the Legislation* (1995) for a summary of the Tribunal of Commissioners' decision and the Court of Appeal's decision in *Palfrey*. See also *CIS 413/1992* which notes the differences that arise from the law of property in Scotland. In *Palfrey* the Tribunal of Commissioners state that the SSAT should have exercised its inquisitorial jurisdiction to call for the documents under which the property was acquired in order to sort out the beneficial ownership. But in *CIS 127/1993* the Commissioner did not find this necessary, since it was not disputed that the house had been conveyed into the names of the claimant and her daughter, and the method of valuation was the same whether the claimant and her daughter actually had equal shares or were deemed to do so by reg.52.

Note *R(IS) 3/96* which contains a useful discussion as to whether the District Valuer's opinion supplied in that case met the requirements of *CIS 391/1992*. The guidance to decision makers suggests that they should obtain an expert opinion on the market value of a deemed share in land/premises. In a case where the other owners will not buy the share or agree to a sale of the asset as a whole, the guidance states that the valuer should not simply assume that a court would order a sale but must consider the particular circumstances and take into account legal costs, length of time to obtain possession, etc. The guidance also says that the expert would need to explain whether on the facts of the case there was any market for the deemed share and indicate how the value of the deemed share had been calculated.

2.404   However, in practice, it seems that the valuations obtained do not always meet such criteria (as noted in *CIS 3197/2003*, see below). See, for example, *R(JSA) 1/02* which was concerned with valuing the claimant's interest in his former matrimonial home. His wife, from whom he was separated and who was in ill-health, continued to live there with their daughter, who had learning difficulties. The valuation obtained by the Jobcentre on a standard form (A64A/LA1) gave the open market value as £30,000 and the claimant's deemed undivided share as £9,200. No reasons were given for this conclusion. The property was leasehold but there was no evidence as to the remaining term of the lease, or as to the condition of the property. There was also no evidence as to the age of the daughter and no consideration as to whether a court would order a sale (which seemed very unlikely, given the purpose for which the property had been acquired and the purpose for which it was being used). The Commissioner, referring to *CIS 191/1994*, holds that there was no evidence that the claimant's capital exceeded £8,000. He stated that everything depended on the facts and the evidence before the tribunal. In this case the valuation evidence was so unsatisfactory as to be worthless. He set out the following guidance on valuation:

> "13. Proper valuation evidence should include details of the valuer's expertise, the basis on which he or she holds him or herself out as able to give expert evidence in relation to the property in question. Where it is the sale of a share in a property which is in issue, the evidence should deal with the valuer's experience in relation to such shares, and their sale. The property, and any leasehold interest, should be described in sufficient detail, including details of the length of any lease, of any special terms in it, and of the location, size and condition of the property, to show that the factors relevant to its value have been taken into account, and the reasons for the conclusion as to the value should be given. A similar approach should be applied to a share of a property, and an explanation should be given of the factors identified as relevant to the valuation, and how they affect it. The expert should also give evidence of any comparables identified, or of other reasons why it is concluded that the share could be sold at any particular price. If there is no evidence of actual sales of such interests, an acceptable explanation of the absence of such evidence should be given.
> 14. I appreciate that, in cases of this kind, this will on occasions be a counsel of perfection which cannot be realised. Where a valuer does not have relevant information, and proceeds upon assumptions, the report should state what is missing, and should also state the assumptions upon which it is based. This will normally give the claimant the opportunity to correct any mistaken assumptions or other errors of fact in the report."

2.405   It will not always be the case that a deemed equal share in a property will be of minimal value, even if the other co-owners are unwilling to sell. As *Wilkinson v Chief Adjudication Officer*, CA, March 24, 2000, reported as *R(IS) 1/01*, illustrates, the purposes for which the joint ownership was established will need to be scrutinised in order to assess whether a court would order a sale. In *Wilkinson* the claimant's mother had died, leaving her home to the claimant and her brother "to do with as they wish". It was accepted that the mother had expressed the hope that the claimant's brother would live in the house with his son when his divorce proceedings in Australia were resolved (although there was nothing in the will to this effect). The claimant contended that the capital value of her half share in the property was of a nominal value only because her brother was unwilling to leave the property and unwilling to sell his share in it. She maintained that a court would not order a sale under s.30 of the Law of Property Act 1925 (repealed with effect from January 1, 1998 and replaced by ss.14 and 15 of the Trusts of Land and Appointment of Trustees Act 1996). But the Court of Appeal, by a majority (Mummery and Potter L.JJ.), disagreed. This was not a case like *Palfrey* where property had been acquired by joint owners for a collateral purpose (*e.g.* for them to live in as long as they wished) and that purpose would be defeated by ordering a sale. On the contrary, this was a case where an order for sale would enable the claimant's mother's wishes, as expressed in her will, to be carried out. Her brother's unwillingness to sell or pay the claimant for the value of her share was in fact having the effect of defeating that testamentary purpose. Evans L.J., however, took the opposite view. He considered that the claimant's share should be valued on the basis that a sale would not be ordered because this would defeat the mother's wish that her son and grandson be allowed to live in the property. As this case illustrates, much will depend on the circumstances in a particular case (and the view that is taken of those circumstances).

The issue was again revisited in *CIS 3197/2003*. The claimant jointly owned a house with her daughter, the daughter having a two-thirds share. The claimant went into a nursing home, leaving the house in the occupation of her daughter and the daughter's disabled child. The daughter would not agree to a sale of the house nor was she willing to buy out the claimant's share. It semed unlikely that a court would order a sale. In view of the Secretary of State's failure to provide proper evidence of the value of the claimant's share the Commissioner found that the value of the claimant's interest was nil. However, he added that tribunals should not approach the matter in this way. If the evidence was incomplete they should adjourn with directions as to the ways in which the evidence should be supplemented and should not decide the case on the burden of proof. Clearly where there has been no attempt to obtain any valuation evidence this should apply. However, if such attempts have been made and the evidence remains inadequate, it is suggested that the burden of proof may need to come into play (and indeed this was the approach taken in both *R(IS) 3/96* and *CIS 417/1992*). For example, in *R(IS) 3/96* it was held that grounds for revising the claimant's award had not been shown in the light of the deficiences in the District Valuer's report.

Note the increased upper and lower capital limits for people permanently in residential care from April 1996 (regs 45(b) and 53(1A), see the note to reg.53) and people aged over 60 or over from April 2001 (regs 45(aa) and 53 (1ZA) (note that as a consequence of the start of the state pension credit scheme on October 6, 2003 the £12,000/£6,000 limits now only apply if the claimant's partner is aged 60 or over; if the claimant has reached the qualifying age for state pension credit (defined in s.137(1) of the Contributions and Benefits Act—the effect of that definition is that the qualifying age is 60 for both men and women until April 2010 after which it will increase by stages to 65 in line with the increase in pensionable age for a woman) he will not be entitled to income support (s.124(1)(aa) of the 1992 Act))).

Calculation of tariff income from capital

53.—(1) [³Except where the circumstances prescribed in paragraph [⁶ (1ZA) or] (1B) apply to the claimant,] where the claimant's capital calculated in accordance with this Part exceeds £3,000 it shall be treated as equivalent to a weekly income of £1 for each complete £250 in excess of £3,000 but not exceeding [²£8,000].
[⁶ (IZA) Where the claimant—

(a) [⁸. . .] has a partner who is aged 60 or over;
(b) is not a person to whom the circumstances prescribed in paragraph (1B) apply; and
(c) has capital which, calculated in accordance with this Part, exceeds £6,000, that capital shall be treated as equivalent to a weekly income of £1 for each complete £250 in excess of £6,000 but not exceeding £12,000.]

[³(1A) Where the circumstances prescribed in paragraph (1B) apply to the claimant and that claimant's capital calculated in accordance with this

2.406

Part exceeds £10,000, it shall be treated as equivalent to a weekly income of £1 for each complete £250 in excess of £10,000 but not exceeding £16,000.

(1B) For the purposes of paragraph (1A) and regulation 45, the prescribed circumstances are that the claimant lives permanently in—

(a) a residential care or nursing home [4. . .] and that home [4. . .] provides board and personal care for the claimant by reason of his old age, disablement, past or present dependence on alcohol or drugs or past or present mental disorder; or

(b) an establishment run by the Abbey field Society including all bodies corporate or incorporate which are affiliated to that Society; or

(c) accommodation provided under section 3 of, and Part II of the Schedule to, the Polish Resettlement Act 1947 (provision of accommodation in camps) where the claimant requires personal care [5 by reason of old age, disablement, past or present dependence on alcohol or drugs, past or present mental disorder or a terminal illness and the care is provided in the home].

[4(d) residential accommodation.]

(1C) For the purposes of paragraph (1B), a claimant shall be treated as living permanently in such home or accommodation where he is absent—

(a) from a home or accommodation referred to in sub-paragraph [4(a), (b) or (d)] of paragraph (1B)—

(i) [7 . . .] in the case of a person over pensionable age, for a period not exceeding 52 weeks, and

(ii) in any other case, for a period not exceeding 13 weeks;

(b) from accommodation referred to in sub-paragraph (c) of paragraph (1B), where the claimant, with the agreement of the manager of the accommodation, intends to return to the accommodation in due course.]

(2) Notwithstanding [3paragraphs (1) [6, (1ZA)] and (1A)], where any part of the excess is not a complete £250 that part shall be treated as equivalent to a weekly income of £1.

(3) For the purposes of [3paragraphs (1) [6, (1ZA)] and (1A)], capital includes any income treated as capital under regulations [1 . . .] 48 and 60 ([1 . . .] income treated as capital and liable relative payments treated as capital).

[3(4) For the purposes of this regulation, the definition of 'residential accommodation" in regulation 21(3) (applicable amounts of income support in special cases) shall have effect as if, after the words 'subject to the following provisions of this regulation", there were inserted' (except paragraphs (4) and (4A)).]

AMENDMENTS

2.407

1. Income Support (General) Amendment No.5 Regulations 1988 (SI 1988/2022), reg.13 (December 12, 1988).

2. Income-Related Benefits (Miscellaneous Amendments) Regulations 1990 (SI 1990/671), reg.5 (April 9, 1990).

3. Income-related Benefits Schemes (Miscellaneous Amendments) Regulations 1996 (SI 1996/462), reg.12(1) (April 8, 1996).

4. Income-related Benefits and Jobseeker's Allowance (Miscellaneous Amendments) Regulations Regulations 1997 (SI 1997/65), reg.8 (April 7, 1997).

5. Income-related Benefits and Jobseeker's Allowance (Amendment) (No. 2) Regulations 1997 (SI 1997/2197), reg.7(5) and (6)(a) (October 6, 1997).

6. Social Security Amendment (Capital Limits and Earnings Disregards) Regulations 2000 (SI 2000/2545), reg.2(1)(c) (April 9, 2001).

7. Social Security Amendment (Residential Care and Nursing Homes) Regulations 2001 (SI 2001/3767), reg.2(1) and Pt I of Sch., para.9 (April 8, 2002).

8. State Pension Credit (Consequential, Transitional and Miscellaneous Provisions) Regulations 2002 (SI 2002/3019), reg.29(3) (October 6, 2003).

DEFINITIONS

"claimant"—see reg.2(1), reg.23(1).
"nursing home"—see reg.19(3).
"residential accommodation"—see reg.21(3).
"residential care home"—see reg.19(3).

GENERAL NOTE

The overall capital limit under reg.45 has been £8,000 since April 1990, but on April 8, 1996 it was raised to £16,000 for claimants living permanently in residential care or nursing homes, residential accommodation or Polish resettlement homes (see reg.45(b) and para.(1B)). For these claimants the tariff income rule only applies to capital between £10,000 and £16,000 (para.(1A)). In addition, on April 9, 2001 the capital limit was increased to £12,000 where the claimant or any partner is aged 60 or over (since October 6, 2003, when state pension credit was introduced, this provision only applies if the claimant's partner is 60 or over; if the claimant has reached the qualifying age for state pension credit (defined in s.137(1) of the Contributions and Benefits Act—the effect of that definition is that the qualifying age is 60 for both men and women until April 2010 after which it will increase by stages to 65 in line with the increase in pensionable age for a woman) he will not be entitled to income support (s.124(1)(aa) of the 1992 Act)) (see reg.45(aa) and para.(1ZA)). In this case the tariff income rule only applies to capital over £6,000. | 2.408

The effect of paras (1), (1ZA) and (1A) is that if the claimant and partner (if any) have capital over £3,000 (£6,000 for claimants within para.(1ZA) or £10,000 for claimants within para.(1B)), but not over £8,000 (£12,000 for para.(1ZA) claimants, £16,000 for para.(1B) claimants), it is treated as producing an income of £1 per week for each complete £250 between the limits, and £1 per week for any odd amount left over. Thus if a claimant (other than one to whom para.(IZA) or (1B) applies) has exactly £6,000, that is treated as producing £12 per week. If he has £4,001, that is treated as producing £5 per week. The actual income from most forms of capital is disregarded under para.22 of Sch.9.

Para. (1B)
See the notes to the definitions of residential care home and nursing home in reg.2(1) and residential accommodation in reg.21 (note the effect of para.(4) which enables people in residential accommodation who are under 18 or not receiving board to benefit from the higher capital limits). Under sub-para.(b) all Abbey field Homes are included whether or not they provide board and personal care. | 2.409

Para. (1C)
This deals with periods of temporary absence from the accommodation for claimants covered by para.(1B). | 2.410

Liable Relatives

Interpretation

2.411   **54.** In this Chapter, unless the context otherwise requires—
"claimant" includes a young claimant;
"liable relative" means–

(a) a spouse or former spouse of a claimant or of a member of the claimant's family;

(b) a parent of a child or young person who is a member of the claimant's family or of a young claimant;

(c) a person who has not been adjudged to be the father of a child or young person who is a member of the claimant's family or of a young claimant where that person is contributing towards the maintenance of that child, young person or young claimant and by reason of that contribution he may reasonably be treated as the father of that child, young person or young claimant;

(d) a person liable to maintain another person by virtue of section 26(3)(c) of the Act [SSAA, s.78(6)(c)] (liability to maintain) where the latter is the claimant or a member of the claimant's family,

and, in this definition, a reference to a child's, young person's or young claimant's parent includes any person in relation to whom the child, young person or young claimant was treated as a child or a member of the family;

"payment" means a periodical payment or any other payment made by or derived from a liable relative including, except in the case of a discretionary trust, any payment which would be so made or derived upon application being made by the claimant but which has not been acquired by him but only from the date on which [¹it could be expected to be acquired were an application made]; but it does not include any payment—

(a) arising from a disposition of property made in contemplation of, or as a consequence of—

   (i) an agreement to separate; or

   (ii) any proceedings for judicial separation, divorce or nullity of marriage;

(b) made after the death of the liable relative;

(c) made by way of a gift but not in aggregate or otherwise exceeding £250 in the period of 52 weeks beginning with the date on which the payment, or if there is more than one such payment the first payment, is made; and, in the case of a claimant who continues to be in receipt of income support at the end of the period of 52 weeks, this provision shall continue to apply thereafter with the modification that any subsequent period of 52 weeks shall begin with the first day of the benefit week in which the first payment is made after the end of the previous period of 52 weeks;

(d) [² . . .]

(e) made—
  (i) to a third party in respect of the claimant or a member of the claimant's family; or
  (ii) to the claimant or to a member of the claimant's family in respect of a third party,
where having regard to the purpose of the payment, the terms under which it is made and its amount it is unreasonable to take it into account;
(f) in kind;
(g) to, or in respect of, a child or young person who is to be treated as not being a member of the claimant's household under regulation 16 (circumstances in which a person is to be treated as being or not being a member of the same household);
(h) which is not a periodical payment, to the extent that any amount of that payment—
  (i) has already been taken into account under this Part by virtue of a previous claim or determination; or
  (ii) has been recovered under section 27(1) of the Act [SSAA, s.74(1)] (prevention of duplication of payments) or is currently being recovered; or
  (iii) at the time the determination is made, has been used by the claimant except where he has deprived himself of that amount for the purpose of securing entitlement to income support or increasing the amount of that benefit;
"periodical payment" means—
(a) A payment which is made or is due to be made at regular intervals in pursuance of a court order or agreement for maintenance;
(b) in a case where the liable relative has established a pattern of making payments at regular intervals, any such payment;
(c) any payment not exceeding the amount of income support payable had that payment not been made;
(d) any payment representing a commutation of payments to which sub-paragraphs (a) or (b) of this definition applies whether made in arrears or in advance,
but does not include a payment due to be made before the first benefit week pursuant to the claim which is not so made;
"young claimant" means a person aged 16 or over but under 19 who makes a claim for income support.

AMENDMENTS

1. Income Support (General) Amendment Regulations 1988 (SI 1988/663), reg.23 (April 11, 1988).   **2.412**

2. Social Security (Working Tax Credit and Child Tax Credit) (Consequential Amendments) Regulations 2003 (SI 2003/455), reg.2 and Sch.1, para.14 (April 6, 2004, except in "transitional cases" and see further the note to reg.17 of the Income Support Regulations).

DEFINITIONS

"the Act"—see reg.2(1).
"benefit week"—*ibid.*
"child"—see 1986 Act, s.20(11) (SSCBA, s.137(1)).
"claimant"—see reg.2(1), reg.23(1).

"family"—see 1986 Act, s.20(11) (SSCBA, s.137(1)).
"young person"—see reg.2(1), reg.14.

GENERAL NOTE

2.413   The rules for liable relative payments do not apply to payments of child support maintenance paid under an assessment carried out in accordance with the Child Support Acts 1991–1995 (reg.25A). They are taken into account as income in accordance with regs 60A to 60D.

"Liable relative"

2.414   Note that the definition for these purposes is not restricted to those who are obliged to maintain others under s.78(6) of the Administration Act, but includes in particular, a former spouse and a person who may reasonably be treated as the father of a child (by reason of contributing to the maintenance of the child).

"Payment"

2.415   The general definition is very wide, including payments not yet acquired which would be made on application (*cf.* reg.51(2)). The general category of "payment" is divided into "periodical payments" (further defined below) and "other payments". This division is important in the following regulations.

The list of exceptions is also very important—

(a) A payment arising from a disposition of property made in connection with an agreement to separate or matrimonial proceedings is not a liable relative payment (LRP). There had been great problems in construing the similar, but not identical, supplementary benefit provision, in particular in deciding when a payment "resulted from" a disposition of property. Although the words here are "arising from," the authoritative settlement of the supplementary benefit problem in *R(SB) 1/89* should apply. The claimant received a payment of £2,500 from her ex-husband pursuant to a county court order. This was a consent order made on the basis that the claimant gave up any claims against her ex-husband's houses. The Tribunal of Commissioners holds that there must be a chain of causation, however short, between the disposition and the payment, and that the prior disposition does not have to be by way of sale. Where a payment is made in discharge of a claimant's proprietary interest (or a claim to such an interest) it results from a disposition of property. Where it is made in discharge of maintenance obligations the payment stands alone and does not result from a disposition. *R(SB) 1/89* approves the result of *CSB 1160/1986* where a husband and wife had a joint building society account. On their separation they agreed to split the account and as a result the husband paid £2,500 to the wife, who was receiving supplementary benefit. It was held that the building society account was "property" and that the agreement to split it was a "disposition." The payment then resulted from a disposition of property. It was not a LRP, and had to be dealt with under the ordinary rules on resources.

(b) Payments made after the liable relative's death are not LRPs.

(c) Gifts up to £250 in 52 weeks do not count as LRPs. In view of para.(f), para.(c) must apply to gifts of money or property.

(d) This paragraph, which was revoked on April 6, 2004 (except in "transitional cases"—see the note to reg.17), excluded payments to which reg.44(2) (payments to residential schools for a child's or young person's maintenance) applied (reg.44(2) was also revoked with effect from April 6, 2004, except in "transitional cases"—see reg.17; see the 2003 edition of this volume for reg.44 and the notes to that regulation). The revocation of reg.44, and in turn this paragraph, are part of the consequential changes that apply from April 6,

2004 (except in "transitional cases"—see the note to reg.17) because of the removal of amounts for children and young persons from the income support scheme; financial assistance to help with the cost of bringing up a child or young person is now to be provided through the child tax credit system, see Vol. IV of this series.

Note that a new disregard has been introduced in place of the provisions formerly in reg.44(2) (see para.25A of Sch.9). Note also para.(e).

(e) Payments from liable relatives to third parties in respect of the claimant or a member of the claimant's family do not count as LRPs if it would be unreasonable for them to do so. Here much of the guidance in *R(SB) 6/88* is still relevant. This indicates that while the factors mentioned must be considered, other relevant factors may also be considered. If the payment is not a LRP, see reg.51(3).

   Similar rules apply to payments to a member of the claimant's family for a third party (and see para.(9)).

(f) Payments in kind are not LRPs. This could be an important factor in benefit planning.

(g) Payments to or in respect of a child or young person who would otherwise be a member of the claimant's household, but is treated as not being in the household by reg.16, do not count as LRPs. See reg.51(3).

(h) Where an "other payment" is being considered, its amount is to be reduced if any of the three categories listed apply. Category (iii) is likely to be particularly important where there is a significant gap between the date of receipt of the payment in question and the date on which the claim for income support is determined. See the notes to reg.51(1) for the difficulties of deciding when a claimant's purpose is to secure or increase entitlement to income support.

"Periodical payment"
This definition is also very wide, as the four categories are alternatives.   2.416

Sub-paras (a) and (b) are relatively straightforward, covering the standard cases where payments are due to be made at regular intervals or a regular pattern has been established.

The effect of sub-para.(d) is that a payment of arrears of payments under (a) and (b), or a payment in advance, also counts as a periodical payment (subject to the final exception). If, however, a regular pattern of payments has ceased to exist and there is no court order or agreement to make regular payments, such a payment cannot be a commutation of payments under sub-paras (a) or (b) (*Bolstridge v Chief Adjudication Officer, The Times*, May 5, 1993). It will be a matter of fact in each case by what date a regular pattern of payments ceases to exist. The facts in *Bolstridge* were that the claimant's ex-husband paid her maintenance of £40 per week on a voluntary basis up to July 31, 1986. He was then made redundant and ceased making payments. In September 1987 her ex-husband made her a payment of £10,500 "in lieu of future maintenance". In July 1988, she claimed income support. The Court of Appeal held that, in the absence of any subsisting contract or outstanding liability, it could not be said that by September 1987, there was an agreement for maintenance of any particular sum or any pattern of regular payment. Therefore, the £10,500 was not a periodical payment. It was an "other payment", to be taken into account under reg.57. Any part of the total amount which fell outside the definition of "payment" (above) would not be taken into consideration at all. In particular, amounts which the claimant had already spent for "legitimate" purposes would be excluded under sub-para.(h)(iii) of the definition.

The intention of sub-para.(c) seems to be that relatively small payments (*i.e.* up to the amount of one week's income support) are to be treated as periodical payments.

The final exception is crucial to the working of the LRP system. If a payment was due to be made before the first benefit week, pursuant to the claim, but is paid in or after that benefit week, it is an "other payment," not a periodical payment. Thus the treatment of arrears will vary according to whether the claimant was or was not in receipt of benefit during the period to which the arrears relate (on which see *McCorquodale v Chief Adjudication Officer*, reported as *R(SB) 1/88*).

Treatment of liable relative payments

2.417 **55.** [¹Subject to regulation 55A and] except where regulation 60(1) (liable relative payments to be treated as capital) applies a payment shall—

(a) to the extent that it is not a payment of income, be treated as income;

(b) be taken into account in accordance with the following provisions of this Chapter.

AMENDMENT

1. Social Security Benefits (Maintenance Payments and Consequential Amendments) Regulations 1996 (SI 1996/940), reg.6(2) (April 19, 1996).

DEFINITION

"payment"—see reg.54.

GENERAL NOTE

2.418 The general rule is that if a payment falls into the definition in reg.54, it is to be taken into account as income. It is only in the limited circumstances described in reg.60(1) that it can be treated as capital, and therefore be much less likely to affect benefit. See also reg.55A.

[¹Disregard of payments treated as not relevant income

2.419 **55A.** Where the Secretary of State treats any payment as not being relevant income for the purposes of section 74A of the Social Security Administration Act 1992 (payment of benefit where maintenance payments collected by Secretary of State), that payment shall be disregarded in calculating a claimant's income.]

AMENDMENT

1. Social Security Benefits (Maintenance Payments and Consequential Amendments) Regulations 1996 (SI 1996/940), reg.6(3) (April 19, 1996).

DEFINITIONS

"payment"—see reg.54.

"relevant income"—see reg.2(c), Social Security Benefits (Maintenance Payments and Consequential Amendments) Regulations 1996 (p.730).

GENERAL NOTE

2.420 See the note to s.74A of the Administration Act in Vol. III of this series.

Period over which periodical payments are to be taken into account

2.421 **56.**—(1) The period over which a periodical payment is to be taken into account shall be—

(a) in a case where the payment is made at regular intervals, a period equal to the length of that interval;

(b) in a case where the payment is due to be made at regular intervals but is not so made, such number of weeks as is equal to the number (and any fraction shall be treated as a corresponding fraction of a week) obtained by dividing the amount of that payment by the weekly amount of that periodical payment as calculated in accordance with regulation 58(4) (calculation of the weekly amount of a liable relative payment);

(c) in any other case, a period equal to a week.

(2) The period under paragraph (1) shall begin on the date on which the payment is treated as paid under regulation 59 (date on which a liable relative payment is to be treated as paid).

DEFINITION

"periodical payment"—see reg. 54.

GENERAL NOTE

If a periodical payment is actually paid at regular intervals, it is to be taken into account for the length of the interval. If it is due to be paid regularly but is not, each payment is spread at the weekly rate of proper payment. In other cases (*e.g.* some payments within sub-para.(c) of the definition of periodical payment) the payment is taken into account for a week.

2.422

The application of reg. 56 to payments under sub-para.(d) of the definition of periodical payment is not straightforward. In *Bolstridge v Chief Adjudication Officer, The Times*, May 5, 1993, it was accepted that reg. 56(1)(b) can be given a sensible meaning only if the word "payment" in that regulation sometimes applies to the commutated payment and sometimes to the payment that was due to be made at regular intervals.

Payments are taken into account from the date on which they are treated as paid under reg. 59.

Period over which payments other than periodical payments are to be taken into account

57.—(1) Subject to paragraph (2), the number of weeks over which any payment other than a periodical payment is to be taken into account shall be equal to the number (and any fraction shall be treated as a corresponding fraction of a week) obtained by dividing that payment [5 by the aggregate] of £2 and the amount of income support which would be payable if the payment had not been made;

2.423

[1(a) [5 . . .]

(b) [5 . . .].]

(2) Where a liable relative makes a periodical payment and any other payment concurrently and the weekly amount of that periodical payment, as calculated in accordance with regulation 58 (calculation of the weekly amount of a liable relative payment), is less than [5 . . .] the aggregate of £2 and the amount of income support which would be payable had the payment not been made

(a) [5 . . .]

(b) [5 . . .]

that other payment shall, subject to paragraph (3), be taken into account over a period of such number of weeks as is equal to the number obtained (and any fraction shall be treated as a corresponding fraction of a week) by dividing that payment by an amount equal to the extent of the difference between the amount [5 as calculated under this paragraph] and the weekly amount of the periodical payment.

(3) If—

(a) the liable relative ceases to make periodical payments, the balance (if any) of the other payment shall be taken into account over the number of weeks equal to the number obtained (and any fraction shall be treated as a corresponding fraction of a week) by dividing that balance by the amount referred to in [⁵ . . .] paragraph (1) [⁵. . .];

(b) the amount of any subsequent periodical payment varies, the balance (if any) of the other payment shall be taken into account over a period of such number of weeks as is equal to the number obtained (and any fraction shall be treated as a corresponding fraction of a week) by dividing that balance by an amount equal to the extent of the difference between the amount referred to in [⁵ . . .] paragraph (2) and the weekly amount of the subsequent periodical payment.

(4) The period under paragraph (1) or (2) shall begin on the date on which the payment is treated as paid under regulation 59 (date on which a liable relative payment is treated as paid) and under paragraph (3) shall begin on the first day of the benefit week in which the cessation or variation of the periodical payment occurred.

AMENDMENTS

2.424

1. Income Support (General) Amendment No. 3 Regulations 1990 (SI 1990/1776), reg.7 (October 15, 1990).

2. Child Benefit, Child Support and Social Security (Miscellaneous Amendments) Regulations 1996 (SI 1996/1803), reg.38 (April 7, 1997).

3. Social Security Amendment (Enhanced Disability Premium) Regulations 2000 (SI 2000/2629), reg.2(b) (April 9, 2001).

4. Social Security Amendment (Carer's Allowance) Regulations 2002 (SI 2002/2497), reg.3 and Sch.2 (April 1, 2003).

5. Social Security (Working Tax Credit and Child Tax Credit) (Consequential Amendments) Regulations 2003 (SI 2003/455), reg.2 and Sch.1, para.15 (April 6, 2004, except in "transitional cases" and see further the note to reg.17 of the Income Support Regulations).

DEFINITIONS

"child"—see 1986 Act, s.20(11) (SSCBA, s.137(1)).
"claimant"—see reg.2(1), reg.23(1), reg.54.
"family"—see 1986 Act, s.20(11) (SSCBA, s.137(1)).
"liable relative"—see reg.54.
"payment"—*ibid.*
"periodical payment"—*ibid.*
"young person"—see reg.2(1), reg.14.

GENERAL NOTE

2.425

This regulation deals with payments other than periodical payments. The basic rule under para.(1) is to spread them at the rate of income support that would have been payable if the payment had not been made, plus £2. Paras (2) and (3) modify this rule where the payment is in addition to periodical payments so as to spread the payments at the rate of the difference between the amount of the periodical payment and the amount identified in para.(1), as long as the periodical payments continue to be made.

See reg.58(5) for the weekly amount to be taken into account.

Note that the amendments made to this regulation with effect from April 6, 2004 (except in "transitional cases"—see the note to reg.17) are as a consequence of the removal of amounts for children and young persons from the income support scheme with effect from April 6, 2004 (except in "transitional cases"). Financial assistance to help with the cost of bringing up a child or young person is now to be provided through the child tax credit system, see Vol. IV of this series, and income support has in effect become an "adults only" benefit. The old form of this regulation (see the 2003 edition of this volume) continues in force for "transitional cases"—see the note to reg.17.

Calculation of the weekly amount of a liable relative payment

58.—(1) Where a periodical payment is made or is due to be made at intervals of one week, the weekly amount shall be the amount of that payment.

(2) Where a periodical payment is made or is due to be made at intervals greater than one week and those intervals are monthly, the weekly amount shall be determined by multiplying the amount of the payment by 12 and dividing the product by 52.

(3) Where a periodical payment is made or is due to be made at intervals and those intervals are neither weekly nor monthly, the weekly amount shall be determined by dividing that payment by the number equal to the number of weeks (including any part of a week) in that interval.

(4) Where a payment is made and that payment represents a commutation of periodical payments whether in arrears or in advance, the weekly amount shall be the weekly amount of the individual periodical payments so commutated, as calculated under paragraphs (1) to (3) as is appropriate.

(5) The weekly amount of a payment to which regulation 57 applies (period over which payments other than periodical payments are to be taken into account) shall be equal to the amount of the divisor used in calculating the period over which the payment or, as the case may be, the balance is to be taken into account.

2.426

DEFINITIONS

"payment"—see reg.54.
"periodical payment"—*ibid*.

GENERAL NOTE

The weekly rate of periodical payments is normally calculated by dividing the payment into weekly bits depending on the intervals between payment dates (paras (1) to (3)). For a commutation of periodical payments, whether in arrears or in advance (which itself comes within the definition of periodical payment), the weekly rate is the appropriate one for the recurring payments.

2.427

Date on which a liable relative payment is to be treated as paid

59.—(1) A periodical payment is to be treated as paid—
  (a) in the case of a payment which is due to be made before the first benefit week pursuant to the claim, on the day in the week in which it is to be paid which corresponds to the first day of the benefit week;
  (b) in any other case, on the first day of the benefit week in which it is due to be paid unless, having regard to the manner in which income support is due to be paid in the particular case, it would be more practicable to treat it as paid on the first day of a subsequent benefit week.

(2) Subject to paragraph (3), any other payment shall be treated as paid—
  (a) in the case of a payment which is made before the first benefit week pursuant to the claim, on the day in the week in which it is paid which corresponds to the first day of the benefit week;

2.428

(b) in any other case, on the first day of the benefit week in which it is paid unless, having regard to the manner in which income support is due to be paid in the particular case, it would be more practicable to treat it as paid on the first day of a subsequent benefit week.

(3) Any other payment paid on a date which falls within the period in respect of which a previous payment is taken into account, not being a periodical payment, is to be treated as paid on the first day following the end of that period.

DEFINITIONS

"benefit week"—see reg.2(1).
"payment"—see reg.54.
"periodical payment"—*ibid.*

GENERAL NOTE

Para. (1)

2.429   This provision effectively applies the ordinary rule for income (see reg.31) to periodical payments. Under sub-para.(a) for the payment still to be a periodical payment it must have been paid as well as been due before the first benefit week pursuant to the claim. Once the benefit week is determined under para.4 of Sch.7 to the Claims and Payments Regulations, prior weeks can be counted off and payments attributed to the first day of each week. Under sub-para.(b), for other periodical payments (which can include many payments of arrears) the crucial thing is the benefit week in which the payment is due, or, if it would be more practicable, a subsequent week. A payment of arrears within the definition of a periodical payment may well have been due in a large number of past weeks, for which benefit has already been paid on the assumption that no LRP had been received. This would seem to trigger the application of s.74(1) of the Administration Act (1986 Act, s.27(1)). Para.28834 of the *Decision Makers Guide* suggests that in such circumstances it is more practicable to take the payment into account from the next benefit week in which the amount of benefit can be adjusted, although the *Guide* does not really face the problem of payments of arrears. If continuing periodical payments are being made, the spreading of a payment of arrears over future benefit weeks could lead to more than one periodical payment being taken into account in the same benefit week. Whether this leaves the claimant better off than if recovery under s.74(1) had been triggered depends on the levels of payment in relation to income support entitlement. It is not at all clear that this solution is "more practicable" than spreading the payment of arrears over the past period to which the arrears related. The latter solution, with the recovery of any overpayment under s.74(1), may be better.

Para. (2)

2.430   This provision applies to all "other payments", including payments of arrears identified in the final exception to the definition of "periodical payment". Here it is the date of actual payment, rather than the date on which payment is due, which is crucial. Sub-para.(a) applies to payments made before the first benefit week pursuant to the claim. Sub-para.(b) applies in all other cases, and allows attribution to a later benefit week than that of payment if that is more practicable.

The result for payments of arrears relating to a period before entitlement to benefit, is that the payment is treated as income to be spread at the rate identified in reg.58 from the date of actual payment. This reverses the result of *McCorquodale v Chief Adjudication Officer* (reported as *R(SB) 1/88*). If this results in one "other payment" being attributed to a benefit week to which another "other payment" has already been attributed, the attribution of the later payment is deferred until the first one runs out (para.(3)).

Liable relative payments to be treated as capital

60.—(1) Subject to paragraph (2), where a liable relative makes a peri-   2.431
odical payment concurrently with any other payment, and the weekly
amount of the periodical payment as calculated in accordance with regulation 58(1) to (4) (calculation of the weekly amount of a liable relative
payment), is equal to or greater than the amount referred to in sub-
paragraph (a) of regulation 57(2) (period over which payments other than
periodical payments are to be taken into account) less the £2 referred to
therein, or sub-paragraph (b) of that regulation, as the case may be, the
other payment shall be treated as capital.

(2) If, in any case, the liable relative ceases to make periodical payments,
the other payment to which paragraph (1) applies shall be taken into
account under paragraph (1) of regulation 57 but, notwithstanding
paragraph (4) thereof, the period over which the payment is to be taken into
account shall begin on the first day of the benefit week following the last one
in which a periodical payment was taken into account.

DEFINITIONS

  "benefit week"—see reg.2(1).
  "liable relative"—see reg.54.
  "payment"—*ibid.*
  "periodical payment"—*ibid.*

GENERAL NOTE

  If a periodical payment at least equals the income support rate that would have   2.432
been payable if the payment had not been made, any other payment made at the
same time is treated as capital. If the liable relative later stops making the periodical
payments the other payment can be tapped as income under para.(2).

[¹*Chapter VIIA*

Child Support

Interpretation

60A. In this Chapter—   2.433
"child support maintenance" means such periodical payments as are
  referred to in section 3(6) of the Child Support Act 1991 [² and shall
  include any payments made by the Secretary of State in lieu of such
  payments];
"maintenance [³ calculation]" has the same meaning as in the Child
  Support Act 1991 by virtue of section 54 of that Act.]

AMENDMENTS

  1. Social Security (Miscellaneous Provisions) Amendment Regulations 1993
(SI 1993/846), reg.3 (April 19, 1993).
  2. Social Security (Child Maintenance Premium and Miscellaneous Amendments)
Regulations 2000 (SI 2000/3176), reg.2(1)(a) (in force in relation to any particular case
on the day on which s.23 of the Child Support, Pensions and Social Security Act 2000

comes into force in relation to that type of case. Note that the commencement provision of these regulations (reg.1) was substituted by reg.4 of the Social Security (Child Maintenance Premium) Amendment Regulations 2004 (SI 2004/98) on February 16, 2004 to provide that the 2000 Regulations come into force as follows: on (i) February 16, 2004 in relation to any particular case in respect of which s.23 CSPSSA 2000 has come into force before February 16, 2004 (ii) where this does not apply, the day on which s.23 comes into force in relation to that type of case; (iii) February 16, 2004 in relation to a person who is entitled to income support/income-based JSA on that date and who receives her first payment of child maintenance made voluntarily whilst entitled to income support/income-based JSA on that date; (iv) in such a case where the day that the first voluntary payment is received is after February 16, 2004, the day the payment is received; (v) February 16, 2004 in relation to a person who makes a claim for income support/income-based JSA on or after that date and receives a payment of child maintenance made voluntarily on or after the date of that claim).

3. Child Support (Consequential Amendments and Transitional Provisions) Regulations 2001 (SI 2001/158), reg.6(2) (in force in relation to any particular case on the day on which s.1 of the Child Support, Pensions and Social Security Act 2000 comes into force in relation to that type of case).

GENERAL NOTE

2.434
For those cases to which the new child support scheme introduced by the Child Support, Pensions and Social Security Act 2000 applies, s.3(6) of the Child Support Act 1991 refers to "periodical payments which are required to be paid in accordance with a maintenance calculation". A "maintenance calculation" is defined in s.54 as "a calculation of maintenance made under this Act and, except in prescribed circumstances, includes a default maintenance decision and an interim maintenance decision".

The new child support scheme is being implemented in stages (see the introductory note at the beginning of the Child Support Act 1991 in Part I of this volume). See reg.10 of the Child Support (Consequential Amendments and Transitional Provisions) Regulations 2001 (SI 2001/158) (p.684) for the saving provision. For the form of reg.60A that continues to apply in cases that have not yet become subject to the new rules, see the 2002 edition of this volume.

[¹Treatment of child support maintenance

2.435
60B. [²Subject to regulation 60E], all payments of child support maintenance shall to the extent that they are not payments of income be treated as income and shall be taken into account on a weekly basis in accordance with the following provisions of this Chapter.]

AMENDMENTS

1. Social Security (Miscellaneous Provisions) Amendment Regulations 1993 (SI 1993/846), reg.3 (April 19, 1993).

2. Social Security Benefits (Maintenance Payments and Consequential Amendments) Regulations 1996 (SI 1996/940), reg.6(4) (April 19, 1996).

DEFINITIONS

"child support maintenance"—see reg.60A.
"payment"—see reg.2(1).

GENERAL NOTE

2.436
Since the definition of "child support maintenance" refers to payments which are required to be made periodically, it appears that payments in commutation of periodical payments, either in advance or in arrears, will be payments of child

support maintenance, providing that there is a subsisting liability under a maintenance calculation (see *Bolstridge v Chief Adjudication Officer, The Times,* May 5, 1993). They then have to be treated as payments of income. See reg.60C(5) for commutation payments. Payments made at the periodical intervals required under the maintenance calculation would be income anyway, but are to be taken into account according to the rules set out in regs 60C and 60D.

All income under Chapter VIIA is taken into account in full in assessing entitlement to income support. There are no disregards. But see reg.60E. Note also that for cases to which the new child support scheme applies (see the note at the beginning of the Child Support Act 1991 in Part I of this volume) there is a £10 disregard of child maintenance payments (see para.73 of Sch.9 and the notes to that regulation).

[¹Calculation of the weekly amount of payments of child support maintenance

60C.—(1) The weekly amount of child support maintenance shall be determined in accordance with the following provisions of this regulation.   2.437

(2) Where payments of child support maintenance are made weekly, the weekly amount shall be the amount of that payment.

(3) Where payments of child support maintenance are made monthly, the weekly amount shall be determined by multiplying the amount of the payment by 12 and dividing the product by 52.

(4) Where payments of child support are made at intervals and those intervals are not a week or a month, the weekly amount shall be determined by dividing that payment by the number equal to the number of weeks (including any part of a week) in that interval.

(5) Where a payment is made and that payment represents a commutation of child support maintenance the weekly amount shall be the weekly amount of the individual child support maintenance payments so commuted as calculated in accordance with paragraphs (2) to (4) as appropriate.

(6) Paragraph (2), (3) or, as the case may be, (4) shall apply to any payments made at the intervals specified in that paragraph whether or not—

(a) the amount paid is in accordance with the maintenance [² calculation], and

(b) the intervals at which the payments are made are in accordance with the intervals specified by the Secretary of State under regulation 4 of the Child Support (Collection and Enforcement) Regulations 1992].

AMENDMENTS

1. Social Security (Miscellaneous Provisions) Amendment Regulations 1993   2.438
(SI 1993/846), reg.3 (April 19, 1993).

2. Child Support (Consequential Amendments and Transitional Provisions) Regulations 2001 (SI 2001/158), reg.6(2) (in force in relation to any particular case on the day on which s.1 of the Child Support, Pensions and Social Security Act 2000 comes into force in relation to that type of case).

DEFINITIONS

"child support maintenance"—see reg.60A.
"maintenance calculation"—*ibid.*
"payment"—see reg.2(1).

GENERAL NOTE

The amendment made to para.(6)(a) by the Child Support (Consequential   2.439
Amendments and Transitional Provisions) Regulations 2001 only applies to those

cases in relation to which the new child support regime introduced by the Child Support, Pensions and Social Security Act 2000 has come into force (see further the note to reg.60A).

The Secretary of State specifies the day and interval by reference to which payments of child support maintenance are to be paid by the liable person (Child Support (Collection and Enforcement) Regulations 1992, reg.4). Paras (2) to (4) work easily when payments of the full amount of the maintenance calculation are made at regular intervals. Then they supply simple arithmetical rules for working out the weekly amount and reg.60D defines when each payment is to be treated as made. If the payments are not made at regular intervals, it is not clear whether para.(4) should apply, taking the interval since the last payment to define the weekly amount, or whether the payment should be treated as a commutation of past maintenance under para.(5). If regular payments are made of less than the maintenance calculation, the effect of para.(6) is that the actual amount paid should be treated as income, not the amount properly due. If later a payment of arrears is made in a lump sum, does para.(5) apply to that payment as a commutation of child support maintenance, or does the definition of child support maintenance mean that para.(5) only applies to payments which are multiples of the payments required to be made under the maintenance calculation? It would seem that the former is intended, because there can be recovery of overpaid income support under s.74(1) of the Administration Act when arrears of child support maintenance are paid only to take account of the period between the effective date of the maintenance calculation and the date when normal periodical payments start (Social Security (Payments on account, Overpayments and Recovery) Regulations 1988, reg.7(1)(b)). In practice, where the parent with care is on income support, it is likely that payments of arrears by an absent parent for periods after normal periodical payments start will be made direct to the Child Support Agency who will retain an amount equal to the income support that would not have been paid if the child support maintenance had been paid on time. But if arrangements for payment direct to the Child Support Agency have not yet been made (*e.g.* where the absent parent has only just fallen into arrears), para.(5) may apply to any payments made in these circumstances.

Para.(5) deals with payments which are commutations of child support maintenance. Although nothing is said expressly, it would seem to cover commutations both in advance or in arrears. There is little problem over payments in advance.

See *CIS/2455/2004* for a discussion of the application of this regulation and the other regulations in this Chapter.

[¹Date on which child support maintenance is to be treated as paid

2.440

60D.—[²(1) Subject to paragraph (2),] a payment of child support maintenance is to be treated as paid—

  (a) [² subject to sub-paragraph (aa),] in the case of a payment which is due to be paid before the first benefit week pursuant to the claim, on the day in the week in which it is due to be paid which corresponds to the first day of the benefit week;

[²(aa) in the case of any amount of a payment which represents arrears of maintenance for a week prior to the first benefit week pursuant to a claim, on the day of the week in which it became due which corresponds to the first day of the benefit week;]

  (b) in any other case, on the first day of the benefit week in which [²it is due to be paid] or the first day of the first succeeding benefit week in which it is practicable to take it into account.]

[²(2) Where a payment to which paragraph (1)(b) refers is made to the Secretary of State and then transmitted to the person entitled to receive it, the payment shall be treated as paid on the first day of the benefit week in which it is transmitted or, where it is not practicable to take it into account in that week, the first day of the first succeeding benefit week in which it is practicable to take the payment into account.]

AMENDMENTS

1. Social Security (Miscellaneous Provisions) Amendment Regulations 1993 (SI 1993/846), reg.3 (April 19, 1993).

2.441

2. Income-related Benefits Schemes and Social Fund (Miscellaneous Amendments) Regulations 1986 (SI 1996/1944), reg.6(7) (October 7, 1996).

DEFINITIONS

"benefit week"—see reg.2(1).
"child support maintenance"—see reg.60A.

GENERAL NOTE

Sub-paragraphs (a) and (b) of para.(1) contain the same rule as in reg.31(1). Para.(1)(aa) clarifies the position (possibly superfluously) where any arrears of child support maintenance are paid that were due before income support was first paid. Para.(2) sets the date when child support maintenance payments that are paid via the Child Support Agency are treated as paid.

2.442

[¹Disregard of payments treated as not relevant income

60E. Where the Secretary of State treats any payment of child support maintenance as not being relevant income for the purposes of section 74A of the Social Security Administration Act 1992 (payment of benefit where maintenance payments collected by Secretary of State), that payment shall be disregarded in calculating a claimant's income.]

2.443

AMENDMENT

1. Social Security Benefits (Maintenance Payments and Consequential Amendments) Regulations 1996 (SI 1996/940), reg.6(5) (April 19, 1996).

DEFINITIONS

"child support maintenance"—see reg.60A.
"payment"—see reg.2(1).
"relevant income"—see reg.2(c), Social Security Benefits (Maintenance Payments and Consequential Amendments) Regulations 1996 (p.700).

GENERAL NOTE

See the note to s.74A of the Administration Act in Vol. III of this series.

2.444

Chapter VIII

[¹⁵ *Students*]

Interpretation

61.—[¹²(1)] In this Chapter, unless the context otherwise requires—
[¹⁸ "academic year" means the period of twelve months beginning on 1st January, 1st April, 1st July or 1st September according to whether the

2.445

course in question begins in the winter, the spring, the summer or the autumn respectively but if students are required to begin attending the course during August or September and to continue attending through the autumn, the academic year of the course shall be considered to begin in the autumn rather than the summer;]

[[13] "access funds" means—

(a) grants made under section 7 of the Further and Higher Education Act 1992 and described as "learner support funds" or grants made under section 68 of that Act [[18] for the purpose of providing funds on a discretionary basis to be paid to students];

(b) grants made under sections 73(a) and (c) and 74(1) of the Education (Scotland) Act 1980; [[18] . . .]

(c) grants made under Article 30 of the Education and Libraries (Northern Ireland) Order 1993, or grants, or grants loans or other payments made under Article 5 of the Further Education (Northern Ireland) Order 1997 in each case being grants, or loans or other payments as the case may be, made for the purpose of assisting students in financial difficulties;] [[18] [[20] . . .]

(d) discretionary payments, known as "learner support funds", which are made available to students in further education by institutions out of funds provided by the Learning and Skills Council for England under sections 5, 6 and 9 of the Learning and Skills Act 2000;] [[20] or

(e) Financial Contingency Funds made available by the National Assembly for Wales;]

[[8]"college of further education" means a college of further education within the meaning of Part I of the Further and Higher Education (Scotland) Act 1992;]

[[8]"contribution" means any contribution in respect of the income [[10]of a student or] of any other person which the Secretary of State [[18], the Scottish Ministers] or an education authority takes into account in ascertaining the amount of the student's grant [[11] or student loan], or any sums, which in determining the amount of a student's allowance or bursary in Scotland under the Further and Higher Education (Scotland) Act 1992, the [[18]Scottish Ministers] or education authority takes into account being sums which the [[18]Scottish Ministers] or the education authority consider that the holder of the allowance or bursary, the holder's parents and the holder's spouse can reasonably be expected to contribute towards the holder's expenses;]

[[8]"course of advanced education" means—

(a) a course leading to a postgraduate degree or comparable qualification, a first degree or comparable qualification, a diploma of higher education or a higher national diploma; or

(b) any other course which is of a standard above advanced GNVQ or equivalent, including a course which is of a standard above a general certificate of education (advanced level), [[21] a Scottish national qualification (higher or advanced higher)];]

"covenant income" means the income [[8]. . .] payable to a student under a Deed of Covenant by a person whose income is, or is likely to be, taken into account in assessing the student's grant or award;

"education authority" means a government department, a local education authority as defined in section 114(1) of the Education Act 1944 (interpretation), [8a local education authority as defined in section 123 of the Local Government (Scotland) Act 1973], an education and library board established under Article 3 of the Education and Libraries (Northern Ireland) Order 1986, any body which is a research council for the purposes of the Science and Technology Act 1965 or any analogous government department, authority, board or body, of the Channel Islands, Isle of Man or any other country outside Great Britain; [16 . . .]

[8"full-time course of advanced education" means a course of advanced education which is [12 . . .]—

(a) [12 . . .] a full-time course of study which is not funded in whole or in part by [17 the Learning and Skills Council for England or by the National Council for Education and Training for Wales] or a full-time course of study which is not funded in whole or in part by the [19Scottish Ministers] at a college of further education or a full-time course of study which is a course of higher education and is funded in whole or in part by the [19Scottish Ministers];

[17(b) a course of study that is funded in whole or in part by the Learning and Skills Council for England or by the National Council for Education and Training for Wales if it involves more than 16 guided learning hours per week for the student in question, according to the number of guided learning hours per week for that student set out—

  (i) in the case of a course funded by the Learning and Skills Council for England, in his learning agreement signed on behalf of the establishment which is funded by that Council for the delivery of that course; or

  (ii) in the case of a course funded by the National Council for Education and Training for Wales, in a document signed on behalf of the establishment which is funded by that Council for the delivery of that course; or]

(c) [12 . . .] a course of study (not being higher education) which is funded in whole or in part by the [19Scottish Ministers] at a college of further education if it involves—

  (i) more than 16 hours per week of classroom-based or workshop-based programmed learning under the direct guidance of teaching staff according to the number of hours set out in a document signed on behalf of the college; or

  (ii) 16 hours or less per week of classroom-based or workshop-based programmed learning under the direct guidance of teaching staff and it involves additional hours using structured learning packages supported by the teaching staff where the combined total of hours exceeds 21 per week, according to the number of hours set out in a document signed on behalf of the college;]

[8"full-time course of study" means a full-time course of study which—

(a) is not funded in whole or in part by [16 the Learning and Skills Council for England or by the National Council for Education and Training for Wales] or a full-time course of study which is not funded in whole or in part by the [19Scottish Ministers] at a college of further education or a full-time course of study which is a course of higher education and is funded in whole or in part by the [[19]Scottish Ministers];

[[16] (b) a course of study which is funded in whole or in part by the Learning and Skills Council for England or by the National Council for Education and Training for Wales if it involves more than 16 guided learning hours per week for the student in question, according to the number of guided learning hours per week for that student set out—

    (i) in the case of a course funded by the Learning and Skills Council for England, in his learning agreement signed on behalf of the establishment which is funded by that Council for the delivery of that course; or

    (ii) in the case of a course funded by the National Council for Education and Training for Wales, in a document signed on behalf of the establishment which is funded by that Council for the delivery of that course; or]

(c) is not higher education and is funded in whole or in part by the [[19]Scottish Ministers] at a college of further education if it involves—

    (i) more than 16 hours per week of classroom-based or workshop-based programmed learning under the direct guidance of teaching staff according to the number of hours set out in a document signed on behalf of the college; or

    (ii) 16 hours or less per week of classroom-based or workshop-based programmed learning under the direct guidance of teaching staff and it involves additional hours using structured learning packages supported by the teaching staff where the combined total of hours exceeds 21 per week, according to the number of hours set out in a document signed on behalf of the college;]

[[12] "full-time student" means a person who is—

(a) aged less than 19 and is attending or undertaking a full-time course of advanced education;

(b) aged 19 or over but under pensionable age and is attending or undertaking a full-time course of study at an educational establishment; or

(c) on a sandwich course;]

[[13] "grant" (except in the definition of "access funds") means any kind of educational grant or award and includes any scholarship, studentship, exhibition, allowance or bursary but does not include a payment from access funds [[21] or any payment to which paragraph 11 of Schedule 9 or paragraph 63 of Schedule 10 applies];]

"grant income" means—

(a) any income by way of a grant;

(b) in the case of a student other than one to whom sub-paragraph (c) refers, any contribution which has been assessed whether or not it has been paid;

(c) in the case of a student to whom [[9] paragraph 1, 2 10, 11 or 12 of Schedule 1B] applies (lone parent or disabled student), any contribution which has been assessed and which has been paid;

and any such contribution which is paid by way of a covenant shall be treated as part of the student's grant income;

[8"higher education" means higher education within the meaning of Part II of the Further and Higher Education (Scotland) Act 1992;]

[3"last day of the course" means the date on which the last day of the final academic term falls in respect of the course in which the student is enrolled;]

"period of study" means—

(a) in the case of a course of study for one year or less, the period beginning with the start of the course [3and ending with the last day of the course];

(b) in the case of a course of study for more than one year, in the first or, as the case may be, any subsequent year of the course, [3other than the final year of the course,] the period beginning with the start of the course or, as the case may be, that year's start and ending with either—

[14 (i) the day before the start of the next year of the course in a case where the student's grant or loan is assessed at a rate appropriate to his studying throughout the year or, if he does not have a grant or loan, where a loan would have been assessed at such a rate had he had one; or]

(ii) in any other case the day before the start of the normal summer vacation appropriate to his course;

[3 (c) in the final year of a course of study of more than one year, the period beginning with that year's start and ending with the last day of the course;]

[20 "periods of experience" means periods of work experience which form part of a sandwich course;]

[13 "sandwich course" has the meaning prescribed in regulation 5(2) of the [20 Education (Student Support) Regulations 2002], regulation 5(2) of the Education (Student Loans) (Scotland) Regulations 2000 or regulation 5(2) of the [20 Education (Student Support) Regulations (Northern Ireland) 2001], as the case may be;]

[8"standard maintenance grant" means—

(a) except where paragraph (b) or (c) applies, in the case of a student attending [12 or undertaking] a course of study at the University of London or an establishment within the area comprising the City of London and the Metropolitan Police District, the amount specified for the time being in paragraph 2(2)(a) of Schedule 2 to the Education (Mandatory Awards) Regulations 1995 ("the 1995 Regulations") for such a student;

(b) except where paragraph (c) applies, in the case of a student residing at his parents' home, the amount specified in paragraph 3(2) thereof;

[18 (c) in the case of a student receiving an allowance or bursary under the Education (Scotland) Act 1980, the amount of money specified as the "standard maintenance allowance" for the relevant year appropriate for the student set out in the Student Support in Scotland Guide issued by the Student Awards Agency for Scotland, or its nearest equivalent in the case of a bursary provided by a college of further education or a local education authority and paid under the Further and Higher Education (Scotland) Act 1992;]

(d) in any other case, the amount specified in paragraph 2(2) of Schedule 2 to the 1995 Regulations other than in sub paragraph (a) or (b) thereof;]

[¹² "student" means a person, other than a person in receipt of a training allowance, who is attending or undertaking a course of study at an educational establishment;]

[¹¹"student loan" means a loan towards a student's maintenance pursuant to any regulations made under section 22 of the Teaching and Higher Education Act 1998, section 73 of the Education (Scotland) Act 1980 or Article 3 of the Education (Student Support) (Northern Ireland) Order 1998 [¹⁸ and shall include, in Scotland, a young student's bursary paid under regulation 4(1)(c) of the Students' Allowances (Scotland) Regulations 1999];

[¹⁸. . .].

[¹² (2) For the purposes of the definition of "full-time student" in paragraph (1), a person shall be regarded as attending or, as the case may be, undertaking a full-time course of study, a full-time course of advanced education or as being on a sandwich course—

    (a) subject to paragraph (3), in the case of a person attending or undertaking a part of a modular course that would be a full-time course of study for the purposes of this Part, for the period beginning on the day on which that part of the course starts and ending—
        (i) on the last day on which he is registered with the educational establishment as attending or undertaking that part as a full-time course of study; or
        (ii) on such earlier date (if any) as he finally abandons the course or is dismissed from it;

    (b) in any other case, throughout the period beginning on the date on which he starts attending or undertaking the course and ending on the last day of the course or on such earlier date (if any) as he finally abandons it or is dismissed from it.

(3) For the purpose of sub-paragraph (a) of paragraph (2), the period referred to in that sub-paragraph shall include—

    (a) where a person has failed examinations or has failed to successfully complete a module relating to a period when he was attending or undertaking a part of the course as a full-time course of study, any period in respect of which he attends or undertakes the course for the purpose of retaking those examinations or that module;

    (b) any period of vacation within the period specified in that paragraph or immediately following that period except where the person has registered with the educational establishment to attend or undertake the final module in the course and the vacation immediately follows the last day on which he is required to attend or undertake the course.

(4) In paragraphs (2), "modular course" means a course of study which consists of two or more modules, the successful completion of a specified number of which is required before a person is considered by the educational establishment to have completed the course.]

AMENDMENTS

2.446   1. Income Support (General) Amendments No.5 Regulations 1988 (SI 1988/2022), reg.14 (December 12, 1988).

    2. Social Security Benefits (Student Loans and Miscellaneous Amendments) Regulations 1990 (SI 1990/1549), reg.5(5) (September 1, 1990).

    3. Income Support (General) Amendment No.4 Regulations 1991 (SI 1991/1559), reg.10 (August 5, 1991).

4. Income Support (General) Amendment Regulations 1992 (SI 1992/468), reg.5 (April 6, 1992).

5. Income-related Benefits Schemes (Miscellaneous Amendments) (No.3) Regulations 1992 (SI 1992/2155), reg.19 (October 5, 1992).

6. Income-related Benefits Schemes (Miscellaneous Amendments) (No.4) Regulations 1993 (SI 1993/2119), reg.16 (October 4, 1993).

7. Social Security Benefits (Miscellaneous Amendments) Regulations 1995 (SI 1995/1742), reg.2 (August 1, 1995).

8. Income-related Benefits Schemes and Social Fund (Miscellaneous Amendments) Regulations 1996 (SI 1996/1944), reg.6(8) (October 7, 1996).

9. Income-related Benefits and Jobseeker's Allowance (Amendment) (No.2) Regulations 1997 (SI 1997/2197), reg.5(5) (October 6, 1997).

10. Social Security (Miscellaneous Amendments) Regulations 1998 (SI 1998/563), reg.4(1) and (2)(e) (April 6, 1998).

11. Social Security Amendment (Students) Regulations 1999 (SI 1999/1935), reg.3(2) (August 30, 1999, or if the student's period of study begins between August 1 and 29, 1999, the first day of the period).

12. Social Security Amendment (Students) Regulations 2000 (SI 2000/1981), reg.5(3) (July 31, 2000).

13. Social Security Amendment (Students and Income-related Benefits) Regulations 2000 (SI 2000/1922), reg.2(2) (August 28, 2000, or if the student's period of study begins between August 1 and 27, 2000, the first day of the period).

14. Social Security Amendment (Students and Income-related Benefits) Regulations 2000 (SI 2000/1922), reg.2(3) (August 28, 2000, or if the student's period of study begins between August 1 and 27, 2000, the first day of the period).

15. Income Support (General) Amendment Regulations 2001 (SI 2001/721), reg.2(b) (March 29, 2001).

16. Social Security (Miscellaneous Amendments) (No.2) Regulations 2001 (SI 2001/652), reg.3(1) and (2)(c) (April 1, 2001).

17. Social Security (Miscellaneous Amendments) (No.2) Regulations 2001 (SI 2001/652), reg.3(3) (April 1, 2001).

18. Social Security Amendment (Students and Income-related Benefits) Regulations 2001 (SI 2001/2319), reg.2(1) and (2)(c) (August 1, 2001).

19. Social Security Amendment (Students and Income-related Benefits) Regulations 2001 (SI 2001/2319), reg.2(3) (August 1, 2001).

20. Social Security Amendment (Students and Income-related Benefits) Regulations 2002 (SI 2002/1589), reg.2(1) (August 1, 2002).

21. Social Security (Students and Income-related Benefits) Amendment Regulations 2004 (SI 2004/1708), reg.5(1) (September 1, 2004, or if the student's period of study begins between August 1 and August 31, 2004, the first day of the period).

DEFINITIONS

"training allowance"—see reg.2(1).
"course of study"—*ibid.*

GENERAL NOTE

"Academic year"
    This definition is important for the purposes of calculating student loan income. **2.447** "Academic year" means a period of 12 months beginning on January 1, April 1, July 1 or September 1, depending on whether the course in question starts in the winter, the spring, the summer or the autumn respectively. For students who begin their course in August or September and continue to attend during the autumn (*i.e.* for most students) the academic year is treated as starting in the autumn—*i.e.* on September 1.

"Grant"

2.448   *R(SB) 20/83* decided that "award" included a loan. However, in *R(IS) 16/95* the Commissioner disagrees with *R(SB) 20/83*. In his view, "award", if given its every-day meaning, particularly in the context of academic grants and awards, implied an outright gift with no liability to repay. Thus the education loan received by the claimant's partner from the Norwegian Government did not fall within reg.61, but was to be taken into account as income under reg.40 (see *R(SB) 7/88*). Reg.66A (concerning the student loan scheme in its then form) had been introduced simply for the removal of doubt and did not indicate that, without it, loans would not count as income. *CJSA 1134/2003*, to be reported as *R(JSA) 4/04*, confirms that a student loan paid to a part-time student (whether properly paid under the student loan scheme or not) constituted income for the purposes of income-based JSA (the same would apply for income support), to be taken into account over the period of the academic year in respect of which it was paid; furthermore the claimant was not enti-tled to the benefit of the disregards in reg.136 of the JSA Regulations (reg.66A of the Income Support Regulations) because this only applied to full-time students.

The September 2004 amendment ensures that education maintenance allowances (EMAs) are excluded from the definition of grant. EMAs are fully disregarded (see para.11 of Sch.9 for the income disregard and see para.63 of Sch.10 for the capital disregard).

"Grant income"

2.449   Note that in most cases a parental contribution is included whether paid or not.

Where a person is due to repay part or all of a student grant because he leaves or is dismissed from his course before it finishes, see regs 29(2B), 32(6A) and 40(3B). But note *Chief Adjudication Officer v Leeves* (November 6, 1998, CA, reported as *R(IS) 5/99*) in the notes to reg.29(2B) and the argument discussed in those notes as to when reg.29(2B) applies. Note also para.61 of Sch.9 under which any grant (or covenant income or student loan or contribution) left over at the end of a person's course is ignored.

"Student" and "Full-time student"

2.450   On July 31, 2000 the existing definition of "student" was substituted and a new definition of "full-time student" was inserted. The latter definition needs to be read in conjunction with paras (2)–(4) which expand upon it.

The aim of these new definitions is to reinforce the Government's policy intention that a full-time student should count as such throughout the duration of his course until he completes or is finally dismissed from or finally abandons it (but note the new provisions relating to "modular courses" (defined in para.(4)) in paras (2)(a) and (3)). It had been felt necessary to introduce these changes following the Court of Appeal's decisions in *Clarke and Faul* and *Webber* (see below). The Government's original pro-posals for change (first mooted in March 1998) were more extensive and were roundly rejected by the Social Security Advisory Committee (SSAC) in their report submitted in May 1998 (for SSAC's report and the Government's statement in reply see Cm 4739 (2000)). SSAC's primary recommendation was that the proposed amendments should be withdrawn and replaced by regulations designed "to provide safety net support for people who are not currently engaged in full-time studies—either through social security (subject to the normal conditions of entitlement) or mandatory grants". Not surprisingly this did not find favour with the Government, although the Secretary of State's reply to SSAC's report did acknowledge "the need to ensure that the inter-action of legislation underpinning [the Government's] overall policy on full-time stu-dents does not result in individual students being denied financial support in certain circumstances". Thus the final version of the amendments to the JSA Regulations includes a provision enabling those full-time students who interrupted their studies because of illness or caring responsibilities but who have now recovered or whose caring responsibilities have ceased to claim JSA. They will be eligible until the earlier of the day before they rejoin their course or the day before the start of their next academic year, provided that they do not qualify for a student grant or loan in this period (see reg.1(3D) and (3E) of the JSA Regulations). (A similar provision was also introduced into the Housing Benefit and Council Tax Benefit Regulations). The Government did not, however, accept one of SSAC's other recommendations, namely, that lone parents students who had completed a substantial part of their full-time course should continue to be eligible for benefit after their youngest child reached 16. The response that "the Government believes that it is reasonable to expect a lone parent who wishes to study full-time to undertake and complete a course of full-time study before the youngest child reaches the age of 16" is not a particularly helpful one.

Note that the definitions of "student" and "full-time student" now encompass a person who is "undertaking" as well as "attending" a course. The stated purpose of the inclusion of the word "undertaking" is to indicate that it is not necessary for the person to be physically present at the relevant educational establishment in order to count as a student.

"Full-time student"

The definition of full-time student is important not just for the purposes of this Chapter of the Regulations, but also because it feeds back in through the additional definition of "period of study" in reg.2(1) to remove most full-time students' entitlement (see reg.4ZA(2) and (3)). Note that those in receipt of a training allowance are excluded from the definition of student and hence full-time student.

Besides those on sandwich courses (see the definition of sandwich course later in para.(1)), there are two categories, depending on whether the person is under 19 or not. A person under 19 is a full-time student if attending or undertaking a full-time course of advanced education. Advanced education is defined earlier in para.(1).

A person of 19 or over (but under pensionable age) is a full-time student if attending or undertaking a full-time course of study at an educational establishment. It does not have to be any particular level. A person of 19 cannot be in relevant education, because that only applies to children or young persons (reg.12).

2.451

"Course of study at an educational establishment"

The reference in the definition of full-time student (and student) is to a course of study, rather than of education, as it was in the Supplementary Benefit (Conditions of Entitlement) Regulations. This probably makes little difference, although it makes it harder to argue that students pursuing degrees purely by research, with no course-work, are not "attending" a course (see *(R(SB) 26/82)*, but pursuing or following it. (Now that the reference is to "attending or undertaking" a course, this argument is no longer open.)

R(SB) 25/87 decides that a pupil barrister is not a student because pupillage is not a course of education, but an assimilation of specific vocational skills by attending on the pupil master. Presumably, a pupil barrister would be said not to be attending a "course of study" (the phrase here) either. *CIS 50/1990* suggests that this approach is not lightly to be extended to other circumstances. The claimant was attending an intensive shorthand and typing course at a commercial training centre. There was little difficulty in deciding that this was a full-time course. The Commissioner holds that since there was active tuition, the claimant was engaged in study, regardless of the technical nature of the skills studied. The centre was within the ordinary meaning of "educational establishment." In *R(IS) 5/97* a person attending the Bar Vocational Course at the Council of Legal Education was a student. *R(SB) 25/87* was clearly distinguishable. See also *CIS 450/1997* which decides that a Project 2000 student nurse came within the definition of "student".

On the meaning of "course", see *R(IS) 1/96*. The claimant was training to be an architect. He had obtained his degree and had to find a year's placement with a firm before undertaking a further two years' study (to be followed by a further year's practical experience) in order to complete his professional training. The Commissioner holds that he was not a student during the year "out". In the Commissioner's view, a course was a "unified sequence of study, tuition and/or practical training . . . intended

2.452

to lead to one or more qualifications obtained on its completion". So if a profession required more than one qualification for which colleges did not provide a single sequence of tuition and/or experience, the person was not engaged on one continuous "course" throughout, but completed one "course" before moving onto another. Thus para.(a) of the then definition (see the 1995 edition of *Mesher and Wood, Income-related Benefits: the Legislation*) of student did not apply to him. Para.(b) also did not apply as the claimant was not on a "sandwich course", since any periods of outside practical experience were not "associated with" his full-time study within the meaning of the Education (Mandatory Awards) Regulations. See also *CIS 576/1994* in which the Commissioner similarly decides that the course is the whole course leading to the qualification and not a separate course each year. Note that a student who passes resits after a year's absence from his course is rejoining the same, not a different, course (*O'Connor v Chief Adjudication Officer and another* [1999] All E.R.(D) 220 (see below)).

On the other hand, *R(JSA) 2/02* holds that where the course of training is separated from the course of examinations it is only the course of training that constitutes the course of study, not the course of examinations, nor some sort of amalgam of both. Thus where a University provided a course of training to prepare the claimant for a course of examinations set and marked by an outside professional institute, the claimant could abandon the University course and cease to be a student for the purposes of JSA, while still being able to pursue his professional qualification.

"Full-time course"

2.453 The question whether the course is full- or part-time is clearly important, since the exclusion from income support does not apply to part-time students who may be eligible for benefit if they fall within any of the categories in Sch.1B.

Note that it is the course which has to be full-time, rather than the claimant's hours of attendance on it (see *R(SB) 40/83, R(SB) 41/83, CSB 176/1987*). If a non-modular course (see below for the position of modular courses under the new rules introduced on July 31, 2000) is full-time, the effect of para.(2)(b) is that the definition of full-time student applies for the entire length of the course, unless the student finally abandons the course or is dismissed from it (see further below). Note *CIS 368/1992* which decided that a student who exercised the option of working in France for a year as part of her course remained a student throughout her four-year course. Her course was continuing, even if in a different form.

Although the distinction between full- and part-time courses is a crucial one, there continues to be no definition of "full-time course", with the exception of certain courses that are referred to in sub-paras (b) and (c) of the definitions of "full-time course of study" and "full-time course of advanced education". In England and Wales, for courses funded totally or partly by the Learning and Skills Council for England or the National Council for Education and Training for Wales, the cut-off for a full-time course is 16 or more "guided learning hours" each week. The number of a person's "guided learning hours" will be set out in his learning agreement with his college (in Wales referred to simply as a document). Guided learning hours are "hours when a member of staff is present to guide learning on a programme including lectures, tutorials and supervised study", as opposed to time spent in private study (*Decision Makers Guide*, para.30040). Note the different definitions that apply in Scotland.

But for courses which are not so funded, whether or not a course is full-time remains to be determined by the circumstances in each case. The educational establishment's description of the course is not conclusive but should be accepted unless challenged by pertinent evidence (*R(SB) 40/83; R(SB) 41/83*).

In *CIS 152/1994* the Commissioner recognised that recent developments in education, and in particular the advent of modular courses, have blurred the distinction between full-time and part-time courses, and that what is in essence the same course can often be accessed on either a full-time or a part-time basis. The claimant had begun a full-time course in 1992, studying 21 and three quarters hours a week. In

1993 he reduced the number of modules he was taking from seven to five, so that his hours of study became 15 a week. The Commissioner states that it is no longer sufficient just to look at the course. The overall circumstances (*e.g.* the hours of study, number of modules, length of time it would take to obtain the qualification on the basis of five as opposed to seven modules at a time, correspondence from the college, fees payable and any relevant information in the college prospectus) therefore had to be examined to ascertain whether the course the claimant was *currently* attending was full or part-time. (But note that it now seems clear that whether a non-modular course is full-time is to be determined by the nature of the course at its start, not according to later changes, see *O'Connor* and *R(IS) 1/00* below. For the position of modular courses under the new rules introduced on July 31, 2000, see below).

A similar approach was taken in *CIS 576/1994*. The claimant's modular degree course could be undertaken on a full-time or part-time basis. He attended on a full-time basis for the first year and then changed to part-time. He became full-time again for the last two terms of the third year. The Commissioner states that para.(a) of the then definition of "student" (see the 1995 edition of *Mesher and Wood, Income-related Benefits: the Legislation*) did not have the effect of turning a course, attendance on which was on a part-time basis, into a full-time course. Whether a person was, or was not, attending a full-time course depended on the facts at the material time. The factors suggested in *CIS 152/1994* were relevant; whether the person had a local authority grant or student loan might also be pertinent since these were not available to part-time students (see the Education (Mandatory Awards) Regulations). The claimant was not a student (as then defined) when he was attending part-time.

An appeal against this decision was dismissed by the Court of Appeal (*Chief Adjudication Officer v Webber* [1997] 4 All E.R. 274, also reported as *R(IS) 15/98*, but for differing reasons. Hobhouse L.J. stated that the definition of "course of study" presupposes that it is possible at the outset to categorise a course as full-time or part-time and that the same categorisation will apply from the start to the end of the course. But that assumption did not accord with the practice of many educational institutions. Many courses allowed students the option of attending on a full- or part-time basis at different stages of the course, as was the case in this appeal. The consequence was that the claimant had *never* been a student (as then defined) because the course on which he was enrolled did not require full-time attendance and so could not be described as full-time. Such an interpretation clearly had significant implications and went considerably beyond that of the Commissioner. Evans L.J. held that the deeming provision in para.(a) of the then definition of "student" could not be relied upon to confer the status of student when this did not in fact exist. In his view, if interpreted in that way the provision created "an anomalous class of people left to destitution without state support of any kind" and he would require "express words of the utmost clarity to persuade [him] that Parliament intended to produce that disgraceful result". Peter Gibson L.J.'s judgment was based on the fact that the definition of "student" at the time in question included the words "throughout any period of term or vacation within it" (which phrase was omitted from August 1, 1995 following the Court of Appeal's decision in *Clarke and Faul*, see below).

The result of these differing approaches was that the position was somewhat unclear. However in *O'Connor v Chief Adjudication Officer and another* [1999] All E.R.(D) 220, also reported as *R(IS) 7/99*, the judges who were in the majority agreed with Hobhouse L.J. that the status of student (as then defined) was determined by the nature of the course at its beginning and distinguished their own decision from that in *Webber* on that basis. Auld L.J. stated that in Mr O'Connor's case his course was a full-time three year course, with no provision for part-time or modular or other flexible arrangements. Although he had been allowed a year's break in order to re-take exams that he had failed, this was not an option of the course when he started it. But if at its start a course could be followed full- or part-time according to the student's preference, the position was different for the reasons given by Hobhouse L.J. in *Webber*.

The consequence therefore seemed to be that a claimant on a course that could not be characterised as full-time at the outset because he could study full- or part-

2.454

2.455

time for different periods of it would not come within the definition of "student" (as then defined). This was confirmed by *R(IS) 1/00*.

In *R(IS) 1/00* the claimant was undertaking a BTEC National Diploma course. When she claimed income support she was studying for 20 hours a week. The college stated that they did not designate courses as full-time or part-time, as students were able to take separate modules to build towards a final qualification. The Commissioner concluded that the express approval by Auld and Swinton L.JJ. in *O'Connor* of the view taken by Hobhouse L.J. in *Webber* had been necessary to the decision in *O'Connor* and so authoritatively established the position. Thus the fundamental question was how the course was characterised at its outset. As Hobhouse L.J. had stated, a course that did not have a fixed and determined character at its commencement and which could be followed on a full-time or part-time basis was not a full-time course. Moreover, in the Commissioner's view it inevitably followed from this approach that the result would be the same even if the claimant's actual attendance throughout had been on a full-time basis.

To determine whether the claimant's course should be treated as full-time, the Commissioner suggested that information would be needed about such matters as the structure of the course (modular or otherwise), the length of time over which it could be completed, whether a student was committed to any particular structure on initial registration and whether it was possible to change from full-time to part-time attendance or vice versa within the same course.

C5/98 (JSA) (a decision of a Northern Ireland Commissioner) also accepted that it was the nature of the course, as determined at the outset, that was relevant, as did *CJSA/836/1998*, although this was not the primary ground of the Commissioner's decision (see further below).

The Commissioner in *C5/98(JSA)* granted the claimant leave to appeal to the Court of Appeal in Northern Ireland but the appeal was dismissed (*McComb v Department for Social Development*, Court of Appeal in Northern Ireland, March 12, 2001). The claimant contended that the tribunal and the Commissioner, in classifying his course as full-time, had failed to take account of its modular nature. The Court agreed that a modular course was not readily distinguishable from a mixed mode one (the university concerned did not classify any course as mixed mode). It then continued: "The critical matter, however, is whether [the claimant] started out on a course of full-time study, even if he had the option of converting at a later stage to part-time by reducing the number of modules." But with respect to the Northern Ireland Court of Appeal this does not seem to fully accord with the approach of Hobhouse L.J. in *Webber* (which has been followed in subsequent British cases, see above). If a claimant has the option of changing to studying on a part-time basis, how can it be said that the course requires full-time attendance, or that it has a fixed and determined character at its commencement? If it does not, then applying Hobhouse L.J.'s approach, it cannot be characterised as full-time at its outset.

On its facts, however, the decision in *McComb* that the claimant's course was full-time would seem correct. Mr McComb had enrolled on a full-time degree course for which he received an education authority grant for the first three years. When he failed to complete the final year's requirements he was allowed to register as an "examination only" student for a fourth year but he remained on the full-time course on which he had originally enrolled. Now see the new rules for modular courses introduced on July 31, 2000, although on the facts of Mr McComb's case the outcome is likely to be the same (see para.(3)(a)).

"Modular courses"

2.456   New rules were introduced on July 31, 2000 which were intended to clarify the position of modular courses. "Modular course" is defined in para.(4). To come within para.(4) a course must simply consist of two or more modules, the successful completion of a specific number of which is required in order for a student to finish the course.

A person attending or undertaking part of a modular course which would be classified as a full-time course will be treated as a full-time student for the period from the day that part of the course begins until the last day he is registered as attending or undertaking that part as a full-time course (subject to earlier final abandonment or dismissal) (para.(2)(a)). This includes any vacation in that period, or immediately following that part of the course, unless the vacation follows the last day on which he is required to attend or undertake the course (para.(3)(b)). It also includes any period that the person attends or undertakes the course in order to retake examinations or a module that he had previously taken on a full-time basis. It seems that this will apply even if the person is now registered as a part-time student.

It will be a question of fact whether a person is attending or undertaking a part of a modular course that counts as a full-time course. Relevant evidence might include the university or college's regulations and registration procedures, the course regulations and course handbook and any other relevant information given to the student about his status. As stated above, the educational establishment's description is not conclusive but should be accepted unless challenged by pertinent evidence (*R(SB) 40/83; R(SB) 41/83*). It should be noted, however, that not all modular courses allow the option of full-time or part-time attendance. Some universities and colleges do not have mixed mode courses but only offer separate full-time and part-time courses, even though the courses are classed as modular. Disputes about whether the part of the modular course (or indeed the whole of the course) that the person is attending or undertaking counts as a full-time course may therefore still continue. If the modular course is a full-time course throughout it would seem to come within sub-para.(a) of para.(2) but may also be covered by sub-para.(b).

However, the importance of these new rules is that for modular courses the deeming of full-time student status only operates during the periods prescribed in paras (2) and (3). It does not apply outside these periods if the student's status has changed to part-time. A student on a part of a modular course which is not classed as full-time and who is not caught by para.(3) may thus be able to claim income support or JSA if he satisfies the normal condition of entitlement for one of these benefits.

"Attending or undertaking [a course] . . . finally abandons . . . or is dismissed from it"

The deeming provision, whereby a person whose non-modular course is full-time **2.457** (as determined at its start, see above under "*Full-time course*") will count as a full-time student until the last day of the course or until he finally abandons or is dismissed from it is now contained in para.(2)(b). Note the separate deeming provision for those on a part of a modular course that is classed as full-time in para.(2)(a) (and note paras (3) and (4); see above for a discussion of these new rules for modular courses).

The predecessor of para.(2)(b) (para.(a) of the former definition of "student", see the 2000 edition of this book, and see the 1995 edition of *Mesher and Wood, Income-related Benefits: the Legislation* for the form of para.(a) that was in force before August 1, 1995) came under close scrutiny in several cases, notably *Chief Adjudication Officer and Secretary of State for Social Security v Clarke and Faul* [1995] E.L.R. 259, *CIS 15594/1996* (appealed to the Court of Appeal as *O'Connor v Chief Adjudication Officer and another* [1999] All. E.R.(D) 220, also reported as *R(IS) 7/99*), *CIS 13986/1996* and *CIS 14255/1996*. For a discussion of these decisions see the 2000 edition of this book (pp.405–6). Note that one of the points decided in those cases, namely that "abandon" in this context meant "abandon permanently" has now received statutory endorsement in para.(2). Dismissal similarly means final dismissal (*CIS 15594/1996*). Note also *Driver v Chief Adjudication Officer* (Court of Appeal, December 12, 1996, reported as *R(IS) 6/97*) which held that a student on a sandwich course whose industrial placement ended prematurely nevertheless remained a student throughout the period of her intended placement.

As a result of those decisions, it seems fairly clearly established that a person whose non-modular course is full-time (as determined at its outset) will count as a full-time student until the last day of the course (subject to any earlier final abandonment or dismissal), regardless of non-attendance on the course for whatever reason. (But see above for the position of modular courses.) Note, however, that a full-time student who has been incapable of work for 28 weeks (or who qualifies for a disability or severe disability premium) will be eligible for income support (reg.4ZA(3)(b) and para.10 of Sch.1B).

In addition, from July 31, 2000, a full-time student who has taken time out of his course with the consent of his university or college because of illness or caring responsibilities, and who has now recovered or whose caring responsibilities have ended, can claim JSA until the day before he rejoins his course or the first day of the following academic year, whichever is the earlier, provided that he is not eligible for a grant or student loan during this period (see reg.1(3D) and (3E) of the JSA Regulations). Note that caring responsibilities in this context is not defined. For the position of pregnant students and JSA, see *Secretary of State for Social Security v Walter* [2001] EWCA Civ 1913, reported as *R(JSA) 3/02* (which overturned the decision in *CJSA 1920/1999*) discussed in the notes to reg.130 of the JSA Regulations. A pregnant student is excluded from income support (see reg.4ZA and Sch.1B; para.14 of Sch.1B which covers pregnant women is not one of the paragraphs applied to students by reg.4ZA(3)(b)). But once the child is born the student may be eligible under reg.4ZA(3)(b) and para.1 of Sch.1B if she is a lone parent.

One other point should be made. Para.(2)(b) refers to "the course" that the full-time student is attending or undertaking. So if a student does finally abandon his full-time non-modular course and then starts a separate part-time course he should not be caught by the deeming provision. In this connection it is interesting to note that para.12 of the Secretary of State's response to SSAC's report on the amendment regulations introduced on July 31, 2000 (Cm 4739 (2000), see above under *"Student"* and *"Full-time Student"*) seems to accept that those changing from full-time to part-time courses are abandoning one course before starting another. Note, however, that this would not appear to assist a claimant who is not attending his course because he has failed exams and is only permitted to return if and when he successfully passes the resits. Although *CIS 13986/1996* decided that a claimant in that situation had been dismissed from his *original* course and if he passed the resit examinations a year later would be joining a *different* course, this was not followed in *CIS 15594/1996(O'Connor)*. The Commissioner's view in *CIS 15594/1996* was that if a person was readmitted after an interval to follow essentially the same programme, that person was returning to the same course. On appeal the Court of Appeal in *O'Connor* decided the substantive issue in *CIS 13986/1996* against the claimant (for further discussion see pp.405–6 of the 2000 edition of this volume).

Differences between income support and JSA definition

2.458   The definitions applying to full-time students under the JSA Regulations take a slightly different form (see the notes to reg.130 of the JSA Regulations).

Since the amendments made to both the Income Support and the JSA Regulations on July 31, 2000 by SI 2000 No. 1981 the differences are less marked. However, in *CJSA 836/1998* (a decision on the pre-July 31, 2000 form) the Commissioner took the view that the differences between the then form of the JSA and income support definitions had a material effect. This was because for the purposes of JSA the provision deeming a person who had started a course to be attending or undertaking it until the last day of the course (or earlier abandonment or dismissal) was contained in the definition of "course of study" in reg.1(3) of the JSA Regulations. Under income support the deeming provision was in the definition of "student" in reg.61. This defined a student as someone who was attending a full-time course and provided that a person who had started on "such a course" (*i.e.* a full-time course) was to be treated as attending it until the last day of the course or earlier abandonment or dismissal. The deeming under the definition of "course of study" in reg.1(3), on the other hand, did not necessarily refer to a full-time course. In the Commissioner's view, therefore, there was nothing in the JSA Regulations that required a person who had started a course on a full-time basis but changed to part-time to be treated as continuing to be a full-time student. Whether the course was full- or part-time was to be determined by looking at the situation at the time in question. But this approach was not followed in *C5/98 (JSA)*. The Commissioner in that case considered that the "it" in the definition of "course of study" in reg.1(3) referred to the course started. The fact that the "deeming" under JSA was contained in the definition of "course of study" rather than the definition of "student" was not material. This point was not dealt with by the Northern Ireland Court of Appeal in the appeal against *C5/98 (JSA)* (*McComb v Department for Social Developmental*, March 12, 2001, see above).

But since the insertion of paras (3A) to (3C) into reg.1 of the JSA Regulations (which provisions parallel paras (2) to (4)) with effect from July 31, 2000 the Commissioner's reasoning in *CJSA 836/1998* no longer applies. This is because the deeming of full-time student status for the entire length of a course (subject to earlier final abandonment or dismissal) is now contained in reg.1(3A)(b) of the JSA Regulations, rather than the definition of "course of study" in reg.1(3).

Note also paras (3D) and (3E) of reg.1 of the JSA Regulations (see the notes to reg.130 of the JSA Regulations). There is no equivalent to these provisions in the Income Support Regulations.

Summary

The position for non-modular courses may thus be summarised as follows. 2.459 Whether or not a person comes within the definition of "full-time student" depends on the nature of his course, as determined at its outset. If the course is not full-time so that the definition of full-time student does not apply, the fact that the person attends the course on a full-time basis throughout would seem to be immaterial (see *CIS 12823/1996*). On the other hand, if the person's course is classified as full-time at its beginning, he will count as a student for the duration of his course (subject to earlier abandonment or dismissal), regardless of his actual mode of attendance on the course.

If the course is a modular one (as defined in para.(4)), the rules in paras (2) and (3) will apply (see above under *"Modular courses"*). Under para.(2)(a), it will be a question of fact whether a student is attending or undertaking a part of a modular course that would be classified as a full-time course. If a modular course is a full-time course throughout it would seem to come within sub-para.(a) of para.(2) but may also be covered by sub-para.(b). However, the importance of these new rules is that for modular courses the deeming of full-time student status only operates during the periods prescribed in paras (2) and (3). It does not apply outside these periods if the student's status has changed to part-time. A student on a part of a modular course which is not classed as full-time and who is not caught by para.(3) may thus be able to claim income support or JSA if he satisfies the normal conditions of entitlement for one of these benefits.

As readers will be aware, the Human Rights Act 1998 came into force on October 2, 2000 (see Vol. III of this series). The claimant in *O'Connor* had relied on the right to education in Art.2 of the First Protocol to the European Convention on Human Rights in support of his argument on irrationality. However, Auld L.J. considered that there was no potential breach of the right to education. This was because, firstly, there were rulings of inadmissibility by the European Commission of Human Rights suggesting that Article 2 was concerned primarily with school, not higher, education. Secondly, Article 2 did not require the State to subsidise a student in his exercise of his right to avail himself of education which it provided. But in view of the anomalous and often arbitrary treatment of students under social security legislation, there may well be further challenges under the Human Rights Act in the future.

"Student loan"

Note *CIS/3734/2004* which confirms that since a claimant does not count as a student until he starts a course, in apportioning his loan income under reg.66A any loan income should be ignored until the beginning of the first term (despite the provision in reg.66A(2)(c)). The Commissioner accepted the Secretary of State's submission that "a student loan can only have an existence for the purposes of the Income Support (General) Regulations 1987 where it is for the maintenance of a student. Until the claimant starts to attend or undertake the course of study . . . [he] is not a student. Until [he] is a student, whatever the point in its administrative path [his] student loan application has reached, it cannot meet the definition of student loan herein and so does not fall to be taken into account as income."

Calculation of grant income

2.460   **62.**—(1) The amount of a student's grant income to be taken into account shall, subject to [³paragraphs [⁷(2) and (2A)]], be the whole of his grant income.

(2) There shall be disregarded from the amount of a student's grant income any payment—

(a) intended to meet tuition fees or examination fees;

(b) [⁴. . .]

(c) intended to meet additional expenditure incurred by a disabled student in respect of his attendance on a course;

(d) intended to meet additional expenditure connected with term time residential study away from the student's educational establishment;

(e) on account of the student maintaining a home at a place other than that at which he resides during his course but only to the extent that his rent [²². . .] is not met by housing benefit;

(f) on account of any other person but only if that person is residing outside of the United Kingdom and there is no applicable amount in respect of him;

(g) intended to meet the cost of books and equipment [⁴. . .] [⁶. . .];

(h) intended to meet travel expenses incurred as a result of his attendance on the course.

[¹⁸(i) intended for the maintenance [²¹. . .] of a child dependant.]

[²¹ (j) intended for the child care costs of a child dependant.]

[⁶(2A) Where a student does not have a student loan and is not treated as possessing such a loan, there shall be excluded from the student's grant income—

(a) the sum of [¹⁹£275] in respect of travel costs; and

[¹²(b) the sum of [²⁰£343] towards the costs of books and equipment,] whether or not any such costs are incurred.]

[¹³[¹⁸ (2B) There shall also be excluded from a student's grant income any grant of £510 in respect of expenditure on travel, books and equipment which is payable under regulation 15(8) of the Education (Student Support) Regulations 2002.]]

(3) [⁹ Subject to paragraph (3B), a student's grant income except any amount intended for the maintenance of [¹⁸ adult] dependants under Part III of Schedule 2 to the Education (Mandatory Awards) Regulations 1999 [¹⁸. . .]] shall be apportioned—

(a) subject to paragraph (4), in a case where it is attributable to the period of study, equally between the weeks [¹⁶ in the period beginning with the benefit week, the first day of which coincides with, or immediately follows, the first day of the period of study and ending with the benefit week, the last day of which coincides with, or immediately precedes, the last day of the period of study];

(b) in any other case, equally between the weeks in the period [16 beginning with the benefit week, the first day of which coincides with, or
immediately follows, the first day of the period for which it is payable
and ending with the benefit week, the last day of which coincides
with, or immediately precedes, the last day of the period for which it
is payable].

[1(3A) [14 Any grant in respect of [18 an adult dependant] paid under
section 63(6) of the Health Services and Public Health Act 1968 (grants in
respect of the provision of instruction to officers of hospital authorities) and]
any amount intended for the maintenance of [18 an adult dependant] under
the provisions referred to in paragraph (3) shall be apportioned equally over
a period of 52 weeks or, if there are 53 benefit weeks (including part-weeks)
in the year, 53.]

[10 (3B) [16 In a case where a student is in receipt of a student loan or
where he could have acquired a student loan by taking reasonable steps but
had not done so,] any amount intended for the maintenance of [18 an adult
dependant] under provisions other than those referred to in paragraph (3)
shall be apportioned over the same period as the student's loan is apportioned or [16, as the case may be, would have been apportioned].]

(4) In the case of a student on a sandwich course, any periods of experience within the period of study shall be excluded and the student's grant
income shall be apportioned equally between [16 the weeks in the period
beginning with the benefit week, the first day of which immediately follows
the last day of the period of experience and ending with the benefit week, the
last day of which coincides with, or immediately precedes, the last day of the
period of study].

AMENDMENTS

1. Income Support (General) Amendment Regulations 1988 (SI 1988/663),   **2.461**
reg.24 (April 11, 1988).
2. Income Support (General) Amendment Regulations 1992 (SI 1992/468), reg.5
(April 6, 1992).
3. Income-related Benefits Schemes (Miscellaneous Amendments) (No.3)
Regulations 1992 (SI 1992/2155), reg.20 (October 5, 1992).
4. Income-related Benefits Schemes and Social Fund (Miscellaneous
Amendments) Regulations 1996 (SI 1996/1944), reg.6(9) (October 7, 1996).
5. Social Security (Student Amounts Amendment) Regulations 1998 (SI
1998/1379), reg.2 (August 31, 1998, or if the student's period of study begins
between August 1, and 30, 1998, the first day of the period).
6. Social Security Amendment (Students) Regulations 1999 (SI 1999/1935),
reg.3(3) (August 30, 1999, or if the student's period of study begins between August
1 and 29, 1999, the first day of the period).
7. Social Security Amendment (Students and Income-related Benefits)
Regulations 2000 (SI 2000/1922), reg.2(4)(a) (August 28, 2000, or if the student's
period of study begins between August 1 and 27, 2000, the first day of the period).
8. Social Security Amendment (Students and Income-related Benefits)
Regulations 2000 (SI 2000/1922), reg.2(4)(b) (August 28, 2000, or if the student's
period of study begins between August 1 and 27, 2000, the first day of the period).
9. Social Security Amendment (Students and Income-related Benefits)
Regulations 2000 (SI 2000/1922), reg.2(4)(d) (August 28, 2000, or if the student's
period of study begins between August 1 and 27, 2000, the first day of the period).
10. Social Security Amendment (Students and Income-related Benefits)
Regulations 2000 (SI 2000/1922), reg.2(4)(e) (August 28, 2000, or if the student's
period of study begins between August 1 and 27, 2000, the first day of the period).

11. Social Security Amendment (Students and Income-related Benefits) Regulations 2001 (SI 2001/2319), reg.3(1) and (3)(c) (August 27, 2001, or if the student's period of study begins between August 1 and 26, 2001, the first day of the period).

12. Social Security Amendment (Students and Income-related Benefits) Regulations 2001 (SI 2001/2319), reg.3(2) and (3)(c) (August 27, 2001, or if the student's period of study begins between August 1 and 26, 2001, the first day of the period).

13. Social Security Amendment (Students and Income-related Benefits) Regulations 2001 (SI 2001/2319), reg.3(4) (August 27, 2001, or if the student's period of study begins between August 1 and 26, 2001, the first day of the period).

14. Social Security Amendment (Students and Income-related Benefits) Regulations 2001 (SI 2001/2319), reg.6 (August 27, 2001, or if the student's period of study begins between August 1 and 26, 2001, the first day of the period).

15. Social Security Amendment (Students and Income-related Benefits) Regulations 2002 (SI 2002/1589), reg.3 (August 26, 2002, or if the student's period of study begins between August 1 and 25, 2002, the first day of the period).

16. Social Security Amendment (Students and Income-related Benefits) Regulations 2002 (SI 2002/1589), reg.4 (August 26, 2002, or if the student's period of study begins between August 1 and 25, 2002, the first day of the period).

17. Social Security Amendment (Students and Income-related Benefits) (No.2) Regulations 2002 (SI 2002/2207), reg.2 (September 2, 2002).

18. Social Security (Working Tax Credit and Child Tax Credit) (Consequential Amendments) Regulations 2003 (SI 2003/455), reg.2 and Sch.1, para.16 (April 6, 2004, except in transitional cases and see further the note to reg.17 of the Income Support Regulations), as amended by Social Security (Working Tax Credit and Child Tax Credit) (Consequential Amendments) (No. 3) Regulations 2003 (SI 2003/1731) (August 8, 2003).

19. Social Security (Students and Income-related Benefits) Amendment Regulations 2004 (SI 2004/1708), reg.2(1) and (3)(c) (September 1, 2004, or if the student's period of study begins between August 1 and August 31, 2004, the first day of the period).

20. Social Security (Students and Income-related Benefits) Amendment Regulations 2004 (SI 2004/1708), reg.2(2) and (3)(c) (September 1, 2004, or if the student's period of study begins between August 1 and August 31, 2004, the first day of the period).

21. Social Security (Students and Income-related Benefits) Amendment Regulations 2004 (SI 2004/1708), reg.3(3) (September 1, 2004, or if the student's period of study begins between August 1 and August 31, 2004, the first day of the period).

22. Social Security (Miscellaneous Amendments) Regulations 2005 (SI 2005/574), reg.3(4) (April 4, 2005).

DEFINITIONS

2.462   "full-time student"—see reg.61(1).
"grant"—*ibid.*
"grant income"—*ibid.*
"period of study"—*ibid.*
"periods of experience"—*ibid.*
"sandwich course"—*ibid.*
"student"—*ibid.*
"student loan"—*ibid.*

GENERAL NOTE

2.463   For students who started their course in or after the 1998/99 academic year, the main source of financial help is the student loan system (see the note to reg.66A). However, they may also be eligible for various additional allowances, which may be paid as grants (for example, if they have a child or a disability). Some of these grants will come under the rules in this regulation.

A student's grant is first to be subject to the disregards listed in paras (2)–(2B). Note that from August 30, 1999 the disregard in para.(2A) only applies if the student does not, and is not deemed to, have a student loan (defined in reg.61(1)): see reg.66A. The disregards referred to in para.(2A) will normally be applied to the student loan (see reg.66A(5)). On para.(2)(h), note that the standard maintenance grant no longer includes a set amount for travel costs (see *R(IS) 7/95* referred to in the note to the previous form of para.(2A) in *Mesher and Wood, Income-related Benefits: the Legislation* (1999)).

The disregard in para.(2)(i) is a general disregard of any payment intended for the maintenance of a child and that in para.(2)(j) is a general disregard of any payment intended for child care costs. Both these disregards were previously contained in para.(2)(i) which was introduced on April 6, 2004 to replace the various disregards for students with child care responsibilities previously contained in para.(2B), except that in sub-para.(b) which became the new form of para.(2B). However the new para.2(i) and the amendments to para.(2B) did not apply in "transitional cases" (*i.e.* those cases in which the claimant is still receiving amounts for his children in his income support—see further the note to reg.17). For "transitional cases" the old form of para.(2B) remained in force. However, the insertion of the new para.(2)(j) with effect from September 1, 2004 (or if the student's period of study begins between August 1 and 31, 2004, the first day of the period), which provides for a general disregard of payments intended for the child care costs of a child dependant, means that the disregards contained in sub-paras. (c), (cc) and (d) of the unamended form of para.(2B) are no longer needed. These have therefore been omitted from the unamended form of para.(2B) with effect from September 1, 2004 (or if the student's period of study begins between August 1 and 31, 2004, the first day of the period) by reg.3(5) and (6)(c) of the Social Security (Students and Income-related Benefits) Amendment Regulations 2004 (SI 2004/1708). See the 2003 edition of this volume and the 2003/2004 Supplement for the unamended form of para.(2B).

Note that the £510 grant (payable to students with dependants) which is ignored under para.(2B) only applied in relation to an academic year that began before September 1, 2003 (the Education (Student Support) Regulations 2002 (SI 2002/195) were revoked by reg.3(1) of the Education (Student Support) (No. 2) Regulations 2002 (SI 2002/3200) with effect from September 1, 2003, and see reg.3(2) of those Regulations).

In *CIS 91/1994* the claimant argued that the disregard for books in para.(2)(g) should be apportioned over 52 weeks. It would then reduce the dependants and mature student elements of her grant that were taken into account in calculating her income support during the summer vacation. But the Commissioner holds that the deduction in sub-para.(g) could only be applied to the basic maintenance grant, as this was clearly the part of the grant which contained provision for books. *R(IS) 7/95* confirms that it is the intention of the grant-making authority, not of the student, that counts under sub-para.(h). *R(IS) 16/95* similarly holds that in the case of the disregard for tuition fees under sub-para.(a), it is the intention of the provider of the payment that has to be considered. The fact that the claimant's partner spent all his grants from the Norwegian Government on tuition fees was irrelevant. Presumably the same approach would also be applied to the disregards in sub-paras (c), (d) and (g).

A grant is normally apportioned over the weeks of the period of study, *i.e.* from the beginning of the academic year to the day before the summer vacation (para.(3)(a)). (The August 2002 amendment to para.(3)(a) is to ensure that the grant income is attributed to complete benefit weeks; see the similar amendments to paras (3)(b) and (4)). Elements of the grant for mature students or dependants under the Mandatory Awards Regulations 1999 were apportioned over 52 weeks (para.(3A)), but only while the person remained a student. *CIS 7/1988* holds that these elements of grant would ordinarily be attributable to the same period as the maintenance grant under the Mandatory Awards Regulations. *CIS 7/1988* is followed (with some reservation) in *R(IS) 1/96*, where the Commissioner points out that under reg.15(1) of the Mandatory Awards Regulations an award comes to an end on the expiry of the course.

This supported the conclusion that in the final year the dependants and mature student elements were, like the ordinary maintenance grant, to be treated as payable for the period up to the day before the summer vacation. After that date the person was no longer a student and reg.62 no longer applied. A grant or bursary for dependants paid to NHS-funded students is also apportioned over 52 weeks (para.(3A)).

2.464   In *R(IS) 15/95* the claimant claimed income support for the summer vacation at the end of the first year of her course. Her grant included a dependants allowance and a single parent's allowance. The Commissioner decides that the single parent element had to be apportioned over 52 weeks. This was because the single parent's allowance was provided for in Sch.4 to the Mandatory Awards Regulations. The effect of Sch.4 was to increase in certain circumstances the amount awarded under Part III of Sch.2 for the maintenance of dependants. Sch.4 on its own awarded nothing. Thus the single parent's allowance was in fact merely an increase of the amount intended for the maintenance of dependants and so fell to be apportioned in accord with para.(3A). Even if this was not the case, the allowance had to be apportioned equally between the weeks in the period in respect of which it was payable (para.(3)(b)). That period was 52 weeks (see paras 12(1) and 20 of Sch.2 to the Mandatory Awards Regulations).

However, if the student's course started on or after September 1, 1998 (August 1, 1998 for Scotland) the grant for dependants is taken into account for the same period as the student loan (this used to apply even if the claimant did not have a student loan but from August 2002 it only applies if the student has received such a loan or could get one by taking reasonable steps) (para.(3B)). This is because under the system for student support introduced from the start of the 1998/1999 academic year (see further the note to reg.66A), the non-repayable dependants element is payable on the same basis as the student loan.

Note that from September 1, 2003 grants for dependants will only be payable in respect of certain adult dependants or a spouse (Education (Student Support) (No. 2) Regulations 2002 (SI 2002/3200), reg.15; the same applies to grants under the Education (Mandatory Awards) Regulations, see para.13(1) of Sch.2 of the 2003 Regulations (SI 2003/1994)). Students with children are expected to apply for child tax credit for help with their costs. In addition, paras (3), (3A) and (3B) have been amended with effect from April 6, 2004 (except in "transitional cases"—see reg.17) so that they only refer to grants in respect of adult dependants. This is as a consequence of the removal of amounts for children and young persons from the income support scheme with effect from April 6, 2004 (except in "transitional cases"). Financial assistance to help with the cost of bringing up a child or young person is now to be provided through the child tax credit system, see Vol. IV of this series. The old form of these provisions (see the 2003 edition of this volume) continues in force for "transitional cases"—see the note to reg.17.

Subject to reg.62, a student's grant will be taken into account as income under reg.40. Thus any relevant disregards in Sch.9 will apply (*R(IS) 16/95*).

For the disregard of any grant (or covenant income, student loan or contribution) left over after a student has completed his course, see para.61 of Sch.9.

Calculation of covenant income where a contribution is assessed

2.465   **63.**—(1) Where a student is in receipt of income by way of a grant during a period of study and a contribution has been assessed, the amount of his covenant income to be taken into account for that period and any summer vacation immediately following shall be the whole amount of his covenant income less, subject to paragraph (3), the amount of the contribution.

(2) The weekly amount of the student's covenant income shall be determined—

   (a) by dividing the amount of income which falls to be taken into account under paragraph (1) by 52 or, if there are 53 benefit weeks (including part weeks) in the year, 53; and

(b) by disregarding from the resulting amount, £5.

(3) For the purposes of paragraph (1), the contribution shall be treated as increased by the amount, if any, by which the amount excluded under [¹regulation 62(2)(h) (calculation of grant income) falls short of the amount for the time being specified in paragraph 7(4)(i) of Schedule 2 to the Education (Mandatory Awards) Regulations 1991 (travel expenditure).]

AMENDMENT

1. Income Support (General) Amendment Regulations 1992 (SI 1992/468), reg. 5 (April 6, 1992). **2.466**

DEFINITIONS

"benefit week"—see reg.2(1).
"contribution"—see reg.61(1).
"covenant income"—*ibid.*
"grant"—*ibid.*
"period of study"—*ibid.*
"standard maintenance grant"—*ibid.*
"student"—*ibid.*

GENERAL NOTE

Although the number of covenants dropped away following the 1988 Budget, some existing covenants may have continued running, perhaps at inadequate levels. **2.467**

If a student has a grant, with a parental contribution assessed, covenant income is only taken into account to the extent that it exceeds the assessed contribution (plus any addition under para.(3)). The definition of covenant income in reg.61 confines it to the payment net of tax. Any excess is spread over the whole year, with a £5 per week disregard.

Covenant income where no grant income or no contribution is assessed

64.—(1) Where a student is not in receipt of income by way of a grant the amount of his covenant income shall be calculated as follows— **2.468**
  (a) any sums intended for any expenditure specified in regulation 62(2)(a) to (f), (calculation of grant income) necessary as a result of his attendance on the course, shall be disregarded;
  (b) any covenant income, up to the amount of the standard mainten-ance grant, which is not so disregarded, shall be apportioned equally between the weeks of the period of study and there shall be disre-garded from the covenant income to be so apportioned the amount which would have been disregarded under [¹regulation 62(2)(g) and (h) and (2A)] (calculation of grant income) had the student been in receipt of the standard maintenance grant;
  (c) the balance, if any, shall be divided by 52 or, if there are 53 benefit weeks (including part weeks) in the year, 53 and treated as weekly income of which £5 shall be disregarded.

(2) Where a student is in receipt of income by way of a grant and no contri-bution has been assessed, the amount of his covenant income shall be calculated in accordance with sub-paragraphs (a) to (c) of paragraph (1), except that—
  (a) the value of the standard maintenance grant shall be abated by the amount of his grant income less an amount equal to the amount of any sums disregarded under regulation 62(2)(a) to (f); and

(b) the amount to be disregarded under paragraph (1)(b) shall be abated by an amount equal to the amount of any sums disregarded under [¹regulation 62(2)(g) and (h) and (2A)].

AMENDMENT

2.469   1. Income Support (General) Amendment Regulations 1992 (SI 1992/468), reg.5 (April 6, 1992).

DEFINITIONS

"benefit week"—see reg.2(1).
"contribution"—see reg.61(1).
"covenant income"—*ibid.*
"grant"—*ibid.*
"grant income"—*ibid.*
"standard maintenance grant"—*ibid.*
"student"—*ibid.*

GENERAL NOTE

Para.(1)

2.470   If the student has no grant, first any sums earmarked for things listed in reg.62(2)(a) to (f) are excluded. Then the amount of covenant income up to the rate of the standard maintenance grant (less the items specified above) is spread over the weeks of the period of study, disregarding items specified in reg.62(2)(g) and (h) and (2A). Then any excess is spread over the whole year with a £5 p.w. disregard.

Para.(2)

2.471   If the student has a grant with no parental contribution, the effect is to spread the covenant income, after topping up any deficiency from the standard maintenance grant, over the whole year, as in para.(1).

Relationship with amounts to be disregarded under Schedule 9

2.472   **65.** No part of a student's convenant income or grant income shall be disregarded under paragraph 15 of Schedule 9 (charitable and voluntary payments) and any other income [¹to which sub-paragraph (1) of that paragraph applies shall be disregarded only to the extent that] the amount disregarded under regulation 63(2)(b) (calculation of convenant income where a contribution is assessed) or, as the case may be, 64(1)(c) (convenant income where no grant income or no contribution is assessed) is less than [²£20].

AMENDMENTS

1. Income Support (General) Amendment Regulations 1990 (SI 1990/547), reg.14 (April 9, 1990).
2. Income-related Benefits Schemes (Miscellaneous Amendments) Regulations 1996 (SI 1996/462), reg.8 (April 8, 1996).

DEFINITIONS

"covenant income"—see reg.61(1).
"grant income"—*ibid.*
"student"—*ibid.*

Other amounts to be disregarded

66.—(1) For the purposes of ascertaining income [¹other than grant   2.473
income, covenant income and loans treated as income in accordance with
regulation 66A], any amounts intended for any expenditure specified in
regulation 62(2) (calculation of grant income) necessary as a result of his
attendance on the course shall be disregarded but only if, and to the extent
that, the necessary expenditure exceeds or is likely to exceed the amount
of the sums disregarded under regulation 62(2) [¹and (2A)], 63(3)
[², 64(1)(a) or (b) and 66A(5) (calculation of grant income, covenant
income and treatment of student loans)] on like expenditure.

(2) Where a claim is made in respect of any period in the normal summer
vacation and any income is payable under a Deed of Covenant which commences or takes effect after the first day of that vacation, that income shall
be disregarded.

AMENDMENTS

1. Income-related Benefits Schemes (Miscellaneous Amendments) Regulations   2.474
1994 (SI 1994/527), reg.5 (April 11, 1994).
2. Social Security Amendment (Students) Regulations 1999 (SI 1999/1935),
reg.3(4) (August 30, 1999, or if the student's period of study begins between
August 1 and 29, 1999, the first day of the period).

DEFINITIONS

"covenant income"—see reg.61(1).
"grant income"—*ibid.*
"student loan"—*ibid.*

GENERAL NOTE

Paragraph (2) will not be of any practical effect, because new covenants are   2.475
unlikely to be made now that the tax advantages have been removed in the 1988
Budget.

[¹Treatment of student loans

66A.—[⁶(1) A student loan shall be treated as income unless it is a hard-   2.476
ship loan in which case it shall be disregarded.

(1A) For the purposes of paragraph (1), "hardship loan" means a loan
made under regulation 21 of the Education (Student Support) Regulations
2000, regulation 12 of the Education (Student Loans) (Scotland)
Regulations 2000 or regulation 21 of the Education (Student Support)
Regulations (Northern Ireland) 2000.

(2) In calculating the weekly amount of the loan to be taken into account
as income—

[¹⁰(a) in respect of a course that is of a single academic year's duration
      or less, a loan which is payable in respect of that period shall be
      apportioned equally between the weeks in the period beginning
      with—
      (i) except in a case where (ii) below applies, the benefit week, the
           first day of which coincides with, or immediately follows, the
           first day of the single academic year;

    (ii) where the student is required to start attending the course in August or where the course is of less than an academic year's duration, the benefit week, the first day of which coincides with, or immediately follows, the first day of the course,

and ending with the benefit week, the last day of which coincides with, or immediately precedes, the last day of the course;]

[⁹(aa) in respect of an academic year of a course which starts other than on 1st September, a loan which is payable in respect of that academic year shall be apportioned equally between the weeks in the period beginning with the benefit week [¹⁰, the first day of which coincides with, or immediately follows, the first day of that academic year and ending with the benefit week, the last day of which coincides with, or immediately precedes,] the last day of that academic year but excluding any benefit weeks falling entirely within the quarter during which, in the opinion of the Secretary of State, the longest of any vacation is taken and for the purposes of this sub-paragraph, "quarter" shall have the same meaning as for the purposes of the Education (Student Support) Regulations 2001;]

(b) in respect of the final academic year of a course (not being a course of a single year's duration), a loan, which is payable in respect of that final academic year shall be apportioned equally between the weeks in the period beginning with [¹⁰. . .]—

    [¹⁰ (i) except in a case where (ii) below applies, the benefit week, the first day of which coincides with, or immediately follows, the first day of that academic year;

    (ii) where the final academic year starts on 1st September, the benefit week, the first day of which coincides with, or immediately follows, the earlier of 1st September or the first day of the autumn term;]

and ending with [¹⁰ the benefit week, the last day of which coincides with, or immediately precedes,] the last day of the course;

(c) in any other case, the loan shall be apportioned equally between the weeks in the period beginning with the earlier of—

    (i) the first day of the first benefit week in September; or

    [¹⁰ (ii) the benefit week, the first day of which coincides with, or immediately follows, the first day of the autumn term,]

and ending with [¹⁰ the benefit week, the last day of which coincides with, or immediately precedes, the last day of June],

and, in all cases, from the weekly amount so apportioned there shall be disregarded £10.]

[⁵(3) A student shall be treated as possessing a student loan in respect of an academic year where—

(a) a student loan has been made to him in respect of that year; or

(b) he could acquire such a loan in respect of that year by taking reasonable steps to do so.

(4) Where a student is treated as possessing a student loan under paragraph (3), the amount of the student loan to be taken into account as income shall be, subject to paragraph (5)—

(a) in the case of a student to whom a student loan is made in respect of an academic year, a sum equal to the maximum student loan he is able to acquire in respect of that year by taking reasonable steps to do so and either—

(i) in the case of a student other than one to whom head (ii) refers, any contribution whether or not it has been paid to him; or

(ii) in the case of a student to whom paragraph 1, 2, 10, 11 or 12 of Schedule 1B applies (lone parent or disabled student), any contribution which has actually been paid to him;

(b) in the case of a student to whom a student loan is not made in respect of an academic year, the maximum student loan that would be made to the student if—

(i) he took all reasonable steps to obtain the maximum student loan he is able to acquire in respect of that year; and

(ii) no deduction in that loan was made by virtue of the application of a means test.

(5) There shall be deducted from the amount of income taken into account under paragraph (4)—

(a) the sum of [^{11}£275] in respect of travel costs; and,

[^{8}(b) the sum of [^{12}£343] towards the costs of books and equipment,] whether or not any such costs are incurred.]]

AMENDMENTS

1. Social Security Benefits (Student Loans and Miscellaneous Amendments) Regulations 1990 (SI 1990/1549), reg.5(7) (September 1, 1990).

2. Income Support (General) Amendment Regulations 1991 (SI 1991/236), reg.9 (March 13, 1991).

3. Income Support (General) Amendment No.4 Regulations 1991 (SI 1991/1559), reg.12 (August 5, 1991).

4. Income-related Benefits Schemes (Miscellaneous Amendments) Regulations 1996 (SI 1996/462), reg.9 (April 8, 1996).

5. Social Security Amendment (Students) Regulations 1999 (SI 1999/1935), reg.3(5) (August 30, 1999, or if the student's period of study begins between August 1 and 29, 1999, the first day of the period).

6. Social Security Amendment (Students and Income-related Benefits) Regulations 2000 (SI 2000/1922), reg.2(5) (August 28, 2000, or if the student's period of study begins between August 1 and 27, 2000, the first day of the period).

7. Social Security Amendment (Students and Income-related Benefits) Regulations 2001 (SI 2001/2319), reg.3(1) and (3)(c) (August 27, 2001, or if the student's period of study begins between August 1 and 26, 2001, the first day of the period).

8. Social Security Amendment (Students and Income-related Benefits) Regulations 2001 (SI 2001/2319), reg.3(2) and (3)(c) (August 27, 2001, or if the student's period of study begins between August 1 and 26, 2001, the first day of the period).

9. Social Security Amendment (Students and Income-related Benefits) Regulations 2001 (SI 2001/2319), reg.4 (August 27, 2001, or if the student's period of study begins between August 1 and 26, 2001, the first day of the period).

10. Social Security Amendment (Students and Income-related Benefits) Regulations 2002 (SI 2002/1589), reg.5 (August 26, 2002, or if the student's period of study begins between August 1 and 25, 2002, the first day of the period).

11. Social Security (Students and Income-related Benefits) Amendment Regulations 2004 (SI 2004/1708), reg.2(1) and (3)(c) (September 1, 2004, or if the student's period of study begins between August 1 and August 31, 2004, the first day of the period).

12. Social Security (Students and Income-related Benefits) Amendment Regulations 2004 (SI 2004/1708), reg.2(2) and (3)(c) (September 1, 2004, or if the student's period of study begins between August 1 and August 31, 2004, the first day of the period).

2.477

461

DEFINITIONS

"academic year"—see reg.61(1).
"benefit week"—see reg.2(1).
"last day of the course"—see reg.61(1).
"student"—*ibid.*
"student loan"—*ibid.*
"year"—*ibid.*

GENERAL NOTE

2.478   The changes made to this regulation on August 30, 1999, and the further changes made on August 28, 2000, reflect the introduction of the new system for student support from the start of the 1998/1999 academic year. The previous system of grants and non-means-tested loans will continue for "existing" students (*i.e.* broadly those who started their course before September 1, 1998 (August 1, 1998 for Scotland)). But "new" students will receive financial support by way of a loan, the first 25 per cent of which will be subject to a means test.

    The basic rule is that if a student is, exceptionally, entitled to income support, the amount of the maximum student loan (defined in reg.61(1)) that he would be entitled to if he applied for it is treated as income, whether he actually applies for the loan or not. But this does not apply in the case of a hardship loan (defined in para.(1A)), which is ignored (para.(1)). The amount of the student loan taken into account will include any assessed contribution, but in the case of lone parent or disabled students only to the extent that any such contribution has actually been paid (para.(4)(a)). However if no loan has been applied for, the amount treated as income will be the maximum student loan without any deduction for unpaid contributions (para.(4)(b)). A deduction of £275 for travel costs and £343 for books and equipment will be made (para.(5)). Note that the amount of the travel disregard is now specified in the regulations as the DfEE have introduced one unified figure for travel costs rather than having differing amounts for those living in the parental home and elsewhere.

    The income so calculated is then apportioned in accordance with the rules in para.(2), with a £10 disregard. Note the definition of "academic year" in reg.61(1). If the student is required to start attending his course during August or September (as will usually be the case) and to continue attending through the autumn, the academic year of the course will be the 12 months starting on September 1. Loans payable for courses of one year's duration or less, or for the final year of a course, are covered by sub-paras (a) and (b) respectively; sub-para.(aa) deals with courses in which the academic year starts other than in the autumn; and sub-para.(c) applies in other cases. The purpose of the amendments made to para.(2) in August 2002 is to ensure that a student loan is apportioned over and attributed to complete benefit weeks.

    Under sub-para.(c), the loan is apportioned over the period from the first benefit week in September, or the benefit week, the first day of which coincides with, or immediately follows, the beginning of the autumn term (whichever is the earlier), to the benefit week, the last day of which coincides with, or immediately precedes the last day of June. In the first year of a course the effect of this rule could be to attribute loan income to a period before the actual start of the claimant's course. But since a claimant does not count as a student until he starts a course, it is suggested that any loan income should be ignored until the beginning of the term. This has now been confirmed by *CIS/3734/2004*. The Commissioner accepted the Secretary of State's submission that "a student loan can only have an existence for the purposes of the Income Support (General) Regulations 1987 where it is for the maintenance of a student. Until the claimant starts to attend or undertake the course of study . . . she is not a student. Until she is a student, whatever the point in its administrative path her student loan application has reached, it cannot meet the definition of student loan herein and so does not fall to be taken into account as income."

    In the final year of the course the period that the loan income is taken into account starts from the benefit week, the first day of which coincides with, or immediately follows, the earlier of September 1 or the first day of the autumn term in a case where the final year begins on September 1; otherwise it starts from the benefit week, the first day of which coincides with, or immediately follows, the first day of that final year. It ends with the benefit week which coincides with, or immediately precedes, the last day of the course (sub-para.(b)).

In the case of courses of one year's duration or less, the period over which the loan is apportioned starts from the benefit week which coincides with, or immediately precedes, the first day of the course in a case where the course begins in August or is for less than one academic year; otherwise it starts from the benefit week, the first day of which coincides with, or immediately follows, the first day of the academic year. It ends with the benefit week, the last day of which coincides with, or immediately precedes, the last day of the course (sub-para.(a)).

Where the academic year starts other than in the autumn, the loan is apportioned over the period which begins with the benefit week, the first day of which coincides with, or immediately follows, the first day of that academic year and ends with the benefit week, the last day of which coincides with, or immediately precedes, the last day of that academic year but excluding any complete benefit weeks within the "quarter" during which the longest vacation falls (sub-para.(aa)). Under the Education (Student Support) Regulations 2001 (since revoked; the regulations currently in force are the Education (Student Support) (No. 2) Regulations 2002 (SI 2002/3200) (Interpretation Act 1978, ss. 17(2)(a) and 23(1), will apply)) a quarter is one of the periods from January 1 to March 31, April 1 to June 30, July 1 to August 31 and September 1 to December 31.

For the apportionment of student loans under the previous form of para.(2) (in force until August 28, 2000), see the note to reg.66(2) in the 2000 edition of this volume.

See reg.40(3A)–(3B) for the position where a student ends the course prematurely.

For the disregard of any student loan (grant or covenant income or contribution) left over after the student has completed his course, see para.61 of Sch.9.

Note also *R(IS) 16/95* and *CJSA 1134/2003*, to be reported as *R(JSA) 4/04*, referred to in the note to "grant" in reg.61. *R(JSA) 4/04* confirms that reg.136 of the JSA Regulations (which is the equivalent of reg.66A) only applies to loans paid to full-time students; thus the student loan paid to the claimant who was a part-time student fell to be taken into account in full without any disregards.

For the treatment of access funds see regs 66B and 68(2) and (3).

[¹ Treatment of payments from access funds

66B.—(1) This regulation applies to payments from access funds that are not payments to which regulation 68(2) or (3) (income treated as capital) applies.

(2) A payment from access funds, other than a payment to which paragraph (3) of this regulation applies, shall be disregarded as income.

(3) Subject to paragraph (4) of this regulation and paragraph 36 of Schedule 9, any payments from access funds which are intended and used for food, ordinary clothing or footwear (which has the same meaning as in paragraph 15(2) of Schedule 9), household fuel, rent for which housing benefit is payable [² or any housing costs] to the extent that they are met under regulation 17(1)(e) or 18(1)(f) (housing costs) [² . . .], of a single claimant or, as the case may be, of [³ his partner], and any payments from access funds that are used for any council tax or water charges for which that claimant or [³ partner is liable] shall be disregarded as income to the extent of £20 per week.

(4) Where a payment from access funds is made—

2.479

(a) on or after 1st September or the first day of the course, whichever first occurs, but before receipt of any student loan in respect of that year and that payment is intended for the purpose of bridging the period until receipt of the student loan; or

(b) before the first day of the course to a person in anticipation of that person becoming a student,

that payment shall be disregarded as income.]

AMENDMENTS

2.480   1. Social Security Amendment (Students and Income-related Benefits) Regulations 2000 (SI 2000/1922), reg.2(6) (August 28, 2000, or if the student's period of study begins between August 1 and 27, 2000, the first day of the period).

2. Social Security Amendment (Residential Care and Nursing Homes) Regulations 2001 (SI 2001/3767), reg.2(1) and Pt I of Sch. para.10 (April 8, 2002).

3. Social Security (Working Tax Credit and Child Tax Credit) (Consequential Amendments) Regulations 2003 (SI 2003/455), reg.2 and Sch.1, para.17 (April 6, 2004, except in "transitional cases" and see further the note to reg.17 of the Income Support Regulations).

DEFINITIONS

"access funds"—see reg.61(1).
"claimant"—see reg.2(1).
"family"—see SSCBA, s.137(1).
"payment"—see reg.2(1).
"single claimant"—*ibid.*
"student"—see reg.61(1).
"student loan"—*ibid.*

GENERAL NOTE

2.481   Reg.66B and the new paras (2) and (3) of reg.68 (added with effect from August 28, 2000) are concerned with the treatment of payments from access funds (defined in reg.61(1)). These funds are administered by individual colleges and universities. An access fund payment (for the definition of "payment" see reg.2(1)) that is paid as a single lump sum will be treated as capital (reg.68(2)). If such a payment of capital is intended and used for items other than food, ordinary clothing or footwear, fuel, housing costs met by income support or housing benefit, council tax or water charges, it is disregarded for 52 weeks from the date of payment (reg.68 (3)). Other payments from access funds are ignored as income unless they are intended and used for food, ordinary clothing or footwear, fuel, housing costs met by income support or housing benefit, council tax or water charges, in which case a disregard of up to £20 applies (this is subject to the overall limit of £20 for this and other payments in para.36 of Sch.9) (reg.66B(2) and (3)). But even if the payment is to cover the cost of food, etc., it will be totally ignored as income if it is intended to bridge a gap before the start of a course or receipt of a student loan (reg.66B(4)).

Note that the amendments made to this regulation (and to reg.68) with effect from April 6, 2004 (except in "transitional cases"—see the note to reg.17) are as a consequence of the removal of amounts for children and young persons from the income support scheme with effect from April 6, 2004 (except in "transitional cases"). Financial assistance to help with the cost of bringing up a child or young person is now to be provided through the child tax credit system, see Vol. IV of this series, and income support has in effect become an "adults only" benefit. The old form of this regulation (see the 2003 edition of this volume) continues in force for "transitional cases"—see the note to reg.17.

Disregard of contribution

67. Where the claimant or his partner is a student and [¹, for the purposes   **2.482**
of assessing a contribution to the student's grant [²or student loan], the
other partner's income has been taken into account, an account equal to that
contribution shall be disregarded for the purposes of assessing that other
partner's income.]

AMENDMENTS

1. Income-related Benefits Schemes (Miscellaneous Amendments) Regulations
1996 (SI 1996/462), reg.10 (April 8, 1996).
2. Social Security Amendment (Students) Regulations 1999 (SI 1999/1935),
reg.3(6) (August 30, 1999, or if the student's period of study begins between August
1 and 29, 1999, the first day of the period).

DEFINITIONS

"claimant"—see reg.2(1), reg.23(1).
"contribution"—see reg.61(1).
"grant"—*ibid.*
"partner"—see reg.2(1).
"student"—see reg.61(1).
"student loan"—*ibid.*

Further disregard of student's income

67A. Where any part of a student's income has already been taken into   **2.483**
account for the purposes of assessing his entitlement to a grant [² or student
loan], the amount taken into account shall be disregarded in assessing that
student's income.]

AMENDMENTS

1. Social Security (Miscellaneous Amendments) Regulations 1998 (SI 1998/
563), reg.4(3) and (4)(e) (April 6, 1998),
2. Social Security Amendment (Students) Regulations 1999 (SI 1999/1935),
reg.3(7) (August 30, 1999, or if the student's period of study begins between August
1 and 29, 1999, the first day of the period).

DEFINITIONS

"grant"—see reg.61(1).
"student"—*ibid.*
"student loan"—*ibid.*

Income treated as capital

68.—[¹(1)] Any amount by way of a refund of tax deducted from a   **2.484**
student's income shall be treated as capital.
[¹ (2) An amount paid from access funds as a single lump sum shall be
treated as capital.
(3) An amount paid from access funds as a single lump sum which is
intended and used for an item other than food, ordinary clothing or footwear (which has the same meaning as in paragraph 15(2) of Schedule 9),
household fuel, rent for which housing benefit is payable, [² or any

housing costs] to the extent that they are met under regulation 17(1)(e) or 18(1)(f) (housing costs) [² . . .], of a single claimant or, as the case may be, of [³ his partner], or which is used for an item other than any council tax or water charges for which that claimant or [³ partner is liable] shall be disregarded as capital but only for a period of 52 weeks from the date of the payment.]

AMENDMENTS

1. Social Security Amendment (Students and Income-related Benefits) Regulations 2000 (SI 2000/1922), reg.2(7) (August 28, 2000, or if the student's period of study begins between August 1 and 27, 2000, the first day of the period).
2. Social Security Amendment (Residential Care and Nursing Homes) Regulations 2001 (SI 2001/3767), reg.2(1) and Pt I of Sch. para.11 (April 8, 2002).
3. Social Security (Working Tax Credit and Child Tax Credit) (Consequential Amendments) Regulations 2003 (SI 2003/455), reg.2 and Sch.1, para.17 (April 6, 2004, except in "transitional cases" and see further the note to reg.17 of the Income Support Regulations.

DEFINITIONS

"access funds"—see reg.61(1).
"claimant"—see reg.2(1).
"family"—see SSCBA, s.137(1).
"payment"—see reg.2(1).
"single claimant"—*ibid.*
"student"—see reg.61(1).

GENERAL NOTE

2.485   On paras (2) and (3), see the note to reg.66A.

Disregard of changes occurring during summer vacation

2.486   **69.** In calculating a student's income [¹ there shall be disregarded] any change in the standard maintenance grant occurring in the recognised summer vacation appropriate to the student's course, if that vacation does not from part of his period of study, from the date on which the change occurred up to the end of that vacation.

AMENDMENT

2.487   1. Social Security Act 1998 (Commencement No.12 and Consequential and Transitional Provisions) Order 1999 (SI 1999/3178 (C.81)), art.3(5) and Sch.5, para.7 (November 29, 1999)

DEFINITIONS

"period of study"—see reg.61(1).
"standard maintenance grant"—*ibid.*
"student"—*ibid.*

PART VI

URGENT CASES

Urgent Cases

70.—(1) In a case to which this regulation applies, a claimant's weekly   2.488
applicable amount and his income and capital shall be calculated in accordance with the following provisions of this Part.

(2) Subject to paragraph (4), this regulation applies to—

[⁵(a) a claimant to whom paragraph (2A) applies (persons not excluded from income support under section 115 of the Immigration and Asylum Act);]

(b) a claimant who is treated as possessing income under regulation 42(3) (notional income);

(c) [¹. . .]

[⁶(2A) This paragraph applies to a person not excluded from entitlement to income support under section 115 of the Immigration and Asylum Act by virtue of regulation 2 of the Social Security (Immigration and Asylum) Consequential Amendments Regulations 2000 except for a person to whom paragraphs 3 and 4 of Part I of the Schedule to those Regulations applies.]

(3) [⁷. . .]

[²(3A)[⁷. . .]

(3B)[⁷. . .]]

(4) This regulation shall only apply to a person to whom paragraph (2)(b) [¹applies, where the income he is treated as possessing by virtue of regulation 42(3) (notional income)] is not readily available to him; and—

(a) the amount of income support which would be payable but for this Part is less than the amount of income support payable by virtue of the provisions of this Part; and

(b) [⁴ the Secretary of State] is satisfied that, unless the provisions of this Part are applied to the claimant, the claimant or his family will suffer hardship.

AMENDMENTS

1. Income Support (General) Amendment No.2 Regulations 1989 (SI 1989/   2.489
1323), reg.16 (October 9, 1989).

2. Income Support (General) Amendment No.3 Regulations 1993 (SI 1993/
1679), reg.2 (August 2, 1993).

3. Social Security (Persons from Abroad) Miscellaneous Amendments Regulations 1996 (SI 1996/30), reg.8(3) (February 5, 1996).

4. Social Security Act 1998 (Commencement No.12, and Consequential and Transitional Provisions) Order 1999 (SI 1999/3178), art.3(5) and Sch.5, para.8 (November 29, 1999).

5. Social Security (Immigration and Asylum) Consequential Amendments Regulations 2000 (SI 2000/636), reg.3(7)(a) (April 3, 2000).

6. Social Security (Immigration and Asylum) Consequential Amendments Regulations 2000 (SI 2000/636), reg.3(7)(b) (April 3, 2000).

7. Social Security (Immigration and Asylum) Consequential Amendments Regulations 2000 (SI 2000/636), reg.3(7)(c) (April 3, 2000).

DEFINITIONS

"the 1971 Act"—see reg.21(3).
"claimant"—see reg.2(1).
"family"—see 1986 Act, s.20(11) (SSCBA, s.137(1)).
"partner"—see reg.2(1).

GENERAL NOTE

Paras (1) and (2)

2.490   The provision for urgent cases outside the normal scope of the income support rules is very restricted. The two categories are certain people "subject to immigration control" and claimants who are treated as possessing income which is due, but has not been paid. In the last case the notional income must not be readily available and the decision-maker must be satisfied that the claimant or his family would suffer hardship if the normal income support entitlement was not brought up to the urgent cases rate (para.(4)). Applicable amounts are adjusted under reg.71, and income and capital rules are in reg.72.

Para. (2A)

2.491   Section 115 of the Immigration and Asylum Act 1999 excludes claimants who are "subject to immigration control" from entitlement to various benefits including income support and income-based jobseeker's allowance with effect from April 3, 2000 (see commentary to reg.21(3)). However, under regs 2(1), (4)(a) and (5) of the Social Security (Immigration and Asylum) Consequential Amendments Regulations 2000 (SI 2000/636) certain groups of people who would otherwise be within s.115 are not excluded from entitlement to income support. The effect of para.(2A) is that people in those categories (other than sponsored immigrants who have been resident in the UK for at least five years and nationals of States which have ratified the ECSMA Agreement or the European Social Charter (see commentary to reg.21(3)) *i.e.* who are within paras 3 and 4 of Pt I of the Schedule to SI 2000/636) receive benefit at the lower "urgent cases" rate.
    Paragraph(2A) covers four categories of claimant:

(1) people who have limited leave to enter or remain in the UK subject to the condition that they should not have recourse to public funds but whose supply of funds from abroad has been temporarily disrupted (see reg.2(1) and para.1 of Pt I of the Schedule to SI 2000/636);

(2) sponsored immigrants who have been resident in the UK for less than five years but whose sponsor (or sponsors) has died (see reg.2(1) and para.2 of Pt I of the Schedule to SI 2000/636);

(3) people who are entitled to or receiving benefit under the transitional protection established by reg.12(1) and (2) of the Social Security (Persons From Abroad) Miscellaneous Amendments Regulations 1996 (see reg.2(4)(a) of SI 2000/636); and

(4) certain people who applied for asylum on or before April 2, 2000 (see regs 2(5) and 12(3) of SI 2000/636)

For categories (1) and (2) see the commentary to reg.21(3).

Pre-April 3, 2000 asylum seekers

2.492   Reg.12(3)–(5) of SI 2000/636 effectively reproduce the former para.(3A), the only additional requirement being that the claim for asylum must have been made on or before April 2, 2000. The authorities on para.(3A) therefore continue to have effect.
    Before February 5, 1996, asylum seekers were entitled to urgent cases payments of income support at all stages from the submission of their initial asylum applica-

tion until the final decision on it was made (including any appeal or representations). The stated justification for the draconian restrictions on the right of asylum seekers to claim benefit introduced by reg.8(3) of the Social Security (Persons from Abroad) Miscellaneous Amendments Regulations 1996 was the Government's belief that "the current benefit arrangements encourage abuses of the asylum system . . . in two major ways: the ready availability of benefits for asylum applicants provides an incentive for people to make unfounded asylum claims . . . both to prolong their stay in the UK and to gain access to benefits; the availability of benefits throughout the asylum process provides an incentive for failed asylum seekers to lodge and prolong unfounded appeals" (para.11 of the DSS's Explanatory Memorandum to the Social Security Advisory Committee, Cm 3062/1996). Despite widespread and highly publicised criticisms of its proposals and SSAC's recommendation that they should be completely withdrawn, the Government pressed ahead (although certain concessions were made, particularly in relation to transitional protection for existing claimants). A challenge to the validity of the regulations was lost in the High Court on March 25, 1996. However, on June 21, 1996, the Court of Appeal (by a majority) struck down as *ultra vires* those parts of the amending regulations which denied income support, housing benefit or council tax benefit to any asylum seeker whose asylum application had not been finally determined (*R. v Secretary of State for Social Security Ex p. Joint Council for the Welfare of Immigrants and Another* [1996] 4 All E.R. 385). The Court held that the regulations were unlawful because they contravened the Asylum and Immigration Appeals Act 1993 by drastically interfering with the rights of asylum seekers under that Act. The Government's speedy response was to introduce amendments to the Asylum and Immigration Bill then going through Parliament in order to validate those parts of the regulations affected by the Court of Appeal's decision. See s.11(1) and (4) of and Sch.1 to the Asylum and Immigration Act 1996 in Part I of this book. The Act came into force on July 24, 1996. Para.2(b) of Sch.1 reinstated paras (3A) and (3B) in their February 5, 1996 form from that date. The consequence was that asylum seekers were only entitled to urgent cases payments on or after July 24, 1996 if they could qualify under para.(3A) or could benefit from the transitional protection in reg.12(1) of the 1996 Regulations (see below).

Under para.(3A) the only categories of asylum seekers who were entitled to urgent cases payments were those who apply for asylum "on arrival" (other than re-entry) in the UK from a country outside the Common Travel Area (see para.(3B)) and those who, while present in Great Britain, applied for asylum within three months of a declaration by the Secretary of State that the country of which they were are a national was going through such a fundamental change of circumstances that they would not normally be ordered to return there (para.(3A)(a) and (aa)). In both cases the application for asylum had to be officially recorded. A declaration under para.(3A)(aa)(i) was made in respect of Zaire on May 16, 1997, for three months; and in respect of Sierra Leone on July 1, 1997, again for a three month period. See below for the position of asylum seekers between February 5 and July 24, 1996.

"On arrival"

It is not entirely clear what "on arrival" in the UK means. (Note that there is no set procedure for applying for asylum; an application does not need to be in writing but can be made orally.) It should be noted that sub-para.(a) simply refers to "on arrival . . . in the UK". It does not refer to arrival *at a port* (or *immigration control*), nor are the words "on arrival" qualified by words such as "immediately" or "on the date of". Moreover the test chosen is that of arrival, rather than the more precise term of "entry" into the UK (for the distinction in domestic law see *R. v Naillie* [1993] A.C. 674). It could therefore be argued that a person who, for example, did not apply for asylum at the port of entry, but immediately after leaving the port went straight to the Immigration Department and made an application there, had applied for asylum "on arrival" in the UK. However, this has not been the approach taken in the Commissioners' decisions that have so far emerged on this issue. The

2.493

Commissioners have recognised the inexact nature of the term "on arrival" but have concluded that it should be interpreted narrowly in the light of the Ministerial statements made while the Asylum and Immigration Bill (now the 1996 Act) was going through Parliament. Thus in *CIS 2719/1997* the Commissioner accepts that sub-para.(a) does not specify at what stage during the process of arriving in this country (disembarkation, passing through immigration control, passing through customs or leaving the port or airport) an application for asylum has to be made. But after having regard to statements made by the Secretary of State in the House of Commons (HC Vol. 281, cols 844 to 879) under the *Pepper v Hart* ([1993] A.C. 593) principle, the Commissioner concludes that the application (or at least an indication of an intention to make an asylum application) had to be made while the claimant was still within the port of arrival. However, it did not necessarily have to be made before clearing immigration control (as had been held in *CIS 143/1997*. In the Commissioner's view, the process of arrival finished when the person arriving left the port of arrival; it did not continue beyond that point. Thus to count under sub-para.(a) an asylum application had to be made before leaving the port; if for whatever reason it was not, sub-para.(a) was not satisfied.

See also *CIS 1137/1997* (heard with *CIS 2719/1997*), the particular facts of which may explain the Commissioner's choice of test for the meaning of "on arrival". In *CIS 1137/1997* the claimant and his mother were escorted through immigration control at Heathrow airport by an agent who then left them at the airport. Later that day they were taken to the office of the Refugee Arrivals Project at Terminal 2. There was no Persian speaker there and neither the claimant nor his mother spoke English. The Project staff placed the claimant and his mother in a hotel for the night and the next morning took them to the Immigration and Nationality Department at Lunar House, Croydon, where claims for asylum were made. The Commissioner directed the new tribunal, in the course of considering whether the claimant had made his asylum application "on his arrival", to make findings on whether the claimant had made contact with anyone acting in the name of the Secretary of State before he left Heathrow airport, whether that contact was recorded by that person, the locus of the Refugee Arrivals Project, whether it had any mandate from the Secretary of State to deal with asylum seekers and whether anyone from the Project contacted an immigration officer in Heathrow on the day of the claimant's arrival.

In *R(IS) 14/99* the Commissioner (who was the same Commissioner who decided *CIS 143/1997*) accepts that the relatively vague term "on his arrival" was used deliberately instead of any more precise term, in order to maintain a level of flexibility. But the degree of flexibility had to be measured in the light of Parliament's clear intention that in the ordinary case of a person arriving at a recognised port of entry with full immigration control and interpretation facilities, the person's entitlement to benefit should depend upon him making an application for asylum at that port. The statements made by the Secretary of State in the House of Commons (HC, Vol. 281, cols 846 to 848) showed a willingness to take account of matters wholly beyond the claimant's control that might make an immediate claim for asylum impossible (*e.g.* the lack of an interpreter). But this did not extend to other matters, such as wrong advice given by an agent to the claimant. The Commissioner did not have to decide in that case whether asylum had to be claimed before the claimant cleared immigration control or left the port of entry. However, he did point to the existence of para.6(2) of Sch.2 to the Immigration Act 1971 (which allows an immigration officer to cancel a notice giving leave to enter within 24 hours of the conclusion of an examination under para.2 of the Schedule), as leaving open the possibility of a person returning to an immigration officer at the port of entry and making a claim for asylum that could be treated as made "on arrival", even though he had originally passed beyond immigration control (and indeed had left the port of entry).

2.494   Thus in some circumstances "clearing immigration control" may be a more extensive concept than that of leaving the port of entry. See also the statement by the Secretary of State in the House of Commons that "People who arrive at an airport or other port of entry with no interpretation facility are told to come back and complete the formalities in a few days' time. They are then treated as if they have just arrived and were making an in-port claim although such a claim is made two or three days later. That flexibility will continue . . ." (col. 846).

CIS 3231/1997 also decides that the test is whether asylum was claimed at immigration control. The Commissioner accepts that if for some reason immigration control was not available, for example because of a strike or the lack of an appropriate interpreter, it would be sufficient if the claim for asylum was made at the first opportunity. In that case the claimant had been smuggled out of Iraq in the back of a lorry; he was sedated throughout the journey until he was put out in London. With the help of his brother he went to an immigration office in Cardiff the next day (although he did not actually claim asylum until he was interviewed by an immigration officer three days later). The tribunal decided that he had claimed asylum "on arrival" because he had done so "as soon as reasonably practicable" after entry into the UK. However the Commissioner holds that this was not the correct test and that a person who was smuggled in and made his asylum claim a day or so later had not claimed asylum "on his arrival".

In *CIS 3231/1997* the Commissioner expressed the view that a person who had gained entry by being smuggled in or otherwise landing unofficially should not be in a better position than a person who had gone through the normal procedures. But it is difficult to see what else a person in similar circumstances to those of the claimant in *CIS 3231/1997* could do. It would certainly seem arguable that while he remained hidden in the lorry the claimant in *CIS 3231/1997* had not "arrived" in the UK in the sense of having made an appearance here (see the *Shorter Oxford English Dictionary* definition of "arrival"); moreover, if he was put out of the lorry (in a confused state) at a point where there were no immigration facilities he would need time to make enquiries as to where to go. Provided that this was done as soon as reasonably practicable, it is difficult to see why this does not come within the latitude that the use of the term "on arrival" was apparently intended by Parliament to achieve. Moreover, Article 31 of the Geneva Convention relating to the Status of Refugees which forbids the imposition of "penalties, on account of their illegal entry or presence, on refugees who, coming directly from a territory where their life or freedom was threatened in the sense of Art.1, enter or are present in [a] territory without authorisation, provided they present themselves without delay to the authorities and show good cause for their illegal entry or presence". In *CIS 4439/1998* (having first raised the issue in *R(IS) 14/99*) the Commissioner decided, following the decision of the High Court in *R. v Uxbridge Magistrates Court Ex p. Adimi* [1999] 4 All E.R. 520, that the refusal of income support could amount to a "penalty" in these circumstances, and that since there is acknowledged to be some ambiguity in the term "on arrival" (see *CIS 2719/1997* and *R(IS) 14/99*) sub-para.(a) should be construed in a manner that is not inconsistent with the UK's international obligations. It is suggested that *CIS 4439/1998* is to be preferred to the more restrictive approach taken by the Commissioner in *CIS 3867/1998* and *CIS 259/1999* where the Article 31 point was not argued (see para.11).

Note that the claimants in *CIS 2719/1997*, *CIS 1137/1997* and *CIS 3231/1997* were granted leave to appeal to the Court of Appeal. However, the appeals were withdrawn; the reasons for this are not known. 2.495

In *CIS/597/1999* (which is in identical terms with *CIS/4889/1999*, *CIS/2003/1999* and *CIS/2511/1999*) the Commissioner, following a comprehensive review of the authorities, holds that the "clearing immigration control" interpretation of "on arrival" was to be preferred to the "port perimeter" test set out in *CIS/2719/1997*. Where the claimant arrives in the UK by Eurostar, this means that the application for asylum must be made to the immigration officer on the train.

The Commissioner also disagrees with the Commissioner in *CIS/4439/1998* and holds that the requirement to claim asylum while clearing immigration control does not amount to the imposition of a "penalty" which would be prohibited by Art.31 of the Geneva Convention relating to the Status of Refugees, that article being concerned solely with "freedom from a penalty in the form of prosecution". However, in *CIS 43/2000* and *CIS 2702/2000*, the Commissioner who decided *CIS 2719/1997* restated his adherence to the "port perimeter" test, notwithstanding the decision in *CIS 597/1999*. In the latter decision he did, however, agree with what had been said in *CIS 597/1999* about the application of Art.31 of the Geneva Convention.

Thus the result of the Commissioners' decisions that have so far emerged on the meaning of the term "on arrival" seems on balance to be that if a person enters the country through a recognised port of entry and does not claim asylum before clearing immigration control (*CIS 143/1997, CIS 3231/1997* and *CIS 597/1999*), or before leaving the port of entry (*CIS 2719/1997, CIS 1137/1997, CIS 40/2000* and *CIS 2702/2000*), he will not come within sub-para.(a). His reasons for not claiming asylum at the port of entry (*e.g.* because he was advised not to do so by an agent) will not be relevant (*CIS 2719/1997* and *CIS 1137/1997*), unless they were wholly outside his control (*R(IS) 14/99* and *CIS 3231/1997*) (*e.g.* lack of an appropriate interpreter, or possibly his state of health). If the person does not pass through (*i.e.* clear) immigration control, *e.g.* because he does not enter the country through a recognised port or because there are no immigration facilities available at the port, it seems that he will be treated as making an application for asylum on arrival as long as the application is made as soon as reasonably practicable after his arrival in the country. As a reported decision, *R(IS) 14/99* commands the assent of a majority of commissioners and should be preferred to *CIS 3231/1997* to the extent that there is a conflict between them.

The jurisprudence at Commissioner level must now be read in the light of two recent decisions of the Court of Appeal. In *Shire v Secretary of State for Work and Pensions* [2003] EWCA Civ 1465 (October 13, 2003) (Lord Woolf L.C.J, Chadwick and Buxton L.J.J.) it was held that the words "on his arrival" in reg.70(3A) did not extend to cover the circumstances of the claimant who had arrived at Gatwick from the Yemen at 10:30 p.m. on August 29, 1999 and did not apply for asylum until August 31, 1999 because she was under the control of the agent who had arranged the documents on which she was admitted to the country. The Court said that a person who uses an agent must be regarded as putting themselves under the control of that agent so that they are responsible for his or her actions unless there is clear evidence of some form of physical duress. The Court did not find it necessary to decide between the "clearing immigration control" and "port perimeter" tests. *Shire* was followed in *Kola and Mirzajani v Secretary of State for Work & Pensions* [2004] EWCA Civ 638 (May 21, 2004) (Kennedy, Jonathan Parker and Dyson L.J J.).

Note also that the arrival must be from a country outside the Common Travel Area. Presumably this refers to the country that the person originally departed from. So the fact that person's flight was via, *e.g.* the Isle of Man, or even that it was diverted there, should not mean that sub-para.(a) does not apply. But what if the person spends a few days in the Isle of Man before coming to the UK? Further, those who apply on "re-entry" are excluded from sub-para.(a). The purpose presumably is to stop people trying to get within this sub-paragraph by leaving the UK for a short time and then making an asylum application at the port of entry on their return. But if the person last visited the UK, *e.g.* some years ago or there is no connection between their departure after the last visit and their arrival on this occasion this would not seem to be a "re-entry", but a *fresh* entry into the UK. In *CIS 265/1999* the Commissioner held that "re-entry" has a non-technical meaning and that the purpose of the provision was to prevent those who had not claimed asylum on arrival from gaining another opportunity to do so. However the Commissioner considered it to be undesirable that he should give general guidance on the interpretation of the phrase and that the law should develop on a case by case basis.

Finally note that there are special rules to provide for the control of entry of foreign nationals through the Channel Tunnel under amendments that have been made to the Immigration Act 1971. The effect of this is that British immigration control extends into the Tunnel and a person who encounters an immigration officer on the train will have passed through immigration control before he has arrived in England.

In *CIS 4510/1998* the Commissioner held that a diplomat who had claimed asylum while still entitled to the protection of the Diplomatic Privileges Act 1964 satisfied the requirements of the former reg.70(3A).

"Upheaval declarations"

The wording of the former para.(3A)(aa) (now reg.12(4)(b) of SI 2000/636) was   **2.496**
considered by the Commissioner in *CIS 3864/1998*. The Commissioner rejected the
claimant's argument (based on the commentary in the 1999 edition of *Mesher and
Wood, Income-related Benefits: the Legislation*) that the words "while present in Great
Britain" applied only to distinguish para.(3A)(aa) from para.(3A)(a) and that it was
therefore not necessary for the asylum seeker to have been present in Great Britain
when the upheaval declaration was actually made. He held that the position of the
words showed that they governed all three of the conditions which followed so that
the asylum seeker must be present in Great Britain when the upheaval declaration is
made, when the subsequent claim for asylum is made and when it is recorded.

Note that head (aa) only covers nationals of the country concerned (as confirmed
in *R. v Secretary of State for Social Security Ex p. Grant*, High Court, July 31, 1997).

"Ceases to be an asylum seeker"

The person's entitlement to urgent cases payments will end when the first deci-   **2.497**
sion is recorded as made on his asylum application (or his application is abandoned)
if this is on or after February 5, 1996 (para.(3A)(b)(i)), or, if that decision was
recorded as made before February 5, 1996 and an appeal is pending by February 5,
1996, or is submitted within the time limits for appeal, on the date that appeal is
determined (para.(3A)(b)(ii)), (but see below for the position between February 5
and July 24, 1996). Sub-para.(b)(ii) will include cases where the time limit for
appealing under r.5 of the 1993 Rules has been extended. The argument that sub-
para.(b) either should be construed as only applying where claims for asylum were
made after February 5, 1996 or was *ultra vires* was rejected by Dyson J. in *R. v
Secretary of State for Social Security Ex p. Vijeikis, Zaheer and Okito* (High Court, July
10, 1997); an appeal against this decision was dismissed by the Court of Appeal on
March 5, 1998.

The DSS's original view was that a decision was recorded by the Immigration
Department on the date it was received by the asylum applicant. Presumably this
was a reference to the date of the letter conveying the decision, or the date of the
interview at which the applicant was informed of the decision. The position is complicated by the fact that the right of appeal is against the immigration decision that
is made as a consequence of the Secretary of State's decision on the asylum application, not the asylum decision itself. These decisions could be made simultaneously or possibly several months apart. But in practice it seems that the Benefits
Agency withdrew benefit from the date it was informed of the Home Office's initial
decision. This often had the consequence that an asylum seeker first learnt of the
refusal of his asylum claim when his benefit stopped, although according to evidence given in *Ex p. Karaoui and Abbad* (see below) since the beginning of
November 1996 it has been the Home Office's practice to inform asylum seekers of
the decision on their claim at the same time as notification is sent to the Benefits
Agency.

The previous controversy as to when an asylum claim "is recorded by the
Secretary of State as having been determined" for the purposes of para.(3A)(b)(i)
has now been settled by the decision of the House of Lords in *R. v Secretary of State
for the Home Department and Secretary of State for Work and Pensions Ex p. Anufrijeva*
[2003] U.K.H.L. 36, HL, June 26, 2003. By a majority (Lords Steyn, Hoffmann,
Millett and Scott of Foscote, Lord Bingham of Cornhill dissenting) it was held that
the paragraph was not satisfied until an asylum seeker had been notified of the Home
Office decision and that income support could not be stopped on the basis of a decision which had been made but not communicated to the claimant. The decision of
the Court of Appeal in *R. v Secretary of State for the Home Department Ex p. Salem*
[1999] Q.B. 805, CA which was to the opposite effect was overruled and, although
they were not expressly referred to in the opinions in the House of Lords, it is clear
that *R. v Secretary of State for the Home Department Ex p. Karaoui and Abbad*, QBD,
The Times, March 27, 1997 and *CIS 1542/2001* are no longer good law.

It would appear (see for example Lord Steyn at paras 23 and 36 of the opinions in *Anufrijeva*) that notification takes place when notice of the Home Office decision is sent to the asylum seeker rather than when s/he receives it.

In *CIS 3418/1998*, the Commissioner held that a pending immigration appeal is "determined" for the purposes of the former regulation 70(3A) as soon as the next decision is made on that appeal, even if further appeals remain open to the claimant. Where the outcome of the appeal is favourable to the claimant, the asylum application is determined when the appeal decision is promulgated, or at any rate once it has been indicated that the Home Secretary will not appeal further, and not on the subsequent date when the Immigration and Nationality Department writes to the claimant to grant indefinite leave to remain as a refugee—see *CIS 1542/2001*, para.6.

If the Home Office's decision is to accept that the person is a refugee (or to grant exceptional leave to remain), he can qualify for income support/income-based JSA under the normal rules (refugees and those with exceptional leave to enter or remain are treated as satisfying the habitual residence test: see reg.21(3), definition of "person from abroad", sub-paras (b) and (c) and the equivalent provision in reg.85 of the JSA Regulations).

Entitlement from February 5 to July 23, 1996

2.498   As a result of the Court of Appeal's decision in *Ex p. JCWI*, asylum seekers were entitled to benefit under the old form of para.(3A) (see the 1995 edition of this book) until July 24, 1996 (it was accepted that the Court of Appeal's judgment was not a "relevant determination" within ss.68 and 69 of the Administration Act and so the limits on backdating did not apply: see AOG Memo Vol 3/90). But unless they qualified under the new form of para.(3A) that entitlement ceased when the Asylum and Immigration Act 1996 reintroduced the parts of the 1996 Regulations that had been declared invalid by the Court of Appeal (para.6(1)(a) of Sch.1 to the Act); see *Ex p. T* below which holds that the transitional protection for asylum seekers entitled to benefit before February 5, 1996 does not extend to those who were only entitled on or after that date. Note that a claim or application for review by a person who qualified for urgent cases payments on or after February 5, 1996 as a result of the Court of Appeal's judgment in *Ex p. JCWI* had to be made before July 24, 1996 (para.6(1)(b) of Sch.1 to the 1996 Act). Note also reg.21ZA, in force from October 15, 1996, which allowed those whose refugee status is subsequently recognised by the Home Office to make a retrospective claim for urgent cases payments for the period they were denied benefit as an asylum seeker. Now see reg.21ZB.

Reg.12(1) and (2) of the Persons from Abroad Regulations 1996

2.499   Reg.12(1) of the 1996 Regulations provides some transitional protection for asylum seekers entitled to benefit before February 5, 1996 (see reg.12(1) of the Social Security (Persons from Abroad) Miscellaneous Amendments Regulations 1996, p.674). The effect of this is that an asylum seeker who was entitled to urgent cases payments before February 5, 1996 under the previous form of para.(3A)(a) will continue to be entitled until he ceases to count as an asylum seeker under sub-para.(b) (see above). *CIS 3108/1997* confirms that the protection in reg.12(1) only extends to the acqusition of asylum seeker status, not its loss.

It was suggested in the 1997 edition of *Mesher and Wood, Income-Related Benefits: the Legislation* that entitlement at some point (not necessarily immediately) before February 5, 1996 should be sufficient. However, in *R. v Secretary of State for Social Security Ex p. Vijeikis, Zaheer and Okito* (High Court, July 10, 1997) Dyson J. held that in order to rely on the transitional protection in reg.12(1) a claimant had to be entitled to benefit *immediately* before February 5, 1996. He reluctantly accepted that the words "those provisions of those Regulations as then in force shall continue to have effect" in reg.12(1) (together with the words "at the coming into force of these Regulations" in the amendment to reg.12(1) introduced by para.5 of Sch.1 to the Asylum and Immigration Act 1996) showed clearly that the paragraph was an ordinary saving clause which only preserved the entitlement of persons who were entitled to benefit at the time when the new rules came into force. A person who once was, but no longer is, entitled to benefit could not be described as a person in respect of whom the provisions "continue" to have effect. Moreover, the wording of reg.12(2) and (3) showed that only those who were currently entitled to or receiving benefit at the time the new rules came into force were protected by the saving provisions in those paragraphs and it would be surprising if the phrase 'before the coming into force of these Regulations" had a different meaning in para.(1) than in the other paragraphs in reg.12. This decision was upheld by the Court of Appeal (*R. v Secretary of State for Social Security, Ex p. Vijeikis and Vijeikeine and Zaheer*, March 5, 1998).

The same conclusion was reached by the Commissioner in *R(IS) 15/99*. The Commissioner decides that he was not bound by Dyson J.'s decision in *Vijeikis* but in his view it was correct. In *R(IS) 15/99* the Commissioner also rejects an argument that the claimant was entitled to income support by virtue of EC Regulation 1408/71. The claimant had argued that he was a "worker" and a "refugee" within Article 1(a) and (d), that income support came within Article 4(2)(a), and so he was entitled to equality of treatment with nationals of the UK by virtue of Art.3(1). However, the Commissioner holds that because he had not exercised the right of freedom of movement within the EU he could derive no assistance from Regulation 1408/71, relying on *Land Nordrhein-Westfalen v Uecker* and *Jacquet v Land Nordrhein-Westfalen* (joined cases C-64/96 and C-65/96). The ECJ had held in that case that Regulation 1612/68 could not apply where there was no movement from one Member State to another and the Commissioner considered that the same reasoning applied to Regulation 1408/71. One of the claimants in *R(IS) 15/99* appealed to the Court of Appeal but his appeal was dismissed (*Krasniqi v Chief Adjudication Officer and the Secretary of State for Social Security*, December 10, 1998, CA reported as part of *R(IS) 15/99*). The Court of Appeal held that Regulation 1408/71 did not apply to a matter which was wholly internal to a single Member State (see *Petit*, Case 153/91, [1992] E.C.R. I-4973).

There has been considerable controversy as to whether an asylum seeker who was **2.500** entitled to income support immediately February 5, 1996 and is therefore entitled to transitional protection under reg.12(1) loses that protection if there is a break in his claim after that date. The issue had been considered by the Court of Appeal in relation to reg.12(3) in *R. v Adjudication Officer Ex p. B* (since upheld by the House of Lords in *M v Secretary of State for Social Security* [2001] UKHL 35) and it had been held that the transitional protection in that paragraph did not survive the end of the claim which was current on February 5, 1996. However, the Court had pointed out that regs 12(1) and (2) dealt with narrower classes of claimant and different benefits from reg.12(3) and that reg.12(3) contained an express provision which continued transitional protection only "until such time as [the claimant's] entitlement to that benefit is reviewed" which had no equivalent in paras (1) and (2). Moreover, for asylum seekers in receipt of income support, to lose transitional protection in such circumstances would create an undesirable incentive not to work because taking a job, possibly of a short duration, would lead to a loss of benefit when that job came to an end which might be greater than the wages which had been earned. In *Yildiz v Secretary for Social Security* (CA, February 28, 2001, reported as *R(IS) 9/01*), the Court of Appeal decided that the transitional protection provided by reg.12(1) did survive a break in entitlement. The Court focussed on Mr Yildiz's status as an asylum seeker. Having "[become] an asylum seeker under regulation [the former] 70(3A)(a) of the Income Support Regulations" by submitting a claim for asylum which remained undetermined on February 5, 1996 the effect of reg.12(1) was that the pre-February 1996 law continued to apply to him until his asylum claim was finally determined notwithstanding any break in entitlement. *CIS 1115/1999* which decided the contrary, *CIS 6258/1999* (which followed *CIS 1115/1999*) and—to the extent that they are inconsistent with the Court of Appeal's decision—*CIS 1077/1999* and *CIS 6608/1999* must be regarded as no longer being good law. In *CJSA 4143/2001*, Mr Commissioner Mesher stressed that *Yildiz* did not decide that a person who claimed asylum before February 5, 1996 was not caught by the rules on persons from abroad which came into force on that date but that "an asylum seeker who was entitled to IS on that basis immediately before February 5, 1996 was not caught by the new rules and remained free of the new rules even if there was a break in entitlement to income support after February 5, 1996". As the claimant in that appeal had not been entitled to income support before February 5, 1996, *Yildiz* did not assist him.

Note the amendment to reg.12(1) made by para.5 of Sch.1 to the 1996 Act with effect from July 24, 1996. This enables those who are no longer members of the claimant's family (*e.g.* a separated partner or a child who is no longer a dependent) to qualify for the transitional protection in their own right. However, the person must have been a member of the claimant's family at the coming into force of the Regulations, *i.e.*, February 5, 1996 (as confirmed in *Ex p. Vijeikis, Zaheer and Okito*). It will also allow members of a couple to "swap the claimant role" without losing the transitional protection.

When the restrictions on asylum seekers' entitlement to benefit were reimposed by the Asylum and Immigration Act 1996 on July 24, 1996, the question arose as to whether the transitional protection in reg.12(1) covered people entitled to benefit prior to July 24, 1996 as a result of the Court of Appeal's judgment in *Ex p. JCWI* or only those entitled before February 5, 1996, the date the regulations originally came into force. The DSS's view was that it did not apply to the former, relying on para.6(1)(a) of Sch.1 to the Act. But it was certainly arguable that since reg.12(1) refers to those entitled to benefit under para.(3A) as in force before the coming into force of the 1996 Regulations (which is July 24, 1996 in relation to para.(3A): see para.2 of Sch.1) and since para.6(2) states that para.6(1) does not apply where a person is entitled to benefit under reg.12(1), that the former were covered. However, in *R. v Secretary of State for Social Security Ex p. T*, March 18, 1997, the Court of Appeal held that reg.12(1) only applied to those entitled to benefit before February 5, 1996. The Act had only "modified" those provisions in the 1996 Regulations which had been declared unlawful in *Ex p. JCWI*, that is, those that related to the denial of income support, housing benefit and council tax benefit. This did not apply to reg.12(1). Ms T's claim for income support which had been made on February 20, 1996 fell under the modified provisions and so para.6(1) of Sch.1 excluded her entitlement to benefit from July 24, 1996.

Reg.12(2) contains transitional protection for sponsored immigrants entitled to income support before February 5, 1996. This continues until the entitlement to income support ends. The claimant must have been entitled to income support immediately before February 5, 1996 for reg.12(2) to apply (*R(IS) 15/99*).

Applicable amounts in urgent cases

2.501   **71.**—(1) For the purposes of calculating any entitlement to income support under this Part—

    (a) except in a case to which [¹ sub-paragraph [¹⁷. . .] (c) or (d)] applies, a claimant's weekly applicable amount shall be the aggregate of—

        (i) 90 per cent of the amount applicable in respect of himself or, if he is a member of a couple or of a polygamous marriage, of the amount applicable in respect of both of them under paragraph 1(1), (2) or (3) of Schedule 2 or, as the case may be, the amount applicable in respect of them under regulation 18 (polygamous marriages); [¹²and where regulation 22A (reduction in applicable amount where the claimant is appealing against a decision [¹³which embodies a determination] that he is not incapable of work) applies, the reference in this head to 90 per cent of the amount applicable shall be construed as a reference to 90 per cent of the relevant amount under that regulation reduced by 20 per cent;]

        (ii) [¹⁹. . .]

(iii) the amount, if applicable, specified in [⁵ Part [¹⁹ . . .] III of Schedule 2 (premiums)]; and

(iv) any amounts applicable under [²regulation 17(1)(e) or, as the case may be, 18(1)(f) (housing costs); [⁴and

(v) the amount of the protected sum which may be applicable to him determined in accordance with Schedule 3A [⁷or, as the case may be, 3B];]

[⁹(vi)[¹⁸. . .]]

(b) [¹⁶. . .]

(c) [¹⁸. . .]

[¹(d) except where sub-paragraph [¹⁷. . .] (c) applies, in the case of a person to whom any paragraph, other than [¹⁴paragraph 16A], in column (1) of Schedule 7 (special cases) applies, the amount shall be 90 per cent of the amount applicable in column 2 of that Schedule in respect of the claimant and partner (if any), plus, if applicable—

(i) [¹⁹. . .]

(ii) any premium under [⁵Part [¹⁹. . .] III of Schedule 2]; and

[² (iii) any amounts applicable under regulation 17(1)(e) or, as the case may be, 18(1)(f)]; [⁴ and

(iv) the amount of the protected sum which may be applicable to him determined in accordance with Schedule 3A [⁷or, as the case may be, 3B].]

[¹⁶(1A)[¹⁸. . .]]

[¹⁶(2) In a case to which paragraph 1 of Part I of the Schedule to the Social Security (Immigration and Asylum) Consequential Amendments Regulations 2000 applies, the period for which a claimant's weekly applicable amount is to be calculated in accordance with paragraph (1) shall be any period, or the aggregate of any periods, not exceeding 42 days during any one period of leave to which that paragraph of that Part of the Schedule to those Regulations applies.]

[¹(3) Where the calculation of a claimant's applicable amount under this regulation results in a fraction of a penny that fraction shall be treated as a penny.]

AMENDMENTS

1. Income Support (General) Amendment Regulations 1988 (SI 1988/663), reg.25 (April 11, 1988).

2. Income Support (General) Amendment No.4 Regulations 1988 (SI 1988/1445), reg.15 (September 12, 1988).

3. Income Support (General) Amendment No.4 Regulations 1988 (SI 1988/1445), Sch.1, para.5 (April 10, 1989).

4. Income Support (General) Amendment No.4 Regulations 1988 (SI 1988/1445), Sch.1, para.13 (April 10, 1989).

5. Family Credit and Income Support (General) Amendment Regulations 1989 (SI 1989/1034), reg.9 (July 10, 1989).

6. Income Support (General) Amendment Regulations 1989 (SI 1989/534), Sch.1, para.8 (October 9, 1989).

7. Income Support (General) Amendment Regulations 1989 (SI 1989/534), Sch.1, para.17 (October 9, 1989).

8. Social Security Benefits (Amendments Consequential Upon the Introduction of Community Care) Regulations 1992 (SI 1992/3147), Sch.1, para.4 (April 1, 1993).

9. Income-related Benefits Schemes (Miscellaneous Amendments) (No. 4) Regulations 1993 (SI 1993/2119), reg.17 (October 4, 1993).

2.502

10. Income-related Benefits Schemes (Miscellaneous Amendments) Regulations 1994 (SI 1994/527), reg.6 (April 11, 1994).

11. Social Security (Persons from Abroad) Miscellaneous Amendments Regulations 1996 (SI 1996/30), reg.8(4) (February 5, 1996).

12. Income Support (General) (Jobseeker's Allowance Consequential Amendments) Regulations 1996 (SI 1996/206), reg.18 (October 7, 1996).

13. Social Security Act 1998 (Commencement No. 9 and Savings and Consequential and Transitional Provisions) Order 1999 (SI 1999/2422), art.3(7) and Sch.6, para.2.

14. Social Security (Immigration and Asylum) Consequential Amendments Regulations 2000 (SI 2000/636), reg.3(8)(a) (April 3, 2000)

15. Social Security (Miscellaneous Amendments) (No. 3) Regulations 2001 (SI 2001/859), reg.3(1) and (3) (April 9, 2001).

16. Social Security Amendment (Residential Care and Nursing Homes) Regulations 2001 (SI 2001/3767), reg.2 and Sch., Pt I, para.12 (April 8, 2002).

17. Social Security Amendment (Residential Care and Nursing Homes) Regulations 2001 (SI 2001/3767), reg.2 and Sch., Pt I, para.12 (as amended by Social Security Amendment (Residential Care and Nursing Homes) Regulations 2002 (SI 2002/398), reg.4(2)) (April 8, 2002).

18. Social Security (Removal of Residential Allowance and Miscellaneous Amendments) Regulations 2003 (SI 2003/1121), reg.2 and Sch.1 para.5 (October 6, 2003).

19. Social Security (Working Tax Credit and Child Tax Credit) (Consequential Amendments) Regulations 2003 (SI 2003 No. 455), reg.2 and Sch.1, para.18 (April 6, 2004, except in "transitional cases" and see further the note to reg.17 of the Income Support Regulation).

DEFINITIONS

2.503   "the 1971 Act"—see reg.21(3).
"child"—see 1986 Act, s.20(11) (SSCBA, s.137(1)).
"claimant"—see reg.2(1).
"couple"—*ibid.*
"family"—see 1986 Act, s.20(11) (SSCBA, s.137(1)).
"nursing home"—see reg.2(1), reg.19(3).
"polygamous marriage"—see reg.2(1).
"residential accommodation"—*ibid.*, reg.21(3).
"residential care home"—*ibid.*, reg.19(3).
"young person"—*ibid.*, reg.14.

GENERAL NOTE

Para. (1)

2.504   The basic rule, with detailed variations, is that 90 per cent. of the applicable amount for the claimant and any partner is allowed, and (from July 1989) all premiums, and housing costs.

Para. (2)

2.505   The form of para.(2) on force before April 3, 2000 only covered reg.70 payments made to people whose funds had temporarily dried up (such payments are strictly time-limited). The form introduced on April 3, 2000 was appararently intended to do the same but its effect is unclear, as pointed out in the 2000 edition. The amendment on April 9, 2001 has however made the position clear. For payments made to asylum seekers, see reg.12(5) of SI 2000/636. Presumably other reg.70 payments continue while the conditions of entitlement are met.

Assessment of income and capital in urgent cases

72.—(1) The claimant's income shall be calculated in accordance with   2.506
Part V subject to the following modifications—
[¹⁰(a) any income other than—
  (i) a payment of income or income in kind made under the
       Macfarlane Trust, the Macfarlane (Special Payments) Trust,
       the Macfarlane (Special Payments) (No. 2) Trust, the Fund,
       the Eileen Trust or the Independent Living Funds; or
  (ii) income to which paragraph 5, 7 (but only to the extent that a
       concessionary payment would be due under that paragraph for
       any non-payment of income support under regulation 70 of
       these Regulations or of jobseeker's allowance under regulation
       147 of the Jobseeker's Allowance Regulations 1996 (urgent
       cases)), 31, 39(2), (3) or (4), 40, 52 or 57 of Schedule 9
       (disregard of income other than earnings) applies,
  possessed or treated as possessed by him, shall be taken into account
  in full not withstanding any provision in that Part disregarding the
  whole or any part of that income;]
  (b) any income to which regulation 53 (calculation of tariff income from
       capital) applies shall be disregarded;
  (c) income treated as capital by virtue of [² regulation 48(1), (2), (3) and
       (9)] (income treated as capital) shall be taken into account as income;
  (d) in a case to which paragraph (2)(b) of regulation 70 (urgent cases)
       applies, any income to which regulation 42(3) (notional income)
       applies shall be disregarded;
  (e) [³. . .].
(2) The claimant's capital calculated in accordance with Part V, but
including any capital referred to in paragraphs 3 and, to the extent that such
assets as are referred to in paragraph 6 consist of liquid assets, 6 [²and,
except to the extent that the arrears referred to in paragraph 7 consist of
arrears of housing benefit payable under Part II of the Act or Part II of the
Social Security and Housing Benefits Act 1982 [SSCBA, Part VII] [¹⁰ or any
arrears of benefit due under regulation 70 of these Regulations or regulation
147 of the Jobseeker's Allowance Regulations 1996 (urgent cases)], 7, 9(b),
19, 30 [⁹, 32 and 47 to 49] of Schedule 10] (capital to be disregarded) shall
be taken into account in full and the amount of income support which
would, but for this paragraph be payable under this regulation, shall be
payable only to the extent that it exceeds the amount of that capital.

Amendments

1. Family Credit and Income Support (General) Amendment Regulations 1988   2.507
(SI 1988/999), reg.6 (June 9, 1988).
  2. Income Support (General) Amendment No.5 Regulations 1988 (SI 1988/
2022), reg.15 (December 12, 1988).
  3. Income Support (General) Amendment No.2 Regulations 1989 (SI 1989/
1323), reg.17 (October 9, 1989).
  4. Income-related Benefits Schemes Amendment Regulations 1990 (SI 1990/
127), reg.3 (January 31, 1990).
  5. Income-related Benefits Schemes and Social Security (Recoupment)
Amendment Regulations 1991 (SI 1991/1175), reg.5 (May 11, 1991).
  6. Income-related Benefits Schemes and Social Security (Recoupment)
Amendment Regulations 1992 (SI 1992/1101), reg.6 (May 7, 1992).

7. Social Security Benefits (Miscellaneous Amendments) (No.2) Regulations 1993 (SI 1993 No. 963), reg.2(3) (April 22, 1993).

8. Income-related Benefits Schemes and Social Security (Recoupment) Amendment Regulations 1993 (SI 1993 No. 1249), reg.4(3) (May 14, 1993).

9. Income Support and Social Security (Claims and Payments) (Miscellaneous Amendments) Regulations 1996 (SI 1996/2431), reg.4 (October 15, 1996).

10. Social Security (Miscellaneous Amendments) Regulations 1998 (SI 1998/563), reg.19(1) (April 6, 1998).

DEFINITIONS

2.508   "the Act"—see reg.2(1).
"claimant"—*ibid.*
"concessionary payment"—*ibid.*
"the Eileen Trust"—*ibid.*
"the Fund"—*ibid.*
"the Independent Living Funds"—*ibid.*
"the Macfarlane (Special Payments) Trust"—*ibid.*
"the Macfarlane (Special Payments) (No. 2) Trust"—*ibid.*
"the Macfarlane Trust"—*ibid.*

GENERAL NOTE

Para. (1)

2.509   This paragraph modifies the ordinary rules on income in urgent cases. All income is to be taken into account, free of any disregards, except for income from the Macfarlane Trusts (haemophiliacs), the Fund, the Eileen Trust or the Independent Living Funds, all forms of housing benefit, council tax benefit, backdated payments of income support under reg.21ZB and the notional income which gives rise to the entitlement to urgent cases payments in cases under reg.70(2)(b). Note the April 6, 1998 amendment which adds social fund payments and concessionary payments for the non-payment of income support under reg.70 or income-based JSA under reg.147 of the JSA Regulations to this list (see the note to para.(2) below). The tariff income from capital under reg.53 is disregarded, but that is of little consequence given para.(2). Under sub-para.(c) several items of income normally treated as capital retain their status as income.

Para. (2)

2.510   The calculation of capital is much as normal. Categories normally disregarded which count for urgent cases purposes are the proceeds of sale of a former home, liquid assets of a business, arrears of certain benefits, certain sums deposited with Housing Associations, refunds of MIRAS tax, training bonuses under £200, payments to compensate for loss of transitional protection and backdated payments of income support, housing benefit and council tax benefit made after recognition of refugee status. But note that the amendment of April 6, 1998 allows any arrears of income support under reg.70 or income-based JSA under reg.147 of the JSA Regulations to be ignored. There had been a problem that if arrears of such payments were paid the claimant could lose entitlement to further awards of urgent cases payments. This had particularly affected asylum seekers where there had been a delay in verifying information, etc.

Once the capital has been calculated a payment for urgent cases is only to be made in so far as it exceeds the amount of capital. There is no £16,000, £8,000, £10,000, £3,000, £500 or £1 exemption.

Reg.72(2) was considered by Commissioner Mesher in the important decision, *CIS/6249/1999*. In that appeal, the claimant received £787.70 in arrears of income support at the urgent cases rate in October 1995. As this was before the amendment to para.(2) effected by SI 1998/563 on April 6, 1998, the receipt of this amount of arrears should immediately have disentitled the claimant from further urgent cases payments and the claimant would therefore have had to spend the arrears on every day living and would have become entitled to income support again about 12 weeks later. Crucially, this would have been before February 5, 1996. However, the Benefits Agency took no steps to review the award of urgent cases payments to the claimant until April 1998 and, on appeal against that decision, the social security appeal tribunal held that the claimant had not been entitled to income support since October 1995. On appeal to the Commissioner, it was held first, that reg.72(2) was *intra vires* s.136(5)(d) of AA 1992 (which empowered the Secretary of State to prescribe "circumstances in which . . . capital is to be treated as income"), and secondly that s.25(1) of AA 1992 granted a power to review if grounds for review existed but did not impose a duty to carry out a review in every such case. In the circumstances of the appeal, the exercise of that power in respect of a past period was an abuse of power (and therefore erroneous in law) because the sole practical effect of such a review was to disadvantage the claimant unfairly by securing retrospectively that he was not in receipt of income support on February 5, 1996 and therefore lost the benefit of the transitional protection established by reg.12(1) of the Social Security (Persons From Abroad) Miscellaneous Amendments Regulations 1996. If the Benefits Agency had taken the correct action at the correct time, the claimant's entitlement to transitional protection would not have been compromised.

For further discussion of *CIS/6249/1999* in relation to the powers to revise and supersede under the Social Security Act 1998, see Vol. III.

[¹PART VII

CALCULATION OF INCOME SUPPORT FOR PART-WEEKS

Amount of income support payable

73.—(1) Subject to regulations 75 (modifications in income) and 76 (reduction in certain cases), where a claimant is entitled to income support for a period (referred to in this Part as a part-week) to which subsection (1A) of section 21 of the Act [SSCBA, s.124(5)] (amount etc. of income-related benefit) applies, the amount of income support payable shall, except where paragraph (2) applies, be calculated in accordance with the following formulae— 2.511

   (a) if the claimant has no income, $\dfrac{N \times A}{7}$;

   (b) if the claimant has income, $\dfrac{N \times (A - I)}{7} - B$.

(2) [⁶. . .]

(3) In this Regulation—

"A", [⁶. . .] means the claimant's weekly applicable amount in the relevant week;

"B" means the amount of any income support, [⁵jobseeker's allowance], [²maternity allowance,] [⁴short-term or long-term incapacity benefit], or severe disablement allowance payable in respect of any day in the part-week;

"I" means his weekly income in the relevant week less B;

"N" means the number of days in the part-week;
"relevant week" means the period of 7 days determined in accordance
with regulation 74.

(4) and (5) [⁶. . .]

AMENDMENTS

2.512   1. Income Support (General) Amendment Regulations 1988 (SI 1988/663),
reg.27 (April 11, 1988).
2. Income Support (General) Amendment No.4 Regulations 1988 (SI 1988/
1445), reg.17 (September 12, 1988).
4. Disability Working Allowance and Income Support (General) Amendment
Regulations 1995 (SI 1995/482), reg.12 (April 13, 1995).
5. Income Support (General) (Jobseeker's Allowance Consequential
Amendments) Regulations 1996 (SI 1996/206), reg.19 (October 7, 1996).
6. Social Security Amendment (Residential Care and Nursing Homes)
Regulations 2001 (SI 2001/3767), reg.2 and Sch., Pt I para.13 (April 8, 2002).

DEFINITIONS

"the Act"—see reg.2(1).
"claimant"—*ibid.*

GENERAL NOTE

2.513   Although the rules set out in regs 73 to 77 do look very complex, they set out a
relatively straightforward method of calculating benefit for part-weeks. See *CIS
706/1997* for an exposition of how these rules operate.

[¹Relevant week

2.514   **74.**—(1) Where the part-week—
(a) is the whole period for which income support is payable or occurs at
the beginning of the claim, the relevant week is the period of 7 days
ending on the last day of that part-week; or
(b) occurs at the end of the claim, the relevant week is the period of 7
days beginning on the first day of that part-week.

(2) Where during the currency of a claim the claimant makes a claim for
a relevant social security benefit within the meaning of paragraph 4 of
Schedule 7 to the Social Security (Claims and Payments) Regulations 1987
and as a result his benefit week changes, for the purpose of calculating the
amount of income support payable—
(a) for the part-week beginning on the day after his last complete benefit
week before the date from which he makes a claim for the relevant
social security benefit and ending immediately before that date, the
relevant week is the period of 7 days beginning on the day after his
last complete benefit week (the first relevant week);
(b) for the part-week beginning on the date from which he makes a claim
for the relevant social security benefit and ending immediately before
the start of his next benefit week after the date of that claim, the relevant week is the period of 7 days ending immediately before the
start of his next benefit week (the second relevant week).

(3) Where during the currency of a claim the claimant's benefit week
changes at the direction of the Secretary of State under paragraph 3 of
Schedule 7 to the Social Security (Claims and Payments) Regulations 1987,
for the purpose of calculating the amount of income support payable for the

part-week beginning on the day after his last complete benefit week before the change and ending immediately before the change, the relevant week is the period of 7 days beginning on the day after the last complete benefit week.]

AMENDMENT

1. Income Support (General) Amendment Regulations 1988 (SI 1988/663), reg.27 (April 11, 1988).

2.515

DEFINITIONS

"benefit week"—see reg.2(1).
"claimant"—*ibid.*

[¹ Modifications in the calculation of income

75.—For the purposes of regulation 73 (amount of income support payable for part-weeks), a claimant's income and the income of any person which the claimant is treated as possessing under section 22(5) of the Act [SSCBA, s.136(1)] or regulation 23(3) shall be calculated in accordance with Part V and, where applicable, VI subject to the following modifications—

2.516

   (a) any income which is due to be paid in the relevant week shall be treated as paid on the first day of that week;
   (b) any income support, [⁴jobseeker's allowance], [²maternity allowance,] [³short-term or long-term incapacity benefit], or severe disablement allowance [³. . .] payable in the relevant week but not in respect of any day in the part-week shall be disregarded;
   (c) where the part-week occurs at the end of the claim, any income or any change in the amount of income of the same kind which is first payable within the relevant week but not on any day in the part-week shall be disregarded;
   (d) where the part-week occurs immediately after a period in which a person was treated as engaged in remunerative work) under regulation 5(5) (persons treated as engaged in remunerative work) any earnings which are taken into account for the purposes of determining that period shall be disregarded;
   (e) where regulation 74(2) (relevant week) applies, any payment of income which—
      (i) is the final payment in a series of payments of the same kind or, if there has been an interruption in such payments, the last one before the interruption;
      (ii) is payable in respect of a period not exceeding a week; and
      (iii) is due to be paid on a day which falls within both the first and second relevant weeks,
   shall be taken into account in either the first relevant week or, if it is impracticable to take it into account in that week, in the second relevant week; but this paragraph shall not apply to a payment of income support, [⁴jobseeker's allowance], [²maternity allowance,] [³short-term or long-term incapacity benefit] or severe disablement allowance [³. . .];
   (f) where regulation 74(2) applies, any payment of income which—
      (i) is the final payment in a series of payments of the same kind or, if there has been an interruption in such payments, the last one before the interruption;

(ii) is payable in respect of a period exceeding a week but not exceeding 2 weeks; and

(iii) is due to be paid on a day which falls within both the first and second relevant weeks,

shall be disregarded; but this sub-paragraph shall not apply to a payment of income support, [⁴jobseeker's allowance], [²maternity allowance,] [³short-term or long term incapacity benefit], or severe disablement allowance, [³. . .]

(g) where regulation 74(2) applies, if the weekly amount of any income which is due to be paid on a day which falls within both the first and second relevant weeks is more than the weekly amount of income of the same kind due to be paid in the last complete benefit week, the excess shall be disregarded;

(h) where only part of the weekly amount of income is taken into account in the relevant week, the balance shall be disregarded.]

AMENDMENTS

2.517   1. Income Support (General) Amendment Regulations 1988 (SI 1988/663), reg.27 (April 11, 1988).

2. Income Support (General) Amendment No. 4 Regulations 1988 (SI 1988/1445), reg.17 (September 12, 1988).

3. Disability Working Allowance and Income support (General) Amendment Regulations 1995 (SI 1995/482), reg.13 (April 13, 1995).

4. Income support (General) (Jobseeker's Allowance Consequential Amendments) Regulations 1996 (SI 1996/206), reg.20 (October 7, 1996).

DEFINITIONS

"claimant"—see reg.2(1).
"Social Security Act"—*ibid.*

[¹Reduction in certain cases

2.518   **76.**—There shall be deducted from the amount of income support which would, but for this regulation, be payable for a part-week—

(a) [² in the case of a claimant to whom regulation 22A (reduction in applicable amount where the claimant is appealing against a decision [³ which embodies a determination] that he is not incapable of work) applies], the proportion of the relevant amount specified therein appropriate to the number of days in the part-week;

(b) where regulation 75(f) (modifications in the calculation of income) applies, one-half of the amount disregarded under regulation 75(f) less the weekly amount of any disregard under Schedule 8 or 9 appropriate to that payment.]

AMENDMENTS

2.519   1. Income Support (General) Amendment Regulations 1988 (SI 1988/663), reg.27 (April 11, 1988).

2. Income Support (General) (Jobseeker's Allowance Consequential Amendments) Regulations 1996 (SI 1996/206), reg.21 (October 7, 1996).

3. Social Security Act 1998 (Commencement No.9 and Savings and Consequential and Transitional Provisions) Order 1999 (SI 1999/2422), art.3(7) and Sch.6, para.2

"claimant"—see reg.2(1).

[¹Modification of section 23(5) of the Act [SSCBA, s.126(5)]

77.—Where income support is payable for a part-week, section 23(5) of   2.520
the Act [SSCBA, s.126(5)] (trade disputes) shall have effect as if the following paragraph were substituted for paragraph (b)—

"(b) any payment by way of income support for a part-week which
apart from this paragraph would be made to him, or to a person
whose applicable amount if aggregated with his—

(i) shall not be made if the payment for the part-week is equal to
or less than the proportion of the relevant sum appropriate to
the number of days in the part-week; or
(ii) if it is more than that proportion, shall be made at a rate equal
to the difference."

AMENDMENT

1. Income Support (General) Amendment Regulations 1988 (SI 1988/663),
reg.27 (April 11, 1988).

DEFINITION

"the Act"—see reg.2(1).

SCHEDULES

SCHEDULE 1

[Revoked by the Income Support (General) (Jobseeker's Allowance Consequential Amendments)   2.521
Regulations 1996 (SI 1996/206), reg.28 and Sch.3 with effect from October 7, 1996.]

SCHEDULE 1A

[Revoked by the Income Support (General) (Jobseeker's Allowance Consequential Amendments)   2.522
Regulations 1996 (SI 1996/206), reg.28 and Sch.3 with effect from October 7, 1996.]

[¹ SCHEDULE 1B   Regulation 4ZA

PRESCRIBED CATEGORIES OF PERSON

Lone parents
1. A person who is a lone parent and responsible for a child who is a member of his   2.523
household.

Single persons looking after foster children
2. A single claimant or a lone parent with whom a child is placed by a local authority or   2.524
voluntary organisation within the meaning of the Children Act 1989 or, in Scotland, the Social
Work (Scotland) Act 1968.

Persons temporarily looking after another person
3. A person who is—   2.525
(a) looking after a child because the parent of that child or the person who usually looks
after him is ill or is temporarily absent from his home; or
(b) looking after a member of his family who is temporarily ill.

Persons caring for another person

2.526   **4.** A person (the carer)—

(a) who is regularly and substantially engaged in caring for another person if—

(i) the person being cared for is in receipt of attendance allowance [². . .] or the care component of disability living allowance at the highest or middle rate prescribed in accordance with section 72(3) of the Contributions and Benefits Act; or

(ii) the person being cared for has claimed attendance allowance [². . .] but only for the period up to the date of determination of that claim, or the period of 26 weeks from the date of that claim, whichever date is the earlier; or

[²(iia) the person being cared for has claimed attendance allowance in accordance with section 65(6)(a) of the Contributions and Benefits Act (claims in advance of entitlement), an award has been made in respect of that claim under section 65(6)(b) of that Act and, where the period for which the award is payable has begun, that person in receipt of the allowance;] [¹⁶ or]

(iii) the person being cared for has claimed entitlement to a disability living allowance but only for the period up to the date of determination of that claim, or the period of 26 weeks from the date of that claim, whichever date is the earlier; or

[²(iiia) the person being cared for has claimed entitlement to the care component of a disability living allowance in accordance with regulation 13A of the Social Security (Claims and Payments) Regulations 1987 (advance claims and awards), an award at the highest or middle rate has been made in respect of that claim and, where the period for which the award is payable has begun, that person is in receipt of the allowance;]

(b) who is engaged in caring for another person and [¹⁰who is both entitled to, and in receipt of,] [¹⁸ a carer's allowance] [¹⁷ or would be in receipt of that allowance but for the application of a restriction under section 7 of the Social Security Fraud Act 2001 (loss of benefit provisions)].

5. A person to whom paragraph 4 applied, but only for a period of 8 weeks from the date on which that paragraph ceased to apply to him.

6. A person who, had he previously made a claim for income support, would have fulfilled the conditions of paragraph 4, but only for a period of 8 weeks from the date on which he ceased to fulfil those conditions.

Persons incapable of work

2.527   **7.** A person who—

(a) is incapable of work in accordance with the provisions of Part XIIA of the Contributions and Benefits Act and the regulations made thereunder (incapacity for work); or

(b) is treated as incapable of work by virtue of regulations made under section 171D of that Act (persons to be treated as incapable or capable of work); or

(c) is treated as capable of work by virtue of regulations made under section 171E(1) of that Act (disqualification etc); or

(d) is entitled to statutory sick pay.

Disabled workers

2.528   **8.** A person to whom [⁵ [⁹ regulation 6(4)(a)]] (persons not treated as engaged in remunerative work) applies.

Persons in employment living in residential care homes, nursing homes or residential accommodation

2.529   **9.** A person to whom [⁵[⁹ regulation 6(4)(d)]] applies.

[¹⁵ Persons who have commenced remunerative work

2.530   **9A.** A person to whom regulation 6(5) (persons not treated as engaged in remunerative work) applies.]

Disabled students

2.531   **10.** A person who is a [¹¹ full-time student] and—

(a) whose applicable amount includes the disability premium or severe disability premium; or

(b) who has satisfied the provisions of paragraph 7 for a continuous period of not less than 196 days, and for this purpose any two or more separate periods separated by a break of not more than 56 days shall be treated as one continuous period.

11. A person who is a [¹¹ full-time student] and who—

(a) immediately before 1st September 1990 was in receipt of income support by virtue of paragraph 7 of Schedule 1 as then in force; or

(b) on or after that date makes a claim for income support and at a time during the period of 18 months immediately preceding the date of that claim was in receipt of income support either by virtue of that paragraph or regulation 13(2)(b),

but this paragraph shall not apply where for a continuous period of 18 months or more the person has not been in receipt of income support.

Deaf students

12. [¹² A person who is a full-time student in respect of whom—

(a) a supplementary requirement has been determined under paragraph 9 of Part II of Schedule 2 to the Education (Mandatory Awards) Regulations 1999;

2.532

(b) an allowance or, as the case may be, bursary has been granted, which includes a sum under paragraph (1)(d) of regulation 4 of the Students' Allowances (Scotland) Regulations 1999 or, as the case may be, under paragraph (1)(d) of regulation 4 of the Education Authority (Bursaries) (Scotland) Regulations 1995, in respect of expenses incurred;

(c) a payment has been made under section 2 of the Education Act 1962;

(d) a grant has been made under regulation 13 of the Education (Student Support) Regulations 2000, or under regulation 13 of the Education (Student Support) Regulations (Northern Ireland) 2000; or

(e) a supplementary requirement has been determined under paragraph 9 of Schedule 6 to the Students Awards Regulations (Northern Ireland) 1999 or a payment has been made under Article 50(3) of the Education and Libraries (Northern Ireland) Order 1986,

on account of his disability by reason of deafness.]

Blind persons

13. A person who is registered as blind complied by a local authority under section 29 of the National Assistance Act 1948 (welfare services) or, in Scotland, has been certified as blind and in consequence he is registered as blind in a register maintained by or on behalf of a regional or islands council, but a person who has ceased to be registered as blind on regaining his eyesight shall nevertheless be treated as so registered for a period of 28 weeks following the date on which he ceased to be so registered.

2.533

Pregnancy

14. A woman who—

2.534

(a) is incapable of work by reason of pregnancy; or

(b) is or has been pregnant but only for the period commencing 11 weeks before her expected week of confinement and ending seven weeks after the date on which her pregnancy ends [¹⁹ where the expected week of confinement begins prior to 6th April 2003 or fifteen weeks after the date on which her pregnancy ends where the expected week of confinement begins on or after 6th April 2003].

[⁶Parental leave

14A.—(1) A person who is—

2.535

(a) entitled to, and taking, parental leave by virtue of Part III of the Maternity and Parental Leave etc. Regulations 1999 in respect of a child who is a member of his household; and

(b) not entitled to any remuneration from his employer in respect of that leave for the period to which his claim for income support relates; and

(c) entitled [²². . .] [²¹ working tax credit, child tax credit payable at a rate higher than the family element,] housing benefit or council tax benefit on the day before that leave begins.

(2) In this paragraph "remuneration" means payment of any kind [²¹ and "family element" means in a case where any child in respect of whom child tax credit is payable is under the age of one year, the amount specified in regulation 7(3)(a) of the Child Tax Credit Regulations 2002 or in any other case, the amount specified in regulation 7(3)(b) of those Regulations] [²² but subject in any case to calculations of those amounts made in accordance with the Tax Credits (Income Thresholds and Determination of Rates) Regulations 2002.]]

[²⁰Paternity Leave

14B.— (1) A person who is entitled to, and is taking, paternity leave and who satisfies either or both of the conditions set out in sub-paragraph (2) below.

2.536

(2) The conditions for the purposes of sub-paragraph (1) are—
- (a) he is not entitled to statutory paternity pay by virtue of Part 12ZA of the Contributions and Benefits Act, or to any remuneration from his employer in respect of that leave for the period to which his claim for income support relates;
- (b) he is entitled to [²². . .] [²¹ working tax credit, child tax credit payable at a rate higher than the family element,] housing benefit or council tax benefit on the day before that leave begins.

(3) In this paragraph "remuneration" means payment of any kind [²¹ and "family element" means in a case where any child in respect of whom child tax credit is payable is under the age of one year, the amount specified in regulation 7(3)(a) of the Child Tax Credit Regulations 2002 or in any other case, the amount specified in regulation 7(3)(b) of those Regulations] [²² but subject in any case to calculations of those amounts made in accordance with the Tax Credits (Income Thresholds and Determination of Rates) Regulations 2002.]]

Persons in education

2.537   **15.** A person to whom any provision of regulation 13(2)(a) to (e) (persons receiving relevant education who are parents, severely handicapped persons, orphans and persons estranged from their parents or guardian) applies.

Certain persons aged 50 who have not been in remunerative work for 10 years

2.538   **16.**—(1) Subject to sub-paragraph (2), a person who on 6th October 1996 or at any time during the eight weeks immediately preceding that date [³ was in receipt of income support and] satisfied the conditions of paragraph 13 of Schedule 1 as in force on that date (persons aged not less than 50 who had not been in remunerative work during the previous 10 years).

(2) If a person to whom sub-paragraph (1) applies ceases to be entitled to income support, and subsequently makes a further claim for income support, this paragraph shall continue to apply to him only if—
- (a) the further claim for income support is made within 8 weeks of the date he ceased to be so entitled; and
- (b) he has not been in remunerative work since he ceased to be so entitled.

[¹⁴ Certain persons aged between 55 and 60 whose spouse has died

16A. A person—
2.539
- (a) who had, as at 9th April 2001, attained the age of 55 but not the age of 60;
- (b) whose spouse died during the period beginning on 9th April 2001 and ending on 9th April 2006; and
- (c) who is claiming income support as a single claimant.]

Persons aged 60 or over

2.540   **17.** [²³. . .].

Refugees

2.541   **18.** A person who is a refugee within the definition in Article 1 of the Convention relating to the Status of Refugees done at Geneva on 28th July 1951 as extended by Article 1(2) of the Protocol relating to the Status of Refugees done at New York on 31st January 1967 and who—
- (a) is attending for more than 15 hours a week a course for the purpose of learning English so that he may obtain employment; and
- (b) on the date on which that course commenced, had been in Great Britain for not more than 12 months.

but only for a period not exceeding nine months.

[⁸**18A.** A person to whom regulation 21ZB (treatment of refugees) applies by virtue of regulation 21ZB(2) from the date his claim for asylum is made until the date the Secretary of State makes a decision on that claim.]

Persons required to attend court

2.542   **19.** A person who is required to attend court as a justice of the peace, a party to any proceedings, a witness or a juror.

Persons affected by a trade dispute

2.543   **20.** A person to whom section 126 of the Contributions and Benefits Act (trade disputes) applies or in respect of whom section 124(1) of the Act (conditions of entitlement to income support) has effect as modified by section 127(b) of the Act (effect of return to work).

Persons from abroad

2.544   **21.** A person to whom [⁸ regulation 70(2A)] (applicable amount of certain persons from abroad) applies.

Persons in custody

22. A person remanded in, or committed in, custody for trial or for sentencing.　　2.545

Member of couple looking after children while other member temporarily abroad

23. A person who is a member of a couple and who is treated as responsible for a child who　2.546
is a member of his household where the other member of that couple is temporarily not present
in the United Kingdom.

**Persons appealing against a decision [⁴ which embodies a determination] that they
　　are not incapable of work**

24. A person—　　2.547
　　(a) in respect of whom it has been determined for the purposes of section 171B of the
　　　　Contributions and Benefits Act (the own occupation test) that he is not incapable of
　　　　work; and
　　(b) whose medical practitioner continues to supply evidence of his incapacity for work in
　　　　accordance with regulation 2 of the Social Security (Medical Evidence) Regulations
　　　　1976 (evidence of incapacity for work); and
　　(c) who has made and is pursuing an appeal against the [⁴ decision which embodies a]
　　　　determination that he is not so incapable.
but only for the period prior to the determination of his appeal.

25. A person—
　　(a) in respect of whom it has been determined for the purposes of section 171C of the
　　　　Contributions and Benefits Act ([⁷ personal capability assessment]) that he is not inca-
　　　　pable of work; and
　　(b) who has made and is pursuing an appeal against the [⁴ decision which embodies a]
　　　　determination that he is not so incapable.
but only for the period [²⁴ beginning with the date on which that determination takes effect
until] the determination of his appeal.

26. A person who on 6th October 1996 was not required to be available for employment by
virtue of regulation 8(2) (persons appealing against decisions [⁴ which embody a determination]
that they are not incapable of work) as modified by the savings provision in regulation 20(1) or
(3) of the Disability Working Allowance and Income Support (General) Amendment Regulations
1995, but only for a period prior to the determination of his appeal.

27. A person who on 6th October 1996 was required to register for employment by virtue of
regulation 11(2) (persons appealing against decisions [⁴ which embody a determination that
they are not incapable of work) as modified by the savings provisions in regulation 20(2) or (3)
of the Disability Working Allowance and Income Support (General) Amendment Regulations
1995, but only for the period prior to the determination of his appeal.

28. A person who is engaged in training, and for this purpose "training" means training for
which persons aged under 18 are eligible and for which persons aged 18 to 24 may be eligible
[¹³ secured by the Learning and Skills Council for England or by the National Council for
Education and Training for Wales] and, in Scotland, directly or indirectly by a Local Enterprise
Company pursuant to its arrangement with, as the case may be, Scottish Enterprise or
Highlands and Islands Enterprise (whether that arrangement is known as an Operating
Contract or by any other name).]

AMENDMENTS

1. Income Support (General) (Jobseeker's Allowance Consequential Amendments)　　2.548
Regulations 1996 (SI 1996/206), reg.22 and Sch.1 (October 7, 1996).

2. Jobseeker's Allowance and Income Support (General) (Amendment)
Regulations 1996 (SI 1996/1517), reg.33 (October 7, 1996).

3. Social Security and Child Support (Miscellaneous Amendments) Regulations
1997 (SI 1997/827), reg.5 (April 7, 1997).

4. Social Security Act 1998 (Commencement No. 9 and Savings and
Consequential and Transitional Provisions) Order 1999 (SI 1999/2422 (C. 61)),
art.3(7) and Sch.6, para.3 (September 6, 1999).

5. Social Security (Miscellaneous Amendments) (No.2) Regulations 1999 (SI
1999/2556), reg.2(7) (October 4, 1999).

6. Income Support (General) Amendment (No.2) Regulations 1999 (SI
1999/3329), reg.2 (January 5, 2000).

7. Social Security (Incapacity for Work) Miscellaneous Amendments Regulations
1999 (SI 1999/3109), reg.6 (April 3, 2000).

8. Social Security (Immigration and Asylum) Consequential Amendments Regulations 2000 (SI 2000/636), reg.3(9) (April 3, 2000).

9. Social Security (Miscellaneous Amendments) Regulations 2000 (SI 2000/681), reg.2(d) (April 3, 2000).

10. Social Security (Miscellaneous Amendments) Regulations 2000 (SI 2000/681), reg.4(1) (April 3, 2000).

11. Social Security Amendment (Students) Regulations 2000 (SI 2000/1981), reg.5(5) and Sch. (July 31, 2000).

12. Social Security Amendment (Students and Income-related Benefits) Regulations 2000 (SI 2000/1922), reg.2(8) (August 28, 2000, or if the student's period of study begins between August 1 and 27, 2000, the first day of the period).

13. Social Security (Miscellaneous Amendments) (No. 2) Regulations 2001 (SI 2001/652), reg.4 (March 26, 2001).

14. Social Security Amendment (Bereavement Benefits) Regulations 2000 (SI 2000/2239), reg.2(2) (April 9, 2001).

15. Social Security (Miscellaneous Amendments) Regulations 2001 (SI 2001/488), reg.5 (April 9, 2001).

16. Social Security (Miscellaneous Amendments) (No.3) Regulations 2001 (SI 2001/859), reg.3(4) (April 9, 2001).

17. Social Security (Loss of Benefit) (Consequential Amendments) Regulations 2002 (SI 2002/490), reg.4 (April 1, 2002).

18. Social Security Amendment (Carer's Allowance) Regulations 2002 (SI 2002/2497), reg.3 and Sch.2 (April 1, 2003).

19. Social Security (Paternity and Adoption) Amendment Regulations 2002 (SI 2002/2689), reg.2(5)(a) (November 24, 2002).

20. Social Security (Paternity and Adoption) Amendment Regulations 2002 (SI 2002/2689), reg.2(5)(b) (December 8, 2002).

21. Social Security (Working Tax Credit and Child Tax Credit) (Consequential Amendments) Regulations 2003 (SI 2003/455), reg.2 and Sch.1, para.19 (April 7, 2003)

22. Social Security (Working Tax Credit and Child Tax Credit) (Consequential Amendments) (No. 3) Regulations 2003 (SI 2003/1731), reg.2(3) (August 8, 2003).

23. State Pension Credit (Consequential, Transitional and Miscellaneous Provisions) Regulations 2002 (SI 2002/3019), reg.29(4) (October 6, 2003).

24. Social Security, Child Support and Tax Credits (Miscellaneous Amendments) Regulations 2005 (SI 2005/337), reg.6 (March 18, 2005).

DEFINITIONS

2.549   "adoption leave"—see reg.2(1).
"attendance allowance"—*ibid.*
"child"—see SSCBA, s.137(1)).
"disability living allowance"—see reg.2(1).
"full-time student"—*ibid.*, reg.61(1).
"lone parent"—see reg.2(1).
"maternity leave"—*ibid.*
"paternity leave"—*ibid.*
"payment"—*ibid.*
"personal capability assessment"—SSCBA s.171C, Incapacity for Work Regs., reg.24.
"single claimant" see reg.2(1).
"student"—*ibid.*, reg.61(1).
"voluntary organisation"—see reg.2(1).

GENERAL NOTE

2.550   As a consequence of the introduction of JSA on October 7, 1996, the income support scheme had to undergo a fundamental restructuring. Income support is no longer available to people who are claiming benefit because they are unemployed. People who have to be available for, and actively seeking, work as a condition of receiving benefit now have to claim JSA. Since October 7, 1996, in order to qualify for income support a person has to fall within a "prescribed category" (see SSCBA, s.124(1)(e) and reg.4ZA). Sch.1B sets out these categories.

See the notes to reg.4ZA for discussion of the position of claimants who may be able to claim either income support or JSA; note also that the raising of the limit for remunerative work for partners to 24 hours a week from October 7, 1996 may mean that some couples will have to decide whether they will gain more by claiming working tax credit.

The categories in Sch.1B broadly resemble most of those in the former Sch.1 (people not required to be available for employment) (revoked on October 7, 1996), but there are some differences. There is no equivalent to paras 12 (Open University students attending a residential course), 18 (discharged prisoners) or 23 (persons taking child abroad for medical treatment) of the former Sch.1. But if people in these circumstances claim JSA they will be treated as available for work (see sub-paras (f), (h) and (c) respectively of reg.14(1) of the JSA Regulations). See the note to para.28 for people in receipt of a training allowance.

Sch.1B provides an exhaustive list of the circumstances in which a person will be entitled to income support. There is no category of analogous circumstances or provision for a reduced rate of benefit on the ground of hardship for people who do not come within these categories (compare the former reg.8(3), see the 1996 edition of *Mesher and Wood, Income-related Benefits: the Legislation*). Moreover, the provision for hardship payments under JSA is considerably restricted (see regs 140–146 (regs 146A to 146D in the case of joint-claim couples) of the JSA Regulations and the notes to those regulations). For the very limited provision for urgent cases outside the normal scope of the income support rules, see reg.70.

A further substantial contraction in the number of people covered by income support occurred on October 6, 2003 when the state pension credit scheme commenced. Claimants who have reached the qualifying age for state pension credit (defined in s.137(1) of the Contributions and Benefits Act—the effect of that definition is that the qualifying age is 60 for both men and women until April 2010 after which it will increase by stages to 65 in line with the increase in pensionable age for a woman) are no longer entitled to income support (see s.124(aa) of the Contributions and Benefits Act 1992). Such claimants now have to claim state pension credit. A claimant whose partner is *entitled* to state pension credit is also ineligible (s.124(g) of the 1992 Act). Thus claimants who are aged 59 or less themselves, but who have partners aged 60 or over, can still claim income support as long as their partners are not actually entitled to state pension credit. The result is that a couple with one member aged over 60 and the other aged under 60 (and who are not already in receipt of state pension credit) can choose to claim either income support or state pension credit (or JSA). It will normally be advantageous to claim state pension credit. For an overview of the state pension credit scheme see the Introduction and General Note at the beginning of the State Pension Credit Act 2002. As a consequence of the introduction of state pension credit para.17 of this Schedule (under which a claimant who had reached 60 was eligible for income support) has been revoked with effect from October 6, 2003.

Note also that the coverage of the income support scheme is likely to be further diminished by the removal of amounts for children and young persons from income support with effect from April 6, 2004 (except in "transitional cases"—see the note to reg.17). Financial assistance to help with the cost of bringing up a child or young person is now to be provided through the child tax credit system, see Vol. IV of this series.

Para.1

See reg.15 for responsibility for a child and reg.16 for membership of the household. Once a child turns into a young person (reg.14) or ceases to be a member of

2.551

the family (SSCBA, s.137(1)), a lone parent ceases to fall under para.1. *CIS 2260/2002* confirms that child in para.1 means a person under 16 and does not include a young person.

Note that the introduction of compulsory interviews for lone parents, with attendance a condition of entitlement to income support, which has been brought in in stages, now (since April 5, 2004) applies to all lone parents aged 18 or over and under 60 who are responsible for a child in their household. See the Social Security (Work-focused Interviews for Lone Parents) and Miscellaneous Amendments Regulations 2000 (SI 2000/1926) (as amended) in Vol. III of this series.

Note also the Social Security (Quarterly Work-focused Interviews for Certain Lone Parents) Regulations 2004 (SI 2004/2244) which provide for certain lone parents in the Extended Schools Childcare Pilot areas to attend mandatory work-focused interviews on a quarterly basis (see Vol III).

Para.2

2.552   Special provision is necessary for foster children because they are not members of the foster-parent's household (reg.16(4)).

Para.3

2.553   This covers a person who is looking after a child because his parent or the person who usually looks after him is ill or temporarily absent, or a member of the family (SSCBA, s.137(1)) who is temporarily ill.

See the note to reg.6(1)(b) on childminders.

In *CIS 866/2004* the claimant argued that she came within para.3(a) because her husband was unable to look after their young child due to his alcohol problems. The child had a long-term disability. However the Deputy Commissioner holds that for para.3(a) to apply either the parent of the child who usually looked after the child or some other person who usually looked after the child had to be ill or temporarily absent. In his view it was only if read in this way that the use of the term "the parent" in para.3(a) rather than "a parent" made sense. On the facts it was the claimant who usually looked after the child, not her husband. Furthermore, para.3(b) did not apply. This was because the child was not temporarily ill but had a long-term disability and the claimant was not looking after her husband. Since the husband could not claim because his application for asylum had been refused the consequence was that the claimant had no obvious means of state financial support other than child benefit.

Paras 4–6

2.554   There is no requirement that alternative arrangements cannot be made. Under para.4(a) the fact of being substantially and regularly engaged in providing care for someone who receives or has been awarded attendance allowance or one of the two higher care components of disability living allowance or who is waiting for a decision on entitlement is enough. In the last case, entitlement to income support under para.4(a) lasts for up to 26 weeks from the date of the claim for attendance/disability living allowance, or until it is decided, whichever is the earlier. For carer's allowance purposes "substantial" is 35 hours a week but *R(IS) 8/02* confirms that there is no such minimum requirement in order for para.4(a) to apply. Under para.4(a) it is simply a question of fact, having regard to the nature and amount of care provided, whether the claimant is "regularly and substantially engaged in caring". The Commissioner in *CSIS 1081/2001* also holds that care covers assistance or supervision arising out of the disabled person's needs and therefore will include domestic tasks that the person is unable to carry out themselves because of their disability, even if such tasks are not carried out in the person's presence. But it would not include travelling time to the person's home in order to provide the care as this is not in itself assistance to the disabled person. On the facts the claimant who went to her parents' home three times each weekday and provided care for 25–30 hours a week fell within para.4(a). It was irrelevant that she was also looking after her daughter (following a back injury) and her granddaughter.

Para.4(b) covers anyone entitled to and in receipt of carer's allowance (or who would be but for the application of a sanction under s.7 of the Social Security Fraud Act 2001 (see Vol. III in this series).

The effect of paras 5 and 6 is that the carer can qualify for income support in the eight weeks after ceasing to meet the conditions in para.4 (note the transitional provision in reg.27(1) of the Income Support (General) (Jobseeker's Allowance Consequential Amendments) Regulations 1996 (p.675)).

Para. 7

This covers people who are incapable of work. A person who is not capable of work will not be entitled to JSA (s.1(2)(f) of the Jobseekers Act). But note reg.55 of the JSA Regulations which allows a JSA award to continue while a person is incapable of work for up to two weeks (subject to a limit of two such periods in any 12 months). On the operation of reg.55, see *CIS 2107/1998* in the notes to reg.55 of the JSA Regulations.

The framework for deciding whether a person is capable or incapable of work is contained in Part XIIA of the Contributions and Benefits Act (ss.171A-G) but the detail is (as usual) in regulations, see in particular the Social Security (Incapacity for Work) (General) Regulations 1995 (SI 1995/311) in Vol. 1 of this series. See also reg.10 of the Social Security and Child Support (Decisions and Appeals) Regulations 1999 (conclusive effect of decision on capacity for work) in Vol. III. But note that reg.10 does not mean that a decision that a person is *not*, or is not to be treated as, incapable of work is of continuing effect. The decision will operate to allow supersession of an award of benefit current at the time it is made but does not operate so as to prevent a person from making a new claim or a further application for supersession. However, in such circumstances reg.28 of the 1995 Regulations (person treated as incapable of work until personal capability assessment (which has replaced the all work test from April 3, 2000) is carried out) may not apply.

Note also the additional ground for supersession in reg.6(2)(g) of the Decisions and Appeals Regulations where the decision is an "incapacity benefit decision where there has been an incapacity determination" (for the definitions of these terms see reg.7A of these regs). But it should be remembered that reg.6(1) provides that the Secretary of State *may* supersede a decision if the grounds are made out. Thus it would seem that this discretion should not be exercised if the medical evidence received by the Secretary of State is not sufficient to justify altering the decision. A new medical opinion is not itself a change of circumstances, although a report which contains new clinical findings or other evidence of an underlying change could be *(R(S) 4/86, R(IS) 2/98)*. In the case of a second or subsequent personal capability assessment where the claimant is contending that there has been no change in his condition, it may therefore still be necessary for a tribunal to see the previous medical advisers' reports in order to consider whether grounds for supersession exist. Moreover, the previous reports are generally available to the medical adviser conducting the examination (and, it seems, the decision-maker). Clearly a tribunal hearing an appeal should have the same information and evidence before it that was available to the person who made the decision under appeal. *CIB 2338/2000* has now held (see also *CIB 1972/2000*) that a tribunal has a duty to call for the previous personal capability assessment papers in cases where the claimant maintains that there has been no improvement since he passed the test on the prior occasion or that his condition is variable. See further Vol. I of this series.

Para.7 covers four categories: those who are incapable of work (sub-para.(a)); those who are treated as incapable of work under regulations made under s.171D of the Contributions and Benefits Act 1992 (see regs 10–15 and 27 of the Incapacity for Work Regulations) (sub-para.(b)); those who are treated as capable of work under regulations made under s.171E(1) of the 1992 Act (see reg.18 of the Incapacity for Work Regulations) (sub-para.(c)); and those who are entitled to statutory sick pay (sub-para.(d)).

2.555

There are two tests for assessing whether a person is incapable of work: the "own occupation test" and the "personal capability assessment" (which replaced the "all work test" from April 3, 2000). For full details of the tests for deciding incapacity for work and of the rules for treating a person as incapable or capable of work see vol. I of this series.

If para.7 does not apply, a decision-maker or tribunal should go on to consider para.8 (*CIS/137/1992, CIS/1997/2002, CIS/1657/2004*, to be reported as *R(IS) 10/05*). In *R(IS) 10/05* the claimant had been in receipt of income support on the ground of incapacity for work but then started working. The Deputy Commissioner points out that since it is possible for a claimant to be working at up to 75 per cent of the capacity of a person without disability and still fall within para.8, the evidential threshold required to raise the possible application of para.8 is relatively low. The fact that a claimant has been incapable of work for a significant period of time but is now working will normally be sufficient to require further investigation. Moreover, even if the issue is not raised by the claimant, it is incumbent upon the decision-maker on behalf of the Secretary of State in his inquisitorial role (see *Kerr v Department for Social Development* [2004] UKHL 23) to consider the claimant's possible alternative bases of entitlement to income support and to ask "the questions it needs to ask" (Baroness Hale at para.62 in *Kerr*). If this is not done it will for the tribunal in exercise of its inquisitorial jurisdiction to consider any such possible alternatives. The Deputy Commissioner rejected the Secretary of State's submission that the tribunal had not erred in failing to consider para.8 because the issue had not been raised by the claimant (see s.12(8)(a) of the Social Security Act 1998). Section 12(8)(a) gave the tribunal a discretion not to consider issues which were not raised by the parties but the decision under appeal was that the claimant was not entitled to income support (*i.e.* that she did not come within any of the prescribed categories) and so the possibility that the claimant might fall within para.8 was inherent in the decision itself.

See also paras 24–27 which apply to claimants who are appealing against a decision that they are capable of work.

Para. 8

2.556
This paragraph covers a person to whom reg.6(4)(a) (person not treated as engaged in remunerative work) applies. Previous editions of this volume suggested that because the wording of this paragraph refers to a "person", it could apply to a claimant who was not actually working but who satisfied the conditions of reg.6(4)(a) (*i.e.* he was not incapable of work but his earnings and hours of work were less (*i.e.* nil) because of his mental or physical disability). However, this suggestion has not found favour with the Commissioners. In *CIS/1657/2004*, to be reported as *R(IS) 10/05*, the Deputy Commissioner follows *CIS/15/1997* and *CIS/1997/2002* in holding that reg.6(4)(a) only applies to a claimant in weeks that he is working.

In *R(IS) 10/05* the Commissioner goes on to point out that there is no definition of what amounts to a mental or physical disability for the purposes of reg.6(4)(a), so whether or not the claimant is mentally or physically disabled will be a question of fact. He adds that there is no requirement that the disability should be severe or evidenced by receipt of a disability benefit. Moreover, by its very nature reg.6(4)(a) only applies to those whose disabilities do not prevent them from working; it is in fact possible for a person still to fall within para.8 if they are working at up to 75 per cent of the capacity of a person without disability. The Deputy Commissioner considered that in deciding whether reg.6(4)(a) applied, a tribunal would need to make findings on the nature of the disability, the hours of work/earnings of the claimant, and the hours/earnings that a claimant without his disability would reasonably expect to work/earn in that employment or comparable employment in the area in order to make the necessary comparison.

R(IS) 10/05 also emphasises that if para.7 does not apply (or no longer applies) because a claimant is doing some work, para.8 should always be considered (see further the note to para.7 above).

Para. 9

See the notes to reg.6(4)(d).

2.557

Para. 9A

See the notes to reg.6(5) to (8).

2.558

Paras 10–12

These paragraphs cover full-time students (defined in reg.61) who contrary to the normal rule can claim income support (see reg.4ZA(2) and (3)). Para.10 applies to a full-time student who qualifies for the disability or severe disability premium (sub-para.(a)) or who has been incapable of work for at least 28 weeks (sub-para.(b)). Two or more periods of incapacity count as one continuous period unless there is a break of more than eight weeks. For the purposes of para.10 note the transitional provision in reg.27(2) of the Income Support (General) (Jobseeker's Allowance Consequential Amendments) Regulations 1996 (p. 675).

2.559

Para.11 continues to protect disabled full-time students who no longer fell under para.7 of the former Sch.1 following its amendment on September 1, 1990. See *CIS 276/1989* on the pre-September 1990 form of para.7, which held that in asking whether the student was unlikely to obtain employment within a reasonable period of time, the period started with the date of claim, not with the end of the course.

Para.12 applies to full-time students who are within the definition of "deaf" for one of the various grant purposes.

Para. 13

Only those registered as blind with the local authority can use this paragraph and the 28 weeks' period of grace on regaining sight. But other categories may be available for the unregistered.

2.560

Para. 14

Sub-para.(a) covers a person who is incapable of work because of pregnancy and sub-para.(b) applies for the 11 weeks before the baby is due and the seven weeks after the pregnancy ends in a case where the expected week of confinement starts before April 6, 2003, or the fifteen weeks thereafter if the expected week of confinement begins on or after that date. In *CIS 542/2001* the issue was the relationship, if any, between sub-para.(a) and para.7. Para.7 covers, *inter alia*, a person who is incapable of work or treated as incapable of work in accordance with Part XIIA SSCBA 1992 or regulations made thereunder. Those regulations include reg.14 of the Incapacity for Work (General) Regulations 1995, the effect of which is that a pregnant woman is to be treated as incapable of work during any period when, because of her pregnancy, there is a serious risk to her health or that of the unborn child if she continues to work. Sub-para.(a), on the other hand, simply requires the woman to be incapable of work due to her pregnancy. The Secretary of State argued that sub-para.(a) had to be read as incorporating the stricter test in reg.14(a). The Commissioner, however, holds that sub-para.(a) stands alone. In his view, if it had been intended that sub-para.(a) was to incorporate the reg.14(a) test, this could have been expressly stated. Furthermore, the provision in para.14 had been included in the Income Support Regulations since they first came into force in 1987 (it had formerly appeared as para.9 of Sch.1). This was several years before the introduction of incapacity benefit and thus supported the conclusion that sub-para.(a) was freestanding and not dependent on any other provision dealing with incapacity. The Secretary of State had relied on s.171A(1) SSCBA 1992 which provides that whether a person is capable or incapable of work is to be determined in accordance with Part XIIA of the Act (thus including reg.14(a)). In the Commissioner's opinion, however, s.171A(1) had to be read subject to the later provisions of the Jobseekers Act 1995 and associated regulations (including s.124(1)(e) SSCBA, inserted by the 1995 Act, which provides that a person is entitled to income support if they fall into

2.561

a prescribed category, and section 40 of the 1995 Act which authorises the making of transitional, consequential and saving provisions). The result is that sub-para.(a) applies to any woman who is incapable of work by reason of pregnancy.

Para.14A

2.562   This covers a member of a couple who is on unpaid parental leave to care for a child who is a member of his household (lone parents are already eligible for income support, as are couples where one member is ill or temporarily absent, see paras 1, 3, and 23). The right to claim parental leave came into effect on December 15, 1999 (for details see the Maternity and Parental Leave etc. Regulations 1999 (SI 1999/3312)). To come within para.14A the person must have been entitled to working tax credit, child tax credit (CTC) payable at a rate higher than the family element (at April 2003 rates (not increased in April 2004 or April 2005) this is £1,090 where any child for whom CTC is payable is under one year old and £545 in any other case), housing benefit or council tax benefit immediately before the leave began. Note also that the claimant must not be getting any kind of payment from his employer during the parental leave (sub-para.(1)(a) and (2)).

Para.14B

2.563   This applies to a person who is entitled to and is on paternity leave and who (i) is not entitled to statutory paternity pay or any other pay from his employer in respect of the paternity leave *or* (ii) was entitled to working tax credit, child tax credit (CTC) payable at a rate higher than the family element (at April 2003 rates (not increased in April 2004 or April 2005) this is £1,090 where any child for whom CTC is payable is under one year old and £545 in any other case), housing benefit or council tax benefit immediately before the paternity leave began. The new rights to paternity leave and adoption leave introduced by the Employment Act 2002 apply where the expected week of confinement or birth is on or after April 6, 2003 (in the case of adoption leave and paternity leave for adopters this applies where a child is either matched or placed for adoption on or after April 6, 2003 (Paternity and Adoption Leave Regulations 2002 (SI 2002/2788, reg.3)).

Para.15

2.564   Since October 7, 1996 the lower age limit for income support is now 16 in all cases (SSCBA s.124(1)(a)). However, the exclusion for 16–18 year olds who are receiving relevant education remains, except for those who fall within reg.13(2). This paragraph enables young people covered by reg.13(2)(a)–(e) to claim income support; a young person to whom reg.13(2)(h) applies will be eligible under para.18. See the notes to reg.13 for the circumstances in which reg.13(2) applies.

Para.16

2.565   Para.13 of the former Sch.1 covered people aged not less than 50 who had not been in remunerative work for 10 years, had been exempt from the reqirement to be available during that time (or who would have been exempt had a claim for income support been made, see *CIS 613/1995* below), and had no prospect of future employment. The provision is not repeated in Sch.1B, but under para.16 a person who was in receipt of income support and satisfied the former para.13 on October 6, 1996, or at any time in the previous eight weeks, will be entitled to income support (note the linking rule in sub-para.(2)). Thus a person who only falls into this category after October 6, 1996 will not qualify for income support on that ground.

Para.13 applied if the person had been exempt from the requirement to be available for 10 years or would have been so exempt "had a claim for income support been made by or in respect of him". In *CIS 613/1995* the Commissioner decides that "in respect of him" referred to where a claim could have been made by the claimant's husband in respect of her. In that case he would have had to satisfy the conditions of entitlement. As his partner she would not have been required to be available for work. Accordingly the claimant satisfied para.13.

In *R(SB) 5/87* it was suggested that to have no prospect of future employment, a person has to have no realistic prospects of securing employment in his working life. It is not necessary to show that the person's prospects are nil, but the test is still strict and merely poor prospects will not do.

Para. 16A

As part of the new system of bereavement benefits that came into effect on April 9, 2001 (see Vol. I of this series), for a transitional five year period new widows and widowers who were aged between 55 and 60 on April 9, 2001 will be entitled to claim income support. This applies if their spouse died on or after April 9, 2001 and they remain single. Para.16A will cease to have effect on April 10, 2006 (see reg.6 of the amending regulations). In addition note the new bereavement premium for such widows and widowers (see para.8A of Sch.2; this premium also applies for JSA—see para.9A of Sch.1 to the JSA Regulations).

A £10 disregard of any widowed mother's or widowed parent's allowance was also introduced on April 9, 2001 (see para.16(g) and (h) of Sch.9 and para.17(d) and (e) of Sch.7 to the JSA Regulations).

2.566

Para. 22

A person required to live in a bail hostel is not "detained in custody" (*R(IS) 17/93*; note the effect of Sch.7, para.9, if a person in a bail hostel is a member of a couple). However, once a person has been charged, he is detained in custody pending trial, even if subsequently no trial takes place (*R(IS) 1/94*). See the notes to "prisoner" in reg.21(3). The definition of prisoner was amended from April 10, 1995 to reverse the effect of *Chief Adjudication Officer v Carr* (reported as *R(IS) 20/95*) which held that a person serving a prison sentence was not "in custody" while on home leave.

2.567

Para. 23

Someone in this situation could not come within para.1 because they would not be a lone parent while the absence of the partner was only temporary, but clearly deserves the same treatment in these circumstances.

2.568

Paras 24–27

There was no equivalent of these paragraphs in the former Sch.1.

Paras 24 and 25 replace the provisions formerly in reg.8(2) and (2A) (revoked on October 7, 1996) and cover those who are appealing against a decision that they are capable of work under the "own occupation test" (para.24) or the "personal capability assessment" (which has replaced the "all work test" from April 3, 2000) (para.25). See Vol. I of this series for full details of these tests and when they apply.

Reg.8(2) had been amended and reg.8(2A) had been introduced on April 13, 1995 as a consequence of the introduction of the new tests for incapacity for work. There was transitional protection for claimants who were pursuing an incapacity appeal and to whom the previous form of reg.8(2) applied on April 12, 1995 and for those who appealed against a decision on incapacity made on or before April 12, 1995. In those cases the old form of reg.8 continued to apply (reg.20(1) and (3) of the Disability Working Allowance and Income Support (General) Amendment Regulations 1995 (see p.670)). Para.26 covers such a person to whom the pre-April 13, 1995 form of reg.8(2) still applied on October 6, 1996. He was eligible for income support (without reduction) pending the determination of his incapacity appeal. See below for when an appeal is determined.

Para.27 provides the same result for a person to whom the pre-April 13, 1995 form of reg.11(2) still applied on October 6, 1996. See the 1996 edition of *Mesher and Wood, Income-related Benefits: the Legislation,* for reg.11 which was revoked on October 7, 1996.

Under para.24, if the claimant's own doctor continues to certify that he is incapable of work while he is pursuing an appeal against the incapacity decision, he will be eligible for income support pending the determination of the appeal. This means the final determination of the appeal, *e.g.* if it is taken to the Social Security

2.569

Commissioner, confirmed in *CIS 2654/1999*. The person does not have to have been in receipt of income support before the incapacity decision was made. If para.24 applies full income support is payable (compare para.25).

If the claimant is appealing against capacity for work on the basis of the personal capability assessment, there is no requirement under para.25 for him to continue to submit medical certificates from his own doctor. This is because they are no longer required once the personal capability assessment has been applied. Again it is not necessary for the person to have been in receipt of income support before the incapacity decision was made. But if para.25 applies, the claimant's income support is reduced by 20 per cent of the appropriate personal allowance for a single claimant of his age until the appeal is determined (reg.22A), unless he is appealing after failing his first all work test or personal capability assessment and immediately before April 13, 1995 he had been incapable of work for 28 weeks or in receipt of invalidity benefit or severe disablement allowance (reg.22A(3); and see the transitional protection in reg.27(3) of the Income Support (General) (Jobseeker's Allowance Consequential Amendments) Regulations 1996 referred to in the note to reg.22A(3)). (If the appeal is successful, the reduction will be repaid.) See above for when an appeal is determined.

In order to receive full benefit, a claimant who is appealing against a failure to satisfy the personal capability assessment will have to sign on as available for work and claim JSA (unless any of the other paragraphs of Sch.1B apply). This could place the claimant in a dilemma if he is maintaining that he is unable to work. The best course may be for him to say to the Job Centre that he has been found capable of work and that he will accept any suitable work having regard to his limitations (see reg.13(3) of the JSA Regulations). However, the fact that he has claimed JSA will not prejudice the appeal about incapacity as it will postdate the decision under appeal (s.12(8)(a) SSA 1998).

It will be noted that both para.24 and para.25 refer to a person who "has made and is pursuing an appeal" against an incapacity decision. There will usually be a gap between the date that the incapacity decision takes effect and the date the appeal is lodged. Can para.24 or 25 apply during this gap? According to the Commissioner in *CIS 2075/2002* the legislation implies that benefit will be paid in respect of the period between such a decision being given and an appeal being brought, at least if the appeal is not late or is admitted despite its lateness (and moreover this also applied where an appeal had been rejected as not duly made but was later reinstated as had occurred in the case before him). He therefore agreed with the Secretary of State that the claimant had remained entitled to income support ever since the decision was made that he was not incapable of work. However, the difficulty was the procedural hurdles created by the Social Security Act 1998 and the Decisions and Appeals Regulations 1999. The question was, if lodging an appeal or having one reinstated retrospectively did affect entitlement to income support, what was the ground for backdating an income support claim or for revision or supersession and from what date was the supersession, if supersession was appropriate, effective? The Commissioner found a solution to this dilemma on the facts of the case before him but suggested that amendments to the Decisions and Appeals Regulations may be needed to adequately cater for decision-making under paras 24 to 27.

However, in *CIS/1614/2004*, to be reported as *R(IS)2/05*, the Commissioner disagreed with *CIS/2057/2002* as in his view the legislation contained no such implication. He held that there was no entitlement to income support under para.25 in the period between the date of the decision that supersedes the award of benefit on the ground that the person is not incapable of work and the date of the appeal against that decision. On the Commissioner's reasoning the same would apply in relation to para.24.

The problems highlighted by these decisions have lead to the amendment made to para.25 with effect from March 18, 2005. This provides that para.25 applies from the date that the determination that the claimant is not incapable of work takes effect. Associated amendments have also been made to the Decisions and Appeals Regulations 1999 (see Vol.III of this series). Two new provisions have been introduced into reg.3 of those regulations: reg.3(7C) which allows for revision of a decision to terminate income support entitlement where that entitlement was ended because the claimant was found capable of work and he appeals that decision; and reg.3(7B) which provides that where the appeal against the incapacity decision is successful the decision to award reduced rate income support under reg.22A can be revised (in practice this has happened and the reduction has been repaid even in the absence of such an express provision). In addition a new reg.6(2)(n) deals with the situation where income support has been disallowed as a result of the incapacity decision and the claimant appeals against that disallowance (as well as the incapacity decision). In the past, if the appeal against the income support disallowance was heard before the appeal against the incapacity decision (and assuming that the claimant did not qualify for income support on any other ground), the tribunal would (unless it adjourned that appeal pending the outcome of the incapacity appeal) be bound to uphold the disallowance decision. If the incapacity appeal subsequently succeeded, there was no provision that enabled the first tribunal's decision upholding the income support disallowance to be revised. However, reg.6(2)(n) of the 1999 Regulations now provides for supersession of the first tribunal's decision in these circumstances; in addition a new reg.7(34) provides that such a supersession takes effect from the date that income support was terminated as a result of the decision that the person was not incapable of work.

Para. 28

2.570

Para.11 of the former Sch.1 applied to a person in receipt of a training allowance. Para.28 only covers a person under 24 who is undergoing Work Based Learning for Young People. However, under reg.170 of the JSA Regulations a person in receipt of a training allowance (in respect of training *other* than that covered by para.28) may qualify for income-based JSA without having to be available for, or actively seek, employment or enter into a jobseeker's agreement.

SCHEDULE 2 **Regulations 17 [³ (1)] and 18**

Applicable Amounts

[³⁵Part I

Personal Allowances

2.571

1. The weekly amounts specified in column (2) below in respect of each person or couple specified in column (1) shall be the weekly amounts specified for the purposes of regulations 17(1) and 18(1) (applicable amounts and polygamous marriages).

Column (1)	Column (2)
Person or Couple	*Amount*
(1) Single claimant aged—	
(a) except where head (b) or (c) of this sub-paragraph applies, less than 18;	(1)(a) [⁶²£33.85];
[²⁸(b) less than 18 who falls within any of the circumstances specified in paragraph 1A;]	(b) [⁶²£44.50];
(c) less than 18 who satisfies the condition in paragraph 11(a);	(c) [⁶²£44.50];
(d) not less than 18 but less than 25;	(d) [⁶²£44.50];
(e) not less than 25.	(e) [⁶⁰£56.20];

Column (1)	Column (2)
Person or Couple	*Amount*
(2) Lone parent aged—	(2)
(a) except where head (b) or (c) of this sub-paragraph applies, less than 18;	(a) [62£33.85];
[28(b) less than 18 who falls within any of the circumstances specified in paragraph 1A;]	(b) [62£44.50];
(c) less than 18 who satisfies the condition in paragraph 11(a);	(c) [62£44.50];
(d) not less than 18.	(d) [62£56.20];
[28(3) Couple—	(3)
(a) where both members are aged less than 18 and—	(a)[62£67.15];
(i) at least one of them is treated as responsible for a child; or	
(ii) had they not been members of a couple, each would have qualified for income support under regulation 4ZA; or	
(iii) the claimant's partner satisfies the requirement of section 3(1)(f)(iii) of the Jobseekers Act 1995 (prescribed circumstances for persons aged 16 but less than 18); or	
(iv) there is in force in respect of the claimant's partner a direction under section 16 of the Jobseekers Act 1995 (persons under 18: severe hardship);	
(b) where both members are aged less than 18 and head (a) does not apply but one member of the couple falls within any of the circumstances specified in paragraph 1A;	(b) [62£44.50];
(c) where both members are aged less than 18 and heads (a) and (b) do not apply;	(c) [62£33.85];
(d) where both members are aged not less than 18;	(d) [62£88.15];
(e) where one member is aged not less than 18 and the other member is a person under 18 who—	(e) [62£88.15]
(i) qualifies for income support under regulation 4ZA, or who would so qualify if he were not a member of a couple; or	
(ii) satisfies the requirements of section 3(1)(f)(iii) of the Jobseekers Act 1995 (prescribed circumstances for persons aged 16 but less than 18); or	
(iii) is the subject of a direction under section 16 of the Jobseekers Act 1995 (persons under 18: severe hardship);	
(f) where the claimant is aged not less than 18 but less than 25 and his partner is a person under 18 who—	(f) [62£44.50];
(i) would not qualify for income support under regulation 4ZA if he were not a member of a couple; and	
(ii) does not satisfy the requirements of section 3(1)(f)(iii) of the Jobseekers Act 1995 (prescribed circumstances for persons aged 16 but less than 18); and	
(iii) is not the subject of a direction under section 16 of the Jobseekers Act 1995 (persons under 18: severe hardship);	
(g) where the claimant is aged not less than 25 and his partner is a person under 18 who—	(g) [62£56.20];
(i) would not qualify for income support under regulation 4ZA if he were not a member of a couple; and	
(ii) does not satisfy the requirements of section 3(1)(f)(iii) of the Jobseekers Act 1995 (prescribed circumstances for persons aged 16 but less than 18); and	
(iii) is not the subject of a direction under section 16 of the Jobseekers Act 1995 (persons under 18: severe hardship).]]	

[²⁸ **1A.**—(1) The circumstances referred to in paragraph 1 are that—
  (a) the person has no parents nor any person acting in the place of his parents;
  (b) the person—
    (i)   is not living with his parents nor any person acting in the place of his parents; and
    (ii) in England and Wales, was being looked after by a local authority pursuant to a relevant enactment who placed him with some person other than a close relative of his; or in Scotland, was in the care of a local authority under a relevant enactment and whilst in that care was not living with his parents or any close relative, or was in custody in any institution to which the Prison Act 1952 or the Prisons (Scotland) Act 1989 applied immediately before he attained the age of 16;
  (c) the person is in accommodation which is other than his parental home, and which is other than the home of a person acting in the place of his parents, who entered that accommodation—
    (i)   as part of a programme of rehabilitation or resettlement, that programme being under the supervision of the probation service or a local authority; or
    (ii) in order to avoid physical or sexual abuse; or
    (iii) because of a mental or physical handicap or illness and needs such accommodation because of his handicap or illness;
  (d) the person is living away from his parents and any person who is acting in the place of his parents in a case where his parents are or, as the case may be, that person is, unable financially to support him and his parents are, or that person is—
    (i)   chronically sick or mentally or physically disabled; or
    (ii) detained in custody pending trial or sentence upon conviction or under sentence imposed by a court; of
    (iii) prohibited from entering or re-entering Great Britain; or
  (e) the person of necessity has to live away from his parents and any person acting in the place of his parents because—
    (i)   he is estranged from his parents and that person; or
    (ii) he is in physical or moral danger; or
    (iii) there is a serious risk to his physical or mental health.
(2) In this paragraph—
  (a) "chronically sick or mentally or physically disabled" has the same meaning it has in regulation 13(3)(b) (circumstances in which persons in relevant education are to be entitled to income support);
  (b) in England and Wales, any reference to a person acting in place of a person's parents includes a reference to—
    (i)   where the person is being looked after by a local authority or voluntary organisation who place him with a family, a relative of his, or some other suitable person, the person with whom the person is placed, whether or not any payment is made to him in connection with the placement; or
    (ii) in any other case, any person with parental responsibility for the child, and for this purpose "parental responsibility" has the meaning it has in the Children Act 1989 by virtue of section 3 of that Act;
  (c) in Scotland, any reference to a person acting in place of a person's parents includes a reference to a local authority or voluntary organisation where the person is in their care under a relevant enactment, or to a person with whom the person is boarded out by a local authority or voluntary organisation whether or not any payment is made by them.]
[³⁵ **2.** [⁵⁹ . . .]]
[¹⁷ **2A.** [⁵⁵ . . .]]

Family Premium

2.572   **3.** [^{59} . . .]

Premiums

2.573   **4.** Except as provided in paragraph 5, the weekly premiums specified in Part IV of this Schedule shall, for the purposes of regulations 17[^{3}(1)](d)[^{3} and 18(1)](e), be applicable to a claimant who satisfies the condition specified in [^{42}paragraphs 8A] [^{10} to 14ZA] in respect of that premium.

    5. Subject to paragraph 6, where a claimant satisfies the conditions in respect of more than one premium in this Part of this Schedule, only one premium shall be applicable to him and, if they are different amounts, the higher or highest amount shall apply.

    [^{58} **6.**—(1) Subject to sub-paragraph (2), the following premiums, namely—

      (a)   a severe disability to which paragraph 13 applies;
      (b)   an enhanced disability premium to which paragraph 13A applies;
      (c)   [^{59} . . .]; and
      (d)   a carer premium to which paragraph 14ZA applies,

may be applicable in addition to any other premium that may apply under this Schedule.

    (2) An enhanced disability premium in respect of a person shall not be applicable in addition to—

      (a)   a pensioner premium under paragraph 9 or 9A; or
      (b)   a higher pension premium under paragraph 10.]

    7.—[^{10}(1) Subject to sub-paragraph (2)] for the purposes of this Part of this Schedule, once a premium is applicable to a claimant under this Part, a person shall be treated as being in receipt of any benefit—

      (a)   in the case of a benefit to which the Social Security (Overlapping Benefits) Regulations 1979 applies, for any period during which, apart from the provisions of those Regulations, he would be in receipt of that benefit; and
      (b)   for any period spent by a claimant in undertaking a course of training or instruction provided or approved by the [^{12}Secretary of State for Employment] under section 2 of the Employment and Training Act 1973 [^{11}, or by Scottish Enterprise or Highlands and Islands Enterprise under section 2 of the Enterprise and New Towns (Scotland) Act 1990,] [^{7}or for any period during which he is in receipt of a training allowance].

    [^{10}(2) For the purposes of the carer premium under paragraph 14ZA, a person shall be treated as being in receipt of [^{49} carer's allowance] by virtue of sub-paragraph (1)(a) only if and for so long as the person in respect of whose care the allowance has been claimed remains in receipt of attendance allowance[^{15}, or the care component of disability living allowance at the highest or middle rate prescribed in accordance with section 37ZB(3) of the Social Security Act [SSCBA, s.72(3)]].]

Lone Parent Premium
    8. [^{29} . . .].

2.574   [^{42} **Bereavement Premium**

    8A.—(1) Subject to sub-paragraphs (2) and (3), the condition is that the claimant—

      (a)   had, as at 9th April 2001, attained the age of 55 but not the age of 60;
      (b)   was in receipt of, but is no longer entitled to, a bereavement allowance under section 39B of the Contributions and Benefits Act in respect of the death of a spouse who died on or after 9th April 2001; and
      (c)   is claiming income support as a single claimant.

    (2) A premium under sub-paragraph (1) shall not be applicable in respect of a claimant who claims income support more than 8 weeks after the last day on which he was entitled to a bereavement allowance.

    (3) Where a claimant to whom a premium under sub-paragraph (1) is applicable, ceases to be entitled to income support or to be a single claimant, a premium under subparagraph (1) shall only again be applicable to that claimant where he claims income support as a single

claimant no more than 8 weeks after the date on which he ceased to be entitled to income support or to an income-based jobseeker's allowance or, as the case may be, to be a single claimant.]

[Pensioner premium for persons under 75
[⁵⁴ **9.** The condition is that the claimant has a partner aged not less than 60 but less than 75.]

Pensioner premium for persons 75 and over
[⁵⁴ **9A.** The condition is that the claimant has a partner aged not less than 75 but less than 80.]]

Higher Pensioner Premium
10.—[⁵⁴ (1) The condition is that—   2.575
  (a) the claimant's partner is aged not less than 80; or
  (b) the claimant's partner is aged less than 80 but not less than 60 and either—
      (i) the additional condition specified in [⁵⁸ paragraph 12(1)(a), (c) or (d)] is satisfied; or
     (ii) the claimant was entitled to, or was treated as being in receipt of, income support and—
          (aa) the disability premium was or, as the case may be, would have been, applicable to him in respect of a benefit week within eight weeks of his partner's 60th birthday; and
          (bb) he has, subject to sub-paragraph (3), remained continuously entitled to income support since his partner attained the age of 60.
(2) . . .]
(3) For the purposes of this paragraph and paragraph 12—
  (a) once the higher pensioner premium is applicable to a claimant, if he then ceases, for a period of eight weeks or less, to be entitled to [⁴¹or treated as entitled to] income support, he shall, on becoming re-entitled to income support, thereafter be treated as having been continuously entitled thereto;
  (b) in so far as [⁵⁴ sub-paragraph (1)(b)(ii) is] concerned, if a claimant ceases to be entitled to [⁴¹or treated as entitled to] income support for a period not exceeding eight weeks which includes his [⁵⁴ partner's] 60th birthday, he shall, on becoming re-entitled to income support, thereafter be treated as having been continuously entitled thereto.
[³³(4) In the case of a claimant who is a welfare to work beneficiary, references in sub-paragraphs (1)(b)(ii), (2)(b)(ii) and (3)(b) to a period of 8 weeks shall be treated as references to a period of 52 weeks.]
[⁴¹ (5) For the purposes of this paragraph, a claimant shall be treated as having been entitled to and in receipt of income support throughout any period which comprises only days on which he was participating in an employment zone programme and was not entitled to income support because, as a consequence of his participation in that programme, he was engaged in remunerative work or had income in excess of his applicable amount as prescribed in Part IV.]

Disability Premium
11. The condition is that—   2.576
  (a) where the claimant is a single claimant or a lone parent, [⁵⁴ . . .] the additional condition specified in paragraph 12 is satisfied; or
  (b) where the claimant has a partner, either—
      [⁵⁴ (i) the claimant satisfies the additional condition specified in paragraph [⁵⁸ 12(1)(a), (b), (c) or (d)]; or]
      (ii) his partner is aged less than 60 and the additional condition specified in [⁵⁸ paragraph 12(1)(a), (c) or (d)] is satisfied by his partner.

Additional condition for the Higher Pensioner and Disability Premiums
12.—(1) Subject to sub-paragraph (2) and paragraph 7 the additional condition referred to   2.577
in paragraphs 10 and 11 is that either—
  (a) the claimant or, as the case may be, his partner—
      (i) is in receipt of one or more of the following benefits: attendance allowance, [¹⁵disability living allowance, [⁵⁰ the disability element or the severe disability element of working tax credit as specified in regulation 20(1)(b) and (f) of the Working Tax Credit (Entitlement and Maximum Rate) Regulations 2002], mobility supplement, [²⁵long-term incapacity benefit] under [²²Part II of the Contributions and Benefits Act or severe disablement allowance under Part III of that Act] [¹but, in the case of [²⁵long-term incapacity benefit] or severe disablement allowance only where it is paid in respect of him]; or

(ii) is provided by the Secretary of State with an invalid carriage or other vehicle under section 5(2) of the National Health Service Act 1977 (other services) or, in Scotland, under section 46 of the National Health Service (Scotland) Act 1978 (provision of vehicles) or receives payments by way of grant from the Secretary of State under paragraph 2 of Schedule 2 to that 1977 Act (additional provisions as to vehicles) or, in Scotland, under that section 46; or

(iii) is registered as blind in a register compiled by a local authority under section 29 of the National Assistance Act 1948 (welfare services) or, in Scotland, has been certified as blind and in consequence he is registered as blind in a register maintained by or on behalf of a regional or islands council; or

[^{26}(b) the claimant—

(i) is entitled to statutory sick pay or [^{27}is, or is treated as, incapable of work,] in accordance with the provisions of Part XIIA of the Contributions and Benefits Act and the regulations made thereunder (incapacity for work), and

(ii) has been so entitled or so incapable [^{27}, or has been treated as so incapable,] for a continuous period of not less than—

(aa) 196 days in the case of a claimant who is terminally ill within the meaning of section 30B(4) of the Contributions and Benefits Act; or

(bb) 364 days in any other case; and for these purposes any two or more periods of entitlement or incapacity separated by a break of not more than 56 days shall be treated as one continuous period; or]

[^{54} (c) the claimant's partner was in receipt of long-term incapacity benefit under Part II of the Contributions and Benefits Act when entitlement to that benefit ceased on account of the payment of a retirement pension under that Act and—

(i) the claimant has since remained continuously entitled to income support;

(ii) the higher pensioner premium or disability premium has been applicable to the claimant; and

(iii) the partner is still alive;

(d) except where paragraph (1)(a), (b), (c)(ii) or (d)(ii) of Schedule 7 (patients) applies, the claimant or, as the case may be, his partner was in receipt of attendance allowance or disability living allowance—

(i) but payment of that benefit has been suspended under the [^{60} Social Security (Attendance Allowance) Regulations 1991 or the Social Security (Disability Living Allowance) Regulations 1991] or otherwise abated as a consequence of the claimant or his partner becoming a patient within the meaning of regulation 21(3); and

(ii) a higher pensioner premium or disability premium has been applicable to the claimant.]

[^{34}(1A) In the case of a claimant who is a welfare to work beneficiary, the reference in sub-paragraph (1)(b) to a period of 56 days shall be treated as a reference to a period of 52 weeks.]

(2) For the purposes of sub-paragraph (1)(a)(iii), a person who has ceased to be registered as blind on regaining his eyesight shall nevertheless be treated as blind and as satisfying the additional condition set out in that sub-paragraph for a period of 28 weeks following the date on which he ceased to be so registered.

(3) [^{26}. . .]

(4) For the purpose of [^{58} sub-paragraph (1)(c) and (d)], once the higher pensioner premium is applicable to the claimant by virtue of his satisfying the condition specified in that provision, if he then ceases, for a period of eight weeks or less, to be entitled to income support, he shall on again becoming so entitled to income support, immediately thereafter be treated as satisfying the condition in [^{58} sub-paragraph (1)(c) and (d)].

[^{4}(5) For the purposes of sub-paragraph (1)(b), once the disability premium is applicable to a claimant by virtue of his satisfying the additional condition specified in that provision, he shall continue to be treated as satisfying that condition for any period spent by him in undertaking a course of training provided under section 2 of the Employment and Training Act 1973 [^{7}or for any period during which he is in receipt of a training allowance].]

[^{25}(6) For the purposes of [^{58} sub-paragraph (1)(a)(i) and (c)], a reference to a person in receipt of long-term incapacity benefit includes a person in receipt of short-term incapacity benefit at a rate equal to the long-term rate by virtue of section 30B(4)(a) of the Contributions and Benefits Act (short-term incapacity benefit for a person who is terminally ill), or who would be or would have been in receipt of short-term incapacity benefit at such a rate but for the fact that the rate of short-term incapacity benefit already payable to him is or was equal to or greater than the long-term rate.]

[^{40} [^{61} . . .]]

Severe Disability Premium

13.—(1) The condition is that the claimant is a severely disabled person.   2.578

(2) For the purposes of sub-paragraph (1), a claimant shall be treated as being a severely disabled person if, and only if—

    (a) in the case of a single claimant[[19], a lone parent or a claimant who is treated as having no partner in consequence of sub-paragraph (2A)]—

        (i) he is in receipt of attendance allowance [[15]or the care component of disability living allowance at the highest or middle rate prescribed in accordance with section 37ZB(3) of the Social Security Act [SSCBA, s.72(3)]], and

       (ii) subject to sub-paragraph (3), he has no non-dependants aged 18 or over [[23]normally residing with him or with whom he is normally residing,] and

      (iii) [[41]no person is entitled to, and in receipt of, [[49] a carer's allowance] under section 70 of the Contributions and Benefits Act in respect of caring for him;]

    (b) [[42] in the case of a claimant who] has a partner—

        (i) he is in receipt of attendance allowance [[15], or the care component of disability living allowance at the highest or middle rate prescribed in accordance with section 37ZB(3) of the Social Security Act [SSCBA, s.72(3)]]; and

       (ii) his partner is also in receipt of such an allowance or, if he is a member of a polygamous marriage, all the partners of that marriage are in receipt thereof; and

      (iii) subject to sub-paragraph (3), he has no non-dependants aged 18 or over [[23]normally residing with him or with whom he is normally residing,]

and either [[41]a person is entitled to, and in receipt of, [[49] a carer's allowance] in respect of caring for only one of the couple or, in the case of a polygamous marriage, for one or more but not all the partners of the marriage or, as the case may be, no person is entitled to, and in receipt of, such an allowance] in respect of caring for either member of the couple or any partner of the polygamous marriage.

[[19](2A) Where a claimant has a partner who does not satisfy the condition in sub-paragraph (2)(b)(ii), and that partner is blind or is treated as blind within the meaning of paragraph 12(1)(a)(iii) and (2), that partner shall be treated for the purposes of sub-paragraph (2) as if he were not a partner of the claimant.]

(3) For the purposes of sub-paragraph (2)(a)(ii) and (2)(b)(iii) no account shall be taken of—

    (a) a person receiving attendance allowance [[15], or the care component of disability living allowance at the highest or middle rate prescribed in accordance with section 37ZB(3) of the Social Security Act [SSCBA, s.72(3)]]; or

    (b) [[21]...]

    (c) subject to sub-paragraph (4), a person who joins the claimant's household for the first time in order to care for the claimant or his partner and immediately before so joining the claimant or his partner was treated as a severely disabled person; [[19] or

    (d) a person who is blind or is treated as blind within the meaning of paragraph 12(1)(a)(iii) and (2).]

[[1](3A) For the purposes of sub-paragraph (2)(b) a person shall be treated [[41]...]

    (a) [[41] as being in receipt of] attendance allowance[[15], or the care component of disability living allowance at the highest or middle rate prescribed in accordance with section 37ZB(3) of the Social Security Act [SSCBA, s.72(3)]] if he would, but for his being a patient for a period exceeding 28 days, be so in receipt;

    (b) [[41] as being entitled to and in receipt of [[49] a carer's allowance] if he would, but for the person for whom he was caring being a patient in hospital for a period exceeding 28 days, be so entitled and in receipt.]]

[[22](3ZA) For the purposes of sub-paragraph (2)(a)(iii) and (2)(b), no account shall be taken of an award of [[49] a carer's allowance] to the extent that payment of such an award is back-dated for a period before the date on which the award is made.]

(4) Sub-paragraph (3)(c) shall apply only for the first 12 weeks following the date on which the person to whom that provision applies first joins the claimant's household.

[[45] (5) In sub-paragraph (2)(a)(iii) and (b), references to a person being in receipt of [[49] a carer's allowance] shall include references to a person who would have been in receipt of that allowance but for the application of a restriction under section 7 of the Social Security Fraud Act 2001 (loss of benefit provisions).]

[[43] Enhanced disability premium

13A.—(1) Subject to sub-paragraph (2), the condition is that the care component of disability living allowance is, or would, but for a suspension of benefit in accordance with regulations under section 113(2) of the Contributions and Benefits Act or but for an abatement as   2.579

505

a consequence of hospitalisation, be payable at the highest rate prescribed under section 72(3) of the Contributions and Benefits Act in respect of—

(a) the claimant; or

[⁵⁴ (b) [⁵⁹ the claimant's partner (if any)] who is aged less than 60.]

(2) An enhanced disability premium shall not be applicable in respect of—

(a) [⁵⁹ . . .]

(b) a claimant who—

(i) is not a member of a couple or a polygamous marriage; and

(ii) is a patient within the meaning of regulation 21(3) and has been for a period of more than [⁵⁶ 52] weeks; or

(c) a member of a couple or a polygamous marriage where each member is a patient within the meaning of regulation 21(3) and has been for a period of more than [⁵⁶ 52] weeks.]

2.580   **Disabled Child Premium**

14. [⁵⁹ . . .]

2.581   [¹⁰**Carer premium**

14ZA.—(1) [¹³Subject to sub-paragraphs (3) and (4),] the condition is that the claimant or his partner is, or both of them are, [⁴¹ entitled to [⁴⁹ a carer's allowance] under section 70 of the Contributions and Benefits Act]

(2) [⁵⁷ . . .]

[⁴¹ [⁴⁸ (3) Where a carer premium is awarded but—

(a) the person in respect of whose care the [⁴⁹ carer's allowance] has been awarded dies; or

(b) in any other case the person in respect of whom a carer premium has been awarded ceases to be entitled [⁵⁷ . . .] to [⁴⁹ a carer's allowance],

the condition for the award of the premium shall be treated as satisfied for a period of eight weeks from the relevant date specified in sub-paragraph (3A) below.

(3A) The relevant date for the purposes of sub-paragraph (3) above shall be—

(a) [⁵⁷ where sub-paragraph (3)(a) applies,] the Sunday following the death of the person in respect of whose care [⁴⁹ a carer's allowance] has been awarded or the date of death if the death occurred on a Sunday;

(b) [⁵⁷ . . .]

(c) in any other case, the date on which the person who has been entitled to [⁴⁶ a carer's allowance] ceases to be entitled to that allowance.]

(4) Where a person who has been entitled to an invalid care allowance ceases to be entitled to that allowance and makes a claim for income support, the condition for the award of the carer premium shall be treated as satisfied for a period of eight weeks from the date on which—

[⁴⁸(a) the person in respect of whose care the [⁴⁹ carer's allowance] has been awarded dies;

(b) [⁵⁷ . . .]

[⁵⁷ (c) in any other case, the person who has been entitled to a carer's allowance ceased to be entitled to that allowance.]]

2.582   [³**Persons in receipt of concessionary payments**

14A. For the purpose of determining whether a premium is applicable to a person [¹² under paragraphs 12 to 14ZA], any concessionary payment made to compensate that person for the non-payment of any benefit mentioned in those paragraphs shall be treated as if it were a payment of that benefit.]

2.583   [⁸**Person in receipt of benefit**

14B. For the purposes of this Part of this Schedule, a person shall be regarded as being in receipt of any benefit if, and only if, it is paid in respect of him and shall be so regarded only for any period in respect of which that benefit is paid.]

[^{37} Part IV

Weekly Amounts of Premiums Specified in Part III   2.584

Column (1)	Column (2)
Premium	*Amount*
15.—(1)[^{29}...]	(1) [^{29}...].
[^{42}(1A) Bereavement Premium.]	[^{42} (1A) [^{63} £25.85]]
[^{54} (2) Pensioner premium for persons to whom paragraph 9 applies.	(2) [^{54}...] [^{63}£78.90];
(2A) Pensioner premium for persons to whom paragraph 9A applies.	(2A) [^{54}...] [^{63}£78.90].
(3) Higher pensioner premium for persons to whom paragraph 10 applies.]	(3) [^{54}...] [^{63}£78.90].
(4) Disability Premium—	(4)
(a) where the claimant satisfies the condition in paragraph 11(a);	(a) [^{63}£23.95];
(b) where the claimant satisfies the condition in paragraph 11(b).	(b) [^{63}£34.20].
(5) Severe Disability Premium—	(5)
(a) where the claimant satisfies the condition in paragraph 13(2)(a);	(a) [^{63}£45.50];
(b) where the claimant satisfies the condition in paragraph 13(2)(b).	(b)
(i) if there is someone in receipt of [^{49} a carer's allowance] or if he or any partner satisfies that condition only by virtue of paragraph 13(3A);	(i) [^{63}£45.50];
(ii) if on-one is in receipt of such an allowance.	(ii) [^{63}£91.00];
(6) [^{59} ...]	(6) [^{59} ...]
(7) Carer Premium—	(7) [^{63}£25.80] in respect of each person who satisfied the condition specified in paragraph 14ZA.]
[^{43} (8) Enhanced disability premium where the conditions in paragraph 13A are satisifed—	(8) (a) [^{59} ...]
	(b) [^{63}£11.70] in respect of each person who is neither—
	(i) a child or young person; nor
	(ii) a member of a couple or a polygamous marriage, in respect of whom the conditions specified in paragraph 13A are satisfied:

Column (1)	Column (2)
Premium	*Amount*
	(c) [[63] £16.90] where the claimant is a member of a couple or a polygamous marriage and the conditions specified in paragraph 13A are satisfied in respect of a member of that couple or polygamous marriage.]

PART V

Rounding of Fractions

2.585   **16.** Where income support is awarded for a period which is not a complete benefit week and the applicable amount in respect of that period results in an amount which includes a fraction of a penny that fraction shall be treated as a penny.

AMENDMENTS

2.586   1. Income Support (General) Amendment Regulations 1988 (SI 1988/663), reg.29 (April 11, 1988).

2. Income Support (General) Amendment No.3 Regulations 1988 (SI 1988/1228), reg.9 (September 12, 1988).

3. Income Support (General) Amendment No.4 Regulations 1988 (SI 1988/1445), reg.19 (September 12, 1988).

4. Income Support (General) Amendment No.5 Regulations 1988 (SI 1988/2022), reg.17(*b*) (December 12, 1988).

5. Income Support (General) Amendment No.5 Regulations 1988 (SI 1988/2022), reg.17(*a*) (April 10, 1989).

6. Income Support (General) Amendment Regulations 1989 (SI 1989/534), reg.5 (October 9, 1989).

7. Income Support (General) Amendment No.3 Regulations 1989 (SI 1989/1678), reg.6 (October 9, 1989).

8. Income Support (General) Amendment Regulations 1990 (SI 1990/547), reg.17 (April 9, 1990).

9. Income Support (General) Amendment No.2 Regulations 1990 (SI 1990/1168), reg.2 (July 2, 1990).

10. Income Support (General) Amendment No.3 Regulations 1990 (SI 1990/1776), reg.8 (October 1, 1990).

11. Enterprise (Scotland) Consequential Amendments Order 1991 (SI 1991/3870, art.9 (April, 1991).

12. Income Support (General) Amendment Regulations 1991 (SI 1991/236), reg.2 (April 8, 1991).

13. Income Support (General) Amendment No.4 Regulations 1991 (SI 1991/236). reg.15 (August 5, 1991).

14. Income Support (General) Amendment No.4) Regulations 1991 (SI 1991/1559), reg.15 (October 7, 1991).

15. Disability Living Allowance and Disability Working Allowance (Consequential Provisions) Regulations 1991 (SI 1991/2742), reg.11(4) (April 6, 1992).

16. Income Support (General) Amendment Regulations 1992 (SI 1992/468), reg.6 (April 6, 1992).

17. Social Security Benefits (Amendments Consequential Upon the Introduction of community Care) Regulations 1992 (SI 1992/3147), reg.2 (April 1, 1993).

18. Social Security Benefits (Miscellaneous Amendments) Regulations 1993 (SI 1993/518), reg.5 (April 1, 1993).

19. Income-related Benefits Schemes (Miscellaneous Amendments) (No.2) Regulations 1993 (SI 1993/1150), reg.3 (May 25, 1993).

[20.]

21. Income-related Benefits Schemes (Miscellaneous Amendments) (No.4) Regulations 1993 (SI 1993/2119), reg.18 (October 4, 1993).

22. Income-related Benefits Schemes (Miscellaneous Amendments) (No.5) Regulations 1994 (SI 1994/2139), reg.30 (October 3, 1994).

23. Income-related Benefits Schemes (Miscellaneous Amendments) (No.6) Regulations 1994 (SI 1994/3061), reg.2(3) (December 2, 1994).

24. Income-related Benefits Schemes (Miscellaneous Amendments) Regulations 1995 (SI 1995/516), reg.24 (April 10, 1995).

25. Disability Working Allowance and Income Support (General) Amendment Regulations 1995 (SI 1995/482), reg.16 (April 13, 1995).

26. Disability Working Allowance and Income Support (General) Amendment Regulations 1995 (SI 1995/482), reg.17 (April 13, 1995).

27. Income-related Benefits Schemes and Social Security (Claims and Payments) (Miscellaneous Amendments) Regulations 1995 (SI 1995/2303), reg.6(8) (October 2, 1995).

28. Income Support (General) (Jobseeker's Allowance Consequential Amendments) Regulations 1996 (SI 1996/206), reg.23 and Sch.2 (October 7, 1996).

29. Child Benefit, Child Support and Social Security (Miscellaneous Amendments) Regulations 1996 (SI 1996/1803), reg.39 (April 7, 1997).

30. Income-related Benefits and Jobseeker's Allowance (Personal Allowances for Children and Young Persons) (Amendment) Regulations 1996 (SI 1996/2545), reg.2 (April 7, 1997).

31. Income-related Benefits and Jobseeker's Allowance (Amendment) (No.2) Regulations 1997 (SI 1997/2197), reg.7(5) and (6)(a) (October 6, 1997).

32. Social Security Amendment (Lone Parents) Regulations 1998 (SI 1998/766), reg.12 (April 6, 1998).

33. Social Security (Welfare to Work) Regulations 1998 (SI 1998/2231), reg.13(3)(a) (October 5, 1998).

34. Social Security (Welfare to Work) Regulations 1998 (SI 1998/2231), reg.13(3)(b) (October 5, 1998).

35. Social Security Benefits Up-rating Order 1999 (SI 1999/264), art.18(3) and Sch.4 (April 12, 1999).

36. Social Security Benefits Up-rating Order 1999 (SI 1999/264), art.18(4)(b) (April 12, 1999).

37. Social Security Benefits Up-rating Order 1999 (SI 1999/264), art.18(5) and Sch.5 (April 12, 1999).

38. Social Security Amendment (Personal Allowances for Children and Young Persons) Regulations 1999 (SI 1999/2555), reg.2(1)(b) and (2)(April 10, 2000).

39. Social Security and Child Support (Tax Credits) Consequential Amendments Regulations 1999 (SI 1999/2566), reg.2(2) and Sch.2, Pt II (October 5, 1999).

40. Social Security (Miscellaneous Amendments) (No.2) Regulations 1999 (SI 1999/2556), reg.2(8) (October 4, 1999).

41. Social Security (Miscellaneous Amendments) Regulations 2000 (SI 2000/681), reg.4 (April 3, 2000).

42. Social Security Amendment (Bereavement Benefits) Regulations 2000 (SI 2000/2239), reg.2(3) (April 9, 2001).

43. Social Security Amendment (Enhanced Disability Premium) Regulations 2000 (SI 2629), reg.2(c) (April 9, 2001).

44. Social Security Amendment (Residential Care and Nursing Homes) Regulations 2001 (SI 2001/3767), reg.2 and Sch., Pt I para.14 (April 8, 2002).

45. Social Security (Loss of Benefit) (Consequential Amendments) Regulations 2002 (SI 2002/490), reg.2 (April 1, 2002).

46. Social Security Amendment (Residential Care and Nursing Homes) Regulations 2001 (SI 2001/3767), reg.2 and Sch., Pt I para.14 (as amended by Social Security Amendment (Residential Care and Nursing Homes) Regulations 2002 (SI 2002/398), reg.4(2)) (April 8, 2002).

47. Social Security Amendment (Personal Allowances for Children and Young Persons) Regulations 2002 (SI 2002/2019), reg.2 (October 14, 2002).

48. Social Security Amendment (Carer Premium) Regulations 2002 (SI 2002/2020), reg.2 (October 28, 2002).

49. Social Security Amendment (Carer's allowance) Regulations 2002 (SI 2002/2497), reg.3 and Sch.2 (April 1, 2003).

50. Social Security (Working Tax Credit and Child Tax Credit) (Consequential Amendments) Regulations 2003 (SI 2003/455), regs 1(5), 2 and Sch.1, para.20(b) (April 7, 2003).

51. Social Security Benefits Up-Rating Order 2003 (SI 2003/526), art.17(3) and Sch.2 (April 7, 2003).

52. Social Security Benefits Up-Rating Order 2003 (SI 2003/526), art.17(5) and Sch.3 (April 7, 2003).

53. Social Security Benefits Up-Rating Order 2003 (SI 2003/526), art.17(4) (April 7, 2003).

54. State Pension Credit (Consequential, Transitional and Miscellaneous Provisions) Regulations 2002 (SI 2002/3019), reg.29(5) (October 6, 2003).

55. Social Security (Removal of Residential Allowance and Miscellaneous Amendments) Regulations 2003 (SI 2003/1121), reg.2 and Sch.1 para.6 (October 6, 2003).

56. Social Security (Hospital In-Patients and Miscellaneous Amendments) Regulations 2003 (SI 2003/1195), reg.3 (May 21, 2003).

57. Social Security (Miscellaneous Amendments) (No.2) Regulations 2003 (SI 2003/2279), reg.2(3) (October 1, 2003).

58. Income Support (General) Amendment Regulations 2003 (SI 2003/2379), reg.2 (October 6, 2003).

59. Social Security (Working Tax Credit and Child Tax Credit) (Consequential Amendments) Regulations 2003 (SI 2003/455), reg.2 and Sch.1, para.20 (April 6, 2004, except in "transitional cases" and see further the note to reg.17 of the Income Support Regulations).

60. Social Security (Miscellaneous Amendments) (No. 2) Regulations 2004 (SI 2004/1141), reg.6 (May 12, 2004).

61. Social Security (Back to Work Bonus and Lone Parent Run-on) (Amendment and Revocation) Regulations 2003 (SI 2003/1589), reg.2(d) (October 25, 2004).

62. Social Security Benefits Up-rating Order 2005 (SI 2005/522), art.16 and Sch.2 (April 11, 2005)

63. Social Security Benefits Up-rating Order 2005 (SI 2005/522), art.16 and Sch.3 (April 11, 2005)

DEFINITIONS

2.587   "attendance allowance"—see reg.2(1).
"benefit week"—*ibid.*
"child"—see 1986 Act, s.20(11) (SSCBA, s.137(1)).

"claimant"—see reg.2(1).
"close relative"—*ibid.*
"couple"—*ibid.*
"disability living allowance"—*ibid.*
"family"—see 1986 Act. s.20(11) (SSCBA, s.137(1)).
"invalid carriage or other vehicle"—see reg.2(1).
"lone parent"—*ibid.*
"mobility supplement"—*ibid.*
"non-dependent"—see reg.3.
"nursing home"—see regs 2(1) and 19(3).
"partner"—see reg.2(1).
"polygamous marriage"—*ibid.*
"preserved right"—see reg.2(1) and 19.
"residential care home"—see regs 2(1) and 19(3).
"single claimant"—see reg.2(1).
"Social Security Act"—*ibid.*
"welfare to work beneficiary"—*ibid.*
"young person"—*ibid.*, reg.14.

GENERAL NOTE

The details of the personal allowances and premiums are at the heart of the income   **2.588**
support system. Their adequacy or otherwise is crucial to the success of the scheme.
The personal allowances can be looked at as a simplified version of the supplementary benefit scale rates (note that there is no long-term rate and no special rate for
pensioners), but the premiums were a new departure in April 1988. Instead of an
attempt, through supplementary benefit additional requirements, to tailor the level
of benefit to the individual needs and circumstances of the claimant and his family,
higher amounts of benefit are now targeted on fairly broad categories of claimant. In
such a structure benefit may be adequate for those with routine and predictable
needs (although of course there is always room for argument about the adequacy of
particular rates), but it is almost impossible to make it adequate for those with
unusually high needs. The Transitional Regulations protected transferring claimants
to some extent, but had the effect, particularly for those with large transitional
additions, of preventing any real increase in benefit for, in some cases, several years.
An improvement of the structure for pensioners was introduced in October 1989 and
for those caring for the disabled in October 1990. Pensioners (other than those who
are the partners of people who are under 60 and who choose to claim income support
rather than state pension credit) were removed from the income support scheme
altogether when state pension credit was introduced on October 6, 2003.

Personal Allowances

Para. 1

This paragraph was amended (and para.1A was introduced) in October 1996 as   **2.589**
a consequence of the changes to income support following the introduction of JSA.

The lower age limit for income support is now 16 (SSCBA, s.124(1)(a)) but a
person is only eligible if he falls into one of the categories prescribed by reg.4ZA and
Sch.1B (s.124(1)(e)). (Note too that a person aged 16–18 in relevant education is
still only entitled to income support in certain circumstances (s.124(1)(d) and
reg.13)). However, the age-break of 18 remains significant as regards the rate of the
personal allowance (and so the immense complexity of sub-para.(3) is retained),
with another very significant break at 25 for single claimants.

For couples, where both partners are aged less than 18, the lower couple rate is
only paid if either a child is a member of the family, or both partners are eligible for
income support, or the non-claiming partner is either eligible for JSA or the subject
of a severe hardship direction under s.16 of the Jobseekers Act 1995 (sub-
para.(3)(a)). If this does not apply but one member of the couple comes within

para.1A (person living away from parents and anyone acting in place of parents in specified circumstances), the personal allowance is the same as the higher rate for a single claimant under 18 (sub-para.(3)(b)), but otherwise only the equivalent of the lower rate for a single claimant under 18 is paid (sub-para.(3)(c)). Where one partner is 18 or over and the other is under 18, the higher couple rate is only paid if the partner under 18 is eligible for income support or income-based JSA or the subject of a JSA severe hardship direction (sub-para.(3)(e)). If this is not the case, the personal allowance is the same as for a single claimant (sub-para.(3)(f)), with another age-break at 25 (sub-para.(3)(g)).

The crucial age for lone parents is 18 (sub-para.(2)(d)). Lone parents of 16 and 17 are always eligible (para.1 of sch.1B) but are paid at a higher rate if they fall within para.1A (person living away from parents and any substitute in certain circumstances) or qualify for a disability premium (sub-para.(2)(b) and (c)).

Single claimants under 18 qualify for the 18–24-year-old rate if they fall within para.1A (sub-para.(1)(b)) or qualify for a disability premium (sub-para.(1)(c)). But for single claimants there is another very significant break at the age of 25 (para.1(1)(e)). This is connected to the absence of any distinction in the personal allowances between householders and non-householders. Instead, the assumptions are made that most single people of 25 and over are responsible for their own households and that most single people under 25 are not responsible for independent households, typically living with parents. Thus a higher rate is paid to those of 25. Both these assumptions are correct, looking at the entire age-groups involved, but clearly have no direct applicability to the needs and circumstances of individuals. Young single claimants were one of the losing groups in the 1988 reforms.

In *Reynolds v Secretary of State for Work & Pensions* [2002] EWHC 426 (Admin), Q.B.D. (Wilson J.), (March 7, 2002) a challenge to the lower rates for those under 25 on the basis that they infringed various provisions of the European Convention on Human Rights (including Art.14 and Art.1 of the First Protocol taken together) was rejected. That decision was upheld by the Court of Appeal and by the House of Lords in *Carson and Reynolds v Secretary of State for Work and Pensions* [2003] EWCA Civ 797, CA (Simon Brown, Laws and Rix L.JJ.) [2005] UKHL 37, HL.

See Sch.7 for special cases, such as hospital patients. From April 1989 there are no special rules for people in board and lodging accommodation and from October 1989 no special rules for residents in most hostels. Special rules for the residents of residential care and nursing homes were abolished on October 6, 2003. For details of the position before that date, see pp. 486–488 of Vol. II of the 2003 Edition.

Para.1A

2.590   This paragraph lists those categories of 16- and 17-year-olds who qualify for the higher rate of personal allowance under para.1(1)(b), (2)(b) and (3)(b). The categories replicate those formerly in paras 6–9A of Part II of Schedule 1A (Sch.1A was revoked on October 7, 1996 as a consequence of the changes to income support following the introduction of JSA).

See sub-para.(2) for definitions. On heads (a), (d) and (e) of sub-para.(1), see the notes to reg.13(2)(c), (e) and (d) respectively. Head (b) is similar to reg.13(2)(dd) but there are some important differences in the wording. Those covered by head (c) are expected to be particularly vulnerable.

Para.2

2.591   Personal allowances for dependant children and young persons were abolished with effect from April 6, 2004. Except in transitional cases (as to which see the note to reg.17), financial help with the cost of supporting and bringing up a child or young person is now provided through child tax credit (see Vol. IV). For details of the position before April 6, 2004, see p.486 of Vol. II of the 2003 edition. In transitional cases the personal allowance for a child or young person was increased to £43.38 from the beginning of the first benefit week after April 11, 2005 by art.16(3) and Sch.2 to the Social Security Benefits Up-rating Order 2005 (SI 2005/522). If the child or young person has been a patient for a period of more than 12 weeks, art.16(7) and Pt.I of Sch.4 reduces the personal allowance to £16.40.

Para.2A

The system of special payments of IS, known as "residential allowances", to people in private or voluntary sector residential care or nursing homes were abolished with effect from October 6, 2003. For details of the position before that date, see pp. 486–488 of Vol. II of the 2003 edition.

2.592

Premiums

Para.3

The family premium was also abolished with effect from April 6, 2004. For details of the position before April 6, 2004, see pp. 488–489 of Vol. II of the 2003 edition and see the note to reg.17 for details of the transitional provisions. For those still entitled to the premium on a transitional basis, it was increased to £16.10 per week from the beginning of the first benefit week following April 11, 2005 by art.16(4) of the Social Security Benefits Up-rating Order 2005 (SI 2005/522).

2.593

Para.4 to 7

These provisions establish the general framework for the other premiums, in paras 9 to 14. Para.4 provides that in each case the premium is applicable to the claimant, although the condition will sometimes relate to the claimant's partner and, in the cases of the pensioner, enhanced pensioner and higher pensioner premiums, can only relate to, the claimant's partner since—with effect from October 6, 2003—people aged 60 or over can no longer be the claimant for income support (see note to s.124(1)(aa) of the Contributions and Benefits Act). The general rule is that only one of these premiums is applicable. If the claimant satisfies the conditions for more than one, the highest is applicable (para.5). But a number of exceptions appear in para.6. The severe disability premium is allowed in addition to any other premium, as is the carer premium; so too is the enhanced disability premium in some cases.

2.594

Many of the conditions for premiums are based on the receipt of other social security benefits. Para.7(1) deals with two situations where, once a premium has been allowed, the person concerned ceases actually to receive the other benefit. It allows entitlement to the premium to continue if the person has only ceased to receive the relevant benefit because of another, overlapping, benefit or is on a government training course or in receipt of a training allowance (the main example being Work Based Learning for Young People, which has replaced Youth Training and other training provision focussed on 16/17 year olds). See para.14B on the meaning of receipt of benefit.

Under para.7(2), the above rules do not allow the carer premium to continue unless the person cared for continues to receive attendance allowance or one of the two higher rates of the care component of disability living allowance.

Para.8A

The bereavement premium was introduced with effect from April 9, 2001 as part of the overall reforms of the former widow's benefits. Although it is available to both men and women, one function of the premium appears to be to provide some compensation to those widows who—but for those reforms—might have received a widow's pension until the age of 65 but who will now only receive a bereavement allowance for 52 weeks under s.39B of the Contributions and Benefits Act (see Vol. I).

2.595

To qualify, a claimant must have been born between April 10, 1941 and April 9, 1946 (inclusive), be claiming IS as a single claimant and to have ceased to be entitled to a bereavement allowance. Under sub-para.(2) the premium is not payable if the IS claim is made more than eight weeks after bereavement allowance ceased. Under sub-para.(3), entitlement to the premium, once established, survives breaks in entitlement to IS of eight weeks or less.

A similar premium also applies to income-based JSA but—at least until April 9, 2006—any claimant who was entitled to it would automatically also fall within paragraph 16A of Sch.1B above and would therefore be entitled to IS without having to sign on.

Para.9 and 9A

2.596   These provisions, together with the increases in the higher pensioner premium under para.15(3), implemented the Government's commitment to give increased help to needy pensioners in October 1989. The ordinary pensioner premium under para.9 was limited to people aged 60 to 74. Para. 9A provided a separate premium for those aged 75 to 79, with a small differential over the ordinary pensioner premium. The effect of reg.14(1D) of the Transitional Regulations was that these increases did not affect any transitional addition in payment. But from April 2001 the differential has been removed. From October 6, 2003, the premium can only be paid where a claimant who is under 60 has a partner who is above that age (or, in the case of the enhanced pensioner premium, is 75 or older) and who is not entitled to state pension credit. Many couples in this position will be better off by claiming state pension credit and the importance of the pensioner premium and enhanced pensioner premium is therefore likely to decline.

Para.10

2.597   From October 6, 2003, the first qualification for the HPP is that the claimant's partner is aged 80 or over. If that is not satisfied, there are another two alternatives, provided that the claimant's partner is at least 60. The first is that the claimant's partner satisfies the disability test in para.12(1)(a), (c), or (d). The second is that the claimant was entitled to, or treated as entitled to, the income support disability premium within eight weeks of the partner's 60th birthday and has remained continuously entitled to income support since that birthday. The requirement that the disability premium was, or would have been applicable to the claimant presumably now means applicable in respect of his or her partner rather than in his or her own right, although sub-para.(1)(b)(ii)(aa) does not actually spell that out. Further, *CIS 458/1992* decides that a premium is not "applicable" unless it actually forms part of the claimant's applicable amount (but see *CIS 11293/1996* in the notes to para.12).

The second alternative is subject to a number of extensions which may assist claimants:

- first, entitlement to income-based JSA is treated as entitlement to income support—see reg.32 of the Income Support (General) (Jobseeker's Allowance Consequential Amendments) Regulations 1996;

- second, sub-para.(5) treats claimants who were participating in an employment zone programme and who were not entitled to income support because, as a result of that participation, they were in remunerative work (see regs.5 and 6) or had income in excess of their applicable amounts as being entitled to income support;

- third, claimants who cease to be entitled to income support for a period of up to eight weeks which includes their partners' 60th birthday are treated by sub-para.(3)(b) as having been continuously entitled to income support when they become re-entitled. Whilst an eight week linking period is better than no linking period at all, this rule is entirely arbitrary. There are many circumstances in which a claimant might cease to be entitled to income support at the time of his or her partner's 60th birthday (for example, receipt of capital from the proceeds of an endowment or retirement annuity policy or an occupational pension) which have nothing to do with the future disability needs of the claimant's partner;

- fourth, if the claimant is a "welfare to work beneficiary" (as defined in reg.2(1)) the eight week period is extended to 52 weeks by sub-para.(4);

- finally, sub-para.(3)(a) provides that once a claimant has become entitled to the HPP, breaks in entitlement to income support of up to eight weeks will not affect entitlement to the premium, despite the concluding words of sub-para.(1)(b)(ii).

Para. 11

The qualification for the DP can be for the claimant personally to satisfy one of the conditions in para.12. If it is the claimant's partner who might qualify, then only para.12(1)(a), (c) or (d), not (b), will do. If the condition is to be satisfied by the claimant's *partner*, s/he must be under 60. If s/he is over 60 then there will be entitlement to the HPP under para.10(1)(b)(i). Following the introduction of state pension credit on October 6, 2003, all income support claimants must be under 60 (see notes to s.124(1)(aa) of the Contributions and Benefits Act).   **2.598**

Para. 12

Sub-para.(1) prescribes four alternative conditions for HPP and DP. Heads (a) and (d) may be satisfied by either the claimant or his or her partner, head (b) may only be satisfied by the claimant. Head (c) contains some criteria which must be satisfied by the claimant's partner and some which must be satisfied by the claimant. As far as possible the conditions are made to depend on decisions already taken by other authorities, so that decision-making here should be routine.   **2.599**

Head (a) applies to receipt of the benefits listed in head (i), provision of or grant towards an invalid carriage, or being registered blind. From April 1990, para.14B defines receipt of benefit in terms of payment, reversing the effect of *R(SB) 12/87*. Long-term incapacity benefit requires 52 weeks of incapacity for work, and has a contribution test. (Previously invalidity pension required only 28 weeks of incapacity.) Note sub-para.(6), the effect of which is to treat a person who is terminally ill as in receipt of long-term incapacity benefit after 28 weeks. Severe disablement allowance is non-contributory, but has an additional (and tough) test of disablement. The extension to all levels of disability living allowance brought in some previously excluded claimants. See sub-para.(2) for blindness, and the notes to para.13 of Sch.1B.

Entitlement to HPP is affected by the discriminatory age limit for claims for long-term incapacity benefit (previously invalidity benefit) that results from the UK's different pensionable ages for men and women (*i.e.* 65 for men, 60 for women; full equalisation of pensionable age will not be achieved until April, 2020) (but see *CIB 13368/1998* below where the entitlement to incapacity benefit derives from an industrial injury or a prescribed industrial disease). (As a result of the ECJ's decision in *Secretary of State for Social Security v Thomas* [1993] E.C.R. I-1247, [1993] 4 All E.R. 556, also reported as *R(G) 2/94*, the discriminatory age limit for initial claims for severe disablement allowance was finally changed on October 28, 1994 (see Social Security (Severe Disablement Allowance and Invalid Care Allowance) Amendment Regulations 1994 (SI 1994/2556).) In *Secretary of State for Social Security and Chief Adjudication Officer v Graham and Others* (Case C-92/94, [1995] 3 C.M.L.R. 169, [1995] All E.R. (EC) 865, also reported as *R(S) 2/95*) the ECJ held that the different treatment of men and women in relation to invalidity benefit was not in breach of EC Directive 79/7 on equal treatment for men and women in matters of social security. The discrimination in the rules for invalidity benefit was permitted under Art.7(1)(a) of the Directive as it was "necessarily and objectively linked" to the UK's different pension ages (see *Thomas*). The Court's reasoning is scanty (compare the Advocate General's Opinion delivered on June 15, 1995). But the judgment has (for the time being at least) put an end to the argument that a discriminatory link to pensionable age for *contributory* (as opposed to non-contributory: see *Thomas*) benefits is unlawful. See the 1995 edition of *Mesher and Wood, Income-related Benefits: the Legislation* for further details of *Graham* (and associated issues) and related European case law on the scope of Directive 79/7. Long-term incapacity benefit is not payable to people over pensionable age (except those who were over pensionable age before April 13, 1995 who remain eligible for up to five years over that age). The consequence of the ECJ's judgment in *Graham* is that this discrimination against women (and its effect on entitlement to HPP) remains (until the pensionable age differential is finally abolished). Note, however, that in *CIB 13368/1996* Commissioner Levenson held that for women who were getting invalidity benefit because of industrial injury or prescribed disease, and who transferred to transitional incapacity benefit (being deemed to satisfy the contribution conditions), the discriminatory age limit was unlawful. Reg.17(4) of the Social Security (Incapacity Benefit) (Transitional) Regulations 1995) fell on the *Thomas*, rather than the *Graham* side of the line. But Commissioner Levenson's decision was, by concession, reversed by the Court of Appeal in *CAO v Rowlands* on June 27, 2000, following the ECJ's decision in *Hepple.*

The current form of head (b) is a consequence of the changes associated with the introduction of incapacity benefit (which replaced sickness benefit and invalidity benefit from April 13, 1995). It is no longer linked to what is now para.7 of Sch.1B (see the 1994 edition of *Mesher and Wood, Income-related Benefits: the Legislation* for notes on the previous form of head (b)), although it employs the same criteria as heads (a), (b) and (d) of para.7. See the notes to para.7 of Sch.1B. The test must now be satisfied for a continuous period of at least 52 weeks before a disability or higher pensioner premium can be awarded under head (b), unless the claimant is terminally ill when the period is 28 weeks. Two or more periods separated by not more than eight weeks (from October 5, 1998, 52 weeks in the case of a "welfare to work beneficiary" (sub-para.(1A)); see the notes to reg.2(1) for when a person counts as a welfare to work beneficiary) count as one continuous period. A person is defined as terminally ill if he is expected to die from a progressive disease within six months. If the person has been incapable of work (or entitled to statutory sick pay) for 28 weeks by the time a decision-maker decides he is terminally ill, head (b) will immediately apply. Before April 13, 1995 the qualifying period under head (b) was 28 weeks. There is some transitional protection, see below. In the case of a couple, head (b) can only be satisfied by the claimant.

A person is entitled to statutory sick pay from the first day of incapacity (even though it is not paid for the first three "waiting days"). Otherwise it is only days on which it is accepted that the claimant is, or is to be treated as, incapable of work in accordance with the rules for determining incapacity for work (see Vol. I of this series) that count. A claimant does not have to be in receipt of income support during the qualifying period, so if a person has been incapable of work for 52 weeks before claiming income support head (b) will immediately apply.

Any days when the claimant is treated as capable of work under the incapacity rules (see Vol. I of this series) will not count, but note the linking rule. A person may be treated as capable of work for a maximum of 6 weeks under reg.18 of the Social Security (Incapacity for Work) (General) Regulations; or indefinitely in other cases. Thus the effect of a decision to treat a claimant as capable of work may (depending on the circumstances) only result in that period not counting towards establishing entitlement to a disability or higher pensioner premium, rather than necessitate a return to square one. If the claimant has already been awarded a premium it will not be payable while he is treated as capable of work. But if this is for eight weeks or less it will apply again immediately after the break. Note also the 52-week linking rule from October 5, 1998 for a claimant who is a "welfare to work beneficiary" (see reg.2(1) and the notes to that regulation).

Note *CIS 15611/1996* which decides that a claimant who had been entitled to a disability premium before going into prison and who continued to be incapable of work while in prison did not have to re-serve the 52 week qualifying period on his release. Although days of disqualification from incapacity benefit during a period of imprisonment did not count as days of incapacity for work under reg.4(1)(b) of the Incapacity Benefit Regulations 1994, this only applied for the purposes of incapacity benefit. The Incapacity for Work (General) Regulations 1995 contained no such provision and so subject to the claimant providing evidence of his incapacity for work throughout his period in prison he was entitled to a disability premium when he reclaimed income support on his release.

If a claimant makes a late claim for a benefit on the grounds of incapacity for work, the days on which it is accepted that he was, or was to be treated as, incapable of work should count under head (b). It does not matter that there is no entitlement to the benefit because the claim is late. See *R(IS) 8/93* (but note the amendments to reg.2(1) of the Social Security (Medical Evidence) Regulations 1976 (SI 1976/615) from April 13, 1995).

In *CIS/2699/2001* Commissioner Mesher considered whether the requirement that a claimant should have been incapable of work for a continuous period of 364 days (or 196 days if terminally ill) could be satisfied on the basis of retrospective medical evidence. He concluded that this was permitted by reg.28(2)(a) of the Social Security (Incapacity for Work) (General) Regulations 1995 and reg.2(1)(d) of the Social Security (Medical Evidence) Regulations 1976. However, by virtue of s. 12(8)(b) of the Social Security Act 1998 (which prohibits a tribunal from considering circumstances arising after the date of the decision under appeal), such medical evidence had to be provided *before* the date of the Secretary of State's decision. This was because under reg.28(2)(a), the production of medical evidence was *itself* a circumstance relevant to the claimant's entitlement and not merely evidence related to some relevant circumstance. In so holding, Commissioner Mesher differed from the decision of Commissioner Rowland in *CIS/4772/2000* in which the point about s.12(8)(b) had not been raised.

There is transitional protection for claimants entitled to a disability premium on April 12, 1995 under head (b) as then in force. See reg.19(2) to (4) of the Disability Working Allowance and Income Support (General) Amendment Regulations 1995 (p.669). The premium will continue to be paid as long as they remain incapable of work (in accordance with the new rules, including the transitional protection). Note the linking rule. In addition, any period immediately before April 13, 1995 during which a claimant satisfied para.5 of Sch.1 as then in force (see the 1994 edition of *Mesher and Wood, Income-related Benefits: the Legislation*) counts towards the qualifying period under head (b).

Heads (c) and (d) apply where receipt of some benefits specified in (a) only ceased because of age limits or going into hospital. The claimant has to remain continuously entitled to income support (or income-based JSA: reg.32 of the Income Support (General) (Jobseeker's Allowance Consequential Amendments) Regulations 1996 (see p. 676) under which entitlement to income-based JSA counts as entitlement to income support for the purpose of satisfying any condition that the person is or has been entitled to income support) and if it is his partner who has ceased to receive long-term incapacity benefit she must still be alive. Note the linking rule in sub-para.(4). Note also sub-para.(6) in relation to incapacity benefit, the effect of which is to treat a person who is terminally ill as in receipt of long-term incapacity benefit after 28 weeks. There is transitional protection for claimants entitled to a higher pensioner premium under the old form of head (c)(i) at any time in the eight weeks before April 12, 1995 (*i.e.* those who transferred to retirement pension from invalidity benefit): see reg.20(4) of the Disability Working Allowance and Income Support (General) Amendment Regulations 1995 (p.670).

CIS 587/1990 exposes a gap in the legislation which has not yet been closed. The claimant transferred from invalidity benefit to retirement pension in 1982. He could not qualify under the old form of head (c) because he had not been continuously entitled to income support since the transfer. If he had delayed the transfer until after April 10, 1988, he would have qualified. The extent of his need at the relevant date (April 1990) was identical under either alternative. See sub-para.(4) for linking rules. Another gap is highlighted by *CIS 458/1992* which holds that the condition that a premium has been applicable requires that it should have been part of the claimant's applicable amount. So where a claimant had been in a residential care home he could not use head (c), because Sch.4 has no provision for premiums. But see *CIS 11293/1996* in the notes to para.4(6) of Sch.3 where the Commissioner holds that housing costs were "applicable" under para.5A(3) of the former Sch.3 if they were potentially applicable.

Para. 13

2.600   The presence of this category is required by s.22(3) of the 1986 Act, now s.135(5) of the Contributions and Benefits Act. The concern which prompted the inclusion of that subsection was that a severely disabled claimant on supplementary benefit might be getting high additional requirements for a range of extra needs (*e.g.* heating, laundry, diet, wear and tear on clothes, etc.), which the ordinary disability premium would go nowhere near matching. However, the conditions for the severe disability premium (SDP) are so tight that very few will qualify. The Independent Living Fund was set up to provide further cash help to the very severely disabled, but its budget was usually fully spent part way through its financial year. The Fund was suspended in 1992. On April 1, 1993, it was replaced by two funds, the Independent Living (Extension) Fund which took over payments to existing beneficiaries and the Independent Living (1993) Fund for new applications.

First note that the SDP can only apply to the claimant, not to his partner. But since a couple has a free choice as to which of them should be the claimant (Claims and Payments Regulations, reg.4) this should not be a problem.

If the claimant has no partner, he first must be in receipt of attendance allowance or one of the two higher rates of the care component of disability living allowance, *i.e.* he must require attention or supervision (sub-para.(2)(a)(i)). Then there must be no non-dependants of 18 or over residing with him (sub-para.(2)(a)(ii)). The addition of the words "with whom he is normally residing" from December 2, 1994 is to reverse the effect of the Court of Appeal's decision in *Bate v Chief Adjudication Officer and Secretary of State for Social Security* on November 30, 1994 (since overturned by the House of Lords: see the notes to reg.3). The effect of sub-para.(3) is that adults in receipt of attendance allowance or one of the two higher rates of care component of disability living allowance or who are registered as blind or treated as blind or carers for the first 12 weeks of residence do not count for this purpose. "Non-dependant" is defined in reg.3. See the notes to that regulation for the intricacies of the definition. Care must be taken to apply the particular form of reg.3 in force at the relevant time. The current version makes it very difficult for the parents with whom an adult claimant is living not to be regarded as non-dependants. Finally, no-one must be receiving invalid care allowance for caring for the claimant (sub-para.(2)(a)(iii)). *R(IS) 14/94* held that where arrears of ICA were awarded, it had been "in payment" for the period covered by the arrears. "In payment" in sub-para.(2)(a)(iii) did not mean timeously in payment. Thus an SDP that had been paid for the same period could be recovered under s.74(4) of the Administration Act (s.27(4) of the 1986 Act). This was despite the fact that the recipient of the SDP and the recipient of the ICA were different people whose requirements and resources were not aggregated for the purposes of income support. The claimant was granted leave to appeal to the Court of Appeal, but the appeal was not proceeded with as the DSS issued internal guidance stating that such overpayments were not to be recovered. Now sub-para.(3ZA) provides that where an award of ICA is made which includes arrears, entitlement to the severe disability premium only ceases from the date the award of ICA is actually made. This should avoid any question of an overpayment of an SDP by reason of a backdated award of invalid care allowance.

If the claimant has a partner, the assumption is that the partner can care for the claimant. So there is an additional qualification that the partner is also in receipt of a qualifying allowance (sub-para.(2)(b)(ii)) or, if not, is registered as blind or treated as blind (sub-para.(2A)). There must be no eligible non-dependants in residence (see above), and at least one of the couple must not have a carer receiving invalid care allowance.

In *R(IS) 22/93* and a number of associated appeals, the Commissioner held that sub-para.(2)(a)(ii) and (iii) were not validly made, since s.22(4) of the Social Security

Act 1986 (now s.135(6) of the Contributions and Benefits Act) only gave power to prescribe conditions relating to a claimant's disability. Section 22(3) (SSSCBA, s.135(5)) requires a severely disabled person's applicable amount to include a special premium. Heads (ii) and (iii) are concerned with the presence of others in the household and the benefit entitlement of other people, which are not connected to the claimant's disability. This cogently argued decision was reversed by the Court of Appeal in *Chief Adjudication Officer v Foster* [1992] Q.B. 31, [1991] 3 All E.R. 846, which held by a majority that the provisions were valid. The House of Lords confirmed this part of the Court of Appeal's decision (*Foster v Chief Adjudication Officer* [1993] A.C. 754, [1993] 1 All E.R. 705, also reported as part of *R(IS) 22/93*). Therefore, the full conditions of para.13 must be applied at all points of its history. See the notes to s.135 of the Contributions and Benefits Act for more details, and see vol III of this series for the power of the Social Security Commissioners and others to determine whether regulations have been validly made.

The premium is high, since it is in addition to DP or HPP (para.6(1)). For a claimant without a partner it is £45.50. For a couple (where both partners have to qualify) it is £45.50 for each of them who does not have a carer with carer's allowance (para.15(5)).

It was argued in *Rider and others v Chief Adjudication Officer*, reported as *R(IS) 10/94*, that for periods before April 1990, (when para.14B was introduced) where a lone parent received attendance allowance in respect of a child under 16, para.13(2)(a)(i) was satisfied. Reg.6(4) of the Social Security (Attendance Allowance) (No. 2) Regulations 1975 made the parent entitled to the attendance allowance in these circumstances. But if the parent, and not the child, were treated as in receipt of attendance allowance, that would mean that a child could never have satisfied the conditions of para.14(b) on the DCP. *R(IS) 10/94* decides that in the context of para.14(b) a child is in receipt of attendance allowance when the child satisfies the prescribed conditions and the meaning must be the same in para.13(2)(a)(i). The introduction of para.14B in April 1990, providing that a person is to be regarded as in receipt of any benefit only where it is paid in respect of that person was to clarify the law, not to change it. The decision in *R(IS) 10/94* was confirmed by the Court of Appeal which held that on an overall comparison of the words "in receipt of" in paras 13(2)(a)(i) and 14(b) (and also para.12(1)(a)(i) in relation to the disability premium), it could be seen that the words were not to be read just as they stood but as importing the additional requirement that the attendance allowance should be payable in respect of the recipient's own needs. Para.13 (and para.12) was concerned only with the needs of claimants and their partners; para.14 only with the needs of children and young persons.

Note that entitlement to a severe disability premium is a question to which the assumption in reg.13(2) of the Decisions and Appeals Regulations 1999 applies (relevant information not in possession of decision-maker deemed to be adverse to claimant).

Para.13A

With effect from April 9, 2001, this paragraph establishes an enhanced disability premium for claimants who (or whose partners or, in transitional cases (see the note to reg.17), members) are younger than 60 and entitled to the highest rate of the care component of disability living allowance. By para.6(2) above the premium may be paid in addition to any other premium except the pensioner, enhanced pensioner and higher pensioner premiums payable under paras 9, 9A and 10.

2.601

In transitional cases, the premium is not payable if the person who is entitled to the highest rate of the care component of disability living allowance is a child or young person with more than £3,000 in capital.

The premium is payable for the first six weeks of any stay in a hospital or similar institution even if payment of disability living allowance has been suspended because of the hospitalisation. If the claimant is a member of a couple or a polygamous marriage, the premium is payable unless both members of the couple or all members of the marriage have been hospitalised for six weeks.

In transitional cases, the enhanced disability premium for a child was increased to £17.71 from the beginning of the first benefit week after April 11, 2005 by Art.16(5) and Sch.3 to the Social Security Benefits Up-rating Order 2005 (SI 2005/522).

Para.14

2.602   Except in transitional cases (as to which see the note to reg.17), the disabled child premium was abolished with effect from April 6, 2004. For details of the position before that date, see p. 496 of Vol. II of the 2003 Edition. In transitional cases the disabled child premium was increased to £43.89 from the beginning of the first benefit week after April 11, 2005 by art.16(5) and Sch.3 to the Social Security Benefits Up-rating Order 2005 (SI 2005/522).

Para.14ZA

2.603   The carer premium (CP) is part of the Government's shift of resources amongst the disabled. It goes to a person who is entitled to carer's allowance, or is treated as entitled to it (sub-para.(2)). The CP may encourage the claiming of carer's allowance (formerly called "invalid care allowance" ("ICA")) against which must be balanced the possible loss of SDP for the disabled person being cared for. See *R(IS) 14/94* above and para.13(3ZA). Under sub-paras (3) and (4) entitlement to the premium continues for eight weeks after ceasing to receive carer's allowance. In cases where carer's allowance is not payable because of the overlapping benefits rules, one of the conditions of entitlement is that the claim for carer's allowance should have been made on or after October 1, 1990. Whether this means the original claim or can also encompass any later claim is not entirely clear. DWP Policy is now that those who established an underlying entitlement to ICA (as it then was) before October 1, 1990 can be paid the premium with effect from April 3, 2000 (see Memo DMG JSA/IS 32). For the legal basis for the advice given in the Memo see *CIS/367/2003*.

Paragraph 14ZA (as it was worded in July 1999) was considered by Mr Commissioner Jacobs in *CIS 4267/2001*. In that case, the claimant had been entitled to ICA and hence—under sub-para.(1)—to a carer premium (CP) immediately before he reached the age of 65. He then ceased to receive ICA because of the operation of the Overlapping Benefits Regulations (*i.e.* presumably because he had begun to receive his state retirement pension) but nevertheless continued to be *treated as* receiving that benefit—and therefore to be entitled to the CP—under sub-para.(2). Subsequently, the person for whom he was caring ceased to be entitled to disability living allowance ("DLA"). If the Overlapping Benefits Regulations had not applied, the claimant would have continued to be entitled to ICA even though he was no longer caring for a severely disabled person (see SSCBA 1992, s.70(6) and reg.11 of the Invalid Care Allowance Regulations) and would therefore have continued to be entitled to a CP under sub-para.(1). However, sub-para.(2) provided that a person who was not *actually* in receipt of ICA could only be *treated as* in receipt of that benefit for as long as the person cared for was in receipt of attendance allowance or the middle or highest rates of the care component of DLA. The Commissioner rejected the argument by the claimant's representative that the income support legislation was in conflict with the ICA legislation and that the latter should be given priority. The legislation simply established different rules for different benefits and there was nothing inconsistent in providing differently for the carer premium and for ICA itself.

The wording of para.14ZA has been clarified by the amendments made by SI 2002/2020 with effect from October 28, 2002.

Para.14A

2.604   In paras 12 to 14ZA receipt of a concessionary (*i.e.* extra-statutory) payment to compensate for non-payment of a benefit is to be equated with actual payment of that benefit.

Para.14B

This important definition of receipt of benefit in terms of payment, not entitlement, reverses the effect of *R(SB) 12/87*. It makes for a further simplification of decision-making. It also ended the argument that it was the parent of a child under 16 who qualified for attendance allowance who received the benefit. See the note to para.13.

2.605

[¹SCHEDULE 3 **Regulations 17(1)(e)
and 18(1)(f)**

HOUSING COSTS

Housing costs

1.—(1) Subject to the following provisions of this Schedule, the housing costs applicable to a claimant are those costs—

(a) which he or, where he is a member of a family, he or any member of that family is, in accordance with paragraph 2, liable to meet in respect of the dwelling occupied asthe home which he or any other member of his family is treated as occupying, and

(b) which qualify under paragraphs 15 to 17.

(2) In this Schedule—

"housing costs" means those costs to which sub-paragraph (1) refers;

"existing housing costs" means housing costs arising under an agreement entered into before 2nd October 1995, or under an agreement entered into after 1st October 1995 ("the new agreement")—

[²⁹ (a) which replaces an existing agreement, provided that the person liable to meet the housing costs—

(i) remains the same in both agreements, or

(ii) where in either agreement more than one person is liable to meet the housing costs, the person is liable to meet the housing costs in both the existing agreement and the new agreement;]

(b) where the existing agreement was entered into before 2nd October 1995; and

(c) which is for a loan of the same amount as or less than the amount of the loan under the agreement it replaces, and for this purpose any amount payable [². . .] to arrange the new agreement and included in the loan shall be disregarded;

"new housing costs" means housing costs arising under an agreement entered into after 1st October 1995 other than an agreement referred to in the definition of "existing housing costs";

"standard rate" means the rate for the time being [²⁶ determined in accordance with] paragraph 12.

(3) For the purposes of this Schedule a disabled person is a person—

(a) in respect of whom a disability premium, a disabled child premium, a pensioner premium for persons aged 75 or over or a higher pensioner premium is included in his applicable amount or the applicable amount of a person living with him; or

(b) [². . .] who, had he in fact been entitled to income support, would have had included in his applicable amount a disability premium, a disabled child premium, a pensioner premium for persons aged 75 or over or a higher pensioner premium.

(4) For the purposes of sub-paragraph (3), a person shall not cease to be a disabled person on account of his being disqualified for receiving benefit or treated as capable of work by virtue of the operation of section 171E of the Contributions and Benefits Act (incapacity for work, disqualification etc.).

2.606

[⁶Previous entitlement to income-based jobseeker's allowance

1A.—(1) Where a claimant or his partner was in receipt of or was treated as being in receipt of income-based jobseeker's allowance not more than 12 weeks before one of them becomes entitled to income support or, where the claimant or his partner is a person to whom paragraph 14(2) or (8) (linking rules) refers, not more than 26 weeks before becoming so entitled and—

(a) the applicable amount for that allowance included an amount in respect of housing costs under paragraph 14 or 15 of Schedule 2 to the Jobseeker's Allowance Regulations 1996; and

2.607

(b) the circumstances affecting the calculation of those housing costs remain unchanged since the last calculation of those costs,

the applicable amount in respect of housing costs for income support shall be the applicable amount in respect of those costs current when entitlement to income-based jobseeker's allowance was last calculated.

(2) Where, in the period since housing costs were last calculated for income-based job-seeker's allowance, there has been a change of circumstances, other than a reduction in the amount of an outstanding loan, which increases or reduces those costs, the amount to be met under this Schedule shall, for the purposes of the claim for income support, be recalculated so as to take account of that change.]

Circumstances in which a person is liable to meet housing costs

2.608   **2.**—(1) A person is liable to meet housing costs where—

(a) the liability falls upon him or his partner but not where the liability is to a member of the same household as the person on whom the liability falls;

(b) because the person liable to meet the housing costs is not meeting them, the claimant has to meet those costs in order to continue to live in the dwelling occupied as the home and it is reasonable in all the circumstances to treat the claimant as liable to meet those costs;

(c) he in practice shares the housing costs with other members of the household none of whom are close relatives either of the claimant or his partner, and

(i) one or more of those members is liable to meet those costs, and

(ii) it is reasonable in the circumstances to treat him as sharing responsibility.

(2) Where any one or more, but not all, members of the claimant's family are affected by a trade dispute, the housing costs shall be treated as wholly the responsibility of those members of the family not so affected.

Circumstances in which a person is to be treated as occupying a dwelling as his home

2.609   **3.**—(1) Subject to the following provisions of this paragraph, a person shall be treated as occupying as his home the dwelling normally occupied as his home by himself or, if he is a member of a family, by himself and his family and he shall not be treated as occupying any other dwelling as his home.

(2) In determining whether a dwelling is the dwelling normally occupied as the claimant's home for the purposes of sub-paragraph (1) regard shall be had to any other dwelling occupied by the claimant or by him and his family whether or not that other dwelling is in Great Britain.

(3) Subject to sub-paragraph (4), where a single claimant or a lone parent is a [15 full-time student] or is on a training course and is liable to make payments (including payments of mortgage interest or, in Scotland, payments under heritable securities or, in either case, analogous payments) in respect of either (but not both) the dwelling which he occupies for the purpose of attending his course of study or his training course or, as the case may be, the dwelling which he occupies when not attending his course, he shall be treated as occupying as his home the dwelling in respect of which he is liable to make payments.

(4) A full-time student shall not be treated as occupying a dwelling as his home for any week of absence from it, other than an absence occasioned by the need to enter hospital for treatment, outside the period of study, if the main purpose of his occupation during the period of study would be to facilitate attendance on his course.

(5) Where a claimant has been required to move into temporary accommodation by reason of essential repairs being carried out to the dwelling normally occupied as his home and he is liable to make payments (including payments of mortgage interest or, in Scotland, payments under heritable securities or, in either case, analogous payments) in respect of either (but not both) the dwelling normally occupied or the temporary accommodation, he shall be treated as occupying as his home the dwelling in respect of which he is liable to make those payments.

(6) Where a person is liable to make payments in respect of two (but not more than two) dwellings, he shall be treated as occupying both dwellings as his home only—

(a) where he has left and remains absent from the former dwelling occupied as the home through fear of violence in that dwelling or by a former member of his family and it is reasonable that housing costs should be met in respect of both his former dwelling and his present dwelling occupied as the home; or

(b) in the case of a couple or a member of a polygamous marriage where a partner is 15 full-time student] or is on a training course and it is unavoidable that he or they should occupy two separate dwellings and reasonable that housing costs should be met in respect of both dwellings; or

(c) in the case where a person has moved into a new dwelling occupied as the home, except where sub-paragraph (5) applies, for a period not exceeding four benefit weeks if his liability to make payments in respect of two dwellings is unavoidable.

(7) Where—

(a) a person has moved into a dwelling and was liable to make payments in respect of that dwelling before moving in, and

(b) he had claimed income support before moving in and either that claim has not yet been determined or it has been determined but an amount has not been included under this Schedule and if the claim has been refused a further claim has been made within four weeks of the date on which the claimant moved into the new dwelling occupied as the home; and

(c) the delay in moving into the dwelling in respect of which there was liability to make payments before moving in was reasonable and—

    (i) that delay was necessary in order to adapt the dwelling to meet the disablement needs of the claimant or any member of his family; or

    (ii) the move was delayed pending the outcome of an application under Part VIII of the Contributions and Benefits Act for a social fund payment to met a need arising out of the move or in connection with setting up the home in the dwelling and either a member of the claimant's family is aged five or under or the claimant's applicable amount includes a premium under paragraph 9, 9A, 10, 11, 13 or 14 of Schedule 2; or

    (iii) the person became liable to make payments in respect of the dwelling while he was a patient or was in residential accommodation,

he shall be treated as occupying the dwelling as his home for any period not exceeding four weeks immediately prior to the date on which he moved into the dwelling and in respect of which he was liable to make payments.

(8) This sub-paragraph applies to a person who enters residential accommodation—

(a) for the purpose of ascertaining whether the accommodation suits his needs; and

(b) with the intention of returning to the dwelling which he normally occupies as his home should, in the event, the residential accommodation prove not to suit his needs,

and while in the accommodation, the part of the dwelling which he normally occupies as his home is not let, or as the case may be, sub-let to another person.

(9) A person to whom sub-paragraph (8) applies shall be treated as occupying the dwelling he normally occupies as his home during any period (commencing with the day he enters the accommodation) not exceeding 13 weeks in which the person is resident in the accommodation, but only in so far as the total absence from the dwelling does not exceed 52 weeks.

(10) A person, other than a person to whom sub-paragraph (11) applies, shall be treated as occupying a dwelling as his home throughout any period of absence not exceeding 13 weeks, if, and only if—

(a) he intends to return to occupy the dwelling as his home; and

(b) the part of the dwelling normally occupied by him has not been let or, as the case may be, sub-let to another person; and

(c) the period of absence is unlikely to exceed 13 weeks.

(11) This sub-paragraph applies to a person whose absence from the dwelling he normally occupies as his home is temporary and—

(a) he intends to return to occupy the dwelling as his home; and

(b) while the part of the dwelling which is normally occupied by him has not been let or, as the case may be, sub-let; and

(c) he is—

    [³⁰ (i) detained in custody on remand pending trial or, as a condition of bail, required to reside—

        (aa) in a dwelling, other than the dwelling he occupies as his home; or

        (bb) in premises approved under section 9 of the Criminal Justice and Court Services Act 2000,

    or, detained pending sentence upon conviction, or]

    (ii) resident in a hospital or similar institution as a patient, or

    (iii) undergoing or, as the case may be, his partner or his dependent child is undergoing, in the United Kingdom or elsewhere, medical treatment, or medically approved convalescence, in accommodation other than residential accommodation, or

    (iv) following, in the United Kingdom or elsewhere, a training course, or

    (v) undertaking medically approved care of a person residing in the United Kingdom or elsewhere, or

     (vi) undertaking the care of a child whose parent or guardian is temporarily absent from the dwelling normally occupied by that parent or guardian for the purpose of receiving medically approved care or medical treatment, or

    (vii) a person who is, whether in the United Kingdom or elsewhere, receiving medically approved care provided in accommodation other than residential accommodation, or

  (viii) a [15 full-time student] to whom sub-paragraph (3) or (6)(b) does not apply, or

    (ix) a person other than a person to whom sub-paragraph (8) applies, who is receiving care provided in residential accommodation; or

     (x) a person to whom sub-paragraph (6)(a) does not apply and who has left the dwelling he occupies as his home through fear of violence in that dwelling [2, or by a person] who was formerly a member of his family; and

  (d) the period of his absence is unlikely to exceed a period of 52 weeks or, in exceptional circumstances, is unlikely substantially to exceed that period.

(12) A person to whom sub-paragraph (11) applies is to be treated as occupying the dwelling he normally occupies as his home during any period of absence not exceeding 52 weeks beginning with the first day of that absence.

(13) In this paragraph—

  (a) "medically approved" means certified by a medical practitioner;

  (b) "patient" means a person who is undergoing medical or other treatment as an in-patient in a hospital or similar institution;

  (c) "residential accommodation" means accommodation—

     (i) provided under sections 21 to 24 and 26 of the National Assistance Act 1948 (provision of accommodation); or

    (ii) provided under sections 13B and 59 of the Social Work (Scotland) Act 1968 (provision of residential and other establishments) where board is available to the claimant; or

   (iii) which is a residential care home within the meaning of that expression in [21 regulation 2(1)] other than sub-paragraph (b) of that definition; or

   (iv) which is a nursing home;

  (d) "training course" means such a course of training or instruction provided wholly or partly by or on behalf of or in pursuance of arrangements made with, or approved by or on behalf of, Scottish Enterprise, Highlands and Islands Enterprise, a government department or the Secretary of State.

Housing costs not met

2.610   **4.**—(1) No amount may be met under the provisions of this Schedule—

  (a) in respect of housing benefit expenditure; or

  (b) where the claimant is in accommodation which is a residential care home or a nursing home except where he is in such accommodation during a temporary absence from the dwelling he occupies as his home and in so far as they relate to temporary absences, the provisions of paragraph 3(8) to (12) apply to him during that absence.

(2) Subject to the following provisions of this paragraph, loans which, apart from this paragraph qualify under paragraph 15 shall not so qualify where the loan was incurred during the relevant period and was incurred—

  (a) after 1st October 1995, or

  (b) after 2nd May 1994 and the housing costs applicable to that loan were not met by virtue of the former paragraph 5A of this Schedule in any one or more of the 26 weeks preceding 2nd October 1995, or

  (c) subject to sub-paragraph (3), in the 26 weeks preceding 2nd October 1995 by a person—

     (i) who was not at that time entitled to income support; and

    (ii) who becomes, or whose partner becomes entitled to income support after 1st October 1995 and that entitlement is within 26 weeks of an earlier entitlement to income support for the claimant or his partner.

(3) Sub-paragraph (2)(c) shall not apply in respect of a loan where the claimant has interest payments on that loan met without restrictions under an award of income support in respect of a period commencing before 2nd October 1995.

[2(4) The "relevant period" for the purposes of this paragraph is any period during which the person to whom the loan was made—

  (a) is entitled to income support, or

  (b) is living as a member of a family one of whom is entitled to income support,

together with any linked period, that is to say a period falling between two such periods of entitlement to income support separated by not more than 26 weeks.]

[⁷(4A) For the purposes of sub-paragraph (4), a person shall be treated as entitled to income support during any period when he or his partner was not so entitled because—

    (a) that person or his partner was participating in an employment programme specified in regulation 75(1)(a)(ii) of the Jobseeker's Allowance Regulations 1996 [¹⁹ , in the Intensive Activity Period specified in regulation 75(1)(a)(iv) of those Regulations or in the Intensive Activity Period for 50 plus]; and

    (b) in consequence of such participation that person or his partner was engaged inremunerative work or had an income in excess of the claimant's applicable amount as prescribed in Part IV.]

(5) For the purposes of sub-paragraph (4)—

    (a) any week in the period of 26 weeks ending on 1st October 1995 on which there arose an entitlement to income support such as is mentioned in that sub-paragraph shall be taken into account in determining when the relevant period commences; and

    (b) two or more periods of entitlement and any intervening linked periods shall together form a single relevant period.

(6) Where the loan to which sub-paragraph (2) refers has been applied—

    (a) for paying off an earlier loan, and that earlier loan qualified under paragraph 15 [⁴during the relevant period]; or

[⁴(b) to finance the purchase of a property where an earlier loan, which qualified under paragraph 15 or 16 during the relevant period in respect of another property, is paid off (in whole or in part) with monies received from the sale of that property;]

then the amount of the loan to which sub-paragraph (2) applies is the amount (if any) by which the new loan exceeds the earlier loan.

(7) Notwithstanding the preceding provisions of this paragraph, housing costs shall be met in any case where a claimant satisfies any of the conditions specified in sub-paragraphs (8) to (11) below, but—

    (a) those costs shall be subject to any additional limitations imposed by the sub-paragraph; and

    (b) where the claimant satisfies the conditions in more than one of these sub-paragraphs, only one sub-paragraph shall apply in his case and the one that applies shall be the one most favourable to him.

(8) The conditions specified in this sub-paragraph are that—

    (a) during the relevant period the claimant or a member of his family acquires an interest ("the relevant interest") in a dwelling which he then occupies or continues to occupy, as his home; and

    (b) in the week preceding the week in which the relevant interest was acquired, housing benefit was payable to the claimant or a member of his family;

so however that the amount to be met by way of [². . .] housing costs shall initially not exceed the aggregate of—

        (i) the housing benefit payable in the week mentioned at sub-paragraph (8)(b); and

        (ii) any amount included in the applicable amount of the claimant or a member of his family in accordance with regulation 17(1)(e) or 18(1)(f) in that week;

and shall be increased subsequently only to the extent that it is necessary to take account of any increase, arising after the date of the acquisition, in the standard rate or in any housing costs which qualify under paragraph 17 (other housing costs).

(9) The condition specified in this sub-paragraph is that the loan was taken out, or an existing loan increased, to acquire alternative accommodation more suited to the special needs of a disabled person than the accommodation which was occupied before the acquisition by the claimant.

(10) The conditions specified in this sub-paragraph are that—

    (a) the loan commitment increased in consequence of the disposal of the dwelling occupied as the home and the acquisition of an alternative such dwelling; and

    (b) the change of dwelling was made solely by reason of the need to provide separate sleeping accommodation for children of different sexes aged 10 or over who belong to the same family as the claimant.

(11) The conditions specified in this sub-paragraph are that—

    (a) during the relevant period the claimant or a member of his family acquires an interest ("the relevant interest") in a dwelling which he then occupies as his home; and

    (b) in the week preceding the week in which the relevant interest was acquired, the applicable amount of the claimant or a member of his family included an amount determined by reference to paragraph 17 and did not include any amount specified in paragraph 15 or paragraph 16;

so however that the amount to be met [²by way of housing costs] shall initially not exceed the amount so determined, and shall be increased subsequently only to the extent that it is necessary to take account of any increase, arising after the date of acquisition, in the standard rate or in any housing costs which qualify under paragraph 17 (other housing costs).

(12) The following provisions of this Schedule shall have effect subject to the provisions of this paragraph.

Apportionment of housing costs

2.611   **5.**—(1) Where the dwelling occupied as the home is a composite hereditament and—

(a) before 1st April 1990 for the purposes of section 48(5) of the General Rate Act 1967 (reduction of rates on dwellings), it appeared to a rating authority or it was determined in pursuance of subsection (6) of section 48 of that Act that the hereditament, including the dwelling occupied as the home, was a mixed hereditament and that only a proportion of the rateable value of the hereditament was attributable to use for the purpose of a private dwelling; or

(b) in Scotland, before 1st April 1989 an assessor acting pursuant to section 45(1) of the Water (Scotland) Act 1980 (provision as to valuation roll) has apportioned the net annual value of the premises including the dwelling occupied as the home between the part occupied as a dwelling and the remainder,

the amounts applicable under this Schedule shall be such proportion of the amounts applicable in respect of the hereditament or premises as a whole as is equal to the proportion of the rateable value of the hereditament attributable to the part of the hereditament used for the purposes of a private tenancy or, in Scotland, the proportion of the net annual value of the premises apportioned to the part occupied as a dwelling house.

(2) Subject to sub-paragraph (1) and the following provisions of this paragraph, where the dwelling occupied as the home is a composite hereditament, the amount applicable under this Schedule shall be the relevant fraction of the amount which would otherwise be applicable under this Schedule in respect of the dwelling occupied as the home.

(3) For the purposes of sub-paragraph (2), the relevant fraction shall be obtained in accordance with the formula—

$$\frac{A}{A+B}$$

where—

"A" is the current market value of the claimant's interest in that part of the composite hereditament which is domestic property within the meaning of section 66 of the Act of 1988;

"B" is the current market value of the claimant's interest in that part of the composite hereditament which is not domestic property within that section.

(4) In this paragraph—

"composite hereditament" means—

(a) as respects England and Wales, any hereditament which is shown as a composite hereditament in a local non-domestic rating list;

(b) as respects Scotland, any lands and heritages entered in the valuation roll which are part residential subjects within the meaning of section 26(1) of the Act of 1987;

"local non-domestic rating list" means a list compiled and maintained under section 41(1) of the Act of 1988;

"the Act of 1987" means the Abolition of Domestic Rates Etc. (Scotland) Act 1987;

"the Act of 1988" means the Local Government Finance Act 1988.

(5) Where responsibility for expenditure which relates to housing costs met under this Schedule is shared, the amounts applicable shall be calculated by reference to the appropriate proportion of that expenditure for which the claimant is responsible.

Existing housing costs

2.612   **6.**—(1) Subject to the provisions of this Schedule, the existing housing costs to be met in any particular case are—

(a) where the claimant has been [²entitled to] income support for a continuous period of 26 weeks or more, the aggregate of—

(i) an amount determined in the manner set out in paragraph 10 by applying the standard rate to the eligible capital for the time being owing in connection with a loan which qualifies under paragraph 15 or 16; and

(ii) an amount equal to any payments which qualify under paragraph 17(1)(a) to (c);

   (b) where the claimant has been [²entitled to] income support for a continuous period of not less than 8 weeks but less than 26 weeks, an amount which is half the amount which would fall to be met by applying the provisions of sub-paragraph (a);

   (c) in any other case, nil.

[²(1A) For the purposes of sub-paragraph (1) [⁶ and subject to sub-paragraph (1B)], the eligible capital for the time being owning shall be determined on the date the existing housing costs are first met and thereafter on each anniversary of that date.]

[⁶(1B) Where a claimant or his partner ceases to be in receipt of or treated as being in receipt of income-based jobseeker's allowance [²⁵ or state pension credit] and one of them becomes entitled to income support in a case to which paragraph 1A applies, the eligible capital for the time being owing shall be recalculated on each anniversary of the date on which the housing costs were first met for whichever of the benefits concerned the claimant or his partner was first entitled.]

(2) Where immediately before 2nd October 1995 a claimant's applicable amount included a sum by way of housing costs in accordance with regulation 17(1)(e) or 18(1)(f), but the claimant had not on that date been entitled to income support for a continuous period of 26 weeks or more, the amount of the housing costs to be met in his case shall, for the balance of the 26 weeks falling after 1st October 1995, be determined in accordance with sub-paragraph (3).

(3) Subject to sub-paragraph (4), where the claimant had on 1st October 1995—

   (a) been entitled to income support for less than 16 consecutive weeks (including the benefit week in which 1st October 1995 falls), any housing costs to be met in his case shall remain at the amount they were before 2nd October 1995 until the end of the 16th consecutive week of that entitlement and shall thereafter be determined as if he had been entitled for a continuous period of 26 weeks;

   (b) been entitled for 16 consecutive weeks or more but less than 26 consecutive weeks (including the benefit week in which 1st October 1995 falls), any housing costs to be met in his case shall be determined as if he had been entitled for 26 weeks.

(4) Sub-paragraph (3) above shall apply in a particular case only for so long as the agreement in respect of which a sum by way of housing costs falls to be met immediately before 2nd October 1995 in accordance with regulation 17(1)(e) or 18(1)(f) remains in force.

Transitional Protection

7.—(1) Where the amount applicable to a claimant by way of housing costs under regulation 17(1)(e) or regulation 18(1)(f) (as the case may be) in the benefit week which includes 1st October 1995 ("the first benefit week") is greater than the amount which, in accordance with paragraphs 6 and 10, is applicable in his case in the next succeeding benefit week ("the second benefit week"), the claimant shall be entitled to have his existing housing costs increased by an amount (referred to in this paragraph as "add back") determined in accordance with the following provisions of this paragraph.

2.613

(2) Where the amount to be met by way of housing costs in the first benefit week is greater than the amount to be met in the second benefit week, then the amount of the add back shall be a sum representing the difference between those amounts.

(3) Where the amount of existing housing costs, disregarding the add back, which is applicable to the claimant increases after the second benefit week, the amount of the add back shall be decreased by an amount equal to that increase, and the amount of the add back shall thereafter be the decreased amount.

(4) Any increase in the amount of the existing housing costs, disregarding the add back, shall reduce the amount of the add back in the manner specified in sub-paragraph (3), and where the amount of the add back is reduced to nil, the amount of the existing housing costs shall thereafter not include any amount by way of add back.

(5) Where a person or his partner—

   (a) was entitled to income support; and

   (b) had an applicable amount which included an amount by way of add back in accordance with this paragraph; and

   (c) ceased to be entitled to income support for a continuous period in excess of 12 weeks,

then, on the person or his partner again becoming entitled to income support, the applicable amount of the claimant shall be determined without reference to the provisions relating to add back in sub-paragraphs (1) to (4).

(6) Where a person whose applicable amount included an amount by way of add back under this paragraph loses the right to have an amount by way of housing costs included in his applicable amount, then where that person's applicable amount again includes an amount by way of housing costs, that amount shall be determined without reference to the provisions relating to add back in sub-paragraphs (1) to (4).

(7) Where the partner of a person to whom sub-paragraph (6) applies becomes entitled to income support and—

(a) his applicable amount includes an amount by way of existing housing costs, and

(b) those housing costs are in respect of payments which were formerly met in the applicable amount of the person to whom sub-paragraph (6) applies,

then the provisions of this paragraph shall apply to the partner as they would if he had been responsible for the housing costs immediately before 2nd October 1995 [²provided the claim is made not more than 12 weeks after the last day of entitlement to housing costs relating to a claim made by the person to whom sub-paragraph (6) applies].

(8) Where in the first benefit week, a claimant's applicable amount included an amount by way of housing costs which was calculated by reference to paragraph 7(1)(b)(ii) of Schedule 3 as then in force (50 per cent. of eligible interest met) then for the purposes of this paragraph, the amount of the add back shall be determined by reference to the amount which would have been applicable on that day if 100 per cent. of the claimant's eligible interest had been met, but only from the benefit week following the final benefit week in which paragraph 7(1)(b)(ii) of Schedule 3 would, had it remained in force, have applied in the claimant's case.

(9) Where the existing housing costs of the claimant are determined by reference to two or more loans which qualify under this Schedule, then the provisions of this paragraph shall be applied separately to each of those loans and the amount of the add back (if any) shall be determined in respect of each loan.

[⁹(10) In the case of a person who is a welfare to work beneficiary, the references in sub-paragraphs (5)(c) and (7) to a period of 12 weeks shall be treated as references to a period of 52 weeks.]

New housing costs

2.614

8.—(1) Subject to the provisions of this Schedule, the new housing costs to be met in any particular case are—

(a) where the claimant has been [²entitled to] income support for a continuous period of 39 weeks or more, an amount—

(i) determined in the manner set out in paragraph 10 by applying the standard rate to the eligible capital for the time being owing in connection with a loan which qualifies under paragraph 15 or 16; and

(ii) equal to any payments which qualify under paragraph 17(1)(a) to (c);

(b) in any other case, nil.

[²(1A) For the purposes of sub-paragraph (1) [⁶ and subject to sub-paragraph (1B),] the eligible capital for the time being owing shall be determined on the date the new housing costs are first met and thereafter on each anniversary of that date.]

[⁶(1B) Where a claimant or his partner ceases to be in receipt of or treated as being in receipt of income-based jobseeker's allowance [²⁵ or state pension credit] and one of them becomes entitled to income support in a case to which paragraph 1A applies, the eligible capital for the time being owning shall be recalculated on each anniversary of the date on which the housing costs were first met for whichever of the benefits concerned the claimant or his partner was first entitled.]

(2) This sub-paragraph applies to a claimant who at the time the claim is made—

[³(a) is a person to whom paragraph 4 or 5 of Schedule 1B (persons caring for another person) applies;]

(b) is detained in custody pending trial or sentence upon conviction; or

(c) has been refused payments under a policy of insurance on the ground that—

(i) the claim under the policy is the outcome of a pre-existing medical condition which, under the terms of the policy, does not give rise to any payment by the insurer; or

(ii) he was infected by the Human Immunodeficiency Virus, and the policy was taken out to insure against the risk of being unable to maintain repayments on a loan which is secured by a mortgage or a charge over land, or (in Scotland) by a heritable security.

(3) This sub-paragraph applies subject to sub-paragraph (5) where a person claims income support because of—

(a) the death of a partner; or

(b) being abandoned by his partner,

and where the person's family includes a child.

(4) In the case of a claimant to whom sub-paragraph (2) or (3) applies, any new housing costs shall be met as though they were existing housing costs and paragraph 6 applied to them.

(5) Sub-paragraph (3) shall cease to apply to a person who subsequently becomes one of a couple.

General exclusions from paragraphs 6 and 8   2.615
    9.—(1) Paragraphs 6 and 8 shall not apply where—
[25 (a) the claimant's partner has attained the qualifying age for state pension credit;]
    (b) the housing costs are payments—
        (i) under a co-ownership agreement;
        (ii) under or relating to a tenancy or licence of a Crown tenant; or
        (iii) where the dwelling occupied as the home is a tent, in respect of the tent and the site on which it stands.
    (2) In a case falling within sub-paragraph (1), the housing costs to be met are—
    (a) where head (a) of sub-paragraph (1) applies, an amount—
        (i) determined in the manner set out in paragraph 10 by applying the standard rate to the eligible capital for the time being owing in connection with a loan which qualifies under paragraph 15 or 16; and
        (ii) equal to the payments which qualify under paragraph 17;
    (b) where head (b) of sub-paragraph (1) applies, an amount equal to the payments which qualify under paragraph 17(1)(d) to (f).

[20 The calculation for loans
    10.—(1) The weekly amount of existing housing costs or, as the case may be, new housing   2.616
costs to be met under this Schedule in respect of a loan which qualifies under paragraph 15 or
16 shall be calculated by applying the formula:—

$$\frac{(A \times B)}{52}$$

where—

A = the amount of the loan which qualifies under paragraph 15 or 16;
B = the standard rate for the time being [27 applicable in respect of that loan].]

General provisions applying to new and existing housing costs
    11.—(1) [2 . . .]   2.617
    (2) Where on or after 2nd October 1995 a person enters into a new agreement in respect of
a dwelling and an agreement entered into before 2nd October 1995 ("the earlier agreement")
continues in force independently of the new agreement, then—
    (a) the housing costs applicable to the new agreement shall be calculated by reference to the provisions of paragraph 8 (new housing costs);
    (b) the housing costs applicable to the earlier agreement shall be calculated by reference to the provisions of paragraph 6 (existing housing costs);
and the resulting amounts shall be aggregated.
    (3) [2Sub-paragraph (2) does] not apply in the case of a claimant to whom paragraph 9
applies.
    (4) Where for the time being a loan exceeds, or in a case where more than one loan is to be
taken into account, the aggregate of those loans exceeds the appropriate amount specified in
sub-paragraph (5), then the amount of the loan or, as the case may be, the aggregate amount of
those loans, shall for the purposes of this Schedule, be the appropriate amount.
    (5) Subject to the following provisions of this paragraph, the appropriate amount is
£100,000.
    (6) Where a person is treated under paragraph 3(6) (payments in respect of two dwellings)
as occupying two dwellings as his home, then the restrictions imposed by subparagraph (4)
shall be applied separately to the loans for each dwelling.
    (7) In a case to which paragraph 5 (apportionment of housing costs) applies, the appropri-
ate amount for the purposes of sub-paragraph (4) shall be the lower of—
    (a) a sum determined by applying the formula—
        P × Q, where—
        P = the relevant fraction for the purposes of paragraph 5, and
        Q = the amount or, as the case may be, the aggregate amount for the time being of any loan or loans which qualify under this Schedule; or
    (b) the sum for the time being specified in sub-paragraph (5).
    (8) In a case to which paragraph 15(3) or 16(3) (loans which qualify in part only) applies,
the appropriate amount for the purposes of sub-paragraph (4) shall be the lower of—
    (a) a sum representing for the time being the part of the loan applied for the purposes spe-
cified in paragraph 15(1) or (as the case may be) paragraph 16(1); or
    (b) the sum for the time being specified in sub-paragraph (5).

(9) In the case of any loan to which paragraph 16(2)(k) (loan taken out and used for the purpose of adapting a dwelling for the special needs of a disabled person) applies the whole of the loan, to the extent that it remains unpaid, shall be disregarded in determining whether the amount for the time being specified in sub-paragraph (5) is exceeded.

[²(10) Where in any case the amount for the time being specified for the purposes of sub-paragraph (5) is exceeded and there are two or more loans to be taken into account under either or both paragraphs 15 and 16, then the amount of eligible interest in respect of each of those loans to the extent that the loans remain outstanding shall be determined as if each loan had been reduced to a sum equal to the qualifying portion of that loan.

(11) For the purposes of sub-paragraph (10), the qualifying portion of a loan shall be determined by applying the following formula—

$$R \times \frac{S}{T}$$

where—

R = the amount for the time being specified for the purposes of sub-paragraph (4);
S = the amount of the outstanding loan to be taken into account;
T = the aggregate of all outstanding loans to be taken into account under paragraphs 15 and 16.]

The standard rate

2.618

12.—[²⁸(1) The standard rate is the rate of interest applicable per annum to a loan which qualifies under this Schedule.

(2) Subject to sub-paragraphs (3), (4) and (6), the standard rate shall be 1.58 per cent. plus—
  (a) the rate announced from time to time by the Monetary Policy Committee of the Bank of England as the official dealing rate, being the rate at which the Bank is willing to enter into transactions for providing short term liquidity in the money markets, or
  (b) where an order under section 19 of the Bank of England Act 1998 (reserve powers) is in force, any equivalent rate determined by the Treasury under that section.

(3) The Secretary of State shall determine the date from which the standard rate calculated in accordance with sub-paragraph (2) takes effect.

(4) Where—
  (a) the actual rate of interest charged on the loan which qualifies under this Schedule is less than 5 per cent. per annum on the day the housing costs first fall to be met, and
  (b) that day occurs before 28th November 2004,
the standard rate shall be equal to that actual rate.

(5) Sub-paragraph (4) shall cease to apply in a particular case to any one or more loans which fall within that sub-paragraph on whichever of the following dates occurs first—
  (a) the date on which the actual rate of interest charged on such a loan is 5 per cent. per annum or higher,
  (b) the anniversary of the date on which the housing costs first fell to be met, or
  (c) where a supersession decision based on a change of circumstances arising on or after 28th November 2004 is made under section 10 of the Social Security Act 1998 (decisions superseding earlier decisions), the date of the change of circumstances.

(6) Where sub-paragraph (4) does not apply to a loan which qualifies under this Schedule, the standard rate shall be 5.88 per cent. until the first date determined by the Secretary of State under sub-paragraph (3).]

Excessive Housing Costs

2.619

13.—(1) Housing costs which, apart from this paragraph, fall to be met under this Schedule shall be met only to the extent specified in sub-paragraph (3) where—
  (a) the dwelling occupied as the home, excluding any part which is let, is larger than is required by the claimant and his family and any child or young person to whom regulation 16(4) applies (foster children) and any other non-dependants having regard, in particular, to suitable alternative accommodation occupied by a household of the same size; or
  (b) the immediate area in which the dwelling occupied as the home is located is more expensive than other areas in which suitable alternative accommodation exists; or
  (c) the outgoings of the dwelling occupied as the home which are met under paragraphs 15 to 17 are higher than the outgoings of suitable alternative accommodation in the area.

(2) For the purposes of heads (a) to (c) of sub-paragraph (1), no regard shall be had to the capital value of the dwelling occupied as the home.

(3) Subject to the following provisions of this paragraph, the amount of the loan which falls to be met shall be restricted and the excess over the amounts which the claimant would need to obtain suitable alternative accommodation shall not be allowed.

(4) Where, having regard to the relevant factors, it is not reasonable to expect the claimant and his family to seek alternative cheaper accommodation, no restriction shall be made under sub-paragraph (3).

(5) In sub-paragraph (4) "the relevant factors" are—

   (a) the availability of suitable accommodation and the level of housing costs in the area; and

   (b) the circumstances of the family including in particular the age and state of health of its members, the employment prospects of the claimant and, where a change in accommodation is likely to result in a change of school, the effect on the education of any child or young person who is a member of his family, or any child or young person who is not treated as part of his family by virtue of regulation 16(4) (foster children).

[[13](6) Where sub-paragraph (4) does not apply and the claimant (or other member of the family) was able to meet the financial commitments for the dwelling occupied as the home when these were entered into, no restriction shall be made under this paragraph during the 26 weeks immediately following the date on which—

   (a) the claimant became entitled to income support where the claimant's housing costs fell within one of the cases in sub-paragraph (1) on that date; or

   (b) a decision took effect which was made under section 10 (decisions superseding earlier decisions) of the Social Security Act 1998 on the ground that the claimant's housing costs fell within one of the cases in sub-paragraph (1),

nor during the next 26 weeks if and so long as the claimant uses his best endeavours to obtain cheaper accommodation.]

(7) For the purposes of calculating any period of 26 weeks referred to in sub-paragraph (6), and for those purposes only, a person shall be treated as entitled to income support for any period of 12 weeks or less in respect of which he was not in receipt of income support and which fell immediately between periods in respect of which he was in receipt thereof.

(8) Any period in respect of which—

   (a) income support was paid to a person, and

   (b) it was subsequently determined [[13]. . .] that he was not entitled to income support for that period,

shall be treated for the purposes of sub-paragraph (7) as a period in respect of which he was not in receipt of income support.

(9) Heads (c) to (f) of sub-paragraph (1) of paragraph 14 shall apply to sub-paragraph (7) as they apply to paragraphs 6 and 8 but with the modification that the words "Subject to sub-paragraph (2)" were omitted and references to "the claimant" were references to the person mentioned in sub-paragraph (7).

Linking rule

14.—(1) Subject to sub-paragraph (2), for the purposes of this Schedule—   2.620

   (a) a person shall be treated as being in receipt of income support during the following periods—

      (i) any period in respect of which it was subsequently [[13]determined] that he was entitled to income support; and

      (ii) any period of 12 weeks or less [[16] or, as the case may be, 52 weeks or less,] in respect of which he was not in receipt of income support and which fell immediately between periods in respect of which

        [[4](aa) he was, or was treated as being, in receipt of income support,

        (bb) he was treated as entitled to income support for the purpose of subparagraph (5) or (5A), or

        (cc) (i) above applies;]

   (b) a person shall be treated as not being in receipt of income support during any period other than a period to which (a)(ii) above applies in respect of which it is subsequently [[13]determined] that he was not so entitled;

   (c) where—

      (i) the claimant was a member of a couple or a polygamous marriage; and

      (ii) his partner was, in respect of a past period, in receipt of income support for himself and the claimant; and

      (iii) the claimant is no longer a member of that couple or polygamous marriage; and

      (iv) the claimant made his claim for income support within twelve weeks [[16] or, as the case may be, 52 weeks,] of ceasing to be a member of that couple or polygamous marriage, he shall be treated as having been in receipt of income support for the same period as his former partner had been or had been treated, for the purposes of this Schedule, as having been;

(d) where the claimant's partner's applicable amount was determined in accordance with paragraph 1(1) (single claimant) or paragraph 1(2) (lone parent) of Schedule 2 (applicable amounts) in respect of a past period, provided that the claim was made within twelve weeks [16 or, as the case may be, 52 weeks,] of the claimant and his partner becoming one of a couple or polygamous marriage, the claimant shall be treated as having been in receipt of income support for the same period as his partner had been or had been treated, for the purposes of this Schedule, as having been;

(e) where the claimant is a member of a couple or a polygamous marriage and his partner was, in respect of a past period, in receipt of income support for himself and the claimant, and the claimant has begun to receive income support as a result of an election by the members of the couple or polygamous marriage, he shall be treated as having been in receipt of income support for the same period as his partner had been or had been treated, for the purposes of this Schedule, as having been;

[7(ee) where the claimant—

(i) is a member of a couple or a polygamous marriage and the claimant's partner was, immediately before the participation by any member of that couple or polygamous marriage in an employment programme specified in regulation 75(1)(a)(ii) of the Jobseeker's Allowance Regulations 1996 [19, in the Intensive Activity Period specified in regulation 75(1)(a)(iv) of those Regulations or in the Intensive Activity Period for 50 plus], in receipt of income support and his applicable amount included an amount for the couple or for the partners of the polygamous marriage; and

(ii) has, immediately after that participation in that programme, begun to receive income support as a result of an election under regulation 4(3) of the Social Security (Claims and Payments) Regulations 1987 by the members of the couple or polygamous marriage,

the claimant shall be treated as having been in receipt of income support for the same period as his partner had been or had been treated, for the purposes of this Schedule, as having been;]

(f) where—

(i) the claimant was a member of a family of a person (not being a former partner) entitled to income support and at least one other member of that family was a child or young person; and

(ii) the claimant becomes a member of another family which includes that child or young person; and

(iii) the claimant made his claim for income support within 12 weeks 1996[16 or, as the case may be, 52 weeks,] of the date on which the person entitled to income support mentioned in (i) above ceased to be so entitled,

the claimant shall be treated as being in receipt of income support for the same period as that person had been or had been treated, for the purposes of this Schedule, as having been.

(2) Where a claimant, with the care of a child, has ceased to be in receipt of income support in consequence of the payment of child support maintenance under the Child Support Act 1991 and immediately before ceasing to be so in receipt an amount determined in accordance with paragraph 6(1)(a)(i) or paragraph 8(1)(a)(i) was applicable to him, then—

(a) if the child support maintenance [23 calculation] concerned is terminated or replaced [13 . . .] by a lower [23 calculation] in consequence of the coming into force on or after 18th April 1995 of regulations made under the Child Support Act 1991; or

(b) where the child support maintenance [23 calculation] concerned is an [23 interim maintenance decision or default maintenance decision] and, in circumstances other than those referred to in head (a), it is terminated or replaced after termination by another [23 interim maintenance decision or default maintenance decision] or by a maintenance [23 calculation] made in accordance with Part I of Schedule 1 to the Child Support Act 1991, in either case of a lower amount than the [23 calculation] concerned,

sub-paragraph (1)(a)(ii) shall apply to him as if for the words "any period of 12 weeks or less" there were substituted the words "any period of 26 weeks or less".

(3) For the purposes of this Schedule, where a claimant has ceased to be entitled to income support because he or his partner is participating in arrangements for training made under section 2 of the Employment and Training Act 1973 or attending a course at an employment rehabilitation centre established under that section, he shall be treated as if he had been in

receipt of income support for the period during which he or his partner was participating in such arrangements or attending such a course.

[7(3ZA) For the purposes of this Schedule, a claimant who has ceased to be entitled to income support because—

    (a) that claimant or his partner was participating in an employment programme specified in regulation 75(1)(a)(ii) of the Jobseeker's Allowance Regulations 1996 [19, in the Intensive Activity Period specified in regulation 75(1)(a)(iv) of those Regulations, in the Intensive Activity Period for 50 plus] [14or in an employment zone scheme]; and

    (b) in consequence of such participation the claimant or his partner was engaged in remunerative work or had an income in excess of the claimant's applicable amount as prescribed in Part IV,

shall be treated as if he had been in receipt of income support for the period during which he or his partner was participating in that programme [19or activity].]

[2(3A) Where, for the purposes of sub-paragraphs [7(1), (3) and (3ZA)], a person is treated as being in receipt of income support, for a certain period, he shall [12, subject to sub-paragraph (3AA),] be treated as being entitled to income support for the same period.]

[12(3AA) Where the appropriate amount of a loan exceeds the amount specified in paragraph 11(5), sub-paragraph (3A) shall not apply except—

    (a) for the purposes of paragraph 6(1) or 8(1); or

    (b) where a person has ceased to be in receipt of income support for a period of 52 weeks or less because he or his partner is a welfare to work beneficiary.]

[7(3B) For the purposes of this Schedule, in determining whether a person is entitled to or to be treated as entitled to income support, entitlement to a contribution-based jobseeker's allowance immediately before a period during which that person or his partner is participating in an employment programme specified in regulation 75(1)(a)(ii) of the Jobseeker's Allowance Regulations 1996 [19, in the Intensive Activity Period specified in regulation 75(1)(a)(iv) of those Regulations or in the Intensive Activity Period for 50 plus] shall be treated as entitlement to income support for the purposes of any requirement that a person is, or has been, entitled to income support for any period of time.]

(4) For the purposes of this Schedule, sub-paragraph (5) applies where a person is not entitled to income support by reason only that he has—

    (a) capital exceeding £8,000; or

    (b) income exceeding the applicable amount which applies in his case, or

    (c) both capital exceeding £8,000 and income exceeding the applicable amount which applies in his case.

(5) A person to whom sub-paragraph (4) applies shall be treated as entitled to income support throughout any period of not [2more] than 39 weeks which comprises only days—

    (a) on which he is entitled to unemployment benefit, [3a contribution-based jobseeker's allowance,] statutory sick pay or incapacity benefit; or

    (b) on which he is, although not entitled to any of the benefits mentioned in head (a) above, entitled to be credited with earnings equal to the lower earnings limit for the time being in force in accordance with [11regulation 8A or 8B] of the Social Security (Credits) Regulations 1975; or

    (c) in respect of which the claimant is treated as being in receipt of income support.

[2(5A) Subject to sub-paragraph (5B), a person to whom sub-paragraph (4) applies and who is either a person to whom [3paragraph 4 or 5 of Schedule 1B (persons caring for another person) applies] or a lone parent shall, for the purposes of this Schedule, be treated as entitled to income support throughout any period of not more than 39 weeks following the refusal of a claim for income support made by or on behalf of that person.

(5B) Sub-paragraph (5A) shall not apply in relation to a person mentioned in that sub-paragraph who, during the period referred to in that sub-paragraph—

    (a) is engaged in, or is treated as engaged in, remunerative work or whose partner is engaged in, or is treated as engaged in, remunerative work;

    [3(b) is a [15full-time student], other than one who would qualify for income support under regulation 4ZA(3) (prescribed categories of person);]

    (c) is temporarily absent from Great Britain, other than in the circumstances specified in regulation 4(2) and (3)(c) (temporary absence from Great Britain).]

(6) In a case where—

    (a) [2sub-paragraphs (5) and (5A) apply] solely by virtue of sub-paragraph (4)(b); and

    (b) the claimant's income includes payments under a policy taken out to insure against the risk that the policy holder is unable to meet any loan or payment which qualifies under paragraphs 15 to 17,

[²sub-paragraphs (5) and (5A)] shall have effect as if for the words "throughout any period of not [²more] than 39 weeks" there shall be substituted the words "throughout any period that payments made in accordance with the terms of the policy".

(7) [². . .]

(8) This sub-paragraph applies—

(a) to a person who claims income support, or in respect of whom income support is claimed, and who—

    (i) received payments under a policy of insurance taken out to insure against loss of employment, and those payments are exhausted; and

    (ii) had a previous award of income support where the applicable amount included an amount by way of housing costs; and

(b) where the period in respect of which the previous award of income support was payable ended not more than 26 weeks before the date the claim was made.

(9) Where sub-paragraph (8) applies, in determining—

(a) for the purposes of paragraph 6(1) whether a person has been [²entitled to] income support for a continuous period of 26 weeks or more; or

(b) for the purposes of paragraph 8(1) whether a claimant has been [²entitled to] income support for a continuous period of 39 weeks or more,

any week falling between the date of the termination of the previous award and the date of the new claim shall be ignored.

[¹⁰(10) In the case of a person who is a welfare to work beneficiary, the references in sub-paragraphs (1)(a)(ii), [¹⁷ (1)(c)(iv),] (1)(d) and (1)(f)(iii) to a period of 12 weeks shall be treated as references to a period of 52 weeks.]

[¹⁸ (11) For the purposes of sub-paragraph (1)(a)(ii), (1)(c)(iv), (1)(d) and (1)(f)(iii), the relevant period shall be—

(a) 52 weeks in the case of a person to whom sub-paragraph (12) applies;

(b) subject to sub-paragraph (10), 12 weeks in any other case.

(12) This sub-paragraph applies, subject to sub-paragraph (13), in the case of a person who, on or after 9th April 2001, has ceased to be entitled to income support because he or his partner—

(a) has commenced employment as an employed earner or as a self-employed earner or has increased the hours in which he is engaged in such employment;

(b) is taking active steps to establish himself in employment as an employed earner or as a self-employed earner under any scheme for assisting persons to become so employed which is mentioned in regulation 19(1)(r)(i) to (iii) of the Jobseeker's Allowance Regulations 1996; or

(c) is participating in—

    (i) a New Deal option;

    (ii) an employment zone programme; or

    (iii) the self-employment route; [¹⁹ or

    (iv) the Intensive Activity Period specified in regulation 75(1)(a)(iv) of the Jobseeker's Allowance Regulations 1996 or the Intensive Activity Period for 50 plus,]

and, as a consequence, he or his partner was engaged in remunerative work or had income in excess of the applicable amount as prescribed in Part IV.

(13) Sub-paragraph (12) shall only apply to the extent that immediately before the day on which the person ceased to be entitled to income support, his housing costs were being met in accordance with paragraph 6(1)(a) [²² 6(1)(b)] or 8(1)(a) or would have been so met but for any non-dependant deduction under paragraph 18.]

[²⁵ (14) For the purpose of determining whether the linking rules set out in this paragraph apply in a case where a claimant's former partner was entitled to state pension credit, any reference to income support in this Schedule shall be taken to include also a reference to state pension credit.]

Loans on residential property

2.621   **15.**—(1) A loan qualifies under this paragraph where the loan was taken out to defray monies applied for any of the following purposes—

(a) acquiring an interest in the dwelling occupied as the home; or

(b) paying off another loan to the extent that the other loan would have qualified under head (a) above had the loan not been paid off.

(2) For the purposes of this paragraph, references to a loan include also a reference to money borrowed under a hire purchase agreement for any purpose specified in heads (a) and (b) of sub-paragraph (1) above.

(3) Where a loan is applied only in part for the purposes specified in heads (a) and (b) of sub-paragraph (1), only that portion of the loan which is applied for that purpose shall qualify under this paragraph.

Loans for repairs and improvements to the dwelling occupied as the home

16.—(1) A loan qualifies under this paragraph where the loan was taken out, with or without security, for the purpose of—

2.622

    (a) carrying out repairs and improvements to the dwelling occupied as the home;

    (b) paying any service charge imposed to meet the cost of repairs and improvements to the dwelling occupied as the home;

    (c) paying off another loan to the extent that the other loan would have qualified under head (a) or (b) of this sub-paragraph had the loan not been paid off,

and the loan was used for that purpose, or is used for that purpose within 6 months of the date of receipt or such further period as may be reasonable in the particular circumstances of the case.

(2) In sub-paragraph (1) "repairs and improvements" means any of the following measures undertaken with a view to maintaining the fitness of the dwelling for human habitation or, where the dwelling forms part of a building, any part of the building containing that dwelling—

    (a) provision of a fixed bath, shower, wash basin, sink or lavatory, and necessary associated plumbing, including the provision of hot water not connected to a central heating system;

    (b) repairs to existing heating systems;

    (c) damp proof measures;

    (d) provision of ventilation and natural lighting;

    (e) provision of drainage facilities;

    (f) provision of facilities for preparing and cooking food;

    (g) provision of insulation of the dwelling occupied as the home;

    (h) provision of electric lighting and sockets;

    (i) provision of storage facilities for fuel or refuse;

    (j) repairs of unsafe structural defects;

    (k) adapting a dwelling for the special needs of a disabled person; or

    (l) provision of separate sleeping accommodation for children of different sexes aged 10 or over who are part of the same family as the claimant.

(3) Where a loan is applied only in part for the purposes specified in sub-paragraph (1), only that portion of the loan which is applied for that purpose shall qualify under this paragraph.

Other housing costs

17.—(1) Subject to the deduction specified in sub-paragraph (2) and the reductions applicable in sub-paragraph (5), there shall be met under this paragraph the amounts, calculated on a weekly basis, in respect of the following housing costs—

2.623

    (a) payments by way of rent or ground rent relating to a long tenancy and, in Scotland, payments by way of feu duty;

    (b) service charges;

    (c) payments by way of rentcharge within the meaning of section 1 of the Rentcharges Act 1977;

    (d) payments under a co-ownership scheme;

    (e) payments under or relating to a tenancy or licence of a Crown tenant;

    (f) where the dwelling occupied as the home is a tent, payments in respect of the tent and the site on which it stands.

(2) Subject to sub-paragraph (3), the deductions to be made from the weekly amounts to be met under this paragraph are—

    (a) where the costs are inclusive of any of the items mentioned in paragraph 5(2) of Schedule 1 to the Housing Benefit (General) Regulations 1987 (payment in respect of fuel charges), the deductions prescribed in that paragraph unless the claimant provides evidence on which the actual or approximate amount of the service charge for fuel may be estimated, in which case the estimated amount;

    (b) where the costs are inclusive of ineligible service charges within the meaning of paragraph 1 of Schedule 1 to the Housing Benefit (General) Regulations 1987 (ineligible service charges) the amounts attributable to those ineligible service charges or where that amount is not separated from or separately identified within the housing costs to be met under this paragraph, such part of the payments made in respect of those housing costs which are fairly attributable to the provision of those ineligible services having regard to the costs of comparable services;

(c) any amount for repairs and improvements, and for this purpose the expression "repairs and improvements" has the same meaning it has in paragraph 16(2).

(3) Where arrangements are made for the housing costs, which are met under this paragraph and which are normally paid for a period of 52 weeks, to be paid instead for a period of 53 weeks, or to be paid irregularly, or so that no such costs are payable or collected in certain periods, or so that the costs for different periods in the year are of different amounts, the weekly amount shall be the amount payable for the year divided by 52.

(4) Where the claimant or a member of his family—

(a) pays for reasonable repairs or redecorations to be carried out to the dwelling they occupy; and

(b) that work was not the responsibility of the claimant or any member of his family; and

(c) in consequence of that work being done, the costs which are normally met under this paragraph are waived,

then those costs shall, or a period not exceeding 8 weeks, be treated as payable.

(5) Where in England and Wales an amount calculated on a weekly basis in respect of housing costs specified in sub-paragraph (1)(e) (Crown tenants) includes water charges, that amount shall be reduced—

(a) where the amount payable in respect of water charges is known, by that amount;

(b) in any other case, by the amount which would be the likely weekly water charge had the property not been occupied by a Crown tenant.

Non-dependant deductions

2.624

18.—(1) Subject to the following provisions of this paragraph, the following deductions from the amount to be met under the preceding paragraphs of this Schedule in respect of housing costs shall be made—

[³¹(a) in respect of a non-dependant aged 18 or over who is engaged in any remunerative work, [³²£47.75];

(b) in respect of a non-dependant aged 18 or over to whom paragraph (a) does not apply, [³²£7.40].]

(2) In the case of a non-dependant aged 18 or over to whom sub-paragraph (1)(a) applies because he is in [²remunerative] work, where the claimant satisfies the [¹³Secretary of State] that the non-dependant's gross weekly income is—

(a) less than [³²£101.00], the deduction to be made under this paragraph shall be the deduction specified in sub-paragraph (1)(b);

(b) not less than [³²£101.00] but less than [³²£150.00], the deduction to be made under this paragraph shall be [³²£17.00];

(c) not less than [³²£150.00] but less than [³²£194.00], the deduction to be made under this paragraph shall be [³²£23.35];

(d) not less than [³²£194.00] but less than [³²£258.00], the deduction to be made under this paragraph shall be [³²£38.20];

(e) not less than [³²£258.00] but less than [³²£322.00], the deduction to be made under this paragraph shall be [³²£43.50]].

(3) Only one deduction shall be made under this paragraph in respect of a couple or, as the case may be, the members of a polygamous marriage, and where, but for this sub-paragraph, the amount that would fall to be deducted in respect of one member of a couple or polygamous marriage is higher than the amount (if any) that would fall to be deducted in respect of the other, or any other, member, the higher amount shall be deducted.

(4) In applying the provisions of sub-paragraph (2) in the case of a couple or, as the case may be, a polygamous marriage, regard shall be had, for the purpose of sub-paragraph (2), to the couple's or, as the case may be, all the members of the polygamous marriage's, joint weekly income.

(5) Where a person is a non-dependant in respect of more than one joint occupier of a dwelling (except where the joint occupiers are a couple or members of a polygamous marriage), the deduction in respect of that non-dependant shall be apportioned between the joint occupiers (the amount so apportioned being rounded to the nearest penny) having regard to the number of joint occupiers and the proportion of the housing costs in respect of the dwelling occupied as the home payable by each of them.

(6) No deduction shall be made in respect of any non-dependants occupying the dwelling occupied as the home of the claimant, if the claimant or any partner of his is—

(a) blind or treated as blind by virtue of paragraph 12 of Schedule 2 (additional condition for the higher pensioner and disability premiums); or

(b) receiving in respect of himself either—

(i) an attendance allowance; or

(ii) the care component of the disability living allowance.
(7) No deduction shall be made in respect of a non-dependant—
    (a) if, although he resides with the claimant, it appears to the [[13] Secretary of State] that the dwelling occupied as his home is normally elsewhere; or
    (b) if he is in receipt of a training allowance paid in connection with a Youth Training Scheme established under section 2 of the Employment and Training Act 1973 or section 2 of the Enterprise and New Towns (Scotland) Act 1990; or
    (c) if he is a full-time student during a period of study or, if he is not in remunerative work, during a recognised summer vacation appropriate to his course; or
    (d) if he is aged under 25 and in receipt of income support [[5]or an income-based jobseeker's allowance]; or
    (e) in respect of whom a deduction in the calculation of a rent rebate or allowance falls to be made under regulation 63 of the Housing Benefit (General) Regulations 1987 (non-dependant deductions); or
    (f) to whom, but for paragraph (2C) of regulation 3 (definition of non-dependant) paragraph (2B) of that regulation would apply; or
    (g) if he is not residing with the claimant because he has been a patient for a period in excess of [[24] 52] weeks, or is a prisoner, and for these purposes—
        (i) "patient" and "prisoner" have the meanings given in regulation 21(3) (special cases), and
        (ii) the period of [[24] 52] weeks shall be calculated by reference to paragraph (2) of that regulation as if that paragraph applied in his case [[31] or
    (h) if he is in receipt of state pension credit.]
(8) In the case of a non-dependant to whom sub-paragraph (2) applies because he is in [[2]remunerative] work, there shall be disregarded from his gross income—
    (a) any attendance allowance or disability living allowance received by him;
    (b) any payment made under the Macfarlane Trust, the Macfarlane (Special Payments) Trust, the Macfarlane (Special Payments) (No.2) Trust, the Fund, the Eileen Trust or the Independent Living Funds which, had his income fallen to be calculated under regulation 40 (calculation of income other than earnings), would have been disregarded under paragraph 21 of Schedule 9 (income in kind); and
    (c) any payment which, had his income fallen to be calculated under regulation 40 would have been disregarded under paragraph 39 of Schedule 9 (payments made under certain trusts and certain other payments).

Rounding of fractions
19. Where any calculation made under this Schedule results in a fraction of a penny, that fraction shall be treated as a penny.]

2.625

Amendments

1. Social Security (Income Support and Claims and Payments) Amendment Regulations 1995 (SI 1995/1613), reg.2 and Sch.1 (October 2, 1995).
2. Social Security (Income Support, Claims and Payments and Adjudication) Amendment Regulations 1995 (SI 1995/2927), reg.5 (December 12, 1995).
3. Income Support (General) (Jobseeker's Allowance Consequential Amendments) Regulations 1996 (SI 1996/206), reg.24 (October 7, 1996).
4. Income-related Benefits Schemes and Social Fund (Miscellaneous Amendments) Regulations 1996 (SI 1996/1944), reg.6(10) (October 7, 1996).
5. Social Security and Child Support (Miscellaneous Amendments) Regulations 1997 (SI 1997/827), reg.6 (April 7, 1997).
6. Social Security (Miscellaneous Amendments) (No.4) Regulations 1997 (SI 1997/2305), reg.2 (October 22, 1997).
7. Social Security Amendment (New Deal) Regulations 1997 (SI 1997/2863), reg.16 (January 5, 1998).
8. Social Security (Non-Dependant Deductions) Regulations 1996 (SI 1996/2518), reg.4 (April 6, 1998).
9. Social Security (Welfare to Work) Regulations 1998 (SI 1998/2231), reg.13(4)(a) (October 5, 1998).
10. Social Security (Welfare to Work) Regulations 1998 (SI 1998/2231), reg.13(4)(b) (October 5, 1998).

2.626

11. Social Security Benefits (Miscellaneous Amendments) Regulations 1999 (SI 1999/714), reg.3 (April 5, 1999).

12. Income Support (General) and Jobseeker's Allowance Amendment Regulations 1999 (SI 1999/1921), reg.2(1) (August 2, 1999).

13. Social Security Act 1998 (Commencement No.12 and Consequential and Transitional Provisions) Order 1999 (SI 1999/3178 (C.81)), art.3(5) and Sch.5, para.9 (November 29, 1999)

14. Social Security Amendment (Employment Zones) Regulations 2000 (SI 2000/724), reg.4(3)(c) (April 3, 2000).

15. Social Security Amendment (Students) Regulations 2000 (SI 2000/1981), reg.5(5) and Sch. (July 31, 2000).

16. Social Security (Miscellaneous Amendments) Regulations 2001 (SI 2001/488), reg.6(a) (April 9, 2001).

17. Social Security (Miscellaneous Amendments) Regulations 2001 (SI 2001/488), reg.6(b) (April 9, 2001).

18. Social Security (Miscellaneous Amendments) Regulations 2001 (SI 2001/488), reg.6(c) (April 9, 2001).

19. Social Security Amendment (New Deal) Regulations 2001 (SI 2001/ 1029), reg.14 (April 9, 2001).

20. Income Support (General) and Jobseeker's Allowance Amendment Regulations 2001 (SI 2001/3651), reg.2(1) (December 10, 2001).

21. Social Security Amendment (Residential Care and Nursing Homes) Regulations 2001 (SI 2001/3767), reg.2(1) and Pt I of Sch., para.15 (April 8, 2002).

22. Social Security (Miscellaneous Amendments) Regulations 2002 (SI 2002/841), reg.6 (April 8, 2002).

23. Child Support (Consequential Amendments and Transitional Provisions) Regulations 2001 (SI 2001/158), reg.6(3) (in force in relation to any particular case on the day on which s.1 of the Child Support, Pensions and Social Security Act 2000 comes into force in relation to that type of case).

24. Social Security (Hospital In-Patients and Miscellaneous Amendments) Regulations 2003 (SI 2003/1195), reg.3(4) (May 21. 2003).

25 State Pension Credit (Consequential, Transitional and Miscellaneous Provisions) Regulations 2002 (SI 2002/3019), reg.29(6) (October 6, 2003).

26. Social Security (Housing Costs Amendments) Regulations 2004 (SI 2004/2825), reg.2(2) (November 28, 2004).

27. Social Security (Housing Costs Amendments) Regulations 2004 (SI 2004/2825), reg.2(3) (November 28, 2004).

28. Social Security (Housing Costs Amendments) Regulations 2004 (SI 2004/2825), reg.2(4) (November 28, 2004).

29. Social Security (Housing Costs Amendments) Regulations 2004 (SI 2004/2825), reg.2(5) (November 28, 2004).

30. Social Security (Housing Benefit, Council Tax Benefit, State Pension Credit and Miscellaneous Amendments) Regulations 2004 (SI 2004/2327), reg.5(a) (April 4, 2005).

31. Social Security (Housing Benefit, Council Tax Benefit, State Pension Credit and Miscellaneous Amendments) Regulations 2004 (SI 2004/2327), reg.5(b) (April 4, 2005).

32. Social Security Benefits Up-rating Order 2005 (SI 2005/522), art.16(6) (April 11, 2005).

DEFINITIONS

2.627   "attendance allowance"—see reg.2(1).
"benefit week"—*ibid.*
"claimant"—*ibid.*
"close relative"—*ibid.*
"couple"—*ibid.*

"course of study"—*ibid.*
"co-ownership scheme"—*ibid.*
"Crown tenant"—*ibid.*
"disability living allowance"—*ibid.*
"dwelling occupied as the home"—*ibid.*
"employment zone"—*ibid.*
"family"—see SSCBA, s.137(1).
"full-time student"—see reg.61(1).
"housing benefit expenditure"—see reg.2(1).
"Intensive Activity Period for 50 plus"—*ibid.*
"lone parent"—*ibid.*
"non-dependant"—see reg.3.
"nursing home"—see reg.19(3).
"partner"—see reg.2(1).
"period of study"—*ibid.*
"polygamous marriage"—*ibid.*
"remunerative work"—see reg.5.
"residential care home"—see reg.2(1).
"self-employment route"—*ibid.*
"single claimant"—*ibid.*
"the Eileen Trust"—see reg.2(1).
"the Fund"—*ibid.*
"the Independent Living Funds"—*ibid.*
"the Macfarlane (Special Payments) Trust"—*ibid.*
"the Macfarlane (Special Payments) (No.2) Trust"—*ibid.*
"the Macfarlane Trust"—*ibid.*
"training allowance"—*ibid.*
"water charges"—*ibid.*
"welfare to work beneficiary"—*ibid.*
"year of assessment"—*ibid.*

GENERAL NOTE

A new Sch.3 came into force on October 2, 1995 which introduced major changes **2.628** to the rules for payment of housing costs by income support. See the notes to Schedule 3 in the 1995 edition of *Mesher and Wood, Income-related Benefits: the Legislation* for details of the previous rules. See also the associated changes to paras 29 and 30 of Sch.9, and Schs 9 and 9A of the Claims and Payments Regulations. Note reg.5(2) of the Social Security (Income Support and Claims and Payments) Amendment Regulations 1995 which preserves the operation of previous saving provisions (see p.672).

The new rules placed further substantial limits on the housing costs that will be met by income support. Since August 1993 this has been increasingly restricted. The upper ceiling for loans, first introduced on August 2, 1993, has been reduced twice and is now (since April 10, 1995) £100,000. Since May 2, 1994, interest on loans taken out or increased while a person was entitled to income support (or caught by the 26 weeks linking rule), which increased his housing costs, has not been met, subject to certain exceptions (note that from October 2, 1995 this only applies to loans taken out for house purchase and not those for repairs and improvements). These limits were in addition to those applying to tenants buying their own homes and the rules concerning excessive housing costs. All these provisions were retained (although there is no longer a separate rule for tenants who buy their own homes, to whom para.4(8) will now apply). However, the new restrictions signified a more fundamental change of approach to the meeting of housing costs by income support.

The main new departure was that no mortgage interest (nor some other housing costs—see below) is to be paid at all for certain periods which vary according to whether the loan or other agreement existed before October 2, 1995 (for the position of replacement loans see below). Interest will also generally be payable at a set rate rather than at the actual rate charged. Interest on arrears of interest (previously payable in limited circumstances, *e.g.* on arrears which accrued during the first 16 weeks of a claim) will not be met, nor will interest on loans for non-approved purposes for separated partners. In addition, the loans for repairs and improvements that qualify were further restricted. There was some transitional protection for existing claimants. Note also that *all* payments of loan interest are now made directly to lenders who participate in the mortgage interest direct scheme; previously such loan interest payments were paid to claimants during the 50 per cent period (see the amendment to para.2 of Sch.9A to the Claims and Payments Regulations).

These changes were introduced as part of the Government's long-term aim of replacing state support with private insurance where possible. According to the Social Security Advisory Committee's (SSAC) report on the proposals (Cm. 2905(1995)), about 10 per cent of all home buyers then had mortgage payment protection insurance (para.16). The DSS's Memorandum to SSAC also referred to the need to simplify the calculation of housing costs (which were responsible for 13.1 per cent of all income support errors in the period April to December 1994). But the Memorandum acknowledged that the introduction of a set rate of interest was also part of a clear policy that the State would not, even in the long-term, take full responsibility for borrowers' commitments (para.36). SSAC recommended that the changes, in particular for existing borrowers, be postponed until April 1996 and made a number of other proposals to mitigate the effect of the new scheme. However, most of the recommendations were rejected. In reply to SSAC, the Government stated that the shift to private insurance for payment of mortgage interest was primarily directed at new loans (*i.e.* those taken out after October 1, 1995). In the Government's view the changes did not increase the need for mortgage insurance for existing borrowers, because most mortgage protection policies do not cover the first two months (under the new rules the waiting period for existing borrowers is eight weeks). But this ignores other important features of the new rules (such as 50 per cent only for the next 18 weeks, interest to be paid at the standard rate, etc.) which also had a major impact on existing borrowers. The concessions made by the Government in response to the widespread criticism of the new restrictions were very limited. Where concessions were made, for example in relation to carers, this generally only resulted in the existing borrower rule being applied, rather than complete exemption from the changes.

In *CIS 16769/1996* the Commissioner rejects the contention that the amending regulations substituting the new Sch.3 were *ultra vires*. In that case the claimant was not entitled to income support on October 1, 1995; he simply had an expectation that if the regulations and any other relevant circumstances did not change, he would be entitled to income support on a new claim made on or after November 7, 1995. In those circumstances there was no question of any accrued right being interfered with by the revocation of the former Sch.3.

In addition, from October 7, 1996, the effect of reg.32 of the Income Support (General) (Jobseeker's Allowance Consequential Amendments) Regulations 1996 (see p.676) should be noted. This provides that entitlement to income-based JSA counts as entitlement to income support for the purpose of satisfying any condition that the person is or has been entitled to income support for any period of time. It also has the same effect where the requirement is that the person is or has been treated as being in receipt of income support. This is obviously important for claimants transferring from JSA to income support. See para.18 of Sch.2 to the JSA Regulations where the transfer is the other way round. Note also para.1A, introduced on October 22, 1997.

Since October 6, 2003 when the state pension credit scheme commenced, claimants who have reached the qualifying age for state pension credit (defined in s.137(1) of the Contributions and Benefits Act—the effect of that definition is that the qualifying age is 60 for both men and women until April 2010 after which it will increase by stages to 65 in line with the increase in pensionable age for a woman) are no longer entitled to income support (see s.124(aa) of the Contributions and Benefits Act 1992). Such claimants now have to claim state pension credit. A claimant whose partner is *entitled* to state pension credit is also ineligible (s.124(g) of the 1992 Act). For an overview of the state pension credit scheme see the Introduction and General Note at the beginning of the State Pension Credit Act 2002. There are no waiting periods for housing costs for state pension credit claimants (as there were not for income support claimants who, or whose partner, were aged 60 or over (see the previous form of para.9(1)(a) of this Schedule in the 2003 edition of this volume). However, for claimants whose former partners were entitled to state pension credit and who transfer to income support note the effect of the linking rule in para.14(14) which was added with effect from October 6, 2003.

Para.1—Housing costs

To be entitled to a sum for housing costs, the claimant, or another member of the family, must be liable to meet any of those costs on the home which are eligible under paras 15–17. Para.2 deals with when a person is "liable to meet" housing costs (which has replaced the more cumbersome "treated as responsible for the expenditure which relates to housing costs"). Whether a person is occupying a dwelling as his home is essentially a question of fact (*CIS 480/1992*).

2.629

CIS 636/1992 (confirmed by the Court of Appeal in *Brain v Chief Adjudication Officer*, December 2, 1993) held in relation to the previous form of Sch.3 that an amount for housing costs was limited to what the claimant was actually required to pay. Under the terms of her mortgage the claimant was not liable to pay any capital or interest so long as the amount outstanding (including accrued interest) did not exceed 75 per cent of the value of the mortgaged property. She was not entitled to an amount for mortgage interest while she was not liable to pay it. The reasoning in that case would also seem to apply to the current form of Sch.3, despite the differences in the wording. See also *CIS 743/1993* in the note to para.2(a).

Note also reg.13(1) of the Decisions and Appeals Regulations 1999 (see Vol. III of this series) which provides that if the Secretary of State considers that he does not have all the relevant information or evidence to decide what housing costs to award, the claim will be decided on the basis of those housing costs that can immediately be awarded.

Housing costs are limited to those specified in paras 15–17. To be doubly sure, para.4(1) excludes housing benefit expenditure and also provides that if a person is in a residential care or nursing home, no housing costs can usually be paid. But if the person is temporarily absent from his home, see para.3(8)–(12) as to when housing costs for that dwelling can continue to be met although the person is in the residential care home, etc.

The categories in paras 15–17 are the same as those listed in para.1 of the former Sch.3 (but note the reduced eligibility of loans for repairs and improvements: see para.16). As far as mortgage interest, payments under a hire-purchase agreement and interest on loans for repairs and improvements are concerned, the question is no longer whether the interest is eligible, but whether the loan qualifies (see paras 15 and 16). Presumably this is at least partly the consequence of introducing a standard rate of interest (see para.12). It also means that the kind of situation dealt with in *R(IS) 11/95* (where the question was whether interest on a replacement loan was eligible where the original loan had been interest free—see p.264 of *Mesher and Wood, Income-related Benefits: the Legislation* (1995)) will no longer be an issue.

Note the restrictions on loans that will be met in paras 4(2)–(12), 11(4)–(11) and 13.

Para.1 contains some important definitions, notably "existing housing costs" and "new housing costs". These are needed because under the new rules no housing costs (subject to certain exceptions: see para.9) are paid at all for certain periods. The length of the period depends on whether the housing costs are "existing" or "new" housing costs. Note the protection for existing claimants in para.6(2)–(4), the expanded linking rules in para.14, that certain claimants with new housing costs are treated as existing borrowers (see para.8(2)–(5)) and the exemptions from the waiting periods in para.9. As before, if the claimant or partner is aged at least 60 (since October 6, 2003 this only applies if the claimant's partner has reached the qualifying age for state pension credit, currently 60; see the note to para.9), "full" housing costs are met from the beginning of the claim. Since para.9(1)(b) only covers miscellaneous housing costs in para.17(1)(d)–(f), this means that the waiting periods and the 50 per cent. rule apply not only to qualifying loans under paras 15 and 16 but also to the housing costs in para.17(1)(a)–(c).

"Existing housing costs" are those which arise under an agreement made before October 2, 1995. (See *R(IS) 5/01* in the note to para.4(2) as to when a loan is incurred.) In addition, exisiting housing costs include those relating to an agreement made after October 1, 1995 if it replaces one made before October 2, 1995 and the specified conditions are met. These conditions were significantly amended with effect from November 28, 2004. Under the previous form of the definition, housing costs relating to a replacement agreement made after October 1, 1995 only counted as existing housing costs if the agreement was between the same parties, in respect of the same property and for a loan of the same amount or less (excluding any arrangement fees). The purpose was solely to cover remortgaging with an existing lender since the policy intention was that the "new housing costs" rules should apply if a "new lending decision" was involved. However, under the new form, it is no longer necessary for the replacement agreement to be between the same parties and in respect of the same property. The new agreement can be with a different lender and/or in respect of a different property, provided that the amount borrowed does not increase. In addition, as long as at least one of the persons liable for the housing costs (not necessarily the claimant) remains the same, the replacement loan can include a change in borrower (*e.g.* a new partner). These changes will alleviate the problems that arose in connection with the old form of the definition of "existing housing costs" referred to in previous editions of this volume (*e.g.* for couples who have separated) to some degree. However, it seems that the amended provision still only allows those who have remortgaged to have had "one bite at the cherry" if their housing costs are to count as existing housing costs. This is because the new agreement has to replace an existing agreement (see head (a)) "where the existing agreement was entered into before 2nd October, 1995" (see head (b)). The effect of this would seem to be that a replacement loan will only qualify as "existing housing costs" if there has only been one such new agreement after October 1, 1995. If the objective of the amended definition is to enable people to "shop around for the best deal" without being penalised if they have to claim income support at some time in the future and thus, according to the Explanatory Memorandum prepared by the Department, to be "more representative of the modern market", the reason for limiting the number of replacement agreements allowed to one is not immediately obvious.

"New housing costs" are those that arise under an agreement made after October 1, 1995, other than one which qualifies as an existing loan.

If a claimant has both an existing and a new agreement, the rules for existing and new housing costs will apply respectively (para.11(2)).

Para. 1A—previous entitlement to income-based JSA

2.630   The effect of this provision is that a claimant who moves from income-based JSA to income support within a linked period (normally 12 weeks but 26 weeks if para.14(2) or (8) apply) will receive the same amount for housing costs on any eligible loan as he did under JSA. The same will apply if it is the claimant's partner who was, or was treated as, getting income-based JSA or who becomes entitled to income support. But if there has been a change in circumstances (other than a reduction in the amount of the loan), the housing costs will be recalculated. A parallel provision has been inserted into Sch.2 to the JSA Regulations that has the same result where the claimant moves from income support to income-based JSA. From October 6, 2003 the same also applies if the claimant moves from income support or income-based JSA to state pension credit (see para.7(4A)–(5) of Sch.2 to the State Pension

Credit Regulations). See also paras 6(1B) and 8(1B) under which the anniversary date for the recalculation of the eligible capital in these circumstances will be the date that the claimant or his partner was first entitled to housing costs under either benefit, or from October 6, 2003, state pension credit.

Para.2—liability to meet housing costs

Para.2 is similar to the former para.3 (although there are some differences in sub-paras (b) and (c)). It defines when a person is "liable to meet housing costs", which has replaced the former "treated as responsible for the expenditure which relates to housing costs". Three situations are specified, to satisfy para.1(1).

2.631

(a) Where the claimant, or any partner, has a liability for housing costs, it must not be to a member of the same household. See *R(SB) 13/82, R(SB) 4/83, CSB 145/1984* and *CSB 463/1986,* and the notes to s.137(1) of the Contributions and Benefits Act 1992.

Where a separated spouse or cohabitee has a joint mortgage with the former partner who has left the home, normally the liability for the mortgage will be a joint and several one (although each case will depend on the exact terms of the mortgage deed or loan agreement). This means that each party will be legally liable for the whole payment. *R(IS) 4/00* confirms that a claimant in this situation where the other party is not paying his share is therefore entitled to housing costs for the total payment. Even if each party is liable separately for a defined share of the payment, then the claimant will in most circumstances of separation be treated as responsible for the other party's share under sub-para.(b), if the other party is not paying this. But if the claimant is only paying half the mortgage interest (even though she is jointly and severally liable), because payments for the other half are being made by someone else, the amount of her housing costs will be restricted to what she actually pays (*CIS 743/1993,* and see *CIS 636/1992* in the note to para.1). See para.5(5).

(b) The wording of this has been changed so that in all cases it has to be reasonable to treat the claimant as liable for the housing costs where the liable person is not meeting them; under the former para.3(1)(b) this was not necessary where it was the person's former partner who was liable for, but not paying, the housing costs. This may not make much difference in practice, as in most cases of separated partners it will probably be reasonable to treat the claimant as liable.

It would not seem to be necessary for the claimant to have continuously lived in the home since the person liable to meet the housing costs failed to meet, or stopped meeting, them. What is required is that the claimant is living in the home and has to meet the housing costs in order to continue to do so when she claims income support. See *Ewens v Secretary of State for Social Security* (Court of Appeal, February 13, 2001, reported as *R(IS) 8/01*) which holds that the phrase "in order to continue living in the dwelling occupied as the home" in para.7(7) of the former Sch.3 (loans for non-approved purposes) did not require that the claimant had continuously lived in the home since her former partner had left (see further the notes to para.7 (transitional protection)).

An example of where the former para.3(1)(b) was applied is *R(IS) 12/94.* The claimant lived with her daughter and grandson. Her daughter had a mortgage on their home. Following the death of her daughter the claimant applied for income support. The daughter's will left the property in trust for her son until he reached 21 (he was then aged seven). The Commissioner holds that "the person" liable can include an incorporeal person such as the estate of a deceased person. The daughter's estate was liable to pay the mortgage but was not doing so. It was reasonable to treat the claimant as liable for the mortgage interest. See also *CH/3013/2003,* to be reported as *R(H) 5/05,* on reg.6(1)(c) of the Housing Benefit Regulations which contains a similar provision to head (b). The Commissioner holds that "person" in reg.6(1)(c) could include a "body of persons corporate or unincorporate" (see s.5 of and Sch.1 to the Interpretation Act 1978). Thus the operation of the provision in reg.6(1)(c) was not excluded by reason only of the fact that it was a limited company who had the legal liability to pay rent under the tenancy agreement (and was not meeting it).

In *CIS 14/1993* the claimant lived with her daughter in a home in their joint names. The daughter took out a hire purchase agreement for a central heating boiler and a cooker. The claimant reimbursed her daughter for half of the hire purchase payments. The claimant argued that she could bring herself within sub-para.(1)(b) because there was a possibility that if the payments were not made, British Gas would apply for a charging order on the home under the Charging Orders Act 1979. The Commissioner holds that for sub-para.(1)(b) to apply, there had to be an immediate threat to the continued occupation of the home, not a theoretical possibility of this in the future. On its particular facts this decision would seem to be correct (the daughter was in fact making the payments). But it is suggested that importing a requirement of an immediate threat to possession into sub-para.(1)(b) is not justified by the wording of the provision and so this decision should be restricted to its particular circumstances.

(c) Only sharing with another member of the same household will do, but see the definition of close relative. This enables sharers to get their proportionate share of housing costs. See para.5(5).

Para.3—occupying a dwelling as the home

2.632 Generally a claimant can only have one home—the one normally occupied (sub-paras (1) and (2)), although in some circumstances two separate units of accommodation may constitute one dwelling (see notes to reg.2(1)). *R(SB) 7/86* holds that premises cannot be "normally occupied as the home" if the claimant has never actually resided in them. However, doubts were expressed about this rule in *CSB/524/1985* and *CIS/4/1990* and it is suggested that the issue will be one of fact in each case. See *CH/2521/2002* and *CH/2957/2004*, to be reported as *R(H) 9/05*, (which concerned reg.5(1) of the Housing Benefit Regulations, the equivalent provision to sub-para.(1)) in the note to the definition of "*dwelling occupied as the home*" in reg.2(1) for further discussion of this question.

2.633 *Sub-paras (3) and (4)*: These give special rules for choosing the home of full-time students (defined in reg.61(1)) with a term-time and a vacation base.

In some circumstances payments will be made for two homes. The limit in para.11(5) will be applied separately to each home (para.11(6)).

2.634 *Sub-para.(5)*: This covers moving into temporary accommodation while repairs are done. There is no limit in sub-para.(5) itself as to how long it can apply. *CIS 719/1994* rejects the AO's argument that para.4(8) of the former Sch.3 (now para.3(10)) applied to restrict the operation of sub-para.(5). The claimant's house had been declared unfit for human habitation in 1989 and he had moved into rented accommodation while the repairs were carried out. These had still not been completed when he claimed income support in December 1992. The Commissioner holds that once the SSAT had found that the claimant was to be treated as occupying the house as his home by virtue of sub-para.(5) they had been right to ignore the fact that he had been absent from that home for more than 52 weeks (which was the limit for temporary absences under para.4(8)). Para.4(8) provided an alternative basis to the bases provided by the other sub-paragraphs for treating a claimant as occupying a dwelling as his home while temporarily absent from it. In taking this approach the Commissioner does not follow *CIS 252/1994* which had reached the opposite conclusion. It is suggested that the construction adopted in *CIS 719/1994* is to be preferred, since the former sub-paras (3)–(8) (now sub-paras (3)–(12)) do seem to deal with specific and distinct situations. The reasoning in *CIS 719/1994* will also apply to para.3 which has a similar structure to that of the former para.4. Although the wording of para.3(10) is different from para.4(8) it is not materially different in relation to this issue. There is also an additional argument, which supports the conclusion of *CIS 719/1994*, although not all its reasoning. Where sub-para.(5) applies, its effect is to define which dwelling a claimant is to be treated as occupying. So long as the same situation prevails, the claimant is not to be treated as absent from that dwelling. Therefore sub-paras (10) and (11) simply do not bite in these circumstances.

Sub-para. (6): This allows payments in three cases where there is an overlap of liability. *R(SB) 7/86* decides that there must be a liability at both the "outgoing" end and the "ingoing" end. It was suggested that a legal liability at the outgoing end might not be necessary, but *CSSB 564/1987* decides that the liability in respect of the old home had to constitute a responsibility for housing expenditure within reg. 14 of the Requirements Regulations. It was argued there that the claimant was liable to make payments to her father as a licensee, but she could not be responsible under reg. 14 because the payment was to another member of the same household (differing from *CSB 865/1986*).

   It is not clear how these principles might apply under the rules for income support. Para. 2 deals with liability (including in sub-para.(a) an exclusion of liability to a member of the same household), but only for housing costs. Items which count as housing costs are those which qualify under paras 15–17 (see para. 1(1) and (2)) and do not include ordinary rent or payments as a licensee to occupy a dwelling. A straightforward application of *CSSB 564/1987* would conclude that there could be no overlap of liability if there was only an obligation to make these kinds of payments at the ingoing end. However, it is necessary to look at the problem to which sub-para.(6) is directed. This is that the "new home" would not ordinarily count as "the dwelling occupied as the home" when the claimant had not moved in, or the family more regularly lived elsewhere (reg. 2(1), sub-para.(1), *R(SB) 7/86*). Sub-para.(6) is to enable the "new home" to be treated as occupied as the home. In the circumstances it does not seem to matter that the liability in respect of the "old home" was not one included as a housing cost, provided that there was a true liability. But the reference in sub-para.(6)(a) and (b) to meeting two lots of housing costs and the definition of "housing costs" in para. 1(2) raise doubts. See sub-para.(7).

   Of the three cases covered, one is fear of violence in the former home or by a former member of the family. This can continue as long as reasonable. The fear of violence leading to the claimant leaving the former home has to be directed against the claimant, not caused by him (*CIS 339/1993*). The second is where one of a couple is a full-time student or on a training course and the double expenditure is unavoidable. This can also continue as long as reasonable. The third is an unavoidable overlap of liability on moving home. What is unavoidable is a matter of fact. This can last for a maximum of four weeks.

   CIS 543/1993 contains some useful guidance as to when head (a) will apply, although its particular facts were highly unusual. The claimant was a former police officer who had been convicted of conspiracy to murder but whose release was later ordered by the Home Secretary. On his release he went to live with his wife in a rented flat. They also owned a house in another part of the country which was let to tenants on an assured shorthold tenancy. The claimant had left this house through fear of violence from gangsters when he was on bail pending trial. The Commissioner points out that head (a) is not restricted to domestic violence and can apply in any case where one of the reasons for the claimant leaving the home was fear of violence in that home. It did not matter if in addition there was a fear of violence in places other than the home. But a fear of violence outside the home, even if in the vicinity of the home, would not suffice. Furthermore, the relevant leaving was the last one before the week to which head (a) might apply. Leaving in this context meant the ending of normal occupation of the home; it should be interpreted broadly as the circumstances of the departure might well be confused and distressing. Moreover, if a person had left, and was currently absent from, a home through fear of violence there, he *remained* absent for that reason, even if during an intervening period the absence was for a different reason (in this case imprisonment).

   Although the claimant in this case was liable to make payments for two dwellings he did not have two lots of income support housing costs as his current accommodation was rented. The Commissioner states that in these circumstances the test in head (a) had to be interpreted as asking whether it was reasonable to meet housing costs for the former dwelling when another dwelling was currently occupied as the person's home. The question of reasonableness had to be determined at the date

2.635

when the adjudicating authority was considering the issue (although what it was reasonable for the claimant to have done at the time could be relevant in deciding this question), and in the light of all the circumstances. These could include among other factors the length of absence, whether it was reasonable to expect the person to take steps to end the liability in respect of the former home (*e.g.*, whether there was a hope of resuming occupation, whether it was practicable to end the liability, his current financial situation and means of support), and the extent to which the liability was in practice being met otherwise than through income support (in this case from the tenants' rent). The conclusion might be different in relation to different weeks.

2.636   *Sub-para. (7)*: This is an important provision allowing a person in certain circumstances to be treated as occupying a dwelling as his home for up to four weeks before moving in. This has consequences for entitlement to housing benefit and may fill in some of the gaps in sub-para.(6). The decision can only be made once the claimant has moved in. Then the claimant can be treated as occupying the dwelling for up to four weeks before the date of the move. The delay in moving while there was a liability to make payments must have been reasonable and fall into one of the three categories set out in sub-para.(7)(c). The categories cover: (i) delay necessary for adaptations for disablement needs; (ii) delay while a social fund application is determined and a member of the family is aged under six, over 59 or is disabled; and (iii) the move is from being a patient or in residential accommodation (see sub-para.(13)).

    On the meaning of "moving in", see *CH/2957/2004*, to be reported as *R(H) 9/05*, discussed in the note to the definition of *"dwelling occupied as the home"* in reg.2(1). The Deputy Commissioner concluded that the claimant had moved in for the purposes of reg.5(6) of the Housing Benefit Regulations (the equivalent provision to sub-para.(7)) when through her agents she had removed all her furniture from her previous home and moved it into her new flat, even though she was not physically present because she was in hospital.

    See para.6(6) of Sch.7 to the Claims and Payments Regulations.

2.637   *Sub-paras (8) to (12)*: These deal with temporary absences from home. See also the definitions in sub-para.(13). These rules were tightened up in April 1995, despite the Social Security Advisory Committee's (Cm. 2783) recommendation that the changes should not proceed, as the Government considered that the previous rules were too generous in some cases. Claimants whose absence began before April 10, 1995 remained subject to the previous temporary absence rule (52 weeks irrespective of the reason for absence: see the 1994 edition of *Mesher and Wood, Income-related Benefits: the Legislation*) while that absence continued. See the Housing Benefit, Council Tax Benefit and Income Support (Amendments) Regulations 1995 (SI 1995/625), reg.7.

    The primary rule is in sub-para.(10). Sub-paras (11) and (12) deal with absences in special cases and there is a separate provision for absences due to trial periods in residential accommodation (sub-paras (8) and (9)).

    Under sub-para.(10) a person is to be treated as occupying the home during any absence of up to 13 weeks. All three of heads (a) to (c) have to be satisfied (see the Northern Ireland decision *R1/91(IS)* and *R(IS) 17/93*). *CIS 613/1997* confirms that as long as all three conditions are satisfied a claimant will be entitled to the benefit of the rule for the first 13 weeks' absence, even if in the event his absence extends beyond that period. This decision also holds that although there is a difference in wording between the previous provision (para.4(8) of the former Sch.3) and sub-para.(10), their effect is the same. *CIS 508/1992* and *CIS 484/1993* hold that the intention to return in head (a) must be an unqualified one. It is not enough for the intention to be contingent on the outcome of an event (such as a partner's admission into the UK: *CIS 508/1992*, or the obtaining of employment: *CIS 484/1993*). The same should apply to sub-para.(11) (see below). On the meaning of "return", see *CH/2957/2004*, to be reported as *R(H) 9/05*, discussed in the note to the definition of *"dwelling occupied as the home"* in reg.2(1). Note that there is no discretion under head (c), as there was before April 1995. If the absence is likely to exceed 13 weeks, the person is not treated as occupying the home from the outset.

Sub-paras (11) and (12) deal with absences for particular reasons. Sub-para.(11)(c) lists those people who can be treated as occupying the home during temporary absences of up to 52 weeks. They are: people remanded in custody pending trial or sentence, and those required as a condition of bail to live at an address away from "home" or in a bail hostel; patients; people (or whose partner, or dependant child, is) undergoing medical treatment or medically approved convalescence in the UK, or abroad (but not in residential accommodation); people providing or receiving (but not in residential accommodation) medically approved care in the UK or abroad; people caring for a child whose parent or guardian is temporarily away from home in order to receive medical treatment or medically approved care; people in residential accommodation, other than on a trial basis; people on a training course (defined in sub-para.(13)(d)) in the UK or abroad; people in fear of violence who are not covered by sub-para.(6)(a); eligible students not covered by sub-paras (3) or (6)(b). Several of the categories refer to "medically approved" care (or convalescence: head (iii)), which is defined in sub-para.(13)(a). According to DSS guidance, some kind of corroboration from a doctor (or nurse) will do, not necessarily in the form of a medical certificate. There does not seem to be any restriction on who can provide the care.

A person in one of the categories in head (c) must also satisfy the conditions in heads (a), (b) and (d). Heads (a) and (b) are the same as heads (a) and (b) in sub-para.(10), except that the use of the word "while" in head (b) confirms that if there has been a letting, the person can satisfy sub-para.(11) when it terminates. On head (a), see *CIS 508/1992* and *CIS 484/1993* above. Under head (d) (as was the case under the pre-April 1995 rule), sub-para.(12) can apply where the absence is unlikely substantially to exceed 52 weeks and there are exceptional circumstances. Presumably a stay in hospital or other circumstances over which the person has no control (which were previously given as examples under the old rule) should qualify.

2.638

In relation to head (d), see *CH 1237/2004* which concerned a claimant who was temporarily absent from her home through fear of violence. The Commissioner decides that the question of whether the absence is unlikely to exceed 52 weeks, or in exceptional circumstances unlikely to substantially exceed that period, in reg.5(8B)(d) of the Housing Benefit Regulations (the equivalent of head (d)) had to be assessed at the date the claimant left her home. Furthermore, whether she continued to satisfy the conditions in reg.5(8B) had to be judged on a week by week basis. The question whether the absence was unlikely to be longer than 52 weeks had to be assessed objectively; the claimant's belief was a factor in deciding, but was not determinative of, this issue.

In *R (Waite) v Hammersmith and Fulham LBC and Secretary of State for Social Security* [2002] EWCA Civ 482, a case on reg.5(8), (8B) and (8C) of the Housing Benefit Regulations (the equivalent of sub-paras.(10) to (12)), the issue was whether the fact that the claimant, who had been released on licence from a sentence of detention at Her Majesty's Pleasure and then recalled to prison, was only entitled to 13 weeks' housing benefit, whereas a person held on remand awaiting trial (or sentence following conviction) was entitled for 52 weeks, violated Art.14 ECHR taken with either Art.8 or Art.1 of Protocol 1. The Court of Appeal dismissed the appeal, holding that the claimant's position was not analogous to that of an unconvicted prisoner (or indeed a convicted prisoner held on remand awaiting sentence). He had been convicted and sentenced whereas an unconvicted person on remand had the presumption of innocence in his favour. Further, in the case of a convicted prisoner on remand he might only have been convicted of a relatively minor offence and not receive a long sentence. But even if this was wrong, the Court accepted that the discrimination between the two groups was justified.

See also *CH 4574/2003* which held that the then form of reg.5(8B)(c)(i) of the Housing Benefit Regulations (the equivalent of the then form of sub-para.(11)(c)(i)) did treat a person required as a condition of bail to live at a specified address away from 'home' differently from a person who was required to live in a bail hostel but concluded that the difference in treatment was within the margin of judgment that was allowed to the legislature and so there was no breach of ECHR. Leave to appeal to the Court of Appeal was granted by the Commissioner on May 25, 2004 (under the name of *Walsh v Peterborough City Council and the Secretary of State for Work and Pensions*) but the appeal was dismissed by consent on February 11, 2005. However, the new form of sub-para.(11)(c)(i) introduced with effect from April 4, 2005 has removed this discrimination (reg.5(8B)(d) of the Housing Benefit Regulations has been similarly amended). The new form applies to a person who is required as a condition of bail to live at an address away from 'home' (sub-head (aa)) as well as a person required to live in a bail hostel (sub-head (bb)).

Sub-paras (8) and (9) apply where a person has gone into residential accommodation (defined in sub-para.(13)(c)) for a trial period with the intention of returning to his own home if the accommodation proves unsuitable. If the person has entered the home for the purpose of, *e.g.*, respite care, or convalescence, the 52 weeks rule, not this one, should apply (see sub-para.(11)(c)(ix)). There will obviously be some grey areas here; as was pointed out to SSAC in the course of their consultation on these rules, the reason given for entry into a residential home may well vary depending on who is asked. Note that, in this case, unlike absences covered by sub-paras (10) and (11), the person does not have to intend to return home within a specified period. He will be treated as occupying his home during the first 13 weeks of the absence, starting with the day he first goes into the residential accommodation (*not* the date his absence from home begins) even if it is likely at the outset that he will be away for longer. However, if he becomes a permanent resident he will lose the benefit of these provisions at that point (regardless of the length of the absence) as he will have ceased to occupy his former home (*CH/1854/2004*). There is no limit on the number of times sub-paras (8) and (9) can apply, so a person will be able to try out different homes. But the 13 weeks is subject to a maximum of 52 weeks for that period of absence. So, for example, if the person has been in hospital for 40 weeks before going into a residential home for a trial period, he will only be treated as occupying his own home for a further 12 weeks.

If the reason for the absence changes, the rule governing absence for the latest reason will apply. The intention is that the absence will count from the first day the person left his own home, not the date the reason changed, except where the special rule for trial periods in residential accommodation applies.

There are no linking rules for any of these provisions (see *R. v Penwith District Council Housing Benefit Review Board Ex p. Burt* (1990) 22 H.L.R. 292 on the equivalent housing benefit provisions). This means that provided the person returns to his own home for a period, he can be treated as occupying his own home for repeated 13 or 52 week absences. As the rules do not specify any length of time for which the person must return to his own home, presumably a very short period (24 hours?) will suffice.

Para. 4—Housing costs not met

2.639 *Sub-para. (1):* This provision is similar to para.5 of the former Sch.3. It excludes housing benefit expenditure and payment of housing costs if a person is in a residential care or nursing home. But if the person in a residential care or nursing home is only temporarily absent from his home see para.3(8)–(12) as to when he can continue to receive housing costs for his home.

Sub-paras (2)–(12) contain the restriction on payment of interest on loans taken out while income support (or, from October 7, 1996, income-based JSA: see reg.32 of the Income Support (General) (Jobseeker's Allowance Consequential Amendments) Regulations 1996, p. 676) is being claimed (or a person is caught by the linking rule; from October 6, 2003 note the effect of para.14(14) where the claimant's former partner was entitled to state pension credit) which was first introduced on May 2, 1994 (see para.5A of the former Sch.3). It stemmed from the Government's concern about possible "upmarketing" at the expense of the benefit system, although no figures were produced as to the numbers of people said to have been exploiting income support by taking on bigger mortgages while on benefit. There may be many reasons why a claimant needs to take out or increase a loan while in receipt of income support (or income-based JSA) which have nothing to do with "upmarketing". Some, but by no means all, of these are catered for by the limited exceptions in sub-paras (8)–(11). Furthermore, as the Social Security Advisory Committee pointed out (Cm. 2537(1994)), "not only has it been Government policy to encourage home ownership, but . . . the rented sector is unable to meet the demands placed on it".

Note the similar rules for state pension credit (see para.5 of Sch.2 to the State Pension Credit Regulations).

Sub-para.(2): This provision contains the basic rule. Note that the restriction now **2.640** only applies to loans (or money borrowed under a hire purchase agreement) for house purchase. Before October 2, 1995 it also applied to *some* loans for repairs and improvements. (See *CIS 14141/1996* which decides that para.5A of the former Sch.3 was not invalid on the ground of irrationality, even though it had the unfair and absurd result of treating claimants with identical needs for housing costs differently. The Commissioner holds that para.5A did prevent claimants with no previous housing costs for loan interest from receiving housing costs for new loans for repairs and improvements, but not claimants who had been receiving housing costs for loan interest.) Sub-para.(2) states that a loan for house purchase will not be eligible if it has been incurred during "the relevant period" (see sub-paras (4)–(5)), and (i) after October 1, 1995, or (ii) after May 2, 1994 and the loan interest was not met under the former para.5A in the 26 weeks before October 2, 1995, or (iii) between April 3, and October 1, 1995 when the person was not entitled to income support but he or his partner became entitled after October 1, 1995 and was entitled within the previous 26 weeks, unless interest on the loan was being met before October 2, 1995 (see sub-para.(3)). (The purpose of heads (b) and (c) of sub-para.(2) is presumably to catch loans which might otherwise escape restriction because the new form of Sch.3 was not retrospective.) But in the case of replacement loans the restriction will only apply to the extent of any increase in the amount loaned (see sub-para.(6)).

It is not entirely clear when a loan is incurred in this context. For example, if a further advance is added to a person's existing mortgage does this constitute incurring a loan, or is it merely increasing a loan that has already been incurred? (It may be that it is the former that is intended; *cf.* sub-para.(6) which catches increases in the amount borrowed in the case of replacement loans.) Will the restriction apply where the terms of an existing mortgage are varied rather than a new agreement entered into (as may happen, *e.g.*, where a couple separate and one member takes over the whole mortgage for which they were previously jointly and severally liable)? In those circumstances it would certainly seem arguable that the loan was incurred when the mortgage was first taken out, not when its terms were changed. It should also be noted that it is the date that the loan was incurred that counts, not the date that the person became liable to meet (see para.2) the housing costs. In *R(IS) 5/01* the Commissioner applies *CIS 2978/1995* in holding that where a claimant came under a legal obligation to pay for a property (as would happen when contracts were exchanged) and the only practical way of doing so was to take up the offer of a loan, in reliance on which the obligation was undertaken, the loan had been incurred at the time that legal obligation arose. Thus since the completion of the purchase of the new property was on May 10, 1994, it was likely that contracts had been exchanged (and the loan incurred) before the restriction on loans taken out while on income support came into force on May 2, 1994. (But apparently exchange and completion did in fact take place on the same day; the claimant appealed to the Court of Appeal on another point, but his appeal was dismissed (*Saleem v Secretary of State for Social Security*, Court of Appeal, January 18, 2001, reported as part of *R(IS) 5/01*), see the note to sub-para.(10) below).

The restriction only applies to loans taken out by the claimant or a member of his family during the claimant's current entitlement to income support or a period of non-entitlement included in "the relevant period" by the operation of sub-para.(4). Note sub-paras (4A) and (5). Note also reg.32 of the Income Support (General) (Jobseeker's Allowance Consequential Amendments) Regulations 1996 (see p.676), the effect of which is that entitlement to income-based JSA will count as entitlement to income support. Although sub-para.(2) does not specifically limit the period during which the loan will not qualify to the claimant's current claim (and any linked period), it is understood that this is the intention. Sub-para.(2) does refer to "the" (not "a") relevant period. Moreover, any other interpretation would have a draconian effect. Thus if entitlement to income support (and income-based JSA) ceases for more than 26 weeks, the claimant should be paid the full amount of his loan interest (at the standard rate: see para.12) if he makes a further claim (subject to the waiting periods (paras 6(1) and 8(1)) and the ceiling on loans (para.11(5)). In addition loans taken out *before* a claimant or his partner claimed income support (or income-based JSA) are not caught (subject to the 26 week linking rule). There are exceptions in sub-paras (7)–(11).

2.641   *Sub-paras (4) and (5)*: Periods of entitlement to income support (or income-based JSA: reg.32 of the Income Support (General) (Jobseeker's Allowance Consequential Amendments) Regulations 1996, see p.676, assuming that this rule can be interpreted as a "requirement" that the person is, or has been, entitled to income support: see reg.32(a)) separated by 26 weeks or less are treated as continuous for the purposes of sub-para.(2). So a loan taken out during a period of 26 weeks or less that falls between two periods of entitlement to income support (and/or income-based JSA) will be subject to the restriction. The 26 weeks is much more stringent than the normal linking rule (now 12 weeks: see para.14(1)). There is also no provision for the restriction to cease to apply if there is a major change of circumstances (*cf.* para.10(2)(b) in the former Sch.3 for tenants who bought their own homes).

The effect of sub-para.(4) is that if a couple who are in receipt of income support (or income-based JSA) separate, the restriction will also apply to the partner who was not the claimant if s/he claims income support (or income-based JSA) within 26 weeks.

Note sub-para.(4A), the effect of which is that any period which the claimant or his partner spends on a New Deal option for 18–24 year-olds or in the Intensive Activity Periods for people aged 25 or over, or 50 plus, during which he (or his partner) is in remunerative work or has an income that is too high to qualify for income support will count as part of the relevant period. Thus even though the claimant (or his partner) may not be entitled to income support (or income-based JSA) for 26 weeks because the claimant (or his partner) is taking part in this kind of New Deal option, or activity, this will not break the running of any relevant period for the purposes of sub-para.(4).

2.642   *Sub-para.(6)*: This will cover the situation where a person moves, or remortgages his home, when only the increase in the amount loaned will be caught by sub-para.(2). Under head (a) the replaced loan must have qualified under para.15 during the relevant period (defined in sub-para.(4); note para.(4A)). The inclusion of the words "during the relevant period" from October 7, 1996 is significant, since sub-para.(2) treats a loan that would otherwise qualify under para.15 because of its purpose as not doing so if it was incurred during the relevant period and at any of the times specified in sub-para.(2). Head (b) was also amended on October 7, 1996. The previous form (see the 1996 edition of *Mesher and Wood, Income-related Benefits: the Legislation*) was potentially quite wide as it merely required that a previous loan (or loans: ss.6(c) and 23(1) of the Interpretation Act 1978) that was secured on another property had been wholly or partly repaid. So it seemed that the earlier loan could, for example, have been for business purposes, or one that was not eligible under sub-para.(2). But under the new form the loan that has been repaid has to be one that qualified under para.15 or 16 during the relevant period (although there is no requirement that it was a secured loan). It does not seem to be necessary for the repaying of the earlier loan and the taking out of the new to be connected in time.

See *R(IS) 20/98* which confirms that the fact that there was a gap (of over two years) between paying off the old mortgage and taking out the new larger one did not remove the claimant's entitlement to housing costs to the extent met on the original mortgage. This was a decision on para.5A(3) of the former Sch.3 (see *Mesher and Wood, Income-related Benefits: the Legislation* (1995)) but the position should be the same under sub-para.(6). Under the former para.5A(3) and (7), if the claimant (or a member of the family) received housing benefit during the gap, it seemed that interest payments could be restricted to the amount of housing benefit payable in the intervening period, even if the second home was cheaper than the first. But this will not be the case under sub-para.(6). If there is no increase (or even a decrease) in the amount of the claimant's new loan, the restriction will not apply, whether or not the claimant receives housing benefit in the intervening period. Sub-para.(8) may, however, come into play in cases where sub-para.(2) does bite and the claimant received housing benefit during the gap.

Thus the effect of sub-para.(6) would seem to be that if a couple who are in receipt of income support (or income-based JSA) separate, and the former home is sold each partner will be entitled to interest on a loan up to the previous amount (*i.e.* each would receive interest on a £30,000 loan if that was the amount of the loan they had as a couple). *CIS 11293/1995* decides that this was the position under the previous rule in para.5A(3) of the former Sch.3. The claimant was jointly and severally liable with her ex-husband for a mortgage of £18,000 on the home in which she lived. She was awarded housing costs on £9,000 only. She then sold that house and moved to a new home which she purchased with a mortgage of £18,000 (the old mortgage having been paid off). The Commissioner holds that she was entitled to interest on £18,000 because the "new liability" under para.5A(3) did not exceed the "former liability". It was the claimant's legal liability that was material, not what had actually been paid as income support housing costs, and she had potentially been liable for all the interest on the original mortgage. The Commissioner disagrees with *CIS 5353/1995* which considered that housing costs were only "applicable" under para.5A(3) if they had actually been met; in his view "applicable" in para.5A(3) meant "potentially applicable". The comparison in sub-para.(6) is between the amount of the old and new *loans*, which wording would seem to achieve the same result as in *CIS 11293/1995*. But if one member of the couple buys a new property without the former matrimonial home being sold, sub-para.(2) will apply and the loan will not be eligible (unless it involved some remortgaging and so sub-para.(6)(a) applies). A new (or increased, but see the note to sub-para.(2) for discussion of when a loan is incurred) loan to buy out the other partner's share will not be met if it is taken out during the relevant period. If the couple were not in receipt of income support (or income-based JSA), the restriction will not apply if the loan for the new property, or to buy out the other partner's share, is taken out before a claim for income support (or income-based JSA), is made (subject to the 26 week linking rule).

Sub-para.(8): A person receiving housing benefit who buys a home will be paid   **2.643** housing costs but only up to the level of the housing benefit payable in the week before the purchase, together with any amount for housing costs that he was being paid that week. *CIS 4712/2002* holds that "payable" in sub-para.(b)(i) referred to entitlement, rather than to the amount actually paid in the week before the purchase. However, the Commissioner added that it was not for the tribunal to determine the level of entitlement but it was for the parties to produce evidence of the correct figure to the tribunal.

Sub-para.(8) covers tenants who buy their own homes as well as those receiving housing benefit who move into owner occupation. The more generous treatment of the former under the rules in para.10(1) and (2) of the former Sch.3 (see the 1995 edition of *Mesher and Wood, Income-related Benefits: the Legislation*, pp. 262 and 269–270) no longer applies. Thus there is no provision, for example, for the restriction to cease to apply if there is a major change of circumstances. There can be an increase in the restricted level equivalent to any subsequent increase in the standard rate (*not* the claimant's actual rate) or in housing costs that are eligible under para.17. But there is no provision for subsequent reductions. So if the standard rate is later lowered or the para.17 housing costs reduce, a claimant can continue to enjoy the partial relief from restriction due to the previous increase (*R(IS) 8/94*). If the housing costs fall below the restricted level the amount payable will be the lower figure (*R(IS) 8/94*).

No reference is made to loans under para.16. Does this mean that if sub-para.(8) applies, no payment will be made for loans for repairs and improvements? This would seem unfair and also illogical in view of the exclusion of para.16 loans from the restriction in sub-para.(2). It is understood that it is not the DSS's intention to preclude payment for loans for repairs and improvements taken out by people covered by sub-para.(8) (or sub-para.(11) where the same point arises). The DSS take the view that because sub-para.(2) only relates to para.15 loans these provisions do not affect para.16 loans at all.

2.644   *Sub-para. (9)*: If the loan is taken out, or increased, to acquire a home to meet the needs of a disabled person, this is exempt from restriction under sub-para.(2) (although the excessive housing costs rule (para.13) and the ceiling on loans in para.11(5) could apply). This provision should cover people wanting to move into sheltered accommodation. Note that the new accommodation only has to be more suited to the needs of the disabled person; there is no requirement that it has been specifically adapted for that person's needs (*CIS 16250/1996*). A person counts as disabled if he qualifies for the disability, disabled child (note that this premium has been abolished since April 6, 2004, except in "transitional cases"— see the note to reg.17), higher pensioner or enhanced pensioner premium, or would do so if entitled to income support, including periods when he is disqualified from receiving benefit or treated as capable of work under the incapacity rules (para.1(3) and (4)). (See Vol. I of this series for more details on the incapacity for work rules.) This definition of a disabled person is quite restrictive and may exclude some people who need care even though they do not, or would not, qualify for these premiums. However, *CIS 13661/1996* confirms that it is an exhaustive definition. The disabled person does not have to be a member of the claimant's family, or to have previously lived with the claimant. However he does have to qualify as a disabled person at the time the loan is taken out (*R(IS) 20/98*).

The scope of this provision is discussed in *CIS 14551/1996*. The Commissioner points out that the fact that new accommodation is more suited to the special needs of the disabled person only has to be *a* reason for its acquisition, not the sole or predominant reason; moreover, the test is whether the new accommodation is more suited, not whether it was reasonable to acquire it. Further, the person's overall mental and physical condition had to be taken into account, not just the condition that triggered the application of the definition of "disabled person". But the person's needs had to stem from a specific disease or bodily or mental disablement to count under this paragraph. The claimant had contended that part of the reason for moving was to alleviate mental stress caused by financial worries. The Commissioner accepts that, for example, moving to smaller or more compact accommodation that is less expensive to heat, or to accommodation that is nearer to a person who can look after the claimant so as to reduce that person's travelling expenses, could come within this provision. But it was the accommodation itself that had to be more suited, not the terms of its acquisition, so moving simply in order to reduce mortgage liability, or so as to take advantage of the exemption from restriction under this provision, would not be covered.

In *CIS 3295/2003* the claimant had moved to the property over a year before she acquired ownership of it. The Commissioner points out that there are no time limits in sub-para.(9), and in particular no requirement of immediacy linking the time of acquisition, the time the loan is taken out, and the time the claimant moves to the property. He states that what is required for sub-para.(9) to apply is (i) that alternative accommodation is acquired; (ii) that it is more suited to the special needs of the disabled person than the accommodation occupied by that person before the acquisition; and (iii) that the loan was taken out to acquire the accommodation. Thus whether sub-para.(9) applies will depend entirely on the circumstances.

Sub-para.(9) only applies to loans to purchase a home. A loan taken out to adapt a home to meet the needs of a disabled person will be eligible under para.16 (see para.16(2)(k) and note para.11(9)).

Sub-para.(10): Increased loans taken out because of a need to move to provide sep- **2.645** arate sleeping accommodation for male and female children aged 10 or over who are members of the claimant's family are exempt (although the ceiling on loans in para.11(5) and the excessive housing costs rule (para.13) could apply).

See *CIS 14657/1996* in which the Commissioner points out that the need to provide separate sleeping accommodation for children of different sexes aged 10 or over may exist before all the children involved reach 10. Action may have to be taken earlier to secure that result by the time the children become 10. *CIS 1068/2003* emphasizes that there must be a need for separate accommodation. *R(IS) 5/01* considered the meaning of the phrase "solely by reason of" in sub-para.(10)(b). In the Commissioner's view, providing separate sleeping accommodation for older children of opposite sexes was not likely to be the only reason but one of a number of reasons for choosing the particular new home. It was therefore necessary to look primarily at the reasons for moving. However, the tribunal in that case had been entitled to con- clude that the main reason for moving was to acquire space generally. The claimant's appeal against this decision was dismissed (*Saleem v Secretary of State for Social Security*, Court of Appeal, January 18, 2001, reported as part of *R(IS) 5/01*). The Court agreed with the Commissioner that it was necessary to focus on the reason for the change of home. Para.(10)(b) would not apply if the operative reason for the change was other than to provide separate sleeping accommodation for children of different sexes aged 10 or over. However, the Court did accept that if this was the sole reason for the change, the fact that the new home brought other advantages would not prevent para.(10)(b) from applying. The Court also rejected an argument that the provision was *ultra vires* on the ground of irrationality.

Sub-para.(11): Claimants who were only receiving para.17 housing costs before they **2.646** purchased their home will have their loan interest met up to the level of their previ- ous housing costs. The rule is similar to that for claimants previously in receipt of housing benefit in sub-para.(8). The restricted level can be increased for subsequent increases in the standard rate or in para.17 housing costs (see the notes to sub- para.(8)).

Para.5—Apportionment of housing costs

Sub-para.(1): This allows the expenditure on premises used for mixed purposes (*e.g.* **2.647** business and domestic) to be apportioned and the part attributable to a private dwelling met (subject to the limit in para.11(7)). Where the "composite hereditam- ment" existed before the community charge came into force the apportionment follows the rateable value of each part of the premises (sub-para.(1)). Where the composite hereditament comes into existence after the advent of the community charge, the apportionment is to follow the current market value of each part (sub- paras (2)–(4)).

On the application of sub-paras (1) and (2) see *CIS 2024/1998*.

Sub-para.(5): In *CIS 743/1993* the Commissioner holds that "responsible" at the end **2.648** of sub-para.(5) did not mean legally responsible (as it did elsewhere in the Schedule), but referred to the proportion of the shared responsibility that a claimant was actu- ally paying. The claimant was jointly and severally liable with her ex-husband under the terms of the mortgage, but only paid half the mortgage interest. She was only entitled to housing costs for the amount she actually paid.

Where para.5 applies, the effect of para.11(7) is that the ceiling on loans is applied to the eligible part of the loan.

Para. 6—Existing housing costs

2.649   Note the restriction on house purchase loans incurred while entitled to income support (or income-based JSA: reg.32 of the Income Support (General) (Jobseeker's Allowance Consequential Amendments) Regulations 1996, see p.676), or while a person is caught by the linking rule in para.4(2)–(12), as well as the limits imposed under paras 11(5) and 13.

2.650   *Sub-para. (1)*: In the case of existing housing costs (defined in para.1(2)), none are payable for the first eight weeks, and only 50 per cent for the next 18 weeks (sub-para.(1)(b) and (c)). Once the claimant has been entitled to income support (and/or income-based JSA: reg.32 of the Income Support (General) (Jobseeker's Allowance Consequential Amendments) Regulations 1996, see p.676) for a continuous period of 26 weeks (note the linking rules in para.14 and in particular the effect of para.14(14) where the claimant's former partner was entitled to state pension credit), "full" housing costs are met (see below). But the waiting periods do not apply if the claimant or partner is aged at least 60 (since October 6, 2003 this only applies if the claimant's partner has reached the qualifying age for state pension credit, currently 60; see the note to para.9), or to housing costs that qualify under para.17(1)(d)–(f), *i.e.*, payments under a co-ownership scheme, by a Crown tenant or in respect of a tent (para.9). In these cases housing costs will be met from the start of the income support claim, although interest on qualifying loans will be calculated at the standard rate. *R(IS) 2/94* rejected the argument that under para.7(1)(b)(i) of the former Sch.3 receipt of income support on *any* claim for a continuous period of what was then 16 weeks was sufficient. The qualifying period recommenced each time a fresh claim for income support was made (subject to the linking rules—see para.14). *CSJSA/125/2004* holds that the waiting periods for housing costs are not in breach of ECHR.

There is no actual equivalent to para.7(2) of the former Sch.3 in the current Schedule. That provision avoided the creation of a "mortgage trap" which could have resulted from the then 50 per cent. rule (see the note to para.7(2) in the 1995 edition of *Mesher and Wood, Income-related Benefits: the Legislation*). Under the current rules the possibility remains that if the result of a nil or 50 per cent. figure for housing costs is that a claimant does not qualify for income support, he will never clock up the necessary weeks of entitlement to qualify for "full" housing costs under sub-para.(1)(a). Para.14(4) to (9) will assist many claimants who could otherwise be caught in this trap, but not all. See the notes to para.14 below.

To calculate the amount of housing costs that are payable under para.6, for loans that qualify under paras 15 or 16 the standard rate (see para.12) is applied to the eligible capital owing for the time being (sub-para.(1)(a)(i)). To this are added the actual payments due for any housing costs in para.17(1)(a)–(c) (*i.e.* ground rent, service charges and rentcharges) (sub-para.(1)(a)(ii)).

"Eligible capital" is not defined, but see paras 4(2)–(12), 11(4)–(9) and 13 for the limits on loans that will be met. What does "eligible capital for the time being owing" mean? Does it just mean the original amount of the loan less any that has been repaid, or could it include an increase in that capital, due, for example, to capitalised interest? The terms of the claimant's mortgage may be relevant here. See, for example, *CIS 146/1993*, where the claimant's mortgage repayments were adjusted annually. Any arrears due to changes in interest rates during the year were capitalised, divided into 12 and added to the monthly instalments for the following year. The Commissioner holds that the capitalised interest was not arrears but part of the interest payable in the following year. Thus it qualified as eligible interest. But the interest on the capitalised interest was to be treated as arrears and so was not payable.

A similar distinction may be relevant to the question of what is the eligible capital owing for the time being, depending on the terms of the mortgage. In *CIS 141/1993* the Commissioner confirmed that for interest to qualify as eligible interest under the former para.7(3), any increase in the capital owing on the loan had to be for the purpose of acquiring an interest in the home. *CJSA 888/1999* similarly so decides in relation to the current provisions. The claimant's mortgage agreement allowed payment of a proportion of the chargeable interest to be delayed for 10 years. At the end of the 10 years the accumulated deferred interest was added to his outstanding loan and interest charged on the new balance. The Commissioner confirmed that interest attributable to the capitalised deferred interest could not be met. See also *R(IS) 14/01* in the note to para.15(1).

2.651   Note that the amount of eligible capital will be recalculated only once a year (sub-paras (1A) and (1B)). See also reg.7(14) of the Decisions and Appeals Regulations 1999 which provides that a supersession due to a reduction in eligible capital will only have effect on the next anniversary of the date the claimant's housing costs were first met. Since reg.7(14) only applies to *reductions* in the outstanding capital, arguably a supersession due to any eligible increase should take effect in the normal way (despite sub-paras (1A) and (1B)). Indeed this is the approach taken in the *Decision Makers Guide* (see para.23508).

See the notes to paras 15 and 16 for which loans are eligible.

The formula for determining the weekly amount of loan interest payable is in para.10. Interest is only met when the claimant is actually required to pay it (*CIS 636/1992 (Brain)* and *CIS 743/1993* referred to in the notes to para.1).

Only interest is covered, not the capital element in loan repayments. There are a number of ways round this deficiency. First, the lender may be prepared to accept repayments of interest only. Second, if the claimant sub-lets part of the home, the first £4 of any payments (plus £10.55, if heating is included) is disregarded (Sch.9, para.19). See also *CIS 13059/1996* referred to below. Contributions to living or accommodation expenses by someone who normally resides with the claimant are disregarded entirely (Sch.9, para.18) (but see para.18 of this Schedule). See also para.20 of Sch.9 for the disregard of board and lodging payments. Payments from others to meet capital repayments (or interest not met by income support or premiums on a mortgage protection or buildings insurance policy) are disregarded (Sch.9, para.30). See *CIS 13059/1996* in the note to para.30 of Sch.9 which decides (contrary to the view expressed in *CIS 82/1993*) that the disregard in para.30(1) can apply to payments made by a tenant (or licensee) of the claimant who lives in his home. Payments from liable relatives would not be disregarded, but if made direct to the lender might be excluded from the liable relative provisions (reg.54). Payments from mortgage protection policies are disregarded to the extent that they cover capital repayments (or interest on a qualifying loan that is not met by income support or the premiums on a mortgage protection or buildings insurance policy) (Sch.9, para.29). See also *R(IS) 13/01* in the note to para.30 of Sch.9.

The cost of premiums on insurance policies connected with the loan is also not met (*R(SB) 46/83*).

There is no longer any provision for the payment of interest on arrears of interest. Under the old rules interest on arrears accrued during a period subject to the 50 per cent restriction was allowed (para.7(6) of the former Sch.3). But there is no such provision in relation to arrears that accrue during the new waiting periods. In addition, interest that accrues on deferred interest loans is no longer covered. Interest on loans for non-approved purposes in the case of separated partners is also no longer met (see para.7(7) of the former Sch.3 for the old rule). But note the transitional protection for existing claimants in regulation 3 of the Income Support (General) Amendment and Transitional Regulations 1995 (p.672, and see note to para.7 below).

2.652   *Sub-paras (2)–(4)*: Under the former Sch.3 the 50 per cent rule only applied for the first 16 weeks of a claim (there was no "nil" period). These subparagraphs contain some protection for claimants in relation to the new 26 weeks rule. If on October 1, 1995 a claimant has been entitled to income support for less than 16 weeks his housing costs will remain the same (even if the interest rate changes), until he has been entitled for 16 weeks when they will be calculated as if he had been entitled for 26 weeks (*i.e.* 100 per cent at the standard rate). If he has been entitled for 16 or more but less than 26 weeks by October 1, 1995, he will be treated as if he had been entitled for 26 weeks. This will cease to apply if the agreement under which those housing costs arise ends. (See also para.7(8), noted below.) Since these provisions only apply where the claimant's income support included an amount for housing costs immediately before October 2, 1995 (see sub-para.(2)), at first sight they did not appear to assist claimants who were not entitled to income support on October 1, 1995 because their income exceeded their applicable amount due to the former 50 per cent rule. It would be possible for claimants who were unemployed or sick, lone parents or carers to rely on paras 14(4)–(6) to treat them as entitled to income support during the 16 weeks and thus to qualify under para.6(3)(a) in that way, but this still left the problem of para.6(2), which seemed to govern the operation of para.6(3).

However, in *CSIS 162/1996* the Commissioner held that if a person is to be treated as entitled to income support for a period, he has benefit weeks and applicable amounts during that period. *CIS 16769/1996* confirms that the effect of this is that para.(2) can apply to a claimant who was not entitled to income support on October 1, 1995 because of the former 50 per cent rule. This was because the calculation of his applicable amount did include a sum by way of housing costs (even though the result of the calculation was that he was not entitled to income support because his income exceeded his applicable amount while only 50 per cent. of his housing costs were included). In addition, note the linking rules in para.14. So, for example, a claimant may still benefit from these provisions if he claims income support after October 1, 1995 but that claim links with a previous claim made before October 2, 1995 which included an amount for housing costs.

Para. 7—Transitional protection

2.653   This paragraph is not straightforward. This at least partly stems from the fact that some of the provisions refer to "housing costs", some to "existing housing costs" and some only to qualifying loans. It contains the following detailed rules. Sub-paras (1) and (2) provide that if a claimant's housing costs under the former Sch.3 in the benefit week which includes October 1, 1995 ("the first benefit week") are more than the amount payable under para.6 in the next benefit week ("the second benefit week") that amount will be increased by the difference between the amount of his housing costs in the first and second benefit weeks, called the "add back" (sub-para.(1) and (2)). Thus if no housing costs are applicable in the week including October 1, 1995, the claimant will not be entitled to any add back. As to whether an amount for housing costs is applicable in the week including October 1, 1995 see *CSIS 162/1996* and *CIS 16769/1996* below. If the claimant has more than one qualifying loan the add back will be calculated separately for each loan (sub-para.(9)). If the claimant's existing housing costs, less the add back, increase after the second benefit week, the add back will be reduced by the amount of any increase until it is reduced to nil when it will cease to apply (sub-paras (3) and (4)). See *Secretary of State for Work and Pensions v Arathoon* [2005] EWCA Civ 942 (Court of Appeal, June 24, 2005) below for the application of this provision in relation to increases in the standard rate under para.12. An allowable increase (compared with the second benefit week—see *Arathoon*) in a loan will reduce the add back (but not if the increase in borrowing is by way of a separate loan). But as existing housing costs include not only mortgage interest but also, for example, ground rent and service charges, will any add back be reduced by increases in such costs? It is understood that this was not the intention and that sub-paras (3) and (4) are really only meant to deal with qualifying loans (despite the reference to "existing housing costs"). Note that where there is more than one loan the reduction of the add back on one will not affect the add back on the other (see sub-para.(9)).

The issue in *CIS 672/2004* was in precisely what circumstances a reduction in the add back under sub-para.(3) took place. The claimant contended that a reduction in the add back only occurred when the amount payable by way of housing costs (ignoring the add back) increased above the amount which was payable in the first week when the new regime applied. The Secretary of State, on the other hand, argued that a reduction occurred whenever (disregarding the add back) there was any increase in the amount payable by way of housing costs. Thus, suppose that the standard rate of interest fluctuated from its initial rate of 8.39 per cent as follows: 7.39 per cent, 8.39 per cent, 7.39 per cent, 8.39 per cent. On the claimant's contention there would be no erosion of the add back because the housing costs had not increased above the amount payable in the first week of the new regime. However, if the Secretary of State's interpretation was accepted, there would have been an erosion of the add back on both occasions when there was a 1 per cent increase in the standard rate of interest. After a thorough analysis of sub-paras.(3) and (4), the Commissioner concludes that the claimant's interpretation was the correct one.

On appeal the Court of Appeal in *Secretary of State for Work and Pensions v Arathoon* [2005] EWCA Civ 942 (June 24, 2005) agreed that there should have been no reduction in a claimant's add back resulting from increases in the standard rate until it exceeded its initial level of 8.39 per cent (which has only occurred once since the introduction of the standard rate on October 2, 1995, namely on December 27, 1998; for a list of the standard rates since October 2, 1995 see p.575 in the 2004 edition of this volume and note that before the new provisions relating to the standard rate came into force on November 28, 2004 (see the note to para.12) there was one further change on September 19, 2004 when the standard rate increased to 5.88 per cent (see reg.2 of SI 2004/2174)). However, the Court disagreed with the Commissioner that only an increase which took the standard interest rate higher than it had ever been before could reduce the add back. The Court held that once there was an increase in housing costs due to the standard interest rate going above 8.39 per cent that increase would serve to reduce the add back (note that as yet this has not occurred again since December 27, 1998). The effect of this ruling is likely to mean that many claimants will have had their add back wrongly calculated as the calculations will have been carried out in accordance with the Department's interpretation of sub-paras (3) and (4). Note that for the purposes of the "anti-test case" provisions (see s.27 of the Social Security Act 1998) the date of the Commissioner's decision was July 5, 2004.

If entitlement to income support (and/or income-based JSA: reg.32 of the Income Support (General) (Jobseeker's Allowance Consequential Amendments) Regulations 1996, see p.676) ceases for more than 12 weeks (from October 5, 1998, 52 weeks where the person or his partner is a "welfare to work beneficiary" (sub-para.(10)); see the notes to reg.2(1) for when a person counts as a welfare to work beneficiary) no add back will be payable on any new claim (sub-para.(5)). In addition, if a person ceases to be entitled to housing costs (for any length of time) the add back is lost (sub-para.(6)). But if that person's partner (or former partner?) claims income support within 12 weeks (from October 5, 1998, 52 weeks in the case of a "welfare to work beneficiary"), including existing housing costs previously met in that person's claim, the partner will have the add back (sub-para.(7)).

Sub-para.(8) provides that if in the first benefit week the claimant had not been in receipt of income support for 16 weeks and so only 50 per cent of his eligible interest was being met under the former para.7(1)(b)(ii), the add back will be calculated as though he was receiving 100 per cent. of his eligible interest at that time (the reference to "on that day" is presumably meant to be "in that benefit week", as confirmed in *CIS 16769/1996*). But any add back will not be paid until the date the claimant would have become entitled to 100 per cent interest if the old rules had remained in force. *CIS 16769/1996* confirms that this is the effect of sub-para.(8), rejecting the Secretary of State's submission that it could only operate if the claimant's 16th and 17th benefit weeks coincided with the first and second benefit weeks as defined in sub-para.(1).

See also para.6(2)–(4) which contains some protection for claimants in relation to the increased waiting period for existing housing costs.

Note the important additional transitional protection for existing claimants in reg.3 of the Income Support (General) Amendment and Transitional Regulations 1995 (p.672). Interest on arrears of interest, on loans for non-approved purposes or for repairs and improvements that are no longer eligible that was included in a claimant's applicable amount for income support on October 1, 1995 will continue to be met for as long as the claimant continues to satisfy the conditions of para.7(6), 7(7) or 8(1)(a) of the former Sch.3 (see the 1995 edition of *Mesher and Wood, Income-related Benefits: the Legislation*) and be in, or treated as in, receipt of income support (and/or, from October 7, 1996, income-based JSA: reg.32 of the Income Support (General) (Jobseeker's Allowance Consequential Amendments) Regulations 1996, see p.676). Note reg.3(3) which provides that only the linking rules in para.14(1)(a), (c) and (e) will apply in these cases. Since the effect of reg.3(2) is to treat these three categories as eligible housing costs under para.15 or 16, the protection in reg.3 will operate separately from the rules for add back in para.7 and will not be affected by them.

2.654 In *Ewens v Secretary of State for Social Security* (Court of Appeal, February 13, 2001, reported as *R(IS) 8/01*) the Court held (disagreeing with the Commissioner) that under para.7(7) of the former Sch.3 it was not necessary for the claimant (i) to have been occupying the dwelling as her home when the non-approved loan was first secured on the dwelling (agreeing with *CIS 450/1993*) or (ii) to have continuously lived in the home after her partner had left. What was required for para.7(7) to apply was that (a) a non-approved loan *e.g.* for business purposes) had been secured on the home (it was immaterial whether either the claimant or her partner were living there at the time); (b) the former partner had lived in the dwelling at some point but had since left; (c) the former partner was not meeting the interest on the loan; and (d) that the claimant was living there when she claimed income support and had to meet the loan in order to continue doing so.

CSIS 162/1996 deals with the relationship between the transitional protection in para.7 and in reg.3 and the question whether the claimant had an applicable amount for housing costs in the week including October 1, 1995. The claimant had been in receipt of income support, including an amount for interest on a loan for repairs and improvements under para.8 of the former Sch.3, until September 20, 1995. He then obtained work but reclaimed income support on October 23, 1995 when his employment ended. His housing costs were calculated under para.16 which resulted in a lower award than on his original claim. But the Commissioner holds that reg.3 applied so that the claimant was entitled to have his housing costs met in accordance with the former para.8. The Commissioner's reasoning was as follows. The claimant fell to be treated as in receipt of income support during the period September 20 to October 23, 1995 under the linking rule in para.14(1)(a)(ii). Since he was to be treated as being in receipt of income support he must also be regarded as being entitled to income support. Consequently he had a "benefit week" in each of the weeks in the gap in his income support claim within the meaning of para.4 of Sch.7 to the Claims and Payments Regulations (see the definition of "benefit week" in reg.2(1)) because he was sufficiently "entitled" to a social security benefit. He also had an applicable amount in those weeks because if a person is to be treated as entitled to, and in receipt of, income support in any particular week, his applicable amount can be ascertained in accordance with Part IV in the normal way. The Commissioner also considered that the transitional protection in reg.3 applied in this case, rather than that in para.7. This was because reg.3 dealt with the particular situation at issue in this case, whereas para.7 was a general provision and operated only where no specific provision applied. The result was that the claimant's income support was not subject to diminution of any "add back" which would have been the case if para.7 had applied. Instead his housing costs would continue to be met in accordance with the former para.8 as long as he remained in, or treated as in, receipt of income support. The AO appealed against this decision to the Court of Session but the appeal was later withdrawn.

See also *CIS 16769/1996* which applies *CSIS 162/1996* in the case of a claimant who was not entitled to income support on October 1, 1995 because his income exceeded his applicable amount due to the rule that only 50 per cent of housing costs were met for the first 16 weeks that applied under the former Sch.3. The result was that he could benefit from the protection in para.6(2)–(4). The Commissioner goes on to deal with the calculation of the claimant's add back in these circumstances.

On para.7(6) of the former Sch.3, which allowed interest on arrears of interest to be met in certain circumstances, note *CIS 8166/1995*. The Commissioner decides that for the former para.7(6)(c) to apply it was not necessary for the mortgage to specifically stipulate that the liability to make payments had been deferred for at least two years. It was sufficient for the terms of the mortgage to result in there being a deferral period of at least two years.

Note also the transitional protection in relation to housing costs for claimants transferring from income support to JSA in reg.87(4) to (6) of and para.18 of Sch.2 to the JSA Regulations.

Para. 8—New housing costs

Note the restriction on house purchase loans incurred while entitled to income support (or income-based JSA: reg.32 of the Income Support (General) (Jobseeker's Allowance Consequential Amendments) Regulations 1996, see p.676), or while a person is caught by the linking rule in para.4(2)–(12) as well as the limits imposed under paras 11(5) and 13.   **2.655**

Sub-para. (1): New housing costs (defined in para.1(2)) are not met until the claimant has been entitled to income support (and/or income-based JSA: reg.32 of the Income Support (General) (Jobseeker's Allowance Consequential Amendments) Regulations 1996, see p.676) for 39 weeks (but see the exceptions in para.9). Note the linking rules in para.14 and in particular the effect of para.14(14) where the claimant's former partner was entitled to state pension credit. The rules for calculating the amount of new housing costs that are payable are the same as for existing housing costs (see the note to para.6(1) above). The drafting of para.8(1)(a) could be improved. It is not clear why sub-para.(1)(a) has not adopted the same format as para.6(1)(a). Presumably it is intended that the amounts in heads (i) and (ii) are to be aggregated but para.8(1)(a) does not exactly say that.   **2.656**

Sub-paras (2)–(5): New housing costs will be treated as existing housing costs for claimants who are eligible for income support as carers, are in custody pending trial or sentence, have been refused payment under a mortgage protection policy because of a pre-existing medical condition or HIV or who are lone parents who have claimed due to the death of, or being abandoned by, a partner (sub-paras (2)–(4)). In the case of a lone parent this will cease to apply if she becomes a member of a couple again (sub-para.(5)). These exemptions from the 39 week waiting period seem very limited. For example, why does head (c) of para.8(2) not extend to all those who are refused payment under a mortgage protection policy, or people who cannot obtain insurance because of their medical condition? Further, sub-para.(3) will only apply if there is a child in the family. A young person (*i.e.* aged 16–18) will not do.   **2.657**

There have been a number of decisions on abandonment in sub-para.(3)(b). *CIS 2790/1998* considers the requirement that the claim for income support was made "because of" being abandoned by a partner. The Commissioner says that although the abandonment need not be the sole cause of the claim for income support, there had to be some causative link between it and the reason for making the income support claim at the time it was made. In that case because of the complexity of events that had happened between the abandonment and the income support claim a year later the claim could not be said to have been made "because of" the claimant's being abandoned. But there was no particular time limit within which a claim had to be made after the abandonment. It was also not necessary for the mortgage in question to be in existence when the abandonment occurred. *CIS/2790/1998* is cited with approval in *Secretary of State for Work and Pensions v W* [2005] EWCA Civ 570, [2005] All ER (D) 256, also to be reported as *R(IS) 9/05* (see further below). The Court of Appeal considered that tribunals should not draw too fine a distinction about what it is that "causes" a claim for income support to be made but should adopt a robust, common-sense approach on causation. See also *CIS 6268/1999* in which the claim for income support was not made until June 1998 although the claimant's husband had left her in May 1997. The Commissioner held that the cause of the income support claim was clear; a claim would not have been made but for the husband's departure and his ceasing to pay the bills.

In *CIS 5177/1997* "abandoned" was given a restrictive meaning by the Commissioner. The claimant's husband had failed to support her financially and had been cruel to her and the children for some months. Her solicitor wrote to him suggesting that he should leave the matrimonial home, which he did shortly afterwards. The Commissioner holds that abandonment in the context of sub-para.(3) was similar to desertion. Thus its essence was (i) physical separation and (ii) an absence of consent to it on the part of the deserted or abandoned partner. The claimant's husband could not be said to have abandoned her because she had (through her solicitor) suggested that he went and the actual separation was by agreement.

However, in *R2/00(IS)* (a Northern Ireland decision) the Commissioner, although agreeing that a separation by agreement would not constitute abandonment, did not accept that the remaining partner necessarily had to oppose the separation. It depended on the circumstances of each case. In the Commissioner's view, for there to be an abandonment there had to be a departure and a relinquishing of responsibility. See also *R(IS) 2/01* which decides that abandonment can include "constructive abandonment". The claimant had moved out of the matrimonial home with her daughter due to her husband's violence. Some ten days later the husband left the house and the claimant moved back into it. The Commissioner holds that if the husband's behaviour had been such as to leave the claimant with little option but to leave the matrimonial home, then there had been a constructive abandonment and this meant that the claimant came within sub-para.(3)(b).

R(IS) 12/99 held that a separation forced upon the parties by the husband's imprisonment did not constitute abandonment within the meaning of sub-para.(3)(b). In the Commissioner's view, deliberate withdrawal of both the husband's society and his financial support was required for the sub-paragraph to apply.

However, *R(IS) 12/99* was distinguished in *CIS/2816/2003* on the ground that the nature of the husband's offences (which were against children) made it impossible for the claimant's husband to live with her and the children. She would not have allowed her children to be put at risk or to be taken from her and therefore she would have been compelled either to leave the matrimonial home or to take steps to have her husband excluded from it. Thus her husband's behaviour amounted to constructive desertion. The Secretary of State appealed against the decision in *CIS/2816/2003* but the appeal was dismissed (*Secretary of State for Work and Pensions v W* [2005] EWCA Civ 570, [2005] All ER (D) 256, also to be reported as *R(IS) 9/05*). The Court of Appeal stated that the term "abandoned" was intended to bear the same meaning as "deserted" has in matrimonial law as between couples. Furthermore, sub-para.(3)(b) was intended to cover cases of "constructive abandonment", that is to say where a claimant and her child or children are effectively forced out of the home by the violence or other unacceptable conduct of her partner. The same was true if, as a result of such conduct, the claimant refused to allow her partner into the home. Imprisonment (or other forms of compulsory separation) could constitute the necessary element of separation for there to be an abandonment (the Court did not agree with *R(IS) 12/99* on that point), but there also had to be an intention to desert. This could be inferred from the husband's conduct in this case, which was such that, despite his apparent wish to return home in due course as noted on the claim form, he must have accepted would not have been allowed to happen. The Court rejected the Secretary of State's submission that the party alleging abandonment had to show that she regarded the relationship as at an end. It was not her mental state that was relevant (on this point see also *R2/00(IS)* above).

CJSA 679/2004 considered the scope of para.7(3) of the JSA Regulations (which is the equivalent of sub-para.(2)(c) (refusal of payment under a mortgage protection policy)). The tribunal had decided that para.7(3) did not apply because the claimant, having been refused payment under the mortgage protection policy, had cancelled it before the date of the JSA claim. But the Comissioner holds that there is no requirement under para.7(3) that the policy must still be in force. In that case the mortgage protection policy had been taken out in connection with the mortgage current at the date of the JSA claim and the claim on it which had been refused because of a pre-existing condition related to the current mortgage. In these circumstances para.7(3) clearly applied.

Para.9—Exclusions from paras 6 and 8

This paragraph does two things. First, it provides for exemption for certain **2.658** claimants from the waiting periods in paras 6 and 8 so that housing costs will be met from the start of the claim (sub-paras (1)(a) and (2)(a)). Interest on qualifying loans will be calculated at the standard rate (see para.12). Before October 6, 2003 sub-para.(1)(a) applied to a claimant who or whose partner was aged 60 or over. However from October 6, 2003 it only applies to a claimant whose partner has attained the qualifying age for state pension credit (defined in s.137(1) of the Contributions and Benefits Act—the effect of that definition is that the qualifying age is 60 for both men and women until April 2010 after which it will increase by stages to 65 in line with the increase in pensionable age for a woman). This is because a person who has reached the qualifying age for state pension credit or whose partner is entitled to state pension credit is not entitled to income support (SSCBA, s.124(1)(aa) and (g)).

Secondly, it also disapplies the waiting periods in relation to housing costs covered by para.17(1)(d)–(f), *i.e.*, payments under a co-ownership scheme, by a Crown tenant or in respect of a tent, so that these are also met from the start of a claim for income support (sub-paras (1)(b) and (2)(b)).

Note the restriction on house purchase loans incurred while entitled to income support (or income-based JSA: reg.32 of the Income Support (General) (Jobseeker's Allowance Consequential Amendments) Regulations 1996, see p.676), or while a person is caught by the linking rule in para.4(2)–(12) as well as the limits imposed under paras 11(5) and 13.

Para.10—Calculation for loans

This contains the formula (referred to in paras 6(1)(a)(i) and 8(1)(a)(i)) for cal- **2.659** culating the weekly amount of interest that will be met on a qualifying loan. Presumably "A" is only intended to refer to the amount of a loan that qualifies under para.15 or 16 to the extent that it comprises eligible capital, although para.10 does not actually say that. The current form of para.10 was introduced to reflect the abolition of MIRAS (mortgage interest relief at source) in April 2000.

Para.11—New and existing housing costs

Sub-para.(2). If a claimant has both an existing and a new agreement, the rules **2.660** for existing and new housing costs will be applied respectively and the amounts aggregated.

Sub-paras (4)–(11): These contain the provisions first introduced in August 1993 **2.661** relating to the ceiling on loans (see the notes to para.7(6B)–(6F) of the former Sch.3 in the 1995 edition of *Mesher and Wood, Income-related Benefits: the Legislation*). For SSAC's report on these changes see Cm. 2272. Sub-paras (4) and (5) provide that there is an absolute limit on the size of loans that can be taken into account in calculating housing costs. The current limit is £100,000 (sub-para.(5)). *CIS 4320/2002* holds that the £100,000 cap on loans was not *ultra vires* nor in breach of ECHR. The Commissioner found that the imposition of a ceiling did come within the ambit of Art.8 but concluded that there had not been a breach of Art.8, or Art.8 in conjunction with Art.14.

If there is more than one loan, all qualifying loans (except any loan taken out to adapt a home for disablement needs (sub-para.(9)) are aggregated and the total amount outstanding is subject to the ceiling (sub-para.(4)). Sub-para.(10) provides that the restriction is to be applied proportionately to each loan where the total outstanding exceeds the ceiling. If a claimant qualifies for loan interest for two homes the limit is applied separately to the loans for each home (sub-para.(6)). If only a proportion of the loan is for a qualifying purpose, or the property is used for mixed purposes (*e.g.* business and domestic), the limit is applied to the proportion of the loan covered by income support (sub-paras (7) and (8)).

If the loan was "to adapt a dwelling" for the needs of a disabled person, that loan is ignored in calculating whether the limit on loans in sub-para.(5) is exceeded (sub-para.(9)). For when a person counts as disabled see para.1(3) and (4) and the note to para.4(9). The disabled person does not have to be a member of the claimant's family. "Adapt a dwelling" is not defined, but this should include the building of an extension, for example. See *CIS 278/1992* and the other decisions referred to in the notes to para.8 of the former Sch.3 on the meaning of reasonable improvements to the home to improve its fitness for occupation in *Mesher and Wood, Income-related Benefits: the Legislation* (1995).

The limit on loans was £150,000 from August 2, 1993 until April 10, 1994, £125,000 from April 11, 1994 to April 9, 1995 and has been £100,000 since April 10, 1995. The rules applied to loans taken out before, as well as those taken out or increased after, these dates, but there was transitional protection for existing claimants (see reg.4 of the Income Support (General) Amendment No. 3 Regulations 1993 (p.668) and reg.28 of the Income-related Benefits Schemes (Miscellaneous Amendments) Regulations 1995 (p.671)). The effect of this is that there is no limit on the existing loans of claimants entitled to income support on August 2, 1993 (or who were treated as entitled by virtue of the linking rules) while their entitlement continues; for claimants who did not qualify for this protection but who were entitled, or treated as entitled, to income support on April 11, 1994, the ceiling on their existing loans is £150,000 while they remain entitled to income support (reg.4). There was similar transitional protection in connection with the reduction of the limit to £100,000 from April 10, 1995 (reg.28). *CIS 12885/1996* confirms that the claimant's entitlement to income support must be continuous; the protection is lost if it ceases for even a single day. (But see the note to para.14(3AA) where the claimant or his partner is a "welfare to work beneficiary".) Note that reg.5(2) of the amending regulations preserves the operation of the respective saving provisions (see the Social Security (Income Support and Claims and Payments) Amendment Regulations 1995 (p.672)). Note also reg.32 of the Income Support (General) (Jobseeker's Allowance Consequential Amendments) Regulations 1996 (see p.676) under which entitlement to income-based JSA counts for the purpose of satisfying a condition that the person is entitled to income support.

The limit applies from the beginning of a claim, so that the 50 per cent for weeks 9 to 26 in the case of existing housing costs applies to the restricted amount of a loan. The ceiling on loans is in addition to the rules on "excessive" housing costs (see para.13) and the restriction on house purchase loans incurred while entitled to income support (or income-based JSA: reg.32 of the Income Support (General) (Jobseeker's Allowance Consequential Amendments) Regulations 1996, see p.676), or while a person is caught by the linking rule (see para.4(2)–(12)). Note that the disregard in para.29 of Sch.9 of payments from mortgage protection policies includes any interest payment on a qualifying loan that is not met by income support; see also the disregard in para.30(1)(b) of Sch.9 and *CIS 13059/1996* in the note to that paragraph.

Para.12—Standard rate

2.662   Interest on eligible loans is paid at the "standard rate". In the past this represented a weighted average of the rates applied by the top 20 building societies calculated by the Financial Services Agency and published monthly by the Office for National Statistics in Financial Statistics Table 7.1L. The trigger for change in the figure was movements of 0.25 per cent or more. However, it was felt that this method was becoming increasingly unrepresentative, due to the fact that many building societies have de-mutualised and become banks and mortgages are now available from a broader range of providers.

Thus with effect from November 28, 2004 a new form of para.12 has been introduced which provides for a change in the method of calculating the standard rate. The new method will use the Bank of England Base Rate plus 1.58 per cent (sub-para.(2)). This will avoid the need to amend the regulations every time the standard rate changes (as happened in the past). According to the Explanatory Memorandum published by the Department, the trigger for change in the standard rate will continue to be movements of 0.25 per cent or more since the Bank of England does not change its base rate by less than 0.25 per cent. However para.12 is silent as to the mechanics of the implementation of any changes. Sub-para.(3) simply provides that the Secretary of State will determine the date from which the new standard rate will be applicable. A footnote in the amending regulations states that the date determined and the standard rate will be available from the Housing Support Division of the Department and will be published on the DWP website at least seven days before the new standard rate becomes applicable. Sub-para.(6) provides that the standard rate will be 5.88 per cent until the first date determined by the Secretary of State under sub-para.(3). At the time of writing, according to the Jobcentre Plus website (*www.jobcentreplus.gov.uk*), a standard rate of 6.33 per cent has been effective from December 5, 2004.

The other change introduced with effect from November 28, 2004 is the phased abolition of the "five per cent rule". Under the old form of para.12, if the actual rate of interest was less than five per cent on the day housing costs were first payable, that rate applied (ignoring any changes in it) until it reached five per cent when the standard rate applied. The effect of sub-paras.(4) and (5) is that this rule no longer applies where housing costs first fall to be met on or after November 28, 2004 and will cease to apply to existing claims on the day the actual rate of interest charged reaches five per cent or more, the anniversary of the date on which housing costs first fell to be met, or whenever a change of circumstances (not necessarily associated with housing costs) occurs, whichever is the earlier.

In *CJSA 232/2003* the claimant contended that the standard interest rate was in violation of Art.14 of ECHR when read with either Art.8 or Art.1 of Protocol 1. The Commissioner was prepared to accept that the standard interest rate might come within the ambit of Art.8 but found that discrimination had not been established and moreover that the standard interest rate was a proportionate response to legitimate aims.

Para.13—Excessive housing costs

This restricts the housing costs that will be met where the accommodation is too   **2.663** large or expensive. These limits are in addition to the ceiling on loans (para.11(4)–(11)), and the restriction on house purchase loans incurred while the claimant is entitled to income support (or income-based JSA: reg.32 of the Income Support (General) (Jobseeker's Allowance Consequential Amendments) Regulations 1996, see p.676), or caught by the linking rule in para.4(2)–(12).

The rules are very similar to those in para.10(3)–(7) of the former Sch.3, but the linking rule in sub-para.(7) is 12, not eight, weeks. Note that there is no equivalent to the former para.10(1)–(2) relating to tenants who buy their homes, as they are now covered by the stricter rules in para.4(8). See the notes to para.10(1)–(2) in the 1995 edition of *Mesher and Wood, Income-related Benefits: the Legislation* for a discussion of the former provisions.

Sub-para. (1): This does not specifically provide for any deduction for the presence of   **2.664** a non-dependant to be made first, before deciding whether the level of housing costs is excessive (unlike the former para.10(3)). But since sub-para.(1) refers to housing costs that fall to be met under this Schedule, this indicates that it is the amount of housing costs net of deductions (and restrictions) that is the relevant figure.

There are three sets of circumstances in which a restriction can be applied. The first is that the home is unnecessarily large for the claimant's family, including any foster children and non-dependants living in the household. An absolutely literal reading of the provision would lead to the result that it does not apply to a single claimant, who does not have a family. *CIS 104/1991* decides that the words must be read as "the claimant and his family (if any)." Any part of the home which is let is ignored in assessing the size of the accommodation against the needs of its occupants. At base is an issue of opinion about what is unnecessarily large. Some common situations caught by this provision (*e.g.* a married couple whose children have left home, or a deserted spouse) may escape under sub-para.(4) or (6).

The second set of circumstances, under head (b), is that the immediate area of the home is more expensive than other areas in which suitable alternative accommodation is available. It is not at all clear how restricted the immediate area might be, but it will probably be more limited than the area under (c). *CSB 1016/1982* suggests that the delimitation of an area is likely to be within the knowledge of tribunals. It must be possible also to identify another cheaper area (using the *CSB 1016/1982* definition) in which suitable alternative accommodation exists. The condition of suitability will limit the distance within which other areas can be sought (*R(IS) 12/91*).

Finally, under head (c), there is a restriction if the outgoings of the home are higher than for suitable alternative accommodation in the area (not the immediate area). In *CSB 1016/1982* (in relation to an earlier formulation of this rule) "area" was said to connote "something more confined, restricted and more compact than a locality or district. It might consist of dwelling houses or flats contiguous to a road or a number of roads, refer to a neighbourhood or even to a large block of flats. It is not capable of precise definition." This approach was commended for the purposes of sub-para.(1) in *CIS 34/1989* and *R(IS) 12/91*.

If sub-para.(1) applies, sub-para.(3) provides that the "amount of the loan" shall be restricted and the excess expenditure over that for a home of suitable size or expense will not be met. The purpose of the reference to "the amount of *the loan*" is not entirely clear, since sub-para.(1) applies to any housing costs met under Sch.3, not just qualifying loans. Sub-paras (4) and (6) contain exceptions to the operation of sub-paras (1) and (3).

R(IS) 9/91 decides that sub-paras (1) and (3) operate in the same way as *R(SB) 6/89* decided that the old reg.21 of the Requirements Regulations did. The excess is not the difference between the actual expenditure and the maximum that would be allowed for a family of similar size in a home of the necessary size or in an acceptably cheaper area. The excess is the difference between the actual expenditure and the housing costs which would be incurred by the claimant in the alternative accommodation. On the facts of *R(IS) 9/91*, the net proceeds of sale of the existing home would have completely covered the cost of acquiring alternative accommodation, so that there would be no income support housing costs. Thus the entire actual expenditure was "excess".

Note also *CJSA 2683/2002*. This holds that in considering the amount of a loan that the claimant would need to obtain alternative cheaper accommodation under sub-para.(3), unsecured loans that became repayable on the sale of the existing home could be taken into account when calculating the net proceeds of sale of that home which could be put towards the alternative accommodation.

2.665   *Sub-para. (4)*: If it is not reasonable to expect the claimant to seek alternative cheaper accommodation, no restriction is to be made at all. It must already have been determined under sub-para.(1) that cheaper alternative accommodation which is suitable exists. All the relevant factors set out in sub-para.(5) must be considered.

Under head (a) the availability of suitable accommodation must be judged objectively (*R(SB) 7/89* and *R(IS) 10/93*). The particular circumstances of the claimant and his family are taken into account under head (b). The reference in head (a) to area is particularly obscure. Does it mean the area in which the home is situated or can it include another area in which suitable accommodation is available? In *CSB 1016/1982* it is suggested that it only governs the level of housing costs, not the availability of suitable accommodation, but it seems to be assumed in *R(SB) 7/89* that it governs both matters.

Sub-para. (5) (b): Brings in all the relevant circumstances, not just those mentioned   **2.666** (*R(SB) 6/89, R(SB) 7/89* and *R(IS) 10/93*). One relevant factor mentioned in *CSB 1016/1982* was that the home had only just come into the claimant's occupation in matrimonial proceedings. In *CSB 617/1988* the claimant was assured by the manager of the local DSS office before she moved from a house with a mortgage of £25,000 to a house with a mortgage of £69,890 that the full interest on the new mortgage would be met by supplementary benefit. Although such an assurance could not bind the AO by creating an estoppel (*R(SB) 14/88*) it was one of the circumstances to be considered. (*CSB 617/1988* is reported as *R(SB) 14/89*, but it is the unreported version that should be referred to, as the reported decision omits the last three paragraphs which are the relevant ones here.)

Financial hardship is also a relevant factor. In *R(SB) 6/89* the invidious financial position the claimant would be put in if she were forced to sell the home in which she had lived for many years before its renovation was complete was relevant. As was the claimant's inability to find a buyer because of the stagnant housing market (*CIS 347/1992*). In that case the claimant had been advised of a price range for selling his home and would suffer financial hardship if forced to sell below that price. In *CIS 434/1992* the not uncommon problem of a negative equity was relevant. A further factor mentioned in *R(SB) 7/89* was that if the claimant sold his home, his lenders would not be prepared to lend to him again, but if the proceeds of sale were not put to purchasing another house, the capital would disentitle him from benefit. Thus rented accommodation may not be a straightforward alternative. *R(IS) 10/93* holds that the inability of the claimant to obtain suitable accommodation is a relevant factor. As in that case, that inability may stem from the fact that the claimant is unable to sell his existing home, despite making all reasonable efforts to do so.

Sub-para. (6): If the restriction is not removed completely under sub-para. (4) there   **2.667** can be a limited exemption here. If the claimant (or a member of the family) was able to meet the financial commitments for the home when they were first entered into, there is to be no restriction under this paragraph (but the ceiling in para.11(5) may apply) for the first six months on income support (and/or income-based JSA: reg.32 of the Income Support (General) (Jobseeker's Allowance Consequential Amendments) Regulations 1996, see p.676) or from the date on which the housing costs are determined on a supersession to be excessive. This should include a person who was a member of the family when the mortgage was taken on (*e.g.* where a couple have separated). The exemption can be extended for up to another six months so long as the claimant uses his best endeavours to obtain cheaper accommodation. What are the best endeavours is an issue of fact. *R(SB) 7/89* holds that a claimant can only be penalised for failing to use his best endeavours if he has been given some advance notice of the necessity to do so. In *R(IS) 13/92* the claimant's housing costs were restricted from the beginning of the claim to £146.85 a week, the amount appropriate to interest on a capital sum of £110,000. At the time the capital and accrued unpaid interest amounted to £696,063.44. The Commissioner agreed that a restriction under sub-paras (1) and (3) was indicated, but on the evidence the claimant was able to meet the financial commitments for the dwelling at the time the mortgage was obtained. Therefore the absence of restriction for the first six months under sub-para.(6) was mandatory. The Commissioner did however consider that the initial improper restriction operated as a notice of the intention to restrict housing costs after the six months under *R(SB) 7/89*. The Court of Appeal in

Secretary of State for Social Security v Julien, The Times, April 21, 1992, also reported as *R(IS) 13/92*, confirmed the Commissioner's decision, saying that the issue is ability to meet the financial commitments, not prudence.

In *CIS 104/1991* the Commissioner takes the approach of *R(SB) 7/89* a little further. He holds that if the claimant could afford the housing commitments when he took them on there cannot be a restriction until there has been an explicit notice in a decision that there may be a restriction in six months' time. The sub-para.(6) meter has to be started explicitly and it has to run for six months. In *CIS 104/1991* only two months notice was given. The claimant had to be allowed another four months and then the question of using the best endeavours to obtain cheaper accommodation had to be explored.

In *CIS 3163/1997* the claimant contended that because there would have to be what was then a review (now a supersession) at the end of any exemption period under sub-para.(6), this meant that on that review a new automatic 26 weeks' exemption from restriction would have to be allowed (with a possible extension for an extra 26 weeks), and so on, on a rolling basis. However, the Commissioner holds that the reference to review in the then form of sub-para.(6) was to the review which first started the sub-para.(6) clock running within any period of income support entitlement. The maximum period for the application of sub-para.(6) was thus 52 weeks from the date of that review (or from the start of entitlement if sub-para.(6) was applied immediately on the award of entitlement). To allow a new automatic 26-week period to start on any review would undermine the manifest purpose of sub-para.(6). However, where after a restriction had been imposed, a decision was made (*e.g.* that sub-para.(4) applied or that the conditions of sub-para.(1) were no longer met) which had the effect of lifting that restriction, but later still it was decided that a restriction should be made, then the review (now supersession) decision reimposing the restriction *did* trigger the operation of sub-para.(6) (*CJSA 2536/2000*).

2.668 *Sub-paras (7) to (9)*: A person can now only requalify for the deferment of a restriction under sub-para.(6) if there is a break in entitlement to income support of more than 12 weeks. Note that the linking rules in para.14(1)(c) to (f) apply.

Para.14—Linking rules

2.669 Note that the amendment made to sub-para.(2) by the Child Support (Consequential Amendments and Transitional Provisions) Regulations 2001 only applies to those cases in relation to which the new child support regime introduced by the Child Support, Pensions and Social Security Act 2000 has come into force. The new child support scheme is being implemented in stages (see the introductory note at the beginning of the Child Support Act 1991 in Part I of this volume). See reg.10 of the Child Support (Consequential Amendments and Transitional Provisions) Regulations 2001 (SI 2001/158) (p.699) for the saving provision. For the form of sub-para.(2) that continues to apply in cases that have not yet become subject to the new rules, see the 2002 edition of this volume.

These rules are particularly important for the waiting periods under paras 6 and 8, but apply throughout the Schedule. Sub-paras (1)–(3) largely reproduce para.7(9), (12) and (11) respectively of the former Sch.3, except that the basic linking period in sub-para.(1) is 12, not eight, weeks. SSAC had recommended 26 weeks because a shorter linking period could act as a disincentive to work in view of the new waiting periods. But note the extended linking period of 52 weeks in some cases—see sub-paras (10)–(13) and the notes to those sub-paragraphs.

Regulation 32 of the Income Support (General) (Jobseeker's Allowance Consequential Amendments) Regulations 1996 (see p.676) should also be noted. This provides that entitlement to income-based JSA counts as entitlement to income support for the purpose of satisfying any condition that the person is or has been entitled to income support for any period of time. It also has the same effect where the requirement is that the person is or has been treated as being in receipt of income support. See para.18(1)(c) of Sch.2 to the JSA Regulations for the converse provision under the JSA rules. Where the claimant's former partner was entitled to state pension credit, see sub-para.(14) below, inserted with effect from October 6, 2003.

Note the new linking rules in sub-para.(1)(ee) and sub-paras (3ZA) and (3B) introduced on January 5, 1998 as a consequence of the "New Deal". The intention is that time spent on the New Deal should not put claimants at a disadvantage in terms of qualifying for housing costs. Thus under sub-para.(3ZA) a claimant is deemed to be in receipt of income support during any period that he stops getting income support because he or his partner is on a New Deal option, or (from April 3, 2000) an employment zone (defined in reg.2(1)) scheme, or (from April 9, 2001) in the Intensive Activity Period of the New Deal for people aged 25 or over or the Intensive Activity Period for 50 plus, that results in him (or his partner) being in remunerative work or having an income that is too high to qualify for income support. In addition, sub-para.(1)(ee) treats a claimant as in receipt of income support for the same period that his partner was in receipt, or treated as in receipt, of income support where the claimant is awarded income support for the couple immediately after either of them has been taking part in one of the three New Deal employment programmes or the Intensive Activity Periods for people aged 25 or over or 50 plus and immediately before this his partner had been getting income support for the couple. See also sub-para.(3B) which treats any period of entitlement to contribution-based JSA immediately before a person or his partner took part in a New Deal employment programme or the Intensive Activity Periods for people aged 25 or over or 50 plus as a period of entitlement to income support. Similar provisions have been inserted into Sch.2 to the JSA Regulations (see para.13(1)(ee) and (3A) of Sch.2; an equivalent of sub-para.(3B) is obviously not needed).

See sub-paras (10)–(13) (and the notes to those sub-paragraphs below) for the situations where the linking period in sub-paras (1)(a)(ii), (1)(c)(iv), (1)(d), and (1)(f)(iii) is 52, rather than the basic 12, weeks.

Sub-para. (3A): The waiting periods in paras 6 and 8 talk in terms of entitlement to income support but the linking rules in sub-paras (1)–(3ZA) refer to deemed receipt of income support. Sub-para.(3A) states that deemed receipt for the purposes of sub-paras (1), (3) and (3ZA) counts as deemed entitlement, to confirm that these linking rules apply to the waiting periods. 2.670

Sub-para. (3AA): Sub-para.(3AA), inserted with effect from August 2, 1999, was considered necessary because the DSS had received advice that the effect of para.14 (since December 12, 1995) had been to provide a linking rule for the payment of interest on loans above the £100,000 ceiling in para.11(5) (although see *CIS 12885/1996* in the note to para.11). The purpose of sub-para.(3AA) is to reaffirm the policy intention that *any* break in claim (however short) will result in the loss of transitional protection for payment of interest on loans above the ceiling. There is an exception for welfare to work beneficiaries (see above) for whom the right to this transitional protection is preserved during their 52 week linking period. A similar amendment has been made to para.13 of Sch.2 to the JSA Regulations. 2.671

Sub-paras (4)–(9): These were new in October and December 1995 and are intended to assist claimants in satisfying the waiting periods. Note also sub-para.(3B) (see above). Sub-paras (4), (5), (5A) and (5B) provide that a person who is not entitled to income support only because s/he has too much capital and/or income will be treated as so entitled for any period (or periods: Interpretation Act 1978, s.6) of up to 39 weeks during which s/he is entitled to unemployment benefit, contribution-based JSA, statutory sick pay or incapacity benefit (or credits), eligible for income support as a carer, a lone parent, or treated as in receipt of income support (and/or income-based JSA: reg.32 of the Income Support (General) (Jobseeker's Allowance Consequential Amendments) Regulations 1996, see p. 676). Note that for these provisions to apply the person must not be entitled to income 2.672

support by reason *only* that he has too much income and/or capital. In *CIS 621/2004* the claimant who was in receipt of incapacity benefit was paid contractual sick pay by his employer until his employment was terminated with three months pay in lieu of notice. Although he was not treated as in remunerative work while he was absent from work while ill (see reg.5(3A)), the effect of reg.5(5) was to treat him as in remunerative work during the three month' notice period. The consequence was that he ceased to fall within sub-para.(4) during the 13 week notice period (and could not take advantage of the linking rule in sub-para.(1)(a)(ii) because the notice period was more than 12 weeks).

Further note that a lone parent includes a person who is responsible only for a young person (*i.e.* aged 16–18) (see reg.2(1)). (But since such a lone parent will not be eligible for income support under para.1 of Sch.1B, she will have to satisfy one of the other paragraphs in Sch.1B in order to come within para.(4).) In the case of carers and lone parents covered by sub-para.(5A) it is necessary for a claim for income support to have been made, the refusal of which fixes the start of the deemed entitlement. The absence of such a requirement in sub-para.(5) would seem to imply that it is not necessary for a claim to have been made for a person to benefit from this provision. This has now been confirmed by *CJSA 4613/2001*. The Commissioner holds that the words "not entitled . . . by reason only of his income" in para.13(5) of Sch.2 to the JSA Regulations (the equivalent of sub-para.(4)) refer to the substantive conditions of entitlement; they do not require a claim for JSA (or income support) to have been made. The Commissioner also holds that in para.13(1)(a)(ii)(bb) of Sch.2 the reference to "sub-paragraphs (5), (6) and (7)" has to be read as meaning "sub-paragraphs (5) and (6) or (7)" in order to make sense (see sub-para.(1)(a)(ii)(bb) above which does use the disjunctive, not the conjunctive).

Although sub-para.(4) states that these rules apply where a person is not entitled to income support only because of excess capital and/or income, sub-para.(5B) also provides that for lone parents and carers covered by sub-para.(5A) the deemed entitlement does not apply if during the relevant period the person would not be entitled to income support because s/he (or any partner) is in remunerative work or s/he is a full-time student (other than one who is eligible for income support) or temporarily absent from Great Britain. Is the effect of this, for example, that if a lone parent finds work after sub-para.(5A) has applied to her for, say, 20 weeks, the deemed entitlement under that sub-paragraph does not apply at all? Although the wording of sub-para.(5B) is not entirely clear, the fact that where the period of work is 12 (or from October 5, 1998, 52 in the case of a "welfare to work beneficiary" (sub-para.(10)) weeks or less the linking rule in sub-para.(1)(a)(ii)(bb) will apply so that the period of work can count under sub-para.(5)(c) indicates that this is not the case and that sub-para.(5B) only applies to the periods when the lone parent or carer is in remunerative work, etc. (Note that because sub-para.(3A) now treats deemed receipt of income support as deemed entitlement for the purposes of sub-paras (1), (3) and (3ZA), such a period of 12 (or 52) weeks or less can in fact count directly under sub-para.(1)(a)(ii)(bb) without having to go via the sub-para.(5)(c) route. This is relevant for JSA. Paragraph 13(6) of Sch.2 to the JSA Regulations contains no equivalent of sub-para.(5)(c), but since such a provision is no longer needed in these circumstances the effect of these rules will be the same for both income support and JSA.) The amendments to sub-para.(1)(a)(ii) introduced on October 7, 1996 have addressed the problem raised in the 1996 edition of *Mesher and Wood, Income-related Benefits: the Legislation* that the linking rule in that sub-paragraph might not have applied because under its pre-October 1996 form the period of deemed receipt had to fall between periods of *receipt* (or deemed receipt) of income support whereas sub-paras (5) and (5A) treat a person as *entitled* to income support. (There was the same potential problem before October 7, 1996 for people who fell within sub-para.(5) and who, for example, worked for a period of 12 weeks or less between two periods of unemployment.) Note that this may not be too much of an issue for carers and many lone parents, for whom new housing costs are treated as existing housing costs (see para.8(2)–(5)). But it could be if, for example, their income disqualifies them until "full" housing costs are payable. In addition, not all lone parents are covered by para.8(3).

Note that if the only reason for non-entitlement to income support is too much income, and the person's income includes payments under a policy taken out to insure against the risk of not being able to meet eligible housing costs, s/he will be treated as entitled to income support for the period that the insurance payments are made (sub-para.(6)).

Sub-paras (8) and (9): If a claim for income support is made by, or in respect of, a person whose payments under a policy to insure against a loss of employment have stopped and who had been getting income support (and/or income-based JSA: reg.32 of the Income Support (General) (Jobseeker's Allowance Consequential Amendments) Regulations 1996, see p.676, and/or, from October 6, 2003, whose former partner had been getting state pension credit: sub-para.(14)) including housing costs within the last 26 weeks, the weeks in between the claims are ignored for the purpose of deciding whether the claimant has been entitled to income support for either the 26 or 39 week qualifiying period.   2.673

Sub-para.(10): The linking period in the case of a "welfare to work beneficiary" is 52 weeks. See the notes to reg.2(1) for when a person counts as a welfare to work beneficiary. This concession is part of the Government's New Deal for Disabled People. The aim of the extended linking period is that the person should not be worse off if he has to reclaim benefit within a year because he (or his partner) has again become incapable of work. For JSA there is a similar extension of the linking period where the claimant's partner is a welfare to work beneficiary (see para.13(12) of Sch.2 to the JSA Regulations).   2.674

Sub-paras (11)–(13): To encourage claimants who have already qualified for housing costs back into work, a 52-week linking period also applies if the following conditions are met. A person must stop getting income support on or after April 9, 2001 because he or his partner has started work or increased his hours of work, is taking steps to get work as an employee or in self-employment under certain Training for Work schemes, or is on a New Deal option, an employment zone programme or the self-employment route, and as a result he or his partner counts as in full-time work or has an income that is too high to be eligible for income support. But the longer linking period will only apply if immediately before entitlement to income support ceased the person's housing costs were being met (or would have been but for any non-dependant deduction) because he had already served the eight, 26 or 39-week waiting period. Thus for claimants who have not yet completed the relevant waiting period for 50 per cent or "full" housing costs when they move into work the linking period remains 12 weeks. For the equivalent JSA provisions see the amendments to para.13(1) and the new sub-paras (13)–(15) of para.13 of Sch.2 to the JSA Regulations inserted with effect from April 9, 2001.   2.675

Note also the "mortgage interest run-on" which has been introduced from April 9, 2001 to allow housing costs to be met for the first four weeks of employment. See the notes to reg.6.

Sub-para.(14): This provides, as referred to above, that for the purposes of the linking rules in this paragraph, if a claimant's former partner was entitled to state pension credit, any reference to income support in this Schedule also includes a reference to state pension credit.   2.676

Para.15—Loans on residential property

Under the new rules the question is no longer whether the interest is eligible, but whether the loan qualifies. Thus the situation dealt with in *R(IS) 11/95* where the   2.677

original loan was interest free (see the notes to para.7(3) of the former Sch.3 in the 1995 edition of *Mesher and Wood, Income-related Benefits: the Legislation*) will no longer be an issue. This paragraph (and para.16) deal with whether a loan is for a qualifying purpose. Note the restrictions on loans that will be met in paras 4(2)–(12), 11(4)–(11) and 13.

Clearly there has to be a loan for para.15 to apply. *CIS 14483/1996* concerned a scheme for Muslims operated by the Albaraka International Bank because the Koran prohibits the payment or charging of interest on money loaned. Under the scheme the claimant and the bank jointly purchased the property; the legal estate vested in the claimant who held it on trust for himself and the bank and the beneficial interest was divided into investment shares. The claimant agreed to purchase a number of shares from the bank each month and to pay the bank an amount of "mesne profit" each month to reflect his use of the bank's share in the property. The Commissioner holds that the mesne profit did not constitute "eligible interest" which could be met under para.7(3) of the former Sch.3 because there was no loan. The agreement was not in the nature of a mortgage but was a form of co-partnership, designed specifically to prevent the payment of interest.

2.678 *Sub-para. (1)*: The loan (or any increase in the loan, *CIS 141/1993*) must either be *for the purpose of acquiring an interest in the home, or paying off another loan which was for an approved purpose*. In the second situation the loan will only qualify to the extent that the old loan would have qualified, on which see *CIS 5110/1999*. In *CIS 5110/1999* the claimant's original loan to purchase his home was for £49,000. He then discharged that loan with a loan from a home loans company. That loan was for £50,470 because it included an acceptance fee of £1,470. Subsequently that loan was replaced by a loan from a building society for £50,450. The Commissioner holds that the whole of the third loan, including the sum representing the home loan company's acceptance fee, fell within sub-para.(1)(b). The claimant had had to pay the fee of £1,470 in order to obtain the £49,000 that he needed to discharge his original loan. The £1,470 therefore qualified as money that had been applied for the purpose of paying off a loan within sub-para.(1)(a).

The cost of acquiring an interest in the home includes besides the purchase price expenses necessary for the purchase, *e.g.* stamp duty, legal fees (see *Decision Makers Guide*, para.23576). Loans include hire purchase agreements (sub-para.(2)). An overdraft facility is a loan for this purpose (see *CIS 6010/1995* in the notes to para.16), as is a debt owing on a credit card (see *CCS 4722/1998* decided under the similar child support provision).

Sub-paras (1)(a) and (b) are not mutually exclusive, so eligible interest can be allowed under both heads (see *R(IS) 6/94* below).

CIS 563/1991 considered when money is being *applied* for an approved purpose. Clearly this is the case if it is spent directly on the purchase price and the legal and other expenses of the purchase. The Commissioner considers that it could also include money used for the purchase of goods or some other interest in property that then formed part of the consideration for the transfer of the interest in the home. However, it does not extend to money that has to be spent on some other purpose as a result of a precondition imposed by some other person, *e.g.* the mortgagee (see *Guest v Chief Adjudication Officer*, April 2, 1998, unreported, CA, below).

"Interest" includes a "further interest": In *R(IS) 7/93*, the claimant had been living in leasehold property for some time and receiving housing costs for the interest on the loan to acquire that interest. He received a further advance to enable him to buy the freehold reversion. It is held that the loan to acquire a further interest was for a qualifying purpose, and it did not matter that he already had one interest. "An interest" in the home should include both legal and equitable interests. In *CIS 465/1994* the Commissioner holds that "acquiring an interest" covers the situation where the owner does not have a present right of possession and takes out a mortgage to buy out sitting tenants so that she can move into the property. The tenants

were statutory tenants under the Rent Act 1977. The Commissioner states that the primary purpose of Sch.3 was to help with the costs of acquiring or keeping a roof over one's head. Interest in sub-para.(1)(a) was not restricted to "an interest in land" in the Law of Property Act sense, although it did contemplate "an interest of a proprietary nature or some closely analogous right of tenure or occupancy similar to that of a true tenant". Moreover, acquiring an interest could include purchasing an interest only for the purpose of extinguishing it (see *R(IS)6/95* in the notes to para.3 of Sch.10 which regards a similar transaction as a sale from the tenant's point of view). The Commissioner distinguished *R(IS) 4/95* (see below) on the ground partly that the right of occupation at issue in that case was not a right of exclusive occupation.

In *CIS 679/1992* a loan taken out to purchase a strip of land to extend the claimant's garden was for the purpose of acquiring an interest in what was, at the date of the claim, the dwelling occupied as the home.   2.679

In *R(IS) 6/94* the claimant and his wife had bought their home in joint names with the help of a mortgage. They were equitable joint tenants. The claimant was made bankrupt and a trustee in bankruptcy appointed. The trustee in bankruptcy sold the claimant's former interest in the home to the claimant's wife. She obtained a mortgage to pay for this and to discharge the original mortgage (among other things). When the claim for income support was made, interest was only allowed on an amount equal to the original loan under sub-para.(1)(b). The Commissioner points out that on the appointment of the trustee in bankruptcy the claimant's estate vested in him and the equitable joint tenancy was severed (*Re Dennis (a Bankrupt)* [1992] 3 W.L.R. 204). It was replaced by an equitable tenancy in common, under which the trustee and the claimant's wife held equal shares. Therefore, when buying the claimant's former interest in the home, his wife was acquiring a further interest in it and the interest on the part of the mortgage advanced for that purpose was payable under sub-para.(1)(a).

When a claimant buys a former partner's interest in the home this will constitute acquiring a further interest in a home (but note para.4(2)–(12)). In *CIS 762/1994* the former matrimonial home was transferred to the claimant on the basis that she paid her ex-husband £5,000 and released him from all liability under the mortgage. The original mortgage had been for £43,200 but had increased to just over £52,300 because of arrears. The bank would not agree to the transfer of the house into the claimant's name unless the arrears were discharged. She therefore took out a second loan for £52,300 to discharge the original loan and the arrears. The AO only awarded housing costs on £43,200. But the Commissioner holds that the claimant was entitled to housing costs on the full amount of the second loan. That loan had been applied in part to acquire the husband's interest in the home, the consideration for which included releasing him from all liability under the mortgage, and in part to pay off the original loan of £43,200, and so the whole of it was eligible. However, if the claimant and partner still count as a couple, the acquisition by one of them of the other's interest in the home, does not come within sub-para.(1)(a). They are one entity for the purposes of income support, and any transaction between them, when together they previously owned the entire interest, does not give rise to housing costs (*R(IS) 1/95*). *R(IS) 4/95* decides that a Class F land charge (registered by a spouse to protect his or her rights under the Matrimonial Homes Act 1983) is not "an interest in the dwelling occupied as the home", but a mere right of occupation (see *Wroth v Tyler* [1974] Ch. 30).

In *R(IS) 18/93* the land certificate of the claimant's home had been deposited with a bank as security for a company loan. When the bank threatened to call in the loan when the company was in trouble, the claimant obtained a mortgage to discharge the debt to the bank. This loan was not for a qualifying purpose. The deposit of the land certificate may have been evidence of the creation of an incumbrance on the claimant's title to the home, but the bank did not acquire an interest in the home. Therefore the mortgage loan was not to acquire the bank's interest. *CIS 336/1993* reaches a similar conclusion. It made no difference that the bank's charge had been created by way of a legal mortgage rather than deposit of the land certificate. By effecting the charge the claimant had not parted with an interest in his home. When he obtained release of the charge he did not acquire any interest.

2.680 See also *R(IS) 14/01*. Under the terms of the claimant's mortgage she paid reduced interest payments during the first three years. The deferred interest was capitalised in another account and at the end of the three years interest was also charged on that sum. The AO refused to include the interest payable on the capitalised interest as part of the claimant's housing costs. The Commissioner accepted that the tribunal had been right to regard the capitalised sum in the second account as a loan as it was in effect a form of secondary financing. However, the sum "lent" to the claimant was not for the purpose of paying interest on the main loan because the interest due on that loan had been reduced. It was lent to allow the claimant to spend money on other things during the first three years. Although this may have had the effect of enabling the claimant to buy the house, this was not sufficient for the loan to qualify under sub-para.(1) (*CIS 3774/1997* not followed). See also *CJSA 888/1999* and *CIS 141/1993* in the note to para.6(1).

R(IS) 11/94 holds that "dwelling occupied as the home" in sub-para.(1)(a) includes any dwelling intended to be occupied as the home, since most properties are acquired before they become a home. If a person acquires a site and then builds a home on it, all the costs connected with the acquisition of the site and the subsequent building work constitute "monies applied" for the purpose of "acquiring an interest" in the home. Such building costs include the value of the claimant's own labour (put in this case at £9,000) and all bank charges (including overdraft interest) necessary to enable the home to be built up to the first day of occupation. However, any interest accruing after the claimant moves into the home is not eligible.

CIS 297/1994 holds that the intention to make the property the home has to be formed at the date of acquisition and implemented as soon as practicable. But it would seem at least arguable that the wording of para.15(1)(a) does not actually require this, and that if the dwelling is now occupied as the home, even if this was not the case, or the intention, at the time the interest was acquired, sub-para.(1)(a) can apply. This has now been confirmed by *CIS 401/1999* which disagrees with *CIS 297/1994*. The Commissioner in *CIS 401/1999* points out that sub-para.(1)(a) is worded in general terms in order to cover a range of circumstances but it plainly covers the typical case in which the dwelling does not become the claimant's home until after the purchase has been completed and the claimant moves in. This showed that sub-para.(1)(a) was concerned with the use of the property at the time entitlement to income support was determined rather than at the time of acquisition. The claimant was therefore entitled to housing costs even though the property she was now living in was not originally acquired as a home.

In *Guest v Chief Adjudication Officer* (April 2, 1998, unreported, CA) it was a condition of the claimant's loan of £85,000 to purchase his home that there would be a further charge of £30,000 on the property in order that the building society could recoup some of its loss in relation to his previous mortgage. The Commissioner held that this "further advance" of £30,000 was simply a transfer of part of the claimant's liability under the earlier mortgage to his new property and that this did not represent the taking out of a loan for the purposes of para.7(3) of Sch.3 (as in force before October 2, 1995). In addition, it did not fall within para.7(3)(a) (now sub-para.(1)(a)), as this did not extend to money which had to be spent on some other purpose as a result of a precondition imposed by some other person (*e.g.* the mortgagee). Para.7(3)(b) (now sub-para.(1)(b)) also did not apply as the provision of alternative security for part of the claimant's pre-existing liability did not amount to "paying off another loan". Moreover, that liability had not been incurred for the purpose of purchasing any interest in his *present* home. The Court of Appeal dismissed the claimant's appeal, holding that no loan as such had been taken out and that the Commissioner's conclusions as to the ambit of para.7(3) were correct.

Head (b) had to be read in the light of the essential purpose of Sch.3, which was to provide housing costs in respect of the dwelling occupied as the claimant's home (*i.e.* his present home). Although there are differences between the former para.7(3) and sub-para.(1), the reasoning in this decision will apply equally to sub-para.(1), as confirmed by *CJSA 4807/2000*. The loans secured on the claimant's home included a loan taken out to purchase a house in which the claimant was living at the time of the loan but which had since been sold. The Commissioner holds that para.14(1)(a) of Sch.2 to the JSA Regulations (the equivalent of para.15(1)(a)) did not apply to a loan that was used to purchase a dwelling which has since ceased to be occupied as the home, even though it was so occupied at the date of the loan.

Sub-para.(3): The proportion of a loan for an eligible purpose defines the proportion of the loan that qualifies under para.15 (subject to the limit in para.11(8)).   2.681

Para.16—Loans for repairs and improvements

Sub-para.(1). Loans for the purpose of repairs or improvements to the home, or   2.682
for service charges to pay for repairs or improvements, or loans to pay off such loans, are eligible (although these have been considerably restricted: see sub-para.(2)). Placing limitations on the meeting of such costs does not breach Art.8 ECHR (respect for private and family life) (*CIS 2056/2002*)). Repairs or improvements to any part of the building containing the claimant's home, *e.g.* the common parts of a block of flats are covered (see sub-para.(2)). *R(IS) 5/96* holds that the loan has to be for repairs or improvements to the home that is currently occupied. Thus the claimant was not entitled to interest on a bank loan for central heating after he moved from that home. "Repairs and improvements" are defined in sub-para.(2). The loan has to be used for the repairs, etc., within six months or some further period. If the loan is not so used, the claimant is not entitled to interest on it even during the six months or any extended period (*CIS 257/1994*). The capital amount of the loan is disregarded under para.8(b) of Sch.10.

CIS 6010/1995 decides that the use of an overdraft facility to finance building works could constitute a taking out of a loan for repairs and improvements. The claimant's builders required immediate payment, so she arranged an overdraft in order to pay them before her improvement grant came through. The AO refused payment of the interest on the overdraft on the ground that an overdraft facility was not a loan. The Commissioner holds that the wide ordinary meaning of "loan" as "money borrowed at interest" applied in this context and this covered the drawing of money on overdraft. There was clear evidence that the bank had agreed to grant the overdraft facility for the specific purpose of financing the building works. The Commissioner leaves open the questions whether a loan would be "taken out" where there was no advance arrangement and whether the required purpose could easily be shown in such circumstances.

Note that the overall limit on loans applies (see para.11(4) and (5) but note the exception in para.11(9)) as well as the general limits in para.13. But the restriction in para.4(2)–(12) (loans incurred while entitled to income support, or income-based JSA; reg.32 of the Income Support (General) (Jobseeker's Allowance Consequential Amendments) Regulations 1996, see p.676) does not apply to loans for repairs and improvements.

Sub-para.(2): There has been a considerable tightening up of the extent to which   2.683
loans for repairs and improvements will be met by income support. To qualify, both repairs and improvements must now be undertaken with a view to "maintaining the fitness of the dwelling for human habitation . . .", *and* be one of the listed measures. This is narrower than para.8(3) of the former Sch.3 under which any major repairs were covered if they were "necessary to maintain the fabric" of the home. Now for repairs to be eligible they must not only maintain the home's fitness for human habitation but also come within heads (a)–(l). The test in the former para.8(3) (that

applied to improvements only) was that of "improving . . . fitness for occupation" (see *CIS 643/1993* which held that if the claimant considered that the work would improve the property this should be accepted, save in the most exceptional cases). The notion of "maintaining" is narrower than "improving" fitness. Moreover, the new criterion of human habitation seems to be an attempt to move away from the particular needs of the claimant in favour of a more "objective" standard (but see the new head (k) which necessarily will involve consideration of the needs of the disabled person concerned).

The most notable omission from the listed measures is the former head (k), "other improvements which are reasonable in the circumstances" (see the notes to para.8(3) of the former Sch.3 in the 1995 edition of Mesher and Wood, *Income-related Benefits: the Legislation* as to the ambit of this provision). But the scope of several others has also been narrowed. For example, provision of heating is no longer covered, only repairs to an existing heating system under head (b) (the use of the word "system" indicates that a replacement boiler, for example, should be covered as *part* of a heating system and see *CIS 15036/1996* below; see also *CIS 781/2002* below); head (j) seems considerably more limited than the former head (f) which referred to improvement in the structural condition of the home; and loans for facilities for storing food are no longer included (head (f)). Cupboards and a refrigerator are such facilities (*R(IS) 16/98*); the Commissioner also holds that a loan for a refrigerator would not in any event be covered by para.16 unless it is a fixture within the home (see *CIS 363/1993*). "Provision of" has replaced "provision or improvement of" in a number of places (reflecting the change in the overall test from "improving" to "maintaning" the fitness of the home). "Provision of" would not seem to be limited to initial installation, but could cover repairs to, or replacement of, an existing facility (see *R. v Social Fund Inspector Ex p. Tuckwood* (High Court, April 27, 1995). *CJSA 5439/1999* has confirmed that provision includes replacement in this context (see also *CIS 2901/2004*). Heads (k) and (l) are new and make provision for these two specific situations. Note that a loan to which the new head (k) applies is ignored for the purposes of the ceiling on loans (para.11(9)).

2.684   On head (1) see *CIS 14657/1996*. The Commissioner points out that the loan has to be taken out "for the purpose" of the relevant improvements. The claimant's loan could therefore fall within head (1) where his daughter was aged 10 but her brother would not reach that age for another year or so because the money was being used for something that was bound to happen in the near future. The Commissioner also decides that the cost of a survey could come within head (j) as reasonably incidental to the carrying out of the work covered by that head. *CIS 1678/1999* goes further than *CIS 14657/1996* in holding that it was not necessary for the provision of separate sleeping accommodation to have been the sole or even the main purpose in taking out the loan. It was enough if it was one of two or more purposes (the claimant had wanted her children to have separate bedrooms from the beginning so as not to disturb each other's sleep). Furthermore, it did not matter how long a time had elapsed between the taking out of the loan and the children's attainment of the age of 10 (the loan in question had been incurred while the claimant was expecting her second child). This was because if there were children of different sexes their need for separate sleeping accommodation was a foreseeable and inevitable future need that was likely to have been in the mind of a claimant extending her house. The Commissioner in *CIS 1678/1999* expressly does not follow *CIS 16936/1996* which had decided that the relevant children must all have been at least 10 years old at the date on which the loan was taken out. However, in *CIS 5119/2001* the Commissioner declines to follow *CIS 1678/1999*. In his view it conflicted with *CIS 14657/1998*. But in any event it conflicted with *CIS 2711/1999* (decided by the same Commissioner as *CIS 14657/1998*). In para.9 of *CIS 2711/1999* the Commissioner had stated that in deciding whether the conditions in head (l) were met it was the circumstances as they stood at the time the loan was taken out and the money was used in carrying out the repairs and improvements that had to be considered, not any later date when a claim for income support was made, or some still later date when during the continuation of a claim a child reached 10. The Commissioner in *CIS 5119/2001* was in complete agreement that the focus had to be on the nature and purpose of the loan at the time when it was taken out rather than any later date. There is therefore a conflict between these various decisions, but the weight of authority would now seem to be that the relevant children must already be 10, or at least within a year or so of becoming 10, when the loan is taken out.

On the meaning of "repairs to existing heating systems" in head (b), see *CIS 781/2002*. The claimant had two storage radiators in her home. She replaced these with a boiler and ten radiators. The Commissioner considered that repairing an existing system meant changing a part of the system that did not work or putting it back into working order. A repair could have as an incidental effect an improvement in the system. But in the circumstances of this case there had clearly been a replacement of the system, not a repair of the existing system.

Note also *CIS 15036/1996* which concerned whether replacement of a central heating boiler came within para.8(3)(h) of the former Sch.3 ("provision of heating, including central heating"). The Commissioner decides that the installation of the new boiler was an improvement which had been undertaken with a view to "improving fitness for occupation" and so came within para.8(3) (it was not contended that it constituted a major repair necessary to maintain the fabric of the home). The fact that the boiler had merely been replaced by its modern equivalent did not matter. The Commissioner refers to *Morcom v Campbell-Johnson* [1956] 1 Q.B. 106 in which Denning L.J. had drawn a distinction between the provision of something new which would constitute an improvement and the replacement of something worn out, albeit with a modern equivalent, which would come within the category of repairs, not improvement. Presumably on the basis of this dictum the replacement of a boiler would also fall within head (b) as it would seem to fulfil the test of maintaining fitness for human habitation. The consequence for the claimant in *CIS 15036/1996* was that the element of her service charge attributable to the new boiler had to be deducted under the former para.9(2)(c) (now para.17(2)(c)).

CIS 2132/1998 also concerns service charges. The claimant had been billed for the cost of renewing a roof over one of the other flats in her block. The Commissioner decides that this did not come within any of the relevant heads in sub-para.(2). Head (g) did not apply as the roof was not part of the dwelling occupied by the claimant as her home. Head (j) was also not applicable, as there was no evidence that the roof had been renewed because of an unsafe structural defect. In addition, although a repair to a roof could, depending on its nature, be a damp-proofing measure, the renewal of a roof did not fall within head (c). In *CIS/2901/2004* (another service charges case), the Commissioner stated that in his view "damp proofing" and "insulation" were terms of art in the building trade which have found their way into ordinary language. As used in head (c), he considered that "damp proofing" was limited to measures taken to prevent rising damp or damp from condensation, and "insulation" in head (g) was similarly restricted to such things as the installation of double-glazing, loft insulation and cavity wall insulation.

Sub-para.(3): See the note to para.15(3).

Para.17—Other housing costs

This provision lists the other miscellaneous housing costs covered by income support (sub-para.(1)(a)–(f), which are the same as para.1(c)–(i) of the former Sch.3 except that the list has been reordered) and contains the conditions for meeting these costs (which are virtually identical to the former para.9, subject to some tidying-up of the wording).

Of these items, the category of "service charges" (sub-para.(1)(b)) is probably of most interest. This phrase is given no special definition. (It does not include an administration fee charged by a lender where mortgage payments are in arrears (*CIS*

2.685

2.686

392/1994).) *CIS 157/1989* suggested that it means charges in respect of a service rendered to a tenant by the landlord. The Tribunal of Commissioners in *R(IS) 3/91* and *R(IS) 4/91* decides that the category can extend to owner-occupiers as well. The essence is the determination and arranging of what would otherwise be left for the occupier to do for himself, on the basis of an arrangement which the terms of occupation of the property make binding on all those with the same interest in the property. However, things within the housing benefit definition of ineligible service charges are excluded (sub-para.(2)(b)). This list covers charges in respect of day-to-day living expenses, a number of personal services and other services "not connected with the provision of adequate accommodation" (see *CIS 1460/1995* below). (Note that in April 2003 the "transitional housing benefit scheme" (see Sch.1B to the Housing Benefit Regulations) which had allowed certain service charges to be met where the claimant was in supported accommodation came to an end; the responsibility for meeting such costs passed to local authorities under the "Supporting People" programme. Payments made by local authorities for such "welfare services" (in Scotland "housing support services") are disregarded (see para.76 of Sch.9 and para.66 of Sch.10)). *CJSA 5493/1999* expresses the view that "adequate" has a looser meaning than fitness for human habitation but is not to be equated with what is desirable; nor is a provision for bad debt connected with the adequacy of accommodation. But a provision for future repairs could be: see *CIS 667/2002* and *CIS 2901/2004* below. Under sub-para.(2)(c) charges for the cost of repairs and improvements, as defined in para.16(2), are also deducted. The narrowing of the scope of para.16(2) will mean a corresponding reduction in the exclusion of service charges under sub-para.(2)(c). For interest on loans for service charges for repairs and improvement, see para.16. If a charge includes fuel charges, deductions are also made (except for charges in respect of communal areas: para.4 of Sch.1 to the Housing Benefit Regulations, confirmed in *CIS 1460/1995*). The standard amounts to be deducted under sub-para.(2)(a) are (from April 2005): heating (apart from hot water), £10.55; hot water, £1.25; lighting, 85p; cooking, £1.25. The standard amounts can be altered on evidence of the actual or estimated charge. Note that since housing benefit expenditure is excluded generally under para.4(1)(a), this means that no service charge, payment of which by a tenant is a condition for the occupation of the home (and therefore within the definition of rent), can count under Sch.3.

In *R(IS) 3/91* a leaseholder's share of the cost of roof repairs was a service charge. The obligation was imposed on the claimant by the conditions of her occupation and the service was connected with the provision of adequate accommodation, so that the exclusion in sub-para.(2)(b) did not bite. In the light of *CIS/2132/1998* and *CIS/2901/2004* (see below) it would seem that the exclusion in sub-para.(2)(c) also does not apply. In *R(IS) 4/91* the claimant, an owner-occupier, had to pay £93 a year to have his cess-pit emptied. The appeal had to be returned to the SSAT for further findings of fact, but it was suggested that if the service was carried out by an outside contractor engaged by the claimant, the cost would not be a service charge.

In *R(IS) 4/92* it was held that sums required to be paid by a tenant under the terms of the lease to reimburse the landlord for the cost of property insurance were a service charge within the principles set out in *R(IS) 3/91* and *R(IS) 4/91*. The Commissioner also found that the landlord's obligation to use any money paid out under the insurance policy as a result of fire on reinstatement of the property meant that the charge was connected with the provision of adequate accommodation. The Commissioner in *CSIS 4/1990* doubted that building insurance was so connected (referring to the earlier decision in *CIS 17/1988* where there was a suggestion to the contrary). The Court of Session in the *McSherry* case (which is the appeal in *CSIS 4/1990*) does not deal with this point. However, in *R(IS) 19/93* the Commissioner agrees with *R(IS) 4/92* and dissents from the suggestion in *CIS 17/1988*. The weight of authority would therefore seem to favour the interpretation taken in *R(IS) 4/92* in relation to payments by tenants to reimburse landlords for the cost of building insurance. But note the effect of para.4(1)(a). In *R(IS) 4/92* the Commissioner made his award subject to enquiries whether the reimbursement of the landlord's insurance premiums would be included in the claimant's rent for housing benefit purposes.

In *Dunne v Department of Health and Social Security* (September 10, 1993), the Court of Appeal in Northern Ireland decided that the building insurance premium paid by the claimant as an owner occupier was not a service charge. Although the claimant was obliged to take out such insurance under the terms of both his building lease and his mortgage, it did not fulfill the test laid down in *R(IS) 3/91* and *R(IS) 4/91*. Such a premium was to be distinguished from payment required to be made to the landlord for building insurance by occupiers of a block of flats which clearly was a service charge. In *Secretary of State for Social Security v McSherry* (March 17, 1994) the property insurance premium at issue was mandatory under the terms of the claimant's mortgage. The Court of Session agrees with the decision in *Dunne*, holding that the omission of insurance premiums from para.1 of the former Sch.3 (in contrast to the express provision for routine maintenance and insurance in the supplementary benefit scheme) was deliberate. (*R(SB) 1/90* holds that although decisions of the Court of Appeal of Northern Ireland are not binding on Commissioners in Great Britain, identically worded provisions operating in both Northern Ireland and Great Britain are to be interpreted uniformly. Decisions of the Court of Session are binding.)

R(IS) 19/93 had come to a similar conclusion. The Commissioner states that the **2.687** claimant's obligation to pay the insurance premium to his building society was not an obligation arising from his interest or estate in the property, but from his mortgage. It was a consequence of the claimant's financial arrangements, not his ownership of the property itself, and thus was not a service charge. In essence, the payment was no different from a house insurance premium paid under an ordinary contract between an owner/occupier and his insurance company (which had been held in *CIS 17/1988* not to constitute a service charge).

The result is that whether the obligation to pay insurance charges or to reimburse a landlord for the payment of insurance premiums constitutes a service charge depends upon it coming within the principles set out in *R(IS) 3/91* and *R(IS) 4/91*. It seems clear that payments required to be made to the landlord from occupiers of a block of flats to cover insurance for the building are a service charge, whereas a building insurance premium payable under the terms of a claimant's mortgage is not. An insurance charge of the kind concerned in *R(IS) 4/92* also constitutes a service charge. On the other hand, an obligation on the claimant to effect insurance under the terms of a lease would not qualify.

CIS 667/2002 considered payments into a reserve fund. The Commissioner referred to *CCS 5242/1995* (a child support case) which had decided that payments into a reserve fund could be eligible as housing costs, although there might have to be an apportionment for any relevant deductions under sub-para.(2). The only relevant deductions in this context were those that were not connected with the provision of adequate accommodation and any amounts for repairs and improvements as defined in para.16(2). The Commissioner acknowledges that because the works for which the reserve fund will eventually be used are not yet known an element of speculation is required. But this could be informed by the following factors: (i) the terms governing the use of the reserve fund or the scope of the landlord's powers under the service charge; (ii) information on how the reserve fund has been used in the past; (iii) details of any work that is planned or anticipated. In this case the only evidence available related to (iii). Future works were to cover roof recovering, repair of a lift, external repointing and redecoration and improvements of the common parts. The Commissioner concluded that none of those constituted a repair or improvement under para.16(2) (see *CIS 2132/1998* in the notes to para.16 in relation to roof renewal) and all related to the provision of adequate accommodation. The consequence was that the whole of the current payment into the reserve fund was an eligible service charge (although in future years the available evidence might justify a different conclusion).

Payments for future maintenance was also one of the issues in *CIS/2901/2004*. The Secretary of State had argued that the cost of replacement windows and roof repairs provided for in the reserve fund were deductible from the service charge under sub-para.(2)(c) as being in respect of the provision of insulation, natural light, damp proofing or the repair of unsafe structural defects. However, this is rejected by the Commissioner who points out that the purpose of a reserve fund is to avoid the need for the repair of unsafe structural defects and that the repeated use of the word "provision" in para.16(2) implies the furnishing of something not already in existence or the replacement of something which no longer functions. He agrees with *CIS/2132/1998* that damp proofing is not the predominant purpose of a roof. However, he goes on to state that in his view "damp proofing" and "insulation" are terms of art in the building trade which have found their way into ordinary language. As used in para.16(2), he considered that the former was limited to measures taken to prevent rising damp or damp from condensation in an existing building, and the latter to such things as the installation of double-glazing, loft insulation and cavity wall insulation to reduce heat loss in an existing building. Furthermore, the contribution to the reserve fund in respect of future window repairs in the claimant's own flat came within the definition of service charge in para.15 of *R(IS) 4/91*. The Commissioner also made the more general observation that even if any of the contingencies itemised in a reserve fund do correspond to the para.16(2) list, what is deductible under sub-para.(2)(c) is the current or recent capital cost of works referred to in para.16(2) incurred within the time prescribed by para.16(1), not the claimant's current contributions to a reserve against such capital costs in the future.

CIS 1460/1995 concerned a service charge for residents of sheltered accommodation for the elderly. The claimant lived in a self-contained bungalow and had the use of communal areas (pathways and gardens) and a communal lounge; the service charge covered the costs of broadly the maintenance of the common areas and the structure of the buildings, as well as a resident warden. The Commissioner accepts that the terms of the appendix to *R(IS) 3/91* and *R(IS) 4/91* as a whole (as opposed to the headnote) made it clear that a service charge was only to be excluded under sub-para.(2)(b) to the extent it related to matters specified as ineligible in para.1 of Sch.1 to the Housing Benefit Regulations; there was no overriding test of connection with the adequacy of the accommodation (see para.1(g) of Sch.1). Where an element of a service charge was not dealt with in sub-paras (a)–(f) of para.1 of Sch.1 so that sub-para.(g) had to be considered, a common sense view had to be taken. In general, where a claimant had a right to use a communal lounge, gardens, etc., services related to those communal areas should be accepted as related to the provision of adequate accommodation. Para. 1 as a whole did contemplate that charges for communal areas could be eligible (see, for example, sub-para.(a)(ii) (laundry facilities), (iii) (children's play area) and (iv) (cleaning of communal areas)). Moreover, if service charges were thought to be excessive, the appropriate control mechanism was para.10 (now see para.13). On the meaning of para.1(g) itself, although it excluded services which related purely to meeting the personal needs of residents, this did not mean that in considering whether a service was related to the provision of adequate accommodation the question of suitability for the personal needs of the residents was not relevant (see Sedley J. in *R. v North Cornwall D C Ex p. Singer and Others* (High Court, November 26, 1993, pp.11–12 of the transcript). Para.1 of Sch.1 did envisage that the personal needs of the claimant could be considered (see sub-para.(a)(iv) on window-cleaning and (c) on emergency alarm systems where the eligibility of a service charge depended on the claimant's personal circumstances). What was connected to the provision of adequate accommodation, including how far the personal needs of residents should be taken into account, was a question of fact in each case (para.17 of the appendix to *R(IS) 3/91* and *R(IS) 4/91*). The Commissioner also deals with the meaning of "sheltered accommodation" (see the definition of "communal area" in para.7 of Sch.1 to the Housing Benefit Regulations which includes rooms of common use in sheltered accommodation). He suggests that the characteristics of such accommodation were the grouping together of individual dwellings, which were offered primarily to those with some special housing need, and where some communal facilites, the employment of a warden and an emergency alarm system, were included. But accommodation could still be sheltered accommodation even without some of these features.

From April 2000 the "transitional housing benefit scheme" (see Sch.1B to the Housing Benefit Regulations) had allowed certain service charges to be met by housing benefit where the claimant was in supported accommodation. However, this came to an end in April 2003 and the responsibility for meeting such costs passed to local authorities under the "Supporting People" programme. Payments made by local authorities for such "welfare services" (in Scotland "housing support services") are disregarded (see para.76 of Sch.9 and para.66 of Sch.10).

CIS/2901/2004 also concerned supported accommodation. The claimant owned a leasehold property in a complex. Under the terms of her lease she had to pay a service charge which covered services in respect of the buildings, gardens and other ground that formed the complex (but not the insides of any dwelling), as well as personal and communal services for herself and the other owners. One of the issues was the proportion of staff salaries and associated administrative costs that were to be attributed to housing related services (and therefore eligible for income support), as opposed to personal care services (which would be met under the "Supporting People" programme). The tribunal had simply accepted the estimate provided by the company that managed the complex. However, the Commissioner set the tribunal's decision aside, stating that it was necessary to make findings on how many hours the staff actually spent providing accommodation-related services (as opposed to personal services). This ratio should then be applied to the other staff-related costs, such as staff advertising. The Commissioner also considered whether payments into a reserve fund could be met as part of the service charge (see above).

On sub-para.(1)(d) (payments under a co-ownership scheme), see *CJSA 5493/1999*.

Sub-para.(1)(a) includes in Scotland payments by way of feu duty. However, note that feu duty was abolished with effect from November 28, 2004 (see the Abolition of Feudal Tenure etc. (Scotland) Act 2002 (Commencement No. 2) (Appointed Day) Order 2003 (SSI 2003/456)).

Para. 18—Non-dependent deductions

Non-dependent is defined in reg.3. The standard deductions depend on whether the non-dependent is in remurative work or not, and the level of earnings (sub-paras (1) and (2)). The same deduction is made for a couple as for a single person (sub-paras (3) and (4)). Note that no deduction is made from the benefit of a claimant who (or whose partner) is blind or who is in receipt of attendance allowance or the care component of disability living allowance for himself (sub-para.(6)). Note also the list in sub-para.(7) of non-dependants for whom no deduction is made. Those covered include those getting a training allowance while on Work Based Learning for Young People (head (b)); students (head (c)); under-25s on income support or income-based JSA (head (d)); those for whom a deduction has already been made from a rent allowance or rebate (head (e)); people who would not count as non-dependents under reg.3(2B) but for reg.3(2C) (*e.g.* co-owners who are close relatives or their partners, where the co-ownership arose after April 11, 1988) (head (f)); patients absent from home for more than 52 weeks, prisoners (head (g)), and people in receipt of state pension credit (head (h)). See also sub-para.(8).

2.688

[¹SCHEDULE 3A   **Regulations 17(1)(g), 18(1)(h)**
and 71(1)(a)(v) and (d)(iv)

PROTECTED SUM

Interpretation

2.689   **1.**—(1) In this Schedule—

[³"eligible housing benefit" means
- (a) for the period of 7 consecutive days beginning on 3rd April 1989, the amount of housing benefit to which the claimant or his partner was entitled in that period which relates to the board and lodging accommodation normally occupied as the home by him or, if he has a partner, by him and his partner;
- (b) for the period of 7 consecutive days beginning on 10th April 1989 or, in a case to which paragraph 7(7)(b) applies, for the period of 7 consecutive days referred to in that paragraph, the amount of the claimant's or his partner's maximum housing benefit determined in accordance with regulation 61 of the Housing Benefit (General) Regulations 1987 (maximum housing benefit) which relates to that accommodation;]

"first week" means the benefit week beginning on a day during the period of 7 days commencing on 3rd April 1989;

"income support" includes any sum payable under Part II of the Income Support (Transitional) Regulations 1987;

"protected sum" means the amount applicable under this Schedule [⁹or by virtue of regulation 87(2) of the Jobseeker's Allowance Regulations 1996] [³to a claimant who in the first week is living in board and lodging accommodation or who or whose partner is temporarily absent in that week from that accommodation];

[³"protected total" means—
- (a) the total of the claimant's applicable amount under regulation 20 (applicable amounts for persons in board and lodging accommodation) in the first week or, in a case to which paragraph 7(7) applies, if the protected person or any partner of his is temporarily absent from his accommodation in that week, the amount which would have fallen to be calculated under that regulation for that week as if there had been no temporary absence; and
- (b) the amount of any eligible housing benefit for the period of 7 consecutive days beginning 3rd April 1989;]

"relevant provisions" means—
- (a) regulation 17(1)(a) to (f) (applicable amounts);
- (b) regulation 18(1)(a) to (g) (polygamous marriages);
- (c) regulation 71(1)(a)(i) to (iv) (urgent cases);
- (d) regulation 71(1)(d)(i) to (iii);
- (e) in relation to a case to which paragraph 17(b)(ii) or (c)(i) of Schedule 7 (persons from abroad) applies, the regulations specified in that paragraph but as if the reference to regulation 17(1)(g) in that paragraph were omitted; or
- (f) in relation to a case to which paragraph 17(d)(i) of that Schedule applies, the regulations specified in that paragraph but as if the reference to regulation 18 were a reference to regulation 18(1)(a) to (g) only; ·

"second week" means the benefit week beginning on a day during the period of 7 days commencing on 10th April 1989.

[³"third week" means the benefit week beginning on a day during the period of 7 days commencing on 17th April 1989.]

(2) For the purposes of this Schedule—

(a) in determining a claimant's applicable amount in his first week, second week or any subsequent benefit week no account shall be taken of any reduction under regulation 22 (reduction in certain cases of unemployment benefit disqualification);

(b) [²except in so far as it relates to any temporary absence to which paragraph 7(7) refers,] where a change of circumstances takes effect in the claimant's second week which, had it taken effect in the first week, would have resulted in a lesser applicable amount in respect of that week, his applicable amount in the first week shall be determined as if the change of circumstances had taken effect in that week.

Protected sum

2. [³Subject to sub-paragraph (2) and the following paragraphs] of this Schedule, where the protected total of a claimant is more than—
    (a) his applicable amount in the second week determined in accordance with the relevant provisions; and
    (b) any eligible housing benefit for the period [³of 7 consecutive days] beginning 10th April 1989,
the protected sum applicable to the claimant shall be an amount equal to the difference.

    [³(2) Where—
    (a) in the second week a claimant's income calculated in accordance with Part V or, as the case may be, VI exceeds the aggregate of his applicable amount determined in accordance with the relevant provisions and X; and
    (b) the amount of income support to which he is entitled in the first week is more than the amount of housing benefit to which he would, but for this subparagraph, have been entitled in the period of 7 consecutive days beginning on 10th April 1989.
the protected sum applicable to the claimant shall, subject to sub-paragraph (3), be an amount equal to X + Y + 10 pence.

    (3) Where a claimant or his partner is, or both are, entitled in the first, second and third weeks to a relevant social security benefit or to more than one such benefit and consequent upon the Social Security Benefits Up-rating Order 1989 the claimant or his partner is, or both are, entitled to an increase in any one or more of those benefits in the third week, the protected sum under sub-paragraph (2) shall be increased by an amount equal to the difference between—
    (a) the amount of benefit or aggregate amount of those benefits to which the claimant or his partner is, or both are, entitled in the third week; and, if less,
    (b) the amount of benefit or aggregate amount of those benefits to which the claimant or his partner is, or both are, entitled in the second week.

    (4) In this paragraph—

    "X" means the sum which, but for sub-paragraph (2), would be the protected sum applicable under sub-paragraph (1);
    "Y" means the amount of the excess to which sub-paragraph (2)(a) refers;
    "relevant social security benefit" means—
        (a) child benefit
        (b) any benefit under the Social Security Act [SSCBA];
        (c) war disablement pension;
        (d) war widow's pension;
        (e) any payment under a scheme made under the Industrial Injuries and Diseases (Old Cases) Act 1975;
        (f) any concessionary payment.]

2.690

Persons not entitled to a protected sum

3. A protected sum shall not be applicable to a claimant where in the first week—

    (a) he is aged under 25 and, if he is a member of a couple, his partner is also aged under 25; and

    (b) he is required to be available for employment for the purposes of section 20(3)(d)(i) of the Act [SSCBA, s.124(1)(d)(i)]; and

    (c) he was not in receipt of supplementary benefit as a boarder on November 24, 1985; and

    (d) none of the conditions in paragraph 16(4) of Schedule 5 (applicable amounts of persons in board and lodging accommodation or hostels) applies to him.

2.691

    [²(2) A protected sum shall not be applicable to a claimant [³unless he, or any partner of his, is entitled to housing benefit for the period of 7 consecutive days beginning 10th April 1989 or, where paragraph 7(7)(b) applies, for the period of 7 consecutive days referred to in that paragraph in respect of] the board and lodging accommodation normally occupied as the home by him, or if he has a partner, by him and his partner.

    (3) Subject to paragraph 7, a protected sum shall not be applicable to a claimant where he changes or vacates his accommodation during the period of 7 consecutive days beginning 10th April 1989.]

Period of application

4. Subject to paragraph 7, the protected sum shall not be applicable to a claimant for more than—

2.692

(a) in the case of a claimant who is a member of a family and that family includes a child or young person and during the first week that family was in accommodation not provided or secured by a local authority under section 63 or 65(2) or (3)(a) of the Housing (Scotland) Act 1987, a period of 52 weeks beginning with the second week;

(b) in any other case, a period of 13 weeks beginning with the second week.

Reduction of protected sum

2.693   5.—(1) Subject to [8sub-paragraphs (2) to (6)], the protected sum shall be reduced by the amount of any increase, in a benefit week subsequent to the second week, in the claimant's applicable amount determined in accordance with the relevant provisions.

(2) Where regulation 22 (reduction in certain cases of unemployment benefit disqualification) [6or regulation 21A (reductions in certain cases of failure to attend courses)] ceases to apply to a claimant and as a result his applicable amount increases no account shall be taken of that increase.

[3(3) Where by virtue of the coming into force of regulation 5 of the Income Support (General) Amendment Regulations 1989 the claimant's applicable amount increases in his benefit week beginning on a day during the period of 7 days commencing on 9th October 1989, no account shall be taken of that increase.]

[5(4) Where a claimant's applicable amount increases because a child or young person mentioned in paragraph (5)(c) of regulation 16 (circumstances in which a person is treated or not treated as a member of the household) is treated as a member of the claimant's household under paragraph (6) of that regulation, the claimant's protected sum shall not be reduced by the amount of that increase unless the child or young person has been treated as a member of the household for a continuous period which exceeds 8 weeks.]

[7(5) Where by virtue of the coming into force of regulation 15(a), (b) or (c) of the Income Support (General) Amendment No. 4 Regulations 1991 a claimant's applicable amount increases in his benefit week beginning on a day during the period of 7 days commencing on 1st October 1991, no account shall be taken of that increase.]

[8(6) Where by virtue of the coming into force of regulation 3(1) and (2) of the Income-Related Benefits Amendment Regulations 1992 a claimant's applicable amount increases in his benefit week beginning on a day during the period of 7 days commencing on 5th October 1992, no account shall be taken of that increase.]

Termination of protected sum

2.694   6. Subject to paragraph 7, the protected sum shall cease to be applicable if—
(a) that amount is reduced to nil under paragraph 5; or
(b) the claimant changes or [2vacates] his accommodation; or
(c) the claimant ceases to be entitled to income support.

Protected persons

2.695   7.—(1) Subject to sub-paragraph (2), for the purposes of this paragraph a protected person is a claimant, where—
(a) in respect of the first week he is entitled to an increase under paragraph 7 of Schedule 5 (applicable amounts of persons in board and lodging accommodation or hostels) because either he or, if he is one of a couple or a member of a polygamous marriage, he or his partner satisfies any of the conditions in paragraph 8 of that Schedule; or
(b) in the first week the claimant or, if he has a partner, either he or his partner—
    (i) is in need of personal care by reason of [2old age,] mental or physical disablement, mental illness, or dependence on alcohol or drugs; and
    (ii) is receiving both board and personal care in accommodation other than a residential care home or nursing home or residential accommodation within the meaning of regulation 21(3) (special cases) [3 . . .]; and
    (iii) is in accommodation which he entered under arrangements for his personal care made by a statutory authority or a voluntary or charitable body and those arrangements are being supervised on a continuing basis by that authority or body; or
(c) he or, if he has a partner, either he or his partner but for his temporary absence from his accommodation for a period not exceeding 13 weeks, which includes the first week, would have satisfied (a) or (b) above.

(2) A claimant is not a protected person if he or, if he has a partner, he or his partner, in the first week, is temporarily living in board and lodging accommodation and that accommodation is not the accommodation normally occupied as the home.

(3) Paragraph 4 shall not apply to a protected person.

(4) Paragraph 6(b) shall not apply to a protected person if:

  (a) he moves to accommodation where he satisfies conditions (i) to (iii) of sub paragraph (1)(b); or

  (b) he becomes a patient within the meaning of regulation 21(3); or

  (c) on his ceasing to be a patient within the meaning of regulation 21(3), either he returns to the accommodation which he occupied immediately before he became a patient, or he moves to other accommodation where he satisfies conditions [²(i) to (iii)] of sub-paragraph (1)(b); or

  (d) in a case to which sub-paragraph (6) applies, on his becoming re-entitled to income support, he is either in the accommodation which he occupied immediately before he ceased to be entitled to income support, or in accommodation where he satisfies conditions (i) to (iii) of sub-paragraph (1)(b).

[³(5) Except where sub-paragraph (7) applies, where a protected sum was applicable to a protected person immediately before he or any partner of his became a patient within the meaning of regulation 21(3) for a period of 14 weeks or less, he shall, subject to sub-paragraph (4)(c), on his or, as the case may be, his partner's easing to be a patient, be entitled to a protected sum equal to—

  (a) the amount by which his protected total exceeds his applicable amount determined in accordance with the relevant provisions in the first benefit week in which his applicable amount ceases to be determined under paragraph 1 of Schedule 7 and either—

    (i) any eligible housing benefit for the period of 7 consecutive days beginning on 10th April 1989; or, if greater,

    (ii) in a case where sub-paragraph (7)(b) applied, any eligible housing benefit for the period of 7 consecutive days referred to in that sub-paragraph; or

  (b) the amount of the protected sum to which he was entitled in the immediately preceding benefit week,

whichever is the lower.

(6) Paragraph 6(c) shall not apply to a protected person who has ceased to be entitled to income support for [⁴a period not exceeding the permitted period determined in accordance with regulation 3A (permitted period)]—

  (a) if immediately before he ceased to be so entitled a protected sum was applicable to him; and

  (b) except where sub-paragraph (7) applies, if during that period the protected person becomes re-entitled, or would by virtue of this sub-paragraph be re-entitled, to income support he shall, subject to sub-paragraph (4)(d), be entitled to a protected sum equal to—

    (i) the amount by which his protected total exceeds his applicable amount determined in accordance with the relevant provisions in the first complete benefit week in which he becomes so re-entitled and either any eligible housing benefit for the period of 7 consecutive days beginning 10th April 1989 or, if greater, in a case to which sub-paragraph (7)(b) applied, any eligible housing benefit for the period of 7 consecutive days referred to in that sub-paragraph; or

    (ii) the amount of the protected sum to which he was previously entitled,

whichever is the lower.

(7) Where a protected person or any partner of his is temporarily absent from his accommodation for a period not exceeding 13 weeks which includes the first or second week (or both)—

  (a) in a case where a protected sum was applicable to the protected person immediately before his or, as the case may be, his partner's return to that accommodation and the full charge was made for the accommodation during the temporary absence, on the protected person's or, as the case may be, his partner's return to that accommodation, the protected person shall be entitled to a protected sum equal to—

    (i) the amount by which his protected total exceeds his applicable amount determined in accordance with the relevant provisions in the first complete benefit week after his or, as the case may be, his partner's return to that accommodation and any eligible housing benefit for the period of 7 consecutive days beginning 10th April 1989; or

    (ii) the amount of the protected sum which was applicable to him in the immediately preceding benefit week,

whichever is the lower;

  (b) in a case where—

    (i) a protected sum has not at any time been applicable to the protected person; or

    (ii) immediately before the protected person's or, as the case may be, his partner's return to that accommodation a protected sum was applicable but a reduced charge was made for the accommodation during the temporary absence.

the protected person on his or, as the case may be, his partner's return to that accommodation shall, subject to sub-paragraph (8), be entitled to a protected sum equal to the amount by which his protected total exceeds his applicable amount determined in accordance with the relevant provisions in the first complete benefit week after his or, as the case may be, his partner's return to that accommodation and the amount of eligible housing benefit for the period of 7 consecutive days beginning on the date determined in accordance with regulation 65 or, as the case may be, 68(2) of the Housing Benefit (General) Regulations 1987 (date on which entitlement is to commence or change of circumstances is to take effect) following that person's return to that accommodation.

(8) Where, in a case to which sub-paragraph (7)(b)(i) applies—

   (a) in the first complete benefit week after the protected person's or, as the case may be, his partner's return to his accommodation the protected person's income calculated in accordance with Part V or, as the case may be, VI exceeds the aggregate of his applicable amount determined in accordance with the relevant provisions and X; and

   (b) the amount of income support to which he was entitled in the first week is more than the amount of housing benefit to which he would, but for this sub-paragraph, have been entitled in the period of 7 consecutive days beginning on the date determined in accordance with regulation 65 or, as the case may be, 68(2) of the Housing Benefit (General) Regulations 1987 following the case may be, his partner's return to that accommodation.

the protected sum applicable shall, subject to sub-paragraph (9), be an amount equal to X + Y + 10 pence.

(9) Where the protected person or, as the case may be, his partner returns to the accommodation in the second week and he or his partner is, or both are, entitled in the first, second and third weeks to a relevant social security benefit or to more than one such benefit and consequent upon the Social Security Benefits Up-rating Order 1989 he or his partner, or both are, entitled to an increase in any one or more of those benefits in the third week, the protected sum under sub-paragraph (8) shall be increased by an amount equal to the difference between—

   (a) the amount of benefit or aggregate amount of those benefits to which the protected person or his partner is, or both are, entitled in the third week; and, if less,

   (b) the amount of benefit or aggregate amount of those benefits to which the protected person or his partner is, or both are, entitled in the second week.

(10) In sub-paragraph (8)—

"X" means the sum which, but for sub-paragraph (8), would be the protected sum applicable in a case to which sub-paragraph (7)(b)(i) applies;

"Y" means the amount of the excess to which sub-paragraph (8)(*a*) refers;

"relevant social security benefit" has the same meaning as in paragraph 3(4).]]

AMENDMENTS

2.696
1. Income Support (General) Amendment No.4 Regulations 1988 (SI 1988/1445), Sch.2 (April 10, 1989).

2. Income Support (General) Amendment No.5 Regulations 1988 (SI 1988/2022), reg.19 (April 10, 1989).

3. Income Support (General) Amendment Regulations 1989 (SI 1989/534), reg.7 and Sch.1 (April 10, 1989).

4. Income Support (General) Amendment No.3 Regulations 1989 (SI 1989/1678), reg.8 (October 9, 1989).

5. Income Support (General) Amendment Regulations 1990 (SI 1990/547), reg.19 (April 9, 1990).

6. Income Support (General and Transitional) Amendment Regulations 1990 (SI 1990/2324), reg.4 (December 17, 1990).

7. Income Support (General) Amendment No. 4 Regulations 1991 (SI 1991/1559), reg.17 (October 1, 1991).

8. Income-related Benefits Amendment Regulations 1992 (SI 1992/1326), reg.3(3) (October 5, 1992).

9. Income Support (General) (Jobseeker's Allowance Consequential Amendments) Regulations 1996 (SI 1996/206), reg.25 (October 7, 1996).

Definitions

"the Act"—see reg.2(1).
"benefit week"—*ibid.*
"board and lodging accommodation"—*ibid.*
"child"—see 1986 Act, s.20(11) (SSCBA, s.137(1)).
"claimant"—see reg.2(1).
"couple"—*ibid.*
"employment"—*ibid.*
"family"—see 1986 Act, s.20(11) (SSCBA, s.137(1)).
"partner"—see reg.2(1).
"polygamous marriage"—*ibid.*
"young person"—*ibid.*, reg.14.

General Note

Sch.3A is made necessary by the removal from the Regulations of the special treat-ment of those in board and lodging accommodation. Before April 1989, such claimants received their board and lodging charge (subject to a maximum amount, and a maximum length of time for some under-25s) plus a personal allowance, but were not eligible for housing benefit. From April 1989, they receive ordinary personal allowances and premiums, but are eligible for housing benefit. Sch.3A provides transitional protection if there is a loss of income for existing claimants, in the form of a "protected sum" to make up the difference.

R(IS) 2/92 holds that to be a protected person within para.7(1)(a) a person must actually have been entitled to an increase of the maximum amount for boarders under para.7 of Sch.5 immediately before the benefit week beginning in the week from April 3, 1989.

[¹SCHEDULE 3B   **Regulations 17(1)(g), 18(1)(h)
and 71(1)(a)(v) and (d)(iv)**

Protected Sum

Interpretation
1.—(1) In this Schedule—

"eligible housing benefit" means—
    (a) for the period of 7 consecutive days beginning on 2nd October 1989, the amount of housing benefit to which the claimant or his partner was entitled in that period which relates to the hostel normally occupied as the home by him or, if he has a partner, by him and his partner;
    (b) for the period of 7 consecutive days beginning on 9th October 1989 or, in a case to which paragraph 6(4) (*b*) applies, for the period of 7 consecutive days referred to in that paragraph, the amount of the claimant's or his partner's maximum housing benefit determined in accordance with regulation 61 of the Housing Benefit (General) Regulations 1987 (maximum housing benefit) which relates to that accommodation.
"first week" means the benefit week beginning on a day in the period of 7 days commencing on 2nd October 1989;
"hostel" means any establishment which immediately before the commencement of this Schedule was a hostel within the meaning of regulation 20(2) (applicable amounts for persons in hostels);
"income support" includes any sum payable under Part II of the Income Support (Transitional) Regulations 1987;
"March benefit week" means the benefit week beginning on a day during the period of 7 consecutive days beginning 20th March 1989;
"protected sum" means the amount applicable under this Schedule [⁷or by virtue of regu-lation 87(2) of the Jobseeker's Allowance Regulations 1996] to a claimant who in the first week is living in a hostel or who or whose partner is temporarily absent in that week from that accommodation;

"protected total" means—
   (a) the total of the claimant's applicable amount under regulation 20 in the first week or, [².. .] if the claimant or any partner of his is temporarily absent from his accommodation [²for a period not exceeding 14 weeks which includes that week], the amount which would have fallen to be calculated under that regulation for that week as if there had been no temporary absence; and
   (b) the amount of any eligible housing benefit for the period of 7 consecutive days beginning 2nd October 1989;
"relevant benefit week" means the benefit week beginning on a day during that period of 7 consecutive days commencing on 9th April 1990;
"relevant provisions" means—
   (a) regulation 17(1)(a) to (f) (applicable amounts);
   (b) regulation 18(1)(a) to (g) (polygamous marriages);
   (c) regulation 71(1)(a)(i) to (iv) (urgent cases);
   (d) regulation 71(1)(d)(i) to (iii);
   [²(dd) paragraph 13 of Schedule 7 (persons in residential accommodation);]
   (e) in relation to a case to which paragraph 17(b)(ii) or (c)(i) of Schedule 7 (persons from abroad) applies, the regulations specified in that paragraph but as if the reference to regulation 17(1)(g) in that paragraph were omitted; or
   (f) in relation to a case to which paragraph 17(d)(i) of that Schedule applies, the regulations specified in that paragraph but as if the reference to regulation 18 were a reference to regulation 18(1)(a) to (g) only;
"second week" means the benefit week beginning on a day during the period of 7 consecutive days commencing on 9th October 1989.

(2) For the purposes of this Schedule—
   (a) in determining a claimant's applicable amount in his first week, second week or any subsequent benefit week no account shall be taken of any reduction under regulation 22 (reduction in certain cases of unemployment benefit disqualification);
   (b) except in so far as it relates to any temporary absence to which paragraph 6(4) refers, where a change of circumstances takes effect in the claimant's second week which, if it had taken effect in the first week, would have resulted in a lesser applicable amount in respect of that week, his applicable amount in the first week shall be determined as if the change of circumstances had taken effect in that week.

Protected sum

2.700   **2.**—(1) Subject to the following provisions of this paragraph and the following paragraphs of this Schedule, where the protected total of a claimant is more than—
   (a) his applicable amount in the second week determined in accordance with the relevant provisions less the amount of any increase consequent on the coming into force of regulation 5 of the Income Support (General) Amendment Regulations 1989; and
   (b) any eligible housing benefit for the period of 7 consecutive days beginning 9th October 1989,
the protected sum applicable to the claimant shall be an amount equal to the difference.
(2) Where—
   (a) in the second week a claimant's income calculated in accordance with Part V or, as the case may be, VI exceeds the aggregate of his applicable amount determined in accordance with the relevant provisions and X; and
   (b) the amount of income support to which he is entitled in the first week is more than the amount of housing benefit to which he would, but for this sub-paragraph, have been entitled in the period of 7 consecutive days beginning on 9th October 1989, the protected sum applicable to the claimant shall be an amount equal to X + Y + 10 pence.
(3) In sub-paragraph (2)—

"X" means the sum which, but for sub-paragraph (2), would be the protected sum applicable under sub-paragraph (1);
"Y" means the amount of the excess to which sub-paragraph (2)(a) refers.

(4) For the period beginning with the claimant's relevant benefit week the protected sum applicable to the claimant shall, subject to sub-paragraph (6), and the following paragraphs of this Schedule, be—
   (a) the total of—
       (i) the amount of the allowance for personal expenses for the claimant or, if he is a member of a family, for him and for each member of his family in the first week

determined, or which, but for any temporary absence, would have been determined, in accordance with paragraph 11 of Schedule 5 as then in force;

    (ii) [³subject to sub-paragraph (7)] the amount of any increase for meals in the first
week determined, or which, but for any temporary absence, would have been
determined, in accordance with paragraph 2 of that Schedule; and

    (iii) the amount or, if he is a member of a family, the aggregate of the amounts deter-
mined in accordance with sub-paragraph (5),

less the aggregate of his applicable amount in the second week determined, or which,
but for any temporary absence, would have been determined, in accordance with the
relevant provisions and, where applicable, the amount of any reduction in the protected
sum made by virtue of paragraph 4 in a benefit week occurring before the relevant
benefit week; or

  (b) the amount of the protected sum which was applicable to him in the immediately preceding benefit week,

whichever is the lower.

(5) For the purposes of sub-paragraph (4)(a), where in the first week the accommodation
charge makes or, but for any temporary absence, would have made, provision or no provision
for meals, as respects each person an amount shall be determined as follows—

  (a) in a case where the provision is for at least three meals a day—
      (i) for the claimant, £17.20;
      (ii) for a member of his family aged 16 or over, £12.50;
      (iii) for a member of the family aged less than 16, £6.25;

  (b) except where head (c) applies, in a case where the provision is for less than three meals
a day—
      (i) for the claimant, £13.85;
      (ii) for a member of his family aged 16 or over, £8.30;
      (iii) for a member of his family aged less than 16, £4.15;

  (c) in a case where the provision is for breakfast only—
      (i) for the claimant, £7.05;
      (ii) for a member of his family, £1.50;

  (d) in a case where there is no provision for meals, for the claimant or, if he is a member
of a family, for the claimant and for the members of his family for whom there is no
such provision, £5.55;

(6) Where in the relevant benefit week the claimant is in, or only temporarily absent from,
residential accommodation, the protected sum applicable to the claimant for the period beginning with that week shall[², subject to the following paragraphs of this Schedule,] be—

  (a) equal to the difference between—
      (i) the amount of the allowance for personal expenses for the claimant or, if he is a
member of a family, for him and for each member of his family in the first week
determined, or which, but for any temporary absence, would have been determined, in accordance with paragraph 11 of Schedule 5 as then in force; and
      (ii) the amount of the allowance for personal expenses for the claimant or, if he is a
member of a family, for him and for each member of his family in the second
week determined, or which, but for any temporary absence would have been
determined, under paragraph 13 of Schedule 7 (persons in residential accommodation),

less, where applicable, the amount of any reduction in the protected sum made by virtue of
paragraph 4 in a benefit week occurring before the relevant benefit week; or

  (b) the amount of the protected sum which was applicable to him in the immediately preceding benefit week,

whichever is the lower.

[³(7) In the case of a member of a family who in the first week is a child aged less than 11,
the amount of any increase for meals under sub-paragraph (4)(a)(ii) shall be either—

  (a) the amount of any such increase in the first week determined, or which, but for any
temporary absence, would have been determined, in accordance with paragraph 2 of
Schedule 5 as then in force; or
  (b) £17.65,

whichever is the lower.]

Persons not entitled to a protected sum

3.—(1) Subject to paragraph 6, a protected sum shall not be applicable to a claimant   **2.701**
where he changes or vacates his hostel during the period of 7 consecutive days beginning 9th
October 1989.

(2) Except where regulation 8(2)(b) of the Housing Benefit (General) Regulations 1987 (eligible housing costs) applies, a protected sum shall not be applicable to a claimant unless he, or any partner of his, is entitled to housing benefit for the period of 7 consecutive days beginning 9th October 1989 or, where paragraph 6(4)(b) applies, for the period of 7 consecutive days referred to in that paragraph, in respect of the hostel normally occupied as the home by him, or if he has a partner, by him and his partner.

(3) A protected sum shall not be applicable to a claimant where—

   (a) he has been or would, but for any temporary absence, have been in the same accommodation in both the March benefit week and the second week, and—

      (i) his applicable amount in both those weeks fell or would have fallen, but for any temporary absence, to be determined under paragraph 13(1) of Schedule 7; or

      (ii) his applicable amount in the second week fell or would have fallen, but for any temporary absence, to be determined under that paragraph and would also have fallen to be so determined in the March benefit week had his stay in that accommodation been other than temporary; or

   (b) his applicable amount in the second week fell or would have fallen, but for any temporary absence, to be determined under that paragraph and would also have fallen to be so determined in the March benefit week had he been in the same accommodation in that week and had his stay in that accommodation been other than temporary[²; or

   (c) his applicable amount in the first week fell or would have fallen, but for any temporary absence, to be determined under regulation 20 but would not have fallen to be so determined in the March benefit week had he been in the same accommodation in that week and had his stay in that accommodation been other than temporary.

(4) For the purposes of sub-paragraph (3), where—

   (a) a claimant's applicable amount in respect of the March benefit week has been determined under paragraph 13(1) of Schedule 7 and it is subsequently determined [⁸ . . .] that it fell to be determined under regulation 20, he shall, notwithstanding [⁸ that determination], be treated as if his applicable amount fell to be determined under that paragraph;

   (b) a claimant has been temporarily absent from his accommodation in the March benefit week and immediately before the period of temporary absence his applicable amount was determined under paragraph 13(1) of Schedule 7, he shall be treated as if his applicable amount would have fallen to be determined under that paragraph during the period of temporary absence notwithstanding that it is subsequently determined [⁸ . . .] that immediately before the period of temporary absence it fell to be determined under regulation 20;

   (c) a claimant has entered his accommodation after the March benefit week, he shall be treated as if his applicable amount, had he been in that accommodation in the March benefit week, would not have fallen to be determined under regulation 20 in that week if the applicable amounts of other claimants in that accommodation in that week were determined otherwise than under that regulation notwithstanding that it is subsequently determined [⁸ . . .] that they fell to be determined under regulation 20.]

Reduction of protected sum

2.702   **4.**—(1) Subject to [⁶sub-paragraphs (2) to (5)], the protected sum shall be reduced by the amount of any increase, in a benefit week subsequent to the second week, in the claimant's applicable amount determined in accordance with the relevant provisions.

(2) Where regulation 22 (reduction in certain cases of unemployment benefit disqualification) [⁴or regulation 21A (reductions in certain cases of failure to attend courses)] ceases to apply to a claimant and as a result his applicable amount increases no account shall be taken of that increase.

[³(3) Where a claimant's applicable amount increases because a child or young person mentioned in paragraph (5)(c) of regulation 16 (circumstances in which a person is treated or not treated as a member of the household) is treated as a member of the claimant's household under paragraph (6) of that regulation, the claimant's protected sum shall not be reduced by the amount of that increase unless the child or young person has been treated as a member of the household for a continuous period which exceeds 8 weeks.]

[⁵(4) Where by virtue of the coming into force of regulation 15(a), (b) or (c) of the Income Support (General) Amendment No. 4 Regulations 1991 a claimant's applicable amount increases in his benefit week beginning on a day during the period of 7 days commencing on 1st October 1991, no account shall be taken of that increase.]

[⁶(5) Where by virtue of the coming into force of regulation 3(1) and (2) of the Income-Related Benefits Amendment Regulations 1992 a claimant's applicable amount increases in his benefit week beginning on a day during the period of 7 days commencing on 5th October 1992, no account shall be taken of that increase.]

Termination of protected sum

5. Subject to paragraph 6, the protected sum shall cease to be applicable if—   2.703
  (a) that amount is reduced to nil under paragraph 4; or
  (b) the claimant changes or vacates his hostel; or
  (c) the claimant ceases to be entitled to income support.

Modifications in cases of temporary absence and loss of entitlement to income support

6.—(1) Paragraph 5(b) shall not apply to a claimant if—   2.704
  (a) he becomes a patient within the meaning of regulation 21(3) (special cases); or
  (b) on ceasing to be a patient within the meaning of regulation 21(3), he returns to the hostel which he occupied immediately before he became a patient; or
  (c) in a case to which sub-paragraph (3) applies, on his becoming re-entitled to income support, he is in the accommodation which he occupied immediately before he ceased to be entitled to income support.

(2) Except where sub-paragraph (4) applies, where a protected sum was applicable to the claimant immediately before he or any partner of his became a patient within the meaning of regulation 21(3) for a period of 14 weeks or less, he shall, subject to subparagraph (1)(b), on his or, as the case may be, his partner ceasing to be a patient be entitled to a protected sum equal to—
  (a) the amount by which his protected total exceeds his applicable amount determined in accordance with the relevant provisions in the first benefit week in which his applicable amount ceases to be determined under paragraph 1 of Schedule 7 and either—
    (i) any eligible housing benefit for the period of 7 consecutive days beginning on 9th October 1989; or, if greater,
    (ii) in a case where sub-paragraph (4)(b) applied, any eligible housing benefit for the period of 7 consecutive days referred to in that sub-paragraph; or
  [³(aa) where the first benefit week in which his applicable amount ceases to be determined under paragraph 1 of Schedule 7 is the relevant benefit week, the amount determined under paragraph 2(4) or, as the case may be, paragraph 2(6), less any reduction under paragraph 4(1) other than a reduction which arises by virtue of his ceasing to be a patient within the meaning of regulation 21(3); or]
  (b) the amount of the protested sum to which he was entitled in the immediately preceding benefit week
whichever is the lower.

(3) Paragraph 5(c) shall not apply to a claimant who has ceased to be entitled to income support for [²a period not exceeding the permitted period determined in accordance with regulation 3A (permitted period)]—
  (a) if immediately before he ceased to be so entitled a protected sum was applicable to him; and
  (b) except where sub-paragraph (4) applies, if during that period he becomes re-entitled, or would by virtue of this sub-paragraph be re-entitled, to income support he shall, subject to sub-paragraph (1)(c), be entitled to a protected sum equal to—
    (i) the amount by which his protected total exceeds his applicable amount determined in accordance with the relevant provisions in the first benefit week in which he becomes so re-entitled and either any eligible housing benefit for the period of 7 consecutive days beginning 9th October 1989 or, if greater, in a case to which sub-paragraph (4)(b) applied, any eligible housing benefit for the period of 7 consecutive days referred to in that subparagraph; or
    [³(ii) where the first benefit week in which he becomes so re-entitled is the relevant benefit week, the amount determined under paragraph 2(4) or, as the case may be, paragraph 2(6), less any reduction under paragraph 4(1) in that benefit week; or
    (iii) where the first benefit week in which he becomes so re-entitled is a week subsequent to the relevant benefit week, the amount which would have been determined under paragraph 2(4) or, as the case may be, paragraph 2(6) had he been entitled in the relevant benefit week, less any reduction under paragraph 4(1) in the benefit week in which he becomes re-entitled; or
    (iv) the amount of the protested sum to which he was previously entitled,]
whichever is the lower.

(4) Where a claimant or any partner of his temporarily absent from his accommodation for a period not exceeding 14 weeks which includes the first or second week (or both)—

(a) in a case where a protected sum was applicable to the claimant immediately before his or, as the case may be, his partner's return to that accommodation and the full charge was made for that accommodation during the temporary absence, on the claimant's or, as the case may be, his partner's return to that accommodation, the claimant shall be entitled to a protected sum equal to—

    (i) the amount by which his protected total exceeds his applicable amount determined in accordance with the relevant provisions in the first complete benefit week after his, or as the case may be, his partner's return to that accommodation and any eligible housing benefit for the period of 7 consecutive days beginning 9th October 1989; or

    (ii) the amount of the protected sum which was applicable to him in the immediately preceding benefit week,

whichever is the lower.

(b) in a case where—

    (i) a protected sum has not at any time been applicable to the claimant; or

    (ii) immediately before the claimant's or, as the case may be, his partner's return to that accommodation a protected sum was applicable to the claimant but a reduced charge was made for the accommodation during the temporary absence,

the claimant on his or, as the case may be, his partner's, return to that accommodation shall, subject to sub-paragraph (5), be entitled to a protected sum equal to the amount by which his protected total exceeds his applicable amount determined in accordance with the relevant provisions in the first complete benefit week after his or, as the case may be, his partner's return to that accommodation and the amount of eligible housing benefit for the period of 7 consecutive days beginning on the date determined in accordance with regulation 65 or, as the case may be, 68(2) of the Housing Benefit (General) Regulations 1987 (date on which entitlement is to commence or change of circumstances is to take effect) following that person's return to that accommodation.

(5) Where, in a case to which sub-paragraph (4)(b)(i) applies—

(a) in the first complete benefit week after the claimant's or, as the case may be, his partner's return to his accommodation the claimant's income calculated in accordance with Part V or, as the case may be, VI exceeds the aggregate of his applicable amount determined in accordance with the relevant provisions and X; and

(b) the amount of income support to which he was entitled in the first week is more than the amount of housing benefit to which he would, but for this sub-paragraph, have been entitled in the period of 7 consecutive days beginning on the date determined in accordance with regulation 65 or, as the case may be, 68(2) of the Housing Benefit (General) Regulations 1987 following his or, as the case may be, his partner's return to that accommodation.

the protected sum applicable to the claimant shall be an amount equal to X + Y + 10 pence.

(6) In sub-paragraph (5)—

"X" means the sum which, but for sub-paragraph (5), would be the protected sum applicable in a case to which sub-paragraph (4)(b)(i) applies;

"Y" means the amount of the excess to which sub-paragraph (5)(a) refers.

(7) The foregoing provisions of this paragraph shall not apply to a claimant if he or, if he has a partner, he or his partner, in the first week is temporarily living in a hostel and that accommodation is not the accommodation normally occupied as the home.]

AMENDMENTS

2.705   1. Income Support (General) Amendment Regulations 1989 (SI 1989/534), Sch.1, para.18 and Sch.2 (October 9, 1989).

2. Income Support (General) Amendment No.3 Regulations 1989 (SI 1989/1678), reg.9 (October 9, 1989).

3. Income Support (General) Amendment Regulations 1990 (SI 1990/547), reg.20 (April 9, 1990).

4. Income Support (General and Transitional) Amendment Regulations 1990 (SI 1990/2324), reg.5 (December 17, 1990).

5. Income Support (General) Amendment No. 4 Regulations 1991 (SI 1991/1559), reg.17 (October 1, 1991).

6. Income-related Benefits Amendment Regulations 1992 (SI 1992/1326), reg.3(4) (October 5, 1992).

7. Income Support (General) (Jobseeker's Allowance Consequential Amendments) Regulations 1996 (SI 1996/206), reg.25 (October 7, 1996).

8. Social Security Act 1998 (Commencement No.12 and Consequential and Transitional Provisions) Order 1999 (SI 1999/3178 (C.81)), art.3(5) and Sch.5, para.10 (November 29, 1999)

GENERAL NOTE

These complex provisions provide transitional protection for those hostel-dwellers who are moved on to housing benefit in October 1989. A full description cannot be given here, but there is a helpful summary on pp.4 and 5 of *Welfare Rights Bulletin* 91 (August 1989).   **2.706**

The main provision is in para.2. Sub-paras (1) to (3) deal with the position from October 9, 1989. For claimants who are residents in or only temporarily absent from a hostel in the week before that date, their protected sum is normally the difference between their applicable amount in that week and their applicable amount plus housing benefit in the following week (para.2(1)). If the claimant's income is too high for entitlement to income support on the ordinary rules there is a special calculation in para.2(2). Note that the transitional protection ceases if the claimant changes or vacates his hostel or ceases to be entitled to income support (para.5) subject to the exceptions in para.6.

Para. 2(4) to (6) deals with protection from April 9, 1990. See *CIS 168/1990* and *CIS 340/1990* on the definition of "hostel" and *CIS 142/1991*.

SCHEDULE 3C

[Revoked by the Social Security (Removal of Residential Allowance and Miscellaneous Amendments)   **2.707**
Regulations 2003 (SI 2003/1121), reg.2 and Sch.1, para.7 with effect from October 6, 2003.]

SCHEDULE 4

[Revoked by Social Security Amendment (Residential Care and Nursing Homes) Regulations 2001   **2.708**
(SI 2001/3767), reg.2 and Sch. Pt I para.16 with effect from April 8, 2002.]

SCHEDULE 7   **Regulation 21**   **2.709**

APPLICABLE AMOUNTS IN SPECIAL CASES

Column (1)	*Column (2)*
Patients	
1. Subject to paragraphs 2, 2A [29 and 3], a person who has been a patient for a period of more than [29 52] weeks and who is—	1.
(a) [29 . . .]	(a) [29 . . .]
(b) a lone parent;	(b) [32£20.50] plus any amounts applicable to him under [31 regulation 17(1)(e), (f) or (g);]

Column (1)	Column (2)

(c) a member of a couple—
   (i) where only one of the couple is a patient or, where both members of the couple are patients but only one has been a patient for that period;
   (ii) where both members of the couple have been a patient for that period;
(d) a member of a polygamous marriage—
   (i) where at least one member of the polygamous marriage is not a patient or has not been a patient for more than that period;
   (ii) where all the members of the polygamous marriage have been patients for more than that period.
	(c)
	   (i) the amount applicable in respect of both of them under regulation 17(1) reduced by [^{32}£16.90];
	
	   (ii) [^{32}£41.00] plus any amounts which may be applicable under [^{31} regulation 17(1)(e), (f) or (g);]
	(d)
	
	   (i) the applicable amount under regulation 18 (polygamous marriages) shall be reduced by [^{32}£16.40] in respect of each such member who is a patient;
	   (ii) the applicable amount shall be [^{32}£20.50] in respect of each such member plus any amounts applicable under [^{31} regulation 18(1)(f), (g) or (h);]

2. A single claimant who has been a patient for a continuous period of more than 52 weeks, where—
   (a) the following conditions are satistfied—
     (i) a person has been appointed to act for him under regulation 33 of the Social Security (Claims and Payments) Regulations 1987 (persons unable to act); and
     (ii) his income support is payable to an administrative officer of the hospital or other institution either as or at the request of the person so appointed; and
     (iii) a registered medical practitioner treating him certifies that all or part of his income support cannot be used by him or on his behalf; or
   (b) those conditions are not satisfied.
	2.
	
	   (a) Such amount (if any) not exceeding [^{32}£16.40] as is reasonable having regard to the views of the hospital staff and the patient's relatives if available as to the amount necessary for this personal use;
	
	   (b) [^{32}£16.40]

2A. A single claimant who is detained in hospital under the provisions of the Mental Health Act 1983, or, in Scotland, under the provisions of the Mental Health (Scotland) Act 1984 or the Criminal Procedure (Scotland) Act 1995,] and who immediately before his detention [^{23} under any of those Acts] was a prisoner.	**2A.** [^{32}£16.40]
3. [^{31}. . .]	**3.** [^{31}. . .]
4. [^{6}. . .]	
5. [^{6}. . .].	
Claimants without accommodation **6.** A claimant who is without accommodation.	**6.** The amount applicable to him under regulation 17[^{3}(1)](a) only.

Column (1)	Column (2)
Members of religious orders 7. A claimant who is a member of and fully maintained by religious order.	7. Nil.

Prisoners
8. A person—
  (a) except where sub-paragraph
    (b) applies, who is a prisoner;
  (b) who is detained in custody
    pending trial or sentence
    following conviction by a court.
	8.
	  (a) Nil;
	
	  (b) only such amount, if any, as
	    may be applicable under
	    regulation 17[^{3}(1)](e).

9. A claimant who is a member of a couple and who is temporarily separated from his partner [^{10}where—
  (a) one member of the couple is—
    (i) not a patient but is resident in a nursing home, or
    (ii) resident in a residential care home, or
    (iii) resident in premises used for the rehabilitation of alcoholics or drug addicts, or
    (iv) resident in accommodation provided under section 3 of and Part II of the Schedule to, the Polish Resettlement Act 1947 (provision of accommodation in camps), or
    (v) participating in arrangements for training made under section 2 of the Employment and Training Act 1973 [^{12}or section 2 of the Enterprise and New Towns (Scotland) Act 1990] or attending a course at an employment rehabilitation centre established under that section [^{12}of the 1973 Act], where the course requires him to live away from the dwelling occupied as the home, or
    (vi) in a probation or bail hostel approved for the purpose by the Secretary of State; and
  (b) the other member of the couple is—
    (i) living in the dwelling occupied as the home, or
    (ii) a patient, or
    (iii) in residential accommodation, or
    (iv) resident in a residential care home or nursing home;]
	9. Either—
	
	  (a) the amount applicable to him as a member of a couple under regulation 17; or
	
	  (b) the aggregate of his applicable amount and that of his partner assessed under the provisions of these Regulations as if each of them were a single claimant, or a lone parent,
	whichever is the greater.

Polygamous marriages where one or more partners are temporarily separated 10. A claimant who is a member of a polygamous marriage and who is temporarily separated from a partner of his, where one of them is living in the home while the other member is—	10. Either—

Column (1)	Column (2)
(a) not a patient but is resident in a nursing home; or (b) resident in a residential care home; or (c) [¹. . .] (d) resident in premises used for the rehabilitation of alcoholics or drug addicts; or (e) attending a course of training or instruction provided or approved by the [¹²Secretary of State for Employment] where the course requires him to live away from home; or (f) in a probation or bail hostel approved for the purpose by the Secretary of State.	(a) the amount applicable to the members of the polygamous marriage under regulation 18; or (b) the aggregate of the amount applicable for the members of the polygamous marriage who remain in the home under regulation 18 and the amount applicable in respect of those members not in the home calculated as if each of them were a single claimant, or a lone parent, whichever is the greater.
[²⁴**Single claimants temporarily in local authority accommodation** **10A.** [³⁰ . . .]	**10A.** [³⁰ . . .]
Couples and members of polygamous marriages where one member is or all are temporarily in local authority accommodation **10B.** [³⁰ . . .]	**10B.** [³⁰ . . .]
Lone parents who are in residential accommodation temporarily **10C.** [³⁰. . .]	**10C.** [³⁰ . . .]]
10D. [¹⁵ . . .]	**10D.** [¹⁵ . . .]
Couples where one member is abroad **11.** [¹¹Subject to paragraph 11A] a claimant who is a member of a couple and whose partner is temporarily not present in [³United Kingdom].	**11.** For the first four weeks of that absence, the amount applicable to them as a couple under regulation 17, [²⁷. . .] [⁹ or 21] as the case may be and thereafter the amount applicable to the claimant in Great Britain under regulation 17 [²⁷. . .] or [⁹ or 21] as the case may be as if the claimant were a single claimant or, as the case may be, a lone parent.
[¹¹**Couple or member of couple taking child or young person abroad for treatment** **11A.** [¹⁵—(1)] A claimant who is a member of a couple where either— (a) he or his partner is, or, (b) both he and his partner are absent from the United Kingdom [¹⁴in the circumstances specified in paragraph (2). (2) For the purposes of subparagraph (1), the specified circumstances are— (a) in respect of a claimant, those in regulation 4(3)(a) to (d); (b) in respect of a claimant's partner as if regulation 4(3)(a) to (d) applies to that partner.]	**11A.** For the first eight weeks of that absence, the amount applicable to the claimant under regulation 17(1) [²⁷. . .] or 21, as the case may be, and, thereafter, if the claimant is in Great Britain the amount applicable to him under regulation 17(1) [²⁷. . .] or 21, as the case may be, as if the claimant were a single claimant, or, as the case may be, a lone parent.

Column (1)	Column (2)

Polygamous marriages where any member is abroad
12. Subject to paragraph 12A, a claimant who is a member of a polygamous marriage where—
    (a) he or one of his partners is, or
    (b) he and one or more of his partners are, or
    (c) two or more of his partners are, temporarily absent from the United Kingdom.
	12. For the first four weeks of that absence, the amount applicable to the claimant under regulations 17 to 21, as the case may be, and thereafter, if the claimant is in Great Britain the amount applicable to him under regulations 18 to 21, as the case may be, as if any member of the polygamous marriage not in the United Kingdom were not a member of the marriage.

Polygamous marriage: taking child or young person abroad for treatment
12A. [¹⁵—(1)] A claimant who is a member of a polygamous marriage where—
    (a) he or one of his partners is,
    (b) he and one or more of his partners are, or
    (c) two or more of his partners are, absent from the United Kingdom [¹⁴in the circumstances specified in paragraph (2).
    (2) For the purposes of subparagraph (1), the specified circumstances are—
    (a) in respect of a claimant, those in regulation 4(3)(a) to (d);
    (b) in respect of a claimant's partner or partners, as the case may be, as if regulation 4(3)(a) to (d) applied to that partner or those partners.]
	12A. For the first 8 weeks of that absence the amount applicable to the claimant under regulations 18 to 21, as the case may be, as if any member of the polygamous marriage not in the United Kingdom were not a member of the marriage.]

[²⁴**Persons in residential accommodation.** 13.—(1) [²⁹ . . .] [³⁰ . . .] (2) [²⁹ . . .]	13.—(1) [³⁰ . . .] 13A. [³⁰ . . .]
Polish Resettlement (2) [²⁹ . . .]	13A. [³⁰ . . .]
[¹⁸**Polish resettlement: Persons temporarily absent from accommodation** 13B. [³⁰ . . .]	13B. [³⁰ . . . [²⁹ . . .]]]
Polish resettlement 14. [⁹. . .]	14. [⁹ . . .]
Resettlement units 15. [⁹. . .]	15. [⁹ . . .]
Persons temporarily absent from a hostel, residential care or nursing home 16. [²⁷. . .]	16. [²⁷. . .]
[²⁵**Partner of a person subject to immigration control** 16A.—(a) A claimant who is the partner of a person subject to immigration control.	[³¹ 16A.—[³¹. . .](a) The amount applicable in respect of the claimant only under regulation 17(1)(a), any amount which may be applicable to him under regulation 17(1)(d) plus the

Column (1)	Column (2)
	amount applicable to him under regulation 17(1)(e), (f) and (g) or, as the case may be, regulation 21.
(b) Where regulation 18 (polygamous marriages) applies and the claimant is a person— (i) who is not subject to immigration control within the meaning of section 115(9) of the Immigration and Asylum Act; or (ii) to whom section 115 of that Act does not apply by virtue of regulation 2 of the Social Security (Immigration and Asylum) Consequential Amendments Regulations 2000; and (iii) who is a member of a couple and one or more of his partners is subject to immigration control within the meaning of section 115(9) of that Act and section 115 of that Act applies to her for the purposes of exclusion from entitlement to income support.]	(b) The amount determined in accordance with that regulation or regulation 21 in respect of the claimant and any partners of his who are not subject to immigration control within the meaning of section 115(9) of the Immigration and Asylum Act and to whom section 115 of that Act does not apply for the purposes of exclusion from entitlement to income support.]
17. [²⁵**Person from abroad**]	**17.** [²⁵ nil]
[²⁴**Persons in residential care or nursing homes who become patients**] **18.** [²⁷. . .]	**18.** [²⁷. . .]
Claimants entitled to the disability premium for a past period **19.** A claimant— (a) whose time for claiming income support has been extended under regulation 19(2) of the Social Security (Claims and Payments) Regulations 1987 (time for claiming benefit); and (b) whose partner was entitled to income support in respect of the period beginning with the day on which the claimant's claim is treated as made under [¹⁹regulation 6(3) of those Regulations] and [¹⁹ending with the day before the day] on which the claim is actually made; and (c) who satisfied the condition in paragraph 11 (*b*) of Schedule 2 and the additional condition referred to in that paragraph and specified in paragraph 12(1)(b) of that Schedule in respect of that period.	**19.** The amount only of the disability premium applicable by virtue of paragraph 11(b) of Schedule 2 as specified in paragraph 15(4)(b) of that Schedule.

Column (1)	Column (2)

[²⁶**Persons who have commenced remunerative work**
19A.—(1) A person to whom regulation 6(5) (persons not treated as in remunerative work) applies.]
	[²⁶**19A.**—(1) Subect to sub-paragraph (2), the lowest of either—
	    (a) the amount determined in accordance with—
	    (i) Schedule 3 (housing costs); or
	    (ii) as the case may be, Schedule 2 to the Jobseeker's Allowance Regulations 1996 (housing costs),
	which was applicable to the claimant or his partner immediately before he or his partner commenced the remunerative work referred to in regulation 6(5)(a); or
	    (b) the amount of income support or, as the case may be, income-based jobseeker's allowance which the claimant or his partner was entitled to in the benefit week immediately before the benefit week in which he or his partner commenced the remunerative work referred to in regulation 6(5)(a) or, where he or his partner was in receipt of a training allowance in that benefit week, the amount of income support or income-based jobseeker's allowance which he would have been entitled to in that week had he not been in receipt of a training allowance.
	    (2) Nothing in sub-paragraph (1) shall prevent any adjustment being made to the amount referred to in (a) or, as the case may be, (b) of that sub-paragraph during the period referred to in regulations 6(6), in order to reflect changes during that period to the amounts prescribed in Schedule 2 [²⁸. . .]or 4 or in this Schedule or to reflect changes in circumstances during that period relating to the matters specified to in sub-paragraph (3).
	    (3) The changes in circumstances referred to in sub-paragraph (2) are changes to the amount of housing costs to be met in accordance with Schedule 3 in the claimant's case occasioned by—
	    (a) the claimant becoming entitled to income support for a continuous period of 26 weeks or more;
	    (b) a change to the standard interest rate; or

Column (1)	Column (2)
	(c) any non-dependant deduction becoming applicable, or ceasing to be applicable. (4) In sub-paragraph (1), a reference to the claimant or his partner being entitled to and in receipt or an income-based jobseeker's allowance or to an amount being applicable to either of them under the Jobseeker's Allowance Regulations 1996 shall include a reference to the claimant and his partner being entitled to, and in receipt of, a joint-claim jobseeker's allowance and to an amount being applicable to that couple under those Regulations.]
Rounding of fractions 20. Where any calculation under this Schedule or as a result of income support being awarded for a period less than one complete benefit week results in a fraction of a penny that fraction shall be treated as a penny.	

AMENDMENTS

2.710   1. Income Support (General) Amendment Regulations 1988 (SI 1988/663), reg.33 (April 11, 1988).

2. Employment Act 1988, s.24(3) (May 26, 1988).

3. Income Support (General) Amendment No.4 Regulations 1988 (SI 1988/1445), reg.23 (September 12, 1988).

4. Income Support (General) Amendment No.5 Regulations 1988 (SI 1988/2022), reg.21 (December 12, 1988).

5. Income Support (General) Amendment No.4 Regulations 1988 (SI 1988/1445), Sch.1, para.1 (April 10, 1989).

6. Income Support (General) Amendment No.4 Regulations 1988 (SI 1988/1445), Sch.1, para.1 (April 10, 1989).

7. Income Support (General) Amendment No.4 Regulations 1988 (SI 1988/1445), Sch.1, para.15 (April 10, 1989).

8. Income Support (General) Amendment Regulations 1989 (SI 1989/534), reg.9 (April 10, 1989).

9. Income Support (General) Amendment Regulations 1989 (SI 1989/534), Sch.1, para.13 (October 9, 1989).

10. Income Support (General) Amendment No.3 Regulations 1989 (SI 1989/1678), reg.11 (October 9, 1989).

11. Income Support (General) Amendment Regulations 1990 (SI 1990/547), reg.21 (April 9, 1990).

12. Enterprise (Scotland) Consequential Amendments Order 1991 (SI 1991/387), art.2 (April 1, 1991).

13. Income Support (General) Amendment Regulations 1991 (SI 1991/236), reg.2(1) (April 8, 1991).

14. Income Support (General) Amendment Regulations 1991 (SI 1991/236), reg.13 (April 8, 1991).

15. Income Support (General) Amendment No.4 Regulations 1991 (SI 1991/1559), reg.19 (October 7, 1991).

16. Social Security Benefits (Amendments Consequential Upon the Introduction of Community Care) Regulations 1992 (SI 1992/3147), Sch.1, para.6 (April 1, 1993).

17. Income-related Benefits Schemes (Miscellaneous Amendments) (No.4) Regulations 1993 (SI 1993/2119), reg.21 (October 4, 1993).
18. Income-related Benefits Schemes (Miscellaneous Amendments) (No.5) Regulations 1994 (SI 1994/2139), reg.31 (October 3, 1994).
19. Income-related Benefits Schemes (Miscellaneous Amendments) Regulations 1995 (SI 1995/516), reg.26 (April 10, 1995).
20. Child Benefit, Child Support and Social Security (Miscellaneous Amendments) Regulations 1996 (SI 1996/1803), reg.40 (April 7, 1997).
21. Income-related Benefits and Jobseeker's Allowance (Amendment) (No. 2) Regulations 1977 (SI 1997/2197), reg.5(7) (October 6, 1997).
22. Social Security (Miscellaneous Amendments) Regulations 1998 (SI 1998/563), reg.8(1) and (2)(c)(ii) (April 6, 1998).
23. Social Security (Miscellaneous Amendments) Regulations 1998 (SI 1998/563), reg.8(3) (April 6, 1998).
24. Social Security Benefits Up-rating Order 2003 (SI 2003/526), art.17(7) and Sch.4 (April 8, 2002).
25. Social Security (Immigration and Asylum) Consequential Amendments Regulations 2000 (SI 2000/636), reg.3 (April 3, 2000).
26. Social Security (Miscellaneous Amendments) Regulations 2001 (SI 2001/488), reg.7 (April 9, 2001).
27. Social Security Amendment (Residential Care and Nursing Homes) Regulations 2001 (SI 2001/3767), reg.2 and Sch., Pt I para.17 (April 8, 2002).
28. Social Security Amendment (Residential Care and Nursing Homes) Regulations 2001 (SI 2001/3767), reg.2 and Sch., Pt I para.17 (as amended by Social Security Amendment (Residential Care and Nursing Homes) Regulations 2002 (SI 2002/398), reg.4(2)) (April 8, 2002).
29. Social Security (Hospital In-Patients and Miscellaneous Amendments) Regulations 2003 (S.I. 2003/1195), reg.3 (May 21, 2003).
30. Social Security (Removal of Residential Allowance and Miscellaneous Amendments) Regulations 2003 (SI 2003/1121), reg.2 and Sch.1 para.8 (October 6, 2003).
31. Social Security (Working Tax Credit and Child Tax Credit) (Consequential Amendments) Regulations 2003 (SI 2003/455), reg.2 and Sch.1, para.21 (April 6, 2004, except in "transitional cases"—see further the note to reg.17 of the Income Support Regulations).
32. Social Security Benefits Up-rating Order 2005 (SI 2005/522), Art.16 and Sch.4 (April 11, 2005)

DEFINITIONS

"child"—see 1986 Act, s.20(11) (SSCBA, s.137(1)).   2.711
"claimant"—see reg.2(1).
"couple"—*ibid.*
"family"—see 1986 Act, s.20(11) (SSCBA, s.137(1)).
"lone parent"—see reg.2(1).
"nursing home"—see reg.2(1), reg.19(3).
"partner"—see reg.2(1).
"patient"—see reg.21(3).
"partner of a person subject to immigration control"—*ibid.*
"person from abroad"—*ibid.*
"polygamous marriage"—see reg.2(1).
"prisoner"—see reg.21(3).
"relative"—see reg.2(1).
"residential accommodation"—see reg.21(3).
"residential care home"—see reg.2(1), reg.19(3).
"single claimant"—see reg.2(1).
"young person"—*ibid.*, reg.14.

GENERAL NOTE

2.712   See the notes to reg.21 and 6(5)—(8).

SCHEDULE 8   **Regulations 36(2), 38(2)**
                                   and 44(6)

SUMS TO BE DISREGARDED IN THE CALCULATION OF EARNINGS

2.713   1. In the case of a claimant who has been engaged in remunerative work as an employed
earner [¹or, had the employment been in Great Britain would have been so engaged]—
            (a) any earnings paid or due to be paid [²in respect of that employment which has
                 terminated]—
                    (i)   [²⁰ . . .]
                    (ii) otherwise than by retirement except earnings to which regulation 35(1)(b) to (e)
                          and [⁵(g) to (i)] applies (earnings of employed earners);
            [¹⁰(b) where—
                    (i)   the employment has not been terminated, but
                    (ii) the claimant is not engaged in remunerative work,
                 any earnings in respect of that employment except earnings to which regulation
                 35(1)(d) and (e) applies; but this sub-paragraph shall not apply where the claimant has
                 been suspended from his employment.]
            [²⁰ **1A.** If the claimant's partner has been engaged in remunerative work as an employed
earner or, had the employment been in Great Britain, would have been so engaged, any earnings paid or due to be paid on termination of that employment by way of retirement but only
if the partner has attained the qualifying age for state pension credit on retirement.]
            [¹⁰**2.**—In the case of a claimant who, before the date of claim—
            (a) has been engaged in part-time employment as an employed earner or, where the
                 employment has been outside Great Britain, would have been so engaged had the
                 employment been in Great Britain, and
            (b) has ceased to be engaged in that employment, whether or not that employment has
                 been terminated,
any earnings in respect of that employment except any payment to which regulation 35(1)(e)
applies; but this paragraph shall not apply where the claimant has been suspended from his
employment.]
            3. In the case of a claimant who has been engaged in remunerative work or part-time employ-
ment as a self-employed earner [¹or, had the employment been in Great Britain would have
been so engaged] and who has ceased to be so employed, from the date of the cessation of his
employment any earnings derived from that employment except earnings to which regulation
30(2) (royalties etc.) applies.
            [⁴**4.**—(1) In a case to which this paragraph applies, [¹⁶£20]; but notwithstanding regulation
23 (calculation of income and capital of members of claimant's family and of a polygamous
marriage), if this paragraph applies to a claimant it shall not apply to his partner except where,
and to the extent that, the earnings of the claimant which are to be disregarded under this
paragraph are less than [¹⁶£20].
            (2) This paragraph applies where the claimant's applicable amount includes, or but for his
being an in-patient [¹⁸ . . .] or in residential accommodation would include, an amount by way
of a disability premium under Schedule 2 (applicable amounts).
            (3) This paragraph applies where—
            (a) the claimant is a member of a couple, and—
                    (i)   his applicable amount would include an amount by way of the disability
                          premium under Schedule 2 but for the higher pensioner premium under that
                          Schedule being applicable; or
                    (ii) had he not been an in-patient [¹⁸ . . .] or in residential accommodation his
                          applicable amount would include the higher pensioner premium under that
                          Schedule and had that been the case he would also satisfy the condition in
                          (i) above; and
            (b) [²⁰ . . .]
            (4) This paragraph applies where—
            (a) the claimant's applicable amount includes, or but for his being an in-patient [¹⁸ . . .] or
                 in residential accommodation would include, an amount by way of the higher pensioner
                 premium under Schedule 2; and
            [²⁰ (b) the claimant's partner has attained the qualifying age for state pension credit;]

(c) immediately before attaining that age [20 . . .] his partner was engaged in part-time employment and the claimant was entitled by virtue of sub-paragraph (2) [20 . . .] to a disregard of [16£20]; and

(d) he or, as the case may be, he or his partner has continued in part-time employment.

(5) [15. . .].

(6) [15. . .].

[6(7) For the purposes of this paragraph—

(a) except where head (b) or (c) applies, no account shall be taken of any period not exceeding eight consecutive weeks occurring—

[20 (i) on or after the date on which the claimant's partner attained the qualifying age for state pension credit during which the partner was not engaged in part-time employment or the claimant was not entitled to income support; or]

(ii) immediately after the date on which the claimant or his partner ceased to participate in arrangements for training made under section 2 of the Employment and Training Act 1973 [7or section 2 of the Enterprise and New Towns (Scotland) Act 1990] or to attend a course at an employment rehabilitation centre established under that section [7of the 1973 Act];

(b) in a case where the claimant has ceased to be entitled to income support because he, or if he is a member of a couple, he or his partner becomes engaged in remunerative work, no account shall be taken of any period, during which he was not entitled to income support, not exceeding the permitted period determined in accordance with regulation 3A (permitted period) occurring on or after the date on which [20 the claimant's partner attains the qualifying age for state pension credit];

(c) no account shall be taken of any period occurring on or after the date on which [20 the claimant's partner, if he is a member of a couple, attained the qualifying age for state pension credit] during which the claimant was not entitled to income support because he or his partner was participating in arrangements for training made under section 2 of the Employment and Training Act 1973 [7or section 2 of the Enterprise and New Towns (Scotland) Act 1990] or attending a course at an employment rehabilitation centre established under that section [7of the 1973 Act].]]

[135. In a case where the claimant is a lone parent and paragraph 4 does not apply, [16£20].]

[116. Where the claimant is a member of a couple—

(a) in a case to which none of paragraphs 4, 6A, 6B, 7 and 8 applies, £10; but notwithstanding regulation 23 (calculation of income and capital of members of claimant's family and of a polygamous marriage), if this paragraph applies to a claimant it shall not apply to his partner except where, and to the extent that, the earnings of the claimant which are to be disregarded under this sub-paragraph are less than £10;

(b) in a case to which one or more of paragraphs 4, 6A, 6B, 7 and 8 applies and the total amount disregarded under those paragraphs is less than £10, so much of the claimant's earnings as would not in aggregate with the amount disregarded under those paragraphs exceed £10.]

[96A.—(1) In a case to which none of paragraphs 4 to 6 applies to the claimant, and subject to sub-paragraph (2), where the claimant's applicable amount includes an amount by way of the carer premium under Schedule 2 (applicable amounts), [16£20] of the earnings of the person who is, or at any time in the preceding eight weeks was, in receipt of [19 carer's allowance] or treated in accordance with paragraph 14ZA(2) of that Schedule as being in receipt of [19 carer's allowance].

(2) Where the carer premium is awarded in respect of the claimant and of any partner of his, their earnings shall for the purposes of this paragraph be aggregated, but the amount to be disregarded in accordance with paragraph (1) shall not exceed [16£20] of the aggregated amount.

6B. Where the carer premium is awarded in respect of a claimant who is a member of a couple and whose earnings are less than [16£20], but is not awarded in respect of the other member of the couple, and that other member is engaged in an employment—

(a) specified in paragraph 7(1), so much of the other member's earnings as would not when aggregated with the amount disregarded under paragraph 6A exceed [16£20];

(b) other than one specified in paragraph 7(1), so much of the other member's earnings from such other employment up to £5 as would not when aggregated with the amount disregarded under paragraph 6A exceed [16£20].]

7.—(1) In a case to which none of paragraphs [94 to 6B] applies to the claimant, [16£20] of earnings derived from one or more employments as—

(a) a part-time fireman in a fire brigade maintained in pursuance of the Fire Services Acts 1947 to 1959;

[23 (aa) a part-time fire-fighter employed by a fire and rescue authority;]

   (b) an auxiliary coastguard in respect of coast rescue activities;

   (c) a person engaged part time in the manning or launching of a life boat;

   (d) a member of any territorial or reserve force prescribed in Part I of Schedule 3 to the Social Security (Contributions) Regulations 1979;

but, notwithstanding regulation 23 (calculation of income and capital of members of claimant's family and of a polygamous marriage), if this paragraph applies to a claimant it shall not apply to his partner except to the extent specified in sub-paragraph (2).

   (2) If the claimant's partner is engaged in employment—

   (a) specified in sub-paragraph (1) so much of his earnings as would not in aggregate with the amount of the claimant's earnings disregarded under this paragraph exceed [16£20];

   (b) other than one specified in sub-paragraph (1) so much of his earnings from that employment up to £5 as would not in aggregate with the claimant's earnings disregarded under this paragraph exceed [16£20].

8. Where the claimant is engaged in one or more employments specified in paragraph 7(1) but his earnings derived from such employments are less than [16£20] in any week and he is also engaged in any other part-time employment so much of his earnings from that other employment up to £5 as would not in aggregate with the amount of his earnings disregarded under paragraph 7 exceed [16£20].

9. In a case to which none of paragraphs 4 to 8 applies to the claimant, £5.

[11**10.** Notwithstanding the foregoing provisions of this Schedule, where two or more payments of the same kind and from the same source are to be taken into account in the same benefit week, because it has not been practicable to treat the payments under regulation 31(1)(b) (date on which income treated as paid) as paid on the first day of the benefit week in which they were due to be paid, there shall be disregarded from each payment the sum that would have been disregarded if the payment had been taken into account on the date on which it was due to be paid.]

11. Any earnings derived from employment which are payable in a country outside the United Kingdom for such period during which there is a prohibition against the transfer to the United Kingdom of those earnings.

12. Where a payment of earnings is made in a currency other than sterling, any banking charge or commission payable in converting that payment into sterling.

13. Any earnings which are due to be paid before the date of claim and which would otherwise fall to be taken into account in the same benefit week as a payment of the same kind and from the same source.

14. Any earnings of a child or young person [21 . . .].

15. [21 . . .].

[11**15A.** In the case of a claimant who—

   (a) has been engaged in employment as a member of any territorial or reserve force prescribed in Part I of Schedule 3 to the Social Security (Contributions) Regulations 1979; and

   (b) by reason of that employment has failed to satisfy any of the conditions for entitlement to income support other than section 124(1)(b) of the Contributions and Benefits Act (income support in excess of the applicable amount),

any earnings from that employment paid in respect of the period in which the claimant was not entitled to income support.]

[14**15B.** [22 . . .]]

[17**15C.** In the case of a person to whom paragraph (5) of regulation 6 (persons not treated as in remunerative work) applies, any earnings.]

16. In this Schedule "part-time employment" means employment in which the person is not to be treated as engaged in remunerative work under regulation 5 or 6 (persons treated, or not treated, as engaged in remunerative work).

AMENDMENTS

2.714   1. Income Support (General) Amendment Regulations 1988 (SI 1988/663), reg.34 (April 11, 1988).

    2. Income Support (General) Amendment No.4 Regulations 1988 (SI 1988/1445), reg.24 (September 12, 1988).

    3. Income Support (General) Amendment No.4 Regulations 1988 (SI 1988/1445), Sch.1, para.8 (April 10, 1989).

    4. Income Support (General) Amendment Regulations 1989 (SI 1989/534), reg.10 and Sch.1 (October 9, 1989).

    5. Income Support (General) Amendment No.2 Regulations 1989 (SI 1989/1323), reg.18 (October 9, 1989).

6. Income Support (General) Amendment No.3 Regulations 1989 (SI 1989/1678), reg.12 (October 9, 1989).

7. Enterprise (Scotland) Consequential Amendments Order 1991 (SI 1991/387), art.2 and 9 (April 1, 1991).

8. Income Support (General) Amendment Regulations 1992 (SI 1992/468), reg.7 (April 6, 1992).

9. Income-related Benefits Schemes (Miscellaneous Amendments) Regula tions 1993 (SI 1993/315), reg.8 (April 12, 1993).

10. Income-related Benefits Schemes (Miscellaneous Amendments) (No.4) Regulations 1993 (SI 1993/2119), reg.22 (October 4, 1993).

11. Income-related Benefits Schemes and Social Fund (Miscellaneous Amendments) Regulations 1996 (SI 1996/1944), reg.6(11) (October 7, 1996).

12. Child Benefit, Child Support and Social Security (Miscellaneous Amendments) Regulations 1996 (SI 1996/1803), reg.41 (April 7, 1997).

13. Social Security Amendment (Lone Parents) Regulations 1998 (SI 1998/766), reg.13 (April 6, 1998).

14. Social Security (Miscellaneous Amendments) (No.2) Regulations 1999 (SI 1999/2556), reg.2(9) (October 4, 1999).

15. Social Security (Miscellaneous Amendments) Regulations 2000 (SI 2000/681), reg.12(a) (April 3, 2000).

16. Social Security Amendment (Capital Limits and Earnings Disregards) Regulations 2000 (SI 2000/2545), reg.3 and Sch. para.2 (April 9, 2001).

17. Social Security (Miscellaneous Amendments) Regulations 2001 (SI 2001/488), reg.8 (April 9, 2001).

18. Social Security Amendment (Residential Care and Nursing Homes) Regulations 2001 (SI 2001/3767), reg.2(1) and Pt I of Sch. para.18 (April 8, 2002).

19. Social Security Amendment (Carer's Allowance) Regulations 2002 (SI 2002/2497), reg.3 and Sch.2 (April 1, 2003).

20. State Pension Credit (Consequential, Transitional and Miscellaneous Provisions) Regulations 2002 (SI 2002/3019), reg.29(7) (October 6, 2003).

21. Social Security (Working Tax Credit and Child Tax Credit)(Consequential Amendments) Regulations 2003 (SI 2003/455), reg.2 and Sch.1, para.22 (April 6, 2004, except in "transitional cases" and see further the note to reg.17 of the Income Support Regulations).

22. Social Security (Back to Work Bonus and Lone Parent Run-on) (Amendment and Revocation) Regulations 2003 (SI 2003/1589), reg.2(d) (October 25, 2004).

23. Fire and Rescue Services Act 2004 (Consequential Amendments) (England) Order 2004 (SI 2004/3168), art.14 (December 30, 2004) (only applies in England).

DEFINITIONS

"benefit week"—see reg.2(1).   2.715
"child"—see 1986 Act, s.20(11) (SSCBA, s.137(1)).
"claimant"—see reg.2(1).
"couple"—*ibid.*
"date of claim"—*ibid*
"employed earner"—*ibid.*
"family"—see 1986 Act, s.20(11) (SSCBA, s.137(1)).
"nursing home"—see reg.2(1), reg.19(3).
"partner"—see reg.2(1).
"polygamous marriage"—*ibid.*
"remunerative work"—*ibid.*
"residential accommodation"—see reg.2(1), reg.21(3).
"residential care home"—see reg.2(1).
"Social Security Act"—see reg.2(1).
"supplementary benefit"—*ibid.*
"young person" *ibid.*, reg.14.

GENERAL NOTE

2.716 Before April 6, 2004 the income (but not the capital) of a child or young person who was a member of the claimant's family was aggregated with the claimant's, subject to the modifications in reg.44. Under the form of this Schedule in force at that time paras 1 to 10 did not apply to children or young persons (see the form of reg.23(2) then in force) and paras 14 and 15 only applied to children and young persons (see the 2003 edition of this volume for the old form of reg.23 and of paras 14 and 15 of this Schedule). However, with effect from April 6, 2004 (except in "transitional cases"—see the note to reg.17), amounts for children and young persons have been removed from the income support scheme; financial assistance to help with the cost of bringing up a child or young person is now to be provided through the child tax credit system, see Vol. IV of this series. As a consequence, the income of a child or young person is no longer aggregated with the claimant's (see the new form of reg.23 and the notes to that regulation) and so the disregards that applied to such income are no longer needed (although note that part of para.14 has been retained). The former disregards do however remain in force for "transitional cases"—see the note to reg.17.

For income support claimants who had an award of child tax credit before April 6, 2004 see reg.7 of the Social Security (Working Tax Credit and Child Tax Credit) (Consequential Amendments) Regulations 2003 (SI 2003/455) (as amended) on p.686 and the notes to that regulation.

Note that from April 9, 2001, the higher earnings disregard in paras 4, 5, 6A, 6B, 7, 8 and 15 (which has been £15 since the commencement of income support) increased to £20.

Paras 1 and 1A

2.717 This disregard is crucial to entitlement following the termination of full time employment (*i.e.* 16 hours or more per week in the case of the claimant, 24 hours or more per week for a partner: reg.5(1) and (1A); references to the "claimant" in Part V of the Income Support Regulations include his partner (if any), unless the context otherwise requires (reg.23(1)). The effect, under sub-para.(a)(ii), is that final payments of wages and salary are disregarded. This means that entitlement can begin immediately, unless a payment in lieu of wages or notice or holiday pay is due or a compensation payment is made. If any of these payments are made, reg.5(5) treats the person as in full-time work for the period covered by the payments (regs 29(3) and (4)). *CJSA/1589/2004* holds that any such holiday pay is to be attributed in terms of days, that is to each of the seven days in a week, not on the basis of "working days" (see further the note to reg.35(1)(d)). Once the period covered by the payments has ended, any money remaining counts as capital (*CIS 104/1989* and *R(IS) 3/93*). The disregard is more extensive if the employment has not terminated but the person is working less than 16 hours a week (or none at all). The old form of para.1(b) applied the disregard if the employment had been "interrupted". In *CIS 301/1989* it was held that a shift from full-time to part-time employment with the same employer was an interruption of "the" employment. If the evidence had supported the replacement of one contract with another this would have been a termination. The new wording should cover this type of situation with less linguistic contortion. The disregard in sub-para.(b) does not apply if the person has been suspended. Payments by way of a retainer (reg.35(1)(e)) are not disregarded under sub-para.(a)(ii) or (b). *R(IS) 9/95* decides that a guarantee payment under s.12 of the Employment Protection (Consolidation) Act 1978 counts as a retainer.

Under the form of sub-para.(a)(i) in force before October 6, 2003 no earnings due on termination of employment were taken into account if the person was retiring at pensionable age. However, since the commencement of the state pension credit scheme on October 6, 2003, claimants who have reached the qualifying age for state pension credit (this is currently 60 but between 2010 and 2020 will gradually rise until it reaches 65, see further the note to s.1(6) of the State Pension Credit Act 2002) or whose partner is entitled to state pension credit are not entitled to income support (SSCBA, s.124(aa) and (g)). There is thus no longer any need for a disregard of a claimant's earnings paid on termination of employment due to retirement at pensionable age. For the disregard of a partner's earnings paid on termination of employment due to retirement see para.1A, inserted with effect from October 6, 2003. Such earnings will be disregarded in full provided that the partner has reached the qualifying age for state pension credit.

Para. 2

There is a more extensive disregard where the person's part-time (*i.e.* less than 16 hours per week (24 hours in the case of a partner): para.16 and reg.5(1) and (1A)) work has stopped before the claim (provided he has not been suspended). On payments within reg.35(1)(e) see *R(IS) 9/95* in the note to para.1. It is not necessary for the employment to have ended. On this, see *R(JSA) 8/03* which concerned a part-time supply teacher who claimed JSA during the school summer holidays. The Commissioner decides that because she did not have a recognisable cycle of work the equivalent disregard in para.2 of Sch.6 to the JSA Regulations applied. However, if a cycle of work has been established, *R(JSA) 2/03* holds that a person is to be regarded as engaged in employment (whether remunerative or part-time) during the whole of the cycle and so the disregard in para.2 will not apply. See further the notes to para.2 of Sch.6 to the JSA Regulations.

If the part-time work ends while the claimant is claiming income support, payments are taken into account as earnings in the usual way.

2.718

Para. 3

When a self-employed person leaves that employment, only royalties or payments for copyright count.

2.719

Para. 4

This provision allows a disregard of £20 between the claimant and any partner, if the claimant meets the basic conditions for a disability premium or if the conditions for the higher pensioner premium are met with the restrictive extra conditions of sub-para.(4). Note that there appears to be a spare "and" at the end of sub-para.(3) as a result of the amendments made on October 6, 2003 consequent upon the introduction of state pension credit.

See the saving provision in reg.4 of the Social Security Amendment (Capital Limits and Earnings Disregards) Regulations 2000 (SI 2000/2545) (p.683) to enable claimants who were entitled to the previous £15 disregard under sub-paras (2) and (3) to meet the condition in sub-para.(4)(c). The saving provision also applies to para.5(4)(c) of Sch.6 to the JSA Regulations.

2.720

Para. 5

If the claimant is a lone parent the first £20 of net earnings are disregarded. Since April 6, 1998 it has not been necessary for the claimant to be receiving the lone parent rate of the family premium under para.3(1)(a) of Sch.2 for this disregard to apply; *all* lone parent now qualify for a disregard under this paragraph, unless they are entitled to a £20 disregard under para.4.

2.721

Para. 6

From October 7, 1996 the previous £15 disregard for long-term unemployed couples aged less than 60 which applied under this paragraph has been replaced by a £10 earnings disregard that applies to all couples. This is the same as the disregard that applies for JSA.

2.722

Paras 6A and 6B

Where the carer premium is payable, the first £20 of the earnings of the carer are disregarded. If the carer does not use up the disregard, what is spare may be applied

2.723

to a (non-carer) partner's earnings under para.6B. Only £5 may be disregarded in this way, except for the employment mentioned in para.7(1).

Para. 7

2.724   Earnings from these activities attract a £20 disregard, but a couple cannot have a total disregard of more than £20.

Para. 9

2.725   The basic disregard of net earnings from part-time work is £5.

Para. 10

2.726   See notes to reg.32(5).

Para. 13

2.727   Where earnings are due before the date of claim, overlaps with payments of the same kind are avoided. See notes to reg.32(5).

Para. 14

2.728   See the note at the beginning of the Schedule. The old forms of paras 14 and 15 continue in force for "transitional cases"—see the note to reg.17. It is not entirely clear why this disregard is being retained.

Para. 15A

2.729   This introduces a new disregard (that also applies for JSA) of earnings paid to a member of the reserve forces while attending training (and therefore not entitled to income support).

Para. 15C

2.730   From April 9, 2001 a claimant who, or whose partner, starts remunerative work (*i.e.* 16 hours or more a week) after either of them has been in receipt of income support or income-based JSA for at least six months will be allowed a four week "mortgage interest run-on" (see further reg.6(5)–(8) and the notes to those provisions). Note that periods when the mortgage interest run-on applies cannot count towards the required six months' continuous entitlement to benefit. Payment of the mortgage interest run-on will be made direct to the claimant, not the lender. The purpose of the run-on is to tackle some of the hurdles (such as the gap between starting work and receiving wages and the wait for in-work benefits) that face people when they begin full-time work. The amount of benefit paid during the run-on period will be the lower of the amount for housing costs that was being met or the income support/income-based JSA that was in payment before the claimant or his partner started work (see further the new para.19A of Sch.7). Para. 15C provides that any of the person's earnings in the run-on period will be disregarded. See also the disregards in para.74 of Sch.9 and para.62 of Sch.10.

SCHEDULE 9   **Regulation 40(2)**

SUMS TO BE DISREGARDED IN THE CALCULATION OF INCOME OTHER THAN EARNINGS

2.731   1. Any amount paid by way of tax on income which is taken into account under regulation 40 (calculation of income other than earnings).

     2. Any payment in respect of any expenses incurred [⁷⁷, or to be incurred,] by a claimant who is—

         (a) engaged by a charitable or [³²voluntary organisation]; or

         (b) a volunteer,

if he otherwise derives no remuneration or profit from the employment and is not to be treated as possessing any earnings under regulation 42(6) (notional income).

     3. In the case of employment as an employed earner, any payment in respect of expenses wholly, exclusively and necessarily incurred in the performance of the duties of the employment.

4. In the case of a payment of statutory sick pay under Part I of the Social Security and Housing Benefits Act 1982 or statutory maternity pay under Part V of the Act [[86]], statutory paternity pay under Part 12ZA of the Contributions and Benefits Act, statutory adoption pay under Part 12ZB of the Contributions and Benefits Act] or any remuneration paid by or on behalf of an employer to the claimant who for the time being is unable to work due to illness or maternity [[86] or who is taking paternity leave or adoption leave]—

    (a) any amount deducted by way of primary Class 1 contributions under the Social Security Act [SSCBA];

    (b) one-half of any sum paid by the claimant by way of a contribution towards an occupational or personal pension scheme.

[[1]**4A.** In the case of the payment of statutory sick pay under Part II of the Social Security (Northern Ireland) Order 1982 [[86], statutory maternity pay under Part XII of the Social Security Contributions and Benefits (Northern Ireland) Act 1992 or a payment under any enactment having effect in Northern Ireland corresponding to a payment of statutory paternity pay or statutory adoption pay]—

    (a) any amount deducted by way of primary Class 1 contributions under the Social Security (Northern Ireland) Act 1975;

    (b) one-half of any sum paid by way of a contribution towards an occupational or personal pension scheme.]

5. Any housing benefit [[103]to which the claimant is entitled] [[41]including any amount of housing benefit to which a person is entitled by virtue of regulation 7B of the Housing Benefit (General) Regulations 1987 (entitlement of a refugee to housing benefit)].

[[88] **5A.**—(1) Any guardian's allowance.]

[[94] **5B.**—(1) Any child tax credit.

(2) Any child benefit.]

6. Any mobility allowance [[18]or the mobility component of disability living allowance].

7. Any concessionary payment made to compensate for the non-payment of—

    (a) any payment specified in [[18]paragraph 6 [[48] or 9]];

    (b) income support [[48] or jobseeker"s allowance].

8. Any mobility supplement or any payment intended to compensate for the non payment of such a supplement.

[[25] **9.** Any attendance allowance or the care component of disability living allowance [[90] . . .].]

[[29]**9A** . . .]

10. Any payment to the claimant as holder of the Victoria Cross or George Cross or any analogous payment.

[[97] **11.**—(1) Any payment—

    (a) by way of an education maintenance allowance made pursuant to—

        (i) regulations made under section 518 of the Education Act 1996;

        (ii) regulations made under section 49 or 73(f) of the Education (Scotland) Act 1980;

        (iii) directions made under sections 12(2)(c) and 21 of the Further and Higher Education (Scotland) Act 1992; or

    (b) corresponding to such an education maintenance allowance, made pursuant to—

        (i) section 14 or section 181 of the Education Act 2002; or

        (ii) regulations made under section 181 of that Act.

(2) Any payment, other than a payment to which sub-paragraph (1) applies, made pursuant to—

    (a) regulations made under section 518 of the Education Act 1996;

    (b) regulations made under section 49 of the Education (Scotland) Act 1980; or

    (c) directions made under sections 12(2)(c) and 21 of the Further and Higher Education (Scotland) Act 1992,

in respect of a course of study attended by a child or a young person or a person who is in receipt of an education maintenance allowance made pursuant to any provision specified in sub-paragraph (1).]

[[83] **11A.** Any payment made to the claimant by way of a repayment under regulation 11(2) of the Education (Teacher Student Loans) (Repayment etc) Regulations 2002.]

12. [[64] . . .].

[[93] **13.**—(1) Any payment made pursuant to section 2 of the Employment and Training Act 1973 (functions of the Secretary of State) or section 2 of the Enterprise and New Towns (Scotland) Act 1990 (functions in relation to training for employment etc.) except a payment—

    (a) made as a substitute for income support, a jobseeker's allowance, incapacity benefit or severe disablement allowance;

    (b) of an allowance referred to in section 2(3) of the Employment and Training Act 1973 or section 2(5) of the Enterprise and New Towns (Scotland) Act 1990;

    (c) intended to meet the cost of living expenses which relate to any one or more of the items specified in sub-paragraph (2) whilst a claimant is participating in an education, training or other scheme to help him enhance his employment prospects unless the payment is a Career Development Loan paid pursuant to section 2 of the Employment and Training Act 1973 and the period of education or training or the scheme, which is supported by that loan, has been completed; or

    (d) made in respect of the cost of living away from home to the extent that the payment relates to rent for which housing benefit is payable in respect of accommodation which is not normally occupied by the claimant as his home.

(2) The items specified in this sub-paragraph for the purposes of sub-paragraph (1)(c) are food, ordinary clothing or footwear, household fuel, rent for which housing benefit is payable, or any housing costs to the extent that they are met under regulation 17(1)(e) or 18(1)(f) (housing costs), of the claimant or, where the claimant is a member of a family, any other member of his family, or any council tax or water charges for which that claimant or member is liable.

(3) For the purposes of this paragraph, "ordinary clothing or footwear" means clothing or footwear for normal daily use, but does not include school uniforms, or clothing or footwear used solely for sporting activities.]

    14. [[34] . . .]

[[10]**15.**—[[29](1) Subject to sub-paragraph (3) and paragraphs 36, 37 and 39, [[39]£20] of any [[84] relevant payment] made or due to be made at regular intervals, except any payment to which sub-paragraph (2) or paragraph 15A applies.]

(2) Subject to [[79]sub-paragraph (3)] and paragraph 39, any [[84] relevant payment] made or due to be made at regular intervals which is intended and used for an item other than food, ordinary clothing or footwear, household fuel, [[98]council tax, water charges,] rent [[103]. . .] for which [[79]housing benefit is payable or] [[16]. . .] any housing costs to the extent that they are met under regulation 17(1) (e) or 18(1)(f) (housing costs) [[79]. . .] [[30]. . .], of a single claimant or, as the case may be, of the claimant or any other member of his family [[98]. . .].

(3) Sub-paragraphs (1) and (2) shall not apply—

    (a) to a payment which is made by a person for the maintenance of any member of his family or of his former partner or of his children;

    (b) in the case of a person to whom section 23 of the Act [SSCBA, s.126] (trade disputes) applies or in respect of whom section 20(3) of the Act [SSCBA, s.124(1)] (conditions of entitlement to income support) has effect as modified by section 23A(b) of the Act [SSCBA, s.127(b)] (effect of return to work).

(4) For the purposes of sub-paragraph (1) where a number of [[84] relevant payments] fall to be taken into account in any one week they shall be treated as though they were one such payment.

(5) For the purposes of sub-paragraph (2) the expression "ordinary clothing or foot wear" means clothing or footwear for normal daily use, but does not include school uniforms, or clothing or footwear used solely for sporting activities.]

[[84] (5A) In this paragraph, "relevant payment" means—

    (a) a charitable payment;

    (b) a voluntary payment;

    (c) a payment (not falling within sub-paragraph (a) or (b) above) from a trust whose funds are derived from a payment made in consequence of any personal injury to the claimant;

    (d) a payment under an annuity purchased—

        (i) pursuant to any agreement or court order to make payments to the claimant; or

        (ii) from funds derived from a payment made,

    in consequence of any personal injury to the claimant; or

    (e) a payment (not falling within sub-paragraphs (a) to (d) above) received by virtue of any agreement or court order to make payments to the claimant in consequence of any personal injury to the claimant.]

[[29](6) [[79]. . .].]

[[25]**15A.**—(1) Subject to the following provisions of this paragraph, in the case of a claimant placed in a residential care home or nursing home by a local authority under section 26 of the National Assistance Act 1948, [[32]sections 13A, 13B and 59(2)(c) of the Social Work (Scotland) Act 1968 or section 7 of the Mental Health (Scotland) Act 1984] any charitable payment or voluntary payment made or due to be made at regular intervals.

(2) This paragraph shall apply only where—

    (a) the claimant was placed in the residential care or nursing home by the local authority because the home was the preferred choice of the claimant, and

(b) the cost of the accommodation was in excess of what the authority would normally expect to pay having regard to the needs of the claimant assessed in accordance with section 47 of the National Health Service and Community Care Act 1990.

(3) [79. . .].

(4) The amount to be disregarded under sub-paragraph (1) shall not exceed the difference between the actual cost of the accommodation provided by the local authority and the cost the authority would normally incur for a person with the particular needs of the claimant.]

[38 **15B.** [90 . . .].]

[35**16.** Subject to paragraphs 36 and 37, £10 of any of the following, namely—

(a) a war disablement pension (except insofar as such a pension falls to be disregarded under paragraph 8 or 9);

(b) a war widow's pension [81 or war widower's pension];

(c) a pension payable to a person as a widow [81 or widower] under the Naval, Military and Air Forces Etc. (Disablement and Death) Service Pensions Order 1983 insofar as that Order is made under the Naval and Marine Pay and Pensions Act 1865 [37 or the Pensions and Yeomary Pay Act 1884], or is made only under section 12(1) of the Social Security (Miscellaneous Provisions) Act 1977 and any power of Her Majesty otherwise than under an enactment to make provision about pensions for or in respect of persons who have been disabled or have died in consequence of service as members of the armed forces of the Crown;

[102(cc) a guaranteed income payment;]

(d) a payment made to compensate for the non-payment of such a pension [102 or payment] as is mentioned in any of the preceding sub-paragraphs;

(e) a pension paid by the government of a country outside Great Britain which is analogous to any of the [102 pensions or payments mentioned in sub-paragraphs (a) to (cc) above];

(f) a pension paid to victims of National Socialist persecution under any special provision made by the law of the Federal Republic of Germany, or any part of it, or of the Republic of Austria.]

[70(g) any widowed mother's allowance paid pursuant to section 37 of the Contributions and Benefits Act;

(h) any widowed parent's allowance paid pursuant to section 39A of the Contributions and Benefits Act.]

17. Where a person receives income under an annuity purchased with a loan which satisfies the following conditions—

(a) that the loan was made as part of a scheme under which not less than 90 per cent. of the proceeds of the loan were applied to the purchase by the person to whom it was made of an annuity ending with his life or with the life of the survivor of two or more persons (in this paragraph referred to as "the annuitants") who include the person to whom the loan was made;

(b) that the interest on the loan is payable by the person to whom it was made or by one of the annuitants;

(c) that at the time the loan was made the person to whom it was made or each of the annuitants had attained the age of 65;

(d) that the loan was secured on a dwelling in Great Britain and the person to whom the loan was made or one of the annuitants owns an estate or interest in that dwelling; and

(e) that the person to whom the loan was made or one of the annuitants occupies the accommodation on which it was secured as his home at the time the interest is paid, the amount, calculated on a weekly basis equal to—

[31(i) here, or insofar as, section 369 of the Income and Corporation Taxes Act 1988 (mortgage interest payable under deduction of tax) applies to the payments of interest on the loan, the interest which is payable after deduction of a sum equal to income tax on such payments at the applicable percentage of income tax within the meaning of section 369(1A) of that Act;]

(ii) in any other case the interest which is payable on the loan without deduction of such a sum.

[32**18.** Any payment made to the claimant by a person who normally resides with the claimant, which is a contribution towards that person's living and accommodation costs, except where that person is residing with the claimant in circumstances to which paragraph 19 or 20 refers.]

[30**19.** Where the claimant occupies a dwelling as his home and the dwelling is also occupied by [32another person], and there is a contractual liability to make payments to the claimant in respect of the occupation of the dwelling by that person or a member of his family—

    (a) £4 of the aggregate of any payments made in respect of any one week in respect of the occupation of the dwelling by that person or a member of his family, or by that person and a member of his family; and

    (b) a further [[104] £10.55], where the aggregate of any such payments is inclusive of an amount for heating.]

[[30]20. Where the claimant occupies a dwelling as his home and he provides in that dwelling board and lodging accommodation, an amount, in respect of each person for whom such accommodation is provided for the whole or any part of a week, equal to—

    (a) where the aggregate of any payments made in respect of any one week in respect of such accommodation provided to such person does not exceed £20.00, 100% of such payments; or

    (b) where the aggregate of any such payments exceeds £20.00, £20.00 and 50% of the excess over £20.00.]

[[1]21.—(1) [[61]Subject to sub-paragraphs (2) and (3)], except where [[61]regulation 40(4)(b) (provision of support under section 95 or 98 of the Immigration and Asylum Act including support provided by virtue of regulations made under Schedule 9 to that Act in the calculation of income other than earnings) or] regulation 42(4)(a)(i) (notional income) applies or in the case of a person to whom section 23 of the Act [SSCBA, s.126] (trade disputes) applies and for so long as it applies, any income in kind;

    (2) The exception under sub-paragraph (1) shall not apply where the income in kind is received from the Macfarlane Trust[[8], the Macfarlane (Special Payments) Trust] [[15], the Macfarlane (Special Payments) (No. 2) Trust][[21], the Fund][[27], the Eileen Trust] [[2] or [[26] the Independent Living Funds]].]

[[61](3) The first exception under sub-paragraph (1) shall not apply where the claimant is the partner of a person subject to immigration control and whose partner is receiving support provided under section 95 or 98 of the Immigration and Asylum Act including support provided by virtue of regulations made under Schedule 9 to that Act and the income in kind is support provided in respect of essential living needs of the partner of the claimant and his dependants (if any) as is specified in regulations made under paragraph 3 of Schedule 8 to the Immigration and Asylum Act.]

22.—(1) Any income derived from capital to which the claimant is or is treated under regulation 52 (capital jointly held) as beneficially entitled but, subject to sub-paragraph (2), not income derived from capital disregarded under paragraph 1, 2, 4, 6 [[3]12 or 25 to 28] of Schedule 10.

(2) Income derived from capital disregarded under paragraph 2 [[3]4 or 25 to 28] of Schedule 10 but [[24]only to the extent of—

    (a) any mortgage repayments made in respect of the dwelling or premises in the period during which that income accrued; or

    (b) any council tax or water charges which the claimant is liable to pay in respect of the dwelling or premises and which are paid in the period during which that income accrued.

(3) The definition of "water charges" in regulation 2(1) shall apply to sub-paragraph (2) with the omission of the words "in so far as such charges are in respect of the dwelling which a person occupies as his home".]

23. Any income which is payable in a country outside the United Kingdom for such period during which there is a prohibition against the transfer to the United Kingdom of that income.

24. Where a payment of income is made in a currency other than sterling, any banking charge or commission payable in converting that payment into sterling.

25.—(1) Any payment made to the claimant in respect of a child or young person who is a member of his family—

    [[20](a) in accordance with regulations made pursuant to section 57A of the Adoption Act 1976 (permitted allowances) [[89] or paragraph 3 of Schedule 4 to the Adoption and Children Act 2002] or with a scheme approved by the Secretary of State under section 51 of the Adoption (Scotland) Act 1978 (schemes for payment of allowances to adopters);

    [[49](b) which is a payment made by a local authority in pursuance of section 34(6) or, as the case may be, section 50 of the Children Act 1975 (contributions towards the cost of the accommodation and maintenance of a child);

    (c) which is a payment made by a local authority in pursuance of section 15(1) of, and paragraph 15 of Schedule 1 to, the Children Act 1989 (local authority contribution to a child's maintenance where the child is living with a person as a result of a residence order);

    (d) which is a payment made by an authority, as defined in Article 2 of the Children Order, in pursuance of Article 15 of, and paragraph 17 of Schedule 1 to, that Order (contribution by an authority to child's maintenance);]]

[100(e)   in accordance with regulations made pursuant to section 14F of the Children Act 1989 (special guardianship support services);]

[94 . . .].

[89 (1A) Any payment, other than a payment to which sub-paragraph (1)(a) applies, made to the claimant in accordance with regulations made under paragraph 3 of Schedule 4 to the Adoption and Children Act 2002.]

(2) [94 . . .].

[94 **25A.** In the case of a claimant who has a child or young person—

(a)   who is a member of his family, and

(b)   who is residing at an educational establishment at which he is receiving relevant education,

any payment made to that educational establishment, in respect of that child or young person's maintenance by or on behalf of a person who is not a member of the family or by a member of the family out of funds contributed for that purpose by a person who is not a member of the family.]

26. Any payment made by a local authority to the claimant with whom a person is [20accommodated by virtue of arrangements made under section 23(2)(a) of the Children Act 1989 (provision of accommodation and maintenance for a child whom they are looking after)] or, as the case may be, [95section 26 of the Children (Scotland) Act 1995] or by a voluntary organisation under [20section 59(1)(a) of the 1989 Act (provision of accommodation by voluntary organisations)] or by a care authority under regulation 9 of the Boarding Out and Fostering of Children (Scotland) Regulations 1985 (provision of accommodation and maintenance for children in care).

27. [46 Any payment made to the claimant or his partner for a person ("the person concerned"), who is not normally a member of the claimant's household but is temporarily in his care, by—

(a)   a health authority;

(b)   a local authority [103 but excluding payments of housing benefit made in respect of the person concerned];

(c)   a voluntary organisation; or

(d)   the person concerned pursuant to section 26(3A) of the National Assistance Act 1948. [73 or

(e)   a primary care trust established under section 16A of the National Health Service Act 1977].]

28. Except in the case of a person to whom section 23 of the Act [SSCBA, s.126] (trade disputes) applies [1or in respect of whom section 20(3) of the Act [SSCBA, s.124(1)] (conditions of entitlement to income support) has effect as modified by section 23A(b) of the Act [SSCBA, s.127(b)] (effect of return to work)], [6any payment made by a local authority [20in accordance with [78 section 17, 23B, 23C or 24A of the Children Act 1989]] or, as the case may be, [96 section 12 of the Social Work (Scotland) Act 1968 or sections 29 or 30 of the Children (Scotland) Act 1995] (local authorities' duty to promote welfare of children and powers to grant financial assistance to persons in, or formerly in, their care).]

[33**29.**—(1) Subject to sub-paragraph (2) any payment received under an insurance policy, taken out to insure against the risk of being unable to maintain repayments on a loan which qualifies under paragraph 15 or 16 of Schedule 3 (housing costs in respect of loans to acquire an interest in a dwelling, or for repairs and improvements to the dwelling, occupied as the home) and used to meet such repayments, to the extent that it does not exceed the aggregate of—

(a)   the amount, calculated on a weekly basis, of any interest on that loan which is in excess of the amount met in accordance with Schedule 3 (housing costs);

(b)   the amount of any payment, calculated on a weekly basis, due on the loan attributable to the repayment of capital; and

(c)   any amount due by way of premiums on—

(i)   that policy, or

(ii)   a policy of insurance taken out to insure against loss or damage to any building or part of a building which is occupied by the claimant as his home.

(2) This paragraph shall not apply to any payment which is treated as possessed by the claimant by virtue of regulation 42(4)(a)(ii) (notional income).

30.—(1) Except where paragraph 29 [50or 30ZA] applies, and subject to sub-paragraph (2), any payment made to the claimant which is intended to be used and is used as a contribution towards—

(a)   any payment due on a loan if secured on the dwelling occupied as the home which does not qualify under Schedule 3 (housing costs);

(b) any interest payment or charge which qualifies in accordance with paragraphs 15 to 17 of Schedule 3 to the extent that the payment or charge is not met;

(c) any payment due on a loan which qualifies under paragraph 15 or 16 of Schedule 3 attributable to the payment of capital;

(d) any amount due by way of premiums on—

(i) [[36] an insurance policy taken out to insure against the risk of being unable to make the payments referred to in (a) to (c) above;] or

(ii) a policy of insurance taken out to insure against loss or damage to any building or part of a building which is occupied by the claimant as his home.

(e) his rent in respect of the dwelling occupied by him as his home but only to the extent that it is not met by housing benefit; or his accommodation charge but only to the extent that the actual charge [[79] exceeds] the amount payable by a local authority in accordance with Part III of the National Assistance Act 1948.

(2) This paragraph shall not apply to any payment which is treated as possessed by the claimant by virtue of regulation 42(4)(a)(ii) (notional income).]

[[50]**30ZA.**—(1) Subject to sub-paragraph (2), any payment received under an insurance policy, other than an insurance policy referred to in paragraph 29, taken out to insure against the risk of being unable to maintain repayments under a regulated agreement as defined for the purposes of the Consumer Credit Act 1974 or under a hire-purchase agreement or a conditional sale agreement as defined for the purposes of Part III of the Hire-Purchase Act 1964.

(2) A payment referred to in sub-paragraph (1) shall only be disregarded to the extent that the payment received under that policy does not exceed the amounts, calculated on a weekly basis, which are used to—

(a) maintain the repayments referred to in sub-paragraph (1); and

(b) meet any amount due by way of premiums on that policy.]

[[29]**30A.**—(1) Subject to sub-paragraphs (2) and (3), in the case of a claimant in a residential care home or nursing home, any payment, whether or not the payment is charitable or voluntary but not a payment to which paragraph 15A applies, made to the claimant which is intended to be used and is used to meet the cost of maintaining the claimant in that home.

(2) This paragraph shall not apply to a claimant for whom accommodation in a residential care home or nursing home is provided by a local authority under section 26 of the National Assistance Act 1948 [[79]. . .].

(3) The amount to be disregarded under this paragraph shall not exceed the difference between—

[[79](a) the claimant's applicable amount; and]

(b) the weekly charge for the accommodation.]

[[19]**31.** Any social fund payment made pursuant to Part III of the Act [SSCBA, Part VIII].]

32. Any payment of income which under regulation 48 (income treated as capital) is to be treated as capital.

33. Any payment under paragraph 2 of Schedule 6 to the Act [SSCBA, s.148] (pensioners' Christmas bonus).

34. In the case of a person to whom section 23 of the Act [SSCBA, s.126] (trade disputes) applies and for so long as it applies, any payment up to the amount of the relevant sum within the meaning of sub-section (6) of that section made by a trade union; but, notwithstanding regulation 23 (calculation of income and capital of members of claimant's family and of a polygamous marriage) if this paragraph applies to a claimant it shall not apply to his partner except where, and to the extent that, the amount to be disregarded under this paragraph is less than the relevant sum.

35. Any payment which is due to be paid before the date of claim which would otherwise fall to be taken into account in the same benefit week as a payment of the same kind and from the same source.

36. The total of a claimant's income or, if he is a member of a family, the family's income and the income of any person which he is treated as possessing under regulation 23(3) (calculation of income and capital of members of claimant's family and of a polygamous marriage) to be disregarded under regulation 63(2)(b) and 64(1)(c) (calculation of covenant income where a contribution assessed)[[11], regulation 66A(2) (treatment of student loans)] [[67], regulation 66B(3) (treatment of payments from access funds)] and [10]paragraphs 15(1)] and 16 shall in no case exceed [[39]£20] per week.

37. Notwithstanding paragraph 36 where two or more payments of the same kind and from the same source are to be taken into account in the same benefit week, there shall be disregarded from each payment the sum which would otherwise fall to be disregarded under this Schedule; but this paragraph shall only apply in the case of a payment which it has not been practicable to treat under regulation 31(1)(b) (date on which income treated as paid) as paid on the first day of the benefit week in which it is due to be paid.

[¹**38.** Any resettlement benefit which is paid to the claimant by virtue of regulation 3 of the Social Security (Hospital In-Patients) Amendment (No. 2) Regulations 1987.

[¹⁵**39.**—(1) Any payment made under the Macfarlane Trust, the Macfarlane (Special Payments) Trust, the Macfarlane (Special Payments) (No. 2) Trust ("the Trusts"), [²¹the Fund][²⁷, the Eileen Trust] or [²⁶the Independent Living Funds].

(2) Any payment by or on behalf of a person who is suffering or who suffered from haemophilia [²¹or who is or was a qualifying person], which derives from a payment made under any of the Trusts to which sub-paragraph (1) refers and which is made to or for the benefit of—

    (a) that person's partner or former partner from whom he is not, or where that person has died was not, estranged or divorced;

    (b) any child who is a member of that person's family or who was such a member and who is a member of the claimant's family; or

    (c) any young person who is a member of that person's family or who was such a member and who is a member of the claimant's family.

(3) Any payment by or on behalf of the partner or former partner of a person who is suffering or who suffered from haemophilia [²¹or who is or was a qualifying person] provided that the partner or former partner and that person are not, or if either of them has died were not, estranged or divorced, which derives from a payment made under any of the Trusts to which sub-paragraph (1) refers and which is made to or for the benefit of—

    (a) the person who is suffering from haemophilia [²¹or who is a qualifying person];

    (b) any child who is a member of that person's family or who was such a member and who is a member of the claimant's family; or

    (c) any young person who is a member of that person's family or who was such a member and who is a member of the claimant's family.

(4) Any payment by a person who is suffering from haemophilia [²¹or who is a qualifying person], which derives from a payment under any of the Trusts to which sub-paragraph (1) refers, where—

    (a) that person has no partner or former partner from whom he is not estranged or divorced, nor any child or young person who is or had been a member of that person's family; and

    (b) the payment is made either—

        (i) to that person's parent or step-parent, or

        (ii) where that person at the date of the payment is a child, a young person or a [⁶⁶ full-time student] student who has not completed his full-time education and has no parent or step-parent, to his guardian,

but only for a period from the date of the payment until the end of two years from that person's death.

(5) Any payment out of the estate of a person who suffered from haemophilia [²¹or who was a qualifying person], which derives from a payment under any of the Trusts to which sub-paragraph (1) refers, where—

    (a) that person at the date of his death (the relevant date) had no partner or former partner from whom he was not estranged or divorced, nor any child or young person who was or had been a member of his family; and

    (b) the payment is made either—

        (i) to that person's parent or step-parent, or

        (ii) where that person at the relevant date was a child, a young person or a [⁶⁶ full-time student] who had not completed his full-time education and had no parent or step-parent, to his guardian,

but only for a period of two years from the relevant date.

(6) In the case of a person to whom or for whose benefit a payment referred to in this paragraph is made, any income which derives from any payment of income or capital made under or deriving from any of the Trusts.]

[²¹(7) For the purposes of sub-paragraphs (2) to (6), any reference to the Trusts shall be construed as including a reference to the Fund [⁹⁹, the Eileen Trust and the Skipton Fund].]]

[³**40.** Any payment made by the Secretary of State to compensate for the loss (in whole or in part) of entitlement to housing benefit.]

[⁴**41.** Any payment made by the Secretary of State to compensate a person who was entitled to supplementary benefit in respect of a period ending immediately before 11th April 1988 but who did not become entitled to income support in respect of a period beginning with that day.

42. Any payment made by the Secretary of State to compensate for the loss of housing benefit supplement under regulation 19 of the Supplementary Benefit (Requirements) Regulations 1983.

43. Any payment made to a juror or a witness in respect of attendance at a court other than compensation for loss of earnings or for the loss of a benefit payable under the benefit Acts.

44. [²³ . . .].]

[⁹**45.** Any community charge benefit.

46. Any payment in consequence of a reduction of a personal community charge pursuant to regulations under section 13A of the Local Government Finance Act 1988 or section 9A of the Abolition of Domestic Rates Etc (Scotland) Act 1987 (reduction of liability for personal community charges) [²³or reduction of council tax under section 13 or, as the case may be, section 80 of the Local Government Finance Act 1992 (reduction of liability for council tax).]

47. Any special war widows payment made under—

    (a) the Naval and Marine Pay and Pensions (Special War Widows Payment) Order 1990 made under section 3 of the Naval and Marine Pay and Pensions Act 1865;

    (b) the Royal Warrant dated 19th February 1990 amending the Schedule to the Army Pensions Warrant 1977;

    (c) the Queen's Order dated 26th February 1990 made under section 2 of the Air Force (Constitution) Act 1917;

    (d) the Home Guard War Widows Special Payments Regulations 1990 made under section 151 of the Reserve Forces Act 1980;

    (e) the Orders dated 19th February 1990 amending Orders made on 12th December 1980 concerning the Ulster Defence Regiment made in each case under section 140 of the Reserve Forces Act 1980;

and any analogous payment made by the Secretary of State for Defence to any person who is not a person entitled under the provisions mentioned in sub-paragraphs (a) to (e) of this paragraph.]

[¹²**48.**—(1) Any payment or repayment made—

    (a) as respects England and Wales, under regulation 3, 5 or 8 of the National Health Service (Travelling Expenses and Remission of Charges) Regulations 1988 (travelling expenses and health service supplies);

    (b) as respects Scotland, under regulation 3, 5 or 8 of the National Health Service (Travelling Expenses and Remission of Charges) (Scotland) Regulations 1988 (travelling expenses and health service supplies).

(2) Any payment or repayment made by the Secretary of State for Health, the Secretary of State for Scotland or the Secretary of State for Wales which is analogous to a payment or repayment mentioned in sub-paragraph (1).

49. Any payment made under regulation 9 to 11 or 13 of the Welfare Food Regulations 1988 (payments made in place of milk tokens or the supply of vitamins).

50. Any payment made either by the Secretary of State for the Home Department or by the Secretary of State for Scotland under a scheme established to assist relatives and other persons to visit persons in custody.]

[¹⁹**51.** Any payment (other than a training allowance) made, whether by the Secretary of State or by any other person, under the Disabled Persons (Employment) Act 1944 [⁹³. . .] to assist disabled persons to obtain or retain employment despite their disability.]

[²³**52.** Any council tax benefit] [⁴¹including any amount of council tax benefit to which a person is entitled by virtue of regulation 4D of the Council Tax Benefit (General) Regulations 1992 (entitlement of a refugee to council tax benefit)].]

[³⁰**53.** Where the claimant is in receipt of any benefit under Parts II, III or V of the Contributions and Benefits Act [³⁴or pension under the Naval, Military and Air Forces Etc. (Disablement and Death) Service Pensions Order 1983], any increase in the rate of that benefit arising under Part IV (increases for dependants) or section 106(a) (unemployability supplement) of that Act [³⁴or the rate of that pension under that Order] where the dependant in respect of whom the increase is paid is not a member of the claimant's family.]

[³¹**54.** Any supplementary pension under article 29(1A) of the Naval, Military and Air Forces etc. (Disablement and Death) Service Pensions Order 1983 (pensions to widows [⁸¹ or widowers]).

55. In the case of a pension awarded at the supplementary rate under article 27(3) of the Personal Injuries (Civilians) Scheme 1983 (pensions to widows [⁸¹ or widowers]), the sum specified in paragraph 1(c) of Schedule 4 to that Scheme.

56.—(1) Any payment which is—

    (a) made under any of the Dispensing Instruments to a widow [⁸¹ or widower] of a person—

        (i) whose death was attributable to service in a capacity analogous to service as a member of the armed forces of the Crown; and

        (ii) whose service in such capacity terminated before 31st March 1973; and

(b) equal to the amount specified in article 29(1A) of the Naval, Military and Air Forces etc. (Disablement and Death) Service Pensions Order 1983 (pensions to widows [⁸¹ or widowers]).

(2) In this paragraph "the Dispensing Instruments" means the Order in Council of 19th December 1881, the Royal Warrant of 27th October 1884 and the Order by His Majesty of 14th January 1922 (exceptional grants of pay, non-efective pay and allowances).]

[⁴¹**57.** Any amount of income support to which a person is entitled by virtue of [⁶² regulation 21ZB] above (treatment of refugees).]

[⁴²**58.** Any payment made under the Community Care (Direct Payments) Act 1996 or under section 12B of the Social Work (Scotland) Act 1968.

59. [⁹³ . . .]

60. [⁹³ . . .]

61. (1) Any payment specified in sub-paragraph (2) to a claimant who was formerly a [⁶⁹student] and who has completed the course in respect of which those payments were made.

(2) The payments specified for the purposes of sub-paragraph (1) are—

    (a) any grant income and covenant income as defined for the purposes of Chapter VIII of Part V;

[⁵⁷(b) any student loan as defined in Chapter VIII of Part V;

    (c) any contribution as defined in Chapter VIII of Part V which—

        (i) is taken into account in ascertaining the amount of a student loan referred to in head (b); and

        (ii) has been paid.]]

[⁷⁵ **62.** [⁹³. . .].]

[⁸² **62A.** [⁹³. . .].]

[⁴⁵**63.** [⁹³. . .].]

[⁵¹**64.**—(1) Subject to sub-paragraph (2), in the case of a person who is receiving, or who has received, assistance under [⁶⁸ "the self-employment route"] , any payment to the person—

    (a) to meet expenses wholly and necessarily incurred whilst carrying on the commercial activity;

    (b) which is used or intended to be used to maintain repayments on a loan taken out by that person for the purpose of establshing or carrying on the commercial activity, in respect of which such assistance is or was received.

(2) Sub-paragraph (1) shall apply only in respect of payments which are paid to that person from the special account as defined for the purposes of Chapter IVA of Part V.]

[⁵³**65.**[⁹³. . .].]

[⁵⁴**66.** Any payment made with respect to a person on account of the provision of after-care under section 117 of the Mental Health Act 1983 or section 8 of the Mental Health (Scotland) Act 1984 or the provision of accommodation or welfare services to which [⁶³ Part III of the National Assistance Act 1948 refers or to which the Social Work (Scotland) Act 1968 refers], which falls to be treated as notional income under paragraph (4A) of regulation 42 above (payments made in respect of a person in a residential care or nursing home).]

67. [*Omitted*]

68. [*Omitted*]

[⁵⁶**69.**—(1) Any payment of a sports award except to the extent that it has been made in respect of any one or more of the items specified in sub-paragraph (2).

(2) The items specified for the purposes of sub-paragraph (1) are food, ordinary clothing or footwear, household fuel, rent for which housing benefit is payable or any housing costs to the extent that they are met under regulation 17(1)(e) or 18(1)(f) (housing costs) [⁷⁹. . .], of the claimant or, where the claimant is a member of a family, any other member of his family, or any council tax or water charges for which that claimant or member is liable.

(3) For the purposes of sub-paragraph (2)—

"food" does not include vitamins, minerals or other special dietary supplements intended to enhance the performance of the person in the sport in respect of which the award was made;

"ordinary clothing and footwear" means clothing or footwear for normal daily use but does not include school uniforms or clothing or footwear used solely for sporting activities.]

[⁵⁹**70.** [¹⁰¹ . . .]]

[⁶⁵**71.** Where the amount of a subsistence allowance paid to a person in a benefit week exceeds the amount of income-based jobseeker's allowance that person would have received in that benefit week had it been payable to him, less 50p, that excess amount.

72. In the case of a claimant participating in an employment zone programme, any discretionary payment made by an employment zone contractor to the claimant, being a fee, grant, loan or otherwise.]

[⁸⁵ [⁹² **73.**—(1) Subject to sub-paragraph (3), any payment of child maintenance where the child or young person in respect of whom the payment is made is a member of the claimant's family except where the person making the payment is the claimant or the claimant's partner.

(2) For the purposes of sub-paragraph (1), where more than one payment of child maintenance—

(a) in respect of more than one child or young person; or

(b) made by more than one person in respect of a child or young person,

falls to be taken into account in any week, all such payments shall be aggregated and treated as if they were a single payment.

(3) No more than £10 shall be disregarded in respect of each week to which any payment of child maintenance is attributed in accordance with regulations 28, 29, 31 and 32 (calculation of income) or regulations 60B to 60D (treatment of child support maintenance).

(4) In this paragraph, "child maintenance" shall have the same meaning as that prescribed for the purposes of section 74A of the Social Security Administration Act 1992 (payment of benefit where maintenance payments collected by Secretary of State) and shall include any payment made by the Secretary of State in lieu of such maintenance.]]

[⁷¹**74.** In the case of a person to whom paragraph (5) of regulation 6 (persons not treated as in remunerative work) applies, the whole of his income.]

[⁷⁶ **75.** Any discretionary housing payment paid pursuant to regulation 2(1) of the Discretionary Financial Assistance Regulations 2001.]

[⁸⁷ [⁸⁹ **76.**—(1) Any payment made by a local authority, or by the National Assembly for Wales, to or on behalf of the claimant or his partner relating to a service which is provided to develop or sustain the capacity of the claimant or his partner to live independently in his accommodation.]

(2) For the purposes of sub-paragraph (1) "local authority" includes, in England, a county council.]

[⁸⁹ **77.** [⁹³ . . .].]

[⁹¹ **78.** [⁹³ . . .].]

AMENDMENTS

2.732   1. Income Support (General) Amendment Regulations 1988 (SI 1988/663), reg.35 (April 11, 1988).

2. Family Credit and Income Support (General) Amendment Regulations 1988 (SI 1988/999), reg.5 (June 9, 1988).

3. Income Support (General) Amendment No.4 Regulations 1988 (SI 1988/1445), reg.25 (September 12, 1988).

4. Income Support (General) Amendment No.5 Regulations 1988 (SI 1988/2022), reg.22 (December 12, 1988).

5. Income Support (General) Amendment No.4 Regulations 1988 (SI 1988/1445), Sch.1, para.9 (April 10, 1989).

6. Family Credit and Income Support (General) Amendment Regulations 1989 (SI 1989/1034), reg.12 (July 10, 1989).

7. Income Support (General) Amendment Regulations 1989 (SI 1989/534), Sch.1, para.15 (October 9, 1989).

8. Income-related Benefits Schemes Amendment Regulations 1990 (SI 1990/127), reg.3 (January 31, 1990).

9. Income Support (General) Amendment Regulations 1990 (SI 1990/547), reg.22(e) (April 1, 1990).

10. Income Support (General) Amendment Regulations 1990 (SI 1990/547), reg.22 (April 1, 1990).

11. Income-related Benefits Amendment Regulations 1990 (SI 1990/1657), reg.5(4) (September 1, 1990).

12. Income Support (General) Amendment No.3 Regulations 1990 (SI 1990/1776), reg.10 (October 1, 1990).

13. Enterprise (Scotland) Consequential Amendments Order 1991 (SI 1991/387), art.2 and 9 (April 1, 1991).

14. Income Support (General) Amendment Regulations 1991 (SI 1991/236), reg.14 (April 8, 1991).

15. Income-related Benefits Schemes and Social Security (Recoupment) Amendment Regulations 1991 (SI 1991/1175), reg.5 (May 11, 1991).

16. Income Support (General) Amendment No.4 Regulations 1991 (SI 1991/1559), reg.20 (October 7, 1991).

17. Social Security Benefits Up-rating (No.2) Order 1991 (SI 1991/2910), art.13(13) (April 6, 1992).

18. Disability Living Allowance and Disability Working Allowance (Consequential Provisions) Regulations 1991 (SI 1991/2742), reg.11(6) (April 6, 1992).

19. Income Support (General) Amendment Regulations 1992 (SI 1992/468), reg.8 (April 6, 1992).

20. Income Support (General) Amendment Regulations 1992 (SI 1992/468), Sch., para.9 (April 6, 1992).

21. Income-related Benefits Schemes and Social Security (Recoupment) Amendment Regulations 1992 (SI 1992/1101), reg.6 (May 7, 1992).

22. Social Security Benefits (Amendments Consequential Upon the Introduction of Community Care) Regulations 1992 (SI 1992/3147), Sch.1, para.7 (April 1, 1993).

23. Income-related Benefits Schemes (Miscellaneous Amendments) Regulations 1993 (SI 1993/315), Sch., para.5 (April 1, 1993).

24. Income-related Benefits Schemes (Miscellaneous Amendments) Regulations 1993 (SI 1993/315), reg.9 (council tax and council tax benefit: April 1, 1993; otherwise April 12, 1993).

25. Social Security Benefits (Miscellaneous Amendments) Regulations 1993 (SI 1993/518), reg.5 (April 1, 1993).

26. Social Security Benefits (Miscellaneous Amendments) (No.2) Regulations 1993 (SI 1993/963), reg.2(3) (April 22, 1993).

27. Income-related Benefits Schemes and Social Security (Recoupment) Amendment Regulations 1993 (SI 1993/1249), reg.4(4) (May 14, 1993).

28. Income Support (General) Amendment No.3 Regulations 1993 (SI 1993/1679), reg.6 (August 2, 1993).

29. Income-related Benefits Schemes (Miscellaneous Amendments) (No.4) Regulations 1993 (SI 1993/2119), reg.23 (October 4, 1993).

30. Income-related Benefits Schemes (Miscellaneous Amendments) Regulations 1994 (SI 1994/527), reg.9 (April 11, 1994).

31. Income-related Benefits Schemes (Miscellaneous Amendments) (No.5) Regulations 1994 (SI 1994/2139), reg.32 (October 3, 1994).

32. Income-related Benefits Schemes (Miscellaneous Amendments) Regulations 1995 (SI 1995/516), reg.27 (April 10, 1995).

33. Social Security (Income Support and Claims and Payments) Amendment Regulation 1995 (SI 1995/1613), reg.4 and Sch.3 (October 2, 1995).

34. Income-related Benefits Schemes and Social Security (Claims and Payments) (Miscellaneous Amendments) Regulations 1995 (SI 1995/2303), reg.6(9) (October 2, 1995).

35. Income-related Benefits Schemes Amendment (No.2) Regulations 1995 (SI 1995/2792), reg.6(3) (October 28, 1995).

36. Social Security (Income Support, Claims and Payments and Adjudication) Amendment Regulations 1995 (SI 1995/2927), reg.6 (December 12, 1995).

37. Income-related Benefits Schemes (Widows, etc. Pensions Disregards) Amendment Regulations 1995 (SI 1995/3282), reg.2 (December 20, 1995).

38. Income Support (General) Amendment Regulations 1996 (SI 1996/606), reg.2 (April 8, 1996).

39. Income-related Benefits Schemes (Miscellaneous Amendments) Regulations 1996 (SI 1996/462), reg.8 (April 8, 1996).

40. Social Security Benefits Up-rating Order 1996 (SI 1996/599), reg.18(13) (April 8, 1996).

41. Income Support and Social Security (Claims and Payments) (Miscellaneous Amendments) Regulations 1996 (SI 1996/2431), reg.5 (October 15, 1996).

42. Income-related Benefits and Jobseeker's Allowance (Miscellaneous Amendments) Regulations 1997 (SI 1997/65), reg.2(3) (April 7, 1997).

43. Income-related Benefits and Jobseeker's Allowance (Amendment) (No. 2) Regulations 1997 (SI 1997/2197), reg.7(7) and (8)(e) (October 6, 1997).

44. Social Security Amendment (New Deal) Regulations 1997 (SI 1997/ 2863), reg.17(7) and (8)(e) (January 5, 1998).

45. Social Security Amendment (New Deal) Regulations 1997 (SI 1997/ 2863), reg.17(9) and (10)(e) (January 5, 1998).

46. Social Security (Miscellaneous Amendments) Regulations 1998 (SI 1998/ 563), reg.7(3) and (4)(e) (April 6, 1998).

47. Social Security (Miscellaneous Amendments) Regulations 1998 (SI 1998/ 563), reg.13(1)(c) (April 6, 1998).

48. Social Security (Miscellaneous Amendments) Regulations 1998 (SI 1998/ 563), reg.15(1) (April 6, 1998).

49. Social Security (Miscellaneous Amendments) Regulations 1998 (SI 1998/ 563), reg.15(2) (April 6, 1998).

50. Social Security (Miscellaneous Amendments) (No.3) Regulations 1998 (SI 1998/1173), reg.4 (June 1, 1998).

51. Social Security (Miscellaneous Amendments) (No.4) Regulations 1998 (SI 1998/1174), reg.6(4) (June 1, 1998).

52. Social Security (Miscellaneous Amendments) (No.4) Regulations 1998 (SI 1998/1174), reg.7(3) and (4)(e) (June 1, 1998).

53. Social Security Amendment (New Deal) (No.2) Regulations 1998 (SI 1998/2117), reg.4(4) (September 24, 1998).

54. Social Security Amendment (New Deal) (No.2) Regulations 1998 (SI 1998/2117), reg.6(2) (September 24, 1998).

55. Social Security Amendment (Educational Maintenance Allowance) Regulations 1999 (SI 1999/1677), reg.2(1) and (2)(e) (August 16, 1999).

56. Social Security Amendment (Sports Awards) Regulations 1999 (SI 1999/ 2165), reg.6(4) (August 23, 1999).

57. Social Security Amendment (Students) Regulations 1999 (SI 1999/1935), reg.3(8) (August 30, 1999, or if the student's period of study begins between August 1 and 29, 1999, the first day of the period).

58. Income Support (General) Amendment Regulations 1999 (SI 1999/ 2554), reg.2(3) (October 4, 1999).

59. Social Security (Miscellaneous Amendments) (No.2) Regulations 1999 (SI 1999/2556), reg.2(10) (October 4, 1999).

60. Social Security Amendment (Education Maintenance Allowance) Regulations 2000 (SI 2000/55), reg.2(1) and (2)(c) (February 7, 2000).

61. Social Security (Immigration and Asylum) Consequential Amendments Regulations 2000 (SI 2000/636), reg.3(12) (April 3, 2000).

62. Social Security (Immigration and Asylum) Consequential Amendments Regulations 2000 (SI 2000/636), reg.3(13) (April 3, 2000).

63. Social Security (Miscellaneous Amendments) Regulations 2000 (SI 2000/ 681), reg.7 (April 3, 2000).

64. Social Security (Miscellaneous Amendments) Regulations 2000 (SI 2000/ 681), reg.12(a) (April 3, 2000).

65. Social Security Amendment (Employment Zones) Regulations 2000 (SI 2000/724), reg.3(3) (April 3, 2000).

66. Social Security Amendment (Students) Regulations 2000 (SI 2000/1981), reg.5(5) and Sch. (July 31, 2000).

67. Social Security Amendment (Students and Income-related Benefits) Regulations 2000 (SI 2000/1922), reg.2(9) (August 28, 2000, or if the student's

period of study begins between August 1 and 27, 2000, the first day of the period).

68. Social Security Amendment (Employment Zones) (No.2) Regulations 2000 (SI 2000/2910), reg.4(1) and (2)(c)(i) (November 27, 2000).

69. Income Support (General) Amendment Regulations 2001 (SI 2001/721), reg.2(c) (March 29, 2001).

70. Social Security Amendment (Bereavement Benefits) Regulations 2000 (SI 2000/2239), reg.2(4) (April 9, 2001).

71. Social Security (Miscellaneous Amendments) Regulations 2001 (SI 2001/488), reg.9 (April 9, 2001).

72. Social Security (Miscellaneous Amendments) (No.3) Regulations 2001 (SI 2001/859), reg.3(5) (April 9, 2001).

73. Social Security (Miscellaneous Amendments) (No.3) Regulations 2001 (SI 2001/859), reg.6(3)(c) (April 9, 2001).

74. Social Security Amendment (New Deal) Regulations 2001 (SI 2001/ 1029), reg.15(10) and (11)(c) (April 9, 2001).

75. Social Security Amendment (New Deal) Regulations 2001 (SI 2001/ 1029), reg.15(12) and (13)(c) (April 9, 2001).

76. Social Security Amendment (Discretionary Housing Payments) Regulations 2001 (SI 2001/2333), reg.2(1)(c) (July 2, 2001).

77. Social Security Amendment (Volunteers) Regulations 2001 (SI 2001/ 2296), reg.2(1) and (2)(c) (September 24, 2001).

78. Children (Leaving Care) Act 2000 (Commencement No.2 and Con sequential Provisions) Order 2001 (SI 2001/3070), art.3(2) and para.(c) of Sch.1 (October 1, 2001).

79. Social Security Amendment (Residential Care and Nursing Homes) Regulations 2001 (SI 2001/3767), reg.2(1) and Pt I of Sch. para.19 (April 8, 2002).

80. Social Security Benefits Up-rating Order 2002 (SI 2002/668), art.16(9) (April 8, 2002).

81. Social Security (Miscellaneous Amendments) Regulations 2002 (SI 2002/ 841), reg.2(4) (April 8, 2002).

82. Social Security Amendment (Employment Programme) Regulations 2002 (SI 2002/2314), reg.3(3) (October 14, 2002).

83. Social Security (Miscellaneous Amendments) (No.2) Regulations 2002 (SI 2002/2380), reg.2(a) ((October 14, 2002).

84. Social Security Amendment (Personal Injury Payments) Regulations 2002 (SI 2002/2442), reg.3(1)(d) and (2)(c) (October 28, 2002).

85. Social Security (Child Maintenance Premium and Miscellaneous Amendments) Regulations 2000 (SI 2000/3176), reg.2(1)(b) (in force in relation to any particular case on the day on which s.23 CSPSSA 2000 comes into force in relation to that type of case).

86. Social Security (Paternity and Adoption) Amendment Regulations 2002 (SI 2002/2689), reg.2(6) (December 8, 2002).

87. Social Security (Miscellaneous Amendments) Regulations 2003 (SI 2003/ 511), reg.2(2) (April 1, 2003)

88. Social Security (Working Tax Credit and Child Tax Credit) (Consequential Amendments) Regulations 2003 (SI 2003/455), reg.2 and Sch.1, para.23(a) (April 7, 2003).

89. Social Security (Miscellaneous Amendments) (No.2) Regulations 2003 (SI 2003/2279), reg.2(4) (October 1, 2003).

90. Social Security (Removal of Residential Allowance and Miscellaneous Amendments) Regulations 2003 (SI 2003/1121), reg.2 and Sch.1, para.9 (October 6, 2003).

91. Social Security (Incapacity Benefit Work-focused Interviews) Regulations 2003 (SI 2003/2439), reg.13(a) (October 27, 2003).

92. Social Security (Child Maintenance Premium) Amendment Regulations 2004 (SI 2004/98), reg.2 (in force on (i) February 16, 2004 in relation to any particular

case in respect of which s.23 CSPSSA 2000 has come into force before February 16, 2004; (ii) where this does not apply, the day on which s.23 comes into force in relation to that type of case; (iii) February 16, 2004 in relation to a person who is entitled to income support/income-based JSA on that date and who receives her first payment of child maintenance made voluntarily whilst entitled to income support/income-based JSA on that date; (iv) in such a case where the day that the first voluntary payment is received is after February 16, 2004, the day the payment is received; (v) February 16, 2004 in relation to a person who makes a claim for income support/income-based JSA on or after that date and receives a payment of child maintenance made voluntarily on or after the date of that claim).

93. Social Security (Miscellaneous Amendments) Regulations 2004 (SI 2004/565), reg.2(3) (April 1, 2004).

94. Social Security (Working Tax Credit and Child Tax Credit) (Consequential Amendments) Regulations 2003 (SI 2003/455), reg.2 and Sch.1, para.23 (except sub-para.(a) (April 6, 2004, except in "transitional cases" and see further the note to reg.17 of the Income Support Regulations).

95. Social Security (Miscellaneous Amendments) (No. 2) Regulations 2004 (SI 2004/1141), reg.4(1) and (2)(c) (May 12, 2004).

96. Social Security (Miscellaneous Amendments) (No. 2) Regulations 2004 (SI 2004/1141), reg.4(3) and (4)(c) (May 12, 2004).

97. Social Security (Students and Income-related Benefits) Amendment Regulations 2004 (SI 2004/1708), reg.5(2) (September 1, 2004, or if the student's period of study begins between August 1 and August 31, 2004, the first day of the period).

98. Social Security (Miscellaneous Amendments) (No. 3) Regulations 2004 (SI 2004/2308), reg.2(1) and (2)(a) (October 4, 2004).

99. Social Security (Miscellaneous Amendments) (No. 3) Regulations 2004 (SI 2004/2308), reg.3(3) and (4)(a) (October 4, 2004).

100. Social Security (Miscellaneous Amendments) (No. 3) Regulations 2004 (SI 2004/2308), reg.4(3) and (4)(a) (October 4, 2004).

101. Social Security (Back to Work Bonus and Lone Parent Run-on) (Amendment and Revocation) Regulations 2003 (SI 2003/1589), reg.2(d) (October 25, 2004).

102. Social Security (Miscellaneous Amendments) Regulations 2005 (SI 2005/574), reg.2(7) and (8)(a) (April 4, 2005).

103. Social Security (Miscellaneous Amendments) Regulations 2005 (SI 2005/574), reg.3(5) (April 4, 2005).

104. Social Security Benefits Up-rating Order 2005 (SI 2005/522), art.16(9) (April 11, 2005).

DEFINITIONS

2.733 "access funds"—see reg.61(1).
"the Act"—see reg.2(1).
"adoption leave"—*ibid.*
"attendance allowance"—*ibid.*
"the benefit Acts"—*ibid.*
"benefit week"—*ibid.*
"child"—see 1986 Act, s.20(11) (SSCBA, s.137(1)).
"the Children Order"—see reg.2(1).
"claimant"—*ibid.*
"contribution"—see reg.61.
"course of study"—see reg.2(1).
"disability living allowance"—*ibid.*
"dwelling occupied as the home"—*ibid.*
"employed earner"—*ibid.*
"employment zone contractor"—*ibid.*
"employment zone programme"—*ibid.*

"family"—see 1986 Act, s.20(11) (SSCBA, s.137(1)).
"full-time student"—see reg.61(1).
"a guaranteed income payment—see reg.2(1).
"Immigration and Asylum Act"—*ibid.*
"Intensive Activity Period for 50 plus"—*ibid.*
"maternity leave"—*ibid.*
"mobility allowance"—see reg.2(1).
"mobility supplement"—*ibid.*
"nursing home"—*ibid.*, reg.19(3).
"occupational pension"—see reg.2(1).
"occupational pension scheme"—see Pension Schemes Act 1993, s.1.
"partner of a person subject to immigration control"—see reg.21(3).
"paternity leave"—see reg.2(1).
"payment"—*ibid.*
"personal pension scheme"—*ibid.*
"qualifying person"—*ibid.*
"remunerative work"—see reg.2(1), reg.5.
"residential care home"—see reg.2(1), reg.19(3).
"retirement annuity contract"—see reg.2(1).
"self-employment route"—*ibid.*
"Social Security Act"—*ibid.*
"special account"—see reg.39A.
"sports award"—see reg.2(1).
"student loan"—see reg.61.
"subsistence allowance"—see reg.2(1).
"the Eileen Trust"—*ibid.*
"the Fund"—*ibid.*
"the Independent Living Funds"—*ibid.*
"the Macfarlane (Special Payments) Trust"—*ibid.*
"the Macfarlane (Special Payments) (No.2) Trust"—*ibid.*
"the Macfarlane Trust"—*ibid.*
"the Skipton Fund"—*ibid.*
"training allowance"—*ibid.*
"voluntary organisation"—*ibid.*
"young person"—*ibid.* reg.14.

GENERAL NOTE

Para. 1

There is no provision in Chap. V itself for deducting tax. So if taxable payments are treated as income under reg.40 a disregard is needed.   2.734

CIS/1067/2004, to be reported as *R(IS) 4/05*, decides that "any amount paid by way of tax" includes tax that is to be paid. The claimant's income support claim had been rejected because her state retirement pension exceeded her applicable amount. Her retirement pension was paid gross, with any tax due being payable by her in a lump sum following the end of the tax year. The claimant produced a forecast from the Inland Revenue, which estimated her likely tax liability for the current year. She contended that this amount should be deducted from her retirement pension. The Commissioner agreed. He held that the disregard in para.1 is not concerned with the time at which tax is paid. It applies to tax which at the date of the benefit decision either has been, or is to be, paid, the only condition being that it is tax on income which is being taken into account under reg.40. The tax to be disregarded is the tax paid or due on the income attributable to the benefit weeks in question, not the tax payable in respect of earlier tax years. Where the tax payable is an annual sum, reg.32(1) provides a method for calculating the weekly amount.

As a consequence of this decision guidance has been issued to decision-makers (DMG Letter 04/05) which states that if a claimant provides evidence, such as a forecast from the Inland Revenue, which shows the tax due on income other than earnings paid to him for the current year, the amount of the estimated tax should be disregarded and the net amount taken into account.

Para. 2

2.735   A payment purely of expenses to a volunteer or someone working for a charity or a voluntary organisation is disregarded unless the person is caught by reg.42(6) on underpaid services. The September 2001 amendment allows an advance payment of expenses to be disregarded. A volunteer is someone who without any legal obligation performs a service for another person without expectation of payment (*R(IS) 12/92*).

Para. 3

2.736   Such payments are not earnings (reg.35(2)), but are income (reg.40(4)). See the notes to reg.35(1)(f) for "wholly, exclusively and necessarily." *CFC 2/1989* might suggest that payments made by the employee for necessary, etc., expenses out of such income are to be deducted from that income. But that is not consistent with the scheme of the legislation and is rejected in *R(FC) 1/90, R(IS) 16/ 93* and *CIS 77/1993*. See the notes to reg.35(2). However, note the effect of the application of the principle in *Parsons v Hogg* to the meaning of "gross earnings" (see the notes to reg.36(3)).

Paras 4 and 4A

2.737   The standard deductions are to be made from contractual or statutory sick, maternity, paternity or adoption leave pay, which are not earnings (reg.35(2)), but are income (reg.40(4)).

Para. 5

See also paras 40, 42, 45, 46 and 52.

2.738   In *CIS 521/2002* the claimant was one of four partners who ran a hotel providing board and lodging accommodation for the homeless. Under reg.37(2)(a) payments received for providing board and lodging accommodation do not count as earnings from self-employment. They count as income under reg.40(4)(a) and thus any appropriate disregard in Sch.9 may apply. The board and lodging charges were primarily met by housing benefit which was paid direct to the partnership. The Commissioner raises the point that such payments would seem to come within para.5 (although he did not have to reach a conclusion on the issue). However, to apply the disregard to direct payments of housing benefit to landlords would draw a line between such landlords and those receiving rent from tenants who had housing benefit paid to them and there seemed to be no reason for such a distinction. For further discussion of *CIS 521/2002* see the note to para.20 below.

Note the April 2005 amendment which is intended to make clear that it is only payments of housing benefit to which the claimant is entitled that are ignored under para.5 and that the disregard does not extend to housing benefit paid direct to the claimant as a landlord. This amendment was made as a result of the Commissioner's decision in *CH/2321/2002* on the ambit of the disregard in para.27(b) (see the note to para.27) but it also deals with the point raised by the Commissioner in *CIS/521/2002*.

Para. 5A

A new disregard of guardian's allowance has been introduced as part of the changes associated with the start of child tax credit in April 2003.

Para. 5B

With effect from April 6, 2004 (except in "transitional cases"—see the note to reg.17), amounts for children and young persons have been removed from the income support scheme; financial assistance to help with the cost of bringing up a child or young person is now to be provided through the child tax credit system, see Vol. IV of this series. As part of the changes associated with the introduction of child tax credit child benefit and child tax credit are ignored (except in "transitional cases—see the note to reg.17).

For income support claimants who had an award of child tax credit before April 6, 2004 see reg.7 of the Social Security (Working Tax Credit and Child Tax Credit) (Consequential Amendments) Regulations 2003 (SI 2003/455) (as amended) on p.686 and the notes to that regulation.

Para. 6

The former mobility allowance or the mobility component of disability living allowance is disregarded. See also paras 7 and 8.

2.739

Para. 9

The general rule is that attendance allowance and the care component of disability living allowance is disregarded.

2.740

However, for most claimants in residential care, attendance allowance and the care component of disability living allowance will normally cease to be payable after a claimant has been a resident in a residential care or nursing home for four weeks. (See *CPAG's Welfare Benefits and Tax Credits Handbook* as to when people in residential care and nursing homes may continue to receive attendance allowance or the care component of disability living allowance without restriction.)

From October 6, 2003 there is no longer any special provision under this paragraph for claimants living in Polish resettlement homes (with the introduction of state pension credit on October 6, 2003, claimants living in Ilford Park Polish Home, the only remaining resettlement home, are unlikely to qualify for income support in any event because of their age). See the 2003 edition of this volume for the form of para.9 in force before October 6, 2003 (and the notes to that paragraph for the other special cases previously dealt with in para.9).

Para. 11

Education maintenance allowances (EMAs) are disregarded in full.

2.741

A national scheme for the payment of EMAs has been introduced from the start of the 2004/5 academic year (this replaces the previous pilot project). EMAs are payable for up to two years to 16–18 year-olds (in some cases for up to three years to 16–19 year-olds) who remain in non-advanced education after the age of 16. Under the national scheme they include weekly payments (depending on income), together with periodic bonuses. The allowance is fully disregarded when calculating entitlement to income support, JSA, working tax credit and child tax credit (as well as housing benefit and council tax benefit). For the capital disregard see para.63 of Sch.10 (the equivalent JSA provisions are in para.12 of Sch.7 and para.52 of Sch.8 to the JSA Regulations). The new form of para.11 has been introduced so that it reflects all the legislation under which EMAs are paid; sub-para.(2) also applies the disregard to payments (*e.g.* scholarships or expenses) which are paid in respect of courses of education to "a child or a young person or a person who is in receipt of an education maintenance allowance" (this wording is necessary because in some cases an EMA can be paid to a person who does not come within the definition of "young person" because he is not under 19).

Para. 11A

As part of the Government's strategy to recruit and retain teachers, s.186 of the Education Act 2002 and the Education (Teacher Student Loans) (Repayment, etc.) Regulations 2002 provide for the reduction/extinguishment of the amount owing on student loans for newly qualified teachers in shortage subjects working in England and Wales. The scheme operates differently depending on where the student loan was originally incurred. For those teachers who took out student loans while living

2.742

in England and Wales the Department for Education and Skills will simply waive repayment. However, for those who took out their loans while living in Scotland, Northern Ireland or another EEA country, annual payments will be made to the teacher over a number of years to enable them to repay the Student Loan Company. Under the new para.11A any such payments are disregarded.

Para. 13

2.743   The new form of para.13 in force from April 1, 2004 has been introduced in order to provide a single disregard of the various allowances, grants and other payments made under s.2 of the Employment and Training Act 1973 or s.2 of the Enterprise and New Towns (Scotland) Act 1990 to people participating in New Deals and other training and welfare to work schemes. Before April 1, 2004 separate disregards had existed in respect of such payments under a number of the provisions in this Schedule. As a consequence of this change, those provisions have been revoked or amended. The revoked paragraphs are paras 59, 60, 62, 62A, 63, 65, 77 and 78; the two paragraphs that have been amended are paras 51 and 70.

Sub-para.(1) provides that payments under s.2 of the 1973 Act or s.2 of the 1990 Act are ignored *unless* they are (i) paid instead of income support, JSA, incapacity benefit or severe disablement allowance (*e.g.*, a New Deal allowance) (sub-para.(1)(a)); (ii) payments of a "bridging allowance" to a young person under s.2(3) of the 1973 Act (s.2(5) of the 1990 Act) (sub-para.(1)(b)); (iii) intended to cover food, ordinary clothing or footwear (defined in sub-para.(3)), fuel, housing costs met by income support or rent for which housing benefit is payable, council tax or water charges while the claimant is on an education, training or other scheme to help "enhance his employment prospects", but not if the payment is a Career Development Loan and the period of education or training in respect of which the loan was paid has ended (sub-paras (1)(c) and (2)); or (iv) paid for living away from home costs which overlap with housing benefit (sub-para.(1)(d)).

A single capital disregard of such payments has also been introduced at the same time. See para.30 of Sch.10. If these payments do count as capital they are only ignored for 52 weeks from the date of receipt.

Para. 15

2.744   The amendments made to para.15 with effect from October 28, 2002 apply the disregard for charitable and voluntary payments to regular payments from funds derived from a personal injury award to the claimant. In the case of the latter, the disregard is applicable whether the payments are made from a trust fund, or under an annuity, or by virtue of an agreement or court order. This new disregard thus ameliorates the problem highlighted by *Beattie v Secretary of State for Social Security*, April 9, 2001, reported as part of *R(IS) 10/01* (see the note to reg.41(2)).

If regular charitable or voluntary payments or payments from funds derived from a personal injury award to the claimant are intended and used for items other than those listed in sub-para.(2) they are disregarded (sub-para.(2)). Note the exceptions in sub-para.(3) and para.39. Otherwise the normal disregard is £20, subject to the overall £20 disregard in para.36 (sub-para.(1)). The purpose of the October 4, 2004 amendment is to clarify that payments for council tax and water charges are subject to the £20 limit on the disregard. It was considered that the previous wording allowed payments for council tax and water charges to be disregarded in full and this is not the policy intention. The provision assumes that such charitable or voluntary payments amount to income. Reg.41(7) treats any periodical payments paid under an agreement or court order to a claimant in consequence of personal injury to him, other than payments deemed to be capital (see reg.48(4)), as income. Irregular charitable or voluntary payments count as capital (reg.48(9)).

In *CH 2820/2003* (which concerned a similar provision in para.13 of Sch.4 to the Housing Benefit Regulations) the Commissioner refers to the fact that the precise purpose for which voluntary payments are made is not always expressed and that it is difficult to anticipate how they will be used or to trace how they have been used.

In such cases the purpose and use of the payments has to be ascertained from the surrounding circumstances. It was reasonable to make three assumptions: (i) that a claimant would give priority to paying for basic essentials and housing costs over other items; (ii) that his applicable amount (excluding any "eligible housing costs" in an income support case) was sufficient to meet the basic essentials; and (iii) that a person making a voluntary payment to the claimant intends the payment to supplement the claimant's other income (ignoring for this purpose possible entitlement to an income-related benefit) and that the claimant receives it on that basis and so pays for basic essentials and housing costs using the other income first and then using the voluntary payment. On that basis a voluntary payment could be presumed to be used for basic essentials and housing costs to the extent that it was necessary to meet the gap between the claimant's "applicable amount" plus any "eligible rent" and his other income (unless the voluntary payment was specifically earmarked for another purpose). Equally, however, it could be presumed to be intended and used for other purposes if the claimant's income exceeded his "applicable amount" plus any "eligible rent". In the present case the claimant's pensions just exceeded his applicable amount plus his rent (the whole of his rent was eligible). The Commissioner therefore concluded that the voluntary payments from his son were intended and used for items other than food, household fuel, rent or ordinary clothing or footwear with the result that they fell to be fully disregarded.

The Secretary of State appealed to the Court of Appeal on the ground that the Commissioner had been wrong to make such general presumptions or assumptions. In *Secretary of State for Work and Pensions v Perkins and Ryedale District Council* [2004] EWCA Civ 1671 the Court agreed that a tribunal should not make assumptions or presume anything. However it could, and should, draw inferences from the facts if they were warranted in the circumstances. The Court concluded that even though the Commissioner had expressed his views in forceful terms, using words such as "presumed" and "assumption", he had not been wrong to reach the conclusion that he did on the facts of this case. He could have drawn the inferences that he did and he had also had the advantage of being able to hear evidence from the claimant at the hearing. The Court therefore dismissed the appeal. Sedley L.J., however, distinguished the second of the Commissioner's assumptions on the basis that this was a mixed question of fact and law. The statutory purpose of the applicable amount was, in broad terms, to quantify the needs to be met and he therefore considered that this purpose could legitimately enter into an inference a tribunal was contemplating drawing about the intended use of a voluntary or charitable payment.

There is no special definition of "charitable" or "voluntary." The words must be applied to whoever makes the payment. In *R. v Doncaster B C Ex p. Boulton, The Times*, December 31, 1992, on the equivalent provision in housing benefit, Laws J. holds that the word "charitable" appearing in a statute providing for the distribution and calculation of legal rights must refer only to payments under a charitable trust, rather than referring to acts done for some generous motive. He finds the legislative purpose to be to allow charities to make payments to claimants knowing that they will not simply reduce the amount of benefit. That decision must be highly persuasive, but does not preempt the income support position.

Laws J. also takes a different view to that expressed in the 1992 edition Mesher, *Income-related Benefits: the Legislation* on the meaning of "voluntary." He holds that it does not refer to a payment which is not compulsory or not legally enforceable, but to a payment for which the person making the payment gets nothing in return. It does not matter that in voluntarily undertaking the payment the person comes under an obligation. The legislative purpose would then be consistent with that for charitable payments. He then had to apply this principle to payments by the National Coal Board in lieu of concessionary coal to a miner's widow. The concessionary coal scheme and the conditions for the payment of cash in lieu, including to widows, is contained in a collective agreement which is incorporated into miners' contracts of employment. Laws J. holds that neither he nor the Housing Benefit Review Board had sufficient evidence of the particular contractual arrangements to be able to conclude that under the principle of *Beswick v Beswick* [1968] A.C. 58 the widow could as administratrix of her husband's estate obtain specific performance of the contract to make payments to his widow. However, he was satisfied that the NCB did receive something in return for payments made under the collective agreement, in the promotion of the efficient running of the coal industry. An element of this purpose was seeing that employees, ex-employees and their spouses were properly looked after. Therefore, he finds that the payments were not voluntary and the disregard did not apply. On this point also, the *Boulton* case cannot be conclusive for income support purposes, but is cogently argued and persuasive. It has been applied to para.15 in *R(IS) 4/94*. In *CIS 702/1991* an annuity had been purchased for the claimant under the terms of her friend's will. It was argued that the payments under the annuity were "voluntary" as in essence there was a gift of them from the friend under the will. It is held that the disregard in para.15 did not apply since the payments under the annuity were contractual in nature. That was consistent with the decision of Laws J. in the *Boulton* case. See also *CIS 492/1992*.

However the irregular payments received by the claimant in *CH/3013/2003*, to be reported as *R(H) 5/05*, from a friend and his parents following his inability to work after a stroke were "voluntary". The friend had written a letter which indicated that the payments from her were by way of a loan to be repaid at some unspecified date. But in the Commissioner's view the payments were made without any clear thought about their legal nature. The overall circumstances showed that no legally enforceable rights or obligations were created by the payments to the claimant and that she obtained nothing in return for the payments. The Commissioner commented that "if something like the maintenance of a relationship of affection or of familial duty on the part of the payer or the creation of a merely moral obligation on the part of the payee, dependent on undefined future developments, takes a case out of the category of "voluntary payment" nothing significant would be left". Thus, applying *Boulton*, since the friend had obtained nothing in return for the payments she made to the claimant by way of loan, they were voluntary payments within the meaning of reg.40(6) of the Housing Benefit Regulations (the equivalent of reg.48(9); it was accepted that the payments were not regular and therefore fell to be treated as capital). The payments from the claimant's parents, where the presumption of gift applied in the absence of evidence to the contrary, also fell within reg.40(6).

If regular payments are not charitable or voluntary or made from funds derived from a personal injury award to the claimant, they count as ordinary income with no disregard.

Para.15A

2.745   Where a claimant is newly placed after April 1, 1993, by a local authority in a residential care or nursing home whose fee is more expensive than would normally be met, charitable or voluntary payments may be disregarded in so far as they make up the difference. This is only so if the reason for the placement is the choice of the claimant.

Para.16

2.746   The £10 disregard under sub-para.(a) only applies if the payment is not fully disregarded under paras 8 or 9.

"War disablement pension" is not defined in either these Regulations or any relevant part of the Contributions and Benefits Act 1992. However, it was defined in s.84(1) of the Social Security Act 1986. When these regulations were first introduced they were made under the 1986 Act. Thus, in the absence of any other definition, the meaning in s.84(1) applies (*CIS 276/1998*; see Interpretation Act 1978, s.11). Section 84(1) defined a war disablement pension as:

"(a) any retired pay, pension or allowance granted in respect of disablement under powers conferred by or under the Air Force (Constitution) Act 1917, the Personal Injuries (Emergency Provisions) Act 1939, the Pensions (Navy, Army, Air Force and Mercantile Marine) Act 1939, the Polish Resettlement Act 1947 or Part VII or s.151 of the Reserve Forces Act 1980;

(b) without prejudice to para.(a) of this definition, any retired pay or pension to which sub-section(1) of s.365 of the Income and Corporation Taxes Act 1970 applies".

The claimant in *CIS 276/1998* was discharged from the RAF on medical grounds and was awarded a service invaliding pension. This pension was exempt from income tax under s.315 of the Income and Corporation Taxes Act 1988 (formerly s.365 of the 1970 Act). The AO treated the pension as an occupational pension. But the Commissioner holds that the concepts of occupational pension and war disablement pension were not mutually exclusive. The claimant's pension clearly fell within para.(b) of the definition in s.84(1) and so it was also a war disablement pension. He was thus entitled to a £10 disregard under sub-para.(a).

On sub-para.(cc), see the note to the definition of *"the Armed Forces and Reserve Forces Compensation Scheme"* in reg.2(1).

Para. 17

If a person takes out one of these schemes for converting the capital value of the home into income, then so much of the annuity as goes to the mortgage interest is disregarded. The conditions are complicated. Only schemes entered by those aged at least 65 count.   2.747

Para. 18

The inter-relationship of this and the following two paragraphs is now much clearer.   2.748
The new form of this paragraph, together with the amendment to para.19, was introduced in April 1995, following the decision in *CIS 82/1993*. The Commissioner held that on the previous wording the dividing line between paras 18 and 19 was not whether a payment for accommodation was made under a contractual obligation, but whether or not the payment was made by a person who normally resided with the claimant. Para.19 only applied where the person did not normally reside with the claimant. (See the 1994 Supplement to *Mesher and Wood, Income-related Benefits: the Legislation* for a summary of the Commissioner's reasoning.) "Normally resides" in para.18 had no special meaning (*cf.* reg.3) and could include someone who was liable to make payments to the claimant for his occupation of the claimant's home. On the facts, the two "lodgers" who shared the claimant's flat, and each paid him £70 per week, did reside with him. The result was that para.18, not para.19, applied. "Payment" could include part of a payment (see reg.2(1)), so the proportion of each payment that went to meeting the "lodger's" living and accommodation costs could be disregarded under para.18 (*CIS 422/1992* followed). The evidence was that the benefit of the outgoings on the flat was shared more or less equally between the three occupants, so the Commissioner divided the rent, water rates and fuel costs by three and added to this the cost of the services provided by the claimant (*e.g.* laundry, routine repairs and replacements). This led to a much larger proportion of each payment (£47) being disregarded, than would have been the case if para.19 applied.

The new form of para.18, and the amendment to para.19, have dealt with most of the difficulties exposed in *CIS 82/1993* regarding the inter-relationship of these two paragraphs. Paras 18, 19 and 20 can now all apply where the person is residing with the claimant, so the problem identified in the 1994 edition of *Mesher and Wood, Income-related Benefits: the Legislation* no longer exists. If para.18 applies, payments by someone who normally resides with the claimant towards his own living and accommodation costs continue to be wholly disregarded. The new wording confirms, as decided in *CIS 422/1992* and *CIS 82/1993*, that it is only payments towards the "lodger's" living expenses that are disregarded (see above). However, para.18 does not apply in the circumstances covered by paras 19 and 20, so that those provisions must be looked at first. The intention is that payments from sub-tenants and licensees should fall within para.19, not para.18 (see below).

If the person making the payment is a non-dependant (see reg.3), note that standard deductions are made from housing costs for the presence of a non-dependant in the household (see para.18 of Sch.3).

Para.19

2.749   Whenever the person occupying the claimant's home has a contractual liability to make payments (an oral agreement will suffice: *CIS 1501/2002*), this paragraph will now apply. This is certainly wide enough to cover income from subtenants and licensees. The disregard is small. People referred to in paras 18 and 20 are no longer excluded, but para.18 does not apply if the circumstances come within para.19 (see above). Although some payments could fall within both para.19 and para.20, it does not matter that there is no provision for choosing between them, for a claimant can simply take advantage of the more generous disregard in para.20 when the conditions of that paragraph are met (*CIS 82/1993*).

In *CIS 82/1993* the Commissioner raised the possibility of whether the disregard in para.30(d) (now para.30(1)(e)) (contribution intended and used towards rent) might apply to payments by a sub-tenant or licensee of a tenant. He accepted the AO's submission that in view of the specific provisions in paras 18, 19 and 20, para.30(d) (now (1)(e)) did not cover such payments, but did consider that legislative clarification of the relationship between para.30 and para.18, 19 and 20 would be useful. It is not clear on the wording of para.30(1)(e) why payments from a subtenant or licensee should be excluded, provided that they are intended and used as a contribution towards rent not met by housing benefit. Payments may be disregarded under more than one paragraph of Sch.9, provided this is not specifically prescribed. Para.30(1)(e) does not refer to payments under paras 18, 19 or 20; the only payments that are specifically excluded from para.30 are those covered by para.29. Indeed this was the approach taken by the Commissioner in *CIS 13059/1996*, who declined to follow *CIS 82/1993* on this point. He decides that para.30 can apply at the same time as any of paras 18 to 20 because paras 18 to 20 are not concerned with the same sort of payments as para.30. Para. 30 makes provision for disregarding payments designed to help meet certain elements of a claimant's housing expenditure, whereas this is not the specific purpose of paras 18 to 20. See further the notes to para.30.

In April 1994 the wording of para.19 was tightened up so that only one disregard per week applies to payments for each licence or subtenancy. On the pre-April 1994 form a separate disregard could have applied to each payment regardless of the period covered by it (*e.g.* daily).

Para.20

2.750   This disregard (and not para.18) applies when a person provides board and lodging accommodation in his home. The post-April 1994 form makes it clear that only one disregard is allowed per week per boarder (see the notes to para.19).

Under reg.37(2)(a) payments received for providing board and lodging accommodation do not count as earnings from self-employment. They count as income under reg.40(4)(a) and thus any appropriate disregard in Sch.9 may apply. In *CIS 521/2002* the claimant was a partner in a board and lodging business run in what was formerly a fully-fledged hotel. As the claimant lived in the hotel (and on the basis that she was to be regarded as living in the whole hotel as her home) para.20 applied. The issue was how her income was to be calculated. The Commissioner holds that the full disregard under sub-para.(b) in respect of each boarder was to be applied to her share of the weekly board and lodging payments. As the Commissioner points out, there is no provision in para.20 for cases of partnerships or for taking into account only a proportion of the total number of persons being provided with board and lodging. The consequence was that the claimant had no income to be taken into account for the purposes of income support. For further discussion of *CIS 521/2002* see the note to reg.37(2). See also the note to para.5 above.

Para.21

Income in kind is normally disregarded but note the exceptions. Earnings in kind are not earnings (reg.35(2)), but are income. There is some scope for benefit planning here, but note *R(IS) 2/98* in the notes to reg.42(6) (notional earnings). On the first exception in sub-para.(1) and on sub-para.(3) see the notes to reg.21(3).

2.751

Para.22

The general rule is that the actual income derived from capital is disregarded as income. It can go to increase the amount of capital under reg.48(4). But income in the categories specified—premises, business assets and trusts of (but not funds held in court that derive from) personal injury compensation (see the note to reg.48(4))— is not disregarded. Where this income is from premises whose capital value is disregarded, any mortgage repayments, water charges and council tax can be set off against it. Mortgage repayments in sub-para.(2)(a) include capital and interest, buildings insurance, and if an endowment policy is a condition of the mortgage, premiums on that policy (*CFC 13/1993*). *CIS 563/ 1991* deals with the situation where both a disregard in the excepted categories and a disregard under some other paragraph of Sch.10 apply. See the notes to reg.48(4) and see also *CIS 2211/2002* and *CIS 929/2000* in those notes.

2.752

Para.24

In *CIS 627/1995* the Commissioner puts forward the view that since para.24 disregards the *cost* of converting a payment into sterling, it was the *gross* sterling equivalent of the claimant's Canadian pension that had to be taken into account (*i.e.* the cost of conversion had to be added back to the net amount paid to the claimant). However, it is respectfully suggested that the purpose of para.24 is not to disregard any banking charge or commission *as a cost*, but simply to ensure that the amount of any banking charge or commission is not included in the income taken into account. Although the wording of para.24 could be clearer, it seems unlikely that the Commissioner's interpretation is the intended one. It is also not the approach taken in the *Decision Makers Guide* (see para.28415).

2.753

Para.25

With effect from April 6, 2004 (except in "transitional cases"— see the note to reg.17) amounts for children and young persons have been removed from the income support scheme; financial assistance to help with the cost of bringing up a child or young person is now to be provided through the child tax credit system, see Vol. IV of this series. As a consequence the disregard in para.25 has been amended with effect from April 6, 2004 (except in "transitional cases"—see the note to reg.17) so that payments made to adopters in respect of a child or young person who is a member of the claimant's family are fully disregarded. The same applies to payments from local authorities towards the maintenance of children by sub-paras (b)–(d). The new form of sub-paras (b)–(d) introduced on April 6, 1998 included such payments from authorities in Northern Ireland (sub-para.(d)). Sub-para.(e) covers payments by local authorities to special guardians (s.115 of the Adoption and Children Act 2002 amended the Children Act 1989 to introduce a new special guardianship order, which is intended to provide permanence for children for whom adoption is not appropriate; the special guardian has parental responsibility for the child but the child's legal relationship with his birth parents is not severed. The special guardianship provisions will come into force on December 30, 2005). For the capital disregard of such payments see para.68A of Sch.10.

The old form of para.25(1) and (2) (see the 2003 edition of this volume), but as amended on October 4, 2004, remains in force for "transitional cases"—see the note to reg.17.

With effect from October 1, 2003, any payment, other than one that falls under sub-para.(1)(a), that is made in accordance with regulations under para.3 of Sch.4 to the Adoption and Children Act 2002 (see the Adoption Support Services (Local

2.754

Authorities) (England) Regulations 2003 (SI 2003/1348) and the Adoption Support Services (Local Authorities (Wales) Regulations 2004 (SI 2004/1011)) that is not in respect of a child or young person who is a member of the claimant's family is ignored in full (sub-para.(1A)). This could apply, for example, to payments made before placing the child with the family. Note that *any* payment made under para.3 of Sch.4 to the Adoption and Children Act 2002 that counts as capital is fully disregarded (see para.68 of Sch.10).

Para. 25A

With effect from April 6, 2004 (except in "transitional cases"—see the note to reg.17) amounts for children and young persons have been removed from the income support scheme; financial assistance to help with the cost of bringing up a child or young person is now to be provided through the child tax credit system, see Vol. IV of this series. Income support has in effect become an "adults only" benefit. Accordingly the income (as well as the capital) of a child or young person who is a member of the claimant's family is not aggregated with the claimant's (see the new form of reg.23(2)) and the income support applicable amount no longer includes any personal allowance for a child or young person, the family premium, the disabled child premium or an enhanced disability premium for a child or young person.

This new disregard is another of the consequential changes that apply from April 6, 2004 (except in "transitional cases"—see the note to reg.17) as a result of the new system. Under this paragraph payments to a boarding school for the maintenance of a child or young person, who is a member of the claimant's family, made by a third party or out of funds provided by a third party are ignored in full (compare the previous form of this provision in reg.44(2) (now revoked, except in "transitional cases"—see the note to reg.17; see the 2003 edition of this volume for reg.44 and the notes to that regulation) which applied when the income of a child or young person who was a member of the claimant's family was, subject to the modifications in reg.44, aggregated with the claimant's (see the old form of reg.23 in the 2003 edition)).

Para. 26

2.755

Payments to foster-parents are disregarded completely. Foster-children are not members of the family (reg.16(4)).

A different form of this provision, referring to the relevant Scottish legislation, applies in Scotland.

Para. 27

2.756

CIS 17020/1996 concerned a local authority scheme for placing disabled people in the carers' own homes. In order to attempt to take advantage of the disregard in para.27 the local authority sent the disabled person a bill for his care and accommodation and then paid the money to the claimant, instead of the disabled person paying the claimant directly. However, the Commissioner decides that para.27 only applied to payments made by a local authority from its own resources. The appropriate disregard was in para.20. He also discusses the meaning of the words "not normally a member of the claimant's household but is temporarily in his care". In his view the word "normally" referred to the period of the membership, not the manner of it. The question of whether the disabled person was temporarily in the claimant's care was one of fact, having regard to the intention of the parties and the length of the stay.

In *CH/2321/2002* (which concerned para.25 of Sch.4 to the Housing Benefit Regulations, the equivalent of para.27), the Commissioner decided that the disregard could apply to payments of housing benefit paid direct to the claimant in respect of a person in their care. However this was not the policy intention; in addition it was felt that this interpretation created an anomaly since the full disregard under sub-para.(b) would not apply where the housing benefit was paid to the tenant and he used it to pay for board and lodging; in that case only the more limited disregard in para.20 would apply. Sub-para.(b) has therefore been amended with effect from April 4, 2005 to exclude payments of housing benefit from the disregard. See also the amendment to para.5.

Para. 28

Regulation 41(3) deems all such payments in trade dispute cases to be income and not capital. Then this disregard does not apply in trade dispute cases. Outside that special situation payments under the legislation (broadly to prevent children going into care, or to support certain care leavers) can be capital or income (*R(SB) 29/85*). Income is disregarded here and capital under para.17 of Sch.10.

2.757

Para. 29

Since October 1995 the proceeds of mortgage protection policies can be used to cover payments in respect of *any* interest on a loan that qualifies under paras 15 or 16 of Sch.3 that is not met by income support, capital repayments on a qualifying loan and any premiums on the policy and any building insurance policy. (Despite the "or" in head (c) the disregard presumably applies to premiums on both types of policy if premiums on both are due). Any excess counts as income. If the loan is not a qualifying loan see para.30. Para. 30 will also be relevant rather than this paragraph where the policy is a general income protection policy taken out only partly to meet housing costs (*R(IS) 13/01*). According to the *Decision Makers Guide* "capital repayments" include not only repayments of capital on a repayment mortgage but also payments into endowment policies, personal equity plans, personal pension plans and other investment plans that have been taken out to repay a mortgage or loan (para.28231). Note reg.7(15) and (16) of the Decisions and Appeals Regulations 1999 which provides that certain changes in the loan interest payable will not lead to an immediate review of the amount disregarded under this paragraph.

2.758

Sub-para.(2) seems merely declaratory as the disregard only applies to payments for housing costs that are not met by income support.

Para. 30

Payments other than those disregarded under para.29 or, from June 1, 1998, para.30ZA, earmarked for these elements of housing expenditure, are ignored (sub-para.(1)). Note that payments from liable relatives are dealt with in reg.54.

2.759

If payments are made for purposes within sub-para.(1)(a) to (e), it should be assumed, in the absence of clear evidence to the contrary, that they are made out of income "intended to be used" for those purposes (*R(IS) 13/01*). See also *CIS 13059/1996* below.

However, *CIS 4255/2002* holds that the disregard under sub-para.(1) does not extend to payments from social security benefits. Benefits such as incapacity benefit, child benefit and invalid care allowance (now carer's allowance) were no more closely connected with or referable to housing costs than to a claimant's expenses generally and thus could not be said to be "intended to be used . . . as a contribution towards" the expenses in sub-para.(1). The necessary connection that had been found to exist in *CIS 13059/1996* (see below) and in *R(IS) 13/01* (because in that case the income protection policy had been taken out a few days after the mortgage from which it could be inferred that there was an intention that income from the policy would be used, if necessary, to pay the mortgage) was not present. A similar approach was taken in *CIS 3911/1998* which held that payments from an occupational pension scheme could not be disregarded under sub-para.(1).

Since October 1995 the disregard extends to payments on *any* loan secured on the home that is not a qualifying loan under Sch.3 (*e.g.* a loan for business purposes) (head (a)); any housing cost that is eligible under Sch.3 to the extent that it is not met by income support (head (b)); capital repayments on a qualifying loan (head c)), and premiums on any buildings insurance policy and (since December 1995) any policy taken out to insure against the risk of not being able to make the payments in heads (a) to (c) (head (d)). On the meaning of capital repayments see the note to para.29.

Note reg.7(15) and (16) of the Decisions and Appeals Regulations 1999 which provides that certain loan interest changes will not lead to an immediate review of the amount disregarded under heads (a) to (c).

CIS 13059/1996 decides (contrary to the view taken in *CIS 82/1993*, see the note to para.19) that sub-para.(1) can apply to payments made by a tenant (or licensee) of the claimant who lives in her home. The claimant's mortgage interest was met by income support but only to the extent of the interest on £125,000 (there was about £160,000 owing on her mortgage). There were two tenants living in her flat. The AO decided that the rent received from the tenants had to be taken into account in calculating the claimant's income support, subject only to the disregard in para.19. However, the Commissioner concludes that para.30 could apply at the same time as para.19 (or para.18 or 20) because these paragraphs were not concerned with the same sort of payments. Paras 18 to 20 were not intended to make specific provision for disregarding payments designed to help meet a claimant's housing costs, whereas para.30 was so intended. Moreover, there was no reason why para.30 should not apply to payments made under a contractual liability. The Commissioner also deals with the meaning of the phrase "payment . . . which is intended to be used and is used as a contribution towards" in para.(1). He rejects the argument that it was only necessary to look at the intention of the claimant. But he holds that it was possible to infer from a tenancy agreement that the tenant intended the landlord to use the rent, so far as necessary, to pay the landlord's own liabilities on the property so that the tenant could continue to occupy it. "Intended" in para.(1) was used in the sense of "designed" or "calculated" and it was necessary to look at the general context in which payments were made in order to ascertain the intention of the parties. The Commissioner also confirms that there was no reason why part of a payment could not be disregarded under para.30 in addition to part being disregarded under any of paras 18 to 20. (See reg.2(1): "payment" includes part of a payment). Thus in addition to the para.19 disregard, a further amount to cover the claimant's mortgage interest that was not met under paras 7 and 8 of Sch.3 as then in force could be disregarded from the rent payments.

The same Commissioner again considered the operation of the para.30 disregard in *R(IS) 13/01*. The claimant had an income protection policy, not a mortgage protection policy, so para.29 did not apply. The Commissioner holds that the difference between the amount the claimant was "due to pay" his building society (rather than the amount actually debited from his mortgage account—see *CIS 632/1992* upheld by the Court of Appeal in *Brain v Chief Adjudication Officer*, December 2, 1993 in the notes to para.1 of Sch.3) and the amount of mortgage interest met by income support, to the extent that the claimant actually made up that difference, could be deducted from the income he received under the income protection policy under heads (a) and (b) of sub-para.(1). In addition, head (c) covered the premiums on his endowment policy because the premiums were "due on a loan attributable to the payment of capital" (following *CIS 642/1992* rather than the approach he had taken in *CIS 13059/1996*). The claimant's building insurance premiums also fell within head (d)(ii). However, the premiums on the income protection policy itself could not be disregarded under para.30. Head (d)(i) did not apply as the policy had not been *taken out* to insure against the risk of being unable to maintain his mortgage payments.

Again, sub-para.(2) seems merely declaratory as the disregard under para.(1) only applies to elements of housing expenditure that are not met by income support.

Para.30ZA

2.760
This provides for a disregard of payments received under so-called "creditor insurance" policies. It will apply to payments received under an insurance policy to cover, for example, hire-purchase payments or loan or similar payments. But any excess above the amount of the payment due, plus any premiums on the policy concerned, counts as income.

Para.30A
Where a claimant is in a residential care or nursing home and the accommodation has not been arranged by a local authority, payments towards the cost of the home's fees are disregarded. The amount ignored is the difference between the claimant's applicable amount and the weekly charge for the accommodation.

2.761

Para.34
This is the compensation for the automatic counting of the "relevant sum" as part of the family's income under s.126(5)(b) of the Contributions and Benefits Act. From April 2005 the relevant sum is £30.50.

2.762

Para.35
See notes to reg.32(5).

2.763

Para.37
See notes to reg.32(5).

2.764

Para.39
The disregard now extends to payments to haemophiliacs from the three trusts, and to non-haemophiliacs from the Fund and the Eileen Trust, and to distributions of income payments to the close family, or to a slightly wider class for the two years following such a person's death. Such distribution of income payments are also ignored if they derive from a Skipton Fund payment (it is understood that no disregard under sub-para.(1) is considered necessary because the Skipton Fund only provides lump sum payments). Any payments from the Independent Living Funds are ignored.

2.765

Para.47
These are the special payments to compensate pre-1973 war widows who had not benefited from amendments to the Armed Forces Pension Scheme. There was a commitment that the payments would not affect means-tested benefits. See paras 54–56.

2.766

Para.51
Payments to a disabled person to assist him to obtain or retain employment under the Disabled Persons (Employment) Act 1994 are ignored. The previous form of this paragraph also referred to payments for this purpose under s.2 of the Employment and Training Act 1973. However from April 1, 2004 a single disregard has been introduced in relation to payments under all s.2 schemes. See para.13.

2.767

Para.53
Increases for dependants who are not residing with the claimant paid with certain benefits (*e.g.* retirement pension) or war pensions are disregarded. Such increases are only paid if the claimant is contributing at least that amount to the maintenance of the dependant.

2.768

Paras 54–56
See para.47. These new disregards arose from the transfer of responsibility for the payment of most pre-1973 war widows' (and widowers') pensions from the Ministry of Defence to the DSS from October 1994.

2.769

Para.57
See the note to reg.21ZB.

2.770

Para. 58

2.771   The Community Care (Direct Payments) Act 1996 allows local authorities to make cash payments in lieu of community care services to disabled people aged 18–65 (payments may continue after 65 if they began before a person's 66th birthday). Such payments are to be ignored.

Paras 59–60

2.772   For the previous form of these paragraphs, which concerned Career Development Loans, see the 2003 edition of this volume. However they have been omitted with effect from April 1, 2004 because from that date para.13 contains a single disregard in relation to payments made under s.2 of the Employment and Training Act 1973 or s.2 of the Enterprise and New Towns (Scotland) Act 1990 to people participating in New Deals and other training and welfare to work schemes. See the note to para.13.

Para. 61

2.773   Any grant or covenant income, student loan or contribution (for definitions see reg.61) left over at the end of a person's course is ignored. See regs 29(2B), 32(6A) and 40(3B) for the position where part or all of a student's grant is repayable because he has left or is dismissed from his course before it finishes.

Paras 62, 62A and 63

2.774   For the previous form of these paragraphs see the 2003 edition of this volume. However they have been omitted with effect from April 1, 2004 because from that date para.13 contains a single disregard in relation to payments made under s.2 of the Employment and Training Act 1973 or s.2 of the Enterprise and New Towns (Scotland) Act 1990 to people participating in New Deals and other training and welfare to work schemes. See the note to para.13.

Para. 64

2.775   (*Note*: this is a new para.64; the previous para.64 is now para.66).
   This disregards any payment to a person, who is on, or has left, the "self-employment route" (defined in reg.2(1)), from his "special account" (defined in reg.39A) if it is (i) to meet expenses wholly and necessarily incurred in his business while on the self-employment route; or (ii) used, or intended to be used, to make repayments on a loan taken out for the purposes of that business. For the treatment of a person's income from "test-trading" while on the self-employment route, see regs 39A to 39D and the note to reg.102C of the JSA Regulations.
   See also the disregard in para.13.

Para. 65

2.776   See the note to paras 62, 62A and 63 above.

Para. 66

2.777   This is the renumbered para.64. See the note to reg.42(4A).

Para. 69

2.778   A "sports award" (defined in reg.2(1)) is ignored, except to the extent that it has been made for any of the items listed in sub-para.(2) (note the definitions in sub-para.(3)). For the disregard where the sports award counts as capital see para.56 of Sch.10 but note that under para.56 the disregard only applies for 26 weeks from the date of receipt. See also reg.6(1)(m) under which a person will be deemed not to be in remunerative work while engaged in activity for which the only payment he is, or will be, receiving is a sports award and reg.37(2)(c) which ensures that the award is not treated as self-employed earnings.

Paras 71 and 72

2.780   See the note to reg.42(5A).

Para. 73

The disregard under this paragraph has been introduced as part of the child 2.781
support reforms under the Child Support, Pensions and Social Security Act 2000.
It replaces the child maintenance bonus scheme under s.10 of the Child Support Act
1995 which allowed income support and income-based JSA claimants receiving
child maintenance to build up a "child maintenance bonus". See the Social Security
(Child Maintenance Bonus) Regulations 1996 (SI 1996/ 3195). The long-delayed
start to the commencement of the new child support scheme finally began on March
3, 2003. The new rules are being implemented in stages, depending on the type of
case (see the note at the beginning of the Child Support Act 1991 in Part I of this
volume). For those cases to which the new regime applies (and for cases where child
maintenance which is not child support maintenance is first paid under an agreement or court order on or after March 3, 2003), s.23 of the 2000 Act repeals s.10 of
the Child Support Act 1995 (see the note to s.10 of the 1995 Act for further details
of the commencement of s.23). Once s.23 has come into force in relation to a particular case, it will no longer be possible for the claimant to accrue a child maintenance bonus. (See reg.4 of the Social Security (Child Maintenance Premium and
Miscellaneous Amendments) Regulations 2000 (SI 2000/3176), as substituted by
reg.2 of the Social Security (Child Maintenance Premium and Miscellaneous
Amendments) Amendment Regulations 2003 (SI 2003/231) (p.739) and the note
at the beginning of the Child Maintenance Bonus Regulations for the transitional
provisions in relation to a bonus that has accrued before s.23 comes into force for a
particular case). Instead, the claimant will be eligible for the disregard under this
paragraph (for the corresponding disregard under JSA, see para.70 of Sch.7 to the
JSA Regulations).

However, it was later recognised that the introduction of the new disregard in this
way had created a potential anomaly. This is because the definition of "child maintenance" is wider for the purposes of the disregard (see below for this definition) than
it is for the bonus (the definition in reg.1(2) of the Child Maintenance Bonus
Regulations does not include payments made voluntarily). Thus the possibility arose
that a non-resident parent could make voluntary payments of child maintenance but
the claimant would qualify for neither the bonus nor the disregard (because s.23 had
not yet commenced in her case). Thus in order to enable the disregard to apply to
such voluntary payments, the commencement provisions in reg.1 of the Social
Security (Child Maintenance Premium) Amendment Regulations 2004 (SI
2004/98), which inserted the current form of this paragraph, provide that it applies,
inter alia, to a person who makes a claim for income support/income-based JSA on
or after February 16, 2004 and receives a payment of child maintenance made voluntarily on or after the date of that claim and to a person who is entitled to income
support/income-based JSA on February 16, 2004 and who receives her first payment
of child maintenance made voluntarily whilst entitled to income support/income-
based JSA on or after that date. "Payment of child maintenance made voluntarily"
is defined in reg.1(4) of those Regulations as a payment of child maintenance made
other than under a court order, under the old or new child support schemes, in accordance with s.28J of the Child Support Act 1991 (voluntary payments in anticipation
of a maintenance calculation under the new child support system), under an agreement or by the Secretary of State in lieu of child maintenance. Note that the commencement provisions in reg.1 of the Social Security (Child Maintenance Premium
and Miscellaneous Amendments) Regulations 2000 (SI 2000/3176), which *inter alia*
inserted the original form of para.73, have also been similarly amended with effect
from February 16, 2004.

The disregard is of up to £10 of any child maintenance payments. No more than
£10 can be ignored in any week, regardless of the number of children in respect
of whom maintenance is paid, or the number of non-resident parents from whom
payments are received (sub-paras (2) and (3)). "Child maintenance" for this purpose
has the meaning prescribed for the purposes of s.74A of the Social Security
Administration Act 1992 (see Vol. III in this series) in reg.2(a) of the Social Security

Benefits (Maintenance Payments and Consequential Amendments) Regulations 1996 (as amended) (see p.721). It also includes any payments made by the Secretary of State in lieu of child maintenance payments. Regulation 2(a) of the 1996 Regulations defines child maintenance as any payment for the maintenance of a child or young person ("young person" has the same meaning as for income support: regs 2(a) and 3(a) of the 1996 Regulations), including payments made under a court order or agreement, a maintenance calculation under the Child Support Act 1991 or voluntarily. Thus, for instance, if payments are made to a third party (*e.g.* if a non-resident parent pays the gas bill), rather than directly to the claimant, the disregard should apply to such payments, if it is reasonable to treat them as payments of child maintenance.

Para. 74

2.782   This provides for the whole of a claimant's income to be disregarded during any "mortgage run-on" period. See the notes to reg.6(5)–(8) as to when this applies. See also the disregards in para.15C of Sch.8 and para.62 of Sch.10 and the note to para.15C.

Para. 75

2.783   Discretionary housing payments can be made by a local authority to housing benefit/council tax benefit claimants who need extra help with their housing or council tax liability. They replaced the previous system of exceptional circumstances payments and exceptional hardship payments with effect from July 2, 2001. Any such payments are ignored as income; for the capital disregard see para.7 of Sch.10.

Para. 76

From April 1, 2003 the responsibility for meeting the cost of housing-related services for people in supported accommodation passed to local authorities under the "Supporting People" programme (between April 2000 and April 2003 under the "Transitional Housing Benefit Scheme" certain service charges for claimants in supported accommodation had been met by housing benefit (see Sch.1B to the Housing Benefit Regulations which ceased to have effect on April 7, 2003)).

This paragraph provides for payments under this programme to be ignored. The previous form of the disregard (see the 2003 edition of this volume) referred to payments from a local authority in respect of "welfare services" within the meaning of s.93(1) or (2) of the Local Government Act 2000 (in Scotland "housing support services" under s.91(1) of the Housing (Scotland) Act 2001). However the form in force from October 1, 2003 has been reworded to remove those legislative references in order to ensure that the disregard covers all payments made under the Supporting People programme.

For the indefinite capital disregard of such payments see para.66 of Sch.10.

Paras 77 and 78

For the previous form of these paragraphs, which concerned the Employment, Retention and Advancement (ERA) scheme and the Return to Work Credit scheme respectively, see the 2003/2004 Supplement to this volume. However these paragraphs have been omitted with effect from April 1, 2004 because from that date para.13 contains a single disregard in relation to payments made under s.2 of the Employment and Training Act 1973 or s.2 of the Enterprise and New Towns (Scotland) Act 1990 to people participating in New Deals and other training and welfare to work schemes. See the note to para.13.

SCHEDULE 10   **Regulation 46(2)**

CAPITAL TO BE DISREGARDED

1. The dwelling occupied as the home but, notwithstanding regulation 23 (calculation of   **2.784**
income and capital of members of claimant's family and of a polygamous marriage), only one
dwelling shall be disregarded under this paragraph.

2. Any premises acquired for occupation by the claimant which he intends to occupy [⁴as his
home] within 26 weeks of the date of acquisition or such longer period as is reasonable in the circumstances to enable the claimant to obtain possession and commence occupation of the premises.

3. Any sum directly attributable to the proceeds of sale of any premises formerly occupied
by the claimant as his home which is to be used for the purchase of other premises intended
for such occupation within 26 weeks of the date of sale or such longer period as is reasonable
in the circumstances to enable the claimant to complete the purchase.

4. Any premises occupied in whole or in part by—

   (a) a partner or relative of [¹²a single claimant or any member of] the family [⁴as his home]
       where that person is aged 60 or over or is incapacitated;

   (b) the former partner of a claimant [² . . .] as his home; but this provision shall not apply
       where the former partner is a person from whom the claimant is estranged or divorced.

[²⁶**5.** Any future interest in property of any kind, other than land or premises in respect of
which the claimant has granted a subsisting lease or tenancy, including sub-leases or
sub-tenancies.]

6.—[¹²(1)] The assets of any business owned in whole or in part by the claimant and for the
purposes of which he is engaged as a self-employed earner or, if he has ceased to be so engaged,
for such period as may be reasonable in the circumstances to allow for disposal of any such asset.

   [¹²(2) The assets of any business owned in whole or in part by the claimant where—

   (a) he is not engaged as a self-employed earner in that business by reason of some disease
       or bodily or mental disablement; but

   (b) he intends to become engaged (or, as the case may be, re-engaged) as a self-employed
       earner in that business as soon as he recovers or is able to become engaged, or re-
       engaged, in that business;

for a period of 26 weeks from the date on which the claim for income support is made, or is
treated as made, or, if it is unreasonable to expect him to become engaged or re-engaged in
that business within that period for such longer period as is reasonable in the circumstances to
enable him to become so engaged or re-engaged.]

[³³(3) In the case of a person who is receiving assistance under [⁴⁴the self-employment route],
the assets acquired by that person for the purpose of establishing or carrying on the commercial activity in respect of which such assistance is being received.

(4) In the case of a person who has ceased carrying on the commercial activity in respect of
which assistance was received as specified in sub-paragraph (3), the assets relating to that activity
for such period as may be reasonable in the circumstances to allow for disposal of any such asset.]

7. [⁵⁵—(1) Subject to sub-paragraph (2),] any arrears of, or any concessionary payment
made to compensate for arrears due to the non-payment of,—

   (a) any payment specified in paragraph 6, [¹⁶8[⁵⁵ or 9]] of Schedule 9 (other income to be
       disregarded);

   (b) an income-related benefit or [²⁸ an income-based jobseeker's allowance,] supplemen-
       tary benefit, family income supplement under the Family Income Supplements Act
       1970 [⁵⁷, working families' tax credit under section 128 of the Contributions and
       Benefits Act, disabled person's tax credit under section 129 of that Act, child tax credit,
       working tax credit,] or housing benefit under Part II of the Social Security and
       Housing Benefits Act 1982;

   [²⁹(c) [⁶⁸ . . .]]

   [⁵⁰(d) any discretionary housing payment paid pursuant to regulation [⁵⁰2(1) of the
       Discretionary Financial Assistance Regulations 2001,]

but only for a period of 52 weeks from the date of the receipt of the arrears or of the
concessionary payment.

   [⁵⁵ (2) In a case where the total of any arrears and, if appropriate, any concessionary payment
referred to in sub-paragraph (1) relating to any one of the specified payments, benefits or
allowances amounts to £5,000 or more (referred to in this sub-paragraph and in sub-paragraph
(3) as the "relevant sum") and is—

   (a) paid in order to rectify, or to compensate for, an official error as defined in regulation
       1(3) of the Social Security and Child Support (Decisions and Appeals) Regulations
       1999, and

(b) received by the claimant in full on or after 14th October 2001,
sub-paragraph (1) shall have effect in relation to such arrears or concessionary payment either for a period of 52 weeks from the date of receipt, or, if the relevant sum is received in its entirety during the award of income support, for the remainder of that award if that is a longer period.

(3) For the purposes of sub-paragraph (2), "the award of income support" means—

(a) the award either of income support or of an income-based jobseeker's allowance in which the relevant sum (or first part thereof where it is paid in more than one instalment) is received, and

(b) where that award is followed by one or more further awards which in each case may be either of income support or of an income-based jobseeker's allowance and which, or each of which, begins immediately after the end of the previous award, such further awards until the end of the last such award, provided that for any such further awards the claimant—

   (i) is the person who received the relevant sum, or

   (ii) is the partner of the person who received the relevant sum, or was that person's partner at the date of his death, or

   (iii) in the case of a joint-claim jobseeker's allowance, is a joint-claim couple either member or both members of which received the relevant sum.]

8. Any sum—

(a) paid to the claimant in consequence of damage to, or loss of the home or any personal possession and intended for its repair or replacement; or

(b) acquired by the claimant (whether as a loan or otherwise) on the express condition that it is to be used for effecting essential repairs or improvements to the home,

and which is to be used for the intended purpose, for a period of 26 weeks from the date on which it was so paid or acquired or such longer period as is reasonable in the circumstances to enable the claimant to effect the repairs, replacement or improvements.

9. Any sum—

(a) deposited with a housing association as defined in section 189(1) of the Housing Act 1985 or section 338(1) of the Housing (Scotland) Act 1987 as a condition of occupying the home;

(b) which was so deposited and which is to be used for the purchase of another home, for the period of 26 weeks of such longer period as is reasonable in the circumstances to complete the purchase.

10. Any personal possessions except those which had or have been acquired by the claimant with the intention of reducing his capital in order to secure entitlement to supplementary benefit or income support or to increase the amount of that benefit.

11. The value of the right to receive any income under an annuity and the surrender value (if any) of such an annuity.

[^{12}**12.** Where the funds of a trust are derived from a payment made in consequence of any personal injury to the claimant, the value of the trust fund and the value of the right to receive any payment under that trust.]

13. The value of the right to receive any income under a life interest or from a liferent.

14. The value of the right to receive any income which is disregarded under paragraph 11 of Schedule 8 or paragraph 23 of Schedule 9 (earnings or other income to be disregarded).

15. The surrender value of any policy of life insurance.

16. Where any payment of capital falls to be made by instalments, the value of the right to receive any outstanding instalments.

17. Except in the case of a person to whom section 23 of the Act [SSCBA, s.126] (trade disputes) applies [^{1}or in respect of whom section 20(3) of the Act [SSCBA, s.124(1)] (conditions of entitlement to income support) has effect as modified by section 23A(b) of the Act [SSCBA, s.127(b)] (effect of return to work)], [^{6}any payment made by a local authority [^{18}in accordance with [^{51}section 17, 23B, 23C or 24A of the Children Act 1989] or, as the case may be, [^{62} section 12 of the Social Work (Scotland) Act 1968 or sections 29 or 30 of the Children (Scotland) Act 1995] (local authorities' duty to promote welfare of children and powers to grant financial assistance to persons in, or formerly in, their care).]

[^{17}**18.** Any social fund payment made pursuant to Part III of the Act [SSCBA, Part VIII].]

19. Any refund of tax which fell to be deducted under section 26 of the Finance Act 1982 (deductions of tax from certain loan interest) on a payment of relevant loan interest for the purpose of acquiring an interest in the home or carrying out repairs or improvements in the home.

20. Any capital which under [^{11}regulation 41 [^{61} . . .] or 66A (capital treated as income [^{61} . . .] or treatment of student loans)] is to be treated as income.

21. Where a payment of capital is made in a currency other than sterling, any banking charge or commission payable in converting that payment into sterling.

[[1]**22.**—[[14](1) Any payment made under the Macfarlane Trust, the Macfarlane (Special Payments) Trust, the Macfarlane (Special Payments) (No. 2) Trust ("the Trusts"), [[19]the Fund] [[23]], the Eileen Trust] [[63], the Independent Living Funds or the Skipton Fund].

(2) Any payment by or on behalf of a person who is suffering or who suffered from haemophilia [[19]or who is or was a qualifying person], which derives from a payment made under any of the Trusts to which sub-paragraph (1) refers and which is made to or for the benefit of—

(a) that person's partner or former partner from whom he is not, or where that person has died was not, estranged or divorced;

(b) any child who is a member of that person's family or who was such a member and who is a member of the claimant's family; or

(c) any young person who is a member of that person's family or who was such a member and who is a member of the claimant's family.

(3) Any payment by or on behalf of the partner or former partner of a person who is suffering or who suffered from haemophilia [[19]or who is or was a qualifying person] provided that the partner or former partner and that person are not, or if either of them has died were not, estranged or divorced, which derives from a payment made under any of the Trusts to which sub-paragraph (1) refers and which is made to or for the benefit of—

(a) the person who is suffering from haemophilia [[19]or who is a qualifying person];

(b) any child who is a member of that person's family or who was such a member and who is a member of the claimant's family; or

(c) any young person who is a member of that person's family or who was such a member and who is a member of the claimant's family.

(4) Any payment by a person who is suffering from haemophilia [[19]or who is a qualifying person], which derives from a payment under any of the Trusts to which sub-paragraph (1) refers, where—

(a) that person has no partner or former partner from whom he is not estranged or divorced, nor any child or young person who is or had been a member of that person's family; and

(b) the payment is made either—

(i) to that person's parent or step-parent, or

(ii) where that person at the relevant date was a child, a young person or a [[43] full-time student] who had not completed his full-time education and had no parent or step-parent, to his guardian,

but only for a period of two years from the date of the payment until the end of two years from that person's death.

(5) Any payment out of the estate of a person who suffered from haemophilia [[19]or who was a qualifying person], which derives from a payment under any of the Trusts to which sub-paragraph (1) refers, where—

(a) that person at the date of his death (the relevant date) had no partner or former partner from whom he was not estranged or divorced, nor any child or young person who was or had been a member of his family; and

(b) the payment is made either—

(i) to that person's parent or step-parent, or

(ii) where that person at the relevant date was a child, a young person or a [[43] full-time student] who had not completed his full-time education and had no parent or step-parent, to his guardian,

but only for a period of two years from the relevant date.

(6) In the case of a person to whom or for whose benefit a payment referred to in this paragraph is made, any capital resource which derives from any payment of income or capital made under or deriving from any of the Trusts.]

[[19](7) For the purposes of sub-paragraphs (2) to (6), any reference to the Trusts shall be construed as including a reference to the Fund [[64], the Eileen Trust and the Skipton Fund].]

23. The value of the right to receive an occupational [[15]or personal] pension.

[[26]**23A.** The value of any funds held under a personal pension scheme or retirement annuity contract.]

24. The value of the right to receive any rent [[26]except where the claimant has a reversionary interest in the property in respect of which rent is due.]]

[[2]**25.** Where a claimant has ceased to occupy what was formerly the dwelling occupied as the home following his estrangement or divorce from his former partner, that dwelling for a period of 26 weeks from the date on which he ceased to occupy that dwelling [[56] or, where that dwelling is occupied as the home by the former partner who is a lone parent, for as long as it is so occupied].

26. Any premises where the claimant is taking reasonable steps to dispose of those premises, for a period of 26 weeks from the date on which he first took such steps, or such longer period as is reasonable in the circumstances to enable him to dispose of those premises.

[⁵**27.** Any premises which the claimant intends to occupy as his home, and in respect of which he is taking steps to obtain possession and has sought legal advice or has commenced legal proceedings, with a view to obtaining possession, for a period of 26 weeks from the date on which he first sought such advice or first commenced such proceedings whichever is earlier, or such longer period as is reasonable in the circumstances to enable him to obtain possession and commence occupation of those premises.]

28. Any premises which the claimant intends to occupy as his home to which essential repairs or alterations are required in order to render them fit for such occupation, for a period of 26 weeks from the date on which the claimant first takes steps to effect those repairs or alterations, or such longer period as is reasonable in the circumstances to enable those repairs or alterations to be carried out and the claimant to commence occupation of the premises.]

[⁴**29.** Any payment in kind made by a charity [⁸or under the Macfarlane (Special Payments) Trust] [¹⁹, the Macfarlane (Special Payments) (No. 2) Trust] [²², the Fund or the Independent Living (1993) Fund].

[⁶⁰**30.** Any payment made pursuant to section 2 of the Employment and Training Act 1973 or section 2 of the Enterprise and New Towns (Scotland) Act 1990, but only for the period of 52 weeks beginning on the date of receipt of the payment.]

31. Any payment made by the Secretary of State to compensate for the loss (in whole or in part) of entitlement of housing benefit.]

[⁵**32.** Any payment made by the Secretary of State to compensate a person who was entitled to supplementary benefit in respect of a period ending immediately before 11th April 1988 but who did not become entitled to income support in respect of a period beginning with that day.

33. Any payment made by the Secretary of State to compensate for the loss of housing benefit supplement under regulation 19 of the Supplementary Benefit (Requirements) Regulations 1983.

34. Any payment made to a juror or a witness in respect of attendance at a court other than compensation for loss of earnings or for the loss of a benefit payable under the benefit Acts.

35. [²⁰ . . .].]

[⁹**36.** Any payment in consequence of a reduction of a personal community charge pursuant to regulations under section 13A of the Local Government Finance Act 1988 or section 9A of the Abolition of Domestic Rates Etc (Scotland) Act 1987 (reduction of liability for personal community charge) [²⁰or reduction of council tax under section 13 or, as the case may be, section 80 of the Local Government Finance Act 1992 (reduction of liability for council tax)] but only for a period of 52 weeks from the date of the receipt of the payment.]

[¹⁰**37.** Any grant made to the claimant in accordance with a scheme made under section 129 of the Housing Act 1988 or section 66 of the Housing (Scotland) Act 1988 (schemes for payments to assist local housing authority and local authority tenants to obtain other accommodation) which is to be used—

    (a)   to purchase premises intended for occupation as his home; or

    (b)   to carry out repairs or alterations which are required to render premises fit for occupation as his home

for a period of 26 weeks from the date on which he received such a grant or such longer period as is reasonable in the circumstances to enable the purchase, repairs or alterations to be completed and the claimant to commence occupation of those premises as his home.]

[¹²**38.**—(1) Any payment or repayment made—

    (a)   as respects England and Wales, under regulation 3, 5 or 8 of the National Health Service (Travelling Expenses and Remission of Charges) Regulations 1988 (travelling expenses and health service supplies);

    (b)   as respects Scotland, under regulation 3, 5 or 8 of the National Health Service (Travelling Expenses and Remission of Charges) (Scotland) Regulations 1988 (travelling expenses and health service supplies);

but only for a period of 52 weeks from the date of receipt of the payment or repayment.

(2) Any payment or repayment made by the Secretary of State for Health, the Secretary of State for Scotland or the Secretary of State for Wales which is analogous to a payment or repayment mentioned in sub-paragraph (1); but only for a period of 52 weeks from the date of receipt of the payment or repayment.

39. Any payment made under regulation 9 to 11 or 13 of the Welfare Food Regulations 1988 (payments made in place of milk tokens or the supply of vitamins), but only for a period of 52 weeks from the date of receipt of the payment.

40. Any payment made either by the Secretary of State for the Home Department or by the Secretary of State for Scotland under a scheme established to assist relatives and other persons to visit persons in custody, but only for a period of 52 weeks from the date of receipt of the payment.

41. Any arrears of special war widows payment which is disregarded under paragraph 47 of Schedule 9 (sums to be disregarded in the calculation of income other than earnings) [²⁵or of any amount which is disregarded under paragraph 54, 55 or 56 of that Schedule], but only for a period of 52 weeks from the date of receipt of the arrears.]

[¹⁷**42.** Any payment (other than a training allowance[⁶⁰ . . .]) made, whether by the Secretary of State or by any other person, under the Disabled Persons (Employment) Act 1944 [⁶⁰ . . .] to assist disabled persons to obtain or retain employment despite their disability.

43. Any payment made by a local authority under section 3 of the Disabled Persons (Employment) Act 1958 to homeworkers under the Blind Homeworkers' Scheme.]

[²⁵**44.** Any sum of capital administered on behalf of a person [³¹. . .] by the High Court [⁵⁸ or the County Court under Rule 21.11(1) of the Civil Procedure Rules 1998], or the Court of Protection, where such sum derives from—

    (a) an award of damages for a personal injury to that person; or

    (b) compensation for the death of one or both parents [³¹ where the person concerned is under the age of 18].]

45. Any sum of capital administered on behalf of a person [³¹. . .] in accordance with an order made under [⁵⁸ section 13 of the Children (Scotland) Act 1995], or under Rule 36.14 of the Ordinary Cause Rules 1993 or under Rule 128 of the Ordinary Cause Rules, where such sum derives from—

    (a) an award of damages for a personal injury to that person; or

    (b) compensation for the death of one or both parents [³¹ where the person concerned is under the age of 18].]

[²⁷**46.** Any payment to the claimant as holder of the Victoria Cross or George Cross.]

[³⁰**47.** Any amount of council tax benefit to which a person is entitled by virtue of regulation 4D of the Council Tax Benefit (General) Regulations 1992 (entitlement of a refugee to council tax benefit), but only for a period of 52 weeks from the date that such an amount is received.

48. Any amount of housing benefit to which a person is entitled by virtue of regulation 7B of the Housing Benefit (General) Regulations 1987 (entitlement of a refugee to housing benefit), but only for a period of 52 weeks from the date that such an amount is received.

49. Any amount of income support to which a person is entitled by virtue of [⁴¹regulation 21ZB] above (treatment of refugees), but only for a period of 52 weeks from the date that such an amount is received.]

[⁴⁸ **50.** [⁶⁰. . .].]

[⁵⁴ **50A.** [⁶⁰. . .].]

[³² **51.** [⁶⁰. . .].]

[³⁵ **52.** In the case of a person who is receiving, or who has received, assistance under [⁴⁴ the self-employment route], any sum of capital which is acquired by that person for the purpose of establishing or carrying on the commercial activity in respect of which such assistance is or was received but only for a period of 52 weeks from the date on which that sum was acquired.]

[³⁶**53.** [⁶⁰. . .].]

54. [*Omitted*]

55. [*Omitted*]

[³⁷**56.**—(1) Any payment of a sports award for a period of 26 weeks from the date of receipt of that payment except to the extent that it has been made in respect of any one or more of the items specified in sub-paragraph (2).

(2) The items specified for the purposes of sub-paragraph (1) are food, ordinary clothing or footwear, household fuel, rent for which housing benefit is payable or any housing costs to the extent that they are met under regulation 17(1)(e) or 18(1)(f) (housing costs) [⁵³. . .], of the claimant or, where the claimant is a member of a family, any other member of his family, or any council tax or water charges for which that claimant or member is liable.

(3) For the purposes of sub-paragraph (2)—

"food" does not include vitamins, minerals or other special dietary supplements intended to enhance the performance of the person in the sport in respect of which the award was made;

"ordinary clothing and footwear" means clothing or footwear for normal daily use but does not include school uniforms or clothing or footwear used solely for sporting activities.]

[^{38}**57.** [^{67}. . .]]

[^{42}**58.** In the case of a claimant participating in an employment zone programme, any discretionary payment made by an employment zone contractor to the claimant, being a fee, grant, loan or otherwise, but only for the period of 52 weeks from the date of receipt of the payment.

59. Any arrears of subsistence allowance paid as a lump sum but only for the period of 52 weeks from the date of receipt of the payment.]

60. *[Omitted]*.

[^{45} **61.** Where an ex-gratia payment of £10,000 has been made by the Secretary of State on or after 1st February 2001 in consequence of the imprisonment or internment of—

    (a) the claimant;

    (b) the claimant's partner;

    (c) the claimant's deceased spouse; or

    (d) the claimant's partner's deceased spouse,

by the Japanese during the Second World War, £10,000.]

[^{46}**62.** In the case of a person to whom paragraph (5) of regulation 6 (persons not treated as in remunerative work) applies, the whole of his capital.]

[^{65} **63.**—(1) Any payment—

    (a) by way of an education maintenance allowance made pursuant to—

        (i) regulations made under section 518 of the Education Act 1996;

        (ii) regulations made under section 49 or 73(f) of the Education (Scotland) Act 1980;

        (iii) directions made under sections 12(2)(c) and 21 of the Further and Higher Education (Scotland) Act 1992; or

    (b) corresponding to such an education maintenance allowance, made pursuant to—

        (i) section 14 or section 181 of the Education Act 2002; or

        (ii) regulations made under section 181 of that Act.

(2) Any payment, other than a payment to which sub-paragraph (1) applies, made pursuant to—

    (a) regulations made under section 518 of the Education Act 1996;

    (b) regulations made under section 49 of the Education (Scotland) Act 1980; or

    (c) directions made under sections 12(2)(c) and 21 of the Further and Higher Education (Scotland) Act 1992,

in respect of a course of study attended by a child or a young person or a person who is in receipt of an education maintenance allowance made pursuant to any provision specified in sub-paragraph (1)].

[^{49}**64.**—(1) Subject to sub-paragraph (2), the amount of any trust payment made to a claimant or a member of a claimant's family who is—

    (a) a diagnosed person;

    (b) the diagnosed person's partner or the person who was the diagnosed person's partner at the date of the diagnosed person's death;

    (c) a parent of a diagnosed person, a person acting in the place of the diagnosed person's parents or a person who was so acting at the date of the diagnosed person's death; or

    (d) a member of the diagnosed person's family (other than his partner) or a person who was a member of the diagnosed person's family (other than his partner) at the date of the diagnosed person's death.

(2) Where a trust payment is made to—

    (a) a person referred to in sub-paragraph (1)(a) or (b), that sub-paragraph shall apply for the period beginning on the date on which the trust payment is made and ending on the date on which that person dies;

    (b) a person referred to in sub-paragraph (1)(c), that sub-paragraph shall apply for the period beginning on the date on which the trust payment is made and ending two years after that date;

    (c) a person referred to in sub-paragraph (1)(d), that sub-paragraph shall apply for the period beginning on the date on which the trust payment is made and ending—

        (i) two years after that date; or

        (ii) on the day before the day on which that person—

    (aa) ceases receiving full-time education; or

    (bb) attains the age of 19,

    whichever is the latest.

(3) Subject to sub-paragraph (4), the amount of any payment by a person to whom a trust payment has been made, or of any payment out of the estate of a person to whom a trust payment has been made, which is made to a claimant or a member of a claimant's family who is—

(a) the diagnosed person's partner or the person who was the diagnosed person's partner at the date of the diagnosed person's death;

(b) a parent of a diagnosed person, a person acting in the place of the diagnosed person's parents or a person who was so acting at the date of the diagnosed person's death; or

(c) a member of the diagnosed person's family (other than his partner) or a person who was a member of the diagnosed person's family (other than his partner) at the date of the diagnosed person's death,

but only to the extent that such payments do not exceed the total amount of any trust payments made to that person.

(4) Where a payment as referred to in sub-paragraph (3) is made to—

(a) a person referred to in sub-paragraph (3)(a), that sub-paragraph shall apply for the period beginning on the date on which that payment is made and ending on the date on which that person dies;

(b) a person referred to in sub-paragraph (3)(b), that sub-paragraph shall apply for the period beginning on the date on which that payment is made and ending two years after that date;

(c) a person referred to in sub-paragraph (3)(c), that sub-paragraph shall apply for the period beginning on the date on which that payment is made and ending—

    (i) two years after that date; or

    (ii) on the day before the day on which that person—

      (aa) ceases receiving full-time education; or

      (bb) attains the age of 19,

    whichever is the latest.

(5) In this paragraph, a reference to a person—

(a) being the diagnosed person's partner;

(b) being a member of the diagnosed person's family; or

(c) acting in the place of the diagnosed person's parents,

at the date of the diagnosed person's death shall include a person who would have been such a person or a person who would have been so acting, but for the diagnosed person being in residential accommodation, a residential care home or a nursing home on that date.

(6) In this paragraph—

"diagnosed person" means a person who has been diagnosed as suffering from, or who, after his death, has been diagnosed as having suffered from, variant Creutzfeldt- Jakob disease;

"relevant trust" means a trust established out of funds provided by the Secretary of State in respect of persons who suffered, or who are suffering, from variant Creutzfeldt-Jakob disease for the benefit of persons eligible for payments in accordance with its provisions;

"trust payment" means a payment under a relevant trust.]

[⁵²**65.** The amount of a payment, other than a war pension within the meaning in section 25 of the Social Security Act 1989, to compensate for the fact that the claimant, the claimant's partner, the claimant's deceased spouse or the claimant's partner's deceased spouse—

(a) was a slave labourer or a forced labourer;

(b) had suffered property loss or had suffered personal injury; or

(c) was a parent of a child who had died,

during the Second World War.]

[⁵⁶[⁵⁸ **66.**— (1) Any payment made by a local authority, or by the National Assembly for Wales, to or on behalf of the claimant or his partner relating to a service which is provided to develop or sustain the capacity of the claimant or his partner to live independently in his accommodation.]

(2) For the purposes of sub-paragraph (1) "local authority" includes, in England, a county council.]

[⁵⁸ **67.** Any payment made under the Community Care (Direct Payments) Act 1996, regulations made under section 57 of the Health and Social Care Act 2001 or under section 12B of the Social Work (Scotland) Act 1968.

68. Any payment made to the claimant in accordance with regulations made under paragraph 3 of Schedule 4 to the Adoption and Children Act 2002.

[⁶⁶ **68A.** Any payment made to the claimant in accordance with regulations made pursuant to section 14F of the Children Act 1989 (special guardianship support services).]

69. [⁶⁰. . .].]

[⁵⁹ **70.** [⁶⁰. . .].]

AMENDMENTS

2.785   1. Income Support (General) Amendment Regulations 1988 (SI 1988/663), reg.36 (April 11, 1988).

2. Income Support (General) Amendment No.2 Regulations 1988 (SI 1988/910), reg.3 (May 30, 1988).

3. Family Credit and Income Support (General) Amendment Regulations 1988 (SI 1988/999), reg.5 (June 9, 1988).

4. Income Support (General) Amendment No.4 Regulations 1988 (SI 1988/1445), reg.26 (September 12, 1988).

5. Income Support (General) Amendment No.5 Regulations 1988 (SI 1988/2022), reg.23 (December 12, 1988).

6. Family Credit and Income Support (General) Amendment Regulations 1989 (SI 1989/1034), reg.12 (July 10, 1989).

7. Income Support (General) Amendment Regulations 1989 (SI 1989/534), Sch.1, para.18 (October 9, 1989).

8. Income-related Benefits Schemes Amendment Regulations 1990 (SI 1990/127), reg.3 (January 31, 1990).

9. Income Support (General) Amendment Regulations 1990 (SI 1990/547), reg.23(*a*) (April 1, 1990).

10. Income Support (General) Amendment Regulations 1990 (SI 1990/547), reg.23(*b*) (April 9, 1990).

11. Social Security Benefits (Student Loans and Miscellaneous Amendments) Regulations 1990 (SI 1990/1549), reg.5(9) (September 1, 1990).

12. Income Support (General) Amendment No.3 Regulations 1990 (SI 1990/1776), reg.11 (October 1, 1990).

13. Enterprise (Scotland) Consequential Amendments Order 1991 (SI 1991/387), arts, 2 and 9 (April 1, 1991).

14. Income-related Benefits Schemes and Social Security (Recoupment) Amendment Regulations 1991 (SI 1991/1175), reg.5 (May 11, 1991).

15. Income Support (General) Amendment No.4 Regulations 1991 (SI 1991/1559), reg.21 (October 7, 1991).

16. Disability Living Allowance and Disability Working Allowance (Consequential Provisions) Regulations 1991 (SI 1991/2742), reg.11(7) (April 6, 1992).

17. Income Support (General) Amendment Regulations 1992 (SI 1992/468), reg.9 (April 6, 1992).

18. Income Support (General) Amendment Regulations 1992 (SI 1992/468), Sch., para.10 (April 6, 1992).

19. Income-related Benefits Schemes and Social Security (Recoupment) Amendment Regulations 1992 (SI 1992/1101), reg.6(8) (May 7, 1992).

20. Income-related Benefits Schemes (Miscellaneous Amendments) Regulations 1993 (SI 1993/315), Sch., para.6 (April 1, 1993).

21. Social Security Benefits (Miscellaneous Amendments) (No.2) Regulations 1993 (SI 1993/963), reg.2(3) (April 22, 1993).

22. Social Security Benefits (Miscellaneous Amendments) (No.2) Regulations 1993 (SI 1993/963), reg.2(5) (April 22, 1993).

23. Income-related Benefits Schemes and Social Security (Recoupment) Amendment Regulations 1993 (SI 1993/1249), reg.4(5) (May 14, 1993).

24. Income-related Benefits Schemes (Miscellaneous Amendments) (No.4) Regulations 1993 (SI 1993/2119), reg.24 (October 4, 1993).

25. Income-related Benefits Schemes (Miscellaneous Amendments) (No.5) Regulations 1994 (SI 1994/2139), reg.33 (October 3, 1994).

26. Income-related Benefits Schemes and Social Security (Claims and Payments) (Miscellaneous Amendments) Regulations 1995 (SI 1995/2303), reg.6(10) (October 2, 1995).

27. Income-related Benefits Schemes (Miscellaneous Amendments) Regulations 1996 (SI 1996/462), reg.11(1) (April 8, 1996).

28. Income Support (General) (Jobseeker's Allowance Consequential Amendments) Regulations 1996 (SI 1996/206), reg.26 (October 7, 1996).

29. Income-related Benefits Schemes and Social Fund (Miscellaneous Amendments) Regulations 1996 (SI 1944), reg.13 and Sch., para.7 (October 7, 1996).

30. Income Support and Social Security (Claims and Payments) (Miscellaneous Amendments) Regulations 1996 (SI 1996/2431), reg.6 (October 15, 1996).

31. Income-related Benefits and Jobseeker's Allowance (Amendment) (No.2) Regulations 1997 (SI 1997/2197), reg.7(9) and (10)(e) (October 6, 1997).

32. Social Security Amendment (New Deal) Regulations 1997 (SI 1997/ 2863), reg.17(11) and (12)(e) (January 5, 1998).

33. Social Security (Miscellaneous Amendments) (No.4) Regulations 1998 (SI 1998/1174), reg.7(7) and (8)(e) (June 1, 1998).

34. Social Security (Miscellaneous Amendments) (No.4) Regulations 1998 (SI 1998/1174), reg.7(9) and (10)(e) (June 1, 1998).

35. Social Security (Miscellaneous Amendments) (No.4) Regulations 1998 (SI 1998/1174), reg.7(11) and (12)(e) (June 1, 1998).

36. Social Security Amendment (New Deal) (No.2) Regulations 1998 (SI 1998/2117), reg.5(2) and (3)(c) (September 24, 1998).

37. Social Security Amendment (Sports Awards) Regulations 1999 (SI 1999/ 2165), reg.6(5) (August 23, 1999).

38. Social Security (Miscellaneous Amendments) (No.2) Regulations 1999 SI 1999/2556), reg.2(11) (October 4, 1999).

39. Social Security Amendment (Education Maintenance Allowance) Regulations 2000 (SI 2000/55), reg.2(3) and (4)(c) (February 7, 2000)

40. Social Security (Miscellaneous Amendments) Regulations 2000 (SI 2000/ 681), reg.9 (April 3, 2000).

41. Social Security (Immigration and Asylum) Consequential Amendments Regulations 2000 (SI 2000/636), reg.3(13) (April 3, 2000).

42. Social Security Amendment (Employment Zones) Regulations 2000 (SI 2000/724), reg.3(4) (April 3, 2000).

43. Social Security Amendment (Students) Regulations 2000 (SI 2000/1981), reg.5(5) and Sch. (July 31, 2000).

44. Social Security Amendment (Employment Zones) (No.2) Regulations 2000 (SI 2000/2910), reg.4(1) and (2)(c)(ii) (November 27, 2000)

45. Social Security Amendment (Capital Disregards) Regulations 2001 (SI 2001/22), reg.2(a) (February 1, 2001).

46. Social Security (Miscellaneous Amendments) Regulations 2001 (SI 2001/ 488), reg.10 (April 9, 2001).

47. Social Security (Miscellaneous Amendments) (No.3) Regulations 2001 (SI 2001/859), reg.3(6) (April 9, 2001).

48. Social Security Amendment (New Deal) Regulations 2001 (SI 2001/ 1029), reg.15(14) and (15)(c) (April 9, 2001).

49. Social Security Amendment (Capital Disregards and Recovery of Benefits) Regulations 2001 (SI 2001/1118), reg.2(1) (April 12, 2001).

50. Social Security Amendment (Discretionary Housing Payments) Regulations 2001 (SI 2001/2333), reg.2(2)(c) (July 2, 2001).

51. Children (Leaving Care) Act 2000 (Commencement No.2 and Consequential Provisions) Order 2001 (SI 2001/3070), art.3(2) and para.(c) of Sch.1 (October 1, 2001).

52. Social Security Amendment (Capital Disregards) (No.2) Regulations 2001 (SI 2001/3481), reg.2 (November 19, 2001).

53. Social Security Amendment (Residential Care and Nursing Homes) Regulations 2001 (SI 2001/3767), reg.2(1) and Pt I of Sch., para.20 (April 8, 2002).

54. Social Security Amendment (Employment Programme) Regulations 2002 (SI 2002/2314), reg.3(4) (October 14, 2002).

55. Social Security (Miscellaneous Amendments) (No.2) Regulations 2002 (SI 2002/2380), reg.2(b) (October 14, 2002).

56. Social Security (Miscellaneous Amendments) Regulations 2003 (SI 2003/511), reg.2(3) (April 1, 2003).

57. Social Security (Working Tax Credit and Child Tax Credit) (Consequential Amendments) Regulations 2003 (SI 2003/455), reg.2 and Sch.1, para.24(a) (April 7, 2003).

58. Social Security (Miscellaneous Amendments) (No.2) Regulations 2003 (SI 2003/2279), reg.2(5) (October 1, 2003).

59. Social Security (Incapacity Benefit Work-focused Interviews) Regulations 2003 (SI 2003/2439), reg.13(b) (October 27, 2003).

60. Social Security (Miscellaneous Amendments) Regulations 2004 (SI 2004/565), reg.2(4) (April 1, 2004).

61. Social Security (Working Tax Credit and Child Tax Credit) (Consequential Amendments) Regulations 2003 (SI 2003/455), reg.2 and Sch.1, para.24(b) (April 6, 2004, except in "transitional cases" and see further the note to reg.17 of the Income Support Regulations).

62. Social Security (Miscellaneous Amendments) (No. 2) Regulations 2004 (SI 2004/1141), reg.3(1) and (2)(c) (May 12, 2004).

63. Social Security (Miscellaneous Amendments) (No. 2) Regulations 2004 (SI 2004/1141), reg.3(3) and (4)(c) (May 12, 2004).

64. Social Security (Miscellaneous Amendments) (No. 2) Regulations 2004 (SI 2004/1141), reg.3(5) and (6)(c) (May 12, 2004).

65. Social Security (Students and Income-related Benefits) Amendment Regulations 2004 (SI 2004/1708), reg.5(3) (September 1, 2004, or if the student's period of study begins between August 1 and August 31, 2004, the first day of the period).

66. Social Security (Miscellaneous Amendments) (No. 3) Regulations 2004 (SI 2004/2308), reg.4(5) (October 4, 2004).

67. Social Security (Back to Work Bonus and Lone Parent Run-on) (Amendment and Revocation) Regulations 2003 (SI 2003/1589), reg.2(d) (October 25, 2004).

68. Social Security (Miscellaneous Amendments) Regulations 2005 (SI 2005/574), reg.3(6) (April 4, 2005).

DEFINITIONS

2.786   "the Act"—see reg.2(1).
"the benefit Acts"—*ibid.*
"child"—see 1986 Act, s.20(11) (SSCBA, s.137(1)).
"claimant"—see reg.2(1).
"dwelling occupied as the home"—*ibid.*
"employment zone contractor"—*ibid.*
"employment zone programme"—*ibid.*
"family"—see 1986 Act, s.20(11) (SSCBA, s.137(1)).
"full-time student"—see reg.61(1).
"Intensive Activity Period for 50 plus"—see reg.2(1).
"lone parent"—*ibid.*
"nursing home"—*ibid.*
"occupational pension"—*ibid.*
"partner"—*ibid.*
"payment"—*ibid.*
"personal pension scheme"—*ibid.*
"policy of life insurance"—*ibid.*
"qualifying person"—*ibid.*
"relative"—*ibid.*
"remunerative work"—*ibid.*
"residential accommodation"—*ibid.*

"residential care home"—*ibid.*
"retirement annuity contract"—*ibid.*
"self-employed earner"—*ibid.*
"self-employment route"—*ibid.*
"sports award"—*ibid.*
"subsistence allowance"—*ibid.*
"supplementary benefit"—*ibid.*
"the Eileen Trust"—*ibid.*
"the Independent Living Funds"—*ibid.*
"the Macfarlane (Special Payments) Trust"—*ibid.*
"the Macfarlane (Special Payments) (No. 2) Trust"—*ibid.*
"the Macfarlane Trust"—*ibid.*
"the Skipton Fund"—*ibid.*
"training allowance"—*ibid.*
"young person"—*ibid.*, reg.14.

GENERAL NOTE

Capital may be disregarded under more than one paragraph of Sch.10 at the same time, or in succession. There is no provision in reg.46(2) or Sch.10 for establishing any order of priority if different paragraphs of Sch.10 are applicable, so the claimant will be entitled to the benefit of the most favourable disregard (this is also the case for Sch.9). The disregards in Sch.10 apply to notional capital (*CIS 25/1990, CIS 81/1991, CIS 562/1992* and *CIS 30/1993*), provided that their conditions are met (*CIS 30/1993*). See the note to para.26.   2.787

In *R(IS) 15/96* the Commissioner expresses the view that claimants should be advised by the Benefits Agency of the existence of relevant disregards so that they can take advantage of them. In that case the claimant had received a criminal injuries compensation award so he could have taken steps to utilise the disregard in para.12.

Para.1

The value of the home is disregarded. Para.3 of Sch.3 contains rules about when a person is or is not to be treated as occupying a dwelling as his home. The fact that Sch.10 did not originally contain paras 25 to 28 gave rise to a number of problems (for which see p.178 of Mesher, *Income Support, the Social Fund and Family Credit: the Legislation* (1988)). The introduction of, in particular, a disregard of the value of premises which are for sale will solve, or at least postpone, many of the problems. See reg.17(f) and (2) to (7) for transitional protection for those excluded from income support from April 11, 1988 to May 29, 1988, and Sch.9, para.41 and Sch.10, para.32.   2.788

On the meaning of "dwelling occupied as the home", see notes to reg.2(1). Para.1 can apply to notional capital (*CIS 81/1991* (although it was not necessary to the decision) and *CIS 30/1993*).

Para.2

The value must be disregarded for the first 26 weeks after the acquisition. Thereafter all the circumstances must be looked at in deciding what is reasonable. There must be some realistic prospect of occupation starting. It might be thought that the requirement that the premises have been "acquired for occupation by the claimant" would exclude some forms of acquisition (*e.g.* inheritance). But according to para.29553 of the *Decision Makers Guide*, a person may acquire premises if he buys, is given or inherits them. "Premises" is to be given a reasonably wide meaning; thus acquiring land on which a person intends to build his home is covered by the disregard (see *CIS 8475/1995* in the note to para.3).   2.789

The income from premises whose value is disregarded under this provision counts as income (Sch.9, para.22), but mortgage repayments, water charges and council tax can be set off against it.

Para. 3

2.790   The sum must be directly attributable to the actual (*R(IS) 4/96*) proceeds of sale of a home, and must be intended for the purchase of another home (not repairs or refurbishment: *R(SB) 14/85; CIS 368/1993*). Money paid out on the surrender of endowment policies that had not been used to repay the claimant's mortgage on his former home was not "directly attributable to the proceeds of sale" of that home (*CFC 2493/1997*). *R(IS)6/95* decides that para.3 is not restricted to circumstances where a claimant is free to sell to a third party but can apply where a statutory tenancy of a home has been surrendered to the landlord. The claimant had sold his home, albeit technically by a surrender rather than a sale, and it was irrelevant to whom he had sold it.

As well as the purchase of a home that is already erected, the disregard also covers buying land and building a house on it (*CIS 8475/1995*). In *CIS 8475/ 1995* the claimant decided to use the proceeds of sale of his former home to buy a plot of land and build a bungalow on it. When he made his claim for income support the sale proceeds were held on deposit. By the date of the tribunal hearing the claimant had used the majority of the proceeds to purchase and clear the land. He had about £10,000 left for materials and labour to build the bungalow. The Commissioner decides that the claimant's intended use of the proceeds of sale fell within para.3. The words "purchase of other premises" in para.3 were to be given a reasonably wide meaning and included the outlay of money in stages to acquire land and build a house on it. This approach was consistent with that adopted in *R(IS) 11/94* in relation to housing costs met by income support (see the notes to para.15 of Sch.3); the Commissioner also agrees with *R(IS) 3/96* that the word "premises" in the first four paragraphs of this Schedule has a similar meaning (see the note to para.4). But the disregard in para.3 only applied to sums of money. Once the claimant had acquired the plot of land, the land and the partly-built bungalow as the work progressed, fell to be disregarded under para.2. On the facts of this case it was reasonable for the period of the disregard under paras 2 and 3 to be extended to 18 months from the date of the claim for income support. The Commissioner comments that in self-build cases a disregard of 12 months rather than six will normally be reasonable.

In *CIS 8475/1995* the Commissioner also makes the point that there is a difference between the wording "is to be used" in para.3 and the tests of intended occupation in, for example, paras 2, 27 and 28. In his view, para.3 required an element of practical certainty as well as subjective intent. This could be shown, for example, by a binding contract for purchase which had not yet been completed, or an agreement "subject to contract" in circumstances where it seemed likely that the money would not be diverted to other purposes. On the facts of that case the Commissioner found obtaining planning permission, placing the purchase in the hands of solicitors and accepting a builder's quote to be sufficient. *CIS 685/1992*, however, decides that it is not necessary, in order for there to be an extension of the primary 26 week period, that an intention to occupy specific premises should have been formed before the end of that period. If the proceeds of sale had not been used at the end of the 26 weeks there was a general discretion for the AO (or SSAT) to allow a longer period for the finding of another home and the completion of its purchase. However, a mere hope that the proceeds might be used at some future date for another home was not sufficient. In *R(IS) 7/01* the Commissioner considers that these two decisions are not irreconcilable and, adopting the approach of *CIS 15984/1996* to the words "to be used", concludes that the test under para.3 is that there must not only be an intention to use the capital to buy another home but also reasonable certainty that it will be used within 26 weeks or such further period as may be reasonable. In *CIS/4757/2003*, the same Commissioner confirms that personal circumstances (such as illness, as in that case, or awaiting the outcome of job applications that might determine the location of the new home as in *CIS/15984/1996*) can justify an extension beyond the 26 weeks. If the claimant can still demonstrate an intention to use the proceeds of sale to purchase another home, and it is reasonably certain that a property will be purchased within a further identifiable period, an extension of time will generally be appropriate.

Note also *CIS/4269/2003* which confirms that there is nothing in para.3 which says that the proceeds of sale must be of the property that was occupied immediately before the property which is to be purchased. The disregard in para.3 can still apply if a claimant who has a sum directly attributable to the proceeds of sale of home A is currently living in home B, providing that the condition that the sum is to be used to purchase home C within 26 weeks (or reasonable longer period) of the sale of home A is met.

In *CIS 222/1992* the claimant intended to use her share of the proceeds of sale of her deceased mother's house to purchase her own council house. The claimant had lived in her mother's house for a short time some 10 years before. The Commissioner rejects the argument that the claimant was entitled to the benefit of the disregard in para.3 because she formerly occupied her mother's home as her home. He finds that the conditions for a purposive construction of para.3 were satisfied (see Lord Diplock at p. 105 in *Jones v Wrotham Park Settled Estates Ltd* [1980] A.C. 74), and holds that para.3 only applied where the claimant had owned the property when she had lived there.

Para.4

In *R(IS) 3/96* the Commissioner rejects a submission from the AO (said to reflect the policy intention) that para.4 applied to disregard premises of any kind and extent. He decides that "premises" in para.4 was to be interpreted in accordance with the definition of "dwelling occupied as the home" in reg.2(1). The first four paragraphs of Sch.10 were all concerned with disregarding the claimant's home or what would be the home if the claimant was in actual occupation, and thus it was entirely consistent for "premises" in paras 2, 3 and 4 to be given a similar interpretation. Thus when the claimant went to live in a residential care home the farmhouse she jointly owned with her husband could be ignored under para.4(b), but not the farmland which had its own access and could have been sold separately.

2.791

"Relative" is defined in reg.2(1). "Incapacitated" is not. Para.29435 of the *Decision Makers Guide* suggests that receipt of incapacity benefit, statutory sick pay, or the disability element of working tax credit (as well as more rigorous benefits like severe disablement allowance, attendance allowance and disability living allowance) or an equivalent degree of incapacity will do. Under supplementary benefit, occupation was held to connote occupation as a residence, not merely as a holiday home (*R(SB) 1/85*). Under sub-para.(b) it does not now matter that the claimant also occupies the home.

Occupation by a former partner does not count if there has been estrangement or divorce, but see the disregard in para.25 in these circumstances. Estrangement is not the same as separation (*CIS/4843/2002*). *CIS/1846/2004*, to be reported as *R(IS) 5/05*, agrees with *R(SB) 2/87* that estrangement has a "connotation of emotional disharmony", whereas separation does not necessarily imply estrangement. However, when a woman talks of being "separated" from her husband, she is not usually referring to physical separation but to a separation prompted by emotional disharmony (presumably the Commissioner would also consider that the same applied if a husband referred to being "separated"!). The essential question was whether the parties had ceased to consider themselves as a couple and not whether, despite that, they continued to maintain friendly relations. In *CH/117/2005*, which concerned the equivalent provision in para.4(b) of Sch.5 to the Housing Benefit Regulations, the Commissioner did not agree with *R(IS) 5/05* that emotional disharmony must necessarily be a feature of estrangement. In his view a couple who have decided that their relationship is at an end could remain the best of friends but would be estranged for the purposes of housing benefit or income support. However, the Commissioner does agree with *R(IS) 5/05* that the central question is whether the couple have ceased to consider themselves as a couple. Thus a couple will not be estranged if they have retained all the indicia of partners apart from physical presence in the same household. However, with respect to the Commissioner in

CIS/117/2005, his approach appears to ignore the fact that sub-para.(b) refers to the claimant's "former partner". A couple who are merely temporarily apart will not have ceased to be partners (see reg.16). It is therefore suggested that there must be at least some element of "emotional disharmony" for sub-para.(b) not to apply. *R(IS)5/05* as a reported decision should in any event be preferred.

In *CIS 231/1991* the claimant had transferred his former home to his parents who were both over 60. When he claimed income support they were living in the home. The Commissioner decides that para.4(a) applied to the former home; the disregard applied to notional, as well as actual, capital.

Para.5

2.792   Before October 2, 1995 the disregard in para.5 applied to "any reversionary interest". The new form is in response to the Court of Appeal's decision in *Chief Adjudication Officer v Palfrey and Others, The Times*, February 17, 1995, also reported as part of *R(IS) 26/95*, which upheld the Tribunal of Commissioners' decision in *CIS 85/1992* that property subject to a tenancy was a reversionary interest and so was to be disregarded. The Commissioners had held that *R(SB) 3/86* (which decided that a reversionary interest was "something which does not afford any present enjoyment but carries a vested or contingent right to enjoyment in the future" and that a landlord's interest in a freehold property was not merely such an interest) was not to be followed. In *CIS 85/1992* the rented property was freehold, but *CIS 563/1991* and *CIS 615/1993* confirmed that the disregard under the previous form of para.5 applied to leasehold property as well.

It was considered that the effect of these decisions was to create an easy loophole which could enable a claimant to have the capital value of property disregarded simply by letting it, and so the new form of para.5 was introduced. Under the new form, the disregard applies to future interests in property but not land or premises which have been let by the claimant. A future interest in property is one that does not take effect immediately. An example would be where the claimant's entitlement only arises on the death of a person who has a life interest in the particular fund or property. Note that for the exception to operate, the lease, etc., has to be granted by the claimant. So, if the tenancy was granted by someone else (*e.g.* before the claimant owned the property) the disregard should still apply.

CIS 635/1994 suggests that the disregard could also apply if the property was subject to an irrevocable licence (rather than a lease or tenancy). The Commissioner expressed doubts as to whether a freehold or leasehold interest in a property subject to a tenancy could be said to be a future interest, but considered that the way the exception was put appeared to assume that it was. This meant that the new disregard might not be limited (as at first sight it seemed to be) to future interests in the sense of interests where there was no right at all until the future event happened. If the consequence is that the new form of para.5 covers situations where the claimant's interest affords no present enjoyment (and is a future interest in that sense) then, leaving aside the exception, the disregard itself may not be significantly different. Indeed it could be argued that a future interest is wider than a reversionary interest as it could include not only an interest that will revert to the claimant but also one that will only take effect in the future. (Note that in *Palfrey* both the Court of Appeal and the Commissioners considered that the capital value of the element of possession involved in a tenanted property fell to be disregarded under para.24 (in its previous form); it was the right to regain possession of the property at the end of the term which was a purely reversionary right that was covered by the old form of para.5.)

2.793   See also *R(IS) 1/97*. The claimant on separating from his wife had agreed that she could remain in the former matrimonial home (which was in his sole name) for her lifetime. There was no written agreement. The Commissioner decides that in the circumstances an irrevocable licence had been granted or could be inferred which gave rise to a constructive trust which in turn made the wife a tenant for life for the purposes of the Settled Land Act 1925. The Commissioner decides that the test laid down in *Ashburn Anstalt v Arnold* [1989] Ch. 1 for imposing a constructive trust, that is, that the owner of the property had so conducted himself that it would be inequitable to allow him to deny the beneficiary an interest in the property, was satisfied. The result was that the claimant's interest in the former matrimonial home was a reversionary one as it did not afford any present enjoyment. If the claimant's interest can similarly be ignored under the new form of para.5 (see above), this decision may have potentially wide implications for separating couples.

Note also *R(IS) 4/96* which decides that a charge on a former matrimonial home which was not to be enforced until the claimant's ex-wife died, remarried or cohabited for longer than six months was not a reversionary interest but gave the claimant a secured debt payable at a future date (see *Re Fisher* [1943] Ch. 377).

See also the amendment to para.24.

Rent from tenanted property, as and when it is received, will generally count as capital, not income (Sch.9, para.22), under reg.48(4). But note the excepted cases, *e.g.*, if the property is up for sale (and so disregarded under para.26). See the notes to reg.48(4) and para.22 of Sch.9 and note *CIS 563/1991* discussed in the note to reg.48(4).

Para.6

The business assets of a self-employed person are primarily disregarded under sub-para.(1) if he is engaged in the business. Para. 28375 of the *Decision Makers Guide* states that a person should be treated as engaged in a business for as long as he performs some work in it (*e.g.* checking stock), even for as little as half an hour a week. Business assets have to be distinguished from personal assets by asking if they are "part of the fund employed and risked in the business" (*R(SB) 4/85*). The income tax and accounting position are factors to be taken into account, but are not conclusive (*CFC 10/1989*), although see *CIS 5481/1997* which emphasises the relevance of accounting practice.

CIS/2467/2003 concerned a self-employed author who received advances on contracting to write a book and subsequent royalties on sales. The Commissioner rejected his argument that money paid by way of advances was not legally owned by him because the advances were repayable if he did not fulfill the contract. In his view the advances fully belonged to the claimant as soon as they were received. He further concluded that the receipts from the claimant's business were capital (see further the note to reg.30) and that they could not be disregarded under para.6. This was because, applying the test in *R(SB) 4/85*, the money was not employed in and risked in the business. The Commissioner rejected the claimant's argument that the ISA into which advances had been paid constituted a long-term reserve fund that underwrote and underpinned his business. It was a Maxi ISA; these are designed for personal savings by investment on a medium and long-term basis. The money in it was thus not employed in the business but in the personal sphere as the proceeds of the business. As the claimant was the business, if things went wrong he might need to draw on the value of the investment but this would represent a putting back into the business of resources from the claimant's personal sphere. The claimant also had a joint account with his wife into which some business receipts were paid and which was used for domestic purposes. The Commissioner emphasised that if a claimant wished to benefit from the disregard in para.6 in relation to money which is not in a separate business account, he must show that there is some positive demarcation between the assets of the business and personal assets. The claimant had failed to do this and the consequence was that none of the capital in his accounts fell to be disregarded under para.6.

R(FC) 2/92 holds that the ownership by an individual of a tenanted house is not a business, although there may come a point, depending on the circumstances, at which the amount of administration and/or activity involved even in the letting out of a single property could amount to self-employment (*CCS 2128/2001*; *CIB 1595/2000* and *CIB 2114/2000*). See also *CFC 4238/1997*. In *CH/4258/2004*, which concerned para.7(1) of Sch.5 to the Housing Benefit Regulations (the equivalent of para.6(1)), the claimant ran a retail business from the ground floor and basement of a building which also included three flats on the upper floors. She purchased the freehold of the whole

2.794

building (as the owner was not prepared to sell the retail part separately). The Comissioner concludes that the flats (which were let to tenants) were not used for the retail business (the fact that one business loan had been used to purchase the whole building did not affect this). Nor, applying *R(FC) 2/92*, were they assets of another business. As a consequence their value counted as the claimant's capital. Note that since October 2, 1995 a property that the claimant has let to tenants is not ignored as a reversionary interest (see the notes to para.5).

In *R(IS) 14/98* although the claimant was only a sleeping partner, the Commissioner decides that she continued to be gainfully employed and so a self-employed earner (s.2(1)(b) of the Contributions and Benefits Act 1992) in the farm business she owned with her son. The claimant had ceased to take an active role, having gone to live permanently in a residential care home, but she remained entitled to a share of the profits and capital and jointly and severally liable for the partnership's losses. Thus her share of the partnership assets, including the farm, fell to be disregarded under para.6. See also *CG 19/1994* where the claimant who had become a partner in her husband's business solely for tax purposes was held to be gainfully employed in the business. But the decision in *R(IS) 14/98* was appealed to the Court of Appeal, which allowed the appeal (*Chief Adjudication Officer v Knight*, April 9, 1997, reported as part of *R(IS) 14/98*). The Court held that for the disregard in para.6 to apply, a financial commitment to a business on its own was insufficient. The claimant had to be involved or engaged in the business in some practical sense as an earner. Thus a sleeping partner in a business managed and worked exclusively by others could not benefit from para.6.

If the claimant ceases to be engaged in the business, the value of the assets is disregarded for a period which is reasonable to allow them to be disposed of. In *CIS 5481/1997* the partnership that the claimant had been involved in had ceased trading. The Commissioner points out that a partnership did not cease to exist when it stopped trading. It ceased to exist when it was dissolved (which might or might not be the same time as it stopped trading). The assets remained business assets until the partnership was dissolved. However, the disregard in para.6 operated while a person was engaged as a self-employed earner for the purposes of the business and for such further time as was reasonable to allow for the disposal of the business's assets. The point when a person ceased to be engaged as a self-employed earner might be at the same time as a partnership ceased trading, or when it was dissolved, or at some other time (*e.g.* see *Knight* above). Thus in considering what was a reasonable time for disposal of assets under para.6 account had to be taken of the obligation on partners to sort out the partnership debts before distributing the assets. This would depend on the terms of any partnership deed or agreement or the Partnership Act 1890, and what was a reasonable period of time might alter if the circumstances changed. The Commissioner also suggested that a tribunal dealing with a case of this kind should include a financially qualified panel member under reg.36(3) of the Decisions and Appeals Regulations 1999 in view of the nature of the issues.

Where the self-employed person is temporarily not engaged in the business because of illness, there is a disregard under sub-para.(2).

Sub-paras.(3) and (4) disregards any assets of a business carried on while a person is participating in the "self-employment route" (defined in reg.2(1)), and, if the person later ceases to be engaged in that business, for a period which is reasonable to allow them to be disposed of. See also para.52 under which any capital acquired for the purposes of such a business is ignored for 52 weeks from the date of receipt.

Note in addition the general disregard of payments made under s.2 of the Employment and Training Act 1973 or s. 2 of the Enterprise and New Towns (Scotland) Act 1990 in para.30.

Income from capital disregarded under para.6 is not disregarded (Sch.9, para.22).

Para.7

2.795   Arrears of benefit which would be income when paid on the proper date retain their character as income (*R(SB) 4/89*). However, if any money is left after the end of the period to which the benefit is attributed as income then this will be capital (see notes to reg.40(1)).

Para.7 applies, under sub-para.(a), to mobility allowance or supplement, attendance allowance and any care or mobility component of disability living allowance, under sub-para.(b), to income support, income-based JSA, disability working allowance, working families' tax credit, disabled person's tax credit, child tax credit, working tax credit, family credit, housing benefit, council tax benefit, supplementary benefit and FIS. (Sub-para.(c) which applied to earnings top-up, a pilot scheme for people in low-paid work who did not have children which came to an end in October 1999, was revoked on April 4, 2005.) From July 2, 2001 it also applies under sub-para.(d) to discretionary housing payments. These are payments that can be made by a local authority to housing benefit/council tax benefit claimants who need extra help with their housing or council tax liability. They replaced the previous system of exceptional circumstances payments and exceptional hardship payments with effect from July 2, 2001.

For these benefits there is a disregard for 52 weeks from the date of receipt under sub-para.(1), unless the more extensive disregard in sub-para.(2) applies.

The effect of sub-para.(2) is that if, on or after October 14, 2001, as a consequence of an official error (as defined in reg.1(3) of the Decisions and Appeals Regulations 1999, see Vol. III of this series), a claimant receives arrears and/or concessionary payment(s) totalling £5,000 or more in relation to any one of the benefits listed in para.(1) ("the relevant sum"), this will be ignored indefinitely while the award during which the payment(s) are made continues, or for 52 weeks from the date of receipt, whichever is the longer. Award for this purpose means the award either of income support or income-based JSA during which the arrears/concessionary payment (or first instalment thereof) was received and includes subsequent awards of income support or income-based JSA, provided that such awards are continuous and that the claimant is either the person who received the relevant sum or the partner of that person, or was his partner at the date of his death, or in the case of joint-claim JSA is a joint-claim couple, either or both of whom received the relevant sum (sub-para.(3)). Thus the sub-para.(2) disregard will not apply and a claimant will be restricted to the 52 week disregard under sub-para.(1) if the relevant sum (or part thereof) was paid before income support/income-based JSA was claimed. It also seems that £5,000 or more must have been paid in respect of one of the listed benefits for the indefinite disregard to apply; payments in relation to more than one of these benefits cannot be aggregated for this purpose. Further, the requirement that a subsequent award should begin immediately after the end of the previous award for the indefinite disregard to continue to apply may cause difficulties, since there can often be a gap between claims when a claimant moves from income support to income-based JSA (or vice versa), unless the new claim is made with alacrity. For the limited circumstances in which claims can be backdated see reg.19 of the Claims and Payments Regulations in Vol. III of this series.

Note also the disregards in paras 38 to 41 and 47 to 49.

Para.8

This meets the problems in *R(SB) 14/81* and para.8(2) of *R(SB) 14/85*. Such sums may not be part of the claimant's capital anyway (see *CSB 975/1985* and the notes to reg.46). **2.796**

R(IS) 6/95 decides that sub-para.(a) only applies where the claimant has suffered damage to, or the loss of, his property against his will, not where he has deliberately brought this about. Thus it did not cover payment received for the surrender of a statutory tenancy of the claimant's home. *CIS 368/1993* rejects the argument that money (in that case proceeds of sale of a previous home) ear-marked for the renovation of the claimant's home came within sub-para.(b). The Commissioner decides that the money had not been "acquired on the express condition" that it was to be used for the renovation, but as a consequence of the sale.

Para.9

Sub-para.(b) gets round the problem in *R(SB) 4/87*. **2.797**

Para. 10

2.798   The supplementary benefit exceptions to the general disregard of the value of personal possessions were wider. Now it is only possessions bought with the intention of reducing capital so as to gain supplementary benefit or income support which count. See the notes to reg.51(1) for "purpose". Note that the corresponding paragraph under JSA (para.15 of Sch.8 to the JSA Regulations) applies if a person has bought possessions with the intention of reducing capital in order to secure entitlement to or increase the amount of JSA *or income support*. That avoids the question that might otherwise have arisen on a claimant transferring from income support to JSA as to whether possessions that had been bought only for the purpose of income support could be caught by para.15 of Sch.8. But para.10 has not been similarly amended.

If the value of personal possessions does count, it is their current market value, less 10 per cent if there would be expenses in selling, which must be included. For the possible problems of double counting and the interaction of this paragraph if personal possessions are not ignored and reg.51(1), see *CIS 494/1990* and *R(IS)8/04*, discussed under *"Deprivation"* in the notes to reg.51(1).

Presumably anything which is not real property is a personal possession. Providing that it is an object and not a right to sue for something, like a debt. But hard lines might have to be drawn between coins and bank-notes (obviously capital) and investments like paintings, stamps, furniture (apparently disregarded). What about gold bars?

Para. 12

2.799   There is an unlimited disregard of the value of a trust fund deriving from payment in compensation for personal injury. This seems particularly generous compared to the treatment of other forms of capital. Note that although para.12 refers to "personal injury to the claimant" the *Decision Makers Guide* originally simply referred to a payment made because of a personal injury (para.29412, although the current paragraph (29415) has subsequently been amended in the light of *R(IS) 3/03*, see below). Presumably this was because under reg.23(1) the capital of the claimant's partner is treated as the claimant's and any reference to the "claimant" is construed for the purpose of Part V of the Regulations as a reference to his partner, unless the context otherwise requires. However, the Commissioner in *R(IS) 3/03* took a more limited view.

In *R(IS) 3/03* the claimant had received compensation in respect of respiratory disease suffered by her husband which had been put in trust. Her husband had died some years previously. The issue was whether the disregard in para.12 applied in the circumstances of this case. It was contended that the reference to "the claimant" in para.12 included a reference to the claimant's partner by virtue of reg.23(1). The tribunal dismissed this argument on the basis that on the facts of this case reg.23(1) did not apply. This was because the personal injury had been suffered by the claimant's husband who was now dead and so had ceased to be her partner (as defined in reg.2(1)). (But is it not arguable that the situation should be looked at as at the date of the personal injury?). The Commissioner, however, considered that it might not in any event be right to treat the reference in para.12 as including a reference to the claimant's partner in the present case. He states:

"11. It appears that the purpose of the concluding part of reg.23(1) is simply that, <u>for the purpose of calculating the partner's capital where it is to be treated as that of the claimant under s.136</u> [SSCBA], references in the detailed provisions of Part V to 'the claimant' are to be treated as references to the claimant's partner. It should be noted that Reg.23 says that references to the claimant are to be treated as references to the partner (*i.e.* the claimant's partner' is <u>substituted</u> for 'claimant' so that the detailed provisions of Part V make sense when applied to calculation of the claimant's partner's capital). It does not say that references to 'claimant' shall be treated as <u>including</u> references to the claimant's partner. In the present case we are not concerned with determining the amount of the claimant's husband's capital which is to be treated as that of the claimant, but with determining the amount of the claimant's own capital, and Reg.23(1) therefore arguably simply has no application."

The Commissioner did state that he was not basing his decision on this reasoning as it had not been argued before him, so it may be that the decision should be restricted to its facts. If the disregard in para.12 only applies where it is the claimant (not his partner) who has suffered the personal injury, this could severely restrict its ambit. Moreover, as the Commissioner acknowledges, the wording of the exemptions from the notional capital rules in reg.5(1) and (2) for trusts derived from personal injury would not seem to be so limited. It seems odd that a parallel approach is not employed in all these provisions.

If there is no trust the amount of compensation counts as capital, even though it is in a solicitor's hands (*Thomas v Chief Adjudication Officer*, reported as (*R(SB) 17/87*; see also *R(IS) 15/96* in the notes to reg.46. But note *CIS 984/2002* which holds that money held by the claimant's solicitor pending quantification of the statutory charge to the Legal Services Commission under s.10(7) of the Access to Justice Act 1999 was not part of the claimant's capital: see further the note to reg.46). If the claimant then transfers the compensation to trustees, the exception in reg.51(1)(a) operates so that he will not be treated as having deprived himself of the capital placed on trust. Although putting money into a trust would normally count as deprivation, to do so in the case of trusts of personal injury compensation would defeat the purpose of para.12. It is not necessary for the trust to be set up before the compensation is received. Furthermore, since para.12 refers to funds "derived" from personal injury compensation, it is certainly arguable that the disregard should also apply even if the compensation was initially used for other purposes before being placed on trust. An example could be if the compensation was used to buy a home but this was later sold and the proceeds of sale put on trust. If the money placed on trust derived (in the sense of "originated") from personal injury compensation, there would seem to be no policy reason why the disregard in para.12 should not apply. The purpose of the disregard is presumably to allow such compensation payments to be used for the person's disablement needs that have arisen as a result of the injury. The fact that the funds have been employed elsewhere for an intermediate period would not seem to affect this policy intention.

CIS 368/1994 decides that the disregard in para.12 applied where the compensation was held and administered by a combination of the Public Trustee and the Court of Protection. In the Commissioner's view, the word "trust" was used to cover the situation where the legal estate was in one person and the beneficial interest in another. It did not matter for the purposes of para.12 whether a particular trust had been set up or whether there was in operation a statutory scheme involving, for example, the Court of Protection. The effect of this decision would seem to be that the disregard in para.12 can apply whether the money is administered by the Court of Protection itself or held in the name of the receiver or the Public Trustee. For further discussion of the position of funds held by the Court of Protection, see *CIS 2011/2003*, to be reported as *R(IS) 9/04*, in the note to reg.46.

Now see paras 44 and 45 which have introduced a specific disregard for funds held in court that derive from damages for personal injury or compensation for the death of a parent. See the notes to paras 44 and 45 and note the October 1997 amendments to those paragraphs. Note also that paras 44 and 45 have not been added to the list of exceptions in reg.48(4). This means that payments to a claimant from funds disregarded under those paragraphs will apparently be treated as capital under the rule in reg.48(4), even if due to their nature (*e.g.* because they are made periodically) they would otherwise count as income. See further the notes to reg.48(4).

Note that "personal injury" includes a disease and any injuries suffered as a result of a disease (*e.g.* amputation of both legs following meningitis and septicaemia), as well as any accidental or criminal injury (*R(SB) 2/89*).

Any payment from the trust will be income or capital depending on the nature of the payment (income from trusts disregarded under this paragraph is one of the excepted cases from the general rule in reg.48(4) that income from capital counts as capital). But note that from October 28, 2002 regular payments from funds derived from a personal injury award to the claimant will be disregarded under para.15 of Sch.9, unless they are used for the items listed in para.15(2), in which case a disregard of £20 (subject to the overall £20 disregard in para.36 of Sch.9) applies. (See reg.41(7) which treats periodic payments paid under an agreement or court order to a claimant in consequence of personal injury to him, other than payments deemed to be capital (see reg.48(4)), as income.) Note also the rules for payments to third parties in regs 42(4) and 51(3). The notional income rule in reg.42(2) (income available on application) and the notional capital rules in reg.51(1) (deprivation of capital) and reg.51(2) (capital available on application) do not apply to trusts of personal injury compensation.

Para.13

2.800   This reverses the result of *R(SB) 43/84*.

Para.14

2.801   The provisions mentioned deal with situations where foreign income or earnings cannot be transmitted to the United Kingdom.

Para.15

2.802   The surrender value of all life insurance policies is disregarded. In supplementary benefit there was a limit of £1,500.

In *R(IS) 7/98* the claimant had placed her capital in an "investment bond". This provided for a low guaranteed minimum death benefit if the investment had not been fully cashed in before death. But it also included, among other surrender options, a "monthly withdrawal plan", under which the claimant received a sum of £75.20 a month by way of partial encashment until the value of the investment was exhausted. The Commissioner decides that the bond fell within the definition of "policy of life insurance" in reg.2(1). For this definition to apply, it was not necessary for death of the investor to be the only contingency under which money was payable (see *CIS 122/1991*), nor was the relative size of the death benefits on one hand, and the investments benefits on the other, relevant (see *Gould v Curtis* [1913] 3 K.B. 84). The value of the bond therefore fell to be disregarded under para.15 (even though its full investment value was obtainable on demand and so would have come within reg.51(2) (capital available on demand), except for para.15). However, in relation to the original decision to purchase the bond, the deprivation rule in reg.51(1) would have to be considered (see *CIS 112/1994* (and *CIS 109/1994*) in the notes to reg.51). Moreover, since the £75.20 monthly payments represented payments of capital by instalments, for as long as the total outstanding under the policy together with any other capital belonging to the claimant exceeded £8,000, such payments would count as income for the period they were paid under reg.41. (See para.16 as regards the right to receive these payments.)

Para.16

2.803   See reg.41(1) and *R(IS) 7/98* in the note to para.15.

Para.17

2.804   Although in ordinary cases the nature of such payments as capital or income depends on general principles of law (*R(SB) 29/85*), in trade dispute cases reg.41(3) secures that they are all treated as income.

Para.20

2.805   This is to avoid double counting. Note that the amendments made to this provision on April 6, 2004 do not apply in "transitional cases"—see the note to reg.17. The amendments were made because with effect from April 6, 2004 (except in "transitional cases"—see the note to reg.17) amounts for children and young persons were removed from the income support scheme (financial support for children and young persons is now to be provided through the child tax credit system, see Vol. IV in this series) and income support became in effect an "adults only" benefit. See the 2003 edition of this volume for the old form of para.20.

Para.22

The disregard now extends to payments to haemophiliacs from the three trusts and to non-haemophiliacs from the Fund, the Eileen Trust and the Skipton Fund, and to distributions of income payments to the close family, or a slightly wider class for the two years following such a person's death. Any payments from the Independent Living Funds are ignored.   **2.806**

Para.23

Accrued rights to receive an occupational or personal pension in the future are often amongst a person's most valuable assets, but they are not capable of being bought or sold, and so have no market value anyway.   **2.807**

Para.23A

See the notes to reg.42(2)–(2C).   **2.808**

Para.24

This paragraph was amended on October 2, 1995 at the same time as the new form of para.5 was introduced. See the notes to para.5. Since the annual amount of the rent due can be used to calculate the value of a tenanted property the amendment will prevent the annual rent (and thus the capital value of the property) from being reduced to nil because of the disregard.   **2.809**

Para.25

This paragraph applies where a claimant has ceased to be part of a couple because of estrangement or divorce and has left what was formerly the home. In these circumstances the claimant may well have an actual or deemed (see reg.52) interest in the dwelling, but no longer be able to get within para.1. But see the notes to reg.52 on disputed matrimonial assets. Divorce is an easily proved event, but estrangement is a less hard edged concept. It has "connotations of emotional disharmony" (*R(SB) 2/87* and *CIS/1846/2004*, to be reported as *R(IS) 5/05*, although *CIS/117/2005* does not consider that emotional disharmony is an essential feature in this context - see further the note to para.4). It is not the same as separation (*CIS/4843/2002*). Since the two people concerned must no longer be partners, there must be more than a temporary absence (and see reg.16). *R(IS) 5/05* and *CIS/117/2005* conclude that the central question is whether the couple have ceased to regard themselves as a couple - see further the note to para.4.   **2.810**

The disregard used to be limited to 26 weeks from the date on which the claimant left the dwelling, with no extension. However, with effect from April 1, 2003 it applies without limit if the former partner who occupies the home is a lone parent. This brings the disregard into line with that which applies for the purpose of housing benefit and council tax benefit.

Para.26

This provision restores some of the effect of the similar supplementary benefit disregard. It will ease some of the problems noted on p. 178 of Mesher, *Income Support, the Social Fund and Family Credit: the Legislation* (1988), but not all of them. It applies if reasonable steps are being taken to dispose of premises. "Premises" in para.26 is to be construed widely and includes land without buildings (*R(IS) 4/97*), preferring *CSB 222/1986* to *CIS 673/1993*). See also *R(IS) 3/96* and *CIS 8475/1995* in the notes to paras 3 and 4. What are reasonable steps must be a question of fact. The Commissioner in *CIS 7319/1995* considers that the test is an objective one. So, if the sale price was totally unrealistic, that attempt at sale should be disregarded and   **2.811** the period of the disregard would not start to run until reasonable steps to dispose of the premises were *first* taken. In his view the period of the disregard must be continuous. *CIS 6908/1995* also confirms that the disregard starts when the claimant first takes steps to dispose of the premises, which may well be before a property is put on the open market. In *CIS/1846/2004*, to be reported as *R(IS) 5/05*, the Commissioner points out that the bringing of ancillary relief proceedings within a divorce suit may have been a necessary preliminary step before a former matriomonial home was put on the market; there also seemed no reason why the para.26 disregard should not apply while arrangements were being made for a former partner to buy the interest of the claimant, which avoided putting the home on the market at all. He added that if the claimant was proposing to buy out the former partner and move back into the matrimonial home herself, the disregard in para.27 might be applicable instead.

The initial disregard is for 26 weeks, but can be extended where reasonable to enable the disposal to be carried out.

In *CIS 562/1992* it is held that the 26 weeks does not run from the beginning of each fresh claim for income support, but from the day on which the claimant first took steps to dispose of the property. On its particular facts (it was several years since the property was first put on the market and the claimant had transferred ownership of it to his son for some time but then taken it back) this decision seems right. However, if a property is up for sale, then is genuinely taken off the market and put up for sale again later, it must be arguable that the time under para.26 runs from the second occasion of taking steps to dispose of the property. As *CIS 2668/1998* and *CJSA 2379/1998* confirms, it will depend on the circumstances of a particular case. In *CIS 6908/1995* the Commissioner accepts that the 26 weeks could run while the property was being disregarded under some other paragraph of Sch.10. But it would often be right to extend the period to a date (at least) 26 weeks after the property had ceased to be disregarded under that other paragraph (because otherwise the effect could be to deprive a claimant of the benefit of para.26). The Commissioner also suggests some of the factors that might be relevant in deciding whether the 26 weeks should be extended. Besides the efforts made by the claimant to dispose of the property, other factors might be the state of the housing market, the claimant's intentions as regards the proceeds of sale, the value of his interest in the property and his ability to borrow money on the strength of that interest. Each case would depend on its own facts.

CIS 30/1993 decides that this disregard cannot apply to notional capital if the claimant has already disposed of the same capital so as to trigger reg.51(1). This is because para.26 is only applicable where the *claimant* is taking steps to dispose of premises. The Commissioner in *CIS 30/1993* acknowledges that this view is different from that taken in some other decisions, but having reviewed these (*R(SB) 9/91*, *CIS 25/1990*, *CIS 81/1991* and *CIS 562/1992*) concludes that the only one in which this question had been central to the appeal was *CIS 25/1990* and in that case the point had not been argued in any detail. He was therefore not bound by it. (*R1/92 (IS)*, a decision of the Chief Commissioner in Northern Ireland, had come to the same conclusion as he had done.) It had been argued on behalf of the claimant that if the property was put up for sale by the actual possessor of it, para.26 should apply. The AO had submitted, first, that the wording of para.26 made it clear that the disregard only applied if the claimant was taking steps to dispose of the premises; second, that the purpose of the disregard in para.26 was to allow the claimant a reasonable time to liquidate assets to provide money to live on. There could be no guarantee that the third party would allow the proceeds of sale to be used to support the claimant and thus there was no reason to delay counting the notional capital. The Commissioner holds that the words of para.26 were plain and unambiguous and could not apply because the claimant could not be taking steps to dispose of what she had already disposed of. This seems unfair in that a claimant deemed to have notional capital may suffer an additional penalty through not being able to benefit from the disregard in para.26. But the Commissioner's conclusion is cogently argued.

Para.27

In these circumstances the claimant will have an interest in the premises, but it would be unfair to count the value of the interest. The initial disregard is for 26 weeks, with an extension as reasonable.

In *CIS 240/1992* the legal advice given to the claimant was that he could not obtain possession of the premises until the end of the current tenancy. The Commissioner states that for para.27 to apply the claimant must be taking steps to obtain possession and rejects a submission that a failure to take steps that were bound to be unsuccessful did not preclude the application of para.27. But in seeking legal advice was not the claimant taking such steps? Para.27 does not require the claimant to have commenced legal proceedings for the disregard to apply; it is sufficient if he has sought legal advice with a view to obtaining possession. Provided that a claimant is willing to commence proceedings immediately the tenancy ends (which did not appear to be the case in *CIS 240/1992*) it is difficult to see what other steps he could take in such circumstances.

Para.28

Since the value of the home is disregarded, this is a limited extension. Then the disregard is for 26 weeks, with an extension as reasonable.

The scope of the similar disregard in para.27 of Sch.5 to the Housing Benefit Regulations was considered in *R. v Tower Hamlets L B C Housing Benefit Review Board Ex p. Kapur, The Times*, June 28, 2000, HC. The claimant, who was in receipt of housing and council tax benefit, owned a house valued at £240,000 which was vacant and unfit for human habitation. He wanted to move into the property and made several unsuccessful attempts to obtain finance to effect repairs to it. The local authority decided that the value of the property could not be disregarded because the steps taken by the applicant to raise finance were merely preparatory and were not steps taken to effect repairs. Scott Baker J. held that this was the wrong approach. He referred to the *Adjudication Officer's Guide* which stated, in relation to the income support disregard in para.28, that steps could include getting a grant or loan to pay for repairs or alterations, employing an architect, getting planning permission or finding someone to do the work, and the date that a person first took such steps could be the date he first started making these inquiries. It was a question of fact as to when the first steps were taken but the Board's approach had been too narrow. Now see paras 29572–6 of the *Decision Makers Guide*.

Para.29

Payments of earnings or other income in kind are disregarded (see regs 35(2) and 40(4) and Sch.9, para.21). Most payments of capital in kind would be personal possessions (see para.10).

Para.30

The new form of this paragraph in force from April 1, 2004 provides a blanket capital disregard of the various allowances, grants and other payments made under s.2 of the Employment and Training Act 1973 or s.2 of the Enterprise and New Towns (Scotland) Act 1990 to people participating in New Deals and other training and welfare to work schemes. However if these payments do count as capital they are only ignored for 52 weeks from the date of receipt.

Before April 1, 2004 separate disregards had existed in respect of such payments under a number of the provisions in this Schedule. As a consequence of this change, those provisions have been revoked or amended. The revoked paragraphs are paras 50, 50A, 51, 53, 69 and 70; the amended paragraph is para.42.

For the income disregard of payments under s.2 of the 1973 Act and s.2 of the 1990 Act see para.13 of Sch.9.

Para.42

These are capital payments from special Department of Employment schemes to assist disabled people, such as the "business on own account' scheme and the "personal reader service."

2.812

2.813

2.814

2.815

Para. 43

2.816   Start-up capital payments under the Blind Homeworkers' Scheme are disregarded, but payments of income are taken into account.

Paras 44–45

2.817   These paragraphs were amended in October 1997 so that the disregard of funds held in court that derive from damages for personal injury is no longer restricted to under 18-year-olds but now applies without age limit. However, where the compensation was awarded for the death of a parent (or parents), the person concerned must be under 18 for the disregard to apply. Death benefits under a pension or insurance policy are not compensation, since this implies the replacement of something lost, whereas such benefits are paid on the basis of a contract made by the deceased (*McAuley v Department for Social Development*, Court of Appeal of Northern Ireland, reported as *R3/01(IS)*).

See para.12 for the disregard of compensation payments for personal injury placed on trust. *CIS 368/1994* decided that the disregard in para.12 applied to compensation for personal injury that was held and administered by the Court of Protection, since in the circumstances such an arrangement amounted to a "trust". (For further discussion of the position of funds held by the Court of Protection, see to be reported as *R(IS) 9/04* in the note to reg.46.) The disregard in para.44(a) will now apply to damages for personal injury held by the Court of Protection (and also the High Court and the County Court, and, under para.45(a), the equivalent Scottish courts), whatever the age of the person. Note that the award must be for injury to that person.

Note that funds disregarded under paras 44(a) and 45(a) are excluded from the notional income rule in reg.42(2) (income available on application) and the notional capital rules in reg.51(1)(c) and (2)(e) (deprivation of capital and capital available on application). Note further that paras 44 and 45 have not been added to the list of expected cases in reg.48(4). This means that payments to a claimant from funds disregarded under para.44 or 45 will apparently count as capital, whatever the nature of those payments. See further the notes to reg.48(4).

"Personal injury" includes a disease and any injuries suffered as a result of a disease (*e.g.* amputation of both legs following meningitis and septicaemia), as well as any accidental or criminal injury (*R(SB) 2/89*).

Para. 49

2.818   See the note to reg.21ZB.

Paras 50, 50A and 51

2.819   For the previous form of these paragraphs see the 2003 edition of this volume. However they have been omitted with effect from April 1, 2004 because from that date para.30 contains a blanket disregard in relation to payments made under s.2 of the Employment and Training Act 1973 or s.2 of the Enterprise and New Towns (Scotland) Act 1990 to people participating in New Deals and other training and welfare to work schemes. But note that if such payments do count as capital they are only ignored for 52 weeks from the date of receipt. See further the note to para.30.

Para. 52

2.820   Any capital acquired for the purposes of a business carried on while a person is participating in the "self-employment route" (defined in reg.2(1)) is ignored for 52 weeks from the date of receipt.

See also the disregard of business assets for people participating in the self-employment route in para.6(3) and (4) and the general disregard of payments made under s.2 of the Employment and Training Act 1973 or s.2 of the Enterprise and New Towns (Scotland) Act 1990 in para.30.

Para.53

See the note to paras 50, 50A and 51 above.   2.821

Para.56

See the note to para.69 of Sch.9. Note that if a sports award (or part of it) counts   2.822
as capital, the payment will only be disregarded for 26 weeks from the date of receipt.

Paras 58 and 59

See the note to reg.42(5A).   2.823

Para.60

This paragraph has not been reproduced as it only related to a pilot scheme to   2.824
reduce under-occupation operating in three London boroughs (Croydon, Haringey
and Newham) from April 3, 2000. It was added by reg.12 of the Social Security
(Payments to Reduce Under-occupation) Regulations 2000 (SI 2000/637) on April
3, 2000 and provided that a payment made under the scheme would be ignored for
52 weeks from the date of payment. The pilot scheme lasted for three years and the
Payments to Reduce Under-occupation Regulations ceased to have effect on March
31, 2003.

Para.61

This allows *ex-gratia* payments of £10,000, made to former Japanese prisoners of   2.825
war or to their surviving spouse, on or after February 1, 2001, to be disregarded
indefinitely.

Para.62

This provides for the whole of a claimant's capital to be disregarded during any   2.826
"mortgage run-on" period. See the notes to reg.6(5)–(8) as to when this applies. See
also the disregards in para.15C of Sch.8 and para.74 of Sch.9 and the note to
para.15C.

Para.63

See the note to para.11 of Sch.9. Note that the new form of para.63 in force from   2.827
the start of the national scheme of education maintenance allowances (EMAs) provides for an indefinite disregard of any part of the EMA that counts as capital.

Para.64

This refers to payments from, or derived from, the government-funded trust funds   2.828
set up to help those who have contracted variant Creutsfeldt-Jakob disease. The disregard extends to distribution of capital to the partner of the "diagnosed person"
(defined in sub-para.(6)), to any child for two years from the date of the payment,
or until he leaves full-time education or becomes 19, if this is later, or to any parent
for two years from the date of the payment.

Para.65

This provides for an indefinite disregard of compensation paid because the   2.829
claimant, his partner, his deceased spouse or his partner's deceased spouse was
forced to work, lost property or suffered personal injury, or was the parent of a child
who died, during the Second World War.

Para.66

See the note to para.76 of Sch.9.

Para.67

This disregard has been introduced to ensure that if payments for community
care services which a local authority makes direct to the person concerned do count
as capital they are not taken into account. For the income disregard see para.58 of
Sch.9.

Para.68

For the regulations under para.3 of Sch.4 to the Adoption and Children Act 2002 see the Adoption Support Services (Local Authorities) (England) Regulations 2003 (SI 2003/1348) and the Adoption Support Services (Local Authorities (Wales) Regulations 2004 (SI 2004/1011)). Any payments to adopters or potential adopters made under these provisions are fully disregarded.

Para. 68A

Section 115 of the Adoption and Children Act 2002 amended the Children Act 1989 to introduce a new special guardianship order, which is intended to provide permanence for children for whom adoption is not appropriate; the special guardian has parental responsibility for the child but the child's legal relationship with his birth parents is not severed. The special guardianship provisions come into force on December 30, 2005. Payments made by local authorities to special guardians are ignored. For the income disregard see para.25(1)(e) of Sch.9.

Paras 69 and 70

For the previous form of these paragraphs, which concerned the Employment, Retention and Advancement (ERA) scheme and the Return to Work Credit scheme respectively, see the 2003/2004 Supplement to this volume. However these paragraphs have been omitted with effect from April 1, 2004 because from that date para.30 contains a blanket disregard in relation to payments made under s.2 of the Employment and Training Act 1973 or s.2 of the Enterprise and New Towns (Scotland) Act 1990 to people participating in New Deals and other training and welfare to work schemes. But note that if such payments do count as capital they are only ignored for 52 weeks from the date of receipt. See further the note to para.30.

Income Support (Liable Relatives) Regulations 1990

(SI 1990/1777)

Made by the Secretary of State under s.166(1) to (3A) of the Social Security Act 1975 and ss.24A(1), 24B(5) and 84(1) of the Social Security Act 1986

Citation, commencement and interpretation

2.830

1.—(1) These Regulations may be cited as the Income Support (Liable Relatives) Regulations 1990 and shall come into force on 15th October 1990.

(2) In these Regulations—

"the Act" means the Social Security Act 1986; and

"the Income Support Regulations" means the Income Support (General) Regulations 1987.

Prescribed amounts for the purposes of section 24A of the Act [SSAA, s.107]

2.831

2.—(1) For the purposes of section 24A of the Act [SSAA, s.107] (recovery of expenditure on income support: additional amounts and transfer of orders) the amount which may be included in the sum which the court may order the other parent to pay under section 24(4) of the Act [SSAA, s.106(2)] shall be the whole of the following amounts which are payable to or for the claimant—

(a) any personal allowance under paragraph 2 of Part I of Schedule 2 to the Income Support Regulations for each of the children whom the other parent is liable to maintain;

(b) any family premium under paragraph 3 of Part II of that Schedule;

(c) any lone parent premium under paragraph 8 of Part III of that Schedule;

(d) any disabled child premium under paragraph 14 of Part III of that Schedule in respect of a child whom the other parent is liable to maintain; and

(e) any carer premium under paragraph 14ZA of Part III of that Schedule if, but only if, that premium is payable because the claimant is in receipt, or is treated as being in receipt, of [¹ a carer's allowance] by reason of the fact that he is caring for a severely disabled child or young person whom the other parent is liable to maintain.

(2) If the court is satisfied that in addition to the amounts specified in paragraph (1) above the liable parent has the means to pay, the sum which the court may order him to pay under section 24 of the Act [SSAA, s.106] may also include all or some of the amount of any personal allowance payable to or for the claimant under paragraph 1 of Part I of Schedule 2 to the Income Support Regulations.

AMENDMENT

1. Social Security Amendment (Carer's Allowance) Regulations 2002 (SI 2002/2497), reg.3 and Sch.2 (April 1, 2003).

Notice to the Secretary of State of applications to alter etc. maintenance orders

3.—(1) For the purposes of section 24B(5) of the Act [SSAA, s.108(5)] (prescribed person in prescribed circumstances to notify the Secretary of State of application to alter etc. a maintenance order) the prescribed person is, and in paragraph (2) below that expression means,—

(a) in England and Wales—
  (i) in relation to the High Court, where the case is proceeding in the deputy principal registry the senior registrar of that registry, and where the case is proceeding in a district registry the district registrar;
  (ii) in relation to a county court, the proper officer of that court within the meaning of Order 1, Rule 3 of the County Court Rules 1981; and
  (iii) in relation to a magistrates' court, the clerk to the justices of that court; and

(b) in Scotland—
  (i) in relation to the Court of Session, the deputy principal clerk of session; and
  (ii) in relation to a sheriff court, the sheriff clerk.

(2) For the purposes of that subsection the prescribed circumstances are that before the final determination of the application the Secretary of State has made a written request to the prescribed person that he be notified of any such application, and has not made a written withdrawal of that request.

GENERAL NOTE

See the notes to ss.107 and 108 of the Administration Act in Vol. III of this series.

2.832

2.833

Income Support (Transitional) Regulations 1987

(SI 1987/1969)

2.834   *These regulations have been omitted in order to save space and because they are now only likely to be relevant to a very few cases. For the full text of these Regulations, see Vol. II of Social Security Legislation 2000.*

Income Support (General) Amendment No. 6 Regulations 1991

(SI 1991/2334)

Made by the Secretary of State under ss. 22(1) and 84(1) of the Social Security Act 1986 and s. 166(1) to (3A) of the Social Security Act 1975

[In force November 11, 1991]

Saving Provision in relation to Severe Disability Premium

2.835   4.—(1) The provisions of this regulation are subject to regulation 5.

(2) Where paragraph (3), (4), (5) or (6) applies to a claimant, sub-paragraph (2)(a)(ii), or, as the case may be, sub-paragraph (2)(b)(iii) of paragraph 13 of Schedule 2 to the General Regulations shall have effect as if the relevant amendment had not been made.

(3) This paragraph applies to a claimant who satisfied both the qualifying conditions in the week immediately preceding 21st October 1991.

(4) This paragraph applies to a claimant—

(a) who satisfied both the qualifying conditions in at least one of the eight weeks immediately preceding 21st October 1991, but did not satisfy either or both of those conditions in the week immediately preceding that date; and

(b) who in a week commencing not more than eight weeks after the date on which he last satisfied both the qualifying conditions, would again have satisfied both those conditions if the relevant amendment had not been made.

(5) This paragraph applies to a claimant—

(a) who ceased to be entitled to income support because he became engaged in remunerative work for a period not exceeding the permitted period determined in accordance with regulation 6 and that period had commenced but had not ended before 21st October 1991; and

(b) who satisfied both the qualifying conditions in the week ending on the day before the first day of that period commenced; and

(c) who in the week which commences on the day immediately following the day on which that period ends, would again have satisfied both the qualifying conditions if the relevent amendment had not been made.

(6) This paragraph applies to a claimant—

(a) who satisfied both the qualifying conditions immediately before he—

    (i) participated in arrangements for training made under section 2 of the Employment and Training Act 1973 or section 2 of the Enterprise and New Towns (Scotland) Act 1990; or

    (ii) attended a course at an employment rehabilitation centre established under section 2 of the Employment and Training Act 1973,

and he had begun the training or joined the course before 21st October 1991 and was still continuing with the training or course at that date; and

(b) who in the week which commences on the day immediately following the last day he attended the training or course, would again have satisfied both the qualifying conditions if the relevant amendment had not been made.

(7) The "qualifying conditions" means the two qualifying conditions set out in paragraph (8)(a) and (b) below.

(8) For the purposes of paragraph (7)—

(a) the first qualifying condition is that the claimant—

    (i) has made a claim for income support which has not been determined, but had it been determined and an award made, his applicable amount would have included severe disability premium; or

    (ii) has a current award of income support and the applicable amount appropriate to that award includes severe disability premium; or

    (iii) has a current award of income support and has before 21st October 1991 made an application in writing in accordance with section 104(2) of the Social Security Act requesting a review of that award, where the ground, or one of the grounds for review, is that—

        (aa) he has become a co-owner with a close relative of the dwelling which he and that close relative jointly occupy as their home; or

        (bb) he has become jointly liable with a close relative to make payments to a landlord in respect of the dwelling which he and that close relative jointly occupy as their home,

    whether or not there are other co-owners or other persons jointly liable to make such payments and, if revised, the applicable amount appropriate to the award includes severe disability premium in respect of a period prior to that date;

(b) the second qualifying condition is that the person is—

    (i) a co-owner, with a close relative, of the dwelling he and that close relative jointly occupy as their home, whether or not there are other co-owners; or

    (ii) jointly liable, with a close relative, to make payments to a landlord in respect of the dwelling he and that close relative jointly occupy as their home, whether or not there are other persons jointly liable to make such payments.

[¹(9) For the purposes of paragraph (8)(b) and regulation 5(2)(b), where a person has satisfied the second qualifying condition, but his circumstances change so that he no longer satisfies it, he shall nonetheless be treated as satisfying it for so long as he is a person to whom paragraph (10) applies.

(10) This paragraph applies to a person—

(a) who was, together with a close relative of his, either a co-owner of, or jointly liable to make payments to a landlord in respect of, the dwelling which he and that close relative jointly occupied as their home; and

(b) who has since become, with that close relative or any other close relative, either—

   (i) jointly liable to make payments to a landlord in respect of that dwelling or any other dwelling; or

   (ii) a co-owner of that dwelling or any other dwelling,

   which he and the close relative jointly occupy as their home (whether or not there are other co-owners, or other persons jointly liable to make such payments).]

AMENDMENT

2.836   1. Income-related Benefits Schemes (Miscellaneous Provisions) Amendment Regulations 1991 (SI 1991/2695), reg.5 (December 27, 1991).

DEFINITIONS

"claimant"—see Income Support Regulations, reg.2(1).
"close relative"—*ibid.*
"dwelling occupies as the home"—*ibid.*
"partner"—*ibid.*
"permitted period"—see reg.6.
"relevant amendment"—see General Note.
"remunerative work"—see Income Support Regulations, reg.2(1).
"Social Security Act"—*ibid.*

GENERAL NOTE

2.837   The "relevant amendment" is the amendment to the definition of non-dependant in reg.3 of the Income Support Regulations with effect from November 11, 1991, by reg.2 of these Regulations (reg.1(3)). These Regulations were made on October 21, 1991, which is why that is the date used in reg.4 to fix the transitional protection. Reg.4 allows existing claimants to continue to receive the benefit of the severe disability premium where they previously met the new conditions for joint occupiers of the home, except that the joint occupation was with a close relative.

Regulation 5 defines when the protection of reg.4 ceases to apply.

Circumstances in which regulation 4 ceases to apply

2.838   **5.**—(1) Regulation 4 shall cease to apply to a claimant, or his partner, on the relevant day and shall not apply on any day thereafter.

(2) The relevant day is the first day after a period of eight consecutive weeks throughout which—

(a) subject to paragraph (3), he is not entitled to income support; or

(b) he is unable to satisfy, or be treated as satisfying, the second qualifying condition.

(3) For the purpose of calculating a period in excess of eight weeks in paragraph (2)(a) above the following periods shall be disregarded—

(a) where the claimant, or his partner, becomes engaged in remunerative work, any period during which he, or his partner, was not entitled to income support, not exceeding the permitted period determined in accordance with regulation 6;

(b) any period during which the claimant, or his partner, was participating in arrangements for training made under section 2 of the Employment and Training Act 1973 or section 2 of the Enterprise and New Towns (Scotland) Act 1990 or attending a course at an employment rehabilitation centre established under section 2 of the Employment and Training Act 1973.

DEFINITIONS

"claimant"—see Income Support Regulations, reg.2(1).
"partner"—*ibid.*
"permitted period"—see reg.6.
"qualifying condition"—see reg.4(7).

Definition of "permitted period" for the purposes of regulations 4 and 5

6.—(1) For the purposes of regulations 4(5) and 5(3)(a), where a claimant has ceased to be entitled to income support because he or his partner became engaged in remunerative work, [¹. . .] the permitted period shall be a period of 12 consecutive weeks. **2.839**

(2) [¹ . . .]

(3) [¹ . . .]

AMENDMENT

1. Income Support (General) (Jobseeker's Allowance Consequential Amendments) Regulations 1996 (SI 1996/206), reg.31 (October 7, 1996).

DEFINITIONS

"claimant"—see Income Support Regulations, reg.2(1).
"partner"—*ibid.*
"relevant education"—see Income Support Regulations, reg.12.
"remunerative work"—see Income Support Regulations, reg.2(1).
"student"—*ibid.*

Income Support (General) Amendment No. 3 Regulations 1993

(SI 1993/1679)

Made by the Secretary of State under ss.135(1), 136(5)(b), 137(1) and 175(1) to (4) of the Social Security Contributions and Benefits Act 1992

[In force August 2, 1993]

2.—(4) In the case of a claimant who was entitled to income support by virtue of regulation 70 of the Income Support Regulations for the benefit **2.840**

week which includes 2nd August 1993, then in respect of each day after that date on which the claimant's entitlement to income support continues, regulation 70 shall continue to apply in his case as if the preceding provisions of this regulation had not been made.

GENERAL NOTE

See the notes to reg.70(3) in the 1995 edition of Mesher and Wood, *Income-related Benefits: the Legislation*. Reg.70(3) was amended by reg.2(1) to (3) of these Regulations on August 2, 1993.

Saving

2.841   **4.**—(1) In the case of a claimant who was entitled to income support for the benefit week which included 2nd August 1993 then, but subject to paragraph (3), in respect of each day after that date on which the claimant's entitlement to income support continues, Schedule 3 to the Income Support Regulations shall continue to apply in his case as if regulation 3 of these Regulations had not been made.

(2) Heads (c) to (f) of sub-paragraph (9) of paragraph 7 of Schedule 3 to the Income Support Regulations shall apply to paragraph (1) above as they apply to sub-paragraph (1) of paragraph 7, but with the modification that for the words "in receipt of income support", wherever they occur, there were substituted the words "entitled to income support" and that the words "Subject to sub-paragraphs (10) and (11)" were omitted.

(3) In its application to any loan taken out or increased after 2nd August 1993 Schedule 3 to the Income Support Regulations shall have effect as amended by regulation 3 of these Regulations.

(4) Paragraphs (1) and (3) above shall apply as from 11th April 1994 as if for the references to "2nd August 1993" wherever they occur there were substituted references to "11th April 1994".

GENERAL NOTE

2.842   See the notes to para.7(6B) to (6F) of the former Sch.3 to the Income Sup-port Regulations in the 1995 edition of *Mesher and Wood, Income-related Benefits: the Legislation*. Para.7 of the former Sch.3 was amended by reg.3 of these regulations on August 2, 1993. See also notes to para.11(4)–(11) of the new Sch.3.

Income-related Benefits Schemes (Miscellaneous Amendments) (No.3) Regulations 1994

(SI 1994/1807)

Made by the Secretary of State under ss. 131(3)(b), 135(1), 137(1) and (2)(i) and 175(1), (3) and (4) of the Social Security Contributions and Benefits Act 1992

[In force August 1, 1994]

2.843   **4.**—(2) The provisions of this regulation shall only apply in the case of a claimant who was entitled to income support on 31st July 1994 where a claim for income support is made or treated as made by or in respect of him after that date, and where those provisions do apply they shall apply from the first day of the period in respect of which that claim is made.

GENERAL NOTE

See the note to the amendment to reg.21(3) of the Income Support Regulations inserted by reg.4(1) of these regulations.　　2.844

Where there is a change of circumstances a claimant may be required to fill in a new claim form for administrative purposes, but this is not necessarily a new or repeat claim. If a person is protected by this provision and there is a review of his claim (*e.g.* because of a change of circumstances) he should continue to have the benefit of that protection.

Disability Working Allowance and Income Support (General) Amendment Regulations 1995

(SI 1995/482)

Made by the Secretary of State under ss. 124(1) (d) (i) and (3), 129(2B) (b) and (c) and (8), 135(1), 137(1) and 175(1), (3) and (4) of the Social Security Contributions and Benefits Act 1992 and s.12(1) of the Social Security (Incapacity for Work) Act 1994

[In force April 13, 1995]

Transitional provisions with respect to the Income Support Regulations

19.—(1) Sickness benefit shall be a qualifying benefit for the purposes of regulation 9(2)(a)(i) of the Income Support Regulations, and for this purpose "sickness benefit" means sickness benefit under section 31 of the Social Security Contributions and Benefits Act 1992 as in force on 12th April 1995.　　2.845

(2) Where the disability premium was applicable to a claimant on 12th April 1995 by virtue of paragraph 12(1)(b) of Schedule 2 to the Income Support Regulations as in force on that date, the disability premium shall continue to be applicable to that claimant for so long as paragraph 12(1)(b)(i) of that Schedule applies to him.

(3) Paragraph (2) shall not apply to a claimant to whom paragraph 12(1)(b)(i) of Schedule 2 to the Income Support Regulations has ceased to apply for a period of more than 56 continuous days.

(4) Where on 12th April 1995 paragraph 5 of Schedule 1 to the Income Support Regulations (persons incapable of work) as in force on that date applied to a claimant, but the disability premium was not applicable to him, that claimant shall be treated for the purposes of paragraph 12(1) of Schedule 2 to the Income Support Regulations as if, throughout the period that paragraph 5 of Schedule 1 had applied to him, paragraph 12(1)(b)(i) of Schedule 2 applied to him.

(5) [² Where it is determined on or after 13th April, 1995] that a claimant fails to satisfy the incapacity for work test, in accordance with regulations

669

made under section 171C of the Contributions and Benefits Act (the all work test), on its first application to the claimant concerned, and the claimant, immediately prior to [¹13th April 1995], was either—

(a) incapable of work and had been so for a continuous period of 28 weeks in circumstances to which paragraph 5 of Schedule 1 of the Income Support Regulations refers (persons incapable of work not required to be available for employment); or

(b) in receipt of invalidity benefit or severe disablement allowance,

then, in a case in which either regulations 8(2A) or 11(2A) of the Income Support Regulations applies (persons not required to be available for employment and registration for employment), notwithstanding regulation 22(1A) and (5A) of the Income Support Regulations (reductions in applicable amounts), the amount of any income support to which the claimant is entitled shall be calculated in accordance with regulation 17 of those Regulations.

[¹(6) Where—

(a) a determination of the amount of a person's benefit has been made in a case to which paragraph (5) of this regulation, as originally made, had effect; and

(b) an appeal to which regulation 8(2A) or 11(2A) of the Income Support Regulations (persons not required to be available or registered for employment) refers, remains outstanding on 2nd October 1995;

the amount of any benefit to which he is entitled shall continue to be determined under paragraph (5), as originally made, until the determination of the appeal.]

AMENDMENTS

2.846   1. Income-related Benefits Schemes and Social Security (Claims and Payments) (Miscellaneous Amendments) Regulations 1995 (SI 1995/2303), reg.8(2) (October 2, 1995).

2. Social Security Act 1998 (Commencement No.9 and Savings and Consequential and Transitional Provisions) Order 1999 (SI 1999/2422 (C.61)), art.3(12) and Sch.11 (September 6, 1999).

Savings with respect to the Income Support Regulations

2.847   **20.**—(1) Where a person was not required to be available for employment on 12th April 1995 by virtue of regulation 8(2) of the Income Support Regulations as in force on that date, that regulation shall continue to apply in that person's case as if regulation 6 of these Regulations had not been made.

(2) Where a claimant was not required to register for employment on 12th April 1995 by virtue of regulation 11(2) of the Income Support Regulations as in force on that date, that regulation shall continue to apply in that claimant's case as if regulation 8 of these Regulations had not been made.

(3) Where a claimant appeals against a decision of an adjudication officer that he is not incapable of work, and that decision was made on or before 12th April 1995, regulations 8 and 11 of the Income Support Regulations shall apply in that claimant's case as if these Regulations had not been made.

(4) Where the higher pensioner premium was applicable to a claimant on, or at any time during the 8 weeks immediately preceding, 12th April 1995 by virtue of paragraph 12(1)(c)(i) of Schedule 2 to the Income Support

Regulations as in force on that date, paragraph 12 of that Schedule shall continue to apply in that claimant's case as if regulation 16 of these Regulations had not been made.

GENERAL NOTE

These transitional and saving provisions relate to some of the amendments made   2.848
to the Income Support Regulations as a consequence of the introduction of incapacity benefit and the new tests for deciding incapacity for work from April 13, 1995. See the notes to reg.22A of, and paras 24–27 of Sch.1B to, the Income Support Regulations.

Reg.19(5) was amended on October 2, 1995 to make it clear that it only applied to people who had been incapable of work for 28 weeks or in receipt of invalidity benefit or severe disablement allowance immediately before April 13, 1995 (and not to people who were so incapable, etc. by the date of the adjudication officer's decision). Reg.19(6) allows payment of full income support under the previous form of reg.19(5) to those whose appeals are outstanding on October 2, 1995 until the appeal has been determined. This should mean the final determination of the appeal, *e.g.*, if it is taken to the Social Security Commissioner.

See the further transitional protection in reg.27(3) of the Income Support (General) (Jobseeker's Allowance Consequential Amendments) Regulations 1996 (p.675).

Income-related Benefits Schemes (Miscellaneous Amendments) Regulations 1995

(SI 1995/516)

Made by the Secretary of State under ss. 123(1)(a) to (c), 128(5), 129(4) and (8), 135(1), 136(3), (5)(a) and (b), 137(1), (2)(c) and (d)(i) and 175(1), (3) and (4) of the Social Security Contributions and Benefits Act 1992

[In force April 10, 1995]

Saving

28.—(1) In the case of a claimant who was entitled to income support for   2.849
the benefit week which included 9th April 1995 then, but subject to paragraph (3), in respect of each day after that date on which the claim-ant's entitlement to income support continues, Schedule 3 to the Income Support Regulations shall continue to have effect as though regulation 25(c) of these Regulations had not been made.

(2) Heads (c) to (f) of sub-paragraph (9) of paragraph 7 of Schedule 3 to the Income Support Regulations shall apply to paragraph (1) above as they apply to sub-paragraph (1) of paragraph 7, but with the modification that for the words "in receipt of income support", wherever they appear, there were substituted the words "entitled to income support" and that the words "Subject to sub-paragraphs (10) and (11)" were omitted.

(3) In its application to any loan taken out or increased after 9th April 1995, Schedule 3 to the Income Support Regulations shall have effect as amended by regulation 25(c) of these Regulations.

DEFINITION

"claimant"—see Income Support Regulations, reg.2(1).

GENERAL NOTE

2.850
See the notes to para.7(6B) to (6F) of the former Sch.3 to the Income Support Regulations in the 1995 edition of Mesher and Wood, *Income-related Benefits: the Legislation*. Para.7(6C) of the former Sch.3 was amended by reg.25(c) of these Regulations on April 10, 1995. See also the notes to para.11(4)–(11) of the new Sch.3.

Social Security (Income Support and Claims and Payments) Amendment Regulations 1995

(SI 1995/1613)

Made by the Secretary of State under ss.135(1), 136(5)(b), 137(1) and 175(1) and (3)–(5) of the Social Security Contributions and Benefits Act 1992 and ss.5(1)(p). 15A(2), 189(1) and (4) and 191 of the Social Security Administration Act 1992

[In force October 2, 1995]

Revocations and savings

2.851
5.—(2) The revocation by paragraph (1) above and Schedule 4 to these Regulations of any provision previously amended or substituted but subject to a saving for existing beneficiaries does not affect the continued operation of those savings.

GENERAL NOTE

See the notes to paras 11(4)–(11) of Sch.3 to the Income Support Regulations.

Income Support (General) Amendment and Transitional Regulations 1995

(SI 1995/2287)

Made by the Secretary of State under ss.135(1), 137(1) and 175(1) and (3) to (5) of the Social Security Contributions and Benefits Act 1992

[In force October 2, 1995]

Transitional protection

2.852
3.—(1) Where a claimant for income support whose applicable amount, in the benefit week which included 1st October 1995, included an amount in respect of the interest on a loan or part of a loan by virtue of paragraph

7(6), 7(7) or 8(1)(a) of Schedule 3 to the Income Support Regulations (housing costs) ("the former paragraphs") as then in force and that loan or part of a loan is not a qualifying loan for the purposes of paragraphs 15 and 16 of Schedule 3 to the Income Support Regulations, paragraphs (2) and (3) shall have effect in his case.

(2) A loan or part of a loan to which paragraph (1) applies shall qualify as a loan to which paragraph 15 or 16, as the case may be, of Schedule 3 to the Income Support Regulations applies, for as long as any of the former paragraphs would have continued to be satisfied had it remained in force and the claimant remains in receipt of income support or is treated as being in receipt of income support.

(3) Heads (a), (c) and (e) of sub-paragraph (1) of paragraph 14 of Schedule 3 to the Income Support Regulations shall apply to paragraph (2) above as they apply to Schedule 3, but as if the words "Subject to sub-paragraph (2)" at the beginning were omitted.

DEFINITION

"claimant"—see Income Support Regulations, reg.2(1).

GENERAL NOTE

See the note to para.7 of Sch.3 to the Income Support Regulations.   2.853

Income-related Benefits Schemes and Social Security (Claims and Payments) (Miscellaneous Amendments) Regulations 1995

(SI 1995/2303)

Made by the Secretary of State under ss.123(1), 124(1)(d), 129(3), 130(2) and (4), 135(1), 136(1) and (3)–(5), 137(1) and (2)(b), (d), (h), (i) and (l) and 175(1) and (3)–(6) of the Social Security Contributions and Benefits Act 1992 and ss.5(1)(h), (i) and (o), 6(1)(h) and (i) and 189 of the Social Security Administration Act

[In force October 2, 1995]

Transitional provision with respect to the Income Support Regulations

8.—(1) In determining whether a claimant is entitled to income support   2.854
on or after 2nd October 1995 and whether he satisfies the provisions of either—
  (a) regulation 4(2)(c)(v) of the Income Support Regulations(temporary absence from Great Britain); or
  (b) paragraph 7 of Schedule 1 to those Regulations (disabled students not required to be available for work);
in a case where the claimant, for a period up to and including 12th April 1995, was continuously incapable of work for the purposes of paragraph 5 of Schedule 1 to the Income Support Regulations, as it was then in force, that period of incapacity shall be treated as forming part of a subsequent period

of incapacity beginning not later than 7th June 1995 to which the provisions referred to in paragraphs (a) or (b) above refer and which is continuous to the date of the determination in question.

DEFINITION

"claimant"—see Income Support Regulations, reg.2(1).

GENERAL NOTE

2.855   See the notes to reg.4(2)(c)(v) of the Income Support Regulations. For para.7 of Sch.1 see the 1996 edition of Mesher and Wood, *Income-related Benefits: the Legislation*.

Social Security (Persons from Abroad) Miscellaneous Amendments Regulations 1996

(SI 1996/30)

Made by the Secretary of State under ss.64(1), 68(4)(c)(i), 70(4), 71(6), 123(1), 124(1), 128(1), 129(1), 130(1) and (2), 131(1) and (3), 135, 137(1) and (2)(a) and (i) and 175(1) and (3)–(5) of the Social Security Contributions and Benefits Act 1992 and s.5(1)(r) of the Social Security Administration Act 1992

[In force February 5, 1996]

Saving

2.856   **12.**—(1) Where, before the coming into force of these Regulations, a person who becomes an asylum seeker under regulation 4A(5)(a)(i) of the Council Tax Benefit Regulations, regulation 7A(5)(a)(i) of the Housing Benefit Regulations or regulation 70(3A)(a) of the Income Support Regulations, as the case may be, is entitled to benefit under any of those Regulations, those provisions of those Regulations as then in force shall continue to have effect [¹ . . .] [² (both as regards him and as regards persons who are members of his family at the coming into force of these Regulations)] as if regulations 3(a) and (b), 7(a) and (b) or 8(2) and (3)(c), as the case may be, of these Regulations had not been made.

(2) Where, before the coming into force of these Regulations, a person in respect of whom an undertaking was given by another person or persons to be responsible for his maintenance and accommodation, claimed benefit to which he is entitled, or is receiving benefit, under the Council Tax Benefit Regulations, the Housing Benefit Regulations or the Income Support Regulations, as the case may be, those Regulations as then in force shall have effect as if regulations 3, 7 or 8, as the case may be, of these Regulations had not been made.

AMENDMENTS

1. Added by the Asylum and Immigration Act 1996, Sch.1, para 5 (July 24, 1996) and repealed by Immigration and Asylum Act 1999, Sch.14 para.113 (April 3, 2000).

2. Social Security (Immigration and Asylum) Consequential Amendments Regulations 2000 (SI 2000/636), reg.12(11)(a) (April 3, 2000).

GENERAL NOTE

See the notes to "persons subject to immigration control" in reg.21(3) and to reg.70 of the Income Support Regulations.

2.857

Income Support (General) (Jobseeker's Allowance Consequential Amendments) Regulations 1996

(SI 1996/206)

Made by the Secretary of State under s.40 of the Jobseekers Act 1995 and ss.124(1)(e), 137(1) and 175(1) to (4) of the Social Security Contributions and Benefits Act 1992.

[In force October 7, 1996]

Transitional provisions

27.—(1) Where on 6th October 1996 or at any time during the eight weeks immediately preceding that date paragraph 4(1) of Schedule 1 to the principal Regulations (persons caring for another person) as in force on that date applied to a claimant, or would have applied to him if he had made a claim for income support the claimant shall be treated for the purposes of paragraphs 5 and 6 of Schedule 1B to the principal Regulations as if, throughout the period that paragraph 4(1) of Schedule 1 applied or would have applied to him, paragraph 4 of Schedule 1B had applied or would have applied to him.

2.858

(2) Where on 6th October 1996 paragraph 5 of Schedule 1 to the principal Regulations (persons incapable of work) as in force on that date applied to a claimant, the claimant shall be treated for the purposes of regulation 4(2)(c)(v) of and paragraph 10 of Schedule 1B to the principal Regulations as if, throughout the period that paragraph 5 of Schedule 1 applied to him, paragraph 7 of Schedule 1B had applied to him.

(3) Where—

(a) a determination of the amount of a person's benefit has been made in a case to which regulation 19(5) of The Disability Working Allowance and Income Support (General) Amendment Regulations 1995 as originally made had effect (amendments consequential on the coming into force of the Social Security (Incapacity for Work) Act 1994: transitional provisions); and

(b) an appeal to which regulations 8(2A) or 11(2A) of the principal Regulations as in force on 2nd October 1995 referred (persons not required to be available or registered for employment), has still to be determined,

regulation 22A(1) of the principal Regulations (reduction in applicable amount where the claimant is appealing against a decision that he is not incapable of work) shall not apply to that person.

"claimant"—see Income Support Regulations, reg.2(1).

GENERAL NOTE

2.859   These transitional provisions relate to the some of the changes made to the income support scheme as a result of the introduction of JSA on October 7, 1996. On para.(3) see the notes to regs 19 and 20 of the Disability Working Allowance and Income Support (General) Amendment Regulations 1995 on p.671 and reg.22A of the Income Support Regulations.

Continuity with jobseeker's allowance

2.860   **32.** In determining whether a person is entitled to income support [¹or is to be treated as being in receipt of income support or whether any amount is applicable or payable—

   (a) entitlement to an income-based jobseeker's allowance shall be treated as entitlement to income support for the purposes of any requirement that a person is or has been entitled to income support for any period of time; and

   (b) a person who is treated as being in receipt of income-based jobseeker's allowance shall be treated as being in receipt of income support for the purposes of any requirement that he is or has been treated as being in receipt of income support for any period of time.]

AMENDMENT

1. Income-related Benefits Schemes and Social Fund (Miscellaneous Amendments) Regulations 1996 (SI 1996/1944), reg.12 (October 7, 1996).

GENERAL NOTE

2.861   Para. (a) of this important provision allows entitlement to income-based JSA to count as entitlement to income support for the purposes of satisfying any requirement that the person is or has been entitled to income support for any period of time. Para. (b) has the same effect where the requirement is that the person is or has been treated as being in receipt of income support. This could be relevant, for example, in relation to waiting periods or the linking rules for payment of housing costs. For the JSA provision see para.18(1)(c) of Sch.2 to the JSA Regulations.

Income-related Benefits and Jobseeker's Allowance (Personal Allowances for Children and Young Persons) (Amendment) Regulations 1996

(SI 1996/2545)

Made by the Secretary of State under ss.128(1)(a)(i) and (5), 129(1)(c)(i) and (8). 135(1). 136(3) and (4), 137(1) and 175(1), (3) and (4) of the Social Security Contributions and Benefits Act 1992 and ss.4(5), 35(1) and 36(1), (2) and (4) of the Jobseekers Act 1995.

[In force April 7, 1997].

Transitional provisions

10.—(1) Where, in relation to a claim for income support, jobseeker's   2.862
allowance, housing benefit or council tax benefit, a claimant's weekly applicable amount includes a personal allowance in respect of one or more children or young persons who are, as at the day before the appropriate date
these Regulations come into force for the purpose of those benefits in
accordance with regulation 1 of these Regulations (referred to in this regulation as "the appropriate date"), aged 11, 16 or 18, the provisions specified
in regulation 2(7) of these Regulations shall have effect, for the period specified in paragraph (2) below, as if regulation 2 of these Regulations had not
been made.

(2) The period specified for the purposes of paragraph (1) above shall be,
in relation to each particular child or young person referred to in that paragraph, the period beginning on the appropriate date and ending—

(a) where that child or young person is aged 11 or 16 as at the day before
the appropriate date, on 31st August 1997;

(b) where that young person is aged 18 as at the day before the appropriate date, on the day preceding the day that young person ceases
to be a person of a prescribed description for the purposes of regulation 14 of the Income Support Regulations, regulation 76 of the
Jobseeker's Allowance Regulations, regulation 13 of the Housing
Benefit Regulations or regulation 5 of the Council Tax Benefit
Regulations.

DEFINITIONS

"child"—see SSCBA, s.137(1).
"claimant"—see Income Support Regulations, reg.2(1).
"young person"—see Income Support Regulations, regs 2(1) and 14.

GENERAL NOTE

See the notes to para.2 of Sch.2 to the Income Support Regulations. Para.2 of   2.863
Sch.2 and para.2 of Sch.1 to the JSA Regulations were amended by reg.2 of these
Regulations on April 7, 1997.

The weekly amount for a person aged not less than 18 in sub-para.(d) of the previous form of para.2 of Sch.2 and para.2 of Sch.1 to the JSA Regulations was
increased to £38.90 from April 7, 1997 (Social Security Benefits Up-rating Order
1997 (SI 1997/543), art.18(4) and 24(4)). The weekly amounts in sub-paras. (a),
(b) and (c) were also increased and were the same as the amounts in sub-paras. (a),
(b) and (c) of the 1997 form of the respective paras.

The Social Security (Immigration and Asylum) Consequential Amendments Regulations 2000

(SI 2000/636)

*Made by the Secretary of State under ss.115(3), (4) and (7), 1235) and (6),
166(3) and 167 of the Immigration and Asylum Act 1999, ss.64(1), 68(4), 70(4),
71(6), 123(1)(a), (d) and (e), 135(1), 136(3) and (4), 137(1) and (2)(i) and*

175(1), (3) and (4) of the Social Security Contributions and Benefits Act 1992, ss.5(1)(a) and (b), 189(1) and (4) and 191 of the Social Security Administration Act 1992, ss.12(1) and (2), 35(1) and 36(2) and (4) of the Jobseekers Act 1995.

[In force April 3, 2000]

GENERAL NOTE

2.864   See commentary to regs 21(3), 21ZB and 70 of the IS Regulations.

Citation, commencement and interpretation

2.865   **1.**—(1) These Regulations may be cited as the Social Security (Immigration and Asylum) Consequential Amendments Regulations 2000.
(2) These Regulations shall come into force on 3rd April 2000.
(3) In these Regulations—
"the Act" means the Immigration and Asylum Act 1999;
"the Attendance Allowance Regulations" means the Social Security (Attendance Allowance) Regulations 1991;
"the Claims and Payments Regulations" means the Social Security (Claims and Payments) Regulations 1987;
"the Contributions and Benefits Act" means the Social Security Contributions and Benefits Act 1992;
"the Council Tax Benefit Regulations" means the Council Tax Benefit (General) Regulations 1992;
"the Disability Living Allowance Regulations" means the Social Security (Disability Living Allowance) Regulations 1991;
"the Housing Benefit Regulations" means the Housing Benefit (General) Regulations 1987;
"the Income Support Regulations" means the Income Support (General) Regulations 1987;
"the Invalid Care Allowance Regulations" means the Social Security (Invalid Care Allowance) Regulations 1976;
"the Jobseeker's Allowance Regulations" means the Jobseeker's Allowance Regulations 1996;
"the Persons from Abroad Regulations" means the Social Security (Persons from Abroad) Miscellaneous Amendments Regulations 1996;
"the Severe Disablement Allowance Regulations" means the Social Security (Severe Disablement Allowance) Regulations 1984.
(4) In these Regulations, unless the context otherwise requires, a reference—
(a) to a numbered regulation or Schedule is to the regulation in, or the Schedule to, these Regulations bearing that number;
(b) in a regulation or Schedule to a numbered paragraph is to the paragraph in that regulation or Schedule bearing that number.

GENERAL NOTE

2.866   With effect from April 7, 2003 the definition of "the Claims and Payments Regulations" was revoked in so far as it related to child benefit and guardian's allowance (reg.43 of and Pt I of Sch.3 to the child Benefit and Guardian's Allowance (Administration) Regulations 2003). The Definition remains in force for the purposes of other benefits.

Persons not excluded from specified benefits under section 115 of the Immigration and Asylum Act 1999

2.—(1) For the purposes of entitlement to income-based jobseeker's allowance, income support, a social fund payment, housing benefit or council tax benefit under the Contributions and Benefits Act, [² or state pension credit under the State Pension Credit Act 2002,] as the case may be, a person falling within a category or description of persons specified in Part I of the Schedule is a person to whom section 115 of the Act does not apply.

(2) For the purposes of entitlement to attendance allowance, severe disablement allowance, [¹ carer's allowance], disability living allowance, a social fund payment or child benefit under the Contributions and Benefits Act, as the case may be, a person falling within a category or description of persons specified in Part II of the Schedule is a person to whom section 115 of the Act does not apply.

(3) For the purposes of entitlement to child benefit, attendance allowance or disability living allowance under the Contributions and Benefits Act, as the case may be, a person in respect of whom there is an Order in Council made under section 179 of the Social Security Administration Act 1992 giving effect to a reciprocal agreement in respect of one of those benefits, as the case may be, is a person to whom section 115 of the Act does not apply.

(4) For the purposes of entitlement to—

(a) income support, a social fund payment, housing benefit or council tax benefit under the Contributions and Benefits Act, as the case may be, a person who is entitled to or is receiving benefit by virtue of paragraph (1) or (2) of regulation 12 of the Persons from Abroad Regulations is a person to whom section 115 of the Act does not apply;

(b) attendance allowance, disability living allowance, [¹carer's allowance, severe disablement allowance, a social fund payment or child benefit under the Contributions and Benefits Act, as the case may be, a person who is entitled to or is receiving benefit by virtue of paragraph (10) of regulation 12 is a person to whom section 115 of the Act does not apply.

[²(c) state pension credit under the State Pension Credit Act 2002, a person to whom sub-paragraph (a) would have applied but for the fact that they have attained the qualifying age for the purposes of state pension credit, is a person to whom section 115 of the Act does not apply.]

(5) For the purposes of entitlement to income support by virtue of regulation 70 of the Income Support Regulations (urgent cases), to job-seeker's allowance by virtue of regulation 147 of the Jobseeker's Allowance Regulations (urgent cases) or to a social fund payment under the Contributions and Benefits Act, as the case may be, a person to whom regulation 12(3) applies is a person to whom section 115 of the Act does not apply.

(6) For the purposes of entitlement to housing benefit, council tax benefit or a social fund payment under the Contributions and Benefits Act, as the case may be, a person to whom regulation 12(6) applies is a person to whom section 115 of the Act does not apply.

[² (7) For the purposes of entitlement to state pension credit under the State Pension Credit Act 2002, a person to whom paragraph (5) would have

2.867

applied but for the fact that they have attained the qualifying age for the purposes of state pension credit, is a person to whom section 115 of the Act does not apply.

(8) Where paragraph 1 of Part I of the Schedule to these Regulations applies in respect of entitlement to state pension credit, the period for which a claimant's state pension credit is to be calculated shall be any period, or the aggregate of any periods, not exceeding 42 days during any one period of leave to which paragraph 1 of Part I of the Schedule to these Regulations applies.]

AMENDMENTS

2.868   1. Social Security Amendment (Carer's Allowance) Regulations 2002 (SI 2002/2497), reg.3 and Sch.2 (April 1, 2003).
        2. State Pension Credit (Transitional and Miscellaneous Provisions) Amendment Regulations 2003 (SI 2003/2274), reg.6 (October 6, 2003).

Transitional arrangements and savings

2.869   **12.**—(1) Paragraph (2) shall apply where, in relation to a claim for income support, a social fund payment, housing benefit or council tax benefit, as the case may be, a person has submitted a claim for asylum on or before 2nd April 2000 and is notified that he has been recorded by the Secretary of State as a refugee within the definition in Article 1 of the Convention relating to the Status of Refugees done at Geneva on 28th July 1951 as extended by Article 1(2) of the Protocol relating to the Status of Refugees done at New York on 31st January 1967.

(2) Where this paragraph applies—

(a) regulation 21ZA of the Income Support Regulations (treatment of refugees) shall continue to have effect as if regulation 3(4)(a), (5) and (9) had not been made;

(b) regulations 4(3C), 6(4D) and 19(8) of the Claims and Payments Regulations shall continue to have effect as if regulation 5 had not been made;

(c) paragraphs 1 and 2 of Schedule A1, paragraph 62 of Schedule 4 and paragraph 51 of Schedule 5 to the Housing Benefit Regulations (treatment of claims for housing benefit by refugees) shall continue to have effect as if regulation 6(5) and (7) had not been made; and

(d) paragraphs 1 and 2 of Schedule A1, paragraph 62 of Schedule 4 and paragraph 51 of Schedule 5 to the Council Tax Benefit Regulations (treatment of claims for council tax benefit by refugees) shall continue to have effect as if regulation 7(5) and (7) had not been made.

(3) Regulation 70 of the Income Support Regulations and regulation 147 of the Jobseeker's Allowance Regulations, as the case may be, shall apply to a person who is an asylum seeker within the meaning of paragraph (4) who has not ceased to be an asylum seeker by virtue of paragraph (5).

(4) An asylum seeker within the meaning of this paragraph is a person who—

(a) submits on his arrival (other than on his re-entry) in the United Kingdom from a country outside the Common Travel Area a claim for asylum on or before 2nd April 2000 to the Secretary of State that it would be contrary to the United Kingdom's obligations under the Convent for him to be removed or required to leave, the United

Kingdom and that claim is recorded by the Secretary of State as having been made before that date; or

(b) on or before 2nd April 2000 becomes, while present in Great Britain, an asylum seeker when—

  (i) the Secretary of State makes a declaration to the effect that the country of which he is a national is subject to such a fundamental change of circumstances that he would not normally order the return of a person to that country; and

  (ii) he submits, within a period of three months from the date that declaration was made, a claim for asylum to the Secretary of State under the Convention relating to the Status of Refugees, and

  (iii) his claim for asylum under that Convention is recorded by the Secretary of State has having been made; and

(c) in the case of a claim for jobseeker's allowance, holds a work permit or has written authorisation from the Secretary of state permitting him to work in the United Kingdom.

(5) A person ceases to be an asylum seeker for the purposes of this paragraph when his claim for asylum is recorded by the Secretary of State as having been decided (other than on appeal) or abandoned

(6)–(8) [*Omitted as applying only to housing benefit and council tax benefit.*]

(9) In paragraphs (4) and (7) "the Common Travel Area" means the United Kingdom, the Channel Islands, the Isle of Man and the Republic of Ireland collectively and "the Convention" means the Convention relating to the Status of Refugees done at Geneva on 28th July 1951 as extended by Article 2(1) of the Protocol relating to the Status of Refugees done at New York on 31st January 1967.

(10) Where, before the coming into force of these Regulations, a person has claimed benefit to which he is entitled or is receiving benefit by virtue of regulation 12(3) of the Persons from Abroad Regulations or regulation 14B(g) of the Child Benefit (General) Regulations 1976, as the case may be, those provisions shall continue to have effect, for the purposes of entitlement to attendance allowance, disability living allowance, [1 carer's allowance], severe disablement allowance or child benefit, as the case may be, until such time as—

(a) his claim for asylum (if any) is recorded by the Secretary of State as having been decided or abandoned; or

(b) his entitlement to that benefit is revised or superseded under section 9 or 10 of the Social Security Act 1998, if earlier,

as if regulations 8, 9, 10 and 11 and paragraph (2) or paragraph (3), as the case may be, of regulation 13, had not been made.

(11) In the Persons from Abroad Regulations—

(a) in paragraph (1) of regulation 12, after the words "shall continue to have effect" there shall be inserted the words "both as regards him as regards persons who are members of his family at the coming into force of these Regulations)"; and

(b) notwithstanding the amendments and revocations in regulations 3, 6 and 7, regulations 12(1) and (2) of the Persons from Abroad Regulations shall continue to have effect as they had effect before those amendments and revocations came into force.

AMENDMENT

1. Social Security Amendment (Carer's Allowance) Regulations 2002 (SI 2002/2497), reg.3 and Sch.2 (April 1, 2003).   **2.870**

SCHEDULE   **Regulation 2**

Persons not Excluded from Certain Benefits under Section 115
of the Immigration and Asylum Act 1999

Part I

2.871   *Persons not excluded under section 115 of the Immigration and Asylum Act from entitlement to*
income-based jobseeker's allowance, income support, a social fund payment, housing benefit or council
tax benefit.

1. A person who—
   (a) has limited leave (as defined in section 33(1) of the Immigration Act 1971) to enter or
       remain in the United Kingdom which was given in accordance with the immigration
       rules (as defined in that section) relating to—
          (i) there being or there needing to be, no recourse to public funds, or
          (ii) there being no charge on public funds,
       during that period of limited leave; and
   (b) having, during any one period of limited leave (including any such period as extended),
       supported himself without recourse to public funds, other than any such recourse by
       reason of the previous application of this sub-paragraph, is temporarily without funds
       during that period of leave because remittances to him from abroad have been dis-
       rupted, provided there is a reasonable expectation that his supply of funds will be
       resumed.

2. A person who has been given leave to enter or remain in, the United Kingdom by the
Secretary of State upon an undertaking by another person or persons pursuant to the immigration rules within the meaning of the Immigration Act 1971, to be responsible for his maintenance and accommodation and who has not been resident in the United Kingdom for a
period of at least five years beginning on the date of entry or the date on which the undertaking was given in respect of him, whichever date is the later and the person or persons who gave
the undertaking to provide for his maintenance and accommodation has, or as the case may
be, have died

3. A person who—
   (a) has been given leave to enter or remain in, the United Kingdom by the Secretary of
       State upon an undertaking by another person or persons pursuant to the immigration
       rules within the meaning of the Immigration Act 1971, to be responsible for his main-
       tenance and accommodation; and
   (b) has been resident in the United Kingdom for a period of at least five years beginning
       on the date of entry or the date on which the undertaking was given in respect of him,
       whichever date is the later.

4. A person who is a national of a state which has ratified the European Convention on Social
and Medical Assistance (done in Paris on 11th December 1953) or a state which has ratified
the Council of Europe Social Charter (signed in Turin on 18th October 1961) and who is lawfully present in the United Kingdom.

Part II

2.872   *Persons not excluded under section 115 of the Immigration and Asylum Act from entitlement to*
attendance allowance, severe disablement allowance, [¹carer's allowance] disability living allowance,
a social fund payment or child benefit.

1. A member of a family of a national of a State contracting party to the Agreement on the
European Economic Area signed at Oporto on 2nd May 1992 as adjusted by the Protocol
signed at Brussels on 17th March 1993.

2. A person who is lawfully working in Great Britain and is a national of a State with which
the Community has concluded an agreement under Article 310 of the Treaty of Amsterdam
amending the Treaty on European Union, the Treaties establishing the European Communities
and certain related Acts providing, in the field of social security, for the equal treatment of
workers who are nationals of the signatory State and their families.

3. A person who is a member of a family of, and living with, a person specified in paragraph 2.

4. A person who has been given leave to enter, or remain in, the United Kingdom by
the Secretary of State upon an undertaking by another person or persons pursuant to the

immigration rules within the meaning of the Immigration Act 1971, to be responsible for his maintenance and accommodation.

AMENDMENT

1. Social Security Amendment (Carer's Allowance) Regulations 2002 (SI 2002/2497), reg.3 and Sch.2 (April 1, 2003).

2.873

Social Security Amendment (Capital Limits and Earnings Disregards) Regulations 2000

(SI 2000/2545)

Made by the Secretary of State under ss.123(1)(a), (d) and (e), 134(1), 136(2) and (5)(b) and (d), 137(1) and 175(1), (3) and (4) of the Social Security Contributions and Benefits Act 1992 and ss.12(4)(b) and (d), 13(1) and (3), 35(1) and 36(1), (2) and (4) of the Jobseekers Act 1995.

[In force April 9, 2001]

Saving

4.—Paragraph 3(4)(c) of Schedule 3 to both the Council Tax Benefit Regulations and to the Housing Benefit Regulations, paragraph 4(4)(c) of Schedule 8 to the Income Support Regulations and paragraph 5(4)(c) of Schedule 6 to the Jobseeker's Allowance Regulations shall have effect as if regulation 3 above had not been made in a case where the claimant was entitled, by virtue of sub-paragraph (2) or (3) of those paragraphs as in force immediately before the coming into force of these Regulations, to a disregard of £15.

2.874

GENERAL NOTE

See the note to para.4 of Sch.8 to the Income Support Regulations. Para. 4 of Sch.8 and para.5 of Sch.6 to the JSA Regulations were amended by reg.3 of and the Sch.to these Regulations on April 9, 2001.

2.875

Child Support (Consequential Amendments and Transitional Provisions) Regulations 2001

(SI 2001/158)

Made by the Secretary of State under s.29(2) of the Child Support, Pensions and Social Security Act 2000.

[In force in relation to a particular case on the date on which s.1 of the 2000 Act comes into force in relation to that type of case]

PART III

SAVINGS

Savings for particular cases

2.876   **10.**—[¹ (Z1) This regulation is subject to the Child Support (Transitional Provisions) Regulations 2000.]

(1) Where, in respect of a particular case there is a maintenance assessment the effective date of which is before the date that these Regulations come into force with respect to that type of case ("the commencement date"), these Regulations shall not apply for the purposes of—

(a) [*omitted*];

(b) the Income Support Regulations, in relation to a person who is entitled to income support for a period beginning on or before the day before the commencement date;

(c) the Jobseeker's Allowance Regulations, in relation to a person who is entitled to a jobseeker's allowance for a period beginning on or before the day before the commencement date; and

(d) [*omitted*].

(2) These Regulations shall not apply with respect to the Income Support Regulations and the Jobseeker's Allowance Regulations in relation to a person who is entitled to income support or a jobseeker's allowance, as the case may be, for a period beginning on or before the day before the commencement date.

AMENDMENT

2.877   1. Child Support (Transitional Provision) (Miscellaneous Amendments) Regulations 2003 (SI 2003/347), reg.2(3) and (4)(b) (March 3, 2003).

GENERAL NOTE

These regulations make amendments to regs 60A and 60C(6)(a) of and para.14(2) of Sch.3 to the Income Support Regulations and to regs 125 and 128(6)(a) of and para.13(2) of Sch.2 to the JSA Regulations. See the note to reg.60A of the Income Support Regulations.

The Social Security (Working Tax Credit and Child Tax Credit) (Consequential Amendments) Regulations 2003

(SI 2003/455)

Made by the Secretary of State under ss.1(1C) and 189(1) of the Social Security Administration Act 1992, ss.22(5), 122(1), 123(1)(a), (d) and (e), 124(1)(e), 135(1), 136(1), (3), (4) and (5), 137(1), 138(1)(a), (2) and (4), and 175(1) and (3) to (5) of the Social Security Contributions and Benefits Act 1992, ss.4(5), 12, 13(2), 35(1), 36(2) and (4) of the Jobseekers Act 1995.

Citation, commencement and interpretation

1.—(1) These Regulations may be cited as the Social Security (Working   2.878
Tax Credit and Child Tax Credit) (Consequential Amendments) Regulations 2003 and this regulation shall come into force on 1 April 2003.

(2) Subject to paragraph (5), in a case where a claimant for income
support—

    (a) has a child or young person who is a member of his family for the pur-
poses of his claim for income support, and

    (b) is awarded, or his partner is awarded, a child tax credit for a period
beginning before 6 April 2004,

regulation 7 shall have effect from the first day of the first benefit week to
commence for that claimant on or after the day from which that award of
child tax credit begins and regulation 2 and Schedule 1 shall have effect from
the first day of the first benefit week to commence for that claimant on or
after 6 April 2004.

(3) Subject to paragraph (5), in a case where a claimant for income
support—

    (a) has a child or young person who is a member of his family for the pur-
poses of his claim for income support, and

    (b) has not been awarded, or his partner has not been awarded, a child
tax credit for a period beginning before 6 April 2004,

regulations 2 and 7 and Schedule 1 shall have effect from the first day of
the first benefit week to commence for that claimant on or after the day on
which his, or his partner's, award of child tax credit begins.

(4) Subject to paragraph (5), in a case where paragraph (2)(a) or (3)(a)
does not apply to a claimant for income support, regulation 2 and Schedule
1 shall have effect from the first day of the first benefit week to commence
for that claimant on or after 6 April 2004.

(5) *[Omitted]*.

(6) Subject to paragraph (9), in a case where a claimant for a jobseeker's
allowance—

    (a) has a child or young person who is a member of his family for the pur-
poses of his claim for jobseeker's allowance, and

    (b) is awarded, or his partner is awarded, a child tax credit for a period
beginning before 6 April 2004, regulation 8 shall have effect from the
first day of the first benefit week to commence for that claimant on
or after the day from which that award of child tax credit begins and
regulation 3 and Schedule 2 shall have effect from the first day of the
first benefit week to commence for that claimant on or after 6th April
2004.

(7) Subject to paragraph (9), in a case where a claimant for a jobseeker's
allowance—

    (a) has a child or young person who is a member of his family for the pur-
poses of his claim for jobseeker's allowance, and

    (b) has not been awarded, or his partner has not been awarded, a child
tax credit for a period beginning before 6th April, 2004.

regulations 3 and 8 and Schedule 2 shall have effect from the first day of
the first benefit week to commence for that claimant on or after the day on
which his, or his partner's, award of child tax credit begins.

(8) Subject to paragraph (9), in a case where paragraph (6)(a) or (7)(a)
does not apply to a claimant for jobseeker's allowance, regulation 3 and

Schedule 2 shall have effect from the first day of the first benefit week to commence for that claimant on or after 6 April 2004.

(9)–(10) *[Omitted].*

(11) In paragraphs (2) to (5) and regulation 7, the expressions "benefit week", "claimant" and "partner" have the same meaning as in regulation 2(1) of the Income Support Regulations and in paragraphs (6) to (9) and regulation 8, the expressions "benefit week" and "partner" have the same meaning as in regulation 1(3) of the Jobseeker's Allowance Regulations.

(12) In these Regulations—

[Omitted].

"the Income Support Regulations" means the Income Support (General) Regulations 1987; and

"the Jobseeker's Allowance Regulations" means the Jobseeker's Allowance Regulations 1996.

2.—6. *[Omitted].*

Income Support—transitional arrangements

2.879

7.—(1) [¹ Subject to paragraph (2) and regulation 31(3) of the Income Support Regulations,] in the case of a claimant for income support who makes a claim, or whose partner makes a claim, for a child tax credit, the Secretary of State shall treat that claimant's income as including an amount equivalent to the amount of child tax credit to which he, or his partner, is entitled for the period specified in pargraph (3).

(2) In a case where a claimant for income support—

(a) has a child or young person who is a member of his family for the purposes of his claim for income support; and

(b) is, or has a partner who is, aged not less than 60.

the Secretary of State shall, [¹ in the benefit week which begins on or includes 5 October 2003, disregard from his income an amount equivalent to the amount of child tax credit to which he is entitled.]

(3) For the purposes of [¹ paragraph (1)], the specified period begins on the first day of the first benefit week to commence for that claimant on or after 7 April 2003, or the date the award of child tax credit begins if later, and ends on the day before the first day of the first benefit week to commence for that claimant on or after 6 April 2004.

(4) In the case of a claimant for income support who applies for an applicable amount under regulation 17 or 18 of the Income Support Regulations on or after 7 April 2003 in respect of a child or young person who is a member of his family, the Secretary of State shall treat that claimant's income as including an amount equivalent to the amount of child benefit to which he, or his partner, is entitled in respect of that child or young person for the period specified in paragraph (5).

(5) For the purposes of paragraph (4), the specified period begins on the first day of the first benefit week to commence for that claimant on or after the date from which his claim includes that applicable amount and ends on—

(a) in a case where the claimant, or his partner, is awarded child tax credit for a period beginning before 6th April 2004, the first day of the first benefit week to commence for that claimant on or after 6 April 2004;

(b) in the case where the claimant, or his partner, is awarded child tax credit for a period beginning on or after 6th April 2004 the first day of the first benefit week to commence for that claimant on or after the day that award of child tax credit begins; or

(c) the first day of the first benefit week in which his applicable amount in respect of that child or young person ends, if earlier.

(6) In the case of a claimant for income support who is entitled, or whose partner is entitled, to child benefit in respect of a child under the age of one year, for the purposes of his claim for income support, the Secretary of State shall disregard from the claimant's income the sum of [² £10.50] in respect of one child only for the period specified in paragraph (7).

(7) For the purposes of paragraph (6), the specified period begins on the first day of the first benefit week to commence for that claimant on or after 7 April 2003 and ends on—

(a) [¹ subject to sub-paragraph (d)] in a case where the claimant, or his partner, is awarded child tax credit for a period beginning before 6th April 2004; the first day of the first benefit week to commence for that claimant on or after 6 April 2004;

(b) [¹ subject to sub-paragraph (d)] in a case where the claimant, or his partner, is awarded child tax credit for a period beginning on or after 6th April 2004, the first day of the first benefit week to commence for that claimant on or after the day that award of child tax credit begins; [¹. . .]

(c) [¹ subject to sub-paragraph (d)] the first day of the first benefit week in which the award of child benefit in respect of that child ends, if earlier in respect of that child or young person ends, if earlier [¹ or

(d) the first day of the benefit week in which the child's first birthday occurs, if earlier.]

AMENDMENTS

1. Social Security (Working Tax Credit and Child Tax Credit) (Consequential Amendments) (No.3) Regulations 2003 (S.I. 2003/1731), reg.6 (August 8, 2003).   **2.880**

2. Social Security (Miscellaneous Amendments) Regulations 2004 (SI 2004/565), reg.11 (April 12, 2004).

Jobseeker's allowance—transitional arrangements

8.—(1) [¹ Subject to regulation 96(3) of the Jobseeker's Allowance Regulations,] in the case of a claimant for jobseeker's allowance who makes a claim, or whose partner makes a claim, for a child tax credit, the Secretary of State shall treat that claimant's income as including an amount equivalent to the amount of child tax credit to which he, or his partner, is entitled for the period specified in pararaph (2).   **2.881**

(2) For the purposes of paragraph (1) the specified period begins on the first day of the first benefit week to commence for that claimant on or after 7 April 2003, or the date that award of child tax credit begins if later, and ends on the day before the first day of the first benefit week to commence for that claimant on or after 6 April 2004.

(3) In the case of a claimant for jobseeker's allowance who applies for an applicable amount under regulation 83 or 84 of the Jobseeker's Allowance Regulations on or after 7 April 2003 in respect of a child or young person who is a member of his family, the Secretary of State shall treat the

claimant's income as including an amount equivalent to the amount of child benefit to which he, or his partner, is entitled in respect of that child or young person for the period specified in paragraph (4).

(4) For the purposes of paragraph (3), the specified period begins on the first day of the first benefit week to commence for that claimant on or after the date from which his claim includes that applicable amount and ends on—

    (a) in a case where the claimant, or his partner, is awarded child tax credit for a period beginning before 6 April 2004, the first day of the first benefit week to commence for that claimant on or after 6 April 2004;

    (b) in a case where the claimant, or his partner, is awarded child tax credit for a period beginning on or after 6 April 2004, the first day of the first benefit week to commence for that claimant on or after the day on which that award of child tax credit begins; or

    (c) the first day of the first benefit week in which his applicable amount in respect of that child or young person ends, if earlier.

(5) In the case of a claimant for jobseeker's allowance who is entitled, or whose partner is entitled, to child benefit in respect of a child under the age of one year, for the purposes of his claim for jobseeker's allowance, the Secretary of State shall disregard from that claimant's income the sum of [²£10.50] in respect of one child only for the period specified in paragraph (6).

(6) For the purposes of paragraph (5), the specified period begins on the first day of the first benefit week to commence for that claimant on or after 7 April 2003 and ends on—

    (a) [¹ subject to paragraph (d)] in a case where the claimant, or his partner, is awarded child tax credit for a period beginning before 6 April 2004, the first day of the first benefit week to commence for that claimant on or after 6 April 2004;

    (b) [¹ subject to paragraph (d)] in a case where the claimant, or his partner, is awarded child tax credit for a period beginning on or after 6 April 2004, the first day of the first benefit week to commence for that claimant on or after the day that award of child tax credit begins [¹. . .]

    (c) [¹ subject to paragraph (d)] the first day of the first benefit week in which the award of child benefit in respect of that child ends, if earlier [¹ or

    (d) the first day of the benefit week in which the child's first birthday occurs, if earlier.]

AMENDMENTS

2.882

1. Social Security (Working Tax Credit and Child Tax Credit) (Consequential Amendments) (No.3) Regulations 2003 (SI 2003/1731), reg.6(1) and (3) (August 8, 2003).

2. Social Security (Miscellaneous Amendments) Regulations 2004 (SI 2004/565), reg.11 (April 12, 2004).

GENERAL NOTE

2.883

These regulations make transitional provisions for IS and JSA claimants who are responsible for a child or young person and who are also awarded child tax credit (see Vol. IV) which was introduced on April 7, 2003.

It is intended that starting from April 6, 2004, IS and JSA will become "adults only" benefits with all means-tested state financial help towards the cost of bringing up a child being met through child tax credit. To this end, reg.2 and Sch.1 and reg.3 and Sch.2 (which are referred to above) amend, respectively, the IS Regulations and the JSA Regulations from that date (except in "transitional cases"—see the note to reg.17 of the Income Support Regulations) so as to abolish the family premium and personal allowances for children and young persons and child-related premiums. Regulations 7 and 8 deal with the period between April 7, 2003 and April 6, 2004. The general rule (reg.7(1), (4) and (5) and 8(1)–(4)) is that child tax credit counts as income for IS and JSA so that the claimant does not receive a double benefit. This is subject to the disregards established by reg.7(6)–(7) and 8(5)–(6)).

Regulations 1(5), (9) and (10) which are not reproduced here amend other regulations with effect from April 7, 2003. Their effect is noted in the text of those regulations where appropriate.

In *CIS 995/2004*, to be reported as *R(IS) 3/05*, the Commissioner acknowledges that there were several problems in working out the meaning of reg.7(1) but on the facts of that case he saw no difficulty in interpreting reg.7(1) as deeming the claimant's income to include the amount equivalent to that contained in the operative award of child tax credit. The main issue was whether the claimant had made a valid claim for child tax credit (the claimant having discovered that he would be better off not claiming child tax credit); the Commissioner decided that an effective claim had been made (for further discussion of this decision see the annotation to reg.5 of the Tax Credits (Claims and Notifications) Regulations 2002 (SI 2002/2014) in Vol. IV of this series).

However, the Commissioner did have to grapple with the meaning of reg.7(1) in *CIS/1064/2004*. The claimant, who had two young children, had been awarded working tax credit and child tax credit for the period April 6, 2003 to April 5, 2004. However she had stopped working, it seems in early August 2003 (it was not exactly clear when). This resulted in a change in the tax credit decisions. The award of working tax credit was stopped and the overpayment of working tax credit that was said to have arisen was set off against the child tax credit that remained payable, leaving very little in payment. However, when calculating her income support the maximum amount of child tax credit was taken into account. The claimant appealed. The tribunal reluctantly dismissed her appeal, deciding that as reg.7(1) used the word "entitled", rather than "paid", and as a person who is in receipt of income support is entitled to the maximum award of child tax credit (see s.7(2) and s.13(1) of the Tax Credits Act 2002 and reg.4 of the Tax Credits (Income Thresholds and Determination of Rates) Regulations 2002 (SI 2002/2008) in Vol.IV of this series), it was the amount of that entitlement that had to be taken into account.

In a very detailed analysis the Commissioner firstly rejects the claimant's contention that reg.7(1) did not apply where a person who already had an award of child tax credit made a claim for income support during the tax year 2003/2004 but only applied where a person who was already in receipt of income support applied for child tax credit. He decided that the order in which the claims were made did not matter. He then went on to consider the application of reg.7(1) in the claimant's case. Identifying the effect of reg.7(1) was, in his view, "a matter of considerable difficulty and complexity". However, he concludes that the most natural reading of reg.7(1) was that it required identification of the amount of child tax credit to which the particular claimant was actually "entitled" week by week during the period that was in question for income support purposes. It did not simply deem the claimant to be receiving the maximum amount of child tax credit for the children for whom she was responsible. However, the question remained of what was meant by "is entitled". The Commissioner concluded that it referred to the amount of child tax credit attributable, in accordance with the most recent award or amended award made by the Board, to the period from the effective date of the award or amended award to the end of the tax year. This result was consistent with the overall scheme of decision-making under the Tax Credits Act 2002. It also had the merit of being consistent with the general principle that the income support scheme was designed to meet financial needs when they arose through a shortfall in resources available at the time in question.

Applying this to the facts of the claimant's case, the Commissioner finds that the Board must have made a decision under s.28(5) of the 2002 Act (because the child tax credit had been reduced to recoup the overpayment of working tax credit), although he thought that there must also have been a use of the duty under reg.12(3) of the Tax Credits (Payments by the Board) Regulations 2002 (*SI 2002/2173*) (see Vol. IV in this series) to adjust the amount of the child tax credit payment in consequence of the amendment of the child tax credit award. Therefore, as there had been an amended award, the effect of reg.7(1) and (3) was that the clamant had to be treated as receiving an amount of income equivalent to the amount of child tax credit to which she was entitled under that amended award. The result was that it was the amount of child tax credit that she was actually receiving that was to be taken into account in calculating her income support. Note that the Commissioner left open how reg.7(1) and (3) applied in a case where the award of child tax credit had not been amended but by some administrative action there had simply been an adjustment of the amount paid without an amendment of the award.

The final question was how much of the amount under the amended child tax credit award was to be taken into account for the period specified in reg.7(1) and (3). The answer to this was to be found in reg.31(3) of the Income Support Regulations, although this did not supply a complete rule for the taking into account of income arising from awards of child tax credit and working tax credit. This was because it does not say how a weekly amount of income is to be derived from the amount of a tax credit award. The Commissioner therefore considered that reg.32 of the Income Support Regulations, substituting for the word "payment" in that regulation the amount of the tax credit award or amended award, should be applied (either directly or by a process of analogy to flesh out reg.31(3)). The period of the most recent child tax credit or working tax credit award had to be considered. Thus, where there had been an amended award, the period over which the amount of the amended award would be taken into account would be only the period after the effective date of the amendment. The weekly amount so calculated had then to be taken into account, but only from the first day of the benefit week identified under reg.31(3). The weekly amount had to be attributed to all the benefit weeks in the period after the effective date of the amendment to the end of the tax year, regardless of the way in which payments of tax credit were actually being made. If a tax credit award was terminated or amended later in the year there would either no longer be any amount to be taken into account or there would have to be a fresh application of reg.31(3)(b) or (c).

The Social Security (Habitual Residence) Amendment Regulations 2004

(SI 2004/1232)

Made by the Secretary of State under ss. 123(1)(a), (d) and (e), 131(3)(b), 135(1) and (2), 137(1) and (2)(i) and 175(1), (3) and (4) of the Social Security Contributions and Benefits Act 1992, ss. 4(5), 35(1) and 36(2) and (4) of the Jobseekers Act 1995 and ss. 1(5)(a) and 17(1) of the State Pension Credit Act 2002

[In force May 1, 2004]

GENERAL NOTE

See the commentary to reg.21 of the Income Support Regulations.

Citation, commencement and interpretation

1.—(1) These Regulations shall be cited as the Social Security (Habitual   2.884
Residence) Amendment Regulations 2004 and shall come into force on 1
May 2004.

(2) In these Regulations—

[*Definitions of "the Council Tax Benefit Regulations" and "the Housing Benefit
Regulations" omitted*]

"the Income Support Regulations" means the Income Support (General)
    Regulations 1987;
"the Jobseeker's Allowance Regulations" means the Jobseeker's
    Allowance Regulations 1996;
"the State Pension Credit Regulations" means the State Pension Credit
    Regulations 2002.

2.—**5.** *[Omitted]*

Transitional arrangements and savings

6.—(1) Paragraph (2) shall apply where a person—   2.885
  (a) is entitled to a specified benefit in respect of a period which includes
      30th April 2004;
  (b) claims a specified benefit on or after 1 May 2004 and it is subse-
      quently determined that he is entitled to that benefit in respect of a
      period which includes 30 April 2004;
  (c) claims a specified benefit on or after 1 May 2004 and it is subse-
      quently determined that he is entitled to such a benefit in respect of
      a period which is continuous with a period of entitlement to the same
      or another specified benefit which includes 30 April 2004;
  (d) claims jobseeker's allowance on or after 1 May 2004 and it is subse-
      quently determined that he is entitled to jobseeker's allowance in
      respect of a period of entitlement to that benefit which is linked to a
      previous period of entitlement which includes 30 April 2004 by
      virtue of regulations made under paragraph 3 of Schedule 1 to the
      Jobseekers Act 1995.

(2) Where this paragraph applies—
  (a) *[Omitted]*;
  (b) regulation 21 of the Income Support Regulations shall continue to
      have effect as if regulation 3 had not been made;
  (c) regulation 85 of the Jobseeker's Allowance Regulations shall continue
      to have effect as if regulation 4 had not been made; and
  (d) regulation 2 of the State Pension Credit Regulations shall continue to
      have effect as if regulation 5 had not been made.

(3) The provisions saved by paragraph (2) shall continue to have effect
until the date on which entitlement to a specified benefit for the purposes of
paragraph (1) ceases, and if there is more than one such specified benefit,
until the last date on which such entitlement ceases.

(4) In this regulation "specified benefit" means income support,
housing benefit, council tax benefit, jobseeker's allowance and state pension
credit.

The Accession (Immigration and Worker Registration) Regulations 2004

(SI 2004/1219)

Made by the Home Secretary, under section 2(2) of the European Communities Act 1972 and section 2 of the European Union (Accessions) Act 2003.

[In force May 1, 2004]

GENERAL NOTE

2.886   See the commentary to reg.21 of the Income Support Regulations.

PART 1

General

Citation, commencement and interpretation

2.887   **1.**—(1) These Regulations may be cited as the Accession (Immigration and Worker Registration) Regulations 2004 and shall come into force on 1 May 2004.

(2) In these Regulations—

(a) "the 1971 Act" means the Immigration Act 1971;

(b) "the 2000 Regulations" means the Immigration (European Economic Area) Regulations 2000;

(c) "accession period" means the period beginning on 1st May 2004 and ending on 30th April 2009;

(d) "accession State worker requiring registration" shall be interpreted in accordance with regulation 2;

(e) "authorised employer" shall be interpreted in accordance with regulation 7;

(f) "EEA State" means a Member State, other than the United Kingdom, or Norway, Iceland or Liechtenstein, and "EEA national" means a national of an EEA State;

(g) "employer" means, in relation to a worker, the person who directly pays the wage or salary of that worker;

(h) "registration certificate" means a certificate issued under regulation 8 authorising an accession State worker requiring registration to work for an employer;

(i) "relevant accession State" means the Czech Republic, the Republic of Estonia, the Republic of Latvia, the Republic of Lithuania, the Republic of Hungary, the Republic of Poland, the Republic of Slovenia and the Slovak Republic;

(j) "self-sufficient person" has the same meaning as in regulation 3 of the 2000 Regulations;

(k) "worker" means a worker within the meaning of Article 39 of the Treaty establishing the European Community, and "work" and "working" shall be construed accordingly.

"Accession State worker requiring registration"

2.—(1) Subject to the following paragraphs of this regulation, "accession State worker requiring registration" means a national of a relevant accession State working in the United Kingdom during the accession period.

2.888

(2) A national of a relevant accession State is not an accession State worker requiring registration if on April 30 2004 he had leave to enter or remain in the United Kingdom under the 1971 Act and that leave was not subject to any condition restricting his employment.

(3) A national of a relevant accession State is not an accession State worker requiring registration if he was legally working in the United Kingdom on 30th April 2004 and had been legally working in the United Kingdom without interruption throughout the period of 12 months ending on that date.

(4) A national of a relevant accession State who legally works in the United Kingdom without interruption for a period of 12 months falling partly or wholly after 30 April 2004 shall cease to be an accession State worker requiring registration at the end of that period of 12 months.

(5) A national of a relevant accession State is not an accession State worker requiring registration during any period in which he is also a national of—

(a) the United Kingdom;

(b) another EEA State, other than a relevant accession State; or

(c) Switzerland.

(6) A national of a relevant accession State is not an accession State worker requiring registration during any period in which he is—

(a) a posted worker; or

(b) a family member of a Swiss or EEA national who is in the United Kingdom as—

(i) a worker, other than as an accession State worker requiring registration;

(ii) a self-sufficient person;

(iii) a retired person; or

(iv) a student.

(7) For the purpose of this regulation—

(a) a person working in the United Kingdom during a period falling before 1 May 2004 was legally working in the United Kingdom during that period if—

(i) he had leave to enter or remain in the United Kingdom under the 1971 Act for that period, that leave allowed him to work in the United Kingdom, and he was working in accordance with any condition on that leave restricting his employment; or

(ii) he was entitled to reside in the United Kingdom for that period under the 2000 Regulations without the requirement for such leave;

(b) a person working in the United Kingdom on or after 1 May 2004 is legally working during any period in which he is working in the United Kingdom for an authorised employer;

(c) a person shall also be treated as legally working in the United Kingdom on or after 1 May 2004 during any period in which he falls within paragraph (5) or (6).

(8) For the purpose of paragraphs (3) and (4), a person shall be treated as having worked in the United Kingdom without interruption for a period of 12 months if he was legally working in the United Kingdom at the beginning and end of that period and any intervening periods in which he was not legally working in the United Kingdom do not, in total, exceed 30 days.

(9) In this regulation—

(a) "retired person" and "student" have the same meaning as in regulation 3 of the 2000 Regulations;

(b) "posted worker" means a person whose employer is not established in the United Kingdom and who works for that employer in the United Kingdom for the purpose of providing services on his employer's behalf;

(c) "family member" means—

(i) in relation to a worker, his spouse and his children who are under 21 or dependent on him;

(ii) in relation to any other person, his spouse and his children who are dependent on him.

PART 2

IMMIGRATION

Amendment of the 2000 Regulations

3. *[Omitted].*

Right of residence of work seekers and workers from relevant acceding States during the accession period

2.889   **4.**—(1) This regulation derogates during the accession period from Article 39 of the Treaty establishing the European Community, Articles 1 to 6 of Regulation (EEC) No. 1612/68 on freedom of movement for workers within the Community and Council Directive (EEC) No. 68/360 on the abolition of restrictions on movement and residence within the Community for workers of Member States and their families .

(2) A national of a relevant accession State shall not be entitled to reside in the United Kingdom for the purpose of seeking work by virtue of his status as a work seeker if he would be an accession State worker requiring registration if he began working in the United Kingdom.

(3) Paragraph (2) is without prejudice to the right of a national of a relevant accession State to reside in the United Kingdom under the 2000 Regulations as a self-sufficient person whilst seeking work in the United Kingdom.

(4) An accession State worker requiring registration shall only be entitled to reside in the United Kingdom in accordance with the 2000 Regulations as modified by regulation 5.

Application of 2000 Regulations in relation to an accession State worker requiring registration

5.—(1) The 2000 Regulations shall apply in relation to an accession State worker requiring registration subject to the modifications set out in this regulation.

(2) An accession State worker requiring registration shall be treated as a worker for the purpose of the definition of "qualified person" in regulation 5(1) of the 2000 Regulations only during a period in which he is working in the United Kingdom for an authorised employer.

(3) Subject to paragraph (4), regulation 5(2) of the 2000 Regulations shall not apply to an accession State worker requiring registration who ceases to work.

(4) Where an accession State worker requiring registration—

(a) begins working for an authorised employer on or after 1st May 2004; and

(b) ceases working for that employer in the circumstances mentioned in regulation 5(2) of the 2000 Regulations during the one month period beginning on the date on which the work begins,

that regulation shall apply to that worker during the remainder of that one month period.

(5) An accession State worker requiring registration shall not be treated as an EEA national for the purpose of the power in regulation 10 of the 2000 Regulations (dependants and members of the household of EEA nationals) to issue a residence permit or a residence document to a relative of an EEA national or his spouse.

(6) An accession State worker requiring registration shall not be treated as a qualified person for the purpose of regulation 15 of the 2000 Regulations (issue of residence permits and residence documents).

Transitional provisions applying to the application of the 2000 Regulations to nationals of the accession States and their family members

6.—(1) Where before 1 May 2004 a qualified person or the family member of a qualified person has been given leave to enter or remain in the United Kingdom under the 1971 Act subject to conditions, those conditions shall cease to have effect on and after that date.

(2) Where before 1 May 2004 directions have been given for the removal of a qualified person or the family member of a qualified person under paragraphs 8 to 10A of Schedule 2 to the 1971 Act or section 10 of the 1999 Act, those directions shall cease to have effect on and after that date.

(3) Where before 1 May 2004 the Secretary of State has made a decision to make a deportation order against a qualified person or the family member of a qualified person under section 5(1) of the 1971 Act—

(a) that decision shall, on and after 1 May 2004, be treated as if it were a decision under regulation 21(3)(b) of the 2000 Regulations; and

(b) any appeal against that decision, or against the refusal by the Secretary of State to revoke the deportation order, made under section 63 of the 1999 Act or section 82(2)(j) or (k) of the 2002 Act before 1 May 2004 shall, on and after that date, be treated as if it had been made under regulation 29 of the 2000 Regulations.

(4) In this regulation—

2.890

2.891

(a) "the 1999 Act" means the Immigration and Asylum Act 1999
(b) "the 2002 Act" means the Nationality, Immigration and Asylum Act 2002;
(c) regulation 6 of the 2000 Regulations shall apply for the purpose of determining whether a person is the family member of another person;
(d) any reference to a qualified person or to the family member of a qualified person is a reference to a person who becomes for the purpose of the 2000 Regulations a qualified person or the family member of a qualified person, as the case may be, on 1st May 2004 by virtue of regulation 3.

PART 3

ACCESSION STATE WORKER REGISTRATION

Requirement for an accession State worker requiring registration to be authorised to work

2.892   **7.**—(1) By way of derogation from Article 39 of the Treaty establishing the European Community and Articles 1 to 6 of Regulation (EEC) No. 1612/68 on freedom of movement for workers within the Community, an accession State worker requiring registration shall only be authorised to work in the United Kingdom for an authorised employer.

(2) An employer is an authorised employer in relation to a worker if—

(a) the worker was legally working for that employer on 30 April 2004 and has not ceased working for that employer after that date;
(b) the worker—
  (i) during the one month period beginning on the date on which he begins working for the employer, applies for a registration certificate authorising him to work for that employer in accordance with regulation 8; and
  (ii) has not received a valid registration certificate or notice of refusal under regulation 8 in relation to that application or ceased working for that employer since the application was made;
(c) the worker has received a valid registration certificate authorising him to work for that employer and that certificate has not expired under paragraph (5); or
(d) the employer is an authorised employer in relation to that worker under paragraph (3) or (4).

(3) Where a worker begins working for an employer on or after 1 May 2004 that employer is an authorised employer in relation to that worker during the one month period beginning on the date on which the work begins.

(4) Where a worker was, before 1 May 2004, issued with leave to enter the United Kingdom under the 1971 Act as a seasonal worker at an agricultural camp and the worker begins working for an employer on or after 1 May 2004 as a seasonal worker at such a camp, that employer is an

authorised employer in relation to that worker during the period beginning on the date on which the work begins and ending on the date on which the worker ceases working for that employer, or on 31 December 2004, which ever is the earlier.

(5) A registration certificate—

(a) is invalid if the worker is no longer working for the employer specified in the certificate on the date on which it is issued;

(b) expires on the date on which the worker ceases working for that employer.

(6) Regulation 2(7)(a) shall apply for the purpose of determining whether a person is legally working on 30 April 2004 for the purpose of this regulation.

Registration card and registration certificate

8.—(1) An application for a registration certificate authorising an accession State worker requiring registration to work for an employer may only be made by an applicant who is working for that employer at the date of the application.

(2) The application shall be in writing and shall be made to the Secretary of State.

(3) The application shall state—

(a) the name, address, and date of birth of the applicant;

(b) the name and address of the head or main office of the employer;

(c) the date on which the applicant began working for that employer;

(d) where the applicant has been issued with a registration card, the reference number of that card.

(4) Unless the applicant has been issued with a registration card under paragraph (5), the application shall be accompanied by—

(a) a registration fee of £50;

(b) two passport size photographs of the applicant;

(c) the applicant's national identity card or passport issued by the applicant's State;

(d) a letter from the employer concerned confirming that the applicant began working for the employer on the date specified in the application.

(5) In the case of an application by an applicant who has not been issued with a registration card under this paragraph, the Secretary of State shall, where he is satisfied that the application is made in accordance with this regulation and that the applicant—

(a) is an accession State worker requiring registration; and

(b) began working for the employer on the date specified in the application,

send the applicant a registration card and a registration certificate authorising the worker to work for the employer specified in the application, and shall return the applicant's national identity card or passport.

(6) In the case of any other application, the Secretary of State shall, if he is satisfied as mentioned in paragraph (5), send the applicant a registration certificate authorising the worker to work for the employer specified in the application.

(7) A registration card issued under paragraph (5) shall contain—

(a) the name, nationality and date of birth of the applicant;

(b) a photograph of the applicant;

2.893

(c) a reference number.

(8) A registration certificate issued under paragraph (5) or (6) shall contain—

(a) the name of the applicant;

(b) the reference number of the applicant's registration card;

(c) the name and address of the head or main office of the employer, as specified in the application;

(d) the date on which the applicant began working for the employer, as specified in the application; and

(e) the date on which the certificate is issued.

(9) Where the Secretary of State receives an application made in accordance with this regulation and he is not satisfied as mentioned in paragraph (5), he shall—

(a) send the applicant a notice of refusal; and

(b) return any documents and fee that accompanied the application to the applicant.

(10) Where the Secretary of State sends a registration certificate or notice of refusal to an applicant under this regulation he shall, at the same time, send a copy of the certificate or notice to the employer concerned at the address specified in the application for that employer.

(11) Certificates and notices, and copies of these documents, sent under this regulation shall be sent by post.

Restriction on employers of relevant accession State workers requiring registration

2.894   **9.** *[Omitted]*.

Community Charges (Deductions from Income Support) (No.2) Regulations 1990

(SI 1990/545)

Made by the Secretary of State under ss.22(3) and 146(6) and Sch.4 para.6 of the Local Government Finance Act 1988.

GENERAL NOTE

2.895   The first version of these Regulations (SI 1990/107) was defective and was replaced.

The Community Charges (Deductions from Income Support) (Scotland) Regulations 1989 (SI 1989/507) made provision for Scotland from April 10, 1989. They have been amended by SI 1990/113 to bring them into line with these Regulations, but are not reproduced.

Citation, commencement and interpretation

1.—(1) These Regulations may be cited as the Community Charges (Deductions from Income Support) (No. 2) Regulations 1990 and shall come into force on 1 April 1990.

(2) In these Regulations, unless the context otherwise requires—

[3. . .];

"the 1986 Act" means the Social Security Act 1986;
[³. . .];
[⁴"the 1998 Act" means the Social Security Act 1998;]
"appropriate social security office" means an office of the Department of Social Security which is normally open to the public for the receipt of claims for income support and includes an office of the [¹Department for Education and Employment] which is normally open to the public for the receipt of claims for [¹jobseeker's allowance and income support];
[⁵"Commissioner" has the meaning it bears in section 39(1) of the 1998 Act;]
[²"contribution-based jobseeker's allowance", except in a case to which paragraph (b) of the definition of income-based jobseeker's allowance applies, means a contribution-based jobseeker's allowance under Part I of the Jobseekers Act 1995, but does not include any back to work bonus under section 26 of the Jobseekers Act which is paid as job-seeker's allowance;]
"couple" means a married or unmarried couple;
"debtor" means a person against whom a liability order has been obtained;
"5 per cent of the personal allowance for a single claimant aged not less than 25" and
"5 per cent of the personal allowance for a couple where both members are aged not less than 18" means, in each case, where the percentage is not a multiple of 5 pence, the sum obtained by rounding that 5 per cent to the next higher such multiple;
"income support" means income support within the meaning of the 1986 Act [¹but does not include any back to work bonus under section 26 of the Jobseekers Act which is paid as income support;]
[²"income-based jobseeker's allowance" means—
(a) an income-based jobseeker's allowance under Part I of the Job-seekers Act 1995; and
(b) in a case where, if there was no entitlement to contribution-based jobseeker's allowance, there would be entitlement to income-based jobseeker's allowance at the same rate, contribution-based job-seeker's allowance;]
but does not include any back to work bonus under section 26 of the Jobseekers Act which is paid as jobseeker's allowance;]
[¹"Jobseekers Act" means the Jobseekers Act 1995;
"jobseeker's allowance" means an allowance under Part I of the Job-seekers Act but does not include any back to work bonus under section 26 of that Act which is paid as jobseeker's allowance;]
"liability order" means an order under regulation 29 of the Community Charges (Administration and Enforcement) Regulations 1989;
"married couple" has the meaning ascribed to it in section 20(11) of the 1986 Act [SSCBA, s.137(1)];
"payments to third parties" means direct payments to third parties in accordance with Schedule 9 to the Social Security (Claims and Payments) Regulations 1987;
"polygamous marriage" means a marriage to which section 22B of the Social Security Act 1986 [SSCBA, s.133] refers;

"single debtor" means a debtor who is not a member of a couple;

[⁷ "state pension credit" means the benefit of that name payable under the State Pension Credit Act 2002;]

[⁶"tribunal" means an appeal tribunal constituted under Chapter I of Part I of the 1998 Act;] and

"unmarried couple" has the meaning ascribed to it in section 20(11) of the 1986 Act [SSCBA, s.137(1)].

(3) Unless the context otherwise requires, any reference in these Regulations to a numbered regulation or Schedule is a reference to the regulation and Schedule bearing that number in the Regulations and any reference in a regulation or Schedule to a numbered paragraph is a reference to the paragraph of that regulation or Schedule having that number.

AMENDMENTS

2.896   1. Social Security (Jobseeker's Allowance Consequential Amendments) (Deductions) Regulations 1996 (SI 1996/2344), reg.6 (October 7, 1996).

2. Social Security (Miscellaneous Amendments) Regulations 1998 (SI 1998/ 563), reg.3(1) and (2)(a) (April 1, 1998). (Note that the commencement date for this provision was amended by Social Security (Miscellaneous Amendments) (No. 2) Regulations 1998 (SI 1998/865), reg.2 (March 20, 1998).)

3. Social Security Act 1998 (Commencement No.12, and Consequential and Transitional Provisions) Order 1999 (SI 1999/3178 (C.81)), art.3(11) and Sch.11, para.1(a).

4. Social Security Act 1998 (Commencement No.12, and Consequential and Transitional Provisions) Order 1999 (SI 1999/3178 (C.81)), art.3(11) and Sch.11, para.1(b) (November 29, 1999).

5. Social Security Act 1998 (Commencement No.12, and Consequential and Transitional Provisions) Order 1999 (SI 1999/3178 (C.81)), art.3(11) and Sch.11, para.1(c) (November 29, 1999).

6. Social Security Act 1998 (Commencement No.12, and Consequential and Transitional Provisions) Order 1999 (SI 1999/3178 (C.81)), art.3(11) and Sch.11, para.1(d) (November 29, 1999).

7. State Pension Credit (Consequential, Transitional and Miscellaneous Provisions) Regulations 2002 (SI 2002/3019), reg.35 (October 6, 2003).

[³[⁴Application for deductions] from income support [⁶, state pension credit] or jobseeker's allowance]

2.897   **2.**—(1) Where a debtor is entitled to income support [⁶, state pension credit] [³or jobseeker's allowance], an authority may apply to the Secretary of State by sending an application in respect of the debtor or, where a liability order is made against a couple in respect of both of the couple, to an appropriate social security office asking the Secretary of State to deduct sums from any amount payable to the debtor, or as the case may be either of the couple by way of income support [³or jobseeker's allowance].

(2) An application from an authority shall be in writing and shall contain the following particulars—

(a) the name and address of the debtor or where the liability order is made against a couple, the names and address of both of them;

(b) the name and place of the court which made the liability order;

(c) the date when the liability order was made;

(d) the total amount of the arrears specified in the liability order;

(e) the total amount which the authority wishes to have deducted from income support [⁶, state pension credit] [³or jobseeker's allowance].

(3) Where it appears to the Secretary of State that an application from an authority gives insufficient particulars to enable the debtor to be identified he may require the authority to furnish such further particulars as may reasonably be required.

(4) [⁵. . .].

(5) [⁵. . .].

(6) [⁵. . .].

AMENDMENTS

1. Social Security (Claims and Payments) Amendment Regulation 1992 (SI 1992/1026), reg.7 (May 25, 1992).

2.898

2. Social Security (Claims and Payments) Amendment (No.3) Regulations 1993 (SI 1993/2113), reg.5 (September 27, 1993).

3. Social Security (Jobseeker's Allowance Consequential Amendments) (Deductions) Regulations 1996 (SI 1996/2344), reg.7 (October 7, 1996).

4. Social Security Act 1998 (Commencement No. 12, and Consequential and Transitional Provisions) Order 1999 (SI 1999/3178 (C.81)), art.3(11) and Sch.11, para.2(1) (November 29, 1999).

5. Social Security Act 1998 (Commencement No. 12, and Consequential and Transitional Provisions) Order 1999 (SI 1999/3178 (C.81)), art.3(11) and Sch.11, para.2(2) (November 29, 1999).

6. State Pension Credit (Consequential, Transitional and Miscellaneous Provisions) Regulations 2002 (SI 2002/3019), reg.35 (October 6, 2003).

DEFINITIONS

"adjudication officer"—see reg.1(2).

2.899

"authority"—see Local Government Finance Act 1988, s.144.

"appropriate social security officer"—see reg.1(2).

"couple"—*ibid.*

"debtor"—*ibid.*

"5 per cent. of the personal allowance for a single claimant aged not less than 25"—*ibid.*

"5 per cent. of the personal allowance for a couple where both members are aged not less than 18"—*ibid.*

"income support"—*ibid.*

"Jobseekers Act"—*ibid.*

"jobseeker's allowance"—*ibid.*

"liability order"—*ibid.*

"payments to third parties"—*ibid.*

"polygamous marriage"—*ibid.*

GENERAL NOTE

R(IS) 3/92 held that if the Secretary of State accepted the validity (*i.e.* the form and content) of an application under para.(2), the AO or SSAT also had to accept it. But where there is an issue as to whether the claimant is a "debtor" (defined in reg.1(2)) at all, the tribunal must satisfy itself that the basic conditions for the operation of the procedure exist: namely that there *is* a subsisting liability order, properly obtained, under which there *is* outstanding a sum due of the amount sought to be deducted from income support (*R(IS) 1/98*). In that case neither the alleged liability order nor any evidence from the local authority confirming that an amount was still due from the claimant had been produced, whereas the claimant had produced evidence which appeared to substantiate that she was in fact in credit on her community charge account. The Commissioner therefore decided that there was no jurisdiction to make any deduction from the claimant's income support in respect of the community charge.

2.900

[¹ Deductions from debtor's income support [² , state pension credit] or jobseeker's allowance

2.901 **3.**—(1) Subject to paragraph (4) and regulation 4, where the Secretary of State receives an application from an authority in respect of a debtor who is entitled to income support [², state pension credit] or income-based job-seeker's allowance and the amount payable by way of that benefit, after any deduction under this paragraph, is 10 pence or more, the Secretary of State may deduct a sum from that benefit which is equal to 5 per cent of the personal allowance—

(a) set out in paragraph 1(1)(e) of Schedule 2 to the Income Support (General) Regulations 1987 or, as the case may be, of Schedule 1 to the Jobseeker's Allowance Regulations 1996 for a couple where—

    (i) a liability order is made; and

    (ii) that benefit is payable, in respect of both members of a couple both of whom are aged not less than 18; and

(b) in any other case, for a single claimant aged not less than 25 set out in paragraph 1(3)(c) of Schedule 2 to the Income Support (General) Regulations 1987 or, as the case may be, paragraph 1(3)(e) of Schedule 1 to the Jobseeker's Allowance Regulations 1996,

and pay that sum to the authority towards satisfaction of any outstanding sum which is or forms part of the amount in respect of which the liability order was made.

(2) Subject to paragraph (3) and regulation 4, where—

(a) the Secretary of State receives an application from an authority in respect of a debtor who is entitled to contribution-based job-seeker's allowance; and

(b) the amount of contribution-based jobseeker's allowance payable before any deduction under this paragraph is equal to or more than one-third of the age-related amount applicable to the debtor under section 4(1)(a) of the Jobseekers Act,

the Secretary of State may deduct a sum from that benefit which is equal to one-third of the age-related amount applicable to the debtor under section 4(1)(a) of the Jobseekers Act and pay that sum to the authority towards satisfaction of any outstanding sum which is or forms part of the amount in respect of which the liability order was made.

(3) Where the sum that would otherwise fall to be deducted under paragraph (2) includes a fraction of a penny, the sum to be deducted shall be rounded down to the next whole penny.

(4) Before making a deduction under paragraph (1) the Secretary of State shall make any deduction which falls to be made in respect of a liability mentioned in any of the following provisions of the Social Security (Claims and Payments) Regulations 1987—

(a) regulation 34A[103] (mortgage interest);

(b) paragraph 3[104] (housing costs) of Schedule 9;

(c) paragraph 5[105] (rent and certain service charges for fuel) of Schedule 9;

(d) paragraph 6[106] (fuel costs) of Schedule 9; and

(e) paragraph 7[107] (water charges) of Schedule 9.

(5) Subject to regulations 5 and 6, a decision of the Secretary of State under this regulation shall be final.

(6) The Secretary of State shall notify the debtor in writing of a decision to make a deduction under this regulation as soon as is practicable and at the same time shall notify the debtor of his right of appeal.]

AMENDMENTS

1. Social Security Act 1998 (Commencement No.12, and Consequential and Transitional Provisions) Order 1999 (SI 1999/3178 (C.81)), art.3(11) and Sch.11, para.3 (November 29, 1999).
2. State Pension Credit (Consequential, Transitional and Miscellaneous Provisions) Regulations 2002 (SI 2002/3019), reg.35 (October 6, 2003).

2.902

Circumstances, time of making and termination of deductions

4.—[²(1) The Secretary of State—

    (a) shall make deductions under regulation 3 only where the debtor is entitled to income support [³ , state pension credit] or jobseeker's allowance throughout any benefit week; and

    (b) shall not determine any application under regulation 2 which relates to a debtor in respect of whom—

        (i) he is making deductions; or

        (ii) deductions fall to be made,

pursuant to an earlier application under regulation 3 until no deductions pursuant to that earlier application fall to be made.]

(2) The Secretary of State shall make deductions from income support [³, state pension credit] [¹or jobseeker's allowance] at a time which corresponds to the payment of income support [³ , state pension credit] [¹or jobseeker's allowance] to the debtor and he shall cease making deductions when—

    (a) a payment to a third party has priority;

    (b) there is insufficient entitlement to income support [³ , state pension credit] [¹or jobseeker's allowance] to enable him to make the deduction;

    (c) entitlement to income support [³ , state pension credit] [¹or jobseeker's allowance] ceases;

    (d) an authority withdraws its application for deductions to be made; or

    (e) the debt in respect of which he was making the deductions is discharged.

(3) Payments shall be made to the authority at such intervals as the Secretary of State may decide.

2.903

AMENDMENTS

1. Social Security (Jobseeker's Allowance Consequential Amendments) (Deductions) Regulations 1996 (SI 1996/2344), reg.9 (October 7, 1996).
2. Social Security Act 1998 (Commencement No.12, and Consequential and Transitional Provisions) Order 1999 (SI 1999/3178 (C.81)), art.3(11) and Sch.11, para.4 (November 29, 1999).
3. State Pension Credit (Consequential, Transitional and Miscellaneous Provisions) Regulations 2002 (SI 2002/3019), reg.35 (October 6, 2003).

2.904

DEFINITIONS

    "adjudication officer"—see reg.1(2).

    "authority"—see Local Government Finance Act 1988, s.144.

    "debtor"—see reg.1(2).

    "income support"—*ibid.*

    "jobseeker's allowance"—*ibid.*

[¹Revision and supersession

2.905   **5.** Any decision of the Secretary of State under regulation 3 may be revised under section 9 of the 1998 Act or superseded under section 10 of that Act as though the decision were made under section 8(1)(c) of that Act.]

AMENDMENT

1. Social Security Act 1998 (Commencement No.12, and Consequential and Transitional Provisions) Order 1999 (SI 1999/3178 (C.81)), art.3(11) and Sch.11, para.5 (November 29, 1999).

[¹ Appeal

2.906   **6.** Any decision of the Secretary of State under regulation 3 (whether as originally made or as revised under regulation 5) may be appealed to a tribunal as though the decision were made on an award of a relevant benefit (within the meaning of section 8(3) of the 1998 Act) under section 8(1)(c) of the 1998 Act.]

AMENDMENT

1. Social Security Act 1998 (Commencement No.12, and Consequential and Transitional Provisions) Order 1999 (SI 1999/3178 (C.81)), art.3(11) and Sch.11, para.5 (November 29, 1999).

Correction of accidental errors

2.907   **7.**—[¹ . . .]

AMENDMENT

1. Social Security Act 1998 (Commencement No.12, and Consequential and Transitional Provisions Order 1999 (SI 1999/3178 (C.81)), art.3(11) and Sch.11, para.6 (November 29, 1999).

Setting aside decisions on certain grounds

2.908   **8.**—[¹ . . .]

AMENDMENT

1. Social Security Act 1998 (Commencement No.12, and Consequential and Transitional Provisions) Order 1999 (SI 1999/3178 (C.81)), art.3(11) and Sch.11, para.6 (November 29, 1999).

Provisions common to regulations 7 and 8

2.909   **9.** [¹ . . .]

AMENDMENT

1. Social Security Act 1998 (Commencement No.12, and Consequential and Transitional Provisions) Order 1999 (SI 1999/3178 (C.81)), art.3(11) and Sch.11, para.6 (November 29, 1999).

Fines (Deductions from Income Support) Regulations 1992

(SI 1992/2182)

Made by the Secretary of State under ss. 24 and 30 of the Criminal Justice Act 1991.

Citation, commencement and interpretation

1.—(1) These Regulations may be cited as the Fines (Deductions from Income Support) Regulations 1992 and shall come into force on 1 October 1992.

2.910

(2) In these Regulations, unless the context otherwise requires—

"the 1971 Act" means the Vehicles (Excise) Act 1971;

"the 1973 Act" means the Powers of the Criminal Courts Act 1973;

[⁴ "the 1998 Act" means the Social Security Act 1998;]

[⁴ . . .];

"application" means an application made under regulation 2 [⁶ . . .] containing the information specified in regulation 3(1);

[⁴ . . .];

"benefit week" has the meaning prescribed in regulation 2(1) of the Income Support Regulations [² or, as the case may be, [⁷ regulation 1(2) of the State Pension Credit Regulations 2002 or] regulation 1(3) of the Jobseeker's Allowance Regulations 1996;]

"the Claims and Payments Regulations" means the Social Security (Claims and Payments) Regulations 1987;

[⁴ "Commissioner" has the meaning it bears in section 39(1) of the 1998 Act;]

[³ "contribution-based jobseeker's allowance", except in a case to which paragraph (b) of the definition of income-based jobseeker's allowance applies, means a contribution-based jobseeker's allowance under Part I of the Jobseekers Act 1995, but does not include any back to work bonus under section 26 of the Jobseekers Act which is paid as jobseeker's allowance;]

"court" means in England and Wales a magistrates' court and in Scotland a court;

"5 per cent. of the personal allowance for a single claimant aged not less than 25" means, where the percentage is not a multiple of 5 pence, the sum obtained by rounding that 5 per cent. to the next higher such multiple;

[² "income support" means income support under Part VII of the Social Security Contributions and Benefits Act 1992, but does not include any back to work bonus under section 26 of the Jobseekers Act which is paid as income support;]

"Income Support Regulations" means the Income Support (General) Regulations 1987;

[³ "income-based jobseeker's allowance" means—

(a) an income-based jobseeker's allowance under Part I of the Jobseekers Act 1995; and

(b) in a case where, if there was no entitlement to contribution-based jobseeker's allowance, there would be entitlement to income-based jobseeker's allowance at the same rate, contribution-based job-seeker's allowance,

but does include any back to work bonus under section 26 of the Jobseekers Act which is paid as jobseeker's allowance;]

[² "Jobseekers Act" means the Jobseekers Act 1995;

"jobseeker's allowance" means an allowance under Part I of the Jobseekers Act but does not include any back to work bonus under section 26 of that Act which is paid as jobseeker's allowance;]

"payments to third parties" means direct payments to third parties in accordance with Schedules 9 and 9A to the Claims and Payments Regulations, regulation 2(4) of the Community Charges (Deductions from Income Support) (No. 2) Regulations 1990 and regulation 2(4) of the Community Charges (Deductions from Income Support) (Scotland) Regulations 1989 [¹and regulation 2 of the Council Tax (Deductions from Income Support) Regulations 1993];

[⁷ "personal allowance for a single claimant aged not less than 25" means—

(a) in the case of a person who is entitled to either income support or state pension credit, the amount for the time being specified in paragraph 1(1)(e) of column (2) of Schedule 2 to the Income Support Regulations; or

(b) in the case of a person who is entitled to an income-based job-seeker's allowance, the amount for the time being specified in para-graph 1(1)(e) of column (2) of Schedule 1 to the Jobseeker's Allowance Regulations 1996;]

"social security office" means an office of the [⁵ Department for Work and Pensions which is open to the public for the receipt of claims for income support or a jobseeker's allowance.] [⁷ "state pension credit" means the benefit of that name payable under the State Pension Credit Act 2002;]

[⁴ "tribunal" means an appeal tribunal constituted under Chapter 1 of Part I of the 1998 Act.]

(3) Unless the context otherwise requires, any reference in these Regulations to a numbered regulation, Part or Schedule bearing that number in these Regulations and any reference in a regulation or Schedule to a numbered paragraph is a reference to the paragraph of that regulation or Schedule having that number.

AMENDMENTS

2.911   1. Deductions from Income Support (Miscellaneous Amendment) Regulations 1993 (SI 1993/495), reg.3 (April 1, 1993).

2. Social Security (Jobseeker's Allowance Consequential Amendments) (Deductions) Regulations 1996 (SI 1996/2344), reg.10 (October 7, 1996).

3. Social Security (Miscellaneous Amendments) Regulations 1998 (SI 1998/563), reg.3(1) and (2)(d) (April 1, 1998). (Note that the commencement date for this provision was amended by Social Security (Miscellaneous Amendments) (No.2) Regulations 1998 (SI 1998/865), reg.2 (March 20, 1998).)

4. Social Security Act 1998 (Commencement No. 12, and Consequential and Transitional Provisions) Order 1999 (SI 1999/3178 (C.81)), art.3(12) and Sch.12, para.1 (November 29, 1999).

5. Secretaries of State for Education and Skills and for Work and Pensions Order 2002 (SI 2002/1397), art.12 and Sch., para.22 (June 27, 2002).

6. Fines (Deductions from Income Support) (Amendment) Regulations 2003 (SI 2003/1360), reg.2(a) (June 20, 2003).

7. State Pension Credit (Consequential, Transitional and Miscellaneous Provisions) Regulations 2002 (SI 2002/3019), reg.32 (October 6, 2003).

[¹Application for deductions from income support [², state pension credit] or jobseeker's allowance]

2.—(1) Where a fine has been imposed on an offender by a court or a sum is required to be paid by a compensation order which has been made against an offender by a court and (in either case) the offender is entitled to income support [², state pension credit] [¹or jobseeker's allowance], the court may, subject to paragraph (2), apply to the Secretary of State asking him to deduct sums from any amounts payable to the offender by way of income support [², state pension credit] [¹or jobseeker's allowance], in order to secure the payment of any sum which is or forms part of the fine or compensation.

2.912

(2) Before making an application the court shall make an enquiry as to the offender's means.

AMENDMENTS

1. Social Security (Jobseeker's Allowance Consequential Amendments) (Deductions) Regulations 1996 (SI 1996/2344), reg.11 (October 7, 1996).
2. State Pension Credit (Consequential, Transitional and Miscellaneous Provisions) Regulations 2002 (S.I. 2002/3019), reg.32 (October 6, 2003).

2.913

DEFINITIONS

"court"—see reg.1(2).
"income support"—*ibid.*
"jobseeker's allowance"—*ibid.*

[¹ Information that the court may require

2A.—(1) Where an application is made the court may require the offender to provide his full name, full address, date of birth, national insurance number and the name of any benefits to which he is entitled.

2.914

(2) For the purposes of this regulation "benefits" means income support, state pension credit or a jobseeker's allowance.]

AMENDMENT

1. Fines (Deductions from Income Support)(Amendment) Regulations 2004, reg.2(a) (December 18, 2004)

Contents of application

3.—(1) An application [¹. . .] shall contain the following information—
  (a) the name and address of the offender, and, if it is known, his date of birth;
  (b) the date when the fine was imposed or the compensation order made;
  (c) the name and address of the court imposing the fine or making the compensation order;
  (d) the amount of the fine or the amount payable by the compensation order as the case may be;
  (e) the date on which the application is made;
  (f) the date on which the court enquired into the offender's means;

2.915

(g) whether the offender has defaulted in paying the fine, compensation order or any instalment of either.

(2) A court making an application shall serve it on the Secretary of State by sending or delivering it to a social security office.

(3) Where it appears to the Secretary of State that an application from a court gives insufficient information to enable the offender to be identified, he may require the court to furnish such further information as he may reasonably require for that purpose.

AMENDMENT

1. Fines (Deductions from Income Support) (Amendment) Regulations 2003 (SI 2003/1360), reg.2(b) (June 20, 2003).

DEFINITIONS

"application"—see reg.1(2).
"court"—*ibid.*
"social security office"—*ibid.*

[¹Deductions from offender's income support [², state pension credit] or jobseeker's allowance

2.916   **4.**—(1) Subject to regulation 7, where—
(a) the Secretary of State receives an application from a court in respect of an offender who is entitled to income support [² , state pension credit] or income-based jobseeker's allowance;
(b) the amount payable by way of that benefit, after any deduction under this paragraph, is 10 pence or more; and
(c) the aggregate amount payable under one or more of the following provisions, namely, paragraphs 3(2)(a), 5(6), 6(2)(a) and 7(3)(a) and (5)(a) of Schedule 9 to the Claims and Payments Regulations, and regulation 2 of the Council Tax (Deductions from Income Support) Regulations 1993, together with the amount to be deducted under this paragraph does not exceed an amount equal to 3 times 5 per cent. of the personal allowance for a single claimant aged not less than 25 years,

the Secretary of State may deduct a sum from that benefit which is equal to 5 per cent. of the personal allowance for a single claimant aged not less than 25 [³ or £5, whichever is the greater amount allowed by sub-paragraphs (b) and (c)] and pay that sum to the court towards satisfaction of the fine or the sum required to be paid by compensation order.

(2) Subject to paragraphs (3) and (4) and regulation 7, where—
(a) the Secretary of State receives an application from a court in respect of an offender who is entitled to contribution-based job-seeker's allowance; and
(b) the amount of contribution-based jobseeker's allowance payable before any deduction under this paragraph is equal to or more than one-third of the age-related amount applicable to the offender under section 4(1)(a) of the Jobseekers Act,

the Secretary of State may deduct a sum from that benefit which is equal to one-third of the age-related amount applicable to the offender under section 4(1)(a) of the Jobseekers Act and pay that sum to the court towards satisfaction of the fine or the sum required to be paid by compensation order.

(3) No deduction shall be made under paragraph (2) where a deduction is being made from the offender's contribution-based jobseeker's allowance under the Community Charges (Deductions from Income Support) (No. 2) Regulations 1990, the Community Charges (Deductions from Income Support) (Scotland) Regulations 1989 or the Council Tax (Deductions from Income Support) Regulations 1993.

(4) Where the sum that would otherwise fall to be deducted under paragraph (2) includes a fraction of a penny, the sum to be deducted shall be rounded down to the next whole penny.

(5) The Secretary of State shall notify the offender and the court in writing of a decision to make a deduction under this regulation so far as is practicable within 14 days from the date on which he made the decision and at the same time shall notify the offender of his right of appeal.]

AMENDMENTS

1. Social Security Act 1998 (Commencement No.12, and Consequential and   2.917
Transitional Provisions) Order 1999 (SI 1999/3178 (C.81)), art.3(12) and Sch.12,
para.2 (November 29, 1999).
2. State Pension Credit (Consequential, Transitional and Miscellaneous
Provisions) Regulations 2002 (SI 2002/3019), reg.32 (October 6, 2003).
3. Fines (Deductions from Income Support) (Amendment) Regulations 2004,
reg.2(b) (December 18, 2004)

Notification of decision

5. [¹ . . .]   2.918

AMENDMENT

1. Social Security Act 1998 (Commencement No.12, and Consequential and
Transitional Provisions) Order 1999 (SI 1999/3178 (C.81)), art.3(12) and Sch.12,
para.2 (November 29, 1999).

[¹Deductions from offender's income support or income-based jobseeker's allowance]

6. [² . . .]   2.919

AMENDMENTS

1. Social Security (Jobseeker's Allowance Consequential Amendments)
(Deductions) Regulations 1996 (SI 1996/2344), reg.13 (October 7, 1996).
2. Social Security Act 1998 (Commencement No.12, and Consequential and
Transitional Provisions) Order 1999 (SI 1999/3178 (C.81)), art.3(12) and Sch.12,
para.2 (November 29, 1999).

DEFINITIONS

"adjudication officer"—see reg.1(2).
"court"—*ibid.*
"5 per cent. of the personal allowance for a single claimant aged not less than 25"—*ibid.*

[¹Deductions from offender's contribution-based jobseeker's allowance

6A. [² . . .]   2.920

AMENDMENTS

1. Social Security (Jobseeker's Allowance Consequential Amendments) (Deductions) Regulations 1996 (SI 1996/2344), reg.14 (October 7, 1996).

2. Social Security Act 1998 (Commencement No.12, and Consequential and Transitional Provisions) Order 1999 (SI 1999/3178 (C.81)), art.3(12) and Sch.12, para.2 (November 29, 1999).

Circumstances, time of making and termination of deductions

2.921   7.—(1) The Secretary of State may make deductions from income support [⁴, state pension credit] [¹or jobseeker's allowance] under [² under regulation 4] only if—

(a) the offender is entitled to income support [⁴, state pension credit] [¹or jobseeker's allowance] throughout any benefit week; and

(b) no deductions are being made in respect of the offender under any other application.

(2) The Secretary of State shall not make a deduction unless—

(a) the offender at the date of application by the court is aged not less than 18;

(b) the offender is entitled to income support [⁴ , state pension credit] [¹or jobseeker's allowance]; and

(c) the offender has defaulted in paying the fine, compensation order or any instalment of either.

(3) The Secretary of State shall make deductions from income support [⁴, state pension credit] [¹or jobseeker's allowance] by reference to the times at which payment of income support [⁴ , state pension credit] [¹or jobseeker's allowance] is made to the offender.

(4) The Secretary of State shall cease making deductions from income support [⁴ , state pension credit] [¹or jobseeker's allowance] if—

(a) there is no longer sufficient entitlement to income support [⁴, state pension credit] [¹or jobseeker's allowance] to enable him to make the deduction;

(b) entitlement to income support [⁴ , state pension credit] [¹or job-seeker's allowance] ceases;

(c) a court withdraws its application for deductions to be made; or

(d) the liability to make payment of the fine or under the compensation order as the case may be has ceased.

[³ (5) The Secretary of State shall not determine any application under regulation 2 which relates to an offender in respect of whom—

(a) he is making deductions; or

(b) deductions fall to be made,

pursuant to an earlier application under that regulation until no deductions pursuant to that earlier application fall to be made.]

(6) Payments of sums deducted from income support [⁴ , state pension credit] [¹or jobseeker's allowance] by the Secretary of State under these Regulations shall be made to the court at intervals of 13 weeks.

(7) Where the whole of the amount to which the application relates has been paid, the court shall so far as is practicable give notice of that fact within 21 days to the Secretary of State.

(8) The Secretary of State shall notify the offender in writing of the total of the sums deducted by him under any application—

(a) on receipt of a written request for such information from the offender; or

(b) on the termination of deductions made under any such application.

AMENDMENTS

1. Social Security (Jobseeker's Allowance Consequential Amendments) (Deductions) Regulations 1996 (SI 1996/2344), reg.15 (October 7, 1996).   **2.922**
2. Social Security Act 1998 (Commencement No.12, and Consequential and Transitional Provisions) Order 1999 (SI 1999/3178 (C.81)), art.3(12) and Sch.12, para.3(a) (November 29, 1999).
3. Social Security Act 1998 (Commencement No.12, and Consequential and Transitional Provisions) Order 1999 (SI 1999/3178 (C.81)), art.3(12) and Sch.12, para.3(b) (November 29, 1999).
4. State Pension Credit (Consequential, Transitional and Miscellaneous Provisions) Regulations 2002 (SI 2002/3019), reg.32 (October 6, 2003).

DEFINITIONS

"adjudication officer"—see reg.1(2).
"authority"—*ibid.*
"benefit week"—*ibid.*
"court"—*ibid.*
"income support"—*ibid.*
"jobseeker's allowance"—*ibid.*

Withdrawal of application

8. A court may withdraw an application at any time by giving notice in writing to the social security office to which the application was sent or delivered.   **2.923**

DEFINITIONS

"application"—see reg.1(2).
"court"—*ibid.*
"social security office"—*ibid.*

[¹Revision and supersession

9. Any decision of the Secretary of State under regulation 4 may be revised under section 9 of the 1998 Act or superseded under section 10 of that Act as though the decision were made under section 8(1)(c) of that Act.]   **2.924**

AMENDMENT

1. Social Security Act 1998 (Commencement No.12, and Consequential and Transitional Provisions) Order 1999 (SI 1999/3178 (c.81)), art.3(12) and Sch.12, para.4 (November 29, 1999).

[¹Appeal

10. Any decision of the Secretary of State under regulation 4 (whether as originally made or as revised under regulation 9) may be appealed to a tribunal as though the decision were made on an award of a relevant benefit (within the meaning of section 8(3) of the 1998 Act) under section 8(1)(c) of the 1998 Act.]   **2.925**

AMENDMENT

1. Social Security Act 1998 (Commencement No.12, and Consequential and Transitional Provisions) Order 1999 (SI 1999/3178 (c.81)), art.3(12) and Sch.12, para.4 (November 29, 1999).

Correction of accidental errors

2.926   **11.** [¹ . . .]

AMENDMENT

1. Social Security Act 1998 (Commencement No.12, and Consequential and Transitional Provisions) Order 1999 (SI 1999/3178 (c.81)), art.3(12) and Sch.12, para.5 (November 29, 1999).

Setting aside decisions on certain grounds

2.927   **12.** [² . . .]

AMENDMENTS

1. Deductions from Income Support (Miscellaneous Amendment) Regulations 1993 (SI 1993/495), reg.3 (April 1, 1993).
2. Social Security Act 1998 (Commencement No.12, and Consequential and Transitional Provisions) Order 1999 (SI 1999/3178 (c.81)), art.3(12) and Sch.12, para.5 (November 29, 1999).

Provisions common to regulations 11 and 12

2.928   **13.** [¹ . . .]

AMENDMENT

1. Social Security Act 1998 (Commencement No.12, and Consequential and Transitional Provisions) Order 1999 (SI 1999/3178 (C.81)), art.3(12) and Sch.12, para.5 (November 29, 1999).

Manner of making applications or appeals and time limits

2.929   **14.** [¹ . . .]

AMENDMENT

1. Social Security Act 1998 (Commencement No.12, and Consequential and Transitional Provisions) Order 1999 (SI 1999/3178 (C.81)), art.3(12) and Sch.12, para.5 (November 29, 1999).

Manner and time for the service of notices etc.

2.930   **15.**—[² . . .]

AMENDMENTS

1. Deductions from Income Support (Miscellaneous Amendment) Regulations 1993 (SI 1993/495), reg.3 (April 1, 1993).
2. Social Security Act 1998 (Commencement No.12, and Consequential and Transitional Provisions) Order 1999 (SI 1999/3178 (C.81)), art.3(12) and Sch.12, para.5 (November 29, 1999).

SCHEDULE 1

TIME LIMITS FOR MAKING APPLICATIONS OR APPEALS

[¹ . . .]   **2.931**

AMENDMENT

1. Social Security Act 1998 (Commencement No.12, and Consequential and Transitional Provisions) Order 1999 (SI 1999/3178 (C.81)), art.3(12) and Sch.12, para.5 (November 29, 1999).

SCHEDULE 2

CONDUCT AND PROCEDURE IN RELATION TO APPEALS AND APPLICATIONS

[¹ . . .]   **2.932**

AMENDMENT

1. Social Security Act 1998 (Commencement No.12, and Consequential and Transitional Provisions) Order 1999 (SI 1999/3178 (C.81)), art.3(12) and Sch.12, para.5 (November 29, 1999).

SCHEDULE 3

FORM

APPLICATION TO SECRETARY OF STATE UNDER THE FINES (DEDUCTIONS FROM INCOME SUPPORT) REGULATIONS 1992

[¹ . . .]   **2.933**

AMENDMENT

1. Fines (Deductions from Income Support) (Amendment) Regulations 2003 (SI 2003/1360), reg.2(c) (June 20, 2003).

Council Tax (Deductions from Income Support) Regulations 1993

(SI 1993/494)

Made by the Secretary of State under ss. 14(3), 97(5), 113 and 116(1) of and Schs 4, paras 1 and 6, and 8, para. 6, to the Local Government Finance Act 1992

Citation, commencement and interpretation

1.—(1) These Regulations may be cited as the Council Tax (Deductions   **2.934**
from Income Support) Regulations 1993 and shall come into force on 1st
April 1993.
   (2) In these Regulations, unless the context otherwise requires—
   [³ "the 1998 Act" means the Social Security Act 1998;]
   [³ . . .]
   "application means an application made under regulation 2 or regulation
      3 containing the information specified in regulation 4;

[³ . . .]

"authority" means—

(a) in relation to England and Wales, a billing authority, and

(b) in relation to Scotland, a levying authority;

"benefit week" has the meaning prescribed in regulation 2(1) of the Income Support (General) Regulations 1987 [¹or, as the case may be, [⁵ regulation 1(2) of the State Pension Credit Regulations 2002 or] regulation 1(3) of the Jobseeker's Allowance Regulations 1996;]

"Claims and Payments Regulations" means the Social Security (Claims and Payments) Regulations 1987;

[³ "Commissioner" has the meaning it bears in section 39(1) of the 1998 Act;]

[² "contribution-based jobseeker's allowance", except in a case to which paragraph (b) of the definition of income-based jobseeker's allowance applies, means a contribution-based jobseeker's allowance under Part I of the Jobseekers Act 1995, but does not include any back to work bonus under section 26 of the Jobseekers Act which is paid as jobseeker's allowance;]

"debtor"—

(a) in relation to England and Wales, has the same meaning as in paragraph 6 of Schedule 4 to the Local Government Finance Act, and

(b) in relation to Scotland, has the same meaning as in paragraph 6 of Schedule 8 to that Act;

"5 per cent. of the personal allowance for a single claimant aged not less than 25" means, where the percentage is not a multiple of 5 pence, the sum obtained by rounding that 5 per cent. to the next higher such multiple;

"income support" means income support within the meaning of the Social Security Contributions and Benefits Act 1992 [¹but does not include any back to work bonus under section 26 of the Jobseekers Act which is paid as income support;]

[² "income-based jobseeker's allowance" means—

(a) an income-based jobseeker's allowance under Part I of the Jobseekers Act 1995; and

(b) in a case where, if there was no entitlement to contribution-based jobseeker's allowance, there would be entitlement to income-based jobseeker's allowance at the same rate, contribution-based jobseeker's allowance,

but does not include any back to work bonus under section 26 of the Jobseekers Act which is paid as jobseeker's allowance;]

[¹ "Jobseekers Act" means the Jobseekers Act 1995;

"jobseeker's allowance" means an allowance under Part I of the Jobseekers Act but does not include any back to work bonus under section 26 of that Act which is paid as jobseeker's allowance;]

"the Local Government Finance Act" means the Local Government Finance Act 1992;

[⁵ "personal allowance for a single claimant aged not less than 25" means—

(a) in the case of a person who is entitled to either income support or state pension credit, the amount for the time being specified in paragraph 1(1)(e) of column (2) of Schedule 2 to the Income Support Regulations; or

(b) in the case of a person who is entitled to an income-based jobseeker's allowance, the amount for the time being specified in paragraph 1(1)(e) of column (2) of Schedule 1 to the Jobseeker's Allowance Regulations 1996;]

"social security office" means an office of the [⁴ Department for Work and Pensions which is open to the public for the receipt of claims for income support or a jobseeker's allowance.]

[⁵ "state pension credit" means the benefit of that name payable under the State Pension Credit Act 2002;]

[³ "tribunal" means an appeal tribunal constituted under Chapter 1 of Part I of the 1998 Act.]

(3) Unless the context otherwise requires, any reference in these Regulations to a numbered regulation or Schedule is a reference to the regulation or Schedule bearing that number in these Regulations and any reference in a regulation or Schedule to a numbered paragraph is a reference to the paragraph of that regulation or Schedule having that number.

AMENDMENTS

1. Social Security (Jobseeker's Allowance Consequential Amendments) (Deductions) Regulations 1996 (SI 1996/2344), reg.17 (October 7, 1996).

2. Social Security (Miscellaneous Amendments) Regulations 1998 (SI 1998/563), reg.3(1) and (2)(c) (April 1, 1998). (Note that the commencement date for this provision was amended by Social Security (Miscellaneous Amendments) (No.2) Regulations 1998 (SI 1998/865), reg.2 (March 20, 1998).)

3. Social Security Act 1998 (Commencement No.12, and Consequential and Transitional Provisions) Order 1999 (SI 1999/3178), art.3(13) and Sch.13, para.1 (November 29, 1999).

4. Secretaries of State for Education and Skills and for Work and Pensions Order 2002 (SI 2002/1397), art.12 and Sch., para.23 (June 27, 2002).

5. State Pension Credit (Consequential, Transitional and Miscellaneous Provisions) Regulations 2002 (SI 2002/3019), reg.33 (October 6, 2003).

2.935

[¹Application for deductions from income support [², state pension credit] or jobseeker's allowance: England and Wales]

2. Where a liability order has been made against a debtor by a magistrates' court and the debtor is entitled to [² , state pension credit] income support [¹or jobseeker's allowance] the billing authority concerned may apply to the Secretary of State asking him to deduct sums from any amounts payable to the debtor by way of income support [² , state pension credit] [¹or jobseeker's allowance] in order to secure the payment of any outstanding sum which is or forms part of the amount in respect of which the liability order was made.

2.936

AMENDMENTS

1. Social Security (Jobseeker's Allowance Consequential Amendments) (Deductions) Regulations 1996 (SI 1996/2344), reg.18 (October 7, 1996).

2. State Pension Credit (Consequential, Transitional and Miscellaneous Provisions) Regulations 2002 (SI 2002/3019), reg.33 (October 6, 2003).

2.937

DEFINITIONS

"debtor"—see reg.1(2).
"income support"—*ibid.*
'jobseeker's allowance"—*ibid.*

[²Application for deductions from income support [², state pension credit] or jobseeker's allowance: Scotland]

2.938   **3.**—(1) Where a levying authority has obtained a summary warrant or a decree against a debtor in respect of arrears of sums payable under paragraph 1(1) of Schedule 8 to the [¹Local Government Finance Act] and the debtor is entitled to income support [² , state pension credit] [²or jobseeker's allowance], the levying authority may, without prejudice to its right to pursue any other means of recovering such arrears, apply to the Secretary of State asking him to deduct sums from any amounts payable to the debtor by way of income support [² , state pension credit] [²or jobseeker's allowance] in order to secure the payment of any outstanding sum which is or forms part of the amount in respect of which the summary warrant or decree was granted.

AMENDMENTS

2.939   1. Social Security (Claims and Payments) Amendment (No.3) Regulations 1993 (SI 1993/2113), reg.6 (September 27, 1993).
    2. Social Security (Jobseeker's Allowance Consequential Amendments) (Deductions) Regulations 1996 (SI 1996/2344), reg.19 (October 7, 1996).
    3. State Pension Credit (Consequential, Transitional and Miscellaneous Provisions) Regulations 2002 (SI 2002/3019), reg.33 (October 6, 2003).

DEFINITIONS

"debtor"—see reg.1(2).
"income support"—*ibid.*
"jobseeker's allowance"—*ibid.*
"Local Government Finance Act"—*ibid.*

Contents of application

2.940   **4.**—(1) An application shall contain the following particulars—
(a) the name and address of the debtor;
(b) the name and address of the authority making the application;
(c) the name and place of the court which made the liability order or granted the summary warrant, or decree as the case may be;
(d   the date on which the liability order was made or the summary warrant or decree granted as the case may be;
(e) the amount specified in the liability order, summary warrant or decree as the case may be;
(f) the total sum which the authority wishes to have deducted from income support [² , state pension credit] [¹or jobseeker's allowance].
(2) An authority making application shall serve it on the Secretary of State by sending or delivering it to a social security office.
(3) Where it appears to the Secretary of State that an application from an authority gives insufficient particulars to enable the debtor to be identified he may require the authority to furnish such further particulars as may reasonably be required for that purpose.

AMENDMENTS

2.941   1. Social Security (Jobseeker's Allowance Consequential Amendments) (Deductions) Regulations 1996 (SI 1996/2344), reg.20 (October 7, 1996).

2. State Pension Credit (Consequential, Transitional and Miscellaneous Provisions) Regulations 2002 (SI 2002/3019), reg.33 (October 6, 2003).

DEFINITIONS

"application"—see reg.1(2).
"authority"—*ibid.*
"debtor"—*ibid.*
"jobseeker's allowance"—*ibid.*
"social security office"—*ibid.*

GENERAL NOTE

On regs 2, 3 and 4 see *R(IS) 3/92* and *R(IS) 1/98* in the notes to reg.2 of the Community Charges (Deductions from Income Support) (No.2) Regulations 1990. *CIS 1725/1997* confirms that *R(IS) 1/98* applies to deductions for council tax arrears as well as those for arrears of the community charge.   2.942

[¹Deductions from debtor's income support [², state pension credit] or jobseeker's allowance

5.—(1) Subject to regulation 8, where—   2.943

(a) the Secretary of State receives an application from an authority in respect of a debtor who is entitled to income support [² , state pension credit] or income-based jobseeker's allowance;

(b) the amount payable by way of that benefit, after any deduction under this paragraph, is 10 pence or more; and

(c) the aggregate amount payable under one or more of the following provisions, namely, paragraphs 3(2)(a), 5(6), 6(2)(a) and 7(3)(a) and (5)(a) of Schedule 9 to the Claims and Payments Regulations together with the amount to be deducted under this paragraph does not exceed an amount equal to 3 times 5 per cent. of the personal allowance for a single claimant aged not less than 25 years,

the Secretary of State may deduct a sum from that benefit which is equal to 5 per cent. of the personal allowance for a single claimant aged not less than 25 and pay that sum to the authority towards satisfaction of any outstanding sum which is or forms part of the amount in respect of which the liability order was made or the summary warrant or the decree was granted.

(2) Subject to paragraph (3) and regulation 8, where—

(a) the Secretary of State receives an application from an authority in respect of a debtor who is entitled to contribution-based job-seeker's allowance; and

(b) the amount of contribution-based jobseeker's allowance payable before any deduction under this paragraph is equal to or more than one-third of the age-related amount applicable to the debtor under section 4(1)(a) of the Jobseekers Act,

the Secretary of State may deduct a sum from that benefit which is equal to one-third of the age-related amount applicable to the debtor under section 4(1)(a) of the Jobseekers Act and pay that sum to the authority towards satisfaction of any outstanding sum which is or forms part of the amount in respect of which the liability order was made or the summary warrant or the decree was granted.

(3) Where the sum that would otherwise fall to be deducted under paragraph (2) includes a fraction of a penny, the sum to be deducted shall be rounded down to the next whole penny.

(4) The Secretary of State shall notify the debtor and the authority concerned in writing of a decision to make a deduction under this regulation so far as is practicable within 14 days from the date on which he made the decision and at the same time shall notify the debtor of his right of appeal.]

AMENDMENTS

1. Social Security Act 1998 (Commencement No.12, and Consequential and Transitional Provisions) Order 1999 (SI 1999/3178 (C.81)), art.3(13) and Sch.13, para.2 (November 29, 1999).
2. State Pension Credit (Consequential, Transitional and Miscellaneous Provisions) Regulations 2002 (SI 2002/3019), reg.33 (October 6, 2003).

Notification of decision

2.944   **6.** [¹ . . .]

AMENDMENT

1. Social Security Act 1998 (Commencement No.12, and Consequential and Transitional Provisions) Order 1999 (SI 1999/3178 (C.81)), art.3(13) and Sch.13, para.2 (November 29, 1999).

[¹Deductions from debtor's income support or income-based jobseeker's allowance]

2.945   **7.** [² . . .]

AMENDMENTS

1. Social Security (Jobseeker's Allowance Consequential Amendments) (Deductions) Regulations 1996 (SI 1996/2344), reg.22 (October 7, 1996).
2. Social Security Act 1998 (Commencement No.12, and Consequential and Transitional Provisions) Order 1999 (SI 1999/3178 (C.81)), art.3(13) and Sch.13, para.2 (November 29, 1999).

[¹Deductions from debtor's contribution-based jobseeker's allowance]

2.946   **7A.** [² . . .]

AMENDMENTS

1. Social Security (Jobseeker's Allowance Consequential Amendments) (Deductions) Regulations 1996 (SI 1996/2344), reg.23 (October 7, 1996).
2. Social Security Act 1998 (Commencment No.12 and Consequential and Transitional Provisions) Order 1999 (SI 1999/3178 (C.81)), art.3(13) and Sch.13, para.2 (November 29, 1999).

Circumstances, time of making and termination of deductions

2.947   **8.**—(1) The Secretary of State may make deductions from [¹income support [³, state pension credit] or jobseeker's allowance under regulation 7 or 7A] only if—
    (a) the debtor is entitled to income support [³ , state pension credit] [¹or jobseeker's allowance] throughout any benefit week;
    (b) no deductions are being made in respect of the debtor under any other application; and

(c) no payments are being made under regulation 2 of the Community Charge (Deductions from Income Support) (Scotland) Regulations 1989 or regulation 2 of the Community Charge (Deductions from Income Support) (No. 2) Regulations 1990.

(2) The Secretary of State shall make deductions from income support [³ , state pension credit] [¹or jobseeker's allowance] by reference to the times at which payment of income support [³ , state pension credit] [¹or jobseeker's allowance] is made to the debtor.

(3) The Secretary of State shall cease making deductions from income support [³ , state pension credit][¹or jobseeker's allowance] if—

(a) there is no longer sufficient entitlement to income support [³ , state pension credit] [¹or jobseeker's allowance] to enable him to make the deduction;

(b) an authority withdraws its application for deductions to be made; or

(c) the debt in respect of which he was making deductions is discharged.

[²(4) The Secretary of State shall not determine any application under regulation 2 or 3 which relates to a debtor in respect of whom—

(a) he is making deductions; or

(b) deductions fall to be made,

pursuant to an earlier application under either of those regulations until no deductions pursuant to that earlier application fall to be made.]

(5) Payments of sums deducted from income support [³ , state pension credit] [¹or jobseeker's allowance] by the Secretary of State under these Regulations shall be made to the authority concerned, as far as is practicable, at intervals not exceeding 13 weeks.

(6) Where the whole of the amount to which the application relates has been paid, the authority concerned shall, so far as is practicable, give notice of that fact within 21 days to the Secretary of State.

(7) The Secretary of State shall notify the debtor in writing of the total of the sums deducted by him under any application—

(a) on receipt of a written request for such information from the debtor; or

(b) on the termination of deductions made under any such application.

AMENDMENTS

1. Social Security (Jobseeker's Allowance Consequential Amendments) (Deductions) Regulations 1996 (SI 1996/2344), reg.24 (October 7, 1996).

2. Social Security Act 1998 (Commencement No.12, and Consequential and Transitional Provisions) Order 1999 (SI 1999/3178 (C.81)), art.3(13) and Sch.13, para.3 (November 29, 1999).

3. State Pension Credit (Consequential, Transitional and Miscellaneous Provisions) Regulations 2002 (SI 2002/3019), reg.33 (October 6, 2003).

Withdrawal of application

9. An authority may withdraw an application at any time by giving notice in writing to the social security office to which the application was sent or delivered.

2.948

[¹Revision and supersession

10. Any decision of the Secretary of State under regulation 5 may be revised under section 9 of the 1998 Act or superseded under section 10 of that Act as though the decision were made under section 8(1)(c) of that Act.]

2.949

719

AMENDMENT

1. Social Security Act 1998 (Commencement No.12, and Consequential and Transitional Provisions) Order 1999 (SI 1999/3178 (C.81)), art.3(13) and Sch.13, para.4 (November 29, 1999).

[¹Appeal

2.950   **11.** Any decision of the Secretary of State under regulation 5 (whether as originally made or as revised under regulation 10) may be appealed to a tribunal as though the decision were made on an award of a relevant benefit (within the meaning of section 8(3) of the 1998 Act) under section 8(1)(c) of the 1998 Act.]

AMENDMENT

1. Social Security Act 1998 (Commencement No.12, and Consequential and Transitional Provisions) Order 1999 (SI 1999/3178 (C.81)), art.3(13) and Sch.13, para.4 (November 29, 1999).

Correction of accidental errors

2.951   **12.** [¹ . . .]

AMENDMENT

1. Social Security Act 1998 (Commencement No.12, and Consequential and Transitional Provisions) Order 1999 (SI 1999/3178 (C.81)), art.3(13) and Sch.13, para.5 (November 29, 1999).

Setting aside decisions on certain grounds

2.952   **13.** [¹ . . .]

AMENDMENT

1. Social Security Act 1998 (Commencement No.12, and Consequential and Transitional Provisions) Order 1999 (SI 1999/3178 (C.81)), art.3(13) and Sch.13, para.5 (November 29, 1999)

Provisions common to regulations 12 and 13

2.953   **14.** [¹ . . .]

AMENDMENT

1. Social Security Act 1998 (Commencement No.12, and Consequential and Transitional Provisions) Order 1999 (SI 1999/3178 (C.81)), art.3(13) and Sch.13, para.5 (November 29, 1999)

Manner of making applications or appeals and time limits

2.954   **15.** [¹ . . .]

AMENDMENT

1. Social Security Act 1998 (Commencement No.12, and Consequential and Transitional Provisions) Order 1999 (SI 1999/3178 (C.81)), art.3(13) and Sch.13, para.5 (November 29, 1999)

Manner and time for the service of notices etc.

16. [¹ . . .]   2.955

AMENDMENT

1. Social Security Act 1998 (Commencement No.12, and Consequential and Transitional Provisions) Order 1999 (SI 1999/3178 (c.81)), art.3(13) and Sch.13, para.5 (November 29, 1999)

SCHEDULE 1

TIME LIMITS FOR MAKING APPLICATIONS OR APPEALS

[¹ . . .]   2.956

AMENDMENT

1. Social Security Act 1998 (Commencement No.12, and Consequential and Transitional Provisions) Order 1999 (SI 1999/3178 (c.81)), art.3(13) and Sch.13, para.5 (November 29, 1999).

SCHEDULE 2

CONDUCT AND PROCEDURE IN RELATION TO APPEALS AND APPLICATIONS

[¹ . . .]

AMENDMENT

1. Social Security Act 1998 (Commencement No.12, and Consequential and   2.957
Transitional Provisions) Order 1999 (SI 1999/3178 (c.81)), art.3(13) and Sch.13, para.5 (November 29, 1999).

Social Security Benefits (Maintenance Payments and Consequential Amendments) Regulations 1996

(SI 1996/940)

Made by the Secretary of State under ss.74A(5) and (6), 189(1) and (3)–(5) and 191 of the Social Security Administration Act 1992 and ss.136(5)(b), 137(1) and 175(1)–(4) of the Social Security Contributions and Benefits Act 1992

[In force April 19, 1996]

Interpretation for the purposes of section 74A of the Act

2. In section 74A of the Act (payment of benefit where maintenance pay-   2.958
ments collected by Secretary of State)—
    (a) "child maintenance" means any payment towards the maintenance of
        a child or young person, including payments made—
        (i) under a court order;

  (ii) under a maintenance [¹ calculation] made under the Child Support Act 1991;
  (iii) under an agreement for maintenance; or
  (iv) voluntarily,
  and for this purpose a "young person" is a person referred to in regulation 3 of these Regulations (persons of a prescribed description);

(b) "spousal maintenance" means any payment made by a person towards the maintenance of that person's spouse, including payments made—
  (i) under a court order;
  (ii) under an agreement for maintenance; or
  (iii) voluntarily;

(c) "relevant income" means—
  (i) any income which is taken into account under Part V of the Income Support Regulations for the purposes of calculating the amount of income support to which the claimant is entitled; or
  (ii) any income which is taken into account under Part VIII of the Jobseeker's Allowance Regulations for the purposes of calculating the amount of jobseeker's allowance to which the claimant is entitled.

AMENDMENT

1. Child Support (Consequential Amendments and Transitional Provisions) Regulations 2001 (SI 2001/158), reg.8 (in force in relation to a particular case from the date on which s.1 CSPSSA 2000 comes into force in relation to that type of case).

Persons of a prescribed description

2.959   **3.** For the purposes of the definition of "family" in section 74A(5) of the Act, a person of a prescribed description is any person who—
  (a) is referred to as a "young person" in the Income Support Regulations by virtue of regulation 14 of those Regulations; or
  (b) is referred to as a "young person" in the Jobseeker's Allowance Regulations by virtue of regulation 76 of those Regulations.

Circumstances in which a person is to be treated as responsible for another

2.960   **4.** A person shall be treated as responsible for another for the purposes of section 74A of the Act if he is treated as responsible for that other person under either regulation 15 of the Income Support Regulations or regulation 77 of the Jobseeker's Allowance Regulations.

Circumstances in which persons are to be treated as being members of the same household

2.961   **5.** Persons shall be treated as members of the same household for the purposes of section 74A of the Act if they are treated as members of the same household under either regulation 16 of the Income Support Regulations or regulation 78 of the Jobseeker's Allowance Regulations.

GENERAL NOTE

For s.74A of the Social Security Administration Act, see Vol. III of this series.
See the note to para.73 of Sch.9 to the Income Support Regulations.

Social Security (Back to Work Bonus and Lone Parent Run-on) (Amendment and Revocation) Regulations 2003

(SI 2003/1589)

Made by the Secretary of State under ss. 123(1)(a), (d) and (e), 130(4), 131(10), 135(1), 136(3) and (5)(b), 137(1) and (2)(d), 175(1) and (3) to (5) of the Social Security Contributions and Benefits Act 1992 and ss. 26, 35(1) and (3) and 36(2) to (5) of the Jobseekers Act 1995 and ss. 1(1), 5(1)(a) and (b), 6(1)(a) and (b), 78(2), 128A(1), 189(1), (4) and (5) and 191 of the Social Security Administration Act 1992

[In force October 25, 2004]

Transitional Provisions

10.—(1) [¹ Subject to the amendments made by paragraphs (2) and (3)],   2.962
the Back to Work Bonus Regulations shall continue to have effect as if
regulation 8 of these Regulations had not been made, in relation to a person
who—

(a) satisfies the requirements of regulation 6 (waiting period) of the Back
to Work Bonus Regulations on 24th October 2004; and either

(b) satisfies regulation 7 (requirements for a bonus) or regulation 17
(persons attaining pensionable age) of the Back to Work Bonus
Regulations on 24th October 2004 but whose claim for a bonus had
not been determined on or before that date; or

(c) satisfies the conditions contained in regulation 7 or regulation 17 of
the Back to Work Bonus Regulations on any day during the period
from 25th October 2004 to 28th January 2005; or

(d) satisfies the conditions contained in regulation 7 or 17 on or before 28th
January 2005 other than the requirement to make a claim within—

(i)   for a person who satisfies the conditions in regulation 7(2), the
period specified in regulation 7(2)(c);

(ii) for a person who satisfies the conditions in regulation 7(3), the
period specified in regulation 7(3)(d);

(iii) for a person who satisfies the conditions in regulation 7(4), the
period specified in regulation 7(4)(c);

(iv) for a person who satisfies the conditions in regulation 7(5), the
period specified in regulation 7(5)(e); and

(v)   for a person who satisfies the conditions in regulation 17, the
period specified in regulation 17(5)

but who satisfies the requirements set out in regulation 23(6) of the Back to
Work Bonus Regulations [¹ , or who makes a claim for a bonus after
28th January 2005 within the appropriate specified period].

(2) For the purposes of paragraph (1), in regulation 1 (citation, commencement and interpretation) of the Back to Work Bonus Regulations—

(a) for the definition of "bonus period" substitute—
" " bonus period" means a period beginning on the first day of entitlement to a qualifying benefit (provided that that day is not after
24th October 2004) in a period of entitlement to a qualifying benefit
which falls after the waiting period and which ends on the last day of
that period of entitlement or on 24th October 2004 whichever of
these two dates is the earlier,";

(b) for the definition of "waiting period" substitute—
" " waiting period" means the period of 91 consecutive days to which
regulation 6 refers, provided that none of those days falls after 24th
October 2004;"

(3) For paragraph (3) in regulation 17 substitute—
"(3) In the case of a person who is entitled to a bonus in accordance with
paragraph (1)—

(a) the bonus period and the period of entitlement to a qualifying benefit
shall end on the date he attained the age of 60, or as the case may be,
pensionable age, whichever is the later, provided that that date is not
after 24th October 2004;

(b) where that date would be after 24th October 2004 the bonus period
and period of entitlement to a qualifying benefit shall be treated as
ending on 24th October 2004."

AMENDMENT

2.963   1. Back to Work Bonus (Amendment) Regulations 2004 (SI 2004/1655), reg.2
(October 25, 2004).

GENERAL NOTE

2.964   Regulation 8 of these Regulations revokes the Social Security (Back to Work
Bonus) (No. 2) Regulations 1996 with effect from October 25, 2004, subject to the
transitional provisions in reg.10. The 1996 regulations contained the detailed (and
complex) rules relating to the back to work bonus scheme which was first introduced
on October 7, 1996 (see s. 29 of the Jobseekers Act). See the 2004 edition of this
volume for the 1996 Regulations and the note to those Regulations. The effect of
reg.10 is to continue the 1996 Regulations in force (as modified by the amendments
in paras (2) and (3)) in order to enable claimants to claim the bonus during a further
period.

Regulation 10(1) provides that a person will be entitled to a back to work bonus
if he has served the 13 week waiting period on October 24, 2004 (note in addition
that the effect of the amended definition of "bonus period" in para.(2)(a) is that no
further bonus can build up after October 24, 2004) and satisfies the conditions for
a bonus to become payable

(i) on October 24, 2004 but his claim has not been decided by that date; or
(ii) on any day during the period from October 25, 2004 to January 28, 2005;
or
(iii) on or before January 28, 2005, other than the need to make a claim within
12 weeks of the relevant triggering event (*i.e.* his ceasing to be entitled to
income support or JSA, his training ending or his separation from his
partner—see reg.7(2) to (5) of the Back to Work Bonus Regulations—or
his reaching the age of 60 if he has ceased to be entitled to income support
or pensionable age if he has ceased to be entitled to JSA—see reg.17(5) of
the Back to Work Bonus Regulations) but who either shows continuous
good cause for the delay in claiming (in which case the time for claiming
can be extended to up to twelve months (see reg.23(6) of the Back to Work
Bonus Regulations), or who makes a claim after January 28, 2005 within

the relevant specified time limit. Presumably this means the specified time limit as extended under reg.23(6) if appropriate, although this is not spelt out.

Thus the net effect of these somewhat convoluted provisions would seem to be that claimants who have served the 13 week waiting period by October 24, 2004 will be able to claim the bonus if they satisfy the conditions of entitlement for a bonus (including making a claim) during the period October 25, 2004 to January 28, 2005 or if they satisfy the other conditions of entitlement during that transitional period and make a claim after January 28, 2005 within the relevant time limit. But they will not be able to build up any further bonus after October 24, 2004.

Social Security (Child Maintenance Bonus) Regulations 1996

(SI 1996/3195)

Made by the Secretary of State under ss.10 and 26(1) to (3) of the Child Support Act 1995, ss.5(1)(p), 6(1)(q), 71(8), 78(2), 189(1), (3) and (4) and 191 of the Social Security Administration Act 1992 and ss.136(5)(b), Benefits Act 1992.

ARRANGEMENT OF REGULATIONS

GENERAL NOTE

These regulations contain the details of the child maintenance bonus scheme that   2.966
was introduced by s.10 of the Child Support Act 1995. As part of the changes to the child support scheme under the Child Support, Pensions and Social Security Act 2000, the child maintenance bonus is being abolished and replaced by a child maintenance "premium". This is in effect a disregard of up to £10 a week of any child maintenance for claimants in receipt of income support or income-based JSA. For details of the disregard see para.73 of Sch.9 to the Income Support Regulations, and the note to that paragraph, and para.70 of Sch.7 to the JSA Regulations.

The long-delayed start to the commencement of the new child support regime finally began on March 3, 2003. The new rules are being implemented in stages, depending on the type of case (see the note at the beginning of the Child Support Act 1991 in Part I of this volume). For those cases to which the new scheme applies (and for cases where child maintenance which is not child support maintenance is first paid under an agreement or court order on or after March 3, 2003), s.23 of the 2000 Act repeals s.10 of the 1995 Act (see the note to s.10 of the 1995 Act for further details of the commencement of s.23). Once s.23 has come into force in relation to a particular case, it will no longer be possible for the claimant to accrue a child maintenance bonus. Instead, the claimant will be eligible for the income support or income-based JSA disregard. See further the note to para.73 of Sch.9 to the Income Support Regulations for other cases in which the disregard applies.

For the transitional provisions where a child maintenance bonus has accrued before s.23 comes into force in relation to a particular case, see reg.4 of the Social Security (Child Maintenance Premium and Miscellaneous Amendments) Regulations 2000 (SI 2000/3176), as substituted by reg.2 of the Social Security (Child Maintenance Premium and Miscellaneous Amendments) Amendment Regulations 2003 (SI 2003/231) (p.739) and see the end of this note.

Since it will be possible for income support and income-based JSA claimants receiving child maintenance to continue to accrue a child maintenance bonus until their case is converted to the new child support regime, s.10 of the Child Support Act and these regulations are being retained in this edition.

There are no notes or definitions after each individual regulation but the following paragraphs contain a brief summary of the main provisions. Most of the relevant definitions are in reg.1, although there also needs to be some reference to the Child Support Acts 1991 and 1995 (by s.27(2) of the 1995 Act expressions in that Act have the same meaning as in the 1991 Act).

2.967 Since April 7, 1997 a person who has a qualifying child (*i.e.* a child, one or both of whose parents are absent parents: see Child Support Act 1991, s.3(1)) living with her, and who is receiving, or (from April 1, 1998) is due ro receive, child maintenance while she (or her partner) is entitled (whether or not benefit is payable: regs 1(7) and 4) to income support or income-based JSA, has been able to build up a child maintenance bonus (reg.4(1)). This is known as the "bonus period". A bonus period can only start on or after April 7, 1997. A bonus period will not run if the child support maintenance assessment is nil since in such a case child support is not payable or being paid (*CIS 3544/2002*). Note that although the definition of "qualifying benefit" in reg.1(4) refers to income support and "jobseeker's allowance", the effect of reg.2(1) is that a bonus can only accrue while the person is entitled to income-based JSA. Note also that for the purpose of accumulating the bonus, days on which entitlement to income support/income-based JSA is at the urgent cases rate because the claimant is treated as possessing income which is due but has not been paid, do not count (reg.4(9)).

Two or more bonus periods separated by one "connected period" (but not more than one: reg.4(5)) can link to form one period (reg.4(2)). A "connected period" is a period of 12 weeks or less, or two years or less throughout which incapacity benefit, severe disablement allowance or invalid care allowance (now carer's allowance) is payable to the person claiming the bonus, or a period throughout which maternity allowance is payable to that person (reg.4(3)).

Child maintenance for the purpose of these regulations includes maintenance paid under an agreement (whether enforceable or not) or a court order (but not spousal maintenance), and deductions from benefit as a contribution towards child maintenance, as well as child support maintenance (reg.1(2)). Note that from April 1, 1998 this includes maintenance, etc., that is payable as well as that which is paid. However, child maintenance is not payable or being paid if the child support maintenance assessment is nil (*CIS 3544/2002*).

For the definition of "child" see s.55 of the 1991 Act which is in effect the same as for the purposes of child benefit (see s.142 of the Contributions and Benefits Act 1992 and the notes to reg.12 of the Income Support Regulations). A qualifying child will be treated as living with the person claiming the bonus during any temporary absence of not more than 12 weeks (reg.4(6)).

The amount of the bonus will be £5 for each benefit week in which at least £5 child maintenance was due (or the amount due for that week if less than £5), or the total amount of child maintenance paid in the bonus period, or £1,000, whichever is the lowest (reg.5). It is not taxable.

The bonus will be payable when the person (or her partner) starts or returns to work (other than a return to work for the same employer where the absence was due to a trade dispute: reg.3(2)), or works more hours, or has increased earnings (this is referred to as "the work condition") and as a result her (or her partner's) entitlement to income support or income-based JSA ceases (reg.3(1)(c) and (d)). From April 1, 1998 the work condition must normally be met within 14 days of the end of the person's bonus period (reg.3(1)(f)(iii)) (under the previous form of reg.3(1)(f) the limit was 14 days of the person ceasing to be entitled to income support/income-based JSA; thus it was possible, for example, for a person whose bonus period had ended because a child had ceased to be a qualifying child but who had remained in receipt of income support/income-based JSA to claim a bonus some considerable time after her bonus period had ended). But if the absent parent dies, ceases to be habitually resident in the UK or is found not to be the parent of the qualifying child(ren), the time limit for satisfying the work condition is 12 weeks from the earliest date on which any of these events occurs; or if the person cares for only one child and that child dies, the time limit is 12 months from the date of death (reg.3(1)(f)(i) and (ii)). A bonus will also be payable if entitlement to income support or income-based JSA ceased for any other reason but the work condition is met within the time limits in reg.3(1)(f) (reg.3(1A)). The work condition has to be satisfied before the penultimate day before the person's 60th birthday (or his 65th birthday if a man and the qualifying benefit was income-based JSA) (reg.3(1)(e)). See reg.8 for the special rules that apply to a person who has reached this age, or is approaching it. Apart from people covered by reg.8(1) and (2), a claim for the bonus has to be made, usually within 28 days of income support/income-based JSA ceasing (regs. 3(1)(a) and 8(5)). For the rules governing claims see regs 10–11; note also reg.13.

In the case of a couple, the person entitled to the bonus is the person with care of 2.968 the child and to whom child maintenance is payable; where this applies to both members of the couple, each of them will qualify for a bonus (reg.9(1) and (2)). If a couple separate, they both count for the purpose of the bonus period as entitled to income support/income-based JSA on the days benefit was being paid to them as a couple (reg.9(5)).

If a person with care of a qualifying child dies, accrued bonus can be passed on to the new person caring for the child if the conditions in reg.7 are met.

The bonus is treated as income support or income-based JSA (s.10(3) of the Child Support Act 1995), depending on which was last in payment in the bonus period (reg.12). Thus decisions on claims can be appealed to a tribunal.

The bonus counts as capital for the purpose of income support and income-based JSA (reg.14). It is disregarded as income for working tax credit and child tax credit (Tax Credits (Definition and Calculation of Income) Regulations 2002 (SI 2002/2006), reg.7, Table 3, paras 13, 16 and 17—see Vol. IV in this series). It also counts as capital for housing benefit and council tax benefit; for these benefits it is disregarded for 52 weeks from the date of receipt.

Transitional provisions following the abolition of child maintenance bonus

These are contained in reg.4 of the Social Security (Child Maintenance Premium 2.969 and Miscellaneous Amendments) Regulations 2000 (SI 2000/3176), as substituted by reg.2 of the Social Security (Child Maintenance Premium and Miscellaneous Amendments) Amendment Regulations 2003 (SI 2003/231) (see p. 739).

The effect of reg.4 is as follows. A person's bonus period will end on the day before "the commencement date" (*i.e.* the date that the child maintenance bonus scheme is abolished in her case) (reg.4(7)(c); for "the commencement date", see reg.1 of the 2000 Regulations)). A child maintenance bonus that has already accrued will still be payable if the person (i) satisfied the work condition and made a claim for the bonus within the time limit (or any extension of the time limit for good cause) before the commencement date but no decision had been made on the claim by that date (reg.4(2)(a)); (ii) is a person to whom the special rules in reg.8(1), (2) or (4) of the 1996 Regulations (people who reach 60 or pension age) applied before the commencement date but, in the case of a person to whom reg.8(1) or (2) applied, her entitlement was not decided by that date, or in the case of a person to whom reg.8(4) applied, she had claimed the bonus but no decision had been made on the claim by that date (reg.4(2)(b) and (c)); or (iii) qualified for the bonus before the commencement date and claimed on or after that date but within the time limit (or any extension of the time limit for good cause) (reg.4(2)(d)). If a person has claimed the bonus but not satisfied the work condition before the commencement date the time limit for meeting the work condition in reg.3(1)(f)(iii) of the 1996 Regulations is extended to one month after the bonus period ends (the time limits in reg.3(1)(f)(i) and (ii) are also adjusted). Where a person has not claimed the bonus nor satisfied the work condition before the commencement date but on the day before that date she (or her partner) was entitled, or treated as entitled, to income support or income-based JSA, and child maintenance was in payment or payable for a qualifying child, the time limit for satisfying the work condition in reg.3(1)(f)(iii) is also one month (and the time limits in reg.3(1)(f)(i) and (ii) are also adjusted) (reg.4(3)–(5)).

Any child maintenance bonus that has accrued before the commencement date in a particular case that is not claimed under the above rules will be lost.

Citation, commencement and interpretation

2.970   **1.**—(1) These Regulations may be cited as the Social Security (Child Maintenance Bonus) Regulations 1996 and shall come into force on 7th April 1997.

(2) In these Regulations—

"the Act" means the Child Support Act 1995;

"applicant", except where regulation 8 (retirement) applies, means the person claiming the bonus;

"appropriate office" means an office of the [³ Department for Work and Pensions];

"benefit week"—

    (a) where the relevant benefit is income support, has the meaning it has in the Income Support (General) Regulations 1987 by virtue of regulation 2(1) of those Regulations; or

    (b) where the relevant benefit is a jobseeker's allowance, has the meaning it has in the Jobseeker's Allowance Regulations 1996 by virtue of regulation 1(3) of those Regulations;

"bonus" means a child maintenance bonus;

"bonus period" comprises the days specified in regulation 4;

[²"child maintenance" means maintenance in any of the following forms—

    (a) child support maintenance paid or payable;

    (b) maintenance paid or payable by an absent parent to a person with care of a qualifying child, under an agreement (whether enforceable or not) between them, or by virtue of an order of a court; or

    (c) maintenance deducted from any benefit payable to an absent parent who is liable to maintain a qualifying child,

which, as the case may be, is paid, payable or deducted on or after 1st April 1998, but does not include any maintenance paid or payable in respect of a former partner];

"couple" means a married or an unmarried couple;

"income-based jobseeker's allowance" has the same meaning as in the Job-seekers Act by virtue of section 1(4) of that Act;

"the Jobseekers Act" means the Jobseekers Act 1995;

"jobseeker's allowance" means an income-based Jobseeker's allowance'

"partner" means where a person, whether an applicant or otherwise,—

    (a) is a member of a married or unmarried couple, the other member of that couple;

    (b) is married polygamously to two or more members of his household, any such member; or

    (c) is a member of a marriage to which section 133(1)(b) of the Social Security Contributions and Benefits Act 1992 (polygamous marriages) refers and the other party to the marriage has one or more additional spouses, the other party;

"work condition" means the condition specified at regulation 3(1)(c).

(3) Expressions used in these Regulations and in the Child Support Act 1991 have the same meaning in these Regulations as they have in that Act.

(4) For the purposes of the Regulations, the qualifying benefits are a jobseeker's allowance and income support.

(5) In these Regulations, where—

    (a) a payment is made in any benefit week by an absent parent to a person with care;

    (b) the absent parent pays both child maintenance and maintenance for the person with care; and

    (c) there is no evidence as to which form of maintenance that payment is intended to represent,

the first £5 of any such payment or, where the amount of payment is less than £5, that amount shall be treated as if it was a payment of child maintenance.

(6) For the purposes of these Regulations, child maintenance is treated as payable where it is paid under an agreement which is not enforceable.

(7) Where a person is entitled to a qualify benefit on any day but no qualifying benefit is payable to her in respect of that day, that person shall be treated for the purposes of these Regulations [¹ other than regulation 4 (bonus period)] as not entitled to a qualifying benefit for that day.

(8) In these Regulations, unless the context otherwise requires, a reference—

    (a) to a numbered section is to the section of the Act bearing that number;

    (b) to a numbered regulation is to the regulation in these Regulations bearing that number;

    (c) in a regulation to a numbered paragraph is to the paragraph in that regulation bearing that number;

    (d) in a paragraph to a lettered or numbered sub-paragraph is to the sub-paragraph in that paragraph bearing that letter or number.

AMENDMENTS

1. Social Security (Miscellaneous Amendment) Regulations 1977 (SI 1997/454), reg.8(2) (April 6, 1997).   **2.971**

2. Social Security (Miscellaneous Amendments) Regulations 1998 (SI 1998/563), reg.2(2) (April 1, 1998). (Note that the commencement date for this provision was

amended by Social Security (Miscellaneous Amendments) (No.2) Regulations 1998 (SI 1998/865), reg.2 (March 20, 1998).)

3. Secretaries of State for Education and Skills and for Work and Pensions Order 2002 (SI 2002/1397), art.12 and Sch., para.29 (June 27, 2002).

Application of the Regulations

2.972

2.—(1) Subject to paragraph (2), these Regulations apply only in a case where on or after 7th April 1997 an absent parent has paid child maintenance in respect of a qualifying child and that maintenance has been—

(a) taken into account in determining the amount of a qualifying benefit payable to the person with care or the partner of that person; or

(b) retained by the Secretary of State in accordance with section 74A(3) of the Social Security Administration Act 1992 (payable of benefit where maintenance payments are collected by the Secretary of State).

(2) Regulation 6 (Secretary of State to issue estimates) applies also where a maintenance assessment has been made but no maintenance has been paid.

(3) No day falling before 7th April 1997 shall be taken into account in determing whether any condition specified in these Regulations is satisfied or whether any period specified in these Regulations commenced.

Entitlement to a bonus

2.973

3.—(1) An applicant is entitled to a bonus where—

(a) she has claimed a bonus in accordance with regulation 10 (claiming a bonus);

(b) the claim related to days falling within a bonus period;

(c) except where paragraph (2) applies, she satisfies the work condition, that is to say, she or her partner takes up or returns to work or increases the number of hours in which in any week she or her partner is engaged in employment or the earnings from an employment in which she or her partner are engaged is increased;

(d) as a result of satisfying the work condition any entitlement to a qualifying benefit in respect of herself and, where she has a partner, her family ceases;

(e) in a case where the qualifying benefit which ceased—

(i) was income support, the person with care has not reached the day before her 60th birthday;

(ii) was a jobseeker's allowance, the person with care has not reached the day before she attains pensionable age,

at the time the work condition is satisfied; and

[²(f) the work condition is satisfied within the period of—

(i) in a case where an applicant with care cares for one child only and that child dies, 12 months immediately following the date of death;

(ii) in a case where the absent parent has—

(aa) died;

(bb) ceased to be habitually resident in the United Kingdom; or

(cc) has been found not to be the parent of the qualifying child or children,

12 weeks immediately following the first date on which any of those events occurs;

(iii) in any other case, 14 days immediately following the day on which the bonus period applying to the applicant comes to an end.]

[[1](1A) In the case of an applicant who satisfies the requirements of paragraph (1)(f) but whose entitlement, or whose partner's entitlement, to a qualifying benefit ceased otherwise than as a result of satisfying the work condition, for sub-paragrph (d) of paragraph (1) there shall be substituted the following sub-paragraph—

"(d) had the work condition been satisfied on the day she, or her partner, was last entitled to a qualifying benefit, that entitlement would as a consequence have ceased."]

(2) A person who is absent from work because of a trade dispute at her place of work and returns to work with the employer she worked for before the dispute began, does not thereby satisfy the requirements of paragraph (1)(c).

(3) In paragraph (2), "place of work", in relation to any person, means the premises at which she was employed.

(4) An applicant is also entitled to a bonus where she satisfies the requirements specified in regulation 8 (retirement).

AMENDMENTS

1. Social Security (Miscellaneous Amendments) Regulations 1997 (SI 1997/454), reg.8(3) (April 6, 1997).
2. Social Security (Miscellaneous Amendments) Regulations 1998 (SI 1998/563), reg.2(3) (April 1, 1998). (Note that the commencement date for this provision was amended by Social Security (Miscellaneous Amendments) (No.2) Regulations 1998 (SI 1998/865), reg.2 (March 20, 1998).)

2.974

Bonus period

4.—(1) A bonus period comprises only days falling on or after 7th April 1997 [[1], other than days to which paragraph (9) applies,] on which—
   (a) the applicant or, where the applicant has a partner, her partner is entitled to, or is treated as entitled to a qualifying benefit whether it is payable or not;
   (b) the applicant has residing with her a qualifying child; and
   (c) child maintenance is either—
       [[2](i) paid or payable to the applicant; or]
       (ii) retained by the Secretary of State in accordance with section 74A(3) of the Social Security Administration Act 1992.

(2) Any two or more bonus periods separated by any one connected period shall be treated as one bonus period.

(3) For the purposes of these Regulations, "a connected period" is—
   (a) any period of not more than 12 weeks falling between two bonus periods to which paragraph (1) refers;
   (b) any period of not more than 12 weeks throughout which—
       (i) [[1]. . .]
       (ii) the applicant ceases to be entitled to a qualifying benefit on becoming one of a couple and the couple fail to satisfy the conditions of entitlement to a qualifying benefit; or
   (c) any period throughout which maternity allowance is payable to the applicant; or

2.975

(d) any period of not more than 2 years throughout which incapacity benefit, severe disablement allowance or [¹ carer's allowance] is payable to the applicant.

(4) In calculating any period for the purposes of paragraph (3) no regard shall be had to any day which falls before 7th April 1997.

(5) Bonus periods separated by two or more connected periods shall not link to form a single bonus period but shall instead remain separate bonus periods.

(6) Where a qualifying child is temporarily absent for a period not exceeding 12 weeks from the home he shares with the applicant, the applicant shall be treated as satisfying the requirements of paragraph (1)(b) throughout that absence.

(7) A bonus period which would, but for this paragraph, have continued shall end—

(a) where the applicant or, where the applicant has a partner, her partner, satisfies the work condition and claims a bonus, on the last day of entitlement to a qualifying benefit to which any award made on that claim applies; or

[¹(b) on the date of death of a person with a care of a qualifying child to whom child maintenance is payable.

(8) In paragraphs (1)(c)(i) and (9) "claimant"—

(a) where the qualifying benefit is income support, means a person who claims income support; and

(b) where the qualifying benefit is a jobseeker's allowance, means a person who claims a jobseeker's allowance.

(9) This paragraph applies to days on which the claimant is a person to whom—

(a) regulation 70 of the Income Support (General) Regulations 1987 (urgent cases) applies other than by virtue of paragraph (2)(a) of that regulation (certain persons from abroad), or

(b) regulation 147 of the Jobseeker's Allowance Regulations 1996 applies other than by virtue of paragraph (2)(a) of that regulation.]

AMENDMENTS

2.976   1. Social Security (Miscellaneous Amendments) Regulations 1997 (SI 1997/454), reg.8(4) (April 6, 1997).

2. Social Security (Miscellaneous Amendments) Regulations 1998 (SI 1998/563), reg.2(4) (April 1, 1998). (Note that the commencement date for this provision was amended by Social Security (Miscellaneous Amendments) (No.2) Regulations 1998 (SI 1998/865), reg.2 (March 20, 1998).)

3. Social Security Amendment (Carer's Allowance) Regulations 2002 (SI 2002/2497), reg.3 and Sch.2 (April 1, 2003).

Amount payable

2.977   **5.**—(1) The amount of the bonus shall be—

(a) subject to the following provisions of this regulation, a sum representing the aggregate of—

(i) £5 for each benefit week in the bonus period in which the amount of child maintenance payable was not less than £5; and

(ii) where in any benefit week in the bonus period the amount of child maintenance payable was less than £5, the amount that was payable;

(b) the amount of the child maintenance paid in the bonus period; or

(c) £1,000.

whichever amount is the least.

(2) [¹ . . .]

(3) So much of any child maintenance paid in excess of the amount either—

(a) declared for the purposes of determining the amount of qualifying benefit payable to the applicant or her partner; or

(b) retained by the Secretary of State in accordance with section 74A(3) of the Social Security Administration Act 1992,

shall be disregarded in determining the amount payable under paragraph (1).

(4)[¹ . . .]

(5) Where but for this paragraph the amount of bonus payable in accordance with paragraph (1) would be less than £5, the amount of the bonus shall be nil.

AMENDMENT

1. Social Security (Miscellaneous Amendments) Regulations 1997 (SI 1997/454), reg.8(5) (April 6, 1997).

2.978

Secretary of State to issue estimates

6.—(1) Where it appears to the Secretary of State that a person [¹ with care], or the partner of such a person, may satisfy the requirments of regulation 3 (entitlement to a bonus) he may issue to [¹ that person] a written statement of the amount he estimates may be payable by way of a bonus in his particular case, and may provide such further statements as appear appropriate in the circumstance, stating the amount he estimates may be payable.

2.979

(2) The issue by the Secretary of State of a statement under paragraph (1) shall not be binding on the adjudication officer when he makes his determination on a claim for a bonus as to—

(a) whether the applicant satisfies the conditions of entitlements to the bonus; and

(b) the amount, in any, payable where the bonus is awarded.

AMENDMENT

1. Social Security (Miscellaneous Amendments) Regulations 1997 (SI 1997/454), reg.8(6) (April 6, 1997).

2.980

Death of a person with care of a child

7.—(1) In a case where—

2.981

(a) the person (A) with care of a[¹ qualifying child to whom child maintenance is payable dies];

(b) on the date of her death, the person (A) was entitled or, where she has a partner, her partner was entitled to a qualifying benefit or had been so entitled within the 12 weeks ending on the date of her death;

(c) after the death, another person (B), who is a close relative of the person (A) and who was not before the death a person with the care of the child, become the person with care; and

(d) that other person was entitled or, where the other person has a partner, the other person or her partner was entitled to a qualifying benefit on the day the person (A) died or becomes entitled to a qualifying benefit within 12 weeks of the day on which the person (A) was last entitled to a qualifying benefit,

then any weeks forming part of the bonus period of the person (A) which was current at the date of her death or within 12 weeks of the date on which she died shall be treated as part of the bonus period of the person (B) to the extent that those weeks are not otherwise a part of her bonus period.

(2) In this Regulation, "close relevant" means a parent, parent-in-law, son, son-in-law, daughter, daughter-in-law, step-parent, step-son, step-daughter, brother, sister, or the spouse of any of the proceeding persons or, if that person is one of an unmarried couple, the other member of that couple.

AMENDMENT

2.982   1. Social Security (Miscellaneous Amendments) Regulations 1997 (SI 1997/454), reg.8(7) (April 6, 1997).

Retirement

2.983   **8.**—(1) In a case where the person with care of the child in respect of whom child maintenance is payable (the applicant) or the applicant's partner, either—
   (a) is entitled to income support on the day before the applicant attains the age of 60; or
   (b) is entitled to a jobseeker's allowance on the day before the applicant attains pensionable age,
the bonus period shall end on the day before the applicant attains 60 or, as the case may be, pensionable age and a bonus shall become payable to the applicant whether or not a claim is made for it.

(2) Where an applicant who ceases to be entitled to a jobseeker's allowance after attaining the age of 60 without satisfying the condition in paragraph (1)(b) above, becomes entitled to [¹ state pension credit] within—
   (a) a period of 12 weeks of him ceasing to be entitled to a jobseeker's allowance, or
   (b) the duration of any connected period to which regulations 4(3) applies which immediately follows such an entitlement and which applies in his case,
he shall be entitled to the bonus as though paragraph (1) were satisfied in his case and his bonus period shall be treated as though it ended on the day he becomes entitled to [¹ state pension credit].

[¹ (2A) In paragraph (2), "state pension credit" means the benefit of that name payable under the State Pension Credit Act 2002.]

(3) No day which falls after the day the bonus period ends in accordance with paragraph (1) or (4) or is treated as ending in accordance with paragraph (2), shall form part of that or any other bonus period.

(4) Paragraph (5) shall apply where—
   (a) the applicant or the applicant's partner—
      (i) ceased to be entitled to income support in the 12 weeks preceding the date of the applicant attaining the age of 60;

(ii) ceased to be entitled to a jobseeker's allowance in the 12 weeks preceding the date of the applicant attaining pensionable age; and

(b) the person who ceased to be so entitled failed to satisfy the requirements of regulations 3(1)(c) to (f).

(5) Where this paragraph applies—

(a) the bonus period shall end on the day entitlement to the qualifying benefit ceased; and

(b) a bonus shall become payable to the applicant, but only where a claim is made for it in accordance with regulation 10 (claiming a bonus).

(6) In this regulation, "applicant" includes, where no claim is made, a person who would have been an applicant had a claim for a bonus been required.

AMENDMENT

1. State Pension Credit (Consequential, Transitional and Miscellaneous Provisions) (No.2) Regulations 2002 (SI 2002/3197), reg.7(1) (October 6, 2003).   **2.984**

Couples

9.—(1) In the case of a couple, the person entitled to the bonus is the person who has the care of the child and to whom child maintenance is payable in respect of that child.   **2.985**

(2) Where each member of a couple has both the care of a child and child maintenance is payable in respect of the child for whom they have care, each of them may qualify for a bonus in accordance with these Regulations where a qualifying benefit ceases to be payable to either of them because one them, whether or not the person to whom the benefit was payable, satisfies the work condition.

(3) A member of a couple to whom paragraph (2) applies shall not qualify for a bonus unless she claims it in accordance with regulation 10 (claiming a bonus).

(4) Subject to paragraph (5), these Regulations shall apply to both members of a couple who separate as if they had never been one of a couple.

(5) In the case of a couple who separate any entitlement to a qualifying benefit of one member of the couple during the time they were a couple shall be treated as the entitlement of both members of the couple for the purpose only of determining whether any day falls within a bonus period.

Claiming a bonus

10.—(1) A claim for a bonus shall be made in writing on a form approved for the purpose by the Secretary of State and shall be made—   **2.986**

(a) not earlier than the beginning of the benefit week which precedes the benefit week in which an award of a qualifying benefit come to an end; and

(b) except in a case to which sub-paragraph [². . .] (d) applies, not later than 28 days after the day the qualifying benefit [¹. . .]ceases; or [¹(c) [². . .]]

(d) in the case of a person to whom regulation 8(4) refers, not later than 28 days after the day the applicant attains the age of 60 or, as the case may be, pensionable age.

(2) A claim for a bonus shall be delivered or sent to an appropriate office.

(3) If a claim is defective at the time it is received, the Secretary of State may refer the claim to the person making it and if the form is received properly completed within one month, or such longer period as the Secretary of State may consider reasonable, from the date on which it is so referred, the Secretary of State may treat the claim as if it had been duly made in the first instance.

(4) A claim which is made on the form approved form the time being is, for the purposes of paragraph (3), properly completed if it is completed in accordance with instructions on the form and defective if it is not.

(5) A person who claims a bonus shall furnish such certificates, documents, information and evidence in connection with the claim, or any questions arising out of it, as may be required by the Secretary of State and shall do so within one month of being required to do so or such longer period as the Secretary of State may consider reasonable.

(6) Where a person who has attained the age of 60 but has not attained pensionable age for the purposes of a jobseeker's allowance ceases to be entitled to a jobseeker's allowance and becomes instead entitled to income support, regulation 8 (retirement) and this regulation shall apply in his case as if he attained the age of 60 on the day he first became entitled to income support.

AMENDMENTS

2.987   1. Social Security (Miscellaneous Amendments) Regulations 1997 (SI 1997/454), reg.8(8) (April 6, 1997).

2. Social Security (Miscellaneous Amendments) Regulations 1998 (SI 1998/563), reg.2(5) (April 1, 1998). (Note that the commencement date for this provision was amended by Social Security (Miscellaneous Amendments) (No.2) Regulations 1998 (SI 1998/865), reg.2 (March 20, 1998)).

Claims: further provisions

2.988   **11.**—(1) A person who has made a claim may amend it at any time by notice in writing received at an appropriate office before a determination has been made on the claim, and any claim so amended may be treated as if it had been so amended in the first instance.

(2) A person who has made a claim may withdraw it at any time before a determination has been made on it, by notice to an appropriate office and any such notice of withdrawal shall have effect when it is received.

(3) The date on which the claim is made shall be—

(a) in the case of a claim which meets the requirements of regulation 10(1), the date on which it is received at an appropriate office; or

(b) in the case of a claim treated under regulation 10(3) as having been duly made, the date on which the claim was received in an appropriate office in the first place.

(4) Where the applicant proves there was good cause throughout the period from the expiry of the 28 days specified in regulation 10(1), for failure to claim the bonus within the specified time, the time for claiming the bonus shall be extended to the date on which the claim is made or to a period of 6 months, whichever is the shorter period.

Payment of bonus

12. A bonus calculated by reference to child maintenance paid during periods of entitlement to a jobseeker's allowance and to income support shall be treated as payable—

    (a) wholly by way of a jobseeker's allowance, where the qualifying benefit last in payment in the bonus period was a jobseeker's allowance; or

    (b) wholly by way of income support, where the qualifying benefit last in payment in the bonus period was income support.

2.989

Payments on death

13.—(1) Where a person satisfies the requirements for entitlement to a bonus other than the need to make a claim, but dies within 28 days of the last day of entitlement to a qualifying benefit, the Secretary of State may appoint such person as he may think fit to claim a bonus in place of the deceased person.

2.990

(2) Where the conditions specified in paragraph (3) are satisfied, a claim may be made by the person appointed for the purpose of claiming a bonus to which the deceased person would have been entitled if he had claimed it in accordance with regulation 10 (claiming a bonus).

(3) Subject to the following provisions of this regulation, the following conditions are specified for the purposes of paragraph (2)—

    (a) the application to the Secretary of State to be appointed a fit person to make a claim shall be made within 6 months of the date of death; and

    (b) the claim shall be made in writing within 6 months of the date the appointment was made.

(4) Subject to paragraphs (5) and (6), the Secretary of State may, in exceptional circumstances, extend the period for making an application or a claim to such longer period as he considers appropriate in the particular case.

(5) Where the period is extended in accordance with paragraph (4), the period specified in paragraph (3)(a) or (b) shall be shortended by a corresponding period.

(6) The Secretary of State shall not extend the period for making an application or a claim in accordance with paragraph (4) for more than 12 months from the date of death, but in calculating that period any period between the date when an application for a person to be appointed to make a claim is made and the date when the Secretary of State makes the appointment shall be disregarded.

(7) A claim made in accordance with paragraph (2) shall be treated, for the purposes of these Regulations, as if made on the date of the deceased's death.

Bonus to be treated as capital for certain purposes

14. Any bonus paid to an applicant shall be treated as capital of hers for the purposes of—

    (a) housing benefit;

    (b) council tax benefit;

    (c) [1 working families' tax credit];

    (d) [2 disabled person's tax credit];

2.991

(e) income support;

(f) a jobseeker's allowance.

AMENDMENTS

2.992   1. Social Security and Child Support (Tax Credits) Consequential Amendments
Regulations 1999 (SI 1999/2566), reg.2(1) and Sch.2, Pt I (October 5, 1999).
2. Social Security and Child Support (Tax Credits) Consequential Amendments
Regulations 1999 (SI 1999/2566), reg.2(2) and Sch.2, Pt II (October 5, 1999).

Social Security (Child Maintenance Premium and Miscellaneous Amendments) Regulations 2000

(SI 2000/3176)

*Made by the Secretary of State under ss.123(1)(a), (d) and (e), 136(3) and
(5)(b), 137(1) and 175(1) and (3) of the Social Security Contributions and
Benefits Act 1992, ss.12(1) and (4)(b), 35(1) and 36(1), (2) and (4) of the
Jobseekers Act 1995, ss.10 and 26(1)–(3) of the Child Support Act 1995 and
s.87(4) of the Northern Ireland Act 1998*

[¹ Citation, commencement and interpretation

2.993   **1.**—(1) These Regulations may be cited as the Social Security (Child
Maintenance Premium and Miscellaneous Amendments) Regulations 2000
and shall come into force—

   (a) in relation to any particular case, on the date on which section 23
       of the 2000 Act comes into force in relation to that type of case
       ("the commencement date");

   (b) in relation to a person who, on or after 16th February 2004—

       (i) makes a claim for income support or an income-based job-
           seeker's allowance; and

       (ii) on or after the date of that claim receives any payment of child
            maintenance made voluntarily,

   on 16th February 2004; or

   (c) in relation to a person who—

       (i) on 16th February 2004 is entitled to income support or an
           income-based jobseeker's allowance; and

       (ii) on or after 16th February 2004 receives any payment of child
            maintenance made voluntarily and that payment is the first
            payment of child maintenance received by that person whilst
            he is entitled to income support or an income-based jobseeker's
            allowance,

   on 16th February 2004 if a payment referred to in head (ii) above is
   received on that day, or on the day on which such a payment is received
   where it is received after 16th February 2004.

   (2) In this regulation—

"the 1991 Act" means the Child Support Act 1991;

"the 2000 Act" means the Child Support, Pensions and Social Security
Act 2000;

"child maintenance" shall have the same meaning as that prescribed for the purposes of section 74A of the Social Security Administration Act 1992;

"an income-based jobseeker's allowance" has the meaning given by section 1(4) of the Jobseekers Act 1995;

"payment of child maintenance made voluntarily" means any payment of child maintenance other than such a payment made—

(a) under a court order;

(b) under a maintenance assessment made under the 1991 Act prior to its amendment by the 2000 Act or under a maintenance calculation made under the 1991 Act after its amendment by the 2000 Act;

(c) under an agreement for maintenance;

(d) in accordance with section 28J of the 1991 Act; or

(e) by the Secretary of State in lieu of child maintenance, including any payment made by the Secretary of State under section 27 of the 2000 Act.]

AMENDMENT

1. Social Security (Child Maintenance Premium) Amendment Regulations 2004 (SI 2004/98), reg.4(1) (February 16, 2004).

Revocations and transitional provisions

[¹ **4.**—(1) Subject to paragraphs (2) to (8) below—   2.994

(a) regulations 2 to 13 of the Social Security (Child Maintenance Bonus) Regulations 1996 ("the Child Maintenance Bonus Regulations");

(b) the Child Maintenance Bonus (Northern Ireland Reciprocal Arrangements) Regulations 1997 ("the Reciprocal Arrangements Regulations");

(c) regulation 8 of the Social Security (Miscellaneous Amendments) Regulations 1997; and

(d) regulation 2 of the Social Security (Miscellaneous Amendments) Regulations 1998,

are hereby revoked.

(2) Subject to paragraph (6) below, the Reciprocal Arrangements Regulations and regulations 2 to 13 of the Child Maintenance Bonus Regulations shall continue to have effect as if paragraph (1) above had not been made in relation to a person—

(a) who—

(i) satisfied the requirements of regulation 10 (claiming a bonus) or, as the case may be, regulation 11(4) (claims: further provisions) of the Child Maintenance Bonus Regulations; and

(ii) satisfied the work condition in accordance with regulation 3(1)(c) of the Child Maintenance Bonus Regulations (entitlement to a bonus: the work condition),

before the commencement date, but whose claim has not been determined before that date;

(b) to whom regulation 8(1) or (2) of the Child Maintenance Bonus Regulations (retirement) applied before the commencement date but whose entitlement has not been determined before that date;

    (c) who—
        (i) satisfied the requirements of regulation 10 or, as the case may be, regulation 11(4) of the Child Maintenance Bonus Regulations; and
        (ii) satisfied the requirements of regulation 8(4) of the Child Maintenance Bonus Regulations,

before the commencement date, but whose claim has not been determined before that date; or

    (d) who—
        (i) satisfied the requirements of regulation 3(1)(b) to (f) of the Child Maintenance Bonus Regulations before the commencement date; and
        (ii) satisfies the requirements of regulation 10 (claiming a bonus) or, as the case may be, regulation 11(4) (claims: further provisions) of the Child Maintenance Bonus Regulations on or after the commencement date.

(3) Subject to paragraphs (5) and (6) below, the Reciprocal Arrangements Regulations and regulations 2 to 6 and 9 to 13 of the Child Maintenance Bonus Regulations shall continue to have effect as if paragraph (1) above had not been made in relation to—

    (a) a person who—
        (i) satisfied the requirements of regulation 10 of the Child Maintenance Bonus Regulations before the commencement date; and
        (ii) has not satisfied the work condition in accordance with regulation 3(1)(c) of the Child Maintenance Bonus Regulations before that date; or

    (b) a person—
        (i) who has not claimed a child maintenance bonus before the commencement date; and
        (ii) to whom the provisions of paragraph (4) below apply on the day immediately before the commencement date.

(4) For the purposes of paragraph (3)(b)(ii) above, the provisions of this paragraph are that—

    (a) the person or, where the person has a partner, her partner is entitled to, or is treated as entitled to a qualifying benefit whether it is payable or not;
    (b) the person has residing with her a qualifying child;
    (c) child maintenance is either—
        (i) paid or payable to the person; or
        (ii) retained by the Secretary of State in accordance with section 74A(3) of the Social Security Administration Act 1992; and
    (d) the person has not satisfied the work condition in accordance with regulation 3(1)(c) of the Child Maintenance Bonus Regulations.

(5) For the purposes of paragraph (3) above, regulation 3 of the Child Maintenance Bonus Regulations shall have effect as if in paragraph (1)—

    (a) the words "no later than the day immediately before the commencement date" were inserted after—
        (i) "dies" in sub-paragraph (f)(i); and
        (ii) "has" where that word first appears in sub-paragraph (f)(ii); and
    (b) for the words "14 days" in sub-paragraph (f)(iii) there were substituted "one month".

(6) For the purposes of paragraphs (2) and (3) above, regulation 4 of the Child Maintenance Bonus Regulations (bonus period) shall have effect as if for paragraph (7) there were substituted the following paragraph—

"(7) A bonus period which would, but for this paragraph, have continued shall end—

(a) where the applicant or, where the applicant has a partner, her partner, satisfies the work condition and claims a bonus, on the last day of entitlement to a qualifying benefit to which any award made on that claim applies;

(b) on the date of death of a person with care of a qualifying child to whom child maintenance is payable; or

(c) on the day immediately before the commencement date, whichever is the earlier."

(7) Nothing in this regulation shall prevent the Secretary of State from issuing a written statement pursuant to regulation 6(1) of the Child Maintenance Bonus Regulations (Secretary of State to issue estimates) to a person who appears to him to satisfy the requirements of regulation 3 of those Regulations.

(8) For the purposes of this regulation "child maintenance" has the meaning given by regulation 1(2) of the Child Maintenance Bonus Regulations (interpretation).]

AMENDMENT

1. Social Security (Child Maintenance Premium and Miscellaneous Amendments) Amendment Regulations 2003 (SI 2003/231), reg.2 (in force, in relation to any particular case, on the date on which s.23 CSPSSA 2000 comes into force in relation to that type of case). **2.995**

GENERAL NOTE

See the note to the Social Security (Child Maintenance Bonus) Regulations 1996. **2.996**

The Children (Leaving Care) (England) Regulations 2001

(SI 2001/2874)

Made by the Secretary of State under ss.23A(3), 23B(5), (6), (8)(c), (10), 23D(2), 23E, 24B(6), 24D(2) and 104(4) of, and paras 19B(2), (3) (7) and (8) of Sch.2 to, the Children Act 1989.

[In force October 1, 2001]

REGULATIONS REPRODUCED

GENERAL NOTE

See the note to reg.2 of the Children (Leaving Care) Social Security Benefits Regulations 2001. **2.998**

Eligible children

2.999   **3.**—(1) For the purposes of paragraph 19B(2)(b) of Schedule 2 to the Act, the prescribed period is 13 weeks and the prescribed age is 14.

(2) A child falling within paragraph (3) is not an eligible child despite falling within paragraph 19B(2) of Schedule 2 to the Act.

(3) A child falls within this paragraph if he has been looked after by a local authority in circumstances where—

(a) the local authority has arranged to place him in a pre-planned series of short-term placements, none of which individually exceeds four weeks (even though they may amount in all to the prescribed period); and

(b) at the end of each such placement the child returns to the care of his parent, or a person who is not a parent but who has parental responsibility for him.

Relevant children

2.1000   **4.**—(1) For the purposes of section 23A(3), children falling within paragraph (2) are an additional category of relevant children.

(2) Subject to paragraph (3), a child falls within this paragraph if—

(a) he is aged 16 or 17;

(b) he is not subject to a care order; and

(c) at the time when he attained the age of 16 he was detained or in hospital and immediately before he was detained or admitted to hospital he had been looked after by a local authority for a period or periods amounting in all to at least 13 weeks, which began after he reached the age of 14.

(3) In calculating the period of 13 weeks referred to in paragraph (2)(c), no account is to be taken of any period in which the child was looked after by a local authority in any of a pre-planned series of short-term placements, none of which individually exceeded four weeks, where at the end of each such placement the child returned to the care of his parent, or a person who is not a parent but who has parental responsibility for him.

(4) For the purposes of this regulation—

(a) "detained" means detained in a remand centre, a young offenders-institution or a secure training centre, or any other institution pursuant to an order of a court; and

(b) "hospital" means—

(i) any health service hospital within the meaning of the National Health Service Act 1977; or

(ii) any mental nursing home being a home in respect of which the particulars of registration are for the time being entered in the separate part of the register kept for the purposes of section 23(5)(b) of the Registered Homes Act 1984.

(5) Subject to paragraph (7), any child who has lived with a person falling within section 23(4) of the Act ("a family placement") for a continuous period of six months or more is not to be a relevant child despite falling within section 23A(2) of the Act.

(6) Paragraph (5) applies whether the period of six months commences before or after a child ceases to be looked after by a local authority.

(7) Where a family placement within the meaning of paragraph (5) breaks down and the child ceases to live with the person concerned, the child is to be treated as a relevant child.

(SI 2001/2189)

The Children (Leaving Care) (Wales) Regulations 2001

(SI 2001/2189)

Made by the National Assembly for Wales under ss.23A(3), 23B(5), (6), (8)(c), (10), 23D(2), 23E, 24B(6), 24D(2) and 104(4) of, and paras 19B(2), (3), (7) and (8) of Sch.2 to, the Children Act 1989

[In force October 1, 2001]

GENERAL NOTE

See the note to reg.2 of the Children (Leaving Care) Social Security Benefits   2.1002
Regulations 2001.

Eligible children

3.—(1) For the purposes of paragraph 19B(2)(b) of Schedule 2 to the   2.1003
Act, the prescribed period is 13 weeks and the prescribed age is 14.

(2) The following categories of children are not to be eligible children despite falling within paragraph 19B(2) of Schedule 2—

(a) any child who has been looked after by a local authority in circumstances where the following conditions apply—
   (i) the local authority has arranged to place the child in a series of short-term placements none of which individually exceeds four weeks (even though they may amount in all to the prescribed period); and
   (ii) at the end of each such placement the child returns to the care of his or her parent, or a person who is not a parent but who has parental responsibility for the child,

(b) [¹. . .]

AMENDMENT

1. Children (Leaving Care) (Amendment) (Wales) Regulations 2002 (SI 2002/   2.1004
1855), reg.2(a) (August 1, 2002).

Relevant children

4.—(1) For the purposes of section 23A(3), the category of children   2.1005
described in paragraph (2) are an additional category of relevant children.

(2) [² Subject to paragraph (2A),] any child aged 16 or 17 (not being subject to a care order) who—

(a) at the time when he or she attained the age of 16 was detained or in hospital; and

(b) had been accommodated by a local authority for a single period of at least 13 weeks ("the single period") or for periods amounting in all to at least 13 weeks ("the aggregate period")where
    (i) the single period or the first period of the aggregate period began after he or she reached the age of 14, and
    (ii) the single period or the aggregate period ended immediately before such detention or admission.

[² (2A) In calculating the period of 13 weeks referred to in sub-paragraph (2)(b), no account is to be taken of any period in which the child was looked after in a series of short-term placements none of which individually exceeds four weeks, where, at the end of each such placement, the child returned to the care of his parent, or a person who is not a parent but who has parental responsibility for him.]

(3) For the purposes of this regulation, "detained" means detained in a remand centre, a young offenders institution or a secure training centre, or any other institution pursuant to an order of a court.

[¹ (4) Subject to paragraph (6), any child who has lived with a person falling within section 23(4) of the Act ("a family placement") for a continuous period of six months or more is not to be a relevant child despite falling within section 23A(2).]

(5) Paragraph (4) applies whether the period of six months commences before or after a child ceases to be looked after by a local authority.

[¹ (6) Where
(a) a family placement within the meaning of paragraph (4) breaks down and the child ceases to live with the person concerned, and
(b) six months have elapsed since that family placement began,
the child is to be treated as a relevant child.]

AMENDMENTS

2.1006
1. Children (Leaving Care) (Amendment) (Wales) Regulations 2002 (SI 2002/1855), reg.2(b) (August 1, 2002).
2. Children (Leaving Care) (Wales) (Amendment) Regulations 2004 (SI 2004/1732), reg.2 (July 23, 2004).

The Children (Leaving Care) Social Security Benefits Regulations 2001

(SI 2001/3074)

Made by the Secretary of State for Work and Pensions under s.6(3), (5), (6) and (7) of the Children (Leaving Care) Act 2000

[In force October 1, 2001]

REGULATIONS REPRODUCED

2.1007   2.   Entitlement to Benefits

Entitlement to Benefits

2.—(1) Section 6 (exclusion from benefits) shall not apply for the pur-   2.1008
poses of entitlement to income support or income-based jobseeker's
allowance where a person—
  (a) falls within subsection (2)(a) or (b) of that section; and
  (b) falls within a category of person prescribed in—
    (i) provided the person is a lone parent, regulation 13(2)(a) (cir-
      cumstances in which persons in relevant education may be enti-
      tled to income support) of;
    (ii) regulation 13(2)(b) of; or
    (iii) paragraph 1, 2, 7, 8, 10, 11, 12, 13, 24 or 25 of Schedule 1B
      (prescribed categories of person) to,
    the Income Support (General) Regulations 1987 ("the Income
    Support Regulations").

(2) Section 6 shall not apply to a person who falls within subsection (2)(a)
or (b) of that section who has not been looked after by a local authority for
the purposes of paragraph 19B of Schedule 2 to the Children Act 1989 on
or after 1st October 2001.

(3) Where a person who falls within subsection (2)(a) or (b) of section 6 is
residing in Scotland but is not supported by a local authority in England or
Wales then, notwithstanding that he has been looked after by such a local
authority for the purposes of paragraph 19B of Schedule 2 to the 1989 Act on
or after 1st October 2001, section 6 shall not apply to that person [[1] provided
that he ceased to be so looked after before 1st April 2004].

(4) In paragraph (1)(b)(i) above, "lone parent" has the meaning it bears
in regulation 2(1) of the Income Support Regulations.

AMENDMENT

1. Social Security (Miscellaneous Amendments) Regulations 2004 (SI 2004/565),   2.1009
reg.12 (April 1, 2004).

GENERAL NOTE

This regulation deals with the exceptions to the exclusion from benefit in s.6 (2)(a)   2.1010
and (b) of the Children (Leaving Care) Act 2000 (see the note to the Children
(Leaving Care) Act 2000). See the Children (Leaving Care) Social Security Benefits
(Scotland) Regulations 2004 (SI 2004/747) below which provide for similar exceptions to the exclusion under s.6(2)(c) of the 2000 Act (as well as defining the scope
of the exclusion under that provision).

Under s.6, an "eligible child" (defined in para.19B of Sch.2 to the Children Act
1989) or a "relevant child" (defined in s.23A of the 1989 Act) is not entitled to
income-based JSA, income support or housing benefit (subss (1), (2)(a) and (2)(b)).
(Such a child would not in any event be entitled to council tax benefit since liability
to pay council tax cannot arise until the age of 18). See also the consequential
amendments to reg.4ZA of the Income Support Regulations and reg.57 of the JSA
Regulations made by the Children (Leaving Care) Act 2000 (Commencement No. 2
and Consequential Provisions) Order 2001 (SI 2001/ 3070) with effect from
October 1, 2001.

Paragraph 19B of Sch.2 to, and s.23A of, the Children Act 1989 were inserted by
ss.1 and 2 respectively of the Children (Leaving Care) Act 2000 (p.180).

Under para.19B, together with reg.3 of the Children (Leaving Care) (England)
Regulations 2001 (SI 2001/2874) ("the English Regulations")/reg.3 of the Children
(Leaving Care) (Wales) Regulations 2001 (SI 2001/2189) ("the Welsh Regulations")

(pp.742–743), an "eligible child" is a 16 or 17 year-old who is being looked after by a local authority and who has, since the age of 14, been looked after by a local authority for a period of at least 13 weeks, or periods totalling at least 13 weeks, which ended after he became 16. But periods of respite care are excluded. Thus the child will not be an eligible child if he has been/is placed in a series of (in England only, pre-planned) short-term placements, none of which exceed four weeks (even if in total they amount to 13 weeks or more), and the child returns to the care of his parent or the person who has parental responsibility for him at the end of each placement.

If the person is an eligible child, the local authority has a duty under para.19B to assess his needs, both while they are still looking after him and after they cease to do so, and to prepare a "pathway plan" for him. In addition, a local authority is required to appoint a personal adviser for each eligible child that they are looking after (para.19C of Sch.2 to the 1989 Act).

2.1011 A "relevant child" is a 16 or 17 year-old who was an eligible child but who is no longer being looked after by a local authority (s. 23A(2) of the 1989 Act). It also includes a 16 or 17 year-old (not subject to a care order) who at the age of 16 was in hospital or detained in a remand centre, a young offenders institution, a secure training centre, or any other institution pursuant to an order of a court, and who immediately before he was in hospital or detained, had, since the age of 14, been looked after by a local authority for a period or periods totalling at least 13 weeks (reg.4(2) to (4) of the English Regulations; reg.4(2) to (3) of the Welsh Regulations). In calculating the 13 weeks any short-term placement which does not exceed four weeks and at the end of which the child returns to the care of his parent or the person who has parental responsibility for him is ignored (reg.4(3) of the English Regulations; reg.4(2A) of the Welsh Regulations). However, a child who has lived with his parent, the person who has parental responsibility for him or, in the case of a child subject to a care order, the person in whose favour a residence order had been made before the care order was made ("a family placement") for at least six months, whether or not the six months started before or after the child stopped being looked after by a local authority, does not count as a relevant child (reg.4(5) and (6) of the English Regulations/reg.4(4) and (5) of the Welsh Regulations); but will do so if the family placement breaks down and the child ceases to live with the person concerned (reg.4(7) of the English Regulations; reg 4(6) of the Welsh Regulations).

If the person is a relevant child, s.23B of the 1989 Act (inserted by s.2 of the 2000 Act) requires the responsible local authority (ie the one who last looked after him (s.23A(4)) to keep in touch with him, prepare a pathway plan and appoint a personal adviser for him, if this has not already been done, maintain him and provide him with suitable accommodation.

Once an eligible or relevant child becomes 18 he ceases to count as such and the exclusion from benefit in s.6 will not apply.

If there is a dispute over whether the s.6 exclusion applies, it may be necessary for decision-makers (and appeal tribunals) to decide whether a child falls within either definition. For this reason the text of the relevant parts of both the English and the Welsh Regulations has been included (see pp.741–744). Clearly information from the relevant social services department will be useful in determining these issues. But if, for example, a local authority has decided that a family placement has broken down with the result that the person concerned is again treated as a relevant child, is a tribunal bound by the local authority decision or can it reach a different conclusion? As this will be largely a question of fact, there seems to be no reason why the tribunal cannot consider this issue in deciding whether the s.6 exclusion applies.

See also the amendments to reg.14 of the Income Support Regulations and reg.76(2) of the JSA Regulations made by the Children (Leaving Care) Act 2000 (Commencement No. 2 and Consequential Provisions) Order 2001 (SI 2001/3070) with effect from October 1, 2001. The result of these amendments is that a person to whom the s.6 exclusion applies cannot form part of a claimant's family for the purposes of income support and income-based JSA.

Exceptions to the s.6 exclusion

The circumstances in which the s.6 exclusion will not apply are set out in reg.2.   **2.1012**
Note firstly that the exclusion only applies to an eligible or relevant child who has been looked after by a local authority on or after October 1, 2001 (para.(2)) (ie it does not apply to a 16 or 17 year-old who left local authority care before that date). It also did not originally apply if an eligible or relevant child who would otherwise be caught by s.6 was living in Scotland, provided that he was not being supported by an English or Welsh local authority (para.(3)). However, this now only applies if the person ceased to be so looked after before April 1, 2004. This is because, with the exception of s.6, the Children (Leaving Care) Act 2000 did not apply to Scotland and so 16 or 17 year-olds who left Scottish local authority care remained potentially entitled to income support, income-based JSA and housing benefit, whether they were in Scotland, England or Wales. However, with effect from April 1, 2004 equivalent legislation has come into force in Scotland and so 16 or 17 year-olds leaving Scottish local authority care will now come within s. 6. See the Support and Assistance of Young People Leaving Care (Scotland) Regulations 2003 (SSI SI 2003/608).
In addition to these general exceptions, para.(1) provides that an eligible child or a relevant child can still qualify for income support or income-based JSA if he is (i) in relevant education and a lone parent (as defined in reg.2(1) of the Income Support Regulations (para.(4)); (ii) in relevant education and severely mentally or physically disabled and unlikely to obtain employment within the next twelve months; or (iii) a lone parent, a single foster parent, incapable of work or appealing against a decision that he is capable of work, a disabled worker within the meaning of para.8 of Sch.1B to the Income Support Regulations, blind, or a student who qualifies for the disability or severe disability premium, or who has been incapable of work for 28 weeks, or who is disabled and comes within para.11 of Sch.1B, or deaf and comes within para.12 of Sch.1B. But note that there is no exception under para.(1) to the exclusion from housing benefit even if the person does fall within any of these categories.

The Children (Leaving Care) Social Security Benefits (Scotland) Regulations 2004

(SI 2004/747)   **2.1013**

Made by the Secretary of State for Work and Pensions under s.6(4), (6) and (7) of the Children (Leaving Care) Act 2000

[In force April 1, 2004]

REGULATIONS REPRODUCED

2.   Entitlement to Benefits (Scotland)

Entitlement to Benefits (Scotland)

2.—(1) For the purposes of section 6(2)(c) of the Children (Leaving   **2.1014**
Care) Act 2000 (exclusion from benefits of persons of a prescribed description)—
  (a) a person of the description set out in paragraph (2) is hereby prescribed unless he is a person to whom paragraph (3)(b) applies; and

(b) a person of the description set out in paragraph (3) is hereby prescribed in relation only to entitlement to housing benefit.

(2) The description of person mentioned in paragraph (1)(a) is a person—

(a) who is less than 18 years of age,

(b) to whom a local authority in Scotland is obliged to provide advice, guidance and assistance in terms of section 29(1) of the Children (Scotland) Act 1995 (duty of local authorities to provide after-care to persons who at the time when they cease to be of school age or at any subsequent time were, but are no longer, looked after by a local authority),

(c) who ceased to be looked after on or after 1st April 2004 and since the age of 14 has been looked after and accommodated for a period of, or periods totaling, 13 weeks or more, and

(d) who either—
   (i) is not living with his family, or
   (ii) is living with his family and is provided with regular financial assistance in terms of that section.

(3) The description of person mentioned in paragraph (1)(b) is a person—

(a) who falls within the description set out in paragraph (2)(a) to (d), and

(b) who also falls within a category of person prescribed in—
   (i) provided the person is a lone parent, regulation 13(2)(a) (circumstances in which persons in relevant education may be entitled to income support) of;
   (ii) regulation 13(2)(b) of; or
   (iii) paragraph 1, 2, 7, 8, 10, 11, 12, 13, 24 or 25 of Schedule 1B (prescribed categories of person) to,
the Income Support (General) Regulations 1987 ("the Income Support Regulations").

(4) In this regulation—

(a) in calculating the period of, or periods, totaling 13 weeks referred to in paragraph (2)(c) no account shall be taken of any pre-planned series of short-term placements, of 4 weeks or less where the person returns to his family at the end of each such placement,

(b) "accommodated" means provided with accommodation by a local authority pursuant to its duties under section 25 of the Children (Scotland) Act 1995 or in compliance with a direction made in a supervision requirement under section 70(3) of that Act, but does not include circumstances where a person has been placed with his family either under arrangements made under section 26(1)(c) of that Act or in compliance with a direction made in a supervision requirement under that Act,

(c) "family" includes any person who has parental responsibility for another person who is less than 18 years of age and any person with whom that other person was living prior to being looked after by a local authority, but does not include a local authority,

(d) "lone parent" has the meaning assigned to it in regulation 2(1) of the Income Support Regulations,

(e) "looked after" has the meaning assigned to it in section 17(6) of the Children (Scotland) Act 1995.

GENERAL NOTE

See the note to the Children (Leaving Care) Act 2000 and the Children (Leaving Care) Social Security Benefits Regulations 2001. The effect of these regulations and s.6 of the 2000 Act is to remove entitlement to income support, income-based JSA and housing benefit for most 16/17 year-old Scottish care leavers with effect from April 1, 2004, thus bringing the rules in Scotland into line with those that already exist in England and Wales. Note that the new rules will only apply to 16/17 year-olds who stop being looked after by a Scottish local authority on or after April 1, 2004 (*i.e.* they do not apply to a 16/17 year-old who left Scottish local authority care before that date). The exceptions to the s.6 exclusion are the same that apply in England and Wales (see the note to the Children (Leaving Care) Social Security Benefits Regulations 2001 (again there is no exception to the exclusion from housing benefit).

Child Support (Maintenance Calculation Procedure) Regulations 2000

(SI 2001/157)

Made by the Secretary of State under various provisions of the Child Support Act 1991

REGULATIONS REPRODUCED

PART 1

GENERAL

PART VIII

REVOCATION, SAVINGS AND TRANSITIONAL PROVISIONS

GENERAL NOTE

2.1016   See the notes to ss.6 and 46 of the Child Support Act 1991 in Part I of this volume for when a reduced benefit decision may be made.

These regulations came into force on March 3, 2003 in relation to those cases to which the forms of ss.6 and 46 substituted by the Child Support, Pensions and Social Security Act 2000 apply from that date. See the note to s.6 as to the cases to which the new forms of ss.6 and 46 apply.

Reg.30(1) of these Regulations revokes the Child Support (Maintenance Assessment Procedure) Regulations 1992 with respect to those cases to which these Regulations apply. For the provisions of the Maintenance Assessment Procedure Regulations that relate to reduced benefit directions, see the 2002 edition of this volume.

Only the regulations necessary to understand how a reduced benefit decision operates are reproduced. There are no notes or definitions after each individual regulation. Most relevant definitions are in reg.8, although there also needs to be some reference to reg.1 and the Child Support Act 1991.

Once a reduced benefit decision is given, the Secretary of State must then apply the reduction in making any initial decision on a claim for income support or income-based JSA and supersede any existing award on a relevant change of circumstances.

2.1017   Regulation 11 specifies that the reduction is to be of a fixed amount for a fixed period. There is no discretion to alter either element whatever the circumstances. The reduction is by 40 per cent of the income support personal allowance for a single claimant aged not less than 25 and will last for three years (reg.11(2)).

From April 2005 the amount of the reduction is £22.48 per week. This amount is subject to reg.12, under which a reduction will be adjusted so as not to reduce the amount of income support or income-based JSA below 10p. A reduced benefit decision is suspended where income support or income-based JSA is payable under the special rules applying to hospital patients or persons in residential accommodation or residential care or nursing homes; if this applies for 52 weeks the reduced benefit decision will cease to be in force (regs. 14 and 15).

A reduced benefit decision will not be given if the parent's, or any partner's, income support or income-based JSA includes a disability, higher pensioner or disabled child premium (note that with effect from April 6, 2004 as a consequence of the removal of amounts for children from income support and income-based JSA the disabled child premium has been abolished, except in "transitional cases"—see the note to reg.17 of the Income Support Regulations; financial support for the cost of bringing up children and young persons is now to be provided through the child tax credit system), or the parent (or any partner) has an award of child tax credit that includes the element for a child/young person with a disability (reg.10).

A reduced benefit decision will be suspended if income support or income-based JSA cease to be payable (reg.13). The balance of the reduction period is applied if benefit becomes payable again within 52 weeks; otherwise the reduced benefit decision will cease to be in force after 52 weeks. The same applies if the sole qualifying child ceases to be a child within the meaning of the Child Support Act 1991 or if the parent stops being the person with care (reg.18). Under reg.16, a reduced benefit decision ceases to be in force if the parent withdraws her request for the Secretary of State not to act, provides the required information or submits to a DNA test, or the Secretary of State, having required the parent to restate her reasons, decides that there are reasonable grounds for her request for him not to act, or income support or income-based JSA cease to be payable for 52 weeks. A reduced benefit decision will also terminate if the decision to issue it is revised or superseded or in the case of a successful appeal.

Only one reduced benefit decision can be in operation at a time (reg.11(8)). However, if an additional qualifying child appears, a further reduced benefit decision can be made which replaces the original one (reg.17(1)).

PART I

GENERAL

Citation, commencement and interpretation

1.—(1) These Regulations may be cited as the Child Support (Maintenance Calculation Procedure) Regulations 2000.

    2.1018

(2) In these Regulations, unless the context otherwise requires—

"the Act" means the Child Support Act 1991;

"date of notification to the non-resident parent" means the date on which the non-resident parent is first given notice of a maintenance application;

[*definitions omitted as not relating to reduced benefit decisions*]

[*Paras (3) and (4) not reproduced*]

(5) These Regulations shall come into force in relation to a particular case on the day on which the amendments to sections 5, 6, 12, 46, 51, [¹ and 54] of the Act made by the Child Support, Pensions and Social Security Act 2000 come into force in relation to that type of case.

AMENDMENT

1. Child Support (Miscellaneous Amendments) Regulations 2002 (SI 2002/1204), reg.6(2) (April 30, 2002).

    2.1019

PART IV

REDUCED BENEFIT DECISIONS

Interpretation of Part IV

8.—(1) For the purposes of this Part—

"applicable amount" is to be construed in accordance with Part IV of the Income Support Regulations and regulations 83 to 86 of the Jobseeker's Allowance Regulations;

    2.1020

"benefit week", in relation to income support has the same meaning as in the Income Support Regulations, and in relation to jobseeker's allowance has the same meaning as in the Jobseeker's Allowance Regulations;

"Income Support Regulations" means the Income Support (General) Regulations 1987;

"Jobseeker's Allowance Regulations" means the Jobseeker's Allowance Regulations 1996;

"parent concerned" means the parent with respect to whom a reduced benefit decision is given;

"reduced benefit decision" has the same meaning as in section 46(10)(b) of the Act; and

"relevant benefit" has the same meaning as in section 46(10)(c) of the Act.

(2) In this Part references to a reduced benefit decision as being "in operation", "suspended" or "in force" shall be construed as follows—

    (a) a reduced benefit decision is "in operation" if, by virtue of that decision, relevant benefit is currently being reduced;

    (b) a reduced benefit decision is "suspended" if—

        (i) after that decision has been given, relevant benefit ceases to be payable, or [¹ the circumstances in regulation 14(4) or 15(4), as the case may be, apply;]

       (ii) at the time the reduced benefit decision is given, [¹ the circumstances in regulation 14(4) or 15(4), as the case may be, apply,] and these Regulations provide for relevant benefit payable from a later date to be reduced by virtue of the same reduced benefit decision; and

    (c) a reduced benefit decision is "in force" if it is either in operation or suspended and cognate terms shall be construed accordingly.

AMENDMENT

2.1021   1. Child Support (Miscellaneous Amendments) (No.2) Regulations 2003 (SI 2003/2779), reg.5(2) (November 5, 2003).

Period within which reasons are to be given

2.1022   **9.** The period specified for the purposes of section 46(2) of the Act (for the parent to supply her reasons) is 4 weeks from the date on which the Secretary of State serves notice under that subsection.

[¹ Period for parent to state if request still stands

2.1023   **9A.** The period to be specified for the purposes of section 46(6) of the Act (period for the parent to state if her request still stands) is 4 weeks from the date on which the Secretary of State serves notice under that subsection.]

AMENDMENT

2.1024   1. Child Support (Miscellaneous Amendments) Regulations 2002 (SI 2002/1204), reg.6(3) April 30, 2002).

Circumstances in which a reduced benefit decision shall not be given

10.— [² (i)] The Secretary of State shall not give a reduced benefit deci-   2.1025
sion where—
   (a) income support is paid to, or in respect of, the parent in question and
       the applicable amount of the claimant for income support includes
       one or more of the amounts set out in paragraph 15(3), (4) or (6) of
       Part IV of Schedule 2 to the Income Support Regulations; or
   (b) an income-based jobseeker's allowance is paid to, or in respect of, the
       parent in question and the applicable amount of the claimant for an
       income-based jobseeker's allowance includes one or more of the
       amounts set out in paragraph 20(4), (5) or (7) of Schedule 1 to the
       Jobseeker's Allowance Regulations [¹ or
   (c) an amount prescribed under section 9(5)(c) of the Tax Credits Act
       2002 (increased elements of child tax credit for children or young
       persons with a disability) is included in an award of child tax credit
       payable to the parent in question or a member of that parent's family
       living with him.]
[²(2) In paragraph (1)(c), "family" has the same meaning as in the
Maintenance Calculations and Special Cases Regulations.]

Amendments

1. Child Support (Miscellaneous Amendments) Regulations 2003 (SI 2003/ 328),   2.1026
reg.7(3) (April 6, 2003).
2. Child Support (Miscellaneous Amendments) Regulations 2005 (SI 2005/785,
reg.5 (March 16, 2005).

**Amount of and period of reduction of relevant benefit under a
reduced benefit decision**

11.—(1) The reduction in the amount payable by way of a relevant benefit   2.1027
to, or in respect of, the parent concerned and the period of such reduction
by virtue of a reduced benefit decision shall be determined in accordance
with paragraphs (2) to (8) below.
   (2) Subject to paragraph (6) and regulations 12, 13, 14, and 15, there
shall be a reduction for a period of 156 weeks from the day specified in the
reduced benefit decision under the provisions of section 46(8) of the Act in
respect of each such week equal to—

$$0.4 \times B$$

where B is an amount equal to the weekly amount in relation to the week in
question, specified in column (2) of paragraph 1(1) (e) of Schedule 2 to the
Income Support Regulations.
   (3) Subject to paragraph (4), a reduced benefit decision shall come into
operation on the first day of the second benefit week following the date of
the reduced benefit decision.
   (4) Subject to paragraph (5), where a reduced benefit decision ("the subsequent decision") is made on a day when a reduced benefit decision ("the
earlier decision") is in force in respect of the same parent, the subsequent
decision shall come into operation on the day immediately following the day
on which the earlier decision ceased to be in force.

(5) Where the relevant benefit is income support and the provisions of regulation 26(2) of the Social Security (Claims and Payments) Regulations 1987 (deferment of payment of different amount of income support) apply, a reduced benefit decision shall come into operation on such later date as may be determined by the Secretary of State in accordance with those provisions.

(6) Where the benefit payable is income support or an income-based jobseeker's allowance and there is a change in the benefit week whilst a reduced benefit decision is in operation, the period of the reduction specified in paragraph (2) shall be a period greater than 155 weeks but less than 156 weeks and ending on the last day of the last benefit week falling entirely within the period of 156 weeks specified in that paragraph.

(7) Where the weekly amount specified in column (2) of paragraph 1(1)(e) of Schedule 2 to the Income Support Regulations changes on a day when a reduced benefit decision is in operation, the amount of the reduction of income support or income-based jobseeker's allowance shall be changed from the first day of the first benefit week to commence for the parent concerned on or after the day that weekly amount changes.

(8) Only one reduced benefit decision in relation to a parent concerned shall be in force at any one time.

Modification of reduction under a reduced benefit decision to preserve minimum entitlement to relevant benefit

2.1028   **12.** Where in respect of any benefit week the amount of the relevant benefit that would be payable after it has been reduced following a reduced benefit decision would, but for this regulation, be nil or less than the minimum amount of that benefit that is payable as determined—

(a) in the case of income support, by regulation 26(4) of the Social Security (Claims and Payments) Regulations 1987;

(b) in the case of an income-based jobseeker's allowance, by regulation 87A of the Jobseeker's Allowance Regulations,

the amount of that reduction shall be decreased to such extent as to raise the amount of that benefit to the minimum amount that is payable.

Suspension of a reduced benefit decision when relevant benefit ceases to be payable

2.1029   **13.**—(1) Where relevant benefit ceases to be payable to, or in respect of, the parent concerned at a time when a reduced benefit decision is in operation, that reduced benefit decision shall, subject to paragraph (2), be suspended for a period of 52 weeks from the date the relevant benefit ceases to be payable.

(2) Where a reduced benefit decision has been suspended for a period of 52 weeks and no relevant benefit is payable at the end of that period, it shall cease to be in force.

(3) Where a reduced benefit decision is suspended and relevant benefit again becomes payable to, or in respect of, the parent concerned, the amount payable by way of that benefit shall, subject to regulations 14 and 15, be reduced in accordance with that reduced benefit decision for the balance of the reduction period.

(4) The amount or, as the case may be, the amounts of that reduction to be made during the balance of the reduction period shall be determined in accordance with regulation 11(2).

(5) No reduction in the amount of benefit under paragraph (3) shall be made before the expiry of a period of 14 days from service of the notice specified in paragraph (6), and the provisions of regulation 11(3) shall apply as to the date the reduced benefit decision again comes into operation.

(6) Where relevant benefit again becomes payable to, or in respect of, a parent with respect to whom a reduced benefit decision is suspended, she shall be notified in writing by the Secretary of State that the amount of relevant benefit paid to, or in respect of, her will again be reduced, in accordance with the provisions of paragraph (3), if she falls within section 46(1) of the Act.

Suspension of a reduced benefit decision [¹ . . .] (income support)

14.—(1) Where a reduced benefit decision is given or is in operation at a time when income support is payable to, or in respect of, the parent concerned [¹ but the circumstances in paragraph (4) apply to her], that decision shall be suspended for so long as [¹ those circumstances apply], or 52 weeks, whichever period is the shorter.   2.1030

(2) [¹ . . .]

(3) Where a case falls within paragraph (1) [¹ . . .] and a reduced benefit decision has been suspended for 52 weeks, it shall cease to be in force.

[¹ (4) The circumstances referred to in paragraph (1) are that—

(a) she is resident in a care home or an independent hospital;

(b) she is being provided with a care home service or an independent health care service; or

(c) her applicable amount falls to be calculated under regulation 21 of and any of paragraphs 1 to 3 of Schedule 7 to the Income Support Regulations (patients).

(5) In paragraph (4)—

"care home" has the meaning assigned to it by section 3 of the Care Standards Act 2000;

"care home service" has the meaning assigned to it by section 2(3) of the Regulation of Care (Scotland) Act 2001;

"independent health care service" has the meaning assigned to it by section 2(5)(a) and (b) of the Regulation of Care (Scotland) Act 2001; and

"independent hospital" has the meaning assigned to it by section 2 of the Care Standards Act 2000.]

AMENDMENT

1. Child Support (Miscellaneous Amendments) (No.2) Regulations 2003 (SI 2003/2779), reg.5(3) (November 5, 2003).   2.1031

Suspension of a reduced benefit decision [¹ . . .] (income-based jobseeker's allowance)

15.—(1) Where a reduced benefit decision is given or is in operation at a time when an income-based jobseeker's allowance is payable to, or in respect of, the parent concerned [¹ but the circumstances in paragraph (4) apply to her], that reduced benefit decision shall be suspended for so long as [¹ those circumstances apply], or 52 weeks, whichever is the shorter.   2.1032

(2) [¹ . . .]

(3) Where a case falls within paragraph (1) [¹ . . .] and a reduced benefit decision has been suspended for 52 weeks, it shall cease to be in force.

[¹ (4) The circumstances referred to in paragraph (1) are that—

(a) she is resident in a care home or an independent hospital;

(b) she is being provided with a care home service or an independent health care service; or

(c) her applicable amount falls to be calculated under regulation 85 of and paragraph 1 or 2 of Schedule 5 to the Jobseeker's Allowance Regulations (patients).

(5) In paragraph (4)—

"care home" has the meaning assigned to it by section 3 of the Care Standards Act 2000;

"care home service" has the meaning assigned to it by section 2(3) of the Regulation of Care (Scotland) Act 2001;

"independent health care service" has the meaning assigned to it by section 2(5)(a) and (b) of the Regulation of Care (Scotland) Act 2001; and

"independent hospital" has the meaning assigned to it by section 2 of the Care Standards Act 2000.]

AMENDMENT

2.1033   1. Child Support (Miscellaneous Amendments) (No.2) Regulations 2003 (SI 2003/2779), reg.5(4) (November 5, 2003).

Termination of a reduced benefit decision

2.1034   **16.** A reduced benefit decision shall cease to be in force—

(a) where the parent concerned—

   (i) withdraws her request under section 6(5) of the Act;

   (ii) complies with her obligation under section 6(7) of the Act; or

   (iii) consents to take a scientific test (within the meaning of section 27A of the Act);

(b) where following written notice under section 46(6)(b) of the Act, the parent concerned responds to such notice and the Secretary of State considers there are reasonable grounds;

(c) subject to regulation 13, where relevant benefit ceases to be payable to, or in respect of, the parent concerned; or

(d) where a qualifying child with respect to whom a reduced benefit decision is in force applies for a maintenance calculation to be made with respect to him under section 7 of the Act and a calculation is made in response to that application in respect of all the qualifying children in relation to whom the parent concerned falls within section 46(1) of the Act.

Reduced benefit decisions where there is an additional qualifying child

2.1035   **17.**—(1) Where a reduced benefit decision is in operation, or would be in operation but for the provisions of regulations 14 and 15, and the Secretary of State gives a further reduced benefit decision with respect to the same parent concerned in relation to an additional qualifying child of whom she is a parent with care, the earlier reduced benefit decision shall cease to be in force.

(2) Where a further reduced benefit decision comes into operation in a case falling within paragraph (1), the provisions of regulation 11 shall apply to it.

(3) Where—

(a) a reduced benefit decision ("the earlier decision") has ceased to be in force by virtue of regulation 13(2); and

(b) the Secretary of State gives a further reduced benefit decision ("the further decision") with respect to the same parent concerned where that parent falls within section 46(1) of the Act,

as long as the further decision remains in force, no additional reduced benefit decision shall be brought into force with respect to that parent in relation to one or more children to whom the earlier decision was given.

(4) Where a case falls within paragraph (1) or (3) and the further decision, but for the provisions of this paragraph, would cease to be in force by virtue of the provisions of regulation 16, but the earlier decision would not have ceased to be in force by virtue of the provisions of regulation 16, the further reduced benefit decision shall remain in force for a period calculated in accordance with regulation 11.

(5) In this regulation "additional qualifying child" means a qualifying child of whom the parent concerned is a parent with care and who was either not such a qualifying child at the time the earlier decision was given or had not been born at the time the earlier decision was given.

Suspension and termination of a reduced benefit decision where the sole qualifying child ceases to be a child or where the parent concerned ceases to be a person with care

18.—(1) Where a reduced benefit decision is in operation and—   2.1036

(a) there is, in relation to that decision, only one qualifying child, and that child ceases to be a child within the meaning of the Act; or

(b) the parent concerned ceases to be a person with care,

the decision shall be suspended from the last day of the benefit week during the course of which the child ceases to be a child within the meaning of the Act, or the parent concerned ceases to be a person with care, as the case may be.

(2) Where, under the provisions of paragraph (1), a decision has been suspended for a period of 52 weeks and no relevant benefit is payable at that time, it shall cease to be in force.

(3) If during the period specified in paragraph (2) the former child again becomes a child within the meaning of the Act or the parent concerned again becomes a person with care and relevant benefit is payable to, or in respect of, that parent, a reduction in the amount of that benefit shall be made in accordance with the provisions of paragraphs (3) to (6) of regulation 13.

Notice of termination of a reduced benefit decision

19. Where a reduced benefit decision ceases to be in force under the pro-   2.1037
visions of regulation 16, 17 or 18 the Secretary of State shall serve notice of this on the parent concerned and shall specify the date on which the reduced benefit decision ceases to be in force.

Rounding provisions

2.1038 **20.** Where any calculation made under this Part results in a fraction of a penny, that fraction shall be treated as a penny if it exceeds one half and shall otherwise be disregarded.

PART VIII

REVOCATION, SAVINGS AND TRANSITIONAL PROVISIONS

Transitional provision—effective dates and reduced benefit decisions

2.1039 **31.**—[*Paras (1) and (2) omitted as not relating to reduced benefit decisions*]

(3) Paragraphs (4) to (7) shall apply where, [¹ immediately before] the commencement date, section 6 of the former Act applied to the parent with care.

(4) [² Where the assessment effective date] is before the prescribed date and on or after the commencement date the parent with care notifies the Secretary of State that she is withdrawing her authorisation under subsection (1) of that section, these Regulations shall apply as if the notification were a request not to act under section 6(5) of the Act.

(5) Where a maintenance assessment was not made because section 6(2) of the former Act applied, these Regulations shall apply as if section 6(5) of the Act applied.

(6) Where a maintenance assessment was not made, section 6(2) of the former Act did not apply and a reduced benefit direction was given under section 46(5) of the former Act, these Regulations shall apply as if the reduced benefit direction were a reduced benefit decision made under section 46(5) of the Act, from the same date and with the same effect as the reduced benefit direction.

(7) Where a maintenance assessment was not made, the parent with care failed to comply with a requirement imposed on her under section 6(1) of the former Act and the Secretary of State was in the process of serving a notice or considering reasons given by the parent with care under section 46(2) or (3) of the former Act, these Regulations shall apply as if the Secretary of State was in the process of serving a notice or considering reasons under section 46(2) or (3) of the Act.

(8) For the purposes of this regulation—

(a) "2000 Act" means the Child Support, Pensions and Social Security Act 2000;

[² "absent parent" has the meaning given in section 3(2) of the former Act;]

[² "assessment effective date" means the effective date of the maintenance assessment under regulation 30 or 33(7) of the Assessment Procedure Regulations or regulation 3(5), (7) or (8) of the Maintenance Arrangements and Jurisdiction Regulations, whichever applied to the maintenance assessment in question or would have applied had the effective date not been determined under regulation 8C or 30A of the Assessment Procedure Regulations;]

"Assessment Procedure Regulations" means the Child Support (Maintenance Assessment Procedure) Regulations 1992;

"commencement date" means with respect to a particular case the date these Regulations come into force with respect to that type of case;

"former Act" means the Act before its amendment by the 2000 Act;

"Maintenance Arrangements and Jurisdiction Regulations" means the Child Support (Maintenance Arrangements and Jurisdiction) Regulations 1992;

"maintenance assessment" has the meaning given in the former Act; and

"prescribed date" means the date prescribed for the purposes of section 4(10)(a) of the Act; [² and

"relevant date" means the date which would be the assessment effective date of the application which is to be proceeded with in accordance with Schedule 3, if a maintenance assessment were to be made.]

(b) references in paragraphs (4) to (7) to sections 6(5), 46(5) and 46(2) and (3) of the Act mean those provisions as substituted by the 2000 Act; and

(c) in the application of the Assessment Procedure Regulations for the purposes of paragraph (4) where, on or after the prescribed date, no maintenance enquiry form, as defined in those Regulations, is given or sent to the absent parent, the Regulations shall be applied as if references in regulation 30—

  (i) to the date when the maintenance enquiry form was given or sent to the absent parent were to the date of notification to the non-resident parent;

  (ii) to the return by the absent parent of the maintenance enquiry form containing his name, address and written confirmation that he is the parent of the child or children in respect of whom the application was made were to the provision of this information by the non-resident parent; and

(d) in the application of the Maintenance Arrangements and Jurisdiction Regulations for the purposes of paragraph (4), where, on or after the prescribed date no maintenance enquiry form, as defined in the Assessment Procedure Regulations, is given or sent to the absent parent, regulation 3(8) shall be applied as if the reference to the date when the maintenance enquiry form was given or sent were a reference to the date of notification to the non-resident parent.

Amendments

1. Child Support (Miscellaneous Amendments) Regulations 2002 (SI 2002/ 1204), reg.6(8) (April 30, 2002).

2. Child Support (Miscellaneous Amendments) Regulations 2003 (SI 2003/ 328), reg.7(7)(b) and (c) (February 21, 2003).

2.1040

Child Support (Maintenance Calculations and Special Cases) Regulations 2000

(SI 2001/155)

Made by the Secretary of State under various provisions of the Child Support Act 1991

REGULATIONS REPRODUCED

PART II

2.1041   CALCULATION OF CHILD SUPPORT MAINTENANCE

4.   Flat rate.

GENERAL NOTE

See the note to s.43 of the Child Support Act 1991.

Flat rate

2.1042   **4.**—(1) The following benefits, pensions and allowances are prescribed for the purposes of paragraph 4(1)(b) of Schedule 1 to the Act—
    (a) under the Contributions and Benefits Act—
            (i)   bereavement allowance under section 39B;
            (ii) category A retirement pension under section 44;
            (iii) category B retirement pension under section 48C;
            (iv) category C and category D retirement pensions under section 78;
            (v)   incapacity benefit under section 30A;
            (vi) [¹ carer's allowance] under section 70;
            (vii) maternity allowance under section 35;
          (viii) severe disablement allowance under section 68;
            (ix) industrial injuries benefit under section 94;
            (x)   widowed mother's allowance under section 37;
            (xi) widowed parent's allowance under section 39A; and
            (xii) widow's pension under section 38;
    (b) contribution-based jobseeker's allowance under section 1 of the Jobseekers Act;
    (c) a social security benefit paid by a country other than the United Kingdom;
    (d) a training allowance (other than work-based training for young people or, in Scotland, Skillseekers training); [⁴ . . .]
    (e) a war disablement pension [³ . . .] within the meaning of section 150(2) of the Contributions and Benefits Act or a pension which is analogous to such a pension paid by the government of a country outside Great Britain [³ [⁴ . . .]
    (f) a war widow's pension or a war widower's pension] [⁴; and

(g) a payment under a scheme mentioned in section 1(2) of the Armed Forces (Pensions and Compensation) Act 2004 (compensation schemes for armed and reserve forces).]

(2) The benefits prescribed for the purposes of paragraph 4(1)(c) of Schedule 1 to the Act are—

(a) income support under section 124 of the Contributions and Benefits Act; and

(b) income-based jobseeker's allowance under section 1 of the Jobseekers Act [² and

(c) state pension credit.]

(3) Where the non-resident parent is liable to a pay a flat rate by virtue of paragraph 4(2) of Schedule 1 to the Act—

(a) if he has one partner, then the amount payable by the non-resident parent shall be half the flat rate; and

(b) if he has more than one partner, then the amount payable by the non-resident parent shall be the result of apportioning the flat rate equally among him and his partners.

AMENDMENTS

1. Social Security Amendment (Carer's Allowance) Regulations 2002 (SI 2002/2497), reg.3 and Sch.2 (April 1, 2003).

2.1043

2. State Pension Credit (Consequential, Transitional and Miscellaneous Provisions) Regulations 2002 (SI 2002/3019), reg.27(3) (October 6, 2003).

3. Child Support (Miscellaneous Amendments) (No.2) Regulations 2003 (SI 2003/2779), reg.6(3) (November 5, 2003).

4. Child Support (Miscellaneous Amendments) Regulations 2005 (SI 2005/785), reg.6(2) (March 16, 2005).

PART III

JOBSEEKER'S ALLOWANCE

Jobseeker's Allowance Regulations 1996

(SI 1996/207)

Made by the Secretary of State for Education and Employment and the Secretary of State for Social Security under various powers in the Jobseekers Act 1995, the Social Security Administration Act 1992 and the Social Security Contributions and Benefits Act 1992

ARRANGEMENT OF REGULATIONS

PART I

GENERAL

PART IA

JOINT-CLAIM COUPLES

PART II

JOBSEEKING

Chapter I

Interpretation

Chapter II

Availability for employment

Chapter III

Actively seeking employment

Chapter IV

Attendance, information and evidence

Chapter V

Jobseeker's agreement

PART III

OTHER CONDITIONS OF ENTITLEMENT

PART IV

YOUNG PERSONS

PART V

SANCTIONS

PART VI

MEMBERSHIP OF THE FAMILY

PART VII

AMOUNTS

PART VIII

INCOME AND CAPITAL

Chapter 1

General

Chapter II

Income

Chapter III

Employed earners

Chapter IV

Self-employed earners

Chapter IVA

Participants in the self-employment route

Chapter V

Other income

Chapter VI

Capital

Chapter VII

Liable relatives

Chapter VIII

Child support

Chapter IX

Full-time students

PART IX

HARDSHIP

PART IXA

HARDSHIP FOR JOINT-CLAIM COUPLES

SCHEDULES

PART I

GENERAL

Citation, commencement and interpretation

1.—(1) These Regulations may be cited as the Jobseeker's Allowance   **3.32**
Regulations 1996.

(2) These Regulations shall come into force on 7th October 1996.

(3) In these Regulations—

"the Act" means the Jobseekers Act 1995;

[[31] "adoption leave" means a period of absence from work on ordinary or additional adoption leave by virtue of section 75A or 75B of the Employment Rights Act 1996;]

[[38] "the Armed Forces and Reserve Forces Compensation Scheme" means the scheme established under section 1 (2) of the Armed Forces (Pensions and Compensation) Act 2004;]

"attendance allowance" means—

(a) an attendance allowance under section 64 of the Benefits Act;

(b) an increase of disablement pension under section 104 or 105 of the Benefits Act (increases where constant attendance needed and for exceptionally severe disablement);

(c) a payment under regulations made in accordance with section 111 of, and paragraph 7(2) of Schedule 8 to, the Benefits Act (payments for constant attendance in workmen's compensation cases);

(d) an increase in allowance which is payable in respect of constant attendance under section 111 of, and paragraph 4 of Schedule 8 to, the Benefits Act (industrial diseases benefit schemes);

(e) a payment by virtue of article 14, 15, 16, 43 or 44 of the Personal Injuries (Civilians) Scheme 1983 or any analogous payment;

(f) any payment based on the need for attendance which is paid as an addition to a war disablement pension;

"benefit week" means a period of 7 days ending on the day which corresponds with the day of the week specified in a notice given or sent to the claimant in accordance with regulation 23 (attendance) [³ requiring him to provide a signed declaration as referred to in regulation 24(6) or, in the case of a claimant who is not normally required to attend in person, on the day which corresponds with the day of the week specified by the Secretary of State in accordance with regulation 24(10) for the provision of a signed declaration,] except—

[⁴ (a) where—

    (i) the Secretary of State requires attendance otherwise than at regular two weekly intervals, or in the case of a claimant who is paid benefit in accordance with Part III, other than regulation 20A, of the Claims and Payments Regulations at the time he provides a signed declaration as referred to in regulation 24(6), the "benefit week" ends on such day as the Secretary of State may specify in a notice in writing given or sent to the claimant;

    (ii) in accordance with an award of income support that includes the relevant day, the "benefit week" ends on a Saturday, the "benefit week" shall end on a Saturday, or on such other day as the Secretary of State may specify in a notice in writing given or sent to the claimant; or

    (iii) in accordance with an award of unemployment benefit that includes the relevant day, the claimant is paid benefit in respect of a period of seven days ending on the weekday specified in a written notice given to him by the Secretary of State for the purpose of his claiming unemployment benefit, and that day is a Saturday, the "benefit week" shall end on a Saturday or on such other day as the Secretary of State may specify in a notice in writing given or sent to the claimant;]

[³ (aa) where the Secretary of State has set a day for payment of a jobseeker's allowance in respect of a claim, but no notice has yet been given or sent to the claimant in accordance with regulation 23, the "benefit week" means a period of 7 days ending on the day which has been set;]

  (b) for the purpose of calculating any payment of income in accordance with Part VIII, "benefit week" also means the period of 7 days ending on the day before the first day of the benefit week following the date of claim or, as the case may be, the last day on which a jobseeker's allowance is paid if it is in payment for [⁴ less than a week,

and in this definition "relevant day" has the meaning it has in the Jobseeker's Allowance (Transitional Provisions) Regulations 1995.] "board and lodging accommodation" means—

  (a) accommodation provided to a person or, if he is a member of a family, to him or any other member of his family, for a charge which is inclusive of the provision of that accommodation and at least some cooked or prepared meals which both are cooked or prepared (by a person other than the person to whom the accommodation is provided or a member of his family) and are consumed in that accommodation or associated premises; or

  (b) accommodation provided to a person in a hotel, guest house, lodging house or some similar establishment,

except accommodation provided by a close relative of his or of any other member of his family, or other than on a commercial basis;

[³² "child tax credit" means a child tax credit under section 8 of the Tax Credits Act 2002;]

[⁷"the Children Order" means the Children (Northern Ireland) Order 1995;]

"Claims and Payments Regulations" means the Social Security (Claims and Payments) Regulations 1987;

"close relative" means, except in Parts II [⁴ . . .] and V, a parent, parent-in-law, son, son-in-law, daughter, daughter-in-law, step parent, step-son, step-daughter, brother, sister, or the spouse of any of the preceding persons or, if that person is one of an unmarried couple, the other member of that couple;

"college of further education" means a college of further education within the meaning of Part I of the Further and Higher Education (Scotland) Act 1992;

"concessionary payment" means a payment made under arrangements made by the Secretary of State with the consent of the Treasury which is charged either to the National Insurance Fund or to a Departmental Expenditure Vote to which payments of benefit under the Act or the Benefits Act are charged;

"co-ownership scheme" means a scheme under which a dwelling is let by a housing association and the tenant, or his personal representative, will, under the terms of the tenancy agreement or of the agreement under which he became a member of the association, be entitled, on his ceasing to be a member and subject of any condition stated in either agreement, to a sum calculated by reference directly or indirectly to the value of the dwelling;

"couple" means a married or an unmarried couple;

"course of advanced education" means—

   (a) a course leading to a postgraduate degree or comparable qualification, a first degree or comparable qualification, a diploma of higher education or a higher national diploma; or

   (b) any other course which is of a standard above advanced GNVQ or equivalent, including a course which is of a standard above a general certificate of education (advanced level), [³⁶ a Scottish national qualification (higher or advanced higher)]

[¹⁶"course of study" means any course of study, whether or not it is a sandwich course and whether or not a grant is made for attending or undertaking it;]

"Crown tenant" means a person who occupies a dwelling under a tenancy or licence where the interest of the landlord belongs to Her Majesty in right of the Crown or to a government department or is held in trust for Her Majesty for the purposes of a government department, except (in the case of an interest belonging to Her Majesty in right of the Crown) where the interest is under the management of the Crown Estate Commissioners;

"date of claim" means the date on which the claimant makes, or is treated as making, a claim for a jobseeker's allowance for the purposes of regulation 6 of the Claims and Payments Regulations;

"disability living allowance" means a disability living allowance under section 71 of the Benefits Act;

[³² . . .]

"dwelling occupied as the home" means the dwelling together with any garage, garden and outbuildings, normally occupied by the claimant as his home including any premises not so occupied which it is impracticable or unreasonable to sell separately, in particular, in Scotland, any croft land on which the dwelling is situated;

"earnings" has the meaning specified, in the case of an employed earner, in regulation 98, or in the case of a self-employed earner, in regulation 100; [39 ....]

..........]

"the Eileen Trust" means the charitable trust of that name established on 29th March 1993 out of funds provided by the Secretary of State for the benefit of persons eligible for payment in accordance with its provisions;

"employment-related course" means a course the purpose of which is to assist persons to acquire or enhance skills required for employment, for seeking employment or for a particular occupation;

[12 "employment zone" means an area within Great Britain designated for the purposes of section 60 of the Welfare Reform and Pensions Act 1999 and an "employment zone programme" means a programme established for such an area or areas designed to assist claimants for a jobseeker's allowance to obtain sustainable employment;

"employment zone contractor" means a person who is undertaking the provision of facilities in respect of an employment zone programme on behalf of the Secretary of State for Education and Employment;]

[35 . . .]

[24 . . .]

"full-time course of advanced education" means a course of advanced education which is [16. . .]—

(a) [16. . .] a full-time course of study which is not funded in whole or in part by [24 the Learning and Skills Council for England or by the National Council for Education and Training for Wales] or a full-time course of study [1 . . .] which is not funded in whole or in part by the Secretary of State for Scotland at a college of further education [1 or a full-time course of study which is a course of higher education and is funded in whole or in part by the Secretary of State for Scotland;]

[24(b) a course of study which is funded in whole or in part by the Learning and Skills Council for England or by the National Council for Education and Training for Wales if it involves more than 16 guided hours per week for the student in question, according to the number of guided learning hours per week for that student set out—

    (i) in the case of a course funded by the Learning and Skills Council for England, in his learning agreement signed on behalf of the establishment which is funded by the Learning and Skills Council for England for the delivery of that course; or,

    (ii) in the case of a course funded by the National Council for Education and Training for Wales, in a document signed on behalf of the establishment which is funded by the National Council for Education and Training for Wales for the delivery of that course; or,]

(c) [16. . .] a course of study (not being higher education) which is funded in whole or in part by the Secretary of State for Scotland at a college of further education if it involves—

    (i)   more than 16 hours per week of classroom-based or workshop-based programmed learning under the direct guidance of teaching staff according to the number of hours set out in a document signed on behalf of the college; or

    (ii) 16 hours or less per week of classroom-based or workshop-based programmed learning under the direct guidance of teaching staff and it involves additional hours using structured learning packages supported by the teaching staff where the combined total of hours exceeds 21 per week, according to the number of hours set out in a document signed on behalf of the college;

"full-time student" means a person, other than a person in receipt of a training allowance, who is—

(a) aged less than 19 and undertaking a full-time course of advanced education or

(b) aged 19 or over but under pensionable age and—

    (i)   attending a full-time course of study which is not funded in whole or in part by [²⁴ the Learning and Skills Council for England or by the National Council for Education and Training for Wales] or a full-time course of study [¹ . . .] which is not funded in whole or in part by the Secretary of State for Scotland at a college of further education [¹ or a full-time course of study which is a course of higher education and is funded in whole or in part by the Secretary of State for Scotland;]

  [²⁴(ii) undertaking a course of study which is funded in whole or in part by the Learning and Skills Council for England or by the National Council for Education and Training for Wales if it involves more than 16 guided hours per week for the student in question, according to the number of guided learning hours per week for that student set out—

      (aa) in the case of a course funded by the Learning and Skills Council for England, in his learning agreement signed on behalf of the establishment which is funded by the Learning and Skills Council for England for the delivery of that course; or,

      (bb) in the case of a course funded by the National Council for Education and Training for Wales, in a document signed on behalf of the establishment which is funded by the National Council for Education and Training for Wales for the delivery of that course; or]

  (iii) undertaking a course of study (not being higher education) which is funded in whole or in part by the Secretary of State for Scotland at a college of further education if it involves—

      (aa) more than 16 hours per week of classroom-based or workshop-based programmed learning under the direct guidance of teaching staff according to the number of hours set out in a document signed on behalf of the college; or

      (bb) 16 hours or less per week of classroom or workshop based programmed learning under the direct guidance of teaching staff and it involves additional hours using structured learning packages supported by the teaching staff where the combined total of hours exceeds 21 per week, according to the number of hours set out in a document signed on behalf of the college;

"the Fund" means moneys made available from time to time by the Secretary of State for the benefit of persons eligible for payment in accordance with the provisions of a scheme established by him on 24th April 1992 or, in Scotland, on 10th April 1992;

[38 "a guaranteed income payment" means a payment made under article 14(1)(b) or article 21(1)(a) of the Armed Forces and Reserve Forces (Compensation Scheme) Order 2005;]

"higher education" means higher education within the meaning of Part II of the Further and Higher Education (Scotland) Act 1992;

"housing association" has the meaning assigned to it by section 1(1) of the Housing Associations Act 1985;

[5"housing benefit expenditure" means expenditure in respect of which housing benefit is payable as specified in regulation 10(1) of the Housing Benefit (General) Regulations 1987 but does not include any such expenditure in respect of which an amount is applicable under regulation 83(f) or 84(1)(g) (housing costs);]

[14 "Immigration and Asylum Act" means the Immigration and Asylum Act 1999;]

"Income Support Regulations" means the Income Support (General) Regulations 1987;

"the Independent Living (Extension) Fund" means the Trust of that name established by a deed dated 25th February 1993 and made between the Secretary of State for Social Security of the one part and Robin Glover Wendt and John Fletcher Shepherd of the other part;

"the Independent Living Fund" means the charitable trust established out of funds provided by the Secretary of State for the purpose of providing financial assistance to those persons incapacitated by or otherwise suffering from very severe disablement who are in need of such assistance to enable them to live independently;

"the Independent Living (1993) Fund" means the Trust of that name established by a deed dated 25th February 1993 and made between the Secretary of State for Social Security of the one part and Robin Glover Wendt and John Fletcher Shepherd of the other part;

"the Independent Living Funds" means the Independent Living Fund, the Independent Living (Extension) Fund and the Independent Living (1993) Fund;

[23"Intensive Activity Period for 50 plus" means the programme known by that name and provided in pursuance of arrangements made by or on behalf of the Secretary of State under section 2 of the Employment and Training Act 1973, being a programme lasting for up to 52 weeks for any one individual aged 50 years or over on the day that he first joined any such programme, and consisting for that individual of any one or more of the following elements, namely assistance in pursuing self-employed earner's employment, education and training, work experience, assistance with job search, motivation and skills training;]

"invalid carriage or other vehicle" means a vehicle propelled by a petrol engine or by electric power supplied for use on the road and to be controlled by the occupant;

"jobseeking period" means the period described in regulation 47 [⁸except where otherwise provided];

"last day of the course" has the meaning prescribed in regulation 130 for the purposes of the definition of "period of study" in this paragraph;

"liable relative" has the meaning prescribed in regulation 117;

"lone parent" means a person who has no partner and who is responsible for, and a member of the same household as, a child or young person;

"long tenancy" means a tenancy granted for a term of years certain exceeding twenty one years, whether or not the tenancy is, or may become, terminable before the end of that term by notice given by or to the tenant or by re-entry, forfeiture (or, in Scotland, irritancy) or otherwise and includes a lease for a term fixed by law under a grant with a covenant or obligation for perpetual renewal unless it is a lease by sub-demise from one which is not a long tenancy;

"lower rate" where it relates to rates of tax has the same meaning as in the Income and Corporation Taxes Act 1988 by virtue of section 832(1) of that Act;

"the Macfarlane (Special Payments) Trust" means the trust of that name, established on 29th January 1990 partly out of funds provided by the Secretary of State for the benefit of certain persons suffering from haemophilia;

"the Macfarlane (Special Payments) (No.2) Trust" means the trust of that name, established on 2nd May 1991 partly out of funds provided by the Secretary of State, for the benefit of certain persons suffering from haemophilia and other beneficiaries;

"the Macfarlane Trust" means the charitable trust, established partly out of funds provided by the Secretary of State to the Haemophilia Society, for the relief of poverty or distress among those suffering from haemophilia;

"making a claim" includes treated as making a claim;

"maternity leave" means a period during which a woman is absent from work because she is pregnant or has given birth to a child, and at the end of which she has a right to return to work either under the terms of her contract of employment or under Part III of the Employment Protection (Consolidation) Act 1978;

"mobility supplement" means any supplement under article 26A of the Naval, Military and Air Forces etc (Disablement and Death) Service Pensions Order 1983 including such a supplement by virtue of any other scheme or order or under article 25A of the Personal Injuries (Civilians) Scheme 1983;

"net earnings" means such earnings as are calculated in accordance with regulation 99;

"net profit" means such profit as is calculated in accordance with regulation 101;

[¹⁵ "the New Deal options" means the employment programmes specified in regulation 75(1)(a)(ii) and the training scheme specified in regulation 75(1)(b)(ii);]

"non-dependant" has the meaning prescribed in regulation 2;

"non-dependant deduction" means a deduction that is to be made under regulation 83(f) and paragraph 17 of Schedule 2;

"nursing home" means—

(a) premises which are a nursing home or mental nursing home within the meaning of the Registered Homes Act 1984 and which are either registered under Part II of that Act or exempt from registration under section 37 thereof (power to exempt Christian Science Homes); or

(b) any premises used or intended to be used for the reception of such persons or the provision of such nursing or services as is mentioned in any paragraph of subsection (1) of section 21 or section 22(1) of the Registered Homes Act 1984 (meaning of nursing home or mental nursing home) or, in Scotland, as are mentioned in section 10(2) ofthe Nursing Homes Registration (Scotland) Act 1938 (interpretation) and which are maintained or controlled by a body instituted by special Act of Parliament or incorporated by Royal Charter;

(c) in Scotland,

(i) premises which are a nursing home within the meaning of section 10 of the Nursing Homes Registration (Scotland) Act 1938 which are either registered under that Act or exempt from registration under section 6 or 7 thereof (general power to exempt homes and power to exempt Christian Science Homes); or

(ii) premises which are a private hospital within the meaning of section 12 of the Mental Health (Scotland) Act 1984 (private hospitals), and which are registered under that Act;

"occupational pension" means any pension or other periodical payment under an occupational pension scheme but does not include any discretionary payment out of a fund established for relieving hardship in particular cases;

"partner" means where a claimant—

(a) is a member of a married or an unmarried couple, the other member of that couple;

(b) is married polygamously to two or more members of his household, any such member;

[19but in so far as this definition applies to a member of a joint-claim couple, it shall only apply to such a member specified in regulation 3E(2)].

"part-time student" means a person who is attending or undertaking a course of study and who is not a full-time student;

[31 "paternity leave" means a period of absence from work on leave by virtue of section 80A or 80B of the Employment Rights Act 1996;]

"payment" includes a part of a payment;

"pay period" means the period in respect of which a claimant is, or expects to be, normally paid by his employer, being a week, a fortnight, four weeks, a month or other longer or shorter period as the case may be;

"period of study" except in Parts II, IV and V means—

(a) in the case of a course of study for one year or less, the period beginning with the start of the course and ending with the last day of the course;

(b) in the case of a course of study for more than one year, in the first or, as the case may be, any subsequent year of the course, other than the final year of the course, the period beginning with the start of the course or, as the case may be, that year's start and ending with either—

[17(i) the day before the start of the next year of the course in a case where the student's grant or loan is assessed at a rate appropriate to his studying throughout the year, or, if he does not have a grant or loan, where a loan would have been assessed at such a rate had he had one; or]

    (ii) in any other case the day before the start of the normal summer vacation appropriate to his course;

(c) in the final year of a course of study of more than one year, the period beginning with that year's start and ending with the last day of the course;

"policy of life insurance" means any instrument by which the payment of money is assured on death (except death by accident only) or the happening of any contingency dependent on human life, or any instrument evidencing a contract which is subject to payment of premiums for a term dependent on human life;

"polygamous marriage" means any marriage during the subsistence of which a party to it is married to more than one person and the ceremony of marriage took place under the law of a country which permits polygamy;

[25 . . .]

"qualifying person" means a person in respect of whom payment has been made from the Fund [37, the Eileen Trust or the Skipton Fund];

"relative" means close relative, grand-parent, grand-child, uncle, aunt, nephew or niece;

"relevant enactment" has the meaning prescribed in [2 regulation 78(9)(a)];

"remunerative work" has the meaning prescribed in regulation 51(1);

"residential accommodation" has the meaning prescribed in regulation 85(4);

[33 . . .]

"residential care home" means an establishment—

(a) which is required to be registered under Part I of the Registered Homes Act 1984 and is so registered, or is deemed to be registered under section 2(3) of the Registered Homes (Amendment) Act 1991 (which refers to the registration of small homes where the application for registration has not been determined); or

(b) run by the Abbeyfield Society including all bodies corporate or incorporate which are affiliated to that Society; or

(c) which provides residential accommodation with both board and personal care and is managed or provided by a body incorporated by Royal Charter or constituted by Act of Parliament other than a local social services authority; or

(d) in Scotland, which is a home registered under section 61 of the Social Work (Scotland) Act 1968 or is an establishment provided by a housing association registered with Scottish Homes established by the Housing (Scotland) Act 1988 which provides care equivalent to that given in residential accommodation provided under Part IV of the Social Work (Scotland) Act 1968; or

(e) which is exempt from registration under Part I of the Registered Homes Act 1984 pursuant to section 1(4)(a) of that Act (exemption from registration in respect of certain homes) because one or more of the residents are treated as relatives pursuant to section 19(4) of that Act;

and in paragraph (c) of this definition "personal care" means personal care for persons in need of personal care by reason of disablement, past or present dependence on alcohol or drugs, or past or present mental disorder

[[17] "sandwich course" has the meaning prescribed in regulation 5(2) of the [[28] Education (Student Support) Regulations 2002] or regulation 5(2) of the Education (Student Loans) (Scotland) Regulation 2000 or regulation 5(2) of the [[28] Education (Student Support) Regulations (Northern Ireland) 2001], as the case may be;]

"self-employed earner" has the meaning it has in Part I of the Benefits Act by virtue of section 2(1)(b) of that Act;

[[18] [30] [36] "self-employment route" means assistance in pursuing self-employed earner's employment whilst participating in—

(a) an employment zone programme; or

(b) a programme provided or other arrangements made pursuant to section 2 of the Employment and Training Act 1973 (functions of the Secretary of State) or section 2 of the Enterprise and New Towns (Scotland) Act 1990 (functions in relation to training for employment etc.);]

"single claimant" means a claimant who neither has a partner nor is a lone parent;

[[37] "the Skipton Fund" means the ex-gratia payment scheme administered by the Skipton Fund Limited, incorporated on 25th March 2004, for the benefit of certain persons suffering from hepatitis C and other persons eligible for payment in accordance with the scheme's provisions;]

[[11] "sports award" means an award made by one of the Sports Councils named in section 23(2) of the National Lottery etc. Act 1993 out of sums allocated to it for distribution under that section;]

[[13] "subsistence allowance" means an allowance which an employment zone contractor has agreed to pay to a person who is participating in an employment zone programme;]

"terminal date" in respect of a claimant means the terminal date in his case for the purposes of regulation 7 of the Child Benefit (General) Regulations 1976;

"training allowance" means an allowance (whether by way of periodical grants or otherwise) payable—

(a) out of public funds by a Government department or by or on behalf of the Secretary of State for Education and Employment, Scottish Enterprise or Highlands and Islands Enterprise [[21], the Learning and Skills Council for England or the National Assembly for Wales]; and

(b) to a person for his maintenance or in respect of a member of his family; and

(c) for the period, or part of the period, during which he is following a course of training or instruction provided by, or in pursuance of arrangements made with, that department or approved by that department in relation to him or so provided or approved by or on behalf of the Secretary of State for Education and Employment, Scottish Enterprise or Highlands and Islands Enterprise [[22] or the National Assembly for Wales],

but it does not include an allowance paid by any Government department to or in respect of a person by reason of the fact that he is following a course of full-time education, other than under arrangements made under section 2 of the Employment and Training Act 1973

[³ or section 2 of the Enterprise and New Towns (Scotland) Act 1990,] or is training as a teacher;

"voluntary organisation" means a body, other than a public or local authority, the activities of which are carried on otherwise than for profit;

"war disablement pension" means a pension payable to a person in respect of disablement—

   (a) under the Naval, Military and Air Forces Etc (Disablement and Death) Service Pensions Order 1983 and any order re-enacting the provisions of that order;

   (b) under the Personal Injuries (Civilians) Scheme 1983, and any subsequent scheme made under the Personal Injuries (Emergency Provisions) Act 1939;

   (c) under any scheme made under the Pensions (Navy, Army, Air Force and Mercantile Marine) Act 1939 or the Polish Resettlement Act 1947 applying the provisions of any such order as is referred to in paragraph (a);

   (d) under the order made under section 1(5) of the Ulster Defence Regiment Act 1969 concerning pensions and other grants in respect of disablement or death due to service in the Ulster Defence Regiment;

   (e) under the order in council of 19 December 1881, the Royal Warrant of 27 October 1884, or the order by His Majesty of 14 January 1922 (exceptional grants of pay, non-effective pay and allowances);

   (f) paid by the Overseas Development Administration and which is analogous to any of the pensions mentioned in the preceding paragraphs;

"war widow's pension" means a pension payable to a woman as a widow under any of the enactments mentioned in the definition of "war disablement pension" in respect of the death or disablement of any person;

[²⁶ "war widower's pension" means a pension payable to a man as a widower under any of the enactments mentioned in the definition of "war disablement pension" in respect of death or disablement of any person;]

"water charges" means—

   (a) as respects England and Wales, any water and sewerage charges under Chapter 1 of Part V of the Water Industry Act 1991;

   (b) as respects Scotland, any water and sewerage charges under Schedule 11 to the Local Government Finance Act 1992;

   in so far as such charges are in respect of the dwelling which a person occupies as his home;

"week" in [⁶ the definitions of "full-time course of advanced education" and of "full-time student" and] [³ Parts III, VI, VII, VIII, IX, X, XI, XII and XIII] means a period of 7 days;

[⁹"welfare to work beneficiary" means a person—

   (a) to whom regulation 13A(1) of the Social Security (Incapacity for Work) (General) Regulations 1995 applies; and

   (b) who again becomes incapable of work for the purposes of Part XIIA of the Contributions and Benefits Act 1992;]

[³² "working tax credit" means a working tax credit under section 10 of the Tax Credits Act 2002;]

[³² . . .]

"year of assessment" has the meaning prescribed in section 832(1) of the Income and Corporation Taxes Act 1988;

"young person" except in Part IV has the meaning prescribed in regulation 76.

[¹⁶ (3A) For the purposes of the definition of "full-time student" in paragraph (3) but subject to paragraph (3D), a person shall be regarded as attending or, as the case may be, undertaking a course of study or as being on a sandwich course—

(a) subject to paragraph (3B), in the case of a person attending or undertaking a part of a modular course which would be a full-time course of study, for a period beginning on the day on which that part of the course starts and ending—

  (i) on the last day on which he is registered with the educational establishment as attending or undertaking that part as a full-time course of study; or

  (ii) on such earlier date (if any) as he finally abandons the course or is dismissed from it;

(b) in any other case, throughout the period beginning on the date on which he starts attending or undertaking the course and ending on the last day of the course or on such earlier date (if any) as he finally abandons it or is dismissed from it.

(3B) For the purpose of sub-paragraph (a) of paragraph (3A), the period referred to in that sub-paragraph shall include—

(a) where a person has failed examinations or has failed to successfully complete a module relating to a period when he was attending or undertaking a part of the course as a full-time course of study, any period in respect of which he attends or undertakes the course for the purpose of retaking those examinations or that module;

(b) any period of vacation within the period specified in that paragraph or immediately following that period except where the person has registered with the educational establishment to attend or undertake the final module in the course and the vacation immediately follows the last day on which he is required to attend or undertake the course.

(3C) In paragraph (3A), "modular course" means a course of study which consists of two or more modules, the successful completion of a specified number of which is required before a person is considered by the educational establishment to have completed the course.

(3D) A full-time student shall not be regarded as undertaking a full-time course of advanced education or a full-time course of study for the period specified in paragraph (3E) if—

(a) at any time during an academic year, with the consent of the relevant educational establishment, he ceases to attend or undertake a course because he is—

  (i) engaged in caring for another person; or

  (ii) ill;

(b) he has subsequently ceased to be engaged in caring for that person or, as the case may be, he has subsequently recovered from that illness; and

(c) he is not eligible for a grant or a student loan (as defined in regulation 130) in respect of the period specified in paragraph (3E).

(3E) The period specified for the purposes of paragraph (3D) is the period, [[29], not exceeding one year,] beginning on the day on which he ceased to be engaged in caring for that other person or, as the case may be, the day on which he recovered from that illness and ending on the day before—

(a) the day on which he resumes attending or undertaking the course; or

[[29](b) the day from which the relevant educational establishment has agreed that he may resume attending or undertaking the course, whichever shall first occur.]

[[25] (3F) For the purposes of these Regulations, where a person's principal place of residence is a residential care home or a nursing home and he is temporarily absent from that home, he shall be regarded as continuing to reside in that home—

(a) where he is absent because he is a patient, for the first [[34] 52] weeks of any such period of absence and for this purpose—

(i) "patient" has the meaning it has in Schedule 5 by virtue of regulation 85; and

(ii) periods of absence separated by not more than 28 days shall be treated as a single period of absence equal in duration to all those periods; and

(b) for the first three weeks of any other period of absence.]

(4) In these Regulations, unless the context otherwise requires, a reference—

(a) to a numbered section is to the section of the Act bearing that number;

(b) to a numbered Part is to the Part of these Regulations bearing that number;

(c) to a numbered regulation or Schedule is to the regulation in or Schedule to these Regulations bearing that number;

(d) in a regulation or Schedule to a numbered paragraph is to the paragraph in that regulation or Schedule bearing that number;

(e) in a paragraph to a lettered or numbered sub-paragraph is to the sub-paragraph in that paragraph bearing that letter or number.

(5) Unless the context requires otherwise, any reference to the claim-ant's family or, as the case may be, to a member of his family, shall be construed for the purposes of these Regulations as if it included in relation to a polygamous marriage a reference to any partner and to any child or young person who is treated as the responsibility of the claimant or his partner, where that child or young person is a member of the claimant's household.

AMENDMENTS

1. Jobseeker's Allowance (Amendment) Regulations 1996 (SI 1996/1516), reg.2 (October 7, 1996). **3.33**

2. Jobseeker's Allowance (Amendment) Regulations 1996 (SI 1996/1516), reg.20 and Sch. (October 7, 1996).

3. Jobseeker's Allowance and Income Support (General) (Amendment) Regulations 1996 (SI 1996/1517), reg.2 (October 7, 1996).

4. Social Security and Child Support (Jobseeker's Allowance) (Miscellaneous Amendments) Regulations 1996 (SI 1996/2538), reg.2(2) (October 28, 1996).

5. Income-related Benefits and Jobseeker's Allowance (Miscellaneous Amendments) Regulations 1997 (SI 1997/65), reg.4(2) (April 7, 1997).

6. Social Security (Miscellaneous Amendments) Regulations 1997 (SI 1997/454), reg.2(2) (April 7, 1997).

7. Social Security (Miscellaneous Amendments) Regulations 1998 (SI 1998/563), reg.5(1) and (2)(f) (April 6, 1998).

8. Social Security Amendment (New Deal) Regulations 1998 (SI 1998/1274), reg.2 (June 1, 1998).

9. Social Security (Welfare to Work) Regulations 1998 (SI 1998/2231), reg.14(2) (October 5, 1998).

10. Social Security and Child Support (Tax Credits) Consequential Amendments Regulations 1999 (SI 1999/2566), reg.2(3) and Sch.2, Pt III (October 5, 1999).

11. Social Security Amendment (Sports Award) Regulations 1999 (SI 1999/2165), reg.2(1) and (2)(e) (August 23, 1999).

12. Social Security Amendment (Employment Zones) Regulations 2000 (SI 2000/724), reg.2(1) (April 3, 2000).

13. Social Security Amendment (Employment Zones) Regulations 2000 (SI 2000/724), reg.2(1) (April 3, 2000).

14. Social Security (Immigration and Asylum) Consequential Amendments Regulations 2000 (SI 2000/636), reg.4(2) (April 3, 2000).

15. Jobseeker's Allowance (Amendment) Regulations 2000, reg.2(2) (March 6, 2000).

16. Social Security Amendment (Students) Regulations 2000 (SI 2000/1981), reg.6(2) (July 31, 2000).

17. Social Security Amendment (Students and Income-related Benefits) Regulations 2000 (SI 2000/1922), reg.3(2) (August 28, 2000, or if the student's period of study begins between August 1 and 27, 2000, the first day of the period).

18. Social Security Amendment (Employment Zones) (No.2) Regulations 2000 (SI 2000/2910), reg.2(3) (November 27, 2000).

19. Jobseeker's Allowance (Joint Claims) Regulations 2000 (SI 2000/1978), reg.2(5) and Sch.2, para.(1) (March 19, 2001).

20. Social Security (Miscellaneous Amendments) (No.2) Regulations 2001 (SI 2001/652), reg.2(a) (March 26, 2001).

21. Social Security (Miscellaneous Amendments) (No.2) Regulations 2001 (SI 2001/652), reg.2(b)(i) (March 26, 2001).

22. Social Security (Miscellaneous Amendments) (No.2) Regulations 2001 (SI 2001/652), reg.2(b)(ii) (March 26, 2001).

23. Social Security Amendment (New Deal) Regulations 2001 (SI 2001/1029), reg.2 (April 9, 2001).

24. Jobseeker's Allowance (Amendment) Regulations 2001 (SI 2001/1434), reg.2(2)(a) (April 1, 2001).

25. Social Security Amendment (Residential Care and Nursing Homes) Regulations 2001 (SI 2001/3767), reg.2 and Sch., Pt II, para.1 (April 8, 2002).

26. Social Security (Miscellaneous Amendments) Regulations 2002 (SI 2002/841), reg.3 (April 8, 2002).

27. Income Support (General) and Jobseeker's Allowance Amendment Regulations 2002 (SI 2002/1411), reg.2 (June 17, 2002).

28. Social Security Amendment (Students and Income-related Benefits) Regulations 2002 (SI 2002/1589), reg.2(3) (August 1, 2002).

29. Social Security Amendment (Intercalating Students) Regulations 2002 (SI 2002/1763), reg.2 (August 1, 2002).

30. Social Security Amendment (Employment Programme) Regulations 2002 (SI 2002/2314), reg.2(2) (October 14, 2002).

31. Social Security (Paternity and Adoption) Amendment Regulations 2002 (SI 2002/2689), reg.3 (December 8, 2002).

32. Income-related Benefits and Jobseeker's Allowance (Working Tax Credit and Child Tax Credit) (Amendment) Regulations 2002 (SI 2002/2402), reg.3 and Sch.2, para.1 (April 6, 2003).

33. Social Security (Removal of Residential Allowance and Miscellaneous Amendments) Regulations 2003 (SI 2003/1121), reg.4 and Sch.2 para.1 (October 6, 2003).

34. Social Security (Hospital In-Patients and Miscellaneous Amendments) Regulations 2003 (SI 2003/1195), reg.6 (May 21, 2003).

35. Social Security (Miscellaneous Amendments) Regulations 2004 (SI 2004/565), reg.5(2) (April 1, 2004).

36. Social Security (Income-Related Benefits Self-Employment Route Amendment) Regulations 2004 (SI 2004/963), reg.2 (May 4, 2004).

37. Social Security (Miscellaneous Amendments) (No. 2) Regulations 2004 (SI 2004/1141), reg.2(a) (May 12, 2004).

38. Social Security (Miscellaneous Amendments) Regulations 2005 (SI 2005/574), reg.2 (April 4, 2005).

39. Social Security (Miscellaneous Amendments) Regulations 2005 (SI 2005/574), reg.6 (April 4, 2005).

DEFINITIONS

"Benefits Act"—see Jobseekers Act 1995, s.35(1).　　　　　　　　　　　3.34
"child"—*ibid.*
"claimant"—*ibid.*
"family"—*ibid.*
"married couple"—*ibid.*
"occupational pension scheme"—*ibid.*
"unmarried couple"—*ibid.*

GENERAL NOTE

See the notes to reg.2(1) of the Income Support Regulations for points on some　3.35
of these definitions, namely, "board and lodging accommodation", "close relative", "dwelling occupied as the home", "occupational pension", "self-employed earner", "self-employment route", "the Skipton fund", "training allowance", "welfare to work beneficiary" and "year of assessment". Otherwise, the significance of particular definitions is dealt with in the notes to the regulations in which they occur.

Note also the additional definitions in reg.3 and the definitions in reg.4 for the purposes of Pt II (jobseeking), Pt IV (young persons), Pt V (sanctions) and various sections of the Jobseekers Act.

On paras (3A) to (3E), see the note to reg.139.

Definition of non-dependant

2.—(1) In these Regulations, "non-dependant" means any person, except　3.36
a person to whom paragraph (2), (3) or (4) applies, who normally resides with the claimant or with whom the claimant normally resides.

(2) This paragraph applies to—

(a) any member of the claimant's family;

(b) a child or young person who is living with the claimant but who is not a member of his household by virtue of regulation 78 (circumstances in which a person is to be treated as being or not being a member of the household);

(c) a person who lives with the claimant in order to care for him or for the claimant's partner and who is engaged for that purpose by a charitable or voluntary organisation (other than a public or local authority) which makes a charge to the claimant or the claimant's partner for the care provided by that person;

(d) the partner of a person to whom sub-paragraph (c) applies.

(3) This paragraph applies to a person, other than a close relative of the claimant or the claimant's partner,—

(a) who is liable to make payments on a commercial basis to the claimant or the claimant's partner in respect of his occupation of the claimant's dwelling;

(b) to whom the claimant or the claimant's partner is liable to make payments on a commercial basis in respect of his occupation of that person's dwelling;

(c) who is a member of the household of a person to whom subparagraph (a) or (b) applies.

(4) Subject to paragraph (5), this paragraph applies to—

(a) a person who jointly occupies the claimant's dwelling and who is either—

(i) a co-owner of that dwelling with the claimant or the claimant's partner (whether or not there are other co-owners); or

(ii) jointly liable with the claimant or the claimant's partner to make payments to a landlord in respect of his occupation of that dwelling; or

(b) a partner of a person to whom sub-paragraph (a) applies.

(5) Where a person is a close relative of the claimant or the claimant's partner, paragraph (4) shall apply to him only if the claimant's, or the claimant's partner's, co-ownership, or joint liability to make payments to a landlord in respect of his occupation, of the dwelling arose either before 11th April 1988, or, if later, on or before the date upon which the claimant or the claimant's partner first occupied the dwelling in question.

(6) For the purposes of this regulation a person resides with another only if they share any accommodation except a bathroom, a lavatory or a communal area but not if each person is separately liable to make payments in respect of his occupation of the dwelling to the landlord.

(7) In this regulation "communal area" means any area (other than rooms) of common access (including halls and passageways) and rooms of common use in sheltered accommodation.

DEFINITIONS

3.37

"child"—see Jobseekers Act 1995, s.35(1).
"claimant"—*ibid.*
"close relative"—see reg.1(3).
"family"—see s.35(1).
"partner"—see reg.1(3).
"voluntary organisation"—*ibid.*

GENERAL NOTE

See the notes to reg.3 of the Income Support Regulations.

[¹Disapplication of section 1(1A) of the Administration Act

3.38

2A. Section 1(1A) of the Administration Act (requirement to state national insurance number) shall not apply—

(a) [² . . .]

(b) to any claim for jobseeker's allowance made or treated as made before 5th October 1998].

AMENDMENTS

1. Social Security (National Insurance Number Information: Exemption) Regulations 1997 (SI 1997/2676), reg.12 (December 1, 1997).
2. Social Security (Working Tax Credit and Child Tax Credit) (Consequential Amendments) Regulations 2003 (SI 2003/455), reg.3 and Sch.2, para.1 (April 6, 2004, except in "transitional cases" and see further the note to reg.83 and to reg.17 of the Income Support Regulations).

DEFINITIONS

"child"—see Jobseekers Act 1995, s.35(1).   **3.39**
"young person"—see reg.76.

GENERAL NOTE

See the notes to s.1(1A)–(1C) of the Administration Act and reg.2A of the Income Support Regulations. Note that in the case of jobseeker's allowance, unlike income support, the requirement to have, or apply for, a national insurance number as a condition of entitlement to benefit does not apply to any claim made or treated as made before October 5, 1998 (para.(b)).

Meanings of certain expressions used in the Jobseekers Act 1995

3. For the purposes of the Act and of these Regulations—   **3.40**
"employed earner" has the meaning it has in Part I of the Benefits Act by
    virtue of section 2(1)(a) of that Act;
[¹"employment", except as provided in regulations 4 and 75, includes any
    trade, business, profession, office or vocation;]
"pensionable age" has the meaning it has in Parts I to VI of the Benefits
    Act by virtue of section 122(1) of that Act.

AMENDMENT

1. Social Security Amendment (New Deal) Regulations 1997 (SI 1997/2863), reg.2 (January 5, 1998).

DEFINITION

"the Benefits Act"—see Jobseekers Act 1995, s.35(1).

GENERAL NOTE

"employed earner". See the note to reg.2(1) of the Income Support Regulations.   **3.41**
"employment". From January 5, 1998 this definition and the definition of "employment" in reg.4 have been amended as a consequence of the introduction of the "New Deal" for 18–24 year-olds. For a brief summary of the New Deal see the notes to reg.75. The amendments remove Pt V of these Regulations and s.19 of the Jobseekers Act 1995 from the list of provisions in reg.4 in which employment only refers to work as an employee and does not include self-employment (unless otherwise stated), employment for the purposes of Pt V and s.19 now being defined in reg.75. This provides that employment for the purposes of those provisions refers to work as an employee, *except* work in which a person is employed while on the Employment, Voluntary Sector or Environment Task Force options of the New Deal (reg.75(4)). But note that this does not apply to s.19(9) in which "employment" simply means employed earner's employment (reg.75(5)). These amendments are needed because people on the Employment option will, and on the Voluntary Sector and Environment Task

Force options may, be employees and thus would otherwise potentially be liable to sanctions of up to 26 weeks under s.19(6) of the Act for refusing or losing, etc. their place on the option. The intention is that the fixed term sanctions of two or four weeks will apply to all people taking part in the New Deal, regardless of whether they are employed or in receipt of an allowance. See further the notes to reg.69.

Note also the definition of employment in s.7(8) of the Act for the purposes of regs 18 to 22.

"*pensionable age*". Pensionable age is 65 for men and for women born after April 5, 1955, and 60 for women born before April 6, 1950 (Pensions Act, 1995, s.126 and Sch.4, Pt I). Women born between April 6, 1950 and April 5, 1955 will reach pensionable age at a date between their 60th and 65th birthday (the exact days are set out in Pt I of Sch.4 to the Pensions Act 1995).

[¹ PART IA

JOINT-CLAIM COUPLES

Prescribed description of a joint-claim couple for the purposes of section 1(4)

3.42   **3A.**—(1) For the purposes of section 1(4), a joint-claim couple shall include any joint-claim couple within the meaning given in section 1(4) of the Act where at least one member [² is aged 18 or over and] was born after [³ 28th October 1957], unless a member of the couple is treated as responsible for a child or young person under regulation 77(3), or the couple has care of a child or young person in one or more of the circumstances mentioned in regulation 78(4), or a child or young person is living with either member of the couple in the circumstances mentioned in regulation 78(8).

(2) In a case where a person would (but for these Regulations) be a member of more than one joint-claim couple, a joint-claim couple means the couple of which he is a member which that person nominates (or in default of such nomination, which the Secretary of State nominates), to the exclusion of any other couple of which he is a member.]

AMENDMENTS

3.43   1. Jobseeker's Allowance (Joint Claims) Regulations 2000 (SI 2000/1978), reg.2(2) (March 19, 2001).

2. Social Security Amendment (Joint Claims) Regulations 2001 (SI 2001/ 518), reg.2(2) (March 19, 2001).

3. Jobseeker's Allowance (Joint Claims) Amendment Regulations 2002 (SI 2002/1701), reg.2(a) (October 28, 2002).

GENERAL NOTE

3.44   The standard JSA picture has been one of a claimant claiming in his own right a contribution-based jobseeker's allowance and of a claimant claiming income-based jobseeker's allowance for himself, and any spouse and/or children, with consequent aggregation of needs and resources. From March 19, 2001, a new dimension was added: the requirement that a "joint-claim couple" make a joint claim for jobseeker's allowance (what in reality is a joint-claim income-based jobseeker's allowance) (s.1(2B)–(2D)). This aspect of the scheme goes beyond the familiar notion of aggregation of needs and resources (although "joint-claim jobseeker's allowance" embodies that too (see ss.3A, 4)) since that traditional model embodies the notion of one partner in a couple being dependent on the other, the latter being the claimant having to fulfil the conditions of entitlement. The "joint-claim couple" aspect goes further than this in that each partner is party to the claim and each must satisfy the conditions of entitlement in s.1(2)(a)–(c) and (e)–(i). In other words, each partner of a joint-claim couple must (i) be available for employment; (ii) have entered into a jobseeker's agreement; (iii) be actively seeking employment; (iv) not be engaged in remunerative work; (v) be capable of work; (vi) not be receiving relevant education; (vii) be under pensionable age; and (viii) be in Great Britain.

The "joint-claim" scheme has, legislatively speaking, required the adaptation of rules designed for a single claimant to deal instead with two people. Of particular note are the provisions for entitlement notwithstanding that one member of the couple does not meet the "labour market conditions" (see JSA Regulations, reg.3D) and the provision enabling one member of the couple to receive a reduced rate jobseeker's allowance where the other is caught by a fixed or discretionary period sanction in s.20A. This makes analogous provision for the application to members of a joint claim couple of the sanctions applicable to claimants under s.19, *e.g.* for non compliance with a jobseeker's direction [fixed period sanction] or for loss of employment through misconduct or for having voluntarily left employment without just cause [discretionary period sanctions].

A "joint-claim couple" is defined in s.1(4) as a married or unmarried couple, of a prescribed description, who are not members of any family that includes someone for whom one of the members of the couple is entitled to child benefit. JSA Regulations, reg.3A gives the prescribed description: initially where one of the members of the couple was born after March 19, 1976, but being 18 or over (reg.3A(1)). From October 28, 2002, subject to reg.3E(2)(l), it covers such a person born after October 28, 1957. Such a couple, however, will not be of a prescribed description if there is a child but no one is as yet entitled to child benefit, because there has been no claim or one has only just been made; if the couple has care of a child or young person as fosterers or with a view to adoption; or if a child or young person is living with the couple when he is away from home while at school (reg.3A(1)).

In short, the central idea of the "joint-claim scheme" is that certain childless   **3.45**
couples–young childless couples at least one of whom is (in the initial scheme under 25, later extended to under 45)—will have to make joint claims for income-based jobseeker's allowance. The change is aimed at preventing benefits dependency at a young age by ensuring that both partners are directly involved in the labour market, so that, for example, each will have to be available for and actively seeking work. Rather than one being the dependant of the other, both members of the couple will be claimants having equal rights and responsibilities.

Jobseekers Act 1995, s.1(4) defines "joint-claim couple" as a married or unmarried couple, of a prescribed description, who are not members of any family that includes someone for whom one of the members of the couple is entitled to child benefit. JSA Regs, reg.3A, as amended from October 28, 2002 gives the prescribed description: where one of the members of the couple was born after October 28, 1957, but being 18 or over. Subject to reg.3E(l), below, it thus now covers a member aged between 18–45. Initially coverage was for those aged between 18 and 25. Such a couple, however, will not be of a prescribed description if:

    (a) under reg.77(3), one of its members is treated as responsible for a child or young person (where no one is as yet entitled to child benefit, for example, because a claim has only just been made);

    (b) the couple has care of a child or young person in one or more of the circumstances mentioned in JSA Regs, reg.78(4) (where they are fosterers or the child has been placed with them for adoption);

    (c) a child or young person is living with the couple in the circumstances mentioned in JSA Regs, reg.78(8) (a child living with the couple when he is away from home while at school).

[¹ Entitlement of a former joint-claim couple to a jobseeker's allowance

3.46   **3B.**—(1) Where a joint-claim couple cease to be a joint-claim couple because they become, or are treated as, responsible for one or more children—

    a) any claim made by both members of that couple for a jobseeker's allowance may be treated as a claim for a jobseeker's allowance made by either member of that couple;

    (b) any award of a joint-claim jobseeker's allowance in respect of that couple may be terminated and may be replaced by a replacement award,

where the conditions specified in paragraph (2) have been complied with.

(2) The conditions specified in this paragraph are that a member of the couple—

    (a) provides such evidence as the Secretary of State may require confirming that the couple are responsible for one or more children; and

    (b) advises the Secretary of State as to which member of the couple is to be the claimant.

(3) The claim by a member of the couple for a jobseeker's allowance referred to in paragraph (1)(a) shall be treated as made on the date on which he and his partner were treated as having claimed a jobseeker's allowance as a joint-claim couple as determined in accordance with regulation 6 of the Claims and Payments Regulations.

(4) In this regulation, "replacement award" shall have the meaning ascribed to it by paragraph 9A of Schedule 1 to the Act.]

AMENDMENT

3.47   1. Jobseeker's Allowance (Joint Claims) Regulations 2000 (SI 2000/1978), reg.2(2) (March 19, 2001).

GENERAL NOTE

3.48   This regulation sets out what happens if a joint claim couple become responsible for a child (and therefore cease to be a joint claim couple—see the definition in reg.3A(1)). The existing joint claim can be treated as a claim by either member of the couple and the joint award of benefit is terminated and replaced by a "replacement award". If the couple wish this to happen, they must provide the Secretary of State with evidence that they have become responsible for a child and notify him as to which member of the couple is to be the claimant.

[¹ Entitlement of a new joint-claim couple to a jobseeker's allowance

3.49   **3C.**—(1) Paragraph (2) shall apply where a couple become a joint-claim couple because the child, or all the children, for which they were responsible have—

    (a) died;

    (b) ceased to be a child or children for whom they are responsible; or

    (c) reached the age of 16 and are no longer receiving full-time education for the purposes of section 142 of the Benefits Act.

(2) In a case to which this paragraph applies—

(a) any claim made by either member of that couple for a jobseeker's allowance may be treated as a claim made by both members of the couple;

(b) any award of an income-based jobseeker's allowance, or a replacement award, in respect of either member of that couple may be terminated and may be replaced by a new award in respect of the couple,

where the conditions specified in paragraph (3) have been complied with.

(3) The conditions specified in this paragraph are that the Secretary of State—

(a) has sufficient evidence to decide whether a new award should be made; and

(b) is informed as to which member of the couple is to be the nominated member for the purposes of section 3B.

(4) The claim by both members of the joint-claim couple for a jobseeker's allowance referred to in paragraph (2)(a) shall be treated as made on the date on which the claim by a member of that couple was treated as made in accordance with regulation 6 of the Claims and Payments Regulations.

(5) For the purposes of paragraphs 6 and 7 of Schedule 2 (housing costs), any award of an income-based jobseeker's allowance which related to the day before the day on which the relevant event specified in paragraph (1) occurred and any new award referred to in paragraph (2)(b) shall be treated as a continuous award of an income-based jobseeker's allowance.

(6) In this regulation, "new award" shall have the meaning ascribed to it by paragraph 9C of Schedule 1 to the Act.]

AMENDMENT

1. Jobseeker's Allowance (Joint Claims) Regulations 2000 (SI 2000/1978), reg.2(2) (March 19, 2001).   3.50

GENERAL NOTE

Reg.3C is the mirror image of reg.3B. The latter regulation sets out what happens when a couple become responsible for a child and therefore cease to be a joint claim couple whereas reg.3C sets out what happens when a couple becomes a joint claim couple because they are no longer responsible for a child. In the circumstances listed in para.(1), any claim by either member of the couple may be treated as a joint claim and any award in favour of either may be terminated and replaced with a joint award.   3.51

[¹ Further circumstances in which a joint-claim couple may be entitled to a joint-claim jobseeker's allowance

3D.—(1) Subject to paragraph (2), a joint-claim couple are entitled to a joint-claim jobseeker's allowance where—   3.52

(a) the members of that couple claim a jobseeker's allowance jointly;

(b) one member satisfies the conditions set out in section 1(2)(a) to (c) and (e) to (i); and

[² (c) the other member satisfies the condition in section 1(2)(e) and (h) but is not required to satisfy the other conditions in section 1(2B)(b) because, subject to paragraph (3), he is a person to whom any paragraph in Schedule A1 applies; and]

(d) the conditions set out in section 3A are satisfied in relation to the couple.

(2) A member of a joint-claim couple who falls within any paragraph in Schedule A1 for the purposes of this regulation for any day in a benefit week shall fall within that category for the whole of that week.

(3) Subject to paragraph (4), paragraph 2 of Schedule A1 (students) may only apply to a member of a joint-claim couple in respect of one claim for a jobseeker's allowance made jointly by that couple in respect of a jobseeking period applying to the other member of that couple.

(4) Notwithstanding paragraph (3), paragraph 2 of Schedule A1 may apply to a member of a joint-claim couple in respect of a further claim for a jobseeker's allowance made jointly by the couple where the couple's previous entitlement to a joint-claim jobseeker's allowance ceased because one member of the couple—

(a) was engaged in remunerative work;

(b) had been summoned to jury service; or

(c) was within a linked period as prescribed in regulation 48(2).]

AMENDMENTS

3.53   1. Jobseeker's Allowance (Joint Claims) Regulations 2000 (SI 2000/1978), reg.2(2) (March 19, 2001).

2. Social Security Amendment (Joint Claims) Regulations 2001 (SI 2001/ 518), reg.2(3) (March 19, 2001).

GENERAL NOTE

3.54   In the circumstances set out in reg.3D, a joint claim couple can be entitled to JSA even though only one of them satisfies the labour market conditions. This applies if one member is in Great Britain, under pensionable age, capable of, available for and actively seeking work, has a jobseekers agreement, and is neither in remunerative work nor receiving relevant education. The other member must be under pensionable age and not in remunerative work and must fall into one of the prescribed categories listed in Sch.A1, namely full-time students, carers, and those who are incapable of work, living in residential care or nursing homes, disabled workers, disabled or deaf students, blind, pregnant, over 60, a refugee, required to attend court, in training and, in certain cases, involved in a trade dispute.

Note that this regulation only dispenses the "failing" member from compliance with the labour market conditions. It is still necessary for the couple to make a joint claim and to meet the requirements of s.3A of the Jobseekers Act 1995.

[¹ Entitlement of a member of a joint-claim couple to a jobseeker's allowance without a claim being made jointly by the couple

3.55   **3E.**—(1) A member of a joint-claim couple is entitled to a jobseeker's allowance if, without making a claim jointly for that allowance with the other member of the couple—

(a) he satisfies the conditions set out in section 1(2) (a) to (c) and (e) to (i);

(b) he satisfies the conditions set out in section 3; and

(c) the other member of that couple fails to meet the conditions of entitlement set out in section 1(2B)(b) and is a person to whom paragraph (2) applies.

(2) This paragraph applies to a member of a joint-claim couple—

(a) who has failed to attend at the time and place specified by the employment officer for the purposes of regulation 6 of the Claims and Payments Regulations;

(b) in respect of whom it has been determined by the Secretary of State that the conditions in section 1(2)(a) to (c) have not been satisfied but only for so long as it has been so determined in respect of that member;

(c) who is temporarily absent from Great Britain;

(d) who is a person from abroad as defined for the purposes of regulation 85 and Schedule 5;

(e) who is subject to immigration control within the meaning of section 115(9) of the Immigration and Asylum Act;

(f) who is over pensionable age;

(g) who is engaged, or has agreed to be engaged, in remunerative work for [² 16 hours or more] per week but less than 24 hours per week;

(h) who has claimed a maternity allowance payable in accordance with section 35 of the Benefits Act or who has claimed statutory maternity pay payable in accordance with Part XII of that Act;

(i) who is or has been pregnant and to whom sub-paragraph (h) does not apply but only for the period commencing 11 weeks before the expected week of confinement and ending seven weeks after the date on which the pregnancy ends [⁴ where the expected week of confinement begins prior to 6th April 2003 or fifteen weeks after the date on which her pregnancy ends where the expected week of confinement begins on or after 6th April 2003];

(j) in respect of whom there is an Order in Council under section 179 of the Administration Act giving effect to a reciprocal agreement which, for the purposes of jobseeker's allowance, has effect as if a payment made by another country is to be treated as a payment of a jobseeker's allowance; [³ . . .]

(k) who is in receipt of statutory sick pay and who, immediately before he became incapable of work, was engaged in remunerative work for 16 hours or more per week; [³ or

(l) where the other member was entitled to an income-based jobseeker's allowance on 27th October 2002, save that this sub-paragraph shall apply only until the day on which he is required to attend at a place specified by an employment officer in a notification given or sent to him.]]

AMENDMENTS

1. Jobseeker's Allowance (Joint Claims) Regulations 2000 (SI 2000/1978), reg.2(2) (March 19, 2001).

2. Social Security Amendment (Joint Claims) Regulations 2001 (SI 2001/518), reg.2(4) (March 19, 2001).

3. Jobseeker's Allowance (Joint Claims) Amendment Regulations 2002 (SI 2002/1701), reg.2(b) (October 28, 2002).

4. Social Security (Paternity and Adoption) Amendment Regulations 2002 (SI 2002/2689), reg.3(3) (November 24, 2002).

3.56

GENERAL NOTE

In the circumstances set out in reg.3E, one member of a joint claim couple can make a standard claim for JSA (*i.e.* not jointly with the other member) as long as s/he meets the labour market conditions and the conditions in s.3 of the Jobseekers Act 1995. The circumstances in which this is possible are listed in para.(2) and are self-explanatory.

3.57

[¹ Transitional case couples: prescribed circumstances and period for the purposes of paragraph 8A(2) of Schedule 1

3.58   **3F.** A transitional case couple shall be entitled to a joint-claim jobseeker's allowance without having made a claim for it jointly for the period beginning on the day on which section 59 of, and Schedule 7 to, the Welfare Reform and Pensions Act 1999 comes into force and ending on the day on which the member of the transitional case couple who was not entitled to an income-based jobseeker's allowance on the coming into force of that Schedule is required to attend at a place specified by an employment officer in a notification given or sent to that member.]

AMENDMENT

    1. Jobseeker's Allowance (Joint Claims) Regulations 2000 (SI 2000/1978), reg.2(2) (March 19, 2001).

GENERAL NOTE.

3.59   Couples where one member was entitled to JSA on March 19, 2001 continue to be entitled until the member who was not entitled is summoned for interview at the Job Centre.

[¹ Supply of information

3.60   **3G.** Where a claim for a jobseeker's allowance has been made jointly by a joint-claim couple, information relating to that claim may be supplied by the Secretary of State to either or both members of that couple for any purpose connected with that claim.]

AMENDMENT

    1. Jobseeker's Allowance (Joint Claims) Regulations 2000 (SI 2000/1978), reg.2(2) (March 19, 2001).

GENERAL NOTE

3.61   This regulation is self-explanatory. Normally information provided in connection with a claim is confidential to the claimant. With a joint claim, the Secretary of State may discuss the claim with either or both claimants.

PART II

JOBSEEKING

Chapter I

Interpretation

Interpretation of Parts II, IV and V

3.62   **4.**—In Parts II, IV and V and, as provided below, the Act—
    "appropriate office" means the office of the Department for Education and Employment which the claimant is required to attend in accordance

with a notice under regulation 23, or any other place which he is so required to attend;

"caring responsibilities" means responsibility for caring for a child or for an elderly person or for a person whose physical or mental condition requires him to be cared for, who is either in the same household or a close relative;

"casual employment" means employment from which the employee can be released without his giving any notice [³except where otherwise provided];

"close relative" means [¹, except in Part IV,] a spouse or other member of an unmarried couple, parent, step-parent, grandparent, parent-in-law, son, step-son, son-in-law, daughter, step-daughter, daughter-in-law, brother, sister, grandchild or the spouse of any of the preceding persons or, if that person is one of an unmarried couple, the other member of that couple;

"elderly person" means a person of over pensionable age;

"employment" in sections 1, 3, 6, 8, 14 [² . . .] and 20 and paragraph 8 of Schedule 1 to the Act and in [²Parts II and IV] means employed earner's employment except where otherwise provided;

"employment officer" means a person who is an employment officer for the purposes of sections 9 and 10;

[³"examination" in relation to a qualifying course means an examination which is specified as an examination related to the qualifying course in a document signed on behalf of the establishment at which the qualifying course is being undertaken;

"made a claim for a jobseeker's allowance" includes treated as having made a claim for the allowance and treated as having an award of the allowance in accordance with regulation 5, 6 or 7 of the Jobseeker's Allowance (Transitional Provisions) Regulations 1996;]

"Outward Bound course" means any course or programme for personal development which is made available to persons who are not in employment by the charitable trust known as the Outward Bound Trust Limited;

"part-time member of a fire brigade" means a person who is a part-time member of a fire brigade maintained in pursuance of the Fire Services Acts 1947–1959;

"pattern of availability" has the meaning given in regulation 7;

[⁴ "period of study" means—
  (a) the period during which the student is regarded as attending or undertaking the course of study; and
  (b) any period of attendance by the student at his educational establishment or any period of study undertaken by the student, in connection with the course, which occurs before or after the period during which he is to be regarded as undertaking the course of study;]

"a person who is kept on short-time" means a person whose hours of employment have been reduced owing to temporary adverse industrial conditions;

"a person who is laid off " means a person whose employment has been suspended owing to temporary adverse industrial conditions;

[³"qualifying course" has the meaning given in regulation 17A;

"term-time" in relation to a qualifying course means the period specified as term-time in relation to a person to whom regulation 17A(2) applies in a document signed on behalf of the establishment at which the qualifying course is being undertaken;

"vacation" in relation to a qualifying course means any period falling within the period of study, which is not term-time;]

"voluntary work" means work for an organisation the activities of which are carried on otherwise than for profit, or work other than for a member of the claimant's family, where no payment is received by the claimant or the only payment due to be made to him by virtue of being so engaged is a payment in respect of any expenses reasonably incurred by him in the course of being so engaged;

"week" in sections 6 and 7 and in Parts II and IV means benefit week except where provided otherwise in Parts II and IV;

"work camp" means any place in Great Britain where people come together under the auspices of a charity, a local authority or a voluntary organisation to provide a service of benefit to the community or the environment.

AMENDMENTS

3.63   1. Social Security and Child Support (Jobseeker's Allowance) (Miscellaneous Amendments) Regulations 1996 (SI 1996/2538), reg.2(3) (October 28, 1996).

2. Social Security Amendment (New Deal) Regulations 1997 (SI 1997/2863), reg.3 (January 5, 1998).

3. Social Security Amendment (New Deal) Regulations 1998 (SI 1998/1274), reg.3 (June 1, 1998).

4. Social Security Amendment (Students) Regulations 2000 (SI 2000/1981), reg.6(3) (July 31, 2000).

DEFINITIONS

3.64   "benefit week"—see reg.1(3).
"child"—see Jobseekers Act 1995, s.35(1).
"couple"—see reg.1(3).
"course of study"—*ibid.*
"payment"—*ibid.*
"pensionable age"—see reg.3.
"voluntary organisation"—see reg.1(3).

GENERAL NOTE

3.65   "*close relative*". See the note to reg.2(1) of the Income Support Regulations.
"*employment*". See the note to the definition of "employment" in reg.3.
"*period of study*". See *R(JSA) 2/02.*

Chapter II

Availability for employment

Exceptions to requirement to be available immediately: carers, voluntary workers, persons providing a service and persons under an obligation to provide notice

3.66   **5.**—[¹ (1) In order to be regarded as available for employment—
(a) a person who has caring responsibilities is not required to be able to take up employment immediately, providing he is willing

and able to take up employment on being given 48 hours' notice; and

(b) a person who is engaged in voluntary work is not required to be able to take up employment immediately, providing he is willing and able—

    (i) to take up employment on being given one week's notice; and

    (ii) to attend for interview in connection with the opportunity of any such employment on being given 48 hours' notice.]

(2) In order to be regarded as available for employment, a person who is engaged, whether by contract or otherwise, in providing a service with or without remuneration, other than a person who has caring responsibilities or who is engaged in voluntary work, is not required to be able to take up employment immediately, providing he is willing and able to take up employment on being given 24 hours' notice.

(3) In order to be regarded as available for employment, a person who is in employed earner's employment and is not engaged in remunerative work and who is required by section 49 of the Employment Protection (Consolidation) Act 1978 to give notice to terminate his contract is not required to be able to take up employment immediately, providing he is willing and able to take up employment immediately he is able to do so in accordance with his statutory obligations.

(4) Where in accordance with regulation 7, 13 or 17 a person is only available for employment at certain times, he is not required to be able to take up employment at a time at which he is not available, but he must be willing and able to take up employment immediately he is available.

(5) Where in accordance with paragraph (1) or (2) a person is not required to be able to take up employment immediately, the [¹ one week,] 48 hour and 24 hour periods referred to in those paragraphs include periods when in accordance with regulation 7 or 13 he is not available.

[¹ (6) In this regulation "week" means any period of seven consecutive days.]

AMENDMENT

1. Jobseeker's Allowance (Amendment) Regulations 2002 (SI 2002/3072), reg.3   **3.67**
(January 1, 2003).

DEFINITIONS

"caring responsibilities": see reg.4.
"employment": *ibid.*
"remunerative work": see regs 1(3) and 51(1).
"voluntary work": *ibid.*
"week": see para.(6).

GENERAL NOTE

The general rule on availability set out in s.6(1) of the Jobseekers Act 1995,   **3.68**
requires that a claimant be willing and able to take up *immediately* any employed earner's employment (on which see s.6(9) of that Act and SSCBA 1992, ss.2(1) and 122(1)). This regulation provides qualifications of and exceptions to that general rule.

Paragraph (4) qualifies the "immediately" condition by requiring that it be related to the claimant's "pattern of availability" (the times at which he is available to take up employment) permitted by regs 7 (enabling restriction of hours to 40 or more), 13 (enabling carers to restrict hours of availability to between 16 and 40 hours to suit caring responsibilities, and the sick/disabled to restrict times and/or hours of availability so far as reasonable in light of physical or mental condition) and 17 (treating as available persons laid off from employment or put on short-time). Paragraph (4) stipulates that a claimant, available only at certain times in accordance with any of those provisions, is not required to be able to take up employment during one of his permitted periods of nonavailability, but must be willing and able to take up employment immediately in one of his spells of availability. In addition, paras (1)–(3) give varying periods of grace within which one must be willing and able to take up employment, to carers, voluntary workers, to other service-providers, and to persons employed for less than 16 hours per week and under a specific statutory obligation to provide notice.

Carers (paras (1), (5))

3.69   A carer (someone "who has caring responsibilities", defined below) is exempt from the requirement to be immediately available, provided that he is willing and able to take up employed earner's employment on being given 48 hours' notice. In *CIS 142/1993* the Commissioner decided that the same phrase (except that the required notice was only 24 hours) in reg.12(1) of the Unemployment, Sickness and Invalidity Benefit Regulations 1983 mean that the notice should only start to run when the claimant would receive notification of the job (in that case by a telephone call from his parents in the evening as he was doing voluntary work during the day). See also para.21236 of the *Decision Makers Guide*. Paragraph (5) makes clear that the 48-hour notice period includes periods of non-availability in accordance with reg.7 or 13. Regulation 7 enables restriction of hours to 40 or more in an pattern of employment agreed with the Employment Service. Under reg.13, so long as he has reasonable prospects of employment despite the restriction, a carer can restrict availability to such hours between 16 and 40 hours per week as his caring responsibilities allow, and for the specific hours those responsibilities allow (reg.13(4), (5), and 8). Regulation 13 also permits anyone to restrict his times and/or hours of availability so far as reasonable in light of his physical or mental condition (reg.13(3)).

A carer (a person "who has caring responsibilities") is someone who has responsibility for a child or for an elderly person or for a person whose physical or mental condition requires him to be cared for. But the child, the elderly person and the person whose condition requires him to be cared for must either be a close relative or in the same household (reg.4). "Close relative" means a spouse or other member of an unmarried couple, parent, step-parent, grandparent, parent-in-law, son, step-son, son-in-law, daughter, step-daughter, daughter-in-law, brother, sister, grandchild or the spouse of any of these persons or, if that person is one of an unmarried couple, the other member of that couple (*ibid.*). On "unmarried couple" see Jobseekers Act 1995, s.35(1) and the note thereto.

Voluntary workers (paras (1), (5))

3.70   A voluntary worker ("a person who is engaged . . . in voluntary work", defined below) is exempt from the requirement to be immediately available, provided that he is willing and able to take up employed earner's employment on being given one week's notice, and to attend for interview in connection with the opportunity of any such employment on being given 48 hours' notice. The "one week" and 48-hour periods include periods when in accordance with reg.7 or 13 he is not available (para.(5)).

"Voluntary work" covers work for an organisation, the activities of which are carried on otherwise than for profit, or work other than for a member of the claimant's family, where no payment is received by the claimant or the only payment due to be made to him by virtue of being so engaged is one in respect of any expenses reasonably incurred by him in the course of being engaged in the work (reg.4). On "family", see Jobseekers Act 1995, s.35(1) and regs 76–78.

Others providing a service (paras (2), (4))

These paragraphs cover those engaged in providing a service, other than carers or   **3.71**
voluntary workers, who are, in any event, more generously treated under para.(1),
examined above. It matters not whether the service is provided by contract or not.
Nor is it material whether the service is or is not remunerated. Those engaged in providing a service do not have to be available immediately. It suffices that they are available on being given 24 hours' notice. That 24-hour period includes periods when,
in accordance with regs 7 or 13, the service-provider is not available (para.(5)).

The provision is similar to, but wider than, its predecessor (USI Regs, reg.12(1)),
which was interpreted in *CU/96/1994*. There Commissioner Skinner considered the
phrase "providing a service with or without remuneration" found both in USI Regs,
reg.12(1) and the JSA provision now under consideration. In *CU/96/1994*,
Commissioner Skinner considered the meaning of the phrase in an appeal by a
claimant who had been found not to be available for work because he was not in a
position to accept a job offer at once, but would require 24 hours' notice in order to
make arrangements for his wife and two teenage children to be able to make their
way to college and school and return from there to home. In setting aside the tribunal decision as erroneous in law, Commissioner Skinner opined that the phrase is
"a wide one", capable of embracing the necessary help given to member's of one's
own family: "The service provided does not have to be for the public, it does not
have to arise under a contract of employment" (para.5). The contrast between the
wording of paras (1) and (1A) (service as a volunteer) (the same contrast as between
paras (1) and (2) of this regulation) reinforced his view, as did the *Shorter Oxford
English Dictionary* definition of "service" as "the action of serving, helping or benefiting: conduct tending to the welfare or advantage of another: an act of helping or
benefiting". That was the sense in which the word was used in para.(1) of the regulation:

> "So consequently if the claimant does an act which helps or benefits a member of
> his family or does something which tends to their welfare or advantage, he can be
> said to be rendering a service. However it must be necessary service not some fan-
> ciful help. No doubt many unemployed peoplemay be able to satisfy that criteria"
> (para.5).

But the claimant taking his children to school could not be a "service" in the sense
of the regulation; it was merely an exercise of parental responsibility, fulfilling a
parental duty rather than rendering a service to his children. Transporting his wife
to and from her nursing course, however, was in law capable of amounting to a
"service":

> "It was something done for the wife's benefit and it does not seem that the
> claimant had any duty or responsibility so to transport her. No doubt it was a
> worthwhile and kindly thing to do, but he did not have to do it, and I accept that
> he could in law provide a service" (para.7).

Commissioner Skinner thought the real restriction on the operation of USI Regs,
reg.12(1) to be the requirement therein that the circumstances be such that it would
not be reasonable to expect the claimant to be ready for suitable employment on less
than 24 hours' notice. That restriction is not embodied in the JSA provision now
under consideration.

Those working less than 16 hours per week and under an obligation to provide notice
(para.(3))

This provision covers claimants, employed in employed earner's employment,   **3.72**
who are not "engaged in remunerative work" and so not precluded from JSA. In
short, it embraces those working but for less than 16 hours a week, who are statutorily obliged to give notice (*i.e.* those continuously employed for one month or
more) ("section 49 of the Employment Protection (Consolidation) Act 1978"
requires a minimum of one week's notice). Such a person is not required to be

available to take up employment immediately, provided he is willing to and can do so immediately his statutory obligations permit. Should that occur during a permitted spell of non-availability under reg.7 or 13, he will not be ruled out by the "immediately" requirement, so long as he is willing and able to take up employment immediately that spell of non-availability ends (para.(4)).

The effect of para.(5)

3.73   In calculating the expiry of the 48-hour period allowed to carers and voluntary workers and also the 24-hour period allowed to other service providers (the groups embraced by paras (1) and (2)), there must be included any period of permitted non-availability under reg.7 or 13. See further the notes on those groups.

Employment of at least 40 hours per week

3.74   **6.**—(1) In order to be regarded as available for employment, a person must be willing and able to take up employment of at least 40 hours per week, unless he has restricted his availability in accordance with paragraph (3) or (4) of regulation 13 or paragraph (2) of regulation 17 or two or more of those provisions.

(2) In order to be regarded as available for employment, a person must be willing and able to take up employment of less than 40 hours per week but not for a greater number of hours per week than the number for which he is available in accordance with paragraph (3) or (4) of regulation 13 or paragraph (2) of regulation 17 or two or more of those provisions.

DEFINITIONS

"employment": see Jobseekers Act 1995, s.35(1); reg.4.
"week": *ibid.*

GENERAL NOTE

3.75   Under the previous regime of benefits for the unemployed, being available for part-time work only did not of itself necessarily preclude availability (*CU109/48(KL); CU22/91*, paras 9, 10). Under JSA, the general rule is different. Section 6(1) states simply that someone is available for employment if willing and able to take up immediately *any* employed earner's employment. But that is subject to qualification and modification by regulations. This regulation stipulates that, normally, in order to be regarded as available for employment, a person must be willing and able to take up employment for a minimum of 40 hours per week, but also be willing to take up employment of less than 40 hours per week. In other words, being available merely for part-time employment (less than 40 hours per week) does not suffice, but to be available one must not only be available for full-time employment (40 or more hours per week) but be willing and able to accept part-time employment (less than 40 hours per week), if offered.

The general rule stated in this regulation is itself subject to exceptions for those in certain protected groups—those covered by reg.13(3) or (4) or reg.17(2)—who are permitted to reduce their hours of availability to a level below 40 per week (*e.g.* to 26 because of caring responsibilities) and cannot be required to take up work for a number of hours below 40 but above that permitted level. The first protected group is the sick/disabled, who can impose *any* restrictions on availability which are reasonable in light of physical or mental condition (reg.13(3). Carers (the second protected group) can restrict their hours to between 16 and 40 per week, so long as they are available for as many hours as their caring responsibilities allow and for the specific hours those responsibilities permit so long as there are reasonable prospects of employment despite the restriction (reg.13(4)). Those in employment but currently kept on short time (defined in reg.4) (the third group) are treated as available for up to 13 weeks so long as they are willing and able to resume that employment (it is obviously beneficial for all concerned to aid their ultimate return to full-time working in that job) and are available for casual employment so that the total number of hours for which they work and are available for casual employment is at least 40 per week (reg. 17).

Despite the general 40 hours per week rule, it would appear, however, that persons who refuse to accept work of less than 24 hours per week cannot be subject to sanctions under s.19(6)(c) [refusal without good cause to accept suitable employment, etc.] or (6)(d) [neglect without good cause to avail oneself of a reasonable opportunity of employment] (see JSA Regs, reg.72(5)(c)). Nor can those able to restrict availability to less than 24 hours per week be subject to sanctions under those provisions for refusing to accept, etc., employment of less than 16 hours per week (*ibid.*).

For availability purposes, "week" means "benefit week": generally the period of seven days ending with the day corresponding to the claimant's "signing"/attendance day (regs 4, 1(3)).

In *CJSA/1434/00*, Commissioner Bano held that reg.6 was not contrary to EEC 　　**3.76** Council Directive 79/EEC as indirectly discriminatory on grounds of sex. He stated:

> "Because regulation 13(4) of the Jobseeker's Allowance Regulations exempts claimants with caring responsibilities from the requirement in regulation 6 to be willing and able to take up employment for 40 hours per week and regulation 13(3) enables claimants with physical and mental disabilities to restrict their availability in any way, provided that the restrictions are reasonable, it has not been possible to identify any category of claimant unable to comply with the 40 hour availability requirement. In the absence of evidence of the existence of any such category, I agree with Ms. Bergmann that compliance with regulation 6 must be regarded as a matter of choice for each individual claimant. The regulation therefore does not create a condition with which a claimant either can or cannot comply, and no statistical comparison of men and women on that basis is therefore possible. The elements necessary to establish a claim of indirect discrimination on a statistical, or demographic, basis in accordance with the approach of the European Court of Justice in *Seymour-Smith* and of the Court of Appeal in *Jones* are therefore lacking in this case, and I therefore consider that the claimant's claim of indirect discrimination on that basis must fail. Having reached that conclusion, I do not consider it necessary to deal with Ms Bergmann's alternative submission that the 40 hour availability rule is objectively justified" (para.14).

Restriction of hours for which a person is available to 40 hours per week

7.—(1) Except as provided in regulation 13 and in regulation 17(2), a 　　**3.77** person may not restrict the total number of hours for which he is available for employment to less than 40 hours in any week.

(2) A person may restrict the total number of hours for which he is available for employment in any week to 40 hours or more providing

(a) the times at which he is available to take up employment (his "pattern of availability") are such as to afford him reasonable prospects of securing employment;

(b) his pattern of availability is recorded in his jobseeker's agreement and any variations in that pattern are recorded in a varied agreement and

(c) his prospects of securing employment are not reduced considerably by the restriction imposed by his pattern of availability.

(3) A person who has restricted the total number of hours for which he is available in accordance with paragraph (2) and who is not available for employment, and is not to be treated as available for employment in accordance with regulation 14, for one day or more in a week in accordance with

his pattern of availability shall not be regarded as available for employment even if he was available for employment for a total of 40 hours or more during that week.

DEFINITIONS

> "employment": see Jobseekers Act 1995, s.35(1); reg.4.
> "pattern of availability": see para.(2)(a).
> "week": see Jobseekers Act 1995, s.35(1); reg.4.

GENERAL NOTE

3.78   For availability purposes, "week" means "benefit week": generally the period of seven days ending with the day corresponding to the claimant's "signing"/attendance day (regs 4, 1(3)).

Para.(1)

3.79   This paragraph reinforces the general rule, stated in reg.6(1), that, save for those in the groups protected by reg.13 (the sick/disabled, carers) and 17(2) (those working short time), in order to be available for employment, one must be willing and able to take up employment of at least 40 hours per week: this paragraph stipulates that a person not in a protected group may not restrict the total number of hours for which he is available to less than 40 hours in any week.

Para.(2)

3.80   Section 6(1) of the Jobseekers Act 1995 stipulates that a person is available for employment if he is willing and able to take up immediately *any employed earner's employment*. This paragraph qualifies the rigour of that by enabling any claimant to set a ceiling at or above 40 hours on the total number of hours for which he is available in any week. This involves the claimant and the Employment Service agreeing a "pattern of availability"—the times at which he is available to take up employment (sub-para.(a))—which must be recorded in his job-seeker's agreement (sub-para.(b)). On jobseeker's agreement, see Jobseekers Act 1995, s.9. Any variation in that pattern must be agreed with the Employment Service and recorded in a varied agreement (on variation see Jobseekers Act 1995, s.10). A ceiling on total hours of availability can only be set in this way if his pattern of availability is such as to afford the claimant reasonable prospects of securing employment and those prospects are not reduced considerably by the restriction imposed by his pattern of availability (sub-paras (a), (c)). The burden of establishing reasonable prospects of employment rests on the claimant (reg.10(2)). In deciding whether he has reasonable prospects of employment, regard must be had in particular to: his skills, qualifications and experience; the type and number of vacancies within daily travelling distance of his home; how long he has been unemployed; what job applications he has made and their outcome (reg.10(1)(a)–(d)). If he also wishes to place restrictions on the nature of the employment he is prepared to accept (under reg.8 or 13(2)), regard must also be had to whether he is willing to move home to take up employment (reg.10(1)(e)).

In *CJSA 1279/98* and *R(JSA) 3/01* (considered in the notes to para.(3), below), Commissioner Levenson, taking a "whole week" approach to this regulation, seems to take the view that if the claimant has not expressly restricted his hours to less than 40 hours per week he must be taken to have restricted them to 40 hours or more so that this paragraph and para.(3) interact, unless some other exception applies, so that non-availability even for one day in a week will preclude availability throughout the benefit week. It may even apply where others effect the restriction (*e.g.* the police taking the claimant into custody). In *R(JSA) 3/01*, however, the Commissioner held that the claimant was saved by reg.13(3): the restriction was reasonable in view of his physical condition (incarceration). That "saving" was rejected as erroneous in law by the Court of Appeal in *CAO v David* (reported in *R(JSA) 3/01*) (see notes to para.(3), below). *David* was applied in *CJSA/5944/99*, another case of someone detained in police custody. See further commentary to reg.14.

Para. (3)

This at first sight baffling provision stresses that a claimant must ensure availabil-   **3.81**
ity each week in accordance with his agreed pattern of availability; failure to be available on one or more days in a week in accordance with the agreed pattern will
preclude entitlement even though the claimant was available for a total of 40 hours
or more in that week unless, with respect to the day(s) of nonavailability the claimant
is protected by a "deemed availability" rule in reg.14. So, if a claimant with an agreed
pattern of availability under para.(2), goes away on a holiday which includes one of
his agreed days of availability without informing the Employment Service and agreeing a revised pattern in accordance with para.(2), this paragraph precludes his availability for the whole of that benefit week, despite his being available for 40 or more
hours spread over the other days of that week (see also AOG para.26231, now DMG
21231); similarly if the day of non-availability arose because the claimant was in
custody (whether police or prison) (*ibid*.).

But what of persons not available on a particular day(s) for similar reasons, but who
do not have a para.(2) pattern of availability (*e.g.* because they are willing to do any
job, whatever hours at any time)? AOG para.26233 (now DMG 21233) advises decision-makers to treat them as not available throughout that week, despite their being
available in the rest of the week for 40 hours or more (if action took them below
40 hours availability reg.6(1) would, of course, rule them non-available). That
preclusion throughout the week clearly cannot be founded on para.(3) which only
applies where a claimant "has *restricted* the total number of hours for which he is available *in accordance with paragraph (2)*" (emphasis supplied). The person away on
holiday may have *de facto* "restricted" his hours but, not having sought or obtained a
revision of his jobseeker's agreement, has not done so "in accordance with paragraph
(2)"; nor has the person in custody who might in any event not properly be regarded
as having restricted his hours as opposed to having them restricted for him by the
action of others which may or may not have been warranted. Clearly such claimants
are not available on the particular days of non-availability (unless the day(s) can be
brought within one of the situations of deemed availability in reg.14). But does this
not mean that, if satisfying the "40 or more hours rule" in reg.6 they should be
regarded as available on the other days of the week and entitled to a proportionate
rate of benefit? The Departmental view on this is apparently that one must read
Jobseekers Act 1995, s.6(1) with s.1 of that Act. Taking that "total" availability rule
("a person is available for employment if he is willing and able to take up immediately any employed earner's employment") with the weekly basis of JSA ("a jobseeker's allowance is payable in respect of a week": s.1(3)), the requirement is that
one be available throughout the week in the absolute terms set by s.6(1), unless specifically relieved from that requirement by means of the concessions set out in the JSA
Regs. dealing with availability: so that, a single unprotected day of non-availability
precludes entitlement for that benefit week. The difficulties with that approach are
that neither s.6 nor s.1 are explicit on that point and that the preclusion for a full week
because of a single day of non-availability for those with a pattern of availability (the
para.(2) situation) is specifically sanctioned by para.(3). That is something which is
arguably suggestive of a view that such a result does not necessarily flow from the
asserted general principles of the Act itself. If this paragraph is thought necessary to
deal with those departing from an agreed pattern of availability (something less than
7 days × 24 hours) whilst complying with the "40 hours rule" in reg.6, surely a similar
specific rule is needed to preclude for the whole week those without such a pattern?
Or is para.(3) there out of an excess of caution to emphasise that the "concession"
afforded by para.(2) is a limited one? In short, while the policy intention may be clear,
if harsh, it is by no means clear that it has successfully been translated into law.

If, however, the whole week preclusion is the correct result, whether on the rules   **3.82**
as currently phrased or on the basis of any newly inserted specific rule similar to

para.(3), it may be appropriate for legislators to consider whether the situations of deemed availability need to be extended. Take the situation of a person unjustifiably arrested and held in custody for one or more days. Should he be precluded from benefit for the whole week, even though available for 40 hours or more? At present it would be difficult to fit the days of non-availability into the deemed availability heads of reg.14, below, save by a generous reading of the "domestic emergency" provision in reg.14(2). Yet the situation has arisen other than through his fault and it seems odd that he should be treated less generously than the person just released from prison, remand centre or youth custody institution (see reg.14(1)(h)). The approach of precluding JSA only for the actual day(s) of non-availability would seem a fairer one in that situation.

Commissioner Levenson has considered the question of approach to reg.7 in two decisions. He supports a "whole week" approach. In *R(JSA) 3/01* he thought it clear that—

> "there is no provision (other than for exceptions that do not apply in this case) to award jobseeker's allowance for parts of the week or to find that a claimant was available for employment during part of a week but not during the rest of the week. The claimant is either available for employment during a particular week or he is not so available" (para.4).

In consequence, as regards holidays, Commissioner Levenson has supported the Department's approach. In *CJSA 1279/98*, the claimant's signing-on day was Tuesday, so that his benefit week ran from Wednesday to Tuesday. He went on holiday, having informed the Jobcentre, from Saturday to Saturday for one week, stating that in that period he would not be available for work. Commissioner Levenson upheld the finding that pursuant to paras (2) and (3) of this regulation, his non-availability even for one day in each of the benefit weeks meant he was not entitled to benefit in either of those weeks. The Commissioner took the view that since he had not restricted his hours of availability to less than 40 hours per week, he must be taken to have restricted them to 40 hours or more under para.(2), so that the preclusive effect of para.(3) came into operation. It is submitted that it could equally be argued that the claimant had not in fact invoked para.(2): the real question should have been whether in each of the weeks in question he was, in the days prior to and after his holiday, available for at least 40 hours (see CPAG, *Welfare Rights Bulletin* 153, at p. 19).

3.83   In *R(JSA) 3/01* the Commissioner dealt with someone in police custody for two days of his benefit week. He held here that, even though someone else imposed the restrictions, that is the police, reg.13(3) protected the claimant from the preclusive effect of reg.7: the restriction (two days in police custody) was reasonable (indeed inevitable) in light of his physical condition which was such that he was not free, legally or practically to leave (para.6). On appeal, however, the Court of Appeal held that Commisioner Levenson had erred in law (*CAO v David* (December 15, 2000, reported in *R(JSA) 3/01*). Simon Brown L.J. said:

> "In short, the Commissioner took the view, first that the expression in regulation 13(3) 'physical or mental condition' is apt to refer not only to some disability on the claimant's part but also to any extraneous physical constraints that may be placed upon him; and second that it is unnecessary under this regulation for the claimant himself to have invoked his 'condition' so as to justify restricting his availability in advance of the week in question; rather the claimant's non-availability can retrospectively be overlooked under this provision.
>
> I have to say that to my mind both limbs of this construction are impossible. The reference to the claimant's 'physical or mental condition' seems to me clearly confined to some personal disability. And it seems to me no less clear that the provision applies prospectively only and specifically with regard to the completion of the jobseeker's agreement. That this is so is surely demonstrated also by regulation 55 which deals with short periods of sickness. . . .

On the Commissioner's approach there would be no need for regulation 55: such a person could instead invoke regulation 13(3) and, notwithstanding his job-seeker's agreement, assert that his availability was restricted by his temporary physical incapacity.

It follows that in my judgment the Commissioner was wrong in his decision and that, so far from resolving the appeal in favour of the claimant (who had not appealed), he should have decided it in favour of the adjudication officer (who had)" (paras 19–22 of the judgment).

Simon Brown L.J. was clearly unhappy with the injustice of the result. He continued: **3.84**

"I cannot, however, simply leave the matter there. . . .

. . . I think it right to touch on certain troubling features of the jobseeker's allowance scheme which this appeal has brought to light.

The first of these relates to the jobseeker's agreement itself. Section 6 of the Act, as noted, requires the claimant to be willing and able to take up employment 'immediately'. That 'immediately' means within a very short space of time indeed is clear not only from the word itself but also from regulation 5 which provides for exceptions to this requirement in the case of those with caring responsibilities or engaged in voluntary work (who need only be willing and able to take up employment on 48 hours' notice) and certain others engaged in providing a service (who get 24 hours' notice). No doubt the requirement for immediate availability allows the claimant time to wash, dress and have his breakfast, but strictly it would seem inconsistent with, say, a claimant's stay overnight with a friend or relative, or attendance at a weekend cricket match, or even an evening at the cinema (unless perhaps he had left a contact number and had not travelled far).

In these circumstances, claimants ought clearly to be wary of entering into an agreement which offers unrestricted availability throughout the entire week, day and night, weekdays and weekends.

The second concern arises even more directly from the circumstances of the present appeal. It is not altogether easy to see why a claimant should lose his weekly jobseeker's allowance merely through being detained by the police. During such detention he must surely be presumed innocent; indeed Mr David, it appears, was never even charged. The case might be one of mistaken identity. The detention here, of course, was for 42 hours. But say it had been for only 12 hours or six hours. It might have been during the day; it might have been during the night. Or the claimant might have been kidnapped and detained by a criminal gang. Or stuck in a train for eight hours. These things happen. Yet under the scheme as it stands the allowance for the week would be forfeit. Miss Lieven for the Secretary of State accepts, indeed asserts, as much. There is, in short, a lacuna in the legislation with regard to unforeseen circumstances. No doubt adjudication officers and, on appeal, tribunals (now the Unified Appeal Tribunal) are generally sensible and realistic about such cases. But this is a field in which claimants are periodically required to make declarations of availability (attended by criminal sanctions) and where strictly no element of discretion is conferred upon those administering the scheme.

These matters seem to me sufficiently troubling to suggest that the Secretary of State ought properly to consider amending the scheme to grant some measure of discretion to adjudication officers to deal with cases like this where a claimant is unavailable for work through unforeseen and excusable circumstances. In the meantime one may hope perhaps for a solution by way of *ex gratia* payments. No doubt cases like this are few and far between but to my mind they ought not simply to be swept under the carpet" (paras 23–28 of the judgment).

David was applied in *CJSA/5944/99*, another case of someone detained in police custody. See further commentary to reg. 14.

Other restrictions on availability

3.85   **8.** Subject to regulations 6, 7 and 9, any person may restrict his availability for employment by placing restrictions on the nature of the employment for which he is available, the terms or conditions of employment for which he is available (including the rate of remuneration) and the locality or localities within which he is available, providing he can show that he has reasonable prospects of securing employment notwithstanding those restrictions and any restrictions on his availability in accordance with regulations 7(2), 13(2), (3), (4) or 17(2).

DEFINITION

"employment": see Jobseekers Act 1995, s.35(1); reg.4

GENERAL NOTE

3.86   Section 6(1) of the Jobseekers Act 1995 states that a claimant is available for employment if he is willing and able to take up immediately *any employed earner's employment*. This regulation mitigates the rigour of that by enabling a claimant to restrict his availability by placing restrictions on the nature of the employment for which he is available, on its terms and conditions (including rate of remuneration) and on the locality or localities within which he is available. The regulation is subject to regs 6, 7 and 9, so the apparent width of this regulation cannot be used to circumvent the limitations imposed by those regulations. This means that he cannot under this regulation restrict hours of work to below 40 (reg.6), his pattern of availability (the times at which he is available to take up employment) must conform with the criteria in reg.7, and no remuneration restrictions are permissible after six months from the date of claim (reg.9). Moreover, restrictions are only allowable under this regulation if the claimant can establish that he has reasonable prospects of securing employment despite these restrictions and any other restrictions imposed under other availability regulations (namely, regs 7(2), 13(2), (3) or (4), 17(2)). Regulation 10(2) emphasises that the burden of establishing this lies on the claimant. In determining whether he has reasonable prospects of employment, regard must be had in particular to: his skills, qualifications and experience; the type and number of vacancies within daily travelling distance of his home; how long he has been unemployed; what job applications he has made and their outcome (reg.10(1)(a)–(d)). If the restrictions include ones on the nature of the employment he is prepared to accept (both regs 8 and 13(2) enable such restrictions), regard must also be had to whether he is willing to move home to take up employment (reg.10(1)(e)). Note that the standard is "reasonable prospects" of employment not the higher standard of "good prospects" (see Commissioner Levenson in *CJSA/4435/1998*).

No restrictions on pay after six months

3.87   **9.** After the expiry of the six month period beginning with the date of claim, a person may not restrict his availability for employment by placing restrictions on the level of remuneration in employment for which he is available.

DEFINITIONS

"date of claim": see reg.1(3).
"employment": see Jobseekers Act 1995, s.35(1); reg.4.

GENERAL NOTE

3.88   Regulations 8 (and possibly 13(3)) allow restrictions as to remuneration in the employment for which a claimant is available. This regulation stipulates that restrictions on the level of remuneration in the employment for which a claimant is available are allowable, if at all, only for maximum of six months beginning with the date of claim. The "date of claim" means the date on which the claimant makes, or is treated as making, a claim for a jobseeker's allowance for the purposes of reg.6 of the Social Security (Claims and Payments) Regulations 1987 (see reg.1(3)).

Reasonable prospects of employment

10.—(1) For the purposes of regulations 7 and 8 and paragraphs (2) and   3.89
(4) of regulation 13, in deciding whether a person has reasonable prospects of securing employment, regard shall be had, in particular, to the following matters—
   (a) his skills, qualifications and experience;
   (b) the type and number of vacancies within daily travelling distance from his home;
   (c) the length of time for which he has been unemployed;
   (d) the job applications which he has made and their outcome;
   (e) if he wishes to place restrictions on the nature of the employment for which he is available, whether he is willing to move home to take up employment.
   (2) It shall be for the claimant to show that he has reasonable prospects of securing employment if he wishes to restrict his availability in accordance with regulation 7 or 8 or paragraph (2) or (4) of regulation 13.

DEFINITION

"employment": see Jobseekers Act 1995, s.35(1); reg.4.

GENERAL NOTE

A number of regulations enabling the claimant to restrict his availability make the   3.90
permissibility of restrictions depend on whether, despite all the restrictions he imposes, he has reasonable prospects of securing employment (see regs 7, 8, 13(2), (4)). Paragraph (2) of this regulation places on the claimant the burden of showing that such is the case. Paragraph (1) of this regulation requires that in deciding the matter of "reasonable prospects", regard must be had *in particular* (the list is thus not exhaustive) to: his skills, qualifications and experience; the type and number of vacancies within daily travelling distance of his home; how long he has been unemployed; what job applications he has made and their outcome (sub-paras (a)–(d)). If the restrictions include ones on the nature of the employment he is prepared to accept (both regs 8 and 13(2) enable such restrictions), regard must also be had to whether he is willing to move home to take up employment (sub-para.(e)). Note that the standard is "reasonable prospects" of employment not the higher standard of "good prospects" (see Commissioner Levenson in *CJSA/4435/1998*).

Part-time students

11.—(1) If in any week a person is a part-time student and   3.91
   (a) he falls within paragraph (2)
   (b) he has restricted the total number of hours for which he is available in accordance with regulation 7(2), [¹ 13(3) or (4)] or 17(2); and
   (c) the hours of his course of study fall in whole or in part within his pattern of availability,
   in determining whether he is available for employment no matter relating to his course of study shall be relevant providing he is willing and able to re-arrange the hours of his course in order to take up employment at times falling within his pattern of availability, to take up such employment

immediately or, if he falls within paragraph (1), (2) or (3) of regulation 5, at the time specified in that paragraph and providing he complies with the requirements of regulation 6.

(2) A person falls within this paragraph if

(a) for a continuous period of not less than 3 months falling immediately before the date on which he first attended the course of study he was in receipt of jobseeker's allowance or incapacity benefit or was on a course of training or he was in receipt of income support and he fell within paragraph 7 of Schedule 1B to the Income Support Regulations or

(b) during the period of 6 months falling immediately before the date on which he first attended the course of study he was

(i) for a period, or periods in the aggregate, of not less than 3 months in receipt of jobseeker's allowance or incapacity benefit or on a course of training or he was in receipt of income support and he fell within paragraph 7 of Schedule 1B to the Income Support Regulations and

(ii) after the period referred to in (i), or in the case of periods in the aggregate, after the first such period and throughout the remainder of the 6 months for which that sub-paragraph did not apply to him, engaged in remunerative work or other work the emoluments of which are such as to disentitle him from receipt of jobseeker's allowance or incapacity benefit or from receipt of income support which would have been payable because he fell within paragraph 7 of Schedule 1B to the Income Support Regulations

and the period of 3 months referred to in sub-paragraph (i) or, as the case may be, the period of 6 months referred to in sub-paragraph (ii), fell wholly after the terminal date.

(3) In this regulation, "training" means training for which persons aged under 18 are eligible and for which persons aged 18 to 24 may be eligible [³ secured in England and Wales by the Learning and Skills Council for England or by the National Council for Education and Training for Wales, and in Scotland, provided] directly or indirectly by a Local Enterprise Company pursuant to its arrangement with, as the case may be, Scottish Enterprise or Highlands and Islands Enterprise (whether that arrangement is known as an Operating Contract or by any other name).

AMENDMENTS

3.92   1. Jobseeker's Allowance and Income Support (General) (Amendment) Regulations 1996 (SI 1996/1517), reg.3 (October 7, 1996).

2. Jobseeker's allowance (Amendment) (No.2) Regulations 1999 (SI 1999/3087), reg.2 (November 30, 1999).

3. Jobseeker's Allowance (Amendment) Regulations 2001 (SI 2001/1434), reg.2(3) (March 26, 2001).

DEFINITIONS

"course of study"—see reg.1(3).
"employment"—see reg.4.
"part-time student"—see reg.1(3).
"pattern of availability"—see regs 4 and 7(2)(a).
"terminal date"—see reg.1(3).

GENERAL NOTE

The effect of this provision, broadly, is to disregard a part-time student's course of **3.93** study when deciding whether he is available for employment, as long as he is prepared and able to re-arrange the hours of his course in order to take up employment, to start work immediately, or on notice if reg.5(1), (2) or (3) applies, and he complies with reg.6. However, it only applies to part-time students who satisfy the conditions in para.(2) and who have restricted the hours they are available under regs 7(2), 13(3) or (4) or 17(2). Note that if a part-time student's hours of study fall completely outside the times he has agreed to be available for work he will not need to rely on this provision as his availability will not be affected.

A part-time student is a person who is undertaking a course of study who is not a full-time student (reg.1(3)). See reg.1(3) for the definitions of "full-time student" and "course of study" and the notes to reg.130. Note the transitional protection in reg.15 of the Jobseeker's Allowance (Transitional Provisions) Regulations 1996 (replacing reg.13 of the 1995 Regulations) for part-time students who were entitled to income support on July 31, 1996 under the "21 hour rule" in the former reg.9(1)(c) of the Income Support Regulations (see, *Mesher and Wood, Income-Related Benefits: The Legislation* (1996).)

This regulation does not apply to a person in relevant education (defined in reg.54(1) and (2), see the notes to reg.54) because such a person is excluded from JSA (s.1(2)(g) of the Jobseekers Act). But note that under reg.54(3) a young person (*i.e* under 19: reg.76) who is a part-time student on a course other than one of advanced education or of a kind within para.(b) of the definition of full-time student in reg.1(3) and who satisfies para.(2) of this regulation does not count as in relevant education (and will not do so after he finishes or leaves his part-time course (reg.54(4))). Thus para.(1) may apply to such a young person.

A part-time student (except a person whose course does not conflict with his permitted pattern of availability) who does not satisfy the conditions in this regulation will probably not be treated as available unless he is prepared to abandon his course in order to take up employment. But note that a pilot scheme ("Workskill") (see the notes to s.29 of the Jobseekers Act) was introduced in some areas from April 1997 (and further extended in September 1997) to allow claimants to study full-or part-time without having to be available for work. See also reg.17A, in force from June 1, 1998, under which a claimant aged 25 or over may be able to attend a full-time employment-related course while continuing to receive JSA.

Para. (2)

The main condition (sub-para.(a)) is that for the whole three months immediately **3.94** before the course the claimant was either in receipt of JSA, incapacity benefit or income support while sick or on Work Based Training for Young People (which has replaced Youth Training and other training focused on 16/17 year olds) (see the definition of training in para.(3)). Receipt of benefit means entitlement to benefit, whether benefit is actually in payment or not (*R(SB) 12/87*). The intention is that the claimant should be primarily unemployed and not simply wishing to continue to study on benefit. A person who leaves school in the summer will not be entitled to JSA until the first Monday in September (see reg.54(2)) and thus will not have had three months on benefit in time to start a course before January.

The three months (or the six months in sub-para.(b), see below) cannot begin until after the "terminal date", that is, after the person has ceased to be treated as in relevant education. If the claimant starts (say in September) a course whose contact hours are below 12, so as to be outside the definition of relevant education (see the notes to reg.54), and after three months on benefit increases the hours, it may be difficult to decide when the claimant first attended "the" course. The official view in the previous edition of the *Adjudication Officer's Guide* (para.25529) (in relation to the 21-hour rule in the former reg.9 of the Income Support Regulations, see *Mesher and Wood, Income-Related Benefits: The Legislation* (1996)) was that a mere change in hours did not mean that a new course was starting, so that the three months' benefit would have been at the wrong time, but that if the subjects taken had changed there would have been a new course.

Under sub-para.(b) a claimant can mix receipt of a relevant benefit, Work Based Training and work over the six months, provided that the relevant benefit and the Work Based Training add up to at least three months.

Volunteers

3.95   [[1] **12.**—(1) Paragraph (2) applies if in any week a person is engaged in voluntary work and—

   (a) he has restricted the total number of hours for which he is available in accordance with regulation 7(2), 13(3) or (4) or 17(2); and

   (b) the hours in which he is engaged in voluntary work fall in whole or in part within his pattern of availability.

(2) In determining whether a person to whom this paragraph applies is available for employment no matter relating to his voluntary work shall be relevant providing—

   (a) on being given one week's notice, he is willing and able to re-arrange the hours in which he is engaged in voluntary work in order to take up employment at times falling within his pattern of availability; and

   (b) on being given 48 hours' notice, he is willing and able to re-arrange the hours in which he is engaged in voluntary work in order to attend for interview at times falling within his pattern of availability in connection with the opportunity of any such employment; and

   (c) he complies with the requirements of regulation 6.

(3) In paragraph (2) "week" means any period of seven consecutive days.]

AMENDMENT

3.96   1. Jobseeker's Allowance (Amendment) Regulations 2002 (SI 2002/3072), reg.4 (January 1, 2003).

DEFINITIONS

   "employment"—see reg.4
   "pattern of availability"—*ibid.* and reg.7(2)(a).
   "voluntary work"—see reg.4.

GENERAL NOTE

3.97   Section 6(1) of the Jobseekers Act 1995 stipulates that a claimant is available for employment if he is willing and able to take up immediately *any employed earner's employment*. This regulation mitigates the rigour of that section as regards determining the availability of a claimant engaged in voluntary work (defined below).

If a person has restricted his hours of availability under reg.7(2), 13(3) or (4) or 17(2), any voluntary work (defined in reg.4) that he does which coincides with the times he has agreed to be available for work will be disregarded when deciding whether he is available for work, as long as he is prepared and able, on one week's notice, to re-arrange the hours in which he is engaged in voluntary work in order to take up employment at times falling within his pattern of availability, and, on 48 hours' notice, to re-arrange the hours in which he is engaged in voluntary work in order to attend for interview at times falling within his pattern of availability in connection with the opportunity of any such employment. He must, however, comply with reg.6. If a person's voluntary work falls outside his permitted pattern of availability this regulation does not apply as his availability will not be affected.

See also reg.5(1) under which a person doing voluntary work only has to be available to take up employment on one week's notice and to attend for interview for such employment on 48 hours' notice.

A claimant is engaged in voluntary work when working for an organisation the activities of which are carried on otherwise than for profit, or for someone other than a member of his family, where he receives no payment by virtue of such engagement or the only payment due for it is one in respect of his reasonable expenses of such engagement (reg.4). For availability purposes, "week" means "benefit week": generally the period of seven days ending with the day corresponding to the claimant's "signing"/attendance day (regs 4, 1(3)).

Additional restrictions on availability for certain groups

13.—(1) In any week a person may restrict his availability for employment in the following ways, if the circumstances set out apply.

3.98

(2) Subject to regulations 6, 7 and 9, a person may impose restrictions on the nature of the employment for which he is available by reason of a sincerely held religious belief, or a sincerely held conscientious objection providing he can show that he has reasonable prospects of employment notwithstanding those restrictions and any restrictions on his availability in accordance with regulation 7(2), 8, paragraph (3) or (4) of this regulation or regulation 17(1) or (2).

(3) A person may restrict his availability in any way providing the restrictions are reasonable in the light of his physical or mental condition.

(4) A person with caring responsibilities may restrict the total number of hours for which he is available for employment to less than 40 hours in any week providing

(a) in that week he is available for employment for as many hours as his caring responsibilities allow and for the specific hours that those responsibilities allow and

(b) he has reasonable prospects of securing employment notwithstanding that restriction and

(c) he is available for employment of at least 16 hours in that week.

(5) In deciding whether a person satisfies the conditions in paragraph (4)(a), regard shall be had, in particular, to the following matters—

(a) the particular hours and days spent in caring;

(b) whether the caring responsibilities are shared with another person;

(c) the age and physical and mental condition of the person being cared for.

GENERAL NOTE

Section 6(1) of the Jobseekers Act 1995 stipulates that a claimant is available for employment if he is willing and able to take up immediately *any employed earner's employment*. This regulation mitigates the rigour of that by enabling certain claimants to impose restrictions on availability without thereby precluding entitlement to JSA. For availability purposes, "week" means "benefit week": generally the period of seven days ending with the day corresponding to the claimant's "signing"/attendance day (regs 4, 1(3)).

3.99

Para. (1)

This makes clear that in any week a claimant may be able to impose restrictions under more than one of the other paragraphs in this regulation; this paragraph reads "may restrict his availability for employment in the following *ways*" (emphasis added by annotator).

3.100

Para. (2)

3.101   A claimant, complying with the dictates of regs 6, 7 and 9, can impose restrictions on the nature of the employment for which he is available because of a sincerely held religious belief or conscientious objection, so long as he can show that he has reasonable prospects of employment despite those and any other restrictions imposed under other availability regulations (namely, regs 7(2); 8, paras (3) and (4) of this regulation, and regs 17(1) and (2)). Regulation 10(2) emphasises that the burden of establishing this lies on the claimant. In determining whether he has reasonable prospects of employment, regard must be had in particular to: his skills, qualifications and experience; the type and number of vacancies within daily travelling distance of his home; how long he has been unemployed; what job applications he has made and their outcome (reg.10(1)(a)–(d)). Since his restrictions include ones on the nature of the employment he is prepared to accept, regard must also be had to whether he is willing to move home to take up employment (reg.10(1)(e)).

Para. (3)

3.102   This provides protection for the sick/disabled: those who are in some way physically or mentally incapacitated and who are unable to take advantage of an incapacity benefit. Under this paragraph, a claimant can restrict his availability *in any way* provided that such restrictions are reasonable in light of his physical or mental condition. If all the restrictions imposed can be so justified, no issue of "reasonable prospects of employment" arises. If, however, restrictions are imposed which require justification under certain other provisions (regs 7, 8 or para.(2) of this regulation), then the claimant has to show that he has reasonable prospects of employment despite the totality of restrictions imposed (including those justified under this paragraph). In such a case, reg.10(2) emphasises that the burden of establishing this lies on the claimant. In determining whether he has reasonable prospects of employment, regard must be had in particular to: his skills, qualifications and experience; the type and number of vacancies within daily travelling distance of his home; how long he has been unemployed; what job applications he has made and their outcome (reg.10(1)(a)–(d)). If the restrictions include ones on the nature of the employment he is prepared to accept (this and regs 8 and 13(2) enable such restrictions), regard must also be had to whether he is willing to move home to take up employment (reg.10(1)(e)). If, however, the only other restrictions imposed are those as a carer on hours and pattern of availability justifiable under para.(4), the reasonable prospects issue focuses only on the restrictions imposed under that paragraph. Note that, in contrast to para.(4), this paragraph sets no minimum on hours of availability; the touchstone is reasonableness in light of physical or mental condition.

This provision is potentially quite wide. It permits *any* restrictions on availability that are reasonable because of the claimant's physical or mental condition. Indeed, in *R(JSA) 3/01*, Commissioner Levenson held that, even though someone else imposed the restrictions, that is the police, reg.13(3) protected the claimant from the preclusive effect of reg.7: the restriction (two days in police custody) was reasonable (indeed inevitable) in light of his physical condition which was such that he was not free, legally or practically, to leave (para.6). On appeal, however, the Court of Appeal held that Commissioner Levenson had erred in law (*CAO v David* (December 15, 2000, reported in *R(JSA) 3/01*). Simon Brown L.J. said:

> "In short, the Commissioner took the view, first that the expression in regulation 13(3) 'physical or mental condition' is apt to refer not only to some disability on the claimant's part but also to any extraneous physical constraints that may be placed upon him; and second that it is unnecessary under this regulation for the claimant himself to have invoked his 'condition' so as to justify retricting his availability in advance of the week in question; rather the claimant's non-availability can retrospectively be overlooked under this provision.
>
> I have to say that to my mind both limbs of this construction are impossible. The reference to the claimant's 'physical or mental condition' seems to me clearly

confined to some personal disability. And it seems to me no less clear that the provision applies prospectively only and specifically with regard to the completion of
the jobseeker's agreement. That this is so is surely demonstrated also by regulation 55 which deals with short periods of sickness. . . .

On the Commissioner's approach there would be no need for regulation 55:
such a person could instead invoke regulation 13(3) and, notwithstanding his jobseeker's agreement, assert that his availability was restricted by his temporary
physical incapacity.

It follows that in my judgment the Commissioner was wrong in his decision and
that, so far from resolving the appeal in favour of the claimant (who had not
appealed), he should have decided it in favour of the adjudication officer (who
had)" (paras 19–22 of the judgment).

Unlike restrictions allowed under regs 7(2), 8, or para.(2) or (4) the claimant does
not have to show under this rule that he still has reasonable prospects of finding work
despite the restrictions. In the case of restrictions on availability imposed under
reg.7(2) or para.(4) the claimant only has to show that he has a reasonable chance
of finding employment despite the limits on his hours permitted under the respective provision. But under reg.8 and para.(2) restrictions that have been allowed
under other provisions, including this paragraph, have to be taken into account in
deciding whether the person still has reasonable prospects of finding work. The consequence seems to be that restrictions under this paragraph will be subject to the reasonable prospects test if combined with other restrictions under reg.8 or para.(2),
despite the clear wording of this paragraph. However, a person with physical or
mental disabilities may well wish to impose limits on, *e.g.*, the nature or the location
of the work for which he is available but only *because of* those disabilities. If that is
the case the correct approach would seem to be for the claim to be considered under
this paragraph alone rather than under a combination of *e.g.* this paragraph and
reg.8. The approach taken by the *Decision Maker's Guide* is to distinguish between
restrictions that are connected with the claimant's disability and those that are not
(para.21449).

Note also that para.(3) is not made subject to any other provisions. Thus, for
example, although restrictions on the rate of pay may only be imposed for six months
under reg.9, the DfEE apparently accepts that restrictions under para.(3) can
include limits on the rate of pay the claimant will accept *after* six months, as long as
the restriction is reasonable in the light of his condition, *e.g.* because of additional
transport costs (see *Welfare Rights Bulletin* 138, p.4).

Paras (4), (5)

These paragraphs provide assistance to a claimant who is a carer ("a person with   **3.103**
caring responsibilities", defined below), enabling him to restrict his total hours of
availability in any week to below 40 hours but not less than 16 hours per week, provided that in that week he is available for employment for as many hours as his caring
responsibilities permit and for the specific hours they allow, and provided that he has
reasonable prospects of employment notwithstanding that restriction (para.(4)). In
determining whether in any week he is available for as many hours as his caring
responsibilities allow and for the specific hours they allow ("the conditions in paragraph (4)(a)"), regard must be had, in particular (the list is not exhaustive), to: the
particular hours and days spent in caring; whether the caring responsibilities are
shared with someone else; the age, physical and mental condition of the person being
cared for by the claimant (para.(5)). In determining whether he has reasonable
prospects of employment (and the burden of establishing this lies on the claimant:
reg.10(2)), regard must be had in particular to: his skills, qualifications and experience; the type and number of vacancies within daily travelling distance of his home;
how long he has been unemployed; what job applications he has made and their
outcome (reg.10(1)(a)–(d)). If the claimant has placed other restrictions on his availability under regs 7, 8 or para.(2) of this regulation, the matter of "reasonable

prospects" must be looked at in the context of the totality of restrictions imposed, although that flows from those other provisions rather than this. If those restrictions include ones on the nature of the employment he is prepared to accept (reg.8 and para.(2) of this regulation enable such restrictions), regard must also be had to whether he is willing to move home to take up employment (reg.10(1)(e)). If, however, the only restrictions imposed apart from those under para.(4) are ones justified under para.(3) of this regulation (reasonable in light of physical or mental condition), the "reasonable prospects" issue would fall to be decided only with regard to the total hours and pattern of availability restrictions imposed under para.(4).

A carer (a person "who has caring responsibilities") is someone who has responsibility for a child or for an elderly person or for a person whose physical or mental condition requires him to be cared for. But the child, the elderly person and the person whose conditions requires him to be cared for must either be a close relative or in the same household (reg.4). "Close relative" means a spouse or other member of an unmarried couple, parent, step-parent, grandparent, parent-in-law, son, step-son, son-in-law, daughter, step-daughter, daughter-in-law, brother, sister, grand-child or the spouse of any of these persons or, if that person is one of an unmarried couple, the other member of that couple (*ibid.*). On "unmarried couple" see Jobseekers Act 1995, s.35(1) and note thereto.

Circumstances in which a person is to be treated as available

3.104   **14.**—(1) A person, other than one [² to whom regulation 15(a), (b) or (c) applies,] shall be treated as available for employment in the following circumstances for as long as those circumstances apply, subject to any maximum period specified in this paragraph—

  (a) notwithstanding regulation 15(a), if he is participating as a full-time student in an employment-related course where participation by him has been approved before the course started by an employment officer, for a maximum of 2 weeks and one such course in any period of 12 months;

  (b) if he is attending a residential work camp, for a maximum of 2 weeks and one such occasion in any period of 12 months;

  (c) if he is temporarily absent from Great Britain because he is taking a member of his family who is a child or young person abroad for treatment, for a maximum of 8 weeks;

  (d) if he is engaged in the manning or launching of a lifeboat or in the performance of duty as a part-time member of a fire brigade or engaged during an emergency in duties for the benefit of others;

  (e) if he is a member of a couple and is looking after a member of his family who is a child while the other member is temporarily absent from the United Kingdom, for a maximum of 8 weeks;

  (f) if he is following an Open University course and is attending, as a requirement of that course, a residential course, for a maximum of one week per course;

  (g) if he is temporarily looking after a child full-time because the person who normally looks after the child is ill or temporarily absent from home or the person is looking after a member of the family who is ill, for a maximum of 8 weeks;

  (h) if he has been discharged from detention in a prison, remand centre or youth custody institution, for one week commencing with the date of his discharge;

  [²(i) if the period beginning on the date of claim and ending on the day before the beginning of the first week after the date of claim is less than 7 days and the circumstances in paragraph (2A) apply, for any part of that period when he is not treated as available for employment under any other provision of this regulation;]

[¹(j) if the award is terminated other than on the last day of a week, for the period beginning with the beginning of the week in which the award is terminated and ending on the day on which the award is terminated;]

(k) notwithstanding regulation 15(a), if he is participating in a programme provided by the Venture Trust in pursuance of an arrangement made by the Secretary of State for the Home Department with the Trust, for a maximum of 4 weeks and one such programme in any period of 12 months;

(l) if he is treated as capable of work in accordance with regulation 55, for the period determined in accordance with that regulation;

[⁵ (ll) if he is treated as capable of work in accordance with regulation 55A, for the period determined in accordance with that regulation;]

(m) if he is temporarily absent from Great Britain to attend an interview for employment and has given notice to an employment officer, in writing if so required by the employment officer, that he will be so absent for a maximum of one week;

(n) if he is a member of a couple [⁴ other than a joint-claim couple] and he and his partner are both absent from Great Britain and a premium referred to in paragraph 10, 11, 12, 13 or 15 of Schedule 1 (applicable amounts) is applicable in respect of his partner, for a maximum of 4 weeks.

[⁴(nn) if he is a member of a joint-claim couple and he and his partner are both absent from Great Britain and a premium referred to in paragraph 20E, 20F, 20G or 20I of Schedule 1 (applicable amounts) is applicable in respect of his partner, for a maximum of 4 weeks;]

[³(o) if—

    (i) he is available for employment, or is treated as such, on the day he makes his claim for a jobseeker's allowance; and

    (ii) the Secretary of State has directed that the prescribed time for claiming a jobseeker's allowance be extended under regulation 19(6) of the Claims and Payments Regulations where the circumstances specified in regulation 19(7)(d) of those Regulations applied in relation to an entitlement to incapacity benefit or an entitlement to income support by virtue of paragraph 7 of Schedule 1B to the Income Support Regulations,

for the period of that extension.]

[⁴(p) if he is temporarily absent from Great Britain in the circumstances prescribed in regulation 50(6B)(a) or (c) for the period of any such temporary absence.]

[⁵ (q) if he is temporarily absent from Great Britain in the circumstances prescribed in regulation 50(6AA) or, as the case may be, (6C).]

(2) A person, other than one to whom regulation 15 applies, shall be treated as available for employment in the following circumstances—

(a) if there is a death or serious illness of a close relative or close friend of his;

(b) if there is a domestic emergency affecting him or a close relative or close friend of his;

(c) if there is a funeral of a close relative or close friend of his;

(d) if he has caring responsibilities and the person being cared for has died;

for the time required to deal with the emergency or other circumstance and for a maximum of one week on the occurrence of any of the circumstances set out in sub-paragraphs (a) to (d), or any combination of those circumstances, and on no more than 4 such periods in any period of 12 months.

[²(2A) A person shall be treated as available for employment under paragraph (1)(i) only if—

(a) where a pattern of availability is recorded in his jobseeker's agreement, or where he has restricted the hours for which he is available in accordance with regulations 13(3) or (4) or 17(2) and that restriction has been agreed with an employment officer, he is available for employment during such of the period referred to in paragraph (1)(i) as he is not treated as available for employment under any other provision of this regulation, in accordance with—

    (i) his pattern of availability or, as the case may be, the hours to which he has restricted his availability in accordance with regulations 13(3) or (4) or 17(2), and

    (ii) any other restrictions he has placed on his availability for employment which will apply in the first week after the date of claim, provided those restrictions have been agreed with an employment officer, and

    (iii) if he falls within regulation 5, that regulation;

(b) where no pattern of availability is recorded in his jobseeker's agreement, he is available for employment during such of the period referred to in paragraph (1)(i) as he is not treated as available for employment under any other provision of this regulation—

    (i) in accordance with any restrictions he has placed on his availability for employment which will apply in the first week after the date of claim, provided those restrictions have been agreed with an employment officer, and

    (ii) for 8 hours on each day falling within that period on which he is not treated as available for employment to any extent under any other provision of this regulation, and

    (iii) if he falls within regulation 5, in accordance with that regulation.]

(3) If any of the circumstances set out in paragraph (1), except those in sub-paragraphs (i) and (j), or any of those set out in paragraph (2) apply to a person for part of a week, he shall for the purposes of regulation 7(1) be treated as available for 8 hours on any day on which those circumstances applied subject to the maximum specified in paragraph (1) or (2), unless he has restricted the total number of hours for which he is available in a week in accordance with regulation 7(2), [¹ 13(4)] or 17(2). If he has so restricted the total number of hours for which he is available, he shall, for the purposes of regulation [¹ 7(1), 13(4) or 17(2)], be treated as available for the number of hours for which he would be available on that day in accordance with his pattern of availability recorded in his jobseeker's agreement, if any of the circumstances set out in paragraph (1) except those in sub-paragraphs (i) and (j) or any of those set out in paragraph (2) applied on that day, subject to the maximum specified in paragraph (1) or (2).

(4) In paragraph (1)(c), "treatment" means treatment for a disease or bodily or mental disablement by or under the supervision of a person qualified

to provide medical treatment, physiotherapy or a form of treatment which is similar to, or related to, either of those forms of treatment.

(5) For the purposes of paragraph (1)(d),

(a) a person is engaged in duties for the benefit of others while—

(i) providing assistance to any person whose life may be endangered or who may be exposed to the risk of serious bodily injury or whose health may be seriously impaired,

(ii) protecting property of substantial value from imminent risk of serious damage or destruction, or

(iii) assisting in measures being taken to prevent a serious threat to the health of the people,

as a member of a group of persons organised wholly or partly for the purpose of providing such assistance or, as the case may be, protection;

(b) events which may give rise to an emergency include—

(i) a fire, a flood or an explosion,

(ii) a natural catastrophe,

(iii) a railway or other transport accident,

(iv) a cave or mountain accident,

(v) an accident at sea,

(vi) a person being reported missing and the organisation of a search for that person.

(6) In paragraph (1), except in sub-paragraphs (i) and (j), and in paragraph (2), "week" means any period of 7 consecutive days.

AMENDMENTS

1. Jobseeker's Allowance and Income Support (General) (Amendment) Regulations 1996 (SI 1996/1517), reg.5 (October 7, 1996).   **3.105**

2. Social Security (Jobseeker's Allowance and Mariners' Benefits) (Miscellaneous Amendments) Regulations 1997 (SI 1997/563), reg.2 (March 11, 1997).

3. Jobseeker's Allowance (Amendment) (No.2) Regulations 1999 (SI 1999/3807), reg.3 (November 30, 1999).

4. Jobseeker's Allowance (Joint Claims: Consequential Amendments) Regulations 2000 (SI 2000/3336), reg.2 (March 19, 2001).

5. Social Security (Income Support and Jobseeker's Allowance) Amendment Regulations 2004 (SI 2004/1869), reg.3(2) (October 4, 2004).

DEFINITIONS

"a joint-claim couple": see Jobseekers Act 1995, s.1(4).   **3.106**
"capable of work": see Jobseekers Act 1995, s.35(2), Sch.1, para.2; reg.55.
"child": see Jobseekers Act 1995, s.35(1).
"close relative": see reg.4.
"couple": see reg.1(3).
"date of claim": *ibid.*
"employment": see Jobseekers Act, s.35(1); reg.4.
"employment officer": see reg.4; Jobseekers Act 1995, s.9(13).
"employment-related course": see reg.1(3).
"engaged during an emergency in duties for the benefit of others": see para.(5).
"family": see Jobseekers Act 1995, s.35(1).
"full-time student": see reg.1(3).
"Great Britain": see Jobseekers Act 1995, s.35(1).
"partner": see reg.1(3).
"part-time member of a fire brigade": see reg.4.

"treatment": see para.(3).
"week" (except in paras (1)(i), (j), (2)): see para.6.
"week" (in paras (1)(i), (j), (2)): see reg.4.
"work camp": see reg.4.
"young person": see regs 1(3), 76.

GENERAL NOTE

3.107   Like its predecessors under the unemployment benefit regime (USI Regs, regs 9–12A), this regulation sets out in paras (1) and (2) a range of situations in which, for the periods specified therein, someone is to be treated as available for employment even though, were it applied to him, he might fail to satisfy the test of availability for work set out in s.6(1) of the Jobseekers Act 1995 as modified by regs 5–17. Generally someone falling within reg.15 (a), (b) or (c)—which require full-time students, prisoners on temporary release and women in receipt of maternity allowance to be treated as not available for employment—cannot avail himself of the protection afforded by this regulation. But paras (1)(a) and (k) provide exceptions in respect of the summer vacation in the situation in which both members of a couple are full-time students and one is treated as responsible for a child or young person (see further annotation to reg.15(a)). Paragraph (3) concerns the situation in which para.(1) protections (other than those in sub-paras (i) and (j)) and para.(2) protections apply only in respect of part of a benefit week (generally the period of seven days ending with the day corresponding to the claimant's "signing"/attendance day; see regs 4, 1(3)). The protection offended by paras (1)(i) only extends to claimants meeting the conditions in para.(2A). The remainder of the regulation contains relevant definitions.

In applying this regulation, careful note should be taken of the specific definition of certain terms (listed under "Definitions", above), in particular the different meanings of "week". One must also remember and maintain the distinction between Great Britain (England, Scotland and Wales) on the one hand, and the United Kingdom (of Great Britain and Northern Ireland) on the other.

Note that where it has been decided that a person is to be treated as available for employment in any benefit week, a subsequent revision or supersession of that decision can embrace also the question whether in that week the person was actually available for employment (Jobseekers Act 1995, s.6(6)). Note further that unlike the position with unemployment benefit, where full benefit remained in payment pending resolution of the issue (see USI Regs, reg.12A), under JSA if there remains an unresolved issue as to the claimant's availability for work there will be no entitlement to benefit, although the person excluded may be eligible for a hardship payment (see JSA Regs, regs 140–146 ("standard" cases) and regs 146A–146D ("joint-claim" couples)).

In *CAO v David* (reported as *R(JSA) 3/01* alongside the decision of Commissioner Levenson, whose reasoning the Court rejected)(see further the commentary to reg.7(3)), the Court of Appeal thought that the scheme of deemed availability should be extended to cover those, like Mr David, unavailable through circumstances beyond their control (detention in police custody). No change has been made to regulation 14 to do so. *David* was applied in *CJSA/5944/99*, another case of someone detained in police custody. Commissioner Angus held that reg.14(1)(h) did not aid the claimant:

"I have come to the conclusion that the submission by the adjudication officer is correct and the wording of sub-paragraph (h) is not apt to describe class of detention establishments which would include the cells in a police station. My reasoning is slightly different from what I understand to be the adjudication officer's and the Secretary of State's representative's reasoning.

11. It seems to me that the three establishments specified in sub-paragraph (h) are all establishments to which a person can be committed by the Court to await

further court procedures or to serve a custodial sentence. Detention in one of those establishments, whether on sentence or on remand, can be prolonged. Detention in a police cell, however, is normally temporary pending charge and the first appearance in court and is normally for not more than 48 hours. Therefore to my mind the police cell is not an establishment in the same genus as the establishments specified in sub-paragraph (h) and regulation 14(1) does not assist the claimant."

Circumstances in which a person is not to be regarded as available

15. A person shall not be regarded as available for employment in the following circumstances—

3.108

  (a) if he is a full-time student during the period of study unless he has a partner who is also a full-time student, if either he or his partner is treated as responsible for a child or a young person, but this exception shall apply only for the period of the summer vacation appropriate to his course and providing he is available for employment in accordance with the provisions of this Chapter or unless he is treated as available in accordance with regulation 14(1)(a) or 14(1)(k);

  (b) if he is a prisoner on temporary release in accordance with the provisions of the Prison Act 1952 or rules made under section 39(6) of the Prisons (Scotland) Act 1989;

[¹(bb) if the period beginning on the date of claim and ending on the day before the beginning of the first week after the date of claim is less than 7 days, for that period, unless he is treated as available for employment for that period in accordance with regulation 14;]

[²(bc) if he is on paternity leave or ordinary adoption leave by virtue of section 75A of the Employment Rights Act 1996;]

  (c) if she is in receipt of maternity allowance or maternity pay in accordance with section 35 or sections 164–171 respectively of the Benefits Act.

AMENDMENTS

1. Social Security (Jobseeker's Allowance and Mariners' Benefits) (Miscellaneous Amendments) Regulations 1997 (SI 1997/563), reg.3 (March 11, 1997).

3.109

2. Jobseeker's Allowance (Amendment) Regulations 2002 (SI 2002/3072), reg.5 (December 13, 2002).

DEFINITIONS

"child": see Jobseekers Act 1995, s.35(1).
"employment": see Jobseekers Act 1995, s.35(1); reg.4.
"full-time student": reg.1(3).
"partner": *ibid.*
"period of study": see reg.4.
"young person": see regs 1(3), 76.

GENERAL NOTE

This regulation excludes certain groups from entitlement to JSA by treating them (whatever would be the reality of the situation applying the standard availability test) as not available for employment. The excluded groups (and the circumstances of their exclusion) are set out below.

3.110

(1) Full-time students (para. (a)).

With one exception, any claimant who is a full-time student (defined in reg.1(3)) is treated as not available for employment throughout the "period of study": the period beginning with the start of the claimant's course of study and ending on its last day or on such earlier date as he abandons it or is dismissed from it (reg.4). Note that the "period of study" includes any period of his attendance at his educational establishment, or any period of study undertaken by him, in connection with his course whether occurring before or after the period of the course (*ibid.* and see further *CJSA/1457/1999*). The exception covers the situation where both claimant and partner are full-time students and one is treated for child benefit purposes as responsible for a child or young person. It only applies, however, during the summer vacation of the claimant's course, and only then if he is actually available for work in accordance with the usual rules on availability or is treated as available under reg.14(1)(a) (when participating in an approved employment-related course) or reg.14(1)(k) (when participating in a Venture Trust programme).

(2) Prisoners on temporary release (para. (b)).

(3) Women receiving maternity allowance (see SSCBA 1992, s.35) or statutory maternity pay (see SSCBA 1992, ss.164–171) (para. (c)).

(4) Claimants in respect of part weeks at the beginning of a claim (para. (bb))

This provides that a claimant is not to be regarded as available for employment (and is therefore excluded from JSA) for a part-week at the beginning of a claim unless he is treated as available for that period by one of the provisions in reg.14, above.

(5) Persons on paternity leave or ordinary adoption leave (para. (bc)).

Further circumstances in which a person is to be treated as available: permitted period

3.111

16.—(1) A person who is available for employment—
(a) only in his usual occupation;
(b) only at a level of remuneration not lower than that which he is accustomed to receive, or
(c) only in his usual occupation and at a level of remuneration not lower than that which he is accustomed to receive

may be treated for a permitted period as available for employment in that period.

(2) Whether a person should be treated as available for a permitted period and if so, the length of that permitted period shall be determined having regard to the following factors—
(a) the person's usual occupation and any relevant skills or qualifications which he has;
(b) the length of any period during which he has undergone training relevant to that occupation;
(c) the length of the period during which he has been employed in that occupation and the period since he was so employed;
(d) the availability and location of employment in that occupation.

(3) A permitted period shall be for a minimum of one week and a maximum of 13 weeks and shall start on the date of claim and in this paragraph "week" means any period of 7 consecutive days.

DEFINITIONS

"date of claim": see reg.1(3).   **3.112**
"employment": see Jobseekers Act 1995, s.35(1); reg.4.
"permitted period": see para.(3).
"week" (in para.(3)): see para.(3).

GENERAL NOTE

Section 6(1) of the Jobseekers Act 1995 stipulates that a claimant is available for   **3.113**
employment if he is willing and able to take up immediately *any employed earner's
employment*. This regulation mitigates the rigour of that by enabling a claimant who has
a usual occupation to be treated, for a permitted period of between one and 13 weeks,
as available for employment even though he is only available for employment in his
usual occupation and/or at his accustomed level of remuneration (paras (1), (3)). Here
"week" in para.(3) means any period of seven days, and the permitted period begins
on the date of claim (para.(3)). Whether a claimant should be so treated and for how
long is to be determined having regard to: his usual occupation and any of his relevant
skills and qualifications; the length of any period of training, relevant to that occupation, which he has undergone; how long he was employed in that occupation and the
length of time elapsed since he was last employed in it; the location and availability of
employment in that occupation. Note also that under reg.20(1), such a claimant can
be treated as actively seeking employment for a corresponding period. Furthermore,
under reg.20(2), someone who has at any time in the 12 months prior to his date of
claim for JSA been engaged in self-employment in his usual occupation, can be treated
as actively seeking employment during the "permitted period" even though he
confines his jobsearch to employment, self-employment, or both, only in his usual
occupation, or only at his accustomed rate of remuneration, or only in his usual occupation and at his accustomed rate. But under the terms of this regulation, he must still
be available for *employment* as opposed to *self-employment*. Whether a claimant has a
usual occupation will be a question of fact looking to his employment history and the
time for which he has followed a particular occupation.

For limitations on the application of this regulation in the case of a claimant laid-
off from employment or working short-time, see reg.17(4).

Laid off and short-time workers

17.—(1) A person who is laid off shall be treated as available for employ-   **3.114**
ment providing he is willing and able to resume immediately the employment from which he has been laid off and to take up immediately any casual
employment which is within daily travelling distance of his home or, if he
falls within paragraph (1) or (2) of regulation 5, at the time specified in that
regulation.

(2)—[¹(a)] A person who is kept on short-time shall be treated as available
for employment, providing he is willing and able to resume immediately the employment in which he is being kept on short-time and to
take up immediately any casual employment which is within daily
travelling distance of his home or, if he falls within paragraph (1) or
(2) of regulation 5, at the time specified in that regulation in the hours
in which he is not working short-time but the total number of hours
for which he works and is available for casual employment must be at
least 40 in any week [¹unless paragraph (b) or (c) applies.

(b) The total number of hours for which a person kept on short-time
works and is available for casual employment may be less than 40 in
any week if that person has imposed restrictions on his availability
which are reasonable in the light of his physical or mental condition;

(c) The total number of hours for which a person kept on short-time works and is available for casual employment may be less than 40 in any week if he has caring responsibilities providing the total number of hours for which he works and is available for casual employment is as many as his caring responsibilities allow and for the specific hours those responsibilities allow and is at least 16 in any week;]

(3) A person shall not be treated as available for employment in accordance with this regulation for more than 13 weeks, starting with the day after the day he was laid off or first kept on short-time.

(4) A person who is laid off or kept on short-time may not be treated as available for employment for a permitted period in accordance with regulation 16, unless he ceases to be laid off or kept on short-time within 13 weeks of the day on which he was laid off or first kept on short time, in which case he may be treated as available for employment for a permitted period ending a maximum of 13 weeks after the date of claim.

(5) In paragraphs (3) and (4), "week" means any period of 7 consecutive days.

AMENDMENT

3.115   1. Jobseeker's Allowance and Income Support (General) (Amendment) Regulations 1996 (SI 1996/1517), reg.6 (October 7, 1996).

DEFINITIONS

"casual employment": see reg.4.
"employment": see Jobseekers Act 1995, s.35(1); reg.4.
"permitted period": see reg.16(3).
"a person who is kept on short-time": see reg.4.
"a person who is laid off ": *ibid.*
"week" (in paras (3), (4)): see para.(5).
"week" (in para.(2)): see reg.4.

GENERAL NOTE

3.116   For up to 13 weeks from the day after he was laid off or put on short time, as the case may be, this regulation enables a claimant who is laid off or kept on short time to be treated as available for employment (paras (1)–(3)). It also sets limitations on treating such a claimant as available for employment during the permitted period under reg.16 (para.(4)). Its aim is to assist for a short period a claimant whose employment has been affected by temporary adverse industrial conditions in the hope that before the end of that period a recovery will mean that he can return to working or to usual hours of working in that employment and thus cease to need JSA.

A claimant who is laid off (para. (1))

3.117   A person is laid off when his employment has been suspended owing to temporary adverse industrial conditions (reg.4). A claimant who is laid off must be treated as available for employment provided (1) that he is willing and able to resume immediately the employment from which he has been laid off, and (2) that he is willing and able to take up, immediately or, if a carer, voluntary worker or person providing a service, within the period of grace afforded by reg.5(1) or (2), any casual employment within daily travelling distance of his home (para.(1)). "Casual employment" means employment from which the employee can be released without giving notice (reg.4).

A claimant who is kept on short-time (para. (2))

A person is kept on short time when his hours of employment have been reduced   **3.118**
owing to temporary adverse industrial conditions (reg.4). Given that the remunerative work exclusion precludes claims by those working 16 or more hours per week
(Jobseekers Act 1995, s.1(2)(e); regs 51–53), the reduction must take the claimant
below that threshold. Nor must his earnings exceed the prescribed amount
(Jobseekers Act 1995, s.2(1)(c); JSA Regs, reg.56), since that also precludes entitlement. A claimant who is kept on short time in an employment must be treated as
available for employment, provided he is willing and able to resume immediately that
employment and to take up, generally immediately, any casual employment within
daily travelling distance of his home in the hours he is not working short time. Usually,
however, the total number of hours for which he works and is available for casual
employment must be at least 40 in any [benefit] week (para.(2)(a), regs 4, 1(3)).
"Casual employment" is employment from which the employee can be released
without giving notice (reg.4). As regards willingness and ability to take up casual
employment, the general requirement "immediately" does not apply to carers, voluntary workers, and those providing a service, who are afforded the appropriate
period of grace in reg.5(1), (2): 48 hours for carers and voluntary workers; 24 hours
for those providing a service (para.(2)(a)). The total hours rule (at least 40) does not
apply to a claimant who has imposed restrictions on his availability which are reasonable in the light of his physical or mental condition (para.(2)(b)). Nor does it apply
to a claimant who is a carer (a person with caring responsibilities as defined in reg.4):
in any week in such a case the total of hours worked and those of availability for casual
employment can be as many hours between 16 and 40 as his caring responsibilities
allow (para.(2)(c)).

Para. (3)

Some claimants will only experience lay off, others only being kept on short time.   **3.119**
For others, short time may be followed by lay off. This paragraph stipulates that,
whichever of these situations is the case, a claimant can only be treated as available
under this regulation for up to 13 weeks from the day after the day he was laid off or
first kept on short time.

Para. (4)

The effect of this is that a claimant who is laid off or kept on short time for   **3.120**
13 weeks cannot then take advantage of the one to 13 weeks permitted period
afforded by reg.16 during which, for example, a claimant can confine his availability to employment in his usual occupation. A claimant, laid off or kept on short time,
can only be eligible for protection under reg.16 if he ceases to be laid off or kept on
short time within the 13-week period afforded by this regulation. If he does so, in
reality by becoming wholly unemployed, he can be treated as available under reg.16
for a permitted period ending no more than 13 weeks from the date of claim. The
date of claim is the date the claimant makes, or is treated as making, a claim for JSA
for the purposes of reg.6 of the Claims and Payments Regulations (reg.1(3)). In
many (but not necessarily all) cases that will be immediately after the day he was first
laid off or put on short time, so that in such a case, for example, a claimant who has
had 10 weeks' protection under this regulation, could get no more than three weeks'
protection under reg.16.

[¹Further circumstances in which a person is to be treated as available: full-time students participating in a qualifying course

17A.—(1) A person to whom paragraph (2) applies shall, notwith-   **3.121**
standing regulation 15(a), be treated as available for employment in accordance with paragraph (3).

(2) This paragraph applies to a person—

(a) who is aged 25 years or over; and

(b) [²subject to paragraph (2A),] who has made a claim for a jobseeker's allowance and has been receiving benefit within a jobseeking period for not less than 2 years as at the date he started, or is due to start, the qualifying course and for the purposes of this paragraph the linking provision set out in regulation 48 shall apply.

[²(2A) A person who has been receiving benefit in accordance with paragraph (b) of the definition of "receiving benefit" in paragraph (7) shall, for the purposes of paragraph (2)(b), be treated as having received benefit within a jobseeking period.]

(3) Subject to paragraph (4), where an employment officer has determined, having regard to the factors specified in paragraph (5), that a person to whom paragraph (2) applies may undertake a qualifying course, that person shall be treated as available for employment in any week in which he is undertaking the qualifying course as a full-time student and—

(a) which falls wholly or partly in term-time, providing he—

   (i) provides evidence, as often as may be required by an employment officer, within 5 days of being so required by the employment officer, consisting of a document signed by him and on behalf of the establishment at which he is undertaking the qualifying course, confirming that he is attending the establishment when required to attend, in such form as may be required by the employment officer; and

  (ii) provides evidence, as often as may be required by an employment officer, within 5 days of being so required by the employment officer, consisting of a document signed by him and on behalf of the establishment at which he is undertaking the qualifying course, confirming that he is making satisfactory progress on the course, in such form as may be required by the employment officer;

(b) in which he is taking examinations relating to the qualifying course; or

(c) which falls wholly in a vacation from the qualifying course, if he is willing and able to take up immediately any casual employment.

(4) In a case where the combined duration of—

(a) any qualifying course, other than one falling within paragraph (6), which a person to whom paragraph (2) applies has previously undertaken in respect of which he was, for any part of such qualifying course, treated as available for employment in accordance with paragraph (3); and

(b) the qualifying course which he is currently undertaking

is more than 1 year, the person shall only be treated as available for employment in accordance with paragraph (3) if he has been receiving benefit within a jobseeking period for not less than 2 years since the last day of the most recent such qualifying course in respect of which he was, for any part, treated as available in accordance with paragraph (3), and for the purposes of this paragraph the linking provision set out in regulation 48 shall apply.

(5) The factors which an employment officer must take into account when determining whether a person may undertake a qualifying course are—

(a) the skills, qualifications and abilities of that person;

(b) whether the course would assist him to acquire new skills and qualifications;

(c) whether he would have to give up a course of study in order to undertake this course;

(d) any needs arising from his physical or mental condition;

(e) the time which has elapsed since he was last engaged in employment as an employed earner or as a self-employed earner;

(f) his work experience;

(g) the number of jobs in the labour market and, if relevant, the local labour market, which require the skills and qualifications which he would acquire on the course; and

(h) any evidence about whether this course or this type of course has facilitated the obtaining by persons of work.

(6) A qualifying course falls within this paragraph if the person had good cause for any act or omission for the purposes of section 19(5)(b) in relation to that course.

(7) In this regulation—

[³ "benefit" means—

(a) income support, unemployment benefit, a jobseeker's allowance or any earnings credited to a person in accordance with regulation 8A or 9A of the Social Security (Credits) Regulations 1975 or which would be credited to a person in accordance with paragraph (1) of that regulation 9A but are not so credited by reason only of the fact that no further earnings are in his case required for the purpose mentioned in that paragraph; or

(b) any earnings credited to a person for unemployment in accordance with regulation 9 of the Social Security (Credits) Regulations 1975 as it applied before 7th October 1996 and]

"receiving benefit" means [²receiving—

    (a) benefit which that person has claimed and received as an unemployed person or in accordance with Part I of the Act [⁴ or in accordance with regulation 9A of the Social Security (Credits) Regulations 1975] or

    (b) income support which that person has claimed and received as an asylum seeker pursuant to regulation 70(3A) of the Income Support Regulations but only to the extent that—

        (i) any periods in respect of which he was in receipt of income support as an asylum seeker pursuant to regulation 70(3A) of the Income Support Regulations link with the jobseeking period which includes the date on which he started, or is due to start, the qualifying course and for this purpose, such periods shall link where they are separated by a period of 12 weeks or less in respect of which he was not in receipt of income support; and

        (ii) he is, at the date he started, or is due to start, the qualifying course, a person to whom paragraph (7A) applies;]

"casual employment" means employment from which the employee can be released without his giving any notice or, if he is required to give notice, employment from which he can be released before the end of the vacation;

"duration" in relation to a qualifying course means the period beginning with the start of the course and ending with the last day of the course;

"jobseeking period" means the period described in regulation 47 and any period treated as a jobseeking period pursuant to regulation 47A;

"last day" in relation to a qualifying course means the date on which the last day of the course falls, or the date on which the final examination relating to that course is completed, whichever is the later;

"qualifying course" means a course which—

(a) is an employment-related course;

(b) lasts no more than 12 consecutive months; and

(c) except where it falls within paragraph (8), is either—

> (i) a course of a description falling within Schedule 2 to the Further and Higher Education Act 1992; or
>
> (ii) a programme of learning falling within section 6 of the Further and Higher Education (Scotland) Act 1992.

[²(7A) Subject to paragraph (7B), this paragraph shall apply in the case of a person—

(a) who—

> (i) is a refugee within the definition of Article 1 of the Convention relating to the Status of Refugees done at Geneva on 28th July 1951, as extended by Article 1(2) of the Protocol relating to the Status of Refugees done at New York on 31st January 1967; or
>
> (ii) has been granted exceptional leave—
>
> > (aa) to enter the United Kingdom by an immigration officer appointed for the purposes of the Immigration Act 1971; or
> >
> > (bb) to remain in the United Kingdom by the Secretary of State; and

(b) who was in receipt of income support as an asylum seeker pursuant to regulation 70(3A) of the Income Support Regulations at any time during the period of 12 weeks immediately preceding the beginning of the jobseeking period which includes the date on which he started, or is due to start, the qualifying course.

(7B) Paragraph (7A) shall include a person who has been recorded as a refugee by the Secretary of State within the definition in sub-paragraph (a) of that paragraph and whose claim for income support was determined in accordance with regulation 21ZA(2) or (3) of the Income Support Regulations (treatment of refugees).]

(8) A course or a programme of learning which is of a standard above that of a course or programme of learning falling within paragraph (c) of the definition of "qualifying course" falls within this paragraph if an employment officer so determines in a particular case.]

AMENDMENTS

3.122
1. Social Security Amendment (New Deal) Regulations 1998 (SI 1998/1274), reg.4 (June 1, 1998).

2. Jobseeker's Allowance Amendment (New Deal) Regulations 1998 (SI 1998/2874), reg.2 (November 24, 1998).

3. Jobseeker's Allowance Amendment (New Deal) Regulations 1999 (SI 1999/3083), reg.2(2) (November 30, 1999).

4. Jobseeker's Allowance Amendment (New Deal) Regulations 1999 (SI 1999/3083), reg.2(3) (November 30, 1999).

DEFINITIONS

"benefit": see para.7.   3.123
"casual employment": *ibid.*
"course of study"—see reg.1(3).
"duration": see para.7.
"employed earner"—see reg.3, SSCBA 1992, s.2(1)(a).
"employment"—see reg.4.
"employment officer"—*ibid.*
"employment-related course"—see reg.1(3).
"examination"—see reg.4.
"full-time student"—see reg.1(3).
"jobseeking period": see para.7.
"last day": *ibid.*
"made a claim for jobseeker's allowance"—see reg.4.
"qualifying course": see paras 7 and 8.
"receiving benefit": see para.7.
"self-employed earner"—see reg.1(3), SSCBA 1992, s.2(1)(b).
"term-time"—see reg.4.
"vacation"—*ibid.*
"week"—*ibid.*

GENERAL NOTE

One element in the New Deal is that of encouraging education in terms of fol-   3.124
lowing an employment related course to acquire new or better skills.
This regulation allows a claimant doing so, in certain circumstances, to be treated
as available for employment. The claimant must be 25 or over, have made a claim
for JSA and been "receiving benefit" (see below) for at least two years within a jobseeking period (the linking provision in regulation 48 applies) as at the start date for
the course, and must be undertaking a qualifying course with the agreement of an
employment officer. A qualifying course is one meeting the criteria set out in para.(7)
read with para.(8): in essence a course of further or higher education (or one at a
level superior to that if an employment officer so determines in a particular case)
which is employment related and lasts no more than 12 months. In determining
whether to agree that a claimant can undertake such a course, an employment officer
must take into account the factors listed in para.(5). Basically, such a claimant must
be treated as available for employment in any week in which he is undertaking such
a course which week falls (i) wholly or partly within term-time (note the evidence
requirements in para.(3)(a) including one with respect to "satisfactory progress"),
or (ii) which is one in which he is taking examinations relating to the course, or
(iii) which falls wholly in a vacation from the course provided in this third case that
he is willing and able to take up immediately any casual employment (defined for
these purposes in para.(7) rather than according to the general definition in reg.(4)
(para.(3)). Note, however, that para.(3) is expressed to be "subject to paragraph
(4)". Paragraph (4) deals with the situation where the claimant has already been
treated as available with respect to one qualifying course and is now undertaking
another. If the combined duration of the two courses is more than a year, then the
claimant cannot be treated as available under this regulation unless he has been
receiving benefit within a jobseeking period for at least two years (the linking provision in reg.48 applies) since the last day of the most recent qualifying course in
respect of which he was for any part of that course treated as available by para.(3) of
this regulation. In short, a claimant can only be treated as available under this regulation for up to one year without having to serve a two year requalification period in
receipt of benefit. Note, however, when looking to the combined duration of qualifying courses that one ignores any course where the claimant had good cause for the
purposes of s.19(5)(b) (neglect to avail himself of a place on a course, refusing to
apply for a vacant place or accept it when offered, giving up such a place or failing

to attend the course) with respect to any act of omission in relation to that course (para.(6)).

3.125   These rules became effective on June 1, 1998. "Receiving benefit" is not just confined to receiving benefit (income support, unemployment benefit or jobseeker's allowance) as an unemployed person or in accordance with Part I of the Jobseekers Act 1995 (para.7). With effect from November 24, 1998, it also covers refugees or persons granted exceptional leave to remain receiving income support as an asylum seeker pursuant to reg.70(3A) of the Income Support Regulations at any time during the 12-week period immediately prior to the beginning of the jobseeking period which includes his start date or anticipated start date on the qualifying course. Such persons must be refugees or persons granted exceptional leave as at that date. Periods of receipt of income support as an asylum seeker link to the jobseeking period if not separated from it by more than 12 weeks, and periods of less than 12 weeks when not receiving income support as an asylum seeker do not "break" the ongoing period in receipt of income support. This enables refugees and persons given, on humanitiarian grounds, exceptional leave to remain in the United Kingdom, to count periods of receipt of income support as asylum seekers towards the two year qualifying period stipulated in para.(2) (see paras (2A), (7), (7A) and (7B)). With effect from November 30, 1999, "benefit" and "receiving benefit" also includes receipt of earnings credited for contributions purposes in respect of unemployment and of persons aged 60 or over.

Note, finally, that during any week in which a person is treated as available under this regulation he will be treated also as actively seeking work. Where the week is during a vacation from the course, he must however show that during that week he has taken such steps as he can reasonably be expected to have to take to have the best prospects of securing the casual employment for which reg.17A requires him to be available (see reg.21A, below).

Chapter III

Actively seeking employment

Steps to be taken by persons actively seeking employment

3.126   **18.**—[¹ (1) For the purposes of section 7(1) (actively seeking employment) a person shall be expected to have to take more than two steps in any week unless taking one or two steps is all that is reasonable for that person to do in that week.]

(2) Steps which it is reasonable for a person to be expected to have to take in any week include—

(a) oral or written applications (or both) for employment made to persons—
  (i) who have advertised the availability of employment; or
  (ii) who appear to be in a position to offer employment;
(b) seeking information on the availability of employment from—
  (i) advertisements;
  (ii) persons who have placed advertisements which indicate the availability of employment;
  (iii) employment agencies and employment businesses;
  (iv) employers;
(c) registration with an employment agency or employment business;
(d) appointment of a third party to assist the person in question in finding employment;

(e) seeking specialist advice, following referral by an employment officer, on how to improve the prospects of securing employment having regard to that person's needs and in particular in relation to any mental or physical limitations of that person;

(f) drawing up a curriculum vitae;

(g) seeking a reference or testimonial from a previous employer;

(h) drawing up a list of employers who may be able to offer employment to him with a view to seeking information from them on the availability of employment;

(i) seeking information about employers who may be able to offer employment to him;

(j) seeking information on an occupation with a view to securing employment in that occupation.

(3) In determining whether, in relation to any steps taken by a person, the requirements of section 7(1) are satisfied in any week, regard shall be had to all the circumstances of the case, including—

(a) his skills, qualifications and abilities;

(b) his physical or mental limitations;

(c) the time which has elapsed since he was last in employment and his work experience;

(d) the steps which he has taken in previous weeks and the effectiveness of those steps in improving his prospects of securing employment;

(e) the availability and location of vacancies in employment;

(f) any time during which he was—

   (i) engaged in the manning or launching of a lifeboat or in the performance of duty as a part-time member of a fire brigade or engaged during an emergency in duties for the benefit of others.

   (ii) attending an Outward Bound course,

   (iii) in the case of a blind person, participating in a course of training in the use of guide dogs,

   (iv) participating in training in the use of aids to overcome any physical or mental limitations of his in order to improve his prospects of securing employment,

   (v) engaged in duties as a member of any territorial or reserve force prescribed in Part I of Schedule 3 to the Social Security (Contributions) Regulations 1979,

   (vi) participating as a part-time student in an employment-related course,

   (vii) participating for less than 3 days in an employment or training programme for which a training allowance is not payable;

(g) any time during which he was engaged in voluntary work and the extent to which it may have improved his prospects of securing employment;

(h) whether he is treated as available for employment under regulation 14;

(i) whether he has applied for, or accepted, a place on, or participated in, a course or programme the cost of which is met in whole or in part out of central funds or by the European Community and the purpose of which is to assist persons to select, train for, obtain or retain employed earner's employment or self-employed earner's employment; and

(j) where he had no living accommodation in that week the fact that he had no such accommodation and the steps which he needed to take and has in fact taken to seek such accommodation.

(4) Any act of a person which would otherwise be relevant for purposes of section 7 shall be disregarded in the following circumstances—
(a) where, in taking the act, he acted in a violent or abusive manner,
(b) where the act comprised the completion of an application for employment and he spoiled the application,
(c) where by his behaviour or appearance he otherwise undermined his prospects of securing the employment in question,
unless those circumstances were due to reasons beyond his control.

(5) In this regulation—
"employment agency" and "employment business" mean an employment agency or (as the case may be) employment business within the meaning of the Employment Agencies Act 1973;
"employment or training programme" means a course or programme the person's participation in which is attributable to arrangements made by the Secretary of State under section 2 of the Employment and Training Act 1973 for the purpose of assisting persons to select, train for, obtain or retain employed earner's employment.

AMENDMENT

1. Jobseeker's Allowance (Amendment) Regulations 2004 (SI 2004/1008), reg.2(2) (April 19, 2004 [new claimants]; October 18, 2004 [existing claimants and existing recipients of jobseeking credits]).

DEFINITIONS

3.127

"employment": see Jobseekers Act 1995, s.7(8); regs 3, 4.
"employment agency": see para.(5).
"employment business": *ibid.*
"employment or training programme": *ibid.*
"employment officer": see reg.4; Jobseekers Act 1995, s.9(13).
"employment-related course": see reg.1(3).
"engaged during an emergency in duties for the benefit of others": see reg.22.
"Outward Bound course": see reg.4.
"part-time member of a fire brigade": *ibid.*
"part-time student": see reg.1(3).
"steps": see para.(2).
"training allowance": see reg.1(3).
"voluntary work": see reg.4.
"week": *ibid.*

GENERAL NOTE

3.128

For the purposes of the Jobseekers Act 1995, in any week a person is actively seeking employment if during that week he takes such steps as he can reasonably be expected to have to take in order to have the best prospects of securing employment (s.7(1)). In its original form, paragraph (1) of this regulation amplified that "touchstone test" by stipulating that a person will be expected to take more than one step on one occasion in any week unless taking one step on a single occasion in the week is all that it is reasonable for that person to do in that week. (see *CJSA/2162/2001*, noted in the commentary to Jobseekers Act 1995, ss.7 and 9). A new version was substituted with effect from April 19, 2004 for new claimants and from October 18, 2004 for those who were existing claimants at April 19 or then in receipt of jobseeking credits. The substitution increased the minimum number of steps that a jobseeker must take to be actively seeking employment from at least two to at least three in a week, unless taking one or two steps is all that it is reasonable to do in that week.

Concerns were expressed by the SSAC (see Cmd 6145) about the lack of need for and the effect of the change at a time of national low unemployment, and against a background of manpower cuts at Jobcentres. Despite this, the change was made. The Secretary of State was of the view that tailored support was an important way to help people return to work but that, in addition to special provision, it was reasonable in a buoyant labour market to increase expectations of the claimant unemployed through measures designed to be adapted to the individual to increase prospects of getting a job more quickly. The positive effects of being in work outweighed any negative effects. Impact on staff resources would be small. General evidence showed that more contact and increased quality job-search, designed to keep people attached to the labour market, were among the most successful and cost effective measures in helping people find work.

The remainder of the regulation supplies further detail to flesh out that "touchstone test" in terms of providing a partial definition of "steps" (para.(2)), stipulating circumstances to be taken into account in determining whether the test is met in any week (para.(3)) and, most controversially, setting out the circumstances in which otherwise relevant acts are to be disregarded (para.(4)). Paragraph (5) provides definitions of certain terms used in this regulation: "employment agency", "employment business" and "employment or training programme". "Week" means "benefit week" (reg.4); that is, generally, the period of seven days ending with the claimant's "signing"/attendance day (reg.1(3)).

Paragraph (2) provides a partial definition of "steps" and thus gives a general indication of the type of action claimants must take in order not to fall foul of the actively seeking work test. The list, albeit much longer than its predecessor (USI Regs, reg.12B) is not exhaustive: the provision reads "steps which it is reasonable to expect a person to have to take in any week *include*" (emphasis supplied by annotator). Regard must still be had to all the steps taken by the claimant to try to get employment: the "touchstone test" remains that in the statute: "such steps as he can reasonably be expected to have to take in order to have the best prospects of securing employment". To determine whether in a particular week any steps taken by a particular claimant satisfy that test, para.(3) requires that regard must be had to all the circumstances of the case, including those specifically there listed. In para.(2) the specifically listed "steps" are:

(a) written and/or oral applications for employment to those who have advertised its availability or who appear to be in a position to offer it;

(b) seeking information on the availability of employment from advertisements, advertisers and employers, or from employment agencies and employment businesses within the meaning of the Employment Agencies Act 1973;

(c) registration with an employment agency or employment business within the meaning of the Employment Agencies Act 1973;

(d) the appointment of a third party to assist the claimant in finding employment (an actor appointing an agent might be an example);

(e) seeking specialist advice, after referral by an employment officer, on how to improve prospects of securing employment having regard to the claimant's needs and in particular any of his physical or mental limitations;

(f) drawing up a curriculum vitae (CV);

(g) seeking a testimonial or reference from a former employer;

(h) drawing up a list of possible employers with a view to seeking information from them on the availability of employment;

(i) seeking information about possible employers;

(j) seeking information on an occupation with a view to securing employment in it.

The statutory touchstone test of actively seeking employment requires the claimant to take in any week "such steps as he can reasonably be expected to have to take in order to have the best prospects of securing employment". To determine whether in a particular week any steps taken by a particular claimant (whether listed in para.(2) or not—that list not being exhaustive) satisfy that test, para.(3) requires

3.129

that regard must be had to all the circumstances of the claimant's case, including those specifically listed. The listed circumstances are:

    (a) his skills, qualifications and abilities;

    (b) his physical or mental limitations (something important to those once on an incapacity benefit who have been found capable of work and must needs look to JSA);

    (c) his work experience and how long he has been employed;

    (d) what he has done in previous weeks to find employment and the effectiveness of that in improving his prospects of finding it;

    (e) what jobs are available and where they are;

    (f) time spent in certain worthwhile activities; lifeboatman or part-time fireman; as someone undertaking duties in an emergency (on which see reg.22); attendance at an Outward Bound course; or, if blind, taking part in a course of training in the use of guide dogs; or participating in training in the use of aids to overcome any physical or mental limitations in order to improve prospects of securing employment; engagement in a prescribed territorial or reserve force; participation as a part-time student in an employment-related course (one whose purpose is to assist persons to acquire or enhance skills required for seeking employment, for a particular occupation or for employment—see reg.1(3)); participating for less than three days in an employment or training programme (as defined in para.(5)) for which a training allowance is not payable;

    (g) engagement in voluntary work and the extent to which it may have improved his prospects of securing employment;

    (h) whether he is treated as available for work under reg.14 (para.(1)(d) of which is in identical terms to para.(f)(i) of this regulation—lifeboatman, part-time fireman, someone undertaking duties in an emergency);

    (i) whether he has applied for, or accepted a place on, or participated in, a wholly or partially centrally or European Community-funded course or programme designed to help people select, train for, obtain and retain employment or self-employment;

    (j) the fact that he is homeless, the steps taken and those that he needed to take to find somewhere to live.

3.130   It must, however, be stressed that this list of particular factors is not exhaustive; regard must be had to all the circumstances of the claimant's case to decide whether he meets the touchstone test, the hallmark of which is flexibility and adaptability to different claimants and different labour markets by setting a general target and allowing flexibility of interpretation and application to the individual case, to decide what should be the appropriate extent of job search for a particular individual at a particular time and place. It is submitted that there will be occasions when there is nothing useful that a particular individual can do in a particular week; he is expected to take "appropriate steps, not fruitless action" (*per* Mr N. Scott, M.P., H.C., Debs., Standing Committee F, col. 271 (February 2, 1989), commenting on the reintroduction of the "actively seeking work" hurdle in the debates on what became the Social Security Act 1989). Might an example for those seeking factory work in a particular industry in a particular town be that industry's "holiday fortnight" when all the factories are closed? The period between Christmas and New Year may spring to mind as an example for some, but clearly not all, claimants, depending on the type of work appropriate to them at that point in their claim. And might another instance be the claimant in a particular area who has, in previous weeks, written to all the relevant employers in the appropriate area and last week received replies stating that his application was on file, there was nothing for him at the moment but he would be contacted "if a vacancy arose". Such a claimant could surely not be expected to contact them all again so soon.

    The aim of the controversial provision in para.(4) was to "enable a person's job-seeking activity to be disregarded if he behaves or presents himself in such a way as deliberately to reduce or extinguish his chance of receiving offers of employment"

(DSS, *Notes on Clauses* [with respect to the Jobseekers Bill]). It provides that an otherwise relevant act of a person is to be disregarded in a number of circumstances unless the circumstances were due to reasons beyond his control: (i) where in taking the act he acted in a violent or abusive manner; (ii) where the act comprised the completion of an application for employment and he spoiled the application; (iii) where, by his behaviour or appearance, he otherwise undermined his prospects of securing the employment in question.

The paragraph, particularly in head (iii) thus involves a more explicit "policing" of behaviour, appearance and, possibly, form-filling competence by Employment Service personnel, decision-makers and tribunals. The concept of "spoiled the application" in head (ii) is by no means crystal clear. The saving for circumstances beyond one's control will presumably protect the dyslexic and the illiterate, but what about the semi-literate? Electoral law, of course, has the concept of the "spoilt ballot paper", which covers the situation in which the voter has, in that context inadvertently, dealt with his ballot paper in such a manner that it cannot conveniently be used as a ballot paper, but whether that in any way provides a valid analogy for "spoiled" in this regulation remains to be seen. On "spoiled", see the remarks of Commissioner Howell in *CJSA/4665/01*, noted in the commentary to Jobseekers Act 1995, s.19(6)(c). Given the aim of the provision, it might have been better for sake of clarity to have worded it "deliberately spoiled". A further sanction for some such behaviour lies in the preclusion of payment of benefit under s.19(6)(c) in respect of the person having, without good cause, neglected to avail himself of a reasonable opportunity of employment; the equivalent provision in the unemployment benefit regime enabled disqualification of a claimant who had attended an interview for a job as a parcel porter in a "dirty and unshaven state" (*R(U)28/55*). Care will have to be taken to avoid applying the provision in a manner discriminatory on grounds of sex or race (*e.g.* to penalise men with long hair or Rastafarians with dreadlocks).

For an interesting consideration of para.4 and Jobseekers Act 1995, s.7(3), see N. Wikeley, "What the Unemployed Need is a Good Haircut . . ." in [1996] 25 I.L.J. 71.

[¹Actively seeking employment in the period at the beginning of a claim

18A.—(1) Paragraph (2) applies in any case [²other than a case which falls   **3.131** within regulation 19(1)(i) or (s),] where the period beginning on the date of claim and ending on the day before the beginning of the first week after the date of claim is less than 7 days.

(2) Where this paragraph applies, a person is actively seeking employment in the period referred to in paragraph (1) if he takes in that period such steps as he can reasonably be expected to have to take in order to have the best prospects of securing employment and in determining whether a person has taken such steps—

(a) the steps which it is reasonable for him to be expected to have to take include those referred to in regulation 18(2); and

(b) regard shall be had to all the circumstances of the case, including those matters referred to in regulation 18(3).]

AMENDMENTS

1. Social Security (Jobseeker's Allowance and Mariners' Benefits) (Miscellaneous   **3.132** Amendments) Regulations 1997 (SI 1997/563), reg.4 (March 11, 1997).

2. Jobseeker's Allowance (Amendment) (No.2) Regulations 1999 (SI 1999/3087), reg.4 (November 30, 1999).

Definitions

Definitions

"employment": see Jobseekers Act 1995, s.7(8); regs 3, 4.
"week": see reg.4.

General Note

3.133   The actively seeking work test in Jobseekers Act 1995, s.7 is expressed in terms of each week. This regulation, inserted with effect from March 11, 1997, adapts that test to cover a part-week at the beginning of a claim, so that a claimant will satisfy the test if in that part-week period he takes such steps as he can reasonably be expected to have to take in order to have the best prospects of securing employment, having regard to all the circumstances of the case including the matters set out in reg.18(3), above. "Steps" include those referred to in reg.18(2), above.

Circumstances in which a person is to be treated as actively seeking employment

3.134   **19.**—(1) A person shall be treated as actively seeking employment in the following circumstances, subject to paragraph (2) and to any maximum period specified in this paragraph—

(a) in any week during which he is participating for not less than 3 days as a full-time student in an employment-related course where participation by him has been approved before the course started by an employment officer, for a maximum of 2 weeks and one such course in any period of 12 months;

(b) in any week during which he is attending for not less than 3 days a residential work camp, for a maximum of 2 weeks and one such occasion in any period of 12 months;

(c) in any week during which he is temporarily absent from Great Britain for not less than 3 days because he is taking a member of his family who is a child or young person abroad for treatment, for a maximum of 8 weeks;

(d) in any week during which he is engaged for not less than 3 days in the manning or launching of a lifeboat or in the performance of duty as a part-time member of a fire brigade or engaged during an emergency in duties for the benefit of others;

(e) if he is a member of a couple, in any week during which he is for not less than 3 days looking after a member of his family who is a child while the other member is temporarily absent from the United Kingdom, for a maximum of 8 weeks;

(f) if he is following an Open University course, in any week during which he is attending for not less than 3 days, as a requirement of that course, a residential course, for a maximum of one week per course;

(g) in any week during which he is for not less than 3 days temporarily looking after a child full-time because the person who normally looks after the child is ill or temporarily absent from home or the person is looking after a member of the family who is ill, for a maximum of 8 weeks;

(h) in the first week after the date of claim if he is treated as available for employment to any extent in that week under regulation 14(1)(h);

[³(i) for any period if he is treated as available for employment to any extent in that period under regulation 14(1)(h);]

[¹(j) [if the award is terminated other than on the last day of a week, for the period beginning with the beginning of the week in which the award is terminated and ending on the day on which the award is terminated;]

(k) in any week during which he is participating for not less than 3 days in a programme provided by the Venture Trust in pursuance of an arrangement made by the Secretary of State for the Home Department with the Trust, for a maximum of 4 weeks and one such programme in any period of 12 months;

(l) in any week during which he is for not less than 3 days treated as capable of work in accordance with regulation 55;

[⁶(ll) in any week during which he is for not less than 3 days treated as capable of work in accordance with regulation 55A;]

(m) in any week during which he is temporarily absent from Great Britain for not less than 3 days in order to attend an interview for employment and has given notice to an employment officer, in writing if so required by the employment officer, that he will be so absent, for a maximum of 1 week;

(n) if he is a member of a couple [⁵ other than a joint-claim couple], in any week during which he and his partner are both absent from Great Britain for not less than 3 days and in which a premium referred to in paragraph 10, 11, 12, 13 or 15 of Schedule 1 (applicable amounts) is applicable in respect of his partner for a maximum of 4 weeks;

[⁵(nn) if he is a member of a joint-claim couple, in any week during which he and his partner are both absent from Great Britain for not less than 3 days and in which a premium referred to in paragraph 20E, 20F, 20G or 20I of Schedule 1 (applicable amounts) is applicable in respect of his partner, for a maximum of 4 weeks;]

(o) in any week during which he is treated as available for employment on not less than 3 days under regulation 14(2);

(p) in any week in respect of which he has given notice to an employment officer, in writing if so required by the employment officer, that—
  (i) he does not intend to be actively seeking employment, but
  (ii) he does intend to reside at a place other than his usual place of residence for at least one day;

(q) in any week during which he is participating for not less than 3 days in an employment or training programme for which a training allowance is not payable;

[²(r) in any week, being part of a single period not exceeding 8 weeks falling within a period of continuous entitlement to a jobseeker's allowance, during which he is taking active steps to establish himself in self-employed earner's employment under any scheme for assisting persons to become so employed—
  (i) where, in Wales, his participation under the scheme is attributable to arrangements made by the Secretary of State under section 2 of the Employment and Training Act 1973,
  (ii) where, in Scotland, the scheme—
    (aa) is established by virtue of arrangements made by Scottish Enterprise or Highlands and Islands Enterprise under section 2(3) of the Enterprise and New Towns (Scotland) Act 1990 or
    (bb) is directly or indirectly provided by, or with financial assistance from, the Secretary of State,

     (iii) where, in England, the scheme is directly or indirectly provided by, or with financial assistance from, the Secretary of State, the Urban Regeneration Agency, an urban development corporation or a housing action trust,

and the single period referred to above shall begin with the week in which he is accepted on a place under the scheme.]

    [⁴(s) for any period if he is treated as available for employment to any extent in that period under regulation 14(1)(o).]

    [⁵(t) if he is temporarily absent from Great Britain in the circumstances prescribed in regulation 50(6B)(a) or (c), for the period of any such temporary absence.]

    [⁶(u) if he is temporarily absent from Great Britain in the circumstances prescribed in regulation 50(6AA) or, as the case may be (6C).]

(2) In any period of 12 months a person shall be treated as actively seeking employment under paragraph (1)(p) only for the number of weeks specified in one of the following subparagraphs—

    (a) a maximum of 2 weeks; or

    (b) a maximum of 3 weeks during which he is attending for at least 3 days in each such week an Outward Bound course; or

    (c) if he is a blind person, a maximum of 6 weeks during which, apart from a period of no more than 2 weeks, he participates for a maximum period of 4 weeks in a course of training in the use of guide dogs of which at least 3 days in each such week is spent in that training.

(3) In this regulation—

"employment or training programme" means a course or programme the person's participation in which is attributable to arrangements made by the Secretary of State under section 2 of the Employment and Training Act 1973 for the purpose of assisting persons to select, train for, obtain or retain employment;

"housing action trust" means a corporation established by an order of the Secretary of State pursuant to section 62(1) of the Housing Act 1988;

"treatment" means treatment for a disease or bodily or mental disablement by or under the supervision of a person qualified to provide medical treatment, physiotherapy or a form of treatment which is similar to, or related to, either of those forms of treatment;

"urban development corporation" means a corporation established by an order of the Secretary of State pursuant to section 135(1) of the Local Government, Planning and Land Act 1980;

"Urban Regeneration Agency" means the agency referred to in section 158(1) of the Leasehold Reform, Housing and Urban Development Act 1993.

AMENDMENTS

3.135   1. Jobseeker's Allowance and Income Support (General) (Amendment) Regulations 1996 (SI 1996/1517), reg.7 (October 7, 1996).

2. Social Security Amendment (New Deal) Regulations 1998 (SI 1998/1274), reg.5 (June 1, 1998).

3. Jobseeker's Allowance (Amendment) (No. 2) Regulations 1999 (SI 1999/3087), reg.5(2) (November 30, 1999).

4. Jobseeker's Allowance (Amendment) (No. 2) Regulations 1999 (SI 1999/3087), reg.5(3) (November 30, 1999).

5. Jobseeker's Allowance (Joint Claims: Consequential Amendments) Regulations 2000 (SI 2000/3336), reg.2 (March 19, 2001).

6. Social Security (Income Support and Jobseeker's Allowance) Amendment Regulations 2004 (SI 2004/1869), reg.3(3) (October 4, 2004).

DEFINITIONS

"a joint-claim couple": see Jobseekers Act 1995, s.1(4).   **3.136**
"capable of work": see Jobseekers Act 1995, s.35(2), Sch.1, para.2; reg.55.
"child": see Jobseekers Act 1995, s.35(1).
"couple": see reg.1(3).
"date of claim": *ibid.*
"employed earner's employment": see Jobseekers Act 1995, s.7(8); SSCBA 1992,
    ss.2, 122(1).
"employment": see Jobseekers Act 1995, s.7(8); regs 3, 4.
"employment officer": see reg.4; Jobseekers Act 1995, s.9 (13).
"employment or training programme": see para.(3).
"employment-related course": see reg.1(3).
"engaged during an emergency in duties for the benefit of others": see reg.22.
"family": see Jobseekers Act 1995, s.35(1).
"full-time student": see reg.1(3).
"Great Britain": see Jobseekers Act 1995, s.35(1).
"housing action trust": see para.(3).
"partner": see reg.1(3).
"part-time member of a fire brigade": see reg.4.
"self-employed earner's employment": see Jobseekers Act 1995, s.7(8); SSCBA
    1992, ss.2, 122(1).
"training allowance": see reg.1(3).
"treatment": see para.(3).
"urban development corporation": *ibid.*
"Urban Regeneration Agency": *ibid.*
"week": see reg.4.
"work camp": *ibid.*
"young person": see regs 1(3), 76.

GENERAL NOTE

Like its predecessor under the unemployment benefit regime (USI Regs, reg.12D),   **3.137**
this regulation sets out in para.(1) a range of situations in which, for the periods specified
therein or in para.(2), someone is to be treated as actively seeking employment, even
though, were it applied to him, he might fail to satisfy the touchstone test of actually
actively seeking work set out in Jobseekers Act 1995, s.7(1) as amplified by reg.18. Note,
however, that where it has been decided that a person is to be treated as actively seeking
employment in any week, a subsequent revision and supersession of that decision can
embrace also the question whether in that week the person was actually actively seeking
employment (Jobseekers Act 1995, s.7(7)). In applying the regulation, careful note
should be taken of the specific definition of certain terms (listed in "Definitions",
above). One must also remember the distinction between *Great Britain* (England,
Scotland and Wales) and the *United Kingdom* (of Great Britain and Northern Ireland).

Further circumstances in which a person is to be treated as actively seeking employment: permitted period

20.—(1) A person to whom paragraph (2) does not apply shall be treated   **3.138**
as actively seeking employment in any week during any permitted period
determined in his case in accordance with regulation 16, if he is actively
seeking employment in that week—

(a) only in his usual occupation,

(b) only at a level of remuneration not lower than that which he is accustomed to receive, or

(c) only in his usual occupation and at a level of remuneration not lower than that which he is accustomed to receive.

(2) A person to whom this paragraph applies shall be treated as actively seeking employment in any week during any permitted period determined in his case in accordance with regulation 16, if he is actively seeking employment, self-employed earner's employment, or employment and self-employed earner's employment in that week—

(a) only in his usual occupation,

(b) only at a level of remuneration not lower than that which he is accustomed to receive, or

(c) only in his usual occupation and at a level of remuneration not lower than that which he is accustomed to receive.

(3) Paragraph (2) applies to a person who has, at any time during the period of 12 months immediately preceding the date of claim, been engaged in his usual occupation in self-employed earner's employment.

DEFINITIONS

3.139 "employment": see Jobseekers Act 1995, s.7(8); regs 3, 4.

"employed earner's employment": see Jobseekers Act 1995, s.7(8); SSCBA 1992, s.2.

"self-employed earner's employment": *ibid.*

"week": see reg.4.

GENERAL NOTE

3.140 Under the Act, all claimants must be available for employment (as opposed to self-employment). For a "permitted period" of up to 13 weeks, a claimant can be treated as available even though he is only available for employment in his usual occupation and/or at his accustomed level of remuneration (reg.16). Paragraph (1) of this regulation enables such a person to be treated as actively seeking employment for that period. Under para.(2), someone who has at any time in the 12 months prior to his date of claim for JSA been engaged in self-employment in his usual occupation can be treated as actively seeking employment during the "permitted period", even though he confines his jobsearch to employment, self-employment or both, only in his usual occupation, or only at his accustomed rate of remuneration, or only in his usual occupation and at his accustomed rate. But he must, of course, still be available for employment as an employed earner. On determining whether a particular claimant can have such a "permitted period" and, if so, its length, see reg.16(2). For limitations on the application of the period in the case of a claimant laid of from, or kept on short time in, his employment, see reg.17(4).

Further circumstances in which a person is to be treated as actively seeking employment: laid off and short time workers

3.141 **21.** A person who has restricted his availability for employment in accordance with regulation 17(1) or, as the case may be, regulation 17(2), shall in any week in which he has so restricted his availability for not less than 3 days be treated as actively seeking employment in that week if he takes such steps as he can reasonably be expected to have to take in order to have the best prospects of securing employment for which he is available under regulation 17.

DEFINITIONS

"employment": see Jobseekers Act 1995, s.7(8); regs 3, 4.
"week": see reg.4.

GENERAL NOTE

Under reg.17, a claimant laid off from employment or put on short time can, for   **3.142**
up to 13 weeks, be treated as available for employment, provided he is willing and
able to resume immediately the employment from which, as the case may be, he is
laid off or kept on short time, and to take up immediately any casual employment
within daily travelling distance of his home. The requirement of immediacy is
modified for carers and volunteers (48 hours' notice) and those providing a service
(24 hours' notice), protected by reg.5(1), (2).
   This regulation stipulates that a claimant who has restricted his availability in that
way for not less than three days in a particular week is to be treated as actively seeking
employment in that week, provided he takes such steps as he can reasonably be
expected to have to take in order to have the best prospects of securing the employment for which, under reg.17, he is available. In short, for up to 13 weeks of short
time or lay off, he can confine his jobsearch to the job with respect to which he has
been laid off or kept on short time and casual employment within daily travelling distance of his home.

[¹Further circumstances in which a qualifying person is to be treated as actively seeking employment: full-time students participating in a qualifying course

21A. A person who is treated as available for employment in accordance   **3.143**
with regulation 17A(3) shall be treated as actively seeking employment in
any week—
   (a) which, in relation to the qualifying course, falls wholly or partly in
       term-time;
   (b) in which he is taking examinations relating to the qualifying course; or
   (c) which falls wholly in a vacation from the qualifying course, if in that
       week he takes such steps as he can reasonably be expected to have to
       take in order to have the best prospects of securing employment for
       which he is available under regulation 17A(3)(c).]

AMENDMENT

1. Social Security Amendment (New Deal) Regulations 1998 (SI 1998/1274),   **3.144**
reg.6 (June 1, 1998).

DEFINITIONS

"employment": see Jobseekers Act 1995, s.7(8); regs 3, 4.
"employed earner's employment": see Jobseekers Act 1995, s.7(8); SSCBA 1992, s.2.
"examination"—*ibid.*
"qualifying course"—*ibid.*, reg., 17A(7).
"self-employed earner's employment": see Jobseekers Act 1995, s.7(8); SSCBA
   1992, s.2.
"term-time"—see reg.4.
"vacation"—*ibid.*
"week"—*ibid.*

GENERAL NOTE

Complementing reg.17A, reg.21A provides that during any week in which a   **3.145**
person is treated as available under reg.17A, he will be treated also as actively seeking

work. Where the week is during a vacation from the course, he must however show that during that week he has taken such steps as he can reasonably be expected to have to take to have the best prospects of securing the casual employment for which reg.17A requires him to be available.

Interpretation of certain expressions for the purposes of regulations 18(3)(f)(i) and 19(1)(d)

3.146

22. For the purposes of regulations 18(3)(f)(i) and 19(1)(d)—

(a) a person is engaged in duties for the benefit of others while—

    (i) providing assistance to any person whose life may be endangered or who may be exposed to the risk of serious bodily injury or whose health may be seriously impaired,

    (ii) protecting property of substantial value from imminent risk of serious damage or destruction, or

    (iii) assisting in measures being taken to prevent a serious threat to the health of the people,

as a member of a group of persons organised wholly or partly for the purpose of providing such assistance or, as the case may be, protection;

(b) events which may give rise to an emergency include—

    (i) a fire, a flood or an explosion,

    (ii) a natural catastrophe,

    (iii) a railway or other transport accident,

    (iv) a cave or mountain accident,

    (v) an accident at sea,

    (vi) a person being reported missing and the organisation of a search for that person.

GENERAL NOTE

3.147
Regulation 18(3)(f)(i) provides that in applying the touchstone test of actively seeking employment to a claimant's jobseeking activity in a week, the fact that a claimant was engaged during an emergency in duties for the benefit of others is one of the circumstances to be taken into account. Under reg.19(1)(d) a claimant so engaged for at least three days in a week is treated as actively seeking work in that week. For the purposes of those provisions, this regulation provides in para.(1) a complete definition of when "a person is engaged in duties for the benefit of others" and in para.(b) an indication of what events can give rise to an "emergency". Paragraph (b) is not, however, exhaustive; it reads "events which may give rise to an emergency *include*" (emphasis supplied by annotator). See further reg.14, where the same definitions are deployed, and the annotations to that provision.

Chapter IV

Attendance, information and evidence

GENERAL NOTE

3.148
The terms and effects of the regulations in this Chapter (regs 23–30) are noted in the annotations to s.8 of the Jobseekers Act 1995 (attendance, information and evidence).

Attendance

23. [¹A claimant shall attend at such place and at such time as an employ-   **3.149**
ment officer may specify by a notification which is given or sent to the
claimant and which may be in writing, by telephone or by electronic means.]

AMENDMENT

1. Jobseeker's Allowance (Amendment) (No. 3) Regulations 2000 (SI 2000/
2194), reg.2(2) (September 11, 2000).

GENERAL NOTE

"sent": In *R(JSA) 1/04*, the claimant had been sent a notice, dated October 8,   **3.150**
2001 calling him for interview on October 25, 2001, but, Commissioner Turnbull
accepted, had probably not received it. The Commissioner held that the proper
interpretation of "sent" in accordance with s.7 of the Interpretation Act 1978, as
applied by s.23 of that Act to subordinate legislation, meant that the claimant was
entitled to prove non-receipt in order to say it had not been "sent" with the consequence that his entitlement to JSA could not be terminated since he had not
"failed to attend" the interview.

In *CJSA/1080/2002*, Commissioner Rowland held that the requirement to attend
as a condition of entitlement to JSA lapses once the claimant has been informed that
his claim for JSA has been rejected. In that case, the letter so informing the claimant
may have been meant to refer only to IBJSA but was so worded that a reasonable
claimant would understand it to reject both her claim for IBJSA and CBJSA.
Accordingly, the tribunal had erred in not considering title to CBJSA: the requirement to attend having lapsed, regs 25 and 26 were inapplicable, so that there was no
limit to the period for which the tribunal could have awarded CBJSA on the appeal.

[¹ Attendance by members of a joint-claim couple

23A. Each member of a joint-claim couple shall attend at such place and   **3.151**
at such time as the employment officer may specify by a notification which
is given or sent to that member and which may be in writing, by telephone
or by electronic means.]

AMENDMENT

1. Jobseeker's Allowance (Joint Claims) Regulations 2000 (SI 2000/1978), Sch.2,
para.2 (March 19, 2001).

GENERAL NOTE

"sent": see *R(JSA) 1/04* noted in the commentary to reg.23, above. On the require-   **3.152**
ment to attend lapsing, see *CJSA/1080/2002* noted in the commentary to reg.23,
above.

Provision of information and evidence

24.—(1) A claimant shall provide such information as to his circum-   **3.153**
stances, his availability for employment and the extent to which he is actively
seeking employment as may be required by the Secretary of State in order
to determine the entitlement of the claimant to a jobseeker's allowance,
whether that allowance is payable to him and, if so, in what amount.

[¹ (1A) A member of a joint-claim couple shall provide such information
as to the circumstances of each or either member of a couple, the availability for employment of each or either member of the couple and the extent

to which each or either member of the couple is actively seeking employment as may be required by the Secretary of State in order to determine the entitlement of the couple to a jobseeker's allowance, whether that allowance is payable to the couple and, if so, in what amount.]

(2) A claimant shall furnish such other information in connection with the claim, or any question arising out of it, as may be required by the Secretary of State.

(3) Where—

(a) a jobseeker's allowance may be claimed by either member of a couple, or

(b) entitlement to a jobseeker's allowance or whether that allowance is payable and, if so, in what amount, is or may be affected by the circumstances of either member of a couple or any member of a polygamous marriage,

the Secretary of State may require the member of the couple other than the claimant to certify in writing whether he agrees to the claimant's making the claim, or that he, or any member of a polygamous marriage, confirms the information given about his circumstances. [¹, and in this paragraph "couple" does not include a joint-claim couple.

(3A) Where entitlement to a joint-claim jobseeker's allowance or whether that allowance is payable and, if so, in what amount, is or may be affected by the circumstances of any member of a polygamous marriage, the Secretary of State may require either member of the joint-claim couple to certify in writing that any member of the polygamous marriage confirms the information given about that member's circumstances.]

(4) A claimant shall furnish such certificates, documents and other evidence as may be required by the Secretary of State for the determination of the claim.

(5) A claimant shall furnish such certificates, documents and other evidence affecting his continuing entitlement to a jobseeker's allowance, whether that allowance is payable to him and, if so, in what amount as the Secretary of State may require.

[¹ (5A) A member of a joint-claim couple shall furnish such certificates, documents and other evidence affecting the continuing entitlement of the couple to a jobseeker's allowance, whether that allowance is payable to the couple and, if so, in what amount as the Secretary of State may require.]

(6) A claimant shall, if the Secretary of State requires him to do so, provide a signed declaration to the effect that—

(a) since making a claim for a jobseeker's allowance or since he last provided a declaration in accordance with this paragraph he has either been available for employment or satisfied the circumstances to be treated as available for employment, save as he has otherwise notified the Secretary of State.

(b) since making a claim for a jobseeker's allowance or since he last provided a declaration in accordance with this paragraph he has either been actively seeking employment to the extent necessary to give him his best prospects of securing employment or he has satisfied the circumstances to be treated as actively seeking employment, save as he has otherwise notified the Secretary of State, and

(c) since making a claim for a jobseeker's allowance or since he last provided a declaration in accordance with this paragraph there has been no change to his circumstances which might affect his entitlement to

a jobseeker's allowance or the amount of such an allowance, save as
he has notified the Secretary of State.

(7) A claimant shall notify the Secretary of State—

(a) of any change of circumstances which has occurred which he might
reasonably be expected to know might affect his entitlement to a jobseeker's allowance [¹ or, in the case of a joint-claim couple, the entitlement of the couple to a joint-claim jobseeker's allowance] or the
payability or amount of such an allowance; and

(b) of any such change of circumstances which he is aware is likely so to
occur,

and shall do so as soon as reasonably practicable after its occurrence or, as
the case may be, after he becomes so aware, by giving notice in writing
(unless the Secretary of State determines in any particular case to accept
notice given otherwise than in writing) to the appropriate office.

(8) Where, pursuant to paragraph (1) [¹ (1A)] or (2), a claimant is
required to provide information he shall do so when he attends in accordance with a [²notification] under regulation 23 [¹ or 23A], if so required by
the Secretary of State, or within such period as the Secretary of State may
require.

(9) Where, pursuant to paragraph (4) or (5) [¹ or (5A)], a claimant is
required to provide certificates, documents or other evidence he shall do so
within seven days of being so required or such longer period as the Secretary
of State may consider reasonable.

(10) Where, pursuant to paragraph (6), a claimant is required to provide
a signed declaration he shall provide it on the day on which he is required
to attend in accordance with a [² notification] under regulation 23 [¹ or 23A]
or on such other day as the Secretary of State may require.

AMENDMENTS

1. Jobseeker's Allowance (Joint Claims) Regulations 2000 (SI 2000/1978), Sch.2,   **3.154**
para.3 (March 19, 2001).

2. Jobseeker's Allowance (Amendment) (No. 3) Regulations 2000 (SI 2000/
2194), reg.2(3) (September, 11, 2000).

GENERAL NOTE

A failure to provide a signed declaration in accordance with reg.25(6) and (10)
means loss of entitlement to JSA (see reg.25(1)(c)). The mere non-furnishing of the
evidence contemplated by the other provisions in reg.24 has no such automatic
preclusive effect, but may, of course, cause a decision-maker or tribunal to doubt
assertions about actively seeking work (see Commissioner Brown in the Northern
Ireland decisions *C1/00–01 (JSA)* and *C2/00–01 (JSA)*, para.35).

Entitlement ceasing on a failure to comply

25.—(1) Subject to regulation 27, entitlement to a jobseeker's allowance   **3.155**
shall cease in the following circumstances—

(a) if [³ a claimant] fails to attend on the day specified in a [² notification]
under regulation 23 [³ or 23A], other than a [² notification] requiring
attendance under an employment programme or a training scheme;

(b) if—

[¹(i) [³ that claimant] attends on the day specified in a [² notification]
under regulation 23 [³ or 23A] but fails to attend at the time

specified in that [² notification] (other than a [² notification] requiring attendance under an employment programme or a training scheme), and the Secretary of State has informed ³ that claimant] in writing that a failure to attend, on the next occasion on which he is required to attend, at the time specified in such a [² notification] may result in his entitlement to a jobseeker's allowance ceasing, and

    (ii) he fails to attend at the time specified in such a [² notification] on the next occasion;

(c) if [³ that claimant] was required to provide a signed declaration as referred to in regulation 24(6) and he fails to provide it on the day on which he ought to do so in accordance with regulation 24(10).

(2) In this regulation, "an employment programme" and "a training scheme" have the meaning given in regulation 75.

AMENDMENTS

3.156   1. Jobseeker's Allowance (Amendment) Regulations 1999 (SI 1999/530), reg.2 (March 25, 1999).

2. Jobseeker's Allowance (Amendment) (No. 3) Regulations 2000 (SI 2000/2194), reg.2(4) (September 11, 2000).

3. Jobseeker's Allowance (Joint Claims) Regulations 2000 (SI 2000/1978), Sch.2, para.4 (March 19, 2001).

DEFINITIONS

"an employment programme": see reg.75.
"a training scheme": see reg.75.

GENERAL NOTE

In *CJSA/3139/2001*, Commissioner Rowland held that someone who attended on the right day but failed to sign the required declaration, could not lose entitlement because of reg.25(1)(a) or (b) but was instead caught by reg.25(1)(c). Here the claimant knew he had to sign on, but left the Jobcentre rather than waiting for a member of staff to return to the enquiries desk. Accordingly, he did not have good cause for the failure to sign.

Time at which entitlement is to cease

3.157   **26.** Entitlement to a jobseeker's allowance shall cease in accordance with regulation 25 on whichever is the earlier of—

(a) the day after the last day in respect of which [⁴ that claimant] has provided information or evidence which [² shows that he continues to be entitled] to a jobseeker's allowance,

(b) if [¹ regulation 25(1)(a) or (b)] applies, the day on which he was required to attend, and

(c) if [¹ regulation 25(1)(c)] applies, the day on which he ought to have provided the signed declaration, provided that it shall not cease earlier than the day after he last attended in compliance with a [³ notification] under regulation 23 [⁴ or 23A].

AMENDMENTS

3.158   1. Jobseeker's Allowance (Amendment) Regulations 1996 (SI 1996/1516, reg.8 and Sch. (October 7, 1996).

2. Jobseeker's Allowance and Income Support (General) (Amendment) Regulations 1996 (SI 1996/1517), reg.9 (October 7, 1996).

3. Jobseeker's Allowance (Amendment) (No. 3) Regulations 2000 (SI 2000/2194), reg.2(5) (September 11, 2000).

4. Jobseeker's Allowance (Joint Claims) Regulations 2000 (SI 2000/1978), Sch.2, para.5 (March 19, 2001).

GENERAL NOTE

In *CJSA/2652/2001*, Commissioner Williams approved the approach in   **3.159**
CJSA/3139/2001, noted in the commentary to reg.25, above. It did not, however, apply to his case. He attempted in the case to elucidate regs 23–26 and, in particular, to make some sense of regulation 26. His approach was, however, overturned on appeal by the Court of Appeal in *Ferguson v Secretary of State for Work and Pensions* (neutral citation: [2003] EWCA Civ 56, reported as *R(JSA)6/03*). Lady Justice Arden, giving the judgment of the Court, stated:

"**38.** I turn to the first of the substantial issues, which I would call the devoid issue. I accept, for the reasons I have already given, the submission of the Secretary of State that there is a clear distinction between regulations 25 and 26. They reflect the enabling power and deal separately with cessation events and the effective date for cessation of a benefit. When we examine regulation 26(a) it is clear that that is directed to ensuring that the claimant only receives benefit for the period in respect of which he fulfils all the conditions of entitlement, otherwise there would be no point in having paragraph 26(a). It is necessary, of course, to fix a date other than that of the cessation event, and regulation 26 has that object because it refers, as I have said, to the earlier of certain events. The purpose of regulation 26(a), in contrast to 26(b) and (c), seems to me clearly to be to fix the date so that the claimant only receives benefit for the period in which he fulfils all the conditions of entitlement and has demonstrated that. As I have said, the proviso confirms that. It is also important to note that, contrary to the conclusion of the Commissioner, regulation 26(a) is dealing with a factual situation; namely, it is establishing the date as the day after the last day in respect of which the claimant provided information or evidence of the requisite kind. It is not dealing in terms with a failure to provide information or evidence; it is directed simply to a factual situation. Had it been intended to deal with a failure to comply with a requirement to produce information or evidence, as it seems to me, it would necessarily have been differently worded.
39. As I see it, the answer to the devoid issue must be that 26(a) does not render 26(b) and (c) devoid of meaning. Circumstances can arise in which no declaration is required, in which case 26(b) and (c) will become operative. Circumstances can also arise where there is a failure to attend and reasonable cause for non-attendance is not shown but the claimant does produce satisfactory evidence of compliance with the conditions. On this point I would turn to the evidence of Mr Anthony Booth, an administrator in the Department for Work and Pensions responsible for certain policy aspects of the JSA. His witness statement is dated 13th November 2002. He says this:

'3. JSA claimants are normally required to attend the Jobcentre each fortnight. They lose entitlement if they fail to do so, unless they can show good cause for the failure within the next five working days. In the second quarter of 2002, about 180,000 JSA claims were terminated in these circumstances.

4. Most of those failing to attend make no contact with the Jobcentre during the five days. Consequently in terminating their entitlement, the Jobcentre has no information as to whether the JSA conditions were satisfied during the preceding fortnight. Entitlement is therefore terminated indefinitely with effect from the day after their last correct attendance.

5. Of those whose entitlement is terminated on a failure to attend, a minority make contact during the next five days but are found not to have good cause for their failure. They can, however, usually show that they satisfied the JSA conditions during the previous fortnight. Their entitlement is therefore terminated with effect from the date of failure only. They are also in a position to make an immediate new claim, so that their period of disentitlement lasts only from the date of failure to the date of renewal. About 30,000 people fell into this category in the second quarter of 2002.'

40. Pausing there, as Keene L.J. pointed out, the date of failure to which Mr Booth referred is the date of failure to attend. So circumstances can arise in which a person fails to attend but produces subsequently, and is accepted as producing, evidence of entitlement, so that paragraph (a) of regulation 26 would not apply.
41. Before I leave Mr Booth's statement on this point, I note that in the next paragraph he draws the conclusion that, although it cannot be substantiated, it is probable that a significant proportion of the people who fail to attend and make no contact with the Jobcentre have in fact ceased to satisfy the JSA entitlement conditions at some point between their last attendance and the date of failure. He adds:

'Paying JSA to them for that period therefore risks making an overpayment.'

42. Therefore, this evidence illustrates that section 26(a) does not render the subsequent paragraphs of that regulation inoperative or ineffective. Regulation 26(a) does not, moreover, provide that the necessary information can only be provided on the specified date for interview or in the window of opportunity permitted by regulation 27.
43. I therefore turn to the next substantial issue of construction, which I will call the analogue issue. That is the question which much concerned the Commissioner. It is as to whether there was a sanction for failure to comply with a requirement under regulation 24(5) to produce information or evidence. As I see it, the answer to this issue has been provided by the Secretary of State's reference to the Social Security and Child Support (Decisions and Appeals) Regulations 1999, from which I have read extracts. Accordingly, there is separate statutory machinery which comes into operation if there is a failure to provide information or evidence and therefore it is not significant, in my judgment, that the failure to provide information or evidence is not a cessation event for the purpose of regulation 25."

3.160 The court also held that the term "evidence" in para.(a) includes the declaration required by regs 24(6) and 25(1)(c) (para.44). Reg.26(c) is not limited to "postal signers" (para.48). Lady Justice Arden considered the conclusion the court had reached to be a "logical one" (para.50). Commissioner Williams had erred in failing

"to give appropriate weight in his conclusion to two important textual points from these Regulations. The first point is that regulations 25 and 26 cover different subject matters. They have a different scope. Regulation 25 deals with cessation events; regulation 26 deals with the effective date of cessation of benefit. In addition, the Commissioner failed, in my judgment, to give appropriate weight to the 'earlier' point. As I see it, regulation 26 compels reference to the earlier of two dates. The court must give effect to those words and apply the regulation so that benefit terminates on whichever of those dates first occurs. It seems to me that the regulation was probably correct to say 'earlier' rather than 'earliest', since only one of the cessation events in paragraphs (b) and (c) of regulation 26 will occur. Once it occurs, the benefit terminates and any subsequent event is irrelevant. Contrary to Mr Ferguson's submission, I cannot treat as subsumed within a failure to attend a failure to provide information or to sign a declaration with which a requirement to attend was coupled. It seems to me that those two matters must be decoupled in order to apply the regulation properly in accordance with its wording.

50. The conclusion which I reach is, in my judgment, a logical one. Entitlement to JSA depends on eligibility. Eligibility depends for one of its requirements on showing entitlement at the end of the 14-day period. On the interpretation which I prefer, benefit will cease as at the date immediately following the last date for which the necessary proof was given if there is a failure to attend in accordance with regulation 25(a) or (b) or a failure to sign a declaration. As Mr Forsdick put it, the Commissioner's construction gives the claimant who is in default an additional two-week period of grace for which he cannot in fact prove eligibility. That seems to me to be contrary to the scheme of the Regulations. In addition, it seems to me to undermine regulations 27 and 28, which give a window of opportunity for five days only provided that the claimant can establish a reasonable cause for nonattendance. As I see it, the Commissioner's construction, with respect to him, was inconsistent with and undermined those regulations. Accordingly, on the main issue of construction I would allow the appeal." (paras 49, 50.)

In *R(JSA)2/04*, Commissioner Rowland considered *Ferguson* and noted that as the Secretary of State submitted in *Ferguson*.

"regulation 26(a) is intended to avoid overpayments by allowing the Secretary of State to terminate promptly an award of jobseeker's allowance in a case where a claimant has failed to 'sign on' and has not shown continued entitlement during the previous fortnight. However, I am satisfied that the language used does not prevent the Secretary of State's decision from being adjusted on revision or appeal if the claimant takes appropriate action within the time allowed under the Social Security and Child Support (Decisions and Appeals) Regulations 1999 and provides the information or evidence before a further decision is made" (para.18).

Where entitlement is not to cease

27.—(1) Entitlement to a jobseeker's allowance shall not cease if [² a claimant] shows, before the end of the fifth working day after the day on which he failed to comply with a [¹ notification] under regulation 23 [² or 23A] or to provide a signed declaration in accordance with regulation 24, that he had good cause for the failure.

(2) In this regulation, "working day" means any day on which the appropriate office is not closed.

3.161

AMENDMENTS

1. Jobseeker's Allowance (Amendment) (No. 3) Regulations 2000 (SI 2000/ 2194), reg.2(5) (September 11, 2000).
2. Jobseeker's Allowance (Joint Claims) Regulations 2000 (SI 2000/1978), Sch.2, para.6 (March 19, 2001).

3.162

DEFINITION

"appropriate office"—see reg.4.

Matters to be taken into account in determining whether a claimant has good cause for failing to comply with a notice under regulation 23 [² or 23A]

28.—(1) Subject to regulation 30, in determining, for the purposes of regulation 27, whether a claimant has good cause for failing to comply with

3.163

a [¹ notification] under regulation 23 [² or 23A] the matters which are to be taken into account shall include the following

(a) whether the claimant misunderstood the requirement on him due to any learning, language or literacy difficulties of the claimant or any misleading information given to the claimant by an employment officer;

(b) whether the claimant was attending a medical or dental appointment, or accompanying a person for whom the claimant has caring responsibilities to such an appointment, and whether it would have been unreasonable, in the circumstances, to rearrange the appointment;

(c) any difficulty with the claimant's normal mode of transport and whether there was any reasonable available alternative;

(d) the established customs and practices of the religion, if any, to which the claimant belongs;

(e) whether the claimant was attending an interview for employment.

(2) In this regulation, "employment" means employed earner's employment except in relation to a claimant to whom regulation 20(2) applies and for the duration only of any permitted period determined in his case in accordance with regulation 16, in which case, for the duration of that period, it means employed earner's employment or self-employed earner's employment.

AMENDMENTS

3.164   1. Jobseeker's Allowance (Amendment) (No. 3) Regulations 2000 (SI 2000/2194), reg.2(5) (September 11, 2000).

2. Jobseeker's Allowance (Joint Claims) Regulations 2000 (SI 2000/1978), Sch.2, para.7 (March 19, 2001).

DEFINITIONS

"caring responsibilities"—see reg.4.
"employed earner's employment"—see regs 3, 4, SSCBA 1992, s.2(1).
"employment officer"—see reg.4.
"self-employed earner's employment"—see regs 1(3), 3, SSCBA 1992, s.2(1).

Matters to be taken into account in determining whether a claimant has good cause for failing to provide a signed declaration

3.165   **29.** In determining, for the purposes of regulation 27, whether a claimant has good cause for failing to comply with a requirement to provide a signed declaration, as referred to in regulation 24(6), on the day on which he ought to do so the matters which are to be taken into account shall include the following—

(a) whether there were adverse postal conditions;

(b) whether the claimant misunderstood the requirement on him due to any learning, language or literacy difficulties of the claimant or any misleading information given to the claimant by an employment officer.

DEFINITION

"employment officer"—see reg.4.

Circumstances in which a claimant is to be regarded as having good cause for failing to comply with a [¹ notification] under regulation 23 [² or 23A]

30. For the purposes of regulation 27, a claimant is to be regarded as   3.166
having good cause for failing to comply with a [¹ notification] under regulation 23 [² or 23A]—
- (a) where, if regulation 5(1) [³ (a) or (b)] applies in his case, he was required to attend at a time less than 48 hours from receipt by him of the [¹ notification];
- (b) where, if regulation 5(2) applies in his case, he was required to attend at a time less than 24 hours from receipt by him of the [¹ notification];
- (c) where he was, in accordance with regulation 14(1)(a)–(g), (k)–(n) or 14(2), treated as available for employment on the day on which he failed to attend;
- (d) where the day on which he failed to attend falls in a week in which he was, in accordance with regulation 19(1)(p) and 19(2), treated as actively seeking employment.

AMENDMENTS

1. Jobseeker's Allowance (Amendment) (No. 3) Regulations 2000 (SI 2000/   3.167
2194), reg.2(5) (September 11, 2000).
2. Jobseeker's Allowance (Joint Claims) Regulations 2000 (SI 2000/1978), Sch.2,
para.8 (March 19, 2001).
3. Jobseeker's Allowance (Amendment) Regulations 2002 (SI 2002/3072), reg.6
(January 1, 2003).

DEFINITIONS

"employment"—see reg.4.
"week"—*ibid.*

Chapter V

Jobseeker's Agreement

GENERAL NOTE

The terms and effects of the regulations in this Chapter (regs 31–40) are noted in   3.168
the annotations to ss.9 and 10 of the Jobseekers Act 1995 as follows:
Section 9 (the jobseeker's agreement): regs 31–36.
Section 10 (variation of jobseeker's agreement): regs 37–40.

Contents of Jobseeker's Agreement

31. The prescribed requirements for a jobseeker's agreement are that it   3.169
shall contain the following information—
- (a) the claimant's name;
- (b) where the hours for which the claimant is available for employment are restricted in accordance with regulation 7, the total number of hours for which he is available and any pattern of availability;

(c) any restrictions on the claimant's availability for employment, including restrictions on the location or type of employment, in accordance with regulations 5, 8, 13 and 17;

(d) a description of the type of employment which the claimant is seeking;

(e) the action which the claimant will take—
   (i) to seek employment; and
   (ii) to improve his prospects of finding employment;

(f) the dates of the start and of the finish of any permitted period in his case for the purposes of sections 6(5) and 7(5);

(g) a statement of the claimant's right—
   (i) to have a proposed jobseeker's agreement referred to [¹ the Secretary of State];
   (ii) to seek a [² revision or supersession] of any determination of, or direction given by, [¹ the Secretary of State]; and
   (iii) to appeal to [³ an appeal tribunal] against any determination of, or direction given by [¹ the Secretary of State] [⁴ following a revision or supersession];

(h) the date of the agreement.

AMENDMENTS

3.170   1. Social Security Act 1998 (Commencement No.11, and Savings and Consequential and Transitional Provisions) Order 1999, Sch.12, para.2 (SI 1999/ 2860 (C.75)) (October 18, 1999).
    2. Social Security Act 1998 (Commencement No.11, and Savings and Consequential and Transitional Provisions) Order 1999, Sch.12, para.1(a) (SI 1999/ 2860 (C.75)) (October 18, 1999).
    3. Social Security Act 1998 (Commencement No.11, and Savings and Consequential and Transitional Provisions) Order 1999, Sch.12, para.1(b)(i) (SI 1999/2860 (C.75)) (October 18, 1999).
    4. Social Security Act 1998 (Commencement No.11, and Savings and Consequential and Transitional Provisions) Order 1999, Sch.12, para.1(b)(ii) (SI 1999/2860 (C.75)) (October 18, 1999).

Back-dating of a Jobseeker's Agreement [¹ . . .]

3.171   **32.** In giving a direction under section 9(7)(c), the [² Secretary of State] shall take into account all relevant matters including—

(a) where the claimant refused to accept the agreement proposed by the employment officer, whether he was reasonable in so refusing;

(b) where the claimant has signified to the employment officer or to the [² Secretary of State] that the claimant is prepared to accept an agreement which differs from the agreement proposed by the employment officer, whether the terms of the agreement which he is prepared to accept are reasonable;

(c) where the claimant has signified to the employment officer or to the [² Secretary of State] that the claimant is prepared to accept the agreement proposed by the employment officer, that fact;

(d) the date on which, in all the circumstances, he considers that the claimant was first prepared to enter into an agreement which the [² Secretary of State] considers reasonable; and

(e) where the date on which the claimant first had an opportunity to sign a jobseeker's agreement was later than the date on which he made a claim, that fact.

AMENDMENTS

1. Social Security Act 1998 (Commencement No.11, and Savings and Consequential and Transitional Provisions) Order 1999, Sch.12, para.3 (SI 1999/2860 (C.75)) (October 18, 1999).
2. Social Security Act 1998 (Commencement No.11, and Savings and Consequential and Transitional Provisions) Order 1999, Sch.12, para.2 (SI 1999/2860 (C.75)) (October 18, 1999).

3.172

Notification of Determinations and Directions under Section 9

33. The claimant shall be notified of—
  (a) any determination of the [¹ Secretary of State] under section 9;
  (b) any direction given by the [¹ Secretary of State] under section 9;

3.173

AMENDMENT

1. Social Security Act 1998 (Commencement No.11, and Savings and Consequential and Transitional Provisions) Order 1999, Sch.12, para.2 (SI 1999/2860 (C.75)) (October 18, 1999).

Jobseeker's Agreement treated as having been made

34. A claimant is to be treated as having satisfied the condition mentioned in section 1(2)(b)—

  (a) where he is permitted to make a claim for a jobseeker's allowance without attending at an office of the [³ Department for Work and Pensions], for the period beginning with the date of claim and ending on the date on which he has an interview with an employment officer for the purpose of drawing up a jobseeker's agreement;

  (b) where, after the date of claim, the claim is terminated before he has an interview with an employment officer for the purpose of drawing up a jobseeker's agreement;

  (c) as long as he is treated as available for employment in accordance with regulation 14 where the circumstances set out in that regulation arise after the date of claim and before he has an interview with an employment officer for the purpose of drawing up a job-seeker's agreement;

  (d) as long as there are circumstances not peculiar to the claimant which make impracticable or unduly difficult the normal operation of the provisions governing, or the practice relating to, the claiming, awarding or payment of jobseeker's allowance;

[¹ (e) where the claimant was in receipt of a training allowance and was, in accordance with regulation 170, entitled to an income-based jobseeker's allowance without being available for employment, having entered into a jobseeker's agreement or actively seeking employment, for the period beginning with the date on which regulation 170 ceased to apply to him and ending on the date on which he has an interview with an employment officer for the purpose of drawing up a jobseeker's agreement.]

[² (f) if he is temporarily absent from Great Britain in the circumstances prescribed in regulation 50(6B)(a) or (c), for the period of any such temporary absence.]

3.174

AMENDMENTS

3.175   1. Jobseeker's Allowance (Amendment) Regulations 1996 (SI 1996/1516), reg.3 (October 7, 1996).
2. Jobseeker's Allowance (Joint Claims) Regulations 2000 (SI 2000/1978), Sch.2, para.9 (March 19, 2001).
3. Secretaries of State for Education and Skills and for Work and Pensions Order 2002 (SI 2002/1397), art.12 and Sch., para.26 (June 27, 2002).

DEFINITIONS

"date of claim": see reg.1(3).
"employment": see regs 3, 4.
"employment officer": see reg.4.
"training allowance": see reg.1(3).

Automatic Back-dating of Jobseeker's Agreement

3.176   **35.** Where a jobseeker's agreement is signed on a date later than the date of claim and there is no reference of that agreement to [¹ the Secretary of State] under section 9(6), the agreement shall be treated as having effect on the date of claim.

AMENDMENT

1. Social Security Act 1998 (Commencement No. 11, and Savings and Consequential and Transitional Provisions) Order 1999, Sch.12, para.2 (SI 1999/2860 (C.75)) (October 18, 1999).

DEFINITION

"date of claim": see reg.1(3).

Jobseeker's Agreement to remain in effect

3.177   **36.** A jobseeker's agreement entered into by a claimant shall not cease to have effect on the coming to an end of an award of a jobseeker's allowance made to him—
(a) where a further claim for a jobseeker's allowance is made within a period not exceeding 14 days; or
(b) in respect of any part of a period of suspension, where—
(i) the Secretary of State has directed under regulation 37(1A) of the Claims and Payments Regulations that payment under an award be suspended for a definite or indefinite period on the ground that a question arises whether the conditions for entitlement to that allowance are or were fulfilled or the award ought to be revised,
(ii) subsequently that suspension expires or is cancelled in respect of a part only of the period for which it has been in force, and
(iii) it is then determined that the award should be revised to the effect that there was no entitlement to the allowance in respect of all or any part of the period between the start of the period over which the award has been suspended and the date when the suspension expires or is cancelled; or
(c) for as long as the claimant satisfies the conditions of entitlement to national insurance credits, other than any condition relating to the existence of a jobseeker's agreement, in accordance with the Social Security (Credits) Regulations 1975.

Variation of Jobseeker's Agreement

37. The prescribed manner for varying a jobseeker's agreement shall be   **3.178**
in writing and signed by both parties in accordance with section 10(2) on
the proposal of the claimant or the employment officer.

<small>DEFINITION</small>

"employment officer": see reg.4.

Direction to vary Agreement: time for compliance

38. The prescribed period for the purposes of section 10(6)(c) shall be   **3.179**
the period of 21 days beginning with the date on which the direction was
issued.

Variation of Agreement: matters to be taken into account

39. In giving a direction under section 10(6)(b) or (d) [¹ the Secretary of   **3.180**
State] shall take into account the preference of the claimant if he considers
that both the claimant's proposals and those of employment officer satisfy
the requirements of section 10(5).

<small>AMENDMENT</small>

1. Social Security Act 1998 (Commencement No. 11, and Savings and
Consequential and Transitional Provisions) Order 1999, Sch.12, para.2 (SI
1999/2860 (C.75)) (October 18, 1999).

<small>DEFINITION</small>

"employment officer": see reg.4.

Notification of Determinations and Directions under Section 10

40. The claimant shall be notified of—   **3.181**
(a) any determination of [¹ the Secretary of State] under section 10;
(b) any direction of [¹ the Secretary of State] under section 10.

<small>AMENDMENT</small>

1. Social Security Act 1998 (Commencement No.11, and Savings and
Consequential and Transitional Provisions) Order 1999, Sch.12, para.2 (SI
1999/2860 (C.75)) (October 18, 1999).

*[Regulations 41–45 were revoked by Social Security Act 1998 (Commencement No. 11,
and Savings and Consequential and Transitional Provisions) Order 1999, Sch.12, para.4
(SI 1999/2860) (October 18, 1999).]*

PART III

OTHER CONDITIONS OF ENTITLEMENT

Waiting days

46.—(1) Paragraph 4 of Schedule 1 to the Act shall not apply in a case   **3.182**
where—

(a) a person's entitlement to a jobseeker's allowance commences within 12 weeks of an entitlement of his to income support, incapacity benefit or [² carer's allowance] coming to an end; or

(b) a claim for a jobseeker's allowance falls to be determined by reference to section 3(1)(f)(ii) (persons under the age of 18).
[¹ or

(c) a joint-claim couple are entitled to a joint-claim jobseeker's allowance in respect of themselves and that paragraph of that Schedule has already applied to one member of that couple in respect of a job-seeking period which is linked to a jobseeking period relating to that member which has commenced by virtue of his having claimed a jobseeker's allowance as a member of that couple;

(d) a joint-claim couple have claimed a jobseeker's allowance jointly within 12 weeks of either member of that couple being entitled to a jobseeker's allowance, income support, incapacity benefit or [² carer's allowance];

(e) a member of a joint-claim couple is both in receipt of a training allowance and the nominated member for the purposes of section 3B.]

(2) In the case of a person to whom paragraph 4 of Schedule 1 to the Act applies, the number of days is 3.

AMENDMENTS

1. Jobseeker's Allowance (Joint Claims) Regulations 2000 (SI 2000/1978), Sch.2, para.10 (March 19, 2001).
2. Social Security (Miscellaneous Amendments) Regulations 2003 (SI 2003/511), reg.3(5) (April 1, 2003).

DEFINITION

"the Act": see reg.1(3).

GENERAL NOTE

3.183   Unemployment benefit was a daily benefit payable in respect of a six-day week. JSA is a weekly benefit. Nonetheless, through para.4 of Sch.1 to the Jobseekers Act 1995, as amplified by this regulation, it deploys the concept of "waiting days", familiar from unemployment benefit but never part of income support, whereby, despite meeting the other conditions of entitlement to JSA, there is no entitlement to it for a number of days (currently three (see para.(2)) but alterable by regulations) at the start of a jobseeking period. On "jobseeking period" and the effect of "linking", see notes to regs 47 and 48 below. Note further that the "waiting days" rule does not apply where the claimant's entitlement to JSA begins within 12 weeks of the ending of his entitlement to income support, incapacity benefit or invalid care allowance, nor where the claim for income-based JSA has to be determined by reference to s.3(1)(f)(ii) (*i.e.* the person is 16 or 17, registered for training but is not being provided with any, severe hardship will result to him if JSA is not paid, and the (Secretary of State directs that s.16 is to apply to him) (para.(1)(a), (b)).

As regards a "joint-claim couple", the waiting days will not have to be served again where the jobseeking period commenced because of a claim as a "joint claim couple" links to a jobseeking period in which one of the members had already served the waiting days (para.(1)(c)). Nor will they need to be served where the joint-claim is within 12 weeks of either member's entitlement to jobseeker's allowance, income support, incapacity benefit or invalid care allowance (para.(1)(d)). Nor do the waiting days have to be served if the nominated member (see Jobseekers Act 1995, s.3B) of the couple is receiving a training allowance (para.(1)(e)).

A sanction imposed under s.19 of the Act (see Part V of these Regulations) will not begin until after any waiting days have been served. But a claimant who is entitled to income-based JSA will qualify for maximum housing benefit and/or council tax benefit during any waiting days (see reg.2(3A)(b) of the Housing Benefit Regulations 1987 and the Council Tax Benefit Regulations 1992 respectively).

Jobseeking period

47.—(1) For the purposes of the Act, but subject to paragraphs (2) and (3), the "jobseeking period" means any period throughout which the claimant satisfies or is treated as satisfying the conditions specified in paragraphs (a) to (c) and (e) to (i) of subsection (2) of section 1 (conditions of entitlement to a jobseeker's allowance).

3.184

(2) Any period in which—

(a) a claimant does not satisfy any of the requirements in section 1(2)(a) to (c), and

(b) a jobseeker's allowance is payable to him in accordance with Part IX (Hardship), [³ or, where the claimant is a member of a joint-claim couple, a jobseeker's allowance is payable in accordance with Part IXA (hardship)]

shall, for the purposes of paragraph (1), be treated as a period in which the claimant satisfies the conditions specified in paragraphs (a) to (c) of subsection (2) of section 1.

[¹(2A) Any period in which a claimant is entitled to a jobseeker's allowance in accordance with regulation 11(3) of the Jobseeker's Allowance (Transitional Provisions) Regulations 1995 shall, for the purposes of paragraph (1), be treated as a period in which he satisfies the conditions specified in paragraphs (a) to (c) and (e) to (i) of subsection (2) of section 1.]

(3) The following periods shall not be, or be part of, a jobseeking period—

(a) any period in respect of which no claim for a jobseeker's allowance has been made or treated as made;

(b) such period as falls before the day on which a claim for a jobseeker's allowance is made or treated as made [². . .];

(c) where a claim for a jobseeker's allowance has been made or treated as made but no entitlement to benefit arises in respect of a period before the date of claim by virtue of section 1(2) of the Administration Act (limits for backdating entitlement), that period;

(d) where—

(i) a claimant satisfies the conditions specified in paragraphs (a) to (c) and (e) to (i) of subsection (2) of section 1; and

(ii) entitlement to a jobseeker's allowance ceases in accordance with regulation 25 (entitlement ceasing on a failure to comply),

the period beginning with the date in respect of which, in accordance with regulation 26, entitlement ceases and ending with the day before the date in respect of which the claimant again becomes entitled to a jobseeker's allowance; or

(e) any week in which a claimant is not entitled to a jobseeker's allowance in accordance with section 14 (trade disputes).

[²(f) subject to regulation 2A, any period in respect of which the claimant is not entitled to a jobseeker's allowance because section 1(1A) of the

Administration Act (requirement to state national insurance number) applies.]

(4) For the purposes of section 5 (duration of a contribution-based jobseeker's allowance) any day—

    (a) which falls within a jobseeking period;

    (b) and either;

        (i) on which the claimant satisfies the conditions specified in section 2 (the contribution-based conditions) other than the conditions specified in subsection (1)(c) and (d) of that section; and

        (ii) on which a contribution–based jobseeker's allowance is not payable to the claimant by virtue of section 19 [4 or on which the claimant is a member of a joint-claim couple and a joint-claim jobseeker's allowance is not payable or is reduced because he is subject to sanctions by virtue of section 20A] [5 or by virtue of a restriction imposed pursuant to section 62 or 63 of the Child Support, Pensions and Social Security Act 2000 [6 or section 7, 8 or 9 of the Social Security Fraud Act 2001] (loss of benefit provisions)];

    (c) which falls within a period which is treated as a period in which the claimant satisfies the conditions specified in paragraphs (a)–(c) of sub-section (2) of section 1, in accordance with paragraph (2),

shall be treated as if it was a day in respect of which he was entitled to a contribution-based jobseeker's allowance.

AMENDMENTS

3.185
1. Social Security and Child Support (Jobseeker's Allowance) (Miscellaneous Amendments) Regulations 1996 (SI 1996/2538), reg.2(4) (October 28, 1996).

2. Social Security (Incapacity Benefit and Jobseeker's Allowance) Amendment Regulations 1999 (SI 1999/2226), reg.3 (September 6, 1999).

3. Jobseeker's Allowance (Joint Claims) Regulations 2000 (SI 2000/1978), Sch.2, para.11 (March 19, 2001).

4. Social Security Amendment (Joint Claims) Regulations 2001 (SI 2001/ 518), reg.2(5) (March 19, 2001).

5. Social Security (Breach of Community Order) (Consequential Amendments) Regulations 2001 (SI 2001/1711), reg.2(4) (October 15, 2001).

6. Social Security (Loss of Benefit) (Consequential Amendments) Regulations 2002 (SI 2002/490), reg.7 (April 1, 2002).

DEFINITIONS

"the Act": see reg.1(3).
"claimant": see Jobseekers Act 1995. s.35(1).
"contribution-based jobseeker's allowance": see ss.35(1), 1(4).
"jobseeking period": see para.(1).

GENERAL NOTE

Paras (1)–(3)
3.186
This regulation, read with reg.48, below and para.3 of Sch.1 to the Jobseekers Act 1995, makes provision which benefits those whose unemployment is intermittent, interspersed with, say, periods of employment, of incapacity for work, of training for work or periods when pregnant, by providing, somewhat after the fashion of unemployment benefit and its notion of "period of interruption of employment" ("PIE"), for the concept of "linking" and "linked periods" whereby apparently

separate jobseeking periods are fused into one and certain periods ("linked periods") do not "break" a jobseeking period.

A "jobseeking period" is, basically, any period throughout which the claimant satisfies (or is treated as satisfying) the conditions of entitlement to JSA set out in Jobseekers Act 1995, s.1(2)(a)–(c) and (e)–(i): available for employment; a current jobseeker's agreement; actively seeking employment; not in remunerative work; not receiving relevant education; under pensionable age; and in Great Britain (para.(1)) (note that reg.49, below, treats certain days as ones meeting those conditions in respect of men over 60 but under pensionable age). Where a hardship payment under Pt IX or IXA (joint-claim couple) of these Regulations is paid to a claimant who does not satisfy a labour market condition (any of the conditions in Jobseekers Act 1995, s.1(2)(a)–(c): availability; actively seeking; jobseeker's agreement), he is to be treated as satisfying them for purposes of applying the above definition of jobseeking period (para.(2)). Note that Transitional Reg.11(3) in para.(2A) is now reg.13(3) of the JSA (Transitional) Regs 1996. Certain periods cannot constitute, or be part of, a jobseeking period: (i) any period in which no claim for JSA has been made or treated as made; (ii) any period before the day on which a claim is made; (iii) a period caught by the 12-month limit on backdating entitlement under s.1(2) of the AA 1992; (iv) a period of disentitlement under regs 25, 26; (v) any week of disentitlement because the claimant is caught by the trade dispute rule in Jobseekers Act 1995, s.14; (vi) any period that the claimant is not entitled to JSA because he has not provided the required information or evidence about his national insurance number or that of any adult dependant included in his claim (para.(3)). Para. (3)(f) will apply to days falling on or after September 6, 1999 but not to any period before that date. The amendment is considered necessary to avoid a possible advantage being gained by a person who makes a further claim to JSA that links to the earlier disallowed claim. Without this provision the jobseeking period formed by the earlier claim would determine what tax years were used to decide entitlement to contribution-based JSA and the claimant would not need to serve the three waiting days on the second claim.

[¹ Jobseeking periods: periods of interruption of employment

[³ **47A.**—(1)] For the purposes of section 2(4)(b)(i) and for determining any waiting days—   3.187

[²(za) where a linked period commenced before 7th October 1996 [³. . .], any days of unemployment which form part of a period of interruption of employment where the last day of unemployment in that period of interruption of employment was no more than 8 weeks before the date upon which that linked period commenced;]

  (a) where a jobseeking period or a linked period commences on 7th October 1996, any period of interruption of employment ending within the 8 weeks preceding that date; or

  (b) where a jobseeking period or a linked period commences after 7th October 1996, any period of interruption of employment ending within the 12 weeks preceding the day the jobseeking period or linked period commenced,

shall be treated as a jobseeking period [²and, for the purposes of paragraph (za), a day shall be treated as being, or not being, a day of unemployment in accordance with section 25A of the Social Security Contributions and Benefits Act 1992 and with any regulations made under that section, as in force on 6th October 1996].]

[³(2) In paragraph (1) "period of interruption of employment" in relation to a period prior to 7th October 1996 has the same meaning as it had in the Benefits Act by virtue of section 25A of that Act (determination of days for which unemployment benefit is payable) as in force on 6th October 1996.]

3.188   1. Social Security and Child Support (Jobseeker's Allowance) (Miscellaneous Amendments) Regulations 1996 (SI 1996/2538), reg.2(5) (October 28, 1996).

2. Jobseeker's Allowance (Amendment) (No. 2) Regulations 1997 (SI 1997/2677), reg.2 (December 1, 1997).

3. Social Security (Miscellaneous Amendments) Regulations 1998 (SI 1998/563), reg.16 (April 1, 1998).

DEFINITION

"jobseeking period"—see reg.47.

Linking periods

3.189   **48.**—(1) For the purposes of the Act, two or more jobseeking periods shall be treated as one jobseeking period where they are separated by a period comprising only—

(a) any period of not more than 12 weeks;

(b) a linked period;

(c) any period of not more than 12 weeks falling between—

(i) any two linked periods; or

(ii) a jobseeking period and a linked period;

[¹(d) a period in respect of which the claimant is summoned for jury service and is required to attend court.]

(2) Linked periods for the purposes of the Act are any of the following periods—

(a) to the extent specified in paragraph (3), any period throughout which the claimant is entitled to [⁸ a carer's allowance] under section 70 of the Benefits Act;

(b) any period throughout which the claimant is incapable of work, or is treated as incapable of work, in accordance with Part XIIA of the Benefits Act;

(c) any period throughout which the claimant was entitled to a maternity allowance under section 35 of the Benefits Act;

(d) any period throughout which the claimant was engaged in training for which a training allowance is payable.

[²(e) a period which includes 6th October [³ 1996] during which the claimant attends court in response to a summons for jury service and which was immediately preceded by a period of entitlement to unemployment benefit.]

[⁴(f) any period throughout which the claimant was participating—

(i) in the [⁷ Self-Employed] Employment Option of the New Deal as specified in regulation 75(1)(a)(ii)(aa);

[⁶(ii) in the Voluntary Sector Option of the New Deal specified in regulation 75(1)(a)(ii)(bb), in the Environment Task Force Option of the New Deal specified in regulation 75(1)(a)(ii)(cc), in the Intensive Activity Period specified in regulation 75(1)(a)(iv) or in the Intensive Activity Period for 50 plus and was not entitled to a jobseeker's allowance because, as a consequence of his participation, the claimant was engaged in remunerative work or failed to satisfy the condition specified either in section 2(1)(c) or in section 3(1)(a).]

[⁵(g) any period throughout which the claimant was participating in an employment zone programme and was not entitled to a job-seeker's allowance because, as a consequence of his participation in that programme, he was engaged in remunerative work or failed to satisfy the condition specified in section 2(1)(c) or in section 3(1)(a).]

[²(2A) A period is a linked period for the purposes of section 2(4)(b)(ii) of the Act only where it ends within 12 weeks or less of the commencement of a jobseeking period or of some other linked period.]

(3) A period of entitlement to invalid care allowance shall be a linked period only where it enables the claimant to satisfy contributions for entitlement to a contribution-based jobseeker's allowance which he would otherwise be unable to satisfy.

AMENDMENTS

1. Jobseeker's Allowance and Income Support (General) (Amendment) Regulations 1996 (SI 1996/1517), reg.15 (October 7, 1996).   **3.190**
2. Social Security and Child Support (Jobseeker's Allowance) (Miscellaneous Amendments) Regulations 1996 (SI 1996/2538), reg.2(6) (October 28, 1996).
3. Social Security (Miscellaneous Amendments) Regulations 1997 (SI 1997/454), reg.2(4) (April 7, 1997).
4. Social Security Amendment (New Deal) Regulations 1997 (SI 1997/2863), reg.4 (January 5, 1998).
5. Social Security Amendment (Employment Zones) Regulations 2000 (SI 2000/724), reg.4(4)(a) (April 3, 2000).
6. Social Security Amendment (New Deal) Regulations 2001 (SI 2001/1029), reg.3 (April 9, 2001).
7. Social Security Amendment (Employment Programme) Regulations 2002 (SI 2002/2314), reg.2(3) (October 14, 2002).
8. Social Security (Miscellaneous Amendments) Regulations 2003 (SI 2003/511), reg.3(5) (April 1, 2003).

DEFINITIONS

"the Act": see s.35(1).   **3.191**
"the Benefits Act": see reg.1(3).
"claimant": see s.35(1).
"employment zone programme": see reg.1(3).
"jobseeking period": see reg.47(1)–(3).
"linked period": see paras (2), (3).
"training allowance": see reg.1(3).
"week": see reg.1(3).

GENERAL NOTE

This regulation, read with reg.47, above, and para.3 of Sch.1 to the Jobseekers Act   **3.192**
1995, above, makes provision which benefits those whose unemployment is intermittent, interspersed with, say, periods of employment, of incapacity for work, of training for work or periods when pregnant, by providing, somewhat after the fashion of unemployment benefit and its notion of "period of interruption of employment" ("PIE"), for the concepts of "linking" and "linked periods" whereby apparently separate jobseeking periods are fused into one and certain periods ("linked periods") do not "break" a jobseeking period.

"Linking", and through it the creation of a single jobseeking period, is important for two reasons: (1) the "waiting days" (see para.4 of Sch.1 to the Jobseekers Act 1995, above) only have to be served once in a jobseeking period; (2) in determining "the relevant benefit year" for purposes of identifying which tax/contribution years have to be looked at in order to ascertain if the claimant satisfies the contribution-record conditions of entitlement to contribution-based JSA (see further annotation to Jobseekers Act 1995, s.2, above).

A "jobseeking period" is, basically, any period throughout which the claimant satisfies (or is treated as satisfying) the conditions of entitlement to JSA set out in Jobseekers Act 1995, s.1(2)(a)–(c) and (e)–(i): available for employment; a current jobseeker's agreement; actively seeking employment; not in remunerative work; not receiving relevant education; under pensionable age; and in Great Britain (Jobseekers Act 1995, s.35(1); reg.47(1)). Where a hardship payment under Pt IX or IXA (joint-claim couple) of these regulations is paid to a claimant who does not satisfy a labour market condition (any of the conditions in Jobseekers Act 1995, s.1(2)(a)–(c): availability; actively seeking; jobseeker's agreement), he is to be treated as satisfying them for purposes of applying the above definition of jobseeking period (reg.47(2)). Certain periods cannot constitute or be part of, a jobseeking period: (i) any period in which no claim for JSA has been made or treated as made; (ii) any period before the day on which a claim is made or before the earliest date in which good cause for a late claim is shown; (iii) a period caught by the 12-month limit on backdating entitlement under s.1(2) of the SSAA 1992; (iv) a period of disentitlement under JA Regs, regs 25, 26; (v) any week of disentitlement because the claimant is caught by the trade dispute rule in Jobseekers Act 1995, s.14; (vi) any period in reg.47(3)(f).

"Linked periods" comprise (i) any period throughout which the claimant is, or is treated as, incapable of work under the Pt XIIA of the SSCBA 1992; (ii) any period throughout which she was entitled to a maternity allowance under s.35 of that Act; (iii) any period throughout which the claimant was engaged in training for which a training allowance is payable; (iv) a period of attendance at court in response to a summons for jury service which includes October 6, 1996 and was immediately preceded by a period of entitlement to unemployment benefit; (v) any period throughout which the claimant was participating in various "Options" of the New Deal (Employment; Voluntary Sector or Environment Task Force); (vi) certain periods of non-entitlement to JSA because of participation in an employment zone programme and (vii) (but only for contributions-conditions purposes—see notes to Jobseekers Act 1995, s.2(1) any period throughout which the claimant was entitled to a carer's allowance under s.70 of the SSCBA 1992 (paras (2), (3)). The New Deal "options" which are included in para.(2)(f) include the Intensive Activity Period and the Intensive Activity Period for 50 plus.

Two or more jobseeking periods "link" and are treated as one jobseeking period where they are separated by a period comprising only (i) one of 12 weeks; (ii) a linked period; (iii) a period of not more than 12 weeks falling between any two linked periods or between a jobseeking period and a linked period; (iv) any period in respect of which the claimant is summoned for jury service and is required to attend court (para.(1)).

Note also s.47A with respect to linking back to a period of interruption of employment precommencement of JSA for purposes of identifying the relevant benefit year for contributions conditions purposes for CBJSA and for determining any waiting days.

Persons approaching retirement and the jobseeking period

3.193

49.—(1) [² Subject to paragraph (5),] the provisions of this regulation apply only to days which fall—

(a) after 6th October 1996; and

(b) within a tax year in which the claimant has attained the age of 60 but is under pensionable age;

and in respect of which a jobseeker's allowance is not payable because the decision of the determining authority is that the claimant—

(i) has exhausted his entitlement to a contribution-based jobseeker's allowance; or

(ii) fails to satisfy one or both the contribution conditions specified in section 2(1)(a) and (b); or

    (iii) is entitled to a contribution-based jobseeker's allowance but the amount payable is reduced to Nil by virtue of deductions made in accordance with regulation 81 for pension payments.

[¹(2) For the purposes of paragraph (1) of regulation 47 (jobseeking period) but subject to paragraphs (3) and (4), any days to which paragraph (1) applies and in respect of which the person does not satisfy or is not treated in accordance with regulation 14, 16, 17, 19, 20, 21 or 34 as satisfying the conditions specified in paragraphs (a) to (c) of subsection (2) of section (1) (conditions of entitlement to a jobseeker's allowance), shall be days on which the person is treated as satisfying the condition in paragraphs (a) to (c) and (e) to (i) of subsection (2) of section (1).]

    (3) Where a person—

    (a) [¹. . .]

    (b) is employed as an employed earner or a self-employed earner for a period of more than 12 weeks,

then no day which falls within or follows that period shall be days on which the person is treated as satisfying those conditions so however that this paragraph shall not prevent paragraph (2) from again applying to a person who makes a claim for a jobseeker's allowance after that period.

    (4) Any day which is, for the purposes of section 30C of the Benefits Act, a day of incapacity for work falling within a period of incapacity for work shall not be a day on which the person is treated as satisfying the conditions referred to in paragraph (2).

[²(5) This regulation shall not apply in respect of any days in respect of which a joint-claim jobseeker's allowance has been claimed.]

AMENDMENTS

1. Jobseeker's Allowance and Income Support (General) (Amendment) Regulations 1996 (SI 1996/1517), reg.16 (October 7, 1996).   **3.194**
2. Jobseeker's Allowance (Joint Claims) Regulations 2000 (SI 2000/1978), Sch.2, para.12 (March 19, 2001).

DEFINITIONS

"claimant": see Jobseekers Act 1995, s.35(1).
"contribution-based jobseeker's allowance": see Jobseekers Act 1995, s.1(4).
"pensionable age": see reg.3.

GENERAL NOTE

This regulation enables men 60 or over but under pensionable age to have days   **3.195**
rank as part of a jobseeking period where under normal rules they would not do so. It is of value to them because of its impact on the waiting days rule (they only have to be served once in a single jobseeking period formed by a jobseeking period continuous in calendar terms or formed as one by the operation of the linking rules: see Jobseekers Act 1995, s.21, Sch.1, paras 3, 4; regs 46, 48). It will also impact on the matter of determining relevant benefit years for purposes of identifying the tax/contribution years pertinent to the contribution conditions for contribution-based JSA and on the matter of requalification for contribution-based JSA (see Jobseekers Act 1995, ss.2, 5). It may also be of assistance with respect to contribution credits in respect of unemployment. Note, however, that this regulation cannot apply to days which are the subject of a claim for joint-claim jobseeker's allowance (subs.(5)).

The days which can rank as part of a jobseeking period under this regulation are ones falling after October 6, 1996, in a tax year in which the claimant is 60 or over and under pensionable age in respect of which JSA is not payable because (i) the claimant has exhausted his title to contribution-based JSA, or (ii) he fails to satisfy either or both of the contribution conditions, or (iii) although he is entitled to contribution-based JSA none is payable because of abatement to nil by pension payments (paras (1), (2)). Days which are ones of incapacity for work within a period, of incapacity for work cannot form part of a jobseeking period in this way (para.(4)) (they will in fact constitute a "linked period" under reg.48(2)(b)). Further, where someone works in employment or self-employment for more than 12 weeks, no day within or after that period can be treated as part of a jobseeking period in this way (para.(3)), but the protection afforded by paras (1) and (2) of the regulation can apply again after such a period when the person makes a claim for JSA (para.(3)).

Persons temporarily absent from Great Britain

3.196   **50.**—(1) For the purposes of the Act, a claimant shall be treated as being in Great Britain during any period of temporary absence from Great Britain—

(a) not exceeding 4 weeks in the circumstances specified in paragraphs (2), (3) and (4);

(b) not exceeding 8 weeks in the circumstances specified in paragraph (5).

(2) The circumstances specified in this paragraph are that—

(a) the claimant is in Northern Ireland and satisfies the conditions of entitlement to a jobseeker's allowance; and

(b) immediately preceding the period of absence from Great Britain the claimant was entitled to a jobseeker's allowance; and

(c) the period of absence is unlikely to exceed 52 weeks.

(3) The circumstances specified in this paragraph are that—

(a) immediately preceding the period of absence from Great Britain the claimant was entitled to a jobseeker's allowance; and

(b) the period of absence is unlikely to exceed 52 weeks; and

(c) while absent from Great Britain, the claimant continues to satisfy, or be treated as satisfying, the other conditions of entitlement to a jobseeker's allowance; and

(d) is one of a couple, both of whom are absent from Great Britain, where a premium referred to in paragraphs 10, 11, 12, 13 or 15 of Schedule 1 (applicable amounts) is applicable in respect of the claimant's partner.

(4) The circumstances of this paragraph are that—

(a) while absent from Great Britain the person is in receipt of a training allowance; and

(b) regulation 170 (person in receipt of training allowance) applies in his case; and

(c) immediately preceding his absence from Great Britain, he was entitled to a jobseeker's allowance.

(5) The circumstances specified in this paragraph are that—

(a) immediately preceding the period of absence from Great Britain, the claimant was entitled to a jobseeker's allowance; and

(b) the period of absence is unlikely to exceed 52 weeks; and

(c) the claimant continues to satisfy or be treated as satisfying the other conditions of entitlement to a jobseeker's allowance; and

(d) the claimant is, or the claimant and any other member of his family are, accompanying a member of the claimant's family who is a child or young person solely in connection with arrangements made for the treatment of that child or young person for a disease or bodily or mental disablement; and

(e) those arrangements related to treatment—
   (i) outside Great Britain;
   (ii) during the period whilst the claimant is, or the claimant and any member of his family are, temporarily absent from Great Britain; and
   (iii) by, or under the supervision of, a person appropriately qualified to carry out that treatment.

(6) A person shall also be treated, for the purposes of the Act, as being in Great Britain during any period of temporary absence from Great Britain where—

(a) the absence is for the purpose of attending an interview for employment; and

(b) the absence is for 7 consecutive days or less; and

(c) notice of the proposed absence is given to the employment officer before departure, and is given in writing if so required by the officer; and

(d) on his return to Great Britain the person satisfies the employment officer that he attended for the interview in accordance with his notice.

[1(6A) A member of a joint-claim couple shall be treated, for the purposes of the Act, as being in Great Britain where he is a member of a transitional case couple as defined for the purposes of paragraph 8A(2) of Schedule 1 to the Act and, as at the date on which Schedule 7 to the Welfare Reform and Pensions Act 1999 comes into force—

(a) he is temporarily absent from Great Britain; or

(b) he has made definite arrangements to be temporarily absent from Great Britain from some future date,

and that member shall be so treated during any such period of temporary absence from Great Britain.

[2(6AA) For the purposes of the Act a claimant shall be treated as being in Great Britain during any period of temporary absence from Great Britain if—

(a) he was entitled to a jobseeker's allowance immediately before the beginning of that period of temporary absence; and

(b) that period of temporary absence is for the purpose of the claimant receiving treatment at a hospital or other institution outside Great Britain where that treatment is being provided—
   (i) under section 3 of the National Health Service Act 1977 (services generally);
   (ii) pursuant to arrangements made under section 23 of that Act (voluntary organisations and other bodies); or
   (iii) pursuant to arrangements made under paragraph 13 of Schedule 2 to the National Health Service and Community Care Act 1990 (National Health Service Trusts—specific powers).]

(6B) A member of a joint-claim couple shall be treated, for the purposes of the Act, as being in Great Britain during any period of temporary absence from Great Britain—

(a) not exceeding 4 weeks where he is in Northern Ireland and the period of absence is unlikely to exceed 52 weeks;

(b) not exceeding 4 weeks where he is in receipt of a training allowance during the period of absence and regulation 170 applies in his case; or

(c) not exceeding 7 days where the absence is for the purpose of attending an interview for employment,

where that member is so temporarily absent as at the date of claim by the other member of that couple.]

[[2](6C) For the purposes of the Act a member of a joint-claim couple ("the first member") shall be treated as being in Great Britain during any period of temporary absence if—

    (a) he and the other member of that couple were entitled to a joint-claim jobseeker's allowance immediately before the beginning of that period of temporary absence; and

    (b) that period of temporary absence is for the purpose of the first member receiving treatment at a hospital or other institution outside Great Britain where that treatment is being provided—

        (i) under section 3 of the National Health Service Act 1977;

        (ii) pursuant to arrangements made under section 23 of that Act; or

        (iii) pursuant to arrangements made under paragraph 13 of Schedule 2 to the National Health Service and Community Care Act 1990.]

(7) In this regulation—

"appropriately qualified" means qualified to provide medical treatment, physiotherapy or a form of treatment which is similar to, or related to, either of those forms of treatment;

"employment officer" means a person who is an employment officer for the purposes of sections 9 and 10.

AMENDMENTS

3.197   1. Jobseeker's Allowance (Joint Claims) Regulations 2000 (SI 2000/1978), Sch.2, para.13 (March 19, 2001).

    2. Social Security (Income Support and Jobseeker's Allowance) Amendment Regulations 2004 (SI 2004/1869), reg.3(4) (October 4, 2004).

DEFINITIONS

"the Act": see reg.1(3).
"appropriately qualified": see para.(7).
"child": see Jobseekers Act 1995, s.35(1).
"claimant": see Jobseekers Act 1995, s.35(1).
"employment": see reg.3.
"employment officer": see para.(7); Jobseekers Act 1995, s.9(13).
"entitled": see Jobseekers Act 1995, s.35(1).
"family": see Jobseekers Act 1995, s.35(1).
"joint-claim couple": see Jobseekers Act 1995, s.1(4).
"Great Britain": see Jobseekers Act 1995, s.35(1).
"training allowance": see reg.1(3).
"week": see reg.1(3).
"young person": see regs 1(3), 76.

GENERAL NOTE

Para. (1)

3.198   Entitlement to JSA is dependent on the claimant being in Great Britain (Jobseekers Act 1995, s.1(2)(i)). This regulation treats a claimant as being in Great Britain during a range of periods of temporary absence from Great Britain, thus rendering him eligible for JSA. On "temporary absence", see notes on Persons Abroad Regulations 1975, reg. 2 in Bonner, Hooker and White, *Social Security Legislation 2002: Vol. I. Non-Means Tested Benefits*. Note, however, that in contrast to that regulation, some of the paragraphs defining the circumstances in which someone is to be treated as if in Great Britain themselves set a requirement that the absence must be unlikely to exceed a specified number of weeks.

Para. (2) read with para. (1) (a)

A claimant entitled to JSA immediately prior to the absence can be treated as being in Great Britain for up to four weeks of temporary absence from Great Britain where the period of absence is unlikely to exceed 52 weeks, he is in Northern Ireland, and satisfies the conditions of entitlement to JSA.

3.199

Para. (3) read with para. (1) (a)

A claimant entitled to JSA immediately prior to the absence can be treated as being in Great Britain for up to four weeks of temporary absence from Great Britain where the period of absence is unlikely to exceed 52 weeks, and during the absence he continues to satisfy or be treated as satisfying the other conditions of entitlement to JSA, provided that the claimant is one of a couple and a premium is applicable to his partner under any of paras 10–13 or 15 of Sch. 1. The relevant premiums are: pensioner premium for persons over 60; pensioner premium for a partner 75 or over; higher pensioner premium; disability premium; and severe disability premium.

3.200

Para. (4) read with para. (1) (a)

A claimant entitled to JSA immediately prior to the absence can be treated as being in Great Britain for up to four weeks of temporary absence from Great Britain provided that while absent he is entitled to a training allowance but training is not being provided so that reg. 170 applies to him. This would appear to limit this provision to claimants under 25.

3.201

Para. (5) read with para. (1) (b)

A claimant entitled to JSA immediately prior to the absence can be treated as being in Great Britain for up to eight weeks of temporary absence from Great Britain where the period of absence is unlikely to exceed 52 weeks, and during the absence he continues to satisfy or be treated as satisfying the other conditions of entitlement to JSA, provided that the claimant (or the claimant and another family member) is (are) accompanying a child or young person of the claimant's family solely in connection with arrangements made for the treatment of that child or young person for a disease or bodily or mental disablement outside Great Britain and during the period of absence, by or under the supervision of someone appropriately qualified to carry out that treatment. "Appropriately qualified" means qualified to provide medical treatment, physiotherapy or a similar or related form of treatment (para. (7)).

3.202

Para. (6)

A person must also be treated as being in Great Britain during a period of temporary absence of up to seven days where the absence is for the purpose of attending an interview for employment, notice (in writing if required) of the absence was given to an employment officer before his departure, and on return he satisfies an employment officer that he attended for the interview in accordance with the notice. An "employment officer" is an officer of the Secretary of State or any other person designated as employment officer by the Secretary of State (para. (7), Jobseekers Act 1995, s. 9(13)); in reality, an officer in the Employment Service.

3.203

Paras (6A) and (6B)

These apply only to members of a joint-claim couple.

Remunerative work

3.204   **51.**—(1) For the purposes of the Act "remunerative work" means—

(a) in the case of [⁵ a claimant], work in which he is engaged or, where his hours of work fluctuate, is engaged on average, for not less than 16 hours per week; and

(b) in the case of any partner of the claimant, work in which he is engaged or, where his hours of work fluctuate, is engaged on average, for not less than 24 hours per week; [¹ and

(c) in the case of a non-dependant, or of a child or young person to whom paragraph 18 of Schedule 6 refers, work in which he is engaged or, where his hours of work fluctuate, is engaged on average, for not less than 16 hours per week,]

and for those purposes, [³ "work" is work] for which payment is made or which is done in expectation of payment.

(2) For the purposes of paragraph (1), the number of hours in which [⁵ a claimant] or his partner is engaged in work shall be determined—

(a) where no recognisable cycle has been established in respect of a person's work, by reference to the number of hours or, where those hours are likely to fluctuate, the average of the hours, which he is expected to work in a week;

(b) where the number of hours for which he is engaged fluctuate, by reference to the average of hours worked over—

(i) if there is a recognisable cycle of work, and sub-paragraph (c) does not apply, the period of one complete cycle (including, where the cycle involves periods in which the person does not work, those periods but disregarding any other absences);

(ii) in any other case, the period of five weeks immediately before the date of claim or the date of [⁴ supersession], or such other length of time as may, in the particular case, enable the person's average hours of work to be determined more accurately;

(c) where the person works at a school or other educational establishment or at some other place of employment and the cycle of work consists of one year but with school holidays or similar vacations during which he does no work, by disregarding those periods and any other periods in which he is not required to work.

(3) In determining in accordance with this regulation the number of hours for which a person is engaged in remunerative work—

(a) that number shall include any time allowed to that person by his employer for a meal or for refreshments, but only where the person is, or expects to be, paid earnings in respect of that time;

(b) no account shall be taken of any hours in which the person is engaged in an employment or scheme to which any one of paragraphs (a) to (h) of regulation 53 (person treated as not engaged in remunerative work) applies;

(c) no account shall be taken of any hours in which the person is engaged otherwise than in an employment as an earner in caring for—

(i) a person who is in receipt of attendance allowance [¹ . . .] or the care component of disability living allowance at the highest or middle rate; or

(ii) a person who has claimed an attendance allowance [¹ . . .] or a disability living allowance, but only for the period beginning with the date of claim and ending on the date the claim is determined or, if earlier, on the expiration of the period of 26 weeks from the date of claim; or

(iii) another person [² and] is in receipt of [⁶ carer's allowance] under Section 70 of the [¹Benefits Act; or

(iv) a person who has claimed either attendance allowance or disability living allowance and has an award of attendance allowance or the care component of disability living allowance at one of the two higher rates prescribed under section 72(4) of the Benefits Act for a period commencing after the date on which that claim was made.]

(4) In the case of a person to whom regulation 22 of the Income Support (General) Amendment No. 4 Regulations 1991 would have applied had he been entitled to income support and not a jobseeker's allowance, paragraph (1)(a) shall have effect as if for the reference to 16 hours there was substituted a reference to 24 hours.

(5) In determining for the purposes of paragraph (4) whether regulation 22 of the 1991 Regulations applies, regulations 23 and 24 of those Regulations shall have effect as if the references to income support included also a reference to income-based jobseeker's allowance.

AMENDMENTS

1. Jobseekers's Allowance (Amendment) Regulations 1996 (SI 1996/1516), reg.9 (October 7, 1996).   3.205

2. Jobseekers's Allowance (Amendment) Regulations 1996 (SI 1996/1516), reg.20 and Sch. (October 7, 1996).

3. Social Security (Miscellaneous Amendments) Regulations 1997 (SI 1997/454), reg.2(5) (April 7, 1997).

4. Social Security Act 1998 (Commencement No.11, and Savings and Consequential and Transitional Provisions) Order 1999 (SI 1999/2860 (C.75)), art.3(1) and (12) and Sch.12, para.5 (October 18, 1999)

5. Jobseeker's Allowance (Joint Claims) Regulations 2000 (SI 2000/1978), reg.2(5) and Sch.2, para.14 (March 19, 2001).

6. Social Security (Miscellaneous Amendments) Regulations 2003 (SI 2003/511) reg.3(4) and (5) (April 1, 2003).

DEFINITIONS

"the Act"—see reg.1(3)   3.206
"attendance allowance"—*ibid.*
"the Benefits Act"—see Jobseekers Act, s.35(1).
"child"—*ibid.*
"claimant"—*ibid.*
"date of claim"—see reg.1(3).
"disability living allowance"—*ibid.*
"earnings"—*ibid.*
"employment"—see reg.3.
"partner"—see reg.1(3).
"payment"—*ibid.*
"week"—*ibid.*
"young person"—*ibid.*, reg.76.

GENERAL NOTE

A person who is in remunerative work is not entitled to JSA (s.1(2)(e) of the Jobseekers Act). This applies to both contribution-based and income-based JSA. For   3.207

income-based JSA there is also no entitlement if a person is a member of a couple whose partner is engaged in remunerative work (s.3(1)(e) of the Jobseekers Act).

Para.(1) contains the basic rule. Remunerative work is work for 16 hours or more on average a week in the case of the claimant (sub-para.(a)), or a non-dependent (see reg.2) or (in "transitional cases"—see notes to reg.83 and reg.17 of the Income Support Regulations) a child or young person who has left school and is treated as in relevant education until the next terminal date (sub-para.(c)). (Whether a non-dependent or such a child or young person is in remunerative work is relevant to income-based JSA: see para.17 of Sch.2 (non-dependent deductions from housing costs) and para.18 of Sch.6 (earnings of a child or young person not disregarded)). But in the case of a partner remunerative work is 24 hours or more a week (sub-para.(b)). Work is remunerative if payment is made for it, or it is done in the expectation of payment. See further the notes to reg.5 of the Income Support Regulations.

Para.(2) is similar to reg.5(2) and (3B) and para.(3)(a) and (b) to reg.5(7) and (6) respectively of the Income Support Regulations. On para.(3)(c) see the note to reg.53 below. Like reg.5(2) of the Income Support Regulations, the opening words of para.(2) suggest a mechanism for determining the hours worked in all cases but sub-paras (a), (b) and (c) do not cover all situations. In particular, a person who works for a regular number of contracted hours seems to fall outside para.(2) and inside para.(1).

The notes to reg.5 of the IS Regulations must, however, be read subject to the decision of the Tribunal of Commissioners in *R(JSA) 4/03*, which held that reg.51(2)(c) of the JSA Regulations (which is in similar terms to reg.5(3B) of the Income Support Regulations) discriminated indirectly against women and could not be objectively justified by reference to factors other than sex and therefore was inconsistent with EC Directive 79/7/EEC (see Vol.III). In consequence reg.51(2)(c) was to be regarded as being of no effect.

For an example of the application of the principles in *R(JSA) 5/03* (and, in particular, the treatment of paid public or extra-statutory holidays falling outside term-time) see the decision of Mr Commissioner Mesher in *CJSA 1638/2003*.

It is important to note that the above decisions were all concerned with JSA, *not* IS. The government conceded that, as had been held by the Court of Appeal in *Hockenjos v Secretary of State for Social Security* [2001] EWCA Civ 624 (CA), JSA was within the material scope of Directive 79/7/EEC. By contrast the ECJ held in C.-63/91 and C.-64/91 *Jackson and Cresswell v Chief Adjudication Officer* [1992] ECR. I-4737 (also reported as an appendix to *R(IS) 10/91*) that IS was *not* within the material scope of the Directive because it provided protection against poverty rather than against any of the risks listed in art.3 of the Directive. Therefore reg.5(3B) of the Income Support Regulations (as interpreted by the HL in *Staffford and Banks*) remains good law even though the equivalent JSA Regulation is of no effect.

Note also that all those who stand to benefit from the disapplication of reg.51(2)(c) will *ex hypothesi* be workers and will therefore inevitably come within the personal scope of the Directive as defined by art.2.

Paras (4) and (5)

3.208   Regs 22 to 24 of the Income Support (General) Amendment No.4 Regulations 1991 (SI 1991/1559) provided transitional protection for existing income support claimants when the limit for remunerative work for income support was reduced from 24 to 16 hours per week in April 1992. The effect of paras (4) and (5) is to continue that protection for claimants on the transfer to jobseeker's allowance.

Persons treated as engaged in remunerative work

3.209   **52.**—(1) Except in the case of a person on maternity leave [⁶, paternity leave, adoption leave] or absent from work through illness, a person shall be treated as engaged in remunerative work during any period for which he is absent from work referred to in regulation 51(1) (remunerative work) where the absence is either without good cause or by reason of a recognised, customary or other holiday.

(2) For the purposes of an income-based jobseeker's allowance, [³ but not a joint-claim jobseeker's allowance] the partner of a claimant shall be treated as engaged in remunerative work where—

(a) the partner is or was involved in a trade dispute; and

(b) had the partner claimed a jobseeker's allowance, section 14 (trade disputes) would have applied in his case; and

(c) the claimant was not entitled to an income-based jobseeker's allowance when the partner became involved in the trade dispute;

and shall be so treated for a period of 7 days beginning on the date the stoppage of work at the partner's place of employment commenced, or if there was no stoppage of work, the date on which the partner first withdrew his labour in furtherance of the trade dispute.

[⁴(2A) For the purposes of a joint-claim jobseeker's allowance, a member of a joint-claim couple shall be treated as engaged in remunerative work where—

(a) he is or was involved in a trade dispute;

(b) had the joint-claim couple of which he is a member claimed a jobseeker's allowance jointly, section 14 (trade disputes) would have applied in the case of one or both members of that couple; and

(c) the joint-claim couple were not entitled to a joint-claim jobseeker's allowance when that member of the joint-claim couple became involved in the trade dispute,

and shall be so treated for a period of 7 days beginning on the date the stoppage of work commenced at that member's place of employment or, if there was no stoppage of work, the date on which that member first withdrew his labour in furtherance of the trade dispute.]

(3) A person who was, or was treated as being, engaged in remunerative work and in respect of that work earnings to which [¹ regulation 98(1)(b) and (c)] (earnings of employed earners) applies are paid, shall be treated as engaged in remunerative work for the period for which those earnings are taken into account in accordance with Part VIII.

[⁵(4)–(6) . . .]

AMENDMENTS

1. Jobseekers's Allowance (Amendment) Regulations 1996 (SI 1996/1516), reg.20 and Sch. (October 7, 1996).

3.210

2. Social Security (Miscellaneous Amendments) (No.2) Regulations 1999 (SI 1999/2556), reg.3 (October 4, 1999).

3. Jobseeker's Allowance (Joint Claims) Regulations 2000 (SI 2000/1978), reg.2(5) and Sch.2, para.15(a) (March 19, 2001).

4. Jobseeker's Allowance (Joint Claims) Regulations 2000 (SI 2000/1978), reg.2(5) and Sch.2, para.15(b) (March 19, 2001).

5. Social Security (Miscellaneous Amendments) Regulations 2001 (SI 2001/488), reg.12(a) (April 9, 2001).

6. Social Security (Paternity and Adoption) Amendment Regulations 2002 (SI 2002/2689), reg.3 (December 8, 2002).

DEFINITIONS

"maternity leave"—see reg.1(3).
"partner"—*ibid.*

"remunerative work"—see reg.51(1).
"trade dispute"—see Jobseekers Act, s.35(1).

GENERAL NOTE

3.211   This provision deems people to be in remunerative work in certain circumstances.

Para. (1)
See reg.5(3) and (3A) of the Income Support Regulations and the notes to those paragraphs. See also the discussion under the heading "Term-time only workers" in the notes to reg.5.

Para. (2)
See the notes to s.15 of the Jobseekers Act.

Para. (3)
Where a person was in remunerative work and any "compensation payment" (defined in reg.98(3)) or (within four weeks of termination or interruption of employment) holiday pay is paid, the person is treated as in remunerative work for the period covered by the payment (see regs 94(2) and (6) to (9) for this period; note reg.94(3) and (4) where both kinds of payment are made).

Persons treated as not engaged in remunerative work

3.212   **53.** A person shall be treated as not engaged in remunerative work in so far as—

(a) he is engaged by a charity or a voluntary organisation or is a volunteer where the only payment received by him or due to be paid to him is a payment which is to be disregarded under regulation 103(2) and paragraph 2 of Schedule 7 (sums to be disregarded in the calculation of income other than earnings);

(b) he is engaged on a scheme for which a training allowance is being paid;

[3(bb) he is receiving assistance [7under the self-employment route]

[5(c) he is in employment, lives in, or is temporarily absent from, a residential care home, a nursing home or residential accommodation and requires personal care by reason of old age, disablement, past or present dependence on alcohol or drugs, past or present mental disorder or a terminal illness;]

(d) he is engaged in employment as—

(i) a part-time member of a fire brigade maintained in pursuance of the Fire Services Acts 1947 to 1959;

[6(ia) a part-time fire-fighter employed by a fire and rescue authority;]

(ii) an auxiliary coastguard in respect of coastal rescue activities;

(iii) a person engaged part-time in the manning or launching of a lifeboat;

(iv) a member of any territorial or reserve force prescribed in Part I of Schedule 3 to the Social Security (Contributions) Regulations 1979;

(e) he is performing his duties as a councillor, and for this purpose "councillor" has the same meaning as in section 171F(2) of the Benefits Act;

   (f) he is engaged in caring for a person who is accommodated with him by virtue of arrangements made under any of the provisions referred to in paragraph 27 or 28 of Schedule 7 (sums to be disregarded in the calculation of income other than earnings), and is in receipt of any payment specified in that paragraph;

   (g) he is—

      (i) the partner of the claimant; and

      (ii) involved in a trade dispute; and

      (iii) not a person to whom regulation 52(2) applies,

      and had he claimed a jobseeker's allowance, section 14 (trade disputes) would have applied in his case;

[⁴(gg) he is—

      (i) a member of a joint-claim couple; and

      (ii) involved in a trade dispute; and

      (iii) not a person to whom regulation 52(2A) applies,

      and had the joint-claim couple of which he is a member claimed a jobseeker's allowance jointly, section 14 (trade disputes) would have applied in the case of one or both members of that couple;]

   (h) he is mentally or physically disabled, and by reason of that disability—

      (i) his earnings are reduced to 75 per cent or less of what a person without that disability and working the same number of hours would reasonably be expected to earn in that employment or in comparable employment in the area; or

      (ii) his number of hours [¹of] work are 75 per cent or less of what a person without that disability would reasonably be expected to undertake in that employment or in comparable employment in the area.

[²(i) he is engaged in an activity in respect of which—

      (i) a sports award has been made, or is to be made, to him; and

      (ii) no other payment is made or is expected to be made to him].

   (j) [*Omitted.*]

AMENDMENTS

1. Jobseekers's Allowance (Amendment) Regulations 1996 (SI 1996/1516), reg.20 and Sch. (October 7, 1996).

2. Social Security Amendment (Sports Awards) Regulations 1999 (SI 1999/2165), reg.7(2) (August 23, 1999).

3. Social Security Amendment (Employment Zones) (No. 2) Regulations 2000 (SI 2000/2910), reg.3 (November 27, 2000).

4. Jobseeker's Allowance (Joint Claims) Regulations 2000 (SI 2000/1978), reg.2(5) and Sch.2, para.16 (March 19, 2001).

5. Social Security Amendment (Residential Care and Nursing Homes) Regulations 2001 (SI 2001/3767), reg.2 and Sch. Pt II, para.2 (April 8, 2002).

6. Fire and Rescue Services Act 2004 (Consequential Amendments) (England) Order 2004 (SI 2004/3168), reg.36(3) (December 30, 2004) (not Scotland or Wales).

7. Social Security (Income-Related Benefits Self-Employment Route Amendment) Regulations 2004 (SI 2004/963), reg.4 (May 4, 2004).

3.213

DEFINITIONS

"the Benefits Act"—see Jobseekers Act, s.35(1).

"earnings"—see reg.1(3).

"employment"—see reg.3.
"partner"—see reg.1(3).
"remunerative work"—see reg.51(1).
"residential accommodation"—see reg.1(3).
"residential allowance"—*ibid.*
"residential care home"—*ibid.*
"nursing home"—*ibid.*
"trade dispute"—see Jobseekers Act, s.35(1).
"training allowance"—see reg.1(3).
"voluntary organisation"—*ibid.*

GENERAL NOTE

3.214   See the notes to reg.6 of the Income Support Regulations. The categories are similar to those in paras (1) and (4) of reg.6 but there are slight differences. On para.(g), see the notes to s.15 of the Jobseekers Act.

Unlike income support (see reg.6(4)(c)), carers are not covered by reg.53. Instead, unless they are "employed as an earner", no account is taken of the hours they spend in caring in deciding whether they are engaged in remunerative work (see reg.52(3)(c)).

There is no equivalent to reg.6(b). So a childminder working 16 or more hours a week (or 24 if she is the partner of a claimant) may count as in remunerative work.

Relevant education

3.215   **54.**—(1) Only full-time education which is undertaken by a child or young person and which is not a course of advanced education shall be treated as relevant education for the purposes of the Act.

(2) A child or young person who is receiving full-time education for the purposes of section 142 of the Benefits Act (meaning of child) or who is treated as a child for the purposes of that section shall be treated as receiving full-time education.

(3) A young person who—

(a) is a part-time student; and

(b) before he became a part-time student fulfilled the requirements specified for a person falling within paragraph (2) of regulation 11 (part-time students); and

(c) is undertaking a course of study, other than a course of advanced education or a course of study of a kind specified in head (i), (ii) or (iii) of the definition of "full-time student" in regulation 1(3),

shall not be treated as receiving relevant education.

(4) A young person to whom paragraph (3) applied and who has completed or terminated his course of part-time study shall not be treated as receiving relevant education.

[[1](5) A young person who is participating in the Full-Time Education and Training Option of the New Deal as specified in regulation 75(1)(b)(ii) shall not be treated as receiving relevant education.]

AMENDMENT

3.216   1. Social Security Amendment (New Deal) Regulations 1997 (SI 1997/2863), reg.5 (January 5, 1998).

DEFINITIONS

"the Benefits Act"—see Jobseekers Act, s.35(1).
"child"—*ibid.*

"course of advanced education"—see reg.1(3).
"course of study"—*ibid.*
"part-time student"—*ibid.*
"young person"—*ibid.*, reg.76.

GENERAL NOTE

Paras (1) and (2)

Under s.1(2)(g) of the Jobseekers Act a person is excluded from JSA if he is in   3.217
relevant education (except if he is in a category who can claim income support while
in relevant education (see regs 57(2) and (4)(a) and reg.61(1)(c)). Paras (1) and (2)
provide an exhaustive test of when a person is to be treated as receiving relevant
education.

Note that only a child or young person (that is, a person aged under 19: see reg.76)
can qualify and that relevant education does not include a course of advanced
education (defined in reg.1(3)). There is a reference over to the child benefit legislation and the reg.54(2) to (4) question is one to which the assumption in reg.15 of
the Decisions and Appeals Regulations 1999 (see Vol. III of this series) applies. If the
Secretary of State considers that he does not have all the relevant information or evidence to decide whether the person should count as in relevant education, he will
proceed on the basis that the child benefit decision would be adverse to the claimant
in the JSA sense.

See on the child benefit test, regs 5 to 11 of the Child Benefit (General)
Regulations 2003 (SI 2003/493) (which revoke and replace the Child Benefit
(General) Regulations 1976) in Vol I of this series. Contact hours of at least 12 per
week are required. See *R(F) 1/93* in which the Commissioner held that supervised
study (in reg.5 of the Child Benefit Regulations 1976) "would normally be under-
stood to import the presence or close proximity of a teacher or tutor". A different
approach is taken in *Flemming v Secretary of State for Work and Pensions* [2002]
EWCA Civ 641, CA, May 10, 2002 (agreeing with the Northern Ireland Court of
Appeal's decision in *Bronwyn Wright-Turner v Department of Social Development*
(January 11, 2002, unreported) in relation to the similar provision in reg.5 of the
Invalid Care Regulations 1976 (see Vol. I of this series) but note that this was in a
different context, namely that of full-time university education. Relevant education
continues through temporary interruptions, like school holidays. When a person
ceases actually to receive relevant education he is treated as doing so (unless he is
in remunerative work of 24 hours or more a week and in certain other circumstances) until the next terminal date after he reaches compulsory school leaving
age, or after he leaves relevant education if he stays on beyond compulsory school
leaving age, or until he reaches 19 if this is earlier. The terminal dates are the
Sunday after the first Monday in January, the first Monday after Easter Monday,
or the first Monday in September. For England and Wales (but not Scotland) there
is now a single school leaving date: the last Friday in June in the school year in
which the child's 16th birthday falls (see the Education (School Leaving Date)
Order 1997 (SI 1997/1970)). Thus in 2005 children in England and Wales who
reach 16 before September 1, 2005 can leave school on Friday, June 24, 2005; their
terminal date will be Sunday, September 11, 2005 and they count as being in relevant education until that date (unless the exceptions apply). For a child who stays
on beyond compulsory school leaving age the three terminal dates are still applicable. There is also the possibility of a person remaining a "child" for an extension
period of 12 weeks beyond the terminal date (or 16 weeks if the terminal date is
the Sunday after the first Monday in September) if he is under 18, registered for
work or training, not in remunerative work of 24 hours or more a week, not in
receipt of income support/income-based JSA in his own right and not on Work
Based Learning for Young People. In England and Wales for a child whose school
leaving date is June 24, 2005, the extension period will be September 12, 2005 to
January 1, 2006.

Note that some claimants may be able to receive income support though in relevant education (see reg.13 of the Income Support Regulations), in which case they may also be eligible for JSA (see above). It will normally be better for most young people to claim income support in these circumstances, so as to avoid the risk of being sanctioned for not complying with the JSA labour market conditions.

Paras (3) and (4)

3.218   Under para.(3) a 16-to18-year-old who is a part-time student (see the definitions of full-time and part-time student in reg.1(3); note also reg.1(3A) to (3E)) undertaking a course other than one of advanced education or of a kind within para.(b) of the definition of "full-time student" in reg.1(3) who satisfies the conditions in sub-para (b) does not count as in relevant education (and will not so count after he finishes or leaves his part-time course (para.(4)). The conditions in para.(3)(b) are that for the three months before he started his course he was in receipt of JSA or incapacity benefit or income support while sick or on Work Based Learning for Young People or in the six months before the course was in receipt of any of these benefits or on Work Based Learning for a total of three months and for the remainder of the time was in remunerative work (see reg.51) or earning too much to be entitled to benefit (in both cases the three and the six months must be after the young person has ceased to be in relevant education).

See reg.11 which may enable such a part-time student to be accepted as available for work even though his hours of study coincide with the times he is required to be available for employment.

Para.(5)

3.219   This provision ensures that a young person (*i.e.* aged under 19) who is on the Full-Time Education and Training option of the New Deal for 18–24 year-olds is not treated as in relevant education.

Short periods of sickness

3.220   **55.**—(1) Subject to the following provisions of this regulation, a person who—

>   (a) [¹ has been awarded a jobseeker's allowance] or is a person to whom any of the circumstances mentioned in section 19(5) or (6) [² or 20A(2)] apply; and
>   (b) proves to the satisfaction of the adjudication officer that he is unable to work on account of some specific disease or disablement; and
>   (c) but for his disease or disablement, [¹ would satisfy] the requirements for entitlement to a jobseeker's allowance other than those specified in section 1(2)(a), (c) and (f) (available for and actively seeking employment, and capable of work),

shall be treated for a period of not more than 2 weeks as capable of work, except where the claimant states in writing that for the period of his disease or disablement he proposes to claim or has claimed incapacity benefit, severe disablement allowance or income support.

(2) The evidence which is required for the purposes of paragraph (1)(b) is a declaration made by the claimant in writing, in a form approved for the purposes by the Secretary of State, that he has been unfit for work from a date or for a period specified in the declaration.

(3) The preceding provisions of this regulation shall not apply to a claimant on more than two occasions in any one jobseeking period or where a jobseeking period exceeds 12 months, in each successive 12 months within that period and for the purposes of calculating any period of 12 months, the first 12 months in the jobseeking period commences on the first day of the jobseeking period.

(4) The preceding provisions of this regulation shall not apply to any person where the first day in respect of which he is unable to work falls within 8 weeks of—

(a) an entitlement of his to incapacity benefit, severe disablement allowance or statutory sick pay; or

(b) an entitlement to income support where the person claiming a jobseeker's allowance satisfied the requirements for a disability premium by virtue of paragraph 12(1)(b) of Schedule 2 to the Income Support Regulations.

[³(5) The preceding provision of this regulation shall not apply to a claimant who is temporarily absent from Great Britain in the circumstances prescribed by regulation 50(6AA) or, as the case may be, (6C).]

AMENDMENTS

1. Jobseeker's Allowance and Income Support (General) (Amendment) Regulations 1996 (SI 1996/1517), reg.17 (October 7, 1996).   3.221

2. Jobseeker's Allowance (Joint Claims) Regulations 2000 (SI 2000/1978), reg.2(5) and Sch.2, para.17 (March 19, 2001).

3. Social Security (Income Support and Jobseeker's Allowance) Amendment Regulations 2004 (SI 2004/1869), reg.3(5) (October 4, 2004).

DEFINITIONS

"capable of work"—see Jobseekers Act, s.35(2) and Sch.1, para.2.
"claimant"—see Jobseekers Act, s.35(1).
"jobseeking period"—see regs 1(3) and 47(1)–(3).

GENERAL NOTE

Para. (1) allows a JSA award to continue while a person is incapable of work for   3.222
up to two weeks (subject to a limit of two such periods in any 12 months (para.(3)) by treating him as capable of work for that period. This does not apply if the person was entitled to incapacity benefit, severe disablement allowance, statutory sick pay or income support with a disability premium on the grounds of his incapacity for work in the eight weeks before the first day that he became unfit for work. Presumably the intention is to avoid a claimant having to chop and change between benefits where his period of incapacity is only likely to be short. However, a person can still choose to claim an incapacity benefit in these circumstances if he wishes to do so.

In *CIS 2107/1998* the claimant who had been in receipt of income-based JSA was advised to claim incapacity benefit when he became unfit for work. This was refused but income support was awarded from a later date. The claimant appealed against the refusal to backdate his income support. The Commissioner states that when a claimant appeals against a gap in benefit, that should be taken as an appeal against *all* the decisions that gave rise to that gap (in this case potentially JSA, incapacity benefit and income support). He also held that the proviso at the end of para.(1) should be construed narrowly in order not to defeat the primacy of the rule in reg.55. In his view the proviso meant that there had to be some written statement by the claimant, other than the claim form for incapacity benefit; moreover, the statement had to make it clear that it applied to the whole period of sickness. The result was that the proviso did not operate in this case and the claimant was entitled to JSA for the two week period after he became ill (which period coincided with the gap in his claim).

On para.(5) see the note to reg.55A.

[¹Periods of sickness and persons receiving treatment outside Great Britain

3.223 **55A.**—(1) A person—

(a) who has been awarded a jobseeker's allowance, a joint-claim job-seeker's allowance or is a person to whom any of the circumstances mentioned in section 19(5) or (6) or 20A(2) apply; and

(b) who is temporarily absent from Great Britain in the circumstances prescribed by regulation 50(6AA) or, as the case may be, (6C); and

(c) who proves to the satisfaction of the Secretary of State that he is unable to work on account of some specific disease or disablement; and

(d) but for his disease or disablement, would satisfy the requirements for entitlement to a jobseeker's allowance other than those specified in section 1(2)(a), (c) and (f) (available for and actively seeking employment and capable of work),

shall be treated during that period of temporary absence abroad as capable of work, except where that person has stated in writing before that period of temporary absence abroad begins that immediately before the beginning of the period of that temporary absence abroad he has claimed incapacity benefit, severe disablement allowance or income support.

(2) The evidence which is required for the purposes of paragraph (1)(c) is a declaration made by that person in writing, in a form approved for the purposes by the Secretary of State, that he will be unfit for work from a date or for a period specified in the declaration.]

AMENDMENT

3.224 1. Social Security (Income Support and Jobseeker's Allowance) Amendment Regulations 2004 (SI 2004/1869), reg.3(6) (October 4, 2004).

GENERAL NOTE

3.225 The purpose of this provision, together with the amendments that have been made to regs 14, 19, 50 and 55, is to enable entitlement to JSA to continue during any period that the claimant (including a member of a joint-claim couple) goes abroad temporarily for the purpose of receiving treatment funded by the NHS. Regulation 55A treats such a person as capable of work, provided that he supplies a written declaration on an approved form that he is unfit for work from a stated date or for a specified period and satisfies the conditions for an award of JSA (other than the requirements of being available for and capable of, and of actively seeking, work). However, he will not be treated as capable of work if he has stated in writing before the absence abroad begins that he has claimed incapacity benefit, severe disablement allowance or income support. Thus a person in these circumstances can choose to remain in receipt of JSA or to claim benefit on the ground of incapacity for work if he wishes to do so.

Prescribed amount of earnings

56.—(1) The prescribed amount of earnings for the purposes of section 2(1)(c) (the contribution-based conditions) shall be calculated by applying the formula— 3.226

$$(A + D) - £0.01$$

where—

A is the age-related amount applicable to the claimant in accordance with section 4(2); and

D is any amount disregarded from the claimant's earnings in accordance with regulation 99(2) (calculation of net earnings of employed earners) or regulation 101(2) (calculation of net profit of self-employed earners) and Schedule 6.

(2) For the avoidance of doubt in calculating the amount of earnings in accordance with paragraph (1), only the claimant's earnings shall be taken into account.

GENERAL NOTE

Under Jobseekers Act 1995, s.2(1)(c), to be entitled to contribution-based JSA, a claimant "must not have earnings in excess of the prescribed amount". This regulation gives the set formula for determining that prescribed amount, which amount is not the same for everyone. The prescribed amount is a level equal to the claimant's personal age-related rate of contribution-based JSA (determined in accordance with Jobseekers Act 1995, s.4 and reg.79) (A in the formula) plus the appropriate disregards from his earnings (D in the formula), minus one penny. 3.227

PART IV

YOUNG PERSONS

Interpretation of Part IV

57.—(1) In this Part— 3.228

"the Careers Service" means a person of any description with whom the Secretary of State has made an arrangement under section 10(1) of the Employment and Training Act 1973 and any person to whom he has given a direction under section 10(2) of that Act;

"child benefit extension period" means

(a) in the case of a person who ceases to be treated as a child by virtue of section 142(1)(a) of the Benefits Act (meaning of child) or regulation 7 of the Child Benefit (General) Regulations 1976 (circumstances in which a person who has ceased to receive full-time education is to continue to be treated as a child)

(i) on or after the first Monday in September, but before the first Monday in January of the following year, the period ending with the last day of the week which falls immediately before the week which includes the first Monday in January in that year;

    (ii) on or after the first Monday in January but before the Monday following Easter Monday in that year, the period ending with the last day of the week which falls 12 weeks after the week which includes the first Monday in January in that year;

    (iii) at any other time of the year, the period ending with the last day of the week which falls 12 weeks after the week which includes the Monday following Easter Monday in that year;

  (b) in the case of a person who was not treated as a child by virtue of section 142(1)(a) of the Benefits Act immediately before he was 16 and who has not been treated as a child by virtue of Regulation 7 of the Child Benefit (General) Regulations 1976 (interruption of full-time education), the period ending with the date determined in accordance with sub-paragraph (i), (ii) or (iii) of paragraph (a) as if he had ceased full-time education on the first date on which education ceased to be compulsory for a person of his age in England and Wales or, if he is resident in Scotland, in Scotland;

and in this sub-paragraph "week" means a period of 7 days beginning with a Monday and "year" means a period of 12 months beginning on 1st January;

"chronically sick or mentally or physically disabled" has the same meaning as in regulation 13(3)(b) of the Income Support Regulations (circumstances in which persons in relevant education may be entitled to income support);

[4 "the Connexions Service" means a person of any description with whom the Secretary of State has made an arrangement under section 114(2)(a) of the Learning and Skills Act 2000 and section 10(1) of the Employment and Training Act 1973 and any person to whom he has given a direction under section 114(2)(b) of the Learning and Skills Act 2000 and section 10(2) of the Employment and Training Act 1973;]

"full-time education" has the same meaning as in regulation 1 of the Child Benefit (General) Regulations 1976;

"suitable training" means training which is suitable for that young person in vocationally relevant respects, namely his personal capacity, aptitude, his preference, the preference of the training provider, the level of approved qualification aimed at, duration of the training, proximity and prompt availability of the training;

"training" in sections 3, 16 and 17 and in this Part except in regulation 65 read with section 7 and except in the phrase "suitable training", means training for which persons aged under 18 are eligible and for which persons aged 18 to 24 may be eligible [5 secured by the Learning and Skills Council for England or by the National Council for Education and Training for Wales and, in Scotland, provided] directly or indirectly by a Local Enterprise Company pursuant to its arrangement with, as the case may be, Scottish Enterprise or Highlands and Islands Enterprise (whether that arrangement is known as an Operating Contract or by any other name);

"treatment" means treatment for a disease or bodily or mental disablement by or under the supervision of a person qualified to provide medical treatment, physiotherapy or a form of treatment which is similar to, or related to, either of those forms of treatment;

[1 "young person" means a person—

  (a) who has reached the age of 16 but not the age of 18;

(b) who does not satisfy the conditions in section 2 or whose entitlement to a contribution-based jobseeker's allowance has ceased as a result of section 5(1); and

(c) who is not a person to whom section 6 of the Children (Leaving Care) Act 2000 (exclusion from benefits) applies.]

(2) A young person falls within this paragraph if he is

(a) a member of a married couple where the other member of that couple
    (i) has reached the age of 18 or
    (ii) is a young person who has registered for employment and training in accordance with regulation 62 or
    (iii) is a young person to whom paragraph (4) applies;

(b) a person who has no parent nor any person acting in the place of his parents;

(c) a person who—
    (i) is not living with his parents nor any person acting in the place of his parents; and
    (ii) immediately before he attained the age of 16 was—

(aa) [² in England and Wales] being looked after by a local authority pursuant to a relevant enactment which placed him with some person other than a close relative of his [² . . .]

(bb) in custody in any institution to which the Prison Act 1952 applies or under [² the Prisons (Scotland) Act 1989; or]

[²(cc) in Scotland, in the care of a local authority under a relevant enactment and whilst in that care was not living with his parents or any close relative.]

(d) a person who is in accommodation which is other than his parental home and which is other than the home of a person acting in the place of his parents, who entered that accommodation—
    (i) as part of a programme of rehabilitation or resettlement, that programme being under the supervision of the probation service or a local authority; or
    (ii) in order to avoid physical or sexual abuse; or
    (iii) because of a mental or physical handicap or illness and he needs such accommodation because of his handicap or illness;

(e) a person who is living away from his parents and any person who is acting in the place of his parents in a case where his parents are or, as the case may be, that person is, unable financially to support him and his parents are, or that person is—
    (i) chronically sick or mentally or physically disabled; or
    (ii) detained in custody pending trial or sentence upon conviction or under a sentence imposed by a court; or
    (iii) prohibited from entering or re-entering Great Britain;

(f) a person who of necessity has to live away from his parents and any person acting in the place of his parents because—
    (i) he is estranged from his parents and that person; or
    (ii) he is in physical or moral danger; or
    (iii) there is a serious risk to his physical or mental health.

[²(3)(a) In England and Wales, any reference in this regulation to a person acting in place of a person's parents includes a reference to—
    (i) where the person is being looked after by a local authority or voluntary organisation which places him with a family, a relative of his, or some other suitable person, the person with whom the

person is placed, whether or not any payment is made to him in connection with the placement; or

    (ii) in any other case, any person with parental responsibility for the child, and for this purpose "parental responsibility" has the meaning it has in the Children Act 1989 by virtue of section 3 of that Act; and

(b) in Scotland, any reference in this regulation to a person acting in place of a person's parents includes a reference to a local authority or voluntary organisation where the person is in its care under a relevant enactment, or to a person with whom the person is boarded out by a local authority or voluntary organisation whether or not any payment is made by it.]

(4) This paragraph applies to

(a) a person who falls under any of the following paragraphs of Schedule 1B to the Income Support Regulations—

Paragraph 1	(lone parents)
Paragraph 2	(single person looking after foster children)
Paragraph 3	(persons temporarily looking after another person)
Paragraph 4	(persons caring for another person)
Paragraph 10	(disabled students)
Paragraph 11	
Paragraph 12	
Paragraph 13	(blind persons)
Paragraph 14	(pregnancy)
Paragraph 15	(persons in education)
Paragraph 18	(refugees)
Paragraph 21	(persons from abroad)
Paragraph 23	(member of couple looking after children while other member temporarily abroad)
Paragraph 28	(persons in receipt of a training allowance);

(b) a person who is a member of a couple and is treated as responsible for a child who is a member of his household;

(c) a person who is laid off or kept on short-time, who is available for employment in accordance with section 6 and Chapter II of Part II read with regulation 64 and who has not been laid off or kept on short-time for more than 13 weeks;

(d) a person who is temporarily absent from Great Britain because he is taking a member of his family who is a child or young person abroad for treatment, and who is treated as being in Great Britain in accordance with regulation 50(1)(b) or whose entitlement to income support is to continue in accordance with regulation 4(3) of the Income Support Regulations and who is not claiming a jobseeker's allowance or income support;

(e) a person who is incapable of work and training by reason of some disease or bodily or mental disablement if, in the opinion of a medical practitioner, that incapacity is unlikely to end within 12 months because of the severity of that disease or disablement.

AMENDMENTS

3.229   1. Children (Leaving Care) Act 2000 (Commencement No. 2 and Consequential Provisions) Order 2001 (SI 2001/3070), art.3(5) and Sch.4.

2. Jobseeker's Allowance and Income Support (General) (Amendment) Regulations 1996 (SI 1996/1517), reg.11 (October 7, 1996).

3. Jobseeker's Allowance (Amendment) (No.2) Regulations 1998 (SI 1998/1698), reg.2 (August 4, 1998).

4. Social Security (Miscellaneous Amendments) (No.2) Regulations 2001 (SI 2001/652), reg.5(a) (April 1, 2001).

5. Social Security (Miscellaneous Amendments) (No.2) Regulations 2001 (SI 2001/652), reg.5(c) (March 26, 2001).

DEFINITIONS

"the Benefits Act"—see Jobseekers Act, s.35(1).
"child"—*ibid.*
"close relative"—see reg.4.
"couple"—see reg.1(3).
"employment"—see reg.4.
"married couple"—see Jobseekers Act, s.35(1).
"a person who is kept on short-time"—see reg.4.
"a person who is laid off "—*ibid.*
"relative"—see reg.1(3).
"voluntary organisation"—*ibid.*

GENERAL NOTE

Para. (1)

"*young person*". To be entitled to income-based JSA, a person must in general be 18 (s.3(1)(f)(i) of the Jobseekers Act). This Part of the Regulations deals with the exceptions to this general exclusion (see s.3(1)(f)(ii) and (iii) of the Jobseekers Act). The lower age limit does not apply to contribution-based JSA, although in practice people below 18 will be unlikely to satisfy the contribution conditions (see s.2(1) of the Jobseekers Act). If a 16-or 17-year-old does qualify for contribution-based JSA, he does not count as a young person for the purposes of this Part.

3.230

The categories of 16- and 17-year-olds who under regs 58–61 are entitled to income-based JSA are similar (but not identical) to those who qualified for income support before October 7, 1996. (16- and 17-year-olds who are entitled to benefit while in relevant education can still claim income support under reg.13 of the Income Support Regulations, see para.15 of Sch.1B to those Regulations.) In *some* cases (see reg.61), a 16- or 17-year-old who is eligible for income-based JSA will also be eligible for income support. Because of the stricter benefit regime associated with JSA, it will usually be better for such a young person to claim income support. If the claimant does not come within one of the prescribed circumstances for JSA there is still the possibility of a severe hardship direction being made by the Secretary of State under s.16 of the Jobseekers Act, which then exempts the young person from the lower age limit (see s.3(1)(f)(ii)).

It is important to remember that satisfying an exception only gets the young person past the age condition for income-based JSA. All the other conditions of entitlement (see ss.1 and 3 of the Jobseekers Act) must be met. In order to meet the labour market conditions the young person will have to (i) register for work and training with the Careers Service (defined in reg.57(1)), or in certain circumstances with the Employment Service, (reg.62); (ii) be available for work, although if he has not been "sanctioned" for a training-related "offence" or refusing a job opportunity or voluntary unemployment or losing a job through misconduct, laid off or put on short-time or accepted an offer to enlist in the armed forces within the next eight weeks, he can restrict his availability to employment where the employer provides "suitable training" (defined in reg.57(1)) (reg.64); (iii) actively seek work and training (reg.65); and (iv) enter into a jobseeker's agreement (reg.66).

Paras (2) to (4)

3.231   See the notes to regs 58–61.

[¹Young persons to whom section 3(1)(f)(iii) or 3A(1)(e)(ii) applies

3.232   **58.** For the period specified in relation to him, a young person to whom regulation 59, 60 or 61 applies shall be regarded as a person within prescribed circumstances for the purposes of section 3(1)(f)(iii) or section 3A(1)(e)(ii) (conditions of entitlement for certain persons under the age of 18).]

AMENDMENT

3.233   1. Jobseeker's Allowance (Joint Claims) Regulations 2000 (SI 2000/1978), reg.2(5) and Sch.2, para.18 (March 19, 2001).

DEFINITION

"young person"—see reg.57(1).

GENERAL NOTE

3.234   This regulation, together with regs 59, 60 and 61, prescribes the circumstances in which, and the periods for which, 16 and 17-year-olds can be exempted from the lower age limit of 18 imposed by s.3(1)(f)(i) of the Jobseekers Act. See the notes to regs 59, 60 and 61.

Young persons in the child benefit extension period

3.235   **59.**—(1) For the period specified in paragraph (2), this regulation applies to a young person who falls within paragraph (2) of regulation 57.

(2) The period in the case of any person falling within paragraph (1) is the child benefit extension period, except where regulation 61(1)(d) or (e) applies.

DEFINITIONS

"child benefit extension period"—see reg.57(1).
"young person"—*ibid.*

GENERAL NOTE

3.236   A 16 or 17-year-old who comes within any of the categories in reg.57(2) is exempt from the ordinary lower age limit for income-based JSA imposed by s.3(1)(f)(i) of the Jobseekers Act until the end of the child benefit extension period, unless reg.61(1)(d) or (e) applies (see below). See reg.57(1) for the definition of the "child benefit extension period" and the notes to reg.54. Note that reg.59 only gets the young person past the age condition for income-based JSA. All the other conditions of entitlement must be met (see the note to the definition of "young person" in reg.57(1)).

The categories in reg.57(2) are broadly the same as those in the former Part II of Sch.1A to the Income Support Regulations (revoked on October 7, 1996) (16-or 17-year-old exempt from the age test for income support during the child benefit extension period). Note, however, the slightly different conditions in reg.57(2)(a)(ii) (the young person must have registered for employment *and* training), and in reg.57(4)(c) and (d).

Reg. 61(1)(d) and (e) apply to a young person who is otherwise eligible for JSA who either cannot register with the Careers Service because of an emergency there (head (d)) or would suffer hardship because of the extra time it would take for him to register at the Careers Service (head (e)). If the young person registers at the Employment Service instead he will be exempt from the lower age limit for the period allowed in reg.61(2)(c) or (d) (normally two weeks if reg.61(1)(d) applies or 5 days in the case of reg.61(1)(e)).

See also regs 60 and 61.

Young persons at the end of the child benefit extension period

60.—(1) For the period specified in relation to him in paragraph (2), this regulation applies to a young person who is—

3.237

  (a) a person who has ceased to live in accommodation provided for him by a local authority under Part III of the Children Act 1989 (local authority support for children and families) and is of necessity living away from his parents and any person acting in place of his parents;

  (b) a person who has been discharged from any institution to which the Prison Act 1952 applies or from custody under the Criminal Procedure (Scotland) Act 1975 after the child benefit extension period and who is a person falling within paragraph (2) of regulation 57.

(2)(a) Except where regulation 61(1)(d) or (e) applies, the period in the case of a person falling within paragraph 1(a) is the period which begins on the day on which that paragraph first applies to that person and ends on the day before the day on which that person attains the age of 18 or the day at the end of a period of 8 weeks immediately following the day on which paragraph 1(a) first had effect in relation to him, whichever is the earlier; and this period may include any week in which regulation 7 of the Child Benefit (General) Regulations 1976 (circumstances in which a person who has ceased to receive full-time education is to continue to be treated as a child) also applies to that person;

  (b) except where regulation 61(1)(d) or (e) applies, the period in the case of any person falling within paragraph 1(b) is the period beginning on the day after he was discharged, and ends on the last day of the period of 8 weeks beginning with the date on which the period began or on the day before the date on which that person attains the age of 18, whichever first occurs.

(3) In this regulation, "week" means any period of 7 consecutive days.

DEFINITIONS

"child benefit extension period"—see reg.57(1).
"young person"—*ibid.*

GENERAL NOTE

This provision is similar to the former reg.13A(4)(c) and (d) of the Income Support Regulations (now revoked). The effect, with reg.58, is to exempt 16-and 17-year-olds from the ordinary lower age limit for income-based JSA (see s.3(1)(f)(i) of the Jobseekers Act) if they leave local authority care and have to live away from their parents and any substitute (para.(1)(a)), or if they have been discharged from custody after the end of the child benefit extension period and one of the conditions in

3.238

reg.57(2) applies (para.(1)(b)). Except where reg.61(1)(d) or (e) applies (see the note to reg.59 above as to when these apply), the exemption lasts for eight weeks, or until the person reaches 18, if sooner (para.(2)). If the exemption is under para.(1)(a), any week in the child benefit extension period can count in the eight weeks (it is understood that this is the intended meaning, although para.(2)(a) refers to reg.7, not reg.7D, of the Child Benefit Regulations).

Note that there is no equivalent to the former reg.13A(4)(a) (incapacity for work and training which is likely to end within 12 months). Such a young person could claim income support: see para.7 of Sch.1B to the Income Support Regulations.

It is important to remember that reg.60 only gets the young person past the age condition for income-based JSA. All the other conditions of entitlement must be met (see the note to the definition of "young person" in reg.57(1)).

See also reg.61.

Other young persons in prescribed circumstances

3.239

61.—(1) For the period specified in relation to him in paragraph (2), this regulation applies to a young person—

(a) who is a person who is laid off or kept on short-time and is available for employment in accordance with section 6 and Chapter II of Part II read with regulation 64;

(b) who is a member of a couple and is treated as responsible for a child who is a member of his household;

(c) who falls within a prescribed category of persons for the purposes of section 124(1)(e) of the Benefits Act and who is not claiming income support;

(d) in whom section 3(1)(f)(ii) [¹or section 3A(1)(e)(i)] does not apply, who is a person falling within paragraph (2) of regulation 57, sub-paragraph (a) or (b) of paragraph (1) of regulation 60 or sub-paragraph (b) or (c) and who is unable to register with the Careers Service [⁴ or the Connexions Service] because of an emergency affecting the Careers Service [⁴or the Connexions Service] and registers with the Employment Service in accordance with regulation 62(2);

(e) to whom section 3(1)(f)(ii) [or section 3A(1)(e)(i)] does not apply, who is a person falling within paragraph (2) of regulation 57, sub-paragraph (a) or (b) of paragraph (1) of regulation 60 or sub-paragraph (b) or (c) and who would suffer hardship because of the extra time it would take him to register with the Careers Service [⁴ or the Connexions Service] and registers with the Employment Service in accordance with regulation 62(3);

(f) who has accepted a firm offer of enlistment by one of the armed forces with a starting date not more than 8 weeks after the offer was made who was not in employment or training at the time of that offer and whose jobseeker's allowance has never been reduced in accordance with regulation 63 or section 19(5)(b) or (c) or section 19(6)(c) or (d) [² or section 20A(2)(b), (c), (f) or (g)] read with regulation 68 or rendered not payable in accordance with section 19(6)(a) or (b) read with Part V.

(2) (a) The period in the case of any person falling within paragraph (1)(a) is the period starting with the date on which he was laid off or first kept on short-time and ending on the date on which he ceases to be laid off or kept on short-time or the day before the day he attains

the age of 18 or at the expiry of the 13 week period starting with the date of the lay off, or date he was first kept on short-time, whichever first occurs;

(b) except where paragraph (1)(d) or (e) applies, the period in the case of any person falling within paragraph (1)(b) or (c) is the period until the day before that person attains the age of 18 or until paragraph (1)(b) or (c) ceases to apply, whichever first occurs;

(c) the period in the case of any person falling within paragraph (1)(d) is the period starting with the date of registration with the Employment Service and ending on the day on which the person is next due to attend in accordance with regulation 23 [³ or regulation 23A] or on the date on which the period calculated in accordance with regulation 59(2) or 60(2) or sub-paragraph (b) would have expired, whichever first occurs;

(d) the period in the case of any person falling within paragraph 1(e) is the period starting on the date of registration with the Employment Service and ending five days after that date or on the day after the day on which he registered with the Careers Service, or on the date on which the period calculated in accordance with regulation 59(2) or 60(2) or sub-paragraph (b) would have expired, whichever first occurs;

(e) the period in the case of any person falling within paragraph 1(f) is the period starting with the date of claim and ending with the day before the day on which he is due to enlist or the day before he attains the age of 18, whichever first occurs.

(3) In this regulation "week" means a period of 7 consecutive days.

AMENDMENTS

1. Jobseeker's Allowance (Joint Claims) Regulations 2000 (SI 2000/1978), reg.2(5) and Sch.2, para.19(a) (March 19, 2001).
2. Jobseeker's Allowance (Joint Claims) Regulations 2000 (SI 2000/1978), reg.2(5) and Sch.2, para.19(b) (March 19, 2001).
3. Jobseeker's Allowance (Joint Claims) Regulations 2000 (SI 2000/1978), reg.2(5) and Sch.2, para.19(c) (March 19, 2001).
4. Social Security (Miscellaneous Amendments) (No.2) Regulations 2001 (SI 2001/652), reg.5(b) (April 1, 2001).

3.240

DEFINITIONS

"the Benefits Act"—see Jobseekers Act, s.35(1).
"the Careers Service"—see reg.57(1).
"child"—see Jobseekers Act, s.35(1).
"couple"—see reg.1(3).
"a person who is kept on short-time"—see reg.4.
"a person who is laid off "—*ibid.*

GENERAL NOTE

This sets out additional circumstances in which a 16 or 17-year-old will be exempt from the lower age limit imposed by s.3(1)(f)(i) of the Jobseekers Act. Para.(1) defines the categories covered and para.(2) the length of the exemption. *Para. (1) (a).* A person who is laid off or on short-time working and who is available for work (see reg.64) will be exempt for up to 13 weeks (para.(2)(a)).

3.241

Para. (1) (b). A person who is a member of a couple and responsible for a child (see regs 77 and 78) is exempt until 18 (except where para.(1)(d) or (1(e) applies, see below) (para.(2)(b)).

Para. (1) (c). A person who falls within para.4ZA of, and Sch.1B to, the Income Support Regulations (which prescribe the categories of people entitled to income support under s.124(1)(e) of the SSCBA), and who is not claiming income support, is exempt until 18 (except where para.(1)(d) or (e) applies, see below) (para.(2)(b)). As the age limit for income support is now 16 (see s.124(1)(a) of the SSCBA, amended with effect from October 7, 1996), it will be better for most young people who come within Sch.1B to claim income support so as to avoid the risk of being sanctioned for not complying with the JSA labour market conditions.

Para. (1) (d) and (e). These sub-paras, do not apply if a severe hardship direction has been made. Except for a young person who is laid off or on short-time (sub-para.(a)) or has accepted an offer to enlist in the armed forces in the next eight weeks (sub-para.(f)), a 16-or 17-year-old who is eligible for income-based JSA must register with the Careers Service (or Connexions Service) for work and training (reg.62). If such a person is unable to register with the Careers Service because of "an emergency affecting the Careers Service" (sub-para.(d)), or would suffer hardship because of the extra time it would take for him to register with the Careers Service (sub-para.(e)), and registers with the Employment Service instead, he will be exempt from the lower age limit for JSA under sub-para.(2)(d) until he is next due to attend (para.(2)(c)) or under sub-para.(e) for up to five days (para.(2)(d)) (or until he ceases to be eligible for JSA under reg.59 or 60 or reaches 18, if this is earlier).

Para. (1) (f). This applies to a person who has accepted an offer (made when he was not employed or in training) to enlist in the armed forces within the next eight weeks and who has never been sanctioned for a training-related "offence" or refusing a job opportunity or voluntary unemployment or losing a job through misconduct. The exemption lasts until he enlists (para. (2)(e)).

Note that reg.61 only gets the young person past the age condition for income-based JSA. All the other conditions of entitlement must be met (see the note to the definition of "young person" in reg.57(1)).

Registration

3.242 **62.**—(1) Except in the circumstances set out in paragraphs (2) and (3) a young person to whom section 3(1)(f)(ii) or (iii) [¹ or section 3A(1)(e)(i) or (ii)] applies other than one falling within regulation 61(1)(a) or (f), must register with the Careers Service [² or the Connexions Service] for both employment and training.

(2) A young person who is unable to register with the Careers Service [² or the Connexions Service] because of an emergency affecting the Careers Service [²or the Connexions Service] such as a strike or fire must register with the Employment Service for both employment and training.

(3) A young person who would suffer hardship because of the extra time it would take him to register with the Careers Service [² or the Connexions Service] must register with the Employment Service for both employment and training.

AMENDMENTS

3.243 1. Jobseeker's Allowance (Joint Claims) Regulations 2000 (SI 2000/1978), reg.2(5) and Sch.2, para.20 (March 19, 2001).

2. Social Security (Miscellaneous Amendments) (No.2) Regulations 2001 (SI 2001/652), reg.5(b) (April 1, 2001).

DEFINITIONS

"the Careers Service"—see reg.57(1)
"employment"—see reg.4.
"training"—see reg.57(1).
"young person"—*ibid.*

GENERAL NOTE

Except for a young person who is laid off or on short-time, or who has never been **3.244** sanctioned for a training-related "offence" or refusing a job opportunity or voluntary unemployment or losing a job through misconduct and has accepted an offer to enlist in the armed forces within the next eight weeks, a 16- or 17-year-old who is exempt from the lower age limit for income-based JSA has to register with the Careers Service (or Connexions Service) for work and training (para.(1)). If such a young person is unable to register with the Careers Service because of an emergency, *e.g.* a strike or fire (para.(2)), or would suffer hardship because of the extra time it would take for him to register with the Careers Service (para.(3)) he has to register with the Employment Service instead. See the note to reg.61(1)(d) and (e) above.

While paras (2) or (3) apply, he will be deemed to have entered into a jobseeker's agreement (reg.66(2)).

See also regs 64 to 66.

Reduced payments under section 17

63.—(1) Except as provided in paragraph (3), the amount of an income- **3.245** based jobseeker's allowance which would otherwise be payable to a young person shall be reduced by[¹, if he is a single person or a lone parent,] a sum equal to 40 per cent of the amount applicable in his case by way of a personal allowance determined [¹ in accordance with paragraph 1(1) or 1(2) of Schedule 1 (as the case may be) or, if he is a member of a couple, a sum equal to 40 per cent of the amount which would have been applicable in his case if he had been a single person determined in accordance with paragraph 1(1) of Schedule 1] for the period set out in paragraph (2) if

  (a) he was previously entitled to an income-based jobseeker's allowance and that entitlement ceased by virtue of the revocation of a direction under section 16 because he had failed to pursue an opportunity of obtaining training or rejected an offer of training;

  (b) his allowance has at any time in the past been reduced in accordance with this regulation or in accordance with regulation 68 because he has done an act or omission falling within section 19(5)(b) or (c) [² or section 20A(2)(b) or (c)] or rendered not payable in accordance with section 19(6)(a) or (b) [² or section 20A(2)(d) or (e)] read with Part V and he has—

    (i) failed to pursue an opportunity of obtaining training without showing good cause for doing so,

    (ii) rejected an offer of training without showing good cause for doing so or

    (iii) failed to complete a course of training and no certificate has been issued to him under subsection (4) of section 17 with respect to that failure;

  (c) he has—

    (i) done an act or omission falling within section 16(3)(b)(i) or (ii) and has not shown good cause for doing so or done an act or omission falling within section 19(5)(b)(i), (ii) or (iv) [⁴ or section 20A(2)(b)(i), (ii), or (iv)] without good cause or done an act or omission falling within section 19(5)(b)(i), (ii), or (iv) [⁴ or section 20A(2)(b)(i), (ii) or (iv)] for which he was regarded as having good cause in accordance with regulation 67(1) and

    (ii) after that act or omission failed to complete a course of training and no certificate has been issued to him under subsection (4) of section 17 with respect to that failure and at the time he did the act or omission falling within subparagraph (i) he was a new jobseeker;

(d) he has—

    (i) failed to complete a course of training and no certificate has been issued to him under subsection (4) of section 17 with respect to that failure or done an act or omission falling within section 19(5)(b)(iii) [⁵ or section 20A(2)(b)(iii)] without good cause or done an act or omission falling within section 19(5)(b)(iii) [⁵ or section 20A(2)(b)(iii)] for which he was regarded as having good cause in accordance with regulation 67(1) and

    (ii) after that failure he has failed to complete a course of training and no certificate has been issued to him under subsection (4) of section 17 with respect to that failure and on the day before the day he first attended the course referred to in sub-paragraph (i) he was a new jobseeker; or

(e) he has failed to complete a course of training and no certificate has been issued to him under subsection (4) of section 17 with respect to that failure and on the day before he first attended the course he was not a new jobseeker; or

(f) he has failed to complete a course of training and no certificate has been issued to him under subsection (4) of section 17 with respect to that failure and he lost his place on the course through his misconduct.

(2) The period shall start with the date on which the first severe hardship direction is made under section 16 after the act or acts referred to in paragraph (a), (b), (c), (d), (e) or (f) of paragraph (1) have taken place and shall end fourteen days later.

(3) In the case of a young person who is pregnant or seriously ill who does an act falling within sub-paragraphs (a)-(f) of paragraph (1), the reduction shall be [¹ if he is a single person or a lone parent] of 20 per cent of the amount applicable in his case by way of a personal allowance [¹ determined in accordance with paragraph 1(1) or 1(2) of Schedule 1 (as the case may be) or, if he is a member of a couple, of 20 per cent of the amount which would have been applicable in his case if he had been a single person determined in accordance with paragraph 1(1) of Schedule 1].

(4) For the purposes of this regulation, "new jobseeker" means a young person who has not since first leaving full-time education been employed or self-employed for 16 or more hours per week or completed a course of train in or failed to complete a course of training and no certificate has been issued to him to show good cause for that failure under subsection (4) of section 17 or done an act or omission falling within section 19(5)(b)(iii) [⁶ or section 20A(2)(b)(iii)] without good cause or done an act or omission falling within section 19(5)(c) [⁶ or section 20A(2)(c)].

(5) A reduction under paragraph (1) or (3) shall, if it is not a multiple of 5p, be rounded to the nearest such multiple or, if it is a multiple of 2.5p but not of 5p, to the next lower multiple of 5p.

AMENDMENTS

1. Social Security and Child Support (Miscellaneous Amendments) Regulations 1997 (SI 1997/827), reg.2 (April 7, 1997).

    3.246

2. Jobseeker's Allowance (Joint Claims) Regulations 2000 (SI 2000/1978), reg.2(5) and Sch.2, para.21(a)(i)(aa) (March 19, 2001).
3. Jobseeker's Allowance (Joint Claims) Regulations 2000 (SI 2000/1978), reg.2(5) and Sch.2, para.21(a)(i)(bb) (March 19, 2001).
4. Jobseeker's Allowance (Joint Claims) Regulations 2000 (SI 2000/1978), reg.2(5) and Sch.2, para.21(a)(ii) (March 19, 2001).
5. Jobseeker's Allowance (Joint Claims) Regulations 2000 (SI 2000/1978), reg.2(5) and Sch.2, para.21(a)(iii) (March 19, 2001).
6. Jobseeker's Allowance (Joint Claims) Regulations 2000 (SI 2000/1978), reg.2(5) and Sch.2, para.21(b) (March 19, 2001).

DEFINITIONS

"full-time education"—see reg.57(1).
"income-based jobseeker's allowance"—see Jobseekers Act, s.1(4).
"training"—see reg.57(1).
"young person"—*ibid.*

GENERAL NOTE

Para. (1)

    Section 20(2) of the Act provides that where a severe hardship direction is in force and the young person has without good cause failed to pursue an opportunity, or rejected an offer, of training or failed to complete a training course, a s.19(5) sanction will not be applied. Instead, the circumstances in which income-based JSA payable under a severe hardship direction will be paid at a reduced rate are set out in this regulation. The reduction is 40 per cent of the appropriate single person or lone parent personal allowance under para.1 of Sch.1, or 20 per cent if the young person is pregnant or seriously ill (not defined) (para.(3)), and lasts for two weeks (para.(2)). If the person is a member of a couple, the same reduction is applied as if he was a single claimant.

    3.247

    The effect of para.(1) is that in some cases, *e.g.* where the person was previously a "new jobseeker," the reduction will only be applied where it is a "second offence". The detailed rules provide for the reduction to be imposed if:

  (i) a previous severe hardship direction was revoked because the person failed to pursue an opportunity, or rejected an offer, of training without good cause (sub-para (a)); or

  (ii) at any time in the past the person's JSA has been subject to a reduction under this regulation, or reg.68 for a training-related "offence" or stopped because of voluntary unemployment or losing a job through misconduct, and then without good cause he fails to pursue an opportunity, or rejects an offer, or fails to complete a course, of training (sub-para. (b)); or

  (iii) while he was a new jobseeker (defined in para.(4)) he failed to pursue an opportunity, or rejected an offer, of training without good cause while a severe hardship direction was in force, or did not avail himself of, or failed to apply for or accept after having been notified of, or failed to attend, a place on a training scheme or employment programme either without good cause, or only with deemed good cause under reg.67(1), and then fails without good cause to complete a course of training (sub-para.(c)); or

  (iv) he has failed to complete a course of training without good cause while a

891

severe hardship direction was in force, or given up a training scheme or employment programme place either without good cause or only with deemed good cause under reg.67(1), and was a new jobseeker (defined in para.(4)) on the day before he started the course, and then fails to complete a course of training without good cause (sub-para. (d)); or

(v) he has failed to complete a course of training without good cause and was not a new jobseeker on the day before he started the course (sub-para.(e)); or

(vi) he has lost his training place through misconduct before finishing the course (sub-para. (f)).

The above is a summary of the very detailed rules in para.(1) but the reader is advised to check the text of the regulation where there is any doubt as to whether a particular sub-paragraph applies.

Para. (4)

3.248   A new jobseeker is a 16- or 17-year-old who since leaving full-time education (see reg.57(1)) has not been employed or self-employed for 16 hours or more a week, or finished a training course, or failed to finish a training course without good cause or given up without good cause or lost through misconduct a training scheme or employment programme place.

Availability for employment

3.249   **64.**—(1) A young person is required to be available for employment in accordance with section 6 and Chapter II of Part II except as provided in paragraphs (2) and (3).

(2) A young person whose jobseeker's allowance has not been reduced in accordance with regulation 63 or in accordance with regulation 68 because he has done an act or omission falling within section 19(5)(b) or (c) or section 19(6)(c) or (d) [¹ or section 20A(2)(b), (c), (f) or (g)] or rendered not payable in accordance with section 19(6)(a) or (b) [¹ or section 20A(2)(d) or (e)] read with Part V and who does not fall within regulation 61(1)(a) or (f) may restrict his availability for employment to employment where suitable training is provided by the employer.

(3) A young person who places restrictions on the nature of employment for which he is available as permitted by paragraph (2) does not have to show that he has reasonable prospects of securing employment notwithstanding those restrictions.

AMENDMENT

3.250   1. Jobseeker's Allowance (Joint Claims: Consequential Amendments) Regulations 2000 (SI 2000/3336), reg.2(8) (March 19, 2001).

DEFINITIONS

"employment"—see reg.4.
"suitable training"—see reg.57(1)

GENERAL NOTE

3.251   In order to be entitled to JSA, a young person has to be available for work under the normal rules (see s.6 of the Jobseekers Act and regs 5 to 17) (para.(1)). However, provided that he is not subject to a sanction under reg.63 or under reg.68 for a training-related "offence" or refusing a job opportunity or voluntary unemployment or losing a job through misconduct, a 16- or 17-year-old can restrict his availability to employment where the employer provides "suitable training" (para.(2)). See reg.57(1) for the definition of suitable training. This does not apply to a young person who has been laid off or is on short-time working, or who has never been sanctioned for a training-related "offence" or refusing a job opportunity or voluntary unemployment or losing a job through misconduct and has accepted an offer to join the armed forces in the next eight weeks. Presumably this is because such a young person is only expected to be unemployed for a short time and so it would not be reasonable to require an employer to provide him with training. The young person does not have to show that he still has reasonable prospects of obtaining work (para.(3)). Note also reg.67(2).

In addition, see regs 62 and 65 to 66.

Active seeking

65.—(1) Subject to the following paragraphs, Section 7 and Chapter III of Part II shall have effect in relation to a young person as if "employment" included "training".

(2) Subject to paragraphs (4) and (5), in order to have the best prospects of securing employment or training a young person can be expected to have to take more than one step on one occasion in any week unless taking one step on one occasion is all that it is reasonable for that person to do in that week, and unless it is reasonable for him to take only one step on one occasion, he can be expected to have to take at least one step to seek training and one step to seek employment in that week.

(3) Subject to paragraph (4), steps which it is reasonable for a young person to be expected to have to take include, in addition to those set out in regulation 18(2)—

(a) seeking training and

(b) seeking full-time education.

(4) Paragraphs (1), (2) and (3) do not apply to a young person falling within regulation 61(1)(a) or (f).

(5) Paragraphs (1) and (2) do not apply to a young person who has had his jobseeker's allowance reduced in accordance with regulation 63 or regulation 68 because he has done an act or omission falling within section 19(5)(b) or (c) or section 19(6)(c) or (d) [¹or section 20A(2)(b), (c), (f) or (g)] or rendered not payable in accordance with section 19(6)(a) or (b) [¹ or section 20A(2)(d) or (e)] read with Part V but paragraph (3) does apply to such a young person.

(6) "Training" in section 7 and in this regulation means suitable training.

3.252

AMENDMENT

1. Jobseeker's Allowance (Joint Claims: Consequential Amendments) Regulations 2000 (SI 2000/3336), reg.2(9) (March 19, 2001).

3.253

DEFINITIONS

"employment"—see reg.4.
"full-time education"—see reg.57(1).
"suitable training"—*ibid.*
"young person"—*ibid.*

GENERAL NOTE

The normal rules in relation to actively seeking work apply to young people (see s.7 of the Jobseekers Act and regs 18 to 22) but they must seek training (which

3.254

means suitable training (para.(6)) as well as work (para.(1)). See reg.57(1) for the definition of "suitable training". They are expected to take more than one step (see reg.18(2)) each week, including at least one step to find work and one to find training, unless it is reasonable to take only one step that week (para.(2)). In the case of a young person, "steps" include, as well as those referred to in reg.18(2), seeking training and seeking full-time education (para.(3)).

These special rules do not apply to a young person who is laid off or on short-time working or who has never been sanctioned for a training-related "offence" or refusing a job opportunity or voluntary unemployment or losing a job through misconduct and has accepted an offer to join the armed forces within the next eight weeks (para.(4)). Presumably this is because they are only expected to be unemployed for a short time and so it would not be reasonable to require them to seek training or education in that time, only work.

Para. (5) appears to provide that a young person whose JSA is subject to a sanction under reg.63 or under reg.68 for a training-related "offence" or refusing a job opportunity or voluntary unemployment or losing a job through misconduct is not required to seek training as well as work, since it states that paras (1) and (2) do not apply to such a person. But this is followed by the somewhat contradictory statement that para.(3) does apply; that is, such a young person *is* required to seek training and full-time education. The policy intention apparently is that a 16 or 17-year-old who has been sanctioned should only be seeking training (and education) with a view to finding work and not as an end in itself.

See also regs 62, 64, 65A and 66.

[¹Attendance, information and evidence

3.255   **65A.** A young person who does not fall within regulation 61(1)(a) or (f) shall, if the Secretary of State requires him to do so, provide, in addition to the declaration specified in regulation 24(6), a declaration to the effect that since making a claim for a jobseeker's allowance or since he last provided a declaration in accordance with this regulation he has been actively seeking suitable training to the extent necessary to give him his best prospects of securing suitable training save as he has otherwise notified the Secretary of State.]

AMENDMENT

1. Jobseeker's Allowance and Income Support (General) (Amendment) Regulations 1996 (SI 1996/1517), reg.12 (October 7, 1996).

DEFINITIONS

"suitable training"—see reg.57(1).
"young person"—*ibid.*

GENERAL NOTE

3.256   This regulation provides that a 16- or 17-year-old may be required to declare that he has been actively seeking suitable training as well as work when he signs on. There is the usual exception from this rule for a young person who has been laid off or is on short-time working, or who has never been sanctioned for a training-related "offence" or refusing a job opportunity or voluntary unemployment or losing a job through misconduct and has accepted an offer to join the armed forces within the next eight weeks.

See also regs 62, 64, 65 and 66.

The jobseeker's agreement

66.—(1) In a jobseeker's agreement with a young person, other than one falling within regulation 61(1)(a) or (f), the following information is required in addition to that prescribed in chapter V of Part II: a broad description of the circumstances in which the amount of the person's benefit may be reduced in accordance with section 17 and regulation 63, or may be rendered not payable in accordance with section 19 [²or section 20A] read with Part V or may be payable at a reduced rate in accordance with sections 19 and 20 [²or sections 20A and 20B] and regulation 68.

3.257

(2) A young person is to be treated as having entered into a jobseeker's agreement and as having satisfied the condition mentioned in section 1(2)(b) as long as the circumstances set out in [¹regulation 62(2) or 62(3) apply.]

AMENDMENTS

1. Jobseekers's Allowance (Amendment) Regulations 1996 (SI 1996/1516), reg.8 and Sch. (October 7, 1996).
2. Jobseeker's Allowance (Joint Claims) Regulations 2000 (SI 2000/1978), reg.2(5) and Sch.2, para.22 (March 19, 2001).

3.258

DEFINITIONS

"jobseeker's agreement"—see Jobseekers Act, s.9(1).
"young person"—see reg.57(1).

GENERAL NOTE

See the notes to ss.9 to 11 of the Jobseekers Act and regs 31 to 45 for the rules relating to jobseeker's agreements.

3.259

Para. (1)
A 16 or 17-year-old has to enter into a jobseeker's agreement as a condition of receiving JSA in the normal way. But the agreement must contain additional information as to the sanctions that can be applied. There is the usual exception from this rule for a young person who has been laid off or is on short-time working, or who has never been sanctioned for a training-related "offence" or refusing a job opportunity or voluntary unemployment or losing a job through misconduct and has accepted an offer to join the armed forces within the next eight weeks.

Para. (2)
A young person will be deemed to have entered into a jobseeker's agreement while he has to register with the Employment Service for work and training instead of the Careers Service due to an emergency or because the extra time involved in registering with the Careers Service would cause him hardship.

Sanctions

67.—(1) Without prejudice to any other circumstances in which a person may be regarded as having good cause for any act or omission for the purposes of section 19(5)(b) [²or section 20A(2)(b)], and in addition to the circumstances listed in regulation 73, a young person is to be regarded as having good cause for any act or omission for the purposes of section 19(5)(b) [² or section 20A(2)(b)] where

3.260

    (a) this is the first occasion on which he has done an act or omission falling within section 19(5)(b) [²or section 20A(2)(b)] and he has not while claiming a jobseeker's allowance failed to pursue an opportunity of obtaining training without good cause or rejected an offer of training without good cause or failed to complete a course of training and no certificate has been issued to him under subsection (4) of section 17 with respect to that training; and

(b) at the time he did the act or omission falling within section 19(5)(b)(i), (ii) or (iv) [³ or section 20A(2)(b)(i), (ii) or (iv)] he was [¹. . .] a new jobseeker or, in the case of an act or omission falling with section 19(5)(b)(iii), [³ or section 20A(2)(b)(iii)] at the time he first attended the scheme or programme he was [¹. . .] a new jobseeker.

(2) Without prejudice to any other circumstances in which a person may be regarded as having good cause for any act or omission for the purposes of section 19(6)(c) or (d) [⁴ or section 20A(2)(f) or (g)], a young person is to be regarded as having good cause for any act or omission for the purposes of section 19(6)(c) or (d) [⁴ or section 20A(2)(f) or (g)] where the employer did not offer suitable training unless he falls within regulation 61(1)(a) or (f) or his jobseeker's allowance has been reduced in accordance with regulation 63 or in accordance with regulation 68 because he has done an act or omission falling within section 19(5)(b) or (c) [⁵or section 20A (2)(b) or (c)] or section 19(6)(c) or (d) [⁴or section 20A(2)(f) or (g)] or rendered not payable in accordance with section 19(6)(a) or (b) [⁶or section 20A(2)(d) or (e)] read with Part V.

(3) For the purposes of this regulation, "new jobseeker" means a young person who has not since first leaving full-time education been employed or self-employed for 16 or more hours per week or completed a course of training or failed to complete a course of training and no certificate has been issued to him to show good cause for that failure under subsection (4) of section 17 or done an act or omission falling within section 19(5)(b)(iii) [⁷ or section 20A(2)(b)(iii)] without good cause or done an act or omission falling within section 19(5)(c) [⁸ or section 20A(2)(c)].

AMENDMENTS

3.261   1. Jobseeker's Allowance and Income Support (General) (Amendment) Regulations 1996 (SI 1996/1517), reg.13 (October 7, 1996).

2. Jobseeker's Allowance (Joint Claims) Regulations 2000 (SI 2000/1978), reg.2(5) and Sch.2, para.23(a)(i) (March 19, 2001).

3. Jobseeker's Allowance (Joint Claims) Regulations 2000 (SI 2000/1978), reg.2(5) and Sch.2, para.23(a)(ii) (March 19, 2001).

4. Jobseeker's Allowance (Joint Claims) Regulations 2000 (SI 2000/1978), reg.2(5) and Sch.2, para.23(b)(i) (March 19, 2001).

5. Jobseeker's Allowance (Joint Claims) Regulations 2000 (SI 2000/1978), reg.2(5) and Sch.2, para.23(b)(ii) (March 19, 2001).

6. Jobseeker's Allowance (Joint Claims) Regulations 2000 (SI 2000/1978), reg.2(5) and Sch.2, para.23(b)(iii) (March 19, 2001).

7. Jobseeker's Allowance (Joint Claims) Regulations 2000 (SI 2000/1978), reg.2(5) and Sch.2, para.23(c)(i) (March 19, 2001).

8. Jobseeker's Allowance (Joint Claims) Regulations 2000 (SI 2000/1978), reg.2(5) and Sch.2, para.23(c)(ii) (March 19, 2001).

DEFINITIONS

"full-time education"—see reg.57(1).
"suitable training"—*ibid.*
"training"—*ibid.*
"young person"—*ibid.*

See the notes to s.19 of the Jobseekers Act for the circumstances in which sanc-   **3.262**
tions may be applied.

Para. (1)
The broad effect of paragraph (1) is to give a "new jobseeker" (see para.(3)) a
second chance in certain circumstances where a sanction might otherwise be
imposed. He will be deemed to have good cause for the purposes of s.19(5)(b) if this
is the first time he has refused or given up, etc. a training scheme or employment
programme opportunity.

Para. (2)
This provides that unless a young person has been sanctioned under reg.63 or under
reg.68 for a training-related "offence" or refusing a job opportunity or voluntary
unemployment or losing a job through misconduct, he will have good cause for failing
to apply for or accept a notified job, or for not taking advantage of a reasonable opportunity of employment if the employer does not offer suitable training (defined in
reg.57(1)). There is the usual exception from this rule for a young person who has
been laid off or is on short-time working, or who has never been sanctioned for a training-related "offence" or refusing a job opportunity or voluntary unemployment or
losing a job through misconduct and has accepted an offer to join the armed forces
within the next eight weeks. See also s.64 which provides that a 16-or 17-year-old may
limit his availability to employment where the employer provides suitable training.

Para. (3)
See the note to reg.63(4).

Reduced amount of allowance

68.—(1) Subject to paragraphs (2) and (4), the amount of an income-   **3.263**
based jobseeker's allowance which would otherwise be payable to a young
person shall be reduced by [¹, if he is a single person or a lone parent,]
a sum equal to 40 per cent of the amount applicable in his case by way of a
peronal allowance determined [¹in accordance with paragraph 1(1) or
1(2) of Schedule 1 (as the case may be) or, if he is a member of a couple
[³(including a joint-claim couple)], sum equal to 40 per cent of the amount
which would have been applicable in his case if he had been a single person
determined in accordance with paragraph 1(1) of Schedule 1] for a period of
two weeks from the beginning of the first week after [²the Secretary of State]'s
decision where the young person has done any act or omission falling within
section 19(5) or within 19(6)(c) or (d) [³or within section 20A(2)(a) to (c),
(f) or (g)], unless the young person reaches the age of 18 before that two week
period expires, in which case the allowance shall be payable at the full rate
applicable in his case from the date he reaches the age of 18.

(2) Subject to paragraph (4), in a case where the young person or any
member of his family is pregnant or seriously ill the amount of an income-
based job-seeker's allowance which would otherwise be payable to the young
person shall be reduced by [¹, if he is a single person or a lone parent,] a sum
equal to 20 per cent of the amount applicable in his case by way of a personal allowance determined [¹ in accordance with paragraph 1(1) or 1(2) of
Schedule 1 (as the case may be) or, if he is a member of a couple, a sum
equal to 20 per cent of the amount which would have been applicable in his
case if he had been a single person determined in accordance with paragraph

1(1) of Schedule 1] for a period of two weeks from the beginning of the first week after [² the Secretary of State]'s decision where the young person has done any act or omission falling within section 19(5) or within 19(6)(c) or (d) [³ or within section 20A(2)(a) to (c), (f) or (g)], unless the young person reaches the age of 18 before that two week period expires, in which case the allowance shall be payable at the full rate applicable in his case from the date he reaches the age of 18.

(3) A reduction under paragraph (1) or (2) shall, if it is not a multiple of 5p, be rounded to the nearest such multiple or if it is a multiple of 2.5p but not of 5p, to the next lower multiple of 5p.

(4) If a young person's claim for an income-based jobseeker's allowance is terminated before the expiry of the period determined in accordance with paragraphs (1) and (2), and he makes a fresh claim for the allowance, it shall be payable to him at the reduced rate determined in accordance with paragraph (1) or (2) for the balance of the time remaining of that two weeks, unless the young person reaches the age of 18 before that two week period expires, in which case the allowance shall be payable at the full rate applicable in his case from the date he reaches the age of 18.

(5) An income-based jobseeker's allowance shall be payable to a young person at the full rate applicable in his case after the expiry of the two week period referred to in paragraphs (1) and (2).

AMENDMENTS

3.264

1. Social Security and Child Support (Miscellaneous Amendments) Regulations 1997 (SI 1997/827), reg.3 (April 7, 1997).

2. Social Security Act 1998 (Commencement No.11, and Savings and Consequential and Transitional Provisions) Order 1999 (SI 1999/2860 (C.75)), art.3(1) and (12) and Sch.12, para.2 (October 18 1999).

3. Jobseeker's Allowance (Joint Claims) Regulations 2000 (SI 2000/1978), reg.2(5) and Sch.2, para.24 (March 19, 2001).

DEFINITIONS

"income-based jobseeker's allowance"—see Jobseekers Act, s.1(4).
"young person"—see reg.57(1).

GENERAL NOTE

3.265

See the notes to s.19 of the Jobseekers Act as to the circumstances in which sanctions may be applied.

The rules as to the amount and duration of a benefit sanction are different from those for adults. A person aged 18 or over who is sanctioned will only be paid JSA (at a reduced rate) if he is in hardship; see regs 140–146. If a young person is "sanctioned" under s.19(5) or (6)(c) or (d), his income-based JSA will continue to be paid but at a reduced rate. (Note that this does not apply if the sanction is imposed under s.19(6)(a) and (b); in such a case the young person will only qualify for JSA if he can show hardship.) The reduction is 40 per cent of the appropriate single person or lone parent personal allowance under para.1 of Sch.1, or 20 per cent if the young person or any member of the family is pregnant or seriously ill. If the person is a member of a couple the same reduction is applied as if he was a single claimant. It lasts for two weeks but will cease if the young person becomes 18 within that time. If the young person stops receiving JSA before the end of the two weeks but then claims JSA again, the reduction will be applied for the unexpired balance of the two-week period or until the person reaches 18.

PART V

SANCTIONS

[¹ Prescribed period for purposes of section 19(2)

69.—(1) The prescribed period for the purposes of [⁴sections 19(2) and 20A(3)] shall be—

   3.266

(a) 2 weeks, in any case which does not fall within [⁹sub-paragraph (b), (c) or (d)] below;

(b) 4 weeks, in any case [²(other than a case where a jobseeker's allowance is determined not to be payable in circumstances relating to the employment programme known as "Gateway to Work" specified in regulation 75(1)(a)(i)(bb))] in which—

  (i) a jobseeker's allowance is determined not to be payable to the claimant in circumstances falling within section 19(5) [⁵or section 20A(2)(a) to (c)], and

  (ii) one of the following circumstances applies—

    (aa) where the determination in (i) above does not relate to one of the New Deal options [⁹or the intensive Activity Period specified in regulation 75(1)(a)(iv)], on a previous occasion the jobseeker's allowance was determined not to be payable to him in circumstances falling within section 19(5) [⁵ or section 20A(2)(a) to (c)], or

    (bb) where the determination in (i) above relates to one of the New Deal options, on a previous occasion the jobseeker's allowance was determined not to be payable to him in circumstances falling within section 19(5) [⁵or section 20A(2)(a) to (c)] that relate to one of those options, [⁹or]

    [⁹(cc) where the determination in (i) above relates to the Intensive Activity Period specified in regulation 75(1)(a)(iv), on a previous occasion the jobseeker's allowance was determined not to be payable to him in circumstances falling within section 19(5) or section 20A(2)(a) to (c) that relate to any intensive Activity Period specified in regulation 75(1)(a)(iv), and]

  (iii) the first date on which the jobseeker's allowance was not payable to him on that previous occasion falls within the period of 12 months preceding the date of the determination mentioned in (b)(i) above;

(c) 26 weeks in any case [³(other than a case where a jobseeker's allowance is determined not to be payable in circumstances relating to the employment programme known as "Gateway to Work" specified in regulation 75(1)(a)(i)(bb))]

  (i) a jobseeker's allowance is determined not to be payable to the claimant in circumstances falling within section 19(5) [⁵ or section 20A(2)(a) to (c)] and the determination relates to an act or omission arising after this regulation comes into force in respect of one of the New Deal options; and

  (ii) on two or more previous occasions a jobseeker's allowance has been determined not to be payable to the claimant in circumstances falling within section 19(5) [⁵ or section 20A(2)(a) to (c)] and each such determination relates to one of the New Deal options; and

(iii) no more than 12 months have elapsed between the beginning of the day on which the determination mentioned in (c)(i) above is made and the beginning of the first day on which a jobseeker's allowance was not payable to the claimant as a result of the determination which most recently preceded it whether the preceding determination is either—

(aa) a determination falling within sub-paragraph (b) (i) to which the circumstances in sub-paragraph (b) (ii)(bb) apply; or

(bb) itself an earlier determination falling within sub-paragraph (c)(i).

[⁹(d) 26 weeks in any case (other than a case where a jobseeker's allowance is determined not to be payable in circumstances relating to the employment programme known as "Gateway to Work" specified in regulation 75(1)(a)(i)(bb)) in which—

(i) a jobseeker's allowance is determined not to be payable to the claimant in circumstances falling within section 19(5) or section 20A(2)(a) to (c) and the determination relates to an act or omission arising after this regulation comes into force in respect of the Intensive Activity Period specified in regulation 75(1)(a)(iv); and

(ii) on two or more previous occasions a jobseeker's allowance has been determined not to be payable to the claimant in circumstances falling within section 19(5) or section 20A(2)(a) to (c) and each such determination relates to any Intensive Activity Period specified in regulation 75(1)(a)(iv); and

(iii) no more than 12 months have elapsed between the beginning of the day on which the determination mentioned in (d)(i) above is made and the beginning of the first day on which a jobseeker's allowance was not payable to the claimant as a result of the determination which most recently preceded it whether the preceding determination is either—

(aa) a determination falling within sub-paragraph (b)(i) to which the circumstances in paragraph (b)(ii)(cc) apply; or

(bb) itself an earlier determination falling within sub-paragraph (d)(i).]

(2) The prescribed period for the purposes of [⁶sections 19(2) and 20A(3)] shall begin—

(a) where, in accordance with regulation 26A(1) of the Claims and Payments Regulations a jobseeker's allowance is paid otherwise than fortnightly in arrears, on the day following the end of the last benefit week in respect of which that allowance was paid; and

(b) in any other case, on the first day of the benefit week following the date on which a jobseeker's allowance is determined not to be payable.

(3) In a case falling within paragraph (1)(c) [⁹or (d)] of this regulation in which—

(a) for the first time a determination is made that for a period of 26 weeks a jobseeker's allowance is not payable to the claimant; and

(b) no further such determination is made; and

(c) the Secretary of State gives notice in writing to the claimant that he is no longer required to participate in any of the New Deal options [⁹or the Intensive Activity Period specified in regulation 75(1)(a)(iv)],

an income-based jobseeker's allowance shall be payable to the claimant during the period specified in paragraph (4) even though section 19[⁷ or section 20A] would otherwise prevent the payment of such an allowance.

(4) The period referred to in paragraph (3) shall—

(a) begin on either—

(i) the day specified in a notice by the Secretary of State [⁹either] as being the day on which the claimant is or was no longer required to participate in any of the New Deal options [⁹or the day on which the claimant is or was no longer required to participate in the Intensive Activity Period specified in regulation 75(1)(a)(iv)]; or

(ii) the day four weeks after the first day on which a jobseeker's allowance was not payable as a result of the first determination mentioned in paragraph (3),

whichever is the later;

(b) end on the last day when a jobseeker's allowance was not payable as a result of the first determination mentioned in paragraph (3); but

(c) not include any period during which a jobseeker's allowance is again determined not to be payable to the claimant in circumstances falling within section 19(5) or (6) [⁸or section 20A(2)].

AMENDMENTS

1. Jobseeker's Allowance (Amendment) Regulations 2000 (SI 2000/239), reg.2(3) (March 6, 2000).

2. Jobseeker's Allowance (Amendment) (No.2) Regulations 2000 (SI 2000/1370), reg.2(2) (June 19, 2000).

3. Jobseeker's Allowance (Amendment) (No.2) Regulations 2000 (SI 2000/1370), reg.2(3) (June 19, 2000).

4. Jobseeker's Allowance (Joint Claims) Regulations 2000 (SI 2000/1978), reg.2(5) and Sch.2, para.25(a)(i) (March 19, 2001).

5. Jobseeker's Allowance (Joint Claims) Regulations 2000 (SI 2000/1978), reg.2(5) and Sch.2, para.25(a)(ii) (March 19, 2001).

6. Jobseeker's Allowance (Joint Claims) Regulations 2000 (SI 2000/1978), reg.2(5) and Sch.2, para.25(b) (March 19, 2001).

7. Jobseeker's Allowance (Joint Claims) Regulations 2000 (SI 2000/1978), reg.2(5) and Sch.2, para.25(c) (March 19, 2001).

8. Jobseeker's Allowance (Joint Claims) Regulations 2000 (SI 2000/1978), reg.2(5) and Sch.2, para.25(d) (March 19, 2001).

9. Social Security Amendment (New Deal) Regulations 2001 (SI 2001/1029), reg.4 (April 9, 2001).

3.267

DEFINITIONS

"claimant": see Jobseekers Act, s.35(1).
"New Deal options": see regs 1(3), 75(1)(a)(ii) and 75(1)(b)(ii).
"week": see reg.75(3).

GENERAL NOTE

This sets the period of sanction (a preclusion of payability of JSA) for non- compliance with a jobseeker's direction or for loss or refusal of a place on a training

3.268

scheme or on an employment programme (see Jobseekers Act, s.19(2) and (5)). This new version of the regulation, inserted with effect from March 6, 2000, makes it crucial to distinguish between sanctions imposed in respect of one of the New Deal options for 18–25 year olds and other "fixed term" sanctions applied under the Jobseekers Act, s.19(5) with respect to jobseeker's directions, other employment programmes or other training schemes. (Note that for people participating in the intensive activity period of the New Deal pilots for people aged 25 or over "employment programme" also means that intensive activity period: see reg.6 of the Social Security (New Deal Pilot) Regulations (SI 2000/3134) in force from November 28, 2000; these Regulations replaced the 1999 New Deal Pilot Regulations (SI 1999/3156) in force from November 29, 1999 to November 28, 2000, which in turn replaced the 1998 New Deal Pilot Regulations (SI 1998/2325) in force from November 30, 1998 to November 29, 1999.)

"New Deal options" means the employment programmes specified in reg.75(1)(a)(ii) [the Employment Option, the Voluntary Sector Option and the Environment Task Force Option] and the training scheme specified in reg.75(1)(b)(ii) [the Full-Time Education and Training Option] (see reg.1(3)). The penalty for a first New Deal "offence" is two weeks. For a second such offence within 12 months of the first, the penalty is four weeks. For a third offence within 12 months of the second offence, the fixed penalty is now 26 weeks. So long as no more than 12 months elapse between "offences" that much enhanced penalty would thereafter apply to the fourth and any subsequent New Deal "offence". The period of sanction begins in most cases on the first day of the benefit week following the date on which it was decided that a sanction should be imposed (para.(2)(b)). However, where benefit is paid otherwise than fortnightly in arrears, the sanction begins on the day after the end of the last benefit week in respect of which JSA was paid (para.(2)(a)). "Benefit week" is defined in a complex fashion in reg.1(3): in its basic form, it is the period of seven days ending with the day of the week specified in the claimant's attendance notice (colloquially, the day corresponding to his "signing on" day). Note that where a 26 week sanction is imposed for the first time and the Secretary of State gives the claimant written notice that he is no longer required to participate in one of the New deal options, then, provided no further 26 weeks sanction under s.19(2) and (5) has meanwhile been imposed, income-based JSA is payable to the claimant even though usually Jobseekers Act 1995, s.19 would preclude its payment because a sanction period was still running (see notes to subss. (2)). The period of payability of income-based JSA begins either four weeks into the sanction period or, if later, the day after that specified in the Secretary of State's notice. It ends at the end of that sanction period, but cannot be paid during the currency of a further sanction under either of Jobseekers Act 1995, s.19(5) or (6) (para.(4)).

As regards sanctions in respect of a jobseeker's direction or other employment programmes or training schemes, the regulation sets the period at four weeks in the case of a claimant falling foul of s.19(5) within 12 months of last having done so (even where the other default was in respect of a New Deal option), otherwise at two weeks. The period begins and ends in accordance with para.(2), as explained above in respect of New Deal options.

Sanctions of discretionary length

3.269   **70.** In determining a period under section 19(3) [¹or section 20A(4)] an adjudication officer shall take into account all the circumstances of the case and, in particular, the following circumstances—

(a) where the employment would have lasted less than 26 weeks, the length of time which it was likely to have lasted;

(b) in a case falling within section 19(6)(a) [²or section 20A(2)(d)] in which the employer has indicated an intention to re-engage the claimant, the date when he is to be re-engaged;

(c) where the claimant has left his employment voluntarily and the hours of work in that employment were 16 hours or less a week, the rate of pay and hours of work in the employment which he left; and

(d) where the claimant left his employment voluntarily or has neglected to avail himself of a reasonable opportunity of employment, any mitigating circumstances of physical or mental stress connected with his employment.

AMENDMENTS

1. Jobseeker's Allowance (Joint Claims) Regulations 2000 (SI 2000/1978), reg.2(5) and Sch.2, para.26(a) (March 19, 2001).   **3.270**

2. Jobseeker's Allowance (Joint Claims) Regulations 2000 (SI 2000/1978), reg.2(5) and Sch.2, para.26(b) (March 19, 2001).

DEFINITIONS

"employment": see reg.4.
"week": see reg.75(2).

GENERAL NOTE

Section 19(4) of the Jobseekers Act 1995 enabled the making of regulations specifying circumstances to be taken, or not to be taken, into account by the 68Secretary of State (and hence the Appeal Tribunal) in determing the preclusive period under s.19(3). This regulation is the product. It provides that the Secretary State (and hence the Appeal Tribunal) must take into account all the circumstances of the case. It further specifies certain particular circumstances to be taken into account, some of which reflect previous Commissioners' decisions on unemployment benefit.   **3.271**

Under the previous regimes of benefits for unemployed people, setting the period of preclusion or disqualification was a matter for the discretion of the statutory authorities guided statutorily only by the maximum limit imposable and otherwise by case law (almost entirely decisions of the Commissioners). As for JSA, s.19 enables the making of regulations specifying circumstances to be taken, or not to be taken, into account by the decision-maker (and hence the tribunal) in determining the preclusive period under s.19(3). This regulation provides that the decision-maker (and hence a tribunal) must take into account all the circumstances of the case. It further specifies the following particular circumstances to be taken into account, some of which reflect previous Commissioners' decisions on unemployment benefit (added in square brackets by the annotator):

(1) Where the employment would have lasted less than 26 weeks, the length of time that it was likely to have lasted must be taken into account [*R(U) 5/54* held that where the employment was due to end after another three weeks anyway, it was right to limit the period of disqualification to three weeks].

(2) In a case of preclusion for loss of employment through misconduct, where the employer has indicated an intention to re-engage the claimant, the date when he is to be re-engaged is to be taken into account. [In *R(U) 10/71* where misconduct had only resulted in suspension from work for four weeks (nonetheless a loss of employment) the disqualification period was limited to that of the suspension, thus adequately protecting the National Insurance Fund against an unjustified claim.]

(3) Where the claimant left voluntarily an employment of 16 hours per week or less, the rate of pay and hours of employment which he left must be taken into account.

(4) There must be taken into account in a voluntary leaving or neglect to avail case ("heads" (b) and (d) of s.19(6)), any mitigating circumstances of physical or mental stress connected with his employment.

Otherwise, the regulation rules nothing out or in. *Its core is that the decision-maker [and hence the tribunal] must take account of all the circumstances of the case.* That was also the central message of Commissioners' decisions on fixing the period of disqualification in unemployment benefit cases. These decisions stressed that the discretion was to be exercised judicially and sensibly, taking due account of all the circumstances, including those relevant to the anterior question of whether disqualification was required at all and the justice and merits of each case (*R(U) 8/74(T)*), bearing in mind the purpose of disqualification; the protection of the National Insurance Fund against avoidable claims (*R(U) 27/52*). Tribunals must indicate in their decisions that they have considered the matter of the appropriate period of preclusion (*R(U) 3/79*). A tribunal's failure to indicate conscious exercise of discretion and to state the facts taken into account in exercising it is an error of law (*R(U) 4/87*).

Voluntary redundancy

3.272   **71.**—(1) A claimant is to be treated as not having left his employment voluntarily—

    (a) where he has been dismissed by his employer by reason of redundancy after volunteering or agreeing to be so dismissed, [1 . . .]

    (b) where he has left his employment on a date agreed with his employer without being dismissed, in pursuance of an agreement relating to voluntary redundancy, [1 or

    (c) where he has been laid-off or kept on short-time to the extent specified in sub-section (1) of section 88 of the Employment Protection (Consolidation) Act 1978, and has complied with the requirements of that section.]

(2) In paragraph (1) "redundancy" means one of the facts set out in paragraphs (a) and (b) of section 81(2) of the Employment Protection (Consolidation) Act 1978.

AMENDMENT

3.273   1. Jobseeker's Allowance (Amendment) Regulations 1996 (SI 1996/1516), reg.5 (October 7, 1996).

DEFINITIONS

    "claimant": see Jobseekers Act, s.35(1).
    "employment": see reg.75(4).
    "redundancy": see para.(2).

GENERAL NOTE

3.274   Section 19(7) of the Jobseekers Act 1995 enables the making of regulations setting out circumstances in which a person who might otherwise be regarded, under the normal rules discussed in the notes to s.19(6) of that Act, as having left employment voluntarily, is to be treated as not having left voluntarily. This regulation is the result, covering a number of instances of voluntary redundancy.

    Regulation 71 provides that a claimant is not to be treated as having left voluntarily, in three situations. First echoing SSCBA 1992, s.28(4)), it protects the claimant who has been dismissed by his employer by reason of redundancy after volunteering or agreeing to be so dismissed. The reference to "dismissal" might be thought unfortunate if it were to perpetuate or risk reopening old controversies on its precise meaning. Were it the sole protective limb, *R(U)3/91* ought probably to be followed to give it a wide meaning. But in any event even affixing the narrower meaning as the appropriate one cannot, given the wording and structure of the new provision, have the same detrimental consequences, since the second limb of reg.71(1) now protects a claimant who has left his employment on a date agreed with his employer *without being dismissed*, in pursuance of an agreement relating to voluntary redundancy. "Redundancy", rather than dismissal, is thus the key limiting factor in these protective limbs. It means one of the facts set out in s.81(2) of the Employment Protection (Consolidation) Act 1978 (now s.139(1),(2) of the Employment Rights Act 1996) (reg.71(2)). That subsection provides two facts: (a) the fact that the employer has ceased, or intends to cease, to carry on that business in the place where the employee [the JSA claimant] was employed; (b) the fact that the requirements of that business for employees to carry out work of a particular kind, or for employees to carry out work of a particular kind in the place where [the claimant] was employed, have ceased or diminished or are expected to cease do diminish.

The third situation of protection afforded by reg.71 embraces the claimant who "has been laid off or kept on short-time to the extent specified in subs.(1) of s.88 of the Employment Protection (Consolidation) Act 1978 (now ss.149–152 of the Employment Rights Act 1996), and has complied with the requirements of that section", thus protecting claimants like the one in *CU/71/94*, and thereby going wider than the range of protections afforded by SSCBA 1992, s.28(4), even when that section was interpreted broadly. Section 88 of the 1978 Act enables a person laid off or kept on short time, to claim a redundancy payment if he serves on his employer written notice of his intention to do so. He must have been laid off or kept on short time either for four or more consecutive weeks or for a series of six or more weeks within a period of 13 weeks prior to service of the notice. To get the s.88 payment, the employee must terminate the contract of employment, and not be dismissed by the employer. See now ss.149–152 of the Employment Rights Act 1996.

Good cause for the purposes of section 19(5)(a) and (6)(c) and (d)

72.—(1) This regulation shall have effect for the purposes of section 19 (circumstances in which a jobseeker's allowance is not payable) [³and section 20A (denial or reduction of joint-claim jobseeker's allowance)].   3.275

(2) Subject to paragraph (3), in determining whether a person has good cause for any act or omission for the purposes of section 19(5)(a) and (6)(c) and (d) [⁴and section 20A(2)(a), (f) and (g)] the matters which are to be taken into account shall include the following—

(a) any restrictions on availability which apply in the claimant's case in accordance with regulations 6, 7, 8 [², 13 and 17A], having regard to the extent of any disparity between those restrictions and the requirements of the vacancy in question;

(b) any condition or personal circumstance of that person which indicates that a particular employment or carrying out the jobseeker's direction would be likely to or did—
   (i)   cause significant harm to his health; or
   (ii) subject him to excessive physical or mental stress;

(c) the fact that the failure to undertake a particular employment or to carry out the jobseeker's direction resulted from a religious or conscientious objection sincerely held;

(d) any caring responsibilities which would, or did, make it unreasonable for the person to undertake a particular employment or carry out the jobseeker's direction;

(e) the time it took, or would normally take, for the person to travel from his home to the place of the employment or to a place mentioned in the jobseeker's direction and back to his home by a route and means appropriate to his circumstances and to the employment or to the carrying out of the jobseeker's direction;

(f) the expenses which were, or would be, necessarily and exclusively incurred by the person for the purposes of the employment or of carrying out the jobseeker's direction, together with any expenses of travelling to and from the place of the employment or a place mentioned in the jobseeker's direction by a route and means appropriate to his circumstances, if those expenses did, or would, represent an unreasonably high proportion of—

    (i) in the case of employment, the remuneration which it is reasonable to expect that he would derive from that employment; or

    (ii) in any other case, the income which he received, or would receive, while carrying out the jobseeker's direction.

(3) For the purposes of paragraph (2)(f), in considering whether expenses did, or would, represent an unreasonably high proportion of remuneration or income, the principle shall apply that the greater the level of remuneration or income the higher the proportion thereof which it is reasonable should be represented by expenses.

[²(3A) Without prejudice to any other circumstances in which a person may be regarded as having good cause for any act or omission for the purposes of section 19(6)(c) and (d) [⁵ and section 20A(2)(f) and (g)], a person to whom regulation 17A(2) applies, in respect of whom an employment officer has determined that he may undertake a qualifying course, and who is undertaking such a course as a full-time student, is to be regarded as having good cause for any act or omission for the purposes of section 19(6)(c) and (d) where—

(a) the act or omission took place within a period of 4 weeks before the end of his qualifying course or of his examinations; or

(b) the employment consists of employment for which he is not required to be available in accordance with regulation 17A(3)(c) unless it is permanent full-time employment.

(3B) In paragraph (3A)(b), "full-time employment" means remunerative work as defined in regulation 51(1)(a).]

(4) Where a person has undergone training for a particular kind of employment for a period of not less than 2 months, he is to be regarded for a period of 4 weeks beginning with the day on which the training ends as having good cause for any act or omission for the purposes of section 19(5)(a) and (6)(c) and (d) [⁴and section 20A(2)(a), (f) and (g)], for—

(a) refusing or failing to apply for, or refusing to accept, employment of any other kind when offered to him;

(b) neglecting to avail himself of a reasonable opportunity of employment of any other kind;

(c) refusing or failing to carry out a jobseeker's direction given to him with a view to assisting him to find employment of any other kind.

(5) A person is to be regarded as having good cause for any act or omission for the purposes of section 19(5)(a) and (6)(c) and (d) [⁴ and section 20A(2)(a), (f) and (g)] if, and to the extent that, the reason for that act or omission—

(a) results from restrictions on availability which apply in the claimant's case for the period permitted in accordance with regulations 16 and 17;

(b) results from the fact that the claimant is, in accordance with regulation 5(1) to (3) and (5), excepted from any requirement to be able to take up employment immediately, or is, in accordance with regulation 5(4), excepted from any requirement to be able to take up employment at a time when he is not available;

(c) [¹. . .]

[¹(5A) A person is to be regarded as having good cause for any act or omission for the purposes of section 19(6)(c) and (d) [⁵and section 20A(2)(f) and (g)] if—

(a) in a case where it has been agreed that the claimant may restrict his hours of availability to less than 24 hours a week, the employment in question is for less than 16 hours a week; or

(b) in a case not falling within sub-paragraph (a), the employment is for less than 24 hours a week.]

(6) Subject to paragraphs (8) and (9), a person is not to be regarded as having good cause for any act or omission for the purposes of section 19(5)(a) and (6)(c) and (d) [⁴ and section 20A(2)(a), (f) and (g)] if, and to the extent that, the reason for that act or omission relates to—

(a) subject to paragraph (7), his income or outgoings or the income or outgoings of any other member of his household, or the income or outgoings which he or any other member of his household would have if he were to become employed or to carry out the jobseeker's direction, or did have whilst carrying out the jobseeker's direction, but for the purposes of this sub-paragraph a person's outgoings shall not include any expenses taken into account under paragraph (2)(f);

(b) the time it took, or would normally take, for the person to travel from his home to the place of the employment, or a place mentioned in the jobseeker's direction, and back to his home where that time was or is normally less than [8,—

(i) during the first 13 weeks of entitlement to a jobseeker's allowance, one hour either way; and

(ii) in all other cases, one hour and thirty minutes either way,

by a route and means appropriate to his circumstances and to the employment, or to the carrying out of the jobseeker's direction, unless, in view of the health of the person or any caring responsibilities of his, that time was or is unreasonable.]

(7) Paragraph (6)(a) shall not apply—

(a) where the claimant has agreed a restriction on the level of remuneration he was prepared to accept under regulations 13(3) and 16; or

(b) the employment is remunerated only by commission.

(8) A person shall be regarded for the purposes of section 19(6)(d) [⁶ and section 20A(2)(g)] as having good cause for neglecting to avail himself of an opportunity of employment unless the situation is a qualifying former employment of that person.

(9) For the purposes of paragraph (8) a situation is a qualifying former employment of any person if—

(a) it is employment with an employer for whom he has previously worked or with an employer who has succeeded that employer; and

(b) not more than 12 months have elapsed between—

(i) the date when he last worked for that employer and

(ii) the date when the question under section 19(6)(d) [⁷ or section 20A(2)(g)] arose or, as the case may be, arises, and

(c) the terms and conditions of employment in the situation are not less favourable than those in the situation which he held when he last worked for that employer.

AMENDMENTS

3.276　　1. Social Security (Miscellaneous Amendments) Regulations 1997 (SI 1997/454), reg.2(6) (April 7, 1997).

2. Social Security Amendment (New Deal) Regulations 1998 (SI 1998/1274), reg.7 (June 1, 1998).

3. Jobseeker's Allowance (Joint Claims) Regulations 2000 (SI 2000/1978), reg.2(5) and Sch.2, para.27(a) (March 19, 2001).

4. Jobseeker's Allowance (Joint Claims) Regulations 2000 (SI 2000/1978), reg.2(5) and Sch.2, para.27(b) (March 19, 2001).

5. Jobseeker's Allowance (Joint Claims) Regulations 2000 (SI 2000/1978), reg.2(5) and Sch.2, para.27(c) (March 19, 2001).

6. Jobseeker's Allowance (Joint Claims) Regulations 2000 (SI 2000/1978), reg.2(5) and Sch.2, para.27(d) (March 19, 2001).

7. Jobseeker's Allowance (Joint Claims) Regulations 2000 (SI 2000/1978), reg.2(5) and Sch.2, para.27(e) (March 19, 2001).

8. Jobseeker's Allowance (Amendment) Regulations 2004 (SI 2004/1008), reg.2(2) (April 19, 2004 [new claimants]; October 18, 2004 [existing claimants and recipients of unemployment credits].

DEFINITIONS

"caring responsibilities": see reg.4.
"employment": *ibid.*
"jobseeker's direction": see Jobseekers Act 1995, s.19(10).
"qualifying former employment": see para.(9).

GENERAL NOTE

3.277　　Jobseekers Act 1995, s.19(5)(a) and (6)(c) and (d) set out circumstances in which JSA is not payable to someone who might otherwise be entitled to it. Each of these preclusive "heads" is subject to a saving for "good cause". "Good cause", however, is no longer a matter regulated solely by principles in case law but has been restricted and regulated by s.19(8) and (9) of that Act and this regulation made pursuant to them. Generally speaking, but subject to the specifics in this regulation (and any other regulations which may be made in that behalf), s.19(9) of that Act provides that no regard is to be paid to the level of remuneration in the employment in question in determining "good cause". This regulation does several things: (i) it specifies certain circumstances in which a person is to be regarded as having "good cause"; (ii) subject to that, it precludes certain reasons ranking as "good cause"; and (iii) sets out a non-exhaustive list of factors to be taken into account in determining the "good cause" issue.

3.278　　*"Good cause" for purposes of Jobseekers Act 1995, s.19(5)(a)—jobseeker's direction*: Regulation 72 stipulates a number of situations in which someone will have good cause for refusing or failing to carry out a jobseeker's direction. For a four-week period after the training ends, someone who has undergone at least two months' training for a particular kind of employment will have good cause for refusing or failing to carry out a direction given to assist him find a different kind of employment (para.(4)). Similarly, during the permitted period (maximum 13 weeks) in which one's availability can be confined to one's usual occupation, there will be good cause for ignoring a direction given to help one find a different sort of job (para.(5)(a)), while those laid off or on short time, will, for a period of up to 13 weeks, have good cause for ignoring a direction given to assist them find work other than casual employment (employment from which they can be released without giving notice) (para.(5)(a)). Those exempt from the requirement to be immediately available (*e.g.* carers, voluntary workers) will have good cause if and to the extent that is the reason for the refusal or failure to carry out the jobseeker's direction (for example, it requires a carer to be somewhere at less than 48 hours' notice or at a time when he is not required, pursuant to the JSA scheme, to be available, for instance, during one of his caring periods) (para.(5)(b)).

Correspondingly, this regulation provides that good cause generally cannot be based on the income or outgoings of himself or any member of his household, or the ones he or any such member would have if he carried out the direction or those he or that member did have whilst he was carrying it out. But here "outgoings" do not include expenses necessarily and exclusively incurred by the claimant for the purposes of carrying out the direction, nor his appropriate travelling expenses in carrying it out (reg.72(6)(a)). Nor can this preclusion apply during his "permitted period" for availability purposes (see further JSA Regs, reg.16) where the claimant has agreed a restriction on the level of remuneration he is prepared to accept, or when such a restriction has been agreed in view of his physical or mental condition pursuant to reg.13(3), or when the type of employment the direction aims to help him find is one rewarded solely by commission (para.(6)(a), (7)). When initially introduced, para.(6)(b) further precluded founding good cause on travelling time of less than an hour each way to and from the place specified in the direction, by a route and means appropriate both to his circumstances and to the carrying out of the direction, unless that time is/was unreasonable in view of his health and any "caring responsibilities" (a term specifically defined in reg.4). This changed from April 18, 2004, for new claimants, and from October 18, 2004 for those who were existing claimants at April 19 or then in receipt of unemployment credits. Like its predecessor, the changed version of paragraph (6)(b) like its predecessor, precludes founding good cause on traveling time of less than a certain length with respect to refusing or failing to carry out a jobseeker's direction (Jobseekers Act 1995, s.19(5)(a)) or to apply for or accept employment to which a jobseeker has been referred by an employment officer (s. 19(6)(c)) or which has been offered in a qualifying former employment (s.19(6)(d)). Where the failure relates to the travelling time between the jobseeker's home and the place of employment or the place mentioned in the jobseeker's direction, a jobseeker will not generally have good cause if the time is less than one hour and thirty minutes either way. During the first 13 weeks of entitlement to a jobseeker's allowance, a jobseeker will not have good cause for such a refusal or failure if the travelling time is less than one hour either way. Previously, in all cases, a jobseeker did not have good cause if the travelling time was less than one hour either way.

Otherwise, so far as matters relevant to this preclusive head are concerned, para.(2) provides the following non-exhaustive list of matters to be taken into account in determining whether the claimant had good cause for his refusal or failure to carry out a jobseeker's direction:

(i) any condition or personal circumstance of the claimant indicating that carrying out the direction did, or would be likely to, cause significant harm to his health or subject him to excessive physical or mental stress (sub-para. (b));

(ii) his failure resulted from a sincerely held religious or conscientious objection (sub-para. (c)) [note that an objection to working in the private sector is too wide to fall within this provision regarding conscientious objections and nor did the tribunal's refusal to include it breach Convention rights: see *R. (on the application of Pattison)* v *Social Security and Child Support Commissioners [2004] EWHC 2370*];

(iii) any caring responsibilities (specifically defined in reg.4) making it unreasonable to carry out the direction; (sub-para. (d));

(iv) travelling time to and from the place specified in the direction by a route and means appropriate both to his circumstances and to the carrying out of the direction (sub-para. (e));

(v) whether necessary expenses of compliance (including appropriate travelling expenses) represented an unreasonably high proportion of the income received or receivable from carrying out the direction, applying the principle that the higher the income the higher the reasonable proportion represented by expenses (sub-para (f) read with para.2).

3.279   *"Good cause" for purposes of Jobseekers Act 1995, s. 19(6) (c)*—: This regulation also stipulates a number of situations in which someone will have good cause for a refusal or failure covered by Jobseekers Act 1995, s.19(6)(c). Where under JSA Regs, reg.17A, an employment officer has determined for availability for work purposes that the claimant can undertake a qualifying course and he is undertaking it as a full-time student, he will have good cause for a failure or refusal which occurred within a four-week period before the end of that course or his examinations (para.(3A)(a)). He will also have good cause where the refusal or failure was in respect of employment for which he is not required to be available under reg.17A(3)(c) (employment falling wholly within vacations from the course), but not where the refusal or failure was in respect of permanent full-time employment (that is, remunerative work as defined in reg.51(1)(a) [work engaged in for 16 or more hours a week] (see para.(3A)(b), (3B)). For a four-week period after the training ends, someone who has undergone for at least two months' training for a particular kind of employment will have good cause for refusing or failing to apply for or refusing to accept a different kind of employment (para.(4)). Similarly, during the permitted period (maximum 13 weeks) in which one's availability can be confirmed to one's usual occupation, there will be good cause for refusal or failure to apply for, or refusal to accept, a different sort of job (para.(5)(a)). While those laid-off or on short time will, for a period of up to 13 weeks, have good cause for refusing, etc., anything other than casual employment (employment from which they can be released without giving notice) (para.(5)(a)). Those exempt from the requirement to be immediately available (*e.g.* carers, voluntary workers) will have good cause if and to the extent that that is the reason for the refusal or failure to apply for or accept employment (for example, it requires a carer to be somewhere at less than 48 hours' notice or at a time when he is not required, pursuant to the JSA scheme, to be available, for instance, during one of his caring periods) (para.(5)(b)). Finally, there is good cause if the employment in question is less than 24 hours a week (modified to less than 16 hours a week where the claimant has been allowed to restrict his availability to less than 24 hours per week [*e.g.* as a carer or as a disabled person: see JA Regs, reg.13(3), (4)]) (para.(5A)).

Correspondingly, this regulation provides that good cause generally cannot be based on the income or outgoings of himself or any member of his household, or the ones he or any such member would have if he took the job. But here "outgoings" do not include expenses necessarily and exclusively incurred by the claimant for the purposes of carrying out the direction, nor his appropriate travelling expenses in carrying it out (para.(6)(a)). Nor can this preclusion apply during his "permitted period" for availability purposes (see further JSA Regs, reg.16), where the claimant has agreed a restriction on the level of remuneration he is prepared to accept, or when such a restriction has been agreed in view of his physical or mental condition pursuant to reg.13(3), or when the employment is one rewarded solely by commission (para.(6)(a), (7)). Paragraph (6)(b) further precludes founding good cause on travelling time of less than an hour each way to and from the employment by a route and means appropriate both to his circumstances and to the employment, unless that time is/was unreasonable in view of his health and any "caring responsibilities" (a term specifically defined in reg.4).

3.280   Otherwise, so far as matters relevant to this preclusive head are concerned, para.(2) provides the following non-exhaustive list of matters to be taken into account in determining whether the claimant had good cause for his refusal or failure covered by s.19(6)(c):

(i) any permitted restrictions on availability applicable in his case under JSA Regs, regs 6–8, 13 and 17A, having regard to the extent of the disparity between those restrictions and the requirements of the vacancy in question (sub-para. (a));

(ii) any condition or personal circumstance of the claimant indicating that a particular employment did, or would be likely to, cause significant harm to his health or subject him to excessive physical or mental stress (sub-para. (b));

(iii) his failure resulted from a sincerely held religious or conscientious objection (sub-para. (c));

(iv) any caring responsibilities (specifically defined in reg.4) making it unreasonable to undertake a particular employment (sub-para. (d));

(v) travelling time to and from the place of employment by a route and means appropriate both to his circumstances and to the employment (sub-para. (e));

(vi) whether necessary expenses of compliance (including appropriate travelling expenses) represented an unreasonably high proportion of the remuneration reasonably expected to be derivable from the employment, applying the principle that the higher the income the higher the reasonable proportion represented by expenses (sub-para. (f) read with para.2).

In *CSJSA/261/1998,* Deputy Commissioner Wright held that the tribunal had erred in law in regarding para.(6)(a) as precluding ever founding good cause in relation to s. 19(6)(c) (failure to apply etc) on journey time. That ignores completely para.(2)(e) and the words of para.(6)(a) itself. Read in combination they mean that "traveling time, and also the means of transport, are to be taken into account unless the time is normally less than one hour [now generally one and a half hours], and even in the latter case it may be taken into account in two particular circumstances [health and caring responsibilities, depending on unreasonableness]" (para.10). The matter of expenses also needs to be taken into account (paras(2)(f) and (3) of the reg.). He agreed with the AO that

"it is relevant to take into account the fact that a person who lives in a remote location will usually have a long journey to and from work. I agree that this may be relevant but would stress that it should be applied with care having regard to the particular circumstances of the case and should certainly not be used as a general consideration in effect calling into question the relevance of travelling time and indeed waiting time in cases where claimants live in remote locations. The underlying question is whether the failure to take employment is voluntary or genuinely based on a good reason. A city dweller may have reason, based upon confidence that he can obtain employment nearer to home, to turn down a job involving very substantial travelling time. Conversely, a country dweller, with little prospect of employment in the immediate locality, may be thought not to have good reason to turn down a job which involves travelling. These things, however, must be a matter of degree to be judged reasonably in the particular circumstances, and in either case the actual extent of travelling time and difficulty must be considered. (Subject, of course, to the provisions in regulation 72 considered above)" (para. 17).

"Good cause" for purposes of Jobseekers Act 1995, s.19(6)(d): This head of disqualification overlaps somewhat with s.19(6)(c). Preclusion is to be imposed where the claimant has neglected to avail himself of a reasonable opportunity of employment. There is now a saving for good cause, on which see also the notes to s.19(6)(c), (8) and (9), and this regulation (as applicable to that head). The submission made in the note to s.19(6)(c) on the relevance of suitability/good cause case law also applies here, so that decisions like *R(U)2/77* which protected the person, who could have had his old job back if he would, contrary to his convictions, join a trade union, would still be relevant. An excusing factor mentioned in *R(U)5/71,* namely, a conscientious objection to a job, connected with religion or morals, is reflected as a factor to be taken into account in determining good cause in para.(2)(c).

Those principles and provisions on determining whether the claimant has good cause for neglecting to avail himself of a suitable offer for employment, can, however,

3.281

only be relevant where the employment in question is a "qualifying former employment" of his, because paras (8) and (9) of this regulation affords protection here which is not available under the other preclusive heads of s.19(5). A claimant is to be regarded as having good cause for neglecting to avail himself of an opportunity of employment unless the situation is a "qualifying former employment" of his (para.(8)). The situation will be such a "qualifying former employment" where it is employment with an employer for whom the claimant had previously worked or with a successor employer, not more than 12 months have elapsed between him last working for that employer and the neglect to avail issue arising, and the terms and conditions of employment in the situation are not less favourable than those in the situation the claimant held when he last worked for that employer (para.(9)). Note that this does not mean that a claimant can with impunity turn down any other situation. The provision provides good cause only with respect to this specific "neglect to avail" head, and does not apply to the preclusive "head" in s.19(6)(c), all of which refer to situations notified to the claimant by an employment officer. Thus, in effect, the qualifying former employment provision allows the claimant to turn down other situations, the opportunity for which has arisen other than through notification by an employment officer. On the assumption that such officers would not put forward positions offering derisory remuneration, the protection afforded by this "qualifying former employment" provision appears designed to allay fears that claimants would be forced through threat of preclusion from benefit into accepting any job, no matter how poorly paid.

Good cause for the purposes of section 19(5)(b)

3.282

73.—(1) This regulation shall have effect for the purposes of section 19 (circumstances in which a jobseeker's allowance is not payable) [⁴and section 20A (denial or reduction of joint-claim jobseeker's allowance)].

(2) Without prejudice to any other circumstances in which a person may be regarded as having good cause for any act or omission for the purposes of section 19(5)(b) [⁵ and section 20A(2)(b)], a person is to be regarded as having good cause for any act or omission for those purposes if, and to the extent that, the act or omission is attributable to any of the following circumstances—

    (a) the claimant in question was suffering from some disease or bodily or mental disablement on account of which—
        (i) he was not able to attend the relevant training scheme or employment programme in question;
        (ii) his attendance would have put at risk his health; or
        (iii) his attendance would have put at risk the health of other persons;
    (b) the claimant's failure to participate in the training scheme or employment programme resulted from a religious or conscientious objection sincerely held;
    (c) the time it took, or would normally have taken, for the claimant to travel from his home to the training scheme or employment programme and back to his home by a route and means appropriate to his circumstances and to the scheme or programme exceeded, or would normally have exceeded, one hour in either direction or, where no appropriate training scheme or employment programme is available within one hour of his home, such greater time as is necessary in the particular circumstances of the nearest appropriate scheme or programme;
    (d) the claimant had caring responsibilities and—
        (i) no close relative of the person he cared for and no other member of that person's household was available to care for him; and

    (ii) in the circumstances of the case it was not practical for the claimant to make other arrangements for the care of that person;
  (e) the claimant was attending court as a party to any proceedings, or as a witness or as a juror;
  (f) the claimant was arranging or attending the funeral of a close relative or close friend;
  (g) the claimant was engaged in—
    (i) the manning or launching of a lifeboat; or
    (ii) the performance of duty as a part-time member of a fire brigade;
  (h) the claimant was required to deal with some domestic emergency; or
  (i) the claimant was engaged during an emergency in duties for the benefit of others;
  [¹(j) the claimant gave up a place on a training scheme or an employment programme and if he had continued to participate in it he would have, or would have been likely to have, put his health and safety at risk.]

[²(2A) Without prejudice to any other circumstances in which a person may be regarded as having good cause for any act or omission for the purposes of section 19(5)(b) [⁵ and section 20A(2)(b)], a person is to be regarded as having good cause for any act or omission for those purposes if—
  (a) the act or omission relates to an employment programme specified in regulation 75(1)(a)(ii) [⁸ or (iv)] or the training scheme specified in regulation 75(1)(b)(ii), and
  (b) he had not, prior to that act or omission, been given or sent a notice in writing by an employment officer referring to the employment programme or training scheme in question ("the specified programme") and advising him that if any of the circumstances mentioned in section 19(5)(b) [⁶ or section 20A(2)(b)] arise in his case in relation to the specified programme his jobseeker's allowance could cease to be payable or could be payable at a lower rate.]

[³(2B) Without prejudice to any other circumstances in which a person may be regarded as having good cause for any act or omission for the purposes of section 19(5)(b) [⁵and section 20A(2)(b)], a person to whom regulation 17A(2) applies, in respect of whom an employment officer has determined that he may undertake a qualifying course, and who is undertaking such a course as a full-time student, is to be regarded as having good cause for any act or omission—
  (a) for the purposes of section 19(5)(b) where the act or omission was in relation to an employment programme and he was, or would have been, required to attend the employment programme at a time which would have prevented him from attending the qualifying course;
  (b) for the purposes of section 19(5)(b)(iii) and (iv) [⁷and section 20A(2)(b)(iii) and (iv)] where—
    (i) the act or omission was in relation to a qualifying course undertaken by him and occurred less than 4 weeks after the first day of the period of study;
    (ii) the act or omission was in relation to a qualifying course undertaken by him and was due to his lack of ability; or
    (iii) the act or omission was in relation to a qualifying course undertaken by him which was not suitable for him;]
  (3) For the purposes of paragraph (2)(i),
  (a) a person is engaged in duties for the benefit of others while—

(i) providing assistance to any person whose life may be endangered or who may be exposed to the risk of serious bodily injury or whose health may be seriously impaired;

(ii) protecting property of substantial value from imminent risk of serious damage or destruction; or

(iii) assisting in measures being taken to prevent a serious threat to the health of the people;

as a member of a group of persons organised wholly or partly for the purpose of providing such assistance or, as the case may be, protection;

(b) events which may give rise to an emergency include—

(i) a fire, flood or an explosion;

(ii) a natural catastrophe;

(iii) a railway or other transport accident;

(iv) a cave or mountain accident;

(v) an accident at sea;

(vi) a person being reported missing and the organisation of a search for that person.

[³(4) For the purposes of paragraph (2B)(b)(iii), a qualifying course is suitable for a person if it is suitable for him in vocationally relevant respects, namely his personal capacity, aptitude, his preference, the level of qualification aimed at, duration of the course and proportion of time, if any, which the person has spent on the training in relation to the length of the course.]

AMENDMENTS

3.283   1. Jobseeker's Allowance (Amendment) Regulations 1996 (SI 1996/1516), reg.6 (October 7, 1996).

2. Social Security Amendment (New Deal) Regulations 1997 (SI 1997/2863), reg.7 (January 5, 1998).

3. Social Security Amendment (New Deal) Regulations 1998 (SI 1998/1274), reg.8 (June 1, 1998).

4. Jobseeker's Allowance (Joint Claims) Regulations 2000 (SI 2000/1978), reg.2(5) and Sch.2, para.28(a) (March 19, 2001).

5. Jobseeker's Allowance (Joint Claims) Regulations 2000 (SI 2000/1978), reg.2(5) and Sch.2, para.28(b) (March 19, 2001).

6. Jobseeker's Allowance (Joint Claims) Regulations 2000 (SI 2000/1978), reg.2(5) and Sch.2, para.28(c) (March 19, 2001).

7. Jobseeker's Allowance (Joint Claims) Regulations 2000 (SI 2000/1978), reg.2(5) and Sch.2, para.28(d) (March 19, 2001).

8. Social Security Amendment (New Deal) Regulations 2001 (SI 2001/1029), reg.5 (April 9, 2001).

DEFINITIONS

"caring responsibilities": see reg.4.

"close relative": *ibid.*

"employment programme": see Jobseekers Act 1995, s.19(10)(c) and reg.75(1)(a).

"part-time member of the fire brigade": see reg.4.

"training scheme": see Jobseekers Act 1995, s.19(10)(c) and reg.75(1)(b).

GENERAL NOTE

3.284   Jobseekers Act 1995, s.19(5)(b) covers: (i) a claimant's neglect to avail himself of a reasonable opportunity of a place on a training scheme or employment programme; or (ii) after an employment officer has notified him of a vacant place on such a scheme or programme, his failure to apply for such a place or to accept it when offered to him; or (iii) his giving up his place; or (iv) his failure to attend having been given a place. In all such cases, there is a saving for "good cause".

As regards "good cause" in s.19(5)(b) of that Act, this regulation, made pursuant to s.19(8) of that Act, merely lists a number of circumstances which, if and to the extent that the act or omission is attributable to them, will constitute good cause for an act or omission relevant to para.(b) of subs. (5). The regulation does not rule out any particular circumstances from ranking as good cause; it lists the circumstances which do so rank "without prejudice to any other circumstances in which a person may be regarded as having good cause for any act or omission" for subs. (5)(b) purposes. Nor does it list factors relevant to deciding the good cause question, again leaving that matter at large and at the discretion of the Secretary of State and/or Appeal Tribunal.

To the extent that they are the basis for the act or omission in question under Jobseekers Act 1995, s.19(5)(b), the circumstances set out in para.(2) constitute good cause. In addition, those in para.(2A) apply in relation to the employment programmes (Employment Option, Voluntary Sector Option, Environment Task Force Option) and the training scheme (Full-Time Education and Training Option) in the New Deal (see reg.75(1)(a)(ii) or (iv) and (1)(b)(ii)). Those in para.(2B), which must be read with para.(4), apply in relation to full-time students undertaking a "qualifying course" (an employment-related course of further or higher education, or a standard above that, lasting no more than 12 months) (see reg.17A).

To the extent that they are the basis for the act or omission in question under para.(b), the following circumstances constitute good cause (the sub-para. letters corresponding to those in para.(2)):

(a) The claimant suffers from a disease or bodily or mental disablement which rendered him unable to attend, or is such that his attendance would have put at risk his health or that of others.

(b) His failure to participate in the scheme or programme resulted from a sincerely held religious or conscientious objection. In *R(JSA)7/03*, Commissioner Bano considered that this sub-paragraph was almost certainly included to bring into the JSA scheme the principles in the unemployment benefit cases and was not intended to extend the exemptions beyond those set out in that case law. In his view:

"a principled objection is not the same as a conscientious objection, and although the claimant objected to the provision of employment programmes by private organisations and to the disclosure of his personal details to a private company, he has not stated that his attendance at the training course would have required him personally to act in a way which was contrary to his ethical or moral principles. I therefore do not consider that the claimant's reasons for not attending the training programme amounted to a conscientious objection (para.17)."

While the list of circumstances in para.(2) is not exhaustive of what may amount to good cause, and while good cause resulting from a state of mind is not necessarily restricted to religious or conscientious objections, instances other than those will be rare. There could be exceptional cases such as where a claimant for reasons of modesty or fear is not able to carry out the direction. However, where the refusal based on a state of mind, existing separately from the refusal, does not arise from religious, ethical or moral convictions, it will be more difficult to make out 'good cause' for the refusal (para.18).

(c) Excessive travelling time from home to the scheme or programme and back by a route and means appropriate both to his circumstances and to the scheme or programme. Where an appropriate scheme or programme is available within one hour of the person's home, travel time of more than an hour each way is excessive. Where no such scheme or programme is available within an hour of his home, however, travelling time is only excessive if it exceeds "such greater time as is necessary in the particular circumstances of the nearest appropriate scheme or programme". Presumably, whether a scheme or programme is available "within an hour of his home or not" is determined on a general basis ignoring particular routes or modes of transport or the particular claimant's circumstances (*i.e.* most people in place X can get to place Y in an hour), otherwise the provision is meaningless.

(d) The claimant had caring responsibilities (specifically defined in reg.4) and the circumstances were such that neither a close relative of the person for whom he cared, nor any other member of that person's household, was available to care for him and such that it was not practical for the claimant to make other arrangements for the person's care.

(e) His attendance at court as a witness, juror or party to any proceedings.

(f) The claimant arranging or attending the funeral of a close relative (specifically defined in reg.4) or close friend.

(g) His engagement in the manning or launching of a lifeboat or in the performance of duties as a part-time member of a fire brigade.

(h) The claimant was required to deal with some domestic emergency.

(i) He was engaged during an emergency in duties for the benefits of others. One can only be engaged in such duties while (i) providing assistance to someone whose life may be endangered or who may be exposed to the risk of serious bodily injury or whose health may be seriously impaired, or (ii) protecting property of substantial value from imminent risk of serious damage or destruction, or (iii) assisting in measures being taken to prevent a serious threat to the health of the people, but in each and every case only as a member of a group organised wholly or partly for the purpose of providing such assistance and/or protection (para.(3)(a)). Events which can give rise to an emergency *include* (*i.e.* the list is not exhaustive): fire, flood, explosion, natural catastrophe, railway or transport accident, cave or mountain accident or an accident at sea, and someone being reported missing and the organisation of a search for him/her (para.(3)(b)). Interpreting identically worded legislation on deemed availability (USI Regs, reg.10), the Commissioner in *CU/113/91* stressed that the list of emergencies was not exhaustive, and nor was the *ejusdem generis* rule appropriate to its interpretation. But the provision was not apt to protect a claimant who was trying to help his hospitalised mother come out of a coma; this was not the type of "emergency" envisaged. Nor, in any event, despite hospitalisation and the consequent presence of hospital staff, could it be said that the claimant was "a member of a group of persons organised", etc. as the provision requires. *Quaere* whether the circumstances, at least if sudden, might come within "domestic emergency" in para.(h), above.

(j) Where the claimant gave up a place on a scheme or programme, his continued participation in it would have, or would have been likely to have, put at risk his health and safety.

3.285   In addition, where the act or omission relevant for para.(2)(b) purposes relates to an employment programme ("Employment Option", "Voluntary Sector Option", "Environment Task Force Option") or the training scheme ("Full-Time Education and Training Option") in the New Deal (see reg.75(1)(a)(ii) and (1)(b)(ii)), a person will have good cause if he had not, prior to the act or ommission, been given written notice by an employment officer referring to the "specified programme" (the relevant Option in the New Deal) advising him that JSA could cease to be payable or be payable at a reduced rate should any of the para.(b) circumstances arise in his case in relation to the relevant Option (see para.(2A))—in short no sanction without being put on notice that such could happen.

Furthermore, where the act or omission relates to an employment programme, certain full-time students (see reg.17A(2)) undertaking a qualifying course will have good cause for the act or omission where they were, or would have been, required to attend the programme at a time which would have precluded attendance at the qualifying course (reg.75(2B)(a)). Essentially a "qualifying course" is an employment-related course of further or higher education, or a standard above that, lasting no more than 12 months (see JSA Regs, reg.17A(7), (8)). As regards sub-para (i) and (ii) of s.19(5)(b) (respectively giving up a place on, or failing to attend, a training scheme, in this case, the qualifying course), such persons will have good cause where the giving up or failing to attend the qualifying course came within the first four weeks of the period of study, or was due to lack of ability, or to the course being unsuitable for the person in vocationally relevant respects (JSA Regs, reg.75(2B)(b), (4)).

Person of prescribed description for the purpose of section 20(3)

74.—(1) Subject to paragraph (2), a person shall be of a prescribed description for the purposes of section 20(3) [¹and section 20B(3)] (exemption from non-payment of jobseeker's allowance) and shall not fall within section 19(6)(b) or (d) [²or section 20A(2)(e) or (g)] if he has neither worked in employed earner's employment, nor has been a self-employed earner, nor been a full-time student nor been in relevant education, during the period of 13 weeks preceding the day of the commencement of the employment.

3.286

(2) For the purposes of paragraph (1), a person shall not be regarded as having—

(a) worked in employed earner's employment; or

(b) been a self-employed earner; or

(c) been a full-time student or been in relevant education;

by reason only of any engagement in an activity referred to in paragraph (3) or by his attendance for a period of up to 14 days at a work camp.

(3) The activities referred to in this paragraph are—

(a) the manning or launching of a lifeboat; or

(b) the performance of duty as a part-time member of a fire brigade.

(4) A trial period in section 20(3) [³and section 20B(3)] means a period of 8 weeks beginning with the commencement of the fifth week of the employment in question and ending at the end of the twelfth week of that employment and for the purposes of this definition in determining the time at which the fifth week of the employment in question commences or at which the twelfth week of that employment ends, any week in which a person has not worked in the employment for at least 16 hours shall be disregarded.

AMENDMENTS

1. Jobseeker's Allowance (Joint Claims) Regulations 2000 (SI 2000/1978), reg.2(5) and Sch.2, para.29(a)(i) (March 19, 2001).

3.287

2. Jobseeker's Allowance (Joint Claims) Regulations 2000 (SI 2000/1978), reg.2(5) and Sch.2, para.29(a)(ii) (March 19, 2001).

3. Jobseeker's Allowance (Joint Claims) Regulations 2000 (SI 2000/1978), reg.2(5) and Sch.2, para.29(b) (March 19, 2001).

DEFINITIONS

"employed earner": see Jobseekers Act 1995, s.35(1); reg.3; SSCBA 1992, s.2(1)(a).

"employment": see reg.4.

"full-time employment": see reg.1(3).

"part-time member of a fire brigade": see reg.4.

"relevant education": see Jobseekers Act 1995, s.35(3), Sch.1, para.14, reg.54.

"self-employed earner": see reg.1(3); SSCBA 1992, s.2(1)(b).

"trial period": see para.(4).
"week": see reg.75(2).
"work camp": see reg.4.

GENERAL NOTE

3.288   Taken together, s.20(3) of the Jobseekers Act 1995 and this regulation protect from preclusion from JSA under the voluntarily leaving employment without just cause head of s.19(6)(b) or under s.19(6)(d) (neglect to avail oneself of a reasonable opportunity of employment) of that Act, certain persons who leave employment voluntarily without just cause at any time during a trial period.

These provisions are designed to encourage to enter or re-enter employment certain persons who may be apprehensive about taking up work, fearful that they might not be able to handle it or that it might prove unsuitable and they might have to leave it. The encouragement is afforded by reducing the fear of preclusion from benefit should their fears be realised and they have to give up the job. An example of such people might be carers who have been out of the job market caring for sick or elderly relatives, but the provisions are by no means so limited. Specifically, the persons protected by the provisions are those who have neither worked in employed earner's employment nor been a self-employed earner, nor a full-time student or in relevant education during the 13-week period preceding the day of commencement of the employment. It is specifically stated that engagement in certain activities does not constitute working in employed earner's employment, being a self-employed earner or having been a full-time student or in relevant education: the manning or launching of a lifeboat; the performance of duty as a part-time member of a fire brigade; or attendance for a period of up to 14 days at a work camp (paras 74(2), (3)). For the definition of "full-time student", see JSA Regs, reg.1(2). For that of "work camp", see reg.4. On "relevant education", see s.35(2), Sch.1, para.14, and reg.54.

"Trial period" is a period of eight weeks beginning with the commencement of the fifth week of the employment in question and ending at the end of the twelfth week of that employment. In determining when the fifth week commences or when the twelfth week ends, one disregards any week in which the claimant worked in the employment for less than 16 hours.

Note that there appears to be no requirement that the claimant has taken up the employment on a "trial basis". Note also that protection is afforded those persons "who leave that employment voluntarily *and without just cause*" (subs. (3), emphasis supplied by annotator). In some circumstances those who leave employment taken on a trial basis because it proves unsuitable may well have just cause for voluntarily leaving, thus obviating the need to rely on this subsection, being protected from preclusion under s.19(6)(b) by the terms of that provision, interpreted in the light of case law on "just cause" from the comparable unemployment benefit context. Since establishing "just cause" may well be more difficult to establish than "good cause" (see further the notes to s.19(6)(b)), such persons would surely also have "good cause" so as to protect them from the "neglect to avail" preclusion in s.19(6)(d).

"Week" is defined for the purposes of this regulation as any period of seven consecutive days (reg.75(2)). That differs from the predecessor "trial period" provisions where week then meant a period of seven days beginning with a Sunday. But even had the new definition then been applicable, it would not have assisted the unfortunate claimant in *R(U)1/92*, since he had only completed the requisite number of "working" as opposed to "seven day" weeks.

[¹ **Person in receipt of a training allowance**

3.289   **74A.**—(1) An income-based jobseeker's allowance shall be payable to a claimant [²other than a member of a joint-claim couple] even though section 19 prevents payment of a jobseeker's allowance to him where the claimant is in receipt of a training allowance and is not receiving training falling within paragraph (2) of regulation 170 but the jobseeker's allowance shall be payable only if and for so long as he satisfies the conditions of entitlement to an income-based jobseeker's allowance other than those which he is not required to meet by virtue of regulation 170.

(2) An income-based jobseeker's allowance which is payable to a claimant in accordance with this regulation shall be payable to him at the full rate applicable in his case.]

[³(3) A joint-claim jobseeker's allowance shall be payable in respect of a joint-claim couple even though section 20A prevents payment of a joint-claim jobseeker's allowance to the couple where a member of that couple to whom that section applies is in receipt of a training allowance and is not receiving training falling within paragraph (2) of regulation 170 but the jobseeker's allowance shall be payable only if and for so long as that member satisfies the conditions of entitlement to a joint-claim jobseeker's allowance other than those which he is not required to meet by virtue of regulation 170.

(4) A joint-claim jobseeker's allowance which is payable to a couple in accordance with this regulation shall be payable to the couple at the full rate applicable to it.]

AMENDMENTS

1. Jobseeker's Allowance (Amendment) Regulations 1996 (SI 1996/1516), reg.7 (October 7, 1996).
2. Jobseeker's Allowance (Joint Claims) Regulations 2000 (SI 2000/1978), reg.2(5) and Sch.2, para.30(a) (March 19, 2001).
3. Jobseeker's Allowance (Joint Claims) Regulations 2000 (SI 2000/1978), reg.2(5) and Sch.2, para.30(b) (March 19, 2001).

3.290

DEFINITIONS

"claimant"—see Jobseekers Act 1995, s.35(1).
"income-based jobseeker's allowance"—*ibid.*, s.1(4).
"training allowance"—see reg.1(3).

GENERAL NOTE

This regulation allows income-based JSA to be paid even though a sanction under s.19 has been imposed if the claimant is getting a training allowance but is not doing Work Based Learning for Young People (which has replaced Youth Training and other training provision focused on 16/17 year olds). See reg.170 which exempts such a claimant from having to satisfy the labour market conditions. Paras (3) to (4) make corresponding provision for joint claim couples.

3.291

[¹Reduced allowance where one member of a joint-claim couple is subject to a sanction

74B.—(1) Where only one member of a joint-claim couple is subject to sanctions for the purposes of section 20A, the rate of jobseeker's allowance payable in respect of the couple for the period of those sanctions shall be calculated in accordance with this regulation.

3.292

(2) Where paragraph (1) applies, a reduced rate of jobseeker's allowance shall be payable to the member of the couple who is not subject to sanctions.

(3) That reduced rate shall be—
(a) in any case in which the member of the couple who is not subject to sanctions satisfies the conditions set out in section 2, a rate equal to the amount calculated in accordance with section 4(1);

(b) in any case where the couple are a couple in hardship for the purposes of Part IXA, a rate equal to the amount calculated in accordance with regulation 146G;

(c) in any other case, a rate calculated in accordance with section 4(3A) save that the applicable amount shall be the amount determined by reference to paragraph 1(1) of Schedule 1 which would have been the applicable amount had the member of the couple who is not subject to sanctions been a single claimant.]

AMENDMENT

3.293   1. Jobseeker's Allowance (Joint Claims) Regulations 2000 (SI 2000/1978), reg.2(5) and Sch.2, para.31 (March 19, 2001).

GENERAL NOTE

See notes to ss.20A and 20B of the Jobseekers Act 1995.

[¹ Interpretation

3.294   75.—(1) For the purposes of section 19 [¹⁰, section 20A] and of this Part:

(a) "an employment programme" means—

  (i) any one of the following programmes of advice, guidance or job search assistance provided in pursuance of arrangements made by the Secretary of State under section 2 of the Employment and Training Act 1973, known as—

    (aa) [¹⁷. . .] week to provide advice and guidance on jobs, training and employment opportunity;

    [⁹(bb) Gateway to Work, being a programme of up to two weeks' duration, consisting of advice and assistance on job search activity and the development of job search skills;]

    (cc) [⁴ . . .]

    (dd) [⁷ . . .]

    (ee) [¹⁷ . . .]

  (ii) any one of the following programmes, provided in pursuance of arrangements made by or on behalf of the Secretary of State under section 2 of the Employment and Training Act 1973 and for which only persons who are aged 18 years or over and less than 26 years immediately prior to entry may be eligible, known as—

    [³(aa) the Self-Employed Employment Option of the New Deal, being a programme which lasts for any individual for up to 26 weeks and which includes for that individual assistance in pursuing self-employed earner's employment;]

    (bb) the Voluntary Sector Option of the New Deal, being a programme which lasts for any individual for up to six months and which includes for that individual employed earner's employment or a work placement combined in either case with training, support and job search;

    (cc) the Environment Task Force Option of the New Deal, being a programme which lasts for any individual for up to six months and which includes for that individual employed earner's employment or a work placement combined in either case with training, support and job search.

[8(iii) an employment zone programme, being a programme established for one or more areas designated pursuant to section 60 of the Welfare Reform and Pensions Act 1999 and subject to the Employment Zones Regulations 2000] [18 or the Social Security (Working Neighbourhoods) Regulations 2004]; [16 and

(iv) the Intensive Activity period, that is to say, the programme known by that name and provided in pursuance of arrangements made by or on behalf of the Secretary of State under section 2 of the Employment and Training Act 1973, being a programme lasting for up to 52 weeks for any one individual aged 25 years or over and less than 50 years on the first required entry date to any such programme, and consisting for that individual of any one or more of the following elements, namely assistance in pursuing self-employed earner's employment, education and training, work experience, assistance with job search, motivation and skills training.]

(b) "a training scheme" means—

(i) a scheme for training for which persons aged less than 18 years are eligible and for which persons aged 18 years or over and less than 25 years may be eligible, [15 secured by the Learning and Skills Council for England or by the National Council for Education and Training for Wales and, in Scotland, provided] directly or indirectly by a Local Enterprise Company pursuant to its arrangement with, as the case may be, Scottish Enterprise or Highlands and Islands Enterprise (whether that arrangement is known as an Operating Contract or by any other name); [2 . . .]

(ii) the scheme, provided in pursuance of arrangements made by or on behalf of the Secretary of State under section 2 of the Employment and Training Act 1973 and for which only persons who are aged 18 years or over and less than 26 years immediately prior to entry may be eligible, known as the Full-Time Education and Training Option of the New Deal, being a scheme which lasts for any individual for up to one year and which includes for that individual some or all of the following, namely education, training, work experience and support in job search [2skills; and]

[2(iii) for the purposes of section 19(5)(b)(iii) and (iv) and section 19(5)(c) [11 and section 20A(2)(b)(iii) and (iv) and section 20A(2)(c)], in relation to a person who has been treated as available for employment to any extent under regulation 17A(3), the qualifying course in respect of which he has been so treated.]

(2) In section 19, except subsection (2) [12and in section 20A, except subsection (3)], and in this Part, except regulation 69 and the first occasion on which the word occurs in regulation 72(5A)(a), "week" means any period of 7 consecutive days.

(3) In section 19(2) [13, section 20A(3)], regulation 69 and the first occasion on which the word occurs in regulation 72(5A)(a), "week" means benefit week.

(4) In section 19, except subsection (9), [14in section 20A] and in this Part, "employment" means employed earner's employment other than such employment in which a person is employed whilst participating in an

employment programme falling within paragraph (1)(a)(ii) [^{16} or (iv) or the Intensive Activity period for 50 plus]; and "employed earner" shall be construed accordingly.

(5) In section 19(9), "employment" means employed earner's employment.]

AMENDMENTS

3.295   1. Social Security Amendment (New Deal) Regulations 1997 (SI 1997/2863), reg.8 (January 5, 1998).

2. Social Security Amendment (New Deal) Regulations 1998 (SI 1998/1274), reg.9 (June 1, 1998).

3. Social Security Amendment (Employment Programme) Regulations 2002 (SI 2002/2314), reg.4(1)(b) (October 14, 2002).

4. Jobseeker's Allowance (Amendment) (No.2) Regulations 1998 (SI 1998/1698), reg.3(a) (August 4, 1998).

5. Jobseeker's Allowance (Amendment) (No.2) Regulations 1998 (SI 1998/1698), reg.3(b) (August 4, 1998).

6. Jobseeker's Allowance (Amendment) (No.2) Regulations 1998 (SI 1998/1698), reg.4 (August 4, 1998).

7. Jobseeker's Allowance (Amendment) (No.2) Regulations 1998 (SI 1998/1698), reg.3(c) (December 1, 1998).

8. Employment Zones Regulations 2000 (SI 2000/721), reg.10 (April 3, 2000).

9. Jobseeker's Allowance (Amendment) (No.2) Regulations 2000 (SI 2000/1370), reg.2(2) (June 19, 2000).

10. Jobseeker's Allowance (Joint Claims) Regulations 2000 (SI 2000/1978), reg.2(5) and Sch.2, para.32(a) (March 19, 2001).

11. Jobseeker's Allowance (Joint Claims) Regulations 2000 (SI 2000/1978), reg.2(5) and Sch.2, para.32(b) (March 19, 2001).

12. Jobseeker's Allowance (Joint Claims) Regulations 2000 (SI 2000/1978), reg.2(5) and Sch.2, para.32(c) (March 19, 2001).

13. Jobseeker's Allowance (Joint Claims) Regulations 2000 (SI 2000/1978), reg.2(5) and Sch.2, para.32(d) (March 19, 2001).

14. Jobseeker's Allowance (Joint Claims) Regulations 2000 (SI 2000/1978), reg.2(5) and Sch.2, para.32(e) (March 19, 2001).

15. Social Security (Miscellaneous Amendments) (No. 2) Regulations 2001 (SI 2001/652), reg.5(c) (March 26, 2001).

16. Social Security Amendment (New Deal) Regulations 2001 (SI 2001/ 1029), reg.6 (April 9, 2001).

17. Social Security Amendment (Employment Programme) Regulations 2002 (SI 2002/2314), reg.4(1)(a) (October 14, 2002).

18. Social Security (Working Neighbourhoods) Regulations 2004 (SI 2004/959), reg.23 (April 26, 2004).

DEFINITIONS

3.296   "benefit week"—see reg.1(3).
"employed earner"—see reg.3.
"qualifying course"—see reg.4.

GENERAL NOTE

Para. (1)

3.297   Para. (1) defines "employment programme" and "training scheme" for the purposes of s.19 of the Jobseekers Act 1995 and regs 69 to 74A. See the notes to s.19(5) of the Jobseekers Act 1995 for discussion of the "offences" in relation to such programmes and schemes that can lead to sanction. The form of this regulation in force from January 5, 1998 distinguishes between the three employment programmes and one training scheme that make up the "New Deal options" for 18–24 year-olds (see para.(1)(a)(ii) and (b)(ii)) and other employment programmes (listed in para.(1)(a)(i)) and training schemes (para.(1)(b)(i)). (Note that for people participating in the intensive activity period of the New Deal pilots for people aged 25 or over, "employment programme" also means that intensive activity period: see reg.6 of the Social Security (New Deal Pilot) Regulations (SI 2000/3134) in force from November 28, 2000 to November 27, 2001 (unless revoked earlier); these Regulations replaced the 1999 New Deal Pilot Regulations (SI 1999/3156), in force from November 29, 1999 to November 28, 2000, which in turn replaced the 1998 New Deal Pilot Regulations (SI 1998/2825) in force from November 30, 1998 to November 29, 1999. See below for a brief summary of the New Deal for 18–24 year-olds. Note also the separate provision in para.(1)(b)(iii), introduced on June 1, 1998, which concerns claimants aged 25 or over who are being treated as available for work under reg.17A while attending a full-time employment-related course (see the notes to reg.17A).

"Training scheme" in para.(1)(b)(i) means Work Based Learning for Young People (in Scotland "Skillseekers") which is the new name for training focused on 16/17 year-olds (replacing Youth Training, Modern Apprenticeships, National Traineeships and other provision). Employment programmes and training schemes change from time to time. See the deletion of sub-heads (bb), (cc) and (dd) and the new form of sub-head (ee) in para.(1)(a)(i) which reflect the changes in the employment programmes that have been made. "Programme Centre Workshop" (see the new form of sub-head (ee)) has replaced Workwise (in Scotland, Worklink) and Restart course, 1–2–1 and Jobfinder have been replaced by Jobfinder Plus, which will similarly consist of a series of interviews. Attendance at Jobfinder Plus interviews is apparently to be enforced by means of the provisions in regs 23 to 30 of the JSA Regulations, rather than by including it in this regulation. The employment programmes that are listed in para.(1)(a)(i) (together with the New Deal options and Work Based Learning for Young People) are the programmes and schemes that are for the time being "compulsory" for the purposes of s.19 (although note that in some areas of the country a claimant could in the past also have been sanctioned for refusing without good cause to take part in a pilot scheme called Project Work; Project Work was abolished in May 1998. For a discussion of the conditions in the JSA (Pilot Scheme) Regulations 1996 (SI 1996/1307) for the imposition of a Project Work sanction see *CJSA 5600/1997*). Under para.(1)(b)(iii), note that a claimant aged 25 or over cannot be required to go on a qualifying course. However, if he is treated as available for employment under reg.17A while attending such a course, he can be sanctioned for failing to attend, or giving up, the course without good cause, or losing his place through misconduct. In addition, it is also possible for an employment officer to issue a jobseeker's direction requiring the claimant to attend a "non-compulsory" programme; if the claimant failed to attend without good cause he could be liable to sanction under s.19(5)(a). For further details of employment programmes and training schemes see CPAG's *Welfare Benefits Handbook* (2004/2005 ed.) and for updated information see *CPAG's Welfare Rights Bulletin*.

On the sanction for refusing, or failing to attend, etc., a New Deal option or other prescribed employment programmes and training schemes in addition see further the notes to reg.69.

The New Deal

The "New Deal" for young people aged 18–24 who have claimed jobseeker's allowance for six months or more is a major component of the Government's Welfare to Work programme. It was introduced in a number of "pathfinder areas" of the country on January 5, 1998 and on a national basis on April 6, 1998. A number of other New Deal programmes are in the process of being implemented: for lone parents, the long-term unemployed and disabled people. (The provision in

3.298

reg.17A to enable claimants aged 25 or over to attend a full-time employment-related course while continuing to receive JSA is one of the measures that are designed to help the long-term unemployed.) For further information on these initiatives see CPAG's *Welfare Benefits Handbook* (2005/2006 ed.) and for updated information see CPAG's *Welfare Rights Bulletin*. Information can also be found at http://www.newdeal.gov.uk

Para. (4)

3.299 The effect of this paragraph is that the claimant will not count as in employment for the purposes of s.19 and this Part of the regulations, even if he has employed status while he is on any of the New Deal options in para.(1)(a)(ii). This means that if the claimant does leave his place on the option voluntarily or loses it through misconduct he will be subject to a fixed sanction under s.19(5)(b) or (c), not the discretionary sanctions under s.19(6)(a) or (b).

PART VI

MEMBERSHIP OF THE FAMILY

Persons of a prescribed description

3.300 **76.**—(1) Subject to paragraph (2), a person of a prescribed description for the purposes of the definition of "family" in section 35(1) of the Act is a person aged 16 or over but under 19 who is treated as a child for the purposes of section 142 of the Benefits Act (meaning of child), and in these Regulations, except in Part IV, such a person is referred to as a "young person".

(2) Paragraph (1) shall not apply to a person who is—

(a) on a course of advanced education;

(b) entitled to a jobseeker's allowance or would, but for section 3(1)(d) of the Act (provision against dual entitlement) be so entitled; or

(c) entitled to income support or would, but for section 134(2) of the Benefits Act (exclusion from benefit) be [² so entitled; or

(d) a person to whom section 6 of the Children (Leaving Care) Act 2000 (exclusion from benefits) applies.]

[¹(3) A person of a prescribed description for the purposes of the definition of "family" in section 35(1) of the Act includes a child or young person in respect of whom section 145A of the Benefits Act applies for the purposes of entitlement to child benefit but only for the period prescribed under section 145A(1) of that Act.]

DEFINITIONS

"the Act"—see reg.1(3).
"course of advanced education"—*ibid.*

AMENDMENTS

3.301 1. Income-related Benefits and Jobseeker's Allowance (Working Tax Credit and Child Credit) (Amendment) Regulations 2002 (SI 2002/2402), reg.3 and Sch.2, para.2 (April 6, 2003).

2. Children (Leaving Care) Act 2000 (Commencement No. 2 and Consequential Provisions) Order 2001 (SI 2001/3070), art. 3(5) and Sch.4.

GENERAL NOTE

This regulation is very similar to reg.14 of the Income Support Regulations, except that para.(2) contains an additional exception that the person must not be entitled to income support in their own right (sub-para.(c)), as well as not receiving advanced education (sub-para.(a)) or entitled to JSA in their own right (sub-para.(b)). Note that para.(1) expressly provides that this definition of "young person" does not apply for the purposes of Part IV (entitlement of 16 and 17-year-olds to JSA). **3.302**

For the circumstances in which a person aged 16 to 18 is treated as a child for child benefit purposes see regs 5–11 of the Child Benefit (General) Regulations 2003 in Vol. I of this series, and the notes to reg.54.

Circumstances in which a person is to be treated as responsible or not responsible for another

77.—(1) Subject to the following provisions of this regulation, a person is to be treated for the purposes of the Act as responsible for a child or young person for whom he is receiving child benefit [¹and this includes a child or young person to whom paragraph (3) of regulation 76 applies.] **3.303**

(2) In a case where a child ("the first child") is in receipt of child benefit in respect of another child ("the second child"), the person treated as responsible for the first child in accordance with the provisions of this regulation shall also be treated as responsible for the second child.

(3) In the case of a child or young person in respect of whom no person is receiving child benefit, the person who shall be treated as responsible for that child or young person shall be—

(a) except where sub-paragraph (b) applies, the person with whom the child or young person usually lives; or

(b) where only one claim for child benefit has been made in respect of the child or young person, the person who made that claim.

(4) Where regulation 78(7) (circumstances in which a person is to be treated as being or not being a member of the household) applies in respect of a child or young person, that child or young person shall be treated as the responsibility of the claimant for that part of the week for which he is under that regulation treated as being a member of the claimant's household.

(5) Except where paragraph (4) applies, a child or young person shall be treated as the responsibility of only one person in any benefit week and any person other than the one treated as responsible for the child or young person under this regulation shall be treated as not so responsible.

AMENDMENT

1. Income-related Benefits and Jobseeker's Allowance (Working Tax Credit and Child Tax Credit) (Amendment) Regulations 2002 (SI 2002/2402), reg. Sch.2, para.3 (April 6, 2003). **3.304**

DEFINITIONS

"the Act"—see reg.1(3).
"benefit week"—*ibid.*
"child"—see Jobseekers Act, s.35(1).
"claimant"—*ibid.*

"week"—*ibid.*
"young person"—see reg.76.

GENERAL NOTE

3.305   The definition of family in s.35(1) of the Jobseekers Act refers to a person being responsible for a child or young person (on which see reg.76). This provision mirrors that in reg.15 of the Income Support Regulations and makes the test of responsibility for a child or young person receipt of child benefit. See the notes to reg.15.

Note however, the decision of the Court of Appeal in *Hockenjos v Secretary of State for Social Security* [2004] EWCA Civ 1749 (on appeal from *CJSA 4890/1998*) that paras (1)–(3) and (5) of this regulation discriminated against men contrary to Art.4 of EC Directive 79/7 (see Vol. III) and that such discrimination was not objectively justifiable. Those provisions therefore could not be applied to Mr Hockenjos or, by implication, any man within the personal scope of that Directive. In such a case, whether or not a child or young person was a member of the claimant's "family" was to be decided by applying the definition in s.35 Jobseekers Act as if reg.77 did not exist, *i.e.*, by asking whether that child or young person was a member of the same household for whom the claimant or any partner was responsible. Applying that test to Mr Hockenjos (who had shared parental responsibility and whose daughters lived with him for substantial parts, though not the majority, of each week under a joint residence order made by a court) there was no doubt that it was satisfied. The effect was that Mr Hockenjos was entitled to JSA for his children on the same basis as if they lived with him full time and, as the "one claimant per child" rule in reg.77(5) was indirectly discriminatory, the fact the Secretary of State might also have to pay income support or JSA for the children to their mother on the same basis did not affect that conclusion. The Secretary of State petitioned the House of Lords for leave to appeal, and decision makers were instructed to defer making decisions in look-alike appeals (see DMG Letter 01/05) pending that application. However, leave to appeal has now been refused.

For the reasons given in the note to reg.15 of the IS Regulations, the *Hockenjos* decision does not apply to income support.

Circumstances in which a person is to be treated as being or not being a member of the household

3.306   **78.**—(1) Subject to paragraphs (2) to (5), the claimant and any partner and, where the claimant or his partner is treated as responsible under regulation 77 (circumstances in which a person is to be treated as responsible or not responsible for another) for a child or young person, that child or young person and any child of that child or young person shall be treated for the purposes of the Act as members of the same household notwithstanding that any of them is temporarily living away from the other members of his family.

[³(1A) Subject to paragraphs (2) and (3), the members of a joint-claim couple shall be treated for the purposes of the Act as members of the same household notwithstanding that they are temporarily living away from each other.]

(2) [⁴Paragraphs (1) and (1A)] shall not apply to a person who is living away from the other members of his family where—

(a) that person does not intend to resume living with the other members of his family; or

(b) his absence from the other members of his family is likely to exceed 52 weeks, unless there are exceptional circumstances (for example the person is in hospital or otherwise has no control over the length of his absence), and the absence is unlikely to be substantially more than 52 weeks.

(3) [⁵ Paragraphs (1) and (1A)] shall not apply in respect of any member of a couple or of a polygamous marriage where—

(a) one, both or all of them are patients detained in a hospital provided under section 4 of the National Health Service Act 1977 (special hospitals) or section 90(1) of the Mental Health (Scotland) Act 1984 (provision of hospitals for patients requiring special security); or

[²(b) one, both or all of them are—

(i) detained in custody pending trial or sentence upon conviction or under a sentence imposed by a court; or

(ii) on temporary release in accordance with the provisions of the Prison Act 1952 or rules made under section 39(6) of the Prisons (Scotland) Act 1989]

(c) [⁶ a claimant] is abroad and does not satisfy the conditions of regulation 50 (persons absent from Great Britain); or

(d) one of them is permanently in residential accommodation or a residential care home or a nursing home.

(4) A child or young person shall not be treated as a member of the claimant's household where he is—

(a) placed with the claimant or his partner by a local authority under section 23(2)(a) of the Children Act 1989 or by a voluntary organisation under section 59(1)(a) of that Act; or

(b) placed with the claimant or his partner prior to adoption; or

(c) in accordance with a relevant Scottish enactment, boarded out with the claimant or his partner, whether or not with a view to adoption; or

(d) placed for adoption with the claimant or his partner pursuant to a decision under the Adoption Agencies Regulations 1983 or the Adoption Agencies (Scotland) Regulations 1984.

(5) Subject to paragraphs (6) and (7), paragraph (1) shall not apply to a child or young person who is not living with the claimant and who—

(a) in a case which does not fall within sub-paragraph (b), has been continuously absent from Great Britain for a period of more than four weeks commencing—

(i) where he went abroad before the date of the claim for a jobseeker's allowance, with that date;

(ii) in any other case, on the day which immediately follows the day on which he went abroad; or

(b) where [¹regulation 50(5)] or paragraph 11 or 13 of Schedule 5 (temporary absence abroad for the treatment of a child or young person) applies, has been continuously absent from Great Britain for a period of more than 8 weeks, that period of 8 weeks commencing—

(i) where he went abroad before the date of the claim for a jobseeker's allowance, on the date of that claim;

(ii) in any other case, on the day which immediately follows the day on which he went abroad; or

(c) has been an in-patient or in accommodation provided under any of the provisions referred to in any of sub-paragraphs (a) to (c) of the

definition of residential accommodation in regulation 85 for a continuous period of more than 12 weeks commencing—

    (i) where he became an in-patient or, as the case may be, entered
that accommodation before the date of the claim for a jobseeker's allowance, with that date; or

    (ii) in any other case, with the date on which he became an in-
patient or entered that accommodation,

and, in either case, has not been in regular contact with either the
claimant or any member of the claimant's household; or

(d) is being looked after by a local authority under a relevant enactment;
or

(e) has been placed with a person other than the claimant prior to adoption, or

(f) is in the care of a local authority under a relevant Scottish enactment;
or

(g) has been boarded out under a relevant Scottish enactment with a
person other than the claimant prior to adoption; or

(h) has been placed for adoption pursuant to a decision under the Adoption Agencies Regulations 1983 or the Adoption Agencies (Scotland)
Regulations 1984; or

(i) is detained in custody pending trial or sentence upon conviction or
under a sentence imposed by a court.

(6) In the case of a person who was entitled to income support immediately before his entitlement to a jobseeker's allowance commenced, sub-
paragraphs (a), (b) and (c) of paragraph (5) [¹shall] each have effect as if
head (i) was omitted.

(7) A child or young person to whom any of the circumstances mentioned
in [¹sub-paragraphs (d), (f) or (i)] of paragraph (5) applies shall be treated
as being a member of the claimant's household only for that part of any
benefit week where that child or young person lives with the claimant.

(8) Where a child or young person for the purposes of attending the educational establishment at which he is receiving relevant education is living
with the claimant or his partner and neither one is treated as responsible for
that child or young person that child or young person shall be treated as
being a member of the household of the person treated as responsible for
him and shall not be treated as a member of the claimant's household.

(9) In this regulation—

(a) "relevant enactment" means the Army Act 1955, the Social Work
(Scotland) Act 1968, the Matrimonial Causes Act 1973, the Adoption
(Scotland) Act 1978, the Family Law Act 1986 and the Children Act
1989;

(b) "relevant Scottish enactment" means the Army Act 1955, the Air
Force Act 1955, the Naval Discipline Act 1957, the Adoption Act
1958, the Matrimonial Proceedings Children Act 1958, the Children
Act 1958, the Social Work (Scotland) Act 1968, the Family Law
Reform Act 1969, the Children and Young Persons Act 1969, the
Matrimonial Causes Act 1973, the Guardianship Act 1973, the
Children Act 1975, the Domestic Proceedings and Magistrates'
Courts Act 1978, the Adoption (Scotland) Act 1978, the Child Care
Act 1980, and the Foster Children Act 1980;

(c) "voluntary organisation" has the meaning assigned to it in the Children
Act 1989 or, in Scotland, the Social Work (Scotland) Act 1968.

1. Jobseeker's Allowance (Amendment) Regulations 1996 (SI 1996/1516), reg.20 and Sch. (October 7, 1996).   **3.307**
2. Jobseeker's Allowance and Income Support (General) (Amendment) Regulations 1996 (SI 1996/1517), reg.18 (October 7, 1996).
3. Jobseeker's Allowance (Joint Claims) Regulations 2000 (SI 2000/1978), reg.2(5) and Sch.2, para.33(a) (March 19, 2001).
4. Jobseeker's Allowance (Joint Claims) Regulations 2000 (SI 2000/1978), reg.2(5) and Sch.2, para.33(b) (March 19, 2001).
5. Jobseeker's Allowance (Joint Claims) Regulations 2000 (SI 2000/1978), reg.2(5) and Sch.2, para.33(c)(i) (March 19, 2001).
6. Jobseeker's Allowance (Joint Claims) Regulations 2000 (SI 2000/1978), reg.2(5) and Sch.2, para.33(c)(ii) (March 19, 2001).

DEFINITIONS

"the Act"—see reg.1(3).   **3.308**
"claimant"—see Jobseekers Act, s.35(1).
"child"—*ibid.*
"couple"—see reg.1(3).
"date of claim"—*ibid*
"family"—see Jobseekers Act, s.35(1).
"nursing home"—see reg.1(3).
"partner"—*ibid.*
"polygamous marriage"—*ibid.*
"residential accommodation"—*ibid.*
"residential care home"—*ibid.*
"young person"—see reg.76.

GENERAL NOTE

This regulation is very similar to reg.16 of the Income Support Regulations.   **3.309**
Unlike the Income Support Regulations, the JSA Regulations make separate reference to the Scottish legislation in the case of provisions that were amended in the Income Support Regulations as a consequence of the Children Act 1989 (see para.(4)(c), para.(5)(f) and (g) and (9)(b)).
See the notes to reg.16 of the Income Support Regulations.

PART VII

AMOUNTS

Weekly amounts of contribution-based jobseeker's allowance

79.—(1) In the case of a contribution-based jobseeker's allowance, the   **3.310**
age-related amount applicable to a claimant for the purposes of section
4(1)(a) shall be—
  (a) in the case of a person who has not attained the age of 18, [¹£33.85]
      per week;
  (b) in the case of a person who has attained the age of 18 but not the age
      of 25, [¹£44.50] per week;
  (c) in the case of a person who has attained the age of 25, [¹£56.20] per
      week.

(2) Where the amount of any contribution-based jobseeker's allowance would, but for this paragraph, include a fraction of one penny, that fraction shall be treated as one penny.

AMENDMENT

3.311   1. Social Security Benefits Up-rating Order 2005, art.23 (SI 2005/522) (April 11, 2005).

DEFINITIONS

"contribution-based jobseeker's allowance": see Jobseekers Act 1995, s.35(1) and s.1(4).
"week": see reg.1(3).

GENERAL NOTE

3.312   If a claimant is entitled to a contribution-based JSA, the first step in calculating the amount payable under Jobseekers Act 1995, s.4(1) is to determine the age-related amount payable to him (s.4(1)(a)). Paragraph (1) of this regulation sets out those amounts, setting the lowest rate for the under-18s, a higher rate for those 18–24, and reserving the highest rate for those 25 and over.

Given the contribution conditions it is difficult to see how anyone under 18 could qualify save in highly unusual circumstances, unless there is an alteration to the rules on when contribution credits can be awarded (see annotations to Jobseekers Act 1995, s.2(1)(a), (b), (2)–(4)). Differential rates for the basic part of benefit seem hard to justify, given that the ability to receive JSA regardless of means (the government's description: see White Paper, para.4.21) rests on the same level of contributions for all, regardless of age (see annotations to s.2). The stated justification—that some 75 per cent of under-25s do not live independently and have fewer financial commitments—*per* Mr R. Evans, Parliamentary Under-Secretary of State, *House of Commons Standing Committee B Debates on the Jobseekers Bill*, col.247—may well be accurate, but the resultant rule paints with too broad a brush, relegates social security contributions very much to the realm of earmarked taxation rather than insurance for the future, and seems more appropriate to a means-tested than a contributory benefit payable in consequence of the insured risk materialising. Nonetheless *R. (on the application of Carson)v Secretary of State for Work and Pensions* ([2003] EWCA Civ 797, [2003] 3 All ER 577) held that the differential treatment of those under 25 was not unlawful discrimination contrary to the HRA and ECHR. Art. 14; the reasons advanced by the Secretary of State for the differential treatment constituted "perfectly reasonable justification".

Paragraph (2) provides with respect to contribution-based JSA that fractions of a penny shall be treated as one penny.

Deductions in respect of earnings

3.313   **80.**—(1) The deduction in respect of earnings which falls to be made in accordance with section 4(1)(b) from the amount which, apart from this regulation, would be payable by way of a contribution-based jobseeker's allowance for any benefit week is an amount equal to the weekly amount of the claimant's earnings calculated in accordance with Part VIII (income and capital).

(2) For the avoidance of doubt, in calculating the amount of earnings for the purposes of this regulation, only the claimant's earnings shall be taken into account.

DEFINITIONS

"claimant": see Jobseekers Act 1995, s.35(1).

"contribution-based jobseeker's allowance": see Jobseekers Act 1995, ss.35(1) and 1(4).

"earnings": see regs 98 (employed earner) and 100 (self-employed earner).

"week": see reg.1(3).

GENERAL NOTE

Section 4(1) of the Jobseekers Act 1995 provides that one calculates the amount of contribution-based jobseeker's allowance payable to a claimant by first determining the age-related amount applicable to him (see reg.79) and then making prescribed deductions from that in respect of (a) earnings (the subject-matter of this regulation) and (b) pension payments (the subject-matter of reg.81). The provisions, subjecting contribution-based JSA to a form of means-testing not applicable to unemployment benefit, represent one of the ways in which the scheme deals with the problem of partial unemployment, where a claimant is working below the 16-hour threshold set for the remunerative work exclusion, whether in employment or self-employment. "Earnings" means those of employed earners (reg.98) and self-employed earners (reg.100). Only the claimant's own earnings count for purposes of contribution-based JSA (para.(2); *cf.* reg.88). Under para.(1), the deduction to be made from the appropriate age-related amount in respect of earnings is an amount equal to the weekly amount of his earnings as calculated in accordance with Pt VIII of these Regulations. Essentially, in the case of an employed earner, one takes account of net earnings less appropriate disregards and, in the case of a self-employed earner, net profit, less appropriate disregards. Note, in this regard, that the range of disregards for purposes of this regulation is narrower than those applicable when calculating earnings for purposes of income-based JSA (does income exceed the applicable amount?) or for purposes of ascertaining whether his weekly earnings exceed the "prescribed amount" for the purposes of reg.56 and the preclusion from entitlement to contribution-based JSA set by the Jobseekers Act 1995, s.2(1)(c) (see regs 99(3) and 101(3), contrasting them with regs 99(2) and 101(2)).

3.314

Payments by way of pensions

81.—(1) The deduction in respect of pension payments from the amount which apart from this regulation would be payable to a claimant by way of a contribution-based jobseeker's allowance for any benefit week shall be a sum equal to the amount by which that payment exceeds or, as the case may be, the aggregate of those payments exceed £50 per benefit week.

3.315

(1A) Where pension payments first begin to be made to a person for a period starting other than on the first day of a benefit week, the deduction referred to in paragraph (1) shall have effect from the beginning of that benefit week.

(1B) Where pension payments are already in payment to a person and a change in the rate of payment takes effect in a week other than at the beginning of the benefit week, the deduction referred to in paragraph
(1) shall have effect from the first day of that benefit week.

(2) In determining the amount of any pension payments for the purposes of paragraph (1), there shall be disregarded—

(a) *[Revoked.]*
(b) *[Revoked.]*
(c) any payments from a personal pension scheme, an occupational pension scheme or a public service pension scheme which are payable

to him and which arose in accordance with the terms of such a scheme on the death of a person who was a member of the scheme in question.

(3) Subject to the provisions of paragraph (2), where a pension payment, or an aggregate of such payments, as the case may be, is paid to a person for a period other than a week, such payments shall be treated as being made to that person by way of weekly pension payments and the weekly amount shall be determined—

(a) where payment is made for a year, by dividing the total by 52;

(b) where payment is made for three months, by dividing the total by 13;

(c) where payment is made for a month, by multiplying the total by 12 and dividing the result by 52;

(d) where payment is made for two or more months, otherwise than for a year or for three months, by dividing the total by the number of months, multiplying the result by 12 and dividing the result of that multiplication by 52; or

(e) in any other case, by dividing the amount of the payment by the number of days in the period for which it is made and multiplying the result by 7.

DEFINITION

"pension payments": see Jobseekers Act 1995, s.35(1).

GENERAL NOTE

3.316   Section 4(1) of the Jobseekers Act 1995 provides that one calculates the amount of contribution-based jobseeker's allowance payable to a claimant by first determining the age-related amount applicable to him (see reg.79) and then making prescribed deductions from that in respect of (a) earnings (the subject-matter of reg.80) and (b) pension payments (the subject-matter of this regulation). There is thus brought into contribution-based JSA the concept of abatement of benefit in respect of payments by way of occupational or personal pension previously applied in unemployment benefit to claimants 55 or over pursuant to the now-repealed SSCBA 1992, s.30.

"Pension payments" are defined in Jobseekers Act 1995, s.35(1) and rules on taking them into account (paras (1), (1A), (1B)), determining a weekly equivalent (para.(3)) and on which payments can be disregarded (para.(2)(c)) are set out in this regulation. The definition of the payments covered is not the same as "payments by way of occupational or personal pension" applicable to unemployment benefit under SSCBA 1992, s.122(1). Nor are the rules in this regulation exactly the same as those which applied to unemployment benefit. Unless falling within the disregarded class (para.(2)(c)), a pension payment must be taken into account once its weekly equivalent (or if several, their aggregate weekly equivalent), determined in accordance with para.(3), exceeds £50, regardless of the age of the claimant.

"Pension payments" are periodical payments made in relation to a person, under a personal pension scheme or, in connection with the coming to an end of an employment of his, under an occupational pension scheme or a public service pension scheme, and also such other payments as may be prescribed in regulations (Jobseekers Act 1995, s.35(1)). A "personal pension scheme" embraces a contract or trust scheme approved under Chapter III of Pt XIV of the Income and Corporation Taxes Act 1988; a personal pension scheme approved under Chapter IV of that Part of that Act; and a personal pension scheme as defined in s.1 of the Pension Schemes Act 1993 ("any scheme or arrangement which is comprised in one or more instruments or agreements and which has, or is capable of having, effect so as to provide benefits, in the form of pensions or otherwise, payable on death or retirement to or in respect of employed earners who have made arrangements with the trustees or managers of the scheme for them to become members of it") (Jobseekers Act 1995, s.35(1)). An "occupational pension scheme" is—

"any scheme or arrangement which is comprised in one or more instruments or agreements and which has, or is capable of having, effect in relation to one or more descriptions or categories of employments so as to provide benefits, in the form of pensions or otherwise, payable on termination of service, or on death or retirement, to or in respect of earners with qualifying service in an employment of any such description or category" (Pension Schemes Act 1993, s.1, applied here by virtue of Jobseekers Act 1995, s.35(1)).

A "public service pension scheme" is—

"an occupational pension scheme [as just defined] established by or under an enactment or the Royal prerogative or a Royal charter, being a scheme (a) all the particulars of which are set out in, or in a legislative instrument made under, an enactment, Royal warrant or charter, or (b) which cannot come into force, or be amended, without the scheme or amendment being approved by a Minister of the Crown or government department."

The term includes—

"any occupational pension scheme established, with the concurrence of the Treasury, by or with the approval of any Minister of the Crown and any occupational pension scheme prescribed by regulations made by the Secretary of State and the Treasury jointly as being a scheme which ought in their opinion to be treated as a public service pension scheme for the purposes of this Act" (Pension Schemes Act 1993, s.1, applied here by virtue of Jobseekers Act 1995, s.35(1)).

In determining the amount of any pension payments for abatement purposes, **3.317** there must be disregarded any payable to the claimant which arose in accordance with the terms of a personal pension scheme occupational pension scheme or a public service pension scheme on the death of someone who was a member of that scheme (para.(2)(c)).

In *R(JSA) 1/01* Commissioner Howell considered the case of a claimant for contribution-based JSA. The claimant was a former civil servant with the Property Services Agency who received annual compensation payments for his redundancy which came about when the agency was sold off to the private sector. These annual payments were not part of his retirement benefits but were "contractual payments made by his private employer, not under any separate funded scheme but out of its own operational assets, in satisfaction of the redundancy terms negotiated with him as part of his contract of employment on transfer of employment to them" (paragraph 6). Clearly these payments were not earnings under regulation 98 since paragraph (2)(b) thereof excludes from the definition of earnings "any periodic sum paid to a claimant on account of the termination of his employment by reasons of redundancy". Following the Court of Appeal in *Westminster City Council v Haywood* [1998] Ch. 377 and Hart J. in *City and Council of Swansea v Johnson* [1999] 2 W.L.R. 683, Commissioner Howell held that the annual payments were ones of occupational pension and subject to the abatement of JSA rules in reg.81. He commented:

"I do not for my part consider there to be any absurdity or inconsistency in this result. Periodical payments under an employer's scheme or arrangement of this type after employment terminates appear to me to have the same essential characteristic of deferred or contingent 'pay' for this purpose, whether the reason is permitted early retirement or premature termination on redundancy. It seems to me consistent to treat both in the same way as 'pension payments' under regulation 81 whether or not they come from the same source. Nor do I find any absurdity or inconsistency in their both being taken into account as pension payments though excluded from counting as 'earnings'. The point of excluding both from the definition of 'earnings' in regulation 98 is not to remove them from the reckoning altogether, but to allow the first £50 a week of these types of payment to be left out of account while continued current earnings left within regulation 80 would be fully deductible" (para.28).

To apply this regulation it is vital to identify the source of the payment. Failure so to do is an error of law (*R(JSA)2/01; CJSA/4316/1998*). It would be helpful if the correspondence from employer to claimant indicated the source of the payment (*R(JSA)2/01*). In *R(JSA)2/01* and *CJSA/4316/1998*, the source of the annual compensation payment was the Civil Service Pension Scheme. Following *R(JSA)1/01* and the statements of Millett L.J. in *Westminster City Council v Haywood* [1998] Ch. 377 at 404–405, this was held, both in *R(JSA)2/O1* and *CJSA/4316/1998*, to fall within the JSA definitions of pension payment, notwithstanding that in *R(JSA)2/01*, the claimant got that compensation payment because he did not get what the civil service scheme called a pension (*R(JSA)2/01*, para.7).

In *R(JSA)6/02*, *R(JSA)1/01* was followed to hold that "three months' redundancy payment" on termination of employment with London and Manchester (Management Services) Limited constituted periodical pension payments abating JSA.

In *CJSA 1542/2000*, Commissioner Rowland followed *R(JSA)6/02* to hold that a lump sum payment amounting to three months' redundancy payment was a pension payment for the purposes of this regulation.

[¹ Income-based jobseeker's allowance

3.318   **82.**—(1) Regulations 83 to [² 85] and 87 apply in the case of an income-based jobseeker's allowance but not a joint-claim jobseeker's allowance.

(2) Regulations 86A to [² 86C] only apply in the case of a joint-claim jobseeker's allowance.]

AMENDMENTS

1. Jobseeker's Allowance (Joint Claims) Regulations 2000 (SI 2000/1978), reg.2(5) and Sch.2, para.34 (March 19, 2001).
2. Social Security Amendment (Residential Care and Nursing Homes) Regulations 2001 (SI 2001/3767), reg.2 and Sch. Pt II, para.3 (April 8, 2002).

Applicable amounts

3.319   **83.** Except in the case of a claimant to whom regulation 84, 85, [¹. . .] or Part X (applicable amounts in other cases and urgent cases) applies, a claimant's weekly applicable amount shall be the aggregate of such of the following amounts as may apply in this case—

   (a) an amount in respect of himself or if he is a member of a couple, an amount in respect of both of them, determined in accordance with sub-paragraph (1), (2) or (3), as the case may be, of paragraph 1 of Schedule 1;
   (b) [³ . . .]
   (c) [² . . .]
   (d) [³ . . .]
   (e) the amount of any premiums which may be applicable to him, determined in accordance with Parts III and IV of Schedule 1 (premiums); and
   (f) any amounts determined in accordance with Schedule 2 (housing costs) which may be applicable to him in respect of mortgage interest payments or such other housing costs as are prescribed in that Schedule.

AMENDMENTS

1. Social Security Amendment (Residential Care and Nursing Homes) Regulations 2001 (SI 2001/3767), reg.2 and Sch., Pt II, para.4 (April 8, 2002).
2. Social Security (Removal of Residential Allowance and Miscellaneous Amendments) Regulations 2003 (SI 2003/1121), reg. 4 and Sch. 2, para. 2 (October 6, 2003).
3. Social Security (Working Tax Credit and Child Tax Credit) (Consequential Amendments) Regulations 2003 (SI 2003/455), reg 3 and Sch. 2, para. 2 (April 6, 2004, except in "transitional cases" and see further the note to this regulation and to reg.17 of the Income Support Regulations).

3.320

DEFINITIONS

"child"—see Jobseekers Act, s.35(1).
"claimant"—*ibid.*
"couple"—see reg.1(3).
"family"—see Jobseekers Act, s.35(1).
"young person"—see reg.76.

GENERAL NOTE

This provision only applies to income-based JSA (reg.82).

3.321

Income-based JSA uses the same formula as income support for calculating the amount of a claimant's benefit, that is, by setting his "applicable amount" against his income. Reg. 83 sets out the categories which go towards the total applicable amount which are the same as those in reg.17 of the Income Support Regulations. See the notes to reg.17. There is no equivalent to reg.17(1)(f) and (g) and (2) to (7) which contain various transitional protection provisions. But note the rules for "transitional supplement" to income-based JSA in reg.87 which preserve the effect of these and other income support transitional protection provisions for JSA claimants who would have been covered by them had they been entitled to claim income support after October 6, 1996 (for claimants entitled to a special transitional addition or transitional addition under the Income Support (Transitional) Regulations before October 7, 1996, see para.(1) of reg.87).

As with income support there are special rules for particular categories, see regs 84 to 86D.

Subject to exceptions in "transitional cases", JSA became an "adults only" benefit on April 6, 2004 with all support for the costs of bringing up children and young persons transferred to child tax credit and regs 83(b) and 84(c) (personal allowances for children and young persons), regs.83(d) and 84(e) (family premium) and para.16 of Sch.1 (disabled child premium) were revoked from that date. At the same time para.15A(1)(b) of Sch.1 was amended to remove the possibility of claiming the enhanced disability premium for a child. For JSA the rules which create "transitional cases" are contained in reg.1(6)—(8) of SI 2003/455 (p.685) and are the same as the rules for income support in reg.1(2)—(4). For a detailed discussion, see the note to reg.17 of the Income Support Regulations.

Polygamous marriages

84.—(1) Except in the case of a claimant to whom regulation 83, [²or 85] (applicable amounts in special cases) [². . .] or Part X or paragraph (2) applies, where a claimant is a member of a polygamous marriage his weekly applicable amount shall be the aggregate of such of the following amounts as may apply in his case—
   (a) the highest amount applicable to him and one of his partners determined in accordance with sub-paragraph (3) of paragraph 1 of Schedule 1 as if he and that partner were a couple;

3.322

(b) an amount equal to the difference between the amounts specified in [¹sub-paragraph (3)(e)] and (1)(e) of paragraph 1 of Schedule 1 in respect of each of his other partners;

(c) [⁴. . .]

(d) [³. . .]

(e) [⁴. . .]

(f) the amount of any premiums which may be applicable to him determined in accordance with Parts III and IV of Schedule 1 (premiums); and

(g) any amounts determined in accordance with Schedule 2 (housing costs) which may be applicable to him in respect of mortgage interest payments or such other housing costs as are prescribed in that Schedule.

(2) In the case of a partner who is aged less than 18 the amount which applies in respect of that partner shall be Nil unless that partner—

(a) is treated as responsible for a child; or

(b) is a person who, had he not been a member of a polygamous marriage, would have qualified for a jobseeker's allowance by virtue of section 3(1)(f)(ii) or section 3(1)(f)(iii) and the regulations made thereunder (jobseeker's allowance for persons aged 16 or 17).

AMENDMENTS

3.323   1. Jobseeker's Allowance (Amendment) Regulations 1996 (SI 1996/1516), reg.20 and Sch. (October 7, 1996).

2. Social Security Amendment (Residential Care and Nursing Homes) Regulations 2001 (SI 2001/3767), reg.2 and Sch., Pt II, para.5 (April 8, 2002).

3. Social Security (Removal of Residential Allowance and Miscellaneous Amendments) Regulations 2003 (SI 2003/1121), reg.4 of and Sch.2, para.3 (October 6, 2003).

4. Social Security (Working Tax Credit and Child Tax Credit) (Consequential Amendments) Regulations 2003 (SI 2003/455), reg.3 and Sch.2, para.3 (April 6, 2004 , except in "transitional cases" and see further the note to reg.83 and to reg.17 of the Income Support Regulations).

DEFINITIONS

"child"—see Jobseekers Act, s.35(1).
"claimant"—*ibid.*
"couple"—see reg.1(3).
"family"—see Jobseekers Act, s.35(1).
"young person"—see reg.76.

GENERAL NOTE

3.324   Reg. 84 contains the special rules for polygamous marriages, but not for other kinds of relationships. There the ordinary living together as husband and wife rule in s.35(1) of the Jobseekers Act applies.

This provision only applies to income-based JSA (reg.82).

Special cases

3.325   **85.**—(1) [⁹ Subject to paragraph (2A)] in the case of a person to whom any paragraph in column (1) of Schedule 5 applies (applicable amounts in special cases) the amount included in the claimant's weekly applicable amount in respect of him shall be the amount prescribed in the corresponding paragraph in column (2) of that Schedule [¹¹. . .].

(2) Except where the amount prescribed in Schedule 5 in respect of a person to whom paragraph (1) applies includes an amount applicable under regulation 83(e) or 84(1)(f) a person to whom paragraph (1) applies shall be treated as not falling within the conditions specified in paragraph 15 of Schedule 1 (severe disability premium).

[⁹(2A) [¹⁰. . .]]

(3) In Schedule 5, for the purposes of paragraphs 1[¹⁰ . . .] and 17 (persons in residential care or nursing homes who become patients), where a person has been a patient for two or more distinct periods separated by one or more intervals each not exceeding 28 days, he shall be treated as having been a patient continuously for a period equal in duration to the total of those distinct periods.

(4) [³ [¹²Subject to paragraphs (4A) and (4B)],] in this regulation and Schedule 5—

[⁷. . .]

[⁷ "partner of a person subject to immigration control" means a person—

(i) who is not subject to immigration control within the meaning of section 115(9) of the Immigration and Asylum Act; or

(ii) to whom section 115 of that Act does not apply by virtue of regulation 2 of the Social Security (Immigration and Asylum) Consequential Amendments Regulations 2000; and

(iii) who is a member of a couple and his partner is subject to immigration control within the meaning of section 115(9) of that Act and section 115 of that Act applies to her for the purposes of exclusion from entitlement to jobseeker's allowance;]

"person from abroad" [⁷ . . .] means a claimant who is not habitually resident in the United Kingdom, [¹ the Channel Islands, the Isle of Man or the Republic of Ireland,] but for this purpose, no claimant shall be treated as not habitually resident in the United Kingdom who is—

(a) a worker for the purposes of Council Regulation (EEC) No. 1612/68 or (EEC) No. 1251/70 or a person with a right to reside in the United Kingdom pursuant to Council Directive No. 68/360/EEC or No. 3/148/ EEC [¹²or a person who is an accession State worker requiring registration who is treated as a worker for the purpose of the definition of "qualified person" in regulation 5(1) of the Immigration (European Economic Area) Regulations 2000 pursuant to regulation 5 of the Accession (Immigration and Worker Registration) Regulations 2004]; or

(b) a refugee within the definition of Article 1 of the Convention relating to the Status of Refugees done at Geneva on 28th July 1951, as extended by Article 1(2) of the Protocol relating to the Status of Refugees done at New York on 31st January 1967; or

(c) a person who has been granted exceptional leave [⁶to enter the United Kingdom by an immigration officer within the meaning of the Immigration Act 1971, or] to remain in the United Kingdom by the Secretary of State [⁸;or

(d) a person who is not a person subject to immigration control within the meaning of section 115(9) of the Immigration and Asylum Act and who is in the United Kingdom as a result of his deportation, expulsion or other removal by compulsion of law from another country to the United Kingdom;]

"patient" means a person (other than a prisoner) who is regarded as receiving free in-patient treatment within the meaning of the Social Security (Hospital In-Patients) Regulations 1975;

"prisoner" means a person who—

(a) is detained in custody pending trial or sentence upon conviction or under a sentence imposed by a court; or

(b) is on temporary release in accordance with the provisions of the Prison Act 1952 or the Prisons (Scotland) Act 1989,

other than a person [⁵who is detained in hospital under the provisions of the Mental Health Act 1983, or, in Scotland, under the provisions of the Mental Health (Scotland) Act 1984 or the Criminal Procedure (Scotland) Act 1995;]

"residential accommodation" means, subject to the following provisions of this regulation, accommodation provided by a local authority in a home owned or managed by that or another local authority—

(a) under sections 21 to 24 of the National Assistance Act 1948 (provision of accommodation); or

(b) in Scotland, under section 13B or 59 of the Social Work (Scotland) Act 1968 (provision of residential and other establishments); or

(c) under section 7 of the Mental Health (Scotland) Act 1984 (functions of local authorities),

where the accommodation is provided for a person whose stay in that accommodation has become other than temporary.

[³(4A) In paragraph (4) "person from abroad" does not include any person in Great Britain who left the territory of Montserrat after 1st November 1995 because of the effect on that territory of a volcanic eruption.

[¹²(4B) In paragraph (4), for the purposes of the definition of a person from abroad no person shall be treated as habitually resident in the United Kingdom, the Channel Islands, the Isle of Man or the Republic of Ireland if he does not have a right to reside in the United Kingdom, the Channel Islands, the Isle of Man or the Republic of Ireland.]

(5) A person shall continue to be treated as being in residential accommodation within the meaning of paragraph (4) if—

(a) he is in, or only temporarily absent from, such residential accommodation, and the same accommodation subsequently becomes a residential care home for so long as he remains in that accommodation; or

(b) on 31st March 1993 he was in, or only temporarily absent from, accommodation of a kind mentioned in regulation 21(3B) to (3E) of the Income Support Regulations.]

(6) A person who would, but for this paragraph, be in residential accommodation within the meaning of paragraph (4) shall be treated as not being in residential accommodation where—

(a) he is under the age of 18 and in the care of a local authority under Part II or III of the Social Work (Scotland) Act 1968 (promotion of social welfare of children in need of care); or

(b) except where he is a person to whom paragraph (5)(b) applies, he is in accommodation where—

(i) no cooked or prepared food is made available to him in consequence solely of his paying the charge for the accommodation or any other charge which he is required to pay as a condition of occupying the accommodation, or both of those charges, or

(ii) such food is actually made available for his consumption on payment of a further charge or charges.

AMENDMENTS

1. Jobseeker's Allowance (Amendment) Regulations 1996 (SI 1996/1516), reg.10(1) (October 7, 1996).

2. Jobseeker's Allowance (Amendment) Regulations 1996 (SI 1996/1516), reg.20 and Sch. (October 7, 1996).

3. Social Security and Child Support (Jobseeker's Allowance) (Miscellaneous Amendments) Regulations 1996 (SI 1996/2538), reg.2(7) (October 28, 1996).

4. Social Security (Miscellaneous Amendments) Regulations 1997 (SI 1997/454), reg.2(10) (April 7, 1997).

5. Social Security (Miscellaneous Amendments) Regulations 1998 (SI 1998/563), reg.8(1) and (2)(d) (April 6, 1998).

6. Social Security (Miscellaneous Amendments) Regulations 1998 (SI 1998/563), reg.18(3) and (4)(d) (April 6, 1998).

7. Social Security (Immigration and Asylum) Consequential Amendments Regulations 2000 (SI 2000/636), reg.4(3)(a) (April 3, 2000).

8. Income-related Benefits and Jobseeker's Allowance (Amendment) Regulations 2000 (SI 2000/979), reg.3 (May 2, 2000).

9. Social Security Amendment (Residential Care and Nursing Homes) Regulations 2001 (SI 2001/3767), reg.2 and Sch., Pt II, para.6 (April 8, 2002).

10. Social Security (Removal of Residential Allowance and Miscellaneous Amendments) Regulations 2003 (SI 2003/1121), reg.4 and Sch.2, para.4 (October 6, 2003).

11. Social Security (Working Tax Credit and Child Tax Credit) (Consequential Amendments) Regulations 2003 (SI 2003/455), reg.3 and Sch.4, para.1 (April 6, 2004, except in "transitional cases" and see further the note to reg.83 and to reg.17 of the Income Support Regulations).

12. Social Security (Habitual Residence) Amendment Regulations 2004 (SI 2004/1232), reg.4 (May 1, 2004).

DEFINITIONS

"child"—see Jobseekers Act, s.35(1).
"claimant"—*ibid.*
"Income Support Regulations"—see reg.1(3).
"nursing home"—*ibid.*
"residential care home"—*ibid.*
"young person"—see reg.76.

GENERAL NOTE

This regulation only applies to income-based JSA (reg.82).

Applicable amounts in special cases are to be as prescribed in Sch.5.

This provision is similar to reg.21 of the Income Support Regulations. See the notes to that regulation.

Where the benefit claimed is JSA and the claimant is an EEA national, the habitual residence test must now be applied in accordance with the decision of the European Court of Justice in *Collins v Secretary of State for Work and Pensions*, ECJ, Case C.–138/02, March 23, 2004 and the subsequent decision of Commissioner Mesher in *CJSA/4065/1999*. Mr Collins was born and brought up in the USA and had American citizenship. He spent one semester studying in the UK in 1978 and had also spent 10 months doing part-time and casual work in London between 1980 and 1981. During that period he acquired Irish nationality. Since 1981 he had worked in the US and Africa but had not worked in the UK. In 1998 he returned to the UK for settlement and, on June 8, 1998, claimed JSA while he looked for work. On July 1, 1998 an adjudication officer decided that he was not habitually resident. Mr Collins' appeal against that decision was referred to the European Court of Justice by the Commissioner. The Court held that the work which Mr Collins had done in the UK in 1980 and 1981 was not sufficiently closely connected to the work he was seeking in 1998 for him to have retained his former status as a "worker" and that he therefore was in the same position—from an EU/EEA law point of view—as someone who had never worked in the UK. On that basis—as noted in the commentary to reg.21 of the Income Support Regulations—the Court held that:

- Mr Collins was not a "worker" for the purposes of Title II of Part I of Regulation 1612/68; and

- Directive 68/630 only accords rights of residence to those already in employment and therefore Mr Collins did not have a right of residence under that provision.

Up to this point, the decision of the Court breaks no new ground. However, in its answer to the third question referred to it, the Court went on to hold that in the light of the establishment (by the Maastricht Treaty) of EU citizenship and of its previous decision in Case C—184/99 *Grzelzyk v Belgium*, it was no longer possible to exclude from the scope of Article 48(2) of the Treaty—which abolishes discrimination based on nationality between workers of the Member States as regards employment, remuneration and other conditions of work and employment (see Vol. III)—a benefit of a financial nature intended to facilitate access to employment in the labour market of a Member State. As the habitual residence test could more easily be met by UK nationals, it disadvantaged nationals of other Member States who had exercised their rights of movement to seek employment and could only be justified if it was based on objective considerations which were independent of the nationality of the persons concerned and proportionate to the legitimate aim of the national provisions. Although Member States were entitled to ensure that there was a genuine link between the person seeking work and the employment market of that State before granting an allowance such as JSA, and although that link might be determined by the fact that the claimant had genuinely sought work in the Member State in question for a reasonable period, a residence requirement could not, if it was to be proportionate, go beyond what was necessary to obtain the objective of ensuring such a link:

> "More specifically, its application by the national authorities must rest on clear criteria known in advance and provision must be made for the possibility of a means of redress of a judicial nature. In any event, if compliance with the requirement demands a period of residence, the period must not exceed what is necessary in order for the national authorities to be able to satisfy themselves that the person concerned is genuinely seeking work in the employment market of the host Member State."

Mr Collins' appeal therefore returned to the Commissioner to decide the issue of justification in accordance with the ruling of the Court. The Commissioner rejected the submissions of counsel for Mr Collins (which were along similar lines to the views expressed in the previous edition) that the answer to the question of whether the claimant was genuinely seeking work was provided by the satisfaction of the other conditions of entitlement to JSA so that there was no justifiable role left for a habitual residence test, or that, in the alternative, the habitual residence test as established by reg. 85 and interpreted by the courts (including the ECJ) did not "rest on clear criteria known in advance" as the ECJ had required. Rather:

> ". . . the application of the residence requirement embodied in the habitual residence test in the JSA legislation and in Article 10a of Regulation 1408/71 is, subject to the proviso mentioned below, justified by objective considerations independent of the nationality of the claimant and proportionate to the legitimate aim in the making of the JSA legislation. The requirement meets the conditions as to proportionality set out in paragraph 72 of the ECJ's judgment in relation to the legitimate aim of establishing that a real or genuine link exists between a claimant and the UK employment market, such as by being satisfied of the genuineness of the claimant's search for work in that employment market."

The proviso referred to is that if, on any day, the answer to the question "has the point been reached on that day that the relevant national authority has become satisfied of the genuineness of the claimant's search for work [in the sense referred to in the next paragraph]?" is answered yes, the result of the normal habitual residence test can no longer be applied in his case.

An important part of the Commissioner's decision is that, for the purpose of assessing whether the habitual residence test is proportional, the genuineness of the claimant's search for work is not established on the basis that s/he satisfies the labour market conditions for entitlement to JSA for a particular week:

> "32. I leave aside for the moment what was said in paragraph 72 of the ECJ's judgment about proportionality, clear criteria and means of redress. The crucial sentence is then this:
>
> > "In any event, if compliance with the [residence] requirement demands a period of residence, the period must not exceed what is necessary in order for the national authorities to be able to satisfy themselves that the person concerned is genuinely seeking work in the employment market of the host Member State."
>
> 33. First, I have no doubt that that sentence does not have the effect that the sole legitimate question to be asked is whether the claimant was genuinely seeking work on any particular day, in the sense merely of taking active and appropriate steps to seek suitable work. The relevant legitimate aim in making the JSA legislation, as identified by the ECJ, is the wish to ensure that there is a genuine link (or in other words a real link) between the claimant and the UK employment market. That is the aim in relation to which proportionality must be tested.
>
> 34. Then, paragraph 69 of the judgment spells out that in pursuance of that aim it is legitimate to award benefit only after it has been possible to establish that such a link exists. And it is plainly accepted in paragraphs 69 and 70 that it is legitimate only to accept that there is such a link at any particular date if there has previously been some sufficiently concrete expression of a connection with the UK employment market. It also seems to me that the notion of a genuine link or a real link carries with it a sense that the link has to have some concrete expression. In that context, I conclude that the pivotal part of the final sentence of paragraph 72 is the reference to what period of residence is necessary for the national authorities to be able to satisfy themselves that the claimant is genuinely seeking work. To be consistent with what has been said earlier, it must be legitimate for the national authorities to say that they are not able to satisfy themselves about the genuineness of a search for work until a proper search has continued for some period. A person may actually take steps to search for work on a particular day and actually have on that day an intention to continue to search diligently for suitable vacancies, but national authorities can legitimately say that they have not been satisfied that the search is genuine until they have seen that the search has been sustained, and in a sufficiently diligent and well-directed form, for some period. The condition of proportionality laid down by the final sentence of paragraph 72 is thus that a residence requirement, in principle appropriate, cannot be applied to deny entitlement to benefit beyond the date at which the relevant national authority has become satisfied of the genuineness of the claimant's search for work."

Applying those principles to Mr Collins' appeal the Commissioner held that Mr Collins had not been habitually resident from June 8, 1998 to July 1, 1998 and, on the assumption that *CIS/3280/2003* and others was correctly decided (as to which see the commentary to reg. 21 of the IS Regulations under the heading '*Habitual residence and "down to the date of decision"*'), would not have become so by July 31, 1998, shortly after which, Mr Collins found work.

Applicable amounts for persons in residential care and nursing homes

3.328   **86.**—[¹. . .]

AMENDMENT

1. Social Security Amendment (Residential Care and Nursing Homes) Regulations 2001 (SI 2001/3767), reg.2 and Sch., Pt II, para.7 (April 8, 2002).

[1Applicable amounts for joint-claim couples

3.329   **86A.** Except in the case of a joint-claim couple where regulation 86B (polygamous marriages), [²or 86C] (special cases) [². . .] or Part X (urgent cases) applies, the applicable amount of a joint-claim couple who are jointly claiming a jobseeker's allowance shall be the aggregate of such of the following amounts as may apply in their case—
    (a) an amount in respect of the joint-claim couple determined in accordance with sub-paragraph (3) of paragraph 1 of Schedule 1;
    (b) [³. . .]
    (c) the amount of any premiums which may be applicable to either or both members of the joint-claim couple, determined in accordance with Parts IVA and IVB of Schedule 1 (premiums); and
    (d) any amounts determined in accordance with Schedule 2 (housing costs) which may be applicable to the joint-claim couple in respect of mortgage interest payments or such other housing costs as are prescribed in that Schedule.]

AMENDMENTS

3.330   1. Jobseeker's Allowance (Joint Claims) Regulations 2000 (SI 2000/1978), reg.2(5) and Sch.2, para.35 (March 19, 2001).
2. Social Security Amendment (Residential Care and Nursing Homes) Regulations 2001 (SI 2001/3767), reg.2 and Sch., Pt II, para.8 (April 8, 2002).
3. Social Security (Removal of Residential Allowance and Miscellaneous Amendments) Regulations 2003 (SI 2003/1121), reg. 4 and Sch. 2, para. 5 (October 6, 2003).

GENERAL NOTE

This regulation applies to income-based JSA only (see reg.82). It makes provision corresponding to reg.83 for joint-claim couples.

[¹Applicable amounts for joint-claim couples: polygamous marriages

3.331   **86B.** Except in the case of a joint-claim couple where regulation 86A, [²or 86C] (special cases) [². . .] or Part X (urgent cases) applies, the applicable amount of a joint-claim couple who are jointly claiming a jobseeker's allowance where either or both members of that couple are members of a polygamous marriage, shall be the aggregate of such of the following amounts as may apply in their case—
    (a) the highest amount applicable to a member of the joint-claim couple and one other member of that marriage determined in accordance with sub-paragraph (3) of paragraph 1 of Schedule 1 as if those members were a couple;
    (b) an amount equal to the difference between the amounts specified in sub-paragraphs (3)(e) and (1)(e) of paragraph 1 of Schedule 1 in respect of each of the other members of the polygamous marriage who are members of that household;

(c) [³ . . .]

(d) the amount of any premiums which may be applicable to a member of the joint-claim couple determined in accordance with Parts IVA and IVB of Schedule 1 (premiums); and

(e) any amounts determined in accordance with Schedule 2 (housing costs) which may be applicable to the joint-claim couple in respect of mortgage interest payments or such other housing costs as are prescribed in that Schedule.]

AMENDMENTS

1. Jobseeker's Allowance (Joint Claims) Regulations 2000 (SI 2000/1978), reg.2(5) and Sch.2, para.35 (March 19, 2001).

2. Social Security Amendment (Residential Care and Nursing Homes) Regulations 2001 (SI 2001/3767), reg.2 and Sch., Pt II, para.8 (April 8, 2002).

3. Social Security (Removal of Residential Allowance and Miscellaneous Amendments) Regulations 2003 (SI 2003/1121), reg.4 and Sch.2, para.6 (October 6, 2003).

3.332

GENERAL NOTE

This regulation applies to income-based JSA only (see reg.82). It makes provision corresponding to reg.84 for joint-claim couples.

[¹Joint-claim couples: special cases

86C.—(1) [²[³Where]] a member of a joint-claim couple is a person to whom any paragraph in column (1) of Schedule 5A applies (applicable amounts in special cases for joint-claim couples), the amount included in the joint-claim couple's weekly applicable amount shall be the amount prescribed in the corresponding paragraph in column (2) of that Schedule.

(2) Except where the amount prescribed in Schedule 5A in respect of a joint-claim couple includes an amount applicable under regulation 86A(c) or 86B(d), a person to whom paragraph (1) applies shall be treated as not falling within the conditions specified in paragraph 20I of Schedule 1 (severe disability premium).

[²(2A) [³. . .]

(3) In Schedule 5A, for the purposes of [³paragraph 1 (patients)], where a person has been a patient for two or more distinct periods separated by one or more intervals each not exceeding 28 days, he shall be treated as having been a patient continuously for a period equal in duration to the total of those distinct periods.

(4) Expressions used in this regulation and in Schedule 5A shall have the same meaning as those expressions have for the purposes of regulation 85 and Schedule 5 save that for the purposes of this regulation and of Schedule 5A, the definition of "person from abroad" in regulation 85(4) shall have effect as if after the words "a claimant" there were inserted the words ",other than a member of a joint-claim couple who is not the nominated member for the purposes of section 3B,".]

3.333

AMENDMENTS

1. Jobseeker's Allowance (Joint Claims) Regulations 2000 (SI 2000/1978), reg.2(5) and Sch.2, para.35 (March 19, 2001).

2. Social Security Amendment (Residential Care and Nursing Homes) Regulations 2001 (SI 2001/3767), reg.2 and Sch., Pt II, para.9 (April 8, 2002).

3.334

3. Social Security (Miscellaneous Amendments) Regulations 2004 (SI 2004/565), reg.6 (April 1, 2004).

GENERAL NOTE

This regulation applies to income-based JSA only (see reg.82). It makes provision corresponding to reg.85 for joint-claim couples.

[¹Applicable amount for a joint-claim couple where a member is in residential care or a nursing home

3.335   **86D.**—[². . .]]

AMENDMENTS

1. Jobseeker's Allowance (Joint Claims) Regulations 2000 (SI 2000/1978), reg.2(5) and Sch.2, para.35 (March 19, 2001).
2. Social Security Amendment (Residential Care and Nursing Homes) Regulations 2001 (SI 2001/3767), reg.2 and Sch., Pt II, para.10 (April 8, 2002).

3.336   GENERAL NOTE

This regulation applied to income-based JSA only (see reg.82). It made provision corresponding to reg.86 for joint-claim couples.

Transitional supplement to income-based jobseeker's allowance

3.337   **87.**—(1) In the case of a person who, before 7th October 1996 was entitled to a special transitional addition or transitional addition in accordance with the Income Support (Transitional) Regulations 1987, the amount of any income-based jobseeker's allowance payable to him shall be increased by an amount equal to those additions, but the increase shall continue to be payable only for so long as the claimant continues to satisfy the requirements imposed in those Regulations for payment of the addition.

(2) A claimant's weekly applicable amount shall include an amount (the "protected sum") equal to any protected sum which would have been applicable in his case under regulation 17(1)(g) or 18(1)(h) of, and Schedules 3A and 3B to, the Income Support Regulations had he been entitled to income support and not a jobseeker's allowance.

(3) In the case of any person who had he been entitled to income support and not a jobseeker's allowance, would in any week have had a higher applicable amount, in accordance with regulation 17(2) to (6A) of the Income Support Regulations, than the amount applicable to him in accordance with regulation 82 or, as the case may be, 83 then that amount shall be substituted for the applicable amount determined under that regulation.

(4) Paragraph (5) applies to a person who, had he been entitled to income support and not a jobseeker's allowance, would have been a person to whom any of the following transitional or savings provisions would have applied—

(a) the Income Support (General) Amendment No.3 Regulations 1993 ("the 1993 Regulations"), regulation 4;
(b) the Income-related Benefits Schemes (Miscellaneous Amendments) Regulations 1995 ("the 1995 Regulations"), regulation 28.

(5) Where this paragraph applies, the amount of housing costs applicable in the particular case shall be determined as if, in Schedule 2—

(a) in a case to which regulation 4(1) of the 1993 Regulations would have applied, paragraph 10(4) to (9) was omitted;

(b) in a case to which regulation 4(4) of the 1993 Regulations would have applied, in [¹paragraph 10(4)] for the reference to £100,000 there was substituted a reference to £150,000; and

(c) in a case to which the 1995 Regulations apply, in [¹paragraph 10(4)] for the reference to £100,000 there was substituted a reference to £125,000.

(6) In determining for the purposes of this regulation whether, if the claimant were entitled to income support—

(a) an amount would be applicable;

(b) an amount would be payable; or

(c) if an amount was payable, the rate at which it would be payable,

any requirement that the person be entitled to income support, or to income support for any period of time, shall be treated as if the reference to income support included also a reference to an income-based jobseeker's allowance.

(7) [²For the purposes of applying paragraph (1), regulation 2A of the Income Support (Transitional) Regulations, and for the purposes of paragraph (6), regulation 3A of the Income Support Regulations shall have effect in accordance with the following sub-paragraphs—]

(a) as if in paragraph (1)(a), after the words "permitted period", there was included the words "subject to paragraph 2A"; and

(b) with the addition after paragraph (1) of the following paragraphs—

"(2A) Subject to paragraph (2B) where the claimant or his partner has ceased to be engaged in remunerative work, the permitted period shall be 8 weeks if—

(a) a jobseeker's allowance [²is not payable] to the claimant in the circumstances mentioned in section 19(6)(a) or (b) of the Jobseekers Act 1995 (employment left voluntarily or lost through misconduct); or

(b) the claimant or his partner has ceased to be engaged in that work within 4 weeks of beginning it; or

(c) at any time during the period of 13 weeks immediately preceding the beginning of that work, the person who has ceased to be engaged in it—

(i) was engaged in remunerative work; or

(ii) was in relevant education; or

(iii) was a student.

(2B) [¹Paragraph (2A)(b) or (2A)(c)] shall not apply in the case of a person who, by virtue of regulation 74 of the Jobseeker's Allowance Regulations 1996, is a person to whom section 19(6)(b) of the Jobseekers Act 1995 does not apply.

(2C) In this regulation, 'remunerative work' means remunerative work for the purposes of the Jobseekers Act 1995."

AMENDMENTS

1. Jobseeker's Allowance (Amendment) Regulations 1996 (SI 1996/1516), reg.20 and Sch. (October 7, 1996).

3.338

2. Jobseeker's Allowance and Income Support (General) (Amendment) Regulations 1996 (SI 1996/1517), reg.20 (October 7, 1996).

DEFINITIONS

"claimant"—see Jobseekers Act, s.35(1)
"Income Support Regulations"—*ibid.*
"remunerative work"—see reg.51(1).

GENERAL NOTE

3.339   This provision only applies to income-based JSA (reg.82).

Paras (2) to (5) preserve the effect of various income support transitional protection provisions for JSA claimants who would have been covered by them had they been entitled to claim income support after October 6, 1996. Para. (1) concerns those who were entitled to a special transitional addition or transitional addition under the Income Support (Transitional) Regulations before October 7, 1996. For the regulations referred to in para.(4) see p.668 and p.671. The effect of those regulations is explained in the notes to para.11((4)–(11) of Sch.3 to the Income Support Regulations.

[¹Minimum amount of a jobseeker's allowance

3.340   **87A.** Where the amount of a jobseeker's allowance is less than 10 pence week that allowance shall not be payable.]

AMENDMENT

1. Jobseeker's Allowance and Income Support (General) (Amendment) Regulations 1996 (SI 1996/1517), reg.21 (October 7, 1996).

PART VIII

INCOME AND CAPITAL

Chapter I

General

Calculation of income and capital of members of claimant's family and of a polygamous marriage

3.341   **88.**—(1) Subject to [³ paragraph] (3) [²and [³regulation] 88ZA (calculation of income and capital of a joint-claim couple)] [³ . . .], the income and capital of a claimant's partner [³. . .] which by virtue of section 13(2) is to be treated as the income and capital of the claimant, shall be calculated in accordance with the following provisions of this Part in like manner as for the claimant; and any reference to the "claimant" shall, except where the context otherwise requires, be construed, for the purposes of this Part, as if it were a reference to his partner [³. . .].

[³(2) Subject to the following provisions of this Part, the income paid to, or in respect of, and capital of, a child or young person who is a member of the claimant's family shall not be treated as the income or capital of the claimant.]

(3) Where at least one member of a couple is aged less than 18 and the applicable amount of the couple falls to be determined under [¹paragraph 1(3)(b), (c), (g) or (h)] of Schedule 1 (applicable amounts), the income of the claimant's partner shall not be treated as the income of the claimant to the extent that—

  (a) in the case of a couple where both members are aged less than 18, the amount specified in paragraph 1(3)(a) of that Schedule exceeds the amount specified in paragraph 1(3)(c) of that Schedule; and

  (b) in the case of a couple where only one member is aged less than 18, the amount specified in paragraph 1(3)(e) of that Schedule exceeds the amount which applies in that case which is specified in [¹paragraph 1(3)(g) or (h)] of that Schedule.

(4) Subject to paragraph (5), where a claimant is married polygamously to two or more members of his household—

(a) the claimant shall be treated as possessing capital and income belonging to each such member [³ . . .]; and

(b) the income and capital of that member [³ . . .] shall be calculated in accordance with the following provisions of this Part in like manner as for the claimant [³ . . .].

(5) Where a member of a polygamous marriage is a partner aged less than 18 and the amount which applies in respect of him under regulation 84(2) (polygamous marriages) is nil, the claimant shall not be treated as possessing the income of that partner to the extent that an amount in respect of him would have been included in the applicable amount if he had fallen within the circumstances set out in regulation 84(2)(a) or (b).

AMENDMENTS

1. Jobseeker's Allowance (Amendment) Regulations 1996 (SI 1996/1516), reg.20 and Sch. (October 7, 1996).

2. Jobseeker's Allowance (Joint Claims) Regulations 2000 (SI 2000/1978), reg.2(5) and Sch.2, para.36 (March 19, 2001).

3. Social Security (Working Tax Credit and Child Tax Credit) (Consequential Amendments) Regulations 2003 (SI 2003/455), reg.3 and Sch.2, para.6 (April 6, 2004, except in "transitional cases" and see further the note to reg.83 and to reg.17 of the Income Support Regulations).

3.342

DEFINITIONS

"child"—see Jobseekers Act, s.35(1).
"claimant"—*ibid.*
"family"—*ibid.*
"joint-claim couple"—see JSA, s.1(4).
"partner"—see reg.1(3).
"polygamous marriage"—*ibid.*
"young person"—see reg.76.

GENERAL NOTE

This regulation contains the basic rule on aggregation of resources which is the same as that in reg.23 of the Income Support Regulations. With effect from April 6, 2004 (except in "transitional cases"—see the note to reg.83 and to reg.17 of the Income Support Regulations), only the income and capital of the claimant's partner is treated as the claimant's.

Under the form of reg.88 in force before April 6, 2004 (the old form continues to apply for "transitional cases"—see the note to reg.83 and to reg.17 of the Income Support Regulations) the income (but not the capital) of a child or young person who was a member of the claimant's family was aggregated with the claimant's (see the 2003 edition of this volume for the old form of reg.88 and the notes to that regulation for further details of the former rules relating to treatment of a child or young person's income and capital). However, with effect from April 6, 2004 (except in "transitional cases") amounts for children and young persons have been removed from income-based JSA; financial assistance to help with the cost of bringing up a child or young person is now to be provided through the child tax credit system, see Vol. IV of this series. As a consequence the new form of para.(2) provides that income paid to, or in respect of, and the capital of, a child or young person does not count as that of the claimant. Note the new disregards of child benefit and child tax credit (see para.6B of Sch.7) (for income-based JSA claimants who had an award of

3.343

child tax credit before April 6, 2004 see reg.8 of the Social Security (Working Tax Credit and Child Tax Credit) (Consequential Amendments) Regulations 2003 (SI 2003/455) (as amended) on p.687 and the notes to that regulation).

See further the notes to reg.23.

The aggregation rule is primarily relevant to income-based JSA (although reg.88 applies to both contribution and income-based JSA), since for contribution-based JSA only the *claimant's* earnings and pension payments are taken into account (see s.2(1)(c) and 4(1) of the Jobseekers Act and regs 56(2), 80(2) and 81).

[¹ Calculation of income and capital of a joint-claim couple

3.344   **88ZA.**—(1) Subject to paragraphs (2) and (4), the income and capital of a joint-claim couple shall be calculated by—

(a) determining the income and capital of each member of that couple in accordance with this Part; and

(b) aggregating the amount determined in respect of each member in accordance with sub-paragraph (a) above.

(2) Where—

(a) a member of a joint-claim couple is aged less than 18;

(b) the other member is aged over 18; and

(c) the applicable amount of the couple falls to be determined under paragraph 1(3)(g) or (h) of Schedule 1 (applicable amounts),

the income of the joint-claim couple shall not be aggregated to the extent that the amount specified in paragraph 1(3)(e) of that Schedule exceeds the amount which applies in that case which is specified in paragraph 1(3)(g) or (h) of that Schedule.

(3) Where a member of a joint-claim couple is married polygamously to two or more members of his household, the joint-claim couple shall be treated as possessing income and capital belonging to each such member and the income and capital of that member shall be calculated in accordance with the following provisions of this Part in like manner as for each member of the joint-claim couple.

(4) Regulations 99(2) and 101(2) in so far as they relate to paragraphs 5,7, 8 and 11 of Schedule 6 (earnings to be disregarded) shall not apply to a member of a joint-claim couple but there shall instead be disregarded from the net earnings of a member of a joint-claim couple any sum, where applicable, specified in—

(a) paragraphs 1 to 4 and 13 to 16 of Schedule 6; and

(b) paragraphs 1 to 6 of Schedule 6A.]

AMENDMENT

3.345   1. Jobseeker's Allowance (Joint Claims) Regulations 2000 (SI 2000/1978), reg.2(5) and Sch.2, para.37 (March 19, 2001).

DEFINITIONS

"joint-claim couple"—see JSA, s.1(4).

"polygamous marriage"—see reg.1(3).

[¹ Income of participants in the self-employment route [². . .]

3.346   **88A.** Chapters II, III, IV, V, VII and VIII of this Part and regulations 131 to 136, 138 and 139 shall not apply to any income which is to be calculated in accordance with Chapter IVA of this Part (participants in the self-employment route [². . .]).]

1. Social Security (Miscellaneous Amendments) (No. 4) Regulations 1998 (SI 1998/1174), reg.3(3) (June 1, 1998).
2. Social Security Amendment (Employment Zones) (No. 2) Regulations 2000 (SI 2000/2910), reg.5(2)(a) (November 27, 2000).

DEFINITION

"self-employment route"—see reg.1(3).

GENERAL NOTE

Regulation 88A takes any gross receipts from trading while on the self-employment route (defined in reg.1(3)) out of the categories of earnings, self-employed earnings and income other than earnings. The rules for liable relative payments, payments of child support maintenance and student income (except reg.137) also do not apply. Any such receipts may only be taken into account in accordance with regs 102A to 102D.

3.347

Liable relative payments

89.—Regulations 94 to [¹ 105], 108 to 115 and Chapter IX of this Part shall not apply to any payment which is to be calculated in accordance with Chapter VII thereof (liable relatives).

3.348

AMENDMENT

1. Social Security (Working Tax Credit and Child Tax Credit) (Consequential Amendments) Regulations 2003 (SI 2003/455), reg.3 and Sch.2, para.7 (April 6, 2004, except in "transitional cases" and see further the note to reg.83 and to reg.17 of the Income Support Regulations).

GENERAL NOTE

See reg.25 of the Income Support Regulations.

Child support

90.—Regulations 94, 96, 97, 103 and 105 and Chapters VII and IX of this Part shall not apply to any payment which is to be calculated in accordance with Chapter VIII of this Part (child support).

3.349

GENERAL NOTE

Reg.90 is to the same effect as reg.25A of the Income Support Regulations and takes payments of child support maintenance, paid under an assessment carried out in accordance with the Child Support Acts 1991 to 1995, out of the categories of income other than earnings and of liable relative payments. (Reg. 90 also provides that the provisions relating to full-time students in Chapter IX do not apply to child support maintenance payments; there is no reference to such income support provisions in reg.25A.) Child support maintenance payments are only to be taken into account for the purposes of JSA in accordance with regs 125 to 129 (which are similar to regs 60A to 60E of the Income Support Regulations).

Calculation of income and capital of full-time students

91.—The provisions of Chapters II to VI of this Part (income and capital) shall have effect in relation to full-time students and their partners subject to the modifications set out in Chapter IX thereof (full-time students).

3.350

DEFINITIONS

"full-time student"—see reg.1(3)
"partner"—*ibid.*

GENERAL NOTE

See reg.26 of the Income Support Regulations.

Rounding of fractions

3.351   **92.**—Where any calculation under this Part results in a fraction of a penny that fraction shall, if it would be to the claimant's advantage, be treated as a penny, otherwise it shall be disregarded.

CHAPTER II

INCOME

Calculation of income

3.352   **93.**—(1) For the purposes of [¹ sections 3(1) (the income-based conditions) and 3A(1) (the conditions for claims by joint-claim couples)] (the income-based conditions) the income of a claimant shall be calculated on a weekly basis—

(a) by determining in accordance with this Part, other than Chapter VI, the weekly amount of his income; and

(b) by adding to that amount the weekly income calculated under regulation 116 (calculation of tariff income from capital).

(2) For the purposes of paragraph (1) "income" includes capital treated as income under regulation 104 and income which a claimant is treated as possessing under regulation 105 (notional income).

AMENDMENT

1. Jobseeker's Allowance (Joint Claims) Regulations 2000 (SI 2000/1978), reg.2(5) and Sch.2, para.38 (March 19, 2001).

DEFINITIONS

3.353   "claimant"—see JSA, s.35(1).
"joint-claim couple"—see JSA, s.1(4).

GENERAL NOTE

This confirms that for the purposes of income-based JSA all resources which come under the description of income, including resources specifically treated as earnings or income, are to be taken into account in the income calculation.

Calculation of earnings derived from employed earner's employment and income other than earnings

3.354–   **94.**—(1) Earnings derived from employment as an employed earner and
3.362   income which does not consist of earnings shall be taken into account over a period determined in accordance with the following paragraphs and at a weekly amount determined in accordance with regulation 97 (calculation of weekly amount of income).

(2) Subject to the following provisions of this regulation, the period over which a payment is to be taken into account shall be—

(a) in a case where it is payable in respect of a period, a period equal to the length of that period;

(b) in any other case, a period equal to such number of weeks as is equal to the number obtained (and any fraction shall be treated as a corresponding fraction of a week) by dividing the net earnings, or in the case of income which does not consist of earnings, the amount of that income less any amount paid by way of tax on that income which is disregarded under paragraph 1 of Schedule 7 (sums to be disregarded in the calculation of income other than earnings), by the amount of jobseeker's allowance which would be payable had the payment not been made plus an amount equal to the total of the sums which would fall to be disregarded from that payment under Schedule 6 [⁴ and Schedule 6A] (sums to be disregarded in the calculation of earnings) or, as the case may be, any paragraph of Schedule 7 other than paragraph 1 of that Schedule, as is appropriate in the claimant's case,

and that period shall begin on the date on which the payment is treated as paid under regulation 96.

[¹(2A) The period over which a Career Development Loan, which is paid pursuant to section 2 of the Employment and Training Act 1973, shall be taken into account shall be the period of education and training intended to be supported by that loan.

(2B) Where grant income as defined in Chapter IX of this Part has been paid to a person who ceases to be a full-time student before the end of the period in respect of which that income is payable and, as a consequence, the whole or part of that income falls to be repaid by that person, that income shall be taken into account over the period beginning on the date on which that income is treated as paid under regulation 96 and ending—

(a) on the date on which repayment is made in full; or

[²(aa) where the grant is paid in instalments, on the day before the next instalment would have been paid had the claimant remained a student; or]

(b) on the last date of the academic term or vacation during which that person ceased to be a full-time student

whichever shall first occur.]

(3) Where earnings not of the same kind are derived from the same source and the periods in respect of which those earnings would, but for this paragraph, fall to be taken into account—

(a) overlap, wholly or partly, those earnings shall be taken into account over a period equal to the aggregate length of those periods;

(b) and that period shall begin with the earliest date on which any part of those earnings would otherwise be treated as paid under regulation 96 (date on which income is treated as paid).

(4) In a case to which paragraph (3) applies, earnings under regulation 98 (earnings of employed earners) shall be taken into account in the following order of priority—

(a) earnings normally derived from the employment;

(b) any compensation payment;

(c) any holiday pay.

(5) Where earnings to which regulation 98(1)(b) or (c) (earnings of employed earners) applies are paid in respect of part of a day, those earnings shall be taken into account over a period equal to a day.

(6) Subject to paragraph (7), the period over which a compensation payment is to be taken into account shall be the period beginning on the date on which the payment is treated as paid under regulation 96 (date on which income is treated as paid) and ending—

    (a) subject to sub-paragraph (b), where the person who made the payment represents that it, or part of it, was paid in lieu of notice of termination of employment or on account of the early termination of a contract of employment for a term certain, on the expiry date;

    (b) in a case where the person who made the payment represents that it, or part of it, was paid in lieu of consultation under section 188 of the Trade Union and Labour Relations (Consolidation) Act 1992, on the later of—

        (i) the date on which the consultation period under that section would have ended;

        (ii) in a case where sub-paragraph (a) also applies, the expiry date; or

        (iii) the standard date;

    (c) in any other case, on the standard date.

(7) The maximum length of time over which a compensation payment may be taken into account under paragraph (6) is 52 weeks from the date on which the payment is treated as paid under regulation 96.

(8) In this regulation—

    (a) "compensation payment" means any payment to which paragraph (3) of regulation 98 (earnings of employed earners) applies;

    (b) "the expiry date" means in relation to the termination of a person's employment—

        (i) the date on which the period of notice applicable to the person was due to expire, or would have expired had it not been waived; and for this purpose "period of notice" means the period of notice of termination of employment to which a person is entitled by statute or by contract, whichever is the longer, or, if he is not entitled to such notice, the period of notice which is customary in the employment in question; or

        (ii) subject to paragraph (9), where the person who made the payment represents that the period in respect of which that payment is made is longer than the period of notice referred to in head (i) above, the date on which that longer period is due to expire; or

        (iii) where the person had a contract of employment for a term certain, the date on which it was due to expire;

    (c) "the standard date" means the earlier of—

        (i) the expiry date; and

        (ii) the last day of the period determined by dividing the amount of the compensation payment by the maximum weekly amount which, on the date on which the payment is treated as paid under regulation 96, is specified in paragraph 8(1)(c) of Schedule 14 to the Employment Protection (Consolidation) Act 1978, and treating the result (less any fraction of a whole number) as a number of weeks.

(9) For the purposes of paragraph (8), if it appears to [³the Secretary of State] in a case to which sub-paragraph (b)(ii) of that paragraph applies that, having regard to the amount of the compensation payment and the level of remuneration normally received by the claimant when he was engaged in the employment in respect of which the compensation payment was made, it is

unreasonable to take the payment into account until the date specified in that sub-paragraph, the expiry date shall be the date specified in paragraph (8)(b)(i).

(10) For the purposes of this regulation the claimant's earnings and income which does not consist of earnings shall be calculated in accordance with Chapters III and V respectively of this Part.

AMENDMENTS

1. Income-related Benefits and Jobseeker's Allowance (Miscellaneous Amendments) Regulations 1997 (SI 1997/65), reg.5(2) (April 7, 1997).   **3.363**

2. Social Security (Miscellaneous Amendments) Regulations 1998 (SI 1998/563), reg.12 (April 6, 1998).

3. Social Security Act 1998 (Commencement No.11, and Savings and Consequential and Transitional Provisions) Order 1999 (SI 1999/2860 (C.75)), art.3(12) and Sch.12, para.2 (October 18, 1999).

4. Jobseeker's Allowance (Joint Claims) Regulations 2000 (SI 2000/1978), reg.2(5) and Sch.2, para.39 (March 19, 2001).

DEFINITIONS

"claimant"—*ibid*, reg.88(1)
"earnings"—see reg.1(3).
"employed earner"—see reg.3, SSCBA, s.2(1)(a).
"full-time student"—see reg.1(3).
"grant income"—see reg.130.

GENERAL NOTE

On paras (1) to (5) see the notes to reg.29(1) to (4A) of the Income Support   **3.364**
Regulations. Under paras (3) and (4) note the differences between the disregards in paras 1 to 3 of Sch.8 to the Income Support Regulations and paras 1 to 4 of Sch.6 to the JSA Regulations (see the notes to Sch.6), and the differences between reg.35 of the Income Support Regulations and reg.98 of the JSA Regulations (see the notes to reg.98).

Note the effect of reg.52(3) where a person who was in remunerative work receives holiday pay which counts as earnings (see reg.98(1)(c)).

Paras (6) to (9)

These provisions define the length of the period for which a "compensation   **3.365**
payment" (defined in reg.98(3)) is to be taken into account. If the person receiving the payment was in remunerative work (see reg.51) he will be treated as in remunerative work for the period covered by the payment (see reg, 52(3)). There is no equivalent to reg.29(4C) of the Income Support Regulations so it seems that a compensation payment made on the termination of part-time employment will be taken into account as earnings for the period covered by the payment.

See *CJSA 5529/1997* in which the effect of para.(6) was that the period to which the claimant's compensation payment was to be attributed ended before it started. On October 1, 1996 the claimant agreed with her employer that her employment would end on December 31, 1996 by way of voluntary redundancy. She was to receive a payment of £41,500 on January 4, 1997, which would not include any sum in lieu of notice. She claimed JSA with effect from January 1, 1997. The Commissioner states that the period for which the compensation period was to be taken into account under para.(6) ended on the "standard date". Under para.(8)(c) the standard date was the earlier of the "expiry date" and what might be termed the "apportionment date". The expiry date in this case was no later than December 31, 1996 because the claimant was entitled to 12 weeks (or three months') notice and the agreement for redundancy had been made on October 1, 1996 (see para.(8)(b)(i)). The result was that there was no period in respect of which the compensation payment was to be taken into account and thus no period during which she was to be treated as in remunerative work after December 31, 1996.

Calculation of earnings of self-employed earners

3.366   **95.**—(1) Except where paragraph (2) applies, where a claimant's income consists of earnings from employment as a self-employed earner the weekly amount of his earnings shall be determined by reference to his average weekly earnings from that employment—

(a) over a period of one year; or

(b) where the claimant has recently become engaged in that employment or there has been a change which is likely to affect the normal pattern of business, over such other period as may, in any particular case, enable the weekly amount of his earnings to be determined more accurately.

(2) Where the claimant's earnings consist of royalties or sums paid periodically for or in respect of any copyright those earnings shall be taken into account over a period equal to such number of weeks as is equal to the number obtained (and any fraction shall be treated as a corresponding fraction of a week) by dividing the earnings by the amount of jobseeker's allowance which would be payable had the payment not been made plus an amount equal to the total of the sums which would fall to be disregarded from the payment under Schedule 6 [¹ and Schedule 6A] (earnings to be disregarded) as is appropriate in the claimant's case.

(3) For the purposes of this regulation the claimant's earnings shall be calculated in accordance with Chapter IV of this Part.

AMENDMENT

3.367   1. Jobseeker's Allowance (Joint Claims) Regulations 2000 (SI 2000/1978), reg.2(5) and Sch.2, para.40 (March 19, 2001).

DEFINITIONS

"claimant"—see Jobseekers Act, s.35(1), reg.88(1).
"earnings"—see reg.1(3).
"self-employed earner"—*ibid*. SSCBA, s.2(1)(b).

GENERAL NOTE

3.368   See the notes to reg.30 of the Income Support Regulations.

Note the more general exception to the rule in para.(1)(a) that is hidden in reg.101(11) which allows the amount of any item of income or expenditure to be calculated over a different period if that will produce a more accurate figure.

Date on which income is treated as paid

3.369   **96.**—(1) Except where paragraph (2) [¹ or (3)] applies, a payment of income to which regulation 94 (calculation of earnings derived from employed earner's employment and income other than earnings) applies shall be treated as paid—

(a) in the case of a payment which is due to be paid before the first benefit week pursuant to the claim, on the date on which it is due to be paid;

(b) in any other case, on the first day of the benefit week in which it is due to be paid or the first succeeding benefit week in which it is practicable to take it into account.

(2) Income support, maternity allowance, short-term or long-term incapacity benefit, severe disablement allowance or jobseeker's allowance shall be treated as paid on the day of the benefit week in respect of which it is payable.

[³ (3) Working tax credit or child tax credit shall be treated as paid—

(a) where the award of that tax credit begins on the first day of a benefit week, on that day, or

(b) on the first day of the benefit week that follows the date the award begins, or

(c) on the first day of the first benefit week that follows the date an award of income-based jobseeker's allowance begins, if later,

until the last day of the last benefit week that coincides with or immediately follows the last day for which the award of that tax credit is made.]

AMENDMENTS

1. Social Security (Miscellaneous Amendments) Regulations 2000 (SI 2000/681), reg.3(2) (April 3, 2000).

2. Income-related Benefits and Jobseeker's Allowance (Working Tax Credit and Child Tax Credit) (Amendment) Regulations 2002 (SI 2002/2402), reg.3 and Sch.2, para.4 (April 6, 2003).

3. Social Security (Working Tax Credit and Child Tax Credit) (Consequential Amendments) (No. 3) Regulations 2003 (SI 2003/1731), reg.4 (August 8, 2003).

3.370

DEFINITIONS

"benefit week"—see reg.1(3)
"child tax credit"—*ibid.*
"working tax credit"—*ibid.*

GENERAL NOTE

See the notes to reg.31 of the Income Support Regulations.

Calculation of weekly amount of income

97.—(1) For the purposes of regulation 94 (calculation of earnings derived from employed earner's employment and income other than earnings), subject to paragraphs (2) to [²(7)], where the period in respect of which a payment is made—

3.371

(a) does not exceed a week, the weekly amount shall be the amount of that payment;

(b) exceeds a week, the weekly amount shall be determined—

(i) in a case where that period is a month, by multiplying the amount of the payment by 12 and dividing the product by 52;

(ii) in a case where that period is three months, by multiplying the amount of the payment by 4 and dividing the product by 52;

(iii) in a case where that period is a year by dividing the amount of the payment by 52;

(iv) in any other case by multiplying the amount of the payment by 7 and dividing the product by the number equal to the number of days in the period in respect of which it is made.

(2) Where a payment for a period not exceeding a week is treated under regulation 96(1)(a) (date on which income is treated as paid) as paid before the first benefit week and a part is to be taken into account for some days only in that week ("the relevant days"), the amount to be taken into account for the relevant days shall be calculated by multiplying the amount of the

payment by the number equal to the number of relevant days and dividing the product by the number of days in the period in respect of which it is made.

(3) Where a payment is in respect of a period equal to or in excess of a week and a part thereof is to be taken into account for some days only in a benefit week ("the relevant days"), the amount to be taken into account for the relevant days shall, except where paragraph (4) applies, be calculated by multiplying the amount of the payment by the number equal to the number of relevant days and dividing the product by the number of days in the period in respect of which it is made.

(4) In the case of a payment of—

(a) maternity allowance, short-term or long-term incapacity benefit or severe disablement allowance, the amount to be taken into account for the relevant days shall be the amount of benefit payable in respect of those days;

(b) jobseeker's allowance or income support, the amount to be taken into account for the relevant days shall be calculated by multiplying the weekly amount of the benefit by the number of relevant days and dividing the product by seven.

(5) Except in the case of a payment which it has not been practicable to treat under regulation 96(1)(b) as paid on the first day of the benefit week in which it is due to be paid, where a payment of income from a particular source is or has been paid regularly and that payment falls to be taken into account in the same benefit week as a payment of the same kind and from the same source, the amount of that income to be taken into account in any one benefit week shall not exceed the weekly amount determined under paragraph (1)(a) or (b), as the case may be, of the payment which under regulation 96(1)(b) (date on which income is treated as paid) is treated as paid first.

(6) Where the amount of the claimant's income fluctuates and has changed more than once, or a claimant's regular pattern of work is such that he does not work every week, the foregoing paragraphs may be modified so that the weekly amount of his income is determined by reference to his average weekly income—

(a) if there is a recognisable cycle of work, over a period of one complete cycle (including, where the cycle involves periods in which the claimant does no work, those periods but disregarding any other absences);

(b) in any other case, over a period of five weeks or such other period as may, in the particular case, enable the claimant's average weekly income to be determined more accurately.

[[1](7) Where income is taken into account under paragraph (2B) of regulation 94 over the period specified in that paragraph, the amount of that income to be taken into account in respect of any week in that period shall be an amount equal to the amount of that income which would have been taken into account under regulation 131 had the person to whom that income was paid not ceased to be a full-time student.]

AMENDMENTS

3.372   1. Income-related Benefits and Jobseeker's Allowance (Miscellaneous Amendments) Regulations 1997 (SI 1997/65), reg.6(2) (April 7, 1997).

2. Social Security (Miscellaneous Amendments) Regulations 1997 (SI 1997/454), reg.2(11) (April 7, 1997).

DEFINITIONS

"benefit week"—see reg.1(3).
"claimant"—see Jobseekers Act, s.35(1), reg.88(1).
"full-time student"—see reg.1(3).

GENERAL NOTE

See the notes to reg.32 of the Income Support Regulations. In relation to para.(5), **3.373** the JSA disregards corresponding to the income support disregards referred to in those notes are in Sch.6, para.13, Sch.7, para.39, Sch.6, para.16 and Sch.7 para.37.

Note that there is no equivalent of reg.32(7) as the JSA rules for the treatment of compensation payments made on the termination of part-time employment are different from those under the income support scheme (see reg.98(1)(b) and (3) and the note to reg.94(6) to (9)).

On calculation of entitlement to income-based JSA for part-weeks, see reg.150.

Chapter III

Employed Earners

Earnings of employed earners

98.—(1) Subject to paragraphs (2) and (3), "earnings" means in the case **3.374** of employment as an employed earner, any remuneration or profit derived from that employment and includes—

(a) any bonus or commission;

(b) any compensation payment;

(c) any holiday pay except any payable more than four weeks after the termination or interruption of employment but this exception shall not apply to a person who is, or would be, prevented from being entitled to a jobseeker's allowance by section 14 (trade disputes);

(d) any payment by way of a retainer;

(e) any payment made by the claimant's employer in respect of expenses not wholly, exclusively and necessarily incurred in the performance of the duties of the employment, including any payment made by the claimant's employer in respect of—

   (i) travelling expenses incurred by the claimant between his home and place of employment;

   (ii) expenses incurred by the claimant under arrangements made for the care of a member of his family owing to the claimant's absence from home;

[¹(f) any payment or award of compensation made under section 68(2), 69, 71(2)(a), 77 or 79 of the Employment Protection (Consolidation) Act 1978 (remedies for unfair dismissal and compensation);

(ff) any payment or remuneration made under section 12, 19 or 47 of the Employment Protection (Consolidation) Act 1978 (guaranteed payments, remuneration whilst suspended from work on medical or maternity grounds);]

(g) any award of compensation made under section 156, 157, 161 to 166, 189 or 192 of the Trade Union and Labour Relations (Consolidation) Act 1992 (compensation for unfair dismissal or redundancy on grounds of involvement in trade union activities, and protective awards).

[³(h) the amount of any payment by way of a non-cash voucher which has been taken into account in the computation of a person's earnings in accordance with regulation 18(22) to (25) of the Social Security (Contributions) Regulations 1979.]

(2) "Earnings" shall not include—

(a) [³ Subject to paragraph (2A),] any payment in kind;

(b) any periodic sum paid to a claimant on account of the termination of his employment by reason of redundancy;

(c) any remuneration paid by or on behalf of an employer to the claimant in respect of a period throughout which the claimant is on maternity leave [⁴, paternity leave, adoption leave] or is absent from work because he is ill;

(d) any payment in respect of expenses wholly, exclusively and necessarily incurred in the performance of the duties of the employment;

(e) any occupational pension;

(f) any redundancy payment within the meaning of section 81(1) of the Employment Protection (Consolidation) Act 1978;

[²(g) any lump sum payment made under the Iron and Steel Re-adaptation Benefits Scheme].

[³(2A) Paragraph (2)(a) shall not apply in respect of any non-cash voucher referred to in paragraph (1)(h).]

(3) In this regulation "compensation payment" means any payment made in respect of the termination of employment other than—

(a) any remuneration or emolument (whether in money or in kind) which accrued in the period before the termination;

(b) any holiday pay;

(c) any payment specified in paragraphs (1)(f)[,¹(ff),] or (g) or (2);

(d) any refund of contributions to which that person was entitled under an occupational pension scheme.

AMENDMENTS

3.375   1. Jobseeker's Allowance and Income Support (General) (Amendment) Regulations 1996 (SI 1996/1517), reg.22 (October 7, 1996).

2. Social Security (Miscellaneous Amendments) Regulations 1997 (SI 1997/454), reg.2(12) (April 7, 1997).

3. Social Security Amendment (Non-Cash Vouchers) Regulations 1999 (SI 1999/1509), reg.2(6) (July 1, 1999).

4. Social Security (Paternity and Adoption) Amendment Regulations 2002 (SI 2002/2689), reg.3(5) (December 8, 2002).

DEFINITIONS

"adoption leave"—see reg.1(3).
"claimant"—see Jobseekers Act, s.35(1), reg.88(1).
"employed earner"—see reg.3, SSCBA, s.2(1)(a).
"family"—see Jobseekers Act, s.35(1).
"maternity leave"—see reg.1(3).
"occupational pension"—*ibid.*
"paternity leave"—*ibid.*

GENERAL NOTE

3.376   Reg. 98 applies to earnings from employment as an employed earner. It is similar to reg.35 of the Income Support Regulations but there are some differences which are referred to below. Otherwise see the notes to reg.35.

Like reg.35(1), para.(1) first provides a general definition of earnings from employment as an employee—any remuneration or profit derived from that employment—and then deems certain payments to be earnings. Para. (2) provides a number of exceptions and Sch.6 lists items which would otherwise count as earnings which are to be disregarded.

Para. (1)

Note that the particular categories that are deemed to be earnings are the same as for income support, except that there is no equivalent of reg.35(1)(b), (c) and (i); instead sub-para.(b) refers to "any compensation payment" (defined in para.(3)). In addition, sub-paras. (f), (ff) and (g) slightly expand on the list of awards of compensation or pay made by an employment tribunal and other payments under the employment protection legislation that are specifically deemed to count as earnings (compare reg.35(1)(g) and (h)). For guarantee payments under income support, see the note to reg.35(1)(e).

3.377

The categories of earnings that can lead to complete disentitlement to JSA under reg.52(3) are those in sub-paras. (b) and (c) (compensation payments, but note the exclusions from the definition in para.(3), and holiday pay). Holiday pay outside the period in sub-para. (c) is capital (reg.110(3)).

See the notes to reg.35(1) for further discussion.

Para. (2)

Sub-paras. (b) and (f) contain two additions to the list of payments that do not count as earnings, which otherwise are the same as for income support. Sub-para. (b) in fact contains the same provision that in the Income Support Regulations is expressed as an exception to reg.35(1)(b). But by placing it within the first part of the para.(2) list the JSA rules make it clear that such periodic redundancy payments although not earnings will count as income (see below). Sub-para. (f) expressly states that redundancy payments "within the meaning of s.81(1) of the Employment Protection (Consolidation) Act 1978" (now section 135 of the Employment Rights Act 1996) are not earnings, nor are lump sum payments under the Iron and Steel Re-adaptation Benefits Scheme (sub-para.(g)). On the meaning of redundancy payment under sub-para. (f) see *CJSA 82/1998* in the notes to reg.35(1) of the Income Support Regulations.

3.378

Note that although the payments listed in para.(2)(a) to (e) are deemed not to be earnings they do count as other income (reg.103(6)). However, income in kind is disregarded (Sch.7, para.22) and so are payments of necessary expenses (Sch.7, para.3). There is no provision for the disregard of the payments in sub-paras (b), (c) and (e). Under sub-paras (f) and (g) redundancy payments and lump sum payments under the Iron and Steel Re-adaptation Benefits Scheme will count as capital.

See the notes to reg.35(2) for further discussion.

Para. (3)

This provision is different from reg.35(3) (see also reg.35(1)(i) and (1A)) of the Income Support Regulations but is based on the previous unemployment benefit rule. It provides a broad definition of a "compensation payment" as "any payment made in respect of the termination of employment" but then lists those payments which are not to count as compensation payments. If a payment is a compensation payment it counts as earnings under para.(1)(b) and can lead to complete disentitlement to JSA in accordance with reg.52(3) for the period covered by the payment (see reg.94(6) to (9) and note *CJSA 5529/1997* referred to in the note to reg.94(6) to (9)).

3.379

Calculation of net earnings of employed earners

99.—(1) For the purposes of regulation 94 (calculation of earnings of employed earners) the earnings of a claimant derived from employment as an employed earner to be taken into account shall, subject to paragraph (2), be his net earnings.

3.380

(2) Subject to paragraph (3), there shall be disregarded from a claimant's net earnings, any sum, where applicable, specified in paragraphs 1 to 16 and 19 of Schedule 6.

(3) [*Omitted as not relating to income-based jobseeker's allowance.*]

(4) For the purposes of paragraph (1) net earnings shall be calculated by taking into account the gross earnings of the claimant from that employment less—

(a) any amount deducted from those earnings by way of—
    (i) income tax;
    (ii) primary Class 1 contributions payable under the Benefits Act; and
(b) one-half of any sum paid by the claimant in respect of a pay period by way of a contribution towards an occupational or personal pension scheme.

DEFINITIONS

3.381   "the Benefits Act"—see Jobseekers Act, s.35(1).
"claimant"—*ibid.* reg.88(1).
"employed earner"—see reg.3, SSCBA, s.2(1)(a).
"occupational pension scheme"—see Jobseekers Act, s.35(1).
"pay period"—see reg.1(3).
"personal pension scheme"—see Jobseekers Act, s.35(1).

GENERAL NOTE

3.382   See the notes to reg.36 of the Income Support Regulations.

One of the issues discussed in those notes is the decision of the ECJ in *Cresswell v Chief Adjudication Officer, Jackson v Chief Adjudication Officer* [1992] E.C.R. I-4737, also reported as *R(IS)10/91*, which held that income support did not come within EC Directive 79/7 or EC Directive 76/207. The position of income-based JSA however seemed to be different. Income-based JSA is clearly directly concerned with one of the risks in Art.3(1) of Directive 79/7, namely unemployment. Furthermore, Directive 76/207 may also be applicable. Further challenges against discriminatory aspects of income-based JSA, such as the lack of a child care costs disregard for part-time earnings, may therefore be possible (although note the final result of the *Meyers* case also referred to in the note to s.36). And now see *Hockenjos v Secretary of State* [2001] EWCA Civ. 624, [2001] 2 C.M.L.R. 51, [2001] I.C.R. 966, in which the Court of Appeal has held that JSA is a unitary statutory scheme to provide against the risk of unemployment. The result is that both contribution-based and income-based JSA are within the scope of Directive 79/7.

Chapter IV

Self-Employed Earners

Earnings of self-employed earners

3.383   **100.**—(1) Subject to paragraph (2), "earnings", in the case of employment as a self-employed earner, means the gross receipts of the employment and shall include any allowance paid under any scheme referred to in regulation 19(1)(r) (circumstances in which a person is to be treated as actively seeking employment: schemes for assisting persons to become self-employed earners) to the claimant for the purpose of assisting him in carrying on his business.

(2) "Earnings" shall not include—

(a) where a claimant is involved in providing board and lodging accommodation for which a charge is payable, any payment by way of such a charge;

(b) any payment to which paragraph 27 or 28 of Schedule 7 refers (payments in respect of a person accommodated with the claimant under an arrangement made by a local authority or voluntary organisation, and payments made to the claimant by a health authority, local authority or voluntary organisation in respect of persons temporarily in the claimant's care).

[[1](c) any sports award.]

AMENDMENT

1. Social Security Amendment (Sports Awards) Regulations 1999 (SI 1999/2165), reg.7 (3) (August 23, 1999).

3.384

DEFINITIONS

"board and lodging accommodation"—see reg.1(3)
"claimant"—see Jobseekers Act, s.35(1), reg.88(1).
"employment"—see reg.3.
"self-employed earner"—see reg.1(3), SSCBA, s.2(1)(b).
"sports award"—see reg.1(3).
"voluntary organisation"—*ibid.*

GENERAL NOTE

See the notes to reg.37 of the Income Support Regulations.
The payments in para.(2)(a) count as income under reg.103(6) but subject to disregards. Para.(2)(b) applies to payments to foster-parents and to people for providing temporary care in their home. These payments are disregarded as income other than earnings under paras 27 and 28 of Sch.7. Para.(2)(b) ensures that they are not treated as earnings. See also reg.53(f).

3.385

Calculation of net profit of self-employed earners

101.—(1) For the purposes of regulation 95 (calculation of earnings of self-employed earners), the earnings of a claimant to be taken into account shall be—

3.386

(a) in the case of a self-employed earner who is engaged in employment on his own account, the net profit derived from that employment;

(b) in the case of a self-employed earner whose employment is carried on in partnership, or is that of a share fisherman within the meaning of regulation 156, his share of the net profit derived from that employment less—

   (i) an amount in respect of income tax and of social security contributions payable under the Benefits Act calculated in accordance with regulation 102 (deduction of tax and contributions for self-employed earners); and

   (ii) one half of any premium paid in the period that is relevant under regulation 95 in respect of a personal pension scheme.

(2) Subject to paragraph (3), there shall be disregarded from a claimant's net profit any sum, where applicable, specified in paragraphs 1 to 16 of Schedule 6.

(3) For the purposes of calculating the amount to be deducted in respect of earnings under regulation 80 (contribution-based jobseeker's allowance:

deductions in respect of earnings) the disregards in paragraphs 5 to 8 and 11 of Schedule 6 shall not apply.

(4) For the purposes of paragraph (1)(a) the net profit of the employment shall, except where paragraph (10) applies, be calculated by taking into account the earnings of the employment over the period determined under regulation 95 (calculation of earnings of self-employed earners) less—

(a) subject to paragraphs (6) to (8), any expenses wholly and exclusively defrayed in that period for the purposes of that employment;

(b) an amount in respect of—
    (i) income tax; and
    (ii) social security contributions payable under the Benefits Act, calculated in accordance with regulation 102 (deductions of tax and contributions for self-employed earners); and

(c) one-half of any premium paid in the period that is relevant under regulation 95 in respect of a personal pension scheme.

(5) For the purposes of paragraph (1)(b), the net profit of the employment shall be calculated by taking into account the earnings of the employment over the period determined under regulation 95 less, subject to paragraphs (6) to (8), any expenses wholly and exclusively defrayed in that period for the purposes of that employment.

(6) Subject to paragraph (7), no deduction shall be made under paragraph (4)(a) or (5) in respect of—

(a) any capital expenditure;

(b) the depreciation of any capital asset;

(c) any sum employed or intended to be employed in the setting up or expansion of the employment;

(d) any loss incurred before the beginning of the period determined under regulation 95;

(e) the repayment of capital on any loan taken out for the purposes of the employment;

(f) any expenses incurred in providing business entertainment.

(7) A deduction shall be made under paragraph (4)(a) or (5) in respect of the repayment of capital on any loan used for—

(a) the replacement in the course of business of equipment or machinery; and

(b) the repair of an existing business asset except to the extent that any sum is payable under an insurance policy for its repair.

(8) [¹The Secretary of State] shall refuse to make a deduction under paragraph (4)(a) or (5) in respect of any expenses where he is not satisfied that the expense has been defrayed or, having regard to the nature of the expense and its amount, that it has been reasonably incurred.

(9) For the avoidance of doubt—

(a) a deduction shall not be made under paragraph (4)(a) or (5) in respect of any sum unless it has been expended for the purposes of the business;

(b) a deduction shall be made there under in respect of—
    (i) the excess of any VAT paid over VAT received in the period determined under regulation 95;
    (ii) any income expended in the repair of an existing asset except to the extent that any sum is payable under an insurance policy for its repair;
    (iii) any payment of interest on a loan taken out for the purposes of the employment.

(10) Where a claimant is engaged in employment as a child-minder the net profit of the employment shall be one-third of the earnings of that employment, less—
 (a) an amount in respect of—
  (i) income tax; and
  (ii) social security contributions payable under the Benefits Act, calculated in accordance with regulation 102 (deductions of tax and contributions for self-employed earners); and
 (b) one half of any premium paid in the period that is relevant under regulation 95 in respect of a personal pension scheme.

(11) Notwithstanding regulation 95 and the foregoing paragraphs, [¹the Secretary of State] may assess any item of a claimant's income or expenditure over a period other than that determined under regulation 95 such as may, in the particular case, enable the weekly amount of that item of income or expenditure to be determined more accurately.

(12) For the avoidance of doubt where a claimant is engaged in employment as a self-employed earner and he is engaged in one or more other employments as a self-employed or employed earner, any loss incurred in any one of his employments shall not be offset against his earnings in any other of his employments.

AMENDMENT

1. Social Security Act 1998 (Commencement No.11, and Savings and Consequential and Transitional Provisions) Order 1999 (SI 1999/2860 (C.75)), art.3(12) and Sch.12, para.2 (October 18, 1999). **3.387**

DEFINITIONS

"the Benefits Act"—see Jobseekers Act, s.35(1).
"claimant"—*ibid.*, reg.88(1).
"earnings"—see reg.1(3), reg.100.
"employment"—see reg.3.
"personal pension scheme"—see Jobseekers Act, s.35(1).
"self-employed earner"—see reg.1(3), SSCBA, s.2(1)(b).

GENERAL NOTE

See the notes to reg.38 of the Income Support Regulations. **3.388**

Deduction of tax and contributions for self-employed earners

102.—(1) The amount to be deducted in respect of income tax under regulation 101(1)(b)(i), (4)(b)(i) or (10)(a)(i) (calculation of net profit of self-employed earners) shall be calculated on the basis of the amount of chargeable income and as if that income were assessable to income tax at the lower rate or, as the case may be, the lower rate and the basic rate of tax less only the personal relief to which the claimant is entitled under sections 257(1), 257A(1) and 259 of the Income and Corporation Taxes Act 1988 (personal reliefs) as is appropriate to his circumstances; but, if the period determined under regulation 95 is less than a year, the earnings to which the lower rate of tax is to be applied and the amount of the personal relief deductible under this paragraph shall be calculated on a pro rata basis. **3.389**

(2) The amount to be deducted in respect of social security contributions under regulation 101(1)(b)(i), (4)(b)(ii) or (10)(a)(ii) shall be the total of—
 (a) the amount of Class 2 contributions payable under section 11(1) or, as the case may be, 11(3) of the Benefits Act at the rate applicable at

the date of claim except where the claimant's chargeable income is less than the amount specified in section 11(4) of that Act (small earnings exception) for the tax year in which the date of claim falls; but if the period determined under regulation 95 is less than a year, the amount specified for that tax year shall be reduced pro rata; and

(b) the amount of Class 4 contributions (if any) which would be payable under section 15 of that Act (Class 4 contributions recoverable under the Income Tax Acts) at the percentage rate applicable at the date of claim on so much of the chargeable income as exceeds the lower limit but does not exceed the upper limit of profits and gains applicable for the tax year in which the date of claim falls; but if the period determined under regulation 95 is less than a year, those limits shall be reduced pro rata.

(3) In this regulation "chargeable income" means—

(a) except where sub-paragraph (b) applies, the earnings derived from the employment less any expenses deducted under paragraph (4)(a) or, as the case may be, (5), of regulation 101;

(b) in the case of employment as a child minder, one-third of the earnings of that employment.

DEFINITIONS

3.390   "the Benefits Act"—see Jobseekers Act, s.35(1).
"claimant"—*ibid.*, reg.88(1).
"date of claim"—see reg.1(3).
"earnings"—*ibid.*, reg.100.
"lower rate"—see reg.1(3).

GENERAL NOTE

See the notes to reg.39 of the Income Support Regulations.

[¹Chapter IVA

Participants in the self-employment route [³ . . .]

Interpretation

3.391   **102A.** In this Chapter—
[² . . .]
"special account" means, where a person was carrying on a commercial activity in respect of which assistance was received under the self-employment route, the account into which the gross receipts from that activity were payable during the period in respect of which such assistance was received.]

AMENDMENTS

3.392   1. Social Security (Miscellaneous Amendments) (No.4) Regulations 1998 (SI 1998/1174), reg.3(4) (June 1, 1998).
2. Social Security Amendment (Employment Zones) (No.2) Regulations 2000 (SI 2000/2910), reg.5(2)(b) (November 27, 2000).
3. Social Security Amendment (Employment Zones) (No.2) Regulations 2000 (SI 2000/2910), reg.5(2)(c) (November 27, 2000).

DEFINITION

"self-employment route"—see reg.1(3).

GENERAL NOTE

For the definition of the "self-employment route" see reg.1(3).
See the note to reg.102C.

[¹ Treatment of gross receipts of participants in the self-employment route [² . . .]]

102B. The gross receipts of a commercial activity carried on by a person   3.393
in respect of which assistance is received under the self-employment route,
shall be taken into account in accordance with the following provisions of this
Chapter.]

AMENDMENTS

1. Social Security (Miscellaneous Amendments) (No. 4) Regulations 1998
(SI 1998/1174), reg.3(4) (June 1, 1998).
2. Social Security Amendment (Employment Zones) (No. 2) Regulations 2000
(SI 2000/2910), reg.5(2)(c) (November 27, 2000).

DEFINITION

"self-employment route"—see reg.1(3).

[¹ Calculation of income of participants in the self-employment route [² . . .]]

102C.—(1) The income of a person who has received assistance under   3.394
the self-employment route shall be calculated by taking into account the
whole of the monies in the special account at the end of the last day upon
which such assistance was received and deducting from those monies—
  (a) an amount in respect of income tax calculated in accordance with
      regulation 102D (deduction in respect of tax for participants in the
      self-employment route [² . . .]).
  (b) any sum to which paragraph (4) refers.
  (2) Income calculated pursuant to paragraph (1) shall be apportioned
equally over a period which starts on the date the income is treated as paid
under paragraph (3) and is equal in length to the period beginning with the
day upon which assistance was first received under the self-employment
route and ending on the last day upon which such assistance was received.
  (3) Income calculated pursuant to paragraph (1) shall be treated as paid—
  (a) in the case where it is due to be paid before the first benefit week in
      respect of which the participant or his partner [³ or, in the case of a
      joint-claim couple, the participant and the other member of the
      couple of which the participant is a member,] first claims a jobseeker's
      allowance following the last day upon which assistance was received
      under the self-employment route, on the day in the week in which it
      is due to be paid which corresponds to the first day of the benefit week;
  (b) in any other case, on the first day of the benefit week in which it is
      due to be paid.
  (4) This paragraph refers, where applicable in each benefit week in respect
of which income calculated pursuant to paragraph (1) is taken into account
pursuant to paragraphs (2) and (3), to the sums which would have been

disregarded under paragraphs 5 to 8, 11 and 12 of Schedule 6 [³ or paragraphs 1, 2, 5 and 6 of Schedule 6A] had the income been earnings.]

AMENDMENTS

3.395   1. Social Security (Miscellaneous Amendments) (No.4) Regulations 1998 (SI 1998/1174), reg.3(4) (June 1, 1998).

2. Social Security Amendment (Employment Zones) (No.2) Regulations 2000 (SI 2000/2910), reg.5(2)(c) (November 27, 2000).

3. Jobseeker's Allowance (Joint Claims) Regulations 2000 (SI 2000/1978), reg.2(5) and Sch.2, para.41 (March 19, 2001).

DEFINITIONS

"benefit week"—see reg.1(3).
"self-employment route"—see reg.1(3).
"joint-claim couple"—see JSA, s.1(4).
"special account"—*ibid*.
"week"—see reg.1(3).

GENERAL NOTE

3.396   This regulation, together with reg.102D, applies to the income from "test-trading" of people who have taken part in the "self-employment route" (defined in reg.1(3)). See also reg.88A which takes any gross receipts from trading while on the self-employment route out of the categories of earnings, self-employed earnings and income other than earnings. The rules for liable relative payments, payments of child support maintenance and student income (except reg.137) also do not apply. Any such receipts may only be taken into account in accordance with regs 102A to 102D.

There are several issues raised by reg.102C that need clarifying. The intention seems to be that, after deducting an amount for income tax in accordance with reg.102D and applying the relevant earnings disregard under paras 5 to 8, 11 or 12 of Sch.6 in each benefit week that would have been applicable if the income had been earnings, the balance of the money in the person's "special account" (defined in reg.102A) at the end of the day on which he ceases to receive "assistance" (not defined) under the self-employment route is to be spread over a period equal in length to the period that the person received such assistance. The period starts on the date that the income is treated as paid under para.(3). Under para.(3)(a), if the income is due to be paid before the first benefit week pursuant to the claimant's (or his partner's) first JSA claim after assistance under the self-employment route finishes, it is treated as paid on the day that corresponds to the first day of the benefit week. In any other case it is treated as paid on the first day of the benefit week in which it is due (para.(3)(b)).

But when is this income due to be paid and what or who determines this? According to the guidance (see AM(AOG)82), it is due to be paid on the day after (i) the person leaves the self-employment route if he is not entitled to JSA or income support immediately after leaving the self-employment route; or (ii) his entitlement to JSA or income support ends if that entitlement stops within 13 weeks of the day after he left the self-employment route; or (iii) the expiry of 13 weeks starting on the day after he left the self-employment route if he is entitled to JSA or income support throughout that period. These rules are presumably part of the terms of the New Deal, since such provisions do not appear in the JSA (or Income Support) Regulations themselves. The 13 weeks "period of grace" in (iii) may perhaps be related to the fact that according to Employment Service guidance a person can continue to receive assistance in connection with trying to establish himself in self-employment for a further 13 weeks after his participation in the self-employment route ends. Presumably the intention is that any profit from his "test-trading" should not affect his benefit entitlement until after that period.

Note also that para.(1) refers to "the whole of the monies" in the person's special account but reg.102B refers to the "gross receipts" of the activity carried on while on the self-employment route. The normal rules for the calculation of earnings of self-employed earners (see regs 100 to 102) do not apply (see reg.88A), although presumably the caselaw on the meaning of "gross receipts" for self-employed earners will be relevant (see the notes to reg.37 of the Income Support Regulations). However, certain sums are ignored in calculating the person's income in his "special account". Thus any payment to him from this account (whether before or after he leaves the self-employment route) will disregarded if it is (i) to meet expenses wholly and necessarily incurred in his business while on the self-employment route; or (ii) used, or intended to be used, to make repayments on a loan taken out for the purposes of that business (see para.62 of Sch.7). See also para.11(3) and (4) of Sch.8, which disregard any assets of the business while the person is participating in the self-employment route and, if the person later ceases to be engaged in that business, for a period which is reasonable to allow them to be disposed of. In addition, any capital acquired for the purposes of the business is ignored for 52 weeks from the date of receipt (para.47 of Sch.8).

See also regs 23A and 39A to 39D of, and para.64 of Sch.9 and paras 6(3) and (4) and 52 of Sch.10 to, the Income Support Regulations which introduce similar provisions for the treatment of income from "test-trading" while on the self-employment route when the person or his partner claims income support.

[¹ Deduction in respect of tax for participants in the self-employment route [² . . .]

102D.—(1) The amount to be deducted in respect of income tax under regulation 102C(1)(a) (calculation of income of participants in the self-employment route [² . . .]) in respect of the period determined under regulation 102C(2) shall be calculated as if—

> 3.397

(a) the chargeable income is the only income chargeable to tax;

(b) the personal reliefs which are applicable to the person receiving assistance under the self-employment route by virtue of section 257(1) 257A(1) and 259 of the Income and Corporation Taxes Act 1988 (personal reliefs) are allowable against that income; and

(c) the rate at which the chargeable income less the personal relief is assessable to income tax is the lower rate of tax or, as the case may be, the lower rate and the basic rate of tax.

(2) For the purpose of paragraph (1), the lower rate of tax to be applied and the amount of the personal relief deductible shall, where the period determined under regulation 102C(2) is less than a year, be calculated on a pro rata basis.

(3) In this regulation, "chargeable income" means the monies in the special account at the end of the last day upon which assistance was received under the self-employment route.]

AMENDMENTS

1. Social Security (Miscellaneous Amendments) (No.4) Regulations 1998 (SI 1998/1174), reg.3(4) (June 1, 1998).   **3.398**

2. Social Security Amendment (Employment Zones) (No.2) Regulations 2000 (SI 2000/2910), reg.5(2)(c) (November 27, 2000).

DEFINITIONS

"lower rate"—see reg.1(3).
"self-employment route"—*ibid.*
"special account"—*ibid.*

GENERAL NOTE

See the note to reg.102C above.   **3.399**

Chapter V

Other Income

Calculation of income other than earnings

3.400

103.—(1) For the purposes of regulation 94 (calculation of income other than earnings) the income of a claimant which does not consist of earnings to be taken into account shall, subject to the following provisions of this regulation, be his gross income and any capital treated as income under [⁶ regulation 104 (capital treated as income)].

(2) There shall be disregarded from the calculation of a claimant's gross income under paragraph (1) any sum, where applicable, specified in Schedule 7.

(3) Where the payment of any benefit under the Act or under the Benefits Act is subject to any deduction by way of recovery, the amount to be taken into account under paragraph (1) shall be the gross amount to which the beneficiary is entitled.

(4) [⁷ . . .]

[⁵ (5) Paragraph (5ZA) applies where—

(a) a relevant payment has been made to a person in an academic year; and

(b) that person abandons, or is dismissed from, his course of study before the payment to him of the final instalment of the relevant payment.

(5ZA) The amount of a relevant payment to be taken into account for the assessment period for the purposes of paragraph (1) in respect of a person to whom paragraph (5) applies, shall be calculated by applying the formula—

$$\frac{A - (B \times C)}{D}$$

where—

A = the total amount of the relevant payment which that person would have received had he remained a student until the last day of the academic term in which he abandoned, or was dismissed from, his course, less any deduction under regulation 136(5);

B = the number of benefit weeks from the benefit week immediately following that which includes the first day of that academic year to the benefit week immediately before that which includes the day on which the person abandoned, or was dismissed from, his course;

C = the weekly amount of the relevant payment, before the application of the £10 disregard, which would have been taken into account as income under regulation 136(2) had the person not abandoned or been dismissed from, his course and, in the case of a person who was not entitled to a jobseeker's allowance immediately before he abandoned or was dismissed from his course, had that person, at that time, been entitled to a jobseeker's allowance;

D = the number of benefit weeks in the assessment period.

(5ZB) In paragraphs (5) and (5ZA)—

"academic year" and "student loan" shall have the same meanings as for the purposes of Chapter IX of this Part;

"assessment period" means the period beginning with the benefit week which includes the day on which the person abandoned, or was dismissed from, his course and ending with the benefit week which includes the last day of the last quarter for which an instalment of the relevant payment was payable to that person and for the purposes of this definition, "quarter" shall have the same meaning as for the purposes of the Education (Student Support) Regulations 2001;

"relevant period" means either a student loan or an amount intended for the maintenance of dependants referred to in regulation 131(5A) or both.]

[²(5A) In the case of income to which regulation 94(2B) applies (calculation of income of former full-time students), the amount of income to be taken into account for the purposes of paragraph (1) shall be the amount of that income calculated in accordance with regulation 97(7) and on the basis that none of that income has been repaid.]

(6) For the avoidance of doubt there shall be included as income to be taken into account under paragraph (1)

[⁴(a) any payment to which regulation 98(2)(a) to (e) or 100(2) (payments not earnings) applies; or

(b) in the case of a claimant who is receiving support under section 95 or 98 of the Immigration and Asylum Act including support provided by virtue of regulations made under Schedule 9 to that Act, the amount of such support provided in respect of essential living needs of the claimant and his [⁶ parter] (if any) as is specified in regulations made under paragraph 3 of Schedule 8 to the Immigration and Asylum Act.]

AMENDMENTS

1. Jobseeker's Allowance and Income Support (General) (Amendment) Regulations 1996 (SI 1996/1517), reg.23 (October 7, 1996). **3.401**

2. Income-related Benefits and Jobseeker's Allowance (Miscellaneous Amendments) Regulations 1997 (SI 1997/65), reg.7(2) (April 7, 1997).

3. Social Security (Miscellaneous Amendments) Regulations 1997 (SI 1997/454), reg.2(13) April 7, 1997).

4. Social Security (Immigration and Asylum) Consequential Amendments Regulations 2000 (SI 2000/636), reg.4(4) (April 3, 2000).

5. Social Security Amendment (Students and Income-related Benefits) Regulations 2001 (SI 2001/2319), reg.5(2) (August 1, 2001).

6. Social Security (Working Tax Credit and Child Tax Credit) (Consequential Amendments) Regulations 2003 (SI 2003/455), reg.3 and Sch.2, para.8 (April 6, 2004, except in "transitional cases" and see further the note to reg.83 and to reg.17 of the Income Support Regulations).

7. Social Security (Miscellaneous Amendments) Regulations 2005 (SI 2005/574), reg.6(3) (April 4, 2005).

DEFINITIONS

"academic year"—see reg.130. **3.402**
"the Act"—see reg.1(3).
"the Benefits Act"—see Jobseekers Act, s.35(1).
"benefit week"—see reg.1(3).
"claimant"—see Jobseekers Act, s.35(1), reg.88(1).
"earnings"—see reg.1(3).
"full-time student"—*ibid.*

"Immigration and Asylum Act"—*ibid.*
"student loan"—see reg.130.

GENERAL NOTE

3.403   On paras (1) to (3) and (5) to (6), see the notes to reg.40 of the Income Support Regulations but in relation to para.(6)(b) note that there is no equivalent to reg.40(5).

Capital treated as income

3.404   **104.**—(1) Any capital payable by instalments which are outstanding on the first day in respect of which an income-based jobseeker's allowance is payable, or, in the case of a [³supersession], the date of that [³supersession], shall, if the aggregate of the instalments outstanding and the amount of the claimant's capital otherwise calculated in accordance with Chapter VI of this Part exceeds £8,000 [⁴or, in a case where regulation 107(aa) applies, £12,000] [¹or, in a case where regulation 107(b) applies, £16,000], be treated as income.

(2) Any payment received under an annuity shall be treated as income.

(3) [⁷ . . .]

(4) Any earnings to the extent that they are not a payment of income shall be treated as income.

[²(5) Any Career Development Loan paid pursuant to section 2 of the Employment and Training Act 1973 shall be treated as income.]

[⁶ (6) Where an agreement or court order provides that payments shall be made to the claimant in consequence of any personal injury to the claimant and that such payments are to be made, wholly or partly, by way of periodical payments, any such periodical payments received by the claimant (but not a payment which is treated as capital by virtue of this Part), shall be treated as income.]

AMENDMENTS

3.405   1. Income-related Benefits and Jobseeker's Allowance (Miscellaneous Amendments) Regulations 1997 (SI 1997/65), reg.3(2) (April 7, 1997).

2. Income-related Benefits and Jobseeker's Allowance (Miscellaneous Amendments) Regulations 1997 (SI 1997/65), reg.3(3) (April 7, 1997).

3. Social Security Act 1998 (Commencement No.11, and Savings and Consequential and Transitional Provisions) Order 1999 (SI 1999/2860 C.75)), art.3(12) and Sch.12, para.5 (October 18, 1999).

4. Social Security Amendment (Capital Limits and Earnings Disregards) Regulations 2000 (SI 2000/2545), reg.2(2)(a) (April 9, 2001).

5. Children (Leaving Care) Act 2000 (Commencement No.2 and Consequential Provisions) Order 2001 (SI 2001/3070), art.3(5) and Sch.4, para.(c) (October 1, 2001).

6. Social Security Amendment (Personal Injury Payments) Regulations 2002 (SI 2002/2442), reg.2 (October 28, 2002).

7. Social Security (Working Tax Credit and Child Tax Credit) (Consequential Amendments) Regulations 2003 (SI 2003/455), reg.3 and Sch.2, para.9 (April 6, 2004, except in "transitional cases" and see further the note to reg.83 and to reg.17 of the Income Support Regulations).

DEFINITIONS

"claimant"—see Jobseekers Act, s.35(1), reg.88(1).
"payment"—see reg.1(3).

See the notes to reg.41 of the Income Support Regulations.

3.406

Paragraph (3) was omitted with effect from April 6, 2004 by reg.3 of and para.9 of Sch.2 to the Social Security (Working Tax Credit and Child Tax Credit) (Consequential Amendments) Regulations 2003 (SI 2003/455), except in "transitional cases" (*i.e.* those cases in which the claimant is still receiving amounts for his children in his income-based JSA—see further the notes to reg.83 and to reg.17 of the Income Support Regulations). For "transitional cases" para.(3) continues in force (see the 2003 edition of this volume for this provision). With effect from May 12, 2004, reg.5 of the Social Security (Miscellaneous Amendments) (No. 2) Regulations 2004 (SI 2004/1141) substituted the words "section 12 of the Social Work (Scotland) Act 1968 or sections 29 or 30 of the Children (Scotland) Act 1995" for the words "section 12, 24 or 26 of the Social Work (Scotland) Act 1968" in para.(3). The effect of this amendment is simply to update the references to the Scottish legislation referred to in para.(3).

Notional income

105.—(1) A claimant shall be treated as possessing income of which he has deprived himself for the purpose of securing entitlement to a jobseeker's allowance or increasing the amount of that allowance, or for the purpose of securing entitlement to, or increasing the amount of, income support.

3.407

(2) Except in the case of—

(a) a discretionary trust;

(b) a trust derived from a payment made in consequence of a personal injury;

[^{1}(c) [^{19} . . .]]

(d) [^{18} working tax credit or child tax credit];

(e) a jobseeker's allowance;

(f) [^{21} . . .]

(g) a personal pension scheme where the claimant is aged under 60; [^{2} or

(h) any sum to which paragraph 42(a) or 43(a) of Schedule 8 (disregard of compensation for personal injuries which is administered by the Court) refers]; [^{5}or

(i) rehabilitation allowance made under section 2 of the Employment and Training Act 1973],

income which would become available to the claimant upon application being made but which has not been acquired by him shall be treated as possessed by him but only from the date on which it could be expected to be acquired were an application made.

[^{1} (2A) [^{19} . . .]]

(3) Where a person, aged not less than 60, is a member of, or a person deriving entitlement to a pension under, a personal pension scheme, and—

(a) in the case of a personal pension scheme other than one referred to in sub-paragraph (b), he fails to purchase an annuity with the funds available in that scheme where—

(i) he defers, in whole or in part, the payment of any income which would have been payable to him by his pension fund holder;

(ii) he fails to take any necessary action to secure that the whole or part of any income which would be payable to him by his pension fund holder upon his applying for it, is so paid; or

(iii) income withdrawal is not available to him under that scheme; or

971

(b) in the case of a contract or trust scheme approved under Chapter III of Part XIV of the Income and Corporation Taxes Act 1988, he fails to purchase an annuity with the funds available under that contract or scheme,

the amount of any income foregone shall be treated as possessed by him, but only from the date on which it could be expected to be acquired were an application for it to be made.

(4) The amount of any income foregone in a case to which either head (i) or (ii) of paragraph (3)(a) applies shall be the maximum amount of income which may be withdrawn from the fund and shall be determined by [9 the Secretary of State] who shall take account of information provided by the pension fund holder in accordance with regulation 7(5) of the Social Security (Claims and Payments) Regulations 1987.

(5) The amount of any income foregone in a case to which either head (iii) of paragraph (3)(a), or paragraph (3)(b) applies shall be the income that the claimant could have received without purchasing an annuity had the fund held under the relevant personal pension scheme been held under a personal pension scheme where income withdrawal was available and shall be determined in the manner specified in paragraph (4).

(6) Subject to paragraph (7), any income which is due to be paid to the claimant but has not been paid to him, shall be treated as possessed by the claimant.

(7) Paragraph (6) shall not apply to—

(a) any amount to which paragraph (8) or (9) applies;

(b) a payment to which section 74(2) or (3) of the Administration Act applies (abatement of prescribed payments from public funds which are not made before the prescribed date, and abatement from prescribed benefits where maintenance not paid); and

(c) a payment from a discretionary trust, or a trust derived from a payment made in consequence of a personal injury.

[12(d) any earnings which are due to an employed earner on the termination of his employment by reason of redundancy but which have not been paid to him.]

(8) This paragraph applies to an amount which is due to be paid to the claimant under an occupational pension scheme but which is not paid because the trustees or managers of the scheme have suspended or ceased payment due to an insufficiency of resources.

(9) This paragraph applies to any amount by which a payment made to the claimant from an occupational pension scheme falls short of the payment to which he was due under the scheme where the shortfall arises because the trustees or managers of the scheme have insufficient resources available to them to meet in full the scheme's liabilities.

(10) [6Any payment of income, other than a payment of income specified in paragraph (10A)], made—

(a) to a third party in respect of a single claimant or in respect of a single claimant or [19 his partner] shall be treated—

(i) in a case where that payment is derived from a payment of any benefit under the Act or under the Benefits Act, [20 a payment from the Armed Forces and Reserve Forces Compensation Scheme,] a war disablement pension or war widow's pension [17 or war widower's pension], as possessed by that single claimant, if it would normally be paid to him, or as possessed [19 by his partner, if it would normally be paid to his partner];

[¹⁰ (ia) in a case where that payment is a payment of an occupational pension or is a pension or other periodical payment made under a personal pension scheme, as possessed by that single claimant or, as the case may be, by [¹⁹ the claimant's partner];]

(ii) in any other case, as possessed by that single claimant [¹⁹ or his partner] to the extent that it is used for the food, ordinary clothing or footwear, household fuel, rent for which housing benefit is payable, or any housing costs to the extent that they are met under regulation 83(f) [¹⁵, 84(1)(g), 86A(d) or 86B(e)], of that single claimant or, as the case may be, [¹⁹ of his partner], or is used for any council tax or water charges for which that claimant or [¹⁹ partner is liable];

[¹⁹ (b) to a single claimant or his partner in respect of a third party (but not in respect of another member of his family) shall be treated as possessed by that single claimant or, as the case may be, his partner, to the extent that it is kept or used by him or used by or on behalf of his partner;]

but, except where sub-paragraph (a)(i) applies and in the case of a person who is, or would be, prevented from being entitled to a jobseeker's allowance by section 14 (trade disputes), this paragraph shall not apply to any payment in kind.

[⁶(10A) Paragraph (10) shall not apply in respect of a payment of income made—

(a) under the Macfarlane Trust, the Macfarlane (Special Payments) Trust, the Macfarlane (Special Payments) (No. 2) Trust, the Fund, the Eileen Trust or the Independent Living Funds;

(b) pursuant to section 19(1)(a) of the Coal Industry Act 1994 (concessionary coal); or

(c) pursuant to section 2 of the Employment and Training Act 1973 in respect of a person's participation—

(i) in an employment programme specified in regulation 75(1)(a)(ii);

(ii) in a training scheme specified in regulation 75(1)(b)(ii); or

[¹⁶ (iia) in the Intensive Activity Period for 50 plus or in the Intensive Activity Period specified in regulation 75(1)(a)(iv); or]

(iii) in a qualifying course within the meaning specified in regulation 17A(7).]

(iv) [*Omitted.*]

[¹¹(d) under an occupational pension scheme or in respect of a pension or other periodical payment made under a personal pension scheme where—

(i) a bankruptcy order has been made in respect of the person in respect of whom the payment has been made or, in Scotland, the estate of that person is subject to sequestration or a judicial factor has been appointed on that person's estate under section 41 of the Solicitors (Scotland) Act 1980;

(ii) the payment is made to the trustee in bankruptcy or any other person acting on behalf of the creditors; and

(iii) the person referred to in (i) and [¹⁹ his partner (if any)] does not possess, or is not treated as possessing, any other income apart from that payment.]

(11) Where the claimant lives in a residential care home or a nursing

home, or is temporarily absent from such a home, any payment made by a person other than the claimant or a member of his family in respect of some or all of the cost of maintaining the claimant [^{19} or his partner in that home shall be treated as possessed by the claimant or his partner].

[^{14}(11A) Where the amount of a subsistence allowance paid to a claimant in a benefit week is less than the amount of income-based jobseeker's allowance that person would have received in that benefit week had it been payable to him, less 50p, he shall be treated as possessing the amount which is equal to the amount of income-based jobseeker's allowance which he would have received in that week, less 50p.]

(12) Where a claimant's earnings are not ascertainable at the time of the determination of the claim or of any [^{9} review or supersession] [^{9}the Secretary of State] shall treat the claimant as possessing such earnings as is reasonable in the circumstances of the case having regard to the number of hours worked and the earnings paid for comparable employment in the area.

(13) [^{13} Subject to paragraph (13A),] where—

(a) a claimant performs a service for another person; and

(b) that person makes no payment of earnings or pays less than that paid for a comparable employment in the area,

[^{9} the Secretary of State] shall treat the claimant as possessing such earnings (if any) as is reasonable for that employment unless the claimant satisfies him that the means of that person are insufficient for him to pay or to pay more for the service [^{13} . . .].

[^{13}(13A) Paragraph (13) shall not apply—

(a) to a claimant who is engaged by a charitable or voluntary organisation or who is a volunteer if the Secretary of State is satisfied in any of those cases that it is reasonable for him to provide those services free of charge;

(b) in a case where the service is performed in connection with—

(i) the claimant's participation in an employment or training programme in accordance with regulation 19(1)(q) [^{16}, other than where the service is performed in connection with the claimant's participation in the Intensive Activity Period for 50 plus or in the Intensive Activity Period specified in regulation 75(1)(a)(iv)]; or

(ii) the claimant's or the claimant's partner's participation in an employment or training programme as defined in regulation 19(3) for which a training allowance is not payable or, where such an allowance is payable, it is payable for the sole purpose of reimbursement of travelling or meal expenses to the person participating in that programme.]

(14) Where a claimant is treated as possessing any income under any of paragraphs (1) to (11) the foregoing provisions of this Part shall apply for the purposes of calculating the amount of that income as if a payment had actually been made and as if it were actual income which he does possess.

(15) Where a claimant is treated as possessing any earnings under paragraphs (12) or (13) the foregoing provisions of this Part shall apply for the purposes of calculating the amount of those earnings as if a payment had actually been made and as if they were actual earnings which he does possess, except that paragraph (4) of regulation 99 (calculation of net earnings of employed earners) shall not apply and his net earnings shall be calculated by taking into account the earnings which he is treated as possessing, less—

(a) an amount in respect of income tax equivalent to an amount calculated by applying to those earnings the lower rate or, as the case may
be, the lower rate and the basic rate of tax in the year of assessment
less only the personal relief to which the claimant is entitled under
sections 257(1), 257A(1) and 259 of the Income and Corporation
Taxes Act 1988 (personal reliefs) as is appropriate to his circumstances; but, if the period over which those earnings are to be taken
into account is less than a year, the earnings to which the lower rate
of tax is to be applied and the amount of the personal relief
deductible under this paragraph shall be calculated on a pro rata
basis;

(b) where the weekly amount of those earnings equals or exceeds the
lower earnings limit, an amount representing primary Class 1 contributions under the Benefits Act, calculated by applying to those
earnings the initial and main primary percentages in accordance with
section 8(1)(a) and (b) of that Act; and

(c) one-half of any sum payable by the claimant in respect of a pay period
by way of a contribution towards an occupational or personal pension
scheme.

(16) In this regulation—

"ordinary clothing or footwear" means clothing or footwear for normal
daily use, but does not include school uniforms, or clothing or footwear
used solely for sporting activities;

"pension fund holder" means with respect to a personal pension scheme
the trustees, managers or scheme administrators, as the case may be, of
the scheme concerned;

"resources" has the same meaning as in section 181 of the Pension
Schemes Act 1993.

AMENDMENTS

1. Child Benefit, Child Support and Social Security (Miscellaneous 3.408
Amendments) (Regulation 1996 (SI 1996/1803), reg.42 (April 7, 1997).

2. Income-related Benefits and Jobseeker's Allowance (Amendment) (No.2)
Regulations 1997 (SI 1997/2197), reg.6 (October 6, 1997).

3. Income-related Benefits and Jobseeker's Allowance (Amendment) (No.2)
Regulations 1997 (SI 1997/2197), reg.7(3) and (4)(f) (October 6, 1997).

4. Social Security Amendment (New Deal) Regulations 1997 (SI 1997/2863),
reg.9 (January 5, 1998).

5. Social Security (Miscellaneous Amendments) Regulations 1998 (SI 1998/563),
reg.6(1) and (2)(f) (April 6, 1998).

6. Social Security Amendment (New Deal) (No.2) Regulations 1998
(SI 1998/2117), reg.2(1) (September 24, 1998).

7. Social Security and Child Support (Tax Credits) Consequential Amendments
Regulations 1999 (SI 1999/2566), reg.2(1) and Sch.2, Pt I (October 5, 1999).

8. Social Security and Child Support (Tax Credits) Consequential Amendments
Regulations 1999 (SI 1999/2566), reg.2(2) and Sch.2, Pt II (October 5, 1999).

9. Social Security Act 1998 (Commencement No.11, and Savings and
Consequential and Transitional Provisions) Order 1999 (SI 1999/2860 (C.75)),
art.3(12) and Sch.12 (October 18, 1999).

10. Social Security Amendment (Notional Income and Capital) Regulations 1999
(SI 1999/2640), reg.2(1)(b) (November 15, 1999).

11. Social Security Amendment (Notional Income and Capital) Regulations 1999
(SI 1999/2640), reg.2(3)(d) (November 15, 1999).

12. Income Support (General) and Jobseeker's Allowance Amendment (No.2) Regulations 1999 (SI 1999/3324), reg.2 (January 7, 2000).

13. Social Security (Approved Work) Regulations 2000 (SI 2000/678), reg.2(1) (April 3, 2000).

14. Social Security Amendment (Employment Zones) Regulations 2000 (SI 2000/724), reg.3(1) (April 3, 2000).

15. Jobseeker's Allowance (Joint Claims) Regulations 2000 (SI 2000/1978), reg.2(5) and Sch.2, para.42 (March 19, 2001).

16. Social Security Amendment (New Deal) Regulations 2001 (SI 2001/1029), reg.7 (April 9, 2001).

17. Social Security (Miscellaneous Amendments) Regulations 2002 (SI 2002/841), reg.3(2) (April 8, 2002).

18. Social Security (Working Tax Credit and Child Tax Credit) (Consequential Amendments) Regulations 2003 (SI 2003/455), reg.3 and Sch.2, para.10(b) (April 7, 2003).

19. Social Security (Working Tax Credit and Child Tax Credit) (Consequential Amendments) Regulations 2003 (SI 2003/455), reg.3 and Sch.2, para.10 (except sub-para.(b)) (April 6, 2004, except in "transitional cases" and see further the note to reg.83 and to reg.17 of the Income Support Regulations).

20. Social Security (Miscellaneous Amendments) Regulations 2005 (SI 2005/574), reg.2(6) (April 4, 2005).

21. Social Security (Miscellaneous Amendments) Regulations 2005 (SI 2005/574), reg.6(4) (April 4, 2005).

DEFINITIONS

3.409
"the Act"—see reg.1(3).
"the Armed Forces and Reserve Forces Compensation Scheme" —*ibid.*"
"the Benefits Act"—see Jobseekers Act, s.35(1).
"child tax credit"—see reg.1(3).
"claimant"—*ibid.*, reg.88(1).
"earnings"—*ibid.*
"family"—Jobseekers Act, s.35(1).
"Intensive Activity Period for 50 plus"—see reg.1(3).
"lower rate"—*ibid.*
"occupational pension"—*ibid.*
"occupational pension scheme"—see Jobseekers Act, s.35(1).
"partner"—see reg.1(3).
"pay period"—*ibid.*
"payment"—*ibid.*
"personal pension scheme"—see Jobseekers Act, s.35(1).
"single claimant"—see reg.1(3).
"subsistence allowance"—*ibid.*
"the Eileen Trust"—*ibid.*
"the Fund"—*ibid.*
"the Independent Living Funds"—*ibid.*
"the Macfarlane (Special Payments) Trust"—*ibid.*
"the Macfarlane (Special Payments) (No.2) Trust"—*ibid.*
"the Macfarlane Trust"—*ibid.*
"training allowance"—*ibid.*
"voluntary organisation"—*ibid.*
"war disablement pension"—*ibid.*
"war widow's pension"—*ibid.*
"war widower's pension"—*ibid.*
"water charges"—*ibid.*
"working tax credit"—*ibid.*
"year of assessment"—*ibid.*

See the notes to reg.42 of the Income Support Regulations. There are some dif-   **3.410**
ferences which are mainly related to the different nature of the two benefits (for
example, there is no equivalent in reg.105 to reg.42(6A)(c), (6B) and (6C) as this
relates to lone parents).

Note that under para.(1) if a person has deprived himself of income he will be
caught by this rule if the purpose of the deprivation was to secure entitlement to or
increase the amount of jobseeker's allowance *or income support*. This avoids the question that might otherwise have arisen on a claimant transfering from income support
to jobseeker's allowance whether a deprivation which had only been for the purposes
of income support could be caught by para.(1).

Modifications in respect of children and young persons

106. [¹. . .]   **3.411**

AMENDMENT

1. Social Security (Working Tax Credit and Child Tax Credit) (Consequential   **3.412**
Amendments) Regulations 2003 (SI 2003/455), reg.3 and Sch.2, para.11 (April 6,
2004, except in "transitional cases" and see further the note to reg.83 and to reg.17
of the Income Support Regulations).

GENERAL NOTE

See the notes to reg.44 of the Income Support Regulations.

Chapter VI

Capital

Capital limit

[¹**107.** For the purposes of section 13(1) [² and (2A)] (no entitlement to   **3.413**
an income-based jobseeker's allowance if capital exceeds a prescribed
amount)—

   (a) except where paragraph [³ (aa) or] (b) applies, the prescribed amount
        is £8,000;
[³ (aa) where the circumstances prescribed in regulation 116(ZA) apply in
        the claimant's case, the prescribed amount is £12,000;]
   (b) in the case to which regulation 116(1B) applies, the prescribed
        amount is £16,000.]

AMENDMENTS

1. Jobseeker's Allowance (Amendment) Regulations 1996 (SI 1996/1516), reg.11   **3.414**
(October 7, 1996).

2. Jobseeker's Allowance (Joint Claims) Regulations 2000 (SI 2000/1978),
reg.2(5) and Sch.2, para.43 (March 19, 2001).

3. Social Security Amendment (Capital Limits and Earnings Disregards)
Regulations 2000 (SI 2000/2545), reg.2(2)(b) (April 9, 2001).

DEFINITION

"claimant"—see Jobseekers Act, s.35(1), reg.88(1).

GENERAL NOTE

3.415   Under s.13(1) of the Jobseekers Act there is no entitlement to income-based JSA if the claimant's capital exceeds the prescribed amount. The limit is the same as it is for income support; that is, for most claimants it is £8,000 (para.(a)), but it is £16,000 for claimants living permanently in residential care or nursing homes, residential accommodation or Polish resettlement homes (para.(b)) and £12,000 if the claimant or any partner is 60 or over (note a claimant over pensionable age defined in reg.3 is not entitled to JSA but will have to claim state pension credit). The capital of a claimant's partner is aggregated with the claimant's (reg.88(1)), but not that of children and young persons (reg.88(2)).

See the notes to reg.45 of the Income Support Regulations.

Calculation of capital

3.416   **108.**—(1) Subject to paragraph (2), the capital of a claimant to be taken into account shall be the whole of his capital calculated in accordance with this Part and any income treated as capital under regulation 110.

(2) There shall be disregarded from the calculation of a claimant's capital under paragraph (1) any capital, where applicable, specified in Schedule 8.

DEFINITION

3.417   "claimant"—see Jobseekers Act, s.35(1), reg.88(1).

GENERAL NOTE

See the notes to reg.46 of the Income Support Regulations.

Disregard of capital of child or young person

3.418   **109.** [¹. . .]

AMENDMENT

3.419   1. Social Security (Working Tax Credit and Child Tax Credit) (Consequential Amendments) Regulations 2003 (SI 2003/455), reg.3 and Sch.2, para.11 (April 6, 2004, except in "transitional cases" and see further the note to reg.83 and to reg.17 of the Income Support Regulations).

GENERAL NOTE

See the notes to reg.47 of the Income Support Regulations.

Income treated as capital

3.420   **110.**—(1) Any bounty derived from employment to which paragraph 9 of Schedule 6 applies and paid at intervals of at least one year shall be treated as capital.

(2) Except in the case of an amount to which section 15(2)(c)(i) (refund of tax in trade dispute cases) applies, any amount by way of a refund of income tax deducted from profits or emoluments chargeable to income tax under Schedule D or E shall be treated as capital.

(3) Any holiday pay which is not earnings under regulation 98(1)(c) (earnings of employed earners) shall be treated as capital.

(4) Except any income derived from capital disregarded under paragraphs 1, 2, 4 to 8, 11 or 17 of Schedule 8, any income derived from capital shall be treated as capital but only from the date it is normally due to be credited to the claimant's account.

(5) Subject to paragraph (6), in the case of employment as an employed earner, any advance of earnings or any loan made by the claimant's employer shall be treated as capital.

(6) Paragraph (5) shall not apply to a person who is, or would be, prevented from being entitled to a jobseeker's allowance by section 14 (trade disputes).

(7) Any payment under section 30 of the Prison Act 1952 (payments for discharged prisoners) or allowance under section 17 of the Prisons (Scotland) Act 1989 (allowances to prisoners on discharge) shall be treated as capital.

(8) [³. . .]

(9) Any charitable or voluntary payment which is not made or not due to be made at regular intervals, other than one to which paragraph (10) applies, shall be treated as capital.

(10) This paragraph applies to a payment—

(a) which is made to a person who is, or would be, prevented from being entitled to a jobseeker's allowance by section 14 (trade disputes);
(b) [³ . . .]
(c) which is made under the Macfarlane Trust, the Macfarlane (Special Payments) Trust, the Macfarlane (Special Payments) (No.2) Trust, the Fund, the Eileen Trust or the Independent Living Funds.

[²(11) Any arrears of subsistence allowance which are paid to a claimant as a lump sum shall be treated as capital.]

AMENDMENTS

1. Social Security (Miscellaneous Amendments) Regulations 1998 (SI 1998/563), reg.14(2) (April 6, 1998).

2. Social Security Amendment (Employment Zones) Regulations 2000 (SI 2000/724), reg.3(2) (April 3, 2000).

3. Social Security (Working Tax Credit and Child Tax Credit) (Consequential Amendments) Regulations 2003 (SI 2003/455), reg.3 and Sch.2, para.12 (April 6, 2004, except in "transitional cases" and see further the note to reg.83 and to reg.17 of the Income Support Regulations).

3.421

DEFINITIONS

"child"—see Jobseekers Act s.35(1).
"the Children Order"—see reg.1(3).
"claimant"—Jobseekers Act, s.35(1), reg.88(1).
"earnings"—see reg.1(3).
"employed earner"—see reg.3, SSCBA, s.2(1)(a).
"family"—see Jobseekers Act, s.35(1).
"the Eileen Trust"—see reg.1(3).
"the Fund"—*ibid.*
"the Independent Living Funds"—*ibid.*
"the Macfarlane (Special Payments) Trust"—*ibid.*
"the MacFarlane (Special Payments) (No. 2) Trust"—*ibid.*
"the Macfarlane Trust"—*ibid.*
"subsistence allowance"—*ibid.*

GENERAL NOTE

See the notes to reg.48 of the Income Support Regulations. Most of the categories deemed to be capital are self-explanatory. They are then disregarded as income (Sch.7, para.34).

3.422

There is no equivalent to reg.48(11) of the Income Support Regulations because the JSA rules for the treatment of "compensation payments" (defined in reg.98(3)) made on the termination of employment differ from those of income support (see the notes to regs 98(3) and 94(6) to (9)).

Calculation of capital in the United Kingdom

3.423

111. Capital which a claimant possesses in the United Kingdom shall be calculated—
  (a) except in a case to which sub-paragraph (b) applies, at its current market or surrender value, less—
    (i) where there would be expenses attributable to sale, 10 percent; and
    (ii) the amount of any incumbrance secured on it;
  (b) in the case of a National Savings Certificate—
    (i) if purchased from an issue the sale of which ceased before 1st July last preceding the first day on which an income-based jobseeker's allowance is payable or, in the case of a [¹ supersession], the date of that [¹ supersession], at the price which it would have realised on that 1st July had it been purchased on the last day of that issue;
    (ii) in any other case, at its purchase price.

AMENDMENT

3.424

1. Social Security Act 1998 (Commencement No.11, and Savings and Consequential and Transitional Provisions) Order 1999 (SI 1999/2860 (C.75)), art.3(12) and Sch.12, para.5 (October 18, 1999).

DEFINITION

"claimant"—see Jobseekers Act, s.35(1), reg.88(1).

GENERAL NOTE

See the notes to reg.49 of the Income Support Regulations.

Calculation of capital outside the United Kingdom

3.425

112. Capital which a claimant possesses in a country outside the United Kingdom shall be calculated—
  (a) in a case in which there is no prohibition in that country against the transfer to the United Kingdom of an amount equal to its current market or surrender value in that country, at that value;
  (b) in a case where there is such a prohibition, at the price which it would realise if sold in the United Kingdom to a willing buyer, less, where there would be expenses attributable to sale, 10 per cent, and the amount of any incumbrance secured on it.

DEFINITION

3.426

"claimant"—see Jobseekers Act, s.35(1), reg.88(1).

GENERAL NOTE

See the note to reg.50 of the Income Support Regulations.

Notional capital

113.—(1) A claimant shall be treated as possessing capital of which he has   3.427
deprived himself for the purpose of securing entitlement to a jobseeker's
allowance or increasing the amount of that allowance, or for the purpose of
securing entitlement to or increasing the amount of income support, except—

(a) where that capital is derived from a payment made in consequence
of a personal injury and is placed on trust for the benefit of the
claimant; or

(b) to the extent that the capital he is treated as possessing is reduced in
accordance with regulation 114 (diminishing notional capital rule);
[¹or

(c) any sum to which paragraph 42(a) or 43(a) of Schedule 8 (disregard
of compensation for personal injuries which is administered by the
Court) refers].

(2) Except in the case of—

(a) a discretionary trust;

(b) a trust derived from a payment made in consequence of a personal
injury;

(c) any loan which would be obtainable only if secured against capital
disregarded under Schedule 8; or

(d) a personal pension scheme; [¹or

(e) any sum to which paragraph 42(a) or 43(a) of Schedule 8 (disregard
of compensation for personal injuries which is administered by the
Court) refers],

any capital which would become available to the claimant upon application
being made but which has not been acquired by him shall be treated as possessed by him but only from the date on which it could be expected to be
acquired were an application made.

(3) [³Any payment of capital, other than a payment of capital specified in
paragraph (3A)], made—

(a) to a third party in respect of a single claimant or [¹⁰ his partner] shall
be treated—

    (i) in a case where that payment is derived from a payment of any
benefit under the Act or under the Benefits Act, [¹² a payment
from the Armed Forces and Reserve Forces Compensation
Scheme,] a war disablement pension or war widow's pension
[⁹ or war widower's pension], as possessed by that single
claimant, if it would normally be paid to him, or as possessed
[¹⁰ by his partner, if it would normally be paid to his partner];

    [⁴(ia) in a case where that payment is a payment of an occupational
pension or is a pension or other periodical payment made under
a personal pension scheme, as possessed by that single claimant
or, as the case may be, by [¹⁰ the claimant's partner];]

    (ii) in any other case, as possessed by that single claimant [¹⁰ or his
partner] to the extent that it is used for the food, ordinary clothing or footwear, household fuel, rent for which housing benefit
[⁸ is payable] or any housing costs to the extent that they are met
under regulation 83(f) [⁶84(1)(g), 86A(d) or 86B(e)] [⁸ . . .], of
that single claimant or, as the case may be, [¹⁰ of his partner], or
is used for any council tax or water charges for which that
claimant or [¹⁰ partner is liable];

[¹⁰ (b) to a single claimant or his partner in respect of a third party (but not in respect of another member of his family) shall be treated as possessed by that single claimant or, as the case may be, his partner, to the extent that it is kept or used by him or used by or on behalf of his partner.]

[³(3A) Paragraph (3) shall not apply in respect of a payment of capital made—

(a) under the Macfarlane Trust, the Macfarlane (Special Payments) Trust, the Macfarlane (Special Payments) (No. 2) Trust, the Fund, the Eileen Trust [¹¹, the Independent Living Funds or the Skipton Fund]; or

(b) pursuant to section 2 of the Employment and Training Act 1973 in respect of a person's participation—

    (i) in an employment programme specified in regulation 75(1)(a)(ii);

    (ii) in a training scheme specified in regulation 75(1)(b)(ii); or

    [⁷ (iia) in the Intensive Activity Period for 50 plus or in the Intensive Activity Period specified in regulation 75(1)(a)(iv); or]

    (iii) in a qualifying course within the meaning specified in regulation 17A(7).]

    (iv) [*Omitted* .]

[⁵(c) under an occupational pension scheme or in respect of a pension or other periodical payment made under a personal pension scheme where—

    (i) a bankruptcy order has been made in respect of the person in respect of whom the payment has been made or, in Scotland, the estate of that person is subject to sequestration or a judicial factor has been appointed on that person's estate under section 41 of the Solicitors (Scotland) Act 1980;

    (ii) the payment is made to the trustee in bankruptcy or any other person acting on behalf of the creditors; and

    (iii) the person referred to in (i) and [¹⁰ his partner (if any)]does not possess, or is not treated as possessing, any other income apart from that payment.]

(4) Where a claimant stands in relation to a company in a position analogous to that of a sole owner or a partner in the business of that company, he shall be treated as if he were such sole owner or partner and in such a case—

(a) the value of his holding in that company shall, notwithstanding regulation 108 (calculation of capital), be disregarded; and

(b) he shall, subject to paragraph (5), be treated as possessing an amount of capital equal to the value or, as the case may be, his share of the value of the capital of that company and the foregoing provisions of this Chapter shall apply for the purposes of calculating that amount as if it were actual capital which he does possess.

(5) For so long as the claimant undertakes activities in the course of the business of the company, the amount which he is treated as possessing under paragraph (4) shall be disregarded.

(6) Where a claimant is treated as possessing any capital under any of paragraphs (1) to (4) the foregoing provisions of this Chapter shall apply for the purposes of calculating the amount of that capital as if it were actual capital which he does possess.

(7) For the avoidance of doubt a claimant is to be treated as possessing capital under paragraph (1) only if the capital of which he has deprived himself is actual capital.

(8) In paragraph (3) the expression "ordinary clothing or footwear" means clothing or footwear for normal daily use, but does not include school uniforms, or clothing or footwear used solely for sporting activities.

AMENDMENTS

1. Income-related Benefits and Jobseeker's Allowance (Amendment) (No.2) Regulations 1997 (SI 1997/2197), reg.6 (October 6, 1997).

3.428

2. Social Security Amendment (New Deal) Regulations 1997 (SI 1997/2863), reg.10 (January 5, 1998).

3. Social Security Amendment (New Deal) (No.2) Regulations 1998 (SI 1998/2117), reg.3(1) (September 24, 1998).

4. Social Security Amendment (Notional Income and Capital) Regulations 1999 (SI 1999/2640), reg.2(1)(b) (November 15, 1999).

5. Social Security Amendment (Notional Income and Capital) Regulations 1999 (SI 1999/2640), reg.2(3)(d) (November 15, 1999).

6. Jobseeker's Allowance (Joint Claims) Regulations 2000 (SI 2000/1978), reg.2(5) and Sch.2, para.44 (March 19, 2001).

7. Social Security Amendment (New Deal) Regulations 2001 (SI 2001/1029), reg.8 (April 9, 2001).

8. Social Security Amendment (Residential Care and Nursing Homes) Regulations 2001 (SI 2001/3767), reg.2(2) and Pt II of Sch., para.11 (April 8, 2002).

9. Social Security (Miscellaneous Amendments) Regulations 2002 (SI 2002/841), reg.3(3) (April 8, 2002).

10. Social Security (Working Tax Credit and Child Tax Credit) (Consequential Amendments) Regulations 2003 (SI 2003/455), reg.3 and Sch.2, para.13 (April 6, 2004, except in "transitional cases" and see further the note to reg.83 and to reg.17 of the Income Support Regulations).

11. Social Security (Miscellaneous Amendments) (No. 3) Regulations 2004 (SI 2004/2308), reg.3(1) and (2)(d) (October 4, 2004).

12. Social Security (Miscellaneous Amendments) Regulations 2005 (SI 2005/574), reg.2(6) (April 4, 2005).

DEFINITIONS

"the Act"—see reg.1(3).

3.429

"the Armed Forces and Reserve Forces Compensation Scheme"—*ibid.*
"the Benefits Act"—see Jobseekers Act, s.35(1).
"claimant"—*ibid.*, reg.88(1).
"family"—see Jobseekers Act, s.35(1).
"occupational pension"—see reg.1(3).
"payment"—*ibid.*
"personal pension scheme"—see Jobseekers Act, s.35(1).
"the Eileen Trust"—see reg.1(3).
"the Fund"—*ibid.*
"the Independent Living Funds"—*ibid.*
"the Macfarlane (Special Payments) Trust"—*ibid.*
"the Macfarlane (Special Payments) (No. 2) Trust"—*ibid.*
"the Macfarlane Trust"—*ibid.*
"the Skipton Fund"—*ibid.*
"single claimant"—*ibid.*
"war disablement pension"—*ibid.*
"war widow's pension"—*ibid.*
"war widower's pension"—*ibid.*
"water charges"—*ibid.*

3.430   See the notes to reg.51 of the Income Support Regulations.

Note that under para.(1) if a person has deprived himself of capital he will be caught by this rule if the purpose of the deprivation was to secure entitlement to or increase the amount of jobseeker's allowance *or income support*. This avoids the question that might otherwise have arisen on a claimant transfering from income support to jobseeker's allowance whether a deprivation which had only been for the purposes of income support could be caught by para.(1).

Diminishing notional capital rule

3.431   **114.**—(1) Where a claimant is treated as possessing capital under regulation 113(1) (notional capital), the amount which he is treated as possessing—

(a) in the case of a week that is subsequent to—

    (i) the relevant week in respect of which the conditions set out in paragraph (2) are satisfied, or

    (ii) a week which follows that relevant week and which satisfies those conditions,

shall be reduced by an amount determined under paragraph (2);

(b) in the case of a week in respect of which paragraph (1)(a) does not apply but where—

    (i) that week is a week subsequent to the relevant week, and

    (ii) that relevant week is a week in which the condition in paragraph (3) is satisfied,

shall be reduced by an amount determined under paragraph (3).

(2) This paragraph applies to a benefit week or part week where the claimant satisfies the conditions that—

(a) he is in receipt of a jobseeker's allowance; and

(b) but for regulation 113(1), he would have received an additional amount of jobseeker's allowance in that benefit week or, as the case may be, that part week;

and in such a case, the amount of the reduction for the purposes of paragraph (1)(a) shall be equal to that additional amount.

(3) Subject to paragraph (4), for the purposes of paragraph (1)(b) the condition is that the claimant would have been entitled to an income-based jobseeker's allowance in the relevant week but for regulation 113(1), and in such a case the amount of the reduction shall be equal to the aggregate of—

(a) the amount of jobseeker's allowance to which the claimant would have been entitled in the relevant week but for regulation 113(1); and for the purposes of this sub-paragraph if the relevant week is a part-week that amount shall be determined by dividing the amount of jobseeker's allowance to which he would have been entitled by the number equal to the number of days in the part-week and multiplying the quotient by 7;

(b) the amount of housing benefit (if any) equal to the difference between his maximum housing benefit and the amount (if any) of housing benefit which he is awarded in respect of the benefit week which includes the last day of the relevant week, and for this purpose "benefit week" has the same meaning as in regulation 2(1) of the Housing Benefit (General) Regulations 1987 (interpretation);

(c) the amount of council tax benefit (if any) equal to the difference between his maximum council tax benefit and the amount (if any) of council tax benefit which he is awarded in respect of the benefit week which includes the last day of the relevant week, and for this purpose "benefit week" has the same meaning as in regulation 2(1) of the Council Tax Benefit (General) Regulations 1992 (interpretation).

(4) The amount determined under paragraph (3) shall be re-determined under that paragraph if the claimant makes a further claim for a jobseeker's allowance and the conditions in paragraph (5) are satisfied, and in such a case—

(a) sub-paragraphs (a), (b) and (c) of paragraph (3) shall apply as if for the words "relevant week" there were substituted the words "relevant subsequent week"; and

(b) subject to paragraph (6), the amount as re-determined shall have effect from the first week following the relevant subsequent week in question.

(5) The conditions referred to in paragraph (4) are that—

(a) a further claim is made 26 or more weeks after—

(i) the date on which the claimant made a claim for a jobseeker's allowance in respect of which he was first treated as possessing the capital in question under regulation 113(1); or

(ii) in a case where there has been at least one re-determination in accordance with paragraph (4), the date on which he last made a claim for a jobseeker's allowance which resulted in the weekly amount being re-determined; or

(iii) the date on which he last ceased to be in receipt of a jobseeker's allowance;

whichever last occurred; and

(b) the claimant would have been entitled to a jobseeker's allowance but for regulation 113(1).

(6) The amount as re-determined pursuant to paragraph (4) shall not have effect if it is less than the amount which applied in that case immediately before the re-determination and in such a case the higher amount shall continue to have effect.

(7) For the purposes of this regulation—

(a) "part-week" has the same meaning as in regulation 150(3);

(b) "relevant week" means the benefit week or part-week in which the capital in question of which the claimant has deprived himself within the meaning of regulation 113(1)—

(i) was first taken into account for the purposes of determining his entitlement to a jobseeker's allowance or income support; or

(ii) was taken into account on a subsequent occasion for the purposes of determining or re-determining his entitlement to a jobseeker's allowance or income support on that subsequent occasion and that determination or re-determination resulted in his beginning to receive, or ceasing to receive, a jobseeker's allowance or income support;

and where more than one benefit week or part-week is identified by reference to heads (i) and (ii) of this sub-paragraph, the later or latest such benefit week or part-week;

(c) "relevant subsequent week" means the benefit week or part-week which includes the day on which the further claim or, if more than one further claim has been made, the last such claim was made.

DEFINITIONS

3.432   "benefit week"—see reg.1(3).
"claimant"—see Jobseekers Act, s.35(1), reg.88(1).
"week"—see Jobseekers Act, s.35(1).

GENERAL NOTE

See the notes to reg.51A of the Income Support Regulations.

Capital jointly held

3.433   **115.** Except where a claimant possesses capital which is disregarded under regulation 113(4) (notional capital), where a claimant and one or more persons are beneficially entitled in possession to any capital asset, they shall be treated as if each of them were entitled in possession [¹to the whole beneficial interest therein in an equal share and the foregoing provisions of this Chapter shall apply for the purposes of calculating the amount of capital which the claimant is treated as possessing as if it were actual capital which the claimant does possess.]

AMENDMENT

3.434   1. Social Security Amendment (Capital) Regulations 1998 (SI 1998/2250), reg.2 (October 12, 1998).

DEFINITION

"claimant"—see Jobseekers Act, s.35(1), reg.88(1).

GENERAL NOTE

3.435   See the notes to reg.52 of the Income Support Regulations.

Calculation of tariff income from capital

3.436   **116.**—(1) [¹Except in a case to which paragraph [⁴ (1ZA) or] (1B) applies,] where the claimant's capital calculated in accordance with this Part exceeds £3,000 it shall be treated as equivalent to a weekly income of £1 for each complete £250 in excess of £3,000 but not exceeding £8,000.
    [⁴ (1ZA) Where the claimant—
    (a) is aged 60 or over or has a partner who is aged 60 or over;
    (b) is not a person to whom the circumstances prescribed in paragraph (1B) apply; and
    (c) has capital which, calculated in accordance with this Part, exceeds £6,000,
that capital shall be treated as equivalent to a weekly income of £1 for each complete £250 in excess of £6,000 but not exceeding £12,000.]
    [¹(1A) In the case of a claimant to whom paragraph (1B) applies and whose capital calculated in accordance with Chapter VI of Part VIII exceeds £10,000, it shall be treated as equivalent to a weekly income of £1 for each complete £250 in excess of £10,000 but not exceeding £16,000.
    (1B) This paragraph applies where the claimant lives permanently in—
    (a) a residential care or nursing home [² . . .] and that home [² . . .] provides board and personal care for the claimant by reason of his disablement, past or present dependence on alcohol or drugs or past or present mental disorder; or

(b) an establishment run by the Abbeyfield Society including all bodies corporate or incorporate which are affiliated to that Society; or

(c) accommodation provided under section 3 of, and Part II of the Schedule to, the Polish Resettlement Act 1947 (provision of accommodation in camps) where the claimant requires personal care [³by reason of old age, disablement, past or present dependence on alcohol or drugs, past or present mental disorder or a terminal illness and the care is provided in the home];

[²(d) residential accommodation.]

(1C) For the purpose of paragraph (1B), a claimant shall be treated as living permanently in such home or accommodation where he is absent—

[⁵(a) from a home or accommodation referred to in sub-paragraph (a), (b) or (d) of paragraph (1B) for a period not exceeding 13 weeks;]

(b) from accommodation referred to in sub-paragraph (c) of paragraph (1B), but intends, with the agreement of the manager of the accommodation, to return to the accommodation in due course.]

(2) Notwithstanding [¹paragraphs (1) [⁴, (1ZA)] and (1A)], where any part of the excess is not a complete £250 that part shall be treated as equivalent to a weekly income of £1.

(3) For the purposes of [¹paragraphs (1) [⁴, (1ZA)] and (1A)], capital includes any income treated as capital under regulations 110 and 124 (income treated as capital and liable relative payments treated as capital).

[¹(4) In its application to this regulation, the definition of "residential accommodation" in regulation 85(4) (special cases) shall have effect as if, after the words "subject to the following provisions of this regulation", there were inserted the words "(except paragraph (6))".]

AMENDMENTS

1. Jobseeker's Allowance (Amendment) Regulations 1996 (SI 1996/1516), reg.12 (October 7, 1996).   **3.437**

2. Income-related Benefits and Jobseeker's Allowance (Miscellaneous Amendments) Regulations 1997 (SI 1997/65), reg.8 (April 7, 1997).

3. Income-related Benefits and Jobseeker's Allowance (Amendment) (No.2) Regulations 1997 (SI 1997/2197), reg.7(5) and (6)(b) (October 6, 1997).

4. Social Security Amendment (Capital Limits and Earnings Disregards) Regulations 2000 (SI 2000/2545), reg.2(2)(c) (April 9, 2001).

5. Social Security Amendment (Residential Care and Nursing Homes) Regulations 2001 (SI 2001/3767), reg.2(2) and Pt II of Sch., para.12 (April 8, 2002).

DEFINITIONS

"claimant"—see Jobseekers Act, s.35(1), reg.88(1)
"nursing home"—see reg.1(3).
"residential accommodation"—*ibid.*
"residential care home"—*ibid.*

GENERAL NOTE

See the notes to reg.53 of the Income Support Regulations.

Chapter VII

Liable relatives

Interpretation

3.438 **117.** In this Chapter, unless the context otherwise requires—
"claimant" includes a young claimant;
"liable relative" means—

(a) a spouse or former spouse of a claimant or of a member of the claimant's family;

(b) a parent of a young claimant or of a child or young person who is a member of a claimant's family;

(c) a person who has not been adjudged to be the father of a young claimant or of a child or young person who is a member of a claimant's family, where that person is contributing to the maintenance of that young claimant, child or young person and by reason of that contribution he may reasonably be treated as the father of that young claimant, child or young person;

(d) a person liable to maintain another person by virtue of section 78(6)(c) of the Administration Act where the latter is the claimant or a member of the claimant's family,

and, in this definition, a reference to a child's, young person's or young claimant's parent includes any person in relation to whom the child, young person or young claimant was treated as a child or a member of the family;

"payment" means a periodical payment or any other payment made by or derived from a liable relative including, except in the case of a discretionary trust, any payment which would be so made or derived upon application being made by the claimant but which has not been acquired by him, but only from the date on which it could be expected to be acquired were an application made; but it does not include any payment—

(a) arising as a consequence of a disposition of property made in contemplation of, or as a consequence of—

(i) an agreement to separate; or

(ii) any proceedings for judicial separation, divorce or nullity of marriage;

(b) made after the death of the liable relative;

(c) made by way of a gift but not in aggregate or otherwise exceeding £250 in the period of 52 weeks beginning with the date on which the payment, or if there is more than one such payment the first payment, is made; and in the case of a claimant who continues to be in receipt of an income-based jobseeker's allowance at the end of the period of 52 weeks, this provision shall continue to apply thereafter with the modification than any subsequent period of 52 weeks shall begin with the first day of the benefit week in which the first payment is made after the end of the previous period of 52 weeks;

(d) [¹ . . .]

(e) made—

(i) to a third party in respect of the claimant or a member of the claimant's family; or

(ii) to the claimant or to a member of the claimant's family in respect of a third party,

where having regard to the nature of the payment, the terms under which it is made and its amount, it is unreasonable to take it into account;

(f) in kind;

(g) to or in respect of a child or young person who is to be treated as not being a member of the claimant's household under regulation 78;

(h) which is not a periodical payment, to the extent that any amount of that payment—

(i) has already been taken into account under this Part by virtue of a previous claim or determination; or

(ii) has been recovered under section 74(1) of the Administration Act (prevention of duplication of payments) or is currently being recovered; or

(iii) at the time the determination is made, has been used by the claimant except where he has deprived himself of that amount for the purpose of securing entitlement to a job-seeker's allowance or increasing the amount of that allowance;

"periodical payment" means—

(a) a payment which is made or is due to be made at regular intervals in pursuance of a court order or agreement for maintenance;

(b) in a case where the liable relative has established a pattern of making payments at regular intervals, any such payment;

(c) any payment not exceeding the amount of jobseeker's allowance payable had that payment not been made;

(d) any payment representing a commutation of payments to which sub-paragraph (a) or (b) of this definition applies whether made in arrears or in advance,

but does not include a payment due to be made before the benefit week in which the claimant first became entitled to an income-based job-seeker's allowance, which was not so made;

"young claimant" means a person aged 16 or over but under 19 who makes a claim for a jobseeker's allowance.

AMENDMENT

1. Social Security (Working Tax Credit and Child Tax Credit) (Consequential Amendments) Regulations 2003 (SI 2003/455), reg.3 and Sch.2, para.14 (April 6, 2004, except in "transitional cases" and see further the note to reg.83 and to reg. 17 of the Income Support Regulations).

DEFINITIONS

"benefit week"—see reg.1(3).

"child"—see Jobseekers Act, s.35(1).

"claimant"—*ibid.*, reg.88(1).

"family"—see Jobseekers Act, s.35(1).

"young person"—see reg.76.

3.439

GENERAL NOTE

See the notes to reg.54 of the Income Support Regulations.

Treatment of liable relative payments

3.440   **118.** Subject to regulation 119 and except where regulation 124(1) applies (liable relative payments to be treated as capital) a payment shall—

      (a) to the extent that it is not a payment of income, be treated as income;

      (b) be taken into account in accordance with the following provisions of this Chapter.

DEFINITION

    "payment"—see reg.117.

GENERAL NOTE

    See the note to reg.55 of the Income Support Regulations.

Disregard of payments treated as not relevant income

3.441   **119.** Where the Secretary of State treats any payment as not being relevant income for the purposes of section 74A of the Administration Act (payment of benefit where maintenance payments collected by Secretary of State), that payment shall be disregarded in calculating a claimant's income.

DEFINITIONS

    "payment"—see reg.117.

    "relevant income"—see reg.2(c), Social Security Benefits (Maintenance Payments and Consequential Amendments) Regulations 1996 (SI 1996/940) (p.721).

GENERAL NOTE

    See reg.55A of the Income Support Regulations and the note to s.74A of the Administration Act in Vol. III of this series.

Period over which periodical payments are to be taken into account

3.442   **120.**—(1) The period over which a periodical payment is to be taken into account shall be—

      (a) in a case where the payment is made at regular intervals, a period equal to the length of that interval;

      (b) in a case where the payment is due to be made at regular intervals but is not so made, such number of weeks as is equal to the number obtained (and any fraction shall be treated as a corresponding fraction of a week) by dividing the amount of that payment by the weekly amount of that periodical payment as calculated in accordance with regulation 122(4);

      (c) in any other case, a period equal to a week.

    (2) The period under paragraph (1) shall begin on the date on which the payment is treated as paid under regulation 123.

DEFINITION

    "periodical payment"—see reg.117.

GENERAL NOTE

    See the note to reg.56 of the Income Support Regulations.

Period over which payments other than periodical payments are to be taken into account

121.—(1) Subject to paragraph (2), the number of weeks over which a payment other than a periodical payment is to be taken into account shall be equal to the number (and any fraction shall be treated as a corresponding fraction of a week) obtained by dividing that payment [⁴ by the aggregate] of £2 and the amount of jobseeker's allowance which would be payable had the payment not been made;

  (a) [⁴ . . .]

  (b) [⁴ . . .].

(2) Where a liable relative makes a periodical payment and any other payment concurrently and the weekly amount of that periodical payment, as calculated in accordance with regulation 122 (calculation of the weekly amount of a liable relative payment), is less than [⁴ . . .] the aggregate of £2 and the amount of jobseeker's allowance which would be payable had the payments not been made [⁴ . . .]

  (a) [⁴ . . .]

  (b) [⁴ . . .]

that other payment shall, subject to paragraph (3), be taken into account over a period of such number of weeks as is equal to the number obtained (and any fraction shall be treated as a corresponding fraction of a week) by dividing that payment by an amount equal to the extent of the difference between the amount [⁴ as calculated under this paragraph] and the weekly amount of the periodical payment.

(3) If—

  (a) the liable relative ceases to make periodical payments, the balance (if any) of the other payment shall be taken into account over the number of weeks equal to the number obtained (and any fraction shall be treated as a corresponding fraction of a week) by dividing that balance by the amount referred to in [⁴ . . .] paragraph (1);

  (b) the amount of any subsequent periodical payment varies, the balance (if any) of the other payment shall be taken into account over a period of such number of weeks as is equal to the number obtained (and any fraction shall be treated as a corresponding fraction of a week) by dividing that balance by an amount equal to the extent of the difference between the amount referred to in [⁴ . . .] paragraph (2), and the weekly amount of the subsequent periodical payment.

(4) The period under paragraph (1) or (2) shall begin on the date on which the payment is treated as paid under regulation 123, and under paragraph (3) shall begin on the first day of the benefit week in which the cessation or variation of the periodical payment occurred.

AMENDMENTS

1. Child Benefit, Child Support and Social Security (Miscellaneous Amendments) Regulations 1996 (SI 1996/1803), reg.43 (April 7, 1997).

2. Social Security Amendment (Enhanced Disability Premium) Regulations 2000 (SI 2000/2629), reg.5(b) (April 9, 2001).

3. Social Security (Miscellaneous Amendments) Regulations 2003 (SI 2003/511), reg.3(4) and (5) (April 1, 2003).

4. Social Security (Working Tax Credit and Child Tax Credit) (Consequential Amendments) Regulations 2003 (SI 2003/455), reg.3 and Sch.2, para.15

3.443

3.444

(April 6, 2004, except in "transitional cases" and see further the note to reg.83 and to reg.17 of the Income Support Regulations).

DEFINITIONS

> "child"—see Jobseekers Act, s.35(1).
> "claimant"—*ibid.*, reg.88(1).
> "family"—see Jobseekers Act, s.35(1).
> "liable relative"—see reg.117.
> "payment"—*ibid.*
> "periodical payment"—*ibid.*
> "young person"—see reg.76.

GENERAL NOTE

See the note to reg.57 of the Income Support Regulations.

Calculation of the weekly amount of a liable relative payment

3.445 **122.**—(1) Where a periodical payment is made or is due to be made at intervals of one week, the weekly amount shall be the amount of that payment.

(2) Where a periodical payment is made or is due to be made at intervals greater than one week and those intervals are monthly, the weekly amount shall be determined by multiplying the amount of the payment by 12 and dividing the product by 52.

(3) Where a periodical payment is made or is due to be made at intervals and those intervals are neither weekly or monthly, the weekly amount shall be determined by dividing that payment by the number equal to the number of weeks (including any part of a week) in that interval.

(4) Where a payment is made and that payment represents a commutation of periodical payments whether in arrears or in advance, the weekly amount shall be the weekly amount of the individual periodical payments so commuted as calculated under paragraphs (1) to (3) as appropriate.

(5) The weekly amount of a payment to which regulation 121 applies (period over which payments other than periodical payments are to be taken into account) shall be equal to the amount of the divisor used in calculating the period over which the payment or, as the case may be, the balance is to be taken into account.

DEFINITIONS

> "payment"—see reg.117.
> "periodical payment"—*ibid.*

GENERAL NOTE

See the note to reg.58 of the Income Support Regulations.

Date on which a liable relative payment is to be treated as paid

3.446 **123.**—(1) A periodical payment is to be treated as paid—
(a) in the case of a payment which is due to be made before the benefit week in which the claimant first became entitled to an income-based jobseeker's allowance, on the day in the week in which it is due to be paid which corresponds to the first day of the benefit week;

(b) in any other case, on the first day of the benefit week in which it is due to be paid unless, having regard to the manner in which jobseeker's allowance is due to be paid in the particular case, it would be more practicable to treat it as paid on the first day of a subsequent benefit week.

(2) Subject to paragraph (3), any other payment shall be treated as paid—

(a) in the case of a payment which is made before the benefit week in which the claimant first became entitled to an income-based jobseeker's allowance, on the day in the week in which it is paid which corresponds to the first day of the benefit week;

(b) in any other case, on the first day of the benefit week in which it is paid unless, having regard to the manner in which jobseeker's allowance is due to be paid in the particular case, it would be more practicable to treat it as paid on the first day of a subsequent benefit week.

(3) Any other payment paid on a date which falls within the period in respect of which a previous payment is taken into account, not being a periodical payment, is to be treated as paid on the first day following the end of that period.

DEFINITIONS

"benefit week"—see reg.1(3).
"payment"—see reg.117.
"periodical payment"—*ibid.*

GENERAL NOTE

See the notes to reg.59 of the Income Support Regulations.

Liable relative payments to be treated as capital

124.—(1) Subject to paragraph (2), where a liable relative makes a periodical payment concurrently with any other payment, and the weekly amount of the periodical payment as calculated in accordance with regulation 122(1) to (4) (calculation of the weekly amount of a liable relative payment) is equal to or greater than the amount referred to in sub-paragraph (a) of regulation 121(2) (period over which payments other than periodical payments are to be taken into account), less the £2 referred to therein, or sub-paragraph (b) of that regulation, as the case may be, the other payment shall be treated as capital.   3.447

(2) If, in any case, the liable relative ceases to make periodical payments, the other payment to which paragraph (1) applies shall be taken into account under paragraph (1) of regulation 121 but, notwithstanding paragraph (4) thereof, the period over which the payment is to be taken into account shall begin on the first day of the benefit week following the last one in which a periodical payment was taken into account.

DEFINITIONS

"benefit week"—see reg.1(3).
"liable relative"—see reg.117.
"payment"—*ibid.*
"periodical payment"—*ibid.*

GENERAL NOTE

See the note to reg.60 of the Income Support Regulations.

Chapter VIII

Child Support

Interpretation

3.448   **125.** In this Chapter—

"child support maintenance" means such periodical payments as are referred to in section 3(6) of the Child Support Act 1991[¹ and shall include any payments made by the Secretary of State in lieu of such payments];

"maintenance [² calculation]" has the same meaning as in the Child Support Act 1991 by virtue of section 54 of that Act.

AMENDMENTS

1. Social Security (Child Maintenance Premium and Miscellaneous Amendments) Regulations 2000 (SI 2000/3176), reg.2(2)(a) (in force in relation to any particular case on the day on which s.23 of the Child Support, Pensions and Social Security Act 2000 comes into force in relation to that type of case. Note that the commencement provision of these regulations (reg.1) was substituted by reg.4 of the Social Security (Child Maintenance Premium) Amendment Regulations 2004 (SI 2004/98) on February 16, 2004 to provide that the 2000 Regulations come into force as follows: on (i) February 16, 2004 in relation to any particular case in respect of which s.23 CSPSSA 2000 has come into force before February 16, 2004; (ii) where this does not apply, the day on which s.23 comes into force in relation to that type of case; (iii) February 16, 2004 in relation to a person who is entitled to income support/income-based JSA on that date and who receives her first payment of child maintenance made voluntarily whilst entitled to income support/income-based JSA on that date; (iv) in such a case where the day that the first voluntary payment is received is after February 16, 2004, the day the payment is received; (v) February 16, 2004 in relation to a person who makes a claim for income support/income-based JSA on or after that date and receives a payment of child maintenance made voluntarily on or after the date of that claim).

2. Child Support (Consequential Amendments and Transitional Provisions) Regulations 2001 (SI 2001/158), reg.7(2) (in force in relation to any particular case on the day on which s.1 of the Child Support, Pensions and Social Security Act 2000 comes into force in relation to that type of case).

GENERAL NOTE

See the note to reg.60A of the Income Support Regulations.

Treatment of child support maintenance

3.449   **126.** Subject to regulation 127, all payments of child support maintenance shall to the extent that they are not payments of income be treated as income and shall be taken into account on a weekly basis in accordance with the following provisions of this Chapter.

DEFINITIONS

"child support maintenance"—see reg.125.
"payment"—see reg.1(3).

GENERAL NOTE

See the note to reg.60B of the Income Support Regulations.

Disregard of payments treated as not relevant income

127. Where the Secretary of State treats any payment of child support 3.450
maintenance as not being relevant income for the purposes of section 74A
of the Administration Act (payment of benefit where maintenance payments
collected by Secretary of State), that payment shall be disregarded in calculating a claimant's income.

DEFINITIONS

"child support maintenance"—see reg.125.
"payment"—see reg.1(3).
"relevant income"—see reg.2(c), Social Security Benefits (Maintenance Payments
and Consequential Amendments) Regulations 1996 (SI 1996/940) (p.721).

GENERAL NOTE

See reg.60E of the Income Support Regulations and the note to s.74A of the
Administration Act in Vol. III of this series.

Calculation of the weekly amount of child support maintenance

128.—(1) The weekly amount of child support maintenance shall be cal- 3.451
culated in accordance with the following provisions of this regulation.
(2) Where payments of child support maintenance are made weekly, the
weekly amount shall be the amount of that payment.
(3) Where payments of child support maintenance are made monthly, the
weekly amount shall be determined by multiplying the amount of the
payment by 12 and dividing the product by 52.
(4) Where payments of child support are made at intervals and those
intervals are not a week or a month, the weekly amount shall be determined
by dividing that payment by the number equal to the number of weeks
(including any part of a week) in that interval.
(5) Where a payment is made and that payment represents a commutation
of child support maintenance, the weekly amount shall be the weekly amount
of the individual child support maintenance payments so commuted as calculated in accordance with paragraphs (2) to (4) as appropriate.
(6) Paragraph (2), (3), or, as the case may be, (4) shall apply to any payments made at the intervals specified in that paragraph whether or not—
  (a) the amount paid is in accordance with the maintenance [¹ calcula-
      tion]; and
  (b) the intervals at which the payments are made are in accordance with the
      intervals specified by the Secretary of State under regulation 4 of the
      Child Support (Collection and Enforcement) Regulations 1992.

AMENDMENT

1. Child Support (Consequential Amendments and Transitional Provisions) 3.452
Regulations 2001 (SI 2001/158), reg.7(2) (in force in relation to any particular case

on the day on which s.1 of the Child Support, Pensions and Social Security Act 2000 comes into force in relation to that type of case).

DEFINITIONS

"child support maintenance"—see reg.125.
"maintenance calculation"—*ibid.*
"payment"—see reg.1(3).

GENERAL NOTE

See the notes to reg.60C of the Income Support Regulations.

Date on which child support maintenance is to be treated as paid

3.453   **129.**—(1) Subject to paragraph (2), a payment of child support mainte-nance is to be treated as paid—

(a) [¹subject to sub-paragraph (aa),] in the case of a payment which is due to be made before the benefit week in which the claimant first became entitled to an income-based jobseeker's allowance, on the day in the week in which it is due to be paid which corresponds to the first day of the benefit week;

[¹(aa) in the case of any amount of a payment which represents arrears of maintenance for a week prior to the benefit week in which the claimant first became entitled to an income-based jobseeker's allowance, on the day of the week in which it became due which cor-responds to the first day of the benefit week;]

(b) in any other case, on the first day of the benefit week in which it is due to be paid or the first day of the first succeeding benefit week in which it is practicable to take it into account.

[¹(2) Where a payment to which paragraph (1)(b) refers is made to the Secretary of State and then transmitted to the person entitled to receive it, the payment shall be treated as paid on the first day of the benefit week in which it is transmitted or, where it is not practicable to take it into account in that week, the first day of the first succeeding benefit week in which it is practicable to take the payment into account.]

AMENDMENT

3.454   1. Social Security and Child Support (Jobseeker's Allowance) (Miscellaneous Amendments) Regulations 1996 (SI 1996/2538), reg.2(8) (October 28, 1996).

DEFINITIONS

"benefit week"—see reg.1(3).
"child support maintenance"—see reg.125.

GENERAL NOTE

See the note to reg.60D of the Income Support Regulations.

Chapter IX

[⁴Students]

Interpretation

3.455   **130.** In this Chapter, unless the context otherwise requires—
[⁷ "academic year" means the period of twelve months beginning on 1st

January, 1st April, 1st July or 1st September according to whether the course in question begins in the winter, the spring, the summer or the autumn respectively but if students are required to begin attending the course during August or September and to continue attending through the autumn, the academic year of the course shall be considered to begin in the autumn rather than the summer;]
[⁵ "access funds" means—

(a) grants made under section 7 of the Further and Higher Education Act 1992 and described as "learner support funds" or grants made under section 68 of that Act [⁷ for the purpose of providing funds on a discretionary basis to be paid to students];

(b) grants made under sections 73(a) and (c) and 74(1) of the Education (Scotland) Act 1980; [⁷ . . .]

(c) grants made under Article 30 of the Education and Libraries (Northern Ireland) Order 1993, or grants, loans or other payments made under Article 5 of the Further Education (Northern Ireland) Order 1997 in each case being grants, or grants, loans or other payments as the case may be, made for the purpose of assisting students in financial difficulties;] [⁷ [⁸ . . .]

(d) discretionary payments, known as "learner support funds", which are made available to students in further education by institutions out of funds provided by the Learning and Skills Council for England under sections 5, 6 and 9 of the Learning and Skills Act 2000;] [⁸ or

(e) Financial Contingency Funds made available by the National Assembly for Wales;]

"contribution" means any contribution in respect of the income [¹of a student or] of any other person which the Secretary of State [⁷, the Scottish Ministers] or an education authority takes into account in ascertaining the amount of the student's grant [²or student loan], or any sums, which in determining the amount of a student's allowance or bursary in Scotland in terms of the Students' Allowances (Scotland) Regulations 1991 or the Education Authority (Bursaries) (Scotland) Regulations 1995, the [⁷ Scottish Ministers] or education authority takes into account being sums which the [⁷ Scottish Ministers] or the education authority consider that the holder of the allowance or bursary, the holder's parents and the holder's spouse can reasonably be expected to contribute towards the holder's expenses;

"covenant income" means the income payable to a student under a deed of covenant by a person whose income is, or is likely to be, taken into account in assessing the student's grant or award;

"education authority" means a government department, a local education authority as defined in section 114(1) of the Education Act 1944, a local education authority as defined in section 123 of the Local Government (Scotland) Act 1973, an education and library board established under article 3 of the Education and Libraries (Northern Ireland) Order 1986, any body which is a research council for the purposes of the Science and Technology Act 1965 or any analogous government department, authority, board or body, of the Channel Islands, Isle of Man or any other country outside Great Britain;

[⁵ "grant" (except in the definition of "access funds") means any kind of educational grant or award and includes any scholarship, studentship, exhibition, allowance or bursary but does not include a payment from access funds [⁹ or any payment to which paragraph 12 of Schedule 7 or paragraph 52 of Schedule 8 applies];]

"grant income" means—

(a) any income by way of a grant;

(b) in the case of a student other than one to whom sub-paragraph (c) refers, any contribution that has been taken into account whether or not it has been paid;

(c) in the case of a student who satisfies the additional conditions for a disability premium in paragraph 14 of Schedule 1 (applicable amounts), any contribution which has been taken into account and which has been paid,

and any such contribution which is paid by way of a covenant shall be treated as part of the student's grant income;

[³ . . .]

[⁸ "periods of experience" means periods of work experience which form part of a sandwich course;]

"standard maintenance grant" means—

(a) except where paragraph (b) or (c) applies, in the case of a student attending [³ or undertaking] a course of study at the University of London or an establishment within the area comprising the City of London and the Metropolitan Police District, the amount specified for the time being in paragraph 2(2)(a) of Schedule 2 to the Education (Mandatory Awards) Regulations 1995 ("the 1995 regulations") for such a student;

(b) except where paragraph (c) applies, in the case of a student residing at his parents' home, the amount specified in paragraph 3(2) thereof;

[⁷ (c) in the case of a student receiving an allowance or bursary under the Education (Scotland) Act 1980, the amount of money specified as the "standard maintenance allowance" for the relevant year appropriate for the student set out in the Student Support in Scotland Guide issued by the Student Awards Agency for Scotland, or its nearest equivalent in the case of a bursary provided by a college of further education or a local education authority and paid under the Further and Higher Education (Scotland) Act 1992;]

(d) in any other case, the amount specified in paragraph 2(2) of the 1995 regulations other than in sub-paragraph (a) or (b) thereof;

[⁶ . . .]

[² "student loan" means a loan towards a student's maintenance pursuant to any regulations made under section 22 of the Teaching and Higher Education Act 1998, section 73 of the Education (Scotland) Act 1980 or Article 3 of the Education (Student Support) (Northern Ireland) Order 1998 [⁷ and shall include, in Scotland, a young student's bursary paid under regulation 4(1)(c) of the Students' Allowances (Scotland) Regulations 1999];

[⁷ . . .]

AMENDMENTS

3.456   1. Social Security (Miscellaneous Amendments) Regulations 1998 (SI 1998/563), reg.4(1) and (2)(f) (April 6, 1998).

2. Social Security Amendment (Students) Regulations 1999 (SI 1999/1935), reg.2(2) (August 30, 1999, or if the student's period of study begins between August 1 and 29, 1999, the first day of the period).

3. Social Security Amendment (Students) Regulations 2000 (SI 2000/1981), reg.6(4) (July 31, 2000).

4. Social Security Amendment (Students and Income-related Benefits) Regulations 2000 (SI 2000/1922), reg.3(3) (August 28, 2000, or if the student's period of study begins between August 1 and 27, 2000, the first day of the period).

5. Social Security Amendment (Students and Income-related Benefits) Regulations 2000 (SI 2000/1922), reg.3(4) (August 28, 2000, or if the student's period of study begins between August 1 and 27, 2000, the first day of the period).

6. Social Security Amendment (Students and Income-related Benefits) Regulations 2000 (SI 2000/1922), reg.3(5) (August 28, 2000, or if the student's period of study begins between August 1 and 27, 2000, the first day of the period).

7. Social Security Amendment (Students and Income-related Benefits) Regulations 2001 (SI 2001/2319), reg.2(1)(a) and (2)(d) (August 1, 2001).

8. Social Security Amendment (Students and Income-related Benefits) Regulations 2002 (SI 2002/1589), reg.2(3)(b) (August 1, 2002).

9. Social Security (Students and Income-related Benefits) Amendment Regulations 2004 (SI 2004/1708), reg.6(2) (September 1, 2004, or if the student's period of study begins between August 1 and August 31, 2004, the first day of the period).

DEFINITIONS

"full-time student"—see reg.1(3).
"sandwich course"—*ibid.*

GENERAL NOTE

See the notes to reg.61 of the Income Support Regulations.   3.457

Under JSA the definitions applying to full-time students are in a slightly different form. The main definitions for the purpose of defining full-time student status are in reg.1(3) (namely "course of advanced education", "course of study", "full-time course of advanced education", "full-time student" and "part-time student"); see also paras (3A) to (3E) of reg.1 which apply for the purposes of the definition of "full-time student". Since the amendments made to both the Income Support Regulations and the JSA Regulations on July 31, 2000 by SI 2000/1981 the differences from income support are less marked.

On the pre-July 31, 2000 form, see *CJSA 836/1996*, discussed in the notes to reg.61 of the Income Support Regulations under "*Difference between income support and JSA definition*". The Commissioner in that case took the view that the differences between the then form of the JSA and income support definitions were material. In his view the result was that for the purposes of JSA the question whether a person was attending or undertaking a full- or part-time course had to be determined by looking at the situation at the time in question (rather than at the commencement of the course, as was the case for income support). (Note that *CJSA 836/1996* was not followed in *C5/98(JSA)* (a Northern Ireland decision)). However, since the insertion of paras (3A) to (3C) into reg.1 (which provisions parallel reg.61(2) to (4) of the Income Support Regulations) with effect from July 31, 2000, the Commissioner's reasoning in *CJSA 836/1998* no longer applies. This is because the deeming of full-time student status for the entire length of a course (subject to earlier final abandonment or dismissal) is now contained in reg.1(3A)(b), rather than the definition of "course of study" in reg.1(3).

Note paras (3D) and (3E) inserted into reg.1 at the same time. (There is no equivalent to these provisions in the Income Support Regulations.) The effect of these provisions is to allow a full-time student who has taken time out of his course with the consent of his university or college because of illness or caring responsibilities (not defined), and who has now recovered or whose caring responsibilities have ended, to claim JSA until the earlier of the day before he rejoins his course or the date the relevant educational establishment has agreed that he can rejoin (subject to a maximum of one year). This does not apply if the person is eligible for a grant or student loan during this period.

In *CJSA 1920/1999* the claimant was a full-time student who had applied for a fixed term leave of absence from her course because she was pregnant. Her claim for JSA was refused because she was deemed to be a full-time student. The Commissioner decided (disagreeing with *CJSA 4890/1998*) that JSA was a single benefit and was within the scope of EC Directive 79/7 (on equal treatment in social security). He also concluded that discrimination against a pregnant student was direct discrimination against women in breach of Art.4 of Directive 79/7, that there was such discrimination under the JSA Regulations and that no justification for that discrimination had been established.

The Commissioner in *CJSA 1920/1999* granted the Secretary of State leave to appeal to the Court of Appeal. But in the meantime on May 2, 2001 the Court of Appeal allowed the claimant's appeal against the decision in *CJSA 4890/1998* (*Hockenjos v Secretary of State*, [2001] E.W.C.A. Civ. 624, [2001] 2 C.M.L.R. 51, [2001] I.C.R. 966). The Court of Appeal held that the Jobseekers Act 1995 had set up a unitary statutory scheme to provide against the risk of unemployment which was covered by Art.3(1)(a) of the Directive. Thus both contribution-based and income-based JSA were within the scope of Directive 79/7.

However the Court of Appeal allowed the Secretary of State's appeal against the decision in *CJSA 1920/1999* (*Secretary of State for Social Security v Walter* [2001] EWCA Civ 1913, *The Times*, December 13, 2001). The Court disagreed with the Commissioner's conclusion that the JSA Regulations directly discriminate against pregnant women, although the question of whether they may indirectly discriminate was left open. Arguments that there is such indirect discrimination, or indeed incompatibility with the Human Rights Act, may therefore be raised in the future.

Calculation of grant income

3.458   **131.**—(1) The amount of a student's grant income to be taken into account shall, subject to paragraphs [⁴(2) and (3)], be the whole of his grant income.

(2) There shall be disregarded from the amount of a student's grant income any payment—

(a) intended to meet tuition fees or examination fees;

(b) intended to meet additional expenditure incurred by a disabled student in respect of his attendance on a course;

(c) intended to meet additional expenditure connected with term time residential study away from the student's educational establishment;

(d) on account of the student maintaining a home at a place other than that at which he resides while attending his course but only to the extent that his rent is not met by housing benefit;

(e) on account of any other person but only if that person is residing outside the United Kingdom and there is no applicable amount in respect of him;

(f) intended to meet the cost of books and equipment [¹ . . .] [³ . . .];

(g) intended to meet travel expenses incurred as a result of his attendance on the course.

[¹²(h) intended for the maintenance [¹⁵. . .] of a child dependent].

[¹⁵(i) intended for the child care costs of a child dependant.]

[³(3) Where a student does not have a student loan and is not treated as possessing such a loan, there shall be excluded from the student's grant income—

(a) the sum of [[13] £275.00] in respect of travel costs; and
[[6](b) the sum of [[14] £343.00] towards the costs of books and equipment,]
whether or not any such costs are incurred.]

[[7][[12] (3A) There shall also be excluded from a student's grant income any
grant of £510 in respect of expenditure on travel, books, and equipment
which is payable under regulation 15(8) of the Education (Student Support)
Regulations 2002.]]

(4) [[4] Subject to paragraph (5A), a student's grant income except for any
amount intended for the maintenance of [[12] adult] dependants under Part
III of Schedule 2 to the Education (Mandatory Awards) Regulations 1999
[[12] . . .]] shall be apportioned—

   (a) subject to paragraph (6), in a case where it is attributable to the
       period of study, equally between the weeks [[10] in the period begin-
       ning with the benefit week, the first day of which coincides with, or
       immediately follows, the first day of the period of study and ending
       with the benefit week, the last day of which coincides with, or imme-
       diately precedes, the last day of the period of study];
   (b) in any other case, equally between the weeks in the period [[10]begin-
       ning with the benefit week, the first day of which coincides with, or
       immediately follows, the first day of the period for which it is payable
       and ending with the benefit week, the last day of which coincides
       with, or immediately precedes, the last day of the period for which it
       is payable].

(5) [[8]Any grant paid under section 63(6) of the Health Services and
Public Health Act 1968 (grants in respect of the provision of instruction
to officers of hospital authorities) and] any amount intended for the maintenance of [[12] an adult dependant] under the provisions referred to in paragraph (4) shall be apportioned equally over a period of 52 weeks, or if there
are 53 weeks (including part-weeks) in the year, 53.

[[4](5A) [[10] In a case where a student is in receipt of a student loan or where
he could have acquired a student loan by taking reasonable steps but had
not done so,] any amount intended for the maintenance of [[12]an adult
dependant] under provisions other than those referred to in paragraphs (4)
and (5), shall be apportioned over the same period as the student's loan is
apportioned or [[10], as the case may be, would have been apportioned]].

(6) In the case of a student on a sandwich course, any periods of experience within the period of study shall be excluded and the student's grant
income shall be apportioned equally between [[10]the weeks in the period
beginning with the benefit week, the first day of which immediately follows
the last day of the period of experience and ending with the benefit week,
the last day of which coincides with, or immediately precedes, the last day
of the period of study].

AMENDMENTS

1. Jobseeker's Allowance (Amendment) Regulations 1996 (SI 1996/1516), **3.459**
reg.20 and Sch. (October 7, 1996).
2. Social Security (Student Amounts Amendment) Regulations 1998 (SI
1998/1379), reg.2 (August 31, 1998, or if the student's period of study begins
between August 1, and 30, 1998, the first day of the period).
3. Social Security Amendment (Students) Regulations 1999 (SI 1999/1935),
reg.2(3) (August 30, 1999, or if the student's period of study begins between
August 1 and 29, 1999, the first day of the period).

4. Social Security Amendment (Students and Income-related Benefits) Regulations 2000 (SI 2000/1922), reg.3(6) (August 28, 2000, or if the student's period of study begins between August 1 and 27, 2000, the first day of the period).

5. Social Security Amendment (Students and Income-related Benefits) Regulations 2001 (SI 2001/2319), reg.3(1) and (3)(d) (August 27, 2001, or if the student's period of study begins between August 1 and 26, 2001, the first day of the period).

6. Social Security Amendment (Students and Income-related Benefits) Regulations 2001 (SI 2001/2319), reg.3(2) and (3)(d) (August 27, 2001, or if the student's period of study begins between August 1 and 26, 2001, the first day of the period).

7. Social Security Amendment (Students and Income-related Benefits) Regulations 2001 (SI 2001/2319), reg.3(4) (August 27, 2001, or if the student's period of study begins between August 1 and 26, 2001, the first day of the period).

8. Social Security Amendment (Students and Income-related Benefits) Regulations 2001 (SI 2001/2319), reg.6 (August 27, 2001, or if the student's period of study begins between August 1 and 26, 2001, the first day of the period).

9. Social Security Amendment (Students and Income-related Benefits) Regulations 2002 (SI 2002/1589), reg.3 (August 26, 2002, or if the student's period of study begins between August 1 and 25, 2002, the first day of the period).

10. Social Security Amendment (Students and Income-related Benefits) Regulations 2002 (SI 2002/1589), reg.4 (August 26, 2002, or if the student's period of study begins between August 1 and 25, 2002, the first day of the period).

11. Social Security Amendment (Students and Income-related Benefits) (No.2) Regulations 2002 (SI 2002/2207), reg.2 (September 2, 2002).

12. Social Security (Working Tax Credit and Child Tax Credit) (Consequential Amendments) Regulations 2003 (SI 2003/455), reg.3 and Sch.2, para.16 (April 6, 2004, except in "transitional cases" and see further the note to reg.83 and to reg.17 of the Income Support Regulations), as amended by Social Security (Working Tax Credit and Child Tax Credit) (Consequential Amendments) (No. 3) Regulations 2003 (SI 2003/1731), reg.6(5)(a) (August 8, 2003).

13. Social Security (Students and Income-related Benefits) Amendment Regulations 2004 (SI 2004/1708), reg.2(1) and (3)(d) (September 1, 2004, or if the student's period of study begins between August 1 and August 31, 2004, the first day of the period).

14. Social Security (Students and Income-related Benefits) Amendment Regulations 2004 (SI 2004/1708), reg.2(2) and (3)(d) (September 1, 2004, or if the student's period of study begins between August 1 and August 31, 2004, the first day of the period).

15. Social Security (Students and Income-related Benefits) Amendment Regulations 2004 (SI 2004/1708), reg.3(4) (September 1, 2004, or if the student's period of study begins between August 1 and August 31, 2004, the first day of the period).

DEFINITIONS

3.460

"grant"—see reg.130.
"grant income"—*ibid.*
"period of study"—see reg.1(3).
"periods of experience"—see reg.130.
"sandwich course"—see reg.1(3).
"student loan"—see reg.130.

GENERAL NOTE

See the notes to reg.62 of the Income Support Regulations.

The disregard in para.(2)(h) is a general disregard of any payment intended for the maintenance of a child and that in para.(2)(i) is a general disregard of any payment intended for child care costs. Both these disregards were previously contained in para.(2)(h) which was introduced on 6, April 2004 to replace the various disregards for students with child care responsibilities previously contained in para.(3A), except that in sub-para.(b) which became the new form of para.(3A). However the new para.2(h) and the amendments to para.(3A) did not apply in "transitional cases" (*i.e.* those cases in which the claimant is still receiving amounts for his children in his income-based JSA—see further the notes to reg.83 and to reg.17 of the Income Support Regulations). For "transitional cases" the old form of para.(3A) remained in force. However, the insertion of the new para.(2)(i) with effect from September 1, 2004 (or if the student's period of study begins between August 1 and 31, 2004, the first day of the period), which provides for a general disregard of payments intended for the child care costs of a child dependant, means that the disregards contained in sub-paras(c), (cc) and (d) of the unamended form of para.(3A) are no longer needed. These have therefore been omitted from the unamended form of para.(3A) with effect from September 1, 2004 (or if the student's period of study begins between August 1 and 31, 2004, the first day of the period) by reg.3(5) and (6)(d) of the Social Security (Students and Income-related Benefits) Amendment Regulations 2004 (SI 2004/1708). See the 2003 edition of this volume and the 2003/2004 Supplement for the unamended form of para.(3A).

Calculation of covenant income where a contribution is assessed

132.—(1) Where a student is in receipt of income by way of a grant during   3.461
a period of study and a contribution has been assessed, the amount of his covenant income to be taken into account for that period and any summer vacation immediately following shall be the whole amount of his covenant income less, subject to paragraph (3), the amount of the contribution.

(2) The weekly amount of the student's covenant income shall be determined—

(a) by dividing the amount of income which falls to be taken into account under paragraph (1) by 52 or, if there are 53 benefit weeks (including part-weeks) in the year, 53; and

(b) by disregarding £5 from the resulting amount.

(3) For the purposes of paragraph (1), the contribution shall be treated as increased by the amount, if any, by which the amount excluded under regulation 131(2)(g) falls short of the amount for the time being specified in paragraph 7(4)(i) of Schedule 2 to the Education (Mandatory Awards) Regulations 1995 (travel expenditure).

DEFINITIONS

"benefit week"—see reg.1(3).
"contribution"—see reg.130.
"covenant income"—*ibid.*
"grant"—*ibid.*
"period of study"—see reg.1(3).
"standard maintenance grant"—see reg.130.

GENERAL NOTE

See the note to reg.63 of the Income Support Regulations.

Covenant income where no grant income or no contribution is assessed

133.—(1) Where a student is not in receipt of income by way of a grant   3.462
the amount of his covenant income shall be calculated as follows—

(a) any sums intended for any expenditure specified in regulation 131(2)(a) to (e), necessary as a result of his attendance on the course, shall be disregarded;

(b) any covenant income, up to the amount of the standard maintenance grant, which is not so disregarded, shall be apportioned equally between the weeks of the period of study and there shall be disregarded from the covenant income to be so apportioned the amount which would have been disregarded under regulation 131(2)(f) and (g) and (3) had the student been in receipt of the standard maintenance grant;

(c) the balance, if any, shall be divided by 52 or, if there are 53 benefit weeks (including part-weeks) in the year, 53 and treated as weekly income of which £5 shall be disregarded.

(2) Where a student is in receipt of income by way of a grant and no contribution has been assessed, the amount of his covenant income shall be calculated in accordance with paragraph (1), except that—

(a) the value of the standard maintenance grant shall be abated by the amount of his grant income less an amount equal to the amount of any sums disregarded under regulation 131(2)(a) to (e); and

(b) the amount to be disregarded under paragraph (1)(b) shall be abated by an amount equal to the amount of any sums disregarded under regulation 131(2)(f) and (g) and (3).

DEFINITIONS

"benefit week"—see reg.1(3).
"contribution"—see reg.130.
"covenant income"—*ibid.*
"grant income"—*ibid.*
"standard maintenance grant"—*ibid.*

GENERAL NOTE

See the note to reg.64 of the Income Support Regulations.

Relationship with amounts to be disregarded under Schedule 7

3.463   **134.** No part of a student's covenant income or grant income shall be disregarded under paragraph 15 of Schedule 7 (charitable and voluntary payments) and any other income to which sub-paragraph (1) of that paragraph applies shall be disregarded only to the extent that the amount disregarded under regulation 132(2)(b) (calculation of covenant income where a contribution is assessed) or, as the case may be, 133(1)(c) (covenant income where no grant income or no contribution is assessed) is less than £20.

DEFINITIONS

"covenant income"—see reg.130.
"grant income"—*ibid.*

GENERAL NOTE

See reg.65 of the Income Support Regulations.

Other amounts to be disregarded

135.—(1) For the purposes of ascertaining income other than grant 3.464
income, covenant income, and loans treated as income in accordance with
regulation 136, any amounts intended for any expenditure specified in regulation 131(2) (calculation of grant income) necessary as a result of the
student's attendance on the course shall be disregarded but only if, and to
the extent that, the necessary expenditure exceeds or is likely to exceed the
amount of the sums disregarded under regulation 131(2) and (3), 132(3)
[¹, 133(1)(a) or (b) and 136(5) (calculation of grant income, covenant
income and treatment of student loans)] on like expenditure.

(2) Where a claim is made in respect of any period in the normal summer
vacation and any income is payable under a deed of covenant which commences or takes effect after the first day of that vacation, that income shall
be disregarded.

AMENDMENT

1. Social Security Amendment (Students) Regulations 1999 (SI 1999/1935),
reg.2(4) (August 30, 1999, or if the student's period of study begins between August
1 and 29, 1999, the first day of the period).

DEFINITIONS

"covenant income"—see reg.130.
"grant income"—*ibid.*
"student loan"—*ibid.*

GENERAL NOTE

See the note to reg.66 of the Income Support Regulations.

Treatment of student loans

136.—[²(1) A student loan shall be treated as income unless it is a hard- 3.465
ship loan in which case it shall be disregarded.

(1A) For the purposes of paragraph (1), "hardship loan" means a loan
made under regulation 21 of the Education (Student Support) Regulations
2000, regulation 12 of the Education (Student Loans) (Scotland)
Regulations 2000 or regulation 21 of the Education (Student Support)
Regulations (Northern Ireland) 2000.

(2) In calculating the weekly amount of the loan to be taken into account
as income—

[⁷(a) in respect of a course that is of a single academic year's duration or
less, a loan which is payable in respect of that period shall be apportioned equally between the weeks in the period beginning with—
(i) except in a case where (ii) below applies, the benefit week, the
first day of which coincides with, or immediately follows, the
first day of the single academic year;
(ii) where the student is required to start attending the course in
August or where the course is of less than an academic year's
duration, the benefit week, the first day of which coincides with,
or immediately follows, the first day of the course,
and ending with the benefit week, the last day of which coincides
with, or immediately precedes, the last day of the course;]

[⁵(aa) in respect of an academic year of a course which starts other than on 1st September, a loan which is payable in respect of that academic year shall be apportioned equally between the weeks in the period beginning with the benefit week [⁷, the first day of which coincides with, or immediately follows, the first day of that academic year and ending with the benefit week, the last day of which coincides with, or immediately precedes,] the last day of that academic year but excluding any benefit weeks falling entirely within the quarter during which, in the opinion of the Secretary of State, the longest of any vacation is taken and for the purposes of this sub-paragraph, "quarter" shall have the same meaning as for the purposes of the Education (Student Support) Regulations 2001;]

(b) in respect of the final academic year of a course (not being a course of a single year's duration), a loan which is payable in respect of that final academic year shall be apportioned equally between the weeks in the period beginning with [⁷. . .]—

[⁷(i) except in a case where (ii) below applies, the benefit week, the first day of which coincides with, or immediately follows, the first day of that academic year;

(ii) where the final academic year starts on 1st September, the benefit week, the first day of which coincides with, or immediately follows, the earlier of 1st September or the first day of the autumn term;]

and ending with [⁷the benefit week, the last day of which coincides with, or immediately precedes,] the last day of the course;

(c) in any other case, the loan shall be apportioned equally between the weeks in the period beginning with the earlier of—

(i) the first day of the first benefit week in September; or

[⁷(ii) the benefit week, the first day of which coincides with, or immediately follows, the first day of the autumn term,]

and ending with [⁷the benefit week, the last day of which coincides with, or immediately precedes, the last day of June],

and, in all cases, from the weekly amount so apportioned there shall be disregarded £10.]

[¹(3) A student shall be treated as possessing a student loan in respect of an academic year where—

(a) a student loan has been made to him in respect of that year; or

(b) he could acquire such a loan in respect of that year by taking reasonable steps to do so.

(4) Where a student is treated as possessing a student loan under paragraph (3), the amount of the student loan to be taken into account as income shall be, subject to paragraph (5)—

(a) in the case of a student to whom a student loan is made in respect of an academic year, a sum equal to the maximum student loan he is able to acquire in respect of that year by taking reasonable steps to do so and either—

(i) in the case of a student other than one to whom head (ii) refers, any contribution whether or not it has been paid to him; or

(ii) in the case of a student who satisfies the additional conditions for a disability premium specified in paragraph 14 of Schedule 1 (applicable amounts), any contribution which has actually been paid to him;

(b) in the case of a student to whom a student loan is not made in respect of an academic year, the maximum student loan that would be made to the student if—

(i) he took all reasonable steps to obtain the maximum student loan he is able to acquire in respect of that year; and

(ii) no deduction in that loan was made by virtue of the application of a means test.

(5) There shall be deducted from the amount of income taken into account under paragraph (4)—

(a) the sum of [^{8}£275] in respect of travel costs; and

[^{4}(b) the sum of [^{9}£343] towards the costs of books and equipment,] whether or not any such costs are incurred.]

AMENDMENTS

1. Social Security Amendment (Students) Regulations 1999 (SI 1999/1935), reg.2(5) (August 30, 1999, or if the student's period of study begins between August 1 and 29, 1999, the first day of the period).

2. Social Security Amendment (Students and Income-related Benefits) Regulations 2000 (SI 2000/1922), reg.3(7) (August 28, 2000, or if the student's period of study begins between August 1 and 27, 2000, the first day of the period).

3. Social Security Amendment (Students and Income-related Benefits) Regulations 2001 (SI 2001/2319), reg.3(1) and (3)(d) (August 27, 2001, or if the student's period of study begins between August 1 and 26, 2001, the first day of the period).

4. Social Security Amendment (Students and Income-related Benefits) Regulations 2001 (SI 2001/2319), reg.3(2) and (3)(d) (August 27, 2001, or if the student's period of study begins between August 1 and 26, 2001, the first day of the period).

5. Social Security Amendment (Students and Income-related Benefits) Regulations 2001 (SI 2001/2319), reg.4 (August 27, 2001, or if the student's period of study begins between August 1 and 26, 2001, the first day of the period).

6. Social Security Amendment (Students and Income-related Benefits) Regulations 2002 (SI 2002/1589), reg.3 (August 26, 2002, or if the student's period of study begins between August 1 and 25, 2002, the first day of the period).

7. Social Security Amendment (Students and Income-related Benefits) Regulations 2002 (SI 2002/1589), reg.5 (August 26, 2002, or if the student's period of study begins between August 1 and 25, 2002, the first day of the period).

8. Social Security (Students and Income-related Benefits) Amendment Regulations 2004 (SI 2004/1708), reg.2(1) and (3)(d) (September 1, 2004, or if the student's period of study begins between August 1 and August 31, 2004, the first day of the period).

9. Social Security (Students and Income-related Benefits) Amendment Regulations 2004 (SI 2004/1708), reg.2(2) and (3)(d) (September 1, 2004, or if the student's period of study begins between August 1 and August 31, 2004, the first day of the period).

3.466

DEFINITIONS

"academic year"—see reg.130.
"student loan"—*ibid.*

3.467

GENERAL NOTE

See the note to reg.66A of the Income Support Regulations.

[¹ Treatment of payments from access funds

3.468

136A.—(1) This regulation applies to payments from access funds that are not payments to which regulation 138(2) or (3) (income treated as capital) applies.

(2) A payment from access funds, other than a payment to which paragraph (3) of this regulation applies, shall be disregarded as income.

(3) Subject to paragraph (4) of this regulation and paragraph 38 of Schedule 7, any payments from access funds which are intended and used for food, ordinary clothing or footwear (which has the same meaning as in paragraph 15(2) of Schedule 7), household fuel, rent for which housing benefit is payable [² or any housing costs] to the extent that they are met under regulation 83(f) or 84(1)(g) (housing costs) [². . .], of a single claimant or, as the case may be, of [³ his partner], and any payments from access funds which are used for any council tax or water charges for which that claimant or [³partner is liable] shall be disregarded as income to the extent of £20 per week.

(4) Where a payment from access funds is made—

(a) on or after 1st September or the first day of the course, whichever first occurs, but before receipt of any student loan in respect of that year and that payment is intended for the purpose of bridging the period until receipt of the student loan; or

(b) before the first day of the course to a person in anticipation of that person becoming a student,

that payment shall be disregarded as income.]

AMENDMENTS

3.469

1. Social Security Amendment (Students and Income-related Benefits) Regulations 2000 (SI 2000/1922), reg.3(8) (August 28, 2000, or if the student's period of study begins between August 1 and 27, 2000, the first day of the period).

2. Social Security Amendment (Residential Care and Nursing Homes) Regulations 2001 (SI 2001/3767), reg.2(2) and Pt II of Sch., para.13 (April 8, 2002).

3. Social Security (Working Tax Credit and Child Tax Credit) (Consequential Amendments) Regulations 2003 (SI 2003/455), reg.3 and Sch.2, para.17 (April 6, 2004, except in "transitional cases" and see further the note to reg.83 and to reg.17 of the Income Support Regulations).

DEFINITIONS

"access funds"—see reg.1(3).
"family"—see JSA, s.35(1)
"payment"—see reg.1(3).
"single claimant"—*ibid.*
"student loan"—see reg.130.

GENERAL NOTE

See the note to reg.66B of the Income Support Regulations.

Disregard of contribution

3.470

137. Where the claimant or his partner is a student and, for the purposes of assessing a contribution to the student's grant [¹ or student loan], the other partner's income has been taken into account, an amount equal to that contribution shall be disregarded for the purposes of assessing that other partner's income.

AMENDMENT

1. Social Security Amendment (Students) Regulations 1999 (SI 1999/1935), reg.2(6) (August 30, 1999, or if the student's period of study begins between August 1 and 29, 1999, the first day of the period).

DEFINITIONS

"claimant"—see Jobseekers Act, s.35(1), reg.88(1).
"contribution"—see reg.130.
"grant"—*ibid.*
"partner"—see reg.1(3).
"student loan"—see reg.130.

GENERAL NOTE

See reg.67 of the Income Support Regulations.

[¹Further disregard of student's income

137A. Where any part of a student's income has already been taken into account for the purposes of assessing his entitlement to a grant [²or student loan], the amount taken into account shall be disregarded in assessing that student's income.]

3.471

AMENDMENTS

1. Social Security (Miscellaneous Amendments) Regulations 1998 (SI 1998/563), reg.4(3) and (4)(f) (April 6, 1998).
2. Social Security Amendment (Students) Regulations 1999 (SI 1999/1935), reg.2(7) (August 30, 1999, or if the student's period of study begins between August 1 and 29, 1999, the first day of the period).

DEFINITIONS

"grant"—see reg.130.
"student loan"—*ibid.*

Income treated as capital

138.—[¹(1)] Any amount by way of a refund of tax deducted from a student's income shall be treated as capital.

[¹(2) An amount paid from access funds as a single lump sum shall be treated as capital.

(3) An amount paid from access funds as a single lump sum which is intended and used for an item other than food, ordinary clothing or footwear (which has the same meaning as in paragraph 15(2) of Schedule 7), household fuel, rent for which housing benefit is payable [²or any housing costs] to the extent that they are met under regulation 83(f) or 84(1)(g) (housing costs) [². . .], of a single claimant or, as the case may be, of [³his partner], or which is used for an item other than any council tax or water charges for which that claimant or [³partner is liable] shall be disregarded as capital but only for a period of 52 weeks from the date of the payment.]

3.472

AMENDMENTS

1. Social Security Amendment (Students and Income-related Benefits) Regulations 2000 (SI 2000/1922), reg.3(9) (August 28, 2000, or if the student's period of study begins between August 1 and 27, 2000, the first day of the period).
2. Social Security Amendment (Residential Care and Nursing Homes) Regulations 2001 (SI 2001/3767), reg.2(2) and Pt II of Sch., para.14 (April 8, 2002).
3. Social Security (Working Tax Credit and Child Tax Credit) (Consequential Amendments) Regulations 2003 (SI 2003/455), reg.3 and Sch.2, para.17 (April 6, 2004, except in "transitional cases" and see further the note to reg.83 and to reg.17 of the Income Support Regulations).

DEFINITIONS

"access funds"—see reg.1(3).
"family"—see JSA, s.35(1)
"payment"—see reg.1(3).
"single claimant"—*ibid.*

GENERAL NOTE

On paras (2) and (3), see the note to reg.66B of the Income Support Regulations.

Disregard of changes occurring during summer vacation

3.473   **139.** In calculating a student's income [¹the Secretary of State] shall disregard any change in the standard maintenance grant occurring in the recognised summer vacation appropriate to the student's course, if that vacation does not form part of his period of study, from the date on which the change occurred up to the end of that vacation.

AMENDMENT

1. Social Security Act 1998 (Commencement No.11, and Savings and Consequential and Transitional Provisions) Order 1999 (SI 1999/2860 (C.75)), Art.3(12) and Sch.12, para.2 (October 18, 1999).

DEFINITIONS

"period of study"—see reg.1(3).
"standard maintenance grant—see reg.130.

GENERAL NOTE

See reg.69 of the Income Support Regulations.

PART IX

HARDSHIP

GENERAL NOTE

3.474   This Part deals with the circumstances in which a hardship payment of JSA will be made. A hardship payment can only be paid if a s.19 sanction has been imposed; or the claimant is waiting for a decision at the beginning of his claim as to whether he satisfies the labour market conditions in s.1(2)(a) to (c) of the Jobseekers Act; or payment of JSA has been suspended because a question has arisen as to whether the claimant satisfies the labour market conditions; or, in the case of a claimant who is in a "vulnerable group" (see reg.140(1)) only, a decision-maker has decided that he does not satisfy the labour market conditions. Hardship payments are not available in any other circumstances.

See reg.140 for the meaning of "hardship". Unless the claimant falls into a vulnerable group (see reg.140(1)), no hardship payment will be made for the first two weeks, however severe the person's hardship. In addition, hardship payments are not available throughout the period of a "New Deal sanction" (see the notes to reg.69), unless the claimant is in a vulnerable group (see regs 140(4A) and 140A). If a hardship payment is made, it will be subject to a 40 per cent or 20 per cent reduction of the appropriate personal allowance for a single claimant (see reg.145). While hardship payments are being paid the claimant must continue to satisfy the other conditions of entitlement for income-based JSA and in addition will be required to sign a declaration of hardship (see reg.143).

See also the notes to s.20(4) to (6) of the Jobseekers Act on hardship payments where a s.19 sanction has been imposed.

Meaning of "person in hardship"

140.—(1) In this Part of these Regulations, a "person in hardship" means   3.475
for the purposes of regulation 141 a claimant, other than a claimant to whom paragraph (3) or (4) applies [⁷or a member of a joint-claim couple and regulation 3E does not apply], who—
  (a) is a single woman—
      (i) who is pregnant; and
      (ii) in respect of whom [⁵the Secretary of State] is satisfied that, unless a jobseeker's allowance is paid to her, she will suffer hardship; or
  (b) is a single person who is responsible for a young person, and [⁵the Secretary of State] is satisfied that, unless a jobseeker's allowance is paid to the single person, the young person will suffer hardship; or
  (c) is a member of a married or unmarried couple, where—
      (i) the woman is pregnant; and
      (ii) [⁵the Secretary of State] is satisfied that, unless a jobseeker's allowance is paid, the woman will suffer hardship; or
  (d) is a member of a polygamous marriage and—
      (i) one member of the marriage is pregnant; and
      (ii) [⁵the Secretary of State] is satisfied that, unless a jobseeker's allowance is paid, that woman will suffer hardship; or
  (e) is a member of a married or unmarried couple or of a polygamous marriage where
      (i) one or both members of the couple, or one or more members of the polygamous marriage, are responsible for a child or young person; and
      (ii) [⁵the Secretary of State] is satisfied that, unless a jobseeker's allowance is paid, the child or young person will suffer hardship; or
  (f) has an award of a jobseeker's allowance which includes or would, if a claim for a jobseeker's allowance from him were to succeed have included, in his applicable amount a disability premium and—
      (i) where the person has an award, a jobseeker's allowance is not payable either because it is suspended or because section 19 (circumstances in which a jobseeker's allowance is not payable) applies in his case; and

(ii) [⁵the Secretary of State] is satisfied that, unless a jobseeker's allowance is paid, the person who would satisfy the conditions of entitlement to that premium would suffer hardship; or

(g) suffers, or whose partner suffers from a chronic medical condition which results in functional capacity being limited or restricted by physical impairment and [⁵ the Secretary of State] is satisfied that—

   (i) the suffering has already lasted, or is likely to last, for not less than 26 weeks; and

   (ii) unless a jobseeker's allowance is paid to the claimant the probability is that the health of the person suffering would, within 2 weeks of [⁵the Secretary of State] making his decision, decline further than that of a normally healthy adult and that person would suffer hardship; or

(h) does, or whose partner does, or in the case of a claimant who is married to more than one person under a law which permits polygamy, at least one of those persons do, devote a considerable portion of each week to caring for another person who—

   (i) is in receipt of an attendance allowance or the care component of disability living allowance at one of the two higher rates prescribed under [²section 72(4)] of the Benefits Act; or

   (ii) has claimed either attendance allowance or disability living allowance, but only for so long as the claim has not been determined, or for, 26 weeks from the date of claiming, [¹ whichever is the earlier; or

   (iii) has claimed either attendance allowance or disability living allowance and has an award of either attendance allowance or the care component of disability living allowance at one of the two higher rates prescribed under section 72(4) of the Benefits Act for a period commencing after the date on which that claim was made,]

and [⁵the Secretary of State] is satisfied, after taking account of the factors set out in [²paragraph (5)] in so far as they are appropriate to the particular circumstances of the case, that the person providing the care will not be able to continue doing so unless a jobseeker's allowance is paid to the claimant; or

(i) is a person or is the partner of a person to whom section 16 applies by virtue of a direction issued by the Secretary of State, except where the person to whom the direction applies does not satisfy the requirements of section 1(2)(a) to (c); or

(j) is a person—

   (i) to whom section 3(1)(f)(iii) (persons under the age of 18) applies, or is the partner of such a person; and

   (ii) in respect of whom [⁵the Secretary of State] is satisfied that the person will, unless a jobseeker's allowance is paid, suffer hardship.

[⁶(k) is a person—

   (i) who, pursuant to the Children Act 1989, was being looked after by a local authority;

   (ii) with whom the local authority had a duty, pursuant to that Act, to take reasonable steps to keep in touch; or

   (iii) who, pursuant to that Act, qualified for advice and assistance from a local authority,

but in respect of whom (i), (ii) or, as the case may be, (iii) above had not applied for a period of three years or less as at the date on which he complies with the requirements of regulation 143; and
(iv) as at the date on which he complies with the requirements of regulation 143, is under the age of 21].

(2) Except in a case to which paragraph (3) [² ...] [⁴or (4A)] applies [⁸ or where the person in hardship is a member of a joint-claim couple and regulation 3E does not apply] a "person in hardship" means for the purposes of regulation 142, a claimant where [⁵the Secretary of State] is satisfied that he or his partner will suffer hardship unless a jobseeker's allowance is paid to him.

(3) In paragraphs (1) and (2) a "person in hardship" does not include a claimant who is entitled, or whose partner is entitled, to income support or [³ a claimant or a partner of a claimant] who falls within a category of persons prescribed for the purpose of section 124(1)(e) of the Benefits Act.

(4) Paragraph (1)(h) shall not apply in a case where the person being cared for resides in a residential care home or nursing home.

[⁴(4A) In paragraph (2), a "person in hardship" does not include a claimant to whom section 19(5)(b) or (c) applies by virtue of any act or omission relating to [⁹ one of the New Deal options or to the Intensive Activity Period specified in regulation 75(1)(a)(iv)]]].

(5) Factors which, for the purposes of paragraphs (1) and (2), [⁵the Secretary of State] is to take into account in determining whether a person will suffer hardship are—
(a) the presence in the claimant's family of a person who satisfies the requirements for a disability premium specified in paragraphs 13 and 14 of Schedule 1 [¹or [¹⁰an element of child tax credit in respect of a child or young person who is disabled or severely disabled within the meaning of regulation 8 of the Child Tax Credit Regulations 2002]];
(b) the resources which, without a jobseeker's allowance, are likely to be available to the claimant's family, the amount by which these resources fall short of the amount applicable in his case in accordance with regulation 145 (applicable amount in hardship cases), the amount of any resources which may be available to members of the claimant's family from any person in the claimant's household who is not a member of his family, and the length of time for which those factors are likely to persist;
(c) whether there is a substantial risk that essential items, including food, clothing, heating and accommodation, will cease to be available to the claimant or to a member of the claimant's family, or will be available at considerably reduced levels and the length of time those factors are likely to persist.

AMENDMENTS

1. Jobseeker's Allowance (Amendment) Regulations 1996 (SI 1996/1516), reg.13 (October 7, 1996).   **3.476**
2. Jobseeker's Allowance (Amendment) Regulations 1996 (SI 1996/1516), reg.20 and Sch. (October 7, 1996).
3. Jobseeker's Allowance and Income Support (General) (Amendment) Regulations 1996 (SI 1996/1517), reg.25 (October 7, 1996).
4. Social Security Amendment (New Deal) Regulations 1997 (SI 1997/2863), reg.11 (January 5, 1998).

5. Social Security Act 1998 (Commencement No.11, and Savings and Consequential and Transitional Provisions) Order 1999 (SI 1999/2860 (C.75)), Arts 3(1) and (12) and Sch.12, para.2 (October 18 1999).

6. Jobseeker's Allowance (Amendment) Regulations 2000 (SI 2000/239), reg.2(4) (March 6, 2000).

7. Jobseeker's Allowance (Joint Claims) Regulations 2000 (SI 2000/1978), reg.2(5) and Sch.2, para.45(a) (March 19, 2001).

8. Jobseeker's Allowance (Joint Claims) Regulations 2000 (SI 2000/1978), reg.2(5) and Sch.2, para.45(b) (March 19, 2001).

9. Social Security Amendment (New Deal) Regulations 2001 (SI 2001/1029), reg.9(1) (April 9, 2001).

10. Social Security (Working Tax Credit and Child Tax Credit) (Consequential Amendments) Regulations 2003 (SI 2003/455), reg.3 and Sch.2, para.18 (April 6, 2004, except in "transitional cases" and see further the note to reg.83 and to reg.17 of the Income Support Regulations).

DEFINITIONS

"attendance allowance"—see reg.1(3).
"child"—see Jobseekers Act, s.35(1).
"claimant"—*ibid.*
"disability living allowance"—see reg.1(3).
"married couple"—see Jobseekers Act, s.35(1).
"partner"—see reg.1(3).
"polygamous marriage"—*ibid.*
"unmarried couple"—see Jobseekers Act, s.35(1).
"week"—see reg.1(3).
"young person"—see reg.76.

GENERAL NOTE

Para.(1)

3.477 This lists those claimants who are eligible for hardship payments without any waiting period (the "vulnerable groups"). Note the exclusion in para.(3) of claimants who (or whose partners) are in a category who can claim income support (claimants who, or whose partners, are entitled to income support would in any event be excluded from JSA under s.3(1)(b) or (c) of the Job-seekers Act).

The categories are:

(i) a single claimant who is pregnant whom the decision-maker accepts will suffer hardship if no payment is made (sub-para.(a));

(ii) a member of a couple, or of a polygamous marriage, where the/a woman is pregnant and the decision-maker accepts that the woman will suffer hardship if no payment is made (sub-paras (c) and (d));

(iii) a member of a couple, or of a polygamous marriage, who is/are responsible (see reg.77) for a child or young person (see reg.76) and the decision-maker accepts that the child or young person will suffer hardship if no payment is made (sub-para.(e));

(iv) a single claimant who is responsible (see reg.77) for a *young person* (*i.e.* a 16-to 18-year-old, see reg.76) and the decision-maker accepts that the young person will suffer hardship if no payment is made (sub-para.(b)). (Note that single people who are responsible for a *child* are not included as they are eligible for income support under Sch.1B to the Income Support Regulations and see para.(3); it would normally be better for such a person to claim income support);

(v) people eligible for a disability premium in their income-based JSA and the decision-maker accepts that the person who qualifies for the disability premium would suffer hardship if no payment is made (sub-para.(f)). In contrast to the other sub-paragraphs, sub-para.(f) refers to a person who "has an award of " JSA which includes a disability premium (or whose claim, if successful, would include a disability premium). The intention would seem to be that this category does not apply if the reason for the non-payment of JSA is that the claimant has failed to satisfy the labour market conditions (in such a case the person would not have an award of JSA and see head (i)). But if such a person having failed to satisfy the labour market conditions then makes a further claim for JSA, arguably he falls within sub-para.(f) because he has made a claim for JSA which were it to succeed would include a disability premium.

(vi) a claimant who, or whose partner, has a chronic medical condition resulting in his functional capacity being restricted by physical impairment which has lasted, or is likely to last, for at least 26 weeks and the decision-maker accepts that in the next two weeks the person's health is likely to "decline further than that of a normally healthy adult" and that that person will suffer hardship if no payment is made (sub-para.(g)). If such a person is incapable of work he will be eligible for income support and so will not qualify for a hardship payment (see para.(3)).

(vii) a claimant who, or whose partner, "devotes a considerable portion of each week" to caring for someone (not in a residential care or nursing home, see para.(4)) who is in receipt of, or (in certain circumstances) has claimed attendance allowance, or the higher or middle rate care component of disability living allowance and the decision-maker accepts that the person will not be able to continue caring if no payment is made (sub-para.(h)). (Note: a person in this situation may well be eligible for income support, see paras 4 to 6 of Sch.1B to the Income Support Regulations);

(viii) a claimant who, or whose partner, is under 18, the subject of a severe hardship direction and who satisfies the labour market conditions (sub-para.(i));

(ix) a claimant who, or whose partner, is under 18, but eligible for JSA and the decision-maker accepts that that person will suffer hardship if no payment is made (sub-para.(j)). (*Note*: a 16 or 17-year-old who is being sanctioned for an "offence" under s.19(5) or s.19(6)(c) or (d) of the Jobseekers Act will automatically be paid a reduced rate of JSA and will not need to rely on this provision: see reg.68.)

(x) a person under the age of 21 who was being looked after by a local authority under the Children Act 1989 (or was the subject of certain other local authority duties under that Act) within the past three years.

See para.(5) for the factors the decision-maker must consider when deciding whether a person will suffer hardship.

Note the requirement under reg.143 for the claimant to sign a written declaration as to why he will suffer hardship if no payment is made.

Para. (2)

If a person does not come within one of the categories listed in para.(1) he will only be entitled to a hardship payment after two weeks (reg.142(2), (4) and (5)) and if the decision-maker accepts that he or his partner will suffer hardship if no payment is made. Note the exclusions in paras (3) and (4A). As regards para.(3), claimants who, or whose partners, are entitled to income support would in any event be excluded from JSA under s.3(1)(b) or (c) of the Jobseekers Act. Para.(4A) excludes claimants who are subject to "New Deal sanctions" (see the note to para.(4A) and reg.140A). See para.(5) for the factors the decision-maker must consider when deciding whether hardship will occur and reg.143 for the declaration the claimant will be required to sign.

3.478

Para. (4A)

The effect of this paragraph is to prevent a claimant who is not in a vulnerable group from having access to hardship payments throughout the period of a "New

3.479

Deal sanction" (even one of four weeks duration). Note reg.140A(2) and (3) where the claimant was already receiving hardship payments when the New Deal sanction was imposed. A New Deal sanction is one that is imposed for an offence under s.19(5)(b) or (c) of the Jobseekers Act in relation to a place on one of the New Deal options. See further the notes to reg.69. For a brief summary of the New Deal for 18–24 year-olds see the notes to reg.75.

Para. (5)

3.480   This lists factors that the decision-maker must consider when deciding whether a person will suffer hardship. The list is not exhaustive and the decision-maker should consider all the circumstances of the claimant and his family (if any). "Hardship" is not defined. The *Decision Makers Guide* suggests that it means "severe suffering or privation", and that "privation means a lack of the necessities of life" (para.35155).

The factors that the decision-maker must consider are whether a member of the claimant's family qualifies for a disability or (in "transitional cases" only—see the note to reg.83 and to reg.17 of the Income Support Regulations) a disabled child premium (sub-para.(a)); other available resources, including those which may be available to the claimant's family from anyone else in the claimant's household (sub-para.(b)); and whether there is a "substantial risk" that the claimant or a member of his family will go without essential items such as food, clothing, heating and accommodation, or that they will be available at "considerably reduced" levels, and if so, for how long (sub-para.(c)).

Sub-para.(a) is straightforward. Under sub-para.(b) the decision-maker has to take into account other resources that are likely to be available to the claimant or his family. Thus income and capital that is normally disregarded (*e.g.* disability living allowance) will be taken into account under sub-para.(b). But note that para.35180 of the *Decision Makers Guide* considers that JSA paid for an earlier period should not be taken into account. (Note that if the decision-maker does decide that the person is in hardship the normal income and capital rules will be applied when calculating the amount of a hardship payment; unlike urgent cases payments there are no special rules for the calculation of income and capital. However, the payment will be reduced by 40 or 20 per cent of the appropriate personal allowance for a single person of the claimant's age: see reg.145.) In addition, if there are any non-dependents (for example, a grown-up son or daughter) living in the claimant's household, any contribution that they might be expected to make will be considered. But the resources have to be available to the claimant. So, for example, if a payment from a pension fund will only be available in four weeks' time, or savings can only be cashed after a period of notice has been given, a hardship payment can be made until these resources become available (see paras 35185 to 35195 of *DMG*). Moreover, money that might be obtainable from credit facilities (*e.g.* a credit card or overdraft) should not be taken into account as such facilities are not resources but only increase the claimant's indebtedness (see para.35196 of *DMG*). The decision-maker also has to consider the length of time for which any other resources are likely to be available. Clearly the longer the period of time that JSA will not be payable (*e.g.* if a sanction of several weeks or months' duration has been imposed) the more likely it is that hardship will occur. Sub-para. (c) gives examples of essential items that the decision-maker should take into account but this does not exclude consideration of other items that may be essential to the particular claimant or a member of his family.

If the claimant is not in hardship when the claim is first made but the decision-maker decides that hardship will be established by a later date, see reg.13 of the Claims and Payments Regulations under which hardship payments can be awarded from that later date, provided this is within three months of the date of claim.

[¹Period when a person is not a person in hardship

3.481   **140A.**—[²(1) A claimant who is not a person in hardship by virtue of regulation 140(4A) shall not be a person in hardship throughout the period beginning on the day on which a New Deal decision has effect by virtue of regulation 69 or, as the case may be, by virtue of regulation 7(8) of the Social Security and Child Support (Decisions and Appeals) Regulations 1999 and ending—

(a) on the last day on which he is required to participate in a New Deal option [⁴or in the Intensive Activity Period specified in regulation 75(1)(a)(iv)]; or

(b) on the day which is 14 days after the day on which the New Deal decision had effect,

whichever is the later.]

(2) Where a claimant who is not a person in hardship by virtue of regulation 140(4A) was a person in hardship for the purposes of regulation 142 immediately before the commencement of the period referred to in paragraph (1), that claimant shall, subject to paragraph (3), again become a person in hardship for the purposes of regulation 142 on the day following the expiration of that period.

(3) A claimant to whom paragraph (2) applies shall not again become a person in hardship for the purposes of regulation 142 if—

(a) the day following the day the period referred to in paragraph (1) expires is a day within a period in respect of which a subsequent New Deal decision applies by virtue of paragraph (1); or

(b) on the day following the expiry of the period referred to in paragraph (1), he is not a person in hardship for the purposes of regulation 142.]

[³(4) In this regulation, "New Deal decision" means a decision that section 19(5)(b) or (c) applies by virtue of an act or omission relating to one of the New Deal options [⁵ or to the Intensive Activity Period specified in regulation 75(1)(a)(iv)].]

AMENDMENTS

1. Social Security Amendment (New Deal) Regulations 1997 (SI 1997/2863), reg.12 (January 5, 1998).

2. Jobseeker's Allowance (Amendment) Regulations 2000 (SI 2000/239), reg.2(5)(a) (March 6, 2000).

3. Jobseeker's Allowance (Amendment) Regulations 2000 (SI 2000/239), reg.2(5)(b) (March 6, 2000).

4. Social Security Amendment (New Deal) Regulations 2001 (SI 2001/1029), reg.10(1) (April 9, 2001).

5. Social Security Amendment (New Deal) Regulations 2001 (SI 2001/1029), reg.10(2) (April 9, 2001).

3.482

DEFINITION

"claimant"—see Jobseekers Act, s.35(1).

GENERAL NOTE

Para.(1) confirms that a claimant who is not in a vulnerable group (see reg.140(1)) and who has incurred a New Deal sanction (see the notes to reg.69) of either two or four weeks' duration will not have access to hardship payments for the first 14 days of that sanction unless the period during which he is compulsorily required to participate in the New Deal comes to an end sooner. See also reg.140(4A). This will be the case even if the claimant might otherwise have been considered to be a person in hardship *i.e.* because this had been accepted in connection with a non-New Deal sanction to which he was already subject. The intention is that in those circumstances the New Deal sanction will take precedence. However, in such a case, once the New Deal sanction expires, the claimant will again become eligible for hardship payments, unless another New Deal sanction immediately takes effect, or he is not a person in hardship for the purposes of reg.142 (*e.g.* because the previous non-New Deal sanction has expired) (paras (2) and (3)).

Circumstances in which an income-based jobseeker's allowance is payable to a person in hardship

3.483

141.—(1) This regulation applies to persons in hardship within the meaning of regulation 140(1), and is subject to the provisions of regulations 143 and 144.

(2) Subject to paragraph (3) a person in hardship [¹, other than a person to whom regulation 46(1) (waiting days) applies, shall be treated as entitled to an income-based jobseeker's allowance for the period beginning with the 4th day of the jobseeking period or,] if later, from the day he first becomes a person in hardship and ending on the day before the claim is determined where [²the sole reason for the delay] in determining the claim is that a question arises as to whether the claimant satisfies any of the conditions of entitlement specified in section 1(2)(a) to (c) [²provided he satisfies the conditions of entitlement specified in paragraph (d)(ii) of subsection (2) of section 1.]

(3) A person in hardship to whom paragraph (2) applies may be treated as entitled to an income-based jobseeker's allowance for a period after the date [¹ . . .] referred to in that paragraph [¹which is applicable in his case] but before the date the statement mentioned in regulation 143(1) is furnished where [³the Secretary of State] is satisfied that the claimant suffered hardship because of a lack of resources during that period.

(4) A person in hardship, except where the person has been treated as not available for employment in accordance with regulations under section 6(4) of the Act shall, subject to the conditions specified in regulation 143 (conditions for hardship payments), be entitled to an income-based jobseeker's allowance without satisfying the requirements of section 1(2)(a) to (c) of the Act provided he satisfies the other conditions of entitlement to that benefit.

(5) An income-based jobseeker's allowance shall be payable to a person in hardship even though payment to him of a jobseeker's allowance has been suspended in accordance with [⁴regulation 16 of the Social Security and Child Support (Decisions and Appeals) Regulations 1999] on the ground that a doubt has arisen as to whether he satisfies the requirements of section 1(2)(a) to (c), but the allowance shall be payable only if and for so long as the claimant satisfies the other conditions of entitlement to an income-based jobseeker's allowance.

(6) An income-based jobseeker's allowance shall be payable to a person in hardship even though section 19 (circumstances in which a jobseeker's allowance is not payable) prevents payment of a jobseeker's allowance to him but the allowance shall be payable only if and for so long as he satisfies the conditions of entitlement to an income-based jobseeker's allowance.

AMENDMENTS

3.484

1. Jobseeker's Allowance and Income Support (General) (Amendment) Regulations 1996 (SI 1996/1517), reg.26 (October 7, 1996).

2. Social Security and Child Support (Jobseeker's Allowance) (Miscellaneous Amendments) Regulations 1996 (SI 1996/2538), reg.2(9) (October 28, 1996).

3. Social Security Act 1998 (Commencement No.11, and Savings and Consequential and Transitional Provisions) Order 1999 (SI 1999/2860 (C.75)), Arts 3(1) and (12) and Sch.12, para.2 (October 18 1999).

4. Social Security Act 1998 (Commencement No.11, and Savings and Consequential and Transitional Provisions) Order 1999 (SI 1999/2860 (C.75)), Arts 3(1) and (12) and Sch.12, para.8 (October 18 1999).

DEFINITIONS

"claimant"—see Jobseekers Act, s.35(1).
"entitled"—*ibid.*

GENERAL NOTE

The circumstances in which hardship payments can be made are set out in this regulation for claimants who can be paid immediately and in reg.142 for claimants who have to wait two weeks. No payment will be made under this regulation or reg.142 unless the claimant has signed the declaration required by reg.143 (but note para.(3) below) and provided information about the person in hardship (see reg.144).

3.485

Para.(2) applies where a question arises as to whether the claimant satisfies the labour market conditions in s.1(2)(a)–(c) of the Jobseekers Act (availability for work, signing a jobseeker's agreement, actively seeking work) when a claim is made. This has to be the only reason for the delay in deciding the claim; hardship payments will not be available if the delay is for some other reason (*e.g.* because there is a question whether the person has too much capital or income). If hardship is established a payment will be made until the claim is decided, except for the first three waiting days (see para.4 of Sch.1 to the Jobseekers Act and reg.46) if these apply. The claimant must continue to satisfy the other conditions of entitlement for income-based JSA in s.3 of the Jobseekers Act. A payment under para.(2) may also be made for the period before the claimant has completed a reg.143 declaration if the decision-maker accepts that he suffered hardship because of "a lack of resources" during that period (para.(3)). Once the decision-maker has decided the claim this paragraph no longer applies but the claimant may be eligible for hardship payments under para.(4).

Para. (4) covers a person who is not entitled to JSA because a decision-maker has decided that he does not satisfy the labour market conditions in s.1(2)(a) to (c) of the Jobseekers Act. But it does not apply if the person is treated as not available for work under reg.15 (full-time students, prisoners on temporary release, women in receipt of maternity pay or allowance, people treated as not available at the start of a claim). The person must be in hardship and continue to satisfy the other conditions of entitlement for income-based JSA. Hardship payments can start from the date of the decision-maker's decision and continue for as long as the person remains in hardship. There is no requirement that the claimant has appealed against the decision-maker's decision. Note that there is no equivalent of this provision in reg.142 (persons eligible for hardship payments after waiting period).

Para.(5) applies where payment of a person's JSA has been suspended because a question has arisen as to whether he satisfies the labour market conditions. The person must be in hardship and continue to satisfy the other conditions of entitlement for income-based JSA. Hardship payments can be made until the suspension is lifted or the decision-maker decides that the claimant does not satisfy the labour market conditions. If the decision goes against the claimant he may be eligible for hardship payments under para.(4).

Under para.(6) a person can be paid hardship payments if a s.19 sanction has been applied, provided that he is in hardship and that he continues to satisfy the other conditions of entitlement for income-based JSA (including the labour market conditions). Payments under para.(6) can last as long as the sanction lasts.

See reg.145 for the amount of a hardship payment.

Further circumstances in which an income-based jobseeker's allowance is payable to a person in hardship

3.486   **142.**—(1) This regulation applies to a person in hardship who falls within paragraph (2) but not paragraph (1) of regulation 140 and is subject to the provisions of regulations 143 and 144.

(2) A person in hardship shall be treated as entitled to an income-based jobseeker's allowance for a period commencing on whichever is the later of—

[¹(a) the 15th day following the date of claim disregarding any waiting days; or]

(b) [¹. . .]

(c) the day the claimant complies with the requirements of regulation 143,

and ending on the day before the claim is determined where [¹the sole reason for the delay] in determining the claim is that a question arises as to whether the claimant satisfies any of the conditions of entitlement specified in section 1(2)(a) to (c) [¹provided he satisfies the conditions of entitlement specified in paragraph (d)(ii) of subsection (2) of section 1.]

(3) An income-based jobseeker's allowance shall be payable subject to paragraph (4) to a person in hardship even though payment to him of a jobseeker's allowance has been suspended in accordance with regulations made by virtue of [²section 21 of the Social Security Act 1998] (suspension of benefit) on the ground that a doubt has arisen as to whether he satisfies the requirements of section 1(2)(a) to (c) but the allowance shall be payable only if and for so long as the claimant satisfies the other conditions of entitlement to an income-based jobseeker's allowance.

(4) An income-based jobseeker's allowance shall not be payable in respect of the first 14 days of the period of suspension.

(5) An income-based jobseeker's allowance shall be payable to a person in hardship even though section 19 (circumstances in which a jobseeker's allowance is not payable) prevents payment of a jobseeker's allowance to him, but the allowance—

(a) shall not be payable under this paragraph in respect of the first 14 days of the period to which section 19 applies; and

(b) shall be payable thereafter only where the conditions of entitlement to an income-based jobseeker's allowance are satisfied.

AMENDMENTS

3.487   1. Social Security and Child Support (Jobseeker's Allowance) (Miscellaneous Amendments) Regulations 1996 (SI 1996/2538), reg.2(10) (October 28, 1996).

2. Social Security Act 1998 (Commencement No.11, and Savings and Consequential and Transitional Provisions) Order 1999 (SI 1999/2860 (c.75)), Arts 3(1) and (12) and Sch.12, para.9 (October 18 1999).

DEFINITION

"claimant"—see Jobseekers Act, s.35(1).

GENERAL NOTE

3.488   See the notes to reg.141. This regulation applies to claimants who do not come within any of the categories listed in reg.140(1) and so have to wait for two weeks before any hardship payments can be made. Note that a claimant who does not come within reg.140(1) and who has incurred a New Deal sanction (see the notes to reg.69) will not have access to hardship payments during the period of that sanction (even if it is for four weeks) (see regs 140(4A) and 140A).

The circumstances in which hardship payments can be made under this regulation are similar to those in reg.141 (the differences are noted below), *except* that there is no provision for payment to claimants who have failed to satisfy the labour market conditions in s.1(2)(a) to (c) (compare reg.141(4)); there is only provision in para.(2) for payment where a question arises when a claim is made as to whether a claimant satisfies the labour market conditions and in para.(3) where a claimant's benefit has been suspended because of doubt as to whether these conditions are satisfied. Once a decison-maker has decided that the person does not satisfy the labour market conditions he will not be eligible for hardship payments if he is not in a "vulnerable group". This is the case even if the claimant is appealing against the decision-maker's decision. Such a person may be eligible for a crisis loan from the social fund but this will be limited to expenses which result from a disaster or items required for cooking or heating (including fireguards) for 14 days from the first day of the benefit week following the disallowance decision, or the day of the decision if it is made on the first day of a benefit week (Social Fund Direction 17(b) and (g)); the person's partner can apply for a crisis loan for living expenses: see Direction 18(2).

Paras (3) and (5) correspond to paras (5) and (6) in reg.141, except that in each case a hardship payment under this regulation is not payable for the first two weeks (see para.(4) and para.(5)(a)). Para.(2) is the equivalent of reg.141(2) except that under this regulation a hardship payment can only be made from the 15th day after the date of claim, or the 18th day if the "waiting days" apply (see para.4 of Sch.1 to the Jobseekers Act and reg.46) or from the day the claimant makes the declaration required by reg.143, whichever is the later. There is thus no discretion in the case of hardship payments under para.(2) of this regulation to make any payment for the period before a reg.143 declaration is signed (compare para.(3) of reg.141).

Conditions for hardship payments

143.—(1) A jobseeker's allowance shall not be payable in accordance with regulation 141 or, as the case may be, 142, except where the claimant has—

    (a) furnished on a form approved for the purpose by the Secretary of State or in such other form as he may in any particular case approve a statement of the circumstances he relies upon to establish entitlement under regulation 141 or as the case may be regulation 142; and

    (b) signed the statement.

(2) The completed and signed form shall be delivered by the claimant to such office as the Secretary of State may specify.

3.489

DEFINITION

"claimant"—see Jobseekers Act, s.35(1).

Provision of information

144. For the purposes of [¹section 20(5) of and] paragraph 10(3) of Schedule 1 to the Act, a claimant shall provide to the Secretary of State information as to the circumstances of the person alleged to be in hardship.

3.490

AMENDMENT

1. Jobseeker's Allowance (Amendment) Regulations 1996 (SI 1996/1516), reg.14 (October 7, 1996).

"claimant"—see Jobseekers Act, s.35(1).

Applicable amount in hardship cases

3.491   **145.**—[¹(1) The weekly applicable amount of a person to whom an income-based jobseeker's allowance is payable in accordance with this Part of these Regulations shall be reduced by a sum equivalent to 40% or, in a case where the claimant or any other member of his family is either pregnant or is seriously ill, 20% of the following amount—]

(a) where he is a single claimant aged less than 18 or a member of a couple or a polygamous marriage where all the members, in either case, are less than 18, the amount specified in paragraph 1(1)(a), (b) or (c), as the case may be, of Schedule 1 (applicable amounts);

(b) where he is a single claimant aged not less than 18 but less than 25 or a member of a couple or polygamous marriage where one member is aged not less than 18 but less than 25 and the other member or, in the case of a polygamous marriage each other member, is a person under 18 who is not eligible for an income- based jobseeker's allowance under section 3(1)(f)(iii) or is not subject to a direction under section 16, the amount specified in paragraph 1(1)(d) of Schedule 1;

(c) where he is a single claimant aged not less than 25 or a member of a couple or a polygamous marriage (other than a member of a couple or polygamous marriage to whom sub-paragraph (b) [²applies]) at least one of whom is aged not less than 18, the amount specified in paragraph 1(1)(e) of Schedule 1.

(2) [¹. . .]

(3) A reduction under paragraph (1) or (2) shall, if it is not a multiple of 5p, be rounded to the nearest such multiple or, if it is a multiple of 2.5p but not of 5p, to the next lower multiple of 5p.

AMENDMENTS

3.492   1. Jobseeker's Allowance (Amendment) Regulations 1996 (SI 1996/1516), reg.15 (October 7, 1996).
2. Jobseeker's Allowance and Income Support (General) (Amendment) Regulations 1996 (SI 1996/1517), reg.28 (October 7, 1996).

DEFINITIONS

"claimant"—see Jobseekers Act, s.35(1).
"couple"—see reg.1(3).
"polygamous marriage"—*ibid.*
"single claimant"—*ibid.*

GENERAL NOTE

Hardship payments of JSA are paid at a reduced rate. The reduction in benefit is 40 per cent of the appropriate personal allowance for a single claimant of that age, or 20 per cent if a member of the claimant's family is pregnant or seriously ill (not defined).

Payments made on account of suspended benefit

3.493   **146.**—(1) This regulation applies to a person to whom—
(a) payments of a jobseeker's allowance have been suspended in

accordance with regulations made under [¹section 21 of the Social Security Act 1998];
(b) an income-based jobseeker's allowance is paid under regulation 141 or 142.
(2) In the case of a person to whom—
(a) this regulation applies; and
(b) payments in respect of the benefit suspended fall to be made, any benefit paid or payable by virtue of regulation 141(5) or 142(3) shall be treated as having been paid on account of the suspended benefit and only the balance of the suspended benefit (if any) shall be payable.

AMENDMENT

1. Social Security Act 1998 (Commencement No.11, and Savings and Consequential and Transitional Provisions) Order 1999 (SI 1999/2860 (C.75)), Arts 3(1) and (12) and Sch.12, para.9 (October 18 1999).

3.494

GENERAL NOTE

This provides that hardship payments made while payment of a claimant's JSA was suspended will be taken into account if it is later decided that the suspension should be lifted, and only the balance of the benefit owing will be paid. In other cases (*e.g.* where hardship payments have been made because of a delay in deciding the claim for JSA) offsetting will be applied under the normal rules (see reg.5 of the Payments on Account, Overpayments and Recovery Regulations).

[¹ PART IXA

HARDSHIP FOR JOINT-CLAIM COUPLES

Meaning of "couple in hardship"

146A.—(1) In this Part of these Regulations, a "couple in hardship" means for the purposes of regulation 146C, a joint-claim couple who are claiming a jobseeker's allowance jointly, other than a couple which includes a member to whom paragraph (3) or (4) applies, where—

3.495

(a) the woman member of the joint-claim couple is pregnant and the Secretary of State is satisfied that, unless a joint-claim jobseeker's allowance is paid, she will suffer hardship; or
(b) one or both members of the couple are members of a polygamous marriage, one member of the marriage is pregnant and the Secretary of State is satisfied that, unless a joint-claim jobseeker's allowance is paid, she will suffer hardship; or
(c) the award of a joint-claim jobseeker's allowance includes, or would, if a claim for a jobseeker's allowance from the couple were to succeed, have included in their applicable amount a disability premium and—
  (i) where the couple have an award, a joint-claim jobseeker's allowance is not payable either because it is suspended or because section 20A (denial or reduction of joint-claim jobseeker's allowance) applies in the couple's case; and
  (ii) the Secretary of State is satisfied that, unless a joint-claim jobseeker's allowance is paid, the member of the couple who would

have caused the disability premium to be applicable to the couple would suffer hardship; or

(d) either member of the couple suffers from a chronic medical condition which results in functional capacity being limited or restricted by physical impairment and the Secretary of State is satisfied that—

    (i) the suffering has already lasted or is likely to last, for not less than 26 weeks; and

    (ii) unless a joint-claim jobseeker's allowance is paid, the probability is that the health of the person suffering would, within two weeks of the Secretary of State making his decision, decline further than that of a normally healthy adult and the member of the couple who suffers from that condition would suffer hardship; or

(e) either member of the couple, or where a member of that couple is married to more than one person under a law which permits polygamy, one member of that marriage, devotes a considerable portion of each week to caring for another person who—

    (i) is in receipt of an attendance allowance or the care component of disability living allowance at one of the two higher rates prescribed under section 72(4) of the Benefits Act; or

    (ii) has claimed either attendance allowance or disability living allowance, but only for so long as the claim has not been determined, or for 26 weeks from the date of claiming, whichever is the earlier; or

    (iii) has claimed either attendance allowance or disability living allowance and has an award of either attendance allowance or the care component of disability living allowance at one of the two higher rates prescribed under section 72(4) of the Benefits Act for a period commencing after the date on which that claim was made,

and the Secretary of State is satisfied, after taking account of the factors set out in paragraph (6) in so far as they are appropriate to the particular circumstances of the case, that the person providing the care will not be able to continue doing so unless a joint-claim jobseeker's allowance is paid; or

(f) section 16 applies to either member of the couple by virtue of a direction issued by the Secretary of State, except where the member of the joint-claim couple to whom the direction applies does not satisfy the requirements of section 1(2)(a) to (c); or

(g) section 3A(1)(e)(ii) (member of joint-claim couple under the age of 18) applies to either member of the couple and the Secretary of State is satisfied that unless a joint-claim jobseeker's allowance is paid, the couple will suffer hardship;

(h) one or both members of the couple is a person—

    (i) who, pursuant to the Children Act 1989, was being looked after by a local authority;

    (ii) with whom the local authority had a duty, pursuant to that Act, to take reasonable steps to keep in touch; or

    (iii) who, pursuant to that Act, qualified for advice or assistance from a local authority,

but in respect of whom head (i), (ii) or, as the case may be, (iii) above had not applied for a period of three years or less as at the date on which the requirements of regulation 146F are complied with; and

(iv) as at the date on which the requirements of regulation 146F are complied with, that member is, or both of those members are, under the age of 21.

(2) Except in a case to which paragraph (3), (4) or (5) applies, a "couple in hardship" means for the purposes of regulation 146D, a joint-claim couple where the Secretary of State is satisfied, after taking account of the factors set out in paragraph (6) in so far as they are appropriate to the particular circumstances of the case, that the couple will suffer hardship unless a joint-claim jobseeker's allowance is paid.

(3) In paragraph (1) and (2), a "couple in hardship" does not include a couple one of whose members is entitled to income support or who falls within a category of persons prescribed for the purposes of section 124(1)(e) of the Benefits Act.

(4) Paragraph (1)(e) shall not apply in a case where the person being cared for resides in a residential care or nursing home.

(5) In paragraph (2), a "couple in hardship" does not include a joint-claim couple where section 20A(2)(b) or (c) applies to either or both members by virtue of any act or omission relating to a New Deal option [²or to the Intensive Activity Period specified in regulation 75(1)(a)(iv)].

(6) Factors which, for the purposes of paragraphs (1) and (2), the Secretary of State is to take into account in determining whether a joint-claim couple will suffer hardship are—

(a) the presence in the joint-claim couple of a person who satisfies the requirements for a disability premium specified in paragraphs 20H and 20I of Schedule 1;

(b) the resources which, without a joint-claim jobseeker's allowance, are likely to be available to the joint-claim couple, the amount by which these resources fall short of the amount applicable in their case in accordance with regulation 146G (applicable amount in hardship cases for joint-claim couples), the amount of any resources which may be available to the joint-claim couple for any person in the couple's household who is not a member of the family and the length of time for which those factors are likely to persist;

(c) whether there is a substantial risk that essential items, including food, clothing, heating and accommodation, will cease to be available to the joint-claim couple, or will be available at considerably reduced levels, the hardship that will result and the length of time those factors are likely to persist.]

AMENDMENTS

1. Jobseeker's Allowance (Joint Claims) Regulations 2000 (SI 2000/1978), reg.2(3) (March 19, 2001).   **3.496**

2. Social Security Amendment (New Deal) Regulations 2001 (SI 2001/1029), reg.9(2) (April 9, 2001).

GENERAL NOTE

This regulation makes provision corresponding to reg.140 for joint-claim couples.

[¹Period when a joint-claim couple is not in hardship

146B.—(1) A joint-claim couple which is not a couple in hardship by   **3.497** virtue of regulation 146A(5) shall not be a couple in hardship throughout the period beginning on the day on which a New Deal decision has effect by virtue of regulation 69 or, as the case may be, by virtue of regulation 7(8) of the Social Security and Child Support (Decisions and Appeals) Regulations 1999 in relation to either or both members of that couple and ending—

(a) on the last day on which a member is required to participate in a New Deal option [²or in the Intensive Activity Period specified in regulation 75(1)(a)(iv)]; or

(b) on the day which is 14 days after the day on which the New Deal decision had effect, whichever is the later.

(2) Where a joint-claim couple who are not a couple in hardship by virtue of regulation 146A(5) was a couple in hardship for the purposes of regulation 146D immediately before the commencement of the period referred to in paragraph (1), that couple shall, subject to paragraph (3), again become a couple in hardship for the purposes of regulation 146D on the day following the expiration of that period.

(3) A joint-claim couple to whom paragraph (2) applies shall not again become a couple in hardship for the purposes of regulation 146D if—

(a) the day following the day the period referred to in paragraph (1) expires is a day within a period in respect of which a subsequent New Deal decision applies by virtue of paragraph (1); or

(b) on the day following the expiration of the period referred to in paragraph (1), they are not a couple in hardship for the purposes of regulation 146D.

(4) In this regulation, "New Deal decision" means a decision that section 20A(2)(b) or (c) applies to a member of a joint-claim couple by virtue of an act or omission relating to one of the New Deal options [³ or to the Intensive Activity Period specified in regulation 75(1)(a)(iv)].]

AMENDMENTS

3.498

1. Jobseeker's Allowance (Joint Claims) Regulations 2000 (SI 2000/1978), reg.2(3) (March 19, 2001).

2. Social Security Amendment (New Deal) Regulations 2001 (SI 2001/1029), reg.10(1) (April 9, 2001).

3. Social Security Amendment (New Deal) Regulations 2001 (SI 2001/1029), reg.10(2) (April 9, 2001).

GENERAL NOTE

This regulation makes provision corresponding to reg.140A for joint-claim couples.

[¹ Circumstances in which a joint-claim jobseeker's allowance is payable where a joint-claim couple is a couple in hardship

3.499

146C.—(1) This regulation applies where a joint-claim couple is a couple in hardship within the meaning of regulation 146A(1) and is subject to the provisions of regulations 146E and 146F.

(2) Subject to paragraph (3), a couple in hardship referred to in paragraph (1), other than a couple in hardship where either or both members are persons to whom regulation 46(1) (waiting days) applies, shall be treated as entitled to a joint-claim jobseeker's allowance for the period—

(a) beginning with the fourth day of the jobseeking period or, if later, from the day the couple first becomes a couple in hardship; and

(b) ending on the day before the claim is determined,

where the sole reason for the claim being determined on that day and not earlier is that a question arises as to whether either or both members satisfy the conditions of entitlement in section 1(2)(a) to (c) provided the joint-claim couple satisfy the conditions set out in section 1(2B)(c).

(3) A couple in hardship to whom paragraph (2) applies may be treated as entitled to a joint-claim jobseeker's allowance for a period after the date referred to in that paragraph which is applicable in their case but before the date of the statement referred to in regulation 146E(1) is furnished where the Secretary of State is satisfied that that couple suffered hardship because of a lack of resources during that period.

(4) A couple in hardship, except where either or both members have been treated as not available for employment in accordance with regulations under section 6(4) shall, subject to the conditions specified in regulation 146E (conditions for hardship payments), be entitled to a joint-claim jobseeker's allowance without both members satisfying the requirements of section 1(2)(a) to (c) provided the joint-claim couple satisfy the other conditions of entitlement to that benefit.

(5) A joint-claim jobseeker's allowance shall be payable to a joint-claim couple who are a couple in hardship even though payment to the couple of a joint-claim jobseeker's allowance has been suspended in accordance with regulations made under section 21 of the Social Security Act 1998 on the ground that a doubt has arisen as to whether either joint-claimant satisfies the requirements of section 1(2)(a) to (c), but the allowance shall be payable only if and for so long as—

(a) the joint-claim couple satisfy the other conditions of entitlement to a joint-claim jobseeker's allowance; or

(b) one member satisfies those conditions and the other member comes within any paragraph in Schedule A1 (categories of members not required to satisfy conditions in section 1(2B)(b)).

(6) A joint-claim jobseeker's allowance shall be payable to a couple in hardship even though section 20A(5)(a) (denial of joint-claim jobseeker's allowance) prevents payment of a joint-claim jobseeker's allowance to the couple or section 20A(5)(b) (reduction of joint-claim jobseeker's allowance) reduces the amount of a joint-claim jobseeker's allowance payable to the couple but the allowance shall be payable only if and for so long as—

(a) the joint-claim couple satisfy the other conditions of entitlement to a joint-claim jobseeker's allowance; or

(b) one member satisfies those conditions and the other member comes within any paragraph in Schedule A1 (categories of members not required to satisfy conditions in section 1(2B)(b)).]

AMENDMENT

1. Jobseeker's Allowance (Joint Claims) Regulations 2000 (SI 2000/1978), reg.2(3) (March 19, 2001).   **3.500**

GENERAL NOTE

This regulation makes provision corresponding to reg.141 for joint-claim couples.

[¹ Further circumstances in which a joint-claim jobseeker's allowance is payable to a couple in hardship

3.501

146D.—(1) This regulation applies to a couple in hardship falling within paragraph (2) but not paragraph (1) of regulation 146A and is subject to the provisions of regulations 146E and 146F.

(2) A couple in hardship shall be treated as entitled to a joint-claim jobseeker's allowance for a period commencing on whichever is the later of—

(a) the 15th day following the date of claim disregarding any waiting days; or

(b) the day on which regulation 146E is complied with,

and ending on the day before the claim is determined where the sole reason for the claim being determined on that day and not earlier is that a question arises as to whether either or both members of that couple satisfy the conditions of entitlement in section 1(2)(a) to (c) provided the joint-claim couple satisfy the conditions set out in section 1(2B)(c).

(3) A joint-claim jobseeker's allowance shall be payable, subject to paragraph (4), to a couple in hardship even though payment to them of a joint-claim jobseeker's allowance has been suspended in accordance with regulations made under section 21 of the Social Security Act 1998 (suspension of benefit) on the ground that a doubt has arisen as to whether either or both members of that couple satisfy the requirements of section 1(2)(a) to (c) of the Act but the allowance shall be payable only if and for so long as—

(a) the joint-claim couple satisfy the other conditions of entitlement to a joint-claim jobseeker's allowance; or

(b) one member satisfies those conditions and the other member comes within any paragraph in Schedule A1 (categories of members not required to satisfy conditions in section 1(2B)(b)).

(4) A joint-claim jobseeker's allowance shall not be payable in respect of the first 14 days of the period of suspension.

(5) A joint-claim jobseeker's allowance shall be payable to a couple in hardship even though section 20A(5)(a) (denial of joint-claim jobseeker's allowance) prevents payment of a joint-claim jobseeker's allowance to them or section 20A(5)(b) (reduction of joint-claim jobseeker's allowance) reduces the amount of a joint-claim jobseeker's allowance payable to them but the allowance—

(a) shall not be payable under this paragraph in respect of the first 14 days of the period to which section 20A applies; and

3.502

(b) shall be payable thereafter only where the conditions of entitlement to a joint-claim jobseeker's allowance are satisfied or where one member satisfies those conditions and the other member comes within any paragraph in Schedule A1 (categories of members not required to satisfy conditions in section 1(2B)(b)).]

AMENDMENT

1. Jobseeker's Allowance (Joint Claims) Regulations 2000 (SI 2000/1978), reg.2(3) (March 19, 2001).

GENERAL NOTE

This regulation makes provision corresponding to reg.142 for joint-claim couples.

[¹ Conditions for hardship payments to a joint-claim couple

146E.—(1) A joint-claim jobseeker's allowance shall not be payable in accordance with regulation 146C or, as the case may be, 146D, except where either member of the joint-claim couple has—

3.503

    (a) furnished on a form approved for the purpose by the Secretary of State or in such other form as he may in any particular case approve, a statement of the circumstances he relies upon to establish entitlement under regulation 146C or, as the case may be, regulation 146D; and

    (b) signed the statement.

(2) The completed and signed form shall be delivered by either member to such office as the Secretary of State may specify.]

AMENDMENT

1. Jobseeker's Allowance (Joint Claims) Regulations 2000 (SI 2000/1978), reg.2(3) (March 19, 2001).

GENERAL NOTE

This regulation makes provision corresponding to reg.143 for joint-claim couples.

[¹ Provision of information

146F. For the purposes of section 20B(5) and paragraph 10(3) of Schedule 1 to the Act, a member of a joint-claim couple shall provide to the Secretary of State information as to the circumstances of the alleged hardship of that couple.]

3.504

AMENDMENT

1. Jobseeker's Allowance (Joint Claims) Regulations 2000 (SI 2000/1978), reg.2(3) (March 19, 2001).

GENERAL NOTE

This regulation makes provision corresponding to reg.144 for joint-claim couples.

[¹ Applicable amount in hardship cases for joint-claim couples

146G.—(1) The weekly applicable amount of the joint-claim couple to whom a joint-claim jobseeker's allowance is payable in accordance with this Part of these Regulations shall be reduced by a sum equivalent to 40% or, in a case where a member of a joint-claim couple is either pregnant or seriously ill or where a member of the joint-claim couple is a member of a polygamous marriage and one of the members of that marriage is pregnant or seriously ill, 20% of the following amount—

3.505

    (a) where one member of the joint-claim couple or the polygamous marriage is aged not less than 18 but less than 25 and the other member or, in the case of a polygamous marriage, each other member, is a person under 18 to whom section 3A(1)(e)(ii) applies or is not subject to a direction under section 16, the amount specified in paragraph 1(1)(d) of Schedule 1;

    (b) where one member of the joint-claim couple or of the polygamous marriage (other than a member of a couple or polygamous marriage to whom sub-paragraph (a) applies) at least one of whom is aged not less than 18, the amount specified in paragraph 1(1)(e) of Schedule 1.

(2) A reduction under paragraph (1) shall, if it is not a multiple of 5p, be rounded to the nearest such multiple or, if it is a multiple of 2.5p but not of 5p, to the next lower multiple of 5p.]

AMENDMENT

1. Jobseeker's Allowance (Joint Claims) Regulations 2000 (SI 2000/1978), reg.2(3) (March 19, 2001).

GENERAL NOTE

This regulation makes provision corresponding to reg.145 for joint-claim couples.

[¹ Payments made on account of suspended benefit

3.506   **146H.**—(1) This regulation applies to a joint-claim couple to whom—
(a) payments of a joint-claim jobseeker's allowance have been suspended in accordance with regulations made under section 21 of the Social Security Act 1998;
(b) a joint-claim jobseeker's allowance is paid under regulation 146C or 146D.
(2) In the case of a joint-claim couple to whom—
(a) this regulation applies; and
(b) payments in respect of the benefit suspended fall to be made,
any benefit paid or payable by virtue of regulation 146C(5) or 146D(3) shall be treated as having been paid on account of the suspended benefit and only the balance of the suspended benefit, if any, shall be payable.]

AMENDMENT

1. Jobseeker's Allowance (Joint Claims) Regulations 2000 (SI 2000/1978), reg.2(3) (March 19, 2001).

GENERAL NOTE

This regulation makes provision corresponding to reg.146 for joint-claim couples.

PART X

URGENT CASES

Urgent cases

3.507   **147.**—(1) In a case to which this regulation applies, a claimant's weekly applicable amount and his income and capital shall be calculated for the purposes of an income-based jobseeker's allowance in accordance with the following provisions of this Part.

(2) This regulation applies in accordance with the following provisions to—
[²(a) a claimant to whom paragraph (2A) applies (persons not excluded from income-based jobseeker's allowance under section 115 of the Immigration and Asylum Act);]

(b) a claimant to whom paragraph (6) (certain persons whose income is not readily available to them) applies.

[³(2A) This paragraph applies to a person not excluded from entitlement to income-based jobseeker's allowance under section 115 of the Immigration and Asylum Act by virtue of regulation 2 of the Social Security (Immigration and Asylum) Consequential Amendments Regulations 2000 except for a person to whom paragraphs 3 and 4 of Part I to the Schedule to those Regulations applies.]

(3) [⁴. . .].

(4) [⁴. . .].

(5) [⁴. . .].

(6) This paragraph shall only apply to a person who is treated as possessing income by virtue of regulation 105(6) and (7) (notional income) where the income he is treated as possessing is not readily available to him; and—

(a) the amount of jobseeker's allowance payable to him otherwise than under this Part is less than the amount of a jobseeker's allowance payable to him under this Part; and

(b) the adjudication officer is satisfied that, unless the provisions of this Part are applied to the claimant, the claimant or his family will suffer hardship.

AMENDMENTS

1. Jobseeker's Allowance (Amendment) Regulations 1996 (SI 1996/1516), reg.10(2) (October 7, 1996).   **3.508**

2. Social Security (Immigration and Asylum) Consequential Amendments Regulations 2000 (SI 2000/636), reg.4(5)(a) (April 3, 2000).

3. Social Security (Immigration and Asylum) Consequential Amendments Regulations 2000 (SI 2000/636), reg.4(5)(b) (April 3, 2000).

4. Social Security (Immigration and Asylum) Consequential Amendments Regulations 2000 (SI 2000/636), reg.4(5)(c) (April 3, 2000).

DEFINITIONS

"claimant"—see Jobseekers Act, s.35(1).

"income-based jobseeker's allowance—see Jobseekers Act, s.1(4).

GENERAL NOTE

There are only two categories who can qualify for urgent cases payments of income-based JSA: claimants who are treated as possessing income which is due but has not been paid and certain people who are "subject to immigration control", and so would otherwise be within s.115 of the Immigration and Asylum Act 1999, but who are not excluded from entitlement to income-based JSA. However, in most circumstances it will be better for the person to claim urgent cases payments of income support rather than income-based JSA so as to avoid the risk of being sanctioned for not complying with the JSA labour market conditions.

See the notes to reg.70 of the Income Support Regulations for further discussion of this provision. Note the exclusions from para.(2A). People who are within paras 3 and 4 of Pt I of the Sch. to SI 2000/636 are eligible for "full-rate" benefit rather than the lower "urgent cases" rate.

Applicable amount in urgent cases

148.—(1) For the purposes of calculating any entitlement to an income-based jobseeker's allowance [² or where the person in hardship is a member of a joint-claim couple and regulation 3E does not apply] under this Part—   **3.509**

(a) except in a case to which sub-paragraph [⁴ . . .] (c) or (d) applies, a claimant's weekly applicable amount shall be the aggregate of—
    (i) 90 per cent. of the amount applicable (reduced where appropriate in accordance with regulation 145 (applicable amount in hardship cases)) in respect of himself or, if he is a member of a couple or of a polygamous marriage, of the amount applicable in respect of both of them under paragraph 1(1), (2) or (3) of Schedule 1 or, as the case may be, the amount applicable in respect of them under regulation 84 (polygamous marriages);
    (ii) [⁶ . . .]
    (iii) the amount, if applicable, specified in Part [⁶ . . .] III of Schedule 1 (premiums);
    (iv) any amounts applicable under regulation 83(f) or, as the case may be, 84(1)(g) (housing costs);
    (v) [⁵ . . .]
    (vi) the amount of any protected sum which may be applicable to him in accordance with regulation 87(2);
(b) [³ . . .]
(c) [⁵ . . .]
(d) except where sub-paragraph [⁴ . . .] (c) applies, in the case of a person to whom any paragraph, other than. [¹ paragraph 13A] in column (1) of Schedule 5 (special cases) applies, the amount shall be 90 per cent. of the amount applicable in column 2 of that Schedule in respect of the claimant and partner (if any), plus, if applicable—
    (i) [⁶ . . .]
    (ii) any premium under Part [⁶ . . .] III of Schedule 1; and
    (iii) any amounts applicable under regulation 83(f) or, as the case may be, 84(1)(g); and
    (iv) the amount of the protected sum which may be applicable to him in accordance with regulation 87(2).
[³ (1A) [⁵ . . .]]]
(2) Where the calculation of a claimant's applicable amount under this regulation results in a fraction of a penny that fraction shall be treated as a penny.

AMENDMENTS

3.510 1. Social Security (Immigration and Asylum) Consequential Amendments Regulations 2000 (SI 2000/636), reg.4(6).
2. Jobseeker's Allowance (Joint Claims) Regulations 2000 (SI 2000/1978), reg.2(5) and Sch.2, para.46 (March 19, 2001).
3. Social Security Amendment (Residential Care and Nursing Homes) Regulations 2001 (SI 2001/3767), reg.2 and Sch., Pt II, para.15 (April 8, 2002).
4. Social Security Amendment (Residential Care and Nursing Homes) Regulations 2001 (SI 2001/3767), reg.2 and Sch., Pt II, para.15 (as amended by Social Security Amendment (Residential Care and Nursing Homes) Regulations 2002 (SI 2002/398), reg.4(5)) (April 8, 2002).
5. Social Security (Removal of Residential Allowance and Miscellaneous Amendments) Regulations 2003 (SI 2003/1121), reg.4 and Sch.2, para.7 (October 6, 2003).
6. Social Security (Working Tax Credit and Child Tax Credit) (Consequential Amendments) Regulations 2003 (SI 2003/455), reg.3 and Sch.2, para.19 (April 6, 2004, except in "transitional cases" and see further the note to reg.83 and to reg.17 of the Income Support Regulations).

DEFINITIONS

"child"—see Jobseekers Act, s.35(1).
"claimant"—*ibid.*
"couple"—see reg.1(3).
"family"—see Jobseekers Act, s.35(1).
"nursing home"—see reg.1(3).
"polygamous marriage"—*ibid.*
"residential care home"—*ibid.*
"young person"—see reg.76.

GENERAL NOTE

See reg.71 of the Income Support Regulations.

[¹ Applicable amount in urgent cases: joint-claim couples

148A.—(1) For the purpose of calculating any entitlement to a joint-claim jobseeker's allowance under this Part—

3.511

  (a) except in a case to which sub-paragraph [² . . .] (c) or (d) applies, a joint-claim couple's weekly applicable amount shall be the aggregate of—

    (i) 90 per cent of the amount applicable (reduced where appropriate in accordance with regulation 146G (applicable amount in hardship cases for joint-claim couples)) in respect of the couple under paragraph 1(3) of Schedule 1 or, as the case may be, the amount applicable in respect of them under regulation 86B (joint-claim couples: polygamous marriages);

    (ii) the amount, if applicable, specified in Part IVA of Schedule 1 (premiums);

    (iii) any amounts applicable under regulation 86A(d) or, as the case may be, 86B(e) (housing costs); and

    (iv) [³. . .]

  (b) [². . .]

  (c) [³. . .]

  (d) except where sub-paragraph [² . . .] (c) applies, in the case of a member of a joint-claim couple to whom any paragraph of Schedule 5A (applicable amounts of joint-claim couples in special cases) applies, the amount shall be 90 per cent of the amount applicable in column (2) of that Schedule in respect of the joint-claim couple plus, if applicable—

    (i) any premium under Part IVA of Schedule 1;

    (ii) any amounts applicable under regulation 86A(d) or, as the case may be, 86B(e) (housing costs).

[² (1A) [³. . .]]

(2) Where the calculation of a joint-claim couple's applicable amount under this regulation results in a fraction of a penny that fraction shall be treated as a penny.]

AMENDMENTS

1. Jobseeker's Allowance (Joint Claims) Regulations 2000 (SI 2000/1978), reg.2(5) and Sch.2, para.47 (March 19, 2001).

3.512

2. Social Security Amendment (Residential Care and Nursing Homes) Regulations 2001 (SI 2001/3767), reg.2 and Sch., Pt II, para.16 (as amended by

Social Security Amendment (Residential Care and Nursing Homes) Regulations 2002 (SI 2002/398), reg.4(3)) (April 8, 2002).

3. Social Security (Removal of Residential Allowance and Miscellaneous Amendments) Regulations 2003 (SI 2003/1121), reg.4 and Sch.2, para.8 (October 6, 2003).

GENERAL NOTE

This regulation makes provision corresponding to reg.148 for joint-claim couples.

Assessment of income and capital in urgent cases

3.513   **149.**—(1) The claimant's income shall be calculated in accordance with Part VIII subject to the following modifications—
[²(a) any income other than—
   (i) a payment of income or income in kind made under the Macfarlane Trust, the Macfarlane (Special Payments) Trust, the Macfarlane (Special Payments) (No.2) Trust, the Fund, the Eileen Trust or the Independent Living Funds; or
   (ii) income to which paragraph 6, 8 (but only to the extent that a concessionary payment would be due under that paragraph for any non-payment of jobseeker's allowance under regulation 147 of these Regulations or of income support under regulation 70 of the Income Support Regulations (urgent cases)), 33, 41(2), (3) or (4) or 42 of Schedule 7 (disregard of income other than earnings) applies,
possessed or treated as possessed by him, shall be taken into account in full notwithstanding any provision in that Part disregarding the whole or any part of that income;]
 (b) any income to which regulation 116 (calculation of tariff income from capital) applies shall be disregarded;
 (c) income treated as capital by virtue of regulation 110(1), (2), (3) and (9) (income treated as capital) shall be taken into account as income;
 (d) in a case to which paragraph (2)(b) of regulation 147 (urgent cases) applies, any income to which regulation 105(6) and (7) (notional income) applies shall be disregarded.

(2) The claimant's capital calculated in accordance with Part VIII, but including any capital referred to in paragraphs 3 and, to the extent that such assets as are referred to in paragraph 11 consist of liquid assets, 11 and, except to the extent that the arrears referred to in paragraph 12 [¹ consist] of arrears of housing benefit payable under Part VII of the Benefits Act or Part II of the Social Security and Housing Benefits Act 1982 [²or any arrears of benefit due under regulation 147 of these Regulations or regulation 70 of the Income Support Regulations (urgent cases)], 12, 14(b), 24 and 32 of Schedule 8 (capital to be disregarded) shall be taken into account in full and the amount of a job-seeker's allowance which would, but for this paragraph be payable under this regulation, shall be payable only to the extent that it exceeds the amount of that capital.

AMENDMENTS

3.514   1. Jobseeker's Allowance (Amendment) Regulations 1996 (SI 1996/1516), reg.20 and Sch. (October 7, 1996).

2. Social Security (Miscellaneous Amendments) Regulations 1998 (SI 1998/563), reg.19(2) (April 6, 1998).

DEFINITIONS

"the Benefits Act"—see Jobseekers Act, s.35(1).
"claimant"—*ibid.*
"concessionary payment"—see reg.1(3).
"the Eileen Trust"—*ibid.*
"the Fund"—*ibid.*
"the Independent Living Funds"—*ibid.*
"the Macfarlane (Special Payments) Trust"—*ibid.*
"the Macfarlane (Special Payments) (No. 2) Trust"—*ibid.*
"the Macfarlane Trust"—*ibid.*

GENERAL NOTE

See the note to reg.72 of the Income Support Regulations. But note the slightly different treatment of income and capital for the purpose of urgent cases payments under income support.

PART XI

PART-WEEKS

Amount of a jobseeker's allowance payable

150.—(1) Subject to the following provisions of this Part, the amount   3.515
payable by way of an income-based jobseeker's allowance in respect of part-week shall be calculated by applying the formula—
(a) where the claimant has no income—

$$\frac{(N \times A)}{7}; \text{or}$$

(b) where the claimant has an income—

$$\frac{(N \times (A - I))}{(7)} - B,$$

where—
    A is the claimant's weekly applicable amount in the relevant week;
    B is the amount of any jobseeker's allowance, income support, maternity allowance, incapacity benefit or severe disablement allowance payable to any member of the claimant's family other than the claimant in respect of any day in the part-week;
    I is the claimant's weekly income in the relevant week less B;
    N is the number of days in the part-week.
[¹ (1A) In relation to a joint-claim couple jointly claiming a joint-claim jobseeker's allowance, paragraph (1) shall have effect as if the references to the claimant were references to the joint-claim couple.
(1B) Where a joint-claim couple become, or cease to be, a joint-claim couple on any day other than on the first day of a benefit week, the amount

payable by way of a joint-claim jobseeker's allowance in respect of that benefit week shall be calculated by applying the formula in paragraph (1).]

(2) Subject to the following provisions of this Part, the amount payable by way of a contribution-based jobseeker's allowance in respect of a part-week shall be calculated by applying the formula—

$$\frac{(N \times X) - Y}{(7)}$$

where—

    X is the personal rate determined in accordance with section 4(1);

    Y is the amount of any widow's benefit, [2 carer's allowance], training allowance and any increase in disablement pension payable in accordance with Part I of Schedule 7 to the Benefits Act (Unemployment Supplement) payable in respect of any day in the part-week;

    N is the number of days in the part-week

(3) In this Part—

"part-week" means an entitlement to a jobseeker's allowance in respect of any period of less than a week;

"relevant week" means the period of 7 days determined in accordance with regulation 152.

AMENDMENTS

3.516   1. Jobseeker's Allowance (Joint Claims) Regulations 2000 (SI 2000/1978), reg.2(5) and Sch.2, para.48 (March 19, 2001).

    2. Social Security (Miscellaneous Amendments) Regulations 2003 (SI 2003/511), reg.3(4) and (5) (April 1, 2003).

DEFINITION

"claimant"—see Jobseekers Act, s.35(1).

Amount of a jobseeker's allowance payable where a person is in a residential care or nursing home

3.517   **151.**—[1 . . .]

AMENDMENT

    1. Social Security Amendment (Residential Care and Nursing Homes) Regulations 2001 (SI 2001/3767), reg.2 and Sch., Pt II, para.17 (April 8, 2002).

Relevant week

3.518   **152.**—(1) Where the part-week—
(a) is the whole period for which a jobseeker's allowance is payable or occurs at the beginning of an award, the relevant week is the period of 7 days ending on the last day of that part-week; or
(b) occurs at the end of an award, the relevant week is the period of 7 days beginning on the first day of the part-week; or
(c) occurs because a jobseeker's allowance is not payable for any period in accordance with section 19 [1or 20A] of the Act (circumstances in which a jobseeker's allowance is not payable), the relevant week is the 7 days ending immediately before the start of the next benefit week to commence for that claimant [2 or the joint-claim couple].

(2) [³ Except in a case to which paragraph (3) applies,] where a person has an award of a jobseeker's allowance and his benefit week changes, for the purpose of calculating the amounts of a jobseeker's allowance payable for the part-week beginning on the day after his last complete benefit week before the change and ending immediately before the change, the relevant week is the period of 7 days beginning on the day after the last complete benefit week.

[⁴ (3) Where a joint-claim couple have an award of a joint-claim jobseeker's allowance and their benefit week changes, for the purpose of calculating the amounts of a joint-claim jobseeker's allowance payable for the part-week beginning on the day after their last complete benefit week before the change and ending immediately before the change, the relevant week is the period of 7 days beginning on the day after the last complete benefit week.]

AMENDMENTS

1. Jobseeker's Allowance (Joint Claims) Regulations 2000 (SI 2000/1978), reg.2(5) and Sch.2, para.50(a)(i) (March 19, 2001).
2. Jobseeker's Allowance (Joint Claims) Regulations 2000 (SI 2000/1978), reg.2(5) and Sch.2, para.50(a)(ii) (March 19, 2001).
3. Jobseeker's Allowance (Joint Claims) Regulations 2000 (SI 2000/1978), reg.2(5) and Sch.2, para.50(b) (March 19, 2001).
4. Jobseeker's Allowance (Joint Claims) Regulations 2000 (SI 2000/1978), reg.2(5) and Sch.2, para.50(c) (March 19, 2001).

3.519

DEFINITION

"benefit week"—see reg.1(3).

Modification in the calculation of income

153. For the purposes of regulation 150 (amount of jobseeker's allowance payable for part-weeks) a claimant's income and, in determining the amount payable by way of an income-based jobseeker's allowance, the income of any person which the claimant is treated as possessing under section 12(4) or [¹ regulation 88(4) or 88ZA(3)], shall be calculated in accordance with Parts VIII, and, where applicable, IX and X subject to the following changes—

3.520

   (a) any income which is due to be paid in the relevant week shall be treated as paid on the first day of that week;

   (b) in determining the amount payable by way of an income-based jobseeker's allowance, any jobseeker's allowance, income support, maternity allowance, incapacity benefit or severe disablement allowance under the Benefits Act payable in the relevant week but not in respect of any day in the part-week shall be disregarded;

   (c) in determining the amount payable by way of a contribution- based jobseeker's allowance, any widow's benefit, [² carer's allowance], training allowance or any increase in disablement pension payable in accordance with Part I of Schedule 7 to the Benefits Act (Unemployment Supplement) which is payable in the relevant week but not in respect of any day in the part-week shall be disregarded;

   (d) where the part-week occurs at the end of the claim, any income or any change in the amount of income of the same kind which is first payable within the relevant week but not on any day in the part-week shall be disregarded;

(e) where the part-week occurs immediately after a period in which a person was treated as engaged in remunerative work under regulation 52 (persons treated as engaged in remunerative work) any earnings which are taken into account for the purposes of determining that period shall be disregarded;

(f) where only part of the weekly amount of income is taken into account in the relevant week, the balance shall be disregarded.

AMENDMENTS

1. Jobseeker's Allowance (Joint Claims) Regulations 2000 (SI 2000/1978), reg.2(5) and Sch.2, para.51 (March 19, 2001).
2. Social Security (Miscellaneous Amendments) Regulations 2003 (SI 2003/511), reg.3(4) and (5) (April 1, 2003).

DEFINITIONS

"the Benefits Act"—see Jobseekers Act, s.35(1).
"claimant"—*ibid.*

Reduction in certain cases

3.521   **154.** The reduction to be made in accordance with Part IX (Hardship) in respect of an income based jobseeker's allowance shall be an amount equal to one seventh of the reduction which would be made under that Part for a week multiplied by the number of days in the part-week.

Modification of section 15(2) of the Act

3.522   **155.**—[¹ (1)] In its application to an income-based jobseeker's allowance [² but not a joint-claim jobseeker's allowance] payable for a part-week, section 15(2)(d) shall have effect subject to the following modification—

"(d) any payment by way of an income-based jobseeker's allowance for that period or any part of it which apart from this paragraph would be made to the claimant—
(i) shall not be made, if the amount of an income-based jobseeker's allowance which would be payable for a period of less than a week is equal to or less than the proportion of the prescribed sum appropriate to the number of days in the part-week;
(ii) shall be at a rate equal to the difference between the amount which would be payable for a period of less than a week and the prescribed sum where that amount would be more than the prescribed sum."

[³ (2) In its application to a joint-claim jobseeker's allowance payable for a part-week, section 15(2)(d) shall have effect subject to the following modification—

"(d) any payment by way of a joint-claim jobseeker's allowance for that period or any part of it which apart from this paragraph would be made to the nominated member for the purposes of section 3B—
(i) shall not be made, if the amount of joint-claim jobseeker's allowance which would be payable for less than a week is equal to or less than the proportion of the prescribed sum appropriate to the number of days in the part-week;
(ii) shall be at a rate equal to the difference between the amount which would be

payable for a period of less than a week and the prescribed sum where that amount would be more than the prescribed sum."]

AMENDMENTS

1. Jobseeker's Allowance (Joint Claims) Regulations 2000 (SI 2000/1978), reg.2(5) and Sch.2, para.52 (March 19, 2001).
2. Jobseeker's Allowance (Joint Claims) Regulations 2000 (SI 2000/1978), reg.2(5) and Sch.2, para.52(a) (March 19, 2001).
3. Jobseeker's Allowance (Joint Claims) Regulations 2000 (SI 2000/1978), reg.2(5) and Sch.2, para.52(b) (March 19, 2001).

3.523

PART XIII

MISCELLANEOUS

Recovery of Maintenance

Recovery orders

169.—(1) Where an award of income-based jobseeker's allowance has been made to a person ("the claimant"), the Secretary of State may apply to the court for a recovery order against the claimant's spouse ("the liable person").

3.524

(2) On making a recovery order the court may order the liable person to pay such amount at such intervals as it considers appropriate, having regard to all the circumstances of the liable person and in particular his income.

(3) Except in Scotland, a recovery order shall be treated for all purposes as if it were a maintenance order within the meaning of section 150(1) of the Magistrates Courts Act 1980.

(4) Where a recovery order requires the liable person to make payments to the Secretary of State, the Secretary of State may, by giving notice in writing to the court which made the order, the liable person, and the claimant, transfer to the claimant the right to receive payments under the order and to exercise the relevant rights in relation to the order.

(5) In this regulation—
the expressions "the court" and "recovery order" have the same meanings as in section 23 of the Act; and
"the relevant rights" means, in relation to a recovery order, the right to bring any proceedings, take any steps or do any other thing under or in relation to the order.

DEFINITION

"claimant"—see Jobseekers Act, s.35(1).

3.525

GENERAL NOTE

See the note to s.23 of the Jobseekers Act.

Persons in receipt of a training allowance

3.526   **170.**—[³ (1) A person who is not receiving training falling within paragraph (2) may be entitled to an income-based jobseeker's allowance without —

   (a)   being available for employment;

   (b)   having entered into a jobseeker's agreement; or

   (c)   actively seeking employment,

if he is in receipt of a training allowance or if he would be in receipt of a training allowance if the Social Security (Breach of Community Order) Regulations 2001 did not prevent the payment of a training allowance to him.]

(2) Training falls within this paragraph if it is training for which persons aged under 18 are eligible and for which persons aged 18 to 24 may be eligible [² secured by the Learning and Skills Council for England or by the National Council for Education and Training for Wales and, in Scotland, provided] directly or indirectly by a Local Enterprise Company pursuant to its arrangement with, as the case may be, Scottish Enterprise or Highlands and Islands Enterprise (whether that arrangement is known as an Operating Contract or by any other name).

AMENDMENTS

3.527   1. Jobseeker's Allowance (Amendment) (No.2) Regulations 1998 (SI 1998/1698), reg.5 (August 4, 1998).

   2. Social Security (Miscellaneous Amendments) (No.2) Regulations 2001 (SI 2001/652), reg.5(c) (March 26, 2001).

   3. Social Security (Breach of Community Order) (Consequential Amendments) Regulations 2001 (SI 2001/1711), reg.2(4)(b) (October 15, 2001).

DEFINITIONS

   "employment"—see reg.4.

   "training allowance"—see reg.1(3).

Trade Disputes

Trade disputes: exemptions from section 15 of the Act

3.528   **171.** Section 15(2) (trade disputes: effect on other claimants) shall not apply to a claimant during any period where—

   (a)   a member of the claimant's family is, or would be, prevented by section 14 from being entitled to a jobseeker's allowance; and

   (b)   that member is—

      (i)   a child or young person; or

      (ii)   [¹incapable of work] or within the maternity period, and for this purpose "the maternity period" means the period commencing at the beginning of the 6th week before the expected week of confinement and ending at the end of the 7th week after the week in which confinement takes place.

AMENDMENT

1. Jobseeker's Allowance (Amendment) Regulations 1996 (SI 1996/1516), reg.20 and Sch. (October 7, 1996).

DEFINITIONS

"child"—see Jobseekers Act, s.35(1).
"claimant"—*ibid.*
"family"—*ibid.*
"trade dispute"—*ibid.*
"young person"—see reg.76.

GENERAL NOTE

See the note to s.15 of the Jobseekers Act.

Trade disputes: prescribed sum

172. The prescribed sum for the purposes of section 15(2)(d) is [¹£30.50].

3.529

AMENDMENT

1. Social Security Benefits Up-rating Order 2005 (SI 2005/522), art.25 (April 11, 2005).

[¹ SCHEDULE A1

CATEGORIES OF MEMBERS OF A JOINT-CLAIM COUPLE WHO ARE NOT REQUIRED TO SATISFY THE CONDITIONS IN SECTION 1(2B)(b)

Interpretation
1. In this Schedule, "member" means a member of a joint-claim couple.

3.530

Member studying full-time
[² **2.**—(1) A member—
  (a) who, at the date of claim, is aged 16 or over but under 19 and is receiving full-time education for the purposes of section 142 of the Benefits Act;
  (b) who, at the date of claim, is a full-time student; or
  (c) to whom (a) or (b) does not apply but to whom sub-paragraph (1A) or (2) does apply.
(1A) This sub-paragraph applies to a member who—
  (a) as at the date of claim—
    (i) had applied to an educational establishment to commence a full-time course of study commencing from the beginning of the next academic term or, as the case may be, the next academic year after the date of claim and that application has not been rejected; or
    (ii) had been allocated a place on a full-time course of study commencing from the beginning of the next academic term or, as the case may be, the next academic year; and
  (b) is either—
    (i) aged 16 or over but under 19 and is receiving full-time education for the purposes of section 142 of the Benefits Act; or
    (ii) a full-time student.
(2) This sub-paragraph applies to a member who has applied to an educational establishment to commence a full-time course of study (other than a course of study beyond a first degree course or a comparable course)—
  (a) within one month of—
    (i) the last day of a previous course of study; or
    (ii) the day on which the member received examination results relating to a previous course of study; and
  (b) who is either—
    (i) aged 16 or over but under 19 and is receiving full-time education for the purposes of section 142 of the Benefits Act; or

3.531

(ii) a full-time student.]

(3) A member to whom any provision of regulation 13(2)(b) to (e) of the Income Support Regulations (persons receiving relevant education who are severely handicapped, orphans and persons estranged from their parents or guardian) applies.

Member caring for another person

3.532   **3.** A member (the carer)—

   (a) who is regularly and substantially engaged in caring for another person if—

      (i)   the person being cared for is in receipt of attendance allowance or the care component of disability living allowance at the highest or middle rate prescribed in accordance with section 72(3) of the Benefits Act; or

      (ii) the person being cared for has claimed attendance allowance but only for the period up to the date of determination of that claim, or the period of 26 weeks from the date of that claim, whichever date is the earlier; or

      (iii) the person being cared for has claimed attendance allowance in accordance with section 65(6)(a) of the Benefits Act (claims in advance of entitlement), an award has been made in respect of that claim under section 65(6)(b) of that Act and, where the period for which the award is payable has begun, that person is in receipt of the allowance;

      (iv) the person being cared for has claimed entitlement to a disability living allowance but only for the period up to the date of determination of that claim, or the period of 26 weeks from the date of that claim, whichever date is the earlier; or

      (v)   the person being cared for has claimed entitlement to the care component of a disability living allowance in accordance with regulation 13A of the Claims and Payments Regulations (advance claims and awards), an award at the highest or middle rate has been made in respect of that claim and, where the period for which the award is payable has begun, that person is in receipt of the allowance;

   (b) who is engaged in caring for another person and who is both entitled to, and in receipt of, [⁴ a carer's allowance].

   4. A member to whom paragraph 3 applied, but only for a period of 8 weeks from the date on which that paragraph ceased to apply to him.

   5. A member who, had he previously made a claim for, and had been entitled to, a jobseeker's allowance, would have fulfilled the conditions of paragraph 3, but only for a period of 8 weeks from the date on which he ceased to fulfil those conditions.

Member incapable of work

3.533   **6.** A member who—

   (a) is incapable of work in accordance with the provisions of Part XIIA of the Benefits Act and the regulations made thereunder (incapacity for work); or

   (b) is treated as incapable of work by virtue of regulations made under section 171D of that Act (persons to be treated as incapable or capable of work); or

   (c) is treated as capable of work by virtue of regulations made under section 171E(1) of that Act (disqualification etc.); or

   (d) is entitled to statutory sick pay.

Members in employment living in residential care homes, nursing homes or residential accommodation

3.534   **7.** A member to whom regulation 53(c) (persons treated as not engaged in remunerative work) applies.

Disabled workers

3.535   **8.** A member to whom regulation 53(h) (persons treated as not engaged in remunerative work) applies.

Disabled students

3.536   **9.** A member who is a student and—

   (a) if he were a single claimant, his applicable amount would have included the disability premium or severe disability premium; or

   (b) who has satisfied the provisions of paragraph 6 for a continuous period of not less than 196 days, and for this purpose, any two or more separate periods separated by a break of not more than 56 days shall be treated as one continuous period.

Deaf students

10. A member who is a student in respect of whom—   3.537
    (a) a supplementary requirement has been determined under paragraph 9 of Schedule 2
        to the Education (Mandatory Awards) Regulations 1999; or
    (b) an allowance or, as the case may be, a bursary has been granted which includes a sum
        under paragraph (1)(d) of regulation 4 of the Students' Allowances (Scotland)
        Regulations 1999 or, as the case may be, the Education Authority Bursaries (Scotland)
        Regulations 1995 in respect of expenses incurred; or
    (c) a payment has been made under section 2 of the Education Act 1962; or
    (d) a grant has been made under regulation 13 of the Education (Student Support)
        Regulations 2000 or under regulation 13 of the Education (Student Support)
        Regulations 2000 (Northern Ireland); or
    (e) a supplementary requirement has been determined under paragraph 9 of Schedule 6
        to the Students Awards Regulations (Northern Ireland) 1999 or a payment has been
        made under article 50(3) of the Education and Libraries (Northern Ireland) Order
        1986,
on account of his disability by reason of deafness.

Blind members

11. A member who is registered as blind in a register compiled by a local authority under   3.538
section 29 of the National Assistance Act 1948 (welfare services) or, in Scotland, has been certified as blind and in consequence, he is registered as blind in a register maintained by or on
behalf of a regional or islands council, but a person who has ceased to be registered as blind on
regaining his eyesight shall nevertheless be treated as so registered for a period of 28 weeks following the date on which he ceased to be so registered.

Pregnancy

12. A member who is a woman and who is incapable of work by reason of pregnancy.   3.539

Members aged 60 or over

13. A member aged not less than 60.   3.540

Refugees

14. A member who is a refugee within the definition in Article 1 of the Convention relating   3.541
to the Status of Refugees done at Geneva on 28th July 1951 as extended by Article 1(2) of the
Protocol relating to the Status of Refugees done at New York on 31st January 1967 and who—
    (a) is attending for more than 15 hours a week a course for the purpose of learning English
        so that he may obtain employment; and
    (b) on the date on which that course commenced, had been in Great Britain for not more
        than 12 months,
but only for a period not exceeding nine months.

Members required to attend court

15. A member who is required to attend court as a justice of the peace, a party to any pro-   3.542
ceedings, a witness or a juror.

Young persons in training

16. A member who is engaged in training and for this purpose "training" means training for   3.543
which persons aged under 18 are eligible and for which persons aged 18 to 24 may be eligible
[³ secured by the Learning and Skills Council for England or by the National Council for
Education and Training for Wales] and, in Scotland, directly or indirectly by a Local Enterprise
Company pursuant to its arrangements with, as the case may be, Scottish Enterprise or
Highlands and Islands Enterprise (whether that arrangement is known as an Operating
Contract or by any other name).

Trade disputes

17. A member who is or would be prevented from being entitled to a jobseeker's allowance   3.544
by virtue of section 14 (trade disputes) but only where that section does not prevent the other
member from being so entitled.]

AMENDMENTS

1. Jobseeker's Allowance (Joint Claims) Regulations 2000 (SI 2000/1978),
reg.2(4) and Sch.1 (March 19, 2001).

2. Social Security Amendment (Joint Claims) Regulations 2001 (SI 2001/ 518), reg.2(6) (March 19, 2001).

3. Social Security (Miscellaneous Amendments) (No.2) Regulations 2001 (SI 2001/652), reg.4 (March 26, 2001).

4. Social Security (Miscellaneous Amendments) Regulations 2003 (SI 2003/ 511), reg.3(4) and (5) (April 1, 2003).

DEFINITIONS

"attendance allowance"—see reg.1(3).
" the Benefits Act"—see Jobseekers Act, s.35(1).
"course of study"—see reg.1(3).
"date of claim"—*ibid.*
"disability living allowance"—*ibid.*
"full-time student"—*ibid.*
"joint-claim couple"—see JSA, s.1(4).
"nursing home"—see reg.1(3).
"remunerative work"—*ibid.*, reg.51(1).
"residential accommodation"—see reg.1(3).
"residential care home"—*ibid.*
"single claimant"—*ibid.*
"student"—see reg.130.
"young person"—see regs 1(3), 76.

GENERAL NOTE

See the note to reg.3D.

Many of the categories are similar to those in Sch.1B to the Income Support Regulations (people eligible for income support). See the notes to that Schedule.

SCHEDULE 1   **Regulations 83 and 84(1)**

APPLICABLE AMOUNTS

[⁹*Part I*

Personal Allowances

1. The weekly amounts specified in column (2) below in respect of each person or couple specified in column (1) shall be the weekly amounts specified for the purposes of regulations 83 [²⁸ 84(1), 86A and 86B] (applicable amounts and polygamous marriages).

(1)	*(2)*
Person or Couple	*Amount*
(1) Single claimant aged—	
(a) except where head (b) or (c) of this sub-paragraph applies, less than 18;	1. (a) [³¹£33.85]
(b) less than 18 who falls within paragraph (2) of regulation 57 and who—	(b) [³¹£44.50]
(i) is a person to whom regulation 59, 60 or 61 applies [¹. . .]; or	
(ii) is the subject of a direction under section 16;	
(c) less than 18 who satisfies the condition in paragraph 13(a) of Part 3;	(c) [³¹£44.50]
(d) not less than 18 but less than 25;	(d) [³¹£44.50]
(e) not less than 25.	(e) [³¹£56.20]
(2) Lone parent aged—	
(a) except where head (b) or (c) of this sub-paragraph applies, less than 18;	2. (a) [³¹£33.85]

(1)	*(2)*
Person or Couple	*Amount*
(b) less than 18 who falls within paragraph (2) of regulation 57 and who—	(b) [³¹£44.50]
(i) is a person to whom regulation 59, 60 or 61 applies [¹. . .]; or	
(ii) is the subject of a direction under section 16;	
(c) less than 18 who satisfies the condition in paragraph 13(a) [²of Part 3];	(c) [³¹£44.50]
(d) not less than 18.	(d) [³¹£56.20]
(3) Couple—	
(a) where both members are aged less than 18 and—	3. (a) [³¹£67.15]
(i) at least one of them is treated as responsible for a child; or	
(ii) had they not been members of a couple, each would have been a person to whom regulation 59, 60 or 61 (circumstances in which a person aged 16 or 17 is eligible for a jobseeker's allowance) applied or	
(iii) had they not been members of a couple, the claimant would have been a person to whom regulation 59, 60 or 61 (circumstances in which a person aged 16 or 17 is eligible for a jobseeker's allowance) applied and his partner satisfies the requirements for entitlement to income support other than the requirement to make a claim for it; or	
[¹(iv) they are married and one member of the couple is a person to whom regulation 59, 60 or 61 applies and the other member is registered in accordance with regulation 62; or	
(iva) they are married and each member of the couple is a person to whom regulation 59, 60 or 61 applies; or]	
(v) there is a direction under section 16 (jobseeker's allowance in cases of severe hardship) in respect of each member; or	
(vi) there is a direction under section 16 in respect of one of them and the other is a person to whom regulation 59, 60 or 61 applies [¹. . .], or	
(vii) there is a direction under section 16 in respect of one of them and the other satisfies requirements for entitlement to income support other than the requirement to make a claim for it;	
(b) where both members are aged less than 18 and sub-paragraph (3)(a) does not apply but one member of the couple falls within paragraph (2) of regulation 57 and either—	(b) [³¹£44.50]
(i) is a person to whom regulation 59, 60 or 61 applies [¹. . .]; or	
(ii) is the subject of a direction under section 16 of the Act;	
(c) where both members are aged less than 18 and neither head (a) nor (b) of sub-paragraph (3) applies but one member of the couple—	(c) [³¹£33.85]
(i) is a person to whom regulation 59, 60 or 61 applies [1. . .]; or	
(ii) is the subject of a direction under section 16;	
(d) where both members are aged less than 18 and none of heads (a), (b) or (c) of sub-paragraph (3) apply but one member of the couple is a person who satisfies the requirements of paragraph 13(a);	(d) [³¹£44.50]
(e) where both members are aged not less than 18;	(e) [³¹£88.15]
(f) where one member is aged not less than 18 and the other member is a person under 18 who—	(f) [³¹£88.15]
(i) is a person to whom regulation 59, 60 or 61 applies [1. . .]; or	

(1)	(2)
Person or Couple	*Amount*

(ii) is the subject of a direction under section 16; and
(iii) satisfies requirements for entitlement to income support other than the requirement to make a claim for it;
(g) where one member is aged not less than 18 but less than 25 and the other member is a person under 18—
   (i) to whom none of the regulations 59 to 61applies; or
   (ii) who is not the subject of a direction under section 16; and
   (iii) does not satisfy requirements for entitlement to income support disregarding the requirement to make a claim for
(h) where one member is aged not less than 25 and the other member is a person under 18—
   (i) to whom none of the regulations 59 to 61 applies; or
   (ii) is not the subject of a direction under section 16; and
   (iii) does not satisfy requirements for entitlement to income support disregarding the requirement to make a claim for it.
	(g) [³¹£44.50]
	
	(h) [³¹£56.20]

2. [³⁰ . . .]
3. [²⁹ . . .]

PART II

Family Premium

3.547 **4.** [³⁰ . . .]

PART III

Premiums

3.548 **5.** Except as provided in paragraph 6, the weekly premiums specified in Part IV of this Schedule shall for the purposes of regulations 83(e) and 84(1)(f), be applicable to a claimant who satisfies the condition specified in [⁴ ¹⁵ paragraphs 9A] to 17 in respect of that premium.

6. Subject to paragraph 7, where a claimant satisfies the conditions in respect of more than one premium in this Part of this Schedule, only one premium shall be applicable to him and, if they are different amounts, the higher or highest amount shall apply.

[¹⁶ **7.**—(1) Subject to sub-paragraph (2), the following premiums, namely—

  (a) a severe disability premium to which paragraph 15 applies;

  (b) an enhanced disability premium to which paragraph 15A applies;

  (c) [³⁰ . . .]; and

  (d) a carer premium in which paragraph 17 applies,

     may be applicable in addition to any other premium which may apply under this Part of this Schedule.

(2) An enhanced disability premium in respect of a person shall not be applicable in addition to—

  (a) a pensioner premium under paragraph 10 or 11; or

  (b) a higher pensioner premium under paragraph 12.]

8.—(1) Subject to sub-paragraph (2) for the purposes of this Part of this Schedule, once a premium is applicable to a claimant under this Part, a person shall be treated as being in receipt of any benefit—

  (a) in the case of a benefit to which the Social Security (Overlapping Benefits) Regulations 1979 applies, for any period during which, apart from the provisions of those Regulations, he would be in receipt of that benefit; and

[³(b) for any period spent by a claimant in undertaking a course of training or instruction provided or approved by the Secretary of State for Education and Employment under section 2 of the Employment and Training Act 1973, or by Scottish Enterprise or Highlands and Islands Enterprise under section 2 of the Enterprise and New Towns

(Scotland) Act 1990 or for any period during which he is in receipt of a training allowance.]

(2) For the purposes of the carer premium under paragraph 17, a person shall be treated as being in receipt of [24 carer's allowance] by virtue of sub-paragraph (1)(a) only if and for so long as the person in respect of whose care the allowance has been claimed remains in receipt of attendance allowance, or the care component of disability living allowance at the highest or middle rate prescribed in accordance with section 72(3) of the Benefits Act.

Lone parent premium
   9. [4. . .]   3.549

[15 Bereavement Premium
   9A.—(1) Subject to sub-paragraphs (2) and (3), the condition is that the claimant—   3.550
- (a) had, as at 9th April 2001, attained the age of 55 but not the age of 60;
- (b) was in receipt of, but is no longer entitled to, a bereavement allowance under section 39B of the Benefits Act in respect of the death of a spouse who died on or after 9th April 2001; and
- (c) is claiming a jobseeker's allowance as a single claimant.

(2) A premium under sub-paragraph (1) shall not be applicable in respect of a claimant who claims a jobseeker's allowance more than 8 weeks after the last day on which he was entitled to a bereavement allowance.

(3) Where a claimant to whom a premium under sub-paragraph (1) is applicable, ceases to be entitled to an income-based jobseeker's allowance or to be a single claimant, a premium under sub-paragraph (1) shall only again be applicable to that claimant where he claims a job-seeker's allowance as a single claimant no more than 8 weeks after the date on which he ceased to be entitled to an income-based jobseeker's allowance or to income support or, as the case may be, to be a single claimant.]

Pensioner premium for persons over 60
   10. The condition is that the claimant—   3.551
- (a) is a single claimant or lone parent who has attained the age of 60; or
- (b) has attained the age of 60 and has a partner; or
- (c) has a partner and the partner has attained the age of 60 but not the age of 75.

Pensioner premium where claimant's partner has attained the age of 75
   11. The condition is that the claimant has a partner who has attained the age of 75 but not   3.552
the age of 80.

Higher pensioner premium
   12.—(1) The condition is that—   3.553
- (a) the claimant is a single claimant or lone parent who has attained the age of 60 and either—
  - (i) satisfies one of the additional conditions specified in paragraph 14(1)(a), (c), (e), (f) or (h); or
  - (ii) was entitled to either income support or income-based jobseeker's allowance [12, or was treated as being entitled to either of those benefits and the disability premium was or, as the case may be, would have been,] applicable to him in respect of a benefit week within 8 weeks of his 60th birthday and he has, subject to sub-paragraph (2), remained continuously entitled to one of those benefits since attaining that age; or
- (b) the claimant has a partner and—
  - (i) the partner has attained the age of 80; or
  - (ii) the partner has attained the age of 60 but not the age of 80, and the additional conditions specified in paragraph 14 are satisfied in respect of him; or
- (c) the claimant—
  - (i) has attained the age of 60;
  - [3(ii) satisfies the requirements of either sub-head (i) or (ii) of paragraph 12(1)(a); and]
  - (iii) has a partner.

(2) For the purposes of this paragraph and paragraph 14—
- (a) once the higher pensioner premium is applicable to a claimant, if he then ceases, for a period of eight weeks or less, to be entitled to either income support or income-based jobseeker's allowance [12 or ceases to be treated as entitled to either of those benefits], he shall, on becoming re-entitled to either of those benefits, thereafter be treated as having been continuously entitled thereto;

(b) in so far as sub-paragraphs (1)(a)(ii) and (1)(c)(ii) are concerned, if a claimant ceases to be entitled to either income support or an income-based jobseeker's allowance [¹² or ceases to be treated as entitled to either of those benefits] for a period not exceeding eight weeks which includes his 60th birthday, he shall, on becoming re-entitled to either of those benefits, thereafter be treated as having been continuously entitled thereto.

[⁸(3) In this paragraph where a claimant's partner is a welfare to work beneficiary, sub-paragraphs (1)(a)(ii) and (2)(b) shall apply to him as if for the words "8 weeks" there were substituted the words "52 weeks".]

[¹² (4) For the purposes of this paragraph, a claimant shall be treated as having been entitled to income support or to an income-based jobseeker's allowance throughout any period which comprises only days on which he was participating in an employment zone programme and was not entitled to—

(a) income support because, as a consequence of his participation in that programme, he was engaged in remunerative work or had income in excess of the claimant's applicable amount as prescribed in Part IV of the Income Support Regulations; or

(b) a jobseeker's allowance because, as a consequence of his participation in that programme, he was engaged in remunerative work or failed to satisfy the condition specified in section 2(1)(c) or in section 3(1)(a).]

Disability premium

3.554   **13.** The condition is that the claimant—

(a) is a single claimant or lone parent who has not attained the age of 60 and satisfies any one of the additional conditions specified in paragraph 14(1)(a), (c), (e), (f) or (h); or

(b) has not attained the age of 60, has a partner and the claimant satisfies any one of the additional conditions specified in paragraph 14(1)(a), (c), (e), (f) or (h); or

(c) has a partner and the partner has not attained the age of 60 and also satisfies any one of the additional conditions specified in paragraph 14.

Additional conditions for higher pensioner and disability premium

3.555   **14.**—(1) The additional conditions specified in this paragraph are that—

(a) the claimant or, as the case may be, his partner, is in receipt [²⁵ the disability element or the severe disability element of working tax credit as specified in regulation 20(1)(b) and (f) of the Working Tax Credit (Entitlement and Maximum Rate) Regulations 2002] or mobility supplement;

(b) the claimant's partner is in receipt of severe disablement allowance;

(c) the claimant or, as the case may be, his partner, is in receipt of attendance allowance or disability living allowance or is a person whose disability living allowance is payable, in whole or in part, to another in accordance with regulation 44 of the Claims and Payments Regulations (payment of disability living allowance on behalf of third party);

(d) the claimant's partner is in receipt of long-term incapacity benefit or is a person to whom section 30B(4) of the Benefits Act (long term rate of incapacity benefit payable to those who are terminally ill) applies;

(e) the claimant or, as the case may be, his partner, has an invalid carriage or other vehicle provided to him by the Secretary of State under section 5(2)(a) of and Schedule 2 to the National Health Service Act 1977 or under section 46 of the National Health Service (Scotland) Act 1978 or provided by the Department of Health and Social Services for Northern Ireland under article 30(1) of the Health and Personal Social Services (Northern Ireland) Order 1972, or receives payments by way of grant from the Secretary of State under paragraph 2 of Schedule 2 to the Act of 1977 (additional provisions as to vehicles) or, in Scotland, under section 46 of the Act of 1978;

(f) the claimant or, as the case may be, his partner, is a person who is entitled to the mobility component of disability living allowance but to whom the component is not payable in accordance with regulation 42 of the Claims and Payments Regulations (cases where disability living allowance not payable);

(g) the claimant's partner was either—

(i) in receipt of long term incapacity benefit under section 30A(5) of the Benefits Act immediately before attaining pensionable age and he is still alive; or

(ii) entitled to attendance allowance or disability living allowance but payment of that benefit was suspended in accordance with regulations under section 113(2) of the Benefits Act or otherwise abated as a consequence of [²the partner] becoming a patient within the meaning of regulation 85(4) (special cases), and in either case the higher pensioner premium or disability premium had been applicable to the claimant or his partner;

(h) the claimant or, as the case may be, his partner, is registered as blind in a register compiled by a local authority under section 29 of the National Assistance Act 1948 (welfare services), or, in Scotland, has been certified as blind and in consequence is registered as blind in a register maintained by or on behalf of a regional or islands council.

(2) For the purposes of sub-paragraph (1)(h), a person who has ceased to be registered as blind on regaining his eyesight shall nevertheless be treated as blind and as satisfying the additional condition set out in that sub-paragraph for a period of 28 weeks following the date on which he ceased to be so registered.

Severe disability premium

15.—(1) In the case of a single claimant, a lone parent or a claimant who is treated as having no partner in consequence of sub-paragraph (3), the condition is that—   **3.556**

(a) he is in receipt of attendance allowance or the care component of disability living allowance at the highest or middle rate prescribed in accordance with section 72(3) of the Benefits Act; and

(b) subject to sub-paragraph (4), there are no non-dependants aged 18 or over normally residing with him or with whom he is normally residing; and

[¹¹(c) no person is entitled to, and in receipt of, [²⁴ a carer's allowance] under section 70 of the Benefits Act in respect of caring for him;]

(2) Where the claimant has a partner, the condition is that—

(a) the claimant is in receipt of attendance allowance or the care component of disability living allowance at the highest or middle rate prescribed in accordance with section 72(3) of the Benefits Act (the "qualifying benefit"); and

(b) the partner is also in receipt of a qualifying benefit, or if he is a member of a polygamous marriage, all the partners of that marriage are in receipt of a qualifying benefit; and

(c) subject to sub-paragraph (4), there is no non-dependant aged 18 or over normally residing with him or with whom he is normally residing; and

(d) either—

(i) [¹¹no person is entitled to, and in receipt of, [²⁴ a carer's allowance] under section 70 of the Benefits Act in respect of] caring for either member of the couple or all the members of the polygamous marriage; or

(ii) a person is engaged in caring for one member (but not both members) of the couple, or one or more but not all members of the polygamous marriage, and in consequence is [¹¹entitled to] [²⁴ a carer's allowance] under section 70 of the Benefits Act.

(3) Where the claimant has a partner who does not satisfy the condition in subparagraph (2)(b), and that partner is blind or treated as blind within the meaning of paragraph 14(1)(h) and (2), that partner shall be treated for the purposes of sub-paragraph (2) as if he were not a partner of the claimant.

(4) The following persons shall not be regarded as a non-dependant for the purposes of sub-paragraphs (1)(b) and (2)(c)—

(a) a person in receipt of attendance allowance or the care component of disability living allowance at the highest or middle rate prescribed in accordance with section 72(3) of the Benefits Act;

(b) subject to sub-paragraph (6), a person who joins the claimant's household for the first time in order to care for the claimant or his partner and immediately before so joining the claimant or his partner satisfied the condition in sub-paragraph (1) or, as the case may be, (2);

(c) a person who is blind or treated as blind within the meaning of paragraph 14(1)(h) and (2).

(5) For the purposes of sub-paragraph (2), a person shall be treated [¹¹ . . .]

(a) [¹¹as being in receipt of] attendance allowance, or the care component of disability living allowance at the highest or middle rate prescribed in accordance with section 72(3) of the Benefits Act if he would, but for his being a patient for a period exceeding 28 days, be so in receipt;

[¹¹(b) as being entitled to and in receipt of [²⁴ a carer's allowance] if he would, but for the person for whom he was caring being a patient in hospital for a period exceeding 28 days, be so entitled and in receipt.]

(6) Sub-paragraph (4)(b) shall apply only for the first 12 weeks following the date on which the person to whom that provision applies first joins the claimant's household.

(7) For the purposes of sub-paragraph (1)(c) and (2)(d), no account shall be taken of an award of [24 carer's allowance] to the extent that payment of such an award is backdated for a period before the date on which the award is made.

(8) A person shall be treated as satisfying this condition if he would have satisfied the condition specified for a severe disability premium in income support in paragraph 13 of Schedule 2 to the Income Support Regulations by virtue only of regulations 4 to 6 of the Income Support (General) Amendment (No. 6) Regulations 1991 (savings provisions in relation to severe disability premium) and for the purposes of determining whether in the particular case regulation 4 of those Regulations had ceased to apply in accordance with regulation 5(2)(a) of those Regulations, a person who is entitled to an income-based jobseeker's allowance shall be treated as entitled to income support.

[20 (9) In sub-paragraphs (1)(c) and (2)(d), references to a person being in receipt of [24 a carer's allowance] shall include references to a person who would have been in receipt of that allowance but for the application of a restriction under section 7 of the Social Security Fraud Act 2001 (loss of benefit provisions).]

[16 Enhanced disability premium

3.557

15A.—(1) Subject to sub-paragraph (2), the condition is that the care component of disability living allowance is, or would, but for a suspension of benefit in accordance with regulations under section 113(2) of the Benefits Act or but for an abatement as a consequence of hospitalisation, be payable at the highest rate prescribed under section 72(3) of the Benefits Act in respect of—

(a) the claimant; or

(b) [30 the claimant's partner (if any)], who is aged less than 60

(2) An enhanced disability premium shall not be applicable in respect of—

(a) [30 . . .]

(b) a claimant who—

(i) is not a member of a couple or a polygamous marriage; and

(ii) is a patient within the meaning of regulation 85(4) and has been for a period of more than [27 52] weeks; or

(c) a member of a couple or a polygamous marriage where each member is a patient within the meaning of regulation 85(4) and has been for a period of more than [27 52] weeks.]

Disabled child premium

3.558

16.—[30 . . .]

Carer premium

3.559

17.—(1) Subject to sub-paragraphs (3) and (4), the condition is that the claimant or his partner is, or both of them are, [11entitled to] [24 a carer's allowance] under section 70 of the Benefits Act.

(2) [28 . . .]

[23 (3) Where a carer premium is awarded but—

(a) the person in respect of whose care the [24 carer's allowance] has been awarded dies; or

(b) in any other case the person in respect of whom a carer premium has been awarded ceases to be entitled [28 . . .] to [24 a carer's allowance],

the condition for the award of the premium shall be treated as satisfied for a period of eight weeks from the relevant date specified in sub-paragraph (3A) below.

(3A) The relevant date for the purposes of sub-paragraph (3) above shall be—

(a) [28 where sub-paragraph (3)(a) applies,] the Sunday following the death of the person in respect of whose care [24 a carer's allowance] has been awarded or the date of death if the death occurred on a Sunday;

(b) [28 . . .]

(c) in any other case, the date of which the person who has been entitled to [24 a carer's allowance] ceases to be entitled to that allowance.]

(4) Where a person who has been entitled to an invalid care allowance ceases to be entitled to that allowance and makes a claim for a jobseeker's allowance, the condition for the award of the carer premium shall be treated as satisfied for a period of eight weeks from the date on which—

[23(a) the person in respect of whose care the [24 carer's allowance] has been awarded dies;

(b) [28 . . .]

[28 (c) in any other case, the person who has been entitled to a carer's allowance ceased to be entitled to that allowance.]

Persons in receipt of concessionary payments

3.560

18. For the purpose of determining whether a premium is applicable to a person under paragraphs 14 to 17, any concessionary payment made to compensate that person for the

non-payment of any benefit mentioned in those paragraphs shall be treated as if it were a payment of that benefit.

Person in receipt of benefit

19. For the purposes of this Part of this Schedule, a person shall be regarded as being in receipt of any benefit if, and only if, it is paid in respect of him and shall be so regarded only for any period in respect of which that benefit is paid.

3.561

PART IV

Weekly Amounts of Premiums Specified in Part III

Premium	Amount	
20.—(1) [⁴. . .]	(1) [⁴ . . .]	**3.562**
(1A) Bereavement Premium]	(1A) [³²£25.85]	
(2) Pensioner premium for persons aged over 60—		
(a) where the claimant satisfies the condition in paragraph 10(a);	(2) (a) [³²£53.25].	
(b) where the claimant satisfies the condition in paragraph 10(b).	(b) [³²£78.90].	
(c) where the claimant satisfies the condition in paragraph 10(c).	(c) [³²£78.90].	
(3) Pensioner premium for claimants whose partner has attained the age of 75 where the claimant satisfies the condition in paragraph 11;	(3) [³²£78.90].	
(4) Higher Pensioner Premium—		
(a) where the claimant satisfies the condition in paragraph 12(1)(a);	(4) (a) [³²£53.25].	
(b) where the claimant satisfies the condition in paragraph 12(1)(b) or (c).	(b) [³²£78.90].	
(5) Disability Premium—		
(a) where the claimant satisfies the condition in paragraph 13(a);	(5) (a) [³²£23.95].	
(b) where the claimant satisfies the condition in paragraph 13(b) or (c).	(b) [³²£34.20].	
(6) Severe Disability Premium—		
(a) where the claimant satisfies the condition in paragraph 15(1);	(6) (a) [³²£45.50].	
(b) where the claimant satisfies the condition in paragraph 15(2)—	(b)	
(i) if there is someone in receipt of [²⁴ a carer's allowance] or [²if any partner of the claimant] satisfies that condition by virtue of paragraph 15(5);	(i) [³²£45.50].	
(ii) if no-one is in receipt of such an allowance.	(ii) [³²£91.00].	
(7) [³⁰ . . .]	(7) [³⁰ . . .]	
(8) Carer Premium.	(8) [³²£25.80] in respect of each person who satisfied the condition specified in paragraph 17.]	
[¹⁶ (9) Enhanced disability premium where the conditions in paragraph 15A are satisfied.]	[¹⁶ (9) (a)[³⁰ . . .] (b)[³² £11.70] in respect of each person who is neither—	
	(i) a child or young person; nor	

Premium	Amount
	(ii) a member of a couple or a polygamous marriage, in respect of whom the conditions specified in paragraph 15A are satisfied;
	(c) [³²£16.90] where the claimant is a member of a couple or a polygamous marriage and the conditions specified in paragraph 15A are satisfied in respect of a member of that couple or polygamous marriage.]

[¹⁴ PART IVA

Premiums for Joint-claim Couples

3.563   **20A.** Except as provided in paragraph 20B, the weekly premium specified in Part IVB of this Schedule shall, for the purposes of regulations 86A(c) and 86B(d), be applicable to a joint-claim couple where either or both members of a joint-claim couple satisfy the condition specified in paragraphs 20E to 20J in respect of that premium.

20B. Subject to paragraph 20C, where a member of a joint-claim couple satisfies the conditions in respect of more than one premium in this Part of this Schedule, only one premium shall be applicable to the joint-claim couple in respect of that member and, if they are different amounts, the higher or highest amount shall apply.

[¹⁶ **20C.**—(1) Subject to sub-paragraph (2), the following premiums, namely—

    (a) a severe disability premium to which paragraph 20I applies;

    (b) an enhanced disability premium to which paragraph 20IA applies; and

    (c) a carer premium to which paragraph 20J applies,

    may be applicable in addition to any other premium which may apply under this Part of this Schedule.

(2) An enhanced disability premium in respect of a person shall not be applicable in addition to—

    (a) a pensioner premium under paragraph 20E; or

    (b) a higher pensioner premium under paragraph 20F.]

20D.—(1) Subject to sub-paragraph (2) for the purposes of this Part of this Schedule, once a premium is applicable to a joint-claim couple under this Part, a person shall be treated as being in receipt of any benefit—

    (a) in the case of a benefit to which the Social Security (Overlapping Benefits) Regulations 1979 applies, for any period during which, apart from the provisions of those Regulations, he would be in receipt of that benefit; and

    (b) for any period spent by a person in undertaking a course of training or instruction provided or approved by the Secretary of State under section 2 of the Employment and Training Act 1973, or by Scottish Enterprise or Highlands and Islands Enterprise under section 2 of the Enterprise and New Towns (Scotland) Act 1990, or for any period during which he is in receipt of a training allowance.

(2) For the purposes of the carer premium under paragraph 20J, a person shall be treated as being in receipt of [²⁴ carer's allowance] by virtue of sub-paragraph (1)(a) only if and for so long as the person in respect of whose care the allowance has been claimed remains in receipt of attendance allowance, or the care component of disability living allowance at the highest or middle rate prescribed in accordance with section 72(3) of the Benefits Act.

Pensioner premium where one member of a joint-claim couple has attained the age of 60

3.564   **20E.** The condition is that one member of a joint-claim couple has attained the age of 60 but not the age of 75.

Higher pensioner premium

20F.—(1) The condition is that one member of a joint-claim couple—   **3.565**
  (a) has attained the age of 60 but not the age of 80, and either the additional conditions
      specified in paragraph 20H are satisfied in respect of him; or
  (b) has attained the age of 60 and—
       (i) was entitled to or was treated as entitled to either income support or an
           income-based jobseeker's allowance and the disability premium was or, as the
           case may be, would have been applicable to him in respect of a benefit week
           within 8 weeks of his 60th birthday and he has, subject to sub-paragraph (2),
           remained continuously entitled to one of those benefits since attaining that
           age; or
      (ii) was a member of a joint-claim couple who had been entitled to, or who had been
           treated as entitled to, a joint-claim jobseeker's allowance and the disability
           premium was or, as the case may be, would have been applicable to that couple
           in respect of a benefit week within 8 weeks of the 60th birthday of either member
           of that couple and the couple have, subject to that sub-paragraph (2), remained
           continuously entitled to a joint-claim jobseeker's allowance since that member
           attained that age.
  (2) For the purpose of this paragraph and paragraph 20H—
  (a) once the higher pensioner premium is applicable to a joint-claim couple, if that member
      then ceases, for a period of 8 weeks or less, to be entitled or treated as entitled to either
      income support or income-based jobseeker's allowance or that couple cease to be enti-
      tled to or treated as entitled to a joint-claim jobseeker's allowance, he shall or, as the case
      may be, that couple shall, on becoming re-entitled to any of those benefits, thereafter be
      treated as having been continuously entitled thereto;
  (b) in so far as sub-paragraph (1)(b)(i) or (ii) is concerned, if a member of a joint-claim
      couple ceases to be entitled or treated as entitled to either income support or an
      income-based jobseeker's allowance or that couple cease to be entitled to or treated as
      entitled to a joint-claim jobseeker's allowance for a period not exceeding 8 weeks which
      includes the 60th birthday of either member of that couple, he shall or, as the case may
      be, the couple shall, on becoming re-entitled to either of those benefits, thereafter be
      treated as having been continuously entitled thereto.
  (3) In this paragraph, where a member of a joint-claim couple is a welfare to work beneficiary, sub-paragraphs (1)(b)(i) and (2)(b) shall apply to him as if for the words "8 weeks"
there were substituted the words "52 weeks".
  (4) For the purposes of this paragraph, a member of a joint-claim couple shall be treated as
having been entitled to income support or to an income-based jobseeker's allowance or the
couple of which he is a member shall be treated as having been entitled to a joint-claim jobseeker's allowance throughout any period which comprises only days on which a member was
participating in an employment zone scheme and was not entitled to—
  (a) income support because, as a consequence of his participation in that scheme, he was
      engaged in remunerative work or had income in excess of the claimant's applicable
      amount as prescribed in Part IV of the Income Support Regulations; or
  (b) a jobseeker's allowance because, as a consequence of his participation in that scheme,
      he was engaged in remunerative work or failed to satisfy the condition specified in
      section 2(1)(c) or the couple of which he was a member failed to satisfy the condition
      in section 3A(1)(a).

Disability premium

20G. The condition is that a member of a joint-claim couple has not attained the age of 60   **3.566**
and satisfies any one of the additional conditions specified in paragraph 20H.

Additional conditions for higher pensioner and disability premium

20H.—(1) The additional conditions specified in this paragraph are that a member of a joint-   **3.567**
claim couple—
  (a) is in receipt of [[26] the disability element or the severe disability element of working tax
      credit as specified in regulation 20(1)(b) and (f) of the Working Tax Credit
      (Entitlement and Maximum Rate) Regulations 2002] or mobility supplement;
  (b) is in receipt of severe disablement allowance;
  (c) is in receipt of attendance allowance or disability living allowance or is a person whose
      disability living allowance is payable, in whole or in part, to another in accordance with
      regulation 44 of the Claims and Payments Regulations (payment of disability living
      allowance on behalf of third party);

(d) is in receipt of long-term incapacity benefit or is a person to whom section 30B(4) of the Benefits Act (long-term rate of incapacity benefit payable to those who are terminally ill) applies;

(e) has been entitled to statutory sick pay, has been incapable of work or has been treated as incapable of work for a continuous period of not less than—

    (i) 196 days in the case of a member of a joint-claim couple who is terminally ill within the meaning of section 30B(4) of the Benefits Act; or

    (ii) 364 days in any other case,

and for these purposes, any two or more periods of entitlement or incapacity separated by a break of not more than 56 days shall be treated as one continuous period;

(f) has an invalid carriage or other vehicle provided to him by the Secretary of State under section 5(2)(a) of, and Schedule 2 to, the National Health Service Act 1977 or under section 46 of the National Health Service (Scotland) Act 1978 or provided by the Department of Health and Social Services for Northern Ireland under article 30(1) of the Health and Personal Social Services (Northern Ireland) Order 1972, or receives payments by way of grant from the Secretary of State under paragraph 2 of Schedule 2 to the Act of 1977 (additional provisions as to vehicles) or, in Scotland, under section 46 of the Act of 1978;

(g) is a person who is entitled to the mobility component of disability living allowance but to whom the component is not payable in accordance with regulation 42 of the Claims and Payments Regulations (cases where disability living allowance not payable);

(h) was either—

    (i) in receipt of long-term incapacity benefit under section 30A(5) of the Benefits Act immediately before attaining pensionable age and he is still alive; or

    (ii) entitled to attendance allowance or disability living allowance but payment of that benefit was suspended in accordance with regulations under section 113(2) of the Benefits Act or otherwise abated as a consequence of either member of the joint-claim couple becoming a patient within the meaning of regulation 85(4) (special cases),

and in either case, the higher pensioner premium or disability premium had been applicable to the joint-claim couple; or

    (i) is registered as blind in a register compiled by a local authority under section 29 of the National Assistance Act 1948 (welfare services), or, in Scotland, has been certified as blind and in consequence is registered as blind in a register maintained by or on behalf of a regional or islands council.

(2) In the case of a member of a joint-claim couple who is a welfare to work beneficiary, the reference in sub-paragraph (1)(e) to a period of 56 days shall be treated as a reference to a period of 52 weeks.

(3) For the purposes of sub-paragraph (1)(i), a person who has ceased to be registered as blind on regaining his eyesight shall nevertheless be treated as blind and as satisfying the additional condition set out in that sub-paragraph for a period of 28 weeks following the date on which he ceased to be so registered.

Severe disability premium

3.568

20I.—(1) The condition is that—

(a) a member of a joint-claim couple is in receipt of attendance allowance or the care component of disability living allowance at the highest or middle rate prescribed in accordance with section 72(3) of the Benefits Act ("the qualifying benefits"); and

(b) the other member is also in receipt of such an allowance, or if he is a member of a polygamous marriage, all the partners of that marriage are in receipt of a qualifying benefit; and

(c) subject to sub-paragraph (3), there is no non-dependant aged 18 or over normally residing with the joint-claim couple or with whom they are normally residing; and

(d) either—

    (i) no person is entitled to, and in receipt of, [24 a carer's allowance] under section 70 of the Benefits Act in respect of caring for either member or the couple or all the members of the polygamous marriage; or

    (ii) a person is engaged in caring for one member (but not both members) of the couple, or one or more but not all members of the polygamous marriage, and in consequence is entitled to [24 a carer's allowance] under section 70 of the Benefits Act.

(2) Where the other member does not satisfy the condition in sub-paragraph (1)(b), and that member is blind or treated as blind within the meaning of paragraph 20H(1)(i) and (2), that

member shall be treated for the purposes of sub-paragraph (1) as if he were not a member of the couple.

(3) The following persons shall not be regarded as non-dependant for the purposes of sub-paragraph (1)(c)—

    (a) a person in receipt of attendance allowance or the care component of disability living allowance at the highest or middle rate prescribed in accordance with section 72(3) of the Benefits Act;

    (b) subject to sub-paragraph (5), a person who joins the joint-claim couple's household for the first time in order to care for a member of a joint claim couple and immediately before so joining, that member satisfied the condition in sub-paragraph (1);

    (c) a person who is blind or treated as blind within the meaning of paragraph 20H(1)(i) and (2).

(4) For the purposes of sub-paragraph (1), a member of a joint-claim couple shall be treated—

    (a) as being in receipt of attendance allowance, or the care component of disability living allowance at the highest or middle rate prescribed in accordance with section 72(3) of the Benefits Act if he would, but for his being a patient for a period exceeding 28 days, be so in receipt;

    (b) as being entitled to and in receipt of [24 a carer's allowance] if he would, but for the person for whom he was caring being a patient in hospital for a period exceeding 28 days, be so entitled and in receipt.

(5) Sub-paragraph (3)(b) shall apply only for the first 12 weeks following the date on which the person to whom that provision applies first joins the joint-claim couple's household.

(6) For the purposes of sub-paragraph (1)(d), no account shall be taken of an award of invalid care allowance to the extent that payment of such an award is back-dated for a period before the date on which the award is made.

[20 (7) In sub-paragraph (1)(d), the reference to a person being in receipt of [24 a carer's allowance] shall include a reference to a person who would have been in receipt of that allowance but for the application of a restriction under section 7 of the Social Security Fraud Act 2001 (loss of benefit provisions).]

[16 **Enhanced disability premium**

20IA.—(1) Subject to sub-paragraph (2), the condition is that the care component of disability living allowance is, or would, but for a suspension of benefit in accordance with regulations under section 113(2) of the Benefits Act or but for an abatement as a consequence of hospitalisation, be payable at the highest rate prescribed under section 72(3) of the Benefits Act in respect of a member of a joint-claim couple who is aged less than 60.

3.569

(2) An enhanced disability premium shall not be applicable in respect of a joint-claim couple where each member of that couple or each member of a polygamous marriage of which one member of that couple is a member, is a patient within the meaning of regulation 85(4) and has been for a period of more than [27 52] weeks.]

Carer premium

20J.—(1) Subject to sub-paragraphs (3) and (4), the condition is that either or both members of a joint-claim couple are entitled to [28 . . .] [24 a carer's allowance] under section 70 of the Benefits Act.

3.570

(2) [28 . . .]

[23 (3) Where a carer premium is awarded but—

    (a) the person in respect of whose care the [24 carer's allowance] has been awarded dies: or

    (b) in any other case the member of the joint-claim couple in respect of whom a carer premium has been awarded ceases to be entitled [28 . . .] to [24 a carer's allowance],

the condition for the award of the premium shall be treated as satisfied for a period of eight weeks from the relevant date specified in sub-paragraph (3A) below.

(3A) The relevant date for the purposes of sub-paragraph (3) above shall be—

    (a) [28 where sub-paragraph (3)(a) applies,] the Sunday following the death of the person in respect of whose care [24 a carer's allowance] has been awarded or beginning with the date of death if the death occurred on a Sunday;

    (b) [28 . . .]

    (c) in any other case, the date on which that member ceased to be entitled to [24 a carer's allowance].]

(4) Where a member of a joint-claim couple who has been entitled to an invalid care allowance ceases to be entitled to that allowance and makes a claim for a jobseeker's allowance

jointly with the other member of that couple, the condition for the award of the carer premium shall be treated as satisfied for a period of eight weeks from the date on which—

[²³(a) the person in respect of whose care the [²⁴ carer's allowance] has been awarded dies;

(b) [²⁸ . . .]

(c) [²⁸ (c) in any other case, the person who has been entitled to a carer's allowance ceased to be entitled to that allowance.]

Member of a joint-claim couple in receipt of concessionary payments

3.571   **20K.** For the purpose of determining whether a premium is applicable to a joint-claim couple under paragraphs 20H to 20J, any concessionary payment made to compensate a person for the non-payment of any benefit mentioned in those paragraphs shall be treated as if it were a payment of that benefit.

Person in receipt of benefit

3.572   **20L.** For the purposes of this Part of this Schedule, a member of a joint-claim couple shall be regarded as being in receipt of any benefit if, and only if, it is paid in respect of him and shall be so regarded only for any period in respect of which that benefit is paid.

PART IVB

3.573   *Weekly Amounts of Premiums Specified in Part IVA*

Premium	Amount
20M.— (1) Pensioner premium where one member of a joint-claim couple is aged over 60 and the condition in paragraph 20E is satisfied.	(1) [³³£78.90].
(2) Higher Pensioner Premium where one member of a joint-claim couple satisfies the condition in paragraph 20F.	(2) [³³£78.90].
(3) Disability Premium where one member of a joint-claim couple satisfies the condition in paragraph 20G.	(3) [³³£34.20].
(4) Severe Disability Premium where one member of a joint-claim couple satisfies the condition in paragraph 20I(1)— (i) if there is someone in receipt of [²⁴ a carer's allowance] or if either member satisfies that condition only by virtue of paragraph [¹⁶ 20I(4)];	(4)(i) [³³£45.50].
(ii) if no-one is in receipt of such an allowance.	(ii) [³³£91.00].
(5) Carer Premium.	(5) [³³£25.80] in respect of each person who satisfied the condition specified in paragraph 20J.]
[¹⁶ (6) Enhanced disability premium where the conditions in paragraph 20IA are satisfied.	(6) [³³£16.90] where the conditions specified in paragraph 20IA are satisfied in respect of a member of a joint-claim couple.]

PART V

Rounding of Fractions

3.574   **21.** Where an income-based jobseeker's allowance is awarded for a period which is not a complete benefit week and the applicable amount in respect of that period results in an amount which includes a fraction of one penny that fraction shall be treated as one penny.

AMENDMENTS

1. Jobseeker's Allowance (Amendment) Regulations 1996 (SI 1996/1516), reg.18   **3.575**
(October 7, 1996).

2. Jobseeker's Allowance (Amendment) Regulations 1996 (SI 1996/1516), reg.20
and Sch. (October 7, 1996).

3. Social Security and Child Support (Jobseeker's Allowance) (Miscellaneous
Amendments) Regulations 1996 (SI 1996/2538), reg.2(11) (October 28, 1996).

4. Child Benefit, Child Support and Social Security (Miscellaneous
Amendments) Regulations 1996 (SI 1996/1803), reg.44 (April 7, 1997).

5. Income-related Benefits and Jobseeker's Allowance (Personal Allowances for
Children and Young Persons) (Amendment) Regulations 1996 (SI 1996/2545),
reg.2 (April 7, 1997).

6. Income-related Benefits and Jobseeker's Allowance (Amendment) (No.2)
Regulations 1997 (SI 1997/2197), reg.7(5) and (6)(b) (October 6, 1997).

7. Social Security Amendment (Lone Parents) Regulations 1998 (SI 1998/ 766),
reg.14 (April 6, 1998).

8. Social Security (Welfare to Work) Regulations 1998 (SI 1998/2231), reg.14(3)
(October 5, 1998).

9. Social Security Amendment (Personal Allowances for Children and Young
Persons) Regulations 1999 (SI 1999/2555), reg.2(1)(b) and (2) (April 10, 2000).

10. Social Security and Child Support (Tax Credits) Consequential Amendments Regulations 1999 (SI 1999/2566), reg.2(2) and Sch.2, Pt III (October 5,
1999).

11. Social Security (Miscellaneous Amendments) Regulations 2000 (SI 2000/
681), reg.4(3) (April 3, 2000)

12. Social Security Amendment (Employment Zones) Regulations 2000 (SI
2000/724), reg.4 (April 3, 2000)

13. Social Security Amendment (Personal Allowances for Children) Regulations
2000 (SI 2000/1993), reg.2 (October 23, 2000).

14. Jobseeker's Allowance (Joint Claims) Regulations 2000 (SI 2000/1978),
reg.2(5) and Sch.2, para.53 (March 19, 2001).

15. Social Security Amendment (Breavement Benefits) Regulations 2000 (SI
2000/2239), reg.3(2) (April 9, 2001).

16. Social Security Amendment (Enhanced Disability Premium) Regulations
2000 (SI 2629), reg.5(c) (April 9, 2001).

17. Social Security Amendment (Joint Claims) Regulations 2001 (SI 2001/ 518),
reg.2(7) (March 19, 2001).

18. Social Security Amendment (Bereavement Benefits) Regulations 2000 (SI
2000/2239), reg.3(2)(c) (April 9, 2001).

19. Social Security Amendment (Residential Care and Nursing Homes)
Regulations 2001 (SI 2001/3767), reg.2 and Sch., Pt II, para.18 (April 8, 2002).

20. Social Security (Loss of Benefit) (Consequential Amendments) Regulations
2002 (SI 2002/490), reg.2 (April 1, 2002).

21. Social Security Amendment (Residential Care and Nursing Homes)
Regulations 2001 (SI 2001/3767), reg.2 and Sch., Pt II, para.18 (as amended by
Social Security Amendment (Residential Care and Nursing Homes) Regulations
2002 (SI 2002/398), reg.4(3)) (April 8, 2002).

22. Social Security Amendment (Personal Allowances for Children and Young
Persons) Regulations 2002 (SI 2002/2019), reg.2 (October 14, 2002).

23. Social Security Amendment (Carer Premium) Regulations 2002 (SI
2002/2020), reg.3 (October 28, 2002).

24. Social Security (Miscellaneous Amendments) Regulations 2003 (SI 2003/
511), reg.3(4) and (5) (April 1, 2003).

25. Social Security (Working Tax Credit and Child Tax Credit) (Consequential
Amendments) Regulations 2003 (SI 2003/455), regs 1(9), 3 and Sch.2, para.20(b)
(April 7, 2003).

26. Social Security (Working Tax Credit and Child Tax Credit) (Consequential Amendments) Regulations 2003 (SI 2003/455), regs 1(9), 3 and Sch.2, para.20(e) (April 7, 2003).

27. Social Security (Hospital In-Patients and Miscellaneous Amendments) Regulations 2003 (SI 2003/1195), reg.6 (May 21, 2003).

28. Social Security (Miscellaneous Amendments) (No.2) Regulations 2003 (SI 2003/2279), reg.3(3) (October 1, 2003).

29. Social Security (Removal of Residential Allowance and Miscellaneous Amendments) Regulations 2003 (SI 2003/1121), reg.4 and Sch.2, para.9 (October 6, 2003).

30. Social Security (Working Tax Credit and Child Tax Credit) (Consequential Amendments) Regulations 2003 (SI 2003/455), reg.3 and Sch.2, para.20 (April 6, 2004, except in "transitional cases" and see further the note to reg.83 and to reg.17 of the Income Support Regulations).

31. Social Security Benefits Up-rating Order 2005 (SI 2005/522), art.24 and Sch.14 (April 11, 2005).

32. Social Security Benefits Up-rating Order 2005 (SI 2005/522), art.24 and Sch.15 (April 11, 2005).

33. Social Security Benefits Up-rating Order 2005 (SI 2005/522), art.24 and Sch.16 (April 11, 2005).

DEFINITIONS

3.576
"attendance allowance"—see reg.1(3).
"the Benefits Act"—see Jobseekers Act, s.35(1).
"child"—*ibid.*
"claimant"—*ibid.*
"couple"—see reg.1(3).
"disability living allowance"—*ibid.*
"family"—see Jobseekers Act, s.35(1).
"invalid carriage or other vehicle"—see reg.1(3).
"lone parent"—*ibid.*
"mobility supplement"—*ibid.*
"non-dependent"—see reg.2.
"nursing home"—see reg.1(3).
"partner"—*ibid.*
"polygamous marriage"—*ibid.*
"preserved right"—*ibid.*
"residential care home"—*ibid.*
"single claimant"—*ibid.*
"welfare to work beneficiary"—*ibid.*
"young person"—see reg.76.

GENERAL NOTE

3.577
Here the details of the personal allowances and premiums for income-based JSA are set out. They follow a similar pattern to those for income support. But there are some differences. These are in relation to the qualifying conditions for the different rates of personal allowance paid where one or both members of a couple are under 18 (see para.1(3)) and the conditions for the pensioner and disability premiums.

See the notes to Sch.2 to the Income Support Regulations for discussion of the personal allowances and premiums where the rules are the same for JSA and income support. The note below just refers to the main differences.

Para.1

3.578
The conditions for the lower and higher rate of personal allowance for 16- or 17-year-olds who are single or lone parents match those that applied under income support before October 7, 1996 (see the 1996 edition of Mesher and Wood,

Income-related Benefits: the Legislation). Similarly JSA, like income support, is paid at a lower rate for single people who are under 25.

But in relation to couples there are some additional categories so that para.1(3) is even more complex than the pre-October 7, 1996 form of para.1(3) of Sch.2 to the Income Support Regulations. See heads (a)(iii), (a)(vii), (f)(iii), (g)(iii) and (h)(iii) where the fact that the other member of the couple would or would not be eligible for income support is an additional means of the couple qualifying or not qualifying for a higher rate. (Should the "and" at the end of head (f)(ii) not be an "or"?) Note also the new categories in heads (a)(iv) and (d).

Paras 2 to 4

For a discussion of when the provisions abolishing JSA personal allowances for children and young persons, and the family premium, come into effect—and the "transitional cases" thereby created—see the notes to reg.83 and to reg.17 of the Income Support Regulations.

3.579

Paras 10 and 11

The conditions for qualifying for a pensioner premium (for the rates see para.20; the premiums are paid at the same rate as the pensioner premiums for income support) differ from the income support rules to reflect the fact that income support claimants must be under 60, whereas JSA claimants must be below pensionable age (which for men is 65) (cf. s.124(1)(aa) of the Contributions and Benefits Act 1992 and s.1(2)(h) of the Jobseekers Act 1995). For the premium under para.10 to be payable the claimant must be 60 or over, or have a partner aged 60–74. If his partner is aged 75–79 the claimant will qualify for the premium under para.11.

3.580

Paras 12 to 14

Similarly, the rules for the higher pensioner and disability premiums differ from those for income support to reflect the fact that to be entitled to JSA the claimant has to be capable of work (s.1(2)(f) of the Jobseekers Act). Thus severe disablement allowance and long-term incapacity benefit (or short-term incapacity benefit at the higher rate payable to people who are terminally ill) remain qualifying benefits for the purpose of these premiums but only where it is the claimant's partner that receives them (see para.14(1)(b) and (d)). See also para.14(1)(g) (and note the differences from para.12(1)(c) of the Income Support Regulations). In addition, there is (obviously) no equivalent to para.12(1)(b) of Sch.2 to the Income Support Regulations (claimant incapable of work for at least 52 weeks or 28 weeks in the case of terminal illness).

3.581

Para.15

Note the saving provision in sub-para.(8). Regs 4 to 6 of the Income Support (General) Amendment (No.6) Regulations 1991 are on pp.664–667.

3.582

SCHEDULE 2   **Regulations 83(f) and 84(1)(g)**

HOUSING COSTS

Housing costs

1.—(1) Subject to the following provisions of this Schedule, the housing costs applicable to a claimant are those costs—

3.583

    (a) which he or, where he is a member of a family, he or any member of that family is, in accordance with paragraph 2, liable to meet in respect of the dwelling occupied as the home which he or any other member of his family is treated as occupying; and

    (b) which qualify under paragraphs 14 to 16.

(2) In this Schedule—

"housing costs" means those costs to which sub-paragraph (1) refers;

"existing housing costs" means housing costs arising under an agreement entered into before

2nd October 1995, or under an agreement entered into after 1st October 1995 ("the new agreement")—

[²⁶ (a) which replaces an existing agreement, provided that the person liable to meet the housing costs—
  (i) remains the same in both agreements, or
  (ii) where in either agreement more than one person is liable to meet the housing costs, the person is liable to meet the housing costs in both the existing agreement and the new agreement;]

(b) where the existing agreement was entered into before 2nd October 1995; and

(c) which is for a loan of the same amount as or less than the amount of the loan under the agreement it replaces, and for the purpose of determining the amount of the loan under the new agreement, any sum payable to arrange the new agreement and included in the loan shall be disregarded;

"new housing costs" means housing costs arising under an agreement entered into after 1st October 1995 other than an agreement referred to in the definition of "existing housing costs"; "standard rate" means the rate for the time being [²³determined in accordance with] paragraph 11.

(3) For the purposes of this Schedule a disabled person is a person—

(a) in respect of whom a disability premium, a disabled child premium, a pensioner premium where the claimant's partner has attained the age of 75 or a higher pensioner premium is included in his applicable amount or the applicable amount of a person living with him; or

(b) who, had he in fact been entitled to a jobseeker's allowance or to income support, would have had included in his applicable amount a disability premium, a disabled child premium, a pensioner premium where the claimant's partner has attained the age of 75 or a higher pensioner premium; or

(c) who satisfies the requirements of paragraph 9A of Schedule 2 to the Income Support [¹Regulations] (pensioner premium for person aged 75 or over).

(4) For the purposes of sub-paragraph (3), a person shall not cease to be a disabled person on account of his being disqualified for receiving benefit or treated as capable of work by virtue of the operation of section 171E of the Benefits Act (incapacity for work, disqualification etc.).

[⁵Previous entitlement to income support

3.584   **1A.**—(1) Where a claimant or his partner was in receipt of or was treated as being in receipt of income support not more than 12 weeks before one of them becomes entitled to income-based jobseeker's allowance or, where the claimant or his partner is a person to whom paragraph 13(2) or (10) (linking rules) refers, not more than 26 weeks before becoming so entitled and—

(a) the applicable amount for income support included an amount in respect of housing costs under paragraph 15 or 16 of Schedule 3 to the Income Support Regulations; and

(b) the circumstances affecting the calculation of those housing costs remain unchanged since the last calculation of those costs,

the applicable amount in respect of housing costs for income-based jobseeker's allowance shall be the applicable amount in respect of those costs current when entitlement to income support was last determined.

[¹⁶ (1A) Where either member of a joint-claim couple was in receipt of or treated as being in receipt of income support not more than 12 weeks before the couple becomes entitled to a joint-claim jobseeker's allowance, or, where either member is a person to whom paragraph 13(2) or (10) (linking rules) refers, not more than 26 weeks before becoming so entitled and—

(a) the applicable amount for income support included an amount in respect of housing costs under paragraph 15 or 16 of Schedule 3 to the Income Support Regulations; and

(b) the circumstances affecting the calculation of those housing costs remain unchanged since the last calculation of those costs,

the applicable amount in respect of housing costs for joint-claim jobseeker's allowance shall be the applicable amount in respect of those costs current when entitlement to income support was last determined.]

(2) Where, in the period since housing costs were last calculated for income support, there has been a change of circumstances, other than a reduction in the amount of an outstanding loan, which increases or reduces those costs, the amount to be met under this Schedule shall, for the purposes of the claim for income-based jobseeker's allowance, be recalculated so as to take account of that change.]

Circumstances in which a person is liable to meet housing costs

2.—(1) A person is liable to meet housing costs where—   3.585
  (a) the liability falls upon him or his partner [¹⁶ or, where that person is a member of a joint-claim couple, the other member of that couple,] but not where the liability is to a member of the same household as the person on whom the liability falls;

  (b) because the person liable to meet the housing costs [¹is not meeting them], the claimant has to meet those costs in order to continue to live in the dwelling occupied as the home and it is reasonable in all the circumstances to treat the claimant as liable to meet those costs;

  (c) he in practice shares the housing costs with other members of the household none of whom are close relatives either of the claimant or his partner, [¹⁶ or, where that person is a member of a joint-claim couple, the other member of that couple,] and
      (i) one or more of those members is liable to meet those costs, and
      (ii) it is reasonable in the circumstances to treat him as sharing responsibility.

(2) Where any one or more, but not all, members of the claimant's family are affected by a trade dispute, the housing costs shall be treated as wholly the responsibility of those members of the family not so affected.

Circumstances in which a person is to be treated as occupying a dwelling as his home

3.—(1) Subject to the following provisions of this paragraph, a person shall be treated as   3.586
occupying as his home the dwelling normally occupied as his home by himself or, if he is a member of a family, by himself and his family and he shall not be treated as occupying any other dwelling as his home.

(2) In determining whether a dwelling is the dwelling normally occupied as the claimant's home for the purposes of sub-paragraph (1) regard shall be had to any other dwelling occupied by the claimant or by him and his family whether or not that other dwelling is in Great Britain.

(3) Subject to sub-paragraph (4), where a single claimant or a lone parent is a full-time student or is on a training course and is liable to make payments (including payments of mortgage interest or, in Scotland, payments under heritable securities or, in either case, analogous payments) in respect of either (but not both) the dwelling which he occupies for the purpose of attending his course of study or his training course or, as the case may be, the dwelling which he occupies when not attending his course, he shall be treated as occupying as his home the dwelling in respect of which he is liable to make payments.

(4) A full-time student shall not be treated as occupying a dwelling as his home for any week of absence from it, other than an absence occasioned by the need to enter hospital for treatment, outside the period of study, if the main purpose of his occupation during the period of study would be to facilitate attendance on his course.

(5) Where a claimant has been required to move into temporary accommodation by reason of essential repairs being carried out to the dwelling normally occupied as his home and he is liable to make payments (including payments of mortgage interest or, in Scotland, payments under heritable securities or, in either case, analogous payments) in respect of either (but not both) the dwelling normally occupied or the temporary accommodation, he shall be treated as occupying as his home the dwelling in respect of which he is liable to make those payments.

(6) Where a person is liable to make payments in respect of two (but not more than two) dwellings, he shall be treated as occupying both dwellings as his home only—
  (a) where he has left and remains absent from the former dwelling occupied as the home through fear of violence in that dwelling or by a former member of his family and it is reasonable that housing costs should be met in respect of both his former dwelling and his present dwelling occupied as the home;

  (b) in the case of a couple or a member of a polygamous marriage where a partner is a full-time student or is on a training course and it is unavoidable that he or they should occupy two separate dwellings and reasonable that housing costs should be met in respect of both dwellings; or

  (c) in the case where a person has moved into a new dwelling occupied as the home, except where sub-paragraph (5) applies, for a period not exceeding four benefit weeks if his liability to make payments in respect of two dwellings is unavoidable.

(7) Where—
  (a) a person has moved into a dwelling and was liable to make payments in respect of that dwelling before moving in; and

  (b) he had claimed a jobseeker's allowance before moving in and either that claim has not yet been determined or it has been determined but an amount has not been included under this Schedule and if the claim has been refused a further claim has been made within four weeks of the date on which the claimant moved into the new dwelling occupied as the home; and

(c) the delay in moving into the dwelling in respect of which there was liability to make payments before moving in was reasonable and—

   (i) that delay was necessary in order to adapt the dwelling to meet the disablement needs of the claimant or any member of his family; or

   (ii) the move was delayed pending the outcome of an application under Part VIII of the Benefits Act for a social fund payment to meet a need arising out of the move or in connection with setting up the home in the dwelling and either a member of the claimant's family is aged five or under or the claimant's applicable amount includes a premium under paragraph 10, 11, 12, 13, 15 or 16 of Schedule 1; or

   (iii) the person became liable to make payments in respect of the dwelling while he was a patient or was in residential accommodation,

he shall be treated as occupying the dwelling as his home for any period not exceeding four weeks immediately prior to the date on which he moved into the dwelling and in respect of which he was liable to make payments.

(8) This sub-paragraph applies to a person who enters residential accommodation—

(a) for the purpose of ascertaining whether the accommodation suits his needs; and

(b) with the intention of returning to the dwelling which he normally occupies as his home should, in the event, the residential accommodation prove not to suit his needs,

and while in the accommodation, the part of the dwelling which he normally occupies as his home is not let, or as the case may be, sub-let to another person.

(9) A person to whom sub-paragraph (8) applies shall be treated as occupying the dwelling he normally occupies as his home during any period (commencing with the day he enters the accommodation) not exceeding 13 weeks in which the person is resident in the accommodation, but only in so far as the total absence from the dwelling does not exceed 52 weeks.

(10) A person, other than a person to whom sub-paragraph (11) applies, shall be treated as occupying a dwelling as his home throughout any period of absence not exceeding 13 weeks, if, and only if—

(a) he intends to return to occupy the dwelling as his home; and

(b) the part of the dwelling normally occupied by him has not been let or, as the case may be, sub-let to another person; and

(c) the period of absence is unlikely to exceed 13 weeks.

(11) This sub-paragraph applies to a person whose absence from the dwelling he normally occupies as his home is temporary and—

(a) he intends to return to occupy the dwelling as his home; and

(b) while the part of the dwelling which is normally occupied by him has not been let or, as the case may be, sub-let; and

(c) he is—

   [[27] (i) required, as a condition of bail, to reside—

      (aa) in a dwelling, other than the dwelling he occupies as his home; or

      (bb) in premises approved under section 9 of the Criminal Justice and Court Services Act 2000, or]

   (ii) resident in a hospital or similar institution as a patient and is treated under regulation 55 as capable of work, or

   (iii) undergoing or, as the case may be, his partner or his dependent child is undergoing, in the United Kingdom or elsewhere, medical treatment, or medically approved convalescence, in accommodation other than residential accommodation, or

   (iv) following, in the United Kingdom or elsewhere, a training course, or

   (v) undertaking medically approved care of a person residing in the United Kingdom or elsewhere, or

   (vi) undertaking the care of a child whose parent or guardian is temporarily absent from the dwelling normally occupied by that parent or guardian for the purpose of receiving medically approved care or medical treatment, or

   (vii) a person who is, whether in the United Kingdom or elsewhere, receiving medically approved care provided in accommodation other than residential accommodation, or

   (viii) a full-time student to whom sub-paragraph (3) or (6)(b) does not apply, or

   (ix) a person other than a person to whom sub-paragraph (8) applies, who is receiving care provided in residential accommodation, or

    (x) a person to whom sub-paragraph (6)(a) does not apply and who has left the dwelling he occupies as his home through fear of violence in that dwelling or by a person who was formerly a member of [¹ his] family, and

  (d) the period of his absence is unlikely to exceed a period of 52 weeks or, in exceptional circumstances, is unlikely substantially to exceed that period.

(12) A person to whom sub-paragraph (11) applies is to be treated as occupying the dwelling he normally occupies as his home during any period of absence not exceeding 52 weeks beginning with the first day of that absence.

(13) In this paragraph—

  (a) "medically approved" means certified by a registered medical practitioner;

  (b) "patient" means a person who is undergoing medical or other treatment as an in-patient in a hospital or similar institution;

  (c) "residential accommodation" means accommodation—

    (i) provided under sections 21 to 24 and 26 of the National Assistance Act 1948 (provision of accommodation); or

    (ii) provided under sections 13B and 59 of the Social Work (Scotland) Act 1968 (provision of residential and other establishments) where board is available to the claimant; or

    (iii) which is a residential care home within the meaning of that expression in regulation 1(3) other than sub-paragraph (b) of that definition; or

    (iv) which is a nursing home;

  (d) "training course" means such a course of training or institution provided wholly or partly by or on behalf of or in pursuance of arrangements made with, or approved by or on behalf of, Scottish Enterprise, Highlands and Islands Enterprise, a government department or the Secretary of State.

Housing costs not met

4.—(1) No amount may be met under the provisions of this Schedule—   **3.587**

  (a) in respect of housing benefit expenditure; or

  (b) where [¹⁶ a claimant] is in accommodation which is a residential care home or a nursing home except where he is in such accommodation during a temporary absence from the dwelling he occupies as his home and in so far as they relate to temporary absences, the provisions of paragraph 3(8) to (12) apply to him during that absence.

(2) Subject to the following provisions of this paragraph, loans which, apart from this paragraph, qualify under paragraph 14 shall not so qualify where the loan was incurred during the relevant period and was incurred—

  (a) after 7th October 1996, or

  (b) after 2nd May 1994 and the housing costs applicable to that loan were not met in income support by virtue of the former paragraph 5A of Schedule 3 to the Income Support Regulations or paragraph 4(2)(a) of that Schedule in any one or more of the 26 weeks [³preceding] 7th October 1996, or

  (c) subject to sub-paragraph (3), in the 26 weeks preceding 7th October 1996 by a person—

    (i) who was not at that time entitled to income support; and

    [¹⁶(ii) who becomes, or whose partner becomes or, where that person is a member of a joint-claim couple, that couple become, entitled to a jobseeker's allowance after 6th October 1996 and that entitlement is within 26 weeks of an earlier entitlement to income support for the claimant or his partner or, as the case may be, either member of the joint-claim couple.]

(3) Sub-paragraph (2)(c) shall not apply in respect of a loan where [¹⁶ a claimant] has interest payments on that loan met without restrictions under an award of income support in respect of a period commencing before 7th October 1996.

(4) The "relevant period" for the purposes of this paragraph is any period during which the person to whom the loan was made—

  (a) is entitled to a jobseeker's allowance, or

  (b) is living as a member of a family one of whom is entitled to a jobseeker's allowance,

together with any linked period, that is to say a period falling between two such periods of entitlement to a jobseeker's allowance, separated by not more than 26 weeks.

[⁶(4A) For the purposes of sub-paragraph (4), a person shall be treated as entitled to a jobseeker's allowance during any period when he [¹⁶, his partner or, where that person is a member of a joint-claim couple, the other member of that couple] was not so entitled because—

  (a) that person [¹⁶, his partner or, where that person is a member of a joint-claim couple, the other member of that couple] was participating in an employment programme specified in regulation 75(1)(a)(ii) [[17], in the Intensive Activity Period specified in regulation 75(1)(a)(iv) or in the Intensive Activity Period for 50 plus]; and

(b) in consequence of such participation that person, [[16], his partner or, where that person is a member of a joint-claim couple, the other member of that couple] was engaged in remunerative work or failed to satisfy the condition specified either in section 2(1)(c) [[16], 3(1)(a) or 3A(1)(a)].]

(5) For the purposes of sub-paragraph (4)—

(a) any week in the period of 26 weeks ending on 7th October 1996 on which there arose an entitlement to income support shall be taken into account in determining when the relevant period commences; and

(b) two or more periods of entitlement and any intervening linked periods shall together form a single relevant period.

(6) Where the loan to which sub-paragraph (2) refers has been applied—

(a) for paying off an earlier loan, and that earlier loan qualified under paragraph 14 [[2]during the relevant period]; or

[[2](b) to finance the purchase of a property where an earlier loan, which qualified under paragraphs 14 and 15 during the relevant period in respect of another property, is paid off (in whole or in part) with monies received from the sale of that property;]

then the amount of the loan to which sub-paragraph (2) applies is the amount (if any) by which the new loan exceeds the earlier loan.

(7) Notwithstanding the preceding provisions of this paragraph, housing costs shall be met in any case where a claimant satisfies any of the conditions specified in sub-paragraphs (8) to (11) below, but—

(a) those costs shall be subject to any additional limitations imposed by the sub-paragraph; and

(b) where [[16] a claimant] satisfies the conditions in more than one of these sub-paragraphs, only one sub-paragraph shall apply in his case and the one that applies shall be the one most favourable to him. [[16], or, as the case may be, to the joint-claim couple of which he is a member].

(8) The conditions specified in this sub-paragraph are that—

(a) during the relevant period [[16] a claimant] or a member of his family acquires an interest ("the relevant interest") in a dwelling which he then occupies or continues to occupy as his home; and

(b) in the week preceding the week in which the relevant interest was acquired, housing benefit was payable to [[16] a claimant] or a member of his family;

so however that the amount to be met by way of housing costs shall initially not exceed the aggregate of—

(i) the housing benefit payable in the week mentioned at sub-paragraph (8)(b); and

(ii) any amount included in the applicable amount of [[16] a claimant] or a member of his family in accordance with regulation 83(f) [[16], 84(1)(g), 86A(d) or 86B(e)] in that week;

and shall be increased subsequently only to the extent that it is necessary to take account of any increase, arising after the date of the acquisition, in the standard rate or in any housing costs which qualify under paragraph 16 (other housing costs).

(9) The condition specified in this sub-paragraph is that the loan was taken out, or an existing loan increased, to acquire alternative accommodation more suited to the special needs of a disabled person than the accommodation which was occupied before the acquisition by [[16] a claimant].

(10) The conditions specified in this sub-paragraph are that—

(a) the loan commitment increased in consequence of the disposal of the dwelling occupied as the home and the acquisition of an alternative such dwelling; and

(b) the change of dwelling was made solely by reason of the need to provide separate sleeping accommodation for children of different sexes aged 10 or over who belong to the same family as [[16] a claimant].

(11) The conditions specified in this sub-paragraph are that—

(a) during the relevant period [[16] a claimant] or a member of his family acquires an interest ("the relevant interest") in a dwelling which he then occupies as his home; and

(b) in the week preceding the week in which the relevant interest was acquired, the applicable amount of [[16] a claimant] or a member of his family included an amount determined by reference to paragraph 16 and did not include any amount specified in paragraph 14 or paragraph 15;

so however that the amount to be met by way of housing costs shall initially not exceed the amount so determined, and shall be increased subsequently only to the extent that it is necessary to take account of any increase, arising after the date of acquisition, in the standard rate or in any housing costs which qualify under paragraph 16 (other housing costs).

(12) The following provisions of this Schedule shall have effect subject to the provisions of this paragraph.

Apportionment of housing costs

5.—(1) Where the dwelling occupied as the home is a composite hereditament and—   **3.588**

(a) before 1st April 1990 for the purposes of section 48(5) of the General Rate Act 1967 (reduction of rates on dwellings), it appeared to a rating authority or it was determined in pursuance of sub-section (6) of section 48 of that Act that the hereditament, including the dwelling occupied as the home, was a mixed hereditament and that only a proportion of the rateable value of the hereditament was attributable to use for the purpose of a private dwelling; or

(b) in Scotland, before 1st April 1989 an assessor acting pursuant to section 45(1) of the Water (Scotland) Act 1980 (provision as to valuation roll) has apportioned the net annual value of the premises including the dwelling occupied as the home between the part occupied as a dwelling and the remainder,

the amounts applicable under this Schedule shall be such proportion of the amounts applicable in respect of the hereditament or premises as a whole as is equal to the proportion of the rateable value of the hereditament attributable to the part of the hereditament used for the purposes of a private tenancy or, in Scotland, the proportion of the net annual value of the premises apportioned to the part occupied as a dwelling house.

(2) Subject to sub-paragraph (1) and the following provisions of this paragraph, where the dwelling occupied as the home is a composite hereditament, the amount applicable under this Schedule shall be the relevant fraction of the amount which would otherwise be applicable under this Schedule in respect of the dwelling occupied as the home.

(3) For the purposes of sub-paragraph (2), the relevant fraction shall be obtained in accordance with the formula—

$$\frac{A}{A+B}$$

where—

"A" is the current market value of the claimant's interest in that part of the composite hereditament which is domestic property within the meaning of section 66 of the Act of 1988;

"B" is the current market value of the claimant's interest in that part of the composite hereditament which is not domestic property within that section.

(4) In this paragraph—

"composite hereditament" means—

(a) as respects England and Wales, any hereditament which is shown as a composite hereditament in a local non-domestic rating list;

(b) as respects Scotland, any lands and heritages entered in the valuation roll which are part residential subjects within the meaning of section 26(1) of the Act of 1987;

"local non-domestic rating list" means a list compiled and maintained under section 41(1) of the Act of 1988;

"the Act of 1987" means the Abolition of Domestic Rates Etc. (Scotland) Act 1987;

"the Act of 1988" means the Local Government Finance Act 1988.

(5) Where responsibility for expenditure which relates to housing costs met under this Schedule is shared, the amounts applicable shall be calculated by reference to the appropriate proportion of that expenditure for which the claimant is responsible.

Existing housing costs

6.—(1) Subject to the provisions of this Schedule the existing housing costs to be met in any   **3.589**
particular case are—

(a) where the claimant has been entitled to a jobseeker's allowance for a continuous period of 26 weeks or more, the aggregate of—

(i) an amount determined in the manner set out in paragraph 9 by applying the standard rate to the eligible capital for the time being owing in connection with a loan which qualifies under paragraph 14 or 15; and

(ii) an amount equal to any payments which qualify under paragraph 16(1)(a) to (c);

(b) where the claimant has been entitled to a jobseeker's allowance for a continuous period of not less than 8 weeks but less than 26 weeks, an amount which is half the amount which would fall to be met by applying the provisions of sub-paragraph (a);

(c) in any other case, nil.

(2) For the purposes of sub-paragraph (1) [⁵and subject to sub-paragraph (3)], the eligible capital for the time being owing shall be determined on the date the existing housing costs are first met and thereafter on each anniversary of that date.

[⁵(3) Where a claimant or his partner ceases to be in receipt of or treated as being in receipt of income support [²² or state pension credit] and one of them becomes entitled to income-based jobseeker's allowance in a case to which paragraph 1A applies, the eligible capital for the time being owing shall be recalculated on each anniversary of the date on which the housing costs were first met for whichever of the benefits concerned the claimant or his partner was first entitled.]

[¹⁶ (4) Where either member of a joint-claim couple ceases to be in receipt of or treated as being in receipt of income support and that couple then become entitled to a joint-claim job-seeker's allowance in a case to which paragraph 1A(1A) applies, the eligible capital for the time being owing shall be recalculated on each anniversary of the date on which the housing costs were first met for whichever of the benefits concerned either member of the couple was first entitled to.]

New housing costs

3.590

7.—(1) Subject to the provisions of this Schedule, the new housing costs to be met in any particular case are—

(a) where the claimant has been entitled to a jobseeker's allowance for a continuous period of 39 weeks or more, an amount—

(i) determined in the manner set out in paragraph 9 by applying the standard rate to the eligible capital for the time being owing in connection with a loan which qualifies under paragraph 14 or 15; and

(ii) equal to any payments which qualify under paragraph 16(⁻)(a) to (c);

(b) in any other case, nil.

(2) For the purposes of sub-paragraph (1) [⁵and subject to sub-paragraph (2A)], the eligible capital for the time being owing shall be determined on the date the new housing costs are first met and thereafter on each anniversary of that date.

[⁵(2A) Where a claimant or his partner ceases to be in receipt of or treated as being in receipt of income support and one of them becomes entitled to income-based jobseeker's allowance in a case to which paragraph 1A applies, the eligible capital for the time being owing shall be recalculated on each anniversary of the date on which the housing costs were first met for whichever of the benefits concerned the claimant or his partner was first entitled.]

[¹⁶(2B) Where either member of a joint-claim couple ceases to be in receipt of or treated as being in receipt of income support and that couple then become entitled to a joint-claim job-seeker's allowance in a case to which paragraph 1A(1A) applies, the eligible capital for the time being owing shall be recalculated on each anniversary of the date on which the housing costs were first met for whichever of the benefits concerned either member of the couple was first entitled to.]

(3) This sub-paragraph applies to a claimant who at the time the claim is made has been refused payments under a policy of insurance on the grounds that—

(a) the claim under the policy is the outcome of a pre-existing medical condition which, under the terms of the policy, does not give rise to any payment by the insurer; or

(b) he was infected by the Human Immunodeficiency Virus,

and the policy was taken out to insure against the risk of being unable to maintain repayments on a loan which is secured by a mortgage or a charge over land, or (in Scotland) by a heritable security.

(4) This sub-paragraph applies subject to [¹sub-paragraph (7)] where a person claims a job-seeker's allowance because of—

(a) the death of a partner; or

(b) being abandoned by his partner,

and where the person's family includes a child.

(5) This sub-paragraph applies to a person who at the time the claim is made is engaged in caring for a person who falls within any of the circumstances specified in [¹heads (i) to (iv) of sub-paragraph (c)] of paragraph (3) of regulation 51 (remunerative work).

(6) In the case of a claimant to whom sub-paragraph (3), (4) or (5) applies, any new housing costs shall be met as though they were existing housing costs and paragraph 6 applied to them.

(7) Sub-paragraph (4) shall cease to apply to a person who subsequently becomes one of a couple.

General exclusions from paragraphs 6 and 7

8.—(1) Paragraphs 6 and 7 shall not apply where—
    (a) the claimant or his partner [^{16} or either member of a joint-claim couple] is aged 60 or over;
    (b) the housing costs are payments—
        (i) under a co-ownership agreement;
        (ii) under or relating to a tenancy or licence of a Crown tenant; or
        (iii) where the dwelling occupied as the home is a tent, in respect of the tent and the site on which it stands.

(2) In a case falling within sub-paragraph (1), the housing costs to be met are—
    (a) where head (a) of sub-paragraph (1) applies, an amount—
        (i) determined in the manner set out in paragraph 9 by applying the standard rate to the eligible capital for the time being owing in connection with a loan which qualifies under paragraph 14 or 15; and
        (ii) equal to the payments which qualify under paragraph 16;
    (b) where head (b) of sub-paragraph (1) applies, an amount equal to the payments which qualify under paragraph 16(1)(d) to (f).

[^{18} The calculation for loans

9. The weekly amount of existing housing costs or, as the case may be, new housing costs to be met under this Schedule in respect of a loan which qualifies under paragraph 14 or 15 shall be calculated by applying the formula—

$$\frac{A \times B}{52}$$

where—
    A = the amount of the loan which qualifies under paragraph 14 or 15;
    B = the standard rate for the time being [^{24} applicable in respect of that loan].]

General provisions applying to new and existing housing costs

10.—(1) Where a person enters into a new agreement in respect of a dwelling and an agreement entered into before 2nd October 1995 ("the earlier agreement") continues in force independently of the new agreement, then—
    (a) the housing costs applicable to the new agreement shall be calculated by reference to the provisions of paragraph 7 (new housing costs);
    (b) the housing costs applicable to the earlier agreement shall be calculated by reference to the [^{1}provisions] of paragraph 6 (existing housing costs);
and the resulting amounts shall be aggregated.

(2) Sub-paragraph (1) does not apply in the case of a claimant to whom paragraph 8 applies.

(3) Where for the time being a loan exceeds, or in a case where more than one loan is to be taken into account, the aggregate of those loans exceeds the appropriate amount specified in sub-paragraph (4), then the amount of the loan or, as the case may be, the aggregate amount of those loans, shall for the purposes of this Schedule, be the appropriate amount.

(4) Subject to the following provisions of this paragraph, the appropriate amount is £100,000.

(5) Where a person is treated under paragraph 3(6) (payments in respect of two dwellings) as occupying two dwellings as his home, then the restrictions imposed by subparagraph (3) shall be applied separately to the loans for each dwelling.

(6) In a case to which paragraph 5 (apportionment of housing costs) applies, the appropriate amount for the purposes of sub-paragraph (3) shall be the lower of—
    (a) a sum determined by applying the formula—

$$P \times Q$$

where—
        P = the relevant fraction for the purposes of paragraph 5, and
        Q = the amount or, as the case may be, the aggregate amount for the time being of any loan or loans which qualify under this Schedule; or
    (b) the sum for the time being specified in sub-paragraph (4).

(7) In a case to which paragraph 14(3) or 15(3) (loans which qualify in part only) applies, the appropriate amount for the purposes of sub-paragraph (3) shall be the lower of—
    (a) a sum representing for the time being the part of the loan applied for the purposes specified in paragraph 14(1) or (as the case may be) paragraph 15(1); or
    (b) the sum for the time being specified in sub-paragraph (4).

3.591

3.592

3.593

(8) In the case of any loan to which paragraph 15(2)(k) (loan taken out and used for the purpose of adapting a dwelling for the special needs of a disabled person) applies the whole of the loan, to the extent that it remains unpaid, shall be disregarded in determining whether the amount for the time being specified in sub-paragraph (4) is exceeded.

(9) Where in any case the amount for the time being specified for the purposes of subparagraph (4) is exceeded and there are two or more loans to be taken into account under either or both [¹paragraphs 14 and 15], then the amount of eligible interest in respect of each of those loans to the extent that the loans remain outstanding shall be determined as if each loan had been reduced to a sum equal to the qualifying portion of that loan.

(10) For the purposes of sub-paragraph (9), the qualifying portion of a loan shall be determined by applying the following formula—

$$R \times \frac{S}{T}$$

where—

R = the amount for the time being specified for the purposes of sub-paragraph (4);

S = the amount of the outstanding loan to be taken into account;

T = the aggregate of all outstanding loans to be taken into account under paragraphs 14 and 15.

The standard rate

3.594
[²⁵ (1) The standard rate is the rate of interest applicable per annum to a loan which qualifies under this Schedule.

(2) Subject to sub-paragraphs (3), (4) and (6), the standard rate shall be 1.58 per cent plus—

(a) the rate announced from time to time by the Monetary Policy Committee of the Bank of England as the official dealing rate, being the rate at which the Bank is willing to enter into transactions for providing short term liquidity in the money markets, or

(b) where an order under section 19 of the Bank of England Act 1998 (reserve powers) is in force, any equivalent rate determined by the Treasury under that section.

(3) The Secretary of State shall determine the date from which the standard rate calculated in accordance with sub-paragraph (2) takes effect.

(4) Where—

(a) the actual rate of interest charged on the loan which qualifies under this Schedule is less than 5 per cent. per annum on the day the housing costs first fall to be met, and

(b) that day occurs before 28th November 2004,

the standard rate shall be equal to that actual rate.

(5) Sub-paragraph (4) shall cease to apply in a particular case to any one or more loans which fall within that sub-paragraph on whichever of the following dates occurs first—

(a) the date on which the actual rate of interest charged on such a loan is 5 per cent per annum or higher,

(b) the anniversary of the date on which the housing costs first fell to be met, or

(c) where a supersession decision based on a change of circumstances arising on or after 28th November 2004 is made under section 10 of the Social Security Act 1998 (decisions superseding earlier decisions), the date of the change of circumstances.

(6) Where sub-paragraph (4) does not apply to a loan which qualifies under this Schedule, the standard rate shall be 5.88 per cent until the first date determined by the Secretary of State under sub-paragraph (3).]

Excessive housing costs

3.595
12.—(1) Housing costs which, apart from this paragraph, fall to be met under this Schedule shall be met only to the extent specified in sub-paragraph (3) where—

(a) the dwelling occupied as the home, excluding any part which is let, is larger than is required by the claimant and his family and any child or young person to whom regulation 78(4) applies (foster children) and any other non-dependants having regard, in particular, to suitable alternative accommodation occupied by a household of the same size; or

(b) the immediate area in which the dwelling occupied as the home is located is more expensive than other areas in which suitable alternative accommodation exists; or

(c) the outgoings of the dwelling occupied as the home which are met under paragraphs 14 to 16 are higher than the outgoings of suitable alternative accommodation in the area.

(2) For the purposes of heads (a) to (c) of sub-paragraph (1), no regard shall be had to the capital value of the dwelling occupied as the home.

(3) Subject to the following provisions of this paragraph, the amount of the loan which falls to be met shall be restricted and the excess over the amounts which the claimant would need to obtain suitable alternative accommodation shall not be allowed.

(4) Where, having regard to the relevant factors, it is not reasonable to expect the claimant and his family to seek alternative cheaper accommodation, no restriction shall be made under sub-paragraph (3).

(5) In sub-paragraph (4) "the relevant factors" are—

    (a) the availability of suitable accommodation and the level of housing costs in the area; and

    (b) the circumstances of the family including in particular the age and state of health of its members, the employment prospects of the claimant and, where a change in accommodation is likely to result in a change of school, the effect on the education of any child or young person who is a member of his family, or any child or young person who is not treated as part of his family by virtue of regulation 78(4) (foster children).

(6) Where sub-paragraph (4) does not apply and the claimant (or other member of the family) was able to meet the financial commitments for the dwelling occupied as the home when these were entered into, no restriction shall be made under this paragraph during the first 26 weeks of any period of entitlement to a jobseeker's allowance nor during the next 26 weeks if and so long as the claimant uses his best endeavours to obtain cheaper accommodation or, as the case may be, no restriction shall be made under this paragraph on [¹¹ supersession] during the 26 weeks from the date of the [¹¹ supersession] nor during the next 26 weeks if and so long as the claimant uses his best endeavours.

(7) For the purposes of calculating any period of 26 weeks referred to in sub-paragraph (6), and for those purposes only, a person shall be treated as entitled to a jobseeker's allowance for any period of 12 weeks or less in respect of which he was not in receipt of a jobseeker's allowance and which fell immediately between periods in respect of which he was in receipt thereof.

(8) Any period in respect of which—

    (a) a jobseeker's allowance was paid to a person, and

    (b) it was subsequently determined on appeal [¹¹, revision or supersession] that he was not entitled to a jobseeker's allowance for that period,

shall be treated for the purposes of sub-paragraph (7) as a period in respect of which he was not in receipt of a jobseeker's allowance.

(9) Heads (c) to (f) of sub-paragraph (1) of paragraph 13 shall apply to sub-paragraph (7) as they apply to paragraphs 6 and 7 but with the modification that the words "Subject to sub-paragraph (2)" are omitted and as if references to "the claimant" were references to the person mentioned in sub-paragraph (7).

Linking rule

13.—(1) Subject to [¹⁶ sub-paragraphs (2) and (2A)] for the [¹purposes] of this Schedule—   **3.596**

    (a) a person shall be treated as being in receipt of a jobseeker's allowance during the following periods—

        (i) any period in respect of which it was subsequently held, on appeal or [¹¹revision], that he was so entitled to a jobseeker's allowance; and

        (ii) any period of 12 weeks or less [¹³ or, as the case may be, 52 weeks or less,] in respect of which he was not in receipt of a jobseeker's allowance and which fell immediately between periods in respect of which

          [²(aa) he was, or was treated as being, in receipt of a jobseeker's allowance,

          (bb) he was treated as entitled to a jobseeker's allowance for the purposes of sub-paragraphs (5), (6) and (7), or

          (cc) (i) above applies;]

    (b) a person shall be treated as not being in receipt of a jobseeker's allowance during any period other than a period to which (a)(ii) above applies in respect of which it is subsequently held on appeal [¹¹, revision or supersession] that he was not so entitled;

    (c) where—

        (i) the claimant was a member of a couple or a polygamous marriage; and

        (ii) his partner was, in respect of a past period, in receipt of a jobseeker's allowance for himself and the claimant; and

        (iii) the claimant is no longer a member of that couple or polygamous marriage; and

        (iv) the claimant made his claim for a jobseeker's allowance within twelve weeks [¹³ or, as the case may be, 52 weeks,] of ceasing to be a member of that couple or polygamous marriage,

    he shall be treated as having been in receipt of a jobseeker's allowance for the same period as his former partner had been or had been treated, for the purposes of this Schedule, as having been;

   (d) where the claimant's partner's applicable amount was determined in accordance with paragraph 1(1) (single claimant) or paragraph 1(2) (lone parent) of Schedule 1 (applicable amounts) in respect of a past period, provided that the claim was made within twelve weeks [^{13} or, as the case may be, 52 weeks,] of the claimant and his partner becoming one of a couple or polygamous marriage, the claimant shall be treated as having been in receipt of a jobseeker's allowance for the same period as his partner had been or had been treated, for the purposes of this Schedule, as having been;

[^{16}(dd) where the applicable amount of a member of a joint-claim couple was determined in accordance with paragraph 1(1) (single claimant) or paragraph 1(2) (lone parent) of Schedule 1 (applicable amounts) in respect of a past period, provided that the claim was made within twelve weeks of the joint-claimant becoming a member of the joint-claim couple, the joint-claim couple shall be treated as having been in receipt of a job-seeker's allowance for the same period as that member of the joint-claim couple had been treated, for the purposes of this Schedule, as having been;]

   (e) where the claimant is a member of a couple or a polygamous marriage and his partner was, in respect of a past period, in receipt of a jobseeker's allowance for himself and the claimant, and the claimant has begun to receive a jobseeker's allowance as a result of an election by the members of the couple or polygamous marriage, he shall be treated as having been in receipt of a jobseeker's allowance for the same period as his partner had been or had been treated, for the purposes of this Schedule, as having been;

[^{6}(ee) where the claimant—

     (i) is a member of a couple or a polygamous marriage and the claimant's partner was, immediately before the participation by any member of that couple or polygamous marriage in an employment programme specified in regulation 75(1)(a)(ii) [^{17}, in the Intensive Activity Period specified in regulation 75(1)(a)(iv) or in the Intensive Activity Period for 50 plus], in receipt of income-based jobseeker's allowance and his applicable amount included an amount for the couple or for the partners of the polygamous marriage; and

    (ii) has, immediately after that participation in that programme, begun to receive income-based jobseeker's allowance as a result of an election under regulation 4(3B) of the Claims and Payments Regulations by the members of the couple or polygamous marriage,

the claimant shall be treated as having been in receipt of a jobseeker's allowance for the same period as his partner had been or had been treated, for the purposes of this Schedule, as having been;]

   (f) where—

     (i) the claimant was a member of a family of a person (not being a former partner) entitled to a jobseeker's allowance and at least one other member of that family was a child or young person; and

    (ii) the claimant becomes a member of another family which includes that child or young person; and

   (iii) the claimant made his claim for a jobseeker's allowance within 12 weeks [^{13} or, as the case may be, 52 weeks,] of the date on which the person entitled to a job-seeker's allowance mentioned in head (i) above ceased to be so entitled,

the claimant shall be treated as being in receipt of a jobseeker's allowance for the same period as that person had been or had been treated, for the purposes of this Schedule, as having been.

(2) Where a claimant, with the care of a child, has ceased to be in receipt of a jobseeker's allowance in consequence of the payment of child support maintenance under the Child Support Act 1991 and immediately before ceasing to be so in receipt an amount determined in accordance with paragraph 6(1)(a)(i) or paragraph 7(1)(a)(i) was applicable to him, then—

   (a) if the child support maintenance [^{20} calculation] concerned is terminated or replaced on [^{11}supersession] by a lower [^{20} calculation] in consequence of the coming into force on or after 18th April 1995 of regulations made under the Child Support Act 1991; or

   (b) where the child support maintenance [^{20} calculation] concerned is an [^{20} interim maintenance decision or default maintenance decision] and, in circumstances other than those referred to in head (a), it is terminated or replaced after termination by another [^{20} interim maintenance decision or default maintenance decision] or by a maintenance [^{20} calculation] made in accordance with Part I of Schedule 1 to the Child Support Act 1991, in either case of a lower amount than the [^{20} calculation] concerned,

sub-paragraph (1)(a)(ii) shall apply to him as if for the words "any period of 12 weeks or less" there were substituted the words "any period of 26 weeks or less".

[¹⁶(2A) Where a joint-claim jobseeker's allowance is payable to one member of a joint-claim couple in accordance with section 3B, both members of the couple shall be treated as receiving, or having received, a jobseeker's allowance for the purpose of this paragraph.

(2B) Where both joint-claimants claiming a jobseeker's allowance in respect of themselves have not been in receipt of a jobseeker's allowance for a period before they became a joint-claim couple, sub-paragraph (1) shall have effect in respect of that couple in relation to the period which is most favourable to the couple for the purposes of this Schedule.]

[⁴(3) For the purposes of this Schedule, where a claimant has ceased to be entitled to a jobseeker's allowance because he or his partner [¹⁶ or, where a claimant is a member of a joint-claim couple, the other member of that couple] is participating in arrangements for training made under section 2 of the Employment and Training Act 1973 or attending a course at an employment rehabilitation centre established under that section, he shall be treated as if he had been in receipt of a jobseeker's allowance for the period during which he or his partner [¹⁶ or, where a claimant is a member of a joint-claim couple, the other member of that couple] was participating in such a course.]

[⁶(3A) For the purposes of this Schedule, a claimant who has ceased to be entitled to a jobseeker's allowance because—

(a) that claimant or his partner [¹⁶ or, where a claimant is a member of a joint-claim couple, the other member of that couple] was participating in an employment programme specified in regulation 75(1)(a)(ii) [¹⁷ in the Intensive Activity Period specified in regulation 75(1)(a)(iv) or in the Intensive Activity Period for 50 plus] [¹²or in an employment zone programme], and

(b) in consequence of such participation the claimant or his partner [¹⁶ or, where a claimant is a member of a joint-claim couple, the other member of that couple] was engaged in renumerative work or failed to satisfy the condition specified either in section 2(1)(c) [¹⁶, 3(1)(a) or 3A(1)(a)],

shall be treated as if he had been in receipt of a jobseeker's allowance for the period during which he or his partner [¹⁶ or, where a claimant is a member of a joint-claim couple, the other member of that couple] was participating in that programme [¹⁷ or activity].]

(4) Where, for the purposes of sub-paragraphs [⁶(1), (3) and (3A)], a person is treated as being in receipt of a jobseeker's allowance, for a certain period, he shall [¹⁰, subject to sub-paragraph (4A),] be treated as being entitled to a jobseeker's allowance for the same period.

[¹⁰ (4A) Where the appropriate amount of a loan exceeds the amount specified in paragraph 10(4), sub-paragraph (4) shall not apply except—

(a) for the purposes of paragraph 6(1) or 7(1); or

(b) where a person has ceased to be in receipt of a jobseeker's allowance for a period of 52 weeks or less because he or his partner is a welfare to work beneficiary.]

(5) For the purposes of this Schedule, sub-paragraph (6) applies where a person is not entitled to an income-based jobseeker's allowance by reason only that he has—

(a) capital exceeding £8,000; or

(b) income exceeding the applicable amount which applies in his case; or

[³(bb) a personal rate of contribution-based jobseeker's allowance that is equal to, or exceeds, the applicable amount in his case; or]

(c) both capital exceeding £8,000 and income exceeding the applicable amount which applies in his case.

(6) A person to whom sub-paragraph (5) applies shall be treated as entitled to a jobseeker's allowance throughout any period of not more than 39 weeks which comprises only days—

(a) on which he is entitled to a contribution-based jobseeker's allowance, statutory sick pay or incapacity benefit; or

(b) on which he is, although not entitled to any of the benefits mentioned in head (a) above, entitled to be credited with earnings equal to the lower earnings limit for the time being in force in accordance with [⁹regulation 8A or 8B of the Social Security (Credits) Regulations 1975].

(7) Subject to sub-paragraph (8), a person to whom sub-paragraph (5) applies and who is either a person to whom regulation 13(4) applies (persons with caring responsibilities) or a lone parent shall, for the purposes of this Schedule, be treated as entitled to a jobseeker's allowance throughout any period of not more than 39 weeks following the refusal of a claim for a jobseeker's allowance made by or on behalf of that person.

(8) Sub-paragraph (7) shall not apply in relation to a person mentioned in that sub-paragraph who, during the period referred to in that sub-paragraph—

(a) is engaged in, or is treated as engaged in, remunerative work or whose partner is engaged in, or is treated as engaged in, remunerative work;

    (b) is treated as not available for employment by virtue of regulation 15(a) (circumstances in which students are not treated as available for employment);

    (c) is temporarily absent from Great Britain, other than in the circumstances specified in regulation 50 (temporary absence from Great Britain).

(9) In a case where—

    (a) sub-paragraphs (6) and (7) apply solely by virtue of sub-paragraph (5)(b), and

    (b) the claimant's income includes payments under a policy taken out to insure against the risk that the policy holder is unable to meet any loan or payment which qualifies under paragraphs 14 to 16,

sub-paragraphs (6) and (7) shall have effect as if for the words "throughout any period of not more than 39 weeks" there are substituted the words "throughout any period that payments are made in accordance with the terms of the policy".

(10) This sub-paragraph applies—

    (a) to a person who claims a jobseeker's allowance, or in respect of whom a jobseeker's allowance is claimed, and who—

        (i) received payments under a policy of insurance taken out to insure against loss of employment, and those payments are exhausted; and

        (ii) had a previous award of a jobseeker's allowance where the applicable amount included an amount by way of housing costs; and

    (b) where the period in respect of which the previous award of jobseeker's allowance was payable ended not more than 26 weeks before the date the claim was made.

(11) Where sub-paragraph (10) applies, in determining—

    (a) for the purposes of paragraph 6(1) whether a person has been entitled to a jobseeker's allowance for a continuous period of 26 weeks or more; or

    (b) for the purposes of paragraph 7(1) whether a claimant has been entitled to a jobseeker's allowance for a continuous period of 39 weeks or more,

any week falling between the date of the termination of the previous award and the date of the new claim shall be ignored.

[8(12) Where the claimant's partner to whom this paragraph applies is a welfare to work beneficiary, sub-paragraphs (1)(a)(ii), [14 (1)(c)(iv),] (1)(d) and (1)(f)(iii) shall apply to him as if for the words "twelve weeks" there were substituted the words "52 weeks".]

[15 (13) For the purposes of sub-paragraph (1)(a)(ii), (1)(c)(iv), (1)(d) and (1)(f)(iii), the relevant period shall be—

    (a) 52 weeks in the case of a person to whom sub-paragraph (14) applies;

    (b) subject to sub-paragraph (12), 12 weeks in any other case.

(14) This sub-paragraph applies, subject to sub-paragraph (15), in the case of a person who, on or after 9th April 2001, has ceased to be entitled to a jobseeker's allowance because he or his partner or, where that person is a member of a joint-claim couple, the other member of that couple—

    (a) has commenced employment as an employed earner or as a self-employed earner or has increased the hours in which he is engaged in such employment;

    (b) is taking active steps to establish himself in employment as an employed earner or as a self-employed earner under any scheme for assisting persons to become so employed which is mentioned in regulation 19(1)(r)(i) to (iii); or

    (c) is participating in—

        (i) a New Deal option;

        (ii) an employment zone programme;

        (iii) the self-employment route; [17 or

        (iv) the Intensive Activity Period specified in regulation 75(1)(a)(iv) or the Intensive Activity Period for 50 plus]

and, as a consequence, he or his partner was engaged in remunerative work or failed to satisfy the conditions specified in section 2(1)(c) or 3(1)(a) or the joint-claim couple of which he was a member failed to satisfy the condition in section 3A(1)(a).

(15) Sub-paragraph (14) shall only apply to the extent that immediately before the day on which the person ceased to be entitled to an income-based jobseeker's allowance or the joint-claim couple of which he was a member ceased to be entitled to a joint-claim jobseeker's allowance, his housing costs were being met in accordance with paragraph 6(1)(a) [19, 6(1)(b)] or 7(1)(a) or would have been so met but for any non-dependant deduction under paragraph 17.]

[22 (16) For the purpose of determining whether the linking rules set out in this paragraph apply in a case where a claimant's former partner was entitled to state pension credit, any reference to income-based jobseeker's allowance in this Schedule shall be taken to include also a reference to state pension credit.]

Loans on residential property

14.—(1) A loan qualifies under this paragraph where the loan was taken out to defray monies applied for any of the following purposes—

    (a) acquiring an interest in the dwelling occupied as the home; or

    (b) paying off another loan to the extent that the other loan would have qualified under head (a) above had the loan not been paid off.

(2) For the purposes of this paragraph, references to a loan include also a reference to money borrowed under a hire purchase agreement for any purpose specified in heads (a) and (b) of sub-paragraph (1) above.

(3) Where a loan is applied only in part for the purposes specified in heads (a) and (b) of sub-paragraph (1), only that portion of the loan which is applied for that purpose shall qualify under this paragraph.

3.597

Loans for repairs and improvements to the dwelling occupied as the home

15.—(1) A loan qualifies under this paragraph where the loan was taken out, with or without security, for the purpose of—

    (a) carrying out repairs and improvements to the dwelling occupied as the home;

    (b) paying any service charge imposed to meet the cost of repairs and improvements to the dwelling occupied as the home;

    (c) paying off another loan to the extent that the other loan would have qualified under head (a) or (b) of this sub-paragraph had the loan not been paid off,

and the loan was used for that purpose, or is used for that purpose within 6 months of the date of receipt or such further period as may be reasonable in the particular circumstances of the case.

(2) In sub-paragraph (1) "repairs and improvements" means any of the following measures undertaken with a view to maintaining the fitness of the dwelling for human habitation or, where the dwelling forms part of a building, any part of the building containing that dwelling—

    (a) provision of a fixed bath, shower, wash basin, sink or lavatory, and necessary associated plumbing, including the provision of hot water not connected to a central heating system;

    (b) repairs to existing heating system;

    (c) damp proof measures;

    (d) provision of ventilation and natural lighting;

    (e) provision of drainage facilities;

    (f) provision of facilities for preparing and cooking food;

    (g) provision of insulation of the dwelling occupied as the home;

    (h) provision of electric lighting and sockets;

    (i) provision of storage facilities for fuel or refuse;

    (j) repairs of unsafe structural defects;

    (k) adapting a dwelling for the special needs of a disabled person; or

    (l) provision of separate sleeping accommodation for children of different sexes aged 10 or over who are part of the same family as the claimant.

(3) Where a loan is applied only in part for the purposes specified in sub-paragraph (1), only that portion of the loan which is applied for that purpose shall qualify under this paragraph.

3.598

Other housing costs

16.—(1) Subject to the deduction specified in sub-paragraph (2) and the reductions applicable in sub-paragraph (5), there shall be met under this paragraph the amounts, calculated on a weekly basis, in respect of the following housing costs—

    (a) payments by way of rent or ground rent relating to a long tenancy and, in Scotland, payments by way of feu duty;

    (b) service charges;

    (c) payments by way of the rentcharge within the meaning of section 1 of the Rent-charges Act 1977;

    (d) payments under a co-ownership scheme;

    (e) payments under or relating to a tenancy or licence of a Crown tenant;

    (f) where the dwelling occupied as the home is a tent, payments in respect of the tent and the site on which it stands.

(2) Subject to sub-paragraph (3), the deductions to be made from the weekly amounts to be met under this paragraph are—

    (a) where the costs are inclusive of any of the items mentioned in paragraph 5(2) of Schedule 1 to the Housing Benefit (General) Regulations 1987 (payment in respect of

3.599

fuel charges), the deductions prescribed in that paragraph unless the claimant provides evidence on which the actual or approximate amount of the service charge for fuel may be estimated, in which case the estimated amount;

(b) where the costs are inclusive of ineligible service charges within the meaning of paragraph 1 of Schedule 1 to the Housing Benefit (General) Regulations 1987 (ineligible service charges) the amounts attributable to those ineligible service charges or where that amount is not separated from or separately identified within the housing costs to be met under this paragraph, such part of the payments made in respect of those housing costs which are fairly attributable to the provision of those ineligible services having regard to the costs of comparable services;

(c) any amount for repairs and improvements, and for this purpose the expression "repairs and improvements" has the same meaning it has in paragraph 15(2).

(3) Where arrangements are made for the housing costs, which are met under this paragraph and which are normally paid for a period of 52 weeks, to be paid instead for a period of 53 weeks, or to be paid irregularly, or so that no such costs are payable or collected in certain periods, or so that the costs for different periods in the year are of different amounts, the weekly amount shall be the amount payable for the year divided by 52.

(4) Where the claimant or a member of his family—

(a) pays for reasonable repairs or redecoration to be carried out to the dwelling they occupy; and

(b) that work was not the responsibility of the claimant or any member of his family; and

(c) in consequence of that work being done, the costs which are normally met under this paragraph are waived,

then those costs shall, for a period not exceeding 8 weeks, be treated as payable.

(5) Where in England and Wales an amount calculated on a weekly basis in respect of housing costs specified in sub-paragraph (1)(e) (Crown tenants) includes water charges, that amount shall be reduced—

(a) where the amount payable in respect of water charges is known, by that amount;

(b) in any other case, by the amount which would be the likely weekly water charge had the property not been occupied by a Crown tenant.

Non-dependant deductions

3.600   **17.**—(1) Subject to the following provisions of this paragraph, the following deductions from the amount to be met under the preceding paragraphs of this Schedule in respect of housing costs shall be made—

[28 (a) in respect of a non-dependant aged 18 or over who is engaged in any remunerative work, [29£47.75];

(b) in respect of a non-dependant aged 18 or over to whom paragraph (a) does not apply, [29£7.40].]

(2) In the case of a non-dependant aged 18 or over to whom sub-paragraph (1)(a) applies because he is in remunerative work, where the claimant satisfies [11 the Secretary of State] that the non-dependant's gross weekly income is—

(a) less than [29£101.00], the deduction to be made under this paragraph shall be the deduction specified in sub-paragraph (1)(b);

(b) not less than [29£101.00] but less than [29£150.00], the deduction to be made under this paragraph shall be [29£17.00];

(c) not less than [29£150.00] but less than [29£194.00], the deduction to be made under this paragraph shall be [29£23.35];

[1(d) not less than [29£194.00] but less than [29£258.00], the deduction to be made under this paragraph shall be [29£38.20];

(e) not less than [29£258.00] but less than [29£322.00], the deduction to be made under this paragraph shall be [29£43.50]].

(3) Only one deduction shall be made under this paragraph in respect of a couple or, as the case may be, the members of a polygamous marriage, and where, but for this sub-paragraph, the amount that would fall to be deducted in respect of one member of a couple or polygamous marriage is higher than the amount (if any) that would fall to be deducted in respect of the other, or any other member, the higher amount shall be deducted.

(4) In applying the provisions of sub-paragraph (2) in the case of a couple or, as the case may be, a polygamous marriage, regard shall be had, for the purpose of sub-paragraph (2), to the couple's or, as the case may be, all the members of the polygamous marriage's, joint weekly income.

(5) Where a person is a non-dependant in respect of more than one joint occupier of a dwelling (except where the joint occupiers are a couple or members of a polygamous marriage),

the deduction in respect of that non-dependant shall be apportioned between the joint occupiers (the amount so apportioned being rounded to the nearest penny) having regard to the number of joint occupiers and the proportion of the housing costs in respect of the dwelling occupied as the home payable by each of them.

(6) No deduction shall be made in respect of any non-dependants occupying the dwelling occupied as the home of the claimant, if the claimant or any partner of his is—

    (a) blind or treated as blind within the meaning of paragraph 14(1)(h) and (2) of Schedule 1 (additional condition for the higher pensioner and disability premiums); or

    (b) receiving in respect of himself either—

        (i) an attendance allowance, or

        (ii) the care component of the disability living allowance.

(7) No deduction shall be made in respect of a non-dependant—

    (a) if, although he resides with the claimant, it appears to [¹¹ the Secretary of State] that the dwelling occupied as his home is normally elsewhere; or

[²(b) if he is in receipt of [³a training allowance paid in connection with a Youth Training Scheme established under section 2 of the Employment and Training Act 1973 or section 2 of the Enterprise and New Towns (Scotland) Act 1990; or]]

    (c) if he is a full-time student during a period of study or, if he is not in remunerative work, during a recognised summer vacation appropriate to his course; or

    (d) if he is aged under 25 and in receipt of [⁴an income-based jobseeker's allowance] or income support; or

    (e) in respect of whom a deduction in the calculation of a rent rebate or allowance falls to be made under regulation 63 of the Housing Benefit (General) Regulations 1987 (non-dependant deductions); or

    (f) to whom, but for paragraph (5) of regulation 2 (definition of non-dependant) paragraph (4) of that regulation would apply; or

    (g) if he is not residing with the claimant because he has been a patient for a period in excess of [²¹ 52] weeks, or is a prisoner, and for these purposes—

        (i) "patient" and "prisoner" respectively have the meanings given in regulation 85(4) (special cases), and

        (ii) the period of [²¹ 52] weeks shall be calculated by reference to paragraph (2) of that regulation as if that paragraph applied in his case [²⁸ or

    (h) if he is in receipt of state pension credit.]

(8) In the case of a non-dependant to whom sub-paragraph (2) applies because he is in remunerative work, there shall be disregarded from his gross income—

    (a) any attendance allowance or disability living allowance received by him;

    (b) any payment made under the Macfarlane Trust, the Macfarlane (Special Payments) Trust, the Macfarlane (Special Payments) (No.2) Trust, the Fund, the Eileen Trust or the Independent Living Funds which, had his income fallen to be calculated under regulation 103 (calculation of income other than earnings), would have been disregarded under paragraph 22 of Schedule 7 (income in kind); and

    (c) any payment which, had his income fallen to be calculated under regulation 103 would have been disregarded under paragraph 41 of Schedule 7 (payments made under certain trusts and certain other payments).

Continuity with income support

18.—(1) For the purpose of providing continuity between income support and a job-seeker's allowance—   3.601

    (a) any housing costs which would, had the claimant been entitled to income support, have been existing housing costs and not new housing costs shall, notwithstanding the preceding provisions of this Schedule, be treated as existing housing costs, and any qualifications or limitations which would have applied to those costs had the award been an award of income support shall likewise apply to the costs in so far as they are met in jobseeker's allowance;

    (b) had the award of a jobseeker's allowance been an award of income support and the housing costs which would then have been met would have included an additional amount met in accordance with paragraph 7 of Schedule 3 to the Income Support Regulations (add back), an amount equal to that additional amount shall be added to the housing costs to be met under this Schedule, but that amount shall be subject to the same qualifications and limitations as it would have been had the award been of income support; and

(c) for the purposes of any linking rule [²or for determining whether any qualifying or other period is satisfied], any reference to a jobseeker's allowance in this Schedule shall be taken also to include a reference to income support.

(2) Any loan which, had the claimant been entitled to income support and not a jobseeker's allowance, would have been a qualifying loan for the purposes of Schedule 3 to the Income Support Regulations by virtue of regulation 3 of the Income Support (General) Amendment and Transitional Regulations 1995 shall be treated also as a qualifying loan for the purposes of paragraph 14 or 15, as the case may be, of this Schedule; and for the purpose of determining whether a claimant would satisfy the provision of regulation 3(2) of those Regulations, a person in receipt of an income-based jobseeker's allowance shall be treated as being in receipt of income support.

Rounding of Fractions

3.602   **19.** Where any calculation made under this Schedule results in a fraction of a penny, that fraction shall be treated as a penny.

AMENDMENTS

3.603   1. Jobseeker's Allowance (Amendment) Regulations 1996 (SI 1996/1516), reg.20 and Sch. (October 7, 1996).

2. Jobseeker's Allowance and Income Support (General) (Amendment) Regulations 1996 (SI 1996/1517), reg.29 (October 7, 1996).

3. Social Security and Child Support (Jobseeker's Allowance) (Miscellaneous Amendments) Regulations 1996 (SI 1996/2538), reg.2(12) (October 28, 1996).

4. Social Security and Child Support (Miscellaneous Amendments) Regulations 1997 (SI 1997/827), reg.4 (April 7, 1997).

5. Social Security (Miscellaneous Amendments) (No.4) Regulations 1997 (SI 1997/2305), reg.3 (October 22, 1997).

6. Social Security Amendment (New Deal) Regulations 1997 (SI 1997/2863), reg.13 (January 5, 1998).

7. Social Security (Non-Dependant Deductions) Regulations 1996 (SI 1996/2518), reg.4 (April 6, 1998).

8. Social Security (Welfare to Work) Regulations 1998 (SI 1998/2231), reg.14(4) (October 5, 1998).

9. Social Security Benefits (Miscellaneous Amendments) Regulations 1999 (SI 1999/714), reg.2(2) (April 5, 1999).

10. Income Support (General) and Jobseeker's Allowance Amendment Regulations 1999 (SI 1999/1921), reg.2(2) (August 2, 1999).

11. Social Security Act 1998 (Commencement No.11, and Savings and Consequential and Transitional Provisions) Order 1999 (SI 1999/2860 (C.75)), Art.3(12) and Sch.12 (October 18, 1999).

12. Social Security Amendment (Employment Zones) Regulations 2000 (SI 2000/724), reg.4(4)(d) (April 3, 2000).

13. Social Security (Miscellaneous Amendments) Regulations 2001 (SI 2001/488), reg.12(b)(i) (April 9, 2001).

14. Social Security (Miscellaneous Amendments) Regulations 2001 (SI 2001/488), reg.12(b)(ii) (April 9, 2001).

15. Social Security (Miscellaneous Amendments) Regulations 2001 (SI 2001/488), reg.12(b)(iii) (April 9, 2001).

16. Jobseeker's Allowance (Joint Claims) Regulations 2000 (SI 2000/1978), reg.2(5) and Sch.2, para.54 (March 19, 2001).

17. Social Security Amendment (New Deal) Regulations 2001 (SI 2001/ 1029), reg.11 (April 9, 2001).

18. Income Support (General) and Jobseeker's Allowance Amendment Regulations 2001 (SI 2001/3651), reg.2(2) (December 10, 2001).

19. Social Security (Miscellaneous Amendments) Regulations 2002 (SI 2002/841), reg.6 (April 8, 2002).

20. Child Support (Consequential Amendments and Transitional Provisions) Regulations 2001 (SI 2001/158), reg.7(3) (in force in relation to any particular case

on the day on which s.1 of the Child Support, Pensions and Social Security Act 2000 comes into force in relation to that type of case).

21. Social Security (Hospital In-Patients and Miscellaneous Amendments) Regulations 2003 (SI 2003/1195), reg.6(4) (May 21, 2003).

22. State Pension Credit (Consequential, Transitional and Miscellaneous Provisions) Regulations 2002 (SI 2002/3019), reg.30 (October 6, 2003).

23. Social Security (Housing Costs Amendments) Regulations 2004 (SI 2004/2825), reg.2(2) (November 28, 2004).

24. Social Security (Housing Costs Amendments) Regulations 2004 (SI 2004/2825), reg.2(3) (November 28, 2004).

25. Social Security (Housing Costs Amendments) Regulations 2004 (SI 2004/2825), reg.2(4) (November 28, 2004).

26. Social Security (Housing Costs Amendments) Regulations 2004 (SI 2004/2825), reg.2(5) (November 28, 2004).

27. Social Security (Housing Benefit, Council Tax Benefit, State Pension Credit and Miscellaneous Amendments) Regulations 2004 (SI 2004/2327), reg.6(a) (April 4, 2005).

28. Social Security (Housing Benefit, Council Tax Benefit, State Pension Credit and Miscellaneous Amendments) Regulations 2004 (SI 2004/2327), reg.6(b) (April 4, 2005).

29. Social Security Benefits Up-rating Order 2005 (SI 2005/522), art.24(7) (April 11, 2005).

DEFINITIONS

"attendance allowance"—see reg.1(3).   **3.604**
"the Benefits Act"—see Jobseekers Act, s.35(1).
"benefit week"—see reg.1(3).
"claimant"—see Jobseekers Act, s.35(1).
"close relative"—see reg.1(3).
"couple"—*ibid.*
"course of study"—*ibid.*
"co-ownership scheme"—*ibid.*
"Crown tenant"—*ibid.*
"disability living allowance"—*ibid.*
"dwelling occupied as the home"—*ibid.*
"the Eileen Trust"—*ibid.*
"employment zone programme"—*ibid.*
"family"—see Jobseekers Act, s.35(1).
"the Fund"—see reg.1(3).
"housing benefit expenditure"—*ibid.*
"the Independent Living Funds"—*ibid.*
"lone parent"—*ibid.*
"the Macfarlane (Special Payments) Trust"—*ibid.*
"the Macfarlane (Special Payments) (No. 2) Trust"—*ibid.*
"the Macfarlane Trust"—*ibid.*
"non-dependant"—see reg.2.
"nursing home"—see reg.1(3).
"partner"—*ibid.*
"period of study"—*ibid.*
"polygamous marriage"—*ibid.*
"remunerative work"—see reg.51(1).
"residential care home"—see reg.1(3).
"single claimant"—*ibid.*
"student"—see reg.130, reg.1(3).
"training allowance"—see reg.1(3).
"water charges"—*ibid.*

"welfare to work beneficiary"—*ibid.*
"year of assessment"—*ibid.*

GENERAL NOTE

3.605   Most of this Schedule is very similar to Sch.3 to the Income Support Regulations, subject to some minor differences in the wording. See the notes to Sch.3. There are a few differences which reflect the fact that a claimant must satisfy the labour market conditions in order to be entitled to JSA. Thus there is no equivalent of para.8(2)(b) of Sch.3 in para.7 (new housing costs); see also the differences in para.3(11)(c)(i) and (ii) (person treated as occupying his home during temporary absences of up to 52 weeks). Note also in para.13 (linking rules) the additional category (from October 28, 1996) in sub-para.(5)(bb): person who is not entitled to income-based JSA because his contribution-based JSA equals or exceeds his applicable amount for income-based JSA; and that a carer in sub-para.(7) is defined by reference to reg.13(4) (person with caring responsibilities, see reg.4 for the definition of "caring responsibilities") rather than being restricted to a person who cares for someone receiving attendance allowance or disability living allowance, etc.

Note that in relation to, for example, satisfying the waiting periods for housing costs, periods during which hardship payments are being made will count, since hardship payments are payments of JSA. In addition, periods when a claimant is sanctioned will count towards the waiting periods, since entitlement to JSA continues during the sanction, even though JSA is not paid. This will be so whether or not a hardship payment is made. But "waiting days" at the beginning of a JSA claim are not days of entitlement. The amendments made on March 19, 2001 are necessary because of the introduction of joint-claim jobseeker's allowance (see the notes at the beginning of the Jobseekers Act 1995 and to s.1(4) of the Act). Obviously there is no equivalent to these amendments in Sch.3 to the Income Support Regulations.

The transitional protection provisions in Sch.3 to the Income Support Regulations have been omitted, but note the effect of para.18(1)(b). Para.18 is important for claimants transferring from income support to jobseeker's allowance. For the equivalent of para.18(1)(c) where the transfer is the other way round, see reg.32 of the Income Support (General) (Jobseeker's Allowance Consequential Amendments) Regulations 1996 (p.676)). See p.672 for reg.3 of the Income Support (General) Amendment and Transitional Regulations 1995 referred to in para.18(2) and see the note to para.7 of Sch.3. Note also the further transitional provisions in reg.87(4) to (6). For the linking rule where the claimant's former partner was entitled to state pension credit, see para.13(16), inserted with effect from October 6, 2003.

Note also that entitlement to either contribution-based or income-based JSA counts towards the waiting periods in paras 6 and 7. As the Commissioner points out in *CJSA 2028/2000* the words used are "a jobseeker's allowance" and so refer to either element of JSA.

SCHEDULE 3

3.606   *[Revoked by the Social Security (Removal of Residential Allowance and Miscellaneous Amendments) Regulations 2003 (SI 2003/1121), reg.4 and Sch.2, para.10 with effect from October 6, 2003.]*

SCHEDULE 4

APPLICABLE AMOUNTS OF PERSONS IN RESIDENTIAL CARE AND NURSING HOMES

3.607   *[Revoked by Social Security Amendment (Residential Care and Nursing Homes) Regulations 2001 (SI 2001/3767), reg.2 and Sch., Pt II para.19 with effect from April 8, 2002.]*

SCHEDULE 4A

APPLICABLE AMOUNT OF A JOINT-CLAIM COUPLE WHERE A MEMBER IS IN A RESIDENTIAL CARE OR NURSING HOME

[Inserted by Jobseeker's Allowance (Joint Claims) Regulations 2000 (SI 2000/1978), reg. 2(5) and Sch. 2, para. 55 with effect from March 19, 2001 and revoked by Social Security Amendment (Residential Care and Nursing Homes) Regulations 2001 (SI 2001/3767), reg. 2 and Sch., Pt II para. 19 with effect from April 8, 2002.]

3.608

SCHEDULE 5   Regulation 85

APPLICABLE AMOUNTS IN SPECIAL CASES

3.609

Column (1)	Column (2)

[⁶Person other than claimant who is a patient
1. Subject to paragraphs [¹²
[¹⁰ and 15]], a person who has been a patient for more than [¹¹ 52] weeks and who is—
  (a) a member of a couple and the other member is the claimant, or
  (b) a member of a polygamous marriage and the claimant is a member of the marriage but not a patient.
	1. (a) the applicable amount for a couple under regulation 83 reduced by [¹³£16.40];
	  (b) the applicable amount under regulation 84 (polygamous marriages) reduced by [¹³£16.40] in respect of each member who is a patient.

2. [¹² . . .]	**2.** [¹² . . .]
Claimants Without Accommodation **3.** A claimant who is without accommodation.	**3.** The amount applicable to him under regulation 83(a) (personal allowance) only.
Members of Religious Orders **4.** A claimant who is a member of and fully maintained by a religious order.	**4.** Nil

Specified Cases of Temporarily Separated Couples
5. A claimant who is a member of a couple and who is temporarily separated from his partner, where—
(a) one member of the couple is—
  (i) not a patient but is resident in a nursing home, or
  (ii) resident in a residential care home, or
  (iii) resident in premises used for the rehabilitation of alcoholics or drug addicts, or
  (iv) resident in accommodation provided under section 3 of and Part II of the Schedule to, the Polish Resettlement Act 1947 (provision of accommodation in camps),
  (v) or participating in arrangements for training made under section 2 of the Employment and Training Act 1973, or section 2 of the Enterprise and
	5. Either—
	
	  (a) the amount applicable to him as a member of a couple under regulation 83; or

Column (1)	Column (2)

New Towns (Scotland) Act 1990 or participating in an employment rehabilitation programme established under that section of the Act of 1973, where the course requires him to live away from the dwelling occupied as the home, or
  (vi) in a probation or bail hostel approved for the purpose by the Secretary of State, and
(b) the other member of the couple is—
  (i) living in the dwelling occupied as the home, or
  (ii) a patient, or
  (iii) in residential accommodation, or
 	
  (iv) resident in a residential care home or nursing home
	
	(b) the aggregate of his applicable amount and that of his partner assessed under the provisions of these Regulations as if each of them were a single claimant, or a lone parent.
	whichever is the greater.

Polygamous Marriages where one or more partners are temporarily separated
6. A claimant who is a member of a polygamous marriage and who is temporarily separated from a partner of his, where one of them is living in the home while the other member is—
  (a) not a patient but is resident in a nursing home; or
 	
  (b) resident in a residential care home; or
  (c) resident in premises used for the rehabilitation of alcoholics or drug addicts; or
  (d) attending a course of training or instruction provided or approved by the Secretary of State where the course requires him to live away from home; or
  (e) in a probation or bail hostel approved for the purpose by the Secretary of State.
	6. Either—
	
	(a) the amount applicable to the members of the polygamous marriage under regulation 84; or
	(b) the aggregate of the amount applicable for the members of the polygamous marriage who remain in the home under regulation 84 and the amount applicable in respect of those members not in the home calculated as if each of them were a single claimant, or a lone parent, whichever is the greater.

Single claimants temporarily in local authority accommodation **7.** [¹⁰ . . .]	**7.** [¹⁰ . . .]
Couples and members of polygamous marriages where one member is or all are temporarily in local authority accommodation **8.** [¹⁰ . . .]	**8.** [¹⁰ . . .]
Lone parents who are in residential accommodation temporarily **9.** [¹⁰ . . .]	**9.** [¹⁰ . . .]
Couples where one member is absent from the United Kingdom **10.** [⁷(1)] Subject to paragraph 11, a claimant who is a member of a couple	**10.** [⁷(1)] For the first four weeks of that absence, the amount applicable to them

Column (1)	Column (2)
and whose partner is temporarily absent from the United Kingdom.	as a couple under regulation 83 [⁹ . . .] as the case may be and thereafter the amount applicable to the claimant in Great Britain under regulation 83 [⁹ . . .] as the case may be as if the claimant were a single claimant or, as the case may be, a lone parent.
[⁷ (2) A claimant who is a member of a joint-claim couple and whose partner is temporarily absent from the United Kingdom— 　(a) in the circumstances prescribed in regulation 50(6A); 　(b) in any other circumstances.]	[⁷ (2) (a) For the first four weeks of that absence, the amount applicable to them as a couple under regulation 83 [⁹ . . .] and thereafter the amount applicable to the claimant in Great Britain under regulation 83 [⁹ . . .] as if the claimant were a single claimant; 　(b) The amount which would be applicable to the claimant under regulation 83 [⁹ . . .] if that claimant was a single claimant for the period commencing on the date of claim and ending on the day after the day on which the partner returns to the United Kingdom.]
Couple or member of couple taking child or young person abroad for treatment 11.—(1) A claimant who is a member of a couple where either— 　(a) he or his partner is, or 　(b) both he and his partner are absent from [¹United Kingdom] in the circumstances specified in sub-paragraph (2), 　(2) For the purpose of sub-paragraph (1), the specified circumstances are— 　(a) the claimant is absent from the United Kingdom but is treated as [⁵available for and actively seeking] employment in accordance with regulations 14(1) and 19(1); 　(b) the claimant's partner is absent from the United Kingdom and regulation 50(5) would have applied to him if he had claimed a jobseeker's allowance.	11. For the first 8 weeks of that absence, the amount applicable to the claimant under regulation 83 [⁸ . . .], as the case may be, and, thereafter, if the claimant is in Great Britain the amount applicable to him under regulation 83 [⁸ . . .], as the case may be, as if the claimant were a single claimant, or, as the case may be, a lone parent
Polygamous marriages where any member is abroad 12. Subject to paragraph 13 a claimant who is a member of a polygamous marriage where— 　(a) he or one of his partners is, or 　(b) he and one or more of his partners are, or 　(c) two or more of his partners are, temporarily absent from the United Kingdom.	12. For the first four weeks of that absence, the amount applicable to the claimant under regulations 84 to 87, as the case may be, and thereafter, if the claimant is in Great Britain the amount applicable to him under regulations 84 to 87, as the case may be, as if any member of the polygamous marriage not in the United Kingdom were not a member of the marriage.

Column (1)	Column (2)
Polygamous marriage: taking child or young person abroad for treatment	
13.—(1) A claimant who is a member of a polygamous marriage where— (a) he or one of his partners is, (b) he and one of his partners are, or [¹(c) two or more of his partners are, absent from the United Kingdom in the circumstances specified in sub-paragraph (2).]	**13.** For the first 8 weeks of that absence, the amount applicable to the claimant under regulations 84 to 87, as the case may be, and thereafter, if the claimant is in Great Britain the amount applicable to him under regulations 84 to 87, as the case may be, as if any member of the polygamous marriage not in the United Kingdom were not a member of the marriage.
(2) For the purposes of sub-paragraph (1) the specified circumstances are— (a) in respect of the claimant, [³ . . .] he is absent from the United Kingdom but is treated as available for and actively seeking employment in accordance with regulations 14(1) and 19(1); or [³(b)] one or more of the members of the polygamous marriage is absent from the United Kingdom and regulation 50(5) would have applied to the absent partner [¹if he had claimed a jobseeker's allowance.]	
[⁶**Partner of a person subject to immigration control** **13A.**	[¹² **13A.**
(a) A claimant who is the partner of a person subject to immigration control.	(a) the amount applicable in respect of the claimant only under regulation 83(a), plus any amount which may be applicable to him under regulation 83(e) or (f) plus the amount applicable to him under regulation 87(2) or (3) or, as the case may be, regulation 85;
(b) Where regulation 84 (polygamous marriages) applies and the claimant is a person— (i) who is not subject to immigration control within the meaning of section 115(9) of the Immigration and Asylum Act; or (ii) to whom section 115 of that Act does not apply by virtue of regulation 2 of the Social Security (Immigration and Asylum) Consequential Amendments Regulations 2000; and (iii) who is a member of a couple and one or more of his partners is subject to immigration control within the meaning of section 115(9) of that Act and section 115 of that Act applies to her for the purposes of exclusion from	(b) the amount determined in accordance with that regulation or regulation 85 in respect of the claimant and any partners of his who are not subject to immigration control within the meaning of section 115(9) of the Immigration and Asylum Act and to whom section 115 of that Act does not apply for the purposes of exclusion from entitlement to jobseeker's allowance;]

Column (1)	Column (2)
entitlement to income-based jobseeker's allowance.]	
Persons from abroad **14.** [⁶ person from abroad]	**14.** [⁶ . . . nil]
[⁶**Persons in residential accommodation** **15.**—(1) [¹¹ A] person in or only temporarily absent from residential accommodation who is—	**15.**—(1) Any amount applicable under regulation 87(2) and (3), plus—
(a) a single claimant;	(a) [¹⁰£77.45] of which [¹⁰£17.50] is for personal expenses;
(b) a lone parent;	(b) the amount specified in sub-paragraph (a) of [¹this] column;
(c) one of a couple;	(c) twice the amount specified in sub-paragraph (a) of this column;
(d) [¹² . . .]	(d) [¹² . . .]
(e) a member of a polygamous marriage.	(e) the amount specified in sub-paragraph (a) of this column multiplied by the number of members of the polygamous marriage in or only temporarily absent from that accommodation.
(2) [¹¹ . . .]	(2) [¹¹ . . .]
Persons temporarily absent from a hostel, residential care or nursing home **16.** [⁸ . . .]	**16.** [⁸ . . .]
Persons in residential care or nursing homes who become patients **17.** [⁸ . . .]	**17.** [⁸ . . .]
[⁷ **Joint-claim couples where a claim is made other than jointly by both members** **17A.** A joint claim couple and one member— (a) is a person to whom regulation 3E(2)(a) applies; (b) is a person to whom regulation 3E(2)(b) applies.]	[⁷ (a) The amount which would be applicable to the claimant under regulation 83 [¹⁰ . . .] if that claimant was a single claimant for the period commencing on the day on which the member of the couple who is not the claimant fails to attend at the time and place specified by the Secretary of State for the purposes of regulation 6 of the Claims and Payments Regulations and ending on the day on which that member does so attend; (b) The amount which would be applicable to the claimant under regulation 83 [¹⁰ . . .] if that claimant was a single claimant.]

Rounding of fractions

18. Where any calculation under this Schedule or as a result of a jobseeker's allowance being awarded for a period less than one complete benefit week results in a fraction of a penny that fraction shall be treated as a penny.

3.610

AMENDMENTS

3.611
1. Jobseeker's Allowance (Amendment) Regulations 1996 (SI 1996/1516), reg.20 and Sch. (October 7, 1996).

2. Jobseeker's Allowance and Income Support (General) (Amendment) Regulations 1996 (SI 1996/1517), reg.30 (October 7, 1996).

3. Social Security and Child Support (Jobseeker's Allowance) (Miscellaneous Amendments) Regulations 1996 (SI 1996/2538), reg.2(13) (October 28, 1996).

4. Child Benefit, Child Support and Social Security (Miscellaneous Amendments) Regulations 1996 (SI 1996/1803), reg.45 (April 7, 1997).

5. Social Security (Miscellaneous Amendments) Regulations 1997 (SI 1997/454), reg.2(15) (April 7, 1997).

6. Social Security (Immigration and Asylum) Consequential Amendments Regulations 2000 (SI 2000/636), reg.4 (April 3, 2000).

7. Jobseeker's Allowance (Joint Claims) Regulations 2000 (SI 2000/1978), reg.2(5) and Sch.2, para.56 (March 19, 2001).

8. Social Security Amendment (Residential Care and Nursing Homes) Regulations 2001 (SI 2001/3767), reg.2 and Sch., Pt II, para.20 (April 8, 2002).

9. Social Security Amendment (Residential Care and Nursing Homes) Regulations 2001 (SI 2001/3767), reg.2 and Sch., Pt II, para.20 (as amended by Social Security Amendment (Residential Care and Nursing Homes) Regulations 2002 (SI 2002/398), reg.4(3)) (April 8, 2002).

10. Social Security (Removal of Residential Allowance and Miscellaneous Amendments) Regulations 2003 (SI 2003/1121), reg.4 and Sch.2, para.11 (October 6, 2003).

11. Social Security (Hospital In-Patients and Miscellaneous Amendments) Regulations 2003 (SI 2003/1195), reg.6 (May 21, 2003).

12. Social Security (Working Tax Credit and Child Tax Credit) (Consequential Amendments) (SI 2003/455), reg.3 and Sch.2, para.20 (April 5, 2004, except in "transitional cases" and see further the note to reg.83 and to reg.17 of the Income Support Regulations).

13. Social Security Benefits Up-rating Order 2005 (SI 2005/522), art.24 and Sch.17 (April 11, 2005).

DEFINITIONS

3.612
"child"—see Jobseekers Act, s.35(1).
"claimant"—*ibid.*
"couple"—see reg.1(3).
"family"—see Jobseekers Act, s.35(1).
"lone parent"—see reg.1(3).
"nursing home"—*ibid.*
"partner"—*ibid.*
"patient"—see reg.85(4).
"person from abroad"—*ibid.*
"polygamous marriage"—see reg.1(3).
"prisoner"—see reg.85(4).
"relative"—see reg.1(3).
"residential accommodation"—*ibid.*
"residential care home"—*ibid.*
"single claimant"—*ibid.*
"young person"—see reg.76.

GENERAL NOTE

3.613
See the note to reg.85.

There are some differences between this Schedule and Sch.7 to the Income Support Regulations, mainly due to the different conditions of entitlement for JSA (see, *e.g.* paras 1 and 2).

[¹ SCHEDULE 5A   **Regulation 86C**

APPLICABLE AMOUNTS OF JOINT-CLAIM COUPLES IN SPECIAL CASES

Column (1)	Column (2)
Patients 1. [⁴ A] joint-claim couple where one member— (a) has been a patient for more than [⁵ 52] weeks; (b) is a member of a polygamous marriage and another member of that marriage who is not a joint-claimant has been a patient for more than [⁵ 52] weeks.	1. (a) The applicable amount under regulation 86A reduced by [⁷ £16.40]; (b) The applicable amount under regulation 86B (polygamous marriages) reduced by [⁷ £16.40] in respect of each member of the polygamous marriage who is a patient.
Joint-claim couple without accommodation 2. A joint-claim couple who are without accommodation.	2. The amount applicable to the couple under regulation 86A(a) (personal allowance) only.
Members of religious orders 3. A joint-claim couple who are both members of and fully maintained by a religious order.	3. Nil.

Specified cases of temporarily separated joint-claim couples
4. A joint-claim couple who are temporarily separated where—
(a) one member is—
  (i) not a patient but is resident in a nursing home;
  (ii) resident in a residential care home;
  (iii) resident in premises used for the rehabilitation of alcoholics or drug addicts;
  (iv) resident in accommodation provided under section 3 of, and Part II of the Schedule to, the Polish Resettlement Act 1947 (provision of accommodation in camps);
  (v) participating in arrangements for training made under section 2 of the Employment and Training Act 1973, or section 2 of the Enterprise and New Towns (Scotland) Act 1990 or participating in an employment rehabilitation programme established under that section of the Act of 1973, where the course requires him to live away from the dwelling occupied as the home; or
  (vi) in a probation or bail hostel approved for the purpose by the Secretary of State, and
	4. Either—
	(a) the amount applicable to the joint-claim couple under regulation 86A; or

3.614

1085

Column (1)	Column (2)

(b) the other member is—
   (i) living in the dwelling occupied as the home;
   (ii) a patient;
   (iii) in residential accommodation; or
   (iv) resident in a residential care home or nursing home.
	(b) the aggregate of the applicable amounts of both claimants assessed under the provisions of these Regulations as if each of them were a single claimant, whichever is the greater.

Polygamous Marriages where one or more members of the marriage are temporarily separated
5. A joint-claim couple where one member is a member of a polygamous marriage and is temporarily separated from a partner of his, where one of them is living in the home while the other member is—
  (a) not a patient but is resident in a nursing home;
  (b) resident in a residential care home;
  (c) resident in premises used for the rehabilitation of alcoholics or drug addicts;
  (d) attending a course of training or instruction provided or approved by the Secretary of State where the course requires him to live away from home; or
  (e) in a probation or bail hostel approved for the purpose by the Secretary of State.
	5. Either—
	(a) the amount applicable to the joint-claim couple under regulation 86B; or
	(b) the aggregate of the amount applicable for the joint-claim couple in respect of the members of the polygamous marriage who remain in the home under regulation 86B and the amount applicable in respect of those members not in the home calculated as if each of them were a single claimant, whichever is the greater.

Joint-claim couples and members of polygamous marriages where one member is, or all are, temporarily in local authority accommodation 6. [⁶ . . .]	6. [⁶ . . .]

Joint-claim couples where one member is absent from the United Kingdom
7. A joint-claim couple where one member is temporarily absent from the United Kingdom—
  (a) in the circumstances prescribed in regulation 50(6B);
 	
  (b) in any other circumstances.
	7.
	
	(a) The amount applicable to them as a couple under regulation 86A [² . . .] for the relevant period prescribed in regulation 50(6B).
	(b) For the first four weeks of that absence, the amount applicable to them as a couple under regulation 86A [² . . .] as the case may be and thereafter the amount applicable to the claimant in Great Britain under regulation 83 [² . . .] as the case may be as if that claimant were a single claimant.

Column (1)	Column (2)

Polygamous marriages where any member of the marriage is abroad
8. A joint-claim couple where one member is a member of a polygamous marriage and—
  (a) he, the other member or one of his partners is;
  (b) he, the other member and one or more of his partners are; or
  (c) the other member and one or more of his partners or two or more of his partners are,
temporarily absent from the United Kingdom.
	8. For the first four weeks of that absence, the amount applicable to the joint-claim couple under regulations 86B to [² 86C], as the case may be, and thereafter, if the joint-claim couple are in Great Britain the amount applicable to them under regulations 86B to [² 86C], as the case may be, as if any member of the polygamous marriage not in the United Kingdom were not a member of the marriage.

Members of joint-claim couples in residential accommodation **9.** [⁴ . . .]	**9.** [⁴ . . .]
Members of joint-claim couples temporarily absent from a hostel, residential care or nursing home **10.** [2 . . .]	**10.** [² . . .]
Members of joint-claim couples in residential care or nursing homes who become patients **11.** [² . . .]	**11.** [² . . .]

Rounding of fractions

12. Where any calculation under this Schedule or as a result of a joint-claim jobseeker's allowance being awarded for a period of less than one complete benefit week results in a fraction of a penny, that fraction shall be treated as a penny.]

3.615

AMENDMENTS

1. Jobseeker's Allowance (Joint Claims) Regulations 2000 (SI 2000/1978), reg.2(5) and Sch.2, para.57 (March 19, 2001).
2. Social Security Amendment (Residential Care and Nursing Homes) Regulations 2001 (SI 2001/3767), reg.2 and Sch., Pt II, para.21 (April 8, 2002).
3. Social Security Benefits Up-Rating Order 2003 (SI 2003/526), art.23(9) and Sch.14 (April 7, 2003).
4. Social Security (Removal of Residential Allowance and Miscellaneous Amendments) Regulations 2003 (SI 2003/1121), reg.4 and Sch.2, para.12 (October 6, 2003).
5. Social Security (Hospital In-Patients and Miscellaneous Amendments) Regulations 2003 (SI 2003/1195), reg.6 (May 21, 2003).
6. Social Security (Miscellaneous Amendments) Regulations 2004 (SI 2004/565), reg.6 (April 1, 2004).
7. Social Security Benefits Up-rating Order 2005 (SI 2005/522), art.24 and Sch.18 (April 11, 2005).

GENERAL NOTE

This regulation makes provision corresponding to Sch.5 for joint-claim couples.

3.616

Sums to be Disregarded in the Calculation of Earnings

3.617   **1.** In the case of a claimant who has been engaged in remunerative work as an employed earner or, had the employment been in Great Britain, would have been so engaged—
  (a) any earnings paid or due to be paid in respect of that employment which has terminated—
    (i) by way of retirement but only if on retirement he is entitled to a retirement pension under the Benefits Act, or would be so entitled if he satisfied the contribution conditions;
    (ii) otherwise than by retirement except earnings to which [²regulation 98(1)(b), (c), (d), (f)[³, (ff)] and (g)] applies (earnings of employed earners);
  (b) where—
    (i) the employment has not been terminated, but
    (ii) the claimant is not engaged in remunerative work,
any earnings in respect of that employment except earnings to which regulation 98(1)(c) and (d) applies; but this sub-paragraph shall not apply where the claimant has been suspended from his employment.

2. In the case of a claimant who, before the date of claim—
  (a) has been engaged in part-time employment as an employed earner or, where the employment has been outside Great Britain, would have been so engaged had the employment been in Great Britain, and
  (b) has ceased to be engaged in that employment, whether or not that employment has terminated,
any earnings in respect of that employment except earnings to which regulation 98(1)(b), (c), (d), (f)[³, (ff)] or (g) applies; but this paragraph shall not apply where the claimant has been suspended from his employment.

3. Any payment to which regulation 98(1)(f) applies—
  (a) which is due to be paid more than 52 weeks after the date of termination of the employment in respect of which the payment is made; or
  (b) which is a compensatory award within the meaning of section 72(1)(b) of the Employment Protection (Consolidation) Act 1978 for so long as such an award remains unpaid and the employer is insolvent within the meaning of section 127 of that Act.

4. In the case of a claimant who has been engaged in remunerative work or part-time employment as a self-employed earner or, had the employment been in Great Britain, would have been so engaged and who has ceased to be so employed, from the date of the cessation of his employment any earnings derived from that employment except earnings to which regulation 95(2) (royalties etc.) applies.

5.—(1) In a case to which this paragraph applies, [⁷£20.00] but notwithstanding regulation 88 (calculation of income and capital of members of claimant's family and of a polygamous marriage), if this paragraph applies to a claimant it shall not apply to his partner except where, and to the extent that, the earnings of the claimant which are to be disregarded under this paragraph are less than [⁷£20.00].

(2) This paragraph applies where the claimant's applicable amount includes, or but for his being an in-patient [⁸. . .] or in residential accommodation would include, an amount by way of a disability premium under Schedule 1 (applicable amounts).

(3) This paragraph applies where—
  (a) the claimant is a member of a couple, and—
    (i) his applicable amount would include an amount by way of the disability premium under Schedule 1 but for the higher pensioner premium under that Schedule being applicable; or
    (ii) had he not been an in-patient [⁸. . .] or in residential accommodation his applicable amount would include the higher pensioner premium under that Schedule and had that been the case he would also satisfy the condition in (i) above; and
  (b) he or his partner is under the age of 60 and at least one is engaged in part-time employment.

(4) This paragraph applies where—
  (a) the claimant's applicable amount includes, or but for his being an in-patient [⁸. . .] or in residential accommodation would include, an amount by way of the higher pensioner premium under Schedule 1; and

   (b)   the claimant or, if he is a member of a couple, either he or his partner has attained the age of 60; and

   (c)   immediately before attaining that age he or, as the case may be, he or his partner was engaged in part-time employment and the claimant was entitled by virtue of sub-paragraph (2) or (3) to a disregard of [⁷£20.00]; and

   (d)   he or, as the case may be, he or his partner has continued in part-time employment.

   (5) [⁶ . . .].

   (6) [⁶ . . .].

   (7) For the purposes of this paragraph—

   (a)   except where head (b) or (c) applies, no account shall be taken of any period not exceeding eight consecutive weeks occurring—

       (i)   on or after the date on which the claimant or, if he is a member of a couple, he or his partner attained the age of 60 during which either was or both were not engaged in part-time employment or the claimant was not entitled to a job-seeker's allowance or income support; or

      (ii)   immediately after the date on which the claimant or his partner ceased to partici-pate in arrangements for training made under section 2 of the Employment and Training Act 1973 or section 2 of the Enterprise and New Towns (Scotland) Act 1990 or to participate in an employment rehabilitation programme established under that section of the 1973 Act;

   (b)   in a case where the claimant has ceased to be entitled to a jobseeker's allowance or income support because he, or if he is a member of a couple, he or his partner becomes engaged in remunerative work, no account shall be taken of any period, during which he was not entitled to a jobseeker's allowance or income support, not exceeding the permitted period, occurring on or after the date on which the claimant or, as the case may be, his partner attained the age of 60;

   (c)   no account shall be taken of any period occurring on or after the date on which the claimant or, if he is a member of a couple, he or his partner attained the age of 60 during which the claimant was not entitled to a jobseeker's allowance or income support because he or his partner was participating in arrangements for training made under section 2 of the Employment and Training Act 1973 or section 2 of the Enterprise and New Towns (Scotland) Act 1990 or participating in an employment rehabilitation programme established under that section of the 1973 Act;

[⁵**6.** In a case where the claimant is a lone parent and paragraph 5 does not apply, [⁷£20.00].

   7.—(1) In a case to which neither paragraph 5 or 6 applies to the claimant, and subject to sub-paragraph (2), where the claimant's applicable amount includes an amount by way of the carer premium under Schedule 1 (applicable amounts), [⁷£20.00] of the earnings of the person who is, or at any time in the preceding eight weeks was, in receipt of [⁹ carer's allowance] or treated in accordance with paragraph 17(2) of that Schedule as being in receipt of [⁹ carer's allowance].

   (2) Where the carer premium is awarded in respect of the claimant and of any partner of his, their earnings shall for the purposes of this paragraph be aggregated, but the amount to be dis-regarded in accordance with sub-paragraph (1) shall not exceed [⁷£20.00] of the aggregated amount.

   8. Where the carer premium is awarded in respect of a claimant who is a member of a couple and whose earnings are less than [⁷£20.00], but is not awarded in respect of the other member of the couple, and that other member is engaged in an employment—

   (a)   specified in paragraph 9(1), so much of the other member's earnings as would not when aggregated with the amount disregarded under paragraph 7 exceed [⁷£20.00];

   (b)   other than one specified in paragraph 9(1), so much of the other member's earnings from such other employment up to £5 as would not when aggregated with the amount disregarded under paragraph 7 exceed [⁷£20.00].

   9.—(1) In a case to which none of paragraphs 5 to 8 applies to the claimant, [⁷£20.00] of earnings derived from one or more employments as—

   (a)   a part-time member of a fire brigade maintained in pursuance of the Fire Services Acts 1947 to 1959;

[¹¹ (aa)   a part-time fire-fighter employed by a fire and rescue authority;]

   (b)   an auxiliary coastguard in respect of coast rescue activities;

   (c)   a person engaged part-time in the manning or launching of a lifeboat;

   (d)   a member of any territorial or reserve force prescribed in Part I of Schedule 3 to the Social Security (Contributions) Regulations 1979;

but, notwithstanding regulation 88 (calculation of income and capital of members of claimant's family and of a polygamous marriage), if this paragraph applies to a claimant it shall not apply to his partner except to the extent specified in sub-paragraph (2).

(2) If the claimant's partner is engaged in employment—

(a) specified in sub-paragraph (1), so much of his earnings as would not in aggregate with the amount of the claimant's earnings disregarded under this paragraph exceed [⁷£20.00];

(b) other than one specified in sub-paragraph (1), so much of his earnings from that employment up to £5 as would not in aggregate with the claimant's earnings disregarded under this paragraph exceed [⁷£20.00].

10. Where the claimant is engaged in one or more employments specified in paragraph 9(1) but his earnings derived from such employments are less than [⁷£20.00] in any week and he is also engaged in any other part-time employment, so much of his earnings from that other employment up to £5 as would not in aggregate with the amount of his earnings disregarded under paragraph 9 exceed [⁷£20.00].

11. Where the claimant is a member of a couple [¹ . . .]—

(a) in a case to which none of paragraphs 5 to 10 applies, £10; but, notwithstanding regulation 88 (calculation of income and capital of members of a claimant's family and of a polygamous marriage), if this paragraph applies to a claimant it shall not apply to his partner except where, and to the extent that, the earnings of the claimant which are to be disregarded under this sub-paragraph are less than £10;

(b) in a case to which one or more of paragraphs 5 to 10 applies and the total amount disregarded under those paragraphs is less than £10, so much of the claimant's earnings as would not in aggregate with the amount disregarded under paragraphs 5 to 10 exceed £10.

12. In a case to which none of paragraphs 5 to 11 applies to the claimant, £5.

13. Notwithstanding the foregoing provisions of this Schedule, where two or more payments of the same kind and from the same source are to be taken into account in the same benefit week, because it has not been practicable to treat the payments under regulation 96(1)(b) (date on which income treated as paid) as paid on the first day of the benefit week in which they were due to be paid, there shall be disregarded from each payment the sum that would have been disregarded if the payment had been taken into account on the date on which it was due to be paid.

14. Any earnings derived from employment which are payable in a country outside the United Kingdom for such period during which there is a prohibition against the transfer to the United Kingdom of those earnings.

15. Where a payment of earnings is made in a currency other than sterling, any banking charge or commission payable in converting that payment into sterling.

16. Any earnings which are due to be paid before the date of claim and which would otherwise fall to be taken into account in the same benefit week as a payment of the same kind and from the same source.

17. Any earnings of a child or young person [¹⁰ . . .].

18. [¹⁰ . . .]

19. In the case of a claimant who—

(a) has been engaged in employment as a member of any territorial or reserve force prescribed in Part I of Schedule 3 to the Social Security (Contributions) Regulations 1979; and

(b) by reason of that employment has failed to satisfy any of the conditions of entitlement to a jobseeker's allowance, other than the condition in section 2(1)(c) (prescribed amount of earnings) or section 3(1)(a) (income not in excess of applicable amount), any earnings from that employment paid in respect of the period in which the claimant was not entitled to a jobseeker's allowance.

20. In this Schedule "part-time employment" means employment in which the person is not to be treated as engaged in remunerative work under regulation 52 or 53 (persons treated as engaged, or not engaged, in remunerative work).

21. In paragraph 5(7)(b) "permitted period" means a period determined in accordance with regulation 3A of the Income Support Regulations, as it has effect by virtue of regulation 87(7) of these Regulations.

AMENDMENTS

3.618

1. Jobseeker's Allowance (Amendment) Regulations 1996 (SI 1996/1516), reg.19 (October 7, 1996).

2. Jobseeker's Allowance (Amendment) Regulations 1996 (SI 1996/1516), reg.20 and Sch. (October 7, 1996).

3. Jobseeker's Allowance and Income Support (General) (Amendment) Regulations 1996 (SI 1996/1517), reg.31 (October 7, 1996).

4. Child Benefit, Child Support and Social Security (Miscellaneous Amendments) Regulations 1996 (SI 1996/1803), reg.46 (April 7, 1997).

5. Social Security Amendment (Lone Parents) Regulations 1998 (SI 1998/766), reg.15 (April 6, 1998).

6. Social Security (Miscellaneous Amendments) Regulations 2000 (SI 2000/681), reg.12(b) (April 3, 2000).

7. Social Security Amendment (Capital Limits and Earnings Disregards) Regulations 2000 (SI 2000/2545), reg.3 and Sch., para.3 (April 9, 2001).

8. Social Security Amendment (Residential Care and Nursing Homes) Regulations 2001 (SI 2001/3767), reg.2(2) and Pt II of Sch., para.22 (April 8, 2002).

9. Social Security (Miscellaneous Amendments) Regulations 2003 (SI 2003/511), reg.3(4) and (5) (April 1, 2003).

10. Social Security (Working Tax Credit and Child Tax Credit) (Consequential Amendments) Regulations 2003 (SI 2003/455), reg.3 and Sch.2, para.22 (April 6, 2004, except in "transitional cases" and see further the note to reg.83 and to reg.17 of the Income Support Regulations).

11. Fire and Rescue Services Act 2004 (Consequential Amendments) (England) Order 2004 (SI 2004/3168), art. 36(4) (December 30, 2004).

DEFINITIONS

"the Benefits Act"—see Jobseekers Act, s.35(1).
"benefit week"—see reg.1(3)
"child"—see Jobseekers Act, s.35(1)
"claimant"—*ibid.*, reg.88(1).
"couple"—see reg.1(3).
"date of claim"—*ibid.*
"employment"—see reg.3
"employed earner"—see reg.3, SSCBA, s.2(1)(a).
"Great Britain"—see Jobseekers Act, s.35(1).
"family"—*ibid.*
"nursing home"—see reg.1(3).
"partner"—*ibid.*
"polygamous marriage"—*ibid.*
"remunerative work"—*ibid*, reg.51(1).
"residential accommodation"—see reg.1(3).
"residential care home"—*ibid.*
"self employed earner"—*ibid.*, SSCSA, s.2(1)(b).
"young person"—*ibid.*, reg.76

GENERAL NOTE

Before April 6, 2004 the income (but not the capital) of a child or young person who was a member of the claimant's family was aggregated with the claimant's, subject to the modifications in reg.106. Under the form of this Schedule in force at that time paras 1 to 13 and 19 did not apply to children or young persons (see the form of reg.88(2) then in force) and paras 17 and 18 only applied to children and young persons (see the 2003 edition of this volume for the old form of reg.88 and of paras 17 and 18 of this Schedule). However, with effect from April 6, 2004 (except in "transitional cases"—see the note to reg.83 and to reg.17 of the Income Support Regulations), amounts for children and young persons have been removed from income-based JSA; financial assistance to help with the cost of bringing up a child or young person is now to be provided through the child tax credit system, see Vol. IV of this series. As a consequence, the income of a child or young person is no longer aggregated with the claimant's (see the new form of reg.88 and the notes to that regulation) and so the disregards that applied to such income are no longer needed (although note that part of para.17 has been retained). The former disregards do

3.619

however remain in force for "transitional cases"—see the note to reg.83 and to reg.17 of the Income Support Regulations.

For income-based JSA claimants who had an award of child tax credit before April 6, 2004 see reg.8 of the Social Security (Working Tax Credit and Child Tax Credit) (Consequential Amendments) Regulations 2003 (SI 2003/455) (as amended) on p.687 and the notes to that regulation.

The disregards in this Schedule are similar to those in Sch.8 to the Income Support Regulations but there are some differences, the main ones being the treatment of earnings where part-time employment has stopped (para.2) and the new disregard in para.3. See the notes to Sch.8.

Note that where the claimant is a member of a couple, unless the £20 disregard in paras 5 to 10 applies (para.6 cannot in fact apply as it only applies to lone parents) the earnings disregard is £10 (para.11). Since October 7, 1996 this has also been the case for income support (replacing the previous £15 earnings disregard for long-term unemployed couples aged less than 60). For a single claimant the earnings disregard is £5 (unless the £20 disregard in paras 5 to 10 applies) (para.12).

Para.1

3.620   As with income support the disregard in para.1 is crucial to entitlement following the termination of remunerative work. The effect of sub-para.(a)(ii) is that final payments of wages are disregarded. This means that entitlement can begin immediately, unless a compensation payment is made (reg.98(1)(b)) or holiday pay (reg.98(1)(c)) is due. If either of these payments are made, reg.52(3) treats the claimant as in remunerative work for the number of weeks covered by the payments (reg.94(2) and (6) to (9)). Note the other earnings that are not disregarded under sub-para.(a)(ii) and see the notes to para.1 of Sch.8.

Para.2

3.621   See the notes to para.2 of Sch.8 to the Income Support Regulations and see *CJSA 2867/1999*. Under JSA the disregard is not more extensive where the claimant's part-time work (defined in para.20) has stopped before the claim. The same disregard applies as in the case of termination of full-time employment under para.1(a)(ii) (but in the case of part-time work it is not necessary for the employment to have ended). Para.2 does not apply if the claimant has been suspended. If the part-time work ends while the claimant is claiming JSA, payments will be taken into account as earnings in the usual way.

In *CJSA 1772/2002* the claimant, a supply teacher who worked part-time, claimed JSA at the beginning of the school summer holidays. The Commissioner accepts that unless it could be shown that the claimant had a cycle of work she had ceased to be engaged in employment at the time of her claim for JSA and so her earnings fell to be disregarded under para.2. Since she worked odd days with a number of schools on an irregular basis a cycle of work could not be established. See also *CIS 914/1997* and *CJSA 2759/1998* in the note to reg.5 of the Income Support Regulations under the heading "*Term-time only workers*" for other examples of circumstances in which a cycle of work had not, or had not yet, been established.

But when a part-time worker does have a recognisable cycle of work, *R(JSA) 2/03* holds that she is to be treated as engaged in part-time work for the whole of the cycle. The Commissioner considered that it would be odd if "engaged in . . . employment" had a different meaning in para.2 from the meaning in para.1 and that although para.20 (definition of "part-time work") was not well-drafted, the reference to reg.52 in his view made it plain that a person was to be regarded as engaged in part-time work in circumstances where she would be engaged in remunerative work if a greater number of hours per week were worked. [Note that in *R(JSA) 2/03* the Commissioner held that the claimant was to be regarded as engaged in part-time employment during the whole of the cycle by virtue of reg.51(2)(c) in accordance with the House of Lords' decision in *Banks v Chief Adjudication Officer* [2001] UKHL 33 (reported as *R(IS) 15/01*). In relation to JSA (although not income support) *R(JSA) 4/03* has since held that reg.51(2)(c) is inconsistent with Directive 79/7/EEC and should be regarded as being of no effect (see the note to reg.51). The consequence is that reg.51(2)(b)(i) applies instead (see *R(JSA) 5/03* in the note to reg.51). However, this does not affect the reasoning in *R(JSA) 2/03* that a part-time worker with a recognisable cycle of work is to be regarded as engaged in employment during the whole of the cycle.] Thus the disregard in para.2 did not apply because the claimant had not ceased to be engaged in part-time employment. The claimant in *R(JSA) 2/03* was paid monthly for a 12 hour working week during term-time only. She had claimed contribution-based JSA and therefore the question was whether any of her earnings fell to be deducted under s.4(1)(b) of the Jobseekers Act (under s.2(1)(c) it is also a condition that the claimant should "not have earnings in excess of the prescribed amount"; the Commissioner did not find it necessary to decide this point in view of his decision on the attribution of her earnings for the purposes of s.4(1)(b) but he did point out that there appeared to be no statutory provision attributing earnings to any particular period for the purposes of s.2(1)(c)). The Commissioner holds, under reg.80(1) and applying *R(IS) 10/95*, that her earnings were paid "in respect of a month" and that under reg.94(2)(a) they were to be taken into account for the period of a month beginning with the first day of the benefit week in which the earnings were due to be paid. The result was that the claimant was not entitled to JSA during the half-term holiday as her earnings exceeded her JSA applicable amount.

Para. 3

Under JSA, any payment for compensation for unfair dismissal under ss.68(2), 69, 71(2)(a), 77 or 79 of the Employment Protection (Consolidation) Act 1978 (the references need to be updated to the Employment Rights Act 1996) is disregarded if it is due to be paid more than 52 weeks after the end of the employment to which it relates (sub-para.(a)). In addition, any unpaid compensatory award under s.72(1)(b) of the 1978 Act where the employer is insolvent is also disregarded (sub-para.(b)).   **3.622**

Para. 20

See *R(JSA) 2/03* in the note to para.2 above.

[¹ SCHEDULE 6A

SUMS TO BE DISREGARDED IN THE CALCULATION OF EARNINGS OF MEMBERS OF JOINT-CLAIM COUPLES

1.—(1) In a case to which this paragraph applies, [² £20]; but notwithstanding regulation 88ZA (calculation of income and capital of members of a joint-claim couple), if this paragraph applies to one member of a joint-claim couple, it shall not apply to the other member except where, and to the extent that, the earnings of the member which are to be disregarded under this paragraph are less than [² £20].   **3.623**

(2) This paragraph applies where the joint-claim couple's applicable amount includes, or but for one member being an in-patient [³ . . .] or in residential accommodation would include, an amount by way of a disability premium under Schedule 1 (applicable amounts).

(3) This paragraph applies where—
  (a) the joint-claim couple's applicable amount would include—
    (i) an amount by way of the disability premium under Schedule 1 but for the higher pensioner premium under that Schedule being applicable; or
    (ii) had a member of that couple not been an in-patient [³ . . .] or in residential accommodation, the higher pensioner premium under that Schedule and had that been the case, the joint-claim couple would also satisfy the condition in (i) above; and
  (b) either member is under the age of 60 and at least one is engaged in part-time employment.

(4) This paragraph applies where—
  (a) the joint-claim couple's applicable amount includes, or but for a member being an inpatient [³ . . .] or in residential accommodation would include, an amount by way of the higher pensioner premium under Schedule 1; and

(b) either member has attained the age of 60; and

(c) immediately before attaining that age either, or as the case may be both, members were engaged in part-time employment and the joint-claimant was entitled by virtue of sub-paragraph (2) or (3) to a disregard of [2 £20]; and

(d) either, or as the case may be both, members have continued in part-time employment.

(5) For the purposes of this paragraph—

(a) except where paragraph (b) or (c) applies, no account shall be taken of any period not exceeding eight consecutive weeks occurring—

    (i) on or after the date on which either member attained the age of 60 during which either member was, or both members were, not engaged in part-time employment or either member was, or both members were, not entitled to a jobseeker's allowance or income support; or

    (ii) immediately after the date on which either member ceased to participate in arrangements for training made under section 2 of the Employment and Training Act 1973 or section 2 of the Enterprise and New Towns (Scotland) Act 1990 or ceased to participate in an employment rehabilitation programme established under that section of the 1973 Act;

(b) in a case where either or both members have ceased to be entitled to a jobseeker's allowance or income support because either member becomes engaged in remunerative work, no account shall be taken of any period during which either or both members were not entitled to a jobseeker's allowance or income support, not exceeding the permitted period, occurring on or after the date on which either member attained the age of 60;

(c) no account shall be taken of any period occurring on or after the date on which either member attained the age of 60 during which either or both members were not entitled to a jobseeker's allowance or income support because either or both members were participating in arrangements for training made under section 2 of the Employment and Training Act 1973 or section 2 of the Enterprise and New Towns (Scotland) Act 1990 or participating in an employment rehabilitation programme established under that section of the 1973 Act.

2.—(1) In a case where paragraph 1 does not apply to a member of a joint-claim couple and subject to sub-paragraph (2), where the joint-claim couple's applicable amount includes an amount by way of the carer premium under Schedule 1 (applicable amounts), [2£20] of the earnings of the person who is, or at any time in the preceding eight weeks was, in receipt of [4 a carer's allowance] or treated in accordance with paragraph 20J(2) of that Schedule as being in receipt of [4 a carer's allowance].

(2) Where the carer premium is awarded in respect of a joint-claim couple, the earnings of each member shall for the purposes of this paragraph be aggregated but the amount to be disregarded in accordance with sub-paragraph (1) shall not exceed [2 £20] of the aggregated amount.

3.—(1) In the case to which neither paragraph 1 nor 2 applies to a member of a joint-claim couple ("the first member"), [2 £20] of earnings derived from one or more employments to which paragraph 9 of Schedule 6 applies but, notwithstanding regulation 88ZA (calculation of income and capital of a joint-claim couple), if this paragraph applies to one member of a joint-claim couple it shall not apply to the other member except to the extent specified in sub-paragraph (2).

(2) If the other member is engaged in employment—

(a) specified in sub-paragraph (1), so much of his earnings as would not in aggregate with the amount of the first member's earnings disregarded under this paragraph exceed [2 £20];

(b) other than one specified in sub-paragraph (1), so much of his earnings from that employment up to £5 as would not in aggregate with the first member's earnings disregarded under this paragraph exceed [2 £20] .

4. Where a member of a joint-claim couple is engaged in one or more employments specified in paragraph 3(1) but his earnings derived from such employments are less than [2 £20] in any week and he is also engaged in any other part-time employment, so much of his earnings from that other employment up to £5 as would not in aggregate with the amount of his earnings disregarded under paragraph 3 exceed [2 £20].

5. In the case of a member of a joint-claim couple who—

(a) has been engaged in employment as a member of any territorial or reserve force prescribed in Part 1 of Schedule 3 to the Social Security (Contributions) Regulations 1979; and

(b) by reason of that employment, the joint-claim couple have failed to satisfy any of the conditions of entitlement to a joint-claim jobseeker's allowance, other than the condition in section 3A(1)(a) (income not in excess of applicable amount), any earnings from that employment paid in respect of the period in which the joint-claim couple were not entitled to a joint-claim jobseeker's allowance.

6.—(1) In a case where none of paragraphs 1 to 5 apply, £10 but, notwithstanding regulation 88ZA (calculation of income and capital of joint-claim couples), if this paragraph applies to one member of a joint-claim couple, it shall not apply to the other member except where, and to the extent that, the earnings of the member which are to be disregarded under this sub-paragraph are less than £10.

(2) In a case where one or more of paragraphs 1 to 5 apply and the total amount disregarded under those paragraphs is less than £10, so much of the earnings of the member of a joint-claim couple as would not in aggregate with the amount disregarded under paragraphs 1 to 5 exceed £10.

7. In this Schedule, "part-time employment" and "permitted period" shall bear the meanings prescribed respectively in paragraphs 20 and 21 of Schedule 6.]

AMENDMENTS

1. Jobseeker's Allowance (Joint Claims) Regulations 2000 (SI 2000/1978), reg.2(5) and Sch.2, para.58 (March 19, 2001).   **3.624**
2. Social Security Amendment (Capital Limits and Earnings Disregards) Regulations 2000 (SI 2000/2545), reg.3 and Sch., para.3 (April 9, 2001).
3. Social Security Amendment (Residential Care and Nursing Homes) Regulations 2001 (SI 2001/3767), reg.2(2) and Pt II of Sch., para.23 (April 8, 2002).
4. Social Security (Miscellaneous Amendments) Regulations 2003 (SI 2003/511), reg.3(4) and (5) (April 1, 2003).

DEFINITIONS

"employment"—see reg.3.
"joint-claim couple"—see JSA, s.1(4).
"joint-claim jobseeker's allowance"—*ibid.*
"nursing home"—see reg.1(3).
"remunerative work"—*ibid.*, reg.51(1).
"residential accommodation"—see reg.1(3).
"residential care home"—*ibid.*

SCHEDULE 7   **Regulation 103(2)**

SUMS TO BE DISREGARDED IN THE CALCULATION OF INCOME OTHER THAN EARNINGS   **3.625**

1. Any amount paid by way of tax on income which is taken into account under regulation 103 (calculation of income other than earnings).

2. Any payment in respect of any expenses incurred [27, or to be incurred,] by a claimant who is—

(a) by a charitable or voluntary organisation; or

(b) a volunteer,

if he otherwise derives no remuneration or profit from the employment and is not to be treated as possessing any earnings under regulation 105(13) (notional income).

3. In the case of employment as an employed earner, any payment in respect of expenses wholly, exclusively and necessarily incurred in the performance of the duties of the employment.

4. In the case of a payment of [36 statutory paternity pay by virtue of Part 12ZA of the Benefits Act, statutory adoption pay by virtue of Part 12ZB of the Benefits Act,] statutory sick pay or statutory maternity pay or any remuneration paid by or on behalf of an employer to the claimant who for the time being is unable to work due to illness or maternity [36 or who is taking paternity leave or adoption leave]—

(a) any amount deducted by way of primary Class 1 contributions under the Benefits Act;

(b) one-half of any sum paid by the claimant by way of a contribution towards an occupational or personal pension scheme.

5. In the case of the payment of statutory sick pay or statutory maternity pay under Parts XI or XII of the Social Security Contributions and Benefits (Northern Ireland) Act 1992 [36, or a payment under any enactment having effect in Northern Ireland corresponding to a payment of statutory paternity pay or statutory adoption pay]—

    (a) any amount deducted by way of primary Class 1 contributions under that Act;

    (b) one-half of any sum paid by way of a contribution towards an occupational or personal pension scheme.

6. Any housing benefit [[51] to which the claimant is entitled].

[[38] **6A.**—(1) Any guardian's allowance.]

[[43] **6B.**—(1) Any child tax credit.

    (2) Any child benefit.]

7. The mobility component of disability living allowance, or any mobility allowance accrued under the repealed section 37A of the Social Security Act 1975.

8. Any concessionary payment made to compensate for the non-payment of—

    (a) any payment specified in paragraph 7 or 10;

    (b) a jobseeker's allowance or income support.

9. Any mobility supplement or any payment intended to compensate for the non-payment of such a supplement.

10. Any attendance allowance or the care component of disability living allowance [[29] . . .].

11. Any payment to the claimant as holder of the Victoria Cross or George Cross or any analogous payment.

[[46] **12.**—(1) Any payment—

    (a) by way of an education maintenance allowance made pursuant to—

        (i) regulations made under section 518 of the Education Act 1996;

        (ii) regulations made under section 49 or 73(f) of the Education (Scotland) Act 1980;

        (iii) directions made under sections 12(2)(c) and 21 of the Further and Higher Education (Scotland) Act 1992; or

    (b) corresponding to such an education maintenance allowance, made pursuant to—

        (i) section 14 or section 181 of the Education Act 2002; or

        (ii) regulations made under section 181 of that Act.

(2) Any payment, other than a payment to which sub-paragraph (1) applies, made pursuant to—

    (a) regulations made under section 518 of the Education Act 1996;

    (b) regulations made under section 49 of the Education (Scotland) Act 1980; or

    (c) directions made under sections 12(2)(c) and 21 of the Further and Higher Education (Scotland) Act 1992,

in respect of a course of study attended by a child or a young person or a person who is in receipt of an education maintenance allowance made pursuant to any provision specified in sub-paragraph (1).]

[[33] **12A.** Any payment made to the claimant by way of repayment under regulation 11(2) of the Education (Teacher Student Loans) (Repayment, etc.) Regulations 2002.]

13. In the case of a claimant to whom regulation 11 (part-time students) applies, any sums intended for any expenditure specified in paragraph (2) of regulation 131 (calculation of grant income) necessary as a result of his attendance on his course.

[[42] **14.**—(1) Any payment made pursuant to section 2 of the Employment and Training Act 1973 or section 2 of the Enterprise and New Towns (Scotland) Act 1990 except a payment—

    (a) made as a substitute for income support, a jobseeker's allowance, incapacity benefit or severe disablement allowance;

    (b) of an allowance referred to in section 2(3) of the Employment and Training Act 1973 or section 2(5) of the Enterprise and New Towns (Scotland) Act 1990;

    (c) intended to meet the cost of living expenses which relate to any one or more of the items specified in sub-paragraph (2) whilst a claimant is participating in an education, training or other scheme to help him enhance his employment prospects unless the payment is a Career Development Loan paid pursuant to section 2 of the Employment and Training Act 1973 and the period of education or training or the scheme, which is supported by that loan, has been completed; or

    (d) made in respect of the cost of living away from home to the extent that the payment relates to rent for which housing benefit is payable in respect of accommodation which is not normally occupied by the claimant as his home.

(2) The items specified in this sub-paragraph for the purposes of sub-paragraph (1)(c) are food, ordinary clothing or footwear, household fuel, rent for which housing benefit is payable, or any housing costs to the extent that they are met under regulation 83(f) or 84(1)(g) (housing costs), of the claimant or, where the claimant is a member of a family, any other member of his family, or any council tax or water charges for which that claimant or member is liable.

(3) For the purposes of this paragraph, "ordinary clothing or footwear" means clothing or footwear for normal daily use, but does not include school uniforms, or clothing or footwear used solely for sporting activities.]

15.—(1) Subject to sub-paragraph (3) and paragraphs 38, 39 and 41, £20 of any [³⁴ relevant payment] made or due to be made at regular intervals, except any payment to which sub-paragraph (2) or paragraph 16 applies.

(2) Subject to [²⁹ sub-paragraph (3)] and paragraph 41, any [³⁴ relevant payment] made or due to be made at regular intervals which is intended and used for an item other than food, ordinary clothing or footwear, household fuel, [⁴⁷ council tax, water charges,] rent for which [²⁹ housing benefit is payable or] any housing costs to the extent that they are met under regulation 83(f) or 84(1)(g) (housing costs) [²⁹. . .], of a single claimant or, as the case may be, of the claimant or any other member of his family [⁴⁷ . . .].

(3) Sub-paragraphs (1) and (2) shall not apply—

    (a) to a payment which is made by a person for the maintenance of any member of his family or of his former partner or of his children;

    (b) to a payment made—

        (i) to a person who is, or would be, prevented from being entitled to a jobseeker's allowance by section 14 (trade disputes); or

        (ii) to a member of the family of such a person where the payment is made by virtue of that person's involvement in the trade dispute.

(4) For the purposes of sub-paragraph (1) where a number of [³⁴ relevant payments] fall to be taken into account in any one week they shall be treated as though they were one such payment.

(5) For the purposes of sub-paragraph (2) the expression "ordinary clothing or footwear" means clothing or footwear for normal daily use, but does not include school uniforms, or clothing or footwear used solely for sporting activities.

[³⁴ (5A) In this paragraph, "relevant payment" means—

    (a) a charitable payment;

    (b) a voluntary payment;

    (c) a payment (not falling within sub-paragraph (a) or (b) above) from a trust whose funds are derived from a payment made in consequence of any personal injury to the claimant;

    (d) a payment under an annuity purchased—

        (i) pursuant to any agreement or court order to make payments to the claimant; or

        (ii) from funds derived from a payment made,

    in consequence of any personal injury to the claimant; or

    (e) a payment (not falling within sub-paragraphs (a) to (d) above) received by virtue of any agreement or court order to make payments to the claimant in consequence of any personal injury to the claimant.]

(6) [²⁹ . . .].

16.—(1) Subject to the following provisions of this paragraph, in the case of a claimant placed in a residential care home or nursing home by a local authority under section 26 of the National Assistance Act 1948, sections 13A, 13B and 59(2)(c) of the Social Work (Scotland) Act 1968 or section 7 of the Mental Health (Scotland) Act 1984 any charitable payment or voluntary payment made or due to be made at regular intervals.

(2) This paragraph shall apply only where—

    (a) the claimant was placed in the residential care or nursing home by the local authority because the home was the preferred choice of the claimant, and

    (b) the cost of the accommodation was in excess of what the authority would normally expect to pay having regard to the needs of the claimant assessed in accordance with section 47 of the National Health Service and Community Care Act 1990.

(3) [²⁹. . .].

(4) The amount to be disregarded under sub-paragraph (1) shall not exceed the difference between the actual cost of the accommodation provided by the local authority and the cost the authority would normally incur for a person with the particular needs of the claimant.

[²**16A.** [²⁹ . . .].]

17. Subject to paragraphs 38 and 39, £10 of any of the following, namely—

    (a) a war disablement pension or war widow's [³¹ or widower's] pension or a payment made to compensate for the non-payment of such a pension, except in so far as such a pension or payment falls to be disregarded under paragraphs 9 or 10;

[⁵⁰(aa) a guaranteed income payment or a payment made to compensate for the non-payment of a guaranteed income payment;]

   (b) a pension paid by the government of a country outside Great Britain which is either—
       (i) analogous to a war disablement pension; or
      (ii) analogous to a war widow's [[31] or widower's]] pension;
    [[50] (iii) or analogous to a guaranteed income payment;]
   (c) a pension paid under any special provision made by the law of the Federal Republic of Germany or any part of it or of the Republic of Austria, to victims of National Socialist persecution.
  [[23](d) any widowed mother's allowance paid pursuant to section 37 of the Benefits Act;
   (e) any widowed mother's allowance paid pursuant to section 39A of the Benefits Act.]

18. Where a claimant receives income under an annuity purchased with a loan which satisfies the following conditions—

   (a) that the loan was made as part of a scheme under which not less than 90 per cent. of the proceeds of the loan were applied to the purchase by the person to whom it was made of an annuity ending with his life or with the life of the survivor of two or more persons (in this paragraph referred to as "the annuitants") who include the person to whom the loan was made;

   (b) that the interest on the loan is payable by the person to whom it was made or by one of the annuitants;

   (c) that at the time the loan was made the person to whom it was made or each of the annuitants had attained the age of 65;

   (d) that the loan was secured on a dwelling in Great Britain and the person to whom the loan was made or one of the annuitants owns an estate or interest in that dwelling; and

   (e) that the person to whom the loan was made or one of the annuitants occupies the accommodation on which it was secured as his home at the time the interest is paid,

the amount, calculated on a weekly basis equal to—

      (i) where, or in so far as, section 369 of the Income and Corporation Taxes Act 1988 (mortgage interest payable under deduction of tax) applies to the payments of interest on the loan, the interest which is payable after deduction of a sum equal to income tax on such payments at the applicable percentage of income tax within the meaning of section 369(1A) of that Act;

     (ii) in any other case the interest which is payable on the loan without deduction of such a sum.

19. Any payment made to the claimant by a person who normally resides with the claimant, which is a contribution towards that person's living and accommodation costs, except where that person is residing with the claimant in circumstances to which paragraph 20 or 21 refers.

20. Where the claimant occupies a dwelling as his home and the dwelling is also occupied by another person and there is a contractual liability to make payments to the claimant in respect of the occupation of the dwelling by that person or a member of his family—

   (a) £4 of the aggregate of any payments made in respect of any one week in respect of the occupation of the dwelling by that person or a member of his family, or by that person and a member of his family; and

   (b) a further [[52] £10.55], where the aggregate of any such payments is inclusive of an amount for heating.

21. Where the claimant occupies a dwelling as his home and he provides in that dwelling board and lodging accommodation, an amount, in respect of each person for whom such accommodation is provided for the whole or any part of a week, equal to—

   (a) where the aggregate of any payments made in respect of any one week in respect of such accommodation provided to such person does not exceed £20, 100% of such payments; or

   (b) where the aggregate of any such payments exceeds £20, £20 and 50% of the excess over £20.

22.—(1) [[19] Subject to sub-paragraphs (2) and (3)], except where [[19] regulation 103(6)(b) (provision of support under section 95 or 98 of the Immigration and Asylum Act including support provided by virtue of regulations made under Schedule 9 to that Act in the calculation of income other than earnings) or] regulation 105(10)(a)(i) (notional income) applies or in the case of a payment made—

   (a) to a person who is, or would be, prevented from being entitled to a jobseeker's allowance by section 14 (trade disputes); or

   (b) to a member of the family of such a person where the payment is made by virtue of that person's involvement in the trade dispute,

any income in kind.

(2) The exceptions under sub-paragraph (1) shall not apply where the income in kind is received from the Macfarlane Trust, the Macfarlane (Special Payments) Trust, the Macfarlane (Special Payments) (No.2) Trust, the Fund, the Eileen Trust or the Independent Living Funds.

[¹⁹ (3) The first exception under sub-paragraph (1) shall not apply where the claimant is the partner of a person subject to immigration control and whose partner is receiving support provided under section 95 or 98 of the Immigration and Asylum Act including support provided by virtue of regulations made under Schedule 9 to that Act and the income in kind is support provided in respect of essential living needs of the partner of the claimant and his dependants (if any) as is specified in regulations made under paragraph 3 of Schedule 8 to the Immigration and Asylum Act.]

23.—(1) Any income derived from capital to which the claimant is, or is treated under regulation 115 (capital jointly held) as, beneficially entitled but, subject to sub-paragraph (2), not income [¹ derived] from capital disregarded under paragraph 1, 2, 4 to 8, 11 or 17 of Schedule 8.

(2) Income derived from capital disregarded under paragraph 2 or 4 to 8 of Schedule 8 but only to the extent of—

    (a) any mortgage repayments made in respect of the dwelling or premises in the period during which that income accrued; or

    (b) any council tax or water charges which the claimant is liable to pay in respect of the dwelling or premises and which are paid in the period during which that income accrued.

(3) The definition of "water charges" in regulation 1(3) shall apply to sub-paragraph (2) with the omission of the words "in so far as such charges are in respect of the dwelling which a person occupies as his home".

24. Any income which is payable in a country outside the United Kingdom for such period during which there is prohibition against the transfer to the United Kingdom of that income.

25. Where a payment of income is made in a currency other than sterling, any banking charge or commission payable in converting that payment into sterling.

26.—(1) Any payment made to the claimant in respect of a child or young person who is a member of his family—

    (a) in accordance with regulations made pursuant to section 57A of the Adoption Act 1976 (permitted allowances) [³⁹ or paragraph 3 of Schedule 4 to the Adoption and Children Act 2002] or with a scheme approved by the Secretary of State under section 51 of the Adoption (Scotland) Act 1978 (schemes for payment of allowances to adopters);

    (b) which is a payment made by a local authority in pursuance of section 50 of the Children Act 1975 (contributions to a custodian towards the cost of the accommodation and maintenance of a child);

    (c) which is a payment made by a local authority in pursuance of section 15(1) of, and paragraph 15 of Schedule 1 to, the Children Act 1989 (local authority contribution to a child's maintenance where the child is living with a person as a result of a residence order);

    [⁷ (d) which is a payment made by an authority, as defined in Article 2 of the Children Order, in pursuance of Article 15 of, and paragraph 17 of Schedule 1 to, that Order (contribution by an authority to child's maintenance);]

    [⁴⁹ (e) in accordance with regulations made pursuant to section 14F of the Children Act 1989 (special guardianship support services);]

[⁴³ . . .]

[³⁹ (1A) Any payment, other than a payment to which sub-paragraph (1)(a) applies, made to the claimant in accordance with regulations made under paragraph 3 of Schedule 4 to the Adoption and Children Act 2002.]

    (2) [⁴³ . . .]

[⁴³ **26A.** In the case of a claimant who has a child or young person—

    (a) who is a member of his family, and

    (b) who is residing at an educational establishment at which he is receiving relevant education,

any payment made to that educational establishment, in respect of that child or young person's maintenance by or on behalf of a person who is not a member of the family or by a member of the family out of funds contributed for that purpose by a person who is not a member of the family.]

27. Any payment made by a local authority to the claimant with whom a person is accommodated by virtue of arrangements made under section 23(2)(a) of the Children Act 1989 (provision of accommodation and maintenance for a child whom they are looking after) or, as the case may be, [⁴⁴ section 26 of the Children (Scotland) Act 1995] or by a voluntary organisation under section 59(1)(a) of the 1989 Act (provision of accommodation by voluntary organisations) or by a care authority under regulation 9 of the Boarding Out and Fostering of Children (Scotland) Regulations 1985 (provision of accommodation and maintenance for children in care).

28. [⁸Any payment made to the claimant or his partner for a person ("the person concerned"), who is not normally a member of the claimant's household but is temporarily in his care, by—

    (a) a health authority;

    (b) a local authority [⁵¹ but excluding payments of housing benefit made in respect of the person concerned];

    (c) a voluntary organisation; or

    (d) the person concerned pursuant to section 26(3A) of the National Assistance Act 1948 [²⁴ or.

    (e) a primary care trust established under section 16A of the National Health Service Act 1977].]

29. Except in the case of a person who is, or would be, prevented from being entitled to a jobseeker's allowance by section 14 (trade disputes), any payment made by a local authority in accordance with [²⁸ section 17, 23B, 23C or 24A of the Children Act 1989] or, as the case may be, [⁴⁵ section 12 of the Social Work (Scotland) Act 1968 or sections 29 or 30 of the Children (Scotland) Act 1995] (local authorities' duty to promote welfare of children and powers to grant financial assistance to persons in, or formerly in, their care).

30.—(1) Subject to sub-paragraph (2), any payment received under an insurance policy, taken out to insure against the risk of being unable to maintain repayments on a loan which qualifies under paragraph 14 or 15 of Schedule 2 (housing costs in respect of loans to acquire an interest in the dwelling, or for repairs and improvements to the dwelling, occupied as the home) and used to meet such repayments, to the extent that it does not exceed the aggregate of—

    (a) the amount, calculated on a weekly basis, of any interest on that loan which is in excess of the amount met in accordance with Schedule 2 (housing costs);

    (b) the amount of any payment, calculated on a weekly basis, due on the loan attributable to the repayment of capital; and

    (c) any amount due by way of premiums on—

        (i) that policy, or

        (ii) an insurance policy taken out to insure against loss or damage to any building or part of a building which is occupied by the claimant as his home.

(2) This paragraph shall not apply to any payment which is treated as possessed by the claimant by virtue of regulation 105(10)(a)(ii) (notional income).

31.—(1) Except where paragraph 30 [¹⁰or 31A] applies, and subject to sub-paragraph (2), any payment made to the claimant which is intended to be used and is used as a contribution towards—

    (a) any payment due on a loan if secured on the dwelling occupied as the home which does not qualify under Schedule 2 (housing costs);

    (b) any interest payment or charge which qualifies in accordance with paragraphs 14 to 16 of Schedule 2 to the extent that the payment or charge is not met;

    (c) any payment due on a loan which qualifies under paragraph 14 or 15 of Schedule 2 attributable to the payment of capital;

    (d) any amount due by way of premiums on—

        (i) an insurance policy taken out to insure against the risk of being unable to make the payments referred to in (a) to (c) above, or

        (ii) an insurance policy taken out to insure against loss or damage to any building or part of a building which is occupied by the claimant as his home;

    (e) his rent in respect of the dwelling occupied by him as his home but only to the extent that it is not met by housing benefit; or his accommodation charge but only to the extent that the actual charge [²⁹ exceeds] the amount payable by a local authority in accordance with Part III of the National Assistance Act 1948.

(2) This paragraph shall not apply to any payment which is treated as possessed by the claimant by virtue of regulation 105(10)(a)(ii) (notional income).

[¹⁰**31A.**—(1) Subject to sub-paragraph (2), any payment received under an insurance policy, other than an insurance policy referred to in paragraph 30, taken out to insure against the risk of being unable to maintain repayments under a regulated agreement as defined for the purposes of the Consumer Credit Act 1974 or under a hire-purchase agreement or a conditional sale agreement as defined for the purposes of Part III of the Hire-Purchase Act 1964.

(2) A payment referred to in sub-paragraph (1) shall only be disregarded to the extent that the payment received under that policy does not exceed the amounts, calculated on a weekly basis, which are used to—

(a) maintain the repayment referred to in sub-paragraph (1); and

(b) meet any amount due by way of premiums on that policy.]

32.—(1) Subject to sub-paragraphs (2) and (3), in the case of a claimant in a residential care home or nursing home, any payment, whether or not the payment is charitable or voluntary but not a payment to which paragraph 16 applies, made to the claimant which is intended to be used and is used to meet the cost of maintaining the claimant in that home.

(2) This paragraph shall not apply to a claimant for whom accommodation in a residential care home or nursing home is provided by a local authority under section 26 of the National Assistance Act 1948 or section 59 of the Social Work (Scotland) Act 1968 [²⁹ . . .].

(3) The amount to be disregarded under this paragraph shall not exceed the difference between—

[²⁹(a) the claimant's applicable amount; and]

(b) the weekly charge for the accommodation.

33. Any social fund payment made pursuant to Part VIII of the Benefits Act.

34. Any payment of income which under regulation 110 (income treated as capital) is in to be treated as capital.

35. Any payment under Part X of the Benefits Act (pensioner's Christmas bonus).

36. In the case of a person who is, or would be, prevented from being entitled to a jobseeker's allowance by section 14 (trade disputes), any payment up to the amount of the prescribed sum within the meaning of section 15(2)(d) made by a trade union.

37. Any payment which is due to be paid before the date of claim which would otherwise fall to be taken into account in the same benefit week as a payment of the same kind and from the same source.

38. The total of a claimant's income or, if he is a member of a family, the family's income and the income of any person which he is treated as possessing under regulation 88(4) (calculation of income and capital of members of claimant's family and of a polygamous marriage) to be disregarded under regulations 132(2)(b) and 133(1)(c) (calculation of covenant income where a contribution assessed), regulation 136(2) (treatment of student loans) [²¹, regulation 136A(3) (treatment of payments from access funds)] and paragraphs 15(1) and 17 shall in no case exceed £20 per [⁴benefit week].

39. Notwithstanding paragraph 38, where two or more payments of the same kind and from the same source are to be taken into account in the same benefit week, there shall be disregarded from each payment the sum which would otherwise fall to be disregarded under this Schedule; but this paragraph shall only apply in the case of a payment which it has not been practicable to treat under regulation 96(1)(b) (date on which income treated as paid) as paid on the first day of the benefit week in which it is due to be paid.

40. Any resettlement benefit which is paid to the claimant by virtue of regulation 3 of the Social Security (Hospital In-Patients) Amendment (No.2) Regulations 1987.

41.—(1) Any payment made under the Macfarlane Trust, the Macfarlane (Special Payments) Trust, the Macfarlane (Special Payments) (No.2) Trust, the Fund, the Eileen Trust ("the Trusts") or the Independent Living Funds.

(2) Any payment by or on behalf of a person who is suffering or who suffered from haemophilia or who is or was a qualifying person, which derives from a payment made under any of the Trusts to which sub-paragraph (1) refers and which is made to or for the benefit of—

(a) that person's partner or former partner from whom he is not, or where that person has died was not, estranged or divorced;

(b) any child or young person who is a member of that person's family or who was such a member and who is a member of the claimant's family.

(3) Any payment by or on behalf of the partner or former partner of a person who is suffering or who suffered from haemophilia or who is or was a qualifying person, provided that the partner or former partner and that person are not, or if either of them has died were not, estranged or divorced, which derives from a payment made under any of the Trusts to which sub-paragraph (1) refers and which is made to or for the benefit of—

(a) the person who is suffering from haemophilia or who is a qualifying person;

(b) any child or young person who is a member of that person's family or who was such a member and who is a member of the claimant's family.

(4) Any payment by a person who is suffering from haemophilia or who is a qualifying person, which derives from the payment under any of the Trusts to which sub-paragraph (1) refers, where

(a) that person has no partner or former partner from whom he is not estranged or divorced, nor any child or young person who is or had been a member of that person's family; and

   (b) the payment is made either—
      (i) to that person's parent or step-parent, or
      (ii) where that person at the date of the payment is a child, a young person or a student who has not completed his full-time education, and had no parent or step-parent, to his guardian,

but only for a period from the date of the payment until the end of two years from that person's death.

(5) Any payment out of the estate of a person who suffered from haemophilia or who was a qualifying person, which derives from a payment under any of the Trusts to which sub-paragraph (1) refers, where—

   (a) that person at the date of his death (the relevant date) had no partner or former partner from whom he was not estranged or divorced, nor any child or young person who was or had been a member of his family; and
   (b) the payment is made either—
      (i) to that person's parent or step-parent, or
      (ii) where that person at the relevant date was a child, a young person or a student who had not completed his full-time education, and had no parent or step-parent, to his guardian,

but only for a period of two years from the relevant date.

(6) In the case of a person to whom or for whose benefit a payment referred to in this paragraph is made, any income which derives from any payment of income or capital made under or deriving from any of the Trusts.

[[48] (7) For the purposes of paragraphs (2) to (6), any reference to the Trusts shall be construed as including a reference to the Skipton Fund.]

42. Any payment made by the Secretary of State to compensate for the loss (in whole or in part) of entitlement to housing benefit.

43. Any payment made to a juror or a witness in respect of attendance at a court other than compensation for loss of earnings or for the loss of a benefit payable under the Act or the Benefits Act.

44. Any community charge benefit.

45. Any payment in consequence of a reduction of a personal community charge pursuant to regulations under section 13A of the Local Government Finance Act 1988 or section 9A of the Abolition of Domestic Rates Etc. (Scotland) Act 1987 (reduction of liability for personal community charges) or reduction of council tax under section 13 or, as the case may be, section 80 of the Local Government Finance Act 1992 (reduction of liability for council tax).

46. Any special war widows payment made under—

   (a) the Naval and Marine Pay and Pensions (Special War Widows Payment) Order 1990 made under section 3 of the Naval and Marine Pay and Pensions Act 1865;
   (b) the Royal Warrant dated 19th February 1990 amending the Schedule to the Army Pensions Warrant 1977;
   (c) the Queen's Order dated 26th February 1990 made under section 2 of the Air Force (Constitution) Act 1917;
   (d) the Home Guard War Widows Special Payments Regulations 1990 made under section 151 of the Reserve Forces Act 1980;
   (e) the Orders dated 19th February 1990 amending Orders made on 12th December 1980 concerning the Ulster Defence Regiment, made in each case under section 140 of the Reserve Forces Act 1980;

and any analogous payment made by the Secretary of State for Defence to any person who is not a person entitled under the provisions mentioned in sub-paragraphs (a) to (e) of this paragraph.

47.—(1) Any payment or repayment made—

   (a) as respects England and Wales, under regulation 3, 5 or 8 of the National Health Service (Travelling Expenses and Remission of Charges) Regulations 1988 (travelling expenses and health service supplies);
   (b) as respects Scotland, under regulation 3, 5 or 8 of the National Health Service (Travelling Expenses and Remission of Charges) (Scotland) Regulations 1988 (travelling expenses and health service supplies).

(2) Any payment or repayment made by the Secretary of State for Health, the Secretary of State for Scotland or the Secretary of State for Wales which is analogous to a payment or repayment mentioned in sub-paragraph (1).

48. Any payment made under regulation 9 to 11 or 13 of the Welfare Food Regulations 1988 (payments made in place of milk tokens or the supply of vitamins).

49. Any payment made either by the Secretary of State for the Home Department or by the Secretary of State for Scotland under a scheme established to assist relatives and other persons to visit persons in custody.

50. Any payment (other than a training allowance) made, whether by the Secretary of State or by any other person, under the Disabled Persons (Employment) Act 1944 [⁴² . . .] to assist disabled persons to obtain or retain employment despite their disability.

51. Any council tax benefit.

52. Where the claimant is in receipt of any benefit under Parts II, III or V of the Benefits Act, any increase in the rate of that benefit arising under Part IV (increases for dependants) or section 106(a) (unemployability supplement) of that Act where the dependant in respect of whom the increase is paid is not a member of the claimant's family.

53. Any supplementary pension under article 29(1A) of the Naval, Military and Air Forces etc. (Disablement and Death) Service Pensions Order 1983 (pensions to widows [³¹ or widowers]).

54. In the case of a pension awarded at the supplementary rate under article 27(3) of the Personal Injuries (Civilians) Scheme 1983 (pensions to widows [³¹ or widowers]), the sum specified in paragraph 1(c) of Schedule 4 to that Scheme.

55.—(1) Any payment which is—
  (a) made under any of the Dispensing Instruments to a widow [³¹ or widower] of a person—
      (i) whose death was attributable to service in a capacity analogous to service as a member of the armed forces of the Crown; and
      (ii) whose service in such capacity terminated before 31st March 1973; and
  (b) equal to the amount specified in article 29(1A) of the Naval, Military and Air Forces etc. (Disablement and Death) Service Pensions Order 1983 (pensions to widows [³¹ or widowers]).

(2) In this paragraph "the Dispensing Instruments" means the Order in Council of 9th December 1881, the Royal Warrant of 27th October 1884 and the Order by His Majesty of 14th January 1922 (exceptional grants of pay, non-effective pay and allowances).

[³**56.** Any payment made under the Community Care (Direct Payments) Act 1996 or under section 12B of the Social Work (Scotland) Act 1968.

57. [⁴² . . .]

58. [⁴² . . .]

59.—(1) Any payment specified in sub-paragraph (2) to a claimant who was formerly a full-time student and who has completed the course in respect of which those payments were made.

(2) The payments specified for the purposes of sub-paragraph (1) are—
  (a) any grant income and covenant income as defined for the purposes of Chapter IX of Part VIII;
[¹⁷(b) any student loan as defined in Chapter IX of Part VIII;
  (c) any contribution as defined in Chapter IX of Part VIII which—
      (i) is taken into account in ascertaining the amount of a student loan referred to in head (b); and
      (ii) has been paid.]]

[²⁵ **60.** [⁴² . . .]].

[³² **60A.** [⁴² . . .].]

[⁶ **61.** [⁴² . . .].]

[¹²**62.**—(1) Subject to sub-paragraph (2), in the case of a person who is receiving, or who has received, assistance under [²² the self-employment route], any payment to that person—
  (a) to meet expenses wholly and necessarily incurred whilst carrying on the commercial activity;
  (b) which is used or intended to be used to maintain repayments on a loan taken out by that person for the purpose of establishing or carrying on the commercial activity,
in respect of which such assistance is or was received.

(2) Sub-paragraph (1) shall apply only in respect of payments which are paid to that person from the special account as defined for the purposes of Chapter IVA of Part VIII.]

[¹³**63.** [⁴² . . .].]

[¹⁴**64.** Any payment which falls to be treated as notional income made under paragraph (11) of regulation 105 above (payments made in respect of a person in a residential care or nursing home).]

65. [*Omitted.*]

66. [*Omitted.*]

[¹⁶**67.**—(1) Any payment of a sports award except to the extent that it has been made in respect of any one or more of the items specified in sub-paragraph (2).

(2) The items specified for the purposes of sub-paragraph (1) are food, ordinary clothing or footwear, household fuel, rent for which housing benefit is payable or any housing costs to the extent that they are met under regulation 83(f) or 84(1)(g) (housing costs) [²⁹ . . .], of the claimant or, where the claimant is a member of a family, any other member of his family, or any council tax or water charges for which that claimant or member is liable.

(3) For the purposes of sub-paragraph (2)—

"food" does not include vitamins, minerals or other special dietary supplements intended to enhance the performance of the person in the sport in respect of which the award was made;

"ordinary clothing and footwear" means clothing or footwear for normal daily use but does not include school uniforms or clothing or footwear used solely for sporting activities.]

[²⁰ **68.** Where the amount of a subsistence allowance paid to a person in a benefit week exceeds the amount of income-based jobseeker's allowance that person would have received in that benefit week had it been payable to him, less 50p, that excess amount.

69. In the case of a claimant participating in an employment zone programme, any discretionary payment made by an employment zone contractor to the claimant, being a fee, grant, loan or otherwise.]

[³⁵ [⁴¹**70.**—(1) Subject to sub-paragraph (3), any payment of child maintenance where the child or young person in respect of whom the payment is made is a member of the claimant's family except where the person making the payment is the claimant or the claimant's partner.

(2) For the purposes of sub-paragraph (1), where more than one payment of child maintenance—

(a) in respect of more than one child or young person; or

(b) made by more than one person in respect of a child or young person,

falls to be taken into account in any week, all such payments shall be aggregated and treated as if they were a single payment.

(3) No more than £10 shall be disregarded in respect of each week to which any payment of child maintenance is attributed in accordance with regulations 93, 94, 96 and 97 (calculation of income) or regulations 126, 128 and 129 (treatment of child support maintenance).

(4) In this paragraph, "child maintenance" shall have the same meaning as that prescribed for the purposes of section 74A of the Administration Act and shall include any payment made by the Secretary of State in lieu of such maintenance.]]

[²⁶**71.** Any discretionary housing payment paid pursuant to regulation 2(1) of the Discretionary Financial Assistance Regulations 2001.]

[³⁷ [³⁹ **72.**—(1) Any payment made by a local authority, or by the National Assembly for Wales, to or on behalf of the claimant or his partner relating to a service which is provided to develop or sustain the capacity of the claimant or his partner to live independently in his accommodation.]]

(2) For the purposes of sub-paragraph (1) "local authority" means—

(a) in relation to England, a county council, a district council, a London borough council, the Common Council of the City of London or the Council of the Isles of Scilly;

(b) in relation to Wales, a county council or a county borough council;

(c) in relation to Scotland, a council constituted under section 2 of the Local Government etc. (Scotland) Act 1994.]

[³⁹ **73.** [⁴². . .].]

[⁴⁰ **74.** [⁴². . .].]

AMENDMENTS

3.626   1. Jobseeker's Allowance (Amendment) Regulations 1996 (SI 1996/1516), reg.20 and Sch. (October 7, 1996).

2. Jobseeker's Allowance and Income Support (General) (Amendment) Regulations 1996 (SI 1996/1517), reg.32 (October 7, 1996).

3. Income-related Benefits and Jobseeker's Allowance (Miscellaneous Amendments) Regulations 1997 (SI 1997/65), reg.2(4) (April 7, 1997).

4. Social Security (Miscellaneous Amendments) Regulations 1997 (SI 1997/454), reg.2(16) (April 7, 1997).

5. Income-related Benefits and Jobseeker's Allowance (Amendment) (No.2) Regulations 1997 (SI 1997/2197), reg.7(7) and (8)(f) (October 6, 1997).

6. Social Security Amendment (New Deal) Regulations 1997 (SI 1997/2863), reg.14 (January 5, 1998).

7. Social Security (Miscellaneous Amendments) Regulations 1998 (SI 1998/563), reg.7(1) and (2)(e) (April 6, 1998).

8. Social Security (Miscellaneous Amendments) Regulations 1998 (SI 1998/563), reg.7(3) and (4)(f) (April 6, 1998).

9. Social Security (Miscellaneous Amendments) Regulations 1998 (SI 1998/563), reg.13(2), (April 6, 1998).

10. Social Security (Miscellaneous Amendments) (No.3) Regulations 1998 (SI 1998/1173), reg.5 (June 1, 1998).

11. Social Security (Miscellaneous Amendments) (No.4) Regulations 1998 (SI 1998/1174), reg.4(a) (June 1, 1998).

12. Social Security (Miscellaneous Amendments) (No.4) Regulations 1998 (SI 1998/1174), reg.4(b) (June 1, 1998).

13. Social Security Amendment (New Deal) (No.2) Regulations 1998 (SI 1998/2117), reg.4(1) (September 24, 1998).

14. Social Security Amendment (New Deal) (No.2) Regulations 1998 (SI 1998/2117), reg.6(1) (September 24, 1998).

15. Social Security Amendment (Educational Maintenance Allowance) Regulations 1999 (SI 1999/1677), reg.2(1) and (2)(f) (August 16, 1999).

16. Social Security Amendment (Sports Awards) Regulations 1999 (SI 1999/2165), reg.6(4) (August 23, 1999).

17. Social Security Amendment (Students) Regulations 1999 (SI 1999/1935), reg.3(8) (August 30, 1999, or if the student's period of study begins between August 1 and 29, 1999, the first day of the period).

18. Social Security Amendment (Education Maintenance Allowance) Regulations 2000 (SI 2000/55), reg.2(1) and (2)(d) (February 7, 2000).

19. Social Security (Immigration and Asylum) Consequential Amendments Regulations 2000 (SI 2000/636), reg.4(9) (April 3, 2000).

20. Social Security Amendment (Employment Zones) Regulations 2000 (SI 2000/724), reg.3(3) (April 3, 2000).

21. Social Security Amendment (Students and Income-related Benefits) Regulations 2000 (SI 2000/1922), reg.3(10) (August 28, 2000, or if the student's period of study begins between August 1 and 27, 2000, the first day of the period).

22. Social Security Amendment (Employment Zones) (No.2) Regulations 2000 (SI 2000/2910), reg.4(1) and (2)(d)(i) (November 27, 2000).

23. Social Security Amendment (Bereavement Benefits) Regulations 2000 (SI 2000/2239), reg.3(3) (April 9 , 2001).

24. Social Security Amendment (Miscellaneous Amendments) (No.3) Regulations 2001 (SI 2001/859), reg.6(3) (April 9, 2001).

25. Social Security Amendment (New Deal) Regulations 2001 (SI 2001/ 1029), reg.12 (April 9, 2001).

26. Social Security Amendment (Discretionary Housing Payments) Regulations 2001 (SI 2001/2333), reg.2(1) (July 2, 2001).

27. Social Security Amendment (Volunteers) Regulations 2001 (SI 2001/ 2296), reg.2 (September 24, 2001).

28. Children (Leaving Care) Act 2000 (Commencement No.2 and Consequential Provisions) Order 2001 (SI 2001/3070), art.3(5) and Sch.4, para.(c) (October 1, 2001).

29. Social Security Amendment (Residential Care and Nursing Homes) Regulations 2001 (SI 2001/3767), reg.2(2) and Pt II of Sch., para.24 (April 8, 2002).

30. Social Security Benefits Up-rating Order 2002 (SI 2002/668), art.22(10) (April 8, 2002).

31. Social Security (Miscellaneous Amendments) Regulations 2002 (SI 2002/841), reg.3(4) (April 8, 2002).

32. Social Security Amendment (Employment Programme) Regulations 2002 (SI 2002/2314), reg.2(5) (October 14, 2002).

33. Social Security (Miscellaneous Amendments) (No.2) Regulations 2002 (SI 2002/2380), reg.3(b) (October 14, 2002).

34. Social Security Amendment (Personal Injury Payments) Regulations 2002 (SI 2002/2442), reg.3 (October 28, 2002)

35. Social Security (Child Maintenance Premium and Miscellaneous Amendments) Regulations 2000 (SI 2000/3176), reg.2(2)(b) (in force in relation to any particular case on the day on which s.23 of the Child Support, Pensions and Social Security Act 2000 comes into force in relation to that type of case).

36. Social Security (Paternity and Adoption) Amendment Regulations 2002 (SI 2002/2689), reg.3(6) (December 8, 2002).

37. Social Security (Miscellaneous Amendments) Regulations 2003 (SI 2003/511), reg.3(2) (April 1, 2003).

38. Social Security (Working Tax Credit and Child Tax Credit) (Consequential Amendments) Regulations 2003 (SI 2003/455), reg.3 and Sch.2, para.23(a) (April 7, 2003).

39. Social Security (Miscellaneous Amendments) (No.2) Regulations 2003 (SI 2003/2279), reg.3(4) (October 1, 2003).

40. Social Security (Incapacity Benefit Work-focused Interviews) Regulations 2003 (SI 2003/2439), reg.16(a) (October 27, 2003).

41. Social Security (Child Maintenance Premium) Amendment Regulations 2004 (SI 2004/98), reg.3 (in force on (i) February 16, 2004 in relation to any particular case in respect of which s.23 CSPSSA 2000 has come into force before February 16, 2004; (ii) where this does not apply, the day on which s. 23 comes into force in relation to that type of case; (iii) February 16, 2004 in relation to a person who is entitled to income support/income-based JSA on that date and who receives her first payment of child maintenance made voluntarily whilst entitled to income support/income-based JSA on that date; (iv) in such a case where the day that the first voluntary payment is received is after February 16, 2004, the day that payment is received; (v) February 16, 2004 in relation to a person who makes a claim for income support/income-based JSA on or after that date and receives a payment of child maintenance made voluntarily on or after the date of that claim).

42. Social Security (Miscellaneous Amendments) Regulations 2004 (SI 2004/565), reg.5(3) (April 1, 2004).

43. Social Security (Working Tax Credit and Child Tax Credit) (Consequential Amendments) Regulations 2003 (SI 2003/455), reg.3 and Sch.2, para.23 (except sub-para.(a)) (April 6, 2004, except in "transitional cases" and see further the note to reg.83 and to reg.17 of the Income Support Regulations).

44. Social Security (Miscellaneous Amendments) (No. 2) Regulations 2004 (SI 2004/1141), reg.4(1) and (2)(d) (May 12, 2004).

45. Social Security (Miscellaneous Amendments) (No. 2) Regulations 2004 (SI 2004/1141), reg.4(3) and (4)(d) (May 12, 2004).

46. Social Security (Students and Income-related Benefits) Amendment Regulations 2004 (SI 2004/1708), reg.6(3) (September 1, 2004, or if the student's period of study begins between August 1 and August 31, 2004, the first day of the period).

47. Social Security (Miscellaneous Amendments) (No. 3) Regulations 2004 (SI 2004/2308), reg.2(1) and (2)(b) (October 4, 2004).

48. Social Security (Miscellaneous Amendments) (No. 3) Regulations 2004 (SI 2004/2308), reg.3(5) (October 4, 2004).

49. Social Security (Miscellaneous Amendments) (No. 3) Regulations 2004 (SI 2004/2308), reg.4(3) and (4)(b) (October 4, 2004).

50. Social Security (Miscellaneous Amendments) Regulations 2005 (SI 2005/574), reg.2(9) (April 4, 2005).

51. Social Security (Miscellaneous Amendments) Regulations 2005 (SI 2005/574), reg.6(5) (April 4, 2005).

52. Social Security Benefits Up-rating Order 2005 (SI 2005/522), art. 24(10) (April 11, 2005).

DEFINITIONS

"access funds"—see reg.130.   3.627
"attendance allowance"—see reg.1(3).
"the Benefits Act"—see Jobseekers Act, s.35(1).
"benefit week"—see reg.1(3).
"board and lodging accommodation"—*ibid.*
"child"—see Jobseekers Act, s.35(1).
"the Children Order"—see reg.1(3).
"claimant"—see Jobseekers Act, s.35(1), reg.88(1).
"concessionary payment"—see reg.1(3).
"contribution"—see reg.130.
"course of study"—see reg.1(3).
"disability living allowance"—*ibid.*
"dwelling occupied as the home"—*ibid.*
"employed earner"—see reg.3, SSCBA, s.2(1)(a).
"employment zone contractor"—see reg.1(3).
"employment zone programme"—*ibid.*
"family"—see Jobseekers Act, s.35(1).
"a guaranteed income payment"—see reg.1(3).
"Immigration and Asylum Act"—*ibid.*
"Intensive Activity Period for 50 plus"—*ibid.*
"mobility supplement"—*ibid.*
"nursing home"—*ibid.*
"occupational pension scheme"—see Jobseekers Act, s.35(1).
"partner"—see reg.1(3).
"partner of a person subject to immigration control"—see reg.85(4).
"payment"—see reg.1(3).
"personal pension scheme"—see Jobseekers Act, s.35(1).
"qualifying person"—see reg.1(3).
"residential care home"—*ibid.*
"self-employment route"—*ibid.*
"the Eileen Trust"—*ibid.*
"the Fund"—*ibid.*
"the Independent Living Funds"—*ibid.*
"the Macfarlane (Special Payments) Trust"—*ibid.*
"the Macfarlane (Special Payments) (No. 2) Trust"—*ibid.*
"the Macfarlane Trust"—*ibid.*
"the Skipton Fund"—*ibid.*
"sports award"—*ibid.*
"subsistence allowance"—*ibid.*
"student loan"—see reg.130.
"training allowance"—see reg.1(3).
"voluntary organisation"—*ibid.*
"war disablement pension"—*ibid.*
"war widow's pension"—*ibid.*
"war widower's pension"—*ibid.*
"young person"—see reg.76.

GENERAL NOTE

The disregards in Sch.7 are the same as those in Sch.9 to the Income Support   3.628
Regulations (with minor adjustments in the wording). See the notes to Sch.9.
The only paragraphs in Sch.9 that were not reproduced in the original Sch.7 were
paras 41 and 42 which related to compensation payments made as a consequence of

the 1988 benefit changes and so were not relevant. In addition, there is no equivalent to para.57 of Sch.9 (backdated payments under reg.21ZB of the Income Support Regulations), but the disregard in para.12 of Sch.8 should apply to such payments.

A single disregard of the various allowances, grants and other payments made under s.2 of the Employment and Training Act 1973 or s.2 of the Enterprise and New Towns (Scotland) Act 1990 to people participating in New Deals and other training and welfare to work schemes has been introduced from April 1, 2004 to replace the separate disregards that had existed in respect of such payments under a number of the provisions in this Schedule (para.14). As a consequence of this change, those provisions have been revoked or amended. The revoked paragraphs are paras 57, 58, 60, 60A, 61, 63, 73 and 74; the paragraph that has been amended is para.50. See further the note to para.13 of Sch.9.

On para.62, see the note to reg.102C.

SCHEDULE 8   **Regulation 108(2)**

CAPITAL TO BE DISREGARDED

3.629   **1.** The dwelling occupied as the home but, notwithstanding regulation 88, (calculation of income and capital of members of claimant's family and of a polygamous marriage), only one dwelling shall be disregarded under this paragraph.

2. Any premises acquired for occupation by the claimant which he intends to occupy as his home within 26 weeks of the date of acquisition or such longer period as is reasonable in the circumstances to enable the claimant to obtain possession and commence occupation of the premises.

3. Any sum directly attributable to the proceeds of sale of any premises formerly occupied by the claimant as his home which is to be used for the purchase of other premises intended for such occupation within 26 weeks of the date of sale, or such longer period as is reasonable in the circumstances to enable the claimant to complete the purchase.

4. Any premises occupied in whole or in part by—
   (a) a partner or relative of a single claimant or of any member of the family as his home where that person is aged 60 or over or is incapacitated;
   (b) the former partner of a claimant as his home; but this provision shall not apply where the former partner is a person from whom the claimant is estranged or divorced.

5. Where a claimant has ceased to occupy what was formerly the dwelling occupied as the home following his estrangement or divorce from his former partner, that dwelling for a period of 26 weeks from the date on which he ceased to occupy that dwelling [²² or, where that dwelling is occupied as the home by the former partner who is a lone parent, for as long as it is so occupied].

6. Any premises where the claimant is taking reasonable steps to dispose of those premises, for a period of 26 weeks from the date on which he first took such steps, or such longer period as is reasonable in the circumstances to enable him to dispose of those premises.

7. Any premises which the claimant intends to occupy as his home, and in respect of which he is taking steps to obtain possession and has sought legal advice or has commenced legal proceedings with a view to obtaining possession, for a period of 26 weeks from the date on which he first sought such advice or first commenced such proceedings, whichever is earlier, or such longer period as is reasonable in the circumstances to enable him to obtain possession and commence occupation of those premises.

8. Any premises which the claimant intends to occupy as his home to which essential repairs or alterations are required in order to render them fit for such occupation, for a period of 26 weeks from the date on which the claimant first takes steps to effect those repairs or alterations, or such longer period as is reasonable in the circumstances to enable those repairs or alterations to be carried out and the claimant to commence occupation of the premises.

9. Any grant made to the claimant in accordance with a scheme made under section 129 of the Housing Act 1988 or section 66 of the Housing (Scotland) Act 1988 (schemes for payments to assist local housing authority and local authority tenants to obtain other accommodation) which is to be used—
   (a) to purchase premises intended for occupation as his home; or
   (b) to carry out repairs or alterations which are required to render premises fit for occupation as his home,

for a period of 26 weeks from the date on which he received such a grant or such longer period as is reasonable in the circumstances to enable the purchase, repairs or alterations to be completed and the claimant to commence occupation of those premises as his home.

10. Any future interest in property of any kind, other than land or premises in respect of which the claimant has granted a subsisting lease or tenancy, including sub-leases or sub-tenancies.

11.—(1) The assets of any business owned in whole or in part by the claimant and for the purposes of which he is engaged as a self-employed earner or, if he has ceased to be so engaged, for such period as may be reasonable in the circumstances to allow for disposal of any such asset.

(2) The assets of any business owned in whole or in part by the claimant where—

    (a) he is not engaged as a self-employed earner in that business by reason of some disease or bodily or mental disablement; but

    (b) he intends to become engaged (or, as the case may be, re-engaged) as a self-employed earner in that business as soon as he recovers or is able to become engaged or re-engaged in that business,

for a period of 26 weeks from the date on which the claim for a jobseeker's allowance is made, or is treated as made, or if it is unreasonable to expect him to become engaged or re-engaged in that business within that period, for such longer period as is reasonable in the circumstances to enable him to become so engaged or re-engaged.

[⁴(3) In the case of a person who is receiving assistance under [¹² the self-employment route], the assets acquired by that person for the purpose of establishing or carrying on the commercial activity in respect of which such assistance is being received.

(4) In the case of a person who has ceased carrying on the commercial activity in respect of which assistance was received as specified in sub-paragraph (3), the assets relating to that activity for such period as may be reasonable in the circumstances to allow for disposal of any such asset.]

12. [²¹—(1) Subject to sub-paragraph (2),] any arrears of, or any concessionary payment made to compensate for arrears due to the non-payment of—

    (a) any payment specified in paragraph 7, 9 or 10 of Schedule 7 (other income to be disregarded);

    (b) a jobseeker's allowance or an income-related benefit under Part VII of the Benefits Act [²³ , working families' tax credit under section 128 of that Act, disabled person's tax credit under section 129 of that Act, child tax credit, working tax credit,];

    [¹(c) [³² . . .]]

[¹⁶(d) any discretionary housing payment paid pursuant to regulation 2(1) of the Discretionary Financial Assistance Regulations 2001,]

but only for a period of 52 weeks from the date of receipt of the arrears of the concessionary payment.

[²¹ (2) In a case where the total of any arrears and, if appropriate, any concessionary payment referred to in sub-paragraph (1) relating to any one of the specified payments, benefits or allowances amounts to £5, 000 or more (referred to in this sub-paragraph and in sub-paragraph (3) as the "relevant sum") and is—

    (a) paid in order to rectify, or to compensate for, an official error as defined in regulation 1(3) of the Social Security and Child Support (Decisions and Appeals) Regulations 1999, and

    (b) received by the claimant in full on or after 14th October 2001,

sub-paragraph (1) shall have effect in relation to such arrears or concessionary payment either for a period of 52 weeks from the date of receipt, or, if the relevant sum is received in its entirety during the award of an income-based jobseeker's allowance, for the remainder of that award if that is a longer period.

(3) For the purposes of sub-paragraph (2), "the award of an income-based jobseeker's allowance" means—

    (a) the award either of an income-based jobseeker's allowance or of income support in which the relevant sum (or first part thereof where it is paid in more than one instalment) is received, and

    (b) where that award is followed by one or more further awards which in each case may be either of an income-based jobseeker's allowance or of income support and which, or each of which, begins immediately after the end of the previous award, such further awards until the end of the last such award, provided that for any such further awards the claimant—

        (i) is the person who received the relevant sum, or

        (ii) is the partner of the person who received the relevant sum, or was that person's partner at the date of his death, or

  (iii) in the case of a joint-claim jobseeker's allowance, is a joint-claim couple either
        member or both members of which received the relevant sum.]

13. Any sum—
  (a) paid to the claimant in consequence of damage to, or loss of, the home or any personal
      possession and intended for its repair or replacement; or
  (b) acquired by the claimant (whether as a loan or otherwise) on the express condition
      that it is to be used for effecting essential repairs or improvements to the home,
and which is to be used for the intended purpose, for a period of 26 weeks from the date on which
it was so paid or acquired or such longer period as is reasonable in the circumstances to enable
the claimant to effect the repairs, replacement or improvements.

14. Any sum—
  (a) deposited with a housing association as defined in section 1(1) of the Housing
      Associations Act 1985 as a condition of occupying the home;
  (b) which was so deposited and which is to be used for the purchase of another home, for
      the period of 26 weeks or such longer period as is reasonable in the circumstances to
      complete the purchase.

15. Any personal possessions except those which have or had been acquired by the claimant
with the intention of reducing his capital in order to secure entitlement to a jobseeker's
allowance or to income support or to increase the amount of those benefits.

16. The value of the right to receive any income under an annuity and the surrender value
(if any) of such an annuity.

17. Where the funds of a trust are derived from a payment made in consequence of any personal injury to the claimant, the value of the trust fund and the value of the right to receive any
payment under that trust.

18. The value of the right to receive any income under a life interest or from a liferent.

19. The value of the right to receive any income which is disregarded under paragraph 14 of
Schedule 6 or paragraph 24 of Schedule 7 (earnings or other income payable in a country
outside the United Kingdom).

20. The surrender value of any policy of life insurance.

21. Where any payment of capital falls to be made by instalments, the value of the right to
receive any outstanding instalments.

22. Except in the case of a person who is, or would be prevented from being entitled to a jobseeker's allowance by section 14 (trade disputes), any payment made by a local authority in
accordance with [¹⁷ section 17, 23B, 23C or 24A of the Children Act 1989] or, as the case may
be, [²⁸ section 12 of the Social Work (Scotland) Act 1968 or sections 29 or 30 of the Children
(Scotland) Act 1995] (local authorities' duty to promote welfare of children and powers to
grant financial assistance to persons in, or formerly in, their care).

23. Any social fund payment made pursuant to Part VIII of the Benefits Act.

24. Any refund of tax which falls to be deducted under section 369 of the Income and
Corporation Taxes Act 1988 (deductions of tax from certain loan interest) on a payment of
relevant loan interest for the purpose of acquiring an interest in the home or carrying out repairs
or improvements in the home.

25. Any capital which under regulation 104 [²⁵ . . .] or 136 (capital treated as income [²⁵ . . .]
and treatment of student loans) is to be treated as income.

26. Where a payment of capital is made in a currency other than sterling, any banking charge
or commission payable in converting that payment into sterling.

27.—(1) Any payment made under the Macfarlane Trust, the Macfarlane (Special
Payments) Trust, the Macfarlane (Special Payments) (No. 2) Trust, the Fund, the Eileen Trust
[²⁹, the Skipton Fund] ("the Trusts") or the Independent Living Funds.

  (2) Any payment by or on behalf of a person who is suffering or who suffered from haemophilia
or who is or was a qualifying person, which derives from a payment made under any of the Trusts
to which sub-paragraph (1) refers and which is made to or for the benefit of—
  (a) that person's partner or former partner from whom he is not, or where that person had
      died was not, estranged or divorced;
  (b) any child or young person who is a member of that person's family or who was such a
      member and who is a member of the claimant's family.

  (3) Any payment by or on behalf of the partner or former partner of a person who is suffering or who suffered from haemophilia or who is or was a qualifying person, provided that
the partner or former partner and that person are not, or if either of them has died were not,
estranged or divorced, which derives from a payment made under any of the Trusts to which
sub-paragraph (1) refers and which is made to or for the benefit of
  (a) the person who is suffering from haemophilia or who is a qualifying person;
  (b) any child or young person who is a member of that person's family or who was such a
      member and who is a member of the claimant's family.

(4) Any payment by a person who is suffering from haemophilia or who is a qualifying person, which derives from a payment made under any of the Trusts to which subparagraph (1) refers, where—

    (a) that person has no partner or former partner from whom he is not estranged or divorced, nor any child or young person who is or had been a member of that person's family; and

    (b) the payment is made either—

        (i) to that person's parent or step-parent, or

        (ii) where that person at the date of payment is a child, a young person or a student who has not completed his full-time education, and has no parent or step-parent, to his guardian,

but only for a period from the date of the payment until the end of two years from that person's death.

(5) Any payment out of the estate of a person who suffered from haemophilia or who was a qualifying person, which derives from a payment made under any of the Trusts to which sub-paragraph (1) refers, where—

    (a) that person at the date of his death (the relevant date) had no partner or former partner from whom he was not estranged or divorced, nor any child or young person who was or had been a member of his family; and

    (b) the payment is made either—

        (i) to that person's parent or step-parent, or

        (ii) where that person at the relevant date was a child, a young person or a student who had not completed his full-time education, and had no parent or step-parent, to his guardian,

but only for a period of two years from the relevant date.

(6) In the case of a person to whom or for whose benefit a payment referred to in this paragraph is made, any capital resource which derives from any payment of income or capital made under or deriving from any of the Trusts.

28. The value of the right to receive an occupational or personal pension.

29. The value of any funds held under a personal pension scheme.

30. The value of the right to receive any rent except where the claimant has a reversionary interest in the property in respect of which rent is due.

31. Any payment in kind made by a charity or under the Macfarlane Trust, the Macfarlane (Special Payments) Trust, the Macfarlane (Special Payments) (No. 2) Trust, the Fund, the Eileen Trust or the Independent Living Funds.

[²⁶ **32.** Any payment made pursuant to section 2 of the Employment and Training Act 1973 or section 2 of the Enterprise and New Towns (Scotland) Act 1990, but only for the period of 52 weeks beginning on the date of receipt of the payment.]

33. Any payment made by the Secretary of State to compensate for the loss (in whole or in part) of entitlement to housing benefit.

34. Any payment made to a juror or a witness in respect of attendance at a court other than compensation for loss of earnings or for the loss of a benefit payable under the Act or under the Benefits Act.

35. Any payment in consequence of a reduction of a personal community charge pursuant to regulations under section 13A of the Local Government Finance Act 1988 or section 9A of the Abolition of Domestic Rates Etc. (Scotland) Act 1987 (reduction of liability for personal community charge) or reduction of council tax under section 13 or, as the case may be, section 80 of the Local Government Finance Act 1992 (reduction of liability for council tax), but only for a period of 52 weeks from the date of the receipt of the payment.

36.—(1) Any payment or repayment made—

    (a) as respects England and Wales, under regulations 3, 5 or 8 of the National Health Service (Travelling Expenses and Remission of Charges) Regulations 1988 (travelling expenses and health service supplies);

    (b) as respects Scotland, under regulation 3, 5 or 8 of the National Health Service (Travelling Expenses and Remission of Charges) (Scotland) Regulations 1988 (travelling expenses and health service supplies),

but only for a period of 52 weeks from the date of receipt of the payment or repayment.

(2) Any payment or repayment made by the Secretary of State for Health, the Secretary of State for Scotland or the Secretary of State for Wales which is analogous to a payment or repayment mentioned in sub-paragraph (1); but only for a period of 52 weeks from the date of receipt of the payment or repayment.

37. Any payment made under regulation 9 to 11 or 13 of the Welfare Food Regulations 1988 (payments made in place of milk tokens or the supply of vitamins), but only for a period of 52 weeks from the date of receipt of the payment.

38. Any payment made either by the Secretary of State for the Home Department or by the Secretary of State for Scotland under a scheme established to assist relatives and other persons to visit persons in custody, but only for a period of 52 weeks from the date of receipt of the payment.

39. Any arrears of special war widows payment which is disregarded under paragraph 46 of Schedule 7 (sums to be disregarded in the calculation of income other than earnings) or of any amount which is disregarded under paragraph 53, 54 or 55 of that Schedule, but only for a period of 52 weeks from the date of receipt of the arrears.

40. Any payment (other than a training allowance [26 . . .]) made, whether by the Secretary of State or by any other person, under the Disabled Persons (Employment) Act 1944 [26 . . .] to assist disabled persons to obtain or retain employment despite their disability.

41. Any payment made by a local authority under section 3 of the Disabled Persons (Employment) Act 1958 to homeworkers assisted under the Blind Homeworkers Scheme.

42. Any sum of capital administered on behalf of a person [2 . . .] by the High Court [24 or the County Court under Rule 21.11(1) of the Civil Procedure Rules 1998], or the Court of Protection where such sum derives from—

    (a) an award of damages for a personal injury to that person; or

    (b) compensation for the death of one or both parents [2where the person concerned is under the age of 18].

43. Any sum of capital administered on behalf of a person [2 . . .] in accordance with an order made under [24 section 13 of the Children (Scotland) Act 1995], or under Rule 36.14 of the Ordinary Cause Rules 1993 or under Rule 128 of the Ordinary Cause Rules, where such sum derives from—

    (a) an award of damages for a personal injury to that person; or

    (b) compensation for the death of one or both parents [2where the person concerned is under the age of 18].

44. Any payment to the claimant as holder of the Victoria Cross or George Cross.

[14 **45.** [26 . . .].]

[20 **45A.** [26 . . .].]

[3**46.** [26 . . .].]

[6**47.** In the case of a person who is receiving, or who has received, assistance under [12 the self-employment route], any sum of capital which is acquired by that person for the purpose of establishing or carrying on the commercial activity in respect of which such assistance is or was received but only for a period of 52 weeks from the date on which that sum was acquired.]

[7**48.** [26 . . .].]

49. [*Omitted.*]

50. [*Omitted.*]

[8 **51.**—(1) Any payment of a sports award for a period of 26 weeks from the date of receipt of that payment except to the extent that it has been made in respect of any one or more of the items specified in sub-paragraph (2).

(2) The items specified for the purposes of sub-paragraph (1) are food, ordinary clothing or footwear, household fuel, rent for which housing benefit is payable or any housing costs to the extent that they are met under regulation 83(f) or 84(1)(g) (housing costs) [19 . . .], of the claimant or, where the claimant is a member of a family, any other member of his family, or any council tax or water charges for which that claimant or member is liable.

(3) For the purposes of sub-paragraph (2)—

"food" does not include vitamins, minerals or other special dietary supplements intended to enhance the performance of the person in the sport in respect of which the award was made;

"ordinary clothing and footwear" means clothing or footwear for normal daily use but does not include school uniforms or clothing or footwear used solely for sporting activities.]

[30 **52.**—(1) Any payment—

    (a) by way of an education maintenance allowance made pursuant to—

        (i) regulations made under section 518 of the Education Act 1996;

        (ii) regulations made under section 49 or 73(f) of the Education (Scotland) Act 1980;

        (iii) directions made under sections 12(2)(c) and 21 of the Further and Higher Education (Scotland) Act 1992; or

    (b) corresponding to such an education maintenance allowance, made pursuant to—

        (i) section 14 or section 181 of the Education Act 2002; or

        (ii) regulations made under section 181 of that Act.

(2) Any payment, other than a payment to which sub-paragraph (1) applies, made pursuant to—

(a) regulations made under section 518 of the Education Act 1996;

(b) regulations made under section 49 of the Education (Scotland) Act 1980; or

(c) directions made under sections 12(2)(c) and 21 of the Further and Higher Education (Scotland) Act 1992,

in respect of a course of study attended by a child or a young person or a person who is in receipt of an education maintenance allowance made pursuant to any provision specified in sub-paragraph (1).]

[[11] **53.** In the case of a claimant participating in an employment zone programme, any discretionary payment made by an employment zone contractor to the claimant, being a fee, grant, loan or otherwise, but only for the period of 52 weeks from the date of receipt of the payment.

54. Any arrears of subsistence allowance paid as a lump sum but only for the period of 52 weeks from the date of receipt of the payment.]

55. *[Omitted.]*

[[13] **56.** Where an ex-gratia payment of £10, 000 has been made by the Secretary of State on or after 1st February 2001 in consequence of the imprisonment or internment of—

(a) the claimant;

(b) the claimant's partner;

(c) the claimant's deceased spouse; or

(d) the claimant's partner's deceased spouse,

by the Japanese during the Second World War, £10, 000.]

[[15] **57.**—(1) Subject to sub-paragraph (2), the amount of any trust payment made to a claimant or a member of a claimant's family who is—

(a) a diagnosed person;

(b) the diagnosed person's partner or the person who was the diagnosed person's partner at the date of the diagnosed person's death;

(c) a parent of a diagnosed person, a person acting in the place of the diagnosed person's parents or a person who was so acting at the date of the diagnosed person's death; or

(d) a member of the diagnosed person's family (other than his partner) or a person who was a member of the diagnosed person's family (other than his partner) at the date of the diagnosed person's death.

(2) Where a trust payment is made to—

(a) a person referred to in sub-paragraph (1)(a) or (b), that sub-paragraph shall apply for the period beginning on the date on which the trust payment is made and ending on the date on which that person dies;

(b) a person referred to in sub-paragraph (1)(c), that sub-paragraph shall apply for the period beginning on the date on which the trust payment is made and ending two years after that date;

(c) a person referred to in sub-paragraph (1)(d), that sub-paragraph shall apply for the period beginning on the date on which the trust payment is made and ending—

(i) two years after that date; or

(ii) on the day before the day on which that person—

(aa) ceases receiving full-time education; or

(bb) attains the age of 19,

whichever is the latest.

(3) Subject to sub-paragraph (4), the amount of any payment by a person to whom a trust payment has been made, or of any payment out of the estate of a person to whom a trust payment has been made, which is made to a claimant or a member of a claimant's family who is—

(a) the diagnosed person's partner or the person who was the diagnosed person's partner at the date of the diagnosed person's death;

(b) a parent of a diagnosed person, a person acting in the place of the diagnosed person's parents or a person who was so acting at the date of the diagnosed person's death; or

(c) a member of the diagnosed person's family (other than his partner) or a person who was a member of the diagnosed person's family (other than his partner) at the date of the diagnosed person's death,

but only to the extent that such payments do not exceed the total amount of any trust payments made to that person.

(4) Where a payment as referred to in sub-paragraph (3) is made to—

(a) a person referred to in sub-paragraph (3)(a), that sub-paragraph shall apply for the period beginning on the date on which that payment is made and ending on the date on which that person dies;

(b) a person referred to in sub-paragraph (3)(b), that sub-paragraph shall apply for the period beginning on the date on which that payment is made and ending two years after that date;

(c) a person referred to in sub-paragraph (3)(c), that sub-paragraph shall apply for the period beginning on the date on which that payment is made and ending—

(i) two years after that date; or

(ii) on the day before the day on which that person—

(aa) ceases receiving full-time education; or

(bb) attains the age of 19,

whichever is the latest.

(5) In this paragraph, a reference to a person—

(a) being the diagnosed person's partner;

(b) being a member of the diagnosed person's family; or

(c) acting in the place of the diagnosed person's parents,

at the date of the diagnosed person's death shall include a person who would have been such a person or a person who would have been so acting, but for the diagnosed person being in residential accommodation, a residential care home or a nursing home on that date.

(6) In this paragraph—

"diagnosed person" means a person who has been diagnosed as suffering from, or who, after his death, has been diagnosed as having suffered from, variant Creutzfeldt-Jakob disease;

"relevant trust" means a trust established out of funds provided by the Secretary of State in respect of persons who suffered, or who are suffering, from variant Creutzfeldt-Jakob disease for the benefit of persons eligible for payments in accordance with its provisions;

"trust payment" means a payment under a relevant trust.]

3.630   [[18] **58.** The amount of a payment, other than a war pension within the meaning in section 25 of the Social Security Act 1989, to compensate for the fact that the claimant, the claimant's partner, the claimant's deceased spouse or the claimant's partner's deceased spouse—

(a) was a slave labourer or a forced labourer;

(b) had suffered property loss or had suffered personal injury; or

(c) was a parent of a child who had died,

during the Second World War.]

[[22] [[24] **59.**—(1) Any payment made by a local authority, or by the National Assembly for Wales, to or on behalf of the claimant or his partner relating to a service which is provided to develop or sustain the capacity of the claimant or his partner to live independently in his accommodation.]

(2) For the purposes of sub-paragraph (1) "local authority" means—

(a) in relation to England, a county council, a district council, a London borough council, the Common Council of the City of London or the Council of the Isles of Scilly;

(b) in relation to Wales, a county council or a county borough council;

(c) in relation to Scotland, a council constituted under section 2 of the Local Government etc. (Scotland) Act 1994.]

[[24] **60.** Any payment made under the Community Care (Direct Payments) Act 1996, regulations made under section 57 of the Health and Social Care Act 2001 or under section 12B of the Social Work (Scotland) Act 1968.

61. Any payment made to the claimant in accordance with regulations made under paragraph 3 of Schedule 4 to the Adoption and Children Act 2002.

[[31] **61A.** Any payment made to the claimant in accordance with regulations made pursuant to section 14F of the Children Act 1989 (special guardianship support services).]

62. [[26]. . .].]

[[25] **63.** [[26]. . .].]

AMENDMENTS

1. Social Security and Child Support (Jobseeker's Allowance) (Miscellaneous Amendments) Regulations 1996 (SI 1996/2538), reg.2(14) (October 28, 1996).

2. Income-related Benefits and Jobseeker's Allowance (Amendment) (No.2) Regulations 1997 (SI 1997/2197), reg.7(9) and (10)(f) (October 6, 1997).

3. Social Security Amendment (New Deal) Regulations 1997 (SI 1997/2863), reg.15 (January 5, 1998).

4. Social Security (Miscellaneous Amendments) (No.4) Regulations 1998 (SI 1998/1174), reg.5(a) (June 1, 1998).

5. Social Security (Miscellaneous Amendments) (No.4) Regulations 1998 (SI 1998/1174), reg.5(b) (June 1, 1998).

6. Social Security (Miscellaneous Amendments) (No.4) Regulations 1998 (SI 1998/1174), reg.5(c) (June 1, 1998).

7. Social Security Amendment (New Deal) (No.2) Regulations 1998 (SI 1998/2117), reg.5(1) (September 24, 1998).

8. Social Security Amendment (Sports Awards) Regulations 1999 (SI 1999/2165), reg.7(5) (August 23, 1999).

9. Social Security Amendment (Education Maintenance Allowance) Regulations 2000 (SI 2000/55), reg.2(3) and (4)(d) (February 7, 2000).

10. Social Security (Miscellaneous Amendments) Regulations 2000 (SI 2000/681), reg.9 (April 3, 2000).

11. Social Security Amendment (Employment Zones) Regulations 2000 (SI 2000/724), reg.3(4) (April 3, 2000).

12. Social Security Amendment (Employment Zones) (No.2) Regulations 2000 (SI 2000/2910), reg.4(1) and (2)(d)(ii) (November 27, 2000).

13. Social Security Amendment (Capital Disregards) Regulations 2001 (SI 2001/22), reg.2 (February 1, 2001).

14. Social Security Amendment (New Deal) Regulations 2001 (SI 2001/1029), reg.13 (April 9, 2001).

15. Social Security Amendment (Capital Disregards and Recovery of Benefits) Regulations 2001 (SI 2001/1118), reg.2(1) (April 12, 2001).

16. Social Security Amendment (Discretionary Housing Payments) Regulations 2001 (SI 2001/2333), reg.2(2)(d) (July 2, 2001).

17. Children (Leaving Care) Act 2000 (Commencement No.2 and Consequential Provisions) Order 2001 (SI 2001/3070), art.3(5) and para.(c) of Sch.4 (October 1, 2001).

18. Social Security Amendment (Capital Disregards) (No.2) Regulations 2001 (SI 2001/3481), reg.2 (November 19, 2001).

19. Social Security Amendment (Residential Care and Nursing Homes) Regulations 2001 (SI 2001/3767), reg.2(2) and Pt II of Sch., para.25 (April 8, 2002).

20. Social Security Amendment (Employment Programme) Regulations 2002 (SI 2002/2314), reg.2(6) (October 14, 2002).

21. Social Security (Miscellaneous Amendments) (No.2) Regulations 2002 (SI 2002/2380), reg.3(c) (October 14, 2002).

22. Social Security (Miscellaneous Amendments) Regulations 2003 (SI 2003/511), reg.3(3) (April 1, 2003).

23. Social Security (Working Tax Credit and Child Tax Credit) (Consequential Amendments) Regulations 2003 (SI 2003/455), reg.3 and Sch.2, para.24(a) (April 7, 2003).

24. Social Security (Miscellaneous Amendments) (No.2) Regulations 2003 (SI 2003/2279), reg.3(5) (October 1, 2003).

25. Social Security (Incapacity Benefit Work-focused Interviews) Regulations 2003 (SI 2003/2439), reg.16(b) (October 27, 2003).

26. Social Security (Miscellaneous Amendments) Regulations 2004 (SI 2004/565), reg.5(4) (April 1, 2004).

27. Social Security (Working Tax Credit and Child Tax Credit) (Consequential Amendments) Regulations 2003 (SI 2003/455), reg.3 and Sch.2, para.24(b) (April 6, 2004, except in "transitional cases" and see further the note to reg.83 and to reg.17 of the Income Support Regulations).

28. Social Security (Miscellaneous Amendments) (No. 2) Regulations 2004 (SI 2004/1141), reg.3(1) and (2)(d) (May 12, 2004).

29. Social Security (Miscellaneous Amendments) (No. 2) Regulations 2004 (SI 2004/1141), reg.3(7) and (8)(b) (May 12, 2004).

30. Social Security (Students and Income-related Benefits) Amendment Regulations 2004 (SI 2004/1708), reg.6(4) (September 1, 2004, or if the student's

period of study begins between August 1 and August 31, 2004, the first day of the period).

31. Social Security (Miscellaneous Amendments) (No. 3) Regulations 2004 (SI 2004/2308), reg.4(7) (October 4, 2004).

32. Social Security (Miscellaneous Amendments) Regulations 2005 (SI 2005/574), reg.6(6) (April 4, 2005).

DEFINITIONS

3.631
"the Benefits Act"—see Jobseekers Act, s.35(1).
"child"—*ibid.*
"claimant"—*ibid.*, reg.88(1).
"concessionary payment"—see reg.1(3).
"dwelling occupied as the home"—*ibid.*
"the Eileen Trust"—*ibid.*
"employment zone contractor"—*ibid.*
"employment zone programme"—*ibid.*
"family"—see Jobseekers Act, s.35(1).
"the Fund"—see reg.1(3).
"the Independent Living Funds"—*ibid.*
"the Macfarlane (Special Payments) Trust"—*ibid.*
"the Macfarlane (Special Payments) (No. 2) Trust"—*ibid.*
"the Macfarlane Trust"—*ibid.*
"the Skipton Fund"—*ibid.*
"occupational pension"—*ibid.*
"partner"—*ibid.*
"payment"—*ibid.*
"personal pension scheme"—see Jobseekers Act, s.35(1).
"policy of life insurance"—see reg.1(3).
"qualifying person"—*ibid.*
"relative"—*ibid.*
"self-employed earner"—*ibid.*, SSCBA, s.2(1))b).
"sports award"—see reg.1(3).
"subsistence allowance"—*ibid.*
"training allowance"—*ibid.*
"young person"—see reg.76.

GENERAL NOTE

3.632
The disregards in Sch.8 are the same as those in Sch.10 to the Income Support Regulations (subject to some reordering and minor adjustments in the wording). See the notes to Sch.10.

Paras 32 and 33 of Sch.10 were not reproduced in the original Sch.8 as they are no longer relevant. There was also no equivalent of paras 47 to 49 of Sch.10, but see para.12 of this Schedule.

Note that in para.15 the disregard of the value of personal possessions does not apply if they have been acquired in order to reduce capital so as to gain jobseeker's allowance *or income support*. This avoids the question that might otherwise have arisen on a claimant transfering from income support to jobseeker's allowance whether if the acquisition had only been for the purposes of income support the disregard in para.15 applies.

A blanket capital disregard of the various allowances, grants and other payments made under s.2 of the Employment and Training Act 1973 or s.2 of the Enterprise and New Towns (Scotland) Act 1990 to people participating in New Deals and other training and welfare to work schemes has been introduced from April 1, 2004 to replace the separate disregards that had existed in respect of such payments under a number of the provisions in this Schedule. As a consequence of this change, those provisions have been revoked or amended. The revoked paragraphs are paras 45,

45A, 46, 48, 62 and 63; the amended paragraph is para.40. However note that if these payments do count as capital they are only ignored for 52 weeks from the date of receipt.

On paras 11(3) and (4) and 47, see the note to reg.102C and on paras 53 and 54, see the note to reg.42(5A) of the Income Support Regulations.

Para. 55

This paragraph has not been reproduced as it only related to a pilot scheme to reduce under-occupation operating in three London boroughs (Croydon, Haringey and Newham) from April 3, 2000. It was added by reg.12 of the Social Security (Payments to Reduce Under-occupation) Regulations 2000 (SI 2000/637) on April 3, 2000 and provided that a payment made under the scheme would be ignored for 52 weeks from the date of payment. The pilot scheme lasted for three years and the Payments to Reduce Under-occupation Regulations ceased to have effect on March 31, 2003.

3.633

Jobseeker's Allowance (Transitional Provisions) Regulations 1996

(SI 1996/2567) (*AS AMENDED*)

For the text of these regulations, omitted here for reasons of space and relative infrequency of use, see Social Security: Legislation 2000:Vol. II: Income Support, Jobseeker's Allowance, Tax Credits and the Social Fund, pp. 1054–1083.

3.634

PART IV

STATE PENSION CREDIT

State Pension Credit Regulations 2002

(SI 2002/1792)

Made by the Secretary of State under s.175(3) to (5) of the Social Security Contributions and Benefits Act 1992, ss.7(4A), 9(4A) and 11(1) and (4) of the Social Security Fraud Act 2001 and ss.1(5), 2(3), (4) and (6), 3(4) to (8), 4(3), 5, 6(2), 7(4) and (7), 9(4) and (5), 12(2) and (3), 15, 16(2) and 17(1) and (2) of the State Pension Credit Act 2002

ARRANGEMENT OF REGULATIONS

PART IV

Loss of benefit

SCHEDULES

PART I

General

Citation, commencement and interpretation

4.6   **1.**—(1) These Regulations may be cited as the State Pension Credit Regulations 2002 and shall come into force on 6th October 2003.

(2) In these Regulations—

"the Act" means the State Pension Credit Act 2002;

"the 1992 Act" means the Social Security Contributions and Benefits Act 1992;

[³ "adoption leave" means a period of absence from work on ordinary or additional adoption leave in accordance with section 75A or 75B of the Employment Rights Act 1996;]

"the appointed day" means the day appointed under section 13(3) of the Act;

[⁷ "the Armed Forces and Reserve Forces Compensation Scheme" means the scheme established under section 1(2) of the Armed Forces (Pensions and Compensation) Act 2004;]

"attendance allowance" means—

(a) an attendance allowance under section 64 of the 1992 Act;

(b) an increase of disablement pension under section 104 or 105 of the 1992 Act;

(c) a payment under regulations made in exercise of the power conferred by paragraph 7(2)(b) of Part II of Schedule 8 to the 1992 Act;

(d) an increase of an allowance which is payable in respect of constant attendance under paragraph 4 of Part I of Schedule 8 to the 1992 Act;

(e) a payment by virtue of article 14, 15, 16, 43 or 44 of the Personal Injuries (Civilians) Scheme 1983 or any analogous payment; or

(f) any payment based on need for attendance which is paid as part of a war disablement pension;

"benefit week" means the period of 7 days beginning on the day on which, in the claimant's case, state pension credit is payable;

"care home" has the meaning it has for the purposes of the Care Standards Act 2000 by virtue of section 3 of that Act [²and in Scotland means a care home service];

[² "care home service" has the meaning assigned to it by section 2(3) of the Regulation of Care (Scotland) Act 2001];

"the Claims and Payments Regulations" means the Social Security (Claims and Payments) Regulations 1987;

"close relative" means a parent, parent-in-law, son, son-in-law, daughter, daughter-in-law, step-parent, step-son, step-daughter, brother, sister, or the spouse of any of the preceding persons or, if that person is one of an unmarried couple, the other member of that couple;

[¹ "the Computation of Earnings Regulations" means the Social Security Benefit (Computation of Earnings) Regulations 1996;

"dwelling occupied as the home" means the dwelling together with any garage, garden and outbuildings, normally occupied by the claimant as his home including any premises not so occupied which it is impracticable or unreasonable to sell separately, in particular, in Scotland, any croft land on which the dwelling is situated;]

"Eileen Trust" means the charitable trust of that name established on 29th March 1993 out of funds provided by the Secretary of State for the benefit of persons eligible for payment in accordance with its provisions;

[⁶ "equity release scheme" means a loan—

(a) made between a person ("the lender") and the claimant;

(b) by means of which a sum of money is advanced by the lender to the claimant by way of payments at regular intervals; and

(c) which is secured on a dwelling in which the claimant owns an estate or interest and which he occupies as his home;]

"the Fund" means moneys made available from time to time by the Secretary of State for the benefit of persons eligible for payment in accordance with the provisions of a scheme established by him on 24th April 1992 or, in Scotland, on 10th April 1992;

"full-time student" has the meaning prescribed in regulation 61(1) of the Income Support Regulations;

[7"a guaranteed income payment" means a payment made under article 14(1)(b) or article 21(1)(a) of the Armed Forces and Reserve Forces (Compensation Scheme) Order 2005;]

"the Income Support Regulations" means the Income Support (General) Regulations 1987;

"the Independent Living Fund" means the charitable trust established out of funds provided by the Secretary of State for the purpose of providing financial assistance to those persons incapacitated by or otherwise suffering from very severe disablement who are in need of such assistance to enable them to live independently;

"the Independent Living Funds" means the Independent Living Fund, the Independent Living (Extension) Fund and the Independent Living (1993) Fund;

"the Independent Living (Extension) Fund" means the Trust of that name established by a deed dated 25th February 1993 and made between the Secretary of State for Social Security of the one part and Robin Glover Wendt and John Fletcher Shepherd of the other part;

"the Independent Living (1993) Fund" means the Trust of that name established by a deed dated 25th February 1993 and made between the Secretary of State for Social Security of the one part and Robin Glover Wendt and John Fletcher Shepherd of the other part;

"the Jobseeker's Allowance Regulations" means the Jobseeker's Allowance Regulations 1996;

"the Macfarlane (Special Payments) Trust" means the trust of that name, established on 29th January 1990 partly out of funds provided by the Secretary of State, for the benefit of certain persons suffering from haemophilia;

"the Macfarlane (Special Payments) (No.2) Trust" means the trust of that name, established on 3rd May 1991 partly out of funds provided by the Secretary of State, for the benefit of certain persons suffering from haemophilia and other beneficiaries;

"the Macfarlane Trust" means the charitable trust, established partly out of funds provided by the Secretary of State to the Haemophilia Society, for the relief of poverty or distress among those suffering from haemophilia;

"patient" means a person (other than a prisoner) who is regarded as receiving free in-patient treatment within the meaning of the Social Security (Hospital In-Patients) Regulations 1975;

[3 "paternity leave" means a period of absence from work on leave in accordance with section 80A or 80B of the Employment Rights Act 1996;]

"pension fund holder" means with respect to a personal pension scheme or retirement annuity contract, the trustees, managers or scheme administrators, as the case may be, of the scheme or contract concerned;

"policy of life insurance" means any instrument by which the payment of money is assured on death (except death by accident only) or the happening of any contingency dependent on human life, or any instrument evidencing a contract which is subject to payment of premiums for a term dependent on human life;

"prisoner" means a person who—

(a) is detained in custody pending trial or sentence upon conviction or under a sentence imposed by a court; or

(b) is on temporary release in accordance with the provisions of the
Prison Act 1952 or the Prisons (Scotland) Act 1989,

other than a person detained in hospital under the provisions of the
Mental Health Act 1983, or in Scotland, under the provisions of the
Mental Health (Scotland) Act 1984 or the Criminal Procedure
(Scotland) Act 1995;

"qualifying person" means a person in respect of whom payment has been
made from the Fund [⁴, the Eileen Trust or the Skipton Fund];

[⁵ "the Skipton Fund" means the ex-gratia payment scheme administered
by the Skipton Fund Limited, incorporated on 25th March 2004, for the
benefit of certain persons suffering from hepatitis C and other persons
eligible for payment in accordance with the scheme's provisions;]

[² "voluntary organisation" means a body, other than a public or local
authority, the activities of which are carried on otherwise than for profit;]

"water charges" means—

(a) as respects England and Wales, any water and sewerage charges
under Chapter 1 of Part V of the Water Industry Act 1991;

(b) as respects Scotland, any water and sewerage charges under
Schedule 11 to the Local Government Finance Act 1992;

in so far as such charges are in respect of the dwelling which a person
occupies as his home;

(3) In these Regulations, unless the context otherwise requires, a member
of a married or unmarried couple is referred to as a partner and both
members are referred to as partners.

(4) In these Regulations, unless the context otherwise requires, a
reference—

(a) to a numbered section is to the section of the Act bearing that number;

(b) to a numbered Part is to the Part of these Regulations bearing that
number;

(c) to a numbered regulation or Schedule is to the regulation in, or
Schedule to, these Regulations bearing that number;

(d) in a regulation or Schedule to a numbered paragraph is to the paragraph in that regulation or Schedule bearing that number;

(e) in a paragraph to a lettered or numbered sub-paragraph is to
the sub-paragraph in that paragraph bearing that letter or number.

AMENDMENTS

1. State Pension Credit (Consequential, Transitional and Miscellaneous Provisions) **4.7**
Regulations 2002 (SI 2002/3019), reg.23(a) (October 6, 2003).

2. State Pension Credit (Consequential, Transitional and Miscellaneous Provisions) (No.2) Regulations 2002 (SI 2002/3197), reg.2 and Sch., para.1 (October 6,
2003).

3. State Pension Credit (Transitional and Miscellaneous Provisions) Amendment
Regulations 2003 (SI 2003/2274), reg.2(2) (October 6, 2003).

4. Social Security (Miscellaneous Amendments) (No. 2) Regulations 2004 (SI
2004/1141), reg.2(a) (May 12, 2004).

5. Social Security (Miscellaneous Amendments) (No. 2) Regulations 2004 (SI
2004/1141) reg.2(b)(iv) (May 12, 2004).

6. Social Security (Housing Benefit, Council Tax Benefit, State Pension Credit
and Miscellaneous Amendments) Regulations 2004 (SI 2004/2327), reg.7(2)
(October 4, 2004).

7. Social Security (Miscellaneous Amendments) Regulations 2005 (SI 2005/574),
reg.2(1) (April 4, 2005).

DEFINITION

"claimant"—see SPCA 2002, s.17(1).

GENERAL NOTE

Para. (1)

4.8   "*appointed day*": This date was October 6, 2003: see State Pension Credit Act 2002 (Commencement No.5) and Appointed Day Order 2003 (SI 2003/1766 (C.75)).

"*care home*": Section 3(1) of the Care Standards Act 2000 provides that "an establishment is a care home if it provides accommodation, together with nursing or personal care" for various categories of person (*e.g.* the ill, the disabled, those with mental disorders and those with alcohol or drug dependency). An establishment is not a care home if it is a hospital, independent clinic or children's home, or if it is excluded by regulations (see Care Standards Act 2000, s.3(3) and Care Homes Regulations 2001 (SI 2001/3965), reg.3)). For the (slightly differently phrased) Scottish definition of "care home", see Regulation of Care (Scotland) Act 2001, s.2. This defines a "care home" as an establishment in which a care home service is provided, *i.e.* accommodation together with nursing, personal care, or personal support for people by reason of their vulnerability or need.

"*close relative*": This definition is in identical terms to that used in reg.2(1) of the Income Support (General) Regulations 1987 (SI 1987/1967; see para.2.25 above), and therefore will presumably be interpreted in the same way. Thus "brother" and "sister" include half-brothers and half-sisters, and persons who are adopted cease to have any legal relationship with their birth family (*R(SB) 22/87*).

"*dwelling occupied as the home*": This also follows the income support definition: see para.2.25 above.

"*full-time student*": For commentary on the complex case law on this term in the context of income support, see paras 2.445–2.459 above.

"*patient*": This is the same definition as used for the purposes of income support (see reg.21(3) of the Income Support (General) Regulations 1987 (SI 1987/1967 and see para.2.180 above).

"*prisoner*": This is also the same definition as used for the purposes of income support (see reg.21(3) of the Income Support (General) Regulations 1987 (SI 1987/1967 and see para.2.183 above).

Para. (2)

4.9   These Regulations adopt the traditional social security approach of treating married and unmarried couples in the same way for the purposes of assessing entitlement to the state pension credit. There is no definition in these Regulations as to what constitutes a married or unmarried couple. However, these terms are defined in the same way as for social security purposes in s.17(1) of the State Pension Credit Act 2002. On the approach to be taken, see the commentary to SSCBA 1992, s.137(1) above.

PART II

Entitlement and amount

Persons not in Great Britain

4.10   **2.** [²—(1) Subject to paragraph (2),] a person is to be treated as not in Great Britain if he is not habitually resident in the United Kingdom, the

Channel Islands, the Isle of Man or the Republic of Ireland, but for this purpose, no person is to be treated as not habitually resident in the United Kingdom who is—

(a) a worker for the purposes of Council Regulation (EEC) No.1612/68 or (EEC) No.1251/70 or a person with a right to reside in the United Kingdom pursuant to Council Directive No. 68/360/EEC or No. 73/148/EEC [²or a person who is an accession State worker requiring registration who is treated as a worker for the purpose of the definition of "qualified person" in regulation 5(1) of the Immigration (European Economic Area) Regulations 2000 pursuant to regulation 5 of the Accession (Immigration and Worker Registration) Regulations 2004]; or

(b) a refugee within the definition in Article 1 of the Convention relating to the Status of Refugees done at Geneva on 28th July 1951, as extended by Article 1(2) of the Protocol relating to the Status of Refugees done at New York on 31st January 1967; or

(c) a person who has been granted exceptional leave to enter the United Kingdom by an immigration officer within the meaning of the Immigration Act 1971, or to remain in the United Kingdom by the Secretary of State; or

(d) a person who is not a person subject to immigration control within the meaning of section 115(9) of the Immigration and Asylum Act 1999 and who is in the United Kingdom as a result of his deportation, expulsion or other removal by compulsion of law from another country to the United Kingdom.

[¹(e) a person in Great Britain who left the territory of Montserrat after 1st November 1995 because of the effect on that territory of a volcanic eruption.]

[²(2) For the purposes of treating a person as not in Great Britain in paragraph (1), no person shall be treated as habitually resident in the United Kingdom, the Channel Islands, the Isle of Man or the Republic of Ireland if he does not have a right to reside in the United Kingdom, the Channel Islands, the Isle of Man or the Republic of Ireland.]

AMENDMENTS

1. State Pension Credit (Transitional and Miscellaneous Provisions) Amendment Regulations 2003 (SI 2003/2274), reg.2(3) (October 6, 2003).

2. Social Security (Habitual Residence) Amendment Regulations 2004 (SI 2004/1232), reg.5 (May 1, 2004).

GENERAL NOTE

It is a fundamental requirement of entitlement to the state pension credit that the claimant "is in Great Britain" (SPCA 2002, s.1(2)(a)). This provision adopts the habitual residence test as defined for the purposes of income support and uses it as an exhaustive means of determining whether a person "is in Great Britain" in the context of the state pension credit. For commentary on the five exceptional categories of claimant who are deemed to be habitually resident in the United Kingdom, see paras 2.158–2.166 above on the parallel provision relating to income support (Income Support (General) Regulations 1987 (SI 1987/1967), reg.21(3), defining a "person from abroad"). The use of different jurisdictions in the definition is less than helpful and may lead to confusion. For example, a person who is both present in and habitually resident in Northern Ireland is clearly, as a matter of constitutional law, not "in Great Britain" for the purposes of s.1(2)(a) of the 2002 Act; this provision

4.11

does not deem such a claimant to be in Great Britain. Accordingly he or she makes his claim under the parallel Northern Ireland legislation. But a pensioner who is habitually resident in Northern Ireland but temporarily in England would presumably fall within s.1(2)(a) without the need to rely on this regulation.

Para. (2)

This provision, added with effect from May 1, 2004, is to the same effect as the parallel changes made to the other means-tested benefit schemes (see *e.g.* Income Support (General) Regulations 1987, reg.21(3G) above). Thus the exception to the habitual residence test is extended by the amendment to para.(1)(a) to include certain persons treated as workers from countries acceding to the European Union from that date in accordance with the Accession (Immigration and Worker Registration) Regulations 2004 (SI 2004/1219). However, the new para.(2) provides that no person shall be treated as habitually resident for the purposes of entitlement to state pension credit unless they have a right to reside in the United Kingdom, the Channel Islands, the Isle of Man or the Republic of Ireland. The SSAC's critical views on these amendments were published in Cm 6181. These amendments are subject to a saving provision for those entitled to pension credit on April 30, 2004: see Social Security (Habitual Residence) Amendment Regulations 2004 (SI 2004/1232), reg.6.

Note also the special dispensation for those temporarily absent from Great Britain (reg.3) and those being treated abroad under NHS provisions (reg.4).

Persons temporarily absent from Great Britain

4.12

3.—(1) A [¹claimant's] entitlement to state pension credit during periods of temporary absence from Great Britain is to continue—
(a) for up to four weeks in the circumstances specified in paragraph (2);
(b) for up to eight weeks in the circumstances specified in paragraph (3).
(2) The circumstances specified in this paragraph are that—
(a) the period of the claimant's absence from Great Britain is unlikely to exceed 52 weeks; and
(b) while absent from Great Britain, the claimant continues to satisfy the other conditions of entitlement to state pension credit.
(3) The circumstances specified in this paragraph are that—
(a) the period of the claimant's absence from Great Britain is unlikely to exceed 52 weeks;
(b) while absent from Great Britain, the claimant continues to satisfy the other conditions of entitlement to state pension credit;
(c) the claimant is accompanying a young person solely in connection with arrangements made for the treatment of that person for a disease or bodily or mental disablement; and
(d) those arrangements relate to treatment—
  (i) outside Great Britain;
  (ii) during the period whilst the claimant is temporarily absent from Great Britain; and
  (iii) by, or under the supervision of, a person appropriately qualified to carry out that treatment.
(4) In paragraph (3)—
(a) "young person" means a person who has not attained the age of 19, is treated as a child for the purposes of section.142 of the 1992 Act and lives with the claimant or the claimant's partner; and
(b) "appropriately qualified" means qualified in providing medical treatment, physiotherapy or a form of treatment which is similar to, or related to, either of those frms of treatment.

AMENDMENT

1. State Pension Credit (Transitional and Miscellaneous Provisions) Amendment Regulations 2003 (SI 2003/2274), reg.2(4) (October 6, 2003).

DEFINITIONS

"appropriately qualified"—see para.(4).   **4.13**
"claimant"—see SPCA 2002, s.17(1).
"young person"—see para.(4).

GENERAL NOTE

This provision is closely modelled on that for income support (see Income Support (General) Regulations 1987 (SI 1987/1967), reg.4 (and see commentary at paras 2.61–2.64 above)). Thus a claimant's entitlement to state pension credit will not be broken by up to four weeks' holiday abroad (para.(1)(a) and (2)). Entitlement can continue for up to eight weeks where the claimant is accompanying a young person abroad for medical treatment (para.(1)(b) and (3)). This latter provision was originally introduced into the income support regulations specifically to deal with claimants accompanying children to the Peto Institute in Budapest.

Persons receiving treatment outside Great Britain

4. [¹—(1)] For the purposes of the Act, a person who is not in Great   **4.14** Britain shall be treated as being in Great Britain during any period in which he is receiving treatment at a hospital or other institution outside Great Britain if the treatment is being provided under section 3 of the National Health Service Act 1977 or pursuant to arrangements made under section 23 of that Act or paragraph 13 of Schedule 2 to the National Health Service and Community Care Act 1990.
  [¹(2) Paragraph (1) applies only where—
  (a) the "person" is the claimant or his partner; and
  (b) the claimant satisfied the conditions for entitlement to state pension credit immediately before he or, as the case may be, his partner, left Great Britain.]

AMENDMENT

1. State Pension Credit (Consequential, Transitional and Miscellaneous   **4.15** Provisions) Regulations 2002 (SI 2002/3019), reg.23(b) (October 6, 2003).

DEFINITION

"claimant"—see SPCA 2002, s.17(1).

GENERAL NOTE

This provision ensures that those pensioners who are being treated in hospitals abroad under NHS arrangements (*e.g.* in France or Germany, as a means of cutting waiting list times for certain types of surgery) retain their entitlement to state pension credit. There is no time limit on the dispensation of the normal rule requiring actual presence in Great Britain where such treatment is being received. The dispensation does not assist a pensioner who happens to fall ill while abroad and obtains treatment overseas.

Persons treated as being or not being members of the same household

4.16   **5.**—(1) A person is to be treated as not being a member of the same household as the claimant if—

(a) he is living away from the claimant and—

    (i) he does not intend to resume living with the claimant; or

    (ii) his absence is likely to exceed 52 weeks except where there are exceptional circumstances (for example the person is in hospital or otherwise has no control over the length of his absence), and the absence is unlikely to be substantially more than 52 weeks;

(b) he or the claimant is permanently in a care home;

(c) he or the claimant is, or both are—

    (i) detained in a hospital provided under [3 the provisions of the Mental Health Act 1983, the Mental Health (Scotland) Act 1984, or the Criminal Procedure (Scotland) Act 1995; or]

    (ii) detained in custody pending trial or sentence upon conviction or under a sentence imposed by a court; or

    (iii) on temporary release in accordance with the provisions of the Prison Act 1952 or the Prison (Scotland) Act 1989;

(d) the claimant is abroad and does not satisfy [3 . . .] regulation 3 (persons temporary absent from Great Britain);

[1(e) either he or the claimant is not in Great Britain and is not treated as being in Great Britain in accordance with regulation 4;

[3(f) he is absent from Great Britain—

    (i) for more than 8 weeks where he is accompanying a young person solely in connection with arrangements made for the treatment of that person for a disease or bodily or mental disablement, and those arrangements relate to treatment outside Great Britain by, or under the supervision of, a person appropriately qualified to carry out the treatment, during the period whilst he is temporarily absent from Great Britain; or

    (ii) for more than 4 weeks in all other cases;]

[2(g) [3. . .]

(h) he is a person subject to immigration control within the meaning of section 115(9) of the Immigration and Asylum Act 1999.]

(2) Subject to paragraph (1), partners shall be treated as members of the same household notwithstanding that they are temporarily living apart.

[3 (3) In paragraph (1)(f) "young person" and "appropriately qualified" shall have the meaning given to them in regulation 3(4).]

AMENDMENTS

4.17   1. State Pension Credit (Consequential, Transitional and Miscellaneous Provisions) Regulations 2002 (SI 2002/3019), reg.23(c) (October 6, 2003).

2. State Pension Credit (Consequential, Transitional and Miscellaneous Provisions) (No.2) Regulations 2002 (SI 2002/3197), reg.2 and Sch., para.2 (October 6, 2003).

3. State Pension Credit (Transitional and Miscellaneous Provisions) Amendment Regulations 2003 (SI 2003/2274), reg.2(5) (October 6, 2003).

DEFINITIONS

"appropriately qualified"—see para.(3) and reg.3(4).
"care home"—see reg.1(2).

"claimant"—see SPCA 2002, s.17(1).
"partners"—see reg.1(3).
"young person"—see para.(3) and reg.3(4).

GENERAL NOTE

This provision is modelled on the parallel rule relating to income support (see Income Support (General) Regulations 1987 (SI 1987/1967), reg.16 (and see commentary at paras 2.121–2.128 above)), although the drafting is a little more straightforward. The starting point is that partners (*i.e.* members of a married or unmarried couple) are treated as members of the same household "notwithstanding that they are temporarily living apart" (para.(2)). In other words, membership of the same household does not cease simply because one partner is temporarily living elsewhere. This basic rule is then subject to the exceptions set out in para.(1), which replicate in part those that apply to income support.

Amount of the guarantee credit

6.—(1) Except as provided in the following provisions of these Regulations, the standard minimum guarantee is—   4.18
  (a) [¹£167.05] per week in the case of a claimant who has a partner;
  (b) [¹£109.45] per week in the case of a claimant who has no partner.
  (2) Paragraph (3) applies in the case of—
  (a) prisoners; and
  (b) members of religious orders who are fully maintained by their order.
  (3) In a case to which this paragraph applies—
  (a) section 2(3) has effect with the substitution for the reference to the standard minimum guarantee in section 2(3)(a) of a reference to a nil amount; and
  (b) except in the case of a person who is a remand prisoner, nil is the prescribed additional amount for the purposes of section 2(3)(b).
  (4) Except in a case to which paragraph (3) applies, an amount additional to that prescribed in paragraph (1) shall be applicable under paragraph (5) if the claimant is treated as being a severely disabled person in accordance with paragraph 1 of Part I of Schedule I.
  (5) The additional amount applicable is—
  (a) except where paragraph (b) applies, [¹£45.50] per week if paragraph 1(1)(a), (b) or (c) of Part I of Schedule I is satisfied; or
  (b) [¹£91.00] per week if paragraph 1(1)(b) of Part I of Schedule I is satisfied otherwise than by virtue of paragraph 1(2)(b) of that Part and no one is entitled to and in receipt of an allowance under section 70 of the 1992 Act in respect of caring for either partner.
  (6) Except in a case to which paragraph (3) applies, an amount additional to that prescribed in paragraph (1) shall be applicable—
  (a) if paragraph 4 of Part II of Schedule I is satisfied (amount applicable for carers);
  (b) in accordance with Part III of Schedule I (amount applicable for former claimants of income support or income-based jobseeker's allowance); or
  (c) except where paragraph (7) applies, in accordance with Schedule II (housing costs).
  (7) This paragraph applies in the case of a person who has been detained in custody for more than 52 weeks pending trial or sentence following conviction by a court.

(8) The amount applicable if paragraph 4 of Part II of Schedule I is satisfied is [¹£25.80] per week, and in the case of partners, this amount is applicable in respect of each partner who satisfies that paragraph.

(9) In the case of a remand prisoner paragraph (6) shall apply as if subparagraphs (a) and (b) were omitted.

(10) In this regulation, "remand prisoner" means a person who, for a period not exceeding 52 weeks, has been detained in custody on remand pending trial or, as a condition of bail, required to reside in a hostel approved under section 27(1) of the Probation Service Act 1993 or, as the case may be, detained pending sentence upon conviction.

AMENDMENT

4.19   1. Social Security Benefits Up-rating Order 2005 (SI 2005/522), art.26(2) (April 11, 2005).

DEFINITIONS

"the 1992 Act"—see reg.1(2).
"claimant"—see SPCA 2002, s.17(1).
"partner"—see reg.1(3).
"prisoner"—see reg.1(2).
"remand prisoner"—see para.(10).

GENERAL NOTE

Para. (1)

4.20   The general conditions of entitlement to state pension credit are set out in s.1 of the SPCA 2002, with the supplementary conditions for the guarantee credit component contained in s.2. The amount of the guarantee credit is the "appropriate minimum guarantee" for claimants with no income and the difference between that figure and the person's income in other cases (s.2(2)). The "appropriate minimum guarantee" is comprised of the "standard minimum guarantee" and such other amounts as may be prescribed. This provision sets out the amount of the "standard minimum guarantee" for individual claimants and couples respectively. The "standard minimum guarantee" therefore performs broadly the same function as the age-related personal allowance taken together with the former pensioner premium in the income support scheme before that was subject to amendments consequential upon the coming into force of the SPCA 2002. This figure is then aggregated together with other prescribed amounts as set out in the remaining paragraphs of this regulation and Sch.1 to these Regulations to produce the "appropriate minimum guarantee" (or applicable amount in income support terms). The calculation used to arrive at the final guarantee credit is then as provided for by s.2(2) of the SPCA 2002, as described above.

Subss. (2) and (3)

4.21   As with income support (see the Income Support (General) Regulations 1987 (SI 1987/1967), Sch.7, paras 7 and 8), prisoners and those fully maintained by their religious orders effectively have no entitlement to the guarantee credit, as their living costs are met from other sources. They also have a nil entitlement to the savings credit (reg.7(3)).

Subss. (4) and (5)

4.22   Section 2(7) of the SPCA 2002, which mirrors SSCBA 1992, s.135(5), requires an additional amount to be prescribed (for the purposes of calculating the "appropriate minimum guarantee") for severely disabled people. The qualifying criteria for this additional amount, which essentially performs the same function as the severe disability premium in the income support scheme, are set out in para.1 of Sch.1 to these Regulations.

Subss. (6)–(10)

Further additional amounts for the purposes of calculating the "appropriate minimum guarantee" are prescribed for carers, former claimants of income support or income-based jobseeker's allowance, and in respect of housing costs. The amount of the carer additional amount is set out in para.(8); the other additional amounts are detailed in Pt III of Sch.1 and Sch.2 to these Regulations respectively. Prisoners and fully maintained members of religious orders are not eligible for such additional amounts. Furthermore, those who have been detained in custody for more than 52 weeks pending trial or sentence following conviction are not eligible for housing costs. Note also that remand prisoners are in any event not eligible for the additional amounts prescribed for carers and for former claimants of income support or income-based jobseeker's allowance (paras (9) and (10)).

4.23

Savings Credit

7.—(1) The percentage prescribed for the purposes of determining—

4.24

(a) the maximum savings credit is 60 per cent;

(b) "amount A" in section 3(4) is 60 per cent;

(c) "amount B" in section 3(4) is 40 per cent.

(2) The amount prescribed for the savings credit threshold is [²£82.05] for a claimant who has no partner and [²£131.20] for a claimant who has a partner.

(3) The maximum savings credit shall be taken to be Nil in the case of—

(a) prisoners; and

(b) members of religious orders who are fully maintained by their order.

[¹(4) If a calculation made for the purposes of paragraph (1)(b) or (c) results in a fraction of a penny, that fraction shall, if it would be to the claimant's advantage, be treated as a penny; otherwise it shall be disregarded.]

AMENDMENTS

1. State Pension Credit (Consequential, Transitional and Miscellaneous Provisions) Regulations 2002 (SI 2002/3019), reg.23(d) (October 6, 2003).

4.25

2. Social Security Benefits Up-rating Order 2005 (SI 2005/522), art.26(3) (April 11, 2005).

DEFINITIONS

"claimant"—see SPCA 2002, s.17(1).

"partner"—see reg.1(3).

"prisoner"—see reg.1(2).

GENERAL NOTE

See annotations to s.3 of the SPCA 2002 for a full explanation as to the calculation of the savings credit. This regulation prescribes the relevant percentages (para.(1)) for the purposes of that calculation, specifies the savings credit threshold for individuals and couples (para.(2)) and excludes prisoners and fully maintained members of religious orders (para.(3)).

Special groups

8. Schedule III shall have effect in the case of members of polygamous marriages and patients.

4.26

"patient"—see reg.1(2).

GENERAL NOTE

Section 12 of the SPCA 2002 enables special provision to be made for members of polygamous marriages. Special provision for patients is authorised by the general regulation-making powers in SSCBA 1992, s.175 which apply in this context by virtue of SPCA 2002, s.19(1).

Qualifying income for the purposes of savings credit

4.27 **9.** For the purposes of section 3 (savings credit), all income is to be treated as qualifying income except the following which is not to be treated as qualifying income—
   (a) working tax credit;
   (b) incapacity benefit;
   (c) a contribution-based jobseeker's allowance within the meaning of section 1(4) of the Jobseekers Act 1995;
   (d) severe disablement allowance;
   (e) maternity allowance;
   (f) payments referred to in regulation 15(5)(d) (maintenance payments).

GENERAL NOTE

WTC and the other benefits and payments listed here are excluded from the definition of qualifying income for the purpose of calculating the savings credit under SPCA 2002, s.3.

Assessed income period

4.28 **10.**—(1) For the purposes of section 6(2)(b) (circumstances in which the Secretary of State is prevented from specifying an assessed income period), the circumstances are—
   (a) in the case of partners, one partner is under the age of 60; or
   (b) state pension credit is awarded, or awarded at a higher rate, because an element of the claimant's retirement provision which is due to be paid to the claimant stops temporarily.
   [²(c) that—
        (i) the Secretary of State has sent the claimant the notification required by regulation 32(6)(a) of the Claims and Payments Regulations; and
       (ii) the claimant has not provided sufficient information to enable the Secretary of State to determine whether there will be any variation in the claimant's retirement provision throughout the period of 12 months beginning with the day following the day on which the previous assessed income period ends.]
   (2) The circumstances prescribed for the purposes of section 7(4) (circumstances in which assessed amounts are deemed not to change) are that—
   (a) the claimant's retirement pension scheme or annuity contract contains no provision for periodic increases in the amount payable; or
   (b) the assessed income comprises income from capital other than income to which paragraph (7) applies.

(3) Paragraphs (4) and (5) do not apply where the assessed amount comprises income from capital.

(4) Where the Secretary of State is informed that the arrangements under which the assessed amount is paid contains provision—

    (a) for the payment to be increased periodically;

    (b) for the date on which the increase is to be paid; and

    (c) for determining the amount of the increase, the assessed amount shall be deemed to increase from the day specified in paragraph (5) by an amount determined by applying those provisions to the amount payable apart from this paragraph.

[³(5) The day referred to in this paragraph is—

    (a) in a case to which paragraph (5A) applies—

        (i) where the first increased payment date is the day on which the benefit week begins, that day;

        (ii) where head (i) does not apply, the first day of the next benefit week which begins after that increased payment date;

    (b) in a case to which paragraph (5A) does not apply—

        (i) where the second increased payment date is the day on which the benefit week begins, that day;

        (ii) where head (i) does not apply, the first day of the next benefit week following that increased payment date.

(5A) This paragraph applies where the period which—

    (a) begins on the date from which the increase in the assessed amount is to accrue; and

    (b) ends on the first increased payment date,

is a period of the same length as the period in respect of which the last payment of the pre-increase assessed amount was made.

(5B) In paragraphs (5) and (5A)—

"increased payment date" means a date on which the increase in the assessed amount referred to in paragraph (4) is paid as part of a periodic payment under the claimant's retirement pension scheme or annuity contract; and

"pre-increase assessed amount" means the assessed amount prior to that increase.]

(6) Except where paragraph (4) applies, the assessed amount shall be deemed to increase—

    [³(a) on the day in April each year on which increases under section 150(1)(c) of the Administration Act come into force if that is the first day of a benefit week but if it is not from the next following such day; and]

    (b) by an amount produced by applying to the assessed amount the same percentage increase as that applied for the purposes of additional pensions under section 150(1)(c) and 151(1) of the Administration Act.

(7) Where the assessed amount comprises income from capital, it shall be deemed to increase or decrease—

    (a) on the first day of the next benefit week to commence [¹on or after] the day on which the income increases or decreases; and

    (b) by an amount equal to the change in the claimant's income produced by applying to his income changes made to the yields capital is deemed to produce, or to the capital amounts, specified in regulation 15(6), or to both if both are changed.

(8) In paragraph (6), "pay day" means the day on which state pension credit is normally paid to the claimant.

AMENDMENTS

4.29   1. State Pension Credit (Consequential, Transitional and Miscellaneous Provisions) Regulations 2002 (SI 2002/3019), reg.23(e) (October 6, 2003).
2. State Pension Credit (Transitional and Miscellaneous Provisions) Amendment Regulations 2003 (SI 2003/2274), reg.2(6) (October 6, 2003).
3. State Pension Credit (Miscellaneous Amendments) Regulations 2004 (SI 2004/647), reg.3(2) and (3) (April 5, 2004).

DEFINITIONS

"the Administration Act"—see SPCA 2002, s.17(1).
"assessed income period"—see *ibid.*
"benefit week"—see reg.1(2).
"claimant"—see SPCA 2002, s.17(1).
"increased payment date"—see para.(5B).
"partner"—see reg.1(3).
"pay day"—see para.(8).
"pre-increase assessed amount"—see para.(5B).
"retirement provision"—see SPCA 2002, ss.7(6) and 17(1).

GENERAL NOTE

4.30   The "assessed income period" is central to the operation of the state pension credit. Recognising that the traditional weekly means test of income support has been an important factor in the relatively low take-up of that benefit amongst pensioners, the government has adopted a very different strategy for state pension credit. Section 6(1) of the SPCA 2002 imposes a duty on the Secretary of State to specify an assessed income period when making a decision on a state pension credit claim. In normal circumstances, the assessed income period is fixed at five years from the date that decision takes effect (SPCA 2002, s.9(1)). The principle then is that changes in the pensioner's income during that period need not be reported and thus any increases in income do not, of themselves, result in disentitlement or run the risk of overpayments accruing. Instead, the claimant's income throughout the five-year period is deemed to be the same as the income at the outset (*ibid.*, s.7(3)), subject to deemed cost of living increases (*ibid.*, s.7(4)).

Para. (1)

4.31   Section 6(2) of the SPCA 2002 provides that the Secretary of State is prevented from specifying a standard assessed income period under s.6(1) in two categories of case. The first is where an assessed income period is already in force in the claimant's case by virtue of an earlier application of the s.6 rule. The second comprises "such other circumstances as may be prescribed" (SPCA 2002, s.6(2)(b)). This paragraph prescribes two such types of case. The first is where the claimant is a member of a couple and one partner is aged under 60. This inevitably increases the likelihood that they are in (or may re-enter) the labour market and so a five year "deeming rule" may be inappropriate. The second is where there has been a temporary cessation of the claimant's retirement provision leading to an award (or higher award) of state pension credit.
Presumably the insertion of reg.10(1)(c) should be read as being preceded by the word "or" at the end of reg.10(1)(b).

Para. (2)

4.32   As explained in the General Note above, the normal rule is that the amount of income fixed at the date of claim (the "assessed amount") is deemed to be the claimant's income throughout the assessed income period, subject to cost of living increases (SPCA 2002, s.7(3) and (4)). The prescribed cost of living increases in a claimant's assessed income do not operate where there is no clause in the claimant's pension scheme or annuity contract which provides for such periodic increases in the amount payable. The assessed amount is also not periodically uprated where it comprises income from capital (except income covered by para.(7) below).

Paras (3)—(5)

Many occupational and personal schemes will include provisions for periodic (typ-   4.33
ically annual) increases in the amount payable, which also specify when such increases are to be paid and how they are to be calculated. Where the Secretary of State is informed that such arrangements exist, then para.(4) enables the claimant's assessed income to be increased accordingly, reflecting such improvements in pension provision. The increase is deemed to apply from the start of the benefit week if the increase under the pension scheme is due to be paid on that day or, failing that, from the start of the next benefit week (para.(5)). For cases not covered by para.(4), see para.(6). These provisions do not apply where the assessed income comprises income from capital (para.(3); see further para.(7)).

Para. (6)

In the event that the pension scheme does not include a provision which meets the   4.34
criteria of para.(4), the default position is that the assessed amount is increased in line with the percentage increase stipulated by the Secretary of State as the amount by which additional pensions are to be increased.

Para. (7)

If the assessed amount comprises income from capital, it is deemed to increase (or   4.35
decrease) in line with the tariff income rule under reg.15(6).

Retirement provision in assessed income period

11. Where an element of a person's retirement provision ceases to be   4.36
payable by one source but—
  (a) responsibility for that element is assumed by another source, income from both those sources shall be treated as income from the same source; or
  (b) in consequence of that element ceasing, income of a different description becomes payable from a different source, that income shall be treated as income of the same description from the same source as the element which ceased to be payable.

DEFINITION

"retirement provision"—see ss.7(6) and 17(1) of the SPCA 2002.

GENERAL NOTE

The purpose of this provision is to ensure that the assessed income period continues notwithstanding the fact that responsibility for a pensioner's retirement provision changes (*e.g.* from one pension provider to another).

End of assessed income period

12. An assessed income period shall end at such time as—   4.37
  (a) the claimant no longer satisfies a condition of entitlement to state pension credit;

(b) payments of an element of the claimant's retirement provision which is due to be paid to him stops temporarily or the amount paid is less than the amount due and in consequence his award of state pension credit is superseded under section 10 of the Social Security Act 1998;

(c) a claimant who has no partner is provided with accommodation in a care home other than on a temporary basis.

DEFINITIONS

"assessed income period"—see SPCA 2002, ss.6, 9 and 17(1).
"care home"—see reg.1(2).
"claimant"—see SPCA 2002, s.17(1).
"partner"—see reg.1(3).
"retirement provision"—see ss.7(6) and 17(1) of the SPCA 2002.

GENERAL NOTE

The normal rule is that the assessed income period will last for five years (SPCA 2002, s.9(1)). The primary legislation provides for various exceptions to this principle, namely where the claimant becomes (or ceases to be) a member of a couple, reaches the age of 65 or (in the case of a couple) where their partner attains 65 (*ibid.*, s.9(4)). This regulation provides for three further circumstances in which that period will end before the expiry of five years—where the claimant no longer satisfies a condition of entitlement (para.12(a)), where there is a fall in income provided by way of retirement provision (para.12(b)), and where a single claimant goes into long-term care (para.12(c)). The underlying thinking is that instead of having to report the multitudinous changes of circumstances required under the income support scheme, state pension credit claimants will only have to report the sorts of significant life changes which have to be reported in any event for state pension purposes (*e.g.* bereavement, remarriage, moving into a care home).

Small amounts of state pension credit

4.38   **13.** Where the amount of state pension credit payable is less than 10 pence per week, the credit shall not be payable unless the claimant is in receipt of another benefit payable with the credit.

DEFINITION

"claimant"—see SPCA 2002, s.17(1).

GENERAL NOTE

This applies the same *de minimis* rule as operates in the income support scheme (Social Security (Claims and Payments) Regulations 1987 (SI 1987/1968), reg.26(4)): see Vol. III).

[¹Part-weeks

4.39   **13A.**—(1) The guarantee credit shall be payable for a period of less than a week ("a part-week") at the rate specified in paragraph (3) if—

(a) the claimant was entitled to income support or an income-based jobseeker's allowance immediately before the first day on which the conditions for entitlement to the credit are satisfied; and

(b) the claimant's entitlement to the credit is likely to continue throughout the first full benefit week which follows the part-week.

(2) For the purpose of determining the amount of the guarantee credit payable in respect of the part-week, no regard shall be had to any income of the claimant and his partner.

(3) The amount of the guarantee credit payable in respect of the part-week shall be determined—
  (a) by dividing by 7 the weekly amount of the guarantee credit which, taking into account the requirements of paragraph (2), would be payable in respect of a full week; and then
  (b) multiplying the resulting figure by the number of days in the part-week,
any fraction of a penny being rounded up to the nearest penny.]

AMENDMENT

1. State Pension Credit (Consequential, Transitional and Miscellaneous Provisions) Regulations 2002 (SI 2002/3019), reg.23(f) (October 6, 2003). **4.40**

DEFINITIONS

"a part-week"—see para.1.
"benefit week"—see reg.1(2).
"claimant"—see SPCA 2002, s.17(1).
"partner"—see reg.1(3).

GENERAL NOTE

This regulation provides for a simple means of ensuring continuity of payment for claimants transferring from income support or income-based jobseeker's allowance to state pension credit. Claimants in such circumstances are entitled to a part-week payment of the guarantee credit to take them up to the start of their first week on state pension credit. This part week payment is paid irrespective of the claimant's income (or that of their partner) (para.(2)). Note that there is no provision for part week payments of the savings credit.

[¹Date on which benefits are treated as paid

13B.—(1) The following benefits shall be treated as paid on the day of the week in respect of which the benefit is payable— **4.41**
  (a) severe disablement allowance;
  (b) short-term and long-term incapacity benefit;
  (c) maternity allowance;
  (d) contribution-based jobseeker's allowance within the meaning of section 1(4) of the Jobseekers Act 1995.
(2) All benefits except those mentioned in paragraph (1) shall be treated as paid on the first day of the benefit week in [² . . .] which the benefit is payable.]

AMENDMENTS

1. State Pension Credit (Consequential, Transitional and Miscellaneous Provisions) Regulations 2002 (SI 2002/3019), reg.23(f) (October 6, 2003). **4.42**
2. State Pension Credit (Consequential, Transitional and Miscellaneous Provisions) (No.2) Regulations 2002 (SI 2002/3197), reg.2 and Sch., para.3 (October 6, 2003).

DEFINITION

"benefit week"—see reg.1(2).

GENERAL NOTE

This provision is a good example of the topsy-turvy principle of statutory drafting. The general rule, as enshrined in para.(2), is that a social security benefit is treated as being paid on the first day of the benefit week in which the benefit is payable. The "benefit week" is the period of seven days beginning on the day in which, in the claimant's case, the state pension credit is payable (reg.1(2)). The exceptions to this general principle are then listed in para.(1). Incapacity benefit, severe disablement allowance and jobseeker's allowance are all normally paid fortnightly in arrears from the date of claim (Social Security (Claims and Payments) Regulations 1987 (SI 1987/1968), regs 24(1) and 26A(1)). Maternity allowance is usually payable on Fridays (Social Security (Claims and Payments) Regulations 1987 (SI 1987/1968), reg.24(4)).

PART III

Income

Calculation of income and capital

4.43   **14.** The income and capital of—
(a) the claimant; and
(b) any partner of the claimant,
shall be calculated in accordance with the rules set out in this Part; and any reference in this Part to the claimant shall apply equally to any partner of the claimant.

DEFINITIONS

"claimant"—see SPCA 2002, s.17(1).
"income"—see *ibid.*, s.15.
"partner"—see reg.1(3).

GENERAL NOTE

On the definition of "income", see SPCA 2002, s.15(1) and regs 15–18 and reg.24 below. On the meaning of "capital", see regs 19–23 below. The normal rules on aggregating the income and capital resources of married and unmarried couples apply to state pension credit as to other means-tested benefits (SPCA 2002, s.5).

The approach to income is rather different to the income support scheme, under which claimants are required to report every element of their income and capital and any changes as they occur. For state pension credit purposes, the categories of income to be disclosed by claimants are set out in SPCA 2002, ss.15 and 16 and in this Part of the Regulations, taken together with Schs IV, V and VI, which deal with disregards and calculation. There is, therefore, no need to report forms of income which are not listed in these statutory provisions (*e.g.* charitable payments and compensation for personal injuries).

Income for the purposes of the Act

4.44   **15.**—(1) For the purposes of section 15(1)(e) (income), all social security benefits are prescribed except—
(a) disability living allowance;
(b) attendance allowance payable under section 64 of the 1992 Act;
(c) an increase of disablement pension under section 104 or 105 of the 1992 Act;
(d) a payment under regulations made in exercise of the power conferred by paragraph 7(2)(b) of Part II of Schedule 8 to the 1992 Act;

(e) an increase of an allowance payable in respect of constant attendance under paragraph 4 of Part I of Schedule 8 to the 1992 Act;
(f) any child special allowance payable under section 56 of the 1992 Act;
(g) any guardian's allowance payable under section 77 of the 1992 Act;
(h) any increase for a dependant, other than the claimant's partner, payable in accordance with Part IV of the 1992 Act;
(i) any social fund payment made under Part VIII of the 1992 Act;
(j) child benefit payable in accordance with Part IX of the 1992 Act;
(k) Christmas bonus payable under Part X of the 1992 Act;
[¹(l) housing benefit;
(m) council tax benefit;
(n) bereavement payment;
(o) statutory sick pay;
(p) statutory maternity pay;
(q) statutory paternity pay payable under Part 12ZA of the 1992 Act;
(r) statutory adoption pay payable under Part 12ZB of the 1992 Act;
(s) any benefit similar to those mentioned in the preceding provisions of this paragraph payable under legislation having effect in Northern Ireland.]

(2) For the purposes of section 15(1)(f) (foreign social security benefits), income includes all foreign social security benefits which are similar to the social security benefits prescribed under paragraph (1).

(3) Where the payment of any social security benefit prescribed under paragraph (1) is subject to any deduction (other than an adjustment specified in paragraph (4)) the amount to be taken into account under paragraph (1) shall be the amount before the deduction is made.

(4) The adjustments specified in this paragraph are those made in accordance with—

(a) the Social Security (Overlapping Benefits) Regulations 1979;
(b) the Social Security (Hospital In-Patients) Regulations 1975;
(c) section 30DD or section 30E of the 1992 Act (reductions in incapacity benefit in respect of pensions and councillor's allowances).

(5) For the purposes of section 15(1)(j) (income to include income of prescribed descriptions), income of the following descriptions is prescribed—

(a) any payment made under article 37 of the Naval, Military and Air Forces, etc. (Disablement and Death) Service Pensions Order 1983;
[⁴(aa) a guaranteed income payment;
(ab) a payment made under article 21(1)(c) of the Armed Forces and Reserve Forces (Compensation Scheme) Order 2005 but only where the condition referred to in article 23(2)(c) is met;]
(b) a pension paid to victims of National Socialist persecution under any special provision made by the law of the Federal Republic of Germany, or any part of it, or of the Republic of Austria;
(c) payments under a scheme made under the Pneumoconiosis, etc. (Worker's Compensation) Act 1979;
(d) payments made towards the maintenance of the claimant by his spouse or former spouse or towards the maintenance of the claimant's partner by his spouse or former spouse, including payments made—
(i) under a court order;
(ii) under an agreement for maintenance; or
(iii) voluntarily;

(e) payments due from any person in respect of board and lodging accommodation provided by the claimant, and for this purpose "board and lodging accommodation" has the same meaning as in paragraph 8(2) of Schedule IV;

(f) payments consisting of royalties or other sums received as a consideration for the use of, or the right to use, any copyright, patent or trade mark; [². . .]

(g) any payment made to the claimant in respect of any book registered under the Public Lending Right Scheme 1982;

[² (h) any income in lieu of that specified in—
    (i) paragraphs (a) to (i) of section 15(1) of the Act, or
    (ii) in this regulation;

(i) any payment of rent made to a claimant who—
    (i) owns the freehold or leasehold interest in any property or is a tenant of any property;
    (ii) occupies part of that property; and
    (iii) has an agreement with another person allowing that person to occupy that property on payment of rent.]

[³(j) any payment made at regular intervals under an equity release scheme.]

(6) For the purposes of section 15(2), a claimant's capital, other than capital disregarded under Schedule V, shall be deemed to yield a weekly income—

(a) in the case of a claimant residing permanently in accommodation to which paragraph (7) applies, of £1 for each £500 in excess of £10,000 and £1 for any excess which is not a complete £500;

(b) in any other case, of £1 for each £500 in excess of £6,000 and £1 for any excess which is not a complete £500.

(7) This paragraph applies to accommodation provided—

(a) in a care home;

(b) in an establishment run by the Abbeyfield Society (including all bodies corporate or incorporate which are affiliated to the Society);

(c) under section 3 of, and Part II of the Schedule to, the Polish Resettlement Act 1947 (provision of accommodation) where the claimant requires personal care;

(d) under sections 21 to 24 of the National Assistance Act 1948 (provision of accommodation), or, in Scotland, under section 13B or 59 of the Social Work (Scotland) Act 1968 or section 7 of the Mental Health (Scotland) Act 1984 (functions of local authorities) where—
    (i) the home in which the accommodation is provided is either owned and managed or owned or managed by a local authority; and
    (ii) the claimant occupies the accommodation other than on a temporary basis.

(8) For the purposes of paragraph (6), a person shall be treated as residing permanently in the accommodation—

(a) except where sub-paragraph (b) applies, notwithstanding that he is absent from it for a period not exceeding 52 weeks;

(b) if it is accommodation to which paragraph (7)(c) applies—
    (i) not withstanding that he is absent from it for a period not exceeding 13 weeks; and

(ii) if he, with the agreement of the manager of the home, intends to return to it in due course.

AMENDMENTS

1. State Pension Credit (Consequential, Transitional and Miscellaneous Provi-   4.45
sions) Regulations 2002 (SI 2002/3019), reg.23(g) (October 6, 2003).
2. State Pension Credit (Transitional and Miscellaneous Provisions) Amendment
Regulations 2003 (SI 2003/2274), reg.2(7) (October 6, 2003).
3. Social Security (Housing Benefit, Council Tax Benefit, State Pension Credit
and Miscellaneous Amendments) Regulations 2004 (SI 2004/2327), reg.7(3)
(October 4, 2004).
4. Social Security (Miscellaneous Amendments) Regulations 2005 (SI 2005/574),
reg.2(2) (April 4, 2005).

DEFINITIONS

"the 1992 Act"—see reg.1(2).
"attendance allowance"—see *ibid.*
"board and lodging accommodation"—see para.(5)(e) and Sch.IV, para.8(2).
"capital"—see SPCA 2002, s.17(1).
"care home"—see reg.1(2).
"claimant"—see SPCA 2002, s.17(1).
"income"—see *ibid.*
"partner"—see reg.1(2).

GENERAL NOTE

Para. (1)
The presumption under SPCA 2002, s.15(1)(e) is that social security benefits   4.46
count as income for the purposes of calculating entitlement to state pension credit.
There is, however, an extensive list of exceptions here. Note also that there are disregards that apply to certain forms of income, as specified in reg.17(7) and Sch.IV
below.

Para. (2)
If income is received in a currency other than Sterling, the value of any payment   4.47
is determined by taking the Sterling equivalent on the date that payment is made
(reg.17(6)).

Para. (3)
The effect of this rule is that payments of prescribed social security benefits are   4.48
taken into account gross, *i.e.* before any deductions are applied (*e.g.* under the Social
Security (Claims and Payments) Regulations 1987 (SI 1987/1968), reg.35 and Sch.9).
This is subject to the exceptions specified in para.(4).

Para. (5)
Section 15(1)(j) is a catch-all provision that enables the Secretary of State to   4.49
prescribe other forms of income not caught by any of the other provisions.

Para. (6)
The tariff income rule for state pension credit is markedly more generous to   4.50
claimants than that which applies in the income support scheme. There are two
important changes. First, the assumed rate of return is halved. The rule for state
pension credit is that the claimant is assumed to receive £1 per week for every £500
or part thereof over the usual threshold of £6,000 (or £10,000 for those in care or
nursing homes). Thus a state pension credit claimant with £10,000 in savings will
have a deemed income of £8 per week from that capital. A person of working age

with £10,000 in capital is excluded from entitlement to income support. Under the rules in operation since April 9, 2001, a pensioner with that amount in savings would have been eligible for the minimum income guarantee but would have had a tariff income under the income support scheme of £16 per week. Secondly, the upper capital limit of £12,000 (or £16,000 for those in residential care and nursing homes) has been abolished. The government expect that 85 per cent of those eligible for state pension credit will not have to disclose their capital at all, as their savings will be below the £6,000 threshold.

Retirement pension income

4.51   **16.** There shall be added to the descriptions of income listed in section 16(1) (retirement pension income) the following [¹paragraphs]—

"(k) any sum payable by way of pension out of money provided under the Civil List Act 1837, the Civil List Act 1937, the Civil List Act 1952, the Civil List Act 1972 or the [¹Civil List Act 1975];
[¹(1) any payment, other than a payment ordered by a court or made in settlement of a claim, made by or on behalf of a former employer of a person on account of the early retirement of that person on grounds of ill-health or disability;]
[²(m) any payment made at regular intervals under an equity release scheme.]"

AMENDMENTS

1. State Pension Credit (Consequential, Transitional and Miscellaneous Provisions) (No.2) Regulations 2002 (SI 2002/3197), reg.2 and Sch., para.3 (October 6, 2003).
2. Social Security (Housing Benefit, Council Tax Benefit, State Pension Credit and Miscellaneous Amendments) Regulations 2004 (SI 2004/2327), reg.7(4) (October 4, 2004).

DEFINITION

"income"—see SPCA 2002, ss.15 and 17(1).

GENERAL NOTE

Readers with republican tendencies will doubtless be reassured to see that pensions paid from the Civil List count as retirement pension income for the purposes of SPCA 2002, s.16(1). More prosaically, payments made by virtue of early retirement on ill-health grounds (other than those ordered by court or agreed under the settlement of a claim) also count.

Calculation of weekly income

4.52   **17.**—(1) Except where paragraph (2) and (4) apply, for the purposes of calculating the weekly income of the claimant, where the period in respect of which a payment is made—
  (a) does not exceed a week, the whole of that payment shall be included in the claimant's weekly income;
  (b) exceeds a week, the amount to be included in the claimant's weekly income shall be determined—
    (i) in a case where that period is a month, by multiplying the amount of the payment by 12 ad dividing the product by 52;
    (ii) in a case where that period is three months, by multiplying the amount of the payment by 4 and dividing the product by 52;

(iii) in a case where that period is a year, by dividing the amount of the payment by 52;

(iv) in any other case, by multiplying the amount of the payment by 7 and dividing the product by the number of days in the period in respect of which it is made.

(2) Where—

(a) the claimant's regular pattern of work is such that he does not work the same hours every week; or

(b) the amount of the claimant's income fluctuates and has changed more than once,

the weekly amount of that claimant's income shall be determined—

(i) if, in a case to which sub-paragraph (a) applies, there is a recognised cycle of work, by reference to his average weekly income over the period of the complete cycle (including, where the cycle involves periods in which the claimant does no work, those periods but disregarding any other absences); or

(ii) in any other case, on the basis of—

(aa) the last two payments if those payments are one month or more apart;

(bb) the last four payments if the last two payments are less than one month apart; or

(cc) such other payments as may, in the particular circumstances of the case, enable the claimant's average weekly income to be determined more accurately.

(3) For the purposes of paragraph (2)(b) the last payments are the last payments before the date the claim was made or treated as made or, if there is a subsequent supersession under section 10 of the Social Security Act 1998, the last payments before the date of the supersession.

(4) If a claimant is entitled to receive a payment to which paragraph (5) applies, the amount of that payment shall be treated as if made in respect of a period of a year.

(5) This paragraph applies to—

(a) royalties or other sums payable as a consideration for the use of, or the right to use, any copyright, patent or trade mark; [¹. . .]

(b) any payment made to the claimant in respect of any book registered under the Public Lending Right Scheme 1982; [¹ and

(c) any payment which is made on an occasional basis.]

(6) Where payments are made in a currency other than Sterling, the value of the payment shall be determined by taking the Sterling equivalent on the date the payment is made.

(7) Income specified in Schedule IV is to be disregarded in the calculation of a claimant's income.

(8) Schedule V shall have effect so that—

(a) the capital specified in Part I shall be disregarded for the purpose of determining a claimant's income; and

(b) the capital specified in Part II shall be disregarded for the purpose of determining a claimant's income under regulation 15(6).

[¹(9) The sums specified in Schedule VI shall be disregarded in calculating—

(a) the claimant's earnings; and

(b) any amount to which paragraph (5) applies if the claimant or his partner is the first owner of the copyright, patent or trade mark or the author of the book registered under the Public Lending Right Scheme 1982.

(9A) For the purposes of paragraph (9)(b), and for that purpose only, the amounts specified in paragraph (5) shall be treated as though they were earnings.]

(10) [¹Subject to regulation [²17B(6)] (deduction of tax and contributions for self-employed earners),] in the case of any income taken into account for the purpose of calculating a person's income, there shall be disregarded—

(a) any amount payable by way of tax;

(b) any amount deducted by way of National Insurance Contributions under the 1992 Act or under the Social Security Contributions and Benefits (Northern Ireland) Act 1992;

(c) [². . .].

[¹(11) In the case of the earnings of self-employed earners, the amounts specified in paragraph (10) shall be taken into account in accordance with paragraph (4) or, as the case may be, paragraph (10) of regulation 13 of the Computation of Earnings Regulations, as having effect in the case of state pension credit.]

AMENDMENTS

4.53   1. State Pension Credit (Consequential, Transitional and Miscellaneous Provisions) Regulations 2002 (SI 2002/3019), reg.23(h) (October 6, 2003).
    2. State Pension Credit (Consequential, Transitional and Miscellaneous Provisions) (No.2) Regulations 2002 (SI 2002/3197), reg.2 and Sch., para.5 (October 6, 2003).

DEFINITIONS

"claimant"—see SPCA 2002, s.17(1).
"Computation of Earnings Regulations"—see reg.1(2).
"income"—see SPCA 2002, s.17(1).

GENERAL NOTE

Para. (1)
4.54   This follows the precedent of income support by providing for the same simple method of converting payments of income into weekly equivalents (Income Support (General) Regulations 1987 (SI 1987/1967), reg.32(1)). This is subject to the special rules for irregular patterns of work (para.(2)) and for payments of royalties and other occasional payments (paras (4) and (5)).

Paras (2) and (3)
4.55   This is yet another variant on the various legislative measures devised to deal with the problematic question of accommodating those with irregular working patterns into a means-tested benefit system. The rule is modelled on but also departs from the traditional income support approach (see Income Support (General) Regulations 1987 (SI 1987/1967), reg.32(6)).

Paras (4) and (5)
4.56   Royalties and other occasional payments are treated as paid in respect of a year, in contrast to the income support rule (Income Support (General) Regulations 1987 (SI 1987/1967), reg.30(2)).

Para. (6)

Any banking charges or commission payable when converting payments of income 　4.57
in other currencies into Sterling are disregarded (Sch.IV, para.16).

Para. (7)

See the annotations to Sch.IV. 　4.58

Para. (8)

Schedule V is divided into two Parts. Part I specifies those forms of capital which 　4.59
are to be disregarded for the purpose of calculating the claimant's income. This
extensive list is modelled on Sch.10 to the Income Support (General) Regulations
1987 (SI 1987/1967). Part II contains a more limited list of categories of capital
which are to be disregarded solely for the purposes of calculating notional income.

Para. (9)

This links to Sch.VI, which carries forward the standard £5, £10 and £20 disre- 　4.60
gards on earnings that apply in the income support scheme to the state pension credit
system. However, there is no hours rule for state pension credit, so it matters not
whether a pensioner is working under or over 16 hours a week.

Para. (10)

This is similar to the income support rule (see Income Support (General) 　4.61
Regulations 1987 (SI 1987/1967), reg.36(3)). The principal difference is that the
income support rule applies to earnings, whereas this rule applies to all income. The
income support rule permits a deduction from earnings representing 50 per cent of
the amount of any occupational or personal pension scheme contributions. The parallel provision for state pension credit purposes is to be found in reg.17A(4A) below.

Para. (11)

See also reg.17B. 　4.62

[¹ Treatment of final payments of income

17ZA.—(1) Save where regulation 13B applies, this regulation applies 　4.63
where—
   (a) a claimant has been receiving a regular payment of income;
   (b) that payment is coming to an end or has ended; and
   (c) the claimant receives a payment of income whether as the last of the
        regular payments or following the last of them ("the final payment").
   (2) For the purposes of regulation 17(1)—
   (a) where the amount of the final payment is less than or equal to the
        amount of the preceding, or the last, regular payment, the whole
        amount shall be treated as being paid in respect of a period of the same
        length as that in respect of which that regular payment was made;
   (b) where the amount of the final payment is greater than the amount of
        that regular payment—
        (i) to the extent that it comprises (whether exactly or with an excess
             remaining) one or more multiples of that amount, each such
             multiple shall be treated as being paid in respect of a period of
             the same length as that in respect of which that regular payment
             was made; and
        (ii) any excess shall be treated as paid in respect of a further period
             of the same length as that in respect of which that regular
             payment was made.

(3) A final payment referred to in paragraph (2)(a) shall, where not in fact paid on the date on which a regular payment would have been paid had it continued in payment, be treated as paid on that date.

(4) Each multiple and any excess referred to in paragraph (2)(b) shall be treated as paid on the dates on which a corresponding number of regular payments would have been made had they continued in payment.

(5) For the purposes of this regulation, a "regular payment" means a payment of income made in respect of a period—

    (a) referred to in regulation 17(1)(a) or (b) on a regular date; or

    (b) which is subject to the provisions of regulation 17(2).]

AMENDMENT

4.64   1. State Pension Credit (Miscellaneous Amendments) Regulations 2004 (SI 2004/647), reg.3(4) (April 5, 2004).

DEFINITIONS

"the final payment"—see para.(1)(c)
"regular payment"—see para.(5).

GENERAL NOTE

4.65   This regulation provides for the treatment of final payments of income. The rule applies whenever the claimant has been receiving a regular payment of income (a term which is wider than it first appears; see para.(5) and below), those payments come to an end and a final payment is made (para.(1)). The basic rule is that where the final payment of income is less than or equal to the previous payment of income, then the whole of the final payment is attributed to the normal period for such payments (para.(2)(a); and see para.(3) for the date on which the final payment may be treated as paid). If, however, the final payment exceeds the usual or 'regular payment', then it is treated as applying to a series of sequential periods, depending on the number of multiples involved (para.(2)(b); and see para.(4) for the dates on which such multiple payments may be treated as paid). Para.(5) defines 'regular payment' by reference to reg.17(1) and (2); the effect of this is that irregular patterns of work may nevertheless give rise to a 'regular payment' for the purpose of this provision (see reg.17(2)(b)(ii)).

[¹ Earnings of an employed earner

4.66   **17A.**—(1) For the purposes of state pension credit, the provisions of this regulation which relate to the earnings of employed earners, shall have effect in place of those prescribed for such earners in the Computation of Earnings Regulations.

(2) Subject to paragraphs [²(3), (4) and 4(A)], "earnings" in the case of employment as an employed earner, means any remuneration or profit derived from that employment and includes—

    (a) any bonus or commission;

    (b) any payment in lieu of remuneration except any periodic sum paid to a claimant on account of the termination of his employment by reason of redundancy;

    (c) any payment in lieu of notice;

    (d) any holiday pay;

    (e) any payment by way of a retainer;

    (f) any payment made by the claimant's employer in respect of expenses not wholly, exclusively and necessarily incurred in the performance

of the duties of the employment, including any payment made by the claimant's employer in respect of—
  (i) travelling expenses incurred by the claimant between his home and place of employment;
  (ii) expenses incurred by the claimant under arrangements made for the care of a member of his family owing to the claimant's absence from home;
(g) the amount of any payment by way of a non-cash voucher which has been taken into account in the computation of a person's earnings in accordance with Part V of Schedule 3 to the Social Security (Contributions) Regulations 2001;
(h) statutory sick pay and statutory maternity pay payable by the employer under the 1992 Act;
(i) statutory paternity pay payable under Part 12ZA of the 1992 Act;
(j) statutory adoption pay payable under Part 12ZB of the 1992 Act;
(k) any sums payable under a contract of service—
  (i) for incapacity for work due to sickness or injury; or
  (ii) by reason of pregnancy or confinement.
(3) "Earnings" shall not include—
(a) subject to paragraph (4), any payment in kind;
(b) any payment in respect of expenses wholly, exclusively and necessarily incurred in the performance of the duties of the employment;
(c) any occupational pension;
(d) any lump sum payment made under the Iron and Steel Re-adaptation Benefits Scheme;
[²(e) any payment of compensation made pursuant to an award by an employment tribunal in respect of unfair dismissal or unlawful discrimination.]
(4) Paragraph (3)(a) shall not apply in respect of any non-cash voucher referred to in paragraph (2)(g).
[²(4A) One half of any sum paid by a claimant by way of a contribution towards an occupational pension scheme or a personal pension scheme shall, for the purpose of calculating his earnings in accordance with this regulation, be disregarded.]
(5) In this regulation "employed earner" means a person who is gainfully employed in Great Britain either under a contract of service, or in an office (including elective office) with emoluments chargeable to income tax under Schedule E.]

AMENDMENTS

1. State Pension Credit (Consequential, Transitional and Miscellaneous Provisions) Regulations 2002 (SI 2002/3019), reg.23(i) (October 6, 2003). **4.67**
2. State Pension Credit (Consequential, Transitional and Miscellaneous Provisions) (No.2) Regulations 2002 (SI 2002/3197), reg.3(1) (October 6, 2003).

DEFINITIONS

"claimant"—see para.(2)(a).
"Computation of Earnings Regulations"—see reg.1(2).
"employed earner"—see para.(5).
"occupational pension scheme"—see SPCA 2002, s.17(1).
"personal pension scheme"—see *ibid.*

GENERAL NOTE

This provides a comprehensive definition of "earnings" for employed earners who claim state pension credit which is independent of the rules contained in the Social Security (Computation of Earnings) Regulations 1996 (SI 1996/2745). In contrast, reg.17B below specifically applies the 1996 Regulations to the assessment of the earnings of *self*-employed earners, subject to certain modifications. The rules governing employed earners in this regulation follow closely (but do not entirely mirror) those that apply to the definition of an employed earner's earnings for the purposes of income support (see Income Support (General) Regulations 1987 (SI 1987/1967), reg.35).

[¹ Earnings of self-employed earners

4.68

17B.—(1) For the purposes of state pension credit, the provisions of the Computation of Earnings Regulations in their application to the earnings of self-employed earners, shall have effect in so far as provided by this regulation.

(2) In their application to state pension credit, regulations 11 to 14 of the Computation of Earnings Regulations shall have effect as if—

[²(za) "board and lodging accommodation" has the same meaning as in paragraph 8(2) of Schedule IV;]

(a) "claimant" referred to a person claiming state pension credit and any partner of the claimant;

(b) "personal pension scheme" referred to a personal pension scheme—
   (i) as defined in section 1 of the Pension Schemes Act 1993; or
   (ii) as defined in section 1 of the Pension Schemes (Northern Ireland) Act 1993.

(3) In regulation 11 (calculation of earnings of self-employed earners), paragraph (1) shall have effect, but as if the words "Except where paragraph (2) applies" were omitted.

(4) In regulation 12 (earnings of self-employed earners)—

(a) paragraph (1) shall have effect;

(b) for paragraph (2), the following provision shall have effect—

"(2) Earnings does not include—

(a) where a claimant occupies a dwelling as his home and he provides in that dwelling board and lodging accommodation for which payment is made, those payments;

(b) any payment made by a local authority to a claimant—
   (i) with whom a person is accommodated by virtue of arrangements made under section 23(2)(a) of the Children Act 1989 (provision of accommodation and maintenance for a child whom they are looking after) or, as the case may be, section 26(1) of the Children (Scotland) Act 1995; or
   (ii) with whom a local authority foster a child under the Fostering of Children (Scotland) Regulations 1996;

(c) any payment made "by a voluntary organisation in accordance with section 59(1)(a) of the Children Act 1989 (provision of accommodation by voluntary organisations);

(d) any payment made to the claimant or his partner for a person ("the person concerned") who is not normally a member of the claimant's household but is temporarily in his care, by—
   (i) a health authority;
   (ii) a local authority;

   (iii) a voluntary organisation;
   (iv) the person concerned pursuant to section 26(3A) of the National Assistance Act 1948; or
   (v) a primary care trust established under section 16A of the National Health Service Act 1977;
(e) any sports award [² being an award made by one of the Sports Councils named in section 23(2) of the National Lottery etc. Act 1993 out of sums allocated to it for distribution under that section]."

(5) In regulation 13 (calculation of net profit of self-employed earners)—

(a) for paragraphs (1) to (3), the following provision shall have effect—

   "(1) For the purposes of regulation 11 (calculation of earnings of self-employed earners), the earnings of a claimant to be taken into account shall be—

   (a) in the case of a self-employed earner who is engaged in employment on his own account, the net profit derived from that employment;

   (b) in the case of a self-employed earner whose employment is carried on in partnership, his share of the net profit derived from that employment less—

   (i) an amount in respect of income tax and of social security contributions payable under the Contributions and Benefits Act calculated in accordance with regulation 14 (deduction of tax and contributions for self-employed earners); and

   (ii) one half of any premium paid in the period that is relevant under regulation 11 in respect of a retirement annuity contract or a personal pension scheme";

(b) paragraphs (4) to (12) shall have effect.

(6) Regulation 14 (deduction of tax and contributions for self-employed earners) shall have effect.]

AMENDMENTS

1. State Pension Credit (Consequential, Transitional and Miscellaneous Provisions) Regulations 2002 (SI 2002/3019), reg.23(i) (October 6, 2003).   **4.69**

2. State Pension Credit (Consequential, Transitional and Miscellaneous Provisions) (No.2) Regulations 2002 (SI 2002/3197), reg.3(2) (October 6, 2003).

DEFINITIONS

"board and lodging accommodation"—see para.(2)(za).
"claimant"—see para.(2)(a).
"Computation of Earnings Regulations"—see reg.1(2).
"dwelling occupied as the home"—see *ibid.*
"personal pension scheme"—see para.(2)(b).
"retirement annuity contract"—see SPCA 2002, s.16(3).

GENERAL NOTE

The earnings of self-employed earners for the purposes of state pension credit are calculated in accordance with the Social Security (Computation of Earnings) Regulations 1996 (SI 1996/2745) (on which see Vol. I in this series), subject to the modifications made by this regulation. Thus the special rule relating to royalties does not apply (para.(3)), as special provision is made for such payments for the purposes of state pension credit (see reg.17(4) and (5)). There is also a more extensive list of disregards to be applied when calculating earnings (para.(4)).

Notional income

4.70   **18.**—(1) A claimant who has attained the qualifying age shall be treated as possessing—

(a) the amount of any retirement pension income—
   (i) to which section 16(1)(a) to (e) applies;
   (ii) for which no claim has been made; and
   (iii) to which he might expect to be entitled if a claim for it were made;

(b) income from an occupational pension scheme which the claimant elected to defer.

(2) Where a person, aged not less than 60, is a person entitled to money purchase benefits under an occupational pension scheme or a personal pension scheme, or is a party to, or a person deriving entitlement to a pension under, a retirement annuity contract, and—

(a) he fails to purchase an annuity with the funds available in that scheme where—
   (i) he defers, in whole or in part, the payment of any income which would have been payable to him by his pension fund holder;
   (ii) he fails to take any necessary action to secure that the whole of any income which would be payable to him by his pension fund holder upon his applying for it, is so paid; or
   (iii) income withdrawal is not available to him under that scheme; or

(b) in the case of a retirement annuity contract, he fails to purchase an annuity with the funds available under that contract,

the amount of any income foregone shall be treated as possessed by him, but only from the date on which it could be expected to be acquired were an application for it to be made.

(3) The amount of any income foregone in a case to which either head (i) or (ii) of paragraph (2)(a) applies shall be the maximum amount of income which may be withdrawn from the fund.

(4) The amount of any income foregone in a case to which either head (iii) of paragraph (2)(a) or paragraph (2)(b) applies shall be the income that the claimant could have received without purchasing an annuity had the funds held under the relevant scheme or retirement annuity contract been held under a personal pension scheme or occupational pension scheme where income withdrawal was available and shall be determined in the manner specified in paragraph (3).

(5) In paragraph (2), "money purchase benefits" has the meaning it has in the Pensions Scheme Act 1993.

(6) A person shall be treated as possessing income of which he has deprived himself for the purpose of securing entitlement to state pension credit or increasing the amount of that benefit.

DEFINITIONS

4.71   "claimant"—see SPCA 2002, s.17(1).
"income"—see *ibid.*
"money purchase benefits"—see para.(5).
"occupational pension scheme"—see SPCA 2002, s.17(1).
"pension fund holder"—see reg.1(2).
"personal pension scheme"—see SPCA 2002, s.17(1).
"qualifying age"—see SPCA 2002, s.1(6).
"retirement annuity contract"—see *ibid.*, s.16(3).
"retirement pension income"—see SPCA 2002, ss.16 and 17(1).

This regulation provides for three types of notional income: certain forms of pension income which have not been applied for or have been deferred (para.(1)), income foregone under a money purchase benefits pension scheme or under a retirement annuity contract (paras (2)–(5)), and cases of income deprivation for the purpose of securing entitlement to (or increasing the amount of) state pension credit (para.(6)). Note also that Pt II of Sch.V lists various forms of capital which are to be disregarded in determining a person's notional income.

4.72

Para. (1)

The general rule is that pension income which the claimant could expect to receive on application is to be deemed to be notional income. The reference to SPCA 2002, s.16(1)(a)–(e) has the effect of confining this provision to various categories of state retirement pension income under the SSCBA 1992 or its Northern Ireland equivalent. Notional income also includes income from an occupational pension scheme which the claimant has chosen to defer. Other forms of income from private pension arrangements may be caught by paras (2)–(5).

Paras (2)–(5)

These provisions mirror those that apply to income support (Income Support (General) Regulations 1987 (SI 1987/1967), reg.42(2A)–(2C); see para.2.315 above).

Para. (6)

This is expressed in the same terms as the notional income and notional capital rules for income support, and so the same principles apply ((Income Support (General) Regulations 1987 (SI 1987/1967), regs 42(1) and 51(1); see paras 2.315 and 2.373 above).

Calculation of capital in the United Kingdom

19. Capital which a claimant possesses in the United Kingdom shall be calculated—

4.73

  (a) except in a case to which paragraph (b) applies, at its current market or surrender value less—
   (i) where there would be expenses attributable to sale, 10 per cent; and
   (ii) the amount of any encumbrance secured on it;
  (b) in the case of a National Savings Certificate—
   (i) if purchased from an issue the sale of which ceased before 1st July last preceding the first day on which state pension credit is payable or the date of determination of the claim, whichever is the earlier, or if there is a subsequent supersession, before 1st July preceding the date of the supersession, at the price which it would have realised on that 1st July, had it been purchased on the last day of that issue; or
   (ii) in any other case, at its purchase price.

  "capital"—see SPCA 2002, s.17(1).
  "claimant"—see *ibid.*

This is in the same terms as the parallel provision in the income support scheme (see Income Support (General) Regulations 1987 (SI 1987/1967), reg.49, and see commentary at para.2.368 above).

4.74

Calculation of capital outside the United Kingdom

4.75   **20.** Capital which a claimant possesses in a country outside the United Kingdom shall be calculated—

(a) in a case where there is no prohibition in that country against the transfer to the United Kingdom of an amount equal to its current market or surrender value in that country, at that value;

(b) in a case where there is such a prohibition, at the price which it would realise if sold in the United Kingdom to a willing buyer,

less, where there would be expenses attributable to sale, 10 per cent, and the amount of any encumbrance secured on it.

DEFINITIONS

"capital"—see SPCA 2002, s.17(1).
"claimant"—see *ibid.*

GENERAL NOTE

4.76   This is in the same terms as the parallel provision in the income support scheme (see Income Support (General) Regulations 1987 (SI 1987/1967), reg.50, and see commentary at para.2.372 above).

Notional capital

4.77   **21.**—[²(1) A claimant shall be treated as possessing capital of which he has deprived himself for the purpose of securing entitlement to state pension credit or increasing the amount of that benefit except to the extent that the capital which he is treated as possessing is reduced in accordance with regulation 22 (diminishing notional capital rule).]

[³ (2) A person who disposes of a capital resource for the purpose of—

(a) reducing or paying a debt owed by the claimant; or

(b) purchasing goods or services if the expenditure was reasonable in the circumstances of the claimant's case,

shall be regarded as not depriving himself of it.]

[¹(3) Where a claimant stands in relation to a company in a position analogous to that of a sole owner or partner in the business of that company, he shall be treated as if he were such sole owner or partner and in such a case—

(a) the value of his holding in that company shall, notwithstanding regulation 19 (calculation of capital), be disregarded; and

(b) he shall, subject to paragraph (4), be treated as possessing an amount of capital equal to the value or, as the case may be, his share of the value of the capital of that company and the foregoing provisions of this Chapter shall apply for the purposes of calculating that amount as if it were actual capital which he does possess.

(4) For so long as a claimant undertakes activities in the course of the business of the company, the amount which he is treated as possessing under paragraph (3) shall be disregarded.

(5) Where under this regulation a person is treated as possessing capital, the amount of that capital shall be calculated in accordance with the provisions of this Part as if it were actual capital which he does possess.]

AMENDMENTS

4.78   1. State Pension Credit (Consequential, Transitional and Miscellaneous Provisions) Regulations 2002 (SI 2002/3019), reg.23(j) (October 6, 2003).

2. State Pension Credit (Consequential, Transitional and Miscellaneous Provisions) (No.2) Regulations 2002 (SI 2002/3197), reg.2 and Sch., para.6 (October 6, 2003).

3. State Pension Credit (Miscellaneous Amendments) Regulations 2004 (SI 2004/647), reg.3(5) (April 5, 2004).

DEFINITIONS

"capital"—see SPCA 2002, s.17(1).
"claimant"—see *ibid.*

GENERAL NOTE

Readers who are well acquainted with the income support system will be familiar with the concept of notional capital, that is capital which the claimant is deemed to possess even though he or she does not actually have such resources. This is, therefore, essentially an anti-avoidance provision in the context of means-tested benefits. Section 15(6) of the SPCA 2002 (which mirrors SSCBA 1992, s.163(5)) provides the legislative authority for such a rule in the state pension credit scheme. The notional capital rule enshrined in this regulation contains some parallels with the equivalent rule in the income support scheme (Income Support (General) Regulations 1987 (SI 1987/1967), reg. 51), but is also different. In particular, the state pension credit rule operates only where there is a deprivation of capital with a view to claiming or increasing entitlement to benefit (para.(1)) or where the claimant is a sole trader or a partner in a business which is a limited company (paras (3) and (4)). There is, therefore, no equivalent to the income support rules governing failures to apply for capital which is available, payments to third parties by someone else on the claimant's behalf or retention of capital received on behalf of a third party (Income Support (General) Regulations 1987 (SI 1987/1967), reg.51(2) and (3)).

Para. (1)

The general rule is expressed in similar terms to Income Support (General) Regulations 1987 (SI 1987/1967), reg.51(1). The Secretary of State must accordingly show that (1) the claimant has deprived him or herself of actual capital, and (2) this was done with the purpose of securing or increasing entitlement to state pension credit. As to (1), the traditional approach has been that "deprive" does not carry a special legal meaning and is a matter of ordinary English (*R(SB) 38/85, R(SB) 40/85*). However, these authorities will have to be applied with some care in the context of state pension credit as, unlike in the income support scheme, para.(2) below gives specific examples of what is not to be regarded as a deprivation. The supplementary benefit and income support case law on the claimant's purpose in making the deprivation will presumably apply equally here given the statutory language is the same in this respect (see commentary at para.2.376 above). There is, however, no express exception for capital for personal injuries compensation held in trust or administered by the court (contrast Income Support (General) Regulations 1987 (SI 1987/1967), reg.51(1)(a) and (c)).

Para. (2)

This is an interesting provision which has no direct parallel in the analogous rule that applies under the income support scheme (Income Support (General) Regulations 1987 (SI 1987/1967), reg.51). That said, it appears to be an attempt to illustrate what is not to be regarded as an act of deprivation. Thus, a disposal for the purpose of either reducing or paying a debt owed by the claimant, or in purchasing goods or services "if the expenditure was reasonable in the circumstances of the claimant's case", is not to be seen as a deprivation. Under the income support scheme, such disposals would be seen as a deprivation and the argument would then revolve around the claimant's purpose in making such a disposal. Typically the claimant would argue that the payment was solely for some other purpose, and not

4.79

4.80

4.81

with a view to claiming or increasing entitlement to benefit. The position under the state pension credit scheme would appear to be different, and perhaps weighted more in favour of the claimant. If the claimant is able to demonstrate that one of the circumstances in para.(2) applies, then there has been no deprivation and the issue as to the claimant's purpose need not be explored. This construction is strengthened by the repeal of the qualifying phrase "Without prejudice to the generality of paragraph(1)" as from April 5, 2004. That amendment also repealed the provision which automatically deemed a disposal by way of a gift to a third party to be a deprivation. However, it remains open to decision makers and tribunals to find that such a gift was a deprivation made with the intent of securing (or increasing) entitlement to pension credit.

Paras (3) and (4)

4.82   These two paragraphs establish an artificial method for dealing with one person companies and analogous enterprises. In summary, the value of the individual's shareholding itself is disregarded (para.(3)(a)), but the claimant is treated as possessing a proportionate share of the company's capital (para.(3)(b)). However, so long as the individual undertakes activities in the course of the business, the amount produced by para.(3)(b) is disregarded (para.(4)). See further the commentary on the parallel provisions in reg.51(4) and (5) of the Income Support (General) Regulations 1987 (SI 1987/1967).

Para. (5)

4.83   As the claimant's capital is to be calculated as though it were actual capital, it follows that notional capital is assumed to yield a weekly income on the basis set out in reg.15(6). It also means that any relevant capital disregards under reg.17(8) and Sch.V must be applied to the notional capital (by analogy with *CIS/231/1991*, discussed at para.2.390 above).

Diminishing notional capital rule

4.84   **22.**—(1) Where a claimant is treated as possessing capital under regulation 21(1) (notional capital), the amount which he is treated as possessing—

(a) in the case of a week that is subsequent to—
   (i) the relevant week in respect of which the conditions set out in paragraph (2) are satisfied, or
   (ii) a week which follows that relevant week and which satisfies those conditions,
   shall be reduced by an amount determined under paragraph (2);

(b) in the case of a week in respect of which sub-paragraph (1)(a) does not apply but where—
   (i) that week is a week subsequent to the relevant week, and
   (ii) that relevant week is a week in which the condition in paragraph (3) is satisfied,
   shall be reduced by the amount determined under paragraph (3).

(2) This paragraph applies to a benefit week where the claimant satisfies the conditions that—

(a) he is in receipt of state pension credit; and
(b) but for regulation [¹21(1)], he would have received an additional amount of state pension credit in that benefit week;

and in such a case, the amount of the reduction for the purposes of paragraph (1)(a) shall be equal to that additional amount.

(3) Subject to paragraph (4), for the purposes of paragraph (1)(b) the condition is that the claimant would have been entitled to state pension credit

in the relevant week, but for regulation [¹21(1)], and in such a case the amount of the reduction shall be equal to the aggregate of—

  (a) the amount of state pension credit to which the claimant would have been entitled in the relevant week but for regulation [¹21(1)];

  (b) the amount of housing benefit (if any) equal to the difference between his maximum housing benefit and the amount (if any) of housing benefit which he is awarded in respect of the benefit week, within the meaning of regulation 2(1) of the Housing Benefit (General) Regulations 1987 (interpretation), which includes the last day of the relevant week;

  (c) the amount of council tax benefit (if any) equal to the difference between his maximum council tax benefit and the amount (if any) of council tax benefit which he is awarded in respect of the benefit week which includes the last day of the relevant week, and for this purpose "benefit week" has the same meaning as in regulation 2(1) of the Council Tax Benefit (General) Regulations 1992 (interpretation).

(4) The amount determined under paragraph (3) shall be re-determined under that paragraph if the claimant makes a further claim for state pension credit and the conditions in paragraph (5) are satisfied, and in such a case—

  (a) sub-paragraphs (a) to (c) of paragraph (3) shall apply as if for the words "relevant week" there were substituted the words "relevant subsequent week"; and

  (b) subject to paragraph (6), the amount as re-determined shall have effect from the first week following the relevant subsequent week in question.

(5) The conditions are that—

  (a) a further claim is made 26 or more weeks after—

    (i) the date on which the claimant made a claim for state pension credit in respect of which he was first treated as possessing the capital in question under regulation [¹21(1)]; or

    (ii) in a case where there has been at least one re-determination in accordance with paragraph (4), the date on which he last made a claim for state pension credit which resulted in the weekly amount being re-determined; or

    (iii) the date on which he last ceased to be in receipt of state pension credit, whichever last occurred; and

  (b) the claimant would have been entitled to state pension credit but for regulation [¹21(1)].

(6) The amount as re-determined pursuant to paragraph (4) shall not have effect if it is less than the amount which applied in that case immediately before the re-determination and in such a case the higher amount shall continue to have effect.

(7) For the purpose of this regulation—

  (a) "relevant week" means the benefit week in which the capital in question of which the claimant has deprived himself within the meaning of regulation [¹21(1)]—

    (i) was first taken into account for the purpose of determining his entitlement to state pension credit; or

    (ii) was taken into account on a subsequent occasion for the purpose of determining or re-determining his entitlement to state pension credit on that subsequent occasion and that determination or re-determination resulted in his beginning to receive, or ceasing to receive, state pension credit;

and where more than one benefit week is identified by reference to heads (i) and (ii) of this sub-paragraph the later or latest such benefit week;

(b) "relevant subsequent week" means the benefit week which includes the day on which the further claim or, if more than one further claim had been made, the last such claim was made.

AMENDMENT

4.85   1. State Pension Credit (Consequential, Transitional and Miscellaneous Provisions) (No.2) Regulations 2002 (SI 2002/3197), reg.2 and Sch., para.7 (October 6, 2003).

DEFINITIONS

"benefit week"—see reg.1(2).
"capital"—see SPCA 2002, s.17(1).
"claimant"—see *ibid*.
"relevant week"—see para.(7)(a).
"relevant subsequent week"—see para.7(b).

GENERAL NOTE

4.86   This diminishing notional capital rule is, in all material respects, identical to that which operates under the income support scheme (Income Support (General) Regulations 1987 (SI 1987/1967), reg.51A). Thus if the amount of notional capital has the effect of removing entitlement to state pension credit altogether, owing to the application of the tariff income rule in reg.15(6) above, that notional capital is to be treated as reducing each week in accordance with para.(1)(b) and (3). In such a case the weekly reduction is by a sum representing the aggregate of the state pension credit which would have been received in the absence of such notional capital plus the proportion of rent and council tax not met by housing benefit and council tax benefit respectively. In other cases, the interaction of the notional capital rule and the tariff income rule will reduce rather than extinguish entitlement to state pension credit. In this type of situation the notional capital is to be treated as reducing each week by the amount by which the state pension credit would be increased in the absence of such notional capital (para.(1)(a) and (2)). Paragraphs (4)–(6) provide for redetermination and recalculation in the event of a fresh claim being made.

Capital jointly held

4.87   **23.** Where a claimant and one or more persons are beneficially entitled in possession to any capital asset they shall be treated as if each of them were entitled in possession to the whole beneficial interest therein in an equal share and the foregoing provisions of this Part shall apply for the purposes of calculating the amount of capital which the claimant is treated as possessing as if it were actual capital which the claimant does possess.

DEFINITIONS

"capital"—see SPCA 2002, s.17(1).
"claimant"—see *ibid*.

GENERAL NOTE

4.88   This provision is essentially in the same terms as the parallel and notoriously problematic provision in the income support scheme (see Income Support

(General) Regulations 1987 (SI 1987/1967), reg.52). However, its impact in the context of state pension credit is likely to be much less as there is no capital rule as such. It will, however, have effect for the purpose of calculating the value of the claimant's capital for the purpose of attributing the deemed tariff income under reg.15(6).

Income paid to third parties

24.—(1) Any payment of income, other than a payment specified in paragraph (2), to a third party in respect of the claimant shall be treated as possessed by the claimant.

4.89

(2) Paragraph (1) shall not apply in respect of a payment of income made under an occupational pension scheme or in respect of a pension or other periodical payment made under a personal pension scheme where—

(a) a bankruptcy order has been made in respect of the person in respect of whom the payment has been made or, to Scotland, the estate of that person is subject to sequestration or a judicial factor has been appointed on that person's estate under section 41 of the Solicitors (Scotland) Act 1980;

(b) the payment is made to the trustee in bankruptcy or any other person acting on behalf of the creditors; and

(c) the person referred to in sub-paragraph (a) and his partner does not possess, or is not treated as possessing, any other income apart from that payment.

DEFINITIONS

"claimant"—see SPCA 2002, s.17(1).
"income"—see SPCA 2002, ss.15 and 17(1).
"occupational pension scheme"—see SPCA 2002, s.17(1).
"partner"—reg.1(3).
"personal pension scheme"—see *ibid.*

GENERAL NOTE

The claimant is deemed to possess income which is paid to a third party by someone in respect of the claimant. This is subject to the exceptions set out in para.(2), which is in identical terms to regs 42(ZA)(d) and 51(3A)(c) of the Income Support (General) Regulations 1987 (SI 1987/1967), which apply to notional income and notional capital respectively for income support purposes.

4.90

[¹Rounding of fractions

24A. Where any calculation under this Part results in a fraction of a penny that fraction shall, if it would be to the claimant's advantage, be treated as a penny; otherwise it shall be disregarded.]

4.91

AMENDMENT

1. State Pension Credit (Consequential, Transitional and Miscellaneous Provisions) Regulations 2002 (SI 2002/3019), reg.23(k) (October 6, 2003).

GENERAL NOTE

This reflects the normal rule for means-tested benefits (see Income Support (General) Regulations 1987 (SI 1987/1967), reg.27).

PART IV

Loss of benefit

Loss of benefit

4.92   **25.**—[*Omitted.*]

GENERAL NOTE

This regulation amends the Social Security (Loss of Benefits) Regulations 2001 (SI 2001/4022); the relevant changes are incorporated in Vol. III in this series.

SCHEDULES

SCHEDULE I   **Regulation 6(4)**

PART I

Circumstances in which persons are treated as being or not being severely disabled

Severe disablement

4.93   **1.**—(1) For the purposes of regulation 6(4) (additional amounts for persons severely disabled), the claimant is to be treated as being severely disabled if, and only if—
(a) in the case of a claimant who has no partner—
  (i)   he is in receipt of attendance allowance or the care component of disability living allowance at the highest or middle rate prescribed in accordance with section 72(3) of the 1992 Act; and
  (ii) no person who has attained the age of 18 is normally residing with the claimant, nor is the claimant normally residing with such a person, other than a person to whom paragraph 2 applies; and
  (iii) no person is entitled to and in receipt of an allowance under section 70 of the 1992 Act ([² carer's allowance]), in respect of caring for him;
(b) in the case of a claimant who has a partner—
  (i)   both partners are in receipt of attendance allowance or the care component of disability living allowance at the highest or middle rate prescribed in accordance with section 72(3) of the 1992 Act; and
  (ii) no person who has attained the age of 18 is normally residing with the partners, nor are the partners normally residing with such a person, other than a person to whom paragraph 2 applies;
  and either a person is entitled to, and in receipt of, an allowance under section 70 of the 1992 Act in respect of caring for one only of the partners or, as the case may be, no person is entitled to, and in receipt of, such an allowance in respect of caring for either partner;
(c) in the case of a claimant who has a partner and to whom head (b) does not apply—
  (i)   either the claimant or his partner is in receipt of attendance allowance or the care component of disability living allowance at the highest or middle rate prescribed in accordance with section 72(3) of the 1992 Act; and
  (ii) the other partner is registered as blind in a register compiled by a local authority under section 29 of the National Assistance Act 1948 (welfare services) or, in Scotland, has been certified as blind and in consequence is registered as blind in a register maintained by or on behalf of a regional or islands council; and
  (iii) no person who has attained the age of 18 is normally residing with the partners, nor are the partners normally residing with such a person, other than a person to whom paragraph 2 applies; and
  (iv) no person is entitled to and in receipt of an allowance under section 70 of the 1992 Act respect of caring for the person to whom head (c) (i) above applies.
(2) A person shall be treated—
(a) for the purposes of sub-paragraph (1) as being in receipt of attendance allowance or, as the case may be, the care component of disability living allowance at the highest

or middle rate prescribed in accordance with section 72(3) of the 1992 Act, for any period—

    (i) before an award is made but in respect of which the allowance is awarded; or

    (ii) not covered by an award but in respect of which a payment is made in lieu of an award;

  (b) for the purposes of sub-paragraph (1)(b) as being in receipt of attendance allowance or the care component of disability living allowance at the highest or middle rate prescribed in accordance section [¹72(3)] of the 1992 Act if he would, but for his being a patient for a period exceeding 28 days, be so in receipt;

  (c) for the purposes of sub-paragraph (1), as not being in receipt of an allowance under section 70 of the 1992 Act for any period before the date on which the award is made.

(3) For the purposes of sub-paragraph (1)(c)(ii), a person who has ceased to be registered as blind on regaining his eyesight shall nevertheless be treated as blind and as satisfying the requirements set out in that sub-paragraph for a period of 28 weeks following the date on which he ceased to be so registered.

Persons residing with the claimant whose presence is ignored

  2.—(1) For the purposes of paragraph 1(1)(a)(ii), (b)(ii) and (c)(iii), this paragraph applies   **4.94** to the persons specified in the following sub-paragraphs.

(2) A person who—

  (a) is in receipt of attendance allowance or the care component of disability living allowance at the highest or middle rate prescribed in accordance with section 72(3) of the 1992 Act;

  (b) is registered as blind in a register compiled by a local authority under section 29 of the National Assistance Act 1948 (welfare services) or, in Scotland, has been certified as blind and in consequence is registered as blind in a register maintained by or on behalf of a regional or islands council;

  (c) is no longer registered as blind in accordance with head (b) but was so registered not more than 28 weeks earlier;

  (d) lives with the claimant in order to care for him or his partner and is engaged by a charitable or voluntary organisation which makes a charge to the claimant or his partner for the services provided by that person;

  (e) is a partner of a person to whom head (d) above applies; or

  (f) is a person who is treated as a child for the purposes of Part IX of the 1992 Act.

(3) Subject to sub-paragraph (4), a person who joins the claimant's household for the first time in order to care for the claimant or his partner and immediately before he joined the household, the claimant or his partner was treated as being severely disabled.

(4) Sub-paragraph (3) applies only for the first 12 weeks following the date on which the person first joins the claimant's household.

(5) A person who is not a close relative of the claimant or his partner and—

  (a) who is liable to make payments on a commercial basis to the claimant or his partner in respect of his occupation of the dwelling;

  (b) to whom the claimant or his partner is liable to make payments on a commercial basis in respect of his occupation of that person's dwelling; or

  (c) who is a member of the household of a person to whom head (a) or (b) applies.

(6) Subject to paragraph 3(3), a person who jointly occupies the claimant's dwelling and who is either—

  (a) co-owner of that dwelling with the claimant or the claimant's [¹partner] (whether or not there are other co-owners); or

  (b) jointly liable with the claimant or the claimant's partner to make payments to a landlord in respect of his occupation of that dwelling.

(7) Subject to paragraph 3(3), a person who is a partner of a person to whom sub-paragraph (6) applies.

  3.—(1) For the purposes of paragraphs 1 and 2, a person resides with another only if they share any accommodation except a bathroom, a lavatory or a communal area, but not if each person is separately liable to make payments in respect of his occupation of the dwelling to the landlord.

(2) In sub-paragraph (1), "communal area" means any area (other than rooms) of common access (including halls and passageways) and rooms of common use in sheltered accommodation.

(3) Paragraph 2(6) and (7) applies to a person who is a close relative of the claimant or his partner only if the claimant or his partner's co-ownership, or joint liability to make payments to a landlord in respect of his occupation, of the dwelling arose either before 11th April 1988, or, if later, on or before the date upon which the claimant or the claimant's partner first occupied the dwelling in question.

PART II

Amount applicable for carers

4.95

4.—(1) For the purposes of regulation 6(6)(a), this paragraph is satisfied if any of the requirements specified in sub-paragraphs (2) to (4) are met.

(2) A claimant is, or in the case of partners either partner is, or both partners are, entitled to an allowance under section 70 of the 1992 Act ([2 carer's allowance]).

(3) Where an additional amount has been awarded under regulation 6(6)(a) but—

(a) the person in respect of whose care the allowance has been awarded dies; or

(b) the person in respect of whom the additional amount was awarded ceases to be entitled or ceases to be treated as entitled to the allowance,

this paragraph shall be treated as satisfied for a period of eight weeks from the relevant date specified in sub-paragraph (4).

(4) The relevant date for the purposes of [1sub-paragraph (3) is]—

(a) the Sunday following the death of the person in respect of whose care the allowance has been awarded (or beginning with the date of death if the death occurred on a Sunday);

(b) where sub-paragraph (a) does not apply, the date on which the person who has been entitled to the allowance ceases to be entitled to that allowance.

5. For the purposes of paragraph 4, a person shall be treated as being entitled to and in receipt of an allowance under section 70 of the 1992 Act for any period not covered by an award but in respect of which a payment is made in lieu of an award.

PART III

Amount applicable for former claimants of income support or income-related jobseeker's allowance

4.96

6.—(1) If on the relevant day the relevant amount exceeds the provisional amount, an additional amount ("the transitional amount") equal to the difference shall be applicable to a claimant to whom sub-paragraph (2) applies.

(2) This sub-paragraph applies to a claimant who, in respect of the day before the relevant day, was entitled to either income support or an income-based jobseeker's allowance.

(3) The relevant day is the day in respect of which the claimant is first entitled to state pension credit.

(4) The provisional amount means the amount of the appropriate minimum guarantee applicable to the claimant on the relevant day but for this paragraph.

(5) The relevant amount means the amount which, on the day before the relevant day, was the claimant's applicable amount—

(a) for the purposes of determining his entitlement to income support; or

(b) for the purpose of determining his entitlement to an income-based jobseeker's allowance,

less any of the following amounts included in it—

(i) any amount determined in accordance with paragraph 2 of Schedule 2 to the Income Support Regulations or paragraph 2 of Schedule 1 to the Jobseeker's Allowance Regulations;

(ii) any amount by way of a residential allowance applicable in accordance with paragraph 2A of Schedule 2 to the Income Support Regulations or paragraph 3 of Schedule 1 to the Jobseeker's Allowance Regulations;

(iii) any amount by way of family premium applicable in accordance with paragraph 3 of Schedule 2 to the Income Support Regulations or paragraph 4 of Schedule 1 to the Jobseeker's Allowance Regulations;

(iv) any amount by way of disabled child premium applicable in accordance with paragraph 14 of Schedule 2 to the Income Support Regulations or paragraph 16 of Schedule 1 to the Jobseeker's Allowance Regulations; and

(v) any amount in respect of a person other than the claimant or his partner by way of enhanced disability premium applicable in accordance with paragraph 13A of Schedule 2 to the Income Support Regulations or paragraph 15A of Schedule 1 to the Jobseeker's Allowance Regulations.

(6) In determining the relevant amount under sub-paragraph (5), the applicable amount shall be increased by an amount equal to the amount (if any) payable to the claimant in accordance with Part II of the Income Support (Transitional) Regulations 1987 (transitional protection) or regulation 87(1) of the Jobseeker's Allowance Regulations (transitional supplement to income-based jobseeker's allowance).

(7) If—

   (a) paragraph 1 of Schedule 7 to the Income Support Regulations or paragraph 1 of Schedule 5 to the Jobseeker's Allowance [¹ Regulations] applied to the claimant or his partner on the day before the relevant day; but

   (b) paragraph 2(2) of Schedule 3 does not apply to the claimant or his partner on the relevant day;

then for the purposes of this paragraph the relevant amount shall be determined on the assumption that the provision referred to in sub-paragraph (7)(a) did not apply in his case.

(8) Subject to sub-paragraph (9), the transitional amount shall—

   (a) be reduced by a sum equal to the amount (if any) by which the appropriate minimum guarantee increases after the relevant day;

   (b) cease to be included in the claimant's appropriate minimum guarantee from the day on which—

      (i) the sum mentioned in head (a) above equals or exceeds the transitional amount; or

      (ii) the claimant or the claimant's partner ceases to be entitled to state pension credit.

(9) For the purposes of sub-paragraph (8), there shall be disregarded—

   (a) any break in entitlement not exceeding 8 weeks; and

   (b) any amount by which the increase in the appropriate minimum guarantee arises solely in consequence of paragraph 2(2) of Schedule 3 ceasing to apply in the claimant's case.

[¹ (10) This sub-paragraph applies where the relevant amount included an amount in respect of housing costs relating to a loan—

   (a) which is treated as a qualifying loan by virtue of regulation 3 of the Income Support (General) Amendment and Transitional Regulations 1995 or paragraph 18(2) of Schedule 2 to the Jobseeker's Allowance Regulations; or

   (b) the appropriate amount of which was determined in accordance with paragraph 7(6C) of Schedule 3 to the Income Support Regulations as in force prior to 10th April 1995 and maintained in force by regulation 28(1) of the Income-related Benefits Schemes (Miscellaneous Amendments) Regulations 1995.

(11) Where sub-paragraph (10) applies, the transitional amount shall be calculated or, as the case may be, recalculated, on the relevant anniversary date determined in accordance with paragraph 7(4C) of Schedule II ("the relevant anniversary date") on the basis that the provisional amount on the relevant day included, in respect of housing costs, the amount calculated in accordance with paragraph 7(1) of Schedule II as applying from the relevant anniversary date and not the amount in respect of housing costs determined on the basis of the amount of the loan calculated in accordance with paragraph 7(4A) of that Schedule.

(12) The transitional amount as calculated in accordance with sub-paragraph (11) shall only be applicable from the relevant anniversary date.]

AMENDMENTS

1. State Pension Credit (Consequential, Transitional and Miscellaneous Provisions) (No.2) Regulations 2002 (SI 2002/3197), reg.2 and Sch., para.8 (October 6, 2003).

                                 4.97

2. State Pension Credit (Transitional and Miscellaneous Provisions) Amendment Regulations 2003 (SI 2003/2274), reg.2(8) (October 6, 2003).

GENERAL NOTE

Schedule I sets out the criteria for the award of additional guarantee credit amounts, on the same basis as under the income support scheme, for severely disabled pensioners (Pt I), for carers (Pt II) and for pensioners with entitlement to transitional additions (Pt III). Regulation 6 is the principal provision governing the guarantee credit and lists the actual weekly amounts for the principal additional elements.

SCHEDULE II   **Regulation 6(6)(c)**

HOUSING COSTS

Housing costs

4.98   1.—(1) Subject to the following provisions of this Schedule, the housing costs applicable to a claimant in accordance with regulation 6(6)(c) are those costs—

(a) which the claimant or, if he has a partner, his partner is, in accordance with paragraph 3, liable to meet in respect of the dwelling occupied as the home which he or his partner is treated as occupying; and

(b) which qualify under paragraphs 11 to 13.

(2) In this Schedule—

(a) "disabled person" means a person—

   (i) aged 75 or over;

   (ii) who, had he in fact been entitled to income support, would have satisfied the requirements of paragraph 12 of Schedule 2 to the Income Support Regulations (additional condition for the Higher Pensioner and Disability Premiums); or

   (iii) who—

      (aa) has not attained the age of 19 and for whom the claimant or his partner is responsible; [²and]

      (bb) is a person in respect of whom disability living allowance is payable or would be payable but for any provision of the Social Security (Hospital In-Patients) Regulations 1975; [²or]

      (cc) is registered as blind in a register compiled under section 29 of the National Assistance Act 1948 (welfare services) or, in Scotland, has been certified as blind and in consequence he is registered as blind in a register maintained by or on behalf of a regional or islands council, or who is within 28 weeks of ceasing to be so registered;

(b) "housing costs" means those costs to which sub-paragraph (1) refers;

(c) "standard rate" means the rate for the time being [⁵ determined in accordance with] paragraph 9.

(3) For the purposes of sub-paragraph (2)(a), a person shall not cease to be a disabled person on account of his being disqualified for receiving benefit or treated as capable of work by virtue of the operation of section 171E of the 1992 Act (incapacity for work, disqualification, etc.).

(4) In this Schedule, "non-dependant" means any person, except someone to whom sub-paragraph (5), (6) or (7) applies, who normally resides with the claimant.

(5) This sub-paragraph applies to—

(a) a partner of the claimant or any person under the age of 19 for whom the claimant or the claimant's partner is responsible;

(b) a person who lives with the claimant in order to care for him or for the claimant's partner and who is engaged for that purpose by a charitable or voluntary organisation which makes a charge to the claimant or the claimant's partner for the care provided by that person;

(c) the partner of a person to whom head (b) above applies.

(6) This sub-paragraph applies to a person, other than a close relative of the claimant or the claimant's partner—

(a) who is liable to make payments on a commercial basis to the claimant or the claimant's partner in respect of his occupation of the claimant's dwelling; [²or]

(b) [² . . .]

(c) who is a member of the household of a person to whom head (a) [² . . .] above applies.

(7) This sub-paragraph applies to—

(a) a person who jointly occupies the claimant's dwelling and who is either—

   (i) co-owner of that dwelling with the claimant or the claimant's partners (whether or not there are other co-owners); or

   (ii) jointly liable with the claimant or the claimant's partner to make payments to a landlord in respect of his occupation of that dwelling;

(b) a partner of a person to whom head (a) above applies.

(8) For the purpose of sub-paragraphs (4) to (7) a person resides with another only if they share any accommodation except a bathroom, a lavatory or a communal area but not if each person is separately liable to make payments in respect of his occupation of the dwelling to the landlord.

(9) In sub-paragraph (8), "communal area" means any area (other than rooms) of common access (including halls and passageways) and rooms of common use in sheltered accommodation.

1164

Remunerative work

2.—(1) Subject to the following provisions of this paragraph, a person shall be treated for the purposes of this Schedule as engaged in remunerative work if he is engaged, or, where his hours of work fluctuate, he is engaged on average, for not less than 16 hours a week, in work for which payment is made or which is done in expectation of payment.

4.99

(2) Subject to sub-paragraph (3), in determining the number of hours for which a person is engaged in work where his hours of work fluctuate, regard shall be had to the average of hours worked over—

    (a) if there is a recognisable cycle of work, the period of one complete cycle (including, where the cycle involves periods in which the person does no work, those periods but disregarding any other absences);

    (b) in any other case, the period of 5 weeks immediately prior to the date of claim, or such other length of time as may, in the particular case, enable the person's weekly average hours of work to be determined more accurately.

(3) Where, for the purposes of sub-paragraph (2)(a), a person's recognisable cycle of work at a school, other educational establishment or other place of employment is one year and includes periods of school holidays or similar vacations during which he does not work, those periods and any other periods not forming part of such holidays or vacations during which he is not required to work shall be disregarded in establishing the average hours for which he is engaged in work.

(4) Where no recognisable cycle has been established in respect of a person's work, regard shall be had to the number of hours or, where those hours will fluctuate, the average of the hours, which he is expected to work in a week.

(5) A person shall be treated as engaged in remunerative work during any period for which he is absent from work referred to in sub-paragraph (1) if the absence is either without good cause or by reason of a recognised, customary or other holiday.

(6) A person on income support or an income-based jobseeker's allowance for more than 3 days in any benefit week shall be treated as not being in remunerative work in that week.

(7) A person shall not be treated as engaged in remunerative work on any day on which the person is on maternity leave [4 , paternity leave or adoption leave] or is absent from work because he is ill.

(8) A person shall not be treated as engaged in remunerative work on any day on which he is engaged in an activity in respect of which—

    (a) a sports award has been made, or is to be made, to him; and

    (b) no other payment is made or is expected to be made to him [2, and for the purposes of this sub-paragraph, "sports award" means an award made by one of the Sports Councils named in section 23(2) of the National Lottery etc. Act 1993 out of sums allocated to it for distribution under that section.]

(9) In this paragraph "benefit week"—

    (a) in relation to income support, has the same meaning as in regulation 2(1) of the Income Support Regulations;

    (b) in relation to jobseeker's allowance, has the same meaning as in regulation 1(3) of the Jobseeker's Allowance Regulations.

Circumstances in which a person is liable to meet housing costs

3. A person is liable to meet housing costs where—

4.100

    (a) the liability falls upon him or his partner but not where the liability is to a member of the same household as the person on whom the liability falls;

    (b) because the person liable to meet the housing costs is not meeting them, the claimant has to meet those costs in order to continue to live in the dwelling occupied as the home and it is reasonable in all the circumstances to treat the claimant as liable to meet those costs;

    (c) he in practice shares the housing costs with other members of the household none of whom are close relatives either of the claimant or his partner, and

        (i) one or more of those members is liable to meet those costs, and

        (ii) it is reasonable in the circumstances to treat him as sharing responsibility.

Circumstances in which a person is to be treated as occupying a dwelling as his home

4.—(1) Subject to the following provisions of this paragraph, a person shall be treated as occupying as his home the dwelling normally occupied as his home by himself or, if he has a partner, by himself and his partner, and he shall not be treated as occupying any other dwelling as his home.

4.101

(2) In determining whether a dwelling is the dwelling normally occupied as the claimant's home for the purposes of sub-paragraph (1) regard shall be had to any other dwelling occupied by the claimant or by him and his partner whether or not that other dwelling is in Great Britain.

(3) Subject to sub-paragraph (4), where a claimant who has no partner is a full-time student or is on a training course and is liable to make payments (including payments of mortgage interest or, in Scotland, payments under heritable securities or, in either case, analogous payments) in respect of either (but not both) the dwelling which he occupies for the purpose of attending his course of study or his training course or, as the case may be, the dwelling which he occupies when not attending his course, he shall be treated as occupying as his home the dwelling in respect of which he is liable to make payments.

(4) A full-time student shall not be treated as occupying a dwelling as his home for any week of absence from it, other than an absence occasioned by the need to enter hospital for treatment, outside the period of study, if the main purpose of his occupation during the period of study would be to facilitate attendance on his course.

(5) Where a claimant has been required to move into temporary accommodation by reason of essential repairs being carried out to the dwelling normally occupied as his home and he is liable to make payments (including payments of mortgage interest or, in Scotland, payments under heritable securities or, in either case, analogous payments) in respect of either (but not both) the dwelling normally occupied or the temporary accommodation, he shall be treated as occupying as his home the dwelling in respect of which he is liable to make those payments.

(6) Where a person is liable to make payments in respect of two (but not more than two) dwellings, he shall be treated as occupying both dwellings as his home only—

    (a) where he has left and remains absent from the former dwelling occupied as the home through fear of violence in that dwelling or of violence by a close relative or former partner and it is reasonable that housing costs should be met in respect of both his former dwelling and his present dwelling occupied as the home; or

    (b) in the case of partners, where one partner is a full-time student or is on a training course and it is unavoidable that he or they should occupy two separate dwellings and reasonable that housing costs should be met in respect of both dwellings; or

    (c) in the case where a person has moved into a new dwelling occupied as the home, except where sub-paragraph (5) applies, for a period not exceeding four benefit weeks if his liability to make payments in respect of two dwellings is unavoidable.

(7) Where—

    (a) a person has moved into a dwelling and was liable to make payments in respect of that dwelling before moving in; and

    (b) he had claimed state pension credit before moving in and either that claim has not yet been determined or it has been determined but—

        (i) an amount has not been included under this Schedule; or

        (ii) the claim has been refused and a further claim has been made within four weeks of the date on which the claimant moved into the new dwelling occupied as the home; and

    (c) the delay in moving into the dwelling in respect of which there was liability to make payments before moving in was reasonable and—

        (i) that delay was necessary in order to adapt the dwelling to meet the disablement needs of the claimant, his partner or a person under the age of 19 for whom either the claimant or his partner is responsible; or

        (ii) the move was delayed pending the outcome of an application under Part VIII of the 1992 Act for a social fund payment to meet a need arising out of the move or in connection with setting up the home in the dwelling; or

        (iii) the person became liable to make payments in respect of the dwelling while he was a patient or was in a care home,

he shall be treated as occupying the dwelling as his home for any period not exceeding four weeks immediately prior to the date on which he moved into the dwelling and in respect of which he was liable to make payments.

(8) This sub-paragraph applies to a person who enters a care home—

    (a) for the purpose of ascertaining whether the accommodation suits his needs; and

    (b) with the intention of returning to the dwelling which he normally occupies as his home should, in the event, the care home prove not to suit his needs,

and while in the accommodation, the part of the dwelling which he normally occupies as his home is not let, or as the case may be, sub-let to another person.

(9) A person to whom sub-paragraph (8) applies shall be treated as occupying the dwelling he normally occupies as his home during any period (commencing with the day he

enters the accommodation) not exceeding 13 weeks in which the person is resident in the accommodation, but only in so far as the total absence from the dwelling does not exceed 52 weeks.

(10) A person, other than a person to whom sub-paragraph (11) applies, shall be treated as occupying a dwelling as his home throughout any period of absence not exceeding 13 weeks, if, and only if—

    (a) he intends to return to occupy the dwelling as his home; and

    (b) the part of the dwelling normally occupied by him has not been let or, as the case may be, sub-let to another person; and

    (c) the period of absence is unlikely to exceed 13 weeks.

(11) This sub-paragraph applies to a person whose absence from the dwelling he normally occupies as his home is temporary and—

    (a) he intends to return to occupy the dwelling as his home; and

    (b) while the part of the dwelling which is normally occupied by him has not been let or, as the case may be, sub-let; and

    (c) he is—

        [8 (i) detained in custody on remand pending trial or, as a condition of bail, required to reside—

            (aa) in a dwelling, other than the dwelling he occupies as his home; or

            (bb) in premises approved under section 9 of the Criminal Justice and Court Services Act 2000,

        or, detained pending sentence upon conviction; or]

      (ii) resident in a hospital or similar institution as a patient; or

      (iii) undergoing or, as the case may be, his partner or a person who has not attained the age of 19 and who is dependent on him or his partner is undergoing, in the United Kingdom or elsewhere, medical treatment, or medically approved convalescence, in accommodation other than in a care home; or

      (iv) following, in the United Kingdom or elsewhere, a training course; or

      (v) undertaking medically approved care of a person residing in the United Kingdom or elsewhere; or

      (vi) undertaking the care of a person under the age of 19 whose parent or guardian is temporarily absent from the dwelling normally occupied by that parent or guardian for the purpose of receiving medically approved care or medical treatment, or

      (vii) a person who is, whether in the United Kingdom or elsewhere, receiving medically approved care provided in accommodation other than a care home; or

      (viii) a full-time student to whom sub-paragraph (3) or (6)(b) does not apply; or

      (ix) a person, other than a person to whom sub-paragraph (8) applies, who is receiving care provided in a care home; or

      (x) a person to whom sub-paragraph (6)(a) does not apply and who has left the dwelling he occupies as his home through fear of violence in that dwelling, or by a person who was formerly his partner or is a close relative; and

    (d) the period of his absence is unlikely to exceed a period of 52 weeks or, in exceptional circumstances, is unlikely substantially to exceed that period.

(12) A person to whom sub-paragraph (11) applies is to be treated as occupying the dwelling he normally occupies as his home during any period of absence not exceeding 52 weeks beginning with the first day of that absence.

(13) In this paragraph—

    (a) "medically approved" means certified by a medical practitioner;

    (b) "training course" means such a course of training or instruction provided wholly or partly by or on behalf of or in pursuance of arrangements made with, or approved by or on behalf of, Scottish Enterprise, Highlands and Islands Enterprise, a government department or the Secretary of State.

Housing costs not met

5.—(1) No amount may be met under the provisions of this Schedule—   **4.102**

    (a) in respect of housing benefit expenditure; or

    (b) where the claimant is in accommodation which is a care home except where he is in such accommodation during a temporary absence from the dwelling he occupies as his home and in so far as they relate to temporary absences, the provisions of paragraph 4(8) to (12) apply to him during that absence.

[1(1A) In paragraph (1), "housing benefit expenditure" means expenditure in respect of which housing benefit is payable as specified in regulation 10(1) of the Housing Benefit

(General) Regulations 1987 but does not include any such expenditure in respect of which an additional amount is applicable under regulation 6(6)(c) (housing costs).]

(2) Subject to the following provisions of this paragraph, loans which, apart from this paragraph, qualify under paragraph 11 shall not so qualify where the loan was incurred during the relevant period and was incurred—

(a) after 1st October 1995, or

(b) after 2nd May 1994 and the housing costs applicable to that loan were not met by virtue of the former paragraph 5A of Schedule 3 to the Income Support Regulations in any one or more of the 26 weeks preceding 2nd October 1995; or

(c) subject to sub-paragraph (3), in the 26 weeks preceding 2nd October 1995 by a person—

    (i) who was not at that time entitled to income support; and

    (ii) who becomes, or whose partner becomes entitled to income support or an income-based jobseeker's allowance after 1st October 1995 and that entitlement is within 26 weeks of an earlier entitlement to income support or an income-based jobseeker's allowance of the claimant or his partner.

(3) Sub-paragraph (2)(c) shall not apply in respect of a loan where the claimant has interest payments on that loan met without restrictions under an award of income support in respect of a period commencing before 2nd October 1995.

(4) The "relevant period" for the purposes of this paragraph is any period during which the person to whom the loan was made—

(a) is entitled to income support, income-based jobseeker's allowance or state pension credit; or

(b) has a partner and the partner is entitled to income support, income-based jobseeker's allowance or to state pension credit;

together with any linked period, that is to say a period falling between two periods separated by not more than 26 weeks in which one of heads (a) or (b) above is satisfied.

(5) For the purposes of sub-paragraph (4), a person shall be treated as entitled to income support or, as the case may be, income-based jobseeker's allowance or state pension credit, during any period when he or his partner was not so entitled because—

(a) that person or his partner was participating in an employment programme specified in regulation 75(l)(a)(ii) of the Jobseeker's Allowance Regulations, in the [²Intensive] Activity Period specified in regulation 75(1)(a)(iv) of those Regulations or in the [²Intensive] Activity Period for 50 plus; and

(b) in consequence of such participation that person or his partner was engaged in remunerative work or—

    (i) in the case of income support, had an income in excess of the claimant's applicable amount as prescribed in Part IV of the Income Support Regulations; or

    (ii) in the case of state pension credit, the claimant's income exceeded the amount of his state pension credit entitlement.

(6) For the purposes of sub-paragraph (4)—

(a) any week in the period of 26 weeks ending on 1st October 1995 on which there arose an entitlement to income support such as is mentioned in that sub-paragraph shall be taken into account in determining when the relevant period commences; and

(b) two or more periods of entitlement and any intervening linked periods shall together form a single relevant period.

(7) Where the loan to which sub-paragraph (2) refers has been applied—

(a) for paying off an earlier loan, and that earlier loan qualified under paragraph 11 during the relevant period; or

(b) to finance the purchase of a property where an earlier loan, which qualified under paragraph 11 or 12 during the relevant period in respect of another property, is paid off (in whole or in part) with monies received from the sale of that property;

then the amount of the loan to which sub-paragraph (2) applies is the amount (if any) by which the new loan exceeds the earlier loan.

(8) Notwithstanding the preceding provisions of this paragraph, housing costs shall be met in any case where a claimant satisfies any of the conditions specified in sub-paragraphs (9) to [²(12)] below, but—

(a) those costs shall be subject to any additional limitations imposed by the sub-paragraph; and

(b) where the claimant satisfies the conditions in more than one of these sub-paragraphs, only one sub-paragraph shall apply in his case and the one that applies shall be the one most favourable to him.

(9) The conditions specified in this sub-paragraph are that—
  (a) during the relevant period the claimant or his partner acquires an interest ("the relevant interest") in a dwelling which he then occupies or continues to occupy, as his home; and
  (b) in the week preceding the week in which the relevant interest was acquired, housing benefit was payable to the claimant or his partner;

so however that the amount to be met by way of housing costs shall initially not exceed the aggregate of—
    (i) the housing benefit payable in the week mentioned at sub-paragraph (9)(b); and
    (ii) any additional amount applicable to the claimant or his partner in accordance with regulation 6(6)(c) in that week,

and shall be increased subsequently only to the extent that it is necessary to take account of any increase, arising after the date of the acquisition, in the standard rate or in any housing costs which qualify under paragraph 13 (other housing costs).

(10) The condition specified in this sub-paragraph is that the loan was taken out, or an existing loan increased, to acquire alternative accommodation more suited to the special needs of a disabled person than the accommodation which was occupied before the acquisition by the claimant.

(11) The conditions specified in this sub-paragraph are that—
  (a) the loan commitment increased in consequence of the disposal of the dwelling occupied as the home and the acquisition of an alternative such dwelling; and
  (b) the change of dwelling was made solely by reason of the need to provide separate sleeping accommodation for persons of different sexes aged 10 or over but under 19 who live with the claimant and are looked after by the claimant or his partner.

(12) The conditions specified in this sub-paragraph are that—
  (a) during the relevant period the claimant or his partner acquires an interest ("the relevant interest") in a dwelling which he then occupies as his home; and
  (b) in the week preceding the week in which the relevant interest was acquired, an additional amount was applicable under regulation 6(6)(c) in respect of the claimant or his partner which included an amount determined by reference to paragraph 13 and did not include any amount specified in paragraph 11 or paragraph 12;

so however that the amount to be met by way of housing costs shall initially not exceed the amount so determined, and shall be increased subsequently only to the extent that it is necessary to take account of any increase, arising after the date of acquisition, in the standard rate or in any housing costs which qualify under paragraph 13 (other housing costs).

(13) The following provisions of this Schedule shall have effect subject to the provisions of this paragraph.

Apportionment of housing costs

6.—(1) Where the dwelling occupied as the home is a composite hereditament and—   4.103
  (a) before 1st April 1990 for the purposes of section 48(5) of the General Rate Act 1967 (reduction of rates on dwellings), it appeared to a rating authority or it was determined in pursuance of subsection (6) of section 48 of that Act that the hereditament, including the dwelling occupied as the home, was a mixed hereditament and that only a proportion of the rateable value of the hereditament was attributable to use for the purpose of a private dwelling; or
  (b) in Scotland, before 1st April 1989 an assessor acting pursuant to section 45(1) of the Water (Scotland) Act 1980 (provision as to valuation roll) has apportioned the net annual value of the premises including the dwelling occupied as the home between the part occupied as a dwelling and the remainder,

the additional amount applicable under this Schedule shall be such proportion of the amounts applicable in respect of the hereditament or premises as a whole as is equal to the proportion of the rateable value of the hereditament attributable to the part of the hereditament used for the purposes of a private tenancy or, in Scotland, the proportion of the net annual value of the premises apportioned to the part occupied as a dwelling house.

(2) Subject to sub-paragraph (1) and the following provisions of this paragraph, where the dwelling occupied as the home is a composite hereditament, the additional amount applicable under this Schedule shall be the relevant fraction of the amount which would otherwise be applicable under this Schedule in respect of the dwelling occupied as the home.

(3) For the purposes of sub-paragraph (2), the relevant fraction shall be obtained in accordance with the formula—

$$\frac{A}{A+B}$$

where—

"A" is the current market value of the claimant's interest in that part of the composite hereditament which is domestic property within the meaning of section 66 of the Act of 1988;
"B" is the current market value of the claimant's interest in that part of the composite
hereditament which is not domestic property within that section.

(4) In this paragraph—

"composite hereditament" means—
    (a) as respects England and Wales, any hereditament which is shown as a composite
    hereditament in a local non-domestic rating list;
    (b) as respects Scotland, any lands and heritages entered in the valuation roll which
    are part residential subjects within the meaning of section 26(1) of the Act of 1987;
"local non-domestic rating list" means a list compiled and maintained under section 41(1)
of the Act of 1988;
"the Act of 1987" means the Abolition of Domestic Rates, Etc. (Scotland) Act 1987;
"the Act of 1988" means the Local Government Finance Act 1988.

(5) Where responsibility for expenditure which relates to housing costs met under this
Schedule is shared, the additional amounts applicable under this Schedule shall be calculated
by reference to the appropriate proportion of that expenditure for which the claimant is
responsible.

The calculation for loans

4.104   7.—(1) The weekly amount of housing costs to be met under this Schedule in respect of a loan
which qualifies under paragraph 11 or 12 shall be calculated by applying the formula—

$$\frac{A \times B}{52}$$

where—

A = the amount of the loan which qualifies under paragraph 11 or 12;
B = the standard rate for the time being [6 applicable in respect of that loan].
[2(2) For the purposes of sub-paragraph (1) and subject to sub-paragraphs (3) and (4A), the
amount of the qualifying loan—
    (a) except where paragraph (b) applies, shall be determined on the date the housing costs
    are first met and thereafter on the anniversary of that date;
    (b) where housing costs are being met in respect of a qualifying loan ("the existing
    loan") and housing costs are subsequently met in respect of one or more further
    qualifying loans ("the new loan"), shall be the total amount of those loans deter-
    mined on the date the housing costs were first met in respect of the new loan and
    thereafter on the anniversary of the date housing costs were first met in respect of
    the existing loan.]
(3) Where the claimant or his partner—
    (a) ceases to be in receipt of or treated as being in receipt of state pension credit; but
    (b) within 12 weeks thereof, one of them subsequently becomes entitled again to the
    credit; and
    (c) sub-paragraph (4) applies,
the amount of the qualifying loan shall be—
        (i) the amount last determined for the purposes of the earlier entitlement; and
        (ii) [2recalculated on the relevant date specified in sub-paragraph (4C)].
(4) This sub-paragraph applies if—
    (a) the earlier entitlement included an amount in respect of a qualifying loan; and
    (b) the circumstances affecting the calculation of the qualifying loan remain unchanged
    since the last calculation of that loan.
[2 (4A) Where—
    (a) the last day on which either the claimant or his partner were entitled to income support
    or to an income-based jobseeker's allowance was no more than twelve weeks before—
        (i) except where head (ii) applies, the first day of entitlement to state pension
        credit; or
        (ii) where the claim for state pension credit was treated as made on a day earlier than
        the day on which it was actually made ("the actual date"), the day which would

have been the first day of entitlement to state pension credit had the claim been treated as made on the actual date; and

(b) sub-paragraph (4B) applies,

the amount of the qualifying loan shall be the amount last determined for the purposes of the earlier entitlement and recalculated on the relevant date specified in paragraph (4C).

(4B) This sub-paragraph applies—

(a) where the earlier entitlement was to income support, if their applicable amount included an amount determined in accordance with Schedule 3 to the Income Support Regulations as applicable to them in respect of a loan which qualifies under paragraph 15 or 16 of that Schedule; or

(b) where the earlier entitlement was to an income-based jobseeker's allowance, if their applicable amount included an amount determined in accordance with Schedule 2 to the Jobseeker's Allowance Regulations as applicable to them in respect of a loan which qualifies under paragraph 14 or 15 of that Schedule; and

where the circumstances affecting the calculation of the qualifying loan remain unchanged since the last calculation of that loan and in this paragraph, "qualifying loan" shall, where the context requires, be construed accordingly.

(4C) The recalculation shall take place—

(a) in a case where sub-paragraph (3) applies, on each subsequent anniversary of the date on which, for the purposes of sub-paragraph (2), housing costs were first met;

(b) in a case where sub-paragraph (4A) applies—

   (i) where housing costs under the earlier entitlement were being met in respect of more than one qualifying loan and the amounts of those loans were recalculated on different dates, on the first of those dates which falls during the award of state pension credit and on each subsequent anniversary of that date;

   (ii) in any other case, on each subsequent anniversary of the date on which housing costs were first met under the earlier entitlement;

(c) in the case of claims for state pension credit made between 6th October 2003 and 5th October 2004 and to which sub-paragraph (4A) does not apply—

   (i) where there are no housing costs to be met as at the date of claim but housing costs are to be met in respect of a qualifying loan taken out after the date of claim, on each subsequent anniversary of the date on which housing costs in respect of that loan were first met;

   (ii) in any other case, on each subsequent anniversary of the date on which the decision was made to award state pension credit.]

[[1](5) Where in the period since the amount applicable under this Schedule was last determined, there has been a change of circumstances, other than a reduction in the amount of the outstanding loan, which increases or reduces the amount applicable, it shall be recalculated so as to take account of that change.]

General provisions applying to housing costs

8.—(1) Where for the time being a loan exceeds, or in a case where more than one loan is to be taken into account, the aggregate of those loans exceeds the appropriate amount specified in sub-paragraph (2), then the amount of the loan or, as the case may be, the aggregate amount of those loans, shall for the purposes of this Schedule, be the appropriate amount.

(2) Subject to the following provisions of this paragraph, the appropriate amount is £100,000.

(3) Where a person is treated under paragraph 4(6) (payments in respect of two dwellings) as occupying two dwellings as his home, then the restrictions imposed by subparagraph (1) shall be applied separately to the loans for each dwelling.

(4) In a case to which paragraph 6 (apportionment of housing costs) applies, the appropriate amount for the purposes of sub-paragraph (1) shall be the lower of—

(a) a sum determined by applying the formula—

$$P \times Q$$

where—

   P = the relevant fraction for the purposes of paragraph 6, and

   Q = the amount or, as the case may be, the aggregate amount for the time being of any loan or loans which qualify under this Schedule; or

(b) the sum for the time being specified in sub-paragraph (2).

(5) In a case to which paragraph 11(3) or 12(3) (loans which qualify in part only) applies, the appropriate amount for the purposes of sub-paragraph (1) shall be the lower of—

(a) a sum representing for the time being the part of the loan applied for the purposes specified in paragraph 11(1) or (as the case may be) paragraph 12(1); or

(b) the sum for the time being specified in sub-paragraph (2).

(6) In the case of any loan to which paragraph 12(2)(k) (loan taken out and used for the purpose of adapting a dwelling for the special needs of a disabled person) applies the whole of the loan, to the extent that it remains unpaid, shall be disregarded in determining whether the amount for the time being specified in sub-paragraph (2) is exceeded.

(7) Where in any case the amount for the time being specified for the purposes of sub-paragraph (2) is exceeded and there are two or more loans to be taken into account under either or both paragraphs 11 and 12, then the amount of eligible interest in respect of each of those loans to the extent that the loans remain outstanding shall be determined as if each loan had been reduced to a sum equal to the qualifying portion of that loan.

(8) For the purposes of sub-paragraph (7), the qualifying portion of a loan shall be determined by applying the following formula—

$$\frac{R \times S}{T}$$

where—

R = the amount for the time being specified for the purposes of sub-paragraph (1);
S = the amount of the outstanding loan to be taken into account;
T = the aggregate of all outstanding loans to be taken into account under paragraphs 11 and 12.

The standard rate

4.106
9.—[⁷ (1) The standard rate is the rate of interest applicable per annum to a loan which qualifies under this Schedule.

(2) Subject to sub-paragraphs (3), (4) and (6), the standard rate shall be 1.58 per cent. plus—

(a) the rate announced from time to time by the Monetary Policy Committee of the Bank of England as the official dealing rate, being the rate at which the Bank is willing to enter into transactions for providing short term liquidity in the money markets, or

(b) where an order under section 19 of the Bank of England Act 1998 (reserve powers) is in force, any equivalent rate determined by the Treasury under that section.

(3) The Secretary of State shall determine the date from which the standard rate calculated in accordance with sub-paragraph (2) takes effect.

(4) Where—

(a) the actual rate of interest charged on the loan which qualifies under this Schedule is less than 5 per cent. per annum on the day the housing costs first fall to be met, and

(b) that day occurs before 28th November 2004, the standard rate shall be equal to that actual rate.

(5) Sub-paragraph (4) shall cease to apply in a particular case to any one or more loans which fall within that sub-paragraph on whichever of the following dates occurs first—

(a) the date on which the actual rate of interest charged on such a loan is 5 per cent per annum or higher,

(b) the anniversary of the date on which the housing costs first fell to be met, or

(c) where a supersession decision based on a change of circumstances arising on or after 28th November 2004 is made under section 10 of the Social Security Act 1998 (decisions superseding earlier decisions), the date of the change of circumstances.

(6) Where sub-paragraph (4) does not apply to a loan which qualifies under this Schedule, the standard rate shall be 5.88 per cent. until the first date determined by the Secretary of State under sub-paragraph (3).]

Excessive Housing Costs

4.107
10.—(1) Housing costs which, apart from this paragraph, fall to be met under this Schedule shall be met only to the extent specified in sub-paragraph (3) where—

(a) the dwelling occupied as the home, excluding any part which is let, is larger than is required by the claimant, his partner (if he has one), any person under the age of 19 and any other non-dependants having regard, in particular, to suitable alternative accommodation occupied by a household of the same size; or

(b) the immediate area in which the dwelling occupied as the home is located is more expensive than other areas in which suitable alternative accommodation exists; or

(c) the outgoings of the dwelling occupied as the home which are met under paragraphs 11 to 13 are higher than the outgoings of suitable alternative accommodation in the area.

(2) For the purposes of heads (a) to (c) of sub-paragraph (1), no regard shall be had to the capital value of the dwelling occupied as the home.

(3) Subject to the following provisions of this paragraph, the amount of the loan which falls to be met shall be restricted and the excess over the amounts which the claimant would need to obtain suitable alternative accommodation shall not be allowed.

(4) Where, having regard to the relevant factors, it is not reasonable to expect the claimant and his partner to seek alternative cheaper accommodation, no restriction shall be made under sub-paragraph (3).

(5) In sub-paragraph (4), "the relevant factors" are—
  (a) the availability of suitable accommodation and the level of housing costs in the area; and
  (b) the circumstances of the claimant and those who live with him, including in particular the age and state of health of any of those persons, the employment prospects of the claimant and, where a change in accommodation is likely to result in a change of school, the effect on the education of any person below the age of 19 who lives with the claimant.

(6) Where sub-paragraph (4) does not apply and the claimant or his partner was able to meet the financial commitments for the dwelling occupied as the home when these were entered into, no restriction shall be made under this paragraph during the first 26 weeks of any period of entitlement to state pension credit nor during the next 26 weeks if and so long as the claimant uses his best endeavours to obtain cheaper accommodation or, as the case may be, no restriction shall be made under this paragraph on review during the 26 weeks from the date of the review nor during the next 26 weeks if and so long as the claimant uses his best endeavours.

(7) For the purposes of calculating any period of 26 weeks referred to in sub-paragraph (6), and for those purposes only, a person shall be treated as entitled to state pension credit for any period of 12 weeks or less in respect of which he was not in receipt of state pension credit and which fell immediately between periods in respect of which he was in receipt thereof.

(8) Any period in respect of which—
  (a) state pension credit was paid to a person, and
  (b) it was subsequently determined that he was not entitled to state pension credit for that period,
shall be treated for the purposes of sub-paragraph (7) as a period in respect of which he was not in receipt of state pension credit.

(9) Any period which falls before the appointed day in respect of which a person was entitled to income support or income-based jobseeker's allowance shall be treated, for the purpose of calculating any period of 26 weeks or as the case may be 12 weeks mentioned in sub-paragraphs (6) and (7), as a period in respect of which he was entitled to state pension credit.

(10) References to state pension credit in sub-paragraphs (6) and (7) shall be treated as including references to income support and income-based jobseeker's allowance in respect of any period which falls immediately before—
  (a) the appointed day; or
  (b) the day the claimant or his partner attains the qualifying age.

Loans on residential property

11.—(1) A loan qualifies under this paragraph where the loan was taken out to defray monies applied for any of the following purposes—   **4.108**
  (a) acquiring an interest in the dwelling occupied as the home; or
  (b) paying off another loan to the extent that the other loan would have qualified under head (a) above had the loan not been paid off.

(2) For the purposes of this paragraph, references to a loan include also a reference to money borrowed under a hire purchase agreement for any purpose specified in heads (a) and (b) of sub-paragraph (1).

(3) Where a loan is applied only in part for the purposes specified in heads (a) and (b) of sub-paragraph (1), only that portion of the loan which is applied for that purpose shall qualify under this paragraph.

Loans for repairs and improvements to the dwelling occupied as the home

12.—(1) A loan qualifies under this paragraph where the loan was taken out, with or without security, for the purpose of—   **4.109**
  (a) carrying out repairs and improvements to the dwelling occupied as the home;
  (b) paying any service charge imposed to meet the cost of repairs and improvements to the dwelling occupied as the home;
  (c) paying off another loan to the extent that the other loan would have qualified under head (a) or (b) of this sub-paragraph had the loan not been paid off,

and the loan was used for that purpose, or is used for that purpose within 6 months of the date of receipt or such further period as may be reasonable in the particular circumstances of the case.

(2) In sub-paragraph (1), "repairs and improvements" means any of the following measures undertaken with a view to maintaining the fitness of the dwelling for human habitation or, where the dwelling forms part of a building, any part of the building containing that dwelling—

(a) provision of a fixed bath, shower, wash basin, sink or lavatory, and necessary associated plumbing, including the provision of hot water not connected to a central heating system;

(b) repairs to existing heating systems;

(c) damp proof measures;

(d) provision of ventilation and natural lighting;

(e) provision of drainage facilities;

(f) provision of facilities for preparing and cooking food;

(g) provision of insulation of the dwelling occupied as the home;

(h) provision of electric lighting and sockets;

(i) provision of storage facilities for fuel or refuse;

(j) repairs of unsafe structural defects;

(k) adapting a dwelling for the special needs of a disabled person; or

(l) provision of separate sleeping accommodation for persons of different sexes aged 10 or over but under age 19 who live with the claimant and for whom the claimant or partner is responsible.

(3) Where a loan is applied only in part for the purposes specified in sub-paragraph (1), only that portion of the loan which is applied for that purpose shall qualify under this paragraph.

Other housing costs

4.110   **13.**—(1) Subject to the deduction specified in sub-paragraph (2) and the reductions applicable in sub-paragraph (5), there shall be met under this paragraph the amounts, calculated on a weekly basis, in respect of the following housing costs—

(a) payments by way of rent or ground rent relating to a long tenancy and, in Scotland, payments by way of feu duty;

(b) service charges;

(c) payments by way of rentcharge within the meaning of section 1 of the Rentcharges Act 1977;

(d) payments under a co-ownership scheme;

(e) payments under or relating to a tenancy or licence of a Crown tenant;

(f) where the dwelling occupied as the home is a tent, payments in respect of the tent and the site on which it stands.

(2) Subject to sub-paragraph (3), the deductions to be made from the weekly amounts to be met under this paragraph are—

(a) where the costs are inclusive of any of the items mentioned in paragraph 5(2) of Schedule I to the Housing Benefit (General) Regulations 1987 (payment in respect of fuel charges), the deductions prescribed in that paragraph unless the claimant provides evidence on which the actual or approximate amount of the service charge for fuel may be estimated, in which case the estimated amount;

(b) where the costs are inclusive of ineligible service charges within the meaning of paragraph 1 of Schedule I to the Housing Benefit (General) Regulations 1987 (ineligible service charges) the amounts attributable to those ineligible service charges or where that amount is not separated from or separately identified within the housing costs to be met under this paragraph, such part of the payments made in respect of those housing costs which are fairly attributable to the provision of those ineligible services having regard to the costs of comparable services;

(c) any amount for repairs and improvements, and for this purpose the expression "repairs and improvements" has the same meaning it has in paragraph 12(2).

(3) Where arrangements are made for the housing costs, which are met under this paragraph and which are normally paid for a period of 52 weeks, to be paid instead for a period of 53 weeks, or to be paid irregularly, or so that no such costs are payable or collected in certain periods, or so that the costs for different periods in the year are of different amounts, the weekly amount shall be the amount payable for the year divided by 52.

(4) Where the claimant or the claimant's partner—

(a) pays for reasonable repairs or redecorations to be carried out to the dwelling he occupies; and

(b) that work was not the responsibility of the claimant or his partner; and

(c) in consequence of that work being done, the costs which are normally met under this paragraph are waived, then those costs shall, for a period not exceeding eight weeks, be treated as payable.

(5) Where in England and Wales an amount calculated on a weekly basis in respect of housing costs specified in sub-paragraph (1)(e) (Crown tenants) includes water charges, that amount shall be reduced—

    (a) where the amount payable in respect of water charges is known, by that amount;

    (b) in any other case, by the amount which would be the likely weekly water charge had the property not been occupied by a Crown tenant.

[¹(6) In this paragraph—

    (a) "co-ownership scheme" means a scheme under which a dwelling is let by a housing association and the tenant, or his personal representative, will, under the terms of the tenancy agreement or of the agreement under which he became a member of the association, be entitled, on his ceasing to be a member and subject to any condition stated in either agreement, to a sum calculated by reference directly or indirectly to the value of the dwelling;

    (b) "Crown tenant" means a person who occupies a dwelling under a tenancy or licence where the interest of the landlord belongs to Her Majesty in right of the Crown or to a government department or is held in trust for Her Majesty for the purposes of a government department except (in the case of an interest belonging to Her Majesty in right of the Crown) where the interest is under the management of the Crown Estate Commissioners;

    (c) "housing association" has the meaning assigned to it by section 1(1) of the Housing Associations Act 1985;

    (d) "long tenancy" means a tenancy granted for a term of years certain exceeding twenty one years, whether or not the tenancy is, or may become, terminable before the end of that term by notice given by or to the tenant or by re-entry, forfeiture (or, in Scotland, irritancy) or otherwise and includes a lease for a term fixed by law under a grant with a covenant or obligation for perpetual renewal unless it is a lease by sub-demise from one which is not a long tenancy.]

Persons residing with the claimant

14.—(1) Subject to the following provisions of this paragraph, the following deductions from the amount to be met under the preceding paragraphs of this Schedule in respect of housing costs shall be made—

    [⁹ (a) in respect of a non-dependant aged 18 or over who is engaged in any remunerative work, £47.75;

    (b) in respect of a non-dependant aged 18 or over to whom paragraph (a) does not apply, £7.40.]

4.111

(2) In the case of a non-dependant aged 18 or over to whom sub-paragraph [²(1)(a)] applies because he is in remunerative work, where the claimant satisfies the Secretary of State that the non-dependant's gross weekly income is—

    (a) less than [¹¹£101.00], the deduction to be made under this paragraph shall be the deduction specified in sub-paragraph (1)(c);

    (b) not less than [¹¹£101.00] but less than [¹¹£150.00], the deduction to be made under this paragraph shall be £17.00;

    (c) not less than [¹¹£150.00] but less than [¹¹£194.00], the deduction to be made under this paragraph shall be £23.35;

    (d) not less than [¹¹£194.00] but less than [¹¹£258.00], the deduction to be made under this paragraph shall be £38.20;

    (e) not less than [¹¹£258.00] but less than [¹£322.00], the deduction to be made under this paragraph shall be £43.50.

(3) Only one deduction shall be made under this paragraph in respect of partners and where, but for this sub-paragraph, the amount that would fall to be deducted in respect of one partner is higher than the amount (if any) that would fall to be deducted in respect of the other partner, the higher amount shall be deducted.

(4) In applying the provisions of sub-paragraph (2) in the case of partners, only one deduction shall be made in respect of the partners based on the partners' joint weekly income.

(5) Where a person is a non-dependant in respect of more than one joint occupier of a dwelling (except where the joint occupiers are partners), the deduction in respect of that non-dependant shall be apportioned between the joint occupiers (the amount so apportioned being rounded to the nearest penny) having regard to the number of joint occupiers and the proportion of the housing costs in respect of the dwelling occupied as the home payable by each of them.

(6) No deduction shall be made in respect of any non-dependants occupying the dwelling occupied as the home of the claimant, if the claimant or any partner of his is—

    (a) registered as blind in a register compiled under section 29 of the National Assistance Act 1948 (welfare services) or, in Scotland, has been certified as blind and in consequence he is registered as blind in a register maintained by or on behalf of a regional or islands council, or who is within 28 weeks of ceasing to be so registered; or

    (b) receiving in respect of himself either—

        (i) an attendance allowance; or

        (ii) the care component of the disability living allowance.

(7) No deduction shall be made in respect of a non-dependant—

    (a) if, although he resides with the claimant, it appears to the Secretary of State that the dwelling occupied as his home is normally elsewhere; or

    (b) if he is in receipt of a training allowance paid in connection with a Youth Training Scheme established under section 2 of the Employment and Training Act 1973 or section 2 of the Enterprise and New Towns (Scotland) Act 1990; or

    (c) if he is a full-time student during a period of study or, if he is not in remunerative work, during a recognised summer vacation appropriate to his course; or

[²(cc) if he is a full-time student and the claimant or his partner has attained the age of 65;]

    (d) if he is aged under 25 and in receipt of income support or an income-based jobseeker's allowance; or

    (e) if he is not residing with the claimant because he has been a patient for a period in excess of [³52] weeks, or is a prisoner; and in calculating any period of [³52] weeks, any 2 or more distinct periods separated by one or more intervals each not exceeding 28 days shall be treated as a single period [¹⁰; or]

[¹⁰ (f) if he is in receipt of state pension credit.]

(8) In the case of a non-dependant to whom sub-paragraph (1) applies because he is in remunerative work, there shall be disregarded from his gross income—

    (a) any attendance allowance or disability living allowance received by him;

    (b) any payment from the Macfarlane Trust, the Macfarlane (Special Payments) Trust, the Macfarlane (Special Payments) (No.2) Trust ("the Trusts"), the Fund, the Eileen Trust or the Independent Living Funds; and

    (c) any payment in kind.

Rounding of fractions

4.112   **15.** Where any calculation made under this Schedule results in a fraction of a penny, that fraction shall be treated as a penny.

AMENDMENTS

1. State Pension Credit (Consequential, Transitional and Miscellaneous Provisions) Regulations 2002 (SI 2002/3019), reg.23(l) (October 6, 2003).

2. State Pension Credit (Consequential, Transitional and Miscellaneous Provisions) (No.2) Regulations 2002 (SI 2002/3197), reg.2 and Sch., para.9 (October 6, 2003).

3. Social Security (Hospital In-Patients and Miscellaneous Amendments) Regulations 2002 (SI 2003/1195), reg.8(2) (May 21, 2003).

4. State Pension Credit (Transitional and Miscellaneous Provisions) Amendment Regulations 2003 (SI 2003/2274), reg.2(9)(a) (October 6, 2003).

5. Social Security (Housing Costs Amendments) Regulations 2004 (SI 2004/2825), reg.2(2) (November 28, 2004).

6. Social Security (Housing Costs Amendments) Regulations 2004 (SI 2004/2825), reg.2(3) (November 28, 2004).

7. Social Security (Housing Costs Amendments) Regulations 2004 (SI 2004/2825), reg.2(4) (November 28, 2004).

8. Social Security (Housing Benefit, Council Tax Benefit, State Pension Credit and Miscellaneous Amendments) Regulations 2004 (SI 2004/2327), reg.7(5)(a) (April 4, 2005).

9. Social Security (Housing Benefit, Council Tax Benefit, State Pension Credit and Miscellaneous Amendments) Regulations 2004 (SI 2004/2327), reg.7(5)(b)(i) (April 4, 2005).

10. Social Security (Housing Benefit, Council Tax Benefit, State Pension Credit and Miscellaneous Amendments) Regulations 2004 (SI 2004/2327), reg.7(5)(b)(ii) (April 4, 2005).

11. Social Security Benefits Up-rating Order (SI 2005/522), art.26(4) (April 11, 2005).

General Note

This Schedule, dealing with housing costs, follows the pattern of the income support scheme (Income Support (General) Regulations 1987 (SI 1987/1967), Sch.3).

SCHEDULE III

Special Groups

Polygamous marriages

1.—(1) The provisions of this paragraph apply in any case to which section 12 (polygamous marriages) applies if the claimant is taken to be "the person in question" for the purposes of that section.

4.113

(2) The following provision shall apply instead of section 3(1)—

"(1) The first condition is that, if the claimant is taken [1 . . .] to be "the person in question" for the purposes of section 12 (polygamous marriages)—
(a) the case is one to which that section applies; and
(b) any one or more of the persons falling within subsection (1)(c) of that section has attained the age of 65.".

(3) The following provision shall apply instead of section 4(1)—

"(1) A claimant is not entitled to state pension credit if, taking the claimant to be 'the person in question' for the purposes of section 12 (polygamous marriages)—
(a) the case is one to which that section applies; and
(b) any one or more of the other persons falling within subsection (1)(c) of that section is entitled to state pension credit.".

(4) The following provision shall apply instead of section 5—

"5. Income and capital of claimant, spouses, etc.

(1) This section applies in any case to which section 12 (polygamous marriages) applies if the claimant is taken to be "the person in question" for the purposes of that section.

(2) In any such case, the income and capital of each of the other persons falling within subsection (1)(c) of that section shall be treated for the purposes of this Act as income and capital of the claimant, except where regulations provide otherwise.".

(5) In regulation 6 (amount of the guarantee credit), for paragraph (1) there shall be substituted—

"(1) Except as provided in the following provisions of these Regulations, in a case to which section 12 (polygamous marriages) applies if the claimant is taken to be "the person in question" for the purposes of that section the standard minimum guarantee is the sum of—
(a) [5£167.05] per week in respect of the claimant and any one spouse of the claimant's; and
(b) [5£57.60] per week in respect of for each additional spouse (whether of the claimant or that spouse) who falls within section 12 (1)(c).".

(6) The maximum savings credit shall be determined on the assumption that the standard minimum guarantee is the amount prescribed for partners under regulation 6(1)(a).

(7) In regulation 7 (savings credit) for paragraph (2) there shall be substituted—

"(2) In any case to which section 12 (polygamous marriages) [3applies] if the claimant is taken to be "the person in question" for the purposes of that section, the amount prescribed for the savings credit threshold is [5£131.20]."

(8) In regulations 3,5, [¹6(8),] 10,12 and 14 and in paragraph [⁴6(5)(b)(v)] of Schedule 1 and in Schedule 2, any reference to a partner includes also a reference to any additional spouse to whom this paragraph applies.

(9) For the purposes of regulation 6(5)(a) and (b), paragraph 1(1)(b)(i) of Part I of Schedule I is satisfied only if both partners and each additional spouse to whom this paragraph applies are in receipt of attendance allowance or the care component of disability living allowance at the highest or middle rate prescribed in accordance with section 72(3) of the 1992 Act.

(10) For the purposes of regulation 6(5)(a), paragraph 1(1)(c) of Part I of Schedule 1 is only satisfied if—

(a) both partners and each additional spouse to whom this paragraph applies all fall within either paragraph 1(1)(c)(i) or paragraph 1(1)(c)(ii); and

(b) at least one of them falls within paragraph 1(1)(c)(ii); and

(c) at least one of them falls within paragraph 1(1)(c)(ii) but not paragraph 1(1)(c)(i); and

(d) either paragraph 1(1)(c)(iv) is satisfied or a person is entitled to and in receipt of an allowance under section 70 of the 1992 Act in respect of caring for one or more, but not all, the persons who fall within paragraph 1(1)(c)(i).

(11) Any reference in this paragraph to an additional spouse to whom this paragraph applies is a reference to any person who is an additional spouse (whether of the claimant's or of a spouse of the claimant's) falling within subsection (1)(c) of section 12 if the claimant is taken to be "the person in question" for the purposes of that section.

Further provisions in the case of patients

4.114

2.—(1) Sub-paragraph (2) applies in the case of—

(a) a claimant who; or

(b) a claimant who has a partner one or both of whom; or

(c) a claimant who is a member of a polygamous marriage one or more of whose members,

is or are a patient, and has or have been a patient for a period exceeding [³. . .] 52 weeks ("long term patient").

(2) In the case of a claimant to whom paragraph (1) applies and who—

(a) has no partner, section 2(3) has effect with the substitution for the reference to the standard minimum guarantee in paragraph (a) of a reference to an amount [³ equal to 20] per cent. of the weekly rate of the basic pension for the time being specified in section 44(4) of the 1992 Act [³ ("the standard reduction")];

(b) has a partner and one of the partners is a long term patient, section 2(3) has effect with the substitution for the reference to the standard minimum guarantee in paragraph (a) of a reference to an amount determined by taking the amount for the time being specified in regulation 6(1)(a) and reducing it by an amount equal to [³the standard reduction];

(c) has a partner and both partners are long term patients, section 2(3) has effect with the substitution for the reference to the standard minimum guarantee in paragraph (a) of a reference to an amount determined by taking the amount for the time being specified in regulation 6(1)(a) and reducing it by an amount equal to twice the sum of the standard reduction;

(d) is a member of a polygamous marriage and one or more members of the marriage are long term patients, section 2(3) has effect with the substitution for the reference to the standard minimum guarantee in paragraph (a) of a reference to an amount determined by taking the amount for the time being specified in regulation 6(1)(a) and (b), as substituted by paragraph 1(5), for the members of the marriage and reducing it by an amount equal to the standard reduction multiplied by the number of members who are long-term patients.

(3) [³. . .]

(4) For the purposes of [³ sub-paragraph (2), the standard reduction] shall be rounded to the nearest 5 pence, 2.5 pence being rounded to the next 5 pence above.

(5) For any period in respect of which sub-paragraph (2) [³ . . .] applies to a claimant, "amount B" in section 3(4) (savings credit) shall have effect with the substitution in paragraph (a) to the appropriate minimum guarantee of a reference to an amount determined—

(a) by taking the amount for the time being prescribed under section 2(4); and

(b) adding to it such amount (if any) as may be applicable in his case in accordance with section 2(3)(b);

and the claimant's income for the purposes of section 3 [¹ shall be determined without regard to any adjustments which fall to be made in accordance with the Social Security (Hospital In-Patients) Regulations 1975.]

(6) In calculating for the purpose of this [³paragraph] periods of [³ . . .] 52 weeks, any periods separated by 28 days or less in which a person is a patient shall link to form one single such period.

AMENDMENTS

1. State Pension Credit (Consequential, Transitional and Miscellaneous Provisions) Regulations 2002 (SI 2002/3019), reg.23(m) (October 6, 2003).

4.115

2. State Pension Credit (Consequential, Transitional and Miscellaneous Provisions) (No.2) Regulations 2002 (SI 2002/3197), reg.2 and Sch., para. 10 (October 6, 2003).

3. Social Security (Hospital In-Patients and Miscellaneous Amendments) Regulations 2002 (SI 2003/1195), reg.8(3) (May 21, 2003).

4. State Pension Credit (Transitional and Miscellaneous Provisions) Amendment Regulations 2003 (SI 2003/2274), reg.2(10) (October 6, 2003).

5. Social Security Benefits Up-rating Order 2005 (SI 2005/522), art.26(5) (April 11, 2004).

SCHEDULE IV   **Regulation 17(7)**

AMOUNTS TO BE DISREGARDED IN THE CALCULATION OF INCOME OTHER THAN EARNINGS

1. In addition to any sum which falls to be disregarded in accordance with paragraphs 3 to 6, £10 of any of the following, namely—

4.116

   (a) a war disablement pension (except insofar as such a pension falls to be disregarded under paragraph 2 or 3);

   (b) a war widow's or war widower's pension;

   (c) a pension payable to a person as a widow [³ or windower] under the Naval, Military and Air Forces, etc. (Disablement and Death) Service Pensions Order 1983 insofar as that Order is made under the Naval and Marine Pay and Pensions Act 1865 or the Pensions and Yeomanry Pay Act 1884, or is made only under section 12(1) of the Social Security (Miscellaneous Provisions) Act 1977 and any power of Her Majesty other wise than under an enactment to make provision about pensions for or in respect of persons who have been disabled or have died in consequence of service as members of the armed forces of the Crown;

[⁴ (cc) a guaranteed income payment;]

   (d) a payment made to compensate for the non-payment of such a pension [⁴ or payment] as is mentioned in any of the preceding sub-paragraphs;

   (e) a pension paid by the government of a country outside Great Britain which is analogous to any of the [⁴ pensions or payments mentioned in sub-paragraphs (a) to (cc) above];

   (f) a pension paid to victims of National Socialist persecution under any special provision made by the law of the Federal Republic of Germany, or any part of it, or of the Republic of Austria.

2. The whole of any amount included in a pension to which paragraph 1 relates in respect of—

   (a) the claimant's need for constant attendance;

   (b) the claimant's exceptionally severe disablement.

3. Any mobility supplement under article 26A of the Naval, Military and Air Forces, etc. (Disablement and Death) Service Pensions Order 1983 (including such a supplement by virtue of any other scheme or order) or under article 25A of the Personal Injuries (Civilians) Scheme 1983 or any payment intended to compensate for the non-payment of such a supplement.

4. Any supplementary pension under article 29(1A) of the Naval, Military and Air Forces, etc. (Disablement and Death) Service Pensions Order 1983 (pensions to widows [³ or widowers]).

5. In the case of a pension awarded at the supplementary rate under article 27(3) of the Personal Injuries (Civilians) Scheme 1983 (pensions to widows [³ or widowers]), the sum specified in paragraph 1(c) of Schedule 4 to that Scheme.

6.—(1) Any payment which is—

   (a) made under any of the Dispensing Instruments to a widow [³ or widower] of a person—

      (i) whose death was attributable to service in a capacity analogous to service as a member of the armed forces of the Crown; and

      (ii) whose service in such capacity terminated before 31st March 1973; and

(b) equal to the amount specified in article 29(1A) of the Naval, Military and Air Forces, etc. (Disablement and Death) Service Pensions Order 1983 (pensions to widows [³ or widowers]).

(2) In this paragraph "the Dispensing Instruments" means the Order in Council of 19th December 1881, the Royal Warrant of 27th October 1884 and the Order by His Majesty of 14th January 1922 (exceptional grants of pay, non-effective pay and allowances).

7. £10 of any widowed parent's allowance to which the claimant is entitled under section 39A of the 1992 Act.

[²**7A.** £10 of any widowed mother's allowance to which the claimant is entitled under section 37 of the 1992 Act.]

8.—(1) Where the claimant occupies a dwelling as his home and he provides in that dwelling board and lodging accommodation, an amount, in respect of each person for whom such accommodation is provided for the whole or any part of a week, equal to—

(a) where the aggregate of any payments made in respect of any one week in respect of such accommodation provided to such person does not exceed £20.00, 100 per cent of such payments; or

(b) where the aggregate of any such payments exceeds £20.00, £20.00 and 50 per cent of the excess over £20.00.

(2) In this paragraph "board and lodging accommodation" means accommodation provided to a person or, if he is a member of a family, to him or any other member of his family, for a charge which is inclusive of the provision of that accommodation and at least some cooked or prepared meals which both are cooked or prepared (by a person other than the person to whom the accommodation is provided or a member of his family) and are consumed in that accommodation or associated premises.

9. If the claimant—

(a) owns the freehold or leasehold interest in any property or is a tenant of any property; and

(b) occupies a part of that property; and

(c) has an agreement with another person allowing that person to occupy another part of that property on payment of rent and—

(i) the amount paid by that person is less than £20 per week, the whole of that amount; or

(ii) the amount paid is £20 or more per week, £20.

10. Where a claimant receives income under an annuity purchased with a loan, which satisfies the following conditions—

(a) that the loan was made as part of a scheme under which not less than 90% of the proceeds of the loan were applied to the purchase by the person to whom it was made of an annuity ending with his life or with the life of the survivor of two or more persons (in this paragraph referred to as "the annuitants") who include the person to whom the loan was made;

(b) that at the time the loan was made the person to whom it was made or each of the annuitants had attained the age of 65;

(c) that the loan was secured on a dwelling in Great Britain and the person to whom the loan was made or one of the annuitants owns an estate or interest in that dwelling;

(d) that the person to whom the loan was made or one of the annuitants occupies the dwelling on which it was secured as his home at the time the interest is paid; and

(e) that the interest payable on the loan is paid by the person to whom the loan was made or by one of the annuitants,

the amount, calculated on a weekly basis, equal to—

(i) where, or insofar as, section 369 of the Income and Corporation Taxes Act 1988 (mortgage interest payable under deduction of tax) applies to the payments of interest on the loan, the interest which is payable after deduction of a sum equal to income tax on such payments at the applicable percentage of income tax within the meaning of section 369(1A) of that Act;

(ii) in any other case the interest which is payable on the loan without deduction of such a sum.

11.—(1) Any payment, other than a payment to which sub-paragraph (2) applies, made to the claimant by Trustees in exercise of a discretion exercisable by them.

(2) This sub-paragraph applies to payments made to the claimant by Trustees in exercise of a discretion exercisable by them for the purpose of—

(a) obtaining food, ordinary clothing or footwear or household fuel;

(b) the payment of rent, council tax or water charges for which that claimant or his partner is liable;

(c)   meeting housing costs of a kind specified in Schedule 2;
(d)   [¹. . .].

(3) In a case to which sub-paragraph (2) applies, £20 or—
   (a)   if the payment is less than £20, the whole payment; or
   (b)   if, in the claimant's case, £10 is disregarded in accordance with paragraph 1(a) to (f), [¹ or paragraph 7] [² or 7A] £10 or the whole payment if it is less than £10.

(4) For the purposes of this paragraph—

"ordinary clothing and footwear" means clothing or footwear for normal daily use, but does not include school uniforms, or clothing and footwear used solely for sporting activities; and

"rent" means eligible rent for the purposes of the Housing Benefit (General) Regulations 1987 less any deductions in respect of non-dependants which fall to be made under regulation 63 (non-dependant deductions) of those Regulations.

12. Any increase in pension under Part IV of the Naval, Military and Air Forces, etc. (Disablement and Death) Service Pensions Order 1983 paid in respect of a dependent other than the pensioner's spouse.

13. Any payment ordered by a court to be made to the claimant or the claimant's partner in consequence of any accident, injury or disease suffered by [²the person] to whom the payments are made.

14. Periodic payments made to the claimant or the claimant's partner under an agreement entered into in [² . . .] settlement of a claim made by [² that person] for an injury suffered by him.

15. Any income which is payable outside the United Kingdom for such period during which there is a prohibition against the transfer to the United Kingdom of that income.

16. Any banking charges or commission payable in converting to Sterling payments of income made in a currency other than Sterling.

[³**17.** Any special war widows payment made under -
   (a)   the Naval and Marine Pay and Pensions (Special War Widows Payment) Order 1990 made under section 3 of the Naval and Marine Pay and Pensions Act 1865;
   (b)   the Royal Warrant dated 19th February 1990 amending the Schedule to the Army Pensions Warrant 1977;
   (c)   the Queen's Order dated 26th February 1990 made under section 2 of the Air Force (Constitution) Act 1917;
   (d)   the Home Guard War Widows Special Payments Regulations 1990 made under section 151 of the Reserve Forces Act 1980;
   (e)   the Orders dated 19th February 1990 amending Orders made on 12th December 1980 concerning the Ulster Defence Regiment made in each case under section 140 of the Reserve Forces Act 1980,
and any analogous payment made by the Secretary of State for Defence to any person who is not a person entitled under the provisions mentioned in sub-paragraphs (a) to (e) of this paragraph.

18. Except in the case of income from capital specified in Part II of Schedule V, any actual income from capital.]

AMENDMENTS

1. State Pension Credit (Consequential, Transitional and Miscellaneous Provisions) Regulations 2002 (SI 2002/3019), reg.23(n) (October 6, 2003).

2. State Pension Credit (Consequential, Transitional and Miscellaneous Provisions) (No.2) Regulations 2002 (SI 2002/3197), reg.2 and Sch., para.11 (October 6, 2003).

3. State Pension Credit (Transitional and Miscellaneous Provisions) Amendment Regulations 2003 (SI 2003/2274), reg.2(11) (October 6, 2003).

4. Social Security (Miscellaneous Amendments) Regulations 2005 (SI 2005/574), reg.2(7) and (8)(d) (April 4, 2005).

4.117

GENERAL NOTE

This Schedule performs the same function in relation to state pension credit as Sch.9 to the Income Support (General) Regulations 1987 (SI 1987/1967) does in the context of income support, although the list of disregards is much less extensive (reflecting the different nature of state pension credit).

4.118

Para. (1)

See Income Support (General) Regulations 1987 (SI 1987/1967), Sch.9, para.16 (although that also includes widowed mother's allowance and widowed parent's allowance: see para.(7)).

Para. (3)

See Income Support (General) Regulations 1987 (SI 1987/1967), Sch.9, para.8.

Paras (4)–(6)

See Income Support (General) Regulations 1987 (SI 1987/1967), Sch.9, paras 54–56.

Paras (7)–(7A)

See Income Support (General) Regulations 1987 (SI 1987/1967), Sch.9, para.16(g) and (h).

Para. (8)

See Income Support (General) Regulations 1987 (SI 1987/1967), Sch.9, para.20.

Para. (9)

This is a more generous provision than the nearest equivalent under the income support scheme. Income Support (General) Regulations 1987 (SI 1987/1967), Sch.9, para.19 provides that, for the purposes of income support, only the first £4 a week of income from a sub-tenant is disregarded (plus a slightly larger prescribed figure where the rent charged includes an amount for heating). This provision grants a state pension credit claimant in similar circumstances a disregard of up to £20 a week on payments from a sub-tenant or licensee.

Para. (10)

See Income Support (General) Regulations 1987 (SI 1987/1967), Sch.9, para.17.

Para. (11)

See Income Support (General) Regulations 1987 (SI 1987/1967), Sch.9, para.15 for the closest equivalent under the income support scheme.

Paras (13)–(14)

These are more generous rules than apply to income support. The rule there is that sums paid by way of personal injuries compensation and held under a trust are disregarded as capital (Income Support (General) Regulations 1987 (SI 1987/1967), Sch.10, para.12), but payments made out of the fund to the claimant count as income or capital in the normal way. The rule for state pension credit is that payments made in compensation for personal injuries under a court order or following a settlement do not count as income. The repeal of the word "final" in the first amendment to para.14 (so that it reads "in settlement of" and not "in final settlement of ") presumably ensures that the benefit of this provision will be gained by pensioners who receive provisional awards of personal injuries damages under the Supreme Court Act 1981, s.32A.

Paras (15)–(16)

See Income Support (General) Regulations 1987 (SI 1987/1967), Sch.9, paras 23–24.

SCHEDULE V   **Regulation 17(8)**

INCOME FROM CAPITAL

PART I

Capital disregarded for the purpose of calculating income

1. Any premises acquired for occupation by the claimant which he intends to occupy as his   **4.119**
home within 26 weeks of the date of acquisition or such longer period as is reasonable in the
circumstances to enable the claimant to obtain possession and commence occupation of the
premises.

[³ **1A.** The dwelling occupied by the claimant as his home but only one home shall be
disregarded under this paragraph.]

2. Any premises which the claimant intends to occupy as his home, and in respect of which
he is taking steps to obtain possession and has sought legal advice, or has commenced legal
proceedings, with a view to obtaining possession, for a period of 26 weeks from the date on
which he first sought such advice or first commenced such proceedings whichever is the earlier,
or such longer period as is reasonable in the circumstances to enable him to obtain possession
and commence occupation of those premises.

3. Any premises which the claimant intends to occupy as his home to which essential
repairs or alterations are required in order to render them fit for such occupation, for a period
of 26 weeks from the date on which the claimant first takes steps to effect those repairs or
alterations, or such longer period as is necessary to enable those repairs or alterations to be
carried out.

4. Any premises occupied in whole or in part—
   (a) by a [⁶ person who is a close relative, grandparent, grandchild, uncle, aunt, nephew or
     niece of the claimant or of his partner] as his home where that person is either aged 60
     or over or incapacitated;
   (b) by the former partner of the claimant as his home; but this provision shall not apply
     where the former partner is a person from whom the claimant is estranged or
     divorced.

5. Any future interest in property of any kind, other than land or premises in respect
of which the claimant has granted a subsisting lease or tenancy, including sub-leases or
sub-tenancies.

6.—(1) Where a claimant has ceased to occupy what was formerly the dwelling occupied as
the home following his estrangement or divorce from his former partner, that dwelling for a
period of 26 weeks from the date on which he ceased to occupy that dwelling or, where the
dwelling is occupied as the home by the former partner who is a lone parent, for so long as it
is so occupied.

(2) In this paragraph—
   (a) "dwelling" includes any garage, garden and outbuildings, which were formerly occu-
     pied by the claimant as his home and any premises not so occupied which it is imprac-
     ticable or unreasonable to sell separately, in particular, in Scotland, any croft land on
     which the dwelling is situated;
   (b) "lone parent" means a person who has no partner and who is responsible for, and a
     member of the same household as, a child; and
   (c) "child" means a person treated as a child for the purposes of Part IX of the 1992 Act.

7. Any premises where the claimant is taking reasonable steps to dispose of the whole of his
interest in those premises, for a period of 26 weeks from the date on which he first took such
steps, or such longer period as is reasonable in the circumstances to enable him to dispose of
those premises.

8. All personal possessions.

9. The assets of any business owned in whole or in part by the claimant and for the purposes
of which he is engaged as a self-employed earner or, if he has ceased to be engaged, for such
period as may be reasonable in the circumstances to allow for disposal of those assets.

[¹ **9A.** The assets of any business owned in whole or in part by the claimant if—
   (a) he is not engaged as a self-employed earner in that business by reason of some disease
     or bodily or mental disablement; but
   (b) he intends to become engaged (or, as the case may be, re-engaged) as a self-employed
     earner in that business as soon as he recovers or is able to become engaged, or re-
     engaged, in that business,
     [³ . . .].]

10. The surrender value of any policy of life insurance.

11. The value of any funeral plan contract; and for this purpose, "funeral plan contract" means a contract under which—

(a) the claimant makes one or more payments to another person ("the provider");

(b) the provider undertakes to provide, or secure the provision of, a funeral in the United Kingdom for the claimant on his death; and

(c) the sole purpose of the plan is to provide or secure the provision of a funeral for the claimant on his death.

12. Where an ex-gratia payment has been made by the Secretary of State on or after 1st February 2001 in consequence of the imprisonment or [²internment] of—

(a) the claimant;

(b) the claimant's partner;

(c) the claimant's deceased spouse; or

(d) the claimant's partner's deceased spouse,

by the Japanese during the Second World War, an amount equal to that payment.

13.—(1) Subject to sub-paragraph (2), the amount of any trust payment made to a claimant or a claimant's partner [³ who is]—

(a) [³ . . .] a diagnosed person;

(b) [³a diagnosed person's partner or] was a diagnosed person's partner at the time of the diagnosed person's death;

(c) [³ . . .] a parent of a diagnosed person, a person acting in place of the diagnosed person's parents or a person who was so acting at the date of the diagnosed person's death.

(2) Where [³ a trust payment is made to]—

(a) [³ a person referred to in sub-paragraph (1)(a) or (b), that sub-paragraph] shall apply for the period beginning on the date on which the trust is made and ending on the date on which [³ that person] dies;

(b) [³ a person referred to in sub-paragraph (1)(c), that sub-paragraph] shall apply for the period beginning on the date on which the trust payment is made and ending two years after that date.

(3) Subject to sub-paragraph (4), the amount of any payment by a person to whom a trust payment has been made or of any payment out of the estate of a person to whom a trust payment has been made, which is made to a claimant or a claimant's partner [³ who is]—

(a) [³ . . .] the diagnosed person;

(b) [³ a diagnosed person's partner or] was a diagnosed person's partner at the date of the diagnosed person's death; or

(c) [³ . . .] a parent of a diagnosed person, a person acting in place of the diagnosed person's parents or a person who was so acting at the date of the diagnosed person's death.

(4) Where [³ a payment referred to in sub-paragraph (3) is made to]—

(a) [³ a person referred to in sub-paragraph (3)(a) or (b), that sub-paragraph] shall apply for the period beginning on the date on which the payment is made and ending on the date on which [³ that person] dies;

(b) [³ a person referred to in sub-paragraph (3)(c), that sub-paragraph] shall apply for the period beginning on the date on which the payment is made and ending two years after that date.

(5) In this paragraph, a reference to a person—

(a) being the diagnosed person's partner;

(b) acting in place of the diagnosed person's parents,

at the date of the diagnosed person's death shall include a person who would have been such a person or a person who would have been so acting, but for the diagnosed person being in a care home.

(6) In this paragraph –

"diagnosed person" means a person who has been diagnosed as suffering from, or who, after his death, has been diagnosed as having suffered from, variant [³ Creutzfeldt]-Jakob disease;

"relevant trust" means a trust established out of funds provided by the Secretary of State in respect of persons who suffered, or who are suffering, from variant [³ Creutzfeldt]-Jakob disease for the benefit of persons eligible for payments in accordance with its provisions;

"trust payment" means a payment under a relevant trust.

14. The amount of any payment, other than a war disablement pension or a war widow's or widower's pension, to compensate for the fact that the claimant, the claimant's partner, the claimant's deceased spouse or the claimant's partner's deceased spouse—

(a) was a slave labourer or a forced labourer;

    (b) had suffered property loss or had suffered personal injury; or

    (c) was a parent of a child who had died, during the Second World War.

15.—(1) Any payment made under the Macfarlane Trust, the Macfarlane (Special Payments) Trust, the Macfarlane (Special Payments) (No.2) Trust ("the Trusts"), the Fund, the Eileen Trust [⁴, the Independent Living Funds or the Skipton Fund].

(2) Any payment by or on behalf of a person who is suffering or who suffered from haemophilia or who is or was a qualifying person, which derives from a payment made under any of the Trusts to which sub-paragraph (1) refers and which is made to or for the benefit of that person's partner or former partner from whom he is not, or where that person has died was not, estranged or divorced.

(3) Any payment by or on behalf of the partner or former partner of a person who is suffering or who suffered from haemophilia or who is or was a qualifying person provided that the partner or former partner and that person are not, or if either of them has died were not, estranged or divorced, which derives from a payment made under any of the Trusts to which sub-paragraph (1) refers and which is made to or for the benefit of the person who is suffering from haemophilia or who is a qualifying person.

(4) Any payment by a person who is suffering from haemophilia or who is a qualifying person, which derives from a payment under any of the Trusts to which sub-paragraph (1) refers, where—

    (a) that person has no partner or former partner from whom he is not estranged or divorced, nor any child who is or had been a member of that person's household; and

    (b) the payment is made either—

        (i) to that person's parent or step-parent, or

        (ii) where that person at the date of the payment is a child or a student who has not completed his full-time education and has no parent or step-parent, to any person standing in the place of his parent,

but only for a period from the date of the payment until the end of two years from that person's death.

(5) Any payment out of the estate of a person who suffered from haemophilia or who was a qualifying person, which derives from a payment under any of the Trusts to which sub-paragraph (1) refers, where—

    (a) that person at the date of his death (the relevant date) had no partner or former partner from whom he was not estranged or divorced, nor any child who was or had been a member of his household; and

    (b) the payment is made either—

        (i) to that person's parent or step-parent, or

        (ii) where that person at the relevant date was a child or a student who had not completed his full-time education and had no parent or step-parent, to any person standing in place his parent,

but only for a period of two years from the relevant date.

(6) In the case of a person to whom or for whose benefit a payment referred to in this paragraph is made, any capital resource which derives from any payment of income or capital made under or deriving from any of the Trusts.

(7) For the purposes of sub-paragraphs (2) to (6), any reference to the Trusts shall be construed as including a reference to the Fund [⁵, the Eileen Trust and the Skipton Fund].

(8) In this paragraph—

"child" means any person treated as a child for the purposes of Part IX of the Contributions and Benefits Act (child benefit);

"course of study" means any course of study, whether or not it is a sandwich course and whether or not a grant is made for undertaking or attending it;

"qualifying course" means a qualifying course as defined for the purposes of Parts II and IV of the Jobseeker's Allowance Regulations;

"sandwich course" has the meaning given in regulation 5(2) of the Education (Student Support) Regulations 2001, regulation 5(2) of the Education (Student Loans) (Scotland) Regulations 2000 or regulation 5(2) of the Education (Student Support) Regulations (Northern Ireland) 2000, as the case may be;

"student" means a person, other than a person in receipt of a training allowance, who is attending or undertaking—

    (a) a course of study at an educational establishment; or

    (b) a qualifying course;

"training allowance" means an allowance (whether by way of periodical grants or otherwise) payable—

(a) out of public funds by a Government department or by or on behalf of the Secretary of State, Scottish Enterprise or Highlands and Islands Enterprise;

(b) to a person for his maintenance or in respect of a member of his family; and

(c) for the period, or part of the period, during which he is following a course of training or instruction provided by, or in pursuance of arrangements made with, that department or approved by that department in relation to him or so provided or approved by or on behalf of the Secretary of State, Scottish Enterprise or Highlands and Islands Enterprise,

but it does not include an allowance paid by any Government department to or in respect of a person by reason of the fact that he is following a course of full-time education, other than under arrangements made under section 2 of the Employment and Training Act 1973 or is training as a teacher [2. . .].

16. [1(1)] An amount equal to the amount of any payment made in consequence of any personal injury to the claimant or, if the claimant has a partner, to the partner.

[1(2) Where the whole or part of the payment is administered—

(a) by the High Court under the provisions of Order 80 of the Rules of the Supreme Court 1965, the county court under Order 10 of the County Court Rules 1981, or the Court of Protection;

(b) in accordance with an order made under rule 131 of the Act of Sederunt (Rules of the Court, consolidation and amendment) 1965, or under rule 36.14 of the Ordinary Cause Rules 1993 or under rule 128 of those Rules; or

(c) in accordance with the terms of a trust established for the benefit of the claimant or his partner,

the whole of the amount so administered.]

17. Any amount specified in paragraphs 18 to 20—

(a) in a case where there is an assessed income period, until the end of that period or until the expiration of one year from the date of payment, whichever is the later; or

(b) in any other case, for a period of one year beginning with the date of receipt.

18. Amounts paid under a policy of insurance in connection with the loss of or damage to the property occupied by the claimant as his home and to his personal possessions.

19. So much of any amounts paid to the claimant or deposited in the claimant's name for the sole purpose of—

(a) purchasing premises which the claimant intends to occupy as his home; or

(b) effecting essential repairs or alterations to the premises occupied or intended to be occupied by the claimant as his home.

20.—(1) Any amount paid—

(a) by way of arrears of benefit;

(b) by way of compensation for the late payment of benefit; or

(c) in lieu of the payment of benefit;

[3 d) any payment made by a local authority (including in England a county council), or by the National Assembly for Wales, to or on behalf of the claimant or his partner relating to a service which is provided to develop or sustain the capacity of the claimant or his partner to live independently in his accommodation.]

(2) In paragraph (1), "benefit" means—

(a) attendance allowance under section 64 of the Contributions and Benefits Act;

(b) disability living allowance;

(c) income support;

(d) income-based jobseeker's allowance;

(e) housing benefit;

(f) state pension credit;

(g) [3 . . .]

(h) [3 an increase of a disablement pension under section 104 of the Contributions and Benefits Act (increase where constant attendance needed), and any further increase of such a pension under section 105 of that Act (increase for exceptionally severe disablement)];

(i) any amount included on account of the claimant's exceptionally severe disablement [3 or need for constant attendance] in a war disablement pension or a war widow's or widower's pension.

[1(j) council tax benefit;

(k) social fund payments;

(l) child benefit;

(m) [3 . . .]

(n) child tax credit under the Tax Credits Act 2002.]

[³**20A.**—(1) Subject to sub-paragraph (3), any payment of £5,000 or more to which paragraph 20(1)(a), (b) or (c) applies, which has been made to rectify, or to compensate for, an official error relating to a relevant benefit and has been received by the claimant in full on or after the day on which he became entitled to benefit under these Regulations.

(2) Subject to sub-paragraph (3), the total amount of any payment disregarded under—
- (a) paragraph 7(2) of Schedule 10 to the Income Support (General) Regulations 1987;
- (b) paragraph 12(2) of Schedule 8 to the Jobseeker's Allowance Regulations 1996;
- (c) paragraph 8(2) of Schedule 5 or paragraph 21A of Schedule 5ZA to the Housing Benefit (General) Regulations 1987; or
- (d) paragraph 8(2) of Schedule 5 or paragraph 21A of Schedule 5ZA to the Council Tax Benefit (General) Regulations 1992,

where the award during which the disregard last applied in respect of the relevant sum either terminated immediately before the relevant date or is still in existence at that date.

(3) Any disregard which applies under sub-paragraph (1) or (2) shall have effect until the award comes to an end.

(4) In this paragraph—

"the award", except in sub-paragraph (2), means—
- (a) the award of State Pension Credit under these Regulations during which the relevant sum or, where it is received in more than one instalment, the first instalment of that sum is received; or
- (b) where that award is followed immediately by one or more further awards which begins immediately after the previous award ends, such further awards until the end of the last award, provided that, for such further awards, the claimant—
  - (i) is the person who received the relevant sum;
  - (ii) is the partner of that person; or
  - (iii) was the partner of that person at the date of his death;

"official error"—
- (a) where the error relates to housing benefit or council tax benefit, has the meaning given by regulation 1(2) of the Housing Benefit and Council Tax Benefit (Decisions and Appeals) Regulations 2001; and
- (b) where the error relates to any other relevant benefit, has the meaning given by regulation 1(3) of the Social Security and Child Support (Decisions and Appeals) Regulations 1999;

"the relevant date" means the date on which the claimant became entitled to benefit under the Act;

"relevant benefit" means any benefit specified in paragraph 20(2); and

"the relevant sum" means the total payment referred to in sub-paragraph (1) or, as the case may be, the total amount referred to in sub-paragraph (2).]

21. Where a capital asset is held in a currency other than sterling, any banking charge or commission payable in converting that capital into sterling.

22. The value of the right to receive income from an occupational pension scheme or a personal pension scheme.

23. The value of a right to receive income from a under a retirement annuity contract.

PART II

[¹**Capital disregarded only for the purposes of determining deemed income**]

24. The value of the right to receive any income under a life interest or from a life rent.

25. The value of the right to receive any rent except where the claimant has a reversionary interest in the property in respect of which rent is due.

26. The value of the right to receive any income under an annuity or the surrender value (if any) of such an annuity.

27. [³ . . .]

28. Where property is held under a trust, other than—
- (a) a charitable trust within the meaning of the Charities Act 1993; or
- (b) a trust set up with any payment to which paragraph 16 of this Schedule applies, and under the terms of the trust, payments fall to be made, or the trustees have a discretion to make payments, to or for the benefit of the claimant or the claimant's partner, or both, that property.

4.120

AMENDMENTS

4.121   1. State Pension Credit (Consequential, Transitional and Miscellaneous Provisions) Regulations 2002 (SI 2002/3019), reg.23(o) (October 6, 2003).

2. State Pension Credit (Consequential, Transitional and Miscellaneous Provisions) (No.2) Regulations 2002 (SI 2002/3197), reg.2 and Sch., para. 12 (October 6, 2003).

3. State Pension Credit (Transitional and Miscellaneous Provisions) Amendment Regulations 2003 (SI 2003/2274), reg. 2(12) (October 6, 2003).

4. Social Security (Miscellaneous Amendments) (No. 2) Regulations 2004 (SI 2004/1141), regs 3(3) and 3(4)(d) (May 12, 2004).

5. Social Security (Miscellaneous Amendments) (No. 2) Regulations 2004 (SI 2004/1141), regs 3(5) and 3(6)(d) (May 12, 2004).

6. Social Security (Housing Benefit, Council Tax Benefit, State Pension Credit and Miscellaneous Amendments) Regulations 2004 (SI 2004/2327), reg.7(6) (October 4, 2004).

GENERAL NOTE

4.122   This Schedule includes many of the same disregards as are to be found in Sch.10 to the Income Support (General) Regulations 1987 (SI 1987/1967). However, the function of the two Schedules is conceptually different. The purpose of Sch.10 in the income support scheme is to provide for disregards to be applied in calculating the claimant's capital with a view to seeing whether the relevant capital threshold is exceeded. The purpose of this Schedule is to specify disregards which apply in the assessment of capital which is then used for calculating the claimant's income under the tariff income rule in reg.15(6), there being no capital rule as such in the state pension credit scheme. That said, the actual drafting of these provisions follows closely the parallel provisions in the income support schemes. But note also that the disregards in this Schedule are subdivided into two categories: those which are disregarded for the purpose of calculating income (Pt I) and those disregarded—which are fewer in number— for the purpose of calculating notional income (Pt II).

Para. (1)
See Income Support (General) Regulations 1987 (SI 1987/1967), Sch.10, para.2. The claimant's own home (Sch.2, para.1 of the 1987 Regulations) is disregarded for state pension credit purposes by para.1A below.

Paras (2)–(3)
See Income Support (General) Regulations 1987 (SI 1987/1967), Sch.10, paras 27–28.

Paras (4)–(5)
See Income Support (General) Regulations 1987 (SI 1987/1967), Sch.10, paras 4 and 5.

Para. (4) provides for the disregard of the value of a second property where that property is occupied by someone who is aged 60 or over or is incapacitated and who is a relative of the pension credit claimant or their partner. Note that the original drafting of para.(4) meant that the disregard applied only if the occupier of the property was a close relative of the pension credit claimant himself (or herself). The amended formulation applies the disregard equally where the occupier is a close relative of the claimant's partner. The original wording reflected a drafting oversight, and the minister has indicated that extra-statutory payments will be considered to anyone who lost out (*Hansard*, HC Debates, vol. 421, col. 140W, May 10, 2004).

Para. (6)
This applies the more generous housing benefit and council tax benefit disregard (see, *e.g.* Housing Benefit (General) Regulations 1987 (SI1987/1971), Sch.5,

para.24) in preference to the more limited disregard in the Income Support (General) Regulations 1987 (SI 1987/1967), Sch.10, para.25. Thus the disregard on a former family home is for 26 weeks where the claimant moves out following a relationship breakdown, and beyond that time if the remaining partner is a lone parent (until such time as that status ceases).

Para. (7)

See Income Support (General) Regulations 1987 (SI 1987/1967), Sch.10, para.26.

Para. (8)

See Income Support (General) Regulations 1987 (SI 1987/1967), Sch.10, para.10 (although the qualification in the income support provision is not repeated here).

Paras (9)–(9A)

See Income Support (General) Regulations 1987 (SI 1987/1967), Sch.10, para.6(1) and (2).

Para. (10)

See Income Support (General) Regulations 1987 (SI 1987/1967), Sch.10, para.15.

4.123

Para. (11)

This has no direct parallel under the income support scheme.

Para. (12)

See Income Support (General) Regulations 1987 (SI 1987/1967), Sch.10, para.61.

Paras (13)–(14)

See Income Support (General) Regulations 1987 (SI 1987/1967), Sch.10, paras 64–65.

Para. (15)

See Income Support (General) Regulations 1987 (SI 1987/1967), Sch.10, para.22.

Para. (16)

Payments in respect of compensation for personal injuries are disregarded for both capital and income purposes (see also Sch.IV, paras 13 and 14). Para.16(2) deals with the specific example of funds held in court: see Income Support (General) Regulations 1987 (SI 1987/1967), Sch.10, paras 44 and 45.

Paras (17)–(19)

These paragraphs are designed to fulfil broadly the same functions as the disregards Income Support (General) Regulations 1987 (SI 1987/1967), Sch.10, paras 3 and 8. These disregards, however, last for one year rather than the "26 weeks or such longer period as is reasonable in the circumstances" qualification that applies under the income support scheme.

Para. (20)

See Income Support (General) Regulations 1987 (SI 1987/1967), Sch.10, para.7.

4.124

Para. (21)

See Income Support (General) Regulations 1987 (SI 1987/1967), Sch.10, para.21. See also reg.17(6).

Para. (22)

See Income Support (General) Regulations 1987 (SI 1987/1967), Sch.10, para.(23).

Paras (24)–(26)

See Income Support (General) Regulations 1987 (SI 1987/1967), Sch.10, paras 13, 24 and 11 respectively.

SCHEDULE VI   **Regulation 17(9)**

SUMS DISREGARDED FROM CLAIMANT'S EARNINGS

4.125

1.—(1) In a case where a claimant is a lone parent, £20 of earnings.

(2) In this paragraph—
   (a) "lone parent" means a person who has no partner and who is responsible for, and a member of the same household as, a child;
   (b) "child" means a person treated as a child for the purposes of Part IX of the 1992 Act.

2. In a case of earnings from employment to which sub-paragraph (2) applies, £20.

(2) This paragraph applies to employment—
   (a) as a part-time fireman in a fire brigade maintained in pursuance of the Fire Services Acts 1947 to 1959;
   [³(aa) as a part-time fire-fighter employed by a fire and rescue authority;]
   (b) as an auxiliary coastguard in respect of coast rescue activities;
   (c) in the manning or launching of a lifeboat if the employment is part-time;
   [¹(d) a member of any territorial or reserve force prescribed in Part I of Schedule 6 to the Social Security (Contributions) Regulations 2001].

[¹2A. Where a person is engaged in one or more of the employments specified in paragraph 2 but his earnings derived from those employments are less than £20 in any week and he is also engaged in any other employment, so much of his earnings from that other employment as would not in aggregate with the amount of his earnings disregarded under paragraph 2 exceed £20.]

[² 2B. Where only one member of a couple is in employment specified in paragraph 2(2), so much of the earnings of the other member of the couple as would not, in aggregate with the earnings disregarded under paragraph 2, exceed £20.]

3.—(1) If the claimant or one of the partners is a carer, or both partners are carers, £20 of any earnings received from his or their employment.

(2) In this paragraph the claimant or his partner is a carer if paragraph 4 of Part II of Schedule I(amount applicable for carers) is satisfied in respect of him.

4.—(1) £20 is disregarded if the claimant or, if he has a partner, his partner—
   (a) is in receipt of—
      (i) long-term incapacity benefit under section 30A of the 1992 Act;
      (ii) severe disablement allowance under section 68 of that Act;
      (iii) attendance allowance;
      (iv) disability living allowance under section 71 to 76 of that Act;
      (v) any mobility supplement under article 26A of the Naval, Military and Air Forces, etc. (Disablement and Death) Service Pensions Order 1983 (including such a supplement by virtue of any other scheme or order) or under article 25A of the Personal Injuries (Civilians) Scheme 1983; or
      [¹(vi) the disability element or the severe disability element of working tax credit under Schedule 2 to the Working Tax Credit (Entitlement and Maximum Rate) Regulations 2002; or]
   (b) is or are registered as blind in a register compiled by a local authority under section 29 of the National Assistance Act 1948 (welfare services) or, in Scotland, has been certified as blind and in consequence is registered as blind in a register maintained by or on behalf of a regional or islands council.

(2) Subject to sub-paragraph (4), £20 is disregarded if the claimant or, if he has a partner, his partner has, within a period of 8 weeks ending on the day in respect of which the claimant first satisfies the conditions for entitlement to state pension credit, had an award of income support or income-based jobseeker's allowance and—
   (a) £20 was disregarded in respect of earnings taken into account in that award;
   (b) the person whose earnings qualified for the disegard in employment after the termination of that award.

(3) Subject to sub-paragraph (4), £20 is disregarded if the claimant or, if he has a partner, his partner, immediately before attaining pensionable age—

    (a) had an award of state pension credit; and

    (b) a disregard under paragraph 4(1)(a)(i) or (ii) was taken into account in determining that award.

(4) The disregard of £20 specified in sub-paragraphs (2) and (3) applies so long as there is no break, other a break which does not exceed eight weeks—

    (a) in a case to which sub-paragraph (2) refers, in a person's entitlement to state pension credit or in employment following the first day in respect of which state pension credit is awarded; or

    (b) in a case where sub-paragraph (3) applies, in the person's entitlement to state pension credit since attaining pensionable age.

(5) [¹. . .].

[¹**4A.**—(1) £20 is the maximum amount which may be disregarded under any of paragraphs 1, 2, 3 or 4 notwithstanding that—

    (a) in the case of a claimant with no partner, he satisfies the requirements of more than one of those paragraphs or, in the case of paragraph 4, he satisfies the requirements of more than one of the sub-paragraphs of that paragraph; or

    (b) in the case of married or unmarried couples, both partners satisfy one or more of the requirements of paragraphs 2, 3 and 4.

(2) Where, in a case to which sub-paragraph (1)(b) applies, the amount to be disregarded in respect of one of the partners ("the first partner") is less than £20, the amount to be disregarded in respect of the other partner shall be so much of that other partner's earnings as would not, in aggregate with the first partner's earnings, exceed £20.]

5. Except where the claimant or his partner qualifies for a £20 disregard under the preceding provisions of this Schedule—

    (a) £5 shall be disregarded if a claimant who has no partner has earnings;

    (b) £10 shall be disregarded if a claimant who has a partner has earnings.

6. Any earnings [¹, other than any amount referred to in regulation 17(9)(b),] derived from any employment which ended before the day in respect of which the claimant first satisfies the conditions for entitlement to state pension credit.

[¹**7.** Any banking charges or commission payable in converting to Sterling payments of earnings made in a currency other than Sterling.]

AMENDMENTS

1. State Pension Credit (Consequential, Transitional and Miscellaneous Provisions) (No.2) Regulations 2002 (SI 2002/3197), reg.2 and Sch., para.13 (October 6, 2003).

2. State Pension Credit (Transitional and Miscellaneous Provisions) Amendment Regulations 2003 (SI 2003/2274), reg.2(13) (October 6, 2003).

3. Fire and Rescue Services Act 2004 (Consequential Amendments) (England) Order 2004 (SI 2004/3168), reg.62 (December 30, 2004).

4.126

DEFINITIONS

"attendance allowance"—see reg.1(2).

"child"—see para.1(2).

"claimant"—see SPCA 2002, s.17(1).

"lone parent"—see para.1(2).

"partner"—see reg.1(3).

"pensionable age"—see SPCA 2002, s.17(1).

GENERAL NOTE

This Schedule performs the same function in relation to state pension credit as Sch.8 to the Income Support (General) Regulations 1987 (SI 1987/1967) does in the context of income support. Thus the standard disregard on earnings is £5 a week for a single claimant and £10 a week for a couple (para.5). There are then various special cases (*e.g.* lone parents, carers, disabled claimants and those active pensioners who are still involved in various emergency services in a part-time capacity) where the disregard is £20 a week. Note that the maximum weekly disregard is £20 even where both members of a couple satisfy one of the tests for the maximum disregard (para.(4A)).

4.127

There is, however, one significant difference from income support: although the same earnings disregards apply, there is no 16-hours rule in the context of state pension credit. On the other hand, the low level of the earnings disregards is hardly an incentive for pensioners (or their partners) to work extra hours.

The typographical error in para.4(2)(b) ("disegard" for "disregard") appears in the original version of the Regulations and, as at the time of writing, has not been corrected.

State Pension Credit (Consequential, Transitional and Miscellaneous Provisions) Regulations 2002

(SI 2002/3019)

PART VII

TRANSITIONAL PROVISIONS

Persons entitled to income support immediately before the appointed day

4.128

36.—(1) This regulation applies in the case of any person (referred to as "the transferee") who—
  (a) immediately before the appointed day, is entitled to income support; and
  (b) attains or has attained the qualifying age on or before the appointed day.

(2) The transferee shall be treated as having made a claim for state pension credit in the period of 6 months immediately preceding the appointed day.

(3) The Secretary of State shall, so far as practicable, decide before the appointed day a claim for state pension credit treated as made under paragraph (2).

(4) A decision of the Secretary of State made in accordance with paragraph (3) may be revised by the Secretary of State at any time within the period of 13 months commencing on the date of notification of the decision if an application is made by the claimant to the Secretary of State or a person acting on his behalf for the decision to be revised.

(5) For the purposes of section 9 (duration of assessed income period), the decision of the Secretary of State takes effect on the of appointed day.

(6) Notwithstanding the provisions of regulation 26B(4) of the Claims and Payments Regulations, state pension credit may in the case of a transferee be payable in arrears if the income support to which he was entitled before the appointed day was paid in arrears.

(7) [² Notwithstanding the provisions of Schedule 3B of the Decisions and Appeals Regulations,] in the case of a transferee to whom paragraph (6) applies, any decision under section 10 of the 1998 Act which—
  (a) supersedes a decision awarding state pension credit to a transferee; and

(b) is made on the ground that there has been a relevant change of circumstances since the decision was made or that it is anticipated that a relevant change of circumstances will occur,

shall take effect from the first day of the benefit week in which the change occurs or is expected to occur.

[² (7A) Notwithstanding the provisions of paragraph (7), where the relevant change of circumstances is that the transferee becomes a patient again within the same benefit week in which he ceased to be a patient, the superseding decision in respect of becoming a patient again shall take effect from the first day of the benefit week following the benefit week in which the change occurs.]

(8) For the purpose of paragraph (7), "benefit week" means the period of 7 days ending on the day on which, in the claimant's case, state pension credit is payable.

(9) Any payment made to a transferee to whom paragraph (10) applies—

(a) in respect of a period falling on or after the appointed day;

(b) which would have been payable under an award of income support but for the coming into force of the Act,

shall be offset against any state pension credit payable under an award on or after 6th October 2003 on a claim treated as made under paragraph (2).

(10) This paragraph applies to a transferee in respect of whom no decision has been made on his claim for state pension credit which is treated as having been made in accordance with paragraph (2).

(11) If the Secretary of State determines that no state pension credit is payable, or that the amount payable is less than the payments referred to in paragraph (9), he shall determine the amount of the overpayment.

(12) The amount of any overpayment determined in accordance with paragraph (11) shall be recoverable by the Secretary of State by the same procedures and subject to the same conditions as if it were recoverable under section 71(1) of the Administration Act.

(13) Where the transferee—

(a) has, immediately before the appointed day, an award of income support payable by direct credit transfer in accordance with regulation 21 of the Claims and Payments Regulations; and

(b) state pension credit is payable or treated as payable to him as from the appointed day,

the state pension credit shall be paid by direct credit transfer into the same bank or other account as the payment of income support; and for this purpose, any application made or treated as made and any consent given or treated as given in relation to the payment of income support shall be treated as made or given in relation to the payment of state pension credit.

(14) Where —

(a) the transferee had immediately before the appointed day an award of income support from which deductions were made or where part of the benefit was paid to a third party in accordance with—

(i) regulation 34A of, and Schedule 9A to, the Claims and Payments Regulations (mortgage interest payments); or

(ii) regulation 35 of, and Schedule 9B to, those Regulations (deductions which may be made and payments to third parties); and

(b) state pension credit is payable or treated as payable to the transferee as from the appointed day, then as from the appointed day, those deductions shall be made from the transferee's state pension credit and those payments of part of the benefit shall continue to be made to the third party in accordance with those provisions.

(15) to (19) [¹ . . .]

AMENDMENTS

4.129   1. Social Security (Hospital In-Patients and Miscellaneous Amendments) Regulations 2003 (SI 2003/1195), reg.9 (May 21, 2003).

2. State Pension Credit (Transitional and Miscellaneous Provisions) Amendment Regulations 2003 (SI 2003/2274), reg.3 (October 6, 2003)

Assessed income period

4.130   **37.**—(1) A person to whom paragraph (2) applies shall have an assessed income period allotted to him by the Secretary of State of at least 5 years but not exceeding 7 years beginning on the day the decision takes effect, unless regulation 10(1) of the State Pension Credit Regulations applies in his case.

(2) This paragraph applies to the first assessed income period specified in respect of a person who—

(a) attains or has attained the age of 65 or whose partner attains or has attained that age on or before the appointed day; and

(b) is awarded state pension credit with effect from the appointed day.

Claims for state pension credit

4.131   **38.**—(1) A claim for state pension credit may be made before the appointed day by a person who is not in receipt of income support at the time the claim is made.

(2) Where the Secretary of State is satisfied that unless there is a change in the claimant's circumstances before the appointed day he will satisfy the conditions for entitlement to state pension credit on that day, then the Secretary of State may —

(a) treat that claim as if made for a period beginning with the appointed day; and

(b) award benefit accordingly, but subject to the condition that the claimant does in fact satisfy those conditions when benefit becomes payable under the award.

(3) A decision under paragraph (2)(b) to award benefit may be revised under section 9 of the 1998 Act if the requirements for entitlement to state pension credit are found not to have been satisfied on the appointed day.

(4) A claim for state pension credit made in the period of 12 months beginning with the appointed day may be treated as made on that day if the claimant satisfied the conditions for entitlement to state pension credit on that day.

(5) A person who does not fall within paragraph (4)—

(a) solely because he does not satisfy the conditions for entitlement to state pension credit on the appointed day; but

(b) does satisfy those conditions on a day after the appointed day but before the day on which the claim is received by the Secretary of State, shall be treated as having made the claim on the day the conditions were first satisfied in his case.

(6) A claim for income support made in the period of 6 months preceding the appointed day may be treated also as a claim for state pension credit if the claimant —

(a) is not entitled to income support; and

(b) has attained the age of 60 on the date the claim is made or will have attained that age on the appointed day.

(7) Paragraphs (2) and (3) shall apply to a claim treated as made under paragraph (6) as they apply to a claim made under paragraph (1).

(8) In the case of a person who—

(a) on the appointed day has attained the qualifying age;

(b) was, within the period of 6 months preceding the appointed day, entitled to income support; and

(c) was not entitled to income support on the day immediately preceding the appointed day,

that person shall be treated as having made a claim for state pension credit for a period beginning on the appointed day.

(9) The Secretary of State may treat a claim for state pension credit made in accordance with paragraph (1) as also a claim for income support made on the same day.

GENERAL NOTE

This Part of these Regulations, which came into force on April 7, 2003, contains **4.132** some key transitional provisions for the introduction of state pension credit. Reg.36 permits existing income support pensioner claimants to be treated as having claimed or having been awarded state pension credit. Reg.38(1) allows advance claims for state pension credit. Under reg.38(4) and (5) all claims made before October 5, 2004 should be backdated to the start of the new scheme on October 6, 2003 or the date that the person first satisfied the conditions for state pension credit, if this is later. (This 12 month automatic backdating rule has now been made a permanent feature of the scheme: see Social Security (Claims and Payments) Regulations 1987 (SI 1987/1968), reg.19 and Sch.4, as amended by Social Security (Claims and Payments) Amendment (No. 2) Regulations 2004 (SI 2004/1821), reg.2). Reg.38(6) provides that a claim for income support made in the six months before October 6, 2003 may also be treated as a claim for state pension credit if the claimant was not entitled to income support and had attained 60 by the date of the claim or by October 6, 2003. Reg.38(8) deems a claim for state pension credit to have been made by a person who had attained 60 by October 6, 2003 and who had been entitled to income support in the six months before October 6, 2003 but was no longer so entitled immediately before that date. Finally reg.37 allows awards of state pension credit made with effect from October 6, 2003 to be for a period of up to seven years, instead of the standard five years (thus avoiding the problem of a large number of awards coming up for renewal at the same time).

PART V

THE SOCIAL FUND

Social Fund Cold Weather Payments (General) Regulations 1988

(SI 1988/1724)

Made by the Secretary of State under ss.32(2A) and 84(1) of the Social Security Act 1986 and s.166(1) to (3A) of the Social Security Act 1975

GENERAL NOTE

The cold weather payments scheme has been in operation since April 1988, but has undergone several changes in that time. The most significant has been that taking effect in November 1991. It stemmed from a general review announced in February 1991, when the temperature conditions were deemed to be triggered for the whole country for two weeks and the weekly amount of the payment was increased from £5 to £6.

Since s.138(2) of the Contributions and Benefits Act (1986 Act, s.32(2A)) provides the merest framework, the changes were made by amendment of these Regulations. There are three main changes from November 1991. First, no separate claim needs to be, or can be, made for a cold weather payment. Entitlement simply depends on a person being in the right category of income support (or, from November 4, 1996, income-based JSA) recipient and on the temperature conditions being triggered for the area in which he lives. Second, the temperature conditions can be triggered by a forecast, rather than waiting for a week of cold weather to have happened. Thus payments can potentially be made at the time that expenditure is needed, not after the event.

Third, the system of attaching areas to weather stations has been revised. It is now based on postcode districts, rather than DSS Local Office areas (which no longer exist under the Benefits Agency) or local government areas. The system can be more discriminating, but some weather stations still cover areas a long way away, and there have been complaints about bizarre differences in treatment within towns and cities. The increase in the number of weather stations from 55 to 70 in November 1996 (now further increased to 72 from November 1997) was intended to assist in improving the sensitivity of the scheme.

The decision to make a payment is made by a decision-maker, but since no claim is possible there will be no notification to a person that a payment will not be made. If a person does not receive a payment to which he thinks he is entitled, it appears that he will have to request a negative decision-maker's decision before there is something to appeal against.

Citation, commencement and interpretation

1.—(1) These regulations may be cited as the Social Fund Cold Weather Payments (General) Regulations 1988 and shall come into force on 7th November 1988.

(2) In these Regulations, unless the context otherwise requires—

"the Act" means the Social Security Act 1986;

"the General Regulations" means the Income Support (General) Regulations 1987;

[⁴"the Meteorological Office" means the Meteorological Office of the Ministry of Defence;]

"child" has the meaning assigned to it by section 20(11) of the Act [SSCBA, s.137(1)];

[²"claimant" means a person who is claiming or has claimed income support;]

"family" has the meaning assigned to it by section 20(11) of the Act [SSCBA, s.137(1)] and for the purposes of these Regulations includes persons who are members of a polygamous marriage;

[²"forecast" means a weather forecast produced by the Meteorological Office [⁴. . .] and supplied to the Department of Social Security on a daily basis

[⁴ between 1st November in any year and 31st March in the following year,] which provides the expected average mean daily temperature for a period of 7 consecutive days;

"forecasted period of cold weather" means a period of 7 consecutive days, during which the average of the mean daily temperature for that period is forecasted to be equal to or below 0 degrees celsius; and for the purposes of this definition where a day forms part of a forecasted period of cold weather it shall not form part of any other such forecasted period;]

"home" means the dwelling, together with any garage, garden and outbuildings normally occupied by the claimant as his home, including any premises not so occupied which it is impracticable or unreasonable to sell separately in particular, in Scotland, any croft land on which the dwelling is situated;

[⁴"income-based jobseeker's allowance" has the same meaning in these Regulations as it has in the Jobseekers Act 1995 by virtue of section 1(4) of that Act;]

"income support" means income support under Part II of the Act [SSCBA, Part VII] and includes transitional addition, personal expenses addition and special transitional addition as defined in the Income Support (Transitional) Regulations 1987;

"married couple" means a man and a woman who are married to each other and are members of the same household;]

"mean daily temperature" means, in respect of a day, the average of the maximum temperature and minimum temperature recorded at a station for that day;

[²"overlap period" means any period of a day or days, where a day forms part of a recorded period of cold weather and also forms part of a forecasted period of cold weather;]

[¹"partner" means one of a married or unmarried couple or a member of a polygamous relationship;] [². . .]

"polygamous marriage" means any marriage during the subsistence of which a party to it is married to more than one person and the ceremony of marriage took place under the law of a country which permits polygamy;

[⁴"postcode district" means a Post Office postcode district [⁵except in the case of any postcode district which is identified with an alpha suffix which shall, for the purposes of these Regulations, be treated as if it forms part of a postcode district which is identified without that suffix]];

"recorded period of cold weather" means a period of 7 consecutive days, during which the average of the mean daily temperature recorded for that period was equal to or below 0 degrees celsius; and for the purposes of this definition where a day forms part of a recorded period of cold weather it shall not form part of any other such recorded period;

[⁴. . .]

[⁴"station" means a station accredited by the Meteorological Office at which a period of cold weather may be forecasted or recorded for the purposes of these Regulations;]

[¹"unmarried couple" means a man and a woman who are not married to each other but are living together as husband and wife.]

[¹(2A) For the purposes of these Regulations, a person shall be treated as a member of a polygamous relationship where, but for the fact that the relationship includes more than two persons, he would be one of a married or unmarried couple.]

(3) In these Regulations, unless the context otherwise requires, a reference to a numbered regulation is to the regulation in these Regulations bearing that number and a reference in a regulation to a numbered paragraph or sub-paragraph is to the paragraph or sub-paragraph in that regulation bearing that number.

AMENDMENTS

1. Social Fund (Miscellaneous Amendments) Regulations 1990 (SI 1990/580), reg.3 (April 9, 1990).   **5.3**

2. Social Fund Cold Weather Payments (General) Amendment No.2 Regulations 1991 (SI 1991/2238), reg.2 (November 1, 1991).

3. Social Fund Cold Weather Payments (General) Amendment (No.2) Regulations 1992 (SI 1992/2448), reg.2 (November 1, 1992).

4. Social Fund Cold Weather Payments (General) Amendment Regulations 1996 (SI 1996/2544), reg.2 (November 4, 1996).

5. Social Fund Cold Weather Payments (General) Amendment Regulations 1997 (SI 1997/2311), reg.2 (November 1, 1997).

GENERAL NOTE

"home:" See the notes to reg.2(1) of the Income Support (General) Regulations under "dwelling occupied as the home".   **5.4**

"forecasted period of cold weather:" The original definition of a "period of cold weather" required it to run from a Monday to a Sunday. Since the test of the average of the mean daily temperature (*i.e.* the average of maximum and minimum temperature for each day) for the seven days being below 0 degrees Celsius is a tough one, to have required also that the weather conformed to calendar weeks would have made the operation of the regulation excessively arbitrary. Thus, any consecutive seven days over which the average temperature test is met will do.

The departure in November 1991 is to include a period where the temperature is forecasted to meet the test. See reg.2 for the interrelationship with periods where the temperature test is actually met. If a day falls into a forecasted period of cold weather it cannot count in any other forecasted period, but it can be part of a recorded period of cold weather (see the definition of "overlap period").

In the cold weather payments scheme under the Supplementary Benefit (Single Payments) Regulations the crucial average temperature was 1.5 degrees celsius, rather than 0 degrees celsius.

"recorded period of cold weather:" See the notes on a forecasted period and the definition of "overlap period."

"unmarried couple" and "married couple:" See notes to s.137(1) of the Contributions and Benefits Act (1986 Act, s.20(11)).

[¹Prescribed description of persons

5.5   **1A.**[⁴—(1)] [⁵Subject to paragraph (3), the] description of persons prescribed as persons to whom a payment may be made out of the Social Fund to meet expenses for heating under section 32(2A) of the Act [SSCBA s.138(2)] is claimants who have been awarded income support [⁴state pension credit] or [³income-based jobseeker's allowance] in respect of at least one day during the recorded or the forecasted period of cold weather specified in regulation 2(1)(a) and either—

(i) whose applicable amount includes one or more of the premiums specified in paragraphs 9 to 14 of Part III of Schedule 2 to the General Regulations [² ⁵ . . .]; or

[(ia) whose applicable amount includes one or more of the premiums specified in paragraphs 10 to 16 of Part III of Schedule 1 to the Jobseeker's Allowance Regulations 1996 [⁵ . . .]; or

[⁴(ib) the person is entitled to state pension credit and is not resident in a care home;] [⁶or

(ic) whose child tax credit includes an individual element referred to in regulation 7(4)(a), (b), (d) or (e) of the Child Tax Credit Regulations 2002; or]

(ii) whose family includes a member aged less than 5.]

[⁴(2) In paragraph (1)(ib), the expression "care home" means an establishment which is a care home for the purposes of the Care Standards Act 2000."]

[⁵(3) Paragraph (1) does not apply to a person who resides in—

(a) a nursing home within the meaning given by regulation 2(1) of the Income Support (General) Regulations 1987;

(b) a residential care home within the meaning given by regulation 2(1) of the Income Support (General) Regulations 1987;

(c) residential accommodation within the meaning given by regulation 21(3) of the Income Support (General) Regulations 1987; or

(d) accommodation provided under section 3(1) of, and Part II of the Schedule to, the Polish Resettlement Act 1947 (provision by the Secretary of State of accommodation in camps).]]

AMENDMENTS

5.6   1. Social Fund Cold Weather Payments (General) Amendment No.3 Regulations 1991 (SI 1991/2448), reg.2 (November 1, 1991).

2. Social Fund Cold Weather Payments (General) Amendment Regulations 1993 (SI 1993/2450), reg.2 (November 1, 1993).

3. Social Fund Cold Weather Payments (General) Amendment Regulations 1996 (SI 1996/2544), reg.3 (November 4, 1996).

4. State Pension Credit (Consequential, Transitional and Miscellaneous Provisions) Regulations 2002 (SI 2002/3019), reg.31 (October 6, 2003).

5. Social Security (Removal of Residential Allowance and Miscellaneous Amendments) Regulations 2003 (SI 2003/1121), reg.3 (October 6, 2003).

6. Social Fund Cold Weather Payments (General) Amendment Regulations 2004 (SI 2004/2600), reg.2 (November 1, 2004).

DEFINITIONS

"the Act"—see reg. 1(2).
"the General Regulations"—*ibid.*
"claimant"—*ibid.*
"family"—*ibid.*
"forecasted period of cold weather"—*ibid.*
"income-based jobseeker's allowance"—*ibid.*
"income support"—*ibid.*
"recorded period of cold weather"—*ibid.*

GENERAL NOTE

Only claimants who have been awarded income support state, pension credit or   5.7
income-based JSA, or who have an award of child tax credit that includes an element
for a disabled, or severely disabled, child or young person, for at least one day in a
period of cold weather (forecasted or recorded) can qualify for a payment. Merely
having underlying entitlement to income support or income-based JSA will not do.
However, only certain claimants meet the conditions prescribed by reg. 1A. The
claimant must either be entitled to state pension credit or his or her income support
or income-based JSA must include one of the pensioner or disability premiums (but
from November 1, 1993, claimants who live in a residential care or nursing home do
not qualify), or there must be a child under five in the household. Since no claim for
a cold weather payment is possible, the DM will identify qualifying claimants and make
a payment automatically.

[¹**Prescribed circumstances**

2.—(1) The prescribed circumstances in which a payment may be made   5.8
out of the social fund to meet expenses for heating under section 32(2A) of
the Act [SSCBA, s.138(2)] are—
  (a) subject to paragraphs [⁵(1A), (1B),] (3), (4) and (5)—
      (i) there is a recorded period of cold weather at a station [³identified]
           in column (1) of Schedule 1 to these Regulations [⁴. . .]; or
      (ii) there is a forecasted period of cold weather at a station [³iden-
           tified] in column (1) of Schedule 1 to these Regulations;
           [⁵ and]
    [⁴(iii) [⁵. . .]
  (b) the home of the claimant is, or by virtue of paragraph (2)(b) is treated
       as, situated in a postcode district in respect of which the station men-
       tioned in sub-paragraph (a)(i) or, as the case may be, (a)(ii) is the des-
       ignated station.]
  (c) [². . .]
  [⁵(1A) For the purposes of paragraph (1)(a)(i), where a station identified
in column (1) of Schedule 1 to these Regulations (in this paragraph and in
paragraph (1B) referred to as "the primary station") is unable to provide
temperature information in respect of a particular day, the mean daily temperature on that day—
  (a) at the alternative station for that primary station specified in column
       (2) of Schedule 2 to these Regulations; or
  (b) where there is no such alternative station specified, at the nearest
       station to that primary station able to provide temperature informa-
       tion in respect of that day,

shall be used to determine whether or not there is a recorded period of cold weather at the relevant primary station.

(1B) For the purposes of paragraph (1)(a)(ii), where the Meteorological Office is unable to produce a forecast in respect of a particular period at a primary station, any forecast produced in respect of that period—

(a) at the alternative station for that primary station specified in column (2) of Schedule 2 to these Regulations; or

(b) where there is no such alternative station specified, at the nearest station to that primary station able to provide temperature information for that period,

shall be used to determine whether or not there is a forecasted period of cold weather at the relevant primary station.]

(2) For the purposes of this regulation—

(a) the station [³identified] in column (1) of Schedule 1 to these Regulations is the designated station for the [⁴postcode districts] [³identified] in the corresponding paragraph in column (2) of that Schedule;

(b) where the home of the claimant is not situated within a [⁴postcode district] [³[⁴ . . .] identified] in column (2) of that Sch., it shall be treated as situated within the [⁴postcode district] [⁴ . . .] nearest to it [³identified] in that column.

(3) Subject to paragraphs (4) and (5) where a recorded period of cold weather is joined by an overlap period to a forecasted period of cold weather a payment under paragraph (1) may only be made in respect of the forecasted period of cold weather.

(4) Where—

(a) there is a continuous period of forecasted periods of cold weather, each of which is linked by an overlap period; and

(b) the total number of recorded periods of cold weather during that continuous period is greater than the total number of forecasted periods of cold weather,

a payment in respect of the last recorded period of cold weather may also be made under paragraph (1).

(5) Where—

(a) a claimant [²falls within the description of persons prescribed in Regulation 1A and] satisfies the prescribed circumstances for a payment under paragraph (1) above in respect of a recorded period of cold weather; and

(b) a payment in respect of the recorded period of cold weather does not fall to be made by virtue of paragraph (4); and

(c) the claimant does not [²fall within the description of persons prescribed in Regulation 1A] above in respect of the forecasted period of cold weather which is linked to the recorded period of cold weather by an overlap period,

a payment in respect of that recorded period of cold weather may also be made under paragraph (1).

AMENDMENTS

5.9   1. Social Fund Cold Weather Payments (General) Amendments No.2 Regulations 1991 (SI 1991/2238) reg.3 (November 1, 1991).

2. Social Fund Cold Weather Payments (General) Amendment No.3 Regulations 1991 (SI 1991/2448), reg.3 (November 1, 1991).

3. Social Fund Cold Weather Payments (General) Amendment (No.2) Regulations 1992 (SI 1992/2448), reg.3 (November 1, 1992).

4. Social Fund Cold Weather Payments (General) Amendment Regulations 1996 (SI 1996/2544), reg.4 (November 4, 1996).

5. Social Fund Cold Weather Payments (General) Amendment Regulations 1997 (SI 1997/2311), reg.3 (November 1, 1997).

Definitions

"the Act"—see reg.1(2).
"the General Regulations"—*ibid.*
"claimant"—*ibid.*
"family"—*ibid.*
"forecasted period of cold weather"—*ibid.*
"home"—*ibid.*
"income support"—*ibid.*
"overlap period"—*ibid.*
"postcode district"—*ibid.*
"recorded period of cold weather"—*ibid.*
"station"—*ibid.*

General Note

Section 138(2) of the Contributions and Benefits Act (1986 Act, s.32(2A)) allows any circumstances to be prescribed. Reg.1A prescribes the categories of income support or income-based JSA recipients who can qualify.   **5.10**

The qualifications under reg.2 have become rather more complex in November 1991. Under para.(1)(a) and (b), a period of cold weather (*i.e.* seven consecutive days) must be either recorded or forecast at the weather station relevant to the claimant's home. If a period of cold weather is forecast, but the forecast turns out to be wrong and there are not seven consecutive days of the necessary temperature actually recorded, the situation is simple. Only the forecast period is relevant. Things become more complicated where there is a recorded period of cold weather which coincides wholly or partly with the forecasted period. While an individual day can only count as part of one recorded period of cold weather or one forecasted period of cold weather (see the definitions in reg.1(2)), it can be part of both a recorded and a forecasted period. There is then an overlap period, again defined in reg.1(2). Since the aim is, if possible, to make the payment before the extra heating is required, the general rule, under para.(3), is that payment is to be made only for the forecasted period. However, that rule would lead to unfairness if, for instance, recorded periods of cold weather come at the beginning and end of a continuous series, with forecasted periods only starting towards the end of the first recorded period and finishing towards the start of the last recorded period. In such circumstances, payments can be made for an extra recorded period over the number of forecasted periods (para.(4)). Also, if the claimant does not qualify under reg.1A for any day of the forecasted period, but does qualify for a day of the recorded period, then a payment can be made for the recorded period (para.(5)).

Prescribed amount

3.[¹ . . .] The amount of the payment in respect of each period of cold weather shall be [²£8.50].   **5.11**

AMENDMENTS

5.12   1. Social Fund Cold Weather Payments (General) Amendment No.2 Regulations 1991 (SI 1991/2238), reg.4 (November 1, 1991).
    2. Social Fund Cold Weather Payments (General) Amendment Regulations 1995 (SI 1995/2620), reg.2 (November 1, 1995).

GENERAL NOTE

5.13   The fixed payment is £8.50 for each week which counts under regs 1A and 2. The amount had been fixed at £5 from 1988, until it was increased to £6 in February 1991, at the same time as the temperature condition was deemed to have been triggered for the whole country for two weeks. It was increased to £7 in November 1994 and became £8.50 in November 1995.

Effect and calculation of capital

5.14   **4.** [¹ . . .]

AMENDMENT

    1. Social Fund Cold Weather Payments (General) Amendment No.2 Regulations 1991 (SI 1991/2238), reg.5 (November 1, 1991).

GENERAL NOTE

There is now no capital limit for cold weather payments.

SCHEDULES

[⁵ **SCHEDULE 1**   **(Regulation 2(1)(a) and (2))**

5.15   IDENTIFICATION OF STATIONS AND POSTCODE DISTRICTS

Column (1)	*Column (2)*
Meteorological Office Station	*Postcode districts*
1. Aberporth	SA35–48, SA64–65. SY20, SY23–25.
2. Andrewsfield	AL1–10. CB 10–11. CM1–9, CM11–24, CM77. CO9. RM14–20. SG1–2, SG9–14.
3. Aultbea	IV21–22, IV26, IV40, IV52–54.
4. Aviemore	AB31, AB33–34, AB36–37. PH18–26.
5. Bedford	LU1–7. MK1–19, MK40–46. NN1–16, NN29. PE19. SG3–7, SG15–19.
6. Bingley	BB4, BB8–12, BB18. BD1–24. DE4, DE45. HD1–9. HX1–7. LS21, LS27, LS29. OL1–5, OL12–16. S32–33, S35–36. SK13, SK17, SK22–23. ST13. WF15–17.
7. Bishopton	G1–5, G11–15, G20–23, G31–34, G40–46, G51–53, G60–62, G64–69, G71–78, G81–84. KA1–26, KA28–30. ML1–5. PA1–27, PA30, PA32.
8. Boltshope Park	DH8–9. DL8, DL11–17. NE19, NE44, NE47–48.
9. Boscombe Down	BA12. RG28. SP1–5, SP7, SP9–11.
10. Boulmer	NE22, NE24, NE61–71. TD12, TD15.
11. Braemar	AB35.

Column (1)	Column (2)
Meteorological Office Station	*Postcode districts*
12. Brize Norton	CV36. GL54–56. OX1–8, OX10–18, OX20, OX25–29, OX33, OX39, OX44, OX49. SN7.
13. Capel Curig	LL24–25, LL41.
14. Cardinham (Bodmin)	PL13–17, PL22–35. TR2, TR9.
15. Carlisle	CA1–11, CA16–17. DG12, DG16. LA6–10, LA22–23. NE49.
16. Cassley	IV27–28. KW11, KW13.
17. Charlwood	BN5–6, BN44. GU5–8, GU26–33, GU35. ME14–20. RH1–20. TN1–20, TN22, TN27.
18. Chivenor	EX22–23, EX31–34, EX39.
19. Coleshill	B1–21, B23–38, B40, B42–50, B60–80, B90–98. CV1–12, CV21–23, CV31–35, CV37, CV47. DY1–14. LE10. WS1–15. WV1–16.
20. Coltishall	NR1–35.
21. Crosby	BB1–3, BB5–7. CH1–8, CH41–49, CH60–66. FY1–8. L1–40. LL11–14. PR1–9, PR25–26. SY14. WA1–2, WA4–12. WN1–6, WN8.
22. Culdrose	TR1, TR3–6, TR10–20, TR26–27.
23. Dundrennan	DG1–2, DG5–7.
24. Dunkeswell Aerodrome	DT6–8. EX1–15, EX24. TA21. TQ1–6, TQ9–14.
25. Dyce	AB10–16, AB21–25, AB30, AB32, AB39, AB41–43, AB51–54. DD8–11.
26. Edinburgh Gogarbank	EH1–42, EH47–49, EH51–55. FK1–21. G63. KY3, KY11–13. PH3–6. TD5, TD11, TD13–14.
27. Eskdalemuir	DG3–4, DG10–11, DG13–14. ML12.TD1–4, TD6–10.
28. Fylingdales	TS13. YO11–18, YO21–22, YO25.
29. Great Malvern	GL1–6, GL10–20, GL50–53. HR1–9. NP15, NP25. SY8. WR1–15.
30. Heathrow	BR1–8. CR0, CR2–8. DA1–2, DA4–8, DA14–18. E1–18. E1W. EC1–4. EN1–11. HA0–9. IG1–11. KT1–24. N1–22. NW1–11. RM1–13. SE1–28. SL0, SL3. SM1–7. SW1–20. TW1–20. UB1–10. W1–14. WC1–2. WD1–7, WD17–19, WD23–25.
31. Herstmonceux, West End	BN7–8, BN20–24, BN26–27.TN21, TN31–40.
32. High Wycombe	HP1–23, HP27. OX9. RG9. SL7–9.
33. Hurn (Bournemouth Airport)	BH1–25, BH31. DT1–2, DT11. SP6.
34. Isle of Portland	DT3–5.
35. Kinloss	AB38, AB44–45, AB55–56. IV1–3, IV5, IV7–20, IV30–32, IV36.
36. Kirkwall	KW15–17.
37. Lake Vyrnwy	LL20–21, LL23. SY10, SY15–17, SY19, SY21–22.
38. Lerwick	ZE1–3.
39. Leuchars	DD1–7. KY1–2, KY4–10, KY14–16. PH1–2, PH7, PH12–14.
40. Linton on Ouse	DL1–7, DL9–10. HG1–5. LS1–20, LS22–26, LS28. S62–64, S70–75. TS1–12, TS14–26. WF1–17. YO1, YO7–8, YO10, YO19, YO23–24, YO26, YO30–32, YO41–43, YO51, YO60–62.
41. Liscombe	EX16–21, EX35–38. PL19–20. TA22, TA24.
42. Loch Glascarnoch	IV4, IV6, IV23–24, IV63.
43. Lusa	IV47–49, IV51, IV55–56.
44. Lyneham	BA1–3, BA11, BA13–15. GL7–9. RG17. SN1–6, SN8–16, SN25–26.
45. Machrihanish	KA27. PA28–29, PA31, PA34, PA37, PA41–49, PA60–76. PH36, PH38–41.
46. Manston	CM0. CT1–21. DA3, DA9–13. ME1–13. SS0–17. TN23–26, TN28–30.
47. Marham	IP24–28. PE12–14, PE30–38.

Column (1)	Column (2)
Meteorological Office Station	*Postcode districts*
48. Newcastle	DH1–7. NE1–13, NE15–18, NE20–21, NE23, NE25–43, NE45–46. SR1–8. TS27–29.
49. Nottingham	CV13. DE1–3, DE5–7, DE11–15, DE21–24, DE55–56, DE65, DE72–75. LE1–9, LE11–14, LE16–19, LE65, LE67. NG1–22, NG25, NG31–34. S1–14, S17–18, S20–21, S25–26, S40–45, S60–61, S65–66, S80–81. ST10, ST14.
50. Pembrey Sands	SA1–8, SA10–18, SA31–34, SA61–63, SA66–73.
51. Plymouth	PL1–12, PL18, PL21. TQ7–8.
52. Rhyl	LL15–19, LL22, LL26–32.
53. St. Athan	BS1–11, BS13–16, BS20–24, BS29–32, BS34–37, BS39–41, BS48–49. CF3, CF5, CF10–11, CF14–15, CF23–24, CF31–36, CF61–64, CF71–72. NP10, NP16, NP18–20, NP26.
54. St. Catherine's Point	PO30, PO38–41.
55. St. Mawgan	TR7–8.
56. Salsburgh	EH43–46. ML6–11.
57. Scilly, St. Mary's	TR21–25.
58. Sennybridge	CF37–48, CF81–83. LD1–8. NP4, NP7–8, NP11–13, NP22–24, NP44. SA9, SA19–20. SY7, SY9, SY18.
59. Shawbury	ST1–9, ST11–12, ST15–21. SY1–6, SY11–13. TF1–13.
60. South Farnborough	GU1–4, GU9–25, GU46–47, GU51–52. RG1–2, RG4–8, RG10, RG12, RG14, RG18–27, RG29–31, RG40–42, RG45. SL1–2, SL4–6.
61. Stornoway Airport	HS1–9.
62. Thorney Island	BN1–3, BN9–18, BN25, BN41–43, BN45. GU34. PO1–22, PO31–37. SO14–24, SO30–32, SO40–43, SO45, SO50–53.
63. Tiree	PA77–78. PH42–44.
64. Tulloch Bridge	PA33, PA35–36, PA38, PA40. PH8–11, PH15–17, PH30–35, PH37, PH49–50.
65. Valley	LL33–40, LL42–49, LL51–78.
66. Waddington	DN1–22, DN31–41. HU1–20. LN1–13. NG23–24. PE10–11, PE20–25.
67. Walney Island	CA12–15, CA18–28. LA1–5, LA11–21.
68. Wattisham	CB9. CO1–8, CO10–16. IP1–23, IP29–33.
69. West Freugh	DG8–9.
70. Wick Airport	IV25. KW1–3, KW5–10, KW12, KW14.
71. Wittering	CB1–8. LE15. NN17–18. PE1–9, PE15–17, PE26–29. SG8.
72. Woodford	BL0–9. CW1–12. M1–9, M11–35, M38, M40–41, M43–46, M50, M90. OL6–11. SK1–12, SK14–16. WA3, WA13–16. WN7.
73. Yeovilton	BA4–10, BA16, BA20–22. BS25–28. DT9–10. SP8. TA1–20, TA23.]

AMENDMENTS

5.16   1. Social Security Cold Weather Payments (General) Amendment Regulations 2000 (SI 2000/2690), reg.2 (November 1, 2000).

2. The Social Fund Cold Weather Payments (General) Amendment Regulations 2002 (SI 2002/2524), reg.2 (November 1, 2002).

3. Social Fund Cold Weather Payments (General) Amendment Regulations 2003 (SI 2003/2605), reg.2 and Sch.1 (November 1, 2003).

4. Social Fund Cold Weather Payments (General) Amendment (No.2) Regulations 2003 (SI 2003/3203), reg.2 (November 28, 2003).

5. Social Fund Cold Weather Payments (General) Amendment Regulations 2004 (SI 2004/2600), reg.3 (November 1, 2004).

DEFINITIONS

"Meteorological Office"—see reg.1(2).
"postcode district"—*ibid.*
"station"—*ibid.*

[²SCHEDULE 2   **Regulation 2(1A)(a)
and 2(1B)(a)**

SPECIFIED ALTERNATIVE STATIONS   5.17

Column (1)	Column (2)
Meteorological Office Station	*Specified Alternative Station*
Charlwood	Kenley Airfield
Coleshill	Church Lawford
Kinloss	Lossiemouth
Linton on Ouse	Church Fenton
St. Athan	Cardiff Weather Centre.]

AMENDMENTS

1. Social Fund Cold Weather Payments (General) Amendment Regulations 1999 **5.18**
(SI 1999/2781, reg.3 and Sch.2 (November 1, 1999).
2. Social Fund Cold Weather Payments (General) Amendment Regulations 2003
(SI 2003/2605), reg.3 and Sch.2 (November 1, 2003).

DEFINITIONS

"Meteorological Office"—see reg.1(2).
"station"—*ibid.*

The Social Fund Winter Fuel Payment Regulations 2000

(SI 2000/729)

Made by the Secretary of State under ss. 138(2) and (4) and 175(1), (3) and (4) of the Social Security Contributions and Benefits Act 1992 and ss. 5(1) (a) and (i), and 189(1) and (4) of the Social Security Administration Act 1992 and s. 16(1) and s. 79(1) and (4) of, and para. 3 of Sch. 5 to, the Social Security Act 1998

[In force April 3, 2000]

GENERAL NOTE

5.19   In November 1997, the Government announced that all pensioner households would receive a one-off payment in the winter of 1998 (and another in 1999) towards their fuel bills. These payments would be in addition to any cold weather payments which might be awarded under the Social Fund Cold Weather Payments (General) Regulations 1998 (above). As is the case under those regulations, no separate claim needs to be made for a winter fuel payment. Entitlement simply depends on the person being ordinarily resident in Great Britain and over pensionable age on at least one day in the "qualifying week" (see reg.1(2)). However, following the decision of the European Court of Justice in Case C–382/98, *R. v Secretary of State for Social Security Ex p. Taylor* (ECJ December 16, 1999) the age for eligibility has been equalised at 60 for both sexes and men aged between 60 and 65 may need to make a retrospective claim for the winters of 1997/1998, 1998/1999 and 1999/2000—see commentary to reg.2. See also ss. 1–6 of the Age-Related Payments Act 2004 in Part I of this volume.

Citation, commencement and interpretation

5.20   **1.**—(1) These Regulations may be cited as the Social Fund Winter Fuel Payment Regulations 2000 and shall come into force on 3rd April 2000.

(2) In these Regulations—

"free in-patient treatment" shall be construed in accordance with regulation 2(2) of the Social Security (Hospital In-Patients) Regulations 1975;

"Income Support Regulations" means the Income Support (General) Regulations 1987;

"qualifying week" means in respect of any year the week beginning on the third Monday in the September of that year;

"nursing home" has the meaning it bears in [³regulation 2(1) of the Income Support Regulations (interpretation)];

"partner" means a member of—

(a) a married or unmarried couple; or

(b) a polygamous marriage;

"residential accommodation" has the meaning it bears in regulation 21(3) of the Income Support Regulations (special cases); and

[⁴ "state pension credit" has the meaning assigned to it by section 1 of the State Pension Credit Act 2002;]

[¹ . . .]

[² (3) Subject to paragraph (3A), in these Regulations a person—

(a) is in residential care if, disregarding any period of temporary absence, he resides in—
   (i) a residential care home;
   (ii) a nursing home;
   (iii) residential accommodation; or
   (iv) accommodation provided under section 3(1) of the Polish Resettlement Act 1947 (provision by the Secretary of State of accommodation in camps),
   throughout the qualifying week and the period of 12 weeks immediately before the qualifying week;

(b) lives with another person if—
   (i) disregarding any period of temporary absence, they share accommodation as their mutual home; and
   (ii) they are not in residential care.

[³(3A) For the purposes of paragraph (3)(a)(i) "residential care home" has the meaning given to that expression by virtue of sub-paragraphs (a), (c) and (d) of that definition in regulation 2(1) of the Income Support Regulations.]

(4) In these Regulations, unless the context otherwise requires, a reference—

(a) to a numbered regulation is to the regulation in these Regulations bearing that number; and

(b) in a regulation to a numbered paragraph is to the paragraph in that regulation bearing that number.

AMENDMENTS

1. Social Fund Winter Fuel Payment (Amendment) Regulations 2000 (SI 2000/2864), reg.2(a)(1) (November 13, 2000).

5.21

2. Social Fund Winter Fuel Payment (Amendment) Regulations 2001 (SI 2001/3375), reg.2(2) (November 2, 2001).

3. Social Security (Removal of Residential Allowance and Miscellaneous Amendments) Regulations 2003 (SI 2003/1121), reg.5 (October 6, 2003).

4. Social Fund Winter Fuel Payment (Amendment) Regulations 2004 (SI 2004/2154), reg.2(a) (September 20, 2004).

Social fund winter fuel payments

[¹2.—(1) Subject to paragraphs (2) and (3) and regulation 3 of these Regulations, and regulation 36(2) of the Social Security (Claims and Payments) Regulations 1987, the Secretary of State shall pay to a person who—

5.22

(a) in respect of any day falling within the qualifying week is ordinarily resident in Great Britain; and

(b) has attained the age of 60 in or before the qualifying week,

a winter fuel payment of—

   (i) £200 unless he is in residential care or head (ii)(aa) applies; or
   (ii) £100 if [³ state pension credit] or an income-based jobseeker's allowance has not been, nor falls to be, paid to him in respect of the qualifying week and he is—
      (aa) in that week living with a person to whom a payment under these Regulations has been, or falls to be, made in respect of the winter following the qualifying week; or
      (bb) in residential care.

(2) Where such a person has attained the age of 80 in or before the qualifying week—

    (a) in paragraph (1)(i), for the sum of £200 there shall be substituted the sum of £300; and

[²(b) in paragraph (1)(ii), for the sum of £100 there shall be substituted the sum of £200, except that—

        (i) where he is in that week living with a person to whom a payment under these Regulations has been, or falls to be, made in respect of the winter following that week who has also attained the age of 80 in or before that week, or

        (ii) where he is in residential care,

    there shall be substituted the sum of £150.]

(3) Where such a person has not attained the age of 80 in or before the qualifying week but he is a partner of and living with a person who has done so, in paragraph (1)(i) for the sum of £200 there shall be substituted the sum of £300.]

AMENDMENTS

5.23   1. Social Fund Winter Fuel Payment (Amendment) Regulations 2003 (SI 2003/1737), reg.2 (September 1, 2003).

    2. Social Fund Winter Fuel Payment (Amendment) (No.2) Regulations 2003, (SI 2003/2192), reg.2 (September 3, 2003).

    3. Social Fund Winter Fuel Payment (Amendment) Regulations 2004 (SI 2004/2154), reg.2(b) (September 20, 2004).

DEFINITIONS

"qualifying week"—see reg.1(2).
"residential care"—see reg.1(3).

GENERAL NOTE

5.24   Reg.2 sets out the two conditions of entitlement to a winter fuel payment. A person qualifies if:

    (a) his 60th birthday is before the end of the "qualifying week"—*i.e.* the week commencing on the third Monday in September (see reg.1(2)). For Winter 2004/05 a claimant must be born on or before September 26, 1944 to qualify. For Winter 2005/06 the date is September 25, 1945; and

    (b) he is ordinarily resident in Great Britain for at least one day in the qualifying week.

People who meet these conditions may nevertheless be excluded from entitlement if reg.3 applies to them.

The availability of winter fuel payments to everyone over 60 is a consequence of the decision of the European Court of Justice in Case C–382/98, *R. v Secretary of State for Social Security Ex p. Taylor* (ECJ December 16, 1999) which held that the former rules linking eligibility to pensionable age (currently 60 for women and 65 for men) discriminated unlawfully against men on grounds of their sex contrary to Directive 79/7 (see Vol. III of this series). Men who were over 60 at any of the qualifying weeks in 1997, 1998 and 1999 and who would have qualified for winter fuel payments under the old law if they had been over 65 can now claim retrospectively. A claim form should be available from local offices and can be downloaded from the DWP website (*www.dwp.gov.uk/publications/dwp/2000/wfuel/retro_claim_form.pdf*).

When the new regulations were first introduced, it was anticipated that payment would be at two rates:

(a) a lump sum of £50 for claimants who are not on income support (now replaced by state pension credit for anyone eligible for a winter fuel payment) or income-based jobseeker's allowance in the qualifying week and who are either in residential care or who live with another person who is also entitled to a winter fuel payment; and

(b) a lump sum of £100 for all other claimants except those in residential care.

The above rates were increased to £75 and £150 respectively by SI 2000/2229 and a further, temporary, increase to £100 and £200 respectively was subsequently made by SI 2000/2997 for the winter of 2000/2001. That temporary increase was made permanent for the winter of 2003/2004. At the same time the higher rates specified in paras. (2) and (3) were introduced for those over 80, or whose partners are over 80.

The requirement that the claimant be "ordinarily resident in Great Britain" must be read subject to EC law. In a series of decisions (*CIS/1491/2004, CIS/1427/2004, CIS/1691/2004, CIS/3685/2004* and *CIS/3197/2004*), Commissioner Rowland has discussed the meaning of ordinary residence and the application of Art.10 of EEC Regulation 1408/71 to claims made by those ordinarily resident in other Member States of the EU. The Commissioner held that it was possible, though very rare, for a person to be ordinarily resident in more than one country so that it was an error of law to proceed on the assumption that because a claimant had become ordinarily resident in one EEA state, s/he could not be resident in another. On the facts of *CIS/1691/2004*, the Commissioner accepted that the claimant, who had only recently moved to France from Great Britain was ordinarily resident in both countries. In circumstances where a claimant has qualified for a winter fuel payment by being ordinarily resident in Great Britain during one qualifying week, Regulation 1408/71 permits him or her to retain that entitlement in subsequent years. It does not, however, permit a claimant who has never been entitled to a winter fuel payment to acquire such an entitlement by ordinary residence in another EEA state. For an extremely technical point (now only of historical significance) about the time limits for claims by those ordinarily resident in another EEA state for the winters of 2000/2001 and 2001/2002, see the decision of the Deputy Commissioner in *CIS/0488/2004* and the discussion of that decision in Pt III of Vol.III.

Persons not entitled to a social fund winter fuel payment

3.—(1) Regulation 2 shall not apply in respect of a person who—   5.25
(a) is in the qualifying week—
  (i) a partner [¹of, and living with, a person] aged 60 or over in the qualifying week to whom [² state pension credit] or an income-based jobseeker's allowance has been, or falls to be, paid in respect of the qualifying week;
  (ii) receiving free in-patient treatment and has been receiving free in-patient treatment for more than 52 weeks; or
  (iii) detained in custody under a sentence imposed by a court; or
(b) subject to paragraph (2), has not made a claim for a winter fuel payment before the 31st March following the qualifying week in respect of the winter following that week.
(2) Paragraph (1)(b) shall not apply where—
(a) a payment has been made by virtue of regulation 4(1) before the 31st March following the qualifying week in respect of the winter following that week; or
(b) regulation 4(2) applies.

Amendments

1. Social Fund Winter Fuel Payment (Amendment) Regulations 2000 (SI   5.26
2000/2864), reg.2(a)(ii) (November 13, 2000).

2. Social Fund Winter Fuel Payment (Amendment) Regulations 2004 (SI 2004/2154), reg.2(c) (September 20, 2004).

"free in-patient treatment"—see reg.1(2).
"qualifying week"— *ibid.*

GENERAL NOTE

5.27   Reg.3 excludes certain people from entitlement to a winter fuel payment even if they fall within reg.2(a) and (b). There are four categories:

(a)   partners of people who were entitled to income support or income-based jobseeker's allowance in the qualifying week (reg.3(1)(a)(i)). This is to prevent double payment;

(b)   people who, in the qualifying week, have been receiving free in-patient treatment (see the notes to reg.21(3) of the Income Support Regulations) for more than 52 weeks (reg.3(1)(a)(ii));

(c)   people serving a custodial sentence in the qualifying week (reg.3(1)(a)(iii)). Note that the reference to "a sentence imposed by a court" excludes those in prison on remand; and

(d)   anyone who does not automatically receive a winter fuel payment under reg.4 and who fails to claim it by March 31 in the following year. There is an exception for refugees to whom reg.4(2) applies. In *CIS 2337/2004*, Mr Commissioner Jacobs held that the time limit in reg.3(1)(b) does not infringe claimants' rights under Art.1 of the First Protocol to the European Convention on Human Rights even when a payment has been made without a claim in respect of previous years. Winter fuel payments are not a contributory benefit and the time limit did not deprive claimants of any rights but merely defined the scope of those rights.

Making a winter fuel payment without a claim

5.28   **4.**—(1) Subject to paragraph (2), the Secretary of State may before the 31st March of the year following the year in which the qualifying week falls make a winter fuel payment under regulation 2 in respect of the preceding winter to a person who (disregarding regulation 3(b)) appears from official records held by the Secretary of State to be entitled to a payment under that regulation.

(2) Where a person becomes entitled to income support [¹ or state pension credit] in respect of the qualifying week by virtue of a decision made after that week that section 115 of the Immigration and Asylum Act 1999 (exclusions) ceases to apply to him the Secretary of State shall make a winter fuel payment to that person under regulation 2 in respect of the winter following the qualifying week.

(3) Subject to paragraph (4), for the purposes of paragraphs (1) and (2) official records held by the Secretary of State as to a person's circumstances shall be sufficient evidence thereof for the purpose of deciding his entitlement to a winter fuel payment and its amount.

(4) Paragraph (3) shall not apply so as to exclude the revision of a decision under section 9 of the Social Security Act 1998 (revision of decisions) or the supersession of a decision under section 10 of that Act (decisions superseding earlier decisions) or the consideration of fresh evidence in connection with the revision or supersession of a decision.

AMENDMENT

1. Social Fund Winter Fuel Payment (Amendment) Regulations 2004 (SI 2004/2154), reg.2(d) (September 20, 2004).

DEFINITION

"qualifying week"—see reg.1(2).

GENERAL NOTE

Reg.4 empowers (but does not oblige) the Secretary of State to make winter fuel pay-   **5.29**
ments on the basis of Benefits Agency records and without an express claim being
made. At the outset, the information in those records is deemed to be sufficient evidence of entitlement or non-entitlement (see reg.4(3)) but reg.4(4) permits the initial
decision to be revised or superseded in the normal way if further information comes to
light. Those who consider themselves to be entitled to a winter fuel payment but do
not receive one automatically may make a claim for it, provided they do so by March
31 in the year following the qualifying week (see reg.3(1)(b)).

Reg.4(2) makes special provision for asylum seekers who are granted refugee status
after the qualifying week and become retrospectively entitled to income support, or
state pension credit, for that week (see the notes to reg.21ZB of the Income Support
Regulations). In such circumstances a winter fuel payment *must* be made. The March
31 deadline for claiming does not apply (see reg.3(2)(b)). In *CIS 2497/2002* an argument was raised that the operation of reg. 4 discriminated indirectly against men on
the grounds of their sex contrary to Directive 79/7/EEC. The evidence was that those
selected by the Secretary of State to receive a winter fuel payment without a claim had
been identified from official records of those receiving social security benefits (including retirement pension) in the qualifying week. As the pensionable age for women is
lower than that for men, it was argued that there would be significantly more women
than men in that category. However, Commissioner Mesher rejected that argument
on the basis that, even if the operation of the rules allowing the Secretary of State to
make payments without a claim was discriminatory, the claimant had not been disadvantaged by reg.4 but by "the overall and identical time-limit [i.e., March 31, after the
winter in question] set for claims and for the making of payments without a claim".

Revocations

5. The Social Fund Winter Fuel Payment Regulations 1998, the Social   **5.30**
Fund Winter Fuel Payment Amendment Regulations 1998 and the Social
Fund Winter Fuel Payment Amendment Regulations 1999 are hereby
revoked.

Social Fund Maternity and Funeral Expenses (General) Regulations 1987

(SI 1987/481)

Made by the Secretary of State under the Social Security Act 1986,
ss. 32(2)(a), 84(1) and 89(1), and the Supplementary Benefits Act 1976, ss. 3,
4 and 34

ARRANGEMENT OF REGULATIONS

PART I

GENERAL

Citation and commencement

5.37 **1.** These regulations may be cited as the Social Fund Maternity and Funeral Expenses (General) Regulations 1987 and shall come into force on 6th April 1987.

Revocation

2. The Social Fund Maternity and Funeral Expenses (General)   **5.38**
Regulations 1986 are hereby revoked.

Interpretation

3.—(1) In these regulations unless the context otherwise requires—   **5.39**
[¹¹"the Act" means the Social Security Act 1986;]
[⁷"the Income Support Regulations" means the Income Support
   (General) Regulations 1987;]
[⁷"the Jobseeker's Allowance Regulations" means the Jobseeker's
   Allowance Regulations 1996;]
[⁹"absent parent" means a parent of a child who has died where—
   (a) that parent was not living in the same household with the child at
      the date of that child's death; and
   (b) that child had his home, at the date of death, with a person who was
      responsible for that child for the purposes of Part IX of the Social
      Security Contributions and Benefits Act 1992;]
"child" means a person under the age of 16 [³or a young person within
   the meaning of regulation 14 of the Income Support [⁷Regulations or,
   as the case may be, of regulation 76 of the Jobseeker's Allowance
   Regulations];]
[¹²"child tax credit" means a child tax credit under section 8 of the Tax
   Credits Act 2002;]
"claimant" means a person claiming a social fund payment in respect of
   maternity or funeral expenses;
[⁶"close relative" means a parent, parent-in-law, son, son-in-law, daughter,
   daughter-in-law, step-parent, step-son, step-son-in-law, step-daughter,
   step-daughter-in-law, brother, brother-in-law, sister or sister-in-law;]
"confinement" means labour resulting in the issue of a living child, or
   labour after [⁴24 weeks] of pregnancy resulting in the issue of a child
   whether alive or dead;
"family" means—
   (a) a married or unmarried couple and any children who are members
      of the same household and for whom one of the couple is or both
      are responsible;
   (b) a person who is not a member of a married or unmarried couple
      and any children who are members of the same household and for
      whom that person is responsible;
   (c) persons who are members of the same household and between
      whom there is a polygamous relationship and any children who are
      members of the same household and for whom a member of the
      polygamous relationship is responsible;
[¹²"family element" means in a case where any child in respect of whom
   child tax credit is payable is under the age of one year, the amount
   specified in regulation 7(3)(a) of the Child Tax Credit Regulations
   2002 or in any other case, the amount specified in regulation 7(3)(b) of
   those regulations;]
[¹ . . .]
"funeral" means a burial or a cremation;
"funeral payment" is to be construed in accordance with regulation 7;
[¹⁰"health professional" means—

(a) a registered medical practitioner;
(b) a midwife, nurse or health visitor registered as a midwife, nurse or health visitor with the United Kingdom Central Council for Nursing, Midwifery and Health Visiting under the Nurses, Midwives and Health Visitors Act 1997;]

[8"immediate family member" means a parent, son or daughter;]

[7"income-based jobseeker's allowance" has the same meaning in these Regulations as it has in the Jobseekers Act 1995 by virtue of section 1(4) of that Act;]

[1 . . .]

"married couple" means a man and a woman who are married to each other and are members of the same household;

"[11Sure Start Maternity Grant] is to be construed in accordance with regulation 5;

[6"partner" means where a person—
(a) is a member of a married or unmarried couple, the other member of that couple;
(b) is married polygamously to two or more members of his household, any such member;]

"occupational pension scheme" has the same meaning as in the Social Security Pensions Act 1975;

[8"prescribed time for claiming" means the appropriate period during which [11Sure Start Maternity Grant] or, as the case may be, a funeral payment, may be claimed pursuant to regulation 19 of, and Schedule 4 to, the Social Security (Claims and Payments) Regulations 1987;]

[1"person affected by a trade dispute" means a person—
(a) to whom section 23 of the Act [SSCBA, s.126] applies; or
(b) to whom that section would apply if a claim to income support were made by or in respect of him;]

[5"responsible person" is to be construed in accordance with regulation [87(1)(a)];]

[1 . . .]

[4 "still-born child" has the same meaning as in section 12 of the Births and Deaths Registration Act 1926 and section 56(1) of the Registrations of Births, Deaths and Marriages (Scotland) Act 1965 as they are amended by section 1 of the Still-birth (Definition) Act 1992;]

"unmarried couple" means a man and a woman who are not married to each other but are living together as husband and wife.

[8(1A) For the purposes of Part III of these Regulations, persons are to be treated as members of the same household where those persons—
(a) are married to each other and are living in the same residential accommodation, residential care home or nursing home as defined for the purposes of the Income Support Regulations or, as the case may be, of the Jobseeker's Allowance Regulations; or
(b) were partners immediately before either or both or any or all of those persons moved permanently into such accommodation or home as is referred to in sub-paragraph (a) above.
and that person is or, as the case may be, those persons are resident in such accommodation or home at the date of death of the person in respect of whom a funeral payment is claimed.]

[12"working tax credit" means a working tax credit under section 10 of the Tax Credits Act 2002].

[¹(2) For the purposes of these Regulations, two persons are to be treated as not being members of the same household in the circumstances set out in regulation 16(2) and (3) [⁷(a) to (d)] of the Income Support [⁷Regulations or, as the case may be, in regulation 78(2) and (3)(a) to (c) of the Jobseeker's Allowance Regulations].]

(3) For the purposes of these Regulations, a person shall be treated as a member of a polygamous relationship where, but for the fact that the relationship includes more than two persons, he would be one of a married or unmarried couple.

(4) In these Regulations, unless the context otherwise requires, any reference to a numbered regulation is a reference to the regulation bearing that number in these regulations and any reference in a regulation to a numbered paragraph is a reference to the paragraph of that regulation bearing that number.

AMENDMENTS

1. Social Fund Maternity and Funeral Expenses (General) Amendment Regulations 1988 (SI 1988/36), reg.2 (April 11, 1988).   **5.40**
2. Social Fund Maternity and Funeral Expenses (General) Amendment Regulations 1989 (SI 1989/379), reg.2 (April 1, 1989).
3. Social Fund (Miscellaneous Amendments) Regulations 1990 (SI 1990/ 580), reg.5 (April 9, 1990).
4. Social Fund Maternity and Funeral Expenses (General) Amendment Regulations 1992 (SI 1992/2149), reg.2 (October 1, 1992).
5. Social Fund Maternity and Funeral Expenses (General) Amendment Regulations 1994 (SI 1994/506), reg.2 (April 1, 1994).
6. Social Fund Maternity and Funeral Expenses (General) Amendment Regulations 1995 (SI 1995/1229), reg.2 (June 5, 1995).
7. Social Fund Maternity and Funeral Expenses (General) Amendment Regulations 1996 (SI 1996/1443), reg.2 (October 7, 1996).
8. Social Security (Social Fund and Claims and Payments) (Miscellaneous Amendments) Regulations 1997 (SI 1997/792), reg.2 (April 7, 1997).
9. Social Fund Maternity and Funeral Expenses (General) Amendment Regulations 1997 (SI 1997/2538), reg.3 (November 17, 1997).
10. Social Fund Maternity and Funeral Expenses (General) Amendment Regulations 2000 (SI 2000/528), reg.2 (March 27, 2000).
11. Social Fund Maternity and Funeral Expenses (General) Amendment Regulations 2000 (SI 2000/528), reg.4 (March 27, 2000).
12. Social Security (Working Tax Credit and Child Tax Credit) (Consequential Amendments) Regulations 2003 (SI 2003/455), reg.6 and Sch.4, para.2 (April 7, 2003).

GENERAL NOTE

Para. (1)

"close relative:" See the note to "close relative" in reg.2(1) of the Income Support   **5.41**
Regulations.

"confinement:" Note that a payment can be made for a stillbirth only if it occurs after the 24th week of the pregnancy (reduced from 28 weeks in October 1992).

"family:" Note that the definition differs slightly from that in s.137(1) of the Contributions and Benefits Act (1986 Act, s.20(11)), which applies for the purposes of income support, family credit and disability working allowance and s.35(1) of the

Jobseekers Act, which applies for the purpose of income-based JSA. So far as married and unmarried couples go, the approach is the same (see the notes to s.137(1)). Para.(2) goes further than the income support/income-based JSA rules by deeming members of a couple not to be members of the same household in these circumstances. Para.(2) does not cover the circumstances in which people are treated as members of the same household (but see para.(1A) where people are in residential care), so that presumably the general law on when membership of a household endures through a temporary absence will apply (see *England v Secretary of State for Social Services* [1982] 3 F.L.R. 222; *Taylor v Supplementary Benefit Officer (R(FIS) 5/85)*; *Santos v Santos* [1972] 2 All E.R. 246). See the note to para.(1A).

Until the amendment in April 1990 the definition of "child" meant that beyond the age of 15 a child could not be part of the family although continuing in secondary education and not entitled to income support in her own right. Thus some 16–18-year-old mothers were excluded from maternity payments. The reference to young persons, as defined in reg.14 of the Income Support (General) Regulations, or, from October 1996, reg.76 of the JSA Regulations, remedies this.

"funeral:" The old form of the Single Payments Regulations on funerals left it unclear whether "funeral" meant the ceremonies or religious services which accompany burial or cremation, or simply "burial." *R(SB)23/86* held that, in that context, it meant the latter. The present definition does make it clear it is the burial or cremation which is covered, rather than any accompanying or religious services.

"prescribed time for claiming:" Claims for a maternity payment may be made from the beginning of the 11th week before the expected week of confinement until three months after the actual date of confinement, or the date of the adoption order in the case of an adopted child, or the date of the parental order under s.30 of the Human Fertilisation and Embryology Act 1990 in the case of a child by a surrogate mother (reg.19 and para.8 of Sch.4 to the Claims and Payments Regulations). The time limit for a funeral payment claim is three months from the date of the funeral (Sch.4, para.9). From April 7, 1997 there is no longer any provision allowing claims to be made outside these time limits. But note that where at the date of claim the claimant has claimed, but not yet been awarded, a qualifying benefit and so the claim for a maternity or funeral payment is refused, if a further claim is made within three months of the qualifying benefit being awarded, it will be treated as made on the date of the original claim, or the date the qualifying benefit was awarded, whichever is later (reg.6(24) and (25) of the Claims and Payments Regulations).

"still-born child:" The definition referred to is "a child which has issued forth from its mother after the twenty-fourth week of pregnancy and which did not at any time after being completely expelled from its mother draw breath or show any other signs of life."

Para.(1A)

The purpose of this paragraph (see also the amendment to para.(2) deleting the reference to reg.16(3)(e) of the Income Support Regulations) is to enable a surviving partner in a home to qualify as "the responsible person" for the purposes of a funeral payment where one or both of them lives or lived in residential care. sub-para.(a) will apply, *inter alia*, where a couple marry whilst in residential care; under this sub-paragraph they must be living in the same residential care or nursing home or residential accommodation. Otherwise, sub-para.(b) requires them to have been a married or unmarried couple before one or both of them moved permanently into residential care.

Provision against double payment

5.42   **4.**—(1) Subject to paragraph (2), no [⁶ Sure Start Maternity Grant] shall be made under these Regulations if such a payment has already been made in respect of the child in question.

(2) Notwithstanding that a [⁶Sure Start Maternity Grant] has been made to the natural mother of a child or to one of her family, a second such payment may, subject to the following provisions of these Regulations, be made to the adoptive parents of the child in question [¹ or to persons who have been granted an order in respect of the child in question pursuant to section 30 of the Human Fertilisation and Embryology Act 1990 (parental orders)].

(3) [²Except in a case to which paragraph (4) applies,] no funeral payment shall be made under these Regulations if such a payment has already been made in respect of the funeral expenses in question [¹or in respect of any [²further] funeral expenses arising from the death of the same person].

[²(4) Notwithstanding paragraph (3), a further funeral payment may be made under these Regulations in respect of any funeral expenses arising from the death of a person in respect of which such a payment has already been made where—

(a) the decision pursuant to which the funeral payment was awarded has been [³revised]; and

(b) [⁵the further amount of the award] as revised [⁴. . .], together with the amount of the funeral payment already paid in respect of the death of that person, does not exceed the amount of any funeral payment which may be awarded pursuant to regulation 7A(2).]

AMENDMENTS

1. Social Security (Social Fund and Claims and Payments) (Miscellaneous Amendments) Regulations 1997 (SI 1997/792), reg.3 (April 7, 1997).

2. Social Fund Maternity and Funeral Expenses (General) Amendment Regulations 1997 (SI 1997/2538), reg.4 (November 17, 1997).

3. Social Security Act 1998 (Commencement No.12, and Consequential and Transitional Provisions) Order 1999 (SI 1999/3178 (C.81)), arts 3(4) and Sch.4, para.(a) (November 29, 1999).

4. Social Security Act 1998 (Commencement No.12, and Consequential and Transitional Provisions) Order 1999 (SI 1999/3178 (C.81)), arts 3(4) and Sch.4, para.(b) (November 29, 1999).

5. Social Fund Maternity and Funeral Expenses (General) Amendment Regulations 1999 (SI 1999/3266), reg.2(2) (January 4, 2000).

6. Social Fund Maternity and Funeral Expenses (General) Amendment Regulations 2000 (SI 2000/528), reg.4 (March 27, 2000).

5.43

DEFINITIONS

"child"—see reg.3(1).
"family"—*ibid.*
"funeral payment"—*ibid.*
"Sure Start Maternity Grant"—*ibid.*

GENERAL NOTE

Paras (1) and (3) contain rules preventing double payments in the case of Sure Start Maternity Grants and funeral payments respectively. Where a funeral payment was for less than the maximum, para.(4) is intended to allow an additional payment to be made on review, subject to the limit on funeral expenses in reg.7A(2) (the words "the amount of the award as revised on that review" in sub-para.(b) presumably refer to the additional, and not the total, award).

Only a lawful payment bars another payment (*CG 30/1990*). So where the first payment was made to the partner of the maternity grant claimant (who was the income support claimant) and not to her, this did not prevent her receiving a payment.

5.44

Paragraph (2) provides an exception in the case of Sure Start Maternity Grants as it allows the adoptive parents of a child, or those who have been granted a parental order of a child by a surrogate mother, to receive a payment although a payment has already been made for the natural mother. *CIS 13389/1996* decides that a person only qualifies as an adoptive parent if he has acquired parental responsibility by means of a court order (see the definition of "adoption order" in s.12(1) of the Adoption Act 1976). The claimant had made an agreement with the child's mother under s.4(1)(b) of the Children Act 1989 which conferred parental responsibility on him. However, this was not, and did not purport to be, an order (court orders for parental responsibility were dealt with under s.4(1)(a)) and so the claimant had not acquired parental responsibility by means of adoption. Since a maternity payment had already been made to the child's mother, para.(1) barred a payment to the claimant.

PART II

PAYMENTS FOR MATERNITY EXPENSES

Entitlement

5.45   **5.**—(1) Subject to regulation 6 and Parts IV and V of these Regulations, a payment to meet maternity expenses (referred to in these regulations as a "[8 Sure Start Maternity Grant]") shall be made only where—

[1(a)   the claimant or the claimant's partner has, in respect of the date of the claim for a [8Sure Start Maternity Grant], been awarded either income support [12state pension credit] [4income-based jobseeker's allowance,] [11working tax credit where the disability element or the severe disability element of working tax credit as specified in regulation 20(1)(b) and (f) of the Working Tax Credit (Entitlement and Maximum Rate) Regulations 2002 is included in the award or child tax credit payable at a rate higher than the family element]; and]

(b)   either—

    (i)   the claimant or, if the claimant is a member of a family, one of the family is pregnant or has given birth to a child [3or still-born child]; or

    (ii)   the claimant or the claimant's partner or both of them have adopted a child not exceeding the age of twelve months at the date of the claim; [5or]

    [5(iii)   the claimant and the claimant's spouse have been granted an order in respect of a child pursuant to section 30 of the Human Fertilisation and Embryology Act 1990 (parental orders); and]

[9(bb)   subject to paragraph (3)—

    (i)   the claimant or partner has received advice on health and welfare matters relating to the child from a health professional; and

    (ii)   where the claim is made before the child is born, the claimant or partner has received advice on health and welfare matters relating to maternal health from a health professional; and]

(c)   the claim is made within the [5prescribed time for claiming a [8Sure Start Maternity Grant].

[3(2) Subject to Part IV of these Regulations, the amount of [8Sure Start Maternity Grant] shall be—

(a) where the claim is made before confinement, [¹⁰£500] in respect of each expected child;

(b) where the claim is made after confinement, [¹⁰£500] in respect of each child, including any still-born child;

(c) where the claim is made after a child has already been adopted, [¹⁰£500] in respect of that child.]

[⁵(d) where the claim is made after an order referred to in paragraph (1)(b)(iii) has already been granted in respect of a child, [¹⁰£500] in respect of that child.]

[⁹(3) Paragraph (1)(bb)(i) shall not apply where a claim is made after the birth of a still-born child.]

AMENDMENTS

1. Social Fund Maternity and Funeral Expenses (General) Amendment Regulations 1988 (SI 1988/36), reg.3 (April 11, 1988).   **5.46**

2. Disability Living Allowance and Disability Working Allowance (Consequential Provisions) Regulations 1991 (SI 1991/2742), reg.10 (April 6, 1992).

3. Social Fund Maternity and Funeral Expenses (General) Amendment Regulations 1992 (SI 1992/2149), reg.3 (October 1, 1992).

4. Social Fund Maternity and Funeral Expenses (General) Amendment Regulations 1996 (SI 1996/1443), reg.3 (October 7, 1996).

5. Social Security (Social Fund and Claims and Payments) (Miscellaneous Amendments) Regulations 1997 (SI 1997/792), reg.4 (April 7, 1997).

6. Social Security and Child Support (Tax Credits) Consequential Amendments Regulations 1999 (SI 1999/2566), reg.2(1) and Sch.2, Pt I (October 5, 1999).

7. Social Security and Child Support (Tax Credits) Consequential Amendments Regulations 1999 (SI 1999/2566), reg.2(2) and Sch.2, Pt II (October 5, 1999).

8. Social Fund Maternity and Funeral Expenses (General) Amendment Regulations 2000 (SI 2000/528), reg.4 (March 27, 2000).

9. Social Fund Maternity and Funeral Expenses (General) Amendment Regulations 2000 (SI 2000/528), reg.3(2) (March 27, 2000).

10. Social Fund Maternity and Funeral Expenses (General) Amendment Regulations 2002 (SI 2002/79), reg.2 (June 16, 2002).

11. Social Security (Working Tax Credit and Child Tax Credit) (Consequential Amendments) Regulations 2003 (SI 2003/455), reg.6 and Sch., para.2 (April 7, 2003).

12. State Pension Credit (Consequential, Transitional and Miscellaneous Provisions) Regulations 2002 (SI 2002/3019), reg.31 (October 6, 2003).

DEFINITIONS

"child"—see reg.3(1).
"claimant"—*ibid.*
"confinement"—*ibid.*
"family"—*ibid.*
"health professional"—*ibid.*
"partner"—*ibid.*
"prescribed time for claiming"—*ibid.*
"still-born child"—*ibid.*

GENERAL NOTE

Para. (1)

From June 11, 2000 maternity payments have been renamed "Sure Start Maternity Grants" and an additional condition of entitlement introduced linking eligibility to the receipt of advice on the health and welfare of the child (and, where the claim is made before the birth, of the mother) from a doctor, midwife, nurse or health visitor. The amount of the payment has been increased from £100 to £200.   **5.47**

By reg.5 of the Social Fund Maternity and Funeral Expenses (General) Amendment Regulations 2000 (SI 2000/528), reg.5 continues to apply in its unamended form where a claim is made and the expected date of confinement and date of birth (or of the adoption order or order under s.30 of the Human Fertilisation and Embryology Act 1990) are on or before June 10, 2000. Where a claim under the old law has already been made on the basis of an expected date of confinement on or before June 10, 2000 and the birth actually takes place after that date a further payment can be made under the new law but, in this case, the amount of the first payment is deducted from the amount which would otherwise be due (see reg.5(2) and (3) of SI 2000/528).

The four conditions specified must all be satisfied for a payment to be made but no needs have to be proved beyond them. Under sub-para. (a) either the person claiming the maternity payment or that person's partner must have been awarded a qualifying benefit. Note that whether or not a claimant has a partner is a matter of law, and whether or not she regards herself as having a partner is not conclusive of that issue—see *CIS/2031/2003* in which Commissioner Levenson advised tribunals that:

"... the question of whether a claimant has a partner is intrinsic to the very question of entitlement to a Grant and in an appeal against a refusal of a Grant which depends on the question of entitlement to a qualifying benefit, a tribunal should always enquire whether the person applying for the Grant has a partner".

In that appeal, the claimant was entitled to a grant because her (undisclosed) partner had been entitled to IS at the relevant date, albeit not in respect of her.

Qualifying benefits are income support, state pension credit, income-based JSA, working tax credit (if the award includes the disability element or severe disability elements—see regs.9, 17, and 20(1)(b) and (f) of the Working Tax Credit (Entitlement and Maximum Rate) Regulations 2003 in Vol. IV) or child tax credit (if it is paid at a rate higher than the family element—in 2004/2005, £545 *per annum* or, if the family includes a child aged less than one year, £1090 (see reg.7(3) of the Child Tax Credit Regulations 2002 in Vol. IV). The original form of this regulation referred to the claimant being "in receipt" of benefit, which probably meant "entitled to receive benefit" (R(SB)12/87). Now the crucial matter is an award, rather than the actual payment of benefit. Although para.(a) talks of the claimant having been awarded benefit, an award which is made after the date of the claim for a maternity payment (e.g. following an appeal or a review) will presumably do, provided that it covers the date of claim. The original form of reg.5 also left unclear the exact date on which this condition had to be satisfied. This is now fixed as the date of claim.

Under sub-para.(b), the issues will normally be simple ones of fact. The October 1992 amendments to reg.3 and this regulation mean that a payment can be made when a child is still-born after a confinement of at least 24 weeks. Note that while a payment can be made in advance of the actual birth of a child to a member of the family, in the case of an adoption or surrogacy one can only be made after the event. See the definition of "family" in reg.3(1) and the notes to s.137(1) of the Contributions and Benefits Act (1986 Act, s.20(11)).

Under sub-para.(bb) (introduced with effect from June 11, 2000) either the claimant or her partner (if she has one) must have received advice on the health and welfare of the child from a "health professional" (as defined in reg.3) before a Sure Start Maternity Grant can be paid. For obvious reasons, this requirement does not apply if the child is still-born (see para.(3)). Where the claim is made before the birth of the child, advice must also have been given about the health of the mother.

Under sub-para.(c), the period within which the claim has to be made begins 11 weeks before the first day of the expected week of confinement and ends three months after the actual date of confinement (or the date of the adoption order, in the case of an adopted baby, or the date of the parental order in the case of a child by a surrogate mother) (Claims and Payments Regulations, Sch.4, para.8). From April 7, 1997 there is no longer any provision allowing claims to be made outside this time limit. But note that under reg.6(24) and (25) of the Claims and Payments Regulations, where at the date of claim the claimant has claimed, but not yet been awarded, a qualifying benefit and so the claim for a maternity payment is refused, if a further claim is made within three months of the qualifying benefit being awarded, it will be treated as made on the date of the original claim, or the date the qualifying benefit was awarded, whichever is later.

In *CIS/1965/2003*, Mr Commissioner Williams held *CIS/13389/1996*, which had decided that a parental responsibility agreement under s.4 of the Children Act 1989 did not amount to adoption within reg.5(1)(b)(ii), remained good law after the coming into force of the Human Rights Act 1998 and the Adoption and Children Act 2002. The same was true of a residence order under s.8 of the 1989 Act. Article 26 of the UN Convention on the Rights of the Child did not alter that conclusion.

In *C1/02-03 (SF)* the Chief Commissioner for Northern Ireland held that the Northern Ireland equivalent of para.(c) did not infringe either Art.6 or Art.8 of the European Convention on Human Rights.

Para. (2)

The amount of the payment is (from June 11, 2000) £200 per child, having been at £100 since April 1990 and £85 for two years before that. This will not go very far. The grant is to be increased to £300 with effect from December 3, 2000 (by SI 2000/2229, see the 2000 Supplement to this volume). Although para.(2) is not expressly made subject to Pt V, reg.12(4) secured that any maternity grant awarded (before its abolition on April 6, 1987) in respect of the same confinement was to be deducted from what would otherwise have been awarded.

Persons affected by a trade dispute

6. Where the claimant or the claimant's partner is a person affected by a trade dispute, a [⁶Sure Start Maternity Grant] shall be made only if—
    (a) in the case where the claimant or the claimant's partner is in receipt of [¹income support], [³ or income-based jobseeker's allowance] the trade dispute has, at the date of the claim for that payment, continued for not less than six weeks; or
    (b) in the case where the claimant or the claimant's partner is in receipt of [⁷working tax credit where the disability element or the severe disability element of working tax credit as specified in regulation 20(1)(b) and (f) of the Working Tax Credit (Entitlement and Maximum Rate) Regulations 2002 is included in the award or child tax credit payable at a rate higher than the family element] the claim in respect of which [⁷working tax credit where the disability element or the severe disability element of working tax credit as specified in regulation 20(1)(b) and (f) of the Working Tax Credit (Entitlement and Maximum Rate) Regulations 2002 is included in the award or child tax credit payable at a rate higher than the family element] was awarded was made before the beginning of the trade dispute [⁷ . . .].
    (c) [⁷ . . .]

5.48

AMENDMENTS

1. Social Fund Maternity and Funeral Expenses (General) Amendment Regulations 1988 (SI 1988/36), reg.4 (April 11, 1988).

2. Disability Living Allowance and Disability Working Allowance (Consequential Provisions) Regulations 1991 (SI 1991/2742), reg.10 (April 6, 1992).

3. Social Fund Maternity and Funeral Expenses (General) Amendment Regulations 1996 (SI 1996/1443), reg.4 (October 7, 1996).

4. Social Security and Child Support (Tax Credits) Consequential Amendments Regulations 1999 (SI 1999/2566), reg.2(1) and Sch.2, Pt I (October 5, 1999).

5. Social Security and Child Support (Tax Credits) Consequential Amendments Regulations 1999 (SI 1999/2566), reg.2(2) and Sch.2, Pt II (October 5, 1999).

5.49

6. Social Fund Maternity and Funeral Expenses (General) Amendment Regulations 2000 (SI 2000/528), reg.4 (March 27, 2000).

7. Social Security (Working Tax Credit and Child Tax Credit)(Consequential Amendments) Regulations 2003 (SI 2003/455), reg.6 and Sch.4, para.2 (April 7, 2003).

DEFINITIONS

"claimant"—see reg.3(1).
"Sure Start Maternity Grant"—*ibid.*
"partner"—*ibid.*
"person affected by a trade dispute"—*ibid.*

GENERAL NOTE

5.50   Para.(a) took over a similar rule which used to be in the Supplementary Benefit (Trade Disputes and Recovery from Earnings) Regulations, but the excluding period is reduced from 11 weeks to six weeks. The crucial date is that of the claim for the Sure Start Maternity Grant. It may sometimes be difficult to tell when a trade dispute started, since the dispute is to be distinguished from the stoppage of work due to it. See reg.3(1) for "person affected by a trade dispute."

Paras (b) and (c) only exclude payments where the claim for family credit or disability working allowance was made after the beginning of the trade dispute.

PART III

PAYMENTS FOR FUNERAL EXPENSES

[¹Entitlement

5.51   **7.**—(1) Subject to the following provisions of this regulation, regulation 8 and to Parts IV and V of these Regulations, a social fund payment (referred to in these Regulations as a "funeral payment") to meet funeral expenses shall be made only where—

(a) the claimant or his partner (in this Part of these Regulations referred to as "the responsible person"), [⁷in respect of the date of the claim] for a funeral payment—

(i) has an award of income support, [⁹state pension credit] income-based jobseeker's allowance, [⁸working tax credit where the disability element or the severe disability element of working tax credit as specified in regulation 20(1)(b) and (f) of the Working Tax Credit (Entitlement and Maximum Rate) Regulations 2002 is included in the award, child tax credit payable at a rate higher than the family element], housing benefit or council tax benefit where, in the case of council tax benefit, that benefit is awarded by virtue of the claimant or his partner having fulfilled the conditions of entitlement specified in section 131(3) to (5) of the Social Security Contributions and Benefits Act 1992 (certain conditions for entitlement to council tax benefit); or

(ii) is a person to whom (by virtue of sub-section (7) of section 131 of that Act) sub-section (6) of that section applies where, on a claim for council tax benefit, the conditions of entitlement specified in section 131(3) and (6) for an award of an alternative maximum council tax benefit are fulfilled;

[²(b) the funeral takes place—
    (i) in a case where the responsible person is a person to whom para-graph (1A) applies, in an EEA State;
    (ii) in any other case, in the United Kingdom,
and for the purposes of this sub-paragraph, "EEA State" means a State which is a contracting party to the Agreement on the European Economic Area signed at Oporto on 2nd May 1992 as adjusted by the Protocol signed at Brussels on 17th March 1993;]

 (c) the deceased was ordinarily resident in the United Kingdom at the date of his death;

 (d) the claim is made within the prescribed time for claiming a funeral payment; and

 (e) the claimant or his partner accepts responsibility for those expenses and—
    (i) the responsible person was the partner of the deceased at the date of death; or
    [²(ii) in a case where the deceased was—
        (aa) a child and there is no absent parent or there is an absent parent who, or whose partner, had an award of a benefit to which sub-paragraph (a) above refers current as at the date of death, the responsible person was the person or the partner of the person responsible for that child for the pur-poses of Part IX of the Social Security Contributions and Benefits Act 1992 as at the date of death; or
        (bb) a still-born child, the responsible person was a parent of that still-born child or the partner of a parent of that still-born child as at the date when the child was still-born; or
    (iii) in a case where the deceased had no partner and (ii) above does not apply, the responsible person was, subject to paragraphs (3) and (4), an immediate family member of the deceased and it is reasonable for the responsible person to accept responsibility for those expenses; or
    (iv) in a case where the deceased had no partner and (ii) and (iii) above do not apply, the responsible person was, subject to para-graphs (3) and (4), either—
        (aa) a close relative of the deceased; or
        (bb) a close friend of the deceased,
and it is reasonable for the responsible person to accept responsibil-ity for those expenses.

(1A) This paragraph applies to a person who is—

(a) a worker for the purposes of Council Regulation (EEC) No.1612/68 or (EEC) No.1251/70;

(b) a member of the family of a worker for the purposes of Council Regulation (EEC) No.1612/68;

(c) in the case of a worker who has died, a member of the family of that worker for the purposes of Council Regulation (EEC) No.1251/70; or

(d) a person with a right to reside in the United Kingdom pursuant to Council Directive No.68/360/EEC or No.73/148/EEC.]

(2) For the purposes of paragraph (1)(e)(iii) and (iv), the deceased shall be treated as having had no partner where the deceased had a partner at the date of death and—

(a) no claim for funeral expenses is made by the partner in respect of the death of the deceased; and

(b) that partner dies before the date upon which the deceased's funeral takes place.

(3) [²Subject to paragraph (4), the responsible person shall not be entitled to a funeral payment where he is an immediate family member, a close relative or a close friend of the deceased and—]

(a) [⁵there are one or more immediate family members of the deceased];

(b) neither those immediate family members nor their partners have been awarded a benefit to which paragraph (1)(a) refers; and

(c) any of the immediate family members to which sub-paragraph (b) above refers was not estranged from the deceased at the date of his death.

(4) Paragraph (3) shall not apply to disentitle the responsible person from a funeral payment where the immediate family member to whom that paragraph applies is—

[⁵(za)a person who has not attained the age of 18;]

(a) a person who [⁵ has attained the age of 18 but not the age of 19] and who is attending a full-time course of advanced education as defined in regulation 61 of the Income Support Regulations or, as the case may be, a person aged 19 or over but under pensionable age who is attending a full-time course of study at an educational establishment;

[⁶(aa) a person in receipt of asylum support under section 95 of the Immigration and Asylum Act 1999;]

(b) a member of, and fully maintained by, a religious order;

(c) being detained in a prison, remand centre or youth custody institution and either that immediate family member or his partner had been awarded a benefit to which paragraph (1)(a) refers immediately before that immediate family member was so detained; [¹⁰. . .]

(d) a person who is regarded as receiving free in-patient treatment within the meaning of the Social Security (Hospital In-Patients) Regulations 1975 or, as the case may be, the Social Security (Hospital In-Patients) Regulations (Northern Ireland) 1975 and either that immediate family member or his partner had been awarded a benefit to which paragraph (1)(a) refers immediately before that immediate family member was first regarded as receiving such treatment.[¹⁰; or

(e) a person ordinarily resident outside the United Kingdom].

(5) In a case to which paragraph (1)(e)(iii) or (iv) applies, whether it is reasonable for a person to accept responsibility for meeting the expenses of a funeral shall be determined by the nature and extent of that person's contact with the deceased.

(6) Except in a case where paragraph (7) applies, in a case where the deceased had one or more close relatives and the responsible person is a person to whom paragraph (1)(e)(iii) or (iv) applies, if on comparing the nature and extent of any close relative's contact with the deceased and the nature and extent of the responsible person's contact with the deceased, any such close relative was—

(a) in closer contact with the deceased than the responsible person; or

(b) in equally close contact with the deceased and neither that close relative nor his partner, if he has one, has been awarded a benefit to which paragraph (1)(a) refers

(c) [⁶. . .];

the responsible person shall not be entitled to a funeral payment under these Regulations in respect of those expenses.

[¹⁰(7) Paragraph (6) shall not apply where the close relative who was in closer contact with the deceased than the responsible person or, as the case may be, was in equally close contact with the deceased—

    (a) was under the age of 18 at the date of death and was the only close relative (apart from any other person who was under the age of 18 at that date) to whom either sub-paragraph (a) or (b) of paragraph (6) applies; or

    (b) is a person ordinarily resident outside the United Kingdom.]

AMENDMENTS

1. Social Security (Social Fund and Claims and Payments) (Miscellaneous Amendments) Regulations 1997 (SI 1997/792), reg.5 (April 7, 1997).

2. Social Fund Maternity and Funeral Expenses (General) Amendment Regulations 1997 (SI 1997/2538), reg.5 (November 17, 1997).

3. Social Security and Child Support (Tax Credits) Consequential Amendments Regulations 1999 (SI 1999/2566), reg.2(1) and Sch.2, Pt I (October 5, 1999).

4. Social Security and Child Support (Tax Credits) Consequential Amendments Regulations 1999 (SI 1999/2566), reg.2(2) and Sch.2, Pt II (October 5, 1999).

5. Social Fund Maternity and Funeral Expenses (General) Amendment Regulations 1999 (SI 1999/3266), reg.2(3) (January 4, 2000).

6. Social Fund Maternity and Funeral Expenses (General) Amendment Regulations 2001 (SI 2001/3023), reg.2 (October 8, 2001)

7. Social Fund (Miscellaneous Amendments) Regulations 2002 (SI 2002/2323), reg.3 (October 1, 2002).

8. Social Security (Working Tax Credit and Child Tax Credit) (Consequential Amendments) Regulations 2003 (SI 2003/455), reg.6 and Sch.4, para.2 (April 7, 2003).

9. State Pension Credit (Consequential, Transitional and Miscellaneous Provisions) Regulations 2002 (SI 2002/3019), reg.31 (October 6, 2003).

10. Social Fund Maternity and Funeral Expenses (General) Amendment Regulations 2004 (SI 2004/2536), reg.3 (October 25, 2004).

DEFINITIONS

    "absent parent"—see reg.3(1).
    "child"—*ibid.*
    "claimant"—*ibid.*
    "close relative"—*ibid.*
    "funeral"—*ibid.*
    "immediate family member"—*ibid.*
    "partner"—*ibid.*
    "prescribed time for claiming"—*ibid.*
    "still-born child"—*ibid.*

GENERAL NOTE

This provision replaced both the contributory death grant, which had stood at £30 for many years, and reg.8 of the Supplementary Benefit (Single Payments) Regulations. In its original form it provided effectively the same level of payment as under the Single Payments Regulations, but under wider conditions.

However, on June 5, 1995, a ceiling was imposed on the amount that can be awarded for a funeral payment. At the same time, a new priority order was introduced for deciding who was to be treated as "the responsible person", and the financial test that is applied where the deceased has more than one surviving close relative was tightened up. There was transitional protection for claims for funeral expenses in respect of a death before June 5, 1995 where the funeral took place by September 5, 1995. In such a case the former rules applied (see the 1995 edition of Mesher and

5.52

5.53

Wood, *Income-related Benefits: the Legislation*). Further minor adjustments were made in October 1996 (see the 1996 Supplement). But this was rapidly followed by another major overhaul of the funeral payments scheme, as a result of which the new form of reg.7 and the new reg.7A were introduced on April 7, 1997. See also the changes to reg.8 made at the same time.

The Social Security Advisory Committee's main recommendation in response to these proposed changes was that rather than seeking to tighten the criteria for entitlement to a payment still further, a new approach to help with funeral costs, possibly involving some form of insurance, needed to be considered. They referred to the evidence presented to them (largely anecdotal) that there was a growing problem of the system failing to meet the costs of a simple funeral. In a highly critical report (Cm. 3585) their main conclusion was that the new rules on eligibility added such complexity that it was doubtful whether they were understandable or workable. They considered that the proposals were "unreasonably intrusive" and that particularly those aspects concerning absent parents and the "immediate family" test appeared "to embody a narrow and inflexible view of family responsibilities which ignores the diversity of present day society and would . . . create inequity as well as delaying payments still further, while investigations are made into the relationships of deceased people". However, with one or two minor exceptions, SSAC's strongly voiced concerns were ignored by the Government. There is transitional protection for claims in respect of a death before April 7, 1997 where the funeral takes place by July 7, 1997 (see Social Security (Social Fund and Claims and Payments) (Miscellaneous Amendments) Regulations 1997, reg.9 on p.1491). In such a case the former rules will apply (see the 1996 edition of *Mesher and Wood, Income-related Benefits: the Legislation*, together with the 1996 Supplement).

Reg.7 deals with entitlement; reg.7A defines the amount of the payment. Note also the deductions that will be made from any award under reg.8 and that entitlement is subject to the £500 or £1,000 capital rule in reg.9.

Para. (1)

5.54   All five conditions specified must be satisfied.

Note that the definition of funeral in reg.3(1) avoids the problems of interpretation revealed in *R(SB) 23/86*. It is the cost of a burial or a cremation which is covered, rather than the accompanying ceremonies.

5.55   *Sub-para. (a)*: An award of housing benefit or council tax benefit to either the claimant or his partner will do, as well as an award of income support, income-based JSA, and working tax credit (if the award includes the disability element or severe disability elements—see regs.9, 17, and 20(1)(b) and (f) of the Working Tax Credit (Entitlement and Maximum Rate) Regulations 2003 in Vol. IV) or child tax credit (if it is paid at a rate higher than the family element—in 2004/2005, £545 *per annum* or, if the family includes a child aged less than one year, £1090 (see reg.7(3) of the Child Tax Credit Regulations 2002 in Vol. IV). The award must be in respect of the date of claim for the funeral payment. See the notes to reg.5(1) and note *CIS 2059/1995*. In that case the claimant's claim for a funeral payment had been rejected on the ground that he was not entitled to income support. However, the consequence of the Commissioner allowing his appeal against the decision refusing income support was that the basis for the rejection of his claim for a funeral payment had gone. Thus the tribunal's decision on that appeal, although sound when it was given, had become erroneous and it too had to be set aside.

On head (ii), para.2005 of the *Social Fund Maternity and Funeral Payments Guide* now states that if alternative maximum council tax benefit (usually known as second adult rebate) is the qualifying benefit, it is the person in respect of whom the second adult rebate has been awarded (*i.e.* the non-householder) who can qualify for a funeral payment, not the householder who receives the council tax benefit (see also para.39116 of the *Decision Makers Guide*). Although the wording of head (ii) is not entirely clear, this approach is logical, since it is the circumstances of the non-householder, not the householder, that warrant the rebate. In *CIS/4531/2004*, Commissioner Levenson criticised the *Guide* and the previous editions of this Volume for failing to make clear that it is not necessary for an award of second adult rebate actually to have been made before the non-householder can qualify for a social fund funeral payment under head (ii). The learned Commissioner correctly points out that the regulation is satisfied as long as the conditions in s.131(3) and (6) of the SSCBA 1992 are satisfied and that it is not necessary that any award of second adult rebate should have been made. On the particular facts of the case no award of second adult rebate had been made to the householder (who was not the responsible person) because she had been awarded CTB at a higher rate. However, the non-householder claimant qualified for a funeral payment because the conditions of an award of second adult rebate were satisfied in respect of him.

The requirement that claimants should be in receipt of a qualifying benefit has been held not to infringe their Convention Rights under the Human Rights Act 1998, see *CIS 3280/2001* and *CIS 1722/2002*. In the latter case, the Commissioner also dismissed a number of other *vires* and human rights challenges to reg.7(1), all of which conspicuously lacked merit.

Sub-para. (b): The previous form of sub-para.(b) required the funeral, *i.e.* the burial or cremation, to take place in the UK (*i.e.* Great Britain and Northern Ireland: Interpretation Act 1978, Sch.1). A new form has finally been introduced following the ECJ's judgment in *O'Flynn v Adjudication Officer*, Case C– 237/94, [1996] All E.R. (EC) 541 (*R(IS) 4/98*). The new rule applies to claims for funeral payments made, or treated as made, after November 16, 1997 (reg.2 of the amending regulations). However, the effect of the ECJ's judgment is to produce a similar result in respect of claims for funeral payments made before that date, since clearly the old form of sub-para.(b) has to be read subject to that judgment. 5.56

Mr O'Flynn was an Irish national resident in the UK. His son died in the UK but the burial took place in Ireland. The ECJ held that the rule that the funeral must take place in the UK indirectly discriminated against nationals of other Member States and so was in breach of Art.7(2) of EC Regulation 1612/68 (social and tax advantages). Migrant workers were more likely to have to arrange for burial in another Member State in view of the links which members of such a family generally maintained with their country of origin. As regards the cost of a funeral in another Member State, there was nothing to prevent the UK from limiting the amount of the payment to the normal cost of a funeral in the UK. The cost of transporting the coffin to a place distant from the deceased's home was not covered in any event. When the case returned to a Commissioner he held that not only had the ECJ decided that the rule was discriminatory but also that it was not objectively justified. Accordingly the rule was to be disapplied and the claimant was entitled to a funeral payment. The amount claimed in that case was limited to the costs incurred within the UK. However, the Commissioner did raise the issue of the costs of transporting a body to another Member State for burial or cremation and the costs of the funeral there. He considered that in relation to transport costs, the approach to be adopted was the same as that taken in *R(IS) 11/91* to transport within the UK (note in particular para.9 of *R(IS) 11/91* as regards transport costs under what is now reg.7A(2)(e)); as regards the funeral costs, in his view expenses incurred in the other Member State had to be dealt with in the same way as if the funeral had taken place in a part of the UK distant from the deceased's home. The Commissioner expressed no opinion on the question of travel costs for the responsible person but note the new reg.7A(2)(f) in force from November 17, 1997. In considering any claim for a funeral in another Member State, adjudicating authorities will of course have to bear in mind the particular form of reg.7 (or 7A) in force at the time of the claim; note that the DWP accepts that the effect of *R(IS) 4/98* should be applied without any restriction (*e.g.* under s.69 of the Administration Act).

The new sub-para.(b) provides that the funeral can take place in any EEA state if the "responsible person" (see sub-para.(a)) is a worker for the purposes of EC Regulations 1612/68 or 1251/70, a member of the family of a worker for the purposes of Regulation 1612/68, a member of the family of a worker who has died and to whom Regulation 1251/70 applied, or a person who has a right to reside in the UK under EC Directives 68/360 or 73/148; otherwise it must take place in the UK. The EEA states are the EU member states (Austria, Belgium, Denmark, Finland, France, Germany, Greece, Republic of Ireland, Italy, Luxembourg, the Netherlands, Portugal, Spain, Sweden and the UK) plus Iceland, Liechtenstein and Norway. It is anticipated that a further ten states (Cyprus, the Czech Republic, Estonia, Hungary, Latvia, Lithuania, Malta, Poland, Slovakia and Slovenia) will join the EU on May 1, 2004. See the notes to the definition of "person subject to immigration control" in reg.21(3) of the Income Support Regulations for discussion of the meaning of "worker" and who has a right to reside under these Directives. Under Art.10 of Regulation 1612/68 the members of the family of a worker include his spouse, his, or his spouse's, children, grandchildren, great grandchildren, etc. who are either under 21 or dependent, parents, parents-in-law, grandparents, grandparents-in-law, etc. if they are dependent, and any other member who is dependent or who was living with the worker before he came to the UK. The same definition applies for the purposes of Regulation 1251/70 (see Art.1 of that Regulation).

Note also that reg.7A(2)(f) no longer restricts eligible travel expenses to those within the UK.

The argument that the rule in sub-para.(b) is unlawful under the Race Relations Act 1976 was rejected in *R. v Secretary of State for Social Security Ex p. Nessa, The Times*, November 15, 1994. Section 75 of the 1976 Act states that the Act applies to acts done by, *inter alia*, ministers, as it applies to acts done by a private person. But Auld J. holds that acts of a governmental nature, such as the making of regulations, were not subject to the control of the 1976 Act as they were not acts of a kind that could be done by a private person. In *CIS/3150/1999* a challenge to the validity of reg.7(1)(b) on the basis that it is *ultra vires* and irrational was rejected and in *CIS 4769/2001* the Commissioner rejected a challenge under the Human Rights Act: the rule was not directly discriminatory and the Commissioner was not persuaded either that there was any indirect discrimination against the claimant, a Muslim of Pakistani origin, or that, if there was such discrimination, it had not been established that it was not objectively justified. The latter decision also rejected a challenge to the former rule which includes relatives of the deceased who are ordinarily resident abroad (and who will therefore never in practice be in receipt of qualifying benefits) in the definition of "immediate family members" for the purposes of reg.7(3) (see below).

The conclusion that reg.7(1)(b) did not infringe the claimant's Convention rights was also reached by Mr Commissioner Howell QC in *CIS 1870/2003*, CIS 2302/2003, *CIS 2305/2003* and *CIS 2624/2003*, but for different reasons: the commissioner took the view that, for the purposes of Article 14, funeral payments did not fall within the ambit of either Article 8, Article 9 or Article 1 of the First Protocol to the Convention because there was no direct link between the making of such payments and the performance by the United Kingdom of its obligation to secure the enjoyment of the freedoms and immunities set out in any of those articles.

5.57   *Sub-para.(c)*: This is a new rule from April 7, 1997. The deceased must be ordinarily resident in the UK at the date of his death. On the meaning of "ordinary residence" see the notes to reg.3(1) of the Family Credit Regulations. The requirement is one of ordinary residence, not presence, so, for example, a claim can be made in respect of a UK resident who dies while on holiday abroad for the cost of the funeral in the UK (although the cost of transporting the body back to the UK would not be covered, except possibly under sub-para.(g) of reg.7A(2)).

5.58   *Sub-para. (d)*: The time limit is specified in para.9 of Sch.4 to the Claims and Payments Regulations as three months from the date of the funeral. From April 7, 1997 there is no longer any provision allowing claims to be made outside this time limit (see the new form of reg.19 of the Claims and Payments Regulations). Thus if the circumstances in *CIS 4931/1995* were repeated (claimant who did not qualify for income support until four months after his wife's funeral because only half his mortgage interest was included in his applicable amount until that date was held to have good cause for a late claim for a funeral payment), there would be no entitlement. But note that under reg.6(24) and (25) of the Claims and Payments Regulations, where a claim for a qualifying benefit has been made but not yet determined when the claim for a funeral payment is made and so the claim is refused, if a further claim is made within three months of the qualifying benefit being awarded, it will be treated as made on the date of the original claim for a funeral payment, or the date the qualifying benefit was awarded, whichever is later.

Para. (1) (e) and paras (2) to (7)

Paragraph (1)(e) introduced major new restrictions on eligibility for a funeral payment by imposing a stricter priority order for deciding who is to be treated as the "responsible person". (See reg.9 of the Social Security (Social Fund and Claims and Payments) (Miscellaneous Amendments) Regulations 1997 (p.1415) for the transitional protection for claims in respect of deaths before April 7, 1997 where the funeral takes place by July 7, 1997). The November 1997 amendments to sub-para.(e) have mainly tidied up the wording in order to clarify the policy intention.

5.59

It is first necessary for the claimant or partner to have accepted responsibility for the costs of the funeral. This may give rise to difficulties if the closest relative lacks the legal capacity to accept a contractual liability to the undertakers. In *C1/01-02(SF)* the Commissioner had to decide whether a 16 year-old boy could legally "accept responsibility" for the expenses of his mother's funeral under the Northern Ireland equivalent of reg.7. She held that, in the particular circumstances of that case (where the claimant was the deceased's eldest child, 16 years old, had become the tenant of the family home and there was no other parent whose whereabouts were known) those expenses were a "necessary" for him so that he was obliged to pay a reasonable price for them under s.3 of the Sale of Goods Act 1979 even though he did not have capacity to make a binding contract to pay them.

Second, unless the deceased is a child or still-born child (see below), the person must have been the deceased's partner at the date of death (head (i)), or, if the deceased had no partner, an "immediate family member" (*i.e.* parent, son or daughter, see reg.3(1)) (head (iii)), or, if there is no immediate family member, another close relative (defined in reg.3(1)) or a close friend (head (iv)). Thus an ex-partner (or someone who is no longer treated as a partner), or the surviving partner in a gay couple (or a relative who is not a close relative) will have to qualify under the category of close friend. According to para.39162 of the *Decision Makers Guide*, in considering whether a person was a close friend of the deceased, the depth of the relationship will be more important than its duration. In *CIS 788/2003* the deceased was a boy who had died at the age of three months. The child's mother was herself a minor and the funeral directors refused to enter into a contract with her for that reason. The child's grandmother therefore undertook responsibility for the expenses and claimed a payment from the Social Fund. In these circumstances, Commissioner Turnbull held that the grandmother could be treated as a "close friend" of the deceased under reg.7(1)(e)(iv). The Secretary of State had argued that as child benefit had been paid to the child's mother, she would have satisfied reg.7(1)(e)(ii)(aa) if she had accepted responsibility for the funeral expenses and therefore that the words "(ii) and (iii) above do not apply" in reg.7(1)(e)(iv) were not satisfied. The Commissioner rejected that argument. Reg. 7(1)(e)(ii) "did not apply" because there was no real possibility of the mother's taking responsibility for the funeral expenses. Neither the existence of a family relationship between the grandmother and the child nor the child's very young age prevented her from being treated as his "close friend" for the purposes of the regulation.

Para.(2) makes specific provision for some very limited circumstances in which the deceased will be treated as having no partner.

Where heads (iii) or (iv) apply, it must be reasonable for the person to accept responsibility for the funeral expenses, which is to be decided by considering the nature and extent of that person's contact with the deceased (para.(5)). *R(IS) 3/98* holds that in deciding this question, regard should be had to the person's relationship with the deceased as a whole and not just during the period immediately preceding the date of death. The claimant had claimed a funeral payment in respect of his late father whom he had not seen for 24 years. He was the only close relative. The Commissioner decides that the lack of contact over the last 24 years did not automatically erase the contact they had had in the preceding 30 years. It was not unreasonable for a son to wish to pay his last respects to his father whatever the reasons for their estrangement. See also *CIS 13120/196* (claimant divorced from the deceased only two weeks before his death after 40 years of marriage), a decision on the form of reg.7(1)(b)(iii) as in force up to June 5, 1995 (although the actual result would be different on the current form of reg.7). The fact that it is reasonable for one person to assume responsibility for the cost of a funeral does not mean that it is not reasonable for someone else to do so (*CIS 13120/196*).

But even if it is reasonable for the person to accept responsibility for the cost of the funeral, the intention is that the person will not be entitled to a funeral payment if there are any immediate family members (other than those who were children (*i.e.* under 19 and receiving relevant education (reg.3(1)) at the date of death) who or whose partners, have not been awarded a qualifying benefit, unless they were estranged from the deceased or one of the limited exceptions in para.(4) applies (para.(3)). "Estrangement" has "connotations of emotional disharmony" (*R(SB) 2/87*) and may exist even though financial support is being provided. In *C1/0102(SF)*, the Commissioner stated that "[m]ere disagreement is not sufficient to constitute estrangement, there must be something akin to treating as a stranger for a sufficient period of time". On the facts of that case estrangement had taken place between the claimant's grandparents and his mother (who had a drink problem) "in that there was a deliberate decision to sever relationships due to the strong disapproval and anger which the grandparents felt about the deceased's drinking and the strong desire which they felt that this lifestyle should change and had to change before any relationships could be resumed."

5.60 The meaning of "estranged from" in ref.7(3)(c) has been further considered in *CIS 4498/2001* in which the claimant's deceased mother had suffered from senile dementia as a result of which she could not communicate with anyone or recognise family members and his sister—the other "immediate family member"—had lived in Australia for 10 years but had returned to Britain on at least three occasions because of her mother's ill-health. Quoting his earlier decision in *CIS 5321/1998*, Mr Commissioner Henty stated:

> " 'The appropriate OED definition of "estranged", accepted in *CIS/5119/97* is, "to alienate in feeling or affection". I might put a gloss on that such as "not to be on speaking terms". The evidence before the tribunal points, I think, not at so much as an alienation of feeling or affection—the emphasis being on "alienation", a concept which involves some form of positive consideration—but a drifting apart which to my mind connotes something short of alienation. Of course a long period of "drifting apart" may lead to the inference that there had been an alienation, but such is not, in my view, the case here".

Those considerations are equally applicable here. Had such a break down in relation occurred before the on set of the mother's incapacity, then estrangement there would have been. But the incapacity by itself is not estrangement, and neither is the fact that the sister had been in Australia for some 10 years."

CIS 5321/1998 was followed in *CIS 4769/2001* (see also the annotations to sub-para.(b) above) in which the Commissioner confirmed that family members who lived abroad (and therefore could not be in receipt of a qualifying benefit) could nevertheless count as immediate family members for the purposes of reg.7(3) (i.e., as reg.7(3) and 7(4) were worded prior to October 25, 2004), and that the operation of that rule did not infringe the claimant's rights under Arts 8 and 14 and 9 and 14 taken together of the European Convention on Human Rights.

In *CIS 1228/2004*, Ms Commissioner Fellner held "that registering a death is [not] enough *in itself* to show that the person who does so *cannot* have been estranged from the deceased" (original emphasis).

The wording of para.(3) is not particularly clear; for example, read literally **5.61**
para.(3)(b) could mean that if *any* such immediate family member has been awarded
a qualifying benefit, para.(3) will not apply. *CIS 2288/1998*, however, confirms that
read as a whole the meaning of para.(3) was clear. A person was not entitled to a
funeral payment if there was at least one other immediate family member who was
not estranged from the deceased and neither that member nor the member's partner
was in receipt of a qualifying benefit. A further point had arisen in *CIS 1218/1998*.
The claimant in that case had applied for a funeral payment in respect of his late
mother. His sister was not in receipt of a qualifying benefit. The tribunal decided
that para.(3)(b) referred to both the claimant and his sister and since he was in
receipt of a qualifying benefit the disentitlement imposed by para.(3) did not apply.
The AO appealed, contending that if the tribunal's interpretation was correct, no
claim would ever be caught by para.(3) since it was a requirement under para.(1)(a)
that the responsible person be in receipt of a qualifying benefit. In addition, there
would be no need to exempt from the operation of para.(3) those immediate family
members listed in para.(4). The Commissioner agreed; in his view the immediate
family members referred to in sub-paras (a) and (b) did not include the responsible
person.

What happens if—as may well be the case even in relatively close families—the
claimant simply does not know whether or not any of the other immediate family
members or close relatives is in receipt of a qualifying benefit: where does the burden
of proof lie? This was one of the issues considered by the House of Lords in the recent
decision in *Kerr v Department for Social Development* [2004] UKHL 23 (Lords Steyn,
Hope of Craighead, Scott of Foscote, Rodger of Earlsferry and Baroness Hale of
Richmond), May 6. 2004. In that case, which concerned the Northern Ireland equivalent of reg.7, the claimant was the eldest of three brothers and a sister who, although
living in the Belfast area, had not been in touch with each other for over 20 years. One
of the brothers died and the claimant was traced by the police and agreed to accept
financial responsibility for the funeral. He claimed a funeral expenses payment which
was refused without any enquiry by the Department into whether the surviving
brother and sister had been awarded a qualifying benefit, an issue which, of course,
the Department was better placed to ascertain than the claimant. The issue was therefore whether Mr Kerr had to prove a negative—that neither his sister or brother were
in receipt of a qualifying benefit—or whether the Department had to show that they
were. Giving the judgment of the House, Baroness Hale said, in a passage which has
profound implications for social security administration generally:

> "61. Ever since the decision of the Divisional Court in *R. v Medical Appeal
> Tribunal (North Midland Region), Ex p Hubble* [1958] 2 QB 228, it has been
> accepted that the process of benefits adjudication is inquisitorial rather than
> adversarial. Diplock J. as he then was said this of an industrial injury benefit
> claim at p 240:
> "A claim by an insured person to benefit under the Act is not truly analogous
> to a lis inter partes. A claim to benefit is a claim to receive money out of the
> insurance funds . . . Any such claim requires investigation to determine
> whether any, and if so, what amount of benefit is payable out of the fund. In
> such an investigation, the minister or the insurance officer is not a party
> adverse to the claimant. If analogy be sought in the other branches of the law,
> it is to be found in an inquest rather than in an action."
> 62. What emerges from all this is a co-operative process of investigation in
> which both the claimant and the department play their part. The depart-
> ment is the one which knows what questions it needs to ask and what infor-
> mation it needs to have in order to determine whether the conditions of
> entitlement have been met. The claimant is the one who generally speaking
> can and must supply that information. But where the information is avail-
> able to the department rather than the claimant, then the department must
> take the necessary steps to enable it to be traced.

63. If that sensible approach is taken, it will rarely be necessary to resort to concepts taken from adversarial litigation such as the burden of proof. The first question will be whether each partner in the process has played their part. If there is still ignorance about a relevant matter then generally speaking it should be determined against the one who has not done all they reasonably could to discover it. As Mr Commissioner Henty put it in decision *CIS/5321/1998*, "a claimant must to the best of his or her ability give such information to the AO as he reasonably can, in default of which a contrary inference can always be drawn." The same should apply to information which the department can reasonably be expected to discover for itself."

In this case, the claim was allowed because the Department had failed to ask Mr Kerr the necessary questions and could not "use its own failure to ask questions which would have led it to the right answer to defeat the claim" (para. 65).

Baroness Hale also addressed the position which would have existed if both the claimant and the Department had done everything which was legally required of them but it had still not proved possible to ascertain the true position? In that case

"66. This will not always be sufficient to decide who should bear the consequences of the collective ignorance of a matter which is material to the claim. It may be that everything which could have been done has been done but there are still things unknown. The conditions of entitlement must be met before the claim can be paid. . . . It may therefore become relevant to ask whether a particular matter relates to the conditions of entitlement or to an exception to those conditions. In this case, the department argues that all the elements, including those in regulation 6(6) [Regulation 7(6) of the GB regulations], are conditions of entitlement, so that the claimant must bear the consequences of ignorance. The claimant argues that the conditions of entitlement are laid down in regulation 6(1), supplemented where relevant by paragraphs (2) and (5) {Regulations 7(1), (2) and (5) of the GB Regulations}. Paragraphs (3) and (4), which go together, and paragraph (6) [paras. (3), (4) and (6) of GB Regulation 7] are exceptions.

67. The structure and wording of the regulation support the claimant's case. Conditions (a), (b), (c) and (d) in regulation 6(1) are clearly established. The claimant qualifies as a "close relative" under condition (e)(iv)(aa) but this also requires that it be reasonable for him to accept responsibility. Under regulation 6(5) the question "whether it is reasonable for a person to accept responsibility for meeting the expenses of the funeral shall be determined by the nature and extent of that person's contact with the deceased". The tribunal decided that it was reasonable for the claimant, as the eldest son who had grown up with his brother, to accept that responsibility, despite the fact that they had not been in contact with one another for many years. That conclusion is not challenged in this appeal, in my view rightly. For the reasons given earlier, there is a strong public interest in encouraging families to take responsibility for the speedy and seemly burial of their deceased relatives.

68. Regulation 6(3) provides that the person who has made himself responsible "shall not be entitled" if there is a more appropriate immediate family member. That this is a disentitling provision is made clear by regulation 6(4), which states that "Paragraph (3) shall not apply to *disentitle* the responsible person" (my emphasis) in the circumstances there set out. In the same way, paragraph 6(6) provides that if there is a close relative who is either in closer contact or in equally close contact and not receiving benefits or having capital, the responsible person "shall not be entitled" to the payment. These paragraphs are therefore worded in terms of exceptions rather than qualifying conditions. If anything, this interpretation is supported by the legislative history given earlier, as the existence of a more suitable relative was added as an exception or qualification to the basic rule.

69.   This, therefore, is a case in which the department should bear the burden of the collective ignorance and pay the claim."

Paragraph (4) sets out the circumstances in which the claimant may remain entitled to a funeral payment even if s/he has an immediate family member who is not in receipt of a qualifying benefit. These are largely self-explanatory and include where the immediate family member is under 18, or in certain types of full-time education, or (in relation to claims made on or after October 8, 2001) in receipt of asylum support, or—in some circumstances—in hospital or in prison. It is interesting to note that although both "full-time course of advanced education" and "full-time course of study" are defined by reg.61 of the IS Regulations, para.(4)(a) only applies the reg.61 definition of the former phrase. Logically this should have the consequence that on this occasion "full-time course of study" has the meaning it would bear in ordinary English usage rather than the, more restrictive, reg.61 meaning. However, it is hard to see why the phrase should have one meaning for IS and another for the Social Fund.

If the deceased was a child, the person entitled to a funeral payment will be the person (or his partner) responsible for the child at the date of death, unless there is an absent parent (defined in reg.3(1)) who (or whose partner) was not receiving a qualifying benefit at the date of death (head (ii)(aa)). In that case (or if there is no parent/person (including any partner) responsible for the child) entitlement to a funeral payment will be decided in accordance with heads (iii) and (iv) and the additional rules in paras (2)–(7). A person is responsible for a child if he is counted as such for the purposes of child benefit.

In the case of a still born child, the rules have been simplified from November 17, 1997 so that a parent (or partner) will qualify for a funeral payment, whether or not there is an absent parent (head (ii)(bb)).

As SSAC commented, these rules could have the effect of placing responsibility for a funeral on a relative who is not prepared to accept it and moreover which cannot be enforced. This may cause particular difficulties, for example, in the case of a deceased child depending on the state of relations between the parent with care and the absent parent.

In the past the "immediate family test" made it difficult to claim a funeral payment where a parent, son or daughter of the deceased was living outside the UK, as they would not be entitled to a UK means-tested benefit. The effect of the rule was therefore (among other things) to disadvantage some members of minority ethnic communities. However, in respect of deaths occurring on or after October 25, 2004, the new para. (4)(e) means that an "immediate family member" who is ordinarily resident outside the United Kingdom is excluded from consideration when applying the condition of disentitlement in para. (3). Moreover, although the surviving partner in a gay couple can qualify for a funeral payment under the category of close friend, the immediate family test may well prevent this in many cases. SSAC recommended that where "interdependence" (shared household with shared expenses) could be shown, such a claimant should be given the same priority as if he or she were the partner (in the social security sense) of the deceased, but in common with most of their other recommendations this was not accepted.

In addition to the above rules, if the responsible person is an immediate family member, another close relative or a close friend, and the deceased had one or more close relatives, the nature and extent of their contact with the deceased will be compared (para.(6)). This is a separate test from deciding whether it is reasonable for the person to have accepted responsibility for the funeral costs (see para.(5)), as confirmed in *R(IS) 3/98*. If any close relative had closer contact the responsible person will not be entitled to a funeral payment (para.(6)(a)). However, where the death occurred on or after October 25, 2004, a close relative who is ordinarily resident outside the United Kingdom is excluded from the test. If the contact was equally close, a payment will also be refused if the close relative (or their partner) is not getting a qualifying benefit (see para.(6)(b)). The former rule (in (sub-para.(c)) that if the contact was equally close, the claimant can be disqualified on the basis that the relative or friend

5.62

had more capital was abolished for claims made on or after October 8, 2001. This ties in with the abolition of the capital rule in reg.9 on the same date. This rule does not apply if the close relative was a child (defined in reg.3(1)) at the date of death (para.(7)). Close contact will be a question of fact in each case. It should be noted that the test involves having regard to the nature as well as the extent of the contact. Thus this will bring in issues of quality as well as quantity. See *CIS 8485/1995* which states that when considering the question of contact with the deceased tribunals should adopt a broad brush, commonsense approach. The amount of time spent with the deceased is only one factor, and the nature of the contact should be judged not just by visits, letters etc but also by the quality of the contact. So if the claimant's half-brother's unpredictable nature had affected his relationship with his late mother, that should have been taken into account in assessing the nature of his contact with her. The guidance given to decision-makers by the *Decision Makers Guide* is that they "should consider the overall nature and extent of the contact with the deceased given the circumstances of the individual. For example, domestic or work responsibilities may prevent a close relative from keeping in regular contact with the deceased but the nature of the contact may be equally as close as a close friend who visited every day." The guidance suggests that factors to be considered include the nature of the relationship, frequency of contact, type of contact, domestic or caring assistance given to the deceased, social outings and holidays, domestic or work responsibilities and estrangements or arguments with the deceased (paras 39181–39182).

The question of how para. (6)(b) applies in the situation where none of the close relatives was in contact with the deceased at all—*i.e.*, whether the phrase "in equally close contact" includes circumstances in which there was an equal lack of contact—was considered, *obiter*, by three members of the House of Lords in the *Kerr* case (above). Lord Scott was of the view that it did not. To read "equally close contact" as meaning "equal contact" was to rewrite the statutory language and to ignore the significance of the words "close" and "in"—one cannot be "in" a "close" lack of contact. Where there was no contact at all, then none of the sub-paras. of para. (6) was applicable. Further, the question was not whether any of the close relatives "had had close contact with the deceased in the past" but "whether they were 'in equally close contact' with him at the time of his death" (paras 26–35). By contrast Lord Hope held (at para.9) that the test in para. (6)(b) was not necessarily limited to the state of affairs which existed at the time of the deceased's death:

> "Regulation 6(6) assumes that where there is "contact" the question of "closeness" is put in issue, however slight or remote in time that may be. I do not find anything in the regulation to indicate that the contact must have been current at, or immediately before, the date of the deceased's death. The period of time during which a comparison of the nature and extent of the contact is to be undertaken is not specified. The conclusion which I would draw from this is that there is no restriction as to the time of this contact. In my opinion the first question which the adjudicator must ask himself is whether the relevant person had any "contact" with the deceased at all at any time. If he did, the question of the relative "closeness" of that contact in comparison with the contact of the responsible person can and must be asked and answered."

Baroness Hale (at para.70), whilst agreeing with Lord Scott that it was "harder to see how "was . . . in equally close contact" can cover contact which ended 20 years earlier", preferred not to express any view on the issue.

"Accepts responsibility" for the funeral costs

5.63   As regards acceptance of responsibility for the expenses, the decision in *CSB 488/1982*, that the fact that someone else makes the arrangements does not mean that the claimant has not taken responsibility for the costs, remains applicable. The *Social Fund Maternity and Funeral Payments Guide* has now been amended (see paras 2109–2113) so that it no longer implies that the test is who is responsible for arranging the funeral. It may be that if the person making the arrangements enters into a direct contractual relationship with an undertaker (rather than as agent for the claimant) that person has taken responsibility for the costs. But it is not necessary for the funeral account to be in the claimant's (or partner's) name. In *CIS 12344/1996* the claimant's son made the funeral arrangements; his mother was unable to do so because of her age and the sudden death of her husband. The bill was in his name and he paid it before the claim for a social fund funeral payment was made. It is held that the son had been acting as agent for his mother and the fact that the account was addressed to him did not detract from this. The claimant had accepted responsibility for the funeral costs. In *R(IS) 6/98* the Commissioner retracts his statement in *CIS 12344/1996* that it was necessary for the undertakers to know of the agency. The concept of the "undisclosed principal" in the law of agency allowed an agency to exist even where this was not disclosed to the third party, provided that the agent had in fact had authority beforehand. But if there was no agency at the time the funeral debt was incurred, it was not open to a person to intervene later and claim to be legally responsible for the debt (although depending on the circumstances a novation may achieve that result, see below).

Such an agency situation should be distinguished from a novation, or transfer, of the contract as occurred in *R(IS) 9/93*. The Commissioner follows *CSB 423/1989* in holding that if another person has initially made a contract with the undertakers the claimant may assume liability for the funeral costs by a novation of the contract under which the claimant assumes the other person's liability and the undertakers release the other person from his liability. The novation requires the consent of all three parties, but no consideration or further payment is necessary. Providing that the claimant comes within one of the heads of what is now in sub-para.(e) and has assumed responsibility for the costs before the decision is made (or possibly before the claim is made) the condition is satisfied. Often, arrangements will be made without thinking about the legal niceties, and a commonsense view should be taken.

[¹Amount of funeral payment

7A.—(1) Subject to paragraphs (4) and (5), regulation 8 and Part IV of these Regulations, the amount of a funeral payment shall be an amount sufficient to meet any of the costs which fall to be met or have been met by the claimant or his partner or a person acting on their behalf and which are specified in paragraph (2), inclusive of any available discount on those costs allowed by the funeral director or by any other person who arranges the funeral.

(2) The costs which may be met for the purposes of paragraph (1) are—

(a) except where sub-paragraph (b) applies, in the case of a burial—

    (i) the necessary costs of purchasing a new burial plot for the deceased, together with an exclusive right of burial in that plot;

    [³(ii) the fees levied in respect of a burial by the authority or person responsible for the provision and maintenance of cemeteries for the area where the burial takes place [⁷, or the fees levied by a private grave-digger,] in so far as it is necessary to incur those fees;]

(b) in the case of a cremation—

    [⁴(i) the fees levied in respect of a cremation by the authority or person responsible for the provision and maintenance of crematoria for the area where the cremation takes place in so far as it is necessary to incur those fees;

    (ia) the cost of any medical references;]

    (ii) the cost of any necessary registered medical practitioner's certificates;

    (iii) the fee payable for the removal of any device as defined for the purposes of the Active Implantable Medical Devices Regulations

5.64

1992 save that where that removal is carried out by a person who is not a registered medical practitioner, no more than £20 shall be met in respect of that fee;

(c) the cost of obtaining any documentation, production of which is necessary in order to release any assets of the deceased which may be deducted from a funeral payment pursuant to regulation 8;

(d) where the deceased died at home or away from home and it is necessary to transport the deceased within the United Kingdom in excess of 50 miles to the funeral director's premises or to the place of rest, the reasonable cost of transport in excess of 50 miles;

[²(e) where transport is provided by a vehicle for the coffin and bearers and by one additional vehicle, from the funeral director's premises or the place of rest to the funeral and—

(i) the distance travelled, in the case of a funeral which consists of a burial where no costs have been incurred under subparagraph (a)(i) above, exceeds 50 miles; or

(ii) the distance travelled, in the case of any other funeral, necessarily exceeds 50 miles,

subject to paragraph (4A), the reasonable cost of the transport provided, other than the cost in respect of the first 50 miles of the distance travelled;

(f) subject to paragraph (4B), the necessary cost of one return journey for the responsible person, either for the purpose of making arrangements for, or for attendance at, the funeral;]

(g) any other funeral expenses which shall not exceed [⁵£700] in any case.

[²(3) All references in paragraph (2)(d) and (e) to 50 miles shall be construed as applying to—

(a) in a case to which paragraph (2)(d) applies, the combined distance from the funeral director's premises or the deceased's place of rest to the place of death and of the return journey;

(b) in a case to which paragraph (2)(e) applies, the combined distance from the funeral director's premises or the deceased's place of rest to the funeral and of the return journey.]

(4) The cost of items and services which may be met under paragraph (2) (a), (d) and (e) shall not be taken to include any element in the cost of those items and services which relates to a requirement of the deceased's religious faith.

[²(4A) Costs shall only be met pursuant to head (i) of sub-paragraph (e) of paragraph (2) to the extent that the cost incurred under that head, together with the cost incurred under paragraph (2)(a)(ii), does not exceed the costs which would have been incurred under paragraph (2)(a)(i) and (ii) and, where appropriate, (e)(ii) if it had been necessary to purchase a new burial plot for the deceased with an exclusive right of burial in that plot.

(4B) Costs shall only be met pursuant to sub-paragraph (f) of paragraph (2) to the extent that those costs do not exceed the costs which would have been incurred in respect of a return journey from the home of the responsible person to the location where the necessary costs of the burial or, as the case may be, cremation, would have been incurred pursuant to paragraph (2)(a) or, as the case may be, (b).]

(5) Where items and services have been provided on the death of the deceased under a pre-paid funeral plan or under any analogous arrangement—

(a) no funeral payment shall be made in respect of items or services referred to in paragraph (2) which have been provided under such a plan or arrangement; and

(b) paragraph (2)(g) shall have effect in relation to that particular claim as if for the sum [⁵£700], there were substituted the sum [⁶£120]

AMENDMENTS

1. Social Security (Social Fund and Claims and Payments) (Miscellaneous Amendments) Regulations 1997 (SI 1997/792), reg.5 (April 7, 1997).

2. Social Fund Maternity and Funeral Expenses (General) Amendment Regulations 1997 (SI 1997/2538), reg.6 (November 17, 1997).

3. Social Fund Maternity and Funeral Expenses (General) Amendment Regulations 1999 (SI 1999/3266), reg.2(4)(a) (January 4, 2000).

4. Social Fund Maternity and Funeral Expenses (General) Amendment Regulations 1999 (SI 1999/3266), reg.2(4)(b) (January 4, 2000).

5. Social Fund Maternity and Funeral Expenses (General) Amendment Regulations 2003 (SI 2003/471), regs 2 and 3 (for deaths occurring on or after April 7, 2003).

6. Social Fund Maternity and Funeral Expenses (General) Amendment (No. 2) Regulations 2003 (SI 2003/1570), reg.2 (for deaths occurring on or after (October 6, 2003).

7. Social Fund Maternity and Funeral Expenses (General) Amendment Regulations 2004 (SI 2004/2536), reg.3(3) (October 25, 2004).

DEFINITIONS

"claimant"—see reg.3(1).
"funeral"—*ibid.*

GENERAL NOTE

This regulation contains the limits on eligible funeral costs. (See reg.9 of the Social Security (Social Fund and Claims and Payments) (Miscellaneous Amendments) Regulations 1997 (p.1298) for the transitional protection for claims in respect of deaths before April 7, 1997 where the funeral takes place by July 7, 1997. See also the note to s.133(1)(a) of the Contributions and Benefits Act.) Note that a funeral payment will be made even if the costs have already been met by the claimant, his partner, or a person acting on their behalf.

A payment can be made for the expenses that are listed in para.(2)(a) to (f) (except for those that have been met by a pre-paid funeral plan or similar arrangement (para.(5)(a)), together with up to £700 for other funeral expenses, or £120 if some of the funeral costs have been met under a pre-paid funeral plan or similar arrangement (paras (2)(g) and (5)(b)). Any element in the burial or transport costs that relates to a requirement of the deceased's religious faith will not be met (para.(4)). See *CSIS 42/1996*, a decision on the previous form of reg.7, which held that a vigil is a requirement of the Roman Catholic faith.

CIS 16192/1996 decided that under the previous form of reg.7 the cost of *either* a cremation *or* a burial was allowed but not both (see reg.7(4)(a) and (b) in the 1996 edition of Mesher and Wood, *Income-Related Benefits: The Legislation*). Thus the cost of the interment of the deceased's ashes following a cremation was not covered, since the disposal of the ashes was not part of the cremation process. The Commissioner in *CIS 12838/1996* took the same view, despite the fact that the former reg.7(4)(a) referred to interment rather than burial; although it was common to speak of the interment (rather than a burial) of the ashes, he concluded that in the context of reg.7(4) interment meant burial without there having been a cremation. Para.(2)(a) has removed this confusion by referring to burial rather than interment; moreover, unlike the former reg.7(4)(a), it excludes cases where sub-para.(b) applies.

The expenses to be covered by para.(2)(g) are not specified but will include items such as a funeral director's fees (including the cost of a coffin which cannot be met

5.65

5.66

under either para.(2)(a) or (b)—see *CIS 2651/2003* and *CIS 2607/2003*), church fees or flowers. But there is no definition of funeral expenses and so any expense that is a funeral expense should be allowed.

Thus, in *CIS/1345/2004*, Mr Commissioner Williams held that "suitable funeral attire" might amount to a funeral expense within sub-para.(g). The test was not, as had been suggested by the Secretary of State, whether the expense was "wholly exclusively and necessarily required for the funeral". There was no basis in law for restricting the scope of the paragraph beyond the words actually used in the sub-para. The only tests for applying reg.7A(2)(g) were:

"(i) Were the expenses in fact funeral expenses that took into account any relevant discounts?

(ii) If so, were the expenses met by the claimant or partner (or will they be)?

(iii) If so, were they of a nature covered by any of the provisions in regulation 7A(2)(a) to (f)?

(iv) If not, do they exceed the set sum?

If they do not, they are allowable."

It should be noted, however, that in *CIS/1924/2004*, Ms Commissioner Fellner held that, although flowers were capable of amounting to a funeral expense within the sub-para., obituary notices and the cost of a memorial stone and flower container were not. There is a clear tension between these two decisions: if the *CIS/1345/2004* test had been applied to the items disallowed in *CIS/1924/2004*, it seems probable that some, at least, would have been allowed.

There is nothing to prevent para.(2)(g) being used to pay for the cost of items or services in paras (2)(a) to (f) that have not been fully met or to cover the cost of a religious requirement.

It will be noted that some of sub-paras (a) to (f) in para.(2) contain an express limitation to "reasonable" costs and some do not (in others the word "necessary" is used). On a previous form of this provision *R(IS) 14/92* considered that the word "reasonable" should be read into the listed categories even where it was not expressed. But in *CIS 6818/1995* the Commissioner concluded that what was said about reasonableness in *R(IS) 14/92* was not an essential part of the decision. He expressed the view (which was also not necessary to *his* decision) that each sub-paragraph in what was then reg.7(2) contained its own complete test and that there was no room for any further conditions to be implied. In view of the quite specific nature of the items or services covered by para.(2)(a)–(f) it is suggested that the approach of *CIS 6818/1995* is to be preferred. Under para.(2)(g) there is no limit on the funeral expenses that are to be met, other than the £700 (or £120) ceiling.

5.67   *R(IS) 11/91* decided that the deceased's "home" (see para.(2)(d)) was the accommodation where he normally lived prior to his death, as opposed to his "home town". *R(IS) 18/98* considered the meaning of "necessary costs of a new or reopened grave" in what was then reg.7(4)(a) (now see para.(2)(a)). The Commissioner decides that the word "necessary" implied that any expense over that which was properly required was to be excluded. However, its effect was not to require the purchase of the cheapest possible plot without regard to any other consideration. Account should be taken of the proximity to the deceased's residence while he was alive and of the deceased's religion, so that, for example a person of the Greek Orthodox faith was entitled to be buried in an area set aside for people of that faith.

Para.(2)d) and (e) allow certain transport costs for distances (*i.e.* the combined distance of the outward and return journey (para.(3)), in excess of 50 miles to be met. The previous form of para.(2)(e)(ii) (now sub-para.(e)(i)) did not appear to allow *any* award where the costs of transport and burial in an existing plot (*i.e.* usually away from where the deceased lived) exceeded the purchase and burial costs of a new plot, plus any necessary transport costs (*i.e.* the costs of burying locally). The effect of the new para.(4A) and para.(2)(e)(i) is that such costs will be met up to the level of the local burial costs.

Para.(2)(f) covers one return journey for the responsible person for arranging the funeral or attending it. The November 17, 1997 form of sub-para.(f) (introduced following the ECJ's judgment in *O'Flynn*, *(R(IS) 4/98)*, see the notes to reg.7(1)(b)) no longer restricts the journey to one within the UK. However, para.(4B) limits the costs that will be met to those of a return journey from the responsible person's home to the place where the funeral costs would have been incurred (although the drafting is not entirely clear, it is understood that the intention is to restrict payment of travel costs to those that would have been incurred if the funeral had taken place in the UK). Note that sub-para.(f) now only covers necessary travel expenses; the previous form referred to "reasonable" expenses. *CIS 16957/1996* decides that although sub-para.(f) refers to a "return journey" it did also apply where the claimant only undertook a single journey (her husband had died away from home and she had travelled home to attend the funeral). Others who are relatives of the deceased may be eligible for a community care grant for the cost of travel to and from a funeral in the United Kingdom (see Social Fund direction 4(b)(ii)). The applicant must be a member of a family containing a claimant in receipt of income support or income-based JSA.

From the amount calculated under reg.7A must be deducted the amounts listed in reg.8. These do not include the value of the deceased's estate, but by virtue of s.78(4) of the Administration Act any funeral payment from the social fund is a first charge on the estate.

If the funeral costs have not been paid at the date of claim any funeral payment is to be made direct to the creditor (Claims and Payments Regulations, reg.35(2)).

Deductions from an award of a funeral payment

8. [⁴—(1) Subject to paragraph (2),] there shall be deducted from the amount of any award which would, but for this regulation, be made under regulation 7 the following amounts:—

5.68

    (a) the amount of any assets of the deceased which are available to the [¹responsible person] (on application or otherwise) or any other member of his family without probate or letters of administration [³or in Scotland, confirmation,] having been granted;

    (b) the amount of any lump sum due to the [¹responsible person] or any other member of his family on the death of the deceased by virtue of any insurance policy, occupational pension scheme, or burial club or any analogous arrangement;

    (c) the amount of any contribution [⁴towards funeral expenses] which has been received by the [¹responsible person] or any other member of his family from a charity or a relative of his or of the deceased[⁴ . . .];

    (d) the amount of any funeral grant, made out of public funds, in respect of the death of a person who was entitled to a war disablement pension.

[⁴(e) in relation to a pre-paid funeral plan or any analogous arrangement—

        (i) where the plan or arrangement had not been paid for in full prior to the death of the deceased, the amount of any sum payable under that plan or arrangement in order to meet the deceased's funeral expenses;

        (ii) where the plan or arrangement had been paid for in full prior to the death of the deceased, the amount of any allowance paid under that plan or arrangement in respect of funeral expenses.

(2) The amount of any payment made under the Macfarlane Trust, the Macfarlane (Special Payment) Trust, the Macfarlane (Special Payments) (No. 2) Trust, the Fund [⁶, the Eileen Trust or the Skipton Fund] [⁵ or under a trust established out of funds provided by the Secretary of State in

respect of persons who suffered, or who are suffering, from variant Creutzfeldt-Jakob disease for the benefit of persons eligible for payments in accordance with its provisions] shall be disregarded from any deduction made under this regulation and for the purpose of this paragraph, "the Macfarlane Trust", "the Macfarlane (Special Payments) Trust", "the Macfarlane (Special Payments) (No. 2) Trust", "the Fund" [⁶, "the Eileen Trust" and "the Skipton Fund"] shall have the same meaning as in regulation 2(1) of the Income Support Regulations.]

Amendments

5.69
1. Social Fund Maternity and Funeral Expenses (General) Amendment Regulations 1994 (SI 1994/506), reg.4 (April 1, 1994).
2. Social Fund Maternity and Funeral Expenses (General) Amendment Regulations 1995 (SI 1995/1229), reg.4 (June 5, 1995).
3. Social Fund Maternity and Funeral Expenses (General) Amendment Regulations 1996 (SI 1996/1443), reg.6 (October 7, 1996).
4. Social Security (Social Fund and Claims and Payments) (Miscellaneous Amendments) Regulations 1997 (SI 1997/792), reg.6 (April 7, 1997).
5. Social Security Amendment (Capital Disregards and Recovery of Benefits) Regulations 2001 (SI 2001/1118), reg.3 (April 12, 2001).
6. Social Security (Miscellaneous Amendments) (No. 2) Regulations 2004 (SI 2004/1141), reg.8 (May 12, 2004).

Definitions

"family"—see reg.3(1).
"occupational pension scheme"—see 1986 Act, s.84(1) (PSA, s.1).
"responsible person"—see reg.3(1).

General Note

Para. (1)
5.70
The amounts specified are to be deducted from the amount calculated under reg.7A. Note the exception in para.(2).

Sub-para. (a): Under the Administration of Estates (Small Payments) Act 1965 certain sums can be distributed from the estate to beneficiaries without a grant of probate or letters of administration. The current limit is £5,000. In addition many statutes regulating Post Office and building society accounts, savings certificates, etc. (but not, after privatisation, Trustee Savings Bank accounts) allow payment to be made after the owner's death. There is a similar power for most social security benefits. For details, see *Halsbury's Laws of England* (4th ed.), Vol. 17, para.970. One problem is that these provisions are generally merely permissive, so that payment cannot be demanded as of right. In *R(IS) 14/91* the Commissioner indicates that in straightforward cases it may be concluded that such an amount is available on application. However, the circumstances (*e.g.* some dispute between next of kin of equal status) may point to the opposite conclusion. *R(IS) 14/91* also decides that evidence of availability of assets from the date of death up to the date of the decision on the claim is relevant. Thus where the claim was made on the date of death, a sum of £1300 in the deceased's building society account was available, although the claimant did not obtain the money until a week later. Nor was that conclusion defeated by the fact that before the decision the claimant had distributed or spent most of the money. Funeral expenses are a first charge on the estate *(R(SB) 18/84)*. If there are liquid assets in the estate, these may be immediately available for funeral expenses regardless of other debts. In *R(IS) 12/93* arrears of attendance allowance for the deceased were paid to the claimant as next-of-kin. The Commissioner holds that the arrears were available. Since they exceeded the cost of the funeral, no award was made.

Sub-para. (b): For this paragraph to apply the amount must be due to the claimant   5.71
or a member of his family (defined in reg.3(1)). Due must mean legally due. Sometimes such a member will have a clear legal entitlement under an insurance policy or a pension scheme. Sometimes trustees may have a discretion as to who should be paid a lump sum. In these circumstances no amount can be legally due until the trustees have exercised that discretion.

Sub-para. (c): This paragraph only applies to sums which have actually been received, presumably at the date of claim, since that is the date specified in reg.7(1), although *R(IS) 14/91* casts doubt on this. Only payments towards funeral expenses from charities or from relatives of the deceased or the claimant's family count. Payments from anyone else do not count, except to the extent that they may increase the claimant's capital. From April 7, 1997, any relevant payments are taken into account in full. But if a contribution is for expenses which are not funeral expenses (*e.g.* clothing to wear to the funeral), it is not included under para.(c).
   CIS 450/1995 decides that a genuine loan from a relative that is legally recoverable is not a "contribution" and is not caught by sub-para.(c).

Sub-para. (d): This paragraph is straightforward.

Sub-para. (e): Any amount payable under a pre-paid funeral plan or similar arrangement will be deducted.

Para. (2)
   No deduction is to be made for payments received from these trusts.

PART IV

EFFECT OF CAPITAL

Effect of capital

   9.—[¹ . . .]   5.72

AMENDMENT

   1. Social Fund Maternity and Funeral Expenses (General) Amendment Regulations 2001 (SI 2001/3023), reg.2(3) (October 8, 2001).

GENERAL NOTE

   The capital rule for sure start maternity grants and funeral payments was abolished for claims made on or after October 8, 2001. For the operation of the rule in relation to claims made before that date, see pp.1467–1470 of Vol. II of the 2001 edition.

Assessment of capital

   10. [¹ . . .]   5.73

AMENDMENT

1. Social Fund Maternity and Funeral Expenses (General) Amendment Regulations 1989 (SI 1989/379), reg.5 (April 15, 1989).

PART V

TRANSITIONAL PROVISIONS

Interpretation of Parts V and VI

5.74   **11.** In this Part and Part VI of these Regulations—
"the Single Payments Regulations" means the Supplementary Benefit (Single Payments) Regulations 1981;
"the Trade Dispute Regulations" means the Supplementary Benefit (Trade Disputes and Recovery from Earnings) Regulations 1980; "the Urgent Cases Regulations" means the Supplementary Benefit (Urgent Cases) Regulations 1981.

Transitional arrangements—maternity payments

5.75   **12.**—(1) Subject to paragraph (2), no maternity payment shall be made in the case where the confinement or adoption occurred before 6th April 1987.
(2) Subject to paragraph (3), a maternity payment may be made, so long as the claimant satisfies the conditions of Part II of these Regulations, in respect of a confinement or adoption which occurred on or after 9th March 1987 but only if the claimant or his partner was or would have been, had a claim been made, entitled to supplementary benefit for any period including 9th March 1987 or beginning after that date which falls before the coming into operation of these Regulations.
(3) No maternity payment shall be made in a case where, in respect of the same confinement or adoption, the claimant or his partner has received or is entitled to a single payment of supplementary benefit by virtue of regulation 7 of the Single Payments Regulations or an additional requirement was applicable by virtue of regulation 7 of the Trade Disputes Regulations.
(4) The amount of a maternity payment shall be reduced by the amount of an award, in respect of the same confinement, of a maternity grant under section 21 of the Social Security Act 1975.

DEFINITIONS

"claimant"—see reg.3(1).
"confinement"—*ibid.*
"partner"—*ibid.*
"Single Payments Regulations"—see reg.11.
"Trade Disputes Regulations"—*ibid.*

GENERAL NOTE

5.76   The general rule, under para.(1), is that maternity payments can only be made for births or adoptions after April 5, 1987. Up to that date reg.7 of the Single Payments Regulations was still in operation. However, the crucial date under those regulations is the date of claim, so that if a claim was not made before April 6, 1987, no payment for maternity expenses under reg.7 can be paid. Therefore, if no single payment has been made (para.(3)) a social fund payment can be made for births or adoptions occurring after March 8, 1987 (para.(2)). The ordinary conditions of regs 4 and 5 must be met, and in addition the claimant or his partner must have satisfied the conditions for entitlement to supplementary benefit for some time between March 9 and April 5, 1987, inclusive.

Note that para.(3) provides a general exclusion when there has already been a single payment or trade dispute payment for the same birth or adoption. Similarly, under para.(4) if there has been an award of maternity grant the £25 is to be deducted from any social fund payment.

Transitional payments—funeral payments

13.—(1) Subject to paragraph (2) no funeral payment shall be made where the deceased died before 6th April 1987.

5.77

(2) Subject to paragraph (3) a funeral payment may be made, so long as the claimant satisfies the conditions of regulation 6, where the deceased died on or after 9th March 1987 but only if the claimant or his partner was or would have been, had a claim been made, entitled to supplementary benefit for any period including 9th March 1987 or beginning after that date which falls before the coming into operation of these Regulations.

(3) No funeral payment shall be made in the case where, in respect of the same funeral, the claimant or his partner has received or is entitled to a single payment of supplementary benefit by virtue of regulation 8 of the Single Payments Regulations or an additional requirement was applicable by virtue of regulation 7A of the Trade Disputes Regulations.

(4) The amount of a funeral payment shall be reduced by the amount of an award, in respect of the same funeral, of a death grant under section 32 of the Social Security Act 1975 unless that grant has been spent on any item in respect of which a funeral payment would otherwise have been made.

DEFINITIONS

"claimant"—see reg.3(1).
"funeral"—*ibid.*
"funeral payment"—*ibid.*
"partner"—*ibid.*
"Single Payments Regulations"—see reg.11.
"Trade Disputes Regulations"—*ibid.*

GENERAL NOTE

The general rule, under para.(1), is that funeral payments can only be made for deaths occurring after April 5, 1987. Up to that date, reg.8 of the Single Payments Regulations was still in operation. But the crucial thing under those regulations is the date of claim and if no claim had been made before April 6, 1987, no single payment could be awarded. Therefore, providing that no single payment or trade dispute payment has been made (para.(3)) a social fund payment can be made for deaths after March 8, 1987. The ordinary conditions of reg.6 must be met, and in addition the claimant or his partner must for some period between March 9 and April 5, 1987, inclusive, have satisfied the conditions for entitlement to supplementary benefit.

5.78

Para.(3) provides a general exception from entitlement. Under para.(4) the amount of a social fund payment is to be reduced by the amount of any death grant awarded, unless the grant has been spent on an item covered by reg.6(2). Presumably in this case, a social fund payment will not be made for that item because the person will not have taken responsibility for that item.

PART VI

CONSEQUENTIAL AMENDMENTS

5.79   *14., 15., and 16. [Omitted.]*

Social Fund Maternity and Funeral Expenses (General) Amendment Regulations 1995

(SI 1995/1229)

Made by the Secretary of State under ss.138(1) and (4) and 175(1), (3) and (4) of the Social Security Contributions and Benefits Act 1992

[In force June 5, 1995]

Transitional provision with respect to deaths occurring before 5th June 1995

5.80   **5.** Where, in respect of a death which occurs before 5th June 1995, a claim is made by the responsible person for funeral expenses from the social fund in respect of a funeral which takes place on or before 5th September 1995, regulations 2 to 4 of these Regulations shall not have effect with respect to that claim.

GENERAL NOTE

5.81   See the notes to reg.7 of the Social Fund Maternity and Funeral Expenses (General) Regulations. Regs 7, 8 and 9 were amended by regs 2–4 of these Regulations on June 5, 1995.

Social Fund Maternity and Funeral Expenses (General) Amendment Regulations 1996

(SI 1996/1443)

Made by the Secretary of State of State under ss.138(1)(a) and (4) and 175(1), (3) and (4) of the Social Security Contributions and Benefits Act 1992

[In force October 7, 1996]

Transitional provision

5.82   **8.** Regulations 2(3) and (4), 5(3) to (7) and 6 of these Regulations shall not have effect with respect to any claim for a funeral payment made before 7th October 1996.

GENERAL NOTE

The regulations referred to in this provision effected amendments to regs 3, 7 and 8 of the Social Fund Maternity and Funeral Expenses (General) Regulations on October 7, 1996.

5.83

The Social Fund Maternity and Funeral Expenses (General) Amendment Regulations 1999

(SI 1999/3266)

Made by the Secretary of State under ss.138(1)(a) and (4) and 175(1), (3) and (4) of the Social Security Contributions and Benefits Act 1992

[In force January 4, 2000]

Citation, commencement and interpretation

1.—(1) These Regulations may be cited as the Social Fund Maternity and Funeral Expenses (General) Amendment Regulations 1999 and shall come into force on 4th January 2000.

5.84

(2) In these Regulations, "the principal Regulations" means the Social Fund Maternity and Funeral Expenses (General) Regulations 1987.

Saving

3.—Where, in respect of a death which occurs before 4th January 2000, a claim is made for funeral expenses from the social fund in respect of a funeral which takes place on or before 4th April 2000, regulations 7 and 7A of the principal Regulations shall apply in respect of that claim as if regulation 2(3) and (4) of these Regulations had not been made.

5.85

GENERAL NOTE

Reg.2 of these Regulations introduced technical amendments to regs 7 and 7A of the Social Fund Maternity and Funeral Expenses (General) Regulations 1987. Reg.3 provides that where the death took place on or before January 3, 2000 and the funeral on or before April 3, 2000 the old wording of regs 7 and 7A(see pp.1084–1094 of the 1999 edition of *Mesher and Wood: Income Related Benefits: The Legislation*) applies.

5.86

The Social Fund Maternity and Funeral Expenses (General) Amendment Regulations 2000

(SI 2000/528)

Made by the Secretary of State under ss.138(1)(a) and (4) and 175(1), (3) and (4) of the Social Security Contributions and Benefits Act 1992

[In force March 27, 2000]

Transitional arrangements

5.87   **5.**—(1) Subject to paragraph (2), these Regulations shall not apply in a case where a claim is made and

       (a) the expected date of confinement;

       (b) the date of birth of the child (including any still-born);

       (c) the date of the adoption order; or

       (d) in the case of a child in respect of whom an order has been granted pursuant to section 30 of the Human Fertilisation and Embryology Act 1990[5], the date of the order,

are both before 11th June 2000.

    (2) Subject to paragraph (3), where a payment has been made on the basis that the expected date of confinement is before 11th June 2000 and the date of birth of that child (including any still-born) occurs after 10th June 2000, a further payment may be made in accordance with these Regulations.

    (3) The amount payable as a consequence of paragraph (2) shall be reduced by a sum equal to the payment already made.

GENERAL NOTE

5.88   See the notes to reg.5 of the Social Fund Maternity and Funeral Expenses (General) Regulations 1987. Regs 3, 4–6 and 9 were amended by regs 2–4 of these Regulations on March 27, 2000.

Social Security (Social Fund and Claims and Payments) (Miscellaneous Amendments) Regulations 1997

(SI 1997/792)

Made by the Secretary of State under ss. 138(1)(a) and (4) and 175(1), (3) and (4) of the Social Security Contributions and Benefits Act 1992 and ss. 5(1)(a), 189(1), (3) and (4) and 191 of the Social Security Administration Act 1992

[In force April 7, 1997]

Transitional provision

5.89   **9.** Where, in respect of a death which occurs before 7th April 1997, a claim is made for funeral expenses from the social fund in respect of a funeral which takes place on or before 7th July 1997, regulations 2, 3(b), 5, 6 and 7 of these Regulations shall not have effect with respect to that claim.

GENERAL NOTE

5.90   See the notes to regs 7, 7A and 8 of the Social Fund Maternity and Funeral Expenses (General) Regulations. Regs 3, 4(3), 8 and 9 of those Regulations were amended and new regs 7 and 7A were inserted by regs 2, 3(b), 5, 6 and 7 of these Regulations on April 7, 1997.

INDEX

Index